THE COLUMBIA ENCYCLOPEDIA OF MODERN DRAMA

THE COLUMBIA ENCYCLOPEDIA OF

Modern Drama

Edited by **GABRIELLE H. CODY** and **EVERT SPRINCHORN**

Volume 2

COLUMBIA UNIVERSITY PRESS

New York

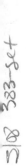

Columbia University Press

Publishers Since 1893

New York   Chichester, West Sussex

Copyright © 2007 Columbia University Press

Library of Congress Cataloging-in-Publication Data

The Columbia encyclopedia of modern drama / edited by

Gabrielle H. Cody and Evert Sprinchorn.

     p.   cm.

     Includes bibliographical references and index.

    ISBN 978−0−231−14032−4 (set : alk. paper)

        978−0−231−14422−3 (v. 1 : alk. paper)

        978−0−231−14424−7 (v. 2 : alk. paper)

    1. Drama—Bio-bibliography—Dictionaries.   2. Drama—

20th century—History and criticism.   3. Theater—History—

20th century— Encyclopedias.   I. Cody, Gabrielle H., 1956–

II. Sprinchorn, Evert.

PN1861 C65 2007

809 2003—dc22   2006051841

∞

Printed in the United States of America

C 10 9 8 7 6 5 4 3 2 1

MACDONALD, ANN-MARIE (1958–)

Ann-Marie MacDonald is a highly recognized and widely respected playwright, actor, and bestselling novelist. In addition to being an international bestseller, her first novel, 1996's epic *Fall on Your Knees*, was the winner of the Commonwealth Writers Prize for Best First Book. MacDonald's second novel, the loosely autobiographical 1950s family saga *The Way the Crow Flies*, was released in 2003 and nominated that same year for CANADA's distinguished Giller prize.

MacDonald's best-known play GOOD NIGHT DESDEMONA (GOOD MORNING JULIET) (1990) parodies several Shakespearean TRAGE-DIES, most specifically *Othello* and *Romeo and Juliet*. Already performed extensively worldwide, this COMEDY successfully incorporates absurdist wordplay, intertextual references to Renaissance texts (often working with William Shakespeare's own dialogue), and same-sex love narratives and playfully invokes several Shakespearean conventions that leave the original tragedies reading more like a feminist-flavored comedy. Among its many accolades, the play was awarded the Governor General's Award, the Chalmers Award, and the Canadian Author's Association Award. As with many of her plays, this comedy invokes feminist issues within a broader satirical context.

Not unlike her young protagonist Madeleine in *The Way the Crow Flies*, MacDonald was born on a Royal Canadian Air Force Base in Baden-Baden, GERMANY (on October 29, 1958), where her father was stationed as a military accountant. The family spent several happy years there before returning to Canada, where Mac-Donald eventually graduated from the National Theatre School of Canada. In addition to growing up Roman Catholic and the frequent relocations because of her father's career, MacDonald's Cape Breton roots have had a significant effect on her storytelling powers and her subject matter. She also credits an early and relentless love of reading as a formative experience of her life.

MacDonald has performed extensively onstage, on television, and in film. Her supporting role in the 1987 feature *I've Heard the Mermaids Singing* garnered her a Genie Award nomination, and she was nominated for a Gemini Award in 1989 as a result of her work in the television film *Where the Spirit Lives*. MacDonald also had a major role in Anne Wheeler's feature film *Better than Chocolate*, a romantic comedy about two lesbians who move in together and the mother-in-law who moves in with them. In her current role as the host of CBC's *Life and Times*, she is seen by television viewers weekly in the award-winning biography program that profiles the lives of famous Canadians. Early in her writing career, in addition to her frequent appearances on Canadian television, MacDonald supported herself writing regularly for television. Her most recent film work is

Cassandra Nicolaou's 2002 feature film *Interviews with My Next Girlfriend*. In 2003 MacDonald married Alisa Palmer, with whom she adopted a baby girl.

[*See also* Gay and Lesbian Drama]

PLAYS: *The Arab's Mouth* (1990); *Goodnight Desdemona (Good Morning Juliet)* (1990); *Nigredo Hotel* (1992); *The Attic, the Pearls and 3 Fine Girls* (1997)

FURTHER READING

Djordjevic, Igor. "*Goodnight Desdemona (Good Morning Juliet)*: From Shakespearean Tragedy to Postmodern Satyr Play." *Comparative Drama* 37, no. 1 (2003): 89–116.

Hengen, Shannon. "Towards a Feminist Comedy." *Canadian Literature* 146 (Autumn 1995): 97–110.

Mackay, Ellen. "The Spectre of Straight Shakespeare." *Canadian Theatre Review* 111 (Summer 2002): 10–15.

"Meet the Writers: Ann-Marie MacDonald." barnesandnoble.com. http://www.barnesandnoble.com/writers/writerdetails.asp?userid =so4JQdx9tR&cid=749287#interview. August 9, 2004 [Print and audio interview with Ann-Marie MacDonald].

L. Bailey McDaniel

MACDONALD, BRYDEN (1960–)

Born in 1960 in Glace Bay, Cape Breton Island, Nova Scotia, Bryden MacDonald became successful in his thirties. Openly homosexual, MacDonald's preoccupation with the marginalization of gay culture influences his plays, which validate diverse sexual identities. MacDonald's breakthrough came in the early 1990s, when his first published play, WHALE RIDING WEATHER (1991), was produced in Toronto, Halifax, and Vancouver. The play received a number of prestigious awards and nominations and has been revived several times since. An aging inner-city "queen," Lyle clings desperately to his young lover, Auto, who gradually tears himself away from the broken-down Lyle's stultifying influence.

The Weekend Healer was produced at Toronto's Factory Theatre in 1994. MacDonald's tendency to depict characters behaving melodramatically is clear. Set in Scarborough, the thirty-one-year-old Lindalou endures a visit to her difficult mother, Betina. On Friday, as Lindalou prepares to return to Cape Breton, her adolescent brother, Curtis, disappears, causing panic. A weekend of agitation, argument, and near hysteria ensues. Although the use of verse dialogue in *Whale Riding Weather* and *The Weekend Healer* may suggest that MacDonald favors poetry over clarity, he is very much a practical dramatist: only three actors are needed for each play, making the plays economically viable for small companies.

MacDonald's first two plays depict the chaos of fragmenting, unconventional families. His third play, *Divinity Bash / Nine Lives* (published 1999), is chaotic on a larger scale. Nothing stays still in the play: walls collapse, as do fixed ideas about society. Intellectually nihilistic, the play is theatrically and thematically descended from the absurdist plays of SAMUEL BECKETT and EUGÈNE IONESCU, from Shakespearean and 19th-century fairy tales, and from Salvador Dali's surrealist paintings. A distinction is drawn between the confusing, deafening world of the present and some imagined, far-off nirvana of peace and tolerance. The play dramatizes the "nine lives" of nine diverse characters—one is an outlandish hermaphrodite prostitute, Glorious. MacDonald's central argument is that lifestyles and sexual identities are necessarily more amorphous and fluid than Canadian conservatives would suggest.

MacDonald personally directed the 2002 production of *Divinity Bash* at the Du Maurier Theatre, Toronto: he has also won acclaim for his direction of work by gay playwrights TENNESSEE WILLIAMS and JOE ORTON (*CAT ON A HOT TIN ROOF* and *What the Butler Saw*). His direction of JUDITH THOMPSON's *Perfect Pie* won a 2002 Ottawa Capital Critics Circle Award. MacDonald has also produced musical shows inspired by popular Canadian musicians: *Sincerely, a Friend* celebrates Leonard Cohen's songs; *When All the Slaves Are Free* celebrates Joni Mitchell's work. MacDonald's most personal musical revue is *Shaking the Foundation*, an homage to the 1980s band Rough Trade, particularly its Carole Pope-written lyrics. Years previously, Pope's honest, upfront lesbianism partly influenced MacDonald's decision to come out. Despite the success of these musical shows and his directing, MacDonald continues to write plays, most recently *The Ecstasy of Bedridden Riding Hood* (2005) and *Beyond the Beaded Curtain* (2005).

MacDonald, a key voice in CANADA's growing canon of gay drama, uses his technical theatrical expertise to great effect when teaching at the National Theatre School of Canada, Montreal.

[*See also* Gay and Lesbian Drama]

PLAYS: *Whale Riding Weather* (1991); *The Weekend Healer* (1994); *Divinity Bash / Nine Lives* (publ. 1999); *The Ecstasy of Bedridden Ridinghood* (2005); *Beyond the Beaded Curtain* (2005)

FURTHER READING

Hastings, To. "Gay and Lesbian Writing." In *Encyclopedia of Literature in Canada*, ed. by William H. New. Toronto: Univ. of Toronto Press, 2002. 418–422.

Martin, Robert K. "Gay Literature." In *The Oxford Companion to Canadian Literature*, ed. by Eugene Benson and William Toye. Toronto: Oxford Univ. Press, 1997. 449–454.

Kevin De Ornellas

MACEDONIA

The proximity of ancient GREECE influenced the cultural life of the Slav tribes that settled in ancient Macedonia. Dionysian Bacchic rites and theatrical performances left deep traces, some of which are still present to this day in the folklore traditions of the Macedonian people. After the Hellenistic and Ilyrrico-Thracian period, Macedonia was for centuries under Roman dominion. Some Roman theatrical repertory was performed in amphitheaters in Macedonian settlements. The antagonism between the Old Slavic pagans and the Byzantine Christians marked the end of one culture and the beginning of another. Even after they accepted Christianity, the Macedonians preserved features of their ancient inheritance. During the five centuries of rule of Macedonia by the Ottoman Empire, between the 14th and the end of the 19th century, there was no theatrical activity in the European sense of the word. Some chamber theater performances were given by traveling showmen, *karagyoz* and *medahi* who entertained in the cafes and tearooms. The *karagyoz* tradition was similar to the Chinese theater of shadows.

During the Macedonian cultural revolution in the 19th century, attempts were made to use the local language and mother tongue in the theater. Theatrical performances played a major role in the Macedonian national emancipation. There were the so-called school theaters, initiated by the important pedagogue, philologist, and playwright Jovan Hadji Konstantinov-Djinot (1821–1882). The primary aim of his playwriting was patriotic and educational.

At the turn of the 20th century, playwright Voidan Chernodrinski (1875–1951), the founder of modern Macedonian theater, brought Macedonian culture under the influence of the theater of the Western world with his *Macedonian Blood Wedding* (1900). This process was also furthered by the regular performances of visiting theaters from Sofia and Belgrade and by the work of the followers of Djinot and Chernodrinski. This significant development was halted during the Balkans wars (1912–1913), when the territory of ethnic Macedonia was divided among BULGARIA, SERBIA, GREECE, and Albania.

During these times the Macedonian people fought for their own independence, a fight that used the theater as a weapon. A whole generation of authors started to write in their mother tongue. The most famous were Marko Cepenkov (1829–1920), Nikola Kirov-Majski (1880–1962), Anton Panov (1905–1968), Risto Krle (1900–1975), and Vasil Iljovski (1902–1995). Their plays were very popular and helped inspire the Macedonians in their struggle and rebellion for freedom. During the 1941–1944 antifascist National Liberation War, a theater of resistance developed, which produced plays such as *Hitler in His Death-Throes* by M. Shulakovski and *Giore of the Five Names* by Vlado Maleski. After 1945 the rapid development of postwar Macedonian theater was the work of a number of gifted playwrights who have embraced various genres and contemporary styles.

One of the most thematically and stylistically innovative is Kole Chashule (1921–), who began with psychological REALISM in *A Twig in the Wind* (1957) and later explored the harsh fate of his nation in *Darkness* (1961), *Whirlpool* (1968), and *Judgement* (1978).

But his work also deals with more universal phenomena such as totalitarianism and dictatorship, bureaucracy, and ALIENATION in *A Partiture for One Miron* (1967) and *As You Please* (1971).

At about the same time the prolific playwright Tome Arsovski (1928–) began his career. Works such as *The Paradox of Diogenes* (1961), *Hoops* (1965), and *A Step Into Autumn* (1969) were characterized by strong social commitment and analysis of social anomalies and their effect on the fate of the individual. In contrast to Arsovski's realism, Branko Pendovski (1927–) cultivated the tragic FARCE and the grotesque. The influence of the Theater of the Absurd is evident in such works as *Flood* (1974), *Travelling* (1978), and *Victim of the Pantheon* (1985). The work of Bogomil Gjuzel (1939–) is marked by a preoccupation with the demystifying of history and showing revolution as a destructive social phenomenon in *Alexiada* (1978), *Apocalypse* (1987), and *Adam and Eve and Job* (1971). Georgi Stalev (1930–) has a special place in contemporary Macedonian theater. He seeks inspiration in the rich tradition of folklore and archetypal myths in his poetic plays *The Wounded Hero* (1971) and *Angelina* (1972).

GORAN STEFANOVSKI (1952–) is a major figure in modern Macedonian drama and one of the most important and widely performed Macedonian playwrights of all time. As a representative of the third wave of 20th-century Macedonian writers, he speaks with a national voice, despite his absorption of Western European influences. In his work he shows his mastery of all the thematic materials that Macedonian drama had previously dealt with, but he is always looking ahead, never content to repeat himself. Stefanovski has an original and up-to-date way of looking at and analyzing the traditional Macedonian templates. His plays include *Jane Zadrogaz* (1974), *Wild Flesh* (1979), *Flying on the Spot* (1981), *Hi-Fi* (1983), *The False Bottom* (1984), *Tattooed Souls* (1985), *The Dishevelled Alphabet* (television serial, 1985), *The Black Hole* (1987), *Long Play* (1988), *Shades of Babel* (1989), and *Chernodrinski Is Coming Home* (1991). *Sarajevo (Tales from a City)* (1992–1993) was an international project that went on an extensive tour across Europe in the summer of 1993, including the London International Theatre Festival (Riverside Studios, Hammersmith) and the Hamburg International Summer Festival. *Bacchanalia* appeared in 1996, *Casabalkan* in 1997, and *Euralien* in 1998. *Euralien*, a huge site-specific project on the themes of alienation and nationalism, was commissioned by Intercult, Stockholm, for the 1998 European Cultural Capital; it was performed by fifty actors and staged by thirteen directors. *Hotel Europa* (2000) was a major European theatrical production and site-specific project, directed by nine Eastern European directors, which toured festivals in Vienna, Bonn, Avignon, Stockholm, and Bologna.

Jordan Plevnes (1953–) has most often dealt with themes from Macedonia's national past and present in *Erigon* (1982), *Mazedonische Zustande* (1984), and *R* (1987). Among other plays and playwrights one should mention *Mara's Wedding*, by Vladimir Kostov (1932–); *Nothing Without Tripholio* (1986), by Rusomir Bogdanovski (1948–); *Showaby Up* (1989) and *Dies Irae* (1990), by Zanina Mircevska (1967–); *The Powder Keg* (1992) and *The Balkans Are Not Dead* (1992), by Dejan Dukovski (1969–); *Whose Are You* (1991), by Sashko Nasev (1966–); *The Porcelain Vase* (1995), by Jugoslav Petrvski (1969–); *A Stake* (1985), by Bratislav Dimitrov (1952–); and *The Night in Which the Lantern Should Not Go Off* (1996), by Trajche Kacarov (1959–).

FURTHER READING

Aleksiev, Aleksandar. *Osnovopoložnici na makedonskata dramska literatura* [Founders of Macedonian Drama]. Skopje: Misla, 1972.

Ilic, Vojislav. *Lice i maska* [Face and Mask]. Skopje: NIO "studentski zbor," 1988.

Siljan, Rade. *Makedonska drama XIX i XX vek* [Macedonian Drama: The Nineteenth and Twentieth Centuries]. Skopje: Makedonska kniga, 1990.

Stefanovski, Risto. *Letopis na makedonskata drama i na teatarot vo Makedonija* [Review of Macedonian Drama and Theatre in Macedonia]. Skopje: Direkcija za kultura i umetnost, 1998.

——. *Teatarot vo Makedonija* [The Theater in Macedonia]. Skopje: Misla, 1990.

Risto Stefanovski

MACHADO, EDUARDO (1953–)

Eduardo Machado is an important contemporary Cuban American playwright many of whose works involve the displacement suffered by his family in the wake of the Cuban Revolution led by Fidel Castro. Born in Havana, CUBA, on June 11, 1953, he and his family fled to Florida after the Cuban Revolution and settled in the San Fernando Valley, close to Los Angeles. A precipitous drop in social standing caused a radical dislocation in the family members.

Machado started as an actor, but in 1977 he became associated with MARIA IRENE FORNES, who mentored his debut into playwriting. He has received three National Endowment for the Arts fellowships and a Rockefeller fellowship and currently heads the playwriting component of Columbia University's Theatre Arts Division.

Machado presents frescoes of large groupings of characters, allowing them to utter the unsayable, even as their greatest obsessions go unspoken. Machado's plays, like ANTON CHEKHOV's, capture onstage the critical point at which momentous political events intersect with and influence intimate family crises. He has authored over twenty-seven plays, such as *Don Juan in NYC* (1988), a baroque epic about a bisexual filmmaker's juggling of loves and career; *A Burning Beach* (1988), a play of political allegory, representing the U.S. takeover of Cuba following the Spanish American War in 1898; and *Havana Is Waiting* (2001), a dramatization of the playwright's return trip to his homeland in 1999.

His best and most representative works, however, are the four plays of The Floating Island series, notably *Fabiola* (1985) and *Broken Eggs* (1984). *Fabiola*, a play in six scenes, encompasses the years of Castro's rise to power through his takeover and eventual embracing of Soviet-style communism. The Marquez family, prosperous factory owners, at first enthusiastically back Castro with money and strategy, since he promises to stand up to the North American giant that has made Cuba a puppet. Cusa, the lady of the house, follows the revolution's progress on the radio, while a cousin, Octavio, bursts on the scene, his fingernails mutilated during a torture session with Batista's thugs. They never imagine being obliged to vacate their home altogether, even as it is confiscated by the government, or having to emigrate. Ultimately, Castro's *milicianos* swarm through the house, triumphantly ordering about their social superiors and toying with knickknacks. The brewing social upheaval is epitomized in the person of Sara, a servant, who is humiliated in the first act by her sister-in-law Clara. This same servant joins the revolution in the second act, refusing to aid the family, who, oblivious to the injustice in which they had been complicit, cannot fathom her disloyalty. In the play's foreground is a web of interpersonal conflicts among family members. Most prominent is the long-term sexual relationship between the two brothers, Osvaldo and the alcoholic Pedro, echoed by the patriarch Alfredo, who keeps a mistress. All these peccadilloes are swept under the carpet—known but unmentioned. Into the sexual and political threads is interwoven the story of Fabiola, Pedro's wife who had died but whose ghost apparently starts records playing and curtains fluttering. She represents the spirit of the carefree, sybaritic Cuba that is being banished forever.

Broken Eggs finds the same family, now displaced in California. The occasion is the wedding of Lizette, the young Americanized daughter, who is trying to bury her Latino roots by marrying the offspring of a Jewish family, the Rifkins. The setting is a waiting room of a "wedding mill" and so in the wings of the main action—the ceremony. Here, off to the side, we see how the family structure and traditional roles have all crumbled. Family members are afflicted by divorce, addictions to cocaine and alcohol, and infidelities. Some members, like the mother, are ineffectually clinging to lost traditions, even as they are forced into greater assimilation. The comic preparations for the wedding and the way they go dizzingly awry yield a parade of quick scenic encounters. Whatever should not happen to make for a successful wedding does happen, which results in a hilarious social FARCE. The title represents the fate of the family victimized by the revolution and the saying "You can't make an omelette without breaking a few eggs." What we see, then, is the dying gasp of Cuba's dynastic grandeur, rendered comic.

[*See also* Avant-Garde Drama; Political Theater in the United States]

PLAYS: *Worms* (1981); *Rosario and the Gypsies* (1982); *The Modern Ladies of Guanabacoa* (1983); *There's Still Time to Dance in the Streets of Rio* (1983); *Broken Eggs* (1984); *Fabiola* (1985); *When It's Over* (with Geraldine Sheman, 1987); *Why to Refuse* (1987); *A Burning Beach* (1988); *Don Juan in NYC* (1988); *Cabaret Bambu* (1989); *Related Retreats* (1990); *Stevie Wants to Sing the Blues* (1990); *In the Eye of the Hurricane* (1991); *Breathing It In* (1993); *Havana Is Waiting* (2001)

FURTHER READING
Machado, Eduardo. *The Floating Island Plays*. New York: Theatre Communications Group, 1991.
Madison, Cathy. "Writing Home." *American Theatre* (October 1991).
Osborn, M. Elizabeth. *On New Ground: Contemporary Hispanic-American Plays*. New York: Theatre Communications Group, 1987.

David Paul Willinger

MACHINAL

In the spring of 1927, SOPHIE TREADWELL attended a sensational trial in which Ruth Snyder, a Long Island housewife, and Judd Gray, her lover, were accused of murdering Snyder's husband; both were found guilty and executed in January 1928. Using the case as a springboard, Treadwell speculated on the circumstances that could have driven Snyder to commit such a violent act.

Described in the text as being a story of "a woman who murders her husband—an ordinary young woman, any woman," *Machinal* offers nine scenes, each depicting "the different phases of life that the woman comes in contact with and in none of which she finds any place, any peace." A nameless, "tender" Young Woman endures a harsh existence: clamoring officeworkers, a repulsive boss, a self-serving mother, an opportunistic lover, and at the end, an insensitive priest. Described by one critic as being "torn along with the current, weak and bruised, too unresourceful to save herself" (Atkinson, 1926), she must contend with marriage to the boss she does not love; momentary, joyful happiness comes in a love affair with a man who later testifies against her after she kills her husband.

When first produced at the Plymouth Theatre on September 7, 1928, Arthur Hopkins's directing and ROBERT EDMOND JONES's set and lighting matched Treadwell's spare, lean script. Brooks Atkinson (1926) described Jones's scenery as creating an atmosphere of "quiet delicacy and beauty" containing "no superfluous detail."

Machinal uses music and sound meant to assault the senses of the audience. Treadwell specifies that before the curtain rises, the audience hears the sounds of office machines that continue throughout the scene and accompany Young Woman's thoughts when the scene goes black; rapidly paced rhythms of machinery underscore and punctuate the clipped, hurried dialogue of officeworkers. When Young Woman attempts to talk with her mother at the dinner table, noise interferes: the buzzer, the janitor's voice, a baby's cry, and conversation coming through an open window. In Young Woman's cell, "the voice of a Negro singing, the whir of an aeroplane flying," and the droning prayers and chants of the priest all lend quiet terror to her last moments.

Reviewers were in accord with their praise of the 1928 showing, comparing the play favorably with ELMER RICE's ADDING

MACHINE and EUGENE O'NEILL's THE EMPEROR JONES and STRANGE INTERLUDE (Dickey, 1999). Oliver M. Sayler described *Machinal* as successfully merging "expressionist form and expressionist content," while Brooks Atkinson (1926) called the production "a triumph of individual distinction, gleaming with intangible beauty." He concluded that "*Machinal* speaks to the mind."

Machinal was produced in London in 1931 under the title *The Life Machine* and in Moscow in 1933. Treadwell, who traveled to Moscow, became the first American playwright to receive royalties from a Soviet production. In recent years, scholarly and critical interest in *Machinal* has grown, aided, in part, by two prominent productions: the New York Shakespeare Festival in 1990 and London's Royal National Theatre in 1993.

[*See also* Expressionism; Feminist Drama in the United States; United States, 1860–1929]

FURTHER READING

Atkinson, J. Brooks. "Against the City Clatter." *New York Times* (September 16, 1926).

Bywaters, Barbara L. "Marriage, Madness, and Murder in Sophie Treadwell's *Machinal*." In *Modern American Drama: The Female Canon*, ed. by June Schlueter. Madison, N.J.: Fairleigh Dickinson Univ. Press, 1990. 97–110.

Dickey, Jerry. "The Expressionist Moment: Sophie Treadwell." In *The Cambridge Companion to American Women Playwrights*, ed. by Brenda Murphy. Cambridge: Cambridge Univ. Press, 1999. 66–81.

Wynn, Nancy. "Sophie Treadwell: Author of *Machinal*." *Journal of American Drama and Theatre* 3 (Winter 1991): 29–47.

Sherry D. Engle

MACIVOR, DANIEL (1962–)

One of CANADA's most popular playwrights, Daniel MacIvor is also well known as an actor. Born in 1962 in Cape Breton, MacIvor has a theater company in Toronto where he now makes his home. With the assistance of producer Sherrie Johnson, da da kamera has become one of Toronto's foremost experimental theater companies.

MacIvor's plays almost always inquire into the nature of the theatrical medium. Self-reflexive performance vehicles, they always remind (and challenge) the audience about their relationship to the stage. In addition to their inquiry into theatrical presence, MacIvor's plays also often deconstruct identity (his plays have been called "postmodern") as character and actor blur and truth and fiction coincide. *Here Lies Henry* (1996), for example, plays on the double meaning of the title: we never really know if Henry is telling the truth. Another one-person show, *House* (1992) explores Victor's storytelling by using the device of a therapy group as the rationale for his inventions.

In their close attention to presence, theatrical and otherwise, MacIvor's plays depend as much on a precise theatrical design as they do on dialogue and text, constantly reminding the audience of an awareness and delight in the "now." Movement is often tightly choreographed; effects such as lighting and sound are integrated into textual choices. As vehicles for actors, his plays present performance challenges. Two of his fairly recent plays, *You are Here* (2002) and *Cul-de-Sac* (2003), are one-person shows that feature twelve and fifteen characters.

In particular, MacIvor's plays often deconstruct masculinity and a compulsory heterosexuality, as in *Never Swim Alone* (1993) and *2-2-Tango* (1992) MacIvor is openly gay, and many of his plays address sexuality. In *Never Swim Alone*, two men directly address the audience in a competition about their relative success, refereed by a girl on a lifeguard tower. As the play unfolds, the story of the girl becomes central to the relationship between the two men and an early childhood trauma. In *2-2-Tango*, the formal nature of the dance becomes a mechanism for exploring the relationship between Jim and James as they fall in love and drift apart.

Primarily trained as a performer, MacIvor usually acts in his own plays, often in one-person shows (*Wild Abandon* [1990], *House*, *Here Lies Henry*), drawing on his own considerable charisma. He also collaborates frequently with other theater artists, such as Daniel Brooks, who often directs his work. He has also written for and collaborated with actor Caroline Gillis. Though he draws on REALISM in *Marion Bridge* (1999) and *The Soldier Dreams* (1997), his most effective and most popular plays are those that challenge theatrical conventions and engage with the unexpected. In recent years, MacIvor has turned more to writing for film: he wrote and acted in *Past Perfect*, in 2002, his first feature film. His plays have garnered a number of awards—*House* and *Here Lies Henry* (Chalmers New Play Awards in 1991 and 1997); *In on It* (Village Voice Obie Award in 2002)—but they have not attracted much attention in academic circles.

[*See also* Gay and Lesbian Drama]

SELECT PLAYS: *See Bob Run & Wild Abandon* (1990); *House* (1992); *2-2 Tango* (1992); *Never Swim Alone* (1993); *This Is a Play* (1993); *Here Lies Henry* (1996); *The Soldier Dreams* (1997); *Theatre Omaha's Production of The Sound of Music* (1998); *Marion Bridge* (1999); *Monster* (1999); *In on It* (2001); *You Are Here* (2002); *Cul-de-Sac* (2003)

FURTHER READING

Knowles, Ric. *Theatre of Form and the Production of Meaning: Contemporary Canadian Dramaturgies*. Toronto: ECW Press, 1999.

MacIvor, Daniel. "This Is an Article." *Theatrum* (September–October 1992): 15–17.

Wallace, Robert. "The Victor(y) of the Subject." Introduction to Daniel MacIvor's *House Humans*. Toronto: Coach House Press, 1992. 7–14.

Wilson, Ann. "Lying and Dying: Theatricality in *Here Lies Henry*." *Canadian Theatre Review* 92 (Fall 1997): 39–41.

Marlene Moser

MACKAYE, PERCY (1875–1956)

When Percy MacKaye delivered the 1897 commencement address to his classmates at Harvard, titled "The Need of Imagination in the Drama of Today," he was already immersed in American theater. Three years earlier, he had lost his father, STEELE MACKAYE, who developed realistic scenography and supported realist drama. Though Percy worked closely with his father and was an enthusiastic promoter of his memory, the younger man was more interested in creating new symbolic and poetic theater. As a playwright, Percy found kinship with modernist designers Edward Gordon Craig and ROBERT EDMOND JONES, the latter a longtime friend of his.

MacKaye was born on March 16, 1875, in New York City. The earliest phase of his career focused on historic verse drama; his first success was with *The Canterbury Pilgrims* (1903), a dramatization of Geoffrey Chaucer's "The Wife of Bath's Tale," mounted in Atlanta. His other verse dramas, including *Jeanne d'Arc* (1906) and *Sappho and Phaon* (1907), were also more successful at university, amateur, and "little" theaters than on the major commercial stages.

His supernatural play *The Scarecrow* (1911) showed similar historic overtones but abandoned the limitations of verse. During its brief New York run, critics remarked that the play was "comparatively free of that pedantic humor which has marred so much of Mr. MacKaye's work." *The Scarecrow* proved to be MacKaye's most enduring play.

MacKaye is most noteworthy for his leadership in the historical and civic pageantry movement in America and for his theories about pageants as communal ritual. Devoted to the sociological purposes of theater, MacKaye worked to develop community performance, with large casts of amateur and professional actors, as a means of fostering social unity. MacKaye declared, "For community drama is nothing else than the technique of neighborliness—the art, *par excellence*, of resolving the estrangement and conflict of social elements into harmony."

MacKaye's first pageant was *The Gloucester Pageant* (1909), a revision of *The Canterbury Pilgrims* presented in Massachusetts with a cast of more than a thousand. *Caliban, by the Yellow Sands* (1916) was a pageant written to commemorate the tercentenary of William Shakespeare's death. Performed in New York (where it drew 15,000 spectators to each of its ten performances) and Boston, *Caliban* had 2,500 actors and featured a performance by Isadora Duncan. Robert Edmond Jones designed *Caliban* as well as *Washington* (1920), *The Evergreen Tree* (1917), and *The Roll Call* (1918).

During the 1920s, MacKaye worked less with historic pageants, seeking instead to promote community spirit by preserving the poetry and folktales of rural America, especially Appalachia; the results were *This Fine Pretty World* (1923) and *Napoleon Crossing the Rockies* (1924).

He also experimented with opera, writing *The Immigrants* (1914) and *Sinbad the Sailor* (1913) on commission by the Boston Opera House and adapting his play *The Canterbury Pilgrims* as an opera for the Metropolitan Opera House.

In 1920 MacKaye was appointed to the American Fellowship in Poetry and Drama at Miami University, Ohio. One of his final writing projects was *The Mystery of Hamlet, King of Denmark* (1943), a tetralogy of plays exploring the larger story of Old Hamlet. MacKaye died on August 31, 1956, in Cornish, New Hampshire.

[See also United States]

PLAYS: *A Maid of Lydon* (1900, with Evelyn Greenleaf); *The Canterbury Pilgrims* (1903); *Fenris the Wolf* (1905); *Jeanne d'Arc* (1906); *Sappho and Phaon* (1907); *Mater* (1908); *The Canterbury Pilgrims* (1909); *The Gloucester Pageant* (1909); *Anti-Matrimony* (1910); *A Garland to Sylvia* (1910); *A Masque of Labor* (1910); *The Scarecrow* (1911); *Chuck: An Orchard Fantasy* (1912); *Gettysburg: A Woodshed Commentary* (1912); *Sam Average* (1912); *Yankee Fantasies: Five One-Act Plays* (1912); *Sanctuary: A Bird Masque* (1913); *Sinbad the Sailor* (1913); *A Thousand Years Ago* (1913); *Tomorrow* (1913); *The Immigrants* (1914); *Saint Louis: A Civic Masque* (1914); *The Antick* (1915); *Caliban, by the Yellow Sands* (1916); *The New Citizenship: A Civic Ritual* (1916); *The Evergreen Tree: A Masque for Christmas* (1917); *The Roll Call* (1918); *The Will of Song* (1919); *Rip Van Winkle* (1920); *Washington: The Man Who Made Us* (1920); *The Cat Boat* (1921); *This Fine Pretty World* (1923); *Napoleon Crossing the Rockies* (1924); *Wakefield* (1932); *The Mystery of Hamlet, King of Denmark* (1943)

FURTHER READING

Brock, D. Heyward, and James M. Welsh. "Percy MacKaye: Community Drama and the Masque Tradition." *Comparative Drama* 6 (1972): 68–84.

Marks, Patricia. "*The Scarecrow*: Percy MacKaye's Adaptation of 'Feathertop.'" *Nathaniel Hawthorne Review* 14, no. 1 (Spring 1988): 13–15.

Potter, Vilma Raskin. "Percy MacKaye's Caliban for a Democracy." *Journal of American Culture* 19, no. 4 (Winter 1996): 71–79.

Quinn, Arthur Hobson. "Percy MacKaye and the Drama as Spectacle." In *A History of the American Drama from the Civil War to the Present Day*. New York: F. S. Crofts, 1936.

Smigel, Libby. "Sophocles and Shakespeare in the Nation's Service: Percy MacKaye's Theory of an American Popular Theatre." *Mid-Atlantic Almanac* 8 (1990): 35–56.

DeAnna M. Toten Beard

MACKAYE, STEELE (1842–1894)

James Morrison Steele MacKaye was born on June 6, 1842, in Buffalo, New York, to the wealthy northern family of Colonel James MacKaye and Emily Steele MacKaye. He traveled to Paris as a young man but returned home to join the Seventh Regiment of the Union army during the Civil War. Although an ardent abolitionist, malaria forced him to resign his original commission, so he returned as a volunteer and worked specifically with companies of black soldiers. Following the war, he returned to Europe and studied acting with François Delsarte in Paris. He later used this knowledge to become one of the earliest exponents of the Delsarte method in the UNITED STATES.

In October 1884 MacKaye founded America's first dramatic school, the Lyceum Theatre School of Acting in New York. His goals for the school were to promote Delsarte's theories of ACTING and to improve the condition of the acting profession in America. He told the first group of students, "Twenty-five years ago, when I desired to go on the stage, there was no school where I could prepare, except the ballet" (MacKaye, 1927). Six months later, in April 1885, MacKaye opened the companion Lyceum Theatre, which debuted with his play *Dakolar*.

MacKaye worked to develop training methods for more believable acting, and he was a supporter of the realistic drama then emerging in Europe. His interest in naturalistic stage illusion and the science of stagecraft was manifest in his many patents for new theater technology, many of which he actually realized. At Madison Square Garden, he created a two-story elevator stage, the "double stage," which made spectacular scene changes of large interior sets possible in less than one minute. MacKaye also redesigned other areas of Madison Square Garden, making the theater more appropriate for the new realistic trends in theater. He removed the proscenium doors, eliminated the forestage, and moved the orchestra pit to create additional seating closer to the stage.

His other theater inventions include air cooling, ventilation and purification systems, fireproofing of scenery, the sliding stage, the floating stage, and technological novelties like the "luxauleator" (curtain of light), the "nebulator" (cloud creator), and devices for creating sun, moon, and rainbow special effects.

MacKaye's most elaborate plans were for the Spectatorium, a theater for "musico-dramatic art" proposed for the 1893 Chicago World's Fair. The Spectatorium was to be enormous: 480 feet long, 380 feet wide, and 275 feet high; the stage opening was to be 150 feet wide and seventy feet high. The planned theater would have seated 10,000 spectators and showcased all of MacKaye's devices for theater spectacle. Because of the size, complexity, and cost of the project, the Spectatorium was never completed. Instead, he and his son PERCY MACKAYE built the Scenitorium, where he staged his final play, *The World Finder* (1894), an elaborate pageant depicting Christopher Columbus's journey to the New World. MacKaye died on February 25, 1894, on a train near Timpas, Colorado.

MacKaye was a prolific writer, publishing many articles during the 1880s about acting theory, new theater technology, and innovative stage design. He also wrote numerous plays, including pageants such as *The Drama of Civilization* (1886), written for Buffalo Bill Cody, and the highly successful MELODRAMA HAZEL KIRKE (1880).

SELECT PLAYS: *Marriage* (1872); *Monaldi* (with Francis Durivage, 1872); *Arkwright's Wife* (with Tom Taylor); *Clancarty* (with Tom Taylor, 1874); *Rose Michel* (1875); *Queen and Woman* (with J. V. Pritchard, 1876); *Twins* (with A. C. Wheeler, 1876); *Won at Last* (1877); *Through the Dark* (1879); *Hazel Kirke* (1880, first produced as *An Iron Will* in 1879); *A Fool's Friend* (1881); *Dakolar* (1885); *In Spite of All* (1885); *The Drama of Civilization* (1886); *Rienzi* (1886); *Paul Kauvar* (first produced as *Anarchy*, 1887); *A Noble Rogue* (1888); *Sir Alan's Wife* (1888); *An Arrant Knave* (1889); *Colonel Tom* (1890); *Money Mad* (1890); *The World Finder* (1894)

FURTHER READING

Fort, Tim. "Steele MacKaye's Lighting Visions for *The World Finder*." *Nineteenth Century Theatre* 18 (Summer–Winter 1990): 35–41.

MacKaye, Percy. *Epoch: The Life of Steele MacKaye, Genius of the Theatre.* New York: Boni & Liveright, 1927.

Ruyter, Nancy Lee Chalfa. "The Delsarte Heritage." *Dance Research* 14 (Summer 1996): 62–74.

Woodard, Debra J. "Steele MacKaye's *Marriage*: The Beginning of a Movement Toward American Realism." *Theatre Survey* 23 (November 1982): 189–195.

DeAnna M. Toten Beard

MACLEISH, ARCHIBALD (1892–1982)

Celebrated poet, playwright, and essayist Archibald MacLeish was born on May 7, 1892, in Glencoe, Illinois. He won Pulitzer Prizes for *Conquistador* (an epiclike chronicle of the conquest of Mexico, 1932), *Collected Poems 1917–1952*, and *J.B.: A Play in Verse* (a redaction of Job, 1958), and his *The Eleanor Roosevelt Story* (film script, 1965) received an Academy Award. He reflected the changing aesthetics and politics of 20th-century America. Two early poems in dramatic form, "Our Lady of Troy" (1917) and *Nobodaddy* (1926) assert the superiority of imagination and self-consciousness in an indifferent universe but stay within the aesthetic boundaries set in his famous poem *Ars Poetica*. While editing at *Fortune* magazine in the 1930s, his writing moved toward more engaged "public speech." In his works a lively mind wrestles rhetorically with the problem of uniting many individuals in one task, family or nation, while retaining individual freedom.

His ballet libretto *Union Pacific* (1934) lauds the Irish and Chinese railroad workers over the so-called empire builders. His first stage play *Panic* (1935) faults the pusillanimous capitalists and the Marxists. Believing a radical Blind Man's prophecy of capitalism's demise, hero J. P. McGafferty loses his ability to lead a chorus of Bankers and save the People in the street. McGafferty, his mistress, bankers, and radicals speak in five-beat lines; the street people, in three-beat lines.

MacLeish's "radio plays"—*Air Raid* (1938) and better THE FALL OF THE CITY (1937), anticipating a blitzkrieg and a conquest—more effectively use the same sprung rhythm and expressionistic place and "characters," plus a narrating Announcer, to demand American mobilization against the fascist forces. *The States Talking* (1941), literally, in verse, justifies the American system over the Axis's. *The American Story: Ten Radio Scripts* (1944) glorified the new continent by excerpting historical narratives of discovery and exploration. His verse plays *The Trojan Horse* (1952) and

This Music Crept by Me Upon the Waters (1953) were both staged after initial broadcasts. While *This Music* laments passing opportunities, he intended the Greek-filled horse that Troy accepts to parallel the monstrously destructive lie of McCarthyism.

J.B. is MacLeish's most appreciated drama. A modern Job, surviving the wager between divine Zuss and diabolic Nickles that triggers the devastation of his life, declares that self-conscious love, not faith or reason, allows him to continue. Critics have faulted MacLeish's plays for their lack of sympathetic characters. *Scratch* (in prose, 1971) argues the balance between freedom and the Union as Daniel Webster, flawed by his vote for the Fugitive Slave Law, defeats the Devil to redeem himself and a sold soul. MacLeish's verse TRAGEDY *Herakles* (1965) is underestimated. Returning from triumphant labors that cleansed the world of monsters, a Nobel-winning scientist and Herakles must face their madness: murdering their wives and sons in metaphor and the myth.

MacLeish died on April 20, 1982, in Boston, Massachusetts.

[*See also* United States]

PLAYS: *Our Lady of Troy* (1917); *Nobodaddy* (1926); *Union Pacific: An American Folk Ballet in One Act and Four Scenes* (1934); *Panic: A Play in Verse* (1935); *The Fall of the City*; *A Verse Play for Radio* (1937); *Air Raid: A Verse Play for Radio* (1938); *The States Talking* (1941); *The American Story: Ten Radio Scripts* (1944); *The Trojan Horse: A Play* (1952); *This Music Crept by Me Upon the Waters: A Play* (1953); *J.B.: A Play in Verse* (1958); *The Secret of Freedom* (1960); *The American Bell* (1962); *The Dialogues of Archibald MacLeish and Mark VanDoren* (1962); *The Eleanor Roosevelt Story* (1965); *Herakles: Verse Play* (1965); *An Evening's Journey to Conway, Massachusetts: An Outdoor Play* (1967); *The Play of Herod* (adaptation of a Medieval Mystery Play, 1968); *Scratch* (1971); *The Great American Fourth of July Parade: A Verse Play for Radio* (1976)

FURTHER READING

Donaldson, Scott, with R. H. Winnick. *Archibald MacLeish: An American Life.* Boston: Houghton, 1992.

MacLeish, Archibald. *A Time to Speak.* Boston: Houghton, 1941 [essays].

Smith, Grover C. *Archibald MacLeish.* Minneapolis: Univ. of Minnesota Press, 1975.

John G. Kuhn

MACLEOD, JOAN (1954–)

Joan MacLeod was born in 1954 in Vancouver, British Columbia. She earned creative writing degrees from the University of Victoria (B.A., 1978) and the University of British Columbia (UBC) (M.F.A., 1981). After graduating from UBC she set off for the Banff School of Fine Arts to attend a six-week-long poetry workshop but soon discovered the adjacent workshop for playwrights and immediately, in her own words, "got hooked." She did not begin writing for the theater until she was thirty-one.

In 1985 the Tarragon Theatre in Toronto, Ontario, readily accepted JEWEL, her first play, and asked MacLeod to join its Playwrights Unit that same year. She became the playwright-in-residence at Tarragon for six years, and after their production of *Jewel* in 1987, her next three plays, *Toronto, Mississippi* (1987), *Amigo's Blue Guitar* (1990), *The Hope Slide* (1992), all premiered at the Tarragon as well. But MacLeod's first produced work for the theater came two years before *Jewel. The Secret Garden*, a libretto based on the classic Victorian novel and written with composer Stephen MacNeff, was presented by Toronto's Comus Music Theatre in 1985 and won MacLeod a Dora Mavor Moore Award for best new musical.

Jewel is a one-act, one-character play that takes place on Valentine's Day in 1985. Marjorie Clifford is a young widow who attempts to reconcile her current and past selves by conversing with her dead husband, a victim of the 1981 *Ocean Ranger* oil-rig disaster. The play received both Dora and Chalmers Award nominations and was later reworked as a radio production titled *Hand of God*.

Although MacLeod's preferred dramatic format is the monologue—and she in fact begins writing each of her plays this way—only *Jewel, The Hope Slide*, and *The Shape of a Girl* (2001) keep as their visual focus the figure of a solitary woman onstage. *The Hope Slide* won the Chalmers Canadian Play Award in 1993. It charts the journey of an actress who, by using her own traveling show about Doukhobors as a vehicle, tries to come to terms with the AIDS epidemic and the death of her best friend. In *The Shape of a Girl* we see a young teenager who again grapples with the idea of senseless death, even though the dead is this time not a loved one but someone she only knows through others. Drawing on MacLeod's own experience as a life-skills mentor, *Toronto, Mississippi* tells the story of a single mother and her mildly mentally handicapped daughter Jhana and the upset this mother-daughter relationship undergoes when Jhana's estranged father, an Elvis impersonator, makes an impromptu appearance.

Amigo's Blue Guitar won the Governor General's Award for drama in 1991 and, like *Toronto, Mississippi*, probes the meaning of family. When a Salvadoran refugee is sponsored to fulfill a college project requirement, neither he nor the British Columbia family he comes to live with anticipate the degree of compassion and frustration that a shift in their respective family dynamics will bring about. *Little Sister* (1994) examines the psychology of eating disorders and in 1995 won the Chalmers Award in the Theatre for Young Audiences category. MacLeod's play *2000* (1996) delves into the world of a middle-aged, middle-class couple who exemplify living at the edge and the anxieties this position necessarily produces.

MacLeod currently lives in Victoria, British Columbia, and teaches in the University of Victoria's Department of Writing.

[*See also* Canada]

PLAYS: *Jewel* (1985, revised 1987); *Toronto, Mississippi* (1987); *Amigo's Blue Guitar* (1990); *The Hope Slide* (1992); *Little Sister* (1994); *2000* (1996); *The Shape of a Girl* (2001); *Homechild* (2006)

FURTHER READING

Leyshon, Glynis. Preface to *The Hope Slide*, by Joan MacLeod. Burnaby: Talonbooks, 1999. 11–13.

McIntyre, Joanna. Preface to *Little Sister*, by Joan MacLeod. Burnaby: Talonbooks, 1999. 47.

Wasserman, Jerry, ed. "Joan MacLeod." In *Modern Canadian Plays: Vol. II*, 4th ed. Vancouver: Talonbooks, 2001. 225–227.

Michelle Lindenblatt

MACLIAMMÓIR, MICHEÁL (1899–1978)

Am I beautiful too? Of course I am. Still beautiful. Look.

—Micheál MacLiammóir *All for Hecuba*, 1946

Micheál MacLiammóir, actor, designer, and author, was born on October 25, 1899, in Willesden, London, as Alfred Willmore. His father dealt in oats for London horse stables. In his autobiographical novel *Enter a Goldfish* (1977), MacLiammóir says that when he first saw his mother with her top off, he wished to have two such beautiful breasts himself, and at his first pantomime, he admired the legs of the actor playing Dick Whittington. OSCAR WILDE became young Alfred Willmore's hero as the homosexual aesthete. At age eleven, he was cast for a part, along with NOËL COWARD, in Lila Field's *Goldfish*, the beginning of a career as a beautiful child star with the nickname "Bubbles." In 1912, he played Oliver Twist opposite Beerbohm Tree. After his voice broke, Willmore, a talented book illustrator, attended art school. Reading W. B. YEATS's essays inspired him with a passion for Celtic aestheticism.

He moved to IRELAND during World War I, joined the Gaelic League, and by 1919 called himself Micheál MacLiammóir from Cork, a second identity he maintained until his death. In the late 1920s, he found work onstage with the traveling Shakespeare company of Anew McMaster, his brother-in-law. There he met his partner and lifelong love, Hilton Edwards, an actor and director. After starting up the first Irish-language theater in Ireland, An Taibhdhearc, which premiered his first play, *Diarmuid agus Grainne* (August 27, 1928), MacLiammóir started a new theater company in Dublin, the Gate, which at first operated out of the Abbey Theatre's studio space ("The Peacock") and later acquired a home at the Rotunda, a prominent city-center building, where the Gate still thrives.

The daring style of Edwards's direction paired with MacLiammóir's glamorous acting and decorative designs won the admiration of Irish audiences. In the 1930s, the Gate shows surpassed those of the Abbey Theatre in production values. MacLiammóir and Edwards gave a uniquely satisfying representation of Denis Johnston's *The Old Lady Says, "No!"* (1929), an expressionist fantasia rejected by the Abbey. MacLiammóir's Hamlet was celebrated in Dublin (he continued to play the part into his mid-fifties), but

it failed to impress London audiences. His acting was often romantic and grandiloquent, not in the more psychological style of his more famous rival, Lawrence Olivier. MacLiammóir plays Iago as a homosexual in Orson Welles's *Othello* (1952), his best acting to be caught on film.

The greatest success of MacLiammóir's many roles and thirteen plays was a one-man show on the life of Wilde, *The Importance of Being Oscar* (1963), which went on a profitable world tour and influenced other shows of the kind, such as Simon Callow's *The Mystery of Charles Dickens* (2000).

MacLiammóir died on March 6, 1978, in Dublin, Ireland. The Dublin funeral of the beloved actor was attended by thousands, including the leaders of the Irish government.

[*See also England*]

PLAYS: *Diarmuid agus Grainne* (1928); *The Ford of the Hurdles* (1929); *Easter 1916* (1930); *Where Stars Walk* (1940); *Dancing Shadows* (1941); *Ill Met by Moonlight* (1946); *Home for Christmas* (1950); *The Importance of Being Oscar* (1963); *Prelude in Kasbek Street* (1973)

FURTHER READING

Barrett, John, ed. *Selected Plays of Micheál MacLiammóir. Irish Drama Selections.* Washington, D.C.: Catholic Univ. of America Press; Gerrards Cross, Bucks.: Colin Smythe, 1995.

Fitz-Simon, Christopher. *The Boys: A Double Biography.* London: Nick Hern, 1994.

MacLiammóir, Micheál. *Enter a Goldfish: Memoirs of an Irish Actor, Young and Old.* London: Thames & Hudson, 1977.

Adrian Frazier

MADAME DE SADE

Madame de Sade (*Sado Kōshaku Fujin*, 1965), a three-act Japanese SHINGEKI play by MISHIMA YUKIO, premiered at his theater company the New Literary Theatre (NLT). The most highly formalized play in Mishima's oeuvre, it presents conversations in the drawing room of Madame de Montreuil, mother of Renee, Marquise de Sade, in the years 1772, 1778, and 1790. Every monologue and conversation is devoted to the attempt to understand who de Sade really is and what *he* means to France, to society, to politics, and to the lives of each of the women. Alphonse, the Marquis de Sade, never appears in the play.

The author himself best states his inspiration and intentions: Reading *The Life of the Marquis de Sade* by Shibusawa Tatsuhiko I was most intrigued by the riddle of why the Marquise de Sade, after having demonstrated such absolute fidelity to her husband during his long years in prison, should have left him the moment that he was at last free. This riddle served as the point of departure for my play, which is an attempt to provide a logical solution.

This play might be described as "Sade seen through women's eyes." I was obliged therefore to place Madame de Sade at the center, and to consolidate the theme by assigning all the other parts to women. Madame de Sade stands for wifely devotion; her mother, for law, society, and morality; Madame de Simiane for religion; Madame de Saint-Fond for carnal desires; Anne, Madame de Sade's younger sister, for feminine guilelessness and lack of principles; and the servant Charlotte, for the common people. I had to involve these people with Madame de Sade and make them revolve around her, with something like the motions of the planets. (Mishima, 1967)

The solution to the riddle that induced Mishima to write the play—why Madame de Sade refused to meet her husband ever again after he left prison—is constructed from Madame de Sade's own convictions and her understanding of what the other women tell her about carnal desire, Christian purity and salvation, and self-preservation. Madame de Sade creates a beautiful, idealized image of her husband, in which "he piles evil on evil, and mounts on top, building a back stairway to heaven" (Mishima, 1967). Her memories of him as a blond, handsome youth are "as if preserved in amber." When told of his current physical decrepitude, she is unwilling to relinquish her fantasies and memories and face the sordid reality of what her husband has become.

Madame de Sade has enjoyed more stage performances than any Mishima play except for *Rokumeikan* and has a strong record of performance abroad. A 1995 survey of fifty-four Japanese theater scholars and critics concluded that *Madame de Sade* is JAPAN's finest 20th-century play.

[*See also Shin Kabuki*]

FURTHER READING

Canby, Vincent. "Theater Review, Mishima's View of Marquis de Sade." *New York Times* (June 9, 1995). http://theater2.nytimes.com/men/theater/treview.html?res=990CE1D9143BF93AA35755C0A963958260

Domoto Masaaki. *Gekijin Mishima Yukio* [Yukio Mishima the dramatist]. Tokyo: Geki Shobo, 1994.

Mishima Yukio. *Five Modern No Plays*. Tr. by Donald Keene. New York: Knopf, 1957.

———. *Madame de Sade*. Tr. by Donald Keene. New York: Grove, 1967.

Laurence Kominz

THE MADMAN AND THE NUN

In the anthill civilization which is coming individualism will be limited like a man in a strait jacket. . . . True artists . . . will be kept in special institutions for the incurably sick and will be, as vestigial specimens of former humanity, the subject of research by psychiatrists.

—Stanisław Witkiewicz, *New Forms in Painting*, 1918

Written in 1923 and first staged in 1924, *The Madman and the Nun* [*Wariat i zakonnica*], or *There Is Nothing Bad Which Could Not Turn Into Something Worse* is one of STANISLAW IGNACY ("Witkacy") WITKIEWICZ's most widely performed dramas. Dedicated to "all the madmen of the world," the play takes as its theme the tyranny of society over the individual. The author himself felt threatened by insanity—an expression of rebellious individuality—and the play may be considered an ironic portrait of the artist.

In *The Madman and the Nun* (the title of one of Witkacy's paintings exhibited in 1921), the creative personality becomes victim of cultural repression when science and state, abetted by religion, form a totalitarian alliance to bring about enforced happiness and social tranquility through psychiatric confinement. Witkacy's decadent poet and drug addict Walpurg exemplifies the destiny of exceptional beings who are locked in padded cells and trapped in ever-widening circles of incarceration by body, family, and society.

The Freudian psychiatrist Grün hopes to cure Walpurg by rendering him normal and restoring him to society lobotomized of the madness that constitutes his genius. The fettered poet (whose consciousness alone is free) and the psychic healer prying into the recesses of his brain are a complementary pair. Grün is both the observing self, voyeuristically watching the instinctual behavior of his alter ego, and the controlling self attempting to curb the explosive creative energy of his double. The doctor alternately provides Walpurg with paper and pencil—tools of creation—and binds his arms in a straitjacket, encouraging his art and yet restricting it. Grün reduces PSYCHOANALYSIS to a mechanistic system for fabricating puppets ready for the anthill society.

As the only way out of imprisonment, Walpurg seduces his nurse (the beautiful Sister Anna), murders one of his doctors, and hangs himself. Here Witkacy introduces a spectacular coup de theater that cancels the seemingly inevitable tragic ending. Stepping over his own corpse lying on the floor, the handsome young Walpurg—an elegantly dressed dandy—enters the cell, bids farewell to his keepers, who are now locked up as insane, and goes off to town with Anna. Witkiewicz's favored device of the risen corpse violates the laws of both nature and conventional dramatic logic; the play subverts its own premises and calls into question the entire rational world that constructs madhouses. Walpurg's feat of dissociation—splitting in two and leaving behind his outer shell—is deeply ambiguous. Has the poet created a new form for himself or merely accepted society's validation of a stereotype? Are his suicide and escape a triumph of mind over matter or a step backward on the treadmill of Eternal Recurrence, repeating the same punitive story?

Pure Form (the modality of the final act) can allow for multiple endings and accommodate contradictory meanings. In the double denouement of *The Madman and the Nun* Witkacy, incorporating Werner Heisenberg's principle of complementarity and Niels Bohr's uncertainty principle, plays bold theatrical tricks on the audience in order to dispose of the dead conventions of stage REALISM along with Walpurg's dead body. Witkacy's protest against psychiatric confinement anticipates strategies of the post-1968 AVANT-GARDE: creative madness, anarchic violence, liberating sexuality, and emancipation through dreams.

[See also Poland]

FURTHER READING

Gerould, Daniel. *Witkacy: A Critical Study of Stanisław Ignacy Witkiewicz as an Imaginative Writer.* Washington, D.C.: Univ. of Washington Press, 1980.

Witkiewicz, Stanisław Ignacy. *The Madman and the Nun.* New York: Applause Books, 1990.

——. *The Witkiewicz Reader,* ed. and tr. by Daniel Gerould. Evanston, Ill.: Northwestern Univ. Press, 1992.

Daniel Gerould

THE MADNESS OF GEORGE III

Late in ALAN BENNETT's play *The Madness of George III,* and film *The Madness of King George,* the recovering King George presses his Lord Chancellor Thurlow to act out the reunion scene of Lear and Cordelia. Hearing George's compassionate rendition of Lear's speech, Thurlow finds the king seems more like himself. George sagely replies, "I have always been myself—I have just learned how to seem. What, what?" George's "what, what?" confirms that his sanity has returned, but his slant on appearance becomes the pivotal metaphor in Bennett's play, a complex, seriocomic drama with political overtones appropriate to both the 18th and 19th centuries.

The Madness of George III chronicles, with poetic license, the troubled rule of George III—known affectionately as "Farmer George" to his subjects because he loved the land and its people. George's monarchy is threatened when he suffers from the neurological disease porphyria, which turns his urine blue and him temporarily demented. The play opens with George angered over the loss of the American colonies. Members of his court, including his faithful wife Queen Charlotte and their fifteen children, cannot help but notice as he descends from a plain, pedantic lord into a sleepless, often delirious paranoid. George surrenders to his irrational fears of a second Noah's Flood and acts out his suppressed erotic fantasies by assaulting the matronly Lady Pembroke, the queen's mistress of robes. The deranged monarch is surrounded by a circle of family, friends, and foes all far madder than he. Consumed by fever, he loses his capacities and his freedom as Parliament brews with disloyalty and upheaval. When sane, George uses the phrase "what, what!" in order to fill the spaces in his conversation. When mad, context disappears, and his problems become paranoia and incessant chatter.

Diagnosing his madness invites problems because, as king, George's actions are beyond questioning. Nonetheless, the fat, petulant, fashionable Prince of Wales ("Prinny"), seeing his father's weakness as an opportunity to control the crown, rallies a slew of supporters including the great orator Charles James Fox. Fox, crazy for power, leads the struggle against the famous British prime minister, Pitt the Younger who, for Ben-

nett, is a sexually repressed alcoholic, aloof, robotic, preoccupied with parsimony, and desperately clinging to his office by utterly denying the king's illness. Secreted away, George is treated by ignorant doctors whose barbaric methods include bleeding, scalding, and restraint. Conspirators deny Charlotte access to George, and the king consequently becomes an isolated, Lear-like figure at the mercy of charlatans and cruelty. Coincidentally, when a new doctor, Dr. Willis, is engaged, the king shows signs of improvement. Yet the king's salvation relies on time and on the support of the most potent medicine—the queen herself.

The play spotlights the power games, family scandals, and personal intrigues that take place under an incapacitated ruler. Within its COMEDY, *Madness* raises provocative questions about leadership and public perception. Bennett challenges viewers to weigh their allegiances, determine when facts are credible, and question whether following impaired authority is prudent.

[See also England, 1940–Present]

FURTHER READING

Bennett, Alan. *The Madness of George III.* London: Faber & Faber, 1992.

Kendle, Burton S. "Alan Bennett." In *Contemporary Dramatists,* ed. by K. A. Berney. 1973. 5th ed., London: St. James, 1993.

Wu, Duncan. *Six Contemporary Dramatists: Bennett, Potter, Gray, Brenton, Hare, Ayckbourn.* London: St. Martin's, 1995.

LynnDianne Beene

MADSEN, SVEND ÅGE (1939–)

Freud: Which story . . . why are you against my theories?
Pirandello: Because you try to make man a rattling machine tied to one single story from which he can't liberate himself.—I think we have innumerable stories inside us from which we choose.
— Act 1, *Naked Masks*

Svend Åge Madsen's work is marked by constant experiments with the possibilities of fiction and an extensive relativism, making him akin to authors like LUIGI PIRANDELLO and Jorge Luis Borges. He is not an easily accessible writer, but his self-reflecting works with their changing narrator perspectives and often very complicated network of parallel actions and stories have nevertheless procured him a large public in DENMARK and abroad, especially in FRANCE. He is primarily known for his novels or antinovels but has also written a good twenty plays for stage and radio—*Svejk in the Third World War* (*Svejk I 3. Verdenskrig,* 1984), *Dr Strangelove* (1985), *The Last Sigh* (*Det sidste suk,* 1986), and *Naked Masks* (*Nøgne masker,* 1987), all four written when he was a dramatist in residence at Århus Theatre.

Naked Masks is a typical Madsen work and one of his most interesting plays, confronting two highly influential cultural personalities of the last century: Pirandello and Sigmund Freud. During this fictive meeting, Madsen also gets an opportunity for self-reflection. Like Pirandello, Madsen does not tell stories only for the stories' sake. He belongs to what Pirandello called the "philosophical" writers who admit solely stories and characters that have been soaked in a particular sense of life—the author's—to acquire from it a universal value. Madsen has a fancy for playing with genres and styles. *Naked Masks* operates on three stylistic levels. On the left part of the stage, representing Pirandello's study, the acting style is "Italian social REALISM"; on the central stage, the ruins of a Greek roman theater in Sicily and the acting place of Pirandello and his theater troupe, the style is "symbolic, playful and theatrical"; and on the right side of the stage, the quay of the Tiber, where Pirandello and Freud confront each other, the style is "COMEDY." The play is also characteristic of Madsen's Chinese box technique and numerous mystifications. At the beginning of *Naked Masks*, a group of actors is planning a play on Pirandello's life in which Freud, who is on a short vacation in Rome, becomes involved with the result that we are continuously left in doubt about when Pirandello is Pirandello or an actor who acts Pirandello and when Freud is the real doctor from Vienna or an actor.

Freud enters the play to solve a problem on the central stage where Pirandello and his actors live in a state of harmony in mutual love to the mystic woman Laura who once was washed ashore like the seaborn Venus. The harmony is broken when Laura's son Doro arrives from the war and claims to know his father's identity. Freud is rapidly changing the play into an Ibsenite TRAGEDY with relentless unveiling of the past, raising doubts about whether the former happy Arcadia can ever be restored.

Madsen makes heavy intellectual demands on his audience, but *Naked Masks* is also an extremely witty play—for example, the two central scenes where Freud and Pirandello relieve each other on the bench of the psychiatrist. In the first confrontation, dealing with the question of whether man is bound to one single story or contains many different stories, Pirandello seems to have the leading hand. Against Freud's Oedipus complex Pirandello comes up with a Robinson Crusoe complex, built on man's fundamental feeling of being totally alone in the world as if he were on an isolated island—a basic situation leaving man free to create himself from scratch without becoming a slave of his past. During this confrontation, Freud listens attentively to Pirandello's interpretations of his dreams as symptoms of his fear of change and longing for creating a new identity for himself. The second confrontation is more complex. Here Freud takes over to prove that Pirandello's relativism is nothing but an escape from responsibility and leaves a still more dizzy Pirandello, who at the end of the play receives his doom from The Unknown, a throughgoing symbolic figure and commentator: "You shall pursue life, reach out for it—and perpetually see it disappear. You shall gain fame and honour—and in your heart know that your works become more and more lifeless, empty and fossilized"—a doom not only applied to Pirandello but also to the postmodernist Svend Åge Madsen?

SELECT PLAYS: *Hopla, We . . . Dot, Dot, Dot* (*Hopla, vi . . . prik, prik, prik,* 1967); *In Reality* (*I virkeligheden,* radio play, 1972); *Kasper in Search of Existence* (*Kasper søger efter tilværelsen,* radio play, 1982); *Svejk in the Third World War* (*Svejk I 3. Verdenskrig,* 1984); *Dr Strangelove* (1985); *The Last Sigh* (*Det sidste suk,* 1986); *Naked Masks* (*Nøgne masker,* 1987); *The Theatre of Death* (*Dødens Teater,* 1987); *The Copyist* (*Kopisten,* 1994)

FURTHER READING

Christoffersen, Erik Exe. *Teaterpoetik* [Theater poetics]. Århus: Klim, 1997.

Gemzøe, Anker. *Metamorfoser i Mellemtiden. Studier i Svend Åge Madsens forfatterskab 1962–1986* [Metamorphosis in the meantime. Studies of Svend Åge Madsen's work 1962–1986]. Holte: Medusa, 1997.

Kela Kvam

MAETERLINCK, MAURICE (1862–1949)

Maurice Maeterlinck was born on August 29, 1862, in Ghent. His greatest contribution was to bring the ideals of the symbolist movement to the dramatic stage. Beneath the surface of a conventional upbringing—Jesuit schooling followed by a degree in law—Maeterlinck consistently nurtured an interest in writing, publishing his first poem in *La Jeune Belgique* in 1883. After graduating from law school in 1885, Maeterlinck moved to Paris, where he befriended poet Stéphane Mallarmé and novelist Villiers de l'Isle Adam, both of whom encouraged Maeterlinck to develop his writing in accord with the burgeoning symbolist movement.

Maeterlinck returned to BELGIUM in 1886, and with the publication of his play *Princess Maleine* (*La Princesse Maleine*) in 1889, he achieved sudden fame. Octave Mirbeau reviewed the as-yet-unperformed script in *Le Figaro* (Aug. 24,1890), proclaiming it "the work of this age most full of genius, and the most extraordinary and most simple as well." Despite his newfound celebrity, Maeterlinck's work was not performed until 1891, when Paul Fort's Théâtre d'Art hesitantly included *The Intruder* at the end of a matinee program. A production of *The Blind* later that year featured a performance by Aurélien Lugné-Poë, who would become an important director of the playwright's work. Traditional plot development was anathema in Maeterlinck's writing, which required exploration of new staging techniques. Lugné-Poë's staging of a single matinee production of *Pelléas and Mélisande* (*Pelléas at Mélisande*) in 1893, for example, was influenced by the moody paintings of Puvis de Chavannes and featured a bare stage separated from the audience by a gauze curtain, lending the action behind it a dreamlike quality. The production was lit unconventionally from above, and the actors spoke with an artificial intonation.

Maeterlinck's works of the 1890s constituted a reaction against naturalist preoccupations. Like other symbolist artists, Maeterlinck explored the ineffable and the mystical, relishing moods of angst and dread. Although Maeterlinck's plays knew little success on the English-speaking stage, their influence was far-reaching. ANTON CHEKHOV was a great admirer of Maeterlinck, recommending his works to the MOSCOW ART THEATRE; VSEVOLD MEYERHOLD turned to Maeterlinck's plays repeatedly to test staging techniques for his "New Drama." In 1902, Claude Debussy's operatic version of *Pelléas and Mélisande* premiered after nine years of preparation, securing Maeterlinck's place in the history of opera. ANTONIN ARTAUD considered Maeterlinck the first to introduce "the diverse wealth of the unconscious" into literature, and some critics view Maeterlinck as a precursor to the Theater of the Absurd. For a time, his works became less pessimistic, as testified by his popular *The Blue Bird* (*L'Oiseau Bleu* 1908), which was twice adapted for film.

In 1911, Maeterlinck won the Nobel Prize for Literature. Shortly thereafter, as a result of his prose work *Death* (*La Mort*), Maeterlinck was placed on the Index of the Catholic Church, and his complete works were prohibited. After 1920, his physical health and literary abilities declined. His marginal position was exacerbated by his move to the UNITED STATES from 1939 to 1946. His last years were spent secluded with his wife, Renée Dahon, in Nice, where his literary output dwindled. Maeterlinck died on May 6, 1949, in Orlamonde near Nice.

[*See also* France; Naturalism; Symbolism]

SELECT PLAYS: *Princess Maleine* (*La Princesse Maleine*, 1889); *The Intruder* (*L'Intruse*, 1891); *The Blind* (*Les aveugles*, 1891); *Pelléas and Mélisande* (*Pelléas at Mélisande*, 1893); *Interior* (*Intérieur*, 1894); *The Death of Tintagiles* (*La Mort de Tintagiles*, 1894); *Monna Vanna* (1902); *The Blue Bird* (*L'Oiseau Bleu*, 1908); *The Betrothal* (*Les Fiançailles*, 1918)

FURTHER READING

Halls, W. D. *Maurice Maeterlinck: A Study of His Life and Thought*. Oxford: Oxford Univ. Press, 1960.

Knapp, Bettina. *Maurice Maeterlinck*. New York: G. K. Hall, 1975.

Konrad, Linn Bratteteig. *Modern Drama as Crisis: The Case of Maurice Maeterlinck*. New York: Peter Lang, 1986.

Daniel Mufson

MAFUNE YUTAKA (1902–1977)

Japanese SHINGEKI and SHINPA playwright, director, novelist, and theater group founder, Mafune Yutaka was born in 1902 to a wealthy landowner and sake brewer in Fukushima, JAPAN. He was adopted in boyhood by a successful businessman and family friend in Hokkaidō. Treated as a common houseboy, Mafune awoke to the ugliness of human nature. He soon fled from his adopted household back to Fukushima.

As a student of English literature at Waseda University in Tokyo, Mafune was introduced to the works of such classic modern Western playwrights as J. M. SYNGE, HENRIK IBSEN, and AUGUST STRINDBERG and to the revolutionary syndicalism of the Irish revolutionary James Connolly. Inspired by Connolly and others, Mafune left school to engage in rural activism in provin-

cial Japan. Mafune's first play, *The Weasel* (*Itachi*, 1931), written while in forced confinement at his father's house, deals with landlord-peasant conflict and was written entirely in the local dialect of Fukushima. *The Weasel*, directed by KUBOTA MANTARŌ at the Sôsakuza in 1934, won critical acclaim that established Mafune's firm foundation as a successful playwright.

Later Mafune turned his pen from a single-minded depiction of the dark, ugly side of human nature to satire, devotedly writing a series of plays in that genre, including *Children of the Sun* (*Taiyō no Ko*, 1936), *The Naked City* (*Hadaka no Machi*, 1936), *The Stranger* (*Mishiranu Hito*, 1936), *Escapade* (*Tonsōfu*, 1937), *Mold* (*Kabi*, 1938), and *Deserted Garden* (*Haien*, 1938), all of which were staged by *shingeki*, *shinpa*, and *shinkokugeki* theater groups; a few were also adapted to film.

The end of World War II marked a critical turning point in Mafune's work. He changed his topics from satiric to human COMEDY, starting with *Nakahashi Household* (*Nakahaski Kōkan*, 1946), which deals with a Japanese family stuck in CHINA after the end of the war. From 1948 on, Mafune was also markedly active in writing scripts for radio drama, such as *Snow*, *The Owl*, *The Sleeping Cat*, and *Winter Chats*.

In the 1950s, he dedicated most of his energies to FARCE, establishing his own studio theater, Mafune Yutaka Library Theatre (Mafune Yutaka Shosai Gekijō) for the production and staging of his own plays. Famed actor-director SENDA KOREYA was a self-styled devotee of Mafune and presented Mafune's plays *The Yellow Room* (*Kiiro no Heya*, 1943) and *Nakahashi Household* in hopes of revitalizing the *shingeki* movement in the early postwar period. Mafune himself directed his plays *Pastorale* (*Den'en*, 1941) and *Farce: The Lightning* (*Farusu: Inazuma*, 1951) for Bungakuza in 1943 and 1952, respectively.

Mafune's plays are conspicuous in their total abstinence from contemporary politics, even during the highly nationalized period of the 1930s and early 1940s, which made them continuously popular with the *shingeki* theater world, Bungakuza in particular.

From 1948 to 1950, Mafune's complete works were published in five volumes. Although widely known in Japan, his work thus far has hardly been critically examined by the English-speaking world. He died in 1977.

SELECT PLAYS: *Winter Geese* (*Kangamo*, 1927); *The Weasel* (*Itachi*, 1931); *Children of the Sun* (*Taiyō no Ko*, 1936); *The Naked City* (*Hadaka no Machi*, 1936); *The Stranger* (*Mishiranu Hito*, 1936); *Escapade* (*Tonsōfu*, 1937); *Deserted Garden* (*Haien*, 1938); *Mold* (*Kabi*, 1938); *Pastorale* (*Den'en*, 1941); *The Yellow Room* (*Kiiro no Heya*, 1943); *Nakahashi Household* (*Nakahashi Kōkan*, 1946); *Farce: The Lightning* (*Farusu: Inazuma*, 1951); *The Loquacious Parrot* (*Ōmu no Gyōzetsu*, 1958); *The Blacksmith on an Solitary Island* (*Kotō no Kajiya*, 1959); *A Life of Zenkō* (*Zenkō no Isshō*, 1963); *Do Not Tread on Flowers* (*Hana wo Fumunakare*, 1964); *A Glass Doll* (*Biidoro Ningyō*, 1965); *Father's Visit to Classwork Day* (*Chihioya no Sankanbi*, 1966); *The Man of Volte-Face* (*Hyōhen Jinbutsu*, 1968)

FURTHER READING

Keene, Donald. *Dawn to the West: Japanese Literature in the Modern Era: Poetry, Drama, Criticism*. New York: Henry Holt, 1984.

Mafune Yutaka. *Mafune Yutaka Senshū* [Selected works of Mafune Yutaka]. Tokyo: Koyama Shoten, 1948–1950.

———. *Mafune Yutaka Rajio Dorama Senshū* [Selected Radio Plays of Mafune Yutaka]. Tokyo: Hōbunkan, 1951.

Powell, Brian. *Japan's Modern Theatre: A Century of Continuity and Change*. London: Japan Library, 2002.

Rokuo Tanaka

MAGGIE AND PIERRE

Maggie and Pierre by LINDA GRIFFITHS and PAUL THOMPSON was first performed in the Backspace at Theatre Passe Muraille in Toronto, in 1979. Originally, the play was wildly successful and enjoyed extensive cross-CANADA touring. Later remounts of the production have frequently been criticized as being dated.

Maggie and Pierre is a unique one-person, three-character play that investigates the intimacies and public image of one of Canada's most famous and infamous political couples, the former Prime Minister Pierre Trudeau and his former wife Margaret Sinclair Trudeau. The play is ambitious in its scope, tracing the development of the relationship between Pierre and Margaret, as well as the rise and decline of Pierre as prime minister of Canada. It is also theatrically demanding, using only one actress to play the three parts: Pierre, Margaret, and Henry (a journalist). Furthermore, it is this aspect that shapes the intimacy of the play itself. This is not simply political satire, or political history, for that matter, although it engages both genres; this is an intimate fantasy of the people who lead the country through one of its most turbulent times in the nation's contemporary history. The portrayal of all three characters by one actress emphasizes the intimacy the play seeks to depict, by physically linking the characters, conversations, internal monologues, and character transformations through the actress's own physicality.

The thematic center of the play is the conflict between public myth and private personae and between Pierre's Cartesian rationality, his learned self-assurance (often interpreted as arrogance) and Margaret's childlike innocence, and her narcissistic attempts to embrace the 1960s counterculture. More simply put, it is a classic drama of the values of the old and the new. According to the play, despite the couple's embrace of liberality, they seem to remain trapped within the limitations of gender, public opinion, and national expectations. In a poignant moment, Margaret is depicted as realizing her own trapped existence as she wanders by the Rideau canal, feeling that she is always being watched, always being corrected: "What's that underneath the water? It looks like wings, like wings beating underneath the water. Pierre would say, 'no, Margaret. It's just the intersection of the wind and the rain causing that configuration on the surface.' But I know it's wings. Is it possible to think if someone is always watching you?"

While Margaret struggles, she might also be speaking on behalf of her husband, who was also subject to the prying and voyeuristic eyes of the Canadian press and public and trapped within the expectations of the mythic status imposed upon him. When he states, "The only way to stay alive is to avoid their wish to define you," Pierre is referring not only to himself but also to the slippery subject of Canadian identity. However, the close degree to which this couple's relationship is monitored by the nation is finally revealed and placed back into private perspective when Pierre learns that his wife has "run off with the Rolling Stones." He invites Henry to "enter his emotional world," an invitation that is in fact impossible. Once the personal anguish of this public man is aired through his prayer, it is no longer possible to hold him in mythical ideal. Trudeau loses the next election, while Maggie is depicted as dancing alone, stopping only to deliver her final monologue, stating that she is Margaret Trudeau, "the woman who gave freedom a bad name." However, her final lines suggest that it was not all for naught, that perhaps if freedom has a price, then it must be paid. She reveals her own recovery from the ordeal when she is able to freely and flirtatiously ask the audience, "Which do you think is my best feature, my legs . . . or my bum?"

FURTHER READING

Maggie and Pierre. Encyclopedia of Canadian Theatre. http://www.canadiantheatre.com/.

Miller, Mary Jane. "*Billy Bishop Goes to War* and *Maggie and Pierre*: A Matched Set." *Theatre History in Canada* 10, no. 2 (1999): 188–198.

Jolene Armstrong

THE MAGISTRATE

The fourth of ARTHUR PINERO's plays to be produced, *The Magistrate* (1885) is a clever three-act FARCE that pokes fun at the absurdities of middle-class British respectability, especially the deceptions that solid guardians of the social order engage in to keep from revealing secrets and unpleasant truths. Pinero's achievement was to draw on the techniques of French farce, but not its risqué subject matter, to create a more lighthearted, distinctly English form of farce.

The play, which takes place in London, revolves around the misadventures of Aeneas Posket, the magistrate of the Mulberry Street Police Court, who is married to a lively widow, Agatha. Mrs. Posket has been keeping her true age from her husband and safeguards her secret by pretending that her nineteen-year-old son from a previous marriage, Cis Farringdon, is only fourteen. This skeleton in the family closet is the occasion for much of the humor in the play and the rather weak mainspring for much of the action. Although he seems actually to believe that he is only fourteen, Cis has an active (although secret) social life and displays a lively interest in gambling, women, and late-night carousing. Playfully, he takes his stepfather on a round of misadventures. While dining at a club after hours, the two are surprised by a police raid and nearly discovered, but they manage to escape, and Posket arrives at his magistrate's room at court the next morning shaken and disheveled. Posket, the model of rectitude, is thrown into confusion when his own wife (who had gone to the same club to meet Colonel Lukyn, an old friend of both, and convince him not to reveal her true age) is brought before him for sentencing, having been taken into custody when discovered in the club after hours. The magistrate, of course, is as guilty as the accused. But in the end, all comes to light and everyone is forgiven.

The initial success of the play revived the failing fortunes of the Court Theatre, where *The Magistrate* was first produced on March 21, 1885 and where it ran for more than 300 performances, a record at the time for a London production. Critics agree that it was *The Magistrate* and two other farces (*The Schoolmistress* and *Dandy Dick*) that Pinero created for the Court Theatre company that made his name. Although the premise of the play is almost preposterous (how can anyone think that Cis is only fourteen?), *The Magistrate* is carefully constructed, and its minor characters are well drawn, revealing Pinero as a conscientious and skilled craftsman.

Early audiences of *The Magistrate*, along with theater critics, greeted the play enthusiastically. A *Boston Herald* review regretted that the play would be on the stage in that city for only three weeks. One critic characterized it as a "lightface" that "never descends for a moment to the level of knockabout farce." Other reviewers called the play "pure fun," "ludicrous, but not silly," and Pinero's "merriest COMEDY," while acknowledging the plot as "the slightest of slight threads." The play has been revived throughout the 20th century.

[*See also* England, 1860–1940]

FURTHER READING

Bratton, J. S. Introduction to *Trelawny of the "Wells" and Other Plays*, by Arthur Wing Pinero. Oxford: Oxford Univ. Press, 1995.

Dawick, John. *Pinero: A Theatrical Life*. Niwot: Univ. Press of Colorado, 1993.

Elaine Brousseau

MAHABIDROHA   See THE GREAT REBELLION

THE MAIDEN STONE

*There is nothing, nothing you cannot be when their eyes are on you.
Nothing.*
—Harriet, Act 1, Scene 6

Premiered at the Hampstead Theatre, London, in 1995, *The Maiden Stone* was the recipient of the inaugural Peggy Ramsay Award. Jean Findlay in *The Scotsman* (1995) calls it a "savage play . . . a wild rumbustious mix of fantasy and fable, birth and death, extreme hardship and bitter cold," and it is certainly the most striking of RONA MUNRO's works in terms of the vigorous interweaving of legend, storytelling, and ballad with an explo-

ration of what it means to be a woman, a mother, and an artist. The dialect in which the Scottish characters speak is expressive, sinuous, but Munro has counted it a handicap to the play's wider success.

Set in northeast SCOTLAND during the 19th century, the play takes place on a series of farm and roadside settings where two wanderers, Harriet, an actress, and Bidie, a traveling woman, meet with their respective family groups. Harriet has come to fulfill a nonexistent engagement at the local castle, while Bidie, sometime farmhand and washerwoman, is also the wet nurse Harriet needs to feed her babies.

The Maiden Stone is a play about transformation, from the legend of the stone by the road, or Harriet sending her reluctant daughter Miriam to beg for food in an assumed character, to wild child Mary's desire to become an actress caught up in Harriet's tales of the transforming power of performance, and Miriam's rejection of her mother's plans for her, to assume the role of a severely conventional schoolteacher. All are choices dearly paid for by the women to become someone of their own choosing.

The action is filled with striking stage pictures; howling winds and snowstorms test the characters, while Bidie's animalistic brood roam the stage, sometimes becoming the ghosts of children long dead, sometimes inhabiting the wild creatures that own the land. *The Maiden Stone* also features some of the most supportive male/female relationships within Munro's writing. Archie, Harriet's loving but weak husband, and Nick, Bidie's occasional lover and soulmate, both provide the women with moments of joy amid the daily struggles for existence. Bidie, both seeking and fearing Nick's fleeting visits, is anchored by her role as mother, providing emotional love and physical nurture for her children, her knowledge of the landscape sustaining them in hard times. Harriet is determined to make an independent life for herself and her children and does not scruple about how this is to be achieved, but she is out of her setting, her education of little use in finding food and shelter, so that she becomes increasingly dependent on others.

The action covers an extended period of time during which Bidie is aged by the rigors of her life, but Harriet is changed totally, from proud, calculating, driven artist to a spent force, broken by one pregnancy too many and the treachery of Miriam. The two women are on journeys that cannot end but with death; and at the last, Harriet hands over her means of escape, her art, to Mary, who leaves for Edinburgh, and Harriet is absorbed into the Maiden Stone of the legend.

FURTHER READING

Horvat, Ksenija, and Barbara Bell. "Sue Glover, Rona Munro and Lara Jane Bunting: Echoes and Open Spaces." In *Contemporary Scottish Women Writers*, ed. by Aileen Christianson and Alison Lumsden. Edinburgh: Edinburgh Univ. Press, 2000. 65–78.

Macdonald, Jan. "Food as Signifier and Symbol in the Work of Contemporary Scottish Women Dramatists." In *A Theatre That*

Matters: Twentieth-Century Scottish Drama and Theatre, ed. by Valentina
  Poggi and Margaret Rose. Milan: Edizioni Unicopli, 2000. 89–110.

Scullion, Adrienne. "Contemporary Scottish Women Playwrights." In
  Modern British Women Playwrights, ed. by Elaine Aston and Janelle
  Reinelt. Cambridge: Cambridge Univ. Press, 2000. 94–118.

Triesman, Susan. "Transformations and Transgressions: Women's
  Discourse on the Scottish Stage." In British and Irish Women
  Dramatists Since 1958, ed. by Trevor R. Griffiths and Margaret
  Llewellyn-Jones. Buckingham: Open Univ. Press, 1993. 124–134.

Barbara A. E. Bell

THE MAIDS

The Maids (Les Bonnes), an intense drama, was the first of JEAN
GENET's plays to reach a wide audience. Originally consisting
of four acts with a large cast (titled The Tragedy of the Confidantes
[La Tragédie des confidentes]), the piece was compressed into a
single act for three players under the dramaturgical guidance
of JEAN COCTEAU, who brought Genet's play to the attention of
Louis Jouvet, an acclaimed actor-artistic director. Jouvet, in
search of a production for his 1947 season, was immediately
drawn to Genet's hypnotic account of two maids rehearsing a
murder.

The play reveals the secret life of Claire and Solange, sisters working as live-in domestics for a glamorous and entitled
young woman known simply as "Madame." During nightly
games in Madame's bedroom, the two young women variously impersonate each other and their mistress, raiding both
the latter's couture-filled closet and litany of admonitions to
play out scenarios of intimidation and rebellion. Fueled by
their fantasies, they conspire to destroy Madame, whose lover
they have denounced in a series of anonymous letters to the
police. But when the lover is suddenly released on bail, the
sisters fear their plot will be discovered and decide to poison
their mistress. Their plan goes awry, however, and Claire,
play-acting as her mistress, deliberately drinks the poison
instead. Solange is left alone to imagine herself as a magnificent murderess liberated from servitude.

The Maids had a "true crime" resonance for its initial audiences, as the play is based on the notorious 1930s case of the
Papin sisters, who tortured, killed, and mutilated the mother
and daughter for whom they worked. But Genet's portrayal of
the maids' stylized rituals of dominance and humiliation is
more of an examination of the psychological violence of imposed
roles than it is of actual physical brutality. Genet biographer
Edmund White (1993) finds echoes of AUGUST STRINDBERG
and Jean Racine in the play's exploration of the master-servant
power dynamic and its use of formal rhetoric to express explosive feeling, as well as the influence of ANTONIN ARTAUD's
Theater of Cruelty. Genet himself cited the Catholic Mass and
the play of children as models for The Maids's alternately hallucinatory and matter-of-fact style.

The Maids premiered in Paris in April 1947, as the curtain-
raiser for JEAN GIRAUDOUX's more decorous The Apollo of Bellac.
Genet's play was a slap in the face of postwar audiences who
were not yet ready to be told that everything they had fought for
was ultimately a sham; with a few exceptions, critics savaged the
play, calling it "crude" and "unhealthy." Hissing and catcalls
interrupted most of its initial run of ninety-two performances.
JEAN-PAUL SARTRE was among the play's earliest and ardent
defenders, calling Genet's play a "Black Mass" that aimed to
"strike at the root of the apparent" and so lay bare the hidden
sadism and despair beneath society's pretenses of civility (Genet,
1954). Sartre also claimed that Genet had envisioned the maids
to be played by men, a bit of apocrypha that influenced directorial approaches for half a century, although Genet later denied
this.

[See also France; Gay and Lesbian Drama]

FURTHER READING

Brooks, Peter, and Joseph Halpern, eds. Genet: A Collection of Critical
  Essays. Englewood Cliffs, N.J.: Prentice-Hall, 1979.

Genet, Jean. The Maids and Deathwatch. Two Plays by Jean Genet. Tr. by
  Bernard Frechtman, with an introduction by Jean-Paul Sartre.
  New York: Grove, 1954.

——. The Selected Writings of Jean Genet. Ed. and with an introduction by
  Edmund White. Hopewell, N.J.: Ecco Press, 1993.

Webb, Richard, comp. File on Genet. London: Methuen Drama,
  1992.

White, Edmund. Genet: A Biography. New York: Knopf, 1993.

Charlotte Stoudt

MAILLET, ANTONINE (1929–)

Canadian playwright and novelist Antonine Maillet was born in
Bouctouche, New Brunswick, in 1929. She is best known for her
work celebrating Acadian life, past and present. Maillet's body of
work includes twelve published plays, fifteen novels, children's
books, television and radio scripts, articles, and translations of
William Shakespeare's Richard III and Twelfth Night. In addition,
Maillet is known nationally and internationally as a keynote
speaker and storyteller par excellence and has taught as a visiting
professor at universities in North America and Europe.

Maillet's writings characteristically showcase Acadian heritage and culture in their story lines. Acadian herself, Maillet
draws from her own background and celebrates the life of this
small but resilient group of Canadians. Originally Acadia (located
roughly in CANADA's Maritime Provinces) was colonized by the
French, but because of the growing threat of Acadian solidarity,
they were displaced by the ruling British in La dispersion or "The
Great Deportation" of 1755. Many Acadians relocated to America,
settling largely in Louisiana, but some returned to their homes
years later. Maillet descends from these hearty people and in her
work makes sure they are not forgotten.

Maillet's works are groundbreaking in that they are written in Acadian French, a language specific to the Acadian people (similar to 17th- and 18th-century French) and one that had, up until Maillet, been solely an oral language. In her works she celebrates Acadian strength and perseverance, giving a body and a voice to a forgotten people. Rather than belaboring the injustice of the past, Maillet's work, though still social criticism, focuses more on the fortitude and ingenuity that helped the Acadians survive against great challenges to their way of life. Maillet champions the Acadian Spirit in its finest form.

The Slattern (La sagouine, 1971), Maillet's most widely known drama, is considered by some critics to be a modern masterpiece, forging new territory in Acadian theater and giving a voice where there formerly was none. Written as a monologue, The Slattern is filled with the musings of an old Acadian scrubwoman as she cleans, all the while thinking about her heritage, what has happened to her people, and the downtrodden state in which they find themselves.

Maillet's writings, particularly her novels, have received much acclaim, earning her such honors as the Prix Champlain for Pointe-aux-coques (Clam Point, 1958), the Canadian Governor General's Award for Fiction for Don l'original (The Tale of Don L'original, 1972), Le Grand Prix de la Ville de Montréal and the Prix France-Canada for Mariaagélas (1973 and 1975), and the Floyd S. Chalmer's Canadian Play Award for The Slattern (1980). She holds the honor of being the first nonnative of FRANCE to win the celebrated Prix Goncourt with her work Pélagie-la-charrette (Pélagie: The Return to a Homeland, 1979). She holds honorary degrees from more than twenty-five universities and has been appointed to national councils for arts and culture in Canada, France, and Monaco. Maillet was appointed Companion of the Order of Canada, Canada's highest civilian honor, for her life's literary work.

PLAYS: The Grimy Ones (Les crasseux, 1968); The Slattern (La sagouine, 1970); Gapi and Sullivan (Gapi et Sullivan, 1973); Évangéline Deusse (1975); Gapi (1975); The Mad Widow (La veuve enragee, 1977); The Middle-Class Gentleman (La bourgeois gentleman, 1978); The Smuggler (La contrebandière, 1981); The Humorous, Horrible, and Terrible Adventures of Panurge, Friend of Pantagruel (Les drolatiques, horrifiques, et epouvantables aventures de Panurge, ami de Pantagruel, 1983); Garroche in Paradise (Garroche en paradis, 1986); Margot the Insane One (Margot la Folle, 1987); William S. (1991)

FURTHER READING

Godin, Jean-Cleo, and Laurent Mailhot, eds. Théâtre Québécois. Montreal: Hurtubise HMH, 1980.

Northwest Passages: Canadian Literature Online. "Antonine Maillet: A Selected Bibliography." http://www.nwpassages.com/bios/maillet2.asp.

Smith, Donald. Voices of Deliverance: Interviews with Quebec & Acadian Writers. Toronto: Anansi, 1986.

Kate Maurer

MAJOR BARBARA

A play by GEORGE BERNARD SHAW, written in 1905 and first performed at the Court Theatre, London, in the same year, Major Barbara has remained a popular and frequently performed play. It is a robust, challenging work that memorably defines the dilemmas that perennially confront reforming idealists when they come to grips with the realities of power in society. Like Saint Joan, her successor in Shaw's dramatic writings, Major Barbara has achieved iconic status as an image of a courageous individual woman pitting her will and faith against the hostile forces of her surrounding world. Equally impressive and enduring as a dramatic image is Shaw's portrait of the munitions manufacturer, Andrew Undershaft, as an unrepentantly successful, engaging but ruthless modern business tycoon.

The action of Major Barbara embodies an imaginatively conceived allegory about different forms of power, bringing into dynamic confrontation with one another the brute force of "money and gunpowder," the spiritual energies of religious idealism, and the civilizing agencies of humanistic culture and philosophy. The intellectual debate in the work is anchored in a human drama involving family loyalties and division, a love affair put to trial in the crucible of ideological conflict, and an intricate pattern of coercive power-play that appears in many areas of action, including the subtly connected subplot about the belligerent Bill Walker. The work is enlivened by searching humor, comic inventiveness, and complex, richly ambiguous characterization.

Having been born into an upper-middle-class family as the daughter of Lady Britomart and her estranged husband Undershaft, Barbara has joined the Salvation Army and is in charge of a shelter in the poverty-stricken district of West Ham in London that is under threat of closure because of lack of funds. Barbara becomes disillusioned when it is revealed that the only way the shelter can be saved is by acceptance of donations from her immensely wealthy father, Undershaft, and Sir Horace Bodger, an owner of whisky distilleries. She suffers a crisis of faith when her jubilant fellow Salvationists, having accepted Undershaft's bounty, follow him offstage in a parody of a Dionysian revel. Undershaft's unconventional ideas, that poverty is a crime, perpetrated by society as a whole, and that the moral virtues can only flourish in a proper economic environment, are underscored by the act 3 visit to his model village of Perivale St. Andrews, which is part of the munitions factory complex.

The play shows the influence on Shaw of William Blake's subversion of conventional ideas of good and evil in such works as The Marriage of Heaven and Hell and Songs of Innocence and Experience and also of the translation of Euripides's The Bacchae by the Australian-born professor of Greek Gilbert Murray, on whom the character of Cusins is modeled. Shaw disclaimed the influence of FRIEDRICH NIETZSCHE on his play in the preface to Major Barbara. But well before 1905 he was aware of the ideas in the German philosopher's work Beyond Good and Evil. The

Nietzschean assault on simplistic categorizations of good and evil, right and wrong, is paralleled in *Major Barbara*.

The development of the play is toward a synthesis of the opposing forces presented in its first two acts. In their final assent to the ideas that "life is all one" and that "the way of life lies through the factory of death" Barbara and Cusins are imaginatively creating a Shavian marriage of heaven and hell. Those who would do good in the world cannot do so by turning their backs on the realities and energies of evil. In recognizing that, for all its virtues, Undershaft's model village of Perivale St. Andrews does not answer all the needs of the human spirit, Barbara rediscovers her sense of religious purpose. There is work for her among the full-fed, snobbish creatures in her father's materialist dream-town. But even as Shaw was writing the play, Undershaft's counterparts in real life were manufacturing the weapons that, within less than a decade, were to be employed in one of the worst wars in human history. The prospect held out in *Major Barbara* of a union of intelligence, spiritual enlightenment, and power was shattered in 1914, and Shaw's wartime work HEARTBREAK HOUSE grimly reflects that fact.

[*See also* Ireland]

FURTHER READING

Albert, Sidney P. "Barbara's Progress." *Shaw: The Annual of Bernard Shaw Studies* 21 (2001).

Crompton, Louis. "*Major Barbara*." In *Shaw the Dramatist*. Lincoln: Univ. of Nebraska Press, 1969.

Gibbs, A. M. "Action and Meaning in *Major Barbara*." In *The Art and Mind of Shaw: Essays in Criticism*. London: Macmillan, 1983.

Grene, Nicholas. "Giving the Devil More than His Due." In *Bernard Shaw: A Critical View*. London: Macmillan, 1984.

Morgan, Margery M. "*Major Barbara*." In *The Shavian Playground*. London: Methuen, 1972.

Wisenthal, J. L. "*Major Barbara*." In *The Marriage of Contraries: Bernard Shaw's Middle Plays*. Cambridge: Harvard Univ. Press, 1974.

A. M. Gibbs

MÅKESPISERE   *See* SEAGULL EATERS

MAKINO NOZOMI (1959–)

Makino Nozomi, Japanese dramatist and artistic director, and head of the theater company Makino Office Productions (MOP), founded in 1984, came to prominence during the upsurge in regional theater activities in JAPAN during the 1990s. A Tokyo resident at present, he attended Dōshisha University in Kyoto, where MOP is located.

Fascinated by the famous 1970s playwright TSUKA KŌHEI's satirical COMEDIES, Makino produced mainly Tsuka's works in the 1980s, especially THE ATAMI MURDER CASE (1973); since the 1990s Makino has focused on writing his own works. He shares with such playwrights as Nagai Ai and Mitani Kōki a reputation for producing well-made plays. He is active both in commercial theater, working with popular television celebrities, and in serious little theater (ANGURA or *shōgekijō*) productions with MOP.

The first notable characteristic of Makino's theater is his preference for historical figures and contexts rather than contemporary social problems. His works treat the dilemma of youth torn between personal desire and national concern during major transitional periods in history, such as the drastic change from the Tokugawa (1603–1868) to the Meiji period (1868–1912). The second striking characteristic of his plays is their pervasive optimism and good humor. His characters live enthusiastically and authentically, however dismal the social circumstances may be. His protagonists include cultural heroes such as outlaw samurai Sakamoto Ryōma in the HAPPY MAN series, poet Yosano Akiko and the literary group surrounding her in *Mother—Do not Laugh* (1994), and novelist Okamoto Kanoko in *Kanojo i*(1997).

His best-known play, *Tokyo Atomic Klub* (1997), for which he won the prestigious Yomiuri Literary Award in 1997, is a fictionalized account of the youth of Nobel Prize winner in physics Tomonaga Shinichirō between 1932 and 1946. It depicts the scientist's life at a boardinghouse with a motley group of residents when he was studying at the Science Research Institute in Tokyo. The play is controversial for depicting without guilt the excitement of scientists over the development of the atomic bomb.

Another work of his about a famous physicist is *Fuyuhiko and the Good Luck Cat* (1997), which received the 1998 Yomiuri Theatre Award. It comically treats the family life of scientist Terada Torahiko (1878–1935), who was also a disciple of novelist Natsume Sōseki. The fictional Terada has difficulty exerting his patriarchal authority over his lively second wife and his rebellious daughter. Having disappointed his wife by canceling a trip, Terada suggests celebrating Christmas at home in the new fashionable Western way by ordering sushi and exchanging presents. It turns out that she is not as resistant to trying Western customs as first appears. In addition, his daughter runs away from home when Terada forbids her to marry a certain young man. This work was produced at the Royal Academy of Dramatic Art, London, in 2001.

Makino received the 2001 Tsuruya Nanboku Drama Award for *Something Far Above* (2000) and the Kinokuniya Theatre Award in the Individual Category for *Red Shirt* (2003).

PLAYS: *HAPPY MAN 2: The Great Shanghai Adventure* (HAPPY MAN 2: *Shanhai Daibōken*, 1990); *HAPPY MAN 3: Goodbye Ryōma* (HAPPY MAN 3: *Sayonara Ryōma*, 1990); *Pisuken* (Pis-ken, 1991); *Angel Eyes* (*Enjeru Aizu*, 1992); *Oldies But Goldies* (*Orudiizu batto Gōrudiizu*, 1993); *MOTHER—Do Not Laugh* (MOTHER—*Kimi Waraitamōkoto Nakare*, 1994); *Fuyuhiko and the Good Luck Cat* (*Fuyuhiko*, 1997); *Kanoko* (1997); *Tokyo Atomic Klub* (*Tokyo Genshikaku Kurabu*, 1997); *Love Suicides at Sonezaki, New Version* (*Shin Sonezaki Shinjū*, 1998); *Something Far Above*

(Takaki Kanomono, 2000); The Black Handkerchief (Kuroi Hankachiifu, 2001); Red Shirt (Aka Shatsu, 2003)

FURTHER READING

Makino Nozomi. Tokyo Atomic Klub (Tokyo Genshikaku Kurabu). Tr. by John D. Swain. In Half a Century of Japanese Theater, Vol. I: 1990s Part I. Tokyo: Kinokuniya, 1999. 327–410.

Senda Akihiko. Butai wa Kataru: Gendai Engeki to Myūjikaru no Mikata [The stage speaks: How to view modern Japanese theater and musicals]. Tokyo: Shūeisha Shinsho, 2002. 100–103.

Mari Boyd

MALAYSIA

Modern Malaysian drama, primarily a post–World War II phenomenon, includes plays in Malay (the national language) as well as English, Mandarin, Tamil, and other languages of this multilingual society. Malaysia's diverse population is also reflected in the characters, themes, settings, and production styles of scripted and performed works. Diversity was already inherent in the Malay opera or *bangsawan* (literally, "nobility"), an improvisational theater that developed as an offshoot of *wayang parsi* (Parsi theater) performed by Indian troupes in Penang in the latter quarter of the 19th century. Especially popular in the 1920s and 1930s, *bangsawan* troupes, performing in Malay, adapted stories from many sources—Arab, Persian, Indian, Malay, Chinese, and Western, such as William Shakespeare—to entertain their broad-based audiences. The progenitor of Malaysia's modern drama, *bangsawan* waned with World War II, as film, radio, and later television gained in popularity.

The 1950s through the 1970s saw the emergence of three distinct forms of modern Malay drama: *sandiwara*, realistic drama, and experimental theater. The first Malay playwrights (1950–1960s), including SHAHAROM HUSAIN, Kalam Hamidy, Ali Aziz, and Usman Awang, wrote *sandiwara* (literally, "drama") scripts that recreated history at a time of rising Malay nationalism, prior to and after independence from ENGLAND in 1957. *Sandiwara* plays also examine the moral dilemmas characters confront in the modern period, especially as they shift from rural to urban settings. Influenced by troupes from INDONESIA as well as Shakespearean models, *sandiwara* playwrights created works that were anticolonialist, antifeudal, and pro-democratic.

Realistic plays, depicting the multifarious social problems challenging the new nation, emerged in the 1960s. Playwrights sought to balance the drive for progress with an appreciation of traditional Malay values. Indonesian authors and Western realists, such as HENRIK IBSEN, were important influences on this modern style. Most realistic authors preferred positive endings that reflect the optimism of a newly independent nation. These social dramas usually focus on the Malay community, with the sitting room of the main characters' household the central locale. Memorable plays that epitomize the era are Awang Had Salleh's For Wiping Away the Tears (Buat Menyapu Si Air Mata, 1963),

Mustapha Kamil Yassin's Tiled Roof, Thatched Roof (Atap Genting Atap Rembia, 1963), and Kalam Hamidy's The Unfortunate Is Lucky (Sial Bertuah, 1963).

Some later realistic works feature unconventional settings, complex intercultural relationships, and/or uncertain endings. Plays such as Usman Awang's Visitors at Kenny Hill (Tamu di Bukit Kenny, 1967) and Anna (1972) by Kemala (né Ahmad Kamal Abdullah) indicate that the optimistic resolutions of earlier realistic drama are no longer guaranteed. Theatrical innovations are at hand.

The third trend is the stylistically inventive plays of the 1970s, which represent a clear break with REALISM. Experimental writers explored the irrational in life in the aftermath of the ethnic riots that occurred in the country on May 13, 1969. During this critical period, as issues of development—social, political, and religious—become more "sensitive," playwrights expressed their concerns symbolically and discretely. They distanced themselves from Western realism and sought to create a clearly Malay style of theater, often combining SURREALISM and traditional Malay performing arts to produce novel stage images. They explored a rich heritage of traditional forms, including *wayang kulit* (shadow puppetry); dance dramas, such as *mak yong*, *menora*, *mek mulong*, and *randai*; trance performances, such as *kuda kepang* and *main puteri*; *dikir barat* (poetic call and response); *boria* (comic sketch and processional), and the *penglipur lara* (traditional storyteller). NOORDIN HASSAN's landmark play IT IS NOT THE TALL GRASS BLOWN BY THE WIND (Bukan Lalang Ditiup Angin, 1970), an allegory of the 1969 ethnic violence, initiated the new production style.

The 1970s "third generation" of Malay playwrights, notably Dinsman, Johan Jaafar, and Hatta Azad Khan, popularized a more abstract, AVANT-GARDE theater. Dinsman's (né Žaruddin Othman) MONODRAMA It Is Not Suicide (Bukan Bunuh Diri, 1974) spotlights a young college student who rejects both secular and religious teachings to find personal truth and God. In Dry Wind (Angin Kering, 1976) and The One (Dia, 1977), Johan Jaafar presents an ironic world in which rich and poor alike futilely pursue illusions and material comfort. In Hatta Azad Khan's futuristic Corpse (Mayat, 1978), a group of nameless individuals confront outsiders who seem responsible for the mysterious disappearance of their deceased friend. However, innovative as the experimental dramatists were, the increasingly esoteric nature of their work created dissonance between artist and audience. Theater attendance diminished.

By the 1980s, there was a decrease in drama activity. As a consequence of fluctuating economic conditions and Islamic revivalism, which affected theater participation, the government significantly reduced its sponsorship of Malay plays. In this artistic vacuum there emerged an English-language theater renaissance.

There had been an active English-language theater in Malaysia prior to 1969, with plays by Edward Dorall, Lee Joo For, Patrick Yeoh, and Syed Alwi. However, in the aftermath of May 13,

Malaysian dramatists felt little incentive to write in English. Since the root cause of the riots was attributed to Malay poverty, the government increased educational and employment opportunities for the Malay community. A national cultural policy sought to establish Malay culture as the foundation culture in the country, with Islam identified as the basis of Malay culture. Although other ethnic groups were acknowledged as playing a relevant cultural role, government funds were mainly channeled to Malay artists.

By the mid-1980s, the cultural atmosphere began to change. Kee Thuan Chye's 1984 *Here and Now*, first performed in 1985, was the harbinger of a renewed English-language drama. The work exposes submerged tensions between Malays and Chinese but ultimately demonstrates the constructive role that theater can play as a catalyst for social integration. Plays by Shakespeare also experienced a comeback on the English, Malay, Mandarin, and Indian stage, beginning with the 1989 production of *Romeo and Juliet*. Although Shakespeare's influence was profound in the early development of Malaysian theater, his plays rarely surfaced on Malaysia's postcolonial stage from the 1960s through most of the 1980s.

During the 1990s, Malaysian theater as a whole flourished once again. The government recommitted substantial support to the performing arts—contributing to English as well as Malay theater. New theater venues opened, including the impressive National Theatre (also called Palace of Culture). New, short Malay comedies, more realistic in form, successfully wooed Malay audiences back to the theater. Large-scale productions of Malay plays, including efforts to revive *bangsawan*, grew increasingly evident. New Malay theater groups, such as The Alternative Stage, a politically and socially attuned company, have also recently emerged. Chinese theater attracts large audiences for productions of Western as well as traditional and modern Chinese plays. Within the Malaysian Indian community, the Temple of Fine Arts is a prominent performing arts organization that draws upon Indian and other artistic sources to create impressive, large-scale productions. Presentations by international troupes have also increased.

Meanwhile, English-language theater comprises a diverse network of artists. Veteran drama critic and director Krishen Jit and the Five Arts Center he co-founded have contributed significantly to this renewed theater trend. The group initially cultivated ethnic plays, such as K. S. Maniam's *The Cord*, a profound tale of Indian immigration to Malaysia, and LEOW PUAY TIN's *Three Children*, an insightful exposé of three troubled Chinese siblings. Then the Center developed multicultural plays, such as *Work and Us*, which highlight the country's diversity through multilingual dialogue. Their 1994 multi-art extravaganza, Maniam's transcultural tour de force *Skin Trilogy*, asks: what is the humanity that ultimately lies beneath the various colors and textures of our skin? Other active English-language companies, which promote new works by engaged writers sensitive to the issues of the day, include the Actors Studio Theatre, Instant Café Theatre, Dramalab, Straits Theatre Company,

and Kuali Works. Malaysia remains blessed with an impressive array of socially and artistically responsive theatrical talent.

FURTHER READING

Abdullah, Ahmad Kamal, et al. "Drama." In *History of Modern Malay Literature*. Kuala Lumpur: Dewan Bahasa dan Pustaka, 1992. 2: 251–328.

Diamond, Catherine. "Parallel Streams: Two Currents of Difference in Kuala Lumpur's Contemporary Theatre." *The Drama Review* 46, no. 2 (T174) (Summer 2002): 7–46.

Ishak, Solehah. *Histrionics of Development: A Study of Three Contemporary Malay Playwrights*. Kuala Lumpur: Dewan Bahasa dan Pustaka and Kementerian Pendidikan Malaysia, 1987.

Ishak, Solehah, and Nur Nina Zuhra (Nancy Nanney). "Malaysia." In *World Encyclopedia of Contemporary Theatre*, ed. by Don Rubin. Toronto: York Univ., 1995. 5: 282–306.

Nur Nina Zuhra (Nancy Nanney). *An Analysis of Modern Malay Drama*. Shah Alam, Malaysia: Biroteks, MARA Institute of Technology, 1992.

Tan Sooi Beng. *A Social and Stylistic History of Popular Malay Opera*. Singapore: Oxford Univ. Press, 1993.

Nancy Nanney

LES MAMELLES DE TIRÉSIAS   See THE BREASTS OF TIRESIAS

MAMET, DAVID (1947–)

David Mamet is one of the UNITED STATES' leading playwrights, as well as one of its most prolific writers in any genre. Since 1969 he has written more than sixty plays, adaptations, screenplays, and books about theater. He has also authored five novels, six children's books, and dozens of essays and magazine articles, many of which have been collected in book form. He has won numerous awards for his writing, including the Pulitzer Prize for Drama for GLENGARRY GLEN ROSS (1984); Obies for AMERICAN BUFFALO and SEXUAL PERVERSITY IN CHICAGO (1976), *Edmond* (1983), and *The Cryptogram* (1995); two Tony Award Nominations for *Glengarry Glen Ross* (1984) and *Speed-the-Plow* (1989); and two Academy Award Nominations for *The Verdict* (1982) and *Wag the Dog*, with Hillary Henkin (1997).

Born on November 30, 1947, in Chicago, Illinois, to a labor lawyer and a schoolteacher who divorced when he was ten years old, Mamet spent his teen years acting in community theater, as well as working a variety of odd jobs, including an oft-cited stint as a waiter in Chicago's noted Second City Comedy Club. He later studied acting at Sanford Meisner's Neighborhood Playhouse in New York City, before earning a bachelor's degree in English literature from Goddard College in Vermont, where he wrote his first play, *Camel*, as his senior thesis. Following his graduation, Mamet returned to New York for a brief period as stage manager of *The Fantasticks*. In 1971, while teaching at Goddard as artist-in-residence, Mamet met actors William H. Macy and Steven Schacter, with whom he would cofound the St. Nicholas Theater Company. Mamet would later say that his decision to become a playwright was clinched by the company's need for nonroyalty material.

Mamet first achieved notoriety as a playwright in Chicago, and his subsequent success in New York and in regional productions helped establish that city's reputation as a center for innovative theater in the 1970s and 1980s. From the New York premiere of his two one-act plays, *Sexual Perversity in Chicago* and *The Duck Variations*, at the OFF-OFF-BROADWAY St. Clements Theater in 1975, Mamet established his reputation as one of the most distinctive voices in contemporary drama. His edgy, rhythmic, and often profane dialogue was hailed by early critics as a highly realistic rendering of the American vernacular, an accurate depiction of the real-life speech of salesmen, con artists, petty thieves, and other working-class characters who inhabit plays such as *American Buffalo* (1975) and *Glengarry Glen Ross* (1983). More recent scholarship, however, suggests that Mamet's characteristic use of language reflects the influence of both his urban Jewish upbringing and his study of existential playwrights such as HAROLD PINTER and SAMUEL BECKETT. "My main emphasis," Mamet told the *Village Voice* in 1976, "is on the rhythm of language—the way action and rhythm are identical. . . . [T]he language we use, its rhythm, actually determines the way we behave, more than the other way around" (Kane, 2001).

While Mamet's early works are fragmentary, consisting of many short scenes strung together around a loose narrative, later plays such as *Speed-the-Plow* (1988) and OLEANNA (1992) are more conventional in form, following a three-act structure. This increased attention to plot and structure is explored at length in his 1998 book *Three Uses of the Knife*. "Dramatic structure," Mamet writes, "is not an arbitrary—or even a conscious—invention. It is an organic codification of the human mechanism for ordering information. Event, elaboration, denouement; thesis, antithesis, synthesis; boy meets girl, boy loses girl, boy gets girl; act one, two, three."

For most of his career Mamet has written screenplays as well as stage plays. Among the many films he has written are *The Postman Always Rings Twice* (1981), *The Untouchables* (1985), and *Hoffa* (1992), as well as film versions of his plays *Glengarry Glen Ross* (1992), *Oleanna* (1994), and *American Buffalo* (1996). Beginning with *House of Games* (1987), Mamet has directed several of his own screenplays, including *Homicide* (1990), *The Spanish Prisoner* (1997), *State and Main* (2000), and *Spartan* (2004). His 1991 book *On Directing Film* advocates the clean, no-frills approach to storytelling that is his cinematic trademark.

Though his career has been made as a writer, Mamet has never strayed far from his roots as a performer. In 1983 he founded the Atlantic Theater Company with actor William H. Macy and a group of New York University acting students. In addition to producing plays on and off Broadway since 1985, the company's Atlantic Acting School has trained hundreds of students in "Practical Aesthetics," their unique approach to acting. Though Mamet

is no longer active in the administration of the school, he published his own thoughts on actor training in the controversial book *True and False: Heresy and Common Sense for the Actor* (1997). In it, Mamet rejects American Method acting in favor of a less emotional approach that emphasizes precision, honesty, and the words of the playwright.

[*See also* United States, 1940–Present]

PLAYS: *Lakeboat* (1970, revised 1980); *The Duck Variations* (1972); *Sexual Perversity in Chicago* (1974); *American Buffalo* (1975); *Reunion* (1976); *Dark Pony* (1977); *A Life in the Theater* (1977); *The Revenge of the Space Pandas* (children's play, 1977); *The Water Engine* (1977); *The Woods* (1977); *Mr. Happiness* (1978); *Lone Canoe, or the Explorer* (1979); *Edmond* (1982); *Glengarry Glen Ross* (1983); *The Shawl and Prairie du Chien* (1985); *Speed-the-Plow* (1988); *Bobby Gould in Hell* (1989); *Oleanna* (1992); *The Cryptogram* (1994); *The Old Neighborhood* (1997); *Boston Marriage* (1999); *Romance* (2005)

FURTHER READING

Bigsby, Christopher, ed. *The Cambridge Companion to David Mamet.* Cambridge: Cambridge Univ. Press, 2004.

Kane, Leslie, ed. *David Mamet in Conversation.* Ann Arbor: Univ. of Michigan Press, 2001.

Mamet, David. *True and False: Heresy and Common Sense for the Actor.* New York: Pantheon Bks., 1997.

———. *Three Uses of the Knife: On the Nature and Purpose of the Drama.* New York: Columbia Univ. Press, 1998.

Henry Bial

MAN AND SUPERMAN

Man and Superman, a play by GEORGE BERNARD SHAW, was written in 1901–1902 and first performed at the Court Theatre, London, in 1905. The work includes an act 3 Dream scene (sometimes performed separately under the title *Don Juan in Hell* and sometimes omitted from performance of the play) and a prefatorial "Epistle Dedicatory" addressed to the theater critic A. B. Walkley, which constitute major expressions of Shaw's ideas about the life force and his creed of creative evolution. When the work was published in 1903, Shaw added a section called "The Revolutionist's Handbook," supposedly written by the gentleman-socialist in the play, Jack Tanner.

The character of Jack Tanner, who is in some respects a Shavian self-portrait, is conceived as that of a modern Don Juan who is the "marked-down prey" rather than the pursuer in the duel of sex. The action of the COMEDY is set in motion with the appointment of the revolutionary Tanner and the old-fashioned liberal Roebuck Ramsden as joint guardians of the guileful Ann Whitefield. A reverse love-chase in motor cars occurs when Tanner, in company with his Wellsian New Man chauffeur Straker, is pursued to the Sierra Nevada by Ann, who has rejected her poet-suitor Octavius. The conflict between Ann, Tanner, and the father-figure Ramsden links the play to the form of the classical New Comedy, in which, typically, systems of patriarchal authority are overthrown by members of a younger generation. But the Shavian twist to this pattern is that, as far as marriage is concerned, Tanner is a reluctant participant in the struggle, maintaining almost to the last his ineffectual resistance to Ann's designs on him as a partner. A skilfully constructed subplot of the comedy brings America and Mathew Arnold into the play's range of satirical subjects.

Wolfgang Amadeus Mozart's *Don Giovanni* is a salient point of reference in the grand debate of the Dream scene, where Tanner turns into a majestic Don Juan engaged in lengthy disputation with the Devil, Ramsden becomes The Statue, and Ann becomes Doña Anna. "The Revolutionist's Handbook" includes a collection of epigrammatic statements, titled "Maxims for Revolutionists," written in a manner resembling the style of the *Maximes* of François de La Rochefoucauld and William Blake's *The Marriage of Heaven and Hell*. Some of the "Maxims for Revolutionists"—for example, "He who can, does. He who cannot, teaches"—are among Shaw's best-known sayings.

In the portrayal of heaven and hell in the Dream scene there are no restrictions of movement between the two states. "People" are perfectly at liberty to come and go as they choose, according to their tastes. But it is made clear that those in hell are certain to find heaven—the home of serious-minded realists, philosophers, poets, and visionaries, the seekers by contemplation of "the inner will of the world"—boring. Hell is the natural home of the seekers of pleasure, happiness, and romance, the shunners of reality, the bon viveurs, the celebrators (like Mozart's Don Juan) of wine, women, and song, the connoisseurs of the fine arts and good taste, the lovers of music, here described as "the brandy of the damned." The Shavian hell is a place "where you have nothing to do but amuse yourself."

Despite the fact that it includes expression of the meliorist philosophy of creative evolution, *Man and Superman* contains some of Shaw's most pessimistic and denunciatory writings about humankind. In the Dream, the Devil describes Man as the most predatory of all the animals and as most skillful in the arts of destruction. And in a section of "The Revolutionist's Handbook" titled "Progress an Illusion," it is argued that history has shown that each attempt at civilization is followed by rapid and disastrous backward slidings into savagery, and each high point of civilization is "but a pinnacle to which a few people cling in giddy terror above an abyss of squalor." The play proper, on the other hand, is generally lighthearted in spirit and contains some of Shaw's finest passages of comic dialogue.

[See also Ireland]

FURTHER READING

Amalric, Jean-Claude. "Shaw's *Man and Superman* and the Myth of Don Juan." *Cahiers Victoriens et Edouardiens* (April 1991).

Crompton, Louis. "Man and Superman." In *Shaw the Dramatist*. Lincoln: Univ. of Nebraska Press, 1969.

Gibbs, A. M., ed. *Bernard Shaw: "Man and Superman" and "Saint Joan": A Casebook*. London: Macmillan, 1992.

A. M. Gibbs

MANN, EMILY (1952–)

I feel the need to tell people's stories and reflect what I see and what I hear. . . . I think it is important, in the end, for me to be, in a way, invisible. I give voice to the voiceless, I give voice to people who are often not heard of, or heard from. Their stories aren't famous enough, they didn't make the tabloids.
—Emily Mann, 1994

American playwright, director, and the artistic director of the McCarter Theatre at Princeton University since 1990, Emily Mann was the preeminent American documentary playwright of the late 20th century. Born on April 12, 1952, in Boston, Massachusetts, Mann grew up under the formidable influence of her historian father Arthur Mann, who taught at Smith College and wrote the biography of New York City mayor Fiorello LaGuardia, a work that led to one of Emily Mann's first theatrical experiences, the musical *Fiorello!*

The knowledge that history and theater can be part of the same endeavor became the basis for Mann's later development of DOCUMENTARY playwriting. Like her father, who also worked on a Holocaust oral history project, Mann began collecting stories. This led her to POLAND, and the kitchen of her best friend's aunt, who, while making chicken soup, described her own Holocaust story. The result was Mann's first play, *Annulla Allen: The Autobiography of a Survivor*, produced in Minneapolis in 1977.

Mann's documentary plays are created from extensive interviews, documents, and newspaper accounts. After the stream of consciousness of *Annulla and Still Life* (1979), a play about the Vietnam War's impact on domestic lives in the UNITED STATES, Mann wrote documentary plays that were more like retrials in the court of public opinion. *Execution of Justice* (1983) and *Greensboro: A Requiem* (1995) respectively reexamined the 1978 murder of Harvey Milk, the first openly gay mayor of San Francisco, and the 1979 murder of five anti–Ku Klux Klan demonstrators during a march in North Carolina. A theme common to all Mann's plays is the ways in which communities have their own unwritten systems of ethics—lawful or unlawful—by which they live.

Mann's plays have appeared on Broadway and at regional theaters, and she is the recipient of a number of awards including the Helen Hayes, Bay Area Theatre Critics Circle, and the HBO New Plays USA Awards for *Execution of Justice*; six Obie Awards including Distinguished Playwriting, Distinguished Direction, and Best Production for *Still Life*; the Greater Los Angeles NAACP (National Association for the Advancement of Colored People) Best Director Award; and The Beverly Hills/Hollywood Area NAACP Award for Best Director for *Twilight: Los Angeles, 1992*. She won the Joseph Jefferson Award for Best Play and Best Direction and the Dramatist Guild's Hull-Warriner Award for Best Play for *Having Our Say* (1994); her screenplay of that drama won the Peabody Award and the Christopher Award. Mann won an Obie for her direction of *All Over* and has been the recipient of Guggenheim and McKnight Fellowships.

[See also Feminist Drama in the United States]

PLAYS: *Annulla Allen: The Autobiography of a Survivor* (1977); *Still Life* (1979); *Execution of Justice* (1983); *Betsey Brown: A Rhythm and Blues Musical* (with Ntozake Shange and Baikida Carroll, 1985); *Having Our Say: The Delaney Sisters' First 100 Years* (1994); *Greensboro: A Requiem* (1995)

FURTHER READING

Mann, Emily. *Testimonies*. New York: Theatre Communications Group, 1997.

———. "In Conversation." *Theatre Topics* 10, no. 1 (2000).

Mann, Emily, and David E. Roessel, eds. *Political Stages: Plays That Shaped a Century*. New York: Applause Bks., 2002.

Carol Martin

LAS MANOS DE DIOS   See THE HANDS OF GOD

MA RAINEY'S BLACK BOTTOM

> White folks don't understand about the blues. They hear it come out, but they don't know how it got there. They don't understand that's life's way of talking. You don't sing to feel better. You sing cause that's a way of understanding life.
> —Ma Rainey, Act 2

AUGUST WILSON'S *Ma Rainey's Black Bottom* opened on October 11, 1984, on Broadway at the Cort Theatre and was an instant success. It ran for 276 performances and marked Wilson's successful Broadway debut. Set in Chicago in 1927, the play focuses on white-owned record companies' exploitation of black musicians.

The play begins with a group of four black studio musicians gathering to wait in the studio for Ma Rainey (who has taken time off from touring to record several songs) to arrive. Through the musicians' conversation, which comprises much of the first act, Wilson reveals that Ma Rainey has been selling well in the South but not in the North and that her style of music is losing its commercial appeal. Wilson draws the distinct personality of each of the four waiting members in detail, and even the way they play their instruments reflects their character. The waiting members are Cutler, the trombone player, who is the leader of the group; Toledo, the well-read piano player; Slow Drag, the upbeat bass player; and Levee, the band's talented but disgruntled trumpet player, who wants to move beyond his role as Ma Rainey's backup. Levee is determined to alter the "jug band" sound of Ma's blues, which he finds reminiscent of minstrel music. Levee has composed his own music and hopes to change the direction of the blues by finding his own voice as an artist.

As a successful commercial artist, Ma Rainey defies the oppressive studio system. However, she is unable to recognize the merits of Levee's efforts and fires him when she first hears his new versions of her standard songs. Unfortunately, Sturdyvant, the white studio owner, ultimately cheats Levee out of his compositions. This element of the play further drives home the TRAGEDY behind the white domination of the studio system that controls the distribution of black music. Levee eventually explodes with a final act of tremendous violence in an effort to reclaim his dignity. The play follows the band's attempt to complete the recording session despite Ma Rainey's problems with the law and the record label. The play ends in tragedy due largely to the intense personal conflicts and power struggles between Ma Rainey and the band.

Charles Dutton made his Broadway debut and earned a Tony nomination for his performance as Levee in the original production. The play was first performed at the Yale Repertory Theatre in New Haven, before coming to Broadway. Through the telling of Ma Rainey's story (the real Ma Rainey was born in 1889 as Gertrude Pridgett and died in 1939), the play also depicts the struggles inherent in developing black music in a white-dominated music industry. In 2002, *Ma Rainey's Black Bottom* enjoyed a revival on Broadway at the Royale Theatre. It was directed by Marion McClinton and starred Charles Dutton and Whoopi Goldberg. *Ma Rainey's Black Bottom* was the first installment of Wilson's ten-play cycle examining the African American experience to reach the stage.

[See also Black Arts Movement; Political Theater in the United States; United States, 1940–Present]

FURTHER READING

Bogunil, Mary L. *Understanding August Wilson*. Columbia: Univ. of South Carolina Press, 1999.

Perlira, Kim. *August Wilson and the African-American Odyssey*. Urbana: Univ. of Illinois Press, 1995.

Wilson, August. *The Ground on Which I Stand*. New York: Theatre Communications Group, 2001.

Ellen Anthony-Moore and Christopher Moore

MARAINI, DACIA (1936–)

One of ITALY's most famous, bestselling contemporary authors, Dacia Maraini was born in 1936 in Florence and began her literary career at the age of twenty-six as a novelist. Her first novel, *The Vacation* (1962), met with unexpected success and signaled the beginning of Maraini's over forty-year career as journalist, scriptwriter, and prize-winning poet, novelist, and playwright.

Influenced by the work of LUIGI PIRANDELLO, Carlo Goldoni, and especially BERTOLT BRECHT, Maraini's plays privilege the word and the text over the image favored by experimental theater. Maraini's theater is double-sided: on the one hand, she offers feminist revisions of the great myths and explores such universal issues as the moral and ethical dimensions of justice. For example, she revisits Aeschylus's The Oresteia in DREAMS OF CLYTEMNESTRA (1978) and the myth of the seducer, Don Juan, in Don Juan (1976), The Gecko (Il Geco, 1987), and Giovanni Tenorio (1988). On the other hand, many of these same plays are simultaneously inspired by contemporary events, such as southern Italian immigration or the student movements of the late 1960s. Thus her writing is linked both to current events and to the mythical or historical roots of current events and grapples with profound and transcendent questions of human existence, human relations, the notion of power, the formation of identity, and the function of the unconscious.

Maraini's career as a playwright started in 1967, when she participated in founding small theater companies, such as Compagnia del Porcospino, La compagnia blu, and Teatroggi. Influenced by the LIVING THEATRE, Maraini's companies performed in the streets and operated shoestring theaters in garages. This was called decentramento, the decentralizing of theater production away from state-funded, bourgeois theaters, which sponsored canonical plays, and toward an autonomous theater that would reach, educate, and be shaped by the working-class audience.

The class struggles of the late 1960s offered not only topics to write about but also a democratization of theater duties. In these theater companies, Maraini learned every aspect of theater production—for example, cleaning, costume repair, lighting, and directing—but shunned acting. All this helped her fare teatro, "to make theater."

By the 1970s Maraini was writing and directing for both street theater and traditional venues. In 1973 she helped to open the famous underground women's theater Teatro della Maddalena, a collaborative theater company devoted to women's issues, which closed in 1990 for lack of funding. Maraini has always been "on the side of women," and women's issues, already evident in her 1960s plays, became central in the 1970s, at the height of the second-wave Italian feminist movement. Maraini's plays denounce sexual violence and oppressive social institutions like the patriarchal family, the Catholic Church, and marriage. They criticize Italy's medical, educational, and penal systems. In the 1970s, theater and activism often united. For example, Maraini fought for and wrote about the right to abortion, which was legalized in 1981 in Italy. Among her most controversial and radical plays, and also one of her most often performed, is the Dialogue Between a Prostitute and Her Client (Dialogo di una prostituta con un suo cliente, 1973), which brings together many of her recurring concerns: prostitution, the dehumanization of the female body, the suppression of female sexuality, and the role of the actress.

One of Maraini's great contributions to Italian theater is her development of complex female characters, fictional and historical, which offer a rich repertoire for actresses tired of stereotypical roles. Maraini has written TRAGEDIES and COMEDIES about women as prostitutes, women as housewives, women as writers, and religious women, many of them transgressive characters. Her innovative Mary Stuart (Maria Stuarda, 1980), about Mary Queen of Scots, continues to be her most performed play. It won the 1980 Lysistrata Prize (International Sitges Festival) and opened in 1987 in New York City at the experimental theater La Mama.

Maraini's plays have enjoyed great international success. Now a world-renowned playwright, Maraini receives many invitations to lecture as more and more translations of her work appear. In fact, much of Maraini's play writing, as she herself points out, is on request, since she no longer has a theater company. One of her more recent plays, The Head-Chopper at Villa Borghese (Il tagliatore di teste a Villa Borghese, 2003), was commissioned for the centennial of the Villa Borghese, located in Rome where Maraini has lived for decades. Her plays, she says, have a life of their own and are being produced all over the world, often without her knowledge. This allows her, after many years of struggling with production, to concentrate on her writing.

PLAYS: Centocelle: The Years of Fascism (Centocelle: Gli anni del fascismo, 1971); Dialogue Between a Prostitute and Her Client (Dialogo di una prostituta con un suo cliente, 1973); Don Juan (1976); Dreams of Clytemnestra (I sogni di Clitennestra, 1978); Mary Stuart (Maria Stuarda, 1980); The Gecko (Il Geco, 1987); Giovanni Tenorio (1988); Crime at the Tennis Club (Delitto, 1994); Love Letters: Unedited Letters by Gabriele D'Annunzio Presented as Theatre (Lettere d'amore: Lettere inedite di Gabriele D'Annunzio rilette in forma teatrale 2002); The Head-Chopper at Villa Borghese (Il tagliatore di teste a Villa Borghese, 2003)

FURTHER READING

Diaconescu-Blumenfeld, Rodica, and Ada Testaferri, eds. The Pleasure of Writing: Critical Essays on Dacia Maraini. West Lafayette, Ind.: Purdue Univ. Press, 2000.

France, Anna Kay, and P. J. Corso, eds. International Women Playwrights: Voices of Identity and Transformation—Proceedings of the First International Women Playwrights Conference, October 18–23, 1988. Metuchen, N.J.: Scarecrow, Press, 1993 [includes discussion by Maraini].

Merry, Bruce. Dacia Maraini and the Written Dream of Women in Modern Italian Literature. Townsville, Australia: James Cook Univ. of North Queensland, 1997.

Picchietti, Virginia. Relational Spaces: Daughterhood, Motherhood and Sisterhood in Dacia Maraini's Writings and Films. Madison, N.J.: Fairleigh Dickinson Univ. Press, 2002.

Weinberg, M. Grazia Sumeli. Invito alla lettura di Dacia Maraini [Invitation to a reading of Dacia Maraini]. Pretoria: Univ. of South Africa, 1993.

Wright, Simona. "Intervista a Dacia Maraini" [Interview with Dacia Maraini]. Italian Quarterly 34 (Winter–Spring 1997): 71–91.

Tommasina Gabriele

MARAT/SADE

Fifteen years after his assassination, the death of Marat is staged by the Marquis de Sade in the Asylum of Charenton, where dissidents and misfits were warehoused during FRANCE's political restoration under Napoleon. Though purely fictional (Marat and de Sade never met), PETER WEISS's play within a play, *The Persecution and Assassination of Jean-Paul Marat as Performed by The Inmates of the Asylum of Charenton Under the Direction of the Marquis de Sade* (*Die Verfolgung und Ermordung Jean Paul Marats dargestellt durch die Schauspielgruppe des Hospizes zu Charenton unter Anleitung des Herrn de Sade*, 1964), is grounded in two historical facts: de Sade did stage theater productions in the asylum (it became fashionable for the Parisian "glitterati" to attend them); and de Sade did deliver a speech commemorating Marat upon his death.

The dramatic tension in Weiss's play occurs through a clever theatrical device: the revolutionary Marat is given the chance to explain and defend his position under the "direction" of his antipode de Sade. The former has been assassinated, and his political legacy is being obliterated by Napoleon Bonaparte; the latter has been "contained" in the asylum where he will eventually die. Neither Marat's nor de Sade's view of the world appears compelling when the play within the play is staged: the social revolution and the revolution of the body have failed. But this is the point of Weiss's play: these revolutions are still to be carried out. Karl Marx and his successors' visions have been realized (as Weiss saw it) in one part of the world, but there the development of the individual to true freedom is prevented by a regressive moral and artistic code. In the other half of the world, the individual is free to experiment in art and with psychoananlytic theories that promise liberation from neuroses and a repressive upbringing, but the individual is kept ignorant of the ultimate cause of his or her oppression, the economic system.

The asylum provides an aesthetic vacuum in which the two worldviews can confront each other as if in a scientific experiment. However, through a series of anachronisms built into the play (Marat speaks of "agents of the stock market" and of those in power as living "in fortresses built of marble and steel"), Weiss indicates that it is not so much the past that is at stake but the present of the two political systems on German soil. In the East, the revolution dictated from above has ended in a German version of Stalinism and the empowerment of a new caste of paranoid petit bourgeois anxiously watching over the privileges they have awarded themselves. In the West, where the promise of individual freedom has ended in pure consumerism, the sociopolitical system tries to keep its customers happy by constantly reinventing itself through new "waves" (e.g., the "eating wave," the "travel wave," the "sex wave"). The asylum indicates the precarious situation of both political systems, which have to keep their own promises alive to justify themselves, while simultaneously having to contain the masses from taking those very promises too far. As the play ends and the inmates threaten to get out of control (they want both "Revolution Revolution" and "Copulation Copulation"), the repressive state apparatus in the form of the nursing staff wields its baton under the command of Coulmier, the director of the asylum.

The play reflects Weiss's view of the author forced to write in a divided world. Marat gets censored in the West; de Sade, in turn, gets censored in the East. Weiss's attempts to combine calls for political revolution with insistence on artistic innovation and his love for historic figures like Leon Trotsky (1879–1940) and Friedrich Hölderlin (1770–1843) (who in his view were working toward the same goal) made Weiss, both literally and intellectually, an exile of both Germanys. Accordingly, the first productions of the play in East (Rostock, 1965) and West GERMANY (West Berlin, 1964) were both inadequate, as they were not able to go beyond the dichotomy between the social revolution and the revolution of the body, finding it necessary to favor one position over the other. Weiss had attempted to preempt such one-sided interpretations by incorporating so many elements of uncertainty into the play that it becomes impossible to say whether the author himself favors one side. De Sade is the director, but he is also an inmate. The inmates play their roles in the play within the play but also their roles as inmates; when they "act insane," they are still playing their parts. Marat gets the opportunity to speak but only as directed by de Sade. The events of 1808 (the time of the play within the play) comment on the events of 1793 (the year of Marat's death), but both sets of events are seen from the perspective of the 20th century. It thus becomes clear that whenever one side appears to be "winning," a new set of historical circumstances could reverse the positions.

FURTHER READING

Chaudhuri, Una. "Marat/Sade and the Politics of Interpretation." In *Reading Plays: Interpretation and Reception*, ed. by Hanna Scolnicov and Peter Holland. Cambridge: Cambridge Univ. Press, 1991. 216–226.

Holderness, Graham. "Weiss/Brook: 'Marat/Sade.'" In *Twentieth-Century European Drama*, ed. by Brian Docherty. New York: St. Martin's, 1994. 162–171.

Sontag, Susan. "Marat/Sade/Artaud." *Partisan Review* 32, no. 2 (1965): 210–219.

Friedemann J. Weidauer

MARBER, PATRICK (1964–)

Patrick Marber's plays are urbane, witty, and sardonic in tone; in terms of content, they represent a departure from the anti–Margaret Thatcher polemics that often dominated the British stage during the previous decade. The work of Marber—along with that of MARTIN MCDONAGH, Joe Penhall, Jez Butterworth—marked the arrival of a new generation of British playwrights, whose work cannot be conveniently placed under any particular label or catchphrase. In contrast to the so-called In-Yer-Face contingent (SARAH KANE, MARK RAVENHILL, ANTHONY NEILSON), Marber's work tends to be more polished and less graphic in tone and subject matter.

Born to a Jewish family in Wimbledon, ENGLAND, in 1964, and educated at Oxford, Marber is a rare specimen in the world of British theater because he came to the stage after establishing a successful career in television and stand-up COMEDY. Marber's break came when the National Theatre decided to produce his first play *Dealer's Choice* in 1995. Much like DAVID MAMET's dissection of the real estate industry in GLENGARRY GLEN ROSS, *Dealer's Choice* is an astute study of a very particular milieu—the Sunday night game of poker. Though ostensibly concerned with gambling, the play is really about male relationships and power struggles.

CLOSER (1997), Marber's follow-up to *Dealer's Choice*, represents the playwright's foray into the gender conflict. Marber's acerbic look at the politics of intimacy was immediately compared to DAVID HARE's *Skylight* and HAROLD PINTER's BETRAYAL. *Closer* examines the genealogy of two couples and their intimate ties—they fall in and out of love, swap partners, and eventually become estranged from each other. Thus, the play's subject matter—infidelity and its effects—is examined from a distance. What is disturbing is not the act of infidelity itself but the aftermath and how the various characters obsessively attempt to remain truthful about their behavior and their motivations. Avoiding didacticism, Marber's play unflinchingly exposes the most brutal aspects of interpersonal relationships.

The third play of Marber's London trilogy, *Howard Katz* (2001), was less well received by the London critics. The play is concerned with a caustic Jewish talent agent who is in the throes of a midlife crisis. Several reviewers compared Marber's tragic hero to Willy Loman of DEATH OF A SALESMAN. However, the comparison is ill chosen because Howard Katz, unlike Willy Loman, is a financially successful dealmaker who is feared and respected. Hence, Marber's TRAGICOMEDY is actually about a man who is bored with success and its rewards. Howard Katz's spiraling self-destruction suggests parallels with Hermann Hesse's *Steppenwolf* and David Mamet's *Edmond* and offers a caustic appraisal of contemporary society—its conception of success, and its mindless veneration of celebrity culture.

Given Marber's interest in sexual politics, it is not surprising that he turned to AUGUST STRINDBERG's MISS JULIE. Marber updates Strindberg's 1888 text by setting the TRAGEDY in a specifically English setting—a country estate just outside of London on the eve of Labour's election victory in 1945. Marber's *After Miss Julie* (1995), which was successfully staged at the Donmar Warehouse in 2003, is an inventive rewrite that boldly dramatizes the Gordian knot of gender, sex, and class conflict that is characteristic of Marber's work.

PLAYS: *After Miss Julie* (1995, 2003); *Dealer's Choice* (1995); *Closer* (1997); *Howard Katz* (2001); *The Musicians* (2004)

FURTHER READING

Droomgoole, Dominic. *The Full Room: An A–Z of Contemporary Playwrighting.* London: Methuen, 2000.

Riggs, Thomas, ed. *Contemporary Dramatists.* 6th ed. Detroit: St. James Press, 1999.

Sierz, Aleks. *In-Yer-Face Theatre British Drama Today.* London: Faber, 2000.

James L. Penner

MARCEL POUSUIVI PAR LES CHIENS *See* MARCEL PURSUED BY HOUNDS

MARCEL PURSUED BY HOUNDS

Unlike the furor with which THE SISTERS-IN-LAW (*Les belles soeurs*) entered Québécois stages, *Marcel Pursued by Hounds* (*Marcel pousuivi par les chiens*, 1992), by MICHEL TREMBLAY, enters the theatrical scene more quietly after Tremblay had already fully established his presence, his characters, and joual as mainstays of Québécois theater. Like Tremblay's oeuvre in general, this play also seeks to depict the working class and underclasses of the Montreal urban landscape in the stark reality of idiomatic joual and unapologetic characters: Marcel as lost innocent, epileptic, possibly insane, but more likely the product of alienation, and Thérèse as alcoholic waitress in a strip club. Marcel is first observed by the "sisters" as running. They discuss the last time they saw him and remark upon the changes in his physicality. He collapses in front of the women, an adolescent of fifteen years old, believing he is being pursued by "the dogs," or the police (but could just as easily be interpreted as the hounds of conscience or traumatic memory), fearing for his life that he will be framed for a murder which he has just witnessed of a stripper. Marcel had gone to the strip club where his sister works in order to borrow money to pay for a pair of sunglasses he bought from a young hustler on the Main. The sunglasses are symbolic of Marcel's desire to view an alternate reality, to escape his painful life. Through the sunglasses, Marcel becomes invisible. While searching for his sister in the back rooms, he happens upon the murder of Carmen in a bathtub by the owner of the club.

This play consists of six characters, four of which are best understood as the three Fates (Rose, Violette, Mauve) and their mother (Florence), who endlessly knit baby booties. Marcel and his sister Thérèse comprise the remainder. The Fates function as an omniscient chorus that describes the state of the characters, offering to the audience an intimacy that Marcel and Thérèse are likely to be incapable of revealing, due to their own traumatized state of being. The presence of such a chorus inspires the audience to recall the grand TRAGEDIES of classical Greek theater, thereby suggesting that the fates of the people of Montreal's Main are players in the same scope of tragedy as the characters of the Greek classical age. Additionally, this play features the reappearance of Marcel and Thérèse from Tremblay's In Detached Parts (En pièces detaches, 1969), in which Thérèse is established as an alcoholic waitress locked into an unhappy marriage with Gérard. Audiences learn in Marcel Pursued that Thérèse was forced to marry due to her premarital pregnancy but that she gives up the child to be raised by a neighbor; she visits the child every day. This play depicts the continuing struggle for survival in a society that functions within outmoded social and moral codes, poverty, and its offspring dysfunctionality; it depicts the meniality of urban life in a working-class neighborhood. It also engages the notion of home and the emptiness when one realizes that one cannot go home to a home that was never there, nor can one return to the safety of childhood if that had also been robbed.

[See also Canada]

FURTHER READING

Moss, Jane. "Québécois Theatre: Michel Tremblay and Marie Laberge." Theatre Research International 21, no. 3: 196–207.

Oddipov, Helene. "French Variation and the Teaching of Québec Literature: A Linguistic Guide to a litterature joualisante." The French Review 67, no. 6 (1994): 944–953.

Usmiani, Renate. Michel Tremblay. Vancouver: Douglas and McIntyre, 1982.

Jolene Armstrong

MARCHESSAULT, JOVETTE (1938–)

A major figure in Québécoise lesbian, feminist, francophone, and native literature, Jovette Marchessault began her career as an artist and sculptor and later wrote prolifically. Many of her French plays and prose works have been translated into English. Although Marchessault has experimented widely with novels that veer between fiction and autobiography and with plays exploring unconventional staging techniques, her themes are consistent. Marchessault lambasts what she perceives as the stifling legacy of Catholic clerical misogyny, masculinist historiography, domestic violence, patriarchy within Quebec, homophobia, and poverty.

A typical strategy in a Marchessault play involves a quest to reclaim some lost paradise. Typically, the characters will be historical women, who examine history, emphasizing their sex's contribution to society—a contribution overlooked in male-dominated histories. The quest for a lost paradise relates to Marchessault's biographical circumstances. Marchessault enjoyed her childhood. After Jovette's Montreal birth, the family moved outside of the city for wartime munitions work. Her grandmother, a half-Indian herbalist, permanently influenced Marchessault—particularly her anger about the destruction of Amerindian civilization. Her father lost his job after the war. At thirteen, Jovette left school (her wide learning is largely the result of autodidacticism) to work in a textile factory. Many

years of unsatisfying, menial jobs followed, giving Marchessault her lifelong affinity with the working classes, particularly with badly paid working-class women.

By 1975, after much traveling in search of her identity and roots, Marchessault was a successful artist and an author. Her first novel, 1975's Comme une Enfant de la Terre (Like a Child of the Earth), won the Prix France-Québec in 1976. Her first play was performed in 1979 at Montreal's Théâtre du Nouveau Monde: its success inspired Marchessault to turn to drama. Night Cows (Les Vaches de nuit, 1978) is a monologue adapted from Marchessault's prose work Triptych Lesbian (Tryptique Lesbien). On the 1980 publication of that work, Marchessault announced her homosexuality publicly. In the play, all divine and earthly power is wielded by nonviolent, responsible females—the women are imagined as responsible, mutually respectful, loving milk cows.

SAGA OF THE WET HENS (La Saga de Poulers Mouillées) was produced at the Tarragon Theatre, Toronto, in 1982. Four historical Quebec women writers meet in an imagined vortex of time and space, celebrating female agency and memories. They dream of future triumphs for women. The Ground Is Too Short, Violette Leduc (La Terre est trop courte, Violette Leduc) was performed by Montreal's Théâtre Experimental des Femmes, also in 1982. This ambitious play features twenty-one characters. Leduc, a real-life friend of JEAN-PAUL SARTRE and Simone de Beauvoir, battles inner demons and social pressures to express herself creatively. Then 1987's Anaïs in the Tail of Comet (Anaïs dans la Queue de la Comète) celebrates the controversial woman of letters Anaïs Nin. Many more plays have followed: The Splendid Voyage of Emily Carr (Le Voyage Magnifique d'Emily Carr) won the Governor General's Award for its production at Montreal's Théâtre d'Aujourd'hui in 1990; The Lion of Bangor (Le Lion de Bangor) was performed at the Théâtre L'Aire de Jeu in 1993. In 2000, Marchessault returned to her theatrical beginnings. The ninety-minute monologue, The Peregrine Cherubnic (La Pérégrin Chérubinique) was performed at Théâtre d'Aujourd'hui by Marchessault's original dramatic collaborator Pol Pelletier.

[See also Canada; Gay and Lesbian Drama]

PLAYS: Night Cows (Les Vaches de nuit, 1978); The Ground Is Too Short, Violette Leduc (La Terre est trop courte, Violette Leduc, 1982); Saga of the Wet Hens (La Saga de poulers mouillées, 1982); Anaïs in the Tail of Comet (Anaïs dans la queue de la comète, 1987); The Splendid Voyage of Emily Carr (Le Voyage magnifique d'Emily Carr, 1990); The lion of Bangor (Le Lion de Bangor, 1993); The Peregrine Cherubnic (La Pérégrin Chérubinique, 2000)

FURTHER READING

Forsyth, Louise. "Jovette Marchessault." In The Oxford Companion to Canadian Literature, ed. by Eugene Benson and William Toye. Toronto: Oxford Univ. Press, 1997. 726–728.

Gaboriau, Linda. "Jovette Marchessault: A Luminous Wake in Space." Canada Theatre Review 43 (1985): 91–99.

Hannan, Annika. "Jovette Marchessault." In *Encyclopedia of Literature in Canada*, ed. by William H. New. Toronto: Univ. of Toronto Press, 2002. 710–711.

Rosenfeld, Martha. "The Development of a Lesbian Sensibility in the Work of Jovette Marchessault and Nicole Brossard." In *Traditionalism, Nationalism, and Feminism: Women Writers of Quebec*, ed. by Paula Gilbert Lewis. Westport, Conn.: Greenwood Press, 1985. 227–239.

Kevin De Ornellas

MARGARET FLEMING

> It is such damn scoundrels as you that make and destroy homes.
> —Doctor Lyn, Act 1

By using a domestic narrative to challenge dual sexual standards and class assumptions, JAMES HERNE introduced a new level of American dramatic REALISM with his play *Margaret Fleming* (1890). The play frankly depicts a woman's response to the discovery that her businessman husband has abandoned a female former employee who has died bearing his child.

No original scripts for *Margaret Fleming* survive; a 1909 fire at the Herne home destroyed all known drafts. Five years later, Katherine Corcoran Herne, the playwright's wife, collaborated with Hamlin Garland to recreate the script from memory.

Philip Fleming seems to embody masculine camaraderie, shrewd business ethics, and paternal benevolence. A series of conversations quickly shows that his prosperity rests precariously on questionable trade practices. Larkin, the family doctor, calls to reveal the Flemings' home life as equally illusory. Philip's former mistress and employee has given birth to Fleming's illegitimate son. Philip rejects responsibility, claiming, "I've done all I could for her." Margaret learns of the child through the mother's sister, nurse to the Fleming's little girl. The mother has refused to name the father. Margaret visits the nurse and sister, arriving just after the woman has died, and learns the truth from a letter to Philip. Shock aggravates the glaucoma that Larkin diagnosed earlier, blinding Margaret. The child cries for food, Margaret sightlessly begins to nurse it, and the act closes as Philip enters the room unnoticed.

The brief final act opens in the Fleming home, following Philip's weeklong absence. He returns to explain that he has been hospitalized after wandering homeless and finally attempting suicide. Margaret urges him to stay and resume his career. She agrees to forgive him but adds that "the wife-heart has gone out of me." She confronts him with his hypocrisy, asking, "Suppose—I—had been unfaithful to you?" Stunned into recognition, Philip vows to regain Margaret's affection. The play ends hopefully; surgery likely will restore Margaret's sight, Philip agrees to raise the child, and reconciliation seems at least possible.

The restored script includes major changes that move it closer to MELODRAMA than earlier accounts suggest. Herne altered the script several times himself, however, with Katherine's collaboration. Prior versions included a seven-year gap before the final act, the boy's death, Margaret's continued blindness, and most significantly, her clear break with the now-alcoholic Philip.

Literary realists and some critics hailed the play, but others attacked it. Garland (1893) called it "one of the most radical plays from a native author ever performed in America," and Herne's comparison to HENRIK IBSEN lasted well into the 20th century. The simulation of Margaret baring her breast to nurse the child shocked many, as did the frank portrayal of illegitimacy and infidelity, and Boston theater owners blocked production. Convinced of the play's value, Herne renovated a hall above the Chickering Piano Company into an intimate space, following ANDRÉ ANTOINE's example. The Hernes' investment and production support led to near insolvency. Ironically, the play that gave Herne lasting fame and his strongest effect on American dramatic realism never made money during his life.

[*See also* United States, 1860–1929]

FURTHER READING

Bucks, Dorothy S., and Arthur H. Nethercot. "Ibsen and Herne's *Margaret Fleming*: A Study of the Early Ibsen Movement in America." *American Literature* 17, no. 4 (January 1946): 311–332.

Garland, Hamlin. "The Future of Fiction," *The Arena* 7 (April 1893): 543.

Hewitt, Barnard. "*Margaret Fleming* in Chickering Hall: The First Little Theatre in America?" *Theatre Journal* 34, no. 2 (May 1982): 165–171.

Knowles, Lawrence John. "Psychological Realism in James A. Herne's *Margaret Fleming*: An Empirical Test." Ph.D. diss., Southern Illinois Univ., 1989.

Pizer, Donald. "An 1890 Account of *Margaret Fleming*." *American Literature* 27, no. 2 (May 1955): 264–267.

——. "The Radical Drama in Boston, 1889–1891." *New England Quarterly* 31 (September 1958): 589–591.

Wegner, Pamela S. "*Margaret Fleming*: James A. Herne's Contributions to American Realism." *New England Theatre Journal* 1, no. 1 (1990): 19–29.

Ron West

MARGOLIN, DEB (1951–)

Deb Margolin, born in Westchester County, New York, in 1951, is an internationally recognized playwright and performance artist whose work has shaped and generated feminist theater in the United States since the early 1980s. Margolin majored in English as an undergraduate at New York University, although during her senior year she had the realization that she "knew nothing about matter" and decided to finish her degree by studying science. In addition to touring the UNITED STATES and Europe as a founding member of SPLIT BRITCHES Theater Company, Margolin has authored seven full-length solo performance pieces, as well as numerous plays, that she has toured throughout the United States.

Margolin launched into the world of performance writing when she joined Lois Weaver and Peggy Shaw to found the groundbreaking lesbian performance group Split Britches. At the time, Weaver and Shaw were working on a show about three women (distant relatives of Weaver's) who had spent their lives in Virginia, living in almost complete isolation. Margolin accidentally became the company's scriptwriter after composing a significant portion of the monologues, scenes, and songs for what would become *Split Britches*, the company's signature piece. The three-woman white, "lesbian" troupe would go on to produce a variety of shows such as *Upwardly Mobile Home, Little Women: The Tragedy, Beauty and the Beast,* and *Lesbians Who Kill,* which have set the stage of lesbian and feminist performance through their witty and audacious deconstructions of canonical texts, cabaret forms, lip synching, vaudeville, and unrelentingly probing explorations of class and gender violence.

Although Margolin's time with Split Britches as a writer, collaborator, and ultimately a performer marked some of the most prolific years of her life, she felt the need to use language to explore other images more closely related to her own experience, "images of divinity and mortality," and images and language that would allow her to engage with her heteronormativity. Margolin's solo performance work attends to the small moments of the everyday, savors ordinary exchanges, and tracks the minutia that enliven and compose our desires. Her work is "a theater of desire"—it is written from the body and is highly erotic. Margolin's work tracks the boundaries between the mimetic and the real, pushes beyond the unspeakable of language, and invents ever more subtle and supple ways for performance to upend commonly held notions of temporality.

Margolin's work has been performed in New York City venues including P.S. 122, HERE Arts Center, Women's Interart Theater, and Dixon Place. Margolin's play *Three Seconds in the Key,* loosely based on her relationship with her son during a recent bout with cancer, was performed by New Georges at the Baruch Performing Arts Center in New York City in 2004. *Index to Idioms,* Margolin's recent performance piece, opened at The Culture Project in 2005. Prior to becoming an instructor in theater studies at Yale University, she was an instructor at universities around the country.

[*See also* Feminist Drama in the United States]

SELECT PLAYS: *Of All the Nerve* (1989); *970-DEBB* (1990); *Gestation* (1991); *Of Mice, Bugs and Women* (1993); *Carthieves! Joyrides!* (1995); *O Wholly Night and Other Jewish Solecisms* (1996); *Critical Mass* (1997); *Three Seconds in the Key* (2004); *Index to Idioms* (2005)

FURTHER READING
Margolin, Deb, and Lynda Hart. *Of All the Nerve: Deb Margolin SOLO.* London and New York: Cassell, 1999.
Vernon, Alexia. "Crossing Over the Line: An Evening with Deb Margolin."

Kerry Moore

MARINETTI, FILIPPO TOMMASO (1876–1944)

Filippo Tommaso Marinetti was a revolutionary force in modernist theater, establishing the AVANT-GARDE in ITALY through his many writings and public activities. He wrote five groundbreaking manifestos: "The Manifesto of Futurist Playwrights" (1911), later published under the title "The Pleasure of Being Booed" (1915); "The Variety Theatre Manifesto" (1913); "The Manifesto of the Dynamic and Synoptic Declamation" (written in 1914, published in 1916); "The Manifesto of Futurist Synthetic Theatre" (1914); and "The Theatre of Surprise" (1921).

Marinetti is widely recognized as a pioneer who called into question turn-of-the-century theatrical conventions and sought to expand the range of possibilities for the genre. According to Marinetti and the futurists, dramatic works should be written onstage, not at the playwright's desk. His theatrical debut took place in Paris in 1909, with *King Revel (aka The Feasting King) (Le Roi Bombance),* and his early years were characterized by a fiercely polemic stance vis-à-vis traditional forms of drama and the bourgeois theater represented by GABRIELE D'ANNUNZIO and his followers. *King Revel* was met with mixed reviews, but the attention it received served to propel the movement and its appeal. The same can be said of the play *Electric Dolls (Poupées électriques),* performed in Turin under the title *The Woman Is Fickle (La donna è mobile)* in January 1909 and later as *Electricity (Elettricità).*

As early as 1910, Marinetti and his followers gathered in cafés for theatrical evenings, called *serate,* which effectively brought their political-poetic agenda to the public. Performances were often preceded by readings of manifestos and poems. Their program resembled a collision course, juxtaposing traditional forms with avant-garde experimentation in every conceivable way, often inspiring violent outbursts among patrons. Futurist theater was also designed to surprise to the point of hilarity, absurdity, and even to cajole spectators out of passivity through a unique blend of improvisation with the mesmerizing effects of constant change and perpetual motion. In its earliest and purest form, ITALIAN FUTURISM under Marinetti had a profound impact on other European movements, most notably DADAISM, SURREALISM, and RUSSIAN FUTURISM.

"Futurist Synthetic Theatre" is a collection of plays written in 1915–1916 by Marinetti and his closest collaborators that reflect the principles of the avant-garde as a programmatic agenda to transform the performing arts. Marinetti maintained that theater must appeal primarily to the senses rather than the intellect, relying on the culture of the music hall and *café-concert.* Based on improvisation and the talent of the performers themselves, this form promised to bring out a new freshness and immediacy that would shake the practice of theater to its foundations.

"The Manifesto of the Dynamic and Synoptic Declamation" offered guidelines for performers, aiming to create the illusion of mechanical beauty through technical agility. "The Theatre of Surprise" (1921) consisted of a touring company directed by

Rodolfo de Angelis that set out to bring every element of debate, novelty, and surprise from the stage to the audience and subsequently to the streets, with the aim of making an indelible mark on the public consciousness. By 1921, however, futurist theater had found itself diluted by new voices, including LUIGI PIRANDELLO, Luigi Antonelli, and Rosso di San Secondo.

With the advent of second futurism in the late 1920s and 1930s, the creative strength of the movement was compromised due to Marinetti's ambivalent attitude toward fascism under Benito Mussolini. The novelty and freshness of the Italian avant-garde and its influence on European culture faded away during the course of World War II, ending with Marinetti's death in 1944 more than three decades after the publication of "The Variety Theatre Manifesto."

SELECT PLAYS: *The Woman Is Fickle (La donna è mobile*, 1909); *Electricity (Elettricità*, 1913); *Zang Tumb Tumb* (1914); *Synthetic Theater (Teatro Sintetico*, 1915–1916); *Theater of Surprise (Teatro della Sorpresa*, 1921); *The Fire Drum (Il tamburo di fuoco*, 1922); *Prisoners (Prigionieri*, 1925); *Volcano (Vulcano*, 1926); *The Ocean of the Heart (L'oceano del cuore*, 1927); *The Prisoners and the Love (I prigionieri e l'amore*, 1927); *Fast Lights (Luci veloci*, 1929); *The Prompter Knot (Il suggeritore nudo*, 1929); *Simultaneous One (Simultanina*, 1931)

FURTHER READING

Antonucci, Giovanni. Lo spettacolo futurista in Italia [The futurist show in Rome]. Rome: Studium, 1976.

Berghaus, Günter. Italian Futurist Theatre, 1909–1944. Oxford: Oxford Univ. Press, 1998.

Kirby, Micheal, and Victoria Nes Kirby. Futurist Performance. New York: PAJ Pubs., 1986.

Daria Valentini

MARRIED TO A CELESTIAL LADY

Married to a Celestial Lady (Tianxian pei, Huangmei xi) by Lu Hongfei is the most famous example of an opera style called *Huangmei xi* (Huangmei opera), which takes its name from its place of origin Huangmei in eastern Hubei Province on the border with Anhui. Huangmei opera is currently most popular in Anhui Province.

Originally a small-scale folk style, Huangmei opera was first brought to Shanghai in the early 1930s. Its heyday was the 1950s, when significant numbers of professional companies and a training system were established, old artists assisted with the rearrangement of traditional items, and scenery was added to performances of items like *Married to a Celestial Lady*. The Chinese Cultural Revolution led to the virtual suspension of Huangmei opera, but it was restored afterward, with fifty-three professional companies operating in 1983. Although the style retains a following, modernization has led to its decline.

According to tradition, the repertoire of the early Huangmei operas was small, with only thirty-six major items and seventy-two minor ones. After 1949, the Chinese Communist Party (CCP) organized Huangmei opera artists to rearrange some of these items to remove the factors they found politically unacceptable and give play to those the CCP favored, such as showing the poor in a favorable light. The CCP also had some new items written to show contemporary life in ways it favored.

Married to a Celestial Lady was among the traditional items. Awarded the first prize in the East China Festival of Tradition Dramas in 1954 and 1955, it is a fairy story based on the historical character Dong Yong of the second century C.E., famed for his filial piety, and has existed in many versions and in many different regional styles.

In the story, Dong Yong is unable to pay for his dead father's funeral, so he borrows the necessary money on condition that he becomes his creditor's slave for three years. The Jade Emperor's Seventh Daughter sympathizes with his plight; she secretly comes to earth and marries him, arranging with the creditor for repayment in embroidery. She weaves enough in one night to enable Dong Yong to shorten his enslavement from three years to a hundred days. However, with the period over, the Jade Emperor forces his daughter to return to heaven, leaving Dong and Seventh Daughter devastated at being compelled to part.

Lu's rearrangement of the piece eliminates the element of destiny and strengthens the hostility to the feudal system of society by showing the TRAGEDY of separation of lovers who have come together not by parents' arrangement but by choice. In older versions, Dong Yong eventually marries the daughter of the family that has enslaved him, but this is removed in the new version. The characterization of the Seventh Daughter brings out her strength as a woman, while Dong Yong is shown as a loyal and pure peasant, both on the side of the people.

[See also China]

FURTHER READING

Lu Hongfei et al. *Tianxian pei* [Married to a Celestial Being]. In *Zhongguo difang xiqu jicheng, Anhui sheng juan* [Collection of Chinese Local Traditional Dramas, Anhui Province], comp. by Chinese Dramatists Association and Anhui Provincial Cultural Bureau. Beijing: Chinese Theatre Press, 1959. 129–193.

Wen Nian. "Huangmeixi" [Huangmei opera] and *Tianxian pei* [Married to a Celestial Being]. In *Zhongguo da baike quanshu, xiqu quyi* [China encyclopedia, traditional theatre and balladry], comp. by Zhang Geng et al. Beijing, Shanghai: China Encyclopedia Press, 1983. 132–133, 390–391.

Colin Mackerras

MARTÍNEZ SIERRA, GREGORIO (1881–1947)

Gregorio Martínez Sierra was a renowned playwright, director, and producer of early-20th-century theater in SPAIN. His career as a playwright started in 1909 with *The Shadow of the Father (La sombra del padre)*. Two years later, Martínez Sierra wrote his most celebrated play, *Cradle song* (*Canción de cuna*, 1911). Later on he not only wrote but also proceeded to direct and produce his own work. Other significant plays by Martínez Sierra include *Mother* (*Mamá*, 1912), *Madame Pepita* (1912), *Dawn* (*Amanecer*, 1915), *Rosina Is Fragile* (*Rosina es frágil*, 1918), *Dream of One Night in August* (*Sueño de una noche de agosto*, 1920), *Don Juan of Spain* (*Don Juan de España*, 1921), and *Triangle* (*Triángulo*, 1930).

A cultivated intellectual with a humanist background, Martínez Sierra married María O. Lejárraga in 1900. They did not have any children, a significant detail in view of the fact that his plays deal mostly with femininity and maternity. According to different critics (Patricia O'Connor, Alda Blanco, and Antonia Rodrigo), María actively collaborated, to put it euphemistically, in the writing of the majority of the plays attributed to Gregorio. He was directly involved in the publication of many literary magazines, such as *Vida Moderna* (1901), *Helios* (1903), and *Renacimiento* (1907). Thereafter, he continuously toured the most important Spanish and Latin American cities with his company. In 1917 Martínez Sierra founded a publishing company, Estrella.

On September 24, 1916, a play written by Martínez Sierra titled *The Kingdom of God* (*El reino de Dios*) premiered in his Eslava Theater in Madrid. This premiere was the beginning of a campaign called "Teatro de Arte" that would completely change the way theatrical staging was done in Spain. Martínez Sierra directed and produced his own plays, as well as works by classical and romantic writers and by contemporary European dramatists. He also helped premiere new performances of plays by consecrated Spanish authors as well as helped launch the careers of promising new playwrights.

Martínez Sierra's most important contribution to Spanish literature harks back to his roles as director and producer, for in these capacities he exercised a tremendous influence. As a playwright he contributed little to the renovation of the theater. His COMEDIES have been classified as conventional and soft, charged with excessive sentimentalism. They portray a cheerful vision of the world in which characters, moved by noble feelings, are inclined to act in a generous way. Nevertheless, the predominance of roles for women in his plays helped expose the female side of social reality in his day. The woman is portrayed as victim and redeemer of masculine power, while the role of mother is always a dignified one in his works. This feminine perspective is inherent in plays like *Mother* and *Cradle Song*, a work that shows the maternal instincts that emerge when some nuns unwittingly adopt a baby girl. Through the protagonist of *The Master of the House* (*El ama de la casa*), Martínez Sierra—or should we say María Martínez Sierra?—intertwines femininity and maternity, thereby affirming that woman and mother are one and the same.

SELECT PLAYS: *The Shadow of the Father* (*La sombra del padre*, 1909); *Cradle Song* (*Canción de cuna*, 1911); *Madame Pepita* (1912); *Mother* (*Mamá*, 1912); *Dawn* (*Amanecer*, 1915); *Rosina Is Fragile* (*Rosina es frágil*, 1918); *Dream of One Night in August* (*Sueño de una noche de agosto*, 1920); *Don Juan of Spain* (*Don Juan de España*, 1921); *Triangle* (*Triángulo*, 1930)

FURTHER READING

Douglas Francés, José. "Gregorio Martínez Sierra." *Hispania* 5–6 (1922–1923).

London, John. *Reception and Renewal in Modern Spanish Theatre: 1939–1963*. Leeds, England: W. S. Maney & Son, 1997.

O'Connor, Patricia W. *Gregorio and Maria Martínez Sierra*. New York: Irvington, 1977.

Reyero Hermosilla, Carlos. *Gregorio Martínez Sierra y su teatro de arte* [Gregorio Martínez Sierra and his theater of art]. Madrid: Fundación Juan March, 1980.

Benito Gómez and Jorge Herreros

MARY NO KUBI   See HEAD OF MARY

MARY QUEEN OF SCOTS GOT HER HEAD CHOPPED OFF

> *I ask you, when's a queen a queen*
> *And when's a queen juist a wummin?*
> —La Corbie, Act 1

Mary Queen of Scots Got Her Head Chopped Off is one of Scottish poet and playwright LIZ LOCHHEAD's most popular plays. Commissioned by the Communicado Theatre Company to mark the 400th anniversary of the death of Mary Stuart, it was first performed at the 1987 Edinburgh Festival, where it won a Scotsman Fringe First Award.

As the title suggests, the play is about Mary Queen of Scots (1542–1587), in history usually presented as a romantically tragic figure, and the suffering heroine of, for example, Friedrich Schiller's play *Maria Stuart* (1800). Lochhead steps away from the popular myth and emphasizes the subjective and constructive nature of historical narrative. Accordingly, she has the chorus-figure La Corbie announce that the setting is SCOTLAND but that "it depends. . . . Ah dinna ken whit like your Scotland is / Here's mines."

The play begins with La Corbie cracking her whip and bringing the historically based characters of Mary, Elizabeth, Darnley, Bothwell, Riccio, and Knox onto stage like animals into a circus arena. The following two acts cover the major events in Mary's life, from the rivalry between her and Queen Elizabeth of England and her struggle with the authoritarian Protestant reformer John Knox, to her marriage with Lord Darnley, the birth of their son James VI, her affair with David Riccio, and finally, her disastrous alliance with Bothwell and the events leading to her imprisonment and execution.

Interestingly, Queen Mary's ending, ironically referred to in the title and especially familiar to Lochhead's Scottish audiences, is not played out. Instead, the final scene illustrates the story's modern bearing by transforming the characters of Elizabeth and

Knox into Wee Betty and Wee Knoxxy, 20th-century children who bully a little Catholic girl named Marie.

Mary Queen of Scots Got Her Head Chopped Off is structured around the juxtaposition of Mary and Elizabeth, "two queens in one island, both o' the wan language—mair or less." The actresses who play the queens also double as their maidservants, emphasizing the interchangeable nature of their situation, because despite their difference in background, character, and appearance, both queens similarly struggle to combine their role as sovereign and woman. For Lochhead, the historical narrative is therefore primarily a framework within which to explore general issues from a modern and essentially feminist viewpoint. Various anachronistic props and symbolic references illustrate the timeless relevance of the play's main themes. Lochhead's John Knox, for example, walks with an Orangeman's gait, a satirical allusion to contemporary events. This illustrates Lochhead's claim that her Mary Queen of Scots is more a metaphor for today rather than a history play.

The enormous energy in Lochhead's play is established mainly through its lively and often humorous dialogues and its great variety in nonnaturalistic performance styles. By means of music and costuming, Lochhead achieves a Brechtian ALIENATION EFFECT, warning her audience, once again, that they are witnesses to a dramatic interpretation and not a historical representation of fact.

FURTHER READING

Crawford, Robert, and Anne Varty, eds. *Liz Lochhead's Voices.*
     Edinburgh: Edinburgh Univ. Press, 1993.
Findlay, Bill, ed. *A History of Scottish Theatre.* Edinburgh: Polygon, 1998.
Fraser, Antonia. *Mary Queen of Scots.* London: Weidenfeld & Nicolson,
     1969.
Gifford, Douglas, and Dorothy McMillan, eds. *A History of Scottish
     Women's Writing.* Edinburgh: Edinburgh Univ. Press, 1997.
Stevenson, Randall, and Gavin Wallace, eds. *Scottish Theatre Since the
     Seventies.* Edinburgh: Edinburgh Univ. Press, 1996.

Astrid Van Weyenberg

MA SEN (1932–)

Ma Sen was born in Mainland CHINA in 1932 and started writing and acting at school in 1949. After he received secondary education, he moved to Taiwan. He received his M.A. degree from National Taiwan Normal University in 1959. He went to Paris to study directing and acting. He received his Ph.D. in sociology from the University of British Columbia in 1977. From 1979 to 1987, he taught at the School of Oriental and African Studies, University of London. In 1987, he joined the faculty of the National Cheng Kung University in Taiwan, as a professor. From 1988 to 1989, he was the chief editor of *Unitas* (*Lienhe Wenhsieh*), a well-known literary journal in Taiwan. After retiring from National Cheng Kung University, he joined the faculty of the Graduate School of Literature at Fou Guang University in Taiwan as a professor. His publications include fiction, prose, film scripts, plays, and scholarly studies of Chinese drama.

Ma's plays influenced the LITTLE THEATER MOVEMENT in the 1980s in Taiwan. His plays and drama criticism have deeply influenced theater, academia, and society in Taiwan, especially from the 1980s to the 1990s. His plays are also well regarded by university drama groups in Mainland China, AUSTRALIA, CANADA, and Taiwan as representative works of the experimental theater in the 1980s.

Ma Sen's play *Flower and Sword* (*Hua Yu Jian*) tells the story of a young person's return to his homeland to visit his father's grave. In this play, Ma Sen used a subconscious dreamlike, symbolist style to describe the tormented young person's desperate attempt to free himself from the voice that has been haunting him all through his adult life. As Martha Cheung and Jane Lai point out in *An Oxford Anthology of Contemporary Chinese Drama* (1997), this play could be interpreted as "the dramatization of a painful attempt to deal with the history of one's origins." Rather than adopting REALISM and NATURALISM, this play is full of stylization in the set, costumes, and acting.

Ma Sen's recent plays are different from his previous one-act plays and include three new kinds of drama: COMEDY, operalike musical, and pictorial drama. Since 1990, Ma Sen has focused more on music and dance, for instance, in his musical *Frogs Play* (*Wa xi*, 2002).

Ma Sen has lived in many countries, including Mainland China, Taiwan, FRANCE, ENGLAND, and MEXICO and these different cultures and languages have inspired his work. As Ma Sen pointed out in *Ma Sen xiju luen ji* (*Ma Sen's dramatic criticism,* 1985), by writing literary works, he attempts to communicate with people as a solitary soul. Ma Sen's research includes the Western and Chinese dramas, in addition to comparing modern Chinese drama in Singapore and Taiwan.

SELECT PLAYS: *The Weak* (*Ruo Zhe*, 1970); *and Frogs* (*Wa xi*, 1970, revil 2002); *A Bowl of Cold Congee* (*Yi Wan Liang Zhou*, 1977); *The Sex Worker Who Works in the Mei Li Hua Pub Saves People in Prostitution* (*Meilihua jiunu jiu fengcheng*, 1990); *We Are All Thieves Who Rob People by Lies* (*Women doushi jinguangdang*, 1995); *Balcony* (*Yangtai*, 2001); *A View Outside of a Window* (*Chuang wai fengjing*, 2001)

FURTHER READING

Hwang, Mei-Shu. *Zhonghua xiandai wenxue daxi—xiju juan*
     [Chinese Modern literature: Volume of drama]. Taipei:
     Guo Go, 1989.
Ma Sen. "Thoughts on the Current Literary Scene." Tr. by Janice
     Wickeri. 1991. http://www.renditions.org/renditions/sps/s_35-36
     .html.
——. *Ma Sen xiju luen ji* [Ma Sen, Dramatic Criticism]. Taipei: E. Y.
     Press, 1985.
——. *Flower and Sword.* Tr. by David E. Pollard. In *An Oxford Anthology of
     Contemporary Chinese Drama,* ed. by Martha P. Y. Cheung and Jane
     C. C. Lai. Hong Kong: Oxford Univ. Press, 1997.

Peng, Yiou-Chuen. "Ma Sen dui huaju xianshi zhuyi chuantong de chaoyue yu huigui" [Ma Sen's transcendence and return to realism in drama]. *Qian Xu* (Hwai Yang College School Newspaper—The Section of Philosophy, Social Science) (March 22, 2000).

Xu, Jing-Cheng. "Ma Sen jinqi xiju (1990–2002) de bian yu bu bian—yi pian gailun" [Change and not-change in Ma Sen's recent plays (1990–2002)]. Ph.D. diss. abstract, Fou Guang University, Taiwan, 2003.

Xu, Xue, and Duo Keng. "Lun Ma Sen dumuju de guannian hexin yu xingshi duchuang" [On the core concept and unique creative form of Ma Sen's one-act play]. *Taiwan Research Journal* 1 (1994).

Iris Hsin-chun Tuan

MASON, BRUCE (1921–1982)

Bruce Mason, born on September 28, 1921, in Wellington, NEW ZEALAND, is New Zealand's first major playwright and a vigorous champion of local theater. He was also an actor, short-story writer, literary and musical critic, and in his later years, the country's leading theater critic—in the mold of ENGLAND's Kenneth Tynan. Mason is best known for his plays examining relations between Maori and Pakeha (New Zealanders of British/European extraction) and his bravura solo works.

Mason's first plays, short realist pieces written for Wellington's Unity Theatre, included *The Bonds of Love* (produced 1953), about a prostitute; *The Evening Paper* (produced 1953), a suburban drama that was subsequently expanded and revised for radio and television as well as the stage; and *The Verdict* (produced 1958), based on a recent murder trial. The full-length *Birds in the Wilderness* (produced 1957), about migration, won first place in the 1958 Auckland Festival competition and had a brief run in London's West End.

Mason's most performed play *The Pohutukawa Tree* (1960) tells the tragic story of an important elder, Aroha Mataira, and her harshly puritanical reaction to her daughter's and son's transgressions. Living in a Pakeha community, Aroha feels greatly shamed, but, ironically, those wrongdoings serve to reunite the children with their tribe. Maori material allowed Mason to cultivate the ornate elocution that characterizes his writing. This is especially marked in *Awatea* (1969, produced 1968), whose second-act hui (tribal conference) provides the occasion for particular rhetorical flourish. *Awatea* and Mason's other Maori plays—*The Hand on the Rail* (produced 1965, published 1987), *Swan Song* (produced 1965, published 1987), and *Hongi Hika* (produced 1968, published 1974/1987)—were initially written for radio and for renowned operatic bass Inia Te Wiata.

Frustrated by the limited opportunity for productions of his plays and inspired by EMLYN WILLIAMS's stage biographies of Charles Dickens and DYLAN THOMAS, in 1959 Mason wrote a solo piece that he could perform himself, without any theatrical trappings. *The End of the Golden Weather* (1962) draws on his childhood in the 1930s Depression, whose grim intrusion into the paradisal world of the beach at Te Parenga signals the end of innocent idealism. The florid writing was matched by the virtuosity of Mason's performance—his orotund voice and grandiloquent gestures—which impersonated some forty characters. In 1987 the play was adapted for a larger cast, and in 1991 it was made into a film.

Mason wrote another five solo plays, giving nearly 2,000 performances, abroad as well as in New Zealand, between 1959 and 1978. They include *To Russia with Love* (produced 1965, published 1981), written and rehearsed in one week when Downstage faced a financial crisis. Other plays are *Zero Inn* (1970), about a hippy rock group, and *Blood of the Lamb* (1981), in which Henry and Eliza Higginson are obliged to reveal to their adult daughter that her father is actually her mother and has lived disguised as a man. Henry's outré persona and language inject into long passages of narration a compensatory theatricality.

SELECT PLAYS: *The Licensed Victualler* (operetta, 1954); *A Case in Point* (1956); *Wit's End* (1956); *The Pohutukawa Tree* (1960); *We Don't Want Your Sort Here* (1963); *The Last Supper* (solo piece, 1965); *The Waters of Silence* (solo piece, 1965); *Awatea* (1969); *Virtuous Circle* (1978); *Courting Blackbird* (solo piece, 1981); *Not Christmas But Guy Fawkes* (solo piece, 1981)

FURTHER READING

Balme, Christopher. "Staging Intertextuality: Alternative Models of New Zealand Culture in Bruce Mason's *Blood of the Lamb*." In *Across the Lines: Intertextuality and Transcultural Communication in the New Literatures in English*, ed. by Wolfgang Klooss. Amsterdam: Rodopi, 1998. 261–270.

Dowling, David. *Introducing Bruce Mason*. Auckland: Longman Paul, 1982.

Harding, Bruce. "Liberal Man Encounters 'Kremlin Man' and Russian Man: The Politics of Exclusion and the Meeting of Minds in Bruce Mason's *Courting Blackbird* and *To Russia, with Love*." *New Zealand Slavonic Journal* (1999): 247–272.

Hedback, Ann-Mari. "Purely Local Signs? Bruce Mason's *The Pohutukawa Tree* and *Awatea*." *Association of Commonwealth Literature and Language Studies* 7, no. 3 (1986): 26–35.

McNaughton, Howard. *Bruce Mason*. Wellington, N.Y.: Oxford Univ. Press, 1976.

Stuart Young

DIE MAßNAHME   See THE MEASURES TAKEN

THE MASTER BUILDER

Just once more, master builder! Do the impossible again!
—Act 3

The Master Builder (*Bygmester Solness*) was the first play HENRIK IBSEN wrote after his return to NORWAY in 1891, and it inaugurates the last period of his work, which ends with the so-called epilogue, WHEN WE DEAD AWAKEN, also including LITTLE EYOLF and JOHN GABRIEL BORKMAN. This final "cycle," and especially *The Master Builder*, is sometimes interpreted as a more or less allegorical meditation on the social and moral conflicts of the artist, sometimes as a modern version of the archetypal tragic myth, and sometimes as Ibsen's critical analysis of the guilt and moral weakness of typical characters in his own contemporary capitalist society.

Halvard Solness, the master builder, started his career as a highly respected builder of churches, but when the family home of his wife was conveniently destroyed in a fire, it became possible for him to climb to the top of the real estate business as a building contractor. This change of career from church building to the building of small houses for common people leaves him, however, with a strong feeling of guilt, since he and his wife Aline also lost their twin sons as a result of the fire. The guilt is augmented by Solness's strained relations with his employees, father and son Brovik, the old man having been overthrown by Solness on his way to the top, whereas the son is held in a subservient position, unable to make a career of his own. One of the consequences of this complex feeling of guilt is Solness's anxiety of being overthrown in his turn by the vitality and force of a younger generation. Into this situation Hilde Wangel enters, a young girl who ten years earlier was so deeply impressed by the flamboyant master builder that she felt it like a seduction and an erotic promise, which she now expects to be redeemed by the master builder. Thus the play develops on three levels. The moral conflict in relation to Aline is deepened but never really solved. The social and moral conflict with Knut and Ragnar Brovik is solved when Solness permits Ragnar to start his own business; but this conflict is never really deepened. More and more the stage is dominated by the enigmatic conversations between Hilde and Solness, partly serious, partly playful, and through and through infused with a strong erotic power. At the end Hilde succeeds in cutting Solness loose from his guilty conscience and in remobilizing his power of imagination and will, so that he is able to repeat the impossible heroic act performed ten years earlier, climbing once more, in spite of his dizziness, as high as he builds. But this victory is also a mortal defeat: having reached the top of the tower of the new house he is building, the master builder falls down and is killed.

No matter how the play is interpreted, Halvard Solness is undoubtedly one of Ibsen's most complex male characters, and Hilde Wangel occupies a distinguished place in the series of equally complex female characters that starts with Furia in *Catilina* (1950), ends with Irene in *When We Dead Awaken*, and includes such enigmatic women as Hjørdis, Gerd, Rebecca West, and Hedda.

FURTHER READING

Binswanger, Ludwig. "Ibsen's The Masterbuilder." In *European Literary Theory and Practice. From Existential Phenomenology to Structuralism*, ed. by Vernon W. Gras. New York: Dell, 1973.

Holtan, Orley I. *Mythic Patterns in Ibsen's Last Plays*. Minneapolis: Univ. of Minnesota Press, 1970.

Saari, Sandra E. "Of Madness or Fame: Ibsen's Bygmester Solness." *Scandinavian Studies* 50 (1978): 1–18.

Atle Kittang

"MASTER HAROLD" . . . AND THE BOYS

"Master Harold" . . . and the boys is the most celebrated play by the highly regarded South African playwright ATHOL FUGARD. Set in 1950 in Port Elizabeth, SOUTH AFRICA, the play offers an unsettling and ultimately harrowing depiction of the corrosive effects of racism and, more specifically, of the institutionalized racism of the apartheid system in South Africa.

The play is set in a tearoom on a wet and dreary afternoon. There are no customers, and two black employees—Sam, a waiter, and Willie, a custodian—are killing time. While carrying on a free-ranging conversation, they practice the dance steps that they hope will enable them to win an approaching ballroom dance contest.

The seventeen-year-old son of the owner, named Hally, arrives at the tearoom. There is an immediate sense of easy camaraderie between him and the two black men. It is gradually revealed that Hally's father is a demanding cripple and an abusive alcoholic and that the two black men have frequently protected Halley from the abuse or have comforted him after he has been abused. In addition, Sam in particular had spent time with Hally, teaching him things that his father has not bothered to teach him, such as how to make and fly a kite. As he has gotten older, Hally has reciprocated by teaching Sam some of the things he has learned in school, at a time when black South Africans were forbidden access to much education. Still, despite his sense of connection to the two men, Hally unself-consciously uses racially derogatory language and seems unaware that Sam and Willie will naturally find it offensive.

Throughout the play, Hally makes uneasy references to his father's pending release from the hospital, where he has had surgery. The play builds steadily to its crisis, a phone call from Hally's father indicating that he is being released from the hospital that very day. Having had a long reprieve from his father's abuse, Hally is pushed to the psychological brink by the inevitability of its resumption.

In a bitterly ironic turn in the play's action, Hally suddenly lashes out at Sam and Willie, transferring his anguish onto them. The pain that this verbal attack causes the two men is so palpable that Hally is forced to recognize that the racism that has pervaded every aspect of his upbringing has made him as unreasonably hateful as his father. He is filled with a terrible self-loathing that overwhelms even his trepidation at his father's return.

FURTHER READING

Beck, Ervin. "Fugard's *Master Harold and the Boys*." *Explicator* 58 (Winter 2000): 109–112.

Jordan, John O. "Life in the Theater: Autobiography, Politics, and Romance in *Master Harold and the Boys.*" *Twentieth Century Literature* 39 (Winter 1993): 461–472.

Post, Robert. "Racism in Athol Fugard's *Master Harold and the Boys.*" *World Literature Written in English* 30, no. 1 (1990): 97–102.

Wertheim, Albert. "Ballroom Dancing, Kites and Politics: Athol Fugard's *Master Harold and the Boys.*" *Journal of the South Pacific Association for Commonwealth Literature* 30 (April 1990): 141–155.

Martin Kich

MÄSTER OLAF   See MASTER OLOF

MASTER OLOF

Master Olof (Mäster Olaf) is the umbrella title for three versions of this historical play, all of them in five acts, by AUGUST STRINDBERG. The first and best known, the so-called prose edition, was written in 1872 and not published until 1881, when it received its premiere at the New Theater in Stockholm. The so-called middle drama, also in prose, is a modified, unsuccessful version of the prose edition. The verse edition, written in 1875–1876, was published in 1878 and first performed in 1890. There is also a fragmentary epilogue to the play, probably written in 1872, then published in 1912.

The action of *Master Olof* takes place in 16th-century SWEDEN, during the reign of Gustav Vasa. Olaus Petri (1493–1552), the play's Master Olof, helps to introduce Lutheranism to Sweden, not realizing at first that he is the king's instrument: Gustav Vasa needs money and backs the Reformation to secure an income for the state by confiscating the property of the Church. Whereas Olof initially believes in cooperation between state and church, the anarchist Gert rejects both. In a classical manner, the reformist is put against the revolutionary. Olof finally joins Gert in his plans to have the king murdered. Caught by the king's men, Gert faces death defiantly, whereas Olof is reprieved after he promises to be loyal to the king.

In his autobiography *I Röda Rummet (In the Red Room,* Part 3 of *The Son of a Servant)* Strindberg comments on this drama of ideas. Strindberg (1996) said that in each historical character we see some aspect of him.

In Olof he would appear as the idealist, in Gustav Vasa as the realist, and in the Anabaptist Gert as the Communard, because he had now discovered that the men of the Paris commune [in 1870–1871] had only applied what Buckle had taught [i.e. the relativity of truth]. Through his three major characters he would express these three principles as three different points of view. To say what he really want[ed] to say he let Gert . . . pretend to be insane, Olof retract his ideas, and Gustav Vasa be right, and no one be wrong. The enemy from the old camp, Hans Brask, he treated with respect, too, as the person who has been right but, who, with the passing of time, had become wrong. For that reason, he had intended to call the play *What Is Truth?* But to get it played both of the tentative titles [the other was *The Renegade*] were rejected for the more indifferent *Master Olof.*

Events that in reality were spread out over more than twenty years are, in the play, compressed into a short period. Many of the characters have hardly more than a name in common with their real counterparts—true, for example, of both Olof and Gert. And the connection between the anabatists and the plot against the king is Strindberg's invention. As a model for the play, Strindberg mentions especially William Shakespeare's *Julius Caesar* with its alternating public and private scenes. Scholars have also pointed to the influence of the tavern scenes in Shakespeare's *Henry IV* and act 2 in *Master Olof.*

Because of its unconventional treatment of historical characters and its straightforward language, the prose version of *Master Olof* met for some time with strong resistance. It is now considered the first modern Swedish drama and is still regularly performed in Sweden.

FURTHER READING

Andersson, Hans. *Strindberg's Master Olof and Shakespeare.* Cambridge, Mass.: Harvard Univ. Press, 1952.

Johnson, Walter. *Strindberg and the Historical Drama.* Seattle: Univ. of Washington Press, 1963.

Lamm, Martin. *August Strindberg.* Tr. and ed. by Harry G. Carlson. New York: Blom, 1971.

Strindberg, August. *The Son of a Servant.* London: Jonathan Cape, 1967.

———. *I Röda Rummet [In the Red Room].* In *Sam lade Verk [Collected Works].* Vol. 21. Stockholm: Stockholm Univ., 1996.

Egil Törnqvist

MATURA, MUSTAPHA (1939–)

Mustapha Matura was born in Trinidad in 1939 and attended the Belmont School. In 1961 he moved to London and started writing in 1966. His theater writing earned him a reputation for biting satire and mordant wit, and he became the first playwright to consider the lives and problems of West Indians living in Britain. One of his earliest works, *Black Pieces,* a series of short plays, was produced in 1970 at the ICA (Institute of Contemporary Art) in London. In the following year, he achieved considerable success with his satirical COMEDY of manners *As Time Goes By.* The play won both the George Devine and the John Whiting awards.

Matura's work featured a variety of characters from his West Indian origins, and he became known for a remarkable talent in reproducing the speech rhythms of his native island. In 1974 he was awarded the Evening Standard Most Promising Playwright Award for *Play Mas,* which premiered at the Royal Court Theatre before moving to the West End with additional productions on OFF-BROADWAY and in Chicago. The first act is set on the eve of Trinidad's independence from Britain while Carnival, the defining cultural event of the island, takes place. The second act takes place some years after independence, and the work is infused with the sense of political crisis and social and cultural change that define that era. The play is one of the few to explore such issues through Carnival, the period of licensed chaos and misrule. Peter Minshall, celebrated and award-winning Carnival creator, designed the costumes for the premiere production. The title of the play is the West Indian term for *playing masquerade*, taking part in Carnival.

In 1978 Matura co-founded the Black Theatre Co-operative with the director Charlie Hanson. The aims of the company were to support and produce work by black writers in Britain. The new company produced *Another Tuesday* (1978), *More, More* (1978), *Welcome Home Jacko* (1979), *A Dying Business* (1980), and *One Rule* (1981). In 1991 the company revived Matura's *Meetings* at the Tricycle Theatre and on tour. It had first been produced in New York City at the Phoenix Theatre in 1981 and at the Hampstead Theatre in London in 1982. In 1983 Matura was the co-writer with Farrukh Dhondy of the first black-created sitcom for British television. The Black Theatre Co-operative continues to produce under a new name, Nitro, and is Britain's oldest, continuously producing company committed to work by black theater artists.

Matura continued to have work produced at the Royal Court Theatre such as *Black Slaves, White Chains* (1975) and *Rum an' Coca Cola* (1976). In 1979 *Independence* opened at the Bush Theatre in a touring production by Foco Novo. *Playboy of the West Indies*, Matura's 1950s Trinidadian rendering of J. M. SYNGE's Irish drama, was first staged at the Oxford Playhouse in 1984 and aired on the BBC in the following year. His use of established plays from the Western canon continued with his *Trinidad Sisters*, his Caribbean take on ANTON CHEKHOV's THREE SISTERS, which premiered at the adventurous Tricycle Theatre in London (1988).

In 1991 the National Theatre premiered Matura's *The Coup—A Play of Revolutionary Dreams* in the Cottesloe Theatre, the first commissioned work by a black writer to be seen in one of the National's main theaters. The farcical piece, while providing genuine insight into West Indian culture, attitudes, and manners, explored the fictional military takeover of government in independent Trinidad and Tobago and featured Matura's favored theme of the contradictions and responsibilities of nationhood.

[*See also* England, 1940–Present]

SELECT PLAYS: *Black Pieces* (1970); *As Time Goes By* (1971); *Play Mas* (1974); *Black Slaves, White Chains* (1975); *Rum an' Coca Cola* (1976); *Another Tuesday* (1978); *More, More* (1978); *Independence* (1979); *Welcome Home Jacko* (1979); *A Dying Business* (1980); *Meetings* (1981); *One Rule* (1981); *Playboy of the West Indies* (1984); *Trinidad Sisters* (1988); *The Coup—A Play of Revolutionary Dreams* (1991)

FURTHER READING

Joseph, May. "Performing the Postcolony: The Plays of Mustapha Matura." In *Late Imperial Culture*, ed. by Roman De La Campa, E. Ann Kaplan, and Michael Sprinker. New York: Verso, 1995.

Lee, Simon. "The Man in the Corner." *Sunday Guardian* (December 19, 1999). http://www.nalis.org.tt/Biography/bio_MustaphaMatura_playwright.htm.

Maslon, Laurence. "Matura Is a Lover of Language: He Captures the Voices and Politics of Trinidad." *American Theatre*, vol. 6, Issue 6, (1989): 56.

Paquet, Sandra Pouchet. "Mustapha Matura's *Playboy of the West Indies*: A Carnival Discourse on Imitation and Originality." *Journal of West Indian Literature* 5, nos. 1–2 (1992): 85–96.

Stone, Judy S. J. *Studies in West Indian Literature and Theatre*. London: Macmillan, 2001 [with a chapter on black British theater].

Lesley Ferris

MAUGHAM, WILLIAM SOMERSET (1874–1965)

A drawing by Bernard Partridge in a 1908 issue of *Punch* depicts William Shakespeare looking worried. He sees a range of playbills, all lauding a young playwright who is so popular that Shakespeare's status is threatened. Shakespeare's rival is W. Somerset Maugham. The drawing seems bizarre today, since many of Maugham's plays were merely ephemeral hits (or misses) in the commercial theaters. Now, Maugham is more renowned for his novels than for his naturalistic plays, which display mastery of characterization, plot development, unpretentious dialogue, and entertaining diversion. His plays are largely forgotten but significant because of the sheer quantity that he produced.

Maugham was born in Paris on January 25, 1874, the youngest son of an English solicitor. By the time that he was ten, both of his parents were dead through illness. Maugham was then reared by Parisian servants and by childless relatives in England. He moved to Heidelberg at sixteen, keen to learn German (his first language was French). There he was influenced by the older John Ellingham Brooks, who seduced him. Maugham was primarily homosexual but later denied that he had ever been gay. After moving back to England when eighteen, he qualified as a doctor but did not practice.

Maugham wrote novels and sought energetically to get his plays staged. His first performed play, about a selfish groom who accepts money from his wife's erstwhile partner, *Marriages Are Made in Heaven*, opened in Berlin in 1902. Maugham's first London production was in 1903, when *A Man of Honour* ran briefly. The play, about a Londoner who marries his pregnant girlfriend, causing misery, attracted some acclaim, but Maugham's commercial clout was established five years later.

Lady Frederick, a COMEDY about an heir whose love for an older woman is resisted by his wealthy family, opened at the Court Theater, London, in October 1907. Immediately popular and critically respected, the play ran for 422 performances. By the summer of 1908, four Maugham plays were running in London: *Mrs. Dot*, *Jack Straw*, *The Explorer*, and *Lady Frederick*—such unprecedented success inspires Shakespeare's anxiety in Partridge's humorous drawing. Capitalizing on his success, enjoying financial and social triumphs, Maugham crafted plays prolifically. His more melodramatic dramas, such as *The Explorer* (1908) and *Smith* (1909), were influenced by HENRIK IBSEN and ARTHUR PINERO. Richard Brinsley Sheridan and OSCAR WILDE influenced his comedies of manners. His 1909 *Penelope*, which ran for 246 performances at London's Comedy Theatre, centers on a clever wife who reacts with calm ingenuity to her husband's cheating, winning him back by letting him learn the follies of his behavior through harsh experience. Maugham's successful plays earned American productions, too, receiving often mixed reactions. Generally, Maugham's plays about English upper-class mores, bourgeois greed and dishonesty, and moneyed but spineless husbands did not translate well to non-British audiences.

After 1910, Maugham's personal life became complex and peripatetic. He married, disastrously, Syrie Wellcome (1897–1945), in America in 1917—divorce came, eventually, in 1929. A thirty-year relationship with Gerald Haxton (1892–1944) began around 1914. Haxton and Maugham traveled widely. Maugham's most lucrative comic plays were written during the early years of his relationship with Haxton. *The Unattainable* (1916) features the amorous dalliances of a widow, Caroline Ashley, who enjoys a love affair with the unmarried Robert Oldham, orchestrating intricate plots to ensure that society does not coerce her into marriage. *Our Betters* premiered in New York's Hudson Theatre in 1917, surviving for 112 performances, despite cool reviews. The play's satire about an American heiress's greed and desire for social enhancement is tough: contemporary reviewers found the play excessively acerbic and cynical. Maugham generates sympathy for neither the American heiress nor the aristocratic family she marries into. Other successful comedies from the period include *Home and Beauty* (1919) and THE CIRCLE (1921). The latter, which compares husband-leaving conduct by women of different generations, ran for 181 performances at London's Haymarket Theatre and has been revived several times. Deft and intricate in its examination of change between generations and its notice of society's gender-based moral values, *The Circle* is regarded as Maugham's most significant and least-dated play. Maugham's last significant comedy was THE CONSTANT WIFE, which failed in London in 1927 but ran for 295 performances at New York's Maxine Elliott's Theatre. Other, more serious 1920s plays work as dramatic companion pieces to Maugham's "exotic" prose works. These include *East of Suez* (1922) and the adultery-focused *The Letter* (1927)—both plays feature Britons living in Asia.

Maugham's later plays were sometimes successful, sometimes not. Maugham stopped being theatrically commercial after 1930, writing his most serious and important plays: his examinations of English society, *For Services Rendered* and SHEPPEY, were not produced in America, indicating their narrow appeal. *For Services Rendered* ran for seventy-eight performances at the Globe Theatre, London, from November 1932. The play dramatizes the post–Great War decline of a once-flourishing, well-off Kent family, the Ardsleys. Morally, physically, and economically maimed by the war, family members endure insanity, disastrous marriages, blindness, terminal illness, and suicide. Their contribution to Britain's war effort is overlooked by an ungrateful nation: the play challenges the value of self-sacrificing "service." John Gielgud directed the production of *Sheppey* at Wyndham's Theatre, London, in 1933. Eighty-three performances were staged, but the play baffled audiences and critics. The plot, about a barber who gives lottery-won money to the poor, alienating his godless, cash-devoted family, is straightforward, but the play, unusually for Maugham who disliked theatrical experimentation, combines NATURALISM with unrealistic SYMBOLISM. Maugham, ahead of his time with *Sheppey*, never wrote another play, although many of his stories were adapted dramatically by other playwrights.

After Haxton's death from tuberculosis in 1944, Maugham's personal and professional status declined. Maugham's reputation for bitterness, vituperation, and denial of truths (such as his homosexuality) was tempered by his many philanthropic gestures and bequeathments. He died in Nice, FRANCE, on December 15, 1965. Maugham's comedies impacted massively upon the commercial theaters of the early-20th century and remain seminal reading for any scholar of that period's dramatic conventions or of crowd-pleasing, theatrical craftsmanship.

[*See also* England, 1860–1940]

SELECT PLAYS: *Marriages Are Made in Heaven* (1902); *A Man of Honour* (1903); *Lady Frederick* (1907); *The Explorer* (1908); *Jack Straw* (1908); *Mrs. Dot* (1908); *Penelope* (1909); *Smith* (1909); *The Unattainable* (1916); *Our Betters* (1917); *Home and Beauty* (1919); *The Circle* (1921); *East of Suez* (1922); *The Constant Wife* (1927); *The Letter* (1927); *For Services Rendered* (1932); *Sheppey* (1933)

FURTHER READING

Bassett, Troy James. "W. Somerset Maugham: An Annotated Bibliography of Criticism." *English Literature in Transition* 41, no. 2 (1998): 133–184.

Connon, Bryan. *Somerset Maugham and the Maugham Dynasty*. London: Sinclair-Stevenson, 1997.

Mander, R., and J. Mitchenson. *Theatrical Companion to Maugham*. London: Rockliff, 1955.

Meyers, Jeffrey. *Somerset Maugham: A Life*. New York: Knopf, 2004.

Rogal, Samuel J. *A Companion to the Characters in the Fiction and Drama of W. Somerset Maugham*. Westport, Conn.: Greenwood Press, 1996.

——. *A William Somerset Maugham Encyclopedia*. Westport, Conn.: Greenwood Press, 1997.

Sanders, Charles. "W. Somerset Maugham." In *Dictionary of Literary Biography*. Vol. 10, Part 2, *Modern British Dramatists, 1900–1945*, ed. by Stanley Weintraub. Detroit: Gale Res., 1982. 22–42.

Kevin De Ornellas

MAYAKOVSKY, VLADIMIR (1893–1930)

Vladimir Mayakovsky was born in Bagdadi, Georgia, on July 7, 1893. Although best known as one of the foremost poets of RUSSIAN FUTURISM, Mayakovsky wrote several important plays. His earliest drama depended heavily on collaboration with other futurist poets and painters.

His first work for the stage, *A Tragedy (Tragediia*, 1913), alternated in repertory with Aleksei Kruchonykh's *Victory Over the Sun.* Although the futurists proclaimed an absolute break with the past, Mayakovsky's *Tragedy* owes much to Greek TRAGEDY and to such immediate predecessors as ALEKSANDR BLOK and NIKOLAI EVREINOV. The influence of Evreinov's MONODRAMA is particularly apparent in the protagonist's fragmented personality, various aspects of which become other characters. Mayakovsky unifies all the disparate aspects of "his" personality through the myth of "himself" as a Christ-like figure, who suffers for all. This production was crucial to the development of futurism. Always experimental in form and genre, Mayakovsky exploited a rather grotesque admixture of mystery play and low, sometimes crude and blasphemous COMEDY in his next play, MYSTERY-BOUFFE (*Misteriia-buff*, 1918). The basic plot concerns a battle between seven pairs of "Clean" bourgeois and seven pairs of "Unclean" proletariat, who survive a cataclysmic flood. Written for the first anniversary of the October Revolution, the play portrays the triumph of the latter, who eventually deposit the "Clean" in hell, reject heaven as their reward, and return to the paradise on earth of communism. VSEVOLOD MEYERHOLD's production, in collaboration with Mayakovsky and with set designs by Kasimir Malevich, had a short run and did not appeal to the conservative aesthetic tastes of the Bolsheviks, despite praise for its "democratic" forms.

Although he greeted the revolution enthusiastically, Mayakovsky became disillusioned and in THE BEDBUG (*Klop*, 1928) created a scathing satire of Soviet bureaucracy and philistinism. In the first half of the play, the protagonist, Prisypkin, mouths Soviet platitudes but leads a profoundly bourgeois existence. His ostentatious wedding deteriorates into a bout of public drunkenness, which leads to a fire that kills everyone but Prisypkin, who cannot be found. Some fifty years pass before his frozen but preserved body is discovered. The remainder of the play focuses on his "resurrected" life in the perfected future and on his alienation from it. Still "contaminated" by irrational impulses, such as love, and parasites, such as bedbugs, he is considered a danger to society and confined to a cage. The pathos of his situation is affecting. Meyerhold's production lent a stylistic brilliance to this, Mayakovsky's most successful play.

In his last play, THE BATHHOUSE (*Bania*, 1930), Mayakovsky goes after Soviet bureaucracy and its stultifying effect on society. The protagonist, Pobedonosikov, rules by red tape, which threatens to obscure the inventor Chudakov's time machine. Nonetheless, Chudakov successfully transports a "Phosphorescent Woman" from the future right into Pobedonosikov's living room. She warns Pobedonosikov that the future will only accept what is consonant with it. It turns out to be resistant to bureaucracy, and the time machine spits out those of the would-be time travelers who are out of step with the future. Despite its sometimes striking language, the play suffers from frequent longueurs. Even Meyerhold could not save it. Coupled with the poet's overwhelming personal crises, the demise of *The Bathhouse* contributed to his suicide soon afterward on April 14, 1930, in Moscow.

Mayakovsky also wrote a number of "agit-plays," or AGITATION-PROPAGANDA plays, as well as plays for the circus.

[*See also* Russia and the Soviet Union]

SELECT PLAYS: *A Tragedy (Tragediia*, 1913); *Mystery-Bouffe (Misteriia-buff*, 1918; revised 1921); *The Bedbug (Klop*, 1928); *The Bathhouse (Bania*, 1930)

FURTHER READING

Briggs, A. D. P. *Vladimir Mayakovsky: A Tragedy.* Oxford: William A. Meeuws, 1979.

Brown, Edward J. *Mayakovsky: A Poet in the Revolution.* Princeton, N.J.: Princeton Univ. Press, 1973.

Markov, Vladimir. *Russian Futurism: A History.* Berkeley: Univ. of California Press, 1968.

Shklovsky, Viktor. *Mayakovsky and His Circle.* Tr. by Lily Feiler. London: Pluto Press, 1972.

Timothy C. Westphalen

MAYAMA SEIKA (1874–1948)

A Japanese novelist, historian, and playwright, Mayama Seika trained as a doctor in his native city of Sendai and briefly practiced in the poverty-stricken rural areas nearby. Conceiving literary ambitions, Mayama, like other young literary hopefuls of the time, gravitated to Tokyo, where he attracted attention with his naturalist stories, particularly those based on the rural poverty that he had witnessed firsthand. His first two plays were naturalist in method, one about a polar explorer desperate to have the world believe him and one about a young man with a hereditary condition, both of which owe something to HENRIK IBSEN.

Mayama's career as a novelist was cut short, however, because he offended the main publishing houses, and from the beginning of 1914 he started a decade in which almost all of his considerable creative output went into SHINPA. Here he willingly applied himself to learning the trade of playwriting in spite of the social stigma attached to a hack playwright's occupation.

In the mid-1920s Mayama came into his own as a literary playwright (with pieces that were hardly performed but were discussed as literature) and as a playwright for *shinkokugeki*, specifically its charismatic leader Sawada Shōjirō. Instead of writing to please *shinpa* actors, Mayama now wrote to challenge Sawada, and the most powerful play to come out of this collaboration/

competition was *Sakamoto Ryôma* (1928). This study of a mid-19th-century political activist shows a man drawn into a historical process (the ending of the feudal era in JAPAN) but at the mercy of his own temperament and developing ideas. Sakamoto, like other Mayama heroes of these years (especially the 10th-century rebel Taira no Masakado in the two plays with his name in the titles), wants just to be a human being (Masakado wants to "live littlely"), but his almost dialectical changes of political commitment make him many enemies, and he is killed.

In the 1930s Mayama, mainly in conjunction with the *kabuki* actor Ichikawa Sadanji II, developed a type of SHIN KABUKI characteristic of himself and much in contrast to that of OKAMOTO KIDŌ (who also worked with Sadanji). Mayama prided himself on his historical research but was not afraid to exaggerate or change emphasis for the sake of the play. His dialogue is dense ("no gaps," commented one *kabuki* actor), and conflicts between characters are expressed in hard-hitting language.

Mayama based his plays on a variety of subjects (including 17th-century prose works by Ihara Saikaku), but history was his first love, and much of his energies in the 1930s went into his ten-play dramatization of the Chūshingura vendetta story (1934–1941). The colorful *Lord Tsunatoyo at His Seaside Estate* (1940) is still popular today. Sukeemon, one of the vendetta members, taunts the future shogun (Tsunatoyo) to his face in a desperate attempt to discover his attitude toward the vendetta. In the last scene, Sukeemon lunges at a figure obscured by a heavy NŌ costume, thinking it is the target of the vendetta, when it is in fact Tsunatoyo himself.

Mayama died in 1948, but his daughter Mayama Miho has over the past thirty years put a whole generation of younger *kabuki* actors through a process of learning to cope with the complex dialogue of her father's plays through her patient but very persistent directing style.

SELECT PLAYS: *Genboku and Choei* (1924); *Sakamoto Ryoma* (1928); *Death of Yoritomo* (*Yoritomo no Shi*, 1932); *Onatsu and Seijūrō* (*Onatsu Seijūrō*, 1933); *The Shogun Leaves Edo* (*Shōgun Edo o Saru*, 1934; the third of the trilogy *Edojō Sōzeme* [*General Attack on Edo*, 1926, 1933, 1934]); *Loyal Retainers in the Genroku Period* (*Genroku Chūshingura*, ten plays, 1934–1941)

FURTHER READING

Ōyama Isao. *Mayama Seika, Hito to Sakuhin*. Tokyo: Bokujisha, 1978.
Powell, Brian. *Kabuki in Modern Japan, Mayama Seika and His Plays*. Basingstoke: Macmillan, 1990.
Tanabe Akio. *Mayama Seika*. Tokyo: Hokuyōsha, 1976.

Brian Powell

MA ZHONGJUN (1957–)

A contemporary Chinese playwright, Ma Zhongjun was born in 1957 in Shanghai, CHINA. Entering a junior high school, he started writing poems and became interested in aesthetics and in literary theory. He was assigned to work in a factory right after graduation. In April 1979, Ma was enrolled in a workshop on playwriting at the Shanghai Municipal Workers' Cultural Center, where he formed a friendship with his classmate Jia Hongyuan.

In 1980 the two of them, in cooperation with Qu Xinhua, wrote a short play titled *There Is Warmth Outside the House* (*Wu wai you re liu*), which won recognition from the Ministry of Culture and garnered a prize as one of the best plays of 1980–1981. Afterward, Ma and Jia Hongyuan co-wrote *Man Wearing National Emblem* (*Dai guohui de ren*, 1981), *Road* (*Lu*, 1981), and *Trendy Red Dress* (*Jie shang liuxing hong qunzi*, 1984). He also collaborated with Qin Peichun in writing the play *Red Room, White Room, Black Room* (*Hong fangjian, bai fangjian, hei fangjian*, 1986), which he also adapted into an award-winning film script. In 1988 he wrote the historical play *The Legend of Old Bawdy Town* (*Lao fengliu zhen*). For a time, he served as a full-time playwright at China Youth Art Theater, but since the mid-1990s, he has been a producer and written several film scripts and television play series.

Notable for his AVANT-GARDE exploration, Ma constantly tries to borrow new ideas and novel theatrical forms from both classical Chinese drama and foreign theater to serve as springboards for expressing the ideas, lives, and pursuits of contemporary Chinese youth. As a one-act play, *There Is Warmth Outside the House* is characteristic of Ma's playwriting practice. Influenced by ARTHUR MILLER'S DEATH OF A SALESMAN in terms of its social concern, the play depicts the lives of the three children of the Zhao family. Suffering the loss of both parents during China's Cultural Revolution, Zhao Changkang, the eldest son, goes to Heilongjiang province to work as a farmer, while his younger brother and sister remain in Shanghai as workers. Pitting the latter two against Changkang in terms of lifestyle and hence different moral attitudes, the play realistically shows the mental lives of the "lost generation" in the post–Cultural Revolution era and their eventual awakening. The play marks a breakthrough with traditional theater by employing a surrealistic depiction of the psychological conflicts among these three characters in a poetic setting. The overall symbolic contrast between the cold inside and the warmth outside suggests two attitudes toward life and two value systems. Because of its novel modes of theatrical expression, the play was a great hit when it was first staged in Beijing in 1980. It has since been regarded as one of the earliest exploration plays during the post–Cultural Revolution period.

SELECT PLAYS: *There Is Warmth Outside the House* (*Wu wai you re liu*, 1980); *Road* (*Lu*, 1981); *Trendy Red Dress* (*Jie shang liuxing hong qunzi*, 1984); *Red Room, White Room, Black Room* (*Hong fangjian, bai fangjian, hei fangjian*, 1986); *The Legend of Old Bawdy Town* (*Lao fengliu zhen*, 1988)

FURTHER READING

Jia Hongyuan and Ma Zhongjun. "Xie *Wu wai you re liu* de tansuo he sikao" [Exploration and thoughts in writing *There Is Warmth Outside the House*]. *Juben* (Play Scripts) 6 (1980).

Lin Kehuan. "Shenhuo yu yishu de re liu—ping *Wu wai you re liu*" [The warmth in life and art: On *There Is Warmth Outside the House*]. *Juben* (Play Scripts) 8 (1980).

Ma Zhongjun. *The Legend of Old Bawdy Town* (*Lao fengliu zhen*). Tr. by Janice Wickeri. In *An Oxford Anthology of Contemporary Chinese Drama*, ed. by Martha P. Y. Cheung and Jane C. C. Lai. Hong Kong: Oxford Univ. Press, 1997. 185–262.

Zhou Yuming. "Liang ge yongyu tansuo de qingnian yeyu zuozhe—jieshao *Wu wai you re liu* de bianju Jia Hongyuan he Ma Zhongjun" [Two amateur playwrights who are bold at exploration: Introducing Jia Hongyuan and Ma Zhongjun, The Two Playwrights of *There Is Warmth Outside the House*] *Juben* (Play Scripts) 8 (1980).

Hongchu Fu and Cai Xingshui

MCDONAGH, MARTIN (1970–)

Wee Thomas was a friendly cat. He would always say hello to you. . . . He won't be saying hello no more, God bless him. Not with that lump of a brain gone.

—Davey, Act 1, *The Lieutenant of Inishmore*

Few dramatists have had as spectacular a debut as Martin McDonagh, whose use of outrageous violence, cruel humor, and melodramatic storytelling has brought him acclaim. He is one of the most discussed writers in world drama: loved by audiences and detested by many critics, his plays provoke strong reactions everywhere they are performed.

McDonagh was born in London in 1970 to Irish parents. His early efforts at playwriting floundered because, McDonagh has stated, his writing was too much influenced by DAVID MAMET and HAROLD PINTER. In an attempt to free himself of this influence, McDonagh decided to write in an exaggerated version of the idiom he had heard during childhood visits to IRELAND.

The result was *The Beauty Queen of Leenane*, a black COMEDY set in rural Ireland, which was premiered in Galway by Druid Theatre Company in 1996. Its success encouraged Druid to premiere two further McDonagh plays the following year when, together with *The Beauty Queen*, his *A Skull in Connemara* and *The Lonesome West* were presented as The Leenane Trilogy. The Trilogy then transferred to Britain, where the Royal National Theatre's production of *The Cripple of Inishmaan* was also playing, earning McDonagh the rare honor of having four of his plays run simultaneously in the West End.

These plays brought McDonagh instant success—but his work was not welcomed universally. His characters are violent and idiotic, and their use of language is engaging but inarticulate. This exposed McDonagh to the accusation that he was reinforcing negative Irish stereotypes. His defenders state that he is in fact critiquing those stereotypes—a fair point but one that fails to deal with the fact that many audiences persist in taking McDonagh's plays as literal representations of Irish life.

The debate about McDonagh's work has been complicated by his high public profile: with a series of outspoken comments and a notorious public argument with the actor Sean Connery, he has antagonized many of his supporters.

The resulting backlash against McDonagh made it difficult for him to have later plays produced, and he provoked much media attention by claiming that the Royal Court and Royal National Theatre had rejected *The Lieutenant of Inishmore*—about a psychopathic Irish terrorist—owing to its political content. Both theaters deny this claim. When that play was finally produced by the Royal Shakespeare Company in 2001, it proved hugely popular, although the debate about the authenticity of McDonagh's Irish characters persisted. McDonagh has stated in response that he considers himself neither Irish nor English— as shown in 2003 when THE PILLOWMAN, a comedy set outside Ireland, was produced in London.

Because McDonagh tends to provoke strong feelings, his work has not received much objective critical attention. This is unfortunate: while his plays show little variation in characterization and language, they are excellent examples of comic storytelling and audience manipulation. But they are, most important, incisive but frequently misunderstood satires of Irish identity.

PLAYS: *The Beauty Queen of Leenane* (1996); *The Cripple of Inishmaan* (1997); *The Lonesome West* (1997); *A Skull in Connemara* (1997); *The Lieutenant of Inishmore* (2001); *The Pillowman* (2003)

FURTHER READING

Feeney, Joseph S. J. "Martin McDonagh: Dramatist of the West." *Studies* 87, no. 345 (Spring 1998).

Kurdi, Maria. *Codes and Masks: Aspects of Identity in Contemporary Irish Plays in an International Context*. Frankfurt am Main: P. Lang, 2000.

Lanters, José. "Playwrights of the Western World: Synge, Murphy, McDonagh." In *A Century of Irish Drama: Widening the Stage*, ed. by Stephen Watt, Eileen Morgan, and Shakir Mustafa. Bloomington: Indiana Univ. Press, 2000.

Merriman, Vic. "Decolonisation: The Theatre of Tiger Trash." *Irish University Review* (Autumn–Winter 1999): 305–317.

Patrick Lonergan

MCGEE, GREG (1950–)

Greg McGee was born in 1950 in Oamaru, NEW ZEALAND. His *Foreskin's Lament* (1980) was hailed by many, including BRUCE MASON, as the Great New Zealand play. Its concern with national identity was stated aggressively in the sixfold "Whaddarya?" ("What are you?") addressed to the audience by the eponymous hero at the final curtain. *Foreskin's Lament* is about rugby union, New Zealand's national game. The first act is set in a changing shed after a local team practice and the second act at the after-match party. The trenchant REALISM of the play—very confrontational in the country's generally intimate theaters—was signaled by the locker room with its "strong smell of liniment" and the players' naked bodies.

Dramatic conflict arises because Clean, a Vietnam veteran and policeman, surreptitiously kicks the captain in the head. As a consequence, loyalties are tested. For coach Tupper, "the town is the team," and the team is, of course, a metaphor for New Zealand society. As fullback, Foreskin is somewhat removed from the rest of the team, his detachment exacerbated by his "univarsity" education. Foreskin's role as commentator culminates in his final harangue, an oratory tour de force, which starts as a parody of an after-match speech and becomes an extravagant lament for the shattered myths of tribal identity.

The play's timeliness was confirmed by the notorious 1981 South African rugby tour of New Zealand. In 1985 McGee actually revised the play, shifting the action from 1976 to the wake of that Springbok tour. He also severely abridged and toned down Foreskin's lament, but the most significant change foregrounded the issue of race: Clean became a Maori as well as a policeman on duty during the tour. The changes were generally deemed injudicious, and later productions reverted to the original text.

As a Junior All Black (national football team) and trialist for the All Blacks, McGee was well qualified to write about rugby; his training as a lawyer served his next play, *Tooth and Claw* (1983), set in a legal office where shady business dealings occur against a background—represented by projections on a screen upstage—of street riots and urban disintegration.

Out in the Cold (1983), based on a short story by McGee, is a situation COMEDY about Judy, a solo mother, who tries to pass as a man in order to secure a job at the local abattoir. The slaughterhouse is a metaphor for the masculine world, whose attitudes Judy attempts to challenge until, inevitably, her true identity is discovered. A television version screened in 1985.

Whitemen (produced 1986), a satirical FARCE about a rugby union committee debating whether to invite a South African team to tour New Zealand again, was judged clumsy, and the large, expensive production was forced to close prematurely. Since then McGee has written almost exclusively for television and film. However, he returned to the stage with *This Train I'm On* (produced 1999), about two lifelong friends facing marital and professional failure.

PLAYS: *Foreskin's Lament* (1980); *Out in the Cold* (1983); *Tooth and Claw* (1983); *Whitemen* (1986); *This Train I'm On* (produced 1999)

FURTHER READING

Black, Sebastian. "Playboys of the South Pacific: The Plays of Greg McGee." *Australasian Drama Studies* 17 (October 1990): 183–202.

Carnegie, David. "The Metamorphoses of Foreskin's Lament." *Australasian Drama Studies* 17 (October 1990): 202–220.

Cordery, Gareth. "Tom Brown's Schooldays and Foreskin's Lament: The Alpha and Omega of Rugby Football." *Journal of Popular Culture* 19, no. 2 (1985): 97–105.

Crawford, Scott. "A National Ethos in Three Dimensions: Rugby in Contemporary New Zealand Fiction." *Arete: The Journal of Sport Literature* 4, no. 1 (1986): 57–72.

Stuart Young

MCGRATH, JOHN (1935–2002)

The theatre can never cause a social change . . . it can be the way people can find their voice, their solidarity and their collective determination.

—Introduction to the Methuen edition of *The Cheviot, the Stag and the Black, Black Oil*, 1981

John McGrath was born in Birkenhead, ENGLAND, in 1935. His death in London in 2002, at the age of sixty-seven, deprived the world of one of its most prolific playwrights and directors who combined intellectual rigor with a commitment to vital, engaging theater. A complete list of his works would include over fifty original plays and about the same quantity of adaptations for theater, film, and television. After Oxford University, McGrath worked for the BBC (1960–1965), notably on *Z Cars*. This police series broke away from the cozy paternalism of shows such as *Dixon of Dock Green* to focus on the social issues underpinning the narrative. Rehearsed for a week, with large casts and multiple sets, and broadcast live, it also provided extensive experience in structuring dramatic action.

A committed socialist, McGrath was at the center of the alternative theater movement in Britain, and in 1971, with his wife Elizabeth Maclennan, he formed 7:84 Theatre Company, named for the statistic that seven percent of the population owned eighty-four percent of Britain's wealth. British alternative theater was divided roughly between those left-leaning groups who played to like-minded and mainly middle-class audiences and those, like 7:84, who sought out audiences who had been ignored by the mainstream, in venues where the commercial theater would not play. They dramatized the issues, political and domestic, that concerned these communities most immediately, from labor disputes to social ills, usually with a more or less unspoken call to action within the play.

McGrath's writing has been compared to BERTOLT BRECHT and DARIO FO in its vigorous utilization of popular theater techniques, such as music, to underpin the political message. It also owed a good deal to Joan Littlewood's work during the 1930s. McGrath extended his ideology to his working methods, continually seeking collective ways of making theater and running his companies. As the 1980s and 1990s saw Britain shift to the Right and public subsidies became scarcer and hedged about with regulation, McGrath came increasingly into conflict with the arts councils.

Throughout what characterized McGrath was his continued commitment to marginalized audiences and venues, when other left-wing playwrights had departed for the commercial stage, and his ability to articulate his ideas. His books *A Good Night Out* and *The Bone Won't Break* are closely argued, yet highly readable, manifestos from a master of popular theater.

Writing in 1992 Christopher Innes, while applauding the "continuing political vitality and popular appeal" of McGrath's work, contrasted his career with that of playwrights such as HOWARD BARKER who had escaped the "stylistic limitations" of AGITATION-PROPAGANDA. Now those "stylistic limitations" may now read differently to a generation whose visual/graphic vocabulary gleefully embraces the cartoon, sampling, popular culture heritage of agit-prop. Indeed, in McGrath's last work, *Hyperlynx* (2002), premiered after his death by Elizabeth Maclennan and directed by their daughter Kate, he demonstrates that his feel for political currents was acute to the last, writing, as Michael Billington in *The Guardian* (August 17, 2002), declared with "a controlled anger and a belief in the validity of personal protest" of the danger that the power of the multinationals will polarize the peoples of the world into violent conflict.

SELECT PLAYS: *Events While Guarding the Bofors Gun* (1966); *Random Happenings in the Hebrides* (1970); *The Cheviot, the Stag and the Black, Black Oil* (1973); *The Games a Bogey* (1974); *Little Red Hen* (1975); *Yobbo Nowt* (1975); *Out of Our Heads* (1976); *The Rat Trap* (1976); *Joe's Drum* (1979); *The Life and Times of Joe of England* (1979); *Blood Red Roses* (1980); *Nightclass* (1981); *Six Men of Dorset* (1984); *All the Fun of the Fair* (1986); *Mairi Mhor* (1987); *Border Warfare* (1989); *John Brown's Body* (1990); *Watching for Dolphins* (1991); *Half the Picture* (1994); *Ane Satire of the Four Estates* (1996); *Hyperlynx* (2002)

FURTHER READING

DiCenzo, Maria. *The Politics of Alternative Theatre in Britain, 1968–1990: The Case of 7:84 (Scotland)*. Cambridge: Cambridge Univ. Press, 1996.

Innes, Christopher. *Modern British Drama 1890–1990*. Cambridge: Cambridge Univ. Press, 1992.

Mackenney, Linda. "The People's Story: 7:84 Scotland." In *Scottish Theatre Since the Seventies*, ed. by Randall Stevenson and Gavin Wallace. Edinburgh: Edinburgh Univ. Press, 1996. 65–74.

McGrath, John. *A Good Night Out. Popular Theatre: Audience, Class and Form*. London: Methuen, 1981.

———. *The Bone Won't Break: On Theatre and Hope in Hard Times*. London: Methuen, 1990.

Patterson, Michael. *Strategies of Political Theatre: Post-War British Playwrights*. Cambridge: Cambridge Univ. Press, 2003.

Barbara A. E. Bell

MCGUINNESS, FRANK (1953–)

Lord, look down on us. Spare us. I love—. Observe the sons of Ulster marching towards the Somme. I love their lives. I love my own life. I love my home. I love my Ulster.

—Kenneth Pyper, Part 4, *Observe the Sons of Ulster Marching Towards the Somme*

Frank McGuinness is the leading Irish playwright of his generation, noted for a powerful body of original plays and adaptations. He was born in 1953 in Buncrana, County Donegal, a town that is politically part of the Republic of IRELAND but geographically within the natural hinterland of Derry City in Northern Ireland. Growing up with a sense of these two different political entities occupying one landscape has clearly had an impact on McGuinness: his work constantly attempts to blend apparent opposites, such as the sacred and the profane, love and hate, masculinity and femininity, and many others.

He began writing plays in 1980, after attending a workshop run by Patrick Mason, who would later direct many of his most successful plays. That workshop resulted in *The Factory Girls*, a celebration of the working-class Donegal culture in which McGuinness was reared. The play was well received when it premiered at the Abbey Theatre in 1982, but its lighthearted tone and formal simplicity gave no indication of the power or subject matter of McGuinness's next major play, OBSERVE THE SONS OF ULSTER MARCHING TOWARDS THE SOMME (1985). A treatment of protestant Irish soldiers fighting in World War I, it strongly challenged social attitudes in both parts of Ireland—and was the play that first brought McGuinness to international attention.

Throughout his subsequent career, McGuinness has continued to rebel against social and theatrical conventions. His response to the 1972 "Bloody Sunday" killing of thirteen Derry civilians by the British army was *Carthaginians* (1988), in which Dido, a drag queen, directs a mock Irish play in a Derry graveyard. For the Royal Shakespeare Company, he produced *Mary and Lizzie* (1989), which presents Karl Marx and Friedrich Engels from the perspective of Engels's Irish maids. For the Royal National Theatre in Britain, he wrote *Mutabilitie* (1997), a play that challenged English audiences by presenting two of their most cherished writers—Edmund Spenser and William Shakespeare—in an unflattering Irish context. And as a gay man living in Ireland—where homosexuality was criminalized until 1992—McGuinness has never shied from presenting homosexuality at the heart of the national experience.

His work is also characterized by a strong interest in relationships—between countries, family members, lovers, and friends. This was most powerfully the case in *Someone Who'll Watch Over Me* (1992), which presented a trio of American, English, and Irish hostages in 1980s Beirut—and it was also a feature of *Dolly West's Kitchen* (1999), a treatment of a family's life during World War II.

Compassionate and courageous, McGuinness's plays have not always been well received—in part because of his often-challenging subject matter, as well as his frequent use of impressionistic theatrical techniques. Yet he remains much respected as one of the liveliest imaginations now working in the theater.

PLAYS: *The Factory Girls* (1982); *Borderlands* (1983); *Baglady* (1985); *Gatherers* (1985); *Observe the Sons of Ulster Marching Towards the Somme*

(1985); *Innocence* (1986); *Rosermsholm* (after Henrik Ibsen; 1987); *Yerma* (after Gabriel García Lorca; 1987); *Carthaginians* (1988); *Peer Gynt* (after Ibsen; 1988); *Times In It* (1988); *Beautiful British Justice* (1989); *Mary and Lizzie* (1989); *The Bread Man* (1990); *Three Sisters* (after Anton Chekhov; 1990); *The House of Bernarda Alba* (after García Lorca; 1991); *The Threepenny Opera* (after Bertolt Brecht; 1991); *Someone Who'll Watch Over Me* (1992); *The Man With the Flower in His Mouth* (after Luigi Pirandello; 1993); *The Stronger* (after August Strindberg; 1993); *The Bird Sanctuary* (1994); *Hedda Gabler* (after Ibsen; 1994); *Uncle Vanya* (after Chekhov; 1995); *The Caucasian Chalk Circle* (after Brecht; 1997); *A Doll's House* (after Ibsen; 1997); *Electra* (after Sophocles; 1997); *Mutabilitie* (1997); *Barbaric Comedies* (after Ramón María del Valle–Inelán, 1999); *Dolly West's Kitchen* (1999); *Miss Julie* (after Strindberg; 1999); *The Storm* (after Aleksandr Ostrovsky; 1999); *Gates of Gold* (2002); *Hecuba* (after Euripedes, 2004); *Rebecca* (after Dane Daphne du Mauries, 2005); *Phaedra* (after Jean Racine, 2006); *Speaking Like Megpies* (2006); *There Came a Gypsy Riding* (2007)

FURTHER READING

Jordan, Eamonn. *The Feast of Famine: The Plays of Frank McGuinness.* Berne: P. Lang, 1997.

Lojek, Helen, ed. *Stages of Mutabilitie.* Dublin: Carysfort Press, 2002.

Murray, Christopher. *Twentieth Century Irish Drama: Mirror Up to Nation.* Manchester: Manchester Univ. Press, 1997.

Roche, Anthony. *Contemporary Irish Drama: From Beckett to McGuinness.* Dublin: Gill & Macmillan, 1994.

Patrick Lonergan

MCNALLY, TERRENCE (1939–)

If a play isn't worth dying for—not to mention months, perhaps years of rewrites and frustration—maybe it isn't worth writing.
—Terrence McNally, 1998

Terrence McNally, whose plays represent an examination of war, homosexuality, AIDS, and obsession, has often been the center of controversy. His first Broadway production, *And Things That Go Bump in the Night* (1964), was condemned by critics for its violence and pessimistic outlook. Although *Lips Together, Teeth Apart* (1991) ran successfully in New York and regionally, it was banned in Cobb County, Georgia, for being "a gay play." The Manhattan Theater Club canceled *Corpus Christi* (1998), a modern retelling of Christ's life from a gay perspective, when threatened with violence. The Theater Club eventually presented the piece after McNally's contemporaries came to his defense and metal detectors were installed at the theater entrance. Yet for four decades, McNally, a four-time Tony Award winner, has managed to sustain a career as one of America's leading dramatists.

Born on November 3, 1939, in St. Petersburg, Florida, and raised in Texas, McNally moved to New York to attend Columbia University. He graduated in 1960 with a bachelor's degree in English literature and saw himself as a journalist who would write the next Great American Novel. Instead, he wrote a play—*This Side of the Door* (1962)—which he sent to the Actors' Studio. As a result, he was asked to join the Studio's Playwrights' Unit, where he learned stagecraft by observing actors and directors in action and working as a stage manager.

Several of his plays were produced in the late 1960s, establishing him as a writer of COMEDIES. His irreverent treatments of volatile topics, such as Vietnam in *Botticelli* (1968) and political assassination in *Witness* (1968), were well received. He achieved his first big commercial success with his FARCE *The Ritz* (1974), for which he also wrote the screenplay. In 1985, *It's Only a Play* was produced, a drama about waiting for first-night reviews that marked a change in McNally's writing style. While it still possesses a satirical tone, the play is more heartfelt than farcical.

Although McNally was not trained in music or dance, both elements are important to his work. He fell in love with opera as a young Catholic schoolboy and views dance as an extraordinary means of expressing love. *Love! Valour! Compassion!* (1994) includes a ballet section, and *Master Class* (1995) is entirely devoted to Maria Callas. In 1992, he collaborated with John Kander and Fred Ebb on *Kiss of the Spider Woman*, winning a Tony Award for Best Book. His dramatic writing includes the books for several other musicals, as well as the libretto for the opera version of *Dead Man Walking* (2000). As a writer who draws inspiration from contemporary cultural concerns, McNally has been strongly influenced by the HIV/AIDS crisis. Although not necessarily a central theme in all of his plays, it undeniably informs the subtexts of his characters. In *Andre's Mother* (1988, whose 1990 PBS version won an Emmy Award), McNally does deal directly with the subject. Written when the UNITED STATES and its theater community were struggling to deal with the crisis, the drama elucidates the impact of AIDS-related deaths on those left behind.

In addition to numerous awards from the theater community, McNally has also been recognized by the Pulitzer Prize Committee.

[See also Gay and Lesbian Drama]

PLAYS: *The Side of the Door* (1962); *The Lady of the Camellias* (1963); *And Things That Go Bump in the Night* (1964); *Next* (1967); *Tour* (1967); *Botticelli* (1968); *Cuba Si* (1968); *Noon* (1968); *Sweet Eros* (1968); *Witness* (1968); *Bring It All Back Home* (1969); *Last Gasps* (1969); *Where Has Tommy Flowers Gone?* (1971); *Let It Bleed* (1972); *Whisky* (1973); *Bad Habits* (1974); *The Ritz* (1975); *It's Only a Play* (1985); *Frankie and Johnny in the Clair de Lune* (1987); *Andre's Mother* (1988); *The Lisbon Traviata* (1989); *Prelude & Liebestod* (1989); *Lips Together, Teeth Apart* (1991); *A Perfect Ganesh* (1993); *The Wibbly, Wobbly, Wiggly Dance that Cleopatterer Did* (1993); *Hidden Agendas* (1994); *Love! Valour! Compassion!* (1994); *Master Class* (1995); *Dusk* (1996); *Corpus Christi* (1998)

FURTHER READING

Bigsby, C. W. E. *Modern American Drama 1945–2000*. Cambridge: Cambridge Univ. Press, 2000.

DiGaetani, John L. *A Search for a Postmodern Theater: Interviews with Contemporary Playwrights*. New York: Greenwood Press, 1991.

Kolin, Philip C., and Colby H. Kullman, eds. *Speaking on Stage: Interviews with Contemporary American Playwrights*. Tuscaloosa: Univ. of Alabama Press, 1996.

MacNicholas, John, ed. *Twentieth-Century American Dramatists: Dictionary of Literary Biography*. Vol. 7. Detroit: Gale Res., 1981.

Zinman, Toby Silverman, ed. *Terrence McNally: A Casebook*. New York: Garland, 1997.

Meghan Duffy

MCPHERSON, CONOR (1971–)

Boredom. Loneliness. A feeling of basically being out of step with everybody else. Fear. Anxiety. Tension. And of course a disposition to generally liking the whole . . . thing of drinking until you pass out.
—John, Part 3, *A Dublin Carol*

Conor McPherson is an Irish dramatist, filmmaker, and director. Most of his work for the stage has been written in the form of monologues, usually presented by deeply flawed and often self-deceptive male characters. His plays represent a moving anatomization of loneliness and masculinity—and are, furthermore, among the finest recent examples of theatrical storytelling.

McPherson's earliest plays were performed in fringe venues in Dublin; his first success was *This Lime Tree Bower* (1995), a series of three interlinked monologues, which he later filmed as *Saltwater*. Produced in Dublin to mixed reviews, the play was more successful when it transferred to London's Bush Theatre—which also produced *St Nicholas* (1997), in which a drunken Irish theater critic falls in with a group of vampires.

McPherson was then commissioned by the Royal Court to write a naturalistic play for an ensemble of actors. The result was *The Weir* (1997), a fiercely moving drama set in a rural Irish pub, in which the local clientele entertain a visitor from Dublin by telling her ghost stories. *The Weir* was very successful, transferring to Dublin and Broadway. It was followed by *A Dublin Carol* (2000), in which an alcoholic undertaker is confronted by his estranged daughter.

While *The Weir* and *A Dublin Carol* appeared to suggest that McPherson has abandoned the monologue, both were strongly dependent on storytelling as a means of representing character. It was therefore unsurprising that McPherson returned to the monologue with *Port Authority* (2001), which presents three generations of dysfunctional Irish males.

In 2001, McPherson became a victim of the kind of lifestyle represented in his plays, when he was hospitalized for pancreatitis associated with heavy drinking. This illness and his subsequent recovery have done nothing to diminish his output: his films *Saltwater* and *The Actors* were released in 2001 and 2003,

and he directed Eugene O'Brien's *Eden* in Dublin and the West End in 2001–2002.

McPherson's reception has not been universally positive. Some commentators regard his representation of women as unsympathetic; others suggest that he needs to explore forms other than the monologue to develop fully as a playwright. McPherson has countered that the monologue offers a uniquely theatrical experience to audiences, who must listen not only to his character's words but also to their silences, unfinished sentences, and slips.

McPherson's contribution to Irish theater is significant. The success of his monologues helped to create an audience for similar work by Enda Walsh, Mark O'Rowe, and others. And although premiered in 1997, *The Weir* was voted by *Irish Times* readers as one of the best Irish plays of the 20th century. This shows the immediacy of the impact of a playwright who has quickly emerged as one of the most exciting young voices in Irish theater.

[See also Ireland]

PLAYS: *Concerning Communication* (1992); *Rum and Vodka* (1992); *A Light in the Window of Industry* (1993); *The Good Thief* (1994); *Inventing Fortune's Wheel* (1994); *The Stars Lose Their Glory* (1994); *This Lime Tree Bower* (1995); *St Nicholas* (1997); *The Weir* (1997); *A Dublin Carol* (2000); *Come on Over* (2001); *Port Authority* (2001); *Shining City* (2004); *The Seafarer* (2006)

FURTHER READING

Grene, Nicholas. *The Politics of Irish Drama: Plays in Context from Boucicault to Friel*. Cambridge: Cambridge Univ. Press, 2000.

Jordan, Eamonn, ed. *Theatre Stuff: Critical Essays on Contemporary Irish Theatre*. Dublin: Carysfort Press, 2000.

Wood, Gerard. *Imagining Mischief*. Dublin: Liffey Press, 2003.

Patrick Lonergan

THE MEASURES TAKEN

BERTOLT BRECHT's *The Measures Taken* (*Die Maßnahme*) premiered in a midnight performance at the Berlin Philharmonic on December 13, 1930. Thematically and aesthetically, it was and remains Brecht's most controversial play.

Four Communist Party agitators, sent by Moscow to CHINA to spread propaganda and foment revolution, return to report that they shot a young comrade and threw his corpse into a lime pit. They submit their case to the Party's judicial organ, the Control Chorus, and reenact, in eight parables, the events leading up to and including the murder. The agitators easily recruit the young comrade to guide them across the border where unrest is rife. However, the same moral outrage at human misery that compels him to swear allegiance to the ABCs of communism and join the underground cell makes the young comrade temperamentally unfit to sustain the deception necessary to maintain Party discipline. Four times he fails to fulfill his charge, and four times he endangers the world revolutionary struggle when his actions threaten to betray the presence of the foreign communist agents. The mercy he shows the coolies in laying stepping stones at their feet as they trudge along the slippery embankment, towing the rice barge upriver, only serves to draw their scorn and to attract the unwanted attention of the overseer. The justice he demands from the police officer, who falsely charges a scab with distributing strike leaflets, draws the ire of the textile workers and undermines worker solidarity. The honor he asserts in refusing to dine with the arms merchant, who proudly proclaims, "I don't know what a man is, I only know his price," undermines the attempt to arm the coolies in the fight against British imperialism. And finally, when, in righteous indignation at the exploitation of the working class, he tears away his mask and calls prematurely for revolution, his howling in the night literally awakens the masses from their slumber, causing them to cry out against the foreign agitators. This final act of betrayal leads to the decision to murder the young comrade as the only means of forestalling the retreat of the Party vanguard. "In the interest of Communism" and "the forward march of the proletarian masses of all nations," the young comrade acquiesces to his own murder.

The discordant sounds of Hanns Eisler's (1898–1962) musical score and the unrhymed, irregular verse of Brecht's libretto symbolize the dissonant social relations under capitalism. Brecht and Eisler drew on disparate poetic and musical traditions (didactic poetry, the Passion oratorio, agit-prop [AGITATION-PROPAGANDA] theater, *actus oratorius*, the brass orchestra, workers choirs, atonal music) to convey the contradiction between Christian virtue and socialist morality. Critical reviews were equally wide-ranging and discordant. While one socialist critic lamented the scriptural overtones of the LEARNING PLAY, another lambasted Brecht for instructing the working class in false ethical dilemmas. Excitement about the new music and new theater for the working class vied with horror at the antihumanistic impulse reflected in the willingness to sacrifice a human life in the service of an ideological end. Despite attempts to elevate the play to the level of a TRAGEDY, the critical consensus sees it as a piece of experimental theater and as part of Brecht's political and artistic journey.

[See also Germany]

FURTHER READING

Cohn, Ruby. " 'Theatrum Mundi' and Contemporary Theater." *Comparative Drama* 1 (1967): 28–35.

Mews, Siegfried, ed. *Critical Essays on Bertolt Brecht*. Boston: G. K. Hall, 1989.

Schoeps, Karl-Heinz. "Brecht's *Lehrstücke*: A Laboratory for Epic and Dialectic Theater." In *A Bertolt Brecht Reference Companion*, ed. by Siegfried Mews. Westport, Conn.: Greenwood Press, 1997. 70–87.

Wirth, Andrzej. "The Lehrstück as Performance." *Drama Review* 43, no. 4 (1999): 113–121.

Kathy Brzovic

MEDOFF, MARK (1940–)

My work is simply a reflection of my own spirit, my fears, sorrows, and fires.
—Mark Medoff, 1980

Mark Medoff was born on March 18, 1940, in Carmel, Illinois, but much of his work focuses on the American Southwest. Medoff's earliest works were written and produced in Las Cruces, New Mexico, during the late 1960s and early 1970s. His early plays reflect the political and social turmoil of America in the late 1960s. In 1973 his play *When You Comin Back, Red Ryder?* brought the playwright an Obie Award, a Drama Desk Award, and national attention. Set in Foster's Diner in the forgotten reaches of New Mexico, the action of the play involves an eclectic group of characters representing a wide range of social backgrounds and takes place in the shadow of the Vietnam War. At the center of the action is Stephen Ryder, a nineteen-year-old cook, who prefers to be called Red. He has ambitions of leaving his small-town existence but appears incapable of pursuing his dream. While all of the patrons are stuck in the diner, a wild Vietnam War veteran named Teddy arrives, saying he is on his way to Mexico. Using a wide variety of clever methods, Teddy aggressively confronts the other characters, uncovering their fears and desires and eventually motivating young Stephen to leave and realize his life's ambition. The play is crafted with wit and insight and formed one portion of *The Hero Trilogy*, which also includes *The Majestic Kid* (1985) and *The Heart Outright* (1986).

In 1977 Medoff met deaf actor Phyllis Frelich at a theater workshop in Rhode Island and began to write a play for her, *Children of a Lesser God* (1979), which was produced on Broadway in 1980. Recognized as a unique and innovative triumph, the drama takes place on an almost bare stage and is set in the mind of teacher James Leeds, chronicling his journey to help a deaf student move forward in her life. Using both spoken and sign language, the play provided a touching and imaginative insight into the world of the deaf. Critically acclaimed and commercially successful, the play ran for 887 performances and won Tony Awards for Best Play, Best Actress (Frelich), and Best Actor (John Rubinstein). Medoff co-adapted the play for the screen (with Hesper Anderson) and received an Academy Award nomination (1986). Other notable collaborations with Frelich include *The Hands of Its Enemy* (1984), *Gila* (1998), and *Road to a Revolution* (2001), which focuses on the riots at the primarily deaf Gallaudet University in Washington, D.C., in the late 1980s.

In 2004 Medoff's play *Prymate* closed after only five official performances on Broadway. The play dealt with issues of race, AIDS, and animal rights; however, Medoff's choice to have an African American male play the role of a violent gorilla caused controversy. "My work is usually issue-driven," acknowledges Medoff (NBlake, 2004). In addition to his success as a playwright, Medoff has worked as an actor, novelist, director of stage and screen, screenwriter, and educator.

[*See also* United States, 1940–Present]

SELECT PLAYS: *The Wager* (1967); *Doing a Good One for the Red Man* (1969); *The Froegle Dictum* (1971); *The Kramer* (1972); *The War on Tatem* (1972); *When You Comin Back, Red Ryder?* (1973); *The Odyssey of Jeremy Jack* (1974); *The Ultimate Grammar of Life* (1974); *The Halloween Bandit* (1976); *The Conversion of Aaron Weiss* (1977); *Firekeeper* (1978); *Children of a Lesser God* (1979); *The Last Chance Saloon* (1979); *The Hands of Its Enemy* (1984); *Kringle's Window* (1985); *The Majestic Kid* (1985); *The Heart Outright* (1986); *Big Mary* (1989); *Stumps* (1989); *The Homage that Follows* (1994); *Crunch Time* (1998); *Gila* (1998); *Showdown on Rio Road* (1998); *Road to a Revolution* (2001); *Tommy J & Sally* (2002); *Gunfighter: A Gulf War Chronicle* (2003); *Prymate* (2004)

FURTHER READING

Erben, Rudolf. *Mark Medoff.* Boise, Idaho: Boise State Univ. Press, 1995.

Green, Blake. "Big, bold, a bit racy." *Newsday,* May 2, 2004. http://www.newsday.com/entertainment/news/ny-ftthe3778468may02,0,5639693.story?coll-ny-nyc-entertainment-headlines

Zachary, Samuel J. *The Dramaturgy of Mark Medoff—Five Plays Dealing with Deafness and Social Issues.* Lewiston, N.Y.: Edwin Mellen Press, 2004.

Ellen Anthony-Moore and Christopher Moore

MEE, CHARLES (1938–)

The defining moment of Charles Mee's life came at the age of fourteen, when what he has described as a vibrant youth was interrupted by a case of polio that would leave him disabled for the rest of his life. In his memoir, Mee finds the roots of his dark, fragmentary writing style in his struggle with his own body: "Intact people should write intact books. . . . That is not my experience of the world. I like a book that feels like a crystal goblet that has been thrown to the floor and shattered."

Mee was born on September 15, 1938, in Evanston, Illinois. After he graduated from Harvard University, he briefly worked on Wall Street before taking a job at the American Heritage publishing company. His first play was produced in 1962 at the Writers' Stage Company, and over the next two years he would have additional plays produced by theaters such as La MaMa E.T.C. He also worked on *The Drama Review* in various editorial capacities from 1963 until 1965, at which point he lost confidence in pursuing a career in the theater. From 1965 until the early 1980s, he was for the most part a historian; he worked as editor of *Horizon,* a magazine on history and the arts, and wrote numerous books on European and American history.

Mee's interest in history and politics did not abate when he returned to playwriting with *The Investigation of the Murder in El Salvador* (1989). Even when adapting numerous Greek TRAGE-DIES, he injected allusions to contemporary events and samples of contemporary texts into the dialogue. Indeed, Mee has referred to his works as assemblages or COLLAGES because they consist in no small part of excerpts taken from numerous texts integrated with material written by himself—and sometimes co-authored by theater ensembles with whom he collaborates. In *The Berlin Circle* (1998), for example, Mee takes the story of BERTOLT BRECHT's THE CAUCASIAN CHALK CIRCLE (which was taken from other sources itself) and imposes its structure on East Berlin just as the Soviet Union is crumbling. His daughter, who has directed Mee's *The Imperialists at the Club Cave Canem* (1988) and *First Love* (2001), has characterized the plays as "blueprints for events" that are "full of excess" in terms of language, movement, themes, and dramaturgical structure. True to his own creative process, Mee (2006) has posted his scripts online and, as part of a "(re)-making project," invited others to take the texts and "pillage" them to build an "entirely new piece out of the ruins."

Mee has worked with some of America's most prominent directors, such as Anne Bogart and Robert Woodruff, and he shared an Obie with director Les Waters for their 2001 collaboration on *Big Love* (1999). As recently as December 2001, however, critic Jeremy McCarter writing for the New York Sun, could complain that Mee's plays deserve "more scrutiny than they've received," singling Mee out as the "rare serious artist whose innovations make his work more popular and more accessible without making it any less serious." Critics such as Robert Brustein have ranked Mee with the likes of WALLACE SHAWN and JOHN GUARE, but few lengthy studies of Mee's work have been published.

[*See also* Avant-Garde Drama, United States; Political Theater in the United States; United States, 1940–Present]

PLAYS: *Vienna: Lusthaus* (1986); *The Imperialists at the Club Cave Canem* (1988); *The Investigation of the Murder in El Salvador* (1989); *Another Person Is a Foreign Country* (1991); *The Constitutional Convention: A Sequel* (1991); *Orestes* (1992); *Agamemnon* (1995); *The Trojan Women: A Love Story* (1996); *The Berlin Circle* (1998); *Big Love* (1999); *bobrauschenbergamerica* (2001); *First Love* (2001); *Limonade Tous Les Jours* (2002)

FURTHER READING

Brustein, Robert. "Varieties of Theatrical Experience." *The New Republic* (December 31, 2001).

Mee, Charles L. *A Nearly Normal Life: A Memoir.* New York: Little, Brown, 1999.

———. *The (re)-making project.* http://www.charlesmee.org/html/prod.html. (Oct. 12, 2006).

Mee, Erin B. "Shattered and Fucked Up and Full of Wreckage: The Words and Works of Charles L. Mee." *The Drama Review* 46, no. 3 (T175) (Fall 2002).

Wilder, Matthew. "Fantasizing About Chuck Mee." *Theatre Forum,* no. 5 (Summer–Fall 1994).

Daniel Mufson

MEI LANFANG (1894–1961)

The best-known Beijing opera *dan* (female) role master and one of the greatest singer-actor-dancers in Chinese history, Mei Lanfang, stage name of Mei Lan, was born in October 1894 in Taizhou county of CHINA's Jiangsu province. His grandfather and father both being well-known opera actors, Mei began studying Beijing opera at the age of eight and made his debut onstage at ten. He joined the Xiliancheng Theatrical Company in 1907 to begin his professional stage career. Thereafter Mei Lanfang played mostly female roles in Beijing operas, but he was a master in *kunqu* as well. In 1913 Mei first toured Shanghai for a professional performance that won him a national reputation. After the start of the second Sino-Japanese War (1937–1945), he went to settle in Hong Kong in protest. He returned to Shanghai in 1942 but did not resume his performance until after World War II in 1945. After 1949, Mei Lanfang served as the first president of China Beijing Opera Academy and performed frequently until his death in August 1961.

Chinese Beijing opera has become globally known, thanks to Mei Lanfang's efforts and his tours in JAPAN, the UNITED STATES, and the former Soviet Union. For his contribution to the art of Beijing opera and to his efforts in introducing the traditional Chinese performing art to the world, Mei was awarded an Honorary Doctor of Philosophy degree by Pomona College and University of Southern California, respectively, during his tour to the United States. While visiting Moscow, he won the praise of such dramatic heavyweights as KONSTANTIN STANISLAVSKY and VSEVOLOD MEYERHOLD.

Mei Lanfang's stage life underwent three periods. From the beginning of his career to 1915, it was the early period of Mei's professional life, when he laid a solid foundation for his later achievement and mainly inherited Beijing operatic tradition. The years from 1915 to the eve of the second Sino-Japanese War marked the middle period of his artistic activities, when he made major reforms to the *dan* roles in Beijing opera by redefining the role of a *qingyi*, the dignified and graceful female, and the role of a *huadan*, the vivacious female. The third and last period followed World War II, when he focused on some of his more successful plays for reinforcements. Plays he performed during this period were frequently made into films.

In his fifty years of stage life, Mei Lanfang played over 100 roles of characters. He revolutionized both stage makeup and costumes and systemized and enriched character gestures, expressions, and poses. He also made innovations in play script and accompanying instrument. Especially praiseworthy was his achievement in incorporating singing, gesticulation, elocution, and acrobatics with dancing in operatic performance. His style of performance won such acclaim over the years that it came to be known as the "Mei Lanfang school." The major plays in his repertoire include *Beauty Defies Tyranny* (*Yu zou feng*), *The Drunken Concubine* (*Gui fei zui jiu*), *Hegemon-King Parts with His Concubine* (*Ba wang bie ji*), and *Scattering Flowers* (*Tian nü san hua*).

FURTHER READING

Hu Shih. *Mei Lan-fang and the Chinese Drama.* Shanghai: Commercial Press, 1931.

Leung, George Kin, et al. *Mei Lan-fang, Foremost Actor of China.* Shanghai: Commercial Press, 1929.

Mei Lanfang. *Hegemon King Says Farewell to His Queen* (*Bawang bieji*). A Beijing Opera play adapted by Mei Lanfang. Tr. by William Dolby. In *Eight Chinese Plays from the Thirteenth Century to the Present*, by Mei Lanfang. New York: Columbia Univ. Press, 1978. 111–137.

Scott, A. C. *Mei Lan-fang: The Life and Times of a Peking Actor.* Hong Kong: Hong Kong Univ. Press, 1971.

Wu, Zuguang, et al. *Peking Opera and Mei Lanfang: A Guide to China's Traditional Theatre and the Art of Its Great Master.* Beijing: New World Press, 1981.

Hongchu Fu

MELODRAMA

One of the misunderstood subjects in theater, melodrama is also one of the most resilient. For many people the word conjures up images of threatened heroines, virtuous heroes, and nefarious villains. It is, however, a more complex and even sophisticated subject.

The term *melodrama* originally comes from the practice of English and French theaters presenting plays with a musical accompaniment. These "melody-dramas" came about as a way to circumvent theater-licensing procedures that restricted non-musical plays to specific theaters.

Music and musical interludes were part of melodrama. They, of course, aided in getting around licensing restrictions. However, it also added a tool for the dramatist or the producer. Music sometimes received use as an underscore to specific scenes. Dramatists used interludes to break the tension of a scene or simply to extend the show's running time. In some cases the interlude was irrelevant to the story line and occurred in order to highlight a specific performer or performers.

Plot, situation, and spectacle rather than well-defined characters drive the plays. The world of the play is a world of poetic justice. The good receive absolution and/or reward; the bad receive their just deserts. A facet of melodrama that evolved over time was spectacle. Producers became increasingly desirous of scenes containing thrilling exploits, scenes where characters performed death-defying deeds. The audiences delighted in the spectacle as well as in the expected "happy ending." The critics, on the other hand, derided melodrama for its non-Aristotelian structure. The observance of the unities was not strict; further, the critics felt, many plot elements depended on wild coincidences and seeming defiance of logic.

Suspense was a major factor in melodrama's hold on its audience. The clever playwright used it to full effect in order to draw his audience into the story. A good example of the "see-saw" battle of good and evil comes from N. Hart Jackson's adaptation of Adolphe D'Ennery and Eugene Cormon's *The Two Orphans* (1874).

Henriette and Louise, the two orphans of the title, arrive in Paris to meet a person who has offered to shelter them. People bent on abducting Henriette for immoral purposes have waylaid him, and they abduct Henriette. Louise, who is blind, hears the scuffle and cries out for her sister. Unfortunately, La Frochard, the villain of the play, hears her and misleads her into thinking La Frochard will aid her in searching for Henriette.

In the second scene DeVaudrey, a disaffected noble more noble than his peers, rescues Henriette. She is now safe, but Louise's singing assists La Frochard in panhandling the streets. Louise begs for relief from this fatiguing task, but La Frochard refuses.

In scene 2 of act 2 a false ray of hope appears. A doctor encounters Louise and La Frochard in the street. He examines Louise's eyes and declares there is the possibility of restoring her sight. He requests she come to his office. La Frochard agrees to this but really does not intend to give up her panhandling racket using Louise. Further heightening the suspense, Henriette almost finds Louise, but DeVaudrey's uncle, who dislikes her, has her arrested. She is taken away by the guards as Louise's voice grows fainter in the background.

Act 3, scene 1, sees Henriette rescued by a girl named Marianne who Henriette did a kind favor for in act 1, scene 1. Marianne is imprisoned along with Henriette. She fears that she will relapse into her old ways if she returns to the world. She accepts Henriette's sentence of exile (arranged under false pretenses by DeVaudrey's uncle) and gives Henriette the pardon she (Marianne) received. In scene 2, Henriette rescues Louise from La Frochard. Both girls have lovers who want them, and the punishment of the evildoers occurs in due course.

PLAYWRIGHTS

What we consider "modern" melodrama derives from the works of the French playwright Guilbert de Pixerécourt (1773–1844). His works achieved great popularity in postrevolutionary FRANCE. His two best-known pieces are *Coelina* (1800) and *The Dog of Montargis* (1814). The first play derives from a novel of the period. The second play is pure melodrama: just before an innocent man's unjust execution, a dog identifies the actual murderer.

One of a dramatist's tricks to keep up suspense is to reveal all, or only part, of the mystery to the audience. In *Coelina* Pixerécourt withholds part of the mystery from the audience. Francisque is a mysterious individual. He is mute and seems fond of Coelina, fond in a paternal way. Truguelin, the villain, has found a way to cheat Coelina of her estate by charging her birth to be illegitimate in a letter to Dufour, Coelina's guardian. Coelina and Francisque are banished. Francisque writes his version of the story in a letter as well. Both the characters in the world of the play and the audience are in quandary. The truth is revealed when Andrevon, the doctor, endorses Francisque's version of the story. Earlier in the play Truguelin avoids the doctor; we find out later that Truguelin was responsible for Francisque's crippling. The doctor's testimony solves the mystery. This set a pattern followed by many melodramas. A character such as a minister, judge, doctor, village elder that most (if not all) members of the community respected for their integrity facilitated the revelation of the truth.

VICTORIEN SARDOU (1831–1908) dominated the French melodrama in the latter half of the 19th century. Many of his plays revolved around misplaced objects, and he, like Eugène Scribe, constructed them in the "well-made play" pattern. In 1900, Giacomo Puccini immortalized his 1887 play *La Tosca* as an opera.

Edward Fitzball (1793–1873), THOMAS TAYLOR (1817–1880), and George R. Sims (1847–1922) are well-known and prolific melodramatists of the English stage. Fitzball had a reputation for the macabre but also wrote melodramas of a nautical theme. *The Inchcape Bell* (1828) and *Jonathan Bradford or, the Murder at the Roadside Inn* (1823) are two of his better-known plays. The latter is an example of so-called cause célèbre (celebrated case) melodrama where the story is taken from a real-life criminal case. Taylor was not as flamboyant as Fitzball but contributed a memorable play to the repertoire: *The Ticket-of-Leave Man* (1863), with the ubiquitous detective Hawkshaw. Sims is most prominent for *The Lights o' London* (1881) and *The Romany Rye* (1882). Both of these plays used the theme of the evils of the metropolis, the former dealing with a falsely accused hero and the latter dealing with the abduction and near murder of the hero. *Romany Rye* also contains a good example of the way logic stretched in melodrama. Two men with murderous intent abduct the hero of *The Romany Rye*. They bring him to a hideout where they leave him in the hands of an old woman who is to knock him out with a sleep potion. However, the old woman cannot bring herself to participate in the hero's demise because he reminds her of her own son. She urges him to fake his unconsciousness, and this allows him to get the drop on his would-be murderers and vanquish them.

The English stage also received translations of plays from France and GERMANY. Besides Pixerécourt's works the German playwright August von Kotzebue (1761–1819) attained translation in ENGLAND. This prolific writer's best-known play *Misanthropy and Remorse* (*Menschenhass und Reue*), written in 1788, shocked its audiences with its radical (for the time) action of having a runaway wife reunited with her husband and children. *The Stranger* (1792) was the title of its English translation, and it played durably for years. A variation of its plot, the errant wife being forgiven and then dying, is found in ELLEN WOOD's adaptation of her own novel EAST LYNNE (1861). It proved very durable in dramatic form.

The American theater has had many playwrights of the melodramatic form. Some received their influence from the

European tradition. Others, especially later, developed a more American point of view.

John Augustus Stone (1800–1834) wrote many plays but is best known for *Metamora* (1829), written for Edwin Forrest. Louisa Medina (c. 1813–1838) was successful as an adapter of novels to the stage. Her best-known one was *The Last Days of Pompeii* (1835), which, with twenty-nine performances, set a record for length of run. Her 1838 adaptation of Robert Bird's novel *Nick of the Woods* contained a spectacular scene of the title character breaking up an attack on some settlers by descending on a cataract in a burning canoe.

George Aiken (1830–1876) wrote the adaptation of *Uncle Tom's Cabin* (1852), which is in most collections. Frank Murdock (1843–1872) wrote DAVY CROCKETT (1872). This play is memorable for the scene where Davy (actually, Davy Junior) saves the villain and the heroine from a pack of wolves by using the "strong arm of a frontiersman" to replace the broken bar on the cabin door.

DIONYSIUS BOUCICAULT (1820–1890) traveled between England and the UNITED STATES, producing plays on both shores. One of his best known is *The Poor of New York* (1858, later renamed *Streets of New York*). This play became *The Streets of London*, *The Poor of Liverpool*, and so on—it took the name of wherever it played.

AUGUSTIN DALY's (1838–1899) plays were famous for their spirited heroines. Daly's UNDER THE GASLIGHT is the first melodrama to feature a rescue from the railroad tracks. The heroine, Laura, driven from her home by the villain's false claim of her illegitimate birth, flees his attempts to abduct her. Seeking the shelter of a shed near a railroad track, an accommodating trainman agrees to lock her in for her protection since the shed also contains tools that need locking up anyway. Snorky, Laura's comic friend, searches for her, but the villain captures him instead. The villain ties Snorky to the tracks as a train sounds in the distance. After the villain leaves, Laura tries in vain against the locked shed door. She remembers the supply of tools. Using an ax, she frees herself and frees Snorky as the train rumbles up.

A similar turn of events occurred in Daly's *The Red Scarf* (1869). This play contained the first rescue from a buzz saw. Again, a heroine rescued the helpless male victim.

WILLIAM GILLETTE's (1853–1937) SECRET SERVICE (1896) was a sturdy Civil War story about a spy who must choose between his mission and his love for a woman. However, one of the most famous Civil War melodramas was SHENANDOAH by BRONSON HOWARD (1842–1908). Written in 1873, it languished until 1888, rescued from oblivion by Charles Frohman. It contained a scene of an advancing army, including some horses, trouping endlessly by a mansion.

Along with William Gillette, DAVID BELASCO (1853–1931) exemplifies the "high road" in melodrama. Belasco was one of the pioneers of electric stage lighting. The brighter stage eliminated the need for broad acting and the use of asides since the stage could be seen clearly from all parts of the house, eliminating any need to "coach" the audience. THE GIRL OF THE GOLDEN WEST (1905) was famous for its attention to the detail of a mining camp. It was also known for a very understated scene where the sheriff discovers the hero's hiding place from drops of blood from the hero's wound landing on the sheriff's handkerchief.

Owen Davis (1874–1956) depended on spectacle and thrill for his dramatics. This style of writing was popular in the era from the 1890s to the late 1910s; its name is "blood and thunder" melodrama. Although Davis later switched over to writing standard dramas, he was a prolific writer of melodrama. One of his most famous plays is *Nellie, the Beautiful Cloak Model* (1907). Nellie triumphed over the villain in the fourth act despite dropping down an elevator shaft, suffering an explosion, and dropping off a bridge in prior acts. His *Through the Breakers* (1899) contained a very subdued thrill scene. The hero, a telegrapher, tied up under the covers of a bed by a villain determined to kill him, is apparently helpless. The hero's partner, not knowing about his captive comrade, is about to leave the hut, which would allow the villain to carry out the murderous plan. However, the hero manages to extricate one hand and tap a message in Morse code on the headboard of the bed. The partner, hearing the message, captures the villain and saves his friend.

GENRES

While there are many types of melodramas, it is difficult to categorize them into concrete genres. Some books on melodrama do this in infinitesimal detail, while others use few categories. They can sometimes be found listed by general locale, example, Western, Railroad, Big City, Military. Sometimes they are broken into smaller groups such as Military being broken into Cavalry, Infantry, Shipboard, and so on. It is more useful to place a play in a larger group that gives a general idea of topic of the play. The genres listed here were likely to show up in most listings and mainly describe plays for the American stage, unless otherwise noted. Each topic is listed with a brief description and some example titles.

MYSTERY MELODRAMAS

Mystery melodramas are plays that contained some form of crime and punishment or detection. These include William Gillette's *Sherlock Holmes* (1898) and Bernard Vieller's *The Trial of Mary Dugan* (1927).

CAUSE CÉLÈBRE MELODRAMAS

Cause célèbre plays derived their story line from actual criminal cases that were current. Edward Fitzball's *Jonathan Bradford, or the Murder at the Roadside Inn* (1823) is a prime example of this type. Sometimes the cases were not fully decided when the plays received presentation. Supposedly, in one such case, the protagonist received a last-minute reprieve on Monday, Wednesday, Friday, and alternating matinees. He went to his fate on Tuesday, Thursday, Saturday, and alternating matinees.

REFORM MELODRAMAS

Reform melodramas plays addressed topics that affected values or morals. *Ten Nights in a Barroom* (William Pratt, 1847) and *The Drunkard* (William Smith, 1844) sermonized on temperance matters. Such plays afforded the person playing the lead with a meaty role since the delirium tremens scenes allowed for extremely broad histrionics. On the other hand, George Aiken's 1852 dramatization of *Uncle Tom's Cabin* (in its antebellum form) spoke against slavery. Later additions such as dances and songs that exhibited the talents of the players entered the production; not all of them were directly relevant to the story line, however.

BIG CITY MELODRAMAS

The big city melodrama style was shared by the English and American stage. It spoke of the attendant evils involved with living in a seemingly corrupt metropolis. The protagonist of George R. Sims's *Lights o' London* is forced to live on the streets of London with his wife, while he is pursued by a villain who seeks to have him imprisoned on false charges. The female protagonist of Augustin Daly's *Under the Gaslight* has lost her social position and must fend for herself in New York while trying to thwart the designs of the villain to exploit her virtue.

HISTORICAL MELODRAMAS

Historical melodramas derive from actual events in American history. *Major André* (1903) and *Nathan Hale* (1898) are about figures from the American Revolution. Both of these plays are by CLYDE FITCH. While the action in some plays occurred with a historical event in the background, like Bronson Howard's *Shenandoah*, the historical melodrama's action received full or partial basis in real people and real events.

SOCIAL MELODRAMA

Social melodrama plays sometimes became satires on certain behaviors others dealt with dramatically. A playwright who wrote in this mode was George Broadhurst (1866–1952). His 1911 play *Bought and Paid For* dealt with a man who felt his money entitled him to treat everything like a possession, including his wife. Bronson Howard's 1887 play *The Henrietta* also commented on a family's obsession with money but in a more humorous way. In the end the most successful member of the family was the ne'er-do-well who made money in the stock market by treating it like a huge gambling game.

NAUTICAL MELODRAMA

Nautical melodrama was unique to the English stage because of its maritime position in the world. *Black Eyed Susan* (Douglas Jerrold, 1829) is one of the most famous of this group. The title character is the wife of the hero. He must risk his life in order to protect her virtue from his own captain.

WESTERN MELODRAMA

Western melodrama was unique to America. Its topics dealt with both the frontier and with the West of contemporary times. David Belasco's *The Girl of the Golden West* was set in a mining camp of the gold rush era. The heroine's love interest was a highway robber, whom she protected from the sheriff.

Frank Murdock's play *Davy Crockett* was far more fantastic in its exploits.

FANTASY MELODRAMA

Fantasy melodrama plays had imaginative settings that departed from the real world or from our own culture. *The Yellow Jacket* (1912) by George C. Hazleton and J. H. Benrimo traced the journey of a young man to attain the yellow jacket of the emperor of CHINA. It contained elements of Chinese theater including an onstage property master. While this play portrayed elements from East Asian culture, racial stereotypes mar the play. An earlier fantasy play is Louisa Medina's *Last Days of Pompeii* (1835). This is set in the ancient Roman city of Pompeii before the volcanic eruption that destroyed it. The protagonists must fight evil powers; however, the volcanic destruction renders everything moot. Plays of this style where the hero's fight against a supernatural power results in Pyrrhic victory were in vogue before the Civil War. Some authorities refer to them as apocalyptic melodramas.

CASTS

The casts of a typical melodrama consisted of stock characters. These include leading men and ladies, heavies, juvenile men and ingenues, comics and soubrettes, characters, and utility players. While the parts of leading man and lady are the same as today, the use of "juvenile" parts has faded into obscurity. These terms referred to roles assumed to be younger adults. Sometimes the juvenile man or the juvenile lady (many times called the ingenue) was the main character; more often, these players acted in support to the leads. (Many stories abound in theater lore about the companies that had juveniles that were almost twice the normal age of a juvenile.)

What is more important to realize about the cast is that they represented virtues or vices. The play was not about the personal sufferings of an individual; it was about the triumph of the virtuous over the evil. Characters in a melodrama were not three-dimensional. Instead, they were "cardboard cutout" portrayals of attributes of good and evil.

CONCLUSION

Melodrama owed its staying power to its ability to deliver a just answer in a perfect world to an inhabitant of a world that seemed unjust or strange. Pixerécourt flourished in the era that followed the Terror in postrevolutionary France. The people of this era had seen their culture transformed in a way that bewildered them. Social structures and values that were once familiar to them changed in ways they did not completely understand. The world of the melodrama, however, offered a catharsis. Here was a world where honesty and virtue triumphed over a clearly defined evil, providing solace to a person living in an age of turmoil. One can find analogies among other eras where melodrama was the theatrical vogue. There was great turmoil in England during the time when French melodrama received translation for the English stage. Parliament underwent a restructuring during this time, and the romantic movement arose in England as well as Europe, which had an effect on the culture.

America was also undergoing upheaval. By the late 1820s the old order of government passed away under the onslaught of Jacksonian democracy. Heroic and apocalyptic melodrama were the order of the day. As the tensions that led to the Civil War grew, melodrama transformed into moral and temperance plays. After the Civil War, other genres rose into place. Sometimes the plays reflected an arcane worldview such as Thomas Dixon's novel made into the play The Klansman.

Heading toward the fin de sieclé from the Civil War, America passed through two major panics and the beginning of the progressive reform movement, which introduced radical (for the time) changes in our society. The old order again transformed, but as the 20th century loomed, changes in theater as well as society began to stir. The American audience matured; consequently, the fare major theaters began offering tended toward the growing REALISM movement. Plays now appeared without happy conclusions; in fact, the endings were not even very tidy. Melodrama trouped on in the form of the "blood and thunder" melodrama, but the venues for that form started to recede.

Many factors contributed to melodrama's loss of ascendancy on the American stage. One of the factors often mentioned is the rise of realism as the dominant standard. While this is not ignorable, it is not the only reason for melodrama's demise. Melodrama, itself, contained the seeds of its own destruction in its increasing need for spectacle as a part of the performance. It became more difficult for stage designers and builders to provide continually increasingly complex effects. The new medium of the film lent itself very neatly to this, however. In addition, film also allowed even more complicated spectacles, which were not possible on the stage.

Boucicault's The Octoroon contains a plot device that made its way into a silent film. The Yankee character Scudder is experimenting with a camera. The film plates of this camera also contain chemicals that cause them to develop themselves after exposure. When the villain, M'Closkey, commits murder in order to steal the letter of credit that can free Zoë (the heroine) from being sold at auction, he stands in front of the camera, not noticing it. He does not know of its activation. This sets the stage for the later revelation, provided by the developed plate, that M'Closkey is the real murderer. This device was later used in Buster Keaton's movie The Cameraman, when the testimony of the villain was disproved by footage from a movie camera accidentally activated.

It was not just the ability of film to deliver spectacle and sensation that caused melodrama's decline; costs of production played a major factor. At the turn of the 20th century, many railroads offered traveling theater troupes special rates for transporting the shows as a way of generating business. As nontheatrical business increased, railroads began to raise rates. Further, nationalization of the railroads during World War I gave priority to war essential freight, which traveling shows were not. Many theater managers learned that the freight on a few cans of film was significantly less than the freight on a theatrical production.

Cost was also a factor with audiences. Tickets for theatrical productions began to rise. Good seats could cost a patron a dollar or two or higher. Most film tickets cost five cents or ten cents, instead.

The melodrama faded away from major venues, replaced by realistic drama, vaudeville, or films. It drifted into circle-stock companies and tent shows. There it enjoyed popularity until the Depression took its toll of those companies. As the minor companies succumbed to financial problems, the "blood and thunder" melodramas transformed into amusing anachronisms. Although its heyday is over, the theater and film still borrow heavily from melodrama's binary "good and bad" world and the use of spectacle.

FURTHER READING

Booth, Michael. English Melodrama. London: Herbert Jenkins, 1965.

Disher, Wilson M. Blood and Thunder: Mid-Victorian Melodrama and Its Origins. London: Frederick Mueller, 1949.

——. Melodrama: Plots that Thrilled. London: Rockliff, 1954.

Rahill, Frank. The World of Melodrama. State Park: Pennsylvania State Univ. Press, 1967.

Vardall, Nicholas A. Stage to Screen. Cambridge: Harvard Univ. Press, 1949.

John M. Bell

MEMOIR

Taking place over the course of a single sweltering Mediterranean afternoon in August 1922, Memoir is playwright JOHN MURRELL's ode both to French actress Sarah Bernhardt and to the enduring and self-deceiving qualities of memory.

At seventy-seven, Bernhardt—la voix d'or (the Golden Voice), the Divine Sarah—the most famous and best-loved actress of her day, finds herself facing only death and obscurity, her life and experiences lost to the crowds. As such, she is busy reworking the second volume of her memoirs, dictating her larger-than-life stories, memories, and adventures to her private secretary and confidante Georges Pitou.

Together in her final few hours, these two relive Bernhardt's past, acting out scenes from Bernhardt's life. We encounter the actress as a shy, frightened child shipped off to a convent, as the wife of a wealthy Greek playboy, as a world-renowned actress called upon by kings.

While Bernhardt never gives up the "starring" role in these memory plays, Pitou gradually begins taking on the role of pivotal figures in the actress's life—he becomes her courtesan mother Judith; Bernhardt's sister, favored daughter Jeanne; the promoter who first brings the actress to the stage, William Jarret; her beloved drug addict womanizing husband, Jacques

Damala; and even OSCAR WILDE, whose special affection for Bernhardt was a source of tremendous pride for the aging heroine.

The melancholy and sometimes whimsical voice of memory in the piece is underscored by the way Bernhardt gradually loses herself in the past. As the fragile sanctuary she has created out of her memories welcomes her home, Bernhardt leaves behind the present reality, finally becoming one with her own memoir.

Murrell's first play, *Memoir* also cemented his place as one of CANADA's preeminent playwrights and earned him a reputation as a writer of lyrical and intellectual sensibilities.

The playwright's decision to frame the piece as a reconstruction of events—acted out and embodied with Bernhardt at center stage and Pitou serving as straight man and foil—rather than as a reliving, adds a dramatic weight to what might otherwise play out as mere device. Instead of coming across as the wandering, bewildered memories of a dying diva, Bernhardt's monologues are bittersweet prose poems: evocative, tender, and rose-colored fragments of a life onstage. Through Pitou, the audience sees how forced are the perspective of these memories, and so are confronted by the inherent fragility and unreliability of all recollection.

The piece initially won first prize in a playwriting competition at the University of Regina, Saskatchewan, in 1976, leading to a full production at the 1977 Guelph Spring Festival in Ontario. Celebrated Irish actress Siobhan McKenna played Bernhardt to Gerald Parkes's Pitou; their acclaimed performances brought the piece to a British tour and an eventual French translation. The Paris production at the Théâtre de l'Oeuvre, starring Georges Wilson and Delphine Seyrig, ran for three years.

Memoir's tremendous success led to a position for Murrell at Canada's famous Stratford Festival and a continuing close association with then-artistic director Robin Phillips.

FURTHER READING

Bernhardt, Sarah. *The Art of the Theatre*. Tr. by H. J. Stenning. 1924.
 Reprint, New York: Blom, 1969.
——. *My Double Life: The Memoirs of Sarah Bernhardt*. Tr. by Victoria
 Tietze Larson. 1907. Reprint, New York: Blom, 1977.
Roberts, Mary Louise. *Disruptive Acts: The New Woman in Fin-de-Siècle
 France*. Chicago: Univ. of Chicago Press, 2002.
Salmon, Eric, ed. *Bernhardt and the Theatre of Her Time*. Westport, Conn.:
 Greenwood Press, 1984.

Daniel Goldberg

THE MEMORANDUM

VÁCLAV HAVEL began to write *The Memorandum* (*Vyrozumeni*) in 1960, shortly after his two years of military service, but the play was not produced until July 25, 1965, at the Theatre on the Balustrade, under the direction of Jan Grossman, the artistic head of the theater. In the meantime, Havel had gained experience by working with two major Czech artists (Jan Werich and Alfred Radok) in other theaters, had joined the Balustrade theatre company, written some short sketches for them, and had his first full-length play produced by them in 1963, *The Garden Party* (*Zahradni slavnost*), which was directed by Otomar Krejča.

The Memorandum takes the techniques and themes of *The Garden Party* to a new, more complex level. A nameless bureaucratic institution becomes the only site of action, the characters acquire more psychological facets, and the action is more elaborately structured. Havel's fascination with the use and abuse of language as a determinant of character and action, a system of signs that becomes more significant than reality, is embodied here in the introduction of a nonsensical artificial language, *ptydepe*. Ostensibly, it is a superior, more scientific language for interoffice communications precisely because it is purged of the emotive imprecisions of human speech; actually, it is a means of gaining power by way of a bizarre series of tactics and manipulations. Grotesquely difficult to learn, it is briefly discarded in favor of traditional language, only to be reconstituted as a new, even more impenetrable language—*chorukor*. Given the sociopolitical climate of the mid-1960s in CZECHOSLOVAKIA, *ptydepe* or *chorukor* could be taken as a metaphor for Marxist-Leninist cant and jargon, but Havel more likely intended it as a symptom of a universal problem: the dehumanization and mechanization of humanity in a postindustrial, cybernetic world.

Speaking in general of his plays, Havel in the 1980s said, "There is a little of the puppet show in them, something of the animated machine." The remark is exemplified in *The Memorandum* not only in some of the comically repetitive behavior of the characters but also in the schematic plot structure, which consists of a cycle of three scenes (each played in a different setting) repeated four times. The action moves through a variety of trivial and major reversals of the main character, Josef Gross, from a position of seeming power to one of thorough humiliation and back again, though his final position is that of an impotent figurehead.

Seemingly a concerned, reasonable person, Gross is an archetypal Havel figure in his instinctual tendency to admit his defeats and flaws but rationalize them in eloquent speeches that seem honest, humble self-critiques but are actually smoke screens masking utter failures of nerve or will. In Gross's case, it is difficult to tell the extent to which such speeches are consciously self-serving or inadvertently self-deceptive. The other characters are deftly differentiated sketches of bureaucratic types, whose habitual behavior patterns precisely capture the mentality and tone of their era and time in Prague, as well as office life universally.

FURTHER READING

Goetz-Stankiewicz, Marketa. *The Silenced Theatre: Czech
 Playwrights Without a Stage*. Toronto: Univ. of Toronto Press,
 1979.

Trensky, Paul I. *Czech Drama Since World War II.* White Plains, N.Y.: M. E. Sharpe, 1978.

Jarka M. Burian

MEN IN WHITE

Written in three months, SIDNEY KINGSLEY's first play was optioned several times over three years before the two-year-old GROUP THEATRE joined with a pair of independent producers to premiere it on Broadway on September 26, 1933. A paean to the medical profession and the dedication required of its practitioners, the play ran for 357 performances, won the Pulitzer Prize, and received a barrage of enthusiastic critical praise.

Kingsley originally called the play *Crisis*; it was retitled toward the end of the Group's intense rehearsals at a summer camp in upstate New York. The new name properly shifted attention from the specifics of Kingsley's rather mechanical plot to the inherent heroism of the doctors, interns, and nurses who populate it. While the large-cast play is rife with social and physical details of the big-city hospital in which it is set, its particulars ultimately coalesce into a canvas of almost mythic dimensions.

The plot revolves around a senior physician and researcher, Dr. Hochberg, and his protégé, Dr. George Ferguson. Ferguson is both caring and brilliant, and Hochberg thinks that with another half-dozen years of work and study he could become truly outstanding. But Ferguson's fiancée, Laura Hudson, chafes at George's long hours and threatens to end their relationship if he does not give up his dream and open a comfortable private practice.

Torn between his calling and his desire for an everyday life, Ferguson tentatively accepts a cynically offered administrative post, in return for which Laura's unscrupulous father will bail the hospital out of its financial difficulties. The young man also has a one-night affair with a sympathetic nurse. The play climaxes after Laura learns of the affair when the nurse, having had a botched back-alley abortion of George's unborn child, is brought to the emergency room and dies. George vows to continue his studies, and Laura ultimately accepts his dedication, though their future together is unclear.

Even those few critics unenthusiastic about the play were enthralled by the production directed by Lee Strasberg. *Men in White* was the young Group's first popular success (ironically so, because many Group members had at first considered the play too conventional to produce); and reviewers applauded the precision ensemble of the acting, notably in the balletic, largely silent emergency-room scene.

Writing in the *New York Times*, Brooks Atkinson expressed the prevailing critical view: *Men in White* was "a good, brave play," reflecting "the theatre fully aware of its varied arts" (Beckerman, 1973). John Mason Brown of the *Evening Post* led the naysayers, calling the work "mildewed in its hokum" (Bailey, 1981). Brown's view is not hard to understand: Laura's party-girl selfishness

and naïveté are badly overdrawn, and several smaller figures (including Laura's father and two contrasting doctors, a pompous quack and a once-promising failure) are barely sketched in. Still, the play's passion, its atmospheric verisimilitude, and its courage in tackling the subject of back-alley abortion decades before *Roe v. Wade* are all admirable.

After winning the Pulitzer, awarded when the Pulitzer advisory committee overruled the recommendation of its critics jury that the prize go to MAXWELL ANDERSON's *Mary of Scotland*, *Men in White* was made into a Metro-Goldwyn-Mayer movie in 1934, with Clark Gable as Ferguson.

[*See also* United States, 1929–1940]

FURTHER READING

Bailey, Paul M. "Sidney Kingsley." In *Dictionary of Literary Biography, Volume 7: Twentieth Century Dramatists*, ed. by John Mac Nicholas. Detroit: Gale Research, 1981.

Beckerman, Bernard, and Howard Siegman. *On Stage: Selected Theatre Reviews from the New York Times, 1920–1970.* New York: Arno Press, 1973.

Clurman, Harold. *The Fervent Years.* New York: Hill & Wang, 1957.

Couch, Nena, ed. *Sidney Kingsley: Five Prizewinning Plays.* Columbus: Ohio State Univ. Press, 1995.

Smith, Wendy. *Real Life Drama: The Group Theatre and America, 1931–1940.* New York: Knopf, 1990.

Clifford A. Ridley

MES YATS V DEREVNYE   *See* A MONTH IN THE COUNTRY

MEXICO

Prior to 1860, theater in Mexico was basically limited to ZARZUELAS (operettas) and *género chico* plays (one-act musicals) imported from FRANCE and SPAIN. However, romantic full-length plays by Victor Hugo (1802–1885), Alexander Dumas (1802–1870), JOSÉ ECHEGARAY (1832–1916), and Duque de Rivas (1791–1865) were also common fare. The only Mexican playwright of the romantic period was Manuel Eduardo de Gorostiza (1789–1851) whose famous satire about the naïveté of youth, *Through Hell and Highwater for You* (*Contigo pan y cebolla*, 1832), captured the attention of all audiences.

From the mid to the late 19th century, theater was produced primarily for commercial reasons and continued to lack autochthony, as was evident in the expectation that actors use a Spanish Castilian accent in order to be hired. While Echegaray's ROMANTICISM was the main influence on the poet and dramatist Manuel José Othón (1888–1906), HENRIK IBSEN's realist drama inspired Federico Gamboa (1864–1939). In addition, the Spanish zarzuela was imitated with great success by José F. Elizondo (1880–1943), whose *Chin-Chun-Chan* (1904) reached a thousand continuous performances.

Mexican theater does not come of age until the late 1920s. Before then, as Kirsten Nigro (1994) has remarked, the dictatorial government of Porfirio Díaz (who governed Mexico from 1876 to 1910) provided little encouragement for local talent. Moreover, the Revolution, which lasted from 1910 to 1920, interrupted almost all theater activity. The main topics of plays performed after the war predictably concerned political events related to the Mexican Revolution. Popular theater consisted of vaudeville-type plays known as *teatro de carpa* (tent shows) or *teatro de revista* (reviews). They were musicals with melodramatic or satiric scenes, which were principally concerned with ridiculing some politician of the period. In 1923, however, seven young men, Carlos Noriega Hope, Víctor Manuel Díez Barroso, Francisco Monterde, José Joaquín Gamboa, Ricardo Parada León, and the Lozano García brothers founded the Unión de Autores Dramáticos. They organized theater conferences and dramatic readings. In 1926 they issued a newsletter urging the public to stop attending the current mediocre spectacles and instead support the new up-and-coming Mexican writers.

The Unión de Autores Dramáticos helped to pave the road for theatrical groups such as Teatro de Ulises, Teatro de Orientación, and Escolares de Teatro. The first two have garnered more attention from U.S. academic circles because of the participation of writers associated with the literary group Contemporáneos. Salvador Novo (1904–1974) and Xavier Villaurrutia (1903–1950) were two of its members who founded Teatro de Ulises in 1928. Other major players included actresses Isabel Corona and Clementina Otero. With financial backing from Antonieta Rivas Mercado (1900–1931)—whose legendary life and infamous suicide at Notre Dame Cathedral Antonio Saura recreates in his film *Antonieta* (1982)—Teatro de Ulises is credited with giving rise to AVANT-GARDE theater in Mexico. According to Julio Jiménez Rueda, playwright and theatrical promoter, the purpose of Teatro de Ulises was to build a small experimental theater where amateur actors would put on the best European plays available for an exclusive audience. They performed plays by EUGENE O'NEILL (1888–1953), JEAN COCTEAU (1889–1963), HENRI-RENÉ LENORMAND (1882–1951), and others, but their selective audiences were not enough to sustain the project for more than two years. Outsiders accused the group of supporting foreign exoticisms and of turning their back on national realities.

In 1931, Escolares de Teatro, founded by Julio Bracho, succeeded Teatro de Ulises with a similar avant-garde project. One of its most memorable performances was *Proteo*, an experimental piece by Francisco Monterde. Teatro Orientación, directed by Celestino Gorostiza (1904–1967), was the last of the series of avant-garde theater groups. It continued to perform translated versions of plays by O'Neill, Cocteau, ANTON CHEKHOV (1860–1904), Moliére (1622–1673), William Shakespeare, J. M. SYNGE (1871–1909), GEORGE BERNARD SHAW (1856–1950), and Nikolai V. Gogol (1809–1852) during its two short runs from 1932 until

1934 and from 1938 to 1939. The main translators were Villaurrutia, Gorostiza, Novo, and Augustín Lazo (1898–1971). During the fourth season, Teatro de Orientación performed plays by Latin American writers. These included *The Boat* (*El barco*) by Carlos Díaz Dufóo Jr. and *Cruel Ifigenia* (*Ifigenia cruel*) by Alfonso Reyes as well as nationalist plays on the Mexican Revolution by Mauricio Magdaleno and Juan Bustillo Oro.

In the 1930s, then, with Celestino Gorostiza and Xavier Villaurrutia at the helm, Mexican theater exhibited interests parallel to those of the surrealists, to ANTONIN ARTAUD's theoretical model, and to LUIGI PIRANDELLO's concept of the relativity of time. According to Ray Williams (1981), the mental processes related to dreams as well as the conscious and the subconscious fascinated Gorostiza. Twenty years later, however, Gorostiza turned toward a theater that is more concerned with social issues.

While Villaurrutia was also mesmerized by the psychology of the individual, he preferred to communicate concepts. Instead of representing social reality, he was more interested in asking, "What is reality?" Between 1933 and 1937 he published five one-act plays under the title *Profane Morality Plays* (*Autos profanos*), which Antonio Moreno considers "ingenious plays of dramatic rhetoric" (Luzuriaga, 1975). His most anthologized plays—and therefore the ones with which U.S. audiences are most familiar—include *Invitation to Death* (*Invitación a la muerte*, written in 1940 and performed in 1947) as well as two one-act pieces: *It Seems a Lie* (*Parece mentira*, 1933) and *What Are You Think?* (*En qué piensas*, 1934). These two plays are about the relativity of time and about the different and unusual perspectives through which life is viewed. Moreover, he situates the characters in surrealistic situations that only seem possible in someone's mind. At the same time that these cosmopolitan writers and artists were putting on their experimental plays, other groups opened the Teatro Murciélago and the Teatro de Ahora with the intention of representing realist national plays with a political content. They were not as concerned with aesthetics and innovation as they were with social reform. Unlike the avant-garde artists, these groups had public support and continued to perform their plays well into the 1940s and 1950s (Nigro, 1994).

The major representative of realist theater writing at the same time was RODOLFO USIGLI (1905–1979), whose play *The Impostor* (*El gesticulador*, written in 1938 and performed in 1947) is required reading in most, if not all, Spanish programs. His play represents the hypocrisy of a postrevolutionary Mexican society. Usigli is also famous for the CORONA TRILOGY. These "antihistorical plays," as he called them, include *Crown of Shadow* (*Corona de sombra*, 1943), *Crown of Fire* (*Corona de fuego*, 1960), and *Crown of Light* (*Corona de luz*, 1963). The first, and best known, depicts the life of Carlota Amalia (1840–1927), the wife of the archiduke of Austria Fernando Maximiliano (1832–67), who was sent by Napoleon Bonaparte to rule Mexico after the French Invasion of 1863. While their reign was short-lived (it lasted only from 1864 until 1867), she outlived him sixty years. And it is precisely the obscurity of these years that Usigli captures in his play.

At the Universidad Nacional Autónoma de México, Usigli taught the works of playwrights who also influenced his own plays such as George Bernard Shaw, Eugene O'Neill, ARTHUR MILLER (1915–2005), and TENNESSEE WILLIAMS (1911–1983). Students of his who went on to become accomplished playwrights include Emilio Carballido, LUISA JOSEFINA HERNÁNDEZ, Jorge Ibargüengoitia, Sergio Magaña, and Héctor Mendoza.

Even though critics usually say that Usigli worked in isolation and never belonged to any literary groups, he did know some of the Contemporáneos. Apparently, between 1935 and 1936, he shared an apartment in New Haven with Villaurrutia when they both received Rockefeller fellowships to study dramatic art and comparative literature at Yale University. Critics attribute Usigli the honor of being the first playwright associated with great theater in Mexico. New groups that appeared after Ulises and Orientación include José de J. Aceves's, Proa Grupo; La Linterna Mágica, directed by Ignacio Retes; Teatro del Arte Moderno, by Jebert Darién and Lola Bravo; Teatro Estudiantil Autónomo, by Xavier Rojas; and later Teatro de la Reforma, under the direction of Seki Sano and Luz Alba.

The government's creation of the Instituto Nacional de Bellas Artes (INBA) in 1946 contributed to the reform of theater as it took charge of combining the dispersed theater organizations and of incorporating Children's Theatre and the School of Drama. It also put theatrical groups from the city and the provinces in contact with each other and organized important theater festivals and well-run theater seasons. Perhaps due to the impulse of the Institute, new theaters begin to open in 1949.

In the 1950s three prominent writers—ELENA GARRO, Octavio Paz, and Juan José Arreola—started a project called Poesía en Voz Alta. The idea was to make poetic theater, but it never produced more than a few works. *Rapaccini's Daughter* (*La hija de Rapaccini*, 1954 or 1956) by Paz is one example. Artists Leonora Carrington and Juan Soriano were also involved in the project.

Critics agree that it is not until the 1960s that Mexican theater broke with traditional Aristotilean theater. This new theater is considered fragmented, rebellious, and even aggressive. External influences are primarily theoretical, especially those of BERTOLT BRECHT (1898–1956), ERWIN PISCATOR (1895–1966), Antonin Artaud (1896–1948), and PETER WEISS (1916–1982). However, critics such as Juan Villegas warn against focusing exclusively on these Western categories because they too easily dismiss the cultural contexts of the plays (Adler, 1999). Some of the playwrights associated with this period are Hugo Arguelles, Luis G. Basurto, Wilberto Cantón, Emilio Carballido, Marcela del Río, Juan García Ponce, Marissa Garrido, Elena Garro, Luisa Josefina Hernández, Jorge Ibargüengoitia, Federico S. Inclán, Vicente Leñero, Sergio Magaña, Hector Mendoza, Rafael Solana, Margarita Urueta, and Maruxa Vilalta.

In addition to the numerous playwrights, the 1960s also produced new dramatic scenes, new theaters, a new audience, and the crowning of creative directors such as Gorostiza, Novo, Xavier Rojas, Fernando Wagner, Seki Sano, Ignacio Retes, and Charles Rooner.

While all of the above are accomplished writers, the one whose name resonates most loudly in theatrical circles is undoubtedly Emilio Carballido. His extensive theatrical production is so varied that it is almost impossible to classify. It covers FARCE, classical TRAGEDY, COMEDY, realistic pieces, conventional theater, surrealist, feminist, and others. His themes range from psychological REALISM to fantasy, and he criticizes the deadening effect of society on the individual. His plays have been translated into many languages and presented all over the world, primarily in Western Europe and throughout Latin America but also in China and some Eastern European countries. The first time his feminist play *A Rose of Two Scents* (*Rosa de dos aromas*, 1986) appeared on the stage in Mexico City, it had a four-year run of uninterrupted performances.

The 1970s produced what Ronald Burgess (1991) calls the *nueva dramaturgia* (new dramatic arts), and it includes playwrights such as SABINA BERMAN, Víctor Hugo Rascón Banda, Pilar Campesino, Carlos Olmos, and Oscar Liera. This generation began to publish their plays between 1967 and 1985. A playwright not included in this generation is Carmen Boullosa, whose plays represent a vital contribution to feminist drama. The playwright who has had by far the most commercial and academic success is Sabina Berman. Her 1992 play *Between Villa and a Naked Woman* (*Entre Villa y una mujer desnuda*) was on stage for two consecutive years, and her most recent *Molière* (2000) and *Happy New Century, Doktor Freud* (*Feliz nuevo siglo, doktor Freud*, 2001) also received wide acclaim.

The 1980s and 1990s brought to the Mexican theatrical scene performance theater, which, according to Beatriz Rizk (2000), is the staging of the performer's personal position on life, art, and society with the intention to bring about social change. One of Mexico's most celebrated performance artists is JESUSA RODRÍGUEZ, who dramatizes her commitment to politics and social change through bodily expressions, technological innovations, and political satire, in her own theatrical space El Hábito and the Teatro la Capilla, which was originally conceived by Salvador Novo in 1954.

FURTHER READING

Adler, Heidryn, and Kati Röttger, eds. *Performance, Pathos, Política—de los sexos* [Performance, Pathos, Policy—of the sexes]. Madrid: Iberoamericana 1999.

Burgess, Ronald. *The New Dramatists of Mexico 1967–1985*. Lexington: Univ. Press of Kentucky, 1991.

Costantino, Roselyn. "Visibility as Strategy: Jesusa Rodríguez's Body in Play." In *Corpus Declecti: Performance Art of the Americas*, ed. by Coco Fusco. New York: Routledge, 2000.

Luzuriaga, Gerardo, and Richard Reeve. *Los clásicos del teatro hispanoamericano* [The classics of Hispano-American theater]. Mexico City: FCE, 1975.

Nigro, Kirsten. "Twentieth-Century Theater." In *Mexican Literature: A History*, ed. by David William Foster. Austin: Univ. of Texas Press, 1994. 212–242.

Rizk, Beatriz J. "El arte del performance y la subversión de las reglas del juego en el discurso de la mujer" [The art of performance and the rules of the game in women's discourse]. *Latin American Theatre Review* 33, no. 2 (Spring 2000): 93–111.

Williams, Ray L. *Teatro del Siglo XX* [Theater of the 20th century]. Madrid: La Muralla, 1981. http://www.faculty.ucr.edu/~williarl/LatinTheater.htm.

Woodyard, George, ed. *The Modern Stage in Latin America: Six Plays*. New York: Dutton, 1971.

Margarita Vargas

ME XIHC CO TEATRO (MXTEATRO)

Me xihc co Teatro (MxTeatro) is a collaborative of multidisciplinary artists, based in Mexico City, whose artistic mission is the manifestation and expression of the ritual art of theater. The company takes its name from the Nahuatl word for "MEXICO": Me (luna/moon) xihc (ombligo/navel) co (lugar/place), roughly translated as "the site of the navel of the moon." Founded in 1991 by theater artists MARÍA MORETT and Alvaro Hegewisch, Me xihc co's critically acclaimed productions, all of which are written or adapted by Morett, include *The Weeping Woman* (La Llorona, 1991), *Mozart and the Elves* (Mozart y los Duendes, 1994), *Death* (Muerte, 1995), *Alarconeando* (1998), *QUIJOTES: Wandering Visions* (QUIJOTES: Visiones itinerantes, 1998), *Crossings: Meeting of the Millennium* (Cruces: Encuentro de milenio, 1999), *Women in Confinement* (Mujeres en el encierro, 2001), and *More Labyrinths* (Más Laberintos, 2003).

The company readily acknowledges its aesthetic debt to the rich tradition of street theater in Latin America. In addition to performing in indoor and outdoor spaces designed specifically for theater, Me xihc co seeks out alternative performance environments such as prisons, parks, plazas, and streets and inaugurates them as theatrical spaces. Company members also participate in educational and community-based programs such as "Theater in Prisons," presenting plays and conducting theater workshops for inmates throughout Mexico.

Death tells the story of three undocumented immigrants, Andres, el Coyote, and el Mojado, who attempt to cross the Mexico–U.S. border in search of a better life but instead meet up with death. The play chronicles the day-to-day struggle of the Mexican people via songs, memories, *danzón* and *lucha libre*. At the same time, *Death* addresses the artist's passionate relationship with death and the acts of ritual and reverence in the face of its great mystery. As the play unfolds, the dead rise up and remember the living, but in doing so, they must cross over to "the other side." They must die in order to be born and be born in order to die. Death is presented onstage as a doorway, a passage to freedom, punishment, or simply departure.

QUIJOTES is a traveling street theater piece designed to be performed over the course of several days in a variety of open-air spaces. It premiered at the 1998 Festival Internacional Cervantino and was performed over the duration of the festival in the streets, plazas, and passageways of Guanajuato. Written by Morett (with poetry by Miguel de Cervantes, Nobel Prize winner José Saramago, Antonio Machado, and others), QUIJOTES is composed of several short "visions" incorporating music, puppetry, and circus techniques such as clowning, juggling, and stilt-walking: an old, tired-out Quijote; a female spear-bearing Quijote on horseback; a Christ-like Quijote, atoning for the end of the world; a blind, lost Quijote guided by the pudgy, ambitious Sancho; an acrobat Quijote, standing on the brink of danger yet filled with hope. The piece, whose visual style is inspired by the paintings of Francisco Goya, Pablo Picasso, and Salvador Dalí, offers a "moveable feast" of images that are at once humorous, grotesque, stately, and lyrical.

Me xihc co's most recent project is *More Labyrinths*, a site-specific theater piece inspired by the texts and images of Sor Juana Inés de la Cruz, Remedios Varo, and Rosario Castellanos. Written and directed by Morett, with sets and costumes by Morett, lighting by Alvaro Hegewisch, and original music by Pablo Flores, *More Labyrinths* opened in October 2003 at the Festival Internacional Cervantino in a co-production with the Instituto Estatal de la Cultura de Guanajuato.

Me xihc co Teatro has toured extensively throughout Latin America, the UNITED STATES, and Europe, appearing at major international arts festivals and collaborting with such international theater artists as MARIA IRENE FORNES, MIGDALIA CRUZ, Ellen Stewart, Peter Schumann, Santiago García, Daniele Finzi, Jordan Simmons, and Cordelia Dvôrák. Since 1998, Me xihc co has been committed to developing binational, bilingual collaborative projects aimed at creating site-specific theater pieces in various Mexican and U.S. cities. This long-term endeavor, whose working title is "Festival Itinerante de Teatro en Espacios Alternativos / Itinerant Site-Specific Theater Festival," involves theater artists from Mexico and the United States, in collaboration with individuals from the participating communities.

Paradoxically, it has been more difficult for Me xihc co Teatro to present its work in Mexico City than throughout the rest of Mexico and abroad. While the Mexican government provides subsidies for large public events such as concerts and parades, financial support for site-specific theater is virtually nonexistent. Morett and Hegewisch admit that their audiences present challenges, as well. They have not purchased tickets, nor have they entered into the tacit agreement, or convention, of silently watching and listening to the performers. They are free to come and go as they please, and talk as loudly as they wish, unless the performance wins over their attention and respect.

Me xihc co Teatro not only accepts but is exhilarated by these challenges. For Morett, her work as a theater artist entails not only an aesthetic and social quest but also the "conquest" of unconventional spaces. Hegewisch emphasizes that street theater allows for the possibility of creating intimacy in public spaces, of sharing these spaces with audiences who have come to the theater "exactly how they are," without the need for an intellectual or cultural pose. In this manner, Me xihc co seeks to touch, challenge, and transform its audiences, many of whom have never before experienced live theater, infusing street theater with passion and the highest level of aesthetic commitment, complexity, and quality.

FURTHER READING

Cruz Barcenas, Arturo. "Para desarrollar el teatro de calle, los artistas deben 'aprender el lenguaje de los lobos' " [In order for street theater to develop, the artists must "learn the language of the wolves"]. La Jornada (October 21, 2003).

Itzcovich, Mabel. "Se puede bailar con la muerte" [It is possible to dance with death]. Clarin (March 8, 2001).

Léon Peña-Villa, Ricardo. "De Amor y Teatro. Interview with María Morett and Alvaro Hegewisch." El Diario/La Prensa (September 1, 2000): 35.

Lipfert, David. Revenue of Muerte and Cruces, by María Morett. CurtainUp (October 29, 2002). http://www.curtainup.com/fringe2000.html.

Deborah Saivetz

MEYERHOLD, VSEVOLOD (1874–1940)

One of the world's greatest and most innovative theater directors, Vsevolod Meyerhold elaborated an AVANT-GARDE poetics of theater that evolved from his early THEATER OF THE GROTESQUE into constructivist theater and finally into the radical October in Theater movement of the early Soviet era. His belief in pure theatricality, as reified in such purely theatrical practices as biomechanics (a theory of acting that privileges the body over the psyche), was combined with a strong sense of the need to bring theater to the forefront of social consciousness.

Born on February 9 (January 28), 1874, in Penza, Meyerhold began as an actor at the newly formed MOSCOW ART THEATRE of Vladimir Nemirovich-Danchenko and KONSTANTIN STANISLAVSKY. Meyerhold quickly distinguished himself, and his performance as Treplev in ANTON CHEKHOV's THE SEAGULL propelled a signature Stanislavsky production. Eventually Meyerhold broke with Stanislavsky over the latter's extreme naturalistic approach and later outlined his own credo of pure theatricality in essays such as "The Naturalistic Theater and the Theater of Mood" (1906) and "A Puppet Show" (1912).

When an invitation to become a shareholder in the Art Theatre was not forthcoming in 1902, Meyerhold took advantage of this fortuitous setback and began his directing career. He proved to be an effective advocate of contemporary European drama. Even though his production of MAURICE MAETERLINCK's The Death of Tintagiles and GERHART HAUPTMANN's Schluck and Jau did not open at Stanislavsky's personally funded Studio Theater, Meyerhold was nonetheless instrumental in introducing not only HENRIK IBSEN and AUGUST STRINDBERG but FRANK WEDEKIND, Maeterlinck, Hauptmann, KNUT HAMSUN, HUGO VON HOFMANNSTHAL, and STANISLAWA PRZYBYSZEWSKA to Russian audiences.

However, Meyerhold's approach crystallized in his productions of the Russian symbolist dramas of ALEKSANDR BLOK, Fyodor Sologub, and their kindred spirit LEONID ANDREEV at the Komissarzhevskaia Theater. His enthusiasm for poetic drama continued through his years as head of the St. Petersburg Imperial opera and drama theaters. Both under and outside the auspices of the Imperial Theaters, Meyerhold staged a great deal more poetic drama, including works by Konstantin Balmont, GABRIELE D'ANNUNZIO, Mikhail Lermontov, and Sologub. It was also at this time in his Meyerhold Studio production of Blok's A PUPPET SHOW and The Unknown Woman that the director first worked out the basic tenets of constructivist theater.

As radical in his politics as in his aesthetics, Meyerhold answered the call of the cultural commissar, ANATOLI LUNACHARSKY, for artists to rally round the Bolshevik flag after the October Revolution. To celebrate the revolution's first anniversary, Meyerhold staged "the first Soviet play," VLADIMIR MAYAKOVSKY's MYSTERY-BOUFFE, and later contributed to the civil war struggle with radical reworkings of Emile Verhaeren's The Dawns (1920), Marcel Martinet / SERGEI TRETYAKOV's World Rampant (1923) and Ilja Erenburg / Jonathan Kellerman's D.E.! (Give Us Europe!) (1924). As self-styled "author of the production" and in response to the Party's demand for REALISM and respect for bourgeois tradition, Meyerhold virtually rewrote classic plays from RUSSIA's past such as ALEKSANDR OSTROVSKY's THE FOREST (1924), Nikolai Gogol's The Inspector General (1926), and Aleksandr Griboedov's Woe from Wit (dubbed Woe to Wit by Meyerhold, 1928) for productions that established his reputation as one of the greatest directors of the 20th century.

Meyerhold continued to collaborate closely on the writing and staging of new, often satirical plays by writers such as NIKOLAI ERDMAN, YURI OLESHA, SERGEI TRETYAKOV, Aleksei Faiko, Vsevolod Vishnevskii, and Ilia Selvinskii. For example, Erdman's The Warrant (1925) and Faiko's Bubus the Teacher (1925) satirized the renaissance of a new bourgeoisie. After Joseph Stalin's seizure of power, criticism of society became "anti-Soviet," but Meyerhold went further and tested the limits in his productions of Mayakovsky's THE BEDBUG (1928) and THE BATHHOUSE (1930). Meyerhold remained undeterred and sought to stage socially critical plays such as Erdman's THE SUICIDE (1932) and Tretyakov's I Want a Baby (1927–1930), which were banned before reaching the stage. Nevertheless, he did succeed in staging Olesha's A List of Assets (1931), which boldly debated the pros and cons of Soviet power. At the same time he collaborated with Soviet dramatists on plays about the

Civil War, Selvinskii's *The Second Army Commander* (1929), and about a potential fascist threat to the Soviet Union, Vishnevskii's *The Last Decisive* (1931), which flaunted Meyerhold's genuine communist credentials in the face of the false ones endorsed by the powers that be.

This conflict came to a head in 1934 with the promulgation of SOCIALIST REALISM as official artistic doctrine, reinforced by rigorous theatrical censorship. Anything vaguely nonrealist was now dubbed "formalist" and, hence, anti-Soviet. At a time when everyone else was writing and staging plays about the Five-Year Plan, Meyerhold's decision to stage a "bourgeois" play, Alexandre DUMAS FILS's *The Lady of the Camellias* (1934), bordered on the suicidal. Under pressure, he sought to rectify matters by staging an ultra-Soviet play based on Nikolai Ostrovskii's novel *How the Steel Was Tempered* (1937). By this time, however, it was too late. His theater was closed, he was arrested in the summer of 1939, arraigned on trumped-up charges, tortured, and executed in prison on February 2, 1940, in Moscow.

[*See also* Russia and the Soviet Union, Russian Symbolist Drama]

FURTHER READING

Braun, Edward. *Meyerhold: A Revolution in Theatre.* 2d ed. London: Methuen, 1995.

Gladkov, Aleksandr. *Meyerhold Speaks, Meyerhold Rehearses.* Tr. and ed. by Alma Law. London: Harwood, 1997.

Hoover, Marjorie L. *Meyerhold: The Art of Conscious Theater.* Amherst: Univ. of Massachusetts Press, 1974.

Leach, Robert. *Vsevolod Meyerhold.* Cambridge: Cambridge Univ. Press, 1989.

Meyerhold, Vsevolod. *Meyerhold on Theatre.* Tr. and ed., with a critical commentary, by Edward Braun. Rev. ed. London: Methuen, 1991.

Rudnitsky, Konstantin. *Meyerhold the Director.* Tr. by George Petrov and ed. by Sydney Schultze. Ann Arbor: Ardis, 1981.

Schmidt, Paul. *Meyerhold at Work.* Austin: Univ. of Texas Press, 1980.

Timothy C. Westphalen

MID-CHANNEL

Drama critic William Archer, who championed HENRIK IBSEN and urged British playwrights to deal with serious subjects in their plays, generously praised the social drama *Mid-Channel* by ARTHUR PINERO, which opened on September 3, 1909, at St. James's Theatre, London. The play tells the story of Zoe Blundell, whose marriage to the bullying stockbroker Theodore Blundell is unravelling and who spends time in the company of men she calls her "tame robins." The play takes place in London and is set in the drawing room of the Blundell household and, five months later, in this same room, in the sitting room of Theodore's apartment, and in the apartment of Leonard Ferris, a younger man who is one of Zoe's admirers.

Zoe has grown tired of her husband of fourteen years, whom she chides for his "elderly ways." After an argument, she travels to ITALY, where she commits the faux pas of writing to Ferris and inviting him to join her in Florence, an indiscretion she hopes will arouse her husband's jealousy. After Zoe's return to London, it looks for a time as though the couple will reconcile. But Theodore is unable to condone his wife's infidelity even though she has forgiven him for the affair he engaged in while she was away. Like Paula Tanqueray in THE SECOND MRS. TANQUERAY, Pinero's most critically acclaimed play, Zoe commits suicide once she realizes that Ferris (who, at Zoe's urging, has gotten engaged) is not in a position to marry her and that her husband will not take her back.

The play's title refers metaphorically to the rough spots in the "mid-channel" of married life that the well-meaning but meddling Peter Mottram, a mutual friend, compares to the shoals that travelers encounter mid-English Channel between Folkestone and Boulogne. Certainly, the storm that can shake a marriage in midlife is one of the themes the play explores. Pinero's real concern, though, is with the hypocrisy of the sexual double standard that looks the other way at the infidelity of husbands but casts adulterous women aside. Pinero also explores the selfishness at the heart of the marital troubles between Zoe and Theodore—and, by extension, the selfishness and barrenness of middle-class life society—although Zoe's attribution of the couple's problems to their decision to remain childless has a false ring to it.

Despite Archer's praise, *Mid-Channel* ran for less than two months in London and was greeted with mixed reviews, both in ENGLAND and, early the following year, in the UNITED STATES. While it was considered to be technically masterful, many critics found the characters to be "brutish" and "vulgar," "unpleasant human beings" whom it was impossible to care about. Appraisal of the play itself ranged from "gloomy" and "sordid" to an acknowledgment that *Mid-Channel* was unpleasant but told the truth. The *New York Daily Tribune* called the play "a sermon" against the sins of society, while another reviewer hailed the play as "a relentless study of real life in the social borderlands" that always interested Pinero. Several reviewers found the play's ending unconvincing, insisting that straying women like Zoe did not have so few options that suicide would have seemed the only resolution to her predicament.

FURTHER READING

Dawick, John. *Pinero: A Theatrical Life.* Niwot: Univ. Press of Colorado, 1993.

Dunkel, Wilbur Dwight. *Sir Arthur Pinero: A Critical Biography with Letters.* Chicago: Univ. of Chicago Press, 1941.

Elaine Brousseau

MIGHTON, JOHN (1957–)

John Mighton was born in Hamilton, Ontario, on October 2, 1957. Mighton is a two-time winner of the Dora Mavor Moore

Award whose plays *Possible Worlds* and *A Short History of Night* won the Governor General's Literary Award for Drama in 1992. After taking up writing in 1987, Mighton wrote five plays over the next seven years while also pursuing a Ph.D. in mathematics from the University of Toronto. Mighton's interests in science are central to each of his plays. SCIENTIFIC AMERICANS (1987), for instance, explores the ethical dilemmas faced by weapons researchers at Los Alamos Laboratory, which produced the atom bomb. *A Short History of Night* (1989) is based on the life of Johannes Kepler and investigates the differences between contemporary scientific attitudes and those of Kepler's era. *Possible Worlds* (1988) enacts the same relationship between the same two characters as it plays itself out in different possible worlds, where "in one world I'm talking to you right now but your arm is a little to the left, in another your interested in that man over there with the glasses, in another you stood me up two days ago. (This philosophical investigation is based in chaos theory, which suggests that even very small events can have very large results so that there are possible worlds where events—perhaps because one might simply have situated his or her arm differently—played out radically different than they did in the world they are aware of.) While less focused specifically on science, *Body and Soul* (1994) examines the social forces that shape human desire, drawing a parallel between the extreme fetishization of necrophiliacs and the increasingly acceptable fixations of cybersex enthusiasts.

Even for a playwright, Mighton has had an eclectically successful career. Since 1995 Mighton's playwriting career, at least, has tapered off; his first play in nine years, *Half Life*, saw preliminary production in 2004. Meanwhile, his credentials in mathematics and playwriting attracted the attention of Matt Damon and Ben Affleck, who hired him to serve as a script consultant for *Good Will Hunting* (1997—which went on to win the Oscar for Best Original Screenplay), leading to his being cast in a minor role in the film.

He has recently published a bestselling book on tutoring children in mathematics, *The Myth of Ability: Nurturing Mathematical Talent in Every Child* (2004), and has started a foundation, JUMP (Junior Undiscovered Math Prodigies). JUMP is simultaneously committed to rejecting the myth that mathematical genius is a matter of genetic inheritance and to bringing the tutoring program that Mighton designed to inner-city children in order to break the cycle of ignorance and poverty. Ironically, his own play *The Little Years* (1995) (as well as *Good Will Hunting*) includes characters who excel at mathematics without any clear indication of the social environment that gave rise to their genius, leaving the reader to suppose that the gift was in their genes. As time passes it will be worth noting whether or not Mighton's later work serves as a rebuttal of his earlier attitude about the roots of scientific genius.

[*See also* Canada]

PLAYS: *Scientific Americans* (1987); *Possible Worlds* (1988); *A Short History of Night* (1989); *Body and Soul* (1994); *The Little Years* (1995); *Half Life* (2005)

FURTHER READING
"John Mighton." In *Encyclopedia of Canadian Theatre*. http://www .canadiantheatre.com/dict.pl?term=Mighton%2C%20John.
"John Mighton Wins $100,000 Theatre Prize." *CBC Arts* (October 25, 2005). http://www.cbc.ca/story/arts/national/2005/10/25/ Arts/siminovitch_051025.html.
Stephenson, Jenn. "Metatheatre and Authentication through Metonymic Compression in John Mighton's *Possible Worlds*." *Theatre Journal* 58, no. 1 (March 2006): 73–93.

Daniel Jernigan

MIHURA, MIGUEL (1905–1977)

Regarded as one of SPAIN's greatest postwar playwrights, Miguel Mihura also distinguished himself as a comic writer, screenplay author, founder of La Ametralladora (1936–1939), and director of La Codorniz (1941–1944). Mihura renovated Spanish theater with his unconventional and irreverently humorous plays. His first and most important work, *Three Top Hats* (*Tres sombreros de copa*, 1932) anticipates the Theater of the Absurd with its irrational style. Because Mihura was unable to stage the play after first writing it, speculations abound regarding the repercussions of this work. His artistic influences include Ramón Gómez de la Serna, Jardiel Poncela, AVANT-GARDE movements, and cinema.

Mihura was born on July 21, 1905, in Madrid, Spain, and spent his childhood and youth in a theatrical atmosphere, as his father was an actor, author, and producer of plays. After *Three Top Hats*, Mihura co-wrote several plays such as *Neither Poor Nor Rich, But All the Opposite* (*Ni pobre ni rico, sino todo lo contrario*, 1939) with Tono and *The Case of the Woman Assassin with Álvaro of the Church* (*El caso de la mujer asesinadita con Álvaro de la Iglesia*, 1946). In part because of the controversial reactions aroused from the critics as well as the public, he decided to focus on writing screenplays, most notably the highly successful and popular film by Luís García Berlanga, *Welcome Mr. Marshal* (*Bienvenido Mr. Marshal*, 1952). In 1952 he returned to the theater, gradually moving away his avant-garde beginnings to more conventional and accessible plays.

As a playwright, Mihura's seminal moment came in 1952 when an amateur experimental theater company performed *Three Top Hats*. Amid critical acclaim and public praise, he was awarded the National Theatre Award for it. *Three Top Hats* tells the story of Dionisio, an average man who spends his last night as a bachelor in a small town hotel. That night he meets an actress from a musical company with whom he falls in love. Paula exposes him to a new world in which fantasy and reality are intertwined, causing Dionisio to question his own mundane and provincial life, which is devoid of fantasy and humor. *Three Top Hats* is innovative not only for its purely verbal humor, which is disorienting, non-conformist, arbitrary, and even surreal, but also for its almost revolutionary subversion of establishment values.

In 1953 Mihura began to produce solo works. His plays of this period can be classified as bourgeoisie COMEDIES, characterized by intrigue, and humor, although fairly distanced from his earlier innovative theater. He received two National Theatre Awards for *My Adored Juan* (*Mi adorado Juan*, 1956–1957) and *Maribel and the Strange Family* (*Maribel y la extraña familia*, 1959). In the latter, a prostitute named Maribel meets Marcelino in a bar. Marcelino, a country widow, has come to Madrid to find a more modern wife. A series of misunderstandings arise among Marcelino's mother and aunt and Maribel's cohorts. *Maribel* is enriched by police intrigue and overtones of mystery, elements that are also prevalent in *The Case of the Woman Assassin* and *Syrup Peach* (*Melocotón en almíbar*, 1958). In 1964, Mihura received the National Literary Award for *Ninette and a Gentleman from Murcia* (*Ninette y un señor de Murcia*), an almost reactionay work that mocks a Spanish political exile in Paris. He stopped writing in 1968 and died on October 28, 1977, in Madrid.

SELECT PLAYS: *Three Top Hats* (*Tres sombreros de copa*, 1932); *Long Live the Impossible!* (*¡Viva lo imposible!* 1939); *Neither Poor Nor Rich, But All the Opposite* (*Ni pobre ni rico, sino todo lo contrario*, 1939); *The Case of the Woman Assassin* (*El caso de la mujer asesinadita*, 1946); *The Case of the Wonderful Lady* (*El caso de la señora estupenda*, 1953); *To Average Light the Three* (*A media luz los tres*, 1953); *The Case of the Gentleman Dressed in Violet* (*El caso del señor vestido de violeta*, 1954); *Sublime Decision!* (*¡Sublime decisión!* 1955); *My Adored Juan* (*Mi adorado Juan*, 1956); *Carlota* (1957); *Syrup Peach* (*Melocotón en almíbar*, 1958); *Maribel and the Strange Family* (*Maribel y la extraña familia*, 1959); *The Villa of Madame Renard* (*El chalet de Madame Renard*, 1961); *The Entertainments* (*Las entretenidas*, 1962); *The Enchanting Dorotea* (*La bella Dorotea*, 1963); *Miracle in the López House* (*Milagro en casa de los López*, 1964); *Ninette and a Gentleman from Murcia* (*Ninette y un señor de Murcia*, 1964); *The Teapot* (*La tetera*, 1965); *Ninette (Modus of Paris)* (*Ninette (Modus de Paris)*, 1966); *The Decent One* (*La decente*, 1967); *Only Love and the Moon Bring Fortune* (*Sólo el amor y la luna traen fortuna*, 1968)

FURTHER READING

Ferreras, Juan Ignacio. *El teatro en el siglo XX (desde 1939)*. [The theater in the 20th century (Since 1939)]. Madrid: Taurus, 1988.

McKay, Douglas. *Miguel Mihura*. Boston: Twayne, 1977.

Pedraza Jiménez, Felipe, and Milagros Rodríguez Cáceres. *Manual de literatura española XIV. Posguerra: Dramaturgos y ensayistas*. [Manual of Spanish literature XIV: Postwar period: Dramatists and essayists]. Pamplona: Cénlit ediciones, 1995.

Esther Lomas-Sampedro

MILLAY, EDNA ST. VINCENT (1892–1950)

"It was unmistakably a youthful work, and very slight," Edna St. Vincent Millay wrote in her preface to the 1932 publication of *The Princess Marries the Page*, "but I thought it rather pretty." "Pretty" always counted with Millay. Effectively constructed, and worthy of its four productions, the play beguiled the senses with the exuberance of Millay's early poetry. A princess (portrayed onstage by Millay) conceals a page from her father, who knows him to be a spy, coyly managing the happy ending one would have wished for this flippantly perceptive poet.

Millay, who was born on February 22, 1892, in Rockland, Maine, was the winner of a Pulitzer Prize for her poetry in 1923, as well as a successful dramatist who, as the "beautiful young actress of the Provincetown theatre," enjoyed the free-swinging life of New York City's Greenwich Village during the 1920s. Millay called *The Princess Marries the Page*, completed while she was a student at Vassar College, class of 1917, "my earliest attempt at play-writing," perhaps forgetting her silly FARCE in rhyming iambic tetrameter titled *Two Slatterns and a King* (1916).

Before the Civil War in the United States, it was expected that serious drama be in verse, and most significant American playwrights adhered to convention. The rise of REALISM, however, virtually banished poetry from the theater, and only with a revival of poetic drama in Europe after 1900 did American poets find their works appreciated onstage. Millay's plays are a striking illustration of the resurgence of poetic drama following World War I, and before a coarsening of moral fibers among later-20th-century generations spawned indifference to subtlety in language, her singular efforts presaged the works of ARCHIBALD MACLEISH and Robert Lowell.

Millay's major dramatic achievement, *Aria da Capo* (1920), was "a bitterly ironic little fantasy," according to Alexander Woollcott in the *New York Times* (Dec 13, 1920), and "the most beautiful and most interesting play . . . in New York." Two simple shepherds interrupt the satirical snipings of Pierrot and Columbine to enact their pastoral scene, which, manipulated by Cothurnus, the Masque of Tragedy, ends with the shepherds killing each other. When the harlequin characters complain of the bodies, Cothurnus advises them to continue their farce: "The audience will forget." Reflecting the emotional atmosphere of Greenwich Village in the 1920s, *Aria da Capo* foreshadows Millay's later defiant poetry, from the impudence of "The Penitent" to the despair of "Justice Denied in Massachusetts."

The Lamp and the Bell (1921), a medieval TRAGEDY in five acts, presents the fate of two women—"a burning lamp" and "a silver bell." *The King's Henchman*, Millay's three-act adaptation of the Tristram and Isolde theme, with music by Deems Taylor, debuted at the Metropolitan in 1927. In her last play, *Conversations at Midnight* (1937), the philosophical ramblings of seven men are underscored by a bitter coda: "O Reason, O ill-starred! / Our single talent."

As Millay evolved from the searching nineteen-year-old who astounded the literary world with "Renassence" to the severe critic of human endeavor, she abandoned the drama. Her dreams were in poetry. Her life was a candle burning brightly—and briefly; she died, already old, on October 19, 1950, in Austerlitz, New York.

[See also United States, 1929–1940]

PLAYS: Two Slatterns and a King (1916); The Princess Marries the Page (1917); Aria da Capo (1920); The Lamp and the Bell (1921); The King's Henchman (1927); Conversations at Midnight (1937)

FURTHER READING
Gould, Jean. The Poet and Her Book: A Biography of Millay. New York: Dodd, Mead, 1970.

Milford, Nancy. Savage Beauty: The Life of Edna St. Vincent Millay. New York: Random House, 2001.

Nierman, Judith. Millay: A Reference Guide. Boston: G. K. Hall, 1977.

Walter J. Meserve

MILLER, ARTHUR (1915–2005)

When Arthur Miller's ALL MY SONS opened on Broadway in 1947, it was obvious that an important new dramatic talent was making his presence felt in the American theater. When DEATH OF A SALESMAN arrived two years later, it was clear that Miller, along with TENNESSEE WILLIAMS, was one of the two major playwrights of post–World War II drama. There have been detractors, of course, but he has remained a force in American letters for more than half a century. In the sixty-six years between 1936, when his undergraduate play No Villain (also known as They Too Arise) won the Hopwood Award at the University of Michigan, and 2002, when Resurrection Blues opened in Minneapolis, Minnesota, he wrote fifteen major plays and a great many one-acts. He also produced film scripts, radio plays, television dramas, libretti, a HENRIK IBSEN adaptation, long and short fiction, an autobiography, a children's book, a great many essays, speeches, and books of reportage (including three with his third wife, the photographer Inge Morath). During that time he lived through—and made dramatic use of—the Depression, World War II and all the wars that followed it, the Red Scare of the 1950s, the turbulence of the 1960s, and the growing and sometimes disturbing international power of the UNITED STATES. He also saw the structure of American theater change from Broadway-centered production to OFF- AND OFF-OFF-BROADWAY and a flourishing regional theater.

EARLY CAREER

Born on October 17, 1915, in New York City, Miller was the second son in an affluent family—his father, a handsome, barely literate, and very successful clothing manufacturer; his mother, a bright, culture-seeking woman, resentful of her arranged marriage but comfortable enough until her husband's business failed in 1929. At that time, the family moved from their fashionable apartment on the south edge of Harlem to Brooklyn into what in Timebends (1987) Miller called "this chicken coop of a

house," a description of a six-room building, presumably miniaturized by memory. His father shriveled into silence; his mother slipped into resentment. So they appear in Timebends, his mosaic of an autobiography. So, too, do they appear at a distance in plays like The American Clock (1979). The plays are full of pairs of brothers, ranging from affectionate to fatally antagonistic in the case of those ur-sibling rivals Cain and Abel, in The Creation of the World and Other Business (1972). Miller's comment on his too-perfect older brother in Timebends ("handsome, clean, and unspeakable in his rectitude") suggests a family connection, which he both denies and confirms when he says of the quarreling brothers in THE PRICE (1968): "The characters were not based on Kermit and me, we were far different from these two, but the magnetic underlying situation was deep in my bones." Oddly enough, there are no sisters in the plays, although that may be because Miller's sister—the actress Joan Copeland—was seven years younger than he, not a central figure and relentless observer as he was of the family's struggles during the Depression that mark so many of his works.

On the other hand, all three of his wives find their way into his plays—notably in AFTER THE FALL (1964). There is nothing surprising in such biographical borrowings since most writers cannibalize their own lives and those of their lovers, spouses, family, and friends; but as a healthy corrective to the titillation of roman à clef, consider a New York Times double interview (November 16, 1980), when The American Clock was about to open in Washington, D.C., in which Miller and his sister (who played Rose Baum) quarreled amiably about what their mother was like until he called an end to the badinage with "She's a character in a play. This is not her biography." Arthur Miller died at home in Roxbury, Connecticut, on February 10, 2005.

The important thing about Miller's use and transformation of his own life is that it gives him an emotional, familial base for the larger ideas about society that characterize his work. In "On Social Plays," published as a preface to the 1955 edition of A VIEW FROM THE BRIDGE, as in a number of other theoretical essays written in the late 1940s and the 1950s, he indicated both his dissatisfaction with the subjective play so popular on Broadway at that time and his impatience with the traditional political play of the 1930s ("an arraignment of society's evils"). For him, the true social play was one that combined a man's social and subjective selves, the public and the private joining to form the whole man. All My Sons and Death of a Salesman, for instance, are both father-son conflicts, and both THE CRUCIBLE and A View from the Bridge are triangle plays, but the power and the substance of all four plays depends on the context in which these generic types are acted out.

Before Miller could get to these plays, which would come to define him as a playwright, he had to escape that "chicken coop" in Brooklyn and get into the capitalized "Outside World" he conjured in a 1955 essay for Holiday ("A Boy Grew in Brooklyn"). He graduated from high school in 1932 at about the time "[a]n invisible vise seemed to be forever closing tighter and tighter" (Miller, 2000). After two years of odd jobs, one in an auto-parts warehouse, memorialized in the one-act play *A Memory of Two Mondays* (1955), he was accepted at the University of Michigan, where he planned to study journalism. With the winning of his first Hopwood Award, he transferred to English and began to study playwriting under Kenneth T. Rowe, "teacher, friend, scholar," as the professor is called in the dedication to *The Theater Essays of Arthur Miller* (1978). In 1937 he won a second Hopwood for *Honors at Dawn* and just missed a third in 1938 with *The Great Disobedience*. None of these early plays has been published, but there were productions in Michigan of *They Too Arise*. With his student work behind him, he graduated in 1938 and returned to New York.

"Shrouding my secret dissociation from their untalented rank," Miller spent six months in the Federal Theatre Project (FTP) among playwrights, whose work, he says in *Timebends*, was "execrable, totally incompetent." Most of the time between his graduation and the end of World War II (he was rejected for service) was spent doing odd literary and nonliterary jobs. The most interesting and least reported was his writing of radio plays. The years of his involvement (1939–1946) was the end of a period of experimentation in the possibilities of radio drama, but Miller was no Norman Corwin, no Arch Oboler, no ARCHIBALD MACLEISH— men who saw radio drama as an artistic challenge. In *Timebends*, Miller dismisses the genre ("more like a form of yelling than writing"). "Still, it was an easy dollar," he says, establishing his credentials as a hack. He wrote for a number of shows—the respected *Columbia Workshop*, for instance, and *Theatre Guild on the Air*—but most of his scripts were written for DuPont's *Cavalcade of America*. The mediocrity of his radio plays, most of which have never been printed, few of which exist on tape, lies perhaps in the speed with which he worked and with the fact that, written in the years leading up to and during the war, they were expected to sound a patriotic note. There are three types: those based on historical figures (Benito Juarez, Giuseppe Garibaldi), those derived from magazine articles about service men and women ("I Was Married in Bataan"), and fictional stories of soldiers. He developed a reputation for efficiency but not for art.

The Golden Years, which might be called the last of his radio plays, was written in 1939 and 1940 and was not intended for radio. A ponderous account of Montezuma's failure to meet the invasion of Hernando Cortés—pockmarked with what Miller calls "purplish passages"—the play disappeared into Miller's trunk and remained unknown until it was resurrected almost fifty years later when BBC Radio gave it a premier performance in 1987. In the introduction to the published version of the play (1989), Miller says that it grew out of his "fear that in one form or another Fascism, with its intensely organized energies, might overwhelm the wayward and self-fixated Democracies" that led to the prewar appeasement of Adolf Hitler. In several of his radio plays—*The Eagle's Nest* (1942), the script about Garib-

aldi, and *The Philippines Never Surrendered* (1945)—there are people at first unwilling to face an impending enemy, but the time and the purpose of the plays make a change of heart inevitable. Montezuma's play came a little earlier and was less a call to arms than a warning about the consequences of inaction. It may have been a too elegant metaphor for contemporary "passivity and its risks," but it is obvious that Miller mainly wanted to create two strong men in inevitable conflict. Unfortunately, each rides his identifying trait so relentlessly that there is more repetition than growth in the characters.

In 1944 Miller was hired by Lester Cowan to visit army camps in search of material for a film script based on Ernie Pyle's wartime reporting. The result—his original script for *The Story of GI Joe* having been passed on to other writers—was his first published book, *Situation Normal*, a diary-essay that tried to understand what sent the soldiers to war. It is a characteristic Miller mix of careful observation and the kind of high-toned ideating that would give an ordinary soldier the willies: "It is terrible to me that everything is so personal; I mean that never in any of these calculations about the soldier can I honestly bring in the socio-political context of this war."

Also in 1944, in an event that had much more to do with Miller's career as a playwright, he had his first Broadway production— *The Man Who Had All the Luck*, which lasted for only four days. He would later tell Mel Gussow (2002) that the play was a nonrealistic play in a naturalistic theater climate: "It's a fable. I think that's what sunk it." Almost sixty years later (2002), the play made its way back to Broadway, where it did markedly better than it had in 1944, but it really belongs with his early work. David Beeves, the play's protagonist, accepts the town's view of his success—that it was all a matter of luck—and, assuming that luck must change, he almost brings disaster on himself and his family until his wife convinces him that a man makes his own luck. This is an early instance of a popular Miller theme, that man is in danger when he succumbs to society's image of him. The theme can be seen also in Miller's novel *Focus* (1945), another, darker fable. When the anti-Semitic Mr. Newman buys a new pair of glasses, his neighbors think that he looks Jewish, and after an increasingly violent series of events, he accepts, even embraces, the identity forced on him.

POSTWAR PLAYS AND POLITICS

Both David Beeves and Mr. Newman reach modified happy endings, the former by rejecting society's definition of his life, the latter by accepting it. In the postwar plays that made Miller's reputation, he returned to the theme with greater sophistication and with fatal consequences to his protagonists. In these plays, whether the characters accepted society's view of what a man should be (Joe Keller in *All My Sons* and Willy Loman in *Death of a Salesman*) or rejected it (John Proctor in *The Crucible* and Eddie Carbone in *A View from the Bridge*), they died of the consequences. In the introduction to *Collected Plays*

(1957), Miller wrote, "It is necessary, if one is to reflect reality, not only to depict why a man does what he does, or why he nearly didn't do it, but why he cannot simply walk away and say to hell with it."

All My Sons opened at the beginning of 1947, when a great many veterans—like Chris Keller in the play—were returning home with a modicum of idealism still intact. They assumed that the world they were returning to was something more than business as usual. For Joe, as he mistakenly says of his dead son Larry, the world "had a forty-foot front, it ended at the building line." A good father, a good husband, he wanted only to save his business to pass on to Chris and to do so was willing to ship out cracked cylinder heads to the air force and to let his business partner take the blame. "I'm his father and he's my son," Joe says, "and if there's something bigger than that I'll put a bullet in my head!" When he learns that for Chris (and the dead Larry) the world was not conterminous with the family ("But I think to him they were all my sons"), he commits suicide, destroying the image of the self-made businessman that defined his life.

All My Sons, the right play for the right moment, ran for 328 performances and garnered a handful of prizes. Its success gave Miller a chance to move to Connecticut and build the studio in which he wrote *Death of a Salesman*, which opened at the beginning of 1949. At the time there was a great deal of argument about whether or not the play was a TRAGEDY—theoretical maundering in which Miller took an active part—but audiences were largely indifferent to the scholarly imbroglio and not at all indifferent to the play itself. It was a remarkable success. It ran for 742 performances, won the Pulitzer Prize, and was performed in countries all over the world. It was even one of the few plays ever chosen by the Book-of-the-Month Club. It became a staple in the curriculum of schools and colleges and has become, with *The Crucible*, one of the most often produced of Miller's plays. The incredible thing is that a character as self-deluding, as lost, as defeated as Willy Loman should have been so widely embraced by playgoers. Miller does not go for pathos; he expects the audience to be moved by Willy, even to identify with him. He is a victim of the American success ethic, beset by conflicting images that feed his double ambition—to be rich and to be well liked. In the Requiem scene that closes the play, Biff says, "He had the wrong dreams." Joe Keller could see through his image just before he shot himself, but Willy goes to his suicide, his dreams still alive, although now not for himself but instead for his son who he assumes will have his "magnificence" when he gets the insurance money. With *Salesman*, Miller eschews the neatness and directness of *All My Sons*, substituting a richness that allows his characters in their comic and painful ways to lie to themselves and to the audience. He replaces the REALISM of the earlier play with a kind of homegrown expressionism that not only permits the viewer to pass through the walls but to see the swirling mix-

ture of past and present, the real and the imagined in the disintegrating mind of Willy. The working title for the play was *The Inside of His Head.*

In 1974 in an article for *New York* magazine ("The Year It Came Apart"), Miller looked back at 1949, the year of the triumph of *Salesman*, and wrote, "An era can be said to end when its basic illusions are exhausted, and my oneness with the Broadway audience was among them." It was true that although his national and international reputation would continue to grow, he would never again have the immediate, electric connection with Broadway that he had when *Sons* and *Salesman* opened. The 1950s would prove to be a time of personal, political, and theatrical problems for him; yet it was the decade in which he wrote *The Crucible*, which, with *Salesman*, was destined to be one of his two most successful plays.

Miller first met Marilyn Monroe in 1950, when he and Elia Kazan, the director who had been an important part of his initial Broadway successes, were in Hollywood to negotiate the production of *The Hook*, a film about corruption on the New York waterfront. In 1956 he divorced Mary Slattery, his wife of sixteen years, and married Monroe, for a short, troubled, and heavily publicized marriage that ended in 1961, the year that the film he wrote for her, *The Misfits*, was released. Plans for *The Hook* fell through under political pressure; Miller's friendship with Kazan collapsed after the director appeared as a friendly witness before the House Un-American Activities Committee (HUAC) in a ritual naming of names that the Committee already knew; and Miller had his own troubles with HUAC in 1956, before which he refused to talk about anyone but himself, a response that led to his conviction, later overturned, for contempt of Congress.

From early in the decade he responded to the political situation in prose pieces and in the theater. In 1950, he adapted HENRIK IBSEN's AN ENEMY OF THE PEOPLE. The story of Dr. Stockmann and his lonely stand for truth had obvious relevance to the climate in which it was produced; and although Miller stuck close to the Ibsen original, the changes he made in some speeches emphasized the contemporary relevance of the piece. More a political gesture than a bid for solid Broadway success, it ran for only thirty-six performances. Three years later in *The Crucible* he found a much more potent analogy. In a lecture at Harvard in 1999, he said, "It would probably never have occurred to me to write a play about the Salem witch trials of 1692 had I not seen some astonishing correspondences with that calamity in the America of the late forties and early fifties" (Miller, 2000). The play was both praised and condemned for its use of the Salem witch trials to attack the investigations of presumed subversives and to show the mixed motives (greed, envy, righteousness) of those who cried "witch" or "Red." John Proctor almost embraces the prevailing atmosphere of Salem, but in the end—a romantic hero of sorts—he chooses death over a false confession. "How may I live without my name?"

Eddie Carbone runs to his death in *A View from the Bridge*, crying, "Now gimme my name." Driven by his undeclared passion for his niece, he betrays her boyfriend to the immigration service, thus violating the standards of his community, and—unlike Proctor who dies to save his sense of self—he dies in an impossible attempt to regain his identity. *View*, originally a one-act play, paired with *A Memory of Two Mondays*, opened on Broadway in 1955 and was rewritten in two acts for a London production in 1956. The play finally found its audience in 1965 in an off-Broadway production that ran for almost two years.

It was 1964 before Miller returned to the New York stage with two new plays—*After the Fall* and *Incident at Vichy*—for the newly formed Repertory Theatre of Lincoln Center. The two very different plays—an excessively long self-analysis full of autobiographical elements and a static work that resembles a roundtable discussion—have similar themes. The protagonists of both search for an understanding of themselves that will allow them to act—Quentin in *Fall* to commit himself to a third marriage, Von Berg in *Vichy* to die in place of another character. In the early plays the quest for identity, for name, was a search for integrity. In the new plays the quest has become an attempt to find a workable definition. In *Fall*, "The action takes place in the mind, thought, and memory of Quentin." The central confrontation is with Maggie, the figure based on Marilyn Monroe, who had died in 1962, but there are scenes (fragments really) with a querulous first wife, with a passive father and an accusatory mother, with old leftist friends whose quarrel over testifying indicates that the situation was more complicated than it seemed in the early 1950s. *Fall* marked Miller's reconciliation with Elia Kazan, who directed it. Quentin, trying to deal with his guilt in all these relationships, ends by generalizing the guilt, making it a murderous fact of human existence. In "Our Guilt for the World's Evil," an essay published in the *New York Times Magazine* shortly after *Vichy* opened, Miller (2000) suggested that Von Berg's martyrdom is gratuitous: "The first problem is not what to do about it, but to discover our own relationship to evil, its reflection of ourselves." The plays are long on argument, short on theatrical action.

One of the most interesting of the Miller plays of the 1960s was *The Price*, which was at once familiar and a happy surprise. Two brothers, both beset by the usual identity problems, meet to dispose of the family furniture. Victor is a policeman who thinks his life meaningless; Walter is a successful surgeon, who has come to distrust that success. They quarrel over who was or was not responsible for their current situations, and they talk until Victor accepts his life. This would be standard Miller if it were not for the character of Gregory Solomon, a ninety-year-old furniture dealer who not only voices the play's theme but embodies it. A wonderfully garrulous man, Solomon is the most successful comic character that Miller ever created.

In 1972 in *The Creation of the World and Other Business*, Miller turned with minimal success to the biblical family for his usual weak father, strong mother, and quarreling sons. They, like God and Lucifer, are comic caricatures, and the play is an unconvincing mix of situation-COMEDY routines, anachronistic jokes, and high-toned philosophical points. The play lasted for only twenty performances on Broadway, and Miller revised it two years later as the book for a musical, *Up from Paradise*, with composer Stanley Silverman. A change of genre did not save one of Miller's weakest plays.

Between 1965 and 1969 Miller served as president of International PEN and continued to work for beleaguered writers after he left office. In 1970 his plays were temporarily banned in the Soviet Union because of his work to free dissidents. It was presumably his activity on the international literary scene that led him to the unusual step of setting a contemporary play outside the United States, *The Archbishop's Ceiling*, which was first performed in Washington in 1977. Set in an unnamed Eastern European country, it concerns a group of writers in relation both to the constant government surveillance of their work and to a young woman who may be intended as a symbol as well as a person. The protagonist, a banned novelist, elects to stay in the country in the face of a possible charge of treason, while two of his friends, including a visiting American writer, take the risk of attempting to smuggle his newest work out of the country. Once again, the ideas and the arguments are more alive than the characters.

Home again and back once more in the 1930s, he wrote *The American Clock*, a panorama of the Depression. It consisted of brief scenes adapted from Studs Terkel's *Hard Times* and two plots involving the Baums, based on Miller's family and his own amorphous relationship to the American Left at the time. After a reading in Seattle in 1979 and a New York production the next year, the play went through many stages, ending finally and happily with Peter Wood's production in 1986 at the National Theatre in ENGLAND, which made fine use of period music. When that production was brought to the United States in 1988, Miller told interviewer Laslie Bennetts of the *New York Times* (July 14, 1988), "The spirit of the whole thing was far grayer on Broadway, but it was never intended that way; it was intended as a six-ring circus, which is what it is now. . . . Onstage it's a kind of vaudeville."

LATER WORK—1980S AND BEYOND

Beyond the recurrent reworkings of *The American Clock*, Miller in the 1980s produced his first play written specially for television, *Playing for Time* (1980), an adaptation of Fania Fenelon's account of a woman's orchestra in a concentration camp that performed to stay alive. He also produced two programs of one-act plays: *Two-Way Mirror* (originally *2 by A.M.*, 1982), consisting of *Elegy for a Lady* and *Some Kind of Love Story*, and *Danger: Memory!* (1987), made up of *I Can't Remember Anything* and *Clara*. He later reworked *Some Kind of Love Story* as a screenplay, turning a largely psychological play into a social satire film, *Everybody Wins*, which was released in 1990 and rapidly disappeared. In 1983, Miller directed *Death of a Salesman* at the People's Art Theater in Beijing, CHINA, and the next year published *Salesman in Beijing*, his account of the experience.

Although Miller's early work remained popular in the 1980s on American stages and—particularly *The Crucible* and *Death of a Salesman*—in American schools, his later work was not well received. Increasingly, he was performed and published in England. America's most famous playwright seemed almost to have become an English one. Perhaps that is why he chose to have *The Ride Down Mount Morgan* (1991) first performed in London. A play not destined to bring glory to either its author or the host country, it is the account of Lyman Felt, the most tedious, self-obsessed, guilt-ridden character in the Miller canon. After an accident, which may have been a suicide attempt, brings both his wives to his bedside, he attempts to justify, or at least define, his behavior ("I've lived my life and I refuse to be ashamed of it!"). He gets in and out of the body cast in which the audience first sees him to observe apparently real scenes or to take part in fantasy ones. A staging note in the published play advises, "The play veers from the farcical to the tragic and back again and should be performed all-out in both directions as the situation demands, without attempting to mitigate the extremes." If mildly eccentric behavior were FARCE and whining garrulity tragedy, which they are not, the note might make a sound point.

In 1993, *The Last Yankee*, expanded from a 1991 version but still a very short play, was performed without an intermission. It concerned two women in a state mental hospital visited by their husbands whose presence exacerbates their condition. Patricia is irritated at Leroy (the titular Yankee) because he will not compromise the quality of his work to increase his income but realizes after watching her fellow patient with her successful but disapproving husband that Leroy is not so bad. It offers a note of hope, but it is not much of a play.

Broken Glass (1994) takes place in 1938, the year of *Kristallnacht*, that carefully organized, spontaneous outbreak of anti-Semitic violence in Nazi GERMANY. Set in Brooklyn, the play concerns the Gellburgs, he an anti-Semitic Jew uneasy about his tenuous place in the largely gentile banking world, she a woman so upset about the news from abroad that it triggers in her hysterical paralysis and a reexamination of her life. The paralysis is presumably a metaphor for their marriage (he is impotent), and the action of the play harks back to early Miller plays as the two characters try to find their way through their self-delusion and mutual distrust, he to acceptance of his Jewishness just before his death, she—depending on which version of the play one sees—to an attempt to struggle to her feet.

Peter Falk, who played the titular hero of *Mr. Peters' Connections* (1998), told a *New York Times* (May 17, 1998) interviewer, "The whole play, and all these people, are in Peters's head." The character enters a derelict building that has been a bank, a res-

taurant, and a nightclub and may be an anteroom to death. Some of the characters with whom he tries and fails to have conversations are clearly dead; others are more ambiguous. All of them are talkative, but the play is essentially a rumination by Peters on the changes that have come to his life and his world as they have to the building.

Falk correctly said that *Mr. Peters' Connections* is a "very funny non-comedy" (id.), a remark that may provide an accidental bridge to *Resurrection Blues* (2002). *Resurrection Blues* could be called an unfunny comedy. In a publicity release (Wilma Theater, June 19, 2003), Miller said, "It's a satiric comedy—you're supposed to laugh. I have to explain that to people because when it's one of my plays, they forbid themselves to laugh." There are not many laugh-aloud lines or scenes, but the play does have a grandly grotesque conceit—comedy at its darkest. In an unnamed country in South or Central America where a civil war has been going on for thirty-eight years, a young revolutionary, whom the people take as the Messiah, has been captured and is to be crucified. An American advertising agency offers millions of dollars for exclusive rights to the crucifixion. The presence of the rebel—never more than a bright light— changes the lives of everyone involved, even curing the impotence of the chief of state. At the end, all the characters except the advertising executive—the revolutionary's friends, his former enemies, the other Americans who have come to film the event—declare their love for the man, but each for his own reason pleads with the rebel simply to disappear, to remain alive in the minds of the people. It is like the end of *Saint Joan* without the Shavian superstructure to support the final irony.

Henri, the millionaire pharmaceutical executive turned scholar and philosopher in *Resurrection Blues*, sees himself as trying to awaken into reality after having slept all his life "in a fog of ideas and a loveless river of words." Such a fog and such a river seem to engulf Miller's plays at their most abstract, but at their finest, the ideas and the words live comfortably with vital characters like Joe Keller, Willy Loman, and Gregory Solomon.

PLAYS: *The Golden Years* (1940); *The Man Who Had All the Luck* (1944); *All My Sons* (1947); *Death of a Salesman* (1949); *An Enemy of the People* (1950); *The Crucible* (1953); *A Memory of Two Mondays* (1955); *A View from the Bridge* (1955); *After the Fall* (1964); *Incident at Vichy* (1964); *The Price* (1968); *The Creation of the World and Other Business* (1972); *The Archbishop's Ceiling* (1977); *The American Clock* (1979); *Playing for Time* (1980); *Two-Way Mirror* (1982); *Danger: Memory!* (1987); *The Ride Down Mount Morgan* (1991); *The Last Yankee* (1993); *Broken Glass* (1994); *Mr. Peters' Connections* (1998); *Resurrection Blues* (2002)

FURTHER READING

Centola, Steven R., ed. *The Achievement of Arthur Miller, New Essays.* Dallas, Tex.: Contemporary Res. Press, 1995.

Gussow, Mel. *Conversations with Miller.* New York: Applause, 2002.

Martin, Robert A., ed. *Arthur Miller, New Perspectives*. Englewood Cliffs, N.J.: Prentice-Hall, 1982.

Miller, Arthur. *The Theater Essays of Arthur Miller*. Ed. by Robert A. Martin. New York: Viking, 1978.

——. *Timebends, a Life*. New York: Grove, 1987.

——. *Echoes Down the Corridor, Collected Essays, 1944–2000*. Ed. by Steven R. Centola. New York: Viking, 2000.

Rigsby, Christopher. *Arthur Miller: A Critical Study*. New York: Cambridge Univ. Press, 2005.

Siebold, Thomas, ed. *Readings on Arthur Miller*. San Diego: Greenhaven Press, 1997.

Weales, Gerald. "Arthur Miller Takes the Air." *American Drama* 5 (Fall 1995): 1–15.

Gerald Weales

MILLER, JOAQUIN (1837–1913)

Born Cincinnatus Hiner Miller on September 8, 1837, on a farm near Liberty, Indiana, Joaquin Miller emigrated to Oregon in 1852 with his family, but in 1854, he left the family farm in Eugene City and traveled to the gold country of California. In 1856, he lived with Indians near Mount Shasta, and late in 1857, he studied briefly at Columbia College. He became a partner in a pony express service running between Idaho and Florence, Oregon, and in 1862 edited the pro-slavery *Democrat-Register* and the more literary *Eugene City Review*. He opened a law practice in Canyon City in 1863, and he served as a judge in Grant County from 1866 to 1869.

Miller published his first volume of poems, *Specimens*, in 1868. His fourth book, *Sons of the Sierras*, led to fame and success, and his narrative study *Life Amongst the Modocs* appeared in 1873. After living on the East Coast for several years, he moved to Oakland, California, and lived there from 1887 until his death on February 17, 1913.

Based on the story "The First Families of the Sierras," *The Danites in the Sierras* opened in New York on August 22, 1877. Written a full generation after the gold rush, Miller gave mature form to the Edenic myth of California, portraying it as a romantic haven. The hero of the play, goes a-courting:

> Say you were waitin' for me, and it will be as if the sun, and the moon, and the stars all together shone out over the Sierras, and made this another Eden, with its one sweet woman in the centre of God's own garden of fruit and flowers.

The honest miners are simple children of the wild, beautiful land that nurtures, sustains, and guides them, while the Danites—avenging religious fanatics from Salt Lake City—are aliens who must be purged from the natural innocence they have invaded.

Forty-Nine (1881) focuses on an old miner who still dreams of striking a vein and filling his baby son's cradle with gold. A young gambler from Illinois heads for California to find a young woman who has inherited an estate in the Santa Clara Valley and who turns out to be a child of nature who hunts chipmunks with a bow and arrow.

Miller's plays recycle the stock characters and situations that BRET HARTE introduced to fiction and the stage: the hopeful old miner, the brash young gambler, the innocent young girl whose wholesome beauty blossoms in the high Sierra, and the villain who schemes to take both the heroine and others' hard-earned wealth. Miller's California is a paradise, an affirmation of hope and dreams where people thrive on honesty, simplicity, and hard work in the clear mountain air, and the repentant shed their sense of burden. They have walked away from the corrupt, complex East, where guile and polished manners prevail, and the long trek to California is the return to the garden, to the prelapsarian utopia of Western myth.

[*See also* United States, 1860–1929]

PLAYS: *The Danites in the Sierras* (1877, with Alexander Fitzgerald); *Forty-Nine: An Idyl Drama of the Sierras* (1881); *Tally-Ho* (1883; unproduced); *An Oregon Idyl* (1910; unproduced)

FURTHER READING

Frost, O. W. *Joaquin Miller*. New York: Twayne, 1967.

Lawson, Benjamin S. *Joaquin Miller*. Boise: Boise State Univ. Press, 1980.

Mayberry, M. Marion. *Splendid Poseur: Joaquin Miller—American Poet*. New York: Crowell, 1953.

Jeffrey D. Mason

MILNE, ALAN ALEXANDER (1882–1956)

Although Alan Alexander (A. A.) Milne is best known as the British author of the Winnie-the-Pooh stories, he was also a prolific writer in other genres, including drama. Among his works are four novels; four books of nonfiction; four collections of poetry; nine story collections; an autobiography called *It's Too Late Now*; and over twenty-five plays.

Milne was born in 1882 in SCOTLAND but raised in London, the son of a preparatory schoolmaster and his wife. Among the early influences on him was the author H. G. Wells, who was one of his childhood teachers and mentors. Educated at Westminster School and Trinity College, Milne became editor of the literary magazine *Granta* during his undergraduate years. Several of his contributions were published in the humor magazine *Punch*, where he later became assistant editor. In 1913 Milne married Dorothy Daphne de Selincourt, and on August 21, 1920, in Chelsea, they had a son they named Christopher Robin. For his first birthday, the boy received an Alpha Farnell teddy bear purchased from Harrod's in London. Both Christopher and his toy would become well known all over the world when Milne's most famous book, *Winnie-the-Pooh*, was published on October 14, 1926. Milne's wife and son were the inspirations for his Winnie-the-Pooh stories, but he did not intentionally write the stories for children and claimed to have no special interest in young people. Although a pacifist, Milne served in the War-wickshire Regiment in FRANCE in World War I. He enjoyed success in all literary genres, particularly in the years between the world wars. His plays, in particular, have been almost completely overshadowed by the success of the Pooh books.

His play *The Fourth Wall* (1928) was made into a film called *The Perfect Alibi*. Before the success of the Pooh books, Milne's plays were performed widely and with great critical acclaim in Great Britain and the UNITED STATES. Today, professional productions of them are rare to nonexistent; however, Milne's plays are still produced in amateur theaters in the English-speaking world.

In 1952 Milne suffered brain damage as the result of surgery and lived the rest of his life as an invalid, reading and enjoying the country. He died in England on January 31, 1956, after a long illness.

[See also England, 1860–1940]

PLAYS: *Worzel-Flummery* (1917); *Belinda* (1918); *The Boy Comes Home* (1918); *Make-Believe* (1918); *The Camberley Triangle* (1919); *Mr. Pim Passes By* (1919); *Mr. Red Feathers* (1920); *The Romantic Age* (1920); *The Stepmother* (1920); *The Truth About Blayds* (1920); *The Dover Road* (1921); *The Lucky One* (1922); *The Artist: A Duologue* (1923); *Give Me Yesterday* (1923); *The Great Boxopp Success* (1923); *Ariadne* (1924); *The Man in the Bowler Hat* (1924); *To Have the Honour* (1924); *Portrait of a Gentleman in Slippers* (1926); *Success: A Play in Three Acts* (1926); *Miss Marlow at Play* (1927); *The Fourth Wall or The Perfect Alibi* (1928); *The Ivory Door* (1929); *Toad of Toad Hall* (1929); *Michael and Mary* (1930); *Four Days Wonder* (1933); *Other People's Lives* (1933); *Miss Elizabeth Bennett* (1936); *Sarah Simple* (1937); *Gentleman Unknown* (1938); *The Ugly Duckling* (1946); *Before the Flood* (1951)

FURTHER READING

Thwaite, Ann. *A. A. Milne: His Life*. London: Faber, 1992.

Wullschlager, Jackie. *Inventing Wonderland: The Lives and Fantasies of Lewis Carroll, Edward Lear, J. M. Barrie, Kenneth Grahame and A. A. Milne*. Detroit: Free Press, 1996.

Connie Ann Kirk

MILNER, ARTHUR (1950–)

Although many of Arthur Milner's plays have not been published, his dramas have been produced throughout Ontario, CANADA, for two decades. Born on July 3, 1950, and raised in Montreal, but living in Ottawa since 1971, Milner has written children's plays, including 1999's *Crusader of the World*, about Shelley, a girl who learns through tough experience about the realities of Third World deprivation. Other genres explored by Milner include the radio play (*The City*, 1991), the collective creation (*Sandinista!*), and the musical (*Joan Henry*, 2003).

Most of Milner's plays were produced by the left-wing Great Canadian Theatre Company (GCTC), Ottawa: he was the GCTC's resident playwright (1978–1991) and artistic director (1991–1995). Two of his plays, *Masada* (1990) and *Learning to*

Live with Personal Growth (1987), both published in important anthologies of Canadian drama, illustrate the variety of Milner's dramatic styles and the seriousness of his plays' politics. *Masada* necessitates only one actor and sparse staging. The play was first performed by the GCTC in January 1990; directed by Steven Bush, *Masada* starred Sally Singal. The character delivers a hurriedly prepared lecture on "The Miracle of Zionism," begins by expressing distaste for counterproductive extremism, but eventually asserts hawkish thoughts that reveal an uncompromising desire for a further expansion of Jewish territory: "It's a nice feeling" to be "in charge" of Palestine, one that Jews should perpetuate, the speaker urges. Appropriating the methods of armies and terrorists is merely an extension of the tactics used by ancient Jews like Moses and the Zealots. The play underlines Milner's discomfort with political belligerence and critiques the racism and sectarianism that facilitates endless killing.

While *Masada* has one long, continuous scene, 1987's four-character *Learning to Live with Personal Growth* has sixty-six very short scenes, dramatizing the fragmentation of Jeff's social consciousness. Motivated, in part, to compensate for a lukewarm marriage, Jeff, gradually, becomes influenced and indeed corrupted by a shallow property investor, Link. Having spent much of his time seeking to help a tired, impoverished single mother, Ginny, Jeff winds up acquiescing in her eviction from a property that he and other investors sell for a handsome profit. By the end of the play, Jeff has given up his job as a social worker and states that poverty can be alleviated by market forces: society will heal, he insists, when taxes are lowered and private enterprise flourishes. Such attitudes, expressed so glibly by Jeff, are anathema to Milner, the GCTC, and its more politically serious audience members.

A onetime president of the Professional Association of Canadian Theatre, Milner continues to write for the stage prolifically, but he has also been involved in the administration and teaching of the arts. In addition to his work with GCTC, he worked as a DRAMATURG for the Banff Centre for the Arts, the Montreal Playwrights Workshop, and the Manitobe Association of Playwrights; he has also taught playwrighting and modern drama at the Universities of Carleton and Concordia. Presently, Milner is an editor of the journal *Inroads*, to which he contributes often controversial articles about culture and national and international politics.

PLAYS: *Cheap Thrill* (1985); *Zero Hour* (1986); *Learning to Live with Personal Growth* (1987); *Masada* (1990); *The City* (1991, radio play); *It's Not a Country, It's Winter* (1998, radio play); *Crusader of the World* (1999); *The Forest* (2001); *Joan Henry* (2003)

FURTHER READING

Filewood, Alan. "Introduction to *Zero Hour* by Arthur Milner." In *The CTR Anthology: Fifteen Plays from Canadian Theatre Review*, ed. by Alan Filewood. Toronto: Univ. of Toronto Press, 1993. 435.

Henighan, Tom. *Maclean's Companion to Canadian Arts and Culture.*
    Vancouver: Raincoast Bks., 2000.
Inroads: The Canadian Journal of Opinion. http://www.inroadsjournal.ca.
Athabasca University. "Arthur Milner." In *Encyclopedia of Canadian
    Theatre.* http://www.canadiantheatre.com/dict.
    pl?term=Milner%2C%20Arthur.

Kevin De Ornellas

MISHIMA YUKIO (1925–1970)

Mishima Yukio was a Japanese novelist and SHINGEKI play-wright. Notorious for his ritual suicide in 1970 after failing to foment a military uprising, Mishima was JAPAN's leading dramatist of the 1950s and 1960s. His sixty-one works for stage and screen span a wide range of genres and styles. Although he mostly wrote realist *shingeki* plays, he also wrote six *kabuki* plays in classical Japanese; Mishima is also recognized as the finest postwar *kabuki* playwright.

As a youth, Mishima (born Hiraoka Kimitake) attended *kabuki* plays every month and the NŌ and *shingeki* occasionally, writing precocious critical essays about almost every play he saw. From *nō* and *kabuki* Mishima developed a love of formalism and of Japan's native tradition that would infuse much of his later theatrical writing. Mishima also admired classical European drama. His favorite play was Jean Racine's *Phèdre*, which he adapted to *kabuki* in 1955. *The Oresteia* and *Heracles* inspired two of his finest *shingeki* plays, *The Tropical Tree* (*Nettaiju*, 1959) and *The Decline and Fall of the House of Suzaku* (*Suzaku Ke no Metsubo*, 1967).

In 1950 Mishima's first "modern *nō*" play, *Kantan*, received critical acclaim at the prestigious Literary Theatre (Bungakuza). Mishima had written nine modern *nō* plays by 1962; many are regarded as his best one-acts. Thanks to early publication in English, these are the Japanese plays most frequently performed abroad. Mishima's *nō* plays take their plots from classical *nō*, but are psychological dramas of love and obsession set in contemporary Japan and intended by Mishima for performance in *shingeki* style.

In 1956 Mishima's three-act romantic MELODRAMA Rokumeikan, produced by the Literary Theatre, and starring the renowned actress Sugimura Haruko, was a huge success, touring Japan for three years. Mishima joined Bungakuza and wrote many successful plays for Sugimura until their bitter falling out in 1964, when he left the company.

Mishima's political and artistic ideals ran counter to the development of postwar Japanese drama. While other dramatists were moving away from traditional constraints toward freedom of expression and eclectic borrowing from various genres, Mishima remained committed to orthodox *kabuki* and *shingeki* plays. Virtually every other dramatist espoused leftist ideals, but Mishima, from the early 1960s, began to champion right-wing nationalist characters and themes. His break with Sugimura and Bungakuza resulted from their refusal to stage his anticommunist *The Harp of Joy* (*Yorokobi no Koto*, 1963–1964). After leaving Bungakuza, Mishima founded two new theater companies. Some of his best long plays he wrote for these companies, including MADAME DE SADE (*Sado Kōshaku Fujin*, 1965), considered his finest play.

In many of his plays Mishima sought to shock, disturb, or even outrage his audiences. His 1955 *Primary Colors* (*Sangenshoku*), which depicts bisexual men kissing, was not performed until 1963. In *The Black Lizard* (*Kuro Tokage*, 1962) Mishima's heroine kills and stuffs beautiful men and women for her museum; in *Madame de Sade* Mishima suggested that murder and depravity could be divine acts; in the modern *nō* play *Yuya* (1967), he argued that deceit makes life beautiful; in *The Decline and Fall of the House of Suzaku* he resurrected emperor worship; in *My Friend Hitler* (*Waga Tomo no Hittora*, 1969), he presented Adolf Hitler as a moderate, rational politician whose purges were justified. These were nightmarish themes for Japanese audiences, but Mishima gilded the horror and pain with gorgeous words, structural elegance, sumptuous sets and costumes, and acting by *shingeki*'s best performers.

Half of Mishima's plays have been performed since his death, and many are presented regularly in theaters in Japan.

[See also Shin Kabuki]

PLAYS: (titles with asterisks were written for *kabuki*) *The Burning House* (*Kataku*, 1949); *The Lighthouse* (*Todai*, 1949); *Kantan* (1950); *Sotoba Komachi* (1952); *Hell Screen** (*Jigoku Hen*, 1953); *The Sardine Seller's Net of Love** (*Iwashiuri Koi no Hikiami*, 1954); *A Blush on the White Hibiscus Blossom: Lady Fuyo and the True Account of' the Ouchi Clan** (*Fuyo no Tsuyu Ouchi Jikki*, 1955); *The Damask Drum* (*Aya no Tsuzumi*, 1955); *The Lady Aoi* (*Aoi no Ue*, 1955); *Rokumeikan* (1956); *Hanjo* (1957); *Steeplechase* (*Daishōgai*, 1957); *Sash Stealing Pond** (*Musume Gonomi Obitori no Ike*, 1958); *The Tropical Tree* (*Nettaiju*, 1959); *The Black Lizard* (*Kuro Tokage*, 1962); *Primary Colors* (*Sangenshoku*, 1963); *The Harp of Joy* (*Yorokobi no Koto*, 1963–1964); *Yoroboshi: The Blind Young Man* (*Yoroboshi*, 1964); *Madame de Sade* (*Sado Kōshaku Fujin*, 1965); *The Decline and Fall of the House of Suzaku* (*Suzaku Ke no Metsubo*, 1967); *Yuya* (1967); *My Friend Hitler* (*Waga Tomo no Hittora*, 1969); *The Terrace of the Leper King* (*Raid no Terrasu*, 1969); *A Wonder Tale: The Moonbow** (*Chinzetsu Yumiharizuki*, 1969)

FURTHER READING
Domoto Masaaki. *Gekijin Mishima Yukio* [Yukio Mishima the
    dramatist]. Tokyo: Geki Shobo, 1994.
Mishima Yukio. *Mishima on Stage: The Black Lizard and Other Masterpieces.*
    Tr. by Laurence Kominz. Ann Arbor: Univ. of Michigan Press, 2001.
Wetmore, Kevin J. "Modern Japanese Drama in English." *Asian Theatre
    Journal* 23, no. 1 (Spring 2006): 179–205.

Laurence Kominz

MISS JULIE

Miss Julie (*Fröken Julie*) is "a naturalistic TRAGEDY" by AUGUST STRINDBERG. Written and published in 1888, it was first performed at the Student Society in Copenhagen in 1889 with Strindberg's wife Siri von Essen as Julie. The editor made a number of changes in the text without Strindberg's permission. It was not until 1984 that modern detection methods allowed the editor's changes to be distinguished from the author's, and the original text was restored. The play was written both for Antoine's Théâtre Libre and for the Scandinavian Experimental Theater Strindberg had just started.

Miss Julie deals with twenty-five-year-old Julie, the daughter of a count, who flirts with her father's valet Jean during the Midsummer Night celebration in the kitchen of the manor house. When the celebrating peasants approach, she and Jean escape to his room, where they have intercourse. Ashamed of having offered herself to someone of a lower station and imagining that she is in love with Jean, Julie agrees to his suggestion that they flee together to SWITZERLAND. But Jean, influenced by Kristin, the cook to whom he is engaged, changes his mind. When it is announced that the count, who has been away visiting friends, has returned, Julie feels trapped. She asks Jean to hypnotize her so that she can muster the courage to commit suicide; she exits, razor in hand.

Miss Julie was written at a manor house not far from Copenhagen, where the Strindbergs lived at the time. The estate belonged to Countess Louise de Frankenau, who was an unmarried eccentric. Everyone believed that her steward, Ludvig Hansen, was her lover. Strindberg, whose conjugal relations with his wife were at low ebb, once or twice made love to Hansen's sixteen-year-old sister Martha. As a result, Hansen tried to blackmail Strindberg by spreading rumors that his sister was pregnant. In the play, Strindberg merged some aspects of Ludvig and Martha Hansen into the figure of Jean. Julie's end was inspired by Swedish writer Victoria Benedictsson's suicide: on the night of July 21, 1888, she cut her throat with a razor at the Hotel Leopold in Copenhagen, following a previous suicide attempt that Strindberg had knowledge of. Like Julie, Benedictsson, who wrote under the male pseudonym Ernst Ahlgren, had been dressed as a boy as a child and taught to ride.

To meet the demands of ÉMILE ZOLA, who had found THE FATHER too abstract, Strindberg was anxious to turn *Miss Julie* into a truly naturalistic drama, which he did: hereditary and environmental circumstances reveal Jean's and Julie's past; the play illustrates the Darwinian survival of the fittest.

Strindberg's naturalistic ambitions did not prevent him from resorting to SYMBOLISM. The setting—a basement kitchen connected with the count's rooms up above via a speaking-tube serving as an intercom—is a telling image of class society. Two highly symbolic dreams—Jean's about rising, Julie's about falling—have social, sexual, and psychological significance. Jean's lust for life versus Julie's longing for death may even make us see the two characters as archetypal incarnations of forces within one and the same person. When Julie's thoroughbred dog Diana mates with the gatekeeper's mutt, this misalliance pre-

pares for Julie's intercourse with Jean. And when Jean slaughters her caged greenfinch, his act anticipates his putting the lethal razor in Julie's hand. More cryptic is the symbolic meaning of Jean's story of how, as a child, he was once caught in the gentry's privy. This story, Evert Sprinchorn (1982) observes,

> becomes the paradigm for Julie's situation in the play itself. She is trapped in the servant's quarters, and also trapped by her own uncontrollable desires. Jean as a child had been forced to crawl through the excrement; now the trapped Julie begs Jean to "lift me out of this awful filth I'm sinking in."

In the play's original preface Strindberg gives numerous reasons for "Miss Julie's tragic fate":

> her mother's "bad" instinct; her father's improper bringing-up of the girl; her own nature and the influence her fiancé's suggestions had on her weak, degenerate brain; also, and more immediately: the festive atmosphere of Midsummer Night; her father's absence; her period; her preoccupation with the animals; the intoxicating effect of the dance; the light summer night; the powerful aphrodisiac influence of the flowers; and finally chance that drives these two people together in a room apart, plus the boldness of the aroused man.

Despite this naturalistic list of hereditary and environmental circumstances, even some of Strindberg's contemporaries found the ending improbable. One of them was the Danish writer and critic Edvard Brandes, who protested: "You do not kill yourself, when there is no danger in sight, and here there is no danger. Perhaps five months from now but not this very night" (Törnqvist, 1988). Brandes refers to a visible pregnancy. The stage history of the play has shown that the more the class difference is accentuated, the more probable is Julie's sense of defiled honor, which in turn justifies the suicide. Yet stressing the class aspect means lessening the rapport with a present-day audience—except in countries where class barriers are still very pronounced. To make the final suicide acceptable from a naturalistic point of view, Strindberg had Jean hypnotize Julie. Yet to save the play as a tragedy, Julie had to choose her death consciously. Thus, by having her walk "*resolutely out through the door,*" Strindberg vaguely suggests that at the end she comes out of her hypnosis.

The famous preface was written shortly after the play was finished. The most important manifesto of NATURALISM in the theater, it is not always trustworthy as a key to the play.

[*See also* Sweden]

FURTHER READING

Bergholz, Harry. "Toward an Authentic Text of Strindberg's *Fröken Julie.*" *Orbis Litterarum* 9 (1954): 167–192.

Carlson, Harry G. *Strindberg and the Poetry of Myth.* Berkeley: Univ. of California Press, 1982.

Karnick, Manfred. *Rollenspiel und Welttheater* [Role Play and World Theater]. München: Wilhelm Fink, 1980.

Sprinchorn, Evert. *Strindberg as Dramatist.* New Haven, Conn.: Yale Univ. Press, 1982.

Törnqvist, Egil, and Barry Jacobs. *Strindberg's Miss Julie: A Play and Its Transpositions*. Norwich: Norvik Press, 1988.

Egil Törnqvist

MISS LULU BETT

ZONA GALE's *Miss Lulu Bett* began life as a bestselling short novel. Producer Brock Pemberton asked Gale to dramatize her novel, a feat she accomplished in a little more than a week. The play, subtitled "An American Comedy of Manners," opened at the Belmont Theatre in New York on December, 27, 1920, to mixed but generally positive reviews. Some critics considered it dull, while others agreed with *New York World* Charles Darnton who recognized that the playwright had captured small-town "people, their talk and manners perfectly." *Miss Lulu Bett* ran some 600 performances on Broadway and on tour, becoming the first play written by a woman to win the Pulitzer Prize. Paramount later turned Gale's COMEDY into a silent film.

Miss Lulu Bett is set in a small midwestern town. The title character is a spinster of thirty-three who does all the work for her sister Ina's querulous family. Lulu's chief nemesis is her brother-in-law Dwight Deacon, a petty tyrant who condescends to all around him. When Dwight's world-traveling brother Ninian arrives for a visit, he recognizes Lulu's plight, and the two are accidentally married in a ceremony that is intended as a joke but turns out to be valid.

Lulu returns to the Deacon home in act 2, announcing that Ninian has a previous wife who may not be dead. At the novel's conclusion, Lulu weds a new suitor, but Gale feared that theater audiences would not accept two marriages in one evening; the original dramatic version has Lulu departing alone with the declaration, "I thought I wanted somebody of my own. Well, maybe it was just myself." Shortly after the play opened, however, Gale capitulated to popular tastes and rewrote the conclusion again, reuniting Lulu with a widowed Ninian. Although Gale defended the new ending, she included both versions of act 3 when she published *Miss Lulu Bett*.

Gale was an outspoken advocate for women's rights, and *Miss Lulu Bett* reveals the plight of women in "Middle America." Lulu's mother is the sardonic Mrs. Bett, a widow who grudgingly accepts her dependence on the "lump" her daughter married. Young Diana tries to elope not because she is in love but to escape her father's sadistic teasing. In a adapts to her situation by enjoying her few wifely prerogatives and echoing her husband's platitudes. Like many single women of the period, Lulu works as an unpaid servant in a relative's home. Ninian does not rescue Lulu; rather, he shows her how capable and badly used she is.

Miss Lulu Bett is remarkable not only for its feminist perspective but also for its deviation from traditional dramatic characterization, structure, and dialogue. As writer Robert C. Benchley (1921) observes, Gale has avoided stock comic figures by giving us "an old lady who is not sweet, and a child who is not cute." The repetitive scenes and banal dialogue were unusual for the time but look forward to techniques that became popular onstage decades later. The success of recent productions of *Miss Lulu Bett* testifies to the enduring importance of its subject as well as Gale's dramatic skill.

[See also Feminist Drama in the United States; United States, 1860–1940]

FURTHER READING

Barlow, Judith E. *Introduction to Plays by American Women, 1900–1930*. New York: Applause Bks., 1985 [volume includes *Miss Lulu Bett*].

Benchley, Robert C. Foreword to *Zona Gale's Miss Lulu Bett: An American Comedy of Manners*. New York: Appleton, 1921.

Derleth, August. *Still Small Voice: The Biography of Zona Gale*. New York: Appleton-Century, 1940.

Schroeder, Patricia R. "Realism and Feminism in the Progressive Era." In *The Cambridge Companion to American Women Playwrights*, ed. by Brenda Murphy. Cambridge: Cambridge Univ. Press, 1999. 31–46.

Shafer, Yvonne. *American Women Playwrights, 1900–1950*. New York: P. Lang, 1995.

Simonson, Harold P. *Zona Gale*. New York: Twayne, 1962.

Judith E. Barlow

MISTERIIA-BUFF   See MYSTERY-BOUFFE

MISTERO   See COMIC MYSTERY

MITCHELL, LANGDON (1862–1935)

Langdon Elwyn Mitchell was born on February 17, 1862, in Philadelphia, Pennsylvania. He received his early education at St. Paul's School in New Hampshire, studied for three years in Dresden and Paris, and studied law at Columbia and Harvard universities. In 1886 he was admitted to the New York bar and later practiced law with the firm of Cadwalader, Wickersham and Taft of Philadelphia.

Despite his legal training, however, Mitchell's primary interest was writing. In 1883, while still at Harvard, Mitchell wrote and published poetry and drama, and in 1885, he published *Sylvian and Other Poems* under the pseudonym John Philip Varley, a step he took to avoid comparison with his father, S. Wier Mitchell, who was a novelist and a poet. Langdon debuted as a professional playwright in 1892 in London, where his play *Deborah* was performed five times at matinees. In that same year, Mitchell married actress Marion Lea, who had performed in productions of HENRIK IBSEN's dramas in London and would later play the role of Vida Phillimore in Mitchell's best-known play *The New York Idea*.

Mitchell came to the public's attention in the UNITED STATES in 1899 when he adapted William Makepeace Thackeray's *Vanity Fair* for the stage. Renamed *Becky Sharp*, the play, which was commissioned by the prominent actress Minnie Maddern Fiske, opened at New York's Fifth Avenue Theatre on September 12, 1899, and ran for nearly two seasons thereafter. Succeeding dramatizations—*The Adventures of François* (1900), an adaptation of his father's novel, and *The Kreutzer Sonata* (1906), which Mitchell adapted from Jacob Gordin's Yiddish rendition of a LYOV TOLSTOY novel—attracted considerably less attention. However, his next attempt, THE NEW YORK IDEA (1906), was both a critical and commercial success.

A brilliant and witty social satire, *The New York Idea* was a critique of Americans' frivolous notions about marriage and their belief that the institution existed solely for their comfort and amusement. The play, written expressly for Minnie Maddern Fiske, revolves around two recently divorced couples, their efforts to find new mates, the confusion and shenanigans that follow, and the resultant insights into Americans' lackadaisical attitudes regarding marriage and divorce. The play was first performed in Chicago and subsequently moved to St. Louis; on November 19, 1906, it opened at New York's Lyric Theatre. Since its debut, *The New York Idea* has been successfully revived a number of times and was mounted in GERMANY by MAX REINHARDT in 1916.

In 1911, Mitchell attempted to repeat the success of *The New York Idea* with *The New Marriage*, but the production was not well received by either critics or the public. His final play, *Major Pendennis* (1916), an adaptation of Thackeray's *Pendennis*, was also poorly received. Following his playwriting career, Mitchell lectured on poetry at the George Washington University, and in 1928 he was appointed Mask & Wig Professor of Playwriting at the University of Pennsylvania. Mitchell died on October 21, 1935, in Philadelphia.

PLAYS: *Deborah* (1892); *In the Season* (1893); *Becky Sharp* (1899); *The Adventures of François* (1900); *The Kreutzer Sonata* (1906); *The New York Idea* (1906); *The New Marriage* (1911); *Major Pendennis* (1916)

FURTHER READING

Gassner, John, ed. *Best Plays of the Early American Theatre: From the Beginning to 1916*. New York: Crown, 1967.

Moody, Richard, ed. *Dramas from the American Theatre, 1762–1909*. Boston: Houghton, 1966.

Price, David M. "Langdon Mitchell: The Man and His Plays." Ph.D. diss., City Univ. of New York, 1978.

Quinn, Arthur Hobson. *A History of the American Drama*. Vol. 2. New York: Appleton, 1927.

John W. Frick

MIYOSHI JŪRŌ (1902–1958)

Miyoshi Jūrō, Japanese SHINGEKI playwright and poet, was born in Saga Prefecture and educated in English literature at Waseda University, where he was first attracted to Marxism. In fact, Miyoshi's work as a dramatist can best be described through his relationship to the proletariat movement in Japanese theater. Early in his career, he founded the magazine *Left-Wing Art* (*Sayoku Geijutsu*), co-founded the "left-wing artist circle," and was a member of the Nihon Proleta Artista Federacio (NAPF) and the Japan Proletariat Theatre League (PROT). Further, his plays of this period were produced by such organizations as the Left-Wing Theatre (Sayoku Gekijō), Tsukiji Little Theatre (Tsukiji Shōgekijō), and Inoue's Theatre Gymnasium (Inoue Engeki Dōjō). Plays such as his second work *The Much-Maimed Oaki* (*Kizu Darake no Oaki*, 1927) and *Who Does the Firing?* (*Kubi o Kiru no wa Dare da*, 1928) define his involvement in the proletariat movement.

However, by the time Miyoshi wrote the Tokugawa-era (1603–1868) tale *The Stabbed Senta* (*Kirare no Senta*, 1934), his dissatisfaction with the politics and formality of the movement was clear. As the introductions and afterwords to his plays testify, Miyoshi had grown disillusioned with the overly politicized and black-and-white view of humanity held by most Marxist writers of the time. For example, in *The Stabbed Senta*, Miyoshi exhibits a career-defining commitment to the fate of the lower classes, particularly rural farmers, which did not necessitate the involvement of the intellectual, Marxist community. *Buoy* (*Bui*, 1940), which has been called a "phantom masterpiece" because of its scant production history, dramatizes Miyoshi's break from orthodox left-wing theater. The play is one of Miyoshi's most autobiographical, as it illustrates both the author's ideological shift and the death of his wife. The hero, Kuga Gorō, a Western-style painter, slowly loses the emotional support of his friends sent to fight in the Sino-Japanese War, the support of his ideologies, and ultimately his wife. Yet, in the end, Kuga emerges with a renewed commitment to life and love.

His break with the proletariat party in part allowed Miyoshi to continue writing during the war, when many writers were either silenced or forced to write propaganda. Though some branded him a collaborationist, Miyoshi himself was deeply conflicted over the war. This complex response became the dominant theme of his postwar work. *The Ruins* (*Haikyo*, 1947), an extended one-act, is populated with a number of characters each representing a different reaction to the war. The play is essentially a lengthy debate over war responsibility, at the heart of which are the retired professor Shibata and his two sons. Miyoshi also brings in numerous characters that serve as reminders, both physically and in their actions, of the desperate times after the war. No resolution follows, and the play ends in a near-violent tension between family members. Other plays during the postwar stage of Miyoshi's career continue this exploration, most notably *I Know Not the Man* (*Sono Hito o Shirazu*, 1948), *Inside the Womb* (*Tainai*, 1949), and *Those Who Committed Crimes* (*Okashita Mono*, 1952).

[See also Japan]

SELECT PLAYS: *The Much-Maimed Oaki* (*Kizu Darake no Oaki*, 1927); *Who Does the Firing?* (*Kubi o Kiru no wa Dare da*, 1928); *Coal Dust* (*Tanjin*, 1930); *The Stabbed Senta* (*Kirare no Senta*, 1934);

Buoy (Bui, 1940); *The Lion* (Shishi, 1943); *The Cliff* (Gake, 1946); *The Ruins* (Haikyo, 1947); *I Know Not the Man* (Sono Hito o Shirazu, 1948); *Inside the Womb* (Tainai, 1949); *Person of the Flames* (Honoo no Hito, 1951); *Those Who Committed Crimes* (Okashita Mono, 1952)

FURTHER READING

Abe Itaru. *Kindai Bungaku no Kenkyū* [Modern literature research]. Tokyo: Ofusha, 1980.

Harada Hiroko. *Aspects of Post-War German and Japanese Drama (1945–1970): Reflections on War, Guilt, and Responsibility.* Lewiston: Edwin Mellen Press, 2000.

Keene, Donald. *Dawn to the West: Japanese Literature in the Modern Era: Poetry, Drama, Criticism.* New York: H. Holt, 1984.

Miyoshi Jūrō. *Miyoshi Jūrō no Shigoto* [The works of Miyoshi Jūrō]. 4 vols. Tokyo: Gakugei Shorin, 1968.

Michael W. Cassidy

MIZU NO EKI   See THE WATER STATION

MNOUCHKINE, ARIANE (1940–)

Ariane Mnouchkine was born on March 3, 1940, in Boulogne-sur-Seine, FRANCE, and is one of the world's preeminent theater directors and a pioneer in transcultural theatrical production. Long associated with the Théâtre du Soleil, which she co-founded in 1964, Mnouchkine is widely recognized for her stylistic eclecticism, innovative staging, and largely egalitarian management style. Since 1970, Théâtre du Soleil has made its home in the Cartoucherie (an abandoned ammunition factory) in the Bois de Vincennes, fifteen minutes outside of central Paris. With its early productions of *The Kitchen*, *The Clowns*, and *1789*, Théâtre du Soleil won its reputation as "the people's theater." Since then, the company has deepened its commitment to producing socially challenging work and, by promoting its productions among trade unions, has attracted factory workers by the busload.

Mnouchkine's directorial approach varies from one production to the next, but it consistently involves stylized athleticism and lavish spectacle. Commedia dell'arte, clowning, and Asian theatrical influences have all found their way into Mnouchkine's work, often combining Western texts with theatrical images taken from Bunraku, *kabuki*, Kathakali, and Sanskrit theatrical traditions. Some of Mnouchkine's strongest influences include JACQUES COPEAU, Jacques Lecoq, Jean Vilar, ANTONIN ARTAUD, Peter Brook, Giorgio Strehler, VSEVOLOD MEYERHOLD, and—despite her impatience with psychological REALISM—KONSTANTIN STANISLAVSKY.

The Théâtre du Soleil has operated as a collective since the start, with each member receiving the same salary. Although performers have come and gone over the years, Mnouchkine values member loyalty and refers to the company in terms of family. While season selections are decided collectively (with ample discussion to work through differences of opinion), Mnouchkine reputedly exercises her authority as necessary to hold the collec-

tive together. Actors join the company as young, enthusiastic amateurs, eager to push themselves to meet Mnouchkine's exacting standards. Mnouchkine describes her approach to rehearsal as a journey into the unknown, for which she provides initial ideas and images, not to prescribe an outcome but to stimulate the actors' thinking. She holds off casting roles right away but lets the actors take turns trading parts until the strongest casting matches emerge. Mnouchkine's directorial approach is exploratory, collaborative, and resistant to the pressures of rushed decisions. She emphasizes the importance of her own, and her actors', efforts at observation, seeing simple watching as the basis for developing the collective's knowledge of the material, mutual trust, informed response, and craft. Rehearsal periods range from six to eighteen months, culminating in a production run of one year.

Selected important productions include *The Kitchen* (*La Cuisine*), by ARNOLD WESKER (1967); *A Midsummer Night's Dream* (*Le Songe d'une Nuit d'Été*), by William Shakespeare (1968); *The Clowns* (*Les Clowns*), jointly created by the Théâtre du Soleil (1969); *1789*, jointly created by the Théâtre du Soleil (1970); *The Age of Gold* (*L'Age d'Or*), jointly created by the Théâtre du Soleil (1975); *Les Shakespeares* [*Richard II*, *Twelfth Night*, *Henry IV*, *Parts One and Two*] (1984); THE TERRIBLE BUT UNFINISHED HISTORY OF NORODOM SIHANOUK, KING OF CAMBODIA (*L'Histoire terrible mais inachevée de Norodom Sihanouk, roi du Cambodge*), by HÉLÈNE CIXOUS (1985); *The Indiade, or the India of Their Dreams* (*L'Indiade, ou l'Inde de leurs rêves*), also by Cixous (1987); *Les Atrides* [consisting of Euripides's *Iphigenia at Aulis* and Aeschylus's trilogy, *The Oresteia*] (1990–1992); and *The Forsworn City, or the Awakening of the Furies* (*La Ville Parjure, ou le réveil des erinyes*), by Cixous (1994).

FURTHER READING

Cohn, Ruby. "Ariane Mnouchkine: Playwright of a Collective." In *Feminine Focus: The New Women Playwrights*, ed. by Enoch Brater. Oxford: Oxford Univ. Press, 1989.

Kiernander, Adrian. *Ariane Mnouchkine and the Théâtre du Soleil.* Cambridge: Cambridge Univ. Press, 1993.

Théâtre du Soleil. http://www.theatre-du-soleil.fr/.

Williams, David. *Collaborative Theatre: The Théâtre du Soleil Sourcebook.* London: Routledge, 1999.

Kristin Johnsen-Neshati

THE MOCK PARLIAMENTS

The Mock Parliaments are a form of political agit-prop (AGITATION-PROPAGANDA) that flourished in CANADA between the early 1890s and 1916, amid campaigns for women's enfranchisement. These plays were put on to raise the profile of suffrage, supply its coffers, and expand public support. To this end, productions were coordinated with petitions to the legislature and provided forums for discussion, lobbying, pamphlet distribution, and signature collection. They were advertised in local papers, covered by reviews, attended by illustrious audiences, and staged in some of Canada's grandest theatrical houses.

Similar plays were produced in America and Britain, like Sophie Louise Wepf Clark's *Entertainment to Make Votes for Women* (1910) and Alison Garland's *The Better Half* (1913). But these were authored by individual playwrights. The Canadian Mock Parliaments were collective creations. They were written and performed by the suffrage movements' most active organizations and most famous proponents, like Nellie McClung, Amelia Yeomans, Cora Hind, Emily Howard Stowe, August Stowe-Gullen, and Lillian Beynon Thomas. There were at least nine discreet plays and thirteen different performances—four in Manitoba, seven in Ontario, and two in British Columbia. The first of these was staged at the Bijou Theatre in Winnipeg on February 9, 1893, by the Women's Christian Temperance Union (WCTU), which was either directly or indirectly involved in most productions. The February 18, 1896, Toronto Mock Parliament was put on by the WCTU and the Dominion Women's Enfranchisement Association. It took place at the Pavillion in Allen Gardens and almost filled the 1,800-seat theater. Canadian historians often mention the 1914 Mock Parliament, especially as it starred Nellie McClung as Premier Roblin of Manitoba. It was produced by the recently formed Winnipeg Political Equality League, filled the large Walker Theatre, and generated enough money to finance the remainder of the provincial suffrage campaign.

The Mock Parliaments are a parodic *canovaccio* (a vague plot outline which is filled in by the various different groups and performers who put it on and common in commedia dell'arte). Their stages imitate a real, historical parliament. The structure of the plays is determined by the routine proceedings of parliament through which the action of the play proceeds. Their central parodic feature is the reversal of roles between men and women. In them, the sex roles of electoral politicians are reversed: we are to imagine that women are in power and have been since the beginning of time. Men are disenfranchised and appear before them to plead for the vote. Typically, the plays are divided into two parts: the first part comprises motions, petitions, orders of the day, and question period and satirizes issues that dominate this first period of women's activism, such as dress reform, temperance, Sunday observance, equal access to the professions, the right to own property and the right to homestead. The second half of the play involves a lengthy debate on the most important of these issues, suffrage. In the only extant version of the debate, the reversal of roles that regulates the action in the first half of the play is suspended. Although heavily weighted in favor of the women suffrage supporters, their arguments fail to convince. The vote is lost, and as it was historically, the fight for political equality continued.

FURTHER READING
Bacchi, Carol Lee. *Liberation Deferred? The Ideas of the English-Canadian Suffragists, 1877–1918.* Toronto: Univ. of Toronto Press, 1983.

Bird, Kym. "Performing Politics: Propaganda, Parody and a Woman's Parliament." *Redressing the Past: The Politics of English-Canadian Women's Drama, 1880–1920.* Montreal: McGill-Queen's Univ. Press, 2003.

Cleverdon, Catherine L. *The Woman Suffrage Movement in Canada.* 2d ed. Toronto: Univ. of Toronto Press, 1974.

Friedl, Bettina, ed. *On to Victory: Propaganda Plays of the Woman Suffrage Movement.* Boston: Northeastern Univ. Press, 1987.

Hirshfield, Claire. "The Suffragist as Playwright in Edwardian England." *Frontiers* 9, no. 2 (1987): 2–6.

McClung, Nellie L. *Purple Springs.* Toronto: Thomas Allen, 1921.

———. *The Stream Runs Fast: My Own Story.* Toronto: Thomas Allen, 1945.

Prentice, Alison, et al. *Canadian Women: A History.* Toronto: Harcourt, 1988.

Kym Bird

MODERNIST DRAMA

When the actors are there they are there and they are there right away.
—Gertrude Stein, "Plays," 1949

Modernist drama should be kept distinct from its cognate, the modern drama or the "New Drama," as it was formerly called, which refers more broadly to drama often associated with the PROBLEM PLAYS of HENRIK IBSEN and GEORGE BERNARD SHAW. Since the term *modern drama* has been so widely used, critics and scholars have often shied away from speaking of a modernist drama, even though modernism is a well-established, if contested, category when it comes to other literary genres such as poetry or the novel. Modernist drama is a drama that subscribes to a set of aesthetic and cultural values prevalent in the late 19th and early 20th centuries. These include an insistence on difficult art works, which distinguishes modernist art from popular, folk, or commercial art; an insistence on the autonomy of art, art's separation from useful or utilitarian endeavors; and a search for new artistic forms.

Taking as a point of departure the category of modernism as it has been used in literary history, one might define those dramas as modernist that were written by writers whose work in other literary genres established them firmly within the modernist canon. T. S. ELIOT, for example, who was central to shaping the concept of modernism, wrote a number of plays, such as MURDER IN THE CATHEDRAL (1935) or *The Cocktail Party* (1950), even though they are less formally innovative than his modernist poems *The Wasteland* and *The Four Quartets* (1922). Other established modernists writing plays include James Joyce, whose only freestanding play, *Exiles* (1918), is less experimental than the dramatic "Circe" chapter in his modernist novel *Ulysses* (1922). Much more genuinely modernist were the plays written by the American poet and novelist GERTRUDE STEIN, who was living near Joyce in Paris. Her dozens of plays, collected in *Geography and Plays* (1922) and *Last Operas and Plays* (1949), violated dramatic form in that they did not follow traditional structure, often did not have characters, and were uninterested in scenic organization. Nevertheless, two of her plays, FOUR SAINTS IN THREE ACTS (1934) and *Mother of Us All* (1947), became the basis for two operas, with music by American composer Virgil Thomson. Many critics have detected sly references to homosexuality in Stein's plays, not unlike the drama of another modernist novelist and fellow Paris expatriate DJUNA BARNES, who is best known for her novel *Nightwood* (1936).

While these writers are not primarily known for their plays, which nevertheless are important texts for the modernist drama, a number of modernists left more lasting marks on dramatic history. The most significant writer in this category is W. B. YEATS. Even though Yeats is primarily known as a poet, he was one of the founding members of the Abbey Theatre in Dublin, which continues to be IRELAND's most important theater. Yeats's plays range from the symbolist *Shadowy Waters* (1906) and plays steeped in Irish mythology, such as the Cuchulain cycle, to contemporary FARCE. Yeats was also significant in his support of other, more political writers of the Irish drama movement such as J. M. SYNGE and SEAN O'CASEY.

While it is easier to classify as modernist plays written by writers who established themselves as modernist in other genres, it is more difficult to transpose the categories organizing modernism from poetry and the novel to drama and the theater. One of the most significant features of modernist literature was the determination to create difficult, experimental works that did not adhere to the conventions of realist art and did not cater to the taste of the audience. The first modernist group of playwrights who treated dramatic conventions and regular theater audiences with contempt were the symbolists: Stéphane Mallarmé, MAURICE MATERLINCK, HUGO VON HOFMANNSTHAL, and ALEKSANDR BLOK. The language of these playwrights is deliberately removed from everyday speech, infused with heightened rhetoric, elaborate images, metaphors, and a tendency toward abstraction, earning their plays the label of "metaphysical theater." Maeterlinck's *Pelleas and Melisande* (1892) takes place in a castle cut off from the rest of the world, and Mallarmé's *Afternoon of a Faun* (1876) is a difficult poetic text with minimal action. Both plays were set to music by Claude Debussy, for opera and ballet, respectively, and it is in these latter forms that they are still performed today.

In defiance of received conventions of drama is a second group of plays, namely philosophical plays, also known as the "drama of ideas." Shaw's philosophical plays, such as MAJOR BARBARA (1905) and MAN AND SUPERMAN (1903), the latter subtitled "A Comedy and a Philosophy," present a mixture of FRIEDRICH NIETZSCHE, Karl Marx, and Charles Darwin, as well as the brand of British socialism known as Fabianism. LUIGI PIRANDELLO's intellectual plays, by contrast, do not so much import existing theories and philosophies into drama as endlessly speculate about the relation between theater and life and

actors and nonactors. They are prime examples of modernist metatheater: theater about theater.

Equally adversarial with respect to the audience was expressionist drama, a movement most fully developed in GERMANY and the UNITED STATES. Expressionist plays are modernist not only because of their themes and their exalted and stylized language but also because they introduced new, episodic structures into the dramatic form. These plays proceeded in loosely connected episodes and scenes without regard for the unities of time, space, and action articulated by Aristotle, considered as ultimate authority for centuries. This disregard was anticipated by AUGUST STRINDBERG, whose A DREAM PLAY (1902) broke with realist and naturalist drama by trying to imitate the structure of dreams. Expressionist forms were continued in surrealist plays, for example, GUILLAUME APOLLINAIRE's THE BREASTS OF TIRESIAS (1918). Indeed, Apollinaire coined the term SURREALISM in his preface to this play. Other playwrights, such as the Polish writer STANISŁAW IGNACY WITKIEWITZ, worked along similar lines without officially belonging to any of these movements.

The significance of expressionist theater lies in the way it responded to modern, industrialized society. The plays of ERNST TOLLER, GEORG KAISER, OSKAR KOKOSCHKA, and REINHARD SORGE present the collision between the individual and early-20th-century masses. Solitary protagonists cannot find their proper place; they are caught in Oedipal struggles with their fathers, with religion, and with modern, industrial society more broadly. In EUGENE O'NEILL's THE HAIRY APE (1922), a worker on a steamship finds himself an outsider everywhere and ends up dying in the arms of a gorilla, whom he had mistaken as his only soul mate. SOPHIE TREADWELL's MACHINAL (1928) likewise responds to the alienation brought about by modern, industrial society, as does ELMER RICE's THE ADDING MACHINE (1923), in which a long-term employee is fired when new and more efficient adding machines are introduced.

Repetitive movements performed on assembly belts changed the way in which the early 20th century conceived of human actions and thus also of acting. The Russian VSEVELOD MEYERHOLD invented a training and performance system called "biomechanics," which was considered an aesthetic response to Taylorism, the system of economizing movements instituted by F. W. Taylor. Similarly interested in mechanized movements was the theater of Italian FUTURISM as well as the theater of the Bauhaus, the latter an institute primarily known for its invention of modernist architecture but whose theatrical activities were significant as well.

The modernist assault on the human actor, the search for a nonhuman theater, also led to a resurgence of marionette and puppet theater. The British director and theorist Edward Gordon Craig polemically called for an "Über-Marionette" to take the place of actors, and a significant number of modernist dramatists, including Maeterlinck, ALFRED JARRY, and FEDERICO

GARCÍA LORCA wrote their most well known plays for marionettes, even though they are now mostly performed by human actors. Others, such as O'Neill and Yeats, recommended that actors should imitate the movements of marionettes.

What fueled these experiments in the theater was the impact of various new media, such as the gramophone and film. Many modernist playwrights and directors, such as JEAN COCTEAU, ANTONIN ARTAUD, SAMUEL BECKETT, and ERWIN PISCATOR, combined film and theater. The most lasting influence on modernist drama, however, was a student of Piscator's, BERTOLT BRECHT, whose work spans from the EXPRESSIONISM of *In the Jungle of the Cities* (1923) to the politically explicit THE MEASURE TAKEN (1930). Brecht managed to gather the various strands of modernist drama and theater—episodic plots, a new conception of acting, the juxtaposition of music and dialogue—and turn them into an entirely new conception of theater.

Modernist drama continues in the work of Beckett, who took many modernist techniques, particularly the critique of the actor and the impact of the media, and turned them into minimalist plays with little action and plot. They also point toward the Theater of the Absurd, the inheritor of modernist drama around midcentury, which continues to influence contemporary playwrights such as HAROLD PINTER.

FURTHER READING

McGuinness, Patrick. *Maurice Maeterlinck and the Making of Modern Drama.* Oxford: Oxford Univ. Press, 2000.

Puchner, Martin. *Stage Fright: Modernism, Anti-theatricality, and Drama.* Baltimore: Johns Hopkins Univ. Press, 2002.

Szondi, Peter. *Theory of the Modern Drama.* Tr. by Michael Hayes. Minneapolis: Univ. of Minnesota Press, 1987.

Williams, Raymond. *Modern Drama from Ibsen to Brecht.* Oxford: Oxford Univ. Press, 1968.

Martin Puchner

MOLNÁR, FERENC (1878–1952)

Ferenc Molnár was born on January 12, 1878, in Budapest, HUNGARY. The most internationally renowned and widely performed Hungarian playwright of the 20th century, Molnár is best known for his many romantic COMEDIES characterized by sophisticated, witty dialogue and expert dramatic construction. He was a master of artifice and surprise. Between 1908 and 1940, sixteen of his plays were produced on Broadway. Richard Rodgers and Oscar Hammerstein's musical *Carousel* is based on his *Liliom* (1909), and several Molnár plays were turned into Hollywood films.

Molnár's emergence as a playwright is inseparable from the growth of his native Budapest into a great fin de siècle metropolis, with an exploding population. Its rapidly expanding middle class demanded a native culture reflecting its newfound cosmopolitanism, and no one was better able to satisfy that demand on the stage than Molnár. Foreign audiences were drawn to the local color of his Hungarian settings, characters, and their temperaments. Molnár's rise to world renown was virtually instantaneous. His first two plays, written in 1902 and 1904, were domestic successes; his third, the comedy *The Devil* (Az ördög, 1907), brought him international celebrity. It contains much of Molnár in a nutshell: the love triangle, the Freudian undertones, and the outlandish idea made to seem perfectly plausible—in this case the appearance onstage of the supernatural title character, whose machinations reveal the sexual impulses lurking behind social decorum. Here, as in general, Molnár subjects his characters to pitfalls that threaten but in the end do not seriously damage their bourgeois morality. Thus he provided his target audiences with just the right amount of titillation.

Variations on his formula can be found in plays such as *The Guardsman* (A testőr, 1910), in which a jealous actor in disguise attempts to seduce his own wife, and *The Play's the Thing* (Játék a Kastélyban, 1926). These plays also evince a favorite subject of Molnár, the psychological advantage of a woman over a jealous man, and feature a frequent Molnár character type: the actor-actress. As a profession, ACTING necessarily depends on dissembling, a skill that can be carried over into "real life." In *The Play's the Thing*, an amorous encounter involving an actress is overheard by her fiancé and a famous playwright, who then writes a play that incorporates the offending scene, thus turning the betrayal into an innocent "rehearsal." This facility of Molnár to manipulate illusion and reality has invited comparisons with LUIGI PIRANDELLO, while OSCAR WILDE and Sigmund Freud are also cited as influences. But literary-minded critics have not always been kind to Molnár, accusing him of a superficiality and sentimentality that thwart social criticism or questions of human destiny. Molnár's *Liliom* comes closest to countering such views. This lower-class love story is an effective blending of REALISM and the supernatural. Its complex hero, a tough with a tender heart, demonstrates the paradoxes of human nature, and his fate is a critique of social injustice.

As Adolf Hitler's clouds were gathering over Europe, Molnár moved to New York City in 1940, where he lived as a celebrated though increasingly isolated and unhappy writer. His life's work includes nearly thirty plays, fiction, essays, memoirs, and reportage. He died on April 2, 1952, in New York City.

SELECT PLAYS: *The Devil* (Az ördög, 1907); *Liliom* (1909); *The Guardsman* (A testőr, 1910); *The Wolf,* a.k.a. *The Phantom Lover* (A farkas, 1912); *The Swan* (A hattyú, 1920); *The Violet* (Az ibolya, 1921); *The Red Mill,* a.k.a. *Mima* (A vörös malom, 1923); *The Glass Slipper* (Az üvegcipö, 1924); *The Play's the Thing* (Játék a kastélyban, 1926); *Olympia* (1928); *One, Two, Three* (Egy, kettö, három, 1929)

FURTHER READING

Czigány, Lóránt. *The Oxford History of Hungarian Literature.* Oxford: Oxford Univ. Press, 1984.

Gergely, Ermo Joseph. *Hungarian Drama in New York.* Philadelphia: Univ. of Pennsylvania Press 1947.

Györgyey, Clara. *Ferenc Molnár*. Boston: Twayne, 1980.

Sárközi, Mátyás. *The Play's the Thing: The Life of Ferenc Molnár*. London: White Raven Press, 2004.

Eugene Brogyányi

MONDRAGÓN AGUIRRE, MAGDALENA (1913–1988)

Magdalena Mondragón was part of the first wave of feminist playwrights to emerge in 20th-century MEXICO. She was born on July 14, 1913, shortly after the start of the Mexican Revolution (1910–1920), in Torreón, Coahuila, Mexico. At the time Mondragón began writing, her country was striving to redefine its national identity. Before establishing herself as a novelist, poet, and playwright, Mondragón wrote for periodicals and eventually became the first female editor of a daily newspaper in Mexico.

Mondragón's theatrical debut, *When Eve Becomes Adam* (*Cuando Eva se vuelve Adán*, 1938) was a great success and was eventually made into a film. It is a realistic and melodramatic piece about a female doctor whose career ambitions lead to a failed marriage.

Though this first play conforms somewhat to social and theatrical norms, Mondragón's subsequent works break from domestic REALISM and reveal the author's feminist outlook. This is evident in plays like *The Siren Who Carried the Sea* (*La sirena que llevaba el mar*, 1945) and *The Lost World* (*El mundo perdido*, 1946). The former dramatizes a woman's desire to leave her husband in order to go live among liberated mermaids, and the latter offers a retelling of Genesis. In *The Lost World*, Adam convinces Eve not eat the apple, only to realize that living forever in Paradise is not all he had hoped. After 2,000 years of boredom, Adam is forced to admit his mistake and apologize to Eve. Both *The Siren Who Carried the Sea* and *The Lost World* draw from Aztec and Christian legends, mixing together two of modern Mexico's major cultural influences.

A later piece, *Because I Feel Like It* (*Porque me da la gana*, 1953), features an aging female snake charmer who decides to have a facelift against her husband's wishes. Only later does she realize that her newly revamped appearance is physically and emotionally stifling to herself and those around her.

PLAYS: *When Eve Becomes Adam* (*Cuando Eva se vuelve Adán*, 1938); *A Boat in the Sea* (*Un barco en el mar*, 1939); *Room for Rent* (*Se alquila cuarto*, 1939); *We Shouldn't Die* (*No debemos morir*, 1944); *The Siren Who Carried the Sea* (*La sirena que llevaba el mar*, 1945); *Whirlwind* (*Torbellino*, 1945); *The Lost World* (*El mundo perdido*, 1946); *Because I Feel Like It* (*Porque me da la gana*, 1953); *The Clash of the Just* (*Choque de los justos*, 1964)

FURTHER READING

"Datos biográficos y críticos sobre la obra de Magdalena Mondragón" [Biographical data and criticism of the work of Magdalena Mondragón]. Introduction to *Dos obras de teatro* [Two theater works], by Magdalena Mondragón. [D.F.]: Grupo América, 1951. 5–9.

Dauster, Frank. "Raising the Curtain: Great Ladies of the Theatre." In *Performance, páthos, política* [Sexes—Performance, pathos, policy of the sexes], ed. by Heidrun Adler and Kati Röttger. Madrid: Iberoamericana, 1999. 23–40.

Del Río, Marcela, ed. Introduction to *Porque me de la gana* [Because I feel like it], by Magdalena Mondragón. New York: Odyssey Press, 1968. vii–xvii.

———. "Especificidad y reconocimiento del discurso dramático femenino en el teatro latinoamericano" [Specificity and recognition of feminine dramatic discourse in Latin American theater]. In *Performance, páthos, política* [Sexes—Performance, pathos, policy of the sexes], ed. by Heidrun Adler and Kati Röttger. Madrid: Iberoamericana, 1999. 41–53.

May Summer Farnsworth

MONODRAMA

A monodrama is a dramatic work written for one actor; by extension it is a work for the theater in which all the characters can be regarded as projections of a single consciousness. As a modern form, the monodrama was created by Jean-Jacques Rousseau with his one-act *Pygmalion* (1771), which combined declamation and pantomime with music. Eighteenth-century musical monodramas were chiefly lamentations by heroines of classical mythology, designed for virtuoso solo performance by talented amateurs. Johann Wolfgang Goethe introduced the genre in Weimar, writing the monodrama *Proserpina* in 1778.

In the 19th century, dramatic monodrama evolved as a psychological form. In GERMANY Richard von Meerheimb published a collection titled *Monodramas of New Form* (*Monodramen neuer Form*, 1882), subtitled *Psycho-Monodramas* (*Psycho-Monodramen*). Scenery and props, like unseen secondary characters, were imaginary. Belgian author Edmond Picard wrote a monodrama titled *Sworn* (*Le Juré*, 1887), accompanied by a theoretical "Lettre sur le monodrame." (letter on the monodrama).

The fin de siècle period invited introspection. William James's stream-of-consciousness, interior monologue in the novel, Henri Bergson's concept of *la durée* (duration), and Sigmund Freud's theory of the unconscious all testify to the period's fascination with subjectivity, which gave rise to monodrame.

French symbolist poets embraced the monodramatic by abandoning the trappings of surface reality for a deeper penetration into the psyche. Calling William Shakespeare the creator of a "theater of the mind alone" and a "drama of the self," Stéphane Mallarmé treats *Hamlet* as a monodrama in which all the secondary characters are emanations of the hero's consciousness.

Rachilde (pen name of Marguerite Vallette-Eymery) created the "cerebral drama" *Madame Death* (*Madame la Mort*, 1891), the second act of which takes place within the brain of a dying man;

and poet Saint-Pol-Roux wrote the monodramatic *Epilogue of the Human Seasons* (*Epilogue des saisons humaines*, 1893) in which all the characters are projections of the psyche of the dying Prince (anticipating by sixty years EUGÈNE IONESCO's *Exit the King*). In Saint-Pol-Roux's *Characters of the Individual* (*Les Personnages de l'individu*, 1893), subtitled "Monodrame," an old man and a young man meet on a bridge over a rushing stream and discuss their lives, only to discover they are the same person at different times. GERHART HAUPTMANN's *Hannele's Journey to Heaven* (1893), AUGUST STRINDBERG's *A DREAM PLAY* (1902) and *To Damascus* (1908), MAURICE MAETERLINCK's *Blue Bird* (1908), and LEONID ANDREEV's *Black Masks* (1908) can all be considered monodramas in part or in whole.

Two leading Russian playwrights of the symbolist period—Fyodor Sologub and NIKOLAI EVREINOV—wrote important theoretical statements about the monodramatic mode. Although he does not use the term, in *The Theatre of One Will* (1908), Sologub proposes a new drama dominated by the personality of the author, arguing, "There are no different people—there is only one single man, only one single Me in the entire universe" (Sologub, 1977). The many speaking roles are parts of a single self.

In his *Introduction to Monodrama* (1909), Evreinov argues that the future of theater lies in monodrama, which he defines as a dramatic performance that strives to convey to the spectator an inner state of mind. At any given moment the spectator should hear, see, and feel what the central character hears, sees, and feels. The task of the monodramatist is thus to turn the spectator into an "imagined" character within the play. In Evreinov's opinion, because the very appearance of the natural world varies according to the mood of the perceiver, the natural setting in monodrama must seem to change as the emotions of the central character change. To illustrate his theory, Evreinov wrote a number of plays in which setting, character, and action are all reflections of a single consciousness.

After SYMBOLISM, the Russian futurists took up monodrama. Velimir Khlebnikov wrote *Mrs. Lenin* (1913), in which all the characters are projections of the consciousness of the heroine; and in VLADIMIR MAYAKOVSKY's first play, *Vladimir Mayakovsky, A Tragedy* (performed in 1913), the characters of the chorus represent different aspects of the hero. Many German expressionist plays of the 1920s are monodramatic. In the 1950s and 1960s SAMUEL BECKETT, Ionesco, and other absurdists further explored and enlarged the genre.

For experimental playwrights, actors, and directors of the late twentieth and early twenty–first centuries monodrama continued to be an AVANT–GARDE theatrical concept that can be put to effective use in solo and in multi–media performance.

[*See also* Expressionism; Futurism; Psychoanalysis]

FURTHER READING

Culler, Dwight A. "Monodrama and the Dramatic Monologue." *PMLA* 90, no. 3 (May 1975): 365–385.

Dana, Joseph. *Le théâtre de la pensée* [The theater of thought]. Rouen: Editions medianes, 1995.

Evreinov, Nikolai. *Introduction to Monodrama* (1909). In *Russian Dramatic Theory from Pushkin to the Symbolists: An Anthology*, ed. by Lawrence Senelick. Austin: Univ. of Texas Press, 1981.

Holmstrom, Kristen Ann. *Monodrama, Attitudes, and Tableaux-Vivants*. Stockholm: Almqvist & Wiksell, 1967.

Senelick, Lawrence. "Moscow and Monodrama: The Meaning of the Craig-Stanislavsky Hamlet." *Theatre Research International* 6, no. 2 (Spring 1981): 109–123.

Sologub, Fyodor. "The Theater of One Will," tr. by Daniel Gerould. *The Drama Review* 21: 4 (T-76, Dec. 1977): 85–99.

Törnqvist, Egil. "Monodrama: Term and Reality." In *Essays in Drama and Theatre. Liber Amicorum Benjamin Hunningher*. Amsterdam: Standaard, 1973.

Daniel Gerould

MONSTROUS REGIMENT

In 1975 Gillian Hanna brought together a group of eleven female actors and musicians from across ENGLAND who were all frustrated with the lack of sizable roles for women and the poor representation of women and their issues on the British stage; they founded Monstrous Regiment, a socialist-feminist collective touring company, dedicated to the creation of new works. The name comes from a misogynist 1558 pamphlet, *The First Blast of the Trumpet Against the Monstrous Regiment of Women*, written by John Knox, a Scottish preacher, attacking both Elizabeth I and Mary Stuart. The company quickly became Britain's most prominent feminist company, touring the art-studio theater circuit. By company policy, female members must outnumber males, and the works they produce must place focus on and highlight women's experiences. In 1981 the company went exclusively female. Monstrous Regiment's first production was commissioned from Chris Bond and Claire Luckham; *Scum: Death, Destruction, and Dirty Washing* (1976) looked at the Paris Commune of 1871 through the eyes of its washerwomen. Other notable productions include CARYL CHURCHILL's *Vinegar Tom* (1976); women's cabarets *Floorshow* (1977) and Bryony Lavery's *Time Gentlemen Please* (1978); *Shakespeare's Sister* (1980), written and performed by Théâtre de l'Aquarium; and FRANCA RAME and DARIO FO's *The Fourth Wall* (1983). Monstrous Regiment also served as a stimulus to women's writing; workshops with the company led to Churchill's TOP GIRLS. After more than twenty-five productions, Monstrous Regiment ceased touring in 1993.

Monstrous Regiment explored several different theatrical forms including cabaret, collage, epic, musical, and performance pieces. Live music quickly became a standard part of their productions. Without a specific process or creative method, Monstrous Regiment's work style evolved according to who was working in the company at any given time, drawing on the available talents within the group. While the company mostly functioned as a collective, the degree of company collaboration and involvement varied according to the project and sometimes the playwright. One of the reasons the company moved into doing cabaret shows was because they had three talented musicians in the company including a composer.

Believing that the "personal is political," the members of Monstrous Regiment confronted sexual stereotypes and inequities first in their company and second on the stage. Committed to facilitating women's ability to be involved in theater, the company ensured that women with family obligations could work according to their availability and provided child care. Seeking to enhance script offerings for women, Monstrous Regiment always made their scripts publicly visible and available to others. In addition to having a feminist leaning, the company also had strong ties to the socialist movement largely because of the personal involvement of its members. When seeking new audiences, Monstrous Regiment made a connection with the trade union movement. At various times during the company's history, however, both the feminist and socialist agendas took a secondary role in their productions as the company struggled to find work of interest to its members.

[See also Political Theater]

FURTHER READING

Hanna, Gillian, ed. *Monstrous Regiment: Four Plays and a Collective Celebration.* London: Nick Hern Bks., 1991.

J. Briggs Cormier

MONTHERLANT, HENRY DE (1895–1972)

Henry-Marie-Joseph-Frédéric-Expedite Millon de Montherlant, playwright, novelist, critic, and public intellectual, would give, throughout his life, the false birthdate of April 21, 1896 (it was actually April 20, 1895), thus reducing his age and linking his birth to the supposed anniversary of the founding of Rome. Such biographical control for public purposes would mark all of his career, including its very end: at the age of seventy-seven, Montherlant would choose the autumnal equinox as the date on which to commit suicide.

Having made an initial reputation as a novelist and essayist, he turned to playwriting with historical dramas produced in Paris during the Occupation. His plays treated issues of spiritual renunciation in ways that could offend neither French citizens nor Nazi occupiers. (He himself wrote on both sides of the political fence and would be lightly sanctioned after the war for collaboration with the Nazis.) Eventually he achieved enough success to become the playwright-in-waiting to the Comédie Française. The refinement of his language was always, and still is, highly praised. During the 1950s, however, his costume dramas came to seem hollow next to the absurdist minimalism of EUGÈNE IONESCO, SAMUEL BECKETT, and ARTHUR ADAMOV.

He left two masterpieces in a neo-Racinian mode—both of them scripts he revised over the course of several decades. The first performed professionally in FRANCE was *Port-Royal* (1954). On a hot August 26 in 1664, the nuns of Port-Royal, the proud Jansenist convent accused of heresy and insubordination, await the verdict of church and court about their survival. The day stretches out in anxious discussion among the nuns—some advocating pragmatic collaboration, others principled martyrdom—until the arrival of the archbishop ends the tension by announcing the dissolution of the convent. The play ends when twelve nuns are selected for removal to another convent, a triage reminiscent of the rounding up of French Jews by Nazi administrators. The position of the convent resembles not only that of France under the Occupation but also Montherlant's own as an individual trying to lead a private life as a homosexual—a personal fact that he believed was the mark of his singular greatness—while sustaining a conventional public life under the gaze of government and society.

The second masterpiece is more overtly autobiographical. *The City Whose Prince Is a Child (La Ville dont le prince est un enfant,* published 1951) opens with Serge Souplier, a fourteen-year-old schoolboy in an all-male Catholic school, being reproached by the Abbot de Pradts, prefect of the school, for conducting a romantic liaison with an older schoolmate, André Sevrais. During the course of the Abbot's reproach to young Souplier, it becomes clear that the Abbot is in love with him—although the Abbot seems blind to his own sexual motivations. Later, after the two schoolmates are caught in a compromising situation, the Abbot decides to expel the older boy for the sake of public morals—but also in order to have young Souplier to himself. In the final act, the Abbot de Pradts and the older boy recreate the opening scene of the play, with the Abbot telling Sevrais that he is being expelled in order to protect young Souplier. But just after Sevrais leaves the Abbot's office, the College Superior enters and, in a superb theatrical stroke, makes the Abbot take the seat previously held by the expelled boy. The Superior then proceeds to reproach the Abbot for being dominated by the same passions as the two schoolboys. The Superior has decided to expel young Souplier in addition to the older Sevrais in order to save the Abbot from his passions—and the Superior also reveals that he, himself, earlier in his career, struggled to overcome his own love for boys. The play ends with the moral and emotional devastation of de Pradts.

Montherlant is still cited as one of France's major 20th-century playwrights, but with little dramaturgical legacy. His critical reputation may yet be revived by queer theory. Posthumous publication of letters and journals revealed a lifetime of pederasty and the hollowness of his claims to prowess on the athletic field, the battlefield, and in the bull ring. He is now viewed as a writer who struggled to reconcile a hidden sexual self with a public role as arbiter of taste and who comes closest to greatness in neoclassical works focusing on the moral power inherent in marginalized solitude. Montherlant died in Paris on September 21, 1972.

PLAYS: *The Exile* (*L'Exil*, written 1914, published 1929, never performed); *Pasiphaé* (written 1928, first performed 1938); *The Dead Queen* (*La Reine morte*, 1942); *Nobody's Son* (*Fils de personne*, 1943); *Malatesta* (published 1946, first performed 1950); *The Master of Santiago* (*Le Maître de Santiago*, 1948); *Daybreak Tomorrow* (*Demain il fera jour*, 1949); *The Ones in Your Arms* (*Celles qu'on prend dans ses bras*, 1950); *The City Whose Prince Is a Child* (*La Ville dont le prince est un enfant*, begun about 1914, published 1951, early amateur performance 1953; first professional performance in English 1953; first professional performance in French in 1967); *Port-Royal* (begun in the early 1940s, first performed 1954); *Brocéliande* (1956); *Don Juan* (1958); *The Cardinal of Spain* (*Le Cardinal d'Espagne*, 1960); *The Civil War* (*La Guerre civile*, 1965)

FURTHER READING
Guicharnaud, Jacques, with June Guicharnaud. *Modern French Theatre from Giraudoux to Genet.* Rev. ed. New Haven, Conn.: Yale Univ. Press, 1967.

Johnson, Robert B. *Henry de Montherlant.* New York: Twayne, 1968.

Sipriot, Pierre. *Montherlant sans masque* [Montherlant without mask]. Paris: Robert Laffont, 1990.

David Pelizzari

A MONTH IN THE COUNTRY

A Month in the Country (*Mesyats v derevnye*) is a COMEDY in five acts by Ivan Turgenev (1818–1883). It was composed in 1854 and published in 1855, but not performed until 1872 because of censorship difficulties. The action is set during the summer of the early 1840s on the country estate owned by Arkady Islayev and his wife, Natalya, who have a ten-year-old son, Kolya. The action revolves around a complex set of relationships involving a family friend and constant visitor to the estate, Rakitin; Kolya's new tutor, Belyayev, who has just taken up his post; and Natalya's seventeen-year-old ward, Verochka. There are subsidiary relationships that echo or mirror the main ones—between a local neighbor Bolshintsov and Verochka, and between the family doctor Shpigelsky and Islayev's mother's companion, Lizaveta Bogdanovna.

The play's running metaphor is of a hothouse for rare plants, where the rarified conditions make the plants susceptible to disease unless carefully protected. Unfortunately, by the time the play opens, a bacillus has entered the hothouse and infected just about everyone, in the shape of the twenty-one-year-old tutor. The door of the hothouse has been opened to admit the "breath of fresh air" that Natalya yearns for, but she did not reckon with the infection of love that the arrival of the energetic young man brings with him, although she is eight years his senior and married (to a man seven years older than herself). Natalya is already the object of the rather wan attentions paid her by the family friend, Rakitin, that pose no threat to the marriage, which is perhaps why Islayev is content to leave them alone together whil he attends to the estate. The fact that he is busy building a dam in the background constitutes another ironic metaphor: the blocking of pent-up feeling.

Belyayev, who is a rather naïve and uncomplicated youth, does not realize the effect he has produced in Natalya, nor does he realize that he is inspiring similar feelings in the adolescent Verochka. The more mature and hitherto bored Natalya, realizing that her ward poses a potential threat, unscrupulously engineers an unsuitable marriage for the young girl with their middle-aged landowning neighbor, Bolshintsov. She also contrives an interview with the unsuspecting Belyayev, during which she makes him aware of her feelings, with consequences that produce precisely what she does not want, namely, his decision to give up his post as tutor and leave, much to the relief of Rakitin. Ironically, the only successful union that the play contemplates at the end is the rather cynical one contrived by the doctor with the mother's companion, as life on the estate reverts to its usual overheated, but stable, condition.

Another analogy that may be said to characterize the action of the play derives from chemistry, whereby a chemical agent (Belyayev) is introduced into a substance in a steady state (the estate) and produces a violent reaction before subsiding. In the detached manner of a chemist, Turgenev merely observes and records the process, in the manner of his friend Gustave Flaubert or ÉMILE ZOLA. His career as a playwright was short-lived and, following the ban placed on *A Month in the Country*, he turned his attention to the novel.

[*See also* Russia and the Soviet Union]

FURTHER READING
Smyrniw, Walter. *Turgenev's Early Works: From Character Sketches to a Novel.* Oakville, ON: Mosaic Press, 1980.

Turgenev, Ivan. *Three Plays.* Tr. by Constance Garnett. London: Cassell & Co., 1934.

——. *Plays.* Tr. by M. S. Mandell, with an Introduction by William Lyon Phelps. Reissue of 1924 edition. New York: Russell & Russell, 1970.

——. *A Month in the Country.* Tr. and Introduced by Isaiah Berlin. London: The Hogarth Press, 1981.

——. *A Month in the Country.* Tr. and ed. by Richard Freeborn. Oxford: Oxford Univ. Press, 1991.

Worrall, Nick. *Nikolai Gogol and Ivan Turgenev.* London: Macmillan, 1982.

Nick Worrall

MOODY, WILLIAM VAUGHN (1869–1910)

Poet and playwright William Vaughn Moody was born on July 8, 1869, in Spencer, Indiana, the son of a riverboat captain who steamed on the Ohio River. His mother was a great lover of arts and literature, and it was soon after her untimely death that Moody began to write poetry. Valedictorian of his high school class, he delivered a speech titled "The Evolution of History" at graduation. After working as a tutor and proctor while studying at Riverview Academy in Poughkeepsie, New York, Moody won a scholarship to Harvard in 1889.

In college, Moody was elected to the board of several literary magazines and won the attention of prominent intellectuals and writers like faculty member George Santayana. After earning a master's degree, Moody taught at Harvard, Radcliffe, and the University of Chicago. His passion for academic life was short-lived, however, and after spending some time editing classical texts, he began to focus more on creative writing. Buoyed by the success of his early poems, which appeared in periodicals such as the *Atlantic Monthly*, Moody devoted himself to writing full-time around 1901.

Moody's first published book was the verse drama *The Masque of Judgement* (1900); in the following year, he published a volume of poems. His next publications included a series of English textbooks, book reviews, verse dramas, and editions of writers such as John Bunyan, Samuel Taylor Coleridge, John Milton, and Homer. Positive reviews encouraged Moody to continue, and he soon began to write dramatic works for the stage.

In 1906, *The Sabine Woman* was produced at the Garrick Theatre in Chicago, then opening at the Princess Theatre in New York with the new title THE GREAT DIVIDE. Telling the story of a woman torn between the formal traditions of her upbringing and the wild passion engendered by her frontier husband, the piece was immediately hailed as a success and a significant contribution to American drama. His next play, *The Faith Healer* (1909), was not as popular with audiences but enjoyed critical acclaim. Moody died on October 17, 1910, in Colorado Springs, Colorado.

Moody's work bridges the stylistic gap between the high romantic lyricism popular in the late 19th century and the Darwinian pragmatics of emerging modernism. His lyrical style reveals a keen sensitivity and intelligence, and his adherence to traditional forms of meter, diction, and syntax reflects his classical education. His plays combine mythic SYMBOLISM with realistic detail in the investigation of contemporary problems. The profound moral and metaphysical questions raised by *The Great Divide* illustrate Moody's engagement in pertinent questions of the day, such as women's rights and the wages of western expansion. Critics speculate that had he not died of a brain tumor in 1910, his work as a dramatist would have rivaled that of EUGENE O'NEILL.

[*See also* United States, 1860–1929]

PLAYS: *The Masque of Judgement: A Masque-Drama in Five Acts and a Prelude* (1900); *The Fire-Bringer* (1905); *The Faith Healer: A Play in Four Acts* (1909); *The Great Divide: A Play in Three Acts* (1909)

FURTHER READING

Brown, Maurice F. *Estranging Dawn: The Life and Works of William Vaughn Moody*. Carbondale: Southern Illinois Univ. Press, 1973.

Hall, Roger A. *Performing the American Frontier, 1870–1906*. Cambridge: Cambridge Univ. Press, 2001.

Halpern, Martin. *William Vaughn Moody*. New York: Twayne, 1964.

Henry, David Dodds. *William Vaughn Moody, a Study*. New York: Folcroft, 1973.

Mason, Daniel Gregory, ed. *Some Letters of William Vaughn Moody*. New York: Houghton Mifflin, 1913.

Quinn, Arthur Hobson. *A History of the American Drama from the Civil War to the Present Day*. New York: F. S. Crofts, 1936.

Leah R. Shafer

A MOON FOR THE MISBEGOTTEN

[A]dawn that won't creep over dirty windowpanes but will wake in the sky like a promise of God's peace in the soul's dark sadness.
—Josie, Act 3

The THEATRE GUILD production of EUGENE O'NEILL's *A Moon for the Misbegotten* closed out of town in 1947; the New York premiere opened on May 2, 1957, with Wendy Hiller as Josie, Franchot Tone as Tyrone, and Cyril Cusack as Phil. After directing revivals in Spoleto, ITALY (1958), and Buffalo, New York (1965), José Quintero staged the 1973 New York production, with Colleen Dewhurst and Jason Robards, that established the play as a landmark. The 1984 Broadway revival featured Kate Nelligan as Josie.

O'Neill's final essay on his family draws the character of Tyrone after Jamie, O'Neill's older brother, as well as his fictional version in LONG DAY'S JOURNEY INTO NIGHT, and the action explores the pain he endured after the death of his mother and his guilt-ridden return to alcoholism. The play adheres to the classical unities of time, place, and action, and it combines comic mischief with the weary resignation of THE ICEMAN COMETH.

The heart of the play is the long night that Josie Hogan passes with James Tyrone. She is the ultimate O'Neill woman—virgin, whore, and mother—so tall and strong that "she is almost a freak." In spite of her show of cynicism, she loves Tyrone, who is "soft and soggy from dissipation," but still with "the ghost of a former youthful, irresponsible Irish charm." He is haunted, turning to drink and Broadway tarts in hopes of dulling the agony of his past, and he goes to Josie in search of solace and an alternative to the deceit that has dominated his life.

Tyrone owns the Hogan farm, so Phil and Josie have cultivated a mischievous relationship with their unlikely landlord. When Josie first greets Tyrone, she observes that he looks so well that he must have stopped at the inn for a morning drink; he addresses her as "the Virgin Queen of Ireland"; and she replies, "[D]on't be miscalling me a virgin. You'll ruin my reputation." The three of them conspire against Harder, a rich, coddled, perpetual undergraduate whom Josie insults openly. Phil returns late that evening from a drinking spree to tell Josie that Tyrone has agreed to sell Harder their farm for three times its worth. Furious with the betrayal, she plans to seduce and compromise Tyrone, but she later learns that he made the deal as a joke just to annoy Harder.

Tyrone drinks to escape the torment of guilt over his mother's death, especially the long railroad journey back from California, when he spent every night with a "blonde pig" of a whore. Josie realizes that his fondest wish is to find forgiveness and peace in death and that her love cannot save him, so as he sleeps in her arms, she marvels, "[I]t's a fine end to all my scheming, to sit here with the dead hugged to my breast, and the silly mug of the moon grinning down, enjoying the joke!" Act 3 closes with O'Neill's Pietà: Josie as the forgiving mother cradling the body of her suffering son. In the end, Tyrone, absolved, walks away to wait for the release he desires.

John McClain praised O'Neill's ability to find poetry in the situation, but Anthony West argued that Tyrone's drunken train ride "can only anchor him in our minds as a grotesque or caricature" (Houchin, 1993). Richard Watts Jr. described the piece as another of "O'Neill's dark and brooding contemplations of our tormented souls [and] a moving, beautiful and shattering play" (Miller, 1973).

[*See also* United States, 1940–Present]

FURTHER READING

Ardolino, Frank. "Irish Myth and Legends in *Long Day's Journey Into Night* and *A Moon for the Misbegotten*." *Eugene O'Neill Review* 22 (Spring–Fall 1998): 63–69.

Garvey, Sheila Hickey. "New Myths for Old: A Production History of the 2000 Broadway Revival of *A Moon for the Misbegotten*." *Eugene O'Neill Review* 24 (Spring–Fall 2000): 121–133.

Hinden, Michael. "O'Neill and Jamie: A Survivor's Tale." *Comparative Drama* 35 (2001–2002): 435–445.

Houchin, John H., ed. *The Critical Response to Eugene O'Neill.* Westport, Conn.: Greenwood Press, 1993.

Manheim, Michael. "O'Neill's Transcendence of Melodrama in *A Touch of the Poet* and *A Moon for the Misbegotten*." *Comparative Drama* 16 (Fall 1982): 238–250.

Miller, Jorden Y. *Eugene O'Neill and American Critic.* Hamden, Conn.: Archon Books, 1973.

Jeffrey D. Mason

MORETT, MARÍA (1964–)

I believe that theater can transform society by functioning as a mirror that not only reflects a particular problem but also allows each audience member to recognize herself in that reflection, in such a way that she becomes filled with questions and energized by the desire to broaden the horizons of her day-to-day world.

—María Morett

María Morett is a playwright, director, actress, and producer. She was born on June 18, 1964, and has lived all her life in Mexico City. Her plays have been performed throughout MEXICO and other Latin American countries, as well as in the UNITED STATES and Europe. She studied playwriting with Hugo Argüelles, OSVALDO DRAGÚN, JOSÉ SANCHIZ SINISTERRA, MIGDALIA CRUZ, and MARÍA IRENE FORNÉS; acting at the Núcleo de Estudios Teatrales with Julio Castillo, Luis de Tavira, Ludwik Margules, and Juan José Gurrola; scene and lighting design with Alejandro Luna; and theater pedagogy with Luis de Tavira at Mexico City's Casa del Teatro.

In 1992, Morett co-founded, with Alvaro Hegewisch, the group ME XIHC CO TEATRO, a company devoted primarily to the creation of site-specific theater. With Me xihc co, she has written and produced *The Weeping Woman* (La Llorona, 1991), *Mozart and the Elves* (Mozart y los duendes, 1994), *Death* (Muerte, 1995), *Alarconeando* (1998), *QUIJOTES: Wandering Visions* (QUIJOTES: Visiones itinerantes, 1998, also co-directed), *Crossings: Meeting of the Millennium* (Cruces: Encuentro de milenio, 1999, also co-directed), *Women in Confinement* (Mujeres en el encierro, 2001, also directed) and *More Labyrinths* (Más laberintos, 2003, also directed).

Women in Confinement, the play for which Morett has received the greatest acclaim, both in Mexico and the United States, was inspired by her experience conducting theater workshops from 1993 to 1997 in the women's prisons of Mexico City and Colombia. Set within the physical confines of an actual prison, *Women in Confinement* explores the notion of female confinement as a labyrinth formed by social, cultural, and archetypal structures of repression. It focuses on the peculiar social contract of supervision that exists in these microcosms, set off from the society at large by prison walls and composed solely of women living "on the edge" who have established among themselves a unique system of behavioral norms and codes of honor. In so doing, they blatantly question the norms of the dominant society—a society that holds itself up as the model to which they must aspire in order to achieve the "miracle" of rehabilitation. The play also addresses, in particular, the condition of the Latin American woman who, in her family and workplace, confronts a complex web of social archetypes that shape her personal, romantic, and professional relationships.

Women in Confinement opened at the 2001 Festival Internacional Cervantino and was then produced at the Universidad Nacional Autónoma de México (UNAM) in Mexico City, completing a run of fifty sold-out performances in April 2002. Deborah Saivetz's English translation of this play was given a staged reading at New York's West End Theater in 2002 and is published in the journal *TheatreForum*. The play has also been translated into German by Cordelia Dvôrák.

Morett has been honored by and awarded grants from Fondo Nacional para la Cultura y las Artes (FONCA) and its "Young Creators" program; the U.S./Mexico Fund for Culture; Residencias Mexico—Colombia; Convocatoria Nacional de Teatro;

the New York International Fringe Festival; Voice & Vision; Arts International; and California's Sol Prize. She is founder and director of Proyecto Ariadna, an international network for the development of alternative art; Mexico's playwright delegate to the Generación Ñ Project of Spain's General Society of Authors and Editors; and a member of the Lincoln Center Theater Directors' Lab, New York's National Conference of Latino Artists (NALAC), and the International Theater School of LatinAmerica and the Caribbean (EITALC). She currently serves as theater consultant for Mexico's Centro Nacional de Artes (CENART).

PLAYS: *The Weeping Woman* (*La Llorona*, 1991); *Mozart and the Elves* (*Mozart y los duendes*, 1994); *Death* (*Muerte*, 1995); *Alarconeando* (1998); *QUIJOTES: Wandering Visions* (*QUIJOTES: Visiones itinerantes*, 1998); *Crossings: Meeting of the Millennium* (*Cruces: Encuentro de milenio*, 1999); *Women in Confinement* (*Mujeres en el encierro*, 2001); *More Labyrinths* (*Más laberintos*, 2003)

FURTHER READING

Barrera, Reyna. Reverend of *Mujeres en el encierro*, by María Morett. *Unomásuno* (February 16, 2002).

Morett, María. *Women in Confinement* (*Mujeres en el encierro*). Tr. by Deborah Saivetz. *TheatreForum* 23 (June 2003): 22–41.

Riveroll, Julieta. "Vuelve metáfora las prisiones" [Prisons become metaphor]. *Reforma* (October 19, 2001): C4.

Saivetz, Deborah. "The Theatrical Labyrinths of María Morett." Introduction to *Women in Confinement* (*Mujeres en el encierro*), by María Morett. Tr. by Deborah Saivetz. *TheatreForum* 23 (June 2003): 18–21.

Deborah Saivetz

MORIMOTO KAORU (1912–1946)

Morimoto Kaoru, Japanese SHINGEKI playwright, was regarded as the most promising young playwright to emerge during the war years. He began as a contributor to *Gekisaku* (*Playwriting*), a journal started by Kishida Kunio (1890–1954) in 1932 as an outlet for what he called "genuine" (meaning not political) Japanese playwrights. Morimoto's first critical success came with the Literary Theatre (Bungakuza), established in 1938 by Kishida and playwrights KUBOTA MANTARŌ (1889–1963) and Iwata Toyoo (1893–1969). Iwata saw real potential in Morimoto and brought him into the company. Their inaugural evening featured four plays, including Morimoto's *A Clever Girl* (*Migoto na Onna*, 1938). The critical reception of this and other Morimoto plays is instructive. Those convinced that theater should take a political approach found Morimoto and his ilk in the Literary Theatre insubstantial and unconnected with real events, while those in agreement with the apolitical approach espoused by Kishida, Kubota, and Iwata found Morimoto to be a truly fresh new talent. He is cited for his clear dialogue, pathos, and portrayal of original attitudes and feelings.

Kishida came to rely increasingly on Morimoto for more than playwriting skills. When, for example, the Literary Theatre attempted to stage Iizawa Tadasu's (1909–1994) *Battle of the Birds and Beasts* (*Chōjū Gassen*) in 1944, a COMEDY satirizing the war effort, government censors served notice that the play was unacceptable. So Kishida tapped the energetic Morimoto, rapidly becoming a leader of the company, to visit the Cabinet Information Office (Naikaku Jōhōkyoku) to plead their case. In fact, most observers regard Morimoto, with his quick grasp and total commitment to the company, as the key person who held the Literary Theatre together and allowed it to operate during the difficult war years. His efforts paid off; though he died young in 1946, the Literary Theatre flourished after the war and continues to this day.

Morimoto was perhaps inadvertently involved in the controversy surrounding Kishida and his position vis-à-vis the war. While Kishida was hardly a warmonger, he accepted a position during the war as head of a patriotic organization of writers. Morimoto, with plays that were not clearly antiwar or leftist, may also have been seen by some as tainted by association. In addition, his signature play, A WOMAN'S LIFE (1945), was in fact commissioned during the war by the Greater East Asia Congress, an arm of the Japanese military that saw benefit in mobilizing writers and sending them to conquered territories.

The play, about a woman who unselfishly serves the family that has adopted her and loyally endeavors to ensure its continued prosperity, resonated with the Japanese people, then in the final throes of a seemingly interminable and tragic war. It went on to become a huge success. Beyond the play's content, Morimoto particularly here and in *Angry Waves* (*Dotō*, 1944), his other notable success, achieved what his mentor Kishida had long sought as the ideal modern theater for JAPAN—lyrical, literary, spoken plays, shorn of the prevailing proletarian inclinations and creating illusion through symbols and images.

SELECT PLAYS: *A Clever Girl* (*Migoto na Onna*, 1938); *The Loyalist Report* (*Kinnō Todoke*, 1943); *Angry Waves* (*Dotō*, 1944); *Folding Fan* (*Ōgi*, 1944); *A Woman's Life* (*Onna no Isshō*, 1945); *A Splendid Family* (*Hanabanashiki Ichizoku*, 1950)

FURTHER READING

Ibaraki, Tadashi. *Nihon Shingeki Shōshi* [A short history of shingeki]. Tokyo: Miraisha, 1980.

Keene, Donald. *Dawn to the West: Japanese Literature in the Modern Era—Poetry, Drama, Criticism*. New York: Henry Holt, 1984.

Morimoto, Kaoru. *Morimoto Kaoru Gikyoku Zenshū* [Complete plays of Morimoto Kaoru]. Tokyo: Bokuyōsha, 1968.

Nihon Kindai Engeki-shi Kenkyūkai, ed. *Nijusseiki no Gikyoku I: Gendai Gikyoku no Tenkai* [Twentieth-century plays I: The world of modern Japanese plays]. Tokyo: Shakai Hyōronsha, 2002.

Powell, Brian. *Japan's Modern Theatre: A Century of Continuity and Change*. London: Japan Library, 2002.

Rimer, J. Thomas. *Toward a Modern Japanese Theatre: Kishida Kunio.* Princeton, N.J.: Princeton Univ. Press, 1974.

John K. Gillespie

MORI ŌGAI (1862–1922)

Mori Ōgai, Japanese novelist, playwright, translator, and critic, was one of the beacons for modernization in the arts of late-19th- and early-20th-century JAPAN. Born Mori Rintarō (Ōgai was a pen name) to a long line of medical doctors, Ōgai spent four years in GERMANY, from 1884 to 1888, studying medicine, frequenting the theater, and reading widely in literature and PHILOSOPHY. Besides maintaining a high-profile public career as a military doctor and bureaucrat (he was promoted to surgeon general of Japan in 1907), he also founded several literary magazines, including *Subaru* (The Pleiades, est. 1909), which published most of his original plays. He was also a frequent contributor to *Kabuki*, a theater magazine edited by his brother Miki Takeji.

Within months after returning to Japan in 1888, Ōgai took issue with the Society for Theatre Reform (Engeki Kairyōkai) by insisting on the need for "backstage poets" to create works of lasting literary value before any work was carried out to improve theater architecture or acting methods. During the 1890s his theater criticism was instrumental in introducing the best of contemporary Western theater to Japanese readers, long before it was possible to stage the plays. A great stylist, Ōgai's translations revolutionized Japan's modern fiction and drama. His translation of HENRIK IBSEN's JOHN GABRIEL BORKMAN, staged by OSANAI KAORU's Free Theatre (Jiyū Gekijō) in 1909, galvanized contemporary Japanese thought and theater. Playwright MAFUNE YUTAKA considered Ōgai's translations a "bible" for younger playwrights learning the craft; they spurred a vogue for one-act drama in the Taishō era (1912–1925).

Drama chiefly interested Ōgai as a medium in which to experiment in literary form and express ideas. A writer of mostly one-act plays, he is credited for creating a modern dramatic idiom; his plays trace the historical development of Japanese, from high classical, poetic diction (*The Jeweled Comb-Box and the Two Urashimas* [*Tamakushige Futari Urashima,* 1902]), through kyōgen (*Nichiren's Street Sermon* [*Nichiren Tsuji-seppō,* 1904]) and the puppet theater (*Purumula,* 1909), to modern colloquial dialogue in such plays as the semiautobiographical *Masks* (*Kamen,* 1909). Ōgai was also first to use modern Japanese in plays with a historical setting, such as *Shizuka* (1909) and *The River Ikuta* (*Ikutagawa,* 1910). Legend and history, rather than modern events, were the basis for most of his drama, which is often criticized for its lack of dramatic tension and expository tone; MAURICE MAETERLINCK, rather than HENRIK IBSEN, was his guide. As in his fiction, Ōgai's plays reflect his social concerns. A staunch member of the establishment in his public life, he was nonetheless a progressive on such issues as socialism, feminism, and the naturalist movement. His heroes and heroines are typically stoics who, in a spirit of defiant resignation, confront their fate: tuberculosis in *Masks,* a merciless ruler in *Shizuka,* and social convention in *The River Ikuta.* Though an advocate of Japan's modernization, he was no slavish imitator of Western ways but sought a middle ground on which Japanese traditions could speak on equal terms with the innovations of European drama.

[*See also* Naturalism; Nō and Kyōgen; Shingeki]

PLAYS: *The Jeweled Comb-Box and the Two Urashimas* (*Tamakushige Futari Urashima,* 1902); *Nichiren's Street Sermon* (*Nichiren Tsuji-seppō,* 1904); *Masks* (*Kamen,* 1909); *Purumula* (1909); *Shizuka* (1909); *The River Ikuta* (*Ikutagawa,* 1910)

FURTHER READING

Bowring, Richard John. *Mori Ōgai and the Modernization of Japanese Culture.* Cambridge: Cambridge Univ. Press, 1979.

Keene, Donald. *Dawn to the West: Japanese Literature in the Modern Era: Poetry, Drama, Criticism.* New York: Henry Holt, 1984.

Mori Ōgai. *Ōgai Zenshū* [Complete works of Ōgai]. 38 vols. Tokyo: Iwanami Shoten, 1971–1975.

———. *Masks.* Tr. by M. Vardaman Jr. In *Mori Ōgai, Youth and Other Stories,* ed. by J. Thomas Rimer. Honolulu: Univ. of Hawaii Press, 1994. 291–311.

Motofuji, Frank T. "Mori Ōgai: Three Plays and the Problem of Identity." *Modern Drama* 9, no. 4 (February 1967): 412–430.

Powell, Brian. *Japan's Modern Theatre: A Century of Continuity and Change.* London: Japan Library, 2000.

Rimer, J. Thomas. *Mori Ōgai.* Boston: Twayne, 1975.

M. Cody Poulton

MORNING'S AT SEVEN

Morning's at Seven is a story play. I think that no matter how much you want to delve into character, the terribly main thing is the plot. You want to know what's happening and how it's going to come out.
—Paul Osborn, 1981

Morning's at Seven is PAUL OSBORN's most successful original work for the theater. Forty years after its 1939 first appearance on Broadway earned a tepid critical and box-office response, it was given a stellar Broadway revival in 1980. The play earned a Tony Award for Osborn as best revival of the 1979–1980 season. Tony Awards were also bestowed on Vivian Matalon as director and David Rounds as best supporting actor in a play. It has been revived regularly by nonprofit theaters across America. Yet it is not always successful: a 2002 Broadway revival with a strong company drew poor reviews and limited audience response.

Morning's at Seven is a conventionally structured, three-act, realistic family COMEDY with a sense of unerring dialogue that forcefully establishes the play's nine characters, reveals their quirky foibles, and can elicit strong laughter from an audience. The characters—a single family of four somewhat batty sisters, their husbands, and progeny—are mostly in their sixties and seventies, plain people who deal with the gentle everyday small problems of life: marriage, fidelity, relationships. Each character has a reversal, that moment when metaphorical lightning strikes, and lives are forever changed.

The action takes place in a small American town late one afternoon in 1939 and continues the following morning. For the 1980 revival the director urged Osborn to let him move the time back to 1922. Matalon says that he felt it "essential for the action to take place during a period of greater innocence in the country's history, during an era of greater simplicity before we had experienced the profound disappointments we were to run upon later—before the shadow of Hitler and the Depression."

Morning's at Seven is set in the adjoining backyards of two houses in an unnamed town. One house belongs to Ted Swanson, his wife Cora, and Cora's spinster sister Aaronetta (called Arry) Gibbs. The other house is occupied by another of Cora's sisters, Ida Bolton, her husband Carl (given to "spells" of failure anxiety), and Homer, their forty-year-old bachelor son hopelessly tied to his mother's apron strings. The fourth Gibbs sister, Esther Crampton, lives in another part of town with her husband David, a retired college professor who snobbishly despises his in-laws. These eight characters are joined by Homer's girlfriend, the thirty-seven-year-old Myrtle Brown.

The seeming tranquility of this tight-knit family is addled by Homer's decision to marry Myrtle after a twelve-year courtship, move out of his parents' house, and strike out on his own. This stunning revelation unbalances the family dynamics, especially as it motivates Cora to demand that Arry leave her house so that she might reclaim her life with Ted. It is no secret in this close-knit family that Arry once had a brief affair with Ted many years ago.

Osborn plucked the play's title from a line of Robert Browning's famous long poem of 1841, *Pippa Passes*: "Morning's at seven; / The hill-side's dew-pearled / The lark's on the wing; / The snail's on the thorn; / God's in his Heaven— / All's right with the world!" When *Morning's at Seven* concludes, Osborn assures us that despite the comic upheavals, all is indeed right in the world of the various Gibbs sisters.

[*See also* United States, 1860–1929]

FURTHER READING

Atkinson, Brooks. "Paul Osborn's 'Morning's at Seven,' a Comedy of American Family Life in a Small Town." *New York Times* (December 1, 1939).

Barnes, Clive. " 'Morning's at Seven': A Hit at Any Hour." *New York Post* (April 11, 1980).

Hinson, Hal. "At Last, Paul Osborn Finds the Rainbow." *Los Angeles Herald Examiner* (December 5, 1981).

Kerr, Walter. "Stage: 'Morning's at 7,' Laughter at Twilight." *New York Times* (April 11, 1980).

Jim Patterson

MOSCOW ART THEATRE AND STUDIOS

The period of the Moscow Art Theatre's greatest success coincided with the reign of Nicholas II (1895–1917), which was both an exciting and tragic period in Russian history marked by rapid economic development and by the intensification of liberal and socialist movements. However, RUSSIA'S defeat in the Russo-Japanese war of 1904–1905, followed by the revolutions of 1905 and 1917, meant that the czar survived at the expense of granting Russia a constitution and a parliament. Inevitably, a reactionary period set in where concession and repression alternated. Nevertheless, the period witnessed an amazing cultural flowering during which Russian intellectual life was lively and pluralistic, as well as receptive to Western influences.

KONSTANTIN STANISLAVSKY (1863–1938) and Vladimir Nemirovich-Danchenko (1859–1943), critic, playwright, and a teacher in the Philharmonic Drama School, met on June 22, 1897, at the Slavic Bazaar restaurant in Moscow and agreed to found the Moscow Art Theatre (MKhAT; Moskovskii Khudozhestvenni Teatr). The theater opened in 1898 with Aleksei Tolstoy's historical TRAGEDY *Tsar Fyodor Ioannovich*. The combination of historical accuracy and theatrical splendor made the production a success. "The historical line" continued with Tolstoy's *Death of Ivan the Terrible* (1899) and *Julius Caesar* (1903). During the first decades of the 20th century, the reception of ANTON CHEKHOV as a playwright was intimately linked to the interpretation of his plays at the MKhAT. THE SEAGULL had been included in the repertoire at Nemirovich's insistence. Stanislavsky wrote the production plan and translated the text into stage terms to create the illusion of scenic life. The premiere in December 1898 was a triumph for the author and the true birth of the new theater. The MKhAT had found its own style, the theater of atmosphere and mood, in the poetic REALISM of Chekhov's plays, which had a tremendous impact on Russian theater and originated a whole new school of ACTING and directing. Foreign directors came to Moscow to learn "the MKhAT manner," and the theater remained unequaled for decades as the home of psychological drama performed as a musical unit within the framework of realistic scenery.

Within a few years, the MKhAT was able to fulfill what Nemirovich regarded as one of its prime functions—the presentation of outstanding contemporary Russian or unfamiliar foreign plays dealing with important social issues. However, fundamental divisions between the two directors began to emerge. For Nemirovich, the basis of a production lay in a detailed literary analysis that was then "illustrated" by the staging. However, he introduced modernistic devices when he staged his beloved HENRIK IBSEN. For Stanislavsky, a production was created in the actual rehearsal period itself, through the active collaboration of actor, director, and designer. Stanislavsky began to stage symbolist drama and started experiments in the studio on Povarskaya Street with VSEVOLOD MEYERHOLD. The studio did not last long, and it was never opened to the public, but it laid the foundation for their future explorations.

Pursuing his notion of a literary theater, Nemirovich emerged as a significant director of "Russian tragedy" in adaptations of Fyodor Dostoevsky's novels. In *The Brothers Karamazov* (1910) he evolved a new form, using a narrator to link scenes, thus breaking the traditional four-act structure. *Nikolai Stavrogin* (1913) was based on Dostoevsky's novel *The Possessed*. After the last symbolist experiment—*Hamlet*, directed in 1911 by Stanislavsky in Gordon Craig's abstract sets—the theater returned to the realistic drama, and in the process, a whole literary generation was ignored even though Nemirovich introduced plays by Aleksei Naidyonov, Aleksei Chirikov, Georgi Yartsev, and Dmitri Merezhkovsky. Stanislavsky was more interested in material for actors' improvisation, and Nemirovich's hope of finding the new psychological drama in LEONID ANDREEV works was not fulfilled. Despite success with audiences, both directors felt the theater to be in decline. In 1912, Stanislavsky established a studio to rejuvenate the true spirit of MKhAT and forge the system of actors' training. In the First Studio, as it was soon called, artistic training owed much to Leopold Sulerzhitsky, a supporter of LYOV TOLSTOY's moral teachings. The studio had talented youth, who would become famous directors. The Studio opened with HERMAN HEIJERMANS's *The Wreck of the "Hope."* Expressionistic notes sounded for the first time on the Russian stage in GERHART HAUPTMANN's *The Festival of Peace* and Henning Berger's *The Flood*, both directed by Evgeny Vakhtangov. Stanislavsky transferred his most innovative work to a series of studios, created as adjuncts to the main stage and often financed by himself. He founded the Second Studio in 1916; the Third, which was a school created by Vakhtangov, in 1920; and the Fourth in 1921. An Opera Studio was started in 1918.

The October Revolution in 1917 was met with indecision and fear by the actors of the MKhAT, most of whom were politically passive. In 1919 all theaters were nationalized. The government conferred the title of academic on the most prominent, including the MKhAT, thus taking these theaters under its protection and giving them special finances. In 1923, censorship appeared, but already, between 1917 and 1922, the theater staged only one production in which Stanislavsky tried to express the spirit of the age—*Byron's Cain* (1920)—but this was not appreciated by audiences. Stanislavsky worked at the First Studio, revising productions prepared by young directors, such as William Shakespeare's *Twelfth Night*. Innovations took place in the three studios, which developed as individual collectives. In the First Studio Evgeny Vakhtangov crossbred psychological realism with theatricalism. AUGUST STRINDBERG's *Erik XIV* was directed by Vakhtangov as a MONODRAMA with stylistic elements of EXPRESSIONISM in which Michael Chekhov acted the tortured monarch. Vakhtangov also directed Chekhov's *The Wedding* at the Third Studio (1921) and Solomon Ansky's THE DYBBUK at the Habima Studio (1922), his work culminating with a production of Carlo Gozzi's *Princess Turandot* (1922). By making the naive fairy tale a celebration of art, Vakhtangov created

a contrast to the cold and dark world of contemporary Moscow. In 1926 the Third Studio became the Vakhtangov Theatre.

Leftist critics condemned MKhAT as a bourgeois theater; Chekhov's plays were dismissed as irrelevant. Only Vladimir Lenin's support and that of ANATOLY LUNACHARSKY, commissar for the arts, saved the theater from destruction. Stanislavsky refused to work with the Studios because of aesthetic differences. One solution to the difficulties was to send the theater on a foreign tour to Berlin, Paris, and the UNITED STATES in 1922–1924 with legendary productions such as *Tsar Fyodor* and Chekhov's plays and with consequences that have influenced Western theater practice to this day. On its return to the Soviet Union, the MKhAT became one of the oases of theatrical culture. Stanislavsky's appeal to the government resulted in being taken under direct government control, and the plenitude of artistic and administrative power was again restored to its directors and founders. In 1923, the First Studio became independent and took the name of the Second Moscow Art Theatre. The Third Studio also became independent, while the Second Studio was merged with the main company. From 1924 to 1928 the Second MKhAT was headed by Michael Chekhov, who created an alternative theater that used symbolic means of expression. The spirituality of his interpretation of *Hamlet* (1924) shook audiences, as did his performance as Senator Ableukhov in a dramatization of *Petersburg* by symbolist writer Andrei Bely. However, frustrated by political interference in his work, Michael Chekhov left Soviet Russia in 1928 to create studios in Europe and America.

The movement of the MKhAT toward contemporary subject matter began with adaptations of new Soviet prose, but Nemirovich also directed new Soviet plays such as Konstantin Trenyov's *The Pugachyov Rebellion* (1925), while Stanislavsky worked on one of the best civil war plays, Vsevolod Ivanov's *Armoured Train 14-69* (1927). Nemirovich worked abroad from 1925 to 1928, while Stanislavsky continued to create the new MKhAT. The most significant and successful production was of DAYS OF THE TURBINS by MIKHAIL BULGAKOV (1926).

In 1928, at the beginning of the Stalinist era, Nemirovich and Stanislavsky were responsible for the defense of MKhAT's traditions. In 1931 it was made directly accountable to the government with the title State Moscow Art Theatre of the USSR. Joseph Stalin awarded the MKhAT his equivalent of "most favored" status, and the theater's past was obliterated when renamed the Gorky Academic Art Theatre in 1932. In the 1930s, the MKhAT enjoyed great popularity. Nemirovich directed Vsevolod Ivanov's *The Blockade* (1929), MAKSIM GORKY's *Enemies* (1933), and Konstantin Trenyov's *Lyubov Yarovaya* (1936). The great Russian realist tradition was identified with the new, optimistic SOCIALIST REALISM, and the theater's tour to Paris in 1937 was intended as a showpiece of this policy. As a result, the best modern plays did not reach its stage. Bulgakov's *Molière* was rehearsed for five years, but Bulgakov and Stanislavsky disagreed over the interpretation and Nemirovich took over. The production opened in 1936 but was soon closed. Bulgakov's *Flight* and NIKOLAI ERDMAN'S *THE SUICIDE*, which Stanislavsky rated highly, were banned. After *Hamlet*, in Boris Pasternak's translation, had been in rehearsal for a long time, it too was banned. Attempts to revive the traditions of psychological drama were made, and in the early 1930s Vladimir Kirshon's *Bread* and Maxim Afinogenov's *Fear* appeared on the MKhAT stage. High points were the adaptations of Tolstoy's novels *Resurrection* (1930) and *Anna Karenina* (1937), directed by Nemirovich. He also directed THE THREE SISTERS (1940), a significant new production of Chekhov's play after almost forty years.

After the 1941–1945 war, the MKhAT was in deep crisis, having long since lost any notion of quality where repertoire was concerned. After the death of Joseph Stalin in 1953, the revival of Russian theater began with Oleg Yefremov and other graduates from the MKhAT drama school. A new studio, the Sovremennik (Contemporary) tried to revive the artistic and ethical ideals of the old MKhAT. In 1970 Yefremov became artistic director of the theater, and even if he was unable to reform the company of 180 actors, he created another company within it and produced modern plays by Mikhail Roshchin, Aleksandr Gelman, and Aleksandr Vampilov. The best young directors were invited, including Lev Dodin, who directed one of the most important productions of the Brezhnev era, *The Golovlyovs*, an adaptation of the classic novel by Mikhail Saltykov-Shchedrin.

In 1987 the huge company was divided into two. Oleg Yefremov stayed at the helm of MKhAT 1, now renamed after Chekhov, and Tatyana Doronina became head of MKhAT 2, which preserved the name of Gorky. Yefremov found a new author, Lyudmila Petrushevskaya, and staged *The Moscow Choir*. He also attained tragic simplicity in his final production—*Three Sisters* (1997). Following Yefremov's death in 1999, he was succeeded as head of MKhAT 1 by Oleg Tabakov.

FURTHER READING

Amiard-Chevrel, C. *Le Théâtre Artistique de Moscou (1898–1917)* [The artistic theater of Moscow]. Paris: CNRS, 1979.

Leach, R., and V. Borovsky, eds. *A History of Russian Theatre.* Cambridge: Cambridge Univ. Press, 1999.

Nemirovich-Danchenko, Vladimir. *My Life in Russian Theatre.* Tr. by John Cournos. London: Geoffrey Bles, 1937.

Sayler, Oliver M. *Inside the Moscow Art Theatre.* New York: Brentano's, 1925.

Slonim, Marc. *Russian Theatre from the Empire to the Soviets.* London: Methuen, 1963.

Smeliansky, Anatoly. *The Russian Theatre after Stalin.* Tr. by Patrick Miles. Cambridge: Cambridge Univ. Press, 1999.

Stanislavsky, Constantin. *My Life in Art.* Tr. by J. J. Robbins. Harmondsworth: Penguin, 1967.

Worrall, Nick. *Modernism to Realism on the Soviet Stage.* Tairov—Vakhtangov—Okhlopkov. Cambridge: Cambridge Univ. Press, 1989.

———. *The Moscow Art Theatre.* New York: Routledge, 1996.

Liisa Byckling

MOSCOW STATE YIDDISH THEATRE

Despite its name, the Moscow State Yiddish Theatre (better known as GOSET, the Russian acronym for Gosudarstvennyi evreiskii teater—literally, State Jewish Theatre) was born in St. Petersburg. It was there that a group that called itself the Jewish Theatrical Society began meeting in 1917 and, in 1919, where the Yiddish Chamber Theater began performing under the direction of Alexander Granovsky. The company began its career with a performance of MAURICE MAETERLINCK's *Blind Men* (*Les aveugles*). The troupe then staged several works by Sholem Asch, a short symbolist work by actor Solomon Mikhoels, and Karl Gutzkow's *Uriel Acosta*. None of these productions was particularly successful; Granovsky had yet to find the directorial voice that would ultimately combine professional discipline, AVANT-GARDE techniques, and the finest talents onstage and backstage that would turn GOSET into one of the most important YIDDISH THEATER companies in the world.

The company would begin to forge its true identity shortly after moving to a small theater in Moscow. The troupe's new incarnation as GOSET began on January 1, 1921, with *An Evening of Sholem Aleichem*, consisting of two one-acts and a monologue by the great comic writer. Granovsky's energetic direction bore the mark of VSEVOLOD MEYERHOLD and of MAX REINHARDT, with whom Granovsky had trained. Marc Chagall, who had not only designed the sets and makeup but also decorated the auditorium with murals, created a unique visual atmosphere; though he worked with the company for only one production, he exerted an influence on its aesthetics all out of proportion with his short tenure.

Though GOSET initially received lukewarm reviews, it enjoyed popular success and soon began looking for a new performance venue. In 1922 it debuted at the Malaia Bronnaia Theatre in Moscow with a revamped version of *Uriel Acosta*. Over the next few years, the company would distinguish itself by reinventing masterpieces by the "classic" Yiddish writers. With its 1922 production of AVROM GOLDFADEN's *The Sorceress* (*Di kishefmakherin*), GOSET showed that it could put a modernist, Soviet stamp on one of the most familiar warhorses of the old Yiddish repertoire. Granovsky commissioned Yekhezkel Dobrushin and Moyshe Litvakov to rework the text, adding such touches as a symbolic funeral for the old Yiddish theater. Composer Joseph Akhron reorchestrated Goldfaden's music, and designer Isaak Rabinovich built a network of platforms and ladders on which the actors scrambled, giving a sense of constant movement.

Later that season, the company again turned to Sholem Aleichem, this time staging his COMEDY *The Big Win* (*Dos groyse gevins*), also known as *200,000*. Granovsky transformed the protagonist Shimele Soroker, a simple tailor who in winning a huge lottery becomes a befuddled nouveau riche, into a traitor to the working class. Granovsky's fanciful visual style was once again evident; a split stage emphasized the split between the classes, and a matchmaker dropped in on the proceedings by parachute.

Among the artists who joined the company to work on 200,000 was composer Lev Pulver, who would stay with GOSET for the rest of its existence.

In the mid-1920s, GOSET offered theater and film audiences a feast of reinvented classics. In the 1925 silent film *Luck* (*Yidishe glikn*; Russian *Yevreiskoe schastie*), Solomon Mikhoels turned Sholem Aleichem's beloved character, the frustrated businessman Menachem Mendl, into a Chaplinesque Little Tramp, and the Sovietized story illustrated the evils of life under the czar. The same period featured stage productions of Granovsky's adaptation of Isaac Leib Peretz's symbolist poetic drama *A Night in the Old Marketplace* (*Baynakht afn altn mark*), which continued the company's assault on traditional life and beliefs, and a dramatization of S. Y. Abramovitsh's novel of a Jewish Don Quixote, *The Travels of Benjamin III* (*Masoes Binyomin hashlishi*). In these productions, actors Solomon Mikhoels and Benjamin Zuskin established themselves as a remarkable team, playing alter egos of the protagonist of Peretz's drama and Benjamin and his sidekick Senderl in *Benjamin III*. Another famed pairing would occur in the company's internationally renowned production of *King Lear* in 1935, where Zuskin played the Fool to Mikhoels's Lear.

GOSET made a fateful trip to Western Europe in 1928, during which Granovsky defected to the West. Mikhoels then took the helm of the company, which for the next several years shifted the emphasis in its repertoire from Yiddish classics to new works by Soviet Yiddish writers like Dovid Bergelson, Peretz Markish, and Moyshe Kulbak. Kulbak's play *Boytre the Bandit* (*Boytre gazlen*, 1936), a blunt portrayal of the Jewish urban underworld, was condemned by the regime, leading to Kulbak's arrest and disappearance into the gulag. This grim response, along with official censure of the company, put GOSET on notice that its style and content had crossed the line of what was considered politically acceptable. The troupe responded by returning once again to Yiddish theater's roots, this time presenting new versions of Goldfaden's nationalistic operettas *Shulamis* and *Bar Kokhba*. Poet Shmuel Halkin's adaptations emphasized the heroism of Jewish characters from the past, the troupe's answer to critiques that regarded *Boytre*'s depiction of gangsters, prostitutes, and cripples as unseemly.

In retrospect, one might argue that such efforts to appease the authorities were only buying time. Though figures like Mikhoels and Zuskin amassed numerous official and unofficial accolades, and Mikhoels served with distinction as a delegate on the Jewish Anti-Fascist Committee during World War II, forging links with Jewish communities in the West, Mikhoels was murdered by a Narodnyi Komissariat Vnutrennikh Del (NKVD) agent in 1948, and Zuskin was arrested later that year; in August 1952, he was shot along with twelve other prominent figures. In 1949, the curtain fell for good on GOSET, a troupe that left a remarkable theatrical legacy. GOSET was among a handful of Yiddish companies, including the Vilna Troupe, the Warsaw Yiddish Art Theatre, and Yung Teater (Warsaw) that used avant-garde theater techniques and rigorous training to create innovative productions that spoke to the concerns of Jewish audiences while attracting a following outside of Yiddish-speaking circles.

[*See also* Russia and the Soviet Union]

FURTHER READING

Berkowitz, Joel, ed. *Yiddish Theatre: New Approaches*. London: Littman Library of Jewish Civilization, 2003.

Picon-Vallin, Béatrice. *Le théâtre juif soviétique pendant les années vingt* [The Soviet Jewish theater during the Twenties]. Lausanne: La Cité-L'Âge d'Homme, 1973.

Sandrow, Nahma. *Vagabond Stars: A World History of Yiddish Theater*. 1977. Reprint, Syracuse, N.Y.: Syracuse Univ. Press, 1999.

Veidlinger, Jeffrey. *The Moscow State Yiddish Theatre*. Bloomington: Indiana Univ. Press, 2000.

Joel Berkowitz

MOSES, DANIEL DAVID (1952–)

Daniel David Moses, a Canadian playwright and Delaware from the Six Nations lands on the Grand River, commits himself to expanding native drama beyond an unhealthy triad of white guilt, ROMANTICISM, and TRAGEDY. Born in Ohsweken, Ontario, CANADA, in 1952, he has produced nearly a dozen dramas since 1988. As playwright, poet, and essayist, Moses acts as an advocate for Canadian Aboriginal writing. He co-edited a widely read anthology of native literature and serves as the artistic directorate of Canada's Native Earth Performing Arts.

Moses objects vigorously to three confines that, he feels, have trapped most native drama. According to Moses, white guilt perpetuates the very wounds drama should work to heal; romanticizing the past prevents meaningful investigation of those wounds; and the climactic structure of conventional Western tragedy dooms all idealistic hopes for the future, purging the very desires that it articulates.

Moses has attempted to transcend each of these in his nearly two decades of theatrical works. *Big Buck City* (1991) portrayed untragic characters, *The Dreaming Beauty* (1990) used the storytelling methods of "youth drama" and the oratory of First Nations theater to reflect on 500 years of history, and his *Indian Medicine Shows* (*Angel of the Medicine Show* [1996] and *Moon and Dead Indians* [1996]) explored the phenomenon of the "vanishing Indian" in binary one-act dramas.

Most critical attention has centered on ALMIGHTY VOICE AND HIS WIFE, which shattered the Aristotelian model of tragedy. The first act depicted the ill-fated marriage of the 19th-century Cree, Kisse-Manitou-Wayou (Almighty Voice), and the daughter of Old Dust (White Girl). It trailed the incidents that lead Almighty Voice to murder and his own ultimate execution. In the second act, White Girl reconciles with her husband's ghost in a variation on the minstrel show. The play ends with a melancholy dance of healing. *Almighty Voice* disrupts commoditization of race, represents natives of thorny character, and provides an experimental landscape to heal the wounds of historical tragedy.

His proactive stance on native drama has sometimes led to controversy. While lecturing on *Coyote City*, he was accused of exploiting native stereotypes (specifically the "drunken Indian"). Moses dismissed the objection as ignorant of his unique theatrical style, but he elsewhere acknowledged that qualities of *The Moon and Dead Indians*, which portrayed white conceit and paranoia regarding "wild Indians," disturbed even him.

Moses never shies from the more unsettling aspects of race hatred and racial self-hatred. He outright rejects the notion of an authentic Indian voice in drama, refusing countless offers to dramatize the stories of other Native Americans. Believing that anecdotal material can never be useful, Moses creates performance canvases that use his own knowledge of history to respond to present social problems. In the words of Robert Appleford, Moses's plays "hold funhouse mirrors up to our desire for 'real Indians' in Canadian theatre" (Appleford, 1993). As winner of the James Buller Memorial Award for Excellence in Aboriginal Theatre (1996), as well as one-act awards from The New Play Centre and Theatre Canada, Moses has sought to craft a theatrical context that is shocking, bitterly aware of burdens of racism, sometimes outrageous, and ever his own.

PLAYS: *Coyote City* (1988); *The Dreaming Beauty* (1990); *Almighty Voice and His Wife* (1991); *Big Buck City* (1991); *Kyotopolis* (1992); *Brebeuf's Ghost* (1996); *Angel of the Medicine Show* (1996); *Moon and Dead Indians* (1996); *City of Shadows* (1998); *Red River* (with Jim Millan, 1998); *The Witch of Niagara* (1998)

FURTHER READING

Appleford, Robert. "The Desire to Crunch Bone: Daniel David Moses and the 'True Real Indian.'" *Canadian Theatre Review* 77 (1993): 21–26.

Knowles, Richard. "'Look. Look Again.' Daniel David Moses' Decolonizing Optics." In *Crucible of Cultures: Anglophone Drama at the End of the New Millennium*, ed. by Marc Maufort and Franca Bellarsi. New York: P. Lang, 2002.

Knowles, Richard, and Monique Mojica, eds. *Staging Coyote's Dream: An Anthology of First Nations Drama in English*. Toronto: Playwrights Canada Press, 2003.

Moses, Daniel David. "How My Ghosts Got Pale Faces." In *Speaking for the Generations: Native Writers on Writing*, ed. by Simon J. Ortiz. Tucson: Univ. of Arizona Press, 1998.

Moses, Daniel David, and Terry Goldie. *An Anthology of Canadian Native Literature in English*. 2d ed. New York: Oxford Univ. Press, 1998.

Ben Fisler

THE MOTHER

BERTOLT BRECHT (1898–1956) started work on *The Mother* (*Die Mutter*) in 1931; it was first performed on January 17, 1932, and would have fourteen performances before Brecht died. Because Brecht kept revising the text, there are three main versions (1933, 1938, 1957). The music for the songs was composed by Hanns Eisler (1898–1962).

Die Mutter is loosely adapted from the Russian novel *Mat* (1906, *Mother*) by MAKSIM GORKY (1868–1936). The novel tells the story of Pavel Vlasova and his mother, Pelagea, during the 1905 revolution in Russia. Brecht retained only the barest plot from Gorky's sentimental and overwritten book, namely, the evolution of Pavel's mother into an ardent supporter of revolution. He also extended the time frame past 1905 up until 1917; the play ends on the eve of the revolution of 1917.

The Mother, however, is not a historical drama. It grew out of what Brecht called the *Lehrstück* (LEARNING PLAY) in which the audience is challenged to find its own solutions to the problems enacted on the stage. Three aspects of learning are presented in *The Mother*. One is the education of the central character, Pelagea Vlasova, who initially wants to have nothing to do with political action but is compelled by circumstances to the insight that only a revolution—violent if need be—can bring economic and social reform. A second theme is the education of others by Pelagea. Using common sense and native wit, she seizes every opportunity to teach others to see through the surface appearances of society and become independent, critical thinkers. Finally, there is the interaction between the play and the members of the audience, who are addressed directly in the songs: "Whose fault is it, if oppression remains? Ours."

The form of the play is derived from the "station drama" often preferred by expressionist playwrights. It consists of fourteen episodes, each of which is structured as a minidrama with events leading to a climax within the act. Continuity for the play is provided by the character of Pelagea and her story and also by the intensification of the revolutionary struggle that becomes evident. At the beginning, only scattered individuals act, but by the end they have become a large, powerful group marching through the streets.

As always with Brecht, the language appears simple but is carefully crafted, as in the chiasmus "What you don't know yourself / You don't know." Because Pelagea's diction is generally so restrained, her one outburst against the Russian men who send their sons into a senseless war stands out for its imagery and intensity: "No animal would offer up its young the way you do yours, without sense or reason, for a bad cause. Your wombs should be ripped out."

The Mother may be taken as a counterpoint to Brecht's more famous MOTHER COURAGE AND HER CHILDREN (*Mutter Courage und ihre Kinder*, 1939–1940). Whereas in *The Mother* the title character learns from her experiences and takes action to end oppression, Mother Courage, who believes she can make a deal with war, learns nothing from her sufferings. Pelagea Vlasova marches at the end with a company of others, but Mother Courage is finally left all alone.

FURTHER READING

Bawey, Petermichael von. "Dramatic Structure of Revolutionary
    Language: Tragicomedy in Brecht's *The Mother*." *CLIO: A Journal of
    Literature, History, and the Philosophy of History* 10 (1980): 21–33. Also
    in *Critical Essays on Bertolt Brecht*. Ed. by Siegfried Mews. Boston:
    G. K. Hall, 1989. 96–106.

Kepa, Ania. "The Relationship of Brecht's *Die Mutter* to Its Sources: A
    Reassessment." *German Life and Letters* 38, no. 3 (1985): 233–248.

Ritterhoff, Teresa. "*Ver/Ratlosigkeit*: Benjamin, Brecht, and *Die Mutter*."
    Brecht Yearbook / Das Brecht-Jahrbuch 24 (1999): 246–262.

Salehi, Eric. "No Brecht-fest in America: Revisiting the Theatre
    Union's 1935 Production of *Mother*." *On-Stage Studies* 21 (1998):
    75–97.

Arnd Bohm

MOTHER COURAGE AND HER CHILDREN

BERTOLT BRECHT wrote *Mother Courage and Her Children* (*Mutter Courage und ihre Kinder*) in SWEDEN in 1939 during his years as a refugee from Nazi GERMANY. The play premiered in Zurich in 1941 and was first produced in Germany in 1949 at the Deutsches Theater in East Berlin under the direction of the author.

Written just as Adolf Hitler and Joseph Stalin were invading POLAND, the play was intended by Brecht as a cautionary tale warning " 'the little person' " against "participation . . . in the catastrophe that everyone then saw on the horizon" (Fuegi, 1972).

The action of the play begins in 1624 during a Protestant recruiting campaign. Mother Courage, who sells supplies to the armies of the Thirty Years' War, enters aboard her wagon, drawn by her sons, Eilif and Swiss Cheese. Next to her sits her mute daughter, Kattrin. Accosted by two recruiting officers, Mother Courage tries to keep her sons from joining up, but while she is behind the wagon selling a belt buckle, Eilif, the brave one, enlists. Thus Brecht illustrates two of the play's major ideas. First, those who feed the war—like Mother Courage—will themselves be devoured by it. Second, in the world of total warfare that exists apart from socialism, human virtue, such as Eilif's bravery, must always be a liability.

Next, Swiss Cheese is undone by his own honesty. He becomes the paymaster for a Protestant regiment, to which he tries to return the cash box during a Catholic attack. He is caught, arrested, and sentenced to death. Mother Courage is offered the opportunity of buying his freedom, but to raise the money she would have to sell the wagon. Torn between economic necessity and maternal instinct, she hesitates too long, and honest Swiss Cheese is executed.

As the years pass, Mother Courage and Kattrin cross and recross war-torn Central Europe. Kattrin is raped, and the wagon is looted. Peace breaks out, threatening business, but brave Eilif continues his wartime behavior and kills a peasant. Now, however, such an act is criminal, and he is condemned to death for it. When he comes to say good-bye to his mother, she is off buying and selling. Thus, without knowing it, she loses another son to the insatiable war.

Reduced to rags and hunger, hauling the wagon like beasts, Mother Courage and Kattrin continue to follow the armies. As Catholics prepare to attack the sleeping town of Halle, Courage goes off to hunt bargains while kindhearted Kattrin learns how the city's children will be slaughtered. She climbs to the top of a shed and begins to beat a drum to warn the victims. Shot dead when she refuses to stop, she nonetheless manages to alert the town. Once again a virtuous child dies as Mother Courage is doing business.

In the last scene Courage arranges her daughter's burial and then, oblivious to the meaning of her losses, harnesses herself to the wagon to resume supplying the war. As another regiment passes by, she calls out her final line, "Hey! Take me with you!"

A great success onstage, *Mother Courage* provoked a level of emotional response that distressed the playwright. Its Swiss premiere elicited press commentary comparing Courage to Niobe, praising her as an exemplar of heartrending maternal vitality. This response contradicted the fundamental premise of Brecht's epic theory: that spectators should regard events onstage with rational detachment. Determined to repel such empathy in future productions, Brecht revised four scenes in the play, increasing the emphasis in each on Courage's mercenary nature and her lack of charity. Thus he would underline her role as the "hyena of the battle field," a ruthless proto-capitalist whose economic self-interest makes war possible. The changes apparently failed to work in the Berlin production eight years later. Staged amid the ruins of an occupied city, this antiwar fable drew full houses and left its audiences in tears. Said a disappointed Brecht, "I do not believe . . . that Berlin . . . understood the play" (Fuegi, 1972). This emotion-laden production was the vehicle that restored Brecht's faded reputation as a playwright and director following his years in exile. The contradiction between theory and practice evident in this paradoxical episode has been an ongoing theme in critical discussions of Brecht's work.

Mother Courage has furnished several of the hallmark images of 20th-century drama: Courage's silent scream as she denies knowing her dead son (a kind of anti-*pieta*); Kattrin's drumming herself to death in mute heroism; and Courage yoked to the wagon, which is both her livelihood and her cross.

[*See also* Epic Theater]

FURTHER READING

Fuegi, John. *The Essential Brecht*. Los Angeles: Hennessey & Ingalls, 1972.
——. *Bertolt Brecht: Chaos, According to Plan*. Cambridge: Cambridge
    Univ. Press, 1987.
White, Alfred D. *Bertolt Brecht's Great Plays*. London: Macmillan, 1978.

Martin Andrucki

MOTHS

ARIFIN C. NOER's *Moths* (*Kapai-Kapai*, 1970) provides an excellent example of how this Indonesian playwright and director used traditional themes and theatrical structures to speak to contemporaries. In this surrealistic play, the main character, Abu, appears in different stages of his life from boyhood to death. His story is framed by a *donggeng* (fairy tale) his mother tells him about a prince who has a magic mirror that protects him from evil, allowing him to marry the princess, living happily ever after. As a child, Abu is transfixed by his mother's tale and wishes to find the mirror to bring some happiness to his own life.

As an adult, Abu is a dehumanized menial worker, at one point identified only by the sound of a bell that rings ". . _ (dot dot dash)." His real life becomes confused with his dreams, in which he is the prince; his dream world and his real world constantly interrupt each other. Abu marries Ijem and has several children, all of whom die. Abu and Ijem are destitute and starving despite years of hard work. They set off to find the edge of the world where Abu believes the magic mirror to be. The Moon, Darkness, and the Bell all conspire with Mother for Abu to meet with his death at the predestined moment in 1980 when he goes through a final door and finds the trick mirror. The play ends with a replaying of the first scene of the play when Abu is a young child being put to sleep by his mother as she tells the fairy tale.

This rather vague fatalistic plot summary does an injustice to the poetic, dreamlike juxtapositions between Abu's grim day-to-day life and his elaborate fantasy world. Arifin's language is rich with metaphors and melodious words and phrases, not unlike traditional Javanese *pantun* (poetry) in which the sound or meaning of the first couplet of a verse influences the second couplet. In contrast to the richness and beauty of its language, a major theme in *Moths* is poverty—not just the poverty of bodies but also a philosophical, theological, and metaphysical poverty of souls. Abu is a messenger who illustrates a spiritual emptiness Arifin perceived in INDONESIA in the late 1960s, an Indonesia that had lost sight of its roots. According to the playwright, this simple story about the prince and his magic mirror is a speculation into an Indonesian conception of happiness, which he found was not clearly formulated etymologically. The play, too, is not clearly formulated but is hazy like a dream, a nightmare, swirling around with reality (fluttering or flailing like a moth attracted to the light), leading inexorably down a path to Abu's death and his rebirth into the cycle again. Abu—which means dust or ash—is from the start, as Mother explains to Darkness in act 1, scene 5, "Like those before, like the others, he too is dead already but doesn't know it yet."

[*See also* Surrealism]

FURTHER READING

Aveling, Harry. Introduction to *Moths*, by Arifin C. Noer. Kuala Lumpur: Dewan Bahasa dan Pusataka, Kementerian Pelajaran, 1974.

Gillitt, Cobina. "Challenging Conventions and Crossing Boundaries: A New Tradition of Indonesian Theatre from 1968–1978." Ph.D. diss., New York Univ., 2001.

Gillitt Asmara, Cobina. "Tradisi Baru: A New Tradition of Indonesian Theatre." *Asian Theatre Journal* 12, no. 1 (1995): 164–174.

Cobina Gillitt

MOUAWAD, WAJDI (1968–)

Wajdi Mouawad was born on October 16, 1968, in a small Lebanese village. His family moved to Paris, FRANCE, when he was eight, and he spent his formative years here. As a young teenager, Mouawad moved with his family again to Quebec, CANADA, and it is here that his interest in theater evolved into a major focus of his life. At age seventeen, Mouawad entered the National School of Theatre of Canada, where he was heavily influenced by theatrical intellectuals like François Ismert. Mouawad graduated from the National School of Theatre of Canada in 1991 and began a successful career as writer, director, and author of more than a dozen works.

Throughout his works, Mouawad's main interest seems to be the duality of humankind's nature and environments. Because of his travels at a young age from war-torn Lebanon to France, Mouawad recognized the paradoxical nature of man: man can be loving and at the same time cruelly self-destructive in warfare. These postmodern duality informs much of Mouawad's works, especially his most famous 1996 play WEDDING DAY AT THE CRO-MAGNONS' (*Journée de noces chez les Cromagnons*).

Mouawad's career took off in 1998, when he was involved in four major productions in Quebec's Festival of Theatre. He received the Quebec's Critics' Circle Award for his plays *Willy Protagoras Locked Up in the Toilets* (*Willy Protagoras enfermé dans les toilettes*, 1993) and *Hands of Edwige at the Time of Birth* (*Les mains d'Edwige au moment de la naissance*, 1994). His plays *Littoral* (1999), *Fires* (*Incendies*, 1999), and *Dreams* (*Rêves*, 1999) all won rich acclaim and praise for Mouawad, and in 1999 his production of *Don Quixote* won best Montreal adaptation. In May 1999 Mouawad was named artistic director of Montreal's Theatre of Quat', where he remained through 2004. Mouawad won the Price of the General Governor of Canada award in 2000 for *Littoral*, and most recently he earned the "Price of Francophone" award in June 2004 by the Company of Authors and Dramatic Type-Setters in Paris, France.

Mouawad's first novel, *Visage Retrouve* (*Found Face*, 2003), explores how an individual builds alternative or parallel universes to escape the painful realities of his/her own world. This concept is mirrored in Mouawad's play *Fires*, in which the psychological pain of warfare results in characters figuratively "burning up." In both, the pain warfare inflicts on individuals becomes too much to bear.

After gaining fame on the Canadian theater scene, Mouawad plans to be more involved in French theater in the future. His new project titled *Forests* (*Forêts*) premiered in March 2006 in Chambéry, France. This work touches on World War I and World War II, just as his previous works are informed by the wars in Lebanon and the Middle East. Not surprisingly, warfare is a major theme in Mouawad's works. Mouawad's close, and often painful, examination of the nature of man defines many of his plays; he confesses that his role as a playwright is to "seek what is not known yet." This perspective allows Mouawad to insightfully explore and expose the darker side of human beings. Undoubtedly, Mouawad will continue his exploration of the human psyche in his future works.

PLAYS: *Part of Hide-and-Seek Between 2 Czechoslovakians at the Beginning of the Century* (1992); *Willy Protagoras Locked Up in the Toilets* (*Willy Protagoras enfermé dans les toilettes*, 1993); *Hands of Edwige at the Time of the Birth* (*Les mains d'Edwige au moment de la naissance*, 1994); *Alphonse* (1996); *Wedding Day at the Cro-Magnons'* (*Journée de noces chez les Cromagnons*, 1996); *Procession of the National Festival* (1997); *Dreams* (*Rêves*, 1999); *Littoral* (1999); *Pacamambo* (2000); *Fires* (*Incendies*, 2003); *A Shell in ON* (2003); *Forests* (*Forêts*, 2006)

FURTHER READING

"The Arts: A Songstress, a Video Artist, a Filmmaker, a Playwright, a Photographer-Director." *Time International* 154, no. 13 (September 27, 1999): 76.

Clarkdon, Adrienne. "Celebrating Literature and Our Collective Life as a Nation." *Canadian Speeches* 14, no. 5 (November–December 2000): 10–12.

Knapp, Bettina L. "Playwrights of Exile: An International Anthology" (book review). *World Literature Today* 72, no. 2 (Spring 1998): 467.

Thaddeus Wakefield

LES MOUCHES   See THE FLIES

MOURNING BECOMES ELECTRA

I'll live along with the dead, and keep their secrets, and let them hound me, until the curse is paid out and the last Mannon is let die!

—Lavinia, Act 4, *The Haunted*

The THEATRE GUILD first produced EUGENE O'NEILL's *Mourning Becomes Electra* on October 26, 1931, with Alla Nazimova as Christine and designs by ROBERT EDMOND JONES.

This trilogy reinterprets Greek TRAGEDY in terms of the aftermath of the American Civil War and explores the themes of community (through a "chorus" of neighbors), family, betrayal, and revenge. Besides following Aechylus's three-part structure and casting pattern in the *Oresteia*, O'Neill works from the Greek precedent by giving strong presence to the sea, the power of the dishonored father, the pervading curse, and the sense of living in a world where ghosts and the furies drive the mortals to a reckoning. From Euripides's *Orestes*, O'Neill took the motif of incest and the compulsion for the individual to justify acts of

violence. At the same time, O'Neill's own experience with a psychoanalyst apparently led to his staging of the Electra complex in Lavinia's painful relationship with her mother and father; the family suffers due to the intensity of the father/daughter and mother/son relationships. The action as purgation therefore develops from both Greek tragedy and Freudian theory.

In the first part, *Homecoming*, General Ezra Mannon returns from the war as Agamemnon returned to Argos from Troy. Waiting at his New England home are his wife Christine (modeled after Clytemnestra) and his daughter Lavinia (Electra). Christine's lover is Adam Brant (roughly corresponding with Aegisthus), a sea captain and Ezra's illegitimate cousin, and they plot to murder Ezra. The general has yearned to return to Christine, but their old resentments keep them apart, while Lavinia assures her father that he is the only man she will ever love. Ezra and Christine quarrel, and when she reveals that she loves Adam, he has an attack of angina. She pretends to provide his medicine but gives him poison from a small box, and Lavinia rushes in to hear her father's last words as he points towards her mother: "She's guilty—not medicine!" When Lavinia finds the little box where it fell on the rug, she realizes the truth.

In the second part, *The Hunted*, Lavinia's brother Orin (Orestes) returns from the war to see the house as a tomb. Christine cannot appease Lavinia, but she has better luck with Orin, who hated his father. Obsessed with death, he tells Lavinia that fighting the war meant "murdering the same man over and over" and realizing that he was killing himself. The women struggle over him, each insisting that Adam is the other's lover. Christine goes to Boston to find Adam on his clipper ship and warn him against Lavinia. Orin shoots Adam dead but cannot help noticing how he resembles his father and himself. He returns to the Mannon home and reveals the murder to Christine, but remorse consumes him when she shoots herself.

In the final part, *The Haunted*, Orin and Lavinia return from a journey to the South Pacific islands, and she coaxes him to stop seeing ghosts; she wants to live openly, and she hopes to marry Peter, one of the local men. Orin broods like his father, working in his study and studying the law of crime and punishment; Lavinia cannot convince him to stop talking of guilt and confession. Orin shoots himself, and Peter rejects Lavinia when she finally confesses that she had sexual relations with a native man in the islands because "I wanted to learn love from him—love that wasn't a sin!" She condemns herself not to die but to live in the Mannon household with the shutters nailed closed, sequestered with her dead, where there can be no rest.

Brooks Atkinson wrote in the *New York Times* (Nov. 1, 1931) that the play

brings the cold splendors of Greek tragedy off the sky-blue limbo of Olympus down to the gusty forum of contemporary life. For the divine omniscience of the gods he substitutes the discovery of modern science, since knowledge is what this civilization pits against the solemn councils of the gods. . . . What makes *Mourning Becomes Electra* his only masterpiece, to my mind, is the cool deliberation with which he has dominated it. The fret and fever of his early work, the truncated thinking, the turgid writing, the elaborate symbolism of masks, the subterfuge of asides, the inarticulation and the collapse into grandiose generalities—have disappeared.

In *The Nation* (Nov. 18, 1931), Joseph Wood Krutch wrote, It is on the other hand—and like all supremely great pieces of literature—primarily about the passions and primarily addressed to our interest in them. . . . [W]hen one does compare it with *Hamlet* or *Macbeth* one realizes that it does lack just one thing and that that thing is language—words as thrilling as the action which accompanies them.

Robert Benchley acclaimed the trilogy as "filled with good, old-fashioned, spine-curling MELODRAMA" (*New Yorker*, Nov. 7, 1931). James A. Robinson (1978) has compared the play's exploration of sin with the work of Nathaniel Hawthorne and its more gothic features with Edgar Allan Poe.

[*See also* Dramatic Cycles; United States, 1860–1929]

FURTHER READING

Chirico, Miriam M. "Moving Fate Into the Family: Tragedy Redefined in O'Neill's *Mourning Becomes Electra*." *Eugene O'Neill Review* 24 (Spring–Fall 2000): 81–100.

Frank, Glenda. "The Tiger as Daddy's Girl." *Eugene O'Neill Review* 19 (Spring–Fall 1995): 55–65.

Houchin, John H. *The Critical Response to Eugene O'Neill*. Westport, Conn.: Greenwood Press, 1993.

Miller, Lisa. "Iphigenia: An Overlooked Influence in *Mourning Becomes Electra*." *Eugene O'Neill Review* 24 (Spring–Fall 2000): 101–112.

Robinson, James A. "The Middle Plays." In *The Cambridge Companion to Eugene O'Neill*, ed. by Michael Manheim. Cambridge: Cambridge Univ. Press, 1998.

Smith, Susan Harris. "Inscribing the Body: Lavinia Mannon as the Site of the Struggle." *Eugene O'Neill Review* 19 (Spring–Fall 1995): 45–54.

Jeffrey D. Mason

MROŻEK, SŁAWOMIR (1932–)

Cartoonist, short-story writer, essayist, filmmaker, actor, and playwright Slawomir Mrożek has been a dominating presence in modern Eastern European theater. He was born on June 29, 1932, in Borzęcin, POLAND. In 1933 his father, a postal employee, moved the family from a nearby village to Cracow, where Slawomir received his schooling and worked as journalist, theater critic, and cartoonist for local newspapers in the mid-1950s (briefly as an ardent believer in Joseph Stalin) before leaving for Warsaw to make his name as a satirist of the absurdities of ideology.

From 1963 he lived in ITALY, FRANCE (as a French citizen since 1968), GERMANY, and MEXICO before returning to Poland in the 1990s. In short, satirical sketches in cabaret style—*Out at*

Sea (*Na pełnym morzu*, 1961), *Striptease* (1961) and *Charlie* (*Karol*, 1961)—Mrożek developed a parable form of drama using model situations, pushed to logical extremes, to explore the operations of power. In the guise of family drama, *Tango* (1964) charts the descent of liberal Europe into totalitarianism; its absurd humor, grotesque characterization, and precise slapstick made it the most widely performed Polish play of the decade.

After Mrożek publicly denounced the invasion of CZECHOSLO-VAKIA, his work was banned in Poland from 1968 to 1973. His plays remained extremely popular in the Polish theater throughout the 1970s and 1980s.

A master parodist, Mrożek subverts Polish national myths and plays with theatrical genres and conventions, without ever committing himself to any single style. Juxtaposing nature and nurture, barbarism and civilization, *The Slaughterhouse* (*Rzeźnia*, 1973) and *The Tailor* (*Krawiec*, 1963; 1977) explore the interdependence of art and violence. *Foxhunt* (*Polowanie na lisa*, 1977) and *Philosopher Fox* (*Lis filozof*, 1977) are witty animal fables, in the manner of Jean de La Fontaine, and concern the seductions of power.

Vatzlav (1970) moves beyond the closed circle of political repression to examine the paradoxes of freedom, and *Emigrés* (*Emigranci*, 1974) deals with the ironies of exile through the symbiotic relationship of an intellectual and a peasant sharing. A fin de siècle COMEDY of manners, *The Hunchback* (*Garbus*, 1975) predicts social unrest and loss of identity in times of conspiracy and paranoiac fear of terrorism. *On Foot* (*Pieszo*, 1980) offers a panoramic view of dislocated lives during World War II, including an apocalyptic artist patterned after STANISŁAW IGNACY WIT-KIEWICZ. *A Summer's Day* (*Letni dzień*, 1984) portrays a competition between two would-be suicides. *Contract* (*Kontrakt*, 1986) pits a dying representative of old European values against a young Eastern European terrorist. *Portrait* (*Portret*, 1987) settles accounts with the fatal legacy of Stalinism; *Widows* (*Wdowy*, 1990) reinstates parable as an existential dance of death; and *Love in the Crimea* (*Miłość na Krymie*, 1993) traces the collapse of Russia through a pastiche of Chekhovian themes.

Mrożek's entire oeuvre gives the portrait of an age scarred by war, communism, and ideological fanaticism. With a cartoonist's bold hand, Mrożek has dissected the power game, showing how human beings terrorize one another and themselves. His sardonic analyses of totalitarianism have had great resonance—political and moral—for audiences in Eastern Europe when public discussion of those issues was possible only in the theater.

Even though the communist regimes have been dismantled, Mrożek's studies of tyranny seem contemporary in their obsession with conspiracy and terrorism and the complex interrelations among art, culture, and power.

PLAYS: *The Professor* (*Profesor*, 1956); *The Police* (*Policja*, 1958); *The Martyrdom of Peter Ohey* (*Męczeństwo Piotra Oheya*, 1959); *The Turkey* (*Indyk*, 1960); *Charlie* (*Karol*, 1961); *Out at Sea* (*Na pełnym morzu*,

1961); *Striptease* (1961); *Kynologist in a Dilemma* (*Kynolog w rozterce*, 1962); *The Party* (*Zabawa*, 1962); *Death of a Lieutenant* (*Śmierć porucznika*, 1963); *The Enchanted Night* (*Czarowna noc*, 1963); *Tango* (1964); *The Foursome* (*Poczwórka*, 1967); *Home on the Border* (*Dom na granicy*, 1967); *The Prophets* (*Testarium*, 1967); *Repeat Performance* (*Drugie danie*, 1968); *Vatzlav* (1970); *Blessed Event* (*Szczęśliwe wydarzenie*, 1971); *The Slaughterhouse* (*Rzeźnia*, 1973); *The Emigrés* (*Emigranci*, 1974); *The Hunchback* (*Garbus*, 1975); *Serenade, Foxhunt, Philosopher Fox* (*Serenada, Polowanie na lisa, Lis filozof*, 1977); *The Tailor* (*Krawiec*, 1977); *Aspiring Fox* (*Lis aspirant*, 1978); *On Foot* (*Pieszo*, 1980); *The Ambassador* (*Ambasador*, 1981); *Alpha* (*Alfa*, 1984); *A Summer's Day* (*Letni dzień*, 1984); *The Contract* (*Kontrakt*, 1986); *The Portrait* (*Portret*, 1987); *Widows* (*Wdowy*, 1990); *Love in the Crimea* (*Miłość na Krymie*, 1993); *The Reverends* (*Wielebni*, 1996); *A Beautiful View* (*Piękny Widok*, 1998)

FURTHER READING

Drama at Calgary 3, no. 3 (1969) [special Mrożek issue].

Esslin, Martin. "An Eastern Absurdist: Sławomir Mrożek, Poland." In *Brief Chronicles*. London: Temple Smith, 1970. 150–161.

Gerould, Daniel. "Contexts for Vatzlav." *Modern Drama* 27, no. 1 (March 1984): 21–40.

Goetz-Stankiewicz, Marketa. "Sławomir Mrożek: The Moulding of a Polish Playwright." In *The Tradition of Polish Ideals: Essays in History and Literature*, ed. by W. J. Stankiewicz. London: Orbis Bks., 1981. 204–225.

Grol-Prokopczyk, Regina. "Sławomir Mrożek's Theatre of the Absurd." *The Polish Review* 24, no. 3 (1979): 45–57.

Klossowicz, Jan. *Mrożek*. Warsaw: Author's Agency, 1980.

Kott, Jan. "Mrożek's Family." In *Theatre Notebook, 1947–1967*, tr. by Bolesław Taborski. New York: Doubleday, 1968. 135–140.

Mrożek, Sławomir. *The Mrożek Reader*. Ed. and intro. by Daniel Gerould. New York: Grove Atlantic, 2004.

Stephan, Halina. *Transcending the Absurd: The Drama and Prose of Sławomir Mrożek*. Amsterdam: Rodopi, 1997.

Daniel Gerould

MRS. WARREN'S PROFESSION

Mrs. Warren's Profession is a play by GEORGE BERNARD SHAW written in 1893 but not licensed for public performance in ENGLAND until 1924. Plans for a performance of the play at J. T. Grein's Independent Theatre in 1894 were not proceeded with, since the play's provocative thematic mix of prostitution and incest guaranteed that an application for a license for public performance would not be granted. Shaw was obliged to make extensive cuts in order to obtain a license for the play to be published in the collection *Plays Pleasant and Unpleasant* (1898). The play was first presented privately by the Stage Society at the New Lyric Club on January 5–6, 1902. At the first performance of the play in the UNITED STATES on October 27, 1905, at the Hyperion Theatre in New Haven, the mayor ordered police to close the theater because of the play's "indecency." The first licensed public production in England was in 1925, when it was presented at the Prince of Wales Theatre, Birmingham, on October 27. The play has been very frequently revived since.

Mrs. Warren's Profession is an unconventional contribution by Shaw to a tradition of 19th-century works initiated by Alexandre Dumas (DUMAS FILS) with his 1848 novel *The Lady of the Camellias* (*La Dame aux camélias*) about the figure of the Woman with a Past, or the Fallen Woman. In 1893, as Shaw was composing *Mrs. Warren's Profession*, OSCAR WILDE and ARTHUR PINERO had presented variations on the theme with their plays *A Woman of No Importance* and THE SECOND MRS. TANQUERAY. In *Mrs. Warren's Profession*, Shaw not only made explicit the subject of prostitution, which is glossed over and glamorized in most works in the tradition to which the play bears a critical relation, but also followed Percy Bysshe Shelley's example in *The Cenci* (1819) of linking incest with corrupt patriarchal systems of wealth and power. In place of the typical beautiful and "tragic" courtesan of works in the tradition, Shaw created in Mrs. Warren a brassy, unrepentant, vital woman with a lively sense of humor who defiantly justifies her "profession" as being the only economically sensible thing to do, given the choices open to her in a society dominated by exploitative capitalist bosses. The wealth she has created from her European chain of high-class brothels has enabled her to live respectably and to send her daughter, Vivie, to Cambridge University, where she has excelled in the mathematics tripos. Both mother and daughter are among the finest portraits of women in Shaw's early plays. The forthright and intelligent Vivie shows many characteristics of the Victorian New Woman, as well as some traces of Shaw's own character and outlook.

The central action of the play revolves around Mrs. Warren's revelations about her past to her daughter. While Vivie at first accepts and admires her mother's account of her profession, she comes to be repelled by it, especially when she discovers that the business is still being carried on and when her mother's disagreeable associate, Sir George Crofts, makes a cynical offer of marriage to her. Crofts is one of two men in the play who are revealed as possibly being the father of Vivie, the other being the Reverend Samuel Gardner, who is the father of Vivie's fiancé Frank. In a powerful final act of the play, Vivie severs her relationship with her mother, after a passionate quarrel between the two, and also breaks off her engagement to Frank. She is last seen throwing a note from Frank into the wastebasket and resolutely getting on with her work in the chambers of her friend Honoria Fraser's actuarial firm in Chancery Lane, London.

[*See also* Ireland]

FURTHER READING

Bullough, Geoffrey. "Literary Relations of Shaw's Mrs. Warren." *Philological Quarterly* 41 (1962): 339–358.

Gibbs, A. M. "The Economics of Love." In *The Art and Mind of Shaw: Essays in Criticism*. London: Macmillan, 1983.

Meisel, Martin. "Courtesans and Magdalens." In *Shaw and the Nineteenth-Century Theater.* Princeton, N.J.: Princeton Univ. Press, 1963.

Peters, Margot. Introduction to *Mrs. Warren's Profession: A Facsimile of the Holograph Manuscript.* New York: Garland, 1981.

A. M. Gibbs

MULATTO

Written in 1930, *Mulatto* was LANGSTON HUGHES's most successful play of the 1930s. It opened in New York at the Vanderbilt Theatre on October 24, 1935. A controversial drama about paternity and race relations in the South, it was, at that time, the longest-running Broadway play by an African American, having played for 373 performances. To Hughes's dismay, Martin Jones, who produced the play for Broadway, altered the original plot. After the New York run, the play was scheduled in 1937 for Philadelphia but was banned for two years by Mayor S. Davis Wilson; it was also banned in Baltimore. In addition to productions in the UNITED STATES, there were performances in such cities as Rome, Paris, Madrid, Tokyo, Rio de Janeiro, and Buenos Aires.

The two-act play set in Georgia centers on Robert Lewis, the son of Colonel Thomas Norwood and Cora Lewis—played by Rose McClendon and later Mercedes Gilbert—who is also the mother of Robert's brother William and sister Sallie. (In Hughes's original version, Sallie goes off to school, but Martin Jones's altered script portrays Sallie as a rape victim.) In act 1, Robert, who has returned from Atlanta, uses his father's car without his permission. Robert is defiant and Norwood domineering, whereas Cora, Sallie, and William are submissive. Norwood learns from the "county politician" Fred Higgins that Robert has defied southern racial codes by speaking up to a white woman clerk in the post office, which could result in a lynching. When Robert returns from taking Sallie to the station, he enters through the front door, initiating a disagreement with his mother and Norwood. Robert claims his status as Norwood's son, calling himself "half-white" and a "Norwood." Robert's defiance comes to a head at the end of act 1 when he refuses to leave by the back door. In act 2, Norwood, angered at Robert's identifying himself as his son, eventually brandishes a gun to warn Robert against using the front door. Robert then strangles him. Shocked and grief stricken, Cora, in a long monologue addressed to the dead Norwood, reiterates, "He was always yo' chile." In the end, she is unable to save Robert, who, followed by the lynch mob, returns to the house.

The controversial play was reviewed by Brooks Atkinson of the *New York Times* (Oct. 25, 1935), who questioned Hughes's skills as dramatist but recognized Hughes's honesty and the play's substance in contrast to other 1935 productions. There were also responses in the *New York Herald Tribune,* the *New York Sun,* the *Brooklyn Daily Eagle,* and the *Newark News,* some of which identified the play's melodramatic elements. However, Winifred

Snell, writing for the *Newark Evening News* (Oct. 25, 1935), faulted producer Martin Jones. African American cultural observer Alain Locke (1983) recognized that Hughes had gone beyond the usual Broadway "formulas." A later reevaluation by Darwin Turner criticized the plot but lauded its departure from the stereotypical tragic mulatto theme. In the 1960s, Webster Smalley (1963) suggested that the play be viewed within the context of melodramatic stage productions of the 1930s.

[*See also* Melodrama]

FURTHER READING

Locke, Alain. "Broadway and the Negro Drama." In *The Critical Temper of Alain Locke: A Selection of His Essays on Art and Culture,* ed. by Jeffrey C. Stewart. New York: Garland, 1983. 240–41.

McLaren, Joseph. *Langston Hughes: Folk Dramatist in the Protest Tradition, 1921–1943.* Westport, Conn.: Greenwood Press, 1997.

Nichols, Charles H., ed. *Arna Bontemps–Langston Hughes Letters, 1925–1967.* New York: Dodd, 1980.

Rampersad, Arnold. *The Life of Langston Hughes.* 2 vols. New York: Oxford Univ. Press, 1986–1988.

Sanders, Leslie Catherine, ed., with Nancy Johnston. *The Plays to 1942: Mulatto to The Sun Do Move. The Collected Works of Langston Hughes.* Vol. 5. Columbia: Univ. of Missouri Press, 2002.

Smalley, Webster, ed. *Five Plays by Langston Hughes.* Bloomington: Indiana Univ. Press, 1963.

Joseph McLaren

MÜLLER, HEINER (1929–1995)

The main impulse is to stir things to their skeleton, to rid them of their flesh and surface.

—Heiner Müller, 1982

Heiner Müller, an outspoken social critic, is considered a close successor of BERTOLT BRECHT in light of his deliberate use of montage techniques and epic narration in the theater. With its multiple visual and auditory effects, Müller's DRAMATURGY presents a dynamic discourse of viewpoints and bodies. Müller is a dialectician, and his synthetic fragments and dramatic collages constitute the main components of a "Dialectic Theater," a theater of oppositional views that aims to sharpen the sensibility and critical engagement of the spectator or reader.

The relationship between the past and the present is essential to Müller and his theater. He espoused the view that older plays must be presented to contemporary audiences in new and innovative productions so as to activate the viewers' thinking. The dramatic work, then, should build a bridge between the past and the present, revising current facts for future knowledge. Accordingly, Müller adapted many plays from various dramatists, including Brecht, in which he reevaluated history to represent contemporary sociopolitical conditions. The new, according to Müller, begins with the destruction of the extant, by renaming things and looking at them in previously unknown ways. In other words, Müller's plays alienate social facts to render them more relevant and interesting to the contemporary spectator. His approach is thus suggestive of the ALIENATION EFFECTS frequently used by Brecht in his theater productions.

Müller's dramas present provocative statements and questions about politics, history, PHILOSOPHY, and the human psyche. They depict multiple power struggles between ideologies, policies, identities, and genders. Though his writing continues to be a challenge to most of his readers, and his provocative and violent images—of such phenomena as nonconformity, lust for rebellion, attacks, and restlessness—often prove too strong for his audiences, his plays have been successfully and repeatedly staged not only in GERMANY but also in different parts of the globe, including FRANCE, SPAIN, ITALY, the NETHERLANDS, the UNITED STATES, Latin America, JAPAN, Korea, GREECE, TURKEY, and the Middle East.

Born January 9, 1929, in Eppindorf, Germany, into a communist household, Müller not only made himself thoroughly familiar with the writings of Karl Marx and Walter Benjamin, but while still a young man, he also read the entire works of Friedrich Schiller and William Shakespeare. When the Nazis came to power in 1933, they arrested and imprisoned Müller's father. The son reflects on this traumatic event in a short autobiographical narrative titled "Der Vater" (1958; The Father), a work that relates Müller's first shocking encounter with national socialism and its horrors.

Following the end of World War II, Müller finished his studies and passed his high school examinations in 1949, after which he tried miscellaneous jobs. He first worked as a clerk in a district administration office and then as an employee in a bookstore. As a result of the latter job, he enjoyed complete access to the works of important German and international writers. Müller began writing professionally in 1956. He worked as a journalist for various newspapers and journals, including *Neue Deutsche Literatur* (New German Literature), became the editor of *Junge Kunst* (Young Art) and the literary adviser for many prominent theaters in East Berlin. After having been turned down twice by Brecht, Müller ironically became dramaturg of the Berliner Ensemble—Brecht's former theater—from 1970 to 1976 and 1992 to 1995. In 1975 Müller traveled for nine months to the United States, during which time he taught as a guest lecturer at the University of Texas in Austin. From 1976 to 1988 he worked as the literary adviser to the Berliner Volksbühne.

Müller received numerous recognitions and major literary awards during his lifetime, including the Heinrich Mann Prize (together with his wife Inge Müller) for *The Scab* (Der Lohndrücker, 1956) in 1959; the Lessing Prize in 1975; the Mülheimer Dramatist Award in 1979; the prestigious Georg Büchner Prize in 1985; the German Democratic Republic's National Prize in 1986; and the European Theater Award in 1991.

Müller's material comes from Germany; in many respects, in fact, it is Germany itself. Even though he defended the ideals of socialism until his death, Müller was critical of the political realities in East Germany. In every piece of his writing, he opposed the views of the East German government and the former national socialist regime, which, through its state-directed cultural policies and its systematic censorship and bans, worked to oppress the artist. Müller's plays always constituted responses to the dysfunctional and violent German socialist state.

Müller's first plays were *Lehrstücke*, "LEARNING PLAYS" or "didactic plays," a form of theater Brecht had created for his working-class actors in the 1930s. These plays were often considered "works in progress" and sought to show the difficulties in establishing a communist society while making use of a dialectic process essential to the plays' productions. Müller's *Lehrstücke* include *The Scab* (Der Lohndrücker, 1956), *The Correction* (Die Korrektur, 1957), *The Resettled Woman or Life in the Country* (Die Umsiedlerin oder Das Leben auf dem Lande, 1961), and *The Construction* (Der Bau, 1963–1964). Through their various proletarian protagonists—for example, the worker Balke, who is supposed to repair a furnace while it is in operation; and Bremer, an old communist who has to fight neglect and mess in his brigade—these texts criticize the extent to which life and labor in "everyday socialism" were based purely on hardship with no recognition for the hard worker, indicating the estrangement, isolation, and destruction of the human being under socialism.

Müller's adaptations constitute the second phase of his writing. To a certain extent, reworking existing plays instead of creating entirely new ones arose out of necessity for Müller, as his plays had started to be banned from the stages of local theaters. In reworking the classics, Müller was able to implant a hidden message into the script by recasting mythical themes into a contemporary setting. Using ancient Greek and Roman cultures as a mask, Müller was able to use dramas such as *Philoctetes* (Philoktet, 1965), *Heracles 5* (Herakles 5, 1966), *Oedipus Rex* (Ödipus Tyrann, 1966), *Prometheus* (1968) and *The Horatian* (Der Horatier, 1968) as political vehicles for hidden but bold and critical renderings. He also adapted many other plays from Shakespeare (*Macbeth*, 1971), Molière (*The Doctor in Spite of Himself* [Der Arzt wider Willen], 1970), and Brecht (*Mauser*, 1970). *Mauser*, considered by many critics to be a particularly significant play in the history of socialist drama, is based on Brecht's THE MEASURES TAKEN (Die Maßnahme, 1931) and criticizes the state's unhesitating use of violence against its own people for the sake of a successful revolution. Müller's favorite play, *Philoctetes*, largely considered to be an antiwar drama, bears thematic similarities to *Mauser*. *Philoctetes* is an extended metaphor for both the prehistory of the human race and the failure of the socialist revolution.

Germania Death in Berlin (Germania Tod in Berlin, 1971), *The Slaughter* (Die Schlacht, 1974), *Tractor* (Traktor, 1974), *Gundling's Life Frederick of Prussia Lessing's Sleep Dream Scream* (Leben Gundlings Prinz Friedrich von Preussen Lessings Schlaf Traum Schrei, 1976), and also his very last play, *Germania 3: Ghosts at Dead Man* (Germania 3. Gespenster am toten Mann, 1995), display both thematic and formal similarities.

They are all based on different phases of German history and draw subtle comparisons between German Democratic Republic (GDR) socialism, national socialism, and Stalinism. They all pose the question whether the "German misery" (a term frequently used by Brecht) continued to exist long after the national socialists were gone. In all five of these plays, Müller experimented with new methods of performance, making frequent use of the surreal and the grotesque. He introduced elements of horror and cruelty echoing ANTONIN ARTAUD combined with undertones of RICHARD WAGNER and SAMUEL BECKETT. The plays constitute a fragmented body consisting of a montage of scenes, of short, independent episodes that form a larger thematic context. The Slaughter emphasizes the horrors of fascism, and its disparate, violent scenes of murder, betrayal, terror, and survival recall the dehumanization during the Third Reich that is also the subject of Brecht's FEAR AND MISERY IN THE THIRD REICH (Furcht und Elend des Dritten Reiches, 1935–1939).

In HAMLETMACHINE (Die Hamletmaschine, 1977) and The Task (Der Auftrag, 1979) as well as in the previously mentioned Gundling's Life Frederick of Prussia Lessing's Sleep Dream Scream, Müller represents power relationships between the aggressor and the oppressed, turning the intellectual's failure into his preeminent theme. In plays such as Quartet (1980; Quartett, based on Choderlos de Laclos's Dangerous Liaisons [1782]) and Despoiled Shore Medeamaterial Landscape with Argonauts (Verkommenes Ufer Medeamaterial Landschaft mit Argonauten, 1982), the focus of the power relationship between the state and its subordinated individuals shifts toward the relentless battle of genders. With this new focus, Müller was able to subject colonialism and its aftermath to new perspectives and to question European civilization from yet another vantage point.

Müller, who usually appeared dressed in black and holding a thick cigar between his fingers, was an internationally acclaimed playwright when he died of cancer in 1995. While he saw himself as Brecht's successor ("I started there, where Brecht had left"), Müller has certainly influenced many other GDR and contemporary German dramatists. While continuously working toward changing cultural policy in the GDR, he was also directly involved in improving the conditions for writers in general. Besides writing and directing plays like a "theater-machine" (a term he himself used), he made numerous appearances on talk shows, gave frequent interviews, wrote and published essays, and never regretted the politically radical viewpoints he espoused. When asked about his thoughts on the unification of the two Germanies, he responded dryly and honestly: "I am not interested in the unification." The GDR, with all its contradictions, was an endless source of material for his works, for example, War Without Slaughter: Life in Two Dictatorships (Krieg ohne Schlacht. Leben in zwei Diktaturen, 1992). Müller saw history as the recurrence of human violence and horror. He was also convinced that the historical and contemporary material offered to him in his own country could be used to show people elsewhere how to avoid repeating similar mistakes. Hav-

ing grasped the universal quality of his material, Müller wrote in order to tell others the story of his nation. Therein lies the reason why people today are curiously interested in listening to what he has to say—be it in the bold statement of a single verse or in the performance of an entire play—even after both the GDR and its most significant playwright are gone. He died on December 30, 1995, in Berlin, Germany.

[See also Postmodernism]

SELECT PLAYS: The Scab (Der Lohndrücker, 1956; co-authored with Inge Müller); The Correction (Die Korrektur, 1957; co-authored with Inge Müller); The Resettled Woman or Life in the Country (Die Umsiedlerin oder Das Leben auf dem Lande, 1961); The Construction (Der Bau, 1963–1964; an adaptation of Erik Neutsch); Philoctetes (Philoktet, 1965; an adaptation of Sophocles); Heracles 5 (Herakles 5, 1966); Oedipus Rex (Ödipus Tyrann, 1966; an adaptation of Sophocles and Friedrich Hölderlin); The Horatian (Der Horatier, 1968); Prometheus (1968; an adaptation of Aeschylus); The Doctor in Spite of Himself (Der Arzt wider Willen, 1970; an adaptation of Molière); Mauser (1970; an adaptation of Brecht); Germania Death in Berlin (Germania Tod in Berlin, 1971); Macbeth (1971; an adaptation of Shakespeare); The Slaughter (Die Schlacht, 1974); Tractor (Traktor, 1974); Gundling's Life Frederick of Prussia Lessing's Sleep Dream Scream (Leben Gundlings Prinz Friedrich von Preussen Lessings Schlaf Traum Schrei, 1976); Hamletmachine (Die Hamletmaschine, 1977; an adaptation of Shakespeare); Fatzer (1978; an adaptation of Brecht); The Task (Der Auftrag, 1979); Quartet (Quartett, 1980; an adaptation of de Laclos); Despoiled Shore Medeamaterial Landscape with Argonauts (Verkommenes Ufer Medeamaterial Landschaft mit Argonauten, 1982); War Without Slaughter: Life in Two Dictatorships (Krieg ohne Schlacht. Leben in zwei Diktaturen, 1992); Germania 3: Ghosts at Dead Man (Germania 3: Gespenster am toten Mann, 1995)

FURTHER READING

Domdey, Horst. Produktivkraft Tod. Das Drama Heiner Müllers [The productive power of death: Heiner Müller's dramas]. Weimar: Böhlau Verlag, 1998.

Eke, Norbert Otto. Heiner Müller. Stuttgart: Reclam, 1999.

Hauschild, Jan-Christoph. Heiner Müller oder Das Prinzip Zweifel. Eine Biographie [Heiner Müller or the principle of doubt: A biography]. Berlin: Aufbau-Verlag, 2001.

Kalb, Jonathan. The Theater of Heiner Müller. Cambridge: Cambridge Univ. Press, 1998.

Schulz, Genia. Heiner Müller. Stuttgart: Metzlersche Verlagsbuchhandlung, 1980.

Teraoka, Arlene Akiko. The Silence of Entropy or Universal Discourse. The Postmodernist Poetics of Heiner Müller. New York: P. Lang, 1985.

Natasa Masanovic

MUNK, KAJ (1898–1944)

Would the day come when the roar of wild swans and the screams of birds of prey in the night are heard again in our sweet country.
—Kaj Munk, 1928

As a dramatist and passionate debater, Kaj Munk was a controversial figure during the interwar years. Born on January 13, 1898, in Maribo, he was early orphaned and grew up in a strongly religious small landowning family in the southern part of DENMARK. Already as a boy he was convinced of having a mission in life, and he was early deeply impressed by Søren Kierkegaard's Christian existentialism. In 1924 he assumed a pastorage in the West Jutland parish Vedersø whose people he depicted with sympathetic insight in the modern miracle play *The Word* (*Ordet*, 1932). To Munk to be a Christian meant "to be in a condition of eternal conflict, conflict with God, with oneself, with the world"—not a bad point of departure for a dramatist.

Munk was quite unique in contemporary Danish theater. His aim was to revive the classical drama of William Shakespeare and Friedrich Schiller and to let loose the great passions on the domestic Danish stage. The hero, the biblical Herod, of his first staged play *An Idealist* (*En Idealist*, 1928) was modeled after William Shakespeare's *Richard III*—a monumental character who did not shrink away from any means to reach his end but at the height of his power was defeated by looking into the clear blue eyes of the infant Christ on his mother's arm.

As a sort of clue to the play, Munk provided the published edition of *An Idealist* with an ironic quotation from Kierkegaard— "Purity of Heart is to will one Thing"—ironic because the quotation is cut off. To Kierkegaard the truly pure of heart will only the good. Herod wills only one thing—power for power's sake—and was crushed by God, the invisible antagonist of most of Munk's plays.

Munk's dramatic heroes are great norm-breaking individuals such as Professor Krater, modeled after famous Danish critic Georg Brandes (*In the Breakers* [*I brændingen*, 1929]); Henry VIII (*Cant*, 1931); and Sigbrit, the manipulating mother of Dyveke, the Danish king Christian II's mistress (*The Dictatoress* [*Diktatorinden*, 1938]). His contempt for democracy made him put his trust in the modern dictators Benito Mussolini and Adolf Hitler as potential saviors of the world from chaos and disruption. Munk was, however, not a blind hero worshipper. In his fictive Mussolini play *The Victory* (*Sejren*, 1936), the chancellor is defeated at the moment he breaks away from peace and attacks a defenseless country. In *He Sits at the Melting Pot* (*Han sidder ved Smeltediglen*, 1938), he had the courage to stand up against the German persecutions of the Jews but is naive enough to believe that anti-Semitism was a passing phenomenon and not the very core of Nazi ideology. He even thought that Hitler might have enjoyed the play.

He Sits at the Melting Pot laid the blame mainly on Hitler's surroundings and did not seriously affect the Godlike status of Der Führer. That did not happen until Hitler's troops invaded Denmark. From then on Munk indefatigably fought against Nazism and all it stood for. He had finally found his mission in real life and went open eyed toward his martyrdom (he was murdered by the Gestapo on January 4, 1944, in Hørbylunde, near Silkeborg). After the liberation, in 1945 the Royal Theatre commemorated Munk by staging his resistance play *Niels Ebbesen* (1942), banned during the occupation but known from Munk's readings and from underground circulation.

PLAYS: *Love* (*Kærlighed* 1926, perfect 1935); *An Idealist* (*En Idealist*, 1928); *In the Breakers* (*I brændingen*, 1929); *Cant* (1931); *The Word* (*Ordet*, 1932); *The Elect* (*De Udvalgte*, 1933); *The Victory* (*Sejren*, 1936); *Pilatus* (1937, written 1917); *The Dictatoress* (*Diktatorinden*, 1938); *He Sits at the Melting Pot* (*Han sidder ved Smeltediglen*, 1938); *Niels Ebbesen* (1942, perfect 1945); *Before Cannae* (*Før Cannae*, 1943)

FURTHER READING

Mitchell, P. M. *A History of Danish Literature*. New York: American Scandinavian Foundation, 1958.

Møller, Per Stig. *Munk*. Copenhagen: Gyldendal, 2000.

Munk, Kaj. *Five Plays by Kaj Munk*. Ed. and tr. by R. P. Keigwin. London: Allen & Unwin, 1953.

Kela Kvam

MUNRO, RONA (1959–)

Audiences out there are very hungry for reflections of women's stories which haven't been told.

—Rona Munro, interview in *Feminist Stages*, 1996

A prolific playwright, Rona Munro has written extensively for film and television as well as for theater. Her television work includes scripts for the cult series *Dr. Who*, while her film scripts include Ken Loach's *Ladybird, Ladybird* (1994) and the Golden Globe–nominated *Aimee and Jaguar* (1999).

Munro was born in Aberdeen, SCOTLAND, in 1959. She began writing plays at school in Aberdeen, and on graduation from Edinburgh University, she worked as a cleaner to support herself as a writer. Her first full-length commission, for the Traverse Theatre, Edinburgh, was *Fugue* (1983), in which a young woman, haunted by a ghost, is played by two actresses, each portraying different aspects of her personality. A residency with Paines Plough Theatre Company followed in 1985 (*Piper's Cave*), but Munro took on a longer-term commitment that same year to the feminist company MsFits, which she formed with fellow Aberdonian Fiona Knowles. Strongly committed to voicing women's stories, MsFits took COMEDY sketches, examining women's lives in a range of small-scale and alternative venues. Munro retired from performing in 1991 but still writes a one-woman show each year for Knowles and values her experience as a performer in shaping her dealings with actors. *Rehab* (2003), her film for the BBC, was workshopped with the actors after research in a drug rehabilitation clinic.

Munro's breakthrough play was the award-winning *Bold Girls* (1991), the story of four women living in Belfast, which quickly established itself and is revived regularly and studied as an important example of feminist playwriting. Munro explores the pressures on the women, from the political situation, from poverty, and from the expectations of a patriarchal society. The play opens in Marie's kitchen, where, throughout the action, she endeavors to fulfill the role of a "good" woman by feeding her children; her neighbors, the mother and daughter Nora and Cassie; the strange girl Deirdre, who invades her home; and even the local sparrows. (Critic Jan Macdonald [2000] has examined the part that food plays in Munro's works.) Deirdre's intrusion into the lives of the "bold girls" on a search for her personal history shakes Marie's existence.

In *Bold Girls* and later plays, notably *Your Turn to Clean the Stair* (1992), *Snake* (1999), and *Iron* (2002), Munro pursues her dissection of a contemporary society crippled by self-delusion. In contrast to her comedic works for *MsFits*, these are serious, often painful examinations of blighted lives, whether in Belfast, a London housing estate (*Snake*), or in prison (*Iron*). In *Iron* two women rediscover each other in a search for "truth" after fifteen years apart. Josie comes to visit her mother, Fay, in prison, where she is serving life for the murder of Josie's father. Josie wants Fay to help her remember her life before the age of eleven, and Fay wants Josie to enable her to "see" outside the confines of the prison. Neither woman is prepared for the impact Fay's "truth" will have on them.

Munro's work, notably *Piper's Cave* and the award-winning THE MAIDEN STONE (1995), is underpinned by images of nature, myth, and legend that arise unbidden or reveal characters' deepest desires. She creates forms that often challenge conventional linear narrative, sliding between time frames or offering alternative stories within the same piece. Above all, it is Munro's mastery of the spoken word that distinguishes her work, whether the dialect of *Maiden Stone* or the jagged REALISM of *Snake*.

SELECT PLAYS: *Fugue* (1983); *Ghost Story* (1985); *Piper's Cave* (1985); *Saturday at the Commodore* (1989); *Bold Girls* (1991); *Your Turn to Clean the Stair* (1992); *The Maiden Stone* (1995); *Snake* (1999); *Iron* (2002)

FURTHER READING

Bain, Audrey. "Loose Canons: Identifying a Women's Tradition in Playwriting." In *Scottish Theatre since the Seventies*, ed. by Randall Stevenson and Gavin Wallace. Edinburgh: Edinburgh Univ. Press, 1996.

Goodman, Lizbeth. *Feminist Stages: Interviews with Women in Contemporary British Theatre*. Amsterdam: Harwood Academic Pubs., 1996.

Horvat, Ksenija, and Barbara Bell. "Sue Glover, Rona Munro and Lara Jane Bunting: Echoes and Open Spaces." In *Contemporary Scottish Women Writers*, ed. by Aileen Christianson and Alison Lumsden. Edinburgh: Edinburgh Univ. Press, 2000.

Macdonald, Jan. "Food as Signifier and Symbol in the Work of Contemporary Scottish Women Dramatists." In *A Theatre That Matters: Twentieth-Century Scottish Drama and Theatre*, ed. by Valentina Poggi and Margaret Rose. Milan: Edizioni Unicopli, 2000.

Scullion, Adrienne. "Contemporary Scottish Women Playwrights." In *Modern British Women Playwrights*, ed. by Elaine Aston and Janelle Reinelt. Cambridge: Cambridge Univ. Press, 2000.

Triesman, Susan. "Transformations and Transgressions: Women's Discourse on the Scottish Stage." In *British and Irish Women Dramatists since 1958*, ed. by Trevor R. Griffiths and Margaret Llewellyn-Jones. Buckingham: Open Univ. Press, 1993.

Barbara A. E. Bell

MURAYAMA TOMOYOSHI (1901–1977)

Murayama Tomoyoshi was a Japanese artist, playwright, director, scene designer, drama theorist, novelist, and children's author. After extensive reading in Western PHILOSOPHY at university, Murayama decided that Marxism offered him the most ideological satisfaction, and he was a leader of left-wing theater in JAPAN throughout his active life. In the 1920s such drama was referred to as the "proletarian drama movement."

Drawing had been a passion of Murayama's from a young age, and on a trip to GERMANY in 1922–1924 he was overwhelmed by theater and contemporary Western art, particularly that of Wassily Kandinsky.

On his return to Japan, Murayama formed an AVANT-GARDE art group that attracted much attention by taking over the recently built Tsukiji Little Theatre (Tsukiji Shōgekijō) for a highly successful evening of experimental theater and dance. At the end of 1924 Murayama was commissioned to design for a mainstream SHINGEKI production of GEORG KAISER's FROM MORNING TO MIDNIGHT; this was his first contact with the *shingeki* movement, and his set became famous as Japan's first constructivist theater design.

Murayama began writing *shingeki* plays in early 1926; his early works are primarily expressionist with compressed, staccato dialogue and sudden changes of plot direction. Although Murayama was already involved in proletarian theater, it took some time for his plays to reflect current demands from leading theorists that plays should embody a sociopolitical objective. By 1927 Murayama had moved closer to what was required ideologically with *Nero in a Skirt* (*Suka-to o Haita Nero*). This is a study of Catherine II of Russia, indicating, through her callousness toward her soldiers and her cruelty toward her lover trying to intercede on their behalf, that imperial institutions (such as Japan had) are undesirable. The censor banned the play. Other plays set abroad and with implied political messages followed.

Record of a Gang of Thugs (*Boryokudanki*, 1929) was described by leading arts theorists as the best proletarian play yet. It portrays a railway strike in CHINA in 1923 and the process by which the strike was broken by a combination of hired gangsters and the military. The play ends in darkness as the soldiers open fire on the strikers, and from the darkness come defiant cries condemning imperialism and militarism and rejoicing in the formation of a national union of railway workers. KUBO SAKAE (1962), later to write the landmark left-wing drama LAND OF VOLCANIC ASH, commented favorably on the balance between the individual and the group, something of great concern to left-wing writers at the time. Murayama's subsequent plays became even more overtly political. In 1932 he was imprisoned, and in 1933 he recanted his Marxism. Although he could no longer be openly active politically, Murayama worked hard in the 1930s to unify the left-wing theater movement and after the war to reestablish it. His main practical theater activity from then on was directing, both for *shingeki* and for SHINPA; in 1974 the theater magazine *Teatoro* awarded him a prize to commemorate his 400th production. Murayama's talent as a director never dimmed, but as a leader he tried to recreate a heroic theatrical past that was increasingly out of touch with postwar Japan.

PLAYS: *Punish My Brother* (*Ani o Basseyo*, 1926); *Nero in a Skirt* (*Suka-to o Haita Nero*, 1927); *Robin Hood* (*Robin Fuddo*, 1927); *Record of a Gang of Thugs* (*Boryokudanki*, 1929); *Oriental Rolling Stock Factory* (*Toyo Sharyo Kōjō*, 1931)

FURTHER READING

Kubo Sakae. *Kubo Sakae Zenshu* [Collected Works of Kubo Sakae]. Tokyo: San'ichi Shobo, 1962. 5: 237–240.

Murayama Tomoyoshi. *Engekiteki Jijoden* [Theatrical autobiography]. 3 vols. Tokyo: Tohosha, 1973.

Nihon Kinclai Engekishi Kenkyūkai, ed. *Nijisseiki no Gikyoku, Nihon Kindai Gikyoku no Sekai* [Plays of the twentieth century: The world of modern Japanese drama]. Tokyo: Shakai Hyōronsha, 1998.

Ōyama Isao. *Kindai Nihon Gikyoku-shi* [History of modern Japanese drama]. Vols. 2–4. Yamagata: Kindai Nihon Gikyoku-shi Kankōkai, 1969–1972.

Shea, George T. *Leftwing Literature in Japan*. Tokyo: Hosei Univ. Press, 1964.

Brian Powell

MURDER IN THE CATHEDRAL

Destiny waits in the hand of God, not in the hands of statesmen.
—The Chorus, Part 1

In 1935, T. S. ELIOT, a convert to the Anglican Church, was commissioned to write a play for the Canterbury Festival of Music and Drama; the verse play, *Murder in the Cathedral*, was the result, and it was first performed in the cathedral's Chapter House, using its pulpit, its great wooden door, and the reverberating acoustics as a profoundly realistic set to celebrate the martyring of Saint Thomas, which happened in 1170 in that very place. The first actor to essay Thomas was Robert Speaight, at the invitation of E. Martin Browne (who would subsequently direct all the premieres of Eliot's plays); all three men were ardent Anglicans.

The play is static, a ritualized pageant rather than a drama, sometimes likened to early Aeschylus, and its strength lies primarily in the splendid poetry of the Chorus—the peasant women of Canterbury who are the greatest problem in production. The play's mystical subject matter creates much of its power: an exploration of the relation of perfect faith to the human will. The play begins too close to the end to create anything like character

development; whatever Thomas was—the wild, profligate friend of the king, who rose from "Cheapside brat" to chancellor and then, in Henry II's drastic miscalculation, archbishop—we have to construct the backstory for ourselves.

Arriving back in ENGLAND after an exile of seven years, Thomas knows the inevitability of his martyrdom; when the Priests welcome him back to Canterbury, Thomas tells them, "All things prepare the event. Watch." And, as though he has conjured them up, the Four Tempters appear; each tempts, and each is rejected without struggle. The Fourth Temptation is the most interesting: the vanity of martyrdom. "What earthly pride, that is not poverty / Compared with richness of heavenly grandeur? . . . I offer what you desire." Act 1 ends as Thomas tells us, "The last temptation is the greatest treason: / To do the right deed for the wrong reason." We have to take it on faith rather than by dramatic discovery that he acquiesces to his death for the right reason.

Following a sermon that forms an interval, act 2 is swift: the Knights arrive and murder Thomas brutally, and the Chorus laments the desecration with "Clear the air! clean the sky! wash the wind!" Instead of ending the play with this high moment, Eliot, modernist that he is, brings the Knights back as spin doctors, making urbane after-dinner speeches in which they justify themselves and implicate the public. The Priests are left to give thanks for a new saint, and the Chorus brings the play to resolution with contrition and prayer to the martyred Thomas. Just as martyrdom is paradoxically both a cause for mourning and rejoicing, so the play sustains typically Eliotic paradoxes: action/passivity, knowing / not knowing, and the Cathedral as deathtrap/haven.

[*See also* United States, 1929–1940]

FURTHER READING

Browne, E. Martin. *The Making of T. S. Eliot's Plays*. Cambridge: Cambridge Univ. Press, 1969.

Donoghue, Denis. *The Third Voice, Modern British and American Verse Drama*. Princeton, N.J.: Princeton Univ. Press, 1959.

Eliot, T. S. *Poetry and Drama*. London: Faber, 1951.

Jones, David E. *The Plays of T. S. Eliot*. London: Routledge, 1960.

Tate, Allen, ed. *T. S. Eliot: The Man and His Work*. New York: Delacorte, 1966.

Tydeman, William. *"Murder in the Cathedral" and "The Cocktail Party."* Houndmills, Basingstoke, Hampshire: Palgrave Macmillan, 1988.

Weales, Gerald. *Religion in Modern English Drama*. Philadelphia: Univ. of Pennsylvania Press, 1960.

Toby Zinman

MURPHY, TOM (1935–)

You came in that door with the audacity of despair, wild with the idea of wanting to soar, and I was the most pitiful of spiritless things.
—JPN King, Scene 7, *The Gigli Concert*

In 2002, the Abbey Theatre in Dublin staged a major retrospective of the career of Tom Murphy. Doing so was an attempt to celebrate the work of one of IRELAND's greatest living playwrights. But it was also an attempt to stimulate international awareness of that work: to the consternation and confusion of Murphy's admirers, his plays have yet to find a significant audience outside of Ireland.

Murphy was born in Tuam, a town in County Galway on Ireland's west coast, in 1935. Throughout the 1950s he worked as a teacher of metalwork and participated actively in Ireland's thriving amateur drama sector, where his interest in theater developed. As he began to attempt writing, he rejected the influence of the canonical Irish works of J. M. SYNGE and SEAN O'CASEY, instead seeking out drama by TENNESSEE WILLIAMS, FEDERICO GARCÍA LORCA, and other international writers. This rejection of traditional Irish writing (which Murphy has since reversed) probably explains why he could not find an Irish theater willing to produce A WHISTLE IN THE DARK, his first professional play. Instead, it became a huge hit in ENGLAND, where it premiered in 1961. A shocking treatment of a violent Irish family living in Coventry, the play laid the ground for much of the English drama of the 1960s, notably HAROLD PINTER's THE HOMECOMING.

The success of A Whistle in the Dark encouraged Murphy to quit his job teaching and to move to London. Yet although his work was occasionally produced during the following decade, he struggled to recapture the success of his debut. His only major achievement was Famine (1968), a challenging treatment of the Irish Famine of 1845–1848, which utilized many of the techniques of BERTOLT BRECHT.

Murphy returned to Ireland in 1970 and began to write regularly for the Abbey Theatre, which staged many of his best plays, such as the surreal The Morning After Optimism (1971). In 1976 The Sanctuary Lamp was accused of anticlericalism and became the most controversial Abbey Theatre production since Sean O'Casey's PLOUGH AND THE STARS debuted in 1926. The hostility that greeted this play caused Murphy to cease writing for a number of years.

Murphy returned to playwriting in the 1980s with a trio of quite remarkable works. The Gigli Concert (1983), Conversations on a Homecoming (1985), and Bailegangaire (1985) are among the finest dramas in the Irish repertoire—but even more remarkable is that they were all produced within only two years. In the Gigli Concert, an Irishman suffering from depression seeks assistance from an English therapist. Conversations is set in a Tuam pub, where a group of friends have met to celebrate the homecoming from America of a successful friend. And in Bailegangaire (an Irish placename, which, translated literally, means "the town without laughter"), an old woman's granddaughters listen to her story about a laughing contest that ends in death. The three plays vary widely in setting, theme, and form, but all place at their center the power of speech, particularly of storytelling.

Murphy continued to write for the Abbey in the 1990s, producing The Wake (1997; adapted from his 1994 novel The Seduction of Morality) and The House (2001), both of which focused on the return of Irish emigrants to Tuam.

One of the most unique aspects of Murphy's work is its musicality, with his dialogue carefully modulated so that character is revealed not only by words but also by sound—meaning that a conversation in a Murphy play can often recreate the harmonies and discordance of a piece of music, without ever appearing unnatural. The level of technical accomplishment in Murphy's plays is for this reason often astonishing.

His subject matter can, however, make for uncomfortable viewing. His plays are uncompromisingly honest in their treatment of depression—from which Murphy has suffered throughout his life—and other forms of human suffering. Yet the beauty of Murphy's plays is that his characters do not defeat adversity, but, through suffering, they transcend it. This transcendence is frequently achieved through artistry, in moments of glorious theatrical transformation—a religious sermon in The Sanctuary Lamp, an operatic aria in the Gigli Concert, through storytelling in Bailegangaire, and song in The Wake.

Whether Murphy's work will acquire international attention is difficult to predict, but it is indisputably deserving of it. His reputation in Ireland is nevertheless secure, and he remains one of the country's most highly esteemed artists.

PLAYS: A Whistle in the Dark (1961); On the Outside (with Noel O'Donoghue, 1962); Famine (1968); A Crucial Week in the Life of a Grocer's Assistant (1969); The Morning After Optimism (1971); The White House (1972); On the Inside (1974); The Vicar of Wakefield (after Oliver Goldsmith, 1975); The J Arthur Maginnis Story (1976); The Sanctuary Lamp (1976); Epitaph Under Ether (after J. M. Synge, 1979); The Blue Macushla (1980); The Informer (after V. C. O'Flaherty, 1981); She Stoops to Conquer (after Goldsmith, 1982); The Gigli Concert (1983); Bailegangaire (1985); Conversations on a Homecoming (1985); A Thief of a Christmas (1985); Too Late for Logic (1989); The Patriot Game (1991); She Stoops to Folly (1995); The Wake (1997); The House (2001); The Drunkard (2003); Alice Trilogy (2005)

FURTHER READING

Grene, Nicholas. The Politics of Irish Drama: Plays in Context from Boucicault to Friel. Cambridge: Cambridge Univ. Press, 1999.

———, ed. Talking About Tom Murphy. Dublin: Carysfort Press, 2002.

Murray, Christopher, ed. Special issue on Tom Murphy, Irish University Review (1987).

O'Toole, Fintan. The Politics of Magic. Dublin: New Island, 1995.

Patrick Lonergan

MURRELL, JOHN (1945–)

Born in Lubbock, Texas, in 1945, John Murrell completed a bachelor of arts degree in drama at the University of Calgary, CANADA, and has subsequently lived for the most part in

Alberta. While he was writing his first plays, he worked as a public school teacher. His first significant successes in the theater came out of his association with the Alberta Theater Projects. Murrell has recently served as the artistic director and executive producer of the Theatre Arts program at the Martha Cohen Theatre of the Epcor Centre for the Performing Arts at the Banff Centre.

In 1998 Murrell's contributions to arts education in Canada were recognized with the Gascon-Thomas Award. In 2002, his lifetime achievements as a dramatist were honored with the Canada Council's Walter Carsen Price for Excellence in the Performing Arts. For three of his plays, he has received the Chalmers Award for the best Canadian play of the year: *Waiting for the Parade* (1977), *Farther West* (1982), and *The Faraway Nearby* (1994).

Murrell's best-known and most highly regarded play may be *Waiting for the Parade*. Set in Calgary during World War II, the play focuses on five women who come together to do volunteer work in support of the war effort. These women have suddenly become defined very much by the ways in which the men in their lives have been categorized because of the war. Catherine's husband is a prisoner of war; Eve's husband is too old to serve; Janet's husband has a job that will keep him out of combat; one of Margaret's sons is serving in the navy, but the other has been put in prison for seeking to undermine the war effort; and Marta's father has been placed in a camp for suspected Nazi sympathizers. The women respond internally and externally to their increasingly conflicted senses of themselves.

In a number of his plays, Murrell has explored the psyches of well-known artists. *Power in the Blood* (1975) is based on the life of the controversial evangelist Amy Semple McPherson. Restaged as *Sarah* in 2002, at the Theater Edouard VII in Paris, MEMOIR (1977) focuses on the efforts of an aging Sarah Bernhardt to complete her autobiography. She relies a great deal on Pitou, her male secretary, who imaginatively acts out the scenes that she is struggling to describe. *October*, which premiered in Toronto in 1988, explores the relationships between three characters—an actress, her Italian lover, and the dancer Isadora Duncan. *The Faraway Nearby* is a treatment of the later life and the aesthetic obsessions of American artist Georgia O'Keefe. *Farther West* depicts the adventures of one of the most colorfully infamous figures of the settlement of western Canadian, the whorehouse madame May Buchanan.

PLAYS: *Metamorphosis* (1970); *Haydn's Head* (1973); *Arena* (1975); *Power in the Blood* (1975); *Teaser* (1975); *A Great Noise, a Great Light* (1976); *Memoir* (1977, published 1978); *Waiting for the Parade: Faces of Women in War* (1977, published 1980); *Bajazet* (1979); *Farther West* (1982, published 1985); *New World* (1984, published 1985); *October* (1988); *Democracy* (1991); *The Faraway Nearby* (1994); *Filumena* (an opera, 2003)

FURTHER READING

Hall, Lynda. "Remembrance of Things Past and Present." *Canadian Theatre Review* 79–80 (Fall 1994): 120–123.

Manthorne, Katherine E. "*The Faraway Nearby*." *American Art* 13, no. 1 (Spring 1999): 2–9.

Salter, Denis. "Ancestral Voices: The (European) Plays of John Murrell." In *On-Stage and Off-Stage*, ed. by Albert-Reiner Glaap and Rolf Althof. St. Johns, Newfoundland: Breakwater, 1996. 201–211.

Martin Kich

DIE MUTTER   See THE MOTHER

MUTTER COURAGE UND IHRE KINDER
See MOTHER COURAGE AND HER CHILDREN

MXTEATRO   See ME XIHC CO TEATRO

MYANMAR   See BURMA

MY HEART'S IN THE HIGHLANDS

Reviewing the opening on April 13, 1939, of *My Heart's in the Highlands* for the *New York Journal American*, John Anderson had trouble focusing his thoughts: "If you squint your eyes and try to understand it, it doesn't make any sense at all, but if you let it alone and let it pry around in your gizzard, it will very likely tug at your heart strings. People seemed to find themselves weeping without knowing what the hell was the matter with them." To this response WILLIAM SAROYAN began his forty years' experience in the theater. Although the play in its initial production ran for only forty-four performances, Saroyan had made his point, as he expressed it in a preface to the published play: "It is better to be a good human being than to be a bad one. It is just naturally better."

Plot is never a dominant feature of Saroyan's art, but neither is character analysis, dramatic conflict, or elaborate crisis. He presents a few people, evokes moods, and manipulates the audience's emotions, and he does this with believable optimism and surprising innocence. In an old house in Fresno, California, a nine-year-old boy named Johnny lives in poverty with his father, an unsuccessful poet, and his grandmother. One day old Jasper MacGregor, an actor, who has run away from an old folks' home, appears at Johnny's house and plays his bugle to the music of Robert Burns's poetry with such plaintive beauty that the neighbors all bring them food. When the people from the old folks' home take MacGregor away, Johnny tries again to con Mr. Kosach, the grocer, for food, but things are bad. Johnny's father tries to pay for groceries with his poems; the real estate man tells them they are being evicted because they are behind in their rent. MacGregor appears after escaping again and dies while playing a scene from King Lear. The new tenants arrive, and Johnny, his father, and grandmother leave. "My heart's in the Highlands, my heart is not here. My heart's in the Highlands a'chasing the deer" (Robert Burns).

In the spring of 1939 the world was in turmoil. Serious men had tried in vain to warn America of the dangers of Adolf Hitler, who in March, in defiance of the Munich agreement of the previous September, completely obliterated CZECHOSLOVAKIA from the map. President Franklin Roosevelt sensed a loss of momentum for his New Deal programs, but there was no doubt that the long recession was ending. People, however, had mixed feelings about their future. Broadway, as always, was catering to a broad scope of audiences. *Hellzapoppin'*, from the previous fall, was going strong. In January GEORGE S. KAUFMAN and MOSS HART replaced *The Fabulous Invalid* with a spectacle suggesting the future—*The American Way*. There were plenty of COMEDIES, but on April 17, 1939, S. N. BEHRMAN would point a finger with NO TIME FOR COMEDY. The public sensed the need for more serious thinking. THORNTON WILDER's OUR TOWN had just closed in New York, and ROBERT SHERWOOD's ABE LINCOLN IN ILLINOIS was still playing at the Plymouth Theatre. In February a new voice of concern appeared in LILLIAN HELLMANN's THE LITTLE FOXES; in March PHILIP BARRY launched his high comedy of Main Line life in THE PHILADELPHIA STORY. Both would run a year on Broadway.

Into this melange of frivolous, serious, demanding, comic, thoughtful, and even irritating drama, Saroyan dropped his whimsical aberration on the impulsive love of beauty among people.

[*See also* United States, 1929–1940]

FURTHER READING

Brown, John Mason. *Broadway in Review*. New York: Norton, 1940.

McCarthy, Mary. *Sights and Spectacles, 1937–1956*. New York: Farrar, Straus, 1956.

Saroyan, William. "How to See." *Theatre Arts* (May 1941): 203–216.

Vernon, Granville. "My Heart's in the Highlands." *Commonweal* 30 (April 28, 1939): 22.

Walter J. Meserve

MY PARTNER

My Partner by BARTLEY CAMPBELL opened on September 16, 1879, at the Union Square Theatre in New York City. The play ran through October 18 before going on tour; there were productions in Berlin (1883) and London (1884).

The play begins with a love triangle between Mary Brandon and two mining partners named Joe Saunders and Ned Singleton. Mary loves both men, but Ned promises to marry her, and she has sexual relations with him. Joe, not suspecting that he and his partner are interested in the same woman, is about to declare his love and propose marriage when he learns the nature of Mary's involvement with Ned; he demands that his recreant partner marry the girl within three days (a nicely arbitrary deadline that invites mishap!) and subsequently dissolves their partnership. Before Ned can keep his promise, he receives a visit from Josiah Scraggs, an old acquaintance and secret enemy of Matthew Brandon, Mary's father. Scraggs suggests that Mary

has been Joe's mistress, and in the ensuing scuffle he picks up a knife and kills Ned. The miners arrest Joe for Ned's murder; months pass, and Mary returns from a mysterious prolonged absence to attest to his character; and Joe suddenly proclaims that they were secretly married in order to ensure the restoration of her father's affections and protect her from Scraggs's slanders. Before the jury can hang Joe, Wing Lee, the stock comic "Chinee" character, produces a torn shirt that incriminates Scraggs, and the lovers look forward to a happy future.

Campbell locates his action in the California landscape; the mountain country is a virtual paradise that confers an Edenic innocence on its inhabitants, where poetic justice flows not from religion or moral abstraction, as in most midcentury MELODRAMA, but from the land itself. Joe refers to "California, where the trees are larger, and men's hearts bigger than anywhere else in all creation," and when young Grace Brandon asks whether there is any place like California, Sam Bowler, her suitor, answers, "Except heaven, and California up here in the mountains is so close to it that none of us want to leave it." The community is upset when circumstances subject Joe, an upright man, to a charge of murder, but when the last-minute discovery saves the victim, it also restores and vindicates the people's faith. Nothing can remain wrong in this Eden; error and transgression settle effortlessly into resolution as the innocent and well-intentioned find ultimate reward. California is the land of kept promises, a garden where dreams grow and hopes flourish.

The *New York Times* (1879) critic described *My Partner* as "a drama of unquestionable power," a combination of COMEDY and melodrama that was "exceedingly fresh and unconventional." The journalist acclaimed the character of Major Britt—orator, politician, stump lawyer, hard drinker—as "original, amusing, and frequently witty . . . Campbell's most valuable contribution to our stage," and he asserted that the play proved "that a woman's shame is excusable as long as a woman is young and innocent."

[*See also* United States, 1860–1929]

FURTHER READING

Bank, Rosemarie. "Frontier Melodrama." In *Theatre West: Image and Impact*, ed. by Dunbar H. Ogden with Douglas McDermott and Robert K. Sarlós. Amsterdam: Rodopi, 1990. 151–160.

Mason, Jeffrey D. "*My Partner* (1879) and the West." In *Melodrama and the Myth of America*. Bloomington: Indiana Univ. Press, 1993.

Meserve, Walter J. "The American West of the 1870s and 1880s as Viewed from the Stage." *Journal of American Drama and Theatre* 3 (Winter 1991): 48–63.

Review of *My Partner*. *New York Times* (September 17, 1879): 5.

Wattenberg, Richard. "Americanizing Frontier Melodrama: From *Davy Crockett* (1872) to *My Partner* (1879)." *Journal of American Culture* 12 (Spring 1989): 7–16.

Jeffrey D. Mason

MYSTERY-BOUFFE

VLADIMIR MAYAKOVSKY wrote his second major dramatic work, *Mystery-Bouffe* (*Misteriia-buff*, 1918; revised 1921), to celebrate the first anniversary of the October Revolution in Russia. Always experimental in his choice of form and genre, Mayakovsky exploited the potential of the mystery play in this work. *Mystery-Bouffe* exhibits a rather grotesque admixture of mystery play and low, sometimes crude and blasphemous, COMEDY.

As in the original mystery plays, the basic plot is simple and straightforward and allows for no confusion between the good and the bad, the right and the wrong. A cataclysmic flood has wiped out humankind, except for seven pairs of the "Clean," who belong to the bourgeoisie, and seven pairs of the "Unclean," who belong to the proletariat. The Clean include politicians like Lloyd George and Georges Clemenceau, while the Unclean tend to be identified by profession and include a miner and a Red Army soldier (the latter introduced in the 1921 version). The play portrays the triumph of the Unclean, who eventually deposit the Clean in hell. The Unclean reject heaven as their reward and return to the paradise on earth of communism.

Reception of the play was often troubled. When Mayakovsky read *Mystery-Bouffe* to the actors of the former Aleksandrinsky Theater, reaction was so negative that the management was forced to reject the play. *Mystery-Bouffe* did find powerful admirers, however. The play's inclusion in the festivities for the first anniversary of the Revolution owes in no small measure to the advocacy of the People's Commissar of Education ANATOLY LUNACHARSKY. Despite such political support, Mayakovsky was reduced to placing a general casting call in a newspaper to drum up voluntary participation. VSEVOLOD MEYERHOLD collaborated with Mayakovsky on this production, and the painter Kasimir Malevich contributed the set designs. *Mystery-Bouffe* had a short run in no small part because it did not appeal to the conservative aesthetic tastes of the Bolsheviks. The play did draw praise, however, for its "democratic" forms. One measure of the problems that plagued the play is to be found in the fact that for the premiere Mayakovsky had to play no fewer than three roles because some of the other actors failed to show up.

When Meyerhold offered to include *Mystery-Bouffe* in the repertory of his theater, Mayakovsky revised the play extensively, and the second version had its premiere at the Third Congress of the Communist Internationale. Meyerhold placed the main action in the middle of the auditorium to great effect.

If *Mystery-Bouffe* was seen by many of Mayakovsky's contemporaries as a work that best encompassed the strivings of the new Soviet society, its reputation has been largely eclipsed since the poet's death. The strength of *Mystery-Bouffe* lies primarily in Mayakovsky's verbal fireworks, while its many weaknesses include its crude ideological slant and its poor characterization. (The latter problem, incidentally, helps to explain the reluctance of actors to participate in the first production.) Moreover, much of Mayakovsky's topical satire has lost all but historic value. Despite these problems, *Mystery-Bouffe* remains an important example of revolutionary drama, from its contempt for the bourgeoisie to its predilection for blasphemy to its absolute faith in the perfect society to come.

[*See also* Russia and the Soviet Union]

FURTHER READING

Brown, Edward J. *Mayakovsky: A Poet in the Revolution*. Princeton, N.J.: Princeton Univ. Press, 1973.

Markov, Vladimir. *Russian Futurism: A History*. Berkeley: Univ. of California Press, 1968.

Mayakovsky, Vladimir. *Plays*. Tr. by Guy Daniels. Evanston, Ill.: Northwestern Univ. Press, 1995.

Terras, Victor. *Vladimir Mayakovsky*. Boston: Twayne, 1983.

Timothy C. Westphalen

NADEEM, SHAHID (1947–)

Born in PAKISTAN in 1947, the year of the partitioning of British INDIA into the new states of India and Pakistan, Shahid Nadeem is the founder and longtime director of Ajoka, a not-for-profit theater in Pakistan that is devoted to the promotion of human rights, political and cultural secularism, and international peace. Imprisoned for his political activism in 1969, 1970, and 1979, Nadeem has been critical of the suppression of civil rights by Pakistan's military regimes and has been a proponent of reconciliation with India. His most recent imprisonment came in 1998, when the Pakistani government pointedly denounced his production of a BERTOLT BRECHT play about Adolf Hitler, THE RESISTIBLE RISE OF ARTURO UI, as a scurrilous attack on its leadership. For much of the last two and a half decades, Nadeem has been forced to live abroad. He has worked for Amnesty International while living in London from 1980 to 1988, in Hong Kong from 1991 to 1993, and later Los Angeles. He has been a Feuchtwanger Fellow and a Getty Scholar, and he has spoken on theatrical topics and political issues in a broad range of venues: for instance, one of his presentations has been titled "Theatre for Social Change in Pakistan: Crossing Frontiers & Breaking Barriers." While he has been abroad, his plays have continued to be staged in Pakistan, but in "guerrilla" productions in underground theaters.

Nadeem has written more than three dozen produced plays. Some were written originally in Urdu or Punjabi, while others were written originally in English. Two collections of the plays in Urdu and Punjabi have been published. Some of his plays have treated historical figures and events, while others have addressed contemporary topics. Bulha (2003) provides a dramatic portrait of the legendary 17th-century Sufi mystic and poet. On the other hand, in Bala King (1998), he delineates the process by which successive Pakistani governments have criminalized free political expression. In Trapped (2001), he depicts the last hours of two men, one Middle Eastern, who are trapped in one of the World Trade Center towers after the terrorist attacks of September 11, 2001.

Perhaps his most frequently and widely produced play, Dukhini (1998) is a bilingual play about the human traffic in women and children across South Asia. It presents the case study of the mistreatment of a Bangladeshi woman illegally transported into Pakistan. Nadeem clearly views the theater as a vehicle for social change. With funding provided by several international arts and cultural foundations, Dukhini has been staged in a large number of Bangladeshi towns and villages as a warning against the empty promises made by those who are conducting the traffic of human beings.

Nadeem has also written eight serial dramas for Pakistani television—though, since 1998, a ban on broadcasting his work has been enforced in Pakistan. In the feature film Mujahid—The Holy Warrior (2004), which he wrote and produced, he focuses on the adjustments facing young Pakistanis whose experiences fighting with the Mujahadeen against the Soviets in Afghanistan has radicalized them politically and culturally and who must now resume their everyday lives in Pakistan. He has also produced two documentaries on human rights efforts in South Asia. His articles on political and cultural topics have appeared in The Far Eastern Economic Review, Index on Censorship, BBC Urdu Service, Zee News, The Leveler (London), The Frontline (Madras), The Daily Times (Lahore), and other Pakistani newspapers including The Herald, The Muslim, and The Newsline.

SELECT PLAYS: A Granny for All Seasons (Aik Thee Nani, 1993); Bala King (1998); Bulha (2003); The Acquittal (Barri, 2001); Border-Border (2001); Dukhini (1998); Sixth River (1992); Third Knock (Teesri Dastak, 2001); Toba Tek Singh; Trapped (2001)

FURTHER READING
Rahman, Maseeh. "Mystic's Life Highlights Fool's World of Fundamentalism." South China Morning Post (January 28, 2004): 12.

Martin Kich

NA DNE See THE LOWER DEPTHS

NAGHIU, IOSIF (1932–2003)

The most outspoken and uncompromising playwright of his generation, Iosif Naghiu published several volumes of plays, most of them banned during the Nicolae Ceauşescu regime in ROMANIA. Only a few of them saw the limelight and enjoyed, as in the case of The Absence (Absenta, 1969) and In One Single Evening (Intr'o Singura Vara, 1974), general acclaim and awards at national theater festivals. In 1982 the unyielding author withdrew his play The Agamemnon Mystery (Misterul Agamemnon) a few days after its opening because of too much meddling with the text. He was ignored for many years, until the opening in 1994 of one of his most interesting plays, The Cell of the Disappeared Poet (Celula poetului disparut). The same year his play The Special Hospital (Spitalul special) received the Best Play of the Year award. Naghiu served until his death as secretary of the Romanian Writers Union. He has remained one of the most respected playwrights who had survived the postcommunist transition.

In The Special Hospital, the author compares the world to a hospital where the injured reformers and the infamous informants who shot them are put in the same room to recover. The hospital director lusts after the shining imported chairs meant for the patients, while the attending physician, Deseara, is investigated as to why she hung two socks of different colors, one red and one orange, on her balcony to dry. She is tortured in the hospital's basement and raped by her superior.

The disappointment with the state of affairs after the 1989 revolution finds its expression in *The Cell of the Disappeared Poet*. Daniel Pana, a former dissident poet, returns to visit the cell where he was tortured and humiliated. The motivation for his return is unclear. In a dialogue with his former jailer, he confesses that now that he is free to write, his pen has run dry, and he has nothing to say. He suffers from a total loss of identity and complete disorientation in a world that appears to him no different from the one before the change. He finds it natural to return to his former prison to "recharge his batteries" by searching for his confiscated poems. Perhaps Naghiu's most disturbing play is *The Window* (*Fereastra*, 1981) in which a crippled old woman spies on the entire town from her chair by the window and sees a tightrope walker falling to his death. She declares the "accident" as a setup. The townspeople are up in arms, and the authorities, through their representative, the Doctor, forbid her to look outside and install a blind man in her armchair. Miraculously, however, the fall occurs over and over in front of the window.

Naghiu's dramatic output, spanning over four decades, encompasses various dramatic modes of expression from SURREALISM to realistic discourse. His characters pursue a tireless quest for absolute justice in a world of shadows where even the strong lose their identity. Like their author, they are uncompromising and are ready to suffer the consequences of taking the high moral road.

SELECT PLAYS: *The Absence* (*Absenta*, 1969); *The Hood Over The Eyes* (*Gluga pe ochi*, 1970); *In One Single Evening* (*Intr-o singura seara*, 1974); *The Window* (*Fereastra*, 1981); *The Agamemnon Mystery* (*Misterul Agamemnon*, 1982); *The Boat Is Full* (*Barca e plina*, 1984); *The Suitcase with Butterflies* (*Valiza cu fluturi*, 1986); *The Execution Will Be Postponed* (*Executia va fi amanita*, 1993); *The Cell of the Disappeared Poet* (*Celula poetului disparut*, 1994); *The Special Hospital* (*Spitalul special*, 1994)

FURTHER READING

Cocora, Ion. *Privitor Ca La Teatru II*. Cluj-Napoca, Romania: Editura Dacia, 1977.

Iosif, Mira. *Teatrul Nostru Cel De Toate Serile*. Bucuresti, Romania: Editura Eminescu, 1979.

Mincu, Dumitru. *Scurta Istorie a Literaturii Romane, IV Perioada Contemporana Dramaturgia Critica*. Bucuresti, Romania: Editura Iriana, 1997.

Naghiu, Iosif. *Celula poetului disparut. Teatru. Colectia Dramaturgia Originala Romaneasca*. Bucuresti, Romania: Editura Expansion, 1994.

Moshe Yassur

NAGY, PHYLLIS (1962–)

Born in New York City in 1962, Phyllis Nagy never intended to become a playwright. She studied music theory and composition at New York University. She had planned to be a poet. Her first play, *Plaza Delores*, was written for a workshop run by a friend and producer in a small theater in Vermont. An early version of BUTTERFLY KISS (1990 revised 1994) was begun while she was studying in the dramatic writing program at New York University; a further draft was written in 1989. Two years later, quitting the work she was doing in real estate and at the *New York Times*, Nagy took part in a two-week residency with the Royal Court in 1991, after which she settled in London permanently.

At the end of the 1980s Nagy's play *Girl Bar* was produced, but its reception was mixed among lesbians who, discomforted, struggled with the way it addressed previously unexplored topics such as obsession with a straight girl and racism within a lesbian community. In ENGLAND, Nagy's career as a playwright immediately became high profile as the Royal Court, backed by the incoming Court director, Stephen Daldry, launched a production of *Weldon Rising* (1992). As co-director of Gay Sweatshop, Lois Weaver (of SPLIT BRITCHES) commissioned Nagy's *Entering Queens* (1993), a piece that confounded expectations for a gay play. Moving out of recognizable structures of identity politics, *Entering Queens* marked a departure from then-current identity politics, radically contesting, rather than celebrating, gay identity. *Butterfly Kiss*, a provocative drama, represents the maternal as a site of violence, daring audiences to consider murder as a loving act. *Disappeared* (1992) examines personal loneliness and the anonymity that accompanies urban life. Next came *The Strip* (1995), a complex dramatization of gender trouble that premiered at the Royal Court Theatre. In *Never Land* (1998), a haunting and poetic play, Nagy returns to the landscape of family emotions, the longing for home, and the sedimentation of prejudice. *The Talented Mr. Ripley* (1998) is an adaptation based on the cult novel by Patricia Highsmith. She first feature film, *Mrs. Harris*, opened in September 2005 in Toronto.

Nagy's experiments with the language of theater widen the scope of theatrical possibility through innovative structures, explosive themes, and transgressive interlacings of cultural, social, and sexual identities. Like Judith Butler, Nagy rehearses and stages acts of gender trouble. Nagy creates characters that rupture the sexual, social, cultural, and national systems that seek to contain the range of their desires. Working with the complex structures of musical composition rather than linear narrative, Nagy's dramaturgical frame politicizes through formal experimentation. Her AVANT-GARDE techniques have tended to create impatience in some audiences who have found the challenges the material presents difficult to comprehend. Not content with mirroring fixed identities, Nagy invents highly imaginative, innovative, and ironic dramas in which characters pass through numerous dis-identifications that challenge fixed notions of identity, exploring the tensions of the performative nature of queer identity without erasing the material and historical reality of our lives. Nagy's plays explore positions of marginality and otherness, provoking us to think outside the fictions that work to regulate and maintain our desires.

[See also Gay and Lesbian Drama; United States, 1940–Present]

SELECT PLAYS: *Butterfly Kiss* (1990 revised 1994); *Awake* (1991); *Disappeared* (1992); *Weldon Rising* (1992); *Entering Queens* (1993); *Trip's Cinch* (1994); *The Scarlet Letter* (1995); *The Strip* (1995); *Never Land* (1998); *The Talented Mr. Ripley* (1998); *The Seagull* (2003)

FURTHER READING

Aston, Elaine. *Feminist Views on the English Stage: Women Playwrights 1990–2000.* Cambridge: Cambridge Univ. Press, 2003.

Edgar, David, ed. *State of Play: Playwrights on Playwriting.* London: Faber, 1999.

Kerry Moore

THE NAME

You don't care. You never listen when I talk to you.
—The Girl, Act 1

JON FOSSE's drama *The Name* (*Namnet*) was written in 1994 and first performed at Den Nationale Scene in Bergen, Norway on May 27, 1995. It has been shown on Norwegian Public Television and performed in theaters all over Europe. In 1996 the play won the Ibsen Prize, which is awarded to works that promote new Norwegian drama.

As a representative example of Fosse's work, *The Name* has a simple story and one-dimensional characters. A young couple arrives at the girl's parents' house. The girl is pregnant and clearly uncomfortable with the situation, while the boy, who has never met her parents before, is left more or less alone with his things: a coat, a suitcase, and a book. The girl's mother is occupied by her bodily pain and the daily trip to the convenience store, and her father is tired because of his work. Only the sister tries to address the stranger, but her communication is childish and helpless. During the play, the girl and the boy try to discuss a name for the child but cannot agree. The girl's old boyfriend turns up, and she flirts with him, while the boy puts on his coat and walks out of the door.

The Name exposes alienation and homelessness. The characters are not able to communicate; their talk is absorbed in an unresponsive void, and they keep uttering the same phrases over and over again or are unable to finish thoughts and sentences. The girl accuses the boy of being uninterested in her and the child and for not listening. In a self-confirming ritual, she repeats the words, "You never listen", "You don't care," while the boy clings to his book. The notion of a home is destroyed by the asocial and unfriendly atmosphere in the parents' house and literally by the couple's lack of a place to live.

As he is not allowed to introduce himself, the boy has no name throughout the play. This namelessness may point to a more fundamental situation, where he hovers between existence and nonexistence. If not directly a persona non grata, he is at least a kind of absent person, a circumstance that is marked by the missing name. This fundamentally philosophical theme is typical of Fosse's work, which persistently raises questions regarding basic human conditions. In this case, also the discussion between the young couple about a name for their child points to an existential dimension of the play.

In order to be adopted into a social, cultural, and linguistic community, each person requires the verbal sign of a name. Thus, the name is a signature, distinguishing an individual from the others, which gives her or him a historical, cultural, or familial context of significance and an opportunity to "fill in," to give meaning to a word. But when the boy suggests "Bjarne" as an "appropriate" name, this implies the complexity of the whole name problematic. Bjarne is the girl's former boyfriend, and the boy's suggestion discloses his jealousy and projects it onto the unborn child. There is a similar irony involving the suggested girl name "Beate," which means "happy."

The Name portrays family life in late modernity and presents an unpleasant state lacking empathy, communication, or any deeper meaning. In the middle of this setting, Fosse situates a linguistic and existential topic connected to a person's name and the irony embedded in our ways of searching and expressing identity and reason in our use of language.

[See also Alienation Effect; Norway]

FURTHER READING

Gran, Anne-Britt. "What Is New in the Norwegian Theatre?" ODIN (2001). http://www.dep.no/odin/english/p30008168/history/032091-991297/dok-bn.html.

Sætre, Lars. "Modernitet og heimløyse. Form og tematikk i *Namnet* av Jon Fosse." In *Norsk litterær årbok* Oslo: Samlaget, 2001. 149–178.

Unni Langås

NAMNET   See THE NAME

NÅR VI DØDE VÅGNER   See WHEN WE DEAD AWAKEN

NATHANSEN, HENRI (1868–1944)

I sometimes think I am a little too much a Jew. I feel too much at home here—inside the walls. But there is something else outside after all—a hole has been cut in the wall—
—Hugo, Act 4, *Inside the Walls*

Henri Nathansen was born into a Jewish family on July 17, 1868, in Hjørring, DENMARK. His literary work is characterized by a permanent conflict between his firm affiliations to his Jewish milieu and a longing to cut his roots. He admired the cosmopolitan Danish critic Georg Brandes, the leader of the modern breakthrough in Scandinavia, but at the same time he thought that Brandes betrayed his Jewish origin and lacked the mental solidarity lying behind the spiritual homelessness of the Jews. As for Brandes, he felt Nathansen more delicate than a soft-boiled egg without a shell.

Nathansen started his literary career as a prose writer but had originally dreamed of becoming an actor. In 1904 he made his debut as a dramatist, and in the following years, he wrote almost exclusively plays. In 1909 he became a stage director at the Royal Theatre, succeeding William Bloch by whose poetic REALISM he was deeply impressed. Nathansen directed most of his plays himself.

Nathansen's by far most famous play is Inside the Walls (Indenfor Murene), first staged in 1912 and still regularly performed. With great warmth Nathansen introduces us to the Levin family, gathered around the Sabbath table with Old Levin, a wealthy stockbroker, presiding at the head as a lovable but conservative and stubborn patriarch, conscious of his race and happy and secure inside the four walls of his home surrounded by his family. The atmosphere is cheerful, but something is not quite as usual. The daughter Esther is belated. She arrives in the middle of the meal from the university, where she, without her father's knowledge but with the tacit accept of her mother, follows the lectures of a young Dr. Herming to whom she is secretly engaged. Esther is an emancipated young lady who compares her secluded home—to her elder brothers "an oasis in the middle of the desert"—with "The Dead Sea." The engagement shocks the old Levins but forces the two pair of parents together. The dinner party in Herming's home leads to a clash of cultures. Prejudices reign on both sides, but the sympathy goes to Old Levin and not to the arrogant and in his heart anti-semitic Herming. Old Levin leaves the party in anger. Esther is split between her love for her fiancé and her loyalty toward her roots, but in the end a happy ending for the two young people seems possible.

By his empathetic description of an old-fashioned Jewish family in Copenhagen, Nathansen has created a Danish classic. In 1988 Inside the Walls was transformed into the musical Esther, with text by Paul Hammerich and music by Bent Fabricius Bjerre, but there is no doubt that the play, representing Danish realism at its best, will outlive the musical on the Danish stage.

When he wrote Inside the Walls, Nathansen could not imagine the horrors that lay ahead. During the occupation he had to flee to Sweden, where, on February 16, 1944, in Lund, he took his own life.

PLAYS: Mother Is Right (Mor har Ret, 1904); The Good Citizen (Den gode Borger, 1907); Daniel Hertz (1908); The Garden of Dana (Danas Have, 1908); The Dream (Drømmen, 1911); Inside the Walls (Indenfor Murene, 1912); The Affair (Affæren, 1913); Dr. Wahl (modeled after Georg Brandes, 1915)

FURTHER READING
Rossel, Sven H., ed. A History of Danish Literature. Lincoln: Univ. of Nebraska Press, 1992.
Wamberg, Niels Birger. "København-forfattere." In Danske digtere i det 20. århundre 3rd ed. vol. 1. Copenhagen: Gad, 1980.

Kela Kvam

NATTEN ÄR DAGENS MOR   See THE NIGHT IS MOTHER TO THE DAY

NATURALISM

In theater and drama, naturalism has two principal meanings. In the broader sense, it is almost synonymous with REALISM. When a distinction is made, naturalism is seen as extreme or intensified realism, a greater fidelity to the minutiae of life, and a deeper descent into the more sordid aspects of life. For instance, one might say that TENNESSEE WILLIAMS's A STREETCAR NAMED DESIRE with its vulgar language and its onstage rape is more naturalistic than ARTHUR MILLER's DEATH OF A SALESMAN. Similarly, HENRIK IBSEN's GHOSTS, in which sexual disease is a prominent motif, is more naturalistic than A DOLL'S HOUSE. Naturalism in this sense claims to encompass more of life than realism.

The other, narrower sense of the word concerns a specific movement in literature, a movement associated with the theories of the French novelist ÉMILE ZOLA. In an age when scientific discoveries were rapidly changing the world, Zola sought to give a scientific basis to the artist's depiction of reality. A naturalist was a scientist, someone who studied the physical world; hence he called his movement naturalism. The main impulse behind it was the growing conviction that everything could be explained in terms of physical laws.

The French critic and philosopher Hippolyte Taine published a lengthy history of English literature (1863) in which he sought to show that creative genius was not some god-given gift but was the result of three factors—heredity, social environment, and the particular moment in history. This approach was in harmony with scientific thinking. He reduced the examination of artistic development to material factors, turning it into a kind of chemistry of genius. In his view, everything had a physical cause, a point he drove home by asserting, in the most quoted phase from his book, that "vice and virtue are products like vitriol and sugar" (Weber, 1960).

Similarly, Claude Bernard in his Introduction à l'étude de la médecine expérimentale (Introduction to the Study of Experimental Medicine, 1865) denied that there was any mysterious force, any so-called vital force, operating in living beings. To Bernard, medicine was both an art and a science, advancing through a series of experiments.

Influenced by Bernard, Zola wanted to make art as scientific as medicine and chose to regard the creative artist as akin to a doctor. In advocating the experimental approach in creative writing, Zola said that all he had to do was replace the word "doctor" by the word "novelist" in order to make his thoughts clear and endow it with the precision of scientific truth. Zola believed that a modern artist would proceed the same way. He called his novel THÉRÈSE RAQUIN (1868) a "surgical autopsy."

Zola described naturalist writers as "those whose method of study is to bring physical nature and human nature as close together as possible, all the while, of course, leaving free the particular temperament of the observer to manifest itself" (Le Naturalism au théâtre [Naturalism in the Theater, 1881]). Art was "a corner of the universe viewed through a temperament" ("Mon Salon" ["My Salon," 1866]).

Many found the naturalist approach profoundly disagreeable, too sordid and unpleasant for artistic expression because it was too physical. Reviewing DUMAS FILS' The Foreigner (L'Étrangère) in 1876, HENRY JAMES (1948) said that the long speeches explaining "love is physics and marriage is chemistry" displayed a "want of perception of certain rudimentary differences between the possible, for decent people, and the impossible" (Saras, 1948).

While the realist claimed objectivity in depicting the world, the naturalist claimed deeper insight into the nature of things. It is in this regard that naturalism becomes more than a artistic movement in the middle of the 19th century. The insistence on seeing heredity and environment as fundamental causes of what we do and of what we are is the basis for nearly all the serious drama of the 20th century.

The triumph of this materialist view of human beings and social life was due mainly to the epoch-making work of Charles Darwin—The Origin of Species. Published in 1859, this work shook the foundations of RELIGION and opened new vistas in PHILOSOPHY. The philosopher Immanuel Kant, in the late 18th century, separated what could be explained by the human mind (phenomena) from what the human mind could never hope to explain (noumena) and gave as an example of the latter the origin of a blade of grass. Yet within 100 years, Darwin offered an explanation.

The consequences were profound and felt everywhere. Some reeled in horror from the world pictured by Darwin, in which the ruling principle was the survival of the fittest. It seemed to give the world over to the brutes, to what the Victorian poet Alfred Tennyson described as "nature red in tooth and claw" ("In Memoriam"). What appalled many, both devout Christians and religious skeptics alike, was the image of a world without a moral system, without some center of meaning and purpose. For the educator Matthew Arnold the world became a place where "ignorant armies clash by night" ("Dover Beach"). For the philosopher FRIEDRICH NIETZSCHE, all discussions of morality and justice became moot. He could write the obituary of God because Darwin had already noticed his passing.

But the defenders of the old faith regrouped their forces and assailed Darwinism at a salient point: in the struggle for survival there seemed to be no way of explaining conscience, which was assumed to be inscribed in man by God. How else could one account for it in a Darwinian world?

Zola attacked this shibboleth of religion in his novel Thérèse Raquin, later adapted into a play, to which he placed as epigraph Taine's words about vice and virtue. If it was possible to explain the origin of life itself in materialistic terms without recourse to a supernatural deity, it should be possible to explain genius (as Taine claimed) and conscience in the same materialistic way. Zola demonstrated without bringing in conscience how a murderous couple could not escape punishment for what seems like a perfect crime. The physical embodiment of retribution is the completely paralyzed mother of the man they killed. She knows their crime but is physically incapable of accusing them. Yet her presence haunts the criminals and feeds their fear that they will betray one another. She is the physical embodiment of their "conscience," which when analyzed "scientifically" turns out to be other people, not something implanted by God.

For Zola, Thérèse Raquin (1867) was an affirmation of determinism as "the supreme law of the universe," in which the connections of physical phenomena "prevent any supernatural agent from interfering to modify the result" (Le Roman Experimental [The Experimental Novel, 1893]).

However, if naturalism was to encompass life fully, it would have to explain the fact that many people were religious and turned to God as a consequence of a physical deed. LYOV TOLSTOY'S THE POWER OF DARKNESS (1886), for example, is a brutally naturalistic play, with murder and infanticide featuring in the plot. But Tolstoy directs the naturalistic action toward a religious conversion, quite the opposite of Zola's TRAGEDY.

HENRIK IBSEN'S GHOSTS (1881) is a naturalistic drama written by a man who was not comfortable with naturalism. The play embodies his conflicted view of scientific determinism. He wanted room for free will, and his heroine Mrs. Alving fights against deterministic forces and tries to free her son Oswald from them. He has cast aside all the old beliefs and is a devotee of life for life's sake, of joie de vivre. But the consequences of it are grave. God does not punish him; implacable physical nature in the form of syphilis does.

AUGUST STRINDBERG considered his play THE FATHER (1887) to be naturalistic, in that his presentation of the battle of the sexes was inspired in part by new revelations in psychology and by recent research in prehistory. So he had reason to hope that Zola would be pleased with it. Zola, however, objected to the abstract nature of the presentation; the characters were closer to being types rather than individualized characters. It was "scientific" in content but not in form.

All the essential elements of naturalism are present in August Strindberg's MISS JULIE (1888). In the preface he enthusiastically embraced what many others thought was the worst aspect of naturalism. "I find the joy of living," he wrote, "in the fierce and ruthless battles of life"—a deliberate echo of the sentiment expressed in the stirring peroration of Darwin's *Origin of Species*: "From the war of nature . . . the production of the higher animals directly follows. There is grandeur in this view of life."

The aristocratic Miss Julie is neurotic and unstable, an unhealthy specimen for the evolution of the species, whereas the lower-class servant Jean is physically strong, rather brutal, and without much of a conscience. In the evolutionary struggle, one of them must give way to the other. Christine, the cook, represents the religious element, here reduced to a minor role. At the end Jean has to yield to another force—not God but his employer, the count, Miss Julie's father. Strindberg recognized the class struggle as one form of the struggle for existence, thus combining Darwin's theory of evolution with Karl Marx's class conflict.

By calling his *Miss Julie* "a naturalistic tragedy," Strindberg challenged conventional esthetic theory, in which naturalism and tragedy were thought to be incompatible with each other. In this view, which was more Christian than Greek, man had free will but was confined by a divine moral order that inevitably made itself felt. The tragic hero was fated to come to an end decided by God (or gods). Strindberg and the naturalists turned that argument on its head, proclaiming that it was only through Darwinism and determinism that tragedy would be possible in the modern age. The gods of ancient tragedy, which nobody any longer believed in, were to be replaced by the forces and laws of nature.

However, those opposed to naturalism countered that the essence of tragedy was not the existence of God but of free will, and if physical life could be reduced to scientific principles, the human being would be entirely deprived of it. And if the human being was seen as the pawn of material forces, a mere specimen in nature's laboratory and not Hamlet's angelic creature, true tragedy was impossible. Darwin's descent of man was a descent into a crude, brutish world with a concomitant loss of beauty and high ideals.

The naturalist's reply to this guided the course of serious drama for the next century. As Strindberg pointed out in a letter of November 12, 1887, determinism in the physical sphere led to indeterminism with regard to moral concepts and ideals (Strindberg, 1996). With man cut loose from the old religious beliefs, he was able to reexamine the basis of morality. He was truly free, and therein lay the basis of modern tragedy.

[*See also* Expressionism; Symbolism]

FURTHER READING

Bernard, Claude. *Introduction à l'étude de la médecine expérimentale.* Paris: J. B. Ballière et fils, 1865.

Innes, Christopher, ed. *A Sourcebook on Naturalist Theatre.* London: Routledge, 2000.

James, Henry. *The Scenic Art: Notes on Acting & the Drama, 1872–1901.* Ed. by Allan Wade. New Brunswick, N.J.: Rutgers Univ., 1948.

"Mon Salon" (1866). Tr. by F. W. J. Hemming, in *From the classicists to the impressionists: Art and Architecture in the Nineteenth Century*, vol. 3 of *A Documentary History of Art*, ed. by Elizabeth Gilmore Holt. N.Y.: Doubleday Anchor, 1966.

Strindberg, August. "On Modern Drama and Modern Theatre." In *Selected Essays*, tr. by Michael Robinson. New York: Cambridge Univ. Press, 1996. 73–86.

Stromberg, Roland N., ed. *Realism, Naturalism, and Symbolism.* New York: Harper & Row, 1968.

Weber, Eugen, ed. *Paths to the Present: Aspects of European Thought from Romanticism to Existentialism.* New York: Dodd, Mead, 1960. Quoting Hod Taine, *History of English Literature*, tr. by H. Van Laun. New York, 1895.

Zola, Émile. *Le Naturalisme au théâtre; les théories et les exemples.* Paris: G. Charpentier, 1881.

——. *Le Roman Experimental.* Paris: G. Charpentier, 1890.

Evert Sprinchorn

NA VSYAKOGO MUDRESTA DOVOL 'NO PROSTOTY *See* THE SCOUNDREL

NEEDLES AND OPIUM

First performed by Quebecer author Robert Lepage in 1991 under the name *Les Aiguilles et l'Opium* in Montreal, *Needles and Opium* was an instant success, despite (or perhaps because of) Lepage's insistence there be absolutely no promotion. This premiere was followed by a highly acclaimed world tour before Lepage then directed actor Marc Labrèche in performances of the one-man show in 1994 and won the Chalmers Award for Best Canadian Play in 1995.

The play is a series of poignant vignettes creating a funeral song to lost love that stirs a mesmerizing examination of the artist's creative processes as revealed through the reconstructed lives of Parisian poet and filmmaker JEAN COCTEAU and jazz trumpeter Miles Davis. Images are more important than text, thus begging the question, Is *Needles and Opium* drama, pure drama, or something more akin to performance art or perhaps even circus? Without a published play script, it remains a germane question, although Lepage is known, as with his other works, for placing the act of writing the script, in terms of sequence, last. He reverses the usual dramatic process, workshopping with collaborators first, and asks: "Doesn't a work's *raison d'être* appear more clearly after it's done?" (Lepage, 1997).

Needles and Opium consists of a scintillating spectacle of live and recorded music; explosions of color and juxtapositions of shadow; montages of documentary footage and text on a Lycra screen; and most notably, a flying harness in which the actor swings and floats in midair between two hypnotically rotating propellers.

Lepage explores the loneliness he suggests prompted not only Cocteau's opium addiction and Davis's heroin habit but his own obsession with an ex-lover—a kind of a biographical amalgam between himself, Cocteau, and Davis with the point of conjunction being Paris, FRANCE. There Davis stayed and suffered in 1949, while Cocteau—miserable after the death of lover Raymond Radiguet—almost simultaneously left Paris for America and Lepage himself suffered a near emotional breakdown after a failed relationship, alone in JEAN-PAUL SARTRE's old Paris hotel room, forty years later. One of the most impressive moments of this grand image maker's work involves a projection of a giant hypodermic syringe finding a vein in Davis's silhouetted arm.

The overall result is an examination of personal loss and how and why an artist must survive the almost unbearable pain and subsequent detoxification from the opioids or whatever balm the artist chooses to assuage the pain. Both Davis and Cocteau found inspiration the moment they stopped taking drugs. Such hurting and recovery enables growth and results in the artist becoming more individualistic. Lepage has opioid use as an ongoing theme in several of his theater works and explains: "If I keep coming back to these drugs, it's because of an experience I had when I was a teenager that left me in a state of depression for almost two years" (Lepage, 1997). His withdrawal from society was eventually dealt with through his dedication to overcoming his own debilitating stagefright on the stage.

As with much of Lepage's work, *Needles and Opium* is difficult to pigeonhole into a single genre. This contemporary theater artist enjoys pushing the boundaries of what many theatergoers would describe as drama and encroaching upon other arenas of artistic endeavor, but always collaboratively. Even with a one-man show such as this, Lepage draws on the genius of numerous backstage and preproduction art technicians and creative minds to shape a piece that, if it is not pure drama, is certainly theater that combines numerous different styles and disciplines to provide an unforgettable dramatic experience.

[*See also* Canada]

FURTHER READING

Dundjerovic, Aleksander. *The Cinema of Robert Lepage: The Poetics of Memory.* New York: Wallflower Press, 2003.

Lepage, Robert. *Connecting Flights: In Conversation with Rmy Charest.* Tr. by Wanda Romer Taylor. London: Methuen, 1997.

Lepage, Robert, and Ex Machina. *The Seven Streams of the River Ota.* London: Methuen Drama, 1996.

D. Bruno Starrs

LES NÈGRES   *See* THE BLACKS

NEILSON, ANTHONY (1967–)

Anthony Neilson, born in Edinburgh, SCOTLAND, in 1967, is usually grouped with the In-Yer-Face playwrights (SARAH KANE, MARK RAVENHILL) who fostered a revival in British playwriting in the mid-1990s. Although the label aptly describes much of

Neilson's work, it has not always served him well because critics often charge that he relies on shock tactics to attract attention and engage his audience. Furthermore, his plays are a catalog of controversial subjects and contemporary iniquities: an encounter with the notorious Düsseldorf Ripper (NORMAL, 1991), a portrait of hypermasculinity that involves the threat of anal rape (*Penetrator*, 1993), and an ethical debate about pornographic images and the need for censorship (*The Censor*, 1997). The latter contains one of Neilson's most notorious scenes: a female director of erotic films defecates onstage to seduce her nemesis—the impotent and repressed censor who is attempting to ban her film. Neilson's willingness to address taboo subjects—and stage them for the full view of the audience—constantly tests the boundaries of what is permitted on the British stage in the era of postcensorship.

Born to a theatrical family in Edinburgh, Neilson was inspired by his parent's participation in the vibrant Scottish theater scene of the 1970s (his father is director Sandy Neilson and his mother is actress Beth Robens). Neilson's first full-length play, *Normal*, debuted in 1991 at the Edinburgh Festival, and his work has remained popular with fringe companies and alternative theaters ever since; his work is also frequently performed abroad (POLAND, SWEDEN, FRANCE, AUSTRALIA, IRELAND, ITALY, and the UNITED STATES).

Neilson often directs his own plays, and much of his work is devised with his actors in the rehearsal period. Neilson's use of improvisation and "group dreaming" in the writing process gives his productions immediacy, unpredictability, and a distinct rawness of tone that has become his theatrical signature. While not denying a desire to *epater le bourgeois* (impress the middle-class man), Neilson has argued that his theatrical aesthetic is rooted in the notion that drama is an experiential mode that must be viscerally felt by the audience. Neilson writes in his introduction to *Plays: 1* (1998): "I'd implore you [theatre artists] not to be reverent. Change them [his plays] as you see fit in whatever time and place you are. Make them better—God knows there's opportunity for that—or better yet, replace my flaws with your own. Above all, make them live and breathe." Neilson's flippant disregard for the sanctity of the written word alludes to his quasi-Artaudian faith in theater as a "lived experience" and his disdain for cerebral theater that offers a detached and rational analysis of social ills.

Though Neilson's subject matter has varied over the last decade, some familiar leitmotifs can be found in his recent works: a fascination with freaks and outsiders (*Edward Gant's Amazing Feats of Loneliness*, 2002), dysfunctional sexual politics à la AUGUST STRINDBERG (*Stitching*, 2002), and the experience of mental illness (*The Wonderful World of Dissocia*, 2004). Neilson has also attempted to show greater range in his oeuvre by experimenting with an Ortonesque FARCE (*The Lying Kind*, 2002), a Victorian freakshow/MELODRAMA (*Edward Gant's*), and an adult pantomime (*The Wonderful World of Dissocia*).

[*See also* England, 1960–Present]

PLAYS : *Normal* (1991); *Penetrator* (1993); *The Year of the Family* (1994); *The Censor* (1997); *Edward Gant's Amazing Feats of Loneliness* (2002); *The Lying Kind* (2002); *Stitching* (2002); *The Wonderful World of Dissocia* (2004)

FURTHER READING

Droomgoole, Dominic. *The Full Room: An A–Z of Contemporary Playwrighting.* London: Methuen, 2000.

Neilson, Anthony. *Plays: 1.* London: Methuen, 1998.

Sierz, Aleks. *In-Yer-Face Theatre: British Drama Today.* London: Faber, 2000.

James L. Penner

NELSON, RICHARD (1950–)

American dramatist Richard Nelson was born in Chicago in 1950 and educated at Hamilton College in New York, where he had fourteen plays produced. The recipient of both Rockefeller and National Endowment for the Arts grants for playwriting, his prolific and sustained career benefited from three occurrences. Appointments as literary manager of the Brooklyn Academy of Music (BAM), associate director of the Goodman Theatre in Chicago, and DRAMATURG of the Guthrie Theatre, Minneapolis, meant sustained work as a writer within ongoing stage companies. Adaptations from Molière, BERTOLT BRECHT, NIKOLAI ERDMANN, Carlo Goldoni, and Pierre-Augustin Beaumarchais saw the writer developing his craft within the context of past masters while producing his own new work. At BAM he met the English stage director David Jones, which led to an ongoing relationship with the Royal Shakespeare Company (RSC) as a commissioned playwright. The long-term work with the RSC was paralleled by Nelson's relationship with Faber & Faber publishers, which meant that, unlike most established American playwrights, Nelson's stage work appeared consistently in published form soon after production.

The early plays centered around two interests: reportage and formal experimentation. *The Killing of Yablonski* (1975), *Conjuring an Event* (1976), and *Jungle Coup* (1978) each had a reporter as protagonist. Contemporary political events figured in his work, in a series of early radio plays: political assassination, Watergate, and so forth. The interaction of dramaturg and playwright resulted in a diversity of DRAMATIC STRUCTURES. *Bal* (1980) was a contemporary transformation of early Brechtian EXPRESSIONISM; *Rip Van Winkle or The Works* (1981) was an exercise in EPIC THEATER; a turn in cartoon AGITATION-PROPAGANDA, *The Return of Pinocchio* (1982), followed; and *An American Comedy* (1983) incorporated elements of 1930s screwball. A further two plays continued the interest in historical events, *Between East and West* (1983) and *Principia Scriptoriae* (1986). These plays, receiving London productions and consolidating his achievements to that point, initiated work with the RSC.

Working with a mélange of directors (David Jones, Roger Mitchell, John Caird, Howard Davies, among others), Nelson was able to begin a series of remarkable, large-cast plays on a variety of topics that allowed for exploration of what he has called "normal, small behavior on a very broad canvas." *Some Americans Abroad* (1989) depicts a group of American academics leading students through an English, cultural-tourist background while fighting out the backbiting problems of status, tenure, and power. A next effort was *Two Shakespearean Actors* (1990), a study of Anglo-American themes and the business of theater itself—its subject being the Astor Place riots in New York City when rival audiences of British actor William Charles Macready and American actor Edwin Forrest (performing *Macbeth* in separate productions) spilled out into the streets. Two further plays demonstrated the growing range: *Columbus and the Discovery of Japan* (1992) and the peculiar *Misha's Party* (1993), written in collaboration with Russian Alexander Gelman, with the 1991 attempted Soviet coup as background. In *The General from America* (1996) Nelson presented events from the American Revolution and Benedict Arnold's transformation from war hero to villainous traitor.

Further work of merit includes smaller-cast plays such as *Life Sentences* (1993) and *New England* (1994), as well as a series of excellent, pensive plays for radio on the BBC. These include *Languages Spoken Here* (1987), *Eating Words* (1989), and *Advice to Eastern Europe* (1990).

[*See also* United States, 1940–Present]

PLAYS : *The Killing of Yablonski* (1975); *Conjuring an Event* (1976); *Scooping* (1976); *Jungle Coup* (1978); *The Vienna Notes* (1979); *Bal* (1980); *Rip Van Winkle or The Works* (1981); *The Return of Pinocchio* (1982); *An American Comedy* (1983); *Between East and West* (1983); *Principia Scriptoriae* (1986); *Languages Spoken Here* (1987); *Roots in the Water* (1988); *Eating Words* (1989); *Some Americans Abroad* (1989); *Advice to Eastern Europe* (1990); *Two Shakespearean Actors* (1990); *Columbus and the Discovery of Japan* (1992); *Life Sentences* (1993); *Misha's Party* (with Alexander Gelman, 1993); *The American Wife* (1994); *New England* (1994); *The General from America* (1996); *Goodnight Children Everywhere* (1997); *Franny's Way* (2001)

FURTHER READING

DiGaetani, John Louis. *A Search for a Postmodern Theater: Interviews with Contemporary Playwrights.* Westport, Conn.: Greenwood Press, 1991.

Nelson, Richard, and David Jones. *Making Plays: The Writer-Director Relationship in the Theatre Today.* London: Faber, 1995.

Savran, David. *In Their Own Words: Contemporary American Playwrights.* New York: Theatre Communications Group, 1988.

Stanley R. Richardson

NETHERLANDS

Dutch drama in the 1860s was heavily influenced by the internationally popular French MELODRAMA. In the 18th century it had followed rules of French neoclassicism, meter and rhyme were used, and declamation was the key ACTING skill. French playwrights remained the role model for Dutch dramatists throughout most of the 19th century. The historical romantic drama of Victor Hugo, the melodramatic works of French dramatists like René Charles Guilbert de Pixérécourt, and well-made plays from both romantic and realist playwrights like Eugène Scribe, VICTORIEN SARDOU, and Alexandre DUMAS FILS were translated for the Dutch stage, providing examples for Dutch dramatists like H. J. Schimmel (1823–1906), Rosier Faassen (1833–1907), and Hendrik Boelen (1825–1900). Schimmel started by writing dramas in verse based on classicist principles but moved gradually through romantic works to more realistic plays. Faassen, who was half French, started as an actor and came to Holland in 1876. He translated several plays and wrote twenty-two of his own. His plays, like *The Black Captain* (*De zwarte kapitein*, 1877) or *Black Griet* (*Zwarte Griet*, 1882), dealt with the lives of ordinary people. He used archetypal characters (for instance, the Stingy Farmer and his Good Wife) set in short, funny, and touching scenes.

But apart from such original Dutch dramatic writing, the imitation and glorification of French drama throughout the bulk of the 19th century appears to have prevented the development of a more mature, indigenous Dutch drama and theater tradition in that period. While Dutch company directors favored translations of French plays, the audience was able to compare the results with the original French interpretations, since French companies came regularly to Amsterdam, The Hague, and Rotterdam. For example, between 1880 and 1890 Sarah Bernhardt's performances of *The Tosca* (*La Tosca*, Sardou), *The Lady of the Camellias* (*La Dame aux Camelias*, Dumas fils), and *Adrienne Lecouvreur* (Scribe) became the standard by which Dutch actresses like Theo Bouwmeester were judged.

As elsewhere in Europe, Dutch 19th-century theater had become an art form for the bourgeoisie. Apart from small subsidies from the royal court, and equally small irregular contributions from the larger cities, the theater was dependent on the box office. As a result, the lower-middle-class melodrama had grown in popularity and importance, influencing the production of plays. "Everything had come to a standstill, except the legs" is an often-quoted expression of Dutch writer Everhardus Potgieter, referring to a popular form of musical entertainment that attracted large audiences. The director's choice of repertoire was made to attract as many spectators as possible.

Around 1865 a group of literary and socially elite bourgeois felt the urge to improve the theater. "In the battle for a National Theater, only joint forces can overcome the problems of distaste, incapacity and routine," claimed J. N. van Hall, a lawyer and writer (1840–1918) (Erenstein, 1996). At the yearly Dutch Language and Literary Congress, he laid the foundation for the Nederlandsch Tooneelverbond (Dutch Theatre Association), by proposing several ways of elevating theater as art form. One of its aims was to encourage the writing of original Dutch drama. Owing to the support of banker and dramatist H. J. Schimmel, this initiative was followed in 1871 by the founding of the the-

atre journal *Het (Nederlandsch) Tooneel* and the creation in 1874 of the first Acting Academy. Schimmel was also one of the initiators of the Vereeniging Het Nederlandsch Tooneel, a theater company that received the title of "Koninklijke" in 1881, due to the support it received from King William III.

Dutch dramatic writing did not, however, live up to these expectations. Critic Leo Simons (1932) described the repertoire of the 1890 season. The four main companies performed approximately 132 different plays in a mix of dramas and COMEDIES, but salon plays and melodramas were the most popular genres, and of the 132, only four original Dutch plays were performed that season.

By 1890, as elsewhere in Europe, realist and naturalist drama had reached the Dutch stages. Translations of HENRIK IBSEN, AUGUST STRINDBERG, and ANTON CHEKOV were available. Performances were presented by the duke of Meiningen and by ANDRÉ ANTOINE. Ibsen's *PILLARS OF SOCIETY* was first performed in 1880, and the Dutch audience reacted positively. Some years later, however, in 1889, there was some commotion over *A DOLL'S HOUSE*, owing to the content, the psychological description of the characters that replaced action, the new acting style, and the realistic scenery. But Ibsen's work became popular. His DRAMATURGY had an immediate influence on directors such as Antoine Jean le Gras. Dramatist HERMAN HEIJERMANS (1864–1924) became the most famous Dutch proponent of NATURALISM.

1900–1945

In the first part of the 20th century, socialist ideology took shape. Workers' unions had their successes in claiming better working conditions through major strikes, for instance, that of the Rotterdam harbor in 1903. Women finally got the right to vote in 1922, after decades of struggle. And in 1920 actors united successfully to achieve a better pension arrangement. In this general atmosphere of changing power, a new generation of writers wished to portray the struggle of life more realistically. Heijermans, a socialist, was one of the few naturalistic Dutch playwrights whose work was performed with success. He depicted the life of the working classes, concentrating on characterization of individuals in a hostile society. There were more Dutch dramatists working in this naturalistic and realistic mode. Josine Simons-Mees (1863–1946) wrote several successful plays like *The Conqueror* (*De veroveraar*, 1906); *Atie's Marriage* (*Atie's huwelijk*, 1907), and *Faith* (*Geloof*, 1924). She was considered to be more subtle in her psychological description of characters than Heijermans. Jan Fabricius (1871–1964) had an enormous oeuvre, among which were *Married by Proxy* (*Met de handschoen getrouwd*, 1907) and *Een ridder kwam voorbij* (1932), which he first wrote in English as *A Knight Passed By* and which was performed in London. Heijermans painted the somber faith of his characters, but Fabricius did the opposite. Although influenced by Heijermans's realistic approach to setting and dialogue, the world of his characters included a way out of their misery.

The rise of REALISM did not banish the melodrama from Dutch stages. And despite the production of a goodly number of local dramatists, Dutch theater managers often preferred plays that were already successful abroad. The system prevented real ensemble work, by providing theaters with too little financial means. Most managers did not look for subtlety or psychological refinement. Therefore, the contribution of the better Dutch dramatists remained limited, to their own frustration.

In the 1920s, actor and director Albert van Dalsum (1889–1979) complained loudly about the level of theater and lack of good drama. He claimed that even the innovations in realistic dramas had disappeared. Under the influence of German EXPRESSIONISM, he pleaded for innovation in theater, with sketchy, explosive use of language, a clear central character, and one-dimensional "types" of characters. He also propounded engaged, political testimony. Plays such as OSKAR KOKOSCHKA's Murder, Hope of the Women (Mörder, Hoffnung der Frauen, 1907) and REINHARD SORGE's The Panhandler (Der Bettler, 1912) were his prototypes. The plays caused discussion but were not performed. After World War I, the political in expressionist drama became more prominent. During the few years that such forms of expressionism were tried out on the Dutch stages, the emphasis lay, however, on the specific form of self expression. Van Dalsum tried to emphasize the political mode, but the Dutch theater companies were not ready for it. When in 1921 the production Friday (Vrijdag) by German dramatist Herbert Kranz was shown, and expressionism was introduced onto the Dutch stage, German expressionism was itself already in decline in GERMANY. August Defresne (1893–1961) is seen as the main Dutch dramatist of that time who, in his work with van Dalsum, developed an expressionistic, contemporary style. The Barge (De woonschuit, 1924) is the first work that demonstrates his conviction that the function of theater is as a testimony of truth. In 1929 van Dalsum and Defresne together founded the Oost-Nederland Toneel in Arnhem, meant to work from expressionistic ideas. Their intentions were mainly sociopolitically oriented, but their plays also focused on the individual. The company existed only for one season. From 1931 van Dalsum became director of the Amsterdamsch Tooneel, where he developed his ideas further.

In the 1930s not much changed for Dutch dramatists. Economic problems made the theater directors even more dependent on box-office revenue and therefore reluctant to experiment. They chose either plays in which audiences could recognize themselves or plays in which great actors could shine. The members of the Bond van Nederlansche Tooneelschrijvers (Organization for Dutch Dramatists) admitted openly at the celebration of their tenth anniversary in 1933 that the situation of Dutch and Flemish dramatists remained in a deplorable state. "In North and South foreign plays supplanted plays from our own soil. Official measures should be taken to protect our art" (Erenstein, 1996). These measures were only taken after World War II.

During the war, theater in the Netherlands functioned in two ways: in the form of official amusement for those who kept performing under the German occupation and in the form of critical protest by theater makers who went underground. In 1940, soon after the occupation started, the department of education, arts, and sciences was replaced by a Departement voor Volksvoorlichting en Kunsten (Department for Education of the People and Arts). Before establishing the Kulturkammer in 1942, the dramaturgy section of this department started censuring plays and performances. Jewish plays, songs, and sketches, as well as English, American, and Russian repertoire were forbidden. Companies had to have their repertoire checked. The aim of the Nazi occupation was to expand German repertoire and to stimulate specific genres of original Dutch drama. By the end of 1944, when it became clear that forces had changed, the interest of the Nazis in infiltrating and influencing Dutch culture had diminished. Liberation was celebrated on May 5, 1945, with the play Free People (Vrij Volk). It was written for the occasion by Anton Coolen (1897–1961), August Defresne, Jeanne van Schaik (1895–1984), and other directors and dramatists who had stayed in hiding during the war. In 1944 some of these same directors, such as Defresne, had surreptitiously published a booklet called Ontwerp voor een regeling van het toneel na de oorlog (Design for a Regulation of Theatre After the War, 1944). They made suggestions for a national policy aimed at preventing the theater from falling back into the commercial situation prior to World War II.

1945–1970

In the years directly following World War II, audiences were eager for entertainment. In 1947 a subsidy system to assist theater makers to develop their artistic ideas without too much dependency on box office was realized. Five companies received national subsidies. In 1969 the number grew to eleven. These companies were to provide society with quality theater, and they had an obligation to tour throughout the country. Companies were also required to produce two productions per season based on Dutch drama. This system was based on the ideological premise that art has an educational function and should be made available for every citizen. The discussion concentrated around how to tackle the issues of geographical (or horizontal) and social (or vertical) spreading of art.

Despite good intentions of stimulating local writing, Dutch theater companies in the 1950s were mainly choosing the international canon. William Shakespeare, Greek TRAGEDIES, Anton Chekov, and Henrik Ibsen were popular, together with new American dramatists including ARTHUR MILLER and TENNESSEE WILLIAMS, as well as the comedies of writers such as ALAN AYCKBORN and GEORGES FEYDEAU. Between 1951 and 1966, about 1,000 premieres took place, but only sixty-one were based on the work of Dutch contemporary dramatists: only six percent. In this period of meager Dutch drama writing, it is striking that a large number of the Dutch plays in the 1950s and 1960s came from writers of literature. Some of them succeeded very well with their experiments. Cees Nooteboom (1933–), later famous for his travel novels, was successful with *The Swans of the Thames* (*De zwanen van de Theems*). It was performed by the premier Dutch company, the Nederlandse Comedie, in 1959. Plays of Harry Mulisch (1927–) (*Tanchelijn*, 1960), Gerard Reve (1923–) (*Commissaris Fennedy*, 1962), and Jan Wolkers (1925–) (*Babel*, 1963) were instantly performed by major Dutch companies. This created a renewed interest in writing drama and a reestimation of the language. But with the exception of HUGO CLAUS, none of these writers remained faithful to drama. The first plays of the Flemish Claus caused a bit of social upheaval. He attacked the hypocrisy in Flemish society and the use of imposed moral systems (for instance, that of the Catholic Church) to suppress human desires and physicality.

In the 1960s some changes occurred. Experimental groups such as Test and Studio, both under the leadership of Kees van Iersel, initiated readings of new drama. In the 1950s van Iersel had introduced absurdist writers (SAMUEL BECKETT and EUGÈNE IONESCO, for example) and had directed several of their plays for television. He organized workshops in order to stimulate young Dutch playwrights to experiment with language. By the second half of the 1960s, the world seemed in turmoil. The political arena, the Vietnam protests, and the student demonstrations in the UNITED STATES, Paris, and Amsterdam influenced a new generation. In 1968 young theater makers rebelled, in what was called Action Tomato after the tomatoes that were thrown in protest. The young theater makers criticized the state of the Dutch theater. Existing production processes were too hierarchical. Engagement with contemporary life was missing, especially in the repertoire of such leading companies as de Nederlandse Comedie and de Haagsche Comedie. They demanded relief from the dominance of the Western canon, wishing to incorporate more experiment and improvisations, utilizing themes arising from the society of their time.

Action Tomato resulted in new production forms. The more collectively run companies that came out of this battle, for instance, the Werkteater, Baal, or Onafhankelijk Toneel, did not necessarily work with written drama. The actor and his or her relation to a theme, a space, or the spectator became as important a signifying element as the text.

1970–PRESENT

Between 1970 and 1990 several attempts were made to improve and inspire Dutch drama writing. Theater critic Ben Stroman wrote his famous book *The Art of Dutch Playwriting: An Attempt To Explain An Absence* (*De Nederlandse toneelschrijfkunst. Poging tot verklaring van een gemis*, 1973). He explained the lack of a Dutch dramatic tradition by describing the centuries of mutual distrust present between the literary and theatrical "scenes." Except for those dramatists who directed their own plays, such as Heijer-

mans, Stroman's analysis was that the literary author dislikes theater and that the theater director mistrusts writers.

But in the 1960s theater was no longer necessarily based on dramatic or literary texts. After Action Tomato, many new, small-scale theater companies arose, and the theater landscape changed. A critical attitude toward society was combined with formal experimentation. Musician Lodewijk de Boer (1937–2004) became a writer and director and emphasized the musicality and rhythm in spoken words. His four-play series *The Family* (1972) became the most famous illustration of the Dutch anti-authoritarian society of the 1970s. Judith Herzberg (1934–) wrote harrowing plays about people coping with life and identity, especially Jewish identity, in plays such as *It Is No Dog* (*Het is geen hond*, 1972), *Malicious Delight* (*Leedvermaak*, 1982), and *Scratch* (*Kras*, 1988). In 1971 Herzberg, as a well-known literary writer, was one of the first to work at the Institute for Research for Dutch Theatre. Then Minister of Culture Marga Klompé had given permission and the finances to create this institute, where writers were invited to develop their drama writing skills, without any pressure to produce.

Collective companies, like Werkteater, created their texts postperformance, as the performances were based on improvisation. Productions like *Happenings* (*Toestanden*, 1972) and *Eveningred* (*Avondrood*, 1974) appealed to new audiences. The company performed at places where they connected to problems of the local people: in a hospital, a prison, or a home for the elderly. The drama was the result of this collective process and not the writing of one specific playwright. A number of groups used similar working methods. Sater and Proloog focused on political and educational subjects; De Salon, Persona, Theater '80, and Spiegeltheater chose feminist themes. Dramatists like Matin van Veldhuizen (1948–) and Frouke Fokkema, who worked with these companies, also developed into directors.

In the midst of these different experiments, the companies Puck and (later) Centrum focused specifically on encouraging Dutch drama writing. In 1974, Peter Oosthoek (1934–) received the Anne Frank Prize for having written and directed six Dutch plays in one season. As artistic director of Centrum, he created space for well-known writers like Hella Haasse (1918–), Dimitri Frenkel Frank (1928–1988), and Mies Bouhuys (1927–) to experiment with the genre. Oosthoek attracted new young talent, among them Ton Vorstenbosch (1949–), who wrote many plays beginning in 1975.

The collective mode of production and the explicit political stances exhausted themselves to some extent by the beginning of the 1980s. Most of these companies dissolved, except for the Werkteater, Maatschappij Discordia, and Onafhankelijk Toneel. By that time, more directors started to write their own plays, for instance: Ger Thijs (1948–), Gerardjan Rijnders (1949–), and Frans Strijards (1952–). They also directed the plays with their own companies. Individual experience is often stressed in these plays. The fact that the director dealt with his own text(s) created possibilities. Many of these plays do not follow traditional Aristotelian dramaturgy or employ textual coherence. Nor are they unambiguous in meaning. Where Thijs writes in the classical tradition (e.g., *Fixtures* [*Winkeldochters*] or *Small Aim* [*Kleine zielen*]), Rijnders creates room for multiple layers of interpretation in the COLLAGE-like performances of his own dramas, for example, *Ballet* (1990) or *Count Your Blessings* (1993). In a postmodern world, he forces the spectator to make individual choices. And in *Hensbergen* (1985) or *Hitchocks Pitchfork* (*Hitchocks Driesprong*, 1985), Frans Strijards plays with the paradox of the illusion of fiction and the fiction of illusion. In the last ten or twenty years, a growing number of dramatist-directors have followed in their footsteps. Koos Terpstra (1955–), Don Duyns (1967–), Peer Wittenbols (1965–), Faul Feld (1958–), and Jeroen van den Berg (1966–) all have their own companies where they can experiment with their own drama. A similar development took place in youth theater. Playwrights like Pauline Mol (1953–), Suzanne van Lohuizen (1955–), Heleen Verburg (1964–), and Esther Gerritsen (1972–) directed their own plays.

In the last ten years a new generation of theater makers chose once again to work in collectives, following the example of companies like Maatschappij Discordia: the Barreland, Dood Paard, Stan, De Roovers. These actors' companies combine high interest in the canon, using and reworking the plays of (for instance) Shakespeare, Chekov, and Beckett according to the respective company's interpretation. Within those groups new dramatists arose, like Oscar van Woensel (1970–) (from Dood Paard). His plays *Who . . .* (*Wie . . .* , 1996), *Between Ourselves* (*Tussen ons gezegd en gezwegen*, 1997), and *Bleat* (*Blaat*, 1998) demonstrate the search for the individual, as is illustrated in this quotation from *Who . . .* : "wie ben ik wie ben jij wie zijn wij wie wie zijn wie ik ben ben ik ik wie jij bent wie wie ik ben ik wij zijn wie wij zijn wie ik" ("who am I are you who are we who who is who am I am I I who are you who who I am I who are who are we am I).

FURTHER READING

Bork, G. J., and P. J. Verkruijsse, eds. *De Nederlandse en Vlaamse auteurs* [The Dutch and Flemish Author]. Leiden: Stichting Digitale Bibliotheek voor de Nederlandse Letteren (dbnl), 2001.

De Leeuwe, Hans, in collab. with Hans Mulder Westerbeek and Hans van Maanen. *International Bibliography of the Dutch and Flemish Theatre.* London: Headley, 1972. Reprinted from *Theatre Research*, vol. XII, no. 2, 1972.

Dubois, Pierre H. *Dutch Art Today, Literature.* Amsterdam: Uitgeverij Contact, 1956.

Erenstein, Robbert, et al., eds. *Een theaterye schiedenis der Nederlanden. Tien eeuwen drama en theater in Nederland en Vlaanderen* [A theater-history of the Netherlands. Ten centuries of drama and theater in the Netherlands and Flanders]. Amsterdam: Amsterdam Univ. Press, 1996.

Kemperink, Mary. *Neederlands toneel in het fin de sciècle, 1890–1900* [Dutch theater at the Fin de Siècle, 1890–1900]. Amsterdam: Amsterdam Univ. Press, 1995.

Ockhuyzen, Ronald. *Een roepende in de polder* [A Voice Crying in the Polder]. Amsterdam: Amsterdam Univ. Press, 1992.

Simons, Leo. *Het drama en het tooneel in hun ontwikkeling, deel V 1875–1930* [The drama and the stage in development, part 5 1875–1930]. Amsterdam: Nederlandse bibliotheek, 1932.

Snijders, Corine Snijders. *Een gebrekkige dialoog? Een onderzoek naar de Nederlandse toneelschrijfkunst in Nederland en Vlaanderen* [An inadequate dialogue? An analysis of the art of Dutch playwriting in the Netherlands and Flanders]. Groningen: Rijksuniversiteit Groningen, 1992.

Stroman, Ben. *De Nederlandsche toneelschrijfkunst: Poging tot verklaring van een gemis* [The art of Dutch playwriting: An attempt to explain an absence]. Amsterdam: Moussault, 1973.

Winkel, J. te. *De ontwikkelingsgang der Nederlandsche letterkunde. Deel 7: Geschiedenis der Nederlandsche Letterkunde in de eerste eeuw der Europeesche Staatsomwentelingen* [The Evolution of Dutch Literature. Part 7: History of Dutch Literature in the age of European Revolutions]. Tweede druk. Haarlem: Erven F. Bohn, 1927.

Worp, J. A. van. *Geschiedenis van het drama en van het tooneel in Nederland. Deel 1 en 2* [History of Drama and Stage in the Netherlands. Parts 1 and 2]. Rotterdam: Fa Langerveld, 1903.

Lucia van Heteren

NEW DRAMATISTS

We were an innocent but heady group of new dramatists that thirty-five years ago climbed to the top of Lindsay and Crouse's Hudson Theatre on West 44th Street week after week to listen to the likes of Maxwell Anderson, Elisa Kazan, Robert Sherwood, Elmer Rice, S. N. Behrman, and Joshua Logan talk about playwriting and theatre.

—Robert Anderson, from the foreword to *Short Pieces from the New Dramatists*, 1985

New Dramatists was established in 1949. It was the UNITED STATES' first development program for playwrights and thus is the oldest, as others have since followed its example throughout the years. Originally an idea of the young dramatist Michaela O'Harra, she produced an initial proposal, the essentials of which have continued in use to century's end. As Robert Anderson noted in an introduction to *Short Pieces from the New Dramatists*, "Young poets are eighteen, young novelists, twenty-five, and young playwrights, thirty-six. I believe it is granted that playwriting is the most difficult form of writing because it is not just writing. It is learning that what is written on the page is only a blueprint" (Chervin, 1985). O'Harra felt that an institutional approach to the development of new writers for the stage was needed.

In her initial proposal, submitted to Dramatist Guild member HOWARD LINDSAY, she suggested a member service organization that would draw on already existing resources (producers, theater companies, agents, etc.) and provide the following opportunities: (1) free tickets for as much attendance in playhouses as possible; (2) informal roundtable discussion of craft with established dramatists, producers, designers, and actors; (3) chances for observation of plays from first read through to opening in New York or closing out of town; and finally (4) script-in-hand workshops in which plays could be discussed, revised or not, and then directed, rehearsed, and performed for a small audience.

Skeptical at first, Lindsay, upon meeting an initial group of potential writers, signed on enthusiastically, and a board was formed with the above cited writers, as well as John Wharton, Richard Rodgers, Oscar Hammerstein, with MOSS HART as president. Describing itself as producing playwrights rather than plays, the organization has continued into the 21st century and has worked with well over 500 playwrights and resulted in productions earning eleven Pulitzer Prizes, twenty-two Tony Awards, fifty Obie Awards, seventeen Drama Desk Awards, and ten Susan Smith Blackburn Awards. Distinguished alumnae over several generations include WILLIAM INGE, William Gibson, JAMES BALDWIN, HORTON FOOTE, JOHN GUARE, ROCHELLE OWENS, MEGAN TERRY, AUGUST WILSON, MAC WELLMAN, ERIC OVERMYER, MARIA IRENE FORNES, JOHN PATRICK SHANLEY, EMILY MANN, Donald Margulies, PAULA VOGEL, and SUZAN-LORI PARKS.

This success resulted in various development programs throughout the country, some independent and some in association with regional theaters, and remains an essential element of theater production in America, allowing fledgling dramatists to learn the business of collaboration and experience the responses of audiences. A negative aspect of the "developmental process" is that some playwrights have felt their plays were "workshopped to death," and others have pointed out the development programs are a way for theaters to throw a little money at "new work," yet rarely do these plays reach the main stage; many never see any full productions at all. Still, some writers have thrived on such a process. TONY KUSHNER's ANGELS IN AMERICA benefited from extensive development before opening in London and finally on Broadway. New Dramatists thus can be described as an essential institution in the history of postwar American drama.

Other developmental programs include Baltimore Playwrights' Festival; Bay Area Playwrights' Festival; New Voices: A Writers' Theatre; O'Neill Playwright Conference; The Playwrights' Center; Playwrights' Platform; Sundance Theatre Laboratory; Theatre West Writers' Workshop; and Women's Work Project.

FURTHER READING

Chervin, Stan, ed. Short Pieces from the New Dramatists. New York: Broadway Play Pub., 1985.

London, Todd, ed. New Dramatists 2000: The Best Plays by the Graduating Class. New York: Smith & Kraus, 2002.

New Dramatists Alumnae Publications Committee, eds. Broadway's Fabulous Fifties: How the Playmakers Made It Happen. Portsmouth, N.H.: Heinemann, 2002.

Stanley R. Richardson

NEW OBJECTIVITY

New Objectivity (*Neue Sachlichkeit*) is one of those slippery aesthetic labels that is almost impossible to grasp firmly and hence manage to fuel considerable theoretical discussion. To be sure, on some points there is consensus. The phrase *Neue Sachlichkeit* itself was put into circulation, if not actually coined, by G. F. Hartlaub (1884–1963), director of an art gallery in Mannheim, when he invited participation in an exhibit on current trends in painting. Hartlaub defined the phrase in contrast to impressionism and EXPRESSIONISM as the work of those artists who were loyal to "positive, tangible reality." The term caught on quickly, spreading from the visual arts to literature and intellectual life. The core meaning articulated a widespread feeling or mood, and by 1925 a reaction had set in against the excesses of expressionism, particularly against the shift toward mythological and fantastic works (as in BERTOLT BRECHT's BAAL [1918]). It also encompassed a new pragmatic attitude toward rebuilding society. The revolutionaries of 1918–1920 had suggested unlimited possibilities for radical change in all spheres of life, but by the early 1920s people wanted calmer, more practical solutions to urgent problems. Hence, some critics have stressed the literal meaning of "Sachlich" as "Sober" and suggested "New Sobriety" as a more accurate translation. (Sokel, 1959).

In the context of literature, the trend led to a renewed investigation of the environment in which people actually lived and worked. The overriding aim was to present "just the facts." For some critics at the time, especially those on the Left, this appeared to be an escapist retreat to 19th-century REALISM, where writers did not operate with political allegiances. The observation could be valid, as in the case of CARL ZUCKMAYER (1896–1977 and his highly successful play *The Merry Vineyard* [*Der fröhliche Weinberg*, 1925]). Others were overtly political, such as FRIEDRICH WOLF (1888–1953) in the hit *Cyanide* (*Cyankali*, 1930), which dealt with abortion. Even those who did not follow a party line produced works that were brutally frank about social conditions, as in MARIELUISE FLEIßER's (1901–1974) exposition of male chauvinism in *Purgatory in Ingolstadt* (*Fegefeuer in Ingolstadt*, 1924) and *Soldiers in Ingolstadt* (*Pioniere in Ingolstadt*, 1928–1929).

The effort to convey objectivity was supported by a style that avoided flowery language and transcribed oral speech. Increasing use was made of direct quotation from documents such as newspapers, so that the audience would be able to check the facts themselves. One playwright whose career and work was not confined to New Objectivity but who learned much from its practitioners was Brecht, especially in terms of integrating DOCUMENTARY material (Brecht clipped newspapers for source material) and in stricter accuracy in the use of historical evidence.

The understanding of New Objectivity has been hampered by a neglect of authors who participated in the rejection of expressionism for an alternative view, including ÖDÖN VON HORVÁTH (1901–1938), Peter Martin Lampel (1894–1965), Günther Weisenborn (1878–1934), Erich Mühsam (1878–1934), and Ilse Langner

(1899–1987). While it seems logical that the new media such as radio and film would have meshed well with the demands for objective representation, research into that conjunction is just beginning.

FURTHER READING

Guenther, Irene. "Magic Realism, New Objectivity, and the Arts During the Weimar Republic." In *Magical Realism: Theory, History, Community*, ed. by Lois Parkinson Zamora and Wendy B. Faris. Durham, N.C.: Duke Univ. Press, 1995. 33–73.

Hermand, Jost. "Unity Within Diversity? The History of the Concept 'Neue Sachlichkeit.'" Tr. by Peter Lincoln and Margaret Lincoln. In *Culture and Society in the Weimar Republic*, ed. by Keith Bullivant. Manchester: Manchester Univ. Press, 1977. 162–182.

McCormick, Richard W. *Gender and Sexuality in Weimar Modernity: Film, Literature, and "New Objectivity."* New York: Palgrave, 2001.

Sokel, Walter H. *The Writer in Extremis: Expressionism in Twentieth-Century German Literature.* Stanford: Stanford Univ. Press, 1959.

Subiotto, A. V. "Neue Sachlichkeit: A Reassessment." In *Deutung und Bedeutung: Studies in German and Comparative Literature Presented to Karl-Werner Maurer*, ed. by Brigitte Schludermann, Victor G. Doerksen, Robert J. Glendinning, and Evelyn S. Firchow. The Hague: Mouton, 1973. 248–274.

Arnd Bohm

THE NEW YORK IDEA

The New York Idea (1906) is a witty, sophisticated satire of the revolving door nature of modern marriage and the relative ease of divorce. Playwright LANGDON MITCHELL had already enjoyed a degree of success with an earlier play, *Becky Sharp*, an adaptation of William Makepeace Thackeray's *Vanity Fair*. The New York Idea centers around two divorced couples—John and Cynthia Karslake and Philip and Vida Phillimore—and the impending marriage of Philip to Cynthia. At the opening of the play, Phillimore's snobbish, proper, aristocratic family is lamenting the fact that the head of their family is marrying a high-spirited, sporty, "unconventional" young woman with a love of horses and racing who is sure to bring disgrace upon their family. Early in the play, the audience also discovers that Cynthia has doubts about being "trapped" in such a family and that John is uncertain about whether he loves or hates his ex-wife.

Mitchell further complicates the action by introducing into the plot a dapper English gentleman, Sir Wilfred Cates-Darby, who is on a quest for an American mate and has no qualms about courting two women (one of them betrothed) simultaneously, proposing to one in front of the other and then, having been discouraged by his first choice, promptly and publicly switching his attentions to the other. When Cynthia decides to go to the race track instead of to her wedding, it is with the intrepid Cates-Darby. Although when compared to the two couples, Cates-Darby is a relatively minor character, he admirably illustrates Mitchell's intimate knowledge of ENGLAND and

English manners and is hardly the caricature of the British aristocrat common on American stages at the time *The New York Idea* premiered.

When Cynthia returns from her race track outing hours late for her wedding, the cultural chasm that divides her from her future husband and in-laws is brought into clear relief by the contrast between her cavalier attitude about the delay of her nuptials and the outrage of the Phillimores. Realizing that marriage to Philip would be a dreadful mistake and spurred by jealousy aroused by Vida Phillimore's flirtation with John, Cynthia, on the verge of exchanging vows, runs away to save her ex-husband from marrying Vida. The Karslakes' subsequent act 4 meeting results in their realization that they still love each other and John's revelation that their divorce was not valid in the first place. With Cynthia no longer available, Cates-Darby turns his full attention toward the vamp, Vida, who had targeted him from the outset.

Because of its vibrant characters, scintillating dialogue, and farcical situations, Mitchell's COMEDY has been compared favorably with the wittiest writing of GEORGE BERNARD SHAW and NOËL COWARD. With Minnie Maddern Fiske as Cynthia, John Mason as Karslake, and Mitchell's wife Marion Lea as Vida Phillimore, *The New York Idea* ran for sixty-six performances at the Lyric Theatre in New York in 1906. It was subsequently produced by MAX REINHARDT at Berlin's Kammerspiel in 1916 and has been revived successfully a number of times.

[See also United States, 1860–1940]

FURTHER READING

Atkinson, Brooks. *Broadway.* New York: Macmillan, 1970.

Moody, Richard, ed. *Dramas from the American Theatre, 1762–1909.* Boston: Houghton, 1966.

Murphy, Brenda. *American Realism and American Drama, 1880–1940.* Cambridge: Cambridge Univ. Press, 1987.

Price, David M. "Langdon Mitchell: The Man and His Plays." Ph.D. diss., City Univ. of New York, 1978.

Wainscott, Ronald. "Plays and Playwrights: 1896–1915." In *The Cambridge History of American Theatre*, ed. by Don B. Wilmeth and Christopher Bigsby. Cambridge: Cambridge Univ. Press, 1999. 278–281.

John W. Frick

NEW ZEALAND

Drama in New Zealand reflects diverse cultural influences and includes both European roots as well as the strong presence of the Maori.

1870–1960

Although Maori performance forms are often emphatically theatrical, there was no Indigenous drama per se in Aotearoa (New Zealand) before Western models were introduced in the 19th century. Before 1920 the most common dramatic forms were FARCE, satire, and MELODRAMA. Writers often drew on the colonial experience—the gold rushes and encounters with the "natives"—and found in the exotic environment the excuse for spectacle, including volcanic eruptions! The most popular of these plays was George Leitch's *The Land of the Moa* (produced 1895, published 1990), in the style of DIONYSIUS BOUCI-CAULT. The scenario is commonplace but interesting for the racial casting: a wily American captain ensnares a Maori chief's beautiful daughter. This was actually typical of local melo-drama: the villains are usually European or American stereo-types, and Maori are portrayed as noble savages sympathetic to British imperialism.

In the 1920s and 1930s playwriting was stimulated by the growth of university and left-wing amateur dramatic societies and by the establishment, in 1922, of a local branch of the Brit-ish Drama League. The influence of GEORGE BERNARD SHAW and JOHN GALSWORTHY is evident in a series of well-made, domestic plays that examine, variously, the experience of Brit-ish immigrants, cultural isolation, and rural monotony and the economic troubles of the Depression. Merton Hodge, who trav-eled to Britain in 1931, had four plays staged in London in the 1930s; the ostensibly Chekhovian *The Wind and the Rain* (1934) played in the West End for three years. There were isolated attempts at EXPRESSIONISM in the 1930s, and Ian Hamilton's antiwar *Falls the Shadow* (1939) was a rare socialist play.

In the postwar years Claude Evans wrote nine light domestic COMEDIES, largely imitative of British models and all staged by Christchurch's Canterbury Repertory Theatre (1946–1961). Established poets Charles Brasch, D'Arcy Cresswell, and Allen Curnow wrote some portentous verse plays, and short-story writer Frank Sargeson also dabbled in drama in the 1930s and again in the 1960s.

Other notable plays during this lean period were spawned by Wellington's progressive Unity Theatre: Kathleen Ross's *The Trap* (1952), a study of three generations of women coping with male exploitation, and the early works of BRUCE MASON. Symp-tomatic of the indifference towards local plays, unless they were endorsed abroad, Stella Jones's *The Tree* (1960), a family homecoming drama in the tradition of EUGENE O'NEILL and ARTHUR MILLER, was toured by the New Zealand Players only after being produced in Bristol in 1957. The Players (1952–1960) was a semiprofessional touring company whose repertoire largely comprised popular British comedies, although it did stage expatriate Douglas Stewart's *Ned Kelly* (1943).

In the late 1950s James K. Baxter, New Zealand's leading poet, turned to drama. His first play, *Jack Winter's Dream* (produced 1958, published 1979), was written for radio, which, along with the British Drama League's one-act play festivals, was the principal sponsor of local drama until the 1970s. Baxter's first stage play, *The Wide Open Cage* (produced 1959, published 1982), produced OFF-BROADWAY in 1962, features alcoholism and prostitution and is characteristically metaphysical. In the late 1960s Baxter

wrote several plays based on biblical and Greek material, for Pat-ric Carey's Globe Theatre in Dunedin.

FURTHER READING

Downes, Peter. *Shadows on the Stage: Theatre in New Zealand—the First 70 Years*. Dunedin: John McIndoe, 1975.

Leitch, George. *The Land of the Moa*. Ed. by Adrian Kiernander. Wellington: Victoria Univ. Press, 1990.

McNaughton, Howard. "Baxter as Dramatist." *Islands* 2 (1973): 184–192.

———. *New Zealand Drama: A Bibliographical Guide*. Christchurch: Univ. of Canterbury Library, 1974.

———. *New Zealand Drama*. Boston: Twayne, 1981.

Mason, Bruce, and John Pocock. *Theatre in Danger: A Correspondence Between Bruce Mason and John Pocock*. Hamilton: Paul's Bk. Arcade, 1957.

Nelson, Erle. "Towards a New Zealand Drama." *Landfall* 17 (1963): 122–134.

Stuart Young

1960–1980

From the late 1960s there was a steady blossoming of New Zealand drama and theater. An important source of this was Wellington's Downstage, founded in 1964. It was the first of a network of professional community theaters established in the main cities, especially in the early to mid-1970s. In its early years, Downstage produced Peter Bland's *Father's Day* (produced 1966) and *George the Mad Ad-Man* (produced 1967); "*Lord, Dismiss Us . . .*" (1967) and *Lines to M* (produced 1969) by Warren Dibble, a radio dramatist; Edward Bowman's *Salve Regina* (produced 1969), which, in a version for television, won the London *Observer* play-writing competition; and Alistair Campbell's *When the Bough Breaks* (1970). Downstage also launched the career of ROBERT LORD.

In 1973 the script advisory service Playmarket was estab-lished. It has also become the chief agent for local playwrights. After an initial workshop in 1974, Playmarket ran a series of biennial workshops, based on the Connecticut and Australian models, from 1980 to 1994; these resumed in 2002. Playmarket also arranges individual workshops.

The collectively devised work of a number of "group" the-aters in the early 1970s exemplified a growing nationalism and interest in local stories. Theatre Action (1971–1977), led by Fran-cis Batten, used the creational methods of French mime teacher Jacques Lecoq for such works as *The Best of All Possible Worlds* (produced 1973), an epic survey of New Zealand's colo-nial history and search for identity. Amamus (1971–1978), founded by Paul Maunder, devised a series of DOCUMENTARY and confrontational pieces, including *The Wall Street Banks in London Have Closed* (produced 1971), about the 1930s Depression; *'51* (produced 1972), about a major waterfront dispute; and *Pic-tures* (produced 1973), about New Zealand's involvement in the

Vietnam War. In 1975 Amamus toured to POLAND (Maunder was an admirer of Jerzy Grotowski) and London with *Gallipoli* (produced 1974), based on an ill-fated Australasian battle in TURKEY in World War I that features prominently in the national psyche. Red Mole (1974–), led by Sally Rodwell and the poet Alan Brunton, created shows, such as *Capital Cabaret Strut* (produced 1977) and *Ghost Rite* (produced 1978), that were a mix of satirical cabaret and phantasmagoric drama. Described by Erika Munk, in *The Village Voice* (1979), as "punk Bread and Puppet," Red Mole spent most of the 1978–1988 period abroad, mainly in New York.

Politically committed playwrights to appear in the 1970s included MERVYN THOMPSON, Craig Harrison, and the particularly polemical Dean Parker. Harrison wrote several satirical COMEDIES dealing with race relations, most notably *Tomorrow Will Be a Lovely Day* (1975). Parker's *Smack* (produced 1974) draws a parallel between drug pushing and capitalism.

More commercially successful were the situation comedies of Gordon Dryland, Joseph Musaphia, and especially Roger Hall. Dryland's light, witty comedies, such as *Fat Little Indians* (produced 1976) and *Unlikely Places* (produced 1979), often feature homosexuality and bisexuality. Musaphia's plays, generally FARCES, deal more thoroughly with sexual unease and maladjustment. They include *Victims* (produced 1973), *Mothers and Fathers* (1977), *Hunting* (produced 1979), and *Shotgun Wedding* (1981). The New Zealand work that has enjoyed the greatest international prominence is Richard O'Brien's "provincial gothic" musical *The Rocky Horror Show* (1974).

FURTHER READING

Black, Sebastian. "'What Kind of a Society Can Develop Under Corrugated Iron?': Glimpses of New Zealand History in New Zealand Plays." *Australasian Drama Studies* 3, no. 1. (1984): 31–52.

Brunton, Alan. *A Red Mole Sketchbook.* Wellington: Victoria Univ. Press, 1989.

Mason, Bruce. *Every Kind of Weather: Selected Writings on the Arts, Theatre, Literature and Current Events in New Zealand, 1953–81.* Ed. by David Dowlin. Auckland: Reed Methuen, 1986.

McNaughton, Howard, ed. *Contemporary New Zealand Plays.* New York: Oxford Univ. Press, 1974.

——. "Drama." In *The Oxford History of New Zealand Literature in English*, ed. by Terry Sturm. 2d ed. Auckland: Oxford Univ. Press, 1998. 321–393.

Munk, Erika. "Burrowing from Without." *The Village Voice* (September 24, 1979): 89.

Rees, Nonnita. "'Getting New Zealand Writing Into Theatres': The Story of Playmarket." *Australasian Drama Studies* 3, no. 1. (1984): 23–30.

Thompson, Mervyn. "Promise and Frustration: New Zealand Playwriting Since 1975." *Australasian Drama Studies* 3, no. 1. (1984): 122–128.

Murray Edmond

1980–PRESENT

The growing confidence of New Zealand drama was evident initially in raw, naturalistic, slice-of-life works, such as GREG MCGEE's "state-of-the-nation" *Foreskin's Lament* (1981), Rore Hapipi's television drama *The Protestors* (produced 1982), and Hilary Beaton's *Outside In* (1984). One of the first feminist plays, *Outside In* documents the tedium and brutality of prison life, portraying the female inmates' entrapment as symptomatic of larger social structures.

The poet Vincent O'Sullivan also turned to the stage with a prison play, *Shuriken* (1985). Examining race and xenophobia, *Shuriken* is based on an incident in 1943, when forty-nine Japanese prisoners were shot by their New Zealand guards. O'Sullivan's other plays include *Billy* (1990) and *Jones and Jones* (1989), which explores the relationship between Katherine Mansfield and Ida Baker and their private alter egos as a music hall duo.

Economic rationalism, which in many respects New Zealand pioneered in the 1980s, took its toll on theater. Funding shifted increasingly from subsidy to sponsorship, and the ethos of a "company" in the community theaters largely disappeared. This resulted in smaller-cast plays and the proliferation of solo shows. Two COMEDIES encapsulated the spirit of the late 1980s, combining a sophisticated, self-conscious use of theatrical forms with savvy commercialism: Stephen Sinclair and Anthony McCarten's *Ladies Night* (produced 1987), about a group of destitute men who become strippers, and Sinclair and Danny Mulheron's *The Sex Fiend* (produced 1989).

Meanwhile, Stuart Hoar's comedy *Squatter* (1988) critiques monetarist economics through a story about the overtaxing of Canterbury farmland in the 1890s. Hoar's plays deal unabashedly with ideas, and their DRAMATURGY is complex, featuring anachronisms and estranging devices. Hoar has written more than twenty plays, including *Yo Banfa* (produced 1993), about Mao Zedong and émigré New Zealander Rewi Alley in China in 1939; *Rutherford* (produced 2000); and *The Face Maker* (produced 2001).

The most important development in the 1990s was the triumphal progress of Maori drama, but other significant playwrights who emerged in this period are Fiona Samuel, Michelanne Forster, and Gary Henderson. Samuel's plays include *The Wedding Party* (produced 1988) and *Lashings of Whipped Cream: A Session with a Teenage Dominatrix* (1995). Like Peter Jackson's film *Heavenly Creatures*, Forster's *Daughters of Heaven* (1992) is based on the notorious 1954 murder by two teenage girls of one of their mothers. Henderson's plays include *Skintight* (produced 1994) and *An Unseasonable Fall of Snow* (produced 1998).

More recently, Toa Fraser and Jacob Rajan have exemplified New Zealand's growing ethnic diversity. Fraser's work, which coincides with the emergence of Pacific Island drama, includes *Bare* (produced 1998), a funky, demotic comedy in which two actors play a range of urban characters; and *No. 2* (produced 1999), in which one actor plays nine roles, mostly members of a south Auckland, Fijian family. Indian Ink, formed in 1996 by actor Jacob Rajan and director Justin Lewis, has produced a trilogy by Rajan that features masks and multiple role-playing: *Krishnan's Dairy* (produced 1997), a solo piece juxtaposing the story of Indian immigrant shopkeepers with the legend of the Taj Mahal; *The Candlestickmaker* (produced 2000), about the physicist Subramanyan Chandrasekah; and *The Pickle King* (produced 2002). Rajan's and Fraser's work has toured extensively and won awards at the Edinburgh Fringe.

FURTHER READING

Black, Sebastian. "Aggressive Laments: New Zealand Theatre in the 1980s." *New Literature Review* 13 (1984): 5–16.

Carnegie, David. "Recent New Zealand Drama." *Journal of New Zealand Literature* 3 (1985): 7–15.

Edmond, Murray. "Lighting Out for Paradise: New Zealand Theatre and the 'Other Tradition.'" *Australasian Drama Studies* 18 (April 1991): 183–206.

Leek, Robert. "Homegrown Drama of the Mid-Eighties." *Journal of New Zealand Literature* 5 (1987): 1–13.

——. "New Drama '86–'87: Various Shades of Laughter." *Journal of New Zealand Literature* 6 (1988): 3–29.

Mann, Philip. "Tragic Power in Vincent O'Sullivan's *Shuriken*." *Australasian Drama Studies* 18 (April 1991): 91–94, 147–158.

O'Donnell, David, and Bronwyn Tweddle. "Toa Fraser: Shifting Boundaries in Pacific Island Comedy." *Australasian Drama Studies* 42 (April 2003): 123–137.

——. "Naked Samoans: Pacific Island Voices in the Theatre of Aotearoa/New Zealand." *Performance Research* 8, no. 1. (2003): 65–73.

Stuart Young

MAORI DRAMA

The burgeoning of Maori drama is one of the most conspicuous and important developments in New Zealand theater since 1990. It is informed by a history of Indigenous people's projects such as assertion of *tino rangatiratanga* (self-determination), reclamation of misappropriated lands, and reconstitution of social and cultural identity. It integrates European dramatic conventions and Maori performance aspects such as *waiata* (song) and *haka* (war-chant). *Marae* (an outdoor meeting area at the heart of a Maori settlement) protocols such as welcome calls, greetings, prayers, and formal farewells are often used.

The development of Maori theater can be traced to the Maori Theatre Trust (1966), none of whose plays were by Maori dramatists. However, actor-directors Don Selwyn and Jim Moriarty, actor and writer Apirana Taylor, and actor George Henare became important figures in Maori drama in the 1980s and 1990s.

The 1975 Land March, when Maori throughout the country protested against the government's land sale policies, is referenced in several plays. Between 1975 and 1990 (the sesquicentennial of the signing of the Treaty of Waitangi—the founding document that established the relationship between Maori and the British Crown), Maori plays—such as *Death of the Land* (produced 1976, published 1991), by Rore Hapipi and Te-Ika-a-Maui Players (1975–1987); *Rise Up! Awaken* (*Maranga Mai*, produced 1979), by the Maranga Mai collective (1979–1980); *The Gospel According to Tane* (produced 1983), by Selwyn Muru and performed by Te Ohu Whakaari (1983–1990); and *Lost, Disappearing Eyes* (*Whatungarongaro*, produced 1990, published 1999), by Roma Potiki and He Ara Hou (1989–1994, 1996)—commented on race relations, social inequality, and cultural ALIENATION. They were created in a context based on Maori social structures and combined Maori oral traditions and ritual, and modern song forms such as rap.

Accompanied by a national acknowledgment of the unique qualities of Maori culture, the late 1980s and 1990s was a period of catalytic activity. Increasingly this activity became associated with Taki Rua-Depot Theatre, a small, cooperatively run professional theater in Wellington, which declared its commitment to the continued growth and development of Maori theater. By 1998 it had ceased to operate as a venue, becoming instead a production company, Taki Rua Productions.

In 1991 *He Reo Hou*, a collection of Maori plays, was published (the first since the publication of Harry Dansey's *Te Raukura* [The Feathers of the Albatross] in 1974). Its publication followed a significant Maori theatrical presence at the 1990 International Festival of the Arts in Wellington. John Broughton's solo play *Michael James Manaia* (1990) further raised the profile of Maori theater: it toured to Edinburgh in 1991, performed by Jim Moriarty.

The mid-1990s saw an expansion in the theatrical adventurousness of Maori dramatists. Apirana Taylor revised BERTOLT BRECHT'S MOTHER COURAGE as *Whaea Kairau* (1999, produced 1995) in the context of the 19th-century New Zealand Wars. By the late 1990s, Taki Rua was touring nationally, performing plays in Maori, and internationally, performing new plays such as novelist Witi Ihimaera's *Woman Far Walking* (2000). Among new playwrights to emerge are Albert Belz and Mitch Tawhi Thomas. In the last few years Taki Rua has also developed Pacific Island plays.

FURTHER READING

Balme, Christopher. "Between Separation and Integration: Contemporary Maori Theatre." *CRNLE Reviews Journal* 1 (1993): 41–48.

Greenwood, Janinka. *History of Bicultural Theatre: Mapping the Terrain.* Research Monograph Series. Christchurch: Christchurch College of Education, 2002.

He Reo Hou: 5 Plays by Maori Playwrights. Wellington: Playmarket, 1991.

Huria, John. "Maa Te Reehia e Kawee." *Playmarket News* 16 (1997): 2–7.

Maufort, Marc. *Transgressive Itineraries: Post-colonial Hybridizations of Dramatic Realism.* Brussels: Peter Lang, 2003.

Mei-Lin Te-Puea Hansen

FEMINIST DRAMA

An explosion of New Zealand women's drama occurred in 1982: RENÉE's *Secrets* was staged; Fiona Farrell's *In Confidence: Dialogues with Amy Bock* was presented at the Women's Studies Association Conference; and at the New Zealand Playwrights' Workshop, Renée's *Breaking Out* received a reading, and Hilary Beaton's realist *Outside In* and Carolyn Burns's *Objection Overruled* were workshopped.

Objection Overruled (1984) is a highly theatrical, mock courtroom drama. An ostensibly unsuspecting, white, middle-class male member of the audience is put on trial for the crime of living, which, it turns out, includes sexual molestation, rape, and incest. The cast plays various roles in improvisations around the accused's life. The audience becomes the jury, and Burns offers two endings, depending on the verdict. Norelle Scott's *Promise Not to Tell* (produced 1984) deals with rape and incest in a much harsher manner, emphasizing the denial and repression of men's violence against women.

New Zealand feminist theater's origins in satirical revues of the mid-1970s, evident in *Objection Overruled* and some of Renée's plays, continues in the work of Jean Betts and Lorae Parry, who have produced significant explorations of gender and sexual desire. Betts and Parry, who also act and direct, were part of the women's cabaret *Hen's Teeth* at Wellington's Circa theater in 1988. This successful enterprise spawned *Digger and Nudger* (produced 1989) and *Digger and Nudger Try Harder* (produced 1990), written by Betts, Parry, and actor Carmel McGlone. It featured a male COMEDY duo, played by Parry and McGlone, searching for the "woman within." The construction of male characters by female performers is also used to unsettle in Stephanie Johnson's *Accidental Phantasies* (produced 1985), a clever, fantastical play about pornography.

Parry's most accomplished play, *Eugenia* (1996), develops this cross-gender theme further. Based on a historical story, it tells of an Italian woman who lived, even married, as a man in Wellington in 1916. This scenario is juxtaposed with a contemporary story of a schoolteacher and her students devising a play about Eugenia. The double plot, with doubled roles, serves to complicate issues of gender construction. *Eugenia* recalls Farrell's *In Confidence*, which celebrates the story of a transvestite confidence trickster who lived in Dunedin in the 1890s.

Parry's *Vagabonds* (2001) also deals with cross-dressing and draws on historical events. A female convict escapes on a boat from AUSTRALIA in the 1850s. Rebuffing the captain's sexual advances, she whips his naked posterior and dons his clothes. Then, in New Zealand, she joins a troupe of traveling players. Parry, whose plays include *Strip* (produced 1988) and *Cracks* (1994), is also credited with writing New Zealand's first notable lesbian play, *Frontwomen* (1993).

Betts's other plays are *Revenge of the Amazons* (1998, produced 1984), a rewriting of *A Midsummer Night's Dream* that reverses the gender of the courtiers, recasts the mechanicals as a female theater troupe, and has Oberon falling for a hard-line feminist Easter bunny; *Ophelia Thinks Harder* (1994), a reworking of *Hamlet*, familiar to feminist theaters elsewhere; and *The Misandrist* (2000), which explores the roles of women in fairy tales.

FURTHER READING

Dale, Judith. "Digger & Nudger Try Harder, and Related Endeavours." *Illusions* 13 (March 1990): 32–33.

——. "Women's Theatre and Why?" *Australasian Drama Studies* 18 (April 1991): 159–182.

——. "Theatre Women's Franchise: Suffrage Year Theatre." *Illusions* 23 (Winter 1994): 36–45.

——. "Performing Identity: Engendering Post-coloniality on Stage." *Illusions* 25 (Winter 1996): 36–43.

White, Helen. "Paths for a Flightless Bird: Roles for Women on the New Zealand Stage Since 1950." *Australasian Drama Studies* 3, no. 2. (1985): 105–143.

Stuart Young

NGEMA, MBONGENI (1955–)

Mbongeni Ngema, born in 1955 in Verulam, South Africa, is a recognized playwright, musician, director, actor, and choreographer.

Ngema made a name in the theater in a career that started with him as a theater-backing guitarist, working with such renowned theater directors in South Africa as Gibson Kente and Barney Simon. In 1979 he started a collaboration with Percy Mtwa, workshopping the play *Woza Albert* (1981)—a highly successful play that employs deep satire to imagine the coming back of Jesus Christ into apartheid South Africa. Offering a critique of political and religious figures in South Africa against a black theological perspective, the play's success is registered as much in its satire as it is in its humor and powerful rendition by two actors full of energy in the songs and dances and the movements that they make use of. Ngema and Mtwa's rendition of *Woza Albert* is captivating not only for the simplicity of the set and its creative use but also in the dexterity of their physical performance mimicking several characters changing from one to the next with the ease and smoothness of seasoned performers.

Indeed, the duo's performance in the play was akin to the powerful performance of the *Island* earlier rendered by the compelling duo of John Kani and Winston Ntshona. *Woza Albert* toured many countries in Europe and the UNITED STATES, winning several awards. Another award-winning play by Ngema was *Asinamali* (1984)—which saw Ngema nominated as Best Director for the Tony Award. The play whose title means "We have no money" is a musical exploration of the rent strikes in the townships of apartheid South Africa in the early 1980s.

Ngema, having made a name in producing successful award-winning musicals, hit the Hollywood big screen when his yet another successful musical play *Sarafina*—which was performed on Broadway between 1988 and 1989 and was nominated for five Tony Awards—was adapted and produced as a film attracting such Hollywood stars as Whoopi Goldberg.

As a musician, Ngema has also recorded music—partly as a score for his plays and movies, working with such renowned musicians as Miriam Makeba and Hugh Masekela. Ngema has been as successful as he has been controversial, in both his artistic productions and his personal life. Accused of being an unapologetic polygamist, his expensively produced *Sarafina 2*, aimed as a musical to combat HIV/AIDS, was criticized as ineffectual and exorbitant. His song "Amandiya"—Zulu for the Indians—recorded in 2002, was also criticized for its lyrics, which were largely seen as racist toward the Indian population in South Africa.

[See also South Africa]

SELECT PLAYS: *Asinamali* (1984); *Sarafina* (1988); *Magic at 4 AM* (1993); *Mama* (1996); *Sarafina 2* (1997); *Nikeziwe* (2005)

FURTHER READING
Barber, Karin. *Readings in African Popular Culture.* Bloomington: Indiana Univ. Press, 1997.
Brown, Roxanne. "*Sarafina!* Young South African Voices Spread Music of Liberation." *Ebony* (February 1990).
Whitaker, Charles F. "The Cultural Explosion—South African Arts." Special issue, Nelson Mandela and the New South Africa. *Ebony* (August 1994).

Bantu Ndung'u

NGUGI WA THIONG'O (1938–)

By the 1980s Ngugi wa Thiong'o's name had become significant as a prominent writer in the literary world, publishing several novels, short stories, and plays, some of which were noted for pricking the consciousness of the political elite, particularly in his country Kenya. He is credited with starting what now is famously referred to as the Literary Revolution that saw the discipline of literature removed from its traditional department of English at the University of Nairobi and established as a department by itself by the beginning of the 1970s.

While it was his writing that saw him sent to detention without trial, after publishing such works as *Petals of Blood*, it was his work at the Kamiirithu Cultural and Educational Centre, where he collaborated with other educationists and villagers to produce plays such as *I Will Marry When I Want* (Ngaahika Ndeenda), that saw him forced into exile in 1982. The work at the Kamiirithu Centre, educational yet using theater as the medium, focused on reexamining colonial history in a postcolonial state that worked to erase rather than uphold the role of the citizenry in the fight against the colonial powers.

Born in 1938, Ngugi's publishing goes back to the 1950s when he was a student at the prestigious Alliance High School in Nairobi, Kenya, where he published his first short story—"Try Witchcraft"—in the school magazine. He has since published several novels, plays, collections of short stories, and critical writings and edited a groundbreaking journal on Gikuyu culture and literature published in Gikuyu. His works have been translated into about thirty languages around the world.

His early works written in English, like *Weep Not Child* (1964), *The River Between* (1965), and *A Grain of Wheat* (1968), depict the conflict of cultures imposed by colonialism engaging with issues such as the role of Christianity, English education, and the oppressive treatment of the colonial and postcolonial state in denying Indigenous people the very land that the colonial settlers had forcefully taken from them. Known mostly as a novelist, Ngugi has written one play, *The Black Hermit* (1972), and co-authored two, *The Trial of Dedan Kimathi* (with Micere Mugo, 1977) and *I'll Marry When I Want* (with Ngugi wa Mirii, 1980). Central to the three plays are conflicts between anticolonial and neocolonial nationalisms in Kenya's history. In all of these plays, Ngugi and his collaborators not only drew attention to the emergence of neocolonialism and its attendant ALIENATION and despair but also theatricalized the protagonist roles the masses of people could play in enhancing their full participation in national politics. Underscoring "decolonization" as a perpetual theme and process, the last two plays particularly highlight modes of historical agency that must be formed to enable Kenya to move forward into a more democratic history. It is indeed Ngugi's participation in writing, co-directing, and organizing communities of disenfranchised Kenyans that led to his subsequent imprisonment and exile.

Ngugi was a leading proponent for calls to reconfigure literature in African languages as well as to reinvigorate their performance cadences. The premise of such a call was to further the thesis of decolonizing African cultures whose political developments were arrested by European colonization and neocolonial dominant cultures. Leading by example, he began to write novels in his native Gikuyu and called for a performance of reading in African languages. His involvement in community-based theater was itself part of immersing himself in reconfiguring Indigenous cultures to stem neocolonial politics as well as to realign Kenya's history on the path to permanent decolonization. His activism also led to his removal as a professor at the University of Nairobi.

While he was never reinstated at the University of Nairobi, where he was chair of the Literature Department, after his detention in 1978, he has, since held several university positions: between 1989 and 1992, he was visiting professor of English and comparative literature at Yale University; from 1992 to 2002 he was the Erich Maria Remarque Professor of Languages at New York University; and he is currently a Distinguished Professor of English and Comparative Literature at the University of California, Irvine, where he is also the director of the International Centre for Writing and Translation.

As a novelist, playwright, and essayist, Ngugi is the recipient of several honors, among which are the Zora Neale Hurston–Paul Robeson Award for artistic and scholarly achievement, 1992; the Gwendolyn Brooks Centre Contributors Award for significant contribution to black literary art, 1994; Fonlon-Nichols Prize, 1996; Distinguished Africanist Award, New York Africa Studies Association, 1996; and the Medal of the Presidency of the Italian Cabinet by the International Scientific Committee of the Pio Manzu International Research Centre, 2002.

[*See also Africa*]

PLAYS: *The Black Hermit* (1972); *The Trial of Dedan Kimathi* (with Micere Mugo, 1977); *I Will Marry When I Want* (*Ngaahika Ndeenda: Ithaako Ria Ngerekano*, with Ngugi wa Mirii, 1977)

FURTHER READING
Cook, D., and M. Okenimpe. *Ngugi wa Thiongo: An Introduction to His Writings*. London: Heineman, 1982.
Lovesey, O. *Ngugi wa Thiongo*. New York: Twayne, 2000.
Robson, C. B. *Ngugi wa Thiongo*. London: Macmillan, 1979.

Bantu Ndung'u

NIETZSCHE, FRIEDRICH (1844–1900)

Among philosophers, probably no one exerted a broader influence on the modern drama than Friedrich Nietzsche, who was born in Röcken, Prussia, on October 15, 1844, and died in Weimar, GERMANY, on August 25, 1900. His examination of the essence of TRAGEDY was a major influence on EUGENE O'NEILL; his reevaluation of moral standards impressed HENRIK IBSEN and AUGUST STRINDBERG; his concept of the superman inspired GEORGE BERNARD SHAW; and his picture of the human being suffering the anguish of freedom anticipated the existentialism of JEAN-PAUL SARTRE and ALBERT CAMUS.

In *The Birth of Tragedy from the Spirit of Music*, published in 1872, Nietzsche argued that drama arose not so much out of efforts to tell a story as out of a desire by humans to make contact with their essential inner being. Ancient Greek tragedy combined instrumental music and song (the chorus) with the word (the actor). The choral song was the primary element, and drama as we know it developed when the actor separated himself from the group. As plot and dialogue became increasingly important, the rational element took over the intuitive element. Thus tragedy lost contact with its roots, a decline represented in Nietzsche's view by the clever skepticism of Euripides, the last of the three great ancient tragedians.

As an explanation of the origins of tragedy, Nietzsche's youthful work was immediately challenged by classical scholars. But its influence was immense because, at a time of shifting values, it set up a dualism that carried one beyond conventional and time-bound ideas of good and evil and schismatic religious doctrines into a realm of something that did seem eternal and all-inclusive. He set Dionysus, the Greek god of intoxication and the god presiding in ancient Athens over tragedy, against Apollo, the god of light and reason. Only through Dionysus can the human being understand what lies beyond the fleeting phenomenon of ordinary existence. This insight leads one to an awareness of the absurdity of existence, producing a *nausea*, a key term in 20th-century existentialism. The wisdom of Dionysus reveals a truth that one cannot live with for long; Apollo's function is to provide the illusion, through art and science, that life does have meaning.

The theory expressed in the essay owes perhaps more to the composer RICHARD WAGNER and the philosopher Arthur Schopenhauer than to Greek tragedy. Wagner's music drama *Tristan and Isolde* overwhelmed the young Nietzsche, and he became, for a while, the composer's ardent disciple. Just as Wagner endeavored to recreate the majesty and spirit of ancient tragedy, so Nietzsche used *Tristan*, in which he saw the union of Dionysus and Apollo as a concrete example of how tragedy can be reborn in the modern age.

The philosophical basis for a reclamation of tragedy lay in Schopenhauer's replacement of a universe that had a direction and a purpose, such as Christian redemption, by a universe without direction or meaning. Schopenhauer put a new spin on the conventional dualism of body and soul, arguing that the true dichotomy was that of the individual and the thing-in-itself, the swirling energy of the universe. The life of the human being consists in a vain effort to impose a meaning on this energy. For Schopenhauer, music was the highest form of art because it did not impose a meaning on human existence; instead, it turned the meaningless energy of the universe against itself and made something beautiful out of it. This pessimistic philosophy with its promotion of the artist and musician above the scientist and the empire builder found a warm response in Wagner and provided a starting point for Nietzsche's own philosophy. In 1870 he wrote, "For me, all that is best and most beautiful is associated with the names Schopenhauer and Wagner."

The belief that the irrational played as great a part in man's life as his reasoning powers was a key element in the romantic imagination. Johann Wolfgang Goethe called it "the demonic" and defined it as that which reason and understanding cannot explain. Nietzsche expanded on this, saying, "Perhaps there is a realm of wisdom . . . from which the logician is excluded. Perhaps art must be seen as the necessary complement of rational discourse?" Here Nietzsche is echoing Schopenhauer: "The musician reveals to us the hidden spirit of the world; he makes himself the interpreter of the profoundest wisdom, while speaking a language that reason does not understand." Nietzsche saw in *Tristan* an example of how the musician revealed the hidden world of the irrational.

Since then there have been attempts by dramatists to penetrate this hidden realm without using music. Probably no dramatist was so much under the spell of Nietzsche as O'Neill in his middle period in such plays as LAZARUS LAUGHED and THE GREAT GOD BROWN.

Nietzsche's other works also influenced dramatists, none more so than *Thus Spake Zarathustra* (1883–1892). In it Nietzsche develops the concept of the superman, the greatly superior individual, who rises above other mortals by forging his own code of morality, his own principles. Bernard Shaw popularized and domesticated this kind of hero in his MAN AND SUPERMAN (1903). But Sartre, the most vocal of the existentialist philosophers, presented the superman in a truly Nietzschean guise, by drawing heavily on *Zarathustra* in his play THE FLIES (1943), a retelling of Aeschylus's *Oresteia*.

[*See also* Philosophy and Drama; Symbolism]

FURTHER READING

Lea, F. A. *The Tragic Philosopher: Friedrich Nietzsche*. New York: Athlone Press, 1993.

Silk, M. S., and J. P. Stern. *Nietzsche on Tragedy*. Cambridge: Cambridge Univ. Press, 1981.

Evert Sprinchorn

THE NIGHT IS MOTHER TO THE DAY

The Night Is Mother to the Day (*Natten är dagens mor*), a four-act display and epilogue by LARS NORÉN, was first performed at the Malmö City Theater in SWEDEN in 1982, then published in 1983. *The Night Is Mother to the Day*, which signified Norén's breakthrough as a dramatist, forms the first part of a family trilogy. The second part is called *Chaos Is God's Neighbor* (*Kaos är granne med Gud*). (The original titles of the two plays are quotations from a poem by the romantic Swedish poet Erik Johan Stagnelius.) The concluding third part is called *The Stillness* (*Stillheten*). Closely related to these three plays and actually preceding them is *The Courage to Kill* (*Modet att döda*), about a traumatic father-son relationship.

Norén's family trilogy is highly autobiographical. In *The Night Is Mother to the Day*, set in the kitchen of a hotel in southern Sweden 1956, we meet four characters: a father (manager of the hotel) and mother, both around fifty, an older son of twenty-six, and a younger one of sixteen. In *Chaos Is God's Neighbor*, set in a hotel lobby in 1961, we virtually meet the same family, although they have other names and are about ten years older. In addition, there is a hotel guest. In *The Stillness*, again set in a hotel lobby, this time in 1968, we meet the same family members, again a little older and with different names. In addition, there is a housekeeper.

While closely patterned on his own family (the age difference between the brothers corresponds, for example, to that between Norén and his elder brother), the family in *The Night* also closely resembles of the family in EUGENE O'NEILL's LONG DAY'S JOURNEY INTO NIGHT, a play highly admired by Norén. Thus in *The Night*, the father is an alcoholic, and the elder son is oedipally attached to his mother while seeking the company of prostitutes. The mother is suffering from incurable cancer. The younger son, David, Norén's alter ego, has spent some time in a mental hospital and fears that he will be sent back to it. Like O'Neill's four-act drama, Norén's play, also in four acts, begins in the morning and ends after midnight that same day in the same room. For Norén, as for O'Neill, the unity of time and place has thematic value, stressing the ambivalent feelings of the family members. To stay in the room they share is painful; to leave it is menacing.

Highly praised in Europe, wherever it has been performed, *The Night Is Mother to the Day* was coolly received when it premiered in the UNITED STATES at the Yale Repertory Theater in New Haven, Connecticut. Mel Gussow (1984), reviewer for the *New York Times*, was outright negative, citing "the play's oppressiveness."

FURTHER READING

Gussow, Mel. "Night Is Mother, New Haven Repertory." *New York Times* (March 14, 1984).

Törnqvist, Egil. "Lars Norén and Eugene O'Neill." In *Small Is Beautiful: Small Countries Theatre Conference*, ed. by Claude Schumacher and Derek Fogg. Glasgow: Theatre Studies Publications, 1990. 63–68.

Van Reis, Mikael. *Det slutna rummet: Sex kapitel om Lars Norén's författarskap 1963–1983* [The Closed Room: Six Chapters on Lars Norén's Authorship 1963–1983]. Stockholm/Stehag: Symposion, 1997. 362–423.

Egil Törnqvist

'NIGHT MOTHER

Written in 1981, MARSHA NORMAN's widely celebrated drama *'Night Mother* explores the subject of suicide. The characters include Jessie Cates, a quiet but determined woman in her late thirties to early forties, and her sturdily assertive mother, Thelma Cates, who is in her late fifties to early sixties. The one-act play takes place during the course of an evening spent in the women's home; the action is in real time, with clocks onstage running throughout the performance. Toward the beginning of the play, Jessie calmly reveals to her mother her intention to shoot herself later that evening. She says that she wishes to prepare Thelma, and it is clear that she is also preparing herself for what she plans to do.

Jessie is deeply unhappy, suffering from a life of personal disappointments and struggles with epilepsy. She feels isolated, trapped in the life she leads with her mother, but has finally found the strength to make her own choice. Jessie's rationale for taking her own life is straightforward: "I'm not having a very good time and I don't have any reason to think it'll get anything but worse," she explains. "I'm tired. I'm hurt. I'm sad. I feel used." Thelma at first dismisses Jessie's announcement as ridiculous but increasingly becomes concerned. What follows is an argument between the two in which truths are revealed, bringing the pair closer than ever together. Thelma attempts to reason with Jessie, growing more and more frantic as Jessie's determination, and her own inability to save her daughter, becomes clear to her. When Jessie finally shuts the bedroom door behind her, and we hear the gun go off, ending her life, Thelma cries, "Forgive me! I thought you were mine!"

In November 1981, 'Night Mother received its first reading at the Circle Repertory Company in New York, and it was first performed in December 1982 by the American Repertory Theatre in Cambridge, Massachusetts, in a production directed by Tom Moore. That production was brought to the John Golden Theatre on Broadway the following year. Reviews broadly praised the work, citing its combination of humor and pathos and powerful impact on its audience, and Norman was heralded as a promising new voice in American playwriting. 'Night Mother ran for just over a year and received four Tony nominations as well as the 1983 Pulitzer Prize for Drama, the Susan Smith Blackburn Prize, the Dramatists Guild's Hull-Warriner Award, and a Drama Desk Award. Norman wrote the screenplay for a 1986 film version of the play, which starred Anne Bancroft and Sissy Spacek

Norman said that she wrote 'Night Mother entirely for herself, during a period of professional frustration, when she decided, "I'm going to write it the way I see it; nobody's going to have anything to say about it. I'm going to do it just for me" (Brown, 1996). Theater scholar Jill Dolan (1991) considered 'Night Mother "one of the first plays written by a woman and addressing women's concerns to gain widespread attention, critical acclaim, and economic success."

[See also Feminist Drama in the United States; United States]

FURTHER READING

Browder, Sally. "I Thought You Were Mine: Marsha Norman's 'Night Mother." In Mother Puzzles: Daughters and Mothers in Contemporary American Literature, ed. by Mickey Pearlman. Westport, Conn.: Greenwood Press, 1989.

Brown, Linda Ginter, ed. Marsha Norman: A Casebook. New York: Garland, 1996.

Demastes, William W. "New Voices Using New Realism: Fuller, Henley, and Norman." In Beyond Naturalism: A New Realism in American Theatre. New York: Greenwood Press, 1988.

Dolan, Jill. "Feminism and the Canon: The Question of Universality." In The Feminist Spectator as Critic. Ann Arbor: Univ. of Michigan Press, 1991.

Harriott, Esther. "Marsha Norman: Getting Out." In American Voices: Five Contemporary Playwrights in Essays and Interviews. Jefferson, N.C.: McFarland, 1988.

Emma Dassori

THE NIGHT OF THE IGUANA

I know people torture each other many times like devils, but sometimes they do see and know each other, you know, and then, if they're decent, they do want to help each other all that they can.
—Hannah Jelkes, Act 2

TENNESSEE WILLIAMS's compelling 1961 drama The Night of the Iguana features a trio of his most memorable characters and a deepening exploration of many of the recurrent themes of his work, particularly the struggle of the spirit over the desires and frailties of the flesh. Williams places emphasis on three principal characters in a lyrical meditation on the nature of God and the struggle of His creatures to find redemption for real or imagined sins.

Set in 1940 on the west coast of MEXICO, The Night of the Iguana finds two groups of travelers in residence at a rundown hotel cradled in a rainforest overlooking the sea. In this steamy Eden, a group of German tourists enthuse about the blitz of London, which, they are certain, will succeed in subjugating the British people to Nazi rule. The other group is a tour of women teachers from Texas escorted by a distracted guide, Lawrence Shannon, an alcoholic ex-priest subsisting under the casual protection of the hotel's owner, Maxine Faulk, a blowsy widow lusting for Shannon. Shannon's libidinous interest, however, has tragically directed itself toward underage women. When he becomes involved with a girl in his parish, a scandal ensues. Shannon renounces his God who, he believes, is a malign deity aggressively pursuing his soul. The revelation of Shannon's renouncement of God has so shocked his congregation that they removed him from his post. He has drifted to Mexico and Maxine, but the lost, tormented Shannon finds momentary redemption when he encounters the deeply spiritual Hannah Jelkes, a wandering artist traveling aimlessly with her ninety-seven-year-old grandfather, Nonno, a "minor" poet grasping to create one last poem. Shannon and Hannah find a momentary respite at the hotel where Hannah, unmarried and touchingly devoted to her grandfather, reaches out to Shannon. Their encounter is briefly liberating for both, a release from their individual constraints symbolized by the sudden escape of a tethered iguana captured by some Mexican boys planning to eat it. The iguana's flight to freedom comes as Nonno completes the poem he has grappled with for twenty years—his most beautiful one, his deeply moved granddaughter exclaims—and he dies, thus achieving the ultimate freedom. Shannon returns to Maxine, while Hannah, now alone and directionless, faces the lonely, barren future stretching before her.

The Night of the Iguana, which was inspired by a 1946 Williams short story, opened at New York's Royale Theatre on December 28, 1961. Under the direction of Frank Corsaro, Iguana won mostly laudatory reviews and a long run. The play's critical and commercial success led to a screen version directed by John Huston.

Critics applauded what several described as a deepening of his themes in The Night of the Iguana, while many later critics consider it his last great drama. Lawrence Shannon is, with the possible exception of Big Daddy in Cat on a Hot Tin Roof and Tom Wingfield of The Glass Menagerie, his most complex male character. In the Williams canon, *The Night of the Iguana* marks a transition from his earlier, larger-scale works. Following *Iguana*, Williams spent the final two decades of his life experimenting with form and language while continuing to explore the terrain between ROMANTICISM and reality.

[*See also* United States, 1940–Present]

FURTHER READING

Adler, Jacob H. "*Night of the Iguana*: A New Tennessee Williams?" *Ramparts* 1, no. 3 (1962): 59–68.

Adler, Thomas P. "Before the Fall—and After: *Summer and Smoke* and *The Night of the Iguana*." In *The Cambridge Companion to Tennessee Williams*, ed. by Matthew C. Roudané. New York: Cambridge Univ. Press, 1997. 114–127.

Leon, Ferdinand. "Time, Fantasy, and Reality in *Night of the Iguana*." *Modern Drama* 11 (1968): 87–96.

Matthews, Kevin. "The Evolution of *The Night of the Iguana*: Three Symbols in the Manuscript Record." *Library Chronicle of the University of Texas* 25, no. 2 (1994): 66–89.

Moritz, Helen E. "Apparent Sophoclean Echoes in Tennessee Williams's *Night of the Iguana*." *Classical and Modern Literature* 5 (1985): 305–314.

Phillips, Rod. " 'Collecting Evidence': The Natural World in Tennessee Williams's *The Night of the Iguana*." *Southern Literary Journal* 32, no. 2 (Spring 2000): 59–69.

James Fisher

THE NIGHT OF THE TRIBADES

The Night of the Tribades (*Tribadernas natt*), "a play from 1889" in two acts by PER OLOV ENQUIST, was published in 1975 and first performed at the Royal Dramatic Theater in Stockholm the same year. When teaching an AUGUST STRINDBERG course at the University of California, Enquist came to the conclusion that Strindberg's MONODRAMA THE STRONGER is a highly autobiographical play, where the absent husband, Bob, corresponds to Strindberg himself; his wife, Mrs. X, to Strindberg's wife Siri von Essen; and Miss Y, who either is or has been Bob's mistress, to Siri's Danish friend Marie David. As appears from his autobiographical novel *A Madman's Defence* (*En dåres försvarstal*), written shortly before *The Stronger*, Strindberg believed that Siri and Marie had a lesbian relationship. In *The Stronger*, this situation is turned into its opposite, two women rivaling for the same man. Strindberg's monodrama, Enquist concluded, is a piece of wishful thinking on the part of the author.

In *The Night of the Tribades*—*tribade* meaning "lesbian"—written in eleven days, Enquist unmasks this highly representative wishful thinking and describes the true situation camouflaged behind it:

two women excluding the man. It is his first and hitherto most successful play; in fact, internationally it was the most acclaimed Swedish play after Strindberg.

Four people have gathered at the Dagmar Theater in Copenhagen on an evening in March 1889 to rehearse Strindberg's new play *The Stronger*. Apart from the author, the individuals are Dane Viggo Schiwe, who is to direct the monodrama; Strindberg's wife Siri von Essen, who is to play Mrs. X, the speaking part; and her Danish friend Marie David, who is to play Miss Y, the silent part. The plot develops from Strindberg's discovery that the hated tribade Marie is to do the part of the mute woman in the world premiere of his play (in reality, the part was played by Anna Pio). His irritation at Marie overrides his jealousy of Schiwe who, he believes, has a liaison with his wife Siri. Most effective and meaningful are the constant switches back and forth between rehearsed lines from *The Stronger* and lines by the characters themselves in this highly metatheatrical drama. At the end, waiting for the man who is to photograph them in connection with the opening of the play, Siri is seen in the middle, flanked by Strindberg and Marie. But when the photographer enters, his and the play's last line is: "The gentleman should stand in the middle." The final photograph becomes a falsified version of the true situation, a version to be passed on to posterity.

"The play explicitly focuses," Shideler (1984) summarizes, "on the male need to dominate women, to be the center of their lives, and on men's sexual insecurity."

[*See also* Sweden]

FURTHER READING

Anderman, Gunilla. "*The Night of the Tribades*: Fact and Fiction in Grez-sur-Loing." In *Documentarism in Scandinavian Literature*, ed. by Poul Houe and Sven Rossel. Amsterdam: Rodopi, 1997. 148–154.

Blackwell, Marilyn Johns. "Ideology and Specularity in Per Olov Enquist's *Tribadernas natt*." *Scandinavian Studies* 67 (1995): 196–215.

Shideler, Ross. *Per Olov Enquist: A Critical Study*. Westport, Conn.: Greenwood Press, 1984.

Törnqvist, Egil. "Playwright on Playwright: Per Olov Enquist's Strindberg and Lars Norén's O'Neill." In *Documentarism in Scandinavian Literature*, ed. by Poul Houe and Sven Rossel. Amsterdam: Rodopi, 1997. 155–164.

Egil Törnqvist

NIHONGDENG XIA DE SHAOBING, HUAJU

See ON GUARD BENEATH THE NEON LIGHTS

NŌ AND KYŌGEN

JAPAN's nō theater is often portrayed as virtually unchanged from the time of its establishment six centuries ago. Yet the modern era has seen a vast transformation in repertoire and influence, both at home and abroad. Nō's founding genius Motokiyo Zeami (1363?–1443?) attempted to preserve his discoveries through secret treatises. When published in 1909, these had a profound influence in reinvigorating this ancient theater.

After World War II, plays that had been considered morally ambiguous, critical of the shogunate, priesthood, or emperor, or too complex were restored in a "revival boom" that continues today. Successful restorations such as *The Burial Mound* (*Motomezuka*, 1951) and *The Burden of Love* (*Koi no Omoni*, 1963) have been assimilated into the official repertoire. *Kyōgen*, the classical COMEDY genre, similarly expanded its repertoire by each of the two existing schools importing works once exclusive to the other and restoring lost works: Shigeyama Sennojō revived the large-cast fantasy *Battle of the Nuts and Fruit* (*Konomi Arasoi*, 1966), a solo *kyōgen Mushroom Hunting* (*Hitori Matsutake*, 1971), and the so-called porno *kyōgen Sleep Reversal* (*Negawari*, 1983), in which two lecherous priests fondle each other instead of the intended young widow.

Modern writers have attempted new works in *nō* style. Plays have been based on classic literature, such as Takahama Kyōshi's *Road to the North* (1944) or Jakuchō Setouchi's *Bridge of Dreams* (*Yume no Ukihashi*, 2001), based on *The Tale of Genji*; legends, such as the marriage of the water-princess and the Chinese Emperor's son in Masaaki Dōmoto's *Drought Dragon-Princess* (*Kasui Ryūnyō*, 1995); historical characters, such as Yōjirō Takita's *Abe no Seimei* (2002); Western religious figures, such as Kichida Rōchi's *The Resurrection of Christ* (*Fukkatsu no Kuraisuto*, 1957); and contemporary issues, such as Tada Toshio's *Well of Darkness* (*Mumyō no Ii*, 1991), about the ethics of brain-death transplants, or Ishimure Michiko's *Shiranui* (2002), concerning Minamata disease.

Kyōgen adaptations and newly written plays draw on fairy tales, legends, horror stories, and literary classics. Tadasu Iizawa's *The Washing River* (*Susugigawa*, 1953), based on the medieval French FARCE *The Washtub*, delineates a henpecked husband's revenge; KINOSHITA JUNJI's folktale play *Tale of Hikoichi* (*Hikoichi Banashi*, 1955) sketches a mischievous goblin; and Hōashi Masami's *The Death-God* (*Shinigami*, 1983) conflates two Grimm tales about a quack doctor. William Shakespeare's *Taming of the Shrew*, *Twelfth Night*, and *Comedy of Errors* have all been staged successfully as *kyōgen*, among other innovative works. Philosopher and "super-kabuki" (SHIN KABUKI) playwright Umehara Takeshi's "super-kyōgen" gives an Aristophanic satiric spin on such contemporary issues as ecological disasters caused by reclaimed land, human cloning, and nuclear war.

Many Westerners have created *nō*-influenced pieces, while *nō* actors, in turn, have adapted Western texts for *nō*. Examples are Kimura Taro's *Woman and Shadow* (*Kage to Onna* 1968), based on PAUL CLAUDEL's play of that name (1923), and Yokomichi Mario's *Hawk Princess* (*Takahime*, 1967), an adaptation of W. B. YEATS's AT THE HAWK'S WELL. There also have been English-language plays written in *nō* style by Richard Emmert, Arthur Little, Janine Beichman, Kenneth Yasuda, and others.

Nō and *kyōgen* experimentation continues annually, although few plays enter the permanent repertory. Moreover, the actors and directors gain immeasurably from their mutually enriching interaction with contemporary artists in other genres.

FURTHER READING

Brandon, James R., ed. *Nō and Kyōgen in the Contemporary World*. Honolulu: Univ. of Hawaii Press, 1997.

Masuda, Shōzō. *Nō to Kindai Bungaku* [Nō and modern literature]. Tokyo: Heibonsha, 1990.

Shigeyama Sennojō. *Kyōgen Yakusha: Hinekure Handaiki* [A Kyōgen actor: A perverse half-life]. Tokyo: Iwanami Shinsho, 1987.

Tada, Tomio. *Nō no Naka no Nō Butai* [The Nō stage inside the brain]. Tokyo: Shinchosha, 2001.

Umehara, Takeshi. *Ōsama to Kyōryū* [King and the dinosaur]. Tokyo: Shinchosha, 2003.

Yokomichi Mario and Seki Kobayashi. *Nō-Kyōgen*. Tokyo: Iwanami Seminar Bks., 1996.

Jonah Salz

NODA HIDEKI (1955–)

Noda Hideki is a Japanese playwright, director, and actor. His career can be divided into two periods, the first leading his troupe, the Dream Wanderers (Yume no Yūminsha), founded in 1976, and the second running his production company, NODA MAP, after his return from ENGLAND in 1993. With the Dream Wanderers, Noda established a distinctive style, influenced by KARA JŪRŌ, that pushed the physicality of 1960s ANGURA theater and the lightly humorous wordplay of the 1970s to higher levels. Noda's style of performance was first viewed with suspicion, but it eventually became the benchmark for theater in the 1980s. Extremely demanding of the actor, Noda's style physicalizes every aspect of the text and has been called "the body that won't stand still."

Noda's first successes were in small theaters (*shogekijo⁻*). One of his early successes, *The Prisoner of Zenda Castle* (*Zenda Jō no Toride*, 1981) was first performed in a little theater on the University of Tokyo campus. After that, he began to produce plays in midsized halls. Other "little theater" companies again followed suit. Noda moved away from the limited production facilities of small theaters to venues that allowed more spectacle. In 1986, he used an indoor arena to produce a trilogy called *Seven Variations on Stonehenge* (*Sutōn Henji Nanahenge*, 1986). Over 26,000 people saw the production in one day. Spectacle still marks his work even though most productions are done in midsized halls.

Noda disbanded the Dream Wanderers in 1992, then spent a year training in England. Instead of a permanent troupe of actors, his production company, NODA MAP, gathers a new group for every play. That has allowed him to work with the best available talent and to use non-Japanese actors and do joint productions abroad. In 2003 he was planning a new production in England based on a Japanese short story.

Another of his early productions was *Young Boy Hunting: Groping in the Pitch Dark* (*Shōnen-gari: Sue wa Ayame mo Shirenu Yami*, 1979). In 1989 he did a production called *The Third Richard* that was an adaptation combining several of William Shakespeare's plays.

Social themes were given more importance after his return from England. His first production was titled *Kiru* (1994) and dealt with cultural imperialism. The sweeping spectacle of the production matched its epic narrative.

The Red Demon Akaoni (*Akaoni*, 1996) deals with xenophobia and the difficulties of intercultural communication. The central character, called Akaoni (red demon) by the locals, is washed ashore in a small village. Akaoni and the villagers cannot communicate, and they view him as a monster. *The Red Demon Akaoni* has been produced in JAPAN, England, and THAILAND with different casts using their native languages.

TABOO (1996) is a critique of Japan's emperor system and theater. A prince is raised thinking he is an idiot. He becomes a NŌ performer, but when he is called to be emperor, the country is plunged into war.

Noda continues to build on a loyal fan base through his use of spectacle, language, and a directing style suited to the shorter attention spans of contemporary audiences.

SELECT PLAYS: *Young Boy Hunting: Groping in the Pitch Dark* (*Shōnen-gari: Sue wa Ayame mo Shirenu Yami*, 1979); *The Prisoner of Zenda Castle* (*Zenda Jō no Toride*, 1981); *Memories of My Little Finger* (*Koyubi no Omoide*, 1983); *Napoleon Preserve* (*Binzume no Naporeon*, 1984); *Revolving Mermaid: What's That You Call Yourself?* (*Kaiten Ningyō: Anata no Namae Nante-no?*, 1984); *Composed of Seven Variations on Stonehenge* (*Sutōn Henji Nanahenge*, 1986); *White Night Valkyrie* (*Bakuya no Warukyūre*); *Comet Siegfried* (*Suisei Jiifuriito*); *Valhalla up in Smoke* (*Waruhara Jōhatsu*)); *Beneath a Cloud of Plastic Cherry Blossoms* (*Kansaku: Sakura no Mori no Mankai no Shita*, 1989); *Kiru* (1994); *The Red Demon Akaoni* (*Akaoni*, 1996); *TABOO* (1996); *Pandora's Bell* (*Pandora no Kane*, 1999); *Oil* (*Oiru*, 2003)

FURTHER READING

Japan Playwrights Association, ed. *Half a Century of Japanese Theater: IV, 1980s, Part 2*. Tokyo: Kinokuniya, 2002.

Kazama Ken. *Shōgekijō no Fūkei* [The little theater landscape]. Tokyo: Chūō Kōronsha, 1992.

Ortolani, Benito. *The Japanese Theatre: From Shamanistic Ritual to Contemporary Pluralism*. Princeton, N.J.: Princeton Univ. Press, 1995.

Powell, Brian. *Japan's Modern Theatre: A Century of Change and Continuity*. London: Japan Library, 2002.

Senda Akihiko. *The Voyage of Contemporary Japanese Theatre*. Tr. by J. Thomas Rimer. Honolulu: Univ. of Hawaii Press, 1997.

John D. Swain

NOER, ARIFIN C. (1941–1995)

Indonesian playwright, director, and actor Arifin C. Noer created plays that combined elements of Western ABSURDISM's text-driven drama and INDONESIA's improvised folk drama. Noer forged a new direction for Indonesian playwriting, drawing significantly from performative structures of his birthplace, Cirebon, West Java. He reshaped traditional idioms to fit into a contemporary audience—an approach that informed all aspects of his plays, from script development to staging. Noer's highly poetic and evocative plays are composed as performances rather than just dramatic literature. He did not merely transpose traditional music and theater; he extracted something closer to its essence.

Noer began his theatrical career as an actor in a study group with W. S. RENDRA in the early 1960s in central Java while studying for his B.A. in state administration. In 1967, after completing his degree, Noer moved to Jakarta, where he founded Teater Ketjil (literally, Little Theatre). He conceived of the group as a laboratory where he and fellow actors could experiment with the workshop model introduced by Rendra, emphasizing process over product. However, unlike Rendra who concentrated on enriching the whole person—intellectually, ethically, and physically—Noer's focus was on cultivating ACTING skills. His breakthrough play was *The Clouds* (*Mega-Mega*, 1969), a surrealistic, dreamlike piece that pushed actors toward alternative acting techniques to the institutionally supported Western ones based on psychological REALISM. The key for Noer and his actors was not in a single acting style but in using whatever was most appropriate to create what he called *teater tanpa batas* (theater without limits). From his eclectic and unconventional approach to acting came productions that were timely and meaningful for the audience on both moral and, covertly, political levels.

Noer was a prolific playwright and director from the 1970s until his death in 1995. He directed all of his original plays including his best-known work MOTHS (*Kapai-Kapai*, 1970) with Teater Ketjil. *The Bottomless Well* (*Sumur Tanpa Dasar*), originally produced in 1964, was revived in 1991 to tour the UNITED STATES as part of the Festival Of Indonesia. *Madun Orchestra* (*Orkes Madun*) (1974, 1976, 1979, 1989) and *Interrogation* (*Interogasi*) (1984, 1990) are other important works. He was also celebrated for his politically relevant stagings of Western plays in translation. These performances were artfully designed to expose social injustices perpetrated by President's Haji Mohammad Suharto's New Order government without being perceived by authorities as critical, which would have led to certain censure. Such adaptations included, among others, CALIGULA by ALBERT CAMUS in 1970, THE FLIES by JEAN-PAUL SARTRE in 1972, and *Macbeth* by EUGÈNE IONESCO in 1975.

Noer was also a leading figure in the Indonesian film industry, first as a scriptwriter and later as an award-winning director. He created both art films and, ironically, government-sponsored propaganda films extolling Suharto's rise to power. His wife Jajang C. Noer played major roles in many of his films as well as producing them.

PLAYS: *The Bottomless Well* (*Sumur Tanpa Dasar*, 1964); *The Clouds* (*Mega-Mega*, 1969); *Moths* (*Kapai-Kapai*, 1970); *Tengul* (1973); *Madekur and Tarkeni or The Madun Orchestra Part I* (*Madekur dan Tarkeni atawa Orkes Madun Bagian Satu*, 1974); *Hilarious* (*Kocak Kecik*, 1975); *Madun Orchestra II: The Hermit Crab* (*Umang-Umang atawa Orkes Madun II*, 1976); *Madun Orchestra IIb: Sandek, the Youth Worker* (*Orkes Madun IIb atawa Sandek Pemuda Pekerja*, 1979); *Interrogation I: In the Shadow of God* (*Interogasi I: Dalam Bayangan Tuhan*, 1984); *Ozone* (*Ozone atawa Orkes Madun IV*, 1989); *Afterbirth* (*Ari-Ari atawa Interogasi II*, 1990)

FURTHER READING

Gillitt, Cobina. "Challenging Conventions and Crossing Boundaries: A New Tradition of Indonesian Theatre from 1968–1978." Ph.D. diss., N.Y. Univ., 2001.

Jit, Krishan. "Indonesia, Modern Spoken Drama." In *Cambridge Guide to Asian Theatre*, ed. by James Brandon. Cambridge: Cambridge Univ. Press, 1992.

Cobina Gillitt

NO EXIT

Generally considered JEAN-PAUL SARTRE's dramatic masterpiece, *No Exit* (*Huis Clos*) was written during the Nazi occupation of FRANCE and has the distinction of being the first play to be produced in liberated Paris in September 1944. It premiered at the Vieux Colombier and ran for more than a year to much acclaim. Sartre and the principal actors had been active in the resistance movement, which, according to Philip Thody in *Jean Paul Sartre—A Literary and Political Study* (1960), "provided additional political reason for the great success which the play enjoyed." While it may not be Sartre's most ambitious stage piece, it is without question his most structurally elegant; its frequent revivals around the world attest to its enduring merit.

Garcin, a South American pacifist journalist, enters his new living quarters, which are decorated in an antiquated Second Empire style. As it turns out, he has been led into his personal room in hell by a valet who finds the usual questions about devils and hot pokers eye-rollingly droll. Garcin is soon introduced to his chamber mates for eternity—Inez, a lesbian with a chip on her shoulder, and Estelle, a pampered bourgeois wife accustomed to male admirers. While Inez knows quite well the reason for her being damned to hell (she drove her lover to murder and suicide), Estelle cannot imagine how she has wound up in such a place—that is, until she reveals that she threw her baby, fathered not by her husband but by her less wealthy lover, out the window. A vicious love triangle soon develops, with Inez angling to gain power over Estelle, who craves only the attention of the sole man in the room.

Sensing the possibility that each roommate has been appointed the unwitting torturer of the others, Garcin requests that they refrain from speaking. The trouble is that he cannot help reviewing his own past with his companions, hoping against hope that fresh perspectives on his actions will render his cruel treatment of his wife and his desertion during wartime as less cowardly acts than they stubbornly appear. Not a chance: death renders all motives inconsequential. "You are—your life, and nothing else" is Inez's pointed formulation, and Garcin will be forced to bear the weight of his shameful mortal choices without extenuation. It is this realization that provokes from him the famous line, "Hell is—other people!" Sartre intends this not so much as a universal condemnation as the inevitable sentiment of a life lived in bad faith.

The DRAMATURGY of *No Exit* has a simple—and savagely ironic—economy. Unlike the bulk of Sartre's literary work, the play resists straining after philosophical import. Its ideas about identity and the complex philosophical distinction between self-honesty and self-dramatization are not imposed but instead fully embodied in a compelling theatrical form. The analysis, in other words, does not arrive in clunky explanatory passages but unfolds dramatically. Though the play fits ERIC BENTLEY's description of Sartre's work as "philosophical MELODRAMA" (Bentley, 1946) it does so not through sensational theatrics but through a natural suspense born out of a chillingly novel situation.

FURTHER READING

Bentley, Eric. *The Playwright as Thinker: A Study of Drama in Modern Times.* New York: Meridian Bks., 1946.

Howells, Christina. *Sartre: The Necessity of Freedom.* Cambridge: Cambridge Univ. Press, 1988.

Kern, Edith, ed. *Sartre: A Collection of Critical Essays.* Englewood Cliffs, N.J.: Prentice-Hall, 1965.

McCall, Dorothy. *The Theatre of Jean-Paul Sartre.* New York: Columbia Univ. Press, 1969.

Murdoch, Iris. *Sartre: Romantic Rationalist.* London: Vintage, 1999.

Sartre, Jean-Paul. *Sartre on Theater.* Tr. by Frank Jellinek. New York: Pantheon Bks., 1976.

Thody, Philip. *Jean-Paul Sartre: A Literary and Political Study.* London: Hamish Hamilton, 1960.

Wood, Philip R. *Understanding Jean-Paul Sartre.* Columbia: Univ. of South Carolina Press, 1990.

Charles McNulty

NORÉN, LARS (1944–)

A theater performance should be like a wound that heals.
—Lars Norén, 1983

One of SWEDEN's leading poets since his debut in 1963, also dramatist, director, and artistic leader of the National Touring Company (Riksteatern) since 1998, Lars Norén has devoted himself almost exclusively to drama since 1980. Astoundingly prolific, he has published some thirty plays and had a number of unpublished ones performed on stage, radio, and television. Although widely translated and staged in northern Europe, Norén has had little response in the Anglo-Saxon world. So far only the short *Munich–Athens* (*München-Athen*, 1983) has been published in English.

After a negative reception of the renaissance drama *The Prince's Bootlicker* (*Fursteslickaren*, 1973), Norén achieved his first success with *The Courage to Kill* (*Modet att döda*, 1980), depicting a traumatic Oedipal parent-child relationship, a recurring theme in Norén's dramatic work. Norén's breakthrough came in 1982 with THE NIGHT IS MOTHER TO THE DAY (*Natten är dagens mor*), where the author's black humor helped to lighten the play's claustrophobic impact. Together with *Chaos Is God's Neighbor* (*Kaos är granne med Gud*, 1983) and *The Stillness* (*Stillheten*, 1986), it forms a family trilogy. Like EUGENE O'NEILL's LONG DAY'S JOURNEY INTO NIGHT, a drama that has had a tremendous impact on Norén, it is highly autobiographical. In the six-hour *The Communion* (*Nattvarden*, 1985), two brothers demonstrate their contrasting attitudes toward their recently dead mother, present on the stage in the form of an urn, while in *Autumn and Winter* (*Höst och vinter*, 1992), which opened in Copenhagen, the family interaction concerns two daughters and their parents. *Hebriana* (*Hebriana*, 1987), first presented in The Hague, and *One-Day Creatures* (*Endagsvarelser*, 1989), which premiered in Kassel, both deal with representatives of a middle-aged "lost generation," caught between their own hopeful past, the spring of 1968, and the darkening future. *And Grant Us the Shadows* (*Och ge oss skuggorna*, 1991) which opened in Oslo, is a play about Eugene O'Neill, his third wife, and his two sons. Set in the living room of the O'Neills on a grim October day in 1949 (O'Neill's sixty-first birthday) from morning to dusk, the play intentionally mirrors *Long Day's Journey Into Night*, demonstrating how the family interaction described in that play (set in 1912) is ironically and fatefully repeated thirty-seven years later. As a semidocumentary "sequel play" to O'Neill's autobiographical masterpiece, *And Grant Us the Shadows* is probably unique in world drama.

While Norén's earlier plays are family oriented, his later ones demonstrate a growing concern for society at large. In *The Leaves in Vallombrosa* (*Löven i Vallombrosa*, 1995), *Bonn* (1991), and *Time Is Our Home* (*Tiden är vårt hem*, 1991), the spiritual discomfort of those living in a welfare state is voiced in Chekhovian polyphony. In the "Dantean" *A Kind of Hades* (*En sorts Hades*, 1994), set in a mental hospital representing Sweden, and in *Personal Circle 3:1* (*Personkrets 3:1*, 1998), a six-hour play and the first part of the trilogy *Death of the Classes* (*Morire di classe*), Norén has attracted large audiences with his shocking descriptions of the outcasts of Swedish society.

Norén has also written a number of radio plays, one of which, *Revenge Aria* (*Hämndaria*), earned him the Prix Italia in 1987. In recent years he has directed some of his own plays as well as plays by others.

In Norén's dramatic universe, the unity of time and place—the closed room—has a fundamental thematic value, stressing the characters' ambivalent feelings about being simultaneously close to each other and yet imprisoned with one another. Confrontation is inevitable; separation—a key concept with Norén—necessary. As with O'Neill, the audience is asked to witness the often strenuous interaction between the characters for a considerable period of time. Writing in a therapeutic era, Norén depicts the hidden workings behind what is pretended. Role-playing, projections, and double-bind mechanisms abound in his psychoanalytically inspired dramatic oeuvre, which demonstrates an acute ear for natural dialogue and subtextual innuendo.

SELECT PLAYS: *The Courage to Kill* (*Modet att döda*, 1980); *Orestes* (1980); *A Terrible Happiness* (*En fruktansvärd lycka*, 1981); *The Night Is Mother to the Day* (*Natten är dagens mor*, 1982); *Chaos Is God's Neighbor* (*Kaos är granne med Gud*, 1983); *Munich-Athens* (*München-Athen*, 1983); *The Communion* (*Nattvarden*, 1985); *The Stillness* (*Stillheten*, 1986); *Revenge Aria* (*Hämndaria*, 1987); *One-Day Creatures* (*Endagsvarelser*, 1989); *Bobby Fischer Lives in Pasadena* (*Bobby Fischer bor i Pasadena*, 1990); *And Grant Us the Shadows* (*Och ge oss skuggorna*, 1991); *Autumn and Winter* (*Höst och vinter*, 1992); *A Kind of Hades* (*En sorts Hades*, 1994); *The Leaves in Vallombrosa* (*Löven i Vallombrosa*, 1995); *Personal Circle 3:1* (*Personkrets 3:1*, 1998); *Terminal* (nine short plays, 2004)

FURTHER READING

Neuhauser, Lotta. "The Intoxication of Insight: Notes on Lars Norén." *Theater* 22 (1990–1991): 89–92.

Osten, Suzanne. "Theatre with Lars Norén: A Working Process for a Director." In *Niet alleen Strindberg: Zweden op de planken* [Not only Strindberg: Sweden on stage], ed. by Egil Törnqvist and Arthur Sonnen. Amsterdam: Holland Festival, 1985. 42–46.

Van Reis, Mikael. *Det slutna rummet: Sex kapitel om Lars Noréns författarskap 1963–1983* [The Closed Room: Six Chapters on Lars Norén's Authorship 1963–1983]. Stockholm/Stehag: Symposion, 1997 [English summary, 503–507].

Egil Törnqvist

NORMAL

The few plays that attract attention at the Edinburgh Fringe Festival tend to contain sensationalist subject matter: ANTHONY NEILSON enhanced the sensational subject matter of his 1991 Fringe play *Normal: The Düsseldorf Ripper* (abbreviated to *Normal* when published) with sensationalism of writing, theatricality, and visceral provocation. *Normal* dramatizes the evil of the notorious Weimar Republic serial killer Peter Kurten. An inexperienced lawyer, Justus Wehner, represents the killer, desperately hoping that he can convince the authorities of his client's insanity. If Kurten is shown to be not in control of his actions, then Wehner can believe that his brutality is not motivated by the evil that Wehner cannot come to terms with. Many theatrical effects are used, including flashback, spectacular lighting, singing, oversized props, and mannequins.

The Fringe production took place at the Pleasance Theatre (subsequently, the play moved to the Finborough Theatre, London), a compact dramatic space. The tininess of the auditorium complemented the performance's claustrophobic milieu, fostering a sense of enclosure that was reminiscent of Fritz Lang's shadowy 1931 film about Kurten. M. Neilson himself directed the three actors. Numerous controversies are raised during the play's thirty-one scenes, including audience voyeurism, prostitution, and the connection between slaughtering animals and slaughtering humans. Three particular issues resonate: the role of society in engendering psychopathic tendencies, the shocking similarities between the outlaw killer and the regular man, and the possible connections between Kurten's killings and Nazism.

Although Neilson makes no claim to explain Kurten's depravity, it is clear that childhood disadvantages contribute to his character. Kurten shocks us with explicit descriptions of sexual climaxes achieved through murderous actions against animals, adults, and children. But his childhood circumstances appear equally shocking: he remembers beatings from an alcoholic father and unavoidable sexual engagements with his mother and sisters. Society is, in part, to blame because the family's abnormality is predicated upon their impoverished confinement in a packed, privacy-free room.

The actors playing Kurten and Wehner are dressed similarly. Wehner, gradually, realizes that he shares some of Kurten's sordid excitements, disgusting himself by becoming excited during Kurten's reminiscences. After seducing Kurten's wife, Frau Kurten—which he is encouraged to do by Kurten, who seeks to demonstrate the ease of temptation—he fantasizes about killing her. This fantasy "killing" is acted out in a six-minute sequence. Wehner's realization that he harbors such beastly desires compromises his claim that Kurten is "not normal."

A connection is drawn between Kurten's murders and those of the Nazis. Kurten's actions, compared to Nazi murders, appear even more "normal." Kurten asserts, "There is no such thing as society." This phrase is often used as a derogatory, shorthand account of the ideology of Margaret Thatcher's right-wing Conservative government of the 1980s. Capitalism can be caricatured as a Darwinian system in which each person fights for himself or herself, disregarding everyone else. Kurten pursues selfish, sick pleasures, careless of all others—that Neilson can draw a connection between him and "normal" capitalists is indeed shocking for any audience.

[*See also* England, 1960–Present; Scotland]

FURTHER READING

Gilbert, Alexander. "Peter Kürten." http://www.crimelibrary.com/serial2/kurten.

Marmion, Patrick. "What I Do Is a Bit Odd" (interview with Anthony Neilson). *The Guardian* (May 13, 2002). http://www.guardian.co.uk/features/story/0,766010,00.html.

McMillan, Joyce. "No Man's Land of Class" (interview with Anthony Neilson). *The Scotsman* (July 31, 2002). http://thescotsman.scotsman.com/s2.cfm?id=822822002.

Reviews of *Normal: The Düsseldorf Ripper*. Theatre Record 11, no. 20 (1991): 1222.

Sierz, Aleks. *In-Yer-Face Theatre: British Drama Today*. London: Faber, 2001.

Wagner, Margaret Seaton. *The Monster of Düsseldorf: The Life and Trial of Peter Kürten*. London: Faber, 1932.

Kevin De Ornellas

NORMAN, MARSHA (1947–)

I feel that we are all working toward one goal, which is the documenting of what it has felt like to be alive in our time. And that we all write the parts of it that we see. You can't possibly do the whole thing so you just do your little part and trust that the assortment of you is great enough to pretty much cover it.
—Marsha Norman, 2000

Born on September 21, 1947, in Louisville, Kentucky, playwright Marsha Norman studied PHILOSOPHY at Agnes Scott College in Decatur, Georgia, and then earned a master's degree at the University of Louisville. Norman's first play, *Getting Out* (1978), was an immediate success. It dramatizes the initial twenty-four hours following a woman's release from prison, as she looks back on her life and ponders a new beginning. Staged by the Actors Theatre of Louisville in 1977, *Getting Out* was produced the following year at the Mark Taper Forum in Los Angeles and OFF-BROADWAY at the Lucille Lortel Theatre and was awarded the John Gassner Medallion, *Newsday*'s Oppenheimer Award, and an American Theater Critics Association Citation. Upon receiving an artist-in-residence playwriting grant from the National Endowment for the Arts, Norman wrote several more plays for the Actors Theatre.

In 1981 Norman moved to New York, where she wrote her most critically acclaimed play, 'NIGHT MOTHER (1982). An exploration of suicide, the play depicts a young woman's last evening spent with her mother, to whom she confesses her intention to take her own life; despite her mother's desperate efforts to dissuade her, the daughter prepares them both for her death. 'Night Mother premiered in December 1982 at the American Repertory Theatre in Cambridge, Massachusetts, and headed to Broadway's John Golden Theatre that March. It won the 1983 Pulitzer Prize for Drama, the Susan Smith Blackburn Prize, and the Hull-Warriner and Drama Desk Awards. The film versions appeared in 1986.

Norman returned to Broadway in 1991 with the musical *The Secret Garden*, for which she wrote both book and lyrics and which won a Tony Award and Drama Desk Award in 1992. *The Red Shoes*, whose book and lyrics she also wrote, followed in 1993. In addition to a substantial body of plays, Norman also wrote a novel, *The Fortune Teller*, as well as scripts for film and television, notably *Face of a Stranger*. She has been a professor of drama at the Julliard School in New York since 1994 and currently serves on the council of the Dramatists Guild.

The influence of the women's liberation movement is evident in Norman's work, which deals chiefly with problems stemming from the political and social oppression of her realistic female characters. Norman's writing is intentionally political: she once stated, "I want to write for a very specific purpose which happens to coincide with what really interests me. It isn't just a political act. It's a political act through and through" (Brown, 1996). Norman's plays are notable for bringing women's issues, and the stories of everyday women in particular, to the stage, something she views as vital: "Clearly women in our culture feel invisible. I feel invisible. I felt invisible as a girl. . . . I write about people you would never see, like me. This has got to change! We have got to get our stories told!" Though women are the primary focus of her writing, Norman's plays have been acknowledged for their ability to reach men and women alike. Speaking of the universality of Norman's work, Robert Brustein praised Norman as "one who speaks to the concerns and experiences of all humankind" (Brustein, 1983).

[See also Feminist Drama in the United States; Political Theater in the United States; United States, 1940–Present]

PLAYS: *Getting Out* (1978); *Third and Oak: The Laundromat* (1978); *Third and Oak: The Pool Hall* (1978); *Circus Valentine* (1979); *Merry Christmas* (1979); *'Night Mother* (1982); *The Holdup* (1983); *Traveler in the Dark* (1984); *Winter Shakers* (1987); *Sarah and Abraham* (1988); *The Secret Garden* (1991); *Loving Daniel Boone* (1993); *The Red Shoes* (1993); *Trudy Blue* (1995)

FURTHER READING

Bigsby, C. W. E. "Marsha Norman." In *Contemporary American Playwrights*. New York: Cambridge Univ. Press, 1999.

Brown, Linda Ginter, ed. *Marsha Norman: A Casebook*. New York: Garland, 1996.

Brustein, Robert. "Don't Read This Review" [review of *'Night Mother*]. *The New Republic* 188 (May 2, 1983): 25–27.

DiGaetani, John L. "Marsha Norman." In *A Search for a Postmodern Theater: Interviews with Contemporary Playwrights*. Westport, Conn.: Greenwood Press, 1991.

Harriott, Esther. "Marsha Norman: Getting Out." In *American Voices: Five Contemporary Playwrights in Essays and Interviews*. Jefferson, N.C.: McFarland & Co., 1988.

Kane, Leslie. "The Way Out, the Way In: Paths to Self in the Plays of Marsha Norman." In *Feminine Focus: The New Women Playwrights*, ed. by Enoch Brater. New York: Oxford Univ. Press, 1989.

Kintz, Linda. *The Subject's Tragedy: Political Poetics, Feminist Theory, and Drama*. Ann Arbor: Univ. of Michigan Press, 1992.

Emma Dassori

NORWAY

19TH-CENTURY DRAMA

Modern Norwegian drama grew out of a national romantic movement that received most of its energy from opposition against continuing Danish hegemony. In 1814 Norway had withdrawn from the union with DENMARK, which had then lasted for more than 400 years. Danish influence in terms of written language and cultural traditions remained strong in mid-19th-century Norway. The theaters had for sometime been dominated by Danish management and Danish actors. Out of the national endeavor in the 1850s came two young theater instructors and dramatic authors, HENRIK IBSEN (1828–1906) and BJØRNSTJERNE BJØRNSON (1832–1910), and at the same time a number of talented Norwegian actors and actresses entered the stage in Bergen and Kristiania (now Oslo). Around 1860 the main source for playwriting was the Old Norse sagas, in particular about the kings of medieval Norway. The heroes of the past were not presented as bloodthirsty vikings but as statesmen and psychologically interesting individuals. Historical plays by William Shakespeare and Friedrich Schiller were important sources of inspiration, as well as the Dane Adam Oehlenschläger's dramatizations of saga material. Representative works in this tradition are Bjørnson's *Sigurd Slembe*, a trilogy (1862), and Ibsen's THE PRETENDERS (1863).

A unique outburst of creativity resulted in two major dramatic poems by Ibsen: BRAND (1866), a forceful criticism of a morally relaxed population, and PEER GYNT (1867), a fabulous romantic version of the medieval morality genre. Both poems reveal Kierkegaardian ideas. The individual is responsible for whatever choice he makes, and the criterion of choice is not common sense or reason but the intensity of feeling; the truth is subjective.

Historical drama faded away due partly to the dwindling of the Danish influence and to a boom period of newspaper distribution. Readers and audiences were drawn to presentations of contemporary issues, and this cleared the ground for the modern domestic drama in prose. Bjørnson led the way, with *The Newly Married Couple* (1865), showing the young wife torn between parents and husband, and in 1875, with *The Editor*, about the power of the press, and A BANKRUPTCY, demonstrating the need for sound ethics in business affairs.

After his "world historical play," EMPEROR AND GALILEAN, spread over ten acts (1873), Ibsen turned to contemporary family life. From 1877 to 1899 he at regular intervals published twelve plays, referred to as the prose cycle, dealing with the moral and psychological problems of modern bourgeois society and exploring the spiritual development of individual characters in a morally problematic family situation. In this series of plays one may perceive a certain similarity with conventions in the well-made play and *pièce à thèse* in the French tradition of Eugène Scribe.

What distinguishes Ibsen's prose plays is the stringency of composition, the inventiveness of plot, the carefully calculated effect of the dialogue, and the metaphorical emphasis suggested by the scenographic expression. In most of them there is a developing sense of unease or longing to become free, often triggered by the appearance of a character from the past or some mysterious stranger, exposing a feeling of guilt or encouraging the idea of a new life, devoid of social conventions. In several of these instances the critical moment of self-realization is a family disaster, a TRAGEDY that could not be avoided. In other cases the central characters are able to get through the crisis and reach an understanding.

Bjørnson also continued to write a number of modern prose plays, and most of them were performed with considerable success. The tragedy BEYOND HUMAN POWER (1883) and the COMEDY Geography and Love (1885) are the ones that have survived longest. Bjørnson was given the Nobel Prize for Literature in 1903. Ibsen never got it; he was not considered sufficiently positive and edifying. Most of his modern prose plays were controversial in Norway, although he was highly respected because of his growing international fame.

The modern prose plays by Ibsen, Bjørnson, and others have been categorized by critics and editors as REALISM, a literature intended to depict the real lives and problems of people. This view, however, is highly debatable. It conceals the fact that even these plays are artful presentations of romantic themes such as heroic individualism, the urge to be free, the resistance to compromise, and the emphasis on subjective truth. The influence of Søren Kierkegaard as well as that of another Dane, the critic Georg Brandes, was considerable.

A number of highly qualified novelists also tried their luck at writing plays but without the same kind of success as Ibsen and Bjørnson. Amalie Skram (1846–1905), whose fiction concentrates on the problems of married women, published Agnete in 1893, a play about a divorced young woman in a bohemian milieu. The man she is attracted to cannot forgive her for a minor offense that her poverty has forced her to commit, and she leaves.

Arne Garborg (1851–1924), critic, poet, and novelist, central in the New Norse language movement, wrote a couple of plays; the most important one is The Teacher (1896). The main character is a farmer and evangelist who wants to practice Christianity the way Jesus did; but he encounters opposition both in his congregation and in his family, mainly because he is blind to the power he exerts over young women who want to be his disciples. In his essays, Garborg introduced contemporary European intellectual movements, most important the vitalist PHILOSOPHY of FRIEDRICH NIETZSCHE, also promoted by the Danish critic Georg Brandes, who deeply influenced Scandinavian intellectuals in the 1880s and 1890s. Following a period of firm belief in science, the age toward the end of the century became more attracted to irrationalist attitudes and cultural pessimism.

The best of KNUT HAMSUN's (1859–1952) six plays reveal the same basically romantic atmosphere as in his early novels, focusing on the dreaming mind of an infatuated outsider, longing for an involvement, and with problematic relations to society. Most important is the dramatic trilogy about the development of Ivar Kareno (1895–1898), who is caught between the will to control his destiny and the insurmountable instincts of life itself.

Hamsun shared much of Nietzsche's vitalism, as did GUNNAR HEIBERG (1857–1929) in some of his early plays. He is considered the most important playwright of his generation. Like Ibsen and Bjørnson, he had some experience as a theater director. His most original plays are The Balcony (1894) and Love's Tragedy (1904). In these plays erotic love is depicted as a force of nature, which human consciousness is unable or unwilling to withstand. In The Balcony the passionate Julie demands adoration and is a ruthless consumer of men. Heiberg started as a disciple of Ibsen, and in one of his plays, King Midas (1890), he turned against Bjørnson's moralist attitude. This made Heiberg the target of antibohemian critics.

20TH-CENTURY DRAMA

Also influenced by the vitalist ROMANTICISM of the 1890s was Hans E. Kinck (1865–1926). His most remarkable dramatic work is the poem The Drover (1908), in the tradition of Ibsen's Peer Gynt, but devoid of allegory.

The most successful comedy of these years, The Fortunate Election (1913), was written by Nils Kjær (1870–1924) in the same year that Norwegian women acquired the right to vote and to be elected to the National Assembly. Kjær's talent for ridiculing political and social phenomena was considerable, and he had limited sympathy for popular traditions and democratic institutions. Seemingly more in line with Ibsen's prose plays were some of the plays by Helge Krog (1889–1962). His first play, The Great We (1919), is a socialist comedy attacking the press for its loyalty to capital owners. In several later plays Krog presented an idealized picture of the modern independent woman in her difficult relations to patriarchal society. Like Heiberg, Krog belonged to the movement of cultural radicalism, which had its intellectual roots in the ideas of Georg Brandes. Highly praised in his time for wit and optimism, Krog's plays are rarely performed today.

Less respectful of Ibsen's poetic heritage and more directly engaged in the ideological use of the theater was NORDAHL GRIEG (1902–1943). He had become a communist during a stay in Moscow, where he studied Soviet film and theater. In OUR POWER AND OUR GLORY (1935)—a political branding of cynical ship owners in times of war—his juxtaposition of scenes influenced by the filmic technique of crosscutting has a striking effect. The Defeat (1937) is a sympathetic presentation of the last days of the Parisian uprising in 1871.

A play that might have been called absurd had it been written in the 1950s is *While We Are Waiting* (1938) by Johan Borgen (1902–1979). The stage is the waiting room of a railway station, where some actors waiting for a train rehearse a play and make other passengers join them. Elements in the play under rehearsal mix with events at the station, creating a Pirandellian effect.

Under the Nazi regime the Germans occupied Norway from 1940 to 1945, making free cultural exchange impossible. Accordingly, conditions for the writing and production of new drama were not favorable. Before the war there had been a strong movement of amateur theater in the country. After the war theatrical activities tended to seek other outlets besides the traditional institutions. Experimental stages, free groups of actors, and regional theaters were established, and the new electronic media became channels for performances. Plays were written and produced locally to commemorate characters and events of local history, and radio and television were effective means of disseminating drama to a mass audience. This did not lead to an immediate increase in dramatic creativity, however.

Postwar attempts to renew the art of drama in various directions include Odd Eidem's (1913–1988) *God's Own Clowns* (1960), a historical play dismantling the dramatic illusion; Johan Borgen's *Day of Liberation* (1963), using music, dance, and pantomime; and Finn Carling's (1925–) *The Bars* (1966), where the characters are caged animals and the human criterion is the capacity for love.

The impulse from BERTOLT BRECHT, who had sought refuge in the UNITED STATES from the Nazi regime in GERMANY, was noticeable in the work of some younger playwrights of the 1960s, most explicitly in the essays and plays of JENS INGVALD BJØRNEBOE (1920–1976). Often using song and pantomime, Bjørneboe sought dramatic effects in extreme confrontations, exploring the ideological roots of evil. In THE BIRD LOVERS (1966), Italian partisans from the war have the chance to take revenge on former Nazi officers, now German tourists in postwar ITALY.

In the 1970s the political use of drama continued, with new social targets. The feminist movement influenced many plays; best known is *Two Acts for Five Women* (1974) by Bjørg Vik (1935–). A reunion of old classmates brings out conflicting views on gender relations, career possibilities, and family problems. Performed in a number of countries, Vik's play may be the most succesful from the 1970s. Roles for women have been relatively scarce in Norwegian drama, a fact that made this play and others focusing on gender and power relations extremely welcome.

Like most 20th-century authors in Norway, Vik has been mainly a writer of fiction. Concentrating on drama, film, and television theater was Sverre Udnæs (1939–1982), who worked as a director both on television and for the stage and wrote several plays, mostly for television. The typical setting for his plays is the living room of the middle-class family, where the characters are unable to communicate with each other. In *Visit Hours* (1976) a young girl is expected to arrive home after a stay at a mental hospital; her family is apprehensive and uncomfortable, and the dramatic tension builds out of unpredictable events.

DOCUMENTARY DRAMA has been less productive in Norway than in many other countries. CECILIE LØVEID's (1951–) best-known play, SEAGULL EATERS, written for radio in 1983, comes close to a documentary radio montage. A number of authentic texts and sound recordings suggest the life of a poor family in Bergen during the war. In Løveid's plays the plot tends to disintegrate, leaving room for poetic elements such as nursery rhymes or allegorical references to animals.

The most successful among the younger generation of playwrights in terms of performances in Norway and abroad is JON FOSSE (1959–). He wrote in other genres before he turned to drama in the 1990s. With their minimalist plot and abrupt, repetitious and dysfunctional dialogue, his plays present partly trivial and partly absurd scenes. The characters seem unable to act or speak coherently. The action is unconventional, though not unrecognizable, suggesting SAMUEL BECKETT's influence. A hundred years after Ibsen's dramatic exposure of malaise in the bourgeois family institution, an important trend in Norwegian drama seems to be the theme of dysfunctional families.

FURTHER READING

Dalgard, Olav. "Norsk etterkrigsdrama" [Norwegian postwar drama]. *Norsk teaterårbok* [Norwegian theater yearbook]. 1975. 25–33.

Garton, Janet, and Henning Sehmsdorf. "Contemporary Norwegian Theatre: An Introduction." In *New Norwegian Plays*, ed. by Janet Garton and Henning Sehmsdorf. Norwich: Norvik Press, 1989. 9–34.

Longum, Leif. "In the Shadow of Ibsen: His Influence on Norwegian Drama and on Literary Attitudes." In *Review of National Literature*. Vol. 12, *Norway*. New York: Griffon House Pubs., 1983. 78–100.

Marker, Frederick J., and Lise-Lone Marker. *The Scandinavian Theatre*. Oxford: Basil Blackwell, 1975.

Asbjørn Aarseth

NO TIME FOR COMEDY

No Time for Comedy by S. N. BEHRMAN opened on April 17, 1939, and ran for 185 performances. The play dramatizes the struggle of a dramatist, on the brink of World War II, to write TRAGEDY rather than his usual sophisticated COMEDY. Sensing he fails at profundity, Gaylord Easterbrook (Laurence Olivier) vows to go to Spain where war is in progress. This time, however, his wife Linda (Katharine Cornell) talks him out of it. The romantic solution, as it is here characterized, is discarded. Instead, she makes the argument that to be an American is to fight to preserve real human values that those at war have lost: "You should stay here, live here where and while it is still possible to live. The more inhuman the rest of the world, the more human we."

Upholding the thematic conflict is a love quartet. In act 1, Philo Smith comes to Linda and informs her that his wife is leading Linda's husband, Gaylord, astray. Amanda Smith does this, he says, by inspiring a man to greatness—in this case, making a tragic playwright out of a comic one. Linda tries to laugh this off, but in act 2 she confronts Amanda, who is sequestering Gay in her library to write on "immortality." The conflict seems to be between Mandy the idealist, who wants men to aspire to great profundity, and Linda the realist, who thinks that they should do what they are good at doing. Linda slowly discovers that Mandy is completely sincere in her desire; Amanda cries when accused of using it as a seductive strategy. Linda realizes that someone who cries real tears and thinks her feelings are noble will be quite difficult to overcome, especially by a realist like herself who sees such things as ACTING.

The third act brings Gay back home to discover Linda's reaction to his new play—which he fears is a failure. He knows she will give him an honest assessment. Gay insists, however, that he will marry Mandy and take her to Spain because he cannot endure Linda's (truthful) criticism any longer. Philo, however, has fallen in love with Linda, but she rejects his cynical vision of the world. Instead, she wins Gay back by proposing that he embark on a new play, one that so inspires him that he drops Amanda and Spain so that he can work on it: "Why don't you write a play about Mandy and me? Two opposite types of women in the life of a man, an artist, a writer—the builder-upper and the breaker-downer—the critical faculty versus the clinging vine—What Every Woman Knows in reverse." Again Behrman struggles for balance between the comic and the tragic, at extremes the cynical and the idealist. In this case, however, he dramatizes that very conflict within the dramatist. The argument is that the comic is the civilized and that America must stand for civilization as the rest of the world is engulfed in chaos.

[See also United States, 1929–1940]

FURTHER READING

Hoy, Cyrus. "Clearings in the Jungles of Life: The Comedies of S. N. Behrman." *New York Literary Forum* 1 (1978): 199–227.

Miller, Jordan Y., and Winifred L. Frazer. *American Drama Between the Wars: A Critical History.* Boston: Twayne, 1991.

David Sauer

NOTTAGE, LYNN (1965–)

Lynn Nottage, an African American playwright born in 1965 and raised in Brooklyn, New York, is a prolific dramatist. Her plays explore longing and desire in relation to the universal search for intimacy. Nottage investigates the fumbling, stumbling, and discoveries that accompany reaching for intimate connections.

Nottage wrote her first play at eight years old and her first musical while attending New York's School of Music and Art,

also known as the "Fame" high school. Nottage graduated from Brown University in 1986 and earned her master of fine arts degree from the Yale School of Drama in 1989. While at Brown, she took a class with playwright PAULA VOGEL, whose *How I Learned to Drive* (1997) launched the Meet the Playwright series. The experience of Vogel's class ignited Nottage's interest in the journey of playwriting.

Before becoming a full-time playwright, Nottage worked for the human rights organization Amnesty International in New York City. In 1993 she reached a crossroads and chose to pursue her art full-time. Nottage self-produced her shows in tiny theaters, often running the soundboard herself. She made critics take note with her ten-minute play *Poof!* (1993), which won the Heideman Award. The play is a meditation on the condition of violence in the home and was produced as a movie for television. Nottage followed that success with her dynamic and complex work *Crumbs from the Table of Joy* (nominated for a National Association for the Advancement of Colored People award) in 1995.

Nottage gave birth to a daughter and lost her mother to Lou Gering's disease in 1997. *Mud, River, Stone* (finalist, Susan Smith Blackburn Prize) was produced in 1998, after which Nottage slowed down her writing for three years in order to raise and care for her young daughter. Nottage wrote her way into OFF-BROADWAY by consistently constructing stories of interruptions, dares, dissonance, and resonance. In 2004, her two latest plays, *Fabulation* and *Intimate Apparel*, were produced. Nottage garnered nominations for both, *Intimate Apparel* winning such prestigious prizes as the Francesca Primus Prize and the Steinberg New Play Award, both granted by the American Theatre Critics Association (ATCA); the New York Drama Critics Circle and Outer Critics Circle for Best Play in 2004; and a Rockefeller grant.

Nottage's plays have been produced off-Broadway and regionally by the Acting Company, Center Stage, Intiman, Playwrights Horizons, Second Stage, Steppenwolf Theatre, Yale Repertory Theatre, and many others. Nottage was awarded playwriting fellowships from Manhattan Theatre Club, New Dramatists, and the New York Foundation for the Arts, where she is a member of their Artists Advisory Board. She received an NEA/TCG (National Endowment for the Arts/Theatre Communications Group, 1999–2000) grant for a residency at Freedom Theatre in Philadelphia. The TCG published an anthology of her plays, *Crumbs from the Table of Joy and Other Plays*, in summer 2004. She is a member of New Dramatists and a visiting lecturer in playwriting at Yale School of Drama.

[See also United States, 1940–Present]

PLAYS: *Poof!* (1993); *Por'Knockers* (1994); *Crumbs from the Table of Joy* (1995); *Mud, River, Stone* (1998); *A Walk Through Time* (2000);

Las Meninas (2001); Becoming American (2002); Snapshot (2002); Fabulation (2004); Intimate Apparel (2004)

FURTHER READING

Brown, Lenora Inez. "Dismantling the Box" (Lynn Nottage interview). American Theatre (July 2001).

"POOF!: A Talk with the Playwright: Lynn Nottage." Kentucky Educational Television. http://www.ket.org/content/ americanshorts/poof/nottage.htm.

Shanté T. Smalls

NOWRA, LOUIS (1950–)

Louis Nowra was born in Melbourne, Victoria, on December 9, 1950, and began his career as a playwright in 1973 with works including the one-act play Albert Names Edward (1977). It was Inner Voices (1977) that identified Nowra as a dramatist of promise and as part of a national theater revival, although he was not always critically embraced because of his preference for international and historical settings. Inner Voices is characteristic of much of his subsequent work. Nowra refers to it, in the preface to the first edition, as "a play which shows a mind under such intense pressure that knowledge and a vision of the world are warped into personal hell. It may be set in Russia; however, a more correct description would set it in the country of the mind."

Visions (1979) is located in Paraguay in the 1860s, and The Precious Woman (1981) is set in CHINA in the 1920s. They are both nonrealistic and epic in style, exploring, as his titles suggest, dream and interior worlds as well as the ethical and emotional conflicts of those in positions of power. Nowra's use of history, like BERTOLT BRECHT's, is never simply literal. "Just as history plays with us, I have played with history," he notes in the introduction to Visions.

With Inside the Island (1981) Nowra turned his attention to specifically Australian themes and settings but even here dislocates time through the use of arcane history and antiheroic perspectives. In the play, a matriarchal farming community in western New South Wales in 1912 is struck by an outbreak of "holy fire"—ergot poisoning from wheat. Nowra is skeptical of Australian mythologies of self-reliance and imperturbability. The Golden Age (1985) also confronts the conflicted, potentially catastrophic implications of the postcolonial legacy.

Nowra returned to the stage with Capricornia (1988), adapted from the novel by Xavier Herbert. The ambling picaresque form gave Nowra a looser style and marks a shift from a mannered, sometimes esoteric magic REALISM to a more vernacular voice. He moves to autobiographical themes for the first time with Summer of the Aliens (1992), set in his Melbourne childhood. Cosi (1992), also staged in the same year, reminisces on Nowra's university student days and sympathetically recounts a production of Cosi Fan Tutti performed by inmates of a mental institution.

Nowra's works offer strong roles for Indigenous actors; Crow (1994), set in wartime Darwin in 1942, describes an Aboriginal woman's fight to regain her title to a tin mine, and Radiance (1993) features three Aboriginal sisters reuniting for their mother's funeral. Like Cosi in 1992, Radiance enjoyed recognition and success as a film adaptation in 1996. Nowra's continuing interest in political dynasties and populist figures is evident in The Incorruptible (1995), based on recent Queensland politics, and The Temple (1993), a broad satire on a self-made entrepreneur.

Nowra has written prolifically for the stage, film, television, radio, and opera and more recently published memoir and nonfiction. His tenacity and originality place him at the forefront of Australian drama even if his unorthodoxy has sometimes muted his recognition.

[See also Australia]

PLAYS: Albert Names Edward (1977); Inner Voices (1977); Visions (1979); Inside the Island (1981); The Precious Woman (1981); The Golden Age (1985); Capricornia (1988); Cosi (1992); Summer of the Aliens (1992); Radiance (1993); The Temple (1993); Crow (1994); The Incorruptible (1995)

FURTHER READING

Gilbert, Helen. "Post-colonial Grotesques: Re-membering the Body in Louis Nowra's Visions and The Golden Age." SPAN 2, no. 36 (1993): 618–634.

Kelly, Veronica, ed. Louis Nowra. Australian Playwrights Monograph Series. Amsterdam: Rodopi, 1987.

——. The Theatre of Louis Nowra. Sydney: Currency, 1998.

Nowra, Louis. "The Shrinking Vision." Island 39 (Winter 1989): 11–20.

Murray Bramwell

OBSERVE THE SONS OF ULSTER MARCHING TOWARDS THE SOMME

The Irish dramatist FRANK MCGUINNESS's plays are characterized by his imaginative engagement with different cultures and ideas. This trait is particularly evident in his third play, *Observe the Sons of Ulster Marching Towards the Somme*, which premiered at the Abbey Theatre in Dublin in 1985.

The play opens with a monologue from a bed-bound old man called Pyper, who asks why, years before, he and his comrades had sacrificed themselves in World War I. The audience is then brought back to 1915, to witness the younger Pyper's initiation into a battalion of eight Ulstermen, who are preparing to fight in France as part of the British army. They do so for many reasons. As Protestants loyal to the United Kingdom, they believe that by fighting in the war they will discourage the English government from awarding IRELAND its independence. It quickly becomes clear, however, that each man is also motivated by other, more private needs and desires.

The action then moves forward several months, to a period in which the eight men are on leave after action, all of them severely traumatized by their experience of war. The stage is divided into four playing areas, each occupied by a pair of the soldiers. This allows McGuinness to explore and celebrate different forms of relationships between men—including a homosexual relationship that has developed between Pyper and one of the other battalion members.

In the play's fourth and final act, the audience is brought to the trenches, to witness the men preparing for the Battle of the Somme—which only Pyper will survive. The play concludes just before the battle begins, which means that this is a war play in which no violence is ever represented onstage. In keeping with the title, the audience observes the eight soldiers marching toward the Somme as the curtain falls.

As a sympathetic portrayal of a group of protestant Ulstermen written by a Catholic playwright, *Observe the Sons of Ulster* is a remarkable exercise in empathy that crosses—and perhaps transcends—the traditional fault lines between Catholic and Protestant, and Nationalist and Unionist, in Ireland. The Battle of the Somme, at which thousands of Ulstermen died, is one of the foundational moments of the Northern Irish state. Representing that battle on the stage of the Abbey Theatre—the beginnings of which were one of the foundational moments of the Republic of Ireland—is a remarkably brave and generous gesture. The play was therefore understood during its 1985 premiere as a commentary on the Northern Irish Troubles. A 1994 Abbey revival, which coincided with the beginnings of the Northern Irish Peace Process, made that commentary even more explicit.

But the play's impact is universal. Its representation of the perseverance of relationships between the eight men is a powerful statement of humanity's ability to find love in a situation of catastrophic violence. This has led to the play being seen as one of the most powerful antiwar dramas in the modern tradition.

FURTHER READING
Jordan, Eamonn. *The Feast of Famine: The Plays of Frank McGuinness.*
    Berne: P. Lang, 1997.
Lojek, Helen, ed. *Stages of Mutabilitie.* Dublin: Carysfort Press, 2002.

Patrick Lonergan

OCAMPO, MARÍA LUISA (1899–1972)

While María Luisa Ocampo was a talented journalist, novelist, poet, and short-story writer, she is most remembered for her prominent place in the history of Mexican theater. Born on November 24, 1899, to middle-class parents in Chilpancingo, Guerrero, MEXICO, Ocampo grew up during the Mexican Revolution (1910–1920). At age twenty-three she launched her dramatic career with the support of the prominent actress María Teresa Montoya with her successful debut of *The Facts of Life* (*Cosas de la vida*, 1923). However, Ocampo's role in the development of Mexican theater is not limited to playwriting. With money she made winning the lottery, she helped form the group La Comedia Mexicana, which operated from 1929 to 1936 with the express purpose of promoting plays by Mexican authors.

The Facts of Life delves into the construction of "woman" within a postrevolutionary Mexican culture that, despite some changes, is still very *machista*. The protagonist, Luisa, is denied access to socially acceptable womanhood and motherhood because of her poverty. Her boyfriend, Rafael, abandons her when she becomes pregnant because his elitist circle disapproves of Luisa. However, the protagonist courageously provides for herself and her child without a man's help. Instead of playing the conventional role of "dishonored woman," Ocampo's heroine becomes a self-assured single mother. The later play *The Corrido of Juan Saavedra* (*El Corrido de Juan Saavedra*, 1929) mixed together folk songs, local legend, and the history of the Mexican Revolution and featured scenery painted by Diego Rivera. Toward the end of her life, Ocampo dedicated herself to library work. She died at the age of seventy-four on August 15, 1974.

SELECT PLAYS: *The Facts of Life* (*Cosas de la vida*, 1923); *The Illusion* (*La quimera*, 1923); *The Bonfire* (*La hoguera*, 1924); *Life Is Crazy After All* (*Al cabo la vida está loca*, 1925); *Wingless* (*Sin alas*, 1925); *The Masks* (*Las*

máscaras, 1926); *You May Leave* (*Puedes irte*, 1926); *Thirst in the Desert*
(*Sed en el desierto*, 1927); *Beyond Men* (*Mas allá de los hombres*, 1929);
The Corrido of Juan Saavedra (*El corrido de Juan Saavedra*, 1929); *Castles
in the Air* (*Castillos en el aire*, 1931); *The House in Ruins* (*La casa en
ruinas*, 1936); *A Woman's Life* (*Una vida de una mujer*, 1938); *The Strong
Virgin* (*La Virgen fuerte*, 1950); *Toward Another Day* (*Al otro día*, 1955)

FURTHER READING

Merlín, Socorro. *María Luisa Ocampo: Mujer de teatro* [María Luisa
    Campo: Theater woman]. Mexico, [D.F.]: Grupo Editorial Lama,
    2000.
Nigro, Kristen. "Theatre, Women, and Mexican Society: A Few
    Exemplary Cases." In *Perspectives on Contemporary Spanish American
    Theatre*, ed. by Frank Dauster. London: Associated Univ. Presses,
    1996. 53–66.
Schmidhuber, Guillermo. *El teatro mexicano en cierne: 1922–1938* [The
    Mexican theater in blossom: 1928–1938]. New York: P. Lang, 1992.

                                                        May Summer Farnsworth

O'CASEY, SEAN (1880–1964)

*That's the Irish People all over—they treat a joke as a serious thing
and a serious thing as a joke.*
—Seumas Shields, Act 1, *The Shadow of a Gunman*

*D'ye know, comrade, that more die o'consumption than are killed in
th' wars? An' it's all because of th' system we're livin' undher?*
—The Covey, Act 4, *The Plough and the Stars*

*We can't give sight to the blind or make the lame walk. We would if
we could. It is the misfortune of war. As long as wars are waged, we
shall be vexed by woe; strong legs shall be made useless and bright
eyes made dark.*
—Susie Monican, Act 4, *The Silver Tassie*

Sean O'Casey was born John Casey at 85 Upper Dorset Street,
Dublin, IRELAND, on March 30, 1880, the youngest of the five
surviving children of Michael and Susan Casey, loyal Protestants
and Unionists, that is, supporters of the union between Great
Britain and Ireland. When Sean's father, a clerk with the Irish
Church Mission, died prematurely in 1886, the family slowly
descended into poverty, though always within a lower-middle-
class environment. As Martin Margulies has shown in *The Early
Life of Sean O'Casey* (1970), O'Casey was later to exaggerate the
nature of his family's poverty. More immediately restricting was
his eye condition, trachoma, which kept him out of school and
limited his formal education to no more than three or four years.
However, his sister Bella's being a grade school teacher, as well
as the scholarly nature of his father, encouraged O'Casey toward
self-education, and he became a wide reader of William Shakespeare, the Bible, and 19th-century drama. He also learned the
Bible by heart at Sunday school, and the *King James Bible* was to be
a lifelong influence on his writing style. When his brother Isaac
pursued an interest in amateur theatricals, the young O'Casey
was drawn toward drama at about age fifteen. Chief among his
literary influences were Shakespeare's plays, which he read vora-
ciously and could quote from liberally, and Victorian MELODRA-
MAS, available in cheap editions, in particular the Irish plays of
DIONYSIUS BOUCICAULT (1820–1890). He saw little professional theater and was almost forty before first attending the
Abbey Theatre. He was always more attracted to popular forms
of entertainment, including vaudeville and music hall.

Failing to hold down a job as junior clerk and probably unfit
to join the army like two of his brothers (Mick and Tom),
O'Casey became a manual worker on the Great Northern Railway in Dublin. He never rose higher than bricklayer's assistant,
and in 1911 he lost his job on the railway for alleged incompetence. By this time he was a member of the Gaelic League and
was known to fellow workers as "Irish Jack" for his fanatical
love of the Irish language and Irish culture. The Gaelic League
provided the college education O'Casey never had. He quickly
brought himself to such proficiency in grammar that he taught
classes in the league and wrote short, satirical pieces in Irish
for the Gaelic League journal. He changed his name to the Irish
version, Seán Ó Cathasaigh, and in 1910 joined and became secretary of the St. Laurence O'Toole's Pipe Band, where he learned
to play the bagpipes and paraded in traditional costume. He
was also a member of the Irish Republican Brotherhood (IRB),
a secret organization dedicated to breaking the colonial domination of Ireland by ENGLAND. But offsetting this development
into ardent nationalism came his interest in socialism. Under
the influence of the charismatic trade union leader Jim Larkin
(1876–1947), who led the Dublin workers into conflict with the
employers in 1913, O'Casey's thinking began to change. He
threw himself into various committees during the 1913 Dublin
Lock-out, which lasted six months, and at the same time wrote
articles for Larkin's *Irish Worker*. Reading GEORGE BERNARD
SHAW's preface to JOHN BULL'S OTHER ISLAND (1904) helped shift
his commitment from nationalism to socialism, and he was
later to say he was a communist all his life. Although he did,
indeed, welcome the October Revolution in RUSSIA in 1917,
O'Casey was never a member of the Communist Party, and his
left-wing politics were always idiosyncratic and tinged with
ROMANTICISM. Yet he retained some of his republican nationalism lifelong and never really resolved the conflict between his
commitment to workers' rights and his love of Ireland.

His early writing, anthologized by Robert Hogan in *Feathers
from the Green Crow* (1962), was mainly nationalist and polemical
in theme and tone. Written for radical newspapers and journals, it called for a militant republican solution to the Ireland-
England problem. In view of O'Casey's subsequent condemnation of war and violence, this early writing seems surprising but
makes clear how from the outset his imagination was politicized. Around 1913, however, the tone of his writing shifted
toward criticism of the bourgeois Volunteers and their narrow
aims. In 1914 he became secretary of the Irish Citizen's Army,
established by Larkin to protect workers, and although he

resigned early on over a dispute with Countess Markiewicz, O'Casey wrote *The Story of the Irish Citizen Army* (1919) as a contribution to the history of events leading up to the 1916 Rising. He disagreed sharply with the aims of James Connolly, the socialist ideologue who assumed leadership of the Irish Citizen Army after Larkin immigrated to the UNITED STATES in October 1914. Connolly joined forces with Patrick Pearse, leader of the Irish Volunteers, to form the insurgents declaring an Irish Republic at the General Post Office in 1916. O'Casey saw this alliance as a betrayal of the working-class movement and believed the Rising was a tragic mistake. It was on this theme that THE PLOUGH AND THE STARS (1925) was to be based.

EARLY PLAYS

After 1916 O'Casey retreated into writing plays. From about 1912 he had been involved with Delia Larkin (1878–1949), Jim's sister, in the Liberty Hall Players, an amateur company dedicated to raising the morale of Dublin workers. He did not write for these Players but formed part of the audience and assisted backstage. He would have seen the work by A. P. Wilson written for the group, AGITATION-PROPAGANDA plays such as *Victims, Poached*, and *The Slough*, although the latter was staged at the Abbey Theatre, which O'Casey did not yet frequent. He submitted a one-act play to the Abbey in 1916, *Profit and Loss*, which was rejected, like the four plays that followed, including *The Harvest Festival* (1919). This three–act play, first published in 1980, and included in the *Complete Plays* (1984), gives a clear idea not only of O'Casey's early commitment to working-class drama but also of the distance he had to travel in order to achieve the status of accomplished Abbey playwright on which his fame largely rests. Recently, the one-act play, *The Cooing of Doves* (1923), which was never staged, has come to light. This rejected piece shows how O'Casey never wasted anything he wrote: it was recycled as act 2 of *The Plough and the Stars*.

His rapid progress in DRAMATURGY was aided by the advice offered by the Abbey directorate who were his readers, WILLIAM BUTLER YEATS, LENNOX ROBINSON, and above all, LADY AUGUSTA GREGORY. It was she who urged him to subordinate politics to characterization. O'Casey, as he now officially called himself, complied and had his first play accepted by the Abbey, THE SHADOW OF A GUNMAN (1922–1923). Its immediate success was followed by that of JUNO AND THE PAYCOCK (1924) and then by the last of the so-called Dublin Trilogy, *The Plough and the Stars*. The availability of a strong Abbey company, which included Sara Allgood, F. J. McCormick, and Barry Fitzgerald, had much to do with the phenomenal popularity of O'Casey's plays, which he tailored to the specific talents of the Abbey players. Because *The Plough and the Stars* inspected the 1916 rising in a subversive, demythologizing style, there was strong opposition from relatives and supporters (mainly women) of the republican "martyrs" who had died in the rising. On the fourth night, organized republicans rioted, and Yeats, as over J. M. SYNGE's PLAYBOY OF THE WESTERN WORLD (1907), summoned the police into the theater to restore order. In a speech from the stage, Yeats rebuked the Dublin audience and assured them that, as with Synge, they had spread the fame of O'Casey worldwide through their attempts to suppress his art and had thereby rocked the "cradle of genius." O'Casey, shocked by the extent of the opposition, agreed to speak at a public lecture given by Hanna Sheehy-Skeffington, a feminist and widow of a pacifist killed during the 1916 rising. In this debate O'Casey came off second-best and soon after left Dublin for London. Although he later asserted that his exile from Ireland stemmed from the hostile reception of *The Plough*, it is clear that his reason for leaving was an invitation to oversee the transfer of the London production of *Juno* from one theater to another. Once in London, although he retained lease of his room in Dublin where all three of his plays had been written (at 422 North Circular Road), having fallen in love with actress Eileen Carey Reynolds, he married in 1927 and settled there.

The story of O'Casey's life and work really divides here. When his next play, the antiwar THE SILVER TASSIE (1927–1928) was rejected by the Abbey Theatre, the ensuing controversy he fomented opened up such a rift that it became impossible for him ever to contemplate returning to live in Ireland. The root of this controversy lay in Yeats's dislike of war poetry and drama about passive suffering, as he called it, and in Yeats's lack of sympathy with the new, experimental drama ushered in by EUGENE O'NEILL and the German expressionists. Act 2 of *The Tassie* was in the expressionist style and was therefore a major departure from the NATURALISM endemic at the Abbey. To Yeats, O'Casey had lost his way and had written about a subject, the 1914–1918 war, of which he had no experience. To O'Casey this was merely an attempt to curtail the freedom of the artist's imagination. Shaw sided with O'Casey, whom he had befriended, but the bitterness of the dispute badly soured the insecure O'Casey and created enmity not only between him and Yeats but also and more painfully with Lady Gregory, who made unavailing attempts at a reconciliation before her death in 1932.

TURN TO LITERARY PLAYS

O'Casey was now without a living theater for which to write. From this point on his plays became literary in style rather than primarily theatrical. Indeed, they were usually published (by his lifelong publishers Macmillan) before production, a factor that inhibited the kind of alterations usual in the collaborative process of theater production. O'Casey became obsessively protective of his texts, usually refusing directors permission to make changes even where cuts and improvements were sensibly suggested. This stubbornness, while principled, tended to maintain O'Casey in the realm of lonely experimenter. He now had a strong dislike for REALISM, dominant in London's West End, and in his public comments and theater criticism, notably in his *The Flying Wasp* (1937), singled out as his two main targets the playwright NOËL COWARD and the drama critic James Agate. These he blamed for creating a public taste hostile to the more experimental work he himself approved. But by such personal attacks O'Casey alienated himself from the theater of his time.

After the production in London of *The Silver Tassie* in 1929, which was a critical but not a financial success, O'Casey spent several difficult years. In 1934 he published *Windfalls*, a collection of poetry, short stories, and two short plays, *The End of the Beginning* (1931–1932) and *A Pound on Demand* (1932). These plays were light FARCES, which he hoped might make a little money on actor-managers' tours. They were favorably reviewed in 1934 by SAMUEL BECKETT, who saw in them the nucleus of O'Casey's tragicomic art, the representation onstage of "chassis" or disorder, through knockabout farce. It can be said that Beckett's own tragicomic WAITING FOR GODOT (1948–1949) showed the influence of O'Casey in this regard, a point David Krause makes in *Sean O'Casey: The Man and His Work* (1975). In 1934 *Within the Gates* (1931–1933), an expressionist play in four acts set in London's Hyde Park, proved too ambitious at the Everyman Theatre and did little better in a new production in New York later that year. Invited out to attend rehearsals, O'Casey made many friends in New York, including the drama critic George Jean Nathan, whose work he greatly admired and who became an important mentor, and Eugene O'Neill, whose MOURNING BECOMES ELECTRA (1928–1930) O'Casey particularly admired. This was to be O'Casey's only visit to America, but its effects were lasting. He loved New York and its people and would have been content, had circumstances allowed, to move there. But his trip was somewhat soured when *Within the Gates* was banned in Boston as a result of Roman Catholic opposition, and its tour had to be canceled.

Toward the end of 1938 the O'Casey family, comprising Eileen and two sons, Breon and Niall, moved from London to Devon, where Shivaun, the last addition to the family, was born in 1939. The motive for this more, partly financial, was mainly so that the children could attend the progressive private school at Dartington Hall. At first, it was thought O'Casey might have a role as playwright-in-association with the Theatre Studio operated at Dartington by Michael Chekhov, nephew of the famous Russian writer, but this plan came to nothing.

As World War II broke out, O'Casey's fortunes were precarious, and he turned to writing his autobiography in a colorful, popular style. Like most of his work, the autobiography, which eventually grew to six volumes, was closely tied to Irish history, for O'Casey saw himself always against the background of those movements that shaped the new Irish State in its genesis. *I Knock at the Door* (published in 1939) and the three volumes that followed took O'Casey's story up to the time he left Ireland, lately arrived at independence. Two more volumes, dealing with his life and career in England, though less interesting, brought the story up to 1954. The autobiographies proved to be bestsellers in the United States and no doubt saved the O'Caseys from pen-

ury. Their dramatic qualities, as the hero moves through the streets of Dublin encountering the great personalities of the day and participating in the cultural movements inaugurated by many of them, became obvious to reviewers, and in due course the early books began to be adapted for the stage.

This development took place mainly in New York, where the themes of the autobiographies appealed to a population for whom O'Casey's overcoming of social and physical handicaps and his realization of his talents in defiance of class restrictions were peculiarly meaningful. These adaptations, by Paul Shyre, followed the two-volume edition of the autobiographies titled *Mirror in My House* (1956). They were more palatable to Cold War audiences than several of the politically informed plays O'Casey wrote in Devon, such as *The Star Turns Red* (1938), an extolling of communism in a text refused publication by Macmillan Ltd., New York (which usually accepted the O'Casey title published by Macmillan London). There is observable in the reception of O'Casey in America in the 1940s and 1950s (a topic yet to be fully explored) a stark contrast between the admiration showered on the democratically informed autobiographies, with their humanistic basis in individual growth, and the hostility shown toward the communist-inspired plays, with their fearless opposition towards Roman Catholicism. This is not to say that the later plays were communist tracts; rather, it is to emphasize how O'Casey's later work divides into the combative, subversive plays, on the one hand, and the genial, if sharply satirical, autobiographies on the other. This division points to a similar split in O'Casey himself between the left-wing intellectual and the popular entertainer.

In England from 1939, this division was less in evidence. For one thing, the autobiographies, although critically admired for the most part (always with some reservations over the style and its Joycean qualities), meant less to a society so secure in its class structures than they did in America. For another, there was in England a persistent interest in poetic drama, aggravated by a sense of guilt over continuing failure to restore it to the popular stage. O'Casey was perceived as a poetic dramatist within the framework of the attempt made by T. S. ELIOT, W. H. AUDEN, and CHRISTOPHER FRY. Thus the fate of *Within the Gates* was lamented, while reviews of the COMEDY *Purple Dust* (1939–1940) and the autobiographical *Red Roses for Me* (1942) usually paid fulsome tribute to the increasing lyricism of O'Casey's dialogue. The London production of *Red Roses* in 1946 proved a rare exception, winning much acclaim, as it did also in New York in 1955–1956. In New York *Purple Dust* had a yearlong run at the Cherry Lane in 1956–1957, though *Cock-a-doodle Dandy* (1948), O'Casey's own favorite, in which fantasy and satire are equally mixed, failed in 1958. When his play about World War II *Oak Leaves and Lavender* (1944) was staged in London in 1947, there was a clear indication that somehow he had missed the historical moment, and this production was a major flop. It seemed that O'Casey, the estranged Irishman living in England's puritanical society, had little to say to English audiences. George Orwell, a hostile witness, reviewing the third volume of the autobiographies, *Drums Under the Windows* (1945), accused O'Casey of living in England under false colors, but the reviewer of the *Collected Plays* in the *Times Literary Supplement* in 1951 got nearer the mark by accusing O'Casey of poor "judgment." By this he probably meant O'Casey's tactless indifference to the expectations of English audiences, although O'Casey took the criticism as a rebuke to his left-wing politics. Either way, from today's perspective, this kind of criticism suggests the AVANT-GARDE nature of O'Casey's later work. In its SYMBOLISM, use of fantasy, and use of absurdity, he was ahead of his time and closer to Beckett than to any British playwright, including JOHN OSBORNE, with whom he began to be compared after 1956. It is no surprise, perhaps, that *Cock-a-doodle Dandy* finally had its English professional premiere at London's Royal Court Theatre, where Osborne had inaugurated a revolution in modern drama. At last, in 1959, it appeared, O'Casey could be seen as part of a general theater of revolt.

RETURN TO IRISH THEATER

In Ireland, meantime, O'Casey was mainly seen as a bête noire. *Windfalls* and the early volumes of the autobiography were banned by the Irish Censorship Board. Reviews in Dublin of subsequent volumes and of the later plays in publications were usually carping, shocked, and ungenerous. The consensus seemed to be that O'Casey had gone sadly astray since leaving the precincts of Dublin, where his art had its roots. The call, none too enthusiastic, was for him to return and renew the wellsprings of lost inspiration. His communism, so flagrantly on parade in the later volumes of autobiography, was much deplored. In 1935 O'Casey was reconciled with Yeats, who then agreed to stage *The Silver Tassie* at the Abbey. There was a storm of opposition to its alleged blasphemous features, and as the Free State under Eamon de Valera became increasingly subservient to the Roman Catholic Church, O'Casey's work became increasingly unacceptable. When *Red Roses for Me* had its premiere in Dublin in 1943, the first O'Casey premiere since *The Plough and the Stars*, the Dublin critics saw it as a great falling-off from his early drama. They insisted on measuring his achievements by the standards of realism he had long neglected. In that context it was brave to the point of foolhardiness on the part of the actor April Cusack to ask O'Casey for *The Bishop's Bonfire* (1954). With Tyrone Guthrie as director, Cusack's own company staged it at the Gaiety Theatre, Dublin, in February 1955. O'Casey declined an invitation to attend; a riot was expected, but in the end the play—another comedy satirical of Ireland's regressive society—was quietly if unenthusiastically received.

The newly established Dublin Theatre Festival then bravely asked O'Casey for his latest play *The Drums of Father Ned* (1957), a gentle comedy of Irish life filtered through memories of the Anglo-Irish War in 1920. Immediately, a controversy arose when the archbishop of Dublin refused to allow the usual solemn votive Mass to inaugurate the festival because of O'Casey's and, indirectly through an adaptation of *Ulysses*, James Joyce's involvement. This was in effect censorship through clerical authoritarianism. As disappointed as he was angry, O'Casey withdrew his play, and following the controversy unleashed, the festival was canceled for 1958. He promptly banned all professional productions of his plays in Ireland, a ban that stood until 1964. O'Casey now felt vindicated in all of his bitterness against Church-dominated Ireland and ended his career as playwright with two further mocking condemnations, *Behind the Green Curtains* (1958–1960) and *Figuro in the Night* (1960). Underlying much of this later work was a glorification of sex, which was one more reason for the puritanical society of the 1950s to find fault with O'Casey.

In the last year of O'Casey's life the American director John Ford visited Dublin to film *Young Cassidy*, based on two of the best books of the autobiography, *Drums Under the Windows* (1945) and *Inishfallen Fare Thee Well* (1949). The script was by British playwright John Whiting and the producers were two American enthusiasts, Robert Emmett Ginna and Robert D. Graff. Sean Connery was cast as Johnnie Cassidy, the character based on O'Casey himself, but when Connery was committed to *Goldfinger* (1964), the role went to Rod Taylor, with other parts going to Maggie Smith and Julie Christie. Released in February 1965 the film, directed more by Jack Cardiff than by Ford, although it simplifies complex areas of O'Casey's life, stands as an interesting if glamorized treatment from a Hollywood perspective.

On the personal level, O'Casey's last years were blighted by the death of his son Niall from leukemia in December 1956, at age twenty-one. O'Casey poured out his grief in a weekly diary spanning four years, published long after his death as *Niall: A Lament* (1991). A collection of stories, essays, and reminiscences, *Under a Colored Cap* appeared in 1962. For decades O'Casey had also been an assiduous letter writer, not only about his work but to ordinary people the world over who consulted him as a sage, and four volumes, edited by his first biographer David Krause, were published between 1975 and 1992. The letters add much information on O'Casey's plays and life. In his later years O'Casey's health deteriorated, as chronic bronchitis and constantly failing eyesight made him virtually a recluse. He died from heart failure in Torbay Hospital, Torquay, Devon, on September 18, 1964, at age eighty-four. After his body was cremated in Torquay, his ashes were scattered at Golder's Green, London.

Assessed some forty years after his death, O'Casey's status as playwright depends mainly on the three early Dublin plays. This is ironic in view of O'Casey's determination to move away from realism and in view of his own belief that his later work was superior. Whereas revivals of the later work, especially of *The Silver Tassie*, still occasionally take place, it is, perhaps sadly, the case that only *The Shadow of a Gunman*, *Juno and the Paycock*, and *The Plough and the Stars* stand today to represent the O'Casey canon. Yet the frequency of revivals in the United States, Britain, and GERMANY (especially before the fall of the Berlin Wall), as well as in Ireland (where the three plays are more often staged than any other play at the Abbey), makes it possible to claim that O'Casey, in spite of his checkered career, is perhaps the greatest Irish playwright of the 20th century. His influence, as a writer whose work favored the tragicomic form, vivid characterization, colorful language, and a state-of-the-nation theme, is to be seen in much Irish drama, from Denis Johnston to BRIAN FRIEL and Beckett. His influence on world drama is another matter. In some respects the work of BERTOLT BRECHT has, through its greater sophistication, had more lasting impact on writers and directors. Nevertheless, it is possible to trace O'Casey's influence on urban tragedy and TRAGICOMEDY from CLIFFORD ODETS to ARTHUR MILLER, and from ARNOLD WESKER to JOHN ARDEN and EDWARD BOND, all of whom have acknowledged admiration and indebtedness.

PLAYS: *The Harvest Festival* (1919); *The Shadow of a Gunman* (1922–1923); *The Cooing of Doves* (1923); *Juno and the Paycock* (1924); *Kathleen Listens In* (1924); *Nannie's Night Out* (1924–1925); *The Plough and the Stars* (1925); *The Silver Tassie* (1927–1928); *The End of the Beginning* (1931–1932); *Within the Gates* (1931–1933); *A Pound on Demand* (1932); *The Star Turns Red* (1938); *Purple Dust* (1939–1940); *Red Roses for Me* (1942); *Oak Leaves and Lavender* (1944); *Cock-a-doodle Dandy* (1948); *Hall of Healing* (1949); *Bedtime Story* (1950); *Time to Go* (1950); *The Bishop's Bonfire* (1954); *The Drums of Father Ned* (1957); *Figuro in the Night* (1960); *Behind the Green Curtains* (1958–1960); *The Moon Shines on Kylenamoe* (1960)

FURTHER READING

Harris, Peter James. *Sean O'Casey's Letters and Autobiographies: Reflections of a Radical Ambivalence.* Trier: Wissenschalftlicher Verlag Trier, 2004.

Kenneally, Michael. *Portraying the Self: Sean O'Casey and the Art of Autobiography.* Gerrards Cross, Bucks: C. Smythe; Totowa, N.J.: Barnes and Noble Bks., 1988.

Kosok, Heinz. *O'Casey the Dramatist.* Tr. by Heinz Kosok and Joseph T. Swann. Gerrards Cross, Bucks: Colin Smythe; Totowa, N.J.: Barnes & Noble Books, 1985.

Krause, David. *Sean O'Casey and His World.* London: Thames & Hudson, 1975.

Murray, Christopher. *Sean O'Casey: Writer at Work: A Biography.* Dublin: Gill & Macmillan, 2004.

Schrank, Bernice. *Sean O'Casey: A Research and Production Sourcebook.* Westport: Greenwood Press, 1996.

Christopher Murray

THE OCCUPATION OF HEATHER ROSE

The Occupation of Heather Rose (1986), WENDY LILL's third play, is a complex work examining the underside of the ostensibly altruistic, as a "white" nurse who means to help the natives of CANADA's north struggles with her continued assumptions of superiority. Heather Rose, a young nurse who goes to work with native peoples at the Snake Lake Reservation, sees herself as an altruistic and dedicated healer. The play is narrated in one long flashback: Heather, returned to southern Ontario, waits for her mentor, Miss Jackson, in order to complain to her about how badly her stint up north has gone.

Heather Rose reveals how the natives fail to welcome her with the open arms she expects. For all her conscious desire to help these people, her redemptive sense of her own mission gives her a kind of messianic arrogance that crumples in the face of the recalcitrance of those whom she purports to help. While talking to the chief of the peoples who live in Snake Lake, Heather Rose screens out the historical factors affecting the present-day condition of the people for whom she is supposed to care. She sees them only in an immediate social context, using cheery, motivational language to try to uplift and energize them. This might work in a suburban white community where the self-image of the people would reflect Heather Rose's. But, as Heather discovers, the Snake Lake people have been so damaged by generations of mistreatment and relegation her optimistic harangues cannot possibly produce their intended effect. Importantly, Heather Rose is not a one-dimensional monster; instead, she is someone who has mistakenly accepted at face value her own privileged assumptions. Her inexperience is one of the factors that causes her to lose her sanity when she comes to understand that she is an intruder, not a source of comfort. This sense of intrusion plays on the double entendre of the "occupation" of the play's title, referring both to Heather Rose's career and to the control of native lands by whites. This double meaning sets the tone for the scrutiny the play casts on customary assumptions of white liberal benevolence.

Much like Lill herself (who spent time as a consultant to the Canadian Mental Health Association among the native communities of northern Ontario), Heather Rose grapples with how to effect change in communities other than one's own. The play, if not a literal self-critique, is certainly highly complex and self-conscious. While the play's focus is on a particular and localized incident, its feminist and political concerns extend more broadly to other communities wrestling with issues of difference, privilege, and multivalent occupations. *The Occupation of Heather Rose* was a finalist for the 1987 Governor-General's Award. In the years since then it has generated considerable academic discussion and many theatrical productions, including several in Canada starring Melanie Miller and one in New York featuring Susan Heafner.

FURTHER READING

Petropoulos, Jacqueline. "Language and Racism: Wendy Lill's *The Occupation of Heather Rose.*" *Canadian Theatre Review* 114 (Spring 2003): 38–41.

Nicholas Birns

THE ODD COUPLE

There's something wrong with this system. . . . I don't think that two single men living alone in a big eight-room apartment should have a cleaner house than my mother.

—Oscar, Act 2

The Odd Couple (1965), NEIL SIMON's third play, has, in its various incarnations, proven to be one of the most successful COMEDIES in the history of the American theater. Based in part on his observations of his own brother and another divorced man trying to live as roommates, the play offered a new twist on Simon's already established style of farcical domestic comedy driven by expertly placed one-liners. Here, instead of newlyweds (as in *Barefoot in the Park*) or a parental family unit (*Come Blow Your Horn*), two middle-aged bachelors end up in a de facto marriage, eventually alienating each other just as they had their former wives.

The action transpires in the New York apartment of sportswriter Oscar Madison who, in the absence of his wife, has visibly degenerated into a slovenly mess. At the opening curtain, he is hosting his usual poker game among friends. One of them, the fussy Felix Ungar, shows up late and suicidal—he, too, has been rejected by his wife, who could no longer put up with his many neuroses. To pacify the dejected Felix, Oscar offers to take him in. Act 2 opens with a brilliant Simon comic tableau—the same apartment, the same poker game, but spotlessly clean and sanitized. Felix has taken over, bringing sterile order to Oscar's locker-room world and taking away much of the fun. In repeating their patterns from their failed marriages, they quickly become a bickering old couple. When Oscar tries to liven things up by arranging a double date with their British neighbors, the Pigeon sisters, Felix's morbid pining for his wife ruins the plans, but he wins the women over anyway with his sensitivity. In act 3 all-out war is declared, as Oscar kicks Felix out and reverts to his old lifestyle. When Felix reappears, it is in the arms of his new roommates, the Pigeon sisters.

After a nerve-wracking out-of-town tryout period (marked by Simon's customarily extensive third-act rewrites), *The Odd Couple* was received with sensational reviews and blockbuster ticket sales on Broadway. The production, directed by Mike Nichols and starring Art Carney and Walter Matthau (for whom Simon wrote the role of Oscar), ran 966 performances. A very successful 1967 film version featured Matthau and Jack Lemmon in Simon's faithful screenplay adaptation. The movie soon led to an television series spin-off, which ran for five seasons (1970–1975) and for decades longer in syndication. For many across the UNITED STATES and the world, the famous roommates will always be personified by the television actors Jack Klugman and Tony Randall, who continued playing the roles for over twenty years in "reunion" episodes, on television commercials, and in stage revivals.

Even Simon himself was not able to leave the play alone. In addition to an all-female version in 1985, he wrote no less than two sequels—the play *Oscar and Felix*, which previewed in Los Angeles in 2002, and the film *The Odd Couple II* (1998), reuniting an aging Lemmon and Matthau in their beloved roles from thirty years earlier.

[*See also* United States, 1940–Present]

FURTHER READING

Bloom, Harold, ed. *Neil Simon*. Philadelphia: Chelsea House, 2002.
Konas, Gary, ed. *Neil Simon: A Casebook*. New York: Garland, 1997.
Koprince, Susan Fehrenbacher. *Understanding Neil Simon*. Columbia: Univ. of South Carolina Press, 2002.
Simon, Neil. *Rewrites: A Memoir*. New York: Simon & Schuster, 1996.

Garrett Eisler

ODETS, CLIFFORD (1906–1963)

Clifford Odets was born on July 16, 1906, in Philadelphia, Pennsylvania; his father was a reasonably successful businessman in printing and advertising, and the family apparently lived an unremarkable middle-class life. Not particularly accomplished in his class work, at seventeen Clifford dropped out of high school, although he had actively participated in dramatic activities and joined the school's literary club. After doing some radio work and acting in the 1920s, he joined THE GROUP THEATRE, appearing in its initial production, PAUL GREEN's *The House of Connelly* (1931), and in SIDNEY KINGSLEY's Pulitzer Prize–winning MEN IN WHITE in 1933.

In 1934 Odets joined the Communist Party, where, by his own admission, he stayed for only a few months. Not surprisingly, his early plays were left wing in their adherence to the Party line. The first, WAITING FOR LEFTY, appeared on Broadway in March 1935 paired with his second play, *Till the Day I Die*, a heavily propagandistic portrayal of a communist cell in GERMANY fighting the Nazis. Poorly written with stereotyped good and bad guys, it was a minor effort.

Lefty's simple stage setting of a row of plain wooden chairs on a bare stage creates the appearance of a union hiring hall, while actors onstage and planted in the auditorium further the audience illusion of attending an actual union meeting. The conditions of the deepening Depression in a society going increasingly awry, causing the assembled taxi drivers to consider a strike, are portrayed by spotlighted vignettes performed in the center of the semicircle of chairs, the most socially significant of which involves the advice given to an actor seeking work that he should read the *Communist Manifesto* or, better yet, go to Russia, where all are equal and everybody calls you comrade. Then, when a messenger rushes in from the audience to announce that the long-awaited leader, Lefty, has been murdered, those onstage and in the audience erupt shouting "Strike! Strike!" as everybody seems ready to rush into the street and man the barricades. *Waiting for Lefty* firmly established Odets as an important writer and a major contributor to the Group Theatre's dramatic PHILOSOPHY and liberal social outlook, remaining even now the most literate, and most effective, of the Depression-era AGITATION-PROPAGANDA (agit-prop) plays.

In AWAKE AND SING! Odets's creation of the Berger family and its struggle against the Depression fit perfectly into the Group's preference for the ensemble style of acting. It also earned him the reputation, not always accurately, as the American ANTON CHEKHOV. In the collective manner of the Russian playwright, there is no leading role, with each character of equal importance, and with virtually no "plot" as such, leading to an emotional climax. Each person's inner struggle is constantly evident, with dialogue preeminent over action. What develops throughout the play, told in Odets's mastery of the Bronx Jewish idiom and his consciously underwritten style, is a keen awareness of each character's inward frustrations in the midst of the debilitating Great Depression, while simultaneously gaining sympathy for and understanding of each individual's predicament.

The conclusion clings to the Group's optimistic philosophy, as young Ralph in the long closing scene proclaims a better future if we can all just "awake and sing" as the prophet Isaiah affirms. The finale may not be entirely convincing, but it does its best to lift things up toward something brighter ahead. Despite Odets's personal beliefs, the communist view is restricted to the old grandfather, who is mostly ignored by the others.

Where Awake and Sing! succeeded as one of Odets's best plays, the next one did not. Paradise Lost, which appeared in December 1935, concerns a once comfortably prosperous family, the Gordons, faced with eviction as the business of Leo Gordon has collapsed in the midst of the Depression because of a partner's embezzlement. The action retains Odets's ensemble style as the family faces and discusses at length their many problems. Meanwhile, the Depression continues to crush down.

The Far Left communist view is limited to a single minor character, but the play remains socially oriented. It concludes, however, with a totally unbelievable closing speech by Leo as he stands with his adoring wife and proclaims the optimism of a better future in which no man will stand alone. The result is a curtain tableau reminiscent of a 19th-century MELODRAMA, and it simply does not work.

In the summer of 1935 Odets went to CUBA on behalf of the American Committee to Investigate Labor and Social Conditions, a rather pointless gesture that gained very little for anybody. Then, disappointed with the failure of Paradise Lost, he left the New York scene and fled to what he hoped were better things in Hollywood. Although he received credit as writer or director on seven films, only one, The General Dies at Dawn in 1936, was of any consequence. Never fitting into the Hollywood scene, Odets returned to New York after only eleven months. In the meantime, however, he had met and married the glamorous Academy Award winner Luise Rainier in 1937 (they divorced in 1940).

Odets's return to Broadway was marked by the Group's successful production of GOLDEN BOY, which opened in November 1937. Now more of a social liberal than a revolutionary, he was still deeply concerned about a society willing to reward brute strength and guile at the expense of honor, decency, or artistic talent. Joe Bonaparte—a talented violinist in a society that cannot support his artistry—is seduced by and succumbs to the sleazy world of professional boxing and its large and instant rewards.

Joe's talents as a skillful boxer rather than a slugging fighter quickly carry him to success, but he clearly does not belong in the fight ring, and he hates himself for being there. When his inward rage turns him, literally, into a killer, he finally destroys himself as well. The end result is not the final-curtain optimism Odets had earlier displayed, as he sends Joe and his girl to their deaths in a speeding car, which society has now permitted him to buy. His broken hands and broken spirit deny him the ability ever to realize his genuine artistic talents, permanently taken from him by a totally insensitive society.

Rocket to the Moon (November 1938) is concerned less with social problems and more with romantic involvement. The Depression is still very much apparent in that Ben Stark cannot afford to buy an air conditioner for his sweltering dentist's office, and his young assistant, Cleo, cannot afford stockings. But all this remains incidental. What matters is Ben's obvious unhappiness in a mostly loveless marriage, driving him inevitably toward Cleo's physical attractions. The brief rocket ride to the moon of their sorry little affair only heightens their mutual loneliness, and Ben realizes that he and his equally frustrated wife must remain together. Once again the optimistic, upbeat conclusion is entirely lacking. The play has an often pathetic intimacy about it, prompting a considerable amount of sympathy for its characters, based almost wholly on personalities and almost not at all on the surrounding social ills.

Odets's next three plays did little to maintain his popular reputation. Night Music (1940), Clash by Night (1941), and an adaptation called The Russian People (1942) can all be safely ignored in the Odets canon. Again, he abandoned New York for Hollywood in 1943, where he remained for the better part of five years.

In 1944 Odets wrote and directed None But the Lonely Heart, a sordid story of life in the slums starring Cary Grant. Deadline at Dawn (1946), a murder mystery, was followed in 1947 by Humoresque, a tearjerker about a tough violinist (shades of Joe Bonaparte) trying to make a living in the Depression, featuring Joan Crawford and John Garfield. Meanwhile, in 1943 Odets married the actress Bette Grayson, with whom he had two children; they divorced in 1951.

By 1948 Odets had returned to New York, and his next play, The Big Knife, opened in February 1949. It was designed to poke fun at Hollywood, but its semiautobiographical outlook prompted one critic to call him a "champ sorehead." However, he regained his reputation in November 1950 with the opening of The Country Girl.

All semblance of social comment and protest is left behind in this story of the alcoholic down-and-out actor whose manager and wife work together to bring him back to the stage. It is a fine character study as the self-pitying Frank Elgin, blaming his wife (who defines herself as a simple country girl and who has not infrequently left him in the past) for all his ills, is eventually straightened out and returns in triumph.

The *Flowering Peach* in December 1954 was Odets's last play. This seriocomic treatment of Noah and the Flood was the only Odets play to be considered for a Pulitzer Prize. This time the antagonist is not society but a demanding and vengeful God who has tapped a seedy reluctant Noah to take on his task of punishing the world. It is a remarkable combination of a serious attempt to discuss man's relationship with his god, at the same time appearing as a kind of clown play replete with Jewish family jokes.

In 1955 Odets left again for Hollywood, and for the last eight years of his life he contributed nothing more to the stage. A screenplay, *Joseph and His Brethren*, was scrapped, but his name did appear in the credits for *Sweet Smell of Success* in 1957 about an ambitious businessman and a powerful columnist. He wrote and directed *The Story on Page One* in 1960, but its story of love and murder and social comment was considered dull and "soapy." His last movie, *Wild in the Country* (1961), with Elvis Presley, brought him little further recognition.

In 1961 Odets was given the Award of Merit for Drama from the American Academy of Arts and Letters. On June 23, 1963, he entered the hospital for ulcer surgery, but on August 14 he died of cancer. He was fifty-seven years old.

A brief note should be made of Odets's appearances on April 24 and May 19–29, 1952, before the House Un-American Activities Committee in its search for communist influences in Hollywood. He freely admitted his early membership in the Communist Party in an almost ritualistic confession. He was never blacklisted and continued his work uninterrupted, saying, "I am against war. I am against Fascism. I am for a third party."

[*See also* United States, 1929–Present]

SELECT PLAYS: *Awake and Sing!* (1935); *Paradise Lost* (1935); *Till the Day I Die* (1935); *Waiting for Lefty* (1935); *Golden Boy* (1937); *Rocket to the Moon* (1938); *Night Music* (1940); *Clash by Night* (1941); *The Russian People* (1942); *The Big Knife* (1949); *The Country Girl* (1950); *The Flowering Peach* (1954)

FURTHER READING

Brennan-Gibson, Margaret. *Clifford Odets, Playwright: The Years from 1906 to 1940*. New York: Atheneum Pubs., 1981.

Cantor, Harold. *Clifford Odets: Playwright-Poet*. Methuen, N.J.: Scarecrow, 1978.

Mendelsohn, Michael. *Clifford Odets, Humane Dramatist*. DeLand, Fla.: Everett-Edwards, 1969.

Murray, Edward. *Clifford Odets: The Thirties and After*. New York: Ungar, 1968.

Shuman, Robert B. *Clifford Odets*. New York: Twayne, 1962.

Weales, Gerald. *Clifford Odets, Playwright*. New York: Pegasus, 1971.

Jordan Miller

OFF- AND OFF-OFF-BROADWAY

After World War II, as television, radio, and film continued their ascendancy over live theater, Broadway successes increasingly tended to be spectacular musicals and conventional dramas. By the end of the century, ARTHUR MILLER would tell Cuban acting students that Broadway had been captured almost exclusively by musicals and pure entertainment and that the few straight plays were limited runs for stars. The situation Miller describes was already well under way in the 1950s and led first to the development of off-Broadway theater, then, a decade later, to the creation of off-off-Broadway.

OFF-BROADWAY THEATER

Off-Broadway began in the early 1950s as a gathering of "New York professional groups actively engaged in theatrical production in places exclusive of the theaters in the Times Square area" (Cordell and Matson, 1959). In 1950 a group of actors leased a defunct cabaret in Greenwich Village, named it Circle in the Square, and produced an in-the-round revival of a semisuccessful Broadway drama *Dark of the Moon*. Circle in the Square continued through the decade, remounting plays by TENNESSEE WILLIAMS, JEAN GIRAUDOUX, John Steinbeck, Truman Capote, FEDERICO GARCÍA LORCA, and ARTHUR SCHNITZLER, which had failed to find Broadway audiences. They were joined in 1952 by the Theatre de Lys (also in Greenwich Village), which mounted a popular 1954 production of the BERTOLT BRECHT–Kurt Weill THE THREEPENNY OPERA; and soon off-Broadway grew to include the Cherry Lane Theatre, the Actors' Playhouse, the Renata Theatre, the Downtown Theatre, the Fourth Street Playhouse, the St. Mark's Playhouse, Greenwich Mews, the Phoenix Theatre, and the venerable Provincetown Playhouse (a holdover from the Little Theater Movement). In 1967 Joseph Papp founded the New York Shakespeare Festival Public Theater to add further institutional solidity to the off-Broadway movement, and that same year Douglas Turner Ward, Robert Hooks, and Gerald Krone started the Negro Ensemble Company to offer an off-Broadway venue for African American plays. Another significant contribution to the development of off-Broadway theater was the 1974 creation of "Theatre Row" on 42nd Street between Ninth and Tenth Avenues. This became a neighborhood of small, nonprofit theaters including Playwrights Horizons, Intar (featuring works by Latino and Latina playwrights), the Acting Company, and the Harold Clurman, SAMUEL BECKETT, and Judith Anderson theaters.

Early off-Broadway dramas typically challenged the conventional fare of Broadway theater, not only by rediscovering artistically worthy Broadway failures but by functioning as a kind of repertory theater for classic European and American dramas (including plays by ANTON CHEKHOV, GEORGE BERNARD SHAW, T. S. ELIOT, William Shakespeare, EUGENE O'NEILL, and SEAN O'CASEY). In addition, off-Broadway offered venues for the emerging Theater of the Absurd: not only its European playwrights—Beckett, EUGÈNE IONESCO, LUIGI PIRANDELLO, and JEAN GENET—but also their American brethren—EDWARD ALBEE, ISRAEL HOROVITZ, and SAM SHEPARD, who would emerge as some of the most influential American playwrights of the 20th century.

From the 1950s onward, off-Broadway drama played an increasingly important role in New York theater. For example, while 1960 was a "disastrous" year for Broadway, according to Daniel Blum (1977), it found off-Broadway "more active than ever," with such productions as Albee's ZOO STORY, a revival of HENRIK IBSEN's HEDDA GABLER, and the premiere of an off-Broadway classic, Tom Jones and Harvey Schmidt's The Fantasticks. Off-Broadway productions soon began to receive Drama Critics' Circle Awards (a 1963 citation for Circle in the Square's The Trojan Women), and its alternative theaters were also the site of the first salvos of the black theater movement, such as AMIRI BARAKA's DUTCHMAN (1964), as well as ADRIENNE KENNEDY's Funnyhouse of a Negro (1964). By 1967, in Blum's opinion, audiences had discovered that the "high-caliber productions . . . flourishing Off-Broadway" were "more exciting fare than Broadway offered"; and by the turn of the 21st century, off-Broadway had established itself as the U.S. center for serious live drama.

OFF-OFF-BROADWAY

While off-Broadway theater started in the early 1950s as an alternative to Broadway theater, in the 1960s off-off-Broadway began to produce even more radical alternatives to mainstream drama. In 1966 Village Voice critic Michael Smith defined off-off-Broadway not simply as a new wrinkle in playwriting but as "a novel form of theater":

> It is amateur theater done largely by professionals. It is theater with no resources but the most sophisticated audience in America. It is both casual community theater and dedicated experimental theater. It is proposing an alternative to an established theater which hardly knows it exists. (Orzel and Smith, 1966)

While off-Broadway theater was a way of producing dramas that could not find a Broadway home because of the changing economics and aesthetics of commercial theater, off-off-Broadway productions were a collective challenge to accepted definitions of theater in general.

Theater historian Arthur Sainer (1997) saw this fundamentally different viewpoint at play in the superrealistic stage presence of the LIVING THEATRE actors who played junkies in JACK GELBER's The Connection (1959). Noting that critic Kenneth Tynan felt the characters of the play "are beyond the reach of drama, as we commonly define the word," Sainer wrote that the apparent passivity of the actors playing heroin addicts was "not passivity at all but an absence of drama," which had to do "not with character being made but with performers ceasing to make performances." According to Sainer, the most notable and ultimately influential element of The Connection was a shift of focus away from the "presence of character," which had been carefully cultivated in American drama, and especially since the advent of KONSTANTIN STANISLAVSKY–style techniques, and to the "presence of performer." To Sainer's eyes, "some essential loosening, . . . some radical loosening of the fabric of drama was taking place before our eyes."

This "loosening of the fabric of drama" would become more pronounced in the 1960s and 1970s with the advent of HAPPENINGS, PERFORMANCE ART, and solo performance, all of which were connected to the development of off-off-Broadway. At Judson Church in Greenwich Village's Washington Square the Judson Poet's Theater produced plays by poets and musicals by the Reverend Al Carmines. At Ellen Stewart's La MaMa Experimental Theatre Club, dozens of new playwrights such as Jean-Claude van Itallie, Julie Bovasso, Sam Shepard, ROCHELLE OWENS, Leonard Melfi, MEGAN TERRY, LANFORD WILSON, MARIA IRENE FORNES, H. M. Koutoukas, and Tom Eyen presented fabric-loosening works directed by Joe Cino, Tom O'Horgan, Marshall Mason, and others. Cino himself started his own theater, the Caffe Cino, joining other off-off-Broadway venues including Theatre Genesis and Theater for the New City. In addition, off-off-Broadway nurtured particular theater groups such as Joseph Chaikin's Open Theatre (whose playwrights included Terry, Van Itallie, and SUSAN YANKOWITZ), Richard Schechner's Performance Group, the Bread and Puppet Theater, and RICHARD FOREMAN's Ontological Hysteric Theater.

SYMBIOSIS AND SELF-SUFFICIENCY

While the distinctions between off-off-Broadway and off-Broadway have always been fluid and somewhat amorphous, the stark, confrontational form and content of early off-off-Broadway plays by Sam Shepard (Chicago, 1965) and Lanford Wilson (The Madness of Lady Bright, 1964) stand in sharp contrast to their later, more accessible works. Off-off-Broadway nurtured Shepard's and Wilson's playwriting as they honed their craft and ultimately achieved Broadway respectability, and this is a mark of the symbiotic relationship that developed among off-off-, off-, and Broadway itself. In other words, for many playwrights off-off-Broadway stages were the first steps on a path that led uptown through off-Broadway theaters to Broadway, and then on to regional theaters and perhaps Hollywood.

On the other hand, by the 1980s off-off-Broadway also had became its own self-sufficient enterprise, offering a secure platform for such playwrights as MAC WELLMAN, Richard Foreman, and ROMULUS LINNEY, whose works remained centered on its stages; as well as The Wooster Group and the Ridiculous Theatre, companies who achieved success and relative stability by pointedly avoiding Broadway, content in their ability to draw crowds to their own downtown theaters. Off-Broadway could also function in the same way.

By the end of the 20th century, the worlds of off-Broadway and off-off-Broadway had been augmented by the solidification of "performance" as its own genre, in such venues as P.S. 122, Dance Theater Workshop, and The Kitchen. New York City remained the center of American theater, but no longer simply because of Broadway, which had long since ceased to be the sole measure of a playwright's success. Instead, a rich array of different types of live theater offered themselves to those audiences inspired enough to choose drama and performance instead of television, film, and the Internet.

[*See also* United States, 1940–Present]

FURTHER READING

Banes, Sally. *Greenwich Village 1963: Avant-Garde Performance and the Effervescent Body.* Durham: Duke Univ. Press, 1993.

Blum, Daniel. *A Pictorial History of American Theatre: 1860–1976.* Rev. 4th ed. New York: Crown, 1977.

Cordell, Richard A., and Lowell Matson, eds. *The Off-Broadway Theatre: Seven Plays.* New York: Random House, 1959.

Miller, Arthur. "A Visit with Castro." *The Nation* 278, no. 2 (2004): 13–17.

Orzel, Nick, and Michael Smith, eds. *Eight Plays from Off-Off Broadway.* New York: Bobbs-Merrill, 1966.

Price, Julia S. *The Off-Broadway Theater.* New York: Scarecrow, 1962.

Sainer, Arthur. *The New Radical Theatre Notebook.* New York: Applause, 1997.

John Bell

OFFENDING THE AUDIENCE

PETER HANDKE's controversial play *Offending the Audience* (*Publikumsbeschimpfung*) premiered in Frankfurt, GERMANY, on June 8, 1966, under the direction of CLAUS PEYMANN. When several offended audience members rushed the stage and began tousling with the actors, the first performance created a sensation in the German theater world. It also established the twenty-three-year-old author as one of the most important, innovative, and provocative writers of postwar German-language literature.

Originally conceived as a manifesto against the established conventions of the theater, *Offending the Audience* provides an important theoretical critique of representational theater, in which a dramatic story is acted out as an enclosed world in front of a hidden audience. Handke's one-act *Sprechstück* (language play) seeks to demolish theater's imaginary fourth wall in a stream of words spoken directly to the audience by four nameless speakers. Using repetition, variation, and contradiction in the rhythmic mode of 1960s beat music, the text penetrates into the psyche of the audience, frustrating—and making them conscious of—their theatergoing habits and expectations: "This

room does not make believe it is a room. The side that is open to you is not the fourth wall of a house. . . . There is no back door. Neither is there a non-existent door as in modern drama. The non-existent door does not represent a non-existent door. . . . This stage is not a world, just as a world is not a stage." Handke's play insists that its audience become the characters in their own play and thereby confront the institutional reality of the theater.

True to its name, *Offending the Audience* ends with the speakers intoning a rhythmic mix of anachronistic and stinging invective. The point of the insults is not to attack a bourgeois and politically complacent theatergoing public as much as an effort to elicit an immediate visceral reaction to words—and thereby completely erase the line between stage and audience. Michael Roloff, who translated the play into English, has suggested it would be more accurate to call the play "Public Insult." In 2000, Roloff recommended that new productions contemporize the insults while still preserving the linguistic rhythms and variation between scathing barbs and quaintly old-fashioned and impersonal diatribe.

Despite its contemptuous critique of classical and contemporary theater conventions, *Offending the Audience* paradoxically continues a centuries-old German theater tradition as much as it tries to depart from it. From Friedrich Schiller's (1759–1805) "moral institution" through BERTOLT BRECHT's EPIC THEATER to the politically charged DOCUMENTARY theater of ROLF HOCHHUTH, HEINAR KIPPHARDT, and PETER WEISS in the 1960s, German playwrights have conceived of theater as an ideal institution for effecting revolutionary social and political change. While Handke's play insists that representational theater is incapable of accurately showing its audience the world outside the theater (either in the form of a problem or a solution), its critique carries on German theater's pedagogical crusade—if now pedantically and obsessively—by dramatizing language's function as a means of social control. Inadvertently, then, *Offending the Audience*'s aesthetic renewal of German drama also renewed the revolutionary potential of the theater.

FURTHER READING

Firda, Richard Arthur. *Peter Handke.* New York: Twayne, 1993.

Handke, Peter. *Offending the Audience. Plays,* 1. Tr. by Michael Roloff. Intro. by Tom Kuhn. London: Methuen Drama, 1997.

Klinkowitz, James, and James Knowlton. *Peter Handke and the Postmodern Transformation: The Goalie's Journey Home.* Columbia: Univ. of Missouri Press, 1983.

Roloff, Michael. "A 30 Year-After Near-Posthumous Note on Peter Handke's 'Public Insult.'" *Translation Journal* 4, no. 3 (2000). http://accurapid.com/journal/13insult.htm.

Schlueter, June. *The Plays and Novels of Peter Handke.* Pittsburgh: Univ. of Pittsburgh Press, 1981.

Jeffrey Schneider

OHASHI YASUHIKO (1956–)

Japanese playwright Ohashi Yasuhiko is a member of the fourth generation of post-1960 "little theatre" (ANGURA and SHŌGEKIJŌ) practitioners and was heavily influenced by TSUKA KŌHEI, foremost representative of the second generation. Tsuka, though shaped by the activism and student unrest of the first generation, forged a playwriting style remarkable for its humorous, ABSURDIST slant on the serious problems of youth. That approach, coupled with the unbridled economic growth of the late-1980s "bubble economy" that fueled widespread pursuit of pleasure, spawned plays concerned less with social reform than with an apolitical, inward-looking journey of self-discovery.

Ohashi's work is visually distinctive for its ingenious stage settings that dazzle spectators with special effects like flowing lava and tossing waves (he majored in electrical engineering). His plays germinate, he maintains, not with an idea or theme but with the performance space, to which he shapes the action in novel ways. To indulge his approach, Ohashi established the Freedom Boat Company (Riburesen) in 1983. Its name combines the Spanish word libre with the Japanese sen or "boat." Written in characters, another meaning emerges: ri means "separation," bu "wind," and re (close to rei) "spirit"—hence, Ohashi defines his theater as indulging in unfettered spiritual journeys to distant shores.

His style is evident in The Red Bird Has Fled . . . (1986), a play based on the worst disaster in aviation history: the 1985 Japan Airlines crash that killed 520 of 524 passengers. The main character is a woman who survived the crash but lost her family. The action occurs ten years after the crash, when Japan Airlines has hired her for a television commercial in an attempt to improve its image and revenues. The undying intensity of feeling for her deceased family empowers her to time warp from the commercial back to the living room of her old home with her family. Ohashi sensitively shows how quickly a heart-rending tragedy, though permanently etched on the bereaved, can fade from mass memory into the black hole of corporate profit.

His signature play is Godzilla (1987), which was awarded the prestigious Kishida Kunio Drama Prize in 1988. Ohashi again uses an actual event as backdrop, this time focusing on the 1986 volcanic eruption on Oshima, an island south of Tokyo. The play opens some time later with a young woman, Yayoi, hiking on the island. She encounters the monster Godzilla, who has been awakened by the volcano, and they fall in love. Members of both families are resistant; steeped in their respective ethnocentric assumptions, each side cites its own common sense and raise the issue of progeny, with great comic effect. At play's end, Yayoi sees her blissful dream fragmented but realizes that such illusions make life possible.

Through Godzilla, a man-made illusion, Ohashi uses this beauty-and-beast love story to plumb the aesthetics of love and suffering, to bemoan the superficiality of the prejudiced mind and the erosion of the ties binding people together. Ohashi senses that only through situations of crisis can he shake his spectators into an awareness of such serious ideas. Contemporary Japanese shingeki playwright INOUE HISASHI has called the work "a masterpiece."

[See also Japan]

SELECT PLAYS: Can't Really Dance (Dansu wa Umaku Odorenai, 1983); The Red Bird Has Fled . . . (Akai Tori Nigeta . . . , 1986); Godzilla (Gojira, 1987); Mind (Maindo, 1989); The Times, Already . . . (Jidai, Sude ni . . . , 1990); Long Long Time Ago (1992); If I Were Born . . . (Tanjōsuru nara . . . 1994); It's the Black Ships! (Kurobune da!, 1995); Anybody Will Do! (Doitsumo Koitsumo!, 1997); Ichirō's Disaster (Ichirō no Sainan, 1999); Subjection 2002 (Sabujekushon, 2002)

FURTHER READING

Ohashi Yasuhiko. Akai Tori Nigeta . . . [The Red Bird Has Fled . . .]. Tokyo: Hakusuisha, 1989.

——. Godzilla. Tr. by John K. Gillespie. In Half a Century of Japanese Theater III: 1980s Part 1, ed. by Japan Playwrights Association. Tokyo: Kinokuniya, 2001.

——. Gojira [Godzilla]. Tokyo: Hakusuisha, 1988.

Senda Akihiko. The Voyage of Contemporary Japanese Theatre. Tr. by J. Thomas Rimer. Honolulu: Univ. of Hawaii Press, 1997.

Watanabe Eriko, et al. Gekisakka Hachinin ni yoru Rojikku Geimu [Mind Games from Eight Playwrights]. Tokyo: Hakusuisha, 1992.

John K. Gillespie

OKAMOTO KIDŌ (1872–1939)

Okamato Kidō (1872–1939) was a Japanese Shin kabuki playwright, theater critic, journalist, and novelist. Okamato's name is synonymous with a certain type of writing for kabuki, one that almost never upset the predilections of kabuki audiences, who would usually be watching classic plays alongside Okamoto's, but could sometimes be modern enough to provoke intellectual comment. Those plays of Okamoto that have survived now appeal to more traditional tastes, unlike the plays of MAYAMA SEIKA, the thinking man's shin kabuki playwright.

Okamoto's father's friendship with Ichikawa Danjūrō IX, the leading kabuki actor of the day, and his own frequent trips to kabuki turned his early literary aspirations toward the theater. Unable to complete his education because of his family's declining fortunes, he became a journalist. He began writing plays during the last years of the 19th century, but in spite of reforms of kabuki spearheaded by the sam Danjūrū, it was still difficult for an outsider to break into the world of kabuki. After some initial failures, Okamoto burst onto the theater scene with TALE OF SHUZENJI (Shuzenji Monogatari, 1911), which—with kabuki actor Ichikawa Sadanji II in the lead—was something of a sensation at its premiere. At a stroke Okamoto was famous as a writer of new-style period dramas. Sadanji, not a skillful actor of traditional *kabuki* roles, had been identified by *kabuki* management as likely to be successful in new plays, with their greater emphasis on dialogue. Okamoto was teamed up with Sadanji and became a full-time playwright.

The decade from *Tale of Shuzenji* was Okamoto's most productive, with plays such as *Onoe and Idahachi* (*Onoe Idahahi*, 1915) and *Love Suicide at Toribeyama* (*Toribeyama Shinjū*, 1915). *Onoe and Idahachi* was consummate theater in its use of stage effects, mainly of natural phenomena, but most interest centered on the main character, Idahachi. As a once-handsome samurai who had botched his love suicide with Onoe, already by the start of the play Idahachi is a depraved executioner, who mistreats and finally kills his former lover. In his defiant rejection of the noble values that he formerly espoused as a samurai, Idahachi broke the mold of the classical double-suicide hero.

The moonlit presuicide scene of *Love Suicide at Toribeyama* is still a favorite with *kabuki* audiences, and Okamoto invests this tenderly romantic story with many features of traditional theater. Hankurō, a samurai in the shogun's bodyguard, falls deeply in love with a young prostitute of infinitely lower status. He commits a crime for which he knows he must kill himself, and she determines to follow him in death. Their mutual farewells have a carefully designed sentimentality that has never failed to engage audiences' emotions.

Generalizing about Okamoto is difficult because, like many regular writers for *kabuki*, his total corpus is huge (around 200 plays) and varied. One feature of his DRAMATURGY that stands out is his abiding concern to show that the complex psychology of samurai characters, expressed principally through the body in classical *kabuki*, could be theatrically effective within the same environment when mediated by dialogue rather than action.

[*See also* Japan; *Shingeki*]

SELECT PLAYS: *Tale of Shuzenji* (*Shuzenji Monogatari*, 1911); *Love Suicide at Toribeyama* (*Toribeyama Shinjū*, 1915); *Onoe and Idahachi* (*Onoe Idahahi*, 1915); *History of Theatre in the Tenpō Era* (*Tenpō Engeki-shi*, 1929); *Araki Mataemon* (1930)

FURTHER READING

Keene, Donald. *Dawn to the West: Japanese Literature of the Modern Era: Poetry, Drama and Criticism.* New York: Holt, Rinehart & Winston, 1984.

Leiter, Samuel L. *New Kabuki Encyclopedia: A Revised Adaptation of Kabuki Jiten.* Westport, Conn.: Greenwood Press, 1997.

Okamoto Keiichi, ed. *Okamoto Kidō Nikki* [Diary of Okamoto Kidō]. Tokyo: Seiabō, 1987–1989.

Ōyama Isao. *Okamoto Kidō, Hito to Sakuhin* [Okamoto Kidō: The man and his works]. Tokorozawa, Saitrama: Gikyokushi Kenkyūkai, 1988.

Brian Powell

OLD STONE MANSION

Playwright MAHESH ELKUNCHWAR refers to *Old Stone Mansion* (*Wada Chirebandi*) as his "flesh and blood" play. It is a close study of relationships among members of a feudal family caught in the turbulent transition toward urbanization and industrialization. The play represents a break from Elkunchwar's earlier symbolic, "experimental" plays in terms of theme, form, and theater.

First performed in Mumbai in 1985 by Kalavaibhav, *Old Stone Mansion* centers on the Dharangaonkar Deshpande family from Vidarbha, a village in Northern Maharashtra representative of villages in postindependence INDIA. Tatyaji, the head of the family, though a Brahmin, has been a farmer. The play begins after his death. Bhaskar, the eldest son and now head of the family, clings to tradition for security and comfort, which it cannot give any more. The second son, Sudhir, has migrated to Mumbai and personifies "modern" life with its opportunities, individualism, and freedom from tradition. The third son, Chandu, exemplifies the suffering of the servile and unprivileged brothers in a traditional setup where brothers cannot marry unless their sisters are married off, where they cannot enter into any other profession apart from the traditional occupation, and where they have to lead a life of endless work and servility. The children from the young generation are rebellious but do not know exactly how to resolve the identity crisis—they take easy ways out. Ranju, the daughter, takes the family gold and elopes with her teacher, while Parag, the son, drops out of school. The mothers, wives, and daughters, whose aspirations for self-reliance, education, and freedom cannot find any fulfillment either in the feudal patriarchal or the modern urban ethos, are caught up in the family drama. Yet it is the women who save the family from immediate disintegration. Family prestige in the village requires performing certain rituals after death, but that requires money that the family does not have. So the mother sells her part of the house to the moneylender, while the eldest daughter-in-law foregoes gold in order to save the honor of her family and her daughter and establishes a connection with the younger daughter-in-law to maintain family ties.

Old Stone Mansion was followed by two sequels because, in Elkunchwar's words, "the characters had entered my home; [and] they wouldn't leave. . . . They continued to live with me and grow" (1989). Elkunchwar wrote *Engrossed on the Shores of a Lake* (*Magna Talyakathi*, 1994) and *End of an Epoch* (*Yuganta*, 1994), which continue the family saga. There is a gap of ten years between the plot of each play. On April 11, 1994, all three plays were performed in succession over the course of eight hours, an experiment that had never been attempted in the Marathi theater.

FURTHER READING

Elkunchwar, Mahesh. *Autobiography.* Calcutta: Seagull Press, 1989.

——. *Old Stone Mansion.* Calcutta: Seagull Press, 1989.

Gokhale, Shanta. *Playwright at the Centre: Marathi Drama from 1843 to the Present.* Calcutta: Seagull Press, 2000.

Maya Pandit

OLD TIMES

First presented in 1971 by the Royal Shakespeare Company, *Old Times* displays HAROLD PINTER's continued interest in power dynamics and language. The play, which opened to critical acclaim, is seen as an improvement on earlier treatments of control, possession, sexuality, and dominance. As Ronald Bryden states in a review for *The Observer*, "On Pinter territory, every question is an attempt to control and every answer a swift evasion." All three characters are in their forties, although the content of their discussion lies twenty years in the past. As they sit together, Kate is the focus of a duel between Deeley, her husband, and Anna, her former roommate. Deeley and Anna battle to possess Kate, using the past to stake their claims and bait each other in a struggle for power. Kate meanwhile switches allegiances and observes silently before staking her own independence at the conclusion of *Old Times*.

As the play opens, Kate and Deeley discuss Kate's recollections of Anna, whom Kate has not seen in twenty years, and Deeley asks many questions about Anna that Kate cannot answer. Anna stands alone upstage, with her back to the audience. The scene then shifts to postdinner discussion, with Anna offering a series of recollections. Deeley's responses are competitive: he suggests that Anna is aging and later attempts to objectify her as a sexual object. Their conversation consists of short sentences interspersed with awkward, charged pauses. Deeley and Anna speak of Kate, who remains quiet, in the third person. The two initiate a musical battle, singing lines from songs with undertones of possession, and then return to reminiscences of Kate. Kate observes their objectification of her, but her protests are ignored. Setting Deeley outside of their connection, Kate begins talking to Anna as if they are still young and living together. Kate leaves the room to take a bath as the lights fade.

In the second act, Deeley recalls meeting Anna years before at a tavern and later looking up her skirt as she sat across from him. They then discuss drying Kate, the object of their competition, after her bath. Deeley attempts to assert his dominance again by remarking that Anna must be forty. Kate enters, wearing a bathrobe, as the other two sing to her. Kate and Anna continue their discussion of past acquaintances, as if still living in the past, until Deeley interrupts to bring Anna to the present. Their conversation grows more contentious until Kate dismisses her husband: "If you don't like it, go." Kate then shifts and presents an image of Anna, dead. The final action takes place in silence. Anna walks away as Deeley begins sobbing. After she returns to recline on the divan, Deeley stops. He walks over to stand above Anna, then returns to lay his head in Kate's lap. Finally he moves away and sits alone in an armchair. The three thus end the play isolated and silent, with connections broken down through their power struggle and Kate's final assertion of individuality.

[See also England, 1960–1980]

FURTHER READING

Cahn, Victor L. *Gender and Power in the Plays of Harold Pinter*. New York: St. Martin's, 1993.

Dukore, Bernard F. *Where Laughter Stops: Pinter's Tragicomedy*. Columbia: Univ. of Missouri Press, 1976.

Gale, Steven H. "Deadly Mind Games: Harold Pinter's *Old Times*." In *Critical Essays on Harold Pinter*, ed. by Steven H. Gale. Boston: G. K. Hall, 1990.

Robin Seaton Brown

OLEANNA

You vicious little bitch. You think you can come in here with your political correctness and destroy my life?
—John, Act 3

Few recent plays have provoked as much controversy as *Oleanna*, DAVID MAMET's scathing exploration of sexual harassment on a college campus. The three-act, two-character play opened at the American Repertory Theatre in Cambridge, Massachusetts, in 1992 and transferred to New York's OFF-BROADWAY Orpheum Theatre later that year. *Oleanna* has been the subject of dozens of scholarly articles and has been produced by professional and university theaters throughout the UNITED STATES, ENGLAND, and CANADA. A film version, directed by Mamet himself, was released in 1994.

The title *Oleanna* refers to a failed 19th-century utopian community, a metaphor for Mamet's depiction of contemporary academia. The play centers on a college professor, John, and his student, Carol. In act 1, Carol has come to John seeking guidance after receiving a poor grade on a paper. John, preoccupied with his ongoing tenure review and his upcoming purchase of a house, offers a variety of opinions and advice on Carol's situation. In act 2, we learn that subsequent to their previous meeting Carol has formally accused John of sexual harassment, which has threatened his chances for tenure. Their second meeting is combative, as both characters strive to define and control the terms of their interaction. Finally, in act 3, the conflict between John and Carol escalates, culminating in physical violence.

Coming in the wake of the October 1991 confirmation hearings for Supreme Court justice Clarence Thomas, *Oleanna* struck a nerve with audiences still struggling to define sexual harassment. Responses to the play tended to be polarized, with critics either praising Mamet's insightful critique of "political correctness" on college campuses or excoriating the play for its perceived misogyny. Those taking the former view point to the unspecified "group" that has advised Carol to file a formal complaint, to her request that certain books be removed from the course syllabus, and to her charge that John's attempt to prevent her from leaving his office at the end of act 2 constitutes attempted rape. Those advocating the view that the play is misogynistic and reactionary argue that Carol is unrealistically aggressive, that she overreacts to trivial slights, and that John's physical attack on her at the end of the play represents a male fantasy of revenge on women who dare claim they have been sexually harassed.

More recent critics have argued that the play is less about the specific issue of sexual harassment than about the general relationship between power, pedagogy, and language. Both characters are at fault, and to attempt to assign blame is as unproductive as it is impossible. Rather, *Oleanna* depicts a system in which power flows to the person who can control the terms of the conversation, a theme prominent in Mamet's earlier work GLENGARRY GLEN ROSS (1983). That power, moreover, becomes an end in itself, with the result that the teacher-student relationship, which ideally should be cooperative, becomes competitive. Carol and John have no hope of achieving reconciliation because each is obsessed with winning the battle of words.

Mamet himself refers to the play as a TRAGEDY, in which John undergoes a reversal of fortune (the loss of his tenured position) and a final moment of recognition (after he loses control and resorts to violence). Despite good intentions from both characters, the ending is, in the playwright's words, "surprising and inevitable."

FURTHER READING

Badenhausen, Richard. "The Modern Academy Raging in the Dark: Misreading Mamet's Political Incorrectness in *Oleanna*." *College Literature* 25, no. 3 (September 1998): 1–19.

Murphy, Brenda. "*Oleanna*: Language and Power." In *The Cambridge Companion to David Mamet*, ed. by Christopher Bigsby. Cambridge: Cambridge Univ. Press, 2004. 124–137.

Norman, Geoffrey, and John Rezek. "Working the Con." In *David Mamet in Conversation*, ed. by Leslie Kane. Ann Arbor: Univ. of Michigan Press, 2001. 123–142.

Skloot, Robert. "*Oleanna*, or, the Play of Pedagogy." In *Gender and Genre: Essays on David Mamet*, ed. by Christopher C. Hudgins and Leslie Kane. New York: Palgrave, 2001. 95–107.

Henry Bial

OLESHA, YURY (1899–1960)

Yury Karlovich Olesha was a Russian prose writer, playwright, and diarist whose works exploring the irreconcilable paradoxes of social upheaval, though few in number, were among the most influential of the early Soviet era. He wrote the drama *The Game of Executioner's Block* (*Igra v plakhu*) in 1920 (published 1921 and 1934 but not produced) and began publishing feuilletons in 1921, although his greatest achievement was the novel *Envy*, printed in 1927 and reworked in 1929 as an independent play, A CONSPIRACY OF FEELINGS (*Zagovor chuvstv*). It was followed by his fairy-tale novel *The Three Fat Men* (*Tri Tolstyaka*), which he published in 1928 and dramatized in 1930. By the

time he completed the original play *A List of Assets* (*Spisok blagodeyanii*) in 1931, his literary career effectively was at an end. Afterward he wrote some screenplays, unfinished plays, and a smattering of stories and essays. He kept a diary from 1929 until his death, portions of which were published posthumously in *Not a Day Without a Line* (1965) and *Book of Farewell* (1999).

Olesha may be seen as an archetype of the refined artist who is left untouched physically but rendered helpless by a totalitarian state. His work reflected the basic conflicts of his age when the needs of the individual were placed second to the requirements of the masses, and practicality and expediency were the new gods. Sincerely attempting to embrace this utilitarian and supposedly egalitarian age, he was disturbed to see the great, though imperfect, human emotions of love, hate, jealousy, vanity, and their corollaries declared obsolete and counterproductive. His speech explaining his point of view at the 1st Congress of the Writers Union of the U.S.S.R. in 1934 was controversial. His works commonly revolved around a tragic rift separating old and new, emotions and reason, creative aimlessness and the pragmatism of progress. Famed for the subtle use of metaphors in his prose, Olesha created slightly contrived and melodramatic but compelling dramas in which characters embody contrasting ideas.

A Conspiracy of Feelings explored a world in which dreamers and poets are marginalized by prudent functionaries. In it one senses Olesha's ardent desire to present all sides with understanding, although his affinity for the "useless" romantic Kavalerov is evident. In *A List of Assets* a Soviet actress seeks freedom of expression in Europe but discovers the crass dictatorship of commerce and dies a disillusioned heroine, shielding a communist protestor from a policeman's bullet. Written for VSEVOLOD MEYERHOLD, it was one of this director's most hotly debated, though short-lived, productions of a contemporary play. The unfinished masterwork *The Death of Zand* (*Smert' Zanda*, c. 1929–1933), about a writer who struggles to overcome his own nature but, in the end, cannot force himself to write to order, was commissioned by the MOSCOW ART THEATRE but produced elsewhere only in 1986. An exception to the rule of Olesha's usual thematic is *The Three Fat Men*, a merry tale about three despots representing wealth, indolence, and gluttony who are overthrown with the aid of itinerant actors. Dramatized for the Moscow Art Theatre, it did not last long in repertory, although it and other dramatizations of the novel were popular throughout the 20th century.

[See also Russia and the Soviet Union]

PLAYS: *The Game of Executioner's Block* (*Igra v plakhu*, published 1921 and 1934); *A Conspiracy of Feelings* (*Zagovor chuvstv*, 1929); *The Death of Zand* (*Smert' Zanda*, unfinished, c. 1929–1933, produced 1986); *The Three Fat Men* (*Tri Tolstyaka*, 1930); *A List of Assets* (*Spisok blagodeyanii*, 1931)

FURTHER READING

Beaujour, Elizabeth K. *The Invisible Land: A Study of the Artistic Imagination of Iurii Olesha.* New York: Columbia Univ. Press, 1970.

Gudkova, Violetta. *Yu. Olesha i Vs. Meyerhold v rabote nad spektaklem "Spisok blagodeyanii"* [Yu. Olesha and Vs. Meyerhold at work on the production of *A List of Assets*]. Moscow: Novoye literaturnoye obozreniye, 2002.

Olesha, Yury Karlovich. *No Day Without a Line: From Notebooks.* Ed. and tr. by Judson Rosengrant. Evanston, Ill.: Northwestern Univ. Press, 1998.

———. *The Complete Plays.* Ed. and tr. by Michael Green and Jerome Katsell. Ann Arbor: Ardis, 1983.

Peppard, Victor. *The Poetics of Yury Olesha.* Gainesville: Univ. of Florida Press, 1989.

Segel, Harold B. *Twentieth-Century Russian Drama from Gorky to the Present.* Rev. ed. New York: Performing Arts Journal Pubs., 1993.

John Freedman

OLSEN, ERNST BRUUN (1923–)

When I write I do not see the lines. I hear them spoken by actors. I am not a writer, I am a man of the theatre.

—Ernst Bruun Olsen, 1977

Ernst Bruun Olsen, born on February 12, 1923, in Nakskov, started his career as an actor and has directed most of his own plays. Like many dramatists of his generation, he made his debut in the radio theater, then an important incubator for new Danish drama. From 1958 until the stunning success of his and the composer Finn Savery's musical *Teenagerlove* in 1962 at the Royal Theatre in Copenhagen Olsen wrote almost exclusively for the radio.

Through the story of the pop star Billy Jack, who on his way to the top betrays his faithful wife and his proletarian background, Olsen satirizes the cynicism and cold speculation of the entertainment industry and the new publicity-driven consumer society. With *Teenagerlove* the Royal Theatre had, according to the critic Svend Kragh-Jacobsen, taken the leap into the musical age with élan, talent, and professional know-how. The musical with Savery's refined mingling of twisted pop and JAZZ attracted a large audience of young people who would probably otherwise never have dreamed of visiting the Royal Theatre.

A strong social and political commitment is the motor of Olsen's dramatic work, including contemporary plays and historical dramas. Among the first are the untranslatable *Bal I den Borgerlige* (1966), the result of a new happy collaboration with Savery, satirizing the working-class takeover of middle-class values; *The Trapped Prometheus* (*Prometheus i saksen*, 1981), a witty and cruel display of the self-censorship of the media; and *Reflections in a Mirror* (*En kvinde spejler sig*, 1995), a woman's reflections on her past and present.

Olsen's inspiration from BERTOLT BRECHT is evident, most clearly in the historical play *The Peaceable* (*De fredsommelige*, 1969),

taking place during the war between DENMARK and SWEDEN (1658–1660) and dealing with the ordinary people in the great men's war. Many of Olsen's historical plays are metaplays, bringing the theater up for discussion: *The Poetic Frenzy* (*Den poetiske raptus*, 1976), leaving the stage to the father of Danish drama, Ludvig Holberg, and his troupe of actors; *Claire Lacombe and the Great Revolution* (*Claire Lacombe og den store revolution*, 1989), introducing an until-then-unknown actress as heroine); and *Betty Nansen on Betty Nansen* (*Betty Nansen på Betty Nansen*, 1991), an homage to the Danish actress and theater manager, performed in the theater she in 1917 named after herself. All three plays deal with the responsibility of the artist and the theater.

Permanent themes in Olsen's plays are the manipulating forces keeping the population in a state of uncritical consumers, and a praise of women as the sex in possession of common sense, honesty, and vigor, which might make the world a better place to live. With an unfailing sense of style, revealing the true man of the theater, Olsen alternates between a richness of forms and techniques.

SELECT PLAYS: *Teenagerlove* (1962); *Bal I den Borgerlige* (1966); *Where Did Nora Go When She Went Out?* (*Hvor gik Nora hen, da hun gik ud,* 1968); *The Peaceable* (*De fredsommelige,* 1969); *The Poetic Frenzy* (*Den poetiske raptus,* 1976); *The Postman from Arles* (*Postbudet fra Arles,* 1974); *The Trapped Prometheus* (*Prometheus i saksen,* 1981); *Claire Lacombe and the Great Revolution* (*Claire Lacombe og den store revolution,* 1989); *Betty Nansen on Betty Nansen* (*Betty Nansen på Betty Nansen,* 1991); *Irene and Her Men* (*Irene og hendes mænd,* 1992); *Reflections in a Mirror* (*En kvinde spejler sig,* 1995)

FURTHER READING

Lundgren, Henrik. "Ernst Bruun Olsen." In *Danske digtere i det 20. århundrede.* Vol. 4. Ed. by Torben Brostrom and Mette Winge. 3d ed. Copenhagen: Gad, 1982.

Rifbjerg, Klaus. "Teenagerlove." *Vindrosen* 1 (1963).

Rubin, Don. *World Encyclopedia of Contemporary Theatre.* Vol. 1, Europe. New York: Routledge, 2001.

Kela Kvam

ON A MUGGY NIGHT IN MUMBAI

On a Muggy Night in Mumbai by MAHESH DATTANI (first performed at the Tata Theatre in Mumbai, INDIA, on November 23, 1998, in a production directed by Lillette Dubey) is the first Indian play to deal openly with issues of homosexuality and to deal sympathetically with questions of love, partnership, trust, and betrayal between gay characters. It shows what happens when members of the gay community are forced into the closet by a hypocritical society.

This bilingual play (in Hindi and English) centers on Kamlesh who, after being dumped by his lover Ed, finds that Ed has proposed to his sister Kiran. It turns out that Ed wants to use his marriage with Kiran to serve as a smokescreen for a continued relationship with Kamlesh. In other words, Ed cannot face being openly gay. The other characters in the play include Bunny, who camouflages his homosexuality with a conventional marriage to a woman, and Ranjit, who has moved to Europe where he can live an openly gay life with his English partner. "Yes, I am sometimes regretful of being an Indian," he says sadly, "because I can't seem to be both Indian and gay." But, he says, he is not ashamed of being gay and accuses Bunny of hiding his shame in marriage. Toward the end of the play Bunny comes to the realization that his wife does not really know him and that the only people who really know him hate him for being a hypocrite. "I have tried to survive. In both worlds," he says. "And it seems I do not exist in either." One of Dattani's strengths as a writer is his ability to use humor to move the audience or to make a point without being sentimental or didactic: "I really wish they would allow gay people to marry," Kiran sighs. "Oh, they do," quips Ranjit. "Only not to the same sex."

Another of Dattani's strengths lies in his ability to intertwine scenes so that each gains depth from the other. The first meeting between Kiran and Ed is intercut with a scene where Kamlesh reveals to Kiran that he loves Ed (without mentioning Ed's name), another scene in which Kiran tells Kamlesh how much she loves Ed, and a fourth scene in which Kamlesh tries to keep Ed from leaving by trying to make him proud (rather than ashamed) of his homosexuality. Time and place collapse in the emotional turmoil caused by a society that forces homosexuality underground.

On a Muggy Night in Mumbai opened to both wildly positive reviews and storm of protest by people wanting to ban a play that condemns society for the way it positions homosexuality. However, it touched many of its audience members deeply: several came up to Dattani after the show and thanked him profusely for writing a play about gay issues. Some of them shared their own stories. The play had a long run in Mumbai and was successfully received when it toured New York. Dattani made the play into a movie called *Mango Souffle*.

[See also Gay and Lesbian Drama]

FURTHER READING

Dattani, Mahesh. *Collected Plays*. 2 vol. New York: Penguin, 2000–2005.

Kumar, T. Vijay. "Dattani Transforms Good Themes Into Good Theatre." *Deccan Chronicle* (Hyderabad) (March 5, 2000).

Malli, Avy. " 'Muggy Night' Raises the Curtain on South Asian Gay Issues." *AsianWeek.com* (June 21–27, 2002). http://www.asianweek.com/2002_06_21/arts_muggynight.html.

"Out of the Closet, on the Screen." *The Hindu* (March 9, 2003). http://www.hinduonnet.com/thehindu/mag/2003/03/09/stories/2003030900660500.htm.

Erin B. Mee

ONCE IN A LIFETIME

In the play *Once in a Lifetime* by Moss Hart and George S. Kaufman, George, Jerry, and May leave vaudeville and head for Hollywood, where they start an elocution school for silent film actors trying to adapt to the "talkies." Herman Glogauer, a blustering boss but actually the helpless slave of the studio he pretends to command, gives them space on his own lot, and George falls in love with Susan, an inept young actress who is just as charming and foolish as he is.

When Glogauer threatens to close the school, George denounces the studio so forcefully that the boss makes him supervisor in charge of all production. George shoots a script Glogauer rejected, but the film garners raves, and even George's impulsive purchase of 2,000 airplanes becomes a stroke of inspiration when every studio decides to make aerial pictures and needs equipment.

George is the king of fools—unable to analyze experience, he takes everything literally, and even his worst blunders become victories. He forgets to turn on the lights for Susan's movie, and the critics praise him for veiling the climax in darkness and stimulating the imaginations of the audience. He compulsively munches Indian nuts on the sound stage, and one critic acclaims the monotonous cracking as a new version of Eugene O'Neill's rhythmic drumbeat in The Emperor Jones.

This Hollywood is full of eager bellboys and cigarette girls who have made pilgrimages in hopes of getting into the movies. Their stories fill a scene set in the lobby of the Hotel Stilton as everyone in town seems to pass through, each involved with his or her private drama and dreams of film glory. The most prominent director is Kammerling, a temperamental German who deserted Reinhardt (who knelt in the Schauspielhaus to beg him not to go) and who obstinately refuses to finish his film until Glogauer finds him an actress who is exactly the right type. Even Glogauer's secretary arrives at the office wearing a black evening dress and pearls in imitation of Elinor Glyn.

The film industry is a world of reverse logic where fools are rewarded and the truly talented go unnoticed. Vail is a skilled playwright whom no one asks to write, and George's movie succeeds due to his own incompetence and Susan's terrible acting. The ultimate statement of Hollywood values occurs when Glogauer accepts George's point of view simply because he makes his case in an emphatic manner. The play is a series of actions that could not possibly happen (but they do), set in a world that could not possibly exist (but it does), populated with characters who could not be alive (but they are). George survives in a crazy mechanism that even the studio boss cannot control, a gizmo that is so unpredictable that only a fool, with his talent for playing the moment without any plan at all, can survive in it.

The play opened on September 24, 1930, with Kaufman in the role of Lawrence Vail. In the *New York Times*, Brooks Atkinson called it "a hard, swift satire—fantastic and deadly, and full of highly charged COMEDY lines."

[*See also* United States, 1929–1940]

FURTHER READING

Gaines, James R. *Wit's End: Days and Nights of the Algonquin Round Table.* New York: Harcourt, 1977.

Goldstein, Malcolm. *George S. Kaufman: His Life, His Theater.* New York: Oxford Univ. Press, 1979.

Hart, Moss. *Act One.* New York: Random House–Vintage, 1959.

Mason, Jeffrey D. *Wisecracks: The Farces of George S. Kaufman.* Ann Arbor: UMI Res. Press, 1988.

Meredith, Scott. *George S. Kaufman and His Friends.* Garden City, N.Y.: Doubleday, 1974.

Teichmann, Howard. *George S. Kaufman: An Intimate Portrait.* New York: Atheneum, 1972.

Jeffrey D. Mason

ONDAATJE, MICHAEL (1943–)

On the island of Sri Lanka (formerly Ceylon), Michael Ondaatje's impressive family name dates back to the 15th century. His descendants include botanists, doctors, lawyers, and plantation owners. Although linked to this rich heritage, Ondaatje's family fortune had nearly evaporated by the time of his birth in Colombo on September 12, 1943, one of four children of Philip Mervyn Ondaatje and Enid Gratiaen Ondaatje. In Ceylon, Ondaatje began his education at St. Thomas College. In 1952, four years following his parents' separation, Ondaatje left St. Thomas College and reunited with his mother in London, ENGLAND. He enrolled at Dulwich College. Not pleased with his English education, Ondaatje joined his older brother Christopher in Montreal, CANADA, in 1962. Two years later, Ondaatje married filmmaker/photographer Kim Jones. The couple became parents to two children, Quintin and Griffin, and legally separated in 1980. Ondaatje received his bachelor of arts degree from the University of Toronto (1965) and his master's degree from Queens University in Kingston, Ontario (1967).

While teaching at the University of Western Ontario in London, Ondaatje began THE COLLECTED WORKS OF BILLY THE KID. Inspired by Ondaatje's childhood memories of playing "Cowboys and Indians," this critically acclaimed piece is an intimate exploration of the legendary outlaw Billy the Kid. It is a fusion of both fact and fiction: a blend of history, biography, and fantasy. A multimedia experience, *The Collected Works* is an assemblage of poems, narratives, and "fabricated" photographs. For this piece Ondaatje was presented the Governor General's Award in 1970. *The Collected Works of Billy the Kid* was brought to the stage at the Stratford Festival in 1973.

In 1976 Ondaatje released *Coming Through Slaughter.* This work illuminates the life of JAZZ-legend Buddy Bolden, believed to be the founding father of jazz. Similar to *The Collected Works of*

Billy the Kid, this piece flows in poetic form and weaves biographical facts into a created backdrop: Ondaatje skillfully integrates the sparse biographical facts of Bolden's life into an appropriate turn-of-the-century New Orleans setting. In the year of its release, *Coming Through Slaughter* was co-winner of the Books in Canada award for first novels (though even Ondaatje himself is hesitant to label the work as a "novel"). *Coming Through Slaughter* was adapted for the stage and first performed in 1980 at Toronto's Theatre Passe Muraille.

In 1992 Ondaatje published *The English Patient*, which received the Booker Prize, the Governor General's Award, and the Trillium Award in the same year. This highly praised, postcolonial work is set in a burned-out villa in Florence, ITALY, near the conclusion of World War II. *The English Patient* tells the story of four companions: a fatally burned Hungarian cartographer (Almasy), a "shell-shocked" Canadian nurse (Hana), a Sikh sapper (Kip), and a thief (Caravaggio). Adapted and directed by Anthony Minghella in 1996, the film verison of *The English Patient* received nine Academy Awards and two Golden Globe Awards in 1997.

Ondaajte resides in Toronto with his wife, Linda Spalding. They edit the literary journal *Brick*.

PLAYS: *The Collected Works of Billy the Kid* (1973); *Coming Through Slaughter* (1980)

FURTHER READING

Barbour, Douglas. *Michael Ondaatje.* New York: Twayne, 1993.

Jewinski, Ed. *Michael Ondaatje: Express Yourself Beautifully.* Toronto: ECW, 1994.

Minghella, Anthony. *The English Patient: A Screenplay.* New York: Hyperion, 1996.

Mundwiler, Leslie. *Michael Ondaatje: Word, Image, Imagination.* Vancouver: Talonbooks, 1984.

Ondaatje, Michael. *The Collected Works of Billy the Kid.* New York: Penguin, 1984.

———. *Coming Through Slaughter.* New York: Vintage, 1996.

Erica Joan Dymond

ONDINE

Based on La Motte-Foqué's 1811 tale, JEAN GIRAUDOUX's *Ondine* (1939), a romantic TRAGEDY, opens with a young water sprite, raised by an old couple, falling in love with Hans, a knight errant. Smitten with her beauty, passion, and natural sexual appeal, and unafraid of her magical powers and mysterious origin, he abandons the dangerous test undertaken for his fiancée Princess Bertha, ignores the warnings of the fishing community, and pledges his love to Ondine. For her part, Ondine is blind to his limitations ("How handsome you are!") and deaf to the admonition of the Old One—her uncle, King of the Sea—that a human husband will inevitably deceive her and thus be punished with death.

When Hans presents his fifteen-year-old bride to the King in the second act, a court entertainment is provided by the Lord Chamberlain, the Superintendent of Theatre, and the Illusionist (her disguised uncle who can control the passage of time). But their fast talk and trickery are more disillusioning than amusing, and Ondine soon discovers her failure to fit into the human world of hypocrisy. Even after lessons in lying, her attempts at pretense prove disastrous. In flash-forward scenes, magically presented by the Illusionist, Hans discovers he has more in common with the all-too-human Bertha than with his sprite spouse.

In the third act, Hans prepares to marry Bertha, with whom he has betrayed Ondine, who has been missing for six months. When Ondine is caught in a fisherman's net and tried for witchcraft, she lies to save Hans from punishment, claiming she betrayed him first. Only when her lie unravels does Hans appreciate her love—and the nonhuman world he has lost. But it is too late. He must die for his infidelity; and as his breath recedes, so does Ondine's memory of their human love and life together.

Like many of Giraudoux's plays, this one explores the union of the ideal (extraordinary Ondine) and the real (ordinary Hans) and comes to the same unhappy conclusion: they are incompatible. Georges Lemaitre in *Jean Giraudoux: The Writer and His Work* (1971) suggests the heroine represents oneness with Nature (she sees clearly in the dark, does not get wet in the rain, sleeps on the surface of the lake, converses with animals and spirits). Thus she flounders in the unnatural, petty world of humans. Their match is doomed to failure, for in any attempt to unite them, the ideal will be compromised, lost. The real will prevail but will not be victorious, as there is no glory in realizing that humans are too limited to accommodate the realm of the imagination.

Produced by Louis Jouvet, *Ondine* began a unanimously acclaimed run at the Athénée in Paris in 1939, which was aborted in 1940 because of the war; but it was revived in 1949. Adapted by Maurice Valency and starring Audrey Hepburn, it opened in New York in 1954 and won the Critics' Circle Award for Best Foreign Play.

[*See also* France]

FURTHER READING

Cohen, Robert. *Giraudoux: Three Faces of Destiny.* Chicago: Univ. of Chicago Press, 1968.

Inskip, Donald. *Jean Giraudoux: The Making of a Dramatist.* London: Oxford Univ. Press, 1958.

Le maitre, Georges. *Jean Giraudoux: The Writer and His Work.* New York: Ungar, 1971.

Reilly, John H. *Jean Giraudoux.* Twayne's World Author Series, No. 513. Boston: Twayne, 1979.

Patricia Montley

ONE DAY IN ASADH

Although the central character of *One Day in Asadh* (*Asadh Ka Ek Din,* 1958) is named after the legendary Sanskrit poet and dramatist Kalidas, the play is not historical—the entire plot is MOHAN RAKESH's invention. The plot centers on the tragic love-relationship of Mallika's selfless love for Kalidas and his self-centered love for her. Through this relationship Rakesh explores two themes. The first is the relationship of the author's creativity to his roots. Mallika and Kalidas live in the backdrop of the Himalayas, among its mountains, valleys, and living creatures. One day a messenger from Ujjaini comes to invite Kalidas to the capital as poet laureate of the state. Kalidas is reluctant to go because somewhere inside he knows he will not be happy if he is cut off from his roots—the mountains, the valleys, its creatures, and of course Mallika. Mallika encourages him to go, and ultimately he does. However, as feared, he feels suffocated in the comfort and luxury of palace life. At the end of the play Kalidas confesses that everything he has written after becoming poet laureate and living in the capital has its roots in his earlier mountainous environment and its creatures. In a poignant speech, he tells Mallika:

> People think that living in that life and atmosphere I have written a great deal. But I know that while living there I wrote nothing. Whatever I wrote was a re-collection of life here. The Himalayas are the backdrop of *Kumarasambhav,* you are the austere Uma. Cut off from his natural environs the creativity of the author gradually dries up. The pain of Yaksha in *Meghdut* is the pain I felt at being separated from you.

Cut off from his natural environment, the author's creativity dries up.

The second theme Rakesh explores is the effect of state patronage on creativity. Patronage may make an artist comfortable, and it may give him exalted status and reputation, but ultimately it suffocates the artist's creativity. Kalidas feels suffocated in the palace and wants to free himself. When he goes back to his village and to Mallika, he hears the cries of Mallika's child. At that moment he realizes time has not stood still in his absence, and it is too late to make a fresh start.

One Day in Asadh was written and published in 1958, and its first major production was done by the theater group Anamika (Kolkata), directed by Shyamanand Jalan. The second major production was directed by Ebrahim Alkazi with the students of the National School of Drama in November 1962, the year he took over the institution as its director. Since then there have been more than sixty productions in various Indian languages including English. In 1968 the play was produced by Mary Washington College, Virginia, in a production directed by Joy Michael.

FURTHER READING

Jain, N. C. "Some Recent Significant Plays." *Enact* 25–26 (January–February 1969).

Nigam, R. L. "*Aadhe Adhure*: A Comment." *Enact* 32–33 (August–September 1969).

Nita, Kumar N. "*Halfway House: A House Divided.*" In *Many Indias, Many Literatures: New Critical Essays,* ed. by Shormishtha Panja. Delhi: Worldview Pubs., 1999.

Rakesh, Mohan. "Why Plays?" *Enact* 13–14 (January–February 1968).

Sethi, J. D. "Rakesh's *Aadhe Adhure:* A Breakthrough." *Enact* 27 (March 1969).

Taneja, Jaidev. *Mohan Rakesh: Rang-shilpa aur pradarshan.* Delhi: Radhakrishan Prakashan, 1996.

Rajinder Nath

O'NEILL, EUGENE (1888–1953)

At the final curtain, there they still are, trapped within each other by the past, each guilty and at the same time innocent, scorning, loving, pitying each other, understanding and yet not understanding at all, forgiving, but still doomed never to be able to forget.

—Eugene O'Neill, letter to George Jean Nathan regarding
Long Day's Journey Into Night, 1940

Eugene Gladstone O'Neill was born on October 16, 1888, at the Barrett House, a hotel on Broadway and 43rd Street, in the heart of the theater district in New York City. His father was James O'Neill (1846–1920), an Irish actor who in 1883 began touring with the Charles Fechter dramatization of ALEXANDRE DUMAS-FILS's novel THE COUNT OF MONTE CRISTO. He cherished the ambition of becoming a Shakespearean actor in the tradition of Edwin Booth, but to his shame he could not resist the lucrative romantic MELODRAMA, and he eventually played Edmond Dantés in over 4,000 performances through 1912. He interrupted his tour to spend just one night with his newborn son and his wife, Ella Quinlan (1857–1922), whose doctor prescribed morphine to help her recover from the delivery, beginning an addiction that would torment her for the rest of her life.

EARLY YEARS, 1895–1915

Eugene spent his first years on tour with his parents, mostly in one-night stands in towns all over the country, and passed summers at their "Monte Cristo" cottage in New London, Connecticut. In October 1895 he enrolled at the St. Aloysius Academy for Boys, a Catholic boarding school in Riverdale, New York, where he served as an altar boy for Sunday Mass and read Rudyard Kipling, Dumas pére, Victor Hugo, and William Shakespeare. On his twelfth birthday, he began studies at the De La Salle Institute in New York City and lived in his family's hotel apartment on West 68th Street near Central Park West. In 1902 he enrolled at the Betts Academy, a nonsectarian boarding school in Stamford, Connecticut. During the summer of 1903 his mother tried to stop taking morphine and, while suffering from withdrawal symptoms, tried to drown herself in the Thames River. In reaction, Eugene refused to attend Mass, and after he returned to Betts for the school year, he started spending his weekends in New York City with his elder brother, Jamie (1878–

1923); the two explored theaters, saloons, and brothels, and Eugene began drinking. He read radical political tracts as well as literature by GEORGE BERNARD SHAW, HENRIK IBSEN, FRIEDRICH NIETZSCHE, and OSCAR WILDE.

On September 20, 1906, he entered Princeton University, but he devoted his energies less to his studies and more to women and drinking (in Trenton, New Jersey, as well as the Hell's Kitchen and Greenwich Village neighborhoods of New York City). In 1907 the university dismissed him for failing to take any final examinations. In the meantime, he read LYOV TOLSTOY; Fyodor Dostoevsky, and MAKSIM GORKY. He took a job as a secretary for a New York mail-order firm and lived in his family's apartment in the Hotel Lucerne on Amsterdam Avenue and 79th Street. In 1909 he met Kathleen Jenkins and secretly married her on October 2, just two weeks before his twenty-first birthday. Soon afterward he traveled to San Francisco and then sailed for Honduras with a mining engineer to prospect for gold. After five months he contracted malaria and returned to New York.

O'Neill took a job as assistant stage manager with his father's tour of *The White Sister,* by Walter Hackett and F. Marion Crawford, and Kathleen bore their son, Eugene Jr., on May 5, 1910. O'Neill saw neither wife nor baby before sailing for Buenos Aires on a Norwegian square-rigged steel bark. He worked a variety of jobs and explored the bars and brothels of the waterfront, and in March 1911 he shipped out as an ordinary seaman on the British freighter *Ikala,* which became the model for the *Glencairn,* the fictional ship on which the playwright set some of his early one-act plays. He returned to New York City and lived for a time at a cheap flophouse run by a man known as "Jimmy the Priest," a place he later fictionalized as the setting for THE ICEMAN COMETH. He sailed for ENGLAND as an ordinary seaman and returned as an able-bodied seaman on the liner *Philadelphia.* Kathleen asked for a divorce, and on December 29 he set up the grounds for the action by arranging for witnesses to view him bedded down with a prostitute.

In 1912 O'Neill attempted suicide with an overdose of sleeping pills, but his roommate saved him, and he became a bit player in his father's vaudeville version of *The Count of Monte Cristo,* touring through Utah and Colorado. In August he became a reporter on the New London *Telegraph,* but he developed a persistent cough in October, and after his illness was diagnosed as tuberculosis, he entered first a public and then a private sanatorium, where he read plays by J. M. SYNGE, GERHART HAUPTMANN, and AUGUST STRINDBERG. By June 3 he was well enough to leave, and he began writing plays. In August 1914 his father paid the costs of publishing *Thirst and Other One Act Plays,* a collection of his work, and in September O'Neill enrolled in GEORGE PIERCE BAKER's playwriting workshop at Harvard University. Although Baker's model was ARTHUR WING PINERO, author of such plays as THE SECOND MRS. TANQUERAY (1903), and the precepts he taught would seem formulaic today, the workshop, initiated in 1909, brought respect to the serious study of playwriting.

O'Neill acquired from Baker the lifelong practice of writing a detailed scenario before attempting the dialogue of a new play.

He spent most of the autumn of 1915 drinking in a bar nicknamed the "Hell Hole" in Greenwich Village, and he met an anarchistic alcoholic named Terry Carlin who in June 1916 took him to Provincetown, Massachusetts, where he met a colony of writers, leftist intellectuals, and genteel bohemians including George Cram "Jig" Cook, playwright SUSAN GLASPELL, radical journalist John Reed, Louise Bryant, and others.

FROM PROVINCETOWN TO NEW YORK, 1916–1925

The Provincetown connection changed O'Neill's life. Led by Cook, a visionary and student of classical Greek culture, in 1915 his new friends had founded the Provincetown Players, which developed from an amateur play-reading troupe to one of the more important companies in the art theater movement that transformed the aesthetic and practice of serious theater in America. In place of the commercial approach that treated plays as commodities and mere entertainment, the art theater sought totality of conception, unity of structure, harmony of impression, freedom of style, simplicity of setting, and artistry in scenic design. Maurice Brown and Ellen Van Volkenberg set the pattern in 1912 when they established the Chicago Little Theater, an amateur troupe that engaged in long rehearsal explorations of the works of such playwrights as Y. B. YEATS, Strindberg, ARTHUR SCHNITZLER, and Euripides. In 1914 Hiram Kelly Moderwell attacked DAVID BELASCO's representationalism in The Theatre of Today, and Sheldon Cheney completed The New Movement in the Theatre and founded Theatre Arts Magazine. In 1915 in Cambridge, Massachusetts, Sam Hume mounted a gallery exhibition of scenic designs, the first such event to elevate theater design to the level of fine art.

On July 28, 1916, the Provincetown Players produced O'Neill's one-act play Bound East for Cardiff. Set in the forecastle of the British tramp steamer Glencairn, the play opens with several men trading stories while a seaman named Yank lies in his bunk dying from injuries consequent to missing his footing on a ladder and falling down in the hold. The men are isolated on the sea, and they resent the wealthy owners who live off their labor and suffering. Driscoll, the Irishman, remembers how Yank saved his life after their former ship sank. The captain of the Glencairn can do nothing to stop the pain or to prevent Yank from spitting up blood. Yank assures Driscoll that he is not sorry to leave the hard life of a sailor, and he can only imagine the pleasure of a home on dry land. He is, in seaman's slang, "bound East for Cardiff," and in the last moments of the play, he dies. The production took place in the company's ramshackle theater set on a wharf, so the waves lapped at pilings as the drama unfolded with Cook as Yank and O'Neill himself in the one-line role of the second mate.

Bound East for Cardiff was the first of four one-act plays that were later known collectively as the S. S. Glencairn. In the Zone (produced October 31, 1917, by the Washington Square Players) takes place in the forecastle again, but now the ship is steaming through a war zone, and the men are fearful of submarines, mines, and especially German spies. The tension and helplessness make them quarrelsome and irritable, and they turn their suspicion on Smitty, who has been behaving furtively and hiding a small black tin box under his mattress. The men find a porthole left open in spite of the blackout routine, and they speculate that Smitty has been signaling to another vessel; they even suspect him of deception because he speaks English too well. They capture him, tie him up, and against Smitty's anguished protests open the mysterious tin box, which turns out to contain a series of love letters that conclude with the woman breaking with him owing to his constant drunkenness. Ashamed, the men free Smitty and turn in for the night. In The Moon of the Caribbees (produced December 20, 1918, by the Provincetown Players), the men relax on the main deck under a full moon in the West Indies. Bella, a bumboat woman, negotiates with their captain to sell them fruit and tobacco, and she quietly arranges to provide other commodities: three shillings for a pint of rum and four shillings for the sexual services of any of the women who accompany her. Most of the men go below to carouse out of sight of the officers, but Smitty remains on deck to dwell on the painful memory of the woman who rejected him for his drinking, and he wonders whether love is no more than what the native women sell to the sailors in the forecastle. The party pours out on deck, and one man plays his accordion while the others dance. The festivities turn into a brawl, and someone knifes Paddy, who knocks himself out when he falls. The mate walks in to restore order and sends Bella off with no money as punishment for selling liquor, and the play ends with Smitty still struggling with his loneliness. THE LONG VOYAGE HOME (1917) depicts the defeat of Olson, a Swedish sailor who hopes to return to his family farm but falls prey to waterfront thugs who drug him and shanghai him aboard an outbound windjammer; it seems that the sea will not let him go.

O'Neill's sea cycle works from the naturalistic conception of man as subject to natural forces, and it shows the influence of Joseph Conrad's The Nigger of the Narcissus. In all four plays, the sea dominates the action, providing the backdrop (sound, light, mood) for the characters and acting as master to the men, who become its vassals and servants. Those who acquiesce survive, but the thoughtful suffer: Yank, Olson, and Smitty betray the sea, which kills or enslaves them.

In the fall of 1916, O'Neill, Cook, and others left Provincetown to open a 140-seat theater, the Provincetown Playhouse, in Greenwich Village, where they produced O'Neill's Bound East for Cardiff, Before Breakfast (1916), Fog (1917), and The Sniper (1917). O'Neill spent the spring and summer of 1917 writing in Provincetown, then he went back to the Hell Hole, corresponded with critic George Jean Nathan (finally meeting him in 1919), and met Agnes Boulton, a writer whom he married on April 12,

1918. The couple settled in Provincetown as the playwright worked on BEYOND THE HORIZON. In May 1919 the O'Neills moved into a converted Coast Guard station at Peaked Hill Bar, a gift from Eugene's father. On October 30 their son Shane was born in Provincetown.

Beyond the Horizon opened on Broadway on February 3, 1920. The play tells the story of two brothers, one who loves the family farm and one who yearns to go to sea, but they trade destinies, with disastrous effect, because the girl who lives next door loves the dreamer instead of the farmer. The farmer succeeds in foreign parts but sacrifices his integrity, while the dreamer marries the girl but drives the farm to ruin and finally dies of consumption. O'Neill developed his ongoing themes of mankind's relationship to the sea and the land and of belonging and displacement; the award of the Pulitzer Prize in June established his reputation. On August 10 his father died of cancer in New London, and his brother, Jamie, swore to stop drinking. On November 1 the Provincetown Players opened THE EMPEROR JONES, which became a major success for both the playwright and the company. The expressionistic action follows Jones's flight through a jungle, where instead of finding safety, he meets his own guilt and fear. Played by Charles Gilpin, Jones was one of the first important roles written for a black actor even though the character is a crap-shooting, arrogant Pullman porter. O'Neill later used his influence to persuade the New York Drama League to break their color line and invite Gilpin to their annual awards dinner.

In 1921 O'Neill became friends with critic Kenneth Macgowan and designer ROBERT EDMOND JONES. June brought the Broadway premiere of Gold, a full-length play O'Neill developed from Where the Cross Is Made (1918). While shipwrecked with his crew on a small coral island, whaling captain Isaiah Bartlett finds an inlaid chest that he believes is filled with gold. He kills two of his men for resisting him, and when a ship comes to rescue them, he buries the chest so he can return to retrieve it in secret. He fits a schooner for the voyage, but he is about to depart from his California home when his daughter tricks him and arranges for her lover, the officer on a steamer, to sail the schooner for him so that he will be forced to remain with his ailing wife. The expedition fails when the ship is lost, but Bartlett refuses to believe the disaster until his son assures him that an anklet from the "treasure" is nothing but brass; at that, the captain shrivels and dies.

ANNA CHRISTIE opened on November 2, 1921, and won the Pulitzer Prize in 1922. A Swedish coal barge captain looks forward to meeting his daughter, who years ago he sent to live with cousins and grow up in wholesome circumstances; however, when she arrives, it is clear that she is a hardened prostitute. They help rescue a sailor from a wrecked steamer, and she falls in love with him. The captain resists the match, and the woman feels she is not good enough for her lover, but in spite of ill feeling on all sides, the three accept each other, the men ship out, and Anna plans to keep a home for them on shore.

In the autumn of 1921 O'Neill met his son, Eugene Jr., eleven years old, for the first time. On February 28, 1922, his mother died in Los Angeles, and Jamie got drunk after having stayed sober for two years. On March 9, the very evening that Jamie brought their mother's body to New York, the Provincetown Players opened THE HAIRY APE. This second expressionist play follows Yank, a stoker on an ocean liner; he is strong, rough, and crude, scorning all sentiment in favor of the raw power he finds embodied in the engines he feeds. After an arrogant rich girl visits the stokehole and finds Yank repulsive, he resolves to find her and confront her. His journey into strange territory takes him to the most refined neighborhood in New York City, to the office of the waterfront chapter of the International Workers of the World, and to the zoo, where he releases a gorilla who crushes him to death in spite of Yank's mischievous thought that they are, at bottom, brothers.

O'Neill bought Brook Farm in Ridgefield, Connecticut, to provide a winter home as an alternative to Peaked Hill Bar. In 1923 the National Institute of Arts and Letters awarded O'Neill a gold medal, and on November 8 Jamie died of complications from heavy drinking. O'Neill did not attend the funeral because he was himself recovering from an alcoholic episode.

By that time Jig Cook had gone to GREECE on a pilgrimage, where he died in 1924, so the Provincetown Players came under the leadership of a triumvirate composed of O'Neill, Macgowan, and Robert Edmond Jones. They formed Experimental Theatre, Inc. and strove for a higher level of professionalism, remodeling the theater and offering both printed playbills and press passes to their productions. During the two years of their administration, they emphasized experimental production more than experimental writing. Overall, from 1916 through 1926, the Provincetown Players presented eighteen of O'Neill's plays.

ALL GOD'S CHILLUN GOT WINGS opened on May 15, 1924, amid hate mail and death threats from the Ku Klux Klan because the play tells the story of a black man (played by Paul Robeson) who marries a white woman. The mayor attempted to close the play and refused to issue permits to the child actors required for the first scene, so director James Light read it aloud to the audience. Although the two leading characters play together easily as children, the woman cannot adjust to the fact of her husband's blackness, and she not only loses her reason; she wrecks his ambition to pass the bar by making it impossible for him to study.

DESIRE UNDER THE ELMS opened on November 11, 1924. Old Ephraim Cabot marries yet again, leading two of his grown sons to conclude that they will never inherit the farm and provoking the youngest, Eben, to determined anger. Abbie seduces her stepson, and when Ephraim promises to give her anything if she will bear him yet another son, she produces a child who is actually Eben's. When her lover resents the baby, she smothers it to prove her love. He summons the sheriff but then chooses to share her guilt, so when the two are arrested, Ephraim is left on the farm, completely alone. The play was subsequently banned in Boston and London in spite of O'Neill offering to replace the word *whore* with *harlot*, and the district attorney for New York City tried to close the play for indecency in 1925. In Los Angeles, the entire cast was tried in court for giving an obscene play.

FROM BERMUDA TO TAO HOUSE, 1926–1946

O'Neill and his family moved to the island of Bermuda, and on January 1, 1925, he swore to stop drinking and smoking but later reneged. On May 14 Agnes bore their second child, Oona. In 1926 O'Neill saw a psychoanalyst and achieved a degree of control over his drinking. With Macgowan and Jones, O'Neill produced THE GREAT GOD BROWN, opening on January 23. The play is O'Neill's first major experiment with masks; Dion cannot appear in public without the personality he wears as a shield, and after he dies, the ordinary conventional Billy Brown takes Dion's masks and lives as both men until he dies from the burden of suffering and vulnerability.

O'Neill spent the summer in Maine, where he met actress Carlotta Monterey, who had played Mildred in *The Hairy Ape*, then returned to Bermuda. In 1927 he initiated a serious relationship with Monterey, which led to an angry correspondence with Agnes and the two lovers traveling together to London, France, China, Saigon, Manila, Singapore, Ceylon, and Egypt. Agnes divorced the playwright, and he married Monterey on July 22, 1929.

In January 1928 the THEATRE GUILD produced two of O'Neill's plays. The first was *Marco Millions*, which develops the conflict between sensitivity and practicality that the playwright explored in *The Great God Brown*. He presents the fabled trader and traveler Marco Polo as a version of an eager American businessman who interprets every commodity and experience in terms of what price he can negotiate for it. The pope tells him, "On the last day one of your seed will interrupt Gabriel to sell him another trumpet," and then he sends him to Cathay, predicting ironically that he will "set an example of virtuous Western manhood" and drive Kublai, the Great Kaan, "to seek spiritual salvation." Kublai finds Marco amusing because he cannot imagine his own death, so he gives him the freedom of his empire in exchange for periodic reports. After fifteen years he realizes that Marco "has not even a mortal soul, he has only an acquisitive instinct. . . . He has lusted for everything and loved nothing." The trader has become a consummate administrator but blithely tramples on Chinese culture and sensibilities. Kublai sends Marco back to Italy but charges him to escort his beloved granddaughter, Kukachin, to Persia, where she is to marry the king. The Kaan's adviser, Chu-Yin, instructs Marco "to look carefully and deeply into the Princess's eyes and note what you see there" on each and every day of the voyage. Kukachin falls in love with the Venetian, who is completely unable to recognize her passion. The news nearly inspires the Kaan to conquer the West for the sole purpose of torturing and dismembering Marco, but he relents. Marco returns to his bourgeois life in Venice, and Kublai mourns Kukachin, who dies of sadness. The cast included Alfred Lunt as Marco Polo, Margalo Gillmore as Princess Kukachin, Dudley Digges as Chu-Yin, and Sanford Meisner as a papal courier.

The second Theatre Guild production was STRANGE INTERLUDE (1928), with Lynn Fontanne as Nina and scenery by Jo Mielziner. In this nine-act epic about a woman and the men who loved her, O'Neill developed his exploration of staging the various levels of personality by writing out the characters' interior monologues for the actors to speak aloud. Although each performance took nearly six hours, including a ninety-minute dinner break, the production ran for seventeen months, led to two touring companies, eventually earned $275,000 (over $3 million in 2006 dollars) for O'Neill, and won the Pulitzer Prize.

A few months later the Pasadena Community Playhouse opened LAZARUS LAUGHED, staged as a vast pageant with over 170 performers, 400 costumes, and 300 masks. Raised from the dead, Lazarus preaches that there is no death, and he responds to all events with warm, all-encompassing laughter. The aged Roman emperor Tiberius fears death and demands that Lazarus repeat the original miracle, and the mad Caligula endeavors without success to learn from Lazarus the secret of everlasting youth.

While visiting Cap d'Ail on the French Riviera in the spring of 1929, O'Neill began working on MOURNING BECOMES ELECTRA. Opening on October 26, 1931, the trilogy interpreted Greek TRAGEDY in American terms, using the Civil War as an analogy for the Greek invasion of Troy and devising counterparts to Agamemnon, Clytemnestra, Electra, Orestes, Aegisthus, and the classical chorus.

In 1932 O'Neill moved to Sea Island, Georgia, to build a home called "Casa Genotta." He became associate editor of George Jean Nathan's new journal *The American Spectator* and contributed a series of three essays on the use of masks in contemporary theater.

> At its best, [the mask] is more subtly, imaginatively, suggestively dramatic than any actor's face can ever be. . . . Why not give all future Classical revivals entirely in masks? Hamlet, for example. Masks would liberate this play from its present confining status as exclusively a "star vehicle." We would be able to see the great drama we are now only privileged to read, to identify ourselves with the figure of Hamlet as a symbolic projection of a fate that is in each of us, instead of merely watching a star giving us his version of a great acting role. We would even be able to hear the sublime poetry as the innate expression of the spirit of the drama itself, instead of listening to it as realistic recitation—or ranting—by familiar actors.

The Theatre Guild produced O'Neill's only COMEDY *Ah Wilderness!*, which opened on October 2, 1933, with George M. Cohan playing the role of Nat Miller, the father. The action takes place on the Fourth of July in 1906 in a town very much like New

London, Connecticut, where O'Neill's family had spent their summers. Richard is O'Neill as he might have been: going on seventeen, just out of high school and bound for Yale, and eager to defy convention. He scorns the Independence Day celebration, telling his father that America is not the land of the free and the home of the brave but the home of the "wage slave ground under the heel of the capitalist class, starving, crying for bread for his children." In addition to reading Thomas Carlyle, Wilde, Shaw, and Ibsen, he has been copying passages of Algernon Swinburne for his fifteen year-old girlfriend, Muriel, but her father finds them so objectionable that he grounds his daughter for a month and forbids her to see Richard again. Still rebelling, the youth visits a bar and drinks with a "swift baby" from New Haven until the owner realizes he is under age and turns him out. He returns home drunk and shocks his family. On the following morning, his mother urges his father to punish him, but before father and son can talk, Richard sneaks out for a clandestine meeting with Muriel on the beach. He tells her all about drinking with what he describes as a chorus girl from New York, and she finally lets him kiss her because the touch will wash off the other girl's kisses. In the last scene, his father reproves him for his earlier folly and tries to explain to him how to handle "certain desires of the flesh" but does no make much progress. The parents leave the boy in the moonlight and enjoy the night together.

On January 8, 1934, the Theatre Guild produced DAYS WITHOUT END, O'Neill's return to some of the concerns and techniques of *The Great God Brown* and *Lazarus Laughed*. He called the piece "the mask, pseudo-Faustian, 'modern miracle play'" and set out to explore the nature of deity. The protagonist is John Loving, whom O'Neill divides into John, a conventional character, and Loving, his double but wearing "a mask whose features reproduce exactly the features of John's face—the death mask of a John who has died with a sneer of scornful mockery on his lips." John was raised as a Catholic but lost his faith when his parents died. He finds happiness in loving his wife, but he worries about what will happen if she dies. His demonic self leads him into an affair with another woman, and the infidelity nearly wrecks his marriage and his life. He writes a novel based on his own life, and when he describes the plot, his wife recognizes her husband and herself, and she walks out into a storm, just like the woman in the story, and catches pneumonia. As she lies at the point of death, John retreats to a church where he struggles with Loving. John prays to Christ on the Cross, and when he accepts his love and forgiveness, Loving is defeated. John receives news that his wife will survive, and he declares, like Lazarus, "Death is dead."

Days Without End marked the end of O'Neill's active involvement in Broadway theater. Early in 1934 his health began to deteriorate; over the next decade he suffered from nervousness, digestive problems and stomach pains, depression, prostate trouble, appendicitis, neuritis, low blood pressure, bronchitis, Parkinson's disease, melancholia, exhaustion, a back injury, and a debilitating tremor. Yet in January 1935 he started working on a cycle of eleven plays he eventually called *A Tale of Possessors Self-Dispossessed*, a project that was to cover the years from 1755 to 1932. In 1941 he met actress Ingrid Bergman and discussed with her the possibility of producing the entire cycle in repertory, but although he wrote several scenarios, he ultimately completed only two of the plays, both produced posthumously: *A Touch of the Poet* (1957) and *More Stately Mansions* (1962).

In 1936 O'Neill left Sea Island and went to Seattle, Washington, where on November 12 he learned that he had won the Nobel Prize for Literature; in his letter of acceptance, he acknowledged the influence of Strindberg on his work. He took temporary lodgings in San Francisco, Berkeley, and Lafayette, and late in 1937 he moved into the newly constructed Tao House, set on 160 acres in the California hills opposite Mount Diablo above what is now Danville.

O'Neill lived at Tao House for over six years, until early 1944, and completed four major, full-length plays in spite of the tremor that made writing more and more difficult, with intermittent periods when he stopped work because of his concern over the progress of World War II. He finished *The Iceman Cometh* in January 1940; HUGHIE, a one-act, in 1942; LONG DAY'S JOURNEY INTO NIGHT in 1943; and both A TOUCH OF THE POET and A MOON FOR THE MISBEGOTTEN in 1944. His small writing study was isolated from the rest of the house, and after spending each long morning working on *Long Day's Journey Into Night*, fighting the tremor to inscribe the dialogue in his meticulously small handwriting, O'Neill would emerge drained and anguished.

In 1943 Oona O'Neill, just eighteen, married Charlie Chaplin in spite of her father's protests. O'Neill's tremor grew worse, making it difficult for him to control a pencil, and because he could not adjust to dictating or to composing at a typewriter, he found himself virtually unable to write. The O'Neills had become increasingly isolated at Tao House after their servants quit to engage in war-related work in 1942, so in 1944 they left to live temporarily at the Huntington Hotel in San Francisco, and the playwright destroyed some of his play manuscripts before moving to New York City in 1945.

The Iceman Cometh opened on October 9, 1946, with scenery by Robert Edmond Jones. The action unfolds in Harry Hope's flophouse, a version of the Hell Hole, and the characters are based on people O'Neill knew there. They drink in search of oblivion, cherishing their dreams of a better tomorrow until Hickey, a regular visitor, walks in to declare that the only way to find happiness is to face life honestly. The flophouse denizens are akin to the damned but still yearning for salvation, while Hickey faces his worst shame, that his wife's love for him has brought her nothing but suffering, and he kills her in order to save her.

FINAL CURTAIN, 1945–1953

O'Neill's last years form a tale of disintegration. He wrote little, if anything, after the war. In 1945 he left a sealed copy of *Long Day's Journey Into Night* in the Random House safe with instructions that it be published twenty-five years after his death and never produced. The Theatre Guild staged *A Moon for the Misbegotten* in 1947, touring from Columbus, Ohio, to Pittsburgh, Detroit, and St. Louis, but they did not bring the play to New York. In 1948 Carlotta walked out on him, but she returned after he got drunk and broke his arm, and they moved to Boston. Eugene Jr. slashed his wrists in 1950, and in the following year, O'Neill broke his leg and Carlotta was incorrectly diagnosed with mental illness; the true cause of her disorientation was overmedication. Fearing that someone else would try to finish his work, the playwright burned the drafts and scenarios of his unfinished cycle plays (unintentionally sparing *More Stately Mansions*), and he died on November 27, 1953, of degeneration of the cerebellum.

O'Neill's reputation blossomed posthumously in the late 1950s, and the director most closely associated with bringing his work back into public view was José Quintero. He revived *The Iceman Cometh* on May 8, 1956, with Jason Robards as Hickey, and six months later (November 7) opened *Long Day's Journey Into Night* (which had its world premiere in Stockholm on February 10, 1956) with Robards and Fredric March. Quintero's subsequent revivals included *Desire Under the Elms* (January 8, 1963) with George C. Scott, Rip Torn, and Colleen Dewhurst; *Strange Interlude* (March 11, 1963) with Geraldine Page as Nina; *Marco Millions* (February 20, 1964) with Hal Holbrook in the title role; *Hughie* (December 22, 1964) with Robards; *A Moon for the Misbegotten* (December 29, 1973) with Dewhurst and Robards; *Anna Christie* (April 14, 1977) with John Lithgow and Liv Ullmann; and *Welded* (June 10, 1981). Harold Clurman directed the premiere of *A Touch of the Poet* (October 2, 1958) with Helen Hayes, and Quintero revived the play (December 28, 1977) with Robards and Geraldine Fitzgerald.

In *Long Day's Journey Into Night*, O'Neill presents his most forthright essay in autobiography, depicting his family in the summer of 1912. The father, the mother, and the two grown sons engage in guilt and recrimination as they deal with their various dependencies on whiskey, on morphine, and on deceit. *A Moon for the Misbegotten* extends the story, following the fall of the older brother as he tries to deal with his guilt over the death of his mother and his own drinking problem, turning to the solace of a woman who knows she cannot save him.

A Touch of the Poet takes place in 1828 and tells the story of Cornelius Melody, the son of an Irish shebeen keeper who rose to be an officer in Wellington's army, had to resign his commission following a duel, and now, to his great shame, keeps a tavern in Massachusetts even while struggling to maintain the appearance of a gentleman. His daughter Sara loves Simon Harford, the son of an aristocratic family, whose father sends a lawyer to negotiate an end to their relationship. Melody, deeply insulted, tries to challenge him to a duel but ends brawling with the servants and thrown in jail. In despair over his crumbling self-image, Melody shoots his beloved mare.

O'Neill's last premiere was *More Stately Mansions*, in its published version as long as *The Iceman Cometh* and *Long Day's Journey Into Night* combined, opening in abridged form at the Kungliga Dramatiska Teatern in Stockholm in 1962. Quintero revived the play (October 31, 1967) at the Ahmanson Theatre in Los Angeles with Colleen Dewhurst as Sara, Arthur Hill as Simon, and Ingrid Bergman as Deborah. Set during 1832–1842, it followed *A Touch of the Poet* in what would have been the cycle. Deborah Harford retreats into her garden, to the refuge of her summerhouse and her daydream of what it would be like to be the mistress of a powerful man. She tells her son Simon the fairy tale of a king who dares not open a door that might lead to his lost realm, so he remains forever dispossessed. Simon contemplates Jean-Jacques Rousseau's conception of man as essentially good but corrupted by property and possession. At Simon's behest, Sara gradually takes control over the Harford empire, and she tries to leave her peasant origins behind in order to displace the Harfords, to live where they have lived and own what they have owned.

O'Neill remains the preeminent American dramatist of the 20th century. He led the theater away from the formulaic melodrama and contrived psychology of the 19th century and set a precedent that led to such playwrights as ARTHUR MILLER, TENNESSEE WILLIAMS, EDWARD ALBEE, SAM SHEPARD, DAVID MAMET, and TONY KUSHNER. Throughout his career he experimented with new ways to explore story, character, relationship, and psychology in stageable terms, moving from NATURALISM to EXPRESSIONISM to masks and interior monologues until he reached the mature, richly realistic plays of his later years. Scholars have analyzed his work in relation to Greek tragedy, Henrik Ibsen, Strindberg, Shaw, Gorky, SAMUEL BECKETT, the art theater movement, melodrama, Freudian psychology, Friedrich Nietzsche, Eastern philosophy, O'Neill's Irish roots, and gender relations. Many have traced the autobiographical nature of his work, all the way from the early one-acts that dramatized his more remarkable youthful experiences to the later plays that depicted his family either overtly or metaphorically. His legacy has expanded the horizons of theater and drama throughout the Western world.

[*See also* United States]

PLAYS: *Before Breakfast* (1916); *Bound East for Cardiff* (1916); *Thirst* (1916); *Fog* (1917); *Ile* (1917); *In the Zone* (1917); *The Long Voyage Home* (1917); *The Sniper* (1917); *The Moon of the Caribbees* (1918); *The Rope* (1918); *Where the Cross Is Made* (1918); *The Dreamy Kid* (1919); *Beyond the Horizon* (1920); *Chris Christopherson* (1920); *Diff'rent* (1920); *The Emperor Jones* (1920); *Exorcism* (1920); *Anna Christie* (1921); *The Straw* (1921); *Gold* (1921); *The First Man* (1922); *The Hairy Ape* (1922); *All*

God's Chillun Got Wings (1924); *The Ancient Mariner* (1924); *Desire Under the Elms* (1924); *Welded* (1924); *The Fountain* (1925); *The Great God Brown* (1926); *Lazarus Laughed* (1928); *Marco Millions* (1928); *Strange Interlude* (1928); *Dynamo* (1929); *Mourning Becomes Electra* (1931); *Ah, Wilderness!* (1933); *Days Without End* (1934); *The Iceman Cometh* (1946); *A Moon for the Misbegotten* (1947); *Long Day's Journey Into Night* (1956); *A Touch of the Poet* (1957); *Hughie* (1958); *More Stately Mansions* (1962)

FURTHER READING

Alexander, Doris. *Eugene O'Neill's Creative Struggle: The Decisive Decade, 1924–1933*. University Park: Pennsylvania State Univ. Press, 1992.

Black, Stephen A. *Eugene O'Neill: Beyond Mourning and Tragedy*. New Haven, Conn.: Yale Univ. Press, 1999.

Bogard, Travis. *Contour in Time: The Plays of Eugene O'Neill*. Rev. ed. New York: Oxford Univ. Press, 1988.

Gelb, Arthur, and Barbara Gelb. *O'Neill*. 1962. New York: Harper, 1974.

Manheim, Michael. *Eugene O'Neill's New Language of Kinship*. Syracuse: Syracuse Univ. Press, 1982.

Pfister, Joel. *Staging Depth: Eugene O'Neill and the Politics of Psychological Discourse*. Chapel Hill: Univ. of North Carolina Press, 1995.

Sheaffer, Louis. *O'Neill: Son and Playwright*. Boston: Little, Brown, 1968.

——. *O'Neill: Son and Artist*. Boston: Little, Brown, 1973.

Wainscott, Ronald H. *Staging O'Neill: The Experimental Years, 1920–1934*. New Haven, Conn.: Yale Univ. Press, 1988.

Jeffrey D. Mason

ONG KENG SEN (1963–)

During the late 1990s, SINGAPORE's Ong Keng Sen emerged as one of Asia's best-known and most influential theater directors on the international stage. Ong's multilingual productions featuring actors from different performance traditions and cultures have challenged existing models of intercultural theater by highlighting rather than minimizing the discontinuities between individual Asian cultures, demonstrating the fiction of any vision of a monolithic Asia.

Initially trained as a lawyer, in 1987 Ong became artistic director of TheatreWorks, a Singaporean theater company founded in 1985. In collaboration with writer Michael Chiang and popular music composer Dick Lee, Ong staged a number of popular Singapore-themed musicals during his first decade at Theatre-Works, including *Beauty World* (1988), *Fried Rice Paradise* (1991), and *Private Parts* (1992). These productions attracted a young, affluent, English-speaking audience to the theater for the first time, building an audience for the company's more adventurous work that followed. By the mid-1990s Ong had already staged a number of works on more challenging themes, including KUO PAO KUN's *Lao Jiu—Ninth Child* (1990) and Singaporean playwright Tan Tarn How's *The Lady of Soul and Her Ultimate "S" Machine* (1993), a political satire.

After returning from graduate study at New York University's Tisch School of the Arts in 1994, Ong's work took a more adventurous approach to staging, content, and structure as he began to create original works with collaborators rather than starting with a completed script. The piece that firmly marked this new way of working was *Broken Birds* (1995), an original, environmental work that sought to excavate the nearly forgotten history of the *karayuki*, the Japanese prostitutes who worked in Singapore during the colonial era. That same year Ong formed the Flying Circus Project, bringing together practitioners of a wide range of Asian performance traditions from throughout the region. Out of these explorations came the international tours of *Lear* (1997), *Desdemona* (2000), and *The Continuum—Beyond the Killing Fields* (2001), which was based on the true story of Cambodian classical dancer Em Theay and others.

In 1999 Ong founded the Arts Network Asia, which sponsors a wide range of collaborations between artists throughout Asia. He was the founding curator of the In Transit Festival at Berlin's House of World Cultures in 2002, while his 2003 production of *The Global Soul—the Buddha Project*, which previewed there, has subsequently toured to Singapore and Europe. His European connections were furthered in 2002, when he directed the site-specific *Search: Hamlet* at a Danish castle, and in 2003, when he served as artist-in-residence at Vienna's Schauspielhaus, where he curated "Myths of Memory" and created two new works. Ong was the first Southeast Asian to direct at the New York Shakespeare Festival with playwright Chay Yew's *A Language of Their Own* (1995), and his staging of *The Silver River* by playwright DAVID HENRY HWANG and composer Bright Sheng was seen by audiences at the 2000 Spoleto Festival and the 2002 Lincoln Center Summer Festival.

SELECT PLAYS: *Broken Birds* (1995); *Descendants of the Eunuch Admiral* (1995); *Six of the Best* (1996); *Destinies of Flowers in the Mirrors* (1997); *Lear* (1997); *Workhorse Afloat* (1997); *Desdemona* (2000); *The Spirits Play: Six Movements in a Strange House* (2000); *The Continuum—Beyond the Killing Fields* (2001); *Search: Hamlet* (2002); *The Global Soul—The Buddha Project* (2003); *The Myths of Memory: Offenes Geheimnis (Open Secret)* (2003); *Sandakan Threnody* (2004); *Geisha* (2006)

FURTHER READING

Bharucha, Rustom. "Consumed in Singapore: The Intercultural Spectacle of Lear." *Yale Theater* 3, no. 1 (Winter 2001): 107–127.

Latrell, Craig. "After Appropriation." *TDR: The Drama Review* 44, no. 4 (Winter 2000): 44–55.

Leverett, James. "Model City/Model Art." *Yale Theater* 32, no. 2 (Summer 2002): 70–75.

Ong Keng Sen. "Encounters." *TDR: The Drama Review* 45, no. 5 (Fall 2001): 126–133.

Oon, Clarissa. *Theatre Life!: A History of English-Language Theatre in Singapore Through the Straits Times (1958–2000)*. Singapore: Singapore Press Holdings, 2001.

Peterson, William. *Theatre and the Politics of Culture in Contemporary Singapore*. Middletown, Ohio: Wesleyan Univ. Press, 2001.

William Peterson

ON GUARD BENEATH THE NEON LIGHTS

On Guard Beneath the Neon Lights (Nihongdeng xia de shaobing, huaju), by Shen Ximeng, Mo Yan, and Lu Xingchen, was one of the best-known plays of 20th-century Chinese spoken drama. This nine-act play was first staged in Shanghai, CHINA, in January 14, 1963, and was well received by the general public and the Chinese government. The Chinese officials praised not only the script but the director, crew, score, and performance, calling it wu hao xi (a play with five excellent elements). Drama critics fully confirmed its success, describing it as leading up to a new direction in military drama. Because of its popularity, it was adapted for the screen by Tian Ma Film in 1964. As anticipated, the film was a big box-office hit. In celebration of the play, many other performing troupes throughout the country staged it in the 1960s.

Primarily based on the true account of a model company of the People's Liberation Army (PLA) in Shanghai, the play depicted the young soldiers from the rural areas fighting against the capturing power of the cosmopolitan while they guarded the bustling Nanjing Road, a place noted for commercial grandeur, nightlife spectacle, and urban vice. Awestruck by the urban scenario and lifestyle, Lieutenant Chen Xi failed to carry on the PLA's tradition of simple living and hard working. He found his rural wife, Chun Ni, incompatible with his new status and unfit for Westernized Shanghai and mistreated her during her visit in Shanghai.

On a parallel with Chen Xi, Tong Anan, a new recruit from the city, did not conform to the military regulations and intended to withdraw from the company upon receiving criticism. Unlike Chen Xi, Sergeant Zhao Dada could not adapt to the metropolitan environment and requested relocation to a battleground. To resolve these troubles, the company commander Lu Dacheng and political supervisor Lu Hua timely engendered class education to increase soldiers' awareness of the hidden dangers beneath the neon lights. The play also showcased a group of Nationalist agents who attempted to destroy Shanghai and murder Tong's sister. This stirred and propelled Chen, Tong, Zhao, and their fellow soldiers into the work of eradicating corrupting forces in the city.

This play trumpets a new model of military drama transforming the traditional presentation of battles and heroic acts into a realistic representation of how New China and its masters reconfigure and reconstruct their power in a new battlefield—the city. Although the play superficially features the confrontation between the Nationalist and the Communist, Chinese tradition and Western influence, the play reveals that the city-rural challenge and transformation is an inevitable task with which the Chinese Communist Party must deal. As one of the early post-1949 dramatic works that touch on the city issues, the play, on the one hand, answers the call of Chinese leaders to associate the rural with the city and presents one such integration. On the other hand, it illustrates a long-practiced pro-village ideology.

The ideology tends to relegate urban history to a subordinate role in the grand narrative of modern China and drives the city into the embattlement of political assertions and economic strategies, and it functions as moral and social criterion evaluating characters' deeds and words in the play. For years, the play has been regarded as both military and urban drama.

FURTHER READING

Esherick, Joseph, ed. Remaking the Chinese City. Honolulu: Univ. of Hawaii Press, 1999.

Haiping Yan. Theater and Society: An Anthology of Contemporary Chinese Drama. Armonk, N.Y.: M. E. Sharpe, 1998.

Zhongguo dangdai wenxue yanjiu ziliao: Ni hong deng xia de shao bing zhuanji [The materials of contemporary Chinese literature studies: The special collection of On Guard Beneath the Neon Lights]. Ed. by the Chinese Department of Nanjing Normal Univ. Nanjing: N.p., 1979.

Ping Fu

ONNA NO ISSHO   See A WOMAN'S LIFE

ON THE JOB

On the Job was the first play by Montreal, CANADA, playwright DAVID FENNARIO, and its success came as a great surprise to the Canadian theater community and Fennario himself. Born in the working-class neighborhood of Pointe Saint Charles, Fennario was a high school dropout who spent several years drifting through short-term jobs, including working in the shipping room of a dress-making factory, an experience he would draw on to create On the Job. Fennario entered Montreal's Dawson College CÉGEP as a mature student in the early 1970s where his English teacher, Sally Nelson, encouraged him to allow the college to publish his journal. Maurice Podbrey, artistic director and co-founder of the Centaur Theatre, read the journal, published as Without a Parachute, and invited Fennario to be writer-in-residence despite the fact that Fennario had never been in a theater in his life. Podbrey's instinct proved astute, and On the Job was the result.

On the Job, originally directed by David Calderisi in 1975, takes place in the shipping room of a Montreal dress factory near Christmas. The workers exchange "French jokes," sing old songs, and pass a bottle of cheap liquor around in expectation of the afternoon off due to the holiday. A late order from a major department store prompts the newly hired manager to cancel the holiday, heightening tension. The French-speaking foreman Rene, whose "tabernac" muttering character borders on stereotype, is the focus of the workers' frustration in the first scenes, especially Gary who seems ready for a fight from the opening scenes. Billy, who has grown children and has worked in the shipping room longer than anyone else, functions as peacemaker, trying to hold on to his job for the next eight years so he can collect his pension. When Billy says, "I don't think there's good people or bad people. There's just people," the feisty Gary responds, "Bullshit." It becomes clear that Rene's Anglophone boss, Shaw, pressures him as much if not more than Rene pressures Gary and the other workers. Ultimately the characters are united in a kind of visceral class consciousness that overrides the timeworn linguistic and cultural antipathy between working-class Montrealers from English- and French-speaking backgrounds. When the short-tempered Gary is fired, the other workers, including Rene, stand by him.

Fennario was to become much more didactic in his later plays, filling his scripts with Brechtian devices such as narrators, historical facts, and direct diatribes against the ruling elite and bourgeoisie. Although politically vague compared to Fennario's later work, the slice of raw, frustrated, masculine life presented in On The Job retains its effectiveness after a quarter century.

Fennario's own story as a poor boy getting his play produced at Montreal's premiere English-language theater made critics, journalists, and the public notice it and him. Fennario was invited to be a guest on CBC television with the urbane and cosmopolitan host Laurier Lapierre. Fennario barely responded to Lapierre's questions, an event alluded to in Fennario's next play Nothing to Lose. Somehow Fennario had managed to make being a monosyllabic Anglo-Quebecer look interesting.

FURTHER READING

Allison, Dianne. "On the Job an Impeccable Performance." Montreal
  Gazette (October 8, 1976).
Fennario, David. Without a Parachute. Toronto: McClelland & Stewart,
  1974.
Zimmerman, Cynthia. The Work: Conversations with English-Canadian
  Playwrights. Toronto: Coach House Press, 1982.

Donald Cameron McManus

ONWUEME, TESS (1955–)

Together we form this moon shape. Lie in ambush surrounding the throne as the men emerge. We together in this naked legion, will salute them in our natural state. Taunting their eyes with their own shame. This naked dance is a last resort women have had over the ages. If our men force us to the wall, we must use it as our final weapon. Unusual problems demand unusual solutions.
—Omu, Movement 5, The Reign of Wazobia

In the prologue to The Reign of Wazobia by Tess Onwueme, the matriarch Omu's proposed strategy of female insurrection against a male campaign to dethrone Anioma Kingdom's feminist sovereign Wazobia represents a provocative semiotic subversion of patriarchy. An army of female bodies, objectified for ages as things of sex, transform *themselves* into political statements against the kingdom's conventional structure of male privilege. Men in Anioma Kingdom in the midwestern region of Ilaaa believe that "serious matters of state concern are too heavy for the brittle heads of women and children." The women's collective defiance of such assumptions by the destabilization of that ulti-

mate gendered signifier of tradition—the monarchy itself—sets the subversive tone of Onwueme's The Reign of Wazobia. First written and published in 1988, when tradition, ritual, and mythology had become key words informing Nigerian anticolonial narratives in dramatic theory and practice, Onwueme's play sought to decolonize the role of women within the nationalist project to establish a more democratic and pluralistic society.

Tess Onwueme attended the universities of Ife and Benin before moving to the UNITED STATES, where she occupies an endowed chair at the University of Wisconsin, Eau Claire. Her plays include *Then She Said It* (2002), *Shakara: Dance-Hall Queen* (2000), *Tell It to Women* (1999), *The Missing Face* (1997), *Riot in Heaven* (1996), *Parables for a Season* (1993), *Legacies* (1989), *Mirror for Campus* (1987), *Ban Empty Barn* (1986), *The Desert Encroaches* (1985), *The Broken Calabash* (1984), and *A Hen Too Soon* (1983). Her plays consistently interrogate conventional modes of representing women as subjects of history and modernity, particularly their resonances within notions of "mythology" and "traditionalism," which the emergent middle classes were obsessed with in Nigeria. Onwueme does not simply incorporate women's stories into existing myths; she goes on to make mythology and mythmaking an unsafe category of social and historical knowledge heavily implicated in the ideologies of patriarchy. She brusquely uses Igbo mythology to subvert the male prerogatives justified by traditional non-Western cultural norms.

Onwueme's plays The Broken Calabash and A Hen Too Soon challenge the institution of marriage as a socializing idiom that enhances female subjugation to patriarchy. Their themes critique marriage as a social contract that inherently suffocates female subjectivity and agency. The Reign of Wazobia goes even further in visualizing women's transition from the marginal citizenship to which they were relegated by Indigenous and foreign traditions to asserting their rights to more proactive citizenship within a democratic framework. The Reign of Wazobia makes a plea for what Onwueme recently called "internal reparations" (for women) as a complement to the compensation for transatlantic slavery demanded by members of the Africa diaspora from contemporary centers of Euro-American modernity (Onwueme, 2002).

The incorporation of the word *Wazobia* in the play's title is deeply contradictory since it is fraught with subversive innuendo. As a neologism, *Wazobia* means "come together," or unity. It is derived from Nigeria's three primary languages—Yoruba, Hausa, and Igbo. Coined by nationalists who believed that the unity of these three ethnic groups guaranteed nationhood, the word continues to be perpetuated by neocolonial nationalists, who also link the preservation of the national union to harmony among the colonially derived ethnic entities. The title *Wazobia* provokes the question of whether the play is a clichéd call to national unity. Before long it becomes apparent that Onwueme has instead subverted a neologism with a postindependence call for unity among women fragmented by patriarchy, ethnicity, and class. It is, however, a vision that equally critiques monolithic political collectives as utopian ideals that are inevitably untenable as long as internal inequities remain within such collectives.

[See also Africa]

SELECT PLAYS: A Hen Too Soon (1983); The Broken Calabash (1984); The Desert Encroaches (1985); The Reign of Wazobia (1988); Legacies (1989); Parables for a Season (1993); Riot in Heaven (1996); The Missing Face (1997); Tell It to Women (1999); Shakara: Dance-Hall Queen (2000)

FURTHER READING

Ajayi-Soyinka, Folabo. "Who Can Silence Her Drums? An Analysis of the plays of Tess Onwueme." In African Theatre. Women. Ed. by Martin Banham, James Gibbs, and Femi Osofisan. With guest editor Jane Plastow. Bloomington: Indiana Univ. Press, 2002.

Bartlett, Juliette E. "Modernity and Tradition in Tess Onwueme's Plays." In Nigeria in the Twentieth Century. Ed. by Toyin Falola. Durham, N.C.: Carolina Academic Press, 2002.

Onwueme, T. O. "Buried in the Rubble: The Missing Face in African Literature." Keynote address at the 28th Annual African Literature Association (ALA) Convention, San Diego, California, April 5, 2002.

Uko, Iniobong I. Gender and Identity in the works of Osonye Tess Onwueme. Trenton, N.J.: Africa World Press, 2004.

Awam Amkpa

OPEN THEATER

The origins of Open Theater (Teatro Abierto) can be traced back to two specific events in 1980 that powerfully illuminate the authoritarian mechanisms of the military dictatorship that devastated ARGENTINA between 1976 and 1983. One of these events, an instance of censorship, occurred when the government's militaristic administration decided to eliminate the department Historia del Teatro Argentino (History of Argentine Theatre) from the Conservatorio Nacional de Arte Dramático (National Conservatory of the Dramatic Arts), under the spurious logic that such theater did not actually exist. This decision came at the end of a long series of unfortunate government interventions within the cultural and educational sectors, including the proliferation of black lists and the shutting down of certain theaters.

The other, an instance of self-censorship, occurred when a group of actors sought the participation of playwright OSVALDO DRAGÚN in composing for them the script that would later become his play To the Rapist (Al violador). Owing to the piece's controversial subject matter—it tells the story of an outcast rapist who becomes a government assassin—and the fear of reprisals, the actors ultimately rejected the project. In this climate of generalized fear, and with the desire to assert the validity of Argentine theater, Open Theater emerged as a form of opposition to the dominant, closed society. Its first season lasted from July 28 to September 21, 1981, and proved a success among critics and audiences alike. Various factors explain this initial success: its substantial media publicity; the fact that most of the pieces were penned by well-known playwrights; the participation of popular television and film actors; and the organization of its performances, composed of twenty brief one-acts, performed thrice daily during—what was for Argentineans—the unusual hour of 6:00 P.M.

Yet it was the burning down of the Teatro del Picadero, home to the series' first performances, that would ensure the memory of Open Theater in the public consciousness. This tragic event in August 1981 was followed by demonstrations of solidarity and support for the series. Among the sixteen theaters that had offered their space to ensure that the series would continue, Open Theater selected the theater Tabarís.

The following year, the series was expanded to reach the entire nation. Yet it was not long before serious methodological, aesthetic, and political objections were raised. The first of these pertained to that season's selection process. Of 412 plays and seventy-five experimental projects, thirty-three and seventeen, respectively, were chosen. Celebrated dramatists like GRISELDA GAMBARO, Eduardo Pavlovsky, and Ricardo Monti were excluded from the series.

As a result, the magazine Humor opened its pages to a public debate, led by writers Mario O'Donnell—also excluded by the judges—and Roberto Cassa. The former accused the organizers of privileging a realist aesthetic that confined the more AVANT-GARDE pieces to the experimental session. The latter responded by asserting that, by his account, the quality of the productions was notably better than those of the previous year.

Yet undoubtedly the greatest weakness plaguing this second season was political in nature. Since the submission deadline was in March of 1982, most of the selected plays were out of touch with the nation's most recent political events. Notably absent was the Falkland Islands War, which marked the undeniable failure and slow death of the military government.

Open Theater's third season's series was organized around the slogan "For a popular theater without censorship" and sought to reflect upon the past seven years of dictatorship. It began with a large parade, where an effigy meant to symbolize censorship was burned. Among this season's most notable characteristics were its strongly collectivist character—seven groups of four authors and four directors contributed to each piece—and the space it made for promising young female artists, as much in the writing as in the directorial realm.

In 1984, twenty-one authors were invited to write on the theme of liberty, and five free cultural workshops were offered in which these scripts would be developed into plays. Yet the majority focused on the traumatic experiences of an authoritarian past. In the process, they displayed a marked inability to imagine society under new, democratic conditions. As a result, the series was canceled at the last moment.

The 1985 season, the series' last, can be divided into three parts. The first, Teatrazo, was an inaugural street festival, held in distinct locations throughout the country. There were performances in plazas, at train and subway stations, in public transportation, and in various stores. Theater groups from all over Latin America were invited to participate, and September 21 of that year was declared the Day of Latin American Theatre. The second, a program called Otros Autores, Otros Directores (Other Authors, Other Directors) consisted of four scriptwriting seminars, overseen by famous playwrights. Finally, Otro teatro (Other Theater) convened groups of writers to explore such delicate issues as the imprisoned and the "disappeared," the state of working-class women, and the marginalized sectors of Buenos Aires' citizens.

Ultimately, then, Open Theater, which began as a frank resistance to military dictatorship, ended up weakened by the changing historical circumstances. In its beginnings it constituted the first cultural manifestation against the regime. Yet it was this very attribute that would lead to the vacillations that marked the development of later seasons and that showed the series to be incapable of reflecting on its role within the context of the transition to democracy. Curiously, while its ambitions grew, attendance dropped. In aesthetic terms, its marked preference for works of a naturalist and realist bent implied an effort to follow existing national theatrical trends that were more relevant in the prior decade than at the dawn of a new era. Nevertheless, its most prominent characteristic was rooted in the ability it demonstrated to mobilize an entire society against the abuses of repression. As such, it occupies a prominent place in the history of Argentine theater.

FURTHER READING

Arancibia, Juana and Zulema Mirkin, eds. *Teatro argentino durante el Proceso (1976–1983)*. Buenos Aires: Vinciguerra, 1992.

Giella, Miguel Angel. "Teatro Abierto 1981." *Volumen I: Teatro Argentino bajo vigilancia*. Buenos Aires: Corregidor, 1991.

Graham-Jones, Jean. *Exorcising History: Argentine Theatre Under Dictatorship*. London: Associated Univ. Presses, 2000.

Taylor, Diana. *Disappearing Acts: Spectacles of Gender and Nationalism in Argentina's "Dirty War."* Durham, N.C.: Duke Univ. Press, 1997.

Villegas, Juan. "Historicizing Latin American Theatre." *Theatre Journal* 41, no. 4 (December 1989): 505–514.

Norberto Cambiasso (Tr. by Gabriel Milner)

OPERA KECOA　*See* THE COCKROACH OPERA

OPTIMISTIC HESKAYA　*See* AN OPTIMISTIC TRAGEDY

AN OPTIMISTIC TRAGEDY

An Optimistic Tragedy (Optimisticheskaya tragediya), written by the Soviet dramatist Vsevolod Vishnevsky (1900–1951) in 1932 and performed the following year, is based on the March 1921 uprising by Soviet sailors of the Baltic fleet on Kronstadt, a naval base on Kotlin Island in the Gulf of Finland, against Bolshevik political domination. Its rhetorical and propagandist form argues for a mode of socialist realist drama of melodramatic and romantic revolutionary hyperbole.

The play dramatizes the conflict as one between anarchism and Party discipline, against a background of foreign military intervention. Most of the action takes place aboard ship and the central conflict is embodied in the persons of the "Chief" of a group of anarchist sailors, whose principal henchman is nicknamed "Gruff" (because of his voice), who are opposed by a woman commissar sent by the Bolsheviks to deal with the anarchists. Her main supporter is a Finnish Communist sailor, Vainonen, who is murdered by "Gruff." Other important issues that the play deals with center on one of the sailors, Aleksei, a first-class seaman with natural leadership qualities, and the commander of the ship, who is a prerevolutionary naval officer of the old school. The play shows how the commissar recognizes that winning over the anarchists involves winning Aleksei for the cause, because of his personal qualities and because his rejection of Bolshevism is based on an ignorance that can be rectified. In this she is successful, as she is in persuading the captain to lend his expertise to the Bolsheviks, even though his hostility to the new regime is unrelenting.

The most dramatic scenes include one in which, threatened with a direct assault on her person by a half-naked sailor, the commissar summarily shoots him dead; a scene in which Aleksei's authority has been so skillfully exploited by the commissar in undermining that of the "Chief" that the former has the latter led away to be shot by his hitherto intimidated followers; and the final scene, where the dying commissar is brought on stage following the successful repulsion of the interventionist forces by the—now united—body of sailors. The final stage direction follows the commissar's last words: "Show them . . . What the navy's made of . . . ," and gives an indication of the play's "revolutionary romanticism" (to use MAKSIM GORKY's phrase) as well as its naïve imperviousness to cynicism: "The regiment stands bareheaded. Every muscle and nerve taut, courage at its peak. The sun is reflected in their eyes . . . A musical call breaks the silence . . . Numberless beings are alive . . . The heart surges with delight at the sight of a world giving birth to people who scorn the old lie about the fear of death. Pulsating arteries. Like the flow of great rivers bathed in light, like the titanic overwhelming forces of nature, terrifying in their mounting strength, there come sounds purged of all melody, raw, crude, colossal—the thunder of cataclysms and the onrushing floods of life."

The stage direction also helps to explain why the "tragedy" is considered "optimistic." Vishnevsky had himself served in the navy during the Civil War and appears to have been permanently attracted to the theme of the Kronstadt rising, writing a play, *The Trial of the Kronstadt Insurrectionists* (1921), and producing the screenplay for Yefim Dzigan's 1936 film, *We Are From Kronstadt*.

[*See also* Russia and the Soviet Union]

FURTHER READING

Maryamov, Alexander. "Vsevolod Vishnevsky at His Best." In *Soviet Literature Monthly* 11 (November 1965).

Segel, Harold B. *Russian Drama from Gorky to the Present.* 2nd ed. Baltimore: Johns Hopkins Univ. Press, 1993.

Vishnevsky, Vsevolod. "Optimistic Tragedy." Tr. by Margaret Wettlin. In *Soviet Literature Monthly* 11 (November 1965).

——. "An Optimistic Tragedy." In *Four Soviet Plays*, ed. by B. Blake. Tr. by H.G. Scott and Robert S. Carr. Reissue of 1937 Moscow edition. New York: Benjamin Blom, 1972.

——. "An Optimistic Tragedy." In *Classic Soviet Plays*, ed. by A. Mikhailova. Tr. by Robert Daglish. Moscow: Progress Publishers, 1979.

Nick Worrall

ORDET   See THE WORD

O REI DA VELA   See THE CANDLE KING

ÖRKÉNY, ISTVÁN (1912–1979)

Master of the modern Hungarian "grotesque," István Örkény is HUNGARY's most influential playwright of the second half of the 20th century. He was born on April 5, 1912, in Budapest. His World War II experiences in a labor brigade at the Russian front and as a prisoner of war influenced his early, naturalistic writing. After a period of prohibition from publishing following the 1956 Hungarian Revolution, he became a celebrated writer of short stories as well as a major playwright.

Örkény brought a startling and innovative point of view to themes current in Hungarian drama of the 1960s and 1970s. This was a period when the communist regime was loosening compulsory artistic norms. Playwrights were increasingly finding ways to express disillusionment with the system holding the country in its grip and with the manifestly failed ideology sustaining that system. The Hungarian grotesque shares a kinship with the work of such playwrights of the region as the Polish SŁAWOMIR MROŻEK, the Czech VÁCLAV HAVEL, and the Romanian MARIN SORESCU. Whereas Western ABSURDISM posits an a priori absurd world that deprives man of a tragic dimension by presenting him as a helplessly flailing being in the wasteland of existence, the grotesque traps its characters in an inscrutable, labyrinthine, and irrational world determined by the nature and structure of society.

THE TOTH FAMILY (Tóték, 1967), Örkény's first grotesque play, is a mordant satire about a family actively participating in its own victimization to achieve what it perceives—mistakenly—as its self-interest. The play anticipates Örkény's other, more absurd treatments of the ambivalent relationship between tyrant and victim. In his last stage work, Screenplay (Forgatókönyv, 1979), the integrity of the protagonist's identity dissipates in the course of a show trial presented as a circus performance. In Stevie in the Bloodbath (Pisti a vérzivatarban, 1969) the title character, played by four actors, represents the national fate. The play is a stylized, carnivallike chronology of modern Hungarian catastrophes, in which Stevie never achieves a coherent identity. He is often simultaneously on antagonistic sides; he is killed only to reappear; at one point he becomes a vacuum, at another the Messiah. The play has been called a pretragedy, since Stevie never achieves the personhood necessary to become a tragic figure.

The question of identity is also at the core of BLOOD RELATIONS (Vérrokonok, 1974) and Key Searchers (Kulcskeresök, 1975), which examine aspects of the national character. The seven characters of Blood Relations are related by the absurdly misdirected focus of their lives: the railroad, which is metaphorical for the cause the nation has wasted its energies on. Each character either loves, hates, dies for, spies for, or is otherwise consumed by the railroad. Key Searchers is about the Hungarian capacity for illusion in an all-too-real world. Örkény's lyrical, realistic COMEDY Catsplay (Macskajáték, 1969), about a sexagenarian love triangle, raises the question of emigration to the comforts of the West versus the dogged determination to stay home.

Örkény was awarded Hungary's two most prestigious literary prizes, the Attila József and the Kossuth. He died on June 24, 1979, in Budapest.

SELECT PLAYS: *The Toth Family* (Tóték, 1967); *Catsplay* (Macskajáték, 1969); *Stevie in the Bloodbath* (Pisti a vérzivatarban, 1969); *Blood Relations* (Vérrokonok, 1974); *Key Searchers* (Kulcskeresök, 1975); *Screenplay* (Forgatókönyv, 1979)

FURTHER READING

Bécsy, Tamás. *Kalandok a drámával, Magyar drámák 1945–1989* [Adventures with Drama, Hungarian Dramas 1945–1989]. Budapest: Balassi Kiadó, 1996.

Czigány, Lóránt. *The Oxford History of Hungarian Literature.* Oxford: Clarendon Press, 1984.

Ézsiás, Erzsébet. *Mai magyar dráma* [Hungarian Drama Today]. Budapest: Kossuth Könyvkiadó, 1986.

Müller, Péter. *A groteszk dramaturgiája* [The dramaturgy of the grotesque]. Budapest: Magvető Könyvkiadó, 1990.

Radnóti, Zsuzsa. *Lázadó dramaturgiák* [Dramaturgies in revolt]. Budapest: Palatinus, 2003.

Eugene Brogyányi

ØRNSBO, JESS (1932–)

Jess: Do plays have to be funny?
Ørnsbo: Yes, otherwise it cannot be serious. There is no regular explanation of the world that is not at the same time a babbling joke. Fun is the antisubstance with which we try to fight the insufferableness of existence. Without fun we could not cope with the most wrong construction of this wrong world.
—Jess Ørnsbo interviewing himself, 1988

Danish playwright and poet Jess Ørnsbo (born on August 26, 1932, in Copenhagen, DENMARK) is the godfather of new

Danish drama, the boom of playwrights that flourished in the 1990s. His point of departure is MODERNISM, especially ABSURDISM. Ørnsbo has managed to be an enfant terrible and provocateur practically from his debut as a playwright in 1968 with *The Dwarf that Disappeared* (Dværgen der blev væk), written in 1962 and premiered at the Student Theatre, which was the period's most significant experimental theater. The inspiration from EUGÈNE IONESCO and SAMUEL BECKETT is clear, but lines can also be drawn to AUGUST STRINDBERG'S CHAMBER PLAYS and from Slavic, especially Polish, literature.

Ørnsbo has a university degree in Slavic philology and has written a doctoral thesis about STANISLAW WITKIEWICZ. But in a broader perspective, an equally strong inspiration comes from the kind of coarse real life he came to know from his childhood in the popular Vesterbro quarter of Copenhagen, including a deep pleasure of absurd linguistic nonsense and appreciation of odd types often from the lower strata of society, a world somewhere between REALISM and SURREALISM. A clamorous scandal arose with Ørnsbo's television play *The Hash-tree* (Hashtræet), written in 1968 and produced in 1973, an absurd prophecy of the bourgeois confrontation with the hippie movement, which was presented in anything but a romantic light, actually as a sect that thought it could fly! For years Ørnsbo had to fight to be performed. And when he was, his universe was almost automatically criticized for being too disgusting, too animalesque, too black, and too disrespectful of ordinary dramaturgical rules.

It was not until the 1990s that his plays were regularly produced. A kind of breakthrough came with *The Trap* (Fælden, 1982) and *The Children After Today* (Børnene derpå, 1984), satirical, absurd COMEDIES about an average couple's existence in a dissolving welfare society, including bizarre fights between parents and children. But it was with *The Wrong Ones* (De forkerte, 1990) that Ørnsbo reached a larger public and almost unanimous critical recognition: a kaleidoscopic, autobiographical story about a family in a Denmark occupied by the Germans during World War II, a remarkable mixture of DOCUMENTARY and grotesque approaches.

The formula father-mother-children is recurrent in Ørnsbo's plays. This matrix is found in plays like *Astma-5* (written 1969, performed 1995), *Mayonnaise* (Majonæse, 1985), and *Ulysses from Vrå* (Odysseus fra Vrå, 1993). Education and family and social life are seen as mechanisms of humiliation and war. Ørnsbo takes the part of the defenseless but without being sentimental. The parents are often more infantile and immature than the children; an immense craving or thirst for affection and tenderness breaks out in its opposite: hatred, revenge, aggression. His principal work from the 1990s THE CLUB (Klubben, 1995) circles around this motif. In 1987 he published a volume of fourteen plays, accompanied by harsh attacks on critics and theater leaders, where he defines theater as "the tear and memory of society."

SELECT PLAYS: *The Dwarf that Disappeared* (Dværgen der blev væk, 1962); *Astma-5* (1969); *Jealousy* (television–play, 1973); *The Serbskij* *Institute* (Serbskij-instituttet, 1973); *The Holy People from Vanløse* (De hellige fra Vanløse, 1978); *The Hobos* (television play, Strejferne, 1979); *Life in Denmark* (Livet i Danmark, 1980); *The Trap* (Fælden, 1982); *The Children After Today* (Børnene derpå, 1984); *Candies in the Kitchen* (television play, Bolsjer i køkkenet, 1985); *Mayonnaise* (Majonæse, 1985); *Love Without Yller* (Kjærlighed uden yller, 1986); *The Wrong Ones* (De forkerte, 1990); *Johny Frankikso* (1991); *13 Square Meters* (13 kvadratmeter, 1991); *Ulysses from Vrå* (Odysseus fra Vrå, 1993); *The Weedy Fellow* (Splejsen, 1993); *The Club* (Klubben, 1995); *No Man's Land* (Ingenmandsland, 1995); *Sewer and Alas* (Kloak og ve, 1996); *Welfare—Violence* (Velfærd–Voldfærd, 1997)

FURTHER READING
Kistrup, Jens. "Playwright for and Against Theatre." *Danish Literary Magazine* 5 (1993).
Theil, Per, and Lise Garsdal. *Hvem der? Scener fra 90erne* [Who's There? Scenes From the 90's]. Copenhagen: Høst og Søn, 2000.

Bent Holm

ORPHEUS

The first important dramatic work by JEAN COCTEAU, *Orpheus* (1926) is based on the myth of the classical lyric poet with whom Cocteau strongly identified. As the artist said of its film adaptation: "It isn't really a film, it is myself, a sort of projection of what really concerns me."

The play is set in contemporary Thrace, with Orpheus and Eurydice imagined as a modern-day bohemian couple. Orpheus, a celebrated poet, has withdrawn from public life in obsessive pursuit of inspiration from the spirit world. As he listens for ghostly communications via a horse, his wife Eurydice breaks a window every day so she can receive a visit from an attentive young glazier, Heurtebise. Eurydice decides to do away with the horse with the help of Aglaonice, a poet and fierce mistress of the Bacchantes. While Orpheus is out, Heurtebise reveals he has brought poison from Aglaonice. But neither can bring themselves to kill the horse, although in the process Heurtebise reveals his magical powers. Disturbed, Eurydice throws him out, but not before sending a letter to Aglaonice in an envelope the latter provided. Too late—the envelope is also poisoned—and Death arrives to take Eurydice to the Underworld and in the process leaves her rubber gloves. Heurtebise advises a bereft Orpheus to put on the gloves and walk through the bedroom mirror to the Underworld.

Orpheus retrieves Eurydice but on condition: if he looks at her, she will die again—this time forever. But neither can endure the strain, and in minutes Orpheus has sent Eurydice to eternal death with a mere glance. A crowd of Bacchantes has gathered outside the house, hungry for blood. Orpheus goes to confront them and is decapitated, although his head continues to cry out for Eurydice. His wife leads his spirit back through the mirror, and they both call for Heurtebise to join them. In the final scene, the three sit down to an otherworldly lunch.

The play is not so much a dramatic narrative as a portrait of the artist's psychological and symbolic vocabulary. Its characters are less memorable than the world in which they move, where an everyday SURREALISM abounds: mirrors are doorways to death, glaziers are really guardian angels in disguise, and literary critics are bloodthirsty Bacchantes. In the midst of this magic, the artist struggles to hear the sound of true poetry—a calling that renders him deaf to the human voices around him. With characteristic ambivalence, Cocteau sees the artist's role as both sublime and absurd, and the play constantly deflates Orpheus's lofty ambitions as much as it celebrates them.

Cocteau wrote *Orpheus* during a deep depression, following the death of his lover Raymond Radiguet in 1924. Ostracized by the surrealists and addicted to opium, the writer's sense of himself as an outcast was only heightened by the play's reception. *Orpheus* opened in Paris on June 17, 1926, to mixed reviews. Many found the play's mix of myth and domesticity tonally confusing, but the play was revived a year later, with Cocteau himself in the role of Heurtebise.

[See also France]

FURTHER READING

Ashton, Dore, ed. *Jean Cocteau and the French Scene*. New York: Abbeville Press, 1984.

Brown, Frederick. *An Impersonation of Angels: A Biography of Jean Cocteau*. New York: Viking, 1968.

Cocteau, Jean. *Orpheus*. Tr. by John Savacool. In *The Infernal Machine and Other Plays*. New York: New Directions, 1963. 97–150.

Charlotte Stoudt

ORTON, JOE (1933–1967)

I'm a believer in original sin. I find people profoundly bad and irresistibly funny.

—Joe Orton, 1986

Born John Kingsley Orton in Leicester, ENGLAND, in 1933, Orton's fame rests on the technical brilliance of his plays, their risqué subject matter, and the sensational nature of his death in 1967 (bludgeoned by his lover Kenneth Halliwell, who then committed suicide). Orton's major works include ENTERTAINING MR SLOANE (1964), LOOT (1966), and *What the Butler Saw* (1969). Other works include *The Ruffian on the Stair* (1964), *The Erpingham Camp* (1966), *The Good and Faithful Servant* (1967), and *Funeral Games* (1968). His first plays *Fred and Madge* (1959) and *The Visitors* (1961) were published for the first time in 1998. His archive is housed at the University of Leicester.

After attending the Royal Academy of Dramatic Art, Orton realized that his talents lay in writing rather than ACTING. Educated and encouraged by Halliwell, he began writing novels with him. Orton's solo work draws on influences as diverse as Ronald Firbank, JEAN GENET, HAROLD PINTER, Greek drama, and Whitehall FARCE. He encapsulated this fusion of farce and TRAGEDY, structure and anarchy, with the comment:

I always say that the theatre is the Temple of Dionysus, and not Apollo. You do the Dionysus thing on your typewriter, and then you allow a little Apollo in, just a little to shape and guide it. (Orton interview with Alan Brien, quoted in Lahr, 1978)

His plays are remarkable for their frank depiction of homosexuality when homosexual acts were still illegal and censored by the Lord Chamberlain. Orton achieved this by inverting society's accepted moral structure, so that outrageous behavior is greeted with equanimity, while the mundane attracts comment. *The Ruffian on the Stair*, for example, opens with a husband telling his wife about his appointment with a man in the toilets at Kings Cross station. She replies, "You always go to such interesting places." *Entertaining Mr Sloane* scandalized audiences with its depiction of a brother and sister sexually sharing the young man who murdered their father. *Loot* was more controversial, satirizing police brutality, Roman Catholicism, and the media's obsession with criminals. *What the Butler Saw* is the pinnacle of Orton's crusade against society's pretensions and represents the perfect fusion of genres. Set in a mental hospital on a set designed for farce (French windows; multiple doors, windows, and cupboards), the play deals with lunacy, incest, adultery, malpractice, and homosexuality.

Orton's life and work epitomize the social and cultural shifts that occurred in Britain in the 1960s. Born working class, his socially ambitious mother saved to send him to an independent school, but in her ignorance, she sent him to a commercial college rather than an academic institution. Her pretensions to grandeur, coupled with the commercial vocabulary Orton learned at school, provided him with a rich seam of COMEDY and dialogue style for his plays.

At the time of his death, Orton was negotiating with the Beatles to write a film for the band (eventually published as *Up Against It*). Choosing Orton was a reflection of his own fame; but it also reflected the growth of the cult of the celebrity as it was being refashioned by working-class provincials like himself and the Beatles. Orton's response to this accolade demonstrates his confidence in his star status; it also epitomizes the "Ortonesque":

Because all teenagers are supposed to imitate the Beatles I mustn't have them doing certain things. I wrote a story, but actually as it turned out, by page 25 they had committed adultery, murder, dressed in drag, been in prison, seduced the daughter of a Priest, I mean the niece of a Priest, blown up a war memorial and all sorts of things like that. (qtd. in Hanson, 1967)

[See also Gay and Lesbian Drama]

PLAYS: *Fred and Madge* (1959); *The Visitors* (1961); *Entertaining Mr Sloane* (1964); *The Ruffian on the Stair* (1964); *The Erpingham Camp* (1966); *Loot* (1966); *The Good and Faithful Servant* (1967); *Up Against It* (1967); *Funeral Games* (1968); *What the Butler Saw* (1969)

FURTHER READING

Bull, J., and F. Gray. "Joe Orton." In *Essays on Contemporary British Drama*, ed. by Hedwig Bock and Albert Wertheim. Munich: Hueber, 1981.

Coppa, F. "Introduction" to *Fred and Madge, The Visitors: Two Plays*, by Joe Orton. London: Nick Hern Bks., 1998.

Hanson, Barry. Interview with Orton on *Crimes of Passion* program, June 1967.

Lahr, J. *Prick Up Your Ears: The Biography of Joe Orton*. London: Allen Lane, 1978.

Orton, J. *The Complete Plays*. London: Methuen, 1976.

——. *The Orton Diaries: Including the Correspondence of Edna Welthorpe and Others*. Ed. by John Lahr. London: Methuen, 1986.

Kate Dorney

OSANAI KAORU (1881–1928)

Osanai Kaoru, Japanese director, critic, translator, and playwright, defined the course of SHINGEKI in the early 20th century. At the Free Theater (Jiyū Gekijō) and the Tsukiji Little Theater (TLT; Tsukiji Shōgekijō), Osanai's productions of modern European classics, as well as new works by Japanese playwrights like MORI ŌGAI, TSUBOUCHI SHŌYŌ, and KUBOTA MANTARŌ, were groundbreaking. Throughout his career he introduced Japanese readers to the latest trends in modern European drama.

While still an undergraduate in English literature at Tokyo University, he became acquainted with Ōgai and SHINPA actor Ii Yōhō, for whose company he served as DRAMATURG from 1904 until 1906, also directing various Western plays. By 1906, growing frustrated with shinpa's resistance to reform, he quit Ii's company and, together with several leading naturalist authors like Tayama Katai and Shimazaki Tōson, established the Ibsen Society to promote the study and production of the Norwegian's plays. Together with kabuki actor Ichikawa Sadanji II, who had returned from an eye-opening tour of Europe in 1907, Osanai founded the Free Theatre; its first production, in 1909, of HENRIK IBSEN's JOHN GABRIEL BORKMAN, was one of the major cultural events of that generation. The Free Theatre trained kabuki actors in modern naturalistic acting techniques, but the TLT, which Osanai opened in 1924 with Hijikata Yoshi and others, forged a complete break with the traditional theater. He alienated many Japanese playwrights in 1924 by his decision to produce at first only Western plays in translation there. Osanai also directed Japan's first radio drama, *In the Mine* (1925), and talkie, *Dawn* (1927). In direction and acting, his models were Gordon Craig and KONSTANTIN STANISLAVSKY; his theory of dramaturgy was indebted to William Archer. He made two extensive study tours abroad, the first to Europe in 1912–1913 and the second to the Soviet Union in 1927–1928.

Osanai wrote more than thirty plays, many of which were adaptations of others' work. He published his first, *The Noncombatant* (*Hisentōin*) in 1904 but considered his real debut as a playwright was *The First World* (*Dai'ichi no Sekai*) which was favorably compared with GERHART HAUPTMANN's *Lonely People*; Sadanji's troupe staged it at the Imperial Theatre in 1921. Osanai's skill in stagecraft shows in his dramaturgy. His plays are tightly structured and feature clear and concise dialogue with few stage directions, demonstrating his belief that drama was primarily a theatrical, not a literary, form. Though he experimented in a variety of styles, ranging from REALISM and EXPRESSIONISM to modern revisions of traditional drama, Osanai always stressed the objective portrayal of human character rather than the explication of any particular theme or ideology. In such plays as *The Master* (*Teishū*, 1925), *The Son* (*Masuko*, 1922; an adaptation of Harold Chapin's *Augustus in Search of a Father*), and *Hades* (*Naraku*, 1926; a work inspired by MAKSIM GORKY's LOWER DEPTHS), he excelled at portraying the lower classes. Osanai rejected kabuki ACTING but staged several daring adaptations of traditional puppet and kabuki plays.

[See also Japan]

SELECT PLAYS: *The Non-combatant* (*Hisentōin*, 1904); *The First World* (*Dai'ichi no Sekai*, 1921); *The Son* (*Musuko*, 1922); *The Master* (*Teishū*, 1925); *Hades* (*Naraku*, 1926); *Kim Okkyun* (1926); *Oda Nobunaga, the Christian* (*Kirishitan Oda Nobunaga*, 1926)

FURTHER READING

Kubo Sakae. *Osanai Kaoru*. Tokyo: Bungei Shunjūsha, 1947.

Osanai Kaoru. *Osanai Kaoru Zenshū* [Complete works of Osanai Kaoru]. 8 vols. Kyoto: Rinsen Shobō, 1976.

Ottaviani, Gioa. "'Difference' and 'Reflexivity': Osanai Kaoru and the Shingeki Movement." *Asian Theatre Journal* 11, no. 2 (Fall 1994): 213–230.

Powell, Brian. *Japan's Modern Theatre: A Century of Continuity and Change*. London: Japan Library, 2002.

M. Cody Poulton

OSBORN, PAUL (1901–1988)

Success, I often feel, can be a very dangerous thing. Up to that moment your whole life, consciously and unconsciously, your thoughts, your dreams, everything you've done, has been concentrated to that one point. And once it is achieved you are rather empty.

—Paul Osborn

Over a career that spanned nearly forty years, Paul Osborn was a flourishing writer of original plays, stage adaptations of novels, and screenplays based on novels and plays or both. He was born on September 4, 1901, in Evansville, Indiana, and grew up in Kalamazoo, Michigan. He received undergraduate and master of arts degrees from the University of Michigan, where for two years he taught English beginning in 1925. He studied playwriting with GEORGE PIERCE BAKER at Yale University in 1928. He stayed for a year and then moved to New York and "just hung around until I got a play on." From 1928, when his first play,

Hotbed, was staged, through the mid-1960s, he wrote almost two dozen scripts that were either produced on the New York stage or filmed by Hollywood studios.

Osborn's most memorable original play is MORNING'S AT SEVEN, a gentle COMEDY of family intrigues. When initially staged in 1939, it was a commercial and critical failure, playing only forty-four performances, but in 1980 it won a Tony Award for best revival of a play on Broadway. It later went on a successful national tour and was produced in London. Osborn's first two original plays produced in New York were not successful. His third, The Vinegar Tree, a sophisticated comedy about free love, performed in 1930, flourished on Broadway, establishing his dramatic credentials. His next original venture, Oliver, Oliver, was poorly received; he then turned to dramatizing novels for the stage. Maiden Voyage, a comic look at the ancient Greek gods, closed in 1957 before reaching Broadway.

While he preferred to write original plays, his greatest talent seemed to be the ability to condense sprawling novels into compact plays and movies without losing the atmosphere of the original work. He brought to these adaptations a keen sense of structure and the ability to adjust characterizations to fit specific actors. His stage adaptations were highly successful—, notably, On Borrowed Time (1938), which ran just short of a year on Broadway, dramatized from the novel by Lawrence Edward Watkin. In the story, a grandfather traps Death in a tree so that he might prolong his life with his much-loved orphaned grandson. A Bell for Adano, based on John Hersey's novel, also had a much-admired Broadway run of 296 performances in 1944. Point of No Return, starring Henry Fonda, dramatized from the novel by J. P. Marquand, was a success of the 1951 season, running for 364 performances.

His screenplays, also based on novels, were usually top-of-the line projects with major stars and produced by such giants as Metro-Goldwyn-Mayer, Warner Brothers, and Twentieth Century-Fox. He was nominated for an Academy Award for his film scripts of John Steinbeck's East of Eden (1955, directed by Elia Kazan) and Sayonara, based on the James Michener novel (1957). In 1982 Osborn received the Laurel Award for Screen by the Screen Writers Guild of America in recognition of his "outstanding contributions to the profession of the screen writer."

His career prospered in New York, London, and Hollywood for well over three decades but ebbed when his eyesight began to fail in the early 1960s. Osborn died on May 12, 1988, in New York City.

[See also United States, 1929–Present]

PLAYS: Hotbed (1928); A Ledge (1929); The Vinegar Tree (1930); Oliver, Oliver (1934); On Borrowed Time (adapted from Watkin's novel, 1938); Morning's at Seven (1939); The Innocent Voyage (adapted from Hughes's novel, 1943); A Bell for Adano (adapted from Hersey's novel, 1944); Point of No Return (adapted from Marquand's novel, 1951); Maiden Voyage (1957); The World of Suzie Wong (from the novel, 1958); Film of Memory (1965); Hot September (musical, adapted from Inges's Picnic, 1965)

FURTHER READING

Botto, Lewis. "Triumph at Twilight." Playbill (June 1980).

Hinson, Hal. "At Last, Paul Osborn Finds the Rainbow." Los Angeles Herald Examiner (December 5, 1981): B1.

Kakutani, Michiko. "40 Years Late, Osborn Has a Hit." New York Times (April 14, 1980): C13.

Jim Patterson

OSBORNE, ALAN (1942–)

Born in 1942 in the former industrial town of Merthyr Tydfil, then and now one of the most deprived areas of Wales, Alan Osborne was educated at Quakers Yard Grammar School. He boxed and swam competitively before studying at Newport College of Art. He trained as a teacher, taught art and architecture in Oxford and London, and returned to Wales in 1975 to teach at Afon Taf, Troed-y-Rhiw. He later gave up teaching to be a full-time artist and writer.

Osborne's first plays explore issues of community and place. They are also explorations of the synergies of different art forms: Terraces (1979), Johnnie Darkie (1981), a "JAZZ opera" set in Tiger Bay, the multicultural docklands of Cardiff, and Tiger, Tiger (1985) are plays that combine music, the visual arts, and performance to which Osborne wrote the libretti, created the set, and wrote some of the music. His first major play Bull, Rock, and Nut won the Play for Wales competition in 1981 and was produced in 1983. In Bull, Rock, and Nut, Osborne juxtaposes the daily emptiness and hopelessness of the terminally unemployed with the pomp of an unseen funeral of the Merthyr-born boxer Johnny Owen. The small-time boxers Rock and Bull and their manager Nut deliberately avoid going to the funeral because they feel cheated by a community that neglects its young people while cheering its dead heroes. Nut's poignant call to "give us the flowers now" can be read as a leitmotif for Osborne's work in general. In Sunshine and in Shadow (1985) begins with the demolition of a house on the poverty-stricken Gurnos council estate in Merthyr that follows a double suicide. The play then explores the reasons behind the suicide and uncovers the sordid lives of bed-bound, drug-dependent Vee, her partner Day, and their children Babes and Ga-ga. The family and the other inhabitants of the estate are hermetically sealed off from mainstream society, whose representatives have embraced the values of Thatcherism and who regard the poverty of the estate dwellers as an illness to be quarantined. Yet there is a pathetic grandness about Vee, who rules her world from her bed, and the play goes some way to reclaim the humanity of the hopelessly deprived. The Redemption Song (1987) is a short, funny play about Mick and Bob, who have invented a toy that might make them rich. However, they are also constantly stoned, and their hazy, enclosed world, in which they are reduced to dreaming of a better world and trying to escape from violent moneylenders, can be read as a social commentary on 1980s Wales.

In the late 1980s and in the 1990s, Osborne returned to music theater. He wrote the libretto for *Forbidden Hymn* (1989) and has been involved in the community theater project *Katerina* (2001), in which Merthyr schoolchildren wrote and staged an opera with the help of members of the Welsh National Opera. Further work includes *Fire Tree* (2002) and *Clockopera* (2002). His artwork has also received numerous exhibitions and is held in many private and public collections.

[*See also* England, 1960–Present]

SELECT PLAYS: *Terraces* (1979); *Johnnie Darkie* (1981); *Bull, Rock, and Nut* (1983); *In Sunshine and in Shadow* (1985); *Tiger, Tiger* (1985); *The Tuscan* (1986); *Redemption Song* (1987); *The Rising* (1987); *Forbidden Hymn* (1989); *The Merthyr Trilogy: Bull, Rock, and Nut; In Sunshine and in Shadow; The Redemption Song* (1998); *Katerina* (Welsh National Opera, 2001); *Clockopera* (Welsh National Opera, 2002); *Fire Tree* (2002)

FURTHER READING

Adams, Gilly. "Give Us the Flowers Now." In *The Merthyr Trilogy*, by Alan Osborne. Cardiff: Parthian, 1998. 9–14.

Heilpern, John. *John Osborne: A Patriot for Us.* London: Chatoo & Windus, 2006.

Osborne, Alan. "Seeing the Possibilities: The Dramatist as Teacher" (interview by Hazel Walford Davies). *New Welsh Review* 41 (Summer 1998): 69–75.

Theatre in Wales [contains information on Welsh theater]. http://www.theatre-wales.co.uk/.

Alyce von Rothkirch

OSBORNE, JOHN (1929–1994)

Most critical opinion concerning British playwright John Osborne tilts toward his lasting importance as a trailblazer for opening up new—and unsettling—themes for the stage, rather than for aesthetic excellence. Yet although under analytic scrutiny his dramas may reveal structural weaknesses, most of his works have an honesty and ardor that lend them impact in the theater.

John James Osborne was born in London on December 12, 1929, son of a barmaid mother he hated (according to his memoirs) and a father (a copywriter) he idolized but who died when Osborne was only twelve years old. Young John was left sufficient funds to attend Belmont College, Devon, but was expelled after punching the headmaster and did not graduate from a university. The combative quality in his personality never abandoned him, and he never hesitated to castigate his four ex-wives (he married five times). Whether the perceived misogyny in his life and works derived from Osborne's closeted homosexuality will remain speculation. Nor did lacerating candor make

Osborne a favorite among his former professional colleagues. But that prickly element in his character added to the overall "angry" public image.

Osborne's first hit, LOOK BACK IN ANGER (1956), gave impetus to an explosive reaction on theater stages against the perceived flaccidity and smug self-satisfaction of leadership establishments of post–World War II Western society. Publicity released by London's Royal Court Theatre at the play's premiere alluded to the "ANGRY YOUNG MEN" symbolized by the play's antihero protagonist Jimmy Porter. That phrase came to represent the frustrated fury of an entire generation of young people caught in a class-dominated society from which there appeared no escape.

When starting out, Osborne dabbled in varied forms of journalism but in 1948 turned to the theater where by 1955 he became a leading actor at the Royal Court. *Look Back* was his fourth play (considered his best) and first hit of many. Successful movies consequently were made of *Look Back* and several other Osborne plays. His works frequently transferred to the UNITED STATES, where they also were warmly applauded. *Look Back, Epitaph for George Dillon* (1957, written with his onetime companion Anthony Creighton), *Inadmissible Evidence* (1964), and THE ENTERTAINER (1957) all received Tony Award nominations, while *Luther* (1961) won in 1964 as Best Play. In addition to stage plays, Osborne wrote eight television dramas and several movie scripts, one of which, *Tom Jones* (1963), won him an Oscar. Two volumes of his autobiography and a few books of literary and cultural commentary rounded out Osborne's writing efforts before his death of diabetic complications in December 1994.

Osborne enjoyed greatest success with his earlier works in which he initiated shock treatment to the British theater through virulent, unvarnished, and unrepentant attacks on the self-absorbed, class-bound English society he observed around him. In his dramas he chronicled the disappointment and disillusionment of his generation and class. Most sharply vitriolic was *Look Back* in which the protagonist Jimmy Porter, educated at a "white-tile" university (not at prestigious Oxford or Cambridge), fires unrelenting salvos at the upper classes represented by his wife, Alison, and her family. *The Entertainer* documented the demise of an earlier way of life—that of the music hall—using that descent as metaphor for ENGLAND. *Inadmissible Evidence* psychologically anatomized the enervating loss of moral fiber in marriage and in business—again, to mirror degeneration in society as a whole. *Luther* portrayed an arch rebel in the field of the religious Establishment during the Reformation, while *A Patriot for Me* (1965) tackled the lethal atmosphere surrounding the homosexual world of the Austro-Hungarian era.

By tackling such controversial issues and assessing responsibility for broken ideals, Osborne swung the door open for a parade of popular contemporary British playwrights who were ablaze with political, social, religious, and usually anticapitalistic zeal, such as EDWARD BOND, JOE ORTON, JOHN ARDEN,

DAVID HARE, HOWARD BRENTON, ARNOLD WESKER, CARYL CHURCHILL, and others.

An important paradox is that although he advocated revolutionary approaches to social problems facing his countrymen, Osborne did not create any startling different dramatic shapes or styles. His themes are expressed in essentially naturalistic modes, leaving more innovative formats to his colleagues such as HAROLD PINTER and TOM STOPPARD.

SELECT PLAYS: *The Devil Inside Him* (1950); *Personal Enemy* (1955); *Look Back in Anger* (1956); *The Entertainer* (1957); *Epitaph for George Dillon* (with Anthony Creighton, 1957); *The World of Paul Slickey* (musical, 1959); *Luther* (1961); *The Blood of the Bambergs* (1962); *A Subject of Scandal and Concern* (1962); *Under Plain Cover* (1962); *Inadmissible Evidence* (1964); *A Patriot for Me* (1965); *A Bond Honoured* (1966); *The Hotel in Amsterdam* (1968); *Time Present* (1968); *West of Suez* (1971); *A Sense of Detachment* (1972); *Place Calling Itself Rome* (1973); *The End of Me Old Cigar* (1975); *Watch It Come Down* (1976); *Try a Little Tenderness* (1978); *Déjàvu* (1992)

FURTHER READING

Hayman, Ronald. *John Osborne*. Rev. ed. London: Heinemann, 1972.

Innes, Christopher. *Modern British Drama: The Twentieth Century*. Cambridge: Cambridge Univ. Press, 2002.

Marowitz, Charles. "Obituary: John Osborne." *TheatreWeek* (January 9, 1995): 24.

Maschler, Tom, ed. *Declarations*. London: Readers Union, 1959.

Page, Malcolm, comp. *File on Osborne*. New York: Methuen, 1988.

Trussler, Simon. *The Plays of John Osborne*. London: Gollancz, 1969.

C. J. Gianakaris

OSHODI, MARIA (1964–)

Maria Oshodi is both a playwright and an actress. She has been included in books that analyze the works of black British authors, but Oshodi describes herself as a mixed-race Anglo-Nigerian Londoner. Oshodi was born on June 9, 1964, in Clapham North. Although she was not born blind, a hereditary eye condition, glaucoma, caused her to lose most of her sight, leaving her with some light and shade perception. In 1997 Oshodi established Extant, co-directed by Damien O'Connor. Extant is recognized as the first performing arts association in the United Kingdom founded and operated by blind arts professionals. The organization seeks to produce works by and about visually impaired people.

Oshodi was asked to write a play about sickle cell anemia in 1986. After some hesitation, she committed to the project, carried out the necessary research, and created what is now known as BLOOD, SWEAT AND FEARS (1988). The play was produced in May 1988 by Harmony Theatre in London. In the preface of *Blood, Sweat and Fears* (1988), published in Yvonne Brewster's *Black Plays: Two* (1989), Oshodi stated that she "felt the need to provide good, strong main characters for young black actors." Thus, black British representation in theater has not always been apparent; however, since the last few decades of the 20th century, blacks have increasingly become key figures in the industry. Oshodi has been instrumental in creating plays that allow for this type of progression.

Prior to writing *Blood, Sweat and Fears* (1988), Oshodi had not taken up issues related to disability. Her first play, *The "S" Bend*, produced as part of the Royal Court Theatre's Young Writers Festival in 1984, focuses on cultural difference within the British black community, and *From Choices to Chocolate* (1986) is set during the 1980s and centers on urban youth in Margaret Thatcher Britain. While attending college, members of the Graeae Theatre Company asked Oshodi to write a play. Oshodi's *Hound* (1992), said to be one of the first professional plays written by a visually impaired playwright and performed by visually impaired people, was the result. The play explores Oshodi's own experiences with guide dog training. *Hound* (1992) toured nationally with the Graeae Theatre Company in 1992 and was published in an anthology titled *Graeae Plays 1: New Plays Redefining Disability*, edited by Jenny Sealey, in 2002. Oshodi earned a bachelor of arts degree in drama and theater from Middlesex University the year *Hound* (1992) was produced.

Other works by her include *Here Comes a Candle* (1989), *Mag-zine* (1990), *Mug* (1990), *Jacks and Kings* (1990), and the untitled script for The Dark exhibition featured at the London Science Museum in 2004. Oshodi completed *Resistance* (2004), based on the true account of Jacques Lusseyran, a blind teenage leader of a resistance movement in Paris during World War II. *Resistance* toured with Extant in spring 2005. Due to writers such as Oshodi, issues that have an impact on blacks have increasingly become the subjects of British plays. Her work has helped make audible the voices of people of color, the disabled, and the disenfranchised.

[See also England, 1980–Present]

PLAYS: *The "S" Bend* (1984); *From Choices to Chocolate* (1986); *Blood, Sweat and Fears* (1988); *Here Comes a Candle* (1989); *Jacks and Kings* (1990); *Mag-zine* (1990); *Mug* (1990); *Hound* (1992); *Resistance* (2004)

FURTHER READING

Aston, Elaine, and Janelle Reinelt, eds. *The Cambridge Companion to Modern British Women Playwrights*. London: Cambridge Univ. Press, 2000.

Oshodi, Maria. *Blood, Sweat and Fears*. In *Black Plays: Two*. Ed. by Yvonne Brewster. London, N.H.: Methuen, 1989.

Sweatman, Sophie. "A Shift in Perspective." *Arberry Profile* (n.d.). http://www.arberryprofile.co.uk/features/?story=yes&id=42.

KaaVonia Hinton

OSOFISAN, FEMI (1946–)

Almost all of my plays, since I became a self-conscious dramatist, have been passionately devoted to it, and dominated by it. In some works I am trying to expose this class failure and probe its causes. In others I am denouncing its corrosive agents, while in others I am ridiculing its antics.

—Femi Osofian, 1998

Femi Osofisan, Nigeria's foremost radical political dramatist, uses his plays to demystify and challenge neocolonial nationalism and oppression in Nigeria and AFRICA. The subjects of his plays are elucidations on existential issues in postindependence Nigeria, particularly to animate his primarily middle-class audiences. After WOLE SOYINKA, Osofisan is Nigeria's leading literary figure whose works are constantly studied in high school and university syllabi and are perhaps the most produced plays by university-based theater artists. Osofisan was born of Christian parents in Erunwon in Nigeria's Ogun state. His education spans the University of Ibadan, Nigeria, the Universite Cheick Anta Diop in Dakar, Senegal, and Universite de Paris III in FRANCE. Osofisan belongs to a cohort of programmatic radical dissidents often impatient with the seeming utopianism of their intellectual forebears such as Soyinka as he mixes Marxism with Negritudism to produce a politically conscious DRAMATURGY.

The majority of Osofisan's plays are deliberate engagements with Soyinka's dramaturgy. Osofisan indicts his generation of educated elites for losing the will of conceptualizing political agency in a world complicated by neocolonialism and large-scale corruption. According to him: "the educated class is at the core of development in any modern economy, and . . . the failure of Nigeria, and in other African countries, is to be traced to the lamentable decadence of that class" (Osofisan, 1998). He thus sees his plays as contributing to a radical decolonizing culture and language by consistently challenging their apparent collusion with Nigeria's neocolonial state:

> I am trying to stir the class out of its customary apathy into combat, provoking it into anger and active resistance. . . . I am constantly, ceaselessly pounding at the educated class, trying to lance, and heal from within, that abscess which Fanon so presciently identified long ago as our distorted consciousness, and which shows itself in collective amnesia and inertia, in cowardice, and an inordinate horror of insurrection. (Osofisan, 1998)

An earlier generation of the educated middle class that led Nigeria's nationalist struggle against English imperialism once imagined Nigeria as a beacon of democracy; such optimism, however, derailed into a political atmosphere of large-scale corruption, military dictatorship, and poverty. The Nigeria Osofisan began to castigate was flushed by windfalls from oil revenue. Demands for the country's crude oil in industrialized economies generated a great deal of material wealth unsupported by any well-organized political vision and infrastructure. The euphoria of postindependence nationalism founded upon unity in diversity did not last too long, particularly for those elements of the middle class who found themselves in a malaise of economic, political, and cultural misadventures. For Osofisan, dramatic literature and theater are discursive forms of challenging social systems in their local and global forms. As the voice of the new disenchanted and more pragmatic bourgeoisie of the 1970s and 1980s, Osofisan distances himself from the utopian ideals of the earlier generation of anticolonial nationalists whose democratic aspirations had failed:

> The older writers represented a watershed, in both the sociohistorical and the purely aesthetic aspects of artistic expression, and it was a watershed from which we had to depart in order to keep our rendezvous with history. These voices, together with their unending mythopoetic narcissism, had to be outgrown and left behind, because when all is said and done, behind their genuinely humane attitude there was always a plea for reactionary or simply impracticable idealist utopia, engaged in the false maze of a tragic cycle. (Osofisan, 1986)

In his hands Yoruba mythology became a tool for subverting European modernity, as well as crafting an intermodernist language of socialism—itself a countercultural tradition within European modernity. Such a combination in his aesthetics pervades the themes of his plays from his earliest *A Restless Run of Locusts* (1975), *The Chattering and the Song* (1976), *Who's Afraid of Solarin?* (1978), *Farewell to a Cannibal Rage* (1986), *Once Upon Four Robbers* (1980), *Esu and the Vagabond Minstrel* (1991), *Birthdays Are Not For Dying* (1990), *Morountodun* (1983), and *Midnight Hotel* (1986), to his more recent *Tegonni* (1994) and *Nkrumah–Ni! . . . Africa–Ni!* (1994).

Thematically, Osofisan's plays describe Nigeria as a historically determined chaos where protagonists must contest and liberate their identities and the national setting from which they can launch political agency. Characters appear as signifiers of social strife, constantly struggling to redefine themselves in an existential dead-end imposed by neocolonial nationalism. The ideological energies of his plays continue to be particularly attractive to university students and professors whose declining fortunes Osofisan constantly refers to in order to prod them from political quiescence and complacency. As one of the most frequently performed playwrights, Osofisan combines a highly innovative theatricality with political outrage against neocolonialism. Music in its residual and emergent mode, dances in their innovatore forms, and storytelling traditions steeped in Yoruba mythology define the aesthetics of all his plays.

SELECT PLAYS: *A Restless Run of Locusts* (1975); *Behind the Ballot Box* (1976); *The Chattering and the Song* (1976); *Who's Afraid of Solarin?* (1978); *Once Upon Four Robbers* (1980); *No More the Wasted Breed* (1983); *Morountodun* (1983); *Farewell to a Cannibal Rage* (1986); *Midnight Hotel* (1986); *Birthdays Are Not for Dying* (1990); *Esu and the Vagabond Minstrel* (1991); *Nkrumah-Ni! . . . Africa-Ni!* (1994); *Tegonni* (1994); *Many Colors Make the Thunder-King* (1997)

FURTHER READING

Amkpa, A. *Theatre and Postcolonial Desires*. London: Routledge, 2003.

Dunton, C. *Make Man Talk True: Nigerian Drama in English Since 1970*. London: Hans Zell, 1992.

Jeyifo, B., ed. *Modern African Drama*. New York: Norton, 2002.

Osofisan, Femi. "The Alternative Tradition: A Survey of Nigerian Literature After the War." In *European-Language Writing in Sub-Saharan Africa*, ed. by A. Gerard. 2 vols. Budapest: Akademiai Kiado, 1986.

———. "'The Revolution as Muse': Drama as Surreptitious Insurrection in a Postcolonial, Military State." In *Theatre Matters: Performance and Culture on the World Stage*, ed. by R. Boone and J. Plastow. Cambridge: Cambridge Univ. Press, 1998.

Richards, S. *Ancient Songs Set Ablaze: The Theatre of Femi Osofisan*. Washington, D.C.: Howard Univ. Press, 1996.

Awam Amkpa

OSTROVSKY, ALEKSANDR (1823–1886)

Aleksandr Ostrovsky, a Russian playwright who came from Moscow's merchant quarter, was born on March 31 (April 23), 1823, in Moscow. He attended but did not graduate from Moscow University and worked for years as a law clerk at Moscow's commercial court. After the success of his first plays he devoted himself to the theater, writing forty-four original plays as well as seven plays in collaboration with other playwrights. He also translated many plays from different languages, including William Shakespeare. His plays are the most remarkable body of drama in Russian. Whereas Aleksandr Griboyedov, Aleksandr Pushkin, Mikhail Lermontov, Ivan Turgenev, and Nikolai Gogol wrote great plays, it was left to Ostrovsky to create a body of Russian drama and a Russian national theater.

Ostrovsky's early plays are slice-of-life realistic "scenes from Moscow life," as some of them are subtitled. His first COMEDY, *A Family Affair* (*Svoi lyudi-sochtyomsya*, 1850), exposes moral cynicism among businessmen. The success story of the emerging class also involves the exposure of shady business tactics. The minimally complicated plot and the traditional mechanics of the play with its "open ending" are characteristic of early Ostrovsky. His REALISM avoids caricature and FARCE since it is based on solid, firsthand knowledge of the life described. The czar agreed with the censor that the play was "immoral," and Ostrovsky was placed under police surveillance, of which he was relieved in the new reign of Alexander II in 1856.

The Poor Bride (*Bednaya nevesta*, 1852) reflects a broad perception of woman's condition, which the critic Apollon Grigoryev declared to be something quite new in Russian literature. The successful production in Moscow and St. Petersburg of *Don't Get Above Yourself* (*Ne v svoi sani ne sadis*, 1853) was a turning point in Ostrovsky's life and in the history of Russian stage. Together with his next two plays—*Poverty Is No Crime* (*Bednost' ne porok*, 1854) and *You Can't Just Live As You Like* (*Ne tak zhivi, kak khochetsya*, 1855)—it reveals Ostrovsky's talent for representing common people and his extraordinary gift for recreating ordinary speech. His plays forced the style of ACTING to shift from extremes of vaudeville and romantic exaltation to a more subdued "natural"

manner, expressing the "spirit of the soil." In *A Lucrative Post* (*Dokhodnoye mesto*, 1857), the two major themes of the power of money and the place of women are conjoined. LYOV TOLSTOY called it Ostrovsky's best play to date, adding: "Just like *A Family Affair*, it contains a strong protest against contemporary manners and mores."

Despite the realistic objectivity claimed by the author, Ostrovsky's plays had important political implications: the despotism that he depicted in family life was a reflection of the police state of Imperial RUSSIA, and reception of his work at the time was definitely shaped by two critics of a sociopolitical bent. Nikolai Chernyshevsky saw in Ostrovsky's early plays an exposure of corruption and the advocacy of a new social order. Nikolai Dobrolyubov called the world of his plays the Dark Kingdom, by which he meant the business world of Moscow with its lack of enlightenment and patriarchal abuse of authority. Ostrovsky created the type of *samodur*, a domestic tyrant and morally limited egotist who tramples on human dignity and freedom. Women are more often the victims of *samodurs* than men. A girl in *Balzaminov's Wedding* (*Zhenit'ba Balzaminova*, 1861) declares: "Men are, in general, more fortunate than women. Woman's misfortune lies in her being always under some authority or other."

Ostrovsky undertook study trips to the Volga region and acquired a rich knowledge of popular speech and beliefs as well as discovering another new world in the kind of provincial Volga town depicted in THE THUNDERSTORM (*Groza*, 1859). The early 1860s brought about a great change in Russia. It began with the abolition of serfdom and the emancipation of the peasants in 1861, followed by administrative and educational reforms and the transformation of old ways of life. Russia changed from a peasant economy into a modern industrial nation. Ostrovsky's later plays reflect these social changes: the declining gentry and the emergence of the new capitalist class. In the view of A. Skabichevsky, the main character in *Easy Money* (*Beshenyye den'gi*, 1870) is "the new type of capitalist-entrepreneur, who undoubtedly will later become the dominant figure of the dark kingdom." *Wolves and Sheep* (*Volk i ovtsy*, 1875) is one of three works showing country estates under the unjust rule of women owners and is a satire of corrupt aristocratic rule. While reflecting a ruthless age of loans and land deals, railroad construction, and the founding of industrial enterprises, it also creates superb comedy of character and situation through skillful development of plot and dialogue.

Complicated plots and surprise endings are typical of the later Ostrovsky. *A Last Sacrifice* (*Poslednaya zhertva*, 1878) negates romantic love and affirms the power of money. *Without a Dowry* (*Bespridannitsa*, 1879) shows greater psychological complexity within a bourgeois ambience and could pass for a play by HENRIK IBSEN. In *Belugin's Marriage* (*Zhenit'ba Belugina*, 1878), the contrast between two lifestyles is acutely moral and with middle-class morality emerging as admirable in comparison with the dishonest aristocratic concern with appearances.

Provincial actors are the main characters in The Forest (Les, 1871) and in several other plays. *Talents and Admirers* (*Talanty i poklonniki*, 1882) is Ostrovsky's best portrayal of theater life, and it is to art that he gives the moral victory. In *Guilty Without Guilt* (*Bez viny vinovatyye*, 1884), Ostrovsky developed a theme frequent in his work—the betrayal of a loving heart—and showed how a heroine survives the blow.

He directed several productions and paid close attention to the rhythms of language, so much so that critics called him "the virtuoso of aural perception." Owing to his example, Russia, unlike most other countries, succeeded in steering clear of the all-pervading school of Eugène Scribe and VICTORIEN SARDOU. The conflicts, everyday speech, and structure of his plays influenced the drama of the next generation, but his successors were minor figures who were not capable of carrying on a vital dramatic tradition. In Russia his plays still provide the bulk of the classical repertoire, along with Shakespeare, and even after perestroika they continue to dominate the Russian repertory. "Only literary works which have had truly popular appeal in their own country have stood the test of time. Such works in the course of time become intelligible and valuable to other nations also, and finally to the whole world," wrote Ostrovsky in "Notes of the Present State of Russian Drama" in 1882. Ostrovsky died on June 2 (14), 1886, in Shchelykovo.

SELECT PLAYS: *It's A Family Affair—We'll Settle It Ourselves*, also known as *A Family Affair* (*Svoi lyudi—sochtyomsya*, 1850); *Don't Sit in Another's Sledge*, also known as *Don't Get Above Yourself* or *Stay in Your Own Lane* (*Ne v svoi sani ne sadis'*, 1853); *A Lucrative Post* (*Dokhodnoye mesto*, 1857); *The Thunderstorm* (*Groza*, 1859); *At a Lively Spot* (*Na boikom meste*, 1865); *Vasilisa Melent'yeva* (written with S. A. Gedenov, 1868); *Enough Stupidity in Every Wise Man*, also known as *Even Wise Men Err* or *The Diary of a Scoundrel* (*Na vsyakogo mudretsa dovol'no prostoty*, 1868); *An Ardent Heart*, also known as *A Burning Heart* (*Goryacheye serdtse*, 1869); *Easy Money* (*Beshenyye den'gi*, 1870); *The Forest* (*Les*, 1871); *The Snow Maiden* (*Snegurochka*, 1873); *Wolves and Sheep* (*Volki i ovtsy*, 1875); *Belugin's Marriage* (written with N. Solovyov, *Zhenit'ba Belugina*, 1878); *Without A Dowry* (*Bespridannitsa*, 1879); *Guilty Without Guilt*, also known as *More Sinned Against Than Sinning* (*Bez viny vinovatyye*, 1884)

FURTHER READING

Cizevskij, Dmitrij. *History of Nineteenth-Century Russian Literature*. 2 vols. Nashville, Tenn.: Vanderbilt Univ. Press, 1974.

Hoover, Marjorie L. *Alexander Ostrovsky*. Boston: Twayne, 1981.

Rahman, Kate Sealey. *Ostrovsky: Reality and Illusion*. Birmingham Slavonic Monographs No. 30 Edgbaston: Univ. of Birmingham, 1999.

Slonim, Marc. *The Epic of Russian Literature*. New York: Oxford Univ. Press, 1950.

Liisa Byckling

ŌTA SHŌGO (1939–)

Ōta Shōgo, Japanese playwright and director active in the ANGURA AND SHŌGEKIJŌ movement since its inception in the 1960s, belongs to the pioneering group of radical theater innovators that includes playwright-directors KARA JŪRŌ and TERAYAMA SHŪJI, director SUZUKI TADASHI, and others. Ōta had all the major characteristics of his radical generation. He was staunchly anti-modern and antirealism, hostile to the establishment, dedicated to tracing the roots of Japanese culture and arts, and experimental in larger-than-life concerns and DRAMATURGY.

After the renewal of the U.S.–Japan Security Treaty in 1960, young theater practitioners like Ōta became increasingly alienated from the established sociocultural institutions of the Old Left and its counterpart in theater, the established SHINGEKI, and sought for new theatrical forms. After withdrawing from Gakushūin (Peers) University, Ōta launched the Theater of Transformation (Tenkei Gekijō, 1968–1988), with Hodojima Takeo, Shinagawa Tōru, and others in 1968. As its artistic head, resident playwright, and director from 1970, Ōta was central in the selection and dissemination of a novel theatrical code attained through an original combination of indigenous culture, traditional theatrical arts, and modern experimental methods that expressed his vision of human existence. Many of the cultural and artistic concepts that underlie Ōta's theatrical vision can be traced to Western existentialism and Zeami Motokiyo's theories of classical NŌ theater.

His artistic aim is to create a theatrical code of divestiture that enables the viewers to distance themselves radically from society and see humans as species traveling through the birth-to-death life cycle. To this end, he applies the "passive power" of silence, slowed-down movement, and empty space. He won the prestigious Kishida Kunio Drama Prize for his partially silent play, *The Tale of Komachi Told by the Wind* (*Komachi Fūden*, 1977). Based on a classical nō play, it is usually produced on a nō stage. His minimalist style was fully developed by 1981, the premier year of his major work The Water Station (*Mizu no Eki*, 1981), which received the 1984 Kinokuniya Theatre Award in the Group Division. This work is the first of a series of silent "Station plays" that illustrates his code of divestiture to its fullest.

In the 1980s, Ōta and his troupe enjoyed a favorable AVANT-GARDE reputation and expanded their activities to function as a cultural force in theater and society. They conducted frequent overseas tours to major cities in both Europe and North America. After disbanding his troupe in 1988 for financial reasons, Ōta has been active as an independent artist, seeking continual transcendence in theater by promoting experimental performance. From 1990 to 2000, he served as the general director of the Fujisawa Civic Theatre in Kanagawa Prefecture, and from 1994 he turned to college theater education. He is presently senior professor at the Kyoto University of Art and Design and head of the International Affairs section of the Japan Playwrights Association.

[See also Japan]

SELECT PLAYS: Nine Scenes on a Bus (Noriai Jidō-sha no Ue no Kokonotsu no Jōkei, 1970); The Tale of Komachi Told by the Wind (Komachi Fūden, 1977); The Water Station (Mizu no Eki, 1981); The Rose of Death (Shi no Bara, 1982) [title changed to The Plastic Rose (Purasuchikku Rōzu)]; The Earth Station (Chi no Eki, 1985); A Thousand Years of Summer (Sennen no Natsu, 1985) [title changed to Wrecked Under the Sun (Natsu no Fune)]; Afternoon Light (Gogo no Hikari, 1986); The Wind Station (Kaze no Eki, 1986); Rainy Sunday (Mizu no Kyūjitsu, 1987); Vacant Lot (Sarachi, 1991); The Sand Station (Suna no Eki,1993); Elements (Eremento,1994); The Water Station 2 (Mizu no Eki 2, 1995); The Water Station 3 (Mizu no Eki 3, 1998); The Arrow: Beckoned (↑ Yajirushi: Sasowarete, 2000)

FURTHER READING

Nishidō Kōjin. Doramachisuto no Shōzō: Gendai Engeki no Zen'ei-tachi [Portraits of dramatists: The avant-garde of modern Japanese theater]. Tokyo: Renga Shobō Shinsha, 2002.

Ōta Shōgo. Geki no Kibō [Hope for drama]. Tokyo: Chikuma Shobō, 1987.

Powell, Brian. Japan's Modern Theatre: A Century of Continuity and Change. London: Japan Library, 2002.

Senda Akihiko. Gekiteki Runessansu: Gendai Engeki wa Kataru [Theatrical renaissance: Modern theater speaks]. Tokyo: Riburopōto, 1983.

———. The Voyage of Contemporary Japanese Theater. Tr. by J. Thomas Rimer. Honolulu: Univ. of Hawaii Press, 1997.

Mari Boyd

OTTAYAN

Ottayan (The Lone Tusker, 1977), by KAVALAM NARAYANA PAN-IKKAR tells the story of Parameshwaran, a kutiyattam performer who, having made a mistake during a performance and losing faith in himself as an actor, escapes to the jungle. As Parameshwaran enters the jungle and says, "Whither shall I go in this wild jungle," the story stops so the actor can elaborate physically, as a kutiyattam actor would, because Ottayan is based on the dramaturgical structure of a kutiyattam performance. A good kutiyattam actor would be able to improvise for at least an hour with this one line. Using mudras (hand gestures), he would describe the trees he sees, the flowers he smells, and the animals he hears; he might, through a technique known in kutiyattam as anukramam (flashback), relive a memory of another time he was in the forest; he might compare the feelings of his character to those of another character in a similar predicament (which would entail telling the other character's story). The difference between kutiyattam and Ottayan is that in kutiyattam, the actor would improvise these elaborations; in Ottayan they are rehearsed and set by the director.

In the jungle, Parameshwaran encounters a wild elephant. Parameshwaran realizes he will be killed unless he does something quickly. He decides to save himself with "a bit of acting"— he decides to transform into an elephant in order to scare off the other elephant. If he succeeds, he will not only have saved his life but also restored his faith in himself as an actor. In Panikkar's production, this transformation is accomplished through behavior: he changes the way he moves and holds his body. In theatrical terms, he behaves "as if" he is an elephant and asks the audience to suspend their disbelief in order to complete the transformation. After Parameshwaran has successfully transformed into an elephant, he gets so absorbed in his role that he continues to dance as an elephant—until he is spotted by the Woodsman and taken to the Woodsman's leader, Moopanar. To escape, Parameshwaran has to prove that he is not an elephant but an actor performing a role: he has to successfully stage a play. Before he proceeds, Parameshwaran tells the Woodsman and Moopanar that there is a prerequisite to the performance of a successful drama:

> Parameshwaran: I shall do drama. But it requires some preparation.
>
> Moopanar: What do you require?
>
> Parameshwaran: Both of you must be ready to see it. Are you ready?
>
> Moopanar: I am ready.
>
> Woodsman: I am also ready.
>
> Parameshwaran: Then half the work is over. . . . Look here, friends, it is not enough on your part to be merely ready to see the play. Watch me closely with your whole mind involved in the performance.

The two woodsmen, and by implication Ottayan's spectators, are being told that the success of the drama depends on the spectators, who must be ready to see the play. More than that, the spectators must be ready to engage. For his dramatic presentation to Moopanar, Parameswaran builds a house (elephants in Kerala are often used in construction, so this is an appropriate action to choose). He narrates the various tasks—"first of all the ground must be cut and made ready"—as he acts them out to the accompaniment of a drum. He lays the foundation, builds a frame, raises the walls, and then secures a beam. But he cannot lift the beam alone, so he turns to the two woodsmen and says: "That is indeed very hard work. . . . Please join in this task." The two woodsmen join the "elephant," and they lift the beam together. Parameshwaran engages the two woodsmen—and the audience—in an act of the imagination as they all work together to create an imaginary reality. This is the real lesson Ottayan has to offer: it offers proof that you can create what you can imagine. The act of watching the play is, for the audience, an exercise for the imagination.

[See also India]

FURTHER READING

Awasthi, Suresh. " 'Theatre of Roots': Encounter with Tradition." TDR 33, no. 4 (1989): 48–69.

Mee, Erin. "Contemporary Indian Theatre, Three Voices." Performing Arts Journal 19 (1997): 1–26.

Panikkar, Kavalam Narayana. *Karimkutty and The Lone Tusker*. Calcutta: Seagull Bks., 1992.

Venu, Ji. *Production of a Play in Kutiyattam*. Trichur: Natanakairali, 1989.

Erin B. Mee

OUR COUNTRY'S GOOD

Written by Timberlake Wertenbaker, *Our Country's Good* is based on the novel *The Playmaker* by Thomas Keneally. It was first produced at London's Royal Court Theatre in 1988. Set in the British colony of AUSTRALIA, where the English transported shiploads of convicts in the late 18th century, the play has the first convicts enacting George Farquhar's *The Recruiting Officer*, ostensibly the first Western theater performance in the colony. The future makers of white Australia, both gaolers and gaolees, are the focus of this play. The gaolers, composed of captains, lieutenants, a reverend, and the Governor General, represent the respectable side of society, while the convicts, both women and men, represent the darker side of human nature at the opening of the play. The idea of good and evil is starkly juxtaposed: as the "respectable" Lieutenant Ralph Clark puts it: "I'm not a convict: I don't sin." (act 1, scene 9). The idea of having the convicts perform Farquhar is Ralph's, and he sets about auditioning the prisoners for parts. The notion of a performance by the prisoners arouses much debate as the majority of the officers think the idea does not hold moral merit and may actually lead the convicts further on the path of wrongdoing.

Wertenbaker's play is a comment on the value of playmaking: its humanizing and moral function. As Captain Arthur Phillip puts it: "Unexpected situations are often matched by unexpected virtues in people." Farquhar's play, with its themes of love and a society divided by its power structures, mirrors the convicts' lives in Wertenbaker's play. The power of theater as a life-changing and life-enhancing process is celebrated in this piece. The notions of the influence of heredity and environment as they affect behavior, the nature of punishment, and the aesthetics of theater are the themes that circumscribe both plays. Both the gaolers and the prisoners are transformed by enacting theater. Ralph, who has regarded all the convict women as disreputable at the opening, sees redeeming qualities in Mary. Their relationship is a landmark in Ralph's previously Victorian sexuality as he sees a woman undressed for the first time. The hint of a modern sensuality in sex is enacted in act 2, scene 9 as Ralph undresses in front of his future wife. The gap between the "respectable" and the "sinners" further closes in act 2, scene 10, which has the gaolers believe an honest convict over and above the word of a drunk and uncertain officer.

The Aborigines, referred to as "savages" and suffering from small pox, function as part of the audience for the convicts' play. While Wertenbaker's play powerfully evokes the notion of the transforming nature of theater especially as practiced in prisons today, its setting in 18th-century Australia seems ambiguous and separatist even as the Aborigines inhabit the margins. As Farquhar's piece begins to the notes of Beethoven's *Fifth Symphony* even as the curtain falls on *Our Country's Good*, it is clear that Wertenbaker's play is primarily about the white presence in Australia. Although there is a lone Aborigine who features as part of the play, commenting on the arrival of the convicts, he does not function as a character in his own right, and Aboriginal heritage and culture are entirely ignored. The words given the Aborigine—"This is a dream which has lost its way. Best to leave it alone" (act 1, scene 2) and "How can we befriend this crowded, hungry and disturbed dream?" (act 2, scene 4)—belie the fact that it was the white presence that has largely ignored and marginalized the Australian natives till this day.

[See also England, 1940–Present]

FURTHER READING

Bimberg, Christiane. "Caryl Churchill's *Top Girls* and Timberlake Wertenbaker's *Our Country's Good* as Contributions to a Definition of Culture." *Connotations: A Journal for Critical Debate* 7 (1998): 399–416.

Davis, Jim. "A Play for England: The Royal Court Adapts *The Playmaker*." In *Novel Images: Literature in Performance*. Ed. by Peter Reynolds. London: Routledge, 1993.

Dymkowski, Christine. " 'The Play's the Thing': The Metatheatre of Timberlake Wertenbaker." In *Drama on Drama: Dimensions of Theatricality on the Contemporary British Stage*. Ed. by Nicole Boireau. New York: St. Martin's, 1997.

Middeke, Martin. "Drama and the Desire for History: The Plays of Timberlake Wertenbaker." In *Anglistentag 1996 Dresden*. Ed. by Uwe Böker and Hans Sauer. Trier: WVT, 1997.

——. "Timberlake Wertenbaker: *Our Country's Good*." In *Kindlers Neues Literatur Lexikon*. Vol. 22. München: Kindler, 1998.

Dimple Godiwala

OUR POWER AND OUR GLORY

The market is looking brighter.
Will there be war in the East?
—The Stock Exchange Man, Epilogue

Back from Moscow in 1934, NORDAHL GRIEG had plans to write a film script focusing on exploitation by the Bergen, NORWAY, shipping companies of sailors during the World War I shipping boom. The Bergen theater persuaded him that his material was eminently suited for the stage. In the Soviet Union, Grieg had studied film directors' use of the technique of crosscutting, and the composition of his play, *Our Power and Our Glory* (*Vår ære og vår makt*, 1935) is clearly influenced by this technique in the constantly changing scenes.

With rising freight rates due to the danger posed by German U-boats and mines, shipowners such as Ditlef Mathiesen and Freddy Bang are more than willing to risk their highly insured ships in the trade between the Allied powers. A salesman, Eilif

Olsen, who aspires to join the rich but lacks the means to speculate, is recruited by a German agent to report on traffic in the North Sea. The British agent, Mr. Cummingham, also employs secret sources of harbor information.

A harbor scene shows sailors saying good-bye to their families before entering the gangway of the *Vargefjell*; the captain receives instructions from the owner; wounded members of a crew rescued from a torpedoed ship are now heading uptown. One of them, the "Swiller," is hired to replace a stoker on board the ship, which is ready to leave.

In act 2, a scene from a U-boat's control room with the Commander and the Lieutenant at the periscope discussing the brutality of war is followed by a scene from the *Vargefjell's* crews quarters, where sailors are chatting about women, when the torpedo strikes; then the scene changes to a restaurant where the shipowners are having a party, bailing their drinks out of a huge silver bowl. In the following scene we see the survivors from the *Vargefjell* in a lifeboat, thirsty and cold, bailing to keep afloat.

In act 3 the spy is being arrested by the police, while the Pastor is bringing sad news to the families of the lost seamen, and Ditlef, who with each ship lost at sea has increased his fortune, is preparing a speech in connection with his donation of an art collection to the city. While the three acts are dated 1917, the epilogue is set in 1935, in the Depression era. The central scene is a lodging for homeless men, many of them unemployed sailors, among them the Swiller, commenting on their present condition, and some of them nostalgic about the old wartime days when jobs were available. The scene finally changes into a tableaulike abstract formation, with the shipowners and a stock exchange figure on the left facing representatives for seamen and workers on the right, with soldiers in the middle.

With its clear political implications as well as the effective use of lighting, musical elements, and harbor sounds, the play is expressionistic and at the same time related to Russian AGITATION-PROPAGANDA drama. Its strong local color also added to a remarkable success in Bergen in 1935, although the shipping circles were generally negative.

FURTHER READING

Naess, Harald S. Introduction to *Five Modern Scandinavian Plays*, ed. by
    Erik J. Friis. New York: Twayne, 1971. 11: 293–298.
Tveita, Jan. *Veier til verket: Om Vår ære og vår makt av Nordahl Grieg*. Oslo:
    Ad Notam Gyldendal 1998.

Asbjørn Aarseth

OUR TOWN

Now you know—that's the happy existence you wanted to go back to. Ignorance and blindness.
    —Simon Stimson, Act 3

THORNTON WILDER'S *Our Town* was first performed at the McCarter Theatre in Princeton, New Jersey, on January 22, 1938, and won the Pulitzer Prize the same year. This is a wise and exquisite play that blends the conventions of time and space. Wilder was known for his vivid characters, potent poetical language, and minimalist sets in which he chose to show much in little. The stage, bare except for a few chairs, tables, and a ladder, adds to *Our Town's* charm and splendor.

By showing how people undervalue life's events, Wilder, in effect, makes those moments monumental. When the play begins, it is 1901. Then it jumps ahead twelve years, back nine years, and ends in 1913. In fact, the play takes place anytime and everywhere. Time rolls forward and backward. It is against this historical background that the fragility of our personal universe becomes evident. As Wilder says, *Our Town* "is an attempt to find a value above all price for the smallest events in our daily life." Not that all the events are small ones in this record of the Gibbs and Webb families and their neighbors in Grover's Corner, New Hampshire; as the titles of the last two acts indicate, there are "Love and Marriage" and "Death."

Private events achieve their pricelessness when contrasted with the turbulent events of history. The Great Depression was in full swing when *Our Town* was first produced. World War I had ended two decades earlier, but World War II was about to begin. The cruel, grotesque dictatorships of Joseph Stalin and Adolf Hitler reigned. Asians, Europeans, and Americans lived under the shadow of destruction. In the UNITED STATES playwrights such as EUGENE O'NEILL and CLIFFORD ODETS were writing dark plays portraying complicated and despairing characters. Wilder's characters found life arbitrary but affirming. Love was worth celebrating, despite inevitable tragedies. Wilder was not attempting to depict realistically the social, economic, and philosophical ferment of his own time. He deliberately breaks the action of the play by having the Stage Manager speak directly to the audience, reminding us that this is a play. His choice of form was to show the sublime and honest moments in everyday people's lives. Time is universal; life is always changing and unfinished. Wilder exposed humanity, not the specific details of a setting in a New England village or a boxed-in stage.

Some critics in the 1930s, responding only to the nostalgic surface of the play, misunderstood Wilder's intent. Marxist literary critic Michael Gold felt Wilder's interest in run-of-the-mill folk was vacuous. Leftist critics preferred heavily propagandist novels and plays that are now mostly forgotten. Wilder's characters sought goodness and meaning in life; and to some critics, goodness is harder to tolerate (onstage) than evil. In *The Woman of Andros* (1930) Wilder writes: "of all forms of genius, goodness has the longest awkward age." Wilder wrote a timeless, eternal masterpiece, not a politically timely drama. As the Stage Manager says, "*something* is eternal. And it ain't houses and it ain't names, and it ain't earth, and it ain't even the stars . . . and that something has to do with human beings."

After all, is it not against a panoramic background—human, earth, cosmic—that the humanity and poignancy of our individual microcosms become clear? To measure minutiae against the vast infinities of creation inspires wonder.

FURTHER READING

Goldstein, Malcolm. *The Art of Thornton Wilder*. Lincoln: Univ. of Nebraska Press, 1965.

Haberman, Donald. *The Plays of Thornton Wilder: A Critical Study.* Middletown, Conn.: Wesleyan Univ. Press, 1967.

Kuner, M. C. *Thornton Wilder: The Bright and the Dark.* New York: Crowell, 1972.

Wilder, Thornton. *Three Plays: Our Town, The Skin of Our Teeth and The Matchmaker*. New York: Harper, 1985.

Meg Walters

OUYANG YUQIAN (1889–1962)

A well-known actor, playwright, drama educator, and one of the founders of modern Chinese drama, Ouyang Yuqian, né Ouyang Liyuan, was born in May 1889 in Liuyang county, Hunan province. He went to study in JAPAN at the age of fifteen and joined the amateur drama troupe Spring Willow Society in 1907. On his return to CHINA in 1911, Ouyang started his drama career by first acting in numerous plays, including Beijing operas, and then directing plays and training young actors and actresses in various drama schools and institutions. He also took an active part in political and cultural activities during the second Sino-Japanese War (1937–1945) by writing Beijing operas and film scripts of anti-Japanese themes and being involved in the activities of the Shanghai Theatrical Circle Salvation Association. After 1949, Ouyang mainly devoted himself to the teaching of dramatic art until his death in September 1962.

Ouyang's contribution to modern Chinese drama is multifaceted. A lover of local operas and Beijing opera when he was young, Ouyang acted in Beijing operas for fifteen years, winning him praise as the equivalent of MEI LANFANG in southern China. He also acted in many modern dramas, including plays by HONG SHEN, CAO YU, and TIAN HAN.

As a drama educator, Ouyang devoted himself to the training of players throughout his life. After his return to China from Japan, Ouyang, together with some of his old friends in Spring Willow Society, founded several drama societies in Shanghai that became forerunners of Chinese modern drama troupes. In 1918 he was invited to Nantong county, Jiangsu province, to establish the earliest school for Beijing opera actors. In 1929 he went to Guangzhou to set up Guangdong Drama Institute where, as head of the school, he taught drama theory and the history of drama and also introduced foreign dramatists and their plays. After 1949, Ouyang continued as an educator of drama by being the president of the Central Academy of Drama until his later years.

As a playwright, Ouyang wrote forty-three modern Chinese plays and forty Beijing and local operas. Well-known Beijing operas that he wrote were mainly historical plays that include

Human Face as Peach Blossom (Renmian taohua, 1920), an adaptation of the play by Kong Shangren (1648–1718) titled *Peach Blossom Fan* (Tao hua shan, 1937), and *Peacock Flies Southeastward* (Kongque dongnan fei, 1946). Influential modern plays include *Virago* (Po fu, 1922), a re-adaptation of *Peach Blossom Fan* (Tao hua shan, 1947), and *Hatred of the Black Slaves* (Hei nu hen, 1959). *Virago* conveys a strong antifeudal theme by extolling individualism and calling for the emancipation of women. *Peach Blossom Fan* was adapted from a play of the same title by Kong Shangren (1648–1718). A full-length play striking a note of patriotism as it relates the tale of romance between a high-class courtesan and an army general in the late Ming dynasty, it is considered by many to be his most mature play. *Hatred of the Black Slave* was adapted from American writer Harriet Stowe's novel *Uncle Tom's Cabin*.

SELECT PLAYS: *Human Face as Peach Blossom* (Renmian taohua, 1920); *Virago* (Po fu, 1922); *After Returning Home* (Huijia yihou, 1924); *Pan Jinlian* (1926); *Peach Blossom Fan* (Tao hua shan, huaju, 1937 and 1947); *Peacock Flies Southeastward* (Kongque dongnan fei,1946); *Hatred of the Black Slaves* (Hei nu hen, 1959)

FURTHER READING

Lehman, James David. "The Rise of Modern Drama in China from Ouyang Yü-ch'ien to Ts'ao Yu." Master's thesis, Univ. of Indiana, 1977.

Ouyang Yuqian. "P'an Chin-lien" [Pan Jinlian]. Tr. Catherine Swatek. In *Twentieth-Century Chinese Drama: An Anthology*, ed. by Edward M. Gunn. Bloomington: Indiana Univ. Press, 1983. 52–75.

Ouyang Yuqian and Ge Congmin. *Ouyang Yuqian*. Beijing: Huaxia chubanshe, 2000.

Su, Guanxin. *Ouyang Yuqian yanjiu ziliao* [Research materials on Ouyang Yuqian]. Beijing: Zhongguo xiju chubanshe, 1989.

Hongchu Fu

OVERMYER, ERIC (1951–)

A play ought to reveal itself slowly, to an audience and its author. This takes patience, and contemporary audiences and critics are impatient, used to a diet of instantly recognizable cliché conventions. I want to be surprised in the theatre. I want theatricality in the theatre. I want charged, shaped, and heightened language.

—Eric Overmyer, 1993

Identified by the *New York Times* as one of the United States's most verbally accomplished playwrights, Eric Overmyer's prolific work spans stage, cinema, and television. In his writings Overmyer has understood that each kind of media requires its own particular style, and his work strives to maximize the specific necessities that each form demands. Despite his success as a television writer and producer, as well as a published poet, Overmyer has not abandoned his theatrical roots but instead continues to explore the power of live drama. In an interview (DiGaetani, 1991) Overmyer said that "one of the strengths of theater is that it accommodates poetry and image and myth and metaphor and other things that great playwrights of the past use."

Overmyer was born on September 25, 1951, in Boulder, Colorado. Although he was raised in Seattle, Washington, and attended Reed College in Portland, Oregon, his travels and experience expanded beyond the Northwest. In the 1980s and 1990s he was literary manager for Playwrights Horizons in New York; an associate artist at Center Stage, Baltimore; a member of New Dramatists, New York City; and an associate artist at the Yale Repertory Theatre in New Haven.

Overmyer's most popular play, *On the Verge* (1985), is a story about three Victorian ladies who set out to explore other countries and then find themselves in the future. The play is about language, relying on visual descriptions and verbal exchanges rather than spectacle to traverse many locales and eras. In his explorations of language, Overmyer uses clichés and banalities to demonstrate how language is debased by slogans and neologisms. *On the Verge* has been produced extensively throughout the United States, CANADA, AUSTRALIA, and ENGLAND and has been translated into French and Norwegian. A second play, *In Perpetuity Throughout the Universe* (1988), was translated into Quebeçois.

Overmyer identifies his most important concerns as language and theatricality. He starts his writing with an image or a notion, rather than a topic. *Native Speech* (1984) is about a disc jockey, but imagery and visual elements transform the play into a work that has aural appeal rather than logical through-lines. This is a common approach in Overmyer's scripts: his primary interest is the poetry of theater, rather than the plot. His growth is revealed in his adaptation of the classic drama *Amphitryon*, the title of which demonstrates Overmyer's sensibilities: *Amphitryon: A Comedy after Kleist by Way of Molière with a Little Bit of Giraudoux Thrown In* (1996). His more recent play *Alki: A Version of Ibsen's Peer Gynt Set in The Pacific Northwest and Points South, Drawn Freehand and Writ Large* (2004) exhibits Overmyer's love for the play of language.

According to Overmyer, his work has been influenced by such novelists as Don Delillo, John Bath, and Ishmael Reed; playwrights who have shaped his work include SAMUEL BECKETT, HAROLD PINTER, and ANTON CHEKHOV. All of these writers reject traditional narrative and rely on the spare theatrical moment and a sense of language. For Overmyer, the ultimate arena for linguistic and visual experimentation is the theater.

[*See also* United States, 1940–Present]

PLAYS: *Native Speech* (1984); *On the Verge, or The Geography of Learning* (1985); *In a Pig's Valise* (musical, 1986); *In Perpetuity Throughout the Universe* (1988); *Hawker* (1989); *On the Road to Jerusalem* (1989); *Don Quixote de la Jolla* (1990); *Kafka's Radio* (1990); *Mi Vida Loca* (a.k.a. *Mi Familia Tropicana*, 1990); *Heliotrope Bouquet by Scott Joplin and Louis*

Chauvin (1991); *Dark Rapture* (1992); *Figaro/Figaro* (1994); *The Dalai Lama Goes Three for Four* (1995); *Amphitryon: A Comedy After Kleist by Way of Molière with a Little Bit of Giraudoux Thrown In* (1996); *Alki: A Version of Ibsen's Peer Gynt Set in The Pacific Northwest and Points South, Drawn Freehand and Writ Large* (2004); *The Lennon Project* (2004)

FURTHER READING

DiGaetani, John L. *A Search for a Postmodern Theater: Interviews with Contemporary Playwrights.* New York: Greenwood Press, 1991.
Guare, John, ed. *Conjunctions 25: The New American Theater.* Annandale-on-Hudson: Bard College, 1995.
Overmyer, Eric. *Collected Plays.* Newbury, Vt.: Smith & Kraus, 1993.

David R. Kilpatrick

OVER OEVNE, ANNET STYKKE   See BEYOND HUMAN POWER

OWENS, ROCHELLE (1936–)

My poetry has much to do with my personal and social identity as a woman in patriarchal culture and resists both in form and idea the absolute power of organized doctrine, principles, and procedure.
—Rochelle Owens

Rochelle Bass Owens was born on April 2, 1936, into a lower-middle-class family in Brooklyn, New York. As the second child of Maxwell Owens, a postal clerk, and Molly, a housewife—who viewed the quest for artistic self-fulfillment as suspect—Owens became interested in art, ballet, and poetry. Although she viewed the discipline required of a dancer to be in accord with her own character, poetry would become the most important form of self-expression to the young girl who saw her gender as a disappointment to her parents and to the woman who used language to underscore the inequities and paradoxes of a patriarchal society.

After graduating from Lafayette High School in 1953, Owens moved to Manhattan, supporting herself with low-paying jobs while briefly studying poetry at The New School, and then acting at Herbert Berghof's HB Studios. She eventually became part of the Beat scene, frequenting Pandora's Box, a popular Greenwich Village café, where she met other artists who would play key roles in the 1960s American AVANT-GARDE. During this period, she met and married David Owens, an artist, salesman, and carpenter. The marriage was annulled in 1959.

Throughout the 1950s, Owens's creative energy was primarily focused on her poetry. Her work began appearing in smaller publications, including *Yugen*, a poetry magazine published by her friend AMIRI BARAKA, then known as LeRoi Jones. However, it was not until the 1960s that Owens achieved artistic success. The burgeoning OFF- AND OFF-OFF-BROADWAY theater culture provided, arguably, a venue for women playwrights and an arena for writers such as Owens whose approach to language was nonconventional. Ironically, it was her imaginative and innovative use of language that was also the most criticized element of her work. Owens, who characterizes herself as a protofeminist, understands this contradiction as indicative of the sexism—which she equates with racism and anti-Semitism—pervading the theater community and American patriarchal culture. She maintains that what theater critics found to be self-indulgent in her work was lauded in the work of SAM SHEPARD and SAMUEL BECKETT.

Although Owens may have received less attention than her male contemporaries, she has received several prizes, including Obie Awards for *Istanboul* (1965), *Futz* (1967), and *Chucky's Hunch* (1982) and an Obie nomination for *The Karl Marx Play* (1973). In addition to receiving honors from the New York Drama Critics Circle and several grants and fellowships, Owens has enjoyed international acclaim with the successful reception of her work at festivals in Edinburgh, Avignon, and Berlin. As an advocate of artistic communities, she helped found the St. Marks Poetry Project, New York Theatre Strategy, and Women's Theatre Council.

In 1962, Owens married George Economou. They eventually moved to Oklahoma, where she taught creative writing at the University of Oklahoma and hosted a weekly radio show. She continues to write and to explore such new forms as poetry performance.

As an artist and a woman, Owens is a risk-taker, eschewing tradition and writing not only, as she stated many years ago, so that "God will not hate you" but also for "truth" and "joy."

[*See also* United States, 1940–Present]

PLAYS: *Futz* (1961); *Beclch* (1968); *Homo* (1968); *Istanboul* (1968); *The String Game* (1968); *Futz* (screenplay, 1969); *Coconut Folksinger* (1974); *Farmer's Almanac* (1974); *He Wants Shih!* (1974); *The Karl Marx Play* (1974); *Kontraption* (1974); *O.K. Certaldo* (1974); *Coconut Folksinger* (radio play, Germany, 1976); *Emma Instigated Me* (1976); *The Colonel* (1977); *Sweet Potatoes* (radio play, 1977); *The Widow* (1977); *Mountain Rites* (1978); *Chucky's Hunch* (1982); *Who Do You Want, Peire Vidal?* (1986); *Oklahoma Too: Rabbits and Nuggets* (television play, 1987); *How Much Paint Does the Painting Need?* (television play, 1992); *Three Front* (radio play, France, 1994); *Black Chalk* (television play, 1994)

FURTHER READING

Aronson, Arnold. *American Avant-Garde Theatre: A History*. Routledge: New York, 2000.

Betsko, Kathleen, and Rachel Koenig. *Interviews with Contemporary Women Playwrights*. New York: Beech Tree Bks., 1987.

Bigsby, C. W. E. *Modern American Drama 1945–2000*. Cambridge: Cambridge Univ. Press, 2000.

Marranca, Bonnie, and Gautam Dasgupta. *American Playwrights: A Critical Survey*. New York: Drama Bk. Specialists, 1981.

Owens, Rochelle. Introduction to *The Karl Marx Play and Others*. New York: Dutton, 1974.

Sarkissian, Adele, ed. *Contemporary Authors Autobiography Series*. Vol. 2. Detroit: Gale Res., 1985.

Meghan Duffy

P

PAGE, LOUISE (1955–)

English playwright Louise Page was born in London in 1955. Influenced at an early age by the plays of William Shakespeare and ARNOLD WESKER, she began writing verse plays at the age of thirteen. From 1973 to 1976 she studied drama and theater arts at Birmingham University, and she received a postgraduate diploma in theater studies from the University of Wales in 1977. At the Birmingham Arts Lab, *Want-Ad* became Page's first play to receive professional production in 1977, and later that year Page obtained her second professional production, for *Glasshouse* in Edinburgh.

In 1978 the Birmingham Arts Lab commissioned her to write a three-actor play for production, and this became *Tissue*, which continues to be her most produced work to this day, perhaps because it takes for its subject matter a woman's confrontation with breast cancer and her subsequent mastectomy, a topic that continues to be current worldwide. With *Tissue*, Page established a reputation as a feminist playwright, due to the play's female-centered subject matter and its episodic structure (the play is made of fifty scenes, in which one actor plays the central character and the other two alternate among numerous others).

Page became Yorkshire Television's Fellow in Drama and Television at the University of Sheffield in 1979. She had two more plays, *Lucy* and *Hearing*, obtain productions, in Bristol and Birmingham, respectively, in 1979, and *House Wives* received a production in Derby in 1981 as she completed her studies at Sheffield. In these plays Page continued to build her reputation as a playwright who writes plays about unremarkable women dealing with the challenges inherent to their ordinary life circumstances in a remarkable way.

In 1982, Page's reputation as a leading contemporary playwright became established. She received the prestigious George Devine Award in 1982, for *Salonika*. This play celebrates of the greater life force elderly people may have than their middle-aged children, represented in the play by a mother-daughter relationship. *Salonika* was produced at the Royal Court Theatre Upstairs in London, and during the following year Page served as the resident writer at the Royal Court Theatre.

Real-Estate (produced by the Tricycle Theatre in London in 1984), like *Salonika*, focuses on the relationship between mother and daughter, but this time the mother and daughter have been separated for twenty years and must confront the tension between past and present in their reunion. *Golden Girls*, written for the Royal Shakespeare Company and produced in 1984, treats the subject of women's worldly ambition through the relationships among a group of female athletes.

Page was awarded the first J. T. Grein Award for Drama in 1985 by the Drama Critics' Circle. In addition to her work for the stage, she has also written extensively for radio and television. Louise has written more than twenty original radio plays, and she served as a scriptwriter for The Archers on BBC Radio-4 for ten years. She currently runs Words4Work, with her husband, writer Christopher Hawes. This series of workshops and seminars assists businesses in improving the standard of their written communications.

[*See also* England, 1960–Present]

SELECT PLAYS: *Glasshouse* (1977); *Want-Ad* (1977); *Tissue* (1978); *Hearing* (1979); *Lucy* (1979); *Flaws* (1980); *House Wives* (1981); *Salonika* (1982); *Falkland Sound/Voces de Mavinas* (1983); *Golden Girls* (1984); *Real-Estate* (1984); *Beauty and the Beast* (1985); *Goat* (1986); *Diplomatic Wives* (1989); *Lily and Colin* (1989); *Adam Was a Gardener* (1991); *Hawks and Doves* (1992); *Like to Live* (1992); *Another Nine Months* (1995); *The Big Adventure* (2002); *Kissing Better* (2003); *Philomel Cottage* (2004)

FURTHER READING

Page, Louise. *Page Plays 1: Tissue, Salonika, Real Estate, Golden Girls*. London: Methuen, 1990.

Turner, Elaine. "Louise Page." In *Contemporary Dramatists*, ed. by K. A. Berney. London: St. James Press, 1993. 516–517.

Antonia Sophia Krueger

PAKISTAN

Drama, in the Western sense of the genre, has had a relatively short history in Pakistan, as in many other Islamic nations in Southwest Asia. As in Arabic, theatrical productions such as dramatic recitals of epic poems or lyric sequences, crude dramatizations of folk tales, musical revues, and puppet shows seem to have a long history in the largely unrecorded history of popular literature in Urdu and Punjabi. But there has been no dramatic tradition in the formal literature in Urdu and Punjabi that is at all comparable in length or scope to the poetic traditions in those languages. And no Pakistani dramatist of anything near the stature and influence of the Egyptian TAWFIQ AL-HAKIM emerged to legitimize drama as a formal literary genre and to establish broad boundaries for the genre within which subsequent dramatists could work.

The first recorded production of a Pakistani play occurred in 1853 with the staging of Mizra Amanat's *The Court of God Indra* (*Inder Sabha*), a musical in Urdu, at the palace of Wajid Ali Shah of Oudh. Within several years, the British deposed Wajid Ali Shah and seized Oudh, but the play outlasted its patron's court by several decades. Its continuing popularity may have inspired enterprising Parsis in Bombay to develop a type of musical theater that became so popular throughout the states of South and Southeast Asia that several professional touring companies were formed. Somewhat formulaically, the so-called Parsi musicals explored romantic themes with carefully modulated shifts between melodramatic crises and comic interludes. Interestingly, the demand for stories was so great that for the first time Urdu playwrights adapted Western plays to their formula, translating some of William Shakespeare's plays. Indeed, even within the constraints of these formulaic plays, some playwrights generated controversy by pushing the limits of popular taste and by exposing seemingly anachronistic customs to implicit criticism.

In the immediate aftermath of the partitioning of British India into the independent states of INDIA and Pakistan, the future for drama in Pakistan seemed to hold vibrant possibilities. At the Government College of Lahore, students founded a dramatic club that presented some plays in English but for the most part Urdu translations of well-known British and continental plays. A decade later, the Pakistani Arts Council, based in Lahore, began producing Urdu versions of more recent and more experimental plays at a theater in its headquarters. The plays proved so popular that, through the Alhamra Drama Group, the Arts Council began offering a full calendar, rather than a seasonal schedule, of productions. In Karachi, in the 1950s, such companies as the Osmania University Old Boys, the British Amateur Society, the Karachi Theater, the Avant Garde Arts Theater, the Drama Guild, and St. Patrick's Dramatic Society presented some remarkable productions of a broad range of classical and modern Western dramas.

In the midst of the dynamic theater scene in Karachi, the first truly noteworthy Urdu dramatist, Khwaja Moinuddin, achieved tremendous celebrity with the staging of his plays *Zawal-e-Hydrabad*, about Indian oppression of Kashmiris, and *La Qile Se Lalukhet*, about the dislocations caused by the partition. The latter debuted in a stadium before an audience of 10,000. Other Pakistani playwrights who produced notable work during this period include Ali Ahmed, whose *Subh Honay Tak* is a loose adaptation of WAITING FOR GODOT; Anwar Knayetullah, whose *Jab Tak Chamkay Sona* is a dramatic treatment of civil unrest in Pakistan; and Yunus Said, whose *The Thing* is a preapocalyptic drama written and staged in English, which synthesizes elements of the symbolist and the absurdist dramatic modes.

Nonetheless, the development of the film and television industries within Pakistan initially undercut dramatic productions in two ways. First, theater owners found it much more profitable to show films than to stage plays; so the number of venues for new plays decreased markedly. Second, television and film work attracted many of the talented people associated with the theater because such work offered greater financial rewards and much broader visibility. Many of the most promising playwrights began to devote much of their energies to writing screenplays and teleplays. Indeed, some became producers and directors as well, and a few began to develop impressive lists of credits as actors. This broad trend was not reversed until the burgeoning popularity of VCRs and DVD players in Pakistani homes caused a precipitous decline in ticket sales at movie houses. Theater owners have subsequently become more interested in staging plays. The political realities in Pakistan have, however, impeded what might otherwise have constituted a major revival of drama in the country's major cities.

Under the series of military regimes that have governed Pakistan for much of the last quarter century, drama has been increasingly associated with political activism, which has typically been characterized as subversive. Much to the displeasure of religious fundamentalists and the authoritarian governments—and counter to prevailing trends in postcolonial literature—many Pakistani dramatists have openly promoted such Western concepts as individual political rights, broad-based economic opportunities, and social progressivism. They have asserted the value of secular and internationalist approaches as alternatives to religious and provincial custom. In the 1970s and 1980s, theater groups such as Ajoka and Lok Rehas have been at the center of a "Parallel Theater" movement that has attracted a good deal of international attention for its defiance of the Pakistani military regimes. Unfortunately, international attention has not protected everyone associated with the groups from retaliation.

Indeed, because the most visible Pakistani playwrights of the last quarter century have been either emigrants or exiles to the United Kingdom or the UNITED STATES, many of the most noteworthy Pakistani plays of the period have been written in English, rather than in Urdu or Punjabi. And those plays originally written in Urdu or Punjabi have, of course, been translated into English as a prerequisite to their production in ENGLAND or the United States. The continued use of English has been a more volatile issue in Pakistan than in India because, compared to the tremendous ethnic and linguistic diversity of India, Pakistan is a relatively homogenous nation. So the very negative associations of English with imperialism and continued Western hegemony have been less counterbalanced in Pakistan than in India by the practical benefits of its being a widely, if not universally, used second language. Ironically, those Pakistani plays produced elsewhere outside of Pakistan have often been translated for Hindi or Bengali productions. So as Pakistani drama has become a medium for political and cultural dissent within Pakistan, it has also been somewhat stigmatized by its association with countries and cultures that have been widely demonized in Pakistan. Although plays by emigres and exiles have been increasingly staged in "GUERRILLA" productions at informal venues in Pakistan's major cities, it remains to be seen whether this drama will evolve into a major force within Pakistani literature or will remain largely a subcategory among the "hyphenated" literatures of the West.

The notable dramatists of this most recent period have produced an increasingly diverse body of work. Rukhsana

Ahmad's *Song for a Sanctuary* (1990) treats domestic violence. Pervaiz Alam's *Safar—The Journey* (2002) concerns the effects of the Partition on a Hindu family that is forced to leave Pakistan and the continuing resonance of the experience in the family's collective memory. Wajahat Ali's *Domestic Crusaders* (2005) chronicles the daily life of a Pakistani-American family. Karim Alrawi's plays *Aliens* (1981), *Before Dawn* (1981), *A Child in the Heart* (1987), *A Colder Climate* (1986), *Crossing the Water* (1991), *Divide and Rule* (1983), *Five in the Lake* (1985), *In Self-Defence* (1983), *Migrations* (1982), *Promised Land* (1988), and *Sink the Pink* (1983) have all been produced in England and have treated overt and subtle manifestations of British racism toward South Asians. Dilip Hiro's *To Anchor a Cloud* (1970) has had significant productions in London and Calcutta. AYUB KHAN-DIN's acclaimed *East Is East* (1997) focuses on the effects of assimilation on the children of Pakistani immigrants to the United Kingdom. HANIF KUREISHI's *My Beautiful Laundrette* (1985) may be most responsible for the current interest in the literature of Pakistani immigrants to the United Kingdom and the United States. SHAHID NADEEM has written more than three dozen produced plays, including *The Suffering One* (Dukhini, 1997), an exposé of the illicit traffic in women and children across South Asia. Ibrahim Quraishi's *Five Streams* (World Premiere 2006) is an experimental, collaborative, multimedia exploration of the dynamic interplay among South Asian Islamic cultures. Saman Shad's *Lingering Voices* (2004) addresses the threats to Pakistani village life posed by uncontrolled development. Imran Shah's *Bunch of Lies* denigrates political corruption in Pakistan through a puppet show. And Bina Sharif's one-woman drama *Afghan Woman* (2002) concerns the oppression of women by the Taliban.

FURTHER READING

Azfal-Khan, Fawzia. "Street Theater in Pakistani Punjab." *The Drama Review* 41(September 1, 1997): 1054–2043.

Brandan, James R., ed. "Pakistan." In *The Cambridge Guide to Asian Theater*. Cambridge: Cambridge Univ. Press, 1993. 211–213.

Enayetullah, Anwar. "Theater in Pakistan." *Pakistan Quarterly* 12, no. 4 (1964): 54–59.

Marek, Jan. "The Impact of Islamic Culture on Urdu Drama." *Die Welt des Islams: International Journal for the Study of Modern Islam* 23–24 (1984): 117–128.

Qadir, Abdul. "Syed Imtiaz Ali Taj: A Pioneer in Modern Urdu Drama." *Perspective: A Monthly Digest Published in Pakistan* 4, no. 10 (1971): 35–37.

Qureshi, M. Aslam. *Wajid Ali Shah's Theatrical Genius*. Lahore: Vanguard, 1987.

Suvorova, A. "Sources of Urdu Drama." In *Proceedings of the Fourth International Conference on the Theoretical Problems of Asian and African Literatures*, ed. by M. Galik. Bratislava, Czechoslovakia: Literary Institute of the Slovak Academy of Sciences, 1983. 213–218.

Martin Kich

PALESTINE

Like all other Arab lands, Palestine was part of the Ottoman Empire from 1516 until the end of Ottoman hegemony in the Near East in 1918. During the 19th century, when cultural activities flourished in Beirut and Cairo, the common assumption is that Jerusalem did not witness an emergence of serious, professional drama activities. According to this assumption, the cultural vacuum was not restricted only to Palestine but extended to the other regions of Greater Syria, which also languished under the deteriorating political, social and economic condition of Ottoman rule. Widespread illiteracy and the lack of national educational institutions contributed to the cultural stagnation in Palestine and Greater Syria, causing the region to trail behind EGYPT and Lebanon and driving many literary historians to judge the pre-1920 cultural atmosphere in Palestine to be one of total backwardness. Yet new research on Palestine contradicts such claims. Rashid Khalidi in *Palestinian Identity: The Construction of Modern National Consciousness* (1997) demonstrates how cultural life and Palestinian identity in late Ottoman Palestine paralleled similar developments elsewhere in the Islamic and Arab world, particularly in neighboring Arab regions. Jerusalem, Khalidi argues, was an important capital district of southern Palestine, where "its importance extended far beyond that. Its schools, newspapers, clubs, and political figures had an impact throughout Palestine, even before the country's British mandate boundaries were established after World War I." In contrast to a picture of total backwardness, one can see distinctive evidence of cultural consciousness and appreciation of drama and world literature, even if at the time these trends may not have been strong enough to reflect political consciousness to the degree later literary production would.

1850–1900

The so-called cultural awakening in Palestine was not only a result of the visiting Egyptian theater troupes but also of the influence of the missionary schools, which promoted education and encouraged Western drama among Palestinians at the beginning of the 19th century. Drama activities in missionary schools were widespread in "Greater Syria" (present-day Syria, Lebanon, Palestine, Jordan), and their numbers increased in the 1910s, especially after the promulgation of Ottoman constitutional rule in 1908.

The influence of these schools, both private and missionary, in Greater Syria is well appreciated. They contributed significantly to the growing cultural and intellectual awareness of the region, strengthening the signs of a budding Palestinian consciousness. Promotion of intellectual and literary activities in Palestine was gaining ground, and this was reflected, in part, in the staging of plays, an activity encouraged by an increasing number of schools. Moreover, local newspapers reported on the school plays and on groups visiting from Lebanon and Egypt, aiming to promote the local troupes and follow their development.

It is clear that a handful of educated Palestinians turned to Western classical literature, such as William Shakespeare and French novels and COMEDIES, especially those of Molière, in the hope of establishing a theater of their own. Bethlehem University professor Qustandi Shomali estimates, despite the lack of documentation for this period, that Palestinians ought to have been aware of the major theatrical trends in Egypt. They may have followed the Egyptian drama that was spreading in the region, or they might have staged plays based on European literature, although the quality of such productions would have suffered from limitations both in form and style. The author provides examples of how the local Palestinian newspapers covered performances of the visiting Egyptian groups of George Abyaḍ and Šayḫ 'Ukāša. He also demonstrates how *Hamlet* was performed in Gaza before World War I.

1920–1948

With the defeat of the Ottoman Empire in World War I, its deteriorating rule in Arab lands came to an end in 1918. Palestine, Transjordan, and IRAQ fell under the British Mandate, while Lebanon and Syria became part of the French Mandate in 1920, the same year Palestine witnessed the first Arab uprising. Political awareness was strengthened after the issue of the Balfour Declaration in 1917, which promised a Jewish National Home in Palestine. Zionist activity in the region and the revival of the economy by the British Mandate, undertaken as part of a scheme to prepare the land for the influx of Zionist immigrants from Europe, were the main elements that contributed to the revitalization of cultural as well as political life in Palestine. Cultural life in general, and Palestinian theater activities in particular, flourished during the British Mandate, stimulated by opening Palestinian national schools and educational institutions, the reactivation of the missionary schools, public libraries, cultural clubs and societies, Christian parish activities, publishing houses, radio stations, newspapers and periodicals, and literary organizations and salons. The changes that took place on the national level, along with external factors, played a major role in stimulating cultural life in Palestine at the time.

The very earliest signs of theatrical activity in Palestine ever mentioned are the shadow play performances known as Ḫayāl aẓ-Ẓill. In the Ottoman province of Syria before World War I, cities like in Damascus, Beirut, Aleppo, Jaffa, and Jerusalem often performed Ḫayāl aẓ-Ẓill plays. The shadow plays presented in Damascus and Beirut contained many Turkish elements, especially in the themes they tackled. The shadow plays in Jerusalem, on the other hand, were mainly carried out during the month of Ramadan as night-time shows when the local troupes had to compete with troupes coming from Syria. After Palestine fell under British rule after World War I, the local cultural tradition of Karakūzk—main character shadow plays—continued during the month of Ramadan.

Another major revival before 1948, combined with theater activities, involved the old Palestinian folk tradition and religious culture. Most famous is the reappearance of al-Ḥakawātī (the storyteller), who used to be seen in coffeehouses telling stories based on folktales and on *A Thousand and One Nights*. Further examples are Šā'ir ar-Rabāba a singer playing the rabāba—a stringed, violinlike instrument with one or three strings; the itinerant Ṣundūq al-'Aǧab, known as the Magic Box or the Box of Wonders, telling folk and historical stories, and religious festivals such the traditional Mawlid, held during the Prophet's birthday, or the Mawālīd (the birthday of the saints), as well as the various entertainment shows presented at night during the fasting month of Ramadan. Other theatrical components could be traced back to the traditional Palestinian peasant dance known as the Dabka, and to the Zaǧal, both of which were performed at special feasts, at wedding celebrations, and at funerals.

External and internal factors also contributed to Palestinian cultural revival. One of the major stimuli for the Palestinian cultural resurgence at the beginning of the twentieth century was the visiting of Palestinian cities by Egyptian, Syrian, and Lebanese theater troupes who performed plays and hence shared their experiences. It appears that the visits of Arab and foreign troupes left an enormous mark on the educated Palestinian youth, moving them to start many ACTING groups of their own. The second most important external factor that contributed to the rebirth of cultural awareness in Palestine is the old foreign missionary schools. In addition, during this period Palestine witnessed the birth of many local amateur theater groups that sprung from schools and were concentrated in the cities of Haifa, Jaffa, Nazareth, Gaza, Jerusalem, and Bethlehem, leaving the southern part of the country untouched. Although these theater activities were very much restricted to individual attempts to cater to local interest, they nevertheless spread out of schools to the various clubs, social associations, cinema houses, and literary salons. It seems that these activities had an impact on the Palestinian public, since many local Palestinian newspapers reported on them.

The establishment of numerous Palestinian associations, including both social institutions and women's associations, was not directly the product of the British Mandate, although the associations grew in number as a reaction to the foreign presence in Palestine. After the promulgation of the Ottoman constitution of 1908, as well as during the British Mandate, many new Palestinian associations came into being and contributed vigorously to political and national awareness, hosting and performing many drama activities. Additionally, many literary salons came into being during this period, in turn giving rise to many Palestinian authors and dramatists like Naǧīb Naṣṣār, Ǧamīl al-Baḥrī. Unfortunately, most of these associations were closed in 1948 after the war that created the state of ISRAEL, since their members were largely among the majority of Palestinians who fled for their lives. The impact of the social and women's institutions and their various activities on the development of both Palestinian cultural life in general and drama in particular is not fully documented. As for the numerous literary salons, they were places to invite the established poets, writers, and dramatists to read their works, hence contributing to the growth of intellectual trends. The most distinguished one was the ad-Daǧānī Literary Salon in Jerusalem, where literary and drama activities were promoted.

The impact of the visiting Egyptian theater groups appears to have been immense during these years. When the Egyptians departed, the local audiences who had flocked to watch their performances and who later constituted the nucleus of the theatergoing Palestinian public bega demanding more local and original Palestinian performances. In spite of the concentration of drama activities mainly in coastal cities, the local troupes there faced many difficulties. For one, they lacked theater venues. Second and more important, the number of productions decreased because the British Mandate authorities did not encourage and even banned many such activities. These activities were regarded as a threat to the mandatory rule and control over Palestine. The ban was reinforced, superficially, on the grounds that theater productions were illegal gatherings and could result in riots, but another reason was the fact the plays dealt indirectly and directly with the theme of losing Palestine to the influx of the immigrant Jews and with the Zionist activities in the region. What is also interesting during this period is the fact that the British Mandate, which started in Palestine in July 1920, issued various restrictive and oppressive rules and laws concerning every aspect of Palestinian daily life: print, publication, distribution of newspapers, transfer of goods, establishing clubs and association, opening shops or libraries. These suppressive measures of the British Mandate were later adopted and are used to the present day by the state of Israel in its occupation of the territories of the West Bank and Gaza Strip.

In general, however, drama and theater activities performed in schools, by associations, or by local troupes are very hard to pin down for further study, since these are so poorly documented. Apart from the name of the troupe and the title of the plays staged, which are mentioned in local newspapers, no further information can be found due to the declaration of the state of Israel and the subsequent flight of Palestinians from their native land to other neighboring Arab countries, where they constituted a nucleus for theatrical activity in the lands in which they exiled. The growth and development of the urban Palestinian middle classes also contributed substantially to the serious attempts to establish professional theater troupes. Some well-to-do families took the initiative to start a serious and professional theater by writing original plays and becoming less dependent on the Western and well-known Egyptian and Lebanese plays that toured the area at the time. Moreover, during the British Mandate, Palestine saw the birth of many educated writers for the theater, such as: Naǧīb Naṣṣār, the owner of al-Karmil newspaper. The first written Palestinian play The Loyalties of the Arabs (Wafā' al-'Arab) is attributed

to him, followed by Ǧamīl al-Baḥrī, Istifān Salīm, Asmā Ṭūbī Naǧwā Faraḥ Qa'wār, Šukrī Sa'īd, and the al-Ǧuzī brothers.

An important early encouragement to theatrical activities in Palestine was the foundation of at least fifteen new local Palestinian newspapers in addition to an-Nafīr, al-Karmil, Ǧarīdat Filasṭīn and az-Zahra. These new papers, launched in the years between 1919 and 1921 and mostly in Haifa and Jerusalem, reported both on theater groups visiting Palestine and on the activities of local theater groups. Moreover, the foundation of Maḥaṭṭat al-Quds or Iḏā'at Filasṭīn (Palestine Broadcasting Station), headed by the well-known Palestinian poet Ibrāhīm Tūqān (1905–1941), and Iḏā'at aš-Šarq al-Adnā (Near East Broadcasting Station), encouraged men of letters, prominent poets, playwrights, and actors—especially women—to broadcast their work.

One of the first professional troupes was Firqat al-Ǧuzī (al-Ǧuzī's Theatre Troupe), established and presided over by Naṣrī al-Ǧuzī from 1930 to 1947, when, after the Nakba, he and his family left Palestine to live in Damascus. He wrote several original plays, but his work was lost during his flight from Palestine, even to the author himself, who does not possess copies of the plays. Naṣrī wrote Truth Prevails (al-Ḥaqq Ya'lū) in 1928. His second social moral play, Leila's Heart (Fu'ād Laylā), came out in 1930, as did his The Burning Candles (aš-Šumū' al-Muḥtariqa). The transition from social to political issues came in 1935 when Naṣrī wrote The Ghosts of the Free (Ašbāḥ al-Aḥrār). The one-act-play dealt with themes such as the danger of the influx of Jews to Palestine, defending the lost land, attacking the ones who sold their land, calling for Arab unity, and defying by force both the British and Zionist presence in Palestine. The play was staged at the YMCA theater in 1935 and in 1936; but due to strict British censorship rule, the play was banned in the city of Ramallah and in the rest of the country. In 1945 Naṣrī al-Ǧuzī became the first Palestinian dramatist ever to write plays for children. Among his ceaseless contributions in this field are The Wisdom of the Judge (Ḏakā' al-Qāḍī); No to the Sale of Land (Lā li-bay'i l-Arāḍi); The Feast of Deportation ('Īd al-Ǧalā'); Palestine, We Shall Not Forget Thee (Filasṭīn lan Nansāki); Loyalty of Friends (Wafā' al-Aṣdiqā'); and Break the Idols! (Ḥaṭimū l-Aṣnām).

Ǧamīl al-Baḥrī is yet another prominent Palestinian figure who contributed significantly not only to journalism but also to the theater movement in Haifa before 1948. Ǧamīl al-Baḥrī owned the journal az-Zahra (The Flower), and the al-Maktaba al-Waṭaniyya (The National Library) published his plays and books in Haifa. In 1919, he published his play His Brother's Murderer (Qātil Aḥīh).

Although the period of the British Mandate over Palestine did see contributions to the revival of cultural activities on all levels, many obstacles caused a slowdown in the development of the Palestinian theater. First was the taboo of women appearing onstage. Generally speaking, in the 1920s and 1930s female roles were performed by men who put on female costumes and makeup and imitated feminine gestures onstage, since real female presence on the stage was limited both by strict Catholic or Muslim teachings and by social circumstances in Palestine. However, with the foundation of the Palestinian Broadcasting Station, women felt more comfortable acting behind the microphone. The second obstacle was the unstable political situation. The demise of the Ottoman Empire, its replacement by the British Mandate, the Balfour Declaration, and the Zionist takeover in the region all contributed to a situation of political instability, not only in Palestine but in the rest of the Arab world as well. Since there was no central national government to speak of, theater arenas, facilities, dramatic schools, and institutions catering to talented youth had no permanent sponsors. This lack of sponsorship had a devastating effect both on the quality of the dramatic work and on the production of original dramatic texts, leading the few Palestinian playwrights who were interested in theater and drama to be dependent on Western texts and literature.

1948–1987

The Palestinian cultural awakening under the British Mandate was silenced abruptly by the 1948 War that established Israel. The 1948 Arab-Israeli war caused panic among Palestinians, causing them to abandon their homes and flee to neighboring Arab countries. The fleeing Palestinians ended up as refugees in Jordan, Lebanon, Syria, Egypt, and the West Bank and Gaza Strip. What took place on the political scene had a negative impact on the development of cultural activities in Palestine. This series of traumatic events is termed *an-Nakba*, the catastrophe.

The greater part of the urban intelligentsia, the traditional and social leaders, and the property owners fled during 1948, causing a state of decline and isolation in cultural activities within Palestine itself (Palestinians in Israel and in the West Bank and Gaza Strip). The immense upset in the wake of the 1948 defeat was that the Palestinian majority in Palestine ended up being the minority in Israel, where the suppressive political climate, as well as the difficult economic and social situation made it nearly impossible for Palestinian writers and poets to be productive. These political and socioeconomic circumstances had a negative effect on the cultural atmosphere in Palestine in general and on theater activities in particular. Thus, all that remained of Palestinian theater as it had been under the British Mandate were a few amateur groups, confined to clubs, associations and schools. Nonetheless, the Palestinian cultural awakening that had existed and flourished in the 1940s was not totally wiped out, although it deteriorated into two separate fragments after 1948: within Israel and outside it.

After 1948, permanent Palestinian residents of the West Bank and Gaza Strip shared the same fate as the refugees. The Hashemite dynastic rule over the West Bank and the Egyptian military one over the Gaza Strip were directed toward suppressing publications of any worthwhile literature of either political or social importance. The direct and suppressive censorship rules forced upon Palestinians by these regimes extended their reach to clubs and educational and social institutions, banning all cultural activities (Ashrawi, 1976). Theatrical performances among Palestinians in the occupied territories were limited in both playwriting and staging, although some cultural and theatrical activities within the framework of summer festivals were held in the West Bank cities of Ramallah and al-Bireh. Another stimulus to theater activities in the 1960s were the several Palestinian plays written in exile by Ghassan Kanafani (1936–1972). In 1964, coinciding with the foundation of the Palestine Liberation Organization (PLO) and the establishment of Ğamʿiyyat al-Masraḥ al-Filasṭīnī (Association of Palestinian Theater) in Damascus, cultural activities were promoted aiming to strengthen Palestinian consciousness.

As for those Palestinians who were uprooted from their homes as a result of the 1948 War, they had to face their daily plight and seek other means by which to survive in the refugee camps, either in the West Bank and Gaza Strip or in the neighboring Arab countries, where they faced, and still do face, an extremely unfavorable political and economical situation. As for Palestinians in Israel, the 1950s did witness a few cultural activities encouraged by the Israeli establishment in an attempt to enhance "positive" cultural activities. With the dispersal of the Palestinian urban cultural elite, it was a few immigrant Jewish poets and writers to Israel, mainly from Iraq, who took it upon themselves to fill the cultural vacuum in Arabic productions. The actual Arabic theater activities in Israel in the 1950s were limited to amateurs and took place mainly in schools. It was only in the 1960s that these theatrical activities started to develop rapidly.

During the 1967 War, the Arab armies involved were defeated, and the West Bank and the Gaza Strip fell under Israeli occupation. The 1967 War was the first time that Palestinians in Israel started meeting fellow Palestinians who had until then been cut off across the Demarcation Line (Green Line) dividing Israel from Jordan and Egypt, respectively. Nonetheless, important plays were published following the war, although most of them were not staged immediately. The prominent contemporary Palestinian poet Samīḥ al-Qāsim (1939–) wrote the verse drama *Qaraqāš* in 1970. Theater activities in the late 1960s and at the beginning of the 1970s can be described as a period when the major stress was on writing new, original dramatic texts as part of an emergence of Palestinian literature in Israel after the 1967 War. In the 1950s, Palestinians in the state of Israel were under "military rule," whereby the Jews and the Arabs were kept separate and the latter were given self-rule only in terms of religious denominations. This explains why theater activities were widely spread in religious clubs and schools.

The restrictions on Palestinians in Israel were finally lifted in November 1966, and thus a minimum of freedom of mobility was granted. This was also the time when Arabs were permitted to be members of the Israeli Histadrut and many other voluntary committees in order to help Palestinians integrate into "Israeli society." As for the Israeli establishment's involvement in the Palestinian cultural arena, it decreased after the 1967 War, following the same failed path as their previous involvement during the 1948–1967 period. The Ministry of Education inaugurated the Arab-Israeli center Bayt al-Karma in Haifa in 1963; in 1962 came the building of the Frank Sinatra Centre in Nazareth. Other signs of involvement by Israeli establishment include the creation of Firqat al-Masraḥ bi-Nādi l-Histidrūt (The Theater Troupe in the Histadrut Club of Nazareth) from 1962 to 1966; al-Masraḥ al-Ḥadīt (The Modern Theater) from 1965 to 1977; al-Masraḥ aš-Šáʿbī (The People's Theater); and the investiture of al-Masraḥ an-Nāhiḍ (The Rising Theater). The revitalization of Palestinian culture was not restricted to the Palestinians in Israel but also extended to the occupied territories, thus contributing another factor to the renewed unity between the two segments of the Palestinian people.

The October War in 1973 was significant, not only in terms of the inter-Palestinian process but also as a boost to Palestinian morale. This marks the period when one starts to talk about Palestinian culture as a whole without making distinctions, especially on the cultural level. One can recall that while the West Bank was under the Hashemite Rule, publication of any worthwhile literature, especially that of social or political significance, was directly suppressed. The situation in Israeli-occupied Palestine was similar: overt and direct censorship, constant control over social and educational institutions, clubs, and all cultural activities, along with relentless political persecution and the lack of freedom of speech were familiar in Israeli-occupied pre-1967 Palestine. Yet the direct Israeli attempts at suppressing worthwhile literature did not succeed entirely and were gradually emasculated by the continuous and persistent attempts and confrontations of the politically committed writers and poets of the area, despite the constant threat of being charged with endangering the "security of the state." The publication conditions were equally discouraging on both sides of the "Green Line" until progressive publishing houses later opened in Israel (Ashrawi, 1976).

The existence of cultural activities in the occupied territories, in Jerusalem, and within Israel set the stage both nationally and internationally for the Palestinian cultural revival of the 1970s. Mostly concentrated in the Ramallah region, this new theater trend attempted to stimulate the theater movement in the occupied territories. It is extremely hard to study the framework, or the nature of the theater troupes of the 1970s, let alone attempt to categorize them in terms of productions, span of life, or the quality of the plays. An important reason is that most of these groups started presenting theater work in the early or mid-1970s, during which time some of them were composed, dismantled, and reformulated under new names. Second, few troupes continued their theater production past the mid-1980s, due to the political situation in Palestine. A third reason is that founders of

the groups either left the troupes forever, ended up creating other troupes, or are no longer participating in theatrical work. Finally, scanty financial resources and the lack of published scripts pose serious problems for the study of this revival.

One very early theatrical event in this revival was the establishment of the ʿĀʾilāt al-Masraḥ (The Family of the Theater) in Ramallah, which later formed the nucleus of Balālīn (Balloons), a theater troupe built around the Bethlehem-born Palestinian director François Abū Sālim and the singer Muṣṭafā al-Kurd from Jerusalem. In 1975, another troupe that left marks on the theater movement assumed the name of Ṣundūq al-ʿAǧab (The Magic Box). The establishment of al-Ḥakawātī Theatre in East Jerusalem in 1977—a joint project of Arab dramatists, directors, and actors from Israel and East Jerusalem—marked an eminent phase in the professionalization of Palestinian theater. al-Ḥakawātī was founded and developed by François Abū Sālim and a group of theater people. Actors, set designers, lighting professionals, and musicians were recruited according to needs. The theater's name alludes to the ancient ḥakawātī, that is the itinerant storyteller who used to wander the country and would appear in places such as cafés and public squares presenting his stories based mainly upon traditional folktales, myths, and legends. Gestures, different voices, a stick, and a tarbouche (a fez hat) would accompany al-Ḥakawātī's tales as means to encourage and motivate his listeners to interact. Muḥammad Maḥāmīd, one of the co-founders of al-Ḥakawātī, affirms that the troupe's aim was to establish a Palestinian theater group that could meet the needs of the Palestinian people by creating a nucleus for a professional theater troupe, strengthening the roots of theater, attracting theater audiences, addressing the burdensome realities of the occupation amidst Palestinian society, and thereby generating a Palestinian national theater. Undertaking to articulate national aspirations to Palestinian society under Israeli occupation, al-Ḥakawātī drew upon various folkloric and traditional sources and incorporated different Western concepts. For lack of suitable, available dramatic texts, and due to a desire to experiment, the act of playwriting and devising characters and dialogues became a collective undertaking by the actors themselves and was based largely upon improvisation. al-Ḥakawātī's having to function under military occupation, Dov Shinar (1987) asserts, including such political constraints as censorship and other forms of control, has been influential in leading the group to the development of a style of collective composition. Plays were created through a process of improvisation on agreed topics; they were not based on prewritten texts. The group claimed that plays were written solely for the benefit of the censorship authorities, "who nevertheless fail from time to time, to grasp the real meaning of the messages" (Shinar, 1987). Thus much variation developed during long months of rehearsal and interaction with the audience until the plays were fully shaped.

A well-known al-Ḥakawātī play is In the Name of the Father, the Mother and the Son (Bismi l-ab wa-l-Umm wa-l-Ibn), which was produced during the 1978–1979 season; another is the play *'Alī, thou Galilean* (*Maḥǧūb Maḥǧūb, Ǧalīlī, yā 'Alī*), written and staged in the 1980–1981 season. In 1984 al-Ḥakawātī presented one of its self-fulfilling prophetic plays, *A Thousand and One Nights of a Stone Thrower* (*Alf Layla wa-Layla min Rāmī l-Ḥiǧāra*). Staged just before the outbreak of the intifada (known in the West as the Uprising), the play pictures the confrontation between a Palestinian youth and Gidi, the Israeli military governor who steals from a magic lamp 'Alā' ad-Dīn. al-Ḥakawātī leased an-Nuzha Cinema building in East Jerusalem for ten years in November 1983 and converted it into the first Palestinian theater in Jerusalem and the West Bank. Local and foreign donations supported the troupe in renovating the building and set it up as their permanent house to host other professional and amateur drama, music, dance groups, and works of local and international artists. The troupe's first performance in the new building was *The Story of the Eye and the Tooth* (*Ḥikāyat al-'Ayn wa-s-Sinn*). This gave al-Ḥakawātī the chance to participate in festivals in Europe, JAPAN and the UNITED STATES.

The outbreak of the intifada on December 8, 1987, imposed a new reality on Palestinian political life; it not only caused the dismantlement al-Ḥakawātī but also led other groups to crumble, thus forcing many groups to search for venues to work in. In addition, the most tangible hindrance was the harsh daily reality of the curfews and roadblocks that prevented many theatergoers from the West Bank and Gaza Strip from entering Jerusalem. The fact that the theater was situated in the heart of Jerusalem was yet another factor making al-Ḥakawātī vulnerable to the Palestinian-Israel contention over control of the city. The dismantling of al-Ḥakawātī Theater troupe at the an-Nuzha Cinema building in the late 1980s led to the adoption of the name of al-Masraḥ al-Waṭanīal-Filasṭīnī (Palestinian National Theater) as the new central framework for the Palestinian theatrical movement. Many professional and amateur groups used to perform on the al-Ḥakawātī stage and included art exhibitions as well as cultural and political debates.

1987–PRESENT

An important turning point for Palestinian theater came about during the long years of the intifada. The intifada began on December 8, 1987 when four Palestinians were killed and seven injured by an Israeli driver in the Gaza Strip. Within a short time, masses of Palestinians in the nearby Jabaliya refugee camp demonstrated against Israeli troops during the funerals, to protest the random, senseless loss of life. Later on, the intifada spread all over the occupied territories. Despite the harsh years of the intifada, Palestinian theater rejuvenated itself in the early 1990s, especially the Palestinian National Theater (PNT) in Jerusalem. The venue held its first Palestinian Festival in December 1990. While Jerusalem's cultural establishment consolidated the status of the city, the rest of the occupied territories were under siege during the festival as a consequence of Iraq's invasion of Kuwait and the ensuing Gulf War. Gaza Strip and the West Bank were isolated from Jerusalem by means of strict checkpoints and roadblocks (which continue to this date).

In 1992, many outstanding plays dealing mainly with the Palestinian plight were produced and performed at Theater Week, held at the PNT. In addition, it also organized various festivals such as Jerusalem Theater Nights in 1998 and 2001. The PNT has also targeted children as its main audience by organizing a yearly puppetry festival from 1989 until 2001, depending on the political situation. In the festivals, various European and Arab troupes performed plays based mainly on fairy tales and including puppets in the form of animals. However, during the intifada, the south of the West Bank and Gaza Strip witnessed such a cultural revival only when the PNT was allowed by the Israeli military to enter into these areas. As for the Palestinians in Israel, they also witnessed many signs of revival, such as the yearly Acre Festivals and the establishment of various theatrical venues.

The cooperation between Palestinians, whether in Israel, in the Gaza Strip, or in the occupied territories, intensified with the Declaration of Principles, which brought an end to the Palestinian intifada with the signing of the Oslo Peace Accords in 1993. Both Palestinians, represented by the Palestinian Liberation Organization (PLO), and Israelis established mutual recognition. Euphoria swept the Gaza Strip and the occupied territories, and various theater activities were launched for some time. Many old troupes resurfaced under new names. Foremost among them is Masraḥ 'Aštār in Ramallah, north of Jerusalem, which targets school children with its program. Another is Masraḥ al-Qaṣaba in Jerusalem and Ramallah. Both of these theaters were active members of various theater troupes in the 1970s. Yet in the aftermath of signing the 1993 Peace Accords between Israel and the Palestinians, and during the last decade of negotiating for a final solution to the question of Palestine, the theater seems to have added to the condition of Palestinians and affected all walks of life.

The difficulties confronting Palestinian theater, however, are immense. Most of the theater troupes complain about the predominance of amateurism and the lack of professional directors, actors, local playwrights, and venues. For most of the troupes, the solution to the shortage of local dramatic texts is adapting from Western literature. In addition, people involved in the theater rank the lack of national financial support as a major obstacle. In the absence of national institutions to support cultural activities, local theater still needs to turn to Western donors. Such has been the case of 'Aštār, 'Inād, and al-Qaṣaba.

It is a fact that foreign funds do guarantee the continuity of theater activities, yet most of the time this support ends up being the only life support offered to contemporary Palestinian theater and art. A great risk thus looms of donors imposing on the troupes, in terms of the selection of texts and, accordingly, the messages conveyed. Ironically, Palestinian theater found itself in a position where it had to recreate settings to face the continuous deteriorating political situation. This feeling was intensified with the al-Aqsa massacres in September 1994 and 1996; recently it was reinforced when the second intifada erupted on September 28, 2000. The continuous violence between the Israelis and the Palestinians and the imposition of curfews, invasions, and assassinations caused the theater to go into yet another period of hybernation, only to rise again.

Currently it is not the Palestinian National Theater taking the lead in Jerusalem but rather al-Qaṣaba, which opened another venue in the city of Ramallah, thus catering to the north of the West Bank, while the south is dominated by various amateur troupes springing from the refugee camps. al-Qaṣaba is the leader in theater activities and has become internationally known. In the last two years, its aim has been to address the daily suffering of its audience. This has been manifested in a collective effort to write and produce *Stories Under Occupation* (2002), and in *Smile, You Are a Palestinian* (2004). Both plays won many awards and were performed in various Arab and European countries. In sum, it seems that the predicament of the Palestinian theater inevitably cannot be divorced from its political context.

FURTHER READING

al-Ġūzī, Naṣrī. Tārīḫ al-Masraḥ al-Filasṭīnī 1918–1948 [The History of Palestinian Theater 1918–1948]. Nicosia: Muassasat Bisan, 1991.

Ashrawi, Hana. *Contemporary Palestinian Literature Under Occupation*. Birzeit: Birzeit Univ. Press, 1976.

Jayyusi, Salma Khadra, ed. *Anthology of Modern Palestinian Literature*. New York: Columbia Univ. Press, 1992.

——, and Roger Allen, eds. *Modern Arabic Drama: An Anthology*. Indianapolis: Indiana Univ. Press, 1995.

Maḥamid, Muḥammad. ʿAbed al-Raʾaf: Masīrat al-Ḥaraka al-Masraḥiyyafī aḍ-Ḍiffa al-Ġarbiyya [The Journey of the theater Movement in the West Bank]. Israel: Tayba, 1989.

Nassar, Hala. *Performing Palestine: A National Arab Theatre*. Florence, Mass.: Interlink Pub. Group, forthcoming.

Sayegh, Anis, ed. al-Mawsuah al-Filasṭiniyah. Al-Qism al-thani: al-dirasat al khaṣṣah [Encyclopedia of Palestine. Second Part, Special Studies]. Beirut: Hayat al-Mawsuah al-Filasṭiniyah, 1990.

Shinar, Dov. *Palestinian Voices: Communication and Nation Building in the West Bank*. Boulder, Colo.: Lynne Riener Pubs., 1987.

Snir, Reuven. "Palestinian Theatre: Historical Development and Contemporary Distinctive Identity." *Contemporary Theatre Review*, Vol. 3, 2 (1995): 29–75.

——. " 'We Were Like Those Who Dream' : Iraqi-Jewish Writers in Israel in the 1950's." *Prooftexts* Vol. 11 (1991): 153–173.

Sulaiman, Mohamed. *The Palestinian Press and the British Mandate Laws* (Arabic). Nicosia: Muassasat Bisan, 1988.

Hala Khamis Nassar

PANIKKAR, KAVALAM NARAYANA (1928–)

Kavalam Narayana Panikkar, born in April 1928 in Kavalam, Kerala, INDIA, is one of the most important figures in the theater of roots movement, a post-independence effort to decolonize the aesthetics of modern Indian theater by challenging the visual practices, performer/spectator relationships, dramaturgical structures, and aesthetic goals of colonial performance—which is to say ways of perceiving, ways of interacting, and ways of structuring experience. Many late 19th-century and early 20th-century productions resisted colonial laws and practices in their subject matter, but the roots movement is important because it challenged colonial culture by reclaiming the aesthetics of performance and addressing the politics of aesthetics. Panikkar has used the *Natyasastra* (a Sanskrit aesthetic treatise), Sanskrit plays, and *kutiyattam* (a way of performing Sanskrit drama) to decolonize the dramaturgical structure, the aesthetics, and the goal of his work. In fact, many of Panikkar's plays, particularly OTTAYAN (*The Lone Tusker*, 1977), are based on the dramaturgical structure of a *kutiyattam* performance.

A *kutiyattam* performance of a Sanskrit play can take anywhere from five to thirty-five nights to complete. On the first night, a character enters, introduces himself by narrating his personal history and some important details from his own life, presents some of the important events leading up to the play, and expands on details found in the first few lines of text. On the second and third nights, the same character (possibly played by a different actor) tells stories connected to, but not found in, the main story of the play. On each successive night another character appears until all the characters have been introduced, each offering his or her own history and version of the story. In this way the story is told and retold from many points of view, the background to the story is fully explored, and the story is made relevant to the audience. On the final night of *kutiyattam*, "the play" is performed. "The play" is only a fraction of the total experience. *Kutiyattam* spectators do not have a "horizontal" experience as they would in Western theater. They do not follow the plot in a linear fashion across time. Instead, they have a series of "vertical" experiences in which they follow the actor as he delves into each moment, exploring it fully at many levels and in many modes. In fact, a *kutiyattam* performance is not the presentation of a text but an elaboration of it—a performer may spend up to three hours illuminating three lines of text by making political and social analogies, exploring emotional associations, and telling related or background stories. Panikkar has adapted this dramaturgical structure for his modern plays and productions. His production of a ten-page play can last for ninety minutes. (Because Panikkar writes his plays for his company Sopanam and directs most of them himself, it is very difficult to separate his playwriting from his DIRECTING.) This process of elaborating on the text is known as *anukirthanam*, or "celebration of [the] mood by stretching it out to enhance the ultimate rasa" (Panikkar, quartered in Mee, 1995).

The goal of Sanskrit drama was to create *rasa*; similarly, Panikkar's goal is to create *rasa*. The word *rasa* has been variously translated as juice, flavor, and essence. It is the aesthetic flavor, or sentiment, that is tasted in or through performance. When food and spices are mixed together in different ways, they create different tastes. Similarly, the mixing of different basic emotions arising from different situations, when expressed through the performer, gives rise to an emotional experience or "taste" in the spectator, which is *rasa*. Panikkar's spectators do not have a cathartic experience while watching his productions but a rasic experience—they savor the emotional essence of the performance.

Panikkar's plays have other similarities to *kutiyattam*. Kutiyattam characters are *alaukika*—not of this world—they are gods, demons, and heroes. Similarly, Panikkar's plays, while they are not about gods or demons, are not kitchen-sink dramas. They are, as he refers to them, "myths for a modern sensibility" (quartered in Mee, 1995). For example, *Aramba Chekkan* (1996), Panikkar's adaptation of the myth of Orpheus and Eurydice, is a cautionary story about the way people take nature for granted. "Aramba" (the name of the Orpheus figure) means "the one who begins," and in the play he represents mankind's discovery of nature. Chekki (the Eurydice figure) is named after an orange forest-flower in Kerala; she personifies the gentle spirit of nature who "blossoms" when she first meets Aramban, then is later destroyed by him. These characters are personifications of ideas. This is true of characters in many of Panikkar's other plays such as *Faust* (1993), which depicts the battle between good and evil, or *Karimkutty* (1983). Karimkutty is a spirit, owned by the magician Kondadimadan. Kondadimadan is in debt to his former student Mantravanan. He repays his debt by selling Karimkutty, an act for which he suffers. The play can be read as a parable about the changing role of the traditional artist in contemporary society or as a parable about someone who sells his power to a wealthy but ignorant outsider (Panikkar, 1992). But it can also be read as a warning to those who think they can, or behave as if they can, own others. It is a critique of the caste system and of class relations. The characters are personifications of thematic ideas.

Many of Panikkar's plays focus on the notion of personal identity and what happens to it in a theatrical context. For example, one of Panikkar's most recent plays, *The Role of Kali* (*Kalivesham*, 2001) deals with a *kathakali* actor (*kathakali* is a classical dance drama from Kerala) who, once "possessed" by his character, cannot escape the effect his character has on him outside the performance.

Panikkar has won many state and national awards for playwriting and directing, including the prestigious Kallidas Samman Award for Theatre (1996). His plays have been presented all over India and in Greece, Japan, Austria, the United States, Russia, and Korea.

SELECT PLAYS: *Witness* (Sakshi, 1964); *Godhead* (Daivathar, 1973); *One's Own Hurdle* (Avanavan Katamba, 1975); *The Lone Tusker* (Ottayan, 1977); *The Black One* (Karimkutty, 1983); *The Domain of the Sun* (Suryasthana, 1984); *The Right To Rule* (Koyma, 1986); *Latent Fire* (Arani, 1990); *Marukidathy* (1991); *Theyyatheyyam* (1991); *The*

Outcast (Poranadi, 1995); *The Man on the Other Side* (Apprakan, 1998); *The Eater of the God of Time* (Kalanetheeni, 2003); *The Role of Kali* (Kalivesham, 2003); *The Girl Who Rolls the Stone* (Kallurutti, 2004)

FURTHER READING

Mee, Erin. "Contemporary Indian Theatre, Three Voices." *Performing Arts Journal* 19 (1997): 1–26.

——. "Folk Philosophy in Kavalam Narayana Panikkar's Poetic Theatre of Transformation, an interview with Kavalam Narayana Panikkar." *Seagull Theatre Quarterly* 7 (1995): 58–61.

Panikkar, Kavalam Narayana. "Aramba Chekkan." In *DramaContemporary: India.* Ed. by Erin B. Mee. Baltimore: Johns Hopkins Univ. Press, 2001.

——. *Karimkutty and The Lone Tusker.* Calcutta: Seagull Books, 1992.

——. *The Right To Rule and Domain of the Sun.* Calcutta: Seagull Books, 1989.

——. "Interview with K. S. Narayana Pillai." In *Contemporary Indian Theatre: Interviews with Playwrights and Directors.* Ed. by Paul Jacob. Delhi: Sangeet Natak Akademi, 1989.

Erin B. Mee

THE PARASITES

Moral lectures can't make a human parasite a useful citizen. But you can exterminate the parasites! You can exterminate them by opening the eyes of the hard-working people to the parasites—and that shall be my social task. Like a fiery fox terrier pursuing rats and mice—in exactly the same way I shall pursue the parasites.
—Johannes, Act 3

CARL ERIK SOYA'S (1896–1983) The Parasites (*Parasitterne*, 1926) takes place in a shabby Copenhagen suburb. When the play opens, we see a young student, Johannes, eagerly studying a tiny hole in the earth overrun with weeds. Through the conversation with his fiancée, we understand that he has at long last found his mission in life: he wants to become an entomologist: to study the life of the insects; and he is now preparing a future treatise about "the parasites of Bombus terrestris" by observing the activities of the bumblebees through a magnifying glass. Johannes is in many ways the alter ego of the author, and in the opening scene playwright Carl Soya introduces the theme of the play—parasites—and the technique used—studying his characters through a magnifying glass.

Parasites are not limited to the world of insects but flourish among humans, too, and Johannes happens to lodge with a fine specimen: Gruesen, a man who behind a jovial and vulgar charm is a ruthless impostor and exploiter of his fellow creatures, among them his imbecile and mentally deranged wife who adores him. *The Parasites* is a picaresque play where the more clever win over the less clever. Gruesen seems to hold a good hand when he takes an elderly and apparently rich "Miss Olsson from America" as a second lodger. By appealing to her sentimental love for children, he asks her to draw up a will for the benefit of his grandchild Evelyne; then, eager to lay hand on the many millions, he intimidates his wife to put rat poison in Miss Olsson's tea. But Gruesen has for once made a miscalculation. Miss Olsson was in fact a poor, lonely person who did not own a thing; moreover, Johannes suspects the true facts and threatens to go to the police. But Gruesen still has a card up his sleeve. He can easily put the blame on his wife and go free. Before the police arrive, however, he is stabbed by her, not because of his deeds but out of jealousy, as she fears he will go to other women while she is in jail. Gruesen dies heroicly without a groan, giving a last farewell to his baby grandchild, the latest offspring of his noble line.

In the preface to the published edition from 1929, Soya called The Parasites a naturalistic play. But Gruesen is hardly an individual character. He is representative of the human parasite, and in the course of the play he grows to monumental size—a monster in a Copenhagen suburban milieu. In 1926, Soya sent the play to the Royal Theatre, where it was accepted but not staged. The first performance took place in 1931 in the Det Sociale Teater, a collective of unemployed actors, in a staging that stressed the grotesque and macabre character of the play. When The Parasites reached the Royal Theatre in 1945, the staging there made the play lose much of its bite.

[See also Denmark]

Kela Kvam

PARASITTERNE See THE PARASITES

PARKS, SUZAN-LORI (1964–)

In 2002 playwright, screenwriter, and novelist Suzan-Lori Parks became the first African American woman to win a Pulitzer Prize for Playwriting. In the years since she started writing plays at Mount Holyoke College, her work has encompassed a variety of styles but has consistently impressed critics and audiences by its rendering of colloquial African American speech as poetic, lyrical language that rapidly swings between humor and pathos.

Parks, daughter of an army officer, was born in 1964 in Fort Knox, Kentucky. She had an itinerant childhood as her father's tour of duty took him through six states before stationing him in GERMANY. Parks has credited her time in Germany with giving her a heightened awareness of the English language while providing her with the experience of being an outsider identified more by her nationality than by her race.

As a student at Mount Holyoke, she took a creative writing class with JAMES BALDWIN, who was instrumental in encouraging her to become a playwright. Influenced by the modernists she read as a major in English and German literature, Parks also looked to ADRIENNE KENNEDY and NTOZAKE SHANGE as examples of writers who broke the confines of psychological REALISM in African American theater.

She moved to New York not long after graduating from college, and the second play she produced there, Imperceptible Muta-

bilities in the Third Kingdom (1989), won her an Obie Award for best new play, as well as a citation by the New York Times's Mel Gussow as the most promising playwright of the year. The production also began Parks's collaboration with director Liz Diamond, who went on to direct the premieres of The Death of the Last Black Man in the Whole Entire World (1990) and THE AMERICA PLAY (1994).

Critic Elinor Fuchs's description of Death of the Last Black Man as "part pageant play, part JAZZ cantata, part Greek TRAGEDY, and always an elegy on the theme of black suffering, loss, and misrepresentation through history" could apply to America Play as well. At the same time, critics such as Robert Brustein championed Parks as one who "avoids the conventions of Black victimology" in works that "portray the humiliation of blacks in white society without complaint or indictment."

Parks's insistence that her "life is not about race," her stated desire to write works as notable for their experimental form as for their content, and her provocative reception by critics such as Brustein made her early plays particularly controversial; critic Shawn Garrett has stated that a planned symposium on Parks in Theater magazine had to be canceled in 1993 because African American critics "objected, in essence, to [Parks's] politics," expressed concern at her appeal to predominantly white audiences, and refused "to go on record with their opinions." Black criticism of Parks reached its height with the 1995 production of Venus, directed by RICHARD FOREMAN; in the African American Review, Jean Young claimed that Parks's portrayal of Saartjie Baartman, a historical figure abducted from South Africa in 1810 and shown through Europe in freak shows that highlighted her large breasts and buttocks, depicted the so-called Hottentot Venus as "complicit in her own horrific exploitation," thereby "diminish[ing] the tragedy of her life as a nineteenth-century Black woman stripped of her humanity at the hands of a hostile, racist society" (Young, 1997).

In her early works, Parks relied consistently on an African American tradition that scholar Henry Louis Gates Jr. has described as "repetition [and] difference." Referred to by Parks herself as "rep and rev," that is to say, "repetition and revision," James Frieze (1998) and other critics have pointed out that the writing technique resonates with jazz compositions in which phrases are repeated in modified forms. Death and resurrection, the evasive presence of history, the motif of digging, and the self-conscious manipulation of racial stereotypes figure prominently in the plays. Of Death of the Last Black Man, Brustein wrote that it was "too densely written for one mind to absorb at a single sitting." After Venus, however, Parks began to show a tendency to use more established dramaturgical conventions, both in terms of structure and language. In the Blood (2006), for example, depicted the desperation of a homeless, single mother trying to raise her children, and it owed as much to BERTOLT BRECHT's THE GOOD WOMAN OF SETZUAN as it did to Nathaniel Hawthorne's Scarlet Letter, which Parks has named as the inspiration for the play.

Parks's screenplay for *Girl 6* was directed and produced by Spike Lee in 1996, and she has also written screenplays for Disney and Jodie Foster. In 2000, she became the head of the dramatic writing program at the California Institute for the Arts in Valencia. She received a prestigious MacArthur Fellowship in 2001. In 2003, Parks published her first novel, *Getting Mother's Body*, to mostly positive reviews. Her latest play *In the Blood* is based on the flooding in New Orleans that resulted from Hurrican Katrina in 2005.

[See also Black Arts Movement; United States, 1965–Present]

PLAYS: *Imperceptible Mutabilities in the Third Kingdom* (1989); *The Death of the Last Black Man in the Whole Entire World* (1990); *The America Play* (1994); *Venus* (1995); *In the Blood* (1999); *Topdog/Underdog* (2002); *Fucking A* (2003); *In the Blood* (2006)

FURTHER READING

Bernard, Louise. "The Musicality of Language: Redefining History in Suzan-Lori Parks's *The Death of the Last Black Man in the Whole Entire World*." *African American Review* 31, no. 4. (Winter 1997).

Drukman, Steven. "Suzan-Lori Parks and Liz Diamond: Doo-a-diddly-dit-dit. An Interview." *The Drama Review* 39, no. 3 (T147) (Fall 1995).

Frieze, James. "*Imperceptible Mutabilities in the Third Kingdom*: Suzan-Lori Parks and the Shared Struggle to Perceive." *Modern Drama*, no. 41 (1998).

Garrett, Shawn-Marie. "The Possession of Suzan-Lori Parks." *American Theatre* (October 2000).

Sellar, Tom. "Suzan-Lori Parks's *Venus*: The Shape of the Past." *TheatreForum*, no. 9 (Summer–Fall 1996).

Young, Jean. "The Re-objectification and Re-commodification of Saartjie Baartman in Suzan-Lori Parks's *Venus*." *African American Review* 31, no. 4 (Winter 1997).

Daniel Mufson

PÅSK *See* EASTER

PÁSKÁNDI, GÉZA (1933–1995)

Géza Páskándi was a prolific Hungarian writer of poetry, fiction, essays, and drama. As a playwright he was at home in ABSURDISM and REALISM. Indeed, some of his historical dramas betray absurdist tendencies.

Born on May 18, 1933, in Szatmárhegy (Viile Satu Mare), Transylvania, as a member of ROMANIA's Hungarian minority of nearly two million, Páskándi was swept up in the government's attempt to crush Hungarian intellectual life in Transylvania following the 1956 Revolution against Soviet domination in neighboring HUNGARY. Páskándi was among the many imprisoned for "nationalist agitation." He spent six years at hard labor, was released in 1963, and moved to Hungary in 1974.

Between the time of his release from prison and his move to Hungary, Páskándi proved a master of a genre that, for reasons of official cultural policy, was relatively new to Hungarian playwrighting. He called his drama "absurdoid" to distinguish it from Theater of the Absurd as practiced in the West. For Páskándi, absurdity does not characterize the human condition as such; rather, it arises out of social realities and is perpetuated by human design or folly. His early absurdoid work includes many droll plays that comment on the ways external authority manipulates its victims into complicity, even against their best interest, and whether or not they are aware of being manipulated.

The play that first brought Páskándi acclaim was *Sojourn* (*Vendégség*, 1969). Set in 16th-century Transylvania, it is about a peculiar relationship between betrayer and betrayed, in which each is open about his purpose and believes he is acting in the best interest of the other and the cause they both believe in. This complex exploration of choice and conduct in situations of coercion was incorporated into a trilogy of "bishop dramas" about Reformation figures, collectively titled *Transylvanian Triptych* (1984). This trilogy examines relations of power from the perspective of the powerless. Another trilogy, *Triptych of the House of Árpád* (1994), about Hungary's first dynasty, deals with the dilemmas of power among the powerful. The difference reflects a shift in Páskándi's focus following his move to Hungary, from the self-awareness of a member of an oppressed minority to a broader national concern. A didactic intent can be detected in these later dramas. At the core of each play is a destructive fraternal struggle, echoing recent history.

Emblematic of Páskándi's ability to create complex allegories is one of his finest late plays, *The Soldiers of Augustus* (*Augustus katonái*, 1992), set during the biblical Slaughter of the Innocents. The Jewish protagonist learns of Herod's plan and must decide whether to declare his newborn a Roman in order to save the child's life. The value of an individual life is pitted against national, religious, and communal survival.

Páskándi returned to his absurdoid roots in his last play, *World's Fair* (*Todogar ajur kvárna*, 1995), in which the once static roadside world of SAMUEL BECKETT's tramps Vladimir and Estragon is now threatened by surges of refugees.

Páskándi was awarded the Attila József and the Kossuth Prizes in Hungary for literature. He died on May 19, 1995, in Budapest.

PLAYS: *No Conductor* (*Kalauz nélkül*, 1967); *The Line* (*A sor*, 1968); *Sojourn* (*Vendégség*, 1969); *The Hiding Place* (*A rejtekhely*, 1972); *I Choose a Tower* (*Tornyot választok*, 1972); *King Kálmán* (*Kálmán király*, 1977); *Residents of the Windmill* (*A szélmalom lakói*, 1981); *Death Bell* (*Lélekharang*, 1986); *The Soldiers of Augustus* (*Augustus katonái*, 1992); *World's Fair* (*Todogar ajur kvárna*, anagram of "Godotra ujra várnak," that is, "they're waiting again for Godot," 1995)

FURTHER READING

Bécsy, Tamás. *Kalandok a drámával, Magyar drámák 1945–1989* [Adventures with drama, Hungarian dramas 1945–1989]. Budapest: Balassi Kiadó, 1996.

Ézsiás, Erzsébet. *Mai magyar dráma* [Hungarian drama today]. Budapest: Kossuth Könyvkiadó, 1986.

Máramarosi, Iza. *Páskándi Géza*. Budapest–Ungvár: Primor és Intermix Kiadó, 1994.

Suto, Andras, and Eugene Brogyanyi, eds. *Dramacontemporary: Hungary: Plays by Andras Suto, Geza Paskandi, Istvan Csurka, Gyorgy Spiro, Mihaly Kornis*. Richmond, Ontario: Hushion House, 1991.

Eugene Brogyányi

PATRICK, JOHN (1905–1995)

John Patrick, one of the most commercially successful dramatists and screenwriters of the mid-20th century, became popular by striving to entertain his audience more than to challenge it. Patrick's dramaturgical craft demonstrated his skills at mixing familiar dramatic and comic elements with a bold theatricality and warm sentimentality. In their time, these qualities endeared Patrick's Broadway plays and films to audiences, but his plays have found consistent production only in collegiate and amateur theaters. The most appreciative critics note that Patrick's dramatic output exudes affection for humanity as evidenced by the richness of his central characters, most of whom are genial, often eccentric survivors whose lives span 20th-century human experience. Detractors, like Harold Clurman, in a 1953 critique in *The Nation*, dismissed Patrick's plays as mere entertainments, "good-natured, liberal, and constantly indulgent."

Born John Patrick Goggan on May 17, 1905, in Louisville, Kentucky, he was abandoned by his parents, John Francis and Mary (Osborn) Goggan, and spent most of his childhood in foster care. In the mid-1920s, Patrick found work as an announcer for RKO Radio in San Francisco, after which he dropped his last name. His writing career began in 1929 when he scripted an impressive 1,100 episodes of *Cecil and Sally*, an NBC radio drama. He also wrote for other regular radio series, but his radio career essentially ended with the outbreak of World War II. After the war, he took courses at Harvard and Columbia Universities, although he never earned a degree.

Hell Freezes Over (1935), Patrick's first play, was poorly received on Broadway and closed after a brief run, but it led Patrick to a three-year stint as a screenwriter for Twentieth Century-Fox. Teamed with various writers, he worked on nineteen film scripts between 1936 and 1939. Returning to the stage in 1942 with *The Willow and I*, a turn-of-the-century gothic drama of the Deep South, Patrick received good reviews, but the play failed commercially. Patrick's breakthrough play, *The Hasty Heart* (1945), won critical acclaim and long runs in New York and London. Set in a British field hospital in Burma, where a nurse encourages the multinational Allied patients to befriend a lonely, dying Scottish soldier, *The Hasty Heart* mixes pathos and humor. *The Hasty Heart* also emphasized basic themes of human dignity and the search for love and connection, all typical of Patrick's plays and films.

Patrick's drama *The Story of Mary Surratt* (1947) had a short run despite critical approval, but his COMEDY *The Curious Savage* (1950) bordered on FARCE and was set in a home for mental patients. It became one of Patrick's most produced works despite a mere month on Broadway. Patrick's farce *Lo and Behold!* (1951) found little favor, but his next play, *The Teahouse of the August Moon* (1953), adapted from Vern Sneider's novel, ran over 1,000 performances on Broadway and was made into a successful 1956 film scripted by Patrick. A satire on the American military's attempt to "Americanize" Okinawa at the end of World War II, *Teahouse* became one of the most frequently produced comedies of its time and Patrick's most honored work. It received the 1954 Pulitzer Prize, the Tony Award as Best Play, and the New York Drama Critics Circle Award. Despite this triumph, Patrick never had a major Broadway success again.

Patrick found considerable success as a screenwriter from the mid-1950s onward with such films as *Three Coins in a Fountain* (1954), *Love Is a Many-Splendored Thing* (1955), *High Society* (1956; a musical adaptation of PHILIP BARRY'S THE PHILADELPHIA STORY with a score by Cole Porter), *Les Girls* (1957), *Some Came Running* (1960), *The World of Susie Wong* (1960), and *The Shoes of the Fisherman* (1968).

As a self-avowed "entertainer," Patrick did not aspire to the serious dramatic goals of contemporaries like TENNESSEE WILLIAMS, ARTHUR MILLER, or EDWARD ALBEE. He was, instead, a forerunner of popular Broadway playwrights like NEIL SIMON, celebrating the status quo with plays that were little more than situation comedies featuring Patrick's warm regard for humanity. Patrick took his own life at age ninety on November 7, 1995, in Del Rey Beach, Florida.

[See also United States]

PLAYS: *Hell Freezes Over* (1935); *The Willow and I* (1942); *The Hasty Heart* (1945); *The Story of Mary Surratt* (1947); *The Curious Savage* (1950); *Lo and Behold!* (1951); *The Teahouse of the August Moon* (1953); *Good as Gold* (1957); *Juniper and the Pagans* (1959); *Everybody Loves Opal* (1961); *It's Been Wonderful* (1966); *Scandal Point* (1967); *Everybody's Girl* (1968); *Love Is a Time of Day* (1969); *A Barrel Full of Pennies* (1970); *Lovely Ladies, Kind Gentlemen* (1970; musical adaptation of *The Teahouse of the August Moon*); *Opal is a Diamond* (1971); *Anybody Out There?* (1972); *The Dancing Mice* (1972); *Macbeth Did It* (1972); *The Savage Dilemma* (1972); *The Enigma* (1973); *Opal's Baby* (1973); *Roman Conquest* (1973); *A Bad Year for Tomatoes* (1974); *Love Nest for Three* (1974); *Sex on the Sixth Floor: Three One-Act Plays: Tenacity, Ambiguity, Frustration* (1974); *Divorce, Anyone?* (1975); *Noah's Animals* (1975); *Opal's Husband* (1975); *People!: Three One-Act Plays: Boredom, Christmas Spirit, Aptitude* (1976); *Suicide, Anyone?* (1976); *The Girls of the Garden Club* (1979); *Opal's Million Dollar Duck* (1979); *That's Not My Father! Three One-Act Plays: Raconteur, Fettucine, Masquerade* (1979); *That's Not My Mother: Three One-Act Plays: Seniority, Reception, Optimism* (1979); *The Magenta Moth* (1983); *Danny and the Deep Blue Sea* (1984); *It's a Dog's Life: The Gift, Co-incidence, The Divorce* (1984)

FURTHER READING

Clurman, Harold. Review of *Teahouse of the August Moon*. *The Nation* (October 31, 1953).

Hall, Michael. "John Patrick: Playwright of the August Moon." Master's thesis, Univ. of Florida at Gainesville, 1972.

Marion, John. "John Patrick." In *Dictionary of Literary Biography 7*, ed. by John MacNicholas. Detroit, Mich.: Broccoli Clark, 1981.

Moe, Christian H. "John Patrick." In *Contemporary Dramatists*, ed. by D. L. Kirkpatrick. 4th ed. London: St. James Press, 1988. 417–418.

James Fisher

PEDRERO, PALOMA (1957–)

Born July 3, 1957, in Madrid, SPAIN, Paloma Pedrero lived the finale of General Francisco Franco's fascist dictatorship, the inauguration of Spain's democratic period, the development of the European Union, and most recently, global terrorism when commuter trains were attacked near Madrid on March 11, 2004. While Pedrero's themes include such sociopolitical events, her interrogation of gender roles distinguishes her theater. With a formation in ACTING, directing, teaching playwriting workshops, and a degree in social anthropology from Madrid's Universidad Complutense, Pedrero is one of a few contemporary Spanish women playwrights to achieve international recognition; she has already seen her plays staged in ENGLAND, the UNITED STATES, COSTA RICA, the Czech Republic, CUBA, and a number of European countries.

Her early plays of the 1980s such as *Lauren's Call* (*La llamada de Lauren*, 1984), *Wolf Kisses* (*Besos de lobo*, 1986), and *The Color of August* (*El color de agosto*, 1987) were relegated to small, marginal Spanish theaters whose budgets provided minimum promotion or distribution of her work. Moreover, as a female writer whose dramas exposed contemporary anxieties about rigid gender conventions within the pluralistic and transitional environment of the early democratic period, critical reviews tended to be subdued or derisive of Pedrero's feminist concerns, in spite of awards some of these plays garnered. These are the very plays, however, that scholars, students, and theater companies in other countries celebrated.

The author's oeuvre ranges from one-act to full-length dramas with a tendency toward verbal economy, linguistic vogue, and poignant humor. Further, the plays display an intensity that confronts, unsettles, and exhilarates audiences who identify with the protagonists' experiences such as defying rigid gender role paradigms (*Wolf Kisses*, *The Color of August*, *Lauren's Call*); brief encounters born of both human desire and the need for compassion (*From Midnight to Dawn* [*De la noche al alba*, 1992], *First Star* [*Una estrella*, 1990]); the social and global realities of terrorism (*Puppies with a Dark Gaze* [*Cachorros de negro mirar*, 1995] and *Ana 3/11* [*Ana el once de Marzo*, 2004]); and self-empowerment (*Wolf Kisses* and *Love Crazy* [*Locas de amar*, 1994]).

During the 1990s, Pedrero began training the next generation of writers and helping them launch their own careers, but it was not until the 21st century that her own playwriting triumphed

with Spanish audiences. *Nights of Passing Love* (*Noches de amor enfímero*, 1989), composed of three one-acts, has attracted the largest and most mainstream audiences. First staged in a small theater in Madrid in 1990, a revised version of *Nights* played at Madrid's prestigious Teatro de Bellas Artes, where spectators filled the theater for almost two months during the winter of 2003. Her healthy number of publications and productions in Spain have affirmed Pedrero's significance within Spanish theater history. Outside of Spain, *Lauren's Call*, *The Color of August*, and *Nights of Passing Love* count among her best-known dramas, and her latest plays have already gained momentum on international stages. In 2006, for example, *Ana 3/11* premiered in both London and New York, while *Midnight's Desire* debuted in Cuba (*Los Ojos de la noche*, 1998). In the same year, *First Kiss* (*Beso a Beso*, 2005) was nominated for nine Premios Max (Spain's equivalent to Broadway's Tony Awards). As an established writer associated with the post-Franco democracy, Pedrero is already shaping Spanish theater of the budding 21st century.

SELECT PLAYS: *Lauren's Call* (*La llamada de Lauren*, 1984); *The Voucher* (*Resguardo personal*, 1985); *Wolf Kisses* (*Besos de lobo*, 1986); *The Color of August* (*El color de agosto*, 1987); *Nights of Passing Love* (*Noches de amor enfímero*, 1989); *First Star* (*Una estrella*, 1990); *Love Crazy* (*Locas de amar*, 1994); *Puppies with a Dark Gaze* (*Cachorros de negro mirar*, 1995); *Aging Quarrels* (*En el túnel un pájaro*, 2004); *Ana 3/11* (*Ana el once de marzo*, 2004); *First Kiss* (*Beso a Beso*, 2005)

FURTHER READING

Leonard, Candyce. "Paloma Pedrero." In *Major Spanish Dramatists: A Bio-critical Guide to the History of Spanish Theatre*, ed. by Mary Parker. Westport, Conn.: Greenwood Press, 2001. 2:337–347.

Perri, Dennis. "Paloma Pedrero's Theater: Seeing Is More Than Believing." *Estreno* 29, no. 1 (2003): 43–48.

Weimar, Christopher B. "Gendered Discourse in Paloma Pedrero's *Noches de amor efímero*." *Gestos* 16 (1993): 89–102.

Zatlin, Phyllis. "From Night Games to Postmodern Satire: The Theater of Paloma Pedrero." *Hispania* 84, no. 2 (May 2001): 193–204.

Candyce Leonard

PEER GYNT

> To be oneself is: to slay oneself.
> —The Button-Molder, Act 5

HENRIK IBSEN's *Peer Gynt* was originally published as a dramatic poem not intended for the stage. The text was performed as a play for the first time in 1876 and has since then enjoyed much success at theaters in an increasing number of countries all over the world. Divided into five acts with dialogues and monologues in rhymed verse, the action covers the life and changing conditions of the main character, a native of Gudbrandsdal, NORWAY, from the age of twenty until he is an old man. He wants to impress his fellow men and is not considered trustworthy. Even his mother is temporarily fooled by his tall-tale inventiveness. After eloping with the bride at a wedding, and then abandoning her, he is outlawed by the community.

Daydreaming about achievements and honor, even aspiring to become emperor, and yet promiscuous, and running away from the consequences of what he has done, he is constantly on the move, exploring new opportunities. This brings him into situations where he is either on the verge of being annihilated, as with the trolls in the mountain hall of Dovre and the encounter with the enigmatic Voice in the dark (act 2), or fooled and robbed, as with the Bedouin girl Anitra in the Sahara (act 4). In act 3 the young girl Solvejg comes to live with him in his cabin in the forest, but the woman in green, daughter of the Dovre Master, appears and claims that he is the father of her child, so Peer chooses to leave, while Solvejg promises to wait for him to return.

Act 4 is staged in North AFRICA with Peer as a middle-aged gentleman moving from Morocco all the way to EGYPT. Here he decides to be a traveling scholar, observing the enigmatic monuments of antiquity. He is approached by Dr. Begriffenfeldt, the German director of the Cairo madhouse, who crowns him to be Emperor of the Self.

Approaching the Norwegian coast (act 5), he survives a shipwreck and starts moving inland, while his morally wretched life comes back to him in retrospective scenes. The Button-molder is instructed by his Master to get hold of Peer's soul; it is to be melted down because of lack of identity. Peer protests and tries in vain to find people who can witness that he has been himself, but all he can get is testimony to the effect that he has been living by the troll motto "Troll, be thyself—enough!" Gradually he realizes that he has not lived up to his moral obligations and that he is doomed to annihilation. At last he arrives with the Button-molder at Solvejg's cabin, and she does not accuse him: he has been himself in her faith, in her hope, and in her love.

Ibsen has added freely to the exploits of the folk hero, changing his character from the bold and helpful hunter of the local traditions into a selfish man whose behavior is dictated by a wish to avoid commitments of any kind and who vainly tries his luck in changing appearances as troll prince, businessman, prophet, scholar. The poem has been regarded in different ways—as a national satire against the Norwegians, as a fairy-tale play about the young, careless suitor approaching the princess, and as a romantic expansion of a medieval morality play, with Johann Wolfgang Goethe's *Faust* as its model. There are arguments in favor of all three concepts, the latter one increasingly demonstrated in the final act.

Key to understanding the difficult act 4 is the section on ancient Egyptian art and religion in Georg Wilhelm Friedrich Hegel's *Aesthetics*. The German philosopher was much studied at European universities in the mid-19th century. He contrasted the symbolic art of the Orient, where animal forms seem to dominate the human element of various sculptures, and the classical art of Greek and Roman origin, where man is triumphing over the animal. Other references to Hegel's PHILOSOPHY are also to be found in the poem, such as his reflections on madness. The Director of the Cairo madhouse, Dr. Begriffenfeldt, may be regarded as a caricature of Hegel.

In act 2 and elsewhere, transformations of a variety of Norwegian folklore figures—for example, trolls with tails and other animal attributes—suggest a mixture of man and animal, corresponding to the enigmas presented by the combined expressions of ancient Egyptian mythology. The imagery of the poem abounds in metaphors and similes involving animal qualities applied to man, most of them aiming at Peer. Not all of these images are easily translated into other languages.

Peer Gynt is not without charm; among foreigners he is often the center of attention, with a talent for entertaining. Intellectually he is not impressive, often facing enigmas but failing to solve them. His monologues are often rich in proverbs and quotations (and misquotations) from the Bible and various other sources, and he may refer to philosophical and moral issues, but rarely in a serious way.

Gradually the story of Peer Gynt turns into an allegory of the ego erring between its lower instincts and its divine essence. For a long time Peer is blind to his own moral imperfections, but following some appalling encounters, such as the madhouse visit and the appearance of the Strange Passenger, he begins to realize that he should lower his aspirations: "among the wild creatures I ought to rank first." Peeling an onion, he is struck by the lack of a core, but he fails to see this as a token of his own spiritual being.

Enigmatic figures, such as the Voice in the dark (generally referred to as the Boyg), the singing statue of Memnon, the Sphinx, the madhouse inmates, can be regarded as mirror appearances, intended to teach Peer the essentials of his own situation. The Button-molder, sent to carry out the judgment, is confronted by Solvejg, the innocent woman, who on the allegorical level can be interpreted as Peer's higher identity. When he finally admits that he is No One, he is ready for the grace mediated through Solvejg. He can sleep and dream; she will be awake.

FURTHER READING

Aarseth, Asbjørn. *Dyret i Mennesket. Et bidrag til tolkning av Henrik Ibsens «Peer Gynt»* [The Beast in Man: A Contribution to the Interpretation of Henrik Ibsen's Peer Gynt.], Bergen o.a., Universitetsforlaget 1975.

——. "Peer Gynt and Hegel's Ideas on Egyptian Art." *Scandinavian Studies* (December 22, 2001).

Collin, Josef. *Henrik Ibsen. Sein Werk—seine Weltanschauung—sein Leben* [Henrik Ibsen. His work—his worldview—his life]. Heidelberg: Carl Winter, 1910.

Fjelde, Rolf. "*Peer Gynt*, Naturalism, and the Dissolving Self." *The Drama Review* 13 (1968): 28–43.

Johnston, Brian. "The Parable of *Peer Gynt*." In *To the Third Empire. Ibsen's Early Drama*. Minneapolis: Univ. of Minnesota Press, 1980. 164–207.

Asbjørn Aarseth

PÉREZ GALDÓS, BENITO (1843–1920)

Benito Pérez Galdós is generally considered SPAIN's greatest novelist. He was also a journalist, translator, and playwright. Born in Las Palmas, Canary Islands, Spain, on May 10, 1843, he was the youngest of ten children in a military family stationed in the Canary Islands. By all accounts the author's mother, María de los Dolores Galdós, was domineering and strict; she may have been Pérez Galdos's model for many strong-willed women in his works such as Doña Perfecta in the novel of the same name (1876). Pérez Galdós concealed his literary interests from her and rebelled against her soon after she sent him to Madrid to study law.

By the time of Pérez Galdós's arrival in Madrid in 1862, Krausism, a liberal PHILOSOPHY named after a minor German philosopher, had taken hold of the Spanish universities. Krausism implored men to live nobly and simply, dedicating themselves to serving and enlightening others. In 1865 Pérez Galdós began his career as a journalist at the Madrid-based La nación, and he would become the editor of the liberal El Debate in 1871. In 1872 he began editing the cultural magazine La Revista de España. While a journalist Pérez Galdós wrote a number of thesis novels between 1867 and 1878 that reflected the influence of Krausism in his work. Beginning in 1881, Pérez Galdós shifted his attention toward writing realist novels that were filled with social criticism of largely urban Madrid society but also included detailed descriptions of the city's customs and hierarchies. Often he would blend his Krausist beliefs with naturalist currents such as those found in the works of ÉMILE ZOLA. In 1889, he was elected to the Royal Spanish Academy. With the publication of forty-six historical novels titled National Episodes (Episodios nacionales, published 1873–1879 and 1898–1912), Pérez Galdós fused his literary talents with his love of Spanish history.

Finally, Pérez Galdós contributed nearly two dozen original or adapted works for the theater beginning in 1892. His most celebrated play Electra premiered in 1901 and was fraught with anticlerical messages as an ultraconservative priest tries to wrestle control over Electra, a young and beautiful woman he deemed convent material, from her modern, liberal cousin. Given the anticlerical context of the post–Spanish American War period, Electra was more a political success than a literary one. In 1914, his native Canary Islands voted him to represent them in the Spanish Parliament despite his deteriorating health and vision. He died in Madrid, Spain, on January 4, 1920.

PLAYS: Reality (Realidad, 1892); Gerona (1893); The Madcap (La loca de la casa, 1893); The Condemned (Los condenados, 1894); The Duchess of San Quintín (La de San Quintín, 1894); Will (Voluntad, 1895); Doña Perfecta (1896); The Festival (La feria, 1896); Electra (1901); Life and Soul (Alma y vida, 1902); Mariucha (1903); Bárbara (1904); Grandpa (El abuelo, 1904); Love and Science (Amor y ciencia, 1905); Pedro Minio (1908); Casandra (1910); Celia in the Depths of Hell (Celia en los infiernos, 1913); Alceste (1914); Sister Simona (Sor Simona, 1915); Solomon the Cheapskate (El tacaño Salomón, 1916); Saint Juana of Castile (Santa Juana de Castilla, 1918)

FURTHER READING

Berkowitz, H. Chanon. Benito Pérez Galdós: Spanish Liberal Crusader. Madison: Univ. of Wisconsin Press, 1948.

Bly, Peter. Galdós's Novel of the Historical Imagination: A Study of the Contemporary Novels. Liverpool, England: Francis Cairns, 1983.

Gilman, Stephen. Galdós and the Art of the European Novel. Princeton, N.J.: Princeton Univ. Press, 1981.

Labanyi, Jo, ed. Galdós. Modern Literatures in Perspective Series. London: Longman, 1993.

Enrique Sanabria

PERFORMANCE ART

I make art about the misunderstandings that take place at the border zone. But for me, the border is no longer located at any fixed geopolitical site. I carry the border with me, and I find new borders wherever I go.
—Guillermo Gomez-Peña, New World Border, 1996

Almost all performance artists appear to share an obsession with some kind of "border zone," the liminal region between this and that art form. The great difficulty presented by even defining the term *performance* has resulted in the grouping together under this rubric of wildly disparate theatrical, quasi-theatrical, and antitheatrical events. One thing can be said: Performance art expresses weariness with traditional boundaries between artistic genres, between elite and popular art, and with the value systems and critical methods of traditional aesthetics. Indeed, it is this very weariness, breeding as it does tremendous innovation and cross-fertilization, that attracts artists, historians, and theorists interested in pushing the envelope.

The term *performance art* was coined initially to describe the collisions between theater, dance, and visual art coming out of Europe, AUSTRALIA, the Americas, and JAPAN in the early 1970s, but the roots of this tradition stretch back to the 1880s. The historical, theatrical AVANT-GARDE's primary aesthetic goal was to combat the rising cultural dictatorship of the middle class by providing an alternative model promoting freedom of thought and action, negating structures of authority (and authorship), and advocating radical revolutionary politics. The avant-garde was not meant to critique the system from within but to attack it from the outside. Their battle cry of *épater le bourgeois!* manifested itself partly as an attempt to shock the audience out of its accustomed aesthetic complacency by undermining their expectations about the relationship of the art object to the consumer in an effort to bring radical social change.

The urge to "break the crust" of conventional aesthetics was enabled by the tradition of politically charged practical joking known as *fumisme*, the "rire jaune" originally associated with the aesthetic innovations of Stéphane Mallarmé and Arthur Rimbaud. Fumisme is a particularly ambiguous form of laughter marked by trangression, subversion, and destruction and is generally acknowledged to be a precursor of Dada and SURRE-

ALISM. *Fumistes* such as the Hydropathes, the practitioners of the Parisian Le Chat Noir, and ALFRED JARRY employed a kaliedoscope of techniques antithetical to mainstream theater conventions, ranging from the base and vulgar to the aggressive and intrusive. FILIPPO TOMMASO MARINETTI, in his 1913 *Variety Theatre,* suggested practical jokes on the audience including smearing mud, gum, or sneezing powder on the seats, selling one seat to ten individuals, giving complimentary seats to the mentally unstable, and so on. These experiments continued to escalate in various forms and with varying degrees of success until the rapid rise of fascism in Europe disrupted the development of radical theater in the 1930s.

This tradition reasserted itself in the experimental theaters emerging in Europe and America in the 1960s and 1970s, led by figures such as Peter Brook, Charles Marowitz, and Richard Schechner, who worked to develop performative events that jeopardized traditional relationships between performer and spectator, dependence on literary dramatic texts, and the Aristotelian devaluing of spectacle. The LIVING THEATRE's 1964 *Mysteries and Smaller Pieces* was a sequence of ritualized behaviors, mostly games; they and other groups, including the OPEN THEATER and the POOR THEATER of Polish director Jerzy Grotowski, searched for the "essential" theatrical experience. Risky body art emerged in the 1970s with the often frightening performances of Vito Acconci, Gina Pane, Adrian Piper, the 1980s work of Orlan (plastic-surgery art that attacks the social construction of beauty and gender identity), and in the 1990s, "posthuman" work synthesizing the human body with a robot's, as in the performances of the Australian artist Stelarc. The emergence of feminist discourse intersected powerfully with avant-garde performance to produce artists like Bobby Baker, Karen Finley, New York's WOW Café, the elaborately stylized art protests of the Guerilla Girls, and the sexually hyperexplicit "speculum" performances of Annie Sprinkle.

In the 1980s, Richard Schechner helped to found PERFORMANCE STUDIES, a new academic discipline to respond to and inspire such innovations. The blurring of conventional boundaries between artistic genres and disciplines coincided powerfully with these experiments. The result was a veritable explosion of experimental performances that did not fit neatly into the traditional definition of "theater." The emergence of postmodernist thought, which eschews the search for "essence" in favor of a romance with surfaces, moved experimental theater closer to the visual arts, particularly in the works of PING CHONG, Meredith Monk, and ROBERT WILSON. Self-reflexive, eclectically hungry, and intensely visual, performance art began to be seen as a logical outgrowth of postmodern discourse. The success of these experiments incited wave after wave of boundary-blurring performance pieces.

By the 1990s, activism and identity politics in performance art embraced ethnicity issues (including the work of Palestinian artist Mona Hatoum), sexuality (Tim Miller's gay-themed solo performances), and disability (as in the dance-based work of Catherine Cole). The Coney Island Sideshow's successful rebirth as a performance art venue gave complex legitimacy to circus-style artists like bearded lady Jennifer Miller. The politically charged work of Guillermo Gomez-Peña and Coco Fusco, who presented themselves outlandishly dressed in an outdoor cage as "undiscovered Amerindians," synthesizes ancient Indigenous performance styles with modern imagery to hyperbolize problems with IDENTITY politics. Performance art also often embraces advances in technology and science, as in the "difficult listening" innovative musical performances of Laurie Anderson, hypnotic with electronically warped sounds and stylized multimedia stage shows.

Performance art, sharing with its avant-garde progenitors a critique of conservatism, found itself under political fire from government censors in the UNITED STATES in the 1990s, when the National Endowment for the Arts radically reduced its funding for performance artists whose work had become controversial. Such criticism made performance art a political pawn in the so-called culture wars of the United States, although similar artists of innovative events are enjoying widespread government funding in Europe and Japan.

[*See also* Deconstruction; Epic Theater; Happenings and Intermedia; Interculturalism; Postmodernism]

FURTHER READING

Banes, Sally. *Subversive Expectations: Performance Art and Paratheatre in New York, 1976–85.* Ann Arbor: Univ. of Michigan Press, 1998.

Carlson, Marvin. *Performance: A Critical Introduction.* London: Routledge, 1996.

Goldberg, RoseLee. *Performance Art: From Futurism to the Present.* Rev. ed. New York: Thames & Hudson, 2001.

Harding, James M., ed. *Contours of the Theatrical Avant-Garde.* Ann Arbor: Univ. of Michigan Press, 2000.

Howell, Anthony. *Analysis of Performance Art: A Guide to Its Theory and Practice.* London: Routledge, 1999.

Scheckner, Richard. *Environmental Theatre.* New York: Hawthorn, 1983.

Michael M. Chemers

PERFORMANCE STUDIES

It is theatre . . . which haunts all performance whether or not it occurs in the theatre.
—Herbert Blau, *The Eye of Prey,* 1987

Performance studies as an emergent scholarly discipline is not a discrete field of study so much as a cross-fertilization of many different disciplines. Coming from theater scholarship and criticism, performance studies as an academic discipline was first proposed by Richard Schechner in 1966, when he expanded the definition of "performance" to include forms of ritualistic social behaviors other than traditional theater and dance, such as sports, games, and festivals. Modern performance studies is very much an outgrowth of this foundational work.

Performance studies allies itself most closely with the fields of cultural anthropology and ethnography, embracing the concept of "cultural performance" envisioned in 1959 by Milton Singer, which suggests that human behavior is largely governed by the acting out of predesigned roles, whether consciously or not. This concept is advanced in the work on "social drama" and ritual developed by Victor Turner, particularly in *From Ritual to Theatre* (1982). Also influential are the cultural anthropologist Clifford Geertz ("Deep Play: Notes on the Balinese Cockfight" [1973] employs performance techniques to analyze social phenomena), folklorist Dell Hynes, and cultural historian Johan Huizinga.

Performance studies engages psychology, sociology, and linguistics as well, particularly the work of Erving Goffman; *The Presentation of Self in Everyday Life* (1959) shows "theatrical" conventions are in play in most social situations. Performance studies is deeply concerned with the relationship between performance and the construction of social and individual identities, a central point for cultural studies and poststructuralist theory. Another concern of performance studies is the ever-widening field of performance that does not fit easily into the broad categories of theater, dance, or other traditional classifications.

Performance studies enables anthropologists, sociologists, psychologists, cultural scholars, and linguists to see the usefulness of theater-related criticism in describing social phenomena. In addition, this growing field has increased the range of events that interest scholars: theme parks, folk festivals, religious displays, sporting events, popular entertainments like circuses and freak shows, and even political demonstrations and riots are seen as extensions of the theatrical activity of humanity.

While many scholars in these cross-pollinated fields are excited by such interdisciplinary opportunities, some critics have been troubled by the blurring of boundaries. Anthropologists, who usually avoid "interference" in the cultures they study, are troubled by the personal involvement of performance theorists in the social phenomena they study. Theater scholars worry that their work is raided for expedience and not engaged fully. Other critics ask, If theater is such a powerful metaphor for human behavior, then what aspect of human interaction is *not* theatrical? If performance studies allows the theatrical metaphor to be overdetermined in this way, it may cease to have relevance at all. These issues and others have resulted in some tension and even suspicion between performance studies and the other fields, a tension that has slowed the development of historical techniques within performance studies.

[*See also* Deconstruction; Epic Theater; Interculturalism; Performance Art; Postmodernism]

FURTHER READING

Carlson, Marvin. *Performance: A Critical Introduction.* London: Routledge, 1996.

Counsell, Colin, and Laurie Wolf. *Performance Analysis: An Introductory Coursebook.* London: Routledge, 2001.

Pollack, Della, ed. *Exceptional Spaces: Essays in Performance and History.* Chapel Hill: Univ. of North Carolina Press, 1998.

Schechner, Richard. *Performance Studies: An Introduction.* New York: Routledge, 2002.

Stern, Carol Simpson, and Bruce Henderson. *Performance: Texts and Contexts.* New York: Longman, 1993.

Stucky, Nathan, and Cynthia Wimmer. *Teaching Performance Studies.* Carbondale: Southern Illinois Univ. Press, 2002.

Michael M. Chemers

PERU

Peru has an active, dynamic theatrical life that transcends the obstacles of political instability, economic hardship, and even violence. Throughout the country there are playwrights and theater groups that create and perform works that reflect national identity. Nowhere is this more true than in Lima, which is not only the political capital of the country but also its cultural center. Much of the theatrical activity in Lima stems from the university groups, the most important of which are the Teatro de la Universidad de San Marcos (begun in 1946 by Guillermo Ugarte Chamorro) and the Teatro de la Universidad Católica (started in 1961), which have encouraged and trained new playwrights. The Teatro Nacional and its director Ruth Escudero have also been instrumental in bringing attention to autochthonous theatrical productions, as have contests such as Concurso Solari Swayne, Teatro Peruano Norteamericano, Hacia Una Dramaturgia Joven, among others, as well as festivals such as Muestras de Teatro Peruano.

Politically and economically, the 1980s were a time of instability in the country as a whole. In the capital, people's lives were daily interrupted by bombs, assaults, assassinations, kidnappings, blackouts, lack of water and other resources, and a constant state of fear. The biggest and most active terrorist group committing the majority of the attacks was Sendero Luminoso, or the Shining Path, a maoist group that was started in the mountains and moved its rebellion toward the cities. One of their most effective strategies was exploding electrical towers, which caused constant blackouts. The roads in and out of the city were dangerous, there were car bombs within the city, and anyone who was perceived to be in a position of authority was a target. Government reprisals were no better and often helped to create militants through a resentment of the heavyhanded methods of dealing with terrorism and of the complete lack of respect for human rights. All of this took place at the same time that hyperinflation and low employment rates added another stress to life in Lima. Economic uncertainty and fear for their safety kept many audiences away from the theaters.

The social upheavals and political violence of the 1980s ushered in an era of theatrical experimentation. The *creación colectiva*, or collective creations, in which several playwrights, with the collaboration of actors and directors, would create a play, often took the place of the individual playwright. These groups were created beginning in the 1950s but became most active in the 1970s and 1980s. In 1953, Reynaldo D'Amore, an Argentinian playwright and director, along with Grégor Díaz and several other playwrights, founded the Club de Teatro de Lima, and in the 1960s Sara Joffré founded Homero Teatro de Grillos, whose most important purpose was the publication of Peruvian theater. These efforts led in the 1970s to the *teatro colectivo*, or *teatro de grupo*, among which the two most well known and influential groups are Cuatrotablas and Yuyachkani, which have a liberal social and political agenda. Other groups are Magia, Alondra, Teatro Del Sol, Clavo y Canela, Yawar, Audaces, and many others. Almost all significant theater in the 1980s in Peru stemmed from the collective groups. The members of many of the groups worked together, traveled together, and organized workshops and even strikes. Their themes were mostly political, and their style experimental. They valued corporal expression over language and group improvisation over the individual playwright. The Movimiento de Teatro Independiente, or MOTÍN, was founded in 1985 and encompassed many theatrical groups in a professional guild. In 1990, MOTÍN was organized into regional divisions to which many playwrights and theater groups belonged and whose goal was to promote a national theater and an emphasis on new theories and praxis.

The new playwrights of the 1990s were active, dynamic, and individual. The resurgence of the importance of the playwright can be attributed to a certain extent to a reaction to the collective creation of the previous decade. Although much relevant and influential work continues to come from those groups, the individual playwright came into the spotlight in the 1990s, after more than a decade. The efforts of the playwrights themselves, as well as of directors and professors at the university theaters, helped to bring about a new generation of very active and productive playwrights. The collective creative movement did, however, influence the manner in which the present playwrights work, in that they are now more involved in the productions and are considered to be in partnership with the actors and director. The most influential of the collective groups remain active, but individual writers are now on the scene: Alonso Alegría, César Vega, Aureo Sotelo, César de María, Sara Joffré, Eduardo Adrianzén, Rafael Dumett, Javier Maraví, Alfonso Santistevan, María Teresa Zúñiga, Delfina Paredes, and Eduardo Valentín are some of the most active authors, according to Luis A. Ramos-García. To that list we can add Claudia Besaccia, Maritza Kirchhausen, and Aldo Miyashiro, among others.

The themes for this new theater of the 1990s are mostly the individual, identity, sexuality, generational conflict, family crises, and feminism. It is surprising, given the political violence of the previous decade, that the playwrights of the 1990s do not often have violent themes, and if they do, they are not generally directly linked to national politics. *The Risk of Living* (El riesgo de vivir), by Lucía Fox Lockert, published in 1982 in the anthology *Voces en escena: Antología de dramaturgas latinoamericanas* (Voices on the stage: Anthology of Latin American Women Play-

wrights), is one of the few graphically violent plays that directly address the problem of terrorism. In the play, a young middle-class woman is taken in by the guerrilla's maoist ideology, without fully understanding the extent of the violence involved. When her cousin and some friends are kidnapped and tortured, she decides to help them, but it is too late. The situation is desperate, and no solution is proposed, but the criticism of the terrorists, the government, and the self-blinded bourgeoisie is evident.

Other plays, such as *Kamikaze! or The History of the Cowardly Japanese Man Kamikaze! o La historia del cobarde japonés* (1999), by César de María, and *Theatrical Wake Función velorio* (2000), by Aldo Miyashiro Ribeiro, confront violence but are also not all that common. In the former, two Japanese brothers during World War II face difficult decisions. One is a cowardly soldier but protects his family at all costs, while the other is capable of fighting and murder but protects only himself. De María himself asserts that this is a commentary on the violence lived during the height of the war with the Shining Path guerrillas, but in removing the action in time and place, he avoids addressing head-on the domestic situation in Peru. In Miyashiro Ribeiro's play the subject is the theater itself and the desperation of a single playwright to get his work produced and receive the attention he feels he deserves. In order to do this, the playwright writes a final scene in which all of the characters actually die: the actors agree to take their own lives during the production. While this may reflect a hyperbolic commentary on the state of the theater in Peru, and illustrates the conflicts between individual characters, it does not directly address the Shining Path terrorists, although it can be argued that the use of murder to attract attention was one of their main strategies. The main themes for Limeño theater today continue to be existential, focusing mostly on the identity of the individual. This can, perhaps, be attributed to the fact that both the playwrights and the public no longer want to reflect on the violence but desire to move on.

Peruvian theater, and in particular Limeño theater, continues to confront obstacles, the greatest of which is a lack of audience, perhaps attributable to the economic problems and the high rate of unemployment that the country still experiences. There have been a few anthologies of Peruvian theater in the past decade, but in all there is not much published theater, and what exists is difficult to find because the editions tend to be limited. The advent of the Internet is helpful in that there are some plays and a great deal of information available online. Theater in Peru, and especially in Lima, is growing in influence and maturing in its search for a national identity. In the coming years there will very likely be continued lively productivity and interest in plays written by local authors.

FURTHER READING

Castro Urioste, José, and Roberto Angeles, eds. *Dramaturgia peruana* [Peruvian dramatic art]. Lima: Latinoamericana, 1999.

Gonzalez Echevarría, Roberto, and Enrique Pupo-Walker, eds. *The Cambridge History of Latin American Literature*. 3 vols. New York: Cambridge Univ. Press, 1996.

Morris, Robert J. *The Contemporary Peruvian Theatre*. Lubbock: Texas Tech Press, 1977.

Oleszkiewicz, Malgorzata. "Muestra Nacional de Teatro: The New Theatre in Peru." *The Drama Review*, TDR 33, no. 3 (Autumn 1989): 10–17.

Ramos-García, Luis. "El discurso de la memoria teatral peruana en los noventa" [Discourse of Peruvian theatrical memory in the 1990s]. LATR (Fall 2000): 173–192.

——. *Voces del interior: Nueva dramaturgia peruana* [Voices of the interior: New Peruvian dramatic art]. Minneapolis, Minn.: Teatro Nacional del Perú, Instituto Nacional de Cultura, 2001.

Sotomayor Roggero, Carmela. *Panorama y tendencias del teatro peruano* [Panorama and trends of the Peruvian theater]. Lima: Herrera, 1990.

Patricia Suppes

PERU, RELIGIOUS THEATER

PERU is a country that celebrates its dual heritage in popular theater, especially during the feast of the patron saint. The faithful perform dance dramas to please and placate the local saint and to assure good health and harvests. The fiesta suspends the daily struggle to survive, enhances the status of the performers, and affirms their collective identity. Adapted from familiar historical and sacred texts, these plays have evolved into a theater of self-affirmation. By reconciling native spirituality with Catholic rituals, the performance summarizes the mestizo (biracial and bicultural) identity of Andean peoples.

Religious theater is communal: financed by community donations, mounted by religious brotherhoods, and performed by working-class people in large outdoor venues. Created collectively from local traditions, the productions feature large troupes, lavish costumes often marked with symbolic images, and ritualized choreography set to live music. In the highlands, the performers tend to be Indians and mestizos; on the coast, these may include Afro-Peruvians. Structurally, the continuous action—without division into scenes—retains pre-Hispanic dramatic form. The scripts are fluid and modified continuously. Some productions are in Spanish, some in Quechua or Aymara, the languages of native Andeans; most are bilingual. Their roots stem from the dance dramas of medieval SPAIN and ancient Peru, which converged when missionary friars used Christian content and native actors, languages, and aesthetics to evangelize the indigenes. Most of today's performances, however, arose in the 1940s as a result of the Indigenous movement to vindicate Aboriginal culture.

The Death of Atahualpa (*La muerte de Atawallpa*), the most-often-performed play in Peru and Bolivia today and during colonialism, portrays the conquest of the Inca from a native perspective. Considered a demigod, the Inca Atahualpa is identified with the Apu, the local protector mountain god. The action begins as various sectors of Inca society greet the royal family with elegant dances and spectacular costumes. The Spanish arrive, capture Atahualpa, and massacre the Quechua soldiers. Pizarro accepts the famous "king's ransom" (two roomsful of silver and one of gold), then baptizes and executes the Inca. After the ritual lament, the Priest proclaims the marriage and miscegenation of Spanish-Andean peoples, and they all dance off into history.

Some scholars date the first conquest play to 1555 in Potosí, now in Bolivia, but two watercolors from 1780s northern Peru provide the oldest proof of age. Conquest plays are more mythic than historical. Sometimes history prevails, and Atahualpa is garroted; in other versions he is decapitated or executed by sword, or the Emperor and Pizarro embrace in reconciliation. Some feature battles on horses reminiscent of the Spanish plays called *Moros y cristianos*. While historical references to conquest dramas abound, the oldest published texts date from 1955 (Bolivia) and 1985 (Peru).

In contrast, *The Little Devils* (*Los diablicos*) hails only from Túcume, a village in north coastal Peru. It depicts the allegorical struggle between good and evil known as "The Dance of the Seven Vices." Hell and the devil were popular themes of missionary theater because holy terror created more converts than compassion. In effect, Lucifer trumped Christ. Like *The Death of Atahualpa*, proof of antiquity comes from a 1780s watercolor. Local lore traces *The Little Devils* to a colonial hoax. At night Spaniards masked as devils emerged from the pyramids nearby and rode through town in a pageant wagon pulled by horses to frighten the natives into accepting Catholicism. This hoax evolved into *The Little Devils*.

The action begins as the devils enter in two columns, a common pre-Conquest choreography. Then each of seven devils recites the evil he embodies: pride, lust, envy, and so on. After reciting the verses, they build a goat and dance in his honor. Occasionally, the Angel interrupts to battle with Lucifer. The Angel defeats him and converts the goat into the "Lamb of God" and the heathens into Christians. In celebration, the Angel invites everyone to dance around the plaza. While there are numerous versions of *Atahualpa*, *The Little Devils* belongs only to Túcume, and the representation has remained relatively stable since its colonial emergence.

The most famous popular production in Peru is the Feast of the Sun (Intiraymi), celebrated in June in Cuzco, the ancient capital of the Inca empire. While this ceremony has dramatic elements, the modern version is a tourist attraction, more commercial than religious.

Religious theater reflects popular worship and societal values; the performers embody the community. On the surface Catholic devotion moves the action, but embedded elements allude to older forms of worship related to Andean sacred geography and the agricultural cycle. The nonverbal performance strategies validate the struggle of workers and farmers to honor their pantheistic worldview. The Apu (Inca mountain god) protects, and Pachamamá (Mother Earth) provides. In contrast, the Catholic saint punishes those who fail to fulfill their ritual obligations. Andean spirituality has many double gods.

Spanish authorities made repeated attempts to extirpate the idolatrous elements from sacred dance dramas, even banning them totally—to no avail. Ritual drama is inextricable to Andean culture. When they did not fume or look the other way, the Spaniards saw happy natives processing dogma into representation. Blinded by what they wanted to see, they failed to perceive the ironic and subversive nuances. In effect, religious theater provided a means for the colonized people to satirize their oppressors and express attitudes deemed dangerous in words. *Los Diablicos*, for example, resemble tricksters, caricatures more laughable than threatening. The small goat looks more like a toy than a weapon. The sword-wielding Angel, symbol of the Church, repeatedly attacks them, not the reverse. The real devils were the Spaniards who resorted to trickery to impose the faith; hell was the abuses of colonialism. In Túcume, the faithful fear the punishments of the Virgin Mary more than the temptations of the devil.

Today's oppressors descend from a caste system that still controls society. Even the conciliatory ending of *The Death of Atahualpa* does not diminish the people's contempt for the invaders. It projects the opulence and dignity of the Inca with stately movements to reaffirm native contributions to national culture. The imperial grandeur confirms the performers' descent from a great civilization and elevates their self-image. Thus conquest plays glorify the Inca past, and *The Little Devils* projects ambiguous images of good and evil. *Atahualpa* is mainly a highland play and *The Little Devils* strictly coastal; together they represent a broad spectrum of religious spectacle in Peru today.

FURTHER READING

Beyersdorff, Margot. *Historia y drama ritual en los andes bolivianos (siglos XVI–XX)*. [History and ritual drama in the Bolivian Andes (16th–20th centuries)]. La Paz, Bolivia: Plural Editores, 1998.

Chang-Rodríguez, Raquel. *Hidden Messages: Representation and Resistance in Andean Colonial Drama*. Lewisburg, Pa.: Bucknell Univ. Press, 1999.

Feliciano, Wilma. *Los diablicos de Túcume: Festividad de la Virgen Purísima* [The Little Devils of Túcume: Holiday of the Purest Virgin]. Lima, Peru, 2002. Spanish/English video.

Millones, Luis. *Dioses familiares: Festivales populares en el Perú contemporáneo* [Familiar gods: Popular festivals in contemporary Peru]. Lima: Fondo Editorial del Congreso del Perú, 1998.

Quintana-Owen, Benito. *The Americas in Spanish Classical Theater: Mythology, Romance, Religion and Politics (Mexico, Peru, Chile)*. Ann Arbor, Mich.: ProQuest/UMI, 2006 [e-book].

Versenyi, Adam. *Theatre in Latin America: Religion, Politics, and Culture from Cortes to the 1980s*. Cambridge: Cambridge Univ. Press, 1993.

Wilma Feliciano

PETA   *See* PHILIPPINE EDUCATIONAL THEATER ASSOCIATION

PETER PAN

The character of Peter Pan first appeared in J. M. BARRIE's novel *The Little White Bird* (1902) and then in a 1904 London stage production *Peter Pan; or, The Boy Who Would Not Grow Up*. After several dramatic and novelistic adaptations of the Peter Pan story, the script was first published as *Peter Pan* in J. M. Barrie's Collected Plays of 1928. *Peter Pan* is a five-act play and is best known as a fantasy for children, although several lines of the dialogue are clearly aimed at adults. The play features an eternally young boy who lives in Never Land with his friends and companions the Lost Boys. Coming into the Darling family nursery, he beckons the Darling children (Wendy, John, and Michael) to fly away with him to Never Land, where Wendy acts as a mother to the Lost Boys, and the group as a whole has many adventures fending off Captain Hook and his pirate crew.

Peter Pan is remarkable for its combination of fantasy and psychological REALISM. Fantasy elements include the famously ageless protagonist Peter and the children's flight to the Never Land with the help of fairy dust. These fantastic situations—perhaps paradoxically—rely on a great deal of NATURALISM and simplicity in the dialogue to achieve their magical effect. Additional character and plot development is provided by an extended preface, prose commentary before each act, and elaborate STAGE DIRECTIONS. A long preface connects the writing and significance of *Peter Pan* to Barrie's relationship with the Llewelyn Davies family. Barrie described his boyish hero as a composite portrait of the five boys of this family: "That is all he is, the spark I got from you." The stage directions to the play, many of which are several paragraphs in length, offer detailed descriptions of the costumes and physical actions of the characters. The stage directions also comment very directly on psychological interactions between characters. As one example, we find in the stage directions the following comment on Wendy's relationship with Peter: "She is too loving to be ignorant that he is not loving enough."

While a fantastic tale for children, the play text also includes social satire primarily aimed at adults, as in the exclamation of Nibs, a Lost Boy: "All I remember about my mother is that she often said to father, 'Oh, how I wish I had a cheque book of my own.'" The innocence of children in the play is often contrasted to a wider world of adult awareness, as we see, for example, in Peter Pan's oblivion to the sexual desire aimed at him by Wendy, Tinkerbell, and Tiger Lily. The play ultimately establishes a sharp line between the realm of adult life and child fantasy, as the Darlings return to their own home and Peter Pan, unable to contemplate a conventional human life, returns to the Never Land.

[*See also* England; Scotland]

FURTHER READING

Carpenter, Humphrey. *Secret Gardens: A Study of the Golden Age of Children's Literature.* Boston: Houghton, 1985.

Gilead, Sarah. "Magic Abjured: Closure in Children's Fantasy Fiction." *PMLA: Publications of the Modern Language Association of America* 106, no. 2 (March 1991): 277–293.

Green, Roger Lancelyn. *Fifty Years of Peter Pan.* London: P. Davis, 1954.

Jack, R. D. S. *The Road to the Never Land: A Reassessment of J. M. Barrie's Dramatic Art.* Aberdeen: Aberdeen Univ. Press, 1991.

Rose, Jacqueline. *The Case of Peter Pan or the Impossibility of Children's Fiction.* Houndsmills, Basingstoke, Hampshire: Macmillan, 1984.

Wilson, Ann. "Hauntings: Anxiety, Technology, and Gender in *Peter Pan.*" *Modern Drama* 43, no. 4 (Winter 2000): 595–610.

Carrie Hintz

THE PETRIFIED FOREST

On May 8, 1934, ROBERT E. SHERWOOD checked into a Reno, Nevada, hotel to wait the required six weeks for a divorce. His past two years had been harrowing, beginning with a European vacation trip with Mr. and Mrs. MARC CONNELLY and spanning the failure of Sherwood's play *Acropolis* (1933) in London, the scandalous behavior of his wife in New York, his near nervous collapse at his English home in Surrey, and a growing involvement with Madeline Connelly. In Reno he passed his time playing tennis, gambling, and enjoying an occasional side trip. One such ride to Carson City inspired him to ask for an office and a typewriter. Four weeks later *The Petrified Forest* was finished, and Sherwood received his divorce in June 1934 and sailed immediately for ENGLAND.

It is 1934—the Depression in the UNITED STATES—and in the lunchroom of the Black Mesa Filling Station and Bar-B-Q, located in eastern Arizona near the Petrified Forest, Gabby explains her dreams of visiting FRANCE, her mother's home, as she waits on a customer, Alan Squier. A disillusioned eastern writer, hitchhiking west, Squier is looking for something worth living for—or dying for. Although Squier soon hitches a ride with a rich couple, they are forced to return by Duke Mantee, a gangster-killer who has evaded a police dragnet and chosen this lunchroom to meet his girlfriend. As they wait, Squier compares himself with Mantee—both individuals, both part of a vanishing race, both symbolically a part of a petrified forest. In a moment of romantic idealism, Squier signs over his life insurance policy to Gabby, who has impressed him with her dreams, and asks Mantee to shoot him before he leaves. As the sheriff's posse closes in, Mantee obliges and flees; Gabby cradles the dying Squier and promises to bury him in the Petrified Forest.

Wanting something to dream about, Depression America found great appeal in this romantic linking of the gunman and the poet. Onstage the play was a brilliant success, almost immediately becoming a popular movie. Man, the intellectual, thought that he could conquer Nature, but Nature struck back with neuro-

ses, and Man—"Homo-Semi-Americanus—a specimen of the in-between age"—now lives in a "world of outmoded ideas," where the idealists are condemned: only the fittest survive. Into this situation Sherwood introduces Mantee, who stimulates a few people to think and to act. At this point, too, Sherwood sensed the garbled expression of his thoughts. Neither Squier nor Mantee is seemingly fit to survive: neither is heroic, and each dies for a woman unworthy of the sacrifice. Although in Squier's statement that he belongs to a "vanishing race" Sherwood attempted to show the disillusionment of his age, he admitted that he lost control of his theme. He liked the first act, he once confessed, but finding no meaningful way to end his play, he resorted to a hokey, melodramatic, and theatrically successful conclusion.

The Petrified Forest ran for seventeen weeks and earned Sherwood $110,000 for movie rights. In June 1935, he and Madeline Connelly were married in Budapest, HUNGARY, where Sherwood saw some drab-looking American chorus girls plodding through their routine at the Club Arizona and found inspiration for another successful play, IDIOT'S DELIGHT.

FURTHER READING

Krutch, Joseph Wood. *The American Drama Since 1918.* Rev. ed. New York: Brazillier, 1957.

Lawson, John Howard. *Theory and Technique of Playwriting.* New York: Putnam's, 1936.

Meserve, Walter J. *Robert E. Sherwood: Reluctant Moralist.* New York: Western Pub. Co., 1970.

Walter J. Meserve

PEYMANN, CLAUS (1937–)

Claus Peymann extensively shaped the profile of German-language theater in the second half of the 20th century, both as a director and as the head of major stages. He was born on June 7, 1937, in Bremen, GERMANY. Without any formal theater training and with BERTOLT BRECHT (1898–1956) as his model, Peymann honed his directorial and political skills during the early 1960s in the flourishing student theater movement, which eventually merged with the student protest movement. A leftist activist, Peymann remained committed to a theater addressing the major issues of the day in a provocative, innovative, and at times confrontational manner. In contrast to the intellectual heaviness that frequently characterizes German theater, Peymann quickly distinguished himself on account of his sense of humor and playful imagination.

From the beginning, Peymann nurtured young and difficult artists in all fields of the theater and continued to work with them throughout his career. His collaborators include the playwrights THOMAS BERNHARD (1931–1989), PETER HANDKE (1942–), ELFRIEDE JELINEK (1946–), HEINER MÜLLER (1929–1995), Gerlind Reinshagen (1926–), and GEORGE TABORI (1914–); the designers Karl-Ernst Herrmann and Ernst Wonder; director and designer Achim Freyer (1934–); and especially his DRAMATURG and co-artistic director Hermann Beil (1941–), who has proved himself the most loyal collaborator as the conceptual and coordinating genius behind Peymann's bold vision and confrontational politics. Unlike most directors at the helm of major theaters, Peymann has consistently worked with other outstanding, internationally acclaimed directors, such as Andrea Breth (1952–), Manfred Karge (1938–), Matthias Langhoff (1941–), and Peter Zadek (1926–). Like Peter Stein (1937–), Peymann developed a core company of actors who have moved with him to the various theaters he has headed over the decades. With little sympathy for psychological NATURALISM, they developed a spare REALISM, inspired by Brecht and transformed by the influence of Heiner Müller and ROBERT WILSON (1941–). In contrast to the exquisite, often preciously self-conscious artistry of Peter Stein's ensemble, Peymann's actors have been more robust and animated by a more visceral joy of performing.

After his early association with the experimental theater collective at Frankfurt's TAT theater, where he premiered Handke's OFFENDING THE AUDIENCE (Publikumsbeschimpfung) and KASPAR, among others, Peymann briefly joined Peter Stein as co-director of Berlin's Schaubühne. Peymann's subsequent directorships of major theaters in Stuttgart and Bochum and, most prominently, of the venerable Viennese Burgtheater were frequently marked by political controversies and public scandals surrounding his aesthetic innovations and political provocations. Asked frequently how he could justify his relentless attacks on the government while accepting full state subsidization of his theaters, Peymann boldly claimed for himself the traditional fool's privilege at the king's court.

One of the early promoters of Brecht's plays at a time when they were boycotted in West Germany and Austria due to the playwright's controversial position in East Berlin, Peymann became artistic director of the Berliner Ensemble in 1999, fifty years after the theater was founded by Brecht and Helene Weigel (1900–1971). Peymann radically broke with the dogmatic legacy of Brecht's successors, only to replace it with his own brand of traditionalism in a repertoire based on previous successes and proven methods with his lifelong collaborators that left little room for genuine innovation.

FURTHER READING

Honegger, Gitta. Thomas Bernhard: The Making of an Austrian. New Haven, Conn.: Yale Univ. Press, 2001.

Koberg, Roland. Claus Peymann. Berlin: Henschel, 1999.

Gitta Honegger

PHILADELPHIA, HERE I COME!

I've stuck around this hole far too long. I'm telling you, it's a bloody quagmire, a backwater, a dead-end! And everybody in it goes crazy sooner or later! Everybody!
—Gar Public, Episode 2

Irish dramatist BRIAN FRIEL's *Philadelphia, Here I Come!* premiered at the Dublin Theatre Festival in 1964, where it was directed by Hilton Edwards, co-founder of Dublin's famous Gate Theatre. It transferred the following year to the Helen Hayes Theatre in New York, where it was an instant hit—and it also achieved much success in its first London production in 1967.

The play is set is set in Ballybeg, a small town in the north of IRELAND, on the night before Gar O'Donnell, a twenty-five-year-old man, is due to immigrate to America. In the course of the play, we learn about Gar's troubled relationship with his father, S.B.—and about his confused attitude to his hometown. The atmosphere of Ballybeg is claustrophobic, emotional stunting, and sexually repressive, but Gar's feelings about leaving home are ambivalent, and throughout the play the audience learns more about the nature and cause of his doubts.

The play's main innovation is its representation of Gar, who is performed by two actors, one portraying his public self, and the other his inner thoughts. Although the action is presented realistically—with the public Gar interacting naturally with the other characters—his private self is visible only to the audience. The contrast between Gar's public utterances and his private thoughts makes the play very funny. But as the narrative develops, the contrast becomes deeply affecting: the audience realizes that Friel has been forced to put the private life of Gar onstage because the public man is too emotionally suppressed to express himself fully. The play's ending is fiercely moving and unnervingly inconclusive: Gar's inner voice asks why he must leave Ireland, and the response of his public self—and the play's last line—is "I don't know. I—I—I don't know."

The play has had lasting significance. It was Friel's first international success, allowing him to set forth interests that have preoccupied him throughout his career, such as the relationship between Ireland and America, the clash between public and private, the connection between REALISM and THEATRICALITY, and the often troubled relationships of fathers and sons. Furthermore, it signaled the emergence of a "second phase" of modern Irish drama. This phase is distinct from the Irish literary revival of WILLIAM BUTLER YEATS, J. M. SYNGE, and SEAN O'CASEY and features such writers as Hugh Leonard, John B. Keane, THOMAS KILROY, TOM MURPHY, and Friel himself. While these writers explored many different themes, all share an interest in charting the disjunction between the traditional Ireland, as represented in the plays of the Revival, and the rapidly industrializing Ireland of the 1960s and later.

However, the play's greatest significance is probably its ongoing popularity with audiences, which can be explained by Friel's skillful combination of humor with a serious treatment of the pain of a young man forced to emigrate.

FURTHER READING

Grene, Nicholas. The Politics of Irish Drama: Plays in Context from Boucicault to Friel. Cambridge: Cambridge Univ. Press, 1999.

Pine, Richard. *Brian Friel and Ireland's Drama*. London: Routledge, 1990.
Maxwell, D.E.S. *Brian Friel*. Lewisburg, Pa.: Bucknell Univ. Press, 1973.

Patrick Lonergan

THE PHILADELPHIA STORY

The Philadelphia Story opened in New York's Shubert Theatre on March 28, 1939, and ran for 417 performances. With this production, playwright PHILIP BARRY solidified his position as the premier creator of high COMEDIES in America and revived the ACTING career of Katharine Hepburn, who had been labeled "box-office poison."

The play explores the world of the megarich Lord family of Philadelphia's Main Line. The action occurs in the twenty-four hours before eldest daughter Tracy is to wed George Kittredge, a major force in the coal-mining industry. Trouble ensues when brother Sandy Lord allows reporters to cover the wedding in exchange for their silence about father Seth Lord's dalliance with a chorus girl. Into this mix, younger sister Dinah and ex-husband C. K. Dexter Haven conspire to prevent what they consider an ill-matched union.

Tracy Lord, Barry's central and signature character, is the quintessential "Barry Girl." She is beautiful, sporty, witty, well read, and wealthy. She strives for excellence in all things and has little patience for any who fall short of this goal. Seth Lord tells her, "You have a good mind, a pretty face, and a disciplined body that does what you tell it. In fact, you have everything it takes to make a lovely woman except the one essential—an understanding heart." Tracy, like many other characters in Barry comedies, must acquire self-awareness and tolerance in order to mature.

Reporter Macaulay Connor and his partner, photographer Liz Imbrie, represent the "regular folks" who are allowed to glimpse the rarified world of the Lord family. Exhibiting popular preconceptions about the rich, Barry allows his audience to make the discovery with Conner "that in spite of the fact that someone's up from the bottom, he may be quite a heel. And that even though someone else's born to the purple, he still may be quite a guy."

The character of Tracy Lord was modeled on Helen Hope Montgomery Scott, a popular Main Line socialite and the wife of Barry's friend, railroad baron Edgar Scott. Also friendly with the Hepburn family, Barry had Katharine in mind to play Tracy from the outset. The cast also included Van Heflin as Macaulay Conner, Joseph Cotton as C. K. Dexter Haven, and Shirley Booth as Liz Imbrie. As Tracy Lord, Hepburn enjoyed her first Broadway success, and she quickly secured the film rights.

The film version of *The Philadelphia Story* remains fairly close to the original; however, modifications were made to increase the role of C. K. Dexter Haven, played by Cary Grant. Jimmy Stewart replaced Heflin as Macaulay Conner. Donald Ogden Stewart's adaptation and George Cukor's direction moved the emphasis of the work toward visual rather than verbal humor. The film was released in 1940, enjoyed a record-breaking $1.3 million profit, and won two Academy Awards.

Philip Barry was at his best when he wrote *The Philadelphia Story*. It is often praised as one of America's finest high comedies.

[See also *Holiday*; United States]

FURTHER READING

Broussard, Louis. *American Drama: Contemporary Allegory from Eugene O'Neill to Tennessee Williams*. Norman: Univ. of Oklahoma Press, 1962.
Gassner, John. "Philip Barry: A Civilized Playwright." In *The Theatre in Our Times: A Survey of the Men, Materials, and Movements in the Modern Theatre*. New York: Crown, 1954.
Roppolo, Joseph Patrick. *Philip Barry*. Twaynes's United States Authors Series. New York: Twayne, 1965.

Judith Midyett Pender

PHILIPPINE EDUCATIONAL THEATER ASSOCIATION

Cecelia Reyes Guidote wrote "Prospectus for the National Theatre of the PHILIPPINES" for her master's degree at the Dallas Theater Center. Returning to Manila in January 1967, she implemented the plan founding the Philippine Educational Theater Association (PETA) with the support of the National Office of Radio and Television, the Citizens' Council for Mass Media, and the United Nations Educational, Scientific, and Cultural Organization (UNESCO). The National Parks Service provided the theater site in Ft. Santiago for the open-air Raha Sulayman theater. The group called for theater in Filipino languages instead of English and saw performance as a tool of education and political awareness. Tickets were inexpensive and shows timed to suit workers' schedules. While the Kalinangan Ensemble for professional production was the most visible aspect of the organization, classes for students, media initiatives, and information dissemination were equally important. Projects in prisons and touring/workshops in the provinces and other Asian countries became the norm.

PETA was a training ground for grassroots political activism and the workshop for a generation of playwrights. First, European plays were adapted to reflect Philippine culture, but soon new works in Indigenous genres became frequent. With ninety percent of its repertory new plays, the company stimulated Philippine dramatic writing. PETA indigenization and stylization weaned audiences from the middle-class REALISM and psychological theater of the 1940s–1960s. PETA was the Filipino participation in the international movement of people's theaters in the 1960s that also brought el Teatro Campesino, Bread and Puppet, and so forth. As in those groups, BERTOLT BRECHT and later AUGUSTO BOAL were significant theoretical influences.

The history of the group falls into three periods. The early years (1967–1972) under Guidote's leadership were a period of self-definition. As Ferdinand Marcos declared martial law in 1972, Guidote was forced to flee the country, but others continued the mission including Lino Brocka, Lutgardo Labad, and Soxie Topacio. From 1972 to 1986 theater became an important tool in building consensus against the government, as PETA and groups inspired by it prepared the downfall of Marcos. With regime change the third phase (1986–present) began. Now the focus moved to diverse issues, from environmental concerns, to examination of the Muslim minorities, to the search for Filipino epics, and to rival of the rich theatrical traditions of Association of Southeast Asian Nations (ASEAN) neighbors. But the momentum and united political resolve of the earlier years were lost. As company members established families, many left the group whose aesthetic of "POOR THEATER" allowed only minimal payment.

An early work was the 1971 staging of Isagani Cruz's *Monster* (*Halimaw*, 1971), which drew on the musical form of ZARZUELA to attack tyrannical power. The 1972 *It Hurts* (*Ai 'Dao*) by MALOU JACOB considered the political situation in the Muslim south. *Juan Tamban* (1979), also by Jacob, showed a social worker whose political consciousness is raised when she studies a street urchin. *Nuclear* (*Nukleyar!*, 1983) and *Nuclear 2* (*Nukleyar II*, 1985) decried nuclear armament and campaigned against power plants. *Oath to Freedom* (*Panata sa Kalayaan*, 1986–1987) by Chris Millado, Al Santos, Rudy Vera, and others depicted the triumph of People Power over the Marcos dictatorship. The 1994 *Linawa* in the Kalinga language dealt with the issues of Chico Dam, championing Indigenous people's rights over the forces of globalization. In *The Long Journey of Radiya M.* (*Ang Mahabang Paglalakbawy ni Radiya Mangadiri*) by Rody Vera, a Filipino *Ramayana* rediscovered Asian roots. *Call Libby Manaoang* (*Tumawag Kay Libby Manaoang*, 2002) and *Libby Manaoag Files* (2003) by Liza Magtoto explored domestic violence and women's reproductive rights by depicting a radio talk show. Choruses of dancing pregnant women belt out their gripes in wacky and wonderful style. Whatever the issue of the day, that is the material of PETA's presentations.

FURTHER READING

Almazan, Elizabeth. *A Case Study of the Philippine Educational Theater Association: Towards a Realization of a National Culture.* Manila: N.P., 1983.

Krishan Jit. "The Philippines: Modern Drama." In *Cambridge Guide to Asian Theatre*, ed. by James Brandon. Cambridge: Cambridge Univ. Press, 1993.

Labad, Lutgardo. *PETA and Brecht: A Story of Friendship.* Weimar: N.P., 1983.

Oath to Freedom. Asian Theatre Journal 8, no. 1 (Spring 1991): 48–88.

Tiongson, Nicanor. *Dulaan: An Essay on Philippine Theater.* Manila: Cultural Center of the Philippines, 1989.

Van Erven, Eugene. *Stages of People Power: The Philippine Educational Theatre Association.* The Hague: Centre for the Study of Education in Developing Countries, 1989.

——. *The Playful Revolution: Theatre and Liberation in Asia.* Bloomington: Indiana Univ. Press, 1992.

Kathy Foley

PHILIPPINES

In spite of conflicting ideologies, most Filipinos today will agree that it is important for the country to forge a consciousness and a culture that would be identifiable as uniquely and proudly Filipino.
—Nicanor Tiongson, *Dulaan: An Essay on Philippine Theater*, 1989

Drama in the Philippines can be divided into Hispanic-influenced, American-influenced, and the postcolonial theater that looks to both Indigenous and international sources for inspiration. While Indigenous and Islamic-influenced song, dance, storytelling, and ritual were widespread by the 16th century, developed dramas first evolved during the long period of Spanish rule (1565–1898).

HISPANIC PLAYS

During colonization, theater was used to convert, focus community emotion, and entertain. Various seasonal religious plays, *komedya* (also called *moro-moro*, *linambay*, *arakyo*), and ZARZUELA are the three significant genres created during the Hispanic period.

Seasonal religious plays, introduced by Catholic missionaries, fall into genres developed in other Spanish colonies. Christmas plays called *panunuluyan* portray Mary and Joseph seeking lodging in Bethlehem in processional performances that conclude in the Church at midnight. Maudy Thursday brings last suppers (*sinakulo*). Holy Week *pasayon* presentations sometimes involve actual crucifixion. Related to pan-Catholic patterns, these performances have remained flashpoints for public display of emotion and have been reinterpreted by modern companies to raise contemporary issues.

Komedya scripts might depict the life of a patron saint as in the *Play of Saint Michael* (*Comedia de San Miguel*), written around 1890 and still staged in Illigan city. Popular stories showed the clash between Muslims and Christians. An example is the *komedya* of St. Helena, which is performed in several towns of Nueva Ecija. It shows St. Helena seeking the true cross, while her son Constantino fights the Moors as a Moorish princess falls in love with a Christian general. After spectacular marches and battles, the defeated Moors convert and the lovers unite (Tiongsan, 1989). Such performances continue to frame ethnic relations between Christians and Muslims. Francisco Baltazar ("Balgtas"; 1788–1862) was a prolific author of this genre, creating over 100 plays. While these are outdoor performances full of spectacle, they helped introduce the idea of a set text as the basis of dramatic performance. *Komedya* started the transition from the purely religious drama toward a more secular theater.

The zarzuela promoted indoor stages, scenic effects, and professional companies. This operatic form rose from the Spanish SAINETE COMEDY and was produced in Spanish. It was introduced in Manila in 1879 by Dario Cespedes, the author of *To Play with Fire* (*Jugar con guego*). In the 1880s Alejandro Cubero's troupe, which featured actress Elisea Raguer, developed many writers and artists of the new genre. Early zarzuela borrowed the romantic plots from komedya but incorporated modern aspects. An 1887 production (*Pascual Bailón*) created a sensation by incorporating the cancan, which brought a scathing pastoral letter from the archbishop of Manila. At the turn of the century, playwrights like the Pampangan writer Mariano Proceso Pabalan (1863–1904) wrote zarzuela in local dialects. His *Ing Magnape* (1900) was an instant success. Severino Reyes (1861–1942) joined the movement, writing in Tagalog. His *RIP* (*Requiescat in Pace*, 1902) called for the burial of the old komedya and support of this "realistic," musical genre. Reyes's work also showed incipient nationalism: his *Without a Wound* (*Walang Sugat*, 1902), created with Fulgencio Tolentino, began a campaign to populate zarzuela with Filipino rather than foreign heroes. A scene where Spanish friars were shot onstage in revenge for torturing patriots marked the transition. The European zarzuela hero was gone; the Filipino took center stage.

Perhaps the most popular zarzuela of all time was *Country Maiden* (*Dalagang Bukid*, 1919), which follows the trials and tribulations of a flower seller and her student suitor. They outwit the lecherous landowner, Don Silvestre, who tries to use the girl's parents' addiction to gambling to gain power over her. The great actress Atang de la Rama rose to prominence playing the lead. From the beginning of the 20th century the zarzuela had become a fully Indigenous genre that captured the hopes and fears of Filipinos. Bicol, Pampangan, Tagalog, and Ilocano language zarzuela abounded. Today zarzuela's spirit lives on in television drama and film.

AMERICAN-INFLUENCED PLAYS

American occupation after 1898 had an immediate impact in theater. As the American colonial authority brutally suppressed opposition of a guerrilla war, playwrights wrote the so-called seditious plays. These patriotic works by young *ilustrados* (the educated elite) were quickly banned by the Americans who recognized the attacks. Playwrights, actors, and producers were arrested and tried. Examples include *Free* (*Malaya*, 1898) by Tomas Remigio; *Golden Chain* (*Tanikalang ginto*, 1902) by Juan Abad; *I Am Not Dead* (*Hindi aco patay*, 1903) by Juan Matapang Cruz; and *Yesterday, Today and Tomorrow* (*Kahapon, ngayon, at bukas*, 1903) by Aurelio Tolentino.

Golden Chain tells of the girl Liwanang ("Light," representing the Philippines) threatened by the Maimbot ("Greedy," representing America). She is saved by K'Ulayaw, representing the revolutionary Filipino. In *Yesterday, Today and Tomorrow*, Inangbayan (Mother Country) and Taga-ilog (Patriot) overcome Chinese rulers, Spanish colonizers, and American military. The last act features a vision of young Filipnos massed to fight behind Taga-ilog, and the play concludes with America granting Filipino freedom (Tiongson, 1989).

Vaudeville called *bodabil* was introduced from America by 1916 and was very popular for almost half a century. The short scenes, songs, dances, and other turns, often modeled on American acts, only lost popularity in the late 1940s.

Modern theater in English developed as it became the medium of instruction. Though there are a few early modern spoken dramas in local languages, the form really developed as a result of English-language productions in the schools. What came to be called "legitimate plays" (i.e., William Shakespeare and authors of the modern Western cannon) were read, produced, and emulated. *A Modern Filipina* (1915) by Jesus Araullo and Lino Castillejo was the first local script in English. It was created at Philippine Normal College (Fernandez, 1987).

This theater developed in the context of higher education. From the 1940s to the 1960s, REALISM waxed. Ateneo de Manila and the University of the Philippines became the major training and performance venues for both Western works and Filipino scripts in English. Wilfred Ma Guerrero (1917–) taught at the University of the Philippines and led its Drama Club for sixteen years from 1947, developing over 100 plays. His work includes *Wanted: A Chaperone* (1940), which deals with traditional customs challenged by modernity. *Forsaken House* (1940) shows a patriarch whose tyranny destroys his children. *Three Rats* (1948) is considered the first Filipino psychological play. Severino Montano (1915–1980), who studied theater at the University of the Philippines and Yale University, established the Arena Theatre at Philippine Normal College, producing almost 200 performances, which toured throughout the country between 1953 and 1964. His major plays are *Parting at Calomba* (1953), *Sabina* (1953), *The Ladies and the Senator* (1953), and *The Love of Leonor Rivera* (1954). The latter probes the passionate love of Rivera for national hero José Rizal, an affair complicated by their marriages to other partners. Alberto Florentino (1931–) was another realist whose plays often featured the poor including *The World Is an Apple* (1954), *Cavort with Angels* (1959), and *Oli Iompan* (1959).

Though noted author NICK JOAQUIN created only a few theatrical works, his *Portrait of the Artist as Filipino* (1951) is the most-produced Filipino play. A memory play set amid the rubble of World War II, it recounts the experience of two sisters and their artist father living in Intramuros, the walled capital of the Hispanic era. The play mourns the loss of the rich Hispanic past in the era of Americanized modernity. Remembrance of things past and documentation of the struggle to survive the Japanese occupation struck a deep chord.

English prevailed through the opening of the Marcos's showcase Cultural Center of the Philippines in 1969, which was celebrated with *Flower Drum Song*. But since the 1970s only a few playwrights have continued to use English. These include Joaquin and Elsa Martinez Coscolluela, whose *In My Father's House* (1987) recounts the disintegration of a family during the Japanese occupation. Other authors rejected the language of colonial rule and returned to Indigenous vernaculars.

POSTCOLONIAL THEATER

Soon a politically engaged and Asian-focused theater would be everywhere. Theater moved from proscenium stagings and psychological realism, taking to the streets and exploring Indigenous styles with BERTOLT BRECHT-influenced approaches. The founding of PETA (PHILIPPINE EDUCATIONAL THEATER ASSOCIATION) by Cecile Guidote-Alvarez led the way. Returning from study in the UNITED STATES, where she wrote a master's thesis titled "Prospectus for a National Theatre of the Philippines" (1964), Guidote inaugurated this company in 1967. PETA has been a major source of new plays for over thirty years. Early works include *It Hurts* (*Ai 'Dao*, 1972), which explored political discontent in Muslim communities of Mindanao. Guidote-Alvarez fled the country to avoid arrest by Ferdinand Marcos's government after the imposition of martial law in 1972 and did not return until 1986. But others continued PETA's work, critiquing the political and social agenda of the government. *The Nation's Worship* (*Pgasambang Bayan*, 1977), written by BONIFACIO ILAGAN and directed by Behn Cervantes, combined street theater, rituals of communion, and singing to examine the plight of peasants and workers under the regime. The playwright was investigated and the director detained. In the 1980s PETA took on environmental issues in the Al Santos-Joey Ayala rock operas *Nuclear* (*Nukleyar!*, 1983) and *Nuclear 2* (*Nukleyar II*, 1984), which campaigned against nuclear power and armaments. In this period, AUGUSTO BOAL's ideas on a Theater of the Oppressed took root, and theater workshops were used by many to probe social and political issues.

Companies resurrected *sinakulo*, *zarzuela* and *pasayon* but infused them with new political content. Virgilio Vitug's *Passion Play of the Nation* (*Sinakulo ning Balen*, 1983), for example, featured a Christ figure, who condemns bribe taking, government corruption, and false uses of RELIGION. MALOU JACOB's *Juan Tamban* (1979) depicts the interaction of Juan, a child who lives on the streets eating cockroaches, and a female social worker who studies him. Her politicization reflected the consciousness raising of the Filipino middle class.

Theater was an important force in the fall of Marcos's government in 1986. *Oath to Freedom* (*Panata sa Kalayaan*, 1986–1987) was PETA's celebration of the success of People Power in displacing the dictatorship. The play mocked the excesses of the regime with extravagant costumes and stylized staging. In the concluding scenes, actors wove cloth together to form a Filipino flag that filled the stage. Theater of the 1970s and 1980s was a cry for justice and freedom, which resulted in political change.

Activism in theater is less highlighted in the last decade. With greater democracy, the issues become less clear-cut, and other media (film, television) are open to writers to express views. However, companies continue to do significant work addressing, for example, the exploitation of Filipino female domestic workers in cities like Hong Kong and SINGAPORE. Environmental and Indigenous people's rights are another theme: Malou Jacobs *Macli-ing* (1988) examined the plight of Cordillera people of the north. A search for Asian roots begun in the 1970s continues in the work of authors like AMELIA LAPENA-BONIFACIO. She, like many of her peers, turned to Asia rather than Europe for theatrical models. *The Journey of Sisa* (*Ang Paglalakbay ni Sisa*, 1976) borrowed from the Japanese NŌ technique to call back the ghost of the mad woman in Rizal's *Touch Me Not* (*Noli me tangere*). In Lapena-Bonifacio's puppet company, she generates many Asian-influenced performances meant for adult as well as child audiences. Other groups have mined Islamic culture of the Islands to create new work. Diamond surveying the theater scene in 1996 saw the "quest for the illusive self" as the unifying theme of the diverse work, while Krishan Jit (1993) noted the retrenchment of the 1990s with loss of a unifying political focus and advent of economic crisis. The Cultural Center of the Philippines 2003 production season included works like Malou Jacob's *Anatomy of Corruption* (*Anatomiya ng Korupsyon*), a COMEDY about petty intrigues and human foibles in a government agency. *Oraciones* by four playwrights (Rene Villanueva, Liza Magtoto, Rody Vera, and Nick Pichay) interprets Filipino-American relations through the characters of the first American secretary of the interior, a Filipina suffragette, a Hukbalahap peasant, and filmmaker Francis Coppola. The Ramon Obusan Folkloric Group presented *Carnival of Manila* (*Carnaval de Manila*), a historical travelogue exploring American intervention in the social, economic, and political lives of Filipinos at the turn of the century. It borrowed from *zarzuela* and *bodabil* for staging.

Playwrights like Jacobs, Lapena-Bonifacio, Tony Perez, Paul Dumol, Rene Villaineuva, and Jose Dalisay and directors like Chris Millardo and Nonon Padilla continue to use the Philippine stage to explore Filipino issues and identity. To do so they utilize the mixed resources that make up Filipino heritage, a culture with both Asian and Western roots. The resulting work is *mestiso*, a mixing of elements that results in something unique.

FURTHER READING

Cultural Center of the Philippines. *CCP Encyclopedia of Philippine Art.*
    Vol. 7, *Philippine Theatre*. Manila: CCP, 1994.

Fernandez, Doreen. "Philippine Theatre After Martial Law." *Asian
    Theatre Journal* 4, no. 1 (1987): 108–114.

——. *Palabras: Essays on Philippine Theatre History*. Quezon: Ateneo de
    Manila Press, 1996.

Hernandez, Thomas. *The Emergence of Modern Drama in the Philippines
    (1898–1930)*. Honolulu: Asian Studies Program, Univ. of Hawaii,
    1976.

Krishan Jit. "The Philippines: Modern Drama." In *Cambridge Guide to Asian Theatre*, ed. by James Brandon. Cambridge: Cambridge Univ. Press, 1993.

Tiongson, Nicanor. *Dulaan: An Essay on Philippine Theatre*. Manila: Cultural Center of the Philippines, 1989.

Kathy Foley

PHILOSOPHY AND DRAMA

The major periods in the history of Western drama have occurred at times of radical changes in philosophical thought. This was true of ancient Greek drama and of the drama of the Renaissance, and it is equally true of the drama of the 19th century.

1860–1960

Western culture underwent a seismic shift around 1800, signaled in politics by the French Revolution, in science by theories about the evolutionary development of life, and in art by an increasing interest in the irrational. Central to this development was the growing belief in material and social progress and in the perfectibility of man. The classic, pre-Christian view that universal history consisted of vast recurring cycles was replaced by a belief that mankind was marching slowly but steadily upward, while the Christian belief that life on earth was a preparation for the life to come yielded slowly to the conviction that earthly existence was an end in itself. Darwin's theory of evolution (his *Origin of Species* was published in 1859), with its implication that life arose out of matter and was not created by an omnipotent god, became, directly or indirectly, a major influence on philosophy. God was increasingly marginalized. When science advanced one step, God retreated one step.

Hegelian Influence

These progressive ideas were implicit in the work of Georg Wilhelm Friedrich Hegel (1770–1831), who quickly came to dominate philosophical thought in northern Europe in the first half of the 19th century. Hegel postulated an immaterial force, the Absolute Spirit, that proceeded by setting up opposition within and against itself. In the popular version of his logic, any idea would immediately by implication give rise to its opposite. An idea A (thesis) inevitably evoked its opposite non-A (antithesis). Out of this clash arose a synthesis B, which in turn would give rise to its opposite; and so on through all of time. These triads could be employed to explain progress in every field, and Hegel's writings covered everything from logic to history, from art to law, from religion to politics.

Hegel caught on because he offered something to just about everybody. Politicians liked him because he made the state the greatest achievement of man. Liberal Christians accepted him because he made spirit the wellspring of all being. Religious skeptics liked him because he sidelined the Christian God. Scientists accepted him because he offered a philosophical basis for evolution. Above all, his philosophy was optimistic.

From this Hegelian fountainhead, three streams flowed forth. The first and broadest one maintained the optimistic spirit, but its very breadth caused it to divide into two lesser streams, one covering society, the other the individual. Karl Marx (1818–1883), whose concept of dialectical materialism is an economic version of the triads, predicted the inevitable reform of human organizations. Henri Bergson (1859–1941) converted Absolute Spirit into the élan vital, the Life Force, and probed into the psychic life of the individual. In Marx matter brought about changes in man's way of living; in Bergson, mind affected matter.

The second current was thoroughly pessimistic. Arthur Schopenhauer (1788–1860) redefined Hegel's Absolute Spirit and argued that progress was an illusion created by human beings to make life bearable.

The third stream was reactionary. The Dane Søren Kierkegaard (1813–1855) in a ferocious sustained assault on Hegel reasserted Christian values and the primacy of the individual over abstract ideas.

Henrik Ibsen's position as father of the modern drama is due in no small measure to the philosophical ideas embedded in his plays. His breakthrough as a thought-provoking author in Scandinavia came with his two poetic dramas Brand (1865) and Peer Gynt (1866), which are imbued with the uncompromising idealism of Kierkegaard, the most discussed and most controversial of contemporaneous thinkers in midcentury Scandinavia.

As a guide to human existence, Hegel's philosophy was, in Kierkegaard's eyes, worthless, since the individual must decide in the present moment between two alternatives (either–or), not on the basis of a future unforeseeable synthesis (both–and). For Hegel, "whatever is, is right"—all part of the ever-evolving spirit. Hegel omitted what was most important, the judgmental factor to which the individual human being contributes. Kierkegaard stressed the freedom of choice that the individual has and also the anguish (angst) that accompanies this freedom. To choose means to commit oneself to an ideal or to a vision; commitment entails sacrifice, the extent of these sacrifices being the measure of the individual's worth. Each decision brings with it consequences that no one can be sure of, since the plan of the universe, whether divine or earthly, pace Hegel, is not knowable.

Kierkegaard's emphasis on the sense of anguish that accompanies freedom of choice led to 20th-century existentialism, but it was first voiced in *Brand*. The hero, a priest, seeks to live the ideal life, a life without compromise, but each crucial decision he is compelled to make brings with it ever greater sacrifices. Eventually, the love of family and of his fellow human beings must yield to the demands of his ideal. At the end he achieves his goal, symbolized by his ascent up a mountain, but he is alone, questioning the path he has taken, and dies in an avalanche, leaving readers to wonder whether Ibsen was praising or damning his hero.

Ibsen followed up *Brand* with *Peer Gynt*, where the hero refuses to make any real commitment and comes to realize in the famous onion scene that there is no core to his being. In act 4 Ibsen caricatured Hegel as Begriffenfeldt, the head of an insane asylum.

Subsequently Ibsen changed his mind about Hegel. His overriding concern was to find some way of reconciling a life based on higher ideals and involving total commitment and sacrifice with a life based on a complacent acceptance of the world as it is. Many of his later plays are based on this conflict between two fundamentally irreconcilable principles. His huge two-part drama EMPEROR AND GALILEAN (1873), which Ibsen himself considered his greatest work, pictured this philosophical conflict as a clash between Christian and pagan values.

In THE WILD DUCK (1884) Ibsen sets Gregers Werle, with his Brandian demands, against Hjalmar Ekdal, the charming and ineffectual dreamer. In the clash between the two, TRAGEDY ensues. Hjalmar's fourteen-year-old daughter, susceptible to Greger's ideals, kills herself, making the complete sacrifice out of love for her father.

It has been argued by Brian Johnston (1992) that all of Ibsen's realistic dramas form a cycle based on Hegel's philosophy, an approach that most readers find too reductive.

SCHOPENHAUER'S LASTING INFLUENCE

The impact that Hegel made on the drama was matched and perhaps surpassed by his antagonist Arthur Schopenhauer. While Kierkegaard assailed Hegel's philosophy as having no value as a guide to living, Schopenhauer attacked the very basis of Hegel's philosophy, the assumption that behind all the phenomena of existence there was a positive, evolving spirit spiraling ever upward.

Schopenhauer said that this helical development was a Hegelian illusion and that the energy driving the universe had no direction and served no purpose. Unhappily he labeled this force, this boundless energy, the will, a term that seemed to imply purpose. This will or energy provides the background to everything that happens in the universe and in everything that humans do. Humans differ from other beings in that they have developed minds that ascribe meaning to the will. But all that man accomplishes, and all that the mind creates, is no more than spume on the waves of a universal ocean, droplets that are cast up and behave for a moment as it they were of individual significance before falling back into the vast immeasurable sea.

Of the major thinkers perhaps Schopenhauer exerted the widest and most lasting appeal on dramatists, who saw a kindred soul in the philosopher. Schopenhauer said that if one seeks the ultimate truth, one turns not to the scientists and the moralists but to the great artists and above all to the great composers. In music the universal energy is mobilized and channeled, not made meaningful (impossible) but made beautiful. He extolled music as the highest of all arts because it expressed the universal will more faithfully than words or pictures could.

The life of the human being consists in a vain effort to impose a meaning on this chaos of energy. Through art the human triumphs over the world will. Instead of being horrified by a confrontation with nothingness, he finds it beautiful and therefore consoling.

This dour view of human endeavor caught on in Europe when the 1848 social revolutions failed, and it made its way into the drama through RICHARD WAGNER. Disillusioned by the crushing of the political radicals in 1848, Wagner increasingly turned his thoughts inward. He discovered Schopenhauer in 1854 and found in him the philosophical basis for *Tristan and Isolde*, a music drama that pictured the inner life, a drama of the soul. Wagner equated love and sex at their most intense with death and the union of the lovers as tantamount to a submission to and reunification with the world will.

This seminal work, built on the dualism of the conscious and unconscious life, the world of appearances as opposed to the universal will, had a tremendous impact on the symbolist writers at the end of the 19th century. What Wagner accomplished through music, putting the life of the soul onstage as directly as possible, the symbolists sought to accomplish using other means. MAURICE MAETERLINCK retold the story of *Tristan and Isolde* in his *Pelléas and Mélisande* (1893). But his attempt to make words do what Wagner's ninety-piece orchestra did was doomed to fail.

GEORGE BERNARD SHAW proclaimed in 1902 that the success of *Tristan* made it apparent that there was "no future now for any drama without music except the drama of thought." For Shaw the drama of emotional effect was "impossible when the dramatist must write in the language of a newspaper reporter."

Not too far removed from Schopenhauer's universal will in the spectrum of philosophical ideas was Charles Darwin's evolutionary appetite. Darwin inevitably influenced all spheres of thought by effectively disposing of the need for any spiritual force in the universe that guided human beings toward some higher end. In place of this teleological view, he offered the possibility of explaining all progress without reference to a higher power. The struggle for existence was the basic drive in the universe, not some supernatural god or abstract spirit. NATURALISM, which pictured the human being as a product of his heredity and environment, provided the literary and dramatic equivalent of Darwinism. Championed by ÉMILE ZOLA, naturalism came to dominate the serious drama in the latter half of the 19th century. Ibsen admitted it into his realistic plays, while AUGUST STRINDBERG (for a while) and ANTON CHEKHOV enthusiastically embraced it.

FRIEDRICH NIETZSCHE became a major influence on the drama because he brought Schopenhauer and Darwin together in one philosophical and cultural concept. Accepting the implications of Darwinism, he famously declared that God was dead. In fact God had been moribund for some time. Johann Wolfgang Goethe in his *Faust* had reduced him to a mere observer; Hegel had transformed God into a pervasive spirit struggling with itself; and Schopenhauer had treated the supreme being along with religion in general as illusions that human beings create in order to avoid facing the great nothingness. Nietzsche spelled out the consequences. If there was no God like the one in the Bible, there was no transcendent moral code to guide human beings. If there was no after life, there was no need for salvation. If there was no meaning to existence in any religious sense, then it follows that the universal, blind will must on the level of the individual be the will to power, exhibited in those superior human beings who in a Darwinian world of struggle determine the course of events in history, in the arts, and in politics. The highest form of human activity is the creation of a superman, who embodies new values and imposes himself in place of God as doer and maker. In his essay on Schopenhauer, Nietzsche conceived of these superior individuals as artist-philosophers.

Along with Darwin, Karl Marx adopted a materialistic approach to progress, dispensing with any higher spirit. The struggle for existence that was the driving force in Darwin was narrowed by Marx into a conflict between social classes, the working men and women and the owners of the means of production. In the drama his impact was felt in the 20th century in the innovative productions of ERWIN PISCATOR and the plays of BERTOLT BRECHT in GERMANY, in the urban dramas of EDWARD BOND in ENGLAND, in the avowedly communist plays of JOHN HOWARD LAWSON in the UNITED STATES, and in the technically venturesome late plays of SEAN O'CASEY in IRELAND, to say nothing of the postrevolution Russian drama.

Arriving on the scene at the end of the 19th century, Bernard Shaw, the most philosophical of the major dramatists, at least in the sense of giving most space to philosophical discussions, could pick and choose from among the great ideas of his predecessors. He created his own system of thought, drawing on Bergson's Life Force, Nietzsche's superman, and Marx's critique of society. He pictured the artist-philosopher in MAN AND SUPERMAN, a coruscating discussion drama, five hours of brilliant talk. Unlike Marx, Shaw believed that the purely materialist approach left the progress of mankind without a motivating force. There had to be something that drives living things in their struggle with one another. He called it the Life Force (after Bergson's élan vital), and he hoped to found a new, up-to-date religion to replace Christianity. His dramatic cycle BACK TO METHUSELAH was intended to be the bible of what he called Creative Evolution. Although Shaw never succeeded is setting up a new church, the lengthy preface to *Methuselah* is one of the most brilliant philosophico-religious essays of the modern period.

Of the major philosophers, Schopenhauer has cast the longest shadow over dramatists, perhaps because of a natural affinity between him and artists in general. He exalted artists above scientists and theologians as thinkers. And his pessimism found a response in those dramatists who confronted the horrors of the 20th century.

Take the case of EUGENE O'NEILL. As a young man, he discovered Nietzsche, and the Apollo-Dionysus dichotomy left deep traces in his plays, especially in THE GREAT GOD BROWN. But in his efforts to find a faith to take the place of Christianity, Nietzsche failed him. After a long absence, he returned to the stage with THE ICEMAN COMETH, his most nihilistic work. Dionysian intoxication here is mere drunkenness.

In the long run, the spirit of Schopenhauer prevailed in O'Neill's dramas. The sea that haunted O'Neill to the extent of being the major symbol in his oeuvre can be seen as Schopenhauer's will. It provides the background to the early sea plays and to ANNA CHRISTIE, in which "dat ole davil, sea" becomes a refrain. The very title of STRANGE INTERLUDE seems to be an allusion to Schopenhauer's belief that the life of the individual is a mere episode between his emergence from the infinite will and his return to it. Perhaps no O'Neill play is more permeated by Schopenhauer's philosophy than LONG DAY'S JOURNEY INTO NIGHT, where once again the sea and the fog form the background—the infinite realm—against which the Tyrones act out their family drama. Edmund's great speech in act 4 is a summing up of O'Neill's own philosophy: "I dissolved in the sea . . . belonged, without past or future, within peace and unity and a wild joy, within something greater than my own life, or the life of Man, to Life itself! To God, if you want to put it that way."

World War II helped to make existentialism the most popular philosophy of the mid-20th century. It made *angst* an English word and brought Kierkegaard out of Scandinavian obscurity. It also produced some significant plays, chiefly those of JEAN-PAUL SARTRE, who advocated a "theater of situation" in place of the conventional "theater of characters" in his 1946 essay, "Forgers of Myths," a theater in which the human being is not defined by his psychological constitution but by the choices he makes in the world of other human beings. The war made Sartre's position, as dramatized in THE FLIES and NO EXIT, seem particularly relevant.

Existentialism and the absurd were both products of the war, but they differed in attitude. Just how much they differed can be seen in comparing SAMUEL BECKETT and Sartre. The absurdist surrendered to meaninglessness, while the existentialist encouraged human beings to act, to forge new worlds. The Sartrean hero is willing to clean the slate of old ideas and move on. Beckett does not do this. He resigns himself, à la Schopenhauer, to an empty universe, without values, without meaning. The last words of Beckett's defining drama WAITING FOR GODOT are, "They do not move."

[See also Absurdism; Apocalyse in Modern Drama; Symbolism]

FURTHER READING
Bentley, Eric. *The Playwright as Thinker*. New York: Harcourt, Brace, 1946.
Peter, John. *Vladimir's Carrot: Modern Drama and the Modern Imagination*. Chicago: Univ. of Chicago Press, 1987.

Johnston, Brian. *The Ibsen Cycle: The Design of the Plays from Pillars of Society to When We Dead Awaken*. Rev. ed. Pittsburgh: Pennsylvania State Univ. Press, 1992.

Williams, Raymond. *Modern Tragedy*. Stanford: Stanford Univ. Press, 1966.

Evert Sprinchorn

1960–PRESENT

During the 20th century, existentialism and drama were closely linked. Existentialist philosophy questioned universal truths, the Enlightenment, and scientific determinism. Søren Kirkegaard, FRIEDRICH NIETZSCHE, Karl Marx, and Martin Heidegger were among the most influential of these philosophers, but JEAN-PAUL SARTRE applied the philosophy to modern drama. His play NO EXIT (*Huis clos*) features three characters trapped in an endless purgatory and reveals that human existence is essentially "being in a situation." SAMUEL BECKETT, whose WAITING FOR GODOT became associated with existentialism, also wrote plays about "being there," a reference to Heidegger's observation that human consciousness is twofold: operating in the functional world and transforming phenomena into ideas and meaning. Existentialist playwrights present humans trying vainly to explain their existence, as in TOM STOPPARD's ROSENCRANTZ AND GUILDENSTERN ARE DEAD.

The Theater of the Absurd focused on images and situations rather than linear narrative. ABSURDISM, however, represented a break from existentialist philosophy by dispensing with the unity of life and thought, revealing fragmented and disjointed lives defined less by morality than by necessity. In addition to Beckett, JEAN GENET (*The Balcony*, *Death Watch*), EUGÈNE IONESCO (*The Chairs*, THE LESSON), and ARTHUR ADAMOV (*The Invasion*, *Parody*) were leading proponents of absurdism. In the UNITED STATES, EDWARD ALBEE attacked that country's postwar optimism and romanticized family structure (*The American Dream*, WHO'S AFRAID OF VIRGINIA WOOLF?), and in ENGLAND, HAROLD PINTER reduced human life to savage games played out in destitute rooms (THE BIRTHDAY PARTY, THE CARETAKER).

Martin Heidegger examined the difference between "presence" and "disclosedness" by distinguishing how we gain knowledge from what is factually "presented" to us. RICHARD FOREMAN's Ontological Hysteric Theater, created during the late 1960s (*Pandering to the Masses: A Misrepresentation*, *Rhoda in Potatoland*), dramatizes this philosophy by creating theater in which the audience is asked to perceive a production from multiple standpoints. Often creating a kind of mirror metaphor in which he doubles this process, Foreman exposes the production mechanism, framing events using repetition, reflection, and focus.

BERTOLT BRECHT and ANTONIN ARTAUD continued to exert influence on post-1960 theater. Brecht, initially influenced by EXPRESSIONISM, drew from Karl Marx's philosophy of dialectics in which society is observed from multiple vantage points and defined by the contradictions among them. Playwrights often used Brecht's concept of "ALIENATION," in which the spectator is drawn skeptically into the artificiality of a performance rather than being swept away by the imposed reality of the play. Numerous plays utilize the Brechtian "epic format." U.S. plays with political themes (*The Serpent*, *Zoot Suit*, *Viet Rock*), British plays about social injustice (*The Romans in Britain*, *Plenty*, *The National Health*), and African plays condemning colonialism (*Bopha!*, *A Play of Giants*) are just a few examples of Brecht's influence on global theater.

Artaud's concept "Theater of Cruelty" integrated perfectly into the revolutionary philosophies of the 1960s. Artaud thought of theater as a shared, cathartic experience between performers and audience. Under the influence of non-Western performance practices, Artaud wrote that "the plague" of Western theater culture had corrupted natural tendencies of performing and should be exorcised. In 1964, Peter Brook devoted a season to Artaud in London with the Royal Shakespeare Company. Brook's production of PETER WEISS's MARAT-SADE merged ritual and text into a "holy" event. Artaud, Brook, Jerzy Grotowski, Richard Schechner, and Eugenio Barba were among many practitioners who used Asian performing traditions (*kabuki*, NŌ, Chinese opera, Balinese dance, shamanism) to develop a philosophy for spiritual transformation. The LIVING THEATRE, committed to revolution and social change, asked the audience to transform themselves into a new consciousness by attaining higher spirituality (*Paradise Now*) or by participating in violence and execution (*Frankenstein*).

POSTMODERNISM had its roots in structuralist philosophy of the 1920s. Using linguistic and literary theories, Roland Barthes, prominent French philosopher and linguist, created a method for "reading theater" through the study of signs. Structuralists believed it was impossible to produce a narrative without reference to an implicit system of rules and meaningful units. In drama, this means that meaning is not fully explicable onstage without exposing the structure of the text. Barthes was critical of mainstream French theater and found Brecht's epic format and the bodies of professional wrestlers and dancers far more dramatically stimulating. Performance artists who use their own bodies as signifiers owe much to Barthes's dialectic between signifier and signified.

Jacques Derrida, often called a "poststructuralist," went a step farther by arguing that true meaning is "differed" and depends on the individual "reading." "DECONSTRUCTION" refuses to accept the idea of construction and suggests that meaning is never absolute: every aspect of a performance is governed by the connotation of words, the textual and peripheral actions onstage, and the primary and secondary meanings of objects. In the United States, the Wooster Group was probably the leading exponent of this philosophy in theater. In *Route 1 & 9*, portions of THORNTON WILDER's nostalgic play OUR TOWN were juxtaposed with a blackface minstrel show, and *L.S.D.* (. . . Just the *High Points*) borrowed portions of ARTHUR MILLER's THE CRUCIBLE to comment on present-day witch hunts. Deconstruction suspends all that we take for granted about language, experience, and human behavior.

Jean-François Lyotard, a French philosopher best known for his book *The Postmodern Condition*, has had an enormous influence on the storytelling aspect of post–1960 drama and theater. Lyotard rejected the grand narratives of modernity, preferring multiple, fragmentary, and discontinuous narratives. Postmodern dramatists often redevelop narratives by using other media and art forms. ROBERT WILSON (*Einstein on the Beach, Civil Wars*) incorporated dance and music and freely juxtaposed time and place to create new texts from theater classics. CARYL CHURCHILL relies on a more conventional dramatic structure than Wilson but nevertheless juxtaposes time, place, and characters. In CLOUD NINE, she satirizes the British colonial ethos by juxtaposing gender roles, historical eras, and performance styles, while in TOP GIRLS she introduces historical characters and transforms them in modern settings.

Many philosophers were critical of racism, particularly racism against black people, and celebrated black culture using terms like *negritude, black consciousness,* and *Black Orpheus*. Negritude, in particular, grew into a philosophy celebrating a cultural consciousness distinct from Western European perceptions. AIMÉ CÉSAIRE, Leopold Senghor, and Jean-Paul Sartre celebrated African culture, conceptualizing a racial essence of African thought. African dramatists drew from the philosophy of Muntu, which celebrates the "force" of living and the belief that there is a central point of thought affecting all living and dead people. Amos Tutuola (*The Palm Wine Drinkard*) and WOLE SOYINKA (*Death and the King's Horseman*) reveal that African philosophy cannot be destroyed by European culture. This philosophy of racial and political empowerment partly inspired the BLACK ARTS MOVEMENT in the United States, which began soon after Malcolm X's assassination in 1965 and featured many black playwrights, most notably AMIRI BARAKA.

During the 1970s and 1980s, feminist playwrights frequently rejected the limitations of realistic linear plots and created new dramatic structures. Simone de Beauvoir's 1949 *The Second Sex* claims that women are not living a life of their own but are objectified through the eyes of the male subject, a key idea for those critical of theater as social institution. Michel Foucault wrote extensively about subjugation, sexual identity, and power and is often cited in feminist thought. The French feminist movement (HÉLÈNE CIXOUS, Julia Kristeva, Luce Irigaray) advocates that women reclaim feminine space by "re-reading" traditional patriarchal myths (such as fairy tales) and develop their sexuality outside of the male gaze. Materialist feminism subverts the patriarchal tendencies of linear plots by establishing gender as social construction rather than biological destiny. The linear structure and realistic style of liberal feminist plays (*Crimes of the Heart,* THE HEIDI CHRONICLES) contrast with the more image-conscious and fragmentary style of materialist plays (*Mineola Twins,* FEFU AND HER FRIENDS).

Queer theory developed out of feminist philosophy, poststructuralism, and GAY AND LESBIAN studies. The theory suggests that sexuality is a complex array of codes and forces and studies how institutional power shapes the ideas of what is normal, essential, or biological. CHARLES LUDLUM and the Ridiculous Theater Company took the theatricality of "queer" behavior to hilarious lengths with plays that parodied famous literary texts through cross-dressing and transpositions of high and low culture (for example, *Bluebeard, Camille*).

By the end of the 20th century, dramatists drew from philosophies including catastrophism, chaos theory, and nihilism. British playwright HOWARD BARKER called for a new theater to replace liberal, humanist, and popular philosophy, a theater "without conscience" where the horror and ugliness of human activity can be freely presented and debated. Chaos theory, used in quantum mechanics, investigates parallel developments across the arts and sciences and emphasizes the unpredictability of natural occurrences. SAM SHEPARD and DAVID RABE endow their characters with random behavior and violent outbursts. Many would argue that nihilism is not a philosophy because it rejects all thought and meaning. In the 1990s a group of young British playwrights, nicknamed "In-Yer-Face" (SARAH KANE, MARK RAVENHILL, ANTHONY NEILSON, PATRICK MARBER, among others), were labeled nihilists because of their subversive way of presenting plays. They used graphic sex, gratuitous violence, humiliated characters, and broken taboos.

Intercultural connections remain at the center of drama's explorations of philosophy after 1960 as philosophies from around the globe are incorporated into dramatic theatrical structures. The state of philosophy and drama today essentially reflects a hybrid of cultures and philosophies.

FURTHER READING

Artaud, Antonin. *The Theatre and Its Double*. New York: Grove, 1958.

Demastes, William W. *Theatre of Chaos: Beyond Absurdism, into Orderly Disorder*. Cambridge: Cambridge Univ. Press, 1998.

Eslin, Martin. *The Theatre of the Absurd*. New York: Anchor Bks., 1961.

Kourany, Janet A., James P. Sterba, and Rosemarie Tong, eds. *Feminist Philosophies*. Englewood Cliffs, N.J.: Prentice-Hall, 1992.

MacDonald, Erik. *Theatre at the Margins: Text and the Post-Structured Stage*. Ann Arbor: Univ. of Michigan. Press 1993.

Norris, Christopher. *Deconstruction Theory and Practice*. London: Routledge, 1991.

Solomon, Robert C., and David Sherman, eds. *The Blackwell Guide to Continental Philosophy*. Oxford: Blackwell, 2003.

Willett, John, ed. and trans. *Brecht on Theatre: The Development of an Aesthetic*. New York: Hill & Wang, 1964.

Chris Olsen

THE PHYSICS

Our science has become terrifying, our research dangerous. . . . We must retract our science, and I have retracted it.

—"Möbius," Act 2

In FRIEDRICH DÜRRENMATT's *The Physicists* (*Die Physiker*), the greatest physicist of all time has become delusional. Tormented by the voice of King Solomon, Wilhelm Heinrich Möbius has spent the last fifteen years in a psychiatric institution in the care of the hunchbacked, eccentric Doctor Mathilde von Zahnd. He shares a suite with two other physicists, "Newton" and "Einstein," who have recently strangled their nurses. Then Möbius strangles his nurse who loves him and has tried to arrange his release from the asylum. All three nurses had stumbled on a secret, which the physicists reveal in the second act. Newton and Einstein, a CIA and KGB agent, respectively, are on secret missions to bring Möbius back to work for their governments. Möbius, however, has no intention of leaving the asylum. He has feigned his delusions in order to have the freedom to research out of view of the scientific community. To this end Möbius is willing to sacrifice his marriage and his reputation, because he has discovered forces that could destroy the world. In a moving speech he convinces the agents to keep up the deception and remain in the asylum for the good of humanity. However, the secret is already out. The doctor, too, has heard the voice of King Solomon and at his orders has been drugging Möbius, copying his manuscripts and exploiting his formulas. "You are mad!" Möbius screams at the doctor, who is poised to rule the world. Insane murderers in the eyes of the law, the physicists are trapped.

Coincidence, the prime mover in Dürrenmatt's dramatic universe, has struck Möbius when he was most certain of success. He has chosen the one asylum in which the doctor was opportunistic, power hungry, and ruthless enough to thwart his plan. But Möbius's greater error lies in trying to retract his science. Dürrenmatt believed that, once conceived, an idea is communal property, because it can always be thought again. There can be no pure research without responsibility for the consequences. Problems that concern everyone can only be solved by everyone. The courageous individual acting alone cannot save society.

In large part the play is a response to BERTOLT BRECHT's THE LIFE OF GALILEO (*Leben des Galilei*, 1955). Heeding Galileo's warning to scientists not to capitulate to governmental authority, Möbius errs to the opposite extreme by fleeing into a supposed ivory tower. A second inspiration for the play was a book Dürrenmatt reviewed in 1956, Robert Jungk's *Brighter than a Thousand Suns*, about the creation of the atomic bomb. Premiering in Zürich on February 21, 1962, at the height of the Cold War, a year after the first manned space flights and only months before the Cuban missile crisis, *The Physicists* is very much a testimony to the angst and pessimism of the time. It joins Brecht's *Galileo* and MICHAEL FRAYN's COPENHAGEN (1998) as one of the most important modern dramas on the moral responsibility of the scientist. With nearly 1,600 performances, it was the most-performed play of the 1962–1963 theater season in German-speaking Europe.

[*See also* Germany]

FURTHER READING

Crockett, Roger A. *Understanding Friedrich Dürrenmatt.* Columbia: Univ. of South Carolina Press, 1998.

Jenny, Urs. *Friedrich Dürrenmatt: A Study of His Plays.* Tr. by Keith Hamnet and Hugh Rorrison. London: Methuen, 1978.

Peppard, Murray. *Friedrich Dürrenmatt.* New York: Twayne, 1969.

Tiusanen, Timo. *Dürrenmatt: A Study in Plays, Prose, Theory.* Princeton, N.J.: Princeton Univ. Press, 1977.

Whitton, Kenneth. *The Theatre of Friedrich Dürrenmatt: A Study in the Possibility of Freedom.* London: Oswald Wolff, 1980.

Roger A. Crockett

DIE PHYSIKER   *See* THE PHYSICS

THE PIANO LESSON

What is you ready for, Berniece? You gonna drift along from day to day. Life is more than making it from one day to another.

—Avery Brown, Act 2

AUGUST WILSON's *The Piano Lesson* was inspired by a 1983 painting, also titled *The Piano Lesson*, by African American artist Romare Bearden. Wilson's play was written in 1986 and first produced the Yale Repertory Theatre in 1988 under the direction of longtime Wilson collaborator Lloyd Richards. It opened on Broadway on April 16, 1990, at the Walter Kerr Theatre. It ran for 328 performances and received widespread critical acclaim.

The drama takes place in Pittsburgh in 1936, at the height of the Great Depression. It tells the story of a brother and a sister forced to confront their responsibilities to the past. Boy Willie appears one day on his sister Berniece's doorstep and wants her to sell their family piano so that he can buy the same Mississippi land that their ancestors once worked as slaves. The piano, beautifully carved with African images by their grandfather, a former slave and carpenter, is a reminder not only of the family's enslavement but a testament to their survival. The carvings depict the history of the family during slavery. Berniece passionately opposes selling the piano. Through this conflict between the practical need of owning land versus the desire to preserve a treasured piece of family history, Wilson deals directly with past family wounds and the legacy they leave for the descendants of slaves.

The play is both poetic and poignant. Wilson intertwines a complex drama about American social history with family relationships. The family dissolves as it decides what to do with the piano and all that it represents. The play also incorporates supernatural elements, which ultimately alter the progress of the story and provide the play with an element of magical

REALISM, when Boy Willie confronts the ghost of Old Sutter who was the slave owner of Willie's family. This confrontation results in Berniece's ability to play the piano again and exorcise the demons, an unusual supernatural element in Wilson's work.

The Piano Lesson is part of Wilson's ten-play cycle about the experience of black Americans throughout the 20th century. The play earned Wilson his second Pulitzer Prize for Drama. In addition to this, The Piano Lesson was awarded a Drama Desk Outstanding New Play Award, a New York Drama Critics' Circle Award for Best Play, a Tony Award for Best Play, and the American Theatre Critics' Outstanding Play Award. Wilson also adapted The Piano Lesson for a television movie. This adaptation earned eight Emmy nominations. It has been suggested by critics that the lovingly carved, thoughtfully adorned piano is a metaphor for black history and that as such it is an element of cultural identity that cannot be sold or overlooked. This would seem to be the lesson Wilson finds in the quotidian life of generations of African Americans.

[See also United States]

FURTHER READING

Bogunil, Mary L. Understanding August Wilson. Columbia: Univ. of South Carolina Press, 1999.

Perlira, Kim. August Wilson and the African-American Odyssey. Urbana: Univ. of Illinois Press, 1995.

Wilson, August. The Ground on Which I Stand. New York: Theatre Communications Group, 2001.

Ellen Anthony-Moore and Christopher Moore

PICKTHALL, MARJORIE (1883–1922)

Canadian writer, poet, and playwright Marjorie Pickthall was born in Gunnersby, Middlesex, ENGLAND, on September 14, 1883. She was a daughter of Arthur C. Pickthall, an electrical engineer, and Helen Mallard. Her family moved to Southwater, Sussex, and then to Toronto in 1889. Pickthall attended St. Mildred's College and Bishop Strachan School. While at Bishop Strachan she sold her first story, "Two-ears," to the Toronto Globe. When she was only seventeen, Pickthall won a Mail and Empire Christmas competition with the poem "O Keep the World for Ever at the Dawn," attracting nationwide attention. She continued to publish poems and short stories in leading periodicals in England, the UNITED STATES, and CANADA. From 1910 to 1912 she worked as an assistant librarian at Victoria College Library in Toronto (currently, the library holds the largest collection of Pickthall's manuscripts and personal papers). In 1912 she moved back to England, near Salisbury, where she lived until 1919. During World War I, she worked as an ambulance driver, a farm laborer, and a library clerk. It was a particularly prolific period in her life. After World War I, she returned to Canada and moved to Vancouver, where she lived until her death on April 19, 1922.

In November 1913 her first collection of poems, A Drift of Pinions, was published by the University Magazine in Montreal. The collection sold out within ten days. Her first novel, Little Hearts, was published two years later, in 1915. Altogether, Pickthall published over 200 short stories, approximately 100 poems, three novels, and a number of articles and essays in journals such as Atlantic Monthly, Harper's, and Scribner's. Pickthall's reputation rests predominantly on her career as a poet, so her play THE WOODCARVER'S WIFE has only recently gained the critical attention it deserves. First produced in Toronto and Montreal and published posthumously in 1923, this one-act modernist verse drama is not typical of Pickthall's rather sentimental poetry. Centered on the love triangle, The Woodcarver's Wife touches on issues of gender, race and eroticism, all charged with violence and intensity that though not easily accessible in the 1920s ultimately became an object of great interest for modern feminist critics.

PLAY: The Woodcarver's Wife (published 1923)

FURTHER READING

Badir, Patricia L. "'So Entirely Unexpected': The Modernist Dramaturgy of Marjorie Pickthall's The Wood-Carver's Wife." Modern Drama 43, no. 2 (2000): 216–245.

Garvin, John William, ed. Canadian Poets. Toronto: McClelland, Goodchild & Stewart, 1916.

Kizuk, Alex. "The Case of the Forgotten Electra: Pickthall's Apostrophes and Feminine Poetics." Studies in Canadian Literature 12 (Winter 1987): 15–34.

Pacey, Desmond. Creative Writing in Canada: A Short History of English-Canadian Literature. Toronto: Ryerson, 1952.

Magda Romanska

PICNIC

Oh, Mom, what can you do with the love you feel? Where is there you can take it?
—Madge, Act 3

WILLIAM INGE's 1953 Pulitzer Prize–winning COMEDY-drama is set on Labor Day in a small Kansas town where the sudden appearance of Hal Carter, a virile young drifter, arouses sexual and emotional undercurrents in three generations of the town's women. Hal is strongly attracted to Madge Owens, local beauty queen, who has been dating Alan Seymour, a bland young man whose family wealth offers the prospect of a secure life. Alan wins the favor of Flo, Madge's mother, who resists Hal, whose presence painfully reminds her of her wayward spouse. She fears that Madge will fall victim to her fate. Flo turns to her feisty widowed neighbor, Helen Potts, but the sharp-tongued old lady seems invigorated by the passion evident between Madge and Hal. Unable to conform to small-town proprieties, Hal's wanderlust is heightened by the whistle of the passing train. Madge, who longs to escape small-town life, grapples with the safe choice of Alan versus her forbidden attraction to Hal.

Picnic also focuses on Rosemary Sidney, a lonely, middle-aged schoolteacher, who feels increasing urgency to find herself a mate. Her only prospect is Howard Bevans, a local merchant, who is not at all certain that he wants marriage. Their seriocomic battle of wills is set against the Hal-Madge-Alan triangle, but it all takes a dramatic turn when the distraught Rosemary literally begs Howard to marry her. Rosemary's desperation encourages Madge to follow her passion for Hal. As the play ends, Madge runs off with Hal, dashing Flo's hopes for her daughter's comfortable future.

The lyrical REALISM of Picnic is, to a great extent, inspired by TENNESSEE WILLIAMS's plays. Featuring elevated poetic language, multiple symbols, and larger-than-life characters, Williams's brand of lyrical realism attracted Inge. Lacking the soaring language typical of Williams, Inge instead demonstrated skill in creating strong characterizations and in depicting the details of small-town midwestern life in the first half of the 20th century. Picnic represents the peak of Inge's dramatic achievement, and it is the strongest evocation of his frequent exploration of the joys and pains of romance and sexuality. Set against the arid surroundings of small-town America, Inge illuminates the crosscurrents of desire and the bittersweet aspects of love, both lost and found.

In 1950 Inge had written a one-act play, Front Porch, which he expanded and renamed Women of Summer before it evolved into Picnic. There was a popular film version in 1955, and it was remade for television in 2003. Despite critical and commercial success, Inge later revised Picnic, shifting the play's focus to the relationship of Rosemary and Howard. Titled Summer Brave it was produced at the Equity Library Theatre in 1973, but the critics were not favorable. The original Picnic remains a classic piece of lyrical realism from the post–World War II Broadway stage.

[See also United States, 1940–Present]

FURTHER READING

Armato, Philip M. "The Bum as Scapegoat in William Inge's Picnic." Western American Literature 10 (1976): 273–282.

Donovan, Robert K. "The Dionysiac Dance in William Inge's Picnic." Dance Chronicle 7 (1985): 413–434.

Lange, Jane W. " 'Forces Get Loose': Social Prophecy in William Inge's Picnic." Kansas Quarterly 18, no. 4 (1986): 57–70.

Smith, Christopher. "Picnic." In Contemporary American Dramatists, ed. by K. A. Berney. Detroit: St. James Press, 1994. 709–711.

Wentworth, Michael. "The Convergence of Fairy Tale and Myth in William Inge's Picnic." Kansas Quarterly 18, no. 4 (1986): 75–85.

James Fisher

PILLARS OF SOCIETY

A citizen's home ought to be like a glass cabinet.
—Rummel, Act 4

After EMPEROR AND GALILEAN (1873), an expansive double drama of world history, HENRIK IBSEN decided to return to contemporary small-town Norwegian society, limited in both space and time. In Pillars of Society (Samfundets støtter, 1877) all four acts take place in the spacious garden room in Consul Bernick's house. The rear wall is entirely of glass, overlooking part of the garden and a street beyond. The device of the glass wall was introduced by BJØRNSTJERNE BJØRNSON in 1875 and developed further by Ibsen. By lowering or raising curtains the distinction between the interior sphere and the world outside is emphasized. The play exploits this scenographic contrast by opposing the complacent atmosphere of the insiders to the unexpected appearance of intruding elements from a larger world.

Arriving on a ship from America is Lona Hessel, once the sweetheart of Karsten Bernick, who was rejected by him for a more profitable alliance with her half sister. With her unconventional approach, Lona causes a stir in the quiet small town. Informed about one or two offenses committed by Bernick in his younger days, and blamed on her brother, who left for America, she is determined to make Bernick confess his misdeeds publicly. Bernick's business management has not been stainless, either. As a shipyard owner he has been eager to have an old vessel hastily repaired, endangering the life of crew and passengers. When he learns that his twelve-year-old son Olaf has boarded the ship as a stowaway, he is seriously concerned.

Business friends of the Consul have prepared a celebration in his honor, to strike back against rumors that undermine his position as a pillar of society. In the last act the curtains are lifted in front of a cheering crowd of townspeople, with music and speeches. The Consul, however, who has just been informed that the ship is held back and his son is safe, does not accept the honor offered him. He is now ready to confess his several offenses, and the celebration is subdued. At the end Bernick honors the women of his family as the pillars of society, but Lona Hessel does not agree: the spirit of truth and the spirit of freedom hold that position.

It has been debated whether Consul Bernick's confession and moral turnaround are credible. Compared to Ibsen's later endings, this one seems rather lighthearted. No doubt, he advanced further in his dramatic art from A DOLL'S HOUSE onward. And yet Pillars of Society became his greatest international success so far, particularly in GERMANY, where it was performed in thirty-one German theaters in 1878.

[See also Norway]

FURTHER READING

Ewbank, Inga-Stina. "Drama and Society in Ibsen's Pillars of the Community." In Drama and Society: Themes in Drama 1, ed. by James Redmond. Cambridge: Cambridge Univ. Press, 1979. 75–97.

McFarlane, James. "Pillars of Society: Comedy, Irony and Deeper Meaning." Contemporary Approaches to Ibsen 8 (1994): 121–129.

Northam, John. "Pillars of Society." In *Ibsen's Dramatic Method*. 1953.
Oslo: Universitetsforlaget, 1971. 40–58.

Asbjørn Aarseth

THE PILLOWMAN

The little boy was just like you said it'd be. I chopped his toes off and he didn't scream at all. He just sat there looking at them. He seemed very surprised. I suppose you would be at that age. His name was Aaron. He had a funny little hat on, kept going on about his mum. God, he bled a lot. You wouldn't've thought there'd be that much blood in such a little boy. Then he stopped bleeding and went blue. Poor thing. I feel quite bad now, he seemed quite nice. . . . But the girl was a pain in the arse. Kept bawling her eyes out. And she wouldn't eat them. She wouldn't eat the applemen, and I'd spent ages making them. It's really hard to get the razor blades inside. You don't say how to make them in the story, do ya?

—Michal, Act 2, Scene 1

MARTIN MCDONAGH's play, first performed in November 2003 at the National Theatre in London, deconstructs the shifting relationship between stories, the storyteller and those to whom stories are told. McDonagh utilizes the familiar narrative tropes of interrogation, flashback, and children's stories to examine the ways in which narratives control, bind, and restrict even as they help us to overcome our isolation and despair.

Set in an unnamed totalitarian state, act 1 opens with its protagonist, Katurian K. Katurian, blindfolded in a police interrogation room. Two policemen question and torture Katurian due to the uncanny resemblance between a series of child murders in his town and the gruesome content of his stories. The similarity between art and life, representation and the real, is made even more problematic given that Katurian's art is conjured from the bizarre experiment conducted by his parents that damaged the mind of his brother Michal when they were both children. Katurian's stories are seductive, first teasing then pulling us into their world. As the tales unfold, they horrifyingly materialize the ways in which children's stories shift from joy to violence, evoke nightmares through words, collapse the known and the familiar, subvert the comforting and innocent, and transform the safe mythology of home into a terrifying locus of violence.

The writer endures the worst critics imaginable—Detective Tupolski, an imaginative, articulate storyteller in his own right, and his violent thug of an assistant, Ariel. What becomes clear, as the unchecked authority of the interrogation proceeds, is that the detectives have stories of their own, stories that serve to underscore the link between state-sanctioned violence and the familial violence of Katurian's narratives. This connection is further elaborated through the play's structure, as the unfolding stories of the interrogation room and Katurian's stories are given theatrical life. The interrogation begins with a familiar theatrical idiom of simultaneously frightening and hilarious exchanges that recall HAROLD PINTER's early menacing COM-EDIES. These scenes are punctuated by Katurian's stories, which come to life as if they are being lifted out of an illustrated children's pop-up book. Katurian's stories abruptly dislocate time and place, pulling us into the psychic space of childhood.

Toward the end of act 1, Michal admits to his brother that he has killed children. A stunned, horrified, and protective Katurian evolves into "The Pillowman," of one of his stories, suffocating his brother to spare him execution by the police. The end of act 1 leaves us desirous to know what happens to the little girl in "The Little Jesus" story. What has Michal done to a little neighborhood girl? We are thus tangled and made complicit with the play's mixture of pleasure and violence in storytelling.

The Pillowman begins with a blindfolded artist and ends with his sight blocked by a black hood over his head, ironic materializations that frame the exploration of the role of the storyteller, artistic responsibility, and the consequences of art as it extends beyond the stage.

[*See also* England, 1960–Present; Ireland]

FURTHER READING
McDonagh, Martin. *The Pillowman*. London: Faber, 2003.
Worthen, Hannah, and H.B. Worthen. "The Pillowman and the Ethics of Allegory." *Modern Drama* 49, no. 2 (2006): 155–173.

Kerry Moore

PIÑERA, VIRGILIO (1912–1979)

One of the most internationally renowned Cuban playwrights, VIRGILIO PIÑERA was born in Cárdenas, CUBA, on August 4, 1912. He led the dramatic theatrical revolution before the political revolution drove him out of the country. In the late 1950s, nightly performances of his plays were performed to large audiences. *Electra Garrigó* (1941) established him as a leading dramatist and contemporary of Carlos Felipe. It adapted the myth of Electra to the disintegrating Cuban bourgeoisie. As the 1960s expanded Cuban drama, he produced *The Fat Guy and the Skinny Guy* (*El flaco y el gordo*, 1959) and *The Philanthropist* (*El filántropo*, 1960). His *Cold Air* (*Aire frío*, 1959) is considered by many Cubans a masterpiece of 20th-century Cuban drama. This autobiographical play portrays several decades of a middle-class Cuban family in transition.

Thematically, his plays portrayed the social and economic evils manifested by the corruption of prerevolutionary regimes. After EUGÈNE IONESCO's THE BALD SOPRANO was staged in 1956, AVANT-GARDE playwrights wrote and staged plays incorporating elements of the Theater of the Absurd. Piñera's plays from the early 1960s until his death in 1979 utilized absurdist elements. He also overtly satirized and challenged the status quo through his oppressed and disenfranchised characters defeated by the new regime. They confront absurd conflicts or challenges that dehumanize each character who must destroy or be destroyed in the final resolution.

Piñera did not address the contradictions of the revolution itself in his early plays. Until the late 1960s, playwrights wrote and staged their works without governmental intervention. In 1961 Fidel Castro's "Words to the Intellectuals" ("Palabras a los intelectuales") initiated a crackdown on artistic expression. Piñera was the only audience member to directly contest Castro among the crowd of intellectuals rounded up for the edict. As a result of Castro's admonition, most playwrights fled the country or stopped writing. Despite censorship and ostracism from the theater community, Piñera, Antón Arrufat, and a few survivors defied the regime and continued to write.

These blacklisted works were rarely published or performed until restrictions were eased in the 1990s. Piñera was most prolific during his later years. An international literary jury awarded him the Casas de las Américas prize in theater for *Two Panicky Old Folks* (*Dos viejos pánicos*) in 1968. Editors in Buenos Aires, where he lived for several years, published several short plays and story collections.

Piñera wrote incessantly, despite the exigencies of the new regime. After devoting his life to the advancement of Cuban arts and letters, he died of a heart attack at home on October 19, 1979. Governmental officials confiscated his manuscripts immediately after his death. Some works were released upon demand by literary scholars and colleagues to be edited and published posthumously. After 1986, the government released plays that were published, including *The Siamese Twins* (*Los siameses*), *The Trip* (*El viaje*), *The Rink* (*El rink*), *Soap Bubbles* (*Pompas de jabón*), *Inermes*, and *A Pick or a Shovel?* (*¿Un pico o una pala?*). Many manuscripts of plays and stories remain in governmental archives, unedited as of 2005.

[*See also* Absurdism]

SELECT PLAYS: *Electra Garrigó* (1941); *False Alarm* (*Falsa alarma*, 1948); *Jesus* (*Jesús*, 1948); *Cold Air* (*Aire frío*, 1959, 1988); *The Fat Guy and the Skinny Guy* (*El flaco y el gordo*, 1959); *The Philanthropist* (*El filántropo*, 1960); *Requiem for Yàrini* (*Réquiem para Yarini*, 1960); *The Wedding* (*La boda*, 1960); *The Servants* (*Los siervos*, 1962); *An Empty Shoebox* (*Una caja de zapatos vacía*, 1968); *Two Panicky Old Folks* (*Dos viejos pánicos*, 1968); *Study in White and Black* (*Estudio en blanco y negro*, 1970); *No* (*El no*, performed 2005)

FURTHER READING

Carrió, Raquel. *Dramaturgia cubana contemporánea* [Contemporary Cuban dramaturgy]. Havana: Editorial Pueblo y Educación, 1988.

de Armas, José R., and Charles W. Steele. *Cuba: Consciousness in Literature*. Miami: Ediciones Univeral, 1978.

Domínguez, Carlos Espinosa. "A Century of Theatre in Cuba: An Introduction to Cuban Theatre." N.d. http://www.repertorio.org/education/pdfs/cubateatro2.pdf.

González-Cruz, Luis F., and Ann Waggoner Aken, trans. *Three Masterpieces of Cuban Drama*. Los Angeles: Green Integer, 2000.

Carole Anne Champagne

PINERO, ARTHUR (1855–1934)

I hope the time will come—is coming—when the Englishman like the Frenchman, will write his play for all nations.
—Arthur Pinero

English actor, director, and playwright Arthur Pinero was knighted (1909) for his contributions to stage literature. Born to middle-class parents of Portuguese Jewish descent, Pinero was sent to work in his father's law offices at the age of ten. As a child Pinero also spent many hours at the Sadler's Wells and the Prince of Wales theaters, where he was introduced to the "cup and saucer" plays of THOMAS WILLIAM ROBERTSON. After his father's retirement, fifteen-year-old Arthur found work as a solicitor's clerk by day and studied elocution at Birkbeck Institute at night. Although he eventually rejected the law profession, the influence of the nine years Pinero spent in solicitors' offices can be seen in many of his plays. Legal details, particularly those related to wills and trusts, and the problem of the law's inequality to women feature prominently in a number of his works.

Pinero excelled in his elocution courses and gained opportunities to perform on tour in Edinburgh and Bristol. During this period Pinero composed his first plays, though none was accepted for performance. In 1874 Pinero abandoned the field of law in order to pursue his childhood dream of ACTING. Actor-manager Henry Irving discovered him in 1876 and engaged him in the company at the Lyceum in London. During his nearly five years at the Lyceum, Pinero gained a reputation as a reliable character actor. Irving also encouraged the budding playwright and staged some of his work. Pinero performed the leading male role in his first produced piece: the one-act *200 £ a Year* was staged at the Globe Theatre on October 6, 1877. His first hit, *The Money-Spinner* (1880), opened in Manchester and later enjoyed a successful run in London.

In 1881 Pinero moved to the Haymarket, where he continued to act and write plays until 1884. Greatly influenced by Haymarket managers Marie and Squire Bancroft, Pinero began to emphasize ensemble work and eschew melodramatic effects in favor of a more intimate, naturalistic approach to drama. He gained notice as an emerging playwright with early FARCES *Imprudence* (1881) and *The Squire* (1881). The play script of *The Squire* illustrates Pinero's conception of his plays in terms of the combined textual, visual, and performance elements of theater. Here, as in his other plays, Pinero included elaborate directions for set design and construction, detailed descriptions of stage business, and specific physical and psychological outlines of his characters.

Between 1882 and 1884 Pinero wrote seven full-length plays, three of them early versions of the marriage PROBLEM PLAY. In 1883 the playwright himself married actress Myra Holme, who had starred in his 1882 play *Girls and Boys*. About this time Pinero established the practice of printing the full script of a new play in order to provide copies for all of the actors. Previously, actors only received "sides"—sections of the text that record cues and give only the speeches of the actor's own role. The result of Pinero's practice was to encourage an ensemble effect and enable the development of realistic acting. During this period, the influential drama critic William Archer (1882) wrote of Pinero as "a thoughtful and conscientious writer with artistic aims, if not yet in command of his artistic means . . . [showing] sufficient promise to warrant a hope that we have in this author a playwright of genuine talent."

After 1884 Pinero's work can be divided into four genres: farce, problem play, social COMEDY, and sentimental comedy. Some of his most skillfully constructed works were his farces for the Court Theatre, all of which took a single social target: the law (THE MAGISTRATE, 1885), the Church (*Dandy Dick*, 1887), politics (*The Cabinet Minister*, 1890), education (*The Schoolmistress*, 1886), and marriage (*The Amazons*, 1893). Pinero's best and most popular Court farce, *The Magistrate*, centers on a woman named Agatha who lies about her age—and the age of her nineteen-year-old son from a previous marriage—in order to wed her second husband, the honest magistrate Mr. Poskett. *The Magistrate* also marks Pinero's first venture into DIRECTING his plays, a practice he continued throughout his career. Following the success of Pinero's London production of *The Magistrate*, he directed a subsequent production in New York in the playwright's only trip to America.

Pinero's reputation as a director was that of a skillful and precise perfectionist who controlled each stage of the production process. As opposed to casting according to convenience or availability, Pinero refused to accept any actor he did not consider to be the best person for the role. He also was one of the first English directors to cast according to physical type. Rehearsal periods for Pinero's productions ran long—sometimes six or seven weeks—and the playwright gave specific direction for line delivery, facial expressions, and stage business. Despite the seeming limitations of this somewhat restrictive approach, Pinero's productions largely received favorable notices from critics and audiences alike.

In 1887 Pinero wrote *The Profligate*, a masterful problem play that was heralded by critics as a breakthrough in English drama. In it, Pinero draws on the melodramatic conventions of coincidence, aside, and soliloquy and appropriates the character of the *raisonneur* from the "well-made play." *The Profligate* centers on a premise that pervaded many of Pinero's later problem plays: a dark secret of the past haunts the protagonist's present and threatens his or her future. More significantly, *The Profligate* addressed the pressing social issue of the sexual "double standard." The plot centers on Lesley Brudenell—an innocent and morally rigid woman who cannot accept the debauched and immoral past of the profligate, Dunstan Renshaw. Initially considered too controversial for performance, *The Profligate* was only produced two years after it was written—and then only after the tragic ending had been revised (the only time Pinero rewrote his work). However, Pinero published the original end-

ing, in which Renshaw is abandoned by Lesley and, believing himself unforgiven for his past sins, commits suicide, dying just as Lesley returns to him.

Pinero's next four "problem plays" all centered on women: THE SECOND MRS. TANQUERAY (1893), *The Notorious Mrs. Ebbsmith* (1894), *Iris* (1901), and MID-CHANNEL (1909). While many critics assumed Pinero modeled his problem plays on those of HENRIK IBSEN, the playwright himself claimed, "When I wrote *The Profligate* I had no knowledge of Ibsen, nor have I, I believe, been influenced in the smallest degree by his works." Although distinctly different in personality, the female protagonists of these psychological studies are all somehow trapped by their relationships with men and rendered powerless by societal expectations and structures—including the law. Most notable among these works is Pinero's masterpiece *The Second Mrs. Tanqueray*. Composed over a two-year span, it was acclaimed as the best English play since Richard Sheridan's *The School for Scandal*.

Other plays of note include Pinero's highly popular "sentimental comedies" *Sweet Lavender* (1888) and *Trelawny of the "Wells"* (1898) and his finest comedy of manners, *The Gay Lord Quex* (1899). *Sweet Lavender*, which was closely modeled on playwright T. W. Robertson's dramatic style, explored social class as a barrier to true love. Pinero's longest-running play *Sweet Lavender* was translated, adapted, and performed on the Continent as well as throughout the English-speaking world. In *Trelawny of the "Wells,"* Pinero sought to recreate the theatrical world of Sadler's Wells and celebrate Robertson's development of early English REALISM. Initially, the play was criticized as "sordidly disagreeable, too destitute of romance or story" (*The Times*, January 21, 1988). Nevertheless, it gained popularity over time, with several revivals and a filmed staging by 1928. The beautifully constructed comedy of manners *The Gay Lord Quex* has been likened to Restoration comedies in its satirical critique of a hypocritical, cynical, and amoral society.

Following a period of extensive but intermittent travel on the Continent, Pinero produced three of his best plays at St. James's Theatre: *His House in Order* (1906), his greatest financial success; *The Thunderbolt* (1908); and *Mid-Channel* (1909). The universally acclaimed 1906 play *His House in Order* features Pinero's satirical critique of snobbery, hypocrisy, and "noble" self-sacrifice. *The Thunderbolt* portrays one middle-class family's hypocrisy and greed as they wrangle over the estate of their recently deceased brother. *Mid-Channel*, one of Pinero's "woman problem plays," chronicles the disintegration of a marriage and the destructive effects of the sexual double standard on a middle-aged wife.

However, after 1910, Pinero's popularity and influence as a playwright began to decline. Pinero's production of *The "Mind the Paint" Girl* (1912)—a satire on the famous Gaiety Girls—was jeered at by audiences and dismissed by critics. Between 1914 and 1918, wartime audiences preferred light entertainment to Pinero's realistic offerings. Late in his career, Pinero began to experiment with form in his plays: *Mr. Livermore's Dream* (1917), *The Enchanted Cottage* (1922), *The Freaks* (1918), and *Dr. Harmer's Holidays* (written in 1923–1924). In 1928, the Garrick Club honored Pinero's contributions to theater on the fiftieth anniversary of his debut as a playwright.

[*See also* England, 1860–1940]

PLAYS: *200 £ a Year* (1877); *Two Can Play at that Game* (1878); *Daisy's Escape* (1879); *Bygones* (1880); *Hester's Mystery* (1880); *La Comete: or, Two Hearts* (1880); *The Money-Spinner* (1880); *Imprudence* (1881); *The Squire* (1881); *Girls and Boys: A Nursery Tale* (1882); *Lords and Commons* (1883); *The Rector* (1883); *The Rocket* (1883); *In Chancery* (1884); *The Iron Master* (1884); *Low Water* (1884); *The Magistrate* (1885); *Mayfair* (1885); *The Hobby-Horse* (1886); *The Schoolmistress* (1886); *Dandy Dick* (1887); *Sweet Lavender* (1888); *The Weaker Sex* (1888); *The Profligate* (1889); *The Cabinet Minister* (1890); *Lady Bountiful: A Story of Years* (1891); *The Times* (1891); *The Amazons* (1893); *The Second Mrs. Tanqueray* (1893); *The Notorious Mrs. Ebbsmith* (1894); *The Benefit of the Doubt* (1895); *The Princess and the Butterfly: or, The Fantastics* (1897); *The Beauty Stone* (with J. Comyns Carr, music by Arthur Sullivan, 1898); *Trelawny of the "Wells"* (1898); *The Gay Lord Quex* (1899); *Iris* (1901); *Letty* (1903); *A Wife Without a Smile: A Comedy in Disguise* (1904); *His House in Order* (1906); *The Thunderbolt* (1908); *Mid-Channel* (1909); *Preserving Mr. Panmure* (1911); *The "Mind the Paint" Girl* (1912); *The Widow of Wasdale Head: A Fantasy* (1912); *Playgoers* (1913); *The Big Drum* (1915); *Mr. Livermore's Dream* (1917); *The Freaks: An Idyll of Suburbia* (1918); *Monica's Blue Boy* (music by Frederic Cowen, 1918); *Quick Work* (1919); *The Enchanted Cottage* (1922); *A Seat in the Park* (1922); *A Private Room* (1928); *Child Man* (1930); *Dr. Harmer's Holidays* (1931); *A Cold June* (1932); *Late of Mockford's* (1934)

SELECT PLAYS: *The Fresh Truffles* (*I nuovi tartufi*, 1865–1866); *Fading Roses* (*Rose caduche*, 1867); *Honor I* (*L'onore I*, 1869); *Rustic Chivalry* (*Carvalleria rusticana*, 1884); *The Porter's Lodging* (*In portineria*, 1885); *The She-Wolf* (*La lupa*, 1886); *After* (*Dopo*, 1886); *Mastro-don Gesualdo* (1889); *Rustic Chivalry* (*Cavalleria rusticana*, 1896); *The Wolf Hunt* (*La caccia al lupo*, 1901); *The Fox Hunt* (*La caccia alla volpe*, 1901); *What's Yours Is Mine* (*Dal tuo al mio*, 1903)

FURTHER READING

Archer, William. *English Dramatists of To-day*. London: Sampson Low, 1882.

Dunkel, Wilbur Dwight. *Sir Arthur Pinero: A Critical Biography with Letters*. Port Washington, N.Y.: Kennikat, 1941.

Fyfe, Sir Hamilton. *Sir Arthur Pinero's Plays and Players*. London: Ernest Benn, 1930.

Griffin, Penny. *Arthur Wing Pinero and Henry Arthur Jones*. New York: St. Martin's, 1991.

Lazenby, Walter. *Arthur Wing Pinero*. New York: Twayne, 1972.

Wearing, J. P. "Pinero the Actor." *Theatre Notebook* 26, no. 4 (Summer 1972).

Leslie A. Dovale

PINGET, ROBERT (1919–1997)

The Swiss-born French novelist and playwright Robert Pinget practiced law in Geneva as a young man. He was born on July 19, 1919, in Geneva, and in 1946 he moved to Paris to study painting but abandoned his studies to travel abroad. Back in FRANCE, he turned from painting to writing, publishing a book of stories, *Entres Fantoine et Agapa* (*Between Fantoine and Agapa*) in 1951. Recognition, however, came late for Pinget; despite finding publishers for his first three novels, they were mostly ignored.

Eventually, Editions de Minuit took a risk on his fourth novel, *Graal Flibuste* (1955) and later reissued his previous three. He soon became associated with the writers of the nouveau roman—Alain Robbe-Grillet, Claude Simon, NATHALIE SARRAUTE, Michel Butor, and others—who rejected the conventions of the traditional novel in favor of techniques that explored subjective experiences of personal anguish, the passage of time, and problems of communication. Throughout his career, however, Pinget resisted particular expectations of genre or identification with any school of writing.

In both fiction and drama, Pinget dealt with personal utterance; for him, writing was synonymous with the human voice. Consequently, he wrote several early plays for radio—*The Crank* (*La Manivelle*), for example, which his friend SAMUEL BECKETT adapted into *The Old Tune* (1960), a favor Pinget returned when adapting ALL THAT FALL and *Embers*. Others he adapted from his fiction. *Architruc* (1961), *Dead Letter* (*Lettre morte*, 1959), and *Clope* (1961) were based on his novels *Baga* (1958), *Le Fiston* (1959), and *Clope au dossier* (1961). Often compared to Beckett, Pinget's plays differ in outlook and manifest an apparent lack of concern for theatrical space and physical action.

Spoken language is the primary impulse of Pinget's drama. His speakers demonstrate his fondness for everyday speech and discourse. His use of language, however, resists the notion that the purpose of drama is to recreate objective reality. Nor do his plays adhere to conventional notions of plot, time, or psychology. They do, however, deploy language in the service of dramatic and comic purpose; his usual tools for achieving his aims are repetition, malapropism, and misunderstanding. His themes emerge from the desire of his characters to satisfy elusive inner needs and their frustrated attempts to understand them. Thus, in *Dead Letter*, Monsieur Levert searches futilely for a letter from the son who abandoned him. Gorman and Cream in *The Old Tune* try to retrieve and verify memories of their shared past. The eponymous characters in *Abel and Bela* (*Abel et Bela*, 1971) struggle in vain to create the text for a play; their failure creates Pinget's success. The drama of the writer-in-process also informs *Identity* (*Identité*, 1972), *Paralchimie* (1973), and the two "Mortin" plays (*About Mortin* [*Autour de Mortin*, 1965] and *Mortin Not Dead* [*Mortin pas mort*, 1986]), which raise the question of what survives after an author's death.

At first, Pinget's project seems pessimistic, for the pattern of his design is the linguistic formation and dismantling of human will, which degenerates into fantasy, or chaos, revealing a negation of self. However, his originality, his humor, and his sincere, soul-searching protagonists mitigate against a thoroughly hopeless vision. Pinget died on August 25, 1997.

PLAYS: *Tous ceux qui tambent* (from Beckett; *All That Fall*, 1957); *Dead Letter* (*Lettre morte*, 1959); *The Old Tune* (based on *The Crank* [*La Manivelle*], 1960); *Here or There* (*Ici ou ailleurs*, 1961); *Architruc* (1961); *Clope* (1961); *The Hypothesis* (*L'Hypothèse*, 1961); *No Answer* (*Le Fiston*, 1961); *About Mortin* (*Autour de Mortin*, 1965); *Abel and Bela* (*Abel et Bela*, 1971); *Identity* (*Identité*, 1972); *Night* (*Nuit*, 1973); *Paralchimie* (1973); *A Bizarre Will* (*Un Testament bizarre*, 1986); *The Chrysanthemum* (*Le Chrysanthène*, 1986); *Crazy Notion* (*Lubie*, 1986); *Dictation* (*Dictée*, 1986); *Mortin Not Dead* (*Mortin pas mort*, 1986); *Sophism and Sadism* (*Sophisne et sadisne*, 1986); *About Nothing* (*De rien*, 1995); *The Beefsteak* (*Le Bifteck*, 1995); *The Ducreux Business* (*L'Affaire Ducreux*, 1995)

FURTHER READING

Esslin, Martin. *The Theatre of the Absurd.* Rev. ed. New York: Doubleday/Anchor, 1969.

Henckels, Robert M., Jr., *Robert Pinget: The Novel as Quest.* Tuscaloosa: Univ. of Alabama. Press, 1979.

Rosmarin, Leonard R. *Robert Pinget.* Twayne's World Authors Series. New York: Twayne, 1995.

Michael D. Kinghorn

PINTER, HAROLD (1930–)

Harold Pinter, winner of the 2005 Nobel Prize in Literature, is often considered by critics to be among the most influential English dramatists of the last half of the 20th century. One overarching reason for such respect is the breadth of his artistic achievements. Pinter has written twenty-nine highly regarded stage plays to date, plus twenty-one screenplays and assorted radio dramas. But he began his theater profession as an actor, also becoming a first-rate stage director with twenty-seven productions to his credit. Additionally, Pinter is a widely published poet and essayist. Finally, he remains a busy political activist who is not afraid to generate controversy. Pinter thus represents a vital man both of the theater and world affairs. In awarding the Nobel Prize, the Swedish Academy said Pinter was an author "who in his plays uncovers the precipice under everyday prattle and forces entry into oppression's closed rooms."

Like many leading authors of post–World War II ENGLAND, Pinter succeeded not through class advantages but despite the lack of them. Born in 1930 in Hackney, a working-class section of East London, Pinter was the only child of a tailor of Portuguese-Jewish heritage. While still a very young boy, he was evacuated several times from London during the German bombings of World War II. Because of his Jewish background, young Pinter was drawn into frequent fistfights on returning to London where an increas-

ingly anti-Semitic, fascist current had emerged. He attended the all-boys Hackney Downs Grammar School from 1942 until 1948 and became attracted there to literature and theater. Pinter acted lead roles in Shakespearean plays while in school, though his interests also included poetry, politics, film, and journalism. Sports were important to Pinter during his school years, as well, including football, cricket, and especially track, a sport where he set school sprint records.

At age eighteen, Pinter entered the Royal Academy of Dramatic Art (RADA) under a scholarship. Feeling out of his depth among more sophisticated students, however, he dropped out and later enrolled at the Central School of Speech and Drama. During that period, Pinter also displayed a strong political consciousness that remained evident in his life and career. On the personal side, when he was eighteen years old and subject to national conscription, he chose the path of conscientious objector rather than serve in the British armed forces—a choice that earned him a fine but not jail. In speeches and in essays he has steadfastly argued on behalf of human rights issues and against politically inspired wars. During the 1990s, when fully established as one of England's premium playwrights, Pinter refused a knighthood because it was proffered by Prime Minister John Major's party whose policies contrasted with Pinter's positions.

Some of his popular playwriting colleagues (DAVID HARE, EDWARD BOND, HOWARD BRENTON) wrote mostly politically charged dramas. But more like TOM STOPPARD and PETER SHAFFER, Pinter created worlds in his plays extending beyond strictly temporal themes. The exceptions include his *One for the Road* (1984), *Mountain Language* (1988), *Moonlight* (1993), and a few other lesser-known works. The "public" persona has not impeded the "artist" in him. As early as 1950, Pinter had his poetry first published. He also began then to perform radio plays over the BBC. His involvement with the legitimate theater took hold, as well, and he toured IRELAND and the English countryside, ACTING William Shakespeare's plays and current dramas. While touring, Pinter met actress Vivien Merchant, whom he married in 1956. They divorced in 1980, at which time he married Lady Antonia Fraser, an aristocrat and noted writer-biographer.

While continuing to write and publish poetry and fiction, Pinter also seriously contemplated potential subjects for plays. A friend in 1957 asked Pinter to write a play based on tone proposed topic. Pinter was acting on tour at the time but in four days wrote the one-act piece *The Room*—his first work for the stage. It proved a success in performance at Bristol University and then at Bristol's Old Vic Theatre. When asked by a commercial producer for other plays, Pinter offered him *The Dumb Waiter* (1959) and THE BIRTHDAY PARTY (1958).

The inquiring producer Michael Codron paid Pinter for the option to stage *The Birthday Party* in Cambridge and in London during the spring of 1958. Most critical response was scathing and audience attendance dismal. Harold Hobson, a critic of *The (London) Sunday Times*, however, recognized evidence beneath the enigmatic surface of the play of "the most original, disturbing and arresting talent in theatrical London" (May 25, 1958). Within two years of its rocky start, *The Birthday Party* was produced again to far better reviews. It played on television and in several large venues including San Francisco—his first play performed in the UNITED STATES.

From our perspective today, we have little difficulty in recognizing the unique strengths of *The Birthday Party*—Pinter's second work and first full-length play. Composed of three conventional acts, the play embeds many of Pinter's dramatic techniques within a permeating atmosphere of eerie menace. The opening act presents traditional exposition but with a twist. A middle-aged couple, Petey and Meg, share their modest English seaside house with a boarder, Stanley. When approached by two strangers in business suits, only Stanley becomes alarmed. Act 2 portrays a wild birthday party, intended to honor Stanley, though it is not his birthday. The idea for the party was suggested by the two outsiders, Goldberg and McCann, and during the festivities it becomes clear the men are there to get Stanley and take him away. The last act depicts Goldberg and McCann assisting an apparently traumatized Stanley into a large black automobile. After the strangers and Stanley are gone, Petey and Meg are left to figure out what has occurred.

Pinter creates a mysterious situation in *The Birthday Party*, wherein Stanley's identity and past history are left blurred. Stanley's explanation that he had been a concert pianist and entertainer does not hold up under questioning. There are hints that Stanley once was associated with McCann and Goldberg, had perhaps broken some company policy, and was to return with them to face some form of justice. But that is supposition, since Pinter's plot refuses to clarify issues of identity or past and future events. The play ends up an intriguing puzzle that audiences are entreated to solve.

Most of Pinter's earlier dramas exhibited techniques derived from ABSURDISM, a theatrical movement popularized by critic Martin Esslin in his influential 1961 book *Theatre of the Absurd*. Average playgoers in 1958 were confused by the absurdist illogicalities and gaps in plot of *The Birthday Party*. Nor had most critics yet become conversant (or comfortable) with absurdism that early in its evolution. Other Pinter features that unsettled audiences were dialogue punctuated with pauses and silences plus sharp innuendo and invective, qualities also found in SAMUEL BECKETT's landmark puzzlers.

From 1958 on, Pinter's career advanced steadily and impressively. His one-act play *The Dumb Waiter* premiered in Frankfurt, GERMANY, in 1959, and his radio drama *A Slight Ache*, written in 1958, was performed in a stage version in London in 1961. *The Dumb Waiter*, almost an extension of *Birthday Party*, shifted to London's Royal Court Theatre following its opening in Germany. Except for being a one-act play, *Dumb Waiter* shares much with *Birthday Party*, especially a pervasive tone of menace and ambiguity. The play revolves around Gus and Ben, two men waiting in a small room; the sole feature of interest in the colorless chamber is a dumb waiter in one wall. Parallels with McCann and Goldberg are obvious, and the two forbidding men are revealed as criminal types, probably hit men on a "job." Little overt action occurs, the chief interest being centered on the distinctions between the two hoodlums. Ben is the no-nonsense leader who receives cryptic messages conveyed through the dumb waiter. The dumb waiter apparatus ultimately becomes catalyst in a life-and-death situation. Gus is less experienced, vulnerable, and nervous about the job ahead. His relative innocence may represent our own discomfort when kept in the dark.

The play features dialogue between the two reflecting their uncertainty about what is expected of them. The answer gradually is divulged to Ben via the dumb waiter that serves as metaphoric messenger from a mysterious, unseen boss. Ironic humor arises when several messages strongly suggest the room once served as a restaurant kitchen where food orders were received. Meanwhile, the audience tries to grasp the significance of the proceedings. Pinter's works typically project an air of uncertainty and puzzlement with spectators drawn into mind games. The goal is to solve the riddle in each play.

Pinter's powerful play THE CARETAKER (1960) opened in London where it enjoyed a run of over 425 performances. It proved to be Pinter's first genuine hit and soon was produced in numerous countries, including the United States. Additionally, it earned prestigious awards for best drama in the United States (i.e., Page One Award of the Newspaper Guild of New York), suggesting that Pinter's specific blend of ambiguous plot, inarticulate speech, and dark menace no longer baffled and irritated audiences. *The Caretaker* was written using naturalistic techniques, though the transparency of the format did not carry over into a clarity of meaning. As in many of Pinter's works, possession of a house or room plays a key role in *The Caretaker*. The beginning point of the story are two brothers, Aston and a younger sibling Mick, who become rivals in winning the support of the down-and-out old Davies whom Aston has saved from a street brawl. Upon bringing Davies to the brothers' home, Aston invites the tramp to stay with them and become caretaker. Mick at first is repulsed by the shabby intruder but reverses course and plays up to Davies, also asking him to stay on.

Ambiguity reigns in *The Caretaker*. Davies clearly is eager to remain in the room furnished him by the brothers, but his identity comes into question. To authenticate who he is, Davies would need to leave the room, with the probability that once gone from the room he would not be permitted back in. Davies's description of himself as cultured is belied by his being smelly and unclean. Aston's seeming kind and benign personality, meanwhile, is thrown into question when he admits having received shock treatments in a psychiatric clinic. Does Aston's confession therefore mean everything he says is false or unreliable? Accepting Aston's declaration at face value, Davies turns his back on Aston, thinking himself superior to anyone who is mentally deficient. Davies then directs his attention to the other brother, only to have Mick reject him. Davies's fatal miscalculation leads to his being exiled from the home he covets.

From one perspective, the brothers' actions appear as an act meant to deliberately mislead the "victim." According to such a view, Pinter consciously plays on his characters'—and audiences'—expectations. The raw truth of the situation is never made clear, and conceivably the brothers are nasty tricksters who waylay gullible strangers. A multiple interpretation of events becomes the prudent approach when dealing with Pinter's dramatic calculus. Paradoxically, in a program note prepared for The Dumb Waiter a month before the opening of The Caretaker, Pinter wrote, "The desire for verification is understandable, but cannot always be satisfied." This play reverberates with countless potential meanings.

By 1962, Pinter was co-directing his latest hit drama The Collection in London with the exciting new director Peter Hall. Pinter's association with Hall climaxed in 1965 when Hall singly directed a first-rate West End production of THE HOMECOMING. Pinter's career seemed at its zenith. The Homecoming combined in a single package nearly all of Pinter's greatest strengths. Already winner of various British awards, The Homecoming production transferring to Broadway earned six 1967 Tony nominations. Among the four actual winners were one for Best Play (Pinter) and one for Best Direction (Peter Hall). A splendidly made filmed version also appeared.

As with most of the works by Pinter, Homecoming offers strong elements of undesignated threats, ambiguity regarding past events, and controversial power struggles—all taking place in a single-room setting with minimal physical action. Dialogue often is opaque, and pauses relate as much information as words. The story is deceptively simple at the surface. Teddy, an English émigré, teaching philosophy at an American college, returns with his English-born wife Ruth to his modest family home in suburban London. Living there are Ted's crusty old father Max (a retired butcher), his benevolent uncle Sam (a chauffeur), and his two brothers Lennie (apparently a pimp) and Joey (part-time boxer). Teddy and his wife are received calmly by his family, odd considering he has been away for six years. Each man living in the house plays a distinct role in the male hierarchy ostensibly ruled over by Max, the tyrannical patriarch. However, the others pay him minimal attention as he harangues and bullies. Lennie displays sly intelligence and evidently is quite successful living off his ladies. Joey trains regularly for a prize fight that will never take place. The full-length play chronicles Ruth's gradual ascension up the family's power network until she takes total command by story's end. Her trump card is serving as the men's sexual companion as well as potentially becoming their profitable whore.

Not all audiences of The Homecoming were amused or entertained. The unexpected and scarcely explained actions in the work were less a problem than the absence of expected moral values. All spectators nonetheless feel the dynamics of a momentous power struggle underlying the drama. Sex and power combine forcefully in Homecoming, making it hard to forget once viewed in the theater.

A new play by Pinter appeared nearly each year during the 1960s, firmly planting him among the era's most popular writers for the stage. His playwriting continued in the 1970s but at an increasingly slower pace. No Man's Land (1975) returned Pinter to the spotlight, followed by his hit BETRAYAL, opening in 1978 at the National Theatre where Pinter had been an associate director. Some familiar stylistic techniques are found here but also a novel structure that proved ideal for expressing a story of marital infidelity. In Betrayal, the playwright turns chronology on its head, starting with the action's conclusion, then staging scenes progressively backward in time. Thus at the play's beginning, two husbands—once best of friends—sit talking about their present lives. From their conversation we learn that Jerry had been unfaithful to Judith with Robert's wife Emma. Succeeding scenes trace events backward chronologically through several stages, back to the play's final scene that depicts when, years earlier, Jerry and Emma first decided to get together and began deceiving their respective spouses.

Sardonic humor occasionally filters through the play, because the mistreated spouse already had discovered the adultery before the guilty parties confessed to it. Power ploys arise as in Pinter's other works, but the ultimate discovery is cautionary: one might not have the exclusive knowledge—hence power—one thinks he has. On several occasions a character is surprised to learn he or she was the last to "know" the facts. Solving the riddle of what is "true" is the play's greatest pleasure, rather than wrestling with metaphysical considerations. Parenthetically, Pinter has admitted to biographers that certain incidents in Betrayal parallel his personal life and led to his divorce from Vivien Merchant.

After Betrayal Pinter wrote no new full-length stage work until Moonlight (1993), Ashes to Ashes (1996), and Celebration (1999). Many of his shorter pieces during the 1980s and early 1990s, as previously noted, reflected urgent political themes then preoccupying him. Pinter's recent health issues make future writing projects uncertain. The appearance of fewer new plays from Pinter to date has not meant reduced activity on his part, however. During the decades of the 1980s and 1990s he pursued careers in acting and DIRECTING while also writing scripts—just as he had as early as the 1960s. As a repertory stage performer before success caught up with him in the 1950s, Pinter toured the English countryside in acting troupes. Once his playwriting career was secure, he acted in and/or directed some of his own works. For example, he acted Mick in The Caretaker (1960), Lenny in Homecoming (1969), Deeley in Old Times (1985), Hirst in No Man's Land (1992–1993), Roote in The Hothouse (1995), Harry in The Collection (1997, 1998), and Nicolas in One for the Road (2001). Pinter also made time for performing in films and television dramas, evidencing another facet of his professional life. Among his films are *The Servant* (1964), *Accident* (1966), *Turtle Diary* (1985), *Mojo* (1997), *Mansfield Park* (1998), and *The Tailor of Panama* (2000).

He has performed in many television plays, such as in his own *A Night Out* (1960), *The Basement* (1967), and *The Birthday Party* (1987), as well as in JEAN-PAUL SARTRE's NO EXIT (*Huis Clos*, 1965), *Rogue Male* (1967), *Langrishe, Go Down* (1978), *Breaking the Code* (1997), Samuel Beckett's *Catastrophe* (2000), and *Wit* (2000). Moreover, Pinter worked in radio beginning as a youth in the early 1950s and has altogether broadcast at least fifteen programs, including readings from his own plays.

But it is with screenwriting that Pinter most parallels his theater endeavors. Most of his acclaimed film scripts are adaptations of major literary works, including his own. The list of Pinter's movie-writing credits is long and impressive. The best known include his own *The Caretaker* (1962), *The Pumpkin Eater* (1963), his *The Servant* (1963), *The Quiller Memorandum* (1965), *Accident* (1966), his *The Birthday Party* (1967), *The Go-Between* (1969), his *The Homecoming* (1969), *The Last Tycoon* (1974), *The French Lieutenant's Woman* (1980), his *Betrayal* (1981), *Turtle Diary* (1984), *The Heat of the Day* (1988), and *The Trial* (1989). Viewers of these movies will instantly recognize how much the films benefit from Pinter's strong scripts.

Playgoers familiar with Beckett's plays built on existentialist premises perceive absurdist elements in Pinter's dramas. Martin Esslin's *Theatre of the Absurd* opened the way for later artistic generations to portray a contemporary world functioning with different assumptions than previously. Values no longer stand unchallenged, and truth no longer is self-evident. Enfeebled language rarely delivers a crystalline message now, leaving the discovery and transmission of "truth" all the more problematic without articulate dialectics. Pinter utilizes absurdist devices—such as omitting crucial information from the plot line—but also has evolved a personal style. Often we term an opaque situation "Pinteresque" in honor of the lack of certitude in his plays. In 1960 program notes, he wrote: "A character on the stage who can present no convincing argument or information as to his past experience, his present behavior or his aspirations, nor give a comprehensive analysis of his motives is as legitimate and as worthy of attention as one who, alarmingly, can do all these things." As for dialogue, Pinter's creed is conveyed in the same program notes: "The more acute the experience, the less articulate its expression." Pauses and silences in dialogue must—and do—convey needed meaning.

Pinter thrusts us into the world of ambiguity conjured in his plays. It is a system where nothing is absolutely true or absolutely false. Menace and mysterious unknowns dominate. Surprises lurk at every turn, and precise comprehension is impossible because no articulate communication is possible. Pinter portrays the world today—as he sees it. Whether called "Pinteresque" or not, we recognize it as our world as well.

SELECT PLAYS: *The Room* (1957); *The Birthday Party* (1958); *The Hothouse* (1958); *A Slight Ache* (1958); *The Dumb Waiter* (1959); *A Night Out* (1959); *The Caretaker* (1960); *The Dwarfs* (1960); *Night School* (1960); *The Collection* (1961); *The Lover* (1962); *The Homecoming* (1964); *Tea Party* (1964); *The Basement* (1966); *Landscape* (1967); *Silence* (1968); *Old Times* (1971); *No Man's Land* (1975); *Betrayal* (1978); *A Kind of Alaska* (1982); *One for the Road* (1984); *Mountain Language* (1988); *The New World Order* (1991); *Party Time* (1991); *Moonlight* (1993); *Ashes to Ashes* (1996); *Celebration* (1999)

FURTHER READING

Billington, Michael. *The Life and Work of Harold Pinter*. London: Faber, 1996.

Bloom, Harold, ed. *Harold Pinter*. Modern Critical Views. New York: Chelsea House, 1987.

Demastes, William W., ed. *British Playwrights, 1956–1995: A Research and Production Sourcebook*. Westport, Conn.: Greenwood Press, 1996.

Dukore, Bernard F. *Harold Pinter*. Modern Dramatists Series. New York: Grove, 1982.

Innes, Christopher. *Modern British Drama: The Twentieth Century*. Cambridge: Cambridge Univ. Press, 2002.

Raby, Peter, ed. *The Cambridge Companion to Harold Pinter*. Cambridge: Cambridge Univ. Press, 2001.

C. J. Gianakaris

PIRANDELLO, LUIGI (1867–1936)

While Luigi Pirandello is certainly among the most studied of 20th-century Italian authors, he remains mysterious and strangely distant, inviting ever more investigation and interpretation. Both his life—divided between the centuries of candlelight and electricity—and his varied texts—literary, theatrical, essays, and personal (letters, confessions, memoirs)—continue to provide a seemingly inexhaustible source for widely different readings by successive generations of readers.

Pirandello was born on June 28, 1867, in a country house known as Il Caos (Chaos), between Sicily's Porto Empedocle and Girgenti (renamed Agrigento by the fascist government in 1927). He was the second of five children.

Though raised in a rural environment defined by his father's occupation as a sulfur miner, with the help of his mother, who understood him completely, Luigi was able to pursue a higher education. He enrolled him in an accounting school and then moved to Palermo to pursue humanistic studies. Later Luigi studied at the University of Rome, then earned his degree in philology (on the dialect of Agrigento) in 1891 in Bonn, GERMANY, where he stayed on for another year as lecturer. During these years Pirandello published several volumes of poetry.

Concerns about his health led him to return to ITALY at the end of 1892. Settling in Rome, he wrote for newspapers and journals while working on his first novel (1901), *L'esclusa* (*The*

Outcast), published serially in 1901 in the daily paper *La tribuna*. Already in 1894 he had published a collection of short stories titled *Amori senza amore* (*Loves Without Love*); the same year he married Antonietta Portulano, the daughter of his father's business partner. He received a teaching appointment in Italian literature at the University of Rome. Several years of peaceful tranquility came to an end with the birth of his third son, Fausto, in 1899, and his wife's nervous breakdown.

Due to Antonietta's illness and the chaotic family situation, to supplement his small teaching stipend Pirandello worked as a private literature tutor, publishing small works here and there; among these his second novel, *The Late Mattia Pascal*, was published between April and June 1904 and again as a serial in the journal *Nuova Antologia*, a work that strongly influenced 20th-century Italian narrative. During this time he published several short-story collections, and in 1908 he published two volumes of essays, *Arte e scienza* (*Art and Science*) and *L'umorismo* (*The Humor*), which articulated the poetic and aesthetic principles of his narrative and theater. Because the short stories sketch out, almost photographically, small vignettes of life, Pirandello thought to translate these photographs into the medium of theater, a more effective mirror of real life. On December 9, 1910, his career as a playwright began: at Rome's Teatro Metastasio two of his one-act plays were performed—one, *The Vise* (*La morsa*), written in 1898 and titled *The Epilogue* (*L'epilogo*), that was based on his short story "The Fear" (*La paura*), the other, *Limes from Sicily* (*Lumíe di Sicilia*), adapted from a short story of the same name. Thereafter he dedicated ever more energy to this new genre, and a strong sign of growing recognition of his dramatic skills came in Milan, on April 19, 1915, when MARCO PRAGA's theater company presented his play *If Not So* (*Se non cosí*) at the Teatro Manzoni. For such a prestigious director to stage this new playwright's play was a great honor. Meanwhile he continued to write novels.

The World War I years were very difficult for Pirandello, because both of his sons, Fausto and Stefano, were soldiers, and the latter was captured and taken prisoner early in the war. This contributed to Antonietta's still deteriorating mental state and in 1919 she was committed to an asylum. Also, Pirandello's mother passed away around this time. Amid these personal crises and sorrows, Pirandello's success in the theater grew as more and more of his works were performed by well-known actors. He wrote many plays in these years: in 1913, *The Doctor's Duty* (*Il dovere del medico*); in 1916, *Think It Over, Giacomino!* (*Pensaci, Giacomino*) and *Liolà*; in 1917, *The Jar* (*La giara*), RIGHT YOU ARE (*If You Think You Are*) (*Cosí è se vi pare*) and *The Pleasure of Honesty* (*Il piacere dell' onestà*); and in 1918, *This Time It Will Be Different* (*Ma non è una cosa seria*) and *The Rules of the Game* (*Il giuoco delle parti*). By the end of the war, Pirandello had definitively moved into the forefront of modern theater both in Italy (*Grafted* [*L'innesto*] and *Man, Beast and Virtue* (*L'uomo, la bestia e la virtú*] in 1919; *All for the Best* [*Tutto per bene*], *As Before, Better than Before*

[*Come prima, meglio di prima*], *Chee-Chee* [*Cecè*], and *Mrs. Morli, One and Two* [*La Signora morli, una e due*] in 1920) and abroad, especially after the opening of SIX CHARACTERS IN SEARCH OF AN AUTHOR (*Sei personaggi in cerca d'autore*) 1921.

But Pirandello's career as a playwright could be conflicted at times. Alongside enthusiastic supporters, both the public and critics were often hostile to his works, as they introduced controversial novelties in conflict with conventional practices in the theater. Reactions after *Six Characters*, in Rome in 1921, were indicative: public outcry against the play and its author was so vehement that Pirandello had to remain backstage and could only leave the theater by a backdoor after everyone else had left. With *Six Characters*, Pirandello gained a name as an important figure in contemporary theater both in Italy and in the wider European world. He had begun to portray on stage the "uneasiness" of representation, dramatizing tensions between the text, the characters, and their author. These metatheatrical developments, in many ways revolutionary, continued to occupy Pirandello for the rest of his career. In 1922, *Henry IV* (*Enrico IV*) and *Clothe the Naked* (*Vestire dli ignudi*) were performed; in 1923, *The Man with the Flower in His Mouth* (*L'uomo dal fiore in bocca*) and *The Life I Gave You* (*La vita che ti diedi*); and in 1924, *Each in His Own Way* (*Ciascuno a suo modo*).

In 1923 Pirandello began to travel abroad, to follow and oversee various productions of his plays, and in 1924 a "Pirandello Season" was produced on Broadway. Then in 1925 he accepted the opportunity to found and direct the Teatro d'Arte di Roma, which sought to promote young and promising playwrights. This position brought him closer to the world and daily lives of actors, giving him a privileged glimpse into and understanding of actors and their experiences. The Teatro d'Arte was also the magical place where Pirandello met Marta Abba, a young Milanese woman who became the company's star actress and with whom the writer would develop an intense and affectionate relationship. After a long period of pain and unhappiness in his marriage and family life, Marta Abba appeared and erased his past. Suddenly, with her youthful presence, she brightened the unhappy life of the writer. In time she would grow into a kind of obsession of his, which exercised a profound influence on his later works. With Marta Abba the female characters in his plays acquired a new, more definite profile and an unmistakable voice, creating the new woman of Pirandellian theater. Before Marta Abba his female characters tended to be diffuse, secondary figures in dramas written largely for male leading roles. These stage women, oppressed by confusions and incapable of finding their own identities, seem inspired by Pirandello's experience with his wife. With Marta Abba the female character becomes the protagonist and is at last capable of dominating the stage in her own right, giving dramatic expression to the conflict between life and form (see below). One can see this total fusion of writer and actress in *Diana and Tuda* (*Diana e la Tuda*, 1926), *The New Colony* (*La nuova colonia*,

1928), and in *As You Desire Me* (*Come tu mi vuoi*, 1930), the play that fits Marta Abba probably better than any other work Pirandello wrote for her. *As You Desire Me* remains even today the most unforgettable example of creative collaboration between a playwright and a performer.

In 1924, after the assassination of socialist leader Giacomo Matteotti, Pirandello joined the Fascist Party, a common enough move of self-preservation for intellectuals in the confusion of the times, but by 1927 Pirandello began to question the decision, and he considered moving elsewhere.

During that three-year period the Teatro d'Arte took Pirandello as a director around the world (touring Europe and South America, provoking everywhere both enthusiasm and criticism), accompanied by Marta Abba. For some time, however, the company's finances had been precarious due to bad administration, and on its return from South America to Italy, collapsing under the weight of debts, it attempted a comeback in November 1927. After the last performances, in Viareggio in August 1928, the Teatro d'Arte company foundered. Pirandello, disillusioned and exhausted, but always eager to begin again, decided to move to Germany, and Marta Abba and her sister Cele went with him.

Though busy with many international duties, his creative activity continued. In 1926 he published the novel *Uno, nessuno e centomila* (*One, None, and One Hundred Thousand*). In 1928–1929, in Berlin, he wrote *Belonging to One or No One* (*O di uno o di nessuno*) and TONIGHT WE IMPROVISE (*Questa sera si recita soggetto*), performed in German at Koenigsberg in 1930, and soon after in Berlin, *Lazarus* (*Lazzaro*, performed in 1929 first in ENGLAND, then in Turin), and for Marta Abba—who by March 1929 had returned to Italy—*As You Desire Me*, which she inaugurated with great success on February 18, 1930, at Milan's Filodrammatici Theater. However, in the Hollywood film version of *As You Desire Me* made two years later, Marta Abba was replaced by a bigger name: Greta Garbo. That same year *Tonight We Improvise* premiered in Germany and Italy. Pirandello also began working on *The Mountain Giants* (*I giganti della montagna*), the play that would occupy him until the end of his life, ultimately remaining unfinished. His last few plays include *To Find Oneself* (*Trovarsi*, 1932), written for Marta Abba; *When You Are Somebody* (*Quando si è Qualcuno*, 1933); *The Fable of the Changeling* (*La favola del figlio cambiato*, 1934); *One Doesn't Know How* (*Non si sa come*, 1935); and *Dream, But Maybe Not* (*Sogno ma forse no*, 1936).

All this literary activity brought him much honorific recognition, including his election to the Accademia d'Italia (1929), and most notably, on December 10, 1934, he received the Nobel Prize for Literature. On December 10 of that year, ill with pneumonia, he died at his house in Rome while working on his last play, *The Mountain Giants*. For his funeral Pirandello left precise instructions requesting an inconspicuous private ceremony:

1) My death should pass in silence. From my friends and enemies, the courtesy not to publicize it in the newspapers, not even the slightest reference. No obituary, no announcements. 2) Once dead, I should not be dressed. Wrap me naked in a sheet. No flowers on the bed. No candles lit. 3) A carriage of the lowest class, that of paupers. Naked. No one is to accompany me, neither relatives nor friends. A carriage, a horse, and a coachman—it's sufficient. 4) Burn me. And my body, once turned to dust, let it be dispersed so that nothing, not even my ashes, will remain. But if this cannot be done, the urn should be brought to Sicily and interred in a rough stone in the countryside of Girgenti where I was born.

These last requests, it would seem, were a dismissive gesture to reigning social conventions in Italy; but it was also something of an implicit criticism of the fascist regime, which Pirandello knew would try to exploit the memorial of his death for its own propagandistic purposes.

From these last requests one can surmise that Pirandello, in his life's conclusion as in his works, wished to convey the message of a life lived without a mask, without concealment, revealing instead its "naked" truth. It is from this perspective that one best approaches his written works as well, beginning with his essays, where Pirandello articulates in theory his vision of life and its representation in writing or on the stage. For central to all his work in different genres is his preoccupation with character, both as a literary or aesthetic fiction and as a problematic psychological entity.

ESSAYS

Early on Pirandello undertook theoretical investigations on fundamental problems of aesthetics and personality. These eventually served as a basis for his theatrical imagination. In essays published in the 1890s the young Pirandello dealt with problems of science and especially psychology. In *Arte e coscienze d'oggi* (*Art and Consciences Today*, 1893) he expresses his interest in Max Nordau's theories, as discussed in his two best-known books *Conventional Lies of Society* (1883) and *Degeneration* (1892), on contemporary moral crises. He attributes some responsibility for humanity's bewilderment to science, which had undermined many traditional points of reference and destabilized conventional measures of value. RELIGION, too, had become largely incapable of answering pressing questions of conscience. This inadequacy is conveyed in his conclusion that certain knowledge about life is no longer possible, only impressions "mutable and various."

In 1900 Pirandello published *Scienza e critica estetica* (*Science and Aesthetic Criticism*; later expanded and reissued in 1908 as *Arte e scienza* [*Art and Science*]), where he discusses the work of psychologist Alfred Binet, *Les altérations de la personalité* (*Deteriorations of the Personality*, 1892), which constituted the basis of a subjective and relativistic mode of knowledge, the direction in which Pirandello's thought was moving. In Binet he finds a concept of the psyche congenial to his view as a dramatic artist: the dissolution of a stable ego image, and the coexistence of and conflict between multiple personalities. Pirandello also found in Binet scientific explanations of that unconscious part of the ego, described as a seat of dark and covert desires, of irrational and instinctive impulses, that unconscious that Sigmund Freud too was exploring in those years. But Binet's theories were enough to fuel Pirandello's own explorations of the kinds of identity crises that random turns of events might provoke. His dramatic plots often hinge on just such scenarios of personality disruption.

In his essay *On Humor*, Pirandello emphasizes the reflexive component, that pause for reflection that intervenes in the genesis of art, explaining how humor brings into art the problem of existence. He observes that if art is ordinarily created in a harmonious form, so that thought conceals itself within the conception of any comic work, reflection serves to analyze and distill perceptions, and this secondary thought process will generate another impression that Pirandello called the "sense of the opposite" (*sentimento del contrario*). To render his idea more concrete, Pirandello sketched a famous example of an elderly woman:

> I see an old lady whose hair is dyed and completely smeared with some kind of horrible ointment; she is all made-up in a clumsy and awkward fashion and is all dolled-up like a young girl. I begin to laugh. I *perceive* that she is *the opposite* of what a respectable old lady should be. Now I could stop here at this initial and superficial comic reaction: the comic consists precisely of this *perception of the opposite*. But if, at this point, reflection intervenes to suggest that perhaps this old lady finds no pleasure in dressing up like an exotic parrot, and that perhaps she is distressed by it and does it only because she pitifully deceives herself into believing that, by making herself up like that and by concealing her wrinkles and gray hair, she may be able to hold the love of her much younger husband—if reflection comes to suggest all this, then I can no longer laugh at her as I did at first, exactly because the inner working of reflection has made me go beyond, or rather enter deeper into, the initial stage of awareness: from the beginning *perception of the opposite*, reflection has made me shift to a *sense of the opposite*. And herein lies the precise difference between the comic and humor. (Pirandello, 1974).

Reflection, then, functions to divide up the various images of perception, every appearance of reality, every form that like a living prison inside each person distances them from an authentic existence and constrains them to mask themselves behind false identities. Following Binet, Pirandello describes the personality as a dynamic equilibrium, a constant oscillation between opposing poles, a struggle among the hopes, forebodings, memories, and perceptions that tend to dominate the personality, in other words, a dichotomy between "life" and "form." Life is that continual flux people are always trying to stop, to fix in definite

forms (concepts, ideas, conditions) in a constant effort to make things coherent and stable. But inside human beings, life's flux continues, formless and undivided, transcending the limits we impose on it to construct a personality. The art of humor searches for the true causes of our behavior, beyond social pretensions, beyond the reasons we provide, which are not as logical as they may often appear. "There are in man four, five souls struggling amongst themselves." It is the task of the humorist, then, to divide out one's fragmentary internal characters into their separate parts and highlight the contradictions among them. On the stage these fragments of personality might become distinct characters, and their interactions, relations, and conflicts the dramatic action itself.

Despite so much dramatization of abstract philosophical theories, Pirandello's interest focuses mainly on the existential crisis of contemporary humanity, deprived of values and reference points to guide them in a chaotic and fragmented world. For this reason also, social life, from a humoristic-relativistic perspective, is always the site of inauthentic existence that conceals and defends itself with lies. From this one may conclude that individuals, in relationship with others, dissimulate and perform roles, or close themselves off either out of ineptitude or out of a need for reassurance or simply out of a desire to be left alone in whatever crystallized form others project upon them. At this point any unpredictable event might cause this form to explode, an eruptive manifestation of the real life that lies beyond the prison of forms and roles that we put on and perform. Many of Pirandello's characters suffer this sort of traumatic experience, and after realizing with pain and surprise the fragmentation of their personality, the characters attain a relativism that refracts into innumerable images, corresponding to and determined by others' perceptions and judgments, which before had led to the loss of identity.

The persisting idea, then, that animates all his works—novels, short stories, and plays—is the drama of inner torments common to the human condition. In particular, it was problems of personality that he continually studied and represented in all its aspects, especially its social dimensions.

NOVELS

For reasons just discussed, Pirandello's novels often explore similar themes as in his short stories and plays. His novels' characters, in fact, often seem to exist in a world that is already a grotesque masquerade of "real" life. His first novel, *The Outcast*, written in 1893–1894 and originally titled *Marta Ajala*, is a dramatic story about a woman cast out of her family after her husband accuses her unjustly of an extramarital affair. Her eventual reacceptance in her family is fraught with irony, however, because by this time she has committed the very sin she was originally accused of. *Il Turno* (*The Turn*, 1895), his second novel, has many humorous touches, and the rules of life are fragmented by unexpected and fortuitous events. His early masterpiece followed, *The Late Mattia Pascal* (1904), the first work to give Pirandello some recognition abroad. It deals with the "double" of a man, Mattia Pascal, whom people believe is dead (therefore "late") but who becomes for awhile Adriano Meis. Here Pirandello's concept of the "sense of the contrary," defined in his essay *On Humor*, seems to have its first creative incarnation. *The Old and the Young*, published between January and November 1909 in the periodical *Rassegna Contemporanea*, Pirandello described as a "novel of Sicily after 1870, very bitter and crowded, which contains the drama of my generation." A historical novel of sorts, it deals with the events of the *Fasci siciliani*, the birth of labor unions and the Banca Romana scandal. The writer describes the dissolution—and disillusion—of the Risorgimento and the disappointments of the young intellectuals who believed in the new socialist movement.

This historical scene is then replaced by the satirical atmosphere of Rome's literary society described in *Her Husband* (1911). Pirandello had to remove the book from circulation to appease the writer Grazie Deledda, who recognized herself in the novel's main character, Silvia Roncella, a strong woman who upends conventional family roles by dominating her husband Giustino Boggiolo. An unfinished revised version was published posthumously under the sarcastically upside-down title *Giustino Roncella, "Maiden Name" Boggiolo*. In *Action!* Pirandello introduces the theme of moviemaking (published in the *Nuova Antologia* in June–August 1915 and reissued ten years later as *The Notebooks of Serafino Gubbio, Cameraman*). Here Pirandello represents the mounting crisis of modern man in relation to the technological apparatus that allows the main character, a cameraman for Kosmograph studios, to see through the camera's lens the fragmentation of human beings, the consequent estrangement of humankind from natural feelings and behavior, which in the end annuls his very being. For professional reasons, Serafino Gubbio comes to identify himself with the hand that turns the movie camera's crank: he views himself as merely a part of the motion picture camera. But in the act of telling his story he recuperates his humanity and destroys the unfeeling mechanism that before had trapped him. *Serafino Gubbio* was an important early literary response to the new artistic and technological mode of cinematic representation, which seemed to transform theatrical productions into mass-produced market commodities.

Returning to themes and formal elements from *Mattia Pascal*, in 1925–1926 Pirandello published in *La Fiera letteraria* the novel *Uno, nessuno e centomila* (*One, Nobody and One Hundred Thousand*). Like the earlier work, it explores ideas about the doubling, even the multiplication, of identity. Here doubling extends to the dissociation of being and appearance for the protagonist Gengè, who realizes that everyone perceives him in their own way, not just in external aspects of appearance, but also that each person has a distinct idea of his character and personality. Hence the title: each person is not "one" but "one hundred thousand" and therefore "nobody." (As Gengè says at one point: "I believe I am, I delude myself that I am one. Instead, I am nobody: for those who see me, I am one hundred thousand, because I appear different in the perceptions of each.") Therefore he conceives the desire to destroy all the false images that other have constructed of him, in order to search for an authentic self concealed in the many masks and "forms" that falsify his true self. The novel's genesis was long and complex. Already in 1922 Pirandello, announcing its imminent publication, suggested an intimate relationship between this new novel and his plays: "This novel should have been the preface to my theatrical works; instead it will be an epilogue." Indeed, he had begun the work much earlier, but his novels had been sidelined in intervening years as theater increasingly occupied his time and energy.

SHORT STORIES

Unlike the longer, more time-consuming novel, the short-story form was a creative outlet for his many ideas, and Pirandello turned to it readily throughout his career, especially as a means for sketching out ideas for the theater. Although critical attention to his short stories has often been overshadowed by greater interest in his plays, it would be unfair to count these among his minor works. In fact, many consider Pirandello a genius of the short story, for his originality, inventiveness, acute introspection, and analysis of characters who often occupy lower social strata: busy officeworkers, petty clerks, corrupt and corrupting lawyers, restless small-time businessmen, small crowds tormented by little problems that make their lives unbearable. They are often like sketch COMEDIES of everyday life, even comedies of errors. Pirandello has with some reason been compared to William Shakespeare for his perceptive representation of quotidian affairs. His characters are men and women incapable of adjusting to reality because their fixations on specific ideas or notions render them unable to follow the continual flux of their lives. Pirandello's master plan was to write 365 short stories, one for each day of the year. Thus the stories are collected under the title *Novelle per un anno* (*Novels for a Year*). But this plan was never achieved—there are only 245—again on account of the overwhelming activity in the theater. Nevertheless, critics have expressed great admiration for his short stories, ranking him among other great artists of the genre, like ANTON CHEKHOV and concluded that he thought of human identity as the product of perception and circumstance. Like mirrors, people reflect the world around them. Pirandello's life and his art symbolize the struggle between one's true self and the selves society imposes. The intensity of their representations display his great talent for sketching rich pictures of life in rapid, urgent and vital dialogues between characters oppressed by adverse destinies from which they cannot escape and against which they are powerless. Nor do their comic aspects avoid caricature and the grotesque. In all this, Pirandello's own experience, which he dissected, subjected to scrutiny, and continually recomposed into different configurations, scenarios, and situations, was critical. Indeed, even before he wrote plays, it was in short stories that Pirandello plumbed the depths of human character, behavior, its rationalizations, and underlying motives. And in moving from prose fiction to dramatic forms, Pirandello often drew ideas first sketched out in his short stories in order to shape his dramas that scrutinize the semblances of reality, casting them into relativity, diffracting it into its constituent parts.

THEATER

To understand Pirandello, one must remember of his career that Pirandello has been identified as an "intellectual" playwright, more interested in ideas than in people, more concerned with abstractions than with their applicability to particular situations. His characters are often attacked for being either puppets manipulated for his own ends or abstractions lacking flesh and blood. The character given the most abstract speeches in any play is usually identified as a *raisoneur* figure (the director), created to represent the playwright's viewpoint and to expound his philosophy.

Pirandello's plays do explore such complex issues as the multiplicity of human personality, the relativity of truth, and the difficulty—if not impossibility—of establishing boundaries between reality and illusion. The focus, however, is usually on the characters' interactions with these concepts, their struggles to deal with the effects such ideas have on their lives. As Pirandello himself wrote, "My works are born from living images, which are the perennial source of art; but these images pass through a filter of concepts that have taken hold of me. Without a doubt no work of art is ever a concept trying to express itself through images; on the contrary, it is an image, often one of life's most vivid images, that, nourishing itself in the travails of my spirit, assumes by itself, for the sole legitimate consistency of the work of art, a universal value." Ideas do not exist in a vacuum for Pirandello, and any attempt to discuss his philosophy at a remove from those characters, treating them as symbols or puppets and not people, risks grave distortion of his work. Pirandello himself, in 1935, a year after winning the Nobel Prize and a year before his death, wrote the following evaluation of his critics: "The world of international literary criticism has been crowded for a long time with numerous Pirandellos—lame, deformed, all head and no heart, gruff, insane and obscure—in whom, no matter how hard I try, I cannot recognize myself, not even in the slightest degree."

The theater was the perfect medium for Pirandello's artistic expression, for what better place to deal with illusion, pretense, and role-playing than where actors assume a role for an audience that accepts them as characters and yet is also aware of their existence as actors? Pirandello realizes that a character's theatricality need not be unexamined or unconscious, that it can be used by its possessor for certain ends. He uses the the-

ater self-consciously in the same way, to examine itself and its relationship to life. Just as the masks and illusions of life need to be examined, with the assistance of the humorist who probes beneath their surfaces, so in the same way the theater, both the mirror of human actions and the source of what it sometimes reflects, must be examined as it is being used to communicate insights into the human activities it imitates. Thus in the plays usually referred to as his theater trilogy—*Six Characters in Search of an Author*, *Each in His Own Way*, and *Tonight We Improvise*—Pirandello pushes theater into modernism by exploring theatrical process and its relationship to the world it mirrors. Although not composed as a trilogy in the usual sense, with continuity of either chronology or plot and character, the three plays form a unity because each is set in the theater and takes theatrical experience as its subject matter and its major metaphor for the author's vision of life.

All three of the theater trilogy plays break through the imaginary "fourth wall" of realistic theater in an attempt to destroy the barrier between auditorium and stage. Although all three include many common dramatic figures, the focus of each work is on one of the three essential components of the process: *Six Characters* emphasizes the subject matter, the characters whose script is dramatized onstage; *Each in His Own Way*, the audience that views the theatrical performance; and *Tonight We Improvise*, the actors who interpret the script and bring it to life for the audience. Despite this difference in perspective for each play, the trilogy as a whole becomes an examination of the relationship between theater and life, their interdependence and interpenetration.

In particular, with *Six Characters*, still his best-known play, Pirandello made a sharp break with his previous work, initiating a revolutionary turn in theater. It opened the window between the stage and audience and eliminated many familiar theatrical trappings. Between 1921, when *Six Characters* premiered, and 1925 the author subjected the play's text to four different revisions. Most important, in 1924 Pirandello added a *Preface*, conceived in a polemical spirit and aimed in part at his critics, as a self-defense and counterargument, and in part at his audience, who had refused to understand his art. The *Preface* now assumes a capital importance. As the key to penetrating the complex Pirandellian world, it is a sure aid to interpreting not only the play that the *Preface* discusses but also most of his work. In the first part of the *Preface* Pirandello discusses his theory of art; in the second he offers a critical interpretation of his play. For its general theoretical statements, the first part is most interesting. Pirandello, servant of "fantasia"—the inventive force—has to interpret what his imagination creates from a universal viewpoint. The imagination has an absolute value, autonomous and present in each author as *nature spontaneously revealed*.

"The mystery of artistic creation," Pirandello writes, "is the same mystery as natural birth." Nature is creative force, and an author is nothing other than a means through which nature labors and produces. An author has but two choices: either accept that nature works through the author as medium, so that the creation of art takes place, or refuse to provide a medium for nature, so that creation is renounced.

In the second part of the *Preface* Pirandello discusses a problem fundamental to *Six Characters* and to other plays of the same period: the conflict between "having form" and "being form." All that "has form" is condemned to continual change, which ends up destroying that form. All that "is form" is immutable and eternal. Every work of art, every character born alive in the mind of an author and fixed in life by means of the word, is form. A character is static in form and never suffers change. A human being, a being who by nature "has form" and changes day by day, is forced to act in different ways. In the *Six Characters* the vision is twofold: the Father, like every other character, is form, but as a human symbol he rebels against the fixity of the form in which he feels himself bound. The father suffers from having been caught in a particular moment of his life and for being judged solely for this. In human affairs there cannot be fixity of form. Nevertheless, all of Pirandello's characters are possessed of this dual force: as characters in themselves they *are form*—immutable and eternal— but as symbols of human beings they *have form*, often fighting against that form's mutability.

These are some of the reasons why Pirandello is considered one of the foremost innovators in 20th-century theater. GEORGE BERNARD SHAW is said to have called the *Six Characters* the most original play ever written, and more than eighty years after its first performance in 1921, the play's power to fascinate is undiminished.

In the author's last creative period, beginning around 1928–1929, Pirandello entrusts his tortured investigations of truth to "myths," as a last hope for coherence, even if illusory, in the face of the relentless fragmentation of forms. The rejection of the world of contingency, against which Pirandello had first reacted with irony and then with dramatic contempt, develops finally into a nostalgic aspiration to a mythic absolute that will generate a new form of fabulous and surrealistic theater. Again, also decisive for this period was his encounter with Marta Abba, the actress for whom he wrote *Diana and Tuda*, *The Wifes' Friend* (1927), and *The New Colony*. Works from this time are suffused with autobiography, reflecting his love for Marta Abba and displaying a depth of emotional expression not found in his earlier work. *The New Colony* is the first stage in his new "mythic theater," in this case a utopian vision of love and basic human solidarity that leads a band of outlaws and a prostitute, La Spera, to take refuge on a deserted island, abandoned by its inhabitants because it might sink into the sea. This ideal community is doomed to fail when "the others" arrive on the island, that is, people already corrupted. An earthquake makes this fallen garden of Eden crumble into the sea, all except the tip of a rock, on which La Spera and her infant son take refuge; it rises up to bear witness to this first miracle of Pirandellian theater.

Society cannot be changed, and only the natural maternal instinct is allowed to survive the final cataclysm.

Pirandello confronts religious dilemmas in *Lazarus* (1929), the second "myth," focusing on the fanatic asceticism that leads Diego Spina to sacrifice himself and his family. The presence of God, however, allows two miracles: Diego is hit by a car and dies but is resurrected thanks to an injection a doctor gives him; and the little daughter Lia, who is paralyzed, miraculously regains her ability to walk.

The third and last "myth," *The Mountain Giants*, intended as a final artistic statement opposing artistic values to the spiritual coarseness of the world, would remain unfinished. In this work, many themes and motives gathered, some giving rise to separate plays, including *As You Desire Me* and *The Fable of the Changeling*. Three worlds stand opposed in the play: that of the Scalognati ("the Unfortunate"), isolated in a villa, at the will of the magician Cotrone (really a stage director who uses theatrical and cinematic devices learned from ERWIN PISCATOR and MAX REINHARDT), where the images of his imagination take shape; that of the Actors, who arrive at the villa with the first actress Ilse wanting to stage a play called *The Fable of the Changeling* (a sly reference to the author's own work); and finally the world of the Giants, personifications of brutal reality who represent the builders of new industry, with huge muscles but hard and thoughtless minds. His eight years of correspondence with Marta Abba testify strongly to the many apprehensions and hopes wrapped up in this last drama, meant as a testament to the power of fantasy and poetry and to the TRAGEDY of art in a brutal modern world. The myth of *The Mountain Giants* was a constant companion through the vicissitudes in the relationship between writer and actress. In a sense, then, the final Marta, the truest Marta, is Ilse (the incarnation of the ultimate sacrifice of self to art) of *The Mountain Giants*, a work that was, by its very nature, unable to be finished, perhaps for reasons above and beyond the death of the author.

PLAYS: *Limes from Sicily* (Lumíe di Sicilia, 1910); *The Vise* (La morsa, 1910); *The Doctor's Duty* (Il dovere del medico, 1913); *If Not So* (Se non cosí, 1915); *Think It Over, Giacomino!* (Pensaci, Giacomino!, 1916); *The Cap to Sonagli* (Il berretto a sonagli, 1917); *The Jar* (La giara, 1917); *Liolà* (1917); *The Pleasure of Honesty* (Il piacere dell'onestà, 1917); *Right You Are (If You Think You Are)* (Cosí è se vi pare, 1917); *The Rules of the Game* (Il giuoco delle parti, 1918); *This Time It Will Be Different* (Ma non è una cosa seria, 1918); *Grafted* (L'innesto, 1919); *Man, Beast and Virtue* (L'uomo, la bestia e la virtú, 1919); *The Patent* (La patente, 1919); *All for the Best* (Tutto per bene, 1920); *As Before, Better than Before* (Come prima, meglio di prima, 1920); *Chee-Chee* (Cecè, 1920); *Mrs. Morli, One and Two* (La Signora Morli, una e due, 1920); *Six Characters in Search of an Author* (Sei personaggi in cerca d'autore, 1921); *At the Gate* (All'uscita, 1922); *Henry IV* (Enrico IV, 1922); *The Imbecile* (L'imbecille, 1922); *Clothe the naked* (Vestire dli ignudi, 1923); *The House with the Column* (L'altro figlio, 1923); *The Life I Gave You* (La vita che ti diedi, 1923); *The Man with the*

Flower in His Mouth (*L'uomo dal fiore in bocca*, 1923); *Each in His Own Way* (*Ciascuno a suo modo*, 1924); *Our Lord of the Ship* (*Sagra del Signore della nave*, 1925); *Diana and Tuda* (*Diana e la Tuda*, 1926); *Bellavita* (1927); *The Wifes' Friend* (*L'amica delle mogli*, 1927); *The New Colony* (*La nuova colonia*, 1928); *Scamandro* (1928); *Belonging to One or No One* (*O di uno o di nessuno*, 1929); *Lazarus* (*Lazzaro*, 1929); *As You Desire Me* (*Come tu mi vuoi*, 1930); *Tonight We Improvise* (*Questa sera si recita a soggetto*, 1930); *To Find Oneself* (*Trovarsi*, 1932); *The Fable of the Changeling* (*La favola del figlio cambiato*, 1934); *When You Are Somebody* (*Quando si è Qualcuno*, 1934); *One Doesn't Know How* (*Non si sa come*, 1935); *Dream, But Maybe Not* (*Sogno ma forse no*, 1936); *The Mountain Giants* (*I giganti della montagna*, unfinished, 1936)

FURTHER READING

Bassnett, Susan. *Luigi Pirandello.* New York: Macmillan, 1983.

Biasin, Gian-Paolo, and Manuela Gieri, eds. *Luigi Pirandello: Contemporary Perspectives.* Toronto: Univ. of Toronto Press, 1999.

Borsellino, Nino. *Ritratti e immagini di Pirandello* [Portraits and Images of Pirandello]. Rome: Laterza, 1991.

Bragaglia, Leonardo. *Interpreti pirandelliani* [Pirandellian Performers]. Rome: Trevi, 1969.

Büdel, Oscar. *Pirandello.* London: Bowes and Bowes, 1966.

D'Amico, Alessandro, and Tinterri, Alessandro, eds. *Pirandello capocomico* [Pirandello, Leader of the Theater Company]. Palermo: Sellerio, 1987.

DiGaetani, John Louis. *A Companion to Pirandello Studies.* Westport, Conn.: Greenwood Press, 1991.

Giudice, Gaspare. *Luigi Pirandello,* Turin: UTET, 1963.

Macchia, Giovanni. *Pirandello o la stanza della tortura* [Pirandello of the Tortured Characters]. Milan: Mondadori, 1981.

Oliver, Roger W. *Dreams of Passion: The Theater of Luigi Pirandello.* New York: N.Y. Univ. Press, 1979.

Pirandello, Luigi. *On Humor.* Tr. by A. Illiano and D. P. Testa. Chapel Hill: Univ. of North Carolina Press, 1974.

Sogliuzzo, A. Richard. *Luigi Pirandello, Director: The Playwright in the Theatre.* New York: Scarecrow, 1982.

Vicentini, Claudio. *Il disagio del teatro* [The Uneasiness of the Theatrical Performance]. Venice: Marsilio, 1993.

Pietro Frassica

PISCATOR, ERWIN (1893–1966)

Erwin Piscator pioneered the "epic" style of theater production, which in his particular case meant highly stylized and mechanized productions featuring wide-ranging social content and communist ideology. Piscator was born on December 17, 1893, in Ulm, GERMANY. After an internship at Munich's Hoftheater, he was drafted into the German army in 1915, serving two years in combat, a radicalizing experience that convinced him that the stage must serve as a platform for left-wing politics. He joined the German Communist Party in 1918 and in 1920 became a founding member of Berlin's Proletarian Theater.

In 1924 he was invited to direct at Berlin's Volksbühne, where he staged Alfons Paquet's (1881–1944) *Flags* (*Fahnen*), a play about labor agitation in Chicago. The first of Piscator's productions to be labeled "epic drama," *Flags* used a revolving stage, presentational ACTING, characterization based on social stereotypes, and projections of scene titles, posters, and newspaper headlines to reveal the relationships between politics and economics that shape daily life. For Piscator the set "would symbolize the social order" (Braun, 1982). In the two years following the success of *Flags*, Piscator staged eleven productions including Paquet's *Tidal Wave* (*Sturmflut*, 1926), a revolutionary fantasy in which he incorporated motion pictures in the mise-en-scène for the first time. Later he adopted a device known as the *Schicksalsbühne*, or "stage of fate," a glass platform lit from beneath that depersonalized the actors performing on it, turning them into projections of historical or social forces.

In 1927 Piscator left the Volksbühne and started his own company, the Piscator Bühne, which was to be housed in a new facility, the famous "Total Theater" designed by Walter Gropius (1883–1969). This project never materialized. Instead the Piscator Bühne was installed at Berlin's Theater am Nollendorfplatz where, in 1928, Piscator staged ERNST TOLLER's *Hoppla, Such Is Life!* (*Hoppla, wir leben!*) and an adaptation of Max Brod (1884–1968) and Hans Reimann's (1889–1969) *Adventures of the Good Soldier Schweik.* The theater's "Dramaturgical Collective" included BERTOLT BRECHT, who collaborated on a number of productions, including the *Schweik* adaptation. Brecht would go on to incorporate many of Piscator's ideas in his own version of EPIC THEATER. The 1929 bankruptcy of the Piscator Bühne marked the end of the major phase of Piscator's career. Following a brief prison term on tax charges, he decamped to RUSSIA in 1931, staying until Joseph Stalin's campaign against "formalism" in the arts made it prudent to move elsewhere.

Piscator settled in New York in 1939, forming a Dramatic Workshop and a Studio Theater at the New School for Social Research. Among his American productions were adaptations of *War and Peace* (1942) and *All the King's Men* (1948). In 1951 he returned to Germany, becoming director of the Freie Volksbühne in West Berlin in 1962. Among the major accomplishments of his last years was the staging of DOCUMENTARY plays by HEINAR KIPPHARDT and PETER WEISS and his production of ROLF HOCHHUTH's *The Deputy* (*Der Stellvertreter*, 1963), which helped restore Piscator to prominence after a period of relative obscurity.

At the height of his career Piscator was a major figure of the cultural Left. His theater was an important asset to the Communist Party, attracting the attention of Berlin-based agents of Stalin who advised him on its affairs. He died on March 30, 1966, in Starnberg, West Germany.

FURTHER READING

Braun, Edward. *The Director and the Stage: From Naturalism to Grotowski.* New York: Holmes & Meier, 1982.

Innes, C. D. *Erwin Piscator's Political Theatre: The Development of Modern German Drama*. Cambridge: Cambridge Univ. Press, 1972.

Piscator, Erwin. *The Political Theatre*. Tr. by Hugh Rorrison. New York: Avon Bks., 1978.

Martin Andrucki

PLATONOV

By scholarly convention, not authorial intention, *Platonov* (1878; also known as *Fatherlessness* and *Play Without a Title*), ANTON CHEKHOV's first large-scale drama, is named after its main protagonist. Found among the playwright's papers after his death, *Platonov* anticipates Chekhov's four major dramas but departs sharply from them in its structure and frequent theatrical clichés. The long, ungainly *Platonov* dwarfs the later plays and lacks the economy of Chekhov's best work. Nonetheless, Chekhov pinned high hopes on this apprentice piece and submitted it to the famous actress Maria Ermolova, hoping for a production at the Maly Theater. Ermolova rejected the play, and the playwright set *Platonov* aside. Its publication in 1923 came nearly twenty years after Chekhov's death.

In *Platonov*, Chekhov treats the breakdown of the old order for the first time in dramatic form. The confrontation between a vital, if uncultured, business class and a failing aristocracy is starker here than in the later work. Vengerovich and Bugrov, two businessmen, lack the moral complexity and self-awareness of a character like Lopakhin in THE CHERRY ORCHARD and garner less sympathy. Likewise, the aristocratic Anna Voinitseva lacks the tragic quality of a Ranevskaia (also in *The Cherry Orchard*) even though both are widows who stand to lose their estates.

The meandering plot threatens to disintegrate at times. Its unity, such as it is, depends on its eponymous protagonist, who issues from a long line of superfluous men, ineffectual members of the intelligentsia burdened by the consciousness of their own inadequacy. Like his literary forebears, Platonov remembers the high hopes of his youth and grapples with the disparity between those aspirations and adult reality. At times, he lashes out at society, and several of his speeches recall the acidic judgments of Aleksandr Griboedov's Chatsky in Griboedov's *Woe from Wit* (1824). Unlike Chatsky, however, Platonov is weak. To the chagrin of his wife Sasha, he loses himself in love affairs. Chekhov's portraits of the highly individuated women with whom Platonov becomes involved constitute one of the play's strengths. Voinitseva's aimless, destructive lust stands in sharp contrast to Maria Grekova's idealism. However, the play's pivotal romance involves Platonov and his first love, Voinitseva's daughter-in-law Sofia, who offers him a new life (a theme characteristic of Chekhov's later work). Platonov is too weak to embrace it, and the culmination of the plot takes on a melodramatic coloration as threats of and attempts at suicide and murder follow one another in quick succession. Despite its overwrought emotionalism, the ending grows organically out of the dramatic material and reflects Chekhov's intuitive grasp of the rules of drama: Sofia cannot abide Platonov's betrayal and, in anger, shoots him.

Although *Platonov* suffers from theatrical clichés and prolixity, it introduces many of Chekhov's most important themes and demonstrates his early mastery of characterization. When he returned to drama years later, he abandoned the play of direct action and sought a new form that would come to fruition in his four masterpieces.

[*See also* Russia and the Soviet Union]

FURTHER READING

Chekhov, Anton. *Platonov*. In *The Oxford Chekhov Vol. 2*, ed. and tr. by Ronald Hingley. New York: Oxford Univ. Press, 1964.

Eekman, Thomas A. "Anton Chekhov and His Play Without a Title." In *Critical Essays on Anton Chekhov*, ed. by Thomas A. Eekman. Boston: G. K. Hall, 1989.

Gilman, Richard. *Chekhov's Plays: An Opening Into Eternity*. New Haven, Conn.: Yale Univ. Press, 1995.

Magarshack, David. *Chekhov the Dramatist*. New York: Hill & Wang, 1960.

Timothy C. Westphalen

THE PLAYBOY OF THE WESTERN WORLD

The Playboy of the Western World, J. M. SYNGE's most famous play, was first produced by the National Theatre Society at the Abbey Theatre on January 26, 1907, under the direction of W. G. Fay, who also played the lead role of Christy Mahon, while Maire O'Neill (Synge's own beloved) took the part of Pegeen Mike, the Playboy's sweetheart. The action of the play takes place in a pub on the Belmullet peninsula of County Mayo in the West of IRELAND, a wild lonely territory. It is night when a stranger, Christy Mahon, caked with mud from long travels by foot, arrives at the pub seeking shelter and a hiding place. The barmaid, Pegeen Mike, and the other townspeople soon get it out of him that he is on the run because he killed his own father with the blow of a loy, a spade for digging potatoes. The people are ready to help nearly any man in flight from the hated British police, but they are especially impressed by a man who had the courage to kill his father.

Christy is hired by Pegeen's father to help out in the pub, and he soon manages to sweet-talk Pegeen out of her engagement with her cousin, the cowardly, priest-fearing Shawn Keogh. Life was never so good for Christy, who had had no idea before that a woman could love him or that he had anything to offer. His triumph is upset by the arrival, with a bloody bandage around his head, of his father, Old Mahon. Before Christy can be exposed as a liar, the Widow Quin—who loves him herself—sends the father off on a false trail. Yet he recognizes his son before he is clear of the town, and the people turn on Christy. Hoping to win their admiration once again, and to keep his beloved Pegeen, he strikes his father a second time, but the townspeople have come to see the difference between a great story and a dirty deed. They tie him up, where he is to stay until he can be hanged by the authorities. But Old Mahon comes back from the dead a second time, and father and son, laughing at what fools there are in Mayo, go prancing off together, leaving Pegeen to wail at the play's curtain that she has "lost the only playboy of the western world." She does not mean, of course, that she has lost Hugh Hefner; the meaning of "playboy" then current was, first, a man who, full of devilry, lives for sport, amusement, and pleasure; second, one who was still full of boy's play; and finally, one who plays many a part.

The riot that greeted the first production of The Playboy of the Western World is the most famous protest by an Irish audience against a play in the 20th century. The uproar was reproduced on a smaller scale in the UNITED STATES in 1911 when the play was taken on tour; some of the players were then arrested for participating in an obscene performance. Initially, in Dublin the outrage focused on a single sentence. In place of Pegeen, the Widow offers Christy herself, a dowry, an escape route, and "finer sweethearts at every waning moon," but he refuses:

> It's Pegeen I'm seeking only, and what'd I care if you brought me a drift of chosen females, standing in their shifts itself maybe, from this place to the Eastern World.

According to LADY GREGORY's telegram to W. B. YEATS, the outbreak occurred precisely at the word "shifts," a ladies' white undergarment. But the audience was already worked into irritation by the comic representation of Irish country people as drunken, swearing, priest-fearing, and fickle. Were such people worthy of self-government? The audience hoped the Irish dramatic revival would aid the home rule movement; this play seemed to damage it.

While changes in the Irish political situation fairly quickly led to the play becoming a favorite in Ireland, it retains its power to disturb and delight. Christy Mahon has patent similarities to Oedipus, Christ, Narcissus, Achilles, and Caesar. The language—especially the love talk—put in the mouths of characters alludes not just to Irish peasant dialect but to François Villon, William Shakespeare, Charles Baudelaire, and the Jacobean playwrights. Along with The IMPORTANCE OF BEING EARNEST and WAITING FOR GODOT, it is one of the classic plays that Ireland has contributed to world literature.

FURTHER READING

Grene, Nicholas. The Politics of Irish Drama. Cambridge: Cambridge Univ. Press, 1999.

Harrington, John. The Irish Play on the New York Stage 1874–1966. Lexington: Univ. of Kentucky Press, 1997.

Kiberd, Declan. Synge and the Irish language. 2d ed. Dublin: Gill & Macmillan, 1993.

Levitas, Ben. The Theatre of Nation: Irish Drama and Cultural Nationalism, 1890–1916. Oxford: Oxford Univ. Press, 2002.

Murray, Christopher. Twentieth-Century Irish Drama: Mirror Up to Nation. Manchester: Manchester Univ. Press, 1997.

Adrian Frazier

PLAY WITHOUT A TITLE   See PLATONOV

PLIEKŠĀNS, JĀNIS   See RAINIS

THE PLOUGH AND THE STARS

Premiered at the Abbey Theatre in Dublin in 1926, The Plough and the Stars is the last and arguably the greatest of SEAN O'CASEY's three Dublin plays, which are sometimes regarded as a trilogy. Like the two plays that preceded it, Plough has a strong base in actuality, this time in the events leading up to the 1916 Rising in Dublin as seen from the vantage point of Dublin's poor. The politics of the play are foregrounded: O'Casey sets out to demythologize 1916 by mocking the romantic notions of heroism and blood sacrifice held by militant republicans such as Patrick Pearse. Underpinning his analysis is the conviction that because it did nothing for the urban poor, the Rising was a tragic mistake. By inference, the play also attacks James Connolly, leader of the working-class Irish Citizen Army, whose flag gives the play its title. As the Covey says in act 1, this flag symbolizes communism and has no place in a mere nationalist struggle.

The power of the play comes from its vivid characterization and poetic language. Some of O'Casey's best-known creations people his tenement setting: Fluther Good, the good-hearted carpenter with a drinking problem; Bessie Burgess, the street vendor with a wicked tongue and a heart of gold; testy Uncle Peter; the fanatical Marxist known as the Covey; and the macabre Mrs. Gogan, whose love of funerals is amply satisfied as the play progresses. O'Casey's rich language is often described as Elizabethan. It is rhetorically elaborate (characters rarely using one word where they can add ten more) and must be understood as the language of an impoverished class for whom rhetoric is a resource and a consolation. The response required is an appreciation of fine phrasing; many of the longer speeches should be regarded as operatic arias.

More experimentally structured than O'Casey's earlier two plays, Plough moves epic-style from the Clitheroes' apartment to a public house, then to the streets during the Rising, and finally to a cramped attic that reflects the end of all hope of liberation. In the domestic setting of act 1, O'Casey highlights the predicament of newly wed Nora Clitheroe, another of his young women whose will drives her toward creating a way of life transcending the limitations imposed by tenement conditions. Nora's opposition to her husband's political ambitions is rooted in her instinctive desire for a home and a recognition that Jack's motive is unacknowledged vanity. The play bears out Nora's point of view as her home is destroyed, she suffers a miscarriage and a breakdown, and the British soldiers, dismissing the Rising as only a bit of a "dog fight," join in the song "Keep the Home Fires Burning" as they occupy the dead Bessie's apartment.

Riots greeted *Plough* on its fourth night at the Abbey, as republican sympathizers, specifically women who had lost menfolk in the Rising, protested in organized opposition to the play. They particularly objected to the public-house scene in act 2, in which the prostitute Rosie Redmond is ironically juxtaposed with the Figure in the Window, recognizably Patrick Pearse (excerpts from whose speeches are used in this scene), and in which the Irish tricolor and the flag of the Irish Citizen Army are introduced. The protesters found the idea of flags in a public house grossly insulting. As the play was disrupted, W. B. YEATS, then managing director of the Abbey, rebuked the audience. Referring to the riots over J. M. SYNGE's PLAYBOY OF THE WESTERN WORLD (1907), Yeats said that O'Casey's fame had been born on that night: "this is his apotheosis." O'Casey had to look up the word in his dictionary when he got home and was alarmed to find he was being placed among the gods.

Plough indisputably placed O'Casey among the great antiwar playwrights of the 20th century. It remains the most frequently staged play in the repertory of the Abbey Theatre. Its qualities as a TRAGICOMEDY have also made it a classic of the international stage, for its use of irony is strongly modernist. Although the politics of the play may cause audiences outside Ireland some difficulty, its solid theatricality invariably renders performances both amusing and moving. In a strange mixture of REALISM, satire, and vaudeville, O'Casey managed to weave a historical tapestry rendering the lives of the poor against a background of a war of liberation.

[*See also* Ireland]

FURTHER READING

Ayling, Ronald, ed. *O'Casey: The Dublin Trilogy*. London: Macmillan, 1985.

Kearney, Colbert. *The Glamour of Grammar: Orality and Politics and the Emergence of Sean O'Casey*. Westport, Conn.: Greenwood Press, 2000.

Lowery, Robert, ed. *A Whirlwind in Dublin: "The Plough and the Stars" Riots*. Westport, Conn.: Greenwood Press, 1984.

Murray, Christopher. *A Faber Critical Guide: Sean O'Casey*. London: Faber, 2000.

Scrimgeour, James R. *Sean O'Casey*. Boston: Twayne, 1978.

Christopher Murray

POLAND

Closely tied to Poland's history, drama has occupied a special position in the cultural life of the country. During long years of foreign domination, drama became a prime force for maintaining national identity, evolving as a metaphoric art that dealt with political, social, and philosophical issues, rather than with private psychological concerns. In the 19th century the forbidden romantic poet-playwrights, living in exile, became revered as seers, but although theater flourished, serious drama, shackled by censorship, stagnated.

PRE–WORLD WAR I DRAMA

Modern Polish drama begins in the late 1890s when writers in the Austrian sector of partitioned Poland, where government control was less severe, came under the influence of new Western European modernist movements—NATURALISM and SYMBOLISM—and participated in the first stagings of previously banned Polish romantic dramas.

It was not the bustling metropolis of Russian-ruled Warsaw but the small ancient city of Cracow that became the breeding ground for a progressive aesthetic movement of cross-fertilization in the arts known as Young Poland. A new theater—the Miejski, built in 1893—introduced the modern repertory of HENRIK IBSEN, AUGUST STRINDBERG, and GERHART HAUPTMANN. Soon Polish writers abroad became caught up in the new trends and came home and embarked on careers as playwrights.

A medical student in Berlin, STANISŁAWA PRZYBYSZEWSKA (1868–1927), frequented the Black Piglet cabaret with Strindberg and Edvard Munch and, influenced by FRIEDRICH NIETZSCHE, developed a theory of "the naked soul" foreshadowing EXPRESSIONISM. In 1898 Przybyszewska settled in Cracow, where he began to edit the innovative artistic journal *Życie* (*Life*). His lurid dramas of hysterical passions leading to murder and suicide, *For the Sake of Happiness* (1900), *The Golden Fleece* (1901), and *Snow* (1903), once widely staged in RUSSIA and championed by VSEVOLOD MEYERHOLD, now seem like fin de siècle period pieces.

GABRIELA ZAPOLSKA (1857–1921) learned the new stagecraft as an actor in Paris at Antoine's Théâtre Libre and Lugné-Poe's Théâtre de l'Oeuvre. She created well-crafted satirical COMEDIES of manners that have never ceased to be popular in the Polish theater. Her masterpiece, *The Morality of Mrs. Dulska* (1906), a tragicomic unmasking of the hypocritical bourgeoisie, became an instant classic. Although disdained by high-bow critics and condemned by the Church, Zapolska was an outstanding European naturalist and the leading woman playwright of her time.

While studying painting in FRANCE, STANISŁAW WYSPIAŃSKI (1869–1907) discovered opera and RICHARD WAGNER. An artist of dual vocation, he approached playwriting with the eye of a painter. Creating his own synthesis of the arts, Wyspiański established the modern Polish tradition of poetic drama rich in powerful images that metaphorically embody complex social and political issues. His landmark drama THE WEDDING (1901) critically reexamines romantic myths about failed rebellion and the role of the artist-intellectual in an oppressed society.

More obscure but equally innovative is the poet Tadeusz Miciński (1873–1918), who shared Wyspiański's notions of the sacred functions of theater and called for drama to return to its origins in the religious mysteries. A mystical sage and pan-Slavist, Miciński wrote a dozen plays designed to unite East and West, reconcile Catholicism with the orthodox faith, and bring Poland and Russia together. The best of his oddly shaped and difficult-to-stage works are *The Revolt of the Potemkin* (1906), a DOCUMENTARY and visionary fantasy on the 1905 mutiny, and *In the Shades of the Golden Palace* (*Basilissa Teophano*, 1909), a dreamlike historical drama about the decadent Byzantine Empire.

Appealing to actors, the naturalistic model of a satirical comedy of manners represented by Zapolska had other skillful exponents, including Jan August Kisielewski (1876–1918), whose *In the Net* (1899) depicts a young girl's attempted rebellion against repressive parents; Tadeusz Rittner (1873–1921), author of ironic dramas about family life, such as *Silly Jacob* (1910); and Włodzimierz Perzyński (1877–1930), best known for his subtle, Chekhovian *Franio's Luck* (1909). But it was Wyspiański's poetic idiom calling for inventive mise-en-scène that became dominant, particularly in the post-1956 years when directors reigned in the Polish theater.

WORLD WAR I ERA

World War I and the Treaty of Versailles, which put Poland back on the map as an independent nation, constituted a major turning point in the evolution of Polish drama. The country and its arts were, for the first time in over 100 years, no longer under foreign domination. The war with the Soviet Union in 1919–1920, successfully waged by strongman Józef Piłsudski, intensified Polish fears of Russian Bolshevism, and the authoritarian government harassed writers, confiscated magazines, and raided theaters suspected of being communist or anarchist.

During twenty years of precarious freedom, new authors attempted to create a dramatic literature attuned to postwar realities of urban life, mechanization, and mass culture. Now that the issue of Polish nationhood appeared settled, writers abandoned the grandiose neo-romantic style and sought for dynamic new forms that could keep pace with the automobile, cinema, and modern psychology. Bruno Winawer (1883–1944) and Antoni Cwojdziński (1893–1972), both physicists by training, developed a genre of light comedy dealing with the impact of science and technology on society, exemplified by Cwojdziński's *Freud's Theory of Dreams* (1937).

The novelist Stefan Żeromski (1864–1925), who began his career as a playwright with *Rose* (1909) and other social dramas, had his greatest success in the theater with *My Little Quail Has Flown Away* (1924), about a utopian scheme for building a cultural center that miscarries because of tangled human passions. Another prewar writer, Adolf Nowaczyński (1876–1944), who had specialized in historical comedies that debunked the great, continued his mockery in the Aristophanic political satire *War for War* (1928). Karol Hubert Rostworowski (1877–1938), author of many prewar historical verse dramas, wrote one powerful

naturalistic TRAGEDY, *The Surprise* (1929), about a peasant woman who unwittingly robs and murders her own son.

In the 1920s and 1930s a protofeminist drama exploring the role of women in society was developed by several leading female authors. The novelist Zofia Nałkowska (1884–1954) wrote *The House of Women* (1930), with an all-female cast, about three generations of a single family. The poet Maria Pawlikowska-Jasnorzewska (1894–1945) contributed subtle psychological comedies: *Egyptian Wheat* (1932), *Heavenly Lovers* (1933), and *Mama's Return* (1935). The actress-turned-playwright Maria Morozowicz-Szczepkowska (1889–1968) reached American audiences with *Monika's Case* (1932), about working women, extramarital sex, single parenting, and abortion, which became the Broadway production and Warner Brothers film *Doctor Monica*.

Despite church and state hostility to experimentation in the arts, a small but vigorous Polish AVANT-GARDE theater with leftist political orientation sprang up during the interwar years. The poet Felicja Kruszewska (1897–1943) created a powerful tragicomic expressionist drama, *A Dream* (1927). The play's hallucinatory visions of the rise of fascism and the heroine's longing for a providential savior spoke directly to Polish audiences about their deepest anxieties.

Witold Wandurski (1891–1934) and Bruno Jasieński (1901–1936) vainly attempted to establish a workers' theater in Poland and later immigrated to the Soviet Union, where, after a warm reception, they were later liquidated during Stalin's purges. Wandurski's *Death on a Pear Tree* (1925) is an antiwar fable about the capture of Death by a crafty peasant. After settling in Moscow where he edited *Literature of the World Revolution*, the futurist Jasieński wrote his *Mannequins' Ball*, in which Parisian fashion dummies stage a revolt against their capitalist masters.

The socialist poet Tadeusz Piper (1891–1969) wrote two experimental plays unstaged in his lifetime: *Six O'clock! Six O'clock!* (1925), which contrasts stage time with real time by inversions of chronological order, and *If There Is No Him* (1933), a drama about loss of identity during a revolution. Undeservedly neglected, Stanisława Przybyszewska (1901–1935) was the author of a brilliant trio of plays about the French Revolution, of which only THE DANTON CASE (1929) was performed, in truncated form, during her lifetime.

The playwright who best captured the turmoil and anxiety of the times was STANISŁAW WITKIEWICZ (1885–1939), but he remained seriously misunderstood and undervalued by his contemporaries. Of his more than thirty plays written between 1918 and 1933, only a handful reached the stage during his lifetime, and few were published. Witkiewicz was rediscovered in the late 1950s, when his works served as an antidote to SOCIALIST REALISM. His breadth of vision, playful dramatic imagination, and seismographic reading of civilization's fault lines now make Witkiewicz a classic of the European avant-garde.

Another major figure of 20th-century Polish literature, novelist WITOLD GOMBROWICZ (1904–1969), was also out of step with his time. He began playwriting with *Ivona, Princess of Burgundia* (1935), a grotesque fairy tale about a persecuted outsider, not performed until 1957. *The Marriage*, a complex exploration of interpersonal mythmaking, was written in 1946 in ARGENTINA, where Gombrowicz was stranded when World War II broke out, published in Paris in 1953, but only produced ten years later. *Operetta*, a history of modern Europe in the form of a musical parody, was written and published in France in 1966 and staged throughout Europe. Because Gombrowicz wrote as a permanent exile critical of the regime, his last two plays could not be performed professionally in Poland until after his death.

WORLD WAR II–1970S

During World War II in Nazi-occupied Poland, no open theater existed, except for collaborationist light entertainment. Most actors refused to appear publicly; instead, clandestine performances were given by conspiratorial groups in private homes. Underground playwriting competitions encouraged new talent, but many young writers were put in concentration camps or killed. The resistance poet and soldier Andrzej Trzebiński (1922–1943) wrote *To Pick Up the Rose* (1942), a grotesque comedy about revolution, Ping-pong, and political power, not long before being shot in a random street execution.

Despite vast physical destruction, especially in Warsaw where not a single theater was left standing, theatrical life was quickly reestablished throughout the country when the war ended. At first the communist government, busy consolidating its control, could not impose ideological conformity on writers. From 1945 to 1949 many Western plays were staged, and prewar playwrights picked up their careers. Jerzy Szaniawski (1886–1970), author of popular whimsical comedies in the 1930s, wrote *The Two Theatres* (1946) about recent war experiences, using the play-within-the-play device to contrast superficial REALISM with a deeper theater of dreams. Catholic playwrights like Jerzy Zawieyski (1902–1969) and Roman Brandstaetter (1906–1987) wrote historical, mythical, and contemporary dramas dealing with moral and metaphysical issues. Karol Wojtyła (1920–2005; the future Pope John Paul II), an actor with the Rhapsodic Theatre, also wrote plays, such as *Our God's Brother* (1947) and *The Jeweler's Shop* (1950), as well as essays on theatrical theory. Each week in a popular Cracow literary magazine, the poet Konstanty Ildefons Gałczyński (1905–1953) created an episode of the Little Theatre of the Green Goose (1946–1950), a miniature nonsense theater that spoofed stage conventions and parodied the myths of Polish and world culture.

This lively diversity in dramatic fare came to an abrupt end in January 1949, when socialist realism was proclaimed the only acceptable style, and later the same year a Festival of Russian and Soviet Drama was instituted to teach Polish playwrights how to write in the Moscow-approved style. All theaters were put under centralized bureaucratic control, Polish romantic dramas were banned, and for the next five years Stalinism ruled over the arts.

With the bloodless October Revolution of 1956, Poland acquired an autonomous policy in the arts. Socialist realism was discarded; formally the arts were free, although censorship of content continued, ruling out truthful presentation of everyday social reality, criticism of the Soviet Union, and treatment of religious or sexual issues that might offend the Catholic hierarchy and upset the delicate church-state balance. The effect of the "thaw" on the theater was extraordinary—the repertory became immense and varied, consisting of some 400 new productions a year, the majority contemporary foreign works.

The public was hungry for plays attuned to modern sensibility. For six years cut off from contact with the West, Polish drama immediately became responsive to foreign influences. Starting with the production of WAITING FOR GODOT in 1957, the previously forbidden Theater of the Absurd was rapidly assimilated by Polish actors, audiences, and writers. Witkiewicz's plays were staged, many for the first time and after battles with the censor.

Theater proved to be the only public arena where national obsessions and grievances could be aired—at least in oblique form. There was a sudden explosion of playwriting. Nearly everyone in the literary world—poets like Zbigniew Herbert (1924–), Stanisław Grochowiak (1934–1976), Tymoteusz Karpowicz (1921–), and Andrzej Bursa (1932–1957), as well as Marxist philosophers like Leszek Kołakowski (1927–)—began writing plays. The flowering of Polish drama after 1956 was made possible by lavish state subsidization, which helped to attract the best talent to the theater. The constant pressure of censorship inclined playwrights to parable and metaphor, devices central to the Polish dramatic tradition. Almost all important new Polish plays were published prior to performance and widely read in the drama magazine *Dialog*, started in 1956 and still published today.

After years of war, occupation, concentration camps, Holocaust, and Stalinist repression, playwrights took an ironic view of ideals and ideologies, including the Polish romantic tradition. In his philosophical allegory *The Names of Power* (1956), Jerzy Broszkiewicz (1922–) scrutinized the arbitrary nature of political power in three scenes set in different historical epochs. The poet Miron Białoszewski (1922–1983) set up a private Theatre Apart (1953–1961) in his apartment where the author and friends gave performances of radical linguistic experiments for invited audiences.

The two playwrights who dominated the Polish stage in the second half of the 20th century were TADEUSZ RÓŻEWICZ (1921–) and SŁAWOMIR MROŻEK (1932–). Although often labeled Theater of the Absurd and compared to SAMUEL BECKETT and EUGÈNE IONESCO, their works, conditioned by history, belong to a native tradition of the grotesque with roots in Witkiewicz,

Gombrowicz, and Gałczyński. Satirist of a totalitarian age in *Tango* (1964) and *Emigrés* (1974), Mrożek reveals the complex bonds between hunter and hunted in a world of illusory freedom where both victim and victimizer use reason to accommodate to unreason. In fragmented open texts that challenge theatrical conventions, like *Card File* (1960) and *White Marriage* (1974), the poet Różewicz probes the terror that lies within, disclosing fear and fascination with eros, self, and the body.

Other outstanding playwrights from the 1960s and 1970s include Ireneusz Iredyński (1939–1985), author of short radio plays and violent neo-naturalistic allegories, such as *A Modern Nativity Play* (1966), about a troupe of actors in a concentration camp giving a Christmas performance, and *An Altar to Himself* (1981), investigating the suicide of an opportunistic party member finally driven by inner demons to revolt against his own degradation. Poet and director Helmut Kajzar wrote innovative plays such as *Pater Noster* (1970) that project dreams in scenic images. Janusz Głowacki (1938–) created satirical comedies in Poland and after 1981 continued his career in New York, writing about Poles abroad in *Hunting Cockroaches* (1984).

POST–1970S

By the late 1970s drama was losing its commanding position at the center of Polish cultural life. As in the West, innovative alternative theaters stopped performing plays; instead, ensembles created their own collaborative spectacles. Official state-supported theaters maintained their broad literary repertories, which no longer spoke to the changing times. No new playwrights with unique voices appeared. The rise of Solidarity, imposition of martial law, and successful battle against communism made public life more exciting than any play. Written drama could not keep up with the drama in the streets.

The underground theater active during martial law in the early 1980s rarely used Polish plays. Oblique metaphoric drama with its hidden codes and allusions lost its power and relevance. Younger spectators preferred a theater of entertainment imitated from the West and flocked to see American-style musicals, such as *Metro* (1992).

After the collapse of communism in 1989 and subsequent abolition of censorship, the Polish theater achieved the freedom for which it had so long struggled. But with its oppositional role eliminated, theater found itself without clear function or direction in a democracy. Since the dismantling of the old system of ideological controls, Polish playwrights have reacted against politics and abandoned the romantic model of national narratives in favor of microsituations and mute existential dramas submerged in everyday life.

Circumstances do not favor the writer. A decentralization of Polish artistic life and proliferation of alternative theaters and festivals have led to ensemble-created works and adaptations of novels and documents rather than new plays. Innovative younger directors show little interest in contemporary Polish playwrights.

At the start of the 21st century, Polish identity and national issues are no longer central concerns of dramatic literature. Personal, not Polish, problems have taken center stage, and psychological realism has made an unexpected comeback. Previously silenced "others" at the margins of society are being given their chance. Polish drama is now attempting to catch up with the latest Western trends by addressing the formerly tabooed subjects of sexuality and the body, gay and lesbian love, and the physically challenged.

Art historian Ingmar Villqist (1960–) has a distinctive new voice, but it sounds no more Polish than does his Scandinavian pseudonym, by which he pays homage to Henrik Ibsen, August Strindberg, PER OLOV ENQUIST, INGMAR BERGMAN, and Lars von Trier, while distancing himself from the Polish romantic tradition. In plays with Scandinavian names and settings like *Helver's Night* (1999), deeply disturbed characters—driven by fear and guilt to violence—face childhood traumas, suffer from AIDS, confront sexual abuse, or deal with complex psychological relationships resulting from their being "different." Villqist has gone back a hundred years to Przybyszewska's and Zapolska's naturalism and psychologism—also a Scandinavian import—but has given it an up-to-date colloquial style and modern "Euro" look.

Other recently staged playwrights making debuts include novelist and German scholar Jerzy Łukosz, whose biographical plays *Mann* and *Hauptmann* treat the artist's relation to the state; actor and director Andrzej Pieczyński, whose *Killing Is Too Good for You* is a family drama of an abused child; and the pseudonymous Amanita Muskaria, author of *Journey to Buenos Aires*, a MONODRAMA about old age as linguistic disintegration. Of an earlier generation, Tadeusz Słobodzianek, whose *Czar Nicholas* and *Prophet Ilya* were highly acclaimed, has written *Dream of a Bedbug, or Comrade Christ*, a sequel to VLADIMIR MAYAKOVSKY's play, in which Prisypkin's return to Moscow is taken as the Second Coming.

FURTHER READING

Braun, Kazimierz. *A History of Polish Theater, 1939–1989: Spheres of Captivity and Freedom.* Contributions in Drama and Theatre Studies, No. 64. Westport, Conn.: Greenwood Press, 1996.

——. *A Concise History of the Polish Theater from the Eleventh to the Twentieth Centuries.* Studies in Theatre Arts, Vol. 21. Lewiston: Edwin Mellen Press, 2003.

Czerwinski, Edward. *Contemporary Theatre and Drama (1956–1984).* Westport, Conn.: Greenwood Press, 1988.

Gerould, Daniel, ed. *Twentieth-Century Polish Avant-Garde Drama.* Ithaca, N.Y.: Cornell Univ. Press, 1977.

Miłosz, Czesław. *The History of Polish Literature.* London: Macmillan, 1969.

Taborski, Bolesław. "Poland." In *Crowell's Handbook of Contemporary Drama,* ed. by Michael Anderson et al. New York: Crowell, 1971. 359–371.

Daniel Gerould and Jadwiga Kosicka Gerould

POLITICAL THEATER IN THE UNITED STATES

Theater advocating political causes is as old as Aeschylus and TRAGEDY. But the special political and economic chaos of the 1930s brought a seeming novelty in form and ideas to the American theater.

GREAT DEPRESSION ROOTS

The trend toward political drama began very early in the 1930s with small theatrical troupes, largely in New York City, that were sponsored by left-wing political groups, such as the Communist Party and various labor unions. They sought to advocate their simple political solutions to the complex social and economic problems of the Great Depression by staging small amateur productions of "agit-props," earnestly satiric skits designed to agitate and propagandize audiences (AGITATION-PROPAGANDA theater). This theatrical format was borrowed from GERMANY and Soviet RUSSIA, where it had developed in the 1920s. The plot lines were episodic, always leading the cartoon characters from political naïveté to left-wing beliefs and, theoretically, sending audiences, thus instructed and agitated, to the revolutionary barricades. The Workers' Laboratory Theatre (WLT) summed up the aim of all agit-prop troupes with a slogan emblazoned on a red banner hanging over its tiny stage: "The Theatre Is a Weapon." But the actors were preaching the class struggle to the converted, and even the converted did not rush to the barricades. There were no right-wing political theaters.

As the agit-props developed in the 1930s, they became more realistic in their subject matter and their characterizations, while still retaining their primary revolutionary message. In 1932, for example, these small troupes, under the aegis of the League of Workers' Theatres (later renamed the New Theatre League), continued to produce agit-props as well as more conventional realistic plays heavily laden with propaganda. Politically concerned actors and directors from professional stages, such as the GROUP THEATER, lent their skills to both agit-props and realistic dramas. While keeping the episodic form of the agit-prop, these professionals, influenced by the traditional realistic drama, transformed the cartoon characters like the "Capitalist" into historical figures like Henry Ford. In *Dimitroff* (1934), an agit-prop about the Reichstag fire, Art Smith and Ella Kazan of the Group Theater developed the same cartoon capitalist into Adolf Hitler and Hermann Goering. Historical events succeeded the theoretical class struggle as subject matter.

By 1935 ordinary people and their everyday problems of survival in the Great Depression became the realistic subject matter of CLIFFORD ODETS's *WAITING FOR LEFTY*. This agit-prop, written and performed by left-wing members of the Group Theater, had its premiere under the aegis of the New Theatre League. Later in 1935 the Group itself staged this play. The message, though a bit subtler than the earlier agit-props, was still class war. When the character Agate led the audience in the call to "Strike," his raised fist—the communist salute—indicated clearly that he was agitating for revolution. In 1936 the New Theatre League continued to alternate between realistic dramas like *Private Hicks* by Albert Maltz and *Hymn to the Rising Sun* by PAUL GREEN and agit-props with humanized characters in the style of *Waiting for Lefty*. The New Theatre League folded in 1940.

In 1933, because most early agit-props had been so unprofessionally staged, a coalition of left-wing groups organized Theatre Union to produce plays OFF BROADWAY, but with the professional sheen of the Broadway stage. Most of the plays were in the realistic style popular on Broadway but with strong leftist themes. *Peace on Earth* (1933) by George Sklar and Albert Maltz was an antiimperialist war drama featuring the conversion of a professor from liberalism to Marxism. *Stevedore* (1934) by Paul Peters and George Sklar, preaching against racism in the South, concluded with a fight between the races in which the white members of a Marxist union rescued the oppressed African Americans. Though Theatre Union presented this ending in a seemingly realistic manner, the rescue was more fantasy than reality. This kind of wish fulfillment was known as "SOCIALIST REALISM." The future as predicted by Marxist theoreticians was shown "realistically" as if it already existed.

Not all of Theatre Union's plays followed socialist realism. FRIEDRICH WOLF's *The Sailors of Cattaro* (1934), translated by Keene Wallis and adapted by Michael Blankfort, concluded with the proletarian sailors being executed for their failed mutiny. This failure was based on history. *Black Pit* (1935) by Albert Maltz told a story of class war in the coal mines, ending in defeat for the miners, but with a prediction that workers would ultimately triumph over their capitalist bosses. The play was advertised as a "proletarian tragedy" because it displayed the fall of a mineworker, but the predicted proletarian triumph was not part of the tragic tradition.

In its next play, MOTHER (1935) by BERTOLT BRECHT as adapted by Paul Peters, Theatre Union tried the experimental form of EPIC THEATER, in which the political lessons taught were more important than the usual emotional empathy generated by the characters and the story of realistic drama. In its episodic form with slogans on signs and slides, *Mother* taught revolution directly to the audience in the manner of the agit-props. But Theatre Union, unwilling to abandon REALISM totally, presented the Russian mother in a sympathetic, emotional way and even added touches of realism by using a real onstage stove boiling real cabbage with its attendant odors emanating out into the audience. Brecht himself, attending a rehearsal, was highly displeased and stormed out of the theater.

Theatre Union's next play was *Bitter Stream* (1936), Victor Wolfson's adaptation of Ignazio Silone's novel *Fontarnara*, an account of Italian peasants who form a union to stop the fascists from stealing their land and water. This play was once again in the realistic format of the company. It was the last play staged at the Civic Repertory Theatre off Broadway before Theatre Union moved to Broadway for its final production: JOHN HOWARD

LAWSON's *Marching Song* (1937). Lawson told the topical story of an autoworkers' union strike that developed into a general strike against evil capitalists and their fascist agents, ending with the triumph of the proletariat. Lawson led the Theatre Union back to socialist realism. The Marxist theoreticians had really recreated 19th-century MELODRAMA, which had been delightfully sent up by W. S. GILBERT in the *Mikado's* epigram, "It's an unjust world, and virtue is triumphant only in theatrical performances." All Theatre Union had done to melodrama was redefine moral virtue as the political power of a radicalized proletariat.

Unlike Theatre Union, the more successful political theaters advocated action much closer to the middle-class aspirations of most Americans, as epitomized by Franklin Roosevelt's New Deal. Larger and broader audiences were more easily persuaded that labor unions—rather than revolution—would alleviate the plight of workers. Reform of labor law was easier to accept than a Soviet America. The theatrical forms of such milder political advocacy did not matter. They could be melodrama, realism, or even experimental agit-props—provided they entertained audiences.

The most entertaining show of the time was *Pins and Needles* (1937–1941), a musical revue advancing the political cause of unionism by means of songs and sketches. It was produced by Labor Stage, which had been organized by Louis Schaeffer as the theatrical arm of the International Ladies' Garment Workers' Union. Satirizing the enemies of labor in the tradition of the agit-prop, the sketch writers—such as Joseph Schrank, Arthur Arent, MARC BLITZSTEIN, and Emanuel Eisenberg—and the composer-lyricist Harold Rome created several editions of the show that were blessed with humor, irony, wit, and sophisticated music. These qualities had eluded most of the dedicated revolutionaries like John Howard Lawson, who tried to write plays to be used as weapons in the class war. *Pins and Needles* preached unionism but never forgot to entertain its audiences with the staples of the musical revue: satiric sketches and singable songs ranging from romantic and sentimental ballads to humorous parodies and patter songs. And the show boasted a chorus line of beautiful working girls. In its long run, first off Broadway and later on Broadway, *Pins and Needles* skewered the enemies of unions ranging from Hitler to Father Coughlin and, later on, from Joseph Stalin to the Daughters of the American Revolution. Most humorously, it also skewered the best of the Marxist playwrights from Bertolt Brecht to Clifford Odets.

The 1930s also saw some political plays offered by theaters that were not founded to advance political causes. For example, the FEDERAL THEATRE PROJECT was established in 1935 by the American government to provide employment for unemployed theater professionals and to provide free entertainment for audiences across America. Headed by Hallie Flanagan, who had staged three agit-props in 1931 at her Vassar College Experimental Theatre, Federal Theatre produced a small percentage of political plays out of a varied repertory of new plays and classic theater. These ranged from an African American *Macbeth* to T. S. ELIOT's MURDER IN THE CATHEDRAL.

But the most exciting productions were those of political plays, especially the living newspapers, a new theatrical genre that aimed to analyze some of the social problems that came to light during the Great Depression. These living newspapers drew on techniques long established by the musical revue with its plotless structure, blackout sketches, and songs. They also drew on the agit-props, movie newsreels, and radio programs to create highly theatrical and politically significant theater. In *Triple-A Plowed Under* (1936) Arthur Arent and his staff writers presented a history of the agricultural depression, focusing on the destruction of the Agricultural Adjustment Administration (AAA) and concluding with the creation of a new Farmer-Labor political party. Arent's *1935* (1936) depicted a wide variety of injustices in American society during the title year. *Injunction Granted* (1936) by Arent and staff was a history of the labor movement in relation to the courts. In its original form, the left-wing political bias was so strong that Hallie Flanagan ordered the production toned down. Arent's next edition of the living newspaper, *Power* (1937), presented a study of the government's creation of electric power by way of the Tennessee Valley Authority (TVA). In *One-Third of a Nation* (1938) Arent depicted the plight of the poor who lacked adequate housing. It was the last living newspaper staged by Federal Theatre.

Although Federal Theatre produced some political plays in more conventional forms like the very successful antifascist *It Can't Happen Here* (1936) by Sinclair Lewis and John C. Moffit, the most inventive theatrical pieces were the living newspapers. But this new dramatic form ceased when the U.S. Congress, fearing the political impact of communist influence on Federal Theatre, cut off its funding. Only one of its many plays, *The Revolt of the Beavers* (1937) by Oscar Saul and Lou Lantz, clearly advocated a communist revolution, even though it was presented in the guise of an allegorical children's fairy tale. But Congress had great fear of communist propaganda.

The Mercury Theatre, founded by Orson Welles and John Houseman, broke away from the Federal Theatre in 1937 when the Works Progress Administration (WPA) canceled the opening of MARC BLITZSTEIN's militantly anticapitalist opera THE CRADLE WILL ROCK. Defying the government and Actors' Equity, Welles and Houseman presented the piece with the singing actors performing among the spectators in the audience and Blitzstein playing the piano accompaniment onstage. There was greater political interest in the defiant producers and performers than in the opera itself with its cartoon characters and its schematic agit-prop format that presented a revolutionary solution to many social evils.

On Broadway there were some political plays sponsored by the THEATRE GUILD, the Group Theatre, the Playwrights' Company, and independent producers. But these were not primarily political theaters. Though dramatists like ROBERT E. SHERWOOD, ELMER RICE, PHILIP BARRY, and MAXWELL ANDERSON presented political themes, they did not advocate any specific political program. Only Clifford Odets of the Group Theatre came close to urging revolution. But after *Waiting for Lefty* (1935) and AWAKE AND SING! (1935), Odets became much less revolutionary in his political themes. The most successful political production on Broadway was *Of Thee I Sing* (1931), a musical COMEDY by GEORGE S. KAUFMAN and Morrie Ryskind, with music by George Gershwin and lyrics by Ira Gershwin. Sending up the entire American political establishment, this show offered satiric laughter and Offenbachian irreverence but not a blueprint for revolution. Playwrights like LILLIAN HELLMAN came close to Marxism, but her message was usually implicit.

Political plays of the 1930s failed to win many converts to any political causes. Since dramatists stacked the premises of their arguments, theatergoers did not follow the political path outlined, unless they had already decided to do so on the basis of their own perceptions of the real world. The most that political theater achieved was to raise questions that might sharpen those perceptions.

FURTHER READING

Clurman, Harold. *The Fervent Years: The Story of the Group Theatre and the Thirties.* New York: Hill & Wang. 1957.

Flanagan, Hallie. *Arena: The History of the Federal Theatre.* New York: B. Blom, 1940.

Goldstein, Malcolm. *The Political Theater: American Drama and Theater of the Great Depression.* New York: Oxford Univ. Press, 1974.

Himelstein, Morgan Y. *Drama Was a Weapon: The Left-wing Theatre in New York, 1929–1941.* New Brunswick, N.J.: Rutgers Univ. Press, 1963.

Levine, Ira A. *Left-wing Dramatic Theory in the American Theatre.* Ann Arbor, Mich.: UMI Res. Press, 1985.

Mathews, Jane DeHart. *The Federal Theatre, 1935–1939: Plays, Relief, and Politics.* Princeton, N.J.: Princeton Univ. Press, 1967.

Weales, Gerald. *Clifford Odets, Playwright.* New York: Pegasus, 1971.

Williams, Jay. *Stage Left.* New York: Scribner's, 1974.

Morgan Y. Himelstein

SECOND HALF 20TH CENTURY

Political theater in the UNITED STATES in the second half of the 20th century reflected the problematic status of political art in the United States, where, unlike Europe, there has been no agreement about its propriety. On one side are playwrights such as DAVID MAMET who believe that "[i]t's not the dramatist's job to bring about social change" (*Three Uses of the Knife*, 1998), and on the other are theater makers such as Bread and Puppet Theater director Peter Schumann, for whom "the arts are political, whether they like it or not" ("Puppetry and Politics," 1986).

This apparently irreconcilable difference is contradicted by a second aspect of political theater in the United States: whenever circumstances become sufficiently dire—during the Depression, World War II, the Vietnam War, the AIDS crisis, and the U.S. war against Iraq—intractable disputes about political art are superseded by an overwhelming sense of its immediate necessity.

By 1940 the United States had witnessed the steady development of an American political theater tradition, which at the beginning of the century included the American Pageant movement, certain aspects of the Little Theater movement, and contemporary African American theater, particularly as promulgated by W. E. B. DuBois. The 1930s saw the largest single experiment in American political theater of the 20th century: the FEDERAL THEATRE PROJECT, which, despite its popularity and its invention of such innovative theatrical techniques as the Living Newspaper, was crushed by conservative members of Congress in 1939. After the United States entered World War II, anti-Nazi plays such as LILLIAN HELLMAN'S 1941 *Watch on the Rhine* and patriotic musicals such as *This Is the Army* (1942, featuring actual servicemen onstage) became popular staples of Broadway theater. As the Cold War superseded World War II, its reverberations could also be felt in mainstream theater, for example, in the 1947 Broadway failure of BERTOLT BRECHT'S THE LIFE OF GALILEO.

Usually the term *political theater* is used to define drama that counters prevailing political ideology by articulating alternative points of view. This was certainly the kind of theater the German director ERWIN PISCATOR promulgated at his Dramatic Workshop in New York City (1939–1951), where among his prize students was Judith Malina. In 1947 Malina joined with Julian Beck to create the LIVING THEATRE, the first, longest-lived, and perhaps most influential American political theater group of the century. The Living Theatre began modestly by performing classic works from the European AVANT-GARDE (JEAN COCTEAU, FEDERICO GARCÍA LORCA, Brecht, and LUIGI PIRANDELLO), but also produced plays by such American writers as GERTRUDE STEIN, William Carlos Williams, and Paul Goodman. Under Malina's direction the company's first performances took place in Manhattan apartments, and although the company soon found OFF-BROADWAY theaters in which to play, it also included street performances and demonstrations as an essential part of its activities, which in the 1950s were influenced by anarchist activism and opposition to atomic weapons.

While the Living Theatre's production of *The Connection* (1959) shocked audiences with its jazz-inflected hipster NATURALISM, *The Brig* (1963) was a political provocation: a head-on critique of American militarism in the middle of the Cold War. The company's production of Kenneth Brown's semiautobiographical story of a military prison in occupied Japan typified the Living Theatre's approach to political art. Directly influenced by the grand theories of Brecht and VSEVOLOD MEYERHOLD, the Malina-Beck production was also profoundly affected by the writings of ANTONIN ARTAUD, who placed great focus on the performance of the individual in crisis. In the 1960s the Living Theatre's radical approach to ACTING, DRAMATURGY, and design led it to produce *Frankenstein* (1965), Brecht's *Antigone* (1966), *Paradise Now* (1968), and *Seven Meditations on Political Sado-Masochism* (1973), which all expressed the company's desire to expand the limits of acting and transgress the boundaries of the Western stage. The Living Theatre became a world-traveling collective whose work caused tumult and furor in Europe, in South America, and across the United States. Members of the Living Theatre were often arrested, and in New York City their performance spaces were shut down by government officials. For many years the company exiled itself in Europe. After the death of Julian Beck in 1985 Hanon Reznikov joined Judith Malina as co-director, and the Living Theatre rerooted itself in New York City and continued work, now under the radar of most theater critics.

The San Francisco Mime Troupe was started by Ronald G. Davis in 1959, a direct outgrowth of the famed Actor's Workshop. The Mime Troupe sought inspiration from Brecht, but also from Italian commedia dell'arte traditions, not only in its use of physical acting and masks, but also in its practice of street performance. The latter caused trouble for the company as early as 1961, when city authorities attempted to prevent the Mime Troupe from passing the hat after performances in San Francisco parks. The Mime Troupe successfully argued its case in court, and free performances in city parks became a hallmark of the company's work. *A Minstrel Show; or, Civil Rights in a Cracker Barrel* (1965) marked the company's turn to contemporary political issues, which continued with a version of Carlo Goldoni's *L'amant militaire* (1967) refocused to examine the Vietnam War. When Davis left the troupe in 1970, it became a collective whose experiments included even further examination of popular theater forms (such as MELODRAMA, detective stories, American musical theater, and science fiction), as well as a continuing interest in Brecht, whose THE MOTHER was a Mime Troupe production of 1973. The Mime Troupe's productions of *The Independent Female; or, A Man Has His Pride* (1970), *The Dragon Lady's Revenge* (1971), *Hotel Universe* (1977), *Americans; Or, Last Tango in Huahuatenago* (1981) and other plays toured widely across the United States and in Europe, but the company kept its connections to San Francisco and park performances, which continue to be the center of its work in the early 21st century.

El Teatro Campesino was founded by LUIS VALDEZ in 1965 after a brief stint with the San Francisco Mime Troupe. El Teatro Campesino's approach to political theater combined the richness of Chicano theater traditions with a desire to tell stories about *campesinos* in short plays called *actos*. In the 1970s and 1980s El Teatro Campesino widened its scope to present an array of brilliantly performed political tragicomedies, including The Great Tent of the Underdogs (*La gracarpa de los Rasquachis*, 1973), The End of the World (*El fin del mundo*, 1975), and *Zoot Suit* (which reached Broadway in 1979), addressing political and social issues of concern to wider American and European audiences.

The Bread and Puppet Theater began in New York City in 1963, when German-born artist Peter Schumann combined his interests in sculpture and dance to create puppet shows that addressed themselves to the same issues and methods other performance forms were tackling. Although early Bread and Puppet shows took place in the context of avant-garde performance in Greenwich Village, Schumann sought to avoid the isolation and exclusivity of the downtown scene by performing in city streets, first with short puppet shows and picture performances, then in community parades supporting Puerto Rican tenants' rights, and ultimately in antiwar protests. In Spanish Harlem in 1966, Schumann and his colleagues created *A Man Says Goodbye to His Mother* with and for the mothers of soldiers serving in Vietnam, a street show that, according to some critics, was the most influential drama of the Vietnam War period. Schumann's large-scale, expressionist-styled puppets came to define street demonstrations of the Vietnam War era, and his more formal shows about the war, including *A Man Says Goodbye to His Mother*, *Fire* (1965), *The Cry of the People for Meat* (1968), *Grey Lady Cantata #2* (1970), and *The Birdcatcher in Hell* (1971), established a new visual vocabulary for American theater. Like the Living Theatre and other political theater groups, Bread and Puppet's theater work achieved much more critical and financial success in Europe than in the United States, but its influence has been global. In 1970 Bread and Puppet moved to Vermont and began a twenty-seven-year tradition of annual *Domestic Resurrection Circuses* at its farm in the town of Glover. The last *Circus* was produced in 1998, but Bread and Puppet continues to perform outdoor shows in Glover, as well as indoor theater spectacles, installations, and street parades around the world.

African American theater has tended to have a political context regardless of the intentions of its makers, at least since W. E. B. DuBois and Alain Locke debated the merits of political art in the 1920s. The Federal Theatre Project deemed Abram Hill and John Silvera's 1938 *Liberty Deferred* (a Living Newspaper about the history of slavery in the United States) too volatile to be performed. Later, ALICE CHILDRESS's *Trouble in Mind* (produced off-Broadway in 1955) focused on the problems of racism as they affect African American actors, but the author's refusal to give the play a happy ending prevented it from advancing to Broadway. In this context the 1959 Broadway success of LORRAINE HANSBERRY'S A RAISIN IN THE SUN stands out as an anomaly. The 1960s rise of a militant African American political activism spawned the Black Theater movement, in which such playwrights as AMIRI BARAKA and ED BULLINS wrote Black Consciousness dramas that articulated specifically African American characters and situations primarily for African American audiences. Baraka forsook the off-off-Broadway theaters of Greenwich Village for stages in Harlem and then in Newark, New Jersey.

Barbara Ann Teer founded the National Black Theatre in Harlem in 1968 to create "Sunday Afternoon Blackenings" and

"Ritualistic Revivals," which were later toured to the Caribbean and Nigeria. Vinnette Carroll, another graduate of Piscator's Dramatic Workshop, founded New York City's Urban Arts Corps in 1967 to encourage young minority theater makers. In 1972 Carroll became the first African American woman to direct a Broadway show: *Don't Bother Me, I Can't Cope*. Even AUGUST WILSON's 1980s Chekhovian dramas of African American life emerged from the Black Theater movement's development in Pittsburgh, and the inevitable political contexts of race in America were clearly at the center of ADRIENNE KENNEDY's abstract dramas, as well as the later works of ANNA DEAVERE SMITH and SUZAN-LORI PARKS.

The 1950s civil rights movement was not often reflected in mainstream American drama, with the major exception of *A Raisin in the Sun*. But when the Vietnam War became a contentious issue in the mid-1960s, off- and off-off-Broadway theaters were both available and inclined to include dramas about the war. The Open Theatre performed MEGAN TERRY's satirical musical *Viet Rock* at La MaMa in 1966; and the following year *Macbird!* (Barbara Garson's treatment of Lyndon Johnson's presidency as a Shakespearean tragicomedy) was another off-Broadway success. Beginning with *The Basic Training of Pavlo Hummel* (1971), Vietnam veteran DAVID RABE wrote a series of plays about the conflict—including STICKS AND BONES (1969) and *Streamers* (1976)—that first appeared at Joseph Papp's Public Theater and then all moved to Broadway. Other Vietnam War dramas, including *The Trial of the Catonsville Nine* (1970) by activist priest and poet Daniel Berrigan, Tom Cole's *Medal of Honor Rag* (1977), LANFORD WILSON's The FIFTH OF JULY (1978), and EMILY MANN's DOCUMENTARY DRAMA *Still Life* (1980), all found audiences off-Broadway and sometimes on Broadway. A signal example of popular Vietnam War theater was *Hair: The American Tribal Love-Rock Musical*, which moved from Papp's Public Theater to Broadway in 1968. *Hair* marked the increasing popularity of the American rock musical, but, more important, reflected the kind of rough, intimate ritual performance that the Living Theatre had been developing for years.

With the end of the Vietnam War in 1975, there was no longer one single issue that uniformly troubled all Americans. Instead, a variety of other concerns presented themselves as dramatic material: continuing questions of racism and the identity of African Americans, Latinos, and other minority groups; U.S. policies in Latin America and other parts of the Third World; large-scale threats to the environment; and issues of personal identity radically defined as women's liberation and gay liberation.

With the emergence of identity politics in the 1970s, the politics of particular theater pieces became more diffuse than during the Vietnam conflict. In New York and San Francisco gay theater makers such as Jack Smith, CHARLES LUDLAM, and George Harris had already embraced what Stefan Brecht would call "queer theatre": outrageously stylized celebrations of homosex-

ual existence drawing upon drag performance traditions and all things "camp" (as Susan Sontag had defined the term in 1964). In 1972 Rosalyn Drexler, MARIA IRENE FORNES, Julie Bovasso, Megan Terry, ROCHELLE OWENS, and Adrienne Kennedy formed the Women's Theater Council, an important step in the developing consciousness of feminist issues in American drama, which continued with those dramatists' plays, as well as in the works of WENDY WASSERSTEIN, NTOZAKE SHANGE, EVE ENSLER, and others.

Another new dramatic form with a strong political element that emerged in the 1970s was solo performance, the development of often autobiographical monologues by SPALDING GRAY, Karen Finley, Eric Bogosian, HOLLY HUGHES, Paul Zaloom, and others connected to the new genre of PERFORMANCE ART. Solo performance sometimes embraced political content, but Gray's approach was typical: in *Swimming to Cambodia* (1985) he succinctly characterized the debacle of the Vietnam War and its murderous spread into Cambodia, but did so as a footnote to the larger story of his ambivalent participation in Hollywood filmmaking. A political debate emerged in 1990 when the "NEA Four"—solo performers Hughes, Finley, John Fleck, and Tim Miller—were denied funding from the National Endowment for the Arts because of their explicit references to sexuality, but the issues of censorship, "indecency," and government funding raised by the controversy lacked the nationwide resonance of the previous decades' struggles over civil rights and Vietnam.

The emergence of HIV/AIDS in the early 1980s sparked another revival of American political theater. The first AIDS drama in New York, William Hoffman's *As Is* (1985), was co-produced off-Broadway by Circle Repertory Company and a gay theater, the Glines, and then moved to Broadway. Shortly thereafter LARRY KRAMER's *The Normal Heart* (1985) opened at Joseph Papp's Public Theater. *The Normal Heart* was a polemic focused on American social, medical, and political establishments that, in Kramer's opinion, were in denial about the AIDS crisis. Other off-Broadway and Broadway AIDS dramas followed, including TONY KUSHNER's ANGELS IN AMERICA, *Part One: Millenium Approaches* (1991), PAULA VOGEL's THE BALTIMORE WALTZ (1992), and TERRENCE MCNALLY's *Love! Valour! Compassion!* (1994).

Significant drama about AIDS also took the form of solo performance. Wooster Group performer Ron Vawter created *Roy Cohn and Jack Smith* (1992) to examine how two idiosyncratic gay men dealt both with AIDS and with their homosexual identity. Tim Miller, Ron Athey, Bill T. Jones, and Ethyl Eichelberger also made noteworthy performances about their personal and political connections to AIDS. But again, as during the Vietnam War years, perhaps the most significant political theater about the subject took place in streets and other public places as ACT UP and other AIDS activists created brilliant interventionist public spectacles that placed AIDS in the middle of American (and worldwide) public discourse.

In the postmodern environment of DECONSTRUCTION and untethered signs, ideological certainties and wholeheartedly felt political positions were suspect; and the celebrated alternative theater makers of the "postmodern" moment—RICHARD FOREMAN, the Wooster Group, ROBERT WILSON—tended to avoid the messiness of outright political, philosophical, and even dramaturgical statements in favor of articulating ambiguity. At the end of the century such uncertainties were countered by Iranian American director Reza Abdoh, whose angry critiques of American culture and intolerant global fundamentalisms, such as *Quotations from a Ruined City* (1994), incorporated existing avant-garde techniques with a clearly politicized and HIV-positive point of view.

At the beginning of the 21st century, and especially after the destruction of the World Trade Center in 2001, many American theater artists once again decided unequivocally that drama and politics had provocative and inspirational links, and once again their efforts ranged from actors' drama—including Tony Kushner's *Homebody Kabul* (2001) and Tim Robbins's *Embedded* (2004)—to such activist organizations as Theaters Against War (THAW, begun in 2002), which by 2004 included over 150 theater groups in New York City alone. However, what is remarkable about American political theater in the 21st century is that it prominently includes the longest-lived theater groups in the United States, which still create theater pieces that reflect the times in which we live. In the summer of 2004 the San Francisco Mime Troupe presented *Showdown at Crawford Gulch*, a critique of George W. Bush and the Iraq War disguised as a western; the Bread and Puppet Theater created its outdoor spectacle *The First World Insurrection Circus* and a proscenium-stage show, *When the World Was on Fire*; and the Living Theatre, as the company put it on its website, performed "street actions in response to the Republican National Convention in New York City."

FURTHER READING

Brecht, Stefan. *Peter Schumann's Bread and Puppet Theatre.* 2 vols. New York: Routledge, 1988.

Cohen-Cruz, Jan, ed. *Radical Street Performance: An International Anthology.* New York: Routledge, 1998.

Colleran, Jeanne, and Jenny S. Spencer, eds. *Staging Resistance: Essays on Political Theater.* Ann Arbor: Univ. of Michigan Press, 1998.

Elam, Harry J. *Taking It to the Streets: The Social Protest Theater of Luis Valdez and Amiri Baraka.* Ann Arbor: Univ. of Michigan Press, 1997.

Sainer, Arthur. *The New Radical Theatre Notebook.* New York: Applause, 1997.

Schumann, Peter. "Puppetry and Politics." *American Theatre* (November 1986): 32–33.

John Bell

POLLOCK, SHARON (1936–)

As one of CANADA's most prolific playwrights, Sharon Pollock's work has also been performed on television, in radio plays, and in feature films. While she has written numerous plays for stage and radio that have been successfully produced, Pollock is probably best known for her stage plays BLOOD RELATIONS (1981; originally titled *My Name Is Lisbeth*), a two-act drama that deals with the real-life murder suspect Lizzie Borden, and *Doc* (1986), a play that explores the difficult relationships between an aging doctor and his family, with the title character based on Pollock's father, physician Everett Chalmers. Often invoking innovative dramatic structure, her plays also frequently interrogate historical subject matter, as with 1976's *The Komagata Maru Incident*, which is based on the true story of Indian Sikh immigrants in 1914 who are refused permission to Canadian land; similarly her more recent *Angel's Trumpet* (2001) follows the relationship of real-life figures Zelda and F. Scott Fitzgerald.

Pollock was born Mary Sharon Chalmers in Fredericton, New Brunswick, in 1936. She did not begin writing her first play, *A Compulsory Option*, until she was pregnant with her sixth child. This first play—sometimes known as *No! No! No!*—went on to win the Alberta Culture playwriting competition in 1971 and was staged the following year at Vancouver's New Play Centre. Since that early theatrical success, Pollock has gone on to win numerous awards and honors, only a few of which include Canada's national literary award, The Governor General's Award, for 1981's *Blood Relations* and again in 1986 for *Doc*; 1987's Canada Australian Literary Award; a Japan Foundation Award in 1995; and the Harry and Martha Cohen award in 1999, which resulted from her major contributions to Calgary theater.

Although Pollock attended the University of New Brunswick, in 1954 she left before graduating to marry Ross Pollock, with whom she had five children, and relocated to Toronto. After separating from Pollock, she and her children returned to Fredericton, and she eventually found work at the Playhouse Theatre. There Pollock performed many jobs, including some work as an actor. By 1966, however, she moved again to Calgary with her children and actor Michael Ball. In Calgary she continued ACTING and writing and earned the Dominion Drama Festival award for her performance in THE KNACK, ANN JELLICOE's play about the bumpy relationships shared by four young people in the 1960s. In addition to Pollock's prodigious career as a playwright and her work as a performer, she has worked as a playwriting instructor, screenwriter, film director, and producer. She has also served as the artistic director at both Theatre Calgary (1984) and Theatre New Brunswick (1988). In 1996 Pollock wrote, produced, and directed the feature film *Everything Relative*. This lesbian comedic drama, dealing with a group of college friends who assemble for a tumultuous weekend reunion, received mixed reviews. For the most part Pollock continues to make Calgary her home base, where she devotes much of her time to supporting Canadian theater and young playwrights.

SELECT PLAYS: *A Compulsory Option* (1970); *Walsh* (1972); *The Komagata Maru Incident* (1976); *The Wreck of the National Line Car*

(1978); *Generations* (1980); *One Tiger to a Hill* (1980); *Blood Relations* (1981); *Doc* (1986); *Fair Liberty's Call* (1993); *Angel's Trumpet* (2001); *End Dream* (2003)

FURTHER READING

Bessai, Diane. "Women Dramatists: Sharon Pollock and Judith Thompson." In *Post-Colonial English Drama: Commonwealth Drama Since 1960*, ed. by Bruce King. London: Macmillan, 1992. 97–117.

Grace, Sherrill. "Creating the Girl from God's Country: From Nell Shipman to Sharon Pollock." *Canadian Literature* 172 (Spring 2002): 92–112.

Nothof, Anne F., ed. *Sharon Pollock: Essays on Her Works*. Toronto: Guernica Editions, 2000.

Zimmerman, Cynthia. *Playwriting Women: Female Voices in English Canada*. Toronto: Simon & Pierre, 1994.

L. Bailey McDaniel

POLYGRAPH

Polygraph, co-created by Robert Lepage and Marie Brassard, uses the lie detector as a metaphor for the tenuous line between truth and fiction. Several story lines intersect, as David Haussman, a German scientist lecturing on criminology and the use of the polygraph, meets Lucie, a young woman in the metro at the scene of a suicide, and they become romantically involved. Their relationship becomes more complicated when it is revealed that François, Lucie's friend, was investigated for a murder years ago by Haussman. Despite passing the polygraph test, François is still haunted by the memory of his friend's death and the investigation and has come to doubt his own innocence. Lucie, an actress, has been cast in a movie about this incident. As the lives of François, Lucie, and David become more involved, the play blurs the line between fiction and truth, constantly manipulating the audience's perspective by collapsing time, replaying key moments, and drawing on a filmic language to foreground how perception shapes truth. Filmic projections of titles mark each of the scenes. Actors shift positions to indicate a classic "top shot" of the corpse, for example, or speed through a choreographed sequence to indicate the passing of time.

As in all of Lepage's work, the play's meaning is created through a complex interplay of images. Realistic scenes from the different story lines are augmented by poetically choreographed moments that accentuate or finish a scene but do not explain it or offer narrative conclusions. Rather, the audience is left to infer meaning. Language becomes just another device for demonstrating the malleability of form: in the first scene of the play, for example, David's speech on Berlin and Lucie's recitation of an autopsy report are intercut, using some of the same lines, and the parallel between the city and the individual is made clear.

Although the play draws on crime drama for its mood and plot, its implications are larger reaching. The play is a meditation on the ephemeral nature of truth, drawing attention to its own manipulation of the audience as viewing positions con-stantly shift. The voyeurism of film and the intrusion of technology are pitted against trust and faith as pacts between human beings. As Michael Sidnell (1990) points out, the play both draws attention to and denies the body's materiality, with a constant attention to the actors' engagement with objects. Perhaps this ambiguity is due, in part, to the collaborative and open-ended nature of the process of creation that Lepage and Theatre Repère drew on in creating this piece. Gyllian Raby, translator for the English version, notes that the script was actually written down in English before French and serves, in some ways, as a temporary record of a piece that is continually evolving. In this way, Lepage makes the experience of his plays a co-creation with his audience. James Brunzli (1999) uses the term "décalage" to describe the displacement that is inherent in Lepage's work: the use of other languages (without translation), the disjunctions between scenes, the estrangement achieved by the manipulation of perspective. In these spaces, the audience finds its engagement.

FURTHER READING

Bunzli, James. "The Geography of Creation: Décalage as Impulse, Process, and Outcome in the Theatre of Robert Lepage." *TDR: The Drama Review: A Journal of Performance Studies* 43, no. 1 (T161) (Spring 1999): 79–103.

Charest, Rémy. *Robert Lepage: Connecting Flights*. Tr. by Wanda Romer Taylor. London: Methuen, 1997.

Donohoe, Joseph I., and Jane M. Koustas, eds. *Theater sans frontières: Essays on the Dramatic Universe of Robert Lepage*. East Lansing: Michigan State Univ. Press, 2000.

Sidnell, Michael. "*Polygraph*: Somatic Truth and an Art of Presence." *Canadian Theatre Review* 64 (Fall 1990): 45–48.

Ziraldo, Cristiana. "Lepage's *Polygraphe* in Italy." *Canadian Theatre Review* 105 (Winter 2001): 16–19.

Marlene Moser

POMERANCE, BERNARD (1940–)

. . . Many people knew the right
better than they knew themselves.
Or any force that moved them silently.
Right eluded them. And came catastrophe.
—Sara Lane, Scene 17, *Quantrill in Lawrence*

Expatriate playwright and poet Bernard Pomerance was born in New York City on September 23, 1940. After graduating from the University of Chicago, Pomerance, then an aspiring novelist, relocated to ENGLAND to write. Attracted by the political commitment and artistic freedom of London's fringe theater scene of the 1970s, he abandoned the novel for playwriting and, with director Roland Rees, co-founded Foco Novo, a radical theater company that took its name from a fictitious group of South American guerrillas in Pomerance's play of the same name. Rees subsequently produced all of Pomerance's work through *The Elephant Man* (1977).

In the UNITED STATES, Pomerance has been known primarily for the highly successful 1979 Broadway debut of *Elephant Man*, which tells the story of John Merrick, a freak show performer in 19th-century London whose body was hideously deformed by neurofibromatosis. Structured in a series of brief episodes, the play traces Merrick's "rescue" from the brutal humiliations of a side show by Dr. Frederick Treves, a rising young London surgeon who provided Merrick with a home at London Hospital, as well as education and entrée into the highest echelons of London society—where Merrick continued to find himself an object of curiosity, study, and revulsion. Under the direction of Jack Hofsiss, *Elephant Man* garnered three Tony Awards in 1979, including Best Play; three Obies; the Drama Desk Award; and the New York Drama Critics' Circle Award. Notoriously media shy, Pomerance flew back to London the night he received the Tony.

While critics have remarked on the apparent influence of BERTOLT BRECHT (whose *Man Is Man* Pomerance adapted) on *The Elephant Man*, the body of Pomerance's work runs a stylistic gamut from NATURALISM to EPIC THEATER and poetic drama. The common thread throughout his writing is a pronounced leftist sociopolitical critique.

Pomerance's work following the *Elephant Man* includes two more historical plays, this time set in the United States. The first of these, *Quantrill in Lawrence* (1980), fictionalizes a particularly nasty piece of Civil War history—the burning of Lawrence, Kansas, one of the war's many atrocities—to bring to the surface the event's archetypal resonances: its cyclic and self-perpetuating violence and its echoes of Cain and Abel. In the introduction to his *Collected Plays* (2001), Pomerance wrote that *Melons* (1985) "was sparked off by reading Geronimo's memoirs and accounts of turmoil instigated on New Mexico pueblos by U.S. authorities, both civil and religious." Concerning the history that underpins *Melons*, Pomerance wrote simply: "after such knowledge, what forgiveness?" In 1987 he returned to his advocacy for Native American rights in a collection of poems titled *We Need to Dream All This Again* (1987), a poetic account of Custer, Crazy Horse, and the Battle for the Black Hills.

Pomerance has dubbed his own playwriting "Left-rationalist" and said in a 1979 *New York Times* interview that "if you point out an error and appeal for the reason, that is a step in the right direction." The function of theater, he suggested, "is some form of social memory. It serves to bring back points that are too volatile, too dangerous to be lived everyday—the skeletons in the closet, the guilt." According to Pomerance, his function as a playwright is to remind the audience of truths known but denied or forgotten: "I'm not bringing hot news My interest in the audience is to remind them of a common thing, and if only temporarily, they do then become a unity, a community."

PLAYS: *High in Vietnam, Hot Damn* (1971); *Hospital* (1971); *Thanksgiving Before Detroit* (1971); *Foco Novo* (1972); *Someone Else Is Still Someone* (1974); *A Man's a Man* (adaptation of the play by Bertolt Brecht, 1975); *The Elephant Man* (1977); *Superhighway* (1978); *Quantrill in Lawrence* (1980); *Melons* (1985); *Hands of Light* (1989)

FURTHER READING

Honegger, Gitta. "How American It Is: Lessons from the Melon Patch." *Theater* 19, no. 2 (1988): 58–64.

Larson, Janet L. "The Elephant Man as Dramatic Parable." *Modern Drama* 26, no. 3 (1983): 335–356.

Owen, Michael. "The Enigmatic Author of the Elephant Man." *New York Times* (February 4, 1979).

Kathryn Syssoyeva

POOR THEATER

No matter how much theater expands and exploits its mechanical resources, it will remain technologically inferior to film and television. Consequently I propose poverty in the theater. . . . The essential concern is finding the proper spectator-actor relationship.
—Jerzy Grotowski, *Towards a Poor Theatre*, 1984

Poor theater is the methodological province, chiefly, of the Polish director and theorist Jerzy Grotowski (1933–1998), who coined the term. He was the director of the Teatr 13 Rzedow (later the Polish Theater Laboratorium) from 1959 to 1979 and, at the end of his life, the Grotowski Workcenter. His most famous production, *Akropolis* (1962), dramatized, through poetry and an extremely physical mise-en-scène, the morbidity and spiritual struggle of Auschwitz inmates.

Caught between the hard line of Stalinism and the recent thaw in church and state relations in Władysław Gomułka's POLAND after Joseph Stalin's death, Grotowski (though trained at Moscow's state theater school) was a controversial artist. Often subjected to censorship, he was relegated to a small provincial theater in Wroclaw, in rural Silesia. With the help of Eugenio Barba and Jean Julien, Grotowski attained international renown in 1966 at Barrault's Theater of Nations in Paris, with another poetic and physical production, *The Constant Prince*. The theory, poor theater, was pronounced in his 1968 book *Towards a Poor Theatre*. *Poor theater* refers to the essential arrangement Grotowski believed theater requires: the audience-performer relationship. All other aspects of production can fall away through a process he called *via negativa*. Theater has no genuine need for costume, scenery, lighting effects, props, music, text, a theater edifice. They are unnecessary unless they contribute to engendering audience participation in the performance on a visceral level. To attain this ideal and to transform this and other theoretical propositions into practice, Grotowski ceased to direct public performances in 1971. His subsequent work in theater was as an advanced pedagogue working on training regimens with professional actors that matured into what he called "actions" and were demonstrated before "witnesses" at the Grotowski Workcenter in Pontederra, ITALY.

He has influenced many contemporary practitioners, notably Eugenio Barba, Peter Brook, ARIANNE MNOUCHKINE, and Richard Schechner. What emerges from the practice of poor theater is the power of the performer's living organism (body and voice) to do the most compelling work in the theater. Text and all nonliving theatrical materials must function as vehicles for an existential depth that transmits from performer to audience. Ideally, Grotowski said, *via negativa* poor theater allows the actor's body to vanish, making his or her impulses visible to the audience. Much work has been done in the spirit of Grotowski that is not necessarily poor theater but rather a kind of "grotowskianism" in which physicality and voice play a prominent role, but mostly for aesthetic affect. Genuine poor theater is not so conscious of itself and is usually the product of a theater group's exigent circumstances or the product of years of experimentation. Grotowski was often more interested in ritual and folk traditions as manifestations of his theories rather than pursuing any interest in mainstream theater.

[*See also* Boal, Augusto; Environmental Theater; Guerrilla Theater; Interculturalism]

FURTHER READING

Barba, Eugenio. *The Land of Ashes and Diamonds; My Apprenticeship in Poland.* Aberystwyth: Black Mountain Press, 1999.

Grotowski, Jerzy. *Towards a Poor Theatre.* Ed. by Eugenio Barba. 1968. Kent: Methuen, 1984.

Kumiega, Jennifer. *The Theater of Jerzy Grotowski.* London: Methuen, 1985.

Richards, Thomas. *At Work with Grotowski on Physical Actions.* London: Routledge, 1995.

Wolford, Lisa. *Grotowski's Objective Drama Research.* Jackson: Univ. of Mississippi Press, 1996.

Seth Baumrin

POPESCU, DUMITRU RADU (1935–)

Born in Păpușa, a village near Oradea, ROMANIA, on August 10, 1935, Dumitru Radu (D. R.) Popescu is considered one of the most prolific and prominent of Romanian writers from the communist era. His literary activity began during the early communist regime and has spanned over four decades and a wide range of genres. His first short story "The Chess Game" ("O partidă de șah," 1954) and his first play *The Mother* (*Mama*, 1960), followed by his first film scenario *A Smile in the Middle of the Summer* (*Un surâs în plină vară*), established his voice in Romanian dramatic literature. An output of more than forty titles followed. Throughout the 1960s and 1970s, his plays achieved widespread success.

In his literary works, Popescu sharply criticizes the transformation of Romanian society under communism of the pre-Ceaușescu era. Many of his plays deal with the cruelly enforced collectivization of private farms during the Stalinist dictator-ship of G. Gheorghiu-Dej. Other plays deal with philosophical and existential questions of the human condition.

In his first play, *The Mother*, a mother, in her dreams, brings her son back from the war, thus restoring the atmosphere of her former harmonious and peaceful family life. In *Cat on the New Year's Eve* (*Pisica în Noaptea Anului Nou*, 1970), one of his most controversial plays, Popescu also uses a family setting in which the father, who had disappeared during the great purges, reappears twenty years later as Santa Claus on New Years Eve. A series of terrible happenings, real or imaginary, punctures the consciousness of the dinner guests, who are forced to reveal their true moral quality. In a complex political-philosophical study, *The Dwarf in the Summer Garden* (*Piticul din grădina de vară*, 1971), Maria, the main character, is convicted of subversive political activity and condemned to death. However, since she is pregnant, the punishment is postponed until she gives birth to a baby boy. Popescu uses the nine-month reprieve to analyze the power play between the victim, a fearless antifascist fighter of strong character, and her tormentors.

Heavily indebted to the surrealists and the absurdist style of the 1960s, his DRAMATURGY oscillates between the unreal and the fantastic, though his plays often are set on the border between the real and the imaginary. Drawn from legends and myths, his characters are a mixture of real people and ghosts from another time and place. Deliberately obscure at times, Popescu's plays defy categorization, and he stands as a unique phenomenon in the modern Romanian theater. Above all, his great success despite his open criticism of communism and the aberrations of those in power remains a mystery. He received prestigious prizes for his plays from the Romanian Academy of Letters and remained for many years the president of the Romanian Writers Union.

SELECT PLAYS: *The Mother* (*Mama*, 1960); *The Summer of Impossible Love* (*Vara Imposibilei Iubiri*, 1966); *Dream* (*Vis*, 1968); *Those Sad Angels* (*Acești ingeri triști*, 1969); *Cat on the New Year's Eve* (*Pisica în Noaptea Anului Nou*, 1970); *The Dwarf in the Summer Garden* (*Piticul din grădina de vară*, 1971); *The Shakespeare Bird* (*Pasărea Shakespeare*, 1973); *The Lame Rabbit* (*Iepurele șchiop*, 1980); *The Pelican Reservation* (*Rezervația de Pelicani*, 1983); *The Angels' City* (*Orașul Ingerilor*, 1985); *A Handkerchief on the Danube* (*O batistă în Dunăre*, 1997)

FURTHER READING

Iosif, Mira. *Teatrul nostru cel de toate serile* [Our Theater of Every Morning]. București, România: Editura Eminescu, 1979.

Micu, Dumitru. *Scurtă istorie a literaturii române. IV. Perioada contemporană dramaturgia critică.* [Short history of Romanian literature. IV. Contemporary period dramatic criticism]. București, România: Editura Iriana, 1997.

Popescu, Dumitru Radu. *Teatru* [Theater]. București, România: Editura Cartea Romanesca, 1974.

Moshe Yassur

POPOVIĆ, ALEKSANDAR (1929–1996)

Aleksandar Popović is one of the most important Serbian dramatists of the second half of the 20th century. Both his biography and the unique features of his works make Popović one of the most interesting and original figures in the history of Serbian drama and theater. With some literary education but no formal qualifications, Popović took up various trades in his youth (which would also be reflected in his works), only to completely devote himself to professional writing for the theater, film, and television in the late 1960s. He was a prolific playwright (considered to have written around forty plays), but as he was a true theater man who wrote plays to be performed onstage, most of his texts have not survived to this day.

When they appeared, in the mid-1960s, the plays of Popović represented a radical change compared to previous trends in Serbian drama. The first thing apparent in them is the break with classical drama: the story is not developed causally, and the characters lack any psychological content. Instead of classical narration, different means of composition are introduced: cyclic events with a semblance of development, sudden and random twists in the plot, and self-sufficient rules of the game.

In terms of genre, Popović's plays can most readily be defined as FARCES (this definition is used by the author himself). The farcical elements in his works are numerous: his portrayal of lower classes of society, situations based on misunderstanding, erotic elements, and fast rhythm. In the view of Mirjana Miočinović, the leading expert on Popović's works, the topics of his farces are not really typical of the genre. Thus, for example, the farce called *Ljubinko and Desanka* (*Ljubinko i Desanka*, 1964) is about the futility of waiting; and this kind of seemingly comical treatment of the topic of waiting (and the impossibility of change) creates an association with SAMUEL BECKETT's *WAITING FOR GODOT*, which had, along with other works of the Theater of the Absurd, an undeniable influence on Popović.

Although Popović's theater is antimimetic, it still sets the outlines of a familiar world. That is the world of Belgrade's pseudo-urban outskirts and its tradesmen, pub owners, and junior clerks. His treatment of this world is not ideologically sharp—all you feel is a very harmless irony. As Slobodan Selenić correctly noted, there were some elements of sharper social criticisms in some later Popović farces; thus, the play *The Development of Bora the Tailor* (*Razvojni put Bore Šnajdera*, 1967) illustrates all the shortcomings of socialist economy: the political interests present, incompetence, irresponsibility, disinterest in work.

The most unique and valuable quality in Popović's plays is his language. The language becomes a dramatic element in its own right and, as such, a factor in character buildup. This language is unique: it is the jargon of different guilds of tradesmen from the city outskirts, which is almost unintelligible to ordinary audiences. Apart from the comic effect, this kind of language creates a bit of BERTOLT BRECHT's distancing effect.

This self-sufficient quality of the language, coupled with the already analyzed deviation from classical narration, is what sets Popović's plays apart from REALISM. In the national context, Popović's works are significant precisely for this radical break with realism.

PLAYS: *Ljubinko and Desanka* (*Ljubinko i Desanka*, 1964); *A 100 Loops Stocking Čarapa od sto petlji*, 1965); *The Development of Bora the Tailor* (*Razvojni put Bore Šnajdera*, 1967); *Lethal Motorcycle Racing* (*Smrtonosna motoristika*, 1967); *The Spawning of Carp* (*Mrešćenje šarana*, 1984)

FURTHER READING

Galonja, Miroslav. "Coffee with Mira: Interview: Aleksandar Popovic, Playwright." *Vreme News Digest Agency*, no. 132 (April 4, 1994). http://www.scc.rutgers.edu/serbian_digest/132/t132-4.htm.

Marjanović, Petar. *Srpski dramski pisci XX stoleća* [The 20th century Serbian playwrights]. Belgrade: Belgrade Drama Faculty, 2000.

——. "The History of Serbian Culture." Serbian Unity Congress. http://www.oea.serbian-church.net/culture/history/ Hist_Serb_Culture/chp/The_Theatre.html.

Miočinović, Mirjana. Foreword to *Izabrane drame* [Selected drama], by Aleksandar Popović. Belgrade: Nolit, 1987.

Selenić, Slobodan. Foreword to *Antologija savremene srpske drame* [Anthology of contemporary Serbian drama]. Belgrade: SKZ, 1977.

Ivan Medenica

PORGY AND BESS

DuBose Heyward is best known for his libretto and songs for *Porgy and Bess*. A humorous newspaper clipping about a black man trying to outrace policemen in a goat cart inspired Heyward's "convincing" novel *Porgy* (1925)—about Charleston's black community in the fictional Catfish Row. DuBose and DOROTHY HEYWARD adapted his novel into the hit play *Porgy* for the THEATRE GUILD (1927), and with George and Ira Gershwin, he revised this into the now more famous "folk opera" (1935). The novel's phonetic spelling of Gullah dialogue becomes less obtrusive in both scripts. Retaining the story and somewhat stereotypical characters, the dramatizations successively reduce the novelist's somewhat patronizing tone. The folk of Catfish Row grow better without commentary and with fewer condescending black jokes.

Catfish Row comes alive Saturday evening with singing and chatter. Jake and Clara lullaby their baby; God-fearing Serena scolds Robbins not to play craps tonight. The cripple Porgy, returning in his goat cart from begging in town, denies being "soft" on Crown's Bess: "When Gawd make cripple, He mean him to be lonely." The big handsome stevedore Crown arrives with Bess for the craps game and, drunk and belligerent, fights with Robbins, killing him with his cotton-hook. As all flee the courtyard, Crown tells Bess he will be back for her. Matriarchal Maria refuses to harbor the "liquor guzzlin' slut," but Porgy does. An unwelcome Bess arrives in Serena's room the next day with Porgy and contributes to the "saucer" burial fund and to singing the spirituals.

Soon Porgy tells Bess, "You is my woman now" and with Maria persuades her to go along to picnic on Kittiwah Island without him. There Crown draws Bess into the palmettos. A week later Porgy prays and conjures to cure the still feverish, delirious Bess. He promises he will not let Crown "handle" her with his "hot han[ds]." The hurricane bell sounds. Terrified residents gather to withstand the "Judgment Day" storm with "shoutings" and spirituals. Crown knocks like Death and barges in, taunting God and Porgy with nasty humor. Clara, spotting Jake's capsized boat, gives Bess their baby and rushes out. Bess's challenge, "Ain't dere no man here?" sends Crown out after her.

When Crown returns for Bess, Porgy kills him. Summoned to identify Crown, Porgy expects the corpse to bleed in its killer's presence. In novel and play, he tries to flee the police in his goat cart. Later learning that Bess left for New York with Sporting Life, in play and libretto Porgy sets out after her in his pathetic cart.

From the era of blackface COMEDY and few serious roles for black actors, Heyward's large-cast plays of *Porgy and Bess* portray one vitally primitive community that resists the incursions of a dominant alien society with resilient dignity. While Duke Ellington debunked the "lampblack Negroisms" and questioned the fit of such "grand music and a swell play, (Morrow, 1935)" history has recognized a "masterpiece of American musical theater." Heyward's public sympathy and "understanding" kept pace with and contributed to white America's slow racial progress.

[*See also* United States]

FURTHER READING

Alpert, Hollis. *The Life and Times of* Porgy and Bess: *The Story of an American Classic.* New York: Knopf, 1990.

Hutchisson, James M. *DuBose Heyward: A Southern Gentleman and the World of Porgy and Bess.* Jackson: Univ. Press of Mississippi, n.d. [c. 2000].

Morrow, Edward. "Duke Ellington on Gershwin's *Porgy.*" *New Theater* (December 1935): 5–6.

Schiff, David. "The Man Who Breathed Life into 'Porgy and Bess.'" *New York Times* (March 5, 2000).

Standifer, James. "The Tumultuous Life of 'Porgy and Bess.'" *Humanities* (November–December 1997): 8–12, 51–54.

John G. Kuhn

POSIBILISMO AND IMPOSIBILISMO

The concepts of *posibilismo* (possibilism) and *imposibilismo* (impossibilism) hark back to a polemic emerged around 1960 between the two playwrights who initiated a radical change in the post–civil war Spanish theater: ANTONIO BUERO VALLEJO and ALFONSO SASTRE. The realist aesthetic proved well suited to the desire of these authors to express a imaginary world that is at the same time profoundly realistic, allowing the use of realist language to convey highly artistic and ideological concepts. Right away a controversy arose between the two supporters of the committed realist theater about the way to denounce the unjust situation in post–civil war SPAIN. Buero, the representative of *posibilismo*, tried in a subtle, indirect way that would take advantage of any oversight by the censors to defend freedom and protest the dictatorship. Sastre, on the other hand, represents *imposibilismo* because he altogether rejected the strategy of referring to Spanish reality in an indirect way. Sastre imbued some of his plays with Marxist ideals—which, to his mind, made them an instrument of revolutionary action. Thus, his plays attempt to do more than represent life or inspire thought. Sastre's plays aimed to incite action.

Numerous authors abandoned their efforts to fight for a different theater. However, the ones that persevered did so with a passionate critical spirit. The different approaches reflected a polemic about submission or resistance to the rules imposed by the system, a polemic that reached its boiling point in 1960 when Sastre published the article "Teatro imposible y pacto social" (Impossible Theater and Social Pact). In the article, Sastre accuses the playwrights Alfonso Paso and Buero Vallejo of conforming to the rules imposed by the control mechanisms of the regime. Indeed, Alfonso kept himself aligned with the *pacto social* (social pact of some intellectuals with the regime) and was able to premiere numerous plays. Buero soon replied to Sastre in another article, "Obligada precisión acerca del 'imposibilismo,'" (Forced Precision About "Impossibilism" [1960]), arguing that there is no such thing as an impossible theater because everything is possible, unless there is a concrete physical obstacle to its realization. Buero concludes that Spain, especially at this time, needed a theater of the possible. He advocated a committed, risky form of theater that found its way not only into scripts but also into performances for the public.

The impact of this academic discussion was so great that the debate between *posibilismo* and *imposibilismo* has become an intrinsic part of the history of 20th-century Spanish theater. The importance of these different attitudes toward theater is reinforced by the fact that the authors identified above played a major role in changing the outlook of post–civil war Spanish theater and also because 1960 marked the birth of a new generation of playwrights, who were thoroughly affected by this polemic. They would soon embrace the commitment and social protest inherited from their realist predecessors and suffer the consequences when theater houses refused to present their plays because of their realist charged content.

FURTHER READING

Buero Vallejo, Antonio. "Obligada precisión acerca del 'imposibilismo.'" [Forced precision about impossibilism]. *Primer Acto* 15 (1960): 1–6.

Delgado, Maria. *Spanish Theatre, 1920–1995: Strategies in Protest and Imagination 3.* Contemporary Theatre Review. Amsterdam: Harwood Acad. Pubs., 1998.

Halsey, Martha T. *Antonio Buero Vallejo.* Twayne's World Authors Series. New York: Twayne, 1973.

O'Leary, Catherine. *The Theatre of Antonio Buero Vallejo: Ideology, Politics and Censorship.* Woodbridge: Támesis, 2005.

Ruiz Ramón, Francisco. "Testimonio y compromiso: Buero Vallejo y Alfonso Sastre" [Testimony and Commitment: Buero Vallejo and Alfonso Sastre]. *Historia del teatro español* [History of Spanish Theater. Twentieth Century]. Siglo XX. Madrid: Cátedra, 1975. 337–420.

Sastre, Alfonso. "Teatro imposible y pacto social" [Impossible theater and social pact]. *Primer Acto* 14 (1960): 1–3.

———. *Anatomía del realismo* [Anatomy of realism]. Barcelona: Seix Barral, 1965.

Schwartz, Kessel. "Posibilismo and Imposibilismo: The Buero Vallejo–Sastre Polemic." *Revista Hispánica Moderna* 34 (1968): 436–445.

Jorge Herreros and Benito Gómez

POSTMODERNISM

Postmodernism has been theorized as a "condition" that led to various cultural, social, and artistic movements. In the sense that it is a "condition," postmodernism refers to the period of late capitalism directly following modernism. Hence, postmodernism might be thought of as a total rejection of the values of modernism. Postmodernism has sometimes been called "antimodernism."

However, "antimodernism" implies a logical progress to history, and it was Jean-François Lyotard (1984) who signaled the beginning of postmodernism in his rejection of "grand narratives"—sometimes called master narratives—or the teleological progression of history. Lyotard saw the postmodern not as a rejection of modernism but as a deepening of modernism's unanswered questions. His critique of history also exposed the dramaturgical structure involved in the writing of history, particularly in conservative Marxism, which implies an ending point to history—part and parcel of the Enlightenment project.

Instead of an end point to history, postmodernism often sees repetition and reiteration as the only certainty. As Herbert Blau (1992) writes, "If we can believe the history of modernism, we are living in the double bind, the history that always repeats itself." For postmodern playwright SUZAN-LORI PARKS history is condemned to repetition, what she calls in her AMERICA PLAY "the great hole of history." This repetition is often termed *pastiche*, a form used because "the producers of culture have nowhere to turn but to the past: the imitation of dead styles," according to Frederic Jameson (1991), "or to the radical cannibalization of the past." The Wooster Group's L.S.D. (. . . Just the High Points) (1985) is a clear example of pastiche, in that the piece collided

Timothy Leary's psychoactive drug experiments with ARTHUR MILLER's THE CRUCIBLE to explore both Leary and John Proctor (the protagonist of The Crucible) as scapegoats of their culture. L.S.D. grew doubly ironic when Miller threatened to sue the Wooster Group for unauthorized use of his play.

In his (re)making project (1992–present), CHARLES MEE uses the repetition of history as a starting point, and he begins with ancient Greek plays and rewrites them to include the language of popular culture. He also does not claim ownership of his plays but invites others to rewrite them by making them available on the Internet. This impulse might derive from Roland Barthes's 1968 essay "The Death of the Author," which he believed signaled "the birth of the reader." The ideology of absolute truth and authorial ownership had been erased.

Postmodern German playwright HEINER MÜLLER embraced this concept in his rewrite of *Hamlet*, titled HAMLETMACHINE (1977), which climaxes in an actress burning a picture of the author. In her 1983 essay "The Death of Character," Elinor Fuchs points to an American postmodernism that moves away from the psychological REALISM of characters and toward a new space where theater itself becomes self-referential. Postmodernism signals the proliferation of identities, a sense of history as repetition, which is often expressed as pastiche, and a movement away from Enlightenment values into a space where personal experience is valued over cultural hierarchies.

[*See also* Deconstruction; Foreman, Richard; Identity Theater; Interculturalism; Performance Art; Performance Studies; Philosophy and Drama]

FURTHER READING

Auslander, Philip. *From Acting to Performance: Essays in Modernism and Postmodernism.* New York: Routlege, 1994.

Birringer, Johannes. *Theatre, Theory, Postmodernism.* Bloomington: Indiana Univ. Press, 1991.

Blau, Herbert. *To All Appearances: Ideology and Performance.* New York: Routlege, 1992.

Fuchs, Elinor. *The Death of Character, Perspectives on Theater After Modernism.* Bloomington: Indiana Univ. Press, 1996.

Jameson, Frederic. *Postmodernism, or the Cultural Logic of Late Capitalism.* Durham, N.C.: Duke Univ. Press, 1991.

Kaye, Nick. *Postmodernism and Performance.* London: Macmillan, 1994.

Lyotard, François. *The Postmodern Condition: A Report on Knowledge.* Tr. by Geoff Bennington and Brian Massumi. Foreword by Frederic Jameson. Minneapolis: Univ. of Minnesota Press, 1984.

Kara Reilly

THE POWER OF DARKNESS

The Power of Darkness (Vlast' t'my), a naturalistic play in five acts by LYOV TOLSTOY, was written in 1886 and published the following year; but because of its uncompromising treatment of murder, adultery, and infanticide, it was banned from performance at the insistence of the Procurator of the Holy Synod. The play's premiere was given, in French, by ANDRÉ ANTOINE at his Theatre Libre in Paris on February 2, 1888, and received with acclaim. Its Russian premiere was staged in St. Petersburg in 1895 by the Literary Artistic Circle headed by ANTON CHEKHOV's friend, publisher Aleksei Suvorin. It was originally written at the request of actor P. A. Denisenko, who was planning a journal devoted to the idea of a "People's Theatre," and Tolstoy based it on the actual trial of one Yefrem Koloskov, details of which the Tula regional prosecutor had communicated to him:

> This was the case of the murder of a peasant girl's new-born child by its father, a distant relative with whom she lived in the same family and in the same house. The peculiar characteristic of the case, aside from the dramatic setting of the murder itself, was the conduct of the murderer, who, racked by conscience, publicly confessed of his own accord to the crime. Later he craved trial and punishment, and, even though he was convicted and sentenced to hard labor, he was pleased with the penalty, considering it as the expiation of his sin.

The play's subtitle, *If the Claw Is Caught—the Whole Bird Is Lost*, is a clue to its moral emphasis—the need to avoid dipping even one's toe into the muddy waters of immorality without risking total immersion—in this case, in lust leading to murder. The "darkness" of the title refers not only to abstract notions of evil but also to the fact that the peasants live in the darkness of ignorance and deprivation as a direct consequence of their social position in 19th-century feudal RUSSIA. The play also portrays the power of ruthless women—in this case, of Anisya, second wife to a sickly husband, Pyotr, whom she poisons with the help of her lover's mother, Matryona. Anisya's motive to do away with her husband, a well-to-do peasant, is to get her hands on his money and to have unrestricted access to Nikita, a good-looking farm laborer in their employ, seven years her junior. Following the murder, of which Nikita is ignorant, Anisya marries him, only to be repulsed by him when he discovers the truth about Pyotr's death. He has already impregnated an orphan girl, whom he now abandons, despite his God-fearing father Akim's plea for him to do the decent thing and marry her. He turns his attention, instead, to Pyotr's sixteen-year-old daughter by his first marriage, Akulina, who is both deaf and mentally retarded. She has a child by him, but since she is betrothed to another, Anisya and Matryona conspire to kill the baby and bury it in the cellar. Nikita crushing the baby's skull with a board is one of the most powerful scenes in 19th-century drama. The denouement occurs at Akulina's wedding when Nikita makes a public confession of his crime and Akim assures him of God's forgiveness.

FURTHER READING

Orwin, Donna Tussing, ed. *Cambridge Companion to Tolstoy*. Cambridge: Cambridge Univ. Press, 2002.
Simmons, Earnest J. *Introduction to Tolstoy's Writings*. Chicago: Univ. of Chicago Press, 1968.
Tolstoy, L. *The Power of Darkness*. In *Plays*, tr. by Louise Maude and Aylmer Maude. 3rd ed. London: Oxford Univ. Press, 1957.
Wilson, A. N. *Tolstoy: A Biography*. New York: Norton, 1988.

Nick Worrall

THE POWER PLAYS

The Power Plays, by Toronto playwright GEORGE F. WALKER, are a loose trilogy featuring a portly antihero named Tyrone Power. He explains in *Filthy Rich* that he has a 1940s movie star's name because his mother was a romantic. Unlike his namesake, this Tyrone Power is sloppy, unromantic, unattractive, and only involved in the plot through the machinations of other characters.

Gossip was first produced in 1977, *Filthy Rich* in 1979, and *The Art of War* in 1983. Until 1977 Walker's plays were staged almost exclusively at Toronto's Factory Theatre Lab, attracting a cult following but not making an impression on the broader regional or international stage. *Gossip* indicated the path Walker was to follow in many subsequent plays. The byplay between FARCE, gritty, often violent REALISM, and social commentary established Walker's predominant style for the next two decades.

Gossip, the first in the series, keeps the social commentary to a minimum. The first image is a minimalist art show at which a murder is committed, indicating that the play is at least as concerned with satirizing art making as commenting on social conditions. There is a vague political corruption plot about a conspiracy to run an illegal mine in a Third World nation, but the plot is overshadowed by the comic absurdity of the characters, relationships, and the film-noire style. Power unravels several murder-conspiracy strands in the dénouement of the play in the style of Sam Spade, Charlie Chan, and a dozen other B-movie detectives. The most surprising thing about *Gossip* is how consistent it is as a mystery, including a satisfying ending for the audience if not for the hero who remains nihilistic and depressive at play's end.

At the beginning of *Gossip*, Power is a journalist who uses his political column as a vehicle for attacking the establishment until his boss, Baxter, insists that he drop the political beat to investigate the murder of "Bitch Nelson" in the art gallery. The caricature of a callous newspaper magnate would return in a much more frightening form years later in Walker's play *Beautiful City*, but the Baxter of *Gossip* is essentially a foil for the hero. *Gossip* is metatheatrical with actor characters and a running gag that actors will do anything for money and an Actors Equity card. The final scene includes outrageous revelations, Baxter pretending to be hopelessly drunk, and a faked murder.

The second *Power Play*, *Filthy Rich*, is substantially more focused than *Gossip*, in part because it takes place entirely in Power's sleazy office. He has quit his job as a journalist and lives in a derelict neighborhood, trying to write a novel. Once again he is unwillingly drawn into the role of private detective, but this time the motivation comes partly from a new character, Jamie Mclean, a young, working-class man who cleans his office and insinuates himself into Power's life as a "positive force." Power is initially hostile toward Jamie, who interrupts his drunken self-pity.

Filthy Rich strikes a delicate balance between social content and COMEDY. Michael Harrison, a candidate for Mayor, has disappeared, and somehow one of Power's old journalist friends is involved. Power has even more threatening foils than in Gossip, such as twin spider-women, Ann and Susan Scott, a coarse, corrupt policeman called Stackhouse, and "one of those killers who really kill" called "The Pig." Power sums up the machinations of the plot near the end as "the obvious becoming mysterious becoming disastrous."

The comedy takes a dark turn when Power's ex-associate turns up dead while trying to deliver blackmail money to Power. The comedy takes an even darker turn when Jamie apparently gets shot dead by Susan Scott. Power seems to have lost both his old and new friend and decides to throw the half million dollars out the window, yelling to the crowd below: "Don't vote for Michael Harrison!" Jamie turns out to be alive, after all, having put blanks in Susan's gun, and tries to stop Power. Despite Jamie's anger at losing the money, the two characters seem genuinely linked in the end.

The Art of War is by far the most didactic of the series, pitting flabby, liberal idealists against ruthless military fanatics and their Third World allies who are unambiguously described as fascists. The urban, film noir backdrop is dispensed with in favor of rural Nova Scotia. Power is the driving force behind the action rather than a naturally passive, unwilling participant, as in the earlier plays. The play begins with a grisly murder, but Power's character seems to have been genuinely rejuvinated by his relationship with Jamie, established in Filthy Rich.

The Art of War is the least comic of the series, and the relationship between Power and his young partner Jamie is less engaging than in Filthy Rich because Power's transformation seems to be complete. The villain of The Art of War is John Hackman, a retired army general who has been reassigned to the Ministry of Culture. At one point Power and Hackman actually debate culture directly, and Walker treads dangerously close to pendantry by allowing his protagonist to step out of character and speak directly for the author. The play's ending is the most depressing in the series because Power's character had seemed to transform into a genuine hero, yet his humanistic scruples are proven inadequate against a villain of Hackman's stature.

As in the end of Filthy Rich there is an ambiguous death scene, but this time it is Jamie who cradles Power in his arms, fearing that Power will die. "I'm tired of losing. It's so depressing" are his final words, and it is difficult not to share his depression. Unlike TRAGEDY in which the death of the hero seems to serve a purpose, Walker avoids pathos by not quite killing Power off, choosing instead to reinforce the futility of his life instead. L. W. Conolly (1987) has praised the tough-mindedness of The Art of War, calling it "an intelligent play that doesn't sit well with the other two," but while The Power Plays do not form a legitimate trilogy, The Art of War would not appear as profound without the perfected farce of its predecessors.

FURTHER READING

Bruckner, D.J.R. "Filthy Rich: A Sleuth Spoof." New York Times (October 8, 1985): 13.

———. "The Art of War." New York Times (April 28, 1987): 13

Conolly, L. W. "Dramatic Trilogies." Canadian Literature, no. 112 (Spring 1987): 110–112.

Walker, Craig Stewart. "George F. Walker: Postmodern City Comedy." In The Buried Astrolabe: Canadian Dramatic Imagination and Western Tradition. Montreal: McGill Univ. Press, 2001. 264–354.

Walker, George F. Shared Anxiety. Toronto: Coach House Press, 1994.

Donald Cameron McManus

POWER VERSUS LAW

Written by Xing Yixun and premiered in 1979 by the China Youth Art Theater in Beijing, Power Versus Law (Quan yu fa) was an immediate success and remained one of the most influential plays in early post-Mao CHINA that addressed the issue of the Chinese Communist Party corruption right after the end of the Cultural Revolution.

Set in 1978, Power Versus Law recounts how Ding Mu, inspired by the party's campaign to reestablish legal systems after the arrest of the Gang of Four, writes a letter to the press exposing the criminal acts of Cao Da, the deputy secretary of the municipal party committee who embezzled public funds for flood victims in order to build his luxurious house. Confident that his past revolutionary record entitles him to special privileges, Cao Da threatens to arrest Ding Mu on the groundless charge that she murdered her husband during the Cultural Revolution to enhance her chances of winning over another man. Under these circumstances, Luo Fang, the newly appointed secretary of the municipal party committee, wins Ding Mu's trust and encourages her to come forward, and she finally succeeds in exposing Cao Da. Unusually in Chinese theater, the play also depicts a courageous news reporter and editor who dare to publish articles against corruption and media censorship, with Luo Fang's support.

The play, which caused a national sensation, raised the topical issue: do those in power have the right to abuse their power and to take reprisals against those who challenge them? Can socialist China practice law and justice against its own members of the ruling party? Unlike other plays of the period, such as Sha Yexin's If I Were for Real, which was criticized for addressing the issue of corruption and privilege, Power Versus Law was praised as a positive example by depicting Luo Fang, the perfect party official, thus providing people with hope for a bright socialist future. But the play also presents a Cao Da whose real-life counterparts were too obvious to miss. Cao Da did not even back down after Luo Fang's well-known central passage: "Don't forget, in this city you're not the foundation but a pillar. You and I both! If we're crooked, people have the right to knock us down. The same applies to those in still higher positions, even in the Central Committee. If anyone breaks the law as you have done, the people have the right to bash him down. Today [holds up the incriminating material] the people are going to bash you!" (act 3). Such a climactic scene cleverly kills two birds with one stone: it satirizes a scoundrel and celebrates an idealized image of Luo Fang, both in the ruling Communist Party, thus winning acceptance from different sectors of society. Many audiences approved Luo Fang's heroism, which offered hope for a better party after the Cultural Revolution, while others pointed to the scarcity of his counterparts in real life. For officials eager to preserve the status quo, he could be used as a cover for their faults and even help establish their new legitimacy. For those inclined to subversive sentiments, he bolstered their conviction that such a paragon could only be found onstage. The play was promoted by the purveyors of official ideology and was also celebrated for its counterdiscourse, appreciated by some audiences attuned to its dichotomies and ironies.

FURTHER READING

Chen, Xiaomei. *Acting the Right Part: Political Theater and Popular Drama in Contemporary China.* Honolulu: Univ. of Hawaii Press, 2002.

——, ed. and intro. *Reading the Right Texts: An Anthology of Contemporary Chinese Drama with a Critical Introduction.* Honolulu: Univ. of Hawaii Press, 2003.

Xing Yixun. *Power Versus Law. Chinese Literature* 6 (1980): 31–91.

Yan, Haiping, ed. *Literature and Society: Anthology of Contemporary Chinese Drama.* Armonk, N.Y.: M. E. Sharpe, 1998. 123–261.

Xiaomei Chen

PRAGA, MARCO (1852–1929)

Marco Praga was born in Milan in 1852, the son of Emilio Praga, a leading member of the Milanese *scapigliatura*, a group of self-styled bohemian writers who opposed the materialistic values of ITALY's newly industrialized society. Marco, on the contrary, like GIUSEPPE GIACOSA, Girolamo Rovetta, and fellow Milanese playwrights Camillo Antona-Traversi and ROBERTO BRACCO, embraced bourgeois society, questioning its moral ideals and examining its effects on the family and on its most vulnerable members, its women. Nearly all of Praga's twenty-two plays deal with love triangles and adulterous relationships celebrating his heroines' ambivalent triumphs over morally bleak situations. His best plays treat the status of women in society with psychological insight approaching that of AUGUST STRINDBERG, HENRIK IBSEN, and ANTON CHEKHOV.

In *The Virgins* (*Le vergini*), which premiered in 1889, three unmarried sisters are called "virgins" with ironic reference to their independent behavior. The youngest sister, disillusioned with society's values, finds an alternative to marriage in a stage career, joining a campany that specializes in light opera. In ONDINE (*L'Ondina*, 1903), however, a young gentleman who has married a former dancer dies in despair of his choice. (An English translation of this play by Denis St. Cyr is available in typescript in the New York Public Library.)

Praga's successful *The Ideal Wife* (*La moglie ideale*) was written for Eleanora Duse, who introduced the play in 1890 in Turin. The play's "ideal wife" simultaneously maintains an affectionate relationship with her husband, who suspects no infidelity, and a passionate affair with her lover. She is the "modern woman," capable of dividing herself between her lover and her home where she enjoys "the emotions, satisfactions, duties and the rights a girl acquires when she becomes wife and mother." The wife's cynical posture is blamed on a society "full of contagious vices, where a woman inhales temptations with the air she breathes, and everything conspires against her humanity." Following the success of *The Ideal Wife*, the composer Giacomo Puccini asked Praga to write a libretto for a new *Manon Lescaut*, but after a disagreement over the opera's third act, Praga withdrew from the project.

In 1923 Eleanora Duse brought Praga's *Closed Door* (*La porta chiusa*) to America. The play's female protagonist is a woman defined by motherhood. Having given up her lover, the father of her son, in order to raise her child in a respectable home, she must also give up her son, who leaves home when he discovers that his birth was illegitimate. "Children," her priest says, "should belong only to the mother; marriage should be abolished, the mother alone is sacred." Performing an English translation of the play by A. S. MacDonald, Duse alternated *Closed Door* with plays by Henrik Ibsen, Tomasso Gallerati-Scotti, and GABRIELE D'ANNUNZIO at the Century Theatre in New York City. Charlie Chaplin reviewed her Los Angeles performance of *Closed Door* enthusiastically.

Praga's theatrical life included his tenure as director-manager of the Manzoni Theater of Milan from 1913 to 1917, where he inaugurated LUIGI PIRANDELLO's *Others' Reason* (*Ragione degli altri*). He was artistic director of Silentium Film of Milan. From 1896 to 1911 he presided over the Italian Society of Authors and Publishers. An anthology of reviews and commentaries abstracted from ten volumes of *Cronache Teatrali* (Theater Reports), published from 1919 to 1929, was edited by Ruggero Rimini and published in 1979. Praga died in Varese in 1929.

PLAYS: *Encounter* (*L'Incontro*, 1883); *The Two Houses* (*Le Due case*, in collaboration with V. Colombo, 1884); *The Friend* (*L'Amico*, 1886); *Giuliana* (1887); *Sorrowful Mother* (*Mater dolorosa*, 1889); *The Virgins* (*Le vergini*, 1889); *The Ideal Wife* (*La moglie ideale*, 1890); *The Sweetheart* (*L'Innamorata*, 1891); *Hallelujah* (*Alleluja*, 1892), *The Spell* (*L'Incanto*, 1892); *The Heir* (*L'Erede*, 1893); *Fair Apollo* (*Il Bell'Apollo*, 1894); *The Mother* (*La Mamma*, 1895); *Doubt* (*Il Dubbio*, 1899); *The Moral of the Tale* (*La Morale della favola*, 1899); *Ondine* (*L'Ondina*,

1903); *The Crisis (La Crisi,* 1904); *The Closed Door (La porta chiusa,* 1913); *The Divorce (Il Divorzio,* 1915); *Orestes, Pilade and Pippo (Oreste, Pilade e Pippo,* 1932)

FURTHER READING

Bondanella, Peter, Julia Conaway Bondanella, and Jody Robin Shiffman, eds. *Dictionary of Italian Literature.* Rev., exp. ed. Westport, Conn.: Greenwood Press, 1996.

Enciclopedia dello Spettacolo [Encyclopedia of theatrical art]. Rome: Maschere, 1954–1962. 7:419–421.

Pullini, Giorgio. *Marco Praga,* Bologna: Cappelli, 1960.

Weaver, William. *Duse: A Biography.* New York: Norton, 1984.

Nancy Dersofi

THE PRETENDERS

> *A man may die for the life work of another; but if he lives, he must live for his own.*
> —Earl Skule, Act 5

HENRIK IBSEN's *The Pretenders (Kongs-Emnerne),* a historical drama in five acts, was first performed at the Christiania Theater in January 1864 under the direction of Ibsen himself. *The Pretenders* takes its material from the period of the civil wars in NORWAY in the 13th century, when the monarchic succession was in dispute and a number of pretenders with varying degrees of legitimacy fought for recognition, among them the play's two protagonists, King Håkon Håkonssøn and Earl Skule. The conflict between Håkon and Skule constitutes the central thematic axis of the play. It reaches its climax after Skule has let himself be proclaimed king of Norway. During the gathering for his inaugural blessing in the Cathedral of Nidaros, Skule's son Peter, blinded by his father's borrowed grand design, steals the shrine of St. Olaf from the cathedral in order to let Skule be consecrated as king according to Church ritual procedures. As a consequence of this blasphemous deed, Skule's opponents are mobilized and his supporters put to flight, and after a dramatic episode in the monastery of Elgeseter, where Skule and his son have arranged a meeting in order to kill Håkon's son, father and son are persuaded by the women of the family to expiate their crime, to walk unarmed out of the monastery, and to let themselves be slain by Håkon's men.

In Ibsen's play Bishop Nikolas is the very incarnation of a cunning intriguer who, since he himself is neither by virtue of birth nor by power of manhood able to become or suited to becoming king, sees it as his mission in life to set in motion a perpetuum mobile, that is to say, to initiate mechanisms that have the effect that none of the other pretenders can ever gain acceptance as the only rightful heir to the throne. Even on his deathbed, he stages a perpetuation of this uncertainty in a masterly piece of orchestration by letting Skule unknowingly burn the letter that would have settled the question regarding Håkon's right to the throne. In this character Ibsen provided a masterful study in the art of compensation psychology.

The relation between Håkon and Earl Skule implies the conflict between a man with an unfailing belief in himself and his own calling and a man who in spite of his excellent abilities has doubts about his legitimate right in the struggle for the throne. The great difference between Håkon and Skule is that while the former has a grand vision he intends to put into effect, the latter is basically a pure medieval power politician with Machiavellian features. King Håkon is the legitimate heir to the throne because he has a vision to unite Norway as kingdom into becoming one "people," while Earl Skule lacks any such vision and would rather copy that of Håkon.

In *The Pretenders* Ibsen breaks the classical unities of time and place. The play comes closer to the romantic drama of the kind one finds represented in William Shakespeare and Friedrich Schiller—with great leaps in time and space, with alternation between crowd scenes and individual appearances, frequent changes of scene, and a large cast.

FURTHER READING

Brynhildsvoll, Knut. "Ibsen's *Pretenders* and Schiller's *Demetrius* Fragment. Similarities and Differences Regarding the Concept of Historic Tragedy." In Astrid Ibsen, *Tragedy, and the Tragic,* ed. by Astrid Sæther. Oslo: Centre for Ibsen Studies, 2003. 73–83.

Kittang, Atle. "*The Pretenders*—Historical Vision or Psychological Tragedy?" In *Ibsen Yearbook.* Olso: Universitets forlag, 1976. 78–88.

Knut Brynhildsvoll

THE PRICE

ARTHUR MILLER's *The Price* opened at the Morosco Theatre in New York on February 7, 1968, and ran for 131 performances. It was played without an intermission. Earlier, during the Philadelphia tryout, it had been done in two acts, which is the way it appears, somewhat deceptively, in published editions. In an author's production note, Miller indicates that although the act designations provide for a place to interrupt the play, "an unbroken performance is preferable." Act 2 opens with the stage direction: "The action is continuous."

Another of the many Miller plays about quarreling brothers, *The Price* brings together Victor and Walter Franz for the first time in sixteen years. They have come to dispose of an attic full of furniture from the house they grew up in—that is, to face their past. In *Timebends* (1987), Miller tells how he discovered the dining room table that had been the center of activity in his childhood home and that it became a prominent part of the discarded jumble onstage at the Morosco; but he also insisted that the characters were not based on him and his brother Kermit. Victor Franz is in a kind of spiritual stasis, haunted by the suspicion that his life and his marriage to Esther have no meaning and that there must be someone or something to blame for his being a police sergeant instead of a successful scientist, for his having sacrificed his career perhaps unnecessarily to his father, broken by the crash and the Depression. Walter, a fashionable surgeon whose losses—a divorce, estrangement from his children, a nervous breakdown—have made him doubt the value of his success is in need of forgiveness for the wrong that he may or may not have done Victor in letting him assume the burden of caring for their father. In the big confrontation scene between them, the talk that Esther so believes in fails to bring them into each other's arms. Walter storms out in anger, but Victor seems to have found his own way to an acceptance of his life as it is. There is so much talk about talk in the play that it is possible to see it not only as still another Miller example of a man's need to face the consequences of his acts but also as a critique of the efficacy of the American fondness for talk as therapy.

The most interesting talker in the play and one of the best and funniest characters in the Miller canon is Gregory Solomon, the ninety-year-old furniture dealer who has come to bid on the contents of the attic. Beginning as a standard Russian-Jewish stereotype, he turns into a formidable comic character—garrulous, crotchety, apothegmatic—whose long scene with Victor shows talk as a human and humanizing activity and leads the younger man to his self-realization. Gregory is both an embodiment of and the voice of a positive power of life: "it's not that you can't believe nothing, that's not hard—it's that you still got to believe it."

[See also United States, 1940–Present]

FURTHER READING

Martin, Robert A., ed., *Arthur Miller, New Perspectives*. Englewood Cliffs, N.J.: Prentice-Hall, 1982.

Miller, Arthur. *Timebends: A Life*. New York: Grove, 1987.

——. *Echoes Down the Corridor, Collected Essays, 1944–2000*. Ed. by Steven R. Centola. New York: Viking, 2000.

Gerald Weales

PRIESTLEY, JOHN BOYNTON (1894–1984)

John Boynton (J. B.) Priestley produced a vast and intimidating body of literature as a novelist, critic, essayist, and screenwriter, but his contributions to drama in the 1930s and 1940s overshadow nearly all his other work. Particularly in his "Time Plays," Priestley sought to relax the naturalistic standards of the British theater through experiments in expressionistic staging, the combination of music and dialogue, and a thematic emphasis on the enduring spiritual and supernatural realities that, he believed, undermine the authority of the visible world.

Priestley was born in 1894 in the wool-manufacturing town of Bradford in Yorkshire, ENGLAND, to a progressive Baptist schoolmaster father and an Irish mother who died shortly after his birth. He enlisted in World War I and served in the trenches in FRANCE, where a mortar bomb badly wounded him. The brutality and muddle of the war haunted Priestley throughout his career. Likewise, the prewar England of his childhood became Priestley's standard for a lost Paradise in plays such as *When We*

Are Married (1938) and *Summer Day's Dream* (1949). After the war, he attended Cambridge University, married the first of his three wives, and moved to London to work as a professional writer.

Priestley established his reputation as a popular literary figure with his bestseller *The Good Companions* (1929), an amiable picaresque about a theatrical troupe in the 1920s. He adapted the novel for the stage as a musical entertainment with Edward Knoblock in 1931 and followed it with the enormously successful DANGEROUS CORNER (1932), a formulaic whodunit with discussions about the indeterminacy of truth that he later dismissed as a "box of tricks." Priestley continued to make use of conventional stage genres to accommodate his metaphysical and political preoccupations in his subsequent plays. The Time Plays, many of which borrow from the detective genre and include *Time and the Conways* (1937), *I Have Been Here Before* (1937), *Johnson Over Jordan* (1939), and arguably AN INSPECTOR CALLS (1945), exemplify Priestley's lifelong inquiry into the nature of temporal perception. In these plays, Priestley popularizes the thought of contemporary time theorists, specifically Russian mystic P. D. Ouspensky and British mathematician J. W. Dunne, while modifying them to fit his own evolving ideas. For Priestley's characters, philosophical discussions about the illusory nature of time and change offer an intellectual consolation that combats the destructive forces of aging, failure, and disillusionment. Alan Conway, for instance, the ineffective younger brother in *Time and the Conways*, maintains hope when his more ambitious siblings crumble because he realizes that any single moment in a life is merely a cross section of a transcendent self that cannot be damaged by passing time.

Priestley often matched his metaphysical speculations with deliberately antinaturalistic staging to find new forms of communicating subjective or supernatural material in a primarily realistic medium. In *Johnson Over Jordan*, a collaboration with Benjamin Britten that incorporates music, masks, and dizzying lighting and set changes, Priestley uncovers the neglected spiritual life of a 20th-century Everyman on the threshold of death. Critics of Priestley's experimental staging have often complained that it seems oddly noncommittal, however, grounded somewhere between NATURALISM and SYMBOLISM. Throughout his career, in fact, Priestley resisted comparisons to AVANT-GARDE theater movements in continental Europe. Priestley's nostalgic regard for Georgian England and its theater mixed uneasily with his calls for artistic, political, and philosophical open-mindedness. Later generations of theatrical reformers typed Priestley as the representative of a complacent, pipe-smoking generation that remained entrenched in the outdated assumptions of the 1930s and 1940s. JOHN OSBORNE levels a particularly aggressive attack at Priestley in LOOK BACK IN ANGER (1956), for instance, when Jimmy Porter characterizes him as "like Daddy—still casting well-fed glances back to the Edwardian twilight from his comfortable disenfranchised wilderness."

His later serious drama is more often concerned with the state of England and the disappearance of a more civilized way of life that flourished before the Cold War and the advent of mass consumer culture. Perhaps his most significant contribution to postwar drama is his theory of "dramatic experience," discussed at length in *The Art of the Dramatist* (1957). According to Priestley, watching a play does not require suspension of disbelief but rather the simultaneous experience of immersive belief and critical disbelief, the sensation that a theatrical production is at once artifice and existential truth. Theater becomes a metaphor for those moments of heightened awareness when one glimpses the life behind appearances as well as the most reliable avenue to that life.

Priestley died of complications related to pneumonia at Kissing Tree House near Stratford-upon-Avon on August 14, 1984, and was given a memorial service at Westminster Abbey. His ashes are in the graveyard of the church at Hubberholme in the Yorkshire Dales.

SELECT PLAYS: *Dangerous Corner* (1932); *I Have Been Here Before* (1937); *Time and the Conways* (1937); *When We Are Married* (1938); *Johnson Over Jordan* (1939); *An Inspector Calls* (1945); *Ever Since Paradise* (1947); *Summer Day's Dream* (1949); *Dragon's Mouth* (1952); *The Glass Cage* (1957)

FURTHER READING

Atkins, John. *J. B. Priestley: The Last of the Sages*. New York: Riverrun Press, 1981.

DeVitis, A. A., and Albert E. Kalson. *J. B. Priestley*. Boston: G. K. Hall, 1980.

Innes, Christopher. "J. B. Priestley: Temporal Dislocation and Transcendence." In *Modern British Drama 1890–1990*. Cambridge: Cambridge Univ. Press, 1992.

Klein, Holger. *J. B. Priestley's Plays*. New York: St. Martin's, 1988.

Priestley, J. B. *The Art of the Dramatist*. London: Heinemann, 1957.

Lawrence Switzky

PRINCESS POCAHONTAS AND THE BLUE SPOTS

Written by Monique Mojica with original music by Alejandra Nunez, *Princess Pocahontas and the Blue Spots* was first fully produced at the Theatre Pass Muraille Backspace in co-production with Nightwood Theatre from February 9 to March 4, 1990. Prior to its formal debut, it was presented as a work in progress at various festivals, including the Groundswell Festival of New Work by Women in November 1989. The play received positive reviews at the time of its performance and has since attracted significant academic interest. Excerpts from the play have been included in various anthologies devoted to Native and feminist writing.

The play explores how dominant Western culture has represented the Native women of North and Central America over the past 400 years, from "storybook Pocahontas" to Malinche, interpreter and strategist for Hernando Cortez, to the "cigar store Squaw." The play's parodic performances of "Indianness" unfix the traditional stereotypes of Native women and enable Mojica to present more nuanced images of Native women. Indeed, in an editorial for the *Canadian Theatre Review* (1991) Mojica addressed the singular importance of Native self-definition: "We must not remain forever the 'other,' either relegated to quaint folklore or elevated to mystic exoticism." With this exhortation in mind, Mojica has iconic figures such as fur-trader woman, mistress, and Indian Princess speak as individuated women. Their stories are set alongside the stories of Contemporary Woman #1 and Contemporary Woman #2 in a way that highlights the connections among women without minimizing the particularity of individual experience. Says Contemporary Woman #1: "I don't want to be mistaken for a crowd of Native women. I am one."

Mojica organized the play into thirteen "transformations, one for each moon in the lunar year." In one of the most affecting scene changes, the satiric humor of the "498th annual Miss North America Beauty Pageant"—won by Princess-Buttered-on-Both-Sides—shifts to the fact-based accounts of murdered American Indian movement activist Anna Mae Aquash and the torture of contemporary Chilean women. The play's two actors each play multiple roles; in the original production, Mojica appeared as Princess Buttered-on-Both-Sides, Pocahontas-Matoaka-Lady Rebecca, and Malinche, while Nunez played such roles as Host, The Blue Spots, Troubador, Spirit-Sister, and Musician. The set design and costuming also reinforce the play's central theme of transformation. Props start out as one thing but become something else. Costumes and props are left to accumulate onstage to remind the audience of the many narratives told; by the play's end the stage is littered with the remnants of all thirteen transformations. The nonlinear structure, the multiple roles, and the repeated transformations of space, time, and characters collectively resist traditional theatrical closure. The play's final stage directions: "*Blind Faith leaps in the dark.*"

[See also Canada]

FURTHER READING

Knowles, Ric. "Translators, Traitors, Mistresses, and Whores: Monique Mojica and the Mothers of the Metis Nations." In *Siting the Other: Revisions of Marginality in Australian and English-Canadian Drama*, ed. by Marc Maufort and Franca Bellarsi. Brussels: Presses Interuniversitaires Europennes, 2001.

Mojica, Monique. *Princess Pocahontas and the Blue Spots*. Toronto: Women's Press, 1991.

———. "Theatrical Diversity on Turtle Island: A Tool Towards the Healing." *Canadian Theatre Review* 68 (Fall 1991): 3.

Tompkins, Joanne. "'Spectacular Resistance': Metatheatre in Post-Colonial Drama." *Modern Drama* 38 (1995): 42–51.

——. "'The Story of Rehearsal Never Ends': Rehearsal, Performance, Identity in Settler Culture Drama." *Canadian Literature* 144 (Spring 1995):144–161.

Andrea R. Stevens

PRIVATE LIVES

Let's savour the delight of the moment. Come and kiss me darling, before your body rots, and worms pop in and out of your eye sockets.
—Elyot Chase, Act 2

NOËL COWARD's *Private Lives* (1931) opened to rave reviews for its comic brilliance and effervescent performances of its stellar cast that included Coward, Gertrude Lawrence, and Laurence Olivier. The play was written over four days while Coward was bedridden in Shanghai with the flu. One critic, writing for *The Tatler* about that original production, wrote that "as a means of topical refreshment it has all the tonic qualities of a first-rate cocktail." Such a description is fitting to describe what is expected of a "Noël Coward play"—acerbic wit, the chaotic upset of good manners, and costumes and sets almost excessive in their expression of wealth and fine taste. Yet *Private Lives*, within its historical context, is an unexpected play, arriving on the scene when, for example, economic depression is creating much more socially conscious playwrighting across the Atlantic by writers such as CLIFFORD ODETS and ELMER RICE. The English had weathered a rough few decades at the dawning of the 20th century, experiencing a waning empire, a lost generation of young men through military conflict, and vastly changing social roles for men and women. While Coward's play only alludes to this background once (with a remark about the *Titanic*), *Private Lives* on one level is about how to respond to things falling apart.

Structurally, the play rejects two central components of drama: plot and closure. Little happens after the end of act 1, when ex-spouses Elyot Chase and Amanda Prynne, after meeting on a shared terrace as each begins their honeymoons with their new partners, Sibyl and Victor, decide to elope together. Act 2 consists of much aimless talk and bickering between Amanda and Elyot in a Paris flat, culminating with the arrival of Sibyl and Victor. The final act is centered on figuring ways out of the "hell of a mess socially" in which the four find themselves, and a proper breakfast slowly deteriorates into argument. Ultimately, Victor and Sibyl explode with rage against one another, neatly mirroring the relationship of their hosts who silently slip out the door together at the end of the play. Rather than maturing Elyot and Amanda, Coward allows their particular brand of passion, alternating between intense lovemaking and equally vituperative quarreling, to become infectious, creating a second pair of loose ends at the play's conclusion.

On the surface, *Private Lives* reflects the younger, wealthy set's rejection of rigid Victorian codes of morality and gender, rebelling against unnatural standards of acceptability since, as Amanda says to Victor, "very few people are completely normal really, deep down in their private lives." They are part of a generation sure that the values they inherited are worn out but unsure of what should replace them. Elyot repeatedly entreats Amanda to adopt his principle of flippancy, to "enjoy the party as much as we can," to "be superficial and pit the poor philosophers," to savor the delight of the moment" before death. Such ways of thinking and behaving drive the play as the characters, in Jean Chothia's words, "use their charm as a way of surviving" with "no commitments to anyone but themselves." Some critics have seen Coward's metaphysics as a forerunner for the sensibility of the Theater of the Absurd and his style as laying the foundation for later "serious" playwrights such as SAMUEL BECKETT, HAROLD PINTER, and EDWARD ALBEE.

[*See also* England, 1860–1940]

FURTHER READING
Kaplan, Joel, and Sheila Stowell, eds. *Look Back in Pleasure: Noel Coward Reconsidered.* London: Methuen, 2000.
Lahr, John. *Coward, the Playwright.* London: Methuen, 1982.
Lesley, Cole. *Remembered Laughter: The Life of Noel Coward.* New York: Knopf, 1976.
Mander, Raymond, and Joe Mitchenson. *Theatrical Companion to Coward: A Pictorial Record of the Theatrical Works of Noël Coward.* 2d ed. London: Oberon Bks., 2000.

Christopher Wixson

PROBLEM PLAY

The term *problem play* was coined by Sydney Grundy (says drama critic William Archer) as the English equivalent of the French *pièce à thèse*, a play with a thesis. *Camille*, the play by DUMAS FILS, proved to be highly controversial because it pictured a courtesan in a favorable light, sacrificing her own happiness for the sake of her young and ardent lover. Théodore Barrière took a sceptical view of the demimonde in his play *Marble Girls* (*Les filles de marbre*, 1853), and two years later, Émile Augier in his *Olympe's Marriage* went on the offensive, arguing that these high-class prostitutes were infiltrating good society and destroying it. Augier's position was that once they have married into a fine family, there was no getting rid of them, except by the most radical means. His courtesan Olympe is in a position to blackmail her husband and to demand whatever she wants. She brazenly outfaces the aged head of the family, who shoots her before killing himself. This ending was meant to be shocking, and if one wishes to make a distinction between a problem play and a thesis play, this is a thesis play. The problem is not debated; it is solved with a pistol shot.

However, most of the plays that dealt with social issues introduced scenes in which there was some discussion pro and con. Often in the problem play, there would be a character, known as a *raisonneur*, in a supporting role, a character who represented the viewpoint of the author.

When Dumas fils took up the subject of disreputable women who make a place for themselves in the best families, as in *The Demi-Monde* (*Le Demi-Monde*, 1855), he presented what amounted to a debate, but with the scales tipped against the unvirtuous woman. In *The Natural Son* (*Le Fils Naturel*, 1858), he dealt with the question of illegitimate sons, arguing that they should be formally recognized as legal heirs in order not to add to the number of uprooted elements in society.

In the preface to the play as published in 1868, he expressed the significance of this new kind of drama. "The old society is collapsing in all respects. All the original laws, all the fundamental institutions, earthly and divine, are being put to the question. Opinions waver and shake, feelings are suspect, the truths of another time tremble before this new wind."

Dumas fils was the true father of the problem play, and from FRANCE it spread to other European nations. In Copenhagen, the young radical critic Georg Brandes in 1871 reprimanded Danish writers for being behind the times, still committed to old religious beliefs and artistic conventions, and he urged them to follow the French example and "submit problems to debate." He had no idea of the impact that simple phrase would have.

In NORWAY, BJØRNSTJERNE BJØRNSON quickly obliged Brandes, producing A BANKRUPTCY (*En fallit*) in 1875, and HENRIK IBSEN reluctantly fell into step with PILLARS OF SOCIETY (1877). For his first venture into the new genre, Ibsen chose financial speculation as his subject (as in a number of French plays, such as Augier's *Maître Guérin*). It was an enormous success both in Norway and in GERMANY. Thereupon Ibsen wrote A DOLL'S HOUSE and GHOSTS, the two most famous (and notorious) of all problem plays.

In Germany, GERHARDT HAUPTMANN achieved notoriety with his study of the degeneration of a family, *Before Sunrise* (*Vor Sonnenaufgang*, 1889). In ENGLAND, OSCAR WILDE, with AN IDEAL HUSBAND, (1895) and ARTHUR PINERO, with THE SECOND MRS. TANQUERAY (1892), proved the commercial value of the problem play, when carefully handled. But the true disciple of the problem play in England was GEORGE BERNARD SHAW, who began his playwriting career with a drama about slum landlords, *Widowers' Houses* (1892). He defined the beginning of modern drama as the discussion scene that ends *A Doll's House* (in the 1913 edition of *The Quintessence of Ibsenism*), and he turned increasingly to a form of drama in which debates swallowed up the plots, producing what are more plays of ideas than plays about people.

The problem play was an outgrowth of REALISM and paved the way for NATURALISM. Many early realistic plays were highly entertaining affairs, meant to appeal to the rising bourgeoisie. Dumas fils, however, wanted the theater to be more than entertaining. In his preface to *The Natural Son* he denounced the apostles of art for art's sake, "three words absolutely devoid of meaning," and called for a useful or utilitarian theater. "Any literature that does not aim at the perfectibility of mankind, at improved morals, at the ideal, in a word, the utilitarian, is a literature stunted and unwholesome, dead at birth."

Problem plays came under attack from two sides. Critics found many of them didactic and inartistic. The characters were often mere stick figures, serving as spokesmen for different positions, and the plays themselves no more than propaganda. Censors condemned many problem plays because they dealt with offensive subjects. To circumvent the government authorities, problem plays were often first performed privately. Such was the case with *Before Sunrise* (incest and degeneracy), EUGÈNE BRIEUX's *Damaged Goods* (*Les Avariés*) (venereal disease), and Shaw's *Widower's Houses* (slum landlords). Shaw's MRS. WARREN'S PROFESSION (prostitution) was given a private performance in 1902 but not allowed to be presented publicly in England until 1925.

The term is usually reserved for and associated with plays written in the 1860–1930 period. In the 1930s, the time of the Great Depression in America, the problem play took the form of DOCUMENTARY DRAMA in which plot and character were less important than hard facts. Authored by Arthur Arent, *One Third of a Nation* dealt with slums in the large cities. An offstage voice calling itself the "Voice of the Living Newspaper" offered much of the factual material and gave the name Living Newspaper to a number of similar productions.

FURTHER READING

Brandes, Georg. "Inaugural Lecture 1873." In *The Theory of the Modern Stage*, ed. by Eric Bentley. Baltimore: Penguin, 1968.

Dumas fils, Alexandre. Préface [Preface] to *Le Fils Naturel* [*The Natural Son*]. In *Théatre complet* [*Complete theater*]. Vol. 3. Paris: Calmann Lévy, 1893.

Henderson, Archibald. "The New Forms." In *The Changing Drama*. New York: Henry Holt, 1914.

Shaw, Bernard. "The Problem Play—A Symposium." In *Shaw on Theatre*, ed. by E. J. West. New York: Hill & Wang, 1958.

Stuart, Donald Clive. "French Realistic Drama. The Problem Play." In *The Development of Dramatic Art*. New York: Appleton, 1928.

Evert Sprinchorn

PROCESSIONAL

JOHN HOWARD LAWSON's *Processional*, subtitled "a jazz symphony of American life," opened on January 12, 1925. Directed by Philip Moeller with scenic design by Mordecai Gorelik, the production ran ninety-six performances.

Processional is a nonrealistic, highly theatrical play set during a labor dispute between West Virginia coal miners and their management. Inspired by JAZZ music and vaudeville, Lawson draws a loose picture of American social concerns in the 1920s. His own Marxist politics are apparent throughout the play, as is his opinion of the bankrupt nature of traditional theater in America: "It is only in the fields of vaudeville and revue," writes Lawson in his preface to the play, "that a native craftsmanship exists."

The play uses theatrical space in unorthodox ways. With the auditorium lights on throughout the show, several characters enter through the audience aisles, including nine musicians, "The Jazz Miners," whose music punctuates the play. *Processional's* plot structure is episodic and fragmented, based more on an evening of vaudeville entertainment than on a traditional stage play, but nonetheless a story is being told.

Isaac Cohen is a Jewish store keeper in a West Virginia coal mining town. In the midst of a violent labor strike, Cohen's daughter Sadie has a sexual encounter with Dynamite Jim, a young country man who has accidentally murdered a soldier sent to squash the strikers. Jim is captured by the Ku Klux Klan and is taken off to be hanged for the murder. Unbeknownst to everyone, Jim is cut down from his lynching ropes by a farmer. Blinded by the Klan's vicious attack but still alive, Jim flees the town.

Time passes, and Sadie discovers that she is pregnant by Jim, a fact that thrills her even as it enrages Cohen and other members of the community. The Klan attacks Sadie, but her father—hidden among their ranks dressed as a Klansman—rescues her. At this moment, Jim surprises everyone by seemingly returning from the dead. He is married on the spot to Sadie, pleasing Cohen and Jim's mother so much that they contemplate marrying each other as well. Suddenly, the pro-labor fighters arrive to triumphantly announce their victory over management and the Klan. The play ends with a rousing procession, the jazz band leading the actors offstage and out through the auditorium.

Cohen is portrayed as a "vaudeville type of Yiddish figure" with a "lisp that makes his caressing voice a little ridiculous." His dual purpose in the play is to act as authoritative figure in Sadie's story and to represent Jewishness onstage as a foil to the other American character types presented. These other Americans include a socialistic Polish immigrant, a glad-handing politician in a tall silk hat, a deaf Civil War veteran, and a minstrel-style "Negro" character. Lawson's use of stereotypes is interesting because while the characters frequently engage in silly dialogue and stage business reminiscent of vaudeville COMEDY, they sometimes show genuine humanity and believability.

In 1937, *Processional* was revived by the FEDERAL THEATRE PROJECT and ran for eighty-one performances.

[*See also* United States]

FURTHER READING

Carr, Gary L. *The Left Side of Paradise: The Screenwriting of John Howard Lawson.* Ann Arbor: UMI Res. Press, 1984.

Hyman, Colette A. *Staging Strikes: Worker's Theatre and the American Labor Movement.* Philadelphia: Temple Univ. Press, 1997.

Mishra, Kshamanidhi. *American Leftist Playwrights of the 1930s: A Study of Ideology and Technique in the Plays of Odets, Lawson, and Sherwood.* New Delhi: Classical Pub. Co., 1991.

Watson, E. Bradlee. *Contemporary Drama: European, English, Irish, and American Plays.* New York: Scribner's, 1941.

DeAnna M. Toten Beard

PROFESSOR BERNHARDI

> It is really terrible that here in Austria all questions of personnel end in the political sphere.
> —Ebenwald, Act 3

Although ARTHUR SCHNITZLER subtitled *Professor Bernhardi* a "comedy in five acts," there is little occasion to laugh at this sociopolitical satire of turn-of-the-century Vienna. Written in 1912, the play premiered in November of the same year in Berlin, even though the director, OTTO BRAHM, was initially skeptical because, he claimed, the issues were Viennese and not pertinent to Berlin. Indeed, the play is about the very politics that barred it from the Viennese stage until 1918, when censorship was lifted after the collapse of the Habsburg monarchy at the end of World War I. The play's political intrigues are intertwined with the anti-Semitism that led to its prohibition in Vienna and also foreshadow attitudes that impelled Adolf Hitler's rise to power in GERMANY and his popularity in Austria.

The plot is set in motion when Professor Bernhardi, the Jewish director of the Elisabethinum Clinic, forbids a Catholic priest to give last rites to a young woman because she is unaware of her impending death. In a euphoric state after surgery for blood poisoning (following a botched illegal abortion), she vainly waits for her fiancé. Bernhardi considers it more ethical to ease her death with illusions than to frighten her—and thereby speed up her demise—with a priestly visitation. He therefore bars the priest from seeing the patient, even though Sister Ludmilla has already announced him. The very knowledge of his presence does indeed hasten her death, as foreseen by Bernhardi.

Bernhardi acts solely on ethical principle, but owing to envy and anti-Semitic agitation, opportunists and conservatives willfully distort his humanist, principled actions as religious interference, turning them into public, political issues in Catholic Austria. The patrons of the clinic subsequently withdraw their support, forcing Bernhardi's suspension. However, his friends and supporters also misunderstand his motives and want to politicize his standpoint for their own ends. Refusing to play any game, Bernhardi remains true to his values. This leads to a trial, during which anti-Semitic forces foment sentiment against him, and he ends up serving a prison term. After his release, public opinion changes, and Bernhardi unwillingly becomes a hero. But because he only wants to return to the clinic and be of service to his patients, this new twist leaves him cold.

Although *Professor Bernhardi* initially focuses on a dying young woman who has violated social mores, the play is more specifically about the machinations that dominate turn-of-the-century

Viennese politics. The Jewish Bernhardi inevitably comes into conflict with the conservative, anti-Semitic Catholic forces that dictate social norms. Yet it is clear that the liberal forces also want to manipulate the protagonist. His principles are suspect not only because he is Jewish but also because those principles undeniably point out the jealousy, small-mindedness, stupidity, and ineptitude that surround Bernhardi and make him a scapegoat. The repercussions of the evil enveloping him mean humiliation and degradation, yet Bernhardi refuses to become a martyr. He refuses to be manipulated by the system, even when a cabinet member, his (former) friend Flint, tries to convince him of the political significance (or potential) of his stance. Bernhardi adheres to his principles at all costs.

[See also Austria]

FURTHER READING

Blickle, Peter. "Die Einlösung subversiven Wirkungspotentials: Die Theaterskandale um Arthur Schnitzlers *Professor Bernhardi* und Rolf Hochhuths *Stellvertreter*" [Redeeming subversive potential effects: The theater scandals surrounding Arthur Schnitzler's *Professor Bernhardi* and Rolf Hochhuth's *The Deputy*]. *New German Review* 10 (1994): 103–118.

Schnabel, Werner Wilhelm. "*Professor Bernhardi* und die Wiener Zensur. Zur Rezeptionsgeschichte der Schnitzlerschen Komödie" [*Professor Bernhardi* and Viennese censorship: On the reception of Schnitzler's comedy]. *Jahrbuch der deutschen Schillergesellschaft* 28 (1984): 349–383.

Weiss, Robert O. "The 'Hero' in Schnitzler's Comedy *Professor Bernhardi*." *Modern Austrian Literature* 2, no. 4 (1969): 30–33.

Elizabeth Ametsbichler

PRZYBYSZEWSKA, STANISŁAWA (1901–1935)

I do not have, I do not want to have a fatherland.
—Stanisława Przybyszewska

The life of Stanisława Przybyszewska, author of three plays about the French Revolution, is a study in dispossession and ALIENATION. Born on October 1, 1901, in Myślenice, POLAND, the illegitimate daughter of Polish modernist novelist and dramatist Stanisław Przybyszewski, she was christened after her father but denied his surname. Given an artistic upbringing in FRANCE and GERMANY by her mother, Aniela Pająk, an impressionist painter who died in 1912, the eleven-year-old Stanisława became a cosmopolitan wanderer, living in Western Europe with friends and relatives.

Back in Poland in 1916, Przybyszewska attended teachers college in Cracow, where she met her internationally famous father whose name she could now adopt. Passionately in search of heroes, she became temporarily infatuated with Przybyszewski but soon grew disillusioned. Her father guided her toward a literary career but played a fatal role by introducing her to morphine, which became an addiction.

In 1922 she moved to Warsaw, where, fluent in German, French, and English, she eked out a living teaching. In 1923, to escape a seemingly predestined isolation, Przybyszewska married a young artist and moved to Danzig, where her husband taught at the Polish high school. She painted and researched the French Revolution, writing her first play, *Thermidor* (1925), in German. Adopting the principles of *neue Sachlichkeit* (NEW OBJECTIVITY), which stressed facts, clarity, and coolness in reaction to expressionistic exaggeration, Stanisława demonstrated that self-discipline and hard work could make her a better artist than her self-indulgent, intuitive father.

After her husband's sudden death in 1925 (from an overdose of morphine), Przybyszewska survived by tutoring but gradually gave up her pupils to have time to write *Ninety-three* (*Dziewięćdziesiąty trzeci*, 1928) and THE DANTON CASE (*Sprawa Dantona*, 1929), preferring to beg from friends and relatives for a meager subsistence. By 1928 she was living in one tiny room, without electricity or plumbing, in wooden school barracks. Racked by hunger, cold, and rheumatic pains, she crawled across the floor, like an "animal at bay in the recesses of its hole." Determined to be a writer, Przybyszewska remained convinced of her own genius and ultimate vindication at the hands of posterity.

Danzig, of divided national character, suited her shattered psyche. She disliked her fellow Poles; the great authors constituting her literary heritage, Pierre Corneille and GEORGE BERNARD SHAW, were French and English. As the Nazis came to power, she realized people like her would be exterminated, but she never considered leaving her cell-like refuge, calling it her "grave."

Eulogizing "this ideal, total *solitude* in which my strength grows invisibly," Przybyszewska desperately needed to share ideas on revolution and her approaching self-extinction. She wrote hundreds of letters, to people both known and unknown to her, in which she describes her artistic vocation, creative struggles, and ceaseless battle for material survival. Written in four languages, sometimes addressed to famous writers, like Thomas Mann, Georges Bernanos, and JEAN COCTEAU, and often unfinished and unsent, Przybyszewska's correspondence (the basis for several stage and television dramatizations of her life) is the autobiography of a mind confronting itself in anguished loneliness and despair, while proudly asserting the cultivation of consciousness as the highest duty. Przybyszewska died of malnutrition and tuberculosis on August 15, 1935, in Danzig, a free city under a League of Nations mandate.

PLAYS: *Thermidor* (1925); *Ninety-three* (*Dziewięćdziesiąty trzeci*, 1928); *The Danton Case* (*Sprawa Dantona*, 1929)

FURTHER READING

Kosicka, Jadwiga, and Daniel Gerould. *A Life of Solitude. Stanisława Przybyszewska*. London: Quartet Bks., 1986.

Jadwiga Kosicka Gerould

PSYCHOANALYSIS

Sigmund Freud, the founder of psychoanalysis, called the unconscious mind "the other showplace," displaying its drama through symptoms, dreams, and artworks. Freud drew his theory of the Oedipus complex from the ancient drama of Sophocles, finding it also in William Shakespeare's *Hamlet*: a universal desire to return to the mother's primal erotic body by killing off the father figure symbolically or physically. Freud's theories influenced many modern dramatists, providing common terms for various aspects of the conscious and unconscious mind that are explored in both psychologically realistic and antirealist dramatic movements. The conflicts of ego (self) with the wayward desires of id (unconscious primary processes), through the social pressures of superego (conscience), can be seen in the struggle of HENRIK IBSEN's heroes with their own destructive idealism, in EUGENE O'NEILL's characters with their "pipe dreams," in the distorted scenery and social traumas of expressionist station plays, in the uncanny imagery and mythic associations of surrealist drama, or in WILLIAM BUTLER YEATS's symbolist figures and AUGUST STRINDBERG's dream plays. The selective REALISM of American dramatists ARTHUR MILLER and TENNESSEE WILLIAMS also reveals the conflict of ego with superego and id, especially through memories and fantasies arising onstage. More recently, PETER SHAFFER, CHRISTOPHER DURANG, ARTHUR KOPIT, and many other dramatists have made psychotherapy the subject of their plays by placing the analyst-patient relationship onstage or parodying the Oedipus complex.

Freudian theory gave tools to Stanislavskian method ACTING for the "given circumstances" of character analysis and for the actor's own "emotional recall." Jungian notions of the collective unconscious and mythic archetypes apply to ANTON CHEKHOV's investigation of psychological gesture. Yet Freud's modernization of Aristotelian "catharsis," from the ancient amphitheater to the therapist's office, also relates to two dramatists who developed the actor-audience relationship in opposite directions: ANTONIN ARTAUD and BERTOLT BRECHT.

Through his surrealist plays and poetic passions about a "Theater of Cruelty," Artaud tried to exorcise the madness of human nature (and of his own psychotic illness) by drawing his audience into the psychic terror of the actor's body onstage, like a martyr "signaling through the flames." But the key here, as Freud discovered through his experiments in psychoanalytic catharsis, is that the devils of id must be consciously interpreted, not just communally expressed. In a similar vein (though not using Freud directly), Brecht moved beyond his early writing of expressionist drama to develop an "EPIC THEATER" that would challenge audience sympathies at strategic points in the plot, making the familiar strange, and to distance spectators toward critical thought and political change (as ALIENATION EFFECT). Brecht attacked Aristotelian sympathy for and fear of the tragic hero's inevitable "fate" as producing a submissive, mimetic audience of "little Oedipuses." While Artaud's cathartic cruelty would merge actor and audience through onstage violence, clarifying primal drives, and prevent such actions in real life, Brecht wanted to cure social ills, not just individual desires, by alienating spectators at certain "gestic" moments in his drama (revealing social attitudes through the semiotic gestures of performance).

Like Brecht's extension of theater's ancient therapeutic power toward modern political change, French psychoanalyst Jacques Lacan expanded Freud's ideas to engage PHILOSOPHY, linguistics, anthropology, and social science in ways that have influenced much of today's poststructuralist theory as applied to stage and screen drama. Lacan himself described the "drama" of the mirror stage, when the infant misrecognizes itself through the "desire of the Other" as an illusory whole self in conflict with its uncoordinated body and fantasies of dismemberment. The Oedipal name of the Father (language and law) intervenes in the child's alienation from its own being through its loss of, yet desire for, the (m)Other, thus bringing the social symbolic order into the family scene—a superego framework for the ego's imaginary mix of fantasy and reality in its struggle with the real of primal id drives. This theater of Oedipal infancy becomes incorporated in the developing human brain, structuring the unconscious (as "discourse of the Other") and replaying through psychotic, perverse, obsessional, or hysterical symptoms throughout life. The interplay of Lacan's symbolic, imaginary, and real orders, revealing the unconscious discourses, desires, and drives of the Other in the Self (as "split subject"), may thus be found in many absurdist, feminist, multicultural, and queer dramas—especially those by SAMUEL BECKETT, EUGÉNE IONESCO, JEAN GENET, HÉLÈNE CIXOUS, CARYL CHURCHILL, ADRIENNE KENNEDY, SUZAN-LORI PARKS, AIMÉ CÉSAIRE, WOLE SOYINKA, MARIA IRENE FORNES, LUIS VALDEZ, DAVID HENRY HWANG, and TONY KUSHNER.

FURTHER READING

Artaud, Antonin. *The Theatre and Its Double.* Tr. by Mary Caroline Richards. New York: Grove, 1958.

Blau, Herbert. *The Audience.* Baltimore: Johns Hopkins Univ. Press, 1990.

Brecht, Bertolt. *Brecht on Theatre.* Tr. by John Willett. New York: Hill & Wang, 1964.

Freud, Sigmund. *The Interpretation of Dreams.* Tr. by James Strachey. New York: Avon, 1965.

Jung, C. G. *Psychological Types.* Tr. by H. G. Baynes. Princeton, N.J.: Princeton Univ. Press, 1971.

Lacan, Jacques. *Écrits: A Selection.* Tr. by Alan Sheridan. New York: Norton, 1977.

Pizzato, Mark. *Edges of Loss: From Modern Drama to Postmodern Theory.* Ann Arbor: Univ. of Michigan Press, 1998.

——. *Theatres of Human Sacrifice: From Ancient Ritual to Screen Violence.* Albany: SUNY Press, 2004.

Mark Pizzato

PUBLIKUMS BESCHIMPFUNG *See* Offending the Audience

LA PUCE À L'OREILLE *See* A Flea in Her Ear

EL PUENTE *See* The Bridge

PUERTO RICO

Before the Spanish conquest, the Taino and Arawak Indians did not have a tradition of the performing arts in their culture. Ritual and ceremonial events incorporated music and dance, but performance such as storytelling and oral folklore was not developed in the native cultures. The Spaniards did not establish a resident performing arts company until they founded Teatro Tapia in 1832.

Alejandro Tapia y Rivera, Puerto Rico's first national playwright, criticized slavery and the Spanish monarchy. His plays were censored and restricted by the Spanish colonial government, but audiences reacted favorably to his dramas. Tapia's plays are still performed today. He wrote *Roberto D'Evreux*, the first authentically Puerto Rican play, in 1856. The popular historical drama moralizes that corrupt ambition is ultimately punished. *Vasco Nuñez de Balboa* (1872) was his last historical drama. Tapia's works include *Cuarterona* (1867), an overt criticism of racism. His *The Lion's Share* (*La parte del león*, 1878) treats the moral and social inequalities in marriage and the innate hypocrisy in defending another person's honor. The literary critic Menéndez Pelayo considered *Bernardo de Palissy* (1857) Tapia's best work. This historical and biographical drama focuses on the Parisian uprising, heroism, imprisonment, and death of Palissy. Tapia incorporated romanticized natural elements and a native Puerto Rican atmosphere to plays unrelated to the island's environment or culture.

Salvador Brau was considered among the best poets of the era. His romantic TRAGEDY *Hero and Martyr* (*Héroe y mártir*, 1871) is a drama in high verse. *The Return Home* (*La vuelta al hogar*) is a romantic COMEDY in verse. His dramatic works were considered second only to those of Tapia. *From the Surface to the Depths* (*De la superficie al fondo*, 1874) was a popular comedy. The quality of his verse echoed the Golden Age dramatic masters, although local color identified his plays as distinctively Puerto Rican.

During the 19th century, the popular *costumbrista* (a slice of Puerto Rican country life) theater depicted common stock characters. Women wrote and produced their own plays, and their works dealt with slavery and female societal roles. Carmen Hernández de Araújo's romantic comedy of mistaken identity is portrayed in her free verse play *Ideal Love* (*Amor ideal*). Eugenio Sánchez de Fuentes y Peláez wrote *Cousin Basilio* (*El primo Basilio*, 1901) about the choice between defending a lover's honor and forgiveness.

After 1898, the UNITED STATES's occupation and political dominance influenced the state of the arts. Luis Llorens Torres, a national poet, wrote *Shout of Lares* (*Grito de Lares*), a protest against U.S. domination. It referred to an 1868 uprising against the Spaniards, but its conflicts and crises parallel the Puerto Rican responses to U.S. occupation.

Manuel Méndez Ballester won first place in the Ateneo Puertorriqueño in 1939 for his play *The Clamor of Furrows* (*El clamor de los surcos*). His work dramatized intense social conflict. *Hilarión* (1943) universalized his tragic protagonist.

In 1940, the Areyto Drama Society was founded by multitalented Emilio Belaval, who served as judge and legislator as well as director and author of diverse genres. *Areyto* referred to the Taino style of ceremonial and ritualistic music and dance. Belaval founded the theater company to create authentic national drama. The University of Puerto Rico engendered and supported the theater troupes Farándula Universitaria and Teatro Rodante to continue Areyto's legacy.

Areyto performed plays by Manuel Méndez Ballester, Martha Lomar, and Fernando Sierra Berdecia. The University of Puerto Rico banned Puerto Rican plays in 1944. The university performed *The Resentful Woman* (*La Resentida*) by Enrique Laguerre. It depicted the peasant unrest against Spanish landowners in 1898. The head of the drama department banned the play, though it was critically acclaimed and well received by audiences. The ban was not lifted until 1956.

José Lacomba and playwright René Marques established the Experimental Theatre in 1951. Playwright Francisco Arriví founded the Instituto de Cultura Puertorriqueña in 1955. René Marqués wrote *The Fanlights* (*Los soles truncos*), and Francisco Arriví wrote *Vegi-Giants* (*Vegigantes*) for the institute's annual theater festivals. Their styles reflect NATURALISM and social REALISM as they examine their society in transition. Naturalism and the harsh reality of midcentury Puerto Rican landowners displaced by the U.S. occupation dominate *The Cart* (*La Carreta*, 1954). Each act depicts the downfall of the idyllic farm family, from the rural mountains to the San Juan slums to the Bronx. The most popular play by Marqués, it is still performed internationally in translation as well as throughout the Spanish-speaking world.

Revolutionary playwrights changed the national drama scene during the 1960s. Luis Rafael Sánchez, the most renowned contemporary playwright, continues the performance of protest. His works incorporated elements of SYMBOLISM and EXPRESSIONISM. His themes expressed Marxist political positions. *The Passion According to Antigona Pérez* (*La pasión según Antígona Pérez*, 1968) exemplified these elements in his retelling of the Antigone myth.

MYRNA CASAS wrote absurdist plays. As a director and playwright, she explored societal roles and sexual identity. She founded Producciones Cisne to produce her plays and international works in translation. Her well-known plays include *Broken Glass in Time* (*Cristal roto en el tiempo*, 1961), *Absurdities in Solitude* (*Absurdos en soledad*, 1963), *Eugenia Victoria Herrera* (1964), and *Three*

(*Tres*, 1974). Her provocative work *El gran circo eukraniano* (1986) was translated and performed internationally as THE GREAT USKRANIAN CIRCUS. This revolutionary work presents actors conscious of their roles mirroring the cross section of society within each audience. Her disjointed plots and dialogue examined social as well as political upheavals during the colonial transition. Casas approaches her themes with humor and metatheater that demands audience involvement. Her work has inspired other theater companies such as El Grupo Teatro del 60 to develop individual styles and novel approaches to performance.

Teresa Marichal is a DRAMATURG active in the Nueva Dramaturgia Puertorriqueña (New Puerto Rican Dramaturgy) theatrical movement. Her works present the opposing dichotomies of Puerto Rican society in conflict. Her trilogy *The Biggest Park in the City* (*El parque más grande de la ciudad*, 1979) explores social inequities. *Midnight Love* (*Amor de medianoche*, 1984) and *Evening Walk* (*Paseo al atardecer*, 1984) restructure traditional roles and incorporate modern technology to demonstrate how mass media and artificial communication alienate the individual. Marichal experimented with several styles to portray the breakdown of communication in contemporary Puerto Rican culture.

Playwright and director Pedro Santaliz founded El Nuevo Teatro Pobre de América (the New Poor Theatre of America), focusing on the working-class San Juan communities. He inspired innovators like José Marquez and Lydia Milagros González. Another community-oriented theater director, Zora Moreno, established Teatro el Gran Quince in 1967. The legacy of these theater companies is close community involvement in the performing arts.

FURTHER READING

Arriví, Francisco. *Máscara Puertorriqueña* [Puerto Rican mask]. Río Piedras, P.R.: Editorial Cultural, 1997.

Birmingham-Pokorny, Elba, ed. *The Demythologization of Language, Gender, and Culture and the Re-Mapping of Latin American Identity in Luis Rafael Sanchez's Works*. Miami: Universal, 1999.

Casas, Myrna. *El gran circo eukraniano: The Great USkranian Circus*. In *Women Writing Women: An Anthology of Spanish-American Theatre of the 1980's*, ed. and tr. by Teresa Cajiao Salas and Margarita Vargas. Albany: SUNY Press, 1997.

Phillips, Jordan B. *Contemporary Puerto Rican Drama*. Madrid: Editorial Playor, 1973.

Sáez, Antonia. *El teatro en Puerto Rico* [The theater of Puerto Rico]. Barcelona: Editorial Universitaria, 1972.

Carole Anne Champagne

A PUPPET SHOW

ALEKSANDR BLOK's *A Puppet Show* (*Balaganchik*, 1906) has proven to be one of the key texts of Russian SYMBOLISM and of MODERNIST DRAMA. The play owes its genesis to a group of Petersburg poets, directors, artists, and musicians who frequented the poet Viacheslav Ivanov's "Tower" and decided to collaborate on a miscellany and a theater, both to be called "Torches." They convinced Blok to write the first play, and VSEVOLOD MEYERHOLD offered to direct. Although the theater came to naught, Meyerhold took the play with him to the Komissarzhevskaia Theater and staged it a year later. This production became a landmark in its own right.

In *A Puppet Show* Blok created a dynamic dramatic language that incorporates theatrical traditions of the past, such as the commedia dell'arte and Greek classical TRAGEDY, but at the same time shapes these traditional elements through devices of estrangement and other modernist techniques that did not become common for decades. Elements of high and low style mix freely, and parody, broadly construed, plays a particularly important role. The play opens with a group of mystics awaiting the arrival of Death, as they might in a play by MAURICE MAETERLINCK. Into their midst stumbles Pierrot, who is looking for his girlfriend Columbine. The mystics treat Pierrot like an idiot; but when Death arrives, her scythe becomes her braid (both words are rendered by *kosa* in Russian), and Death becomes Columbine. Pierrot's happiness is short-lived as Harlequin barges in and steals Columbine away. A character claiming to be the Author of the play interrupts to complain that he had intended a love story; but he is summarily yanked offstage. Pierrot next appears in the middle of a RICHARD WAGNER set and recounts how Columbine turned to cardboard. In quick succession, three couples follow and declaim about love. A Clown sticks his tongue out at the last couple and receives a knock on the head from a wooden sword for his trouble. He falls over the footlights and cries, "I'm haemorrhaging cranberry juice." Harlequin enters as coryphaeus of a chorus. He soon jumps through the scenery into a void. Death reappears but turns into Columbine at Pierrot's approach. The now jubilant Author tries to unite the lovers and opines that despite all obstacles everything has been made right. However, the scenery flies up, and all the characters, including the now-embarrassed Author, run off. Only Pierrot remains, and he closes the play with a lament about lost love.

Meyerhold matched Blok's innovations and here began to elaborate the THEATER OF THE GROTESQUE. Nikolai Sapunov's set design and the poet Mikhail Kuzmin's musical score contributed importantly to the mood of the piece. Response to the first performance was stormy; however, no one could ignore the production. Blok and Meyerhold had wrought a new theatrical language.

Meyerhold returned to *A Puppet Show* in 1908 and again in 1914. Like the 1906 production, the 1914 production at the Tenishevsky school proved to be important because it was in this double bill of *A Puppet Show* and Blok's third lyric drama *The Unknown Woman* that Meyerhold first began to work out the basic tenets of constructivist theater.

[*See also* Russia and the Soviet Union]

FURTHER READING

Blok, Aleksandr. *A Puppet Show.* In *Aleksandr Blok's Trilogy of Lyric Dramas: A Puppet Show, The King on the Square, and The Unknown Woman,* ed. and tr. by Timothy C. Westphalen. London: Routledge, 2003.

Kot, Joanna. "Aleksandr Blok's *The Puppet Show.*" In *Distance Manipulation: The Russian Modernist Search for a New Drama.* Evanston, Ill.: Northwestern Univ. Press, 1999.

Pyman, Avril. *The Life of Aleksandr Blok. Vol.1, The Distant Thunder 1880–1908.* Oxford: Oxford Univ. Press, 1979.

Stelleman, Jenny. "Balaganchik." In *Aspects of Dramatic Communication: Action, Non-action, Interaction (A. P Chekhov, A. Blok, D. Charms).* Amsterdam: Rodopi, 1992.

Westphalen, Timothy C. *Lyric Incarnate: The Dramas of Aleksandr Blok.* London: Harwood Acad. Pubs., 1998.

Timothy C. Westphalen

PURGATORY

Purgatory, a one-act verse play by W. B. YEATS, was first performed at the Abbey Theatre on August 9, 1938, with sets (a bare tree and a ruined house) designed by his daughter Anne Yeats. It was Yeats's last play during his lifetime at the Abbey, a theater he had been instrumental in establishing in Dublin, IRELAND. There are two characters, an old man and his son, both wanderers, who come at night upon a ruined house. The old man explains his theory that souls in Purgatory come back to familiar spots and relive their transgressions until the consequences of their crimes are at an end. At first bored by all this talk, the uneducated son is intrigued by the old man saying that it was in that house that he was born. His mother had been the lady of the house, and his father was a drunken groom in the stable. It had been a wonderful house, but one night, when the old man was just sixteen, in drunkenness his father had set the house on fire. He confesses that in the burning house, he killed his own father, executed him for the capital crime of destroying a great house. Then, however, a window in the house is lit, and the figure of his mother appears, awaiting her drunken groom, for this is the night, relived again and again, in which he conceived the child who is now an old man witnessing the primal scene. Horrified, he hears the hoof beats of the groom's horse, hears him climb the stair. Caught up in this ghostly drama, the old man does not at first notice that his own boy is sneaking away with his purse. Cold-bloodedly, hoping to end the consequences of his mother's sin, and end her weird Purgatory, he stabs the boy to death, using the knife with which he had long ago killed his father. However, his hope to have purified his mother's soul is dashed, as at the play's end we hear once more the hoof beats of his father's horse, as he rides once more to the bedroom of the big house.

The verse in the play—an unrhymed tetrameter—has the stark simplicity of Yeats's best poetry. It is both Sophoclean and conversational. The subject matter was clear to its first audience: the play was the Protestant poet's protest against the destruction of landlords' "Big Houses" over the previous twenty years all across the Irish Free State. The old gentry were not wanted by the citizens of the new Catholic democracy. Even Coole Park—LADY GREGORY's house and Yeats's summer residence for decades—had had its pictures and furniture sold off by an in-law, and the house itself was demolished as of no interest or value except for its building stones. More horrifyingly, the play puts the blame for the decline of Irish civilization on misalliance, the marriage of aristocrats and common people, and suggests that bad marriages pollute a family and taint the genetic heritage of the "race."

With sex and murder at its heart, and a weirdly deranged but beautifully articulated eschatology for its spine, *Purgatory* is an astonishingly compact and disturbing verse play. It was admired by, and influential upon, T. S. ELIOT (who imagined it "solved the problem of speech in verse") and SAMUEL BECKETT (who may have found interesting the picture of endless repetitions of the dead in life).

FURTHER READING

Clark, David R. *W. B. Yeats and the Theatre of Desolate Reality.* Dublin: Dolmen Press, 1965.

Foster, R. F. *W. B. Yeats, a Life: The Arch-poet, 1915–1939.* Oxford: Oxford Univ. Press, 2003.

Welch, Robert. *The Abbey Theatre 1899–1999.* New York: Oxford Univ. Press, 1999.

Worth, Katharine. *The Irish Drama of Europe from Yeats to Beckett.* Atlantic Highlands, N.J.: Humanities Press, 1978.

Adrian Frazier

PURIMSHPIL

Purimshpil (plural Purimshpiln) is a play or monologue performed on Purim, the Jewish holiday commemorating the Persian Jews' narrow escape from annihilation at the hands of the vizier Haman, thanks to the efforts of the court Jew Mordecai and his niece Esther, queen to King Ahasuerus. The events are chronicled in the Book of Esther, read annually on Purim; the joyous holiday is also celebrated by festive meals, excessive drinking, and the temporary carnivalesque suspension of certain talmudic prohibitions and prejudices, most notably against theatrical activity.

Though the essence of the Purimshpil may have originated from the ritual degradation of Haman during the reading of the Book of Esther, the term *Purimshpil* was first used to describe late medieval satiric poetry read during Purim, often during the festive meal. Purimshpiln, in both their poetic and dramatic form, are often parodies of the Book of Esther, but other common themes include the binding of Isaac, the selling of Joseph, the Exodus from Egypt, and David and Goliath, as well as aspects of contemporary Jewish life. The Purimshpil did not develop into a group performance until the birth of humanism and secular theater in Renaissance ITALY. Though the strong anti-Semitic content of medieval mystery plays had provided little for Jews to imitate or admire, the rise of Lutheranism in GERMANY led to a new form of popular secular theater, the Fastnacht play, which provided a more hospitable model, though Jews would still tie their theatrical performance to the traditional holiday.

The first known Jewish play, *An Eloquent Marriage Farce* (*Bedihuta De-Kiddushin*), by Jehuda ben Sommo, was performed during Purim in 1531, but its language of composition—Hebrew—was hardly comprehensible to mass Jewish audiences. Soon, Jewish imitations of the Fastnacht plays started to appear in the YIDDISH vernacular, using the same biblical themes as the Fastnacht plays but also weaving in later rabbinic literature. Like the Fastnacht plays, the Purimshpiln were performed in private homes or taverns by students or apprentices, with scant scenery. A prankster figure, called the *loyfer*, *shrayber*, or *payats*, introduced the characters, content, and moral; narrated; and asked for reward at the end. The later Staatsaktionnen, popularized in Germany in the 17th century, introduced a jester as an actual character in the drama, who took the role of Mondrish in the Jewish plays. Over time the distinctions between Mordecai and Mondrish became blurred, and all the characters became increasingly grotesque. The *Akhashveyrosh-Shpil* (about a king named Akhashveyrosh), the most popular Purimshpil of the 18th century, is replete with cursing, sexual innuendo, and scatological humor. In 1708, a manuscript was publicly burned by the Frankfurt elders who banned the genre, to little avail. This vulgarity underscores the fact that the Purimshpil was principally a folk genre.

More formal renditions of Purimshpiln existed, particularly during the Jewish Enlightenment, in which the Purimshpil was "reformed" along with other aspects of traditional Jewish society, yet these plays were still farcical and retained at least one grotesque character, usually representing the traditional Jew in need of or beyond enlightening. Just as other limitations were relaxed during Purim, the Purimshpil gave the player and audience the chance to transgress socially by ridiculing more powerful members of society and created a channel for social criticism. At the most basic level, Purimshpiln gave people ordinarily bound to a strict behavioral code a chance for ritual release, which may account for why the Purimshpil lives on today most vibrantly among Hasidim.

FURTHER READING

Belkin, Ahuva. *Ha-Purim shpil: 'Iyunim ba-te'atron ha-Yehudi ha-'amami* [The Purimshpil: Studies in Jewish folk theater]. Jerusalem: Bialik Institute, 2002.

———. "The 'Low' Culture of the Purimshpil." In *Yiddish Theatre: New Approaches*, ed. by Joel Berkowitz. Oxford: Littman Library of Jewish Civilization, 2003.

Zinberg, I. *A History of Jewish Literature*. Vol. 7. New York: Ktav, 1975. 301–344.

Alyssa Masor

PYGMALION

Pygmalion: A Romance in Five Acts, a play written in 1912 by GEORGE BERNARD SHAW, was first performed in GERMANY (in translation) at the Hofburg Theater, Vienna, in 1913, and in ENGLAND at His Majesty's Theatre, London, on April 11 in the following year. The work presents a richly comic version of the classical myth about Pygmalion, who creates a sculpture of a woman of ideal beauty that comes to life. The Pygmalion figure in Shaw's play is Henry Higgins, a voluble professor of phonetics partly modeled on Shaw's friend the Oxford University philologist and phonetician Henry Sweet.

In a wager with his colleague Colonel Pickering, Higgins undertakes to turn a cockney flower girl, Eliza Doolittle, into a plausible replica of a Duchess by teaching her how to speak English in the manner of the upper classes. After a perilous test of Higgins's phonetic indoctrination, which ends with Eliza's sensational lapse into cockney with the expression "not bloody likely," the experiment reaches a triumphant conclusion at an ambassadorial reception, which occurs offstage in the original play. The cast includes Eliza's father, Alfred Doolittle, who also undergoes a transformation, from dustman to millionaire public speaker, and Freddy Eynesford-Hill, an ardent admirer of Eliza.

The end of the work has been subjected to numerous revisions by Shaw and the adapters of the play for musical COMEDY and film. In the first text of the play published in 1916, the action closes with Eliza's disdainful response to Higgins's casual order to buy him a new tie and gloves: "Buy them yourself." Higgins is left onstage chuckling and rattling his change in his pockets after confidently telling his mother: "She'll buy em all right enough." Some passages in the play's dialogue undeniably tend to encourage the presumption of an eventual marriage between Higgins and Eliza. But there are compelling arguments for saying that the ingredients of Cinderella romance are a foil to a tougher line of narrative, the closure of which is represented by Eliza's declaration of defiance. This makes *Pygmalion* a play not about the growth of love between master and pupil but about the pupil's regaining, through struggle, of her independent IDENTITY, in the same way that the classical sculptor's creation comes to life. In the portrayal of Higgins, Shaw created humorous suggestions of a Victor Frankenstein-like absorption in scientific experiment without proper regard for the consequences, a thematic motif developed in a different key in the chilling sketch of a character actually named Pygmalion, a creator of "synthetic men," in part 5 of Shaw's later work BACK TO METHUSELAH.

In an Epilogue written in 1915 for the first edition of the play and a revised ending for the 1939 Standard Edition, Shaw attempted to resolve the teasing ambiguities about his portrayal of the tempestuous Higgins-Eliza relation by firm announcements that Eliza's eventual marriage partner was Freddy, rather than the "confirmed bachelor" Higgins. In the highly successful musical comedy based on the play, *My Fair Lady* (1956), and the 1964 film of that name, the narrative is resolved according to the Cinderella romance formula.

FURTHER READING

Bauschatz, Paul. "The Uneasy Evolution of *My Fair Lady* from *Pygmalion*." *Shaw: The Annual of Bernard Shaw Studies* 18 (1998): 181–198.

Bentley, Eric. *Bernard Shaw.* 2d British ed. London: Methuen, 1967.

Gibbs, A. M. "The End of Pygmalion." In *The Art and Mind of Shaw: Essays in Criticism.* London: Macmillan, 1983.

A. M. Gibbs

Q

QUAN YU FA *See* POWER VERSUS LAW

THE QUARE FELLOW

The Quare Fellow was Irish dramatist BRENDAN BEHAN's first professionally produced play. Set in an Irish prison on the night before an inmate's execution, it draws heavily from Behan's own experiences as a prisoner in Britain and IRELAND.

The play premiered in November 1954 at the Pike Theatre in Dublin but first came to international attention two years later, when Joan Littlewood directed it for Theatre Workshop at Stratford East. It subsequently transferred to the West End and toured widely thereafter. Its success may be explained by the play's powerful condemnation of capital punishment—which was much debated in Britain and Ireland during the 1950s. But audiences also responded positively to its skillful combination of farcical humor with TRAGEDY.

Behan wrote *The Quare Fellow* in the early 1940s while imprisoned for shooting an Irish detective. His first draft was written in Irish as *Casadh Súgáin Eile* (*The Twisting of Another Rope*). This title played on Douglas Hyde's 1901 *The Twisting of the Rope* (*Casadh an t-Súgain*), which was one of the key plays of the Irish Dramatic Revival. It was renamed *The Quare Fellow*, a Dublin slang expression for an unusual person, shortly before it opened at the Pike.

The opening scenes introduce us to the prisoners and warders and are full of witty dialogue and visual COMEDY, focused mainly on the antics of Dunlavin—one of the only prisoners who is identified by name. This humor gradually gives way to a mounting sense of dread, as the execution approaches. Prisoners and guards are shown interacting, but their dialogue is a mask for their preoccupation with the fate of the condemned man. The audience is not required to focus on plot—very little actually happens onstage—but on the characters' mostly unexpressed feelings about the execution.

The play's focal point is Regan, a disillusioned warder. His cynicism is unsurprising: almost every inmate executed in the prison had asked that Regan guard them for their final night, and this responsibility has gradually eroded his faith in the prison system. Behan uses Regan to suggest that prison has not reformed anyone but that, on the contrary, the dread created by executions, combined with the boredom of prison life, has corrupted warders and prisoners alike. Most of these characters act entirely out of self-interest, and Behan shows brilliantly how the prison system reinforces their amorality.

The Quare Fellow is an interesting mix of tradition and innovation. Behan's use of fast-witted characters, drawn largely from Dublin's working class, owes much to SEAN O'CASEY's 1920s

Dublin trilogy. But the play is also an example of the absurdist plays that followed World War II: its central character is never named or shown onstage, and the play is, among other things, a dramatization of stultifying boredom. Behan was therefore exploring ground that would later be occupied by SAMUEL BECKETT and others. This makes *The Quare Fellow* a fascinating bridge between early- and later-20th-century Irish drama.

[*See also* Absurdism]

FURTHER READING

Kearney, Colbert. *The Writings of Brendan Behan*. Dublin: Gill & Macmillan, 1977.

Mikhail, E. H., ed. *The Art of Brendan Behan*. New York: Barnes & Noble, 1979.

Simpson, Alan. *Beckett and Behan and a Theatre in Dublin*. London: Routledge & Kegan Paul, 1962.

Patrick Lonergan

THE QUEEN AND THE REBELS

In his most compelling plays UGO BETTI dramatizes a quest into the self, projecting onto the stage the "bewildering incongruity between our existence and what it ought to be according to our soul's aspiration." *The Queen and the Rebels* (*La regina e gli insorti*, 1949), staged in Rome in 1951 and in New York in 1982, is a telling example of Betti's oeuvre. It has the appearance of a political drama taking place at the end of a successful revolution. Yet if it is viewed as a political play, one should rightfully lament its lack of political REALISM, as Walter Kerr in the *New York Times* (October 10, 1982) and Brendan Gill in *The New Yorker* (October 11, 1982) did when reviewing the Broadway production.

Betti rejects realistic depiction: his play is without temporal or geographical specificity, and the revolutionary representatives in it are too rhetorically stylized to be believable. The revolution is only a background to the redemption of Argia, the heroine, who in the extremity of her circumstance is forced to face herself and her life experience. In the play's fourth act the last pronouncements of the rebel Amos speak more of the soul's dark demons than of any aspiration for an improved social order. One should remember, in other words, that *The Queen and the Rebels* is "set"—as E. Martin Browne indicates in his introduction to *Three European Plays* (1965)—"in an atmosphere of the mind expressed by a place unlocalized except insofar as the play's story demands."

The drama is shaped according to the classical unities: the confrontation of the protagonist's destiny in one room from dusk to dawn. Naturally, the audience is aware of the SYMBOLISM of the night—the time of the brooding owl and the searching into the shadow—and the dawning light of self-discovery. What is more striking and to the point, however, is that the night is the time of the horrific—of spies, betrayals, executions, and deaths—suggesting a nightmare.

In act 1 the rebels are looking for the wife of the former dictator, the woman known as the Queen, since a counterrevolution could be mounted around her. Were she captured, she would be tortured to reveal the names of the rebels' enemies. Disguised as a peasant woman, she is among some travelers stopped at the frontier; so, too, is Argia, a prostitute, who has led a life of utter abjection.

In act 2 Argia recognizes the Queen and learns that she is not at all the courageous and dignified figure everyone thinks she is. At first Argia is outraged but later, feeling pity for her, helps her escape. By confronting the Queen, Argia has seen herself.

In act 3 Argia is *mistaken* for the Queen. Amused, she assumes the role and plays it very convincingly. But in act 4, Argia, not being able to prove who she is, in a Pirandellian feat, *becomes* the Queen. She feels free at last. As she declares before her execution: "I am as I would always have wished to be." She has solved the incongruity between her existence and her soul's aspiration.

[*See also* Italy]

FURTHER READING

Betti, Ugo. *Three Plays by Ugo Betti*. Tr. and with foreword by Henry Read. New York: Grove, 1958.

Browne, E. Martin. *Three European Plays*. London: Penguin, 1965.

Gatt-Rutter, John. "Ugo Betti: The Whore as Queen." In *Writers & Politics in Modern Italy*. New York: Holmes & Meier, 1974. 17–21.

Wadsworth, Frank W. "Ugo Betti and *The Queen and the Rebels*. Magnanimous Despair." *Drama Survey* 1 (1961): 165–177.

Emanuele Licastro

QUESTA SERA SI RECITA A SOGGETTO

See TONIGHT WE IMPROVISE

R

RABE, DAVID (1940–)

Choosing to write a play is some kind of surrender. . . . I sit and work and suddenly the door opens and out it comes. I used to be scared of it. And what I've learned over the years is not to try to shape it or control it.

—David Rabe, 1984

David Rabe began his writing career as a journalist, but by the early 1970s he was counted among the most promising young playwrights in America. Rabe was born on March 10, 1940, in Dubuque, Iowa. After receiving a bachelor of arts degree from Loras College in 1962, he enrolled at Villanova University to pursue a master's degree in theater. In 1965 Rabe withdrew from the program and was drafted into the U.S. Army to serve in Vietnam as part of a hospital-support unit. After completing his tour of duty in 1966, he returned to Villanova and earned his master's degree in 1968.

His military experience was the clear inspiration for the plays that first brought him to national attention. *The Basic Training of Pavlo Hummel* was produced in 1971 by Joseph Papp at the Public Theatre in New York City. It was followed almost immediately at the Public by STICKS AND BONES later the same year. In this play, a family loosely based on characters from the television sitcom *The Adventures of Ozzie and Harriet* (1952–1966) is nearly destroyed when eldest son David returns home after being blinded in Vietnam. The success of *Sticks and Bones* prompted Papp to risk a production on Broadway, for which Rabe won the 1972 Tony Award for Best Play. *The Orphan* (1973) was intended to complete his "Vietnam trilogy." Inspired by the *Oresteia* of Aeschylus, *The Orphan* draws parallels between the war and the atrocities of Charles Manson's "family"; however, critics regard *Streamers* (New York Drama Critics Award, 1976), in which a soldier awaiting deployment to Vietnam is killed in a dispute over his friend's sexuality, a better culmination of the trilogy.

Although Rabe eventually departed from military themes, his plays can be characterized by their "population(s) of lost people" (as critic Howard Stein put it), whose failed attempts to integrate often result in the deaths of the individuals themselves, as with Pavlo Hummel, David Nelson (*Sticks and Bones*), Billy (*Streamers*), or Phil (*Hurlyburly* [1984]—Tony Award for Best Play, 1985). Those whom the status quo does not destroy remain existentially adrift, either unaware of, or cynically unconcerned by, the pointlessness of their lives; however, these dark undercurrents are belied by Rabe's humorous and naturalistic dialogue. In *Hurlyburly*, for example, which chronicles the drug-fueled debauchery of two West Hollywood casting directors and their associates, the energetic (at times, frenetic) activity with which Rabe fills the stage often froths over into violence, and the misogyny apparent in the speech and actions of some of his male characters has vexed some feminist critics. Nevertheless, Rabe is often compared favorably with EUGENE O'NEILL for having dramatized American life in the second half of the 20th century as effectively as O'Neill dramatized the first half.

[See also United States, 1940–Present]

PLAYS: *The Basic Training of Pavlo Hummel* (1971); *Sticks and Bones* (1971); *The Orphan* (1973); *In the Boom Boom Room* (1973–1974); *Burning* (1974); *Streamers* (1976); *Hurlyburly* (1984); *Goose and Tomtom* (1986); *Those the River Keeps* (1994); *A Question of Mercy* (1997); *Corners* (1998); *The Dog Problem* (2001); *The Black Monk* (2002, based on a novella by Anton Chekhov)

FURTHER READING

McDonough, Carla J. *Staging Masculinity: Male Identity in Contemporary American Drama.* Jefferson, N.C.: McFarland, 1997.

Savran, David. *In Their Own Words: Contemporary American Playwrights.* New York: Theatre Communications Group, 1988.

Schroeder, Eric James. *Vietnam, We've All Been There: Interviews with American Writers.* Westport, Conn.: Praeger, 1992.

Zinman, Toby Silverman, ed. *David Rabe: A Casebook.* New York: Garland, 1991.

Bill Conte

RADRIGÁN, JUAN (1937–)

Lucho por la culturalidad, creo que en el campo de la cultura tenemos las armas necesarias para vencer ampliamente.
(I fight for the expansion of culture, I think that in the field of culture we have the necessary weapons with which to overcome broadly.)

—Juan Radrigán

On September 11, 1973, CHILE's democratic government was overthrown by a brutal military regime. In 1980, the dictatorship institutionalized its political, economic, and cultural models with the passing of a new national constitution. The 1980s were marked by a series of mass rebellions and protests. One of the most creative and effective spaces for mobilization throughout this period was found within the cultural arena. It is within the margins of cultural defiance that Juan Radrigán became one of the most influential playwrights of resistance. Born in Antofagasta and raised in a working-class family, Radrigán never attended school and taught himself how to read and write.

For twenty years he worked in the textile industry, becoming a labor union president and leader. With the abrupt change of government in 1973, Radrigán was blacklisted and was no longer able to find steady work within the textile industry. Radrigán began selling books in Plaza Almagro, publishing poetry and short stories before he fell "inexplicably" into theater at the age of forty-three. Radrigán's first two plays, *Testimonies of the Deaths of Sabina* (*Testimonios de las muertes de Sabina*, 1979) and *Consummate Deeds* (*Hechos consumados*, 1981), performed by his group Compañía de Teatro Popular El Telón, caused an uproar on the Chilean cultural scene. For many observers, Radrigán's plays demonstrated marginal realities not present in the dictatorship's "official culture." Radrigán's characters and story lines reflected a reality that belied the modernization and false economic stability that the regime pronounced as true. Instead, Radrigán's dramatization of everyday life emphasized the explicit poverty, injustice, and violence that marginal sectors suffered throughout Chile. Using popular dialect, Radrigán's characters transformed the common person into a tragic hero, immersed in an implacable world, where only moments of happiness and hope existed. *Consummate Deeds* went on to win the Critics' Circle Award for Best Play in 1981 and was presented throughout Chile, Latin America, Europe, and the UNITED STATES.

In 1982 he toured *The Bull by Its Horns* (*El toro por las astas*) in Latin America and later at the International Theatre Festival in Nancy, FRANCE; this play also received a Critics' Circle Award for Best Play and the Municipal Award for Theater that same year. In 1986, he presented *The Human Dispute* (*La contienda humana*) in Dormont, GERMANY, which was followed by a bilingual Chilean-German co-production of *Ballad of Those Condemned to Dream* (*Balada de los condenados a sonar*, 1987) in Munich. In 1997 he was awarded the APES Best Playwright award for *Parabola of the Drunk Ghosts* (*Parábola de los fantasmas borrachos*) and later, in 1999, the José Nuez Martín Prize from Universidad Católica. In 2001, Radrigán premiered *The Exile of the Naked Woman* (*El exilio de la mujer desnuda*), which critically examined Chile's transition to democracy; this play was given the Municipal Theater Award in 2002. Later that year, the Academy of Fine Arts in Chile honored Radrigán for his dramatic trajectory. In 2003 he finished *Panic to Two Voices* (*Pánico a dos voces*), a play about SAMUEL BECKETT and WAITING FOR GODOT.

Currently, Radrigán is a faculty member of the Universidad de La República and Arcis University; he instructs a dramatic workshop on weekends and is working on the most bitter play of his career, *Hope* (*Esperanza*), which is about a man who always dreams about but never attains happiness.

SELECT PLAYS: *Testimonies of the Deaths of Sabina* (*Testimonios de las muertes de Sabina*, 1979); *Consummate Deeds* (*Hechos consumados*, 1981); *Mournful Drumroll for Wolves and Lambs* (*Two Monologues and a Dialogue*) (*Redoble fúnebre para lobos y corderos* [*Dos monólogos y un diálogo*], 1981); *The Bull by Its Horns* (*El toro por las astas*, 1982); *The Madman and the Sad Woman* (*El loco y la triste*, 1982); *The Human Dispute* (*La contienda humana*, 1986); *Ballad of Those Condemned to Dream* (*Balada de los condenados a soñar*, 1987); *The Desolate Prince* (*El príncipe desolado*, 1998); *Mapuche Medea* (*Medea Mapuche*, 2000); *The Exile of the Naked Woman* (*El exilio de la mujer desnuda*, 2001)

FURTHER READING

El loco y la triste [*Soulmates of the Fringe*]. *Pinochet Watch* 48 (April 17, 2003). http://www.tni.org/pin-watch/watch48.htm.

Muñoz, Diego, et al., eds. *Poetica de la población marginal: Teatro poblacional Chileno: 1978–1985. Antología crítica.* Vol. 3. Minneapolis: Prisma Ins., 1987.

Pulgar, Leopold. "Juan Radrigán drásticamente valora el teatro nacional" *La Tercera* (August 6, 2000): 56.

Vidal, Hernán. *Cultural nacional Chilena, critica literaria y derechos humanos.* Minneapolis: Institute for the Study of Ideologies and Literature, 1989.

Lissette Olivares

RAIN FROM HEAVEN

Rain from Heaven by S. N. BEHRMAN debuted December 24, 1934, produced by the THEATRE GUILD, and ran for ninety-nine performances. This play veers closer to politics and darkness than Behrman's others. His theory in a prefatory note is that such a story makes TRAGEDY comprehensible to people, while a famine in Russia that kills three million is not. "The truth is that these vast lapses from civilization are so continuous, so wearisomely repetitious, that they become literally unimaginable and boring." But in this early play on the topic, Behrman tries to make the Jews in concentration camps comprehensible on a human scale by bringing one victim of them to an English country house.

The seemingly conventional high COMEDY is set in Lady Lael Wyngate's living room where Rand Eldridge has returned from six months in Antarctica, intending to propose to her. His brother, wealthy banker Hobart Eldridge, warns Rand against her—not for her private life but for her political life. She is not there to welcome them but has gone to London to collect another refugee. She works for relief of Germany's victims while Hobart is negotiating with Lord Abercrombie to start their own imitation of Hitler Youth Corps with Rand as its figurehead. Adolf Hitler is never mentioned in the play; instead, the fascist is the rich American who thinks Lael and her refugees must be communists—though they are not. At the end of the act, when Rand declares his love, hesitating over a query about her "private life," Lael responds, "I mean your assumption that as long as I'm sexually monogamous, no other foible I might have could matter to you. . . . Your psyche, my dear Rand, is sex-ridden. It's obsessed. It's maggoty with possessive desire."

In the second act, she realizes that Rand is also completely naive about politics; she is conscious of world affairs, refugees, fascism; he looks for the unchartered world and does not even realize how his brother is using his fame. Lael and Hobart discuss her recognition, but she resolves not to tell Rand about his brother. At the end of the act, she and new refugee Hugo Willens discover their attraction for each other. In the third act, she is wrongly accused of a previous affair with Hugo by Hobart's jealous wife, who in fact was in love with Hugo years before; and Rand jealously explodes with anti-Semitic remarks about Hugo.

But as Lael and Hugo recognize their love for each other, Hugo realizes he had been too much a dilettante. "Behind this decorative curtain I was forced to discover that there is a harsh reality. Well, I must investigate this further." With this recognition he realizes he must give up the comfort of her home and love: "I see now that there is only one thing left: To destroy the inhuman—to discover humanity." Thus setting an early paradigm for all the love and honor conflict plays and movies of World War II, Hugo forsakes love to return to Germany to fight against the Nazis.

[*See also* United States, 1929–1940]

FURTHER READING

Goldstein, Malcolm. *The Political Stage: American Drama and Theater of the Great Depression.* New York: Oxford Univ. Press, 1974.

Rabkin, Gerald. *Drama and Commitment.* Bloomington: Indiana Univ. Press, 1964.

David Sauer

RAINIS (1865–1929)

Rainis (the pseudonym for Jānis Pliekšāns) is the dominant figure in the evolution of 20th-century Latvian poetry and drama. His achievement in Latvian literature is often compared to Johann Wolfgang Goethe's accomplishment in German literature.

Born on September 11, 1865, in Varslavāni, a rural district of Dunava, LATVIA, the son of a prosperous tenant of estates, Rainis studied law at the University of Petersburg in RUSSIA. After periods of diverse employment (lawyer, journalist, editor of a social democratically oriented daily), followed by imprisonment and exile, Rainis married the famous Latvian poet and playwright Aspazija (Elza Rozenberga) and turned to literature professionally. In prison he translated Goethe's masterpiece *Faust*, the translation being highly innovative for the time. It influenced the development of Latvian literary language. Rainis died on September 12, 1929, in Majori near Riga, Latvia.

Rainis revived verse drama in the 20th century. Though largely based on mythology or Latvian history, Rainis's fifteen plays (including the dramatic poem *The Daugava*) betray his own moral and religious concerns. Rainis's point of departure is the value of the human soul in itself. Human greatness in his plays is measured not only by heroic deeds but also by high moral standards. Ability to make sacrifices and forgive is often inherent in most inconspicuous and worthless individuals—like Antiņš in *The Golden Steed* (Zelta zirgs, 1909) or Baiba in *Blow, Wind!* (Pūt, vējiņi!, 1914). In these plays, which abound in motifs of folklore, Rainis endeavors to revive the metrical form diction and structure of Latvia n folk songs.

Formally, Rainis rejected the dominant theatrical REALISM and found precedents in the symbolist drama and fin de siècle neo-ROMANTICISM. His play *Fire and Night* (Uguns un nakts, 1905) is the most outstanding example of SYMBOLISM and neo-romantic allegory in Latvian literature. Making a periphrase of *Lāčplēsis* (1888), a Latvian epic by Andrejs Pumpurs, Rainis sets forth the fundamental principle of his poetry: an old song to new tunes. The story in his plays is frequently borrowed from historically or geographically distant contexts: Orpheus and Eurydice in *I Played, I Danced* (Spēlēju, dancoju, 1915), Romeo and Juliet in *Indulis and Ārija* (Indulis un Ārija, 1912), and biblical myth in *Joseph and His Brothers* (Jāzeps un viņa brāļi, 1919). In *Fire and Night* Rainis joins ancient saga and Latvian history to contemporary issues—national liberation and independence. The protagonist Bearslayer (Lāčplēsis) embodies the mighty power of a cultural hero and fights for the freedom of his beloved Laimdota—a symbol of Latvia. His strivings are threatened by Teutonic invaders and traitors, as well as The Dark Knight who associates with the powers of evil. However, the most innovative character is Spīdola—ever-changing beauty and spiritual activity, which is neither good nor evil, an archetypical character that exemplifies Rainis's idea about the mobility, dynamism, and transformability of symbols.

Joseph and His Brothers is Rainis's most personal play. It presents the irreconcilable conflict between the individual and society in accordance with the Nietzchsean conception of the absolute value of individuality and of the individual's loneliness. Although reconciliation and fulfillment are the essence of Rainis's conception of life, in *Joseph and His Brothers* he finally shows that they belong to the mystical beyond, outside the confines of this life.

Rainis fulfills two of the principal goals of modern theater: the return to myth and ritual and the creation of a total spectacle. His plays have been extensively staged within Latvia.

PLAYS: *Half Idealist* (Pusideālists, 1903); *Fire and Night* (Uguns un nakts, 1905); *Girts Vilks* (1907); *The Golden Steed* (Zelta zirgs, 1909); *Indulis and Ārija* (Indulis un Ārija, 1912); *Blow, Wind!* (Pūt, vējiņi!, 1914); *I Played, I Danced* (Spēlēju, dancoju,1915); *The Daugava* (Daugava, 1919); *Joseph and His Brothers* (Jāzeps un viņa brāļi, 1919); *The Little Raven* (Krauklītis, 1920); *Ilya of Murom* (Iļja Muromietis, 1923); *The King of Flies* (Mušu ķēniņš, 1923); *Love Stronger than Death* (Mīla stiprāka par nāvi, 1927); *The Witch of Riga* (Rīgas ragana, 1928); *Dog and Cat* (Suns un kaķe, 1928)

FURTHER READING

Straumanis, Alfreds, ed. *The Golden Steed: Seven Baltic Plays.* Prospect Heights, Ill.: Waveland Press, 1979.

——, ed. "Latvian Drama." In *Baltic Drama: A Handbook and Bibliography.* Prospect Heights, Ill.: Waveland Press, 1981.

——, ed. *Fire and Night: Five Baltic Plays.* Prospect Heights, Ill.: Waveland Press, 1986.

Valda Čakare

A RAISIN IN THE SUN

*Mama, it is a play that tells the truth about people, Negroes and life
and I think it will help a lot of people to understand how we are just
as complicated as they are—and just as mixed up—but above all,
that we have among our miserable and downtrodden ranks—people
who are the very essence of human dignity.*

—Lorraine Hansberry, 1959

LORRAINE HANSBERRY completed her best-known work, *A
Raisin in the Sun*, in 1957. A touchstone for the play was the hostile reception her own family had received when they moved
into a "white" Chicago neighborhood in 1938. The play focuses
on an economically disadvantaged extended black family's struggle to emerge both figuratively and literally from their overcrowded
and stifling socioeconomic conditions. Following successful
performances in New Haven, Philadelphia, and Chicago, the
play opened on Broadway on March 11, 1959, at the Ethel Barrymore Theatre to critical acclaim, followed by a run of 538 consecutive performances. It garnered for Hansberry the first
Drama Critics' Circle Award given to a black writer. Directed by
Lloyd Richards, the first African American to direct a Broadway
play, *Raisin* featured an ensemble of actors who would all play
major roles in African American theater in the years to come:
Claudia McNeil as Mama, Sidney Poitier as Walter Lee, Ruby
Dee as Ruth, and Diana Sands as Beneatha. Louis Gossett, Ivan
Dixon, Glynn Turman, Douglas Turner Ward, and Lonnie Elder
III also had roles in the play, and Ossie Davis would eventually
replace Poitier as Walter Lee.

Raisin is first and foremost a play about the impact of social
injustice and inequality on black family relations, and it ties a
black American family's struggle to African liberation struggles through the character Asagai. The play exposes the bitterness wrought by centuries of deferred dreams, while stressing
the celebration of black family unity based on a long-standing
tradition of resistance and endurance.

When *Raisin* opens, Big Walter, the head of the household,
has died, and his extended family is awaiting an insurance
check from the policy Big Walter had the foresight to take out
before his death. Each of the adult family members has ideas
about how to spend the $10,000. The son, Walter Lee, wants to
start his own business, his wife Ruth longs for better living
conditions for her growing family, Walter Lee's sister Beneatha
wants to go to medical school, and Mama Lena wants the
money to answer all their dreams. Lena Younger uses part of
the money as a downpayment on a house in a white neighborhood, because homes in black neighborhoods cost twice as
much. In a gesture of respect, she gives the remainder of the
funds to Walter Lee, directing him to deposit part of it for
Beneatha's education. But Walter Lee gives the money to a hustler to invest in a shady business venture. Bilked and disgraced,
Walter Lee is tempted to accept the offer of an all-white neighborhood association to move into the Youngers' new home.
However, Walter Lee rejects the offer and claims the Youngers'

right—in the name of his ancestors—to live in the neighborhood of their choosing. The play ends with the family preparing to move into the new home. An alternative followed the
Younger family to their new home, where they faced the anger
and violence of their white neighbors.

Hansberry's realistic play represents the African American
quest for the American dream and equal economic opportunity
access, while capturing the spirit of the civil rights movement of
the time. It also deals with black women's issues, through Ruth's
contemplation of an abortion and Beneatha's refusal of Asagai's
marriage proposal and her desire to attend medical school. While
the Youngers' unity relates to universal themes of family struggle,
their opposition to racial and economic discrimination makes the
play more specific to black Americans. Hansberry believed that by
dealing with specific stories, one created universal themes.

The play was adapted for a film in 1961 and won a special
award at the Cannes Film Festival. In 1974, Robert Nemiroff produced the Tony Award–winning musical version of the play,
which he dubbed *Raisin*, and in 1987 Danny Glover and Esther
Rolle starred in an American Playhouse production of *A Raisin in
the Sun* that included material excised from the original production. A 2004 Broadway revival, starring Phylicia Rashad, Audra
McDonald, and Sean Combs, earned Rashad a Tony award for
Best Actress, making her the first African American to receive
that prize. Now considered a classic of American theater, *A Raisin in the Sun* has been translated into over thirty languages.

[*See also* United States, 1940–Present]

FURTHER READING

Carter, Steven R. *Hansberry's Drama: Commitment Amid Complexity.*
  Urbana: Univ. of Illinois Press, 1991.

Cheney, Anne. *Lorraine Hansberry.* New York: Twayne, 1984.

Kappel, Lawrence, ed. *Readings on* A Raisin in the Sun. San Diego:
  Greenhaven, 2001.

"Lorraine Hansberry: Art of Thunder, Vision of Light." Special issue,
  Freedomways: A Quarterly Review of the Freedom Movement 19 (1979).

Wilkerson, Margaret B. "*A Raisin in the Sun*: Anniversary of an
  American Classic." In *Performing Feminisms: Feminist Critical Theory
  and Theatre*, ed. by Sue-Ellen Case. Baltimore: Johns Hopkins
  Univ. Press, 1990.

Lovalerie King

RAKESH, MOHAN (1925–1972)

Madan Mohan Guglani, better known to the literary world as
Mohan Rakesh, was born on January 8, 1925, in Amritsar,
INDIA, in a lower-middle-class family. Son of a lawyer who left
him an orphan at the age of sixteen, brought up by his mother
and sister, he was educated in Amritsar and Lahore (now in
PAKISTAN). He taught in two colleges and one school, edited a
short-story magazine, and finally decided to devote himself
fully to writing.

It is difficult to ascertain whether he started writing first in fiction or in drama, but there is no denying the fact that he was one of three leading lights of a radical literary movement Nai Kahani (New Short Story) that completely transformed the character of Hindi short story. Along with Rajendra Yadav and Kamleshwar (very important and significant contemporary fiction writers in Hindi), he brought the make-believe, romantic short story down to earth and made it an expression of life as it is lived and experienced in the immediate present. What he did in short-story writing he did when it came to writing plays. The subjects he chose for his plays were so interwoven with the reality and life of our times that they brought a proverbial fresh breeze to Hindi theater.

Before Rakesh, Hindi drama used the language of literature. It was meant to be read. In other words, as far as theater is concerned, it was a dead language. Rakesh evolved a dramatic language of theater.

Before Rakesh, Hindi plays were pure entertainment, dealing either with mythology or historical romance. They had highly idealistic themes, and their characters were therefore blatantly didactic and unidimensional, completely devoid of any relationship with contemporary reality. There was no attempt to explore the complexity of life. In 1958 Rakesh changed all that with his first play ONE DAY IN ASADH (Asadh Ka Ek Din), which won first prize in a competition organized by the Sangeet Natak Akademi (the National Academy of Music, Dance, and Drama). One Day in Asadh is the first modern Hindi play.

In One Day in Asadh, Rakesh deals with the relationship of the author to his roots and the relationship between state patronage and creativity. Shyamanand Jalan's production of One Day in Asadh for the theater group Anamika (Kolkata) in 1961 and Ebrahim Alkazi's production for the National School of Drama (Delhi) in 1962 established Rakesh's reputation as the first modern Hindi playwright of immense potential and significance. For the first time Jalan was able to direct a play that demanded not a surface treatment but an in-depth study of a complex character. This resulted in a very sensitive and imaginative production whose impact was further enhanced by great ensemble ACTING. Alkazi's production was done environmentally, in a small space in the compound of a house.

Rakesh wrote only three and a half full-length plays. After One Day in Asadh came The Great Swans of the Waves (Lehron Ke Rajhans, 1963; New Version, 1966), HALFWAY HOUSE (Adhe Adhure, 1969), and the incomplete The Ground Beneath One's Feet (Pair Tale Ki Zameen, 1972), which he was working on when he died.

All of Rakesh's plays center around the man-woman relationship, but it is evident that this theme served as a vehicle for larger statements on other aspects of the human condition. For example, in The Great Swans Rakesh also deals with two conflicting worldviews: material and spiritual. Nand, the protagonist of the play, is attracted to his beautiful wife Sundari. But he feels equally the pull of Buddha's PHILOSOPHY. He says that when he

is with Sundari, he longs for Buddha, and when he is with Buddha, he pines for Sundari. He is a divided self, unable to belong wholly to either the world of Sundari (material) or the world of Buddha (spiritual). Rakesh's play Halfway House is about the tragic collapse of values in the Indian middle-class world.

Rakesh's oeuvre is small, but his reputation and significance are immense because he revolutionized Hindi theater to such an extent that no other playwright of his status has emerged on the scene even thirty-five years after his death on December 3, 1972, in New Delhi.

PLAYS: One Day in Asadh (Asadh Ka Ek Din, 1958); The Great Swans of the Waves (Lehron Ke Rajhans, 1963); Halfway House (Adhe Adhure, 1969); The Ground Beneath One's Feet (Pair Tale Ki Zameen, 1972, incomplete)

FURTHER READING

Jain, N. C. "Some Recent Significant Plays." Enact 25–26 (January–February 1969).

Nigam, R. L. "Aadhe Adhure: A Comment." Enact 32–33 (August–September 1969).

Rakesh, Mohan. "Why Plays?" Enact 13–14 (January–February 1968).

Sethi, J. D. "Rakesh's Aadhe Adhure: A Breakthrough." Enact 27 (March 1969).

Shormishtha Panja, Kumar, and N. Nita. "Halfway House: A House Divided." In Many Indias, Many Literatures: New Critical Essays, ed. by Delhi: Worldview Pubs., 1999.

Rajinder Nath

RAMA V (1853–1910)

King Chulalongkorn, known as Rama V, the fifth ruler of the current Chakri Dynasty, had a significant impact on the development of modern drama in THAILAND. He was educated by English teachers like Anna Leonowens and Daniel Beach Bradley and traveled extensively to Europe in 1897 and 1907, where he saw plays, ballets, operas, and even Isadora Duncan. So he understood European theater as well as being fundamentally versed in traditional Thai models that were part of royal life. He was, therefore, able to combine ideas from both in his work, creating new genres that both reflected his straightforward personality and were suited to the needs of the new Thai social environment.

While young he wrote plays and directed his younger brothers in entertainments for the Thai new year in April. His first scripted play was Dance Drama of Talok (Rabam Talok, 1868) a short COMEDY performed by famous comedians. Another play of unknown date is the adaptation of a work by his father, Dance Drama of the Rain (Bot Lakon Jab Rabam), set in the heavens, depicting thunder and lightning to welcome rain. He initiated "spoken drama" (lakon phud), a genre where speech prevails over dance/music, when he wrote the verse play based on The Arabian Nights, Sleep-Awakening (Nitra Chakrit) for New Year's eve in 1879, later adding songs to highlight selected scenes. His 1882 Play of Prince Inao (Bot Jeraja Lakon Inao) was a spoken drama in prose where the dancers delivered set dialogue rather than following the standard practice where performers improvised the text themselves. His satiric *Wong Tewarat* (1884) was a parody on a traditional play of the same name. Another work, *To Bet Not to Be Angry* (*Panan Ngod Khwam Grot*, 1889), has been lost.

His final work *Ngo Pa* (1906) is his best and breaks with tradition. This love triangle in a Negrito village has ethnographic elements based on the king's knowledge of a tribe in Patalung that he had learned as a child from his Negrito page Kanang. While sick the monarch wrote the play in eight days. His introduction clarifies that he will not follow the rules of traditional theater. *Ngo Pa* is the cornerstone of modern drama in Thailand.

The play broke traditional constraints in many ways. Despite its comic moments it ends with the death of the three lovers onstage. Death scenes, especially of protagonists onstage, were rare. The leading characters were commoners and from a marginalized group rather than the standard princes and princesses. The costumes and vocabulary reflected the Negrito reality. While the play retained aspects of classical theater, it evoked an earthy tone suited to the story. The delightful play continues to be performed annually on October 23, the anniversary of the author's death in 1910.

In addition to his work as a playwright, the king prompted other members of the royal family to create theater that would serve his social reform as well as mounting traditional works. He began the practice of royalty patronizing public theaters rather than confining viewing to the royal palace. His presence was valued by the public, who flocked to the theater for such events. His innovations were continued by his successors.

PLAYS: *Dance Drama of Talok* (*Rabam Talok*, 1868); *Dance Drama of the Rain* (*Bot Lakon Jab Rabam*, n.d.); *Sleep Awakening* (*Nitra Chakrit*, 1879); *Play of Prince Inao* (*Bot Jeraja Lakon Inao*, 1882); *Wong Tewarat* (1884); *To Bet Not to Be Angry* (*Panan Ngod Khwam Grot*, 1889); *Ngo Pa* (1906)

FURTHER READING

Rutnin, Matani. *Dance, Drama, and Theatre in Thailand: The Process of Development and Modernization.* Chiang Mai: Silkworn, 1996.

Virulrak, Surapone. *The Evolution of Thai Performing Arts in Bangkok Period 1782–1934.* Bangkok: Chulalongkorn Univ. Press, 2002 [in Thai].

———. *Performing Arts in the Reign of King Rama V.* Bangkok, Chulalongkorn Univ. Press, 2004 [in Thai].

Surapone Virulrak

RAME, FRANCA (1929–)

By all accounts, Franca Rame has theater in her blood. She made her first stage appearance in her mother's arms when she was eight days old. Rame was born in 1929 to a Northern Italian family who had been itinerant performers for three centuries. Her heritage is rooted in the improvisational comic theater of commedia dell'arte, developed in ITALY in the mid-1500s and characterized by masked figures and stylized characters, like Harlequin and Pulcinella. Rame's family's theatrical repertoire of story lines and other formulas were useful to both Rame and her future husband and theater partner, Nobel laureate DARIO FO. Fo and Rame married in 1954 and have been so indivisibly involved in political activities and theatrical collaborations since then that Dario Fo acknowledged receipt of the Nobel Prize for Literature in 1997 on both their behalf.

Rame has devoted her life and theater work to the exposure of corruption and injustice at home and abroad, even at personal risk to herself. Until 1950 she worked in her father's theater company, then in variety shows and revues. By the mid-1950s, she was performing in plays and on television. Rame slowly shed her reputation as a beautiful but vacuous blond actress through her political activities and professional achievements, achieving international recognition in her own right with the 1977 publication of *All House, Bed and Church* (*Tutta casa, letto e chiesa*, partially translated in FEMALE PARTS), on the crest of the Italian women's movement of the 1970s.

Drawing from slapstick, popular theater, political satire, and the comic-grotesque literary tradition, the Fo-Rame plays criticize political corruption and religious hypocrisy. From the beginning, their DRAMATURGY demonstrates a Marxist concern with the condition of the proletariat and poor in Italy and abroad. During the feminist movements of the 1970s, their plays also begin to focus on the subaltern condition of women, although Rame did not agree with feminist separatism. Other targets of their theatrical satire are controversial current events and cultural phenomena such as the economic boom, consumerism, and modern capitalism.

Rame and Fo have always refused blind allegiance to any authority or political position. For example, although in 1960 Rame became a member of the Partito Comunista Italiano (PCI, the Italian Communist Party), Rame and Fo soon began to satirize the bureaucracy of the PCI, which resulted in the PCI's withdrawal of support for the team (Behan, 2000). Melding theater and political activism, Rame and Fo took their performances outside of traditional venues into occupied factories and onto the streets during the political struggles of the late 1960s to 1970s. This resulted in intense censorship, arrests, and police presence during their shows. As early as 1962, their television variety show *Canzonissima* was censored, and the team was kept off the air until 1977, despite their fame throughout Italy.

Such persecution did not hinder Rame, who founded and ran Soccorso Rosso (Red Aid) to aid 10,000 prisoners. In 1973, the persecution culminated in Rame's being kidnapped, tortured, and raped in a van by neofascists supported—according to a 1998, post-Nobel investigation—by the police. She writes of this in her powerful play *The Rape* (*Lo stupro*, 1982). She performs this piece often and includes it in *Sex? Thanks, Don't Mind If I Do!* (*Sesso? Grazie, tanto per gradire*, 1994) This monologue is coauthored with Fo and their son Jacopo and is based on Jacopo's book on sex education for young people. As recently as 1994, the play was censored, and anyone under eighteen was not permitted to attend.

Although in the mid-1970s Rame's name finally began to appear in co-authorship with Dario Fo, it is difficult to separate their work. The issue of authorship reflects their theater's collaborative modus operandi and Rame's own literary development. The improvisational nature of their comic theater hinges on the contributions, comments, and criticisms of the actors and the response of the audience. Rame has had a central role from the start as Fo's closest critic, who revises, edits, archives, and prepares their plays for publication. Critics point out that Fo's plays would probably not have survived without Rame. Fo himself underscores Rame's importance in the development of the female character. He admits that he would not have been able to write such "solid female characters" without her; in fact, he declares that "they are written *with* Franca." Most critics consider the one-woman monologues in *Female Parts* to be primarily of her invention, and some critics also include *Heroin* (*L'Eroina*), about drugs, and *The Fat Woman* (*La donna grassa*), about human isolation in contemporary times, both in *Let's Talk About Women* (*Parliamo di donne*, 1991). In sum, Rame has been called "one of the three best epic actresses in the world." To this we must add Rame's many accomplishments as gifted editor and playwright.

SELECT PLAYS: *Female Parts* (partial translation of *Tutta casa, letto e chiesa*, 1981); *The Rape* (*Lo stupro*, 1982); *Open Couple* (*Coppia Aperta*, 1983); *Let's Talk About Women* (*Parliamo di donne*, 1991); *Sex? Thanks, Don't Mind If I Do!* (*Sesso? Grazie, tanto per gradire*, 1994)

FURTHER READING

Behan, Thomas. *Dario Fo: Revolutionary Theater*. Sterling, Va.: Pluto Press, 2000 [also discusses Rame].

Farrell, Joseph. *Dario Fo and Franca Rame: Harlequins of the Revolution*. London: Methuen, 2001.

Mitchell, Tony. *Dario Fo: People's Court Jester*. London: Methuen, 1999 [also discusses Rame].

Montgomery, Angela. "The Theatre of Dario Fo and Franca Rame: Laughing All the Way to the Revolution." In *Twentieth–Century European Drama*, ed. by Brian Docherty. New York: St. Martin's Press, 1994.

Valeri, Walter, ed. *Franca Rame: A Woman on Stage*. West Lafayette, Ind.: Bordighera, 2000.

Wood, Sharon. "*Parliamo di donne*: Feminism and Politics in the Theater of Franca Rame." In *Dario Fo: Stage, Text, and Tradition*, ed. by Joseph Farrell and Antonio Scuderi. Carbondale: Southern Illinois Univ. Press, 2000.

Tommasina Gabriele

RASGA CORAÇÃO   See BREAK THE HEART

RATTIGAN, TERENCE (1911–1977)

As a popular playwright Terence Rattigan dominated the English stage from the mid-1930s to the mid-1950s. An advocate of the well-made play (with a clear beginning, middle, and end), emphasis on character more than plot, and attention to the sensibilities of his audience, Rattigan was a supreme craftsman in both COMEDY and serious drama. The most dramatic moments in his plays are often a triumph of the carefully placed understatement, leading the audience either to laughter or tears. His popularity waned in the 1960s and 1970s, but since his death in 1977 he has come to be acknowledged as one of the finest English-speaking playwrights of the 20th century.

Terence Mervyn Rattigan was born in Kensington, London, on June 9, 1911. Terence's father Frank was a diplomat and spent much time abroad with mother Vera, so Terence and his older brother Brian were raised in large part by their paternal grandmother, Lady Rattigan. Terence attended Hornbye's School in Surrey and in 1925 matriculated to Harrow School, Middlesex, on scholarship, where he entered his first of a lifelong series of mostly closeted homosexual relationships. Rattigan read history at Trinity College, Oxford, but never completed his degree, having decided to leave school to attempt to make his way as a professional playwright.

Rattigan's father was not pleased with his son's choice of career but agreed to fund his son with £200 per year for a two-year trial. If by the end of that time Terry had not found sufficient success to make his own way financially as a playwright, the boy would leave playwriting for a more secure profession, such as diplomacy. Rattigan's first play to be produced, *First Episode*, was written with his current roommate Philip Heimann and earned Rattigan £100 in royalties, but as he had already spent £200 on a preview run, he had to consider it a financial loss. During the following year Rattigan invested much time on an adaptation of *A Tale of Two Cities* in collaboration with John Gielgud, but the projected production of the play fell through when Gielgud decided not to compete with another adaptation of the novel that was running at that time. As his second year neared a close, Rattigan submitted another script, at that time called *Gone Away*, to Bronson Alberry, the producer who had intended to produce *A Tale of Two Cities*, in the hope that the man would consider producing this alternative.

Retitled *French Without Tears* (1936), in a pun upon the name of the stage director, Harold French, and in reference to the play's setting in a French language-study resort, *Gone Away* delighted audiences and many critics, running for a record-setting 1,030 performances at the Criterion Theatre. The play deals with the arrival of a predatory female among a crowd of undergraduate men at a resort in FRANCE where they have gone to improve their French-speaking skills and the comedic rivalry for her attentions that follows. The financial success of this play introduced Rattigan to a luxurious standard of living, which became in part an incentive for his future composition of screenplays, although theater always remained his primary love. But Rattigan would never entirely cease to measure his success as a playwright by the size of his royalties, a legacy of his original bargain with Frank Rattigan.

Another measure of success as a playwright for Rattigan was range of genre. Rattigan intended the play following *French Without Tears* to prove his ability to write serious drama as well as light comedy. *After the Dance* (1939) deals with an unhappy love triangle, a topic that was always to run through Rattigan's plays. The plot culminates in the suicide of Joan Scott-Fowler, the central female character, upon her realization of how completely she and her husband have misunderstood each other in their attempts to love. In contrast to the extraordinary run of *French Without Tears*, this play ran for only sixty performances. Weeks after *After the Dance* closed, war broke out in Britain. Rattigan's next two plays, *Follow My Leader* (1940), a satire on Adolf Hitler's GERMANY, and *Grey Farm* (written in collaboration with Hector Bolith, 1940), closed within weeks of their openings, and Rattigan began consulting Dr. Keith Newman, a well-respected psychiatrist, for depression.

Upon the recommendation of Dr. Newman, Rattigan joined the Royal Air Force. *Flare Path*, produced at the Apollo Theatre in 1942, dramatized the culture Rattigan found in military life and rejuvenated his self-esteem through critical praise and a run nearly two years long. In the play three couples face different challenges in love within the context of the World War II British air force. Once again in this serious drama, the central character Patricia must choose between two loves—an attractive ex who has returned to her life after years of absence and her duller air-fighter husband.

While the Sun Shines (1943) and *Love in Idleness* (1944) marked a return to comedy for Rattigan. The FARCE of *While the Sun Shines* centers on three men's attempts to win the affections of beautiful and sensible Elizabeth, a member of the Women's Air Force, and with it Rattigan once again broke records, with a run of 1,154 performances. *Love in Idleness* starred the famous stage couple Alfred Lunt and Lynne Fontanne.

The Winslow Boy (1946), based upon a famous court case of the Edwardian era, has become the play for which Rattigan has perhaps been best remembered. A boy is wrongly accused of stealing a five-shilling postal note and expelled from the Royal Naval Academy where he is enrolled. His family rallies around him and obtains with some difficulty the services of a famous barrister, and they win the court case that clears the boy's name. The restrained precision with which Rattigan builds the suspense of a court drama, in which not a single scene takes place in court, is masterful. The play ran for more than a year at the Lyric Theatre in London and was followed by two one-acts Rattigan had written with actor John Gielgud in mind for the central characters.

Playbill: The Browning Version and Harlequinade was a production of two of a trilogy of one-acts Rattigan wrote with the intention of attempting a dramatic build in which the interruption of a traditional intermission was unnecessary because of a shorter duration. The third of the plays, *High Summer*, was discarded as inferior to the others. THE BROWNING VERSION is a terse portrait of a disappointed classics scholar whose dismal life is brightened by a student's presentation to him of a secondhand copy of Robert Browning's translation of the *Agamemnon* of Aeschylus. *Harlequinade* parodies the backstage life of a theatrical couple closely resembling Alfred Lunt and Lynne Fontanne.

By this time, to his chagrin, Rattigan had earned a label among critics and other playwrights as a popular writer for entertainment. In a letter to the *New Statesman and Nation* in 1950, he defended his work and criticized plays of ideas, which he considered propaganda rather than art. He created a fictional audience member, Aunt Edna, whose response to theater must be a measure of its effectiveness, to illustrate his argument. (Rattigan elaborated further upon Aunt Edna, an elderly, proper, middle-class spinster, in the preface to the second volume of his *Collected Works* published in 1953.) SEAN O'CASEY, GEORGE BERNARD SHAW, CHRISTOPHER FRY, and others responded to his letter with their own contrasting arguments, and Rattigan's reputation as a merely popular playwright grew rather than diminished.

After his exploration of a shorter form in *Playbill*, Rattigan expanded his repertoire to include the epic form in *Adventure Story* (1949), based upon the life of Alexander the Great. Another comedy, *Who Is Sylvia?* (1950), preceded Rattigan's most deeply personal play, THE DEEP BLUE SEA (1952). A response to the suicide of Rattigan's former lover Kenneth Morgan, *The Deep Blue Sea* opens upon the scene of a woman's suicide—unsuccessful, we learn as the play progresses. In the play Rattigan articulates more clearly and poignantly than he had previously the anguish that contrasting styles of loving can bring to relationships. The rawness and depth of emotion presented in the central character Hester Collyer has led many theater historians to hypothesize that Hester may have been originally written as Hector.

Separate Tables (1954), two one-acts that take place in the same hotel and emphasize different characters from among the guests, marked the height of Rattigan's popularity and the conclusion of his reign upon the stage. Following the 1956 opening of JOHN OSBORNE's LOOK BACK IN ANGER and the advent of the "kitchen sink" drama, Rattigan became relegated to the ranks of old-fashioned playwrights who clung to an outmoded style of writing. His seven future plays would fail to reach the popularity and former acclaim his former plays had enjoyed. He died of bone marrow cancer on November 30, 1977, in Hamilton, Bermuda.

With the contemporary dismissal of plays of ideas and renewed appreciation for virtuosity of form and depth of characterization, since the late 1990s Rattigan has been experiencing a renewed popularity among critics, historians, and audiences.

[*See also* England]

FURTHER READING

Darlow, Michael, and Gillian Hodson. *Terence Rattigan: The Man and His Work*. London: Quartet Bks., 1979.

Rusinko, Susan. *Terence Rattigan*. Twayne's English Author Series 366. Boston: Twayne, 1983.

Wansell, Geoffrey. *Terence Rattigan*. London: Fourth Estate, 1995.

Young, B. A. *The Rattigan Version: The Theatre of Character*. New York: Atheneum, 1988.

Antonia Sophia Krueger

RAVENHILL, MARK (1966–)

A graduate in English and drama studies from Bristol University (1987), Mark Ravenhill (born in West Sussex, ENGLAND, in 1966) was catapulted to fame as well as notoriety by his first full-length play, *Shopping and Fucking* (1996). Controversy was provoked not only by the indecent title but also by the abjectness of his characters, the combination of passionless sex with consumerism and violence, and the seeming total lack of "normal" humanist values. A play that depicted homosexual outcasts, drug addicts, and self-mutilating and masochistic characters was prone to cause a stir, and yet Ravenhill's postmodern urban underworld and his use of timely gadgets such as CCTV and video could lay claim to a "new REALISM" appropriate to the 1990s. In 1997, he became literary director of Paines Plough and also worked on the BBC cult televison series *This Life*.

His next three plays were experimental works with strong, yet playful intertextual tendencies. *Faust Is Dead* (1997) is a free updating of the Faust myth, turning the saga of an aging scholar who sells his soul to the devil into an episode in the life of a star philosopher (like Michel Foucault), who announces the end of history on televison. The existentialist gets wedged between the software heir Pete, who has stolen his father's Chaos program and who observes everything through the lens of his video camera, and the self-mutilating teenage boy Donny, who finally kills himself without managing to overcome the boundaries of his own virtuality: his suicide remains as unreal as any television event.

Sleeping Around (1998), which Ravenhill wrote in teamwork, is a contemporary version of ARTHUR SCHNITZLER's classic REIGEN (*La Ronde*). It depicts a chain of superficial sexual encounters, pointing out the meaninglessness of commodified love in a busy consumer culture. *Handbag* (1998) again uses a famous precursor text (OSCAR WILDE's THE IMPORTANCE OF BEING EARNEST) to examine the incessant but unsuccessful human search for meaning and intimacy in life. The juxtaposition of lesbian spouses who conceive a child with a male couple with Victorian repression and sentimentality highlights the loss of the nurturing instinct in an emotionally stunted and selfish society.

Some Explicit Polaroids (1999), based on ERNST TOLLER's 1927 play *Hurrah, This Is Life!* (*Hoppla, wir leben!*), seems to stress a more humanistic tone by representing the world weariness and anger of those deemed "trash" by society. And yet all characters share the same muddled values, the loss of all old certainties of political or moral belief. To enhance their lack of a clearly shaped IDENTITY, the play uses prefabricated language, deploys the phrases and gadgets of contemporary life, from psychobabble and computer language to the idea of the polaroid camera that produces instantly gratifying but short-lived works in a media-oriented culture.

In his black COMEDY with songs, *Mother Clap's Molly House* (2001), Ravenhill weaves together two times zones: London 1726, showing a haberdashery turned into a transvestite meeting house, and London 2001, showing a present-day gay fetish party. The play originated in Ravenhill's discovery of an 18th-century gay subculture of same-sex clubs and uses songs in the cabaret style of the German socialist revolutionary BERTOLT BRECHT's THE THREEPENNY OPERA. Ravenhill, who is open about being "queer" and HIV positive, celebrates the diversity of a human sexuality that defies classification, but the play also questions the fashionableness of modern gay existence, which has become a lifestyle that suits consumer capitalism.

Totally Over You (2003) is based on Molière's *The Invaluable Ridiculous Ones* (*Les précieuses ridicules*), relocating the plot in the context of modern celebrity culture and showing teenage girls dumping their boyfriends for members of a fashionable boy's group—who of course are none other than these former boyfriends. Again this play, geared for teenaged actors and audience, deals with the possibility of intimacy and love in a dehumanized consumer culture where reality and virtuality have become indistinguishable. It remains to be decided whether Ravenhill is merely the enfant terrible purveying a sensationalist Theater of Cruelty or the profoundly moral and socialist playwright who wittily and ironically sums up the zeitgeist and who explores the darker social reality of the homeless, the addicted, and the outcast.

[*See also* Gay and Lesbian Drama]

FURTHER READING

Sierz, Aleks. *In-Yer-Face Theatre: British Drama Today*. London: Faber, 2001.

——. "In-Yer-Face Theatre: Mark Ravenhill and 1990s Drama." *Anglistik & Englischunterricht* 64 (2002): 107–121.

Svich, Caridad. " 'Commerce and Morality in the Theatre of Mark Ravenhill." *Contemporary Theatre Review: An International Journal* 13 (2003): 81–95.

Wandor, Michelene. *Post-war British Drama: Looking Back in Gender*. London: Routledge, 2001.

Heike Grundmann

RAYSON, HANNIE (1959–)

The early work of Hannie Rayson (born in Melbourne, Victoria, AUSTRALIA, on March 31, 1959) reflects her background both as an actor and as a member of the experimental Theatreworks ensemble. Rayson received a bachelor of arts degree (University of Melbourne, 1977) and diploma in dramatic art (Victoria College of the Arts, 1980). *Room to Move* (1985) is episodic and antirealist in form and, like *Mary* (1985), which deals with the experiences of a Greek Australian girl, is the product of an intensely collaborative process.

With *Hotel Sorrento* (1990), however, Rayson establishes the mode that has come to define her distinctive voice in Australian theater: more conservative in form but richer and broader in scope and squarely focused on the analysis of close relationships in the context of powerful cultural metaphors—of the representation of female experience and of Australia in the context of its colonial past. The play, later made into a film, has the classic realistic plot structure and explores the patterns of enduring love and deep resentment in the feelings of the three sisters. At the same time, though, Rayson invokes a broad canvas of national and class IDENTITY. The humble seaside home at Sorrento suggests an Australia that was past—simpler, gentler, but also insular and constrictive. The disintegration of the family is marked by the death of Wal, the father, and the choice of two of the sisters to live overseas, reflecting the painful loss of connectedness that can accompany a growing sophistication.

Falling from Grace (1994) explores another set of female relationships, this time concerning three friends, and also the effects of liberal feminism on the behavior and attitudes of the men in their lives.

Rayson's subsequent work has added another dimension, an overarching political concern. However, only in the least successful of them, the apocalyptic FARCE on economic rationalism, *Competitive Tenderness* (1996), does the subject of the controversy dwarf the complex interactions of the human characters caught up in it. *Life After George* (2000, winner of the Victorian Premier's Literary Award 2001), set in the new "corporatized" university, is less concerned to expose the destructive compromises that academics might be forced to make than to comment on the effects those choices have on the personas they presented and their intimate relationships. Rayson's skill in writing intelligent conversation was critical here, as in *Hotel Sorrento*, in probing beneath the disguises and self-deceptions of people who can be witty and seem acute about their lives.

The public issue in *Inheritance* (2003) is the disintegration and impotent rage of rural Australian societies, and its scale of action is appropriately larger with two big families at the center of the conflict, the vastness of the land to be inherited, and in the metaphorical reach of the language. Rayson again represents a culture on the cusp of change and explores, subtly, the psychological responses that this induces. *Inheritance* offers a parable for contemporary Australia, both in the country's clinging to the shreds of its white colonial past and in its failure to acknowledge fully the darker aspects of that history—the notion that an Aboriginal man might inherit the land once roamed by his own people is incomprehensible to most of the people of the play and encases the action in multiple ironies.

SELECT PLAYS: *Mary* (1985); *Room to Move* (1985); *Hotel Sorrento* (1990); *Falling from Grace* (1994); *Competitive Tenderness* (1996); *Life After George* (2000); *Inheritance* (2003); *Two Brothers* (2005)

FURTHER READING

Fensham, Rachel, and Denise Varney. *The Doll's Revolution: Australian Theatre and the Cultural Imagination*. With Maryrose Casey and Laura Ginters. Melbourne: Australian Scholarly, 2005.

Varney, Denise. "The Desire to Affirm and Challenge: An Interview with Hannie Rayson." *Australasian Drama Studies* 42 (April 2003): 146–160.

——. "Hannie Rayson's *Life After George*: Theatrical Intervention and Public Intellectual Discourse." *Australasian Drama Studies* 42 (April 2003): 161–176.

Peter Fitzpatrick

RAZNOVICH, DIANA (1945–)

Diana Raznovich was born in Buenos Aires, ARGENTINA, in 1945. Unlike many of her contemporaries, Raznovich's artistic trajectory is characterized by a strong sense of humor—she occasionally wrote comic strips, as well—and by a particular attention to issues of social norms.

She began her career in Enrique Escope's theater seminar, working from improvisatory pieces she developed herself. In her early plays *Jumping Jack* (*El buscapiés*, 1968) and *There's Only One Plaza* (*Plaza hay una sola*, 1968), she began developing some of her favorite dramatic techniques: an inversion of spatial-temporal coordinates, the use of fragmentation and discontinuity, and her unique brand of humor, equally predisposed to bursts of laughter, reflection, pity, and even bitterness.

Forced, like so many of her contemporaries, to flee her native country during the violent political unrest of the 1970s, Raznovich sought refuge in SPAIN. Her play *Marcello the Repairman*

(*Marcello el mecánico*) premiered in 1978 and was restaged in 1983 as *Garden in Autumn* (*Jardín de otoño*). It is the story of two middle-aged spinsters who, fascinated by the protagonist of a soap opera, kidnap the actor, only to discover that the television character is nothing like the pitiful actor who portrays him. Generally assumed to be a simple criticism of mass culture, the play's focus centers on the sexual attraction between the two friends and the need—amidst the prejudices of an authoritarian and chauvinistic society—to suppress their feelings by projecting them onto the television screen.

The first season of OPEN THEATER (Teatro Abierto) saw the premiere of her work *Confusion* (*Desconcierto*, 1981). It is a brief monologue given by pianist Irene della Porta, who plays a soundless piano and establishes a sort of pact with her audience avid to "hear" a silent concert. *Confusion* (the title, *Desconcierto*, plays on the Spanish word for *concert*, "concierto") criticizes art that renounces any moral obligations to become a fetishized commodity and is a denunciation of the degradation that women with artistic aspirations suffer in a misogynistic society. The play also expresses indignation toward intellectuals and audience members who are complicit with the censorship, lies, and terror under the military dictatorship of those years.

In later works, Raznovich deepens her criticism to denounce prescribed social norms. Such is the case in *The Matriz Household* (*Casa Matriz*, 1988), a virulent but humorous invective against the construction of motherhood as the most sacred role to which a woman should aspire. In *Backwards and Forwards* (*De atrás para adelante*, 1996), Raznovich recounts the misfortunes of a well-to-do family that falls on hard times and has to depend on its transsexual son to recover the estate.

Throughout her work, Raznovich strives to deconstruct socially accepted behavior and identities, both sexual and normative. She accomplishes this task through the liberating and unprejudiced force of laughter. In this way, her work aspires to create a society where all individuals can find their place without submitting to normative conventions.

SELECT PLAYS: *Jumping Jack* (*El buscapiés*, 1968); *There's Only One Plaza* (*Plaza hay una sola*, 1968); *El guardagente* (1970); *Texasina Wheelbarrow* (*Texas en carretilla*, 1971); *The Mishap* (*El contratiempo*, 1973); *Confusion* (*Desconcierto*,1981); *Garden in Autumn* (*Jardín de otoño*, 1983); *Autographs* (*Autógrafos*, 1984); *The Matriz Household* (*Casa Matriz*, 1988); *Personal Effects* (*Efectos personales*, 1988); *Of the Waist Down* (*De la cintura para abajo*, 1993); *Backwards and Forwards* (*De atrás para adelante*, 1996); *Divine Machines* (*Máquinas divinas*, 1996); *Fast-food at Death's Speed* (*Fast Food a la velocidad de la muerte*, 1996)

FURTHER READING

Glickman, Nora. "Parodia y desmitificación del rol femenino en el teatro femenino de Diana Raznovich." *Latin American Theatre Review* 28, no. 1 (Fall 1994): 89–100.

Taylor, Diana. "Combatiendo el fuego con frivolidad: los actos desafiantes de Diana Raznovich." In *Defiant Acts: Four Plays by Diana Raznovich.* Ed. by Diana Taylor and Victoria Martinez. Lewisburg, P.A.: Bucknell Univ. Press, 2002.

——. *Disappearing Acts: Spectacles of Gender and Nationalism in Argentina's "Dirty War."* Durham, N.C.: Duke Univ. Press, 1997.

——. "The Theater of Diana Raznovich and Percepticide in *El Desconcierto*." In *Latin American Women Dramatists: Theater, Texts, and Theories,* ed. by Catherine Larson and Margarita Vargas. Bloomington, I.N.: Indiana Univ. Press, 1998.

——, and Roselyn Constantino, eds. *Holy Terrors: Latin American Women Perform.* Durham, N.C.: Duke Univ. Press, 2004.

Norberto Cambiasso (Tr. by Gabriel Milner)

READING HEBRON

JASON SHERMAN's most controversial, and perhaps best, play *Reading Hebron* premiered at Theatre Factory in Toronto, CANADA, in 1996. A documentary-based examination of Arab-Israeli relations, *Reading Hebron* brings back Sherman's theatrical stand-in, Nathan Abramowitz (the protagonist of THE LEAGUE OF NATHANS). Nathan is attempting to investigate the Israeli inquest into the murder of thirty Arabs in a mosque by Baruch Goldstein. The play's action alternates between dramatized bits of transcript from the inquest (reminiscent of PETER WEISS's THE INVESTIGATION) and Nathan's encounters along the way with librarians, the Palestinian Information Office, conspiracy theorists, and real-life personalities: in one scene, Nathan invites Noam Chomsky, Hanan Aswari, and Edward Said, along with the 1970s television character Rhoda Morgenstern, to a Passover seder.

The climax of the play is a poem Goldstein wrote as a child, wishing for peaceful reconciliation. Like all of Sherman's best writing, the tone of *Reading Hebron* can switch from mordant to hilariously funny to tragic, in an instant. Actors morph between characters and levels of reality from line to line. Sherman ultimately seems to skewer all sides for using the conflict to advance personal and political agendas. Michael Healey, who played Nathan in the premiere, described Sherman as "an equal-rights abuser. He attacks soft-thinking liberals, but also soft-thinking rightists. He has no time for the glib, self-satisfied or self-righteous, regardless of political stripe. Jason goes after them, and so does Nathan—and Nathan turns the gun on himself as much as anyone else. The play is about developing a point of view that actually means something to you, that costs you something." The result is one of the most complex, incisive, and theatrically vital examinations of the Israeli-Palestinian conflict.

The play's development reflected Sherman's writing process. Sherman originally set out to write a play about the inquest but became frustrated by the difficulties he encountered in getting access to research materials. Trying to get a handle on the material, he revived back the character of Nathan Abramowitz. He then took the materials he had gathered into a workshop with actors, a director, and a DRAMATURG, discussing the material at the table and creating scenes and characters from those discussions and improvisations. This process is quite similar to the way ENGLAND's JOINT STOCK THEATRE GROUP developed plays, most notably CARYL CHURCHILL's CLOUD NINE, and is a process Sherman uses frequently in his writing.

In Canada, the play has had critically successful productions in both English and French. The Theatre Factory production moved to OFF-BROADWAY, where it received strong national press.

[See also Documentary Drama]

FURTHER READING

Friedlander, Mira. "Reading Hebron." Variety (January 6, 1997).

Lawless, Jill. "Anxiety Meets Absurdity in Hebron Drama."
   http://www.jewishbulletin.ca/archives/Feb04/archives04Feb27–06.html.

Sherman, Jason. Jason Sherman: The Plays. Toronto, Canada:
   Playwrights Canada Press, 2001.

Walter Bilderback

REALISM

In the philosophical sense, realism is the opposite of idealism. Realism meant a denial of the metaphysical world as having any absolute being in and by itself. The realistic drama arose in the first half of the 19th century as a continuation of the romantic opposition to classic art. The latter meant imitating ancient models, which in drama meant Greek TRAGEDY and Latin COMEDY.

The new approach was to turn to life itself for inspiration, not to ancient models or to vague abstractions (ideals). The rise of realism was concurrent with developments in politics, science, and PHILOSOPHY. The term as used in art seems to have been coined by the critic Champfleury in writing about Gustave Courbet's painting The Burial at Ornans in 1850. Courbet called his first one-man exhibit "Le Réalisme" in 1855, and he clearly understood the far-reaching effects of the new movement. "Realism is the negation of the ideal and of everything that follows from it. It is only in that way that one can arrive at the emancipation of reason, the emancipation of the individual, and at last, at democracy."

The romantic view was that somehow the good, the true, and the beautiful were all one and the same. Realism questioned this esthetic trinity and saw the true and the beautiful as often separate. The question was, Does one go to the theater to face the facts of life or to escape them? Why go to the theater to see a workingman's hovel onstage, or an alcoholic in a drunken stupor, when one might be amused by clever remarks in a comedy? The answer was obvious to anyone who was disturbed by prevailing conditions in society. Courbet, who devoted a huge canvas to a painting of a stone mason, opted for the truth: "I am not only a socialist, but also a democrat and a republican, in a word,

a partisan of revolution and above all a realist, that is, a sincere friend of the real truth" (letter in 1851). When invited to a Courbet one-man show in 1867, the French statesman and conservative politician Adolphe Thiers responded, "He's too fond of truth; it isn't good to love truth that much."

The best defense of realism against the romantic insistence that a work of art must first of all be beautiful was expressed by Hamlin Garland, American realist novelist, in the 1890s: "The realist . . . sees life in terms of what it might be, as well as in terms of what it is; but he writes of what is, and, at his best, suggests what is to be, by contrast. . . . He aims to hasten the age of beauty and peace by delineating the ugliness and warfare of the present; but ever the converse of his picture rises in the mind of the reader" (Garland, 1960).

The theater was slower than the other arts to embrace realism, in part because the theater was thought of as primarily a place of escape and fantasy, not as a place of truth, and in part because it was difficult to put realistic sets onstage. Improvements in set design and in stage lighting, especially the introduction of gas lighting, promoted the realistic drama.

It prevailed because of the rise of the middle class. The bourgeoisie wanted to see themselves onstage, and their concerns had more to do with money matters and marriage arrangements than affairs of honor and duels. As the middle class became better educated, they wanted something more challenging than the simplicities of MELODRAMA or the bombast of romantic, poetic drama. They wanted to hear their kind of speech, see their kind of social manners, and watch a story occurring in drawing rooms and salons instead of palaces and wild nature.

Playwrights like DUMAS FILS and Emile Augier in FRANCE promoted the realistic drama by dealing with social problems, such as that of the demimonde, while in ENGLAND the actor-playwright-director T. W. ROBERTSON wrote true-to-life dialogue and made the minutiae of daily life, such as the serving of tea, theatrically interesting. In Scandinavia, BJØRNSTJERNE BJØRNSON scored a success with his realist plays and paved the way for his rival dramatist, HENRIK IBSEN. With the worldwide and lasting triumph of the latter's A DOLL'S HOUSE (1879), in which psychological depth was added to the shallow characters of the French plays, the realistic drama came to dominate the stages of the Western world.

[See also Naturalism; Problem Play; Socialist Realism]

FURTHER READING

Garland, Hamlin. Crumbling Idols. Cambridge: Harvard Univ. Press, 1960.

Stromberg, Roland N., ed. Realism, Naturalism, and Symbolism. London: Macmillan, 1968.

Weber, Eugen, ed. Paths to the Present: Aspects of European Thought from Romanticism to Existentialism. New York: Dodd, 1960.

Evert Sprinchorn

THE REAL THING

Love is loving them at their worst.

—Henry, Act 2

First produced in 1982 in London, published the same year and again in 1983 with revisions, TOM STOPPARD's COMEDY *The Real Thing* plumbs the nature of authentic love, finding that, unlike authentic art, the "real thing" in matters of the heart may hinge on a lover's acceptance of impurity and dishonesty. Known for his displays of epigrammatic wit, paradox, and formal daring, Stoppard established with *The Real Thing* his talent for writing about passion and the tribulations of marital love.

In its first scene, *The Real Thing* stages a play within a play: Max, a character in *The House of Cards*, confronts his wife Charlotte with evidence of her adultery. Max behaves with cool, nearly cynical, detachment, and he and his unrepentant wife break up. This scenario in which a husband discovers his wife's adultery will return twice more in *The Real Thing*, with each occurrence contrasting the torturous consequences of infidelity in real life with its fictionalized portrayal in the glossy, unconvincing *The House of Cards*. The play within a play allows Stoppard to probe the distinction between "real" and "inauthentic" emotion.

The Real Thing focuses on Henry, who is the author of *The House of Cards* and the husband of Charlotte (the actress from the play). Henry has an affair with Annie, the wife of Max (the actor from *The House of Cards*). Finding Henry's handkerchief in Annie's car, Max demands an explanation from his wife. When Annie admits to adultery, Max—quite unlike his poised character in *The House of Cards*—submits to rage and grief. Divorcing their spouses, Annie and Henry wed. Annie has an affair with Billy, a young actor and her co-star in a Glasgow production of John Ford's *'Tis a Pity She's a Whore*. Convinced of Annie's infidelity, Henry challenges her on it. Unlike in the earlier scenes of adultery confronted, the result is not the dissolution of a marriage. Rather, Annie continues her affair. Henry resigns himself to a condition of "dignified cuckoldry." Though the breach of faith shakes him to the core, the authentic love he feels for Annie requires him to tolerate her philandering.

The play's subplot involves Annie's championing of Brodie, a soldier who is imprisoned for six years after he commits arson during an anti-nuclear-missile demonstration. Annie hopes to reawaken public interest in the case and to win Brodie a reduced sentence by producing a play that he has written behind bars. She convinces Henry to rewrite the propagandistic and incompetent play. The subplot investigates the connection between authenticity and craftsmanship in literature, with Henry, in a much-praised speech, comparing a well-wrought play to a cricket bat and Brodie's work to a "lump of wood . . . trying to be a cricket bat."

In 1984, *The Real Thing* won five Tony Awards, including Best Play, and in 2000 garnered the Tony for best revival.

[*See also* England, 1980–Present]

FURTHER READING

Jenkins, Anthony, ed. *Critical Essays on Tom Stoppard*. Boston: G. K. Hall, 1990.

Nadel, Ira Bruce. *Tom Stoppard: A Life*. New York: Palgrave Macmillan, 2002.

Nikolai Slywka

REANEY, JAMES (1926–)

James Reaney was born in Stratford, Ontario, CANADA, in 1926. He graduated from Stratford Collegiate Institute (where he acted in plays) in 1944 and completed his undergraduate work at the University of Toronto, where he wrote poems and short stories and studied under the famed critic Northrop Frye, whose theories of SYMBOLISM and language were to be a great influence. Reaney received a doctorate from Toronto in 1958, completing a thesis (directed by Frye) that explores the influence of Edmund Spenser on W. B. YEATS. (He later wrote about the university's history in his play *The Dismissal* [1978].) Reaney attained literary fame early, winning the Governor General's Award for poetry with *The Red Heart* in 1949. He married the poet Colleen Thibodeau in 1951. Reaney turned to theater in the 1950s.

The most successful of Reaney's early plays was *The Killdeer* (1962), set, like most of Reaney's work, in a small Ontario town. Harry must circumvent several obstacles, including his own self-doubt, to demonstrate his love for Rebecca, who is the titular "killdeer"—a bird that both augurs a storm and deliberately attracts a predator so as to distract that predator from her young. Rebecca is accused of murdering Clifford, the dark manipulator of the developmentally retarded Eli Fay, the man who Rebecca unwillingly marries. Harry, in a detective subplot, must exonerate Rebecca of Clifford's murder and bring about their fulfilled love. The play, with a complicated and symbolically laden plot, has had an inconsistent stage history, but its strengths—a strongly felt rural setting and an imaginative, original plot—established Reaney as a preeminent Canadian dramatist.

In midcareer, Reaney wrote the ambitious trilogy *The Donnellys*. Extending across several generations of an Irish-Canadian family living near London, Ontario, from 1834 to 1974, *The Donnellys* is a saga of family secrets and unexpected violence. The trilogy, published as a complete unit in 1983, is composed of *Sticks and Stones* (1975), *The St. Nicholas Hotel, Wm. Donnelly, Prop.* (1976), and *Handcuffs* (1977). The Donnellys are brought down by fate, injustice, and antagonisms they have themselves provoked. Told through a combination of foreshadowing and flashbacks, the trilogy uses elemental interactions to provide a sense of primordial fear and stunted yearning.

Given his extensive literary background, Reaney's drama is strikingly lacking in verbosity or linguistic flamboyance; rather, his plays depend on a sense of ritual and litanylike repetition. In addition to the plays for which he is widely recognized, Reaney has written plays for children as well as opera libretti. *The Story of the Gentle Rain Food Co-op* (1997) is a COMEDY gently satirizing environmental and ecological movements. Although differing in tone from Reaney's other works, it resembles them in the ways in which language, generated by interpersonal situations, is the ground of dramatic meaning.

Reaney has taught English at the University of Western Ontario and the University of Manitoba. In 1966 he established a workshop for theatrical experiments in London, Ontario, and from 1969 to 1979 he edited and printed *Alphabet: The Iconography of the Imagination*. In addition to experimental COLLAGES for radio, he has coauthored (with Jon Beckwith) three operas, *Night Blooming Cereus* (1960), *The Shivaree* (1982) and *Crazy to Kill* (1988).

SELECT PLAYS: *The Killdeer* (1960); *Night Blooming Cereus* (opera, with Jon Beckwith, 1960); *One-Man Masque* (1960); *Colours In the Dark* (1969); *Listen To The Wind* (1972); *Apple Butter* (1973); *Sticks and Stones* (1975); *Baldoon* (with C. H. Gervais, 1976); *The St. Nicholas Hotel, Wm. Donnelly, Prop.* (1976); *Handcuffs* (1977); *The Dismissal* (1978); *Th Shivaree* (opera, with Jon Beckwith, 1978); *Crazy To Kill* (opera, with Jon Beckwith, 1989); *The Story of the Gentle Rain Food Co-op* (1997)

FURTHER READING

Dragland, Stan. "James Reaney's 'Pulsating Dance in and Out of Forms.'" In *The Human Elements: Critical Essays*, ed. by David Helwig. Ottawa: Oberon Press, 1978.

Grandy, Karen. "Playing with Time: James Reaney's *The Donnellys* as Spatial Form Drama." *Modern Drama* 38, no. 4 (Winter 1995): 462–474.

Nicholas Birns

LA REGINA E GLI INSORTI See THE QUEEN AND THE REBELS

REIGEN

I'm also working now at times—ten dialogues, a colorful series; but never has there been something this unperformable.
—Arthur Schnitzler, 1897

Reigen (*La Ronde*), a cycle of ten erotic dialogues written in 1896–1897, permanently propelled ARTHUR SCHNITZLER onto the "scandalous," but also prominent, stage of fin de siècle European theater. Schnitzler was doubtful about how *Reigen* would be received, so he published it in a private edition in 1900 for friends only. In 1903 three of the dialogues (fourth, fifth, and sixth) were performed in Munich, but the whole cycle did not premiere until 1920 in Berlin. The ensuing trial against the play in 1921 justified Schnitzler's initial skepticism; and hoping to avoid further scandal, accusations of pornography, and anti-Semitic harassment, the playwright withdrew permission to have the drama performed in 1922, a ban that kept *Reigen* off German-speaking stages until 1982.

This best known of Schnitzler's plays functions as a social COMEDY and presents a paradigm for the gender relationships seen throughout his works. The ten scenes depict a round dance of sexuality that encompasses Vienna's social spectrum and is reminiscent of the medieval dance of death. The cycle begins with the prostitute and a soldier, continues with the soldier and a parlor maid, the parlor maid and a young gentleman, the young gentleman and a young wife, the young wife and her husband, the husband and a "süßes Mädel" (sweet young thing), the "süßes Mädel" and a poet, the poet and an actress, the actress and a count; and the last scene completes the round dance with the count and the prostitute. In every scene except the last, the dialogue between the couple frames their sexual intercourse, which is indicated in the text by a series of dashes. Reflecting the transitory nature of love and life and the universality of sexuality, each couple in *Reigen* pursues a fleeting union. No one takes the relationship seriously, as is evident by the changing couple constellations of each scene. Each character is involved in the tantalizing pursuit of the moment, and the dialogues reveal the diverse intentions, desires, and mores of each partner. The verbal exchanges constitute the action of the play, while they unmask social practice and formalities, just as the young wife unveils her face or the partners disrobe as they violate social convention. Schnitzler thus exposes the hypocrisy, deception, lies, lust, and superficiality permeating all social classes.

Seemingly, social boundaries are crossed in the pursuit of this elusive intimacy. Yet there is a noticeable difference in each character's behavior between the "before" and "after" intercourse dialogue, which undeniably reflects the social status of those involved. Each character—identified only by "type" and no name—plays a role befitting his or her social station: from crude seduction to naive yielding to pedantic fulfillment of duty to intellectualizing "love" to feigned sensuality to jadedness; from unconscious instinct, through desire for adventure, to game and seduction—to insensibility. The social order that determines the progression of the play necessarily establishes as well as reflects its intellectual and psychological structure. The scandal caused by *Reigen* undeniably reveals just how acutely Schnitzler touched the core (or raw nerve) of his society—and certainly confirms his reservations about making the play accessible to the general public.

FURTHER READING

Otis, Laura. "The Language of Infection: Disease and Identity in Schnitzler's *Reigen*." *The Germanic Review* 70, no. 2 (1995): 65–75.

Pfoser, Alfred, Kristina Pfoser-Schweig, and Gerhard Renner, eds. *Schnitzlers Reigen. Zehn Dialoge und ihre Skandalgeschichte* [Schnitzler's *Reigen*: Ten dialogues and their scandalous history]. Vol. 1, *Der Skandal. Analysen und Dokumente* [The scandal: Analyses and documents]. Vol. 2, *Die Prozesse: Analyse und Dokumente* [The trials: Analysis and documents]. Frankfurt: Fischer, 1993.

Schneider, Gerd K. "The Reception of Arthur Schnitzler's *Reigen* in the Old Country and the New World: A Study in Cultural Differences." *Modern Austrian Literature* 19, nos. 3–4 (1986): 75–89.

Elizabeth Ametsbichler

REINHARDT, MAX (1873–1943)

One of the most prolific, versatile, and influential directors of the 20th century, Max Reinhardt was among the first to realize RICHARD WAGNER's (1813–1883) vision of *Gesamtkunstwerk* ("total artwork") through his integration of drama, music, and spectacle in immense productions employing modern scenic and lighting technology. One ready measure of Reinhardt's impact lies in the number of his productions—over 500—and the more than thirty theaters and theater companies he oversaw.

Born Max Goldmann on September 9, 1873, in Baden, AUSTRIA, Reinhardt began his career as an actor, joining the Deutsches Theater in Berlin under the direction of OTTO BRAHM in 1894. After eight years of Brahm's NATURALISM, the playful and poetic Reinhardt was eager to break away. He founded a cabaret, "Schall und Rauch" (Sound and Smoke), in 1901 and by 1903 was simultaneously directing the Kleines Theater and the Neues Theater, thus instituting the now universal practice of dividing a company's season between large and small spaces.

His first major directorial success came in the Neues Theater in 1905 with *A Midsummer Night's Dream*, a production that discarded the "heavily pictorial" approach of the 19th century. Reinhardt went on to direct twenty-two plays by William Shakespeare in productions marked by free-flowing action and a symbolist approach to scenery, creating "the characteristic style of Shakespearian performance for the twentieth century" (Styan, 1982). In 1906 Reinhardt bought the Deutsches Theater as well as the Kammerspiele, a chamber theater next door. There he directed a season of modern plays, notably HENRIK IBSEN's *GHOSTS* with sets by the expressionist painter Edvard Munch (1863–1944). In 1910, Reinhardt staged two events that would establish his reputation for theatrical spectacle: *Sumurun*, a pantomime based on *Tales from the Arabian Nights*, and a massive production in the Circus Busch of *Oedipus Rex*. The latter was an early version of Reinhardt's idea of the "Theater of the Five Thousand," performances of civic and religious drama for large audiences that would recapture the spirit of the Greeks and the Middle Ages. Reinhardt further developed this idea in 1911 with circus productions of *The Oresteia* and *Everyman* and later with the creation of the Großes Schauspielhaus in Berlin. Also in 1911 he directed *The Miracle* by Karl Vollmoeller (1878–1948), a pseudomedieval religious spectacle with a company of 1,800 artists and technicians that premiered in London and was produced throughout the world for the next twenty years.

In 1920, Reinhardt moved from Berlin to Austria where, with Richard Strauss (1864–1949), Bruno Walter (1876–1962), and HUGO VON HOFMANNSTHAL, he inaugurated the Salzburg Festival. Reinhardt staged Hofmannstal's *Everyman* on the steps of the Salzburg cathedral and Johann Wolfgang Goethe's *Faust* in the riding academy of the old imperial army. Meanwhile, he continued to mount intimate productions of smaller plays by classical and contemporary dramatists.

Born a Jew, Reinhardt was forced out of German-speaking Europe by the Nazis. He settled in the UNITED STATES, dividing his time between Hollywood and New York. Reinhardt also staged a number of plays in New York where, shortly after his seventieth birthday, on October 31, 1943, he died in New York City.

[*See also* Germany]

FURTHER READING

Braun, Edward. *The Director and the Stage: From Naturalism to Grotowski*. New York: Holmes & Meier, 1982.

Leiter, Samuel L. *From Stanislavsky to Barrault: Representative Directors of the European Stage*. New York: Greenwood Press, 1991.

Sayler, Oliver M., ed. *Max Reinhardt and His Theatre*. Tr. by Mariele S. Gudernatsch et al. New York: Brentano's, 1926.

Styan, J. L. *Max Reinhardt*. Cambridge: Cambridge Univ. Press, 1982.

Martin Andrucki

RELIGION AND DRAMA

Drama has intimate historic links with religious rites and sanctified celebratory events for cultures East and West, so "religious drama" could be considered redundant. However, considering the period since 1870, the phrase has acquired a distinct, if malleable, meaning deriving both from subject matter and from intended effect.

Two voices are outstanding in the emergence and continuing vitality of this theater tradition. Søren Kierkegaard, monumental theologian for modern consciousness, in *Purity of Heart* (1948) refers to the prompter, the actor, and the audience as theater roles with significance for both drama and worship. He insists the preacher or play/playwright—not God—is the prompter; the actor is each member of the congregation. Observing each role player on eternity's stage in the role of audience is God. Thus the effect of the work on each onlooker is essential to the designation of a drama as religious and worship as relevant.

That assumption is underscored by GEORGE BERNARD SHAW as pioneer genius of religious drama. "My conscience is the genuine pulpit article; it annoys me to see people comfortable when they ought to be uncomfortable; and I insist on making them think in order to bring them to a conviction of sin. If you don't like my preaching you must lump it. I really cannot help it."

THE INFLUENCE OF SOCIAL GOSPEL

The resurgence of religious drama that began in the late 19th century in America and ENGLAND emerged primarily as part of what came to be known as the "social gospel" in Western

Christian history rather than emphasis on classic dramatic heritage linking theater with appeasement of the gods.

Up to the middecades of the 20th century, the revival of interest in liturgy and medieval mystery plays, the emergence of the ecumenical movement after decades of denominational tensions in international missions, and the early reluctance of organized religion to tackle difficult intellectual problems over the Bible or religion "versus" science together created a turbulent new climate for believers of all persuasions.

With respect to theater, the atmosphere was hospitable for plays whose "message" was vindication of the lonely, pious, or dedicated conscience in conflict with authority, allegiance, or duty to established cultural norms. One respected theater producer-scholar observed: "For the man who finds no solace in the church, its metaphors become meaningless, and he must search elsewhere for satisfaction. Then the theatre moves back into providing alternative ritualistic experience."

In other words, religious drama incarnates a dramatic, even sacred "demilitarized zone" between two authorities or opposing powers. One is the institutional source of traditional rituals such as the established or majority religion or state law and custom. The other varies. Cultural crises such as economic injustice, racism, and changing sexual mores are examples. Subjective psychosocial tensions such as anxiety or the quest "to find who I am" vie with objective political issues such as unjust war, restricted civil liberties, and exploited and disenfranchised minorities.

While the form could still be described as propaganda, broadly defined, it is definitely not restricted to iconic revival and reenactment of saintly lives or historic holy myths. Indeed, it is questionable whether the subjection of sacred text and histories to the implicitly positivist process of iteralistic modern staging and performing is not subversive to understanding and experiencing faith as an authentic alternative within scientific consciousness.

To be sure, staging the quest for divine inspiration and celebration of eternal truths present significant theatrical challenges, with audience reactions more often cerebral than heartfelt. Nevertheless, religious drama shares valiant, occasionally moving witness to the value and virtue of human rites as well as humane rights. Even though worldly powers almost invariably win the day, conscience has its say, and audiences may nurture an embattled faith in values that transcend authoritarian materialism.

One seminal stimulus for the rising tide of religious drama is arguably a still astonishingly popular novelistic parable by a South Dakota farmer-preacher's son with a flair for journalism. After New England college and seminary training, Charles M. Sheldon, embarking on a lifetime pastorate at Central Congregational Church, Topeka, Kansas, preached and then published in 1896 a series of sermons that ranks with *Uncle Tom's Cabin* as catalyst of public enthusiasm for what became known as "social Christianity."

Sheldon's *In His Steps: What Would Jesus Do?* has doubtless surpassed its mid-20th-century record of thirty million copies in every language. Though adapted for film and repeatedly for the stage, Sheldon originally penned lively dialogue and action to punctuate the imaginative, naive tract featuring varied heroes, villains, romances, and martyrdoms in serial format. The work, widely reprinted in the UNITED STATES and abroad after a copyright flaw released it into the public domain, triggered a deluge of melodramatic social mission fiction challenging Gilded Age verities, such as *If Christ Came to Chicago*, by British journalistic crusader William T. Stead, and *The Inside of the Cup*, by respected British novelist Winston Churchill.

The sentimental, soul-stirring morality tale is relevant not only because it remains a bestseller amid myriad popular propaganda focused on social unrest. More important, it clearly highlights the definitive characteristics of religious drama.

TYPES OF RELIGIOUS DRAMA

The dominant thrust is evangelistic prophetic fervor to challenge, if not reform, superpersonal powers and institutions. The prevailing motif is pietistic emphasis on individual conversion and consecration in the face of near-hopeless odds. The justifying message is communication of the experience of redemption that transcends injustice and counters evil. Overall the motivating energy for the production is to deliberately blur the distinction between audience and congregation, to convert onlookers into an informal group of pilgrims sharing hopeful belief, skeptical faith, pessimistic irony—if only for a profoundly artistic and apocryphal theatrical moment.

Among the more than forty works by Shaw, at least five set standards that could exemplify *prophetic, pietistic,* or *apocryphal* religious dramas. Furthermore, in comic spirit and clever insight, which brighten all his plays, he represents what CHRISTOPHER FRY (in THE LADY'S NOT FOR BURNING) illuminates as a factor that might draw any COMEDY into the domain of religious drama.

> For God's sake, shall we laugh? . . . For the reason of laughter, since laughter is surely the surest touch of genius in creation. . . . If you had been making man, stuffing him full of such hopping greed and passions that he has to blow himself to pieces as often as he conveniently can manage it, would it also have occurred to you to make him burst himself with such a phenomenon? That same laughter is an irrelevancy which almost amounts to revelation.

ARMS AND THE MAN and MAJOR BARBARA illustrate prophetic religious drama with endearing characters who confront war and culturally pervasive war-support resources. SAINT JOAN and *Androcles and the Lion,* notwithstanding their insightful and authoritative introductions, exemplify the imaginative, if not inspirational, models to which pietistic religious drama legitimately aspires.

As for apocryphal religious drama, Shaw the irrepressible iconoclast himself proclaimed his Utopian Ring–like cycle of five plays in one, BACK TO METHUSELAH, a "world classic." Shaw noted: "There is no real hope in impossible Utopias. I had to resort to a power which, as it exists and is in daily operation, can easily be conceived as capable of evolutionary intensification. This power is called Awe." His Utopians court catastrophe by stifling hope with the despair through which awe operates, all but wrecking civilization in the hurry to mend it.

Shaw never failed to suggest some new alternative panacea for the icons his plays wittily demolished. In this case, he summarized his redemptive vision: "The history of modern thought now teaches us that when we are forced to give up the creeds by their childishness and their conflicts with science, we must either embrace Creative Evolution or fall into the bottomless pit of an utterly discouraging pessimism."

But it is less that quaint evolutionary faith that justifies calling the work apocryphal than the sweeping scope of the play, Shaw's convicted refusal "to abandon all hope in a world of angry apes and perish in despair," and significant production footnotes. Professional manager Sir Barry Jackson felt enough audience rapport and support at his Birmingham Repertory Theatre presentation to exult in a modestly profitable subsequent London run and ultimately to initiate festival formats by founding one in 1929 at Malvern, largely to produce Shaw.

From the viewpoint of his lofty plays (and prefaces) opens a horizon with an abundance of prophetic, pietistic, and more recently, apocryphal works—a realm of religious drama bursting the narrow bounds of didactic, moralistic, pageantary propaganda illustrating holy books and sacred visionaries.

Two volumes of anthologies, introduced by Marvin Halverson, former head of the now-defunct Department of Worship and the Arts of the National Council of Churches of Christ in the U.S.A., include several examples of the prophetic (volume 1) and of the pietistic (volume 3). The publication of the series included in volume 2 more than twenty samples of medieval mystery cycles and constituted (along with an academic program of lectures and productions at New York City's Union Theological Seminary) a high point of the religious drama landscape in the mid-20th century.

Prominent landmarks among prophetic works are HENRY ARTHUR JONES's *Saints and Sinners*; BERTOLT BRECHT's THE LIFE OF GALILEO and *Lamp Unto My Feet* by Barrie Stavis about the same subject; HENRIK IBSEN's ENEMY OF THE PEOPLE; T. S. ELIOT's *The Rock* and MURDER IN THE CATHEDRAL; ARTHUR MILLER's ALL MY SONS and THE CRUCIBLE; *Inherit the Wind* by JEROME LAWRENCE AND ROBERT E. LEE; and JAMES BALDWIN's *Blues for Mister Charlie*. What John Mason Brown called the "indignant" tone of Hallie Flanagan's innovative "living newspaper" theater appropriately characterizes all these works and merits reference in this context to those experimental plays exploring social, economic, and political dislocation. As social ethics challenged a theology of individualized personal piety, so these socially conscious works stirred controversy and helped extend the boundaries of issues and plays that could be called religious.

A genre of dramatic presentations focused on alcoholism, drug addiction, family abuse, or other dislocating social problems and presented to target audiences under those threats or at religious institutions by the nonprofit body "Plays for Living" stems from this source. They as well as far more popular, less widely known presentations are related as much to morality plays as to television sitcoms.

Radicalized art in the streets, part of strident Black Power social reform energy in the 1960s, helped galvanize what in the 1920s had become known as the Chitlin Circuit of entertainers for a segregated target audience: southern and midwestern U.S. blacks. The vigorous successor to that varied roster of actors, comics, and musicians now features broadly played MELODRAMAS laced with gospel songs and comic caricature that highlight for urban black audiences everyday ghetto problems— gang violence, drug culture, disintegrating families, offspring unwanted and deserted.

Almost exclusively publicized through church bulletins or radio talk and financed in cash by often shady sources, these productions flourish largely outside the domain of culturally mixed audiences, dramatizing on- and offstage preacher/pusher conflict in the still strongly churchgoing black communities that make these productions outstandingly profitable. Righteous fury to move souls fuels playwrights and performers; hearty audience call and response in voice and gesture recalls the enthusiasm of congregations as a holy communion deeply moved. The exuberance of a playgoing experience so poignant, prophetic, and hilarious, as well as so insistent on the indomitable power of prayerful will in one dedicated soul, justifies reference to Adrian Williamson's *My Grandmother Prayed for Me*, a notably popular example of this circuit.

In not just glorifying the masses but actually appealing to them—as Henry Louis Gates Jr. eloquently noted about circuit shows—such productions vividly demonstrate how theater can buoy and rededicate racially and ethnically varied minority target audiences. Aesthetic reservations notwithstanding, such works sanctify their tribulations and hallow their dogged commitment to keep the faith and keep on keepin' on. Aesthetic reservations notwithstanding, finally this visceral sanctity is what sometimes compromises but absolutely marks all forms of religious drama.

Unquestionably the hardiest and most prolific is the pietistic form with its emphasis on individual conscience, conversion, and conviction in the context of historic conflicts with and martyrs to the status quo as well as shadowed soul treks defiantly hopeful, if often bleak or doomed. Resonant with medieval miracle, mystery, and morality play traditions, the effect of these works is to strengthen individual commitment by reaffirming faith and events that witness to divine presence in human history. The more artistically satisfying and durable create characters out of which all-too-familiar scenarios and myths spring afresh.

The Passing of the Third Floor Back by Jerome Jerome, John Edward Masefield's *Coming of Christ*, Charles Rann Kennedy's *The Terrible Meek*, and Dorothy L. Sayers's radio play for the BBC *The Man Born to Be King* all focus on the historical Jesus, his associated friends or enemies, and their latter-day reflections in terms calculated to engage audiences and foster personal faith in the war-torn decades before the mid-20th century. *Saint Mark's Gospel*, a one-actor performance, originally conceived by Alec McCowen in the mid-1970s, was a stunning reminder that in the hands of an accomplished performer unadorned religious texts and saintly characters can enthrall an audience, recalling the simplest hearthside theater compact of lively narrator and rapt listeners.

The legendary, unprecedented MAX REINHARDT production of *The Miracle* demonstrated early in the 20th century on international tour scale the validity of that assumption. It surely underlies the attraction for generations of tourists for the hoary pageantary enactment of Jesus' life at Oberammergau (notwithstanding objections to anti-Semitism) and accounts for the popularity of the Bible as a resource for contemporary professional storytellers.

Certain works in the musical theater tradition that are updated translations of religious texts and traditions such as *Joseph and His Technicolor Dreamcoat*, *Godspell*, *Jesus Christ Superstar*, and *Your Arms Too Short to Box with God* are also examples of spectacles more theatrically sophisticated than pageants but still reflecting the liturgical assumption of music and parable messages delivered to a largely passive body of individual observers whose response remains personal and private.

AUGUST STRINDBERG's *To Damascus*, J. M. BARRIE's *The Boy David*, T. S. ELIOT's *THE FAMILY REUNION*, MARC CONNOLLY's *THE GREEN PASTURES*, EUGENE O'NEILL's *LAZARUS LAUGHED*, Fry's *A Sleep of Prisoners* and *The Lady's Not for Burning*, ARCHIBALD MACLEISH's *J. B.*, and ROBERT BOLT's *A Man for All Seasons* are among soul-searching works that fire the conscience and refresh the visionary. TERRENCE MCNALLY's *Love! Valour! Compassion!* and *A Perfect Ganesh* and DAVID HARE's *Racing Demon* are funny, acid, post-Christian summons for loners to brave the culture war zones girded in street smarts, fired with spirit to share, chastened by sorrow and loss. These works evoke the potency of personal conversion and the embrace of uncertain destiny as a dynamic scenario to stir the soul, whether in settings of theater, religious revival arenas, or political conventions.

SOUL SEARCHING IN THE 21ST CENTURY

It is a fascination as unlikely as awe to lose its power and charm. Even amid 21st-century globalism marked by interfaith dialogue as well as transnational scientific agnosticism, appealing dramatic conflict still lies in the instinct to imitate a lonely quest for a less selfish soul, whether through self-denial and service or through self-critical embrace of the success ethic. The different drummer is assured of a leading role as long as aggressive individualism remains a civilized priority.

Surely symptomatic of multiple cataclysmic threats that plague human civilization particularly since the advent of nuclear power, a third form of play springs from social-ethical and theological sources and yet is distinctive enough from most earlier 20th-century religious drama to be called apocryphal.

Primarily it is the effectively blurred contrast between audience and congregation that sets these works apart. However much both seek to be enlightened, audiences want to be amused, touched, seduced from their disbelief, whereas congregations want to be absolved, healed, helped to restrain their unbelief. If audiences have stars in their eyes, congregations have souls on their sleeves.

Despite these polarities, both bodies of onlookers welcome inspiration, even if it discomforts them. And who can deny the evangelical dimensions of engaging theatergoers by choral recitation of the Lord's Prayer, gospel choir music, or startling and liturgically resonant stage effects experienced (approvingly or pessimistically) at SAMUEL BECKETT's *WAITING FOR GODOT*, BRIAN FRIEL's *Dancing at Lughnasa*, JEAN ANOUILH's *The Lark*, Fr. Daniel Berrigan's *Trial of the Catonsville Nine*, Lee Breuer's *Gospel at Colonus*, and TONY KUSHNER's *ANGELS IN AMERICA*?

The latter work, epochal in its treatment of AIDS and related homosexual themes also brutally exposed in BENT and Daniel Kramer's various works, accentuates the priority of rededicating as well as challenging the audience. A glimpse of the sublime through and beyond conflict, agony, death, and despair is the apocryphal goal to which these plays aspire.

If their authors lack Shaw's confidence that he achieved it, they at least shy away from solutions all too quickly antiquated and irrelevant. With determination as wry as it is exuberant, they prefer faithful, comradely resolution in the face of imponderables. In the process the audience of onlookers in the darkened auditorium is called to see and feel new light, a primarily collective rather than private individual vision incarnating hope against hope for reconciliation, if not redemption.

Though none of these aspire to the majestic sweep of Peter Brook's works about religion and power glimpsed through fiction and legend as well as holy books and characters of diverse world faiths, they share the conviction that the line between public and performer, between objective plot and communal ritual, should at least be obscured, even if it can never quite disappear. Only perhaps THORNTON WILDER's *OUR TOWN* (which according to one critic belied comment as much as the Twenty-third Psalm) hauntingly provokes such audience soul stirring.

Yet its still, small voice, in contrast to *The Maharabata* or Peter Brook's three latest plays based on Islam, Hinduism and Christianity (*Tierno Bokar*, *The Death of Krishna*, and *The Grand Inquisitor*), shares the perspective of Brook's Sufi mystic character Bokar in his reply to a pupil's question, "What is God?" That answer suggests the paradox that ensures the survival of religious drama in the face of believers and skeptics alike: "God is an embarrassment to human intelligence. Because if you affirm

His existence, you cannot prove it. But if you deny His existence, you deny your own existence."

[See also Philosophy and Drama]

FURTHER READING

Eversole, Finley, ed. *Christian Faith and the Contemporary Arts.* Nashville, Tenn.: Abingdon, 1957.

Houghton, Norris. *The Exploding Stage Introduction to Twentieth Century Drama.* New York: Weybright & Talley, 1971.

Religious Drama 1: Five Plays. Intro. by Marvin Halverson. New York: Meridian Bks., 1957.

Religious Drama 2: Twenty-one Medieval Mystery and Morality Plays. Intro. by E. Martin Browne. New York: Meridian Bks., 1958.

Religious Drama 3: An Anthology of Modern Morality Plays. Intro. by Marvin Halverson. Cleveland: World Pub., 1959.

Speaight, Robert. *The Christian Theatre.* New York: Hawthorn Bks., 1960.

Frank Lloyd Dent

RENDRA (1935–)

Indonesian playwright, director, actor, and poet, Rendra is the most influential figure in Indonesian modern theater and the most recognized literary and artistic personality in contemporary INDONESIA. Born on November 7, 1935, in Solo, Central Java, Rendra's Catholic parents christened him Willibrordus Surendra Rendra, which he shortened to W. S. Rendra in the 1950s. In 1970 he converted to Islam, changing his name to Wahyu Sulaiman before dropping the "W. S." altogether. He is now known only as Rendra.

During the repressive years of President Haji Mohammad Suharto's New Order (1966–1998), Rendra was the most overtly political theater artist. He was jailed, placed under house arrest, banned, stoned, and bombed. He had to struggle to obtain permission to perform. Well read, articulate, and even mystical in his private life, Rendra's public persona is flamboyant and charismatic. His overriding concern has been maintaining his personal beliefs.

After studying Western literature in Yogyakarta, and at Harvard and New York University in the early 1960s, he entered the American Academy of Dramatic Art in New York in 1964. Rendra returned to Yogyakarta in 1967, establishing his communal Bengkel Teater (literally Theater Workshop or Garage). There he introduced a new method of actor training to Indonesia—a workshop headed by a playwright/director/actor/"guru" who concentrates on process-oriented approaches to theater rather than the Western REALISM taught by Indonesia's national theater academies.

Rendra's Mini Word plays (*Bip Bop, Rambat, Rate Rata,* and *Piiipppp,* 1968) were groundbreaking movement pieces based on dialogue-free, improvisatory exercises called Beautiful Movements. At their core, these were pieces protesting social condi-

tions and conventional theater practice. Rendra drew upon indigenous theatrical elements that, until that time, had been kept separate from modern theater. His numerous adaptations of Western classical and modern plays—including *Oedipus Rex* (1969, 1987), *WAITING FOR GODOT* (1970), *Macbeth* (1970, 1976), *Hamlet* (1971, 1975, 1976, 1994), *Lysistrata* (1974, 1976, 1979, 1991), and *Antigone* (1974)—are significant. Rendra recontextualizes these works to mirror local social conditions.

Rendra became known internationally after he was banned from mounting plays in Yogyakarta following *The Mastodon and the Condors* (*Mastodon dan burung kondor,* 1973), which told the story of an idealistic young student poet (played by Rendra) entangled in an uprising for educational reform against a repressive dictator. Rendra continued his "pamphlet theatre" in Jakarta with THE STRUGGLE OF THE NAGA TRIBE (*Kisah perjuangan suku Naga,* 1975). Using the structure of a traditional *wayang* (shadow puppet) play, this script depicts a village under threat due to a foreign mining project. In 1975, the same year he was banned from performing in Central Java, Rendra was awarded the Jakarta Academy Arts Award. In 1978, following a reading of protest poetry where two ammonia bombs were thrown into the crowd, Rendra was placed under house arrest for three months. He was banned from performing anywhere from 1978 until 1986, when he staged his spectacular seven-hour *Prince Reso* (*Panembahan Reso*) in Jakarta.

SELECT PLAYS: *Bip Bop* (1968); *Aswar's World* (*Dunia Aswar,* 1971); *The Mastodon and the Condors* (*Mastodon dan burung kondor,* 1973); *The Struggle of the Naga Tribe* (*Kisah perjuangan suku Naga,* 1975); *The District Secretary* (*Sekda,* 1977); *Prince Reso* (*Panembahan Reso,* 1986); *The Ritual of Solomon's Children* (*Selamatan anak cucu Sulaiman,* 1988)

FURTHER READING

Gillitt, Cobina. "Challenging Conventions and Crossing Boundaries: A New Tradition of Indonesian Theatre from 1968–1978." Ph.D. diss., New York Univ., 2001.

Gillitt Asmara, Cobina. "Tradisi Baru: A New Tradition of Indonesian Theatre." *Asian Theatre Journal* 12, no.1 (Spring 1995): 164–174.

Morgan, Anne-Marie. "Three Approaches to Modern Theatre in Jakarta in the 1990s: Rendra, Putu Wijaya and Ratna Sarumpaet." *Australasian Drama Studies* 27 (1995): 70–85.

Verburgt, Ron. "'I Am Because You Are; You Are Because I Am': An Interview with Rendra." *Australasian Drama Studies* 25 (October 1994): 6–16.

Cobina Gillitt

RENDRA, W. S.   *See* RENDRA

RENÉE (1929–)

Renée (born on July 19, 1929, in Napier, NEW ZEALAND) has written a large number of plays that, through a variety of forms, address the oppressions of gender in conjunction with class and even race (she has Maori ancestry: Ngati Kahungunu and Scots).

She worked for many years as an actor and director of community theater.

Her first play, *Setting the Table* (1982), broadcast on radio before being staged at Auckland's Mercury Theatre in 1982, placed her in the vanguard of feminist theater in New Zealand. Set in the kitchen of some women who help at a refuge for victims of domestic and sexual abuse, *Setting the Table* examines the use of violence by women, after an angry husband follows one of the workers home. Interwoven in the action are rehearsals for a satirical feminist revue.

Renée is best known for her trilogy about the women in a working-class family between the 1870s and the 1950s. Resilient and resourceful, Renée's heroines exemplify the contribution women have made to the development of New Zealand. *Wednesday to Come* (1984) concerns the crisis faced by four generations of women when the family breadwinner commits suicide in a relief camp during the 1930s Depression.

In *Pass It On* (1986), the two adolescents of *Wednesday to Come*, Jeannie and Cliff, have grown up, and the play focuses on the role of women in the 1951 Waterfront Dispute. In contrast to the NATURALISM of the earlier play, *Pass It On* has a documentary style: it is episodic and more didactic. The final play, *Jeannie Once* (1990), steps back in time, to present Granna of *Wednesday to Come* as a young woman, recently arrived from IRELAND and newly widowed, working to establish herself as a dressmaker in Victorian Dunedin. Among the other women struggling to create a life in the colonial outpost are an oppressed wife of a Presbyterian minister, her Maori servant, and an Irish music hall singer and former male impersonator. As well as the world of music hall, the play evokes the MELODRAMA characteristic of the theater of the period.

Renée's other plays include *Breaking Out* (1982), about efforts to establish a women's center; *Groundwork* (1985), a didactic piece about lesbian visibility and the effects of the 1981 Springbok rugby tour on five women; *Secrets: Three Short Plays for Two Women* (1982); *Belle's Place* (1987), a lesbian play; *Touch of the Sun* (1990), a COMEDY about two middle-aged sisters sorting through their dead mother's wardrobe; *Missionary Position* (1991), about Greta Garbo, Marilyn Monroe, and Marlene Dietrich, three bag ladies seeking refuge in a fantasy film-star world; and *Te Pouaka Karaeke: The Glass Box* (1992), her most overt exploration of Maori identity. She has also written for television but since 1993 has devoted herself primarily to writing novels.

PLAYS: *Breaking Out* (1982); *Secrets: Three Short Plays for Two Women* (1982); *Setting the Table* (1982); *What did you do in the war, Mummy?* (1982); *Asking for It* (1983); *Wednesday to Come* (1984); *Groundwork* (1985); *Pass It On* (1986); *Belle's Place* (1987); *Born to Clean* (1987); *Form* (1990); *Jeannie Once* (1990); *Touch of the Sun* (1990); *Missionary Position* (1991); *Pink Spots and Mountain Spots* (1992); *Te Pouaka Karaeke: The Glass Box* (1992); *Tiggy Tiggy Touch Wood* (1992); *Heroines, Hussies and High High Flyers* (1993)

FURTHER READING

Beatson, Peter. "Passing It On" [interview with Renée]. *Sites* 16 (Autumn 1988): 24–36.

Black, Sebastian. "Renée, *Wednesday to Come* and *Pass It On*." *Australasian Drama Studies* 12–13 (1988): 190–195.

McCurdy, Claire-Louise. "Feminist Writer Renée: All Plays Are Political." *Women's Studies Journal* 1, no. 2 (April 1984): 61–72.

Payne-Heckenberg, Pamela, and Tony Mitchell. "Interview: Renée." *Australasian Drama Studies* 10 (April 1987): 21–28.

Tompkins, Joanne. "What We Want and What We Get: Renée's *Jeannie Once*." *Hecate* 20, no. 2. (1994): 243–250.

Warrington, Lisa. "A Life Long Affair: Renée Writing for the Theatre. Commentary/Interview." *Australasian Drama Studies* 18 (April 1991): 70–90.

Stuart Young

RESINO, CARMEN (1941–)

Born in Madrid on November 25, 1941, Carmen Resino stands out as one of SPAIN's most prolific and innovative playwrights and novelists with a career that spans forty years of uninterrupted productivity. *The President* (*El presidente*, 1968) heads her literary credits that today include over two dozen dramatic works and nine novels. Resino is an active scholar, teacher, and writer with degrees in history and dramatic arts as well as a founding member and first elected president (1986) of the Spanish Women Playwrights' Guild. Although her theater has been widely published and has attracted national and international critical acclaim, few of her plays have been staged in Spain owing to the endemic lack of financial support and theater space accessible to contemporary dramatists, particularly women.

Resino's theater is original and defies simple classification. Through a prismatic aesthetic approach, Resino integrates elements pertaining to the school of REALISM or of the absurd in order to create a multidimensional reality that is tangible and elusive, critical and philosophical, realistic and bizarre. Oftentimes, the dramatist includes music and dance as integral facets of the drama, thus blurring the conventional parameters between straight and musical theater. Although she rejects the feminist label, the majority of her works reveal a feminist critical underpinning that is reflected both in her strong women characters and in the selection of controversial themes. Among her many considerations, Resino underscores the abuse and imbalance of power between the social classes and the sexes, which have defined the course of history and have caused immeasurable suffering and damage to the dynamic of personal relationships.

Given the author's predilection for history, it is not surprising that so many of her plays center on a particular historic or legendary character or anecdote set in Spain or abroad. The dramatist is less concerned with historical precision of facts, however, and more interested in restoring vitality, sensuality, and immediacy to a particular moment of the past. Her characters are well defined and generally avoid stereotypes or idealizations. Even so, they bear a close resemblance in colloquial language, gestures, and attitudes to the ancestral national *picaros* that populated Spain's most authentic and popular literary genre. They live in a reality fraught with injustice and cruelty that often demands the sacrifice of ideals for the privilege of survival. Regardless of whether they are among the survivors or the defeated, these characters embody a wide spectrum of human nature's flaws, virtues, and contradictions that have not changed over time. Frequently, their individual destinies are differentiated by little more than fortuitous circumstance or varying degrees of success or failure. Nevertheless, they are resourceful and clever and undaunted by the challenge to etch out an identity and reclaim independence from the whims of dispassionate gods.

Herein lies the essence of Resino's theater: it is defined not so much by the heroic or tragic outcomes of conflicts as by the revelations of universal truths about the human condition and experience. Resino's theater is provocative and unsettling, but it provides powerful lessons that transcend time and national boundaries.

SELECT PLAYS: *The President* (*El presidente*, 1968); *The Thirst* (*La sed*, 1980); *Mother, the Child Isn't Crying!* (*¡Mamá, el niño no llora!* 1982); *Ulysses Is Not Returning* (*Ulises no vuelve*, 1983); *There Are No More Waltzes* (*Ya no hay valses*, 1985); *New History of the Princess and the Dragon* (*Nueva historia de la princesa y el dragon*, 1988); *Personal and Not Transferable* (*Personal e intransferible*, 1988); *The Actress* (*La actriz*, 1990); *Auditorium* (*Auditorio*, 1990); *Formula Three* (*Fórmula tres*, 1990); *Impossible dialogues* (*Diálogos imposibles*, 1990); *Margarita, the Beautiful* (*La bella Margarita*, 1990); *Professor Schneider's Secret Enemy* (*El oculto enemigo del profesor Schneider*, 1990); *The Beauty Merchants* (*Los mercaderes de la belleza*, 1992); *The Erotic Dreams of Elizabeth Tudor* (*Los eróticos sueños de Isabel Tudor*, 1992); *Pop and French Fries* (*Pop y patatas fritas*, 1992); *Under Suspicion* (*Bajo sospecha*, 1995); *The Girls from Saint Ildefonso* (*Las niñas de San Ildefonso*, 1996); *Spanish West* (1996); *The Reception* (*La recepción*, 1997); *It's the Others* (*Son los otros*, 2001); *The Orchestra* (*Orquesta*, 2002)

FURTHER READING

Buedel, Barbara Foley. "Rewriting Herstory in Carmen Resino's *Los eróticos sueños de Isabel Tudor*: When Fiction Is 'Truer' than 'History.'" *West Virginia Philological Papers* 46 (2000): 77–83.

Gabriele, John. "Estrategias feministas en el teatro breve de Carmen Resino." *Letras Femeninas* 21, no. 1 (Summer 1995): 85–95.

Lamartina-Lens, Iride. "A New Look at Familiar Faces: Carmen Resino's *Ulises no vuelve* and María José Ragué-Arias' *Clitemnestra*." *Romance Languages Annual* 1 (1990): 495–499.

——. "Introducción al teatro de Carmen Resino." In *Testimonios del Teatro Español: 1950–2000.* Vol. 1, ed. by Candyce Leonard and Iride Lamartina-Lens. Ottawa: Girol Bks., 2002. 141–142.

Leonard, Candyce. "Re-writing/Re-presenting Textual/Sexual Gender Roles in Twentieth-Century Female-Authored Spanish Drama." In *Un Escenario Propio/A Stage of Their Own*, ed. by Kirsten Nigro and Phyllis Zatlin. Ottawa: Girol Bks., 1998. 27–35.

Iride Lamartina-Lens

THE RESISTIBLE RISE OF ARTURO UI

The Resistible Rise of Arturo Ui (*Der aufhaltsame Aufstieg des Arturo Ui*, 1941), published in the critical edition of BERTOLT BRECHT's (1898–1956) works under the revised title *The Rise of Arturo Ui* (*Der Aufstieg des Arturo Ui*), was one of several projects undertaken in exile by Brecht as resistance against the Nazi dictatorship. The common purpose of these projects was to educate people, especially Americans who could not draw upon direct experiences, about the true nature of fascism, while at the same time giving encouragement to those who were fighting to defeat the Nazis. As things turned out, *The Resistible Rise of Arturo Ui* was not to be performed until its premiere in Stuttgart in November 1958.

The play is a political allegory, with obvious correspondences: Arturo Ui=Adolf Hitler (1889–1945); Dogsborough=Paul von Hindenburg (1847–1934); gangsters=fascists; Chicago=GERMANY. In the guise of telling the story of how the mob boss Arturo Ui exploits a cauliflower monopoly as the springboard to power, Brecht presents the history of Hitler's rise in the 1920s through to the annexation of Austria. No one can fail to decode the allegory because at the end of each scene the historical event is glossed explicitly through signboards, a device Brecht often used to prod the audience into critical reflection.

The name Arturo Ui goes back to Brecht's notes as early as 1934 for a satire on the "Life and Deeds of Giaocoma Ui from Padua," set in the Italian Renaissance. But the concept of analyzing the politics of capitalism from the perspective of the gangster underworld had attracted Brecht even earlier, when he adapted John Gay's (1685–1732) *The Beggar's Opera* (1728) into THE THREEPENNY OPERA (*Die Dreigroschenoper*, 1928). There are evident parallels between the rise of Arturo Ui and the reign of Mack the Knife, from their tendency to pathos to their cold cunning when it comes to money and power. However, the main point of both plays is to show that the participants are actors in, not directors of, the historical process. Those who are really in charge are no more visible onstage than in real life. As Arturo Ui himself succinctly states: "Might belongs to those who pay."

The Resistible Rise of Arturo Ui is the work of a mature playwright in full command of his techniques. The dialogue in verse echoes and reworks classical dramas (William Shakespeare, Friedrich Schiller, Johann Wolfgang von Goethe) in a brilliant language adequate to contemporary needs. The bombast of political rhetoric is disarmed by moments in which individuals express an awareness of their lives with poignant simplicity. The last line of Roma's monologue—"No one will hear you. No one heard me"—indicts not just Ui but all tyrants. The fact that Ui could not help having become the boss signals that the political allegory rests on the foundations of a TRAGEDY.

FURTHER READING

Atkins, Robert. " 'Und Es Ist Kein Gott Außer Adolf Hitler': The
   Biblical Motifs in Brecht's *Arturo Ui* and Related Works as
   Political Counter-Propaganda." *Modern Language Review* 85
   (1990): 373–387.

Bathrick, David. "A One-Sided History: Brecht's Hitler Plays." In
   Literature and History, ed. by Leonard Schulze and Walter Wetzels.
   Lanham, Md.: Univ. Press of America, 1983. 181–196.

Grenville, Anthony. "Idealism Versus Materialism in the
   Representation of History in Literature: The Dictator Figure in
   Thomas Mann's 'Mario und der Zauberer' and Brecht's 'Der
   aufhaltsame Aufstieg des Arturo Ui.' " *Journal of European Studies*
   17 (1987): 77–105.

Humble, M. E. "The Stylisation of History in Bertolt Brecht's *Der
   aufhaltsame Aufstieg des Arturo Ui.*" *Forum for Modern Language Studies*
   16 (1980): 154–171.

Schürer, Ernst. "Revolution from the Right: Bertolt Brecht's American
   Gangster Play *The Resistible Rise of Arturo Ui.*" In *Critical Essays on
   Bertolt Brecht*, ed. by Siegfried Mews. Boston: G. K. Hall, 1989.
   138–154.

Arnd Bohm

RETURN OF THE PRODIGAL

The second full-length play by St. John Hankin (Edward Charles) is an ironic updating of the prodigal son parable that reflects the incompatibility of Christian charity with Edwardian materialism. Eustace Jackson, the titular prodigal, having run through the £1,000 with which he was sent off to AUSTRALIA several years earlier, is found prostrate on the doorstep of his home in the village of Chedleigh. His reappearance jeopardizes the ambitions of the parvenu Jacksons, most of which involve keeping up appearances for the upcoming parliamentary elections, in which his father, Samuel, will stand as a Conservative, and for the Faringfords, impoverished aristocrats with a daughter whom his brother, Henry, hopes to marry. Much of the play's conflict centers on Eustace's unwillingness and inability to work and the challenge this poses to his family's cherished middle-class beliefs, particularly that industriousness is the chief measure of social worth. Samuel is outraged when Eustace demands an allowance to support him for the rest of his life, but he capitulates when Eustace threatens to go to a workhouse, which would endanger his father's reputation, or to drown himself, which would quash his brother's chances for marriage. The prodigal departs with the guarantee of £250 a year and a promise never to return.

The Return of the Prodigal is, in part, a response to Hall Caine's *The Prodigal Son*, a Drury Lane MELODRAMA (adapted from Caine's novel) that also had its first production in 1905. Hankin eschews Caine's facile sentimentality by parodying the conventions of the parable: his prodigal is unrepentant, his father unforgiving, while the "fatted calf" becomes a tepid and imper-

sonal breakfast and the clothing of the prodigal a tailor's bill for Eustace's suits that Samuel refuses to pay. The play is also an occasion for satirical jabs at the outmoded conventions of Edwardian life, from the mystification of the middle classes by a titled nobility that lacks money, property, and influence to the boredom induced by postprandial musicales. Hankin reserves his last two acts, however, for an extended and discomfiting examination of predatory capitalism and its human costs from the prodigal's outsider perspective. Eustace delivers several set-piece speeches on the logical outcomes of a "survival of the fittest" market, in which the weak (and poor) are leeches on the success of the strong and wealthy and, as Eustace cynically posits, ought to be slaughtered wholesale by the government for the health of ENGLAND. The play is littered with stories of bad speculations, failed business ventures, and widowed wives without any means of supporting themselves; through these secondhand accounts, Hankin suggests that the suffering that attends failure in a competitive society is not limited to one character or family. Hankin also rejects the possibility that individuals can reform themselves to fit the demands of their environment. The play's epigraph from Heraclitus, "Character is Fate," is echoed in a late speech by Eustace, "The real tragedy is what one is. Because one can't escape from that." His constitutional unsuitability for work forces Eustace into the predatory position of blackmailing his own family, much as the Faringfords prey on the Eustaces for wealth, the Eustaces on the Faringfords for status, and Samuel and Henry on other mills to stay in business. In 1905, this overtly Darwinian critique was unusual in a stage play and unheard of in a "COMEDY."

The Return of the Prodigal opened the second season of the Royal Court Theatre in 1905, and it embodies many of the philosophies of the "New Drama" that premiered there: an emphasis on stage NATURALISM, an "open-endedness" that neither resolves the central conflicts nor allows audience sympathy to rest with one character or position, a brief investigation of the role of women in modern society, and a dedication to exposing the unrealistic conventions of the West End theater and the middle-class audiences that attended it. Unlike many of his fellow playwrights, however, Hankin refuses to identify a program that might address the problems he documents; his play is not as much special pleading for outcast prodigals as it is an unflinching look at the consequences of economic Darwinism. It has only enjoyed a modest success on the British stage, and critics of the play, then and now, have faulted it for didactic exposition that occasionally breaks character, though it has been praised for its bitter humor and trenchant social commentary. *The Return of the Prodigal* returned to the Royal Court in 1907, and there was a revival in 1948 at the Globe Theatre with John Gielgud in the title role. Although it has never received a major production in the UNITED STATES, it was a popular and critical success at the Shaw Festival in repertory during the 2001 and 2002 seasons.

[See also England]

FURTHER READING

Andrews, Alan. "Unhappy Endings: An Essay on *The Return of the Prodigal*."
   In *Shaw and His Contemporaries: Four Plays*, ed. by Denis Johnston.
   Oakville: Mosaic Press and the Academy of the Shaw Festival, 2001.

McDonald, Jan. *The "New Drama" 1900–1914: Harley Granville Barker, John
   Galsworthy, St. John Hankin, John Masefield*. London: Macmillan, 1986.

Phillips, William H. *St. John Hankin: Edwardian Mephistopheles*.
   Cranbury: Associated Univ. Presses, 1979.

Lawrence Switzky

REZA, YASMINA (1959–)

When "ART" ("Art," 1994) opened at Wyndham's Theatre in London in 1995, Yasmina Reza became the first French author to play a West End commercial theater in forty years. "Art" had already played in fifty continental theaters, forty of them German. It would soon be translated into many languages and play in venues around the world. Audiences everywhere reacted to the play's spare, razor-sharp dialogue and its unusual focus on the friendship of three heterosexual males, a friendship plunged into crisis when one of them buys a minimalist painting.

Born in 1959, Reza credits her background as an actress (she trained at the Jacques Lecoq school) with giving her the sensitivity to write actor-friendly plays: "Most writers don't know that actors are never better than in the pauses or in the subtext. They give the actors too many words. In a play, words are parentheses to the silences. They're *useful* for the actors, but only that; they aren't the whole story."

Playgoers who saw her first play, *Conversations After a Burial* (*Conversations après un enterrement*, 1987), were treated to a study in subtly modulating moods. At rise, mourners are gathered stiffly around an open grave: a father's death after a long illness leaves his adult children choked with grief. Over the course of the play the audience comes to understand that the children have been choking on something else for many years, an inchoate mass of resentments they can neither swallow nor reject but must work through.

Reza set her second play, *Winter Crossing* (*La Traversée de l'hiver*, 1989), on a hotel terrace in the Alps in autumn. Under a guise of easy sociability, the few guests staying at the hotel make subtle emotional demands on each other. Their need is not so much to communicate as to commune, to be part of something. When caught in the fact of need, they cover themselves by pointing out that they are only on vacation; they will soon be off to someplace else.

Conversations and *Winter Crossing* each have six characters and are modeled on chamber music—specific string quintets are even mentioned in the dialog. Reza's third play, *The Unexpected Man* (*L'homme du hazard*, 1992, though first produced after "Art" in 1995), used a radically different arrangement: two characters,

no entrances, no exits—two inner monologues that resonate in a closed railway compartment. One belongs to a prominent novelist pushing sixty, an acrid man sensing the wane of his creative abilities yet still possessed of a reckless imagination. Opposite him is a handsome widow of about fifty. In the first twenty-seven pages of the published text, the lines are not spoken in the compartment but voiced to the audience directly from the characters' minds. Long before the novelist, the audience discovers (1) that the woman has recognized him, (2) that he is her favorite author, and (3) that she has got his latest novel in her handbag. The play follows the serpentine path of their mutual self-introductions.

After the enormous success of "Art", Reza hesitated before returning to the theater; she wrote two novels and a book of memoirs. Her fifth play, *Life X 3* (*Trois versions de la vie*, 2000), cycles through three variations on a botched dinner party to show how a change in attitude can provoke a change of fortune. An astrophysicist has invited a senior colleague and his wife to dinner. The night before, he and his wife are putting their offstage child to bed and planning what to serve when the doorbell rings: the other couple has come a day early. The evening goes rapidly downhill as all four characters fall to insulting each other. In the second version, the senior colleague and the astrophysicist's wife are having an affair. In the third version, the astrophysicist is more in control of himself (and his situation) and more optimistic. The improvised evening goes much better, though the play stops short of declaring that attitude is destiny.

The restlessness of some of Reza's characters is prefigured in her family history; her paternal ancestors were forced from SPAIN when, as Jews, they declined to become Catholic. They later had to leave Persia when they refused to become Muslim.

PLAYS: *Conversations After a Burial* (*Conversations après un enterrement*, 1987); *Winter Crossing* (*La Traversée de l'hiver*, 1989); *The Unexpected Man* (*L'homme du hazard*, 1992); "Art" (1994); *Life X 3* (*Trois versions de la vie*, 2000); *A Spanish Play* (*Une pièce espagnole*, 2004)

FURTHER READING

Reza, Yasmina. *Hammerklavier* [Memoirs and reflections]. Tr. by Carol
   Cosman and Geraldine Touzeau-Patrick. New York: Braziller,
   2000.

Riding, Alan. "If 'Art' Is for Art's Sake, It's Also a Career Lift for Its
   French Creator." *New York Times* (November 28, 1996): C11.

Schneider, Robert. "Yasmina Reza: Writing in a Major Key"
   [interview]. *American Theatre* (November 1998).

Robert Schneider

RIANTIARNO, NANO (1949–)

Nakula Riantiarno (Nano) was born in Cirebon, West Java, on June 6, 1949, the fifth of seven children, whose father was a railway clerk. His first stage experience occurred in 1966 when performing in CALIGULA produced by a group in Cirebon.

In 1968 Nano entered the National Theatre Academy of INDONESIA (ATNI) in Jakarta. At ATNI he studied with Teguh Karya. ATNI taught the theory of Western theater based on KONSTANTIN STANISLAVKY's principles of REALISM; Nano studied books on ARTHUR MILLER and BERTOLT BRECHT. Teguh selected Nano for an ACTING course he unofficially opened on the campus. ATNI later prohibited the course; its activities were moved to Jakarta's Hotel Indonesia, where Teguh, with Nano and other students, established Teater Populer (Popular Theater) in 1968. His wife Ratna Riantiarno became a major actress for the group and responsible for managing aspects of business and production.

During the period with Teguh (1968–1975), Nano acted in plays and began playwriting and directing while acquiring acumen in theater management. In 1975 he traveled around Indonesia for six months, seeking inspiration from the traditional (wayang) and popular (ludruk and ketoprak) performing arts. Nano aspired to a theater alternative to realism offering art, PHILOSOPHY, politics, and entertainment. On March 1, 1977, Nano established Teater Koma (Coma Theater).

Most plays written by Nano during the Haji Mohammad Suharto administration were subjected to authoritarian dictates. Performances were monitored by intelligent agencies, censored, shut down, and Nano was constantly interrogated, but not one play was banned outright. After the performance in 1985 of THE COCKROACH OPERA (Opera Kecoa), every play required special permission before it was staged. Themes of plays are often infused with issues of corruption, collusion, and nepotism within a repressed society plagued by poverty rendering it powerless to confront authoritarian rule.

Chinese IDENTITY was suppressed in Nano's play Sampek Engtay (1988), based on a Chinese story. Chinese symbols onstage were forbidden; the appearance of the traditional Chinese lion dance (barongsai) was banned. Nano was interrogated in 1990 while performances of Succession (Suksesi) proceeded; the play was eventually closed. Set in a fictitious kingdom, Suksesi, one of the king's five children, had ambitions for the throne. The play reflected on the issues of President Suharto's succession and his nepotism.

After the Suharto regime fell in October 1998, Nano maintained a political stance with The Constipation Opera (Opera Sembilit), the story of a nation restricted by overbloated leadership. The nation's politics in 2001 are the subject of The Republic of Bagong (Republik Bagong), set in the context of the wayang shadow play, satirizing the ineptness of leadership coupled with the proliferation of new political parties. Nano often returns to plays in the repertoire, believing theater is a journey without periods but filled with commas—hence the name Teater Koma.

SELECT PLAYS: House of Paper (Rumah Kertas, 1977); Time Bomb (Bomb Waktu, 1982); The Cockroach Opera (Opera Kecoa, 1985); Julini's Opera (Opera Julini, 1986); Buriswara Conglomerate (Konglomerat Buriswara,

1987); Sampek Engtay (1988); Transvestites Accuse (Banci Gugat, 1989); Succession (Suksesi, 1990); The Primadonna Opera (Opera Primadona, 1993); The White Snake Opera (Opera Ular Putih, 1994); Semar Accuses (Semar Gugat, 1995); Greedy Love (Cinta yang Serakah, 1996); The Constipation Opera (Opera Sembilit, 1998); President of the Birds (Presiden Burung, 2001); The Republic of Bagong (Republik Bagong, 2001)

FURTHER READING

Junarto, Herry Gendut. Teater Koma: A Portrait of Indonesian Tragedy and Comedy [Potret tragedi dan komedi manusia Indonesia]. Jakarta: Grasindo, 1997.

Schwarz, Adam. A Nation in Waiting: Indonesia in the 1990's. Sydney, Australia: Allen & Unwin, 1994. 167–168.

Vatikiotis, Michael R. J. Indonesian Politics Under Suharto. New York: Routledge, 1993.

Zurbuchen, Mary. "Images of Culture and National Development in Indonesia: The Cockroach Opera." Asian Theatre Journal 7, no. 2 (1990): 127–149.

Ian Jarvis Brown

RICE, ELMER (1892–1967)

Born Elmer Leopold Reizenstein on September 28, 1892, in New York City, Elmer Rice was once ranked second only to EUGENE O'NEILL in importance to the American theater. A prolific writer, he is best remembered today for just two of his plays— THE ADDING MACHINE (1923) and STREET SCENE (1929)—each demonstrating radically different theatrical styles.

Rice studied at the New York Law School, but while working as a law clerk, he became interested in writing plays. His first produced work, The Passing of Chow-Chow, won a dramatic writing competition at Columbia University in 1913.

Rice's first real success as a playwright came with On Trial (1914). Murder trial witnesses testify as their memories are dramatized before the audience in what would now be called flashbacks. In the earliest use of what is now a standard dramatic technique in film and television, the memory scenes take the audience further and further back into the events that led to the murder.

The Adding Machine is a landmark of American EXPRESSIONISM, reflecting the growing interest in this highly subjective and nonrealistic form of modern drama. Rice's style of expressionism was influenced by Eugene O'Neill's THE HAIRY APE; both authors draw heavily upon American urban stereotypes in character and dialect. Yet O'Neill shows his expressionistic hero, Yank, to be a fundamentally decent man who has become unbalanced by a conflict between his sense of IDENTITY in mechanized society and how he is perceived by others, while Rice depicts his protagonist, Mr. Zero, as the epitome of all human vulgarity in the modernized world. Unlike O'Neill, Rice's brand of expressionism is comic. The Adding Machine and The Hairy Ape share anxiety about the soul of the modern working man, a central theme of expressionist theater.

The *Adding Machine* also displays the American expressionist use of exaggeration and grotesqueness in speech, characterization, sound, and visual presentation. The THEATRE GUILD produced the play with designs by the innovative scenographer Lee Simonson, who created a nightmarish larger-than-life adding machine that the protagonist worked with his entire body, an element not called for in Rice's text.

Rice collaborated with Hatcher Hughes, of the Morningside Players, to write *Wake Up Jonathan* (1921), an unmemorable MELODRAMA that starred Minnie Maddern Fiske. He later collaborated with Dorothy Parker on *Close Harmony* (1924), a satiric COMEDY of manners, and with PHILIP BARRY on *Cock Robin* (1928), a comic mystery. These plays found a larger audience in the growing amateur and little theater market than on Broadway.

Street Scene is set on the front stoop and adjacent sidewalk of a New York City tenement; the play features dozens of characters who drift in and out to create slice-of-life NATURALISM. To heighten the local color, Rice's characters use a variety of immigrant and working-class dialects. The play is an excellent example of tastes and trends of American drama in the period. Like the plays of the highly successful naturalistic theater of director-playwright DAVID BELASCO, *Street Scene* is tinged with melodrama; there is a love triangle and sensationalized crime of passion. Yet, like SIDNEY HOWARD's THEY KNEW WHAT THE WANTED, the play ends unromantically. Furthermore, the play emphasizes social reality and portrays sympathetic New York Jewish characters, both suggesting a kinship between Rice and CLIFFORD ODETS.

Street Scene explores themes of brutality and sympathy, and violence and nurturing, all in the style of naturalism. The central theme is much the same as in *The Adding Machine*—the detachment caused by overmechanized urban living. However, *Street Scene* suggests greater optimism for humanity, offering more glimpses of tenderness and genuine affection.

Rice himself directed *Street Scene*, which ran for over six hundred performances. In his autobiography, the playwright described the opening:

> At the final curtain there were cheers. The curtain went up and down so many times that I lost count. . . . As the demonstration continued, there were cries of "Author!" I did not want to appear, for I think a play should speak for itself. But, as the cries and the urgings of the actors became more insistent, I went on and said a few words in praise of the cast. The curtain came down, the house lights went up; it was over at last. (Rice, 1963)

The play won the Pulitzer Prize that year and was made into a successful movie in 1931; Rice later collaborated with Kurt Weill and LANGSTON HUGHES on the musical version.

In the early 1930s, Rice wrote and produced a string of unsuccessful shows, including *We, the People* (1933), *Judgment Day* (1934), and *Between Two Worlds* (1934). In 1934, he announced his retirement from the theater. He soon became interested,

however, in creating a theater organization he called the Theatre Alliance, which helped inspire the FEDERAL THEATRE PROJECT. In 1935, Rice briefly served as head of the New York regional Federal Theatre Project but resigned in protest of the censorship of *Ethiopia*, a Living Newspaper performance.

In 1938, Rice again abandoned semiretirement for a recently begun New York theatrical venture, The Playwrights' Company. Founded in 1937 by ROBERT SHERWOOD, MAXWELL ANDERSON, SIDNEY HOWARD, and S. N. BEHRMAN, the organization's purpose was to foster growth in the work of American playwrights. This was not a repertory theater with a company of resident actors but a commercial theater dedicated to the work of its playwrights, and it produced five new Rice plays in ten years. *Flight to the West* (1940) was a commentary on totalitarian government. Set on board an airplane carrying a variety of World War II refugees and a Nazi diplomat, the play's dialogue and action are highly dialectical and propagandistic, reflecting Rice's strong political views. Predictably, the play pleased audiences and critics who shared Rice's perspective but alienated others.

In the early 1940s, Rice worked for the Hollywood film industry, most notably writing the screenplay for *Holiday Inn* (1942), starring Bing Crosby and Fred Astaire. His last few plays met with only moderate success on Broadway. Rice died on May 8, 1967, in Southampton, ENGLAND.

[*See also* United States]

PLAYS: *On Trial* (1914); *The Passing of Chow-Chow* (1916); *The House of the Free* (one-act, 1917); *For the Defense* (1919); *Wake Up Jonathan* (with Hatcher Hughes, 1921); *The Adding Machine* (1923); *Close Harmony* (with Dorothy Parker, 1924); *Cock Robin* (with Philip Barry, 1928); *See Naples and Die* (1929); *Street Scene* (1929); *The Subway* (1929); *Counsellor-at-Law* (1931); *The Left Bank* (1931); *Black Sheep* (1932); *The House in Blind Alley* (1932); *We, the People* (1933); *Between Two Worlds* (1934); *The Home of the Free* (one-act, 1934); *Judgment Day* (1934); *Not for Children* (1936); *American Landscape* (1938); *Flight to the West* (1940); *Two on an Island* (1940); *A New Life* (1943); *Dream Girl* (1945); *Street Scene* (musical version, with Kurt Weill and Langston Hughes, 1947); *The Grand Tour* (1951); *The Winner* (1954); *Cue for Passion* (1958); *Love Among the Ruins* (1963)

FURTHER READING

Durham, Frank. *Elmer Rice*. New York: Twayne, 1970.

Hogan, Robert. *The Independence of Elmer Rice*. Carbondale: Southern Illinois Univ. Press, 1965.

Palmieri, Anthony F. R. *Elmer Rice: A Playwright's Vision of America*. Rutherford, N.J.: Fairleigh Dickinson Univ. Press, 1980.

Rice, Elmer. *Minority Report: An Autobiography*. New York: Simon & Schuster, 1963.

Vanden Heuvel, Michael. *Elmer Rice: A Research and Production Sourcebook*. Westport, Conn.: Greenwood Press, 1996.

Wixson, Christopher. "Everyman and Superman: Assimilation, Ethnic Identity, and Elmer Rice's Counsellor-at-Law." American Drama 8, no. 1 (Fall 1998): 59–74.

DeAnna M. Toten Beard

RICHARDSON, JACK (1935–)

For my part, I find most theatre dreadful. It is full of totems, taboos, and rituals that should have passed with the Paleolithic Age. It has served as an outlet for man's most sentimental estimates of himself.

—Jack Richardson, 1962

In the early 1960s Jack Richardson was hailed as one of America's most promising young playwrights, attracting critical notice for plays that mirrored the cynicism and disaffection of his generation. His works are notable for their intellectual exploration of philosophical issues, logical construction, and Shavian dialogue.

Richardson was born on February 18, 1935, and raised in New York City. Following a brief stint in summer stock and a three-month course in ACTING at the American Theatre Wing, Richardson enlisted in the army. Serving from 1951 to 1954, he was stationed in Korea, Frankfurt, and Paris (where he briefly attended the University of Paris). Following his discharge from the army, Richardson completed a philosophy degree at Columbia University, then returned to Europe to pursue graduate work at the University of Munich on an Adenauer Fellowship in Germanic Studies.

When Richardson returned to the UNITED STATES in 1958, he turned his attention to the theater. When his first play *The Prodigal* debuted at the OFF-BROADWAY Downtown Theatre on February 11, 1960, twenty-four-year-old Richardson became a critical sensation. Termed "the most brilliantly written new play to come out since the end of World War II" by critic George Wallwarth, *The Prodigal* is an existentialist rendering of the story of Orestes. Richardson depicts his young protagonist as a reluctant hero, forced by societal expectations to avenge the murder of his father Agamemnon. Winner of an Obie Award and a Drama Desk Award, the play's success spurred reviewers to herald Richardson, alongside EDWARD ALBEE, ARTHUR KOPIT, and JACK GELBER, as one of the bright new stars of the American theater.

Gallows Humor (1961), Richardson's second off-Broadway production, pairs two short plays that share a common theme. In them, Richardson returned to the theme of man at the mercy of social institutions. A TRAGICOMIC indictment of capital punishment, the play solidified Richardson's reputation as a philosophical commentator in the vein of FRIEDRICH DÜRRENMATT and JEAN-PAUL SARTRE.

Richardson's subsequent plays failed to attract the critical success of his early efforts. In *Lorenzo* (1963) Richardson again explored the theme of the futility and destructiveness of war, this time during the Italian Renaissance. Opening on Broadway at the Plymouth Theatre on February 14, 1963, the production ran for only four performances. *Xmas in Las Vegas* (1965), a darkly comic play about a compulsive gambler, also had a brief and unsuccessful Broadway production. An unpublished play, *As Happy as Kings*, attracted little notice when it was produced by New Theatre Workshop in 1968.

As the American theater became increasingly experimental and politically vocal in the late 1960s, the abstract rhetoricism of Richardson's plays failed to satisfy public tastes or producers' commercial aims. Following the disappointing reception of his Broadway productions, Richardson turned his focus to critical writing and fiction. A screenplay, *Juan Feldman*, was published in 1968. His novels include *The Prison Life of Harris Filmore* (1965) and *Memoirs of a Compulsive Gambler* (1980), an autobiographical exploration of Richardson's private obsession with gambling. His dramatic criticism and essays have been regularly featured in many national publications, including the *New York Times*, *Esquire*, and *Commentary* magazine.

[*See also* England, 1940–Present]

SELECT PLAYS: *The Prodigal* (1960); *Gallows Humor* (1961); *Lorenzo* (1963); *Xmas in Las Vegas* (1965); *As Happy as Kings* (1968)

FURTHER READING

Callens, Johan. *Double Binds: Existentialist Inspiration and Generic Experimentation in the Early Work of Jack Richardson*. Amsterdam: Rodopi, 1993.

Lumley, Frederick. *New Trends in 20th Century Drama*. New York: Oxford Univ. Press, 1967.

Richardson, Jack. "Jack's First Tape: A Self Interview." *Theatre Arts* 46 (March 1962): 64–65, 73–77.

——. "On Reviewing Plays." *Commentary* (September 1966).

Wellwarth, George. *The Theater of Protest and Paradox*. New York: New York Univ. Press, 1964.

Debra Charlton

RIDERS TO THE SEA

Riders to the Sea, a TRAGEDY uniquely in one-act by J. M. SYNGE, was first performed at Molesworth Hall, Dublin, on February 25, 1904, by the Irish National Theatre Society, with Honor Lavelle in the role of Maurya (it was later played by Sara Allgood) and W. G. Fay as her last son Bartley, the only man in her family of a husband and six sons not yet lost to the sea, though he would be drowned as well by the end of this short play. The play is the only one by Synge that is set on the Aran islands, where his long stays had given him plots, a feeling of kinship with the people, and an ear for poetic peasant speech that influenced all his dramatic work. The great line with which Mauryra, bereaved a seventh time, ends the play—"No man at all can be living forever, and we must be satisfied"—was translated by Synge from a letter in Irish sent him by a friend on the island. The language of the play is less capricious and imaginative than that of Synge's other plays. The action is simple, doom-laden, and devastating. As one son's body is being identified by knit of the sweater on his back, and boards are being gathered for his coffin (painfully, there are no nails to be found on the island, so his burial must wait), the last son—taking a pig for sale to the mainland—refuses his mother's pleading not to leave, because of a bad omen she has noticed, and goes off to his death.

Upon hearing the manuscript play read out by Synge, W. B. YEATS cried out, "Sophocles! No, Aeschylus!" The sense of a primal world of humans nobly living in relation to nature and family, and accepting fate and human limitation, makes the comparison with Aeschylus apt, in spite of the play's brevity and precise localization. Among one-act plays in the English language, it is a classic. Its performance in Dublin humbled Synge's critics, who found much to criticize in the rest of his plays.

[See also Ireland]

FURTHER READING

Paulin, Tom. "Riders to the Sea: A Revisionist Tragedy?" In Interpreting Synge, ed. by Nicholas Grene. Dublin: Lilliput, 2000.

Thornton, Weldon. J. M. Synge and the Western mind. Gerrards Cross, Bucks.: Colin Smythe, 1979.

Watson, George J. Irish Identity and the Literary Revival: Synge, Yeats, Joyce and O'Casey. London: Croom Helm; New York: Barnes & Noble, 1979.

Adrian Frazier

RIGHT YOU ARE

Right You Are (Così è, se vi pare), a play in three acts written by LUIGI PIRANDELLO in 1917, premiered in Milan (ITALY) at the Olympia Theater on June 18, 1917, and is based on Pirandello's short story "Mrs. Frola and Mr. Ponza, her son-in-law." In Right You Are, speech, more than actions, constitutes the essence of this play that inaugurated the so-called cerebralism of the Sicilian playwright's works.

On the outskirts of an unidentified provincial town, in contemporary Italy, a married civil servant, Mr. Ponza, rents a small apartment. He also rents an apartment for his mother-in-law in a downtown building where Mr. Agazzi, Mr. Ponza's head clerk, lives with his wife, Amalia, and daughter, Dina. The gossip in the building is that not only does Mr. Ponza never allow his wife out; he also prohibits her from seeing her mother. The Agazzis, Lamberto Laudisi (Amalia's brother), and other friends, demand an explanation. They rule out the possibility of a relationship between Mrs. Frola and her son-in-law, and later she justifies Mr. Ponza's actions, saying that he wants to be the sole recipient of his wife's love. This explanation is invalidated by Mr. Ponza's statement that Mrs. Frola's daughter, his first wife, died four years before, causing Mrs. Frola's craziness. According to Mr. Ponza, Mrs. Frola believed she saw her daughter when she saw him with his new wife, and out of consideration for his mother-in-law's

mental health, he decided to let her believe it. Again Mrs. Frola undermines Mr. Ponza's credibility, saying that he no longer recognized his wife when she returned from a forced temporary separation that was caused by his brutal physical love. Attempts to attain truth through official documents are foiled by an earthquake that took place years before in the Ponzas' hometown. Ultimately the Prefect, the highest state representative in the city, orders Mr. Ponza, his subordinate, to bring Mrs. Ponza. She enters the room, her face heavily veiled, and says she is Mr. Ponza's second wife, the daughter of Mrs. Frola, no one to herself: she is who others want her to be.

Laudisi's comments remind readers of the pointless quest for one-dimensional facts. While it is excessive to identify him as the voice of the author, Laudisi's words insert a theme crucial to Pirandello: the impossibility of identifying truth. The poignant description of Mr. Ponza as a brute, prey to instincts, who loved his wife too ardently, might suggest, besides Mr. Ponza's sanity or insanity, that the puzzling intellectual game Pirandello is accused of setting up is not his goal. In fact, Pirandello's characters err when they rely too much on intellect. Theories about Mrs. Ponza's identity produce opinions that contradict themselves, trapping the inquisitors in a sterile logic to which anti-intellectualism could provide an escape.

Since 1922 Right You Are was among the first of Pirandello's plays considered for production in the UNITED STATES. It was eventually performed in December 1926 at Cornell University. It then opened in New York on February 23, 1927, with Edward G. Robinson and Morris Carnovsky and thereafter enjoyed continuous success. The play immediately became a trademark of Pirandello's style.

FURTHER READING

Dombroski, Robert S. "Laudisi's Laughter and the Social Dimension of Right You Are (If You Think So)." Modern Drama 16 (1973): 337–346.

Kroha, Lucienne. "Behind the Veil: A Freudian Reading of Pirandello's Così è (se vi pare)." Yearbook of the Society for Pirandello Studies 12 (1992): 1–23.

Stefano Giannini

RINGWOOD, GWEN PHARIS (1910–1984)

To read The Collected Plays of Gwen Pharis (1982) is to be impressed by the variety and scale of this seminal Canadian dramatist's achievements. The collection contains naturalistic, one-act pieces, epic, large-cast, full-length productions, historical musicals, and children's plays. Ringwood also published a novel, Younger Brother (1959; another novel, Pascal, remains unpublished), and numerous critical articles, poems, and short stories.

Ringwood was born in Anatone, Washington, on August 13, 1910. In 1913 her family moved north from Washington State to Lethbridge, Alberta; later they moved close to Magrath. Ringwood's father was an agriculturalist; her mother was a schoolteacher; her three brothers died early—two of them in World

War II. Gwen attended schools in Calgary, Edmonton, and Montana and studied at the Universities of Montana, Alberta, and North Carolina, excelling in dramatic study. Ringwood began to write in the 1930s. At the University of Alberta, she wrote thirteen Sheila Marriot–directed radio plays. Having worked for Sterling Haynes, who was promoting Albertan theater, Ringwood had been inspired to begin a productive career.

Geraldine Anthony, Ringwood's biographer and primary supporter, organizes her dramatic canon into three sections: early prairie plays, Alberta folklore plays, and dramas of social protest. The early, one-act prairie play STILL STANDS THE HOUSE (1938) is regarded as Ringwood's triumph—unlike her other plays, most of which are forgotten, *Still Stands the House* continues to be performed regularly. The play is fraught with images and instances of death, as the inhabitants of a rural house battle with extreme weather, environmental pressures, and conflicting personal motivations. This play, like other, generically similar works, including *One Man's House* (1938) and *Pasque Flower* (1939), was produced in the late 1930s, under the patronage of Frederick Koch of the Playmakers School, University of North Carolina at Chapel Hill.

Ringwood returned to Alberta in 1939—the year of her marriage to medical practitioner John Brian Ringwood—and wrote plays concerning that region's folklore. These plays vary from gentle COMEDIES to raucous FARCES. Many of these 1940s and 1950s plays represent immigrant communities: French and Ukrainian settlers mingle with established Canadians. *The Courting of Marie Jenvrin* (1941), about a canny, much-coveted girl, the rodeo-based *Stampede* (1945), and *Widger's Way* (1952), which follows the adventures of a diffident Albertan farmer, are examples of these entertainments.

The Ringwoods moved to Williams Lake, British Columbia, in 1953. Ringwood became preoccupied with social injustices, concerns that are articulated through her drama. Her concern for native people's welfare is evident in *Maya* (1959), *The Stranger* (1971, a rewrite of *Medea*), *The Lodge* (1976), and *The Furies* (1980), all of which feature Indian protagonists wronged by whites. Ringwood's last plays focus on the challenges facing elderly people. In *The Lodge*, the aging Jasmine surveys with horror her family's scramble to inherit her wealth. Ringwood had known for some time that her cancer was incurable (she died in Williams Lake, British Columbia, on May 24, 1984); it is small wonder, then, that her final plays, such as *Garage Sale* (1981), are haunted by anxieties about old age, physical decline, and the loss of mental control. With plays involving the elderly as well as youngsters, and those neither young nor old, Ringwood's drama communicates to every age range.

[*See also* Canada]

SELECT PLAYS: *The Dragons of Kent* (1935); *Blacksmith* (1938); *Still Stands the House* (1938); *Pasque Flower* (1939); *The Courting of Marie Jenvrin* (1941); *The Jack and the Joker* (1944); *The Drowning of Wasyl*

Nemichuk or A Fine Colored Easter Egg (1948); *Widger's Way* (1952); *Lament for Harmonica or Maya* (1959); *The Road Runs North* (1967); *The Deep Has Many Voices* (1968); *The Stranger* (1971); *The Lodge* (1975); *A Remembrance of Miracles* (1975); *Mirage* (1979); *The Furies* (1980); *The Garage Sale* (1981)

FURTHER READING

Anthony, Geraldine. *Gwen Pharis Ringwood*. Boston: G. K. Hall, 1981.

Benson, Eugene. "Gwen(dolyn Margaret) Pharis Ringwood." In *International Dictionary of Theatre-2: Playwrights*, ed. by Mark Hawkins-Day. Detroit: St. James Press, 1994. 806–808.

Lister, Rota Herzberg. "Gwen Pharis Ringwood." In *The Oxford Companion to Canadian Theatre*, ed. by Eugene Benson and L. W. Connolly. Toronto: Oxford Univ. Press, 1989. 486–489.

Ringwood, Gwen Pharis. *The Collected Plays of Gwen Pharis Ringwood*. Ed. by Enid Rutland. Ottowa: Borealis Press, 1982.

"Ringwood Talks About Her Life and Work." In *Stage Voices*, ed. by Geraldine Anthony. New York: Doubleday, 1978. 90–110.

University of Calgary Libraries. Special Collections Division. *The Gwen Pharis Ringwood Papers: An Inventory of the Archive at the University of Calgary Libraries*. Compiled by Marlys Chevrefils, Shirley A. Onn, and Apollonia Steele. Ed. by Jean M. Moore and Jean F. Tener. Calgary: Univ. of Calgary Press, 1987.

Wagner, Anton. "Gwen Pharis Ringwood Rediscovered." *Canadian Theatre Review* 5 (1975): 63–69.

Kevin De Ornellas

RIP VAN WINKLE

Are we so soon forgot when we are gone.
—Rip Van Winkle

In the summer of 1860, the 19th-century American comic star Joseph Jefferson revised several old versions of Washington Irving's *Rip Van Winkle* and premiered it in Washington, D.C., on November 5. He subsequently commissioned the playwright and actor DIONYSIUS BOUCICAULT to produce a new version, which opened in London on September 4, 1865, and in New York on September 3, 1866. Jefferson continued to perform and "improve" the Boucicault version until his retirement in 1904. The resulting text is a collaborative work among Jefferson, his predecessors in the role, and Boucicault.

Rip Van Winkle begins in the village of Falling Waters, New York, "set amid . . . unmistakable Hudson River scenery." Rip, once a prosperous man, has wasted his fortune on drink. Derrick von Beekman, to whom Rip has mortgaged his lands, was once the suitor of Rip's wife, Gretchen. Derrick hopes to win Gretchen again and to get Rip to sign a deed conveying the property to him. Rip enters, surrounded by children. Derrick reads an incomplete version of the deed to the illiterate Rip. Later, however, Rip tests whether Meenie's playmate Hendrick can read, discovers the deceit, and does not sign the deed.

In the second act, the shrewish Gretchen throws Rip out of the house into a storm. The third act—Jefferson's greatest contribution is to the play—consists of a monologue in which Rip meets the spirits of Hendrick Hudson and his crew, drinks their magic liquor, and falls asleep for twenty years.

In the fourth act, Rip awakens, an aged man, and returns to Falling Waters, where he barely recognizes the town he left, now transformed by the American Revolution. Gretchen is married to Derrick, who is also attempting to get Meenie to give up hoping that Hendrick, now a sailor, will return and trying to force her to marry his ne'er-do-well nephew Cockles.

Because no one recognizes Rip, Jefferson was able to deliver one of his most famous poignant lines: "Are we so soon forgot when we are gone." Just as the mob is about to drive the old man from the village, Hendrick reappears to save him. Rip meets his daughter Meenie, and when she does not know him, he delivers yet another of his "hits": "My child looks in my face, and don't know whom I am!" Meenie, however, rushes into his arms, shouting, "I do! Father!" Hendrick proves that Derrick von Beekman is a fraud, Rip's property is restored, Meenie and Hendrick are united, and Gretchen goes back to Rip and even offers him a drink. Jefferson ended the play with Rip's famous toast: "I'll drink your good health, and your families, and may they all live long and prosper."

Rip's foibles disguise his inner goodness so that when he is punished for drinking by sleeping through twenty years of his life, the late-19th-century audience sympathized with an old man in a new world, his sense of bewilderment and nostalgia marching their own discomfort in the rapid industrialization of post–Civil War America.

[See also United States]

FURTHER READING

Bloom, Arthur. *Joseph Jefferson, Dean of the American Theatre.* Savannah, Ga.: Frederic C. Beil, 2000.

Jefferson, Joseph. *The Autobiography of Joseph Jefferson.* New York: Century, 1889.

Johnson, Stephen. "Joseph Jefferson's Rip Van Winkle." *The Drama Review* 26 (Spring 1982): 4–20.

Arthur W. Bloom

THE RISE OF ARTURO UI See THE RESISTIBLE RISE OF ARTURO UI

RIVERA, JOSÉ (1955–)

Transactions between the mundane and the extraordinary are not merely a literary technique, but a mirror of intractable reality.
—Michiko Kakutani

A Puerto Rican–born playwright noted for reflecting daily reality through poetry and dreams, Jose Rivera, born in San Juan in 1955, moved to the UNITED STATES when he was four years old and for many years was part of the only Hispanic family in his neighborhood. While his family's lack of money and education made him intensely conscious of issues of IDENTITY and belonging, the rich culture he received at home offered him a way to articulate and reconcile such problems.

Writing predominantly in the Latin American style of magic REALISM, Rivera notes that his faith in the supernatural was passed down through generations of a rural family who had little education in the formal sense and who traditionally explained life's dramas through superstition and magic. The family stories about their ancestors that he heard while growing up made no distinction between fantasy and reality. One of his favorite memories is his grandfather's tale of a conquistador in full armor, astride a white horse, bursting out of a tree that the old man had climbed as a boy. Rivera uses this tradition to mirror the challenges of being Hispanic in the United States. His journey as a playwright has been an endeavor to reconcile the contradictions of being caught between two cultures.

Early plays, *The Promise* (1988) and *Each Day Dies with Sleep* (1989), were written in reaction to the negative portrayals of Latinos in popular American culture. Rather than following the tendency to articulate the Puerto Rican experience through harsh realism and urban drug culture, Rivera's plays merged imagination and reality to offer a subjective focus on Latino culture in a small, semirural environment, with an emphasis on family, sexuality, spirituality, and the occult.

Rivera's later plays continue to offer a subconscious interweaving of people and episodes close to his own life but attempt to present a broader vision. The Obie Award–winning *Marisol* (1992) expands on the interior nightmare of the Latino experience to express the chaos caused by the breakdown of social interaction. *Marisol* ("Mary-alone") tells the story of a young middle-class Puerto Rican woman left alone in the Bronx when her guardian angel sheds her wings to wage war against a senile God. Without spiritual protection, the world disintegrates into an apocalyptic nightmare. The disappearance of the moon, ecological disasters in Ohio, and Nazi skinheads torching tramps in parks provide surreal reflections of anxieties such as loneliness and loss of compassion that Rivera believes plague modern life. Other notable plays, *Cloud Tectonics* (1995) and *References to Salvador Dalí Make Me Hot* (2000), also expose the stark truths of life through extreme hallucinatory metaphors. Influenced by the Columbian novelist Gabriel García Márquez, *Cloud Tectonics* examines the way love seems to make time stand still when a man rescues a beautiful young hitchhiker from the rain. The woman claims she is fifty-four and has been pregnant for two years.

Although Rivera has spent much of his career working in film and television, he continues to write for the stage. His recently produced work *Adoration of the Old Woman* (2002) is perhaps his most political to date, blending Latin magic realism with straightforward Western realist drama to directly tackle the question of Puerto Rican independence.

[See also Puerto Rico]

PLAYS: *The House of Ramon Iglesia* (1983); *The Promise* (1988); *Each Day Dies with Sleep* (1989); *Marisol* (1992); *The Crooked Cross* (1994); *Flowers* (1994); *Gas* (1994); *Tape* (1994); *A Tiger in Central Park* (1994); *The Winged Man* (1994); *Cloud Tectonics* (1995); *The Street of the Sun* (1996); *Maricela de la Luz Lights the World* (1997); *Sueño* (1998); *References to Salvador Dalí Make Me Hot* (2000); *Sonnets for an Old Century* (2000); *Adoration of the Old Woman* (2002); *Massacre (Sing to Your Children)* (2004); *School of the Americas* (2004); *Six Billion Devils* (2004)

FURTHER READING

"José Rivera." In *Dictionary of Literary Biography*. Vol. 249, *Twentieth-Century American Dramatists*, 3d series, ed. by Christopher Wheatley. Detroit: Gale, 2002.

Rivera, José. *Marisol and Other Plays*. New York: Theatre Communications Group, 1997.

——. *References to Salvador Dalí Make Me Hot and Other Plays*. New York: Theatre Communications Group, 2003.

Simons, Tad. "José Rivera: We All Think Magically in Our Sleep." *American Theatre* 10 (July 1993).

Svich, Caridad. " 'An Urgent Voice for Our Times.' An Interview with José Rivera." *Contemporary Theatre Review* 14, no. 4 (November 2004): 83–89.

Olivia Turnbull

ROAD

Road, JIM CARTWRIGHT's first play, was premiered at London's Royal Court Upstairs and was such an immediate success that it transferred first to the main house, then later into the West End, and was subsequently toured nationally. The play's structure is episodic, a tour during one night of a street in a run-down northern town, with a guide called Scullery linking the mostly self-contained scenes, sometimes with other characters encountered on the street. The play's opening features a variety of characters preparing for their night out; aggression and poverty are the keynotes. But this is not straight reportage; the first two scenes end with characters directly ("blankly") addressing the audience: "Fucking long life in' it?" The first half of the play also features monologues from Molly, a baby-talking, nostalgic old lady; the "Professor," whose "anthropological study of 'Road'" has led to his losing everything; Skin Lad, a reformed skinhead who tells of how he found the dharma; and Jerry, a nostalgic middle-aged man who "can't see how that time could turn into this time." The half ends with Joey and Clare, two young lovers who starve themselves to death.

Many productions immediately vary the tone with Cartwright's interval material, which features Scullery singing karaoke in the theater bar, and the "Beatoven" disco playing for the "Erotic clutch" (Sheena, Tina, and Maureena), until one of them injures her back. The second half begins after the pubs shut. Helen brings a nearly unconscious soldier back to her place, where he is sick. Valerie's monologue tells of the disintegration of her marriage under the pressure of unemployment. Brian and Marion's drunken flirting turns sour when they are interrupted by his daughter Linda; as Brian storms out, she tells the audience, "POOR LITTLE ME!" The play ends with a good-bye from Scullery after four passionate monologues building to a communal chant, after "you drink, you listen to Otis, you get to the bottom of things and you let rip."

Focusing on *Road* as a "state of the nation" play, besides reducing the necessity to engage with its staging dispossession and loss two decades on, runs the risk of missing the demotic power of Cartwright's language, the emotional charge of his shifts into and out of direct address, and his gifts in rapidly establishing situation and character, particularly in monologue. Critics write of the generosity of Cartwright's vision as much as its grimness. This fusion shows most clearly in the characters' mordant wit and in the play's use of music. Molly is given a pathetically childlike soliloquy; but the action later stops when she "sings a beautiful old Lancashire folk tune." If the play's opening to the sound of Judy Garland's "Somewhere Over the Rainbow" is quickly revealed to be grimly ironic, its cathartic conclusion is built upon the directness and power of Otis Redding's "Tenderness."

[See also England]

FURTHER READING

Cohn, Ruby. *Retreats from Realism in Recent English Drama*. Cambridge: Cambridge Univ. Press, 1991.

Peacock, D. Keith. *Thatcher's Theatre: British Theatre and Drama in the Eighties*. Westport, Conn.: Greenwood Press, 1999.

Sadler, Geoff. "Road." In *Contemporary British Dramatists*. London: St. James, 1994.

Stephen Longstaffe

ROBERTO ZUCCO

BERNARD-MARIE KOLTÈS's last play, *Roberto Zucco* (1989), completed shortly before his death, is based on the life and death of Italian serial killer Roberto Succo. Escaping from an Italian prison, where he was serving a life sentence for killing his parents, Succo remained at large in FRANCE for several years, committing more murders, including a French police officer, and evading French and Italian authorities. Finally captured in 1988, he attempted to escape by climbing on the roof of the Treviso prison, where he spent hours throwing bricks at the guards and screaming at the journalists assembled with television cameras. Koltès, whose interest in Succo began when he saw a "wanted" poster with a series of photographs in the Parisian subway, watched the live television broadcast of Succo's standoff and said in an interview with *Le Monde* on September 26, 1988: "His trajectory is unbelievable; he is an exemplary killer. . . . A mythic creature, a hero, like Samson and Goliath."

Koltès's play transforms the figure of the serial killer away from its violent and sensational excess toward a mode of representation that pays special attention to the dilemma of a dehumanized hero trapped in the gaze of a society that constructs him according to its fantasies of aggression. Confronted with his imminent death, Zucco reaches a certain lucidity from knowing that, like Sisyphus, he is condemned to be "the futile laborer of the underworld," the voice that needs to articulate a certain ineffable metaphysics of despair. But, as ALBERT CAMUS said of Sisyphus, "if this myth is tragic, that is because its hero is conscious"; it is such mortal knowledge that makes Zucco dramatize the world around him.

Borrowing from a film noir editing style, the play is divided into fifteen sequences that end in a mythical image of a sublime ascension toward the sun. Zucco becomes an actor who stages four spectacular murders: the mother (strangled), the father (thrown from a window), the police officer (stabbed with a knife), and the innocent child (shot with a revolver). His antihero's histrionics are a way for Koltès to expose the absurdity of the human condition and the perversity of rebelling against it. The play reveals the contradictions inherent in the representation of elemental evil: extreme brutality is often accompanied by a sense of absence and loss, and in Koltès's world, a bloody killer can be as charmingly lyrical as a young poet. The spectator or reader is moreover denied the satisfaction of knowing the psychological motivations behind the crimes, thus thwarting realist desires to draw causal links between childhood pathology and adult monstrosity.

Roberto Zucco combines Albert Camus's existential angst with the violence of JEAN GENET's theater and a Brechtian sense of ALIENATION and distancing. However, it carries the particular signature of the author: the combination of witty parody with poetic virtuosity. *Roberto Zucco* premiered in 1990, directed by Peter Stein at Berlin's Schaubühne a year after its author's death. The first French production was at Théâtre National Populaire of Villeurbanne, directed by Bruno Boeglin in 1991.

FURTHER READING

Crimp, Martin, tr. *Roberto Zucco*, by Bernard-Marie Koltès. London: Methuen, 1997.

Koltès, Bernard–Marie. *Une part de ma vie, entretiens, 1983–1989* [A Part of My Life, Interviews, 1983–1989]. Paris: Les Editions de Minuit, 1999.

Nash-Siedlecki, Robert Eoin. "Review of *Robert Zucco* [New Federal Theatre, New York, N.Y.]." *American Theatre* (April 1995).

Ubersfeld, Anne. *Bernard-Marie Koltès*. Arles: Actes Sud, 2001.

Donia Mounsef

ROBERTSON, THOMAS WILLIAM (1829–1871)

You see, there is one capital thing in being a dramatist. There is no competition. Nowadays there are no dramatic authors—so they say.
—Jack Randall, Act 1, *Birth*

Thomas William Robertson's plays are often referred to as "cup-and-saucer" drama, and he was one of the earliest British playwrights to represent the middle-class lifestyle realistically on the Victorian stage. Although to later generations his plays seem melodramatic, making use of types, asides, and soliloquies, these plays mark a distinct change in the staging practices of the theater and a definite move toward visual REALISM and social awareness. He paved the way for the late-19th-century social dramas like those of ARTHUR PINERO and GEORGE BERNARD SHAW. He was born into an acting family in 1829 in Newark-on Trent, Notts, ENGLAND, and was on the stage in early childhood. Because he began his career as an actor, his plays hinge heavily on characterization, staging, and settings. He created his characters from his observations of people and their everyday lives.

Robertson's early writing career comprised many adaptations and translations of French plays that influenced his playwriting. He was thoroughly familiar with the form of the well-made play, and this structure influenced the development of his later writing. While adapting and translating, he worked as drama critic for the *Illustrated Times*, and in 1864 he successfully staged *David Garrick*, another adaptation from the French.

Robertson's most important works came out of the time he spent working with the Marie and Squire Bancroft in London in the 1860s. They were devoted to maintaining a small and intimate theater that shunned the star system, and he was set on creating a domestic drama that was an honest representation of his world. Their 1860s productions were characterized by modern costuming, working sets, and the use of real furniture and props. In 1865 they produced *Society*, rejected by many London theaters, thereby setting the tone for the rest of the decade. While still including shallow stereotypes and contrived plotlines, this COMEDY of the goings-on at a gentlemen's club and the newly rich trying to break into the upper social classes represented a move away from the sentimentality of the MELODRAMA and a true picture of modern life.

He followed *Society* with *Ours* in 1866. Written specifically for the Bancrofts, this play marked the first time he was to write a play with a venue and company in mind. By the time he wrote his best-known play CASTE in 1867, Robertson was familiar enough with the group of actors that he was able to write parts with specific actors in mind. The play is constructed on the characters and situation as opposed to the plot. His characters moved away from the stock characters in melodramas to more complex and multifaceted creations reflecting contemporary life. Robertson included specific directions not just for the staging of the play but also for the characters' movements, gestures, and expressions. *Caste* shows the audience characters as they go through the simple routines of everyday life. These mundane actions coupled with the naturalness of conversations delivered as if the characters were speaking to each other rather than for the benefit of an audience together characterize the six plays Robertson wrote for the Bancrofts. It is on these three plays and *Play* (1868) *School* (1869), and *The M.P.* (1870) that his reputation rests.

Robertson died in 1871 in South Hampstead, England, at the age of forty-two. His death left a vacuum in British drama that would not be filled until the 1890s. The social dramas of the last decade of the century are the natural extension of the changes he effected in a small theater in London. His use of real working stage properties—windows with glass, doors with locks, food, and drink—were an early step toward stage realism.

[See also England, 1860–1940]

SELECT PLAYS: *Faust and Marguerite* (1854); *The Half Caste; or, The Poisoned Pearl* (1856); *Peace at Any Price!* (1856); *David Garrick* (1864); *Constance* (1865); *Society* (1865); *Ours* (1866); *Caste* (1867); *For Love* (1867); *Play* (1868); *Home* (1869); *School* (1869); *Birth* (1870); *The M.P.* (1870); *War* (1871)

FURTHER READING

Barrett, Daniel. *T. W. Robertson and the Prince of Wales's Theatre.* New York: P. Lang, 1995.

Pemberton, T. E. *The Life and Writings of T. W. Robertson.* London: R. Bentley & Son, 1893.

Robertson, T. W., and Thomas W. S. Robertson. *The Principal Dramatic Works of Thomas William Robertson with Memoir by his Son.* London: Sampson Low, Marston, Searle & Rivington, Samuel French, 1889.

Savin, Maynard. *Thomas William Robertson: His Plays and Stagecraft.* Providence, R.I.: Brown Univ. Press, 1950.

Angela Courtney

ROBINS, ELIZABETH (1862–1952)

I am conscious that in talking and writing to my nearest and most trusted friends I sometimes suppress and I sometimes embroider.
—Elizabeth Robins

Elizabeth Robins was born on August 6, 1862, in Louisville, Kentucky. She grew up in Zanesville, Ohio, after her mother was committed to a psychiatric institution. Elizabeth went to Vassar to study medicine but in 1880 moved to New York City and became a member of the Boston Museum Company, James O'Neill's traveling company.

In 1885 Robins married George Richmond Parks, an actor. In 1887, Parks committed suicide by jumping into the Charles River, using theatrical armor to weigh himself down. He wrote Robins, saying, "I will not stand in your light any longer" and signed, "Yours in death."

In 1888 Robins traveled to ENGLAND, which she soon adopted as her permanent residence. She played many roles, such as Claire de Cintre in HENRY JAMES's *The American*, but by the 1890s she had discovered HENRIK IBSEN. Her interest in naturalistic theater led to her involvement in producing because she found the actor-manager system confining. Robins produced and acted in several of Ibsen's plays, including Hedda in HEDDA GABLER, Nora in *A DOLL'S HOUSE*, and Hilda Wangel in THE MASTER BUILDER.

In 1896 she organized the Henrik Ibsen–JOSÉ ECHEGARAY subscription series to raise money for the productions of LITTLE EYOLF and Echegaray's *Mariana*. In the following year, William Archer joined her in forming the New Century Theatre to sponsor nonprofit productions such as JOHN GABRIEL BORKMAN and PEER GYNT. During the 1890s, while Robins was active in theater, she began a new career as a writer. Under the pseudonym C. B. Raimond, she saw four of her novels published. She also collaborated with Florence Bell on the play *Alan's Wife*, and after her successful novel *The Open Question* (1898), Robins's pen name became widely known.

In 1900, Robins went to Alaska in search of her brother, who had joined the gold rush. The journey was an important event in her life as she wrote two novels, *The Magnetic North* (1904) and *Come and Find Me* (1908), and several short stories based on her experiences. In November 1902, she made her final appearance as an actress in Mrs. Humphrey Ward's *Eleanor*. She devoted more time to writing and to her growing interest in issues of women's equality. In 1907 a new play by Robins, *Votes for Women*, opened in London, and shortly thereafter, her novelization of it, *The Convert* (1907), was published. She wrote many articles in support of women's suffrage, and the 1913 publication of *Way Stations* brought together a collection of her articles and speeches about suffrage.

In 1908 Robins met Octavia Wilberforce, who became her lifelong companion. Robins's interest in feminism continued throughout the 1920s. In 1924, she published *Ancilla's Share*, a collection of essays on sexism that also addressed the problem of racism and the possibilities for pacifism. Robins died on May 8, 1952, in Brighton, England.

PLAYS: *Alan's Wife* (with Florence Bell, 1893); *Votes for Women; A Play in Three Acts* (1907)

FURTHER READING

Gates, Joanne E. *Elizabeth Robins, 1862–1952: Actress, Novelist, Feminist.* Tuscaloosa: Univ. of Alabama Press, 1994.

Gates, Joanna E., and Victoria J. Moessner, eds. *Alaska-Klondike Diary of Elizabeth Robins, 1900.* Anchorage: Univ. of Alaska Press, 1999.

John, Angela V. *Elizabeth Robins; Staging a Life.* London: Routledge, 1995.

Brian Sajko

ROBINSON, LENNOX (1886–1958)

I've felt for so many years like a bad actor cast for a part far too heroic for his talents, I haven't had technique enough for it, I haven't in any way been big enough for it, the audience has realized at last what I realized years ago.
—The Big House, Scene 4

I think I'd like it better if they [Irish Catholics] hated us [Irish Protestant landowners]. That at least would make me feel that we had power, that we counted for something; it's very hard to forgive toleration.
—The Big House, Scene 2

Esmé Stuart Lennox Robinson, playwright and Abbey Theatre manager, was born on October 4, 1886, in Douglas, County, Cork, IRELAND, the son of a stockbroker who had become a Protestant clergyman in middle age. Robinson was a sickly child unable to attend school regularly but was naturally bookish. At twenty-one, he attended an Irish National Theatre Society production of CATHLEEN NI HOULIHAN at the Cork Opera House, an event that turned him toward Irish nationalism and playwriting. His first play, The Clancy Name, appeared the following year, 1908, at the Abbey Theatre. Thereafter, he consistently produced well-constructed, realistic, and mildly satirical plays about town life in rural Ireland, a dramatic model imitated by T. C. Murray and R. J. Ray, which came to be known as "Cork REALISM." This style dominated the Abbey repertoire up to the arrival of SEAN O'CASEY's work.

After the death of J. M. SYNGE, W. B. YEATS named Robinson as director of the Abbey Theatre in 1909. Robinson spent a season attending plays and shadowing HARLEY GRANVILLE-BARKER at London's Royal Court Theatre and then took over play direction at the Abbey from 1910 to 1914, and from 1918 to the mid-1930s.

Robinson's output as a playwright was not limited to the realistic well-made play. He wrote a number of effective "state of the nation" dramas in the revolutionary second decade of the century. Patriots (1912) concerns the diminishment of the Irish republican movement in the midst of growing middle-class prosperity; The Lost Leader (1918) laments the absence of a figure like Charles Stewart Parnell in the postrevolutionary chaos of Irish politics. Robinson's whimsical COMEDIES, like The White-headed Boy (1916) and Drama at Inish (1933), pleased audiences at the time and continue to be revived, especially by the amateur theater movement in Ireland, which Robinson did much to organize. The driving force behind the Dublin Drama League (1919–1929), founded in order to bring non-Irish experimental plays to the Abbey stage, Robinson himself benefited by the work of LUIGI PIRANDELLO and ANTON CHEKHOV. The Big House (1926) resembles THE CHERRY ORCHARD in its beautiful rendering of the end of an aristocracy. Robinson put into this play his own sadness as a Protestant Irish patriot marginalized after the triumph of that national cause he had himself promoted.

While Yeats's hope that Lennox Robinson would fill the shoes of Synge were never to be fulfilled, Robinson served Yeats, LADY GREGORY, and the Abbey Theatre faithfully. He trained other playwrights, tended to the theatrical and cultural health of Ireland, and wound up being the custodian of the history of the Irish dramatic revival. He edited Lady Gregory's Journals (1946) and wrote Ireland's Abbey Theatre, 1899–1951 (1951), modestly assigning greatness everywhere but to himself. Robinson died on October 14, 1958, in Dublin, Ireland.

SELECT PLAYS: The Clancy Name (1908); The Cross Roads (1909); Harvest (1910); Patriots (1912); The Dreamers (1915); The Lost Leader (1918); Crabbed Youth and Age (1922); The Round Table (1922); Never the Time and the Place (1924); Portrait (1925); The Big House (1926); The Far-Off Hills (1928); Ever the Twain (1929); All's Over Then (1932); Drama at Inish (1933); Church Street (1934); Killycreggs in Twilight (1937)

FURTHER READING

Clarke, Brenna Katz, and Harold Ferrar. The Dublin Drama League 1918–1941. The Irish Theatre Series. Dublin: Dolmen Press, 1979.

Murray, Christopher. Selected Plays of Lennox Robinson. Washington, D.C.: Catholic Univ. of America Press, 1982.

O'Neill, Michael J. Lennox Robinson. New York: Twayne, 1964.

———. Twentieth-Century Irish Drama: Mirror Up to Nation. Manchester: Manchester Univ. Press, 1997.

Adrian Frazier

RODRIGUES, NELSON (1912–1980)

Brazilian playwright Nelson Rodrigues was born in Recife, BRAZIL, and raised in Rio de Janeiro, where he initiated a life-long career as a journalist. When his first play, The Woman Without Sin (A mulher sem pecado), premiered in 1942, Brazilian theater was extremely conservative, limited mostly to COMEDY of manners and vaudeville. The Woman Without Sin introduced new dramatic procedures and themes that the author would develop along a total of seventeen plays. Such dramatic output would establish the modernization of Brazilian theater.

The great novelty of the play was the presentation of the life of the mind, as the delusions of its demented protagonist were concretely enacted onstage. In his second work, WEDDING GOWN (Vestido de noiva, 1943), Rodrigues would carry such innovation much further. Most of the action takes place within the traumatized mind of the heroine, who agonizes in a hospital. The script establishes three planes: memory, hallucination, and reality. Through the meanderings of thoughts, reminiscence, and dreams framed in a dry, stark context of external reality, we watch the gradual emerging of a story of emotional violence and bitter social commentary.

Wedding Gown took Brazilian theater by storm. It was produced by an amateur company, Os Comediantes, and staged by Polish director Zbigniew Ziembinski, one of many European theater professionals escaped from the war who brought Brazilian theater up to date with the trends of contemporary AVANT-GARDE.

Despite the overwhelming acclaim of Wedding Gown, Rodrigues was to be subsequently execrated by audiences and critics and banned by the official censorship. His next plays Family Album (Álbum de família, 1946), Black Angel (Anjo negro, 1947), Lady of the Drowned (Senhora dos afogados, 1947), and Dorotéia (1949) dealt with explosive themes such as incest and family crime as an attempt to explore the mythic realms of the collective unconscious. The style totally departed from strict REALISM, favoring instead anti-illusionistic devices, poetic atmosphere, the absurd, and the grotesque. The author himself called it teatro *desagradável* (unpleasant theater), for, in his own words, these were "pestilent fetid works, capable of themselves of producing typhus and malaria in the audience."

After a brief return to the investigation of the stream of consciousness in the monologue *Waltz Number 6* (*Valsa número 6*, 1951), *The Deceased* (*A falecida*, 1953) marks a total veering in Rodrigues's dramatic style. From then on he would write mostly in the realistic mode, developing an acute observation of the social milieu—the Rio society, its human types and mores—with a focus on the impoverished suburban areas.

As a consequence of his new phase Rodrigues was reconciled with the general public and the intelligentsia. Yet he continued to innovate with dramatic narrative, rejecting superficial NATURALISM and experimenting with daring theatrical procedures that enhanced his illustration of social reality. His themes and subjects did not become more palatable as he insisted on taboo topics, sensational and provocative situations, aberration, degradation, and extreme violence.

In his social dramas, Rodrigues, although avoiding direct political commentary, was undoubtedly intent on denouncing the hypocrisy and corruption of bourgeois society. Through his slices of life, Rodrigues sought to meditate on the misery of the human condition. Eventually he became Brazil's most important and influential playwright.

PLAYS: *The Woman Without Sin* (*A mulher sem pecado*, 1942); *Wedding Gown* (*Vestido de noiva*, 1943); *Family Album* (*Álbum de família*, 1945); *Black Angel* (*Anjo negro*, 1946); *Lady of the Drowned* (*Senhora dos afogados*, 1947); *Dorotéia* (1949); *Waltz Number 6* (*Valsa número 6*, 1951); *The Deceased* (*A falecida*, 1953); *Forgive Me for You Betraying Me* (*Perdoa-me por me traíres*, 1957); *Widow yet Virtuous* (*Viúva, porém honesta*, 1957); *The Seven Kittens* (*Os sete gatinhos*, 1958); *Golden Mouth* (*Boca de ouro*, 1959); *Kiss on the Pavement* (*Beijo no asfalto*, 1960); *Cute but a Tramp* (*Bonitinha, mas ordinária*, 1962); *All Nudity Shall Be Punished* (*Toda nudez será castigada*, 1965); *Anti-Nelson Rodrigues* (*Anti-Nelson Rodrigues*, 1973); *The Serpent* (*A serpente*, 1978)

FURTHER READING

Clark, Fred M. *Impermanent Structures: Semiotic Readings of Nelson Rodrigues' Vestido de Noiva, Album de Fami 'lia, and Anjo Negro.* Chapel Hill: Univ. of North Carolina Press, 1991.

George, David Sanderson. *The Modern Brazilian Stage.* Austin: Univ. of Texas Press, 1992.

——. "Nelson Rodrigues: Life and Works." In *Latin American Writers:* Supplement I, ed. by Carlos A. Solé. New York: Scribner, 2002.

Rohter, Larry. "Reawakening the Giant of Brazil." *New York Times* (December 17, 2000). http://www.stanford.edu/group/brazil/html/dorarticle.html.

Souto, Carla. *Nelson "Trágico" Rodrigues.* Rio de Janeiro: Editora de Ilha, 2001.

Luiz Arthur Ferreira Freire Nunes

RODRÍGUEZ, JESUSA (1957–)

Jesusa Rodríguez, born in Mexico City in 1957, one of MEXICO's most well known artists and activists, prefers existence on the margins of official cultural production. Director, actress, performance artist, scenic designer, entrepreneur, and committed activist feminist, this "chameleon" moves seemingly effortlessly across the spectrum of cultural forms. Rodríguez's *espectáculos* (as both spectacles and shows) challenge traditional classification, crossing boundaries with ease: from elite to popular to mass, from Greek TRAGEDY to cabaret, from pre-Columbian cosmology to opera, from revue, sketch, and "CARPA" to performative acts within political projects.

On the stage, Rodríguez draws from numerous performance traditions, many indigenous to Mexico. Constant in her productions are humor, satire, parody, and linguistic play. Her work regularly features gender bending and interaction with spectators. She chooses forms that render corporeal and thus visible the tensions among the ideological, religious, social, political, and economic discourses operating on and through the individual and collective human body.

Rodríguez trained professionally with director Julio Castillo (1978–1980) at a time when, in Mexican mainstream theater, a director ruled as ultimate authoritative voice over the written and performative text. She adopted Castillo's collaborative and cooperative style that engages the participation of the production team—actors, playwright, director, designers, and technicians. Rodríguez established, with her partner collaborator, Argentine-born composer, musician, and vocalist Liliana Felipe, her own creative space in Mexico City, first in 1980, El Cuervo, then in 1990, El Hábito and the adjacent theater La Capilla.

Evidencing her boundless energy, from 1990 to 1997 Rodríguez and Las Divas (a theater collective she founded, 1983) produced some 200 shows including sixty-eight FARCES, seventy-five "musicals," and innumerable cabaret shows. In many works, Rodríguez performs the constructed nature of master narratives, often by placing center stage women of history and myth whose images and symbolic value embody the battle to control meaning, knowledge, and truth: among them are Aztec goddess Coatlicue; 17th–century nun Sor Juana Inés de la Cruz; Frida Kahlo; La Malinche (translator/partner of conquistador Hernán Cortés); Evita Perón; Marilyn Monroe; Madonna—Mother of God and pop-culture superstar; and Barbie.

Rodríguez collaborates internationally, most recently on the award-winning *A Book of Hours* (1999) with Ruth Maleczech and New York–based Mabou Mines—for which she and Felipe received an Obie for Best Actor. *A Book of Hours* draws parallels between women's confinement and repression in colonial Catholic reformatories, their abuse in maquila factories, and the murder and disappearance of almost 300 young women since the early 1990s in Juárez, Mexico. In 1997 she received a Rockefeller Fellowship to complete her film adaptation of Wolfgang Amadeus Mozart's *Così fan tutte*.

An outspoken feminist, her playscripts, song lyrics, caricatures, and open letters appear regularly in *debate feminista*, one of Latin America's most important feminist journals. She protests against the many faces of institutionalized corruption in Mexico. She promotes the human rights of gays, women, children, prostitutes, indigenous, and other disenfranchised groups and AIDS awareness in the face of the pope's reiteration of the sinfulness of condoms. Her theater bar El Hábito frequently hosts nongovernmental organizations (NGOs), the Zapatistas from Chiapas, feminists, and environmental groups. Rodríguez speaks publicly and rallies activism through emails and speeches and placards that make it into Mexico City's newspapers. Despite several apprehensions and trips to the police station, Rodríguez remains unwavering in her commitment to orchestrating civic participation.

Rodríguez's "ten commandments" include mandates to battle the Catholic Church and ignorance in its myriad manifestations, to mock capitalism's excesses and their effects on a consumption-driven society, and to fight censorship imposed from without and within the individual. She renders corporeal the sociopolitical systems and discourses that operate on *real* bodies and generate *real* violence. Rodriguez's energy is amazing and her commitment nonnegotiable, always interrogating the nature, site, and motive of the politics of representation.

SELECT PLAYS: *How's the Night Going, Macbeth? (¿Cómo va la noche, Macbeth?* 1981); *Don Giovanna* (adaptation of opera by Mozart, 1983–1987); *The Council of Love (El concilio de amor,* an adaptation of Oskar Panizza, 1988, 1995); *Crime (Crimen,* an adaptation of Marguerite Yourcenar, 1989, 1992); *La Malinche on God TV (La Malinche en Dios TV,* 1991); *The Sky Down Below. Pre-Hispanic Cabaret (Cielo de abajo. Cabaret prehispánico,* 1992); *Goddess Diana, Housewife (La Diana casadera,* 1993); *Victims of Neoliberal Sin (Víctimas del pecado neoliberal,* 1994); *Sor Juana in Almaloya Prison (Sor Juana en Almaloya,* 1995); *Barbie and the Devil* (1996); *The Count of Orgasm (El conde del orgasmo,* 1996); *Las horas de Belén: A Book of Hours* (with Liliana Felipe, Ruth Maleczech, and New York–based Mabou Mines, 1999)

FURTHER READING

Costantino, Roselyn. "Jesusa Rodríguez: An Inconvenient Woman." *Women and Performance. A Journal of Feminist Theory* 11, no. 2 (2000): 183–212.

Costantino, Roselyn, and Diana Taylor, eds. *Holy Terrors: Latin American Women Perform.* Durham, N.C.: Duke Univ. Press, 2003.

Roselyn Costantino

ROMAINS, JULES (1885–1972)

Born Louis Farigoule on August 26, 1885, in Saint-Julien-Chapteuil, FRANCE, Jules Romains began using his nom de plume at age nineteen and legally adopted it in 1953. A prolific, successful, and prominent poet, playwright, novelist, and essayist, Romains is best remembered today for his novel cycle *Men of Good Will* (twenty-seven volumes in French, published between 1932 and 1946) and his dark COMEDY *Dr. Knock, or the Triumph of Medicine (Knock ou Letriomphe de la médecine,* 1924). Despite his election to the Académie Française in 1946, his reputation declined in the years following World War II because of his political and literary conservatism. He espoused Franco-German rapprochement in the face of Adolf Hitler and publicly championed European civilization as the only hope for the world in the epic poem *The White Man* (1937). As a result, many contemporary readers' only encounter with Romains may be the excerpts used by AIMÉ CÉSAIRE in his *Discourse on Colonialism,* where he is used as an example of well-meaning French racism.

As a dramatist, Romains worked predominantly with directors from the Vieux-Colombier school, and he looked to ÉMILE ZOLA and Victor Hugo as models. His stage works tended to fill the adventurous end of Boulevard theater, and in the 1920s he had a string of hits, of which only *Dr. Knock* has retained its theatrical vigor. In North America, it was very popular in university and small theater settings into the 1970s, and it remains a standard school text in France. Romains died on August 14, 1972, in Paris.

Dr. Knock gets its energy from its ideas and from the opportunities the title role offers an actor. Dr. Knock, a quack, agrees to buy the provincial practice of Dr. Parpalaid in quarterly installments. In the first act, he discovers that the locals rarely receive medical attention and only pay their bills at Michaelmas, which has just past. He realizes he has been conned but accepts the challenge. The second act shows him rebuilding the practice: he hires the town crier to announce that he will offer free medical consultations. Through skillful questioning and ambiguous responses, he convinces the townspeople that they are suffering a variety of severe diseases; the wealthier the person, the more expensive the course of treatment. In the third act, Parpalaid returns for his first payment to find the town transformed. Knock's reputation has spread to the extent that the town's only hotel has been converted into a hospital for out-of-town patients. By the end of the play, even the skeptical Parpalaid has been convinced that he needs treatment.

The theme of medical quackery puts *Dr. Knock* within a long tradition of French playwriting, dating back to Molière. But most critics agree that medicine is merely a pretext. Many explanations of the play's true theme have been put forth, including the notion that Knock's triumph presaged the rise of European fascism. (The Nazis banned productions in GERMANY.) But it is hard to see Knock as wholly villainous: as Louis Jouvet suggested in an essay honoring the twenty-fifth anniversary of the play's premiere, *Dr. Knock* "demonstrates and lays bare the manufacture of new needs" (1956). Knock capitalizes on the frustrations and vanity of the townspeople, but he in turn generates and shares a great deal of income with them. Today, the play retains its satiric potential in an age when the notion of therapy is dominant.

SELECT PLAYS: *The Army in the Town* (*L'armée dans la ville*, 1911);
Donogoo-Tonka, or the Miracles of Science (*Donogoo-Tonka ou Les miracles
de la science*, 1920); *Old Cromodeyre* (*Cromedeyre-le-Vieil*, 1920);
Dr. Knock, or the Triumph of Medicine (*Knock ou Le triomphe de la médecine*,
1924); *Mr. Trouhadec* (*Monsieur le Trouhadec*, 1924); *Le Trouhadec's
Wedding* (*Le mariage de Le Trouhadec*, 1924); *The Dictator* (*Le dictateur*,
1926); *Jean le Malfranc* (1926, revised as *Musse, or the School for
Hypocrisy* [*Musse ou l'école de l'hypocrisie*, 1930]); *Volpone* (1928,
adaptation of German adaptation by Stefan Zweig); *The Moroccan
Lunch* (*Le déjeuner marocain*, 1929); *Boen, or the Possession of Goods* (*Boen
ou La possession des biens*, 1930); *The Disguised King* (*Le roi masqu*,
1930); *Barbazouk* (published 1963)

FURTHER READING

Boak, Denis. *Jules Romains.* New York: Twayne, 1974.

Dunning, A. J. "*Knock or the Triumph of Medicine.*" European Community
Quality of Life Programme Project: Science, Fiction, and Science-
Fiction (November 4, 2003). http://www.fictionethics.org/aps/Paper/2.

Jouvet, Louis. "Director's Preface to *Dr. Knock.*" In *From the Modern
Repertoire: Series Three,* ed. by Eric Bentley. Bloomington: Indiana
Univ. Press, 1956.

Knapp, Bettina. *Louis Jouvet: Man of the Theatre.* New York: Columbia
Univ. Press, 1957.

Romains, Jules. *Dr. Knock.* English version by Harley Granville-Barker.
In *From the Modern Repertoire: Series Three,* ed. by Eric Bentley.
Bloomington: Indiana Univ. Press, 1956.

Walter Bilderback

ROMANIA

Archeological excavations and early documents attest to proto-
theatrical cults, rituals, and ceremonies practiced by the ancient
Dacians as early as the 5th century B.C. Herodotus, in Book Four,
describes the cult of the god Zalmoxis in which a messenger is
appointed to ask favor of the god in the name of the community.
In his journeys, the Greek historian Xenophon, around the year
399 B.C., mentions war dances with magical significance performed during royal banquets, including the miming of conquest over the enemy. The king himself participated in some of
these dance rituals.

To this very day one can see in rural areas remnants of ancient
rituals, such as the *Paparude*, the rain dance, performed in times
of drought. Groups of youths, decked in branches, walk through
the fields, splashing water all over their bodies, loudly invoking
the heavens to bring down rain. At Christmas, one can still see in
marketplaces and the outskirts of the big cities the dance of the
Capra. A group of men, dressed in bear skins, is led by a disguised
young man, dressed up with a wooden goat head whose jaw he
claps in the rhythm of the accompanying music band. Of the same
ancient origin is the *Calusari* dance popular in the province of Moldavia. Once a year, players gather dressed in women's clothes,
wearing cloth masks over their faces and crowns of twigs on their
heads, talking like women while carrying wooden swords.

Literary Romanian drama arrived on the cultural scene relatively late, though the Romanian language is rooted in antiquity.
The Romanian language developed from a fusion between
indigenous Dacian elements, Roman colonial importations,
and later Slavic and Turkish influences. However, the dominant
component of Romanian is Latin. Dacia, approximately the area
of present-day Romania, was overtaken by the Romans under
Emperor Trajan, between A.D. 101 and A.D. 106 as one of the last
Roman colonies. The Roman occupation lasted until A.D. 275,
during which time, at least at the outset, Geto-Dacian and Latin
languages seemed to coexist, the latter emerging eventually as
the dominant language. After the Roman occupation and during
the following 600 years of the great migrations, this area suffered the invasions of numerous tribes, such as the Avars, Van-
dals, Visigoths, Ostrogoths, Huns, Slavs, and others. Despite all
these influences and the long period of Ottoman rule, the Romanian language maintained its Latin character. Throughout the
centuries, including the 18th century, Romanian survived as the
language of common intercourse but lacked status. Greek was
the prevailing language among the elite and in the schools for
the children of the boyars, while Slavonic was the prevailing
liturgical language.

The relatively late acceptance of Romanian as a vehicle for
artistic expression among the cultural elite might explain the
late appearance of Romanian drama as a literary genre. It was not
until around 1840, when a group of young writers and poets
emerged and responded to the call for the creation of a national
literature, that the Romanian language attained its legitimate
place in the people's consciousness. Writers such as Vasile Alecsandri (1818–1890), Costache Negruzzi (1808–1868), Gheorghe
Asachi (1788–1869), and I. Eliade Radulescu (1802–1872) and
the poet Mihai Eminescu (1850–1889), to name only a few, were
imbued with the romantic ideas of nationhood. Inspired by the
revolutionary fervor of the 1848 Pan-European nationalistic aspirations, they began to write plays aiming to satisfy the demand
for a repertory with which to establish a national theater. The
first Romanian newspapers had already begun to appear, such as
the *Curierul Romanesc* and *Albina Romaneasca* (1829). The establishment of *The Philharmonic Society* in 1833 and training conservato-
ries in the main cities, such as in Bucharest (1834) and in Iassi
(1836), paved the way toward the development of fledgling theatrical endeavors. Visiting theater and opera companies from
ITALY, FRANCE, GERMANY, and RUSSIA influenced and inspired
local talents. The actors Costache Caragiale and Matei Millo were
emboldened to take the stage and play in Romanian, provoking
the opposition of the aristocracy and upper classes disdainful of
the national language and preferring to speak Greek or French.

It is against this status quo that Vasile Alecsandri aimed his
criticism. In *Chirita in Provincie* and *Iassi in Carnaval*, to name only
two of his many plays, he pokes fun at the affectations and social
mores of the landowners and upper classes. The establishment of
the first National Theater in Bucharest (1852), followed by the

National Theatre in Iasi, enabled the further development of dramatic literature and encouraged the production of original plays. Writers now began to see writing for the stage as a national duty; Gheorghe Asachi and the actors Matei Millo and Costache Caragiale were the most notable. However, Alecsandri captured the tone of his time best and ushered in the appearance on the Romanian stage of ION LUCA CARAGIALE (1850–1912), the playwright belonging to a venerable theatrical dynasty. Although he wrote only six plays, with his efforts the Romanian stage reached a pinnacle of Romanian dramatic literature. Caragiale, like Alecsandri before him, lampooned social and political mores with poignant sarcasm in his satires. Plays such as *The Lost Letter* and *A Stormy Night* aroused the ire of the political powers against him. He died in self-imposed exile in Berlin. Today, the National Theatre in Bucharest bears his name, and his plays are a staple in the repertory of every Romanian theater.

After Caragiale and continuing into the 20th century, including the period between the two world wars, the Romanian theater and drama developed a strong basis in Romanian culture. In major cities, such as Iassi, Timisoara, and Cluj, government-supported National Theaters with a permanent staff presented a steady repertory of original plays and translations from the best of the world dramatic literature. In many smaller cities, municipal repertory theaters played a major part in the cultural life of the city. It is during this period that Romanian original drama and Romanian playwrights gained recognition. Bucharest became an acknowledged European theatrical capital.

After independence in 1877 from Turkish rule and the consolidation of the Romanian principalities into a monarchy, professional theater companies offered a repertory in languages other than Romanian for other ethnic populations, such as Hungarians and Germans. In 1876 the beginnings of the YIDDISH THEATER were established under AVROM GOLDFADEN (1840–1908) in Iassi, Moldavia. This theater became an important cultural and educational venue for the Jewish community that survived World War II. As the Teatrul Evreiesc de Stat (Jewish State Theatre), it has remained an almost continuous presence in Bucharest; it is one of several government-supported theaters for ethnic minorities.

After World War I, theater and dramatic literature experienced an intensive surge of activity. Modeled on the French, German, and Russian drama, the Romanian repertory began to modernize. Interaction of intellectuals with Western culture became more intense. For example, Tristan Tzara (1896–1963), the founder of DADAISM, made his name beyond the borders of Romania. In the words of Marian Popescu, a contemporary scholar and drama critic, "The 1930s is one of the most interesting periods of modern Romanian theater. It is the time of open confrontation between a growing nationalism and a strong cosmopolitan movement towards European values of the day. Camil Petrescu (1894–1957), a major playwright and essayist, Haig Acterian (1904–1943), director and organizer, a

younger friend of Gordon Craig, are important for their effort to modernize Romanian theater in terms of structure, artistic profile and repertory." It is also a time when a long list of playwrights—among them Mihail Sorbul (1885–1966), Victor Ion Popa (1895–1946), Victor Eftimiu (1889–1972), Lucian Blaga (1895–1961)—experimented with modern techniques of expression and staging. Sorbul caused quite a stir already in 1916 with his tragic COMEDY *The Red Passion* (*Patima Rosie*), due to its subject and new writing technique. A play about a fatal love triangle, the scenes follow each other in a volley of rapid succession without any psychological ratiocination. Influenced by EDMOND ROSTAND and MAURICE MAETERLINK, Eftimiu spins in his *Spinning Tales* (*Insir'te margarite*) a fairy tale about an emperor and a princess in search of true love who run away from under the wedding canopy, in search of Fat Frumos, the handsome rider on the white horse.

With the appearance in 1938 of Michael Sebastian (1907–1945), playwright, writer, essayist, Romanian dramatic literature reached another pinnacle in terms of style and dramatic structure. In his plays, only four in number—he was killed in a road accident after the war, at the height of his popularity—Sebastian, like ANTON CHEKHOV, describes the ennui of provincial life and the machinations of politics and the press. In his first play, *Vacation Games* (*Jocul De-a Vacanta*, 1938), the protagonist, vacationing in a mountain resort, tries to block the obnoxious daily routines and petty squabbles among the other vacationers—without success. His second play, *A Star Without a Name* (*Steaua Fara Nume*), opened in 1944 under the assumed name Victor Mincu to hide Sebastian's Jewish identity. Mona, a beautiful woman, fed up with her way of easy life and gambling, runs away from the gambling table at the casino and from her lover. She finds herself in a forsaken little town, where she spends the night with the local astronomy teacher, who had discovered a new star, whereas she discovers a new love. However, the next morning brings her back to reality. Her lover finds her, and she leaves with him in his luxurious car because "no star ever strayed from its path"; the teacher is left to continue his stargazing. Both plays were successes in their own time. Today, hardly a season passes without one of his plays produced in at least one theater in the country.

Like Tristan Tzara before him, EUGÈNE IONESCO, too, left Romania for Paris before World War II and wrote in French. His roots are in Romanian literature as well, particularly that of Caragiale and Romanian surrealists such as Urmuz (1883–1923), B. Fundoianu-Fondane (1898–1944), and dadaist Tristan Tzara (1896–1963).

After the communist takeover of Romania in 1947, the theater was enlisted to serve the propaganda machine. More than forty theater companies were established throughout the country on the model of the Soviet theater system. Six of these theaters attained the level of national theaters. Yet plays were censored, many productions banned, and the writers kept under scrutiny.

Major playwrights, such as DUMITRU RADU POPESCU (1935–), Theodor Mazilu (1930–1980), Dumitru Solomon (1932–2003), IOSIF NAGHIU (1932–) and MARIN SORESCU (1936–1997), though abiding under pressure to the canon of SOCIALIST REALISM, found ways to circumvent the harsh censorship. Playwrights, in the best tradition of SURREALISM, succeeded in creating a kind of language that was understood only by the public, while the authorities did not or pretended not to understand. A tacit complicity between the authors and the censorship evolved that enabled many important productions to see the light on the stage. Otherwise, the permission and subsequent success of a play like *Iona*, by Marin Sorescu, would be hard to explain. The play, portraying a fisher trapped in the belly of the fish, is a transparent allegory of the nation caught in a reality from which the only escape is suicide.

Since the fall of communism in 1989, Romanian dramatic literature has undergone a renaissance. Enjoying the new freedom from censorship and closer contact with the West, a young generation of playwrights is experimenting with post-absurd-surrealist modes of expression. Among the best known are Horia Garbea (1962–), Radu Macrinici (1964–), Alina Mungiu-Pippidi (1964–), Alina Nelega (1960–), Saviana Stanescu (1967–), and Vlad Zografi (1960–); Matei Visniec (1956–), who left Romania before the Revolution, lives in Paris and writes in French. The new Romanian Theatre Union (UNITER) is also encouraging new playwrights through its yearly "Best Play" competition and the publication of winning plays. Yearly festivals in major cities give playwrights more venues to present their work. Despite present economic hardships, theaters have public funding from the central government as well as the municipalities; private theater enterprises are emerging; and dramatic writing finds an appreciative public.

[*See also* Tragicomedy]

FURTHER READING

Alterescu, Simion, Redactor responsabil, et al. *Istoria Teatrului inRomania. De la Inceputuri Pina La 1848.* Vol. I. Bucharest: Editura Academiei Republicii Socialiste Romania, 1965.

Calinescu, George. *Istoria Literaturii Romane. Compendiu.* Bucharest: Editura Pentru Literatura, 1968.

Cazaban, Ion. "Romanian Theatre: Brief History." Institute for Cultural Memory, Bucharest. http://www.cimec.ro/Teatre/cazaban_eng.htm.

Micu, Dumitru. *Scurta Istorie A Literaturii Romane IV. Perioada Contemporana Dramaturgia Critica.* Bucharest: Editura Iriana, 1997.

Popescu, Marian. *Oglinda Sparta: Teatrul Romanesc Dupa 1989.* Bucharest: Editura Unitext, 1997.

———. *The Stage and the Carnival: Romanian Theatre After Censorship.* Bucharest: Colectia Mediana Collection, Editura Paralela 45, 2000.

Stefanova, Kalina, ed. *Eastern European Theatre after the Iron Curtain.* New York: Routledge, 2000.

Moshe Yassur

ROMANTICISM

The arts in general, and not theater alone, have been swamped a number of times by waves rolled forward by the romantic imagination—in reaction to previous overdoses of classicism. The romantic movement that began around the 1830s and remained influential until nearly the end of the century could count on some of FRANCE's most gifted younger authors. Victor Hugo made a large dent in French awareness with his preface to *Cromwell* (but not with the play itself) in 1827 when he was twenty-five—and a larger dent in 1830 with *Hernani*—in this case, outstandingly with the play itself; Alexandre Dumas père won deep appreciation with *Henri III and His Court* when he was twenty-seven; Alfred de Musset with a run of *proverbes dramatiques* between 1835 and 1843, from the ages of twenty-five to thirty-three; and Alfred de Vigny remained prominent as a poet even after he wrote plays, one of which, *Chatterton*, told of the brief, sad life of British poet Thomas Chatterton, who comitted suicide when he was only seventeen. The oldest member of this unofficial club of romantics, Alphonse Lamartine, composed some narrative poems for reading aloud rather than staging, but not until the ripe age of forty-six. George Sand joined the theater romantics relatively late in her astoundingly fruitful career—her works amounted to a collected edition of 105 volumes. Honoré de Balzac also came to the drama relatively late, at the age of forty, but after a parade of some of the finest longer fiction of the century, including *The Human Comedy* (*La Comédie humaine*), a gathering of novels that continues to amaze readers and inspire other writers. These seven names wrote at the heart of 19th-century romanticism, though their works still win reprintings in a score of languages.

Not that the old distinctions between classical and romantic hold up any longer. Hugo helped drive them out of separated existence. In our contemporary theater, the makers (who include writers, directors, actors, and spectators alike) prefer their plays in mixed forms. Hugo's preface to *Cromwell* sets forth improvements he intended to bring about by mixing opposites. "The modern muse will look at things with greater breadth of vision. . . . everything in creation is not *beautiful* from the standpoint of mankind, the ugly exists beside the beautiful, the misshapen beside the graceful, the grotesque beside the sublime, evil with good, darkness with light." Hugo does not pretend he has invented a new literature. He draws on instances of mixed sublime and grotesque from William Shakespeare, Euripides, and other ancients, and despite their reputations as classicists, he shows that funny and serious have long been interwoven by literary masters.

The romanticism practiced by the seven names above and their imitators sometimes drew on pastoral COMEDY for some of their creative thinking: flirtations between lusty but easily heartbroken shepherds and coy shepherdesses, all of whom may have stopped maturing mentally long before they reached juvenility, on the understanding that children and, even more, childishness represent an innocence suited to a rural landcape. If a titled gentleman came within attacking range of the very young women's charms, he was liable to be won over by several at once, not unlike the Indian Bharata Natyam dancers in their roles of nubile maidens and in their pursuit of the god Shiva—or like the two rural demoiselles who eat up the dishonest vows articulated by Molière's Don Juan. The authors reinvented historical backgrounds and populated them with political leaders and rebels. They equipped the men with extravagant emotions and speeches, like those of Hernani and Ruy Blas borrowed in their fervor from earlier periods of romanticism. Since women in public life at that time were rarely associated with political leadership, the female roles were, as a rule, vapid compared with Shakespeare's, Friedrich Schiller's, HENRIK IBSEN's, GEORGE BERNARD SHAW's, Pierre Corneille's, Jean Racine's, Molière's, and even those of the most colorful romantic playwright of the following French generation, EDMOND ROSTAND's in The Romanesques (1894), CYRANO DE BERGERAC (1897), and The Young Eagle (L'Aiglon, 1900).

How can one interpret the word romanticism today? Does it have any connection with Rome? Any affiliation with Romanesque architecture's half- semicircular arches and portals? Any hint of Romanies, offensively called gypsies? Or Romania from where the Romanies are said to have initially arrived in the West? What about that mushy word romance? All these nouns appear to have had some bearing on what the word means and what it implies. Even one of the extended derivatives, romanesque, has at least one valid denotation, a classification of buildings constructed after the Roman Empire dominated Europe but before the gothic style took over. But the double syllable romance, apart from its Tin Pan Alley and Hollywood soundings, has too many hopelessly untraceable, often contradictory meanings, from "fantasy" to "spoken in Provence" or "sort of Catholic." It has come down to a word both too thin and too plump to be trusted. But since Victor Hugo tried to unite two warring factions, the blur of romanticism has served more literary purposes than most critics who recruited it could have guessed at. To look up the entry "romanticism" in the index of nearly any book of criticism, either a personal bill of gripes or a collection of assembled essays, is to end up admiring the word for its versatility.

FURTHER READING

Frye, Northrop, ed. Romanticism Reconsidered. New York: Columbia Univ. Press, 1963.

Gleckner, Robert, and Gerald Enscoe, eds. Romanticism: Points of View. Englewood Cliffs, N.J.: Prentice-Hall, 1962.

Praz, Mario. The Romantic Agony. London: Oxford Univ. Press, 1933.

Albert Bermel

ROMERIL, JOHN (1945–)

John Romeril, born in Melbourne, Victoria, AUSTRALIA, on October 26, 1945, has been one of Australia's most prolific playwrights since 1969, having written alone or in collaboration more than forty-five works for the theater. He rose to prominence with the New Wave drama of nationalistic and political fervor in Melbourne, his first plays revealing stylistic and thematic trends that were to interest him for many years. I Don't Know Who to Feel Sorry For (produced 1969) and Mrs. Thally F (1971) portray struggling working-class characters, while Chicago Chicago (1969–1970) and He Can Swagger Sitting Down (produced 1972) are vigorous satires on American politics. Meanwhile, Romeril contributed a string of AGITATION-PROPAGANDA (agit-prop) street theater pieces for the Australian Performing Group (APG), ranging from protest pieces against censorship and the Vietnam War to purpose-made didactic plays for performances in workplaces.

He remained the APG's principal playwright until 1980. Among his most significant works for the APG were: Marvellous Melbourne (with Jack Hibberd, 1970), a pastiche of a Victorian MELODRAMA blending historical events with present-day satire and songs; Bastardy (produced 1972), a play about racism; Carboni (1980), a MONODRAMA retelling one of Australia's formative early political events through the voice of its contemporary chronicler; and The Floating World (produced 1974). The latter deals with ex-prisoner of World War II, Les Harding, who accompanies his wife on a cruise to JAPAN (the land of his brutal captors) many years later. In short scenes, stand-up comedy routines, increasingly horrific flashbacks, and hallucinatory monologues, Harding deteriorates to the point of madness in a graphic illustration of Australians' xenophobic attitudes toward Asia.

Romeril is a much more versatile playwright than the tag "political playwright" might suggest; he has written plays, on commission, across the full spectrum of Australian theater. He has written about many aspects of Australian life and about different regions for various state theater companies, including Top End and Lost Weekend (both produced 1989) and many plays for major young people's theaters. Plays for students have dealt with the aspirations of youth, environmental concerns, and the notorious outlaw-hero Ned Kelly in The Kelly Dance, a participatory promenade play in the form of a bush dance for Flinders University in 1984.

Music-theater has been another of his ongoing interests. He wrote: Jonah (produced 1985) with composer Alan John, a play with songs about an early-20th-century Sydney identity; History of Australia—The Musical (with several others), an ambitious attempt to render historian Manning Clark's six-volume history of Australia in commercial musical form in 1988; and later Black Cargo (produced 1991) with composer Irine Vela, a chamber opera about a historical incident on the Melbourne docks. He has also turned his hand to writing for puppetry, notably with Love Suicides (produced 1997), an accomplished modern adaptation from 18th-century Japanese playwright Chikamatsu Monzaemon for Company Skylark and Playbox Theatre Company after living in Japan in the early 1990s on an Australia Council Creative Fellowship.

Romeril continues to support emerging artists and groups with dramaturgical assistance.

[See also Australia, New Wave Drama]

SELECT PLAYS: *I Don't Know Who to Feel Sorry For* (1969); *Chicago Chicago* (1969–1970); *Marvellous Melbourne* (with Jack Hibberd, 1970); *Mrs Thally F* (1971); *Bastardy* (1972); *He Can Swagger Sitting Down* (1972); *The Floating World* (1974); *The Hills Family Show* (with Jack Hibberd and Bill Hannan, 1975); *The Dudders* (with John Timlin, 1976); *Mickey's Moomba* (1979); *Carboni* (1980); *The Kelly Dance* (1984); *Jonah* (with Alan John, 1985); *History of Australia—The Musical* (1988); *Lost Weekend* (1989); *Top End* (1989); *Black Cargo* (with Irine Vela, 1991); *Reading Boy* (1991); *Doing the Block* (1994); *Love Suicides* (1997); *Kate 'n' Shiner* (1998); *Miss Tanaka* (2001)

FURTHER READING

Griffiths, Gareth, ed. *John Romeril*. Amsterdam: Rodopi, 1993.

Harrison, Wayne. "John Romeril." In *Companion to Theatre in Australia*, ed. by Philip Parsons and Victoria Chance. Sydney: Currency Press, 1995.

Hutchinson, Garrie. "*The Floating World*: Unruly Masterpiece." In *Contemporary Australian Drama*, ed. by Peter Holloway. Rev. ed. Sydney: Currency Press, 1987.

Geoffrey Milne

LA RONDE See REIGEN

ROSENCRANTZ AND GUILDENSTERN ARE DEAD

Wheels have been set in motion, and they have their own pace, to which we are . . . condemned. Each move is dictated by the previous one—that is the meaning of order.
—Guildenstern, Act 2

When TOM STOPPARD's serious COMEDY *Rosencrantz and Guildenstern Are Dead* first was performed in August 1966 as part of the Edinburgh Festival fringe, the theater world took immediate notice. Initial reviews sparked eager interest, and within eight months *Rosencrantz and Guildenstern* was staged by the prestigious National Theatre in London. Stoppard was just shy of thirty years old.

Rosencrantz and Guildenstern puzzled and intrigued London audiences. Critics recognized the play's uniqueness, honoring it with the John Whiting and Evening Standard Drama Awards. With little delay the play transferred to New York that autumn, gaining more enthusiastic reaction. It received eight 1968 Tony nominations and won four awards, including for Best Play. Since coming on the scene, *Rosencrantz and Guildenstern* has been revived countless times, a favorite of amateurs and professional groups alike.

Central to the work are the two title characters—Guildenstern and Rosencrantz—who play minor roles in William Shakespeare's famous *Hamlet*. Most action involves events only tangentially connected to Shakespeare's drama, while Stoppard's duo protagonists carry on unclear, ambiguous lives as escapees from *Hamlet*. A costume drama, the play is placed in a quasi-Elizabethan setting. The protagonists are discovered on a country road on their way to respond to an unspecified summoning. Spectators familiar with *Hamlet* realize it is Claudius who has sent for the two young men who are friends of Hamlet. But Guildenstern and Rosencrantz are oblivious to the host story from which they have been derived.

Action takes the form of a physical and psychic pilgrimage for the two. On the surface level, they follow clues leading them to Elsinore, where they encounter Claudius, Gertrude, and Hamlet. On a deeper level, however, they are grasping for clarifying facts to fill in their blank life histories. On their journey the two several times meet up with a band of traveling players—also retained from *Hamlet*. The actors are traveling to the palace to entertain and hence perhaps have firmer knowledge concerning events around them. But whereas Rosencrantz and Guildenstern yearn for some certitude in their dilemma—that is, roaming the countryside in search of their identities—the players have learned to live without absolutes. As the lead player tells them, "Uncertainty is the normal state. You're nobody special."

The lives of the two questing courtiers intersect several times with the murderous events in Shakespeare's source play, including a final scene on a boat sailing them to ENGLAND and their prescribed doom. The play concludes with the two pilgrims apparently killed off but enjoying no greater knowledge about themselves than at the beginning.

Most commentary points to absurdist drama as inspiration for Stoppard's play. The absence of background concerning the protagonists' lives and the lack of clarity regarding the meaning of events parallel the plays of SAMUEL BECKETT, key representative of absurdist theater—a type of contemporary theater defined in Martin Esslin's 1961 book *Theatre of the Absurd*. Moreover, Stoppard was a confessed admirer of Beckett.

In 1990 Stoppard completed a film of *Rosencrantz and Guildenstern*, which he wrote and directed. It earned the Golden Lion at the Venice Film Festival that year.

[See also Absurdism]

FURTHER READING

Berlin, Normand. "*Rosencrantz and Guildenstern Are Dead*: Theatre of Criticism." *Modern Drama* 16, no. 3 (September 1973): 269–277.

Delaney, Paul. *Tom Stoppard: The Moral Vision of the Major Plays*. London: Macmillan, 1990.

Gianakaris, C. J. "Absurdism Altered: *Rosencrantz and Guildenstern Are Dead*." *Drama Survey* 7 (1968–1969): 52–58.

Gussow, Mel. *Conversations with Stoppard*. New York: Grove, 1996.

Innes, Christopher. *Modern British Drama: The Twentieth Century*. Cambridge: Cambridge Univ. Press, 2001.

Kelly, Katherine E., ed. *The Cambridge Companion to Tom Stoppard.*
Cambridge: Cambridge Univ. Press, 2001.

C. J. Gianakaris

ROSMERSHOLM

It's joy that enobles the mind, Rebecca.

—Johannes Rosmer, Act 2

HENRIK IBSEN's *Rosmersholm,* called *White Horses* in the first draft, was published in Copenhagen, DENMARK, on November 23, 1886. Immediate reviews censured it for being not so fascinating to read and not so dramatic to stage. However, the play was performed in Bergen, Kristiania, Gothenburg, Stockholm, and Berlin within six months of its publication. Ibsen saw its German performance, which took place on April 6, 1886.

Ibsen had traveled to NORWAY in the summer of 1885 in the heat of a sociopolitical change in the parliamentary system. While he believed that the recent reforms in Norway were inadequate and immature, he also confessed to Georg Brandes that the experiences of his journey, the impressions he received, and the observations he had made had had a disturbing effect on him. Therefore, he decided to sculpt these contradictory experiences into *Rosmersholm.* Thus the play may be considered as an arena for debate about the pragmatic demands of the public, on the one hand, and the idealistic world of intellectuals, on the other.

John Rosmer, the only heir to Rosmersholm, has left his position as a pastor, and after the tragic death of his wife Beate, he continues to live chastly with Rebecca West, a bohemian woman from Finnmark in the far north who has had a sexual relationship with her stepfather. Rebecca supports Rosmer in his program of bestowing nobility of character on people. We learn later in the play that Rebecca had charmed Beate into believing that Rosmer and she had an affair. To avoid any future scandals for her husband, Beate had drowned herself in the mill-race. This house of tradition is visited by two local political activists, the conservative Kroll and the radical Mortensgaard. Both of them turn out to be opportunists, however, who want to have Rosmer on their sides as a means to furthering their own purposes. Rosmer gives up his Enlightenment program as he discovers himself entangled in a web of deceit. Rebecca, on the other hand, who is now close to achieving her aim, which is to become Rosmer's wife, discovers that she cannot go any further because Rosmersholm's lethargic impact on life has killed desire in her. Torn between love and remorse and lured by Brendel, Rosmer's former teacher and now an itinerary tramp, the former pastor and Rebecca choose to go the same way Beate went.

The play's dramatic force is enhanced by the uncanny presences of Brendel as well as the balance created between realistic and symbolic levels, an example of which is the subtle parallel between Rebecca's white shawl and the idea of the white horse.

The venerable mansion of Rosmersholm is an arena where the old values affect the mentality of those who dwell there. Apparently a MELODRAMA of love and intrigue against the background of serious sociopolitical changes, the play highlights the polemics of new energies: free love, sexual and political dominance, atheism, opportunism, attitudes that do not recognize moral and cultural inhibitions. Thus the play may be read as Ibsen's confirmation of the need for reshuffling of values crucial for a new age.

FURTHER READING

Beyer, Edvard. "Social Themes and Issues in *Ghosts, Rosmersholm* and *John Gabriel Borkman.*" In *Ibsen Year Book.* Oslo: Univ. Press, 1978. 9–13.

Van Laan, Thomas F. "Art and Structure in *Rosmersholm.*" *Modern Drama* 6 (1963): 150–163.

Wells, Marie. "Ghosts and White Horses: Ibsen's *Gengangere* and *Rosmersholm* Revisited." *Scandinavica* 37, no. 2 (1998): 197–214.

Astrid Sæther

ROSS, CREE IAN (1968–)

Cree Ian Ross was born in McCreary, Manitoba, CANADA, in 1968. His Aboriginal ties stem from both his Saulteaux mother and his Metis father, and it is from this heritage that his writing finds both strength and meaning. Reared in the Metis community of Kinosota and the Saulteaux reserves of Fairford and Winnipeg, Ross learned early in life that poverty was not always a choice.

Originally a science student at the University of Manitoba, Ross graduated with a bachelor of arts degree with a major in film. He worked numerous odd jobs including delivering newspapers, pumping gas, and selling clothes before first finding success with commentaries raising issues reflecting current sociopolitical conditions affecting First Nations. Whether the issue involved poverty, racism, substance abuse, corruption, or self-government, his often humorous addresses encouraged understanding to the largely misunderstood world of the Aboriginal. He used humor as a vehicle of change to expose serious issues, to entice individual intellectual response, and to encourage the formation of new perspectives to old stereotypes.

His plays, likewise, present characters with Everyman qualities exploring and criticizing not simply First Nation issues but issues relatable universally when examined in the larger, global context. Winning the Governor General's Literary Award for Drama in 1997, Ross achieved Canada's highest literary honor for his play *fareWel,* garnering the distinction as the only Nations writer to have received the prestigious award.

The plot of *fareWel* centers on how the absence of welfare checks affects a native reserve. While Ross clearly offers a critique of self-government, he is also offering a demonstration on separate ways to go about change. He encourages the non-Aboriginal to see this story not as an underlying rejection of self-government simply because the idea of self-government dissolves once the welfare checks turn up again. Instead, Ross offers to both the Aboriginal and the non-Aboriginal a demonstration that change will only come about when change occurs as a community.

His plays reflect settings and characters deeply steeped in Aboriginal culture, yet Ross lightly treads upon the spiritual distinctions of Aboriginal writing. His occasional touch upon the presence of another reality or spirit world serves only as a peripheral device, thus allowing his unique voice and native perspective to provide the opportunity to entertain, to unify, and to educate.

SELECT PLAYS: *fareWel* (1996); *The Gap* (2001); *The Illustrated History of the Anishnawbe People* (2001)

FURTHER READING

Lutz, Hartmut. *Contemporary Challenges: Conversations with Canadian Native Authors.* Saskatoon: Fifth House, 1991.

Roberts, David. "Native Drama 'Hits Close to Home.'" *Globe and Mail* (October 21, 1998): A16.

Taylor, Drew. "Story-telling to Stage: The Growth of Native Theatre in Canada." *Drama Review* 41, no. 3 (1997): 140–152.

Christine Marie Hilger

ROSSUM'S UNIVERSAL ROBOTS   See R.U.R.

ROSTAND, EDMOND (1868–1918)

Edmond Rostand, born on April 1, 1868, in Marseille, FRANCE, a playwright, poet, and man of letters, sought to revive the spirit of ROMANTICISM that characterized the French theater of the 1830s and 1840s as exemplified by the work of Victor Hugo. During Rostand's youth, NATURALISM and REALISM in the novel and the theater (in the hands of, among others, ÉMILE ZOLA in France) had come to the foreground of European intellectual and artistic life. For Rostand, this scientific and sociological focus was unduly confining; his sensibility (like Hugo's, a romantic one but also connecting back to the glory days of 17th-century French neoclassical theater) led him to create verse dramas of considerable wit, scope, and ambition.

His first major theatrical success was a fanciful tale of young love, *The Romancers* (*Les Romanesques*, 1894), most famous today as the inspiration for the long-running OFF-BROADWAY musical *The Fantasticks*. In 1897, Rostand wrote the play that secured his reputation, and which has come to typify his quest to revive the spirit of romantic, poetic drama: CYRANO DE BERGERAC. The title role of the long-nosed philosopher-swordsman-poet was written for Constant Coquelin, one of the leading actors of the day; the setting, Paris in the mid-17th century, allowed Rostand to link his work with Pierre Corneille, Jean Racine, and Molière, each representing a different apotheosis of French verse drama. The stylistic range of *Cyrano*, veering from mordant satire to

exuberant COMEDY to high romance to near-tragic pathos, thoroughly repudiates the clinical tonality of which naturalism was accused by those who did not favor it.

Rostand's next major play, *The Eaglet* (*L'aiglon*, 1900), treated the life of Napoleon's son and allowed the great actress Sarah Bernhardt to continue an association with the playwright's work that she had begun some five years earlier in *The Faraway Princess* (*La princesse lointaine*, 1895). After the success of *The Eaglet*, in 1901 Rostand became the youngest member ever elected to the prestigious Académie Française. In somewhat fragile health and unable, as a reigning celebrity, to find quiet or privacy in Paris, he moved to a country estate in Cambon. There he had the opportunity to observe the social organization of farm animals and wrote what many consider his last masterpiece, *Chanticleer* (*Chantecler*, 1910), epitomized by the title character's boast: "I stagger, / Dazzled to behold myself all drenched in red / And at having, by myself, the rooster, made the sun get out of bed." Although *Chanticleer* and *The Eaglet* have not achieved the permanence of *Cyrano de Bergerac* in the theatrical repertoire, they are esteemed, especially in the Francophone world, for the beauty of their verse and the amplitude of their sentiments.

During his final years, his fame secure and his health less so, Rostand wrote nothing else for the theater that was produced in his lifetime, though during the war he composed patriotic verse. The enigmatic *Don Juan's Last Night* (*La dernière nuit de Don Juan*) was produced and published posthumously and was not embraced enthusiastically. Rostand died on December 2, 1918, in Paris during—and quite possibly because of—the worldwide flu epidemic.

SELECT PLAYS: *The Romancers* (*Les Romanesques*, 1894); *The Faraway Princess* (*La princesse lointaine*, 1895); *Cyrano de Bergerac* (1897); *The Good Samaritan* (*La Samaritaine*, 1897); *The Eaglet* (*L'aiglon*, 1900); *Chanticleer*, (*Chantecler*, 1910); *Don Juan's Last Night* (*La dernière nuit de Don Juan*, published posthumously in 1921)

FURTHER READING

Amoia, Alba. *Edmond Rostand*. Boston: G. K. Hall, 1978.

Lloyd, Sue. *The Man Who Was Cyrano: A Life of Edmond Rostand, Creator of Cyrano de Bergerac.* London: Unlimited Pub., 2003.

Rostand, Edmond. *Cyrano de Bergerac*. Tr. and adapted for the modern stage by Anthony Burgess. New York: Applause Theatre and Cinema Bks., 1996.

Rick Davis

ROUTES AND ESCAPE ROUTES

In this play I have tried to delve deep into the issues raised by, and within, the Dalit movement. For me the most important thing is to reach out to people with what I feel about the Dalit movement and Dalit issues. . . . May be I am less of a playwright [than an activist]. But people are not interested in listening to speeches.

That is why I chose this path—writing plays. I might be derided as a didactic writer. But that doesn't affect me in the least.

—Datta Bhagat

Routes and Escape Routes (Wata Palwata, 1986) is the third major play by DATTA BHAGAT. It was written in a workshop organized by Theatre Academy, Pune, INDIA, in 1972 and was first performed in December 1987 at the Tilak Smarak Mandir, Pune, in a production directed by Sudhir Mungi. It became a milestone in both Marathi theater and Dalit theater because of its thought-provoking and mature treatment of the Dalit / upper-caste conflict and because this conflict was presented on the established Marathi stage for the first time.

Routes and Escape Routes dramatizes the conflict between three characters that represent different positions within the Dalit movement, represented by three generations, each articulating their vision of the future of the Dalit movement. The oldest generation is represented by Kaka, a staunch Ambedkarite who represents the old guards, uneducated but devoted followers of Babasaheb Ambedkar. Satish, his nephew and a college professor, represents the post-Ambedkar generation of Dalit intellectuals who are "assimilated" in the mainstream logic of rationality and the rule of law. Arjun, a radical student leader, personifies and articulates the most contemporary phase of the Dalit movement; for him the IDENTITY politics of his community is more important than larger issues of the politics for social transformation or ethics and morality. The play revolves around the issue of distribution of houses built by the government for flood-affected people. When Kaka and Arjun realize that the houses are illegally being claimed by upper-caste people, they decide to forcibly occupy them for people of their particular Dalit community who have no roof on their head. There is police oppression, innocent deaths, and utter devastation, and the fiery young Dalit leader resorts to unethical practices that erode the very foundation of the struggle. What he has claimed as an "all-out war, even greater than the two world wars" ends as a whimper, a subservience to corruption. The revolutionary act ends up as the poor fighting the poor, and the ruthless political establishment project themselves as a benevolent agency.

Routes and Escape Routes asks: What is the future of the Dalit movement? What kind of movement is it becoming? What does it stand for? What are its methods of achieving success? Structurally, the play is a series of discussions among the three men—very little actually happens onstage. Bhagat focuses on the intellectual transformation of the characters. He focuses—both structurally and thematically—on the importance of listening to another person and of being able to hear and acknowledge another person's point of view. Consequently, Bhagat does not want the mise-en-scène to overwhelm the production and interfere with an audience's ability to listen to the characters.

The play also raises questions about savage caste politics and language. Satish's wife Hema, born Brahmin but married to a Mahar, asks: "If you call someone a Mahar, that's an insult! And what if you call someone a Brahmin? Is that supposed to be an honour?"

FURTHER READING

Bhagat, Datta. *Routes and Escape Routes.* In *DramaContemporary:India,* ed. by Erin B. Mee. Baltimore, Md.: Johns Hopkins Univ. Press, 2001.

"Marathi Theatre." Mumbai Theatre Guide.com.

   http://www.mumbaitheatreguide.com/dramas/features/
   marathi_theatre1.asp.

Maya Pandit

ROWLANDS, IAN (1964–)

Ian Rowlands was born in 1964 in Porth, Rhondda Cynon Taf, Wales. He grew up in the predominantly English-speaking Rhondda Valley, but he was educated through the medium of Welsh. He trained as an actor at the Royal Welsh College of Music and Drama in Cardiff. He is the artistic director of the English-language company Theatr y Byd and artistic coordinator of the Welsh-language company Theatr Bara Caws. Rowlands has also written extensively for radio and television, including *A Light in the Valley,* which won the Royal Television Society Award for Best Regional Drama in 1999. Other writings include programs for British Broadcast Corporation Radio Education.

As a writer, Rowlands is concerned with what he calls a "theatre of ideas." Indebted to commedia dell'arte, Rowlands is more interested in a drama that discusses issues and generates debate than in a naturalist representation of character development. Therefore, his drama has consistently been antirealist, and he is known for his verbal ingenuity. Although his themes often seem whimsical, Rowlands has been consistently political in his writing. His caustic wit is leveled against certain self-denigrating and defeatist tendencies in Wales. The two main characters in *Love in Plastic* (1996), Man and Woman, illustrate this: Woman, an actress, has perfected lying about her background because she is ashamed of her Welsh upbringing, and Man has taken morbid introspection to its logical conclusion and laminated his house in plastic, only leaving it occasionally in a space suit. The play is set in a Swansea restaurant in which the waiter tries to capitalize on an invented Welsh tradition, which, however, fails to bring in the crowds. *Love in Plastic* was specifically written to be staged within an art installation created by Tim Davies at the Glynn Vivian Art Gallery in Swansea, thus illustrating Rowlands's ongoing interest in exploring the synergies between different art forms.

Glissando on an Empty Harp (1994) plays on well-worn Welsh stereotypes: two tramps live on the Thames embankment in an image that illustrates the postcolonial relationship between the metropolis and Wales. Emrys is the romantic, effusive Welshman who can come up with complicated Welsh verse at the drop of a hat, and Eric is the English-language, working-class writer who is identified with South Walian industrial culture and literature. Both try but fail to take advantage of Dora, who gives birth to a (Pan) Dora's box of possibilities.

Blue Heron in the Womb (1998) criticizes a stultifying, old-fashioned Welsh nationalism through a discussion of gender relations. *Marriage of Convenience* (1997), a hastily written autobiographical play, which was originally booked in ten community venues but which has since had over a hundred performances and won the Angel Award at the Edinburgh Festival and The Dublin Dry Gin Award for Best Production at the Dublin Festival, is a MONODRAMA that skillfully interweaves the deeply meaningful symbology of mountain and valley with the development of the character, who slowly learns to accept the bicultural nature of himself and his bilingual country. Together with EDWARD THOMAS, Rowlands has been influential in shaping the cultural climate of postdevolution Wales.

SELECT PLAYS: *The Sin-Eaters* (1992); *Solomon's Glory* (1993); *Glissando on an Empty Harp* (1994); *The Ogpu Men* (1994, radio play); *Love in Plastic* (1996); *Marriage of Convenience* (1997); *Blue Heron in the Womb* (1998); *New South Wales* (1999); *Mor Tawel / Pacific* (2001); *Butterfly* (2006)

FURTHER READING
Davies, Hazel Walford. "Theatre as Exorcism" [interview]. *New Welsh Review* 44 (Spring 1999): 70–75.
Rowlands, Ian. "Marriage of Convenience." *One Man, One Voice.* Ed. David Adams. Cardiff: Parthian, 2001.
———. "The Ogpu Men." *Act One Wales: Thirteen One Act Plays.* Ed. Phil Clark. Bridgend: Seren, 1997.
———. *A Trilogy of Appropriation: Three Plays (Blue Heron in the Womb, Love in Plastic, Glissando on an Empty Harp).* Cardiff: Parthian, 1999.
Theatre in Wales [contains information on Rowlands and Welsh theater]. http://www.theatre-wales.co.uk/.

Alyce von Rothkirch

ROYAL GUESTS

Mexican author LUISA JOSEFINA HERNÁNDEZ has produced or published some 100 plays and novels. Her most famous dramas *Fallen Fruit* (*Los frutos caídos*, 1955) and *Royal Guests* (*Los huéspedes reales*, 1958) delve into the psyches of two educated women who sacrifice their happiness to the machista mentality of older relatives. In *Fallen Fruit* the antagonist is an uncle; in *Royal Guests* it is the mother. Despite aggressive campaigns to assert their autonomy, the heroines ultimately yield. Stymied by their internalized patriarchal values, they become accomplices in their own oppression. Ironically, these limits also diminish men and in *Royal Guests* even have the power to annihilate.

Royal Guests begins as Cecilia, the protagonist, faces a forced marriage. Jealous of the relationship between her husband and daughter, the mother, Elena, arranges to marry her off to Juan Manuel, a shameless chauvinist. Cecilia detests her fiancé even before discovering his infidelity but fails to perceive her desire for Ernesto, her father. Their banter about "impossible love" and mutual address as "señor" and señora" voice forbidden passions, the Electra Complex. Delusional about becoming her father's wife, Cecilia rejects the overtures of another young suitor. Instead she begs Ernesto to keep her with him; her language and gestures are charged with sexual innuendo. Shamed by his depravity and emasculated by his wife, Ernesto refuses to intercede. On Cecilia's wedding night, Elena makes sexual advances toward Ernesto, confident that she has eliminated her rival. Tension mounts as Ernesto slaps his wife to repel her. Predictably the new marriage fails. After a disastrous honeymoon, Juan Manuel returns Cecilia to her family. In the final confrontation Cecilia admits to her father that her dream may be a fraud but fantasizes about their future. Desperate about his loss of dignity and impotent to control his daughter's advances, Ernesto runs out and shoots himself, forcing mother and daughter to share their hatred and loss forever.

Structurally, *Royal Guests* has ten scenes composed of escalating confrontations between characters driven by irrational passions. As in classical drama, they are unconscious of their tragic flaws. Cecilia resembles Electra: a woman who loves her father deeply and loathes her mother. Irony foreshadows the denouement. The threatened suicide of Juan Manuel's jilted lover, who comes to the nuptial ceremony, prefigures the suicide of the father who does not attend. When Ernesto talks about an illness that contaminates him, Cecilia thinks about Elena, not about their own polluted relationship. Isabel's warnings (Cecilia's confidante) echo the counsel for moderation of the Greek chorus. Obeisance to destructive cultural values—arranged marriages—warps society. By nature a good person, Cecilia's hatred and hopelessness debase her; she derives perverse pleasure in her misery and certain defeat. Her references to the red carnation by each place setting at the wedding banquet suggests that the "royal guests" of the title will witness her blood sacrifice.

Like the Electra myth, *Royal Guests* acts out an appalling reality: incest. This triangle of forbidden passions and petty rivalries exposes the noxious results of honoring unjust traditions. Ernesto's suicide casts off those irrational emotions. A social system that imposes abnegation, tolerates hypocrisy, and ignores incest perverts all of society. In MEXICO, Hernández implies, the powerlessness of women and the double standard of sexual morality for men and women exacerbate these morbid timeless relationships.

FURTHER READING
Dauster, Frank. "The Ritual Feast: A Study in Dramatic Forms." *Latin American Theatre Review* 9, no. 1 (Fall 1975): 5–9.
de Valdés, María Elena. *The Shattered Mirror: Representations of Women in Mexican Literature.* Austin: Univ. of Texas Press, 1998.

Fox-Lockert, Lucía. "Luisa Josefina Hernández." In *Women Novelists in Spain and Spanish America*. Metuchen, N.J.: Scarecrow, 1979. 241–259.

Krugh, Janis Lynne. "Solitude and Solidarity: Major Themes and Techniques in the Theater of Luisa Josefina Hernández." Ph.D. diss., Univ. of Pittsburgh, 1986.

Magnarelli, Sharon. "Una entrevista con Luisa Josefina Hernández." *Alba de América* (July 1989): 395–404.

——. "Sub/In/Di-Verting the Oedipus Syndrome in Luisa Josefina's *Los huéspedes reales*." *Inti: Revista de Literatura Hispánica* 40–41 (Fall 1994– Spring 1995): 93–112.

Wilma Feliciano

RÓŻEWICZ, TADEUSZ (1921–)

These are almost trivial details, but it is out of trivial details that our life is constituted.

—Tadeusz Różewicz

Poet, short-story writer, and playwright, Tadeusz Różewicz deals with controversial moral and social issues in experimental dramatic form. He has created an "open DRAMATURGY" that offers play text as work in progress to be completed by actors and director.

Born on September 10, 1921, in Radomsk, POLAND, he was the son of a minor court official. Różewicz edited a school magazine where his first poems appeared. During the German occupation he worked as messenger, clerk, and carpenter's apprentice. A member of the noncommunist resistance (Home Army), in 1943–1944 he served in a partisan unit, editing an underground journal. His elder brother was executed by the Gestapo. After the war he completed his secondary education and studied art history in Cracow. With the publication of *Faces of Anxiety* (1947) and other volumes of verse, Różewicz became established as a major poet.

His first performed play, *The Card Index* (*Kartoteka*, 1960), introduced an innovative fragmented structure that expressed postwar sensibility. His anonymous antihero's experiences of ALIENATION and loss were communicated through a radical new aesthetic that took Auschwitz as its basic premise and repudiated ideology, moral judgment, and intellectual speculation as empty abstractions. Abandoning beauty, noble sentiments, and high-flown language, Różewicz affirmed the bare facts of human existence as the only truth in a universe devoid of the absolute or transcendent. A memory play of startling discontinuities, *Card Index* mixes the farcically grotesque and the lyrical in a montage of shards and shreds, combining citations from classics with advertisements, news items, and nursery rhymes.

Subsequent dramas explore social maladjustment and marginality, disintegration of community, and artists' ludicrous position in a world of kitsch. Satirical repetition of clichés in *The Laocoon Group* (*Grupa Laokoona*, 1961) exposes the inauthenticity of art in an age of mechanical reproduction and mass culture. "The scenario of a play," *The Funny Old Man* (*Śmieszny sta-* *ruszek*, 1964) consists of a rambling speech of self-defense by a lonely old man accused of child molestation. Incapable of producing anything new (even aided by a poodle named Mephisto), the great "poet laureate" in *On All Fours* (*Na czworakach*, 1971) spends his days crawling on the floor accompanied by admirers, interpreters, and biographers.

Faced with increasing difficulty in writing plays, Różewicz has devised a new kind of script (half treatise and polemic with his predecessors) in which extended stage directions serve as commentary interrupting action and disintegrating dramatic form. *The Interrupted Act* (*Akt przerywany*, 1964)—coitus, artistic creation, section of a drama?—cannot be completed; conflict looms between the idea of the play and impossibility of its stage realization. Set amidst the rubble of civilization where life goes on after the apocalypse, *The Old Woman Broods* (*Stara kobieta wysiaduje*, 1968) is an open score for theater that invites collaboration by theater artists.

Różewicz's "poetic REALISM" reaches its high point in *White Marriage* (*Białe małżeństwo*, 1974), a body-centered parody of fin-de-siècle sexual obsession seen through the eyes of two pubescent girls, and *The Trap* (*Pułapka*, 1982), a study of Franz Kafka's sexual and familial entanglements viewed from a Holocaust perspective. Following a path leading from ANTON CHEKHOV through Kafka to SAMUEL BECKETT, Różewicz has sought out those empty spaces between events where interior dramas are played out.

SELECT PLAYS: *The Card Index* (*Kartoteka*, 1960); *The Laocoon Group* (*Grupa Laokoona*, 1961); *The Witnesses, or Our Little Stabilization* (*Świadkowie albo nasza mała stabilizacja*, 1963); *The Funny Old Man* (*Śmieszny staruszek*, 1964); *The Interrupted Act* (*Akt przerywany*, 1964); *Gone Out* (*Wyszedł z domu*, 1965); *Spaghetti and the Sword* (*Spaghetti i miecz*, 1967); *Birth Rate* (*Przyrost naturalny*, 1968); *The Old Woman Broods* (*Stara kobieta wysiaduje*, 1968); *On All Fours* (*Na czworakach*, 1971); *Dead and Buried* (*Do piachu*, 1972); *A Funeral Polish Style* (*Pogrzeb po polsku*, 1972); *White Marriage* (*Białe małżeństwo*, 1974); *The Departure of the Hunger Artist* (*Odejście głodomora*, 1976); *Theatre of Inconsistencies* (*Teatr niekonsekwencji*, 1979); *The Trap* (*Pułapka*, 1982)

FURTHER READING

Filipowicz, Halina. *A Laboratory of Impure Forms: The Plays of Tadeusz Różewicz*. Westport, Conn.: Greenwood Press, 1991.

Kott, Jan. "A Very Polish Card Index." In *Theatre Notebook 1947–1967*. Tr. by Bolesław Taborski. Garden City, N.J.: Doubleday, 1968. 131–134.

Vogler, Henryk. *Różewicz*. Warsaw: Author's Agency, 1976 [in English].

Jadwiga Kosicka Gerould

RUDALI

Although the final script is credited to USHA GANGULI, *Rudali* was developed in workshops with several other Bengali play- and screenwriters and the occasional input of Mahasweta Devi, who wrote the novel from which the play is adapted. Ganguli took the several Bengali scripts that emerged from the workshops and compiled them into one play.

Mahasweta Devi's novel centers on Sanichari, a poor, exploited, low-caste village woman struggling to survive in a rich-eat-poor world. The novel is a critique of the nexus between the socioeconomic and religious systems in place in Sanichari's village. One by one, Sanichari's relatives die, and she is unable to cry. She is so worried about the cost of the rituals surrounding death that she does not have the time or energy to mourn: she cannot *afford* to mourn. In Sanichari's village, when a member of a wealthy family dies and there are not enough women in the family to mourn, mourners are hired—the more *rudalis* (hired mourners), the greater the family's prestige. Grief and mourning are commodified. Sanichari goes into business as a *rudali*, and the novel ends with a triumphantly subversive act: she arrives at a funeral with so many *rudalis* in tow that the heirs know nothing will be left of their inheritance. Sanichari has not only given employment to every woman she can find; she has bankrupted a rich family.

Ganguli's play shifts the emphasis slightly from class to gender; Sanichari represents not an oppressed class but an oppressed woman. Ganguli says her play is about "all" of us and that Sanichari represents "women in general." Anjum Katyal (who translated the play into English) notes that in Mahasweta Devi's novel the upper classes exploit the lower classes, whereas in Ganguli's play men exploit women. Nonetheless, Ganguli's play retains Devi's economic critique. Ganguli sees the biggest difference between the novel and the play in the ending: she feels that Devi's ending is too optimistic and therefore untruthful. "Truth has to be bitter and uncompromising," she says. "So was my end." At the end of Ganguli's play, Sanichari is alone onstage: she clearly misses her only real friend, Bikhni, who is now dead. In spite of her sorrow, she resolutely decides to go on.

Rudali opened in Kolkata on December 29, 1992, with Ganguli directing and playing the role of Sanichari. It played for months to packed houses.

[*See also* India]

FURTHER READING

Ganguli, Usha. *Rudali*. Kolkata: Seagull, 1997.

Katyal, Anjum. "The Metamorphosis of Rudali." *Seagull Theatre Quarterly* 1 (1994): 5–11.

——. "The Metamorphosis of Rudali." In *Muffled Voices: Women in Modern Indian Theatre*. Delhi: Shakti Bks., 2002.

Mee, Erin, ed. *DramaContemporary: India*. Baltimore, Md.: Johns Hopkins Univ. Press, 2001.

"Rudali: Questions of Language and Audience." *Seagull Theatre Quarterly* 1 (1994): 12–24.

"Rudali: The Making of a Production." *Seagull Theatre Quarterly* 1 (1994): 25–34.

Erin B. Mee

RUGYENDO, MUKOTANI (1949–)

Mukotani Rugyendo, a poet, playwright, and journalist, was born in Kigezi, southwest of Uganda, in 1949 and attended the University of Dar es Salaam, graduating with a bachelor of arts degree, honors, in literature and theater arts in 1973. He later received a diploma in journalism after attending the International Institute for Journalism in Berlin, GERMANY.

Rugyendo has worked mainly as a newspaper and magazine editor, rising to the rank of the group managing editor at the Madhvani Group—which publishes *New Vision*, Uganda's leading daily newspaper. He has also worked as a book-publishing editor. Currently Rugyendo is a senior media and communication adviser for the Uganda Debt Newtwork—an activist consortium of nongovernmental organizations (NGOs) advocating the reduction of Uganda's international debt.

Rugyendo's artistic work includes poetry published in anthologies including *Singing with the Night* (1977) and *An Introduction to East African Poetry* (1974), both anthologies published by Heinemann in London. As a dramatist Rugyendo has published a collection of plays under the title *The Barbed Wire and Other Plays*, published by Heinemann in 1977 in the African Writers Series.

Rugyendo's drama is experimental in the sense that it attempts to grapple with the realities of postcoloniality soon after the exit of the occupying colonial empire, issues of land redistribution, ethnic animosity, and political upheavals caused by or resulting in military takeover. In the same way, the experimentation of Rugyendo's drama fits within the paradigm of manifest searches of African popular theater in the 1960s and 1970s. In his play *The Contest* (1977), Rugyendo indeed reminds his readers or performers that the play is an experiment that is supposed to encourage the participation of the audience, as he argues participation is what makes African theater popular. The play employs as its artistic technique "heroic recitation," a performance form found among the tradition of ethnic communities in western Uganda.

The Contest's deceivingly simple plot of two characters vying to win over a girl is enhanced by songs and dances well known to the audience, which encourages audience participation. The two main characters, Hero 1 and Hero 2, display their performance prowess through song and dance but, most important, through their mastery of oral presentation. Their speeches are enlivened by well-selected proverbs, imagery, metaphor, and storytelling. As Rugyendo has said in the "Production Notes" to the play, the play "attempts to exploit"—with a good measure of success— "the concentrated rhythm and magic which are part and parcel of the theatre in traditional African conditions."

PLAYS: *The Barbed Wire* (1977); *The Contest* (1977)

FURTHER READING

Gikandi, Simon. *Encyclopedia of African Literature*. New York: Routledge, 2002.

Rugyendo, Mukotani. *Barbed Wire and Other Plays.* Oxford: Heinemann, 1997.

Bantu Ndung'u

R.U.R.

KAREL ČAPEK completed R.U.R. (*Rossum's Universal Robots*) in the spring of 1920, and the play was published in the fall of that year. It was first performed by an amateur group in a provincial Czechoslovakian theater on January 2, 1921. Its official premiere in Prague's National Theatre occurred on January 25, 1921, directed by Vojta Novak and designed by Bedřich Feuerstein. It was a great success, and within little more than a year it was being performed throughout Europe and in the UNITED STATES, the first Czech play to receive such acclaim.

The story involves a corporate enterprise based on the biochemical manufacture of humanlike beings to relieve humanity of all labor. The Robots are without feeling, reason, or the ability to reproduce but perform all tasks with minimal supervision. With thousands being shipped internationally every day, this utopian project succeeds beyond expectations until several unforeseen developments occur: People no longer have to work; they no longer seem to produce offspring; and therefore humanity seems in danger of extinction. Moreover, acting on a compassionate impulse, the daughter of the firm's president persuades the chief scientist of the project to alter the critical formula of the manufacturing process in order to make the Robots more human, which inexorably leads to their agitation, organization, and revolt. They proceed to destroy all humans except the original creators of the project, who barricade themselves in their headquarters in a final stand, hoping to negotiate with the Robots by selling them the secret formula of their manufacture, which is critical for the Robots' own survival. In the meantime, however, Helena, who wanted to make the Robots more human, has destroyed the formula. All the remaining humans except one, a philosophic member of the production team, are wiped out, and he is unable to solve the Robots' crisis of survival. Then he becomes aware that two of the Robots, male and female, are not only drawn to each other but are willing to sacrifice themselves for each other. In their love he sees a new Adam and Eve, as the play ends.

Despite dramaturgical and logical flaws, the play has not only a provocative premise but also lively, theatrically suspenseful action and sharply drawn characters. Moreover, the play's philosophic issues have maintained their viability and relevance. The idea that man's greatest achievements may have the power to destroy him is a challenging one. Similarly, the confrontation of various points of view in the play regarding technology, industrialism, and capitalist commerce has an almost Shavian quality. Čapek himself found the heart of the play in the scenes of the besieged human survivors: "a handful of people await their end with heads erect; human heroism is my beloved ideal and indeed it's what attracted me to this material. . . . I wasn't concerned with Robots but with people." By the same token, the miracle of the two Robots who are to start a new human race was intended to illustrate the sheer will to live, "that creative will . . . that great endurance, that optimistic foundation of the human race."

[*See also* Czechoslovakia]

FURTHER READING

Bradbrook, Bohuslava R. *Karel Čapek: In Pursuit of Truth, Tolerance, and Trust.* Portland, Oregon: Sussex Acad. Press, 1998.

Harkins, William E. *Karel Čapek.* New York: Columbia Univ. Press, 1962.

Jarka M. Burian

RUSSELL, WILLY (1947–)

Playwright, composer, and lyricist Willy (William Martin) Russell was born in Whiston near Liverpool, ENGLAND, on August 3, 1947. One of the most performed English dramatists of the 20th century, his success is remarkable considering his background.

The son of a factory worker, Russell spent his initial school years in the English educational system's D-stream. While still at school, though, he realized that he wanted to be a writer, a desire he initially suppressed as impractical. He left school at fifteen, and to avoid working in a factory, he trained, at his mother's suggestion, to be a ladies' hairdresser.

He pursued this career for six years with little enjoyment, though it helped him to develop an ear for the speech of working-class Liverpudlian people, particularly women. His ability to create authentic-sounding dialogue and his eye for detail are characteristic features in his work.

In order to secure a career that would allow him time to write, Russell returned to school at the age of twenty. In 1970 he started training as a teacher. While at St. Katharine's College of Higher Education in Liverpool, he studied drama and started writing plays. On the strength of his early works the Liverpool Everyman Theatre commissioned him to rewrite a documentary on the Beatles. Russell agreed to the project but on condition that he could write his own piece.

The result was his first major success, the musical *John, Paul, George, Ringo . . . and Bert.* It ran for a year in London's West End and won two awards for the best musical of 1974. Its success allowed Russell to give up teaching and concentrate on writing full-time.

Russell's biggest success *Educating Rita*—a modern-day Pygmalion story about a hairdresser who wants to further her education—came in 1980. Commissioned by the Royal Shakespeare Company, the play ran for three years in the West End to rave reviews. It was named best COMEDY of 1980 by the Society of West End Theatre and by 1983 was the fourth most popular play on the British stage. In 1983 it was turned into a film that earned three Oscar nominations and the British Academy's top award.

The year 1983 also saw the reappearance of his reworked musical *Blood Brothers*. A Liverpudlian *West Side Story*, *Blood Brothers* was voted the best musical of 1983. It has subsequently become one of London's longest-running musicals.

Russell struck gold again in 1986 with *Shirley Valentine*. The story of a frustrated housewife seeking self-fulfilment, this one-woman play enjoyed a long run in both the West End and on Broadway, with Pauline Collins winning both the Society of West End Theatres (SWET) and Tony Awards for Best Actress. The play was turned into a movie in 1989.

Russell's plays draw on his personal experiences, and this gives authority to the voice of the British working class that features so strongly in his work. His plays celebrate the goodness of man and compassionately reflect the aspirations of ordinary people struggling against injustice, their surroundings, and shattered dreams.

SELECT PLAYS: *Keep Your Eyes Down* (1971); *Playground* (1972); *Sam O' Shanker* (1972); *When the Reds* (1973, adaptation of Alan Plater's play, *The Tigers Are Coming-O.K.?*); *John, Paul, George, Ringo . . . and Bert* (1974); *Breezeblock Park* (1975); *One for the Road* (1976); *Our Day Out* (1976); *Stags and Hens* (1978); *Educating Rita* (1980); *Blood Brothers* (1981); *One Summer* (1983); *Shirley Valentine* (1986)

FURTHER READING

Anon. "Willy Russell." BBC—Books. http://www.bbc.co.uk/arts/ books/author/russellw/.

Gill, John. *Willy Russell and His Plays: Including an Exclusive 70 Page Interview with Willy Russell*. Merseyside, England: Countyvise Ltd., 1996.

Goodey, Jan. "Blood Brother." *The Insight.co.uk* (July 2001). http://www.nigelberman.co.uk/feature2_july.htm.

Jones, Chris. "Willy Russell." In *British Playwrights, 1956–1995: A Research and Production Sourcebook*, ed. by William W. Demastes. Westport, Conn.: Greenwood Press, 1996.

McClellan, Mel. "John, Paul, George, Ringo . . . and Bert Lloyd? Willy Russell's Folk Credentials." BBC—Radio 2. http://www.bbc.co.uk/ radio2/folk/features/feat_willyrussell.shtml.

Gregory Hacksley

RUSSIA AND THE SOVIET UNION

Drama developed more slowly in Russia than in other major cultures. The first original plays appeared in the mid-1700s when Aleksandr Sumarokov and others began imitating neo classical TRAGEDY, William Shakespeare, and Molière. Modern COMEDY dates to Denis Fonvizin (*The Brigadier*, 1769, produced 1780; and *The Minor*, 1782), while the inception of modern drama and tragedy may be attributed to Aleksandr Pushkin (*Boris Godunov*, 1825, produced 1870; and the four Little Tragedies, 1823–1830). But the popularity of theater encour-

aged furious activity among writers even if most were epigones of fashionable Europeans. Several seminal works established the tradition: Aleksandr Griboyedov's caustic comedy *Woe from Wit* (1824), Nikolai Gogol's satirical comedy *The Inspector General* (1836), Mikhail Lermontov's tragedy *The Masquerade* (1836, produced uncensored 1862), and Ivan Turgenev's drama *A MONTH IN THE COUNTRY* (1850, produced 1872). Despite the hindrance of censorship (*Boris Godunov*, *The Masquerade*, and *A Month in the Country* were performed in their entirety only after long delays), by midcentury Russia could boast of a dynamic ACTING and performance tradition whose repertoire included a handful of major plays.

REINFORCING THE TRADITION, 1860–1898

Aleksandr II came to power as a reformer in 1855 and between 1858 and 1862 loosened bans on theater criticism (see the discussion of Russian and Soviet dramatic criticism below) and independent theatrical organizations, although the Third Department, or political police, retained far-reaching powers, and theater remained a state monopoly. By freeing the serfs in 1861, he drastically altered the social structure and fueled growing populist convictions among the educated classes. Several plays appeared reinforcing the endemic Russian styles of grotesque satire and realistic drama, one of whose tasks was to be critical of social, if not political, tendencies. These included works by writers best known as novelists: Aleksei Pisemsky's drama *A Bitter Fate* (1859, produced 1863), Mikhail Saltykov-Shchedrin's acrid satires *The Death of Pazukhin* (1857, produced 1889) and *Shadows* (c. 1862–1865, produced 1914), and LYOV TOLSTOY's anti-emancipation and antinihilist satire *A Contaminated Family* (written for the Maly Theater 1864, not produced). Aleksandr Sukhovo-Kobylin's trilogy of grotesque satires—*Krechinsky's Wedding* (1855), *The Case* (1861, produced 1882), and *The Death of Tarelkin* (1869, produced 1900)—was of major importance. This unique trio of works exploring corruption and the unstable nature of human IDENTITY significantly darkened the comic genre that Gogol had developed before him and that would transform in new directions in the 20th century. Since many of this era's plays were under complete or partial bans, their full impact was felt only later. This was especially true of Sukhovo-Kobylin, whose works were staged relatively freely for a short time in the 1920s and then again, aside from a few productions in the mid-20th century, only after the late 1980s.

Many of this era's works can be attributed to the "liberal" or "democratic" tendency in drama, also called "critical REALISM," which emerged in the 1860s and 1870s and held sway beyond the end of the century. It grew stronger following the assassination of Aleksandr II on March 13, 1881, by the extremist Will of the People political group. Although the quantity of plays produced on progressive themes was large, relatively few survived their own era. Leaving even less trace for posterity, though enjoying some popularity, were conservative plays rebutting liberal tendencies. In this period Russian drama and theater became a key platform for the public discussion of ethics and social ills. Some of the most productive writers were Viktor Dyachenko, who wrote a few plays in the 1830s but blossomed as the author of socially aware MELODRAMAS in the 1860s; Aleksei Potekhin, who excelled in comedies and dramas about peasants and lowly clerks; the prolific Viktor Krylov, whose comedies and dramas observed contemporary urban and village life; and Pisemsky, whose dramas, comedies, and historical plays exhibited a strong social conscience.

Historical drama had been a part of Russian theater from the start, but it enjoyed a resurgence in the 1860s. Forty new historical plays were staged between 1862 and 1881, among which the works of Nikolai Chayev and Dmitry Averkiyev were especially successful though soon forgotten. The genre's finest proponent was the poet Aleksei Konstantinovich Tolstoy (not a relative of Lyov Tolstoy and commonly known by his initials A. K.), whose trilogy—The Death of Ioann the Terrible (1867), Tsar Fyodor Ioannovich (1868, produced 1898), and Tsar Boris (1870, produced 1881)—is still popular. Tolstoy followed the lead of Pushkin in Boris Godunov, writing primarily in lucid, modern language and shunning direct parallels with contemporary affairs in favor of exploring the origins of historical events. Tolstoy, whose Don Juan (1862) is also still performed, was famous for creating, with his cousins Aleksei, Aleksandr, and Vladimir Zhemchuzhnikov, the fictitious figure Kozma Prutkov, the "author" of humorous verses, sayings, and short plays. These eccentric parodies, though seldom performed, left a mark that was reflected in the development of 20th-century drama.

ALEKSANDR OSTROVSKY, who wrote his first play in 1846 and wrote prolifically until his death in 1886, overshadowed his contemporaries and most who have followed with the scope and quality of his work. His family chronicles and dramas, tragedies, folklore-based dramas, comedies from the Moscow merchant milieu, and comedies from the theatrical world established the standard of excellence in most genres. He wrote historical dramas that were popular in their time, although they were eclipsed subsequently by his dramas and comedies. In the social drama A Profitable Post (1857), the provincial tragedy The Storm (1859), the social satire Enough Simplicity for Every Wiseman (often rendered in English as The Diary of a Scoundrel, 1868), and the so-called backstage comedies THE FOREST (1871), Talents and Admirers (1882), and Guilty Without Guilt (1884), the secret of his success was evident: his extraordinary ear for language, his precise understanding of the Russian mentality, and his unsurpassed ability to create compelling characters. With his insightful portrayals of women struggling with social constraints, he created more great roles for women than any Russian dramatist before or since. An advocate of writer's and actor's rights, and a co-founder of one of Moscow's first private theater circles in 1865, he helped hasten the repeal of the state monopoly in theater in 1882.

The 1880s and 1890s formed an era of growing disillusionment with a stagnant political and social culture—sometimes called "the time out of joint"—although the reflection of that in drama remained relatively tame. Some of the top dramatists were Ippolit Shpazhinsky, the author of social melodramas and historical plays; Yevtikhy Karpov, who explored life in the villages and factories; Pyotr Boborykin, who had begun writing on timely social themes in 1858 and remained popular to the end of the century; Pyotr Nevezhin, who began writing plays with Ostrovsky in 1880 and whose most successful was the melodrama Second Youth (1887), about a family torn apart when the husband tries to leave his wife for his mistress; and Pyotr Gnedich, who debuted in 1881 with In a Village and had a string of successes lasting to 1912 with some forty plays including Lackeys (1907), revealing submerged intrigues in an aristocratic household. Also prominent was Vladimir Nemirovich-Danchenko, the future co-founder of the MOSCOW ART THEATRE, who wrote his first play in 1881 but had his greatest impact as a writer in the 1890s following the success of A New Business (1890), a comedy about a man who spends fortunes establishing enterprises that invariably fail. Dramatists now were often perceived more as craftsmen than artists, and actors often wrote plays themselves. Significant among these were the St. Petersburg actor Aleksandr Trofimov (real name: Ivanov), whose plays combining satire and NATURALISM were staged often in the 1880s, and the great romantic actor of Moscow's Maly Theater Aleksandr Sumbatov-Yuzhin, whose prolific writing career spanned six decades from 1877 to his death in 1926.

The plays of Lyov Tolstoy may be seen as the culmination of the "critical realism" of the second half of the 19th century and the first major example of psychological realism that subsequently became one of the great strengths of Russian drama and theater. They embodied a depth of purpose and skill of craft that were surpassed among his immediate predecessors only by Ostrovsky. Months after finishing the first of several short didactic plays he wrote over the years, he completed his first major drama, THE POWER OF DARKNESS, in 1886 (produced in FRANCE in 1888, in Russia in 1895). This harrowing tale of the deadening, hopeless world of the peasant, in which murder leads to repentance, raised the drama of morality, PHILOSOPHY, and social criticism to new heights. The comedy The Fruits of Enlightenment (1889) contrasted the natural and useful wisdom of the peasants with the faulty knowledge of the nobility, while the drama The Living Corpse (1900, produced 1911) explored the excruciating spiritual journey of a man who could not live by society's rules. Tolstoy worked on his fourth, unfinished, major drama The Light Shines in the Darkness, another dark exposé of a spiritually inclined man besieged by a bankrupt social order and a nagging wife, from 1884 into the first decade of the 20th century (produced 1918). Although most of these plays were not accessible to the public for some time due to censorship, they were known in artistic circles and exerted considerable influence. Tolstoy's moralistic style can seem tendentious today, but its role in the development of Russian psychological drama cannot be overstated, and his plays continue to be staged regularly.

FERMENT AND CHANGE, 1898–1917

ANTON CHEKHOV began writing PLATONOV, his first dramatic work, in 1878; he wrote ten comic one-act plays between 1884 and 1891; and his first major play, THE SEAGULL, was produced, unsuccessfully, in 1896. But in truth this seminal figure of world drama belongs to the 20th century. It was the revival of The Seagull in 1898 by KONSTANTIN STANISLAVSKY at the newly founded Moscow Art Theatre that both signaled the true discovery of Chekhov as a playwright and established the style of subtle, realistic drama that would dominate much of world theater for the next century. Three more masterworks followed: UNCLE VANYA (1899), THE THREE SISTERS (1901), and THE CHERRY ORCHARD (1904). Set in the countryside and illuminating the intertwining lives of extended groups of family, friends, and neighbors united primarily by their alienation, these plays unmistakably owed a debt to Turgenev's A Month in the Country. From the beginning, controversy attended the Stanislavsky productions, which established Chekhov's reputation as the bard of melancholy and resignation. Chekhov adamantly rejected this, although he confused matters as much as he clarified them by attaching the designation of "comedy" to The Cherry Orchard, a work that ends with a dying servant trapped in a locked house on a formerly splendorous estate that was squandered by its ineffectual owner. Chekhov had proven in his stories and novellas that he was a writer of sublime understatement and psychological acumen, but he was also a master of irony, undercutting pathos and solemnity at every turn. These qualities, along with his formal innovations, are what gave him such a strikingly modern sensibility when compared even to such contemporaries as Tolstoy or MAKSIM GORKY. Formally, Chekhov brought stage speech closer to its natural counterpart by employing pauses, half phrases, and non sequiturs in a way that made the actor's intonation and behavior as important in carrying meaning as the words themselves. It is a trademark of Chekhov's drama that characters often hide their true thoughts behind the words they speak.

Gorky is frequently mentioned alongside Chekhov, by whom he was influenced and with whose plays his own were produced at the Moscow Art Theatre. But his drama is closer to the more didactic works of Tolstoy and, on a lower level, to the formulaic socially oriented plays of the 1860s to 1880s. His best-known play THE LOWER DEPTHS (1902)—about lowlifes in a flophouse—is characteristic of his output for its moralizing, sentimentality, and characters who are less human portraits than patent functions. His best play arguably is SUMMERFOLK (1904), an effective Chekhovian facsimile about aimless people passing time at a country dacha. In time, his plays came to resemble Ostrovsky's studies of despotic families dominated by patriarchs or matriarchs. These included Vassa Zheleznova (first version 1910, second version 1936), The Zykovs (1918), Yegor Bulychyov and Others

(1932), and Dostigayev and Others (1933). None, however, shared Ostrovsky's wit, insight, and craft.

The mood and themes of many plays in the first years of the new century were heavily colored by political developments—strikes, demonstrations, student unrest, the assassination of two ministers of the interior (1902 and 1904) and of the Grand Duke Sergei (1905). Semyon Yushkevich, Yevgeny Chirikov, David Aizman, Sergei Naidyonov, and LEONID ANDREEV, though not unified stylistically, belonged to a group of writers published by the Znaniye (Knowledge) publishing house, which was headed by Gorky. Chirikov (The Jews, 1904), Yushkevich (The King, 1906), and Aizman (The Thorn Bush, produced in France in 1906) touched on themes combining problems facing Jews and the acute political turmoil gripping the country. With Gorky's help, Chirikov's Ivan Mironych (1905), a Chekhovian tale of a man trapped in his own private world, and Yushkevich's Miserere (1910), a symbolist-tinged work reflecting the despairing outlook of that era, were produced at the Moscow Art Theatre, and both men continued to write with marginal success until the Revolution of 1917. Naidyonov's Vanyushin's Children (1901), one of the most celebrated plays of its time and still produced today, was a wicked exposé of a despotic, self-destructive family that echoed the national crisis. The aborted Revolution of 1905 drastically altered the atmosphere in all of the arts. Some writers, like Yushkevich, became more bitter, while Naidyonov was among those who abruptly began writing escapist material such as the comedy The Pretty Girl (1907). He continued writing plays until his death in 1922, eventually returning to civically minded topics, although he never again matched his early success.

Pessimism and decadence were prominent in the early 20th century, as evidenced in the plays of Andreev and the neonaturalist Mikhail Artsybashev, who gained fame with lurid stories and novels (especially Sanin, 1907) depicting rape, lechery, and cynicism. His drama Jealousy (1913) exposed the brutish underpinnings of cultured society, while War (1914), The Law of the Savage (1915), and Enemies (1916) served cocktails of sex, hysteria, and murder. The fuzzy topics of free love, debauchery, and disillusionment were developed to varying degrees by Osip Dymov in Nju (1909), Ilya Surguchyov in The Business Firm (1913), and Nikolai Grigoryev-Istomin in The Kedrov Sisters (1914). Olga Kotylyova, under the pseudonym of O. Mirtov, wrote female responses to this type of play in The Small Woman (1915) and The Predator (1916). Andreev stood at the pinnacle of the writers toiling in this field in part because his work exceeded the limits of shock or scandal. In the unreal, philosophical dramas THE LIFE OF MAN (1907) and Anathema (1909), he showed his debt to the symbolists. In Anfisa (1910) and Yekaterina Ivanovna (1912), he directed a coldly abstract gaze at the sordid details of family and conjugal life. In the circus-based melodrama HE WHO GETS SLAPPED (1915), which enjoyed success in Europe and the UNITED STATES, he examined the illusory nature of reality. Staged at most major theaters and by most major directors, including Stanislavsky and VSEVOLOD MEYERHOLD, Andreev was arguably the most popular playwright of the 1910s.

The rapid capitalization and industrialization of Russia in the 1880s and 1890s had created the conditions for a public seeking tame, palatable fare. This niche was filled in part by veterans such as Ippolit Shpazhinsky, Alexander Yuzhin-Sumbatov, Petr Boborykin, Vladimir Nemirovich-Danchenko, and Nikolai Gnedich, although Ignaty Potapenko, who debuted as a dramatist in 1893, was the standard bearer of this era's mainstream dramatic entertainment. His numerous plays in the first decade of the new century offered affirmative drama and comedy mixing optimism and didacticism in equal measure. Natalya Persiyaninova was a pioneering female dramatist who enjoyed success with such FARCES as The Lady Philanthropist (1901) and The Barren Flower (1903). Other writers with box-office hits were Viktor Ryshkov, Vladimir Aleksandrov, Lev Urvantsov, whose Vera Mirtsev (1915) was a rip-roaring detective story, and Yury Belyayev, whose comedies Confusion, or the Year of 1840 (1905), The Red Tavern (1911), and The Lady from Torzhok (1912) were ironic stylizations of Russian life in the 18th and 19th centuries. Also working with stylizations of the past, but with more aesthetic pretension, was NIKOLAI EVREINOV. A champion of paradox, parody, and mystification, he was an enemy of all things realistic who admitted a debt to the parodies of Kozma Prutkov. He staged many of his own short plays (Backstage of the Soul, also known as The Theatre of the Soul, 1912; The Kitchen of Laughter, 1914; The Fourth Wall, 1915) at the Crooked Mirror cabaret in Petersburg. His A Merry Death (1909) and The Main Thing (1921), borrowing heavily from the commedia dell'arte, enjoyed success in France, ITALY, and the United States, paving the way for him to immigrate to Paris in 1925. Aleksei Tolstoy, a distant relative of Lyov Tolstoy, and who is best known as a historical novelist, updated the traditions of Gogol and Ostrovsky with comedies in the 1910s, turning to historical themes after the Revolution. Boris Zaitsev in Fidelity (1909), The Lanin Estate (1914), and Ariadne (1916) employed an elegiac, Chekhovian sensibility lacking in action and distinct heroes.

A unique feature of the early 20th century, commonly known as the Silver Age and dominated in Russia, as elsewhere, by modernism, was the number of major poets who wrote verse dramas; ALEKSANDR BLOK, Nikolai Gumilyov, VLADIMIR MAYAKOVSKY, Velimir Khlebnikov, Marina Tsvetayeva, and Mikhail Kuzmin among them. These writers, to quote Chekhov's Treplev in The Seagull, were seeking "new forms" with which to counteract the naturalism of the Moscow Art Theatre. The most methodical were the Russian symbolists (see the discussion of Russian symbolist drama below) who wrote not only plays but criticism and theory. Of them, Blok was the central figure, the founder of Russian lyrical drama and the author of THE PUPPET SHOW (also known in English as The Fairground Booth, 1906), an influential revolt against realistic theater and a self-referential play in which the Author is thrown out of his own

work by the commedia dell'arte characters, and The Unknown Woman (1914), which grew out of one of Blok's short poems. Both were among the important early productions of Meyerhold, who staged many of the symbolists. This alliance also was important for the development of Russian stage design, which, along with writers and directors, began to break loose of realistic forms (see the discussion of Russian and Soviet theater design below). As Michael Green (1986) has noted, the symbolists had no intention of writing Lesedramen; their plays were "highly theatrical creations in a new style that demanded a new style of production." This held true for poets from other groupings as well and explains why, Meyerhold notwithstanding, their production histories are so meager. Of the Acmeist Gumilyov's eight major plays drawn from exotic ancient cultures, only Don Juan in Egypt (1913), Gondla (1917, produced 1920) and The Child of Allah (unfinished production 1916) were staged in semi-amateur theaters. (Gumilyov was shot by the Soviets in 1919.) Mikhail Kuzmin had many of his nearly forty sketches, ballets, pantomimes, and plays produced in clubs and cabarets between 1910 and the 1920s, but few were performed in large venues and fewer still were produced a second time. This author of exquisite verse was the first open homosexual in Russian letters, which may have contributed to the fact that his fascinating The Comedy of Alexis, Man of God (1908, produced 1914) and Venetian Madcaps (1914) have been ignored. Marina Tsvetayeva, influenced like Gumilyov by Pushkin's economy, was the author of eight extant, finely tuned plays written between 1918 and 1927, none of which was staged before she committed suicide in 1941. Her six "romantic" plays, including The Adventure (1919), based on the figure of Casanova, were set in the 16th to 18th centuries. Her tragedies Ariadne (1924, published 1927) and Phaedra (1928) were drawn from antiquity. The futurist Mayakovsky reimagined biography as theater in A Tragedy (1913), which was performed on a double-bill with the extravagant futurist opera Victory Over the Sun by the poet Aleksei Kruchenykh, and wrote the first play reflecting the impact of the October Revolution in the satirical MYSTERY-BOUFFE (1918, revised 1921). The sometime futurist and always experimental Velimir Khlebnikov wrote about two dozen, often brief, dramas, including the ironic Marquise Dezes (c. 1909–1911), observing a gathering of decadent sophisticates; Death's Mistake (1915), in which Death is defeated at a comically grim ball; and Nocturnal Search, reproducing the random speech of a police search in the dark (1921). The Hag's Children (c. 1911–1913), an epic work combining prose and poetry, reflected the creation of the world and its knowledge. None of these works violating the tenets of realism and built on neologisms and word and sound play, were produced; few were published. Also leaving plays of note were several novelists and poets associated with the symbolists: Innokenty Annensky's Thamyris Kitharodos (1906, produced posthumously 1916) was based on a theme from Sophocles; Zinaida Gippius, author of four plays, wrote Sacred Blood (1901), a symbolist reworking of

Hans Christian Andersen, and the once-popular melodrama *The Green Ring* (1915); Vyacheslav Ivanov wrote the tragedies *Tantal* (1905) and *Prometheus* (1919); Aleksei Remizov wrote *The Devil's Comedy* (1907), *The Tragedy of Judas, Prince of Iscariot* (1908), and others; Fyodor Sologub wrote *The Triumph of Death* (1907) and some dozen others; Dmitry Merezhkovsky contributed the historical tragedies *Pavel I* (1908), *Tsarevich Aleksei* (1920), and others.

EARLY SOVIET DRAMA, 1917–1930

Mayakovsky's *Mystery-Bouffe* ushered in the revolutionary age, although, in reality, it was a false start for the new era in drama because the political, economic, and social chaos of the civil war (1918–1921) following the Revolution marginalized the arts. This was a time when the task of finding food and shelter overshadowed everything else: one year after Blok died of malnutrition, Khebnikov died of starvation in June 1922 even as his so-called transrational supernovella *Zangezi*, an epic drama about a poet encountering nature and the gods before dying, was published. It was performed once in a Petrograd museum in 1923 (with the constructivist artist Vladimir Tatlin in the title role), then ignored until produced in the United States in 1986 and Russia in 1992. Another poet whose verse dramas were disregarded was Sergei Yesenin, author of *Pugachyov* (1921, produced 1965) and *The Land of Scoundrels* (1925, produced in POLAND 1967). Theaters in the immediate postrevolutionary period relied on the established repertoire with rare exception.

Vladimir Ilich Lenin's colleague in exile ANATOLY LUNACHARSKY was named the first Soviet People's Commissar of Education immediately after the Revolution. This erudite critic and competent playwright set the tone for cultural activity until removed from his post in 1929. Early in Lunacharsky's term, Lenin established the New Economic Policy (NEP, 1921–1928), a liberalization of private enterprise that facilitated the emergence of new theaters, clubs, and cabarets, a public with expendable income to frequent them, and therefore, a market for new texts. NIKOLAI ERDMAN, whose dark comedies *The Warrant* (1925) and THE SUICIDE (c. 1929–1930, produced in SWEDEN 1969) portended the crisis of the individual in Soviet society, honed his skills in this milieu where satire and topicality were kings. It gave rise to a nebulous, short-lived phenomenon known as NEP satire in which shady characters and petty crooks were alternately heroes and objects of scorn. The leading NEP satires were Boris Romashov's *The Soufflé* (1925), about a wheeler-dealer whose grandiose moneymaking scheme caves in; MIKHAIL BULGAKOV's *Zoya's Apartment* (1926), about a brothel masquerading as a dress shop; and Mayakovsky's THE BEDBUG (1929) and THE BATHHOUSE (1929). Plays of various styles reflected the complex forces affecting Soviet society in the 1920s. Bulgakov's drama THE DAYS OF THE TURBINS (1926) treated the story of a family aligned with the White Army; Aleksei Faiko's *Yevgraf, Seeker of Adventures* (1926) followed a lyrical, melancholy barber as he encountered the strange goings-on of NEP-time Moscow; Valentin Katayev's vaudeville

The Squaring of the Circle (1928) spoofed the new notion of communal apartments in which multiple families shared tight living quarters; Aleksandr Bezymensky's verse comedy *The Shot* (1929) satirized the excesses of bureaucracy. The pathos of the new Soviet hero was explored in Vladimir Bill-Belotserkovsky's civil war drama *The Storm* (1923); Lyudmila Seyfulina's *Virineya* (1925), about revolutionaries in Siberia; Konstantin Trenyov's *Lyubov Yarovaya* (1926), portraying a female communist who abandons her counterrevolutionary husband; Boris Lavrenyov's *The Break* (1927), about the revolutionary coming of age of a sailor and an officer; and Vsevolod Ivanov's *Armored Train No. 14–69* (1927), in which a White Army officer is prevented from running his train through Red Army territory.

A parallel development was the constellation of plays examining the increasingly complicated social role of intellectuals and professionals. Among these were Aleksei Faiko's melodrama *Man with Portfolio* (1927), in which a professor commits suicide when he realizes he is out of step with his age; two by YURY OLESHA, A CONSPIRACY OF FEELINGS (1929), depicting a clash between people of practical and poetic natures, and *A List of Assets* (1931), in which an actress seeks creative freedom abroad; and two by Aleksandr Afinogenov, *The Oddball* (1929), a lyrical treatment of a factory administrator seeking to increase productivity, and *Fear* (1931), a response to *Man with Portfolio*, in which a professor opposing communist rule changes his mind.

After Joseph Stalin consolidated power in 1927, the relative freedoms of the previous half-decade began fading. Thus this era is characterized by the appearance of many talented writers whose plays were banned and whose careers and/or lives were crippled or cut short: Mayakovsky committed suicide in 1930; Erdman wrote no major plays after 1930; Olesha completed no major plays after 1931; Bulgakov faced increasing problems with the censor when a ban was placed on his tragic farce FLIGHT (1928, produced 1957), about White Russians fleeing the country. Isaac Babel, the great short-story writer, had some success with *Sunset* (1928), his comedy about the Jewish community in Odessa, but his only other play *Maria* (1935), about the dying out of the aristocracy, was not produced for decades. He was executed in prison in 1941. SERGEI TRETYAKOV, who often wrote lively, openly didactic plays about foreign revolutionaries, had varying levels of success with *Are You Listening, Moscow?* (1923), *Gas Masks* (1924), and especially, *Roar China!* (1926), about two Chinese coolies who were executed by the captain of an English gunboat for a murder they did not commit. His *I Want a Child*, a communist treatment of positive eugenics in which a young woman sets herself the goal of having a healthy, intelligent baby fathered by a worker, was rehearsed by Meyerhold in 1928 but produced in GERMANY only in 1980. He committed suicide in prison in 1939. Yevgeny Zamyatin, the famous author of the anti-utopian novel *We*, wrote eight plays, including *The Fires of St. Dominic* (1922, not produced) and *The Flea* (1925), a dramatization of "Lefty," Nikolai Leskov's story about an artisan of miraculous talent that remains popular today. He immigrated to France in 1931. Emigration in the fifteen years following the Revolution deprived Russian theater of many noteworthy playwrights, including Dymov, Yushkevich, Chirikov, Surguchyov, Zaitsev, Evreinov, and Vyacheslav Ivanov. Vladimir Nabokov, who immigrated to Europe in 1919, published nine plays between 1923 and 1938, although their production histories are scant.

Some nonconformist writers associated with important literary movements—the Serapion Brothers and the Obyedineniye Realnogo Isskustva (OBERIU)—composed plays whose historical value still overshadows their impact in theater. Lev Lunts, the prime theoretician for the Serapions, wrote four plays before his untimely death at the age of twenty-three in 1924: the philosophical tragedy *Outside the Law* (1921); a fantastic treatment of the revolution called *The Apes Are Coming!* (1923); the neo-romantic tragedy *Bertrand de Born* (1923); and *The City of Truth* (1924), which is defined by Harold B. Segel as "the most unequivocally antiutopian play of the 1920s" (Segel, 1993). *Outside the Law* was produced a handful of times in Europe, but the proper discovery of Lunts has yet to occur. Better known is DANIIL KHARMS, a founding member of OBERIU, which brought together a small group of writers whose works were steeped in irony and incongruity. Their preference for brevity and nonsense revealed a kinship with the dramatic jokes of Kozma Prutkov and form the basis of what is known today as the Russian absurd. Kharms's *Yelizaveta Bam* (1928) was rediscovered by Russian theaters in the 1990s, as were plays by Aleksandr Vvedensky, most notably *Christmas at the Ivanovs'* (1938), a cheerfully eccentric tale of a family of children aged one to eighty-two who die around the Christmas tree after one of them is beheaded by their nanny. The debut of the OBERIU occurred with a poetry reading on January 24, 1928, and its last meeting was a reading at a Leningrad University dormitory in spring 1930, after which it was attacked in the press. Kharms and Vvedensky died in prison.

THE AGE OF STALIN, 1930–1953

The period between 1928 and 1930 was characterized by fierce competition among such literary groups as the Constructivists, LEF (Left Front of Art), OBERIU, Pereval (Mountain Pass), and especially, RAPP (Russian Association of Proletarian Writers), the most militant of them all and the one most closely aligned with the Communist Party. By 1930 RAPP effectively had achieved the dissolution of all competitors, although by 1932 it, too, was perceived with suspicion in the Communist Party and was disbanded itself. In its place, the Party moved to establish an official Writers Union, and throughout 1932 and 1933 a new term, SOCIALIST REALISM, began to appear in discussions of art. When the First Congress of the Writers Union of the U.S.S.R. was held in 1934, socialist realism—a nebulous concept that meant in practice that artists were expected to represent Soviet life as communist authorities wished to see it—was proclaimed the official style of all literary activity. The Great

Purges of 1936–1937 decimated the Soviet Union's ranks of intellectuals and professionals, striking deeply at every aspect of society, from the military to the arts. The sum of these events not only drastically altered the topics writers could explore but radically affected who would do the writing.

Many of the era's best playwrights fell silent by choice or by force. It is telling that Boris Pasternak spent much time from the late 1930s to the early 1950s translating Johann Wolfgang Goethe's *Faust* and the plays of Shakespeare, while a play he began writing in 1942 was left unfinished. The prose stylist Andrei Platonov, the satirist Mikhail Zoshchenko, and the unjustly forgotten Aleksandr Kopkov wrote plays but were ignored. Platonov, the author of nearly a dozen dramas, had only a handful of children's plays produced from 1936 to 1941. His major satires (*The Organ Grinder*, c. 1929–1931; *High Voltage*, 1932; *Fourteen Red Huts*, c. 1931–1938) were not produced in his lifetime. Zoshchenko wrote some sixteen one-act and full-length plays, but only *Respected Citizen* (1930), the wicked spoof of an odious Party hack who falls from grace, was produced briefly. Kopkov, the author of four known plays, was produced in his lifetime only with *Tsar Potap* (1939), a family drama in the style of Gorky or Lyov Tolstoy about a severe patriarch. His highly respected satires *Get Him!* (1931, published 1993), lampooning inept bureaucrats in the cultural sphere, and *Elephant* (1932, produced 1967), a send-up of a collective farm, only appeared long after he died in 1942 at age thirty-five during the Leningrad Blockade. ALEKSEI ARBUZOV emerged as an exception to the rule. He wrote some plays of note in the first half of the 1930s, then soared to stardom in 1939 with *Tanya*, a simple tale about a young woman whose world falls apart when she subordinates her life to that of her husband. His heartfelt dramas about people making hard personal choices and living with the consequences made him one of the most important Soviet playwrights from the 1930s to the 1980s.

The 1930s were perceived officially as a heroic age, and dramatists reflected that in their work. Vsevelod Vishnevsky's AN OPTIMISTIC TRAGEDY (1933) was significant for its pathos-laden story of a female commissar taking charge of anarchist sailors and organizing them into a Red Army unit before dying of battle wounds. Other plays by Vishnevsky employing epic heroism to illustrate aspects of the Revolution were *The First Cavalry Army* (1930), *The Final Decisive Battle* (1931), *Battle in the West* (1933), depicting the communist struggle in Germany, and *Unforgettable 1919* (1949). The poet Ilya Selvinsky, who wrote nearly a dozen tragedies, comedies, and historical plays between 1929 and 1957, had his most important success with his self-styled tragedy *The Second Army Commander* (1929), a Civil War drama that for the first time showed conflict among communists as opposed to between the Reds and the Whites. Also appealing to patriotism and displaying political consciousness were Nikolai Pogodin, Vladimir Kirshon, Vsevolod Ivanov, Leonid Leonov, and Boris Lavrenyov, most of whom began writing in the 1920s and continued prolifically through the 1950s and into the 1960s. Pogodin was a founder of the so-called industrial drama with *Tempo* (1929), dramatizing the fast pace of work in a factory; *Aristocrats* (1934), about the positive effects of forced labor on the White Sea Canal; and *Kremlin Chimes* (1942), where an avuncular Lenin convinces a reticent engineer to apply his talents to the building of the Soviet state. Kirshon, executed in prison in 1938, was a Party bureaucrat whose *The Rails Are Humming* (1928) was among the first plays to feature workers and whose *Grain* (1930) explored the conflict between two competing Party bureaucrats in a rural setting. Ivanov and Leonov, best known as novelists, plumbed the revolutionary theme in dramatizations of their own prose.

The start of World War II (called the Great Patriotic War in Russia) on June 22, 1941, ushered in a decade of changes in dramatic styles, although little of the era's output, like that of the preceding period, was of lasting artistic value. The grand heroism of the previous decade was maintained in the numerous plays written to bolster morale at home and at the front, although the "optimistically tragic" inclination was now replaced by a homespun simplicity in the characters and their manner of resolving problems. Following the war, which ended on May 9, 1945, many plays sought to illuminate the problems of the rapidly escalating Cold War. Joining the list of prominent active writers from the 1930s were Konstantin Simonov, Aleksandr Kron, Aleksandr Shtein, and The Brothers Tur (collective pseudonym of Leonid Tubelsky and Pyotr Ryzhei), often in collaboration with Lev Sheinin. Simonov, a poet, novelist, war journalist, and Communist Party functionary, was central among them. His wartime dramas *The Russian People* (1942), *Wait for Me* (1943) and *So Shall It Be* (1944) mixed the themes of national heroism and individual cares, while his postwar play *The Russian Question* (1946), about an honest American journalist who cannot find a publisher for his sympathetic book about the Soviet Union, was a prime example of drama giving voice to Party viewpoints. Leonov's *The Invasion* (1942) was another of the most celebrated plays of the war period.

By the late 1940s, state policies had nearly destroyed Russian drama. This was acknowledged tacitly in a Party resolution, "On the Repertory of Dramatic Theaters and on Measures for its Improvement," issued August 26, 1946. It included the requirements that theaters stage no less than two new Soviet plays each season, that they limit the number of "foreign bourgeois" plays produced, and that they encourage writers to explore politically expedient topics. By the early 1950s a cautious debate had begun about the "theory of conflictlessness"—that is, under socialist realism as enforced by Party bureaucrats there theoretically could be no conflict between positive representatives of Soviet society, while the introduction of negative characters was all but forbidden. This naturally had an especially detrimental effect on comedies, of which remarkably few were produced throughout the 1930s and 1940s. Valentin Katayev had several successes

with frothy comedies, as did Vasily Shkvarkin in *Child of Another* (1933), his most famous work about a budding actress who breaks with her family and boyfriend when they suspect her of being pregnant; *Spring Review* (1937), a comedy about student life; and *A Simple Girl* (1937), the love story of a housemaid in a communal apartment. His satirical *The Terrible Trial* (1939) features a crooked-mirror gallery of bribe-takers, crooks, and bureaucrats that shows the faint influence of Alexander Sukhovo-Kobylin, which may explain why it did not do well in this "heroic" age. The most distinctive comic dramatist to emerge in these years was YEVGENY SHVARTS, who evolved his own form of fantastic, fairy-tale satire. However, his three major works—*The Naked King* (1934, produced 1960), *The Shadow* (1940), and *The Dragon* (1944), all of which revile people wielding power—were produced freely only after 1960.

THAW, STAGNATION, AND PERESTROIKA, 1953–1991

The death of Stalin on March 5, 1953, engendered sweeping changes in Soviet society. The ensuing period, commonly known as the Thaw (*ottepel'*), takes its name from a novel published in 1954 by Ilya Erenburg. Nikita Khrushchev's so-called secret speech denouncing Stalin on February 25, 1956, at the 20th Communist Party conference further encouraged liberalization in the arts, which not only triggered a rise in the quality of new works but facilitated the tentative "rehabilitation" of reputations that had been destroyed over the previous twenty years. Parallel to this liberalization process was a slow reaction among hard-line conservatives that eventually led to the sacking of Khrushchev as general secretary of the Communist Party in 1964, a signal that the advances of the Thaw were in danger. On August 20, 1968, the Soviet army invaded CZECHOSLOVAKIA to stop growing calls for change in that communist satellite state. The Thaw now was over, and a new era, subsequently known as the Period of Stagnation (*zastoi*), began under the leadership of Leonid Brezhnev.

The 1950s saw the return of the personal element to dramatic literature, giving rise to what the scholar Konstantin Rudnitsky (2000) called "honest, but modest realism" and what the critic Mark Shcheglov called "plays of life." Where the pathos of the last two decades had concentrated on the needs and demands of society and its institutions, some writers now focused on the individual, occasionally in exposés of dishonest communist authorities, and the problems facing youth. Viktor Rozov, Leonid Zorin, and Aleksandr Volodin led this trend. Rozov, the author of over twenty plays, had a string of hits that were instrumental in defining the outlook and moral tone of the era: *Good Luck!* (1954) explored teenagers unwilling to live by the tenets of their parents; *In Search of Happiness* (1957) showed young people rejecting materialism in favor of spirituality; *The Unfair Fight* (1960) pitted a hopeful husband and bride-to-be against harping parents; *The Social Director* (1964) examined a man whose life was broken when he left Moscow to escape arrest; *The Reunion* (1966) showed former schoolmates who have not lived up to their youthful ideals. Rozov's lyrical and deeply moving *Alive Forever* (written 1943 as *The Serebriisky Family*, produced 1956 and filmed 1957 as *The Cranes Are Flying*) treated the theme of honor, honesty, and duty among young soldiers during World War II and was one of the single most important works of its time. His late play *Hoffmann* (1991, produced 1995) was a dramatization of prose by E. T. A. Hoffmann.

Zorin, who debuted with *Youth* (1952), nearly became the first casualty of the Thaw when his anticorruption drama *The Guests* (banned 1954, revived 1988) was attacked vehemently. This had a residual effect on his reputation for most of the Soviet period, as he frequently clashed with the censor while enjoying success with audiences. The author of over forty plays and still active in the early 21st century, he worked in the genres of comedy, lyrical drama, and historical drama: *The Good-Natured Ones* (1958), a melancholy comedy, was an exposé of second-rate scientists; *Friends and Years* (1961), spanning the years 1934 to 1961, uncovered the moral compromises of a generation; *The Decembrists* (1967) and *The Tsar's Hunt* (1974) reconsidered elements of Russian history; and *Pokrovskiye Gates* (1974) observed the teeming life in a Moscow apartment house. Zorin's most famous work, *A Warsaw Melody* (1967), showed the adverse effect of politics on personal lives when a Polish woman cannot marry the Russian man she loves. His sequel *Aftertaste* (1998) revisited the pair fifty years later and revealed a common quality of his work, the primacy of ideas over believable drama.

Volodin, who wrote over a dozen plays, may have been the best playwright to emerge in the 1950s. More than most, he experimented with form, using cinematic effects of close-ups and scene shifts and, in some parable plays, developing a fairy-tale atmosphere. *Factory Girl* (1955) showed a young woman who ran afoul of the Komsomol, or Communist Youth League; *Five Evenings* (1959), his most enduring drama, focuses on a middle-age pair renewing a relationship after surviving many hardships; *The Lizard* (1969) portrayed prehistoric tribes that ostensibly do not understand each other; *Dulcinea of Toboso* (1970) modernized the Don Quixote myth, a crucial one in Russian culture, by positing Aldonza Lorenzo and Alonso Quijano as common people ready and willing to take on the responsibility of becoming myths.

Also of note in the 1950s was Aleksandr Galich, who achieved popularity with several youth-oriented works between 1954 and 1959 before he abandoned drama and was forced to emigrate in 1974 because of the popular, straight-talking songs he wrote throughout the 1960s. His *Sailor's Silence* (c. 1945–1956, produced 1988), touching on the Jewish theme in a provincial town, caused his first serious clash with the authorities.

Although the Period of Stagnation was hard on art—Vasily Aksyonov called the 1970s "the iron decade"—a grim stubbornness could be discerned in the way the best playwrights clung to challenging topics and sought to avoid copying set dramatic formulas. They transformed the Soviet models and wrote some of the best drama since the 1920s. Edvard Radzinsky gained

fame in the West in the 1990s with books popularizing Russian history, although his lasting reputation will rest on his plays. He debuted with the first of several youth-oriented plays in 1958, but his penetrating explorations of women, *104 Pages About Love* (1964) and *A Little Bit About a Woman* (1968), established his importance. *A Film Is Shot* (1965) was his first of many plays to treat the problem of the artist and society. On the threshold of the 1970s he began writing parables using historical or literary sources: *The Seducer Kolobashkin* (1968) took off from the Faust myth; *Don Juan Continued* (1978) revealed Leporello usurping his master's place after spending 3,000 years as a servant; *Conversations with Socrates* (1975), *Lunin, or the Death of Jacques, Written in the Presence of the Master* (1986), and the tragifarce *Theater in the Times of Nero and Seneca* (1986) showed the symbiotic relationship of jailers and the jailed. *The Last Night of the Last Tsar* (1996) was closer in spirit to the popular prose of the 1990s than the philosophical plays of the 1970s and 1980s.

Aleksandr Vampilov, who drowned in 1972 in an accident on Lake Baikal two days short of his thirty-fifth birthday, left a handful of the best plays of the Soviet period. *Farewell in June* (1966, reworked 1972) told of a student who must choose between love and a university career; *The Elder Son* (1969) was a comedy with deep dramatic undertones about a young hooligan pretending to be a middle-aged man's long-lost son; *Duck Hunting* (1967, produced 1976) was a dark drama about an aimless, bitter man of no principles; and *Last Summer in Chulimsk* (1971, produced 1973) observed a teenage girl whose hopes of romantic love go awry. Of his approximately dozen one-act plays or short scenes, most of which are known collectively as *Provincial Anecdotes*, the most frequently produced are *An Incident with a Paginator* and *Twenty Minutes with an Angel* (produced 1972). Although Vampilov drew inspiration from the Russian realistic and comic traditions, he has his own unique diction, and his plays "cannot be treated as warmed-over Chekhov or Gogol" as Alma Law has noted in her preface to *Aleksandr Vampilov: The Major Plays* (1996).

Aksyonov, a novelist who has lived primarily in the United States since being forced into emigration in 1980, is the author of five plays employing satire, grotesque, and fantasy of which *Always for Sale* (1965) alone was produced in the Soviet Union. The intriguing, unorthodox nature of such plays as *Your Murderer* (1964), an "anti-alcoholic comedy" set in the tropics, and *Aristophaniana with Frogs* (1968), bringing together Dionysius, Pushkin, Shakespeare, and a poet of the 30th century, suggest their production histories may yet be written. According to Daniel Gerould, in the preface to his translation of *Your Murderer* (2000), Aksyonov's drama reestablished contact with "the great line of Russian and early Soviet satirists, starting with Gogol, Sukhovo-Kobylin, and Saltykov-Shchedrin and continuing through Mayakovsky, Erdman and Bulgakov." Also remaining within the literary tradition, but outside of the theatrical process, were Andrei Amalrik, the author of several, OBERIU-style, absurdist plays written between 1963 and 1975, and the poet Joseph Brodsky, whose verse drama *Marble* was published in the West in 1984. Brodsky was "allowed" to emigrate in 1972; Amalrik in 1976.

Arbuzov continued writing quality plays, including *It Happened in Irkutsk* (1959) and *My Poor Marat* (1965), vastly different dramas about the redemption of two men through their love of a single woman; *The Choice* (1971), whose two acts explore possible divergent outcomes in a man's life based on choices he could have made in his youth; and *Cruel Games* (1978), about twenty-somethings finding a purpose in life.

Mikhail Roshchin contributed several plays of resonance: *The Old New Year* (1967, produced 1973), a comedy about two neighboring families, one on the way up, the other not; *Valentin and Valentina* (1971), a melodrama about two teenagers engaged to be married; *A Husband and Wife Rent an Apartment* (1976), in which a married couple battle the obstacles of Soviet life; *The Remodeling Job* (1975), in which the renovation of an apartment stands as a metaphor for the renewal of human souls; and *The Echelon* (1975), about women being evacuated from Moscow in 1941. His *Pearly Zinaida* (c. 1976, produced 1986), a satire about a novelist whose wife will not leave him in peace to write, and *The Silver Age* (2001), a drama about young and old intellectuals in 1949, did not match earlier successes.

Grigory Gorin, showing the influence of Shvarts, created fantastic, satirical parables, often based on other works or well-known historical topics: *Til* (1970), drawn from the Till Eulenspiegel tale; *Forget Herostratus* (1972), based on the Greek arsonist; *The House that Swift Built* (1980), based on the English satirist; and others. His popular *Memorial Prayer* (1989) was a reworking of Shalom Aleichem's stories with a nod to *Fiddler on the Roof*.

Viktor Slavkin, the author of some well-crafted absurdist one-act plays, made his mark in large part thanks to Anatoly Vasilyev, a legendary director in the making, who staged the full-length, hyperrealistic *A Young Man's Grown-Up Daughter* (1979), which brings together old schoolmates who loved jazz and American culture and are bound by former conflicts and attachments, and *Cerceau* (1985), in which friends spend time at a dacha with mixed results. The closer Slavkin's characters clung to the minutiae of life, the farther they were distanced from meaning, satisfaction, and happiness. All of these writers' plays revealed glimpses of a society in the process of slow disintegration.

Parallel to this tendency were writers preserving the established Soviet model in dramatizations of moral, social, or political issues, although they, too, had their share of censorship problems. Mikhail Shatrov debuted in 1954 with plays about students and workers but is best known for his revisionist historical dramas: *The Bolsheviks* (1967), *Thus Shall We Win!* (1981), *The Dictatorship of Conscience* (1986), and *The Peace at Brest-Litovsk* (1987). The journalist Genrikh Borovik stirred passions with politically charged chronicles such as *Interview in Buenos Aires* (1975), on the events in Chile. Aleksandr Gelman, working in the genre of "industrial drama," had impact with *Protocol of a Conference* (1975), *Back Channels* (1977), and *We, the Undersigned* (1979).

Plays didactically exploring conflicts of ideology and conscience taking place in factories or at construction sites were the specialty of Afanasy Salynsky, Aleksandr Misharin, Ignaty Dvoretsky, Gennady Bokarev, Nikolai Miroshnichenko, and others. Significant sociologically, few had lasting artistic value. As a reaction, top directors such as Georgy Tovstonogov, YURY LYUBIMOV, Anatoly Efros, Lev Dodin, and Kama Ginkas often ignored traditional plays, staging instead dramatizations of prose and poetry. In his memoirs (*Le feu sacré* [*Crowned Fire*], 1985), Lyubimov explained he had "no intention of staging contemporary plays by authors who were distinguished above all by their mediocrity and their profound ignorance of the reality of the stage."

Perestroika, meaning "restructuring," entered the international vocabulary shortly after Mikhail Gorbachev ascended to power in 1985. His efforts to instigate social and political reform began slowly but eventually unleashed a demand for change that, in 1991, swept away Gorbachev, the Communist Party, and the Soviet Union as a nation. A turning point for the arts was the period of 1988–1989, when the censorship directives ceased to be enforced. As the upheavals of perestroika, with its policy of glasnost, or "openness," gripped Russia, Aleksei Shipenko became a cult figure by writing plays laced with irreverent cynicism and sexual and lexical freedom. Rock 'n' roll, which had been a semi-illegal, mostly underground activity, was treated in his *The Observer* (1981), *The Death of Van Halen* (1987), and *Octopus's Garden* (1990). *Natural Governance in Shambala* (1989) and *From the Life of Kamikaze* (1991) revealed an interest in Buddhism and experimental form. Shipenko became a prominent dramatist in Germany to which he immigrated in 1991, although his work has been neglected in Russia since then.

Venedikt Yerofeyev was a cult figure of the Period of Stagnation, famous for *Moscow-Petushki*, a philosophical prose poem about drunken rides on a commuter train that was dramatized with great success in the West as *Moscow Stations* in the 1990s. His wicked tragedy *Walpurgis Night, or, the Steps of the Commodore* (1985, produced 1989) depicted an asylum in which all of the inmates die.

A trio of women, Lyudmila Petrushevskaya, Lyudmila Razumovskaya, and Nina Sadur, bridged the gap dividing the Period of Stagnation from the new independent Russia that emerged after Boris Yeltsin became the first Russian president in 1991. Petrushevskaya, a short-story writer who had trouble being published, wrote some of the most resonant plays—often in one act—of the 1970s and 1980s: *Music Lessons* (1973, produced 1978), *Cinzano* (1973, produced 1978), *Love* (1974, produced 1981), and *Three Girls in Blue* (1980, produced 1985), among them. Harsh, if not cynical, in her plots dissecting the trivia of daily life and usually focusing on the plight of women, she employed a natural diction that prompted admirers to call her a poet of authenticity, while detractors accused her of recording conversations overheard in public toilets.

Razumovskaya was almost merciless in her exploration of women whose escape routes were cut. *Dear Yelena Sergeyevna* (1980), about a schoolteacher driven to suicide by corrupt students, her relentless modern version of *Medea* (1981, produced 1989), and *Your Sister and Captive* (1990, produced in FINLAND 1994), a reconsideration of the duel between Mary, Queen of Scots and Elizabeth I, were compelling modern tragedies. *St. Vladimir Square* (1994), the rocky love story of two aging, forgotten people, and *Homeward* (1995), about dark and light angels among eight children, moved away from the classical catharsis of her earlier work.

Sadur's short plays delved into mystical worlds inhabited by weirdos, fiends, and lowlifes: *The Eccentric Woman* (1982, produced 1987) observes two crotchety hags in a potato field; *Ride On* (1983, produced 1987) pits a suicidal man against an abusive train engineer who will not run his train over him; *The Power of Hair* (1984) records the conversations of a man's individual strands of hair as they observe his every move. Increasingly, Sadur wrote full-length original plays based on classical Russian sources, usually including evil spirits as key characters. These included *Devilish Delights* (also known as *Pannochka*, 1986), based on Gogol's "Viy," a supernatural tale of witches and demons in a church; *Cathedral Folk* (1992), based loosely on Nikolai Leskov's chronicle about the flawed inhabitants of a religious community; and *Brother Chichikov* (1996), a reworking of Gogol's *Dead Souls* that posits Chichikov as a Russian immigrant encouraged by a she-devil to return home to a country she assures him has changed.

NEW RUSSIAN DRAMA, 1991–PRESENT

The collapse of the Soviet infrastructure in the late 1980s and early 1990s, followed by unprecedented historical disclosures and rapid social change, briefly eclipsed the power of art to shock or entertain. People stayed home from theaters in droves to watch the high drama of history unfolding on television while the country's economic system ground to a halt. Meanwhile, paralysis set in among playwrights and critics of the older generation, most of whom had dreamed of freedom but did not know how to respond when it arrived. Some, like Gelman and Roshchin, ceased writing for years. Petrushevskaya returned to writing prose, now that she could be published. Shipenko emigrated. This situation was exacerbated as theaters raced to rediscover a century of neglected drama and patently ignored contemporary writers. Thus arose the great myth of the post-Soviet period, repeated obtusely into the early 21st century, that no one was writing plays of value.

In fact, many new writers appeared in the late 1980s, many more in the 1990s. Some, such as Nikolai Kolyada, Mikhail Ugarov, Yelena Gremina, Olga Mukhina, and Maksim Kurochkin, were destined to have substantial impact. Before that happened,

several plays entered the public consciousness from various sources. Two of Aleksandr Solzhenitsyn's four plays written between 1951 and 1960 debuted onstage: *The Love-Girl and the Innocent* (later titled *The Republic of Labor*, 1954, produced 1991) and *The Victors' Feast* (1951, produced 1995), a "comedy" about anti-Stalin sentiment in the army during World War II. The novelist and screenwriter Friedrich Gorenstein, living as an immigrant in Germany from 1980 to his death in 2002, contributed *Infanticide* (1985, produced 1991), a historical drama about Peter the Great's murder of his son. Sergei Kokovkin, an actor whose *Five Corners* (1981) established his reputation, had success with *Come to Me* (1989), a mystical drama about a mother whose daughter died at birth, and *The Simpleton* (1968, produced 1994), a parable about power, fear, deception, and freedom set in a theater. A pair of writers in their twenties debuted with two of the biggest hits of the time: Daniil Gink's *Bald/Brunet* (1991) observed the battles of an aging musician with his scornful, inner voice; Aleksei Burykin's *Nijinsky* (1993) offered a poetic meditation on the nature of genius and art.

By mid-decade, the gap between those writing and those claiming nothing was being written had grown enormous. Aleksandr Galin, who had huge success with *Retro* (1981), about lonely aging people, and *Stars in the Morning Sky* (1987), about prostitutes during the 1980 Moscow Olympic Games, updated the traditional genre of Soviet social drama with comedies depicting the clash of Russian and foreign cultures. *Sorry* (1992) brought a middle-aged man back to his former sweetheart in Moscow from emigration in Israel; *The Title* (1993) depicted a gold-digging Russian girl who marries an unsuspecting Italian; *Anomaly* (1997) examined puppeteers encountering Russian mafiosi who are propped up by foreigners; *The Competition* (1999) described a contest for Russian girls hoping to work in Singapore. Kolyada, a former actor who wrote his first play in 1986, had written thirty-seven by 1994 (sixty-eight by the year 2000), by which time he was famous not only in Russia but in Europe. In *Murlin Murlo* (1990), *We are Riding, Riding, Riding to Distant Lands* (1996), and *Go Away, Go Away* (1999), he explored people struggling with poverty, loneliness, and disillusionment. Within that atmospheric field he was among the first Russian playwrights to deal with homosexuality in *The Slingshot* (1993), about a war veteran abandoned by his mother, and *The Oginski Polonaise* (1994), in which a woman returns to visit Russia after immigrating to the United States. A tireless editor and educator, Kolyada has conducted an influential playwriting course in his hometown of Yekaterinburg since 1994. Several of his students have achieved international acclaim, including Oleg Bogayev with *The Russian National Postal Service* (1997), about a lonely pensioner hallucinating about meetings with historical figures, and Vasily Sigarev, whose *Plasticene* (2001), examining the violence and homosexuality a schoolboy encounters, and *Black Milk* (2002), portraying a bickering pair of con artists at a commuter train station, have had success in ENGLAND.

Nadezhda Ptushkina had written some fifty plays before her first, *By the Light of Others' Candles* (1995), a tightly woven TRAGI-COMEDY pitting an aging literary critic against a carefree young woman, was produced. Her treatment of the biblical Rachel-Leah story, *The Little Lamb* (1996), catapulted her to stardom, which she has maintained with slick, titillating melodramas about the difficulties women face. Her *As She Lay Dying* (1998), a comedy of errors about a lonely middle-aged woman and her cantankerous old mother, was performed in over fifty Russian theaters in 2001. Others striking a nerve were Stepan Lobozyorov, whose comedy *Family Portrait with Stranger* (1992), about strife breaking out in a home when a stranger enters it, ran in forty-five Russian theaters in 1997; Aleksei Slapovsky, whose *The Little Cherry Orchard* (1993) spoofed the Russian underworld with a nod to Chekhov; and Pyotr Gladilin, whose plays invariably employ the fantastic, as in the tragicomic *The Moth* (2003), where a teenage soldier turns into a woman in order to avoid combat.

Gremina, who wrote her first play in 1984, broke through with *Behind the Mirror* (1994), a study of Catherine the Great falling in love with a young man at the age of fifty, and *The Sakhalin Wife* (1996), the account of prisoners on Sakhalin Island before a visit by Chekhov. Ugarov is the author of sensitive, witty plays that show a deep love for words and are often set in the past. *Doves* (1988, produced 1997) examined a young monk who became one of the False Dmitrys in the 17th century; *The Newspaper "Russian Invalid," Dated July 18 . . .* (1994) portrayed a man in prerevolutionary times who preferred not to leave his apartment; *Deadbeat* (1995) was an opaque, lyrical piece revealing secrets about a constellation of people; *The Green Cheeks of April* (1994, produced 1999) comically observed Lenin in the Swiss countryside before the Revolution. Ugarov's breakthrough was *Oblomov* (2002), an original play reinterpreting the 19th-century novel by Ivan Goncharov. In 2000, the husband and wife Gremina and Ugarov opened Teatr.doc, a playhouse that showcases the genre of verbatim or DOCUMENTARY DRAMA. Its first significant success was Ivan Vyrypaev's *Oxygen* (2002), a male-female dialogue about people seeking breathing room in the modern world, which quickly attracted attention throughout Europe.

In the late 1990s, the gap between popular and critical acceptance began closing. Instrumental in that development were Mukhina, Yevgeny Grishkovets, and Kurochkin. Mukhina's *Tanya-Tanya* (1996), a poetic, dreamy piece about loneliness and sexual energy running amok at a countryside dacha, was a watershed for marking the debut of a major writer and generating a groundswell of opinion refuting the myth that no one was writing plays. Her next work, *YoU* (1997), whose title punned on the Russian letter "yu" and the English personal pronoun, confirmed the presence of a significant new talent. This ambitious, enigmatic work observed the interaction of several generations of urban dwellers as an unidentified war raged around them. Grishkovets's *How I Ate a Dog* (1997), a monologue about a man's service in the navy, quickly made him something of a pop star.

Subsequent monologues about inept, adorable young men, including *Simultaneously* (1998) and *Dreadnoughts* (2001), about a man's fascination with battleships, developed his self-proclaimed genre of "new sentimentalism." He wrote *The Notes of a Russian Traveler* (1999), *Winter* (2000), about two lonely soldiers sent on a mission into the woods, and *Planet* (2001), about a man who cannot make contact with the woman he loves, for two-actor casts. Kurochkin, a native of Kiev who lives in Moscow and writes in Russian, burst onto the scene with *Stalowa Wola* (1998, produced 2001), the winner of the prestigious Russian Anti-Booker award for experimental drama in 1998. This unorthodox play, set near the Polish location of the title, identified Kurochkin's key characteristics: experimentation with anachronisms and cross-cultural themes in the form of epic myths. His *Kitchen* (2000), a poetic, phantasmagoric, and complex historical stew joining modern Russians and the heroes of the Nibelungenlied, was the most hotly debated drama of the post-Soviet period. Author of over a dozen plays, he has creatively adapted works by others: *Imago* (2002) recast GEORGE BERNARD SHAW's PYGMALION as a tale of a dump-dwelling woman overwhelming a pompous professor; *In the Retina* (2002) transformed a story by Sigizmund Khrzhizhanovsky about a man who becomes lost in the retina of his sweetheart's eye.

The opening of the Playwright and Director Center with Yelena Isayeva's biblical-based verse tragedy *Judith* (1998) marked a turning point, for now there was a venue dedicated to developing new writing. Run by veterans Roshchin and Aleksei Kazantsev, who established his reputation with the youth and family dramas *Old Home* (1978) and *Anton and Others* (1982), the Center helped launch many noteworthy playwrights, Sigarev, Kurochkin, and Ugarov among them. A production here of MARK RAVENHILL's *Shopping and Fucking* was of major importance. Others occasionally associated with the Center were Kseniya Dragunskaya, whose *The Latest News in Menswear* (1998), *The Sensation of a Beard* (2002), and *The Apple Thief* (2003) were atmospheric looks at women's experiences; and the Presnyakov Brothers, Oleg and Vladimir, whose *Terrorism* (2002), about the source of violence in society, and *Captive Spirits* (2003), an ironic comedy about the poets Aleksandr Blok and Andrei Bely, signaled the appearance of a new dramatic voice.

Several noteworthy writers remained outside the mainstream. Mikhail Volokhov, a Paris resident since the 1980s, delved into homosexuality, AIDS, drugs, and cannibalism in texts replete with obscenities, one of the last taboos in Russian artistic culture. His *Playing Dead Man's Bluff* (1988, produced 1994) and *The Great Comforter* (1996) were staged in Russia. The novelist Vladimir Sorokin plumbed similar territory in *Dismorphomania* (1995), a *Romeo and Juliet* takeoff set in an asylum, and *Dostoevsky-Trip* (1999), in which addicts pop pills named after Russian writers and have hallucinations based on their works. His *Pel'meny* (1990) was one of several works forming the basis for Lev Dodin's famous production *Claustrophobia* (1994).

Viktor Korkiya revived the rich tradition of verse plays based on historical or literary myths in *The Mystery Man, or, I Am Poor Soso Dzhugashivili* (1988), a farce about Stalin and his chief of the secret police Lavrenty Beria, and the lyrical *Don Quixote and Sancho Panza on the Island of Taganrog* (2001), observing mutations of Miguel de Cervantes's characters in Chekhov's hometown. The AVANT-GARDE director Klim (pseudonym of Vladimir Klimenko) imaginatively reworked *Romeo and Juliet* as *Juliet and Her Romeo* (1999) and the fictions of Carlos Castaneda as a searing hymn to the transformational powers of theater in *The Active Side of Endlessness* (2001).

[*See also* Futurism, Russian]

FURTHER READING

Freedman, John. *Moscow Performances: The New Russian Theater 1991–1996.* Amsterdam: Harwood Acad. Pub., 1997.

Green, Michael. *The Russian Symbolist Theatre.* Ann Arbor, Mich.: Ardis, 1986.

Kasack, Wolfgang. *Dictionary of Russian Literature Since 1917.* Tr. by Maria Carlson and Jan T. Hedges. Bibliographical Revision by Rebecca Atack. New York: Columbia Univ. Press, 1988.

Law, Alma H., and C. Peter Goslett, eds. *Soviet Plays in Translation. An Annotated Bibliography.* New York: Graduate School and University Center of the City Univ. of New York, 1981.

Leach, Robert, and Victor Borovsky, eds. *A History of Russian Theatre.* Cambridge: Cambridge Univ. Press, 1999.

Rudnitsky, Konstantin. *Russian and Soviet Theatre: Tradition and the Avant-Garde.* Tr. by Roxane Permar. Ed. by Lesley Milne. London: Thames & Hudson, 2000.

Russell, Robert. *Russian Drama of the Revolutionary Period.* Totowa, N.J.: Barnes & Noble, 1988.

Segel, Harol B. *Twentieth-Century Russian Drama from Gorky to the Present.* Rev. ed. New York: Performing Arts Journal Pubs., 1993.

Slonim, Marc. *Russian Theater from the Empire to the Soviets.* New York: Collier, 1961.

Terras, Victor, ed. *Handbook of Russian Literature.* New Haven, Conn.: Yale Univ. Press, 1990.

Varneke, B. V. *History of the Russian Theatre, Seventeenth Through Nineteenth Century.* Tr. by Boris Brasol. Rev. and ed. by Belle Martin. 1951. New York: Hafner, 1971.

Zelinsky, Bodo, ed. *Das russische Drama* [The Russian drama]. Dusseldorf: Bagel, 1986.

John Freedman

DRAMATIC CRITICISM

There was little in the way of dramatic criticism in Russia before the late 19th century. The abolition of the Imperial Theatre Monopoly in 1882 gave rise to a proliferation of independent theaters and drama productions, one consequence of which was the appearance of the specialized theatrical journal. The late 19th century also saw the arrival of the professional drama critic, the way being led, during the 1880s, by Aleksandr Bazhenov and Apollon Grigor'yev, the latter editing the first magazine devoted exclusively to the theater, *Antrakt* (*Intermission*). Another leading figure was Sergei Flyorov, who led an assault on the old repertoire of the Imperial Maly Theatre and spoke out for the new naturalist drama. In this he was supported by Nikolai Efros, who published monographs on productions of ANTON CHEKHOV and MAKSIM GORKY at the MOSCOW ART THEATRE. Another important figure at the beginning of the 20th century was Aleksandr Kugel, who edited the magazine *Teatr i iskusstvo* (*Theatre and Art*) and who championed the symbolist drama, which was displacing the NATURALISM of dramatists such as Gorky.

After the revolution, the Communist Party took the theater and the role of the dramatic critic very seriously. It organized theatrical "sections" within government-controlled artistic organizations such as NARKOMPROS (an acronym for the People's Commissariat of Enlightenment), which was headed by ANATOLI LUNACHARSKY, himself no mean drama critic. Theater research faculties were established within artistic institutions in both Moscow and Leningrad in the comparatively liberal climate of the 1920s, but critical responses to productions were carefully monitored by the Party. Freedom of critical expression was gradually eroded during the late 1920s and 1930s, culminating in the foundation, in 1937, of the theatrical organ of the Soviet Ministry of Culture, *Teatr* (*Theater*), which published the opinions of officialdom on matters dramatic and theatrical.

The heyday of Soviet dramatic criticism was undoubtedly the 1920s, and outstanding among Moscow-based critics was Pavel Markov, who doubled as literary manager of the Moscow Art Theatre, and Boris Alpers, literary manager of the Theatre of the Revolution from 1921 to 1924. Markov published influential work on Soviet drama, the Moscow Art Theatre, and as late as the 1970s, four volumes of dramatic criticism. Alpers produced a groundbreaking study of VSEVOLOD MEYERHOLD's theater, *Teatr sotsialnoi maski* (*The Theatre of the Social Mask*) in 1931 and wrote widely on 19th- and 20th-century Russian drama. The Petrograd (later Leningrad) branch of drama criticism was spearheaded by Aleksei Gvozdev, who specialized in the Western European repertoire and encouraged Soviet dramatists to learn from their non-Soviet counterparts. Another important critic based in Leningrad was Adrian Piotrovsky, a powerful advocate of nonprofessional theater who came into conflict with authority. If these critics were creative, the destructive power of the dramatic critic was apparent in the role played by Platon Kerzhentsev, a leading light of the Proletarian Culture (Proletkult) movement, who hounded suspect practitioners even to extinction.

Leading critics of the 1930s and 1940s included Grigory Boiadzhiyev, an expert on French drama, and Iosif Yuzovsky, who published important work on Gorky and socialist realist drama of a kind that caused him to fall foul of authority. Soviet productions of William Shakespeare were chronicled by Mikhail

Morozov from the 1930s to the 1950s, his mantle descending to Aleksandr Anikst and, subsequently, to Aleksei Bartoshevich, who also wrote about English productions of Shakespeare for a Soviet readership.

Konstantin Rudnitsky was the outstanding drama critic of the postwar period, which also saw an unprecedented number of female practitioners enter the ranks, including Tat'yana Bachelis (his wife). Rudnitsky wrote a pioneering study in 1969 of the stage productions of Vsevolod Meyerhold, who had been rehabilitated in 1955, and he subsequently published several volumes of criticism on Soviet drama and practice. Among leading female critics of the period were Inna Solov'yova, Marianna Stroyeva, Yelena Polyakova, Anna Obraztsova (who also published studies of GEORGE BERNARD SHAW and OSCAR WILDE), and Natalya Krymova. More recently, Marina Dmitrievskaya founded the *Peterburgsky teatral'ny zhurnal* (*Petersburg Theatrical Journal*) in 1992, the thirty-second issue of which appeared during 2003. Her counterpart in Moscow, Valery Semenovsky, established the journal *Moskovsky nablyudatel'* (*Moscow Observer*), which survived from 1991 to 1998. In the year 2000 he also revived the journal *Teatr*, which had suspended publication during the 1990s.

Other recent influential figures have been Vladimir Frolov, whose *The Falming Muse of Satire* (*Muza plamennoi satiry*, 1988) rediscovered the work of DANIIL KHARMS, NIKOLAI ERDMAN, Andrei Platonov, and others; and Anatoly Smelyansky, who inherited Markov's post as literary manager of the Moscow Art Theatre and some of whose critical writings, like those of Rudnitsky, have appeared in English.

FURTHER READING

Khaichenko, G. A., ed. *Istoriya sovyetskogo teatro-vedeniya 1917–1941* [History of Soviet theatre studies 1917–1941]. Moscow: Nauka, 1981.

Markov, Pavel. *The Soviet Theatre*. London: Gollancz, 1934.

Morozov, Mikhail M. *Shakespeare on the Soviet Stage*. Tr. by David Magarshack, with an intro. by J. Dover Wilson. London: Soviet News, 1947.

Rudnitsky, Konstantin. *Russian and Soviet Theatre: Tradition and the Avant-Garde*. Ed. by Lesley Milne. Tr. by Roxanne Permar. London: Thames & Hudson, 1988.

Smeliansky, Anatoly. *The Russian Theatre After Stalin*. Tr. by Patrick Miles, with a foreword by Laurence Senelick. Cambridge: Cambridge Univ. Press, 1999.

Solovyova, Inna. "The Theatre and Socialist Realism." In *A History of the Russian Theatre*. Ed. by Robert Leach and Victor Borovsky. Cambridge: Cambridge Univ. Press, 1999.

Nick Worrall

SET DESIGN

The 20th-century in Russia saw a revolution in stage design, perhaps unparalleled worldwide and inspired in its early decades by the antirealist experiments of European AVANT-GARDE artists, by the theories of Georg Fuchs, Adolphe Appia, and RICHARD WAGNER, by a renewed interest in the theaters of classical Greece, medieval Europe, and William Shakespeare, and by a rediscovery of popular performance techniques. But first and foremost, modern design represented a rejection of the standard 19th-century practice of reusing stock set pieces in favor of conceiving productions from scratch.

That idea was central to the work Viktor Simov, who between 1898 and 1906 designed every production at the MOSCOW ART THEATRE and was crucial to the evolution of its early style. Working in close collaboration with KONSTANTIN STANISLAVSKY, he pioneered stage NATURALISM in Russia, seeking by meticulous research and expeditions to make sketches and to collect authentic materials to create a faithful illusion of reality. He greatly advanced the conception of a setting as a lived-in space, though frequently suggesting the world beyond, and developed lighting to marry three-dimensional structures and painted features. But his designs for MAKSIM GORKY's THE LOWER DEPTHS (1902) and for the works of ANTON CHEKHOV (1898–1904) were criticized for having swamped their content with excessive detail, and his attempts to recreate reality were soon at odds with both modernist trends in Europe and in Russia, with the aspirations of the World of Art Group, whose members (like Mstislav Dobuzhinsky and Aleksandr Golovin) sought to realize in the theater their ideals of life-made-art.

Dobuzhinsky's sets for A MONTH IN THE COUNTRY (1909), in which Stanislavsky first implemented his famous ACTING "system," stressed symmetry and balance in reflecting a central theme—man's desire to master nature—and, by creating a sense of containment, accorded with the director's desire to minimize movement and gesture and focus on inner emotions. For VSEVOLOD MEYERHOLD's production of Molière's Don Juan (1910), Golovin covered the orchestra pit with a semicircular apron, decorated a false proscenium with ornate borders in the motifs and colors of the fully illuminated auditorium, and by these means, enveloped the audience in the splendor of Louis XIV's Versailles. He similarly united stage and spectators for Mikhail Lermontov's *Masquerade* (1917), also directed by Meyerhold The silent movement of exquisitely decorated drops, revealing lavish settings for each of ten episodes, suggested a remorseless progress toward death and delirium—a central theme of a production interpreted by some as a requiem for the Romanovs—and thus wedded form to meaning.

In the postrevolutionary era, when political fervor and governmental support for theater encouraged further experimentation, a similar fusion of form, space, structure, and rhythm was variously achieved by the Constructivists, like Aleksandra Ekster, Lyubov Popova, Varvara Stepanova, Aleksandr Vesnin, and the brothers Georgii and Vladimir Stenberg. Constructivism, inspired by industrial design and architecture, and by notions of a socialist world transformed by mechanization, marked a decisive shift from artist-painter to artist-builder.

For Aleksandr Tairov's production of OSCAR WILDE's *Salomé* (1917), Ekster created a complex cubist landscape, whose sculptural lines, like the varied textures, fabrics, and painted decorations of her costumes, harmonized rhythmically with the actors' movements. Mobile lighting and fluid red and blue drapes set the mood of each scene, reflecting Salomé's vacillating emotions. Her set for his *Romeo and Juliet* (1921)—a fractured structure of bridges, balconies, and cascading and fan-shaped steps—accentuated the swirling motions of actors, whose sumptuous, multilayered costumes were reflected in tinfoil mirrors. Popova, incorporating ladders, slides, and windmill sails in her freestanding, skeletal set, for Meyerhold's *The Magnanimous Cuckold* (1922), made space dynamic. Wheels turning at different speeds enhanced the acrobatic movement of actors, trained in his "biomechanics," and dressed in identical blue uniforms (*prozodezhda*). In his *Tarelkin's Death* (1922), Stepanova gave them uniforms decorated with lines and dots, which in their various groupings created living, rhythmic patterns. Her setting included mobile and portable pieces, a wheeled structure—part cage, part mincing machine—and furniture that produced unpredictable effects: a table that collapsed and sprang back, a stool that fired pistol shots. These "performing" props, at once comic and disturbing, underlined the theme of police torture and the overall effect of a terrifying circus.

In 1923 for Tairov's production of *Phaedra* Vesnin broke the stage floor into three steeply raked planes; crimson and gold drapes suggested the sails and rigging of a ship riding between sea and sky. Layered costumes, trailing capes, huge headdresses, and high-heeled *cothurni* complemented their wearers' statuesque movement, broad gestures, and exaggerated style. By contrast, in *The Man Who Was Thursday* (1923) he filled the whole proscenium opening with a multileveled structure, incorporating moving walkways, elevators, and flashing neon signs that accompanied the frenzied pace of the chase sequences. The Stenbergs' sets for Tairov's "EUGENE O'NEILL cycle" indicated locations sparsely but precisely, combining geometric outlines with realist detail. In THE HAIRY APE (1926) an oceanliner shown in cross section facilitated political critique by contrasting the elegance of the upper decks with the hell endured by stokers below. In DESIRE UNDER THE ELMS (1926), Abbie's petty, tragic life was contained by heavy pillars, in gloomy low-ceilinged rooms, and in ALL GOD'S CHILLUN GOT WINGS (1929) geometric shapes created dark, towering buildings at a crossroads between black and white ghettos.

Throughout Joseph Stalin's rule, such experimentation was discouraged and REALISM promoted as the model; the suppression of artistic freedom led to monotony and stagnation. Innovation reappeared, however, in the 1950s and 1960s. Valentin Lalevich, Nikolai Sasunov, Viktor Durgin, and Valerii Levental' defied the sacrosanct style of staging Chekhov in Anatolii Efros's controversial productions of THE SEAGULL (1966), THE THREE SISTERS (1967), and THE CHERRY ORCHARD (1975), and

David Borovsky's work became a vital cog in YURY LYUBIMOV's theatrical machine at the Taganka. Incorporating central metaphors, his designs were at once simple and ingeniously multifunctional. Key props acquired the status of living beings: the now-legendary flying pendulum for Jerzy Stawinski's *Rush Hour* (1969), the moving curtain for *Hamlet* (1971), and the hallucinatory moving door for *Crime and Punishment* (1979).

Russian set design since has remained consistently innovative. Successive generations continue to experiment in the dual tradition of naturalism and overt THEATRICALITY, often acknowledging their debts by scenic "quotations."

FURTHER READING

Aronson, Arnold. "The Scenography of Chekhov." In *The Cambridge Companion to Chekhov*, ed. by Vera Gottlieb and Paul Allain. Cambridge: Cambridge Univ. Press, 2000. 134–148.

Bowlt, John E. "Constructivism on the Russian Stage." *Performance Arts Journal* 1, no. 3 (Winter 1977): 62–84.

——. *Russian Stage Design: Scenic Innovation 1900–1930.* Jackson: Mississippi Museum of Modern Art, 1982.

Gray, Camilla. *The Russian Experiment in Art 1863–1922.* Rev. ed. London: Thames & Hudson, 2000.

Rudnitsky, Konstantin. *Russian and Soviet Theatre: Tradition and the Avant-Garde.* London: Thames & Hudson, 1988.

Van Norman Baer, Nancy, ed. *The Art of Enchantment: Diaghilev's Ballets Russes, 1909–1929.* San Francisco: Fine Arts Museum of San Francisco, 1989.

——, ed. *Theatre in Revolution: Russian Avant-Garde Stage Design 1913–1935.* London: Thames & Hudson, 1991.

Ros Dixon

RUSSIAN SYMBOLIST DRAMA

Although Russian symbolist drama owes a debt to the earlier French and Belgian symbolist tradition of the *lesedrama*—plays primarily intended to be read rather than staged—it developed independently and exerted an enormous influence on both MODERNIST DRAMA and theater.

Russian symbolist drama may be said to begin in earnest with Valerii Briusov's article "Unnecessary Truth" (1902), in which the poet attacks the verisimilitude of realist and realistic theater, arguing instead for stylization. The plays that followed Briusov's manifesto betray an acquaintance with NATURALISM and also with HENRIK IBSEN, AUGUST STRINDBERG, GERHART HAUPTMANN, HUGO VON HOFMANNSTHAL, STANISŁAWA PRZYBYSZEWSKA, and FRANK WEDEKIND, with the French symbolists, particularly Stéphane Mallarmé and Auguste Villiers d'Isle Adam, and with the Belgian MAURICE MAETERLINCK.

Nonetheless, native Russian dramatic traditions, especially the humorous play (*shutochnaia p'esa*), proved more formative. Such playwrights as Vladimir Solov'ev and Koz'ma Prutkov (the latter being the fictional creation of Aleksei Tolstoy and the brothers Zhemchuzhnikov) employed devices later identified by the formalists as defamiliarization or estrangement (*ostranenie*), which revealed to the symbolists a more complex dramatic discourse. Whereas the discourse of European symbolist plays tends toward the monologic, Solov'ev and Prutkov demonstrated how boundaries between playwright, actor, and audience could be broken down.

The implications of this approach became apparent in the productions that the great director VSEVOLOD MEYERHOLD staged at the Komissarzhevskaia Theater in St. Petersburg and that included key symbolist plays, such as ALEKSANDR BLOK's A PUPPET SHOW (1906) and Fyodor Sologub's *Triumph of Death* (1907). The early plays are notable for their dualism, their grotesque admixture of high and low styles, and their incorporation of elements of various theatrical traditions, such as Greek TRAGEDY and the Italian commedia dell'arte. Harlequinades proved durable as evidenced by such works as Blok's *The Unknown Woman* (1906) and Mikhail Kuzmin's *The Venetian Madcaps* (1915).

Other symbolists approached drama from a different direction and sought the renewal of theater in the cathartic art of Greek classical tragedy and drama. Viacheslav Ivanov, in his plays *Tantalus* (1905) and *Prometheus* (1916), sought a renewal of Dionysian drama. The poet Innokenti Annenskii drew largely on the tradition of satyr plays for such lyrical dramas as *Thamyros Kitharodos* (1913). Others found inspiration in folk sources and in religious traditions, such as hagiography. Of particular note are Kuzmin's *On Alexis, Man of God* (1907) and Aleksei Remizov's *Devil's Comedy* (1907) and *The Tragedy of Judas, Prince of Iscariot* (1908).

Over time, many of the symbolists moved toward what Blok called "healthy REALISM," which often expressed itself in quasi-historical subjects. In such plays as Blok's *Song of Fate* (1908) and *The Rose and the Cross* (1913), Sologub's *The Gift of the Wise Bees* (1907), *Vanka the Steward and Jehan the Page* (1908), and *Hostages of Life* (1912), and Zinaida Hippius's *The Green Ring* (1914), the playwrights sought to make their plays work on a realistic plane as well as on a symbolic one.

The influence of Russian symbolist drama proved to be immense and affected a wide range of later playwrights, including YEVGENY SHVARTS and Marina Tsvetaeva and futurists including VLADIMIR MAYAKOVSKY. In their use of intimate forms, the symbolists paved the way for DANIIL KHARMS and the OBERIU (Association for Real Art, founded 1927). Although symbolist dramas themselves have exerted only a limited influence abroad, many of their techniques have become an integral part of the modernist vocabulary, thanks to the spread of Meyerhold's practices.

[*See also* Symbolism]

FURTHER READING

Clayton, J. Douglas. *Pierrot in Petrograd: Commedia dell'Arte/Balagan in Twentieth-Century Russian Theatre and Drama.* Montreal: McGill-Queen's Univ. Press, 1993.

Gerould, Daniel. *Symbolist Drama: An International Collection.* Baltimore, Md.: Johns Hopkins Univ. Press, 1985.

Green, Michael, ed. and tr. *The Russian Symbolist Theatre: An Anthology of Plays and Critical Texts.* Ann Arbor, Mich.: Ardis, 1986.

Kalbouss, George. *The Plays of the Russian Symbolists.* East Lansing, Mich.: Russian Language Journal, 1982.

Moeller-Sally, Betsy F. "The Theater as Will and Representation: Artist and Audience in Russian Modernist Theater, 1904–1909." *Slavic Review* 57, no. 2 (Summer 1998): 350–371.

Pyman, Avril. *A History of Russian Symbolism.* Cambridge: Cambridge Univ. Press, 1994.

West, James D. *Russian Symbolism: A Study of Vyacheslav Ivanov and the Russian Symbolist Aesthetic.* London: Methuen, 1970.

Timothy C. Westphalen

RUTHERFORD AND SON

GITHA SOWERBY's three-act play *Rutherford and Son* premiered at a Court Theatre matinée in January 1912 and then transferred to two further London theaters, achieving 133 performances. Its American premiere was at Little Theatre, New York, in 1912. Following its broadcast on BBC radio in 1952, the drama was rediscovered in the 1980s and revived at the Royal National Theatre, London, in June 1994, in a production directed by Katie Mitchell and starring Bob Peck. It thus became one of the most successful plays of the historic decade of feminist theater interrupted by World War I. Like its predecessor at the Court, ELIZABETH ROBINS's play *Votes for Women!*, Sowerby's play featured "New Women" and engaged with the current debate over marriage, motherhood, and women's self-fulfilment, initiated in the theater by HENRIK IBSEN. However, although it was hailed at the time as a "suffrage play," *Rutherford and Son* does not deal directly with the agitation for the vote; its protagonists are not suffragettes. Unlike Robins, Sowerby emulated Ibsen's studies of the intense and suffocating domestic tyranny that seethed behind the suffrage campaign. Her originality lies in providing an enduring and remarkably astute analysis of capitalist patriarchy.

"Rutherfords" is a family firm, a Tyneside glass manufacturers, dominated by a despot who also runs his motherless family as a system based on financial bargaining and the control of power rather than on love. The plot demonstrates him bullying his three adult children and manipulating his foreman. He emasculates his sons and humiliates his daughter; alienated, they leave home for good. Ideologically colonized, his sister and foreman faithfully continue to submit to his domination. The one person to stand up to him is the modern outsider, his working-class daughter-in-law, who uses his baby grandson as a bargaining ploy to escape the grind of office work. Although Sowerby claimed that the story was "imaginary," it clearly drew on her own background. Her father had run Sowerby and Co., a glass-manufacturing firm on Tyneside founded by his grandfather. The play's striking REALISM is due partly to her ear for language, especially regional dialect, and to her bleak socioeconomic analysis but also to the credible subtlety of her portrait of the industrialist John Rutherford, to whom she attributes considerable charm, dynamism, and ingenuity, as well as ruthlessness.

It is fitting that the play should have been mentioned by Emma Goldmann in *The Social Significance of Modern Drama* (1914), though few would now agree with her judgment that "the Rutherfords are fighting a losing game." Contemporary audiences are more likely to agree with critics like Linda Fitzsimmons and Sheila Stowell, who regard the play as a plea for the self-empowerment of women in the face of patriarchal tyranny. As Julie Holledge (1981) indicates, the most forceful speech is made by the spinster daughter, exiled for asserting her sexual independence by initiating a cross-class extramarital relationship with her father's foreman. She denounces Rutherford as "a man that'd take the blood of life itself and put it into the works."

FURTHER READING

Gardner, Viv, and Susan Rutherford, eds. *The New Woman and Her Sisters: Feminism and Theatre, 1850–1914*. Hemel Hempstead: Harvester Wheatsheaf, 1992.

Goldmann, Emma. *The Social Significance of the Modern Drama*. Boston: R. G. Badger, 1914.

Holledge, Julie. *Innocent Flowers: Women in the Edwardian Theatre*. London: Virago, 1981.

Sowerby, Githa. *Rutherford and Son*. In *New Woman Plays*, ed. by Linda Fitzsimmons and Viv Gardner. London: Methuen, 1991. 133–189.

Stowell, Sheila. *A Stage of Their Own: Feminist Playwrights of the Suffrage Era*. Manchester: Manchester Univ. Press, 1992.

Claire M. Tylee

RYGA, GEORGE (1932–1987)

CANADA lost one of its most challenging, honest, and courageously committed writers when George Ryga passed away on November 18, 1987, in Summerland, British Columbia, from stomach cancer. Ryga did, however, leave an oeuvre impressive in its breadth: his published works consist of plays, television and radio scripts, films, novels, poetry, journal articles, and short stories. There are also a large number of works still unpublished, most of which can be found in the University of Calgary Archives. The subject matter of Ryga's writing ranges widely, often dealing with his Canadian-Ukrainian heritage, but also coming from his travels in Europe, MEXICO, and CHINA, frequently delving into mythology. Further, Ryga left

a legacy of resistance, for both in his work and in his life he strove to make constant challenges to provoke change for the better.

Ryga was born on July 27, 1932, in Deep Creek, a small Ukrainian farming community in Northern Alberta. His early education was in a one-room schoolhouse built when he was seven, and Ryga completed the eighth grade by the age of thirteen, despite the challenge of learning English. He went on to take correspondence courses, as well as to borrow books en masse from the University of Alberta. By fifteen he was writing regularly, and at sixteen his essay "Smoke" won him a scholarship to the Banff School of Fine Arts. After winning the scholarship for a second year he produced a poem critical of the Korean War and was not invited back for a third year by his sponsors.

Even later, Ryga was always known to find joy in his connection to the land. He relocated the family home to Summerland in the Okanagan valley of British Columbia so he could grow enough to feed his family while he wrote. In fact, the primary breadwinner of the household was his partner, Norma, while most of Ryga's nonwriting income was from seasonal labor, such as fruit picking. This was made somewhat more difficult by the fact that Ryga was missing three of the fingers on his right hand from an adolescent workplace accident.

Ryga's background most certainly played a part in his politics; as a young man he joined his father working with the Communist Party, though after seeing firsthand the effects of these politics in Eastern Europe, Ryga became more of a free-association socialist. He was what Antonio Gramsci referred to as an "organic intellectual": an artist arising out of a particular context—in this case, a rural Canadian—who produces art that challenges the complacent norms of an unequal social hierarchy.

Ryga is best known for his play *The Ecstasy of Rita Joe* (1967). However, *Rita Joe* was not his most popular play; *Grass and Wild Strawberries* (1968) played to larger houses. Nor did Ryga consider *Rita Joe* his best play; *A Letter to My Son* (1981) was his favorite. What these works all have in common, though, is their focus on normally marginal members of society: the native in *Rita Joe*, the countercultural hippie in *Grass*, and the Ukrainian farmer in *Letter*.

SELECT PLAYS: *Indian* (1964); *Nothing But a Man* (1966); *The Ecstasy of Rita Joe* (1967); *Grass and Wild Strawberries* (1968); *Just an Ordinary Person* (1968); *Compressions* (1969); *Captives of the Faceless Drummer* (1971); *Paracelus* (1972); *Sunrise on Sarah* (1972); *Portrait of Angelica* (1973); *Last of the Gladiators* (1976); *Ploughmen of the Glacier* (1976); *Seven Hours to Sundown* (1976); *Jeremiah's Place* (1978); *Laddie Boy* (1978); *Prometheus Bound* (1978); *A Letter to My Son* (1981); *One More for the Road* (1985)

FURTHER READING

Hoffman, James. *The Ecstasy of Resistance: A Biography of George Ryga.* Toronto: ECW Press, 1995.

Innes, Christopher. *Politics and the Playwright: George Ryga.* Toronto: Simon & Pierre, 1985.

Ryga, George. *The Athabasca Ryga.* Ed. by E. David Gregory. Vancouver: Talonbooks, 1990.

——. *Summerland.* Ed. by Ann Kujundzic. Vancouver: Talonbooks, 1992.

——. *George Ryga: The Other Plays.* Ed. by James Hoffman. Vancouver: Talonbooks, 2004.

University of Calgary Libraries. Special Collections Division. *The George Ryga Papers: George Ryga fonds, Renée L. Paris fonds, George Ryga & Associates fonds.* An Inventory of the Archive at the University of Calgary Archive. Comp. by Juanita Walton and Sandra Mortensen. Ed. by Marlys Chevrefils and Apollonia Steele. Calgary: Univ. of Calgary Press, 1995.

Derek Irwin

SAALBACH, ASTRID (1955–)

The things are not coherent. They happen in leaps and repetitions, in that strangely manic way, that can drive you completely crazy. It is illogic and untruthful to create a coherent form.

—Astrid Saalbach, 1986

Born on November 29, 1955, in Søborg, DENMARK, playwright Astrid Saalbach trained as an actor at the Danish National Theatre School from 1975 to 1978. She is one of the most significant playwrights of her generation, having been performed at the most important theaters, been honored with a number of rewards, and been translated into more than ten languages. She also writes novels and short stories.

Fragility, with almost neurotic fear of (inner) chaos and of loss, was from the beginning a leitmotif. Her style was to a high degree realistic, like in her stage debut in 1985 in *The Invisible Town* (*Den usynlige by*), about conflicts and tensions at an old people's home; this play implied a social criticism and caused a debate of how old people are being treated. As time went on, Saalbach changed her way of writing toward more scattered and metaphoric forms. Two examples are the BOTHO STRAUSS–like *Morning and Evening* (*Morgen og aften*, 1993), which became the first part of a trilogy about modern society, and *The Blessed Child* (*Det velsignede barn*, 1996), described by critic Jette Lundbo Levy writing for the newspaper *Information* as "an end-game in the shape of a mystery about the last decades of our civilization."

Characteristic is the complexity of realistic and nightmare-like situations, criticism of culture, mythological fragments, and surrealistic episodes, and an almost literary language in the dialogues and monologues. *The Cold Heart* (*Det kolde hjerte*, 2001) is a modern version of *The Little Match Girl* by Hans Christian Andersen, but in Saalbach's work, the girl is a junkie who, just before dying, imagines herself at a royal court that resembles the actual Danish royal family. The play was criticized for being uninspired and mechanical in its satire. *The End of the World* (*Verdens ende*, 2003) is a dream-like story about a woman who gets lost in a world that has gone out of control.

Ashes to Ashes. Dust to Dust (*Aske til aske. Støv til støv*, 1998) is the most successful of her texts. It is a modern version of the Medea myth, combined with a crime plot based on a real murder story, and includes a number of scenes that in different ways relate to the function of the human brain. The story concerns the brain specialist Michael, his wife Charlotte, and their two children. They part, Michael begins a relation with his colleague Nina, but for the children's sake, Michael and Charlotte reunite. In the end Nina kills Charlotte and the children and sets fire to their house. This plot is intermingled with a number of situations that have no apparent relation to the linear story, in a constant playing with associations and layers of fiction, sometimes satirical, sometimes (sur)realistic. In the end some of these episodes seem to take place in the mind of Charlotte in the moment of her death.

PLAYS: *Traces in the Sand* (*Spor i sandet*, radio drama, 1981); *The Confirmation* (*Bekræaftelsen*, radio drama, 1982); *A World that Fades Away* (*En verden der blegner*, television drama, 1984); *The Dance Lesson* (*Dansetimen*, 1986); *The Invisible City* (*Den usynlige by*, 1986); *Myung* (television drama, 1989); *Time of the Miracles* (*Miraklernes tid*, 1990); *Morning and Evening* (*Morgen og aften*, 1993); *The Blessed Child* (*Det velsignede barn*, 1996); *Ashes to Ashes, Dust to Dust* (*Aske til aske, støv til støv*, 1998); *The Cold Heart* (*Det kolde hjerte*, 2001); *The End of the World* (*Verdens ende*, 2003)

FURTHER READING

Bille, Karen-Maria. "Tradition without Context." *Danish Literary Magazine* 6 (1994).

Szatkowski, Janek. "Af jord er du kommet" [From Dust You Have Come]. In *Teaterlegeringer* [Theatrical Alloyings], ed. by Andersen and Lehmann. Århus: Aarhus Universitetsforlag, 1998.

Theil, Per, and Lise Garsdal. *Hvem der? Scener fra 90erne* [Who's There? Scenes from the 90's]. Copenhagen: Høst og Søn, 2000.

Bent Holm

SADO KÔSHAKU FUJIN   See MADAME DE SADE

LA SAGA DES POULES MOUILLÉES   See SAGA OF THE WET HENS

SAGA OF THE WET HENS

Saga of the Wet Hens (*La Saga des poules mouillées*) is the first full-length play written by Québecois author JOVETTE MARCHESSAULT. The first production of the play, directed by Michelle Rossignol, premiered at the Théâtre du Nouveau Monde in Montreal, CANADA, on April 24, 1981. The English version, translated by Linda Gaboriau, was staged at Toronto's Tarragon Theatre in February 1982.

A feminist fantasia set in the Promised Land in the North of the Americas, the play assembles four of Québec's celebrated women writers: Laure Conan, Germaine Guèvremont, Gabrielle Roy, and Anne Hébert. Together, they share life stories and speak of hardships endured under patriarchal institutions. They explore their most vivid dreams, their worst nightmares, and other products of a repressed feminine unconsciousness. Aroused by passionate discussion, the women partake in a voluptuous feast. Inverting the sexist rituals of the Last Supper, they sanctify those normally excluded from the event: women who bake the communion bread and prepare the festive meal. They pool creative energies and prepare to write a history of forgotten women. They cluck, spread their wings, and give birth to a new dynasty of wet hens.

Propelled by a central concern of feminists in the male-dominated art world of the 1970s and 1980s, *Saga* attempts to reclaim an occluded history of female creativity. Rather than subordinating these recovery efforts to a documentary-like search for historical truth, Marchessault eschews REALISM, turning instead to the saga, a narrative form that freely mixes the mythic and the real. Her play exhibits a structural openness; its nonlinear construction presents a series of tableau verses. Marchessault's use of language is densely imagistic, giving the play a lyrical quality. Although the poetic style of *Saga* draws upon familiar conventions in Québec theater, reviewers in English Canada have found it unnecessarily opaque. Several critics of the Tarragon production dismissed her imagery as confusing and weighty, revealing a potential anglocentric bias in their reception of the play.

In its exploration of women's mythology, *Saga* can be situated within a wider feminist movement that aimed to retrieve lost female archetypes and culture. The third verse, for example, is dedicated to Ursa Major, the Great Mother Bear and Mother of the Skies. The play was strongly influenced by Gloria Feman Orenstein's essay on the reemergence of the Great Goddess in the visual arts. To the contemporary critic, Marchessault's Goddess figures and her appeals to a generalized "women's culture" may look like a naive form of essentialism. Critics might see the play as reinforcing patriarchal associations of women with nature, especially when female creativity is linked to biology (menstrual blood and mother's milk). Yet the enduring value of Marchessault's play lies in this body-centered imagery. It aims to redress the abjection of women's bodies and to return to women their diverse physical desires. *Saga* appeals to a universal femininity; at the same time, it shows women's bodily liberation to be vital particularly in Québec, a province traditionally dominated by paternalistic Catholic values.

FURTHER READING
Gaboriau, Linda. "Jovette Marchessault: A Luminous Wake in Space." *Canadian Theatre Review* 43 (Summer 1985): 91–99.
Harris, Norma. "Magic of Wet Hens Misdirected." *Globe in Mail* (February 20, 1982): E9.
Orenstein, Gloria Feman. "The Reemergence of the Archetype of the Great Goddess in Art by Contemporary Women." *Heresies* 2, no. 1 (Spring 1978): 74–84.

Laura Levin

SAINETE

A Spanish comedy of manners, usually in one act, a sainete depicts the life and customs of lower- and working-class characters. Historically, most sainetes have been set in the poor neighborhoods of southern Madrid, SPAIN, although works set in small villages or in rural Andalusia are not uncommon.

The sainete developed in the 17th and 18th centuries as a short piece to be played either during the intermission or at the conclusion of a larger dramatic work. The genre disappeared at the beginning of the 19th century as the taste for shorter pieces declined. The revival of the sainete in the last third of the 19th century was built on two cornerstones. The first was the development of the "theater by hours" system, wherein theater impresarios took to staging three or four shorter works per evening instead of one full-length play, thus allowing them to earn more money by charging separate admissions for each work. The second factor in this revival was the introduction of musical numbers into the sainete, introduced in 1880 when Federico Chueca contributed music to Ricardo de la Vega's *Lola's Song* (*La canción de la Lola*). These lyric sainetes used the music of cafés and dance halls, such as waltzes, polkas, and mazurkas, to reflect the popular ambiance depicted in the plays. The best known modern sainetes, such as Vega and Tómas Bretón's *The Festival of Our Lady of the Dove* (*La verbena de la paloma*, 1894) or José López Silva, Carlos Fernández-Shaw, and Ruperto Chapí's *The Mischievous Lass* (*La Revoltosa*, 1897), are of the lyric variety.

The form of the sainete used throughout the 19th century was modeled directly upon the 18th-century work of Ramón de la Cruz (1731–1794), the acknowledged master of the genre. The key feature of the sainete is that its dramatic impetus does not stem from either the plot or the characters of the play, but from its depiction of daily life and customs. Thus, the dramatic interest is in what otherwise would be termed local color: the use of language, especially slang terms and colloquialisms, details of dress, and depictions of local festivals. The characters are either stock types (the jealous suitor, the lecherous old man) or are defined by solely by their occupation (night watchmen, washerwomen, street vendors). In addition, the characters depicted are of humble station: the action centers on the working class or the peasantry, while the bourgeoisie and the aristocracy turn up infrequently and usually as figures to be mocked. The plot is always comic and usually revolves around a simple romantic conflict. This emphasis on the depiction of the life of the lower classes often led 19th-century critics to equate the sainete with the naturalist movement in literature.

The popularity of the sainete declined in the period after 1910 as the theater by hours gave way once more to full-length plays. Nonlyrical sainetes virtually disappeared, while lyrical works increasingly resembled in form and content full-fledged ZARZUELAS: their length grew to encompass a full evening, and as a result plot and characterization began to take precedence over the traditional depictions of daily life.

FURTHER READING
Barce, Ramón. "El sainete lírico (1880–1915)" [The Lyric Sainete (1880–1915)]. In *La música española en el siglo XIX* [Spanish Music in

the Nineteenth Century], ed. by Emilio Casares Rodicio and Celsa Alonso González. Oviedo: Univ. of Oviedo, 1995. 195–244.

Espín Templado, María Pílar. *El teatro por horas en Madrid (1870–1910)* [The Theatre by Hours in Madrid, 1870–1910]. Madrid: Instituto de Estudios Madrileños, 1995.

Membrez, Nancy Jane Hartley. "The *teatro por horas*: History, Dynamics and Comprehensive Bibliography of a Madrid Industry, 1867–1922 (*género chico, género ínfimo* and Early Cinema)." Ph.D. diss., Univ. of California, Santa Barbara, 1987.

Clinton D. Young

SAINT FRANCES OF HOLLYWOOD

Described as "sledgehammer satire" when it premiered at Alberta Theatre Project's "playRites '94" festival in Calgary (February 5, 1994), SALLY CLARK's dark COMEDY *Saint Frances of Hollywood* dramatizes the life of Hollywood legend Frances Farmer (1913–1970). It ranks among Clark's most ambitious plays.

Following the premier, which featured Megan Leitch in the demanding title role, Clark rewrote the play for production at Toronto's Canadian Stage Theatre (January 17, 1996) with Thea Gill as Farmer. The new version was published by Talon books that year. The play continues to receive professional productions across North America; it often receives amateur and school productions as well, including productions at Edmonton's Walterdale Playhouse (April 25, 2001) and the University of Manitoba's Black Hole Theatre Company (March 11, 2003), owing in part to its lengthy character list, twenty-nine in all.

Through fifty-one quick-paced scenes, the partly biographical, partly fictional account traces Farmer's precocious childhood from the age of sixteen to a bitter "better-to-burn-out-than-fade-away" exit at fifty-six. The first act follows Farmer's meteoric rise to stardom in the 1930s with the GROUP THEATRE (*Golden Boy, Thunder Rock*) and on the silver screen (*Come and Get It, Rhythm on the Range, Son of Fury*); it then stages her falling out with the stage and film industries, the critics, and consequently, her controlling mother Lillian. The second act stages her controversial incarcerations at Washington's Western State Hospital at Steilacoom during the 1940s, where she underwent hydrotherapy, electroshock treatments, and likely a lobotomy. It concludes with Farmer's bewildered appearance on the quiz show, *This Is Your Life*, and her death alongside her later-life partner, Jean Ratcliffe.

Clark's play explores the suspicion that Farmer's repeated incarcerations were more than just products of a chauvinistic film industry sick of dealing with a strong-willed leading lady, or even the inability of Farmer to cope with the roller coaster of celebrity status. Rather, they were part of a government conspiracy to take out of the public eye a woman whose one-time trip to Russia and associations with The Group forever implicated her among subversive communist influences in America. The play unapologetically explores the ludicrous and life-threatening pressures of public scrutiny, as well as the pressures placed upon Farmer by her "celebrity mom," who signed her daughter's commitment papers.

Clark portrays Farmer as a strong-willed saint who fought for her blond-bombshell heroines to speak their minds, even when producers and scripts demanded otherwise. She paid the ultimate price: the erasure first of her will (in rehearsals and film shoots), then of her body and mind (in experimental therapy), and finally of her life.

In dealing with what Clark calls the "primary obsessions of the 20th century—atheism, Communism, media manipulation, and psychiatry," *Saint Frances of Hollywood* suggests that the "modern Saint" is one whose faith is in herself, fighting against blind authority to the end. Everyone has had "one of those days"; Frances Farmer had one of those lives.

[*See also* Canada]

FURTHER READING

Friedlander, Mira. "Saint Frances of Hollywood." *Variety* (February 26 to March 3, 1996): 181.

Garebian, Keith. "Fraught with Background." *Books in Canada* 27, no. 4 (May, 1998): 24.

Wagner, Vit. "Frances Farmer Saga Stirs Emotions." *Toronto Star* (January 21, 1996, final ed.): F7.

Robin C. Whittaker

SAINT JOAN

Saint Joan: A Chronicle Play in Six Scenes, and an Epilogue, by GEORGE BERNARD SHAW, was written and first performed at the Garrick Theater, New York, in 1923. The first performance in ENGLAND was at the New Theatre, London, in 1924. As early as 1913 Shaw had announced his intention to "do a Joan play some day" in a letter from Orleans to Mrs. Patrick Campbell. Frequent uses of Joan of Arc as an icon in pre–World War I suffragette agitation, together with her beatification in 1909 and canonization in 1920, had raised the level of public interest in her in the years leading up the composition of *Saint Joan*.

The play gained immediate acclaim. In a notice of the first New York production, Italian dramatist LUIGI PIRANDELLO declared it "a work of poetry from beginning to end." English critic J. I. M. Stewart later described *Saint Joan* as "certainly Shaw's outstanding play, conceivably the finest and most moving English drama since *The Winter's Tale* or *The Tempest*." Dissenting voices about the merits of the work in the 1920s included that of T. S. ELIOT, who subsequently, however, admitted that he may have been influenced by Shaw in the writing of his own play MURDER IN THE CATHEDRAL. The international success of the play was probably a factor in the decision to award Shaw the 1925 Nobel Prize for Literature.

Shaw described his treatment of the story of the 15th-century warrior-saint as a portrayal of "the romance of her rise, the tragedy of her execution, and the comedy of the attempts of posterity to make amends for the execution." In the composition of the play, Shaw drew extensively on translations of the records of Joan's trial in T. Douglas Murray's *Jeanne d'Arc* (1902). The dramatic action follows Joan's fortunes from securing permission to visit the Dauphin and his granting her the leadership of the French forces against the English, to her capture, trial, and burning at the stake in Rouen. The mainly comic Epilogue shows Joan and a procession of others visiting the Dauphin in a dream, twenty-five years after her execution, when, ironically, her sentence had been set aside.

The play counters sentimental and melodramatic 19th-century fictional accounts of Saint Joan, while at the same time borrowing structural patterns found in previous popular dramatizations of her legend. In the early scenes Shaw presents Joan as pert, forthright, energetic, and managing, but as the play develops he provides her with a powerful and authoritative voice, as in her final speech in Scene V and in many of the speeches during her trial at Rouen (which is the subject of Scene VI). In reference to her reliance on direct inspiration from God and her clash with established ecclesiastical authority, Shaw associated Saint Joan with the dawning of Protestantism.

A controversial feature of the play is the partly sympathetic treatment of the Catholic Inquisition: one of Shaw's most conspicuous departures from history is apparent in the portrayal of the Bishop of Beauvais, Pierre Cauchon, whom the play treats as far more benevolently motivated toward Joan than historical records indicate. But such criticism does not detract from the strength of the work as an imaginative interpretation of Joan's story and as an exploration of the self-justifying strategies of human systems of authority.

FURTHER READING

Bertolini, John. "Imagining Saint Joan." In *Shaw's Plays in Performance. Shaw: The Annual of Bernard Shaw Studies,* 3, ed. by Daniel Leary. Philadelphia: Pennsylvania State Univ. Press, 1983.

Gibbs, A. M., ed. *"Man and Superman" and "Saint Joan": A Casebook.* London: Macmillan, 1992.

Stewart, J. I. M. Chapter on Shaw. In *Eight Modern Writers, Oxford History of English Literature,* vol. 12. Oxford: Oxford Univ. Press, 1963.

Tyson, Brian. *The Story of Shaw's "Saint Joan."* Kingston and Montreal: McGill–Queen's Univ. Press, 1982.

A. M. Gibbs

UNE SAISON AU CONGO   *See* A SEASON IN THE CONGO

SAKATE YŌJI (1962–)

Sakate Yōji, Japanese playwright, was born in Okayama and majored in Japanese literature at Keio University in Tokyo. His lineage in the fourth generation of post-1960 "little theater"

(ANGURA AND SHŌGEKIJŌ) playwrights is clear. As a student he joined the theater group Transposition 21 (Ten'i 21), founded by Yamazaki Tetsu, a key member of the second generation, who had begun his career with the Situation Theatre (Jōkyō Gekijō) of KARA JŪRŌ, stalwart of the first generation. Sakate was influenced by Yamazaki's journalistic style of theater, which dramatized actual events. He established his own company, Phosphorescence Troupe (Rinkōgun), in 1983.

Sakate's approach is partly shaped by the considerable anxiety in JAPAN sparked by several unsettling events: the 1991 Gulf War, Japan's "bubble economy" that burst later that year, the Great Hanshin Earthquake, and the Aum Shinrikyō sarin gas incident in 1995, among others. He is also reacting to a strain of the third generation, embodied in the noisy, frenetic plays of NODA HIDEKI and others in the 1980s, who had turned the humor and youth-oriented topics of their second-generation mentor TSUKA KŌHEI into virtual *manga* (comic books) on stage. Their approach, Sakate felt, was devoid of social relevance and had worn thin. He opted for calmer expression, anchoring his plays in historical events and social trends to encourage consideration of current, often delicate, public issues.

For example, the bombing of a Korean Airlines plane informs *Tokyo Trial* (*Tōkyō Saiban,* 1988), a lesbian discovering her identity propels *Come Out* (*Kamu Auto,* 1989), and problems of the U.S. military in Okinawa underlie *Demise of the Okinawa Milk Plant* (*Okinawa Miruku Puranto no Saigo,* 1998). He links the issues of garbage disposal and the Aum Shinrikyō cult in *Breathless* (*Buresuresu*), which won the Kishida Kunio Drama Prize in 1991. In *Epitaph for the Whales* (*Kujira no Bohyō,* 1993), Sakate dramatizes a touchy subject in Japan, where forced compliance in 1988 to a worldwide whaling ban was considered unfair. The play's structure adapts a traditional NŌ technique, the principal action occurring within a dream of Ikkaku, youngest brother of a whaling family. In the dream, Ikkaku's brothers, who died when their ship sank, return and reflect on their lives. Regarding themselves as the transformed bodies of whales, the brothers lay bare their plight: if they cannot hunt whales, who are they? Underscoring their common identity, Ikkaku states that humans and whales are the only mammals that commit suicide. As his dream ends, his brothers revert to the sea as whales. Sakate thus treats the demise of whaler and whale equally.

Sakate attempts to recover social relevance by even-handedly giving voice to all parties, oppressed or not, and exposing injustices. Still, his work is less overtly political than eminently dramatic; he is known as an outstanding storyteller. And in plays like *Come Out, Breathless,* and *Epitaph,* Sakate questions the very nature of theater and reveals a metatheatrical vision. Theater should not conform to what society condones but should instead transform the spectator, bound by set social assumptions, into a new sense of self—a transformation absolutely required, he is convinced, for theater to be even minimally dramatic.

SELECT PLAYS: *A Dangerous Story* (Kiken na Hanashi, 1988); *Tokyo Trial* (Tōkyō Saiban, 1988); *Come Out* (Kamu Auto, 1989); *Breathless* (Buresuresu, 1991); *The Capital of the Kingdom of the Gods* (Kamigami no Kuni no Shuto, 1993); *Epitaph for the Whales* (Kujira no Bohyō, 1993); *Sōseki and Hearn* (Sōseki to Haan, 1997); *The Boiling Point of the Sea* (Umi no Futten, 1998); *Demise of the Okinawa Milk Plant* (Okinawa Miruku Puranto no Saigo, 1998)

FURTHER READING

Nihon Kindai Engeki-Shi Kenkyūkai, ed. *Nijusseiki no Gikyoku III: Gendai Gikyoku noHenbō* [Twentieth-Century Plays III: The Metamorphosis of Modern Japanese Plays]. Tokyo: Shakai Hyōronsha, 2002.

Sakate, Yōji. *Buresuresu/Kamu Auto* [Breathless/Come Out]. Tokyo: Jiritsu Shobō, 1991.

——. *Epitaph for the Whales* [Kujira no Bohyō]. Tr. by Yuasa Masako. In *Haifa Century of Japanese Theater I: 1990s Part 1*, ed. by Japan Playwrights Association. Tokyo: Kinokuniya, 1999. 103–172.

Senda, Akihiko. *Nihon no Gendai Engeki* [Contemporary Theatre of Japan]. Tokyo: Iwanami Shoten, 1995.

John K. Gillespie

SAKHARAM BINDER

In 1972 when VIJAY DHONDOPANT TENDULKAR wrote *Sakharam Binder*, the Marathi (INDIA) theater audience revered the institution of marriage and considered sexuality a taboo subject. The obedient, subservient wife sacrificing her life for the well-being of her errant husband, children, and family was a popular character on the Marathi stage. *Sakharam Binder* broke this tradition.

The play revolves around Sakharam, a binder by profession and a Brahmin by caste. Sakharam ridicules the institution of marriage: the fake respectability of married men and their double standards as they cheat on their wives. He is unmarried and frankly admits that he is a whoremonger and a drunkard. But he is honest and his logic is simple: a man needs sex and housekeeping, a woman needs security. Marriage legitimizes these needs, but it creates gutless men who cheat on their wives. There is no chance for a man to be honest in marriage. So Sakharam rejects marriage in favor of a system of contractual cohabitation with single deserted women. He expects his women to be subservient to him as the owner of the house, to live with him as a wife, and to provide him with every service, including sex—an expectation disturbingly similar to the advice a Hindu bride would get. There is no emotional involvement whatsoever. His expectations are, in fact, no different from traditional Hindu husbands. But unlike a Hindu husband, he does not impose anything on the women. Then two women enter his life: Laxmi, a typical religious Hindu wife who has been deserted by her husband, and Champa, the rebel wife of an impotent police constable whom *she* has deserted out of sheer contempt. The violent passions that arise out of fanatic

religiosity, sexual possession, and violent jealousy weave a terrible net that catches Sakharam.

Tendulkar inverts the stereotypes of the weak, docile, and religious housewife (a role-model for a high-caste Hindu woman) and the sexually hungry, unruly wife (a detestable "Other"). The meek housewife Laxmi reduces Sakharam to impotence and manipulates him into killing Champa, while Champa's aggressive physicality and drunken bouts actually hide a sympathetic and anguished heart. Champa's death, however, seems inevitable.

Sakharam Binder seriously threatened middle-class morality, and that, combined with the violence on stage, the image of a woman drinking, and the obscenity of the dialogue, brought a storm of protest from the Censor Board and from audiences.

FURTHER READING

Bhalla, Neela. *Ghasiram Kotwal: Essays and Annotations.* Delhi: Worldview Publications, 2002.

Gokhle, Shanta. *Playwright at the Centre: Marathi Drama from 1843 to the Present.* Calcutta: Seagull, 2000.

Pandey, Sudhakar, and Freya Barua, eds. *New Directions in Indian Drama.* Delhi: Prestige Books, 1994.

Tendulkar, Vijay. *Collected Plays in Translation.* Delhi: Oxford Univ. Press, 1983.

——. *Vijay Tendulkar.* Delhi: Katha, 2002.

Maya Pandit

SALACROU, ARMAND (1899–1989)

One of the most successful French playwrights of the 20th century, Armand Salacrou, born on August 9, 1899, in Rouen, FRANCE, wrote over thirty plays, which were performed in both AVANT-GARDE and commercial theaters over nearly fifty years and were directed by the most notable directors of the period, including Aurélien Lugné-Poe, Jean-Louis Barrault, and Charles Dullin (who directed and acted in several of his premières). From his early surrealist-inspired short works, such as *The Plate Breaker* (Le Casseur d'assiettes) and *The Glass Ball* (La Boule de verre) (which was the basis and inspiration for ANTONIN ARTAUD's JET OF BLOOD), to his later plays, Salacrou shared the driving existential concerns of younger contemporaries such as JEAN-PAUL SARTRE and JEAN ANOUILH. His plays, distinguished by outstanding technical skill, dramatize the plight of individuals caught between metaphysical pessimism, liberal humanism, and individual desire.

Salacrou's work reflects his lifelong attempt to reconcile personal freedom and sociopolitical commitment, an awareness of the absurd, and a need for meaning. Having decided at an early age (after reading a scientific explanation of the universe) that God did not exist, Salacrou was determined to find direction for his life and was drawn to both artistic creation and engagement with leftist politics. As a youth before World War I, he wrote for the socialist paper *L'Humanité* and for the communist

Internationale. However, after swiftly making a small fortune with an advertising company in the 1930s, he just as quickly sold the business to devote the whole of his life not to politics, but to playwriting. After a brief period in the armed forces in World War II, he worked for the underground Resistance press alongside Sartre.

His plays vary in dramatic form according to their central thematic concerns, resulting in an oeuvre that employs theatrical modes as diverse as SURREALISM, FARCE, NATURALISM, vaudeville, EXPRESSIONISM, and psychological REALISM. Some plays, such as the masterly *Histoire de rire*, begin as sharp, spirited farces, but they inevitably have undercurrents of excruciating ontological uncertainty that bring them closer to AUGUST STRINDBERG than to NOËL COWARD. *The Unknown Woman of Arras* (*L'Inconnue d'Arras*) splinters linear time in expressionistic fashion by dramatizing the fraction of a second in a man's mind before the bullet he has just fired enters his brain. *Poof*, an enormously successful *comédie-ballet*, reflects Salacrou's own short commercial career in the story of a salesman who discovers the secret of advertising, rises to the top of the business, and then, unable to live in a world he has marketed successfully, leads the campaign for his own downfall. *Nights of Wrath* (*Les Nuits de la colère*), demonstrating the social perspective of BERTOLT BRECHT and the theatrical awareness of LUIGI PIRANDELLO, dramatizes characters in the French resistance movement evaluating the ultimate significance of their lives.

Trapped by the insoluble dilemma of the need for faith and the inability to believe, Salacrou's characters wrestle with the attempt to create a stable identity, always undermined by a reliance on others to remain stable themselves. A reluctant belief in determinism, a painful desire for purity, intense sexual jealousy, and a pervasive comedic anguish populate Salacrou's thematically consistent and distinctive oeuvre. He died on November 23, 1989, in Le Havre.

PLAYS: *Accessory Store* (*Magasin d'accessoires*, c. 1923); *Circus Story* (*Histoire de Cirque*, 1923); *The Plate Breaker* (*Le Casseur d'assiettes*, 1923); *The Thirty Tombs of Judas* (*Les Trente Tombes de Judas*, 1923); *The Glass Ball* (*La Boule de verre*, 1924); *The Bridge of Europe* (*Le Pont de l'Europe*, 1925); *Shore Leave* (*Tour à terre*, 1925); *Patchouli, or, the Disorders of Love* (*Patchouli, ou Les Désordres de l'amour*, 1927); *Atlas Hotel* (*Atlas-Hôtel*, 1929); *The Frenzied Ones* (*Les Frénétiques*, 1929); *The Good Life* (*La Vie en rose*, 1931); *A Free Woman* (*Une Femme libre*, 1933); *Poof* (1933); *The Unknown Woman of Arras* (*L'Inconnue d'Arras*, 1935); *A Man Like the Others* (*Un Homme comme les autres*, 1936); *The World Is Round* (*La Terre est ronde*, 1937); *When the Music Stops* (*Histoire de rire*, 1939); *Marguerite* (*La Marguerite*, 1941); *The Fiancés of Le Havre* (*Les Fiancés du Havre*, 1942); *The Soldier and the Witch* (*Le Soldat et la sorcière*, 1943); *The Lenoir Archipelago, or, One Must Not Touch Immobile Things* (*L'Archipel Lenoir, ou Il ne faut pas toucher aux choses immobiles*, 1945–1947); *Nights of Wrath* (*Les Nuits de la colère*, 1946); *Why Not Me?* (*Pourquoi Pas Moi?* 1947); *God Knew It, or, Life Isn't Serious* (*Dieu le savait, ou La Vie n'est pas sérieuse*, 1950); *No Entry, or, The Ages of Life* (*Sens Interdit, ou Les Âges de la Vie*, 1952); *God's Guests* (*Les Invités du Bon Dieu*, 1953); *Too Honest a Woman, or, It's All in the Way You Say It . . .* (*Une Femme trop honnête, ou Tout est dans la façon de le dire*, 1953); *The Mirror* (*Le Miroir*, 1954); *Boulevard Durand* (1959); *Like Thistles* (*Comme les chardons*, 1964); *The Black Street* (*La Rue noire*, 1966)

FURTHER READING

Hobson, Harold. *French Theatre Since 1830*. London: John Calder, 1978.

Knowles, Dorothy. *French Drama of the Inter-War Years*. London: George G. Harrap & Co. Ltd., 1967.

Looseley, David. *A Search for Commitment: The Theatre of Armand Salacrou*. Exeter: Univ. of Exeter Press, 1985.

Silenieks, Juris. *Themes and Dramatic Forms in the Plays of Armand Salacrou*. Lincoln: Univ. of Nebraska Studies, 1967.

Ubersfeld, Annie. *Armand Salacrou: Textes de Salacrou, points de vue critiques, témoinages, chronologie, bibliographie, illustrations* [Armand Salacrou: Texts by Salacrou, Critical Viewpoints, Testimonies, Chronology, Bibliography, Illustrations]. Paris: Seghers, 1970.

Kimberly Jannarone

SALVATION NELL

Salvation Nell opens with an unforgettable depiction of Sid McGovern's Empire Bar, a dive in New York City's Hell's Kitchen. When it premiered in 1908, American audiences had never before witnessed such a destitute scene or characters. Penned by young playwright EDWARD SHELDON, *Salvation Nell* contributed to the rise of REALISM on the American stage. Perhaps EUGENE O'NEILL said it best when he wrote that *Salvation Nell* "first opened my eyes to the existence of a real theater" (Barnes, 1957).

In the midst of this lower-class bar culture, Nell works scouring floors and emptying spittoons. Nell's boyfriend, Jim, becomes jealous of the men in the bar, and in a drunken rage beats a man to death. Consequently, Nell loses her job. With Jim in jail, she and her unborn baby become homeless. Desperate, Nell considers a job in a nearby brothel. Just as Nell descends into the underworld, Maggie from the Salvation Army intervenes. At the crossroad between vice and salvation, Nell chooses the latter and becomes known as Salvation Nell.

For eight years, Nell struggles as a single mother while working for the Salvation Army. Released from prison, Jim appears at Nell's apartment with foolish plans to make quick money. When Nell refuses to be a part of his criminal life, he strikes her and flees. In spite of Jim's violence, Nell does not lose hope. The play concludes with a moving speech by Nell in which she proclaims that love "always forgives an' waits with open arms fer every wanderin' sinner to come an' know the joy that lasts for all eternity!" Hearing these words, Jim seeks salvation and reconciles with Nell.

Scenic designers Ernest Gros and Frank Dodge also shaped the pioneering realism in Sheldon's text. Some critics claimed that *Salvation Nell*'s realistic scenery had surpassed well-known director DAVID BELASCO's creations. Producer Harrison Grey Fisk, utilizing an almost photo-documentary approach, bought Sid Empire's bar in Hell's Kitchen and literally reassembled it on stage. Similarly, the design team achieved the much-celebrated recreation of Cherry Street tenement dwellings by photographing the slum area and meticulously copying it onstage. The elaborate set decoration, with real fire escapes, lampposts, and hung laundry, took over twenty-four hours to assemble.

Some reviews suggested that *Salvation Nell*'s realistic artistry surpassed photography. Still others critiqued the play precisely because it was too realistic, calling it "slum realism" (Corbin, 1909). But if the play did portray the lower depths, it had an allure for upper-class audiences, who, as one article put it, took delight in "go[ing] slumming" (Review of *Salvation Nell*, *Everybody's Magazine* 20 [1909], 420.) *Salvation Nell* enjoyed a successful run of seventy-one performances and was subsequently chosen as the best play of 1908 by John Gassner.

[*See also* United States, 1860–1929]

FURTHER READING

Barnes, Eric Wollencott. *The High Room: A Biography of Edward Sheldon.* London: W. H. Allen, 1957.

Cohn, Art. "*Salvation Nell*: An Overlooked Milestone in American Theatre." *Educational Theatre Journal* 9 (1957): 11–22.

Corbin, John. "The Drama of the Slums." *Saturday Evening Post* (March 20, 1909): 15.

Dale, Alan. "Mrs. Fiske at Her Best—Play Held Audience Amazed." *New York American* (December 5, 1908).

"'Salvation Nell': A Theatrical Report on Life in the Slums." *New York Times* (November 22, 1908): VI:7.

Katie N. Johnson

SAMFUNDETS STØTTER   *See* PILLARS OF SOCIETY

SÁNCHEZ, FLORENCIO (1875–1910)

Born in Montevideo, Uruguay, in 1875, Florencio Sánchez is inextricably linked with the origins of Argentine theater. Frustrated with the political confrontations between *blancos* (whites) and *colorados* (people of color) that plagued his native country, he sought temporary refuge in BRAZIL, where he supported the uprising of a leader of the Partido Blanco (White Party) against the Uruguayan government.

Beginning in 1900, he took up residence in Buenos Aires and became a leading figure in the city's bohemian circle. It was among this group that he expounded the libertarian ideals that he would try to capture shortly thereafter in his dramatic work. Sudden success came in 1903 with *My Son the Doctor* (*M'hijo el dotor*), in which explored the generational conflict between the father (Olegario) and his son (Julio). The father espouses an unbending traditional morality typical of the Creole farmer that clashes sharply with the liberalism of the son, who is anxious to elude individual responsibility.

Notable among his other rural dramas is *The Hill Down There* (*Barranca Abajo*), the tragic story of the elderly Zoilo, who loses his land, his honor, his family's respect, and ultimately his life. In this way, Sánchez comments upon the inevitable dissolution of the old *modus vivendi* of the gaucho in the countryside of the Río Plata. In *The Foreigner* (*La Gringa*), he sounds a note of optimism with the final reconciliation that occurs between Creole natives (Cantalicio) and immigrants (Nicola), precipitated by the love of their respective children, Próspero and Victoria.

The issue of immigration is seen in his pieces that are set in cities, such as *The Eviction* (*El desalojo*). Occasionally, as well, he paints dramatic portraits of urban plight and life under conditions of extreme poverty—*Canillita*, *Marta Gruni*, and *False Money* (*Moneda falsa*). In other instances, Sánchez describes the economic decline of the middle class and the moral degradation that results from it. Such is the case in *In Family* (*En familia*), detailing the fruitless struggles of a quixotic son to save his family from disaster. To a lesser extent, *The Dead* (*Los Muertos*) also portrays a topsy-turvy home, with the father demoralized by alcoholism and a finale marked by a violence that is rare among the Uruguayan's dramatic work. *Our Children* (*Nuestros hijos*), on the other hand, denounces the cynical submissiveness to social conventions on the part of the well-to-do with such paroxysm that it seems to undercut the playwright's very thesis.

With considerable creative energy and social values inspired by Anarchist trends, Sánchez was ARGENTINA's prodigal son of his era. He deftly expressed an unparalleled realist style and thereby liberated the drama of the Río Plata from the inoffensive *costumbrismo* (customs and manners) in which it had been mired for so long. Attentive to the injustices of his era, he nevertheless maintained a certain faith in progress—undoubtedly the product of positivist convictions that were soon to be embraced by many others. Ultimately, Sánchez's influence proved fundamental to the development of Argentine theater. A handful of his plays, written with a deliberate urgency and force, had enough of an impact that the first decade of the 20th century came to be known as "the golden age of native theater." Sánchez died of tuberculosis—far from his beloved Río de la Plata—in Milan, ITALY, at the end of 1910.

PLAYS: *Canillita* (1903); *My Son, the Doctor* (*M'hijo el dotor*, 1903); *The Foreign Girl* (*La gringa*, 1904); *Poor People* (*La pobre gente*, 1904); *The Dead* (*Los muertos*, 1905); *Down the Cliffs* (*Barranca abajo*, 1905); *With Family* (*En Familia*, 1905); *Health Rights* (*Los derechos de la salud*, 1907); *Our Children* (*Nuestros hijos*, 1907); *Marta Gruni* (1908)

FURTHER READING

Giusti, Roberto. *Florencio Sánchez: Su vida y su obra* [Life and Works]. Buenos Aires: Agencia Sudamericana de Libros, 1920.

Imbert, Julio. *Florencio Sánchez: Vida y creación* [Life and Works]. Buenos Aires: Schapire, 1954.

Murena, H. A. "La pugna contra el silencio: Florencio Sánchez" [The Struggle against Silence: Florencio Sánchez]. In *El pecado original de América* [America's Original Sin]. Buenos Aires: Sur, 1954.

Richardson, Ruth. *Florencio Sánchez and the Argentine Theatre*. New York: The Hispanic Institute in the United States, 1933.

Rojas, Ricardo. "El teatro de Florencio Sánchez." *Nosotros V*, no. 27 (April 1911).

Viñas, David. Prologue to *M'hijo el dotor*. Buenos Aires: Huemul, 1964.

Norberto Cambiasso (Tr. by Gabriel Milner)

SANCHIS SINISTERRA, JOSÉ (1940–)

José Sanchis Sinisterra, born on June 28, 1940, in Valencia, SPAIN, is one of the most renowned Spanish playwrights of the last quarter of the 20th century. In his multifaceted career he has performed the various roles of director, professor, speaker, researcher, collaborator, and promoter of theatrical publications dedicated to theater and culture in general. A writer in constant process of renewal, Sanchis Sinisterra has pursued an ideologically novel theater discourse that is consistently concerned with formal expression and the construction of the dramatic text. Key influences on his work have been theoretical movements such as the Aesthetics of Reception as well as HAROLD PINTER's concept of ludic theater. Sanchis Sinisterra invites the spectator to participate through the imaginary, thereby modifying theatrical codes of spectatorial reception. His plays are sophisticated negotiations of popular consumerist productions and AVANT-GARDE theater. As a member of the so-called Generation of 1982, a group of university-trained playwrights whose first works coincided with the transition to democracy in Spain, he shares an interest in cultivated yet non-elitist formal innovations, intertextuality, subversion of traditional values and ethics, humor as instrument of social critique, and generational disenchantment.

Involved in theater from a young age, Sanchis Sinisterra began creating and directing diverse independent and university theater groups in 1957. In 1960 he traveled to Paris with a scholarship from the French Institute of Valencia. Through this transcendental experience, Sanchis Sinisterra would discover drama theorists that would have a permanent impact on his career, such as Jean-Louis Barrault, Louis Jouvet, ANTONIN ARTAUD, Jean Villar, and BERTOLT BRECHT. After 1966 he combined his theater activity with his university scholarship. In 1977 he founded *Teatro Fronterizo* (Border Theatre) as an aesthetic alternative to and an ideological critique of bourgeois theater. There he directed and staged original plays as well as adaptations of narrative and dramatic texts. In 1980 he wrote, staged, and published his first emblematic work, *Ñaque o de piojos y actores*, whose explicit references to Bertolt Brecht also appear in later works. Since 1988 he has been the director of *Beckett Room* (*Sala Beckett*), which later became the base for *Teatro Fronterizo* and a center for alternative theater in Barcelona. Among his many prizes, the most noteworthy is the National Award in 1990.

¡Ay, Carmela! was staged with tremendous success on November 5, 1987, in Zaragoza and went on to numerous Spanish, European, and U.S. cities, and was eventually adapted to the cinema by Carlos Saura. The play's formal innovations pay homage to Brecht and SAMUEL BECKETT, while its sociopolitical critique invokes his own *Teatro Fronterizo*. The motif of travel, intertextuality, metatheater, and the use of consciously vulgar humor fill this piece. *¡Ay, Carmela!* relates the tragic-comic story of Carmela and Paulino, two second-rate performers who accidentally cross enemy lines while in search of some sausage in the next town. They agree to perform in front of the national troops and adapt their performance accordingly. Carmela loses her life when, led by an irrational impulse, she makes common cause with the prisoners who are sentenced to death and are attending their performance. Paulino, on the other hand, saves his life by submitting to the nationalists in a humiliating way.

SELECT PLAYS: *Tú, no importa quién* (1962); *Midas* (1963); *Demasiado frío* (1965); *Algo así como Hamlet* (1970); *Tendenciosa manipulación del texto de La Celestina de Fernado de Rojas* (1974); *Ñaque o de piojos y actores* (1980); *El retablo de Eldorado* (1984); *¡Ay, Carmela!* (1986); *Crímines y locuras del traidor Lope de Aguirre* (1986); *Pervertimento y Otros gestos para nada* (1986); *El canto de la rana* (1987); *Los figurantes* (1988); *Perdida en los Apalaches* (1990); *Naufragios de Alvar Nuñez* (1991); *Mísero Prospero* (1992); *Valeria y los pájaros* (1992); *Bienvenidas* (1993); *El cerco de Leningrado* (1993); *Dos tristes tigres* (1993); *Marsal Marsal* (1994); *El lector por horas* (1996); *La raya del pelo de William Holden* (1999)

FURTHER READING

Ferreras, Juan Ignacio. *El teatro en el siglo XX (desde 1939)* [The Theater in the Twentieth Century (Since 1939)]. Madrid: Taurus, 1988.

Huerta Calvo, Javier. *Historia del teatro español II. Del siglo XVIII a la época actual* [History of Spanish Theater]. Madrid: Gredos, 2003.

Pedraza Jiménez, Felipe, and Milagros Rodríguez Cáceres. *Manual de literatura española XIV. Posguerra: dramaturgos y ensayistas.* Pamplona: Cénlit ediciones, 1995.

Ruiz Ramón, Francisco. *Historia del teatro español. Siglo XX* [History of Spanish Theater. Twentieth Century]. Madrid: Cátedra, 1977.

Sanchis Sinisterra, José. *¡Ay, Carmela! El lector por horas*. Madrid: Austral, 2000.

Esther Lomas-Sampedro

SÁNDOR, MALENA (1913–1968)

For Malena Sándor the theatre was her passion and religion; her past, her present and her future, her sacrifice and her ambition.
—Silvina Bullrich, "Lo que pude decir," 1969

Malena Sándor was born María Elena James de Terza on December 31, 1913, and she died prematurely of an asthma attack on October 4, 1968. While she was not the first woman to write for the Argentine stage, she was definitely the most successful female playwright to emerge in early 20th-century ARGENTINA.

Her plays consistently debuted in Buenos Aires, received honors, and featured some of the city's best-known actors and directors.

Like most of domestic COMEDIES of her day, Sándor's works primarily dramatized contemporary urban scenarios and relied on mainstream conventions to draw in the spectator. Yet rather than the typical escapist storyline, she offered a glimpse of Argentine society as seen through a feminist lens. Sándor's first two plays, the one-act *Daddy, I'm Getting a Divorce* (*Yo me divorcio papa*, 1937) and the full-length *A Free Woman* (*Una mujer libre*, 1938), both criticize antidivorce laws. *A Free Woman* won the prestigious Premio Nacional de Cultura and was adapted to the cinema in a French-Italian coproduction. The subsequent play, *Penelope No Longer Knits*, is a feminist revision of the *Odyssey* in which the once-devoted wife quits waiting patiently at home for her cheating husband to return. *She and Satan* (*Ella y Satán*, 1948), may have been influenced by Sándor's predecessor, the poet Alfonsina Storni, who attempted to cross over into theater in the late 1920s. Like Storni's controversial play, *The Master of the World* (*El amo del mundo*, 1927), *She and Satan* revolves around the relationship between the rich, egotistical Claudio and his poor but dignified lover, Márgara. *An Almost-Believable Story* (*Una historia casi verosímil*, 1966), Sándor's last play, takes place on Mars, demonstrating how ridiculous the social conflicts on Earth seem when viewed from another planet.

PLAYS: *Daddy, I'm Getting a Divorce* (*Yo me divorico, papa*, 1937); *A Free Woman* (*Una mujer libre*, 1938); *I'm the Strongest* (*Yo soy la más fuerte*, 1943); *Your Life and Mine* (*Tu vida y la mía*, 1945); *Penelope No Longer Knits* (*Pelélope no teje*, 1946); *The Bird Man* (*El hombre de los pájaros*, 194?*); *She and Satan* (*Ella y Satán*,1948); *The Answer Was Given* (*La respuesta fue dada*, 1956); *The Gods Return* (*Los dioses vuelven*, 1958); *A Boy Named Daniel* (*Un muchacho llamado Daniel*, 1961); *An Almost-Believable Story* (*Una historia casi verosímil*, 1966)

FURTHER READING

Bullrich, Silvina. "Lo que no pude decir" [What cannot be said]. In *Teatro Completo* [Complete Plays] by Malena Sandor, ed. by Edmundo Guiburg. Buenos Aires: Editorial Talía, 1969.

Dauster, Frank. "Raising the Curtain: Great Ladies of the Theatre." In *Performance, pathos, política de los sexos* [Performance, Pathos, Politics of the Sexes], ed. by Heidrun Alder and Kati Röttger. Madrid: Iberoamericana, 1999. 23–40.

Farnsworth, May Summer. "The Well-Made (Feminist) Play: Malena Sándor's Comic Innovations on the Argentine Stage in the 1930s and 1940s." *Latin American Theatre Review* 37, no. 1 (2003): 61–73.

Jones, Willis Knapp. *Behind Spanish American Footlights*. Austin: Univ. of Texas Press, 1966.

May Summer Farnsworth

SANGSHUPING JISHI   See THE CHRONICLE OF SANGSHUPING

SARATOGA

Damn travelling for pleasure.
—Remington, Act 2

Saratoga, or, Pistols for Seven, BRONSON HOWARD's first professional production, opened in New York on December 21, 1870, at AUGUSTIN DALY's Fifth Avenue Theatre. For its day, the five-act play's 101-night run showed remarkable success, especially for a debut, earning Howard $175 per week. Considered one of his "social plays," *Saratoga* also established Howard's interest in the American business class, the group he explored throughout his career. Frank Marshall's British adaptation, produced by Charles Wyndham, opened as *Brighton* at London's Court Theatre on May 25, 1874. In ironic contrast to Howard's consistent respectability, Wyndham's version earned critic William Archer's (1882) denunciation for vulgarity, specifically for a woman character's remark, inserted in the adaptation, that implied she preferred a husband sleep nude. Wyndham produced the play in GERMANY as *Seine Erste und Einzige Liebe*; it was possibly the first German production of an American play.

Howard drew on America's reviving interest in the European COMEDY of manners for his cynical view of American socialites at play. The script's greatest weakness lies in Howard's attempt to combine COMEDY, FARCE, and social commentary, resulting in a script that lacks direction. The play also shows an early knack for dialogue and comic development, however, which offsets its shortcomings.

Set in the title's literal watering hole, *Saratoga* follows the romantic misadventures of Bob Sackett. The farcical story line merely forms a unifying device that Howard uses to set American and English social pretensions at each other, leaving both looking foolish at best. The competition is scattered through the story, interspersed with apparently tangential scenes that mock moral and racial hypocrisy; although carefully drawn, they often have little to do with Sackett's predictable escapades.

Simultaneously engaged to four women, Sackett finds himself at Saratoga's Congress Springs, where his fiancées all have arrived and become close friends. As he attempts to avoid exposure, Sackett realizes he actually loves one of them. Inevitably, his deception disintegrates, and he risks dueling four men. Sackett's solution contrives to avoid violence, reconcile one marriage, instigate two others, and ensure his own. In the process, Howard overturns contemporary notions of women's modesty and propriety and attempts to develop a sense of their cleverness and independence. Ultimately, however, notions of the women's insight and self-determination narrow to matters of marital choice.

In a broader sense, *Saratoga* reflects its society most strongly in the side events that Howard distributes throughout Sackett's story. In his treatment of African American characters, Howard reveals and may even subtly denounce white bigotry in the postemancipation era. Though the black servant characters speak in exaggerated dialect, referring to themselves repeatedly as "we culled gemmen at Saratoga," their voice carries a double-edged sense of observation with potential for mockery. Howard also develops a slightly ambiguous sense of the black servants' awareness of their independence. Though possibly playing for laughs, he repeatedly records the hypocritical limits to black freedom, most notably when Sackett addresses the servants as "Fellow American citizens— . . . of African descent."

Saratoga has enjoyed various American revivals, and the Royal Shakespeare Company produced it 1978.

[*See also* United States, 1860–1929]

FURTHER READING

Archer, William. *English Dramatists of Today*. London: Sampson Low, 1882.

Bloomfield, Maxwell. "Mirror for Businessmen: Bronson Howard's Melodramas, 1870–1890." *Midcontinent American Studies Journal* 5 (Fall 1964): 38–49.

Felheim, Marvin. "Bronson Howard, 'Literary Attaché.' " *American Literary Realism* 2 (Summer 1969): 174–179.

Frerer, Lloyd Anton. *Bronson Howard, Dean of American Dramatists*. Lewiston, N.Y.: Edwin Mellen Press, 2001.

Gottlieb, Lois C. "The Antibusiness Theme in Late Nineteenth Century American Drama." *The Quarterly Journal of Speech* 64 (1978): 415–426.

Quinn, Arthur Hobson. *A History of the American Drama from the Civil War to the Present Day*, Vol. 1. New York: F. S. Crofts, 1943. 40–65.

Ron West

SARDOU, VICTORIEN (1831–1908)

Born in Paris on September 5, 1831, Victorien Sardou studied medicine and later taught math, literature, and history; he worked as a journalist from 1850–1860. His first play, *The Student's Tavern* (1854), was a miserable failure, but by 1861 four of his works had been produced to some acclaim, and during that single year, five were running simultaneously. One of these, A SCRAP OF PAPER, secured the playwright's lifelong popularity.

The author of some seventy plays, Sardou has been referred to as the 19th century's ultimate showman. He possessed an acute theatrical sense, understanding his audience as a crowd that was to be entertained, and he rarely sought to do more. Although Sardou found inspiration in contemporary morality, DUMAS FILS saw him as a rival whose plays lacked moral instruction; for Sardou, change was not the object of art. In his stagecraft, if not in his social politics, he was nearly perfect: he practiced drama as a combination of literary artifice and carpentry, and as a formula in which plot took precedence over character. Sardou hybridized previous styles, organizing them under the structure of the well-made play and reinforcing the virtuosity of plot. His plays are not matters of character motivation, but of dramatic causation, mosaics of convenient moments that disregard unity of action: incident is heaped upon incident, consis-

tently disguising the principal action, which only emerges in a manufactured denouement, often involving an inert object like the titular scrap of paper or a fan in *Tosca*. Sardou bore no illusions about the shallowness of his social observations: his characters are caricatures, drawn very broadly and literally— he sketched types he saw around Paris, preferring general form to precise detail. His characters float on his plots much as his sketches floated on paper.

Sardou was praised for giving spectators what they wanted, without shocking, scolding, or duping them. For him, suspense relied on the tenuousness of scenes whose action consists of misunderstandings one question away from being resolved, or objects one step away from being found. However much he courted popular taste, he did not compromise his art, and he often turned to the current historical moment for inspiration. For example, when Baron Haussmann was redesigning the streets of Paris, Sardou gave *The New House*, a satire of an architect's ambitions. When civil discord was brewing around the Franco-Prussian War, he wrote *Homeland* and *Hate*. Turning his attention to spectacle toward the end of his career, Sardou successfully presented *Robespierre*, a historical extravaganza with a cast of sixty-nine, plus some two hundred and fifty extras. *Dante* included a cast of forty-nine and the most advanced stage effects of the period. Although the 1880s saw a rise in interest in the psychological implications of NATURALISM, Sardou weathered its influence by redefining the COMEDY of intrigue with wit, imagination, and endless vigor.

Although critics have panned Sardou for shallow investigation, lack of originality, vulgarity, and a DRAMATURGY of contrivance and implausability, his works were widely produced across Europe and in America during his lifetime. He was an architect more than a student of modern manners, and his technical virtuosity has rarely been matched. Sardou died in Marly-le-Roi, on November 8, 1908.

[*See also* France]

SELECT PLAYS: *The Students' Tavern* (*La taverne des étudiants*, 1854); *The First Arms of Figaro* (*Les premières armes de Figaro*, 1859); *The Nervous People* (*Les gens nerveux*, 1859); *Our Friends* (*Nos intimes*, 1860); *A Scrap of Paper* (*Les pattes de mouche*, 1860); *The Strong Women* (*Les femmes fortes*, 1860); *Progress* (*Les ganaches*, 1862); *The Black Devils* (*Les diables noirs*, 1863); *The Neighbor's Apples* (*Les pommes du voisin*, 1864); *The Benoîton Family* (*La famille Benoîton*, 1865); *The Old Boys* (*Les vieux garçons*, 1865); *The New House* (*Maison neuve*, 1866); *Our Good Villagers* (*Nos bons villageois*, 1866); *Seraphine* (*Séraphine*, 1868); *Homeland* (*Patrie*, 1869); *Fernande* (1870); *Rabagas* (1872); *Hatred* (*La haine*, 1874); *Diplomacy* (*Dora*, 1877); *Daniel Rochat* (1880); *Let's Get a Divorce!* (*Divorçons*, 1880); *Odette* (1881), *Fedora* (*Fédora*, 1882); *Theodora* (*Théodora*, 1884); *Georgette* (1885); *The Crocodile* (*Le crocodile*, 1886); *La Tosca* (*Tosca*, 1887); *Cleopatra* (*Cléopâtre*, 1891); *Thermidor* (1891); *Madame Shameless* (*Madame Sans-Gêne*, 1893); *Gismonda* (1898); *Pamela* (*Paméla*, 1898);

Robespierre (1899); *Dante* (1903); *The Track* (*La piste*, 1906); *The Affair of the Poisons* (*L'affaire des poisons*, 1907)

FURTHER READING

Chandler, Frank Wadleigh. *The Contemporary Drama of France*. Boston: Little, Brown, 1920.

Doumic, René. *Portraits d'écrivains* [Portraits of Writers]. Paris: Librairie Académique, 1911.

Filon, Augustin. *The Modern French Drama*. Tr. by Janet E. Hogarth. London: Chapman and Hall, 1898. Originally published as *De Dumas à Rostand: esquisse du mouvement dramatique contemporain* [From Dumas to Rostand: Sketch of the Contemporary Dramatic Movement]. (Paris: A. Fayard & cie, 1898).

Mauris, Maurice. *French Men of Letters*. New York: Appleton, 1880.

Matt Di Cintio

SAROYAN, WILLIAM (1908–1981)

I seem to insist that people are good, that living is good, that decency is right, that good is not only achievable but inevitable—and there does not appear to be any justification for this.

—William Saroyan, in a preface to *Don't Go Away Mad*, 1949

Probably the best clue to understanding the writings of William Saroyan can be found in the statement above from *Don't Go Away Mad* (1949), a play set in a hospital for incurable diseases. An honest eccentric whose view of life was at once exciting, exasperating, and penetrating in its abrupt simplicity, Saroyan believed in dreams. As Joe, the protagonist in THE TIME OF YOUR LIFE, says: "I believe in dreams sooner than statistics." Understandably, such an approach to humanity coupled with Saroyan's happy-go-lucky vision of the theater utterly befuddled his critics. Yet the play won both the Pulitzer Prize and the Drama Critics' Circle Award. Saroyan, characteristically, refused the Pulitzer Prize on the grounds that the commercial world should not patronize art.

Born on August 31, 1908, in Fresno, California, Saroyan was the child of Armenian immigrants. At his father's death in 1911, poverty forced his mother to place her children in an orphanage for five years. Reunited with his family in an Armenian neighborhood where physical work was glorified, Saroyan revealed his individuality in his determination to become a writer. When he published the story "The Daring Young Man on the Flying Trapeze" in 1934, which brought him international attention, he quit his job. He made his greatest contributions to American literature and the theater between 1934 and 1943, when he was inducted into the army and married.

Saroyan's fascination with the stage began in 1939 and never ended, although after World War II, audiences had generally lost interest in all but a few of his early plays. MY HEART'S IN THE HIGHLANDS (1939) seemed to startle everyone. While theatrical offerings during the 1930s ranged from such entertainments as Ann Nichols's sentimental COMEDY ABIE'S IRISH ROSE (1937) to JOHN HOWARD LAWSON's aggressive Marxism, there was a pervading political atmosphere that Saroyan's plays whimsi-

cally shattered. Interested in fantasy rather than mobilization, he found discipline of any kind—political, social, or aesthetic—quite beyond him. Seemingly at odds with everything the theater was then promoting, he touched something in that amorphous condition of humanity in ways that held tremendous appeal. With unbounded faith in the goodness of people, he insisted on beauty in life.

Before going into the army, Saroyan had seen ten of his plays produced and four of them favorably received. *My Heart's in the Highlands* opened on April 13, 1939, with the oldest message in the world, according to Saroyan: "It is better to be a good human being than to be a bad one." *The Time of Your Life* opened at the Shubert Theatre in October and quickly became a modern American classic. In *Love's Old Sweet Song*, 1940, Saroyan continued his optimistic saga, centering on a family of migrant workers from Oklahoma who settle on a woman's lawn in Bakersfield, California. *The Beautiful People*, 1941, again exploited the sweetness of people. In all of these plays, the plots are so sketchy and improbable that their insignificance seems basic, yet the compelling emotions they evoke reveals Saroyan as a master of the showman's art.

After the war, plagued by marital upheavals, gambling, and other personal problems, Saroyan essentially lost his theater audience. Only *The Cave Dwellers* (1957), in which a group of virtuous people squat in an old theater building (representing the world) and discover that all is good, reached Broadway. From 1944 through 1980, he produced or published twenty-eight more plays, plus a number of television and radio plays, all reflecting his bouyant optimism and sentimentality but falling short of his prewar efforts. Saroyan, however, remained a remarkably prolific writer, mainly publishing novels and reminiscences. At a time when optimism and innocence were becoming suspect in America, he created a brave new world without much else. He died on May 18, 1981, in Fresno, having outlived much of his fame, and left much of his fortune to the William Saroyan Foundation.

[See also United States, 1920–1940]

PLAYS: *My Heart's in the Highlands* (1939); *The Hungerers* (1939); *The Time of Your Life* (1939); *The Great American Goof* (1940); *Hero of the World* (1940); *Love's Old Sweet Song* (1940); *The Ping-Pong Game* (1940); *Radio Play* (1940); *Something About a Soldier* (1940); *A Special Announcement* (1940); *Subway Circus* (1940); *Sweeney in the Trees* (1940); *Across the Board on Tomorrow Morning* (1941); *The Beautiful People* (1941); *Hello, Out There* (1941); *Jim Dandy* (1941); *The People with Light Coming Out of Them* (1941); *There's Something I Got to Tell You* (1941); *The Agony of Little Nations* (1942); *Bad Men in the West* (1942); *Coming Through the Rye* (1942); *Elmer and Lilly* (1942); *Opera, Opera* (1942); *The Poetic Situation in America* (1942); *Razzle Dazzle, or, The Human Opera* (1942); *Talking to You* (1942); *Get Away Old Man* (1943); *Sam's Ego House* (1947); *A Decent Birth, A Happy Funeral* (1949); *Don't Go Away Mad* (1949); *The Son* (1950); *The Slaughter of the Innocents*

(1952); *The Oyster and the Pearl* (1953); *A Lost Child's Fireflies* (1954); *Once Around the Block* (1956); *The Cave Dwellers* (1957); *Ever Been in Love with a Midget* (1957); *The Accident* (1958); *Cat, Mouse, Man, Woman* (1958); *The Dogs, or, The Paris Comedy* (1960); *Sam, the Highest Jumper of Them All* (1960); *Settle Out of Court* (with Henry Cecil, 1960); *High Time Along the Wabash* (1961); *Ah Man* (1962); *The Doctor and the Patient* (1963); *The Handshakers* (1963); *The Playwright and the Public* (1963); *This I Believe* (1963); *Chris Sick, or, Happy New Year Anyway* (1969); *Making Money* (1969); *The New Play* (1970); *Armenians* (1974); *The Rebirth Celebration of the Human Race at Artie Zabala's Off-Broadway Theatre* (1975); *Assassinations* (1979); *Jim, Sam and Anna* (1979); *Play Things* (1980)

FURTHER READING

Calonne, David Stephen. *William Saroyan: My Real Work Is Being.* Chapel Hill: Univ. of North Carolina Press, 1973.

Floan, Howard Russell. *William Saroyan.* New York: Twayne Publishers, 1966.

Foard, Elizabeth C. *William Saroyan: A Reference Guide.* Boston: G. K. Hall and Co., 1989.

Lee, Lawrence, and Barry Gifford. *Saroyan: A Bibliography.* New York: Harper & Row, 1984.

Nathan, George Jean. *The Magic Mirror.* New York: Alfred Knopf, 1960.

Whitmore, Jon. *William Saroyan: A Research and Production Source Book.* Westport, Conn.: Greenwood, 1995.

Walter J. Meserve

SARRAUTE, NATHALIE (1900–1999)

Nathalie Sarraute first became known as a novelist associated with the *nouveau roman* (new novel) movement. A group of postwar writers, including Alain Robbe-Grillet, Michel Butor, ROBERT PINGET, and MARGUERITE DURAS, sought to define a new REALISM for the novel. They renovated the form with their use of spare or elliptical language, first-person narration, and modern psychology. Because their explorations often depicted dramatically charged studies of interior states of being, it was natural for some of the "new novelists," most notably Duras, Sarraute, and Pinget, to extend their methods to dramatic form.

Born Nathalie Tcherniak in RUSSIA on July 18, 1900, Sarraute spent her childhood in Russia and FRANCE. She received a degree in English from the Sorbonne in Paris and married Raymond Sarraute in 1923. Her first major work, a series of short sketches entitled *Tropisms* (*Tropismes*, 1937) offers a clue how to read her other works. "Tropism" refers to an involuntary response—negative or positive—that an organism makes when stimulated. Sarraute saw this scientific concept as emblematic of all human interaction. All of her works—whether play, novel, or sketch—are, on one level, representative studies of banal experience that nevertheless demonstrate how the subtlest shifts in perception can cause great impacts.

Portrait, her second novel, was published in 1946, and featured a preface by JEAN-PAUL SARTRE in which he coined the term *anti-novel* to describe Sarraute's writing. This term could describe her plays as well. Anti-Aristotelian and antitheatrical, they are hazy slips of dramatic landscape. Her first play, tellingly titled *The Silence* (*Le Silence*), was published in 1964 and first performed three years later at the Théâtre de France, starring the grande dame of Parisian theater, Madeleine Renaud. It features a carefully nuanced world devoid of plot. Six of the seven characters are nameless, differentiated only as Woman 1, Woman 2, Man 1, and so forth. Voices stream in from unknown sources; small wonder that most of Sarraute's plays have been performed as radio dramas.

Her next play, *The Lie* (*Le Mensonge*) was broadcast in 1966. *Isma* (*Izzum*) was produced in 1973, *It Is Beautiful* (*C'est beau*) in 1975, and *It Is There* (*Elle est là*) 1980. Among these works, the only play to feature named characters is *The Lie*. Her last play, *For a Yes or a No* (*Pour un oui ou pour un non*) was performed as a radio drama in 1982. Sarraute died in Paris on October 19, 1999.

Sarraute's plays do not feature fantastic plots or romantic liaisons, nor do they reside in the brash, vertiginous worlds that her absurdist contemporaries created. Sarraute prefers to dwell in hidden layers, in sub-conversations, interior landscapes, and communicative silences. Perhaps because of her interest in the subtle and mundane, she received virtually no attention at the beginning of her career. In time, however, French critics embraced her austere vision, and her works began to be translated and performed worldwide. Her semiautobiographical novel *L'Enfance* (*Childhood*), published in 1983, was adapted for the stage and performed in New York City.

PLAYS: *The Lie* (*Le Mensonge*, 1967); *The Silence* (*Le Silence*, 1967); *Isma* (*Izzum*, 1970); *It's Beautiful* (*C'est beau*, 1975); *It Is There* (*Elle est là*, 1978); *For a Yes or a No* (*Pour un oui ou pour un non*, 1982)

FURTHER READING

Besser, Gretchen Rous. *Nathalie Sarrautre.* Boston: Twayne, 1979.

Knapp, Bettina. *Nathalie Sarraute.* Amsterdam: Rodopi, 1994.

Sarraute, Nathalie. *Childhood.* Tr. by Barbara Wright. London: Calder, 1984.

Sarraute, Nathalie, with Simone Benmussa. *Nathalie Sarraute, quêtes-vous?* [Nathalie Sarraute, Who are you?]. Paris: Folio, 1987.

Sarraute, Nathalie. *Tropisms.* Tr. by Maria Jolas. New York: George Braziller, 1963.

Kate Bredeson

SARTRE, JEAN-PAUL (1905–1980)

Widely considered the most popular philosopher in the two decades following World War II, Jean-Paul Sartre was also a playwright, novelist, biographer, and essayist of enormous cultural prominence. His elevated status, as Iris Murdoch noted in her fine book *Sartre—Romantic Rationalist* (1990), derives less from his standing as professional metaphysician than from his role as spokesperson for existentialism, a philosophical movement he helped turn, along with ALBERT CAMUS, into a mid-20th-century literary phenomenon. His plays—perhaps even more than his novels and certainly more than his philosophical essays—were critical in introducing existentialism to a broad public. Yet his reliance on more conventional DRAMATURGY (ranging from staid drawing-room drama to sensational MELODRAMA) places him at a level below his most admired contemporaries, such as BERTOLT BRECHT, SAMUEL BECKETT, and JEAN GENET, all of whom elaborated innovative theatrical forms for their radical visions.

Born on June 21, 1905, in Paris, FRANCE, Sartre grew up in the home of his maternal grandfather, a professor of German language at the Sorbonne. (His father died before he was born.) Sartre graduated first in his class from the prestigious École Normale Supérieure in 1929 with a doctorate in PHILOSOPHY. (Simone de Beauvoir, his short-term paramour and lifelong intellectual companion, ranked second in the same class.) After the university, Sartre served in the French Army from 1929 to 1931 before taking a position as a provincial schoolmaster at Le Havre. His academic career brought him to Berlin, GERMANY, where he studied the works of the German philosopher Edmund Husserl, whose theory of phenomenology was a crucial step in the development of existentialism, as well as the writings of Martin Heidegger, which significantly advanced existentialism from its phenomenological beginnings.

After shuffling through various provincial teaching positions, Sartre finally obtained an academic position in Paris, where he published *Nausea* (1938), a novel that contains the central preoccupations of his own existential thought. Written in diary form, the work tracks the alienated existence of Antoine Roquentin, a character who plunges headlong into the absurdity of human existence, confronting such quintessential Sartrean ideas as the contingency of phenomenon, the lack of relationship between language and reality, and the semiredemptive nature of art. Most important, however, is the protagonist's queasy recognition of humanity's fundamental freedom. Through the course of his depressive mental journey, Roquentin comes to see that, deprived of metaphysical purpose, our lives are our own responsibility, and that only our bad faith or false social conformity prevents us from accepting our autonomous birthright.

Nausea was soon followed by a collection of short stories, *Le Mur* (*The Wall*, 1939), which established Sartre's reputation as the Left Bank intellectual of the day. His literary rise, however, was delayed by the start of World War II. Sartre was taken prisoner with his military unit in 1940 and spent nine months in a German prison camp, where he continued his philosophical studies and even wrote a play for his fellow prisoners. Having falsified his military papers to show that he was unfit for service, he was sent back to France, where he joined the Resistance movement. But political commitment for Sartre meant first and foremost literary production, and the German Occupation turned out to be one of his most prolific periods. During these difficult years he managed not only to write his major philosophical work, *Being and Nothingness* (1943), but also to have two of his most important plays produced in Paris, THE FLIES (*Les Mouches*, 1943) and NO EXIT (*Huis Clos*, 1944).

The Flies, Sartre's first professionally performed play, was directed by Charles Dullin at the Théâtre de la Cité–Sarah Bernhardt in Paris. A retelling of Orestes' revenge against his mother, the drama recasts the ancient myth from a TRAGEDY of fate into a tragedy of freedom. Orestes not only *consciously* chooses to kill his mother Clytemnestra and her lover Aegistheus in retaliation for the murder of Orestes' father Agamemnon, he willingly assumes full responsibility for his decision in the hope that by embracing his "criminal" act, he can liberate the people of Argos from their submissive penitence. Though *The Flies* engages many of the core philosophical precepts of Sartrean freedom, the work spoke more powerfully to its original audience as a political commentary on Vichy France. Though the piece, like much of Sartre's dramatic writing, can seem plodding and overly didactic, it continues to resonate beyond its historical circumstances, offering a stirring advocacy of the necessity of resistance over collaboration in the face of authoritarian oppression.

Considered Sartre's dramatic masterpiece, *No Exit* was the first play to be produced in liberated Paris. Presented at the Vieux Colombier in September 1944, the tightly constructed one-act examines three characters that, confined together in the afterworld, are forced to contend with each other's assessments of their own shameful pasts. The notion that existence precedes essence—or as one character puts it, "You are your life, and nothing else"—takes on a grim finality as exculpatory aims and motives can no longer lighten the burden of the weak and wicked choices the trio made during their previous lives. The refusal to get false validation from one of his fellow damned chambermates provokes the journalist Garcin to utter the oft-quoted Sartrean line, "Hell is other people!" For Sartre the sentiment is not so much universal as it is symptomatic of a life lived in bad faith.

Sartre's other major plays include *The Victors* (*Morts sans sepulture*, 1946), *The Respectful Prostitute* (*La Putain respectueuse*, 1946), *Dirty Hands* (*Les Mains Sales*, 1948), *The Devil and the Good Lord* (*Le Diable et le Bon Dieu*, 1951), an adaptation of Dumas's *Kean* (1953), *Nekrassov* (1955), THE CONDEMNED OF ALTONA (*Les Séquestrés d'Altona*, 1959), and an adaptation of Euripides' *Trojan Women* (*Les troyennes*, 1965). Though consistently written in modern prose and marked by naturalistic dialogue, his dramatic oeuvre varies stylistically, borrowing freely from Greek tragedy, the well-made play, and bourgeois melodrama. In all cases, however, Sartre's theater is rooted in action, as opposed to character, which should come as no surprise given that his philosophy concerns itself more with concrete deeds than abstract desires. For Sartre existence implies the exercise of freedom. Accordingly, he envisioned a "theater of situations," in which a character is defined by his or her behavior within an often-violent set of extreme circumstances.

Sartre tends to organize his scenarios dialectically around complex social and political issues. For example, in *The Respectful Prostitute*, he tackles the hierarchical system of race and class in American society by ironically exploring the relationship of a white prostitute and a black man falsely accused of raping her. In *The Devil and the Good Lord*, he investigates contemporary religious hypocrisy through an atheistic parable set in Reformation Germany. But no matter the era in which the play is set, Sartre believed that the dramatized conflict should shed light on modern social dilemmas (*Sartre on Theater*, "On Dramatic Style," 1976).

Though Sartre's political solidarity inevitably rested with those whose freedom had been curtailed by history, his literary response was rarely programmatic or rigidly ideological. Sartre (1976) once compared the theater "to a sort of ring in which people battle for their rights." While his melodramatic dramaturgy doesn't quite aspire to Georg Wilhelm Friedrich Hegel's ideal of tragedy as "the collision of equally justified powers" (1998), Sartre can't help allowing the human element to complicate simplistic moral pictures. In *Dirty Hands*, for example, the character of Hugo is an assassin whose crime was ostensibly committed for political reasons, yet flashbacks reveal that the motive may have been muddled by chance and misunderstanding. Did Hugo shoot his victim for compromising communist ideology or for wounding his friend's fragile sexual ego? Ambiguity provokes more questions than definitive answers. In *The Condemned of Altona*, the protagonist who has been living in voluntary confinement in his father's house turns out be both a Nazi hero and someone whose entire life has been cruelly determined by historical and family pressures. In short, he is both perpetrator and casualty—a life that can only *reasonably* culminate in suicide.

Sartre was awarded the Nobel Prize for Literature in 1964, which he declined, claiming, "A writer must refuse to allow himself to be transformed into an institution." Sartre's radicalism, however, ultimately failed to manifest itself on the level of artistic form. As Martin Esslin observes in *The Theater of the Absurd* (1962), "While Sartre or Camus express the new content in the old conventions, the Theater of the Absurd goes a step further in trying to achieve a unity between its basic assumptions and the form in which they are expressed." Sartre may have been one of the most incisive admirers of Genet's theater (his biography, *Saint Genet*, is certainly an existential classic), but he was unable to stage a similar dramaturgical rebellion on the level of THE MAIDS and THE BALCONY. Instead, he deployed more orthodox dramatic structures to give trenchant analyses of 20th-century political, social, and philosophical quagmires, and for that he has earned a rightful place in the canon of modern drama. Sartre died on April 15, 1980, in Paris.

PLAYS: *The Flies* (*Les Mouches*, 1943); *No Exit* (*Huis Clos*, 1944); *The Respectful Prostitute* (*La Putain respectueuse*, 1946), *The Victors* (*Morts sans sepulture*, 1946); *Dirty Hands* (*Les Mains Sales*, 1948); *The Devil and the Good Lord* (*Le Diable et le Bon Dieu*, 1951); an adaptation of Dumas's *Kean* (1953); *Nekrassov* (1955); *The Condemned of Altona* (*Les Séquestrés d'Altona*, 1959); an adaptation of Euripides' *Trojan Women* (*Les troyennes*, 1965)

FURTHER READING

Bentley, Eric. *The Playwright as Thinker*. San Diego: Harcourt Brace Jovanovich, 1946.

Esslin, Martin. *The Theatre of the Absurd*. London: Eyre Methuen, 1962.

Hegel, G. W. F. *Aesthetics: Lectures on Fine Art, Volume II*. Tr. by T. M. Knox. Oxford: Clarendon Press: 1998.

Howells, Christina. *Sartre—The Necessity of Freedom*. Cambridge: Cambridge Univ. Press, 1988.

Kern, Edith, ed. *Sartre—A Collection of Critical Essays*. Englewood Cliffs, N.J.: Prentice Hall, 1965.

Murdoch, Iris. *Sartre—Romantic Rationalist*. London: Vintage, 1999.

McCall, Dorothy. *The Theatre of Jean-Paul Sartre*. New York: Columbia Univ. Press, 1969.

Sartre, Jean-Paul. *What Is Literature?* Tr. by Bernard Frechtman. London: Methuen, 1950.

——. *Sartre on Theater*. Tr. by Frank Jellinek. New York: Pantheon Books, 1976.

——. *Basic Writings*. Ed. by Stephen Priest. London: Routledge, 2001.

Thody, Philip. *Jean-Paul Sartre—A Literary and Political Study*. London: Hamish Hamilton, 1960.

Wood, Philip R. *Understanding Jean-Paul Sartre*. Columbia: Univ. of South Carolina Press, 1990.

Charles McNulty

SARUMPAET, RATNA (1949–)

Ratna Sarumpaet, INDONESIA's leading female playwright and director, was born in Tarutung, North Sumatra, in 1949, but moved to Jakarta as a teenager to attend the Catholic University. A performance of W. S. RENDRA's *The Barzanji Chant* (*Kasidah Berzanji*, 1969) inspired her to study in his Workshop Theatre. She acted with Rendra and other leading theater artists in the early 1970s, taking inspiration from communal living, group improvisations, and staging, which indigenized foreign works by using regional costumes and performance techniques. In 1974 she founded her own production company, One Red Stage (Satu Merah Panggung). Just converted to Islam, she directed her own adaptation of Omar Khayyam's *Rubayat*, then versions of *Hamlet* and *Romeo and Juliet* using Batak cultural elements in 1975. Like many discouraged Indonesian theater artists, she turned to writing for film and television in the late 1970s. She returned to theater in 1989 with indigenous stagings of *Othello* and JEAN ANOUILH's ANTIGONE.

In the early 1990s, Sarumpaet began researching political persecution of women by the Indonesian government. In 1992, she wrote and produced a documentary on women's roles in Indonesian development, which the national television network refused to air. In May 1993, Marsinah, a young East Javanese woman, was sexually mutilated and murdered several days after leading a strike at the factory where she worked. A group of soldiers was arrested, but the Indonesian court (a far from independent judiciary) deferred justice. Marsinah became a symbol of the Suharto government's crimes, hypocrisies, and underlying corruption. Drawing from this real-life outrage, Sarumpaet wrote her best-known work: *Marsinah: Songs from the Underworld* (*Marsinah: Nyanyian dari Bawah Tanah*, 1993). Sarumpaet herself speaks through the character of Marsinah from beyond the grave in accusation of President Suharto. With this piece and a related series of monologues called *Marsinah Accuses* (*Marsinah Menggugat*, 1997), Sarumpaet changed from a purveyor of Western classics into an agitational performance artist of *Reformsi*, the Indonesian reform movement. Imprisoned several times in the mid-1990s for organizing political demonstrations, she became a popular celebrity after Suharto's resignation in 1998.

Although Sarumpaet is best known for her Marsinah plays, she wrote several other works denouncing Suharto between 1994 and 1998, and since his fall she continues to portray injustices that still plague Indonesia. In 2000 she wrote *Alia, Wound on the Doorstep to Mecca* (*Alia, Luka Serambi Mekah*), depicting the ongoing confrontation between freedom fighters and the Indonesian military in Aceh. In 2001 she wrote *In the Long Darkness* (*Dalam Kegelapan Panjang*) about the children of communist parents who were stigmatized after the anticommunist massacres that brought Suharto to power in 1965. Despite activism on the behalf of women's issues, Sarumpaet does not identify herself as a feminist (a controversial term in Indonesia). Rather, she feels compelled to call attention to crimes against humanity.

PLAYS: *Rubayat of Omar Khayam* (1974); *Marsinah: Songs from Beneath the Earth* (*Marsinah: Nyanyian dari Bawah Tanah*, 1993); *Muning's Blood* (*Darah Muning*, 1993); *The Final Celebration* (*Pesta Terakhir*, 1994); *Shackled* (*Terpasung*, 1995); *Marsinah Accuses* (*Marsinah Menggugat* 1997); *The King* (*Sang Raja*, 1998); *Alia: Wound on the Doorstep of Mecca* (*Alia: Luka di Serambi Mekah*, 2000); *In the Long Darkness* (*Dalam Kegelapan Panjang*, 2001)

FURTHER READING

Bodden, Michael. "Workers' Theatre and Theatre About Workers in 1990s Indonesia." *RIMA* (*Review of Indonesian and Malaysian Affairs*) 31, no. 1 (1997): 51–61.

Morgan, Anne-Marie. "Three Approaches to Modern Theatre in Jakarta in the 1990s: Rendra, Putu Wijaya and Ratna Sarumpaet." *Australasian Drama Studies* 27 (1995): 70–85.

Sarumpaet, Ratna, and Robyn Fallick. *Marsinah: A Song from the Underworld*. Canberra: Aberrant Genotype Press, 1998.

Sarumpaet, Ratna, and Barbara Hatley. "A Woman Dares to Speak: Ratna Sarumpaet." In *Performing Women/Performing Feminisms: Interviews with International Women Playwrights*, ed. by Joanne Tompkins and Julie Holledge. Brisbane: Australasian Drama Studies Association, 1997.

Sarumpaet, Ratna, and John H. McGlynn. "Marsinah Accuses." *Manoa* 12, no. 1 (2000): 155–66.

Evan Darwin Winet

SASTRE, ALFONSO (1926–)

Alfonso Sastre is one of the most controversial figures in contemporary Spanish theater, owing as much to his political views as to his dramatic work. His ideological leanings and political affiliation with the Communist Party led to a number of problems with Francisco Franco's censorship, and as a result, many of his works were neither published nor performed in SPAIN. Sastre proposes to subvert the very notion of theater through his writings, criticism, theoretical work, and participation in experimental groups. Since the end of the Franco dictatorship, Sastre has achieved greater recognition for his creative work, receiving on two occasions the National Prize for Theater—the first in 1985 for *The Fantastic Tavern* (*La Taberna Fantastica*, 1966) and the second in 1993 for *Jenofa Juncal, the Red gipsy of Jaizkibel Mount* (*Jenofa Juncal, la roja gitana del monte Jaizkibel*, 1983). The most notable influences in his work are JEAN-PAUL SARTRE, Karl Marx, RAMON DEL VALLE-INCLAN, and BERTOLT BRECHT.

Sastre was born on February 20, 1926, in Madrid. His career as a dramatist began in 1945 with the experimental group Arte Nuevo (New Art), a group that emerged as a reaction to the bourgeois theater of the day and a desire for conceptual renewal. In 1950 with Jose M. De Quinto, he founded El Teatro de Agitacion Social (Theater of Social Unrest), in whose manifesto he proclaims that the social is superior to the aesthetic. Because both he and his wife Eva Forest were incarcerated on different occasions for their political activities, his theater was censored and hardly performed in Spain. Consequently his works were only published and performed in Chile, SWEDEN, Cuba, ITALY, and VENEZUELA. In 1960 he created the Grupo de Teatro Realista (Realistic Theater Group), whose guiding principle was to act upon reality by modifying it. Since 1977 he resides in Basque country, where he continues his untiring intellectual labor, yet without renouncing his revolutionary convictions.

His evolution as a playwright runs parallel to the evolution of his political views, which ranges from a rejection of bourgeois society to revolutionary militance. His initial theater of the 1940s, characterized by symbolist, vanguardist, and existential themes, broke with Spanish theater of the time in both content and form. After this experimental phase, Sastre's theater of the 1950s developed a concern with social issues and revolutionary struggle, although it remained anchored in existential themes. Implicating the viewer, his plays force spectators to face the social reality that constitutes their world.

The debut of *Squads Toward Death* (*Escuadra hacia la muerte*) in 1953 marked a milestone in the history of postwar Spanish theater and represented Sastre's definitive arrival as a playwright. Beginning in 1962, he increased his experimentation with form without altering substantively the ideological underpinnings of his work. Sastre refers to these works as "complex TRAGEDIES," a fusion of the *esperpento* of Valle-Inclan and epic drama. He structures these plays in scenes with a relationship that is more ideological than narrative and a language that is colloquial and often "offensive" slang. Since 1985 his plays have presented a greater freedom of dramatic construction, are full of magical and fantastic elements, and are noticeably less ideological in content. In *¿Dónde estás, Ulalume, dónde estás?*, he expresses his wish to end his dramatic career, but nontheless, he resumed dramatic writing in 1993 with a series of hybrid, humorous COMEDIES, *Rain of Angels Over Paris* (*Lluvia de ángeles sobre París*, 1993–1994) and a detective trilogy *Strange Crimes* (*Los crímenes extraños*, 1996–1997).

PLAYS: *The Sound of Death* (*Ha sonado la muerte*, 1946); *Somnambulant Comedy* (*Comedia sonámbula*, 1946); *Uranium 235* (*Uranio 235*, 1946); *Load of Dreams* (*Cargamento de sueños*, 1948); *Squad Toward Death* (*Escuadra hacia la muerte*, 1953); *The Gag* (*La mordaza*, 1954); *Nocturnal Assault* (*Asalto nocturno*, 1958–1959); *In the Net* (*En la red*, 1961); *M. S. V. (Blood and Ash)* (*M.S.V. [La sangre y la ceniza]*, 1965); *The Fantastic Tavern* (*La taberna fantástica*, 1966); *Roman Chronicles* (*Crónicas romanas*, 1968); *Exercises of Terror* (*Ejercicios de terror*, 1970); *Askatasuna!* (1971); *The Dark Comrade* (*El Camarada oscuro*, 1972); *The Fantastic Tragedy of the Gipsy Celestina* (*Tragedia fantástica de la gitana Celestina*, 1977–1978); *Spectral Análisis of a Commando at the Service of the Proletarian Revolution* (*Análisis spectral de un Comando al servicio de la Revolución Proletaria*, 1978); *Now It's No Joke* (*Ahola no es de leíl*, 1979); *Jenofa Juncal, the Red gipsy of Jaizkibel Mount* (*Jenofa Juncal, la roja gitana del monte Jaizkibel*, 1983); *Men and Their Shadows* (*Los hombres y sus sombras*, 1983); *The Infinite Trip of Sancho Panza* (*El viaje infinito de Sancho Panza*, 1983–1984); *The Tale of the Reform, or What the Hell Is Going on Here?* (*El cuento de la reforma o ¿Qué demonios está pasando aquí?* 1984); *The Last Days of Emmanuel Kant Told by Ernst Theodor Amadeus Hoffman* (*Los últimos días de Emmanuel Kant contados por Ernesto Teodoro Amadeo Hoffman*, 1984–1985); *Unexpected Revelations About Moses* (*Revelaciones inesperadas sobre Moisés*, 1988); *Too Late for Philoctetes* (*Demasiado tarde para Filoctetes*, 1989); *Where Are You, Ulalume, Where Are You?* (*¿Dónde estás, Ulalume, dónde estás?* 1990); *Rain of Angels Over Paris* (*Lluvia de ángeles sobre París*, 1993–1994); *Strange Crimes* (*Los crímenes extraños*, 1996–1997)

FURTHER READING

Bryan, Avril T. *Censorship and Social Conflict in the Spanish Theatre. The Case of Alfonso Sastre*. Washington, D.C.: Univ. Press of America, 1982.

Ferreras, Juan Ignacio. *El teatro en el siglo XX (desde 1939)* [The Theater in the Twentieth Century (Since 1939)]. Madrid: Taurus, 1988.

Huerta Calvo, Javier. *Historia del teatro español II. Del siglo XVIII a la época actual* [History of Spanish Theater II. From the 18th Century to the Present Epoch]. Madrid: Gredos, 2003.

Pedraza Jiménez, Felipe, and Milagros Rodríguez Cáceres. *Manual de literatura española XIV. Posguerra: dramaturgos y ensayistas* [Handbook on Spanish Literature 14. Postwar: Playwrights and Essayists]. Pamplona: Cénlit ediciones, 1995.

Ruiz Ramón, Francisco. *Historia del teatro español. Siglo XX* [History of Spanish Theater. Twentieth Century]. Madrid: Cátedra, 1977.

Esther Lomas-Sampedro

THE SATIN SLIPPER

PAUL CLAUDEL's *The Satin Slipper* (*Le Soulier de satin*) is a ten-hour epic drama set in the age of Spanish exploration in the late 16th century. The play was written from 1919 to 1924 and first produced in 1943. It centers on the unconsummated passion shared by the conquistador Don Rodrigue and the noble lady Doña Prouhèze, who are perpetually separated by political and moral circumstances. The play is divided into four "days" rather than acts, has over sixty named characters, and combines elements of medieval public performance, fairground burlesque, and Elizabethan history plays. As in the medieval mysteries, Roman Catholic theology not only governs its psychological motivations but also fills the stage with guardian angels and emblematic visions.

Day One. Doña Prouhèze is in love with Don Rodrigue but married to an aged nobleman, Don Pélage, who governs Spanish territories in AFRICA; all three are in SPAIN when the play opens. Prouhèze wishes to be rescued from her marriage by Rodrigue, but she also vows never to betray her husband—a vow she enacts by offering one of her satin slippers to a statue of the Virgin Mary.

Day Two. Pélage and the King of Spain have now made Prouhèze governor of Mogador in Morocco on the African coast, where she must fight the Moors and govern despite the presence of a lustful second-in-command, Don Camille. The King of Spain, to test Prouhèze's moral strength, sends Rodrigue to Mogador to invite her to return to Spain, but she refuses because of her marital and imperial duties.

Day Three. Ten years later, Rodrigue is Viceroy of the New World. He receives a letter which Prouhèze had written from Mogador in a moment of weakness ten years before, asking him to rescue her. He abandons his conquests to do so, but, arriving at Mogador, discovers that Prouhèze will, once more, not leave with him. After being widowed by her first husband, she had yielded in marriage to Don Camille, by whom she now has a daughter, Doña Seven-Swords. Prouhèze gives Seven-Swords into Rodrigue's protection, but stays to die in the explosion of the Mogador fortress during battle with the Moors.

Day Four. After ten years of changing fortune, Rodrigue now sails the oceans in poverty selling holy images. The Spanish King brings him back to court to offer him the governorship of the British Isles, but it is a false offer, since the recent sinking of the Spanish Armada means Spain will never govern Britain. Rodrigue accepts the trick offer, but with such arrogance that the King imprisons him. Rodrigue ends his life in misery as a slave, knowing that Prouhèze's daughter Doña Seven-Swords survives to marry John of Austria, opening a new era in European history.

The play was premiered at the Comédie-Française in 1943 during the Nazi Occupation in a production by Jean-Louis Barrault, who shortened the text for a two-part presentation on consecutive evenings; Arthur Honegger composed the incidental music. There have been few complete productions since. In 1987, Antoine Vitez produced the full text at Avignon, and in 2003, two other full productions were seen in Paris. But the size of the play and its pro-Catholic, pro-colonial, and anti-Islamic worldview makes revival difficult.

Claudel's use of multiple theatrical traditions to stage an epic story would influence the work of Peter Brook, ARIANE MNOUCHKINE, and Robert LePage. The play is remembered now for its fairy-tale title, in which the satin slipper symbolizes both the resolve to remain upright in a fallen world and the longing for an eternally absent beloved.

[See also France; Religion and Drama]

FURTHER READING

Cahiers Renaud-Barrault, No. 100: A propos du Soulier de Satin
    [Renaud-Barrault Notebooks, No. 100: About the Satin Slipper].
    Paris: Gallimard, 1980.

Claudel, Paul. The Satin Slipper, or The Worst Is Not the Surest. Tr. by
    Fr. John O'Connor. London: Sheed & Ward, 1931.

Guicharnaud, Jacques, with June Guicharnaud. Modern French Theatre
    from Giraudoux to Genet, Rev. Ed. New Haven: Yale Univ. Press, 1967.

Knapp, Bettina L. Paul Claudel. New York: Ungar, 1982.

Lioure, Michel. L'Esthétique dramatique de Paul Claudel. Paris: Armand
    Colin, 1972.

David Pelizzari

SATOH MAKOTO (1943–)

Satoh Makoto, Japanese playwright and director, was a leader of the LITTLE THEATER MOVEMENT (ANGURA AND SHŌGEKŌ) that rebelled against SHINGEKI in the 1960s. Central to Satoh's concerns is the question of whether the political and religious extremism that motivates wars, revolutionary movements, and terrorism can achieve its purpose of realizing human redemption. All evidence suggests that it cannot, Satoh concludes, but there is something admirable about the quest.

Satoh's fascination with and skepticism of political extremism comes from his early life experience. His great-uncle Anami Korechika was the fanatical Army Minister in 1945 who opposed JAPAN's surrender and committed suicide rather than capitulate. Satoh learned from his example both the power and the disastrous consequences of political and religious fanaticism.

Although not a Christian, Satoh attended a Christian primary school. In high school, he read St. Augustine and Kierkegaard and majored in Western philosophy at Waseda University before transferring to the Actors Theatre Training School (Haiyūza Yōseijo), from which he graduated in 1965. His class's graduation project was a production of THE HEAD OF MARY, TANAKA CHIKAO's Catholic drama about Nagasaki survivors.

Satoh founded the Freedom Theatre (Jiyū Gekijō) in 1966 with classmates Kushida Kazuyoshi, Yoshida Hideko, and Saitō Ren. In 1969, the Freedom Theatre joined the June Theatre (Rokugatsu Gekijō) to form Theatre Center 68/69 (Engeki Sentaa 68/69), also known as the Black Tent Theatre (BTT). His cofounders of the Freedom Theatre left the BTT in 1971, but Satoh remained. During the 1970s, the BTT produced almost exclusively works that Satoh wrote and directed. He now serves as professor of directing at Tokyo Art University.

Satoh began exploring the themes of war, revolution, terrorism, and human redemption from his earliest plays. Ismene (1966) deals with war through the eyes of a child mystified by the bellicose political machinations of her elders. My Beatles (Atashi no Biitoruzu, 1967) concerns the legacy of Japan's colonization of Korea.

From 1969 to 1971, Satoh was engaged in writing a group of plays that interrogate the idea of revolution. Nezumi Kozō: The Rat (Nezumi Kozō Jirokichi, 1969), for which Satoh was awarded the Kishida Kunio Drama Prize, deals with the notion of revolution in Japanese history. The Dance of Angels Who Burn Their Own Wings (Tsubasa o Moyasu Tenshi-tachi no Butō, 1970) is a critical response to PETER WEISS's MARAT/SADE and concerns revolution in the Western context.

Abe Sada's Dogs (Abe Sada no Inu, 1975), The Phantom and the Cinema (Kinema to Kaijin, 1976), and The Killing of Blanqui, Spring in Shanghai (Buranki-goroshi Shanhai no Haru, 1979) together comprise The World of Shōwa: A Comedy, which occupied Satoh throughout the 1970s. The plays concern the unintended but far-reaching and catastrophic consequences of the unsuccessful coup d'état attempted by fanatical army officers on February 26, 1936. All of these plays are musicals in the spirit of BERTOLT BRECHT's THE THREEPENNY OPERA and are headed with epigraphs from Walter Benjamin. They share Brecht's dark cynicism and Benjamin's faith in the possibility of redemption.

Satoh's most recent play, The Absolute Airplane (2003), deals with the terror attacks of September 11, 2001, and is addressed to the lead hijacker, Mohammed Atta. The play continues Satoh's theme of intense ambivalence toward political and religious fanatics.

SELECT PLAYS: Ismene (1966); My Beatles (Atashi no Biitoruzu, 1967); Nezumi Kozō: The Rat (Nezumi Kozō Jirokichi, 1969); The Dance of Angels Who Burn Their Own Wings (Tsubasa o Moyasu Tenshi-tachi no Butō, with Yamamoto Kiyokazu, Saitō Ren, and Katō Tadashi, 1970); Ah, Nezumi Kozō (Aa Nezumi Kozō Jirokichi, 1971); Abe Sada's Dogs (Abe Sada no Inu, 1975); The Phantom and the Cinema (Kinema to Kaijin, 1976); The Killing of Blanqui, Spring in Shanghai (Buranki-goroshi Shanhai no Haru, 1979); Night of Night's Night (Yoru to Yoru no Yoru, 1981); The Sinking of the Titanic (Taitanikku Chinbotsu, 1985); The Absolute Airplane (Zettai Hikōki, 2003)

FURTHER READING

Goodman, David G. "Satoh Makoto and the Post-Shingeki Movement in Japanese Contemporary Theatre." Ph.D. diss., Cornell Univ., 1982.

——. *Fuji-san Mieta: Satoh Makoto ni Okeru Kakumei no Engeki* [Mt. Fuji Perceived: The Revolutionary Theatre of Satoh Makoto]. Tokyo: Hakusuisha, 1983.

Satoh Makoto. *Ismene*. Tr. by David G. Goodman. In *Alternative Japanese Drama: Ten Plays*, tr. and ed. by Robert T. Rolf and John K. Gillespie. Honolulu: Univ. of Hawaii Press, 1992: 327–362.

——. *Nezumi Kozō: The Rat*. Tr. by David G. Goodman. In *After Apocalypse: Four Japanese Plays of Hiroshima and Nagasaki*, ed. by David G. Goodman. Cornell East Asia Papers 71. Ithaca, N.Y.: Cornell East Asia Program, 1994. 249–319.

——. *My Beatles*. Tr. by David G. Goodman. In *The Return of the Gods: Japanese Drama and Culture in the 1960s*, ed. by David G. Goodman. Cornell East Asia Papers 116. Ithaca, N.Y.: Cornell East Asia Program, 2003. 177–223.

——. "Zettai Hikōki" [The Absolute Airplane]. *Serifu no Jidai* [Age of Drama] 3 (Summer 2003): 6–28.

Satoh Makoto, et al. *The Dance of Angels Who Burn Their Own Wings*. In *The Return of the Gods: Japanese Drama and Culture in the 1960s*, ed. by David G. Goodman. Cornell East Asia Papers 116. Ithaca, N.Y.: Cornell East Asia Program, 2003.

David G. Goodman

SAVED

> Yer never killed yer man. Yer missed that. Gives you a sense
> a perspective. I was one a the lucky ones . . .
> —Harry, Scene 12

Saved by EDWARD BOND premiered at the English Stage Company (ESC) in 1965. The theater reverted to a private club after its managers were denied licenses to produce Bond's *Saved* and JOHN OSBORNE's *A Patriot of Me*. The Lord Chamberlain brought and won a suit against the ESC, but the resulting controversy persuaded Parliament to abolish government censorship in 1968, which had been in effect in ENGLAND since 1737.

Bond and his play received overnight notoriety after the first private performance primarily because of a shocking scene in which a baby is stoned to death by its father and several of his friends. Bond was attacked by critics and *Saved* denounced in its beginning as sensational, offensive, decadent, and preoccupied with the exhibit of disgusting cruelty. However, today the violence within the play is no longer seen as violence for its own sake but as an expression of the cultural poverty for which society is more responsible than the individual. Within *Saved*, Bond depicts violence rising from the unequal distribution of power and opportunity afforded the lower classes of London. He places the urban poor center-stage in this drama and turns their ordinary corrupted speech into powerful rhythms of poetry. As the playwright aggressively pursues his truth through human bru-

tality, the lives of his characters become a nightmare. After censorship was lifted, largely as a result of plays such as *Saved*, the Royal Court staged an entire season of Bond plays. Soon after *Saved* and Bond's play *Narrow Road to the Deep North* toured Europe under British Council auspices, exposing the writers' concerns about a world in which a lack of compassion breeds a callous society that accepts the horrific as normal.

Saved takes place within the poverty of South London and centers on Len and his attachment to Pam, who like her family and friends has been denied any knowledge of the concept of love or compassion. The dialogue of the play is delivered through a thick dialect of stunted gutter-talk depicting the inherent deprivations of the London youths characterized in the work. The frustrations of the population boil over into acts of mindless savagery owing to a lack of opportunity to seize alternatives. Within the play only the character of Len grasps the notions of kindness and loyalty. After a brief and barren sexual experience with Pam, Len moves in with Pam and her family despite her hostility toward him. He befriends her father Harry, becomes sexually attracted to her adulterous mother Mary, and embraces Pam's infant from an earlier affair. He endures the smoldering anger within the household while Pam attempts every available means to drive him from her life. He is filled with emotional hunger and she with indifferent cynicism throughout the play. Pam feels nothing for her unwanted child and does not mourn its savage murder by Fred, the father. Len continues to remain with her after the death of the child, Fred's trial and release, and Pam's desperate efforts to rid herself of him.

The title of the play, *Saved*, refers to the final image of the play: Len is mending a broken chair for the family. It is a poetic metaphor delivered in silence voicing the playwright's hopes for the moral regeneration of a desolate society.

FURTHER READING

Brockett, Oscar, and Franklin J. Hildy. *History of the Theatre*, 9th ed. Boston: Allyn and Bacon, 2003.

Cornish, Roger, and Violet Ketels, eds. *Landmarks of Modern British Drama: The Plays of the Sixties*, Vol. 1. London: Methuen, 1985.

Hay, Malcolm, and Phillip Roberts. *Bond: A Study of His Plays*. London: Methuen, 1980.

Marla Dean

SCHMIDHUBER DE LA MORA, GUILLERMO (1943–)

Guillermo Schmidhuber de la Mora has published more than thirty plays and prose works. Many critics identify Schmidhuber as part of the *nueva dramaturgia* (new DRAMATURGY) generation. This new generation, which dates from the mid-1980s, follows two generations of Mexican playwrights. The dramatists of this third generation search for theater that adopts a more critical perspective than that of their predecessors, who strived for innovations in techniques and themes. Interestingly,

Schmidhuber does not consider himself a participant of this third generation of Mexican playwrights, perhaps since for the most part he follows the spirit of the first generation of Mexican dramaturges in his quest for more universal innovations.

In his early production, his best-known pieces are *The Human Cathedral* (*La catedral humana*, 1973–1974), for which he was awarded the Premio de la Sociedad de Escritores de México in 1978, *The Futile Heroes* (*Los héroes inútiles*, 1979), and *The Heirs of Segismundo* (*Los herederos de Segismundo*, 1980). The latter play received both the Premio Nacional de Bellas Artes de Literatura and the Premio Literario del Gobierno de Zacatecas. In these early works he experiments with several techniques that he will later master and apply with acute astuteness and reflection. *The Theft of Moctezuma's Headdress* (*El robo del penacho de Moctezuma*, 1981), *The Day Mona Lisa Stopped Smiling* (*El día que Mona Lisa dejó de sonreír*, 1985), and *Quartet of My People* (*Cuarteto de mi gentedad*, 1985) belong to his second phase of production. These are works that address the Mexican and Latin American diaspora. *In the Lands of Columbus* (*Por las tierras de Colón*, 1985–1986) received the Premio "Letras de Oro" from the University of Miami in 1987. More recently he published *The Grandmothers' Armoires* (*El armario de las abuelas*, 1989–1990), *The Secret Friendship of Juana and Dorothy* (*La secreta amistad de Juana y Dorotea*, 1998), *Obituary* (*Obituario*, 1999), and a two-volume compilation of his most stellar plays entitled *Thirteen Chances on Theater* (*Trece apuestas al teatro*, 1999), which includes a FARCE titled "Dramasutra." These later pieces are more abstract in nature and reveal how Schmidhuber plays with concepts of time and space. Many of his plays have been translated into English, French, and German.

Schmidhuber's extensive scholarship includes articles and texts on literary criticism and dramaturgy, and he has contributed extensively to the criticism of Latin American and Peninsular Theater. One of his most significant projects was the discovery of two manuscripts written by Sor Juana Inés de la Cruz.

Schmidhuber's dramaturgy has been described as demonstrating a constant zeal for human liberty through theatrical elements. Schmidhuber holds that the ever-present dilemma of the playwright and the dramatic genre is to strive to dominate time. According to Schmidhuber, a gifted playwright balances the effectiveness of dialogue with astute use of didascalia and proper placement of pauses so that the reader/spectator has the means to recognize that each character thinks in addition to speaking (Schmidhuber, 1998).

In elaborating upon dramaturgy and the role of the playwright, Schmidhuber affirms that, in general, the theater of today initiates an effort to privilege subjective perspectives and images, while other mediums such as television, cinematography, or photography demonstrate preference toward more objective images. He defines theater in three parts: "Theater means three things to me: theater as performance, theater as dramaturgical creation, and theater as cosmos" (Schmidhuber, 1998). Schmidhuber demonstrates a sincere concern for the future of dramaturgy. From his perspective, an alarming number of contemporary dramatic pieces are driven by a director's vision and/or commercial potential rather than a true attempt at the application of dramaturgical prowess.

In turning his attention toward Mexican and Latin American theater, he calls for a change toward more intellectual productions of his contemporaries and of future dramaturges of the region. Schmidhuber defines the challenge of trying to reinterpret the concept of time as a playwright's *raison d'être*, a trial that he has applied in his own works. He clarifies that dramaturgy "is also living the risk of trying to achieve the impossible" (Schmidhuber, 1998).

[See also Mexico]

PLAYS: *Our Sir Quetzalcóatl* (*Nuestro Señor Quetzalcóatl*, 1979); *The Futile Heroes* (*Los héroes inútiles*, 1981); *The Heirs of Segismundo* (*Los Herederos de Segismundo*, 1981); *Lacandonia* (1982); *The Theft of Moctezuma's Headdress* (*El robo del penacho de Moctezuma*, 1982); *We Are All King Lear* (*Todos somos el rey Lear*, 1982); *The Day Mona Lisa Stopped Smiling* (*El día que Mona Lisa dejó de sonreír*, 1987); *In the Lands of Columbus* (*Por las tierras de Colón*, 1987); *The Fifth Voyage of Christopher Columbus* (*El quinto viaje de Colón*, 1992); *The Secret Friendship of Juana and Dorothy: A Play in Seven Scenes* (*La Secreta Amistad de Juana y Dorotea: Obra de Teatro en Siete Escenas*, 1998); *Thirteen Chances on Theater: First Volume and Second Volume* (*Trece apuestas al teatro: Volúmen Primero y Segundo* 1999)

FURTHER READING

Burgess, Ronald D. *The New Dramatists of Mexico, 1967–1986*. Lexington: Univ. Press of Kentucky, 1991.

Martínez, Christine D. "El valor de la libertad en el teatro de Guillermo Schmidhuber de la Mora" [The Value of Liberty in the Theater of Guillermo Schmidhuber de la Mora]. *Latin American Theater Review*, 24, no. 1 (Fall 1990): 29–39.

Montañez, Carmen. "Guillermo Schmidhuber: el dramaturgo y su obra" [Guillermo Schmidhuber: The Playwright and His Works]. *Ariel*, 8 (1992): 56–62.

Schmidhuber, Guillermo. *El Ojo Teatral: 19 lecturas ociosas* [The Theatrical Eye: 19 Leisurely Readings]. Guanajuato: Ediciones la Rana, 1998.

Lourdes Betanzos

SCHNITZLER, ARTHUR (1862–1931)

I have often asked myself in wonder where you could have found this or that secret knowledge which I was able to discover only after arduous examination of the object and ended feeling envious of the poet for whom I have always had the deepest admiration.

—Sigmund Freud in a letter to Arthur Schnitzler, May 8, 1906

The culturally fertile and decadently reckless atmosphere of Vienna, AUSTRIA, in the death throes of the obsolete Habsburg Empire, set the stage for Arthur Schnitzler's life and works. Born on May 15, 1862, in Vienna, into an upper-class Jewish family, he was introduced early to the cultural and intellectual pursuits of the privileged, in part because his father, Johann, was a well-known laryngologist whose patients were often performers. Arthur was thus exposed to the stage and began to write plays at a young age.

Although Johannes Schnitzler encouraged his son's artistic tendencies, he did not approve of literature as a profession for him. Accordingly, Arthur studied medicine and became a physician whose specialties were in dermatology, sexually transmitted diseases, and larynx ailments. His medical journal articles reflect his avid interest in psychology (including experimentation with hypnosis), as do his dramas such as ANATOL (1881–1891) and *Paracelsus* (1898). The fascination with psychology plays such an integral part in Schnitzler's artistic works that they can also be described as studies of the human psyche, as acknowledged by Sigmund Freud (1856–1939) himself, who referred to Schnitzler as his alter ego. Although writing increasingly became a priority for Schnitzler (whose heart was set more on the pursuit of aesthetic and bohemian pleasures than on medicine), he waited until after his father's death in 1893 to resign his position at Vienna's Poliklinik and enter private practice, which afforded him greater opportunities for writing and other aesthetic interests. Because of his medical training, however, Schnitzler approached writing not only with an aesthetic sensibility, but also with the diagnostic eye of a clinician.

At the very minimum, fin-de-siècle Vienna formed the background to all of Schnitzler's work and provided him with abundant material, even if the historical time and place of his texts were occasionally elsewhere. Schnitzler's Vienna has been characterized as a place of frivolity, lightheartedness, and passion combined with the deadly serious. The construction of the Ringstrasse (the grand boulevard that connected the city with its suburbs) in the latter half of the 19th century and its flamboyant, eclectic array of architectural styles signaled not only the extension of the city's boundaries but also an expansion of its identity. While Vienna retained much of its Baroque character, architectural, artistic, literary, philosophical, and scientific experimentation was thriving throughout the city. It was a hotbed of European modernism: home to Freud's PSYCHOANALYSIS; Arnold Schönberg's (1874–1951) atonal music; Ludwig Wittgenstein's (1889–1951) philosophy; urban modernism and Otto Wagner's (1841–1918) functional architecture; and Gustav Klimt (1862–1918) and his fellow Secessionist artists. Vienna also inspired the literary circle called Jung Wien (Young Vienna), a loosely knit group of young men whose meeting place, Café Griensteidl, was located just behind the Hofburg, the imperial Habsburg palace. Schnitzler formed lasting friendships with many of the Jung Wien writers, who included HUGO VON HOFMANNSTHAL, Richard Beer-Hofmann (1866–1945), and Hermann Bahr (1863–1934). The intellectual exhilaration attending the city's social and cultural modernization was also accompanied by dramatic political change and economic turbulence.

For much of Schnitzler's life, Vienna was the capital of the Austro-Hungarian Empire and under the rule of the Habsburgs, who clung firmly to the status quo as they tried to maintain their fading power. The ethnic unrest that besieged the outer territories of the Empire was also felt in the multiethnic capital—and ultimately around the world—as the 1914 assassination of the Habsburg Crown Prince, Franz Ferdinand, in Sarajevo plunged Europe into World War I. Austria's First Republic, which succeeded the disbanded Habsburg empire at the conclusion of the war, was plagued from the outset with conflict among rival political factions as it struggled with hyperinflation and economic depression that led to intolerable social conditions. Economic misery, in turn, exacerbated Austrian anti-Semitism, which had grown increasingly acute in the latter part of the 19th century, particularly among the less privileged and undereducated classes of the overwhelmingly Catholic country. Austrian politicians effectively used anti-Semitic resentments to agitate and manipulate the masses, finding a convenient and identifiable scapegoat to blame for the interwar misery.

As John Simon writes in his "Foreword" to Schnitzler's *Night Games*, "An empire in its decline is the breeding ground for both a heartbreakingly true art and for epicurean, even convulsively decadent, pursuits" (viii). Indeed, the nervousness, restlessness, and agitation so palpable at the time are vividly captured in Schnitzler's dramas. His early plays—*Anatol*, LIEBELEI (1894), and REIGEN (*La Ronde*, 1896–1897), for example—brilliantly present the themes of Eros and Thanatos, sexual love and death. In Schnitzler's works, Eros and Thanatos impart a sense of the precariousness and, on many levels, meaninglessness of life, such that deceit and lies, betrayal and hypocrisy are the norm in relationships. The characters in Schnitzler's works recognize the fragility, brevity, and futility of life; therefore, they engage in power struggles and pursue erotic fulfillment in an effort to find meaning, if only momentarily. The evanescence of the moment thus becomes a preoccupation, and in seeking a diversion from their hopeless and frightening reality, they escape into fantasy and self-deception, "into art, into the attitude of the distanced spectator, even into suicide; at last also into concentration on the immediate, unmediated moment" (Reinhart Müller-Freienfels, in Simon, ix).

Although much secondary literature focuses on Schnitzler's explorations of sexuality and eroticism, his work also deals extensively and perceptively with other important sociopolitical issues of the time, including the anti-Semitism, political intrigue, and bigotry so poignantly portrayed in PROFESSOR BERNHARDI (1912). The opportunism, fueled by envy and anti-Semitism, that ultimately placed in jail the fictional Bernhardi, the impeccably ethical and successful director of the Elisabethium Clinic, was a very real possibility in turn-of-the-century Vienna. Indeed, the drama's plot line was inspired by the political intrigues Schnitzler's own father had faced as director of the city's Poliklinik. The prevalent anti-Jewish sentiment of the time was also frequently reflected in the critical reception of Schnitzler's work.

Even though turn-of-the-century Vienna provided vital subject matter for Schnitzler, the range of issues and motifs he portrays extends far beyond that specific time and place, as illustrated by the several historical plays he wrote. In *Paracelsus*, for example, Schnitzler uses the scientist and the city of Basel at the beginning of the 16th century as vehicles for exploring the contemporary interest in hypnosis. The title character hypnotizes his former lover Justina in front of her husband Cyprian to reveal her unconscious. However, even Paracelsus, the manipulator of the situation, becomes alarmed when the boundaries between illusion and reality grow murky as a result of the unknown lurking beneath the surface.

Another historical play, *The Green Cockatoo* (*Der grüne Kakadu*, 1898), is set in Paris on the eve of the French Revolution of 1789. However important the historical setting and political overtones of this one-act play, the drama also presents many of Schnitzler's favorite themes and motifs, including the intermingling of illusion and reality and a play within a play. The action takes place in Prospere's basement pub, The Green Cockatoo, which metaphorically underscores the political aspect of the play, that is, viewing the revolution from below. Overtly, the action centers on the playacting that goes on in the pub. The characters range from aristocrats and bourgeois guests (who comprise the audience) to actors (who play criminal parts) to actual criminals, and the playacting consists of the "criminals" telling about their crimes and tantalizing the audience. The intermingling of social classes also mixes fiction with fact, and "truth" remains illusive. The action climaxes when Henri, Prospere's best actor, claims to have killed the Duke of Cadignan because of his affair with Henri's new bride. Prospere knows the affair is real and thus reacts in shock. When Cadignan arrives at the pub, Henri, suspecting the truth, really does kill him, and so becomes a hero of the revolution that is occurring outside/above the pub, even though his motives are anything but political.

Several of Schnitzler's historical dramas examine the topic of war and peace through themes that are often identified as his usual bill of fare: the dubious boundaries between *Sein und Schein* (reality and appearance), gender interactions, and the psychology of the soul. In *Beatrice's Veil* (*Der Schleier der Beatrice*, 1899), for instance, 16th-century Bologna is threatened by an impending siege. This five-act play in verse, which reflects its Renaissance-era setting, explores the effects that dreams have on the conscious mind; it also examines the psychological reactions of Bologna's trapped citizens to imminent TRAGEDY. One possible escape route is suicide, which the title character and her lover decide to take. Beatrice, however, loses her nerve and, while fleeing, forgets her veil in the room where her lover has died. She must return for the veil because it is from her husband, Bologna's ruling Duke. The couple's marriage underscores the sense of doom confronting the city, as well as the power of dreams: Beatrice had dreamed that the Duke would

marry her, a commoner, and in the chaos and orgiastic mood of a city under siege, dream becomes reality.

Set around the middle of the 18th century, *The Way to the Pond* (*Der Gang zum Weiher*, 1921) is an explicit political statement on war and patriotism. Mayenau, a former chancellor to the emperor, is called on for his diplomatic skills, and the play depicts a one-man effort to stem prowar sentiments and avert war that is ultimately unsuccessful. *The Young Medardus* (*Der junge Medardus*, 1909), which Schnitzler called "a dramatic history" (the place and time are Vienna in 1809), examines the Napoleonic wars between France and Austria. The longest of his plays and the one with the most complex cast of characters, it demonstrates how conscious intentions are subverted by unconscious desires when Medardus, set on revenging his sister's suicide, actually—and unknowingly—thwarts an assassination attempt on Napoleon Bonaparte.

The illusiveness of appearance and reality is also embodied in the character of the *süßes Mädel*—a pretty, young, unmarried woman from the suburbs (that is, from the lower classes)—of whom Schnitzler is often viewed as the creator. But because character of the "sweet young thing" was already present in the popular dramas and COMEDIES of Johann Nestroy (1801–1862), it would be more accurate to credit Schnitzler with establishing her notoriety. She is a central character in his works, appearing alongside the actresses, bored housewives, prostitutes, and society ladies, and often functions to expose social mores and double standards. In *Liebelei*, for example, Christine ignores the rules of the flirtation game and really does fall in love with the young gentleman Fritz, who in the end, dies in a duel arising from his affair with a married woman. Christine realizes that she was simply a plaything, a pleasant diversion for Fritz, and the implication is that she subsequently commits suicide, highlighting the social and gender inequities of the society. Social bias and hypocrisy are evident in *The Legacy* (*Das Vermächtnis*, 1898) as well, a drama in which a good bourgeois son reveals on his deathbed his secret life to his parents and elicits a reluctant promise from them to take in and care for his *süßes Mädel*, Toni, and their son. The parents only agree because they consider their grandson to be their son's legacy, and they never accept Toni. Thus, when the child subsequently dies, they no longer feel tied to their promise. Toni flees, most probably escaping into death.

The theater was often the setting for Schnitzler's plays, providing an ideal venue for depicting gender discrimination and the double standards inherent in the society. In *Free Game* (*Freiwild*, 1896), Anna Riedel is an aspiring young actress who dreams about performing in the theaters of Vienna one day, but must begin her career by acting in summer provincial theaters where she is expected to "entertain" the military officers stationed there after theater performances. When she refuses the advances of a lieutenant and the friend who comes to her defense is subsequently killed in a duel, she is forced to abandon her career. It is clear that to become a successful actress, she would have to compromise her sense of morality. *The Fairy Tale* (*Das Märchen*, 1891) epitomizes the double standards: Fanny Theren has become the successful actress that Anna Riedel in the later play would hope to become; in the process, Fanny has had lovers. Hence, when the open-minded poet Fedor Denner, whom she loves, claims to believe that women have the same rights as men, she remains hopeful that he will accept her. Although he loves her, he ultimately cannot overcome the social stigma of Fanny's past and abandons her.

At the heart of Schnitzler's work is his skepticism about language and its usage. It is evident that he—as well as many of his contemporaries—distrusted the adequacy of words for communication. Indeed, he was fully aware of how words are often misconstrued; how they can be used to distort or hide the truth; or simply, how a character's personality or psychological perspective can prohibit understanding those around him or her. As early as *Anatol*, this distrust of language is evident when, for example, in the scene "Questioning Fate" (Die Frage an das Schicksal), Anatol has hypnotized Cora but refuses to ask the burning question—Has she been faithful to him?—because any answer could be variously interpreted. "Yes" could indeed mean that she is true (and truthful), but perhaps only in the very moment. What about yesterday or tomorrow? On another level, the pantomime *Pierette's Veil* (Der Schleier der Pierette, 1910) epitomizes the questionable role of language by not using any at all. Intentional or not, miscommunication and confusion ensue in Schnitzler's works because words are inadequate and imprecise. The title of his last series of one-act plays, *Comedy of Words* (Komödie der Worte, 1914), and of his posthumously published fragment, *The Word* (Das Wort), reflect the author's continued skepticism in light of the paradox that words are nothing, but "we have nothing but words" (*Comedy of Words*). Schnitzler repeatedly attempts to address and counter this paradox through irony.

This brief summation of various plays reveals a complex image of the author, an image underscored by his critical reception. Schnitzler is the physician who, with a clinician's eye, recorded the excesses of his times, including his own. He is also the writer-dramatist who suffused his work "with a poet's hypersensitive perception" (Simon, ix); the Anatol-look-alike, that dashing, young, upper-class melancholic who pursued "sweet young things" and married women alike; the unhappily married man who cannot prevent his daughter's suicide; and the well-known personality who is the target of anti-Semitic prejudice and thus an outsider, despite his professional success and upper-class social position.

Schnitzler's works provide critical commentary on a vast number of issues. He dissects his society by observing the mundane and the ordinary; he finds the vanity, greed, concupiscence, and double standards endemic to turn-of-the-century Vienna. With a masterful ear for dialogue, he skillfully weaves his observations into tantalizing plots full of fantasy, illusion, and theatricality. A prolific author, Schnitzler wrote twenty full-length and seventeen one-act plays, as well as numerous short stories and novellas, two novels, an autobiography (*My Youth in Vienna* [Jugend in Wien, 1915–1920]), and aphorisms. He was also the coeditor of his father's medical journal and kept a diary (ten volumes in all) that chronicles his (love) life, work, and times, as do the numerous letters exchanged between him and friends, many of which have been published.

As a dramatist, Schnitzler often felt attacked and misunderstood by critics, by the public, and even by friends who wrote reviews critical of his work. Yet, he was an enormously successful playwright whose works were and still are regularly performed throughout Austria, Germany, and Central Europe. His texts have also been adapted for numerous films; Stanley Kubrick's (1928–1999) *Eyes Wide Shut* (1999), for example, is based on Schnitzler's *Dream Story* (Traumnovelle, 1925). One hundred years after fin-de-siècle Vienna, Schnitzler occupies a prominent place in the literary canon and continues to fascinate and intrigue contemporary audiences with his diagnoses of social disintegration. He died on October 21, 1931, in Vienna, Austria.

SELECT PLAYS: *Anatol* (1888–1891); *Anatol's Megalomania* (Anatols Größenwahn, 1891); *The Fairy Tale* (Das Märchen, 1891); *The Eccentric One* (Die überspannte Person, 1894); *Flirtations* (Liebelei, 1894); *One-thirty* (Halbzwei, 1894); *Free Game* (Freiwild, 1896); *La Ronde* (Reigen, 1896–1897); *The Green Cockatoo* (Der grüne Kakadu, 1898); *The Legacy* (Das Vermächtnis, 1898); *The Mate* (Die Gefährtin, 1898); *Paracelsus* (1898); *Beatrice's Veil* (Der Schleier der Beatrice, 1899); *New Year's Night* (Sylvesternacht, 1900); *Living Hours* (Lebedige Stunden, 1900–1901); *Marionettes* (Marionetten, 1901–1904); *The Lonely Way* (Der einsame Weg, 1903); *The Call of Life* (Der Ruf des Lebens, 1905); *Intermezzo* (Zwischenspiel, 1905); *Countess Mizzie, or, The Family Reunion* (Komtesse Mizzi, oder, der Familientag, 1907); *The Young Medardus* (Der junge Medardus, 1909); *Undiscovered Country* (Das weite Land, 1910); *Professor Bernhardi* (1912); *Comedy of Words* (Komödie der Worte, 1914); *Fink and Fliederbusch* (Fink und Fliederbusch, 1916); *The Sisters, or, Casanova in Spa* (Die Schwestern, oder, Casanova in Spa, 1917); *The Way to the Pond* (Der Gang zum Weiher, 1921); *Comedy of Seduction* (Komödie der Verführung, 1923); *In the Play of Summer Breezes* (Im Spiel der Sommerlüfte, 1928)

FURTHER READING

Arnold, Heinz Ludwig, ed. *Arthur Schnitzler. Text + Kritik 138/139*. Munich: Ed. Text u. Kritik, 1998.

Gay, Peter. *Schnitzler's Century: The Making of Middle-Class Culture, 1815–1914*. New York: Norton, 2002.

Lorenz, Dagmar C. G., ed. *A Companion to the Works of Arthur Schnitzler*. Rochester, N.Y.: Camden House, 2003.

Perlmann, Michaela L. *Arthur Schnitzler*. Stuttgart: J.B. Metzler, 1987.

Simon, Anne-Catherine. *Schnitzlers Wien* [Schnitzler's Vienna]. Vienna: Pichler, 2002.

Simon, John. "Foreward" to *Night Games and Other Stories and Novellas* by Arthur Schnitzler, tr. by Margaret Schaefer. Chicago: Ivan R. Dee, 2002.

Yates, W. E. *Schnitzler, Hofmannsthal, and the Austrian Theatre.*
New Haven: Yale Univ. Press, 1992.

Elizabeth Ametsbichler

SCIENTIFIC AMERICANS

Scientific Americans was written by JOHN MIGHTON, who won the Governor General's Literary Award for Drama for *A Short History of Night*. Mighton received a Ph.D. in mathematics from the University of Toronto, and this interest in science is central to his plays.

Scientific Americans explores the ethical dilemmas faced by weapons researchers at Los Alamos Laboratory, which produced the first atom bomb. The central scientific concept of the play is control theory, which seeks to understand how one can manipulate the parameters affecting the behavior of a given system to produce a desired outcome. The play focuses on two scientists: Jim, whose specialty is electromagnetic radiation, and his fiancée, Carol, who is working on artificial intelligence. Jim has recently taken a job with Los Alamos, and at the beginning of the play, it is clear that Jim has taken the job primarily because both the facilities and working environment allow him to pursue whatever creative work he desires. Meanwhile, Carol worries that Jim will inevitably work on first-strike weaponry, even as Jim continually assures that her that he won't since he is free to work on whatever he pleases.

He, in turn, is often assured (perhaps too often) that this is the case by General Bergen, who explains to Jim, "You can't force creativity. Half the people in your group aren't even working on weapons research. We want you to follow whatever ideas come to you, no matter how wild." However, while the environment at Los Alamos is fairly relaxed, this proves to provide more pressure to produce new ideas (even the most mundane of which are recognized as having military applications), and soon enough Jim is introduced to various weapons projects.

Meanwhile, he begins to defend the work done at Los Alamos to the point that Carol points out that he is beginning to sound like them. After playing a key role in finalizing the plans for the stealth bomber (a first-strike weapon if ever there was one), Carol leaves Jim and Jim attempts suicide. At this point, Jim's inspiration is Carol, and that he can no longer be successfully manipulated to function without her. This fact is metaphoric of the larger dilemmas pointed out by the play, which is devoted to examining the relationship between technological advancement as beneficial to society, on the one hand, and potentially lethal on the other. Even as each and every scientist at Los Alamos has ideal conditions under which they are likely to be the most creative, they also are involved in the production of weapons that could destroy this very same environment that gives rise to their creativity—even as Jim inevitably destroys his relationship with Carol.

When Carol finally corners Jim to try and understand what it was that led him to work on the stealth aircraft, Jim disagrees with her assumption that it was ego, explaining, rather, that he did it because it was easy. The play is ultimately entirely pessimistic about the weapons industry, as even those with the best intentions are seen as all too easily coerced to do its bidding.

[*See also* Canada]

FURTHER READING

Athabasca University. "John Mighton." *The Encyclopedia of Canadian Theatre,* http://www.canadiantheatre.com/dictpl?term=John%20Mighton (Accessed August 29, 2004).

Athabasca University. "A Short History of Night." *Encyclopedia of Canadian Theatre,* http://www.canadiantheatre.com/dict.pl?term=A%20Short%20History%20of%20Night (Accessed December 21, 2006).

Daniel Jernigan

SCOTLAND

"I am very fond of the drama," claimed the Satanic Mr. Bolfry. Early critics of the genre would not have been surprised. *Mr. Bolfry: A Play in Four Scenes* (1943), by JAMES BRIDIE, pseudonym of the most eminent modern Scottish dramatist, Glasgow physician Osborne Henry Mavor (1888–1951), reversed prevailing opinions in its claims that establishment Presbyterianism was underwritten by hell. But Bolfry's support both of drama and of the Scottish religious consensus was subtly ironic. The play was satirizing the force that had perhaps more than any other condemned and undermined the stage. In the aftermath of the Scottish Literary Renaissance of the 1920s and 1930s, the dearth of Scottish dramatic writing was being explained by reference to the Calvinism that had, critics contended, decimated Scottish cultural expression. Arguing that the Presbyterians had been right, that drama did indeed reek of sulphur, and that the Presbyterians had been wrong, for their creed also smacked of hell, *Mr. Bolfry* equivocated on a fundamental and long-standing argument in Scottish cultural history, but implied that Presbyterians and dramatists had far more in common than they dared believe.

Whatever the competing explanations for its absence, critics of Scottish culture agree that drama is the least developed of the Scottish muses. Throughout its history, drama has existed in a fragile and often uncertain relationship with the values of the Scottish establishment and its literary tradition's prioritization of poetry and prose. Edwin Muir, in his biography of John Knox (1929), compared the dramatic glories of Jacobean ENGLAND with the sterility and poverty of Scottish culture in the same period. His argument, amplified by succeeding generations of critics, was straightforward: Scottish Calvinism had dampened—indeed, distorted—Scottish cultural expression. Scottish culture had never recovered from the Reformation's prioritization of the English language over Scots and Gaelic, nor from the removal of the Edinburgh court, with all its opportunities for patronage, to London with the Union of the Crowns in 1603.

Ideas that the Reformation was intrinsically hostile to drama need, however, to be qualified. In his *History of the Reformation* (1644), John Knox referred to drama as a medium of religious change; George Buchanan, tutor to the young James VI and I, prepared several neo-Latin works on biblical themes; and David Lindsey's *Ane Satire of the Three Estatis* (1540) was a robust discussion of the corruption of the late medieval church in vigorously dense Scots. Despite this lively beginning, however, the Scottish church was increasingly influenced by English Puritanism's hostility to drama. Throughout the 17th and 18th centuries, suspicion grew of credible links between Satan and the stage. Edinburgh's Carrubber's Close Theatre, operated by Alan Ramsay, was one of several shut down in the aftermath of the Licensing Act of 1737. Yet, at the same time, Scottish dramatic writing achieved some resounding successes. John Home's *Douglas* (1756) achieved considerable popular appeal, with performances generating the ultimate accolade: "Whaur's yer Wullie Shakespeare noo?" (Walker). Home's career as a clergyman made his dramatic success all the more ironic. Perhaps Bolfry had been right.

Whatever the implications of Home's writing, historians of Scottish drama agree that *Douglas* was the final curtain call for a dramatic tradition that was revived only at the end of the 19th century. This is not to imply that Scottish theater was dead for a century and a half. Despite the very recent establishment of permanent theaters, 19th-century Scotland enjoyed a strong theatrical tradition. Throughout the 19th century, Scottish drama offered a "cornucopia of riches" (Cameron). Scotland's place in the Romantic imagination created an "insatiable" demand for plays about Scotland and the Scots throughout Britain. In Scotland, the prosperous, pursuing their sentimental nationalism at the stage if not the ballot box, indulged their patriotic nostalgia in Edinburgh's Theatre Royal between 1810 and 1851. Theatre Royal's distinctive national drama often took the form of adaptations of the works of prose writers such as Sir Walter Scott. This was a theater with national purpose, but it provided, largely, "a drama . . . without dramatists" (Craig and Stevenson). Those writers who did engage with the challenge of drama typically lost their nerve when it came to the Scots language. John Galt, James Hogg, and Scott each demonstrated a facility for Scots expression in their prose and poetry; but faced with the opportunity of the stage, they each opted for English. Nor was the situation much better away from the national theater, where the less prosperous indulged their interest in patriotic whimsy in the music halls. There, nightly long programs offered a range of productions in a vein that would be immortalized in the 20th century by Sir Harry Lauder. Adaptations of Robert Burns's long narrative poem *Tam O' Shanter*, for example, included a panto-

mime and a harlequinade alongside at least five plays, some of which took astonishing liberties with the text. Trading on stereotypes and capitalizing on the popularity of Burns, Britain's network of music halls presented as many dangers as opportunities for the dramatic expression of Scottish life.

Scotland's national theater entered something of an eclipse, however, after 1870, when the new railway network allowed recently premiered theatrical work to move quickly from London to the provinces. The railway network simultaneously consolidated London's position as the center of the theatrical world and robbed Scottish theater of its independent status. With theaters increasingly depending on London-based companies, fewer Scottish plays were required, and those Scottish dramatists who chose to continue to write began to write more obviously for the market.

But not everyone was content to pander to the values of the age. The end of the 19th century witnessed something of a revival of the CLOSET DRAMA. Among the most prestigious closet dramatists were John Davidson and William Sharp, who would achieve greater fame as the novelist and philosopher Fiona MacLeod, but was also president of the London Stage Society. Opinions vary as to the merit of this writing. Hugh MacDiarmid would hail Davidson's *Robert the Bruce* as Scotland's best historical play. This interest in history would be developed by Professor Robert Buchanan, who published closet dramas on James I and William Wallace. Serious drama was also cultivated by another Robert Buchanan, who was responsible for a series of successful adaptations from classic novels. His *Sophia* (1886) was adapted from *Tom Jones*, and *The Sixth Commandment* (1890) from *Crime and Punishment*. The adaptation of successful novels was clearly market driven, but the relationship between novel and drama was not always one way: Robert Louis Stevenson's *Deacon Brodie* (1884) reads like a first draft for *Dr. Jekyll and Mr. Hyde* (1886). Another successful novelist would be better known as the most important dramatist at the beginning of the 20th century. J. M. BARRIE (1860–1937) enjoyed the success of *Walker, London* (1892) and *The Professor's Love Story* (1894) but made his reputation by the success of *The Little Minister* (1897). By overseeing the stage adaptation of his own novel, Barrie made great advances in its presentation of form and content.

If Barrie represents Scottish drama at its most profitable, his work also demonstrates the provincialism of the Scottish stage. Although he was Scotland's most important dramatist at the beginning of the 20th century, his plays were produced in London and New York—never in Scotland. Paradoxically, Barrie's work is suffused with Scottish themes, although his whimsical and often parochial national vision has been identified as providing for the false consciousness of the *kailyard* (cabbage patch) writers. At the end of the 19th century, Scottish plays performed by Scottish actors using the Scots language were largely restricted to the *geggies*, the transportable theaters that moved among the market towns.

Scottish theater embraced a new radicalism at the beginning of the 20th century. In 1900 Scotland could boast thirty-two theaters, but their number had risen to fifty-three within ten years. While major writers continued to depict Scotland as the landscape of the Romantic imagination, new companies were formed and new plays were published with explicit class and urban concerns. In the period between the wars, the Scottish Community Drama Association dominated Scottish theater. Their annual festival of one-act plays generated immense popular interest: in 1926, only four years after its foundation, the festival attracted over three hundred entries. One outstanding play from this period was Joe Corrie's *In Time o' Strife* (1927). Indeed, the vitality of this creative energy challenges Muir's (1936) claim that Scotland had "no great burst of poetic drama." Ironically, he was living through it, though it is fair to admit that the work of John Brandane, Robert McLellan, Alexander Reid, and Robert Kemp has, in general, not worn well.

The distinctive MODERNIST sensibility cultivated by the Scottish renaissance drew explicit comparisons with IRELAND. The success of the Abbey Theatre in Dublin encouraged the Scottish Repertory Theatre in Glasgow and provided momentum for the formation of the Scottish National Players. Whereas the productions of the Scottish National Players tended to favor rural themes, the Unity Theatre, established in 1941, drew on the political interests of its members to focus its energies on themes relevant to the urban situation of a Scotland at war. Unity assisted the establishment of the Edinburgh Festival Fringe by producing plays without official approval at the first Edinburgh Festival in 1947.

In the same period, James Bridie was doing his utmost to become Scotland's answer to GEORGE BERNARD SHAW. He founded the Citizens' Theatre in Glasgow in 1943, the first dependable outlet for local dramatic writing; he founded the Royal Scottish Academy of Music and Drama in 1950; he was chairman of the Scottish Arts Council; and he authored forty-two plays. He was known for his subtle and enquiring Scottish mind and was considered one of the most intellectually fertile contributors to Scottish literature in any genre. Yet Scottish dramatists have been reluctant to pick up his mantle. Ironically, it was in the Church of Scotland's Assembly Hall in Edinburgh that Scottish drama was re-energized. The situation of Tyrone Guthrie's ground-breaking production of David Lindsay's *Satire* was iconic. In the very heart of the establishment that had sponsored, then cauterized, Scottish drama, Lindsay's *Satire* finally convinced audiences that the Scots language had the power in drama that the writers of the Scottish Renaissance in the 1920s had recognized in poetry and prose.

Dramatic renewal reflected the artistic implications of a wider cultural crisis in Scotland. Cinema and the advent of television had decimated the music hall tradition and educated Scottish audiences to an appreciation of a drama that had little local connection. By 1970, only fifteen theaters remained in Scotland, though other stages existed elsewhere. With a growing appreciation of political distance from London, Scottish writers embraced an increasing nationalism. Theater, with other literary genres, was increasingly reflecting political debate and popular change. JOHN MCGRATH founded the 7:84 THEATRE COMPANY in 1971, and a Scottish 7:84 in 1973. The company's name was a deliberate polemic: McGrath sourced the numbers in an economic statistic that ascribed 84 percent of British wealth to 7 percent of the total number of taxpayers. The company's first hit confirmed its political commitments. THE CHEVIOT, THE STAG AND THE BLACK, BLACK OIL (1973), a collaborative production, developed a *ceilidh*-house style of theater, mixing music and dance with story and song. Its popularity was immense, revitalizing David Lindsay's political commitment with a dramatic verve that saw the company lead the way in touring the Highlands and Islands with their warning of transnational capitalism. Subsequent productions saw 7:84 pushing audiences into an international awareness and a new skepticism about nostalgic visions of Scottish history. This AGITATION-PROPAGANDA drama was developed by a 7:84 off-shoot, WILDCAT, founded in 1978 to retain left-wing commitments while being less overtly orientated toward the working classes.

But the political and cultural commitments of these companies could not disguise the fact that 20th-century drama had grown increasingly marginalized. The outlook at the end of the 1970s, in the aftermath of the scotching of nationalist hopes at the failure of the devolution referendum, seemed bleak. But, as the plays in Alasdair Cameron's *Scot-Free: New Scottish Plays* (1990) demonstrate, Scottish drama flourished in the 1980s. Writers found new confidence in utilizing the Scots language and new confidence in dealing with the past. Tony Roper's *The Steamie* (1987), first staged by Wildcat, appeared to offer audiences the kind of sentimentality critics thought they had left behind with the early 20th-century kailyard—until they realized the play's comment on the decimation of the older urban communities to make way for the soul-less and crime-stricken high-rise developments. Cameron's voicing of women's experience was developed in LIZ LOCHHEAD's MARY QUEEN OF SCOTS GOT HER HEAD CHOPPED OFF (1987), a powerful, searching examination of gender and sectarianism in the contemporary imagination. In *Mary Queen of Scots*, Scottish history met its nemesis. Gender issues were now as important as national concerns.

Drama in the 1990s confirmed the dearth of a nationally focused drama. The newer and more successful writers moved far beyond Glasgow's "smiles better" development campaign and the promise of its status as European City of Culture in 1990. While television drama was now taking time to reflect distinctively Scottish interests and concerns, a national cinema has emerged to address international audiences. *Braveheart* (directed by Mel Gibson, 1995) and *Trainspotting* (directed by Danny Boyle, 1996) may not reflect the "polar twins of the Scottish muse," but they certainly suggest the variety and vitality of Scottish interests in cinema's international market.

Perhaps John Home's Shakespearian status was never likely to emerge. But now, at the beginning of the 21st century, Scottish drama has finally demonstrated its return to the potential recognized by David Lindsay. The Reformation is an ironic place to begin the recovery of the national stage—but perhaps, after all, Mr. Bolfry was right.

FURTHER READING

Cameron, Alasdair. "Scottish Drama in the Nineteenth Century." In *The History of Scottish Literature*, ed. by Cairns Craig. Aberdeen: Aberdeen Univ. Press, 1988. Vol. III, 429–441.

Craig, Cairns, and Randall Stevenson, eds. *Twentieth-Century Scottish Drama: An Anthology*. Edinburgh: Canongate, 2001.

Findlay, Bill, ed. *History of Scottish Theatre*. Edinburgh: Polygon, 1998.

Hutchison, David. "Scottish Drama, 1900–1950." In *The History of Scottish Literature*, ed. by Cairns Craig. Aberdeen: Aberdeen Univ. Press, 1987. Vol. IV, 163–177.

McDonald, Jan. "Scottish Women Dramatists Since 1945." In *A History of Scottish Women's Writing*, ed. by Douglas Gifford and Dorothy McMillan. Edinburgh: Edinburgh Univ. Press, 1997. 494–513.

Muir, Edwin. *Scott and Scotland: The Predicament of the Scottish Writer*. London: Routledge, 1936.

Stevenson, Randall, and Gavin Wallace, eds. *Scottish Theatre Since the Seventies*. Edinburgh: Edinburgh Univ. Press, 1996.

Walker, Marshall. *Scottish Literature Since 1707*. London: Longman, 1996.

Crawford Gribben

THE SCOUNDREL

The Scoundrel (*Na vsyakogo mudretsa dovol'no prostoty*, 1868)—also known as *Even Wise Men Err* or *Even a Wise Man Stumbles*, as well as *The Diary of a Scoundrel*—is a COMEDY in five acts by ALEKSANDR OSTROVSKY in which a young man, Glumov (the name is associated with "making fun of"), who is determined to rise in the world by any means necessary.

Glumov insinuates himself into his uncle Mamayev's good graces. Mamayev is well-disposed toward Glumov and, on his advice, the young man even pretends to love Mamayev's wife, Kleopatra, a society coquette. Mamayev also introduces Glumov to "a young man of importance," Gorodulin, for whom he writes a speech of "liberal" sentiment, and to General Krutitsky, "an old man of importance," for whom Glumov ghost-writes a "conservative" tract with equal facility. Glumov next adopts a pose of religiosity he does not feel so he will be introduced to a widow, Turusina, who is seeking a virtuous fiancé for her richly dowered niece, Mashenka. Glumov pretends to love Mashenka to get his hands on her fortune. However, when a now jealous Kleopatra goes to his apartment, she finds and steals Glumov's diary, to which he has confided the most unflattering comments on his protectors. She makes the contents of the diary public and thus frustrates the marriage. Although this results in Glumov's banishment from society, Krutitsky foresees that he will eventually be recalled, because everyone needs a Glumov in some way or other.

Like a picaresque hero of 18th-century fiction, Glumov exposes to ridicule one milieu after another, from the merchant class to high society. But above all, he prostitutes his own gifts by putting them at the service now of this, now of that opinion. Glumov is a "wise man" who, with his talents for sale, still makes the one unwise mistake that causes his downfall. The word *mudrets* (a wise person) was in common parlance among political sages in post-emancipation RUSSIA (i.e., following the liberation of the serfs in 1861). In an ironic sense, Glumov's patrons are also wise men: Mamayev with his advice to all and sundry, Gorodulin with his liberal remedies, and Krutitsky with his conservative wisdom. Themes of deception, role-playing, and self-delusion are not merely examples of Ostrovsky's depiction of mid-19th-century Russian society, but involve the portrayal of complex human behavior. Glumov talks to a civil servant about the role-playing required by his profession: "Don't think, unless you are ordered to. Laugh, whenever your boss fancies he's cracked a joke. Do all the thinking and work for your boss, while at the same time convincing him with all the humility you can manage that it's his . . ." Examples of hypocrisy make for a number of delightfully comic passages, and Ostrovsky exploits to the full the device of dramatic irony.

Glumov reappeared as a mischief-maker in Ostrovsky's later play *Easy Money*, and the character became an archetype when Mikhail Saltykov-Shchedrin incorporated him in his *A Contemporary Idyll* (1877–1883). The Soviet Russian critic, Vladimir Lakshin, noted that Ostrovsky had written "a political comedy with deep sociophilosophic meaning." The play's satire has proven relevant to later times as well. It was among the thirteen most frequently staged of all Ostrovsky's plays for fifty years after the playwright's death and is frequently revived to this day.

FURTHER READING

Hoover, Marjorie L. *Alexander Ostrovsky*. Boston: Twayne Publishers, 1981.

Ostrovsky, Alexander. *The Diary of a Scoundrel*. Adapted by Rodney Ackland. London: Marston, 1948. Also in Vol. 2 of *The Modern Theatre*, ed. by Eric Bentley (Garden City: Doubleday, 1955). Also published as *Too Clever by Half* (New York: Applause Theatre Book Publications, 1988).

——. *The Scoundrel*. In *Five Plays*. Tr. and ed. by Eugene K. Bristow. New York: Western Publishing Co., 1989.

Rahman, Kate Sealey. *Ostrovsky: Reality and Illusion*. Birmingham Slavonic Monographs No. 30. Birmingham: Univ. of Birmingham, 1999.

Liisa Byckling

A SCRAP OF PAPER

In *A Scrap of Paper* (1860), VICTORIEN SARDOU achieves a high-water mark of dramatic craft through rigorous and imaginative application of the principles of the pièce bien faite or well-made play, developed and perfected by his chief model, Eugène Scribe. Although well-made play structure has been widely applied, from serious social criticism to historical drama to FARCE, *A Scrap of Paper* reveals a perfect union of structure and subject in a play that owes much to the COMEDY of manners of earlier generations.

The situation is romantic and social: three years prior to the play's action, lovers Prosper and Clarisse were forced apart by Clarisse's arranged marriage to Vanhove; on the night they parted, Clarisse wrote him a final love letter and placed it, according to their custom, under a statue in the drawing room. After a scene in which the household servants explain the prior action, Prosper returns (illustrating the late point of attack common to the form) under a mandate to marry and pays court to Clarisse's sister Marthe, who is in love with a shy, young student Paul. The love letter (or "scrap of paper") is discovered under the statue, undisturbed, and after an elaborate but polite struggle in full view of the assembled company, Prosper gains possession of it, to Clarisse's considerable chagrin. Clarisse then enlists her free-spirited friend Suzanne to retrieve the letter from Prosper; accordingly, she pays a visit to Prosper's rooms, in the course of which they begin to fall in love.

The stolid Vanhove, suspicious of the sudden increase in the level of romantic tension (and unaware that he is a character in the middle of the rising action of a well-made play), arrives at Prosper's lodging in search of his wife. Finding Suzanne there, he conceives the notion (which turns out to be correct in the end) that Suzanne is in love with Prosper, and he promises to further their alliance.

Suzanne, meanwhile, has found the scrap of paper; she convinces Prosper to burn it, and he does so by using it as a match to light a lamp; but he throws the burning paper out the window where, extinguished and still legible, it falls into the hands of one Thirion, amateur entomologist. He uses it to wrap a rare beetle that he has discovered while out hunting with Vanhove, which brings the scrap of paper back into Vanhove's house. Paul finds it and uses the reverse side to write a love note to Marthe; at dinner, the paper is revealed to all, but Vanhove's misunderstanding that Suzanne and Prosper are in love turns out to carry the day—and to be the truth—so all ends happily for the two pairs of lovers, as Paul and Marthe are now free to marry as well.

Despite Sardou's considerable and exceedingly formulaic machinations, the play retains its ability to charm through his bravura skills at the plotting and at drawing the lively characters of Prosper and Suzanne. Though GEORGE BERNARD SHAW coined the term *Sardoodledom* to deride the playwright's contrivances, we may find ourselves agreeing with the 1886 verdict of Joseph Jefferson, the American actor: "Among modern plays I consider *The Scrap of Paper* by Victorien Sardou to be the most ingenious of all. If Sardou only had heart he would be one of the greatest dramatists that ever lived."

FURTHER READING

Brockett, Oscar, and Robert R. Findlay. *Century of Innovation: A History of European and American Theatre and Drama Since 1870.* Englewood Cliffs, N.J.: Prentice-Hall, 1973.

Sardou, Victorien. *A Scrap of Paper.* Tr. by Léonie Gilmour. In *Camille and Other Plays,* ed. by Stephen S. Stanton. New York: Hill and Wang, 1957. Also see Stanton's excellent introduction to the dramaturgy of the well-made play as practiced by Scribe, Sardou, Augier, and Dumas *fils.*

Shaw, George Bernard. *Dramatic Opinions and Essays.* London: Constable & Co., 1909.

Rick Davis

THE SCREENS

The first French production of JEAN GENET's three-and-a-half-hour panorama of the Algerian War of Independence caused riots in and around the Odéon Theatre, Paris, in April 1966. Light bulbs, eggs, smoke bombs, and bits of metal were hurled at the actors. Right-wing commando protestors stormed the stage, sometimes rappelling down from the upper balcony to do so. Night after night, the fire curtain had to be lowered while artistic director Jean-Louis Barrault (who was in the cast) appealed to the audience for order. An amendment was introduced in the Chamber of Deputies to reduce the Odéon's subsidy by 270,000 francs, the cost of the production.

In Genet's intricate conception, over ninety characters inhabit a seventeen-scene fresco of Algeria fighting for its independence from FRANCE. Colonists, missionaries, Arab insurgents, prostitutes, peasants, and French paratroopers are locked in rituals of incomprehension that are violent and sordid on both sides. At the center of the action, the humanity of an Arab named Saïd, affianced to an ugly woman because he's too poor to afford a desirable wife, slowly erodes: he beats his wife, he steals, he betrays his countrymen to the French. His mother tries to help him, even after her death, but Saïd is beyond the aid of the living or the dead—nor can he be bothered to take sides in their quarrels. He sends himself off with a scatological remark before being gunned down by Arab insurgents, a traitor dispatched in a glorious light of self-realization.

Although the raw language, politically sensitive theme, and unflattering depiction of the military incensed many, the play's vivid poetry of image, action, and word impressed even its critics. As in Genet's preceding plays, characters seem mesmerized by their own images and insensitive to the suffering of others. The titular screens—some painted, some white, some black—serve as décor but also reveal (and conceal) the status of the characters who move behind them. In each scene, Genet calls for everyday objects to set off the brightly painted screens: a wheelbarrow, a galvanized basin, a watering can. At the moment of death, characters plunge through papered screens only to return to the stage (albeit on a lower platform) to comment on the actions of the living. Through a cruel succession of crimes, rebellions, and revolutions, the colonists see their clothes tatter, even as they wear more decorations to cover the scraps. A sergeant's cruelty makes him glow in the dark. A lieutenant is shot by a sniper; his men see him off by farting in the dead officer's face. "It's a duty we have to perform. Even if he isn't buried in Christian earth, at least he'll breathe the air of home as he dies . . ."

The original production was directed by Roger Blin, with costumes, grotesque makeup, and a multilevel set by André Acquart. Given its incendiary themes and its massive production costs, *The Screens (Les Paravents)* is seldom revived, although Joanne Akalaitis directed a production at the Guthrie Theatre in Minneapolis, Minnesota, in 1989.

FURTHER READING

Dichy, Albert, and Lynda Peskine. *La Bataille des Paravents: Théâtre de l'Odéon, 1966* [The Battle over the Screens: The Odeon Theater, 1966]. Paris: IMEC., 1991.

Genet, Jean. *Selected Writings.* Hopewell, N.J.: Ecco, 1995.

Sartre, Jean-Paul. *Saint Genet, Actor and Martyr.* Tr. by Bernard Frechtman. New York: Random House, 1983.

White, Edmund. *Genet: A Biography.* New York: Vintage Books, 1994.

Robert Schneider

THE SEAGULL

The first of ANTON CHEKHOV's four dramatic masterpieces, *The Seagull (Chaika,* 1895) marks a key departure in the playwright's development. Having long felt fettered by the so-called well-made play that dominated the Russian stage at that time, Chekhov had battled with its conventions in earlier dramas such as PLATONOV and IVANOV. From his point of view, conventional requirements, such as a dramatic event at each curtain, inhibited the portrayal of real life and nurtured theatrical artifice for its own sake. Such considerations led the playwright away from the play of direct action and toward the play of indirect action. More and more Chekhov eschewed overt dramatic conflict and relied more heavily on mood and atmosphere to reveal the unspoken psychological drama that unfolds among his characters. It is this tendency that has led some commentators to speak of Chekhov's literary impressionism.

Although Chekhov is far removed from Sigmund Freud, the psychological drama of *The Seagull* is fundamentally Oedipal in nature, but Oedipal in the same sense that the core conflict in *Hamlet* is Oedipal. Like Hamlet, Konstantin Treplev vies for the affections of his mother, from whom he is estranged. Not only

do his emotional needs put him in conflict with his mother's consort, Boris Trigorin, but so do his aspirations: Trigorin's reputation as an established author evokes a peculiar anxiety of influence in Treplev, who dreams of becoming a writer. This tension is further exacerbated when his love interest, Nina Zarechnaia, becomes interested in Trigorin. Despite this emotionally charged atmosphere, these tensions do not result in overt dramatic confrontation. An excellent example arises in Chekhov's handling of Treplev's suicide, which occurs offstage following a few resigned remarks he makes before exiting. Compare this with the ending of *Ivanov,* in which the main character delivers a quasi-heroic speech before rushing away just far enough from his wife and the other characters to shoot himself in front of them.

Indeed, *The Seagull* is remarkable for the absence of set pieces and soliloquies. (In this sense, it is important that Treplev is no Hamlet.) As a result, greater emphasis is naturally placed on the ensemble and on the interplay among the actors. (It is perhaps this quality that made the play so attractive to KONSTANTIN STANISLAVSKY.) The absence of soliloquies should not obscure Chekhov's innovative use of language. Whereas his predecessors had depended heavily on direct discourse, Chekhov emphasized unmarked speech and highlighted what remained unspoken. Chekhov's discourse concerns the failure to communicate. His concern for theatrical discourse becomes evident at other levels as well. By introducing Treplev's quasi-symbolist play into *The Seagull,* Chekhov draws attention to the metatheatrical discourse of the play; that is, the give and take between different theatrical languages.

That such an innovative and complex text posed problems for its first interpreters comes as no surprise. Several explanations for the failure of *The Seagull* at the Aleksandrinsky Theater in St. Petersburg in 1896 have been advanced. Some critics attribute it to the company's inability to render Chekhov's innovative discourse in the language of the old theatrical tradition, which the playwright had abandoned but to which the troupe still adhered, despite the participation of forward-looking actors and actresses like Vera Komissarzhevskaia, who played the role of Nina. Others have laid blame at the feet of the critics and the audience, who had come to see a benefit performance and were looking to be entertained.

In contrast, the success that Konstantin Stanislavsky and Vladimir Nemirovich-Danchenko enjoyed with *The Seagull* at the newly formed MOSCOW ART THEATER in 1898 owed much to a fortunate convergence of Chekhov's poetics and their own. Stanislavsky's emphasis on ensemble work was consonant with Chekhov's approach to characterization. Schooled in NATURALISM and the most innovative drama of the preceding generation, the remarkable cast, which included Chekhov's future wife Olga Knipper as Irina Arkadina and VSEVOLOD MEYERHOLD himself as Treplev, had an innate feeling for Chekhov's language. Perhaps just as important, the Art Theater's audience came to support a company that existed independently, outside of the Imperial Theater system. Their openness played no small role in the play's success. Chekhov himself, however, remained skeptical about Stanislavsky's approach to The Seagull. In particular, he expressed concern about the slow tempo of the performance and about the naturalistic effects the director employed.

The influence of The Seagull has been immense and was felt almost immediately after the Art Theater production. It played no small part in the development of Russian symbolist drama. Chekhov's evocation of mood and atmosphere, the enigmatic quality of the seagull as a symbol, and his new metatheatrical poetics exercised a decisive influence on the Symbolists. Thanks to the foreign tours of the Moscow Art Theater, the play has proven equally influential in Europe and the United States.

[See also Russia and the Soviet Union]

FURTHER READING

Balukhaty, S. D., ed. "The Seagull" Produced by Stanislavsky—Production Score for the Moscow Art Theatre by K. S. Stanislavsky. Tr. by David Magarshack; introduction by S. D. Balukhaty. London: Dennis Dobson, 1952.

Chekhov, Anton. The Seagull. Tr. by Michael Frayn, with commentary and notes. London: Methuen Student Editon, 2002.

Gilman, Richard. Chekhov's Plays: An Opening into Eternity. New Haven: Yale Univ. Press, 1995.

Peace, Richard. Chekhov: A Study of the Four Major Plays. New Haven and London: Yale Univ. Press, 1983.

Winner, Thomas G. "Chekhov's Seagull and Shakespeare's Hamlet: A Study of a Dramatic Device." In Anton Chekhov's Plays, tr. and ed. by Eugene K. Bristow. New York: W.W. Norton & Co., 1977. 341–48.

Timothy C. Westphalen

SEAGULL EATERS

You eat sea gulls? Excellent dish. Freedom personified brought down from heaven. Bang!
—Theater Director, Part 1

Seagull Eaters (Måkespisere, 1982), a radio drama by CECILIE LØVEID, had its premiere on Norwegian radio in 1982 and was published along with two other plays in 1983 in Måkespisere; Tre spill for radio og scene. The play was Løveid's breakthrough as a playwright and became an immediate success. The play is lyrical and modernistic, with a documentary style to the plot based in World War II during the German occupation of NORWAY. The main character in the drama is Kristine Larsen. Scenes from her childhood and youth are depicted, starting in Bergen in 1939. Kristine wants to become an actress and opposes the roles her parents, her fiancé, the society, and the language itself has prepared for her. She reaches her goal, but the price turns out to be high.

Seagull Eaters is a COLLAGE, a composition of dialogues and scenes telling the story about, and reflecting over, Kristine Larsen's struggle for the life she wants. A children's choir comments on Kristine and her story. Contours of a tragic plot become gradually visible. The peripety is Kristine's surrender to Olsen, a Nazi sympathizer. The main conflict can be found in the question of how a woman can free herself from oppressive cultural traditions and norms and yet achieve the love she needs. "It gets tiring to play tragedies all by yourself." Kristine is also represented as teller of her story in the drama, suggesting that inside the drama she finally will achieve a true voice of her own.

Intertextuality is another important concept for the drama; different texts and literary traditions are employed and referenced throughout. Henriette Schønberg Erken's Stor Kokebok (1895), for a long time the main cookbook for housewives in Norway, is an important background text. Erken reads selected passages from her book at strategic moments in the drama. The quotes represent advice about how to kill, pluck, singe, prepare, and serve birds—and seem also to describe how to deal with young women. An early reply from Kristine leads to this interpretation: "I love reading the cookbook. Suspense and drama. How to cut animals' throats, fry hens, slaughter geese . . ." A main point in the play is to make visible a certain language code in which tame birds, like goose and hen, serve as metaphors for females. Wild birds, like the seagull, and in general predators, often function as metaphors for males. In this way language itself puts Kristine's project of self-liberation in perspective.

The play is usually interpreted as a protest against traditional views of women and womanhood. The language theme supports this feministic theme. The drama also contains a cultural critique and a political dimension: upper-class people as well as Nazis can also be regarded as seagull eaters.

Seagull Eaters was awarded the Prix Italia in 1983 and has since been produced by, among others, German, Swedish, and French radio companies.

FURTHER READING

Garton, Janet. Norwegian Women's Writing 1850–1990. London & Atlantic Highlands, N.J.: Athlone, 1993. 220–221.

Garton, Janet, and Henning Sehmsdorf. New Norwegian plays. Norwich, England: Norvik Press, 1989. 28–30.

Markussen, Bjarne. "Hverdagslige katastrofer" [Everyday Catastrophes] and "Måkespisere" [Seagull Eaters]. In Livsritualer. En bok om Cecilie Løveids dramatikk [Rituals of Life: A Book on Cecilie Løveid's Dramatic Writings], ed. by Merete Morken Andersen. Oslo: Gyldendal, 1998.

Tjønneland, Eivind. "Fabelens fragmentering—noen strøtanker om Cecilie Løveids Måkespisere" [The Fragmentation of Fabula—Some Incidental Thoughts on Cecilie Løveid's Seagull Eaters]. Nordica Bergensia 17 (1998): 29–37.

Alvhild Dvergsdal

SEARS, DJANET (1959–)

Born in London, England, on August 23, 1959, Djanet Sears is a dynamic and versatile figure in Canadian theater. Although most renowned for playwriting, Sears has excelled as an actress, director, scholar, and pedagogue. At fifteen Sears left ENGLAND, where she had been raised by Guyanese and Jamaican parents, and moved to Saskatoon, Saskatchewan, CANADA. After studying at York University, she moved to Toronto to begin an acting career. Sears acted in the first production of her first self-penned play, *Afrika Solo*, which was staged in 1989 at Factory Theatre; a subsequent CBC radio adaptation (which Sears also acted in) brought Sears's explorations of class, gender, and race to a wider audience. *Afrika Solo*, a MONODRAMA, is a semiautobiographical narrative about a character seeking IDENTITY in Canada. Sears has always attended to her own multicultural identity. Feeling partially British, Caribbean, and Canadian, Sears looks to AFRICA as her ancestral and spiritual home: she was christened Janet, but visited a town near Mali called Djanet, felt an affinity with the place and people, and changed her name.

Sears's 1990s plays include *Double Trouble*, *Shakes*, and *Who Killed Katie Ross*. Before 2003's ADVENTURES OF A BLACK GIRL IN SEARCH OF GOD, Sears's best-known play was *Harlem Duet*, which she directed at the Tarragon in Toronto in 1997. The play is a bold prequel to William Shakespeare's *Othello*. Othello is married to Billie; although both are black, the couple is divided on the race issue. Othello cares little for black identity and even seeks to pass for white; Billie, on the other hand, is fiercely antiwhite. *Harlem Duet*, which is enlivened by a blues soundtrack, reworks *Othello* so radically and effectively that Sears's work has become acclaimed by Shakespearean scholars and enthusiasts. One significant aspect of *Harlem Duet* is that there are no white characters; although we are to imagine Mona (Othello's next wife) just offstage, the play illuminates black characters' concerns exclusively. Sears has claimed that some negative reaction to her plays derives from a white discomfort at seeing a stage peopled exclusively with "others," with nonwhites. The number of awards that Sears received for *Harlem Duet* may indicate that white critics and audiences are quite ready to accept an all-black cast.

Sears's commitment to articulating the black voice through theater is not limited to the promotion of her own work. An energetic campaigner for the efficacy and legacy of black Canadian theatrical writing, Sears celebrates the history of black dramatic writing. She is the artistic director of the AfriCanadian Playwrights' Conference Festival and has produced accessible anthologies of black Canadian playwriting. The two volumes of *Testifyn'* collect works of Lorena Gale, Andrew Moodie, and George Seremba, among others. In effect, Sears has constructed the first major canon of black Canadian dramatic texts. Sears continues to write acclaimed plays of her own, as well as to promote previous achievements by African Canadian dramatists and to encourage first-time writers, particularly through her

drama teaching at University College, University of Toronto, where she is an adjunct professor.

PLAYS: *Afrika Solo* (1989); *Who Killed Katie Ross* (1994); *Harlem Duet* (1997); *The Adventures of a Black Girl in Search of God* (2003)

FURTHER READING

Holledge, Julie, and Joanne Tompkins. *Women's Intercultural Performance*. London: Routledge, 2000. 195–196.

Kidnie, M. J. "There's Magic in the Web of It: Seeing Beyond Tragedy in *Harlem Duet*." *Journal of Commonwealth Literature* 36, no. 3 (2001): 29–44.

Knowles, Ric. "Othello in Three Time." In *Shakespeare in Canada: A World Elsewhere*, ed. by Diana Brydon and Irena R. Makaryk. Toronto: Univ. of Toronto Press, 2002. 371–394.

Sears, Djanet. *Afrika Solo*. Toronto: Sister Vision Press, 1990.

——. *Harlem Duet*. In *Adaptations of Shakespeare: A Critical Anthology*, ed. by Daniel Fischlin and Mark Fortier. London: Routledge, 2000. 285–317.

——. *Testifyin': Contemporary African Canadian Drama*, Vols. One and Two. Toronto: Canada Playwrights Press, 2000 and 2003.

Wasserman, Jerry. "Djanet Sears." In *Encyclopedia of Literature in Canada*, ed. by William H. New. Toronto: Univ. of Toronto Press, 2002. 1031.

Kevin De Ornellas

A SEASON IN THE CONGO

The second of AIMÉ CÉSAIRE's three "epics of decolonization" (after *The Tragedy of King Christophe*, 1963), *A Season in the Congo* (1966) depicts in three turbulent acts the final months of historical figure Patrice Lumumba, who briefly served as the first prime minister of the Independent Congo (later known as the Republic of Zaire, and now called the Democratic Republic of Congo).

Much as Georg Büchner used the historical record to critique the French Revolution in *Danton's Death*, Césaire drew heavily on actual events, figures, and recorded speeches to explore the viability of the African independence movement of the early 1960s. Independence from BELGIUM was granted to the Congo in June 1960; Lumumba created a coalition government with President Joseph Kasavubu and Defense Secretary Mobutu Sese Seko (renamed Kala Lubu and Mokutu, respectively). In the play, the charismatic Lumumba is immediately beset by foreign resistance in the form of European economic interests and American policymakers fearful that the Congo will appeal to the Soviet Union for help, and by internal conflicts in the form of long-simmering tribal interests personified by Mokutu and Msiri. A grotesque chorus of bankers, speaking in mock-Alexandrine verse, abets the secession of the Katanga province, known for its rich copper, diamond, and uranium deposits. Lumumba secures the assistance of a United Nations peacekeeping force (in the person of historical figure Dag Hammarsköld), but its stance of neutrality allows Belgian arms and soldiers to pour into the country and further divide the Congolese people. Stripped of his position and placed under house arrest, Lumumba attempts a final march to power but is killed by Katangese rebels and white mercenaries—a murder arranged by Mokutu.

Lumumba attempts too much too soon for his people, but as the playwright predicts, in death, "he will be even more fearsome." Insisting that his play was a poetic TRAGEDY and not a Marxist tract, Césaire has stated that his theater "is not an individual or individualistic theater, it is an EPIC THEATER for it always presents the fate of a whole community." *Season* is ultimately more Brechtian in its stage techniques—short scenes of alternating scale and tone, didactic speech and song, radio news briefs, etc.—than in its outlook. *Season* carries forward cultural traditions from African DRAMATURGY with the figure of The Sanza Player, a sometimes ironic, sometimes lyrical commentator and sparring partner to Lumumba, who represents, with his use of African proverbs and jokes, "the good or good common sense of the people." The Sanza Player has the last word: as the curtain falls, he steps forward to sing ". . . a beginning is only a beginning / And if we're going to do this thing / Let's not do it by halves . . ." This reminds us, as does the title itself, that other seasons will come for both the Congolese people and the ideals of pan-African solidarity for which Lumumba lived and died.

Under the direction of Jean-Marie Serreau, *A Season in the Congo* received its premiere at the Venice Biennale of 1967, before transferring to the Théâtre de L'Est Parisien, a community cultural center in the heart of a working-class district of Paris.

[*See also* Africa; France]

FURTHER READING

Benimadhu, P. "*Une Saison au Congo*: Problématique de la décolonisation" [*A Season in the Congo*: Issues of Decolonization]. *Indian Cultural Review* (1980): 33–46.

Brichaux-Houyoux, Suzanne. *Quand Césaire Écrit, Lumumba Parle. Édition commentée de "Une Saison au Congo"* [When Césaire writes, Lumumba speaks. Critical edition of *A Season in the Congo*]. Paris: Éditions L'Harmattan, 1993.

Césaire, Aimé. *A Season in the Congo*. Tr. by Ralph Manheim. New York: Grove Press, 1968.

Hale, Thomas A. "Aimé Césaire: A Bio-Bibliographical Note." *Callaloo* 17 (1983): 134–136.

Rowell, Charles H. "It Is Through Poetry That One Copes With Solitude: An Interview with Aimé Césaire." *Callaloo* 38 (1989): 49–67.

Sekora, Karin. " 'Il y avait un tabou à lever.' Intertextualité dans *Une Saison au Congo* d'Aimé Césaire" ["There's a taboo to lift." Intertextuality in *A Season in the Congo* by Aimé Césaire]. *Œuvres et Critiques* 19, no. 2 (1994): 243–265.

Lam-Thao Nguyen

THE SECOND MRS. TANQUERAY

Killed herself? Yes—yes. So everybody will say. But I know—I helped to kill her. [She beats her breast] If only I had been merciful!
—Ellean, Act 4, Scene 1

ALFRED WING PINERO's *The Second Mrs. Tanqueray* is one of the best-known late Victorian PROBLEM PLAYS. In tracing a fallen woman's failed attempt at reformation and exposing society's sexual double standard, Pinero both reflects and challenges Victorian conventions of gender and respectability. When this play was first produced in 1893, it was widely criticized for immorality and the sense of unpleasantness that pervades the tale; however, it has since been seen as one of the first truly literary plays of the Victorian period. Mrs. Patrick Campbell, who played Paula Tanqueray in the original production, was widely praised for her performance. Despite lighting effects that emphasized Aubrey Tanqueray as the hero, audiences and critics alike seemed to view Campbell as the star of the play. Indeed, *The London Times* (May 29, 1893) review of this production calls Paula "a masterpiece of execution by author and actress alike."

The play opens in Aubrey Tanqueray's bachelor lodgings. Aubrey is hosting a dinner to announce his marriage and bid farewell to his closest friends. Aubrey's first marriage to a reserved Roman Catholic was unhappy, but when she was dying, he promised to have their daughter reared in a convent. As a result, he has almost no relationship with Ellean. Believing that his daughter has decided to take her vows, Aubrey has decided to marry Paula, an adventuress who has been ill-used by the many men with whom she has been linked. He believes, through patience and a respectable marriage, he will eventually be able to return Paula to society.

Trouble arises when Ellean changes her mind about becoming a nun and comes to live with her father and his new wife in Highercombe, the rural home Aubrey had shared with her mother. Although Aubrey shields her from Paula's past, Ellean senses something in Paula that prompts her to withhold her affection, something the older woman desperately craves. Ellean's reserve, Paula's jealousy, and the isolation in which they live have combined to divide Paula and Aubrey. A visit from her vulgar friends underscores the fact that Paula's character has grown, but she cannot offer Ellean the social advantages appropriate to the girl's class position. Against Paula's wishes, Aubrey sends Ellean to Paris with a friend of the family, further alienating his wife. In Paris, Ellean falls in love with Captain Ardale and returns unexpectedly to obtain her father's blessing. Ellean has forgiven Ardale for his dissolute past, but when it is revealed that he was involved with Paula, she cannot forgive her stepmother. Feeling that she has lost any chance of winning the girl's love and believing that she will soon become a distasteful burden to her husband, Paula retires to her room and commits suicide. Ellean's final lines emphasize the play's message about the injustice of society's sexual double standard.

[*See also* England, 1860–1940]

FURTHER READING

Pinero, Arthur Wing. *The Second Mrs. Tanqueray, Trelawny of the 'Wells' and Other Plays.* Ed. and introduction by J. S. Bratton. Oxford and New York: Oxford Univ. Press, 1995.

"St. James's Theatre." [Review of *The Second Mrs. Tanqueray* by Arthur Wing Pinero.] *The Times* (May 29, 1893): 8.

Robin A. Werner

SECRET SERVICE

The grandfather of all spy thrillers and a star vehicle for its author, *Secret Service* by WILLIAM GILLETTE was first produced on May 13, 1895, in Philadelphia with Maurice Barrymore in the leading role. It then re-opened on October 5, 1896, in New York City with Gillette himself as Thorne. Subsequent productions ran in Boston, London, Paris, Hartford, and San Francisco, and Gillette played the lead in 1,791 performances.

Richmond is under siege during the Civil War. Lewis Dumont, of the United States Secret Service, has infiltrated the city disguised as Captain Thorne of the Confederate Artillery. He loves Edith Varney, the daughter of a Confederate general. She has succeeded in obtaining a special commission for him to assume command of the telegraph office, which attracts the suspicion of Benton Arrelsford of the Confederate Secret Service, who knows that someone has been using the telegraph system to subvert the Southern cause. Arrelsford has captured Dumont's brother, Henry, and tries to use him as bait to expose "Thorne," but the Yankee exploits the set-up to receive a message from Henry and then to make it appear that he has recaptured the prisoner in an escape attempt. In the play's climactic scene, "Thorne" manages to send part of Henry's message in spite of Arrelsford's efforts to stop him; Edith uses the special commission to save "Thorne" from Arrelsford's arrest, knowing full well that "Thorne" is an enemy agent; and the Yankee, torn between his love for Edith and his loyalty to the North, finally cuts the message short. Later, "Thorne" returns to the Varney home for one last conversation with Edith, and Arrelsford's men capture him. They are about to send him before the firing squad when General Randolph arrives to inform Arrelsford that "Thorne" never sent the subversive message and that the Confederate battle strategy has succeeded. "Thorne" is sent to prison as Edith swears her love.

A secondary story line concerns the comic romance between Caroline Mitford and young Wilfred Varney, who aspires to join his father on the front line in spite of his mother's objections.

Gillette was considered courageous by some for daring to make his hero a spy. William Dean Howells (1897) wrote, "The atmosphere of the piece is Confederate, and the patriotism is for the bad cause which the playwright does not make us wish well in making us sympathize with the generous devotion of so many of his brave people to it." *The Athenæum* (May 22, 1897) review reported:

What is most remarkable of all, Mr. Gillette demands and forces our sympathy for treachery, and holds up loyal and constant service to ridicule, if he does not present it as positive villainy. . . . That Mr. Gillette contrives to interest us in the proceedings of [Thorne and Edith] shows how well he judges the pulse of the public.

The 1977 Broadway Theatre Archive video version of the play, based on a 1976 production by the Phoenix Theatre, features John Lithgow in the Gillette role with Meryl Streep as Edith and Mary Beth Hurt as Caroline.

[*See also* Melodrama; United States, 1860–1929]

FURTHER READING

Cullen, Rosemary, and Don B. Wilmeth. *Plays by William Hooker Gillette.* Cambridge: Cambridge Univ. Press, 1983.

Howells, W. D. "Life and Letters." *Harper's Weekly* 41 (January 30, 1897): 107.

Nichols, Harold J. "William Gillette: Innovator in Melodrama." *Theatre Annual* 31 (1975): 7–15.

Jeffrey D. Mason

SEI PERSONAGGI IN CERCA D'AUTORE

See SIX CHARACTERS IN SEARCH OF AN AUTHOR

SENDA KOREYA (1904–1994)

Senda Koreya, Japanese SHINGEKI stage director, actor, translator, and producer, became JAPAN's foremost interpreter of BERTOLT BRECHT. Senda was a mainstay of *shingeki*'s reestablishment after World War II, a leader of the Actors Theatre Company (Haiyūza), and directed plays until his death. Senda Koreya (Sendagaya Korean) is the name he took in 1923 after being mistaken as a Korean and beaten by Japanese vigilantes near Sendagaya, Tokyo, in the chaos following the Great Kanto Earthquake. Senda, a committed socialist who took part in some of the most important artistic and political developments in modern Japanese drama, always had a political dimension to his work.

In 1924, his knowledge of foreign languages landed Senda a job in on the editorial staff of the newly formed Tsukiji Little Theatre (Tsukiji Shōgekijō). He soon began acting. Throughout his life, Senda agreed with the founders of the Tsukiji Little Theatre, who felt that that traditional Japanese theater forms were anachronistic and detrimental to the development of a socially relevant drama.

In addition to the hectic production schedule at the Tsukiji Little Theatre, Senda was active in proletarian theater. He left the Tsukiji Little Theatre in 1926 to devote his entire energy to the proletarian movement. In 1927, he went to GERMANY and was accepted into leftist director ERWIN PISCATOR's Piscatorbühne, but soon left to join a smaller amateur group run by workers. During four and half years in Germany, Senda became a socialist and learned many techniques of agit-prop theater that he brought back in Japan in 1931. While in Germany he made trips to Moscow to see productions by KONSTANTIN STAN-ISLAVSKY and VSEVOLOD MEYERHOLD. However, his main influence was Brecht, and in 1932, he produced the first Japanese language adaptation of THE THREEPENNY OPERA.

Socialism was a particular target of Japan's right-wing government until the end of World War II, and Senda was jailed briefly upon his return from Germany. Although not a member of the Communist Party, Senda recanted his socialist beliefs in 1942 to secure his third release from prison. He trained the actors who became the Actors Theatre. After the war, the company trained many actors and steadily built an audience base while producing both Japanese and Western plays. Senda directed William Shakespeare and ANTON CHEKHOV, not to mention Brecht and ABE KŌBŌ. Senda both translated and directed the original Japanese productions of most of Brecht's major works. He also directed most of Abe's plays from 1955 to 1965.

Although the Actors' Theatre was part of the left-wing coalition that opposed the renewal of the U.S.–Japan security Treaty, by the 1960s, shingeki was labeled as establishment, commercialized theater against which younger practitioners were rebelling. A group of younger actors split from the company in 1971. Senda, however, as the leader of the Actors Theatre, maintained his artistic and political beliefs and continued an active presence in Japanese theater.

FURTHER READING

Goodman, David. *Japanese Drama and Culture in the 1960s: The Return of the Gods.* Armonk, N.Y.: M.E. Sharpe, 1988.

Ortolani, Benito. *The Japanese Theatre: From Shamanistic Ritual to Contemporary Pluralism.* Princeton: Princeton Univ. Press, 1995.

Powell, Brian. *Japan's Modern Theatre: A Century of Change and Continuity.* London: Japan Library, 2002.

"Senda Koreya: An Interview," *Concerned Theatre Japan* 1, no. 1 (1970): 47–79.

Senda Koreya. *Mō Hitotsu no Shingekishi* [One More History of Shingeki]. Tokyo: Chikuma Shōbō, 1975.

Senda Koreya and Fujita Fujio. *Gekihaku: Senda Koreya* [Theatre Confessions: Senda Koreya]. Tokyo: Orijin Shuppatsu Sentaa, 1995.

John D. Swain

LA SEÑORA EN SU BALCÓN *See* THE LADY ON HER BALCONY

SENS DE LA MORT *See* CALIGULA

LES SÉQUESTRÉS D'ALTONA *See* THE CONDEMNED OF ALTONA

SERAFÍN ÁLVAREZ QUINTERO *See* ÁLVAREZ QUINTERO, JOAQUIN

SERBIA

The beginning of the history of Serbian drama can be marked by an interesting coincidence. HENRIK IBSEN died in 1906, the same year that the most important Serbian Ibsen-style naturalist play appeared. The play in question is *Our Sons (Naši sinovi)*, and its author, Vojislav Jovanović Marambo, is the only true representative of NATURALISM in the history of Serbian drama. Marambo does not belong to the group of classic authors readily performed today, but the historical importance of his works is beyond doubt: at the time it was written, his small opus represented a sharp break with the then-dominant trend of well-made plays. The naturalist characteristics of *Our Sons* and other Marambo plays are typical of the genre: an authentic depiction of the social setting (the family, financial circles, or the press) and topics such as the breakup of the middle-class family unit, poverty as a source of moral downfall, and the destruction of progressive ideals under outside pressure.

Between the two world wars (1918–1941), Serbian drama did not experience the transformation that, under the influence of European modernist trends, was underway in other genres of Serbian literature. Theater scholar Mirjana Miočinović is of the opinion that this is because the Belgrade National Theatre, a sluggish institution with a national and social mission, was not a suitable place for the development of new dramatic trends, and Belgrade had no other theaters at the time. The theater's management followed the rules of traditional esthetics and the demands of contemporary market, neither conducive to artistic experiment.

Continuity in drama development is also reflected in the fact that during the period Branislav Nušić (1864–1938) was still the leading Serbian playwright. Nušić started his playwriting career in late 19th century when he wrote his first COMEDIES, *Member of Parliament (Narodni poslanik*, 1883) and *The Suspect (Sumnjivo lice*, 1887), under the influence of Nikolai Gogol's social satire. In the modern period, Nušić's work entered a mature phase that would conclusively affirm his position as the preeminent writer in the history of Serbian comedy and drama. His most important works during this period include *The Minister's Wife (Gospođa ministarka*, 1929), *The Mourning Family (Ožalošćena porodica*, 1934), and his last play, *The Deceased (Pokojnik*, 1937).

Nušić's comedies depict petty bourgeois circles whose inertia and sluggishness are suddenly broken by a dramatic event. The event throws the characters off balance, and they begin to have certain ambitions (gaining political power, amassing a fortune, social recognition, and so forth) far beyond their otherwise modest intellectual and business capabilities. These characters thus become the epitomes of the negative social phenomena and psychological traits that the comedy aims to criticize: greed, love of power, or upstart mentality. The best example of this is the character of Živka in *The Minister's Wife*, a humble housewife who undergoes a complete transformation when her husband becomes a government minister and who, seeking to be recognized in high society, makes a circus both of herself and her house.

However, the criticism of negative character traits and/or social phenomena is never too sharp in Nušić's comedy. The social setting in them is not portrayed with the authenticity of a naturalist play, and the desire to create a comic effect is so predominant that these comedies often contain some elements of lighter genres. Some contemporary critics therefore believe that Nušić's attitude to his comic characters is too benevolent. A sharper note of criticism, amounting to resignation in the face of man's helplessness against an immoral world, is present in Nušić's last play, *The Deceased*, which can thus only conditionally be classified as a comedy.

In the Serbian drama and theater between the two world wars, tradition easily dominates innovation—and this balance of power has, with brief exceptions, been a constant in Serbian culture. Thus it is important to mention some dramatists and plays that brought a breath of MODERNIST DRAMA into the Serbian theater of the period. One of these is *The Mask* (*Maska*, 1918) by Miloš Crnjanski (1893–1977), a leading Serbian poet and novelist. The play, which the author classified as a poetic comedy, is poetic not only because it was written in verse, but also because it creates a lyrical feeling of melancholy, resignation, and being thwarted. In view of the fact that the main character commits suicide in the end, *The Mask* is not a real comedy: the comedy lies in the contrast between the tragic fates of some characters and the frivolous world of 19th-century Vienna ballrooms where the play is set. The main theme of this gloomy drawing-room comedy is the fear of death stemming from the knowledge that youth and beauty must inexorably fade.

Two other modernist undertakings in this period are the plays *The Centrifugal Dancer* (*Centrifugalni igrač*, 1929) by Todor Manojlović and At "*The Eternal Tap*" (*Kod "Večite slavine*," 1938) by Momčilo Nastasijević. The former takes place in a nonspecified European resort, its characters are stylized, and the plot revolves around a love story that is ruined by a young man's desire to be free. The mood is elegiac, and the main point is mystical: cosmic ties bring together people separated by distance or death. The play At "*The Eternal Tap*" is unique for its free composition, which breaks up the chronology of the narration: the prologue and epilogue take place in the present, whereas the main plot is set in the past, and the action is presented from the end to the beginning. The reverse development is justified because the origin of the fatal love between the main characters is found at their birth: they are brother and sister. Its dark, psychoanalytical treatment of sexuality and its authentically presented social setting bring some naturalistic elements into this drama.

The first decade after World War II (1945–1955) did not yield any significant plays. The artistic inferiority of the plays written in the period stemmed mostly from the new political situation. With the communist system's ideological control of art, the works of the early communist period were written in the spirit of SOCIALIST REALISM, with a clear political message based on the "good guys and bad guys" stereotype. In this decade the authors who managed to break the constraints of propaganda were rare; they include, primarily, the Pirandellian dramas of Josip Kulundžic.

The first major turnaround happened in 1956 when two new playwrights, Đorđe Lebović and Aleksandar Obrenović wrote, *The Heavenly Squad* (*Nebeski odred*). Based partially on personal experience (Lebović spent two years in German concentration camps), they wrote a play about a group of Auschwitz prisoners who agreed to work on the cremation of their fellow sufferers to prolong their lives by three months. Slobodan Selenic notes the paradox that, after a decade of official swearing by REALISM, *The Heavenly Squad* was the first truly realistic play. Apart from the critical depiction of a monstrous situation, this play has some higher philosophical and anthropological content. In discord with the prevalent propaganda of optimism, this play poses some essential questions about human nature, the limits of ordeal, and the relativity of moral principles in inhumane situations.

Echoes of contemporary tendencies in world drama begin to appear in Serbia only in the early 1960s. It is interesting to note that ABSURDISM did not have a great impact (with the exceptions listed below), but the philosophical or polemic plays of French authors JEAN-PAUL SARTRE, ALBERT CAMUS, JEAN ANOUILH, and JEAN GIRAUDOUX, which most frequently used myths to pose modern intellectual issues, exerted great influence on the Serbian drama at the time. There are at least two explanations for this kind of influence. First, official Yugoslav policy began to be more open to the West in the 1960s, thus making Western literary influence acceptable. Second, a reinterpretation of classical myths provided good cover for tackling current political and ethical issues.

The most prominent representative of this trend was Jovan Hristić, who used the classical myths of Orestes and Oedipus, following Sartre's model, to raise important moral and philosophical issues. Whether one should avoid his or her human responsibilities to keep a clear conscience is addressed in *Clean Hands*, (*Čiste ruke*, 1960)—a polemic response to Sartre's *Dirty Hands*. Whether revenge has any point if the wrongdoers are no longer the same people they once were, when one needs to bring to mind recollections of their earlier selves is addressed in *Orestes* (1961). In contrast to Hristić, Velimir Lukić did not use existing myths but created his own, and not for the purpose of raising philosophical issues but, using the language of fairy-tale-like FARCE, to address the problems of power, in *The Long Life of King Oswald* (*Dugi život Kralja Osvalda*, 1962) and *The Affair of Innocent Annabelle* (*Afera nedužne Anabele*, 1969). Lukić's plays are structured according to a strict pattern: there is always a rebellion against tyranny that appears absurd in the end, as this world is irredeemably evil. This kind of radical pessimism, as Slobodan Selenić correctly notes, has a paradoxical consequence—it encourages social conformism.

A special place in this trend is reserved for an excellent play *Banović Strahinja* (1963), written by one of the leading intellectuals of the time, Borislav Mihajlović Mihiz. Setting aside Hristić's classical myths and Lukić's imaginary myths, Mihiz found the source for this play in the Serbian medieval mythology. The inspiration of Mihiz is not so much reminiscent of Sartre's existentialism as of the sharp polemics of Shaw. The action is focused around Banović Strahinja, a knight who decides to forgive his wife's infidelity, going against the political interests of his wife's family. His is a brave struggle for deeper moral principles and the right to decide his own fate.

As we have already mentioned, the influence of the theater of absurd on the Serbian drama was much lighter. Some of it can be found in the works of ALEKSANDAR POPOVIĆ (1929–1996), although he is probably the most original Serbian dramatist. His plays break with the classical drama: there is no causality in the plot development, and the characters lack psychological content. The main dramatic tool in these plays is language—the jargon of various guilds from the city outskirts, which apart from providing the comic effects, also gives the plays some of BERTOLT BRECHT's distancing effect. Popovic's plays are classified as farces, although their topics are not always typical of the genre: thus the topic of *Ljubinko and Desanka* (*Ljubinko i Desanka*, 1964) is the futility of waiting, similar to SAMUEL BECKETT's tragic FARCE *WAITING FOR GODOT*.

Faint echoes of the theater of absurd can also be found in the works of Dušan Kovačević, a leading contemporary Serbian dramatist. His comedies always start with a typical setting and the development of a realistic situation, and then, by various dramatic means, turn toward the absurd. In *Marathon Runners Run the Lap of Honour* (*Maratonci trče počasni krug*, 1973), we encounter the Topalović family, consisting of several generations of male members (all the women in the family having passed away), the eldest being 126 years old, his son 102, his grandson seventy-nine, and so on. Since the Topalović family are a destructive and dangerous group, the great span of generations becomes a strong metaphor for the criminal patriarchal world. What characterizes the comedies of Dušan Kovačević is that they do not deal with social deviations typically found in absurdist drama; on the contrary, they examine the lasting anomalies of the Serbian national being. This is why, although he has been called the heir of Nušić, Kovačević is much more bitter than his great predecessor. His other important works are *Radovan III* (1973), *The Assembly Centre* (*Sabirni centar*, 1982), *Balkan Spy* (*Balkanski špijun*, 1983), *The Professional* (*Profesionalac*, 1990), and *Larry Thompson, A Youth's Tragedy* (*Lari Tompson, tragedija jedne mladosti*, 1996).

The great poet Ljubomir Simović started writing plays relatively late in his career, and with only three works performed, created one of the most important opuses in the history of Serbian drama. In the play *Hassan Agha's Wife* (*Hasanaginica*, 1973), the author takes the material from national mythology to treat it in a modern way: this poetic depiction of frustrated longing (both the erotic and the longing for motherhood) also raises the problems of sexual frustration in marriage and the right of individual choice. *A Miracle in 'Šargan'* (*Čudo u 'Šarganu,'* 1975) portrays, through a strange mixture of rough realism and poetic SYMBOLISM, the pathetic world of an outskirts tavern and develops the idea that suffering is the only pivotal point of a man's character. *The Šopalović Traveling Company* (*Putujuće pozorište Šopalović*, 1985) is set during World War II, when a troupe of traveling actors tries to perform in an occupied city. The main theme of the play, the relationship between the real and theatrical reality, raises several essential questions: Is it moral to work in the theater during a war? Where is the borderline between the theater and reality? Can theater change the world?

The last decade of the 20th century saw a dramatic increase in the number of interesting authors. The most important new figure in the Serbian drama at the end of the 20th century, and the only woman mentioned so far, is Biljana Srbljanović. Her dramatic form is an unusual combination of a complex and metaphorical structure and an elliptical and withering dialogue. She turns a sharp focus on, and then proceeds boldly to dismantle the disastrous cultural models (machismo, nationalism, and gerontophilia) at the foundation of all wars and misfortunes in former Yugoslavia. Her dramas from the 1990s sharply criticize the tyranny of the Slobodan Miloševic regime: *The Belgrade Trilogy* (*Beogradska trilogija*, 1997), *Family Stories* (*Porodične priče*, 1988), and *The Fall* (*Pad*, 2000). Her new plays—*Supermarket* (2001) and *America, Part II* (*Amerika, drugi deo*, 2003)—examine the most current phenomena of the contemporary world, a united Europe and the UNITED STATES.

FURTHER READING

Jovićević, Aleksandra. "Milošević i njegovi savremenici" [Milošević and His Contemporaries]. *Teatron Magazine* 119/120. Belgrade: Serbian Theatre Museum, 2002. 19–32.

Marjanović, Petar. *Srpski dramski pisci XX stoleća* [The 20th Century Serbian Playwrights]. Belgrade: Faculty of Drama Arts, 2000.

Miočinović, Mirjana. Foreword to *Drama između dva rata* [Drama between the Two World Wars]. Belgrade: Nolit, 1987.

———. Foreword to *Aleksandar Popović, Izabrane drame* [Aleksandar Popović. Selected Plays]. Belgrade: Nolit, 1987.

Medenica, Ivan. "Srpske i druge drame" [Serbian and Other Plays]. *Teatron Magazine* 119/120. Belgrade: Serbian Theatre Museum, 2002. 7–18.

Selenić, Slobodan. "Savremena srpska drama" [Contemporary Serbian Drama]. Foreword to *Antologija savremene srpske drame* [Anthology of contemporary Serbian drama]. Belgrade: SKZ, 1977.

Stamenković, Vladimir. Foreword to *Dušan Kovačević, Izabrane drame* [Dušan Kovačević. Selected Plays]. Belgrade: Nolit, 1987.

Ivan Medenica

SERJEANT MUSGRAVE'S DANCE

You can't cure the pox by further whoring.

—Private Attercliffe, Act 3

JOHN ARDEN's reputation continues to be determined by *Serjeant Musgrave's Dance*. The play was not an immediate commercial or critical success, despite opening at the Royal Court Theatre in October 1959 with esteemed personnel: Lindsay Anderson produced, Dudley Moore wrote the music, and Jocelyn Herbert designed the elaborate staging. However, the Royal Court run lasted for only twenty performances, and the theater was, on average, only twenty percent full.

The play's fame grew in the 1960s, largely owing to significant productions directed by Peter Brook (Théâtre de l'Athenée, Paris, 1963), Jane Howell (in a Royal Court revival, 1965), Herbert Blau (Actors Company of San Francisco, 1965), and Ed Sherrin (Arena, New York, 1966). The play was performed regularly for the rest of the century, and it has found its way onto schoolchildren's examination syllabi. Fully aware of the disparity between *Serjeant Musgrave's* fame and the commercial failure of most of his other plays, Arden has commented ruefully that *Musgrave* "pays the bills." The play continues to be performed. In 2003 Sean Holmes directed a production at Greenwich Theatre, London: Holmes asserted that the revival of *Musgrave* was intimately associated with the then recent American and British declaration of war against Iraq. Indeed, *Serjeant Musgrave's Dance* is a play that, without crass emoting or grandstanding, decries the brutality of war.

Arden's antiwar convictions are rather hidden by the play's incapacity to allow the audience to feel empathy for any of the characters. At this stage of his playwriting career, Arden was highly influenced by BERTOLT BRECHT's alienating devices. Rather than presenting a series of rounded characters, Arden constructs two sets of dialectically opposed types: Musgrave and his fellow soldiers, deserters from the British Army, who are intent on broadcasting the horrors of war to spread their pacifist message, and the residents of the northern English mining town where Musgrave's men visit seek proactive military action, some of whom want to break a strike, while others want to perpetuate the disorder.

Arden does not allow any sympathy to develop for either the doves or the hawks: each "side" is as reprehensible as the other. Musgrave, with single-minded arrogance, strives to make the consequences of military fighting material and real for the civilians. Using shock tactics, he displays the skeleton of a favorite son of the town and, in the play's extraordinary climax, climbs onto a stage and points a Gatling gun at his audience; the play's audiences also have this machine gun pointed toward them. Musgrave's actions result in violent chaos, making the play's thesis very clear: pacifistic drives must be expressed by peaceful means; physical fighting will inspire only further fighting. The pivotal comment that expresses this moral is made by Private Attercliffe, the character who comes nearest to fulfilling any criteria for common sense: "You can't cure the pox by further whoring." Critics tend to over-complicate *Serjeant Musgrave's Dance*, but for two generations of theater goers, Arden's lesson about the contradictory folly of pacifists using physical force has been clear and stirring.

[*See also* England, 1940–Present]

FURTHER READING

Arden, John. *Serjeant Musgrave's Dance*. London: Methuen, 1960.

Bruster, Douglas. "Why Read Arden." In *John Arden and Margaretta D'Arcy: A Casebook*, ed. by Jonathan Wike. New York: Garland, 1995. 41–50.

Counts, Michael L. "John Arden." In *British Playwrights, 1956–1995: A Research and Production Sourcebook*, ed. by William W. Demasters. Westport and London: Greenwood Press, 1996. 3–14, especially 5.

Hunt, Albert. *Arden: A Study of His Plays*. London: Methuen, 1974. 52–63.

Malick, Javed. *Towards a Theater of the Oppressed: The Dramaturgy of John Arden*. Ann Arbor: Univ. of Michigan Press, 1995. 73–99.

Russell Taylor, John. *Anger and After: A Guide to the New British Drama*. London: Methuen, 1962. 72–82.

Kevin De Ornellas

SERUMAGA, ROBERT (1939–1980)

Robert Bellamino Serumaga was born in 1939 and brought up by a single mother, a situation that was uncommon in Uganda at that time. He grew to become a man of many talents and achievements: from an economist, to a politician, to a successful theater artist and writer. Renowned as East AFRICA's "renaissance writer," his artistic work survived through the turbulent times of politically unstable Uganda.

Serumaga attended Makerere University in Uganda and later went to Trinity College in Dublin, where he received a master's degree in economics; while in Europe, he worked in drama at the British Broadcasting Corporation (BBC). The experience of working at the BBC was useful when he went back to Uganda in 1966 and cofounded the semiprofessional theater company, Theatre Limited, which later changed its name to Abafumbi. Abafumbi produced performances that toured various parts of the world including Jamaica, the Netherlands, Germany, the Philippines, France, and the United States, among others. In his political career, Serumaga served as an economist in Uganda's government and later became minister of commerce under President Yusuf Lule.

In his first novel, *Return to the Shadows*, Serumaga used humor and cynicism to deal with the political and social upheavals of an African country struggling to hold together soon after colonialism. On returning home to Africa, the main character, an economist, has to deal with the agonies of the reality of a military coup in his home country, and in his determination to play his role in all these, he is caught between insecure ideals and the realities of power. These issues remain the focus of the plays he wrote later.

The innovation of his playwriting was in his blending of song, dance, and movement almost to the point of supplanting dialogue, particularly in his highly acclaimed *Renga Moi*, a play in which the innovative use of movement without dialogue can be read as an artistic style employed to satirize and ridicule the brutal politics of Idi Amin. Influenced by artistic innovations and revivals of indigenous performance traditions around the continent, Serumaga was opposed to the widening chasm between the popular masses and the neocolonial governments. Like NGUGI WA THIONG'O, WOLE SOYINKA, and TSEGAYE GABRE-MEDHIN, Serumaga studiously tried to politicize his art by creating highly engaging theatrical spectacles and language in his drama. He dedicated his life to creating plays that metaphorically called the people to return to decolonizing their nations from neocolonial dictators. Tortured in prisons, in 1980 Serumaga became Uganda's example of a political artist who used his drama to contest dictatorship. Fearing for his life, he went into exile during Idi Amin's presidency, and he was to die in exile in 1980.

PLAYS: *A Play* (1962); *The Elephants* (1971); *Renga Moi* (1972); *Amayirikiti* (1974); *Majangwa* (1974)

FURTHER READING

Cook, D. *African Literature: A Critical View*. London: Longman, 1977.

Irele, A. *The African Experience in Literature and Ideology*. London: Heineman, 1981.

Bantu Ndung'u

7:84

The 7:84 Theatre Company took its name from a statistic announced in *The Economist* magazine in 1966: 84 percent of the United Kingdom's wealth was held by 7 percent of the population. The original 7:84 company was an English group formed in 1971, but the Scottish offshoot of the company has proved more enduring and successful. The Scottish 7:84 Theatre Company was formed in 1973 by JOHN MCGRATH and Elizabeth and David MacLennan. The company was brought together to produce a new play, THE CHEVIOT, THE STAG, AND THE BLACK, BLACK OIL. This play, which compared the 19th-century clearance of the Scottish Highlands for sheep-farming with the modern offshore oil boom, was designed to include the kind of rural and working-class community deterred by traditional middle-class theater going. *The Cheviot* was modeled after a *ceilidh*—a traditional form of Highland celebration—and addressed (and included) its audience with songs, music, drama, and forthright political analysis. The first production was a tremendous success among audiences and led to 7:84 securing funding from the Scottish Arts Council for future works.

The first wave of plays put on by both the English and Scottish 7:84 companies during the 1970s were inspired by the success of *The Cheviot*. They were politically motivated dramas with a strong socialist agenda, but refused the bland assurances of either conventional left-wing (or Scottish nationalist) politics. Such plays cemented 7:84's strengths in popular drama, a form normally overlooked by the importance of Brechtian EPIC THEATER to politically minded dramatists. The company broke down the conventions of NATURALISM, but also took care to graft themselves onto existing popular modes of entertainment such as the *ceilidh* and pantomime.

Faced with criticism that 7:84 productions were becoming formulaic, the Scottish company varied their output with a series of revivals of popular drama in the early 1980s. These included plays such as Joe Corrie's *In Time o' Strife*, first produced in 1927 by the Fife Miner Players, and Ena Lamont Stewart's feminist view of working-class life, *Men Should Weep* (1947). The revivals were a success and were incorporated into 7:84's touring repertory.

The 1980s, however, saw what would become a recurring theme throughout the rest of 7:84's history. For as much as they put on successful productions, the company could not survive without subsidy, primarily from central government via the Arts Councils. The problem was worse for the English 7:84, which folded when its funding was entirely withdrawn in 1984. To protect the Scottish company's funding, McGrath resigned in 1988, and the company took a more politically emollient direction toward new drama and personal politics. But even the establishment of a devolved, and (left-wing) Labour-dominated Scottish Parliament in 1999 seems to have done little prevent recurrent crises in 7:84's funding. The company continues, however, with a vigorous program of political theater and a strong commitment to disenfranchised communities and minority groups.

[See also England, 1940–Present; Scotland]

FURTHER READING

DiCenzo, Maria. *The Politics of Alternative Theatre in Britain, 1968–1990: The Case of 7:84 (Scotland)*. Cambridge: Cambridge University Press, 1996.

McGrath, John. *A Good Night Out: Popular Theatre: Audience, Class and Form*. London: Methuen, 1981.

Mackenney, Linda. "The People's Story: 7:84 Scotland." In *Scottish Theatre Since the Seventies*. Ed. by Randall Stevenson and Gavin Wallace. Edinburgh: Edinburgh University Press. 65–72.

MacLennan, Elizabeth. *The Moon Belongs to Everyone: Making Theatre with 7:84*. London: Metheun, 1990.

Gavin Miller

SEVEN KEYS TO BALDPATE

Written, published, and produced in 1913, *Seven Keys to Baldpate* by George M. Cohan is typical of the popular farcical COMEDIES that Cohan churned out during his heyday and is considered to be his best and most lucrative play. It "thrilled Broadway audiences during a year-long run," subsequently moving to Cohan's Grand Opera House in Chicago as well as touring for another three seasons, remaining a favorite with summer stock and amateur companies until well after World War II.

Like many of Cohan's plays, *Seven Keys to Baldpate* is adapted from another work, in this case a novel of the same title by Earl Derr Biggers, also published in 1913. Subtitled "A Mysterious Melodramatic Farce," the play is set in the isolated mountain resort of Baldpate Inn, now closed for the season, on a wintry night, with a storm raging outside. To this desolate place comes William Hallowell Magee, writer of popular dime-store novels, who has made a $5,000 bet with the inn's owner, Hal Bentley, that he can hack out a novel in twenty-four hours. Magee plans to begin work precisely at midnight, certain that he will be undisturbed, as the inn's caretaker has provided him with the only key to the place. "You're positively certain that this key is the only key to Baldpate in existence?" asks Magee, to which Quimby replies, "Yes, sir; I'm sure."

Magee settles down to work but is soon interrupted by the surreptitious entry of a stranger, who places a large stash of money in the safe and who, when confronted by Magee, insists that his is the only key to Baldpate. This intruder is followed by a series of others, including crooked politicians, a murderer, a ghost, corrupt policemen, and blackmailers—all of whom claim to possess the sole key to the Inn. At the end, the criminals turn out to be a group of actors who have put on this performance at Bentley's whim to prove "how perfectly improbably and terrible those awful stories you've been writing would seem if such things really and truly happened." Still, Magee wins the bet by turning this play-within-a-play into the promised novel, appropriately titled *Seven Keys to Baldpate*.

Cohan leaves to the audience the question of whether the events of the play actually occurred or they reflect the novel Magee is writing. One critic noted, "The improbabilities are so well sustained that no one can guess how it will all turn out," but *New York Times* (October 19, 1913) reviewer Adolph Klauber suggested the author underrated the audience's ability to put the pieces together, noting that the epilogue would be illuminating enough to clarify the joke. Still, that was a minor point: Klauber praised Cohan's play as "the exceptional entertainment of the season" for its originality, ingenuity, and adroit handling of "flamboyant MELODRAMA." The huge success of this play, along with Cohen's theatrical virtuosity as an actor, songwriter, and vaudevillian, helps illuminate why Cohen exerted such a profound influence on Broadway in the early decades of the 20th century.

[*See also* United States, 1860–1929]

FURTHER READING

Cohan, George M. *Twenty Years on Broadway and the Years It Took to Get There.* Westport, Conn.: Greenwood, 1925.

Morehouse, Ward. *George M. Cohan: Prince of the American Theatre.* New York: Lippincott, 1943.

McCabe, John. *George M. Cohan: The Man Who Owned Broadway.* Garden City, N.Y.: Doubleday, 1973.

Karen Blansfield

THE SEVEN STREAMS OF THE RIVER OTA

One fascinating aspect of French Canadian Robert Lepage's *The Seven Streams of the River Ota* is its authorship; Methuen Drama attributes the copyright to Lepage and his twelve-member creative ensemble Ex Machina. Expecting devastation and misery in post-atomic-bombed Hiroshima on his first visit to JAPAN, Lepage found instead robust, sensual vitality, and on his return to Quebec in January 1994, he commenced collaborative work in which the physical set, consisting of a wooden rectangle, was the starting point for development of script, plot, and characters, rather than the opposite, more traditional process of playwriting in which stage design is one of the last elements. Through improvisation and egalitarian discussion, the "writing" of psyche preceded scene, and a script was set down only days before its premiere full-length performance in Quebec on May 17, 1996. Additionally, an original adaptation of a scene from GEORGES FEYDEAU's *The Lady of Maxim* was devised and included by the cast. In *Seven Streams*, as Karen Fricker wrote, "the actors *are* the authors."

Seven Streams exists in three separate versions of three, five, and eight hours' duration, and while entire characters and plotlines are excised from the shorter versions, the resounding theme of mirror opposites remains a constant. The polarities of East and West, male and female, TRAGEDY and COMEDY, death and rebirth are illustrated through the mirror motif and the recurring theme of photography. An American soldier, Luke O'Connor, is sent to document the after-effects of the World War II atomic bomb assault on Hiroshima, but he encounters love and respect for a *Hibakusha* (a scarred survivor), Nozomi. His assignment is to photograph physical damage to housing, but instead the soldier is confronted by Nozomi's stoic request to document her physical deformity. Coin-operated photo booths also figure prominently as *Seven Streams* demonstrates that, like a mirror, a photograph is a reflection of you, but it is not you. Other issues touched on include suicide, AIDS, marital infidelity, Nazi anti-Semitism, and of course French nuclear testing in the Pacific. The set's mirrors transform, metaphorically and literally, into doorways to alternative understandings of these controversial subjects.

Another interesting aspect of *Seven Streams* is its reliance on technology, particularly the use of video projection, with which the on-stage actors interact and, apparently, dexterously manipulate. Supertitles are used to translate the occasional passages of Japanese, German, and Québecois French, but many scenes are devoid of speech entirely. Other scenes in this multimedia spectacle are played out in silhouette or by life-sized puppets.

In a way, the authorship question of who wrote, owns, or takes responsibility for *Seven Streams* is the question of who wrote, owns, or takes responsibility for Hiroshima and many more of the ills of late-20th-century humanity. Despite the breadth and gloom of its subject material, *Seven Streams* is an uplifting epic on survival over resignation, forgiveness over blame, and collaboration over auteurism. When Nozumi's scars initially repulse O'Connor, she asks, "Is it my ugliness?" He responds, suggesting generic Western ownership and responsibility, "No . . . it's mine."

[*See also* Canada]

FURTHER READING

Dundjerovic, Aleksandar. *The Cinema of Robert Lepage: The Poetics of Memory.* London, New York: Wallflower Press, 2003.

Lepage, Robert, and Ex Machina. *The Seven Streams of the River Ota.* London: Methuen Drama, 1996.

Feydeau, Georges. *Théatre Complet* [Complete Plays]. Paris: Editions du Bélier, 1948–1956.

D. Bruno Starrs

SEWELL, STEPHEN (1953–)

Stephen Sewell—born in Sydney, New South Wales, AUSTRALIA, March 13, 1953—has been a giant on the periphery of mainstream Australian theater for more than a quarter of a century. Sewell received a bachelor of science degree from the University of Sydney in 1974.

At first his status as troublesome outsider was defined in terms of a "new internationalism," which in the late 1970s was eagerly anticipated by some critics as an overdue antidote to the coarsely comic, aggressively Australian male plays that characterized the "new wave." *Traitors* (1979), with its treatment of the grim atrocities of Stalinism, and *Welcome the Bright World* (1982), with its esoteric references to nuclear theory in the course of probing the moral compromises made by Jewish physicists in Nazi Germany, proclaimed a challenging writer who was actually interested in ideas and history. This was not in itself a misleading impression, but the assumption that those intellectual passions had little to do with contemporary Australian life proved well wide of the mark.

What characterizes Sewell's theater is a refusal to compromise. It is apparent in pragmatic matters like the length of his plays and the size of his casts as well as in the fierceness of his politics and his readiness to shock his audiences. His interest is in people in extremity. The stakes are always high in the confrontations of his plays, and while historical police-states guarantee a certain level of intensity, Sewell's major writing has found it as much in his own society. The three blockbuster plays that he wrote in the 1980s—*The Blind Giant Is Dancing* (1983), *Dreams in an Empty City* (1986), and *Hate* (1988)—all find that vein and open it relentlessly in a mixture of savagely apocalyptic satire, proselytizing zeal, and moral fury. The subjects are local and specific: *Blind Giant* deals with political corruption, particularly in the left wing of the Australian Labor Party; *Dreams* is about the moral bankruptcy of the new plutocracy; and *Hate* invokes both and directs them particularly to the ways in which Australia's power elites have denied their responsibility to the remnants of indigenous culture. In each case the real enemy is despair, promoted by the politics of cynicism and only refutable by a spiritual fervor that is equally absolute. In each of the plays the local references are broadened, and the voice of outrage channeled and controlled, by powerful organizing metaphors: the Faustus myth in *Blind Giant*, the temptation and crucifixion of Christ in *Dreams*, and the trappings of Greek TRAGEDY in *Hate*.

Sewell's work in the 1990s shrinks in scale, reflecting the smaller repertoire of the subsidized theater. Some bold flourishes remain, like the phantasmagoric fable *King Golgrutha* (1991), but the close-up intensity of plays like the two-hander *Sisters* (1991) and *The Sick Room* (1999) is more characteristic of this decade. Sewell turned increasingly to writing for film. In 2003, though, the appearance of *Myth, Disaster and Propaganda in Nazi Germany and Contemporary America*, every bit as confronting and provocative as its title promises, marked the triumphant return of the familiar Sewell and of an individual voice that still demands attention in the Australian theater.

SELECT PLAYS: *Traitors* (1979); *Welcome the Bright World* (1982); *The Blind Giant Is Dancing* (1983); *Dreams in an Empty City* (1986); *Hate* (1988); *King Golgrutha* (1991); *Sisters* (1991); *The Sick Room* (1999)

FURTHER READING

Australasian Drama Studies 14 (1989). This special issue contains four articles on Sewell.

Carroll, Dennis. *Australian Contemporary Drama from 1909,* 2nd ed. Sydney: Currency Press, 1995.

Fitzpatrick, Peter. *Stephen Sewell: The Playwright as Revolutionary.* Sydney: Currency Press, 1993.

McCallum, John. "The World Outside: Cosmopolitanism in the Plays of Nowra and Sewell." *Meanjin* 43 (1984): 286–96.

Peter Fitzpatrick

SEXUAL PERVERSITY IN CHICAGO

First produced by the Organic Theater Company in Chicago in 1974, DAVID MAMET's one-act *Sexual Perversity in Chicago* is regarded by most critics as the play that launched Mamet's long and distinguished playwriting career. Named Best Chicago Play of 1974, *Sexual Perversity* was subsequently produced OFF-OFF-BROADWAY in 1975 at St. Clements Theatre in New York, where it was paired with a shorter Mamet piece, *The Duck Variations* (both plays directed by Albert Takazauckas). After a successful run at St. Clements, the production transferred to the off-Broadway Cherry Lane Theatre, where it earned an Obie Award as the Best New American Play of the 1975–1976 season. The play has become a staple of regional and university theater production and was the basis of the 1986 film *About Last Night* . . . .

The play chronicles the on-again, off-again courtship of Dan and Deborah, two urban singles in their twenties. Through a series of brief, episodic scenes—some as short as five or six lines—spanning approximately nine weeks, we see Dan and Deborah meet, become sexually intimate, move in together, and break up. Along the way, their relationship is complicated, and eventually sabotaged, by the advice they receive from their respective friends: Bernie, a loud-mouthed chauvinist, and Joan, an acerbic kindergarten teacher.

The focus of the play, however, is not on the boy-meets-girl plotline, but on the satiric and explicit dialogue with which all four characters discuss (or, more often, avoid discussing) their sexual and emotional needs. While some critics derided the play's lack of narrative coherence and its less-than-flattering depiction of women, virtually all agreed that Mamet demonstrated a gift for capturing the rhythm and wit of 1970s urban culture in all its vulgarity and cynicism. "Mamet's extraordinary promise," wrote Ross Wetzsteon in the *Village Voice*, "resides not so much in his insights into male-female relationships . . . as in the exhilarating perfection of the language with which he expresses it" (2001).

Mamet himself has suggested that the characters' deft use of language functions as a defense mechanism that prevents them from achieving true intimacy. Dan's humor, Deborah's cynicism, Joan's intellectualism, and Bernie's overbearing profanity are all responses to the insecurity caused by the shifting gender expectations of the 1970s. Unclear about what is expected of them in this new sexual landscape, the characters deal with their frustration and alienation by articulating elaborate and ill-conceived rationalizations for their behavior. They do not talk *to* one another so much as they talk *at* one another. The failure of these articulations either to resolve or to explain the differences between men and women is demonstrated by the play's ending, where we see the two male characters just as they were at the beginning, engaged in a banal and denigrating discussion of women and their body parts.

Critics in New York and London responded less enthusiastically to later revivals of *Sexual Perversity*, suggesting that, in an age when frank language about sex is commonplace, the play has lost some of the shocking force it carried when it premiered. Yet few plays have so adeptly and unflinchingly satirized the spirit of their era.

[*See also* United States, 1940–Present]

FURTHER READING

Bigsby, Christopher, ed. *The Cambridge Companion to David Mamet.* Cambridge: Cambridge Univ. Press, 2004.

Blansfield, Karen. "Women on the Verge, Unite!" In *Gender and Genre: Essays on David Mamet*, ed. by Christopher C. Hudgins and Leslie Kane. New York: Palgrave, 2001. 125–142.

Dean, Anne. *David Mamet: Language as Dramatic Action.* Rutherford, N.J.: Fairleigh Dickinson Univ. Press, 1990.

Kane, Leslie. *David Mamet in Conversation.* Ann Arbor: Univ. of Michigan Press: 2001.

Wetzsteon, Ross. "David Mamet: Remember That Name." In *David Mamet in Conversation*, ed. by Leslie Kane. Ann Arbor: Univ. of Michigan Press, 2001. 9–15.

Henry Bial

THE SHADOW OF A GUNMAN

Subtitled *A Tragedy in Two Acts*, *Shadow of a Gunman* by Sean O'Casey is more TRAGICOMEDY than TRAGEDY, and the reviewers of the first Abbey production (April 1923) complained of the excessive amount of COMEDY that endangers the tragic mood. But it is actually the blend of the comedic and the serious that lends *Gunman* its modern, ever-relevant impact.

It concerns Donal Davoren, a would-be poet who shares a room in a Dublin tenement with a door-to-door salesman, Seumas Shields. The time is 1920, when the Anglo-Irish War of Independence was raging and ordinary citizens could feel "sure of your life nowhere now." Davoren is mistaken by the other residents of the house for an IRA (Irish Republican Army) gunman on the run because of his reclusive lifestyle; out of vanity and because the good-looking Minnie Powell regards him as a hero, he allows the myth to grow around him. Against Shields's advice, Davoren flirts recklessly with Minnie and ignores the little man, Maguire, who arrives to leave a bag in the room for safe keeping and then vanishes.

While Davoren strives to find privacy for his writing, a neighbor, Gallogher, arrives accompanied by others, including Minnie, looking for Davoren's approval of a letter Gallogher has written to the IRA for redress against noisy children in the tenement. In an amusing scene, Davoren is put in the position of literary critic capable of correcting Gallogher's flamboyant style while agreeing to forward the ridiculous letter to the IRA. That night, as Davoren and Shields lie awake discussing the street warfare that terrorizes them, the house is raided by the Black and Tans. The two men panic, fearing the reputation of the dreaded British auxiliary force. Davoren's real character begins to emerge as he searches for the incriminating letter from Gallogher. Minnie bursts in and ask if he has any arms she might hide in her room. An inspection of the bag left by Maguire reveals a cache of Mills bombs. Davoren goes to pieces while Minnie, emerging as the real hero, takes away the bag.

Contrary to expectations, the Black and Tans search Minnie's room as well as terrifying everyone else in ways that bring out comic reactions. Davoren and Shields cower in their room as the bombs are found and Minnie is arrested. She is heard in the street crying, "Up the Republic!" and gunfire is sounded. A neighbor enters to say Minnie has been shot in an IRA ambush while jumping off the truck. In his ensuing shock, Davoren recognizes that Minnie sacrificed herself for a worthless man.

LADY GREGORY told O'Casey that his strong point was characterization. Here he introduces a gallery of colorful characters from lower-class urban life and lets them individually impress themselves on the audience without necessarily being tied into a plot. Yet behind the entertainment lie the enduring themes of identity, authenticity, and role-playing. The play endures also as an intense exploration of the politics of survival.

[See also Ireland]

FURTHER READING

Kearney, Colbert. *The Glamour of Grammar: Orality and Politics and the Emergence of Sean O'Casey.* Westport, Conn.: Greenwood Press, 2000. 49–74.

Murray, Christopher. *A Faber Critical Guide: Sean O'Casey.* London: Faber and Faber, 2000. 21–52.

Schrank, Bernice. " 'You needn't say no more': Language and the Problem of Communication in Sean O'Casey's *The Shadow of a Gunman.*" In *The Dublin Trilogy: A Casebook,* ed. by Ronald Ayling. London: Macmillan, 1985. 67–80.

Christopher Murray

SHAFFER, PETER (1926–)

Peter Levin Shaffer was born in Liverpool, England, on May 15, 1926, seconds after his identical twin Anthony, who like Peter was also to become a Tony award–winning playwright. After his education at London's St. Paul's School and Cambridge University, Shaffer shuttled between New York City and England, working at various jobs including music critic. During the early 1950s, Shaffer published three mystery novels, two written in collaboration with his twin. He also wrote two probing television dramas and a BBC radio play. Each concerned seminal moral issues, as did his first stage hit, *Five Finger Exercise* (1958), whose worldwide acclaim convinced him to follow a life in the theater.

Peter Shaffer has carved out an individual path among his contemporaries. His earliest works, including *Five Finger Exercise,* use dramatic REALISM. But mostly he uses realism to underpin highly theatricalized formats. Existentialist thought appeared in Shaffer's work without the Absurdist enigmatic plots. Drawing on a similar questioning of God's existence, Shaffer acknowledges His presence but as an unreliable figure with little inherent benevolence. Time and again in Shaffer's powerful dramas, protagonists seek validation of God. All end up disappointed and disillusioned, just as are Absurdist heroes.

Three of Shaffer's dramas—*Royal Hunt of the Sun, Equus,* and *Amadeus*—and two of his comedies—*Black Comedy* and *Lettice & Lovage*—enjoyed extended runs in London and New York. *Equus* and *Amadeus* took Best Play Tony awards in 1975 and 1981, respectively, and *Black Comedy* and *Lettice & Lovage* were nominated for Tonys in 1967 and 1990, respectively. Films were made

of *Royal Hunt, Equus* (Oscar nomination), and *Amadeus* (eight Oscars). Verbal articulateness and dazzling theatrical structures have remained Shaffer's great strength and earned him a knighthood in 2001.

The serious plays expand on questions regarding godhead and human conduct. Pizarro in *Royal Hunt* admits he is "god-hunting," but through Atahuallpa discovers the Incan Sun God is as false a deity as any European God. In *Equus,* the psychiatrist Dysart finds that his book-learning cannot "account for me," in the Horse-God's insistent call. *Amadeus* presents a war between an "unjust" God and Salieri, Mozart's court rival who refuses to accept God's arbitrariness.

Tied into the issues of deity are fundamental contradictions between personal morality and social norms. Shaffer shapes crucial conflicts between what FRIEDRICH NIETZSCHE termed the Apollonian and Dionysian in human nature. The Apollonian impulse is that which seeks orderliness and perfection; the Dionysian represents the more creative, often chaotic, self-expressive drive. Pizarro seeks order and understanding of godhead, and Atahuallpa represents unlimited actions based on religious power. Dysart is Apollonian, redirecting Alan's psyche toward society's norms, away from the wild Dionysian spirit who creates a horse-god to worship. Salieri in *Amadeus* expects ordered justice from god; Mozart is depicted as uninhibitedly Dionysian in violating standards of society. Shaffer implies that elements of both, in balance, make for the ideal individual and society, though such integration is difficult to attain.

[See also England, 1940–Present]

SELECT PLAYS: *Five Finger Exercise* (1958); *The Private Ear* (1962); *The Public Eye* (1962); *The Royal Hunt of the Sun* (1964); *Black Comedy* (1967); *White Lies* (revised as *The White Liars,* then as *White Liars,* 1967); *Equus* (1973); *Shrivings* (originally *The Battle of Shrivings,* 1974); *Amadeus* (1979); *Lettice and Lovage* (later *Lettice; Lovage,* 1988); *Yonadab* (1989); *Whom Do I Have the Honour of Addressing?* (radio play, later stage play, 1989); *The Gift of the Gorgon* (1993)

FURTHER READING

Cooke, Virginia, and Malcolm Page, comp. *File on Shaffer.* London and New York: Methuen, 1987.

Gianakaris, C. J. *Peter Shaffer.* London and New York: Macmillan and St. Martin's, 1992.

——, ed. *Peter Shaffer: A Casebook.* New York and London: Garland Publishing, 1991.

Innes, Christopher. *Modern British Drama: The Twentieth Century.* Cambridge: Cambridge Univ. Press, 2002.

Klein, Dennis A. *Peter Shaffer.* In *Twayne English Authors,* rev. ed. Boston: G.K. Hall, 1993.

Plunka, Gene A. *Peter Shaffer: Roles, Rites, and Rituals in the Theatre.* Rutherford, N.J.: Fairleigh Dickinson Univ. Press, 1988.

C. J. Gianakaris

SHANGE, NTOZAKE (1948–)

I'm a consciously feminist person. I use tools that are available to me as a feminist reconstructing history. I don't understand when things are glossed over by misogynist historians and intellectuals, "the experts." Everything I write and have written comes from being a woman-centered person.

—Ntozake Shange, 1990

American playwright, poet, and novelist Ntozake Shange was born on October 18, 1948, in Trenton, New Jersey, as Paulette Williams to an upper-middle-class African American family. Her intellectually stimulating childhood led her to Barnard College, where she graduated with a degree in American studies in 1970. Three years later she gained a master's degree in the same subject from the University of California, Los Angeles, after which she began to teach and perform in the San Francisco area.

Deeply influenced by feminism and the civil rights movement, Shange rocked a generation of gender relations with her most famous play, *for colored girls who have considered suicide / when the rainbow is enuf*, in which she portrays the pain and humiliation of African American women at the hands of African American men. The will to survive and transform the internal divisions wrought by a racist society gave inspiration and strength to women and men of all walks of life. In all her plays, Shange portrays the ways in which African Americans have suffered tremendous sacrifice to achieve the equality that should be a birthright.

Equal to her explosive content is Shange's experimental dramatic form of the "choreopoem," which combines music, dance, poetry, and a narrative that progresses through sequential monologues. Shange attacks the formality and structures of white culture with her self-invented orthography, which results in her characters speaking colloquial and firebrand English. In 1971 she adopted two words from the Xhosa language of the Zulu people as a new name: Ntozake, meaning "she who comes with her own thing," and Shange, "she who walks like a lion."

Shange's awards include a 1977 Obie, the Outer Critics Circle Award, an AUDELCO Award, and the Mademoiselle Award for *for colored girls who have considered suicide/when the rainbow is enuf*; a Guggenheim fellowship in 1981; and an Obie for her adaptation of BERTOLT BRECHT's MOTHER COURAGE AND HER CHILDREN, performed at the New York's Public Theatre.

[See also Black Arts Movement; Political Theater in the United States, 1940–Present]

PLAYS: *for colored girls who have considered suicide/when the rainbow is enuf* (1975); *Where the Mississippi Meets the Amazon* (1977); *Boogie Woogie Landscapes* (1978); *Black and White Two Dimensional Planes* (1979); *spell #7* (1979); *Mother Courage and Her Children* (adapted from the play by Bertolt Brecht, 1980); *A Photograph: Lovers in Motion* (1981); *Bocas* (1982); *Educating Rita* (1983); *From Okra to Greens: A Different Kind of Love Story* (1985); *Three Views of Mount Fuji* (1987); *Betsey Brown: A Rhythm and Blues Musical* (co-authored with

Emily Mann, 1989); *Love Space Demands: A Continuing Saga* (1991); *I Heard Eric Dolphy in His Eyes* (1992)

FURTHER READING

Lester, Neal A. "At the Heart of Shange's Feminism: An Interview." *Black American Literature Forum* 24, no. 4 (Winter 1990).

Richards, Sandra A. "Conflicting Impulses in the Plays of Ntozake." *Black American Literature Forum* 17, no. 2 (Summer 1983).

Timpane, John. "The Poetry of a Moment: Politics and the Open Form in the Drama of Ntozake Shange." In *Modern American Drama: The Female Canon*, ed. by June Schlueter. Rutherford, N.J.: Fairleigh Dickinson Univ. Press, 1990.

Carol Martin

SHANLEY, JOHN PATRICK (1950–)

This play is dedicated to everyone in the Bronx who punched me or kissed me, and to everyone whom I punched or kissed.

—Dedication of *Danny and the Deep Blue Sea*, 1984

Playwright, screenwriter, and director John Patrick Shanley, born October 13, 1950, in New York City, is best known for his Oscar-winning screenplay for *Moonstruck* (1987). Dubbed by *Moonstruck*'s director, Norman Jewison, as the bard of the Bronx, Shanley's most celebrated works for theater also reflect his New York upbringing and have achieved most consistent success OFF-BROADWAY.

Of growing up in an Italian Catholic family in New York City's East Bronx, Shanley commented (in an interview with Robert Coe, 2005), "I grew up in a violent place where people did not communicate well, but where there were big feelings and big longings, and I remember that some of the most interesting people were also the most doomed, because they had no tools to save themselves." After completing a degree in educational theater at New York University and serving in the Marines, Shanley wrote his first play, *Danny and the Deep Blue Sea* (1984), while working as a bartender.

The majority of Shanley's plays reflect his experiences. Typically set in and around cafés and bars in New York City, they are populated by damaged individuals who are disillusioned with life and unable to discover their reasons for being. The protagonists are often romantic dreamers who discover that reality fails to live up to the idealized expectations of their youth. As they approach middle age, they find themselves trapped in an embittered state of limbo. Shanley has frequently characterized this malaise as "the big funk," a term he also used for the title of a 1990 play.

Despite the specificity of his mise-en-scène, Shanley's plays are philosophical dramas that examine metaphysical problems. Through the lives of his characters, Shanley holds the mirror up to the soul in an attempt to examine the perennial problems humanity inflicts on itself. The problems are tackled head-on and the issues clearly underlined through explicit dialogue, blatant symbolism, and occasionally high COMEDY. In the allegorical TRAGICOMEDY *The Big Funk* (1990), Jill is an insecure middle-class woman who is constantly involved in dysfunctional relationships with inappropriate men. When she is first introduced, she is sitting at a bar and has been physically covered in grease by her date—a metaphor for the way she allows herself to be constantly smeared through low self-esteem. Similarly, the virginal status of the protagonist in *Savage in Limbo* (1985) reflects her loneliness in life, and *Kissing Christine* (1997) involves a woman whose dreams of becoming a dancer ended when she literally fell into a hole. The quack psychiatrist in *Psychopathia Sexualis* (1998) who is unable to cure his patient of his fetish for argyle socks is called Dr. Block.

Most of Shanley's dramas are "talking-head" plays, in which the protagonists attempt to break past the inadequacy of their lives through straight talking and rigorous PSYCHOANALYSIS. Interestingly, given the metaphysical nature of their problems and the psychoanalytic means by which they try to solve them, Shanley's characters are often working-class individuals who, no matter what their profession, speak the everyday street vernacular of New York City cab drivers and plumbers. While appropriate to the mise-en-scène, the distinctiveness of such dialogue also results from and reflects upon the limitations of their lives. Consequently, when these individuals attempt to articulate their need for more in life, their vocabulary is often insufficient to express the enormity of their vision.

Shanley has experimented with a variety of styles ranging from SURREALISM to formalism, with settings as diverse as the Wild West and seaside towns. His more recent works reflect such diversity. In DOUBT (2004), he returns to the familiar territory of his youth. Set in a Catholic school in the Bronx in the 1960s, the play examines a nun's suspicions about a priest's relationship with a schoolboy. *A Sailor's Song* (2004) is a surreal love story set in an imagined seaside town, where the characters dance to Johann Strauss.

[*See also* United States, 1940–Present]

PLAYS: *Welcome to the Moon* (1982); *Danny and the Deep Blue Sea* (1984); *The Dreamer Examines His Pillow* (1985); *Savage in Limbo* (1985); *Women of Manhattan* (1986); *All For Charity* (1987); *Italian-American Reconciliation* (1988); *The Big Funk* (1990); *Beggars in the House of Plenty* (1991); *Four Dogs and a Bone* (1993); *Missing/Kissing* (1996); *Psychopathia Sexualis* (1996); *Cellini* (2001); *Where's My Money?* (2001); *Dirty Story* (2003); *Doubt* (2004); *Sailor's Song* (2004)

FURTHER READING

Coe, Robert. *The Evolution of John Patrick Shanley.* Theater Communications Group (November 2004). http://www.tcg.org/publications/at/Nov04/shanley.cfm

Shanley, John Patrick. *13 by Shanley: Thirteen Plays by John Patrick Shanley.* New York: Applause American Masters Series, 1992.

——. *Four Dogs and a Bone and The Wild Goose.* New York: Dramatists Play Service, 1995.

——. *Missing/Kissing: Missing Marisa, Kissing Christine.* New York: Dramatists Play Service, 1997.

——. *Psychopathia Sexualis.* New York: Dramatists Play Service, 1998.

Olivia Turnbull

THE SHAPE OF THINGS

The action of NEIL LABUTE's *The Shape of Things* opens in a museum in a "conservative midwestern town," in front of a naked sculpture of God that has been, at the request of influential members of the community, altered: its bare crotch has been covered with a fig leaf. It is here, in front of this censored sculpture, that Adam, a college student and part-time security guard at the museum, encounters Evelyn, an art student who intends to restore the sculpture to its true form by spray-painting a penis on the makeshift fig leaf.

After a flirtatious banter, Adam and Evelyn decide to date, but the implicit conditions of their nascent relationship—that Adam must modify many aspects of his lifestyle—soon become explicit and cause a radical change in Adam's self-perception. Indeed, Evelyn's suggestions—to lose weight and work out, to cut his hair, to change the way he dresses, and so on—imbue Adam with an unprecedented degree of confidence that turns out to be both a gift and a curse. Although he begins to feel better and more comfortable around women, he also becomes more easily agitated and, in a scene occurring offstage, cheats on Evelyn with his best friend's girlfriend. Only when he severs ties with his best friend and discovers, at a public demonstration, that he is merely an art project—a walking, talking, breathing sculpture that Evelyn has been manipulating for her degree—does he reflect on the type of person he has quickly become. At the play's close we find him alone in the auditorium, exploring the art exhibit Evelyn has manufactured out of various videotapes—some recorded secretly—and Adam's personal belongings.

Labute's frequent, overt allusions to the fall of humankind, especially as portrayed and problematized in John Milton's *Paradise Lost*, serve in part as an open invitation for spectators to compare *The Shape of Things* with the countless retellings of the Genesis narrative. In the play's protagonists we see Labute's take on the Adam and Eve figures and the power games they play. Although one may at first sympathize with Adam's fate—his life becomes public domain—one is quick to realize that, as in other versions of the Fall, Adam could not be forced into any action; Evelyn may have coaxed him into refashioning himself, but Adam always had a choice. Evelyn, in the play's penultimate scene, reminds her audience—and also Labute's audience—of this: "[Adam's] free will was always at the forefront of each decision. [I] coaxed, made suggestions, created the illusion of interest and desire, but never said 'please do this.'"

Juxtaposing this speech about free will with the recognition that Labute deliberately omitted the supernatural characters of the Genesis narrative—the tempting serpent and the punishing

God—we find in *The Shape of Things* an overwhelmingly secular realm, one that places power and its consequences solely in the hands of human beings. Therefore, the play can only end in "silence [and] darkness."

[*See also* England, 1940–Present]

FURTHER READING

Istel, John. "Who Is Neil Labute and Why Is He Saying Those Terrible Things About You?" *American Theatre* 18, no. 9 (November 2001): 38–42.

Jays, David. "The Shape of Things (Films)." *Sight & Sound* 14, no. 1 (January 2004): 57–58.

Lahr, John. "The Makeover Artist." *New Yorker* 77, no. 16 (June 16, 2001): 170–171.

Macnab, Geoffrey. "Loving London." *Sight & Sound* 17, no. 7 (July 2004): 79.

David L. Orvis

SHARED EXPERIENCE THEATRE

In the past twenty-eight years since its 1975 founding by Mike Alfreds, Shared Experience Theatre has established itself as one of Britain's most inventive and enduring alternative theater companies, producing an eclectic body of work including novel adaptations, experiments with classic dramas, and new scripts. Its focus has been on the power of the physical presence of the actor and the process and possibilities of storytelling. It was Shared Experience's work in the 1970s that sparked the reinvigoration of the British interest in stage adaptations of literature with their landmark productions of *Arabian Nights* (1975) and Charles Dickens's *Bleak House* (1977), which was itself a major influence on the Royal Shakespeare Company's famed *Nicholas Nickleby* (1981). Under the artistic leadership of Mike Alfreds, the actors employed the narrative of the novel as a wellspring of theatrical possibility, transforming themselves through the slightest of physical gestures. These experiments paved the way for the subsequent physical theater boom in the 1980s and 1990s, enabling new innovations by companies such as Cheek By Jowl, Théâtre de Complicité, and Method and Madness.

From the late 1980s, under the joint artistic direction of Nancy Meckler and subsequently, Polly Teale, Shared Experience has earned international acclaim for its passionate and visceral novel adaptations, including productions such as *Anna Karenina* (1992), *Mill on the Floss* (1994), *War and Peace* (1996), *Jane Eyre* (1997), and later, Angela Carter's *The Magic Toyshop* (2001) and E. M. Forster's *A Passage to India* (2002). The company is predominantly woman-centered, experimenting with stories that create space for female experience and understanding of the world. With Meckler and Teale, the company's approach to novel adaptation continues to be as innovative as Alfreds's methods during the early years of the London Fringe, yet takes a significantly different path. The style is distinctly and power-fully physical and "expressionistic"; the company excels in revealing the inner, subjective experience of the characters. Thus, rehearsals are an exploration of what the story feels like, rather than what it looks like in reality. The company explores this sensory approach to drama by examining characters' secret, inner worlds through image and movement. The company is interested in theater that expresses those areas of human experience that are inside our heads, the world of images, memory, and hidden thoughts.

The director, along with the actors, designers, movement directors, and other practitioners, all contribute to discovering the images of a theater piece. The creative focus is on finding physical ways to release people together to create a new language to tell a story. The use of ritualized gestures, split characters, and the physicalization of characters' fantasies and dreams have all become hallmarks of the Shared Experience approach. With these tools, Meckler and Teale have cracked open the secrets hidden inside the heart of the novel for the British stage. Through the interweaving of text, gesture, and movement, the cultural pasts within the novels are rediscovered, explored, and reconstructed anew. Through the living memory of the actors' bodies, cultural memories are reimagined and redefined, offering a particular "reading" of a novel, a touchstone for a way to stage a cultural past and an understanding of the world.

[*See also* England, 1940–Present]

FURTHER READING

Alfreds, Mike. "A Shared Experience: The Actor as Story-Teller." *Theatre Papers* 6 (1979–1980): 1–24.

——. *Shared Experience: 1975–1984*. London: Shared Experience, 1985.

Alfreds, Mike, and Clive Barker. "Shared Experience: from Science Fiction to Shakespeare." *Theatre Quarterly* 10, no. 39 (1981): 12–22.

Gardner, Lyn. *Shared Experience: Past & Present*. 2000. Shared Experience Theatre website, http://www.setheatre.co.uk/ (Accessed August 26, 2003).

Goodman, Lizbeth. *Feminist Stages: Interviews with Women in Contemporary British Theatre*. London and New York: Harwood Academic Publishers, 1996. 103–106.

Hay, Malcom. "Shared Experience." *Plays and Players* (April 1985): 8–11.

Lustig, Vera. "Hidden Riches." *Plays and Players* (March 1990): 7–9.

Rea, Kenneth. "The Theatre of Mike Alfreds." *Drama* 1, no. 163 (1987): 3–8.

Stephenson, Heidi, and Natasha Langridge. *Rage and Reason: Women Playwrights on Playwriting*. London: Methuen, 1997.

Kristin A. Crouch

SHARMA, TRIPURARI (1956–)

Tripurari Sharma (born in Delhi, INDIA) graduated from the National School of Drama in Delhi in 1979, when the political street theater movement was gaining momentum. Not all of

Sharma's work is street theater, but her work does reflect the concerns and agendas of the movement. She has dealt with a broad range of topics: communalism, the effect of the dollar on the Indian economy, governmental corruption, and rape. Sharma's work takes several forms: she and her company, Alarippu (Blossoming), perform plays in the streets and conduct theater workshops with children, she develops plays and productions collectively in community workshops, and she redirects classical plays in mainstream theater spaces. Sharma is dedicated to giving voice to those who are not often heard and to political issues that are not being discussed. In conversation, as well as in her methods of work and in her productions, Sharma is not interested in providing answers or solutions to problems. She is more interested in opening dialogue, presenting multiple points of view, and providing a forum for exchange.

Sharma is perhaps best known for the scripts she develops collectively. She first developed such a script in 1979 when she was asked by a group of factory workers in Nagda to create a production about working conditions. Because no extant script was appropriate, the group created the play by using acting exercises to extend and develop stories told by the factory workers. Sharma claimed that one of the mistakes she made was writing the script down: since most of the actors could not read, writing made their own words alien to them. Since then she has never written down her community-created scripts.

Later, Sharma was approached by the women's group Manushi to conduct a workshop with college girls. They created a piece about how it feels to be "not exactly discriminated against, but treated differently" (qtd. in Mee, 1997). Sharma wanted to include a scene in which the women felt uncomfortable or threatened by men while waiting for a bus. Concerned that it would not be taken seriously if she replicated the scene realistically, she did the scene without any men at all, shifting the focus onto the women and how they felt. "I learnt then," she says, "the necessity of going beyond REALISM and abstracting from an experience what may be the essence" (Sharma, 2002). While creating the piece, many of the women expressed anger, sorrow, and bitterness. In some situations, Sharma says, "you don't have to do anything—you don't have to probe, you don't have to make [the actors] become aware of their anger, you just have to create the space" for them to speak (qtd. in Mee, 1997).

When UNICEF asked Sharma to run some workshops as part of a communication package designed to educate people about leprosy and to deal with prejudices blocking the diagnosis and effective treatment of the disease, she ended up writing *The Wooden Cart* (*Kaath Ki Gaadi*), one of her best-known pieces. Sharma developed the play from interviews conducted with patients and from workshops with paramedical doctors. After one of her workshops in a leprosy-prone area, a villager stepped into the playing space to say: "I'm cured of leprosy, and I'm saying this so that [others] who might be hiding [their disease] will see that there is no reason to hide." In that moment Sharma realized that theater is a forum. "It's not so important for the play to say everything, the fact that you bring something out in the open in itself sends out vibrations which are in some way liberating, and get people talking. Earlier I felt it was necessary to put everything about the issues into the play, to make everything clear, but the fact that you create this forum is itself an event, and it leads to many other kinds of events" (qtd. in Mee, 1997).

Sharma later worked with performers in *khayal* (operatic drama with dance, popular in Rajasthan), *nautanki* (operatic drama performed in Rajasthan, Uttar Pradesh, and Punjab), *tamasha* (a popular entertainment of Maharashtra, performed in Marathi), and *pandavani* (a genre of musical storytelling that originated in the Chhattisgarh region of Madhya Pradesh) to see how they can portray women in new ways in these four traditional genres. Her project is designed to address the issue of gender, but also to address the unequal relationship created between urban theater artists and practitioners of traditional performance in situations where urban artists take elements of traditional performance and use them in productions that are performed exclusively for urban audiences on proscenium stages.

When asked whether she thought she could change anyone's mind through performance, Sharma said:

It's very difficult to measure how people change by seeing plays. I believe there is a basic goodness in people, and I feel that if a play points out something positive, it appeals to that positiveness in them. . . . If they didn't get support from outside, then the negative which exists would get strengthened, which is why I feel it is important, even if I am unable to measure, or to feel that I'm doing a very important social service by changing people's minds, [to keep working,] because somewhere it will strengthen something positive, which will have an effect. . . . I don't think . . . that in forty-five minutes you can change a forty-five year experience, but I feel that it adds to something somewhere—it gives people something to think about and keep in mind. (qtd. in Mee, 1997)

Sharma's strength as a writer lies in presenting "other" points of view in ways that cannot be ignored: she provides a place in which people can listen to each other and exchange views.

SELECT PLAY: *The Wooden Cart* (*Kaath Ki Gaadi*)

FURTHER READING

Katyal, Anjum. "Playwright, Director, Activist: An Interview with Tripurari Sharma." *Seagull Theatre Quarterly* 20/21 (1999): 99–132.

Mee, Erin. "Tripurari Sharma: Out in the Open." *Performing Arts Journal* 55 (1997): 12–19.

Sharma, Tripurari. *The Wooden Cart.* In *Drama Contemporary: India*, ed. by Erin Mee. Baltimore: Johns Hopkins University Press, 2001.

——. "Unfinished Journeys." In *Muffled Voices*, ed. by Lakshmi Subramanyam. Delhi: Shakti Books, 2002.

Erin B. Mee

SHAW, GEORGE BERNARD (1856–1950)

Playwright, novelist, critic, and political activist George Bernard Shaw was born at 3 Upper Synge Street (later renamed 33 Synge Street), Dublin, IRELAND, on July 26, 1856. He was the third child of the marriage of George Carr Shaw (1814–1885), a grain merchant who had begun his career as a civil servant in the Dublin Four Courts, and Lucinda Elizabeth (Bessie) Shaw (née Gurly, 1830–1913), an accomplished musician who played leading roles as a mezzo-soprano in operatic productions in Dublin and later became a teacher of singing in London. The two other children of the marriage were Shaw's elder sisters, Lucinda Frances (1853–1920), who became a star singer in musical COMEDIES, and Elinor Agnes (1855–1876), who died from tuberculosis at the age of twenty. Shaw's family belonged to a large clan of Irish Shaws, some of whom rose to positions of great eminence in the social, political, and judicial systems of the Protestant Ascendancy regime as lawyers, bankers, merchants, soldiers, and members of parliament. One of the clan, Sir Robert Shaw (1774–1849), established a large estate at Bushy Park, Terenure, Dublin, which the playwright visited during his childhood. The prosperous and powerful Bushy Park Shaws were the point of contrast in the playwright's famous description of his immediate family's position in the social scale as belonging to a class of "the Shabby Genteel, the Poor Relations, the Gentlemen who are No Gentlemen" (Shaw, 1930).

Shaw's accounts of his family background, which have generally been uncritically adopted and elaborated upon by biographers, are questionable on several grounds. Shaw presented his parents' marriage as having been a disastrous and loveless relationship from the outset, following his mother's alleged discovery on the honeymoon that she had married an alcoholic, and her return in total disillusionment to a domestic "hell" in Dublin. There is strong documentary evidence (including a revealing and largely unpublished collection of fifteen affectionate and good-humored letters written by his father to his mother in the summer of 1857) suggesting that the early years of the marriage may well have been quite happy, and that the son probably exaggerated both the extent of his father's drinking problem and of the family's poverty. For reasons which can only be guessed at, Shaw was impelled to create in his autobiographical writings and correspondence a picture of his own rise to success from a background of miserable failure and familial dysfunction. His parents' marriage did eventually break up—amicably, according to Shaw's childhood friend, Mathew McNulty—but this was not until 1873, as Shaw was turning seventeen. Shaw omitted mention in his autobiographical writings of the keen and intelligent interest his father took in the writing of his early novels.

Shaw revered his "wonderful mother," as a Fabian contemporary described her, Bessie Shaw. The style of a scrap of her autobiographical writing describing her extremely strict piano lessons as a child in Dublin suggests a spirited lady with a keen sense of humor. Scattered reports by Shaw of her comments about various people show that she was also an incisive and shrewd judge of character. Katharine Tynan (1913) said of her that "like her son, she was very witty, very satirical." Although he was full of praise for her in some ways, Shaw also presented some very negative views about his mother, saying that she had "no comedic impulses" (contradicting comments by several others as well as Tynan) and that she was lacking in ordinary maternal feeling. But his mother's continued interest in and concern about her children, her prolonged grieving over the death of her daughter Agnes, whose spirit she tried to reach in séances, and the eighteen years of companionable relations she had with Shaw when he was living in her house in London before his marriage in 1898, cast doubt on the son's perceptions. Psychobiographical accounts of Shaw suggesting that he was emotionally maimed by lack of maternal love in childhood are based on questionable evidence and tend to lead to reductive and simplistic explanations of his life and achievements, and of his engagement with emotional issues both in his life and art.

Although he presented a largely negative view of his father, Shaw did assert that his own comedic spirit and delight in comic anticlimax was inherited from him. The young Shaw was strongly influenced by two other father figures, a Rabelaisian maternal uncle, Walter Gurly, a ship's surgeon, who frequently entertained the household with ribald tales and limericks, and George Vandeleur Lee, a conductor, musical entrepreneur and exponent of a method of voice production, who founded a Dublin Amateur Musical Society in 1852. Bessie Shaw collaborated with Lee in his musical enterprises, and from 1866 until 1873, the Shaws shared with Lee a summer cottage on Dalkey Hill and a house at 1 Hatch Street, Dublin. The idea pursued by some commentators that Lee was the biological father of Shaw through an illicit affair with his mother is based entirely on circumstantial evidence and is rendered improbable by other evidence, which includes Shaw's physical resemblance to relatives on the Carr Shaw side of the family.

As a schoolboy, Shaw was a gifted and well regarded student (coming top in English and Latin on two recorded occasions and receiving a certificate for good conduct on another), but he heartily detested the several schools he attended in and around Dublin, and counted as the three "colleges" of his "university" Lee's Musical Society, the National Gallery of Ireland, and the hillside of Dalkey Hill, with its splendid views of sea and sky. He was keenly interested in art, and attended classes in freehand drawing in 1870. He grew up in a musical household, and the knowledge and love of music that Shaw developed in his childhood profoundly influenced his entire creative career. John Bunyan, Charles Dickens, and William Shakespeare were prominent among the authors of his boyhood reading, and they remained a permanent part of the Shavian mental landscape. He was also powerfully impressed in his childhood by the charismatic figure of Mephistopheles in Charles Gounod's Faust. On the whitewashed walls of his room at Torca Cottage in Dalkey,

Shaw painted watercolor frescoes of Mephistopheles "as the patron saint of sceptics and deriders," explaining to a would-be biographer that at this time, "for the most part my intellectual attitude & affectation was Mephisthophelean." His admiration for the oddly assorted childhood heroes of Mephistopheles and John Bunyan, and his Mr. Valiant for Truth, foreshadow the peculiar combination in the adult Shaw of jesting iconoclast and world-betterer with a sense of religious mission.

In 1873, Bessie Shaw departed from Ireland with her two daughters, and established herself as a music teacher in London. Bernard Shaw remained in Dublin in lodgings with his father until 1876, working as an office boy, and later cashier, in the "highly respectable" estate management firm owned by C. Uniacke Townshend, a distant relative of the family into which Shaw married in 1898. A precipitating factor in Shaw's own decision, just before his twentieth birthday in the summer of 1876, to join his mother in London was the death of his sister Elinor Agnes. Immediately after hearing this news he traveled to London, and then to Ventnor on the Isle of Wight, where Agnes died and is buried. The main reasons Shaw (1930) gave in later writings for his decision to migrate to London were that it was "the literary centre of the English language," and that "every Irishman who felt that his business in life was on the higher planes of the cultural professions felt that he must have a metropolitan domicile and an international culture: that is, he felt that his first business was to get out of Ireland."

Despite his self-exile, Shaw remained an Irishman in spirit. He tended to view matters from an Irish rather than English perspective, and many of his dramatic and nondramatic writings are concerned with Irish subjects. After his departure at the age of nineteen in 1876, he did not return to Ireland until July 1905, but thereafter made quite frequent visits, enjoying especially the West of Ireland, where he and his wife Charlotte stayed at times with LADY GREGORY at Coole Park and at the Great Southern Parknasilla Hotel in County Kerry. Some of his play SAINT JOAN (1923) was written at the Parknasilla Hotel, and Shaw was staying there during the production of his playlet The Shewing-up of Blanco Posnet at the Abbey Theatre in 1909. Shaw was involved with W. B. YEATS in the founding of the Irish Academy of Letters in 1932, with Shaw as its first president. In 1946 he was honored by being made a Freeman of Dublin.

In his early years in London, Shaw attempted to establish himself as a novelist, with the rapidly executed writing of five remarkable works: Immaturity (1879), The Irrational Knot (1880), Love Among the Artists (1881), Cashel Byron's Profession (1882–1883), and An Unsocial Socialist (1883). The novels, which contain substantial components of autobiography and anticipations of many themes in Shaw's dramatic works, presented humorously critical, angular, and wry analyses of the class system and social mores of contemporary English society, and penetrating reflection on contemporary political and social issues. They were rejected with monotonous regularity by leading English publishers as unsuitable for the reading public of the day. The serial publication of An Unsocial Socialist in the monthly magazine To-Day in 1884 led to Shaw's meeting and association with William Morris. It was through Morris that Shaw met W. B. Yeats in 1888 and Florence Farr in 1890, and he formed a close friendship with Morris's daughter, May. Cashel Byron's Profession, which became his most commercially successful novel, was serialized in To-Day in 1885–1886. The Irrational Knot and Love Among the Artists were published serially in Mrs. Annie Besant's magazine Our Corner in 1885–1887 and 1887–1888, respectively. Immaturity was first published, in a more extensively revised form than Shaw revealed, in 1930 with an important autobiographical preface.

During his early years in London, Shaw was heavily dependent on his mother and father for support, although he did have a period of employment with the fledgling Edison Telephone Company, and gained some small income from ghost-writing articles of music criticism for Vandeleur Lee in The Hornet, and occasionally from other forms of casual employment. Beginning in October 1880 with his joining of the Zetetical Society, he became involved with numerous literary, philosophical, political, and economic societies and study groups. He claimed that he was converted to the cause of Socialism after hearing a speech in 1882 by Henry George, the American author of Progress and Poverty. When his close friend William Archer first observed Shaw in the Reading Room of the British Museum early in 1883, he found the young man with "pallid skin and bright red hair and beard . . . day after day, poring over Karl Marx's Das Kapital and an orchestral score of Wagner's Tristan und Isolde" (Archer, 1931). In 1884 Shaw joined the recently formed Fabian Society, of which he was soon to become one of the leading committee members and trumpeters of its gradualist Socialist principles. His membership in the Fabian Society further developed his already established association with two of the Society's leading figures, Sidney and Beatrice Webb. He became renowned for his superb performances as a "platform spellbinder" and was much in demand as a speaker on political and social topics.

Shaw had numerous love affairs and philanderings with women during his early London days, beginning with a lengthy and tempestuous relationship with Alice Lockett, a young woman he met at his uncle Walter Gurly's house in Leyton. Although he described himself as an "incorrigible philanderer," he was often, like the Don Juan in his early short story "Don Giovanni Explains," the object of pursuit, rather than the pursuer in love affairs. He was also a critic of the conventional ideas of love and romance prevalent in Victorian fiction and social life. On his twenty-ninth birthday, he surrendered his virginity to an Irish widow, Mrs. Jane ("Jenny") Patterson, who subsequently became extremely possessive, and fiercely jealous of her chief rivals Mrs. Annie Besant and the actress Florence Farr. An early play, The Philanderer (1893), draws on Shaw's experiences in this triangular relationship.

Shaw had a gift for forming meaningful and mostly long-lasting relationships with both men and women. In the case of his relations with women, tensions frequently arose from the clashes that occurred between his ideal, probably influenced by Percy Bysshe Shelley, of free, disinterested friendship between people and the claims of possession normally created in sexual relationships. These tensions were strongly evident in his personal life and reflected in his early creative writing. But, as his own testimony and correspondence with Mrs. Patterson indicate, Shaw greatly enjoyed the experience of heterosexual intercourse and was evidently a successful and passionate, if sometimes reluctant, lover.

It was not until 1898, when he was forty-two, that he relinquished his bachelorhood and on June 1 married a wealthy Irish heiress, Charlotte Payne-Townshend, whom he had met through her association with Sidney and Beatrice Webb, and who had been deeply impressed by Shaw's writings. The marriage was preceded by a lengthy period of courtship, during which Shaw alternated between moods of deepening affection for Charlotte and unwillingness to commit himself to marriage, largely out of anxiety about his own reliability in relationships with women. The marriage was finally decided upon during a time when Shaw suffered a serious breakdown in health partly caused by the pressure of his work and partly by a necrosis of a bone in the foot, which eventually required an operation. He attended his wedding on crutches, and thereafter went through a lengthy period of convalescence, during which he wrote his play *Caesar and Cleopatra* (1898).

There is clear evidence in Shaw's correspondence with Charlotte that during their courtship they engaged in a good deal of physical intimacy in the form of kisses and embraces. It is impossible to determine precisely what became of the sexual side of their relationship after marriage, but as she told T. E. Lawrence (Lawrence of Arabia) in 1927, Charlotte was averse to the idea of having children. Shaw gave as the reason for their deciding on a nonsexual marriage the fact that at her age—she was married at forty-one—a pregnancy would have been dangerous. So the marriage was possibly unconsummated and was without issue. After the wedding, Charlotte, who had inherited a large fortune from her father, an Irish property owner and successful investor, and her mother settled on Shaw an annuity of £300 per annum. This was an important financial arrangement since Shaw did not begin to make a really substantial income from his writings until late in the Edwardian period. The mostly amicable and affectionate marriage of companionship between Shaw and Charlotte lasted until her death in 1943. Shaw engaged in numerous flirtations and affairs with other women during his marriage, the most serious of which in the early years of the marriage were those with Erica Cotterill and the actress Mrs. Patrick (Stella) Campbell. His correspondence with American actress Molly Tompkins suggests that their relationship may have been physically consummated in Italy when he was in his early seventies.

Shaw first began to establish his literary reputation in the field of journalism, as a music, art, and theater critic and book reviewer in various London periodicals. In this sphere he was assisted in obtaining appointments by his friend, the first English translator of HENRIK IBSEN, William Archer, who wrote of Shaw's outstanding qualities as a music critic that, "he had a peculiar genius for bringing day-by-day musical criticism into vital relation with aesthetics at large, and even with ethics and politics—in a word with life" (Henderson, 1911). The same virtue of cross-fertilization between various fields of interest is present in the trenchant and witty theater criticism he wrote for Frank Harris's *Saturday Review* in the 1890s. Shaw described his series of amusing and often devastating reviews of the theatrical entertainments of the day as "a siege laid to the theater of the 19th century" (Shaw, 1906). A special target of attack was the so-called well-made play among whose most notable practitioners were French dramatists VICTORIEN SARDOU and Eugene Scribe; Shaw coined the term Sardoodledom as an epithet for their mechanical and artificial plotting. He was also a trenchant critic of pseudo PROBLEM PLAYS such as ARTHUR PINERO's *The Notorious Mrs. Ebbsmith* and THE SECOND MRS. TANQUERAY, which he saw as exploiting the sensational value of topical subjects, such as the situation of the "fallen woman" and the female revolt against male authority, only to end up by endorsing fundamentally conservative Victorian positions. The plays of Ibsen were invoked by Shaw as a foil to the comparative banality of much of the late 19th-century drama in ENGLAND. On July 18, 1890, he delivered a lengthy expository lecture on Ibsen at a meeting of the Fabian Society at St. James's Restaurant in London, which was subsequently published in expanded form as "The Quintessence of Ibsenism" (1891). Another early cultural hero of Shaw's was RICHARD WAGNER, about whom he wrote "The Perfect Wagnerite" (1898), a treatise on *The Ring*.

Shaw's career as a publicly performed playwright began in 1892, with the completion of his *Widowers' Houses* and its first production by J. T. Grein's Independent Theatre Company at the Royalty Theatre, Soho. By 1896 he had completed the seven plays that were gathered together under the title *Plays Pleasant and Unpleasant* (1898), and by the end of the century he had completed three further works that were published under the title *Three Plays for Puritans* in 1901. *Widowers' Houses* and the third play in the *Plays Unpleasant* group, MRS. WARREN'S PROFESSION (1893), reflect Socialist politics more explicitly than any of Shaw's later dramatic works. In these plays, the outward behavioral forms of bourgeois society, its codes of ladylike and gentlemanly behavior and its rules of good taste and decency, are seen as part of a conspiracy that conceals underlying, and underpinning, systems of brutal exploitation of labor and conditions of human degradation. Slum tenant houses owned by ruthless landlords, chains of brothels, and factories with appalling working conditions are focal points in these exposures of the dark underside of Victorian gentility and prosperity.

ARMS AND THE MAN, the first of the *Plays Pleasant* group, had its premiere in 1894, with W. B. Yeats's *The Land of Heart's Desire* as a curtain-raiser, at Florence Farr's Avenue Theatre in London. The first authentic notes of Shavian satirical laughter have been rightly traced by one commentator to the treatment of Dr. Paramore's absurd medical experiments in the second play of the *Plays Unpleasant* group, *The Philanderer*. In the *Plays Pleasant* group, Shaw's comic powers were further developed with a series of plays in which twists of fortune in personal relations, flirtations and love affairs, and satire on idealized conceptions of romance and heroism loom larger than social, economic, and political themes. While retaining a sharp edge of thematic originality and unorthodoxy, these plays tend to sport with follies rather than with crimes. The crowning work of this period was *You Never Can Tell* (1895–1896), one of the richest of the early comedies and a work that contains a good deal of masked autobiography.

In *Three Plays for Puritans*, Shaw conducted a two-edged critical campaign. On the one hand, he attacked narrow and unimaginative conceptions of RELIGION—the wrathfully vindictive and appropriately named Mrs. Dudgeon in *The Devil's Disciple* (1896) is an epitome of joyless and rigid Puritanism. On the other hand, Shaw himself took a Puritanical stance in these plays in his subversion of the conventions of sentimental romance and in his critique of the idolatry of love. In *Caesar and Cleopatra*, he developed the interest in historical subjects and in towering historical figures that had earlier been displayed in a one-act play about Napoleon, *The Man of Destiny* (1895).

At the turn of the century, Shaw began the composition of MAN AND SUPERMAN (1901–1902), a major work in which he first announced his new "religion" of Creative Evolution. He was strongly influenced in the formation of his ideas about Creative Evolution and the Life Force by the writings on evolution of Samuel ("Erewhon") Butler, who, believing that Charles Darwin had "banished mind from the universe," wrote numerous polemics against his theories of evolution. Other influences on Shaw's ideas included FRIEDRICH NIETZSCHE and Arthur Schopenhauer. Shaw later associated his Life Force theories with the idea of the Élan Vital propounded by Henri Bergson, though Bergson himself was evidently not comfortable with Shaw's understanding of his theory. ("It is not qvite zat," Bergson is reported to have interjected when he listened to Shaw expounding Bergsonian theory at a luncheon in the French philosopher's honor in London in 1911 [Russell, 1956]).

In Shaw's view, evolution is a series of experiments by the Life Force toward the creation of more and more highly organized forms of life. Individuals can contribute to this process by the exercise of imagination, will, and intelligence. The meliorist and teleological thrust of these ideas is counterbalanced in *Man and Superman*, and elsewhere in Shaw's writings, by deeply pessimistic and skeptical reflections on the human species and by ironic comedy. One of the sections of the Handbook attached

to the published text of *Man and Superman* and headed "Progress an Illusion" describes history as marked by continual relapses of humanity into conditions of savagery, and the Devil in the Dream scene of the play itself delivers a Swiftian diatribe in which man is described as the most destructive and predatory of all the animals.

Shaw's ascendancy to the position of leading dramatist of his day in England, with a strongly developing international reputation, began in the first decade of the 20th century. From 1904 to 1907 he was engaged in a highly successful partnership with the actor-manager HARLEY GRANVILLE-BARKER and with J. E. Vedrenne at the Court Theatre in Sloane Square. Eleven of Shaw's plays were presented at the Court during this period, including the new works JOHN BULL'S OTHER ISLAND (1904), *How He Lied to Her Husband* (1904), MAJOR BARBARA (1905), and *The Doctor's Dilemma* (1906). A command performance of *John Bull's Other Island* at 10 Downing Street before King Edward VII was a significant mark of Shaw's elevation in public esteem.

After the Court seasons, Shaw made increasingly bold experiments in the discussion-play form with *Getting Married* (1907–1908) and *Misalliance* (1909). In contrasting style was the strongly plotted action in the play-within-the play of *Fanny's First Play* (1910–1911) and *Androcles and the Lion* (1911), the latter combining elements of pantomime and action-packed historical drama. In *Fanny's First Play*, which had an all-time record first run for Shavian plays of 622 performances, Shaw settled old scores with some of his newspaper theater critics by introducing easily recognizable satirical caricatures of them into a frame-play that surrounds the work supposedly written by Fanny O'Dowda, a student at Cambridge and member of the Cambridge Fabian Society, who has written a revolutionary play quite at odds with the expectations of her old-fashioned father, Count O'Dowda. The culmination of Shaw's success in the pre–World War I period was reached in 1912 with the composition of the comic classic, PYGMALION, in which middle-class morality and the artificiality of class divisions are among the subjects of satire in a dramatic narrative that follows the transformation of a cockney flowerseller into a duchess by speech training from a professor of phonetics. The play became the basis of the highly successful musical *My Fair Lady*.

Apart from his continued activities as a dramatist, Shaw was in the vanguard of action in numerous political, social, and cultural causes during the Edwardian and early Georgian period. He was closely involved in the agitation for women's suffrage in the Edwardian years and in fact had delivered a speech supporting women's suffrage as early as April 26, 1892, at a stormy meeting in St. James's Hall, London. His book *The Quintessence of Ibsenism*, published in the previous year, contained a lively attack on the Victorian conception of the womanly woman. In March 1907 he spoke in favor of women's suffrage at a meeting in Queens Hall, London, under the auspices of the National Union of Women's Suffrage Societies, and in the following year, in company with his wife Charlotte and his cousin Georgina ("Judy") Gillmore, he joined one of the largest suffragette demonstrations ever held in London. His Edwardian playlet, *Press Cuttings*, which presents satirical portraits of different types of female antisuffragette figures, was written to be presented at the Court Theatre in aid of the London Society for Women's Suffrage and was later performed in tandem with Cicely Hamilton and Christopher St. John's prosuffrage play *How the Vote Was Won*. While he was an unwavering supporter of equality for women, and many of his plays created fine portraits (and role models) of emancipated women, the female characters in some works, such as *Candida* (1904), *Misalliance* (1909), and HEARTBREAK HOUSE (1916–1917), reflect the angel–demon dichotomy in Victorian constructs of the feminine.

Another cause vigorously pursued by Shaw in the Edwardian years was his campaign against the system of stage censorship. Shaw had clashed with the censorship system in England in the 1890s with his play *Mrs. Warren's Profession*, for which a license for public performance was impossible to obtain and which he had to revise extensively for its publication in 1898. The play was not licensed for public performance in England until 1924. In the Edwardian period two of his shorter plays, *The Shewing-up of Blanco Posnet* and *Press Cuttings*, were banned from public performance. In the face of opposition from the authorities of Dublin Castle, Lady Gregory and W. B. Yeats collaborated in mounting a production of *Blanco Posnet* at the Abbey Theatre. On opening night, August 25, 1909, representatives of virtually all the major newspapers in England as well as journalists from Frankfurt and Milan were present. Also in the audience was James Joyce, who reviewed the play for *Piccolo della Sera*, Trieste. The production was a triumph and regarded as a major victory in the struggle for the independence of Ireland from the English censorship system.

In the years leading up to the First World War, Shaw had two relationships with women that severely strained his marriage to Charlotte and had important consequences for his creative work. Erica Cotterill, a woman in her early twenties, cousin of Rupert Brooke and daughter of a Socialist schoolmaster, became infatuated with Shaw in 1905. An attractive, intelligent, and uninhibited woman with considerable gifts as a creative writer, she pursued Shaw to his and Charlotte's homes in Adelphi Terrace and Ayot St. Lawrence, where she showered him with caresses, declarations of love, and marriage proposals. Shaw's eventual rejection of these approaches did not prevent him from drawing on the relationship in the composition of *Getting Married* (1907–1908), *Misalliance* (1909), and in the conception of the "spiritual marriage" between the ancient Captain Shotover and the young Ellie Dunn in *Heartbreak House*.

His love affair with the "perilously bewitching" Mrs. Patrick Campbell began in 1912. Unlike the affair with Ellen Terry, which was entirely conducted by correspondence, that with Stella Campbell involved frequent clandestine visits to her house and a good deal of unconsummated physical intimacy. The relationship reached a crisis in the late summer of 1913 when Stella ran away from a meeting, evidently intended by Shaw to bring the affair to sexual consummation, in a hotel at a seaside resort in Kent. In April of the following year, during rehearsals for *Pygmalion*, in which she played Eliza, Stella married George Cornwallis-West, who left her in 1919. The captivating, witty, and perceptive, but often exasperating, character of Stella Campbell influenced Shaw in his creation of the characters of Hesione in *Heartbreak House* (1916–1917), the Serpent in BACK TO METHUSELAH (1918–1920), and Orinthia in *The Apple Cart* (1928).

Immediately after the outbreak of World War I, Shaw wrote a polemical essay, "Common Sense About the War" (1914), in which he attacked the official British rationale for entry into the struggle and described the war itself as, essentially, a clash between rival imperial powers brought on by Junker militarists on both sides of the English Channel. The essay caused outrage in England and various groups ostracized its author. His major creative achievement in the War years was *Heartbreak House*, a work written in the atmosphere of apocalyptic doom evoked by Zeppelin air raids on civilian targets in London and other English cities. The horror and carnage of the War (which Shaw witnessed first hand when he was invited to visit the Front in 1917) also left a deep imprint on the postwar cycle of plays on evolutionary themes, *Back to Methuselah*.

A pinnacle of international fame and recognition in Shaw's career was reached in the 1920s with the triumphant success on both sides of the Atlantic of his new play, *Saint Joan*, and the 1925 Nobel Prize for Literature. *Saint Joan* was described by fellow playwright LUIGI PIRANDELLO in 1924 as "a work of poetry from beginning to end" ("Pirandello Distills Shaw," *New York Times*, Jan. 13, 1924). Some controversy has surrounded the play in later critical commentary, but it has retained its high reputation in the theater. The title role has been played by many of the 20th century's most celebrated actresses, and the work has influenced playwrights as diverse as T. S. ELIOT and BERTOLT BRECHT. A further accolade for Shaw came in 1929 with the founding, in his honor, of the Malvern Festival, a series of annual theater festivals in which new and revived Shavian works were the major attraction. Shaw's "political extravaganza" *The Apple Cart* was one of the offerings at the first festival. His long silence as a playwright between *Saint Joan* and *The Apple Cart* is partly explained by the fact that he was writing a major political treatise, "The Intelligent Woman's Guide to Socialism and Capitalism" (1928), in the intervening years.

During the last twenty-five years of his life, Shaw continued to be vigorously productive as a playwright. Many of the late plays are remarkable for their experimental formal characteristics and for exotic scenarios that reflect an increasing interest in Eastern and other non-European religions and cultures. Plays such as *On the Rocks* (1933), about conditions in England at the beginning of the Great Depression, and *Geneva* (1938) reveal, with the accompaniment of a great deal of farcical comedy, a sense of near despair on Shaw's part about national and international political organizations. Other plays, however, such as *The Simpleton of the Unexpected Isles* (1934), *The Millionairess* (1935), and *Buoyant Billions* (1946–1948) contain some qualified reaffirmations of faith in life's continually renewed prospects of change, surprise, and wonder. Shaw's last completed dramatic work was the puppet play *Shakes Versus Shav* (1949), in which Shakespeare and Shaw engage in a battle royal of fisticuffs and quotations. A "little comedy," *Why She Would Not*, was written in 1950, but Shaw evidently regarded this work as unfinished. He died a few months after his ninety-fourth birthday, on November 2, 1950, following an illness precipitated by a fall in his garden at Ayot St. Lawrence, Hertfordshire. Shaw's final illness and death attracted huge media attention throughout the world, and when the death was announced, theater audiences in various places stood in silence, and the lights on Broadway were dimmed in tribute. Shaw's birthplace in Dublin has been restored to resemble its probable appearance in the mid–19th century and was opened to the public in 1993. His country residence in England, "Shaw's Corner" at Ayot St. Lawrence, is also open to the public under the auspices of the British National Trust. New productions of his plays are regularly presented in the annual Shaw Festival at Niagara-on-the-Lake in CANADA.

Shaw once described himself as being "up to the chin" in the life of his time, and this comment is borne out by the extraordinary range of his activities and associations. As his own fame grew, and even earlier in some cases, he came into contact in one way or another with a remarkable number of leading figures in the long period of history through which he lived. The normal round of his life came to include such events as exchanging correspondence with LYOV TOLSTOY; entertaining Winston Churchill and his mother to lunch; proposing a toast to Albert Einstein at a dinner in his honor; meeting Joseph Stalin in company with the first British woman Minister of Parliament, Nancy Astor; and having lunch with Charlie Chaplin, Marion Davies, Louis B. Mayer, and Clark Gable in Hollywood, before going on to stay with Randolph Hearst.

None of his other public activities impeded Shaw's prolific output as a playwright, author, and political activist. He wrote twenty-eight full-length plays (counting the five-play cycle *Back to Methuselah* as one work), nineteen playlets, and the puppet play *Shakes versus Shav*. In addition to his five early novels, he wrote a very large number of other nondramatic works in the form of music, theater, and art criticism, treatises, prefaces, essays, and tracts. He is estimated to have written more than a quarter million letters and several thousand contributions to periodicals.

Most of the plays of Shaw's early and middle period, up to and including *Heartbreak House*, were developed from the mould of late 19th-century NATURALISM. Some radical departures from naturalism occurred in this period, in the dream scene of

Man and Superman, for example, and in the pantomime form of several scenes in *Androcles and the Lion* (1912). With *Back to Methuselah*, Shaw entered into a final phase of his playwriting career in which fantastic characterization and incident become increasingly common. *Back to Methuselah* has a time span from the Garden of Eden to the year A.D. 31,920, and much in this work resembles science fiction and utopian and dystopian fable. Later plays, such as *Too True to Be Good* (1931) and *The Simpleton of the Unexpected Isles* contain equally extravagant ingredients. The characters in Shaw's early and middle plays are generally drawn with great psychological insight and lively individuation; in later works, characterization tends toward allegory, and in the case of the political plays, cartoon.

During his lifetime Shaw achieved almost legendary status as playwright, pundit, and wit. In the 1930s his partly sympathetic public comments about European Fascist leaders (which were not completely cancelled by his lampooning of them in *Geneva*), his unqualified support of Russian Communism under Stalin, and public bewilderment about the intellectual directions of some of his new plays led to a decline in his popularity. But his profile as a public figure and commentator on social issues remained high. As a writer of lucid, effective, and vivacious critical and expository prose, Shaw has only a handful of rivals in the English literary tradition. He had an extraordinary ability to bring abstract philosophical, economic, and political subjects to life, an unerring instinct for the natural rhythms of English, and an inexhaustible fund of apt allusion and lively illustration of ideas. As a born iconoclast he employed these gifts successfully in the exposure of humbug and hypocrisy in his time and in the subversion of sanctimonious and sentimental value systems. While he declared his intellectual affiliations with crusading revolutionaries and "artist philosophers" such as Bunyan, Shelley, and William Blake, he was much more influenced by the comic muse than any of these mentors.

As a playwright Shaw made a major contribution to the renovation of the 19th-century dramatic tradition in England, which had been dominated by a vigorously flourishing but intellectually unchallenging medley of FARCES and MELODRAMAS, pièces bien faites, historical costume dramas, pseudo problem plays, grandiose productions of Shakespeare, and other forms of theatrical entertainment. Shaw's work brought a new dimension of vital engagement with fundamental ideological and cultural assumptions as well as a unique combination of comic inventiveness and critical intelligence. In 1924 T. S. Eliot described Shaw as "the intellectual stimulant and the dramatic delight of twenty years" ("Commentary," *Criterion III* [October 1924]). W. B. Yeats in his *Autobiographies* (1954) declared that from the moment in 1894 when Shaw delivered a brilliant repartee to a member of the first-night audience of *Arms and the Man*, he became "the most formidable man in modern letters." (To a man who uttered a single boo from the gallery amid the laughter and cheers from the rest of the audience at a curtain call after the performance, Shaw responded: "My dear fellow I quite agree with you, but what are we two against so many" [*Collected Letters*, Vol. 1, 1965].) Less favorable remarks about Shaw by both Eliot and Yeats have contributed to his neglect and downgrading in the mainstream of 20th-century literary criticism.

In theatrical circles and in the broad public domain, Shaw's standing as a major dramatist has not been seriously questioned, and a large number of his works have become a seemingly permanent part of the international repertory of modern classics. His reputation in academic circles has remained controversial and uncertain, despite the existence of a very large body of generally favorable critical writing that has included, in the period since the end of World War II, more than forty book-length studies.

Shaw's plays engage in entertaining and exciting ways with social, political, moral, and philosophical issues, and that quality is an important part of their attraction and interest. But, as he rightly maintained, whatever ideas they may deal with, his dramatic works were not written as "economic essays" but as "plays of life, character, and human destiny." This is what makes the tag "drama of ideas," which is sometimes attached to them, misleading as a pointer to the experiential character of Shaw's works as scripts for the theater. Typically, the end of a play by Shaw leaves not the sense of a proven thesis but an awareness of open-ended possibilities and irreducible complexity. In the development of action in the plays, reason and theory are generally swept aside by human vitality, instinct, and impulse. His characterization, especially in the early and middle works, is distinguished by its depth, subtlety, and rich humor. Some of the plays contain a good deal of talk—a fact about which Shaw occasionally makes even his dramatis personae complain—but the talk is generally closely related to dramatic action. In the theatrical domain, as his sometimes very critical friend Beatrice Webb acknowledged, Shaw is an artist to the tips of his fingers. Like his character Ann Whitefield in *Man and Superman*, Shaw is "one of the vital geniuses."

PLAYS: *Widowers' Houses* (1892); *Mrs. Warren's Profession* (1893); *The Philanderer* (1893); *Arms and the Man* (1894); *Candida* (1894); *You Never Can Tell* (1895–1896); *The Devil's Disciple* (1896); *Caesar and Cleopatra* (1898); *Captain Brassbound's Conversion* (1899); *Man and Superman* (1901–1902); *John Bull's Other Island* (1904); *Major Barbara* (1905); *The Doctor's Dilemma* (1906); *Getting Married* (1907–1908); *Misalliance* (1909); *Fanny's First Play* (1910–1911); *Androcles and the Lion* (1912); *Pygmalion* (1912); *Heartbreak House* (1916–1917); *Back to Methuselah* (1918–1920); *Saint Joan* (1923); *The Apple Cart* (1928); *Too True to Be Good* (1931); *On the Rocks* (1933); *The Simpleton of the Unexpected Isles* (1934); *The Millionairess* (1934–1935); *Geneva* (1936–1938); *In Good King Charles's Golden Days* (1938–1939); *Buoyant Billions* (1945–1946)

FURTHER READING

Archer, C. *William Archer: Life, Work and Friendships*. London: George Allen & Unwin, 1931.

Evans, T. F. *Shaw: The Critical Heritage*. London: Routledge & Kegan Paul, 1976.

Gibbs, A. M. *Bernard Shaw: A Chronology*. London & New York: Palgrave, 2001.

——. *Bernard Shaw: A Life*. Gainesville: Univ. Press of Florida, 2006.

Henderson, Archibald. *Bernard Shaw: His Life and Works*. London: Hurst & Blackett, 1911.

Holroyd, Michael. *Bernard Shaw*, 4 vols. New York: Random House, 1988–1992.

Laurence, Dan H. *Bernard Shaw: A Bibliography*. Oxford: Oxford Univ. Press, 1983.

Morgan, Margery. *File on Shaw*. London: Methuen Drama, 1990.

Peters, Margot. *Bernard Shaw and the Actresses*. Garden City, N.Y.: Doubleday, 1980.

Russell, Bertrand. *Portraits from Memory*. New York: Simon & Schuster, 1956.

SHAW: The Annual of Bernard Shaw Studies. University Park, Penn.: Pennsylvania. State Univ. Press.

Shaw, Bernard. *Dramatic Opinions and Essay*. New York: Brentano's, 1906.

——. *Immaturity*. London: Constable, 1930.

——. *Sixteen Self Sketches*. New York: Dodd, Mead & Company, 1949.

——. *Collected Letters*, 4 vols, ed. by Dan H. Laurence. New York: Dodd, Mead & Co., 1965–1988.

——. *The Bodley Head Bernard Shaw: Collected Plays with Their Prefaces*, 7 vols. Ed. by Dan H. Laurence. London: Max Reinhardt, 1971–1974.

——. *Shaw's Music*, Vols. I–III. Ed. by Dan H. Lawrence. London: Bodley Head, 1981.

——. *Bernard Shaw: The Diaries 1885–1897*, 2 vols. Ed. by Stanley Weintraub. University Park: Penn State Univ. Press, 1986.

——. *Shaw: Interviews and Recollections*. Ed. by A. M. Gibbs. Iowa City: Univ. of Iowa Press, 1990.

——. *The Drama Observed*. Ed. by Bernard Dukore. University Park: Penn State University Press, 1993.

——. *The Matter With Ireland*, 2nd ed. Ed. by Dan H. Laurence and David Greene. Gainesville: Univ. Press of Florida, 2001.

Tynan, Katharine. *Twenty-Five Years: Reminiscences*. London: Smith Elder, 1913.

Yeats, William Butler. *Autobiographies*. London: Macmillan, 1954.

A. M. Gibbs

SHAWN, WALLACE (1943–)

American playwright and actor Wallace Shawn was born on November 12, 1943, in New York City, and educated at Harvard University and Oxford. Shawn's father was the renowned William Shawn, editor-in-chief of the *New Yorker*, and Wallace grew up in a prosperous world of literary sophistication and liberal political ideas. A self-consciousness about the privileges he had been born into was to haunt, inform, and drive Shawn's writing for the theater, and produced a spare, economic, and clear DRAMATURGY, while also resulting in intellectual complexity and subtle, moral ambiguity.

Shawn's career as a playwright began in obscurity, despite social and family connections. His day job was operating a Xerox machine, and he wrote plays that were neither produced nor published. Then a mixture of obscure presentations in prestigious venues resulted in a lucrative career as a film actor and a growing, if controversial, reputation as a dramatist. Obscenity entered the work at this time. Shawn's turn toward the subject of sex created in a new tension between play and audience. For example, the Obie-Award winning *Our Late Night* (1975), directed by Andre Gregory for the Manhattan Project, was set in a smart, stylish urban flat rife with salacious dialogue and orgiastic narrations. The play's action includes sex acts and vomiting, and was described by Brendan Gill in the *New Yorker* as "ribald and joyous"; Shawn himself saw the production as "upsetting and horrifying." *A Thought in Three Parts* (1975) and *Marie and Bruce* (1978), both with London and New York productions, continued the pornographic element and the often vicious exploration of urban, heterosexual couples.

Critics have suggested that with *Aunt Dan and Lemon* (1985) Shawn began to give up on traditional dramatic structure altogether, largely dispensing with dialogue and plot and depending instead on direct address. *The Fever* (1991), which followed, certainly bolsters this contention. Originally conceived as a piece to be presented in apartments to small groups, the two-hour monologue was performed initially by Shawn himself in both private and public venues. Finally *The Designated Mourner* (1995), using three vivid characters, continues mostly in direct address. Some critics have suggested that the plays are not theatrical at all. This perhaps ignores the reason for Shawn's reduction of dramaturgy to single, speaking voices: the result is a focus on content.

Aunt Dan and Lemon posits one character that admires the Nazis for their successful efficiency in the extermination of Jews and another who admires Henry Kissinger and his courage in overseeing the bombing of North Vietnam. *The Fever* confronts well-to-do, sophisticated audiences with their connection to ongoing torture and killings in remote Third World countries. *The Designated Mourner* depicts a futuristic Gotham City replete with a totalitarian oligarchy, a rioting underclass, and the death of the last man who can read and care about literature. Each of these plays has resulted in critical outrage and audiences shouting back at the stage. However, the three plays must be acknowledged for their formal accomplishment and their sustained and relentless examination of central moral, ethical issues. They provoke thought. Shawn also wrote with Andre Gregory the screenplay for *My Dinner With Andre* (1981).

[See also United States, 1940–Present]

PLAYS: *In the Dark* (libretto, 1975); *Our Late Night* (1975); *A Thought in Three Parts* (1976); *The Mandrake* (after Machiavelli, 1978); *Marie and Bruce* (1978); *My Dinner With Andre* (with Andre Gregory, 1980; film released 1981); *The Music Teacher* (libretto, 1983); *Aunt Dan and Lemon* (1985); *The Fever* (1990–1991); *The Designated Mourner* (1996)

FURTHER READING
Billington, Michael. "Fascism Echoes Patrician Culture." *Manchester Guardian* (April 25, 1996).
Brustein, Robert. "Two Couples," a review of *Marie and Bruce*. *New Republic* (April 5, 1980).
King, W. D. *Writing Wrongs: The Work of Wallace Shawn*. Philadelphia: Temple Univ. Press, 1997.
"Shawn, Wallace." In *Contemporary Dramatists*. Ed. by James Vinson. New York: St. Martin's Press, 1977.

Stanley R. Richardson

SHA YEXIN (1939–)

Sha Yexin was born in July 1939 in Nanjing, CHINA, to parents of Hui muslin. His father, a grocery store owner who had many clients among actors and actresses, encouraged Sha to learn Peking opera at an early age, an experience that influenced his future career choice. At sixteen Sha's first short story appeared in *Jiangsu Literature and Art* (*Jiangsu wenyi*). In 1959 he was admitted to East China Normal University. After graduating in 1961, he was selected for a two-year graduate program in dramatic literature at Shanghai Drama Academy. Since 1963 Sha has been the scriptwriter for Shanghai People's Art Theatre. His first theatric piece, the one-act COMEDY *A Penny* (*Yifen qian*, 1965) was staged in 1965, but as with a majority of Chinese artists, Sha's career was unexpectedly suspended for ten years during the Cultural Revolution (1966–1976).

He rose to prominence again soon after that period of repressive censorship and political terrorism. His first political satire, *The Impostor* (*Jiaru woshi zhende*), premiered in Shanghai in 1979 and was an immediate success. The play confronts the myth of social and economic equality under communism and exposes with comic ambiguity the social as well as material privileges party officials enjoyed in post–Cultural Revolution China. Based on the news that a young man assumes the identity of the son of a high government official in an attempt to obtain special favors reserved for the political elite, the play applies classic comic mechanisms such as dramatic irony and mistaken identity to its advantage. At the same time, Sha uses the play-within-a-play structure framed by Nikolai Gogol's *The Inspector General*. The play begins with a character addressing the audience in a Brechtian manner, saying Gogol's play is delayed because an important guest, a high-ranking official, has not yet arrived. The interruption of normal scheduling coincidentally imitates real life situations, particularly in the theater, during and after the Cultural Revolution. Stratified admission for cultural exhibits and theatrical performance was common during that period. The protagonist is therefore compelled to present himself as someone else to be admitted to the privileged group in the theater and on the stage. Structured comparisons and associations thus blurred the boundaries between audience and players. The audience is invited not only to audit Gogol's and Sha's play but also to observe the similar drama that unfolds in their everyday reality. The protagonist is banished from the stage when his true identity is discovered, yet the play on the stage continues, as does the real-life drama outside the theater. The play triggered a heated debate on whether the stage should highlight only positive or uplifting images of Chinese society. The Impostor, apparently not confined by the socialist realist didacticism, was shelved after three months of stage performances. Nonetheless, it signals a transition from post-Mao to contemporary political culture.

Apart from illuminating the unprivileged and the ordinary in Chinese society, Sha's "everyday" approach embraces issues such as gender relations and family life versus ideology. Starting in 1980 with Mayor Chen Yi (Che Yi shizhang), Sha continues his exegesis of the everyday with The Secret History of Marx (Marx mishi, 1983) and the historical play Qiang Qing and Her Husbands (Qiang Qing he tade zhangfumen, 1991), both of which show the personal facet behind the glamorous public image of spiritual or political leaders. Sha critiques both Marx and Mao as individuals, focusing on the misogyny they exhibit in their in family life.

SELECT PLAYS: A Penny (Yifen qian, 1965); The Impostor (Jiaru woshi zhende, 1979); Mayor Chen Yi (Che Yi shizhang, 1980); History of Marx (Marx mishi, 1983); Jesus, Confucius and John Lennon (Yesu, Kong zi, Pi-tou-shi Lienong, 1988); Qiang Qing and Her Husbands (Qiang Qing he tade zhangfumen, 1991)

FURTHER READING

Chen, Xiaomei, ed. Reading the Right Text: An Anthology of Contemporary Chinese Drama. Honolulu: Univ. of Hawaii Press, 2003. Contains Sha's play Qiang Qing and Her Husbands.
——. Acting the Right Part: Political Theatre and Popular Drama in Contemporary China. Honolulu: Univ. of Hawaii Press, 2002.
——. Occidentalism: A Theory of Counter-Discourse in Post-Mao China, 2nd ed. New York: Rowman and Littlefield, 2002.
Sha Yexin. "The Impostor (If I Were You)" [Jiaru wo shi zhende]. Tr. by Daniel Kane. In Trees on the Mountain: An Anthology of New Chinese Writing, ed. by Stephen C. Soong, et al. Hong Kong: Chinese Univ. Press, 1984. 333–369.

Donghui He

SHELDON, EDWARD (1886–1946)

Edward Sheldon was born on February 4, 1886, into a wealthy Chicago family and was fascinated by the theater from earliest childhood. At eighteen he enrolled at Harvard, where he attended GEORGE PIERCE BAKER's playwriting class. Soon after his graduation in 1907, he began work on SALVATION NELL, a daring, realistic drama featuring a scrubwoman's triumph over her environment through membership in the Salvation Army. It opened on Broadway in 1908 and established Sheldon as a force to be reckoned with in an era when socially conscious plays were rarely seen on the American stage. EUGENE O'NEILL

(1988) later wrote to him, "Your Salvation Nell, along with the work of the Irish Players on their first trip over here, was what first opened my eyes to the existence of a real theater as opposed to the unreal—and to me then, hateful—theater of my father, in whose atmosphere I had been brought up."

Three sociorealistic plays followed: The Nigger (1909) dramatized racial problems in the South through the story of a white Southern politician who discovers that he has an African American grandmother. The Boss (1911) focused on machine politics. The High Road (1912) examined the issues of women's rights and political corruption. By age twenty-six, Sheldon was regarded by many of his contemporaries as the most gifted and ambitious of serious-minded American playwrights.

To those who knew him, Sheldon's talent as a playwright was equaled by his personal charm and by his ability to offer sympathetic advice. Warm, open, incurably romantic, with patrician good looks and a probing intelligence, he became artistic advisor to numerous actors and actresses. Ironically, Sheldon's concern for his friends in the theater led him to depart from social REALISM to devote himself to a series of romantic vehicle plays in many ways similar to the commercial COMEDIES and dramas that ruled Broadway at the time. The most successful of these was Romance (1913). It became an American and international phenomenon; the London production ran for 1,049 performances.

In 1915, at age twenty-nine, Sheldon was stricken abruptly with the first symptoms of what would prove to be progressive and crippling rheumatoid arthritis. Within a decade he was permanently bedridden, and by 1931 he was paralyzed and blind.

After his health began to fail, Sheldon devoted himself largely to adaptations and collaborations. He adapted Peter Ibbetson (1917) and The Jest (1919) for John Barrymore; in the mid-1920s he collaborated with SIDNEY HOWARD on Bewitched (1924) and with Charles MacArthur on Lulu Belle (1926).

The severity of his illness forced Sheldon to retire in 1930. He endured his infirmity with serene grace and regularly provided friendship and advice to the many playwrights and actors who made the pilgrimage to his New York penthouse apartment. He advised ROBERT E. SHERWOOD and THORNTON WILDER on a number of plays including ABE LINCOLN IN ILLINOIS and OUR TOWN. Sheldon died on April 1, 1946, in New York City.

[See also United States, 1860–1929]

PLAYS: Salvation Nell (1908); The Nigger (1909); The Boss (1911); The Princess Zim-Zim (tour, 1911); Egypt (tour, 1912); The High Road (1912); Romance (1913); The Garden of Paradise (adaptation, 1914); The Song of Songs (adaptation, 1914); Camille (adaptation, 1917); Peter Ibbetson (adaptation, 1917); Redemption (adaptation, 1918); The Jest (adaptation, 1919); Richard III (adaptation, 1920); The Lonely Heart (tour, 1921); The Czarina (adaptation, 1922); Bewitched (with Sidney Howard, 1924); The Proud Princess (with Dorothy Donnelly, 1924); Lulu Belle (with Charles MacArthur, 1926); The Age of Innocence (adaptation, with Margaret Ayer Barnes, 1928); Jenny (with

Margaret Ayer Barnes, 1929); *Dishonored Lady* (with Margaret Ayer Barnes, 1930)

FURTHER READING

Barnes, Eric Wollencott. *The Man Who Lived Twice*. New York: Scribner's, 1956.

Cohen Albert. "Salvation Nell: An Overlooked Milestone in American Theatre." *Educational Theatre Journal* 9 (March 1957): 11–22.

Jasper, Lawrence. "Edward Sheldon." In *American Playwrights, 1880–1945: A Research and Production Sourcebook*, ed. by William W. Demastes. Westport, Conn.: Greenwood Press, 1997.

O'Neill, Eugene. *Selected Letters of Eugene O'Neill*. Ed. by Travis Bogard and Jackson R. Bryer. New Haven: Yale Univ. Press, 1988.

Ruff, Loren K. *Edward Sheldon*. Boston: Twayne, 1982.

——. "Edward Sheldon: Theatrical Spokesman in the Progressive Era," *Southern Theatre*, 20, no. 3 (Summer 1977):

Michael A. Morrison

SHENANDOAH

First produced in 1888, when the nation was beginning to heal old wounds, *Shenandoah* by BRONSON HOWARD builds from two intersectional romances arranged in a symmetrical pattern: Robert Ellingham of the 10th Virginia is in love with Madeline, whose brother, Kerchival West of Sheridan's cavalry, is in love with Robert's sister, Gertrude.

The men are West Point graduates, professionals who care about patriotism, loyalty, and honor more than the specific politics that divide them; Kerchival assures his friend that "one of us will be wrong in this great fight, but we shall both be honest in it." Not one of the lovers argues a sectional position to the point of jeopardizing friendship or romance, and Howard interprets the war itself as a courtship gone awry, so love and war become metaphors for each other. The action presents the South as a tempestuous woman whom the masculine North must dominate but without desecration, while the lovers' courtships mimic military tactics.

The villain, Thornton, is neither Northerner nor Southerner but a Copperhead whose loyalty is artificial and so untrustworthy. Within the play's strict and narrow bounds of honor, he compromises Constance, the wife of General Haverhill, and insults Thornton; the incident leads to a duel that leaves Thornton scarred and resentful. Kerchival later captures him, confiscates a miniature of Constance he is carrying, and then falls in an ambush; an officer finds the miniature in his pocket and gives it to Haverhill, who concludes that his wife has betrayed him with Kerchival. After the war, only a letter from Haverhill's dead son reveals the truth: Thornton took the miniature from him while he was a prisoner, and both Kerchival and Constance are innocent. All who fought honorably are reconciled.

The theatrical climax of the play is the Battle of Cedar Creek, when Sheridan rode his black horse to restore the morale of the Union troops, who reverse their retreat and win the day.

The *New York Times* praised the verisimilitude of the production—the crowds, the battle noises, the torch signals, and Sheridan's ride—but assured its readers that "the battle for the Nation is kept in the background, and the battle of a few human hearts is the subject of the play" (Sept. 10, 1889). The *New York Dramatic Mirror* noted, "Heroism instead of partisanship is its theme, and there is an even-handed recognition of the bravery of Northern and Southern men that will make the play just as acceptable in South Carolina as it will be in Boston" (Wheeler, 1889). *Harper's New Monthly Magazine* (June 1890) observed, "For our own selfish pleasure we could have wished to have no pursued and doubted wife in the piece. We believe that the pursuit of wives by villains is so very uncommon in our society as to be scarcely representative or typical, where there is any pursuit of the kind, the energy and initiative of our women would rather imply that it is the pursuit of villains by wives."

[See also United States, 1860–1929]

FURTHER READING

Bloomfield, Maxwell. "Mirror for Businessmen: Bronson Howard's Melodramas, 1870–1890." *Midcontinent American Studies Journal* 5 (Fall 1964): 38–49.

Felheim, Marvin. "Bronson Howard, 'Literary Attaché.'" *American Literary Realism* 2 (Summer 1969): 174–179.

Gottlieb, Lois C. "The Antibusiness Theme in Late Nineteenth Century American Drama." *The Quarterly Journal of Speech* 64 (1978): 415–426.

Mason, Jeffrey D. "Shenandoah (1889) and the Civil War." *Melodrama and the Myth of America*. Bloomington: Indiana Univ. Press, 1993. 155–86.

Ryan, Pat G. "The Horse Drama, With Supernumeraries: Bronson Howard's Semi-Historical Shenandoah." *Journal of American Drama and Theatre* 3 (Spring 1991): 42–69.

Wheeler, Andrew C. ["Nym Crinkle"]. Review of *Shenandoah*. *New York Dramatic Mirror* (September 14, 1889). In *Theatre U.S.A. 1665 to 1957*, ed. by Bernard Hewitt. New York: McGraw-Hill, 1959. 254–56.

Jeffrey D. Mason

SHEPARD, SAM (1943–)

The stories my characters tell are stories that are always unfinished, always imagistic—having to do with recalling experiences through a certain kind of vision. They're always fractured and fragmented and broken. I'd love to be able to tell a classic story, but it doesn't seem to be part of my nature.

—Sam Shepard, 1984

Sam Shepard is arguably the most influential and critically acclaimed playwright of his generation. Coming of age in the 1960s, he created a distinctive mode of experimental drama that displayed a unique fusion of language, myth, and stage action, and drew on the period's political and cultural energies to redefine what was "American" about American drama. His many awards include eleven *Village Voice* Obies for plays written between 1965 and 1982, and a special Obie for Sustained Achievement in 1980; the New York Drama Critics' Circle Award for *A Lie of the Mind* in 1985; the Pulitzer Prize for Drama for BURIED CHILD in 1979; the Golden Palm Award at the 1984 Cannes Film Festival for his screenplay for Wim Wenders's *Paris, Texas*; and the Gold Medal for Drama from the American Academy of Arts and Letters in 1992. His prolific writings include over fifty full-length and one-act plays, ten screenplays, as well as poetry and short stories. Shepard maintains a longstanding relationship with the Magic Theatre in San Francisco, and during its 1996–1997 season, New York's Signature Theatre devoted its entire season to staging seven of his works.

Born Samuel Shepard Rogers III on November 5, 1943, in Fort Sheridan, Illinois, to a military family, Shepard spent his youth constantly on the move, finally settling down for high school in Duarte, a small town in Southern California, where his father bought an avocado farm. He was nicknamed Steve to distinguish him from his father and was brought up Episcopalian in a strict home environment. His mother was a schoolteacher, and his father was a World War II fighter pilot who finished college through the GI Bill and became a Fulbright Scholar. And yet Shepard's "Old Man" also was an often violent alcoholic whose presence and absence would haunt much of Shepard's writing.

Young Steve held many jobs: he was a "hot walker" at the Santa Anita Race Track (walking horses after their morning exercise) as well as a sheepshearer, herdsman, and orange picker. As a member of the 4-H Club, he won awards at the Los Angeles County Fair. Shepard considered a career as a veterinarian and enrolled in a local community college, but soon drifted into theater, acting in campus productions of *Harvey* and THE SKIN OF OUR TEETH and writing his first play, *The Mildew*. According to Shepard, the greatest influence on his writing at this time was SAMUEL BECKETT's *WAITING FOR GODOT*.

Bored with school and anxious to escape his dysfunctional family, Shepard answered a newspaper ad to join a Christian drama group, the Bishop's Company Repertory Players, and spent almost a year performing a range of plays—from A. A. MILNE to CHRISTOPHER FRY—in churches across the country. "It really gave you a sense of the makeshift quality of theater and all the possibilities of doing it anywhere. That's what turned me on most of all," Shepard recalled; "I realized suddenly that anyone can make theater. . . . You just make it with a bunch of people. That's still why I like it" (Shewey, 1997). Although his name had been handed down to him through seven generations, Steve Rogers seized his acting debut as an opportunity to reinvent himself as Sam Shepard.

Arriving in New York City in 1963, Shepard roomed in the East Village with Charles Mingus, Jr. (son of the JAZZ bassist and composer), who guided him through the bohemian art scene and got him a job as a busboy at the Village Gate, where they regularly heard such jazz greats as Eric Dolphy and Nina Simone and such comedians as Woody Allen and Flip Wilson. Ralph Cook, a waiter at the Gate, started Theater Genesis at St. Mark's Church-in-the-Bowery, dedicated to producing new plays. Shepard's one-acts, *Cowboys* and *The Rock Garden*, were premiered there on October 16, 1964. *Village Voice* critic Michael Smith, an advocate for OFF-OFF-BROADWAY theater, was one of the first to recognize Shepard's talent and noted in his review of the one-acts that Shepard was "working with an intuitive approach to language and dramatic structure and moving into an area between ritual and NATURALISM, where character transcends psychology, fantasy breaks down literalism, and the patterns of ordinariness have their own lives" (October 22, 1964). The off-off-Broadway experimental theater movement of the 1960s was well underway, responding to the theatrical innovations of Beckett, ANTONIN ARTAUD, JEAN GENET, EUGÈNE IONESCO, and HAROLD PINTER, as well as the political theater of BERTOLT BRECHT. It nurtured interdisciplinary exploration among poets, actors, musicians, and artists and rejected the rules and values of traditional commercial theater. "Everything influence[d] me," Shepard remembered of that time, "Art wasn't a career or anything intellectual—it was a much more active, playful thing, a way to inhabit a life" (Kakutani, 1984).

During this first phase of his career, until the mid 1970s, Shepard wrote many short plays and had them regularly performed at La Mama, Caffé Cino, the Judson Poets' Theatre, and other Village venues, sometimes acting in or directing them. The predominant form of these plays was a COLLAGE of extended monologues, vivid images, and often ritualistic stage action. *Fourteen Hundred Thousand* (1966) is a good example: here Tom and Donna are building a bookcase for her 140,000 books, with help from Ed, Mom, and Pop. While Tom and Donna install the shelves, they argue and cover each other in paint; Mom and Pop recite passages about a great snowfall and plans for a linear city from the books they have been carrying. The others join in, and finally Tom, Donna, and Ed hum "White Christmas." The play is not held together by plot or character, but instead by a pattern of action, language, sound, and light changes, similar to Donna's method of collecting books: "Without concern for what they're about or what they mean to me and who wrote them when. Just in terms of size and shape and color." The real-time process of experiencing texture, form, rhythm, and image is the pleasure. As Michael Smith astutely commented at that time, "All Sam's plays use the stage to project images: they do not relate to the spectator by reflecting outside reality. . . . rather they relate to reality by operating directly on the spectator's minds and nerves" (Shewey, 1997).

From his early plays on, Shepard's writing has been influenced by Joseph Chaikin's experimental Open Theatre (1963–1973). Shepard contributed material to their productions of *Terminal*, *Nightwalk*, and *Re-Arrangements*. Chaikin and the Open Theatre made collage-like ensemble pieces of highly distilled images, music, sound, and movement. One of their techniques was the "transformation," by which actors abruptly switched personas or styles of acting from scene to scene or moment to moment, freed from the need for psychological motivation. "Instead of the idea of a whole character," Shepard wrote in his note to actors for *Angel City* (1976), "with logical motives behind his behavior into which the actor submerges himself, he should consider instead a fractured whole with bits and pieces of character flying off a central theme . . . more in terms of collage construction or jazz improvisation." The transformation became a major theme and structural device of Shepard's own work, in which characters are preoccupied with inventing roles and identities, and actors are required to shift quickly between realistic and highly stylized modes of performance. Chaikin and Shepard sustained their working relationship until Chaikin's death in 2003; they collaborated on several theater pieces including *Tongues* (1978), *Savage/Love* (1979), and *The War in Heaven* (1983) in which they both also appeared as performers.

Shepard's analogies to music and improvisation are apt, since the works of his second phase have been informally termed his "rock and roll plays," featuring titles reminiscent of rock groups of the period: these include *Melodrama Play* (1967), *Forensic and the Navigators* (1967), *Operation Sidewinder* (1970), *Mad Dog Blues* (1971), *The Unseen Hand* (1970), and the culmination of this period, *The Tooth of Crime* (1972). Shepard was a drummer and guitarist for two progressive bands, the Holy Modal Rounders and the Moray Eels, and he wrote songs and extended music riffs directly into many of his plays using the discursive, improvisational feeling of a jam session to inform their structure and pacing. The plays are populated by visionaries—shamans, cowboys, artists, criminals, rock stars, space aliens, and mythic figures (like MAE WEST or Paul Bunyan)—who seek psychic freedom but often end up being spiritually co-opted by a corrupt society. "You got the genius," the Gambler tells Cody in *Geography of a Horse Dreamer* (1974), but "somebody else got the power."

The subversive and liberating qualities of rock drove Shepard's language to a high pitch of visceral power. This is particularly true of *The Tooth of Crime*, in which a violent duel between the aging rock star Hoss and the upstart Crow is fought in torrents of invented language from the worlds of rock music, drugs, car racing, politics, Mafia wars, and old movies. By the late 1960s, Shepard's work was getting more mainstream exposure with productions of *La Turista* (1966) at London's Royal Court Theatre in 1969 and *Operation Sidewinder* at Lincoln Center's Vivian Beaumont Theatre in 1970. Although his rock music connections included collaborations with Patti Smith and Bob Dylan, Shepard was conscious of his commitment to a theater audience: after attending a revival concert by The Who, Shepard quipped, "It took me a long time to give up the fantasy that a play could ever have the same unanimous impact as a piece of music" (Shewey, 1997).

Although many of his characters pride themselves on being "escape artists," during Shepard's third playwriting phase he sought more directly to explore his own past, particularly his troubled relationship with his father. Unlike most of his previous work, the full-length plays of this period—including CURSE OF THE STARVING CLASS (1976), *Buried Child* (1978), TRUE WEST (1980), FOOL FOR LOVE (1982), and *A Lie of the Mind* (1985)—are written in a more realistic style. They are "family plays," located at the intersection of family bonds and cultural myths, and set against the backdrop of the American West. "I thought for years it was boring . . . to write about the family," Shepard concedes, "but the interesting thing about taking real blood relationships is that the more you start to investigate those things as external characters, the more you see they're also internal characters. The mythology has to come out of real life, not the other way round" (Freeman, 1985).

Although mining deeply disturbing elements of American family life, including incest and murder, these plays are infused with Shepard's mordant humor and arresting images. The characters are ravaged by loneliness, delusions, and guilt, and crave attention; the father figures are wizened and spent and marked by violence, while their children confront the past and seek an elusive sense of truth. "I drive on the freeway every day," says Austin in *True West*, "I swallow the smog. I watch the news in color. I shop in Safeway. . . . there's no such thing as the West anymore! It's a dead issue!" Set in Southern California or the Midwest, the plays are nostalgic for a West that promised the best of the American Dream, but Shepard's characters find themselves psychologically and spiritually adrift in a contemporary landscape of suburban developments and failing farms. The endings of the plays bring no closure or catharsis: Tilden confronts the family with the corpse of the dead infant in *Buried Child*, the rival brothers of *True West* are locked in a threatening stalemate, and the other plays end in images of fire. "The stories my characters tell are stories that are always unfinished, always imagistic," insisted Shepard, ". . . I'd love to be able to tell a classic story, but it doesn't seem to be part of my nature" (Kakutani, 1984).

In addition to his accomplishments as a writer, Shepard has acted in more than thirty films (including *Days of Heaven, Resurrection, Raggedy Man,* and *Fool for Love*) and garnered an Oscar nomination for his portrayal of Chuck Yeager in *The Right Stuff* (1983).

[*See also* United States, 1940–Present]

SELECT PLAYS: *The Rock Garden* (1964); *Chicago* (1965); *4-H Club* (1965); *Icarus' Mother* (1965); *Fourteen Hundred Thousand* (1966); *La Turista* (1966); *Red Cross* (1966); *Forensic and the Navigators* (1967); *Melodrama Play* (1967); *Operation Sidewinder* (1970); *The Unseen Hand* (1970); *Cowboy Mouth* (with Patti Smith, 1971); *The Tooth of Crime* (1972); *Action* (1974); *Geography of a Horse Dreamer* (1974); *Angel City* (1976); *Curse of the Starving Class* (1976); *Suicide in B-Flat* (1976); *Buried Child* (1978); *Tongues* (with Joseph Chaikin, 1978); *Savage/Love* (with Joseph Chaikin, 1979); *True West* (1980); *Fool for Love* (1982); *A Lie of the Mind* (1985); *States of Shock* (1991); *Simpatico* (1994); *The Late Henry Moss* (2001); *The God of Hell* (2005)

FURTHER READING

Bottoms, Stephen J. *The Theatre of Sam Shepard.* New York: Cambridge Univ. Press, 1998.

Dugdale, John, ed. *File on Shepard.* London: Methuen, 1989.

Freeman, Samuel G. "Sam Shepard's Mythic Vision of the Family." *New York Times* (December 1, 1985).

Kakutani, Michiko. "Myths, Dream, Realities—Sam Shepard's America." *New York Times* (January 29, 1984).

Marranca, Bonnie, ed. *American Dreams: The Imagination of Sam Shepard.* New York: Performing Arts Journal Publications, 1981.

Roundané, Matthew, ed. *The Cambridge Companion to Sam Shepard.* Cambridge: Cambridge Univ. Press, 2002.

Shewey, Don. *Sam Shepard.* New York: Da Capo Press, 1997.

Wilcox, Leonard, ed. *Rereading Shepard: Contemporary Critical Essays on the Plays of Sam Shepard.* New York: St. Martin's Press, 1993.

Mary Fleischer

SHEPPEY

Sheppey premiered at Wyndham's Theatre, London, in 1933 in a production directed by John Gielgud and starring Ralph Richardson as the eponymous hero. Based on an early short story, this play was rather different from W. SOMERSET MAUGHAM's previous stage successes. Dramaturgically, for example, it owed much to the morality play and its locus was the urban working class.

The play, which is set in contemporary London, centers on the barber John Miller, known to all as Sheppey because of his birth on the Isle of Sheppey in Kent, who works in a fashionable Jermyn Street barbershop. He is a jovial and engaging character, the heart of the business and the center of the life of the shop where the first act is set.

The plot—or more accurately the character study—really begins when Sheppey learns that he has won a sweepstake prize of £8,500. Immediately his place in the world shifts. The proprietor of the barbershop offers him a partnership that would secure his financial and social future as well as reward his skills and valuable role in the business. Instead, Sheppey decides to resign and give away the money to those poorer and more needy than himself. The decision leads to conflict with his family, with the medical establishment (who interpret his generosity as an indication of madness and wish to see him in an asylum), and even with those he tries to help, such as the thief and the aging whore Bessie Legros. After experiencing an extraordinary and disturbing vision of Death, who appears to both Sheppey and the audience in the guise of Bessie, Sheppey dies.

The play references the morality play, and Sheppey and his psychological journey are not to be read as a realistic drama or black COMEDY. His journey is mythic, and the figures he meets are personifications of values and positions, not fully realized characters. As characters rail and argue against Sheppey, the play considers whether a good man, or even a good act, can exist unpunished in modern society. Sheppey himself is an odd combination of an Everyman figure traversing an increasingly hostile world and a Christ-figure tempted and teased by demons and vice before he finally falls victim to a cruel and decidedly un-Christian world. This style of drama was to achieve some significant success in the decade to come through the writing of CHRISTOPHER FRY, T. S. ELIOT, and JAMES BRIDIE, but in 1933 it proved too much of a change of direction for Maugham's audiences, and it achieved only limited success.

Sheppey was Maugham's final play. Although he lived until 1966, his subsequent output was in prose form and he never again wrote drama.

[See also England, 1860–1940]

FURTHER READING

Cordell, Richard. *Somerset Maugham: A Biographical and Critical Study.* London: Heinemann, 1961.

Curtis, Anthony. *The Pattern of Somerset Maugham: A Critical Portrait.* London: Hamish Hamilton, 1974.

——. *Somerset Maugham: Writers and Their Work.* Windsor: Profile Books, 1982.

Morgan, Ted. *Somerset Maugham.* London: Jonathan Cape, 1980.

Rogal, Samuel J. *A William Somerset Maugham Encyclopedia.* Westport, Conn., and London: Greenwood Press, 1997.

Whitehead, John. *W. Somerset Maugham: The Critical Heritage.* London: Routledge, 1987.

Adrienne Scullion

SHERMAN, JASON (1962–)

Jason Sherman was one of the most highly regarded Canadian playwrights at the start of the 21st century. His plays combine biting wit and almost Borscht-belt humor with a keen interest in historical, political, and moral questions. Theatrically, Sherman's plays are striking for the way he makes actors shift characters and time frames (some bridging centuries) instantaneously.

Born on July 28, 1962, in Montreal, CANADA, to parents who emigrated from ENGLAND following World War II, Sherman graduated from York University. Starting out as an editor and journalist, he switched to playwriting in his mid-twenties and first achieved prominence in Canada with his third play, THE LEAGUE OF NATHANS (1992), which was co-produced by Orange Dog and Theatre Passe Muraille and won the Chalmers Award. This play about three Jewish-Canadian friends named Nathan and their changing relationships to Judaism and Israel over more than a decade introduced Sherman's dramatic alter ego, Nathan Abramowitz, who reappears in his controversial DOCUMENTARY-based READING HEBRON (Factory Theatre, 1996), based on the 1994 massacre of thirty Arabs, the subsequent Israeli inquest, and Sherman/Abramowicz's attempts to research the inquest.

Other notable plays include the political mystery/thriller *Three in the Back, Two in the Head* (1994), an indictment of covert actions by the UNITED STATES and a metaphor for the economic and political domination of Canada by its neighbor to the south, which won the Governor General's Award for Drama; *Patience* (1998), a contemporary retelling of the Job theme, which won another Chalmers Award; and *It's All True* (2001), about Orson Welles's 1937 production of MARC BLITZSTEIN's musical THE CRADLE WILL ROCK. These three plays premiered at the Tarragon Theatre, where Sherman was playwright-in-residence from 1992 to 1999, working frequently with director Richard Rose and DRAMATURG and director Brian Quirt.

Sherman is known for the collaborative nature of his playwriting. His preferred method is to work with director, actors, and dramaturg in workshops, starting either with a working draft of a new play or (as in the case of *Reading Hebron*) research material, discussing motivation and plot, rewriting or cutting-and-pasting on the spot.

A number of his plays have been performed in the United States, in New York as well as in regional theater, often to strong critical acclaim, but none has moved on to Broadway. Like many Canadian writers, he feels his chances for financial success have been limited by what he has described as a "double colonial status" of English-language Canadian drama in relationship to both Broadway and London. In later years he has worked on a wide range of adaptations. *An Acre of Time*, from a book by Phil Jenkins, is an ambitious effort to combine a surveyor's attempt to come to terms with the drowning death of her young daughter with an exploration of Canadian history. He has also adapted ANTON CHEKHOV and ARTHUR SCHNITZLER, and current projects include adaptations of *The Brothers Karamazov*, BERTOLT BRECHT's THE LIFE OF GALILEO, and S. Ansky's THE DYBBUK.

PLAYS: *A Place Like Pamela* (1991); *To Cry Is Not So* (1991); *The League of Nathans* (1992); *The Merchant of Showboat* (1993); *What the Russians Say* (1993); *Three in the Back, Two in the Head* (1994); *Reading Hebron* (1996); *The Retreat* (1996); *Patience* (1998); *It's All True* (1999); *An Acre of Time* (2001); *Reigen/La Ronde* (adaptation of Schnitzler, 2001); *Absolutely Chekhov: The Old Business* (2002); *Remnants (a fable)*, (2003); *The Message* (unproduced)

FURTHER READING

The Canadian Encyclopedia, www.thecanadianencyclopedia.com.

Encyclopedia of Canadian Theatre, www.canadiantheatre.com.

Sherman, Jason. *Jason Sherman: The Plays*. Toronto: Ediciones Boreal, 2001. (Contains *League of Nathans*; *Three in the Back, Two in the Head*; *The Retreat*; *Reading Hebron*; *Patience*; and *It's All True*. Introduction by Urjo Kareda.)

——. *An Acre of Time*. Toronto: Playwrights Union of Canada, 2001.

Walter Bilderback

SHERMAN, MARTIN (1938–)

Born in Philadelphia, Pennsylvania, on December 22, 1938, Martin Sherman, the gay playwright of Russian Jewish parentage, wrote many plays before his 1979 breakthrough, BENT, and his 1980 move to ENGLAND. After growing up in Camden, New Jersey, and studying at Boston University in the late 1950s, he acted in and contributed to the writing of many amateur plays. His first full-length, individually written play, produced when Sherman was the playwright-in-residence at Mills College, Oakland, California, was the 1963 rock musical *A Solitary Thing*. Music is often significant in his plays. Sherman's writing career began to flourish with his move to England.

Before 1980, Sherman was appreciated more in Britain than in the UNITED STATES. The theatrical fortunes of *Passing By* illustrate the difficulties that Sherman faced in the United States. Written in 1972, the play was not performed until 1974, and that in a New York production that irritated Sherman. The play is a serious intervention on behalf of the gay community, one that insists that partners in gay relationships can support one another with the same loving intensity that is possible in heterosexual families. Set in the New York studio apartment of the artistic Toby, *Passing By* dramatizes the improbable romance between Toby and the sportsmanlike Simon. Toby's plans to move to Paris are wrecked by Simon's declining health. The seriousness of the play was undermined by actors who, Sherman claims, cowardly camped up the homoeroticism of the piece, lest they become too identified with homosexuality.

Better revivals of *Passing By* were produced in the United States after Bent made Sherman's name, but Sherman noted that a 1975 London production, directed by Drew Griffiths and starring Simon Callow as Toby, dignified the uncompromising, serious homosexuality of his text. This Almost Free Theatre production convinced Sherman that his plays would be better received in England, and most of his later plays were premiered in England. Sherman is often self-effacingly humorous about the mixed fortunes of his plays in America. Remarking on a flat, 1976, OFF-BROADWAY production of *Cracks*, a "whodunit" parody in which Sherman infuriates the audience by not revealing the murderer's identity, Sherman noted "the stunning spectacular sound of silence. You could hear a pin drop. You shouldn't hear a pin drop in COMEDIES."

Since the enduring triumph of *Bent* and his move to England, Sherman's plays have attracted first-class actors. He is renowned for writing substantial roles for women as well as for gay male leads. For example, various productions of the 1985 play about the dancer Isadora Duncan, *When She Danced*, have been illuminated by the energies of, among others, Elizabeth Ashley, Sheila Gish, and Vanessa Redgrave. *Rose*, written in 1999, is a one-actress dramatization of the necessarily peripatetic life of the eighty-year-old Rose, a Jewish veteran of a traumatic century. Olympia Dukakis thrived in the role of Rose, attracting warm reviews for her Nancy Meckler–directed performances in

London and New York. Although Sherman spends a lot of time writing for the screen, he remains a potent force in both British and U.S. theatrical landscapes.

[See also Gay and Lesbian Drama]

PLAYS: *Passing By* (1974); *Cracks* (1975); *Soaps* (1975); *Rio Grande* (1976); *Bent* (1979); *Messiah* (1982); *When She Danced* (1985); *Madhouse in Goa* (1989); *Some Sunny Day, Rose* (1999); *The Boy from Oz* (2003)

FURTHER READING

Boles, William C. "Martin Sherman." In *The Dictionary of Literary Biography*, Vol. 228: *Twentieth-Century American Dramatists, Second Series*, ed. by Christopher J. Wheatley. Detroit: Gale, 2000. 230–240.

Cott, Thomas. "A Conversation with Martin Sherman." www.lct.org/calendar/platform_detail.cfm?id_event=90216083 (Accessed October 5, 2006).

Dace, Tish. "Martin Sherman." In *Contemporary American Dramatists*, ed. by K. A. Berney. Detroit: St. James Press, 1994. 533–536.

Hischak, Thomas S. *American Theatre: A Chronicle of Comedy and Drama, 1969–2000*. Oxford: Oxford Univ. Press, 2001.

Sherman, Martin. *Passing By*. In *Gay Plays*, ed. by Michael Wilcox. London: Methuen, 1984.

——. *Plays 1*. London: Methuen, 2003.

——. *Rose*. New York: Samuel French, 2002.

Sierz, Aleks, *In-Yer-Face Theatre: British Drama Today*. London: Faber and Faber, 2001. 157–168.

Kevin De Ornellas

SHERRIFF, ROBERT CEDRIC (1896–1975)

English playwright, screenwriter, and novelist Robert Cedric (R.C.) Sherriff is best known for the play JOURNEY'S END (1928), a boldly realistic play about front-line soldiers that drew on his own experiences as an officer in the trenches in World War I.

Sherriff—who was born on June 6, 1896, at Hampton Wick, Middlesex—served as a captain in the East Surrey Regiment during World War I and had a career in his father's insurance business before the remarkable and international success of his seventh play, *Journey's End*, allowed him to become a full-time writer.

His early work for the theater was produced in the amateur sector before the Stage Society produced a play that had been rejected by commercial managements across London. *Journey's End* was presented for just two performances—at the Apollo Theatre in a production directed and designed by James Whale and featuring Laurence Olivier in the lead role of Stanhope. The critical response was very positive. The influential critic James Agate gave over his entire week's radio broadcast to the play, and its reputation was secured. The success of the initial short run by the Stage Society led to the commercial production of *Journey's End* at the Savoy Theatre in 1929 (where it ran for more than 590 performances), a highly successful Broadway production in the same year (some 485 performances), and a film version also directed by Whale in 1930.

Although touched by a whiff of MELODRAMA, *Journey's End* captured a distinctive and, at the time, unfamiliar authenticity about the wartime experience of a generation of young men. Its clear-eyed and generally unsentimental approach to the horrors of the trenches marked it as something highly original, and it was an influential catalyst for a raft of new serious dramatic writing about the war.

Disappointed by the reception of his next play—the rather quaint and certainly overly naturalistic rustic COMEDY *Badger's Green* (1930)—and financially secure as a result of *Journey's End*, Sherriff studied briefly at New College, Oxford, before being invited by Whale to Hollywood to write the screenplay for *The Invisible Man* (1933). There followed a further brief term at Oxford before he returned to writing full time for both stage and screen.

Sherriff never again achieved the success of *Journey's End* but still maintained a high-profile career. He wrote well-crafted, popular thrillers, including *Miss Mabel* (1948) and *Home at Seven* (1950); the ghost story, *The White Carnation* (1953); historical dramas such as *St. Helena* (1935) on Napolean and *The Long Sunset* (1955) on Roman Britain. The last of these was first produced on radio but subsequently produced by Barry Jackson at the Birmingham Rep and Bernard Miles at the London Mermaid. Sherriff also produced assured and bankable screenplays for the British film industry, including the scripts for *Goodbye Mr. Chips* (1936), *The Four Feathers* (1939), *Odd Man Out* (1945), and *The Dam Busters* (1955). His plays, however, fell increasingly out of step with modern sensibilities, and his last drama, *A Shred of Evidence* (1960), was a critical disaster, despite a successful provincial tryout.

Journey's End had a short-lived Broadway production in 1939 but was revived in London in 1972 and again in 1998 with Samuel West in the leading role of Stanhope. Sherriff's autobiography, *No Leading Lady*, was published in 1968, and he died at Kingston Hospital, Kingston-upon-Thames, on November 13, 1975.

[See also England, 1860–1960]

SELECT PLAYS: *The Woods of Meadowside* (1922?); *Profit and Loss* (1923); *Cornlow-in-the-Downs* (1924?); *Mr. Bridie's Finger* (1926); *Journey's End* (1928); *Badger's Green* (1930); *Windfall* (1933); *Two Hearts Doubled* (1934); *St. Helena* (1935); *Miss Mabel* (1948); *Dark Evening* (1949); *Home at Seven* (1950); *The Kite* (1952); *The White Carnation* (1953); *The Long Sunset* (1955); *The Telescope* (1957); *A Shred of Evidence* (1960)

FURTHER READING

Barker, Clive, and Maggie B. Gale, eds. *British Theatre Between the Wars*. Cambridge: Cambridge Univ. Press, 2000.

Pellizzi, Camillo. *The English Drama: The Last Great Phase*. London: Macmillan, 1935.

Sherriff, R. C. *No Leading Lady: An Autobiography*. London: Gollancz, 1968.

Adrienne Scullion

SHERWOOD, ROBERT E. (1896–1955)

Born into a New York family of wealth and social position on April 4, 1896, Robert E. Sherwood was destined for a Harvard education, but his indifference to academic discipline prompted him to leave that university in 1917, when the United States entered World War I. Rejected by the U.S. Army because of his height (six feet seven inches), he enlisted in the Canadian Black Watch Battalion, to be gassed and wounded in France and discharged in early 1919. Back in New York he wrote for *Vanity Fair* (1919–1920), reviewed movies for *Life*, and associated with those clever writers and playwrights then holding forth at the Round Table in the Algonquin Hotel, who were to draw international attention to American drama.

At Harvard Sherwood enjoyed writing for the *Lampoon* and the *Hasty Pudding*, which produced his youthful effort *Barnum Was Right* (written with Samuel P. Sears). Throughout his life Sherwood confessed to a love for "hokum"—a love that would also be a constant annoyance because, as he also confessed, he always started his plays with a "big message and ended up with nothing but good entertainment." Building on his military service and his consequent hatred of war, he began his Broadway career with an ostensibly antiwar play, *The Road to Rome* (1928). Concerned with the "human equation," which Sherwood considered more beautiful than war, the play addressed the question: Why did Hannibal not destroy Rome when he had the opportunity? But it was not a pacifist argument that deterred Sherwood's Hannibal; it was a beautiful woman. In *Reunion in Vienna* (1932), Sherwood intended to satirize the conflict of science and humanity in the guise of a cuckolded and presumably intellectual psychiatrist, but audiences enjoyed only the rollicking, bed-rolling FARCE and its two excellent actors, Alfred Lunt and Lynn Fontanne.

In THE PETRIFIED FOREST (1935), Sherwood again attempted to express the despair of the vanishing intellectual, "Homo-Semi-Americanus—a specimen of the in-between age," but again created first-rate theatrical entertainment linking the gunman and the poet. Sherwood's antiwar sentiments resurfaced in IDIOT'S DELIGHT (1936), set in an Italian resort hotel where a song-and-dance troupe and various guests are stranded as war breaks out. The horror of conflict is expressed as a German scientist excoriates the "obscene maniacs" whom he feels he must join, while a Frenchman rages against the "League of Death"—the munition makers of the world. Yet Sherwood's romantic plot line again undercut his serious theme as falling bombs brought down the final curtain. Not until ABE LINCOLN IN ILLINOIS (1938) did Sherwood manage to avoid hokum in dramatizing that period of Lincoln's life leading to his presidential candidacy.

As Lincoln found 1861 a terrible year to be president, so was 1938 a time of anguish for Sherwood, who struggled with the contradictory virtues of national interest and pacifism. Finally, in *There Shall Be No Night* (1940), he demanded that people "stand up and fight for their freedom against forces of atavistic despo-

tism." A brilliant stage success, this play won a third Pulitzer Prize for Sherwood, both *Idiot's Delight* and *Abe Lincoln in Illinois* having received the award. For the student of theater as an instrument of propaganda, it demonstrates that Franklin Delano Roosevelt did well to select Sherwood as his speech writer and director of the overseas branch of the Office of War Information. Unfortunately, after this climactic period in Sherwood's life, he was unable to write successfully for the stage. Again and again he made the attempt: *The Rugged Path* (1945), *Miss Liberty* (with Irving Berlin, 1949), *Small War on Murray Hill* (1957). During the postwar years his best efforts were his historical study *Roosevelt and Hopkins* (1948), for which he received his fourth Pulitzer Prize, and the movie script for *The Best Years of Our Lives* (1946).

As a dramatist, Sherwood believed that the theater should perform two essentially equal functions: to entertain and to reveal reality. An extremely persuasive idealist, he tried to accomplish both and—because critics could not comprehend the serious purpose within the framework of his plays—inevitably failed. In only one play did he attempt to express his message unadorned by his glittering wit: choosing fifth century B.C. for *Acropolis* (1933), he pitted practical men of war against thoughtful men concerned with life and beauty. The play was not successful on stage, however, and Sherwood was never able to write a satisfactory revision. Trying to believe Socrates' confession "that there are no final answers," Sherwood realized that he was incapable of resting comfortably on paradox or ambiguity. Constantly frustrated in his attempt to dramatize his "human equation," he found the simple and direct platform he required only once in his life—in his writing of *There Shall Be No Night*. An honest man and a remarkably skillful writer of MELODRAMA, Sherwood constantly attempted to live up to the demands of both life and the theater.

[*See also* United States]

PLAYS: *A White Elephant* (1916); *Barnum Was Right* (1918); *The Love Nest* (from the story by Ring Lardner, 1927); *The Road to Rome* (1927); *The Queen's Husband* (1928); *This Is New York* (1930); *Waterloo Bridge* (1930); *Reunion in Vienna* (1931); *Acropolis* (1933); *The Petrified Forest* (1935); *Idiot's Delight* (1936); *Tovarich* (from the play by Jacques Deval, 1936); *Abe Lincoln in Illinois* (1938); *There Shall Be No Night* (1940); *The Rugged Path* (1945); *Miss Liberty* (music by Irving Berlin, 1949); *Second Threshold* (completion of a play by Philip Barry, 1951); *Small War on Murray Hill* (1957)

FURTHER READING

Brown, John Mason. *The Worlds of Robert E. Sherwood: Mirror to His Times, 1896–1939*. New York: Harper & Row, 1965.

———. *The Ordeal of a Playwright: Robert E. Sherwood and the Challenge of War*. New York: Harper & Row, 1970.

Meserve, Walter J. *Robert E. Sherwood: Reluctant Moralist*. New York: Western Publishing Co., 1970.

Sahu, N. S. Theatre of Protest and Anger: Studies in Dramatic Works of Maxwell Anderson and Robert E. Sherwood. Blaby Leicester, England: Advent Books, 1988.

Shuman, R. Baird. Robert E. Sherwood. New York: Twayne, 1964.

Walter J. Meserve

SHIMIZU KUNIO (1936–)

Shimizu Kunio, Japanese playwright, was born and raised in Niigata near the Sea of JAPAN and entered Waseda University in 1956 to study design. In Waseda's atmosphere, simmering with leftist initiatives and AVANT-GARDE theater experimentation, Shimizu was coaxed into his brother's small theater group and soon abandoned design. Like most of his contemporaries, he was swept up in the fervor surrounding the renewal of the U.S.–Japan Mutual Security Treaty in 1960, though political inclinations are hardly evident in his work. Unlike many other students, however, he actually graduated, completing his senior thesis on TENNESSEE WILLIAMS, whose dialogue he cites as influential in his plays. Shimizu has been versatile beyond theater, writing film scenarios (for the noted director Hani Susumu), television documentaries (on the 1963 Miike coal mine incident that inspired his play Those Days), and fiction (nominated for the Akutagawa Prize in 1988).

Shimizu's budding career took off in 1969 when Such a Serious Frivolity (Shinjō Afururu Keihakusa, 1968) was staged by Ninagawa Yukio at the Art Theatre Shinjuku Bunka (an important space also for Shimizu's contemporaries BETSUYAKU MINORU, TERAYAMA SHŪJI, and KARA JŪRŌ). Shimizu's collaboration with Ninagawa has been particularly fruitful. They founded Modern Man's Theatre (Gendaijin Gekijō) in 1969, and Ninagawa has directed many Shimizu plays. In 1976, Shimizu established his own company, Winter Tree Troupe (Mokutōsha), with his wife, the actress Matsumoto Noriko. His plays have garnered respected awards, including the Kishida Kunio Drama Prize in 1974 for When We Go Down That Heartless River (Bokura ga Hijō no Taiga o Kudaru Toki, 1972), the Kinokuniya Drama Award in 1976 for Night, Night of Youth That Raises My Hackles with Screams and Anger (Yoru yo Ore o Sakebi to Sakage de Mitasu Seishun no Yoru yo), and the Teatoro Theatre Award in 1990 with Little Brother! A Message to Sakamoto Ryōma from Otome, His Older Sister (Otōto yo–Ane, Otome kara Sakamoto Ryōma e no Dengon). He is one of the pivotal playwrights—and the most literary—to emerge from the counterculture of the 1960s.

Shimizu's work traffics in the gaps between reality and illusion, change and decay, present and past, or memory of the past, always with overtly realistic dialogue. He often refracts his principal concerns through the lenses of memory as affected by the endemic social disorientation of the era. The issue in Those Days (Ano Hitachi, 1966), for example, is how to deal with the amnesia afflicting coal miners after an accident—by re-creating the past exactly as it was, including the miners' relationships, or by abandoning the effort as impossible and starting anew? Re-creating the past is at best confusing—whose account is one to believe?—but ignoring it can leave one rootless. Shimizu regards identity as rooted in relationships, but recognizes that the unsettled nature of relationships in our helter-skelter age virtually precludes apprehending one's identity through them. That is the crux of The Sand of Youth, How Quickly (Seishun no Suna no Nan to Hayaku, 1980), for example, in which the characters are confused about whether and how they may be related. Two of them, Older Man and Man, might be the same person at different stages on life's way. Yet, caught in the jetlag wrought by blinding change, the best they can do is to conclude uncertainly that they are merely "passing strangers" with themselves. Relationships are up for grabs and identity remains elusive.

SELECT PLAYS: Tomorrow I'll Put Flowers There (Ashita Soko ni Hana o Sasō yo, 1960); Those Days (Ano Hitachi, 1966); Such a Serious Frivolity (Shinjō Afururu Keihakusa, 1968); When We Go Down That Heartless River (Bokura ga Hijō no Taiga o Kudaru Toki, 1972); By Illusion His Heart Pushed to Madness–Our Masakado (Maboroshi ni Kokoro mo Sozoro Kuruoshi no Warera Masakado, 1975); Night, Night of Youth That Raises My Hackles with Screams and Anger (Yoru yo Ore o Sakebi to Sakage de Mitasu Seishun no Yoru yo, 1976); The Dressing Room (Gakuya, 1977); Older Sister, Burning Like a Flame (Hi no yō ni Samishii Ane ga Ite, 1978); My Spirit Is the Sparkling Water (Waga Tamashii wa Kagayaku Mizu Nari, 1980); Sand of Youth, How Quickly (Seishun no Suna no Nan to Hayaku, 1980); Tango at the End of Winter (Tango–Fuyu no Owari ni, 1984); Dreams Departed, Orpheus (Yume Sarite, Orufe, 1986); Little Brother!—A Message to Sakamoto Ryōma from Otome, His Older Sister (Otōto yo–Ane, Otome kara Sakamoto Ryōma e no Dengon, 1990)

FURTHER READING

Ozasa, Yoshio. Contemporary Plays and Playwrights [Dōjidai Engeki to Gekisakkatachi]. Tokyo: Gekishobō, 1980.

Rolf, Robert T., and John K. Gillespie, tr. and eds. Alternative Japanese Drama: Ten Plays. Honolulu: Univ. of Hawaii Press, 1992.

Scholz-Cionca, Stanca, and Samuel L. Leiter, eds. Japanese Theatre and the International Stage. Leiden: Brill, 2001.

Senda, Akihiko. Gekiteki Runessansu–Gendai Engeki wa Kataru [Theatrical Renaissance: The Modern Theatre Speaks]. Tokyo: Riburopōto, 1983.

——. The Voyage of Contemporary Japanese Theatre. Tr. by J. Thomas Rimer. Honolulu: Univ. of Hawaii Press, 1997.

Shimizu Kunio. Tango in Winter. Adapt. by Peter Barnes. London: Amber Lane Plays, 1991.

John K. Gillespie

SHINGEKI

Shingeki (literally "new theater") refers to the international style of theatrical modernism and the movement to establish it in JAPAN. Shingeki shares with modern theaters everywhere a common repertory of plays; a set of conventions regarding ACTING, DIRECTING, and staging; and assumptions about the nature of reality that are essentially rationalistic, secular, and tragic.

Shingeki was born out of a rupture with the premodern theater tradition. During the late 19th century, numerous attempts were made to create a modern theater from traditional forms, especially *kabuki*. These attempts failed, however, because the basic characteristics of *kabuki*, including its use of male actors to play female roles (*onnagata*), its emphasis on song and dance, its plethora of supernatural characters, and its ahistorical understanding of time, were incompatible with rational, scientific modernism. The trauma of this rupture with tradition haunted and shaped the *shingeki* movement.

The transition to an authentically modern theater in Japan came after the Russo-Japanese War (1904–1905) with the discovery of the work of HENRIK IBSEN. Ibsen had been introduced to Japan in 1889 by the writer MORI ŌGAI, and a collection of eight of his social plays, including ENEMY OF THE PEOPLE and A DOLL'S HOUSE, had been published in 1901. It was not until 1907, however, when an Ibsen Society was founded, counting among its members many of the most prominent intellectuals of the day, that interest in Ibsen began in earnest. Japan had become an industrialized society with all its attendant problems, and Ibsen's social criticism, the intense inner struggles of his characters, the naturalness of his language, and the nontheatricality of his staging seemed supremely pertinent to the Japanese condition.

The first troupe to produce an Ibsen play was the Free Theater (Jiyū Gekijō), which premiered JOHN GABRIEL BORKMAN on November 27, 1909. Named after ANDRÉ ANTOINE's Théâtre Libre, the Free Theater was founded by OSANAI KAORU and the *kabuki* actor Ichikawa Sadanji II and sought to retrain professional actors like Sadanji in modern techniques. "Our purpose in establishing the Free Theater was none other," Osanai proclaimed to a thrilled audience on opening night. "It was in order to live!" (Soda, 1999). Creating a modern theater in Japan was not simply a technical matter; it was a life and death struggle to come to terms with the modern world.

The 1911 production of A DOLL'S HOUSE by the Literary Arts Society (Bungei Kyōkai) was, if anything, even more significant. Founded in 1906 by TSUBOUCHI SHŌYŌ, a prominent literary theorist, professor of English literature, and translator of William Shakespeare, and the young critic Shimamura Hōgetsu, the Literary Arts Society was reorganized in 1909, when Tsubouchi built a theater and acting school on the grounds of his Tokyo estate to train amateurs as modern theater actors. One of these amateurs, Matsui Sumako, caused a sensation with her portrayal of Nora in A Doll's House. Not only did her performance establish her as Japan's first modern actress, but it galvanized the modern Japanese women's movement and contributed to the foundation the same year of the Blue Stocking Society (Seitō), Japan's first feminist organization.

Many writers experimented writing Ibsen-style plays during the 1910s. These included well-known authors like Mushakōji Saneatsu, KIKUCHI KAN, YAMAMOTO YŪZŌ, and Tanizaki Junichirō. Not everyone was happy with the new realistic drama,

however. Tsubouchi disbanded the Literary Arts Society in 1913 because he could not accept the new direction; and writers like IZUMI KYŌKA wrote many popular plays infused with the supernatural.

The carnage of World War I and the shock of the Russian Revolution made the need to deal with historical reality and the inability of *kabuki* to do so clearer than ever. In Europe, AVANT-GARDE movements from EXPRESSIONISM to DADAISM and Constructivism to Proletarian theater emerged to modify orthodox REALISM and interpret the new situation. The Tsukiji Little Theatre (Tsukiji Shōgekijō) was the vehicle for these trends in Japan. Founded in 1924 by Osanai Kaoru and Hijikata Yoshi, the Tsukiji was both Japan's first theater building devoted exclusively to modern plays and a production company. Disillusioned by years of failed attempts to reconcile *kabuki* with modern theater, Osanai announced just prior to its opening that for the first two years the Tsukiji would produce only translated foreign works. "Above all, the enemy we must fight against . . . is the traditional theater, that is, *kabuki* drama," Osanai later told his actors. "We must first wage war on this tradition. We must destroy *kabuki* patterns, we must create completely separately our own theater art, new and free" (Osanai, 1975; emphasis in the original). Osanai's controversial decision alienated many of Japan's native playwrights, but by the time it staged its first Japanese work in March 1926, the Tsukiji had mounted forty-four productions of plays by a wide range of Western playwrights—including Ibsen, ANTON CHEKHOV, MAURICE MAETERLINCK, KAREL ČAPEK, GEORG KAISER, GEORGE BERNARD SHAW, AUGUST STRINDBERG, Roman Rolland, and LUIGI PIRANDELLO—and it trained an entire generation of modern theater actors, directors, playwrights, dramaturgs, and designers.

If there was any challenge to the Tsukiji's supremacy in Japan's modern theater, it came from the native playwrights it excluded. Foremost among these was Kishida Kunio, who had returned to Japan in 1923 after spending two years studying in Paris with JACQUES COPEAU and the Vieux Colombier company. With the publication of *Old Toys* (*Furui Omocha*) in 1924, Kishida emerged as the leader of the playwrights Osanai had so alienated. Over the next decade and a half, Kishida would write dozens of mostly one-act plays that were almost devoid of action and had no particular "message" but plumbed the psychology of the alienated modern Japanese. "One does not write a play in order 'to say something,'" Kishida famously asserted. "One 'says something' in order for there to be a play" (Abe, 1980). In 1932, Kishida founded *Playwriting* (*Gekisaku*) magazine and mentored younger playwrights, including TANAKA CHIKAO, Uchimura Naoya, and MORIMOTO KAORU. In 1937, along with Kubota Mantarō and Iwata Toyoo, Kishida founded the Literary Theatre (Bungakuza), which continues to perform today.

Following Osanai's untimely death at the age of forty-seven on December 25, 1928, the Tsukiji company dissolved into warring factions. The basic line of division was between politically engaged and literary groups. The politically oriented faction coalesced around Hijikata Yoshi; the designer, playwright, and director Murayama Tomoyoshi; and the playwright KUBO SAKAE. The literary faction centered on Kishida Kunio and *Playwriting* magazine.

Factionalism was exacerbated by the increasingly repressive political environment. The Asia-Pacific War began with the Manchurian Incident on September 18, 1931, and government repression of political dissent steadily increased through the decade until, in August 1940, the leaders of the left-wing theater movement, about a hundred people in all, were arrested *en masse* and their troupes ordered to disband. Because it resisted this pressure and realized a theater of social concern along the lines defined by Ibsen, Kubo Sakae's LAND OF VOLCANIC ASH (*Kazanbaichi*, 1937–1938), staged in 1938, is often cited as the pinnacle of Japanese playwriting in the prewar period. The monumental seven-act work with a cast of more than fifty characters and an expansive vision depicts the complex social and economic life of a contemporary agricultural village in Hokkaido, tying its local conditions into national and international trends. Although flawed, the play largely succeeds in realizing Kubo's ideal of achieving "a unification of scientific theory and poetic form" (Kubo, 1993).

From 1940 to 1942, Kishida Kunio collaborated with the war effort as head of the cultural section of the Imperial Rule Assistance Association, and during the conflict, many erstwhile left-wing *shingeki* artists promoted Japan's "holy war" as members of propagandistic mobile theater companies. In the postwar period, however, it was not these wartime activities that were remembered but *shingeki*'s prewar legacy of social concern and activism, and the movement's prestige soared to unprecedented heights. The movement reconstituted prewar alliances in three major troupes, the People's Art Theatre (Mingei), the Actors Theatre (Haiyūza), and Kishida's Literary Theatre. By the mid-1950s, the differences among these troupes were less significant than their commonalities, and together they constituted a theatrical establishment, enforcing a modernist orthodoxy.

KINOSHITA JUNJI, MISHIMA YUKIO, and ABE KŌBŌ were among the most important *shingeki* playwrights to emerge in the postwar period. Kinoshita inherited the realist legacy of Kubo Sakae, and his plays *Turbulent Times* (*Fūrō*, 1939–1947) and *Between God and Man* (*Kami to Hito to no Aida*, 1970) display this influence. Mishima, whose modern work was often performed by the Literary Theatre, also wrote for *kabuki* and NŌ. His *Modern Nō Plays* (*Kindai Nōgaku Shū*, 1956) recast the nō classics as one-act plays. His most renowned modern plays, MADAME DE SADE (*Sado Kōshaku Fujin*, 1965) and *My Friend Hitler* (*Waga Tomo Hittoraa*, 1968) explore the relationship between art and evil. Abe Kōbō, who worked with the Actors Theatre for many years, is best known for plays like FRIENDS (*Tomodachi*, 1967), which can be compared with the work of HAROLD PINTER.

After 1960, *shingeki* came under increasing pressure from a new postwar generation, who vehemently attacked it and created a post-modern, post-*shingeki* alternative theater popularly known as ANGURA. Today, the word *shingeki*, which once denoted the most advanced experimental theater, is often used pejoratively to describe a form that once flourished but is now quaint and out of date.

FURTHER READING

Abe Itaru. *Kindai Gekibungaku no Kenkyū* [Studies in Modern Dramatic Literature]. Tokyo: Ōfūsha, 1980.

Havens, Thomas R. H. *Artist and Patron in Postwar Japan: Dance, Music, Theater, and the Visual Arts, 1955–1980*. Princeton, N.J.: Princeton Univ. Press, 1982.

Horie-Webber, A. "Modernisation of the Japanese Theatre: The Shingeki Movement." *Modern Japan Aspects of History, Literature and Society*. Ed. by W. G. Beasley. Univ. of California Press, 1975.

Kano, Ayako. *Acting Like a Woman in Modern Japan: Theater, Gender, and Nationalism*. New York: St. Martin's Press, 2001.

Kishida, Kunio. *Five Plays by Kishida Kunio*. Expanded ed. Ed. by David G. Goodman. Cornell East Asia Papers 51. Ithaca, N.Y.: Cornell East Asia Program, 1995.

Kubo Sakae. *Land of Volcanic Ash*. Rev. ed. Tr. by David G. Goodman. Cornell East Asia Papers 40. Ithaca, N.Y.: Cornell East Asia Program, 1993.

Osanai Kaoru. *Osanai Kaoru Zenshū* [Complete Works of Osanai Kaoru]. Vol. 6. Kyoto: Rinsen Shoten, 1975.

Powell, Brian. *Japan's Modern Theatre: A Century of Continuity and Change*. London: Japan Library, 2002.

Rimer, J. Thomas. *Toward a Modern Japanese Theatre: Kishida Kunio*. Princeton, N.J.: Princeton Univ. Press, 1974.

Soda Hidehiko. *Osanai Kaoru to Nijisseiki Engeki* [Osanai Kaoru and Twentieth Century Theater]. Tokyo: Bensei Shuppan, 1999.

David G. Goodman

SHIN KABUKI

Shin kabuki simply means "new *kabuki*." These plays, mainly historical dramas, represent *kabuki*'s attempt to survive in the modern age as a living theater. Classical *kabuki* was characterized by numerous highly styled conventions of music, posing, movement, and voice. For historical plays, authenticity was not an issue.

Kabuki fans resisted attempts by the actor Ichikawa Danjūrū to vary the popular conventions by introducing some historical verisimilitude in the 1880s. His *katsureki-geki* (living history plays), written by KAWATAKE MOKUAMI, were the forerunners of *shin kabuki* plays in their abandonment of certain presentational methods. In the 1890s TSUBOUCHI SHŌYŌ and MORI ŌGAI established the right of drama to be discussed as literature; their efforts and those by others of like mind prepared the ground for *shin kabuki* proper.

Tsubouchi wrote what are considered the first *shin kabuki* plays, starting with *A Leaf of Paulownia* (*Kiri Hitoha*) in 1894–1895. Concerning the decline and fall of the house of Toyotomi at the beginning of the 17th century, this play had to wait ten years before it was first performed (in 1904), but from this time a range of playwrights (including Matsui Shōyō and Takayasa Gekkō) wrote regularly for kabuki.

Shin kabuki playwrights, writing for classically trained kabuki actors, had to decide how far to go in expressing their dramas through words (thereby broadening the spectrum of responsive spectators and intensifying the psychological shading). OKAMATO KIDŌ tried to avoid diluting the audience's classical theatrical experience. Hasegawa Shin let his wandering gambling heroes speak for themselves as they upheld their own code of honor and protected the weak. MAYAMA SEIKA, by contrast, sometimes immobilized kabuki actors' bodies with lengthy dialogue, but often he achieved a balance between stretching his actors and allowing them to do what they did best.

Okamoto and Mayama were still performed after the war, while other prewar playwrights such as Uno Nobuo and HŌJŌ HIDEJI continued writing for kabuki. In the 1950s the style of shin kabuki playwriting changed as novelists, inexperienced in the practical kabuki theater, wrote for spectators whose kabuki attendance was less regular than had been customary. Funahashi Seiichi wrote a dreamlike adaptation of the 11th-century classic Tale of Genji (Genji Monogatari, 1951–1954), and Osaragi Jirō's Nobunaga in His Young Days (Wakaki Hi no Nobunaga, 1953) was a sensitive portrait of the 16th-century warlord Oda Nobunaga. MISHIMA YUKIO, the famous novelist, had a number of plays performed by kabuki.

In the 1980s the kabuki actor Ichikawa Ennosuke III further advanced shin kabuki with his "super kabuki." Beginning in 1986 with Yamato Takeru, about a 4th-century Japanese hero, Ennosuke speeded the action and introduced recorded accompaniment (including contemporary music). These spectacles (seven so far), in which Ennosuke built on his previous work in restoring much of kabuki's former stage "business," have brought new audiences into kabuki theaters.

Shin kabuki in all its manifestations has demonstrated to kabuki actors that their traditional acting skills can be applied to a wide range of theater. At the beginning of the 21st century, kabuki actors are in many cases involved in a greater variety of performance genres than ever before.

[See also Japan]

FURTHER READING

Kagayama Naozō. Shin Kabuki no Sujimichi [The Method of Shin Kabuki]. Tokyo: Bokujisha, 1967.

Keene, Donald. Dawn to the West: Japanese Literature of the Modern Era: Poetry, Drama and Criticism. New York: Henry Holt, 1984.

Leiter, Samuel L. New Kabuki Encyclopedia: A Revised Adaptation of Kabuki Jiten. Westport, Conn.: Greenwood, 1997.

——, ed. A Kabuki Reader: History and Performance. Armonk, N.Y.: M. E. Sharpe, 2002.

Powell, Brian. Kabuki in Modern Japan: Mayama Seika and His Plays. Basingstoke: Macmillan, 1990.

——. Japan's Modern Theatre: A Century of Continuity and Change. London: Japan Library, 2002.

Brian Powell

SHINPA

JAPAN's first overture toward a modern theater, shinpa was created in the 1880s as a kind of AGITATION-PROPAGANDA theater for the Liberal Party by Sudo Sadanori and KAWAKAMI OTOJIRŌ. Early in its history, it was called sōshi shibai or shosei shibai, "radical theater" or "student theater," indicating its political and amateur tendencies. By the early 1890s, Kawakami's roughhousing, realistic style earned it the name shinpa, "new school," as opposed to the "old school" (kyūha) of kabuki, but Kawakami later preferred to call it "straight drama" (seigeki), in emulation of the European spoken theater that he and his wife, Kawakami Sadayakko, helped introduce to Japan.

Sudo Sadanori's student theater could never compete with Kawakami, but in 1891 another actor, Ii Yōhō, with backing from playwright and theater reformist Yoda Gakkai, founded a nonpolitical theater company, called Seibikan, whose style would rival and eventually overcome Kawakami's. The Seibikan and its successor the Seibidan maintained the use of female impersonators (onnagata) and kabuki-style offstage music, eventually ensuring that shinpa settled into a form closer to kabuki than to modern theater. But by the early 1900s, it had surpassed kabuki in topicality and was riding a crest of popular and critical success.

Shinpa won large audiences with dramatizations of melodramatic fiction by such popular writers as Ozaki Kōyō, IZUMI KYŌKA, and Tokutomi Roka, attracting first-rate playwrights. It commissioned MORI ŌGAI's first play, The Jeweled Comb Box and the Two Urashimas (Tamakushige futari Urashima, 1902), and both OSANAI KAORU and MAYAMA SEIKA served several years as shinpa dramatists. But even during its heyday, critics called shinpa to task for pandering to popular sentiment, its MELODRAMA, amateurish acting, and lack of a critical engagement with social and political issues. The European plays it staged were adaptations rather than authentic translations, and experiments in mixing live theater with film (rensageki), by actor/directors like Inoue Masao (1881–1950) were dismissed by some as "the REALISM of train whistles." (Inoue was one of the many shinpa actors who starred in early Japanese film.) By 1910, the foundations of shingeki, a truly modern, Westernized theater, were laid down by reformists like TSUBOUCHI SHŌYŌ and Osanai Kaoru.

But great performances by onnagata like Kitamura Rokurō and Hanayagi Shōtarō and actresses like Mizutani Yaeko ensured shinpa a popular following long after it had ceased to be the cutting edge of theatrical innovation. Its scripts remained strong well into the 1930s, thanks in large part to the work of playwrights like Kawaguchi Matsutarō, KUBOTA MANTARŌ, MAFUNE YUTAKA, YAMAMOTO YŪZŌ, and MIYOSHI JŪRŌ.

After 1945, the various smaller *shinpa* troupes amalgamated into Gekidan Shinpa (the *shinpa* company). Faced with the loss by the 1970s of a great generation of actors, *shinpa* maintained its appeal with guest appearances by *kabuki* stars Kataoka Niza-emon XV and Bando Tamasaburō V, but today relies on a repertory of plays mostly from before 1945. It celebrated its one hundredth anniversary in 1988 with sold-out houses, indicating that there is still a popular following for melodrama, and continues to reinvent itself by inviting guest directors like Kanō Yukikazu from the neo-*kabuki* company Hanagumi Shibai.

[*See also* Shingeki; Shin Kabuki]

FURTHER READING

Hagii Kōzō. *Shinpa no Gei* [The Art of Shinpa]. Tokyo: Tōkyō Shoseki, 1984.

Kano, Ayako. *Acting Like a Woman in Modern Japan: Theater, Gender, and Nationalism.* New York: Palgrave, 2001.

Keene, Donald. *Dawn to the West: Japanese Literature in the Modern Era: Poetry, Drama, Criticism.* New York: Henry Holt, 1984.

Komiya Toyotaka. *Life and Culture in the Meiji Era.* Vol 2: Music and Drama. Tr. and adapt. by Donald Keene and Edward Seidensticker. Tokyo: Obunsha, 1956.

Powell, Brian. *Japan's Modern Theatre: A Century of Continuity and Change.* London: Japan Library, 2002.

Yanagi Eijirō. *Shinpa no Rokujūnen* [Sixty Years of Shinpa]. Tokyo: Kawade Shobō, 1948.

M. Cody Poulton

SHI WU GUAN, KINGQU See FIFTEEN STRINGS OF CASH

SHŌJO KAMEN See THE VIRGIN'S MASK

SHORE ACRES

> Them free thinkers is hard to get shut of. They're dangerous to young folks' religion.
> —Josiah Blake, Act 1

Opening as *Shore Acres Subdivision* at Chicago's McVicker's Theatre on May 23, 1892, and retitled *Uncle Nat* after the first week, the play barely covered expenses in its initial run. However, later productions as *Shore Acres*, including a five-year tour, made playwright JAMES A. HERNE a millionaire. Begun in 1888 as *The Hawthornes*, the play actually predates MARGARET FLEMING and illustrates Herne's increasing interest in social issues. Revisions, however, relied on sentimentality, melodramatic plot devices, and external realism for effect and audience appeal.

Confrontation between youth and tradition join a conflict between urban and rural values to drive the romantic COMEDY. The script indirectly engages feminism and Herne's suspicion of business and repressive religious fundamentalism, but those concerns remain secondary to the domestic and romantic ele-

ments. Central to the play's popularity, Herne's creation of Uncle Nathaniel Barry also updated the traditional Yankee character.

Martin Barry, a traditional patriarchal tyrant, forbids his independently minded daughter Helen to see the free-thinking young doctor, Sam Warren, because he intends to marry her to Josiah Blake, the local businessman who has persuaded him to risk his farm on a vacation property boom. Martin mortgages the property to Blake, who plans to divide it into speculative vacation lots. The family's consequent forced relocation to Boston will include Martin and Nathaniel's mother, who will be disinterred and reburied there. Helen refuses Blake's proposal and leaves for the West with Warren. A storm rises as the couple's boat sails, and the enraged Martin tries to stop Nathaniel from lighting the farm's lighthouse to warn the boat from foundering on the rocks. Nathaniel subdues his younger brother and struggles, near collapse, to climb the tower stairs. The scene shifts to reveal the storm-tossed passenger boat nearing the rocks; in the distance, a light gradually moves up the lighthouse windows, and the beacon alerts the vessel in time.

The final act brings the now-married couple back at the moment Martin learns his speculation has failed and ruined him. The investment company has collapsed, forcing the now impoverished Blake to demand payment or foreclosure. Reconciliation with the couple, motivated by their child, seems to pose a hazardous solution when Warren offers to cover the debt by mortgaging their home. Nathaniel's long-overdue soldier's pension solves the problem, and he pays the debt on condition that Martin sign the farm over to his wife. Following the general resolution, Herne leaves Nathaniel on stage alone for a silent prolonged scene, in which he secures the house for the night, then exits upstairs, satisfied.

Herne altered the script radically to meet the producer's condition for its premier. The original lacked Nathaniel's last-minute rescue, and the upbeat revisions clashed with Herne's growing commitment to REALISM. Consequently, Herne's original indictment of land speculation and bigotry shifted to a romantic comedy that focused on Nathaniel's stylized rural character. The realistic actions in the final scene, though clearly sentimental, produced a highly unconventional ending that producers resisted. Herne restored the scene for the Boston production, drawing audience approval and mixed critical response.

[*See also* United States, 1860–1929]

FURTHER READING

Cather, Willa. "James A. Herne's *Shore Acres*." In *The World and the Parish: Willa Cather's Articles and Reviews, 1893–1902*, Vol. 1, ed. by William M. Curtin. Lincoln: Univ. of Nebraska Press. 469–471.

Durham, Weldon B. "James A. Herne." In *American Playwrights, 1880–1945*, ed. by William W. Demastes. Westport, Conn.: Greenwood, 1995. 145–155.

Eich, Louis M. "The Stage Yankee." *Quarterly Journal of Speech* 27, no. 1 (February 1941): 16–25.

Jones, Betty Jean. "James A. Herne: The Rise of American Stage Realism." Ph.D. diss., Univ. of Wisconsin, Madison, 1983.

McConachie, Bruce A. "Herne, *Shore Acres* and the Family in the Tradition of the Irish-American Theater." *Theatre Studies* 30 (1984): 17–28.

Ron West

SHUZENJI MONOGATARI See TALE OF THE SHUZENJI

SHVARTS, YEVGENY LVOVICH (1896–1958)

Yevgeny Lvovich Shvarts was a Russian playwright, screenwriter, prose writer, and diarist based in Leningrad whose dramatic satires, written in the style of the fairy tale or fantasy story, were among the most popular of the post-Stalin period in the Soviet Union. After spending a short time acting, he began working in the 1920s in the field of children's literature as an author, an editor, and occasionally performer of his own sketches and poems. Shvarts's first produced play, *Underwood* (*Undervud*, 1929), combined fairy-tale and realistic characters and established the pattern for most of his subsequent works, the best of which were clever, daring spoofs of tyrants and the docile subjects who help them remain in power. In *A Common Miracle* (*Obyknovennoye chudo*, 1954), a magician salvages a young couple's love and turns the king into a bird so he will fly away. Shvarts had notable success writing plays for puppet theater in the 1930s and 1940s.

Censorship problems dogged Shvarts from the beginning (*Underwood* was banned after a short run) and rarely let up thereafter. His major plays—*The Naked King* (*Goly Korol'*), *The Shadow* (*Ten'*), and *The Dragon* (*Drakon*), written in 1934, 1940, and 1944, respectively—had extended success only in the 1960s. The minor *One Night* (*Odna noch'*), uncharacteristically a realistic account of people enduring the Leningrad Blockade, was written in 1942 but staged only in 1975. Films based on Shvarts's scripts were made in the 1930s and 1940s, but the peak of his popularity in cinema occurred between the late 1950s and the late 1970s, when the number of films made from his plays and scripts was so high that his literary legacy had a major influence on that period's style of political satire. Despite a boom in publications of his works around the time that the Soviet Union collapsed in 1991, interest declined somewhat in Shvarts's drama when the need declined in Russia to express daring truths in veiled, indirect ways—commonly called "Aesopian language."

The Naked King, in which a swineherd and a princess salvage their love by humiliating her royal father when he plans to give her in marriage to a neighboring ruler, and *The Shadow*, about a kind scholar whose shadow begins living its own evil life, drew on Hans Christian Andersen fairy stories for character and plot. *The Dragon*, about a monster that assumes human form and has despotically ruled a town for four hundred years, was derived in part from the Arthurian legend of Sir Lancelot. Written during the rise and reign of Nazism in GERMANY, these plays go beyond Soviet satire. Shvarts's drama, though full of fantasy, was grounded in a philosophical belief that the nature of oppression, which always conjoins the tyrant and the tyrannized, is universal. Some commentators find links between Shvarts and European strains of metaphorical and/or EPIC drama as expressed in the works of JEAN GIRAUDOUX, BERTOLT BRECHT, JEAN ANOUILH, FRIEDRICH DÜRRENMATT, HEINER MÜLLER, and others.

[See also Russia and the Soviet Union]

SELECT PLAYS: *On Contemporary Youth* (*O sovremennoi molodyozhi*, not produced, 1927); *Three and a Half* (*Tri s poltinoi*, with Veniamin Kaverin, not produced, 1929); *Underwood* (*Undervud*, 1929); *Island 5-K* (*Ostrov 5-K*, 1932); *Nonsense* (*Pustyaki*, 1932); *The Treasure* (*Klad*, 1933); *The Adventures of Hohenstaufen* (*Pokhozhdeniya Gogenshtaufena*, 1934); *The Naked King* (*Goly Korol'*, 1934; produced 1960); *A Ceremonial Conference* (*Torzhestvennoye zasedaniye*, 1935); *Brother and Sister* (*Brat i sestra*, 1936); *Little Red Riding Hood and the Gray Wolf* (*Krasnaya shapochka i sery volk*, 1938); *Puppet City* (*Kukol'ny gorod*, 1939); *The Snow Queen* (*Snezhnaya koroleva*, 1939); *The Shadow* (*Ten'*, banned 1940, revived 1960); *The Tale of Lost Time* (*Skazka o poteryannom vremeni*, 1940); *Beneath the Limetrees of Berlin* (*Pod lipami Berlina*, with Mikhail Zoshchenko, 1941); *The Distant Land* (*Dalyokii krai*, 1942); *One Night* (*Odna noch'*, 1942, produced 1975); *The Dragon* (*Drakon*, banned 1944, revived 1962); *The Tale of the Courageous Soldier*, also known as *Tsar Vodokrut* (*Skazka o khrabrom soldate*, 1946); *Ivan the Saintly Workman* (*Ivan chestnoi rabotnik*, not produced, 1947); *100 Friends*, also known as *Magicians* (*Sto druzei*, aka *Volshebniki*, 1947); *A Common Miracle* (*Obyknovennoye chudo*, 1954); *Two Maples* (*Dva klyona*, 1954); *The Tale of the Newlyweds* (*Povest' o molodykh suprugakh*, 1957)

FURTHER READING

Golovchiner, Valentina. *Epicheskii teatr Yevgeniya Shvartsa* [The Epic Theater of Yevgeny Shvarts]. Tomsk: Tomsk Univ., 1992.

Loseff, Lev. *On the Benificence of Censorship: Aesopian Language in Modern Russian Literature*. Tr. by Jane Bobko. Munich: Otto Sagner in Kommission, 1984.

Metcalf, Amanda J. *Evgenii Shvarts and His Fairy-Tales for Adults*. Birmingham Slavonic Monographs, 8. 1979.

Segel, Harold B. *Twentieth-Century Russian Drama from Gorky to the Present*. Rev. ed. New York: Performing Arts Journal Publications, 1993.

Shvarts, Yevgeny Lvovich. *The Naked King, The Shadow and The Dragon*. Tr. with an intro. by Elisaveta Fen. London: Boyars, 1976.

Shvartz, E. *Three Plays*. Intr. and notes by Avril Pyman. New York: Pergamon Press. 1972.

John Freedman

SIGURJONSSON, JOHANN (1880–1919)

Johann Sigurjonsson was born on June 19, 1880, at Laxamýri, ICELAND, and died on August 31, 1919, in Copenhagen, DENMARK.

After years of veterinary studies in Copenhagen, Sigurjonsson quit the university to become a full-time writer, a poet and a playwright. Since few people master Icelandic, he decided to write simultaneously in Danish and Icelandic to gain a wider audience.

He made his debut with the realistic drama *Dr. Rung*, a play about a scientist who risks his own life while experimenting with a new medicine he has discovered. The form is conventional, but the language is not especially realistic. In fact, Sigurjonsson, a fine poet in his own right, had been influenced by the neo-romantic movement that emerged in literature as a revolt against the down-to-earth REALISM, and perhaps made a stronger mark in poetry.

His poetic sensibility was all the more obvious in his next play, *The Farmer at Hraun* (*Bondinn a Hrauni*) first performed in Reykjavik in 1908, and a few years later in Denmark. Again a moral conflict is at the core of the action, a problem well known to the Icelanders when the migration from the old farms to the villages took place. An earthquake symbolizes the strong emotions of the characters.

Strong dramatic emotion is also characteristic of his next drama, *Eyvind of the Mountains* (*Fjalla-Eyvindur*), which had its first performance in Reykjavik in 1911 and subsequently was produced in some twenty cities in Europe and North America. Again his setting is Iceland, this time based on a well-known tale of outlaws in the 18th century; the approach, however, is modern, with strong psychological conflicts carrying the action. The first act confronts love and moral conscience (the lover turns out to be a thief); the second act, love and money and social recognition. In the third act, the heroine sacrifices the love for her child for the love of the outlaw she has followed to the mountains, and in the last act, love is confronted with yet another basic instinct, hunger. The language is poetic, somewhat in the vein of the Irishmen J. M. SYNGE and W. B. YEATS. The play was filmed by the Swede Victor Sjöström in 1917–1918. No less dramatic passion characterizes Sigurjonsson's next play, *The Wish* (*Galdra-Loftur*), which also traveled widely, including Paris, after its first production in Reykjavik in 1914. This powerful portrayal of a youngster with the ambition of trying to master the powers of darkness in order to be able to do some undefined good deeds is bustling with scenic life, even if some critics have claimed that its construction leaves something to be desired.

Sigurjonsson's last play, *The Liar* (*Mörður Valgarðsson*), was based on episodes from Njals saga and never found the same response with the audience, not least the Icelanders who prefer the original.

Sigurjonsson died young, but the expectations he awakened in Europe are evident in the following quotation of the French critic Leon Pineau in *La Revue Scandinave* 1914: "Now the name Sigurjonsson is associated with Ibsen, Björnson and Strindberg; one day perhaps it will surpass them all."

PLAYS: *Dr. Rung* (published 1905, staged 1940); *The Farm at Hraun* (*Bondinn á Hrauni, Gaarden Hraun*, 1908); *Eivind of the Mountains* (*Fjalla-Eyvindur*, published under the Danish title *Bjerg-Ejvind og harts Hustru*, 1911); *The Wish* (*Galdra-Loftur*, published under the Danish title *Onsket*, 1914); *The Liar* (*Mörður Valgarðsson*, published and staged under the Danish title *Lögneren*, 1917)

FURTHER READING

Einarsson, Sveinn, *Íslensk leiklist II* [Icelandic Theater II]. Reykjavík: Hið íslenska bókmenntafélag, 1996.

Jónsson, Jón Viðar. *Kaktusblómið og nóttin* [Cactus Blossom and Night]. Akureyri: Hólar, 2004.

Toldberg, Helge. *Johann Sigurjonsson*. Copenhagen: Rasmus Fischers Forlag, 1965.

Sveinn Einarsson

THE SILVER TASSIE

Although famously rejected by W. B. YEATS and the Abbey Theatre in 1928, SEAN O'CASEY's *The Silver Tassie* has established itself as one of the great antiwar plays of the 20th century. Its successful transformation into an opera by Mark Antony Turnage in 2000 would appear to acknowledge its continuing appositeness in modern times. The title comes from a love song by Robert Burns.

The plot concerns a footballer, Harry Heegan, who wins the cup (the eponymous Silver Tassie) for his local team before being shipped to the front in France during the 1914–1918 war. There he is seriously wounded. When he returns in a wheelchair and an operation fails to cure his paralysis, his world falls apart. He loses his girlfriend Jessie to his friend Barney, who saved his life on the battlefield. At the victory dance in the football club, soured and angry, Harry gets into a fight with Barney and crushes the Silver Tassie beneath the wheels of his chair as a symbol of his despair. He and his comrade Teddy, blinded in the war, are sent home while the dance (symbolizing life) goes on without them.

The play was controversial because of the style O'Casey adopts in act 2, which is set in the war. The play shifts from the familiar REALISM of act 1 into EXPRESSIONISM to show as in a dream the dehumanization of war. As O'Casey put it in the fifth book of his autobiography, *Rose and Crown* (1949), he intended to "show the garlanded horror of war . . . in a new way." Instead of plot there is atmosphere; instead of characters there are types and men in masses; instead of realistic dialogue there is poetic chant and a rough kind of poetry. Also in act 2 is a deliberate use of blasphemy to underline the blasphemy of war itself. Harry is not visibly present in this act, although he may be deemed to be part of the mass of exhausted soldiers. The remaining two acts of the play are in a different style. Yeats's main objection to the play was that it lacked artistic unity; GEORGE BERNARD SHAW disagreed vehemently with Yeats and saw the *Tassie* as "a hell of a play," intensifying from act to act.

A second objection Yeats launched at the play was that it did not reflect O'Casey's direct experience in the way his earlier plays had done: he had not personally known the horrors of the 1914–1918 war and so wrote propaganda. In the controversy that arose with Yeats about the play, O'Casey declared that an artist does not necessarily have to experience first-hand what he writes about. The imagination can penetrate minds, hearts, and conditions without direct knowledge and thereby create from secondary sources. This was the principle on which O'Casey based his later plays, which were written in exile in ENGLAND about an IRELAND with which he no longer had direct contact.

In 1935, after they were reconciled, Yeats accepted *Tassie* for production at the Abbey. As Ireland was then undergoing a rapid shift to conservatism and virtually to a church-dominated state, the play met fierce opposition from Roman Catholics and was taken off after a week. This fresh controversy convinced O'Casey that there was no future in a changing Ireland, and he never again offered a new play to the Abbey. But the *Tassie*, though it will always be a challenging text, endures as a powerful representation of "the war to end all wars."

FURTHER READING

Kleiman, Carol. *Sean O'Casey's Bridge of Vision: Four Essays on Structure and Perspective.* Toronto: Univ. of Toronto Press, 1982. 21–48.

Kosok, Heinz. *O'Casey the Dramatist.* Gerrards Cross: Colin Smythe; Totowa, N.J.: Barnes & Noble, 1985. 94–113.

Krause, David. *Sean O'Casey: The Man and His Work.* Rev. ed. New York: Macmillan, 1975. 94–131.

Schrank, Bernice. "Reception, Close Reading and Re-Production: The Case of Sean O'Casey's *The Silver Tassie.*" *Canadian Journal of Irish Studies* 26, no. 2 (Fall 2000)/27, no. 1 (Spring 2001): 34–48.

Scrimgeour, James. *Sean O'Casey.* Boston: Twayne, 1978. 111–128.

Christopher Murray

SIMARD, ANDRE (1945–)

Gymnast, acrobatic choreographer, aerial visionary—such is the reputation of Canadian theater artist Andre Simard. Born in Montréal, Québec, in 1945, Simard has spent the past thirty years perfecting his craft and earning a place as one of the world's most innovative and important practitioners of the "circus arts." The key to his success has been a career-spanning practice in three distinct fields: fine arts, elite sports, and circus.

Simard pursued studies at the Graphic Arts Institute in Montreal while training to compete in the 1972 Munich Olympic Games. He previously competed at several World Championships before being named Senior Canadian Champion (1969, 1970, 1971) and Senior Pan-American Champion (1971). His work has appeared in the productions of Cirque du Soleil, the National Circus School in Montreal, and his own company, Studio de Creation les Gens d'R.

Simard's distinctive style is characterized by constant, fluid motion, evocative of ballet. His role is that of a technician, assessing his performers and guiding them toward making impossible acts of aerial movement seem simple. The key to this approach is a focus on "biomechanics"—for Simard, the principles of muscular action and mechanics, as used in advanced sports training, are as essential as aesthetics to the creation of acrobatic works of art.

Simard has trained prospective gymnasts and acrobats in a number of roles, coaching and teaching students both for competition (as Head Coach of the men's section for the Canadian National Gymnastics team from 1981 to 1987) and for the circus (at schools in FRANCE as well as at the National Theatre School in Montreal and Cirque du Soleil). In 1989, Simard coached the Mouvance trapeze duo (Hélène Turcotte and Luc Martin) to a gold medal at the Festival Mondial du Cirque de Demain in Paris, the first Canadians to have won.

In 1995, he founded Les gens d'R with the goal of experimenting with artistic expression through aerial movement. The company combines theater, music, circus, dance, and the plastic arts to create a kind of acrobatic dance, and performs at festivals and theaters around the world. Their most recent project is the innovative showcase piece, *Échos* (2002), now on an international tour. Since 1997, Simard has served as Aerial Designer and Research and Development Coordinator of aerial techniques for the Cirque du Soleil productions of *La Nouba* (1998), *O* (1998), *Dralion* (1999), *Varekai* (2002), and *Zumanity* (2004).

A wizard of technique, Simard is responsible for several innovative practices considered revolutionary in the contemporary circus arts. In 1994, Simard created Aerial Silk acrobatics, working with French contortionist Isabelle Vaudelle. In Aerial Silk, trapeze artists move through the air suspended by or swinging from lengths of fabric. The effect is fluid and kinetic, the performers seeming to soar through space. In 1989, working with the National Circus School, he developed a security system for trapezes and other aerial swings, that are now considered indispensable in any high-flying act.

[*See also* Canada]

SELECT PLAYS: *Mouvance* (1989); *Ephemeral* (*Éphémère*, 1995); *Trails of the Nazca* (*Les pistes de Nazca*, 1995); *The Nave* (*La Nef*, 1996); *Echoes* (*Échos*, 2001)

FURTHER READING

Babinski, Tony. *Cirque Du Soleil: 20 Years Under the Sun—An Authorized History.* New York: Harry N. Abrams, 2004.

Bartlett, Roger. *Introduction to Sports Biomechanics.* London: E&FN Spon, 1997.

Vial, Veronique. *Varekai: Cirque du Soleil.* New York: Harry N. Abrams, 2003.

——. *O: Cirque du Soleil at Bellagio.* New York: PowerHouse Books, 2001.

Wangh, Stephen. *An Acrobat of the Heart: A Physical Approach to Acting Inspired by the Work of Jerzy Grotowski.* New York: Vintage Books, 2000.

Daniel Goldberg

SIMON, NEIL (1927–)

I think any comment that you make about the way people live can be serious. That is what I try to do. I do it through the medium of comedy, but I don't do it just to evoke a laugh from an audience. I do it also to show them how absurdly we all live our lives. To me, that is the point that I try to make in all the works.

—Neil Simon, 1969

One of the most prolific and successful playwrights of the American theater, Neil Simon practically defined COMEDY on Broadway in the latter half of the 20th century. The author of twenty-eight produced plays, five musicals, and twenty-three films, his legacy continues to influence comedy writers in all genres.

Simon was born in New York City on July 4, 1927. He early acquired the nickname "Doc" and started writing comedy with his older brother Danny after World War II, first for CBS radio and then for Phil Silvers, Sid Caesar, and other stars of the Golden Age of live television—a world he would look back on in his 1993 play *Laughter on the 23rd Floor.* The brothers also began writing material for the theater, including the review *New Faces of 1956.*

It was not until 1961 that Simon had a full-length play of his own produced—*Come Blow Your Horn,* a semiautobiographical story of two adult brothers trying to escape the yoke of their overweening parents. While critical opinion of its dramatic substance varied, uproarious audience response to Simon's sharp one-liners and build-up of farcical tensions was already palpable. The same proved true with *Barefoot in the Park* (1963), featuring newcomers Robert Redford and Elizabeth Ashley as bickering young newlyweds. Buoyed by these early successes, Simon followed with an impressive succession of hit comedies well into the next decade: THE ODD COUPLE (1965), which won a first Tony award; *The Last of the Red Hot Lovers* (1969); *The Prisoner of Second Avenue* (1971); and *The Sunshine Boys* (1972). The humor in all these shows derived from Simon's highly obsessive, usually cantankerous, characters being thrown into extreme conflicts with each other amid the tumult of New York City life.

Meanwhile, a more serious side of his work was beginning to emerge, as well—first in the opening act of the mini-trilogy *Plaza Suite* (1968) and then in *The Gingerbread Lady* (1970), about an alcoholic celebrity. *God's Favorite* (1974), *Chapter Two* (1977), and *I Ought to Be in Pictures* (1980) featured somewhat autobiographical writer-protagonists suffering through romantic and family relationships. Although these plays were not devoid of wit, the laughs were now based more on character than on FARCE, and audiences generally supported Simon's transition to a more sober brand of comedy-drama. Some experiments— an adaptation of ANTON CHEKHOV stories, *The Good Doctor*

(1973), and the Sholem Alechem–inspired tale *Fools* (1981)— were less popular. Critics increasingly berated Simon for abandoning his gift for light comedy in favor of misguided concepts and increasingly sentimental indulgences.

He rebounded, though, with his popular autobiographical trilogy—*Brighton Beach Memoirs* (1983), *Biloxi Blues* (1985), and *Broadway Bound* (1986)—which traced the lovably neurotic Eugene Morris Jerome and his family through the Depression, World War II, and after. These plays were hailed as Simon's most satisfying mix of comedy and sentiment. Similar praise soon followed (as did another Tony and a Pulitzer Prize) for the bittersweet period drama *Lost in Yonkers* (1991).

The 1990s confronted Simon with a changing theater landscape. The dark sex comedy *Jake's Women,* a fantasy play in which he stretched beyond REALISM for the first time, closed out of town—a first for a Simon play—before finally coming to Broadway in a heavily revised 1992 production. In 1995 *London Suite* became the first of his plays not to open on Broadway after its producers decided on a safer, less expensive OFF-BROADWAY run. Even on Broadway the middling reception for *The Dinner Party* (2000), *45 Seconds from Broadway* (2001), and especially the nostalgic drama *Proposals* (1997) indicated Simon was still more appreciated for laughs than for meaning, and further, that even his sense of humor was no longer the box office gold it used to be.

Wavering critical reception notwithstanding, honors have certainly not eluded Simon, who has been awarded a total of four Tony Awards (including one for lifetime achievement), the Kennedy Center Honor in 1995, and even a Broadway theater named after him in 1983. As a LIBRETTIST he wrote the book for such Broadway musicals as *Sweet Charity* (1966), *Promises, Promises* (1969), and a 1993 adaptation of his 1977 film, *The Goodbye Girl.*

The sheer longevity of Simon's career is a testament to the underlying craft of his work and to his continued willingness to challenge himself in both form and content. Yet a new direction was signaled in *Rose's Dilemma* (2003), loosely based on the historical relationship between Dashiell Hammet and LILLIAN HELLMAN. A famously obsessive tinkerer and perfectionist whose first memoir was appropriately entitled *Rewrites,* Simon is a writer who has always taken comedy very seriously.

[*See also* United States, 1940–Present]

PLAYS: *Catch a Star!* (co-writer, 1955); *New Faces of 1956* (co-writer, 1956); *Come Blow Your Horn* (1961); *Little Me* (1962); *Barefoot in the Park* (1963); *The Odd Couple* (1965); *Sweet Charity* (1966); *The Star-Spangled Girl* (1966); *Plaza Suite* (1968); *Promises, Promises* (1968); *The Last of the Red-Hot Lovers* (1969); *The Gingerbread Lady* (1970); *The Prisoner of Second Avenue* (1971); *The Sunshine Boys* (1972); *The Good Doctor* (1973); *God's Favorite* (1974); *California Suite* (1976); *Chapter Two* (1977); *They're Playing Our Song* (1979); *I Ought to Be in Pictures* (1980); *Fools* (1981); *Brighton Beach Memoirs* (1983); *Biloxi Blues* (1985); *The Odd Couple* (female version, 1985); *Broadway Bound* (1986); *Rumors* (1988); *Lost in Yonkers* (1991); *Jake's Women* (1992); *The Goodbye Girl*

(1993); *Laughter on the 23rd Floor* (1993); *London Suite* (1995); *Proposals* (1997); *Hotel Suite* (2000); *The Dinner Party* (2000); *45 Seconds from Broadway* (2001); *Oscar and Felix* (2002); *Rose's Dilemma* (2003)

FURTHER READING

Bloom, Harold, ed. *Neil Simon*. Philadelphia: Chelsea House Publishers, 2002.

Konas, Gary, ed. *Neil Simon: A Casebook*. New York: Garland Publishers, 1997.

Koprince, Susan Fehrenbacher. *Understanding Neil Simon*. Columbia: Univ. of South Carolina Press, 2002.

Simon, Neil. *The Play Goes On: A Memoir*. New York: Simon & Schuster, 1999.

———. *Rewrites: A Memoir*. New York: Simon & Schuster, 1996.

Garrett Eisler

SINGAPORE

The small, densely populated island nation of Singapore, situated at the tip of the Malaysian peninsula, possesses a wide range of theater traditions that reflect its ethnic, cultural, and linguistic diversity. Colonized by the British until 1959, Singaporeans today use English as the language of business, government, and education. The country has a sizable ethnic Chinese majority (77.2 percent), followed by Malays (14.1 percent), Indians (7.4 percent), and Eurasians.

Before the post-independence government began encouraging the widespread use of English, Singaporeans typically supported theater in their respective mother tongues, which include English, Malay, the Indian languages of Tamil and Malayalam, and numerous Chinese dialects. Among Chinese Singaporeans the many forms of *jingju* (known as Chinese Opera in the West) in the dialects of Hokkien, Teochew, and Cantonese were heavily patronized, though their future today is less secure. Also popular was the street theater of amateur troupes performing on portable, raised stages, a tradition that today is largely limited to the eighth month of the Chinese lunar calendar.

Popular among ethnic Malays in the colonial era was the musical form of *bangsawan*, which featured stereotypical characters and elaborate sets and costumes. Indian Singaporeans supported a range of dance-drama traditions, and in the postwar era the South Indian form of *bharata natyam* has become increasingly popular.

During the late 1960s and early 1970s as Singapore's ruling People's Action Party (PAP) began to place the country on a firm capitalist footing, many in the Chinese-speaking community sought to use theater to question the country's rush toward modernization and urbanization. Playwright and practitioner KUO PAO KUN (1939–2002) was the most prominent artist to use theater in this fashion, resulting in his detention by the government from 1976 to 1980, effectively quashing the tradition of political protest theater. During the 1960s, English-language theater struggled to find an authentically Singaporean voice as the first post-independence generation of playwrights continued to rely on British models of dramatic construction and language use. A few early pioneers of English-language drama persisted, the most notable being Lim Chor Pee and Goh Poh Seng, both of whom penned relatively naturalistic plays set against the backdrop of contemporary Singapore. The 1980 production of Robert Yeo's political play *One Year Back Home*, though considerably less polemical than Kuo's Chinese-language work, marked a significant milestone in that it tackled contemporary political and social issues using an English that moved a step closer to the rhythms of Singaporean speech.

During the 1980s a number of new companies were created by young theater artists who were committed to using the medium to entertain, challenge, and provide a window into Singaporean life. Under the leadership of Artistic Director ONG KENG SEN, TheatreWorks (founded in 1985) expanded the audience for English-language theater by offering a number of popular Singapore-themed musicals by lyricist Michael Chiang and composer Dick Lee. The company provided a model for greater professionalism in theater and contributed to raising the overall standards of Singaporean theater. Director Alvin Tan and playwright Haresh Sharma used their company, The Necessary Stage, to create and stage plays dealing with concrete social concerns. The Practice Performing Arts School, which Kuo Pao Kun had established in 1965 with his wife, choreographer Goh Lay Kuan, formed its own company in 1986, and in 2001 created a three-year full-time professional training program for actors, the Theatre Training and Research Programme (TTRP). Other groups—such as Action Theatre, HI! Theatre, Singapore Repertory Theatre (SRT), and the late William Teo's influential Asia-in-Theatre Research Centre—are just a few of the many that have made significant contributions to the field.

Malay-language theater companies include Teater Kami, Teater Ekamatra, and the Teater Artistik, as well as the group Sriwana, which presents traditional Malay performance forms. The Indian companies Agni Koothu, Kairalee Kala Nilayam, and the Ravindran Drama Group reflect the concerns of that community. A number of companies produce work in Mandarin, either occasionally or exclusively, including Page to Stage Studio under Artistic Director Lim Jen Erh, Goh Boon Teck's Toy Factory Ensemble, and Ang Gey Pin's Theatre OX.

From the mid-1980s to the mid-1990s, the number of plays that were able to find producing organizations, venues, and potential audiences greatly increased. Kuo Pao Kun's dramatic monologues THE COFFIN IS TOO BIG FOR THE HOLE (1984) and *No Parking on Odd Days* (1986) set a high standard for theatrical writing while reaching both English- and Mandarin-speaking audiences. The colorful character of Emily, the proud and iron-fisted matriarch in STELLA KON's monologue *Emily of Emerald Hill* (Singapore premiere, 1985), has become the country's best-known dramatic persona, and the play continues to be Singapore's most frequently produced work. Other noteworthy playwrights include Ovidia Yu, Tan Tarn How, Russell Heng Hiang-Khng, Haresh Sharma, Eleanor Wong, and Malaysian LEOW PUAY TIN. Though Singaporean theater continues to be subject to censorship, the boundaries of expression have expanded considerably since the 1980s.

Increasingly Singaporean theater has toured overseas, primarily to international arts festivals. TheatreWorks' Artistic Director Ong Keng Sen has been a significant presence in the export of a performance practice that involves bringing together Asian artists from different cultures and traditions to create new work based loosely on a dramatic text or theme. Among the more significant touring works created in this manner are *Lear* (1997) and *Desdemona* (2000).

Partly as a consequence of this shift away from the text, opportunities for Singaporean playwrights to have their work professionally produced have declined. TheatreWorks' Singapore Writer's Lab, which nurtured playwrights in the early 1990s, has ceased functioning, and Stella Kon, as well as many of the promising younger playwrights in the generation that followed her, have stopped writing for the theater. Compounding the loss is the death in 2001 of Kuo Pao Kun, the country's most respected theater practitioner and playwright. The career of Singaporean-born Chay Yew, who has built a highly successful playwriting career largely in the UNITED STATES, reinforces the perception that Singapore is a difficult country in which to produce plays that deal with challenging themes. Two of his finest and most critically acclaimed works, *Porcelain* (1993) and *A Language of Their Own* (1995), deal unflinchingly with gay sexuality and have not been produced in Singapore.

FURTHER READING

Jit, Krishen. "Modern Theatre in Singapore: A Preliminary Survey." *Tenggara* 23 (1989): 201–226.

Krishnan, Sanjay, ed. *9 Lives: 10 Years of Singapore Theatre*. Singapore: The Necessary Stage, 1997.

Leverett, James. "Model City/Model Art." *Yale Theater* 32, no. 2 (Summer 2002): 70–75.

Lim Chor Pee. "Is Drama Non-Existent in Singapore?" *Temasek* 1 (January 1964): 42–44.

Oon, Clarissa. *Theatre Life!: A History of English-Language Theatre in Singapore through the Straits Times (1958–2000)*. Singapore: Singapore Press Holdings, 2001.

Peterson, William. *Theatre and the Politics of Culture in Contemporary Singapore*. Middletown, Conn.: Wesleyan Univ. Press, 2001.

William Peterson

SIRCAR, BADAL (1925–)

Badal Sircar (formal name, Sudhindra Sircar) was born in 1925 and was educated as an engineer, specializing in urban planning. But after working for a while as a town planner in ENGLAND and Nigeria, Sircar eventually found his true voca-

tion in the theater as playwright and director, administrator, and performer.

And Indrojit (EBONG INDROJIT, 1962) was Sircar's first play, and it remains his most famous. While working in Nigeria, however, Sircar wrote a number of plays including *Remaining History* (*Baki Itihas*, 1965), *Delirium* (*Pralap*, 1966), *Thirtieth Century* (*Tringsha Shatabdi*, 1966), and *Mad Horse* (*Pagla Ghora*, 1967). His work focused on the pointlessness of human existence and the responsibility of the middle class in a world of increasing violence, inhumanity, and conformity.

In 1967 Sircar formed his own theater company, Shatabdi. During the first five years of its existence, Shatabdi produced a number of his plays, but then the group became inactive. This prompted Sircar to question the limitations of the proscenium stage: the way it creates a passive observer who can see from only one angle, the concomitant push toward REALISM, and the need for expensive sets, lights, costumes, and make-up. More importantly, however, Sircar began to question the social limitations of a theater that depended on ticket sales, and therefore on a middle-class audience. He began to develop *anganmancha* (literally, courtyard stage) or Third Theatre, in which he combined the thematic sophistication of socially committed urban theater with the direct communication of rural performance forms such as *jatra*. In 1969 Sircar reorganized Shatabdi, and they began performing in found spaces both indoors and outdoors, taking theater to the people.

He discovered that his Third Theatre required a different dramaturgical structure, a different approach to acting, and allowed for a different relationship between production and participant. Sircar himself describes his goals: "I have been trying to break through this system of 'story' and 'characters' and in my plays 'theme' and 'types' respectively began to replace them gradually. Working on the Third Theatre I began discovering new possibilities of using . . . words addressed directly to spectators more than 'dialogue' between stage characters, using physical 'acting' more than 'language.' . . . Third Theatre liberated from the bondages of stage, auditorium, lighting, sets, props, . . . is very much feasible. We found that theatrical experience rather than narration of a story is more relevant to the Third Theatre for it affords much more directness in communication than the conventional proscenium."

Shatabdi first made use of the arena stage with their productions of *Sagina Mahato* (based on the life of a Nepali trade union leader) and *Spartacus* (based on Howard Fast's play) in the early seventies. Since then, under the continuing leadership of Badal Sircar, Shatabdi has gone on to present some of the most important Bengali plays in the Third Theatre mode, including *Michhil* (The Procession, 1974) and *Bhoma* (1976), which was written and produced collectively with members of a village.

[See also India]

SELECT PLAYS: *And Indrojit* (*Ebong Indrojit*, 1962); *The Other History* (*Baki Itihaas*, 1964); *Remaining History* (*Baki Itihas*, 1965); *Delirium* (*Pralap*, 1966); *Thirtieth Century* (*Tringsha Shatabdi*, 1966); *Mad Horse* (*Pagla Ghora*, 1967); *Procession* (*Michhil*, 1972)

FURTHER READING

Bharucha, Rustom. *Rehearsals of a Revolution: The Political Theater of Bengal.* Honolulu: Univ. of Hawaii Press. 1983.

Crowe, Brian, and Chris Banfield. *An Introduction to Post-Colonial Theatre.* Cambridge: Cambridge Univ. Press, 1996.

Pandey, Sudhakar, and Freya Barua, eds. *New Directions in Indian Drama.* Delhi: Prestige Books, 1994.

Sircar, Badal. *The Third Theatre.* Calcutta: (self-published), 1978.

——. *The Changing Language of Theatre.* Delhi: Indian Council for Cultural Relations, ca. 1982.

——. *Three Modern Indian Plays.* Delhi: Oxford Univ. Press, 1989.

——. *Voyages in the Theatre: Shri Ram Memorial Lectures, 1992.* Calcutta: BIT Blits, 1992.

——. *Ebong Indrajit,* tr. by Girish Karnad. In *Modern Indian Drama: An Anthology,* ed. by G. P. Deshpande. Delhi: Sahitya Akademi, 2000.

Sudipto Chatterjee

SISTERS IN LAW

Sisters in Law (*Les belles soeurs*), written by MICHEL TREMBLAY in 1968, features a cast of fifteen women of all ages and personalities. The group of women includes sisters, sisters-in-law, friends, and neighbors from the Fabre neighborhood (Tremblay's own neighborhood) in Montréal, CANADA. The plot is more concerned with character development than action; however, the main action in the play revolves around the event of Germaine Lauzon's windfall of a million stamps that need to be glued into books so that she can trade the stamps for new household items featured in a catalog.

The stamps become the source of envy for some of the women, who are as underprivileged as Germaine but not so lucky. While the women stick the stamps into the stamp booklets, they discuss their lives, loves, relationships, hopes, children, money, jealousies, church, pregnancy, family, and bingo. Germaine does not realize that her stamps are being pocketed by the women until near the end of the play. Her discovery of this thievery and betrayal initiates a brawl, and the stamps are scattered over the stage. This play offers little in the way of redemption, but instead a glimpse of the toughness and roughness, alienation and isolation of working-class people at the time.

When *Sisters in Law* premiered in 1968, the play stirred controversy and discussion on a grand scale. Hailed as the first true Québecois play, *Sisters in Law* drew attention to working-class women in a working-class neighborhood in Montréal. They speak in a working-class idiom of French, called *joual*, liberally dotted with scatological and liturgical curse words. The play's language inspired some critics to hotly condemn the play, and

others to praise the arrival of a true theater of Québec that did not apologize for its characters' identity, nor try to imitate continental French. While *joual* is technically a dialect of standard French, in the theater it is not simply a dialect; the use of *joual* is a savvy political move on Tremblay's part and reveals the playwright's own desire to see Québec dramas portray the real Québec, not the fictionalized, folkoric, authorized identity frequently imitated and imposed upon it by colonial ideals. Indeed, Tremblay even refused translation rights of the play until after the Separatists' Parti Québécois took power in the province in 1976, fearing that until then, the threat to Québecois culture was too real to allow other languages to appropriate the plays.

In addition to the language controversy, the characters themselves drew attention because they speak about working-class interests, which drew criticism that the play celebrated vulgarity, profanity, mediocrity, and a cultural decline (*joual* also features many Anglicisms); alternatively, detractors of the play saw the entry of *joual* upon the stage as a sign of defeat and alienation. Yet, others saw the play as a victory and as a revolutionary voice that celebrates the real Québec and displays an identity finally freed from colonial influence.

Even if the play's language suggests an assertion of cultural identity, the play itself enacts fatigue and alienation. The phrase *maudite vie plate* (damn senseless life) is the dominant theme of the play, revealing the emotional and spiritual starvation of the working-class women in this neighborhood, as does their lack of solidarity as a community.

FURTHER READING

Moss, Jane. "Québécois Theatre: Michel Tremblay and Marie Laberge." *Theatre Research International* 21, no. 3 (1996): 196–207.

Oddipov, Helene. "French Variation and the Teaching of Québec Literature: A Linguistic Guide to a *litterature joualisante.*" *The French Review* 67, no. 6 (1994): 944–953.

Usmiani, Renate. *Michel Tremblay.* Vancouver: Douglas and McIntyre, 1982.

Jolene Armstrong

SISTER XIANGLIN

The Yue opera (Yueju) play *Sister Xianglin* (also translated as *Xianglin's Wife*) (*Xianglin sao*), an adaptation of the great left-wing writer Lu Xun's short story "The New Year's Sacrifice" ("Zhufu," 1924), premiered in May 1946 in the Mingxing Theater in Shanghai. The play was scripted and directed by Nan Wei (1921–1989), and noted actress Yuan Xuefen (1922–) played the title role.

The play tells a tragic story of an unfortunate peasant woman who has married twice and been widowed twice. Both of her husbands died in sickness and poverty, and wolves consumed her only son. Local superstitions have convinced her that she is to be blamed for her loved ones' misfortunes, owing to her bad karma from previous lives. A fellow servant at the household of Master Lu, where she works as a domestic helper, tells her that, after she dies, the King of the Underworld will cut her into two halves so that she may serve her two husbands in the other world. Villagers scorn her as bringing bad luck to whatever she might touch. For the same reason, Master Lu eventually fires her. Wandering in the streets with a beggar's stick in her hand, she asks people passing by, "Tell me, does the soul exist after a person dies?" No one seems able to answer her question, and people try to avoid her. Cold and hungry, she perishes in the streets one New Year's eve.

Lu Xun's work had rarely been adapted for stage, owing both to its political sensitivity and to the difficulties of translating Lu Xun's artistry, its nuance and rich meaning, into stage performance. This was the first time since the mid-1930s that a story by Lu Xun was put on stage, at a time when Lu Xun's work had become even more politically sensitive than ever on the eve of an all-out civil war between the Nationalist Party and the Communist Party. Because of this, a lowbrow theater as Yue opera for the first time in its history attracted attention from the leftist cultural elite. Under the invitation of Lu Xun's widow Xu Guangping, and out of their respect for the master Lu Xun, a group of left-wing intellectuals including TIAN HAN, HONG SHEN, Huang Zuolin, Shi Dongshan, Fei Mu, Zhang Junxiang, LI JIANWU, Ding Cong, and Hu Feng attended the show. Hardly expecting that a "vulgar" local opera was able to do justice to Lu Xun's work, they were nonetheless impressed by the performance. Tian Han, for example, profusely praised the performance: "This is from real life, humanistic, accurate, and convincing" (Xuesheng juwu bu, 1946: p. 186).

The play also caught the attention of the Nationalist Government and eventually made Yue opera a site of political contention between the two political rivals during the ensuing Civil War (1946–1949). From the conflict emerged an alliance between the Yue opera actresses and left-wing intellectuals: These intellectuals helped make the actresses media icons, while Yue opera in turn provided these men access to the realm of popular entertainment and thereby to a large population characterized by relatively low literacy, political apathy, and indifference to intellectual discourse.

Yuan Xuefen and her colleagues at the Shanghai Yue Opera House reworked and restaged the play in 1962 and again in 1977, making it a classic in the Yue opera repertoire. In 1978, the play was filmed in a joint project by the Shanghai Film Studio and the Hong Kong Phoenix Studio.

[See also China]

FURTHER READING

Jiang, Jin. "Women and Public Culture: Poetics and Politics of Women's Yue Opera in Republican Shanghai, 1930s–1940s." Ph.D. diss. Stanford Univ., 1998.

Shanghai Yueju Yuan, comp. Shuoxi lunyi: Shanghai Yueju Yuan jianyuan sanshi zhounian wutai yishu wenxuan [Discussing the arts of the theater: Selected essays on the art of the stage on the thirtieth anniversary of the founding of Shanghai Yue Opera Institute]. Shanghai: Shanghai Yueju Yuan, 1985.

Xuesheng juwu bu, comp. Xuesheng jinian kan [Memorial issue of Xuesheng Company]. Shanghai: Xuesheng juwu bu, 1946.

Yuan Xuefen. "Chong yan Xianglin sao" [Restaging Sister Xianglin]. In Xianglin Sao [Sister Xianglin]. [1960 version] Yueju [Yue opera script]. Original story by Lu Xun. Adapted by Wu Sheng, Zhuang Zhi, Yuan Xuefen, and Zhang Guifeng. Shanghai: Shanghai wenyi chubanshe, 1978.

Zhang Lihui and Gao Yilong. Yuan Xuefen de yishu daolu [The artistic path of Yuan Xuefen]. Shanghai: Shanghai wenyi chubanshe, 1984.

Jin Jiang

SITI COMPANY

ANNE BOGART and SUZUKI TADASHI founded the Saratoga International Theatre Institute (now simply known as SITI) in 1992 to explore international collaboration in contemporary theater in the United States. Originally envisioned as a summer institute, SITI has grown into a year-round program based in New York City with a summer season in Sarasota Springs, New York. The company is a collaborative, ensemble-based company whose three ongoing investigations include the creation of new work, the training of young theater artists, and international collaboration. Of more than twenty company productions, some of their most noted include Small Lives/Big Dreams (1994), Culture of Desire (1997), Cabin Pressure (1999), and the trilogy on American artists Bob (1998), Room (2000), and Score (2002).

As a collaborative company, SITI creates new works, usually conceived and directed by Bogart, the artistic director, and performed by the SITI Company. For the creation of the trilogy Bob, Room, and Score, based on the lives of ROBERT WILSON, Virginia Woolf, and Leonard Bernstein, respectively, the company looked to these artists' original words. Bogart pulled together text from interviews, letters, recorded interviews, and so forth. The raw text, after being explored in workshops by the actors, was crafted into a script by Irish writer Jocelyn Clarke. During rehearsal, all members of the company including actors and designers contribute to the creation of the performance, producing a truly company-created show.

Noted for their strong physical style, the SITI Company utilizes two unique training systems—Viewpoints and the Suzuki Method. Founded by choreographer Mary Overlie, Six Viewpoints is a system for exploring time and space in postmodern dance. Bogart adapted Overlie's work for actors. Viewpoints enhances an ensemble's ability to work together spontaneously and intuitively. As a communication and improvisational tool, Viewpoints allows the SITI Company to create bold, highly theatrical work in a short period of time. The Suzuki Method comes from the company's cofounder, internationally acclaimed director Suzuki Tadashi, and his work with the Suzuki Company of Toga (SCOT). The Suzuki Method emphasizes strength and seeks to enhance the actor's ability to be fully present emotionally and physically in each moment of a performance. The combination of these two training systems makes the SITI Company unique in their approach to actor training and to the creation of new work, where the physicality of the production assumes as important a role as the text.

Fully committed to training young theater artists, members of the SITI Company are faculty members at The Julliard School and Columbia University in New York City, where they teach sessions in the fall and spring. They also offer an intensive summer workshop and teach master classes at universities around the country.

SITI has performed and taught around the country and world at places such as The Wexner Center for the Arts (Columbus, Ohio); The Walker Arts Center (Minneapolis, Minnesota); The Miami Light Project (Florida); UCLA Performing Arts Center; Portland Institute of Contemporary Art (Oregon); The Hebbel Theater (Berlin); Theater Archa (Prague); The Beckett Theater (Ireland); and international theater festivals in Paris, Holland, Poland, and Edinburgh.

[*See also* United States, 1960–Present]

FURTHER READING

Bogart, Anne. *A Director Prepares: Seven Essays on Art and Theatre.* London: Routledge, 2001.

Dixon, Michael Bigelow, and Joel A. Smith, eds. *Anne Bogart: Viewpoints.* Lyme, N.H.: Smith and Kraus, 1995.

Suzuki Tadashi. *The Way of Acting: The Theatre Writings of Tadashi Suzuki.* Tr. by J. Thomas Rimer. New York: Theatre Communications Group, 1986.

J. Briggs Cormier

SIX CHARACTERS IN SEARCH OF AN AUTHOR

Six Characters in Search of an Author (*Sei personaggi in cerca d'autore*) by LUIGI PIRANDELLO premiered in Rome, ITALY, on May 9, 1921, in the Theater Valle with Vera Vergani and Luigi Almirante. The performance was a fiasco, with the audience sharply divided between heated supporters and detractors. It opened in Milan on September 27 in the Theater Manzoni with astounding success. From that moment Pirandello's name was linked to this play, making a nationally acclaimed playwright into the international figure who changed theater and theatergoers' expectations forever.

During the rehearsal of a play by Pirandello, six unnamed characters—Father, Mother, Son, Step-daughter, Boy, and Little Girl—enter the theater and approach the Manager, claiming that their author had created but subsequently abandoned them. Forever trapped in the form of defined characters, they are looking for an author to allow them to enact their drama. Hoping to convince the director to stage their story, the Father, Step-daughter, and Mother tell their vicissitudes. Despite contradictory statements, their story unfolds as follows: After the birth of her Son, the humble Mother falls in love with her husband's secretary. Realizing their affinity, the Father lets her go. The new couple has three children: the Step-daughter, Boy, and Little Girl. Unbeknown to the Father, however, the secretary's death has plunged the family into dire economic straights. They return to the city, where the Mother becomes a tailor employed by Madame Peace (Madame Pace) in a shop that is also a brothel. The Step-daughter also works in the brothel until she and the Father, without recognizing each other, prepare to embrace. The Mother, seeing them together, stops their encounter.

The horrified Father decides to house the Mother and her three children. The Son, however, who had stayed with his Father, does not accept this arrangement. While the mother wants to beg her Son to forgive her desertion, tragedy befalls: the Little Girl drowns in a small pool and the boy shoots himself. Amid confusion between questions of reality or fiction, the Manager puts an end to the unresolved story. Cloaked in darkness, the Step-daughter runs toward the exit.

Written between October 1920 and January 1921, the idea for this play stayed with Pirandello for many years. He had written two short prose-pieces—in 1911 "The Tragedy of a Character," and in 1915 "Conversations with Characters"—that suggest the idea Pirandello was grappling with for a novel. In *Six Characters* Pirandello pulls together themes from his past and ideas that will develop in the immediate future. RIGHT YOU ARE is the older play that posits the first elements to be developed in Six *Characters, Each in His Own Way,* and TONIGHT WE IMPROVISE: the trilogy, as he defined it, of the "theater in the theater," a metatheatrical reflection on the factors that make theatrical representation possible. *Six Characters* ushered in modern theatrical themes and practices, which were shocking at the time: audiences entered the theater to find the curtain up, the stage still under construction, activity and dialogue on the stage and in the auditorium, dissecting the relationship between art and life, between form and life. Thus Pirandello expresses his discomfort with the author's creative process, cautioning about the difficult transition from life experience to the actor's rendition of art. He criticizes the Manager and his actors for their attention to technical details and their lack of insight into the author's process of creation. As Pirandello states in his *Preface* to the 1924 edition, we will always face the "inherent tragic conflict between life (which is always moving and changing) and form (which fixes it, immutable)." Even theater cannot guarantee the fulfillment of characters' desires: the Son denies the drama that makes him a character, the Mother wants to enact the scene with her Son that never happened, but both fail. The COMEDY illustrates the vain attempt to stage the characters' drama, while the incomprehension that surrounds them is fully exposed.

The first English version was staged in London on February 27, 1922. The play opened in New York on October 30, 1922, at the Princess Theater with Moffatt Johnston, Margaret Wycherly,

Florence Eldridge, and Ernest Cossart, and it was followed by innumerable representations in the United States and world-wide. Memorable is the the April 10, 1923, production in Paris by Georges Pitoëff with the Comédie des Champs-Élysées.

FURTHER READING

Bentley, Eric. "A Translator's Introduction." *Six Characters in Search of an Author*, English Version and Introduction by Eric Bentley. New York: Signet Classic, 1998. vii–xvii.

Lorch, Jennifer. *Pirandello. Six Characters in Search of an Author*. Cambridge: Cambridge Univ. Press, 2005.

Pirandello, Luigi. "Pirandello Confesses: Why and How He Wrote 'Six Characters in Search of an Author.'" *Virginia Quarterly Review* 1 (April 1925): 36–52. Reprinted as "Author's Preface." In *Naked Masks: Five Plays by Luigi Pirandello*, ed. by Eric Bentley. New York: E.P. Dutton and Co., 1952.

Stefano Giannini

SIZWE BANSI IS DEAD

Sizwe Bansi Is Dead by ATHOL FUGARD opens with Styles, a photographer, in a sparse studio reading a newspaper. He critiques some news articles and extrapolates on others, such as the visit of American directors to Ford Motor Factory. During the monologue, Styles not only reveals how he became an independent entrepreneur and photographer, but also the kind of social setting that made photography and representation crucial to daily living in apartheid SOUTH AFRICA. For him, a photograph is both a witness to despair and a dream of transcending alienation.

Styles's long monologue is interrupted by a knock from a rather over-dressed man who introduces himself as Robert Zwelinzima, who desires a photograph for his wife in the home-lands. The scene changes through an epistolary device in which Robert dictates a letter to his wife to accompany his photograph. In the flashback Robert becomes Sizwe and Styles his friend Buntu whom he is visiting to help with acquiring a passbook. Both men go out to a shebeen for a drink and afterward discover a body in a dump. On searching the body they find the dead man had a valid passbook with the name Robert Zwelinzima. The rest of the play is Buntu's attempt to persuade Sizwe to take over the identity of the dead man. It is not an easy task for Sizwe to change his name; the play becomes another ludic frame within which Fugard and his collaborators, John Kani and Winston Ntshona, beg the question about what a name means in a subject-less world. The play switches back to Styles's studio, where Sizwe, now Robert, poses for his photograph—suit, tie, hat, pipe in one hand and cigarette in the other.

Sizwe's dilemma once again illustrates the existential themes in Fugard's plays. As Sizwe, Robert—or indeed any black man in apartheid South Africa—is by law simply an object of labor and oppression. Styles does not spare him any limits of black subjectivity. It is, however, not a fatalistic play. Rather in docu-menting the despair, the play underscores the latent and possible overthrow of the present by a more egalitarian future that guarantees subjectivity and effective citizenship for the black population.

Being part of Fugard's collaborative work with the Serpent Players, this play, like *The Island*, draws attention to the "challenge and response" model he used in writing some of his plays. Fugard and his collaborator-actors use their personal experiences to produce metaphors of being, belonging, and becoming. With John Kani and Winston Ntshona as the most consistent members of the group, Fugard developed stories through improvisations in which the actors brought their realities to explore human determination in the face of social marginalization.

Athol Fugard is no doubt one of AFRICA's most versatile and productive playwrights whose works, particularly during apartheid, exposed the atrocities of South Africa's political realities to the world. Against the backdrop of his past works that form an archive of cultural engagements with an alienating political and cultural context, it will be interesting to see how Athol Fugard responds to the new existential issues emerging in post-apartheid South Africa.

FURTHER READING

Orkin, M. *Drama and the South African State*. Manchester: Manchester Univ. Press, 1991.

Vandenbroucke, R. *Truths the Hand Can Touch*. New York: Theatre Communications Group, 1985.

Walder, D. *Athol Fugard*. London: Macmillan, 1984.

Awam Amkpa

THE SKIN OF OUR TEETH

When you're at war you think about a better life: when you're at peace you think about a more comfortable one.
—Mr. Antrobus, Act 3

THORNTON WILDER's *The Skin of Our Teeth* (1942) was first performed at Plymouth Theatre in New York on November 18, 1942, and won the Pulitzer Prize the following year. This play reinforces the idea that people are who they are because of the trials and tribulations wrought by generation after generation. Great minds from our past shaped history, philosophy, and all of humanity. In the *The Skin of Our Teeth*, all of human history is reduced to the experiences of a New Jersey family named Antrobus—derived from the Greek word for man, *anthropos*. Their ordinary lives are altered by the extreme and arbitrary conditions of nature, as well as by free will. The action covers three periods: the Ice Age, the Great Flood, and a Catastrophic War. In each environmental and/or historical disaster, fragile humans manage to survive by the skin of their teeth.

The American audiences of World War II had very few, if any, theatrical experiences that employed such an absurd plot and bizarre settings to convey serious content. This fantastic parable deals with humankind's age-long struggle to achieve civilization and save the human race from extinction. The human race, despite the destructive powers of natural disasters or the brutalities of fascism, communism, and Nazism, somehow manages to survive. World wars can destroy; people can be forced to live underground, but peace will come again. Man's destiny is his own to forge.

The two main struggles are those caused by nature and those caused by people themselves. People cannot avoid natural catastrophes, but they do have the free will to choose good or evil. Mr. and Mrs. Antrobus represent *reason*, whereas the vain Sabina epitomizes *passion*, especially lust for erotic pleasure or political power. Henry (Cain), through his murderous nature, represents pure evil and wicked passion. No single character represents love, yet the Antrobus family unit does perform some loving deeds such as sharing their hearth with refugees and refusing to enter the ark without Henry. Through clever staging and characters, especially Sabina, Wilder includes the audience as part of the Antrobus (human) family. Finally, there is one experience and one memory. The present is then both real and imaginary, past and future.

In its first productions in 1942, Americans found *The Skin of Our Teeth* highly entertaining and rather zany, if not downright crazy. The play is, however, basically a parody of vaudeville and stock company productions. On that superficial level the play is both hilarious and effective. However, if the audience simply views *The Skin of Our Teeth* superficially, the theatergoer misses Wilder's deeper messages. As Wilder (1957) himself stated, the play "mostly comes alive under conditions of crisis." Wilder wrote this play for Americans and bomb-scarred European audiences. Over sixty years later, it has been performed on every continent in the world. Since economic crisis, despair, natural disaster, terrorism, and war have hardly disappeared from our global society, *The Skin of Our Teeth* promises to remain a vital part of the world's theater experience.

[*See also* United States, 1920–1940]

FURTHER READING

Goldstein, Malcolm. *The Art of Thornton Wilder*. Lincoln: Univ. of Nebraska Press, 1965.

Haberman, Donald. *The Plays of Thornton Wilder: A Critical Study*. Middletown, Conn.: Wesleyan Univ. Press, 1967.

Kuner, M. C. *Thornton Wilder: The Bright and the Dark*. New York: Thomas Y. Crowell, 1972.

Wilder, Thornton. *Three Plays: Our Town, The Skin of Our Teeth and The Matchmaker*. New York: Harper, 1957.

Meg Walters

THE SKRIKER

If she can't guessing game and safety match my name then I'll take her no mistake no mister no missed her no mist no miss no me no.
—The Skriker

CARYL CHURCHILL's *The Skriker*, a one-act play which premiered at the Royal National Theatre in London in 1994, is an audacious reimagining of the traditional superstitions, folk tales, and fairy tales of the British Isles into a modern urban setting. Figures such as the Kelpie (part-man, part-horse, a shapeshifter who seduces young women while in human form and lures them to their deaths), Jenny Greenteeth (a fairy who lurks beneath green scum at the edges of deep water to drown children), the Brownie (a helpful if unpredictable household spirit), and Rawheadand-BloodyBones (a nursery goblin who waits in dark cupboards) constantly swirl about, overlapping and underlying the story proper: the tale of two girls who run away into the deep dark city, without so much as sprinkling breadcrumbs behind them, but with something sinister in pursuit. Neither Lily nor Josie—the former sweet but ineffectual, and very pregnant; the latter more streetwise but unstable, and responsible for the death of her own baby before the play begins—have the resources to protect themselves from a menacing environment or from the very needy spirit who attaches itself to their lives.

In folklore, the Skriker is "a shapeshifter and death portent," a creature that wanders the woods at night emitting piercing shrieks. In Churchill's play it hounds Josie and Lily through a series of shifting identities; it speaks in a charged and dizzying language that is also in continual metamorphosis, from catch-phrase to catch-phrase and from cliché into old tale into obscenity, most dazzlingly in the five-page monologue that starts the play: "Don't put your hand in the fountain pen and ink blot your copy catching fishes eyes and gluesniffer. So he puts his hand in and wail whale moby dictated the outcome into the garden maudlin. . . . I'll give you three wishy washy. An open grave must be fed up you go like dust in the sunlight of heart. . . . Ready or not here we come quick or dead of night night sleep tightarse."

The Skriker feeds off its young hosts—"now I've some blood in my all in veins"—but it is far from all-powerful: the Skriker is "ancient," but it is also "damaged" and must operate in a world it no longer understands and that no longer recognizes its kind. There are humorous scenes in which the Skriker tries to figure out things like television and sleep. Traditionally, fairies and humans have never really gotten along, yet they can't quite leave each other alone. It is a compulsive relationship: "When you've lost her," Josie says of her addictive acquaintance, "you want her back."

The Skriker is a cautionary tale about urban survival and about humanity set on self-destruction. Linguistically it resembles the powerfully fractured verbal experimentation of *Blue Kettle* (1997), and thematically it anticipates the all-inclusive world war of people, animals, and seemingly inanimate objects in FAR AWAY (2000). *The Skriker* is a play where language and folk tales break free from any comfortable associations, and where young and vulnerable things go missing, or become very, very lost in the dark.

[*See also* England, 1940–Present]

FURTHER READING

Bradley, Ben. "A Land of Fairy Tales Creepily Come True." *New York Times* (May 16, 1996): C15. [Review of New York production.]

Rabillard, Sheila, ed. *Essays on Caryl Churchill: Contemporary Representations.* Winnipeg: Blizzard Publishing, 1998.

Remshardt, Ralf Eric. "The Skriker." *Theatre Journal* 47, no. 1 (March 1995): 121. [Review of London production.]

Kevin Ewert

SLOVAKIA

Modern Slovak drama started to develop under adverse circumstances as part of the Austro-Hungarian empire at the beginning of the 20th century. Its founder Jozef Gregor Tajovský (1874–1940) successfully combined principles of traditional realistic drama with deep insight into the inner world of his characters, both in his one-acts, *Sin* (Hriech, 1911) and *In Service* (V službe, 1911), and in his full-length plays, *New Life* (Nový život, 1901) and *Estates-Mistakes* (Statky-zmätky, 1909).

In his traditional COMEDIES and satires, Ivan Stodola (1888–1977) criticizes opportunism, snobbery, and the reactionary views of the middle-class bourgeoisie in contrast to the bravery of the simple man in *Jožko Púčik and His Career* (Jožko Púčik a jeho kariéra, 1931) and *Ants and Crickets* (Mravci a svrčkovia, 1943).

Modernists Vladimír Hurban Vladimírov, known as VHV (1884–1950), and Július Barč-Ivan (1909–1953) represented a trend more connected with artistic movements of the period, especially SYMBOLISM and EXPRESSIONISM. In *Záveje* (Snowdrifts, 1913) and *Milica Nikoličová* (1922), VHV depicts the tragic situation of his heroines in harsh times and circumstances. The visionary *Matka* (Mother, 1943) by Barč-Ivan, author of philosophical dramas, is unique in its combination of realism and mysticism; in *Dvaja* (A Couple, 1945) the fog of the dusky mountains symbolizes the impossibility of escaping one's own conscience.

Tanec nad plačom (Dance at Cry, 1943), an anti-illusionist allegory in verse by Peter Zvon, pseudonym of Vladimír Sýkora (1913–1942), aims verbal and situational comedy, parody, and black humor at the totalitarian regime. *Jánošík* (1941) by Mária Rázusová-Martáková (1905–1964), another major play in verse, uses national mythology dealing with robbery to comment on the situation in the Slovak state from 1939 to 1945.

The next generation of dramatists made their debuts during the war, before the communist take-over in 1948. Marked by the war and inspired by EXISTENTIALISM, they wrote model dramas of ethical conflicts. These include the formally innovative plays of Štefan Králik (1919–1983): *The Last Obstacle* (Posledná prekážka, 1946) and *A Play without Love* (Hra bez lásky, 1946); the dramas with expressive contradictory characters of Leopold Lahola, the pseudonym of Arje Friedmann (1918–1968): *Four Sides of the World* (Štyri strany sveta, 1948) and *Assassination* (Atentát, 1949); and the plays of PETER KARVAŠ (1920–1999): *Meteor* (1945) and *Return to Life* (Návrat do života, 1946).

This promising development was cut short by the dogmas of SOCIALIST REALISM. Slovak drama freed itself from such schematism only at the end of 1950s and into the 1960s when Karvaš wrote his best plays. Ivan Bukovčan (1921–1975) returned to the model of the situation drama containing strong social criticism in his plays *An Ostrich Party* (Pštrosí večerok, 1967) and *Before the Cock Crows* (Kým kohút nezaspieva, 1969). Leopold Lahola's *Inferno* (1960) belongs to the same current, whereas his *Spots on the Sun* (Škvrny na slnku, 1955) shows a certain affinity with absurdist drama.

In the 1960s a new group of dramatists, who would dominate the coming decades, emerged as a result of the political liberalization creating an opening for influences from abroad, especially the AVANT-GARDE and theater of the absurd. The structure of drama was further loosened, and alternative theater developed. Dramatists pictured the everyday problems of modern man and woman in socialist society, thereby documenting its gradual decline. *Sawdust* (Piliny, 1965) by Rudolf Skukálek (1931), the groundbreaking Slovak absurdist play, is a devastating critique of the totalitarian regime. Playful, absurd, intellectual humor that remains accessible characterizes the productions of the legendary comedians Milan Lasica (1940–) and Július Satinský (1941–2002) in *Not Waiting for Godot* (Nečakanie na Godota, 1967), *Soirée* (1968), and *A Day of Joy* (Deň radosti, 1986). Igor Rusnák (1936–) gained attention with *Good Night, Foxes* (Líšky, dobrú noc, 1964), depicting the conflict of generations and values.

In the sixties Stanislav Štepka (1944–), a folk humorist, started to write for his famous Radošinské naivné divadlo (Radošina Naïve Theater). Ľubomír Feldek (1936–) wrote untraditional plays for puppet theater and poetic plays that contain growing social criticism: *A Metaphor* (Metafora, 1977), *Jánošík according to Vivaldi* (Jánošík podľa Vivaldiho, 1979), and *A Rehearsal* (Skúška, 1989). Karol Horák (1943–), who came from the experimental theater of poetry, succeeded in the repertory theaters with his plays *A Man between Wars* (Medzivojnový muž, 1984), *Apocalypse according to Janko* (Kráľ) (Apokalypsa podľa Janka [Kráľa], 1994), and *The Music* (La musica 2000). Rudolf Sloboda (1938–1995) proved his dramatic talent with *Armagedon on the Grb Hill* (Armagedon na Grbe, 1993) and *A Stepmother* (Macocha, 1995), which are brilliant examples of playful magical REALISM. Poetic symbolism and existentialism color the plays of Božena Čahojová (1949–), including *Studňa* (A Well, 1989) and *Cesta pre bosých* (A Road for the Barefooted Ones, 1993).

The realistic counterpoint of this generation is represented by Peter Kováčik (1936–) in *A Pub under the Green Tree* (Krčma pod zeleným stromom, 1976), Osvald Zahradník (1932–) in *A Solo for Striking Clock* (Sólo pre bicie [hodiny], 1972), and Ján Solovič (1934–) in *Meridián* (1974).

At the end of the 1980s, a new postmodern generation began to shape the development of Slovak drama. It is still a text-based playwright's theater, but one of many voices and styles, informed by existentialism, post-absurd drama, and HAPPENINGS. The dramatic works are more fragmented than ever before, the scenes loosely connected by association, and the language highly subjective, using puns, neologisms, and slang. At the Stoka Theatre, productions are created collectively under the direction of Blaho Uhlár (1951–). The playful and often absurd dramatic texts, such as *Eo ipso* (1994), *Monodramas* (*Monodrámy*, 1997), and *Let's Get out of Here* (*Hetstato*, 2000), are homogeneous in style. The Stoka has given rise to the bizarre surreal humor of Laco Kerata (1961–) in *Woolfishness* (*Zvlčenie*, 1994) and *Dinner Above Town* (*Večera nad mestom*, 1995).

GUnaGU is a popular text-based theater that is home to Viliam Klimáček (1958–), who uses poetic language and images in his multilayers dramas *Mária Sabína* (1995) and *The Gothic* (*Gotika*, 1996). Some plays at GUnaGU have been created collectively, such as the mafia comedy *English Is Easy, Csaba Is Dead* (2001). Other successful postmodernists include well-known theater directors like Martin Čičvák (1975–), with *Frankie Is O.K., Peggy Is Fine and the House Is Cool* (*Dom, kde sa to robí dobre*, 1995), Jozef Gombár (1973–) with *Hugo Carp* (*Hugo Karas*, 1999), and Silvester Lavrík (1964–) with *Katarína* (1996). Roman Olekšák (1978–), with his "cool" play *Negativists* (*Negativisti*, 2001), is an adherent of the poetics of the new drama.

Although there are many notable new Slovak plays, they are less likely to be staged in the established repertory companies than in the past. Because of the changed social status of theater in the postcommunist era, the major companies are afraid to run risks. Opportunities for new drama are greater in the fringe theaters.

FURTHER READING

Karvaš, Peter. *Zamyšlení nad dramatem* [Thinking about Drama]. Praha: Československý spisovatel, 1964.

———. *Zamyšlení nad dramaturgií* [Thinking about Dramaturgy]. Praha: Československý spisovatel, 1969.

Pašteka, Július. *Pohľady na slovenskú dramatiku, divadlo a kritikuI.* [Views on Slovak Drama, Theatre and Criticism], Vol. I. Bratislava: Národné divadelné centrum, 1998.

Slovník slovenských spisovateľov [Slovak Writers Dictionary]. Praha: Libri, 1999.

Vrbka, Stanislav. *Cestami slovenskej drámy.* [Byways of Slovak Drama]. Bratislava: Divadelný ústav, 1969.

Juraj Sebesta

SMITH, ANNA DEAVERE (1950–)

I take the words I can get and try to occupy them. Using the idea that my grandfather gave me—"If you say a word often enough it becomes you"—I borrow people for a moment, by borrowing their words.

—Anna Deavere Smith, 2000

Anna Deavere Smith is an acclaimed monologist and a leading performance artist in the United States. An African American playwright and performer, she has developed a form of DOCU-MENTARY theater that combines journalism and social commentary to investigate cultural conflict. With tape recorder in hand, Smith gathers dramatic material by conducting numerous interviews compiled from men and women across a range of age, racial, and economic differences. Verbatim excerpts are then memorized and used as texts for one-woman shows.

Fires in the Mirror: Crown Heights, Brooklyn and Other Identities (1992) addressing the problem of racial healing in contemporary America, was her first solo performance to receive wide recognition. This one-woman docudrama had its premiere at the New York Shakespeare Festival, won an Obie Award, and was nominated for a Pulitzer Prize the same year. The violent circumstances that inspired the play occurred in August 1991 when the Grand Rebbe of the Lubavitcher sect of Hasidic Jews was returning to Crown Heights, Brooklyn. A car from his motorcade jumped the curb and killed an African American child, Galvin Cato. In retaliation for what some African Americans perceived as the murder of a helpless child by the Hasidim, a nearby group of black youths surrounded a Hebrew scholar, Yankel Rosenbaum, and stabbed him to death. These events sparked three days of widespread arson and rioting in which citizens, police, and journalists were beaten.

Performing at the Public Theatre a year later, Smith recreated the events of Crown Heights based on taped interviews taken from the residents of the neighborhood, street people, journalists, academics, and artists. She then edited the interviews, reconstructing the crisis based on these subjective accounts. Mimicking the vocal and physical patterns of her informants, the artist refracted the events through a series of personal monologues that made evident the group's racial, sexual, and generational tensions. Through categories like "Hair," "Wigs," "Ovens," "Race," "Rage," and "Rhythm," the tragedy was retold through the experience of blacks, Caribbeans, Jews, Gentiles, men, and women. What emerged from the performance was a multiplicity of perspectives rarely expressed within black–Jewish dialogue.

Twilight: Los Angeles, 1992 (1993) is a similar form of theater forged in the aftermath of the race riots in Los Angeles following the initial verdict in the Rodney King case. The civil disturbance occurred when four white police officers who had been accused of severely beating a black man, Rodney King, were legally acquitted of any wrong-doing. Smith created a performance from the interviews of nearly two hundred people, including relatives of King, an ex-gang member, jury members, an uncalled witness to the beating, and Los Angeles Police Department personnel including former chief Daryl F. Gates. The performance received an Obie Award and was nominated for a Tony Award.

Both *Fires in the Mirror* and *Twilight: Los Angeles* are part of a series of performances begun in the early 1980s called *On the Road: A Search for American Character* in which the performer interviews people and later performs using their words. The project's main objective was to find the character of America in the way people speak. These are plays about the relationship between language and IDENTITY. Smith was specifically interested in how the language of an individual reflects the character of a group.

House Arrest (1998) chronicles her observations of political life in Washington, D.C., based on historical texts as well as interviews with politicians, historians, and journalists during the 1996 presidential campaign. This play examines the relationship between the American presidency, the press, and national identity. Unlike her previous one-woman performances, this play was performed by a multiracial group cast. Her latest work, *Piano* (2000), is about race, class, and exploitation in an affluent Cuban family on the eve of the Spanish-American War.

Smith's provocative plays enable communication across trenchant racial divides when media coverage of events frequently exacerbates communal tensions. Rather than dramatizing a singular and objective viewpoint, Smith looks at contentious events from multiple perspectives. Her performances are fragmented and often end abruptly, allowing the audience to create their own interpretation. Her lauded series of one-woman plays is a unique genre of documentary theater, one that explores race, community, and character based on interviews with diverse people from communities in crisis.

[*See also* Performance Art; United States, 1940–Present]

SELECT PLAYS: *On the Road: A Search for American Character* (1982); *Aunt Julia's Shoes* (1983); *Aye, Aye, Aye, I'm Integrated* (1984); *Charlayne Hunter Gault* (1984); *Building Bridges Not Walls* (1985); *Chlorophyll Post-Modernism and the Mother Goddess: A Convers/Ation* (1988); *Voices of Bay Area Women* (1988); *Gender Bending: On the Road, Princeton University* (1989); *From the Outside Looking in* (1990); *Gender Bending: On the Road, University of Pennsylvania* (1990); *On Black Identity and Black Theatre* (1990); *Fragments* (1991); *Identities Mirrors and Distortions* (1991); *Fires in the Mirror: Crown Heights, Brooklyn and Other Identities* (1992); *Twilight: Los Angeles, 1992* (1993); *House Arrest* (1997); *Piano* (2000)

FURTHER READING

Fitzgerald, Sharon. "Anna of a Thousand Faces." *American Visions.* (October–November 1994): 14–15.

Martin, Carol. "Anna Deavere Smith: The Word Becomes You: An Interview." In *A Sourcebook of Feminist Theatre and Performance,* ed. by Carol Martin. London: Routledge, 1993. 185–204.

Pelligrini, Ann. *Performance Anxieties: Staging Psychoanalysis, Staging Race.* New York: Routledge, 1997.

Reinelt, Janelle. "Performing Race: Anna Deavere Smith's 'Fires in the Mirror.'" *Modern Drama* (Winter 1996): 609.

Schechner, Richard. "Anna Deavere Smith: Acting as Incorporation." *TDR: The Drama Review* 37, no. 4 (1993): 63–64.

Smith, Anna Deavere. *Talk To Me: Listening Between the Lines.* New York: Random House, 2000.

                                                    Molly Castelloe

---

SNART KOMMER TIDEN *See* SOON THE TIME WILL COME

SOCIALIST REALISM, SOVIET UNION

Officially adopted at the First Congress of Soviet writers in 1934, socialist realism was a prescriptive term for the way in which Soviet literature, drama, and criticism were to be created. Writers were required to reflect a socialist view of history and social development and to serve the interests of the Party. The theater, as a state institution and a tool of propaganda, should play an important role in the construction of communism.

Using readily comprehensible subject matter, dramatists were to eschew abstract, symbolic, and other forms pejoratively termed "formalist" in favor of a realistic style. Indeed, by a rewriting of theater history, socialist realism was promoted as the heir of a performance tradition conceived as exclusively realist (going back to Mikhail Shchepkin and successfully developed by the MOSCOW ART THEATRE). However, since the Soviet Union was to be seen as moving inexorably toward a brighter, happier, prosperous future, the dominant tone of drama must be optimistic. Thus, it was necessary, and indeed "more realistic," not only to stress what was positive in the present but also to point the way forward.

Not surprisingly, factories, farms, and laboratories provided the settings and themes for many plays of the time, since the introduction of socialist realism coincided with the end of the First Five Year Plan (1928–1932), which had seen the creation of a centrally controlled command economy, the development of heavy industry, and the collectivization of agriculture. More importantly, artists (Joseph Stalin's "engineers of the soul") used metaphors of reforging or the smelting of new alloys to depict this process as they were expected to promote the idea of a "New Soviet Man," the product (according to current evolutionary theories) not of nature but of an improving society. Many plays centered on idealized protagonists (sometimes scientists) who journeyed through doubt toward political conviction. Others demonstrated how courage and self-sacrifice in the present would ensure the eventual triumph of ideals. Some, demanding monumental settings, celebrated events from Revolutionary history and the Civil War; others foresaw the heroism of the Soviet people in future conflicts.

MAKSIM GORKY lent socialist realism the considerable weight of his authority as a theorist and playwright, and other leading dramatists whose works merit study, at least as documents of an era, include Vsevolod Vishnevsky, Nikolai Pogodin, Aleksandr Kirshon, and Aleksandr Afinogenov. But in general the theory produced many third-rate plays, with predictable plots and pasteboard characters who were little more than parrots of Party propaganda. The silencing of more innovative writers and directors, the imposition of state and self-censorship, the need to write to formulae, and nonsensical notions such as Nikolai Virta's "conflictless drama," had a disastrous effect on the development of Russian theater. After Stalin's death, the more liberal policies of Khrushchev's thaw allowed greater innovation from a new generation of writers, but until the early 1980s, the terminology of socialist realism was still employed, by conservative critics and in Party literature, as a means of censuring "formalist" directors and writers.

FURTHER READING

Blake, Ben, ed. *Four Soviet Plays*. New York: Benjamin Blom, 1972. Reissue of Lawrence & Wishart, 1937. (Includes Vishnevsky's *An Optimistic Tragedy*, Pogodin's *Aristrocrats*, and Maksim Gorky's *Yegor Bulychov and Others*).

Lyons, Eugene, ed. *Six Soviet Plays*. New York: Greenwood Press, 1968. Reissue of Houghton Mifflin 1934. (Includes Kirshon's *Bread*, Pogodin's *Tempo*, and Afinogenov's *Fear*).

Russell, Robert. *Russian Drama of the Revolutionary Period*. Basingstoke: Macmillan, 1988.

Segel, Harold B. *Russian Drama from Gorky to the Present*, rev. ed. Baltimore and London: Johns Hopkins Univ. Press, 1993.

Solovyova, Inna. "The Theatre and Socialist Realism, 1929–1953." In *A History of Russian Theatre*, ed. by Robert Leach and Victor Borovsky. Cambridge: Cambridge Univ. Press, 1999. 325–357.

Vaughan, James C. *Soviet Socialist Realism*. London: Macmillan, 1973.

Ros Dixon

SOCIALIST REALISM OUTSIDE THE SOVIET UNION

Based on the writings of Karl Marx, Friedrich Engels, and Vladimir Lenin, socialist realism proposes that drama advocate a positive view of socialist society utilizing a realistic style easily understood by the masses. As communism spread throughout Europe, Asia, and the world during the 20th century, socialist realism became the dominant mode. Theater mirrored Soviet writers such as MAKSIM GORKY, Alexander Pushkin, and Fyodor Dostoevsky; KONSTANTIN STANISLAVSKY was the model for ACTING. Socialist realism tended to feature positive heroes who relinquish personal gain for the betterment of the community.

In the German Democratic Republic (GDR), paradigms based on the Soviet model were developed in writers' conferences sponsored by the Socialist Unity Party of GERMANY from 1947 to 1963. In 1947 the first Stanislavsky school was established by Maxim Vallentin, Ottofritz Gaillard, and Otto Lang to train actors and writers in the state-sponsored approach. Early works of HEINER MÜLLER (particularly *The Scab* in 1956 and *The Correction* in 1958) complied with state mandates, though they remained critical of the dogmatic form. Volker Braun, THOMAS BRASCH, and CHRISTOPH HEIN also presented positive views of socialist society, despite their formal experimentation. Although theater artists in the GDR (including BERTOLT BRECHT) accepted the premises of socialist realism, issues of form remained unresolved.

In Eastern Europe the most important proponent of socialist realism was Hungarian Georg Lukács, who proposed that art should present the "objective essence of reality." His greatest critic was Brecht, who rejected the notion that art must be limited to one style. The debate among Brecht, Lukács, and others took place between 1952 and 1956, resulting in a model that allowed for some formal experimentation. The Yugoslav Drama Theatre, founded in Belgrade in 1947 by Bojan Stupica, adopted the style of the MOSCOW ART THEATRE. The doctrine of socialist realism in POLAND was in force from 1949 to 1956 and yielded works best described as Stalinist, given their views on sacrificial contributions to the state: *The Germans* (1949) by Leon Kruczkowski, *Nothing Unusual* (1950) by Adam Tarn, and *House of Cards* (1953) by Emil Zegadlowicz.

After Communism spread to Mainland CHINA in 1949, drama was placed under the Ministry of Cultural Affairs, and socialist realism became the only acceptable form. Under Mao, traditional plays were revised or banned, and techniques such as stage attendants and stylized movement were abolished. New works were written to replace the "harmful" and "backward" ones. Of these, *The Red Lantern* (1964), *Taking Tiger Mountain by Strategy* (1964), and *On the Docks* (1967) are the most important.

Dramas loosely based on the Soviet model appeared on New York stages during the 1930s. The Theatre Union staged Brecht's THE MOTHER in 1932, and the GROUP THEATRE brought radical theater to Broadway in 1934–1935 with productions such as AWAKE AND SING! and WAITING FOR LEFTY. Socially conscious dramas (though short of true socialist realism) have been written by Albert Bein, MARC BLITZSTEIN, Harold Rome, and ARTHUR MILLER. Seldom written or produced since the mid-20th century, social realist dramas have been virtually absent from world theater since the decline of communism in the West.

FURTHER READING

Ermolaev, Herman. "Socialist Realism." In *Marxism and Communism in Western Society*, Vol. 8. New York: Herder & Herder, 1972.

Huettich, H. G. *Theatre in the Planned Society: Contemporary Theatre in the German Democratic Republic*. Chapel Hill: Univ. of North Carolina Press, 1978.

Lahusen, Thomas, and Evgeny Dobrenko, eds. *Socialist Realism Without Shores*. Durham, N.C.: Duke Univ. Press, 1997.

Levine, Ira. *Left-Wing Theory in the American Theatre*. Ann Arbor, Mich.: UMI Research Press, 1985.

Steve Earnest

I SOGNI DE CLITENNESTRA See THE DREAMS OF CLYTEMNESTRA

DER SOHN See THE SON

SOLÓRZANO, CARLOS (1922–)

An artist of *mestizo* (mixed blood) origins, Guatemalan Carlos Solórzano fuses diverse art forms to create a stylized drama of existential despair that is universal in content and Indo-Hispanic in its theatricality to challenge social and religious norms. He grew up among the oligarchy surrounded by millions of starving Indians under a military dictatorship, moved to MEXICO in 1939 to study at the National University, married, and became a playwright, drama critic, and professor. The paradox between the privilege and misery of his early life assumed center stage in his drama, and priests, patriarchs, and tyrants became the antagonists.

Solórzano's major plays, THE HANDS OF GOD (Las manos de Dios), The Puppets (Los fantoches), and The Crucified (El crucificado), combine religion and politics to question the authority of church and state. In The Hands of God (1956), the heroine tries to rescue her brother from an unjust imprisonment, a metaphor for the fear of God. The Puppets: A Mime-Drama for Marionettes (1958) depicts Solórzano's vision of the human condition: The characters are wired with explosives. Periodically, the old Puppet Maker and his daughter, a child masked as "Smiling Death" (la muerte catrina) explode a puppet to make room for the new ones he creates. The Crucified: A Tragic Farce (1958) is a provocative play-within-a-play. The young men who portray Christ and his disciples in the Passion become so drunk that they crucify the actor, a tragedy not unknown in Mexican villages.

Similarly, Solórzano's other plays challenge the oligarchy and God. And Death Brought Forth the Light (La muerte hizo la luz, 1951) denounces despots. Doña Beatriz, the luckless woman (Doña Beatriz, la sin ventura, 1952), recounts the life of the first female governor of the Americas. A volcanic eruption, symbolic of her repressed sexuality, destroys her utopian Catholic society; only the mestiza survive. The Sorcerer (El hechicero, 1954) portrays the search for the Philosopher's Stone. Mea culpa (1958) and The Angel's Forty Winks (El sueño de un angel, 1960) are rituals of confession that annihilate the human spirit. The Shoe (El zapato, 1966) plays out an Oedipal relationship, and in Crossroads (Cruce de vías, 1959), a man falls in love with the sensuous voice of a woman but recoils when he sees her wizened face.

Solórzano's drama charts the key points of life: birth, consciousness, and death. His characters seek God but find only silence. Instead of consolation, religious myths terrorize them; the rites do not deliver the promised transcendence. Unable to reconcile faith and reason, people suffer in solitude. As the protagonist of The Hands of God discovers, once humans discard their illusions of immortality, they cast off their fear of damnation. Beatriz redeems her soul to determine her destiny now, not in some unattainable afterlife. The winner of numerous prizes and honors, Solórzano has also written two novels and significant drama history and criticism that enhance his prominence in Latin American drama.

FURTHER READING

Feliciano, Wilma. El teatro mítico de Carlos Solórzano [The Mythic Theater of Carlos Solórzano]. Mexico City: Univ. Nacional Autónoma de México, 1995.

Rivas, Esteban. Carlos Solórzano y el teatro hispanoamericano [Carlos Solór-zano and the Hispanic American Theater]. Mexico: Anahuac, 1970.

Quackenbush, L. Howard. Devotas irreverencias: el auto en el teatro latinoamericano [Irreverent Devotions: The Miracle Play in Latin American Theater]. Mexico: Univ. of Tlaxcala, Brigham Young Univ., and D. M. Kennedy Center for International Studies, 1998. 88–95.

Solórzano, Carlos. Teatro [Theater]. Mexico City: Univ. Nacional Autónoma de México, 1992.

——. Crossroads and Other Plays by Solórzano. Tr. and ed. by Francesca Colecchia. Rutherford, N.J.: Farleigh Dickenson Univ. Press, 1993.

Versényi, Adam. Theatre in Latin America. Cambridge: Cambridge Univ. Press, 1993. 129–32.

Woodyard, George. "Theater of the Absurd in Spanish-America." Comparative Drama 3 (1969): 183–192.

Wilma Feliciano

THE SON

This drama is incarnation. The indirect route of the Created to reach his archetype; the play of the Son to his Father, the prologue of the Citizen to his Country.
—Walter Hasenclever, 1916

Literary EXPRESSIONISM's rebellion against Wilhelmine GERMANY's repression of the essential human was articulated in calls for brotherhood, humanity, freedom, and individual vision. In the playbill to the 1916 Prague premiere of The Son (Der Sohn, 1914), WALTER HASENCLEVER explains that the twenty-year-old Son's "revolt of the spirit against reality" is projected not by way of causal or mimetic representations of reality, but through the "soul" of the individual. The generational rage of youth betrayed by the historical crisis of the First World War resonated powerfully in postwar productions of The Son, beginning with the 1918 public premiere in Mannheim, thanks to the directorial and lighting strategies of Richard Weichert and Ludwig Sievert, respectively. Unlike the realist staging for the 1916 Prague and Dresden premieres, in Mannheim the Son's psychic landscape was projected into abstract images and symbolic events as he progressed from his immature and vitalist beginnings to the expressionist "New Man." Combined with Ernst Deutsch's overly expressive ACTING style for the 1918 Berlin performance, The Son became a dramatic sensation.

The influence of the Sturm und Drang is apparent in the generational conflict and political connotations of the play, although prewar expressionist dramas such as The Son were more focused on Nietzschean personal realization and transforming societal attitudes than on real-world politics. The drama's challenge to psychological REALISM and German NATURALISM is seen in the juxtaposition of verse, prose, monologues, and hymnic reveries to highlight the Son's inner development and ecstatic rejection of familial and Wilhelmine tyranny as he surpasses the limitations of social types cast around him, including the Tutor, the Friend, and the Father.

After failing his high school examinations despite the best efforts of the Tutor, the Son rejects his Father's tyrannical hold on him at the end of act 2 and escapes house arrest with the aid of a mysterious Friend. The Friend's hypnotic powers enable the Son to address a gathering at the "Club for the Preservation of Joy" in act 3, where he reveals his father's injustices and denounces the world of the Father to wild applause and the singing of the Marseillaise, the song of the French Revolution. In act 4 the Son continues his journey into manhood at the side of the prostitute Adrienne, and then surpasses the nihilistic decadence of the Friend who commits suicide. But whether the Son is destined to new horizons beyond the world of the Father is unclear, since he has failed, as he states in act 4, "after so many stations . . . to do something completely." He owes his successes as a leader to the hypnotic powers of the Friend, and as he steels himself to kill his Father, the ultimate revolutionary act, the Father dies on the spot of a stroke. The play ends with the Son's ecstatic emotional embrace of his role as the "New Man," although this remains vaguely defined: "My mind is fully creative on this day. / With me for what is vital to unite / I have not shunned Death's eternal might. / Now man's great power to proclaim / Toward freedom, is my heart's new aim!"

FURTHER READING

Hoelzel, Alfred. *Walter Hasenclever's Humanitarianism: Themes of Protest in His Works.* New York: Lang, 1983.

Löb, Ladislaus. " 'The Second Time as Farce?' Hasenclever's *Der Sohn* and Schiller's *Don Carlos.*" *The Modern Language Review* 88, no. 2 (1993): 375–388.

Schurer, Ernst, ed. *German Expressionist Plays (The German Library: Vol. 66).* New York: Continuum Publ. Co., 1997. [Includes *The Son,* tr. by H. Marx.]

Sheppard, Richard William. "Unholy Families: The Oedipal Psychopathology of Four Expressionist Ich-Dramen." *Orbis Litterarum* 41, no. 4 (1986): 355–383.

Spreizer, Christa. *From Expressionism to Exile: The Works of Walter Hasenclever (1890–1940).* Rochester, N.Y.: Camden House, 1999.

Christa Spreizer

SÖNDAGSPROMENADEN See THE SUNDAY PROMENADE

A SONG AT TWILIGHT

He has never had the courage or the humility to face the fact that it was not whom he loved in his life that really mattered, but his own capacity for loving.
—Carlotta, Act 2

A Song at Twilight is the first play in a trilogy by NOËL COWARD entitled *Suite in Three Keys* (with *Shadows of the Evening* and *Come into the Garden Maud*). All three are set in a hotel room in Switzerland, and each requires a cast of four. Written in 1965, the first London production of *A Song at Twilight* took place in April 1966 at Queen's Theatre to good reviews with Coward in the role of the main character, Hugo Latymer.

The title refers to Johann Wolfgang von Goethe's warning against self denial. This is the pivot on which this essentially moral melodramatic play turns. Sir Hugo Latymer is a celebrated elderly satirical writer with a secret that he is desperate to conceal from his public. The play opens with Latymer's wife Hilde on the phone, stressing to his agent Latymer's right to control his reputation.

The preservation of Latymer's reputation is central to the play. When in act 1 Latymer has dinner with ex-lover Carlotta Gray, it is because of his reputation that he denies her permission to use his old love letters in her autobiography. Carlotta accepts this but tells him before the curtain falls that she has his love letters to the "only true love of your life," the dead Perry Sheldon, Latymer's male secretary whom he had spurned many years earlier.

Act 2 begins with a shift in power from Latymer to Carlotta. Latymer is desperate to preserve his heterosexual public image, while Carlotta is determined to make him admit his hypocrisy and dishonesty in pretending to be heterosexual.

Homosexuality moves to the foreground and is hotly debated. Into this crossfire a slightly tipsy Hilde returns from a dinner engagement. Carlotta confronts her about Latymer's sexuality. Hilde admits her knowledge of her husband's homosexuality but stays loyal to him despite Carlotta pointing out that Latymer has exploited her.

After further verbal fencing, the play ends with Carlotta surrendering the Sheldon letters to Latymer. In a reciprocal gesture Latymer gives her permission to use his letters in her memoirs. Hilde escorts Carlotta out, and Latymer's isolation is emphasized as he sits reading the letters Carlotta has left him. It is apparent from the stage directions that he is "deeply moved." Hilde does not seat herself next to him when she returns. The play ends in isolation and regret as the curtain falls with them apart.

Although a review in *The Times* on April 15, 1966, stated that the play "seems, beyond question, to be based on the last years of SOMERSET MAUGHAM," a parallel might as successfully be drawn between Latymer and Coward. In *A Song at Twilight* Coward comes as close to confronting his own homosexuality on stage as he ever did in any of his plays. The plea for homosexual tolerance in the play is clear, but Coward, like Latymer, cannot successfully articulate his own vulnerability, possibly because of his own concern with his public reputation.

[See also England, 1960–1980]

FURTHER READING

Elsom, John. *British Post-War Theatre.* London: Routledge and Kegan Paul, 1981.

Lahr, John. *Coward the Playwright.* London: Methuen Ltd., 1982.

Lesley, Cole. *The Life of Noel Coward.* London: Jonathan Cape, 1976.

Morley, Sheridan. *A Talent to Amuse.* London: Heinemann, 1969.

Weightman, John. "Theatre: On Not Appreciating Mr. Coward." *Encounter* (27 July 1966).

Gregory Hacksley

SOON THE TIME WILL COME

I try to buy time, so one has time to have time.
—Hilbert, Act 1

Staged in 1998 and published in 1999, *Soon the Time Will Come* (*Snart Kommer Tiden*) marked a turning-point in the career of LINE KNUTZON and a remarkable success for two seasons at the Dr. Dantes Aveny Theatre in Copenhagen. It went on to tour throughout DENMARK.

This play is characterized by a more complex DRAMATURGY and less focus on youth and more on couplehood than in Knutzon's earlier plays. "When you are in your twenties you hunt a lot of dreams, and at a certain point you have realized them all. . . . there is nothing more to dream about. Now you find yourself in reality! That is a shell shock. What then? You can have a concrete fear of death. . . . It becomes serious. Serious-serious." The couplehood of main characters Rebekka and Hilbert has all but dissolved, and they ought to divorce. Even though time apparently has not passed, they nevertheless suddenly have children. Hilbert has hired a house-maid Oda as a birthday present to Rebekka, so that she may have time to have time. Ambiguous "Little Oda" presents herself as descendant of an entirely childless family. Rebekka fears that Oda has come to kill her and her children. Nevertheless, she orders Oda to arrange her thirty-fifth birthday party; they expect their daughter, the Knutte-child, to come. Even Rebekka's former lover John and his fiancée Ingrid are guests. Knutte turns up; she is fifty-five years old!

The second act is the birthday party. Gradually it becomes apparent that the characters have lived their lives without having noticed nor remembered. It is in fact Rebekka's eighty-fifth birthday, she has had her divorce, Ingrid and Hilbert have had an affair, and so forth. Time is dissolved; things that have happened, happen, fifty years have passed and at the same time they have not. It is not my fault that you have to die, says the Knutte-child. Rebekka declares that although her and Hilbert's relationship is impossible, she cannot control her love for him: "I love you when I hate you." "Take good care of me," says the Knutte-child, and she disappears in a white light.

Some critics had reservations concerning the second act (actually, the second act was written during the rehearsals). Me Lund wrote in *Berlingske Tidende* that Knutzon's plays "have meant a kind of revolution for Danish theater. But as a matter of fact they were also chaotic and philosophically immature. She is still no methodical person in terms of dramaturgy. But the decisive difference between *Soon the Time Will Come* and the rest of her oeuvre—and what we could call one of the most happy quantum leaps in Danish drama—is that Line Knutzon as a playwright has obtained so much distance from her material that she now seems to control her effects and is able, in the middle of the chaotic satire of life style, to insist on small poetic oases, pure monologues that hit precisely and deeply in significant existential scruples."

FURTHER READING

Hesselaa, Birgitte. *Vi lever i en tid. Line Knutzons dramatik* [We live in a time. Line Knutzon's Plays]. Copenhagen: Borgen, 2001.

Theil, Per, and Lise Garsdal. *Hvem der? Scener fra 90erne* [Who's There? Scenes from the 90's]. Copenhagen: Høst og Søn, 2000.

Bent Holm

SORESCU, MARIN (1936–1996)

Marin Sorescu belongs to the generation of writers and poets who emerged during post–World War II communist ROMANIA that shares many common traits in thematics and style. In Sorescu's writings, one feels above all the sense of entrapment and the despair of "no exit" from a suffocating atmosphere in which words, written or spoken, are suspicious and censored.

In addition to many volumes of poetry, Sorescu also wrote nine plays. Three of them—JONAH (*Iona*, 1968), *The Verger* (*Paracliserul*, 1970), and *The Origin* (*Matca*, 1973)—belong stylistically to the Theater of the Absurd, reminiscent of EUGÈNE IONESCO and SAMUEL BECKETT. These plays deal with humanity's search for the Absolute in an alienated society in times of existential uncertainties. Sorescu makes use of metaphoric language with frequent references to religious and mythical symbols.

Other important plays—such as *The Chill* (*Raceala*, 1976), *The Third Stake* (*A Treia Teapa*, 1980), and *Shakespeare's Cousin* (*Varul Lui Shakespeare*, 1990)—belong to a cycle of historical dramas, written in Brechtian EPIC-dramatic style. In these plays, Sorescu evokes the Romanian past for parallels and analogies to the present. For example, *The Third Stake* brings to the stage the 15th-century Romanian cruel despot, Vlad, the Impaler (Vlad Tepes), nicknamed Dracul (Bram Stoker's model for *Dracula*), engaged in his 1461 campaign against Turkish domination under Mehmed II. The stage is strewn with victims, each impaled on a stake, who endure their fate stoically—a symbol, perhaps, of the cross the nation is bearing in silence, or a veiled allusion to the dictatorship in the playwright's own time. In the end, Vlad impales himself on the third stake. *Shakespeare's Cousin*, a five-act play in the historical cycle, is a meditation on the condition of the artist in an ungrateful society. A prologue presents the philosophical theme: life as a play in perpetual rehearsal with changing settings. "We stumble blindly upon the same play which we try to rewrite and in which the lines are dictated to us and uttered eternally by bygone generations." Sorescu presents William Shakespeare as harassed by his contemporaries, implying a parallel to the modern playwright being plagued by the authorities, who keep demanding "full page declarations." Censorship spares nobody; even Yorick's skull risks being impaled on a stake if it continues to utter the forbidden.

Jonah is Sorescu's first play and the most important. It enjoyed instant success when it appeared in 1968 and established its author as a major player on the Romanian stage. The play, a poetic monologue on the human condition, is a cry from the depth, expressing the world's existential angst. As in the Bible, Jonah is trapped in the belly of the big fish, but here the similarity ends. Knife in hand, he tries unsuccessfully to carve a hole in the fish in an attempt to escape. Like the little fish with which he plays in his aquarium, Jonah feels played upon by blind forces from which only his suicide provides liberation.

PLAYS: *Jonah* (*Iona*, 1968); *The Verger* (*Paracliserul*, 1970); *The Matrix* (*Matca*, 1973); *Medusa's Raft* (*Pluta Medusei*, 1974); *Nerves Do Exist* (*Exta Nervi*, 1974); *The Chill* (*Raceala*, 1976); *The Third Stake* (*A treia Teapa*, 1980); *Shakespeare's Cousin* (*Varul Lui Shakespeare*, 1990); *The Fighter on Two Fronts* (*Luptatorul Pe Doua Fronturi*, 1981)

FURTHER READING

Cocora, Ion. *Privitor Ca La Teatru II* [Onlooker at the Theater]. Cluj-Napoca, Romania: Editura Dacia, 1977.

Iosif, Mira. *Teatrul Nostru Cel De Toate Serile* [Our Daily Theater]. Bucharest: Editura Eminescu, 1979.

Sorescu, Marin. *Iona, A Treia Teapa, Varul Shakespeare* [Jonah, The Third Stake, Shakespeare's Cousin]. Prefata de Dumitru Micu. Nota Biobibliografica de Virginia Sorescu [Preface by Dumitru Micu. Bibliographic Note by Virginia Sorescu]. Bucharest: Editura Minerva, 1993.

——. *Varul Shakespeare Si Alte Piese. Teatru* [Shakespeare's Cousin and Other Plays]. Bucharest: Cartea Romanesca, 1992.

Moshe Yassur

SORGE, REINHARD JOHANNES (1892–1916)

Reinhard Johannes Sorge, one of the earliest German expressionist poets and dramatists, based his works on his own aspirations and experiences. Born on January 29, 1892, in Rixdorf, Berlin, GERMANY, the son of a Protestant building inspector, Sorge worked as a clerk and bank apprentice after his father's mental breakdown in 1905. Following his father's death in 1908, he attended courses in Greek philology at the University of Jena before abandoning his studies to become a poet and dramatist.

His earliest poems, although influenced by the Sturm und Drang and the Romantic movements, as well as by Stefan George (1868–1933) and Richard Dehmel (1863–1920), are not lyrical compositions but rather hymnic proclamations steeped in Sorge's deep religious convictions. Early dramatic attempts, such as the one-scene *Zarathustra* (1911) and *Antichrist* (1911), demonstrate the tensions and contradictions Sorge felt between the ecstatic mysticism of one devoted to God and the iconoclastic, FRIEDRICH NIETZSCHE-inspired teachings that so informed the expressionist generation. After experiencing a vision in 1912, Sorge converted to Roman Catholicism in 1913, thus breaking with his Protestant upbringing and Nietzschean philosophy. In 1912 he received the Kleist Prize for his most famous drama, the five-act *The Beggar* (*Der Bettler*, 1912), considered the first expressionist play.

In the autobiographical *Der Bettler*, expressionist characteristics—such as an episodic structure, a rejection of psychological REALISM, ecstatic verse, and character types instead of individuals—illustrate the Poet's "dramatic mission" to found a new theater to renew both himself and society. In a bold advance of staging and dramatic structure, Sorge calls for the Poet to be illuminated from steep angles to highlight his lofty potential, in contrast to representative social figures that appear as barriers or facilitators in his quest. Such revolutionary staging and lighting strategies, realized during the 1917 Berlin premiere, serve to blur the boundaries between subject and object as realistic scenes shift to evocations of a vision-like state of being. But after a series of events, including poisoning his mentally deranged father to alleviate his torment, which also allows the Poet to break from his origins to "create anew," the protagonist experiences only the everyday. In the end his mission to unify art and life eludes him, and he is able to speak "through symbols of eternity" only within the confines of his own play. He accepts his fate as a beggar and social outcast in his drive to renew himself and the world.

Whereas in *Der Bettler* the Poet is still seeking transcendence to become the expressionist New Man, in Sorge's second full-length play, *Guntwar: The School of a Prophet* (*Guntwar. Die Schule eines Propheten*, 1914), he has already taken on the role of a modern prophet who will work tirelessly toward the ecstatic unity of humankind. The play culminates in an apocalyptic vision of Judgment Day, followed by the rise of a new generation illuminated by God's grace. Sorge also wrote two Biblical plays before his untimely death in 1916: *King David* (*König David*, 1916) and *Christ's Victory* (*Der Sieg des Christos*, 1916). Sorge was preparing for theological training to enter the priesthood as World War I began. He volunteered for military service and died of wounds suffered at the battle of Ablaincourt-Somme on July 20, 1916, in France.

[See also Expressionism]

SELECT PLAYS: *Guntwar: A Development* (*Guntwar. Ein Werden*, 1911); *The Beggar: A Dramatic Mission* (*Der Bettler. Eine dramatische Sendung*, 1912); *Guntwar: The School of a Prophet* (*Guntwar. Die Schule eines Propheten*, 1914); *Metanoeite: Three Mysteries* (*Metanoeite. Drei Mysterien*, 1915); *Christ's Victory: A Dramatic Vision* (*Der Sieg des Christos. Dramatische Vision*, 1916); *King David* (*König David*, 1916)

FURTHER READING

Cardullo, Bert, and Robert Knopf, eds. *Theater of the Avant-Garde, 1890–1950: A Critical Anthology*. New Haven: Yale Univ. Press, 2001. 207–260.

Lincoln, Peter. "Aspects of Sorge's Imagery: A Reappraisal of His Position Within Expressionism." *German Life and Letters* 34, no. 4 (1981): 374–384.

Shearier, Stephen. "Modernist Consciousness and Mass Culture: Alienation in *Der Bettler* by Reinhard Sorge." *German Studies Review* 11, no. 2 (1988): 227–240.

Sheppard, Richard William. "Unholy Families: The Oedipal Psychopathology of Four Expressionist Ich-Dramen." *Orbis Litterarum* 41, no. 4 (1986): 355–383.

Christa Spreizer

LE SOULIER DE SATIN   See THE SATIN SLIPPER

SOUTH AFRICA

South African literature has developed in four broad stages: the colonial period, extending to the outbreak of World War II, in which most work was either derivative or of local interest; the nationalist period, through the 1940s and 1950s, which was increasingly dominated by the Afrikaners; the period of protest, from the 1960s through the 1980s and the overthrow of the apartheid system, during which some South African authors gained major international reputations; and the immediate post-apartheid period, extending through the present, in which the full diversity of voices in the reconstituted nation have sought expression but, not surprisingly, have not yet found a focal subject with the resonance of revolt. South African drama had a rather negligible presence in the first two stages of this literary history, but became a major force for both cultural and political change during the protest period.

The first recorded production of a South African play occurred in 1838, with the Graham's Town Amateur Company's performance of Andrew Geddes Bains's *Kaatje Kekkelbeck or Life among the Hottentots*. But for the most part, the Calvinistic religions of the Dutch colonials caused them to view theater-going as a vice. Still in the 1910s and 1920s, missionaries to the black African communities began to use simple plays based on Bible stories that illustrated moral lessons as a tool to reach converts. At the Marianhill missionary station, Father Bernard Hess went so far as to stage some plays derived from Zulu folk tales, as well as some secular light COMEDIES.

It is not surprising, then, that in the late 1920s and the early 1930s, the first theatrical troupes in South Africa were organized in the black townships. Most notable were the Methethwe Lucky Stars and the Bantu Dramatic Society. Although both emphasized productions that represented facets of Bantu cultural traditions and social life, the Bantu Dramatic Society pointedly supported the efforts of black playwrights. In the 1950s, another very influential group, the Orlando Boy's Club Dramatic Society, was formed. Johannesburg's black district, Sophiatown, became a lively and volatile center of black theatrical work, providing a stimulating juncture of black cultural and criminal life comparable to New York's Harlem during the 1920s. Innovations in theater were closely linked to new directions in music and dance. Long after Sophiatown and other black districts were cleared to create greater separation between the white and black populations, several highly regarded productions have sought to capture their vibrant place in South Africa's cultural and social history. One of these, *Kat and the Kings* (1999), by David Kramer and Taliep Peterson, received the Laurence Olivier Award for the best new musical produced in London.

The first black playwright of real note was Herbert Dhlomo, who emerged as a singular voice in the 1940s. His play *The Girl Who Killed to Save* (1936) draws on a historical incident to present anticolonial themes within a truly dramatic frame. It is generally acknowledged to be the first published play by a black South African. By the 1950s, however, the apartheid laws would effectively remove black playwrights, actors, and directors from international and even national view. Under the apartheid laws, plays by black playwrights could not be staged, and black actors could not perform in white theaters. Publishers were prohibited from producing books, including plays, written by blacks. Nevertheless, Dhlomo's example inspired other black dramatists, most notably Lewis Nkosi, whose achievements, like Dhlomo's, may never be fully appreciated. In his first produced play, *The Rhythm of Violence* (1964), Nkosi treats the volatile racial tensions very near the surface of daily life in Johannesburg. His most notable later play has been *Malcolm* (1972).

Within little more than a half-century of their bitter defeat in the Boer War, the Afrikaners had achieved a predominant position in the political, economic, and cultural life of South Africa. Their sense of self-determination found expression in a brief renaissance of nationalistic (that is to say, white) South African literature, particularly that written in Afrikaans. In the late 1940s, the segregated National Theater was created, in part, to provide a venue that would encourage playwriting by white South Africans. Guy Butler received some attention for his plays *The Dam* (1953) and *The Dove Returns* (1956), and N. P. Van Wyk Louw, a university professor and a literary critic of some note, wrote the creditable verse drama *Germanicus* (1956), as well as *The Plume's Seed Blows Far* (*Die pluimsaad waai ver*, 1966), about the Boer War.

During the 1950s, however, the South African theatrical production that received the most international notice was the musical *King Kong* (1959), which resulted from the collaboration of whites and blacks. Some white producers and playwrights had been willing to risk government persecution and social ostracism because of their involvement in integrated theatrical productions. In the early 1950s, Ian Bernhardt helped to organize the Bareti Players, a black theatrical troupe that sought to honor both European dramatic traditions and black South African folk traditions. A decade later, Bernhardt guided the establishment of the Union of South African Artists and its offshoot, the African Music and Drama Association. *King Kong* was the culmination of the latter group's promotion of South African experiments with JAZZ, indigenous musical forms, and musical theater.

From the 1960s onward, almost all noteworthy drama in South Africa, including that written in Afrikaans, was at least indirectly critical of the national retrenchment into the ever more strictly enforced system of racial apartheid. Among the dramatists writing in Afrikaans, Andre Brink continues to be a major figure. Known primarily as a novelist outside of South Africa, Brink has consistently produced work for the theater for more than three decades. His plays, many of which have been translated into English, include: The Bond around Our Hearts (Die band om ons harte, 1959); Caesar (1965); The Guardian Angel (Die beskermengel, 1962); Bagasie: Triptiek vir die toneel (which includes Die koffer, Die trommel, and Die tas, 1965); Elsewhere Fine and Warm (Elders mooiweer en warm, 1970); The Rebels (Die Rebelle: Betoogstuk in nege episodes, 1970); Die verhoor: Verhoogstuk in drie bedrywe (1975); Knots in the Cable (Kinkels innie kabel: 'n verhoogstuk in elf episodes, an adaptation of William Shakespeare's Much Ado About Nothing, 1971); Afrikaners Make Merry (Afrikaners is plesierig, two one-act plays, 1973); Pavane (1974); The Hammer and the Witches (Die hamer van die hekse, 1976); Toiings on the Long Road (Toiings op die langpad, 1979); and Die Jogger (1997). In his plays, as in his novels, Brink has focused on the strains of living within a society that has institutionally justified terrible injustice and that treats any demonstration of moral doubt as dissent.

Other noteworthy plays by white dramatists that critically examined the effects of apartheid were David Herbert's A Kakamas Greek (1960) and Basil Warner's Try for White (1959), both of which treat the risks of being "colored" and trying to pass for white, and Lewis Sowden's The Kimberly Train (1959), which focuses on an interracial romance.

Yet, undoubtedly, the major voice in South African drama of the protest period and, indeed of any period, has been ATHOL FUGARD. Some have asserted that he is the most important writer in any genre that South Africa has ever produced. Others have argued that he is the most important dramatist writing in English of the last quarter of the 20th century, if not of the entire post–World War II period. Certainly his achievement has been widely recognized. The awards that he has received have included Tony Award nominations for best drama, for SIZWE BANZI IS DEAD and The Island (1975), for A Lesson from Aloes (1981), for "MASTER HAROLD" . . . AND THE BOYS (1982), and for THE BLOOD KNOT (1986); the Drama Desk Award and New York Drama Critics Circle Award for best play (1983) and the Evening Standard Award (1984), all for "Master Harold" . . . and the boys; the New York Drama Critics Circle Award for A Lesson from Aloes (1982); an Obie Award for Boesman and Lena (1971); a Plays & Players Award for best new play for Sizwe Banzi Is Dead (1973); the London Theatre Critics Award (1974); the Commonwealth Award for contribution to the American theater (1984); the Drama League Award (1986); the New York Drama Critics Circle Award (1988); and the Helen Hayes Award for direction (1990). His work has been not only widely reviewed but also the subject of much formal criticism.

The son of a British father and an Afrikaner mother, Fugard grew up in a household in which racial separatism was embraced by his expressive but volatile father and quietly undermined by his barely educated but highly principled mother. At the center of his plays is the presence, or the absence, of a common sort of decency that forces one to recognize the inhumanity in racial prejudice. To great emotional effect, the plays gradually reveal the competing capacities within each individual for human understanding and for self-absorbed but socially conditioned meanness. Every character confronts his or her own versions of this fundamental tension, often while being forced to recognize it or deal with it in another character. Each play is like a box of gears of different sizes in which the sprockets engage imperfectly or sometimes hardly at all. Fugard's plays address national and even universal themes, but do so through the very immediately realized relations between completely credible individual characters.

More than Fugard's plays themselves, however, his whole attitude toward the theater transformed it into a force for social change in South Africa. From the initial production of his first staged play, No Good Friday (1956), he featured black South Africans not only as actors in his plays but in every aspect of their production. He has consistently acknowledged that he found his voice as a dramatist by submerging himself in the black theater movement that was beginning to develop in Johannesburg and by working collaboratively with black playwrights, actors, and directors. His collaborations with John Kani and Winston Ntshona, in particular, very much defined his early work and the subsequent emphases in his career. Typically Fugard's early plays were performed in front of integrated audiences in out-of-the-way and sometimes improvised theaters. Yet, even the initial performances of plays such as The Blood Knot, which focuses on two mixed-race brothers, one of whom has much lighter skin, had a profound social impact across all segments of South African society. When such transformative events are ignored in the mainstream media, the credibility both of that media and of the social assumptions that it supports are undermined, giving hope to the oppressed and adding to the uneasiness of the oppressors. In South Africa, the apartheid system was undermined not only by revolutionary expression, which can be suppressed, but also by self-expression, which can never be silenced.

Fugard's reputation both owed a debt to and to some extent legitimized what became known as the township theater movement. In the 1960s and 1970s, black townships had few entertainment venues, and the government treated any sort of black self-expression as potentially seditious. Traveling theatrical troupes moved within and among the black townships, performing in improvised theaters and providing an underground cultural and political forum for black South Africans and for some white playwrights committed to the end of apartheid. Often, these traveling troupes ceased to exist when their main players were arrested, then were reconstituted when those players were released from police custody.

The most legendary figure among those involved in the township movement was Gibson Kente, based in the Transvaal. Recruiting mostly inexperienced actors to play the supporting roles, Kente himself played the leads in efficient but spare productions of such plays as *Can You Take It*, *The Jazz Prophet*, *Laduma*, *Mama and the Load*, *Manana*, and *Sikalo*. Two of Kente's protégés, Percy Mtwa and MBONGENI NGEMA, created *Woza Albert!*, a musical tour de force that proceeds from the premise that Jesus Christ has returned to earth in racially divided South Africa. Through the efforts of Barney Simon, the artistic director of the influential Market Theater, the play was eventually staged in the United Kingdom and the UNITED STATES, then toured internationally. Widely acclaimed, the play has been honored with the Fringe First Award at the Edinburgh Festival, the British Theatre Association Award, the Los Angeles Drama Critics Award, the San Francisco Bay Area Theatre Critics Circle Award, and the Obie Award. Mtwa later wrote *Bopha!* (1986), and Ngema later wrote the acclaimed musical *Sarafina* (1987) about the student uprising of 1976.

Maishe Maponya was the driving force behind the Bahumutsi Drama Group that used a church auditorium in Soweto as its main venue. Maponya's *Gangsters* (1985) shows the linkage between poetry and violent resistance to racial oppression. His other works have included *The Cry* (1976), *Peace and Forgiveness* (1977), *Umongikazi* (1983), *Bring Back the Drums* (1986), *The Valley of the Blind* (1986), *Jika* (1986), *The Hungry Earth* (1979), and *Western Deep Levels* (1994), the last of which dramatizes conditions in South Africa's mines.

Some of the other noteworthy theater troupes were the Imitha Players in East London, the Inkhwezi Players in Grahamstown, and the Shah Theatre Academy in Durban. In the 1970s, several troupes produced creative adaptations of classic plays in the Western canon. The Phoenix Players developed *Phiri*, an adaptation of Ben Jonson's *Volpone* set in a South African township. Working with the Theater Workshop Company in Durban, Welcome Msomi created *Umabatha*, a Zulu version of *MacBeth*. At the other end of the spectrum, one of the most iconoclastic of these theater troupes was the Junction Avenue Theatre Company, which staged improvisational plays such as *The Fantastical History of a Useless Man*, *Randlords and Rotgut*, and *Tooth and Nail*. In 1979, this company dramatized the issues involved in a strike by the Food and Canning Workers Union in a play called *The Sun Will Rise for the Workers*. The play proved so successful that the company developed a dozen other dramas addressing labor-related issues.

In the 1970s, as a complement to the township theater movement, several multiracial theaters were opened in South African cities, most notably the Space Theater in Capetown, the Stable Theater in Durban, and the Market Theater in Johannesburg. Those who operated these theaters defied apartheid at a time when the government had committed itself to using any means necessary to suppress dissent. Therefore, these theaters always faced a precarious future, relying on the government's hesitancy to provoke further international condemnation by completely censoring artistic expression. Often, rather than simply forcing the closing of the theaters, the authorities attempted to undermine them less directly by stigmatizing those involved in the productions, by intimidating those who might wish to attend performances, and by disrupting the performances themselves. The Space Theater passed through several sets of owners who were committed to keeping it open at all costs, but it finally did become clear that it would be prohibitively costly to continue to operate it. Before it closed, the Space Theater staged FATIMA DIKE's *The Sacrifice of Kreli* (1976). Initially staged at the theater during the Soweto uprising, the play would become the first by a South African black female dramatist to be published in book form. It focuses on a Xhosa king who chose exile over enslavement and thereby demonstrated the multiform nature of resistance to racial oppression.

The Market Theater in Johannesburg did outlast apartheid, in large part because Fugard's plays of the period were staged there: *A Lesson from Aloes* (1978), *"Master Harold" . . . and the boys* (1982), *The Road to Mecca* (1984), *A Place with the Pigs* (1987), *My Children! My Africa!* (1989), and *Playland* (1992). Although the earliest and most recent of these plays premiered at the Market Theater, the plays of the 1980s were staged first in the United States, and the attention they received overseas then made it difficult for the government to prohibit their staging in South Africa. Strict prohibitions were maintained, however, against publishing or distributing printed copies of Fugard's work. Ironically, in the postapartheid period, some critics have argued that the attention paid to Fugard's achievement has, in effect, diminished the recognition of the work of those black dramatists who have come to the fore under apartheid and in its aftermath. Although it may often be true that critics tend to focus on a major figure at the expense of some of his or her contemporaries, these complaints about the attention to Fugard's work typically seem to have more to do with Fugard's being white than with his being over-rated. Given the moral force of his vision, the risks that he accepted in giving it dramatic expression, and his promotion of the contributions of blacks to the development of South African theater, it seems a serious misrepresentation to assert that he has to any degree exploited the conditions under apartheid to enhance his own reputation.

In addition to plays by Gibson Kente, Maishe Maponya, Welcome Msomi, Percy Mtwa, and Mbongeni Ngema, the Market Theater also staged and first brought to broader attention the work of many other significant dramatists, including Reza de Wet (*Crossing*), P. G. du Plessis (*Siener in die Suburbs*, 1981), Kessie Govender (*Working Class Hero*, 1976), Zanemvula ("Zakes") Mda and Deon Opperman (*Dear Mrs. Steyn*, 1999), Paul Slabolepszy (*Saturday Night at the Palace*, 1984), Adam Small (*Kanna's Homecoming* [*Kanna hy kō hystoe*], 1965), Bartho Smit (*The Maimed* [*Die verminktes*], 1961), and Pieter-Dirk Uys (*Paradise Is Closing Down*,

1989). Perhaps the most prolific of these playwrights has been Matsemela Manaka, whose plays have included *Egoli: City of Gold* (1979), *Blues Afrika Café* (1980), *Vuka* (1981), *Mbumba* (1984), *Children of Asazi* (1986), *Domba, the Last Prince* (1986), *Pula* (1986), *Size* (1987), *Toro* (1987), *Koma* (1988), *Gorée* (1989), *Ekhaya: Coming Home* (1991), *Ekhaya: Museum over Soweto* (1991), and *Yamina* (1993). But the most important of these playwrights may ultimately be Zanemvula ("Zakes") Mda, whose plays have included *We Shall Sing for the Fatherland* (1973), *The Hill* (1978), *The Road* (1982), *The Nun's Romantic Story* (1992), and *The Dying Screams of the Moon* (1995). Mda has also written highly regarded novels and poetry.

Ironically, the Market Theater floundered financially after the end of apartheid. The rising crime rates in South Africa's cities reduced the audiences at downtown theaters and other cultural venues much more sharply than the secret police had been able to do. In addition, the relaxed restrictions on many forms of entertainment meant that drama no longer enjoyed the advantages that it had had under apartheid, when it had become not only the primary medium for undermining apartheid but also the preeminent form of entertainment.

In the postapartheid period, the following playwrights have produced noteworthy work: Fiona Coyne, Craig Freimond, Nazli George, Rajesh Gopie, Mark Lottering, Mondi Mayepu, Xoli Norman, Oscar Petersen, Lesego Rampolokeng, and Heinrich Reisenhofer. Although it is difficult to generalize about what has been the most wide-ranging and stylistically varied body of work ever produced for the South African theater, these playwrights have tended to focus on the causes and effects of social issues such as the AIDS epidemic, violent street crime, deepening impoverishment, ethnic tensions, and the appeal of various kinds of political extremism. The profound impact of the AIDS epidemic on all segments South African society was reinforced to the South African theater community when Gibson Kente announced that he had been diagnosed with AIDS and ultimately died of the disease.

FURTHER READING

Barrios, Olga. "Commitment and Performance in Black South African Theatre under Apartheid." *New England Theatre Journal* 11 (2000): 19–46.

Fourie, Lorraine. "The Early Days of South African Theatre." *South African Digest* 12 (October 1979): 14–16.

Frank, Heike. *Role-Play in South African Theatre.* Bayreuth, Germany: Thielmann and Breitinger, 2004.

Fuchs, Anne. "The New South African Theatre: Beyond Fugard." In *Post-Colonial English Drama: Commonwealth Drama since 1960*, ed. by Bruce King. New York: St. Martin's, 1992. 165–180.

———. "The Body of Change and the Changing Body in the Plays of Junction Avenue Theatre Company." In *South African Theatre as/and Intervention*, ed. by Marcia Blumberg and Dennis Walder. Amsterdam: Rodopi, 1999. 127–135.

Horn, Andrew. "South African Theater: Ideology and Rebellion." *Research in African Literatures* 17 (Summer 1986): 211–233.

Larlham, Peter. "The Impact of the Dismantling of Apartheid on Theatre in South Africa." *South African Theatre Journal* 6 (September 1992): 43–48.

Maree, Cathy. "Resistance and Remembrance: Theatre during and after Dictatorship and Apartheid." *South African Theatre Journal* 12 (May–September 1998): 11–33.

Oliphant, Andries. "Isolate the Enemy: Community and Conflict in Popular Theatre." *South African Theatre Journal* 6 (September 1992): 18–29.

Peterson, Bhekizizwe. "Apartheid and the Political Imagination in Black South African Theatre." *Journal of Southern African Studies* 16, no. 2 (1990): 229–245.

Schauffer, Dennis. "The South African Indian Contribution to the Developing Concept of an Indigenous South African Theatre." *South African Theatre Journal* 6 (September 1992): 84–92.

Sitas, Ari. "Description of a Struggle: South African Theatre since 1970." *World Literature Today* 70 (Winter 1996): 83–87.

"South African Theater." *South Africa.info.* http://www.southafrica .info/ess_info/sa_glance/culture/drama.htm (Accessed October 5, 2006).

Spitczok von Brisinski, Marek. "Rethinking Community Theatre: Performing Arts Communities in Post-Apartheid South Africa." *South African Theatre Journal* 17 (2003): 114–128.

Steadman, Ian. "Stages in the Revolution: Black South African Theater since 1976." *Research in African Literatures* 19 (Spring 1988): 24–33.

Steadman, Jim. "Performance and Politics in Process: Practices of Representation in South African Theatre." *Theatre Survey* 33 (November 1992): 188–210.

Steinberg, Carol, and Malcolm Purkey. "South African Theater in Crisis." *Theater* 25, no. 3 (1995): 24–37.

Martin Kich

SOWERBY, GITHA (1876–1970)

Little is known about Githa Sowerby's life. She was born on October 6, 1876, in Gateshead, Durham, was raised there, moved to London, married John Kendall (who died in 1952), and died in London on June 30, 1970. With her sister, the illustrator Millicent Sowerby, she produced numerous, unexceptional children's books.

Sowerby was lauded during the 1910s, owing to the commercial and critical success of her 1912 play, RUTHERFORD AND SON. On the basis of that play's call for emancipatory politics, Emma Goldman (1914) called her a "genius," asserting that Sowerby's "exceptional maturity is a phenomenon rarely observed." Since the 1980s, theatrical revivals and reprints of *Rutherford and Son* have boosted Sowerby's reputation, which rests solely on that one play. The texts of her subsequent full-length plays—*A Man and Some Women* (1914), *Sheila* (1917), *The Stepmother* (1924), and *The Policeman's Whistle* (1934)—have never been published and have been rarely performed. *Sheila* was poorly received and ran for only seventeen performances at St James's Theatre, London. The New Theatre run of *The Stepmother* was equally unsuccessful. The other two full-length plays were never performed.

However, the one-act *Before Breakfast* was performed in 1912 and published in 1913, and six theatrical pieces for children were published in 1910. The quality of both *Before Breakfast* and the *Little Plays for Little People* collection indicates that scholars of Sowerby's work should not limit themselves to *Rutherford and Son*. Performed as a curtain-raiser over sixty times at The Playhouse during 1912, *Before Breakfast* is set in Sir George Linton's house in London's Belgrave Square. The play shows the cold and unsocial conditions under which servants work and satirizes both the servants' acquiescence in the class system and the hypocrisy of rich people's calls for equality. The bad-tempered, reactionary servant, Mrs. Gray, demands extra productivity from her hapless young colleague, Jinny, and condemns "these new-fangled ideas—socialism or whatever they call it." Sir George's son, the rakish young George, calls himself a "socialist" and excoriates Jinny's servile demeanor. But, reverting to snobbery, he lambasts gossip-spreading journalists for consulting "footmen and kitchen maids." George's damaging, class-crossing relationship with Jinny's sister is revealed and he flees in self-interest. With earthy dialogue, *Before Breakfast* is fast-paced and strikes its targets sharply.

The *Little Plays for Little People* also show dramatic deftness. *Bearskin* reads like a happily ending *King Lear*. Old Woodcutter is abused by two selfish daughters but nursed by the hard-working Beauty. She agrees to marry the unprepossessing Bearskin so that her family will receive money, and she is rewarded when Bearskin is revealed as a handsome prince. The callousness of Woodcutter, who cherishes only material comforts, scarcely deserves Beauty's loyalty. *Fortunatus and Cassandra* approvingly dramatizes two siblings' refusal to be impoverished. After visiting Fortune's Castle, the young heroes reject notions of chance and fate, and acquire riches for their hitherto impoverished Grandparents. The moral is that the downtrodden should fight for improvements to their lives. Thus, this children's piece, together with *Before Breakfast*, is as central to Sowerby's oeuvre as *Rutherford and Son*.

[*See also England, 1860–1940*]

SELECT PLAYS: *Before Breakfast* (1912); *Rutehrford and Son* (1912); *A Man and Some Women* (1914); *Sheila* (1917); *The Stepmother* (1924); *The Policeman's Whistle* (1934)

FURTHER READING

Gardner, Viv. "Introduction." In *New Woman Plays*, ed. by Linda Fitzsimmons and Viv Gardner. London: Methuen, 1991. vii–xv.

Goldman, Emma. *The Social Significance of Modern Drama*. Boston: Richard G. Badger, 1914. 235–249.

Sowerby, Githa. *Little Plays for Little People*. London: Henry Frowde and Hodder & Stoughton, 1910.

——. *Before Breakfast: A Comedy in One Act*. London and New York: Samuel French, 1913.

——. *Rutherford and Son*. Ed. by Linda Fitzsimmons. London: Methuen, 1994.

Kevin De Ornellas

SOYA, CARL ERIK (1896–1983)

What else am I than a rather intelligent petit bourgeois, walking around extracting laws from what happens—happens with him and around him? Does not everything I have written—plays, novels, short stories, essays—contain a thought, picked up from Soya's philosophy of life or one may say: his cracker-barrel philosophy.

—Carl Erik Soya, 1972

Carl Erik Soya started his career as an *enfant terrible* of the contemporary Danish theatre. He was a rebel against the middle-class milieu to which he belonged. His father was an admired, but rather conventional painter of idyllic watercolors. Soya, on the contrary, saw it as his mission to prick holes in the idyllic surface and unveil the hypocrisy and double standards behind the respectable façade, but he did not totally break away from the liberal conservatism of his youth. His most original plays were written in the 1930s and 1940s; whereas later ones can seem a little repetitive. Satire and a marvelous sense for dialogue are Soya's strengths as a dramatist.

Soya's first play, THE PARASITES (*Parasitterne*, published 1929), was too controversial for The Royal Theatre, which preferred to stage his more harmless *The Laughing Maiden* (*Den leende Jomfru*, 1930). *The Laughing Maiden* explored sexual taboos, a recurrent theme in Soya's work.

In 1935, the same year as KJELD ABELL's *The Melody That Got Lost* ran in Riddersalen Theater, Soya's *Umbabumba* was performed in a private Copenhagen theater. Both plays are revue COMEDIES, but whereas Abell kept within the compass of the petty bourgeois family, Soya made the political world his stage. The play takes place in a primitive African state—Abell designed the imaginative jungle décor for the performance—in which Benito Mussolini, Adolf Hitler, and well-known Danish and European politicians are portrayed under pseudonyms such as Muga, Toto, and Wunga. Soya uses a parable technique popularized by BERTOLT BRECHT, which he might have known from the playwright's *Rise and Fall of the City of Mahagonny* (*Aufstieg und Fall der Stadt Mahagonny*, 1927–1929), performed in Copenhagen three years earlier. After indirect German pressure, The Royal Theatre abandoned plans to stage *Umbabumba*. His novel *A Visitor* (*En Gæast*, 1941), which portrays a family tyrannized by an enormous insect, was banned and Soya was interned by the German occupation forces. In 1945 he was forced to flee to SWEDEN.

Soya's plays are pervaded by moral indignation. With misanthropic delight he exhibits the hideous sides of human nature, but his growing fascination with PSYCHOANALYSIS made him more conciliatory toward his fellow creatures. In *Who Am I?* (*Hvem er jeg?*, 1932), a modern Everyman learns to cope with his destructive instincts when he is guided through his unconscious by Doctor Paprika, a Freudian psychoanalyst, magician, and mountebank.

During the 1940s Soya's plays became more philosophical, dealing with questions such as fate and guilt and discussing whether life is predetermined or a matter of pure coincidence. In a tetralogy that includes *Pieces of a Pattern* (*Brudstykker af et Mønster*, 1940), *Two Threads* (*To Traade*, 1943), *Thirty Years Respite* (*30 Aars Henstand*, 1944), and the satiric drama *Free Choice* (*Frit Valg*, 1948), Soya illuminated the question from different angles without providing any answers. He also changed style to what he called a neo-REALISM, which he felt allowed room for the accidental and the unpredictable.

[See also Denmark]

SELECT PLAYS: *The Parasites* (*Parasitterne*, published 1929); *The Laughing Maiden* (*Den leende Jomfru*, 1930); *Who Am I?* (*Hvem er jeg?*, 1932); *Lord Nelson Drops the Fig Leaf* (*Lord Nelson læagger Figenbladet*, 1934); *Umbabumba* (1935); *My Top Hat* (*Min høje hat*, 1939); *Pieces of a Pattern* (*Brudstykker af et Mønster*, 1940); *Two Threads* (*To Traade*, 1943); *Thirty Years Respite* (*30 Aars Henstand*, 1944); *After* (*Efter*, 1947); *Free Choice* (*Frit Valg*, 1948); *In the Summer Night* (*I den lyse Nat*, 1956); *Petersen in the Land of the Dead* (*Petersen I Dødsriget*, 1957); *The Departed Jonsen* (*Afdøde Jonsen*, 1966); *Only a Falling Tile* (*Bare en Tagsten*, 1966); *The Family Kristensen* (*Familien Kristensen*, 1970)

FURTHER READING

Bredsdorff, Elias, ed. *Contemporary Danish Plays: An Anthology*. London: Thames and Hudson, 1955.

Mitchell, P. M. *A History of Danish Literature*. 2nd ed. New York: Kraus-Thomson Organization, 1971.

Wamberg, Niels Birger. *Soya*. Copenhagen: Borgen, 1966.

Kela Kvam

SOYINKA, WOLE (1934–)

Wole Soyinka, born in 1934 in the Yoruba town of Abeokuta, is widely acknowledged as AFRICA's most accomplished dramatist. Educated at University College, Ibadan, and Leeds University, ENGLAND, Soyinka was a play reader for the Royal Court Theatre in London and has been a director, actor, teacher, and writer in Nigeria.

Using traditions established in Africa's other modern literary forms, Soyinka's plays portray themes of nationalist and transnational crises while embodying penetrating philosophical, political, and metaphoric investigations of African cultures. No other African combines political activism, inventive art, and philosophical analyses with so much eloquence and elegance, energy and intellectual rigor, as does this 1986 Nobel laureate in literature. Soyinka's works focus on a decolonizing attitude toward emergent and residual tyrannies, whether local or global. They

seek to create a space for radical constructions of postcolonial IDENTITY that endows people with "the simultaneous act of eliciting from history, mythology and literature, for the benefit of both genuine aliens and alienated Africans, a continuing process of self-apprehension whose temporary dislocation appears to have persuaded many of its non-existence or irrelevance in contemporary world reality" (Soyinka, 1976, x–xi).

Soyinka's notions of postcolonial identity and agency permeate his versatile body of works spanning well over five decades from the late 1950s; for purposes of cataloguing, they may be placed under three broad but fluid categories. Plays such as *Dance of the Forests* (1960), *Kongi's Harvest* (1965), *The Lion and the Jewel* (1959), *Trials of Brother Jero/Jero's Metamorphosis* (1974), *Opera Wonyosi* (1981), *Play of Giants* (1984), *Requiem for a Futurologist* (1983), *From Zia with Love* (1992), *The Beatification of Area Boy* (1995), and *King Ubaku* (2001) may be classified as political satire. Others including *The Strong Breed* (1962), *Madmen and Specialists* (1971), *The Road* (1965), *The Bacchae of Euripides* (1973), and *Death and the King's Horseman* (1976) may qualify as metaphysical drama. The third category, political street theater skits, is numerous and includes *Before the Blackout*, *After the Blowout*, *Priority Projects*, *Trials and Tribulations*, and *Rice*. Soyinka fashioned the satire of his political sketches into a low-budget film titled *Blues for a Prodigal* and a long-playing record labeled *Unlimited Liability Company*.

Throughout his plays and philosophical pronouncements, Soyinka has consistently sought an adequate language of resistance through an aesthetic comprising mythology, politics, and activism. Such an attitude is best understood through his seminal essay "The Fourth Stage" and eloquently illustrated by his play *Death and the King's Horseman*. "The Fourth Stage" was first published in an anthology of essays dedicated to the Renaissance scholar G. Wilson Knight in 1969 and later presented as one of a series of lectures at Churchill College, Cambridge. As a philosophical statement, the essay broke controversial new ground by calling for a revision of how cultural and political agencies are envisioned in Africa, particularly as its overlapping modernities sometimes freeze the dynamics of change on the continent. The essay, which elicited varied critical responses from within and outside Africa, suggests that Soyinka's DRAMATURGY, although inherently political, does not conform to prescriptive models for knowing or describing individual and collective political identities. In the dramatist's own words:

> I have been preoccupied with the process of apprehending my own world in its full complexity, also through its contemporary progression and distortions. . . . For after (or simultaneously with) an externally directed and conclusive confrontation on the continent must come a reinstatement of the values authentic to that society modified only by the demands of a contemporary world. (Soyinka, 1976, ix)

To apprehend his world, Soyinka in the "Fourth Stage" takes his readers and audiences into the tripartite structure of Yoruba cosmology—the worlds of the unborn, the living, and their ancestors. In such a structure, the acts of being born, of living, and of dying are seen as natural processes of transition. The birth of a child is an occasion for celebration, as is the death of an old person. The world of the living is an arena for reparations through sacrifices, rituals, and mythology. Soyinka, however, complicates and subverts the triplicity of the Yoruba world by suggesting a fourth stage, which he insists should be the most sought and fundamentally most fulfilling of all transitions. This fourth stage catalyzes social action; rather than a simple movement from one point to the other, it is a process that summons a consciousness for change without necessarily naming the manner of such change beyond its immediate anticolonial directions. According to Soyinka, such consciousness can happen in the worlds of the living, the ancestors, and even the unborn. The goal of the fourth stage is disalienation as a constant process of deconstructing domination and seeking a language of equity and justice.

To support his thesis on the fourth stage as the ultimate act of using culture to stimulate subjectivity, Soyinka delves into a Yoruba legend describing the origin of the world. According to this legend, a supreme deity called Orisa-Nla, whose life symbolized the cosmic stability of the world, was struck while tending his garden with a rock thrown by his servant Atunda—thereby the holy symbol of cosmic unity was shattered into a thousand and one pieces. Soyinka had earlier celebrated this rebellion in a poem called "Idanre": "All hail saint Atunda, first revolutionary / Grand iconoclast at genesis and the rest is logic" (Soyinka, 1968, 83).

Returning to the legend in "The Fourth Stage," Soyinka explains that the fragments of the disintegrated symbol of cosmic wholeness signify various godheads in the Yoruba pantheon, thereby assigning them different but complementary metaphysical functions in the mythologies of Yorubas. He goes on to explain that the dusts of cosmic disintegration formed the world of human beings. Consequently Atunda's insubordinate act led to the physical formation of two divided worlds: those of the gods and of human beings. Alienated and impassioned by a desire for cosmic wholeness, the helplessness of these disparate worlds was symbolized by the huge gulf separating them. Soyinka summons up frightening metaphors to underscore not only the enormity of the alienating gulf between these two worlds, but also of the impending violence that promised to attend any act of transgression in either world. The physical gulf and the social alienation between gods and human beings that it symbolized became a factor of constant concern for the gods, in particular, as they tried in vain to fulfill various functions bestowed on them by Orisa-Nla's parts. One of the more daring of their number, characterized simultaneously by creative and destructive impulses, became a prominent actor in his persistent quest to span the chasm between the gods and the humans. That god, Ogun, drew iron ore from the core of the earth to construct a

bridge. Leading a brigade of other gods, as Ogun walked the bridge in search of disalienation, he was thwarted by the violence of natural elements guarding the structure. Dismembered, but not with the finality of disintegration experienced by Orisa-Nla, Ogun was reconstituted and came back to enact his walk many times more. As a regenerative principle, this god's indefatigable pursuit of disalienation made him attractive enough for the dramatist to adopt him as his "patron saint."

Soyinka's use of the legend of Ogun in "The Fourth Stage" illustrates the sociopolitical themes and aesthetic features that characterize much of the playwright's dramatic legacy. It is his conception of TRAGEDY and the notion of agency it incorporates that has made "The Fourth Stage" the subject of intense scrutiny as a marker of Soyinka's dramatic style.

For Soyinka, tragedy is a song of lamentation expressing conditions of alienation and stimulating intense motivations for change. The tragic, for him, does not signify paralysis nor blind adherence to constituted mythology; rather it is a situation that sets up ontological certainties only to destabilize them to enable creativity and the pedagogy of self-reproduction. In developing what he calls African Tragedy, Soyinka proposes an aesthetic principle in which the direction of tragic art is to provoke a catharsis not to terrorize and consign a community to fatalism, but rather to hyper-sensitize the community to conditions of inequity and prompt the harnessing cultural resources to achieve disalienation. As Ogun's perseverance suggests, what makes this approach to a constructive, socially activist tragedy unique is its stress on repetitive, cyclical, and perpetual action as the essence of agency and anticolonial subjectivity.

"The Fourth Stage" challenged the assumptions of the West by depicting seamless transitions between past, present, and future and between the worlds of gods and of humans. Yet, its epistemological challenge to European modernity did not translate into an automatic endorsement of the supposed purity or supremacy of indigenous mythology. Instead, in a neocolonial context, Soyinka's approach suggests that the quest for decolonizing social and political identities must go beyond essentializing pristine traditions and structures conveniently remembered and kept intact through mythology. Unlike the anticolonial nationalisms of such movements like Negritudism and Afrocentrism, he urges the development of a consciousness of power relations within and between discourses of domination. To Soyinka, mythology, as an ideological and epistemological resource, is a site not for canonizing tradition and arresting social development, but for energizing the human spirit's desire for self and communal reproduction. As Soyinka himself states, the purpose of the tragic paradigm is to signify human beings as socially active and acting beings. The value of Yoruba mythic tragedy lies in its symbolic representations of the essence of human subjectivity and social agency, the impulse to act:

To act, the Promethean instinct of rebellion, channels anguish into a creative purpose which releases man from a totally destructive despair, releasing from within him the most energetic, deeply combative inventions which, without usurping the territory of the infernal gulf, bridges it with visionary hopes. (Soyinka, 1976, 146)

Soyinka's use of the tragic paradigm of Yoruba mythology to define notions of subjectivity and issue calls for positive social change emerges most distinctly in his classic play, *Death and the King's Horseman*. It is also this work that most clearly illustrates his use of tradition as a site for inter-modernist and intra-modernist struggles for the signs of agency.

SELECT PLAYS: *The Lion and the Jewel* (1959); *Dance of the Forest* (1960); *The New Republican* (1964); *Before the Blackout* (1965); *Kongi's Harvest* (1965); *The Road* (1965); *The Bacchae of Euripides* (1973); *Death and the King's Horseman* (1976); *Requiem for A Futurologist* (1983); *Before the Deluge* (1991); *A Scourge of Hyacinths* (1991); *From Zia with Love* (1992); *Beatification of Area Boy* (1995); *Boy Soldier* (1997); *Travel Club* (1997); *Document of Identity* (1999); *King Babu* (2001)

FURTHER READING

Dunton, Chris. *Make Man Talk True: Nigerian drama in English Since 1970*. London : Hans Zell, 1992.

Soyinka, W. *Idanre and Other Poems*. New York: Hill and Wang Publishers, 1968.

——. *Myth, Literature and the African World*. Cambridge: Cambridge Univ. Press, 1976.

Awam Amkpa

SPAIN

The development of modern Spanish theater can be divided into three broad periods. The first consists of dramas produced between 1860 and 1936, ending with the start of Spain's devastating Civil War. The second period spans the nearly four decades of the dictatorial regime of Francisco Franco, beginning with his ascent to power in 1939 and ending with his death in 1975. The third includes the post-Franco transition to democracy during the last twenty-five years of the 20th century and continues into the new millennium.

MODERN SPANISH THEATER BEFORE THE SPANISH CIVIL WAR: 1860–1936

Spain's theater at the end of the 19th and beginning of the 20th centuries developed three concurrent but distinct styles, ranging from traditional bourgeois high comedies and thesis plays, to the satirical and often lowbrow COMEDY of the *teatro por horas* (theater by the hour), to the experimental dramas of Spain's most important intellectuals. Although these three classes of dramatic production coincide historically, they differ greatly in both form and function.

Traditional commercial playhouses targeting middle-class audiences primarily produced thesis dramas and drawing room comedies that served to reinforce established social norms. Any criticism of Spanish society invariably fell comfortably within the boundaries of middle-class morality, limited to such themes as the condemnation of vice or the privileging of love, honor, and fidelity over brute lust and materialism. JOSÉ ECHEGARAY (1832–1916), whose melodramatic, neoromantic plays dominated the commercial theater scene in Spain during the last half of the 19th century, was the most popular dramatist of his time. He penned more than eighty plays, including THE GREAT GALEOTO (El gran galeoto, 1881) and *The Son of Don Juan* (El hijo de Don Juan, 1892), and won the Nobel Prize for Literature in 1904. His popularity inspired other playwrights to follow his lead, such as Joaquín Dicenta (1863–1917), whose social drama *Juan José* (1895) remains one of Spain's most frequently performed plays. However, Echegaray's popularity would not be matched until 1894, with the first works of the extraordinarily successful and prolific JACINTO BENAVENTE (1866–1954). Among his more than 170 plays, Benavente's two most acclaimed dramas are the 1907 play *The Bonds of Interest* (Los intereses creados), which drew from the commedia d'ell arte tradition to satirize a society based on hypocrisy and corruption, and the 1913 rural drama *The Ill-beloved* (La malquerida), dealing with themes of blind passion and forbidden love in a brilliantly crafted murder mystery. Although Benavente's style differed significantly from the melodramatic tendencies of Echegaray's works, exhibiting a more natural dialogue and an emphasis on the psychological depth of the characters, the large majority of his work still falls within the boundaries of traditional bourgeois theater. Benavente also won the Nobel Prize in 1922.

Alongside the melodramatic and often moralistic *alta comedia* of Echegaray and the later, more realistic dramas of Benavente, another style of theater also developed. At the end of the 19th century, a number of playhouses in Madrid were dedicated exclusively to *teatro por horas*, presenting a wide variety of comic or satiric one-act plays and sketches, with or without music, which employed the colorful language and stereotyped characters of the working class. These short plays, based on the tradition of the SAINETE and *entremes* of Spain's Golden Age, became known as the *género chico* or "little genre." One of the most popular and critically acclaimed writers of *género chico* plays was Carlos Arniches (1866–1943), with his one-act *cuadros de costumbres* (life portraits) like *The Saint of the Isidra* (El santo de la Isidra, 1898) and later more experimental and socially critical *comedias grotescas* (grotesque comedies) such as *Miss Trevélez* (La señorita de Trevélez, 1916).

However, while commercial playhouses, both traditional and *teatro por horas*, catered to "una España satisfecha consigo misma [a self-satisfied Spain]" (Ruiz Ramón, 1997), many of Spain's literary elite began to challenge bourgeois social norms with experimental plays that questioned the rigid moral structure and adherence to social convention that characterized so much of Spanish theatrical production of the era. BENITO PÉREZ GALDÓS (1843–1920), best known for his realist novels that called into question Spain's restrictive middle class values, brought that same commitment to REALISM and serious social issues to the

Spanish stage with plays such as *Reality* (*Realidad*) in 1892 and *Electra* in 1901. In many ways, Galdós's dramatic works represent a bridge between commercial theater and the more experimental and innovative drama of Generation of '98 writers like Miguel de Unamuno (1864–1936), Azorín (1873–1967) and Jacinto Grau (1877–1958), whose plays demonstrated a preoccupation with the decline of Spanish society, a rejection of the blatant commercialization of conventional Spanish theater, and a desire to explore more universal problems of the human condition.

RAMÓN DEL VALLE-INCLÁN (1866–1936), one of Spain's most innovative and influential writers, shared the concerns of his fellow Generation of '98 authors and rejected the naturalist tradition in favor of a more epic and universal style with his symbolist trilogy *The Savage Comedies* (*Comedias bárbaras*, 1907–1922). His later dramas, called *esperpentos*, moved away from epic theater to incorporate grotesque and absurdist tendencies that anticipated the work of playwrights like ANTONIO ARTAUD of the mid–20th century. The concept of the *esperpento*, a grotesque representation of the distortion, degradation, and inhumanity of Spanish society, is explicitly laid out in the dramatist's 1920 play BOHEMIAN LIGHTS (*Luces de Bohemia*) and reiterated a year later in *The Horns of Don Friolera* (*Los cuernos de Don Friolera*).

FEDERICO GARCÍA LORCA (1898–1936) was the other monumental figure in the world of Spanish theater in the years leading up to and including the Spanish Civil War. Spain's best-known playwright, Lorca joined Valle-Inclán and Unamuno in his rejection of facile commercial theater and searched for new methods to revitalize Spain's dramatic tradition. His early works treat universal issues through experimental dramas that incorporate the techniques of European movements such as SYMBOLISM and SURREALISM, while his trilogy of rural TRAGEDIES BLOOD WEDDING (*Bodas de Sangre*, 1933), YERMA (1934), and THE HOUSE OF BERNARDA ALBA (*La casa de Bernarda Alba*, 1936) brings together the vanguard techniques of earlier plays and a sharp criticism of narrow-minded Spanish society, demonstrating the tragic consequences of its restrictive social conventions. Lorca's brilliant career as dramatist and poet was cut short when he was executed by nationalist forces at the start of the Civil War.

The outbreak of hostilities between Nationalist and Republican forces in 1936 saw the end of a period of great vitality in Spanish theater. Although dramatic activity continued during the war, primarily in the form of AGITATION-PROPAGANDA plays in support of the Republican cause by playwrights like Rafael Alberti (1902–1999) and Max Aub (1902–1972), many of Spain's most important prewar dramatists either died or went into exile between 1936 and 1939.

SPANISH THEATER UNDER THE FRANCO REGIME: 1939–1975

The first decade of Francisco Franco's regime saw little dramatic production of any consequence. Commercial theater continued to cater to the comfortable middle class with evasionist dramas that ignored the devastating effects of the recent conflict. The plays emphasized realistic characters, plot, and dialogue and served to reinforce accepted social norms, much as their prewar predecessors did. Some of the more successful writers of this type of escapist drama were Joaquín Calvo Sotelo (1905–1993) with his 1954 play *The Wall* (*La muralla*), José María Pemán (1898–1981), who wrote historical verse dramas and contemporary moralist plays, and Julia Maura (1910–1970), one of the few Spanish women playwrights to find significant success during the Franco era. Whereas some exiled playwrights, like Aub and Alberti, continued to write dramas critical of the Spanish situation, ANTONIO BUERO VALLEJO (1916–2000) was the first to address the social problems of postwar Spain from within the country with his 1949 drama *The Story of a Staircase* (*Historia de una escalera*). Despite the severe censorship imposed by the dictatorship, Buero Vallejo continued to address both universal themes and current problems with plays that combined social commitment and innovative dramatic techniques. *The Maids of Honour* (*Las meninas*, 1960), *The Skylight* (*El tragaluz*, 1967), and *The Sleep of Reason* (*El sueño de la razón*, 1970), among others, made him Spain's premiere playwright of the postwar era.

A contemporary of Buero, ALFONSO SASTRE (1926–) employed expressionist and symbolist techniques to protest tyranny and violence in plays like *The Condemned Squad* (*Escuadra hacia la muerte*, 1954) and *Night Assault* (*Asalto nocturno*, 1959), though all of his work was severely censored during the dictatorship. Other significant figures in the development of Spanish theater under Franco include Carlos Muñiz (1926–), who also employed expressionist techniques to criticize Spanish society in *The Inkwell* (*El tintero*, 1960), Lauro Olmo (1923–1994), whose use of stark realism in plays like *The Shirt* (*La camisa*, 1962) and *English Spoken* (1968) highlighted the desperate situation of Spain's working classes, José Martín Recuerda (1925–), whose *esperpento*-like plays such as *The Savages in Puente San Gil* (*Las salvajes en Puente San Gil*, 1963) revealed the narrow-mindedness and hypocrisy of Andalusian society, and Jaime Salom (1925–) whose combination social realism and innovative dramatic technique appears in *The Dolphins* (*Los delfines*, 1969). MIGUEL MIHURA (1905–1979) demonstrated the potential for similar innovation in comic theater with the debut in 1952 of *Three Top Hats* (*Tres sombreros de copa*), an absurdist comedy originally written in 1932, which advocates personal freedom in the face of restrictive social norms. However, Mihura's later works appear to have more in common with the well-made plays of bourgeois commercial theater of the time.

The work of FERNANDO ARRABAL (1932–) in the last decades of the Franco dictatorship is also significant to the study of postwar Spanish theater, although the dramatist spent much of that time in FRANCE, and the majority of his plays have debuted there. Arrabal's most acclaimed play, THE ARCHITECT AND THE EMPEROR OF ASSYRIA (*El arquitecto y el emperador de Asiria*, 1967), with its emphasis on circularity, role-playing, and the diametric opposition of creation and destruction, reveals the profound influence of both absurdist techniques and the Panic Theatre movement of the 1960s. ANA DIOSDADO (1938–) emerged as a promising playwright in the waning years of the dictatorship as well, with her 1973 play Yours for the Asking (Usted también podrá disfrutar de ella), which exposed the personal and commercial exploitation of women in Spanish society.

The death of Francisco Franco in 1975 marked a crossroads for Spain's theatrical production with the elimination of censorship and the opportunity for greater freedom of expression on stage. Although almost all of the significant playwrights of the Franco period would continue to work after the fall of the dictatorship, the new political and social circumstances of post-Franco democracy provoked significant changes in the landscape of Spanish theater.

CONTEMPORARY SPANISH THEATER: 1975 TO PRESENT

The lifting of censorship restrictions produced two radically different reactions in the world of Spanish theater in the years immediately following Franco's death. Numerous important and previously suppressed works by Lorca, Valle-Inclán, Alberti, and Buero Vallejo and some new material by established playwrights like Buero Vallejo were presented; at the same time a flood of poor quality plays of a political or blatantly sexual nature also appeared. However, support for the fine arts was part of the new political agenda in the transition to a democratic Spain, and the late 1970s and early 1980s saw the establishment of several important governmental institutions dedicated to the furtherance of the dramatic arts, including the National Centre for Drama, the General Administration of Theatre and Spectacle, and the Centre for Theatre Documentation. In addition, a number of literary prizes were established during the last decades of the century to encourage the creation and production of new drama.

In addition to the continued presence of recognized dramatists like Buero Vallejo and Martín Recuerda, the 1980s saw the emergence of a new generation of playwrights that included a significant number of women writers, including CARMEN RESINO (1941–), who had started to publish shortly before Franco's death, PALOMA PEDRERO (1957–), and Concha Romero (1945–). Some significant dramatists among their numerous male counterparts include José Luis Alonso de Santos (1942–), Ernesto Caballero (1957–), and Fermín Cabal (1948–). The dramas produced by this new generación democrática—such as Pedrero's Lauren's Call (La llamada de Lauren, 1985), Romero's A Scent of Amber (Un olor a ámbar, 1983), Caballero's Squash (1986), Cabal's Dragonfly (Caballito del Diablo, 1983), and Alonso de Santos's Going Down to Marrakech (Bajarse al moro, 1985)—treat contemporary problems of individual sexuality, drug abuse, racial and social intolerance, and women's issues with realist techniques, although frequently that realism is interrupted by incursions into dream worlds or the juxtaposition of reality and fiction on stage.

These breaks with the realist mode anticipate the techniques of the next wave of Spanish playwrights to appear in the 1990s. Among these postmodern dramatists are Sergi Belbel (1963–), Itziar Pascual (1967–), and Lluïsa Cunillé (1963–), who writes in Spanish and Catalán and is widely recognized as one of Spain's best new playwrights. All have plays whose postmodern perspective is characterized by a sense of ideological and historical relativism, the absence of universal truths, and the radical experimentation with form and language that in many ways recalls the grotesque distortion of the esperpento and other AVANT-GARDE techniques. Frequently their dramas take the form of monologue—like Belbel's 1987 collection Elsa Schneider, Pascual's 1999 Postcard from the Sea (Postal del mar [Holliday Aut]), and Cunillé's 1995 Pedestrians (Vianants)—revealing the conflicting desires for individual self-expression and a core cultural identity (Parker), as well as the pressures of a market economy that requires innovative, often hybrid techniques and/or minimalist approaches to facilitate production. However, whether realist or experimental, this youngest generation of Spanish dramatists seems to continue in the tradition of its most talented predecessors, working to explore and expose the problems of a modern, or postmodern, Spain.

FURTHER READING

Edwards, Gwynne. Dramatists in Perspective: Spanish Theatre in the Twentieth Century. Cardiff: Univ. of Wales Press, 1985.

Ferreras, Juan Ignacio. El teatro en el Siglo XX (desde 1939) [Theatre in the Twentieth Century (since 1939)]. Madrid: Taurus, 1989.

Holt, Marion P. The Contemporary Spanish Theater (1949–1972). Boston: Twayne, 1975.

Parker, Mary, ed. Modern Spanish Dramatists: A Bio-Bibliographical Sourcebook. Westport, Conn.: Greenwood Press, 2002.

Ruiz Ramón, Francisco. Historia del teatro español. Siglo XX. [A History of Twentieth-Century Spanish Theatre], 11th ed. Madrid: Cátedra, 1997.

Heather Campbell-Speltz

SPEWACK, BELLA (1899–1990)

SPEWACK, SAM (1899–1971)

As Jewish immigrants who began their writing careers in the newspaper business and achieved their greatest success with a musical adaptation of William Shakespeare, the husband-and-wife duo of Sam and Bella Spewack were among the top COMEDY writers of the 1930s and 1940s, shuttling comfortably between Broadway and Hollywood and between straight plays and musicals. Other than a facility for gag-writing, their work was marked by no particular style; the subject of each piece dictated the tone.

Their backgrounds were remarkably similar. Each came to the United States as a child and grew up in New York: Sam was born on September 16, 1899, in Ukraine and graduated from Columbia University; Bella, who was born on March 25, 1899, in

ROMANIA, was educated through high school, Each became a newspaper reporter. They married in 1922, pursued individual careers as foreign correspondents for New York papers, and had their first Broadway play produced in 1928. It was a failure, as were three more before *Boy Meets Girl* delighted audiences and critics in 1935. A Hollywood satire with a firm grounding in experience (the Spewacks had written the screenplay for the 1934 film *The Cat and the Fiddle*), BOY MEETS GIRL ran for an impressive 669 performances.

Three years later, the Spewacks dusted off their 1932 comedy *Clear All Wires* and proposed it to Cole Porter as the basis for a musical. The result, *Leave It to Me*, was a mild satire about a U.S. ambassador to Moscow trying desperately to get himself recalled. Although a modest success, it is chiefly remembered as the show in which Mary Martin became a star singing "My Heart Belongs to Daddy."

After a Hollywood hiatus that produced two successful scripts, *My Favorite Wife* and *Weekend at the Waldorf*, the Spewacks again teamed with Porter for what would become their (and his) biggest triumph, *Kiss Me, Kate*. Bella, whose contribution to the project was larger than her husband's, initially resisted the idea of turning Shakespeare's *The Taming of the Shrew* into a musical, but relented after she conceived of it is a play-within-a-play set among a troupe of Shakespearean actors.

Porter, too, had to be persuaded to do the musical, and the creative process was marred by an ongoing feud between Bella and coproducer Arnold Saint Subber. When the show opened in 1948, however, it was an immediate smash, eventually running for 1,077 performances and winning the Tony Award as the season's best musical, plus individual Tonys for Porter and the Spewacks. Often revived, it has become a staple of musical repertory.

In 1953, the year *Kiss Me, Kate* became a Metro-Goldwyn-Mayer film, the Spewacks had their last Broadway critical success. Adapted from a play by Albert Husson and set in French Guiana at Christmas, 1910, *My Three Angels* is a sweetly amusing fable about a family of French expatriates whose affairs of money and the heart are set right by a trio of lovable convicts working around the house. It had a respectable run but did not make money. After one final Broadway failure in 1955, the couple never collaborated again, although Sam wrote two further unsuccessful comedies on his own. Sam died on October 14, 1971, in New York; Bella died on April 27, 1990, also in New York.

[*See also* United States]

SELECT PLAYS: *The War Song* (1928); *Clear All Wires* (1932); *Boy Meets Girl* (1935); *Leave It to Me* (1938); *Kiss Me, Kate* (1948); *Two Blind Mice* (Sam alone, 1949); *My Three Angels* (1953); *Festival* (1955)

FURTHER READING

McBrien, William. *Cole Porter: A Biography*. New York: Alfred A. Knopf, 1998.

Mordden, Ethan. *Beautiful Mornin': The Broadway Musical in the 1940s.* New York: Oxford Univ. Press, 1999.

Spewack, Bella. *Streets: A Memoir of the Lower East Side*. New York: The Feminist Press at the City Univ. of New York, 1995.

Clifford A. Ridley

SPIRÓ, GYÖRGY (1946–)

Unique among contemporary Hungarian playwrights, György Spiró has opened a series of windows onto an era of transition: out of the bane of Communism and into the bane of uncertainty. His plays reveal the crisis of the community, connecting the contemporary individual with history.

Born in Budapest, HUNGARY, on April 4, 1946, Spiró's first success, *The Impostor* (1982), a tribute to a previous generation of playwrights, falls within a tradition that assumes the efficacy of human action. The play is about a great 19th-century Warsaw actor making a guest appearance at the Polish theater in Vilnius, a city suffering under Russian oppression. On stage, the actor changes the end of *Tartuffe* into a criticism of the Czar, then vanishes, leaving the Poles with a sense of triumph.

Chickenhead (1985) is a major contribution to a generational shift in Hungarian drama. Spiró came of age in the seemingly hopeless stasis of the Soviet Bloc. The playwrights of his generation, bearing no responsibility for the events that got them into this situation, viewed their world with the clarity of outsiders, and their work is based on the absence of a moral order that could give meaning to human action. Set in the depths of urban decay, the naturalistic *Chickenhead* ends in a meaningless murder. The fragmentary dialogue reflects a level of consciousness that complicates questions of personal responsibility. The issue of the then-socialist society's responsibility for such conditions is less complicated.

After the 1989 change of regime, Spiró's work reveals a civil society that won its freedom but lost its moral footing after decades of subservience. In two satiric plays he tackles the ruthlessness of the new capitalism. In *Latest Zrinyiade* (1991), a 16th-century military hero, reincarnated in modern times, becomes a tycoon. *Racket* (1996) is a nightmarish FARCE about a town where the only virtue is selfishness. These plays take place in a world in which the time-honored role of the intellectual has been all but devalued. This is the theme of *Dobardan* ("good day" in Serbo-Croatian; 1994), in which an engineer tries to adopt a Bosnian orphan as an act of human solidarity, only to be abandoned by his wife and daughter and to lose the respect and support of the outside world.

Spiró's masterly portrayals of the losers and aggrieved in a region savaged by history is evident in his latest plays. *Quartet* (1996) is a homecoming of sorts. Alienated by life in the West, a man returns to Budapest after a forty-year absence, seeking the community and human connections he remembers from boyhood. Instead, he finds a society at least as atomized and alienating as the one he left behind. The issue of Jewish identity in Hungary is the subject of two recent Spiró plays. Set in 1941, *Blackout* (2001) shows how not even the sincere and deep love of a married couple can survive the brutality of history. The legacy of that history is examined in *Soap Opera* (1998). As a playwright, Spiró is the most dedicated chronicler of the current, rapidly changing era in Hungary.

SELECT PLAYS: *Evening Program* (Esti műsor, 1981); *The Impostor* (Az imposztor, 1982); *The Garden* (A kert, 1983); *Chicken Head* (Csirkefej, 1985); *Latest Zrinyiade* (Legújabb Zrinyiász, 1991); *Good Day* (Dobardan, 1994); *Racket* (Vircsaft, 1996); *Quartet* (Kvartett, 1996); *Domestic Bliss* (Honderű, 1997); *Soap Opera* (Szappanopera, 1998); *Blackout* (Elsötétítés, 2001)

FURTHER READING

Bécsy, Tamás. *Kalandok a drámával, Magyar drámák 1945–1989* [Adventures with Drama, Hungarian Dramas 1945–1989]. Budapest: Balassi Kiadó, 1996.

Ézsiás, Erzsébet. *Mai magyar dráma* [Hungarian Drama Today]. Budapest: Kossuth Könyvkiadó, 1986.

Radnóti, Zsuzsa. *Lázadó dramaturgiák* [Dramaturgies in Revolt]. Budapest: Palatinus, 2003.

Eugene Brogyányi

SPLIT BRITCHES

Split Britches was formed in 1980, three years after the chance meeting of its two founding members, Peggy Shaw (who was then performing with the all-male drag group Hot Peaches) and Lois Weaver (performing with Spiderwoman, a multiethnic feminist performance group). Their first play, entitled *Split Britches*, premiered at the Allcraft Center, St. Marks Place, New York City, in 1980. Shaw and Weaver spent the next year developing this production with performance artist DEB MARGOLIN. The second Annual WOW Festival (1981) premiered their final version of *Split Britches*. The three collaborated on plays such as *Beauty and the Beast* (1982), *Upwardly Mobile Home* (1984), *Little Women* (1988), and *Lesbians Who Kill* (1992). These projects placed them at the center of the feminist and lesbian radical performance culture.

Split Britches continued to dismantle the male and female binaries by reconsidering the performance of IDENTITY and power relations through their representations of femme and butch in collaboration with performance artists such as BlooLips (*Belle Reprieve*, 1991) and Stace Makishi (*Salad of the Bad Cafe*, 2000). As such, one might liken their work to Charles Ludlum's Ridiculous Theatrical Company. Like Ludlum's characters, Split Britches allow for multiple sexual identities to be played out on the stage. The characters of Split Britches plays are not defined as transvestite roles as Ludlum's characters often are. But what the two companies do share is the making of plays in which characters perform the spectrum of politics, gender, and sexuality that are a vital part of the queer community.

Perhaps no work demonstrates their bold theatrical arsenal better than *Dress Suits for Hire* (1987), a play spun out of an East Village myth about two sisters who live in a rental clothing store until one is murdered by a topless bar owner named Little Peter. A collaboration with playwright and performance artist Holly Hughes, this "dyke-noir" premiered at P.S. 122 in New York City. *Dress Suits* carries the Split Britches tradition of employing different performance genres (such as folklore, autobiography, pulp fiction, erotic fantasy, and cabaret) to create a sociocultural montage of contradictory realities that shatters metaphors of gender and sexuality.

Now in their twenty-fifth year, Split Britches has won Best Ensemble from *The Villager* in 1985 and the Obie in 1991 for their collaboration with BlooLips on *Belle Reprieve*. Shaw herself has earned two Obies for acting (Deelux in *Dress Suits*, 1988; *Menopausal Gentleman*, one-woman show, 1999). In 1991, Weaver became the co-Artistic Director of Gay Sweatshop in ENGLAND and has since directed Shaw and Hughes in their one-woman shows as well as created her own performance piece entitled *Faith and Dancing*. Margolin has gone on to create a career as a solo performance artist, penning and performing works assembled in the collection *Of All the Nerve: Deb Margolin*, edited by Lynda Hart. Her work earned her the Obie for Sustained Excellence in Performance for the year 1999–2000.

Split Britches's legacy to American theater can be traced through new theater festivals including *Throws Like a Girl* (Austin, March 2005), which celebrates and promotes the work of female American theater artists, through the success of performers with whom Shaw and Weaver have collaborated, and through the emergence of other gender- and norm-challenging theater companies such as FIVE LESBIAN BROTHERS. Split Britches plays are an invaluable part (and intervention into) Modern American drama and culture.

[*See also* Gay and Lesbian Drama; United States, 1940–Present]

FURTHER READING

Case, Sue-Ellen. *Split Britches*. New York: Routledge, 1996.

Davy, Kate. "Reading Past the Heterosexual Imperative: 'Dress Suits to Hire.'" *The Drama Review* 33, no. 1 (1989): 153–170.

Dolan, Jill. "Performance, Utopia, and the 'Utopian Performative.'" *Theater Journal* 53, no. 3 (2001): 455–479.

Hart, Lynda, and Deborah Margolin. *Of All the Nerve*. New York: Cassell Academic, 1999.

Hart, Lynda, and Peggy Phelan. *Acting Out: Feminist Performances*. Ann Arbor: Univ. of Michigan Press, 1993.

Shaw, Peggy, Deborah Margolin, and Lois Weaver. "Split Britches: A True Story." *Women and Performance* 4, no. 2 (1989): 68–95.

Jessica Kaplow Applebaum

SPÖKSONATEN See THE GHOST SONATA

SPRAWA DANTONA See THE DANTON CASE

SPREADING THE NEWS

Spreading the News, a one-act COMEDY by LADY GREGORY (Isabella Augusta Persse), was first performed by the Irish National Theatre Society on the opening night of the Abbey Theatre, Dublin, IRELAND, in a double-bill with *On Baile's Strand* by W. B. YEATS, on December 27, 1904. It became a popular and often revived play in the repertory of the Abbey. The plot is laid in the imaginary village of Coon in the West of Ireland, a setting used in a number of Gregory's plays. The characters—a policeman, magistrate, women shopping for goods or selling them in the market, and so forth—speak a version of Hiberno-English Gregory invented and called Kiltartan. The idiom influenced the stage-speech of JOHN MILLINGTON SYNGE's plays.

The story is characteristic of early Abbey plays in its folk simplicity. A casual remark by Mrs. Fallon that her often unfortunate husband Bartley had "gone up the road following Jack Smith with a hayfork" is changed as it is told by one person to another, as in a game of Chinese whispers, until it becomes a racy tale that Bartley Fallon has killed Jack Smith with a fork and run off to America with Smith's wife. Although no one was less likely to commit the daring crimes of adultery and murder—he is far too feckless—Fallon is about to be sent to prison by the new magistrate (on the look-out for Irish atrocities), when the whole tale unravels with the arrival of Jack Smith. The speed and agility with which the collective fantasy is built up makes the play enjoyable to act and to watch.

The play is all words, but not a word is wasted. Its representation of an "innocent people" who escape poverty by collaboratively inventing a richer world of fantasy had its impact on other Irish dramatists. This analysis of the Irish temperament, for instance, is also found in THE PLAYBOY OF THE WESTERN WORLD and BRIAN FRIEL's TRANSLATIONS. The Irish characters in the play are not deeply satirized—they are themselves conscious that they have no other business but minding other people's business—but they are made to appear so lovable that the comedy can appear condescending.

FURTHER READING

McDiarmid, Lucy, and Maureen Waters, eds. *Lady Gregory: Selected Writings*. New York: Penguin, 1995.

Saddlemyer, Anne, and Colin Smythe, eds. *Lady Gregory: Fifty Years After*. Gerrards Cross, Buckinghamshire: Colin Smythe, 1987.

Adrian Frazier

SPRING AWAKENING

FRANK WEDEKIND's *Spring Awakening* (*Frühlings Erwachen: Eine Kindertragödie*, 1891) was first produced by MAX REINHARDT in 1906 in Berlin, fifteen years after it was written. Even so, the text had to be severely modified to meet standards of decency. Despite all the obstacles and precautions (Wedekind paid for the drama's publication with his own funds), *Spring Awakening* has remained one of Wedekind's best-known and longest-running plays.

Wendla Bergmann has just turned fourteen, and her mother is reluctant to explain the facts of life to her. Meanwhile, Melchior Gabor and Moritz Stiefel discuss their first experiences with "masculine stirrings." Melchior promises Moritz to elucidate the secrets of human reproduction in an essay. Soon after, Melchior and Wendla meet in the woods, where he agrees to her request to be beaten; during a subsequent meeting in a hayloft, the two have intercourse. Moritz, in the meantime, has failed his school examinations and asks Melchior's mother to finance his fleeing to America. Moritz fears his own parents' reaction and threatens suicide if Frau Gabor denies his request. She does just that, however, and Moritz shoots himself on the riverbank. Moritz's father disowns him at the funeral, and the school authorities decide to expel Melchior: His essay on procreation is seen as the cause of Moritz's demise and as a potential threat to the school. Melchior's father convinces Frau Gabor that she has been too liberal in raising their son, who is then sent to a reformatory to learn discipline and "moral principles." At news of Wendla's pregnancy, her mother swiftly arranges an abortion, which leads to Wendla's death.

Following his escape from the reformatory, Melchior stumbles across the headstones of Moritz and Wendla and blames himself for the deaths. An apparition of a headless Moritz appears, beckoning Melchior to join the dead and mock the living. He is interrupted, however, by a Masked Man who convinces Melchior to follow him—and thus affirm life—as the drama ends.

Spring Awakening lacks a traditional dramatic development of conflict and resolution; the scenes are largely self-contained and loosely connected. Critics have compared Wedekind's drama to Georg Büchner's (1813–1837) *Woyzeck* (written 1836–1837, published 1879) in its form and use of language. *Spring Awakening* is considered Wedekind's break with NATURALISM and a precursor to EXPRESSIONISM. Although subtitled "A TRAGEDY," the drama does not follow traditional principles of the genre and should also be seen in its relationship to COMEDY.

Spring Awakening offers a scathing attack on the social institutions of the Wilhelmine era. Parents are portrayed as prudish and selfish; schoolmasters caricatured as vain, pedantic, and strict beyond reason; the church aloof and literal in its use of scripture; the reformatory brutal and impersonal. The children submit to natural sexual impulses partly in defiance, partly in ignorance of societal expectations. Scenes of masturbation, sadomasochism, intercourse, homosexual intimacy, suicide—and even reading *Faust*—stand in stark contrast to the "moral world order" and bourgeois bliss imagined by the adults.

The Masked Man (played by Wedekind in the original production), who defines "real" morality as the product of both (individual) desire and (objective) duty, ultimately acts as a kind of arbiter between the polarized entities of individual vitalism and social repression.

[See also Germany]

FURTHER READING

Boa, Elizabeth. The Sexual Circus: Wedekind's Theatre of Subversion. Oxford: Blackwell, 1987.

Lewis, Ward B. The Ironic Dissident: Frank Wedekind in the View of His Critics. Columbia, S.C.: Camden House, 1997.

Pickerodt, Gerhart. Frank Wedekind: Frühlings Erwachen [Frank Wedekind: Spring Awakening]. Frankfurt: Diesterweg, 1984.

Wagener, Hans, ed. Erläuterungen und Dokumente. Frank Wedekind: Frühlings Erwachen [Commentary and Documents. Frank Wedekind: Spring Awakening]. Stuttgart: Reclam, 1980.

Martins Masulis

STAGE DIRECTIONS AND STAGE SETS

Plays written and printed before the 19th century contained very few stage directions. They became important in the early MELODRAMA, which featured much more physical action than classical drama. Often the directions in the ACTING versions were technical and intended for actors, not readers. "In the side flat, R.2E, is the door" meant the door was in the piece of painted canvas placed at the second entrance (for the actors) at the right side of the stage (from the actor's point of view). The rise of the realistic drama, with the replacement of the wings and flats with more solid scenery and the positioning of furniture about the stage, called for more direction. Similarly, as acting became more life-like, instructions for the actor became more detailed. The directions for the tea party in CASTE (1867) by T. W. ROBERTSON, who was a director as well as an actor, afford a fine example of the change that was taking place.

HENRIK IBSEN was largely responsible for bringing about this change. Much of his income came from the printed play, and his stage directions were intended to aid the reader as much as the actor. (His directions are from the audience's point of view, as are EUGENE O'NEILL's). The very lengthy descriptions in GEORGE BERNARD SHAW's early plays show the extent to which he had readers in mind.

Those stage directions having to do with what the eyes see often have a much more powerful effect on the viewer than on the reader, who after reading the direction once may easily forget it. The conscientious reader will draw a sketch of the scene as a reminder of what the stage looks like. A visual symbol will have a much greater and longer lasting impact on the stage than on the page. In Shaw's Candida, Titian's painting of the Assumption of the Virgin has a central place in the set, serving as a constant, at times subliminal, reminder of the psychological rela-

tionship of the two principal characters, the adolescent Eugene and the motherly Candida.

Portraits can afford a way of keeping the past always present in the action. The portrait of the murdered man in ÉMILE ZOLA's THÉRÈSE RAQUIN is as inescapable as the punishment that will come to the murderers. In Ibsen's HEDDA GABLER, every time our eye glimpses the portrait of Hedda's father in the uniform of a general, we are reminded of how much this manly woman owes to him. In Ibsen's ROSMERSHOLM, "the walls are hung with past and recent portraits of clergymen, officers and officials in their robes and uniforms," powerful visual symbols of the spell cast by family tradition and established society, the dead still present among the living. O'Neill in MOURNING BECOMES ELECTRA uses portraits for the same purpose but intensifies the stage effect: "In the flickering candlelight the eyes of the Mannon portraits stare with a grim forbiddingness."

The Christmas tree in the first act of Ibsen's A DOLL'S HOUSE establishes the warm atmosphere of a happy home. When we see it in the next act stripped of its decorations, we sense that Nora's marriage is in trouble. If Ibsen (who had a painter's eye) had not introduced the bare, unadorned tree, an insightful designer would have.

O'Neill's stage directions seem too numerous, encumbering the text. "Lavinia trying to break away from her, half putting her hands up to her ears," "Then suddenly—with a strange jealous bitterness": directions like this seem to belong in a novel, not a playscript. Many actors resent being dictated to in this way, but when they violate O'Neill's directions, the ear catches a false note. O'Neill grew up in the theater and he knew how to create the effect that he wanted.

The original production of THE ICEMAN COMETH (1946), which O'Neill himself saw through rehearsals, had a set designed by his long-time friend ROBERT EDMOND JONES that perfectly captured the thrust of the plot. The first two acts took place in the back room of the tavern, but in the third act, as the characters made their feeble attempts to rid themselves of their pipe dreams, the set showed the barroom close to the street, with some light coming in. When the play is staged in the round, as it often is, that highly suggestive movement toward the light is lost.

In the best set designs, thanks either to the dramatist or the designer or to both, the whole set serves a symbolic function. In Shaw's HEARTBREAK HOUSE, the room represents part of "an old-fashioned high-pooped ship," and all the talk in the play about the ship of state running aground has a visual backing. In AUGUST STRINDBERG's THE DANCE OF DEATH, the set is a round room in a fortress, underscoring both the plight of the main characters, a man and wife trapped in an unhappy marriage, and the circular form of the plot. For ARTHUR MILLER's DEATH OF A SALESMAN, Jo Mielziner devised a unit set that memorably captured the subjective nature of the drama. SAMUEL BECKETT's set for WAITING FOR GODOT is as visually eloquent as Beckett's text.

O'Neill complained that no one had ever realized the set for DESIRE UNDER THE ELMS as he wished it. His own sketch shows what he wanted, a visual equivalent of what he describes in words: the elms "bend their trailing branches down over the roof. . . . There is a sinister maternity in their aspect, a crushing, jealous absorption."

One of the most striking visual effects in modern drama occurs at the end of Ibsen's GHOSTS. After nearly three acts of rain, the sun bursts forth as Oswald goes insane. This is also one of the most cruelly ironic effects in drama, since the sun symbolizes the joy of life that Oswald has lived for and believed in.

Stage props (properties) are sometimes emblematic of what the whole play is about. The songbird in a cage in Strindberg's MISS JULIE, the pistol in *Hedda Gabler*, and the seagull in ANTON CHEKHOV's play THE SEAGULL are virtual stand-ins for the main characters. Some props bring to light what is buried in the dialogue (SUBTEXT). The cigar that Nora lights for Dr. Rank in *A Doll's House* and the fire poker that Candida holds in her hand in Shaw's play (act 3) were especially potent symbols in an age of sexual repression.

Sound can be hauntingly effective in the theater. The foghorns in LONG DAY'S JOURNEY INTO NIGHT conjure up an image of the fog surrounding the house and of a family drifting away from reality. The sound of a breaking string in Chekhov's THE CHERRY ORCHARD and of axes chopping down the trees well up from the very heart of the drama.

[*See also* Dramatic Dialogue]

FURTHER READING

Ashley, Leonard R. N. "A Note on Stage Directions." In
    Nineteenth-Century British Drama, ed. by Leonard R. N. Ashley.
    New York: Scott, Foresman, 1967. 18–21.

Evert Sprinchorn

STAGE DOOR

A play in three acts by GEORGE S. KAUFMAN and EDNA FERBER, *Stage Door* was first produced by Sam H. Harris on October 22, 1936, at the Music Box Theatre in New York. It was directed by Kaufman himself, starred Margaret Sullavan, and ran for 169 performances.

The play is set in the Footlights Club in New York City, a residence for aspiring stagestruck women. A few lucky ones work on Broadway, but this is during the Depression and jobs are scarce; most spend months working as a salesclerks in department stores or dancing in nightclubs. One leaves for Hollywood. Another has intimate relations with a rich married man and leaves the Club. Still another, penniless and discouraged, commits suicide.

With a cast of twenty-one women and eleven men, the story revolves around Terry Randall. In one sense, it is Terry's success story, as she gains both work and marriage in the end. Terry holds to her dream, earning her living elsewhere, and finally gets "a really fine" play to star in. Its producer-to-be is David Kingsley, also stagestruck, working as a Hollywood agent in New York. Terry and David have been dating for several months, and at the end of the play, they find themselves in love and working together for theater.

One issue implanted in *Stage Door* is its playwrights' unmistakable attitude toward Hollywood. Terry twice giving up a chance to become a movie star is contrasted with Keith Burgess, a radical playwright with whom Terry had worked writing a play for a year. The play opens on Broadway starring another woman, and when Keith becomes successful, he moves to Hollywood with a $2,000-a-week contract, as so many other talented playwrights did during this period. After a year's stay, Keith comes back, but says he's signed up "for another year." He is described by Terry's friend Judith as "one of those fellows started out on a soapbox and ended up in a swimming pool." Before he left for Hollywood, Keith told Terry, "I'll write their garbage in the daytime, but at night I'll write my own plays," but he didn't keep his promise. Terry dismisses him: "When you walked out on me a year ago, you walked out on yourself, too."

Terry's roommate, Jean Maitland, shares this attitude. Jean left for Hollywood a year ago, became a big movie star, and returns to New York to star on Broadway. However, after two weeks' rehearsal, she's found unable to act, and Hollywood executives decide to sell the play to David with Terry to star in it.

These gibes at Hollywood notwithstanding, *Stage Door* was turned into a very successful film, as so many of Ferber's novels and plays were. For stage and screen, *Stage Door* proved a good vehicle for actors to show their talents, portraying, with much laughter and music, young women's realistic choices, valid in any profession.

[*See also* United States, 1929–1940]

FURTHER READING

Gilbert, Julie. *Ferber: Edna Ferber and Her Circle*. New York: Applause,
    1999.
Goldstein, Malcolm. *George S. Kaufman: His Life, His Theater*. New York:
    Oxford Univ. Press, 1979.
Shafer, Yvonne. *American Women Playwrights 1900–1950*. New York:
    Peter Lang, 1997.

Misako Koike

STANISLAVSKY, KONSTANTIN (1863–1938)

Born on January 5, 1863, in Moscow, Konstantin Stanislavsky was the son of a rich factory owner. He saw his task as both actor and director to bring together the creative actor, as defined by Russian realistic traditions, and the organically conceived production as staged by the Meiningen troupe. In 1898 he founded the MOSCOW ART THEATER (MAT) with Vladimir Nemirovich-Danchenko, and together they headed the MAT for forty years.

A new theatrical language was created by Stanislavsky and Nemirovich-Danchenko in ANTON CHEKHOV's THE SEAGULL (1898), for which Stanislavsky wrote the production plan. Stanislavsky, who did not at first understand the play, discovered that detailed physical action revealed the inner state of thought and emotion. Creating the illusion of life, Stanislavsky also revealed the novelty of Chekhov's dialogue, which he called the SUBTEXT, the repressed emotion underlying conversation. The method elaborated in Chekhov's plays was applied to other realistic playwrights, but proved inimical to TRAGEDY and to the work of William Shakespeare, both of which were seldom directed by Stanislavsky at the MAT and, usually, with qualified success.

He emphasized historical authenticity in drama by Aleksei Tolstoy (1898). In LYOV TOLSTOY's THE POWER OF DARKNESS (1902), he reproduced a peasant environment, although the tragic spirit of the drama became buried under a wealth of naturalistic detail. DIRECTING MAKSIM GORKY's first plays, Stanislavsky was interested in their depiction of modern life rather than the political views of the author, and this approach turned *The Merchant Class* (1901) into a dreary family history, *Children of the Sun* (1905) into a benign portrait of the intelligentsia, and THE LOWER DEPTHS (1902) into a combination of NATURALISM with ROMANTICISM. HENRIK IBSEN's AN ENEMY OF THE PEOPLE (1901) was the most successful of Stanislavsky's four Ibsen productions. Critics saw affinities between his own personality and that of Dr. Stockmann in Ibsen's play, with his passionate idealism, the same commitment to truth, as well as an understanding of the COMEDY of character.

His excursions into symbolist theater led to interesting, yet never wholly satisfactory, attempts to stage works by MAURICE MAETERLINCK, LEONID ANDREEV, and KNUT HAMSUN, while Stanislavsky's own unfinished play, *The Comet* (1908), shows the influence of Russian SYMBOLISM. Attempts to stage ALEKSANDR BLOK's poetic plays *Song of Destiny* and *The Rose and Cross* continued for years, but because Stanislavsky found they contradicted his concept of human nature, he never staged them. Soon after beginning to elaborate his system of actors' training, he staged Ivan Turgenev's A MONTH IN THE COUNTRY (1909) as a laboratory experiment designed to capture "the inner life of the human spirit" in a psychological manner. In order to broaden the Theatre's experience, he invited Edward Gordon Craig to stage *Hamlet* (1911) and "World of Art" designer Aleksandr Benois to direct and design productions of Molière's *The Imaginary Invalid* (1913) and Carlo Goldoni's *The Mistress of the Inn* (1914), among others.

In the crisis at the MAT during World War I, Stanislavsky saw the creation of studios as a means of establishing a new generation of directors and actors. He welcomed the 1917 revolution "as the miraculous liberation of RUSSIA," despite its involving the expropriation of the Alekseyev factories and the loss of his personal fortune. His production of Lord Byron's *Cain*, in 1920, reflected the pain of revolution and civil war. During the years 1918–1922, Stanislavsky continued to play major roles for new popular audiences, taught "the system," and directed new, or revived old, productions. He led foreign tours to Berlin, Paris, and the UNITED STATES in 1922–1924, with consequences for ACTING and stage production in America that reverberate to this day. Back in Moscow, he reinvigorated stage REALISM with productions of ALEKSANDR OSTROVSKY's *An Ardent Heart* (1926) and Pierre Beaumarchais's *The Marriage of Figaro* (1927). He supported MIKHAIL BULGAKOV by codirecting DAYS OF THE TURBINS (1926), and he welcomed the same dramatist's FLIGHT, although this was banned before production. Vsevolod Ivanov's *Armoured Train 14–69* (1927) confirmed MAT's status as a Soviet theater, although this was something of a sell-out by Stanislavsky, who did not favor SOCIALIST REALISM in the arts.

Searching for contemporary writers, he directed controversial social satires such as Valentin Kataev's *The Embezzlers* and Leonid Leonov's *Untilovsk* (both in 1928). He also coproduced Aleksandr Afinogenov's *Fear* (1931), Ostrovsky's *Talents and Admirers* (1933), and collaborated, unhappily, with Bulgakov on productions of the latter's *Molière* (1936) and his dramatization of Nikolai Gogol's *Dead Souls* (1932), in all of which he pursued pure acting achievement unencumbered by production values. The production of Molière's *Tartuffe*, on which he worked exhaustively, was premiered in 1939 after his death on August 7, 1938, in Moscow. Stanislavsky, a life-long Christian, was buried in the Novo-Devichy monastery graveyard in Moscow, but his grave was not allowed a cross until 1994.

FURTHER READING

Amiard-Chevrel, C. *Le Theatre Artistique de Moscou (1898–1917)* [The Moscow Art Theatre]. Paris: CNRS, 1979.

Benedetti, Jean. *Stanislavski, a Biography*. London: Methuen, 1988.

Carnicke, Sharon Marie. *Stanislavsky in Focus*. Harwood: Amsterdam, 1998.

Rudnitsky, Konstantin. *Russian and Soviet Theatre: Tradition and the Avant-Garde*. Tr. by Roxanne Permar. London: Thames & Hudson, 1988.

Slonim, Marc. *Russian Theatre from the Empire to the Soviets*. London: Methuen, 1963.

Smeliansky, Anatoly. *Is Comrade Bulgakov Dead? Mikhail Bulgakov at the Moscow Art Theatre*. Tr. by A. Tait. London: Methuen, 1993. An abridged version by the author of his *Mikhail Bulgakov v Khudozhestvennom teatre* [Mikhail Bulgakov at the Art Theatre], 2nd ed. Moscow: Iskusstvo, 1989.

Stanislavski, Constantin. *My Life in Art*. Tr. by J. J. Robbins. Harmondsworth: Penguin Books, 1967.

Worrall, Nick. *The Moscow Art Theatre*. London and New York: Routledge, 1996.

Liisa Byckling

DEN STARKARE See THE STRONGER

STEFANOVSKI, GORAN (1952–)

Goran Stefanovski (born on April 27, 1952, in Bitola, MACEDO-NIA) received his bachelor of arts degree in English language and literature at the Faculty of Philology in Skopje. He then studied DRAMATURGY at the Faculty of Dramatic Arts in Belgrade. He was awarded a master's degree in 1979 upon presentation of his dissertation entitled *Stage Directions as the Foundation of the Theatre of* SAMUEL BECKETT. He worked as a script editor in the Drama Department of the Macedonian Television from 1974 to 1978. He was an assistant professor at the Philological Faculty in Skopje (1978–1986) and a full professor of dramaturgy at the Faculty of Dramatic Arts in Skopje (1986–1998). Later, in Canterbury, ENGLAND, he taught scriptwriting at the Canterbury Christ Church University College and at Kent University. He is a member of the Macedonian Academy of Arts and Sciences and a member of the Macedonian PEN Center.

Stefanovski is a crucial representative of modern Macedonian dramatic writing and one of the most important and widely performed Macedonian playwrights of all time. As a representative of the third wave of Macedonian writers, he did not lose his national voice, despite his European influences. In his plays he masterfully covers every thematic aspect that Macedonian drama had dealt with before him, but he is always looking ahead and never returning to ground that he has already covered. Stefanovski has an original and modern way of looking and analyzing the Macedonian traditional templates.

Stefanovski is the winner of major national and international writing awards. His play *Sarajevo* was published in the United Kingdom in *Storm* magazine and in the United States in *Performing Arts Journal* and *Balkan Blues*. BkMk Press published *HI-FI & The False Bottom* in 1985.

PLAYS: *Jane Zadrogaz* (1974); *Wild Flesh* (1979); *Flying on the Spot* (1981); *Hi-fi* (drama, 1983); *The False Bottom* (1984); *The Dishevelled Alphabet* (television serial, 1985); *Tattooed Souls* (1985); *The Black Hole* (1987); *Long Play* (1988); *Shades of Babel* (1989); *Chernodrinski Is Coming Home* (1991); *Sarajevo (Tales from a City)* (1992–1993); *Bacchanalia* (1996); *Casabalkan* (1997); *Euralien* (1998); *Hotel Europa* (2000)

FURTHER READING

Šeleva, Elizabeta. *Otvoreno pismo: Studii za Makedonskata literatura i kultura* [Open Letter: Studies for Macedonian Literature and Culture]. Skopje: Magor, 2003.

Todorovski, Gane. *Podaleku od zanesot, poblisku do bolot. Beleski kon Divo meso vo knigata Jane Zadrogaz; Divo meso od Goran Stefanovski* [Faraway from Ecstasy, Closer to Pain. Notes about *Wild Flesh* in the book *Jane Zadrogaz*; *Wild Flesh* from Goran Stefanovski]. Skopje: Misla, 1981.

Risto Stefanovski

STEIGERWALD, KAREL (1945–)

Born April 11, 1945, in Vacíkov near Příbram, CZECHOSLO-VAKIA, Karel Steigerwald is another Czech playwright who came to the theater after schooling at the Prague Film Academy. In the Normalization period after 1968, he found that theater offered a greater degree of freedom for a writer than film, television, or even radio. The four plays that made his reputation as a biting critic of contemporary Czech society in the 1980s were written for the Drama Studio in Ustí nad Labem. They indirectly attack the short-sightedness, compromises, self-delusions, and hypocrisy of Czechs in the Normalization years, although none of the plays is set in that era.

Tartar Fair (*Tatarská pouť*, 1979, first produced in 1988) is set in the years bridging the 1950s and 1960s. A young narrator, himself a well-meaning compromiser, describes the struggles of his father to remain true to his essentially upright principles while being pressured and manipulated by a local official. Formally, the play is interesting for its fluid treatment of time from present to past. *Period Dances* (*Dobové tance*, 1980) shifts the action back to 1852, when Hapsburg authorities were investigating the actions of various townspeople during the failed revolution of 1948. Those who have done the most boasting about their revolutionary activity are the ones who quickly back off and try to find a scapegoat, glibly rationalizing their lack of backbone. *Foxtrot* (1982) presents a much broader picture, the years of the First Republic, 1918–1938. *The Neapolitan Disease* (*Neapolská choroba*, 1984, first produced in 1988) takes place in a field hospital in a forest at an unspecified time after some cataclysmic event. The surviving regime is corrupt and fatally self-deluded, and the ordinary people, including medical professionals, are weak if not incompetent. In all these plays, the dominant tone of satiric COMEDY in a realistic frame ranges from the mildly farcical to the grotesque.

In *Sorrow, Sorrow, Fear, the Noose and the Pit* (*Hoře, hoře, strach, oprátka a jáma*, 1990), comedy and satire are virtually nonexistent. The play transcends Steigerwald's focus on Czech society; it evokes the victims of European totalitarianism from the 1930s through the 1980s through a group of wandering refugees. Time and place and identity are in constant flux, and actors assume a variety of archetypal roles. In *Nobel* (1994), grotesque satiric comedy with a dark undertone is once again aimed at specifically Czech targets, now in the new Czech Republic. The characters are no longer victims of a Communist system but of their own illusions and deformed values.

Journalism has been Steigerwald's main activity in recent years, but not exclusively. *Play Comedy* (*Hraj komedii*, 2000) focuses on contemporary Czech society with a clear plot and distinct characterizations. He presents the new millennium as an age of rampant media distortions of truth and exploitation of personalities, including those of three actresses whose pasts harbor controversial activities in the Communist era. Steigerwald's moral stance is as sharp as ever as he questions the truth of historic events and human motivations.

SELECT PLAYS: *Tartar Fair* (*Tatarská pouf*, 1979); *Period Dances* (*Dobové tance*, 1980); *Foxtrot* (1982); *Neapolitan Disease* (*Neapolská choroba*, 1984); *Sorrow, Sorrow, Fear, the Noose and the Pit* (*Hoře, hoře, strach, oprátka a jáma*, 1990); *Nobel* (1994); *Play Comedy* (*Hraj komedii*, 2000)

FURTHER READING
Burian, Jarka M. "Czech Theatre, 1988: Neo-Glasnost and Perestroika," *Theatre Journal* 41, no. 3, Performance in Context (October 1989): 381–395.

Jarka M. Burian

STEIN, GERTRUDE (1874–1946)

Gertrude Stein was born on February 3, 1874, in Allegheny, Pennsylvania. As a child Stein lived in Europe until her wealthy German-Jewish family relocated to Oakland, California, when she was five. She led a privileged and independent childhood, reading prodigiously and frequently attending opera and theater. She attended Radcliffe (then Harvard Annex), studied psychology with William James, and attended medical school at Johns Hopkins before expatriating to Paris with her brother Leo. There, she became a prescient collector of modern painting (Paul Cezanne, Henri Matisse, Pablo Picasso), the hostess of an enormously influential salon, the life-partner of Alice B. Toklas, an icon of the AVANT-GARDE, and the author of more than six hundred literary works. She achieved commercial success at age fifty-nine and was lionized by the media and public during her lecture tour of the United States in 1934. Although her celebrity outshone her artistic achievements in the popular imagination, Stein's subversive, experimental writing has influenced the generations after her, and scholars and theater practitioners have become increasingly interested in her work.

Although her best-known work, *The Autobiography of Alice B. Toklas*, is a straightforward if whimsical narrative, her importance as a writer comes from the thoroughness and breadth of her experiments in a wide range of genres. Important texts include her massive novel *The Making of Americans*, a cubist-inspired series of portraits called *Tender Buttons*, as well as a number of texts that bring together her singular poetic voice with her interests in philosophy, psychology, language, and the rhythms of consciousness. Her style affects a naiveté that is analogous to fauvism in art, a complexity and multidimensionality that gives her affinities with the cubists, and a penchant for strategies of nonmeaning that link her with DADAISM. Her mixture of lush poetry and cryptically encoded eroticism anticipates both progressive queer writing and language poetry.

Stein's eighty plays, many of which remain unproduced, constitute modernism's most thoroughgoing departure from dramaturgical conventions, completely re-imagining our expectations of story, incident, and time, and dismissing entirely conventional notions of character and dialogue. With few exceptions, her plays take place in a "continuous present" in which they are perpetually in a state of beginning and their revision is a frequent subject of the plays themselves. In later plays, like FOUR SAINTS IN THREE ACTS, she expanded her aesthetic to include the notion of the play as landscape. While the theoretical dimension of her playwriting is heady and abstract, the texts themselves pay earthy, sensuous homage to the everyday, often incorporating letters, advertisements, and lists and characters from history, from her life, and from the newspapers. Her lecture/essay "Plays" is one of the most searching and vigorous theoretical documents of the modern theater.

Stein, who died on July 27, 1946, in Paris, FRANCE, has had a crucial influence on the development of American avant-garde theater; her plays have been produced by the LIVING THEATRE, Judson Church, The Wooster Group, ANNE BOGART, James Lapine, RICHARD FOREMAN, and ROBERT WILSON. Her influence is also keenly felt in the writing of her contemporary THORNTON WILDER as well as Lee Breuer, SUZAN-LORI PARKS, and David Greenspan, and her notion of the play as landscape paved the way for environmental theater, site-specific theater, and performance art.

[See also United States, 1860–1940]

SELECT PLAYS: *Geography and Plays* (1922); *Operas and Plays* (1932); *Four Saints in Three Acts* (music by Virgil Thomson, 1934); *Byron, A Play* (1935); *Doctor Faustus Lights the Lights* (1938); *In Savoy, or, Yes Is for a Very Young Man* (1945); *The Mother of Us All* (music by Virgil Thomson, 1947); *Last Operas and Plays* (edited by Carl Van Vechten, 1949)

FURTHER READING
Dydo, Ulla. *Gertrude Stein: The Language That Rises, 1923–1934.* Evanston, Ill.: Northwestern Univ. Press, 2003.

Marranca, Bonnie. *Ecologies of Theater.* Baltimore: Johns Hopkins Univ. Press, 1996.

Robinson, Marc. *The Other American Drama.* New York: Cambridge Univ. Press, 1994.

Ryan, Betsy Alayne. *Gertrude Stein's Theatre of the Absolute.* Ann Arbor: UMI Research Press, 1984.

Stendhal, Renate, ed. *Gertrude Stein in Words and Pictures.* Chapel Hill, N.C.: Algonquin, 1994.

Mark Lord

STERNHEIM, CARL (1878–1943)

Just why Carl Sternheim has been so ignored in the English-speaking world is a difficult yet significant question. Born on April 1, 1878, in Leipzig, GERMANY, it was there he had a first round of popularity that began with the staging of THE UNDERPANTS, also translated as *The Bloomers* (*Die Hose*, 1911), and only ended when his plays were banned during World War I. His revival picked up right after 1945, when *The Snob* (*Der Snob*, 1914) was one of the first plays to be performed in occupied Berlin, and plays from the cycle *Scenes from the Heroic Life of the Middle Classes* (*Aus dem bürgerlichen Heldenleben*) continue to be popular.

Cynics might point to the dearth of home-grown German COM-EDIES as the reason for Sternheim's standing; the ready supply of genuine comedies in English would explain why he has not been imported.

Even in Germany, however, Sternheim's reception has been one-sided, consisting mainly of the comedies played with a light touch. (He is frequently compared to Molière). Other plays by Sternheim, such as *Tabula Rasa* (1916) about political struggles among factory workers, or *Uznach School* (*Die Schule von Uznach*, 1926), a hilarious send-up of Neue Sachlichkeit (NEW OBJEC-TIVITY), are relatively unknown.

One factor shaping Sternheim's reception is that he cannot be easily classified as belonging to a specific movement. He was nei-ther a decided expressionist nor consistent in his political views, despite an involvement with the leftists around the periodical *The Action* (*Die Aktion*). Another obstacle is Sternheim's idiosyncratic style of language, which omits verbs and modifiers, inverts syn-tax, and operates with bizarre similes. For example, the title character in *Paul Schippel, Esq.* (*Bürger Schippel*, 1913) says of him-self: "Was yesterday yet a hare which fearfully crouched in the cabbage. Is now however such colossal activity alive that knives grow from my toes, sabres from my teeth." Unlike the language experiments of EXPRESSIONISM, which were mainly confined to poetry and came in small doses, Sternheim's make extended demands on audiences.

A clue to understanding Sternheim may lie in the fact that one of his last plays, before he went into exile and fell silent, was about OSCAR WILDE, the prototypical dandy. Dandyism as a philosophy presumes that style is substance. Sternheim's worlds are ones in which surface appearances are all there is. Hence, in *The Underpants*, Theobald Maske is so outraged when his wife displays her underpants in public because he knows that cloth-ing makes identities in contemporary society. Audiences want to laugh at such notions, but if fashion is everything, then all con-flicts turn on matters of taste without any governing moral stan-dards. That, as Sternheim saw all too clearly, meant that the choice between good and evil had become irrelevant. The impli-cations become clear in *Uznach School*, where the headmaster of the girls' school reduces them to objects according to the latest fashion so that they will be marketable products. Although Sternheim could not foresee the rise of the Nazis to power, he too was alert to the dangers Walter Benjamin (1892–1940) saw in the aestheticization of politics. In short, the triumph of fashion would turn into the triumph of the will. He died on November 3, 1942, in Brussels, Belgium.

SELECT PLAYS: *The Underpants* (*Die Hose*, 1911); *The Strong Box* (*Die Kassette*, 1912); *Paul Schippel, Esq.* (*Bürger Schippel*, 1913); *The Snob* (*Der Snob*, 1914); *The Candidate* (*Der Kandidat*, adapted from Flaubert, 1914); *1913* (1915); *Tabula Rasa* (1916); *The Grouser* (*Der Stänker*, 1917); *The Mask of Virtue* (*Die Marquise von Arcis*, after Diderot's *Jacques le Fataliste et son maitre*, 1918); *The Contemporary Unbound* (*Der*

entfesselte Zeitgenosse, 1920); *The Adventurer* (*Der Abenteurer*, 1922); *The Good-for-Nothing* (*Der Nebbich*, 1922); *The Fossil* (*Das Fossil*, 1925); *Oscar Wilde* (1925); *Uznach School* (*Die Schule von Uznach*, 1926); *John Pierpont Morgan* (1930)

FURTHER READING

Chick, Edson M. "Sternheim's *1913* as Satire: Fantasy and Fashion." In *Studies in the German Drama: A Festschrift in Honor of Walter Silz*, ed. by Donald H. Crosby and George C. Schoolfield. Chapel Hill: Univ. of North Carolina Press, 1974. 213–224.

Dedner, Burghard. *Carl Sternheim*. Boston: Twayne, 1982.

Gittleman, Sol. "Sternheim, Wedekind, and Homo Economicus." *The German Quarterly* 49, no. 1 (1976): 25–30.

Hays, Michael. "Carl Sternheim's Don Juan: An Artist in Search of His Art." *The Germanic Review* 53, no. 3 (1978): 115–123.

Myers, David. "Carl Sternheim: Satirist or Creator of Modern Heroes?" *Monatshefte* 65 (1973): 39–47.

Sternheim, Carl. *The Underpants*. Adapted by Steve Martin. New York: Theia/Hyperion Books, 2002.

Williams, Rhys W. "Carl Sternheim's Image of Marx and His Critique of the German Intellectual Tradition." *German Life & Letters* NS 32 (1978–1979): 19–29.

Arnd Bohm

STICKS AND BONES

That's what I am—a young . . . blind man in a room . . . in a house in the dark, raising nothing in a gesture of no meaning toward two voices who are not speaking.
—David, Act 1

Composed and redrafted between 1969 and 1971, *Sticks and Bones* is the second play of DAVID RABE's Vietnam trilogy. It pre-miered at Villanova University in 1969 and debuted in New York City at the Public Theatre in 1971, following the success of Rabe's first professionally produced work, *The Basic Training of Pavlo Hummel*, earlier that year. For a time, both plays were run-ning simultaneously, which was remarkable because no play-wright besides William Shakespeare had had more than one work produced at the Public at the same time. Producer Joseph Papp later moved the play to Broadway, and in 1972, *Sticks and Bones* received the Tony Award for Best Play.

Although the crisis is precipitated by the homecoming of David, a soldier blinded in the Vietnam War, *Sticks and Bones* is not a condemnation of war, but rather an indictment of racism, reli-gious hypocrisy, and moral decay thinly camouflaged by the veneer of middle-class American respectability. The principal characters are named after the Nelsons, whose ideal (and real) television family appeared weekly on the American Broadcasting Corporation network (*The Adventures of Ozzie and Harriet*, 1952–1966). David is haunted by memories of war and of his relation-ship with a "yellow girl," Zung. Though David abandoned her, the indelibility of his memories is signified by the girl's ghostly pres-ence in the home. The family becomes increasingly disturbed by

David's isolation, obsessions, and apparent loathing of them all. His mother, Harriet, summons Father Donald, a Catholic priest, to intervene, but David repudiates him violently.

David remains unrepentant about his relationship with the "alien" Zung, an Asian prostitute whom his loved ones consider a cultural and moral monstrosity. Unable to disguise its repugnance toward his miscegenation, the family comes to view David as a contaminant who threatens to undermine the household, which represents white, middle-class America. The family saves itself by encouraging David to cut his wrists with a razor they provide; in the end, they surround David as he bleeds to death in the living room, while brother Ricky plays an up-tempo tune on his guitar. Walter Kerr observes that David had "already described this home as his coffin. . . . if the people in it could ever see themselves, they would see that there was no one there. Why shouldn't he be as dead as they are?"

Sticks and Bones was scheduled to air on the Columbia Broadcast System in March, 1973, as part of a series of televised versions of plays produced by Joseph Papp; however, network chairman William S. Paley abruptly cancelled the program. American prisoners of war recently had begun to return home, and network affiliates feared that the broadcast would be too "abrasive." Eventually, the play was aired but without commercial sponsorship. Though topical and controversial in its day, a revival by the Actors' Theatre of Washington did not "take a 1996 audience to any surprising new places," according to Nelson Pressley of the *Washington Times*.

[*See also* United States, 1940–Present]

FURTHER READING

Epstein, Helen. *Joe Papp: An American Life*. Cambridge and New York: Da Capo Press, 1996.

Rabe, David. "Introduction." In *The Basic Training of Pavlo Hummel/Sticks and Bones: Two Plays by David Rabe*. New York: Viking Press, 1973.

Shaw, Marilyn, and Jeniffer Terry. *Vietnam, Perspectives & Performance: Two Plays About Real People Affected by the Legacy of the Vietnam Conflict*, 2nd ed. Cedar Falls, Iowa: Association for Textual Study & Production, 1996.

Zinman, Toby Silverman, ed. *David Rabe: A Casebook*. New York and London: Garland Publishing, 1991.

Bill Conte

STILL STANDS THE HOUSE

GWEN PHARIS RINGWOOD's one-act *Still Stands the House* (1939) was one of the first plays to present the Canadian prairie experience. It is still considered one of the finest examples of Canadian folk drama ever written. The play has an authentic feel because Ringwood drew on her firsthand experiences of growing up on the Alberta prairie. The play also contains rich symbolism and carefully crafted, poetic language, reminiscent of JOHN MILLINGTON SYNGE and SEAN O'CASEY.

The setting is the main room of a small farmhouse situated in a remote area of the Alberta prairie. The room is furnished in an austere manner. The one bright spot in the room is a bunch of blooming hyacinths. A blizzard rages outside. The play opens with Ruth Warren discussing the possible sale of the farmhouse with real estate agent Arthur Manning. Ruth is twenty-six, pretty and vibrant. She is also pregnant and longs to move closer to town. Hester Warren, Ruth's sister-in-law, then enters the room. She is forty years old with a very stern demeanor. Hester becomes extremely angry when she discovers that Manning was inquiring about purchasing the farm. Hester says that she will not allow the farm to be sold. She has lived in this farmhouse her entire life and has strong ties to it. She has even maintained her father's room exactly as it was at the time of his death six years previous. She deeply resents Ruth. Hester asks whether the lanterns have been filled, and Ruth insists that she will fill them "in a minute."

Bruce returns home. He is a rugged man of about thirty. He and Ruth exit to the kitchen, and while they are out of the room, Hester angrily crushes one of the hyacinth stalks on the table, symbolically killing the life Ruth is trying to inject into the house. When Ruth and Bruce return, the two discuss selling the farm. At first, Bruce resists, but Ruth begs him to reconsider for their unborn child's sake. Bruce finally agrees. He then takes a lantern and goes out into the blizzard to check on a mare that may have her foal that night. Suddenly, Ruth realizes with horror that she has forgotten to fill the lanterns. Bruce will lose his way in the blizzard and freeze to death. Ruth decides she must go after him. Hester offers to fill the other lantern while Ruth is getting ready. Hester does not fill the lantern, however, and sends Ruth out into the blizzard with an almost empty lantern where both she and Bruce will now meet their deaths. Hester then hallucinates that her father is in the room, and she calmly reads to him from the Bible as the blizzard continues to swirl outside.

In this one-act, Ringwood presents the struggle of the resolute human spirit against the unyielding forces of nature. No matter what, Hester and the house will remain on the prairie forever. She will not abandon her roots. *Still Stands the House* is still being performed today, a testament to its quality and timelessness.

[*See also* Canada]

FURTHER READING

Anthony, Geraldine. *Gwen Pharis Ringwood*. Boston: Twayne Publishers, 1981.

Ringwood, Gwen Pharis. *The Collected Plays of Gwen Pharis Ringwood*. Ed. by Enid Delgatty Rutland. Ottawa: Borealis Press, 1982.

Beth A. Kattelman

STOPPARD, TOM (1937–)

Tom Stoppard, arguably Britain's foremost dramatist at the start of the 21st century, happened to be born Czech, not English. His earliest years, like those of many others displaced by World War II, were traumatic. Qualities discernible in his plays often reflect a consciousness formed by early imprinting experiences. For instance, his years in journalism enrich crucial scenes on journalistic ethics in *Night and Day*. His serving as theater critic lends authority to *The Real Inspector Hound*. *Indian Ink* distinctly benefits from his having lived in India during his youth. Several marriages and alliances in Stoppard's life elicit honest, sometimes painful observations about love in *The Real Thing*. His early indoctrination into ABSURDISM through SAMUEL BECKETT clarifies the techniques behind ROSENCRANTZ AND GUILDENSTERN ARE DEAD. Stoppard's fascination with natural laws of physics and mathematics energize plays like *Hapgood* (quantum physics) and ARCADIA (Fermat's Last Equation). Few events from his life are left unmined. Stoppard's eclectic themes and wildly varied theatrical structures are readily identifiable as his by theatergoers and critics.

FIRST STEPPING STONES

In July of 1937, Tomas Straussler (his natal name) was born to Eugen and Martha Straussler in Zlin (Moravia), CZECHOSLO-VAKIA. The senior Straussler was a physician with the Bata shoe firm, one of the largest employers in the region. On March 14, 1939—the day the Nazis invaded Czechoslovakia—the entire Straussler family left with other Jewish families working for Bata and headed for the company's factories in SINGAPORE. Before he ever mastered the Czech language, Tomas was introduced to English at a British school in Singapore. At four years old, Tomas, his older brother Peter, and his mother were evacuated to INDIA because of the Japanese invasion. His father remained behind, however, and was killed.

The brothers attended an English-speaking boarding school in Darjeeling from 1943 until 1946. Their mother, then managing a local Bata shoe store, in 1945 married a British Army officer named Kenneth Stoppard. After moving his new family to England, the senior Stoppard officially adopted his two stepsons, thereby giving them the Stoppard surname. As a youth Stoppard attended school in Nottinghamshire and Yorkshire when the family moved to Bristol. He left school at seventeen to become a journalist on Bristol's *Western Daily Press*, later switching to the *Bristol Evening News*.

At twenty-three in 1960, Stoppard faced a crossroads. He chose to quit his full-time work as journalist and try writing plays. To help stay afloat financially, he wrote two columns a week as a freelancer. That year he wrote a play called *A Walk on the Water* (revised as *Enter a Free Man* in 1968). The 1960s as a whole proved productive for him; he wrote a great number of works in a great variety of genres. Between 1960 and 1961 he wrote the one-act play *The Gamblers* and *The Stand-Ins* (later revised as *The Real Inspector Hound*). He became drama critic at London's *Scene* magazine for two years (1962–1963), during which time his play *A Walk on the Water* was telecast, and two tele-

vision plays (*I Can't Give You Anything But Love, Baby* and *Funny Man*) were written though not produced. The year 1964 overflowed with writing: Three short stories were published, two BBC (British Broadcast Corporation) radio plays were aired (*The Dissolution of Dominic Boot* and "*M*" *Is for Moon Among Other Things*), the unproduced television play *This Way Out with Samuel Boot* was penned, and—while in Berlin on a Ford Foundation grant—his earliest work, *A Walk on the Water*, was staged in Hamburg, GERMANY. He also wrote the one-act piece *Rosencrantz and Guildenstern Meet Lear*.

Stoppard garnered further success in 1965. His play *The Gambler* (in two-act form) received its first staging at Bristol University, and his teleplay *A Paragraph for Mr. Blake* (adapted from a short story) was broadcast. Several episodes written for a BBC World Service drama series also were aired. The year 1966 found Stoppard at the threshold of a major career in writing. During that single year he published the novel *Lord Malquist and Mr. Moon*, aired a radio play, *If You're Glad I'll Be Frank*, televised *A Separate Peace*, and staged a translation (co-authored) of SLAWOMIR MROŽEK's play *Tango* produced by the Royal Shakespeare Company. Most noteworthy of all, *Rosencrantz and Guildenstern Are Dead* was produced by the Edinburgh Festival Fringe. With so many fertile seeds spread so broadly, there was no way Stoppard could be ignored in the theater world.

A WATERSHED IN STOPPARD'S CAREER

Kenneth Tynan, influential theater critic and literary manager for England's National Theatre, read a rousing review of the Edinburgh staging of *Rosencrantz and Guildenstern*. On that basis, he telegraphed Stoppard requesting a script.

Within a year the COMEDY was produced at the National (1967). After the National's production of *Rosencrantz and Guildenstern* transferred to Broadway that same year, it earned 1968 Tony Awards for Best Play, Producer, Scenic Design, and Costumes. Altogether it received eight nominations—an amazing accomplishment for a beginner in the theater. British critics jumped aboard, as well, honoring the comedy with the John Whiting Award and the Evening Standard Drama Award. Positive reviews in 1967 also came for his plays *Teeth* and *Another Moon Called Earth* televised on BBC television; likewise for his BBC radio play *Albert's Bridge*. The prolific Stoppard became the toast of London and New York, based on an ingenious spin-off of William Shakespeare's *Hamlet*—his chief calling card.

There was little let-up in his productivity the following year. Both *Enter a Free Man* (revised from *A Walk on the Water*) and *The Real Inspector Hound* were given productions, while *Neutral Ground* appeared on television. Newly formatted *Albert's Bridge* and *If You're Glad I'll Be Frank* were staged in 1969, while his radio play *Where Are They Now?* was aired. Additionally, an earlier work, *The Dissolution of Dominic Boot*, was expanded to become *The Engagement* and was seen both in the movies and on television. In 1971 his stage works *After Magritte* and *Dogg's Our Pet* were produced.

Stoppard's pace quickened by 1972 with several new or reworked pieces. Stoppard's intricate and innovative play *Jumpers* was staged by London's National Theatre, and *Artist Descending a Staircase* was heard on the radio in Great Britain. New York City saw productions that year of *The Real Inspector Hound* and *After Magritte*. Stoppard turned to stage directing in 1973 with GARSON KANIN's comedy *Born Yesterday*, the same year his adaptation was staged of FEDERICO GARCÍA LORCA's grim THE HOUSE OF BERNARDA ALBA. New York productions of two of his works were mounted, *Jumpers* and *Enter a Free Man*, making 1974 a landmark year. Equally consequential for his career was the Royal Shakespeare Company's staging of TRAVESTIES, a work many still consider among his very finest. Stoppard turned to film and television in 1975. His adaptation of Jerome K. Jerome's *Three Men in a Boat* appeared on British television, as did a co-authored play (with Clive Exton), *The Boundary*. More important, however, was the transfer to New York of *Travesties* in 1975. The following year *Travesties* copped two Tonys, including Best Play. Stoppard's career was becoming rooted in the UNITED STATES as well as in England.

He continued writing plays over the next few years, during which period two directions became dominant. First, he toyed with the myriad spin-off possibilities of Shakespeare's dramas, and second, he began expressing increased political concern through his writing. In 1976 Stoppard spun out an agile knock-off of Shakespeare titled *The (15 Minute) Dogg's Troupe Hamlet*, performed outside the newly opened National Theatre home on London's South Bank. A revival of *Jumpers* in fact was chosen to launch the new National's inauguration. His play *Dirty Linen* moved to London's West End (comparable to New York's Broadway for commercial theater). Shakespeare reappears on Stoppard's radar in 1979 with tours in England and the United States of *Dogg's Hamlet, Cahoot's Macbeth*, a teasing work with political undercurrents.

STOPPARD AS POLITICAL MAN

From the mid-1970s through the mid-1980s, political themes infiltrated his theatrical work. Specifically, Stoppard was aggrieved by terrible injustices stemming from Soviet rule of Eastern Europe—in particular, in his native Czechoslovakia. In 1976 he spoke out publicly against Soviet mistreatment of dissidents in the Russian-controlled Iron Block countries. By the next year, a group of Czech intellectuals—including Czech dramatist VÁCLAV HAVEL—published a declaration of dissent titled Charter 77 that became a rallying call to fight Soviet domination. It also led to the imprisonment of many involved, Havel among them. Stoppard visited Czechoslovakia and published his findings regarding the iron-fisted repression of all dissidents. Direct results of these experiences were several works by Stoppard for the stage and for television. In 1977 his television drama *Professional Foul* documented the house arrest of a fictionalized Czech writer who must smuggle the "truth" about his nation to the outside world. That same year, Stoppard's extraordinary, innovative

play *Every Good Boy Deserves Favour* (built around a musical mnemonic) showcased a boy being separated from his politically dissident father. The plot paralleled an actual case behind the Iron Curtain. Making the work even more original was Stoppard's inclusion of a full symphonic orchestra on stage to serve as a character along with the actors. The world-renowned conductor and composer Andre Previn composed music specifically for the orchestra. The work was first performed in the United States the following year.

Every Good Boy was staged on several more occasions, with its protest theme eliciting support from the Western world, as Stoppard became more deeply immersed in speaking out about persecuted Czech dissidents and Soviet Jews. He served as chairman of the worldwide movement leading to the release of a boy in the U.S.S.R. to join his mother. In 1980 Stoppard traveled to Munich to participate in a protest over the imprisonment of Havel. When Polish leader Lech Walesa and his Solidarity protest union were forcibly detained by the puppet government in Poland, Stoppard wrote a television drama, *Squaring the Circle* (1982), about the Solidarity movement. Four years later Stoppard participated in a rally protesting the restrictions placed by the Soviets on 10,000 Russian Jews seeking to emigrate. Ironically, upon the demise of the Communist rule, both Havel and Walesa were to become presidents of their respective nations.

Another display of a politicized Stoppard exists in his powerful 1978 drama *Night and Day*. The year before, a union representing journalists in England argued for a closed shop. A former journalist himself, Stoppard saw problems regarding freedom of expression in the union position, and he wrote publicly of his opposition. This experience has parallels to *Night and Day*, in which the plot centers on two contrasted journalists, only one whose sole cause is to report the truth. Stoppard does not reveal passionate views on usual Marxist-Capitalism themes, as have some playwriting peers in England (e.g., DAVID HARE, HOWARD BRENTON, JOHN ARDEN, ARNOLD WESKER, and EDWARD BOND). But his writings and pronouncements verify a firm conscience, leading him to do battle in political arenas that mean the most to him.

STOPPARD'S MULTIPLE THEATRICAL INTERESTS

Movies always were vital in the career of Tom Stoppard. His output of fine film scripts accelerated in the 1970s just as his plays were establishing his overall reputation. It also was the time he became active politically. A simple listing of his original film plays include *The Romantic Englishwoman* (1975), co-authored with Thomas Wiseman, and *Brazil*, for which he received an Academy Award nomination in 1985. Stoppard has uncredited contributions to screenplays for Steven Spielberg's movies *Always* and *Indiana Jones and the Last Crusade* in 1989, and he wrote the screenplay for *Rosencrantz and Guildenstern Are Dead*, released in 1991. That movie took the Golden Lion medal at the Venice Film Festival. Not all his attempts succeeded for revising his own plays as movies. His 1995 adaptation of *Hapgood* remains unfilmed, and efforts to adapt *Arcadia* for the screen have not met with success so far. His 1994 full-length animated movie version of *Cats* to date remains unproduced, as well.

His banner year was 1999. Stoppard and co-author Marc Norman shared an Academy Award for the film script of *Shakespeare in Love*—a movie that earned a total of seven Oscars, including Best Picture. That year, he co-authored *Vatel*, a French film released the following year. Meantime, Stoppard adapted to film numerous works written by others including Vladimir Nabokov's novel *Despair* (1978) and Graham Greene's novel *The Human Factor* (1980). For the 1987 movie *Empire of the Sun* (directed by Steven Spielberg), Stoppard adapted J. G. Ballard's novel by that name. His movie scripts adapted from John le Carre's spy novel *The Russia House* (1990), from E. L. Doctorow's novel *Billy Bathgate* (1991), and from Robert Harris's novel *Enigma* (2000) were successfully filmed. Certain of his completed screenplays, though, have not been filmed. His 1988 movie script adapted from Laurens van der Post's novel *A Far Off Place* has not made it to the screen; likewise, his film version of Nicholas Mosley's novel *Hopeful Monsters* (1993).

Clearly, Stoppard evidences a lively mind ever searching for other writers' works to adapt. Throughout his career he has not hesitated to consider novels and plays to adapt for the stage, as well as for film. His original use of Shakespeare's *Hamlet* is an early case in point. During the decade he was active responding to Soviet oppression, Stoppard often turned to adapting for the stage. As is true of his adapted movie scripts, his stage adaptations have proven popular. His first staged adaptation (1973) was Federico García Lorca's *The House of Bernarda Alba*. His *Undiscovered Country* (1979) and *On the Razzle* (1981) were taken from German plays by ARTHUR SCHNITZLER and Johann Nestroy, respectively. The German Schnitzler again was Stoppard's source for an adaptation of *Dalliance* (1986), and Stoppard freely reworked *Rough Crossing* (1984) from the Hungarian Ferenc Molnár's *Play at the Castle*. More recently, Stoppard's version of ANTON CHEKHOV's THE SEAGULL was produced in 1997, directed by Peter Hall. If you were to count Stoppard's translations as adaptations, other staged adaptations would include his 1966 translation (with Nicholas Bethell) of Mrożek's *Tango*, his 1983 translation of the libretto for Sergei Prokofiev's opera *The Love for Three Oranges*, and his 1987 translation of Havel's *Largo Desolato*.

ASCENDING THE LADDER OF SUCCESS

Even though involved in selected political actions from the mid-1970s on, Tom Stoppard sustained a line of uncompromisingly fine dramas. Not all were popular with all audiences, and dramatic adaptations became more common, as noted. In 1982 Stoppard's new romantic comedy THE REAL THING was produced in London to strong reviews. Later, in New York with a different cast, a tidal-wave response led to almost a clean sweep. *The Real Thing* earned five 1984 Tony Awards from its seven nominations,

including Best Play, Best Lead Actor, and Best Lead Actress. No other Stoppard play has won so many top honors on Broadway. Coincidentally, a 1999 revival of *Real Thing* led to three Tony Awards in 2000, including Best Play Revival.

The drama *Hapgood* (1988), in contrast, was coolly received in London and scarcely better in New York despite a revised script. The play remains one of Stoppard's rare disappointments. Coincidence or not, most of Stoppard's writing gravitated toward movies and television for a while, as noted above. All that changed in 1993 with the staging of his mind-teasing comedy *Arcadia* at the National Theatre. *Arcadia* enjoyed an extended run in London at the National Theatre and then in the West End. Its transfer to Broadway also was successful, earning it three Tony nominations, though no awards. *Indian Ink*, a stage version of his radio play *In the Native State*, opened in 1995 to strong reviews, suggesting that Stoppard had another winning streak going. His INVENTION OF LOVE (1997) at the National Theatre reinforced the judgment that he was back in top form. That show's shift to Broadway brought it five 2001 Tony nominations, including two wins, but not for Best Play. With the stunning success of the film *Shakespeare in Love*, which he helped write, Stoppard became arguably the most successful dramatist writing at the start of the new millennium.

Nor has Tom Stoppard slowed down, despite a shower of accolades. His most recent theatrical endeavor is an ambitious trilogy called THE COAST OF UTOPIA. Opening in 2002 at London's National Theatre, the three self-contained plays—*Voyage*, *Shipwreck*, and *Salvage*—constitute a biographical, political, and psychological chronicle beginning with events in 1852. Initial critical reaction has been only lukewarm, though audiences have appreciated the vastness of the enterprise it represents.

A FINAL, BRIEF OVERVIEW

From the above survey, it is evident Stoppard masters a myriad of topics in his plays, while shaping them into highly unique structures. Certain standout qualities define Stoppard's writing, with language and wit near the top. Only an acute intellect could write such razor-sharp dialogue imbued with engaging wit. Also central in Stoppard's writing arsenal is an irrepressible willingness to try out new modes and patterns. The variety of formats is extensive. Ultimately, the final effect is one of theatrical playfulness.

More constrained works such as *Night and Day* and *The Real Thing* hew closer to conventional NATURALISM in form. Deft plotting generates some surprises, all the same, such as cleverly planted ambiguities in *Real Thing*. *Travesties*, set in a Zurich library, offers a fictional conjunction of world famous figures—James Joyce, Vladimir Lenin, and Tristan Tzara (co-founder of DADAISM). Their personae are brilliantly interwoven by the writer to produce laughter and provoking thought. *Arcadia* and *The Invention of Love*, to a lesser extent, marvelously braid different time coordinates to reveal connections between different generations.

Rosencrantz and Guildenstern delights using escapees from *Hamlet* as pilgrims seeking to understanding life and self. Their tenuous lifeline to a "mother ship" is their connection to Shakespeare's "real" drama *Hamlet*. The spin-off construct leads to a fresh style of theatrical narrative. *Every Good Boy Deserves Favour* transforms an orchestra into a character in the plot. Before Stoppard, such outrageous technical experiments were scarcely imaginable.

Thanks to an imagination of enormous breadth and a derring-do rare in today's theater, Tom Stoppard continues to amuse, entertain, and—importantly—provoke serious thinking.

[*See also* England, 1940–Present]

SELECT PLAYS: *A Walk on Water* (1960, revised as *Enter a Free Man*, 1968); *The Gamblers* (one-act play, 1960–1961); *The Stand-Ins* (1960–1961, revised as *The Real Inspector Hound*, 1968); *Rosencrantz and Guildenstern Meet King Lear* (one-act play, 1964); *Rosencrantz and Guildenstern Are Dead* (1966); *Albert's Bridge and If You're Glad I'll Be Frank* (revised radio plays, staged together, 1969); *After Magritte* (1970); *Dogg's Our Pet* (1971); *Jumpers* (1972); *Travesties* (1974); *Dirty Linen* (1976); *The [15 Minute] Dogg's Troupe Hamlet* (1976); *Every Good Boy Deserves Favour* (1977); *Night and Day* (1978); *Dogg's Hamlet, Cahoot's Macbeth* (1979); *Undiscovered Country* (adapted, 1979); *On the Razzle* (adapted, 1981); *The Real Thing* (1982); *Rough Crossing* (adapted, 1984); *Dalliance* (adapted, 1986); *Artist Descending a Staircase* (revised radio play, 1988); *Hapgood* (1988); *Arcadia* (1993); *Indian Ink* (1995); *The Invention of Love* (1997); *The Coast of Utopia* (trilogy of *Voyage*, *Shipwreck*, and *Salvage*, 2002); *Rock 'n' Roll* (2006)

FURTHER READING

Billington, Michael. *Stoppard: The Playwright*. London: Methuen, 1987.

Bloom, Harold, ed. *Tom Stoppard: Modern Critical Views*. New York: Chelsea House Publishing, 1986.

Jenkins, Anthony. *The Theatre of Tom Stoppard*. Cambridge: Cambridge Univ. Press, 1987.

Kelly, Katherine E. *The Cambridge Companion to Tom Stoppard*. Cambridge: Cambridge Univ. Press, 2001.

Londré, Felicia Hardison. *Tom Stoppard*. Modern Literature Series. New York: Frederick Unger, 1981.

Sammells, Neil. *Tom Stoppard: The Artist as Critic*. London: Macmillan, 1988.

C. J. Gianakaris

STOREY, DAVID (1933–)

Born in Wakefield, Yorkshire, England, on July 13, 1933, David Storey studied at the Wakefield College of Art and the Slade School of Fine Art in London, from which he received a diploma in 1956. While enrolled at the Slade School, Storey played rugby professionally for the Leeds club. Throughout his writing career, in both his plays and his novels, there has been a dramatic and thematic tension between the compulsive athlete and the reflective artist.

Other recurring subjects in Storey's work have included the tensions in working class life, most specifically the tension between the need to remain connected to one's background and the need to exceed the usual expectations of someone from that background; the forces in contemporary life that oppress individuality and the corrosive ramifications of that oppression; the tension between the values associated with stoicism and those associated with revolt; and the thin line between the iconoclast and the misfit.

Storey has received many honors for both his plays and for his novels. For *The Restoration of Arnold Middletown* (1966), which treats the maddeningly dreary life and prospects of a married school teacher, Storey received the *Evening Standard* award for most promising playwright. For *The Contractor* (1969), a comic allegory involving the erection of a tent for a wedding, he received the London Theatre Critics award, the Variety Club of Great Britain's Writer of the Year award, and a New York Drama Critics Circle Award. For *Home* (1970), a drama set in a mental hospital that presents broad-reaching social commentary and has underlying allegorical elements, he received the *Evening Standard* drama award, the New York Drama Critics Circle Award, and a nomination for the Tony Award. And for *The Changing Room* (1971), which explores the comradery among the members of a rugby team, he received a New York Drama Critics Circle award and a Tony nomination.

For his novels, Storey has received the Macmillan Award for *This Sporting Life* (1960), the Geoffrey Faber Memorial Award for *Pasmore* (1972), and the Booker Prize for *Saville* (1977).

[*See also* England, 1940–Present]

SELECT PLAYS: *The Restoration of Arnold Middletown* (first produced 1966, first published 1967); *The Contractor* (produced 1969, published 1970); *In Celebration* (1969); *Home* (1970); *The Changing Room* (1971); *Cromwell* (1973); *The Farm* (1973); *Life Class* (produced 1974, published 1975); *Mother's Day* (produced 1976, published 1977); *Early Days* (1980); *Sisters* (produced 1978, published 1980); *Phoenix* (1984); *The March on Russia* (1989); *Caring* (1992); *Stages* (1992)

FURTHER READING

Hutchings, William. *The Plays of David Storey: A Thematic Study*. Carbondale: Southern Illinois Univ. Press, 1988.

Hutchings, William, ed. *David Storey: A Casebook*. Garland Reference Library of the Humanities; Casebooks on Modern Dramatists, No. 1293. New York: Garland, 1992.

Liebman, Herbert. *The Dramatic Art of David Storey: The Journey of a Playwright*. Contributions in Drama and Theatre Studies, No. 71. Westport, Conn.: Greenwood, 1996.

Quigley, Austin E. "The Emblematic Structure and Setting of David Storey's Plays." *Modern Drama* 22 (1979): 259–276.

Reinelt, Janelle. "The Central Event in David Storey's Plays." *Theatre Journal* 31 (1979): 210–220.

Solomon, Rakesh H. "Man as Working Animal: Work, Class, and Identity in the Plays of David Storey." *Forum for Modern Language Studies* 30, no. 3 (July 1994): 193–203.

Martin Kich

STOREY, RAYMOND (1956–)

Raymond Storey was born in Orillia, Ontario, CANADA, in 1956. He developed a love of theater very early. He wrote his first play when he was in the fourth grade, and as a teenager he was active in his high school plays, summer stock, and community theater. When he was seventeen, Storey attended a summer theater program at York University, where he made such an impression that he was offered early admission to York's theater department. Unfortunately, he did not have the grade point average to enter York, so he enrolled in the National Theatre School in Montreal. Storey experienced a very contentious time at the theater school and was asked to leave. He then moved to Toronto, where he worked as a part-time actor and full-time bartender.

In 1979 he moved to Edmonton and began to write plays. In 1980 he became playwright-in-residence for the Theatre Network. That same year he began his collaboration with composer John Roby. Their first production was *Country Chorale*, which premiered at the Blyth Festival in 1982. The two would continue their successful collaboration with two more musicals, *The Girls in the Gang*, which premiered in 1987, and *The Dreamland*, which premiered at in 1989. *Girls in the Gang* won the Dora Mavor Moore Award for Outstanding New Revue/Musical in 1988.

Storey's plays are based strongly in character. His *Saints & Apostles* is a contemporary love story in which the characters must cope with the complication of HIV infection, and *Cheek to Cheek* is about a relationship that develops on the Trocadaro Ballroom dance floor between a shy widower and a waitress. Both plays received the Sterling Award for Outstanding New Play. His critically acclaimed piece, *The Last Bus*, also relies heavily on relationships for its effect. The piece deals with the relationship between a young widow and her dead husband's best friend. The ability to write succinct dialogue that still reveals the complexity of his characters is what has most captivated audiences, and it is this skill for which he has received the most praise among critics.

Storey sets many of his plays and musicals in the past. *Cheek to Cheek* is set in the 1960s, and *Girls in the Gang* chronicles the women who were involved with the notorious, bank-robbing Boyd gang of the 1950s. Another of his award-winning plays, *The Glorious Twelfth*, involves an encounter between Ku Klux Klan recruiters and a rural Ontario family that takes place in 1927. The piece won the Dora Mavor Moore Award for Outstanding New Play.

One of Storey's most ambitious pieces to date is *The Dreamland*, a musical collaboration with John Roby. The piece is a large musical with a cast of twenty-seven people. The story opens in 1966 on the day of an auction to sell memorabilia from The Dreamland dance pavilion. Rose, the owner of building, is on hand for the sale, and her memories of The Dreamland's heyday are triggered by the event. The rest of the play jumps between the 1930s and the 1960s. The musical premiered at the Blyth Festival. It received critical acclaim and is recognized as one of the best Canadian musicals. Storey's most recent play is *Lulie the Iceberg*, an adaptation of a book written by Her Imperial Highness Princess Takamodo of Japan.

SELECT PLAYS: *Country Chorale* (1982); *Angel of Death* (1984); *The Girls in the Gang* (1987); *The Last Bus* (1987); *The Dreamland* (1989); *Cheek to Cheek* (1990); *Saints & Apostles* (1990); *God and the Big Blue Chair* (1991); *In Principle* (1991); *Adventures in Turning Forty* (1992); *The Glorious Twelfth* (1992); *South of China* (1997); *Lulie the Iceberg* (2001)

FURTHER READING

Citron, Paula. "Unlikely Duo Make Beautiful Musicals." *Toronto Star* (April 12, 1991): D-2.

Playwrights Union of Canada. *Who's Who in the Playwrights Union of Canada*, 3d. ed. Toronto: Plawrights Union of Canada, September, 1997. 130.

Wagner, Vit. "Toronto 'Piousness' Gives Playwright a Pain." *Toronto Star* (February 17, 1989): D-16.

Beth A. Kattelman

THE STORY OF BUTTERFLY LOVERS

The Story of Butterfly Lovers (Liang Shanbo yu Zhu Yingtai, Zhejiang yueju) by Xu Jin is the best-known romantic folk story in Chinese cultural history, comparable as the Chinese equivalent of *Romeo and Juliet*. As an oral folk legend, the folk story had its origins somewhere around A.D. 400 in the Jin Dynasty, although most of what has been transmitted to the contemporary audience was recorded from the Song Dynasty or later because very little was recorded on paper as the legend passed through the Six Dynasties, the Sui Dynasty, and the Tang Dynasty. For Chinese people, the romantic folk legend is the perfect love story in which both lovers remain faithfully devoted to each other until death. The tale also presents two eternal themes: the fundamental gender inequality in imperial CHINA and the utter absence of individual freedom in marriage and the resulting suffering of young people under feudal rites and family rules. The tale underwent changes throughout its long history of transmission, performance, and interpretation.

The folk tale has been interpreted for the stage many times. The version staged by the Yueju Opera (also known as Shaoxing Opera) is the most popular and successful theatrical rendition in modern China; it was produced as a film adaptation in 1953. In this version, talented and beautiful Zhu Yingtai dresses as a boy to study at boarding school and falls in love with her classmate Liang Shanbo. Liang proposed to the Zhu family only to find out that they have arranged her marriage to another man. Liang dies of love-sickness soon after. On her wedding day and on the way to the bridegroom's home, Zhu visits Liang's tomb, which was cracked by a sudden thunderbolt. She entered the tomb to be reunited with her lover. The two were then transformed into a pair of dancing butterflies, a traditional symbol of lovers.

The Butterfly Lovers was first staged as Yueju Opera in 1945 by the legendary actresses Yuan Xuefen and Fan Ruijuan. In 1951, it was restaged by the Eastern China Yueju Opera Troupe with Huang Sha as director, Xu Jin as playwright, Chen Jie and Xue Yan as composers of its musical score, and Xing Xi and Su Shifeng as stage designers. Fan Ruijuan played Liang Shanbo, and Fu Quanxiang played Zhu Yingtai. It won numerous prizes at the First National Festival of Classical and Folk Drama in 1952, including screenplay, acting, musical score, choreography, and stage design. In 1953, it was adapted into the first colored regional opera film by Shanghai Film Studio, codirected by Sang Hu and Huang Sha, and screenplayed by Xu Jin and Sang Hu. Yuan Xuefen played Zhu Yingtai, and Fan Ruijuan played Liang Shanbo. The 1953 adaptation focuses on the themes of gender equality and freedom of marriage, which was excellent propaganda for the Marriage Law of May 1950 that enacted equal rights of men and women and outlawed arranged marriages.

FURTHER READING

Yang Hsien-yi and Gladys Yang, tr. *Love under the Willows* [Liu yin ji]. Peking: Foreign Languages Press, 1956.

Mackerras, Colin. *Chinese Drama: A Historical Survey.* Beijing: New World Press, 1990.

Munro, Stanley, tr. and ed. *The Eternal Love: The Story of Liang Shanbo and Zhu Yingtai.* Singapore, Kuala Lumpur, and Hong Kong: Federal Publications, 1991.

Hongwei Lu

STRANGE INTERLUDE

Oh, Mother God, grant that I may some day tell this fool the truth!
—Nina, Act 7

Strange Interlude by EUGENE O'NEILL was first produced by the THEATRE GUILD on January 30, 1928, with designs by Jo Mielziner and featuring Lynn Fontanne as Nina.

Nina mourns Gordon, her lover who was killed flying in the war; she feels guilty for not having had sexual relations with him before he left. Through Nina's predicament, O'Neill explores the conflict between passion and conventional morals; her "body ached" but her "cowardly brain" prevailed and she remains "Gordon's silly virgin." Eager to give of herself in any way she can, she becomes a nurse.

After Nina's father dies, Ned Darrell, the ironic physician, believes that Nina should seek treatment for what he perceives as a self-sacrificial martyr complex, but she decides to marry brash young Sam Evans. Pregnancy fulfills her; where her face was once strangely fascinating, all that remains are "her unchangeably mysterious eyes." In a naturalistic plot device, Sam's mother explains that insanity runs in Sam's father's family—Sam himself was an "accident" after his parents spent the evening drinking and dancing—so Nina has an abortion but then becomes pregnant by Ned. Sam feels so guilty over not giving Nina a child that he's ready to offer her a divorce, but when Ned tells him he's to be a father, his hope is rekindled.

After young Gordon is born, the relationships among Nina, Sam, Ned, and Charles Marsden, an old family friend, are fraught with guilt, resentment, and suspicion, and Nina is quite aware that all three of the men are in love with her: "I feel their desires converge in me." Twenty years later, Nina envies her son both his youth and his fiancée Madeline. Ned has managed to liberate himself from his obsession with Nina, and although he prevents her from telling Madeline the truth about Gordon's paternity, she reveals the truth to the shocked Marsden. Sam suffers a massive stroke and dies several months later, leaving the others to deal with their memories.

In this play, O'Neill broke new ground by writing out the characters' interior monologues, which the actors performed in a series of full-stage freezes. Like the voice-overs of later films, the monologues revealed exactly what the people were thinking, so they were able to disclose thoughts and feelings to the audience without conveying them to each other. We hear their fears, conflicts, and anxieties as they make their way through their overt interactions. The ideas of Sigmund Freud were not yet common knowledge in the United States, so the play introduced many in its audience not only to frank exploration of abortion and adultery but also to a psychological perspective on inner turmoil and the contradictory complexity of personality. O'Neill raised the question of outward behavior deriving from inner neurosis.

O'Neill also explores his interest in how to stage the development of a character through time. Nina begins as striking and athletic, "tall with broad square shoulders, slim strong hips and long beautifully developed legs." A year later, "her eyes try to armor her wounded spirit with a defensive stare of disillusionment." When first pregnant, "her face has a contented expression, there is an inner calm about her." In her second pregnancy, "there is a triumphant strength about her expression, a ruthless self-confidence in her eyes." Another year, and "she looks noticeably older, the traces of former suffering are marked on her face." Eleven years later, Nina is thirty-five, "in the full bloom of her womanhood. . . . Her eyes are tragically sad in repose and her expression is set and mask-like." After another ten years, her hair is white, she wears too much make-up, and "her face is thin, her cheeks taut, her mouth drawn with forced smiling." In her last scene, twenty-six years after her first, "resignation has come into her face, a resignation that uses no make-up, that has given up the struggle to be sexually attractive and look younger." Throughout, all men wish to become part of her, and they regard her as mother, whore, and metaphor for the sea; she is especially the Jungian mother to whom each man strives to return.

The *New York Herald Tribune's* critic Percy Hammond (February 5, 1928) called the monologues "more of a whip than a cushion to our imagination." Barrett H. Clark praised O'Neill's "extraordinary gift for understanding and laying bare some of the complexities of the human mind and heart" (Houchin, 1993). Joseph Wood Krutch, also writing for the *New York Herald Tribune* (March 11, 1928), argued that O'Neill had put Freudian psychology to effective use, and acknowledged the spoken thoughts as taking the drama into territory formerly restricted to the novel.

Despite a performance time of nearly six hours, including a ninety-minute dinner break, the play ran for seventeen months, led to two touring companies, earned $275,000 (nearly $3 million in 2002 dollars) for O'Neill, and won the Pulitzer Prize. José Quintero directed the 1963 Actors Studio Theater revival with Geraldine Page; the 1985 Broadway revival featured Glenda Jackson.

[*See also* United States, 1860–1929]

FURTHER READING

Gross, Robert F. "O'Neill's Queer Interlude: Epicene Excess and Camp Pleasures." *Journal of Dramatic Theory and Criticism* 12 (Fall 1997): 3–22.

Houchin, John H. *The Critical Response to Eugene O'Neill.* Westport, Conn.: Greenwood Press, 1993.

——. "Eugene O'Neill's 'Woman Play' in Boston." *Eugene O'Neill Review* 22 (Spring–Fall 1998): 48–62.

Kennicott, Leigh. "Asides in O'Neill's *Strange Interlude*: An Empirical Study." *On-Stage Studies* 20 (1997): 48–64.

Mandl, Bette. "Gender as Design in *Strange Interlude*." *The Eugene O'Neill Review* 19 (Spring–Fall 1995): 123–28.

Murphy, Brenda. "O'Neill's America: The *Strange Interlude* between the Wars." In *The Cambridge Companion to Eugene O'Neill*, ed. by Michael Manheim. Cambridge: Cambridge Univ. Press, 1998. 135–147.

Wolff, Tamsen. " 'Eugenic O'Neill' and the Secrets of *Strange Interlude*." *Theatre Journal* 55 (May 2003): 215–234.

Jeffrey D. Mason

STRAUSS, BOTHO (1944–)

That a people wishes to assert its moral laws against another and is prepared to sacrifice blood to do so is something we no longer understand and, in our liberal-libertarian self-delusion, view as false and damnable.

—Botho Strauss, 1993

Born on December 12, 1944, in Naumburg-Saale, GERMANY, Botho Strauss is one of the most important playwrights of the contemporary German stage. The author of many novels and essays, he is best known for his complex, often surreal plays. Strauss has always shied away from publicity. He does not attend his premiers, nor does he appear in person to receive the literary prizes he has been awarded. He studied German and sociology in Cologne and Munich before becoming a theater critic and, in 1967, editor of the influential German magazine *Theater heute* (*Theater Today*). In 1970, Strauss became DRAMATURG at Berlin's Schaubühne am Halleschen Ufer and worked with the artistic director Peter Stein (1937–) for several years. He currently lives in Berlin, Germany.

The disruption of reality, fears of being lost, and the intrusion of the supernatural into everyday life constitute prominent themes in Strauss's plays. The atmosphere in his dramas is often gloomy, reminiscent of the German Romantic tradition. A member of the upper middle class and its culture-loving elite, Strauss criticizes this group time and again. His characters often function well in their familiar surroundings but become frightened and lost when confronted with unknown situations.

Big and Little (*Gross und klein*, 1978), Strauss's best known play, depicts a woman who is lost in time and place, suffering because she cannot understand the world and its lack of sensitivity and hope. *Kalldewey, Farce* (1981) questions current psychoanalytical approaches when a couple succumbs to obscure therapists and is driven into a surreal world. In *The Park* (*Der Park*, 1983) Strauss uses characters from William Shakespeare's *Midsummer Night's Dream*. The fairies Oberon and Titania enter our world, only to learn that humans cannot understand the beauty of the fairy world and are lost in reality.

In such plays as *The Tour Guide* (*Die Fremdenführerinm*, 1986), *The Visitors* (*Die Besucher*, 1988), *Seven Doors* (*Sieben Türen*, 1988), and *Time and the Room* (*Die Zeit und das Zimmer*, 1988), Strauss presents characters whose reality is changed and who cannot adjust to the new circumstances. A teacher in *The Tour Guide*, for example, falls in love with a tour guide in Greece, whom he eventually murders because she does not share his feelings.

Strauss's pessimistic approach reaches new heights in *Final Chorus* (*Schlußchor*, 1991), a drama exploring the shattered dreams of Germans upon the fall of the Berlin Wall. A chorus arbitrarily shouting the word "Germany" throughout the play underscores the individual tragedies and criticizes the nationalistic tendencies flaring up at the time. Strauss revisits this topic in *The Balance* (*Das Gleichgewicht*, 1993), set in Berlin in 1992, when the problems of a united Germany appeared insolvable. The play depicts an social order imbalanced not only by increased prices in Eastern Germany but also because the fall of Communism leaves the Germans with a blank set of values.

Strauss is considered a major representative of New Subjectivity, a literary movement seeking to deconstruct misconstrued and alienated notions of Western subjectivity. Strauss, however, departs from the deconstructivist conclusion that humankind is inevitably destined to a form of subjectivity in which the self is rendered homeless.

Strauss's controversial reputation stems in large part from his essay "Swelling Bock Song" ("Anschwellender Bocksgesang," 1993) in which he condemns leftist political views and positions himself politically and culturally on the Right, while simultaneously trying to distance himself from right-wing extremism.

SELECT PLAYS: *The Hypochondriacs (Die Hypochonder, 1972); Familiar Faces, Mixed Feelings (Bekannte Gesichter, gemischte Gefühle, 1974); Reunion Trilogy (Trilogie des Wiedersehens, 1976); Big and Little (Groß und klein, 1978); Kalldewey, Farce (1981); The Park (Der Park, 1983); The Tour Guide (Die Fremdenführerin, 1986); Seven Doors (Sieben Türen, 1988); Time and the Room (Die Zeit und das Zimmer, 1988); Visitors (Besucher, 1988); Angela's Clothes (Angelas Kleider, 1991); Final Chorus (Schlußchor, 1991); Balance (Das Gleichgewicht, 1993); Ithaca (Ithaka, 1996); Jeffers—Act I and II (Jeffers—Akt I und II, 1998); A Kiss of Forgetting (Der Kuß des Vergessens, 1998); Similar Ones (Die Ähnlichen, 1998); Fantasy of Lot (Lotphantasie, 1999); The Idiot and His Wife Tonight in Pancomedia (Der Narr und seine Frau heute abend in Pancomedia, 2001); Unexpected Return (Unerwartete Rückkehr, 2001)*

FURTHER READING

Adelson, Leslie A. *Crisis of Subjectivity: Botho Strauß's Challenge to West German Prose of the 1970s.* Amsterdam: Rodopi, 1984.

Calandra, Denis. *New German Dramatists.* New York: Grove Press, 1983.

DeMeritt, Linda C. *New Subjectivity and Prose Forms of Alienation: Peter Handke and Botho Strauß.* New York: Lang, 1987.

Englhart, Andreas. *Im Labyrinth des unendlichen Textes: Botho Strauß' Theaterstücke 1972–1996* [In a Labyrinth of Endless Texts: The Plays of Botho Strauss]. Tübingen: Niemeyer, 2000.

Willer, Stefan. *Botho Strauß zur Einführung* [An Introduction to Botho Strauss]. Hamburg: Junius, 2000.

Britta Kallin

STREERUWITZ, MARLENE (1950–)

Shakespeare doesn't interest me. What is interesting about Shakespeare is the interest the contemporary theater has in him. Reactionary males roar on all political levels draped in rich costumes. Therefore, I take his characters and put them in different contexts, to show who Romeo really was: someone who speaks sweetly in the bedroom but is a warmonger like all the other aristocrats of his time.

—Marlene Streeruwitz, 1995

Born on June 28, 1950, in Baden, AUSTRIA, Marlene Streeruwitz studied art history and Slavic language and literature in Vienna, writing a dissertation on Russian drama. She worked as a journalist, directed theater and radio plays, and lectured at the universities of Tübingen and Frankfurt. In 1996, Streeruwitz received the literary prize of the Austrian Government's Cultural Division, and in 2000 she was writer-in-residence at the University of Illinois at Chicago.

Streeruwitz's first successes on the German-language stage were productions of *Waikiki-Beach* (1992) and *New York, New York* (1993). Critics identify intertexuality, montage, feminist undertones, and a Brechtian approach as major characteristics of Streeruwitz's dramas. Her plays are critical of mainstream culture and capitalist tendencies, highlighting her feminist intentions by questioning gender roles.

In *Waikiki-Beach*, Streeruwitz's most successful play to date, the mayor's wife and her lover realize that their love is coming to an end when suddenly a homeless couple is beaten to death by skinheads who walk onto the scene. Three housewives appear on stage and comment on the action as if walking through an art exhibition. The use of the unperturbed onlooker is present in a number of Streeruwitz's plays, including *Sloane Square* (1992) in which tourists watch as a group of punks torment one of their own. *New York, New York* takes place in a public restroom in Vienna where a pimp beats a prostitute unconscious while the cleaning lady, Mrs. Horvath, watches without interfering.

Streeruwitz's plays are marked by violence, fantasy-world references, and literary allusions. In her dramas, she repeatedly quotes such authors as William Shakespeare (1564–1616), Goethe (1749–1832), Heinrich von Kleist (1777–1811), and HUGO VON HOFMANNSTHAL (1874–1929). In *Ocean Drive* (1993), for example, a play in which an actress meets a journalist on a glacier, Streeruwitz uses scenes from Shakespeare's *Richard III* and Hofmannsthal's COMEDY *The Difficult Man (Der Schwierige,* 1921). Streeruwitz also integrates characters from television shows and other forms of popular culture into her dramas. In *Bagnacavallo* (1993), for instance, Tick and Trick (i.e., Huey and Dewey), two of Donald Duck's nephews, appear on stage.

Streeruwitz's plays often present images causing the audience to question the banalities of life. In *Elysian Park* (1993) three nurses push strollers containing old men instead of babies. The scenes are then interrupted by Streeruwitz's recurring figure of a homeless person. In *Tolmezzo* (1994) an Austrian Jewish woman, having survived persecution by the Nazis, returns to Vienna from her U.S. exile only to find that the mindset of Austrians in the 1990s has not changed as much as she had hoped. The woman then gets entangled in a television-like game show where she competes with Barbie dolls.

Dentro (1995) is a retelling of Shakespeare's *King Lear,* presenting the audience with a syphilitic king who sexually abuses his daughters. *Boccaleone* (1999) discusses the abuse of asylum seekers, ill patients, and dead corpses by a Viennese company in a science-fiction world. In *Sapporo* (2002), Streeruwitz comments upon the current political situation in Austria using the 1972 Olympic games in Sapporo, Japan, as a backdrop.

Since the mid-1990s, Streeruwitz has also published numerous critically acclaimed novels. She currently lives in Vienna, Austria, and Berlin, GERMANY.

SELECT PLAYS: *New York, New York (1987); Brahm's Square (Brahmsplatz, 1990); Sloane Square (1992); Waikiki-Beach (1992); Bagnacavallo (1993); Elysian Park (1993); Ocean Drive (1993); Tolmezzo (1994); Dentro (1995); Boccaleone (1999); Sapporo (2002)*

FURTHER READING

Fuchs, Christian, ed. *Theater von Frauen: Österreich* [Theater by Women: Austria]. Frankfurt: Eichborn, 1991.

Hempel, Nele. *Marlene Streeruwitz: Gewalt und Humor im dramatischen Werk* [Violence and Humor in Her Dramatic Works]. Tübingen: Stauffenburg, 2001.

Kallin, Britta. "In Brecht's Footsteps or Way Beyond Brecht? Brechtian Techniques in Feminist Plays by Elfriede Jelinek and Marlene Streeruwitz." *Communications from the International Brecht Society* 29, nos. 1–2 (2000): 62–66.

Streeruwitz, Marlene. *New York: New York.* Tr. by Udo Borgert and Laura Ginters. In *Women's Words, Women's Works: An Anthology of Contemporary Austrian Plays by Women.* Ed. by Udo Borgert. Riverside, Calif.: Ariadne Press, 2001.

Britta Kallin

A STREETCAR NAMED DESIRE

Whoever you are—I have always depended on the kindness of strangers.
—Blanche, Scene 11

A Streetcar Named Desire, TENNESSEE WILLIAMS's searing, lyrical 1947 drama, explores the tragic mental disintegration of the deeply troubled Blanche DuBois. For many critics, Williams reached the pinnacle of his achievement as a dramatist with this poetic study of a fragile, mentally unstable woman unable to cope with the losses of her past, her present reduced circumstances, and the realities of the world that are in stark conflict with her frequent retreats into romantic illusion. "I want magic," Blanche insists, but the colored paper lanterns she hangs to dim and soften the light around her does not keep reality, as represented by the brutality of her animalistic brother-in-law, Stanley Kowalski, from exposing and destroying her.

Blanche is a faded middle-aged woman whose delicate manner suggests the sheltered upbringing of a Southern aristocrat. She arrives in the steamy French Quarter of New Orleans on the streetcar named Desire, seeking the home of her only sister, Stella, and Stella's husband, Stanley. Blanche is distressed to discover Stella married to a man Blanche regards as beneath her in class. That Stella's home is merely a cramped flat in a rough, rundown neighborhood exacerbates Blanche's distress.

Despite the fact that she is nearly destitute and in need of a safe haven with Stella, Blanche cannot resist being mockingly critical of Stanley's crude ways. Blanche's affected air of superiority and Stanley's low-brow vulgarity strain relations in the close quarters of the flat. Stanley's coworker, Mitch, a gentle man who lives with his ailing mother, is attracted to Blanche's sensitivity and charm. She encourages a relationship with Mitch in hopes that a marriage with him will provide safety and security, carefully hiding her age and the harsh facts of her life behind a variety of illusory effects. The intense sexual bond between Stanley and Stella disturbs Blanche, and she is horrified when she learns that Stella is pregnant. Despite the impending arrival of a child, and to Stanley's intense annoyance, Stella allows Blanche to stay on with them. He demands to know the status of Belle Reve, the family home, half of which, he believes, belongs to Stella—and, thanks to the "Napoleonic code," to him. When Blanche admits that the property has been lost because the expenses of caring for dying family members depleted their funds, Stanley is unconvinced. He secretly contacts a friend in Blanche's hometown and learns that she has been sexually promiscuous. Worse yet, she was fired from her high school teaching job on the suspicion of an inappropriate relationship with a male student, culminating in her departure from town.

Blanche is also troubled by the past. The memory of her young husband, Alan, whom she caught in bed with a man, haunts her. Alan shot himself in shame, and the incidents surrounding his death continually replay themselves in her turbulent mind as her hold on reality grows more and more tenuous. Blanche's attraction to inappropriately young men is demonstrated by a brief encounter with a newspaper delivery boy, but Williams makes it clear that the heartbroken, guilt-ridden Blanche is in a futile search for the young husband she has lost.

When Stanley tells Mitch of Blanche's background, Mitch at first refuses to accept it. He drunkenly confronts Blanche and finally sees through the illusions in which she has enveloped herself. Blanche's hopes of a marriage are dashed as Mitch flees. When Stella goes to the hospital to give birth, the animosity between Stanley and Blanche explodes and he sexually assaults her. Unhinged by this trauma, Blanche is subsequently unable to convince Stella of the rape. As Mitch watches helplessly, Stella reluctantly goes along with Blanche's commitment to a mental institution. As the play ends, Blanche is escorted away by a nurse and doctor, to whom she sadly states, "I have always depended on the kindness of strangers." As Blanche departs, Stella's passions drive her back to Stanley's arms, despite her lingering suspicions that Blanche's version of events may be true.

Under the direction of Elia Kazan, the original cast of *A Streetcar Named Desire* was led by Jessica Tandy. Her Blanche exposed the contradictions and complexities of a woman who is at once fragile and strong, sensitive and cruel, damaged and poetic. Tandy's performance was matched by Marlon Brando's star-making interpretation of Stanley, an image of potent and overt male sexuality previously unseen on the Broadway stage. The play's frankness smashed taboos that had been firmly in place in American theater, bringing to serious drama the possibility of exploring themes and attitudes previously unavailable to dramatists.

A Streetcar Named Desire was awarded the 1948 Pulitzer Prize for Drama, as well as numerous other honors and critics' awards, and it was filmed in 1951 with most of its original stage cast, including Karl Malden as Mitch and Kim Hunter as Stella, under Kazan's direction. Vivien Leigh, in an Academy Award-winning performance (Malden and Hunter also won Oscars), replaced Tandy on screen, but Brando again played Stanley, and his performance launched him as one of the iconic male stars of post–World War II Hollywood films. *A Streetcar Named Desire* has been revived frequently on both stage and screen.

Critics and audiences have consistently ranked *A Streetcar Named Desire* as one of the three greatest American plays, along with EUGENE O'NEILL's *LONG DAY'S JOURNEY INTO NIGHT* and ARTHUR MILLER's *DEATH OF A SALESMAN*. Its enduring qualities—Williams's poetic language, his sensitive and haunting depiction of his characters, and the play's bold themes—contrive to keep *Streetcar* a constant presence on stages throughout the world.

[See also United States, 1940–Present]

FURTHER READING

Adler, Thomas P. *A Streetcar Named Desire: The Moth and the Lantern.* Boston: Gale, 1990.

Bloom, Harold, ed. *Tennessee Williams's A Streetcar Named Desire (Modern Critical Interpretations).* New York: Chelsea House, 1988.

Hurrell, John D., ed. *Two Modern American Tragedies: Reviews and Criticism of Death of a Salesman and A Streetcar Named Desire.* New York: Scribner's, 1961.

Kolin, Philip C. *Williams: A Streetcar Named Desire.* New York: Cambridge Univ. Press, 2000.

Kolin, Philip C., ed. *Confronting Tennessee Williams' A Streetcar Named Desire: Essays in Critical Pluralism.* Westport, Conn.: Greenwood Press, 1992.

Miller, Jordan Y., ed. *Twentieth Century Interpretations of "A Streetcar Named Desire."* Englewood Cliffs, N.J.: Prentice-Hall, 1971.

James Fisher

STREET SCENE

Street Scene by ELMER RICE opened at the Playhouse in New York on January 10, 1929, in a production directed by the playwright and designed by Jo Mielziner. In obvious imitation of Greek drama, Rice keeps the action of *Street Scene* in a public outdoor space and limits the time of the play to about twenty-four hours. The play has been called dull, undramatic, socially conscious, and compassionate; the disparity of critical appraisal results from Rice's combination of naturalistic elements within a melodramatic plot.

The play is set entirely on the sidewalk and front steps of a New York City tenement. Rice describes the building in a lengthy stage direction that includes details about ambient sound that underscore the entire play: "the distant roar of El trains, automobile sirens, and the whistles of boats on the river . . . musical instruments, a radio, dogs barking and human voices." Thus, Rice creates an impression that we are witnessing events in a very particular time and place. Adding to this spectacle is the vast number of people who fill the stage with bustling city activity. The script calls for more than sixty characters, most of whom are named and given unique attributes, representing a variety of ages and ethnicities in working-class New York. Their diverse

dialects further contribute to the naturalism Rice is trying to achieve.

Against the backdrop of this working-class neighborhood, Rice's characters engage in acts of ordinary life: reading the newspaper on the front stoop, arguing over politics, walking to the grocery store, and gossiping, mostly about the budding romance between Irish Rose Maurrant and Jewish Sam Kaplan. Sam is studying to be a lawyer, and his family worries that his interest in Rose might distract him from his education.

A darker subject of local gossip is the affair between Rose's mother, Anna, and the milkman, Steve Sankey. Rose's father, Frank, becomes suspicious of his wife and ultimately murders Anna and Sankey in the family's apartment. He flees but is quickly caught by the police, and a grief-stricken Rose announces her plans to get out of New York and find a new life for herself and her younger brother, Willie.

Sam offers to give up his career plans and follow her: "I don't care what I do. I'll be a day laborer; I'll dig sewers—anything. Rose, don't leave me!" He professes his love for Rose and argues that they belong to one another. After the recent violence in her family, however, Rose does not believe this claim of romantic love: "I don't think people ought to belong to anybody but themselves. I was thinking, that if my mother had really belonged to herself, and that if my father had really belonged to himself, it never would have happened." Rose leaves, the play ends, and the bustle of life on the street resumes without her.

A film version of *Street Scene* was released in 1931, and the play was set to music by composer Kurt Weill and poet LANGSTON HUGHES in 1947.

[See also United States, 1860–1929]

FURTHER READING

Chametzky, Jules. "Elmer Rice, Liberation, and the Great Ethnic Question." In *From Hester Street to Hollywood: The Jewish-American Stage and Screen,* ed. by Sarah Blacher Cohen. Bloomington: Indiana Univ. Press, 1983.

Murphy, Brenda. "The Final Integration: Innovations in Realistic Thought and Structure, 1916–1940." In *American Realism and American Drama: 1880–1940.* Cambridge: Cambridge Univ. Press, 1987.

Rabkin, Gerald. "Elmer Rice and the Seriousness of Drama." In *Drama and Commitment: Politics in the American Theatre of the Thirties.* Bloomington: Indiana Univ. Press, 1964.

Rice, Elmer. *Minority Report: An Autobiography.* New York: Simon and Schuster, 1963.

DeAnna M. Toten Beard

STRICTLY DISHONORABLE

Maybe good women are good because . . . because it takes two to be bad . . . and they can't find anybody.
—Isabelle, Act 3

Strictly Dishonorable by Preston Sturges opened at New York's Avon Theatre on September 18, 1929, and ran for 557 performances. Brock Pemberton and Antoinette Perry staged the play, and Brooks Atkinson called it a "well-nigh perfect COMEDY" (New York Times, Sept. 19, 1929).

Henry and his fiancée, Isabelle, enter a New York speakeasy for a nightcap before heading home to New Jersey. Henry is rude to everybody and dominates Isabelle, an innocent southern belle. Gus, the Count Di Ruvo, arrives to the sound of operatic music. Isabelle rhapsodizes about Tino Caraffa's singing, and she is overwhelmed to learn that Gus is Tino Caraffa. While Henry is outside handling a parking problem, Gus and Isabelle dance and become mutually infatuated. When Henry returns, he demands Isabelle leave with him, but she refuses. Gus offers Isabelle accommodations for the night in his apartment.

Isabelle: What are your intentions toward me?

Gus (smiling): Strictly dishonorable, Isabelle.

In Gus's apartment above the speakeasy, he and Isabelle experience their first tentative moments. The Judge arrives, intent on saving Isabelle from Gus and herself. Gus leaves to deal with a visitor, while the Judge urges Isabelle to "look well before the leap." Isabelle declares, "Don't you think it's better to be very happy for a little while . . . than never to be happy at all?" When Gus returns, he prepares Isabelle for bed in a very provocative scene for its day. As Isabelle trembles, Gus says, "Life is beautiful . . . and its most beautiful moments are called . . . love. They are very rare, my Isabelle, such moments as this . . . to be accepted tenderly . . . and without fear." He carries her to bed and leaves, seeking accommodations upstairs with the Judge.

The next morning, the Judge congratulates Isabelle for coming to her senses and sending Gus away the night before. Later, Gus arrives while Isabelle is in the shower, tells the Judge of his desire to marry Isabelle, and leaves to dress at the Judge's place. Henry comes to apologize. Gus returns and tells Isabelle that he considered marrying her but knows he would be inconsiderate to ask her to travel so much because of his career. Believing that he is merely being gentlemanly, Isabelle resigns herself to marrying Henry and leaves. To drown their sorrow, the Judge heads to his apartment for liquor but returns with Isabelle instead.

The dialogue is full of subtle humor and irony. The Judge displays fatherly wisdom and wit. Isabelle is a complete woman with both passion and determination. Gus, the debonair man of the world with a heart of gold, finds his ideal woman.

The play offers the choices of staying safe and secure or experiencing and growing with the world. Isabelle has led a very sheltered life, and her future with Henry promises to be unsatisfying. In contrast, she is offered the risky possibility of traveling the world with Gus. Some see in this the clash between advocates of American isolationism and advocates of America accepting a role in world affairs. *Strictly Dishonorable* was Sturges's major stage success before his film career began.

[See also United States, 1929–1940]

FURTHER READING

Curtis, James. *Between Flops: A Biography of Preston Sturges*. New York: Limelight Editions, 1984.

Jacobs, Diane. *Christmas in July: The Life and Art of Preston Sturges*. Berkeley: Univ. of California Press, 1992.

Sturges, Preston. *Preston Sturges*. New York: Simon and Schuster, 1990.

Robert Lewis Smith

STRINDBERG, AUGUST (1849–1912)

No particular form shall bind the author, for the theme dictates the form.

—August Strindberg, 1908

A pioneering Swedish playwright, novelist, short story writer, essayist, and poet, August Strindberg produced truly innovative work also as a painter and photographer, whereas his explorations in the field of natural science have met with more skepticism. Although his prose works and his poetry have renewed and expanded Swedish literature and language, and although he is now regarded as one of the world's outstanding letter writers, it is as a dramatist that he has had the greatest international impact.

The new edition of Strindberg's *Collected Works*, soon to be completed, will consist of about seventy-two volumes. The recently published edition of his letters runs to twenty-two volumes. In addition there is a huge number of manuscripts, most of them in the Strindberg Collection of the Royal Library in Stockholm.

From his earliest works, Strindberg's life and letters are closely interwoven and constantly cross-fertilizing each other. Unlike HENRIK IBSEN, his foremost Scandinavian rival in the field of drama, Strindberg led a very varied life. He married and divorced three times, had five children, and frequently moved from one place to another and one country to another. He also had a tendency immediately to put on paper what he experienced and let it remain there unchanged. At the same time, he frequently experienced what he was writing as exceedingly real.

Johan August Strindberg was born in Stockholm, SWEDEN. His father, with whom he had a difficult relationship, was a steamboat broker. His mother, to whom he was very attached, was a waitress before she married. When she died and his father remarried, Strindberg, at the age of thirteen, found himself confronted with a hated stepmother. After various unsuccessful occupations—university studies in Uppsala, journalism, teaching, translating, acting—Strindberg became an assistant at the Royal Library. In 1877 he married the Finland-Swedish noblewoman Siri von Essen, recently divorced from Baron Carl Gustav Wrangel. Siri was to bear him two daughters and a son.

Having made himself known to the Swedish establishment as a "seducer of the youth" because of his outspokenness in various matters, including sexual, Strindberg chose to go into voluntary exile with his family in 1883; they stayed mainly in FRANCE, SWITZERLAND, GERMANY, and DENMARK. After his divorce from Siri in 1891, Strindberg married the Austrian journalist Frida Uhl, whom he had met in Berlin, in 1893. They had a daughter. This marriage was informally dissolved by the time Strindberg moved to Paris a year later. Here he devoted himself to alchemy, occultism, and attempts to make gold. He also experienced a series of mental crises, usually designated as the Inferno crisis after his novel by that title. In 1899 he returned to Sweden and settled in Stockholm for the rest of his life.

In 1901 he married the Norwegian actress Harriet Bosse, with whom he had one daughter. Harriet was to take leading parts in many of his plays. Although the marriage was dissolved in 1904, Strindberg retained an intimate relationship to her—at times telepathically—for several years thereafter. In 1908 he moved from their common flat to a newly built apartment house, which he called the Blue Tower. This last domicile is now part of the Strindberg Museum. At the end of his life he initiated what is known as the Strindberg Feud, a debate on various aspects of Swedish social, political, and cultural life. Although never awarded the Nobel Prize for literature by the Swedish Academy, he was offered a substantial gift by forty thousand people when he turned sixty-three, and in the evening the Stockholm Workers' Union hailed him in a torchlit procession below his balcony. Against his wishes, he was given what amounted to a state funeral, but in conformance with his wishes, his grave in Stockholm is among those of the common people, "not in the rich people's part, the market of vanity."

It has been said of Strindberg that "no one has a shorter way from the blood to the ink," and his gigantic output seems to bear this out. When asked about his working habits three years before his death, he said that when writing he first felt comfortably feverish, then ecstatic. Sometimes, he added,

> I believe I'm a kind of medium, for it happens so easily, half unconsciously, with little calculation! But it lasts only for three hours (usually between 9 and 12 A.M.). And when it's over, "it's just as boring again!" until next time. But it doesn't come when ordered and not when it suits me. . . . Most often and most successfully after huge crashes. (Strindberg, 1909)

While "watchmaker" Ibsen would spend many months on each of his plays, Strindberg usually finished his admittedly often shorter dramas in a matter of weeks, sometimes days. He believed in the value of swift and spontaneous writing and did not care much about rewriting or proofreading. Even when he, himself, could not quite understand why he had inserted a passage or even a character, he would tend to let it remain as written, trusting that it must have had a meaning at the time of writing. This does not mean that he rigidly insisted that actors should stick to his text at all costs. Strindberg's rich language with its associative leaps and bold imagery is an enormous challenge for the translator. Even the titles present problems. His

Oväder has been rendered in English as Storm, The Storm, The Thunderstorm, Storm Weather, Stormy Weather, and Thunder in the Air.

Strindberg's spiritual development follows a meandering pattern, as could be expected from a man who regarded changeability as a sign of vitality and constancy as akin to sterility. Brought up in an atmosphere of evangelical pietism within the Lutheran state church, Strindberg at an early age found himself more in sympathy with the liberal unitarianism of Theodore Parker. At an early stage he was also, like many other Scandinavians, deeply influenced by the Danish philosopher Søren Kierkegaard's severe demands for taking a clear either-or standpoint, a standpoint given dramatic force in Ibsen's BRAND and, indirectly, in his PEER GYNT, plays much admired by Strindberg.

During the politically oriented 1880s, he felt attracted first to anarchism, then, influenced by Jean-Jacques Rousseau's criticism of civilization, to agrarian socialism—this in contrast to the industrial socialism promoted by the Social Democrats.

Through the Dane Georg Brandes, the dominating critic in Scandinavia at the time, he came in contact with FRIEDRICH NIETZSCHE's ideas. Influenced also by the aristocratic writer-colleague Verner von Heidenstam, he now exchanged his former sympathy for the lower classes for admiration of the superman. Applying a Darwinian perspective, he argued that male power in society was a natural result of a long evolution, and that women could have no right to the same position after only a few decades. Sharing Nietzsche's misogyny, impressed by the Italian criminologist Cesare Lombroso, and seeing it as his task to fight the emancipation movement, Strindberg became an intense hater of what he called half-women: women who by competing with men were traitors to their own sex. This, however, did not prevent him from arguing for a great amount of equality between the sexes and from marrying only career women. Strindberg's views about "the woman question" alienated him from the radical writers of the 1880s, who called themselves Young Sweden and who had earlier regarded him as their leader. A sharp observer of human behavior and fearing for his own sanity, Strindberg was at this period also an avid reader of psychiatric literature. Arguing that "the naturalist has erased guilt along with God," he became for a while an atheist (Strindberg, 1888). But the feeling of guilt remained.

The Inferno crisis in the mid-1890s meant a break with Nietzschean ideals. Far from being dead, God, usually referred to as the Powers, now came to rule both his life and his writing. Along with Arthur Schopenhauer, he tried to accept that life means suffering. Nourished by Emanuel Swedenborg, who was to be his most important spiritual guide for the rest of his life, he even at times welcomed the suffering, seeing it either as a punishment for sins committed in a former existence or as an ordeal to make him worthy of a better life after death. In his later years, he often explicitly referred to life a purgatory or hell from which we are released when we die, or a nightmare from which we awaken at the moment of death. With Swedenborg he believed in "correspondences" between the earthly existence and the life beyond.

Strindberg's religion had more room for a punishing Jehovah than for a Christ who suffers for believers. "Can God forgive?" he once asked and characteristically answered: "Yes, when he has punished."

Often describing his protagonists as innocently suffering scapegoats, he early discovered the pleasure of martyrdom. In his autobiography *The Son of a Servant* (*Tjänstekvinnans son*) are several episodes showing how Johan, his alter ego, consciously or unconsciously strives to be treated unjustly so that those victimizing him will suffer from pangs of conscience and repent.

NONDRAMATIC WORK

Although he first wrote plays, Strindberg's breakthrough came in 1879 with the novel *The Red Room* (*Röda rummet*), subtitled "Scenes from the lives of artists and writers," a satirical attack on the humbug in various parts of society in the spirit of Charles Dickens and Mark Twain, propelled by the dissatisfaction with the parliamentary reform of 1866. Borrowing its title from the room in a Stockholm restaurant where a group of artist-bohemians used to assemble, *The Red Room* now counts as the first modern Swedish novel in both content and style.

The attack on Swedish society was continued, even more violently, in the pamphlet *The New Nation* (*Det nya riket*, 1882).

In the two-volume cultural history *The Swedish People* (*Svenska folket*, 1882), Strindberg argues that the history of Sweden is essentially the history of its people, not the history of its kings as the lauded historian and writer Erik Gustav Geijer had maintained.

A great number of short stories, later collected under the title *Swedish Fates and Adventures* (*Svenska öden och äventyr*), may be seen as the often successful result of his historical research for *The Swedish People*.

Strongly opposed to the emancipation movement and its supporters, notably his rival in the field of drama, Henrik Ibsen, whom he liked to belittle as "the Nora man," Strindberg in 1884 published a collection of short stories entitled *Married* (*Giftas*). In these he describes upper-class women, with good humor, as lazily profiting from their breadwinning husbands. "A Doll's House" (*Ett dockhem*) was intended as a healthy antidote to Ibsen's famous play. Officially because of his blasphemous comments on Holy Communion in "The Rewards of Virtue" (*Dygdens lön*) but presumably from an attempt of feminists to silence him, Strindberg was brought to trial. He was acquitted, but the event left its mark. In *Married II* (*Giftas II*, 1885), a much more sarcastic volume than the first one, he took revenge on the bluestockings.

The most explicitly autobiographical of Strindberg's many semiautobiographical works is the four-part novel *The Son of a Servant*, subtitled "The Story of the Development of a Soul." The first two parts were written and published in 1886, the third part appeared in 1887, the fourth not until 1909. Skeptical about the value of fiction, Strindberg in the eighties encouraged everyone to write about the life one knows best, one's own. In *The Son of a Servant* he set the good example. Although the work shows an inclination to describe the past somewhat in the light of his marital problems at the time of writing and although it is not always true to the facts, it remains one of the truly important *documents humains* in its effort to relate its central figure Johan (Strindberg's first Christian name) to the social and intellectual context of his time.

The Defense of a Madman was written in French in 1887–1888 under the title *Le plaidoyer d'un fou*, first published in German as *Die Beichte eines Thoren* in 1893, published in French in 1895, and much later rendered into Swedish as *En dåres försvarstal*. It is a passionate roman à clef about Axel's and Maria's (i.e., August's and Siri's) difficult relationship. The book has been called a detective novel in the reverse, meaning that both crime and criminal are more enigmatic at the end than at the beginning.

In his most popular work, *The People of Hemsö* (*Hemsöborna*, 1887), a tragicomic novel bringing the enterprising mainlander Carlsson to the rural population of the Stockholm archipelago, Strindberg depicts the resulting controversies and excels in naturalistic descriptions of people and nature.

This is true also of the more serious novel *By the Open Sea* (*I havsbandet*, 1890), set in the same area but this time with a Nietzschean superman doomed to destruction.

Short stories and essays written and published around 1890 reveal the Nietzschean ideology Strindberg embraced at the time as well as more original ideas that were to prove very fruitful in his dramatic work. The titles are telling: "The Battle of the Brains" (*Hjärnornas kamp*), "Hallucinations" (*Hallucinationer*), "Nemesis Divina," "Mysticism—So far" (*Mystik—tills vidare*), and "Psychic Murder" (*Själamord*), the last being an analysis of Ibsen's ROSMERSHOLM.

The so-called Inferno crisis is documented in the Parisian *Inferno* (1897) and *Legends* (*Légendes*, 1898), both written in French. Even more than in most of his other works, it is in these generically unusual works difficult to determine the distinction between fact and fiction. In these highly original works the narrating I sees the world through a pre-Kafkian lens.

Alone (*Ensam*, 1903) is a contemplative, highly autobiographical novella, thematically related to the chamber play *Thunder in the Air*, about a lonely man's sharing, in his imagination, the lives of others living in the same apartment house.

Quite different is the mood in *Black Banners* (*Svarta fanor*, 1907) a roman à clef that violently satirizes several well-known Swedes, especially his former friend, the writer Gustaf af Geijerstam. It caused a tremendous scandal and made it even more difficult for Strindberg to be accepted by the establishment.

The Scapegoat (*Syndabocken*) and *The Roofing Feast* (*Taklagsöl*), both published in 1907, are two powerful novellas. In the latter Strindberg approaches the interior monologue technique later made famous by James Joyce.

In *The Occult Diary* (*Ockulta dagboken*) we have a remarkable day-to-day record of thoughts, events, emotions and, not least, works by himself and others that occupied Strindberg in the period 1896–1908.

Closely related to this are the four *Blue Books* (*Blå böckerna*, 1907–1912). In page-long pieces, Strindberg here deals with a broad spectrum of topics—linguistics, natural science, astronomy, religion, philosophy, history, geography, among others—in an extremely subjective way. Strange coincidences, correspondences, and other signs from the Powers are discovered everywhere.

Although Strindberg was usually skeptical about poetry and spent little time on it, the efforts he did make were innovative. He was one of the first Swedes to write in free verse. In his best known poem, "The Boulevard System" (*Esplanadsystemet*), he welcomes the tearing down of old buildings to make room for new ones, a "Darwinian" standpoint that was to return in the preface to *Miss Julie*.

DRAMATIC WORK

"The secret of all my stories, novels, tales," Strindberg wrote late in his life, "is that they are dramas. . . . when the theaters closed their doors on me for long periods of time, I hit upon the idea of writing my dramas in epic form—for future use" (In a letter to Emil Schering, May 6, 1907). The statement explains the dramatic quality of Strindberg's prose works and corroborates that he was at heart a dramatist. His propensity for drama has to do with his tendency to experience the world in terms of conflict, whether based on gender, class, intelligence, morality, or religion. Writing in general and playwriting in particular, he declared in an interview toward the end of his life, was a blissful escape from merely living: "Only then am I alive!" (Strindberg, 1909).

The first preserved play by his hand, *The Freethinker* (*Fritänkaren*, 1870), an immature CLOSET DRAMA published under pseudonym, demonstrates his skepticism against Christ's *satisfactio vicaria*, a view that was to stay with him throughout his life.

In *The Outlaw* (*Den fredlöse*, 1871), a one-act play set in 12th-century Iceland, several themes that were later to occupy Strindberg can be sensed, notably the power struggle both between God and man and between man and woman, the latter in its characteristic Strindbergian form of the love-hate relationship.

National-historical drama being a popular genre at the time, Strindberg chose to write a play about MASTER OLOF, Sweden's Martin Luther, hoping in this way to increase his chances of getting the play produced. His hopes were quickly dashed when The Royal Theater rejected the play. Written in prose rather than verse, containing a number of anachronisms, and showing little respect for and similarity to the real-life counterparts of the portrayed characters, the play in no way agreed with what was considered appropriate for an historical drama. Nine years after it was written, a new version was successfully produced, signified Strindberg's breakthrough as a dramatist. It is now generally recognized as the first important Swedish drama. Much later the playwright was to summarize his dramatic technique in all the historical plays "from the first *Master Olof*" as follows:

> My purpose was, as it was my teacher William Shakespeare's, to depict human beings both in their greatness and their triviality; not to avoid the right word; to let history be the background and to compress historical periods to fit the demands of the theater of our time by avoiding the undramatic form of the chronicle or the narrative. (Strindberg, 1967)

Both a revised prose version and a verse version of the play were rejected by the theaters.

Having married a woman with histrionic ambitions, Strindberg wrote several plays in which Siri could play prominent roles. The first of them is *The Secret of the Guild* (*Gillets hemlighet*, 1880), thematically somewhat related to Ibsen's THE MASTER BUILDER, a comparison unflattering for Strindberg, who certainly did not build his play masterfully. Playing in the 15th century, it is a somewhat declamatory "COMEDY" about the rivalry between Jacques and Sten concerning the completion of Uppsala cathedral.

A more central part than in this drama was intended for Siri in *Sir Bengt's Wife* (*Herr Bengts hustru*, 1882), set in the early 16th century. The play is of interest mostly as the first drama in which Strindberg discusses "the woman question." Like Ibsen's Nora, Margit wants to divorce her husband. But unlike the end in A DOLL'S HOUSE, Strindberg's play ends with a couple determined to stay together.

Written as a Christmas play for children, *Lucky Per's Journey* (*Lycko-Pers resa*, 1882) combines childish fairy elements derived from Hans Christian Andersen and Dickens with social satire more intelligible for adults. As the title indicates, it is a pilgrimage drama owing much to Ibsen's *Peer Gynt*. As such it anticipates the composition of the post-Inferno station dramas.

With *Comrades* (*Kamraterna*, 1888), about the rivalry between two Parisian artists who are also husband and wife, Strindberg began writing in the present. The battle between the sexes is here fought between Bertha and her husband Axel, a name Strindberg often gives to his alter egos. Bertha is a woman who, lacking a personality of her own, figuratively sucks the blood of her husband. She is the first in a row of the dramatist's vampires.

Strindberg's international breakthrough came with THE FATHER (*Fadren*, 1887), a study in what he called psychic murder. Though characterized as naturalistic by Strindberg himself, possibly in a hope to get ÉMILE ZOLA interested in it (a hope that was not fulfilled) the play has subjectivism in common with the post-Inferno dramas.

In his following three one-act plays, like *The Father* limited to one setting, Strindberg reduced the number of characters further to suit the meager means at his disposal when, after the model of ANDRÉ ANTOINE's Théâtre Libre, he tried to create a Scandinavian Experimental Theater. The attempt failed. But the plays are among the most vigorous that ever came from his pen.

Best known is MISS JULIE (Fröken Julie, 1888), the most frequently performed of all Strindberg's plays. Here and in other contemporary work Strindberg reveals his fascination with hypnosis. Almost as famous as the play itself is the preface to it. In this play, and even more in CREDITORS (Fordringsägare, 1889), is provided a useful summary of what NATURALISM meant in the theater at that time.

Although Strindberg never became an out-and-out naturalist and, as in his essay "On Modern Drama and Modern Theater" (1890), rejected what he called petty naturalism—the concern for life-like veracity—the eleven one-act plays he wrote between 1888 and 1892 are usually referred to as naturalistic. Considering the author's personal situation at the time, it is not surprising that matrimonial relations play a central role. The cynical tone in these plays has much in common with the French comédie rosse.

A congruence of playing time and scenic time characterizes THE STRONGER (Den starkare, 1890), Pariah (Paria, 1890), The First Warning (Första varningen, 1893), and The Bond (Bandet, 1893); in all four the unity of place is also strictly observed. Contrary to what is often assumed, Miss Julie is marked by a certain discrepancy between the playing time (an hour and a half) and the scenic time (around twelve hours). This discrepancy is disguised by having dancing peasants invade the kitchen. Time seems extended. There is no need for a curtain. As a consequence, the illusion of the spectator is never broken. To indicate that we are dealing with representative cases rather than individuals—the scientific pretensions of naturalism are evident here—Strindberg in these plays often designates his characters merely by blood or other relationship (father, daughter, son-in-law), sometimes by profession, and sometimes by abstraction (Mr. X, Miss Y).

Based on a short story by Strindberg's contemporary Ola Hansson, Pariah is at once a detective story (Strindberg was fascinated by Edgar Allan Poe) and a human vivisection. As is clarified by the scenery, Mr. X and Mr. Y are playing an intellectual and moral game of chess. Both are unpunished criminals. In Nietzschean fashion, Strindberg's directions depict Mr. X as a superman and Mr. Y as a pariah. Still frequently performed, the play's outdated Lombrosian racism presents problems for present-day directors.

More strictly than any of his other one-act plays, The Bond follows the slice-of-life formula. Although the trial in the play does not conform with legal practice in Sweden at the time, as a description of a marital conflict over the care of the couple's single child after their divorce, the play has hardly lost its actuality. Moreover, here as often elsewhere, Strindberg indicates that behind husband and wife, the first man and woman can be discerned, and that the trial in the last instance is a metaphor for a cruel world order.

Comedy was hardly Strindberg's genre. When he nevertheless provides his quite successful Playing with Fire: Comedy in One Act (Leka med elden: Komedi I en akt, 1893), with this generic subtitle, we must realize that it is a rather black comedy. In later correspondence (a letter to Svea Åhman, January 31, 1908), he indicates that TRAGICOMEDY might have been a more suitable designation and that the play is "a very serious comedy, where the characters hide their TRAGEDY behind a certain cynicism." Strindberg varies the traditional erotic triangle by letting both husband and wife be attracted by their friend, who functions as a kindler for their nearly extinguished marital passion. Given the chance to marry the wife whom he claims to love, the friend fails to live up to the high morals he has earlier preached to the others and takes to his heels.

After a break of six years, Strindberg returned to playwriting with the first part of his trilogy To DAMASCUS (Till Damaskus I–II, 1898, 1900), a milepost in modern drama. From now on the battle fought in his plays was not so much between human intellects or even sexes as between the protagonist and the Powers. Strindberg's problem was now how to make this interiorized form of drama theatrically arresting. He did it in To Damascus by turning the protagonist's surroundings into semiprojections of himself (they are quite realistic and recognizable), a logical subjectivism by an author who kept insisting that you know only one self, your self. Strindberg did not at first understand how revolutionary his play was; he was too close to it.

ADVENT (1899) makes a striking change from idyll to nightmare, reflected visually, as the double protagonists begin to see themselves not as they appear, even to themselves, but as they are. Thematically related is CRIMES AND CRIMES (Brott och brott, 1899). Set in contemporary Paris, it deals with the relationship between evil deeds and evil thoughts.

With The Saga of the Folkungs (Folkungasagan, 1899), Strindberg returned to historical drama, a genre he would cultivate for many years. Starting with this drama, set in the Middle Ages, he was to proceed chronologically for the next seven plays. The Saga of the Folkungs, though rich in atmosphere, suffers from having a weak hero. King Magnus is a Christlike victim, more sinned against than sinning.

In GUSTAV VASA (1899), often considered the best constructed of the historical dramas, Strindberg instead settled for a powerful protagonist who struggles with the question of whether God sanctions the cruel deeds he feels forced to commit in the national interest. The play follows a pattern that Strindberg applies in several of his post-Inferno dramas: the protagonist (almost always a man) makes himself guilty of hubris, is punished for this by the Powers, then is forgiven.

The last bit, forgiveness, is lacking in ERIK XIV (1899), which ends with the imprisonment of the king and the struggle among his inheritors for the throne, a chaotic situation apparently meant to illustrate the madness of life.

Gustav Adolf (1900), named after the 17th-century king who defended Protestantism against the Catholics in Germany, is Strindberg's longest and one of his least successful plays.

Syncretism being its message, he called it, after Gotthold Lessing, his *Nathan the Wise*. Those who regard Strindberg as anti-Semitic, an easily defendable opinion, will be confused to find that the play's noblest character is a Jew. Despite efforts to see it as a pre-Brechtian EPIC drama, it remains an unwieldy play.

All the more compact is EASTER (*Påsk*, 1901), which Strindberg himself called a chamber play. In its combination of seasonal and religious resurrection, it is one of Strindberg's most poetical dramas, largely because of its thematically central character, the Christlike Eleonora, a part that has proved exceedingly difficult to recreate adequately on the stage.

On the surface, the famous THE DANCE OF DEATH (*Dödsdansen*, 1900), named after the medieval idea of Death dancing with the living, seems to signify a return to the naturalistic dramas of the 1880s: one realistic set, three characters, marital strife. On the other hand, the hubris–nemesis pattern—atheistic self-glorification punished by the imminence of death—defines it as a post-Inferno drama.

The Crownbride (also called *The Bridal Crown*; *Kronbruden*, 1902), a folkloristic drama inspired by Swedish ballads and set in the heart of Sweden, deals with Mats and Kersti and their feuding families; Kersti's murder of her newborn child; her agonized conscience, manifest in her visions of specters and mythical figures; and her final atonement for her crime.

CARL XII (also called *Charles XII*, 1901) is very different from the other historical plays. It is largely a mood drama focusing on the enigmatic and laconic king, whom Strindberg contemptuously liked to call "the destroyer of the nation." The sense of ominous waiting is broken when Strindberg in a loosely integrated act shows Carl quarreling with three archetypal women. Strindberg has him killed in a Swedenborgian manner worthy of a tragedy: mysteriously, from Above.

Thanks to Harriet Bosse, for whom the play was written, Strindberg included *Queen Christina* (*Kristina*, 1903) in his series on Swedish royalty. Daughter of Gustav II Adolf, who fought the Catholics in Germany, and of a German mother, Kristina betrays her father when she converts to Catholicism. In his rather unhistorical portrait of the queen, Strindberg stresses her egocentricity, her childishness, and her role-playing faculties: she is an actress on the throne.

Gustav III is known in Swedish history as a king who cared for the arts. Himself a dramatist, he was especially interested in theater. Fittingly, he was assassinated at a bal masqué in the opera. In *Gustav III* (1903), Strindberg chose to describe instead a situation a few years earlier when Gustav, after a badly planned war against Russia, was threatened with a coup d'etat by the nobility. Stressing the king's histrionic qualities, the complicated plot, in the tradition of the well-made play, shows him as a major role-player surrounded by an ingratiating court. Anckarström, who was later to murder the king and who is negatively presented in the history books, is symptahetically portrayed in this drama. His hatred of the king, it is indicated, is that of

someone who had fallen victim as a young man to Gustav's homosexuality.

Next to THE GHOST SONATA, A DREAM PLAY (*Ett drömspel*, 1902) is undoubtedly Strindberg's most original and seminal contribution to modern drama. As it opens we see the Daughter and a growing castle, symbol both of the growing of the world and of man's growing in the course of his life. On top of the roof is "a flower-bud resembling a crown," a good example of Strindberg's ability to vitalize imagery. When the Daughter at the end enters the burning castle to return to her heavenly Father, "the bud on the roof bursts open into a giant chrysanthemum." The whole play takes place in the time it takes for the chrysanthemum, symbol of divine grace, to bloom. In line with the play's leitmotif of waiting and hoping, it is a boldly visual and deeply meaningful way to compare life on earth with budding and death with blooming.

Strindberg's last important contribution to world drama came with his CHAMBER PLAYS written for his and August Falck's Intimate Theater (1907–1910), with its small and rather primitively equipped stage, youthful semiprofessional ensemble, and intimate 161-seat venue. Far from being plotless, these plays are so complicated that they are almost impossible to unravel—deliberately so, for the plots have largely a metaphoric importance. They show us an intricate web of more or less incomprehensible human relations to make us sense that this is precisely what life is. So in these plays, plot becomes theme. It is precisely the theme orientation of these plays, their dense texture, their combined verbal and visual leitmotifs, that explains their pioneering nature. Each of them—*Thunder in the Air* (*Oväder*, I, 1907), *The Burned House* (also called *After the Fire*; *Brända tomten*, II, 1907), *The Ghost Sonata* (*Spöksonaten*, III, 1907), *The Pelican* (*Pelikanen*, IV, 1907), and *The Black Glove* (*Svarta handsken*, V, 1909)—is given an opus number to remind us of the connection between this truly new drama form and chamber music. It is no coincidence that Strindberg in this period had friends playing string quartets in his apartment. Music forms an important integral element in many of his later plays.

Strindberg's last play, the station drama *The Great Highway* (*Stora landsvägen*, 1909), was regarded by the author as a closet drama, but despite mixing prose and verse has nonetheless proved quite stageable.

Strindberg's international reputation as a dramatist is usually connected with two enterprises. Before the so-called Inferno crisis in the mid-1890s, he is an eminent representative of naturalistic drama. His famous preface to *Miss Julie* is generally recognized as the most important manifesto of the movement. After the Inferno crisis, he writes his pre-expressionistic plays, in which the protagonists are more in conflict with themselves and with what Strindberg termed the Powers than with each other. Strindberg's other contributions to modern drama—the one-act plays, the fairy plays, the historical dramas—have received considerably less attention and recognition. Yet German specialist on the one-act play Diemut Schnetz (1967) unequivocally states that "since Strindberg's theoretical debut in 1889, the one-act play must be considered an independent genre." As for the plays about Swedish royalty, we would have to go back to Shakespeare to find a counterpart.

The Swedes were slow in recognizing the significance of Strindberg's dramatic work, sixty-two plays. *Master Olof*, now recognized as the best Swedish play to date, was not performed until nine years after it was written. *Miss Julie*, his best-known play, had to wait eighteen years for a professional Swedish performance. Many of the plays had their world premières abroad, in Germany, Austria, Denmark, even Finland. The first staging of *A Dream Play* was a fiasco. The chamber plays, first performed at Strindberg's own Intimate Theater, did not fare well with the critics. With few exceptions, notably some of the historical plays, Strindbergian drama was not palatable to the Swedes. Not until the German-speaking countries had discovered their true value did the situation change. It was especially MAX REINHARDT's guest performances in Sweden with *A Dream Play* and *The Ghost Sonata* that drew attention to them. Reinhardt stressed the nightmarish aspect of these plays; Olof Molander, long the leading Strindberg director in Sweden, was influenced by Martin Lamm's biographical readings and opted for more realistic, recognizably Swedish scenery while retaining a dreamlike quality. The trademark of INGMAR BERGMAN, the most prominent Strindberg director in recent decades, is an almost bare, "universal" stage on which the actors and their faces are presented primarily through the lighting.

In the years around World War I, Strindberg was, except for Shakespeare, the most frequently performed playwright on the German stage. The young dramatists who were to shape expressionistic drama received their decisive inspiration from his post-Inferno dramas, notably the dream plays and the chamber plays. While the naturalistic plays are still the ones most frequently performed, it is the pre-expressionistic plays that have had the greater impact upon later drama, whether expressionist, surrealist, or absurdist.

Numerous playwrights have recognized their indebtedness to Strindberg. One of them, EUGENE O'NEILL, in 1924, declared him "the greatest interpreter in the theater of the characteristic spiritual conflicts which constitute the drama—the blood—of our lives today" (Deutsch and Hanau, 1931).

PLAYS: *The Freethinker* (Fritänkaren, 1870); *The Outlaw* (Den fredlöse, 1871); *Master Olof* (Mäster Olof, verse version, 1878, 1890; prose version, 1881); *The Secret of the Guild* (Gillets hemlighet, 1880); *Lucky Per's Journey* (Lycko-Pers resa, 1882, 1883); *Sir Bengt's Wife* (Herr Bengts hustru, 1882); *The Father* (Fadren, 1887); *Comrades* (Kamraterna, 1888, 1905 in Austria); *Miss Julie* (Fröken Julie, 1888, 1889 in Denmark); *Creditors* (Fordringsägare, 1889); *Pariah* (Paria, 1890, 1889 in Denmark); *Simoom* (Samum, 1890); *The Stronger* (Den starkare, 1890, 1889 in Denmark); *The Keys of Heaven* (Himmelrikets nycklar, 1892,

1927 in Germany); *The Bond* (Bandet, 1893 in Germany, 1902 in Germany); *Debit and Credit* (Debet och kredit, 1893 in Germany, 1900 in Germany); *The First Warning* (Första varningen, 1893); *In the Face of Death* (Inför döden, 1893 in Germany); *Motherly Love* (Moderskärlek, 1893 in Germany, 1894 in Germany); *Playing with Fire* (Leka med elden, 1893 in Germany); *To Damascus I–II* (Till Damaskus I–II, 1898, 1900); *Advent* (1899, 1915 in Germany); *Crimes and Crimes* (Brott och brott, 1899, 1900); *Erik XIV* (1899); *Gustav Vasa* (1899); *The Saga of the Folkungs* (Folkungasagan, 1899, 1901); *The Dance of Death* (Dödsdansen, 1900, 1905 in Germany); *Gustav Adolf* (1900, 1903 in Germany); *Charles XII* (Carl XII, 1901, 1902); *Easter* (Påsk, 1901); *Midsummer* (Midsommar, 1901); *The Bridal Crown* (Kronbruden, 1902, 1906 in Finland); *A Dream Play* (Ett drömspel, 1902, 1907); *Swanwhite* (Svanevit, 1902, 1908 in Finland); *Gustav III* (1903, 1916); *Queen Christina* (Kristina, 1903, 1908); *To Damascus III* (Till Damaskus III, 1904, 1922); *The Burned House* (Brända tomten, 1907); *The Ghost Sonata* (Spöksonaten, 1907, 1908); *The Pelican* (Pelikanen, 1907); *Thunder in the Air* (Oväder, 1907); *The Black Glove* (Svarta handsken, 1909); *The Great Highway* (Stora landsvägen, 1909, 1910)

FURTHER READING

Dahlström, Carl. *Strindberg's Dramatic Expressionism*, 2nd ed. Ann Arbor: Univ. of Michigan Press, 1968.

Deutsch, Helen, and Stella Hanau, eds. *The Provincetown: A Story of the Theatre*. New York: Farrar & Rinehart, 1931.

Lamm, Martin. *Strindbergs dramer* [Strindberg's Plays], Vols. 1–2. Stockholm: Albert Bonniers Förlag, 1924–1926.

——. *August Strindberg*. Tr. and ed. by Harry G. Carlson. New York: Blom, 1971.

Meyer, Michael. *Strindberg: A Biography*. New York: Random House, 1985.

Ollén, Gunnar. *Strindbergs dramatik* [Strindberg's Plays]. Stockholm: Sveriges Radios förlag, 1982.

Schnetz, Diemut, *Der moderne Einakter*. Bern: Francke, 1967.

Sprinchorn, Evert. *Strindberg as Dramatist*. New Haven: Yale Univ. Press, 1982.

Steene, Birgitta. *August Strindberg: An Introduction to His Major Works*. Stockholm: Almqvist & Wiksell International, 1982.

Strindberg, August. Preface to *Fröken Julie* [Miss Julie]. Stockholm: Jos. Seligmanns, Strindberg, August 1888.

——. "August Strindberg om sig själv" [August Strindberg about himself], *Bonniers månadshäften* (January 1909).

——. *Open Letters to the Intimate Theatre*, tr. by Walter Johnson. Seattle: Univ. of Washington Press, 1967.

Törnqvist, Egil. *Strindbergian Drama: Themes and Structure*. Stockholm: Almqvist & Wiksell International, 1982.

Egil Törnqvist

THE STRONGER

The Stronger (Den starkare), a MONODRAMA by AUGUST STRINDBERG, was written in 1888–1889, published in 1890, and first performed at the Dagmar Theater in Copenhagen, DENMARK, in

1889. It describes the random meeting of two actresses who are rivals for the same man, Bob. The meeting takes place in a café on Christmas Eve. In the course of the short play both the recipient and the single speaker, Mrs. X, married to Bob, discover that the silent character, Miss Y, has been, and perhaps still is, Bob's mistress. Strindberg has designed the two ladies as professional parallels and social contrasts. Mrs. X is employed at the Grand Theater, where Bob has an important position, and she has three children in her marriage with him. Miss Y is unmarried, has no children and is no longer employed at the house in question.

Impressed by the French *quart d'heure* plays, Strindberg wrote *The Stronger* for the Scandinavian Experimental Theater he was trying to launch in the late 1880s, and it is likely that he intended not only the part of Mrs. X but also that of Miss Y for his own wife, the Finn-Swedish actress Siri von Essen. In performances in SWEDEN, Siri could play the speaking part; in performances in the other Scandinavian countries, she could play the mute one. The play may well have been written to demonstrate that the monologue need not be excluded from naturalist drama.

The criticism of both the text and the performances based on it has focused on the question of how the title should be interpreted: Who is the stronger? For a long time critics were inclined to ascribe the strength to the speaking character, Mrs. X. But in more recent productions, the silent Miss Y has come over as the stronger person. At times the strength has been so evenly distributed between the two women that spectators could arrive at different conclusions.

Strindberg was himself divided on this issue. When commenting on the play sixteen days before it was staged, he remarked that "the heroine does not say a word." A few days before the opening of the play, he gave his wife Siri, who was to play the first Mrs. X, written instructions on how she should act the part. Mrs. X, he now declared, is "the stronger, i.e. the softer. For the rigid person breaks, whereas the pliable one bends—and rises again." Compare this to Mrs. X's line close to the end of the play: "You couldn't learn from others, you couldn't bend—and therefore you broke like a dry reed—but I didn't!"

The Stronger has had a strong impact on later drama. It inspired EUGENE O'NEILL's early monodrama *Before Breakfast*, PER OLOV ENQUIST's "counter-drama" THE NIGHT OF THE TRIBADES, and INGMAR BERGMAN's film *Persona*. Its reverberations can be sensed also in HERMAN HEIJERMANS's Dutch piece *Boredom* (*Verveling*), in JEAN COCTEAU's *La voix humaine*, and in SAMUEL BECKETT's KRAPP'S LAST TAPE.

FURTHER READING

Törnqvist, Egil. "Monodrama: Term and Reality." In *Essays on Drama and Theatre*, ed. by Paul Binnerts, et al. Amsterdam: Moussault, 1973. 145–158.

———. *Strindbergian Drama: Themes and Structure*. Stockholm: Almqvist & Wiksell, 1982. 64–70.

———. *Ibsen, Strindberg and the Intimate Theatre: Studies in TV Presentation*. Amsterdam: Amsterdam Univ. Press, 1999. 127–133.

Egil Törnqvist

THE STRUGGLE OF THE NAGA TRIBE

The Struggle of the Naga Tribe (*Kisah Perjuangan Suku Naga*, 1975, published in English in 1979) by Indonesian playwright-director W. S. RENDRA, debuted in Jakarta, INDONESIA, in 1975, but was banned in other cities. The production grew out of undercover fieldwork Rendra and the Bengkel Teater (literally, Workshop Theater) conducted in Wonoroto in Central Java detailing the social injustices experienced by cotton farm laborers. This play has great historical importance in modern Indonesian drama: not only does it represent a daring critique of the repressive dictatorship under President Soeharto, but, by using traditional performance elements in a contemporary play, it provides a model for freeing Indonesian modern drama from the constraints of its Western-influenced theatrical conventions.

The Struggle draws upon the structure of Javanese *wayang* (puppet theater, masked theater, and dance drama) that includes stories from the *Mahabharata*, a Hindu epic. The play begins with a prologue by a *dalang* (puppeteer), who announces: "This story does not—I stress once again, does not—take place in Indonesia. So don't get uptight and censor the story." Rather, it takes place in the mythical kingdom Astinam, a reference to Astina from the *Mahabharata*. This prologue is followed by the *sabrangan*, scenes that introduce the ogres who live overseas; then *jejer*, or audience scenes, in which the main characters are presented and their kingdoms are described; and the play concludes with the *adegan perang* or battle scenes. Also in the tradition of *wayang*, *The Struggle* was accompanied by original music of a *gamelan* (percussive orchestra).

Astinam is ruled by Sri Ratu, the Queen, and run by the Prime Minister, Cabinet, and Parliament. They are plagued by diseases, the physical manifestations of sick souls. There are two ogre choruses: one of machines symbolizing dehumanized workers who live by mantras of money and the other of bumbling foreign ambassadors. Sri Ratu and her cronies are intoxicated by development. They argue that progress must include foreign aid and capital investments and silence internal criticism. The Queen orders implementation of a foreign mining project that will displace the Naga tribe from their village. Unlike the rulers and ogres, the Naga tribe's existence is marked by "the unity of soul and body" that keeps them in tune with nature.

During the final battle scenes over the future of the village, war is waged with words as weapons. Through clever verbal play, Abisavam, leader of the Naga tribe, twists the government representatives' arguments. Cultures must not be annihilated in the name of economic development. Participation in government programs must allow for more than contributing to the GNP, and these so-called superiors are representatives of the people and should act in the public's interest rather than for an elite few. Finally, under increasing pressure not to create an international incident, it is decided to implement the mining project but not to process the copper *in situ*, which spares the Naga village. The play ends with the *dalang*, who delivers a direct challenge to the audience to defend the need for balance.

FURTHER READING

Gillitt, Cobina. "Challenging Conventions and Crossing Boundaries: A New Tradition of Indonesian Theatre From 1968–1978." Ph.D. diss., New York Univ., 2001.

Lane, Max. "Introduction." In *The Struggle of the Naga Tribe*. New York: St. Martin's Press, 1979.

Verburgt, Ron. "'I Am Because You Are; You Are Because I Am': An Interview with Rendra." *Australasian Drama Studies* 25 (October 1994): 6–16.

Cobina Gillitt

STUFF HAPPENS

DAVID HARE's play *Stuff Happens* opened at London's National Theatre on September 1, 2004. A huge cast dramatizes events leading up to the 2003 invasion of IRAQ. Characters include real-life politicians, ordinary westerners, and Iraqis. Some dialogue is lifted directly from speeches recorded in the media; other dialogue was written by Hare, as he imagined events occurring behind closed doors. A character called simply Actor functions as a chorus, explaining the scenes' significance and delivering factual information chosen to advance Hare's argument. The play is a determined polemic against what Hare argues was a hasty, unjustified war caused by a short-sighted American drive to topple a second-rate dictator, Saddam Hussein.

Donald Rumsfeld, former U.S. Secretary of Defense, is afforded particular scorn. The play's title is lifted from an offhand remark he makes about lawlessness and looting in post-invasion Baghdad. "Stuff happens," he casually tells a journalist. Privately, Rumsfeld relishes a "war on terror": "That way we can do anything," he asserts gleefully. President George W. Bush, although not crudely caricatured as a toxic, witless thief, as he often is in anti-Republican satire, is vilified for sidelining the cautious Colin Powell. Powell presciently notes that there is "Ten times more excitement about going in [to Iraq] than there is about how the hell we get out," but his warnings are ignored by his senior government colleagues.

However, *Stuff Happens* is very much a play written for Britons, as indicated by cameos from middle-ranking British politicians and by a joke about the company, Railtrack, which Americans surely would not comprehend. British Prime Minister Tony Blair is lambasted virulently. He supports Bush's hawkish determination to pursue an invasion of Iraq, even though he knows that no weapons of mass destruction have been located by United Nations inspectors. Blair cares more about party politics than about the long-term consequences of military action.

Like Bush—who, it is noted, lost the popular vote in the 2000 Presidential election—Blair has contempt for public opinion. The Actor tells of a worldwide, antiwar demonstration by "a hundred million protestors." These masses are ignored. The invasion proceeds. Months later, David Kay, heading a group seeking Saddam's elusive weapons, notes ruefully that he has found nothing: "I've barely found lunch." Although facetious, Kay's reference to food illuminates a major division between the West and the Iraqis, material ease. The Iraqis endure serious poverty, whereas western politicians seem always to be eating "fried chicken, cornbread, mashed potatoes," "being served by waiters in white coats," and being "at lunch with editors." The Actor remarks that Bush's family retreat has "sixteen hundred acres of oak groves, cattle, creeks, and freshly stocked ponds."

The life of elite westerners is gilded, argues Hare, whereas "Iraqis have been crucified" by "Saddam's sins, by ten years of sanctions, and then this [invasion]." The haves of the world despise and exploit the have-nots. Hatred of "lesser" peoples such as Iraqis, Hare argues, ensures that decisions made about intervening in "lesser" nations' affairs will depend only on the interests of western elites. This darkly pessimistic play's underlying assumption is that democracy is limited, because populations cannot stop administrations from pursuing irresponsible aggression.

[See also England, 1940–Present]

FURTHER READING

Billington, Michael. Review of *Stuff Happens*. *The Guardian* (September 11, 2004). http://www.guardian.co.uk/arts/politicaltheatre/story/0,,1302327,00.html.

Blix, Hans. "Reviewing Myself." *The Guardian* (September 14, 2004). http://www.guardian.co.uk/arts/features/story/0,,1304248,00.html.

Boon, Richard. *About Hare: The Playwright and the Work*. London: Faber and Faber, 2003. 1–56.

Cook, Robin, and Polly Townbee, et al. "For or Against." *The Guardian* (September 21, 2004). http://www.guardian.co.uk/arts/politicaltheatre/story/0,13298,1296666,00.html.

Hanks, Robert. Review of *Stuff Happens*. *The Independent* (September 14, 2004).

Hare, David. *Stuff Happens*. London: Faber and Faber, 2004.

Hiley, Nicholas. Review of *Stuff Happens*. *The Times Literary Supplement* (September 17, 2004): 20.

Patterson, Michael. *Strategies of Political Theatre: Post-War British Playwrights*. Cambridge: Cambridge Univ. Press, 2003. 125–137.

Kevin De Ornellas

SUBTEXT

The term *subtext* refers to the thought or feeling that is hidden behind the spoken words of the play. The term came into use through the instructive writings of the Russian actor and director

KONSTANTIN STANISLAVSKY. He developed his ideas about sub-text in large part while staging ANTON CHEKHOV's plays. In December 1919 in a lecture delivered at the Art Theatre in Moscow, Stanislavsky spoke of "undercurrents in the text [*podvodnae techenie*]," saying that the principal ideas flowed with these under-currents. The term subtext entered the English language through Elizabeth Reynolds Hapgood's translation of Stanislavsky's *Building a Character* (1949).

In the first act of Chekhov's THE THREE SISTERS, the unhappily married Masha says she is bored and will not stay for her sister's nameday party. Then Officer Vershinin enters and the conversation becomes quite lively. Masha takes off her hat and says she has decided to stay after all. The subtext behind her line, "I'm staying for lunch," is that she has fallen in love with Vershinin. She is not fully aware of what has happened, but her change of mind and her gesture of taking off her hat reveal what is in the subtext. It is up to the actress to convey to the audience what the line by itself does not say.

Of course, actors before Stanislavsky were well aware of the need to convey more than what is stated in a line of dialogue. They called it ACTING "between the lines," and it meant the use of an inflection or a facial expression to evoke more than the single reading the dialogue itself offered. With the advent of subtle dramatists like HENRIK IBSEN and Chekhov, however, so much meaning lay beneath the lines that their playscripts were compared to icebergs, ninety percent of the meaning lying beneath the surface. In psychologically complicated and subtle plays, the main theme that unites the scenes—what Stanislavsky called the through-line—lies in the subtext, and often it runs wide and deep.

When reading a play it is easy to ignore the subtext, since the plot moves forward above it, while in a good performance the actor or director will bring it unexpectedly to light. Even an experienced theater person can miss much that lies in the written text. When the English actor and director HARLEY GRANVILLE-BARKER saw the MOSCOW ART THEATRE staging of Chekhov's THE CHERRY ORCHARD, he remarked that reading "the play afterwards was like reading the libretto of an opera, missing the music." As an example of the kind of "music" that Stanislavsky provided, one can study his production book for Chekhov's THE SEA GULL, which has been published.

In didactic or propaganda plays, the subtext barely exists. In the discussion plays of GEORGE BERNARD SHAW, for example, there is virtually no subtext, as Stanislavsky uses the word. Subtexts exist mainly in realistic or naturalistic plays, where, as in real life, much of what is going on in the minds of the characters is revealed in speech inflections and body language.

In acting the major roles in Ibsen, James Huneker said the actor "must reconstruct a living human from a mere bone of a word. These words seem detached, seem meaningless, yet in action their cohesiveness is unique; dialogue melts into dialogue, action is dovetailed to action, and fleeting gestures reveal a state of soul. Ibsen does not read as well as he acts. He is extremely difficult to interpret for the reason that the old technic of the actor is inadequate" (*Iconoclasts*, 1905).

The subtext may in many instances be difficult to interpret. A reader of novels will usually have gestures and hidden thoughts explained. Such a reader may wonder why Chekhov could not be more helpful and tell in a stage direction that Masha's boredom has turned to love. But a naturalistic dramatist may provide only what the audience would see and hear. Either the dramatist expects fine actors and directors to make the subtext available or he or she expects the wiser sort in the audience to figure out what is going on.

What is one to make of Dr. Chebutykin's dropping of the clock in act 3 of Chekhov's *The Three Sisters*? To begin to understand the subtext, the viewer must have in mind the fact that the clock belonged to the sisters' mother and that Chebutykin had once been in love with her. Disappointed in love, he has become a cynical old man, a dog in the manger, who envies the happiness that others may feel.

Perhaps no play has a deeper subtext than Ibsen's ROSMER-SHOLM, with commentators still trying to discern what is going on in its murkiest depths. Heroine Rebecca West has hesitated at nothing to win the love of Rosmer, even removing his wife from the scene through a kind of psychological murder. Yet when he proposes marriage, she staggers and says that is not possible. What is going on in her mind, subconscious or unconscious, is still the subject of debate among scholars as they minutely examine the text. The force of her reaction indicates that she has been caught off guard and that his proposal has set off a subterranean earthquake; she herself does not know what is happening in the depths of her soul. As James Huneker wrote in 1905, "Not a half-dozen actresses on the globe have grasped the complex skeins of Rebecca West's character, and grasping them have been able to send across the footlights the shivering music of her soul. . . . It is a new virtuosity, a new fingering of the dramatic keyboard, that is demanded" (*Iconoclasts*).

[*See also* Dramatic Dialogue; Stage Directions and Stage Sets]

FURTHER READING

Huneker, James. *Iconoclasts: A Book of Dramatists*. New York: Charles Scribner's Sons, 1905.

Stanislavsky, Konstantin. *My Life in Art*. Tr. by G. Ivanov-Mumjiev. Moscow: Foreign Languages Publishing House, 1958.

Stanislavsky, Constantin. *An Actor Prepares*. Tr. by Elizabeth Reynolds Hapgood. New York: Routledge, 1945.

Evert Sprinchorn

SUDDENLY LAST SUMMER

I think we ought at least to consider the possibility that the girl's story could be true . . .
—Dr. Cukrowicz, Scene 4

Suddenly Last Summer, a long TENNESSEE WILLIAMS one-act grotesquerie originally performed on a double-bill, *Garden District*, with Williams's one-act, *Something Unspoken*, was first staged OFF-BROADWAY in 1958. It offers perhaps the darkest vision of all Williams's plays; set in a sinister primeval garden on a crumbling Southern gothic estate owned by the imperious Violet Venable, *Suddenly Last Summer*'s gruesome portrait of a predatory universe—as represented by a monstrous Venus flytrap dominating Mrs. Venable's garden—examines madness, homosexuality, family dysfunction, the artistic temperament, even cannibalism.

Mrs. Venable intends to employ her vast wealth to arrange for her disturbed niece, Catherine Holly, to undergo a lobotomy. The previous summer, Catherine accompanied Sebastian, Mrs. Venable's poet son, on a European tour during which Sebastian died under mysterious circumstances. Catherine's version of Sebastian's demise outrages Mrs. Venable for, as Catherine ultimately explains, he was a promiscuous homosexual whose only interest in Catherine was as bait for prospective lovers. In past years, Mrs. Venable had accompanied Sebastian on his annual tour, so the implication of Catherine's account is that Mrs. Venable served a similar purpose when she was still able to attract young men. Mrs. Venable's romanticized view of herself as muse for Sebastian's writing drives her to want to silence Catherine permanently. She makes a lucrative offer to the financially strapped Lion's View Hospital if one of its surgeons, Dr. Cukrowicz, will perform the lobotomy aimed at expunging Catherine's version of Sebastian's death. Despite considerable pressure, Cukrowicz refuses to accommodate Mrs. Venable's wishes until he has examined Catherine. He manages to draw out the partially blocked Catherine, who finally recalls the ghastly events in their entirety. Sebastian, she divulges, died at Cabeza del Lobo as a result of a cannibalistic attack by a mob of young men he had sexually exploited. As the recounting of this horror releases Catherine from her disturbed state, the defeated Mrs. Venable descends into madness.

Williams's frequent use of grotesque elements is at its most florid in this play, with savage images of predatory birds gutting baby turtles on the Galapagos Islands and depictions of Sebastian as the martyred Saint Sebastian. In some respects, *Suddenly Last Summer* is an American Grand Guignol, but one that employs its horrors in service of Williams's recurrent themes of the struggle for survival of the fragile or artistic soul in a brutal cosmos. The unseen Sebastian is both victim and victimizer, whereas the ruthless Mrs. Venable is a victimizer who fails to prevail over Catherine, her vulnerable prey. In many respects, *Suddenly Last Summer* employs imagery Williams first explored in his 1950 novella, *The Roman Spring of Mrs. Stone*, and the use of a central character as both victim and victimizer was typical of many of his works, none more effectively than Blanche DuBois of A STREETCAR NAMED DESIRE.

Suddenly Last Summer was well received by critics in its original production, which opened at New York's York Theatre on January 7, 1958, although many considered it a minor work by a major playwright. It remains one of Williams's most frequently produced plays, and it has been filmed twice, in 1959 for the screen and in 1993 for television.

[See also United States, 1940–Present]

FURTHER READING

Clum, John M. "The Sacrificial Stud and the Fugitive Female in *Suddenly Last Summer, Orpheus Descending*, and *Sweet Bird of Youth*." In *The Cambridge Companion to Tennessee Williams*, ed. by Matthew C. Roudané. Cambridge: Cambridge Univ. Press, 1997. 128–146.

Gross, Robert F. "Consuming Hart: Sublimity and Gay Poetics in *Suddenly Last Summer*." *Theatre Journal* 47 (1995): 229–251.

Konkle, Lincoln. "Puritan Paranoia: Tennessee Williams's *Suddenly Last Summer* as Calvinist Nightmare." *American Drama* 7, no. 2 (Spring 1998): 51–72.

Parker, Brian. "A Tentative Stemma for Drafts and Revisions of Tennessee Williams's *Suddenly Last Summer*." *Modern Drama* 41, no. 2 (Summer 1998): 303–326.

Saddik, Annette J. "The (Un)Represented Fragmentation of the Body in Tennessee Williams's 'Desire and the Black Masseur' and *Suddenly Last Summer*." *Modern Drama* 41, no. 3 (Fall 1998): 347–354.

Sofer, Andrew. "Self-Consuming Artifacts: Power, Performance, and the Body in Tennessee Williams's *Suddenly Last Summer*." *Modern Drama* 38 (1995): 336–347.

James Fisher

SUDERMANN, HERMANN (1857–1928)

Gag us, stupefy us, shut us up in harems or in cloisters—and that perhaps would be the best. But if you give us our freedom, do not wonder if we take advantage of it.
—Magda, Act 4, *Heimat*

Together with GERHART HAUPTMANN, Hermann Sudermann brought NATURALIST drama to the German stage. During the 1890s and early 1900s, Sudermann was the more popular of the two playwrights, but today he is essentially forgotten. Sudermann was born on September 30, 1857, and raised in Matziken, East Prussia (currently Macikai, LITHUANIA). After studying at the University of Köningsberg, he moved to Berlin where he continued his university studies while earning his living as a tutor and journalist. Sudermann's first success as an author came with the psychological novel *Frau Sorge* (*Dame Care*, 1887).

In October 1889, just ten days after Hauptmann's breakthrough with BEFORE DAYBREAK (*Vor Sonnenaufgang*) at Berlin's Freie Bühne (Free Stage), Sudermann's first play, *Honor* (*Die Ehre*, 1889), premiered on the same stage and became an instant success. *Honor* is set in a typical Berlin building in which an upper-class family (the Mühlingks) lives in the *Vorderhaus* (the front building), and a lower-class family (the Heineckes) in the *Hinterhaus* (the building behind). The main character, Robert Heinecke, is employed by the Mühlingks and returns from a business trip to find his own family in a degraded state of affairs. His sister is prostituting herself to the Mühlingks's son to receive singing lessons. As part of his attempt to escape the constraints of his lower-class background, Robert has adopted the honor code of the corrupted bourgeoisie and thus challenges the son to a duel. But Robert's honor code is proven false by the intervening Count Trast, who serves as the voice of reason in the play.

With its emphasis on heredity and the environment, its detailed STAGE DIRECTIONS, and its depiction of class conflict, prostitution, alcoholism, and female emancipation, *Honor* is a typical naturalist drama. Yet the happy ending in which Count Trast talks Robert out of the duel and then provides him with a new job and a bright future is considered a fairy-tale conclusion inappropriate for a naturalist play. Moreover, the drama's structural progression from a marked beginning to a climax and a happy denouement deviates from the paradigmatic naturalist slice-of-life DRAMATURGY. Sudermann's second play, *The Destruction of Sodom* (*Sodoms Ende*, 1891) depicts the degenerate lifestyle of Berlin's artistic circles and was banned by the authorities on account of its graphic content.

In *Magda* (*Heimat*, 1893), Sudermann's most famous play, he takes the theme of female emancipation further than his naturalist contemporaries HENRIK IBSEN or Hauptmann. Whereas they portrayed the plight of women in an oppressive male-dominated society, Sudermann presents a woman who has managed to combine her life as a single mother with a successful career. The play begins with the main character, Magda, a world famous singer, returning to her home after a seventeen-year absence. Magda had been forced to leave at age eighteen when she refused to marry the man her father had arranged for her. Upon her return, it appears as if a reconciliation could be possible. But when Magda's father discovers that she has an illegitimate child, he considers his honor destroyed and is prepared to kill his daughter. Before being able to carry out his misdeed, however, he dies of a stroke.

Magda must be seen in the tradition of the German *bürgerliches Trauerspiel* (bourgeois TRAGEDY), a tradition in which a young woman frequently becomes pregnant and is then sacrificed by her family in order preserve their honor. Sudermann is the first to subvert the conventions of this tradition by having the father, not the daughter, be the victim of the old order. The success of *Magda* resulted not only from the appealing and fast-moving plot, but also from the fact that some of the most famous actresses of the time, including Sarah Bernhardt (1844–1923) and Eleanora Duse (1849–1924), played the role of Magda.

In other plays, Sudermann continued his use of naturalist themes. *The Joy of Living* (*Es lebe das Leben*, 1902) is a drama about adultery and corrupt politics in Wilhelminian GERMANY. *The Fires of St. John* (*Johannisfeuer*, 1900) depicts one of the naturalists' central themes, determinism; the drama poses the question whether a gypsy girl brought up by a well-to-do farming family can escape the genetic heritage of a degenerate mother.

As was the case with Hauptmann, it was OTTO BRAHM who promoted Sudermann. However, Brahm valued Hauptmann's talents more than Sudermann's, despite the fact that Sudermann's plays were his top box office hits. Following his initial successes, Sudermann was treated poorly by literary critics, including a group led by Alfred Kerr (1867–1948). In a move that served to worsen the situation, Sudermann mounted a counterattack in several articles. More recent scholars, however, have argued that Sudermann's works deserve renewed attention, not only because of their masterful techniques and important contributions to the development of naturalist drama, but also because these plays have far more depth and poetic beauty than has been acknowledged to date.

Sudermann died on November 21, 1928, in Berlin, Germany.

SELECT PLAYS: Honor (Die Ehre, 1889); The Destruction of Sodom (Sodoms Ende, 1891); Magda (Heimat, 1893); The Battle of the Butterflies (Die Schmetterlingsschlacht, 1895); The Vale of Content (Das Glück im Winkel, 1896); St. John the Baptist (Johannes, 1898); The Fires of St. John (Johannisfeuer, 1900); The Joy of Living (Es lebe das Leben, 1902); Stormbrother Socrates (Der Sturmgeselle Sokrates, 1903); Stone among Stones (Stein unter Steinen, 1905); Morituri (1910)

FURTHER READING

Rix, Walter T., ed. Hermann Sudermann. Werk und Wirkung [Work and Reception]. Würzburg: Köningshausen und Neumann, 1980.

Whitinger, Raleigh. "Self-Consciousness in Die Ehre: A Revised View of Hermann Sudermann's First Drama." Journal of English and Germanic Philology 89, no. 4 (1990): 461–474.

Kerstin T. Gaddy

THE SUICIDE

The Suicide (*Samoubiitsa*, ca. 1929–1930), a tragic COMEDY by NIKOLAI ERDMAN, is one of the most banned and most important plays of the Soviet period. It was rehearsed at the MOSCOW ART THEATER (1931–1932) and the Meyerhold Theater (1932) but dropped by both when prohibitions issued between 1930 and 1932 were not rescinded. Attempts to stage it during the Thaw around 1957 and 1965 failed before rehearsals began, as did efforts to publish it in 1933 and 1968. The world premiere took place in 1969 in Göteborg, SWEDEN, after the text was smuggled to CZECHOSLOVAKIA. A planned 1968 production in Prague was halted when Soviet troops occupied that city. Interest in the play swept through GERMANY in the 1970s, ENGLAND in the late 1970s and early 1980s, and the UNITED STATES in the early 1980s. It was first performed in RUSSIA at Moscow's Satire Theater in 1982 but banned after six performances. The Perestroika-era revival of that same production in 1987 was followed by dozens of stagings throughout the Soviet Union.

The play focuses on Semyon Podsekalnikov, whose name suggests he has been "cut down" or "hooked" like a fish, while echoing the name Podkolyosin from *The Marriage* by Nikolai Gogol, who was a major influence on Erdman. Yearning for a quiet life but depressed by his failure to find work, the antihero Podsekalnikov is nearly driven to suicide through a series of comic misunderstandings and immoral schemes. The idea is not his but arises when his wife wonders aloud if he might kill himself. Kalabushkin, an unscrupulous neighbor, turns this "information" into an evil money-making plan. He "sells" the potential suicide to disenfranchised individuals—an intellectual protesting political tyranny, a writer opposing the repression of art, a priest lamenting the demise of religion, a prostitute mourning the death of romanticism—who hope to draw attention to their causes by convincing Podsekalnikov to name them in his suicide note.

The notion of dying for a grand cause "brightens" Podsekalnikov's "miserable, inhuman life," and he resolves to kill himself, although cowardice saves him. It does not save Fedya Petunin, a youth whom we never see but who is inspired to commit suicide off-stage by stories about Podsekalnikov's intentions. Petunin technically is the title character (the noun of the Russian original refers to a person rather than the act), and his shadowy presence in the finale injects TRAGEDY, tainting Podsekalnikov's survival.

In the dialogue Erdman employs rhythm, rhyme, oratorical technique, and puns as might a poet. Meanwhile, Podsekalnikov's humorous attempts to make sense of his predicament cause him to utter undiluted truths that were deemed treasonable by Soviet authorities and that remain subversive in most modern societies. Thus, language transcends mere style, becoming an element of the play's themes. Characters often commit actions not because they intend to but because someone's unguarded words establish an almost incontrovertible chain of events. Language in *The Suicide* is a powerful instrument that, if wielded carelessly, may have tragic consequences. Podsekalnikov is a victim of those who would promote their causes with his death, but the unseen Petunin may be considered a victim of Podsekalnikov's failure to take responsibility for his own words.

[*See also* Vsevolod Meyerhold]

FURTHER READING

Erdman, Nikolai. *The Mandate and The Suicide.* Tr. by Marjorie Hoover, George Genereux, Jr., and Jacob Volkov; intr. by Hoover and Genereux. Ann Arbor, Mich.: Ardis, 1975.

——. *The Suicide.* Tr. by Peter Tegel. London: Pluto Press, 1981.

——. *The Suicide.* Adapt. and Tr. by Eileen Thalenberg and Alan Richardson. Oakville, Canada: Mosaic Press, 1992.

——. *The Major Plays of Nikolai Erdman: The Warrant and The Suicide.* Tr. and ed. by John Freedman. Amsterdam: Harwood Academic Publishers, 1995.

Freedman, John. *Silence's Roar: The Life and Drama of Nikolai Erdman.* Oakville, Canada: Mosaic Press, 1992.

John Freedman

SUMMER AND SMOKE

So that is your high conception of human desires. What you have here is not the anatomy of a beast, but a man. And I—I reject your opinion of where love is, and the kind of truth you believe the brain to be seeking!—There is something not shown on the chart.

—Alma Winemiller, Scene 8

TENNESSEE WILLIAMS's 1948 drama won only moderate critical approval under Margo Jones's direction in its original production, but the play featured one of Williams's quintessential heroines, Alma Winemiller, effectively portrayed by Margaret Phillips. The back-to-back triumphs of Williams's THE GLASS MENAGERIE in 1945 and A STREETCAR NAMED DESIRE in 1947 somewhat obscured the merits of *Summer and Smoke*, a disappointment that kept Williams revising the play well into the 1970s.

The character of Alma is another variation on the sexually repressed, dysfunctional heroines of Williams's oeuvre, a woman caught between the social constraints of rigid era and her own passions. *Summer and Smoke* offers a poetic examination of the tension between the desires of the body and the longings of the spirit, a frequent theme in Williams's greatest plays. That tension is poignantly embodied in Alma, a character whose persona falls somewhere between the fragile, asexual Laura Wingfield of *The Glass Menagerie* and the hysterical, promiscuous Blanche DuBois of *A Streetcar Named Desire*.

Alma lives in the straightjacket of rigid Christian morality in Glorious Hill, Mississippi, a small Southern town in 1916. She is the pure-minded daughter of the distant, pompous Rev. Winemiller and his mentally disturbed wife whose problems stem, in part, from the stifling repressions of their lives. Although she is keeping company with the effeminate Roger Doremus, Alma is powerfully drawn to the virile, sexually liberated Dr. John Buchanan, her next-door neighbor. Williams uses Alma and John to debate the differences between spiritual love and carnality. John's credentials as a doctor and his worldliness lead him to conclude that spiritual love does not exist and that sex is merely a matter of biology. He spends much of his time drinking and indulging himself at a local brothel. Alma is shocked by John's behavior, which she equates with bestiality; for her, love is in the meeting of minds and in a mutual appreciation of beauty and goodness.

Alma longs to find a fulfilling spiritual love, but gets little guidance from her family. Her fear (and expectation) of sinking into arid spinsterhood or a lifeless marriage to Roger incites a crisis in her attitudes. She has rejected John's advances and lectured him on morality, but when she can resist him no longer it is too late. She learns that John has changed his views and plans to marry an innocent young woman from a local family. This revelation sends Alma into an emotional tailspin that ends with her seduction of a strange man in the local park.

Some critics described the play as an allegory of good (Alma) versus evil (John), but others found it a rehashing of themes Williams had explored to greater effect in earlier plays, particularly *A Streetcar Named Desire*. Williams's own dissatisfactions with this talky, structurally conventional work led him to revise the play in 1976. Renaming it *The Eccentricities of a Nightingale*, Williams maintained the central strengths of *Summer and Smoke*—its characters, language, and central theme—while streamlining the play's language and structure. Despite a fine production featuring Blythe Danner and Frank Langella, *The Eccentricities of a Nightingale* ran only briefly at New York's Morosco Theatre before being filmed for television. *Summer and Smoke* had previously been filmed in 1961 under the direction of Peter Glenville, with Geraldine Page as Alma and Laurence Harvey as John.

Summer and Smoke, along with its revision *The Eccentricities of a Nightingale*, is a significant work in Williams's canon not only because Alma is an essential figure in his gallery of dramatic heroines, but also because the play amplifies Williams's career-long obsessions with the survival of fragile beings and the conflict of body and spirit.

[*See also* United States, 1940–Present]

FURTHER READING

Adler, Thomas P. "Before the Fall—and After: *Summer and Smoke* and *The Night of the Iguana*." In. *The Cambridge Companion to Tennessee Williams*, ed. by Matthew C. Roudané. New York: Cambridge Univ. Press, 1997. 114–127.

Brooking, Jack. "Directing *Summer and Smoke*: An Existentialist Approach." *Modern Drama* 2 (February 1960): 377–385.

Clum, John M. "From *Summer and Smoke* to *Eccentricities of a Nightingale*: The Evolution of the Queer Alma." *Modern Drama* 39 (Spring 1996): 31–50.

Kramer, Richard E. "*Summer and Smoke* and *Eccentricities of a Nightingale*." In *Tennessee Williams: A Guide to Research and Performance*, ed. by Philip C. Kolin. Westport, Conn.: Greenwood Press, 1998. 80–89.

Sahayam, V. Sam. "How Broadway Proved Williams Wrong: A Comparative Study of *The Eccentricities of a Nightingale* and *Summer and Smoke*." In *A Mosaic of Encounters*, ed. by Desai Mutalik, V. K. Malhotra, T. S. Anand, and Prashant K. Sinha. New Dehli: Creative, 1999. 15–20.

James Fisher

SUMMERFOLK

Summerfolk (*Dachniki*), a play in four acts by MAKSIM GORKY, was written and first performed in 1904 but turned down by Nemirovich-Danchenko for the MOSCOW ART THEATRE, much to Gorky's disgust. It was premièred in November in St. Petersburg at Vera Komissarzhevskaya's theater with Komissarzhevskaya as Varvara. A new departure in social setting for Gorky, *Summerfolk* focuses on the professional intelligentsia. It is part of his on-going dialogue with ANTON CHEKHOV's plays, particularly with THE CHERRY ORCHARD, and represents an attempt to fire the intelligentsia into social and political action.

Set in a summer village of dachas (wooden villas) a commutable distance from a large town, the play centers on a lawyer, Basov, his wife, Varvara, and their less-than-happy marriage. The inhabitants of the dachas—lawyers, architects, doctors, writers, and entrepreneurs—represent the range of views in the educated professional classes of the period. The wealthy, complacent Basov and his colleagues are juxtaposed with a radical female doctor, Marya Lvovna, and the easy-going but free-thinking entrepreneur, Dvoietochiye. These people spend their summer in poetry readings, picnics, casual love affairs, and amateur theatricals.

Their prize guest Shalimov, a famous writer, deeply disappoints his once ardent fan, Varvara, while his all-male talk with her husband, which is dismissive of women, causes her to take a hard look at her own marriage. Irritated by the idle ways of the group and their complacent politics, Marya Lvovna confronts them with their social responsibilities and urges them to use their gifts for the betterment of RUSSIA. For this she is branded a troublesome woman. She has also fallen in love with Varvara's brother, Vlas, who is the same age as her own daughter, Sonia, which provides an opportunity for all kinds of antifemale prejudice to be voiced. In the end Varvara, her eyes opened to their indolent lifestyle and insulted by her husband's behavior, walks out on her marriage and joins forces with Marya Lvovna, Vlas, Sonia, and Dvoietochiye.

Echoes of HENRIK IBSEN as well as Chekhov are evident in this play. Varvara takes Henrik Ibsen's Nora (A DOLL'S HOUSE, 1886) a step further by upgrading her marital rebellion to a social and political one, while Marya Lvovna's rhetoric is a broadside at the lack of social conscience among Chekhov's gentrified intellectuals. *Summerfolk* also places "the woman issue" at the forefront. The characters who take the brave steps are principally women (Vlas is as yet a young, but forthright, apprentice lawyer, and Dvoietochiye has already made his millions). Varvara, Marya, and Sonia are set against a series of complacent women whose main interests focus on children, love affairs, and obscure poetry.

Also evident in this play is a conscious THEATRICALITY and a melodramatic thread that infuse the structure and content: an amateur production on an open-air stage is being prepared in the background; a young student in love with Varvara attempts suicide. Gorky uses these devices to accentuate the artificial lifestyle and lack of concern shown by this group for Russian social injustice, which he sees as the real issue. As Varvara states: ". . . we do nothing and we talk much too much . . ." Glimpsed in his two earlier plays, *Philistines* and THE LOWER DEPTHS, Gorky's COMEDY is here generated at the expense of the middle-class intelligentsia, often laughable in their crass behavior and delusions of idealism. For the first time Gorky displays the political power of his blend of satire and MELODRAMA, which together verge on the grotesque, in the presentation of his negative characters.

FURTHER READING

Gorky, M. *Summerfolk*. Adapt. by Nick Dear from a literal tr. by Vera Liber. London: Faber and Faber, 1999.

Harussi, Yael. "Realism in Drama: Turgenev, Chekhov, Gorky, and Their Summer Folk." *Ulbandus Review* 2, no. 2 (1982): 131–148.

Marsh, Cynthia. "Gorky and Chekhov: A Dialogue of Text and Performance." *The Slavonic and East European Review* 77, no. 4 (1999): 601–619.

Rischbieter, Henning. "Peter Stein's Gorky—A Review of *Summerfolk* in West Berlin." *Yale Theatre*, 7, no. 2 (Gorky Issue), 1976.

Cynthia Marsh

THE SUNDAY PROMENADE

The Sunday Promenade (*Söndagspromenaden*), a "play in three acts and an epilogue" by LARS FORSSELL, was first performed at the Royal Dramatic Theater in Stockholm, SWEDEN, in 1963 and published the same year. The title of the play, Forssell's most successful to date, refers to the promenade that Justus Coriander and his family take around their dinner table every Sunday. According to Forssell himself, this unusual Sunday habit is based on what really happened in his own family—which does not exclude the possibility that the work of HJALMAR BERGMAN has served as a further inspiration.

Coriander is a grocer in a small and dull Swedish town at the turn of the century. He has invented the Sunday promenade to escape the dreary confines of small-town life. Justus, we learn, is "a poet," "an actor," "a real rascal." While walking round the table with their picnic baskets, the participants imagine themselves to be in "God's free nature." They describe what they see and sing a song especially composed for the occasion. In this way the contrast between fantasy and reality is illustrated in a slightly absurdist manner.

A rudimentary erotic plot keeps the play together. It concerns Angelica, Coriander's daughter, and Abraham (one of Forssell's Christian names), his goodhearted clerk. Both are set off from Coriander's verbose fantasies, Angelica by being deaf-mute, Abraham by being unimaginative.

Other contrasts concern ideological differences. Pitted against Coriander's dream about the beauty of life—a dream about the *present* that can come true only through separation from the world at large—are the dream of the vicar about a heavenly paradise and the dream of Carl Michael, Coriander's invalid Marxist son, about a true brotherhood on earth, once the world revolution has been accomplished. These two dreams, however different, are similar in their concern for the *future*. In the words of Corrigan:

> For Justus Coriander the only acceptable reality is the moment of here and now, which he attempts to shape and control with his extraordinary imaginative powers. The future is always to be feared because in its unpredictability it can always get out of control.

What Justus attempts is to conquer time: "Time is our enemy. Let's not talk about anything but *now*. *Now* we're alive, *now* we exist." When Coriander by the fictive campfire asks his mother to tell a story, she tells about "The Man Who Wanted to Murder Time." The only way to murder time, to be set free, it appears from the story, which is a premonition of Coriander's fate, is to kill oneself.

This Sunday, as it grows dark outside—a thunderstorm is coming—the participants turn into soldiers reciting nostalgic monologues in blank verse the night before a decisive battle. The thunder and lightning that follow stem not from the clouds but from the cannons of two armies.

Suddenly something unusual happens. Carl Michael has an attack and loses consciousness. For a moment not only the promenaders but also the spectators are uncertain as to whether this is simulated or real. When they realize that it is real, the family rushes to help the stricken boy, whereas Justus struggles to keep the fiction alive even at the expense of his son's life. When told that "this is no game now, Mr. Coriander," he breaks down. Promising God that if the boy's life is saved, he will go to Mongolia as a missionary, Justus declares: "I've been a dreamer, now I'm going to face reality." Carl Michael's life is saved, and true to his promise, Justus sets out with his family for Mongolia.

In the Epilogue, seven years later, we learn that Coriander has been killed by the Mongolians and that his last words before they cut out his tongue were: "I didn't know the world was that big." Confronted with brutal reality, all the dreams have been destroyed. The only one who survives the journey to the Far East is Abraham, the most unimaginative character in the play.

The Sunday Promenade, Forssell (1977) said, "deals with man's tragic lack of consciousness, a lack which causes his destruction." Corrigan points in the same direction when claiming that in the play "the disengaged man is revealed as a betrayer who is ultimately betrayed." Even so, "there is something almost noble in his impossible quest."

FURTHER READING

Corrigan, Robert W. "Introduction." In *The New Theatre of Europe 3: Four Contemporary Plays from the European Stage*. New York: Dell, 1965. 23–29.

Forssell, Lars. *Teater I–II* [Theater I–II]. Lund: Cavefors, 1977.

Syréhn, Gunnar. *Osäkerhetens teater: Studier i Lars Forssells dramatik* [The Theater of Uncertainty: Studies in Lars Forssell's Plays]. Uppsala: Lundequistska, 1979. 137–180.

Törnqvist, Egil. "Lars Forssell: *Söndagspromenaden* (1963)." In *Svenska dramastrukturer* [Swedish Drama Structures]. Stockholm: Prisma, 1973. 128–158.

Egil Törnqvist

SURREALISM

Surrealism, pure psychic automatism, which has the aim of expressing, whether verbally, in writing, or by other means, the actual functioning of thought outside of any control of reason and beyond all aesthetic or moral preoccupation.

—André Breton, *Manifesto of Surrealism*, 1924

Opposed, on principle, to creating works of art, surrealism nevertheless has left an indelible influence on the visual, cinematic, and theatrical arts. Motivated less by the desire to produce objects than to liberate "the marvelous," the surrealists worked from the early 1920s until after World War II to establish creative processes that relied not on reason and form, but on chance, the logic of dreams, and the provocative power of paradox. Their movement, begun in Paris and rapidly expanded throughout Europe, AFRICA, and the Americas, was a collective search for the means of permanent personal, social, and creative revolution, grounded in opposition to bourgeois values of positivism, logic, and REALISM.

Surrealism claimed a wide but coherent family of influences. In its early days, what the leader of the movement, André Breton, labeled the "intuitive epoch" (1919–1925), inspiration was drawn mostly from literature and the arts, with an emphasis on eccentric visionary figures, including Comte de Lautréamont, Arthur Rimbaud, Stéphane Mallarmé, Charles Baudelaire, ALFRED JARRY, the Marquis de Sade, and earlier AVANT-GARDE movements such as SYMBOLISM, FUTURISM (Italian), and DADA-ISM. One scientific figure, however, profoundly shaped the surrealist vision: Sigmund Freud. Later, as surrealism became more involved with the sociopolitical world in its second, or "reasoning," epoch (after 1925), figures such as Karl Marx, Georg Wilhelm Friedrich Hegel, and Pancho Villa entered the vocabulary. Throughout their decades of investigation and creation, the surrealists remained committed to the power of the image, the fusion of dream and reality, and "the revolution of the mind."

Surrealism emphasized collective activity, and its history is one of intensely shared pursuits as well as painful divergences of principle. Its organization, with endless periodicals, pamphlets, meetings, and manifestos, set the stage for future movements that worked across genres and disciplines, such as lettrism and situationism. The common ground, defined by André Breton (1896–1966) and shared by Philippe Soupault (1897–1990), Louis Aragon (1897–1982), Robert Desnos (1900–1945), Paul Éluard (1895–1952), and others in the *Manifesto of Surrealism* (1924), was belief in "the superior reality of certain forms of association neglected heretofore, in the omnipotence of dream, and in the

disinterested play of thought." Their attraction to the unknown drew from both the Symbolist idea of *noumenon* as well as Sigmund Freud's proposition that the unconscious is much bigger than the conscious. They sought to unleash the powers of the imagination by creating conditions favorable to extra-logical events, teaming trance, hypnotism, seances, and occult and scientific experiments with extensive investigations of automatic composition. Essential to this "arranged derangement of the senses" was the creation of games such as the Exquisite Corpse (in which each person supplies one part of a sentence, and the whole is revealed only at the end). Banishing reason and premeditation from the creative process was the underlying goal of all surrealist endeavors, and working in collaboration (to prevent the preponderance of any one vision) was encouraged; many surrealist works are signed collectively, or not at all. Surrealism had several journals under its editorial control, including two runs of the antiliterary *Littérature* (1919–1924), the more politically engaged *La Révolution surréaliste* (1924–1929), and *le Surréalisme au service de la révolution* (1930–1933).

The second, "reasoning," epoch of surrealism centered on revolution in all forms, introducing an explicitly political bent. Opposition to fascism and an antitotalitarian, anticolonial stance led them to ally themselves with the French Communist Party, with whom they collaborated on several projects; this, however, led to perpetual disputes over the possibility of functioning within a political framework. Surrealism sought a political role throughout its existence: many members joined the Party, some to renounce surrealism; gallons of ink were spilled on surrealism's relationship to politics, the war, and revolution; and Breton began a project with Leon Trotsky, whom he met in exile in MEXICO in 1928, to unite writers in opposition to totalitarianism. Through it all, surrealism tried to reconcile its desire for "total revolution" with the widespread social and political upheavals of the time without becoming merely a polemic, a party tool, or succumbing to one way of thinking that would necessarily close the doors to others. The insistence on the freedom of the imagination (and writing and creation) always inserted itself as a wedge between the surrealist project and complete political commitment.

The search for uncharted territories of the mind led the surrealists to a set of concerns that unified their stylistically diverse output: the transcription of dreams, revelation of the unconscious, fusion of dream and reality, paradox, *l'amour fou*, and CHANCE. They formulated not an aesthetic but a process (Aragon [1928]: "Surrealism is not a refuge from style"), with, however, characteristic results. In literary experiments, automatic writing generated stories with alogical progression, surprising juxtapositions, and heavy emphasis on imagery, beginning in 1919 with the first purely automatic text, *The Magnetic Fields*, cowritten by Soupault and Breton. In photography, Man Ray led the quest for new methods of producing images (such as rayographs); in visual art, Max Ernst invented frottage (rubbing over a textured surface) and grottage (scraping the canvas) and mastered COLLAGE; Breton, Jean Arp, and Francis Picabia extended the Dadaist use of found objects; and several artists, notably André Masson, employed automatic drawing. Some artists used the art work as a provocative image for the audience: René Magritte's disconcertingly juxtaposed images invite imaginative leaps, and Salvador Dalì's "paranoiac critical" method promotes the idea that the forcefully creative viewer can realize the "true" reality of any image. In surrealist cinema, dreamlike logic dictated the flow of images, often shocking (Luis Buñuel and Salvador Dalì's Un Chien Andalou [The Andalusian Dog, 1928]), mysterious (ANTONIN ARTAUD and Germaine Dulac's The Seashell and the Clergyman, 1928), or inexplicably beautiful (Fernand Léger's Ballet Mécanique, 1923). In all art works, surrealism tended to mix genres: a canvas might hold poetry, sculpture, collage, photography, and found objects.

Surrealism's period of activity in the theater was brief, 1919 to 1925. Inspired by Dada in Zurich and its program to rouse a complacent public, the soon-to-be surrealists, headed by Breton, aligned themselves with Tzara, who had moved to Paris to promote Dada in 1920. The Dadas provided valuable experience in the new world of inciting audiences and creating audaciously unacceptable performances, but the surrealists soon broke from Dada's "merciless iconoclasm." The dozen or so plays produced by members of the surrealist circle were created during this period, including works by Breton and Soupault (If You Please, 1920, and You Will Forget Me, 1920), Roger Vitrac (Free Entry, 1922, and The Mysteries of Love, 1923), Aragon (At the Foot of the Wall, 1923, and The Mirror Wardrobe One Fine Evening, 1923), and Artaud (JET OF BLOOD, 1924). They shared a pervasive emphasis on imagery, visual and verbal, over plot and character, abandoning rational communication in favor of evoking a new kind of poetry in theater. But surrealist theater as such was short-lived; as opposed to creating a new dramatic aesthetic as to participating in a bourgeois commercial enterprise, surrealists began reprimanding members for their interest in drama.

Nevertheless, much theater created around this period clearly embodies surrealist goals. One of the first recognizable pieces of surrealist theater was Parade (1917), a work written by JEAN COCTEAU, commissioned by Diaghilev with the command: "Astonish me!" The result was a ballet danced by the Ballets Russes, with music composed by Erik Satie and sets and costumes by Pablo Picasso. GUILLAUME APOLLINAIRE, the "patron saint of Surrealism," is credited with coining the term "surrealism" when he described the production with the same word, sur-réaliste, he used for his production of THE BREASTS OF TIRESIAS (also 1917): "When man wanted to create walking, he created the wheel, which doesn't resemble a leg. In the same way, he has created Surrealism without knowing it." In both pieces, as well as Cocteau's 1921 The Wedding on the Eiffel Tower, dramatic events flowed without regard to logical progression; imagery and surprise took precedence over story. The text became a springboard for a theatrical event relying more heavily on design, movement, and sound than on narrative and reason. Sets, costumes, and actors often merged, creating a moving mise-en-scène that itself gave the event meaning.

Many theater artists have nourished themselves on surrealist drama and theater; the first works of Artaud, ROGER VITRAC, and ARMAND SALACROU (especially Circus Story, 1923, and The Glass Ball, 1924) helped liberate the dramatic event from the confines of a narrative-bound premise. Surrealism also inspired postwar dramatists including EUGÈNE IONESCO, JEAN GENET, FERNANDO ARRABAL, STANISLAW WITKIEWICZ, and RAMON DEL VALLE-INCLÀN. Imagery and dream structure have infiltrated modern drama as surely as they have visual and commercial culture; dream sequences can be found on Broadway as easily as in experimental theater or a music video. While the surrealist project centered more on revolution than on art, its wide-ranging investigations into the unconscious have led to the now common joining of the "real" and the "unreal" and the preponderance of dream syntax in modern art, confirming Breton and Paul Eluard's (1929) poetic insight: "In the poet / . . . / It is intelligence, waking that kills; / It is sleep that dreams and sees clearly."

FURTHER READING

Aragon, Louis. Traité du style. Paris: Gallimard, 1928.

Balakian, Anna. Literary Origins of Surrealism: A New Mysticism in French Poetry. New York: King's Crown Press, 1947.

Breton, André. What Is Surrealism? Selected Writings. Ed. and intro. by Franklin Rosemont. New York: Pathfinder, 1978.

Breton, André, and Paul Eluard. "Notes sur la poésie" [Notes on poetry], La Révolution surréaliste, no. 12 (December 1929): 53–55.

Gershman, Herbert S. The Surrealist Revolution in France. Ann Arbor: Univ. of Michigan Press, 1969.

Matthews, J. H. Theatre in Dada and Surrealism. Syracuse: Syracuse Univ. Press, 1974.

Melzer, Annabelle. Latest Rage the Big Drum: Dada and Surrealist Performance. Ann Arbor: UMI Research Press, 1980.

Nadeau, Maurice. The History of Surrealism. New York: Macmillan, 1968.

Polizzotti, Mark. Revolution of the Mind. New York: Farrar, Straus and Giroux, 1995.

Zinder, David G. The Surrealist Connection: An Approach to a Surrealist Aesthetic of Theater. Ann Arbor: UMI Research Press, 1976.

Kimberly Jannarone

SUSPECT CULTURE

Since its inception in 1990, Suspect Culture has proved itself to be one of SCOTLAND's most energetic and inventive experimental groups, constantly evolving and seeking out new ways of working and creating theater. Unlike conventional artistic structures, the work of Suspect Culture is the product of the collective imaginations of artistic director Graham Eatough, DRAMATURG DAVID GREIG, and musical director Nick Powell. Originally founded in ENGLAND while Eatough and Greig were students at

Bristol University, the company has maintained permanent residence in Glasgow, Scotland, since the mid-1990s. This Scottish base of operations reflects one of the company's key missions. Not only did Greig wish to explore the roots of his Scottish childhood, but the artistic and cultural links available between Scotland and Europe allow the company to bypass geographical boundaries and to investigate the connections between local, national, and global concerns.

Suspect Culture is well-known for its unique collaborative working methods, in addition to the unusual form and techniques with which the productions are presented. Rehearsals for a Suspect Culture production never begin with a completed script. Instead, all members of the production team—designers, directors, and performers—contribute to the process of devising a show from inception to opening. The production team, for example, may meet in a small arts centre on the Isle of Mull to explore a variety of possible theatrical languages, including space, gesture, music, movement, and video technology. Coproductions and workshops with a variety of local and international venues and artists extend and rejuvenate their theatrical influences and impulses. One key example that suggests the benefits of such international networking includes a production of *The Golden Ass* (1998), codirected by Graham Eatough and Brazilian director Mauricio Paroni De Castro, and devised by the entire Suspect Culture team in collaboration with Sergio Romano, a leading Italian actor, and a group of eight young people from the local Gorbals community in Glasgow. Other tours have taken the company throughout Scotland, as well as England, Ireland, Spain, Germany, and Italy.

These collaborations, as well as the content and form of the productions, are focused on the connections and possibilities between places, people, and ideas. Recurring thematic obsessions such as "home," "belonging," "memory," and "loss" fuel the group's artistic imagination. In addition, many of the shows are set in stations, airports, hotels, and at borders—all public locations where people might arrive, depart, meet for a moment of intimacy, hide, or escape. Here the performers enact the desire to connect and communicate, as well as the attempts and failures to make contact with another human soul. The action is postmodern and fragmented in form: episodic scenes, snatches of dialogue, repeated catch-phrases, nameless characters, subversive gestures, and layers of dislocated images emanating from video screens all express a theatrical world of constantly shifting identity and endless possibilities.

Notable performances since 1995 include *One-Way Street* (1995), *Airport* (1996), *Timeless* (1997), *Mainstream* (1997), and *Lament* (2002). From a Fringe First award for *Stalinland* at the 1992 Edinburgh Festival to the achievement of four-year funding from the Scottish Arts Council in 1998 and Lottery Funding in 2000, Suspect Culture represents a healthy combination of artistic and financial health that is possible through a spirit of theatrical transformation and renewal.

FURTHER READING

Carter, Pamela, ed. Suspect Culture Web site [online]. Opticski, Designer. http://suspectculture.com/ (Accessed August 26, 2003).

Cavecchi, Mariacristina. "Suspect Culture: The Process Is the Thing." In *A Theatre That Matters: Twentieth-Century Scottish Drama and Theatre*, ed. by Valentina Poggi and Margaret Rose. Milano: Edizioni Unicopli, 2000. 209–223.

Greig, David. "Internal Exile." *Theatre Scotland* 3, no. 11 (1994): 8–10.

——. "One-Way Street." In *Scotland Plays*, ed. by Philip Howard. London: Nick Hern, 1998.

——. *Casanova: A Suspect Culture Text*. New York: Faber and Faber, 2001.

Kristin A. Crouch

SUTHERLAND, EFUA THEODORA (1924–1996)

We didn't need to persist in that maddening blind alley of drama that begun with William Shakespeare and ended with Sheridan. . . . I wanted to create theatre which would obtain its strength and inspiration from Ghanaian life.
—Efua Theodora Sutherland, 1962

Efua Theodora Sutherland is undeniably the chief pioneer of contemporary Ghanaian theater. One of the few female African playwrights, her contributions to Ghanaian theater and culture are well known. Born in Cape Coast in the central region of Ghana, her mother died in a truck accident when Efua was only five months old, and she was left in the care of her maternal grandmother. After her basic education in Cape Coast, she won a scholarship to train as a teacher at the St. Monica's Training College at Asante Mampong. She was so impressed by the nuns who ran the training college that she would have herself become a nun, had her grandmother not intervened. After nearly six years of teaching, she went to Homerton College, Cambridge University, where she earned a BA degree. She then spent another year at the School of Oriental and African Studies in London, where she specialized in African languages, English linguistics, and drama.

She returned to Ghana in 1950 to continue her teaching career and was soon caught up by her great interest in creating a better society for her people through appropriate cultural education. Soon after Ghana's independence in 1957, she together with others presented the idea of a National Theatre Movement, which was to serve as a cultural institution that would fuel the new nation's rapid development. She was also a founder of the Ghana Society of Writers, and under her direction, the Ghana Experimental Theatre Company was created in 1958. Sutherland's vision was to create an authentic Ghanaian theater that was not merely a replica of the European models introduced by the colonialists. Her research and experimentation resulted in what she called *Anansegoro* or Ananse play, a unique dramatic form that drew its inspiration from traditional storytelling. The classic example of *Anansegoro* is her play *The Marriage of Anansewa*.

Driven by her desire to see a flourishing theater in Ghana, she mobilized funds from the Ford Foundation and the Government of Ghana to build the Ghana Drama Studio, which was designed to conform to the demands of African theater practice. This studio provided the needed performance space for Kusum Agromba, a full-time drama company, The Drama Studio Players, and the Workers' Brigade Drama Group, all of which enjoyed her creative leadership. When in 1963 Sutherland joined the Institute of African Studies as a Research Associate, she handed the Drama Studio to the University of Ghana to be used as "an extension division of the School of Music Dance and Drama," now the School of Performing Arts.

In 1993, the Drama Studio was demolished to make way for The National Theatre building, but a replica of the old structure was rebuilt at the School of Performing Arts, which has been named after Sutherland in recognition of her contributions to Ghanaian Theater. Among her many achievements are her village theater project at Atwia, which was the subject of the ABC television documentary "Araba: The Village Story" in 1967. Her published plays include *Edufa* (London: Longman, 1967), *Foriwa* (Accra-Tema: Ghana Publishing Corporation, 1971), and *Vulture! Vulture!* and *Tahinta: Two Rhythm Plays for Children* (Accra: Ghana Publishing House, 1968). Her other plays include *Blood Is Mysterious*, *The Rumor Monger's Fate*, *God's Time Is the Best*, *Love for Your Neighbor*, and *Ananse and the Dwarf Brigade* (all 1971).

Her commitment to the welfare of children led her to establish the Ghana National Commission on Children, which she chaired from 1983 to 1999. She received recognition and sponsorship for her work from the Ghanaian Government as well as some major international agencies, including the Valco Trust Fund, UNESCO, UNICEF, and the Rockefeller Foundation. The University of Ghana honored her with a degree of Doctor of Laws in recognition of her commitment to the development of dramatic arts and her efforts on behalf of children.

[See also Africa]

SELECT PLAYS: *Edufa* (1962); *Tahinta* (1968); *Vulture! Vulture!* (1968); *Ananse and the Dwarf Brigade* (1971); *Blood Is Mysterious* (1971); *Foriwa* (1971); *God's Time Is the Best* (1971); *Love for Your Neighbor* (1971); *The Marriage of Anansewa* (1971); *The Rumor Monger's Fate* (1971)

FURTHER READING

Anyidoho, K., and J. Gibbs, eds. *FonTomFrom: Contemporary Ghanaian Literature, Theater and Film*. Amsterdam and Atlanta: Rodopi, 2000.
"Ghana Gains a Living Theatre." *Drum* (February 1962): 19–21.

Awo Mana Asiedu

SUZUKI SENZABURŌ (1893–1924)

With their focus on infidelity, sexual perversion, and crime, Japanese playwright Suzuki Senzaburō's plays typically highlight extreme and abnormal states of human behavior. His work reflects the decadence of Taishō (1912–1925) Japanese culture and in many respects resembles the stories and plays of his contemporary, Tanizaki Jun'ichirō.

Born in Tokyo, Suzuki wrote classical poetry and discovered *kabuki* in his teens. In 1913 he won an important drama prize, the Mitsukoshi Award, launching his career as a playwright. The following year, he began work at Genbunsha, a publishing house where he remained an editor until the company folded in 1923, financial victim of the Great Kantō earthquake. Suzuki honed his critical skills writing reviews under a variety of pseudonyms for several leading theater magazines, including *Theatre Arts Illustrated* (*Engei Gahō*) and *New Theatre Arts* (*Shin Engei*). Between 1913 and 1924, he wrote twenty-two plays, of which only fourteen are included in his *Complete Plays*; his first anthology was published in 1920. His plays were staged in practically every theatrical style then current: SHIN KABUKI, *Shinkokugeki*, SHINPA, and SHINGEKI. He produced his best work in the last two years of his life, while bedridden from the illness that was to take his life.

Suzuki's earlier dramas tend to be rather contrived and superficial, focusing on the twisted acts of his protagonists, like the sadistic Imura in *Auto da Fé* (1921), who paints his mistress tied to a stake and attempts to set her alight when he discovers that she has fallen in love with his student. Suzuki's later plays, however, demonstrate considerable subtlety in their psychological portrayal of character, great economy in dramatic structure, and witty, piquant dialogue. The shocking events that drive *The Valley's Depths* (1921), a one-act play in twelve short scenes, pale compared with the shattering self-awakening of Toshiyo, whose desperate acts of murder and suicide seem both natural and inexorable. *Two Widows* (1922) avoids sensationalism altogether in plumbing the relationship between two women, Reiko and Tokiko, and the man who had been Reiko's husband and Tokiko's lover.

Though most of Suzuki's plays were set in contemporary times, the works that have endured most are set in the Edo period (1603–1868) and were written for *kabuki* actors. His death at age thirty-one stopped short a brilliant career, but his masterpiece, *Koheiji Lives* (1924), remains one of the great Japanese plays of the 20th century. It has been filmed twice and staged countless times. Based on *kabuki* dramas by Tsuruya Nanboku IV and KAWATAKE MOKUAMI, *Koheiji Lives* stripped away every extraneous detail from the earlier versions that would detract from his themes of infidelity, obsessive love, and mortal fear. Suzuki demonstrated here how a playwright could take traditional materials and create modern, fully rounded, and psychologically compelling characters.

[See also Japan]

SELECT PLAYS: *Father to the Foreigner's Whore* (*Rashamen no chichi*, 1919); *Auto da Fé* (*Hiaburi*, 1921); *The Valley's Depths* (*Tanisoko*, 1921);

Two Widows (*Futari no Mibōjin*, 1922); *The Confessions of Jirōkichi* (*Jirōkichi Zange*, 1923); *Koheiji Lives* (*Ikite Iru Koheiji*, 1924)

FURTHER READING

Oyama Isao. *Kindai Nihon Gikyokushi* [A History of Modern Japanese Drama], Vol. 2, *Taishō era*. Yamagata: Kindai Nihon Gikyokushi Kankōkai, 1969.

Suzuki Senzaburō. *Suzuki Senzaburō Gikyoku Zenshū*; [Complete Plays of Suzuki Senzaburō]. Osaka: Puratonsha, 1925.

——. "Burning Her Alive" (*Hiaburi*). In *New Plays from Japan*, tr. by Yozan Iwasaki and Glenn Hughes. London: Ernest Benn, 1930. 109–125.

——. "Living Koheiji." In *The Passion and Three Other Japanese Plays*, by Mushanokōji Saneatsu, tr. by Noboru Hidaka. Westport, Conn.: Greenwood Press, 1971 (Originally published 1933). 25–54.

M. Cody Poulton

SUZUKI TADASHI (1939–)

Suzuki Tadashi began his career while a student at Waseda University during the turbulent period of the 1960s, when many Japanese artists and intellectuals manifested their resistance to the war in Vietnam, in particular because American forces involved in the conflict were stationed in JAPAN and Okinawa. Suzuki was the cofounder, with playwright BETSUYAKU MINORU, of the Waseda Little Theatre (Waseda Shōgekijō) in 1966. The group soon became one of the most important companies promoting new styles of politically oriented playwriting and acting, producing a number of works now considered classics of the postwar Japanese stage, including works by Betsuyaku, KARA JŪRŌ, and an early success of Suzuki himself, the collage play *On the Dramatic Passions I* (*Gekiteki maru mono o megutte I*, 1970). When this play's second part was written and performed as *On the Dramatic Passions II*, Suzuki began his collaboration with the remarkable actress Shiraishi Kayoko, who would perform central roles in a number of his most important productions.

In 1974, the first version of one of Suzuki's most respected adaptations, his version of *The Trojan Women* of Euripides, was performed in Tokyo. The production has been revised and restaged several times and been presented internationally. The production revealed Suzuki's mature style, which he defined in an interview in 1982 as "a sense of corpus—the relationship between the word and the body. . . . The classical Japanese theater shows us that the word is a kind of gesture, and thus I have been working in this mode. Japanese words, all of them, involve this sense of body— they are very physiological, very close to the Japanese sense of corpus" (Beeman, 1982, 89). Suzuki's training technique for actors involves the use of a strong physical presence combined with elements from classical Japanese theater performance to create a new and powerful stage energy. Suzuki has trained actors from a number of countries, and many non-Japanese have participated in his productions, often speaking in their native language.

Other notable productions adapted from Greek TRAGEDY include *Oedipus*, *The Bacchae*, *Dionysus*, and *Clytemnestra*.

In 1976 Suzuki took his troupe to the village of Toga, in Toyama Prefecture in the mountains of central Japan, where he founded the Suzuki Company of Toga (SCOT), presenting during summer festivals both his own productions and work by visiting companies. During the rest of the year, his group frequently toured both in Japan and abroad. In 1988 his powerful *The Tale of Lear*, based on William Shakespeare, involved an all-male cast, using actors from four leading American repertory companies who trained with Suzuki before touring with the production.

In recent years, Suzuki has worked with two other outstanding creative artists: the architect Arata Isozaki, with whom he has collaborated on the design of several contemporary theaters, and the American director ANNE BOGART, founding a company dedicated to bringing Suzuki's vision and training methods to American students and performers. In recent years, Suzuki has extended his activities into the field of production, working closely with the Shizuoka Performing Arts Center and other groups in Japan.

SELECT PLAYS: *The Folkloric Analysis of the Lower Depths* (*Donzoko ni okeru minzoku-gaku-teki bunseki*, 1968); *On the Dramatic Passions I, II, and III* (*Gekiteki maru mono o megutte I, II, and III*, 1969–1972); *Re-Dyed and Later Appearance* (*Somekaete gonichi no omemie*, 1971); *Don Hamlet* (1972); *The Tale of Lear* (1974); *The Trojan Women* (*Toroia no onna*, 1974); *Night and Clock* (*Yoru to tokei*, 1975); *Night and Feast I* (*Utage no yoru*, 1976); *The Bacchae* (1978); *Clytemnestra* (*Higeki: Atereusu ke no hōkai*, 1980); *The Chekhov* (1989); *Dionysus* (1990)

FURTHER READING

Allain, Paul. *The Art of Stillness: The Theatre Practice of Tadashi Suzuki*. New York: Palgrave Macmillan, 2003.

Beeman, William O. "The Word Is an Act of the Body" (Interview of Suzuki Tadashi), *Performing Arts Journal* 6, no. 2 (1982): 88–92.

Carruthers, Ian, and Takahashi Yasunari. *The Theatre of Suzuki Tadashi*. Cambridge and New York: Cambridge Univ. Press, 2004.

Suzuki Tadashi. *The Way of Acting: The Theatre Writings of Suzuki Tadashi*. Tr. by J. Thomas Rimer. New York: Theatre Communications Group, 1986.

J. Thomas Rimer

SWEDEN

Around 1860 Sweden was still a largely agrarian, fairly poor country with an ethnically, lingustically, culturally, and religiously homogeneous population. Its citizens were born into the Lutheran state church and most of them stayed there. The country played a dominant role in its somewhat strained union with "brother country" NORWAY, established in 1814, under their common Swedish king until the union was peacefully dissolved in 1905.

Politically, modern Sweden was shaped in 1866 when a parliamentary system replaced the four estates. The throne retained a certain power that has gradually diminished until, in recent decades, it fulfills a purely symbolic role. Universal suffrage, first for men, then for women, was introduced in the period from 1907 to 1921. The industrial revolution came late, but after World War I industry began to be Sweden's major source of income.

Related to this development is the emergence of the Social Democratic party. From 1932 until the present day, the Social Democrats have dominated Swedish politics. Gradually the Swedish welfare state, popularly called "the people's home," was created, a development profiting from the fact that the country has known no war since 1815. Unlike most other European countries, Sweden retained its somewhat dubious neutrality even during World War II. Since the 1960s the country has known an increasing influx of immigrants. Its former homogeneity has been replaced by pluriformity. Because of its nonalliance policy, Sweden has been able to play a modest international role after World War II, not least because of the commitment of Prime Minister Olof Palme, assassinated in Stockholm, the Swedish capital, in 1986 by a still unidentified murderer. In a shrinking, globalized world, Sweden has come closer to the rest of Europe and is now a member of the European Union.

A nation blessed with peace for decades, knowing few indigenous turmoils, and with a strong lyrical tradition, Sweden cannot boast any drama of significance until AUGUST STRINDBERG wrote his MASTER OLOF in 1872. From that time Strindberg overshadows all and influences most dramatists in Sweden. No Swede either during this period or after can compete with the author of THE FATHER, MISS JULIE, A DREAM PLAY, or THE GHOST SONATA, to mention only a few of his most famous plays.

What can modern Swedish drama offer? Until World War I, not very much. Gertrud by Hjalmar Söderberg (1869–1941) and Johan Ulfstjerna by Tor Hedberg (1862–1931), both from 1907, are among the few plays from this period that have proved restageable.

Gertrud, best known through Carl Dreyer's film adaptation, is a well-constructed drama in which the title figure is placed in relation to three men: her past love, dramatist Gabriel Lidman; her husband, politician Gustav Kanning; and her present love, proletarian composer Erland Jansson. The theme, formulated by Lidman—"I believe in the lust of the body and the incurable loneliness of the soul"—has become proverbial.

Johan Ulfstjerna (translated by Helga Colquist, 1921), inspired by Eugen Schauman's assassination of the Russian governor in Finland, is a realistic, Ibsenite play with a tragic protagonist and a firmly handled plot. The theme concerns the imbalance between words and deeds; when this imbalance is resolved—i.e., when Ulfstjerna matures enough to be able to shoulder his son's responsibility and murder the tyrant—the drama reaches its conclusion. Hedberg is also known as a writer of witty COMEDIES, a genre not very popular in Sweden, that mildly satirize all things Swedish, as in The National Monument (Nationalmonumentet, 1923).

At the end of the World War I, new signals were heard in HJALMAR BERGMAN's short Marionette Plays (Marionettspel, 1917) and PÄR LAGERKVIST's one-act trilogy The Difficult Hour (Den svåra stunden, 1918; i.e., the moment of dying). In Bergman's Mr. Sleeman Is Coming (Herr Sleeman kommer 1917), as in his other marionette plays, the idea that we are pulled by unseen strings is featured. Next to this fatalistic idea is another one: "born as human beings, we grow old as trolls." With Swedenhielms (1925), a COMEDY about a supposedly very Swedish family, Bergman reached the broad public. Lagerkvist's trilogy is supported by the manifesto "Modern Theater" (Modern teater), which rejects Ibsenite drama in favor of Strindberg's post-Inferno plays. The author here, in expressionistic fashion, pleads for stylization, visualization of inner processes, and concentration on "a single emotion, the intensity of which constantly keeps growing."

In the 1930s the economic depression, the threat of Nazism, and the ambition to turn Sweden into a social welfare state promoted a topical kind of drama. With his novella THE HANGMAN (Bödeln, 1933), successfully dramatized a year later, Lagerkvist was one of the first writers in Scandinavia to warn against the dictatorship and racism in GERMANY. But the play is primarily a timeless drama, indicated by the fact that the Hangman, the tool of evil, straddles its two parts, the first set in the Middle Ages, the second in modern times.

The expressionist trend is continued in a sociopolitical spirit by Rudolf Värnlund (1900–1945), whose The Holy Family (Den heliga familjen, 1932) is the first Swedish play to deal seriously with workers' conditions and issues.

Unlike Värnlund, whose plays never found much response in the theater, Vilhelm Moberg (1898–1973) has been exceedingly popular. His essential contribution concerns another social category, farmers. The first to give a convincing dramatic depiction of Swedish rural life in The Wife (Hustrun, 1928), Moberg continued to draw inspiration from this area in several other plays including Fulfillment (Mans kvinna, 1943). His dramatizations of his novels Ride This Night! (Rid i natt!, 1941), set in the 16th century to disguise its anti-Nazi message to the Swedish censor, and A Time on Earth (Din stund på jorden, 1967) have reached large audiences.

Impulses from Franz Kafka and French existentialism are apparent in STIG DAGERMAN's debut play, The Condemned (Den dödsdömde, 1947). Dagerman's fear is related to Lagerkvist's anguish. In this neo-expressionistic drama, he deals with a man who is sentenced to death, released when it appears that he is innocent, and who after having killed a woman, is returned to prison to await capital punishment. Psychologically, the action is about a man's attempt to make his social persona fit his experience of himself. Existentially, it concerns our collective guilt for the atrocities in the world.

INGMAR BERGMAN, later to become world renowned as a theater and film director, started as a dramatist. Finding little favor with the theater critics, he turned to film script writing and, especially, directing. In recent years he has written dialogue that is unspecified with regard to medium. As a director, he has taken considerable interest in the plays of Björn-Erik Höijer (1907–1996), whose *Isak Juntti Had Many Sons* (*Isak Juntti hade många söner*, 1954), a drama about religious puritanism and burning sensuality in isolated northern Sweden, is considered his best play.

The break from illusionism became quite obvious when, in the mid-1960s, it was combined with a strong social and political commitment. At the time of the Vietnam war, left-wing groups in Sweden found theater an effective means of attacking what they considered American infiltration in southeast Asia. AGITATION-PROPAGANDA theater became the standard fare of the so-called independent groups, a powerful way to bring Marxism to the people and promote the idea of a global classless society. The playwrights now literally placed themselves in the theater and wrote their plays more or less together with those who were to produce and act in them. The most memorable result are three plays about the Swedish situation for which Kent Andersson (1933–) was mainly responsible: *The Raft* (*Flotten*, 1967), *The Home* (*Hemmet*, 1967), and *The Sandbox* (*Sandlådan*, 1968). *The Home*, written with Bengt Bratt (1937–), effectively attacks the situation in Swedish homes for old people. We witness a series of tableaux, connected in their criticism of the welfare state. Each character has a story to tell; the stories are acted out by the others who, in this way, keep playing different roles. We are often taken from a painful present to an idyllic past. The break with illusionism appears in the absence of scenery and in the inclusion of songs which, in the manner of EPIC THEATER, place the events in a wider social and political perspective, indicating, for example, that the home for old people actually represents Sweden, where the average lifetime was and is nearly the longest in the world.

In a period characterized by rapid technical development within the theater, enabling directors to handle light and sound in radically new ways, the verbal element has become marginalized. Dramatists have swept aside dialogue to make room for directors, the true creators of theatrical events.

Nevertheless, a few playwrights have helped to put Sweden on the international map in their endeavor to create a theater in which the word still plays a central role. There is the poet and playwright LARS FORSSELL, the novelist and playwright PER OLOV ENQUIST, and the poet and dramatist LARS NORÉN.

Forssell has been writing plays of various kinds—contemporary and historical drama, comedy, FARCE, MONODRAMA—for several decades. French ABSURDISM and Brechtian epic theater have influenced him to create a poetry *of* the theater rather than merely *in* the theater. The most prominent Swedish playwright in the 1950s and 1960s, Forssell combines playfulness with stylization. His best play, the TRAGICOMEDY *THE SUNDAY PROM-*ENADE (*Söndagspromenaden*, 1963), has been successful on both stage and screen. Forssell has also tried his hand at historical drama in, for example, *The Madcap* (*Galenpannan*, 1964), a play set in the early 19th century about the deposed and exiled Gustav IV Adolf of Sweden.

Per Olov Enquist had an immediate international success with his semi-DOCUMENTARY play *THE NIGHT OF THE TRIBADES* (*Tribadernas natt*, 1975), dealing with Strindberg-the-male, caught between his wife Siri and her friend Marie David, who oppose the roles he has written for them and who finally reject him. Another semi-documentary, *Rainsnakes* (*Från regnormarnas liv*, 1981), about Hans Christian Andersen and the theatrical Heiberg couple, has been almost equally successful.

Showing a marked inclination to portray famous writers—he is also responsible for a television series about Strindberg, a film about KNUT HAMSUN, and a stage play about Selma Lagerlöf—Enquist has met with some opposition from critics who deny the biographical correctness of his portraits. Enquist obviously here permits himself the same freedom as Strindberg did when portraying Swedish monarchs.

Of all the modern Swedish playwrights, August Strindberg excepted, Norén has received the greatest international recognition. Especially in Holland and Germany, his plays, now amounting to more than thirty, have been frequently staged.

Having devoted himself to poetry for a long time, Norén had his breakthrough as a dramatist with NIGHT IS MOTHER TO THE DAY (*Natten är dagens mor*), opening in 1982 and published the year after, to be followed by two more plays about virtually the same family. These plays, modelled on EUGENE O'NEILL's LONG DAY'S JOURNEY INTO NIGHT, deal with the complicated interaction between four family members locked together in one room, much as the couple in Strindberg's THE DANCE OF DEATH, the play Norén selected for his debut as a director in 1993. Frequent repetitions of snatches of dialogue increase the sense—also for the audience—of being closed in. No escape is possible until the masks have been dropped. The theatrical event becomes a therapeutic experience for both characters and spectators.

The most successful playwrights of the last two decades include Agneta Pleijel (1940–), Staffan Göthe (1944–), Stig Larsson (1955–), and Jonas Gardell (1963–). Agneta Pleijel's *Summer Nights* (*Sommarkvällar på jorden*, 1986; translated by James Mark, 1992) is the account of three sisters and their husbands who meet every summer in the summer house of their childhood. Recalling both Chekhov's THREE SISTERS and Ingmar Bergman's *Cries and Whispers*, Pleijel's works are more concerned with topical gender problems.

Staffan Göthe has written plays both for adults and children. His much acclaimed *A Stuffed Dog* (*En uppstoppad hund*, 1986), the second play in a trilogy about the fate of a family, shows a sensitivity for theater that may ascribed to his experience as an actor.

Stig Larsson's debut drama, the three-act mini-play *Red Light* (*Röd gubbe*, translated by Duncan Foster, 1992), records the somewhat Beckettian or Pinteresque conversations between Jim and Tim, Tim and Tom, and Jim and Tom while waiting for a traffic light to change. His *MD* (i.e., Managing Director, *VD*, 1987), a rather farcical play about power, was a hit when produced at the Royal Dramatic Theater.

Jonas Gardell, an outstanding stand-up comedian, writes tragicomedies about ordinary, unsuccessful people. His *Polar Bears* (*Isbjörnarna*, 1990) is an entertaining and sad family drama in which the characters at times address the audience directly.

In vast but thinly populated Sweden (currently only about nine million people live there), regional theater has become increasingly important. Regional theater heightens the communal feeling that otherwise tends diminish with increasing mobility and urbanization.

Thus the director of *The Great Wrath* (*Den stora vreden*, 1988), based on Sven Viksten's stage adaptation of Olof Högberg's regional novel of the same title, published in 1906, chose to have the exceedingly long play performed in an old steel factory, an environment directly related to the theme of the play; during the intermission, the audience was offered food from the region.

Internationally significant is the Swedish contribution to children's theater. Ever since it became an independent branch of the Stockholm City Theater, Unga Klara has devoted itself to this kind of theater. Rejecting the traditional fairy plays, the group has systematically attempted to do new plays that reflect the children's point of view, their needs and problems. The artistic leader, Suzanne Osten (1944–), never tires of declaring that children, even more than women, form a repressed group in society. Both as a playwright and as a director, she has devoted much attention to the problems of both groups. If parents get divorced, children often blame themselves for it. Osten, who like Lars Norén is psychoanalytically oriented, wishes to relieve children of their guilt feelings by expressing their "right to their own experiences in dramatic form." Her highly successful *Medea's Children* (*Medeas barn*, 1975), a "child tragedy" cowritten with Per Lysander (1944–) and inspired by Euripides' *Medea*, describes how two children experience their parents' divorce.

The theater debate, more lively and more in rapport with foreign impulses from the 1960s, has concerned such matters as the location of performances in or outside traditional theaters, the repertoire—a *smörgåsbord* for every taste or an ideologically consistent fare and the balance of native and foreign plays, whether the dramatist is active or passive in relation to the performers, the director's right to make changes in the text, whether rehearsals are open or closed to the public, the role of the audience, the position of the theater critic (Ingmar Bergman marked his standpoint by physically attacking one of them)—and the choice of medium.

The conditions for Swedish dramatists to get their plays produced are favorable. Stockholm boasts a greater number of theaters per capita than any other city in the world, and The National Touring Company (Riksteatern), founded in 1933, is the largest single theater anywhere. On the other hand, a comparison between the plays performed (as listed by Bengt Liljenberg in his survey of the relationship of theaters and theater critics to the plays written and staged in Sweden) and those published, reveals that few dramas, except those by a handful of playwrights, have found their way to the printer. Reading drama is obviously not a favorite occupation with the Swedes.

Apart from the stage, there is radio and television. Since its beginning in 1925, Swedish radio has been the largest producer of drama in the country, including drama written especially for the theater of the ear. Many playwrights made their debut as radio dramatists. With his *Pilot from the Moluccas* (*Lotsen från Moluckas*, 1935), a lyrical play about Magellan's circumnavigation of the earth, Nobel Prize winner Harry Martinson (1904–1978) wrote a radio play that is now considered a classic. Another radio classic is Hjalmar Bergman's adaptation of his own novel *God's Orchid* (*Markurells i Wadköping*; the novel was published in 1919, the play was broadcast on January 1, 1930, and staged August 16, 1930). In the 1940s radio drama became a concept. The two leading writers for this medium, Sivar Arnér (1909–1997) and Björn-Erik Höijer (1907–1996), wrote many plays for broadcasting. Previously a successful novelist, Arnér later limited himself to this medium. In his *Lonely on the Headland* (*Ensam på udden*, 1949), one of the most medium-oriented Swedish radio plays, Arnér cleverly knew how to make stream-of-consciousness dramatically arresting.

When regular television was introduced in Sweden in the mid-1950s, the opportunities for dramatists further increased, especially while the TV Theater produced a play every week. Swedish television drama was born in 1955 when Werner Aspenström's (1918–1997) *The Noose* (*Snaran*), written directly for the new medium, was published and produced. For quite some time Aspenström was the most frequently produced television dramatist. Ingmar Bergman showed an early interest in the new medium when producing his own *The Rite* (*Riten*, 1969) on television, a play about three artists and their censor. And long before his plays found favor in the theater, Lars Norén elicited strong response through the small screen with his *Amala, Kamala* (1971), a play about colonialism, racism, and western man as a thinly disguised brute.

FURTHER READING

Anderman, Gunilla. "Contemporary Swedish Theatre: An Introduction." In *New Swedish Plays*, ed. by Gunilla Anderman. Norwich: Norvik Press, 1992. 9–32.

Brandell, Gunnar, and Jan Stenkvist. *Svensk litteratur 1870–1970* [Swedish Litterature 1870–1970], Vol. 2. Stockholm: Aldus, 1975. 271–294.

Hallingberg, Gunnar. *Radiodramat: Svensk hörspelsdiktning-bakgrund, utveckling och formvärld* [The Radio Drama: Its Background,

Development and Structure with Reference Mainly to Radio Playwriting in Sweden]. Stockholm: Sveriges Radios förlag, 1967. English summary, 251–263.

Liljenberg, Bengt. *Svenska stycken efter Strindberg: Anteckningar kring den svenska scendramatiken och dess författare 1910–1960* [Swedish Plays after Strindberg: Annotations around Swedish Stage Drama and Its Authors, 1910–1960]. Stockholm: Carlsson, 1990.

———. *Dramat, dramatikerna och verkligheten: Anteckningar kring den svenska scendramatiken och dess författare 1960–1990* [The Drama, the Dramatists and the Reality: Annotations around Swedish Stage Drama and Its Authors, 1960–1990]. Stockholm: Carlsson, 2000.

Marker, Frederick J., and Lise-Lone Marker. *A History of Scandinavian Theatre.* Cambridge: Cambridge Univ. Press, 1996. 193–342.

Törnqvist, Egil. "20th Century Drama in Sweden." In *20th Century Drama in Scandinavia*, ed. by Johan Wrede, et al. Helsinki: Univ. of Helsinki, 1979. 43–50.

Warme, Lars G., ed. *A History of Swedish Literature.* Lincoln: Univ. of Nebraska Press, 1996.

Egil Törnqvist

SWITZERLAND

Any discussion of Swiss drama and theater requires a brief overview of Switzerland's history and unique cultural diversity. Modern Switzerland consists of 15,941 square miles and is home to approximately seven million Swiss, of whom seventy percent speak German, eighteen percent French, ten percent Italian, and one percent Romansh. The country's linguistic and cultural plurality renders the notion of a singularly "Swiss" drama moot. Swiss-German playwrights must decide whether to write in standard High German (and thus be able to reach German-speaking audiences beyond Switzerland's borders) ør in *Schwyzerdüütsch*, the Swiss-German dialect consisting of many Alemannic versions differing in grammar, phonology, syntax, and vocabulary.

Historically, Switzerland grew together over centuries because the cantons found favor with a free and democratically oriented society, unlike any of the surrounding monarchies. Switzerland had neither royal courts nor their attending cultural centers, which served to attract artists. In fact, the Calvinist and Zwingli protestant traditions came to spurn the theater. *Festspiele* (folk pageants) became a political tool for unifying the culturally diverse Swiss, and the open-air pageant performed by amateurs in Swiss-German dialect became Swiss theater. Drama in High German was considered a cultural import.

HISTORY OF SWISS DRAMA

To understand contemporary Swiss-German plays, one must understand the unique evolution of drama in Switzerland. Early Swiss drama emerged from the church. Religious leaders used drama to expand and augment the liturgy. Evidence of this drama, as early as 1300, is to be found in the monasteries of Muri (Aargau) and Einsiedeln. These early religious dramas eventually found their way into towns in the form of Passion plays in which the townspeople participated in coproductions with church authorities. Thus, the folk theater was born. Renward Cysat (1545–1614) was perhaps the most successful example of a cantonal clerk who authored and directed Passion plays in the medieval tradition. The Jesuits reclaimed the Passion plays for the church, establishing a Jesuit Theatrical Center in Fribourg. Although they banned the open-air performances in Lucerne in 1677, the folk theater had by then taken root. Political, moral, and religious issues relating to Swiss sovereignty constituted prevalent themes of folk drama. *Wilhelm Tell*, authored by an unknown playwright, first performed around 1511 and repeatedly thereafter, attests to the popularity of folk theater.

The Swiss intellectual centers of Basel, Bern, Geneva, and Zurich remained opposed to theater well into the Enlightenment. Beyond Switzerland's borders, by contrast, the theater flourished, promoting the growth of professional actors and acting companies whose performances in Switzerland whetted the Swiss appetite for drama. Enlightened Swiss luminaries such as Johann Jakob Bodmer (1698–1783) firmly believed that it was better to read dramas than to see them on stage. The Puritan disposition persisted. In Catholic Lucerne, the Enlightenment influenced the locals to reject the Jesuit influence. Josef Ignaz Zimmermann (1737–1797), a former Jesuit schoolteacher, created an enlightened version of *Wilhelm Tell—A Tragedy* (*Wilhelm Tell—ein Trauerspiel*, 1777), which served Friedrich Schiller (1759–1805) as a source for his definitive reworking of the material. Schiller's *Tell* (1805) would become the Swiss national epic.

THE BIRTH OF MODERN SWISS DRAMA

In the 19th century, Swiss merchants who became enamored of theater companies while traveling abroad returned home to help establish theaters in their own country. The leading playwrights of the day were Johann Wolfgang von Goethe (1749–1832), Gotthold Ephraim Lessing (1729–1781), and Schiller. Their dramas required professional actors from GERMANY and AUSTRIA, since Switzerland did not have professionally trained actors of its own. The language of the stage thus became High German, leading to the breach that persists today between the Swiss professional stage, on which one hears High German, the language of "high culture," and the popular theater, where the Swiss-German dialect *Schwyzerdüütsch* predominates.

The prose author Gottfried Keller (1819–1890) originally planned to become a playwright and even wrote one dramatic fragment, *Therese* (1849). However, Keller channeled his dramatic energies into his novellas because he understood how difficult it would be to have his dramas published and performed in a climate unsupportive of highbrow drama in High German. The Puritan principle of utility persisted well into the 19th century; the Swiss were not willing to fund the arts. Since Keller sought to live from his writing, he turned to the literary journals of the day, in which he published his novellas. Keller's "Das

Schillerfest am Mytenstein" ("Tribute to Schiller," 1860), delivered at the dedication of the Swiss National Monument to Schiller (for his *William Tell*), envisioned great pageants staged by large acting companies composed of average citizens participating in patriotic Swiss dramas that they themselves would have written and performed. Although his works do include descriptions of such festivals and pageants, Keller himself never wrote a script for one.

The pageants envisioned by Jean-Jacques Rousseau (1712–1778) and Keller did take place in late-19th-century Switzerland. Swiss government officials viewed these pageants and folk festivals as a means of instilling in the culturally diverse Swiss a patriotic fervor for Switzerland that would transcend their French, German, Italian, or Romansh heritage. The discrepancy between popular theater in dialect and professional theater in High German evolved into a debate over the ideological position of Swiss theater in the national context. Switzerland's industrial revolution did not produce large urban centers, so the folk element in cultural life remained strong. Swiss Nobel laureate Carl Spitteler (1845–1924) took up Keller's lament in 1889, arguing that there would be no Swiss-German stage if a compromise could be reached between the professional stage and Swiss audiences. Spitteler criticized the peculiar Swiss inclination to subjugate aesthetic concerns to patriotic purpose. Amateur folk theater was so popular because it is one-third artistic and two-thirds patriotic.

The establishment of the Bernese Heimatschutztheater (Theater for the Protection of the Homeland), an amateur folk theater, for the 1914 National Exposition confirms Spitteler's analysis. This theater staged pageants that revived historical themes and promoted a national Swiss heritage. By 1950, some 130 plays had been published by Franke in Bern for this theater alone. Successful TRAGEDIES such as Paul Haller's (1882–1920) *Marie und Robert* (1916) possessed universal appeal and had international potential, had it not been written in Haller's Aarguaer dialect. The Swiss rejected expressionist theater, the international AVANT-GARDE, and other forms of modern drama as imported highbrow culture.

THE WAR YEARS: THE 1930s AND 1940s

Switzerland in the 1930s suffered as much economically as the rest of Central Europe. Despite some 85,000 unemployed by the mid-1930s, the Swiss were less inclined to the radical totalitarian solutions sought by their neighbors. While some Swiss demanded forced economic intervention and a suspension of constitutional powers, they remained in the minority and were soundly defeated in a 1935 plebiscite. The political storm gathering beyond Switzerland in the north and the south raised the level of Swiss patriotic fervor, influencing the climate for the arts and fueling the continued subjugation of aesthetic concerns to the demand for cultural patriotism. The economic and political situation was hardly conducive to the fledgling theater industry.

Jakob Bührer (1882–1975) was one of the most productive Swiss playwrights in the 1930s and 1940s, writing some thirty dramas, numerous dramatic sketches, and one-act plays. At least seven of his dramas were staged in Swiss-German professional theaters, while others were performed by amateurs. Bührer composed satires and COMEDIES in dialect, social dramas, and period pieces (*Zeitstücke*) in High German. His 1923 *Ein neues Tellenspiel* (*A New Tell Play*) sought to reveal the unheroic in the *Tell* material. Bührer viewed literature as a means of questioning social practices. His play *The Picket Makers* (*Die Pfahlbauer*, 1932) prepared the viewer to recognize exploitation in the workplace. Subordinating aesthetics to the political message, Bührer intended his works as critiques of the Swiss bourgeoisie. His *The Life of Galileo Galilei* (*Galileo Galilei*, 1933) aimed to unmask the hero that Galileo had become and present a common, innocent, aging human being with all his human frailties. Historical drama, Bührer maintained, should (re-)discover the truth.

Cäsar von Arx (1895–1949) is the only Swiss dramatist of the first half of the 20th century whose plays are still occasionally performed in amateur and professional theaters. No other playwright had so many of his plays regularly staged in Switzerland between 1930 and 1950, and no other Swiss dramatist before FRIEDRICH DÜRRENMATT had so many works performed on prominent international stages. Arx's first major success was *History of General Johann August Suter* (*Geschichte vom General Johann August Suter*, 1929), in which Arx dramatizes the life of the famous adventurer from Basel (1803–1880) in twelve scenes. Continuing with heroic themes, Arx authored *The Treason of Novara* (*Der Verrat von Novara*, 1933), an historical three-act VOLKSSTÜCK (popular drama) in classical style set in 1500. The drama relates the woeful tale of an Urner farmer who struggles to keep his homestead. Arx transforms the historically unsavory figure Erni Turmann into a solid, God-fearing, aspiring hero. In selecting Swiss historical material, Arx made a political statement. *The Treason of Novara* became Arx's greatest success on German stages, with some fifty-four productions before all of Arx's work was banned there in March 1941. During the 1940s, Arx became the official Swiss pageant author and was asked to write the *Federal Pageant* (*Bundesfestspiel*) of 1941, commemorating the 650th anniversary of the founding of Switzerland. Arx's oeuvre reveals innovative and creative experimentation with modern dramatic forms. He wrote both folk pageants and high dramas, preferring intellectual openness to the excesses of Swiss cultural patriotism.

The Haus am Pfauen, the main stage of the Zurich Schauspielhaus, gained a reputation during the war years as the last free bastion of German-language theater. Well-known actors and directors came from Germany and Austria to seek refuge in Zurich to continue their work. Arx was a staunch supporter of these émigrés. Some of the productions, such as Goethe's *Götz von Berlichingen* (1773) or Schiller's *Don Carlos* (1787) and *Wilhelm Tell*, helped the Swiss to articulate their own fears concerning

Swiss sovereignty. BERTOLT BRECHT's MOTHER COURAGE AND HER CHILDREN (Mutter Courage und ihre Kinder, 1939–1940), THE LIFE OF GALILEO (Leben des Galilei, 1939), and THE GOOD WOMAN OF SETZUAN (Der gute Mensch von Sezuan, 1939–1940) all premiered in Zurich, as did GEORG KAISER's Private Tanaka (Der Soldat Tanaka, 1940).

SWISS-GERMAN DRAMA IN THE POSTWAR YEARS

After the war most of the emigrant playwrights returned to their former stages. Friedrich Dürrenmatt and MAX FRISCH emerged as the new Swiss-German playwrights who would dominate the theater scene for the next few decades. In Dürrenmatt's THE VISIT OF THE OLD LADY (Der Besuch der alten Dame, 1956), wealth purchases justice. THE PHYSICISTS (Die Physiker, 1962) raises questions about the social responsibilities of the scientist. Both of these plays became part of the international German repertoire. The dramas of Dürrenmatt's contemporary Max Frisch, including The Great Wall of China (Die chinesische Mauer, 1946), The Firebugs (Biedermann und die Brandstifter, 1958) and ANDORRA (1957), thematize the responsibility of private individuals who must make important public decisions. Both Dürrenmatt and Frisch set universal themes in provincial Swiss settings that have both local and international appeal. The two playwrights worked closely with the Zurich Schauspielhaus. For the first time in the history of Swiss drama, one can speak of a symbiosis between the playwright and the theater.

The Swiss public had grown accustomed to the repertoire of Swiss heroes and the theme of freedom that comprised an important part of the cultural defense and permeated productions during World War II. In the postwar period Dürrenmatt and Frisch sought to break this complacency. In his 1954 novel Stiller (I'm not Stiller), Frisch creates a remarkably dramatic scene in which the sculptor Stiller destroys all of the plaster figures and busts in his atelier, in effect obliterating the false images and past idols as if to invite a new, critical beginning. The Switzerland known for its neutrality, its thriftiness, its cleanliness, and its magnificent landscapes contrasted sharply with the other Switzerland known for its ruthless entrepreneurs, its commerce in weaponry, its bank secrets, and its unwillingness to discuss its recent history.

A younger wave of Swiss authors, including Hansjörg Schneider (1938–), Urs Widmer (1938–), and Thomas Hürlimann (1950–), began to re-examine and deconstruct Swiss icons, images, and historical themes in search of the truth. Women's suffrage also came to Switzerland in 1971 and brought several female voices, most notably the poet Erica Pedretti (1930–), the essayist and novelist Laure Wyss (1913–2002), and the novelist Gertrud Leutenegger (1948–), whose autobiographical Dusk (Vorabend, 1975) became a much revered early feminist text. Once again it was Frisch who led the way in 1971 with his slim volume Wilhelm Tell: A School Text (Wilhelm Tell für die Schule) in which he desconstructs the Tell myth. Following Frisch's lead,

Herbert Meier (1928–) questions contemporary Swiss politics in Stauffer-Bern (1975). Thomas Hürlimann explores the problematic past of Switzerland during World War II in his play Grandfather and Half Brother (Grossvater und Halbbruder, 1981) in which a village extradites a Jewish refugee, supposedly Adolf Hitler's half brother, and his host. Hansjörg Schneider, perhaps inspired by the rebellious youth in Zurich, dramatizes the Swiss generation gap in Indian Summer (Altweibersommer, 1984).

To celebrate the 700th anniversary of Switzerland, Herbert Meier was commissioned by the Government Council of Schwyz to write an open-air pageant. The resulting Festspiel, written in High German, was titled Mythen-Play (Mythenspiel, 1991) after the two mountains (die Mythen) that tower over the cantonal capital Schwyz and form the backdrop for the pageant. Following a traffic accident, the main character Teiler seeks to find his companion Barbara. In his search he stumbles upon Swiss ghosts, historical figures, traditions, and Swiss myths, realizing through these encounters that the moral and ethical development of his world has little in common with the enduring dreams and ideals of the ancient Swiss. Hence, the double meaning of the title Mythenspiel, which literally translates as "playing with myths." Meier brought together professional drama in High German with the atmosphere of the folk pageant to stage a production performed by both professional and amateur actors.

Maja Beutler (born 1936) is the first known female Swiss playwright. Her Lady Macbeth Doesn't Wash Her Hands Anymore (Lady Macbeth, wäscht sich die Hände nicht mehr, 1992) premiered at the Zurich Schauspielhaus in 1994. Beutler's title evokes images of William Shakespeare's character repeatedly washing her hands to cleanse herself of the immense guilt she feels toward her husband and all those who have perished because of her greed and quest for power. Beutler transports Shakespeare's figure into modern-day Switzerland. Hetti Bickel, Beutler's Lady Macbeth, decides on her fiftieth birthday to transform the life she leads with her enormously successful entrepreneurial husband; he lives only for Matchless Chemical, the firm he created. Hetti locks him up at home to prevent him from flying to Hamburg and carrying out the corporate takeover scheduled for that day. She then deals mockingly with company business and persuades him to take his vast fortune and escape with her to begin a new life on a new continent where his endless work would not stand between them. Beutler's Hetti possesses none of the guilt of her Shakespearean predecessor. She is a modern Lady Macbeth who takes control of her husband's life and overcomes the tragedy of her marriage, transforming it into a vision of a better existence.

Staged in 2000 in front of the monastery at Einsiedeln, the site where Swiss theater began, Thomas Hürlimann's The Einsiedler World Theater (Das Einsiedler Welttheater, 2000) blends Calderón de la Barca's (1600–1681) 1641 play with such contemporary Swiss concerns as globalization, xenophobia, the exploitation of the average citizen by the government and the wealthy, and the economic violation of sacred places and traditions. The author who calls the six characters to life speaks Spanish, and the characters themselves speak a mixture of *Schwyzerdüütsch* and High German. These characters explore questions of faith and bemoan the condition of the world, and true to the original, even the monks question how God could allow such catastrophes to occur. The figures on stage experience the transitory nature of life, running from birth to death in a play that has no acts, but instead five scenes representing four seasons and the Plague, the equivalent of a five-act classical drama framed by a prologue and an epilogue. With Hurlimann's play, the now-secularized Swiss theater returned to where it began, the religious setting of the monastery at Einsiedeln.

FURTHER READING

Amstutz, Hans, Ursula Käser-Leisibach, and Martin Stern. *Schweizertheater 1930–1950* [Swiss Theater 1930–1950]. Zurich: Chonos, 2000.

Bänziger, Hans. *Frisch und Dürrenmatt* [Frisch and Dürrenmatt]. Bern: Franke, 1960.

Delecretaz, Anne-Lise, Daniel Maggetti, Michael Pfister, Vincenzo Todisco, and Lucia Walther, eds. *Schriftstellerinnen und Schriftsteller der Gegenwart* [Contemporary Swiss Authors]. Aarau: Sauerländer, 2002.

Demetz, Peter. *Postwar German Literature*. New York: Pegasus, 1970.

Geissler, Rolf. *Zur Interpretation des modernen Dramas* [Interpreting Modern Drama]. Frankfurt: Arche, 1971.

Gut, Katrin. *Das vaterländische Schauspiel* [The Homeland Play]. Freiburg: Universitätsverlag Freiburg, 1996.

Matt, Peter von. *Die tintenblauen Eidgenossen* [The Ink-Stained Swiss Federalists]. Munich: Hanser, 2001.

Mittenzwei. Werner. *Das Zürcher Schauspielhaus 1933–1945* [The Zurich Theater 1933–1945]. Berlin: Henschelverlag, 1979.

Müller, Eugen. *Schweizerische Theatergeschichte* [History of Swiss Theater]. Zürich: Oprecht, 1944.

Rüedi, Peter, ed. *Neue Theaterstücke aus der Schweiz* [New Plays from Switzerland]. Frankfurt/M: Eichborn, 1991.

Schläfer, Beate. *Theater in Switzerland*. Tr. by Eileen Walliser-Schwarzbart. St. Gallen: Stehle Druck, 1994.

Szene Schweiz—Scene Suisse—Scena Svizzera—Scena Svizra [The Swiss Scene], Nos. 1–18. Basel: Schweizerische Gesellschaft für Theaterkultur [For Swiss Theater Culture], 1973–1991.

Theater.ch. www.theater.ch (Accessed October 5, 2006).

Richard R. Ruppel

SYMBOLISM

The reaction against the rationalism of the eighteenth century has mingled with a reaction against the materialism of the nineteenth century, and the symbolical movement, which has come to perfection in Germany in Wagner, in England in the Pre-Raphaelites, and in France in Villiers de L'Isle Adam and Mallarmé, and has stirred the imagination of Ibsen and D'Annunzio, is certainly the only movement that is saying new things.

—W. B. Yeats, "The Celtic Element in Literature," 1897

Symbolism in the broad sense of having a sign represent something other than what it appears to be—one thing standing for another—is as old as art itself. But at the end of the 19th century there sprang up in FRANCE among artists and writers a special form of symbolism characterized by its emphasis on the spiritual and the otherworldly. This movement began as a strong reaction against the NATURALISM of ÉMILE ZOLA. In 1886 just when naturalism had firmly established itself as the mode of advanced drama, the poet Jean Moréas published a manifesto in which he declared that the essential aim of symbolism "is to objectify the subjective"—not to subjectify the objective, which is what Zola did and what the impressionist painters did.

Interviewed by a French journalist in the early 1890s, when the symbolists were much talked about, HENRIK IBSEN drew a distinction between his own use of symbols in a play like THE MASTER BUILDER (1892) and Zola's practice. He found Zola's novel *Germinal* (1885) to be a symbol "of vertiginous depth, the like of which I know not. . . . But the symbols of Zola are the result of the general action; they are the conclusion of the drama. My symbols are the beginning, the premises. They are the raison d'être of things. They contain reality, while those of Zola are explained by reality" (Bigeon, 1893).

Paul Fort, aided by poets like Stéphane Mallarmé and Paul Verlaine, established a theater devoted to antinaturalist plays. In 1891, when he staged MAURICE MAETERLINCK's one-act *The Intruder* (*L'Intruse*), he announced that his Théâtre d'Art would henceforth be devoted to the symbolist drama. "From now on it will be supported by the masters of the new school, Mallarmé, Verlaine, Jean Moréas. . . . At the end of March we shall present the first Symbolist production for the benefit of Verlaine and the admirable symbolist painter Paul Gauguin" (Robichez, 1957).

Zola employed symbols generously in his naturalistic novels, but his symbols made no connection with the world of the spirit. The mine in *Germinal* could represent the exploitation of the worker in a capitalist society, and the locomotive in *La Bete humaine* (1890) could stand for the sexual mania of the engineer. But the connection was between two things that existed on the materialistic and scientific plane. The naturalists, placing their faith in science and materialism, had drained soul and spirit from the universe; the symbolists wanted to bring them back.

Actually they had been there all along, but had been submerged in the drama and theater by naturalism. In the long view naturalism could be seen as an upstart movement, new on the scene, whereas the ideas of the symbolists had a very long history. They could draw on the mystic teachings of Emanuel Swedenborg, the philosophy of Arthur Schopenhauer, the poems of Charles Baudelaire, the musical dramas of RICHARD WAGNER. What they had in common was the belief that the inner life of the human being was more significant than his outer, social life. The esoteric, antisocial position of the symbolists in its most extreme form was expressed by Villiers de l'Isle Adam in his drama *Axel* (1890): "As for living, our servants will do that for us."

From the technical point of view, the problem was how to capture this inner life by means that had to rely on physical instruments. The poet Mallarmé said in 1891 that the soul could not be grasped directly, and consequently it would have to be suggested: "To name an object means to suppress three quarters of the pleasure. . . . Our dream should be to suggest the object" (1945).

The method was that of correspondences. The physical world was a forest of symbols to the imaginative artist, symbols that could conjure up the world of the soul as vividly as a painting could bring before one's eyes the train station in Paris. As Vincent Van Gogh said, "To express hope by some star, the eagerness of a soul by a sunset radiance. Certainly there is no delusive realism in that; but isn't it something that actually exists?" (1945).

If the aim of symbolism was to put one in contact with the spiritual, then the art of preference would be music. The German philosopher Schopenhauer made it the highest of all the arts. Through music it was possible to enter the spiritual realm almost directly. Wagner's music dramas, especially *Tannhäuser*, *Lohengrin*, and *Tristan and Isolde*, became exemplars for the French symbolists because those works combined words and music, resulting in something more apprehensible than pure sound and, as with Van Gogh, bringing together the physical and the spiritual. Wagner's music in *Tristan* is the world will, the ceaseless meaningless energy of the universe out of which the whole drama of desire and death arises.

In the drama, the aims of symbolism were set forth most clearly by Maeterlinck in his essay "The Tragic in Daily Life" (in its first version, it was a review of Ibsen's *The Master Builder*) He argued for a drama with a minimum of action, since action prevented the soul from manifesting itself. For Maeterlinck, Hamlet is most himself not when fighting the duel but when soliloquizing. Man lives most deeply when he is quiet, still, letting the shadows fall upon him, exposed to the subtle eternal forces that impinge on his being as quietly as the moonlight strikes a blade of grass. Active, he cannot feel nor comprehend those eternal forces that emanate from the center of the universe.

A drama without action is pretty much a contradiction in terms. The result was static drama, a drama with a slender plot and little action. What one hoped to see in the theater was a state of soul, a term that Wagner used in describing his music dramas. The efforts of some dramatists to do away with what had always appeared to be the heart and soul of drama constitutes one of the most significant developments in the theater of the 20th century.

In this interior drama there was no violent conflict, no escape from a dangerous situation, no clearly presented issue or controversy to be discussed, no problem that might be resolved by a sudden decision or event—in a word, no drama in the conventional sense. Instead the symbolist play put on the stage a region with forces beyond those of reason or intelligence. The atmosphere of the work became primary and the plot secondary.

Maeterlinck's best play, *Pelléas and Mélisande*, staged in 1893, borrows its plot of illicit love more from Wagner's *Tristan* than from Dante Alighieri's tale of Paola and Francesca, substituting repetitious and incantatory dialogue for the master's music. Inevitably, someone had to put the music back in, which Claude Debussy accomplished in his operatic version of Maeterlinck's play.

In the theater, symbolism found less fertile ground than in the other arts. Paul Fort struggled to find a style of acting and stage design that would somehow represent the soul as convincingly as a realistic play represented everyday existence. The problem lay in the very physical presence of the actor; the immaterial spirit and the physical body were at odds. As Maeterlinck pointed out in 1890, a symbol consists in an irradiation outward from some center. But when the actor comes on stage, the rays converge on him or her and on the present moment. The symbol is shattered and the spirit dies. The attempts by Aurélien Lugné-Poe at his Théâtre de l'Oeuvre in Paris to create a symbolist stage by putting the actors behind a scrim, disembodying them, and having them declaim or chant their lines as if part of a liturgy were doomed to fail. For Pierre Quillard's *The Girl with Cut-off Hands* (*La Fille aux Mains Coupées*, March 1892) at Theatre d'Art, a gauze scrim was set up just behind the footlights. For a production of the Bible's *Song of Songs* (*Cantiques de Cantiques*, in an adaptation by P.-N. Roinard, December 1991) at the same theater, an attempt was made to break through the material plane by synesthesia: the vowels i and o were stressed, the music was in the key of C, the set was in purple, while the smell of frankincense filled the auditorium. These efforts only served to call attention to the problem rather than to solve it.

Although the early symbolists wrote for a small coterie and worked on the fringe of the arts, they are now seen as having been on the cutting edge. Their ideas encouraged experimentation among both dramatists and stage designers. Through innovative artists like Gordon Craig and Adolphe Appia, the realistic stage was dematerialized and theater art forever revolutionized. Dramatists who found the realistic theater inhospitable to their view of the world and too crass for the expression of the spiritual side of existence found encouragement in the Symbolist experiments.

Living in Paris in the mid-1890s, AUGUST STRINDBERG breathed the heady atmosphere of the symbolist AVANT-GARDE and reinvented himself as a dramatist with a strikingly original play, TO DAMASCUS (Part 1, 1898). In it he solved the Maeterlinckian paradox of the physical actor on a symbolic set by making the lead character symbolic, along with all the other objects and props on stage, with the rays radiating from him. He existed as a symbol among other symbols. Everything was seen from his perspective. He moved through a series of sharply divided scenes (or stations, as in medieval religious plays) as he felt the effect of forces he could not explain. Furthermore, Strindberg constructed a story line that brought the hero back to his starting point. This gave the impression that the hero's pilgrimage had been as much imagined as experienced in reality.

The symbolist experiments made a twofold contribution to the development of drama and theater. They offered playwrights the possibility of creating a drama of inwardness, in which the essential human being, stripped of temporal qualities, could be portrayed. They suggested that a drama with little action could be theatrically effective. And they freed the imagination of stage designers, allowing them to imbue even realistic sets with a visual poetry. The techniques required by symbolist drama in order to gain contact with the soul could be applied to plays that were not symbolist in the Maeterlinckian way but more like Zola. The naturalist ANTON CHEKHOV, for instance, could be staged to emphasize the obvious symbolism (in the conventional sense) in THE CHERRY ORCHARD.

Even for skeptical playwrights who had doubts about the existence of a soul, the symbolists provided instructive examples of how a play could present a state of mind in which actions lacked adequate motivation. SAMUEL BECKETT'S WAITING FOR GODOT, thought of as revolutionary, fits in perfectly with the symbolist theories. Lacking action, rich in symbols, it is a static drama par excellence. HAROLD PINTER'S early plays, like EDWARD ALBEE'S, are symbolist too, in their technique, in their small action, their going beyond the realm of logic and reason, creating an apparently realistic scene that seems to float over a submerged realm beyond logic and reason.

[*See also* Dramatic Structure; Russia and the Soviet Union, Russian
    Symbolist Drama]

FURTHER READING

Bigeon, Maurice. "Profils scandinaves: Henrik Ibsen" [Scandinavian
    Profiles: Henrik Ibsen], *Le Figaro* (January 4, 1893).
Deak, Frantisek. *Symbolist Theater: The Formation of an Avant-Garde.*
    Baltimore: Johns Hopkins Univ. Press, 1993.
Jasper, Gertrude R. *Adventure in the Theatre.* New Brunswick, N.J.:
    Rutgers Univ. Press, 1947.
Mallarmé, Stéphane. *Oeuvres complètes.* Ed. Henri Mondor and
    G. Jean-Aubry. Paris: Gallimard, 1945.
McGuiness, Patrick. *Maurice Maeterlinck and the Making of Modern
    Theatre.* Oxford: Oxford Univ. Press, 2000.
Robichez, Jacques. *Le Symbolisme au théâtre: Lugné-Poe et les debuts
    de l'oeuvre.* Paris: L'Arche, 1957.
Van Gogh, Vincent. *Van Gogh: A Self-Portrait.* Ed. by W. H. Auden.
    New York: Dutton, 1963.

                                                                Evert Sprinchorn

SYNGE, JOHN MILLINGTON (1871–1909)

*One has, on one side, Mallarmé and Huysmans producing this [rich,
poetic] literature [of towns]; and on the other hand Ibsen and Zola
dealing with the reality of life in joyless and pallid words. On the
stage one must have reality, and one must have joy, and that is
why the intellectual modern drama has failed, and people have
grown sick of the false joy of the musical comedy, that has been
given to them in place of the rich joy found only in what is superb
and wild in reality.*

—J. M. Synge, Preface to *The Playboy of the Western World*,
    1911

Playwright John (Edmund) Millington Synge was born on April 16, 1871, in a suburb south of Dublin, IRELAND, to an Anglo-Irish family with a distinguished record of service in law, government, and the Protestant church; another branch of the family were considerable landowners in County Wicklow. His father, a barrister, died a year after J. M. Synge, his youngest son, was born; his mother was an evangelical Protestant. Of his brothers, one became a missionary in China, one an engineer who emigrated to Argentina, and the third a land agent, collecting rents from tenantry during a period of agitation against landlordism in Ireland. Synge's mother, older sister, and grandmother wondered what would become of the youngest son, who showed little inclination to follow a profession or to worship with the rest of his pious family.

A frequently ailing child, his schooling was irregular. He enjoyed hiking, fishing, and practicing amateur naturalism in the mountains of County Wicklow. His reading in the works of Charles Darwin at age fourteen had a profound impact on his view of life. At age sixteen, he began studying the violin. At Trinity College, Dublin (1889–1892), he studied the Irish language in the School of Divinity. He also attended the Royal Irish Academy of Music and in 1891 joined the Academy orchestra. In July 1893, he went to live in GERMANY, the better to advance his ambition to become a professional musician; from January 1894, he studied piano and violin in Wurzburg. In 1895, he settled in Paris, and studied Old Irish at the Sorbonne. A shift in his interests from music to literature is manifest in his first critical writings published in journals.

During the years spent in Europe (1893–1902), Synge returned to summer in Wicklow with his mother. On such a visit in 1894, he fell in love with a neighbor of the same faith as his mother, a Plymouth Brethren, Cherrie Matheson. In 1896 and 1897 she declined his proposals of marriage, on the grounds that she could not wed an unbeliever. Still, Synge clung to his unbelief with the sincere conviction of an evangelical.

In 1896, Synge met Maud Gonne and W. B. YEATS in Paris. They first encouraged him to join the Irish League in Paris, but after attending a few meetings, he resigned because he did not want to become "mixed up with a revolutionary and semi-military movement" for Irish independence from Britain. The second gave him significant advice. Envying Synge his knowledge of Irish, the poet said he should go to the Aran Islands, live there as one of the people, and express a life that had never been given expression. Synge could not, Yeats warned, make a triumph writing cosmopolitan journalism in Paris. In 1897, Synge fell seriously ill once again, this time evidently from the Hodgkin's disease that within twelve years would end his life.

In May 1898 Synge visited Inishmore ("big island"; the other two Aran islands are Inishere, "little island," and Synge's favorite, Inishman, "middle island"). On his return to the mainland, he stayed with LADY GREGORY at her country house, Coole Park, just when Yeats, Gregory, and Edward Martyn were planning the Irish Literary Theatre. Although he had as yet written no plays, Synge was from the start aware of and interested in the Irish dramatic revival. Urged by Yeats and Gregory to collect folklore on the Aran Islands, Synge returned there in the summers from 1899 to 1902. While he did not collect a great deal of folklore, he did gather observations for a rather modernist essay in aesthetic anthropology, "The Aran Islands" (not published until 1907). During this period, he continued to spend winters in Paris and the intervening periods with his mother in Wicklow.

It was in Wicklow in June 1902, following the first productions by the Irish National Dramatic Society (CATHLEEN NI HOULIHAN and Deirdre) that Synge began to write plays in a Hiberno-English dialect—his earlier, unfinished play, When the Moon Has Set, was a drawing-room discussion play. For the rest of the summer, the plays came rapidly: IN THE SHADOW OF THE GLEN, RIDERS TO THE SEA, and The Tinker's Wedding. A casual remark by the author after the plays' performances suggested he had picked up this poetical use of local speech by listening through the floorboards to the talk of servants in the kitchen of his mother's Wicklow house. In fact, he had for years been doing literal translations from Old Irish that preserved its characteristic circumlocutions, and he had studied the literary uses of Hiberno-English by Douglas Hyde in The Love Songs of Connaught (1893) and Lady Gregory in Cuchulain of Muirthemne (1902).

The values Synge found in Irish country life, or that he deposited there, clearly owe something to his involvement in modern European letters. He saw Aran through the eyes of the exoticizing popular French novelist Pierre Loti, particularly Loti's writings about a Breton fishing community. An awareness of love in the embrace of death gives Loti's impressionist pictures of the passing of a form of life a unique quality of melancholy. Synge too inhabited the borders of cultures: on Aran, he was a witness from and messenger to the modern metropolis.

From his start as a playwright, Synge had a deliberate ambition to conceive of works that were not merely local or national entertainments, but literary works assuming a place in the history of European literature. The prefaces to his plays, though brief, affiliate his plays with the writings of Molière, Ben Jonson, Charles Baudelaire, and François Villon, and contrast them with the plays of HENRIK IBSEN, whose "joyless and pallid" language Synge disliked. Yet In the Shadow of the Glen is patently influenced

by Ibsen's A DOLL'S HOUSE, and When the Moon Has Set, his unperformed country-house play, is clearly modeled on GHOSTS. Ibsen's AN ENEMY OF THE PEOPLE possibly affected Synge's oppositional conception of the relation of the artist to society.

As a Protestant, the brother of a land agent, a friend of Yeats, and a dropout of Maud Gonne's Irish League, Synge was under some suspicion by members of the Irish National Theatre Society and its audience, when Yeats, president of that society, imposed Synge's plays on them. Prior to the first production of In the Shadow of the Glen (on October 8, 1903), the play was more than once criticized in the Dublin press as "not Irish." The story of a Wicklow wife who carries on with a young farmer behind the back of her aged husband was, to the minds of the audience, unsavory. Wholly unacceptable was the ending in which this woman goes out the door scot-free with an itinerant. Synge felt he had written a love letter to the people and a hymn to freedom and the great world, but the play was taken as an offensive and sectarian insult to Irish women and family structure. Suspicion of Synge lingered throughout his lifetime.

His second play to be performed, Riders to the Sea (on February 25, 1904), was so solemn, noble, and woeful that it was spared criticism. After an audience has been moved to tears, it is unlikely to express outrage. But The Well of the Saints, his first production to be held at the new Abbey Theatre (on February 4, 1905), with characters in costumes designed by English artist Charles Ricketts, was again abused for being overly melancholy and un-Catholic. Set in Wicklow, this three-act play tells of an old blind couple, Martin and Mary Doul, whose sight is restored by a traveling saint. People had always told them they were a lovely man and wife; now they learn this was a joke. With their sight restored, they cannot beg charity but have to work. In the last act, their blindness begins to return, and they prevent the saint from curing them once again: for them, imagination is better than reality. The language of the play is the most elaborately patterned and poetical of all Synge's plays, and its moodiness and philosophical theme are suggestive of the works of MAURICE MAETERLINCK.

Synge was sorely wounded by the reception of The Well of the Saints. With his next play, he promised to give his audience something to make them really hop. This was PLAYBOY OF THE WESTERN WORLD, premiered on January 26, 1907. The play is by a long distance Synge's masterpiece and one of the classics of Irish theater. Many complete drafts of the play exist, and it is plain that Synge toiled over each scene, each speech, and each phrase in each speech. The cast has splendid parts: the scratching and itching but bonny barmaid, Pegeen Mike; her romancing tramp Christy Mahon, who is born out of his own and the villagers' imaginations as a hero; Pegeen's father, Michael James Flaherty, a pub owner with an Homeric talent in oaths; Old Mahon, the undead father of Christy, who is funny in the head and full of meanness; Shawn Keogh, Pegeen's cousin and fiancée who is terrified of Father Reilly; and the Widow Quin, who killed her own husband with a rusty pick and now would like to pair off with Christy. The Abbey company at the time were perfect for the play—including great actors like Sara and Molly Allgood, W. G. and Frank Fay, Arthur Sinclair, and J. M. Kerrigan—and the play was a perfect vehicle to make the most of their talents. But the audience rioted throughout the first week of performances in protest at Synge's extravagant satire of human folly. He had truly made them hop.

Even at the time of the *Playboy*'s production, Synge was a very sick man with tumors developing in his neck. His Hodgkin's disease was reaching its final stages. He was hoping to be able to go on because he had at last found love. He was engaged to the woman who played Pegeen Mike in *The Playboy*, Molly Allgood (stage name, Maire O'Neill). Yet death was clearly inevitable. His last two years were spent working on an unfinished dramatization of the Irish saga about Deirdre, a beautiful young woman betrothed to aging King Conchubar. She elopes instead to Scotland with a young man, Naisi, and his brothers. Lured back to Ireland after seven years by a promise of forgiveness from the king, the brothers are set upon and killed. Before the king can enjoy his prize, Deirdre kills herself with a knife. Throughout the play, the lovers try to justify the sufficiency of their present happiness in the knowledge that it will be short and end in sudden death. This was in fact the very situation of Synge and Molly Allgood. After Synge's death on March 24, 1909, in Dublin, she was the first to play the part of Deirdre. Both cast and audience found the event unbearably sad.

Synge's COMEDY and richness of language were an influence on all subsequent Irish playwrights, especially SEAN O'CASEY. His vivid sense of both joy and death, and his pleasure in the art of theater, had an impact on SAMUEL BECKETT. His seriousness about his art, even in the face of death, made a lasting impression on W. B. Yeats.

PLAYS: *In the Shadow of the Glen* (1903); *Riders to the Sea* (1904); *The Well of the Saints* (1905); *The Tinkers' Wedding* (1906); *Playboy of the Western World* (1907); *Deirdre of the Sorrows* (1909)

FURTHER READING

Greene, David H., and Edward M. Stephens. *J. M. Synge 1871–1909.* Rev. ed. New York: New York Univ. Press, 1989.

Grene, Nicholas, ed. *Interpreting Synge*. Dublin: Lilliput, 2000.

McCormack, W. J. *Fool of the Family: A Life of J. M. Synge.* London: Weidenfeld and Nicolson, 2000.

Watson, G. J. *Irish Identity and the Literary Revival: Synge, Yeats, Joyce and O'Casey.* 2nd ed. Washington, D.C.: Catholic Univ. of America Press, 1994.

Adrian Frazier

T

TABORI, GEORGE (1914–)

George Tabori (born on May 24, 1914, in Budapest, HUNGARY, then a part of the Austro-Hungarian Empire), a Jewish British citizen, is one of the most prolific playwrights and directors in contemporary GERMANY and AUSTRIA.

After moderate success as the author of novels and film-scripts (such as Alfred Hitchcock's *I Confess* [1953]) in post–World War II Hollywood, and following a short theater career in New York City, he relocated to Europe in 1971. Tabori has written more than thirty original plays, as well as several adaptations, and he has frequently directed at renowned theaters in Austria and Germany. For Tabori, the roles of playwright and director have always been intertwined.

Tabori was an apprentice in Berlin when the Nazis rose to power, forcing him into exile. During World War II he worked as a journalist, a BBC broadcaster, and an intelligence officer for the British MI5, and, while stationed in the Middle East, he began writing prose. After becoming a British citizen in 1947, he continued his writing career in the UNITED STATES. Tabori's first plays date from the early 1950s, the time of his collaboration with Lee Strasberg's Actors Studio. Under the influence of Strasberg, Tabori developed his directing principles (improvisation in particular) and became a savvy playwright. His early plays introduce issues of identity, exile, and race relationships; they also identify Tabori's role models (e.g., *Brecht on Brecht* [1960]). The premiere of *The Cannibals* (1968) constituted a turning point in Tabori's career and life: he has lived and worked in German-speaking Europe ever since.

Telling the story of concentration-camp inmates conflicted as to whether to eat the remains of one of their own, *The Cannibals* failed in the United States, but its European premiere (West Berlin, 1969) initiated Tabori's success on the German-language stage. *The Cannibals* is the first of his so-called Holocaust plays; here Tabori uses the theater as a place of remembrance. *The Cannibals* presents the difficulties of maintaining human dignity in the face of extinction, and the drama questions seemingly stable victim-perpetrator constellations through the use of black humor, music, dance, and numerous allusions to the Theater of the Absurd. Although Tabori has written three other Holocaust plays, *My Mother's Courage* (*Mutters Courage*, 1979), *Jubilee* (*Jubiläum*, 1983), and *Mein Kampf* (1987), the themes and methods first introduced in *The Cannibals* have recurred throughout his career—for example, in *Weisman and Copperface: A Jewish Western* (*Weisman und Rotgesicht: Ein jüdischer Western*, 1990), a play that examines race relations in the United States, and in his highly experimental adaptations of works by such authors as BERTOLT BRECHT (THE RESISTIBLE RISE OF ARTURO UI, 1972), Franz Kafka

(*The Hunger Artists, Die Hungerkünstler*, 1977), William Shakespeare (*Shylock-Improvisations, Ich wollte meine Tochter läge tot zu meinen Füßen und hätte die Juwelen in den Ohren*, 1978), and Fyodor Dostoevsky (*The Grand Inquisitor, Der Großinquisitor*, 1992). In most of his plays Tabori returns to the vexing question of victims and perpetrators, arguing that these positions are interchangeable. The genesis of Tabori's works is unique in that he writes his plays in English as prose texts. Collaborator Ursula Grützmacher-Tabori translates them for publication, and Tabori finalizes the dramatic text after a play's premiere. He has frequently appeared as an actor in smaller parts in his plays and, since the 1990s, also in films. Throughout his career Tabori has created actors' workshops modeled on Strasberg's project, for example, Bremer Theater Lab and Vienna Circle. He currently lives in Berlin, Germany.

SELECT PLAYS: *Brecht on Brecht* (1960); *The Cannibals* (1968); *Niggerlovers* (1969); *Pinkville* (1970); *The Resistible Rise of Arturo Ui: A Gangster Spectacle* (1972); *The Hunger Artists* (*Die Hungerkünstler*, 1977); *Shylock-Improvisations* (*Ich wollte meine Tochter läge tot zu meinen Füssen und hätte die Juwelen in den Ohren*, 1978); *My Mother's Courage* (*Mutters Courage*, 1979); *Jubilee* (*Jubiläum*, 1983); *Mein Kampf: Farce* (1987); *Weisman and Copperface: A Jewish Western* (*Weisman und Rotgesicht: Ein jüdischer Western*, 1990); *Goldberg Variations* (*Goldberg-Variationen*, 1991); *The Grand Inquisitor* (*Der Grossinquisitor*, 1992); *Ballad of a Wiener Schnitzel* (*Die Ballade vom Wiener Schnitzel*, 1996)

FURTHER READING

Feinberg, Anat. *Embodied Memory: The Theatre of George Tabori*. Iowa City: Univ. of Iowa Press, 1999.

Höyng, Peter, ed. *Verkörperte Geschichtsentwürfe: George Taboris Theaterarbeit—Embodied Projections on History: George Tabori's Theater Work*. Tübingen: Francke, 1998.

Russell, Susan. "George Tabori." In *Reference Guide to Holocaust Literature*, ed. by Thomas Riggs. Detroit: St. James Press, 2002.

Birgit Tautz

TAKARAZUKA REVUE COMPANY

Takarazuka Revue Company is an all-female theater company begun as the Takarazuka Girls' Opera (Takarazuka Shōjo Kageki) in 1914 at Takarazuka, a spa town in Hyōgo Prefecture. It was the inspiration of railroad tycoon Kobayashi Ichizō. To expand suburban development by increasing the use of his new railway, he planned Takarazuka as an attractive leisure place for affordable family entertainment and education.

The first public pool in JAPAN was remodeled as the art deco Paradise Theater (Paradaisu Gekijō). It was built within the Takarazuka Family Land, Japan's first amusement park. The initial idea of the Girls' Opera was based on the boys' chorus popular at an Osaka department store, and educated girls were recruited from middle-class families.

The Takarazuka Music School was founded in 1919 upon the principles of Kobayashi Ichizō's maxim "Purely, Righteously, Beautifully" (kiyoku, tadashiku, utsukushiku), giving two years of training in Western and Japanese performing arts. All Takarazuka performers are the school's graduates, who maintain a strict senior-junior hierarchy throughout their careers. Today, only girls from the ages of fifteen to eighteen are entitled to apply, and successful candidates must remain unmarried until after their last performance. Both men and women serve as the company's playwrights, directors, conductors, and orchestra.

Male impersonators (otokoyaku) are the stars; the female leads are called musumeyaku. The company, affiliated with the school, has five troupes of about eighty students each: Flower (1921), Moon (1921), Snow (1924), Star (1934), and Cosmos (1998). This enables the company to offer a wide repertory of musicals and shows year-round, including original scenarios, autobiographical interpretations such as J.F.K. (1995) and Michelangelo (Mikeranjero, 2000), adaptations from William Shakespeare's dramas, as well as other classics such as Johann Wolfgang von Goethe's Faust (Tenshi no Bishō, Akuma no Namida, 1989) and The Tale of Genji (Genji monogatari, 1919), and realizations of comic-book (manga) stories such as The Rose of Versailles (Berusaiyu no bara, 1974). The troupes perform simultaneously in the Takarazuka Grand Theater, the Tokyo Takarazuka Theater, and the Bow Hall and on tour in Japan or, occasionally, abroad. During World War II flamboyant Takarazuka performances were banned, and the government restricted the repertory. The Tokyo Takarazuka Theatre was taken over by American occupation forces as the Ernie Pyle Theatre until 1955.

Although it began by staging Japanese fairy tales in modified kabuki style, Takarazuka has been in many respects responsible for introducing foreign culture to the Japanese masses. The first revue production, Mon Paris (Mon Pari, 1927), was written by Tatsuya Kishida, followed by the more spectacular Parisette (Parizēto, 1930) by Tetsuzō Shirai, who established the Takarazuka revue style. The company learned melody and choreography from abroad, importing trendy elements such as speedy rhythms and geometrical compositions. Popular French chansons, such as those by Mistinguette, and visual extravaganzas in the manner of Florenz Ziegfeld were adopted.

An exclusive Takarazuka satellite channel, Sky Stage, started in 2002.

PLAYS: *The Tale of Genji (Genji monogatari, 1919; revised versions, 1952, 1981, 2000); Mon Paris (Mon Pari, 1927; revised version, 1947); Parisette (Parizēto, 1930); Romeo and Juliet (Romio to Juriēto, 1933; revised versions, 1950, 1979, 1990); Red Flower of Tahiti (Minami no Aishū, 1947; revised versions, 1964, 1988); The Story of Gubijin and Kōu* (Gubijin, 1951; revised versions, 1955, 1974); Brilliant Thousand Rhythm (Karei naru Senbyōshi, 1960; revised version, 1999); West Side Story (Uesuto Saido monogatari, 1968; revised version, 1999); Nova Bossa Nova (Noba bosa noba, 1971; revised versions, 1976, 1999); The Rose of Versailles (Berusaiyu no bara, 1974; revised versions, 1975, 1976, 1989, 1990, 1991, 2001); Gone with the Wind (Kaze to tomo ni sarinu, 1977; revised versions, 1984, 1988, 1994, 2002); Faust (Tenshi no Bishō, Akuma no Namida, 1989); Black Jack (Buraku Jaku, 1994); J.F.K. (1995); Elizabeth (Erizabēto, 1996; revised versions, 1998, 2003); Michelangelo (Mikeranjero, 2000)*

FURTHER READING

Kawasaki, Kenko. *Takarazuka: Shōhi-shakai no supekutakuru* [Takarazuka: The spectacle of the consumer society]. Tokyo: Kōdansha, 1999.

Kobayashi, Ichizō. *Takarazuka mampitsu* [Notes on Takarazuka]. Osaka: Hankyū Dentetsu, 1980.

Parker, Helen, S. E. "The Men of Our Dreams: The Role of the Otokoyaku in the Takarazuka Revue." In *Japanese Theatre and the International Stage*, ed. by Stanca Scholz-Cionca and Samuel L. Leiter. Leiden: Brill, 2001. 242–254.

Rimer, J. Thomas. *Culture and Identity: Japanese Intellectuals During the Interwar Years*. Princeton: Princeton Univ. Press, 1990.

Robertson, Jennifer. *Takarazuka: Sexual Politics and Popular Culture in Modern Japan*. Berkeley: Univ. of California Press, 1998.

Ueda, Shinji. *Takarazuka: Hyakunen no yume* [Takarazuka: A hundred-year dream]. Tokyo: Bungei Shunju, 2002.

Makiko Yamanashi

TALE OF SHUZENJI

Tale of Shuzenji (Shuzenji monogatari) is a Japanese play by OKAMATO KIDŌ in one act and three scenes, taking approximately one and a quarter hours in performance. The author published it in a literary magazine early in 1911, and a kabuki company premiered it in May of the same year with Ichikawa Sadanji II in the lead part of Yashaō. Yashaō is a carver of wooden masks commissioned by patrons, thus fulfilling a role similar to that of a portrait sculptor today. An enormous popular success, the production cemented the relationship between Sadanji and the playwright, and this lasted until they both died at the end of the 1930s. The play has been regarded as a model for the genre of Japanese drama known as SHIN KABUKI—plays written by authors living in and aware of the modern age but aiming to use the acting skills of kabuki actors.

Tale of Shuzenji starts on a low key, as many kabuki plays do, with two sisters discussing their futures. They are the daughters of Yashaō, whose profession would have been kept in the family; one daughter sees being the wife of a conscientious craftsman positively, while the other, Katsura, has ambitions to escape such a dull life and serve at court. Their father, Yashaō, is late with a commission for the shogun, Yoriie, because his mask of Yoriie, however many times he carves it, has an aura of death about it.

Katsura, against her father's wishes, shows the mask to Yoriie, who is delighted with it and at the same time falls in love with her. An idyllic evening walk by a stream, during which the shogun utters words of great tenderness to his new lover, is interrupted by the appearance of assassins sent to kill him. Katsura dons the mask to decoy the killers and is mortally wounded. The play ends as Yashaō, confirmed by these events in his belief in the truthfulness of his art, sketches his daughter's dying face.

While Yashaō's seeming heartlessness at the end may have reflected contemporary concerns about the link between art and life, it was the shogun's poetic verbalization of his love for Katsura that caught the mood of the times. Okamato had sensed the poetic potential of a play about the mask when he had seen it on a visit to the Shuzen Temple, and in this play he can be seen in a line from the Japanese romantic poets of the 1890s and their preoccupation with modern, mutually dignified love, expressed through poetry. The play, still very popular, has lost its feeling of fresh romanticism as attitudes toward relations between the sexes have changed, but in 1911 some of Yoriie's lines became catchphrases. *Tale of Shuzenji*, like several of Okamato's plays, while new at the time of its premiere, has settled easily into regular *kabuki* programs, where authentic interaction between stage and auditorium still derives more from familiarity than from novelty.

[See also Japan]

FURTHER READING

Leiter, Samuel L. *New Kabuki Encyclopedia: A Revised Adaptation of "Kabuki Jiten."* Westport, Conn.: Greenwood Press, 1997.

Nihon Kindai Engekishi Kenkyūkai, ed. *Nijisseiki no gikyoku I: Nihon kindai gikyoku no sekai* [Twentieth century plays I: The world of modern Japanese plays]. Tokyo: Shakai Hyōronsha, 2002.

Unno Mitsuko, ed. *You Mean to Say You Still Don't Know Who We Are?* Ashiya, Japan: Personally Oriented, 1976.

Brian Powell

THE TALE OF TEEKA

Like many of MICHEL MARC BOUCHARD's plays, *The Tale of Teeka* draws directly on scenes and events from his own childhood. In an interview with Richard Ouzounian, Bouchard relates, "I saw so many kids beaten; it was tragic. . . . People without education. It is a transmission: Violence goes from generation to generation. If someone is hurt, then they will have to hurt someone else." That idea, the concept of the generational consequences of violence, forms the themes of *The Tale of Teeka*.

First produced in June 1991 under its original French title, *L'histoire de l'oie*, *The Tale of Teeka* premiered at the annual Rencontres internationales théâtre et jeunes spectateurs in Lyon, FRANCE. It was a work almost five years in the making. In 1986 Daniel Meilleur encouraged Bouchard to write a play for young audiences; years later, what Bouchard describes as "the most minimalist of all my plays; fewer words and more emphasis on the power of evocation" resulted. Despite its audience of children, *The Tale of Teeka* deals with one of Bouchard's most controversial subjects—child abuse—and it does so directly, without flinching from the gravity of its subject. Set in 1955, in rural Quebec, CANADA, the play portrays hereditary violence. The play takes place with a storm on the horizon, a storm symbolic of the suffering of both the child and the adult Maurice, the pain and fear that neither can fully escape. It has only three characters, the adult Maurice, the child Maurice, and the puppet goose Teeka, manipulated by the adult Maurice. The adult Maurice acts as the play's narrator and speaks to the audience directly; to the child Maurice, the goose Teeka is not a puppet but a playmate, his only source of friendship. Maurice's parents never make an appearance in the play, but they are nonetheless present as a constant background of fear and imminent violence. Physically abused by his parents, at one point Maurice strips to reveal the bruises coloring his body. He has begun to see that pain as coinage in a frightening, bizarre system of barter and exchange; whenever he is hurt, he receives something—a cap, cake, a costume—in return. The story takes place during a short interval when Maurice's parents are away from the house; in their absence he invites his pet goose Teeka into his room. Yet when they return unexpectedly, Maurice reacts out of fear and replicates upon Teeka the same violence that he himself has experienced, breaking her neck and killing her. He comments, "I can't help it, Teeka. That's the way things are." For Maurice, a child, violence has become accepted and expected, a fury that still corrupts and torments the adult Maurice, who can only hope for a long-awaited peace and calm. The play has been very well received by critics and audiences alike, who have called it touching, haunting, and unforgettable.

FURTHER READING

Bouchard, Michel Marc. *The Tale of Teeka*. Tr. by Linda Gaboriau. Burnaby, B.C.: Talonbooks, 1999.

Graeber, Laurel. "A Story of a Boy and His Goose." *New York Times*, late edition, East Coast (January 30, 1998): E2:41.

Ouzounian, Richard. "Playwright in Character." *Toronto Star* (Canada) (January 25, 2004).

Winter S. Elliott

TALES FROM THE VIENNA WOODS

Is the theater a site for art, an aesthetic realm, or is the stage supposed to present an increasing number of "problem pieces" which have to be endured with displeasure and often in agony?
—Letter to the editor (Rheinische Post) in response to a 1971 production of *Tales from the Vienna Woods*

ÖDÖN VON HORVÁTH is best known for rejuvenating the VOLKSSTÜCK tradition, and *Tales from the Vienna Woods* (*Geschichten aus dem Wiener Wald*) is his best-known *Volksstück*. Completed in the summer of 1931, the "*Volksstück* in three parts" premiered at the Deutsches Theater in Berlin on November 2, 1931, shortly after Horváth had received the prestigious Kleist Prize. Well received by both critics and the general public, the play enjoyed a successful thirty-seven-performance run before closing on December 10, 1931. A number of theaters in GERMANY and AUSTRIA had announced plans to stage the drama shortly after its Berlin premiere, but those productions never materialized because of political circumstances. Indeed, the fascist threats to democracy that the drama depicts and decries were in large part responsible for the fact that *Tales from the Vienna Woods* was not performed again until after the end of World War II.

Taking its title from a Johann Strauss waltz, *Tales from the Vienna Woods* evokes expectations of carefree Viennese gemütlichkeit and lighthearted entertainment. Strauss's music does, in fact, punctuate the dramatic action (together with other waltzes and beloved Viennese folk songs), but rather than reaffirming the imperial elegance of the ballroom or the gay tone of the operetta, *Tales of the Vienna Woods* confronts its audience with a slow and brutal dance of death, performed by the petit bourgeois residents of a "quiet street in Vienna's Eighth District" shortly before the imposition of Engelbert Dollfuß's Austrofascist dictatorship.

Unable to understand the actual causes of their socioeconomic misery after the loss of World War I and the collapse of the Habsburg monarchy, the residents of the "quiet street" mobilize themselves to immobilize Marianne, the only character in the drama who seeks an alternative to the economic, physical, and emotional brutality of the petit bourgeois milieu. As part of her single-handed attempt to put an end to this violence, Marianne breaks her engagement to the neighborhood butcher (literal and figurative) Oskar in favor of a relationship with the financially parasitic Alfred, who has just ended a relationship with the neighborhood tobacconist, Valerie. In attempting to break out of the predetermined role of wife to the "boy next door," Marianne indicts tradition and threatens the authoritarian structure of the patriarchal family. Consequently, a series of grotesque dramatic events ensues, intended to render Marianne, in the words of her fiancé Oskar, "unfit for combat."

The neighborhood ultimately succeeds in collectively bringing about Marianne's forced surrender, and thus a return to the formal configurations with which the drama began. The content of the characters' relationships, though, has necessarily been transformed, since a reimposition of the status quo ante could only be achieved through an intensification of physical and psychological violence, the complete debasement of Marianne, and the death of her young son.

Tales of the Vienna Woods premiered in Austria in 1948, causing the first theater scandal of the Second Republic. For a newly reconstituted nation intent on perpetuating the myth of Austria as the "first victim" of Nazi Germany, there was little enthusiasm among the general population for a drama that represented Austrians as brutal, narrow-minded, and self-pitying victimizers.

FURTHER READING

Brzovic, Kathy, and Craig Decker. "The Struggle for Stasis in Ödön von Horváth's *Geschichten aus dem Wiener Wald*." *German Studies Review* 13, no. 3 (1990): 391–404.

Genno, Charles N. "'Kitsch' Elements in Horváth's *Geschichten aus dem Wiener Wald*." *German Quarterly* 45, no. 2 (1972): 311–323.

Horváth, Ödön von. *Geschichten aus dem Wiener Wald: Mit einem Kommentar von Dieter Wöhrle*. With commentary by Dieter Wöhrle. Frankfurt am Main: Suhrkamp, 2001.

Krischke, Traugott, ed. *Materialien zu Ödön von Horváths "Geschichten aus dem Wiener Wald"* [Materials on Ödön von Horváth's *Tales from the Vienna Woods*]. Frankfurt am Main: Suhrkamp, 1972.

Craig Decker

TALKING HEADS

I didn't say anything.
—Graham, "A Chip in the Sugar"

Talking Heads is a series of six monologues written by ALAN BENNETT for the BBC in 1987. Despite their uniform bleakness, the plays, filmed for television, were an immediate critical and popular success. The broadcasts attracted large viewing figures and much acclaim for the writer and performers; the scripts and audio- and videotapes have sold well ever since. Bennett repeated the winning formula in 1998, when six more monologues were written and broadcast as *Talking Heads 2*.

The original one-character plays all last about half an hour, are filmed with a static camera, and feature the characters speaking directly to the audience, narrating stories that illuminate their present state of stasis. All the characters endure quiet desperation, unaware of the full extent of their desperate loneliness and isolation. Ephemeral moments of extremely funny irony are invariably crushed by tragic pathos. Bennett himself plays the role of the series' sole male "talking head," Graham, in "A Chip in the Sugar." This middle-aged character speaks about his relationship with his mother, a relationship that seems too intimate. Graham feels threatened when Frank Turnbull, a former beau of his mother, arrives. Self-aggrandizing and criminally inclined, Turnbull pontificates witlessly about issues such as immigration and mental health. Faced with the outsider's rudeness and bigotry, Graham is weak, failing to intervene. His catchphrase is "I didn't say anything."

Maggie Smith plays Susan in "Bed Among the Lentils." Susan, a vicar's wife, is a recovering alcoholic. The monologue surprises, because Susan's bitterness is directed at an unlikely party—she resents the fact that her troubles are exploited by her pious husband, who uses them to preach a sort of Christian morality tale. Susan, when drinking, was exploited sexually by a young Asian shopkeeper, but she has no bitterness about these seedy encounters—she "loved every minute." In "A Lady of Letters"

Patricia Routledge plays Irene Ruddock, a prison-bound woman whose sole "real friend" is her pen, with which she writes meddling letters of trivial complaint and of serious allegation. Julia Walters plays the youngest "talking head," Lesley, a third-rate actress who is naïvely persuaded to perform in the nude for a cheap, tacky movie, all the while deluding herself that she embodies acting "professionalism." The financially devastated widow in "Soldiering On," Muriel, is played by Stephanie Cole.

The most remarkable monologue, and the one that features the most extraordinary performance, is "A Cream Cracker Under the Settee." The elderly Doris, played by Thora Hird (1911–2003), cannot admit awareness of her physical deterioration. She has injured herself by attempting to clean her house, having ignored advice to rest. The physical impairment is matched by Doris's emotional emptiness, caused by the death of her husband, Wilfred, and memories of her dead, prematurely born, only child. Immobilized by leg pain and mental anguish at the monologue's end, Doris receives an offer of assistance, but rejects it. The doom that will envelop Doris will arrive long before it will conquer Bennett's other, equally bereft "talking heads."

[See also England]

FURTHER READING

Bennett, Alan. The Complete Talking Heads. London: BBC Worldwide, 1998.

Bull, John. Stage Right: Crisis and Recovery in British Contemporary Mainstream Theatre. Basingstoke: Macmillan, 1994.

Kendle, Burton S. "Alan Bennett." In Contemporary Dramatists, ed. by K. A. Berry. 5th ed. London: St. James Press, 1993. 44–47.

O'Mealy, Joseph H. Alan Bennett: A Critical Introduction. New York: Routledge, 2001.

Wolfe, Peter. Understanding Alan Bennett. Columbia: Univ. of South Carolina Press, 1999.

Kevin De Ornellas

TALLY, TED (1952–)

If you overhear an audience's comments, inevitably you'll hear something that breaks your heart.

—Ted Tally, 1981

Ted Tally's theatrical writing is characterized by the ability to imagine absurd or surreal situations in which normative rules no longer apply. Born on April 9, 1952, in Winston-Salem, North Carolina, Tally studied acting as an undergraduate at Yale and playwriting at the Yale School of Drama, from which he graduated in 1974.

With his drama *Terra Nova*, Tally joined the cadre of promising playwrights who emerged from Yale during the 1970s. The play was first produced as a student production in the spring of 1977 and received its professional premiere at the Yale Repertory Theatre. Tally's tale of the existential questions surrounding the fate of Robert Falcon Scott's trek to the South Pole was drawn from the explorer's letters and journals. The race to the South Pole became, in Tally's hands, a journey through the mind of Scott, who made it to the pole only to discover that he had lost the competition to Norwegian Roald Amundsen. The doomed adventurer perished a short distance from a base camp during his return journey. Within a few years the play had received upwards of 100 productions around the world, although plans for a Broadway showing never materialized. When it was finally produced in New York in 1984, Tally received an Obie Award for playwriting, and the following year he was awarded a Guggenheim Fellowship.

Tally's subsequent work delineated the foibles, concerns, and longings of contemporary society. In *Hooters* (1978) two young men shed their false bravado and come of age in the course of sexual and philosophical encounters with two women in their mid-twenties. In *Coming Attractions* (1983) Tally presaged the increasing linkage between celebrity and crime in the story of a small-time bank robber who, with the help of a theatrical agent, becomes a cult hero as the "Halloween Killer." As the robber's fame begins to wane, he plots to kill Miss America. The work garnered Tally an Outer Critics' Circle Award for Best New American Play. Tally's ability to combine trenchant sociological observation with honest sentiment was showcased in *Little Footsteps* (1986), in which a yuppie couple at the frantic juncture of parenthood struggle with their own self-absorption. After their marriage is torn apart by the impending arrival of their child, they divorce, only to reconcile when Ben, the husband, sneaks back into their apartment during a christening celebration to recite prayers over his son in a renewed awareness of his Jewish heritage.

Tally has also worked inventively in shorter theatrical forms. A compilation of his sketches from the 1970s, *Silver Linings* (several of which had appeared in the 1978 OFF-BROADWAY review *Word of Mouth*), appeared in print in 1983. Tally then displayed his flair for adaptation with *Taxi from Hell*, a reworking of Bud Abbott and Lou Costello's "Who's on First?" routine, which appeared off-Broadway in *Urban Blight* (1988). After *The Gettysburg Sound Bite* (1989), his imagining of Abraham Lincoln in the grip of three contemporary political handlers, Tally turned his focus to screenwriting, a form in which he found great success, winning an Academy Award for his adaptation of *Silence of the Lambs*. In 1991 Tally said about this shift, "It's a chance to have a wider exposure, a wider audience and to be less subject to the whim of critics."

[See also United States]

PLAYS: *Night Mail and Other Sketches* (1977); *Terra Nova* (1977); *Hooters* (1978); *Word of Mouth* (1978); *Silver Linings* (review sketches from the 1970s); *Coming Attractions* (with music by Jack Feldman and lyrics by Feldman and Bruce Sussman, 1983); *Little Footsteps* (1986); *Taxi from Hell* (1988); *The Gettysburg Sound Bite* (1989)

FURTHER READING

Andreach, Robert J. "Tally's *Terra Nova*: From Historical Journals to Existential Journey." *Twentieth Century Literature* 35 (1989): 65–73.

Klaver, Elizabeth. "Coming Attractions: Theater and the Performance of Television." *Mosaic: A Journal for the Interdisciplinary Study of Literature* 28, no. 4 (December 1995): 111–127.

Louis Scheeder

TAMARA

Tamara, written by Canadian playwright JOHN KRIZANC, is a fictionalized account of an encounter between Italian poet and soldier GABRIELE D'ANNUNZIO and the Polish painter Tamara De Lempicka. First performed in Toronto in 1981, *Tamara* takes place between January 10 and 11, 1927, at D'Annunzio's country estate. The complex, almost operatic story lines follow each of the play's ten characters over the two-day period as they spy on and betray each other.

D'Annunzio has been placed under house arrest by Italian dictator Benito Mussolini. He has filled his home with a bizarre bevy of guests and servants in order to pass the time, including Aélis Mazoyer, head of household; Luisa Baccara, a pianist; Aldo Finzi, a Fascist policeman; Mario Pagnutti, the chauffeur; and Gian Francesco de Spiga, a composer. Each of the characters has very clear objectives in the play: Aélis, a lesbian, is trying to seduce Carlotta Barra, a dancer who is seeking a letter of recommendation from D'Annunzio. Aldo, a Jew, has been ordered to keep an eye on D'Annunzio's activities by Mussolini, but desperately wants to return to Rome and his former position in Il Duce's government. Mario is actually the son of the Duke of Milan and is in the house to convince D'Annunzio to escape Italy and fight on the side of the Communists.

Tamara is considered a form of ENVIRONMENTAL THEATER, and audience members attending a performance of the play are asked to choose a character to physically follow through the play. The theatrical space resembles a huge country mansion in order to provide the necessary space for the scenes. At intermission and at the end of the evening the spectators can meet and confer on what they have witnessed.

Though the play is performed mainly in a representational style, where the audience views the play as outside observers, there are presentational moments. The rules of the "game" are presented directly to the audience by Dante Fenzo, the valet and an ex-gondolier, and Finzi at the beginning of the evening's performance, as though the spectators are guests in the house. Participants must follow a number of strict rules, including never passing through closed doors and never being found without the passports that serve as programs and provide a copy of the guidelines they must follow. At the top of the second act Finzi discovers an audience member without a passport and takes her into the hallway to be interrogated.

Since audience members are chasing actors around a multileveled facility (the Park Avenue Armory in New York City, for example), anything can happen to make the event seem very "intimate." Productions of *Tamara* allow audience members the opportunity to see what is often only intimated in other plays—what is going on behind the scenes.

[*See also* Canada]

FURTHER READING

De Lempicka-Foxhall, Kizette, Baroness, and Charles Phillips. *Passion by Design: The Art and Times of Tamara De Lempicka.* New York: Abbeville Press, 1987.

Woodhouse, John. *Gabriele D'Annunzio: Defiant Archangel.* Oxford: Oxford Univ. Press, 2001.

Jamie Skidmore

TANAKA CHIKAO (1905–1995)

Tanaka Chikao was a Japanese SHINGEKI playwright. Three concerns run through his work: his deep fascination with Roman Catholicism, his quest to express Catholic theology in Japanese dramatic dialogue, and the sense of absurdity born of the realization that this might ultimately be impossible.

Tanaka's fascination with Catholicism originated in his upbringing in Nagasaki, JAPAN's most Christian city, and developed with his study of French literature at Keio University in Tokyo, where he matriculated in 1923. Of the French dramatic literature he studied, Tanaka was particularly impressed with the plays of Charles Vildrac. Tanaka attended the inaugural performances of the Tsukiji Little Theater (Tsukiji Shōgekijō) in 1924, but he identified more strongly with the vision of the playwright Kishida Kunio, who advocated a less theatrical, more spiritual kind of theater. Kishida was inspired by the devoutly Catholic French director JACQUES COPEAU, with whom he had studied in Paris in 1921–1922. Although Kishida never espoused Christianity, his plays, which focus on the inner workings of the human spirit, suggested to Tanaka a way to pursue his religious and existential questions through the medium of drama. Tanaka joined Kishida's Modern Theater Institute (Shingeki Kenkyūzho) in 1927; he was a regular contributor to *Playwriting* (*Gekisaku*) magazine, which Kishida established in 1932; and he joined Kishida's Literary Theater (Bungakuza) when it was founded in 1937. Tanaka's wife, the playwright Tanaka Sumie, and their children were baptized in 1952. He himself formally converted to Catholicism in 1989.

Tanaka's first contribution to *Playwriting* was an article on theatrical dialogue; and *Mother* (*Ofukuro*, 1933), his first play, was a one-act etude intended to illustrate his thoughts. The problem of how to communicate ideas through dramatic dialogue remained an abiding concern throughout Tanaka's life, and he authored two theoretical studies on the subject: *Logique du récit* (*Mono-iu jutsu*, 1949) and the two-volume *Introduction to* the *Theory of Dramatic Style* (*Gekiteki buntairon josetsu*, 1978). He taught at the Actors Theater Training School (Haiyūza Yōseijo) and at the Tōhō Academy (Tōhō Gakuen). SATOH MAKOTO was among his many students.

Tanaka's career as a dramatist began in earnest after World War II. Catholic themes were apparent from the outset, but Tanaka struggled to find a way to express these in a Japanese setting. His well-received 1953 play *Education* (*Kyōiku*) is set in France with a cast of French characters.

It was in THE HEAD OF MARY (*Maria no kubi*, 1959), a play about Catholic survivors of the atomic bombing of his native Nagasaki, that Tanaka finally found a way to make his theology credible in a Japanese context. The play is widely regarded as his finest work. Even after his death in 1995, however, his widow continued to complain that the Christian dimension of the play had never been understood in Japan.

The sense of absurdity that characterizes many of Tanaka's works comes, in part at least, from his sense of the incommensurability of Christian ideas and Japanese language and culture. Tanaka studied *kyōgen* and used its techniques in plays such as *Arai Hakuseki* (1968) to convert his sense of futility to humor.

[See also Nō and Kyōgen]

SELECT PLAYS: *Mother* (*Ofukuro*, 1933); *The Limit of the Clouds* (*Kumo no hatate*, 1947); *Education* (*Kyōiku*, 1953); *Tales of Hizen* (*Hizen fudoki*, 1956); *The Head of Mary* (*Maria no kubi*, 1959); *Chidori* (1960); *Arai Hakuseki* (1968); *The Prison Diary of Yaoya Oshichi* (*Yaoya Oshichi hitoya nikki*, 1974)

FURTHER READING

Hayashi Hirochika. "Tanaka Chikao *Maria no Kubi*" [Tanaka Chikao's Head of Mary]. In *Nijusseiki no gikyoku II: Gendai gikyoku no tenkai* [Twentieth-century plays II: The development of contemporary (Japanese) playwriting], ed. by Nihon Kindai Engekishi Kenkyūkai. Tokyo: Shakai Hyōronsha, 2002.

Rimer, J. Thomas. "Four Plays by Tanaka Chikao." *Monumenta Nipponica* 31, no. 3 (1976).

Tanaka Chikao. *The Head of Mary*. Tr. by David G. Goodman. In *After Apocalypse: Four Japanese Plays of Hiroshima and Nagasaki*. Cornell East Asia Papers 71. Ithaca, N.Y: Cornell East Asia Program, 1994.

Wetmore, Kevin J. "The Cross and the Bomb: Two Catholic Dramas in Response to Nagasaki." *Journal of Religion and Theatre* 1, no. 1 (Fall 2002). http://www.fa.mtu.edu/~dlbruch/rtjournal/vol_1/no_1/wetmore.html.

David G. Goodman

TANVIR, HABIB (1923–)

Director, playwright, and poet Habib Tanvir (born on September 1, 1923, in Raipur [Chhattisgarh], INDIA) is perhaps the most popular and revered figure of contemporary Indian theater. He moved to Bombay in 1943 to explore a career in films. In Bombay he became associated with the left-wing cultural movement committed to the cause of a radical and egalitarian rearrangement of society. Tanvir became an active member of the organizations that spearheaded that movement—Indian People's Theatre Association and the Progressive Writers' Association.

Moving to Delhi in 1954, Tanvir began his career in theater. He worked with a repertory theater group called Hindustani Theatre and had his first major success with AGRA BAZAAR (1954). In 1956 he went to ENGLAND to study theater at the Royal Academy of Dramatic Arts and the Bristol Old Vic. He traveled extensively throughout Europe. In Berlin he saw several of BERTOLT BRECHT's productions, which had a lasting impact on him, further reinforcing his left-wing predilections and enhancing his understanding of the social and political potential of theater. Returning to Delhi in 1958, he produced *The Clay Cart* (*Mitti ki Gadi*) (Shudraka's Sanskrit classic in Hindi) for Hindustani Theatre. A year later he married the actress Monica Mishra, and together they founded a professional company called Naya Theatre, which is distinguished from other professional theater groups by its cast of more or less illiterate but remarkably skillful village actors.

Disregarding the dominant practice of imitating European models of theater, Tanvir started a long quest for a distinctly indigenous performance idiom. His theater incisively blends tradition and modernity, folk creativity and skills with a modern critical consciousness. It is this rich blend that makes his work important and memorable. His actors have their background in the traditional Chhattisgarhi dramatic form called *nacha* and bring with them its energy and skills. Nonetheless, Tanvir's plays are not *nacha* productions. A *nacha* performance, which usually lasts through the night, is an improvisatory and arbitrary string of a variety of short and discrete pieces of entertainment interspersed with song and dance sequences. Tanvir's plays, on the other hand, are thematically and structurally coherent and complex. The songs and dances he employs are integral to the fabric of the action and, in a style reminiscent of Brecht, function as an important element in the play's overall argument. Fully alert to the historical and cognitive limitations of folk forms, Tanvir allows his own modern consciousness and political understanding to interact with the traditional energies and skills of his performers. His project, from the beginning, has been to harness elements of the folk traditions as a vehicle and make them yield new, contemporary meanings in order to produce a theater that has a distinctly Indian flavor. In fact, his excellent adaptations of THE GOOD WOMAN OF SETZUAN (*Shaajapur ki Shantibai*, 1978) and *A Midsummer Night's Dream* (*Kamdeo ka Apna, Basant Ritu ka Sapna*, 1993) would not be possible without this rich and creative fusion of modern consciousness and traditional Indian performance styles and rhythms. In these plays he has worked close to the original text and has written songs that reproduce the rich imagery and humor of William Shakespeare's poetry and the complex ideas of Brecht. However, he took meticulous care to fit his words to traditional folk tunes of Chhattisgarh.

Tanvir included some Chhattisgarhi folk performers in the cast of *The Clay Cart*, but by the early 1970s his interest in these artists and in their traditional form *nacha* had led to a sustained involvement with them. Two significant productions came out of this involvement: a delightful farcical COMEDY called *Gaon ka Naam Sasural, Mor Naam Damad* (which literally translates as "The Village Named In-Laws' Place, My Name Son-in-Law"), which was improvised by dovetailing three distinct *nacha* skits; and his famous masterpiece, CHARANDAS THE THIEF (*Charandas Chor*). Ever since then, although he has occasionally worked with urban groups, his main work has been with the Naya Theatre and the folk artists with whom he has staged a rich variety of memorable productions, from traditional tales, Sanskrit classics, and contemporary Indian plays to adaptations of Molière, Shakespeare, Brecht, and Stefan Zweig.

Given the huge economic and social chasm that divides the urban and the rural parts of India, the attitude of the powerful urban elite to the traditional cultural forms of the disadvantaged villagers tends to be exploitative or, at best, patronizing. However, Tanvir's approach to folk culture is neither. He takes special care not to privilege his own educated consciousness over the creativity of his unschooled actors (in fact, he eschews elaborate production values in order to highlight the work of the performers). In his work the two usually meet and interpenetrate as equal partners in a collaborative endeavor. For example, Tanvir blends his poetry and all its complex thought content with the traditional folk and tribal music, allowing the former to retain its own imaginative and rhetorical power and complexity, but without in any way devaluing or destroying the latter. Every major production of his goes through a protracted and painstaking process of joint explorations, experimentations, and improvisations before it reaches the public.

SELECT PLAYS: *Chess Pieces* (*Shatranj ke Mohre*, adaptation of a short story by Munshi Premchand, 1951); *Agra Bazar* (1954); *After Me* (*Mere Baad*, 1968); *The Village Named In-Laws' Place, My name Son-in-Law* (*Gaon ka Nao Sasural, Mor Nao Damaad*, 1972); *Charandas the Thief* (*Charandas Chor*, 1974–1975); *Kalarin the Courageous* (*Bahadur Kalarin*, 1977–1978); *Shantibai of Shajapur* (*Shajapur ki Shantibai*, adaptation of Bertolt Brecht's *The Good Woman of Setzuan*, 1978); *Sone Sagar* (1979); *Lala Shohratrai* (adaptation of Moliere's *Le Bourgeois Gentlehome*, 1981); *The Immortal Tale of Hirma* (*Hirma ki Amar Kahani*, 1986); *Kamdoe ka Apna, Basant Ritu ka Sapna* (adaptation of William Shakespeare's *A Midsummer Night's Dream*, 1993); *The Road* (*Sadak*, 1994); *A Woman Called Hypatia* (*Ek Aurat Hypatia Bhi Thi*, 1999); *The Royal Blood* (*Rajrakt*, adaptation of Rabindranath Tagore's works, 2006)

FURTHER READING

Irvin, Polly, ed. *Directing for the Stage*. Brighton: RotoVision, 2003.

Malick, Javed. "Habib Tanvir: The Making of a Legend." *Theatre India* 2 (November 2000): 93–102.

Rea, Kenneth. "Theatre in India: The Old and the New." Pts. 3 and 4. *Theatre Quarterly* 8, no. 32 (1978): 47–66; 9, no. 34 (1979): 53–65.

Tanvir, Habib. "An Interview with Reeta Sondhi." In *Contemporary Indian Theatre*. Delhi: Sangeet Natak Akademi, 1989.

——. " 'It Must Flow'—A Life in Theatre." *Seagull Theatre Quarterly* 10 (June 1996): 3–38.

——. "My Milestones in Theatre: Habib Tanvir in Conversation." In *Charandas Chor*. Calcutta: Seagull Books, 1996.

Javed Malick

TARDIEU, JEAN (1903–1995)

A poet, art critic, and dramatist, Jean Tardieu targeted the arts, society, and language itself in his playful sketches. Many of them can be viewed as either poetry or drama, and he emphasized their ambiguity with titles such as *A Voice Without Anyone* (*Une voix sans personne*) or *Poems to be Played* (*Poèmes à jouer*).

Born on November 1, 1903, in Saint-Germain-de-Joux, FRANCE, Tardieu began writing poetry before he was ten years of age, and he wrote a one-act verse play in Molière's style at fifteen. At the age of seventeen, however, Tardieu suffered a mental breakdown he later described as severing him psychologically from the rest of the world. Although he went on to have a distinguished public career in literature and radio broadcasting, he avoided writing about the giant political issues that marked 20th-century France. Instead, he mischievously investigated everyday behavior, as though describing bourgeois life on a planet where he did not live. Tardieu died in Créteil on January 27, 1995.

His most famous play is the one-act COMEDY *One Word for Another* (*Un mot pour un autre*, 1950). The play purports to show a linguistic epidemic that struck the "fortunate classes" in the great cities of France about 1900. Because of this plague, middle-class citizens arbitrarily substitute one word for another in their conversations without any awareness that they are speaking nonsense. The dramatic situations in the play are so conventional, however, that the audience understands every word. The maid begins by announcing, "The postern has just eliminated the fodder" instead of "The postman has just delivered the mail." The lady of the house responds, "You may drain" rather than "You may go." When confronted by the women he is betraying, the leading man shouts, "But this is perspiration!" instead of "But this is a conspiracy!" As the linguistic substitutions build, the lines come close in spirit to the cinematic babble of Groucho Marx.

In *The Sonata and the Three Gentlemen; or, How to Talk Music* (*La sonate et les trois messieurs, ou, Comment parler musique*, 1959), three gentlemen share banalities about a piece of classical music they have just heard. They repeat, interrupt, prolong, and double each other's phrases. As their conversation continues, changing tempo and volume, it re-creates the effects of the music they are describing. The sketch mocks the middlebrow trio, because these amateur critics are less original then they think, but it also ennobles them, because the result of their exchange is more beautiful than they know.

Tardieu wrote no single dramatic work of standard length. Although his insistence on the hollowness of everyday language has inspired comparisons with SAMUEL BECKETT and EUGÈNE IONESCO, his work, unlike theirs, is cheerful. Tardieu's cultivation allows him to poke fun at the middle classes, the audience most likely to appreciate his humor, and at those, like himself, who make their living as teachers. In this, his theater participates in the French aesthetic subgenre of mock pedagogy—one to which composers such as Claude Debussy (in *Doctor Gradus ad Parnassum*, 1908) and Maurice Ravel (in *L'enfant et les sortilèges*, 1925) and writers such as GUILLAUME APOLLINAIRE (in *Le bestiaire*, 1911) and Raymond Queneau (in *Exercices de style*, 1947) have all made contributions with the same playful virtuosity as Tardieu.

SELECT PLAYS: *Who Goes There? (Qui est là?, 1949); One Word for Another (Un mot pour un autre, 1950); Subway Lovers (Les amants du métro, 1952); A Voice Without Anyone (Une voix sans personne, 1956); The Alphabet of Our Life (L'A.B.C. de notre vie, 1959); The Sonata and the Three Gentlemen; or, How to Talk Music (La sonate et les trois messieurs, ou, Comment parler musique, 1959); Three People Who Entered Paintings (Trois personnes entrées dans des tableaux, published 1969); An Evening in Provence; or, The Word and the Outcry (Une soirée en Provence, ou, Le Mot et le cri, 1976)*

FURTHER READING

Debreuille, Jean-Yves, et al., eds. *Oeuvres de Tardieu* [Tardieu's works]. Paris: Gallimard, 2003. [In addition to Tardieu's works, contains letters, interviews, photographs, and criticism by prominent literary critics.]

Esslin, Martin. *The Theatre of the Absurd.* Garden City, N.Y.: Anchor Bks., 1969.

Noulet, Émilie. *Jean Tardieu.* Paris: Seghers, 1964.

Pronko, Leonard Cabell. *Avant-Garde: The Experimental Theater in France.* Berkeley: Univ. of California Press, 1962.

Tardieu, Jean. *Oeuvres* [Works]. Ed. by Jean-Yves Debreuille. With Alix Turolla–Tardieu and Delphine Hautois. Paris: Gallimard, 2003.

David Pelizzari

TAYLOR, DREW HAYDEN (1962–)

Drew Hayden Taylor (born in Curve Lake First Nations, Ontario, CANADA, in 1962), an Ojibway writer, film director, and journalist, is, next to TOMSON HIGHWAY, one of the most successful Native playwrights in Canada today. After graduating from Seneca College with an honors diploma in radio and television broadcasting, he began his theater career in 1988 as playwright-in-residence for Native Earth Performing Arts in Toronto, for which he also served as artistic director from 1994 to 1997. Ever since his first play, *Toronto at Dreamer's Rock* (1989), which won him the the Chalmers Canadian Play Award in 1992, Taylor has been a leading voice not only in the Native North American arts scene, but in theater worldwide, with more than sixty-five professional productions on a global scale.

While many minorities use theater for a therapeutic reenactment of oppression and trauma, using pungent, violent imagery to create an awareness of political injustice, the hallmark of Drew Hayden Taylor's dramatic work is the use of humor. Often referred to as the "NEIL SIMON of Native Theatre," Taylor counterbalances colonial experience and stereotypes with witty dialogues "to show that we all weren't oppressed, depressed, or suppressed." At the same time, his COMEDIES never fail to go beneath the surface, probing into themes of Native IDENTITY, family, community, and intercultural dialogue. This combination is best illustrated by the "Blues Quartet," a series consisting of *The Bootlegger Blues* (1990; honored in 1992 with the Canadian Authors' Association Literary Award for Best Drama), THE BABY BLUES (1995), and *The Buz'Gem Blues* (2001), with another sequel to be published.

Besides comedies, Taylor's storytelling on stage includes a wide variety of themes and genres, ranging from kitchen-sink drama to experimentalism. In addition to his plays for young audiences (*The Boy in the Tree House* or *Girl Who Loved Her Horses*), he also uses the stage for sensitive political discussions, as in *Education Is Our Right* (1990) or his trilogy on forced adoption (*Someday*, 1991; *Only Drunks and Children Tell the Truth*, which won the Dora Mavor Moore Award in 1996; and *400 Kilometres*, 1999).

With *AlterNatives*, as in all of his plays, negotiations of identity are interlinked with a consistent questioning of power mechanisms and injustice, regardless of hierarchies, political correctness, or ethnic background. Aiming at universal human understanding across cultural differences, Taylor frequently mocks essentialism and replaces rigid categories of authenticity with irony and playful self-definition: "I've often tried to be philosophical about the whole thing. I have both white and red blood in me: I guess that makes me pink." His skillful interweaving of specific political issues with universal values into dramatic celebrations of tolerance and respect gained him the James Buller Award for Best Playwright in 1997.

In addition to theater, Taylor's versatility extends into popular collections of essays (*Funny, You Don't Look Like One: Observations of a Blue-Eyed Ojibway I–IV* (1998, 1999, 2002, 2004), short stories (*Fearless Warriors*, 1998), film documentaries (*Redskins, Tricksters and Puppy Stew*, 2000), and well-known television productions such as *The Beachcombers* or *North of Sixty*. Drew Hayden Taylor currently lives in Toronto.

SELECT PLAYS: *Toronto at Dreamer's Rock (1989); The Bootlegger Blues (1990); Education Is Our Right (1990); Pictures on the Wall (1990); Someday (1991); A Contemporary Gothic Indian Vampire Story (1992); The All Complete Aboriginal Show Extravaganza (1994); The Baby Blues (1995); Girl Who Loved Her Horses (1995); Only Drunks and Children Tell the Truth (1996); AlterNatives (1998); 400 Kilometres (1999); Toronto@ Dreamer's Rock.com (1999); The Boy in the Tree House (2000); The Buz'Gem Blues (2001); Sucker Falls: A Musical About the Forest and the Demons of the Soul (2002); Raven Stole the Sun (2004)*

FURTHER READING

Däwes, Birgit. "An Interview with Drew Hayden Taylor." *Contemporary Literature* 44, no. 1 (Spring 2003): 1–18.

Geiogamah, Hanay, and Jaye T. Darby, eds. *American Indian Theater in Performance: A Reader.* Los Angeles: UCLA American Indian Studies Center, 2000.

Glaap, Albert-Reiner. "Drew Hayden Taylor's Dramatic Career." In *Siting the Other: Re-visions of Marginality in Australian and English-Canadian Drama,* ed. by Marc Maufort and Franca Bellarsi. Brussels: P. Lang, 2001. 217–232.

Nunn, Robert. "Drew Hayden Taylor's AlterNatives: Dishing the Dirt." In *Crucible of Cultures: Anglophone Drama at the Dawn of the New Millennium,* ed. by Marc Maufort and Franca Bellarsi. Dramaturgies 4. Brussels: P. Lang, 2002. 209–217.

——, ed. *Drew Hayden Taylor: Essays on His Works.* Toronto: Guernica, 2005.

Taylor, Drew Hayden. "Storytelling to Stage: The Growth of Native Theatre in Canada." *Drama Review* 41, no. 3 (Fall 1997): 140–152.

Birgit Däwes

TAYLOR, THOMAS (1817–1880)

Born at Bishop-Wearmouth, a suburb of Sunderland, ENGLAND, on October 19, 1817, Thomas Taylor was a son of a successful brewer and a mother with a keen wit. After attending the Grange in Sunderland, Taylor entered Trinity College in 1837, where he received a bachelor of arts degree in 1840, with honors in the classics and mathematics, followed by a fellowship and eventually a master's degree. From 1845 to 1847 Taylor left Trinity to become a professor of English at London University College. He studied law at the Inner Temple and then served in various positions on the Board of Health. He retired from public service in 1871 and spent the remainder of his life in his already-flourishing literary career.

Taylor was always active in England's literary scene. He was involved in writing articles for various magazines and newspapers from the very beginning and served as the editor of *Punch* from 1874 to 1880. His criticism on art and drama earned him much popularity, but his dramas brought him greater fame and money. In the thirty-five years of Taylor's writing career, he produced over seventy plays. He also served as editor for the autobiographies of B. R. Haydon and C. R. Leslie and for Mortimer Collins's posthumous *Pen Sketches.* Some contemporary critics accused Taylor of lowering his literary standards to please popular demand of the day. The taste of his audience seemed to affect what and how Taylor wrote.

Many of Taylor's dramas were adaptations of plots from other sources, which fact earned him a small reputation for plagiarism and unoriginality. Taylor often turned to French stories for his dramas, as in THE TICKET-OF-LEAVE MAN (1863). He also adapted novels such as *Uncle Tom's Cabin* (1852) and *A Tale of Two Cities* (1860) for stage performance. In addition to his continual borrowing of plots, Taylor often worked in collaboration with other writers and actors to write dramas. This allowed Taylor to fit the characters in his plays to certain actors, but also led to strained work relationships. He most enjoyed working on historical plays such as *Joan of Arc* (1871) or *Anne Boleyn* (1876). Taylor's play *Our American Cousin* was the performance Abraham Lincoln attended the night he was assassinated. Tom Taylor died on July 12, 1880, in Lavender Sweep, Wandsworth, England.

Since his day Taylor's works have dropped in popularity. Actor and drama critic Wayne Turney writes, "Fifty years after his death, Taylor's output was excoriated as representative of the worst defects of mid–Nineteenth Century British playwriting," demonstrating the ever-changing expectations of a writer's audience. Today there is still little interest in Taylor and his prolific playwriting career.

SELECT PLAYS: *Diogenes and His Lantern* (1849); *Philosopher's Stone* (1850); *The Vicar of Wakefield* (1850); *Masks and Faces* (1852); *Uncle Tom's Cabin* (1852); *The King's Rival* (1854); *Two Loves and a Life* (1854); *Still Waters Run Deep* (1855); *The Contested Election* (1859); *The Overland Route* (1860); *A Tale of Two Cities* (1860); *Our American Cousin* (1861); *The Ticket-of-Leave Man* (1863); *New Men and Old Acres* (1869); *Joan of Arc* (1871); *Anne Boleyn* (1876)

FURTHER READING

Granville-Barker, Harley, ed. *The Eighteen-Seventies.* Great Neck, N.Y.: Core Collection Bks., 1978.

Moses, Montrose, ed. *Representative British Dramas: Victorian and Modern.* Boston: Little, Brown, 1925.

Turner, Paul. *Victorian Poetry, Drama, and Miscellaneous Prose, 1832–1890.* Oxford: Oxford Univ. Press, 1990.

Chad Lawrence McLane

TEATRO ABIERTO   *See* OPEN THEATER

TEATRO BUFO   *See* BUFO THEATER

TEATRO DE ARENA DE SÃO PAULO   *See* ARENA THEATER OF SÃO PAULO

TENDULKAR, VIJAY (1928–)

As a writer I feel fascinated by the violent exploiter-exploited relationship, and [I] obsessively delve deep in to it instead of taking a position against it. That takes me to a point where I feel that this relationship is eternal, a fact of life however cruel, and will never end.

—Vijay Tendulkar, 1992

Vijay Dhondopant Tendulkar is one of the founders of modern Marathi and Indian theater. He has also been an accomplished journalist, novelist, translator, and filmscript and short-story writer. He has twenty-eight plays, twenty-four one-act plays, eleven children's plays, seventeen filmscripts, one novel and many short stories, and several translated plays to his credit. He wrote his first short story at the age of six and his first play at the age of eleven. He was born on January 7, 1928, in a lower-middle-class family in Mumbai Maharashtra, INDIA; his formal education came to an end when he joined the Quit India movement and left school in answer to Mahatma Gandhi's call to boycott schools.

Tendulkar's plays signified a break from three dominant traditions of the then-contemporary Marathi theater: Sangeet Rangabhumi (a music–drama popular from 1890 to 1930 based on mythological and folk stories in which classical, semi–classical, and folk music is blended with acting), the politically motivated Indian People's Theatre Association (IPTA) theater, and the commercial popular drawing-room drama. His plays deal mainly with unequal power relations between people and the violence dished out to the powerless by the powerful. Tendulkar's early plays, The Householder (Grihastha, 1955), An Island Called Man (Manus Nawache Bet, 1958), I Won, I Lost (Mi Jinklo, Mi Harlo, 1963), and Crows' School (Kavlyanchi Shala, 1963), deal with the alienation of sensitive lower-middle-class individuals in an increasingly urbanized and industrialized society. At the same time he was experimenting with humorous satirical political plays such as Encounter in Umbugland (Dambadweepcha Mukabla, 1968).

However, his first major play, Silence! The Court Is in Session (Shantata! Court Chalu Ahe, 1968), sent shock waves in Marathi society. The play takes the form of a mock trial in which an unmarried schoolteacher is persecuted by her middle-class friends and colleagues because she has dared to assert her individualism and challenge the moral dictates of a patriarchal society by getting pregnant before marriage. The play attacks hypocritical patriarchal attitudes toward women that glorify motherhood only when it carries the stamp of male "legitimacy," and it exposes the double standards of a rigid community. Moreover, the play dramatizes the hierarchy of power in the institution of family, and the fierce psychological violence that people are capable of.

With his next play, SAKHARAM BINDER (1972), Tendulkar challenges the superiority of Brahmin males and the sexual and moral codes of the middle class. In fact, Tendulkar challenged conventional wisdom so much that the play was banned by the Censor Board (a remnant of the Dramatic Performances Act of 1876, which empowered the government to prohibit dramatic performances that were "scandalous, defamatory, seditious, obscene or otherwise prejudicial to the public interest"). Sakharam is a crude, violent, yet honest Brahmin who eschews traditional marriage in favor of contractual cohabitation with a single woman who agrees to be sexually, morally, and ethically subservient in exchange for food, clothing, and shelter: a replica of traditional marriage shorn of its romantic trappings. The play reveals the institution of marriage as a form of sexual, moral, and religious depravity.

With GHASHIRAM KOTWAL (1972), the most provocative and innovative theater text of its time, Tendulkar scaled new heights of creativity and controversy. Ghashiram presents a unique blend of history, politics, and myth. Tendulkar integrates a gruesome story of political intrigue with popular entertainment, music, and dance.

The Vultures (Gidhade, 1974, which was originally written before Silence!), is a departure from the NATURALISM of Silence! It shows the violent disintegration of an urban family as one defenseless woman and her equally defenseless illegitimate brother-in-law struggle against a pack of middle-class vultures in their unending quest for power and property. The Vultures exposes the violence, avarice, and sexual degradation of the middle class and evoked strong reactions not only among more conventional theatergoers, but from the Censor Board.

Tendulkar's later plays explored the same themes in different domains. Kamala (1981) was based on a real-life media story in which a journalist actually bought a village girl from a flesh market and presented her at a press conference. Written in a naturalistic mode, the play presents the story of journalist Jaising Jadhav, outwardly committed to humanistic values, but inwardly committed to market values of sales, advertising, self-promotion, and profiteering. He buys a tribal woman in a sale and presents her in a press conference to expose the vacuity of the government's claims to egalitarian policies and development of underprivileged people, especially women. Of course, his real intention is to get a promotion; he does not care what will happen to the woman. Kamala exposes the ruthless power politics of the media and journalism's exploitation, violence, and complete indifference to the suffering of others, but it also demonstrates how a woman is treated as an object of possession, sale, enjoyment, and domestic comfort.

A Friend's Story (Mitrachi Goshta, 1982) is the first play on an Indian stage to explore issues encountered by lesbian women. It presents the sensitive story of a lesbian girl and her relationship to the girl she loves and the boy who is her friend. The play has evoked intense reactions from people for whom the subject is taboo, and from feminists who believe that Tendulkar has projected a stereotypical image of lesbians.

Tendulkar's most recent significant play is Gift of a Daughter (Kanyadaan, 1983), in which he exposes the romantic myths of intercaste marriage in a caste-ridden society. In Gift of a Daughter an upper-caste Brahmin girl from a so-called progressive family marries a young Dalit man, only to discover that there is a world of difference between them. The marriage becomes a battleground of caste ideologies, and the girl suffers terrible violence, as if to atone for violence done to the Dalits. This play dramatizes the intellectual confusion of a casteist society.

Tendulkar's powerful characterization, his precise, economical, and intense dialogues, the extremely well-knit structure of his plays, and his formal experimentation are unique in the history of modern Indian theater. He is one of the most controversial figures of his time, and his dramatic genius has given a new direction not only to the Marathi stage but Indian theater as well.

SELECT PLAYS: *The Householder (Grihastha,* 1955); *An Island Called Man (Manus Nawache Bet,* 1958); *Crows' School (Kavlyanchi Shala,* 1963); *I Won, I Lost (Mi Jinklo, Mi Harlo,* 1963); *Encounter in Umbugland (Dambadweepcha Mukabla,* 1968); *Silence! The Court is in Session (Shantata! Court Chalu Ahe,* 1968); *Ghashiram Kotwal* (1972); *Sakharam Binder* (1972); *The Vultures (Gidhade,* 1974); *Kamala* (1981); *A Friend's Story (Mitrachi Goshta,* 1982); *Gift of a Daughter (Kanyadaan,* 1983)

FURTHER READING

Gokhale, Shanta. *Playwright at the Centre: Marathi Drama from 1843 to the Present.* Calcutta: Seagull, 2000.

Tendulkar, Vijay. *Collected Plays in Translation.* New Delhi: Oxford Univ. Press, 2003.

——. *Ghashiram Kotwal.* Tr. by Jayant Karve and Eleanor Zelliot. Calcutta: Seagull, 2002.

——. *Vijay Tendulkar.* New Delhi: Katha, 2001.

Maya Pandit

TERAYAMA SHŪJI (1935–1983)

A Japanese experimental playwright, poet, director, filmmaker, photographer, novelist, memoirist, and cultural critic, Terayama Shūji has been called by many scholars the most significant Japanese dramatist and poet of his generation.

His influences included the Comte de Lautreamont, Georges Bataille, ANTONIN ARTAUD, and IZUMI KYŌKA. Though he died at forty-seven, Terayama produced at least forty-six plays, nineteen films, ten radio dramas, four teleplays, and a yearlong pseudodocumentary radio series. He and his troupe the Peanut Gallery (Tenjō Sajiki, inspired by Marcel Carné's film *Children of Paradise,* where "paradise" refers to the cheapest balcony seats) garnered prestigious film and theater awards. Nevertheless, he was accused of creating pornography (*Directions to Servants* [*Nuhikun,* 1979]), advocating student rebellion (book, play, and film *Throw Away Your Books, Go Out Into the Streets* [*Sho–o suteyō, machi e deyō,* 1967]), and inciting children to murder adults (radio play *Adult Hunting* [*Otona–gari,* 1960] and film *The Emperor Tomato Catsup* [*Tomato kechappu kōtei,* 1970]).

Terayama's style is theatricalist and antirealistic. Early works, THE HUNCHBACK OF AOMORI (*Aomori–ken no semushi otoko,* 1967), *Inugami: The Dog God* (*Inugami,* 1969), and the film *Cache-Cache Pastoral* (*Den'en ni shisu,* 1974), are surreal, poetic, nostalgic, often cruel evocations of childhood in remote, northeastern Aomori. Semiautobiographical elements include rural superstitions, shamanism, mystical Buddhist rituals, blind female mediums, itinerant circus performers, abandoned children, his father's death in World War II, and, most important, his love-hate relationship with his possessive, seductive mother. Images of mother-son incest and matricide abound.

Although not overtly political, Terayama's works display ambivalence toward American dominance and JAPAN's loss of national identity after World War II. His first play, *Blood Is Standing Asleep (Chi wa tatta mama nemutte iru,* 1960), features a gang of teenage anarchists, JAZZ, suicide, and rape-turned-to-love. *The Hunchback of Aomori* transforms the tale of Oedipus into a metaphor for Japan's cultural rape by America. *La Marie-Vison (Kegawa no Marī,* 1967; revised 1970), a bizarre COMEDY about a male transvestite "mother" obsessed with Hollywood, blasphemes Christianity. *We're All Riding on a Circus Elephant (Jidai wa sākasu no zō ni notte,* 1969) lampoons American cultural icons, movies, and sports while warning against a headlong race toward worldwide catastrophe.

Heretics (Jashūmon, 1971) depicts toxic, incestuous families featuring helpless sons, suffocating mothers, hypocritical virgins, and seductive, castrating, even murderous prostitutes. Characters from Japanese folktales or popular culture fruitlessly seek meaning and identity. At the conclusion the actors break out of character, destroy the set, and exhort the audience to transform reality with imagination. In *Heretics* and other plays (*The Crime of Dr. Galigari* [*Garigari hakase no hanzai,* 1969]; *The Origin of the Blood of a Certain Family* [*Aru kazoku no chi no kigen,* 1973]; *A Journal of the Plague Year* [*Ekibyō ryūkōki,* 1975]); terrified audience members were plunged into total darkness, forcibly separated into tiny, curtained rooms, or carried off to become slaves on stage. In Europe *Heretics* caused hysteria, fistfights, and police intervention.

By the mid-1970s Terayama had rejected lyrical poetry and written scripts. He created citywide "town dramas" featuring chance encounters, improvisation, and spectacles such as burning airplanes (*Man-Powered Plane Solomon* [*Jinriki hikōki Soromon,* 1970]; *Knock* [*Nokku*], co-written with KISHIDA RIO, 1975). His book *The Labyrinth and the Dead Sea: My Theatre* (*Meiro to Shikai: Waga engeki,* 1976) justified his artistic tactics.

[See also Shingeki]

SELECT PLAYS: *Blood Is Standing Asleep (Chi wa tatta mama nemutte iru,* 1960); *The Crime of Miss Fatty Oyama (Ōyama Debuko no hanzai,* 1967); *The Hunchback of Aomori (Aomori-ken no semushi otoko,* 1967); *La Marie-Vison (Kegawa no Marī,* also known as *Mink Marie* or *Maria in Furs,* 1967); *Throw Away Your Books, Go Out Into the Streets (Sho–o suteyō, machi e deyō,* 1967); *The Crime of Dr. Galigari (Garigari hakase no hanzai,* 1969); *Inugami: The Dog God (Inugami,* 1969); *We're All Riding on a Circus Elephant (Jidai wa sākasu no zō ni notte,* 1969); *Man-Powered Plane Solomon (Jinriki hikōki Soromon,* 1970); *Heretics (Jashūmon,* 1971); *Run, Melos (Hashire Merosu,* 1971); *Opium War (Ahen sensō,* 1972); *Blind Man's Letter (Mōjin shokan,* 1973); *The Origin of the Blood of a Certain Family (Aru kazoku no chi no kigen,* 1973); *A Journal of the Plague Year (Ekibyō ryūkōki,* 1975); *Knock (Nokku,* co-written with Kishida Rio, 1975); *Shintokumaru: Poison Boy (Shintokumaru,* co-written with Kishida Rio, 1978); *Bluebeard's Castle (Aohigekō no shiro,* 1979); *Directions to Servants (Nuhikun,* 1979); *Lemmings (Remingu,* 1979; variant version, 1982); *One Hundred Years of Solitude (Hyakunen no kodoku,* 1981)

FURTHER READING

Rolf, Robert T., and John K. Gillespie, trs. and eds. *Alternative Japanese Drama: Ten Plays*. Honolulu: Univ. of Hawaii Press, 1992.

Senda, Akihiko. *The Voyage of Contemporary Japanese Theatre*. Tr. by J. Thomas Rimer. Honolulu: Univ. of Hawaii Press, 1997.

Sorgenfrei, Carol Fisher. *Unspeakable Acts: The Avant-Garde Theatre of Terayama Shūji and Postwar Japan*. Honolulu: Univ. of Hawaii Press, 2005.

Terayama Shūji. *Inugami: The Dog God*. Tr. by Carol Fisher Sorgenfrei. *Asian Theatre Journal* 11, no. 2 (1994): 163–190.

——. *La Marie-Vison* [*Kegawa no Marī*]. Tr. by Carol Fisher Sorgenfrei. In *Half a Century of Japanese Theatre*, vol. 6, ed. by Japan Playwrights Association. Tokyo: Kinokuniya, 2004.

——. *Terayama Shūji no gikyoku* [Collected plays of Terayama Shūji]. 9 vols. Tokyo: Shichōsha, 1969–1987.

Carol Fisher Sorgenfrei

THE TERRIBLE BUT UNFINISHED STORY OF NORODOM SIHANOUK, KING OF CAMBODIA

When *The Terrible but Unfinished Story of Norodom Sihanouk, King of Cambodia* (*L'histoire terrible mais inachevée de Norodom sihanouk, roi du Cambodige*) opened in September 1985 after months of preparation, HÉLÈNE CIXOUS's two-part, eight-hour epic was the first wholly new play (not an adaptation) by a single author the Théâtre du Soleil had done since its arrival at the Cartoucherie fifteen years earlier. Cixous, who taught William Shakespeare at the University of Paris, had already helped ARIANE MNOUCHKINE's troupe with its Asian-influenced Shakespeare cycle. Now she applied the same dramaturgical tools to a gory chapter of modern history. The hero of the play, following in the footsteps of Shakespeare's Richard II and Prince Hal, was Norodom Sihanouk, whose career as prince, king, and political leader in and out of exile traces CAMBODIA's fortunes and misfortunes from 1955 to 1979. Extensive research underlay every aspect of the production. The program contained six folio pages of notes and chronology in addition to the credits: twenty-four actors playing forty-four named characters, over seventy parts in all.

The first part is stately and diplomatic, though livened by the ghost of Sihanouk's father dressed as a temple deity. The second half chillingly recounts the horrors of the American bombing, the Khmer Rouge regime, and Cambodia's occupation by the Vietnamese. Each four-hour evening was broken by a Cambodian-style meal served in the Cartoucherie's lobby, redecorated with a giant map of Southeast Asia. The people of Cambodia seemed to be watching the action: 640 figurines surrounded the playing area, dressed as soldiers, monks, and peasants. Among the more than 100 musical instruments played by music director Jean-Jacques Lemetre and his assistant, Pierre Launay, was a special electroacoustic instrument called the "percuphone" designed to imitate the whine of a jet engine or the percussive sound of heli-

copter blades. Georges Bigot, as Sihanouk, soliloquized like a Cambodian Hamlet. To drive the point home, Cixous included explicit references to Shakespeare in the text. When Sihanouk and his minister, Penn Nouth, are gazing at the stars, Penn Nouth asks, "Which star is William Shakespeare, my Lord?" Later, when the pair is under house arrest by the Khmer Rouge, they play Hamlet's game of "very like a whale" (in English), with Khmer Rouge leader Khieu Samphan unwittingly taking Polonius's part. The two men use Hamlet's jibes to covertly affirm their intellectual independence in the face of Khmer Rouge lies about the suffering they see around them. Fervently idealistic and relentlessly self-controlling, the Khmer Rouge are smiling and affable, forever willing to break flesh on the wheel of ideology and swear that they are doing it out of love.

Cixous summarizes the five-year nightmare of their regime by showing two peasant women huddled over a candle rehearsing the Marxist slogans they will be required to recite at the next "political education meeting"—no guns, no barbed wire, just naked terror. The immense scale of the piece permitted interesting actor doubling. Andrés Pérez Araya's Zhou En Lai seemed to be an older and wiser version of the same actor's Khieu Samphan. Serge Poncelet brought contrasting styles of malevolence to the roles of Henry Kissinger and Pol Pot. Bigot's Sihanouk presented a complex mixture of vanity, insouciant humor, and outraged humanity. The play received productions in Germany in 1990 and North America in 2001.

[*See also* France]

FURTHER READING

Barret, Gisele, et al. "Hélène Cixous: Théâtre du Soleil." *Jeu* (Montreal) 39 (1986): 131–153. [Interview.]

Cixous, Hélène. *The Terrible but Unfinished Story of Norodom Sihanouk, King of Cambodia*. Tr. by Juliet Flower MacCannell, Judith Pike, and Lollie Groth. European Women Writers Series. Lincoln: Univ. of Nebraska Press, 1994.

Hotte, Véronique. "Une Témérité tremblante." *Théâtre/Public* 68 (March–April 1986): 22–25. [Interview.]

Shawcross, William. *Sideshow: Kissinger, Nixon and the Destruction of Cambodia*. New York: Simon & Schuster, 1979. [Source used by Cixous and Mnouchkine.]

Williams, David. "The Terrible but Unfinished Story of Norodom Sihanouk, King of Cambodia." *Drama Review* 40, no. 3: 198–200. [Review.]

Robert Schneider

TERRY, MEGAN (1932–)

It's worth it to make a life in art. I want to tell everybody it's possible and it's worth it. I've lived long enough now to see what happens to people who don't follow their hearts.

—Megan Terry, 1987

Because many of her plays highlight women's experiences, Megan Terry has been referred to as the mother of feminist theater. In

Approaching Simone (Obie Award, 1970) and *Mollie Bailey's Travel-ing Family Circus* (1983) she presents resilient women who refuse to be bound by the restrictions of their societies. Yet Terry does not see herself as the feminist movement's spokeswoman and instead defines herself as a humanist who uses the theater as "a terrific catalyst" for sparking discussions of critical issues that shape human existence.

Born Marguerite Duffy on July 22, 1932, in Seattle, Washing-ton, Terry became enamored of the theater at an early age, became part of the Seattle Repertory, and was taught acting and stagecraft by Florence and Burton James. Terry credits the way she constructs her plays to her early interest in design and her discovery of the concepts of Edward Gordon Craig and Adolphe Appia. She attributes her view of theater as a political space to the Jameses' involvement in the Progressive Party.

By the time she moved to New York in 1956, she had become Megan Terry, the playwright. Her first New York production, *Ex–Miss Copper Queen on a Set of Pills* (1963), was presented by the Playwrights' Unit at the Cherry Lane Theatre. Director Joseph Chaikin and critic Michael Smith, who attended the premiere, were impressed by Terry's work and asked her if she would be interested in becoming part of a group conceived as an alterna-tive to commercial theater. She agreed, and the Open Theatre was established.

Terry's association with Chaikin and the Open Theatre was instrumental in the development of her signature style—trans-formations—which evolved from an improvisation exercise and involves rapid changes of identity, place, and emotion. While this technique was important to the Open Theatre's goal of cre-ating an alternative to psychological-realist conventions and circumventing typecasting, it was particularly useful to Terry. She departed from the structures of dramas of the 1950s, allow-ing spectators to supply their own meanings to what they were viewing. She also provided actors with opportunities to explore numerous characters, styles, and interactions, which included examining the idea of fixed IDENTITIES and gender roles.

By the mid-1960s Terry had created a substantial body of work that not only included her transformation plays—*Eat at Joe's* (1964), *Calm Down Mother* (1965), *Keep Tightly Closed in a Cool Dry Place* (1965), *Comings and Goings* (1966), *Viet Rock* (1966), and *Babes in the Bighouse* (1974)—but also more conventional realis-tic dramas such as the original version of *Hothouse* (1953–1958). However, it was not until the success of *Viet Rock*, presented by the Open Theatre at Café La Mama, that Terry gained promi-nence. Developed in a six-month workshop where the actors and playwright worked through the conflicts surrounding the highly contested Vietnam War, *Viet Rock* evolved into the first rock musical.

In 1973, after co-writing the Open Theatre's *Nightwalk* with SAM SHEPARD and Jean-Claude van Itallie, Terry moved to Nebraska to become playwright-in-residence at the Omaha Magic Theater (OMT). In addition to *Babes in the Bighouse* (1974),

a critique of oppressed/oppressor relationships in a women's prison, her association with OMT produced *American King's English for Queens* (1978), an exploration of violence through lan-guage; and *Goona Goona* (1979), an examination of domestic vio-lence, among numerous other plays for the stage and television. Her commitment to experimenting with new forms to explore crucial social issues has never diminished.

[*See also* Feminist Drama in the United States; United States]

SELECT PLAYS: *Ex-Miss Copper Queen on a Set of Pills* (1963); *Eat at Joe's* (1964); *Calm Down Mother* (1965); *Keep Tightly Closed in a Cool Dry Place* (1965); *The Gloaming, Oh My Darling* (1966); *Viet Rock: A Folk War Movie* (1966); *The People vs. Ranchman* (1967); *Approaching Simone* (1970); *Babes in the Bighouse* (1974); *Hothouse* (1974); *Goona Goona* (1979); *Mollie Bailey's Traveling Family Circus, Featuring Scenes from the Life of Mother Jones* (music by Jo Anne Metcalf, 1983); *Do You See What I'm Saying?* (1990); *Breakfast Serial* (1991); *Sound Fields* (1992)

FURTHER READING

Betsko, Kathleen, and Rachel Koenig. *Interviews with Contemporary Women Playwrights.* New York: Beech Tree Bks., 1987.

Breslauer, Jan, and Helene Keyssar. "Making Magic Public: Megan Terry's Traveling Family Circus." In *Making a Spectacle: Feminist Essays on Contemporary Women's Theatre,* ed. by Lynda Hart. Ann Arbor: Univ. of Michigan Press, 1989.

Keyssar, Helene. *Feminist Theatre: An Introduction to Plays of Contemporary British and American Women.* New York: Grove, 1985.

Marranca, Bonnie, and Gautam Dasgupta, eds. *American Playwrights: A Critical Survey.* New York: Drama Book Specialists, 1981.

Savran, David, ed. *In Their Own Words: Contemporary American Playwrights.* New York: Theatre Communications Group, 1988.

Schlueter, June. "Megan Terry's Transformation Drama: *Keep Tightly Closed in a Cool Dry Place* and the Possibilities of Self." In *Modern American Drama: The Female Canon,* ed. by June Schlueter. Rutherford, N.J.: Fairleigh Dickinson Univ. Press, 1990.

Meghan Duffy

TESICH, STEVE (1943–1996)

Born Stoyan Tesich on September 29, 1943, in Titovo Uszice, Yugoslavia, present-day SERBIA, playwright Steve Tesich immi-grated to East Chicago, Indiana, with his family in 1957, at the age of fourteen, speaking no English. In 1965 he graduated from Indiana University, having majored in Russian literature, and he began to write for the theater during his graduate stud-ies at Columbia University. In 1979 he turned to screenwriting, winning an Oscar for his first effort, *Breaking Away*. Between 1981 and 1986 he produced five more screenplays: *Eyewitness, Four Friends, The World According to Garp, American Flyers,* and *Eleni.* After *Eleni* Tesich returned to writing for the theater. He also wrote two novels, *Summer Crossing* (1982) and the posthumously published *Karoo* (1998), a COMEDY about the film industry.

Tesich, who became a U.S. citizen in 1961 at the age of eighteen, began his career writing loving comedies about the social concerns of his adopted nation. *Division Street* (1980) typifies the mood of Tesich's early work: in his own words, "allegro con sentimento." Set in an immigrant Chicago neighborhood, *Division Street* is populated by a motley crew from the margins of American society. The characters are in flight from former lives whose loss, paradoxically, they mourn: Chris, an ex–civil rights activist, dodges the painful consciousness of his lost idealism. His landlady, Mrs. Bruchinski, "a Black woman with a Polish accent," is in perpetual mourning both for the mysterious disappearance of her infant son many years earlier and for the mysterious passing of 1960s radicalism. Betty, a policewoman, had been a 1960s radical known as "Bomber Kellogg." Yovan, a Serbian émigré, prints menus "on mimeo machine" by day, but at night produces a one-man newspaper called *Serbian Sun*. "I write powerful stuff," he says: "I write, America, wake up. People need you. My friends. They give up. They go back to the old country. So I write: fooey on you, you chupped liver patriots. . . . Stuff like that I write. Leaflets too." Tesich's flair for satire notwithstanding, *Division Street* is a paean to hope, and all is resolved in a comedic happy end: brothers find sisters, lovers are united, Mrs. Bruchinski's lost baby boy proves to be policewoman Betty, a new movement is born, and the entire cast, "the lost tribe of the American Dream," comes together in a rousing chorus of "America the Beautiful."

With the passage of time, Tesich's plays took on a darker hue. World events of the early 1990s and U.S. involvement in them—the civil war in Yugoslavia, the 1991 American invasion of Iraq—precipitated a political and spiritual crisis for Tesich, and such later works as *The Speed of Darkness* (1989) and *On the Open Road* (1992) are darkly comic meditations on war, morality, and spirituality. His Beckettian *On the Open Road* is set in "a time of Civil War" in "a place of Civil War"; it begins with the looting of unspecified cultural artifacts and ends with the crucifixion of the thieves.

In the early 1990s Tesich wrote a series of articles that criticized the Gulf War and exposed what he believed to be a campaign of deliberate misrepresentation of the political realities of the Balkans and the "selective condemnation" of the Serbs. He was particularly concerned with the role of public relations firms in manipulating public opinion. His articles remained unpublished, circulated on the Internet by his sister, Nadja Tesich. Steve Tesich died in Sydney, Nova Scotia, on July 1, 1996, of a heart attack at the age of fifty–two.

[*See also* United States, 1940–Present]

PLAYS: *The Carpenters* (1970); *Lake of the Woods* (1971); *Baba Goya* (1973); *Gorky* (1975); *Passing Game* (1977); *Touching Bottom (The Road, A Life, Baptismal)* (1978); *Division Street* (1980); *The Speed of Darkness* (1989); *Square One* (1990); *On the Open Road* (1992); *Arts and Leisure* (published posthumously, 1997)

FURTHER READING

Coen, Stephanie. "Steve Tesich." *American Theatre*, 9, no. 4 (July 1992): 26.

Horton, Andrew. "An Interview with Steve Tesich." *New Orleans Review* 11, nos. 3–4 (Fall–Winter 1984): 80–87.

Ringnalda, Don. "The Theatre of Doing It Wrong, Getting It Right." In *Fighting and Writing the Vietnam War*. Jackson: Univ. Press of Mississippi, 1994.

Kathryn Syssoyeva

THAILAND

Thailand is a Southeast Asian Buddhist country with a long and strong theater tradition. The origin of the Thai people is not clear, but their movement into Southeast Asia, where they took power from the Mon and Khmer by the 15th century, is documented. The major historical periods are named after the royal capitals Sukhothai (1238–1350), Ayudhya (1350–1767), and Ratnakosin (1782–present).

The earliest known drama in Thailand, *manora*, originated in the 14th century and has been practiced to the present. A performance includes a musical prelude, an opening incantation, solo dances, songs, skits, and finally a play. Today *manora* has become intermixed with *lakon jatri* (*jatri*, sorcerer), a form named for troupe heads who were felt to have great spiritual power. Both genres have been transformed: singers in Western costume croon romantic lyrics to Western band accompaniment, and skits and comic routines abound. Another interrelated form is *lakon nok*, literally "outside-the-palace play," which was an all-male dance-drama until the mid-19th century, when women began appearing in female roles. It remains popular, and performances may be held for cremations or at events such as the king's birthday. The *Ramakien*, the Thai version of the Hindu *Ramayana*, or legendary stories are presented in this form.

Other popular forms are the *nang talung* (small-puppet theater), which originally was based on *Ramayana* stories, but now tells a variety of tales, and *likay*, an improvised genre developed about 100 years ago that is a popular presentation of stories of princes and princesses in melodramatic style in which the dialogue is improvised. Song and dance skills are a prerequisite for performers. Spectacular costumes, especially of the male lead, and elaborate stage effects help reinforce the continuing popularity of this form. The dazzling artists, beautifully made up and clothed in sequins, silk, and glittering stones, light up the night on open-air stages. Singing and talent in melodramatic improvisation are crucial for successful performers. Another popular theater form is *mawlum luong*, found in northeast Thailand. It uses local dialect. Music traditionally is provided by a panpipe or *kaen*. Today modern amplification, Western instruments, and pop music are popular innovations in Lao areas.

Court performance included *nang yai* (large leather puppets), *khon* (all-male masked dance-drama), and *lakon nai* (all female dance-drama, or inside-the-palace performance). Today *nang yai* is maintained at temples such as Wat Khanon in Ratchaburi Province, and *khon* and *lakon* are performed regularly by the national theaters and by university groups. Many innovations in court performance occurred in the 19th and 20th centuries.

After the reign of Rama IV, King Mongkut (1851–1868), strict division of the sexes in theater forms ended. Males were allowed to dance with the ladies (traditionally spouses of the monarch), and female dancers were allowed to perform on public stages. A new type of puppetry began in the same period. Performances of classical plays were begun with three-dimensional puppets called *hun*, an innovation of the late 1800s. Today *hun lakon lek* is presented by the Joe Louis Puppet Theatre, a troupe that performs nightly in Bangkok's Suan Lum Night Market for tourist audiences. The group is made up of family members of Sakorn Yangkiosod, also known as Joe Louis (1923–), who carries on the tradition developed by the troupe of Krae Suppanawich.

Royalty were the major authors of the late 19th and early 20th centuries. *Lakon dukdamban* was an innovation of the RAMA V (King Chulalongkorn) period (1868–1910) in which actors delivered their own lines rather than relying on a sung chorus or improvisation. The use of proscenium stages and scenic devices made *lakon dukdamban* a popular form. Rama V is also the author of important plays such as *Ngo Pa* (1906) that depicted commoners and ethnic minorities. His work broke new theatrical ground, bringing greater REALISM to the theater, and he is credited with the first spoken drama (*lakon phud*) where text prevails over music and dance. His work set the course for 20th-century writing, and his signature work, *Ngo Pa*, is presented annually on the anniversary of his death.

Another genre developed in the 19th century was *lakon phantang* ("thousand-ways theater," or mixed-genre experiments), which combines local legends from the *sebha*, a rhymed storytelling tradition, with classical dance presentation. Prince Naradhip developed *lakon rong*, an all-female opera from the 19th century. He adapted plots from English musicals to Thai dance-style performance.

Rama VI (King Vajiravudh), who reigned from 1911 to 1925, wrote texts for many *lakon phud*. Schooled in ENGLAND, he wrote spoken dramas based on Western models and built a Western-style theater in his residence. Selected plays by him are presented annually at the Vajiravudh Center. He also wrote many plays for various types of traditional theater.

Spoken drama (*lakon phud*) is taught and produced today in universities such as Chulalongkorn and Thamasat and by amateur groups. Playwrights usually support themselves by other professions, including television and advertising. Performances usually run for only a few weeks. SOMPOP CHANDRAPRABHA (1919–1987), author of many stage and television plays, was a soil engineer who rose to prominence after World War II with his historical dramas, costumed in period style. In the 1970 and 1980s the highest production values were found in the Montienthong Theatre in the Montien Hotel in Bangkok. This group's performers generally earn their living doing television drama and in Thai-language films.

During the 1980s productions by this foremost spoken-drama troupe tended toward social satire. *Lady Amarapa* (*Khunying Amarapa*) by Satit Chaimano and Apidol Wangthawisap in 1986 showed a social-climbing rich woman trying to buy a noble title. *Puchai Naya*, an adaptation of *Boys in the Band* by Seri Wongmontha in 1986 and 1987, was the most successful production.

At the turn of the 21st century the Patravadi Theatre in Thonburi was active in producing Thai modern drama. Graduates of the theater programs at Thamasat and Chulalongkorn produce there and in other venues. The Thai Cultural Center currently presents various modern and traditional works in its large and small theaters. The National Theatre specializes in traditional theater performance. The Bangkok Theatre Festival, founded in 2002, is an annual celebration of performance in which young artists in theater, dance, and puppetry come together each November to celebrate the vibrant theater arts of Thailand today.

FURTHER READING

Chandavij, Natthapatra, and Promporn Pramualratana. *Thai Puppets and Khon Masks*. Bangkok: River Bks., 1998.

Foley, Kathy. "Thailand." In *The Cambridge Guide to Asian Theatre*, ed. by James Brandon. Cambridge: Cambridge Univ. Press, 1993.

Rutnin, Mattani. *Dance, Drama, and Theatre in Thailand: The Process of Development and Modernization*. Chiang Mai: Silkworm Bks., 1996.

——, ed. *The Siamese Theatre*. Bangkok: Siam Society, 1975.

Virulrak, Surapone. *The Evolution of Thai Performing Arts in the Bangkok Period, 1782–1934* (in Thai). Bangkok: Chulalongkorn Univ. Press, 2000.

——. "Theatre in Thailand Today." *Asian Theatre Journal* 7, no. 1 (1990): 95–105.

Wenk, Klaus. *Thai Literature: An Introduction*. Bangkok: White Lotus, 1995.

Yupho, Danhit. *The Khon and Lakon: Dance Dramas Presented by the Department of Fine Arts*. Bangkok: Dept. of Fine Arts, 1963.

Surapone Virulrak

THEATER OF THE ABSURD   See ABSURDISM

THEATER OF THE GROTESQUE

The Theater of the Grotesque was born on May 29, 1916, the date of the premiere of *The Mask and the Face* by LUIGI CHIARELLI (1880–1947), subtitled *A Grotesque in Three Acts*. The other writers in the style were Luigi Antonelli (1882–1942), Enrico Cavacchioli (1885–1954), and Rosso di San Secondo (1887–1956), although LUIGI PIRANDELLO (1867–1936), with plays such as RIGHT YOU ARE (If You Think So!), can take his place, at least temporarily, alongside them.

The season of grotesque theater was brief, if intense. It was the only school of playwrights ITALY has produced, and the fact that the moving spirits were writers was already a revolution in a national theater traditionally dominated by actors. There was little agreement, then or now, over what exactly the essence of the grotesque was. Unlike their more revolutionary contemporaries, the futurists, grotesque writers did not issue manifestos, but some traits and beliefs can be identified. Their most evident shared feature was the negative one of a contemptuous dismissal of all that goes under the name of "bourgeois theater," but since that too is a nebulous concept, it scarcely aids clarity. None, again unlike the futurists, had any interest in experimenting with new forms, but all used the standard three-act format to ridicule or satirize conventional beliefs, and all showed some interest, common enough at the time, in the aesthetics of puppet theater. Perhaps their most important innovation was the merging of the previously rigorously separate categories of COMEDY and TRAGEDY, and in this they were undoubtedly precursors of a common trend in 20th-century theater. Finally, they were intrigued by the clash between the mask, the expectations imposed by society, and the face, that is, the spontaneous urge that was part of personality. This clash is central to Pirandello's theater.

Writers of grotesque theater were obsessed by the same themes as the despised bourgeois writers—adultery, conjugal infidelity, and the eternal triangle of husband, wife, and lover—but they reversed the conventional outcome. In Chiarelli's seminal play Paolo brags that of course as a husband he would kill his wife if she were unfaithful, but when the infidelity is proven, he cannot bring himself to do the deed and resorts to the desperate expedient of faking her death and having himself put on trial for murder. The mask of ferocious but respectable machismo conflicts with the face of meek devotion to a wife he still loves. Rosso di San Secondo attempted to forge poetic theater from grotesque material in Marionettes, What Passion!, while Antonelli introduced fantasy into the treatment of the adultery theme in The Man Who Met Himself. Luciano believes himself uxoriously happy until, after a disaster, his wife is found dead in the arms of her lover. He is transported to an enchanted island where humans can meet their younger selves, but finds that the youthful Luciano spurns the wise counsel of the older self. The refrain is that there is no escaping destiny.

The problem for the grotesque writers themselves was that they had set off in search of a brave new theatrical world, but while they had identified the wrong path, they had not the boldness, or talent, to cut a wholly new path of their own. By the mid-1920s grotesque theater had vanished from the scene.

[See also Futurism, Italian]

FURTHER READING

Angelini, Franca. Il teatro del Novecento da Pirandello a Fo. Bari: Laterza, 1990.

Ferrante, Luigi. Teatro italiano grottesco. Bologna: Cappelli, 1964.

Livio, Gigi, ed. Teatro grottesco del Novecento. Milan: Mursia, 1965.

Pullini, Giorgio. Teatro italiano del Novecento. Bologna: Cappelli, 1971.

Joseph Farrell

THEATER OF THE OPPRESSED   See BOAL, AUGUSTO

THEATER OF URGENCY

At the turn of the 20th century Spanish theater needed urgent reinvigoration. While experimental theater was flourishing in Europe, the Spanish urban bourgeoisie favored popular entertainments such as light opera and cabaret. In the early 1930s Luis Araquistain (La batalla teatral [The theatrical battle], 1930) and Ramón J. Sender (Teatro de masas [Theatre of masses], 1931) urged a break with commercial theater and theorized current European innovations.

With the proclamation of the Second Republic, playwrights such as María Teresa León and Rafael Alberti, inspired by the "theater of urgency" that was being practiced by BERTOLT BRECHT and ERWIN PISCATOR in GERMANY's Weimar Republic, aimed for a theater that would educate the masses politically and would be a collaborative effort between authors, audiences, designers, and directors. To that effect, the Republican government subsidized theatrical projects such as the Teatro del Pueblo, a component of the Misiones Pedagógicas, and popular and university theater troupes such as La Barraca, directed by FEDERICO GARCÍA LORCA and Eduardo Ugarte, and El Búho, directed by Max Aub. They brought the theater to the masses by performing plays from the golden age (16th and 17th centuries). Other working-class amateur companies performed in casas del pueblo (town halls). Their repertory included SAINETES, juguetes cómicos, and ZARZUELAS, as well as original plays and contemporary European plays created for or adapted to the social needs of the working class.

Immediately after the military rising, theaters were collectivized by the main unions, Confederación Nacional de Trabajo (CNT) and Unión General de Trabajadores (UGT). The theater of Misiones Pedagógicas and La Barraca "gave way to more radical, propagandistic theater aimed at stirring the sentiments of antifascism in the working classes. . . . The Alliance of Antifascist Intellectuals poured resources into creating 'theaters of urgency' and 'guerrillas' to inspire the soldiers at the front and the citizens at home with revolutionary doctrines" (Holguín, 2002). Rafael Alberti's manifesto "Theater of Urgency" urged writers to create short and effective plays whose simple staging could easily adapt to the war circumstances. Alberti and León headed the theatrical troupe called

Nueva Escena. It performed in public squares and villages, and writers such as Alberti, Manuel Altolaguirre, José Bergamín, Rafael Dieste, and Juan Chabás provided much of the staged material. The Teatro de Arte y Propaganda, directed by María Teresa León, revived and adapted classical works that could best be adapted to the revolutionary spirit of the Republic, such as *Fuenteovejuna* by Lope de Vega and *Numancia* by Miguel de Cervantes. The troupe Guerrillas de Teatro performed its pieces on the war front and in factories in order to stir antifascist sentiments, as well as to entertain. In his essay "Theater of Circumstances" Max Aub called on writers to adapt their artistic creation to the special circumstances. Republican troupes also performed ad hoc plays that explicitly used drama to present clear messages to their audiences about how they should act in wartime (Holguín, 2002). Some of the most relevant plays of urgency written and performed during the war years include *Pedro López García* (1936) by Max Aub, *Shepherd of Death: Drama in Four Acts* (*Pastor de la muerte: Drama en cuatro actos*, 1937) by Miguel Hernández, and *Numancia* (1937) and *Cantata of the Heroes and the Fraternity of the Peoples* (*Cantata de los héroes y la fraternidad de los pueblos*, 1938) by Rafael Alberti.

[*See also* Spain]

FURTHER READING

Alberti, Rafael. "Teatro de urgencia." In *Literatura sobre la guerra civil: Poesía, narrativa, teatro, documentación: La expresión estética de una ideología antagonista*. Suplementos de Anthropos 39 (June 1993): 109–110.

Aub, Max. "Teatro de circunstancias." In *Max Aub y la vanguardia teatral: Escritos sobre el teatro, 1928–1938*, ed. by Manuel Aznar Soler. Valencia: Universidad de Valencia, 1993. 216.

Bilbatúa, Miguel. "El teatro durante la segunda república y la guerra civil." In *Literatura y Guerra Civil*. Almería: Instituto de Estudios Almerienses, 1987.

Holguín, Sandie. "Spanish Civil War: Culture on the Battlefield." In *Creating Spaniards: Culture and National Identity in Republican Spain*. Madison: Univ. of Wisconsin Press, 2002. 168–194.

Preston, Paul. "Theater as Secularized Religion: Return to the Golden Age." In *¡Comrades! Portraits from the Spanish Civil War*. London: Fontana Press, 1999. 79–117.

Isolina Ballesteros

THÉÂTRE DU GRAND-GUIGNOL

The Théâtre du Grand-Guignol (1897–1962), the notorious home of grisly and erotic theatrical displays, was tucked away in a former chapel at the end of an alley in the Montmartre district of Paris, FRANCE. Tourists flocked to the theater to witness the latest titillating feats of gore, accompanied primarily by middle-class women with queasy husbands in tow, as well as heads of state. The theater boosted its popularity by assuring audiences that a doctor would be on hand at every performance. Indeed, spectators fainted on an average of two per night, and countless others rushed out of the theater to vomit in the alley.

Despite its reputation for sensationalism, the Grand-Guignol traces its origins to several well-established artistic influences: NATURALISM, MELODRAMA, and the "well-made play." Oscar Méténier, a former police secretary, founded the Grand-Guignol after collaborating with ANDRÉ ANTOINE on plays he wrote for the Théâtre Libre, which he had co-founded in 1887. Méténier was drawn to the stories of the underclass, particularly those that showed the poor as victims of bourgeois morality. Méténier perfected the *rosse* (vicious) play, a short piece of fifteen minutes or less inspired by local crime stories in the newspaper (*faits divers*). Méténier's brand of naturalism was for many too hard to stomach, but it was honest in a way impossible for melodrama or the "well-made play": it presented a world of unpredictable endings.

Méténier's name for the theater derives from the popular marionette character whose name, Guignol, was also used to refer to marionette shows in general. Méténier saw his as a theater for adults, in which live actors would attack each other with a level of cruelty traditionally reserved for puppets such as Punch and Judy. He devised a structure for heightening suspense by alternating COMEDY and horror throughout an evening's program, a format he called *la douche écossaise* (the hot and cold shower). When Méténier passed the leadership of the Grand-Guignol on to Max Maurey in 1898, the character of the theater shifted from a forum for exploring social reality to a bona fide theater of horror.

Under Maurey, considered the true father of the Grand-Guignol, the theater departed from its roots with the Théâtre Libre. Maurey sought to purge his audience's Aristotelian feelings of pity and fear by thrilling them with displays of violence and illicit sexuality. Rape, murder, incest, and acts of madness and mutilation were regularly enacted and made convincing through the special effects of Paul Ratineau and the use of fresh animal parts, delivered daily by local butchers.

André de Lorde, known as the "Prince of Terror," began writing plays for the Grand-Guignol in 1901. His childhood fascination with death and admiration of Edgar Allan Poe prepared him for a twenty-five-year association with the theater, during which he wrote over 100 plays. The company's success was due largely to the convincing portrayals of the actors, the most celebrated of whom was Paula Maxa, who earned the title "the most assassinated woman in the world." Maxa developed a reputation for her bone-chilling scream, which caused sufficient strain in performance to cost her her voice.

In the following years, leadership of the Grand-Guignol passed through several hands, and the theater's future became less certain. Although the theater maintained its popularity even after World War I, mounting financial problems coincided with competition from cinema. Also significant in the company's decline was the fact that with universal recognition of the real-life horrors of World War II, critical and popular opinion rejected the Grand-Guignol as irrelevant and diversionary.

Although the theater's last performance was held in 1962, the influence of the Grand-Guignol extended into the German cabaret, into 20th-century dramatic theory, and far into contemporary film.

FURTHER READING

Antona-Traversi, Camillo. *L'histoire du Grand Guignol*. Paris: Librairie Théâtrale, 1933.

Gordon, Mel. *The Grand Guignol: Theatre of Fear and Terror*. Rev. ed. New York: Da Capo, 1997.

Hand, Richard J., and Michael Wilson. *Grand-Guignol: The French Theatre of Horror*. Exeter: Univ. of Exeter Press, 2002.

Kristin Johnsen-Neshati

THEATRE GUILD

During fifty of the 20th century's early and middle years, the Theatre Guild transformed and elevated the American theater experience. It lifted the professional production of plays from the previous stage diet of mostly box-office-driven MELODRAMA and FARCE to a landmark era in the dramatic arts and did much to shape a new American audience.

The Theatre Guild probably was inevitable in that the need for such an enterprise, along with the enthusiasms, skills, and personalities required to implement it, was at hand. In 1919, when the Guild staged its first play (*Bonds of Interest*, by Nobel Prize winner JACINTO BENAVENTE), others also were producing plays, notably Mare Klaw and Abraham Lincoln Erlanger and the Shubert brothers (Lee, Sam S. and Jacob J.), who were almost entirely commercial before the Guild decided to do something about artistic quality. Previous pioneers in artistic merit were the short-lived but admirable Provincetown Players and the Washington Square Players. The idea of taking plays to other American cities was not new, although doing it with original New York stars and companies became a Guild hallmark. The Guild's membership plan, selling seasons of plays to subscribers across the country, was innovative. So were the practices of bringing dramas of merit from Europe and providing a stage for America's emerging playwrights. Further, the Guild staged more plays and musicals than any other production company: 220 in fifty years. The *Theatre Guild on the Air*, sponsored by United States Steel Corporation (U.S. Steel), pioneered drama on the radio with a series of 316 plays. It ran from 1945 to 1953. Also for U.S. Steel, but this time on television, the Guild produced 245 plays in the ten years from 1953 to 1963.

Outweighing these achievements was the artistic impact of the Guild on the American theater as a whole. In 1944 drama critic John Gassner, Sterling Professor of Playwriting and Dramatic Literature at Yale, wrote about the Guild's "revolution against the prevailing commercialism and lack of taste in the American theater (Nadel, 1969)":

A correct estimate of the Guild's position after its first decade (1929) would have included the realization that the revolution was over. The Guild ceased to be revolutionary because its cause had triumphed. Largely as a result of the example set by the Theatre Guild, Broadway management became hospitable to plays of intellectual caliber and unconventional DRAMATURGY. It became possible to produce any kind of drama in New York. In time, the gap between a typical "Guild play" and a typical "Broadway play" became narrower, and in the case of literate and sophisticated COMEDY, often imperceptible. In the 1930s, in fact, it became customary among the young to regard the Theatre Guild as a bastion of conservatism. (qtd. in Nadel, 1969)

If there was a magical moment when the Theatre Guild began, it was on the evening of December 18, 1918, when Lawrence Langner joined Philip Moeller and Helen Westley over a bottle of wine in the basement of the Brevoort Hotel on lower Fifth Avenue in New York City. Langner, who had built miniature stage sets and produced make-believe plays as a child in his native Wales, was as dedicated to theater as he was to his livelihood career as a patent attorney in America. Westley was an actress and a graduate of the American Academy of Dramatic Arts. Moeller already was launched as a playwright and stage director. At a second meeting they were joined by Theresa Helburn, who became the Guild's play reader and later co-executive director along with Langner. Also present were stage designer Lee Simonson, a painter before he became involved in the living theater, and Maurice Wertheim, who, like Langner, followed a career outside the theater and was good at handling money. These became the six co-directors of the Guild and ran it for many years. Helburn, Simonson, and Wertheim previously had attended Professor GEORGE PIERCE BAKER's '47 Workshop at Harvard, a breeding ground for some of the finest dramatic talent of the 20th century. The six also had been involved with or aware of the experimental Washington Square Players (1914–1918) and, around 1916, the Provincetown Players, best remembered for having introduced the dramas of the young EUGENE O'NEILL. Helburn and Langner guided the Guild for the greater part of its fifty years of play production; thereafter the organization was headed by Armina Marshall, Langner's widow, and his son, Philip Langner. In 1969 Philip took the Guild into movies with his production of *Slaves* and produced the last Guild play, the musical *Darling of the Day*, in 1969.

Names matter much in measuring the Guild's impact on American drama, not only play titles but names of playwrights, directors, actors, designers, costumers, and the others involved in selecting a script and bringing it to the stage. The Guild was not the first to produce the plays of O'Neill, but it did premiere eight of his works in succession as he wrote them: *Marco Millions*, STRANGE INTERLUDE, *Dynamo*, MOURNING BECOMES ELECTRA, *Ah, Wilderness!*, DAYS WITHOUT END, THE ICEMAN COMETH, and *A MOON FOR THE MISBEGOTTEN*. The Guild helped popularize GEORGE BERNARD SHAW's plays with American audiences, staging nineteen productions of them between 1920 and 1958.

Among Guild playwrights were ELMER RICE, SIDNEY HOWARD, FRANZ WERFEL, PHILIP BARRY, MAXWELL ANDERSON, ROBERT E. SHERWOOD, S. N. BEHRMAN, THORNTON WILDER, WILLIAM SAROYAN, TERENCE RATTIGAN, TENNESSEE WILLIAMS, CHRISTOPHER FRY, SEAN O'CASEY, WILLIAM INGE, JEAN ANOUILH, PETER SHAFFER, and HAROLD PINTER. There also were works by William Shakespeare, AUGUST STRINDBERG, HENRIK IBSEN, LUIGI PIRANDELLO, Ivan Turgenev, Molière, ANTON CHEKHOV, and William Congreve. In 1943 the Guild raised the American musical to a new level with Richard Rodgers and Oscar Hammerstein's *Oklahoma!*, which was a box-office triumph as well. Another production that made musical history was George and Ira Gershwin and DU BOSE and DOROTHY HEYWARD's operatic PORGY AND BESS.

FURTHER READING

Krutch, Joseph Wood. *The American Drama since 1918: An Informal History.* New York: Random House, 1939.

Langner, Lawrence. *The Magic Curtain: The Story of a Life in Two Fields, Theatre and Invention.* New York: Dutton, 1951.

Nadel, Norman. *A Pictorial History of the Theatre Guild.* New York: Crown, 1969.

Norman Nadel

THEATRICALITY

The term *theatricality* appears to have entered the English language during the 19th-century when it was used, in a pejorative sense, by Thomas Carlyle to suggest the false or ephemeral: "By act and words he strives to do it; with sincerity, if possible, failing that, with theatricality" (1837) and later, in a specifically theatrical context, "I remember once taking her to Drury Lane Theatre. Of the theatricality itself that night, I can remember absolutely nothing" (1866). In ENGLAND, by the 1860s *theatricality* would have been defined in relation to an increasingly naturalistic norm represented by the work of someone like THOMAS WILLIAM ROBERTSON and in terms of the kind of spectacle on display at a large theater such as Drury Lane that staged popular MELODRAMA. As the theater began to turn away from a dominant NATURALISM at the turn of the 20th century, and with the accompanying rise of the role of the director, theatricality itself began to assume the status of a norm. A classic example is that of a 19th-century play, ALEKSANDR OSTROVSKY's THE FOREST, as directed by VSEVOLOD MEYERHOLD in 1924, when two conventionally realistic love scenes were conceived in a remarkably imaginative theatrical manner. The first, between young lovers, was set on a rotating swing typical of a Russian fairground (also called giant stride) where the nature of the couple's ecstasy was communicated by their ever-increasing upward trajectory; the second, between a traveling comedian and a rather plain housekeeper, was staged astride a blatantly phallic seesaw, with the postclimactic moment suggested by the contemplative cigarette-smoking comedian at the lower end and the raucously satiated housekeeper, legs akimbo, at the upper.

The origins of theatricality in our sense may be said to hark back to the Greeks. Although they would not have understood our use of the term, theatricality defined most aspects of Greek theater. Its amphitheater location may be said to have dictated its style, from the use of masks, declamatory verse speaking, raised buskins or *cothurni*, and a dancing and chanting chorus to the use of mechanical devices for displaying the dead and flying in the gods. The medieval stage was also characterized by an innate theatricality, whether this took the form of "simultaneous staging," or staging "in the round," or street performance on elaborately decorated processional pageant wagons. The Elizabethans inherited a good deal of their own theatricality from the medieval miracle and morality plays, nowhere more so than in a play such as Christopher Marlowe's *Dr. Faustus* with its devils and fireworks. The form of the open-air Elizabethan theater lent itself to heightened effects both of speech and performance. The fact that Philip Henslowe's properties list included "one city of Rome" alongside "a cauldron for the Jew" seems indicative of a power to prompt imaginative extension and seduce with startling effects. Quite different in their appeal to a changed constituency were the spectacular transformation scenes engineered in the Jacobean court masque through the deployment of vast financial resources and the importation of foreign machinery. These baroque spectacles were to dominate the European stage well into the 19th century, when they were adapted to stage melodramas that appealed to less sophisticated palates.

From the mid-19th century, a dominant middle class began to demand a form of theater that answered a need for its own manners and mores to be reflected in unproblematic theatrical terms. The naturalistic norms that this kind of theater inspired gave rise to a modern sense of "theatricality," defined as anything that challenged this kind of photographic verisimilitude. In the realms of ACTING, production, stage configuration, and illumination, the antinaturalist movement was spearheaded by the likes of Edward Gordon Craig, RICHARD WAGNER, Georg Fuchs, and Adolphe Appia. The replacement of candlelight and gaslight by electricity gave rise to all kinds of opportunities for an atmospherically enhanced theatricality, while 20th-century directors such as MAX REINHARDT, Meyerhold, and ERWIN PISCATOR substituted theatricality in place of a realism that they felt had little to do with the fundamentals of performance or production. Meyerhold and Craig were also inspired by non-European theatrical forms that represented an essential theatricality in terms of their alien traditions of acting and staging—in particular the theater of JAPAN—which also influenced the poet and dramatist W. B. YEATS. Meyerhold also looked for inspiration to popular forms such as the puppet show, pantomime, and harlequinade, as well as to nonstandard locations such as fairground and circus, while his biomechanical theories were predicated on physically demonstrative acting principles hostile to psychological REALISM.

Other European practitioners who found inspiration in the East were theorists such as ANTONIN ARTAUD, influenced by Balinese theater, whose notion of a Theatre of Cruelty was a far cry from the European norms of realistic representation espoused by the likes of KONSTANTIN STANISLAVSKY, whose early work at the MOSCOW ART THEATRE tended to emphasize the values and methods of an essentially naturalistic approach to the stage. Dramatists such as AUGUST STRINDBERG (in his late plays), ALFRED JARRY, and others who belonged to "MODERNIST" movements such as SYMBOLISM, SURREALISM, and EXPRESSIONISM tended to embrace theatricality through a desire to contest bourgeois expectations and create a heightened stage world in which the intensities of dream states and the overtly grotesque predominated. More recently the drama of so-called absurdists such as EUGÈNE IONESCO and SAMUEL BECKETT took theatricality to be a sine qua non in asking audiences to accept a language of light, sound, and image that rendered the inanimate stage world as articulate as the animate.

Antonin Artaud's seminal work *The Theatre and Its Double* found expression in productions by ARIANE MNOUCHKINE that aimed to assault the senses of an audience. Peter Brook mounted a Theatre of Cruelty season and staged Artaud-influenced productions during the 1950s and 1960s that sought to destroy the barriers between the proscenium and the audience in startling and unexpected ways. His 1970s production of *A Midsummer Night's Dream* and his later staging of the Hindu epic the *Mahabharata* were also characterized by intense forms of theatrical expressiveness and the use of unorthodox settings. Brook also sought inspiration in non-Western forms of theater, whereas, in Japan, Yukio Ninagawa produced a reverse effect by marrying styles of NŌ, *kabuki*, and Bunraku with Western performance traditions and a Western repertoire in mold-breaking productions of William Shakespeare and Greek TRAGEDY.

In RUSSIA, with the rediscovery of Meyerhold's legacy after his post-Stalinist rehabilitation, the tradition of theatricality (which his compatriots Yevgeni Vakhtangov, Aleksandr Tairov, and Nikolai Okhlopkov also espoused) was taken up by YURY LYUBIMOV from the mid-1960s onwards at the Moscow Taganka Theater and in former Soviet Georgia by Robert Sturua and the Rustaveli Theater. Their productions in English of works by Fyodor Dostoevsky, Shakespeare, and ANTON CHEKHOV served to demonstrate that critical outrage could still be excited by any divergence from perceived norms and expectations. Meanwhile, in Eastern Europe the champions of theatricality tended to hail from POLAND, represented in their most extreme form by Jerzy Grotowski and Tadeusz Kantor with productions such as *Akropolis* and *Dead Class*, which derived their visceral force and powerful imagery from the Nazi death camps and a historical world composed (or decomposed) of the living dead.

In Western Europe the example of BERTOLT BRECHT as dramatist, theorist, and theater director has been preeminent. While his theory of EPIC THEATER, by laying stress on the theatrical as opposed to the illusionist, did not foreground theatricality per se, Brecht's own production of THE CAUCASIAN CHALK CIRCLE combined heightened styles of masked performance with production elements that represented the quintessence of theatricality. The literary scholar and Brecht expert, Ronald Gray, recalled the stunning effect reminiscent of Oriental theater produced by the appearance of a Georgian mountain village painted on a silken backdrop suddenly cascading against the cyclorama before billowing to a standstill. The Brecht-influenced Italian director Giorgio Strehler displayed comparable panache in his productions of THE THREEPENNY OPERA and a vibrantly physical *A Servant of Two Masters* realized within the conventions of his native commedia dell'arte.

In North America and CANADA the work of ROBERT WILSON and Robert Lepage embraced forms of PERFORMANCE ART where text was more often than not made subservient to striking visual effects. Both redefined the imaginative possibilities of theater through the introduction of other media that extended the boundaries of stage illusion and also redefined the role of the actor as executant and stage instrument in a manner first imagined by Gordon Craig as the "übermarionette." Experimental theater companies such as Julian Beck and Judith Malina's LIVING THEATRE, as well as the Wooster Group, also chose to stretch the limits of pure theatricality in the wake of otherwise dissimilar predecessors such as the Bread and Puppet Theater and El Teatro Campesino, which were responsible for reviving the carnivalesque tradition of outdoor performance. This last found its British exemplar in the Welfare State International troupe, while the People Show and Théâtre de Complicité collectives succeeded in refining an AVANT-GARDE theatrical poetics to rival the best of their American and European counterparts.

There have also been individual performance strategies that promoted theatricality for its own sake within otherwise conventional contexts. The example of British actor Laurence Olivier seems exemplary. Whether riding the drop curtain and descending from the flies as Mr. Puff in Sheridan's *The Critic* or, as Coriolanus, falling to his "death" from a raised platform from which he hung suspended by his ankles, his style was in the bravura tradition of someone like Henry Irving. Gordon Craig, writing in 1930, recalled the startling force of Irving's first entry in *The Bells*, with its preparatory buildup, his sudden appearance, and, especially, his delivery of the line "It is I!" in the manner of Japanese nō as a plosive "t'sI!" that "thrilled, and was intended to thrill," eliciting "a hurricane of applause."

Perhaps the last word should be left to Peter Brook: "Make the invisible appear from the visible: if something abnormal is to come forth, what is normal must exist first. Then you heighten it. That's where theatricality comes in."

FURTHER READING

Burns, Elizabeth. *Theatricality: A Study of Convention in the Theatre and in Social Life.* London: Longman, 1972.

Davis, Tracy, and Thomas Postlewait, eds. *Theatricality.* Cambridge: Cambridge Univ. Press, 2003.

Feral, Josette, ed. "Theatricality Issue: The Rise and Fall of Theatricality." *Substance: A Review of Theory and Literary Criticism* 31, nos. 2&3 (2002).

Huxley, Michael, and Noel Witts, eds. *The Twentieth-Century Performance Reader.* 2nd ed. London: Routledge, 2002.

Innes, Christopher. *Avant Garde Theatre, 1892–1992.* London: Routledge, 1993.

Schneider, Rebecca, and Gabrielle Cody. *Re:direction: A Theoretical and Practical Guide.* London: Routledge, 2002.

Nick Worrall

THÉRÈSE RAQUIN

The novel *Thérèse Raquin* (1867) was ÉMILE ZOLA'S first literary success. It became a runaway best-seller, despite charges of pornography from conservative critics who rejected its detailed and—for the period—frank examination of the sex drive and its lack of an authorial condemnation of the characters. Inspired by a newspaper account, Zola's tale concerns its eponymous heroine, a half-African orphan, and Laurent, her lover. Driven by lust, Laurent and Thérèse murder her boring and semi-invalid husband, Camille. They marry and settle into the dreary shop on the Passage du Pont Neuf where Thérèse and Camille had lived with his mother. The murder, however, has killed their passion, and they sink into mutual recrimination and hatred, while Madame Raquin sinks into paralysis. Eventually each plans to murder the other on the same night; when they discover their mutual designs, Thérèse and Laurent commit suicide together.

The critical attacks on the novel led Zola to write a preface for the second edition (1868), which serves as a manifesto for literary NATURALISM. In it Zola argues for a dispassionate, "scientific" approach to literature. He acknowledges a "total absence of soul" in the work, having chosen to "seek within them the animal . . . and then take scrupulous note of their sensations and their actions. I simply carried out on two living bodies the same analytical examination that surgeons perform on corpses."

Some critics defied Zola to attempt to bring this story to the stage. In 1873 he found an opportunity. Produced at the Théâtre de la Renaissance, his adaptation attempted to demonstrate the theories of naturalism on the stage, but was a box-office failure, receiving scathing critical attacks. Zola expressed ironic thanks, noting that the attacks gave the novel the praise it had been denied six years earlier.

Although it has received frequent revivals in the 20th century and contemporary adaptations by writers as diverse as Neal Bell and CHARLES LUDLAM, as a play *Thérèse Raquin* pales in comparison with the works HENRIK IBSEN, AUGUST STRINDBERG, GERHART HAUPTMANN, and even HENRY BECQUE were soon to produce. Zola eliminates the authorial substitute of the *raisonneur* from the play, but is unable to find dramatic equivalents for the novel's great strengths: its descriptive interlinking of the characters' psychology with the physical environment in which they find themselves and the power of time's passage on the consciences of the two murderers. Compressed to four acts, which respect the unities of time and place, his characters recite events and psychological states between discursive domino games and sensational events, including Madame Raquin's onstage stroke and miraculous recovery of her voice, which allows her, like a deus ex machina, to pronounce the moral judgment on the couple, a pronouncement that provokes their mutual suicide. To a contemporary audience, the result is closer to a hybrid of MELODRAMA and EXPRESSIONISM than to REALISM. In his later collaborations with William Brusnach, Zola consciously catered to the tastes of Boulevard audiences, sometimes with international success, as with *L'assommoir*. Still, *Thérèse Raquin* remains his most important work, a genuinely experimental provocation to a new image of theatrical realism.

FURTHER READING

Brown, Frederick. *Zola: A Life.* New York: Farrar Straus Giroux, 1995.

Carter, Lawson A. *Zola and the Theater.* New Haven: Yale Univ. Press, 1963.

Zola, Émile. *Thérèse Raquin* (novel). Tr. by Andrew Rothwell. Oxford: Oxford Univ. Press, 1992.

——. *Thérèse Raquin* (play). Tr. by Pip Broughton. London: Oberon, 1989.

Walter Bilderback

THEY DON'T WEAR BLACK TIE

Written by GIANFRANCESCO GUARNIERI at the age of twenty-two, *They Don't Wear Black Tie* (*Eles não usam black-tie*) was not only an immediate—and enduring—success among the critics and the audience when staged by the ARENA THEATER OF SÃO PAULO in 1958, but also a turning point in the history of Brazilian theater. For the first time in Brazilian drama, the working class was the protagonist of a play. Not only that, but the plot revolved around the preparation of a labor strike.

Intertwining the personal and the political, *They Don't Wear Black Tie* confronts the social and economic problems of the urban working class in BRAZIL through the story of a single family living in a favela (shantytown) in Rio de Janeiro. Otávio, the father, is a factory metalworker involved with the organization of a strike. Aware of the political dimensions of the workers' struggle, he is a man of solid character and convictions, always ready to do what is best for the collective. Romana, the mother, helps the household economy by working as a laundress. With a pragmatic view of life, she makes free use of her sharp tongue, but is compassionate and loving in her own way. Working in a grocery store, Chiquinho, the younger son, is a lively character in the first flush of his awakening sexuality and is inseparable from his girlfriend, Terezinha. Tião (played by Guarnieri), the older son, raised outside the favela by relatives with better social status, also works in the factory and has a hard time adapting to the poor life in the favela. He dreams of a better life in the city, and his individualistic behavior ultimately pits him against his father, his co-workers, and the community of the favela.

The strike sets father and son on opposing sides. Otávio leads the workers in the picket lines and is arrested by the police. Tião, afraid of losing his job—and jeopardizing his plans to marry his pregnant girlfriend, Maria—betrays the workers by breaking the strike. The conflict between the two generations is also an ideological one, for Otávio sees in Tião the petit bourgeois ideology of the relatives who raised him. Choosing his own interests over the interests of the striking collective, Tião ends up alone. Thrown out of the house by his father, he soon discovers that Maria would rather raise the child on her own than leave the favela to follow him to the city.

Although the play deals with broad issues such as class struggle and social inequality, Guarnieri's characters are never stereotypical, but complex, well-developed personages. *They Don't Wear Black Tie* was a breakthrough both in its theme and in its aesthetic, changing forever the way that theater companies and audiences alike regarded Brazilian plays. In sharp contrast to the Teatro Brasileiro de Comédia (Brazilian Comedy Theater), the most important theater company at that time, whose repertoire and staging techniques were "imported" from Europe and the UNITED STATES, Guarnieri's play inaugurates the process of "brazilianizing" the theater, which became Arena's distinctive mark. He brought to the theater the political effervescence of the moment, marked by nationalistic debates and the emergence of a new social landscape born out of the large industrialization and economic development that took place during President Juscelino Kubitschek's term (1956–1961).

The play employs a style that Guarnieri defines as critical REALISM. Influenced by the Italian neorealist cinema, especially that of Roberto Rossellini and Vittorio de Sica, Guarnieri captures daily life in the slum in a series of "snapshots": fast-paced short scenes jump-cut together using counterpoints from one scene to the next. The realism is intensified by the use of the broken syntax of the popular parlance. Achieving a rare balance between the power of social denunciation and artistic excellence, *They Don't Wear Black Tie* established Guarnieri as one of the most important Brazilian playwrights.

After long runs in São Paulo and Rio de Janeiro, and many awards, the play traveled throughout the country and was also performed in Argentina, Uruguay, Chile, and Germany with great success. Guarnieri died in 2006.

FURTHER READING

George, David S. *The Modern Brazilian Stage.* Austin: Univ. of Texas Press, 1992.

Guarnieri, Gianfrancesco. *O melhor teatro de Gianfrancesco Guarnieri.* 2nd ed. São Paulo: Global, 2001.

Magaldi, Sábato. *Um palco brasileiro: O Arena de São Paulo.* São Paulo: Brasiliense, 1984.

Peixoto, Fernando. "Entrevista com Gianfrancesco Guarnieri." In *Teatro em movimento.* 2nd ed. São Paulo: Hucitec, 1986.

Prado, Décio de Almeida. *Apresentação do teatro brasileiro moderno: Crítica teatral, 1947–55.* São Paulo: Martins, 1956.

Rubin, Don, and Carlos Solórzano, eds. *The World Encyclopedia of Contemporary Theatre: The Americas.* New York: Routledge, 1996.

Ana Bernstein

THEY KNEW WHAT THEY WANTED

First presented on February 24, 1924, in the Garrick Theatre in New York City, *They Knew What They Wanted* by SIDNEY HOWARD won the Pulitzer Prize for Drama in 1925. The leading actors—Pauline Lord as Amy, the San Francisco waitress turned mail-order bride; Richard Bennett as Tony, the old wine grower who tricks the young waitress into agreeing to marry him; and Glenn Anders as Joe, the handsome young handyman—apparently had much to do with the play's original success; for years after the play closed, critics praised specific line deliveries and blocking moves.

In *They Knew What They Wanted* Howard depicted genuine Americans exposing their frailties while providing insight into a unique American sense of morality. The play was remarkable not for the love triangle or the key crisis, but for the characters' simple resolve and emotional response to the unforeseen challenges of life.

Howard wrote the play while living in Venice, ITALY, in 1923, and he employed a simple plot that he credited to Dante Alighieri's legend of Paolo and Francesca. In the festive opening set in the Sonoma wine country of northern California, Tony is about to be married to Amy, his mail-order bride. As they await her arrival, preparations are finalized and exposition is presented. Immigrant Tony, worried about his age and appearance, has deceived his beloved by sending her a picture and description of his handyman, the "sloppy, beautiful, and young" Joe. Once she is committed, Tony is confident that she will stay. On her arrival, she balks at the deception and soon lands in Joe's welcoming arms. When Tony is unable to walk after an accident, each of the three decides to make the most of the situation. Although Amy has become pregnant with Joe's baby, Tony freely forgives her, stating, "What you done was mistake in da head, not in da heart. . . . Mistake in da head is no matter." In that single line Tony has managed to change Amy's perception of him. She no longer feels trapped and manipulated. Instead, she sees that he is innately decent and needs her love to survive. Deeply moved by his compassion, she agrees to stay with him. Although she may prefer to be with someone young and handsome like Joe, she needs the security and love Tony can offer. Tony wants a family he can call his own, so he willingly accepts responsibility for Amy's child. Their "slight" adjustments allow each person to save his or her dignity and maintain the life he or she wants. The play's title is very apt because each character ultimately realizes what he or she really wants.

Amy's infidelity and Tony's acceptance of it reversed the theatrical convention of male infidelity quickly forgiven by a female character. Alexander Woollcott called the play "a colorful piece cut from the fabric of American life." George Jean Nathan, although not enthusiastic, called it a "praiseworthy attempt." Arthur Hornblow found it morally objectionable; it was well written but failed to "raise the standards of good morals, good taste, and good manners." Frank Loesser adapted the play into a musical titled *The Most Happy Fella* (1956).

FURTHER READING

Coleman, Willis. "He Knew What He Wanted." *Theatre Magazine* (September 1925): 10+.

Corbin, John. "He Knew What He Wanted." *Saturday Review of Literature* (March 24, 1934): 569–570.

Craven, Bernard H. "Sidney Howard: The Man and His Plays." Master's thesis, Univ. of California, Los Angeles, 1950.

Gewirtz, Arthur. "Sidney Howard." In *American Playwrights, 1880–1945: A Research and Production Sourcebook*, ed. by William W. Demastes. Westport, Conn.: Greenwood Press, 1995. 171–182.

White, Sidney Howard. *Sidney Howard.* Boston: Twayne, 1977.

Andrew Longoria

THEYYATHEYYAM

KAVALAM NARAYAN PANIKKAR'S *Theyyatheyyam* (first performed by the Sopanam company in 1991) is the quintessential example of a play belonging to the theater of roots movement in INDIA, which "liberated" modern Indian theater from Western REALISM (Awasthi, 1989). *Theyyatheyyam* means the *theyyam* of a theyyam. Theyyam is a colloquial expression meaning "god." It is also the name given to a ritual dance performed in northern Kerala to propitiate any one of a number of gods who protect human beings from natural hazards, or dead local heroes who have been deified. The theyyam, or deity, is propitiated through the dancer, who is thought to literally embody the spirit of the deity and is referred to as "the man who takes the form of god" (Ashley, 1979).

Theyyatheyyam, which is based on a true story, begins with a group of villagers gathering for a Paranki theyyam. The theyyam begins with the telling of Paranki's story. Highly simplified, the story is that a foreigner named Paranki, attracted to a local woman named Poonkanni, decides to use his magic powers to abduct her. When the villagers reach the point in their story where Paranki kidnaps Poonkanni, a Policeman interrupts with "Stop this retelling of an antiquated, unsophisticated, village tale! Who wants it?

Where is the murderer?" The narrator (who sings much of his role), thinking that the Policeman does not understand the concept of theater, attempts to explain that they are telling a story:

NARRATOR (SINGER): There is no murderer here. Just a robber. Paranki is a kidnapper.

POLICEMAN: Not him! Where is Ramunni? He is a cold-blooded murderer!

NARRATOR (SINGER): No, you are wrong. Ramunni [in the role of Paranki] kidnapped Poonkanni.

POLICEMAN: I'm not talking about a play, I'm serious. Ramunni killed the landlord Mekkantala. Why don't you tell that story?

So the villagers switch stories and begin to tell the (real and therefore arguably more relevant) story of Ramunni and Mekkantala. Mekkantala tries to seduce Ramunni's girlfriend Kannipoo while she is working in the fields. Ramunni rescues her, but later Mekkantala tries to rape her. Ramunni rescues her by killing Mekkantala, and Ramunni and Kannipoo escape together. However, Ramunni is a theyyam dancer who is ritually obligated to perform the role of Paranki theyyam, so he returns to the village and begins his performance. Just when Ramunni transforms into a theyyam, when he is possessed by the deity Paranki, the villagers kill Paranki. Thus both Ramunni and Paranki are killed: Paranki was killed and later deified, Ramunni as Paranki is killed and deified, and in effect the remurdered Paranki becomes the theyyam of his own theyyam, or theyyatheyyam.

Ramunni is an example of the type of theyyam who is an incarnation of people killed unfairly and later deified "by a guilt-ridden society." In Panikkar's view, this type of theyyam is a reminder of "unjust actions in an unequal society [and] the dance itself is an act of appeasement." Marxist theater director SAFDAR HASHMI objects to the use of traditional performance in modern theater because he claims that it brings with it "the traditional content with its superstition, backwardness, obscurantism, and its promotion of feudal values" (quoted in van Erven, 1992). *Theyyatheyyam* proves the opposite: here Panikkar uses theyyam (a traditional performance) to critique the whole notion of deification. That the villagers themselves have killed the person they deify adds an additional irony to the play.

Theyyatheyyam has been performed by Panikkar's company Sopanam to packed houses in a wide variety of venues ranging from villages in Kerala to proscenium stages in Delhi. It is still in the Sopanam repertory.

FURTHER READING

Ashley, Wayne. "Teyyam Kettu of Northern Kerala." TDR 23, no. 2 (1979): 99–112.

Awasthi, Suresh. " 'Theatre of Roots': Encounter with Tradition." TDR 33, no. 4 (1989): 48–69.

van Erven, Eugene. *The Playful Revolution: Theatre and Liberation in Asia.* Bloomington: Indiana Univ. Press, 1992.

Erin B. Mee

THIRD SISTER LIU

Third Sister Liu (*Liu Sanjie*) is a song drama (*geju*) composed in CHINA in the late 1950s by a team of artists, including Niu Xiu, Huang Yongcha, and Zeng Zhaowen. One day, when Liu Sanjie is going by boat with her elder brother to relations, retainers of the local rich man Mo Huairen accost them. Mo is widely hated as an overlord but wants to use his money and power to entice Liu Sanjie to be his concubine and sends a matchmaker with his proposal. Liu responds that she will agree if he can find people who can win a song competition against her. Mo invites three eminent scholars to compete against Liu Sanjie, but she defeats them. He responds by getting song banned. Despite her resistance, she ends up defeated and rides up to heaven on a fish.

There are records of a real historical figure called Liu Sanjie (Third Elder Sister Liu) or Liu Sanmei (Third Younger Sister Liu), who lived in what is now Guangxi in the early 8th century and was a wonderful folksinger. There are also many legends about her in Guangxi and Guangdong. In the late 1950s a team of researchers and artists looked for material about her and created a drama in a small-scale folk style of northern Guangxi called *caidiao*, which was performed by the Liuzhou Municipal Caidiao Troupe in 1959. In 1960 it was presented at a major festival of dramas on the theme of Liu Sanjie held in the Guangxi capital Nanning. The team then rearranged their piece into the style of song drama. It was also made into a film in 1960. It was banned during the Cultural Revolution, but was revived very soon after.

One special feature of *Third Sister Liu* is its association with ethnic minorities, especially the Zhuang, who are the most populous of China's minorities and whose main home is Guangxi. Liu Sanjie herself was a Zhuang and is so portrayed both in the *caidiao* and in the song drama. Huang Yongcha is a Zhuang artist. Although both *caidiao* and song drama are basically Han drama forms, *Liu Sanjie* has incorporated Zhuang tunes and other features.

Geju features song, including Chinese elements, but is not in traditional Chinese opera style. *Third Sister Liu* is fairly typical of song dramas, especially in the period before the Cultural Revolution, in the Chinese elements of its music, plot, and performance. It is also typical in emphasizing the ideological side in the plot and characterization. For instance, the drama gives play to Liu Sanjie's poor class background and her Zhuang ethnicity, as well as her courage in resisting feudal authority. At the same time, the writers have stressed Mo Huairen's selfishness, wickedness, and stupidity. The lesson is that the poor and oppressed, especially women and minorities, are the good people who contribute to society, while the rich overlords are the negative characters.

FURTHER READING

Liang Tingwang Nong Xueguan. *Zhuangzu wenxue gaiyao* [Essentials of Zhuang literature]. Nanning: Guangxi People's Press, 1991.

Mackerras, Colin. *China's Minority Cultures: Identities and Integration Since 1912.* Melbourne: Longman; New York: St. Martin's, 1995.

Third Sister Liu [*Liu Sanjie*]. Tr. by Yang Xianyi and Gladys Yang. *Chinese Literature* 2 (1961): 53–110. Also, Peking: Foreign Languages Press, 1962.

Yang Liangcai, Tao Lifan, and Deng Minwen. *Zhongguo shaoshu minzu wenxue* [The literatures of China's minority nationalities]. Beijing: People's Press, 1985.

Colin Mackerras

THIRTY DAYS IN SEPTEMBER

Thirty Days in September by MAHESH DATTANI (first performed at the Prithvi Theatre, Mumbai, on May 31, 2001, in a production directed by Lillette Dubey) is about the effects of incest and childhood sexual abuse on women and children. The play was commissioned by Recovering and Healing from Incest (RAHI), a Delhi-based support center for middle- and upper-middle-class survivors. When RAHI approached Dattani, it gave him three mandates:

> The play would articulate the experiences of women survivors and talk about how their lives and relationships are affected as a result of their abuse. It would give the message that no matter what these effects are, recovery is possible when women begin to honor themselves and supportive spaces are provided for them to access [. . . and it would] fulfill the vital purpose of breaking the silence and exposing the myths that surround incest, its perpetrators and its victims and survivors in our society. (Dattani, 2002)

Dattani's play is based on the stories and testimony of incest survivors. These stories were shaped into a single piece that centers around Mala, a young woman caught in behavior she is desperately trying to understand and isolated by memories no one will acknowledge. The other characters are Mala's mother Shanta, whose advice is "If you forget it ever happened, you won't have anything to hide," and "I forget. I forget everything. Be like me"; Deepak, Mala's understanding and helpful fiancé; and Mala's uncle. As the play unfolds, we find out that Mala's uncle raped Shanta when they were children. Shanta survived by looking at a large picture of the god Krishna: when no one else would protect her, she "looked to Him. I didn't feel anything. I didn't feel pain, I didn't feel pleasure. . . . He helped me. By taking away all feeling." As a result, she did not want her husband to touch her, and he left when Mala was a child. Mala's uncle began to support them and to rape Mala, and the play makes it clear that Shanta ignored the rape of her daughter to ensure a roof over her head, and because she had learned to survive by being silent. The title of the play comes from the rhyme Mala chants while her uncle is raping her: thirty days have September, April, June, and November.

Now Mala cannot sustain a long-term relationship. At one point, while having coffee with Deepak, she claims that another man is looking at her breasts, only to admit minutes later that she is lying. When Deepak asks why she would lie, she says, "If he had looked at me, I would have felt—I would have felt—truly alive." Deepak tells her to get some help. After some therapy Mala says, "I can smile . . . for the first time. . . . I hear sounds I never cared to hear before—birds, temple bells. . . . My senses are working again. I can touch this chair and feel the chair touch me." Although she continues to be haunted by the memory of her uncle—an overlapping scene between Mala and her uncle and Mala and Deepak is an emotionally wrenching demonstration of the ways the past continues to be present—she makes enormous progress and regains control of her life.

Audiences attended the play in droves, and critics praised it: "Dattani transforms good themes into good theatre," wrote one reviewer (Kumar, 2000).

FURTHER READING

Dattani, Mahesh. *Collected Plays.* 2 vols. New York: Penguin, 2000–2005.

——. *Thirty Days in September.* New Delhi: RAHI, 2002.

Kumar, T. Vijay. "Dattani Transforms Good Themes Into Good Theatre." *Deccan Chronicle* (Hyderabad, March 5, 2000).

Erin B. Mee

THIYAM, RATAN (1948–)

Writer and director Ratan Thiyam, born in 1948 in Manipur, INDIA, is part of the theater of roots movement. However, while Thiyam's work is tied to a theatrical movement that spans the nation, it is deeply and specifically anchored in Manipuri culture.

Manipur was an independent kingdom until it was overrun by the Burmese in 1819. Seven years later Manipur liberated itself from the Burmese with the help of the British East India Company, which then gradually took on the role of colonizer. But when the Republic of India was established in 1947, and when it claimed all former British territories as its own, including Manipur, many Manipuris felt that they had been unconstitutionally subsumed under the new nation. Since the 1960s demands for self-determination have grown in number and in violence. Today the Indian army is a constant presence in Manipur's capital city, Imphal, and violence has become part of everyday life. Under these conditions it is hardly surprising that many of Thiyam's productions are about war and the power-hungry politicians who wage it.

Thiyam's 1986 adaptation of *Antigone* (*Lengshonnei*) focuses on the personal behavior of politicians. Kreon is the archetypal father figure, and Haemon the archetypal son. When Kreon looks at Haemon, he fails to see an adult but perceives instead the child he used to sing lullabies to; when Haemon looks at his father, he sees a man who has grown old physically without growing any wiser. Thiyam focuses on the human tragedy that creates the political one. "The presence of the army in our country and the presence of a revolutionary people is a result brought on by political leaders," he reasons. "So my thinking goes directly to those political leaders and to how they are failing to handle the situation properly."

Thiyam's *The Final Beatitude* (*Uttar Priyadarshi*, 1996), which has toured India, THAILAND, and the UNITED STATES, is a play about a man's attempt to control his own ego and his own violent urges. Thiyam says that it is also "a play about peace, about non-violence, about the growing attitude of waging war and about the effect of war: What happens to this world, and who are the sufferers?" *The Final Beatitude* is a plea to think seriously about how violence will affect the next generation. Thiyam's most famous play, ARMY FORMATION (*Chakravyuha*, 1984), is about a young warrior sacrificed on the battlefield by his own uncle.

When he started the Chorus Repertory Theatre, Thiyam's mission was to evolve "an indigenous theatre idiom, employing the arts and lore of Manipur" (Jacob, 1989). He asked his father to provide him with gurus of the martial art thang-ta, *pung cholum* (acrobatic dance with drums), *ras lila* (devotional dance), and *wari leeba* (oral storytelling). Thiyam's actors are so well trained that they do not speak their lines, they growl, sing, shriek, whisper, and whine; they do not walk across the stage, they jump, writhe, glide, and stomp. His productions are visually poetic and aurally muscular, making dazzling use of sound, music, rhythm, and color. Thiyam's work engages all the senses—it is total theater.

Thang-ta, meaning "the art of the sword and the spear," forms the backbone of Thiyam's training program. Thang-ta exercises teach flexibility and balance, the ability to coordinate breath and movement, and relaxation. The basic exercises are a practice for the regulation of energy without tension, but they also teach inner awareness—the adjustment and readjustment of the body, using senses other than sight (the one we usually rely on when dealing with appearance). For Thiyam, thang-ta has the added benefit of teaching all these things without giving the actor a particular form. "There are other methods of training," he says, but many of them also give the actor a movement vocabulary that is specific to the particular genre. "An actor becomes a great performer when he is 'shapeless' and can mould his body and mind to fit any role" (Thiyam, 1989).

Pung cholum literally means drum dance. It is an acrobatic dance in which the dancer accompanies himself on the drum. Because the dance begins as a soft whisper and builds to a thunderous climax, pung cholum teaches rhythm and dynamics. More than that, it teaches the actor to be a musician, as well as a dancer (and most of Thiyam's actors play instruments during performances), to coordinate the rhythm and the movement, and to use the body as an instrument.

The actors get their vocal agility and strength through their training in wari leeba, which literally means storytelling (wari, story; leeba, to tell). Thiyam describes it as a form that "paints pictures through words" (Souvenir Program, 1989). Wari leeba storytellers stay seated and use no gestures, so they have only their voices to communicate the denotative and connotative meaning of the words and the emotional import of the story. Thiyam has worked with a number of different wari leeba teachers (*ojhas*) because each has a different strength. Some storytellers are particularly skilled at describing warfare. Others excel at comedy or romance. Wari leeba develops an awareness of vocal equipment, tone, inflection, pitch, diction, nuance, vocal coloration, and vocal imagination. Thiyam insists that his actors not simply speak, but deliver the lines he has written.

Thiyam has directed more than fifty productions for his company, including *Man Doesn't Die by Bread Alone* (1978), *Procession of Man* (*Mee Pareng*, 1979), and *Imphal Imphal* (1982), which he also wrote. Thiyam received the Sangeet Natak Akademi Award for direction in 1987 and the Padma Shri in 1988. His productions have toured to JAPAN, Thailand, the United States, the former Soviet Union, AUSTRALIA, and NEW ZEALAND. His production of *Chakravyuha* won Edinburgh's Fringe First Award in 1987.

FURTHER READING

Jacob, Paul, ed. *Contemporary Indian Theatre: Interviews with Playwrights and Directors.* Delhi: Sangeet Natak Academi, 1989.

Katyal, Anjum. "Of War and Peace: The Theatre of Ratan Thiyam." *Arts International* (Winter 1999): 39–43.

Mee, Erin. "Star of India." *American Theatre Magazine* (July/August 2000).

Souvenir Program for the Nehru Shatabdi Natya Samaroh. Delhi: Sangeet Natak Akademi, 1989.

Thiyam, Ratan. "The Audience Is Inside Me." *Seagull Theatre Quarterly* 14/15 (1997): 62–72.

——. *Chakravyuha.* Calcutta: Seagull Bks., 1998.

——. "Interview with Kavita Nagpal." In *Contemporary Indian Theatre.* Delhi: Sangeet Natak Akademi, 1989.

——. "Uttar-Priyadarshi: Theatre of Manipur." *International Gallerie* 2, no. 2 (1999): 41–49.

Erin B. Mee

THOMAS, AUGUSTUS (1857–1934)

Something in man's constitution . . . makes the theatre necessary.
—Augustus Thomas, 1918

Augustus Thomas was born on January 8, 1857, in St. Louis, Missouri. He served as a page in the Missouri House of Representatives and the U.S. Congress and worked for several railroads. After several years of amateur acting with the Marion Place Dramatic Club in St. Louis, he wrote his first full-length play, *Alone* (1875), for that group. In 1878 he joined his future father-in-law's law office, but left in 1881 for a position at St. Louis's Pope Theatre. He worked for several theater companies and newspapers before landing his first New York position in 1888. *The Burglar* (1889), his first New York production, was a big success and resulted in a position with A. M. Palmer revising and adapting foreign plays.

Although Thomas wrote FARCES and political, socioeconomic, psychological, and psychic plays, he is probably best known for his American regional plays. *Alabama* (1891) advocates reconciliation of American sectional differences by combining northern energy and money with southern resources. *In Mizzoura* (1893) breaks with theatrical tradition by presenting authentic unconventional characters, including both a sheriff and a thief competing for the attention of a woman, all in detailed and realistic settings and situations. *Arizona* (1899) depicts the desolation of the alkali southwestern desert as cowboys and cavalry prepare to leave for Cuba and the Spanish-American War. *Oliver Goldsmith* (1900) is a costume COMEDY about the title character's conception for *She Stoops to Conquer.* *The Capitol* (1895) is a political play that discusses the corrupting influence industry and religion can have on politics. *New Blood* (1894), a socioeconomic play, advocates the responsible use of money, a national concern of the 1890s. Reflecting contemporary public interest, *The Witching Hour* (1907) incorporates telepathy and hypnosis. Regardless of subject, Thomas's plays presented authentic American characters facing contemporary American issues.

In essays and the prefaces to his plays Thomas promulgated his dramatic theories, which were informed by his psychic studies, and explained his process of play construction. For him, the audience's subconscious mind was stimulated by the play's conflict and stirred emotionally to action. He believed that the dramatist must tap the collective subconscious through visualization and suggestion. He reasoned that when a person's subconscious mind has two thoughts, one from another person, such as a dramatist, and the other from the individual, the stronger idea will rise to the conscious mind. Thus dramatists are a social moral force. Thomas's belief in the importance of emotion over the conscious mind typically gave his plays a quiet aspect. Unlike his contemporaries, who used spectacle and typically followed an explosive climax with an immediate curtain, Thomas often dropped the curtain at quiet moments of intense inner emotions.

In 1914 Thomas was awarded the Gold Medal for his lifetime achievement in drama from the American Academy of Arts and Letters and subsequently received several honorary degrees. He was a major dramatist in changing the American theater from one that merely adapted foreign plays to one that presented a uniquely American drama. Consequently, he was one of the most important American playwrights before EUGENE O'NEILL. Thomas died on August 12, 1934, near Nyack, New York.

[See also United States, 1860–Present]

SELECT PLAYS: *Alabama* (1891); *In Mizzoura* (1893); *New Blood* (1894); *The Capitol* (1895); *Arizona* (1899); *Oliver Goldsmith* (1900); *On the Quiet* (1901); *The Earl of Pawtucket* (1903); *The Other Girl* (1903); *Mrs. Leffingwell's Boots* (1905); *The Witching Hour* (1907); *The Harvest Moon* (1909); *As a Man Thinks* (1911); *The Copperhead* (1918); *The Cricket of Palmy Days* (1919)

FURTHER READING

Davis, Ronald J. *Augustus Thomas*. Boston: Twayne, 1984.

Thomas, Augustus. *The Print of My Remembrance*. New York: Scribner, 1922.

Robert Lewis Smith

THOMAS, DYLAN (1914–1953)

Dylan Marlais Thomas was born in Swansea, Wales, in 1914, the son of Florence and D. J. Thomas, a grammar-school master at Swansea Grammar School, where Dylan was a pupil between 1925 and 1931. After leaving school, he spent fifteen months as a junior reporter at the *South Wales Daily Post* before becoming a full-time writer.

Thomas is more famous for his poetry, but constant money worries forced him to seek freelance work at the BBC. In the early 1940s he did documentary work for BBC Radio and, from 1945 onwards, some journalistic work. His creative work for radio includes the monologue *Quite Early One Morning* (recorded in 1944 and first broadcast in 1945), which, with hindsight, reads like a sketch for his most famous "play for voices," *Under Milk Wood* (1954). Another early piece is the short radio play *Return Journey* (first broadcast in 1947), which was produced by P. H. Burton, Richard Burton's mentor. In this piece the narrator, Thomas's alter ego, travels back to Swansea to rediscover his youth and to look for any traces he might have left behind. It is a reminiscence that is at once comic and nostalgic and invokes a prewar Swansea before it was destroyed by Nazi bombers.

From 1950 Thomas was working on a radio play called *The Town That Was Mad*, which was later to become *Llareggub* and then *Under Milk Wood*. The form of the play, its meandering narrative voice that takes the listener from character to character, and its succession of character studies in lieu of plot development are anticipated in *The Londoner* (1945), a radio documentary about the Jacksons, a working-class family in London. Indebted to James Joyce's *Ulysses*, *Under Milk Wood* describes twelve hours in the life of the West Walian village of Llareggub (a linguistic joke to be appreciated when the word is read backwards), delving into dirty, usually sexual, secrets in an amoral village and focusing on the eccentricities of characters such as Captain Cat, Hugh Pugh, the imaginary wife murderer, or the dangerously innocent Reverend Eli Jenkins. Its power, however, resides in Thomas's use of language: he uses an almost hypnotic lyrical descriptive prose, guidebook pastiche, allusions, slapstick, and other forms. Thomas read the unfinished play for the first time in Cambridge, Massachusetts, on May 3, 1953, on a tour of campus readings. He finished the play just in time for the live recording on May 14 in New York in which he read "First Voice" and took three more parts. Revisions of the play continued throughout the summer, and the script was finally delivered to the BBC on October 15, 1953. It was first broadcast on January 25, 1954, with Richard Burton reading "First Voice." The broadcast was posthumous; Dylan Thomas died on November 9, 1953, after a bout of heavy drinking. The exact circumstances of his death remain unclear. *Under Milk Wood* has since been transferred to the stage and is regularly revived.

RADIO PLAYS: *Quite Early One Morning* (1945); *Return Journey* (1947); *Under Milk Wood* (1954)

FURTHER READING

Davies, James A. *A Reference Companion to Dylan Thomas*. Westport, Conn.: Greenwood Press, 1998.

Davies, Walford. *Dylan Thomas*. Milton Keynes: Open Univ. Press, 1986.

Ferris, Paul. *Dylan Thomas: The Biography*. New ed. London: Dent, 1999.

Lewis, Peter. "The Radio Road to Llareggub." In *British Radio Drama*, ed. by John Drakakis. Cambridge: Cambridge Univ. Press, 1981. 72–110.

Thomas, Dylan. *The Broadcasts*. Ed. by Ralph Maud. London: Dent, 1991. [A comprehensive collection of Dylan Thomas's work for radio.]

Tremlett, George. *Dylan Thomas: In the Mercy of His Means*. London: Constable, 1991.

Alyce von Rothkirch

THOMAS, EDWARD (1961–)

Playwright and director Edward (Ed) Thomas was born in 1961 in Abercraf, Wales, and grew up in one of the Welsh-speaking communities in the Swansea Valley in southern Wales. He studied English at University College, Cardiff, and worked in London fringe theater before forming his own theater company, Y Cwmni (later Fiction Factory), in Wales in 1988. Thomas has always stressed the collaborative nature of the playwriting process, and his plays are closely identified with actors such as Richard Lynch and Russell Gomer. The first production of Y Cwmni, HOUSE OF AMERICA (1988), was an instant success because it articulated the spirit of profound cultural resignation in the face of Anglo-American economic and cultural domination in the 1980s in a vivid, angry, and exciting idiom. In later plays Thomas left the conventions of stage REALISM behind and turned to nonrealist, experimental forms as a strategy to create a "theatre of possibilities," which imaginatively articulated a new Welsh self-confidence.

Echoing historian Gwyn A. Williams's famous dictum in *When Was Wales?* that "Wales is an artefact which the Welsh produce," Thomas's plays are part of a conscious political effort to write a new national narrative, a "new mythology" for Wales. In *Flowers of the Dead Red Sea* (1991) the central characters, Mock and Joe, symbolize the cultural amnesia and defeatism Thomas had diagnosed in *House of America*. This play ends, however, with an invocation of the memory of a distinct Welsh culture and the power of art to "save culture." In *East from the Gantry* (1992) the story of a tumultuous marriage becomes caustic social commentary. *Song from a Forgotten City* (1995) imagines Wales as a metropolis, "a place where something good might happen." *Gas Station Angel* (1998) employs magic-realist techniques to enable the characters to tell their own stories and to give them the opportunity to imagine their own future. In this play the traditional hero narrative is subverted in favor of a tapestry of voices in which imagination has the power to change the scenery and thus the world in which the characters are situated. Especially *Gas Station Angel* can be fruitfully disseminated in the context of postcolonial drama.

Thomas's work for the theater has been mainly in English, with the exception of the surreal *Adar heb Adenydd* (1989), which was subsequently reworked as *The Myth of Michael Roderick* (1990). However, he works as a writer and director for the Welsh-language television channel S4C. Later he wrote the script for *Mwy na Phapur Newydd* (1990) and directed the televised version of the acclaimed play *Hunllef yng Nghymru Fydd* by the Welsh-language playwright Gareth Miles (1990). His work for the cinema includes the screenplay for the film *House of America* (1997) and the unsuccessful *Rancid Aluminium* (1999). Thomas still writes for television and returned to the stage with *Who Are You Looking At?* (2004) and the multimedia performance *Rain Dogs* (2002), collaborations with the musician Mike Brookes and actor and director Mike Pearson.

SELECT PLAYS: *House of America* (1988); *Adar heb Adenydd* (1989); *The Myth of Michael Roderick* (1990); *Flowers of the Dead Red Sea* (1991); *East from the Gantry* (1992); *New Wales Trilogy* (1992); *Envy* (1993); *Hiraeth/Strangers in Conversation* (1993); *Song from a Forgotten City* (1995); *Gas Station Angel* (1998); *Rain Dogs* (with Mike Brookes and Mike Pearson, 2002); *Stone City Blue* (2004); *Who Are You Looking At?* (with Mike Brookes and Mike Pearson, 2004)

FURTHER READING

Davies, Hazel Walford, ed. *State of Play: Four Playwrights of Wales.* Llandysul: Gomer, 1998.

Rhys, Martin. "Keeping It in the Family: *Change* by J. O. Francis, *The Keep* by Gwyn Thomas and *House of America* by Ed Thomas." In *Dangerous Diversity: The Changing Faces of Wales*, ed. by Katie Gramich and Andrew Hiscock. Cardiff: Univ. of Wales Press, 1998. 150–177.

Theatre in Wales [contains information on Welsh theater]. http://www.theatre-wales.co.uk/.

Thomas, Edward. *'95–'98 Selected Work: Song from a Forgotten City, House of America, Gas Station Angel.* Cardigan: Parthian, 2002.

——. *Three Plays: House of America, Flowers of the Dead Red Sea, East from the Gantry.* Bridgend: Seren, 1994.

——. "Wanted: A New Welsh Mythology." *New Welsh Review* 27 (Winter 1994/1995): 54–61. [Interview with Hazel Walford Davies.]

Williams, Daniel. "Harry Secombe in the Junkshop: Nation, Myth and Invention in Edward Thomas's *House of America* and David Mamet's *American Buffalo*." *Welsh Writing in English: A Yearbook of Critical Essays* 4 (1998): 133–158.

Alyce von Rothkirch

THOMAS, GWYN (1913–1981)

Writer, dramatist, broadcaster, and television personality Gwyn Thomas was born in 1913 in Cymmer, Rhondda Cynon Taf, Glamorgan, Wales, into an English-speaking Rhondda mining family as the youngest of twelve children. His father was often unemployed, and he grew up in the climate of severe poverty that characterized industrial southern Wales in the depression of the 1920s and 1930s, an experience that was to inform most of his writing. He won a scholarship to St. Edmund Hall, Oxford, to study modern languages, but constant financial difficulties and an alienation from what the committed socialist Thomas perceived as the upper-class, High Tory atmosphere of Oxford contributed to a deep sense of isolation. He experienced periods of unemployment and worked in adult education in ENGLAND and Wales. From 1942 he worked as a grammar-school teacher of French and Spanish in Cardigan and Barry before retiring from teaching to devote himself to writing full-time in 1962.

A prolific writer, Thomas wrote novels (for example, *All Things Betray Thee*, 1949), stage plays, plays and features for radio and television and published two collections of essays (*A Welsh Eye*, 1964, and *A Hatful of Humans*, 1965) and "an autobiography of sorts," *A Few Selected Exits* (1968). His radio play *Gazooka: A Rhondda Reminiscence* (1952) is in many ways characteristic of Thomas's work: written with eloquence, humor, and a great fondness for his characters, who reappear in other radio plays, it captures the idiom of the Rhondda valley as it depicts the exploits of the striking miners as they marched and countermarched about the valleys in rival bands, often dressed up in carnival dress, in the summer of the general strike in 1926. The positive reception of radio plays such as *Gazooka* fueled Thomas's interest in playwriting. His plays, like his other writing, usually deal with working-class life in southern Wales in the first half of the 20th century. Because he writes about the valleys' singular culture characterized by a failing mining industry, the last remnants of nonconformist dogma, and a strongly socialist Laborism, his material is often grim. Yet he treats it with a rare humor and an eye for the more absurd, farcical characteristics of the community he describes and identifies with. THE KEEP (1960) deals with the peculiarly claustrophobic atmosphere of a Rhondda family home in the 1950s. *Jackie the Jumper* (1963) is a historical play about the Merthyr Rising of 1831. In other plays, such as *Loud Organs* (1962) and *Sap* (1974), he moved away from stage REALISM to a form that incorporated nonrealist and music-hall elements.

Once described as the "greatest talker in the world," Gwyn Thomas became a television personality in the 1960s, contributing to various programs as an entertainer, but also as an eloquent spokesman for his native southern Wales. Thomas's health began to fail in the late 1960s because of a combination of diabetes and heavy drinking. He died in 1981 in Cardiff University Hospital shortly before his sixty-eighth birthday. He is remembered as one of the most original, witty, and eloquent "characters" of the Welsh literary scene.

PLAYS: *Gazooka: A Rhondda Reminiscence* (radio–play, 1952); *The Keep* (1960); *Loud Organs* (1962); *Jackie the Jumper* (1963); *Return and End* (based on the life of Aneurin Bevan, c. 1963, unpublished); *The Loot* (1965); *Sap* (1974, unpublished); *The Breakers* (1976, unpublished); *Testimonials* (1979, unpublished)

FURTHER READING

Parnell, Michael. Introduction to *Three Plays*, by Gwyn Thomas. Bridgend: Seren, 1990. 7–21.

——. *Laughter from the Dark: A Life of Gwyn Thomas*. Bridgend: Seren, 1997.

Thomas, Gwyn. *A Few Selected Exits*. Bridgend: Seren, 1985.

——. "Gazooka: A Rhondda Reminiscence." In *Act One Wales: Thirteen One Act Plays*, ed. by Phil Clark. Bridgend: Seren, 1997. 44–69.

——. *Three Plays*. Ed. by Michael Parnell. Bridgend: Seren, 1990. [*The Keep, Jackie the Jumper, Loud Organs.*]

Alyce von Rothkirch

THOMPSON, JUDITH (1954–)

Judith Thompson (born in Montreal, Quebec, CANADA, in 1954) is one of Canada's preeminent playwrights. Trained as an actor with the National Theatre School, Thompson is acutely attuned to the voices of her characters. She often speaks of her artistic process as a kind of channeling of the voices that come from the chaos and the collective unconscious that she sees around her. The characters that inhabit her work are often marginalized, dispossessed people. As Urjo Kareda says in the introduction to a collection of Thompson's work, *The Other Side of the Dark* (1989), "Judith Thompson hears the poetry of the inarticulate and the semi-literate."

This poetry often finds shape in a monologue, which can function as a kind of signature for the character, giving the audience access to the inner turmoil of the characters. For Thompson's characters often find themselves in extreme circumstances: in the throes of birth, death, rage, murder, and betrayal. They inevitably undergo struggles with their own demons, often resulting in fearful transformations. A devastating sense of loss and hollowness haunts them, and for this reason, perhaps, her work lends itself to psychoanalytic interpretations. As Robert Nunn suggests, the extreme behavior of her characters is often traced to a primary loss in the separation from the mother, compounded by the loss enacted by the acquisition of language and entrance into a symbolic order. Although Thompson's plays can be read in this vein, they also offer cogent social critique. Her characters, especially in the early plays, are often of a lower class and are struggling to maintain a sense of dignity in a world that constantly misjudges them.

Thompson's plays range in style from the REALISM of THE CRACKWALKER (1980) to the daisy-chain, imaginative play of LION IN THE STREETS (1990). Although her plays are without exception emotionally draining and highly dramatic, there is a clear comic vein and irony in her work as she punctures moments of crisis with moments of levity and the bizarre. Her work relies on a binary division of the world, which she then proceeds to overturn. This ambiguous space, both terrifying and liberating, is often represented by a character who has an epileptic seizure (Rose in *I Am Yours* [1987], Patsy in *Perfect Pie* [2000]). The "identity panic" that ensues, as Thompson calls it, recurs throughout her plays as her characters struggle to find stability in a fundamentally unstable world. Yet the endings of her plays often exhibit an abiding sense of regeneration.

Thompson has twice won the Governor General's Award for drama (for *White Biting Dog* [1984] and *The Other Side of the Dark*). She has also won the Floyd S. Chalmers Canadian Play Award for *I am Yours* and *Lion in the Streets*. In 2005, she was named an Officer of the Order of Canada. Thompson frequently directs the premieres of her own plays, often at Tarragon Theatre in Toronto. She is a professor at the University of Guelph where she teaches playwriting and acting. Thompson has also written for radio, television, and film. She adapted Susan Swan's novel, *The Wives of Bath*, for the film *Lost and Delirious* and wrote the screenplay for *Perfect Pie*. She has also adapted and directed HENRIK IBSEN's HEDDA GABLER.

SELECT PLAYS: *The Crackwalker* (1980); *White Biting Dog* (1984); *Pink* (1986); *I Am Yours* (1987); *Tornado* (1989); *Lion in the Streets* (1990); *White Sand* (1991); *The Yellow Canaries* (1992); *Sled* (1997); *Perfect Pie* (2000); *Habitat* (2001); *Capture Me* (2004); *Enoch Arden, by Alfred Lord Jabber and His Catatonic Songstress* (2005); *The Palace of the End* (2006)

FURTHER READING

Adam, Julie. "The Implicated Audience: Judith Thompson's Antinaturalism in *The Crackwalker, White Biting Dog, I Am Yours* and *Lion in the Streets*." In *Women on the Canadian Stage: The Legacy of Hrotsvit*, ed. by Rita Much. Winnipeg: Blizzard, 1992.

Canadian Theatre Review 89 (Winter 1996). [Judith Thompson casebook.]

Harvie, Jennifer. "(Im)Possibility: Fantasy and Judith Thompson's Drama." In *On-stage and Off-stage: English Canadian Drama in Discourse*, ed. by Albert-Reiner Glaap with Rolf Althof. St. John's: Breakwater, 1996.

Knowles, Ric, ed. *Judith Thompson*. Toronto: Playwrights Canada Press, 2005.

——, ed. *The Masks of Judith Thompson*. Toronto: Playwrights Canada Press, 2006.

——. *The Theatre of Form and the Production of Meaning: Contemporary Canadian Dramaturgies*. Toronto: ECW Press, 1999.

Nunn, Robert. "Judith Thompson's Marginal Characters." In *Siting the Other: Re-visions of Marginality in Australian and English-Canadian Drama*, ed. by Marc Maufort and Franca Bellarsi. Brussells: P. Lang, 2001.

——. "Spatial Metaphor in the Plays of Judith Thompson." *Theatre History in Canada* 10, no. 1 (Spring 1989): 3–29.

Thompson, Judith. *The Other Side of the Dark: Four Plays*. Toronto: Coach House Press, 1989.

Marlene Moser

THOMPSON, MERVYN (1936–1992)

A coal miner, a university lecturer, and a director, Mervyn Thompson co-founded Christchurch's Court Theatre and was its co-director from 1971 to 74 and director of Wellington's Downstage in 1975–1976. He introduced the specialist drama program at the University of Auckland, teaching there from 1977 to 1989. A controversial figure, he passionately advocated a NEW ZEALAND theater that is "an exciting and compelling witness to all ourselves instead of a pale reflection of some of them" (*Selected Plays*, 1984).

The expressionistic, semiautobiographical play *First Return* (1974) alternates between realistic scenes in London and distorted boyhood memories as the protagonist attempts to come to terms with himself and his IDENTITY as a New Zealander. The play includes songs, drawing on the world of music hall, vaudeville, and the fairground, whose influence became pronounced in all of Thompson's drama.

Subsequent plays extend Thompson's concern with identity and national issues. Sharing the political commitment of groups such as Theatre Action and Amamus, Thompson similarly sought to confront New Zealanders with those parts of their history that they too readily repress. A rumbustious "semi-documentary" play with music, *O! Temperance!* (1972) traces the history of the temperance movement in New Zealand. Signaling a recurring concern to bring together cast and audience, the play takes the form of a meeting in a community hall in 1919. At the end the characters urge the audience to sign pledges.

Thompson's emphasis on music developed into the "song-play," in which the entire play is conveyed through song. *Songs to Uncle Scrim* (produced in 1976, published in 1984), with composer Stephen McCurdy, evokes the 1930s Depression, while *Songs to the Judges* (produced in 1980, published in 1984), with composer William Dart, perhaps Thompson's greatest accomplishment, was inspired by Maori land protests. With the theater as a mock courtroom, presided over by a cartoonish judge, *Songs to the Judges* catalogs the legal chicanery, from 1841 onwards, whereby Maori were dispossessed of their lands and heritage.

Having acted roles in his plays, including the judge in *Songs to the Judges*, in 1984 Thompson wrote and performed the solo work *Coaltown Blues*, which draws heavily on his childhood on the South Island's remote west coast. The Performer tells of his upbringing in a poor coal-mining community, his father's violence, and his mother's deteriorating sanity and eventual suicide. This narrative is set against national events, beginning hopefully with the election of the first Labor government in 1935 and ending with the 1951 Waterfront Dispute, which signaled the repression of the unions.

Thompson's other musical works include *A Night at the Races* (1977), co-written with Yvonne Blennerhassett Edwards and composed by Andrew Glover, and *The New Zealand "Truth" Show* (produced in 1982, published in 1992), devised with Auckland University students. The former celebrates the second in the triad of national pursuits, rugby, racing, and beer, and turns the theater into a race meeting. The second looks at the way the (in)famous weekly newspaper *Truth* mediated New Zealand history over a period of sixty years. Other plays are *Lovebirds* (1992), *Jean and Richard* (1992), and *Passing Through* (1991), another solo autobiographical piece, which recounts Thompson's experiences in the theater.

[See also Documentary Drama]

PLAYS: *First Return* (1974); *O! Temperance!* (1974); *Songs to Uncle Scrim* (with Stephen McCurdy, 1976); *Songs to the Judges* (with William Dart, 1980); *A Night at the Races* (with Yvonne Blennerhassett Edwards and Andrew Glover, 1981); *The New Zealand 'Truth' Show* (1982); *Coaltown Blues* (1984); *Children of the Poor* (adapted from the novel by John A. Lee, 1989); *Jean and Richard* (1992); *Lovebirds* (1992); *Passing Through* (1992)

FURTHER READING

Boire, Gary. "Resistance Moves: Mervyn Thompson's *Songs to the Judges*." *Australian and New Zealand Studies in Canada* 6 (Fall 1991): 15–26.

Corballis, Dick. "Interview with Mervyn Thompson." *Sites* 29 (Spring 1994): 71–97.

Dowling, David. "Mervyn Thompson." *Landfall* 34 (December 1980): 307–313. [Interview with Thompson.]

McNaughton, Howard. "Negotiating Marae Performance." *Theatre Research International* 26, no. 1 (2001): 25–34.

Thompson, Mervyn. *Selected Plays*. Dunedin: Pilgrims South Press, 1984.

——. "The Song Is Sung: Mervyn Thompson and Music Theatre." *Music in New Zealand* 9 (Winter 1990): 38–43.

Stuart Young

THOMPSON, PAUL (1940–)

Evolving from Rochdale College—the 1970s Toronto attempt at a "free university"—was what would become one of the original alternative theaters in Canadian dramatic history, Theatre Passe Muraille. At the helm of this groundbreaking theater company, and having found his feet as technical director—alongside founding artistic director Martin Kinch—was Paul Thompson.

Born in Charlottetown, Prince Edward Island, on May 4, 1940, Thompson grew up in southwestern Ontario, where he attended the University of Western Ontario from 1959 to 1963. After graduating with a B.A. with honors in English and French, Thompson moved to Paris (1964) and studied at the Sorbonne on a scholarship he had received from the French government. During his education at the Sorbonne Thompson immersed himself in European theater, attending up to twenty plays a month. While absorbing the French theatrical experience (which would later influence his studies on French AVANT-GARDE theater practitioner ANTONIN ARTAUD), Thompson forged an artistic relationship with director Roger Planchon. Thompson joined Planchon as *stagiare* (an unpaid apprentice director) before returning to Ontario in 1965, where he spent the next year working towards his M.A. in French with a specialization in theater.

Upon receiving his master's degree, Thompson returned to Paris and joined Planchon's company in Lyons in 1965. Having absorbed the European (and particularly French) theatrical style, Thompson returned to CANADA in 1967. Eventually he would facilitate the creation of a Canadian style. Awaiting him in Canada were many young Canadian actors and writers who—having learned the ropes via the British, American, and European canon—were eager to crystallize a Canadian style with Canadian content. The aim was to generate work that spoke to a Canadian community and expressed the time, place, and interests of those who created, as well as those who witnessed, the theater.

In the spring of 1967 Thompson had the opportunity to work with a variety of young Canadian talent, having been hired as assistant director at the Stratford Festival. After his second season Thompson left the company to pursue his interest in creating plays based on the collective heritage he shared with the Canadian audience. What evolved out of this interest was collective creation, a Canadian theatrical form influenced by the work of European theatrical innovators. Collective creation (as it was called by those who practiced it) forged a method by which to develop a uniquely Canadian repertoire based on the Canadian experience.

Thompson's first effort through collective creation was 1970's *Notes from Quebec*, an adaptation of Jean-Claude Germaine's *Duigidi Duigidi Ha Ha Ha!* Following that were *Doukhbors* and *Free Ride* in 1971. In 1972 Thompson guided the creation of *The Farm Show*, which involved a cast of six relocating to the rural community of Clinton, Ontario, to create a performance that reflected the lives and hardships of its residents. Between 1970 and 1993 Thompson served at the helm of close to thirty collective creations that functioned to cultivate a Canadian dramatic language based in the experiences and sensibilities of those Canadians, both rural and cosmopolitan.

SELECT PLAYS: *Notes from Quebec* (adapted from Jean Claude Germaine's *Duigidi Duigidi Ha Ha Ha!*, 1970); *Doukhbors* (1971); *Free Ride* (1971); *The Farm Show* (1972)

FURTHER READING

Conolly, L. W., ed. *Canadian Drama and the Critics*. Toronto: Talonbooks, 1995.

Healey, Michael. *The Drawer Boy*. Toronto: PUC Play Service, 1999.

Rudakoff, Judith, ed. *Dangerous Traditions: A Theatre Passe Muraille Anthology*. Toronto: Blizzard, 1992.

Sarah Cervinka

THE THREEPENNY OPERA

Based on John Gay's *The Beggar's Opera* (1728) and first produced in Berlin in 1928, *The Threepenny Opera* (*Die Dreigroschenoper*) has a score by Kurt Weill (1900–1950) and a book and lyrics usually attributed to BERTOLT BRECHT—though a number of sources credit Brecht's associate Elisabeth Hauptmann (1897–1973) with having contributed more to the text than Brecht himself.

The opening-night triumph of *The Threepenny Opera* has become one of the legendary events of 20th-century theater. Beset by multiple difficulties, the production seemed destined for disaster. Instead, *The Threepenny Opera* became the sensation of the season, playing to sold-out houses and spawning a Berlin bar dedicated solely to the performance of its music. From GERMANY its success spilled over to the rest of Europe and eventually reached America. Of all the works in the Brecht canon, *The Threepenny Opera* has come closest to penetrating the popular consciousness. In fact, its signature song, "The *Moritat* of Mack the Knife" ("Die Moritat von Mackie Messer") rose to the number two spot on American popular music charts in 1959.

Set in a wholly imaginary Victorian London on the eve of "the coronation," the action centers on the conflict between Jonathan Peachum, who operates a stable of professional beggars, and Macheath, known as Mackie the Knife, the head of a gang of thieves and murderers. Peachum's daughter, Polly, whose pretty legs are one of her father's chief commercial assets, has fallen for Mackie and married him. An outraged Peachum determines to eliminate this threat to the family business by having Mackie arrested and hanged. Tiger Brown, the Chief of Police and Macheath's best friend, at first resists Peachum's efforts. But when Peachum threatens to disrupt the coronation if Mackie is not punished, Brown capitulates. Just before Mackie is to be hanged, however, a messenger from the Queen arrives with a pardon for Mackie, ending the drama on a sardonically happy note.

The staging of *The Threepenny Opera*, with its projected scene titles and its use of stylized lighting changes to mark the beginnings and endings of "operatic" moments, reflects the influence of Brecht's concurrent membership in the "dramaturgical collective" of ERWIN PISCATOR, a pioneer of the "EPIC" style. Such ALIENATION EFFECTS go hand in hand with Brecht's attempt to redefine opera in Marxist terms. *The Threepenny Opera* is a sustained travesty of bourgeois art and morals. Its sleazy characters and slangy music mock the nobility and uplift of conventional opera, while its amiably cynical portrayal of thieves, exploiters, and sexual predators suggests that they are no different from the middle-class businessmen who patronize the theater. According to Brecht, conventional opera exists to "impose" its reactionary social "views as it were incognito" through the illusion-making machinery of the stage (Willett, 1964). The spectator is thereby rendered passive and uncritical. In contrast, the projected titles and intrusive lighting effects of *The Threepenny Opera*, together with the criminality of its bourgeois characters, are meant to shock the spectator into a double critical awareness: of the artifice of the stage and of the contradictions of the social world.

FURTHER READING

Brecht, Bertolt. *Brecht on Theatre.* Ed. and tr. by John Willett. New York: Hill & Wang, 1964.

——. *The Threepenny Opera.* Tr. by Desmond Vesey and Eric Bentley. New York: Grove, 1964.

Speirs, Ronald. *Brecht's Early Plays.* Atlantic Highlands, N.J.: Humanities Press, 1982.

Martin Andrucki

THREE SISTERS

In *Three Sisters* (*Tri sestry*, 1900), the third of ANTON CHEKHOV's four dramatic masterpieces, the playwright continued the exploration of a radically new poetics he had begun in THE SEAGULL and UNCLE VANYA. Having abandoned the conventions of the so-called well-made play that preceded him, Chekhov turned to what critics have described as plays of indirect action. His decision to abandon heroic action as such sounded a death knell for heroes, who are replaced in Chekhov's work by ordinary characters. As the title itself suggests, *Three Sisters* has not one heroine, but many. One consequence of this shift is a greater emphasis on the ensemble of characters in the play.

Another consequence is that what is not said or done often proves just as important as what is said or done. An obvious example arises in the scene between Irina and Tuzenbakh that precedes the duel in which he is killed. The absence of a good-bye heightens the pathos of a parting that will be final. In other instances Chekhov employs language that is devoid of semantic meaning and that seems to say nothing at all, yet turns out to signify matters of great moment. When, for example, Masha and Vershinin fall in love, they acknowledge their interconnectedness through a vocalized melody. To Masha's "tram-tam-tam" Vershinin answers, "Tam-tam!" The meaning of this exchange is enhanced with each repetition, and at different times it signals first an affirmation of their love and later a secret code by which they identify and hail one another. Despite the enormous import of these utterances, their meaning remains largely hidden from the other characters. Chekhov also exploits trivial and seemingly meaningless phrases to similar effect. The famous phrase "Balzac was married in Berdichev," which seems to tumble randomly from Chebutykin's lips as he casually reads the newspaper, falls into this category. On the surface, it seems to have little relevance to the play; however, on closer inspection, it offers telling commentary on the argument about happiness that precedes it. The absence of meaning proves illusory.

Chekhov uses absence and displacement in larger ways to shape the play's themes. The problem of nostalgia begins with the absence of deceased parents. The three sisters recall how much grander, how much livelier, how much fuller life was when their parents, and especially their father, were alive. To them, the name-day party of act 1 seems a ghostly affair compared with parties their parents had thrown. In many ways their shared nostalgia for Moscow grows out of this familial longing. Their pining for other people and other times suggests a failure to define the present in its own terms, which in turn leads to the diminution of their lives that is a kind of violence that they do themselves and that makes them vulnerable to the manipulation of others. In fact, the play's metabasis, or reversal of fortune, arises from this vulnerability. The sisters and Andrei are susceptible to the machinations of Natasha and Protopopov for this reason and lose their home as a consequence. It is worth noting that the greatest absence of all, yet the most terrifying presence, is Protopopov's. His presence is signaled by a series of metonymies: the birthday cake he sends to Irina in act 1, the arrival of his carriage offstage in act 2.

Perhaps because Chekhov put so much emphasis on absences, the metonymic relation of the characters to the objects around them assumes an unusual significance in *Three Sisters*. Almost every character is associated with one or more objects, and those objects bear a clear relation to the characters' emotional dilemmas: Chebutykin's newspaper and notepad highlight his forgetfulness and aimless approach to knowledge, Andrei's violin becomes a means of escape from a life he cannot tolerate, Natasha's gauche green belt reflects her petit bourgeois values, and no amount of perfume can prevent the hands of Tuzenbakh's killer, Solyony, from smelling like a corpse. In other words, ordinary, everyday objects attain a significance that verges on the symbolic. This becomes particularly clear in the relation between the three sisters, particularly Masha, and the grand piano. Despite all that is negative in their lives, the three sisters retain a creative impulse that is closely allied to the determined optimism they express at the end of the play.

Although Chekhov considered giving *Three Sisters* to the renowned actress Vera Komissarzhevskaia, in the end he opted for a production at the MOSCOW ART THEATRE. The premiere took place on January 31, 1901, with a stellar cast: Chekhov's soon-to-be bride Olga Knipper played Masha, the future director VSEVOLOD MEYERHOLD performed the role of Tuzenbakh, and the Art Theatre's director KONSTANTIN STANISLAVSKY acted the part of Vershinin. Although *Three Sisters* was not the bombshell *The Seagull* had been, it enjoyed increasing success with each performance. The following season Chekhov himself participated in rehearsals and supervised the staging of the fire scene in act 3.

[*See also* Russia and the Soviet Union]

FURTHER READING

Brahms, Caryl. *Reflections in a Lake: A Study of Chekhov's Four Greatest Plays.* London: Weidenfeld & Nicolson, 1976.

Bristow, Eugene K. "Circles, Triads, and Parity in *The Three Sisters.*" In *Chekhov's Great Plays: A Critical Anthology,* ed. by Jean-Pierre Barricelli. New York: New York Univ. Press, 1981. 76–95.

Chekhov, Anton. *Three Sisters*. Tr. by Michael Frayn. London: Methuen, 2003.

Gilman, Richard. *Chekhov's Plays: An Opening Into Eternity*. New Haven: Yale Univ. Press, 1995.

McVay, Gordon. *Chekhov's "Three Sisters."* London: Bristol Classical Press, 1995.

Timothy C. Westphalen

THREE TALL WOMEN

The happiest moment? Coming to the end of it, I think, when all the waves cause the greatest woes to subside.
—"A," Act 2

Three Tall Women, which premiered at the English Theater in Vienna, AUSTRIA, in 1991, marked EDWARD ALBEE's return to prominence in mainstream theater writing after a decade of relative inactivity and comparative obscurity. The play was awarded the Pulitzer Prize for Drama (1994) and the Drama Critics' Circle, Lucille Lortel, and Outer Critics' Circle awards for best play.

In act 1 we meet three women who initially appear to be three separate characters who are linked in some way: "A" is a frail ninety-two-year-old woman in need of care, spending her remaining days in an elegantly furnished room; "B" is a fifty-two-year-old woman in the middle of her career; "C," the youngest, at twenty-six, is a legal representative who has come to sort out the old woman's estate. In act 2, however, it is clear that these three represent the same woman at different stages of her life.

The youngest woman cannot accept that she could ever become as bitter and opinionated as her older counterparts; the middle woman is in a state of confused optimism, unable to comprehend or accept that her son simply left home with no explanation. During the play we witness the painful scene of her emotional breakdown. The old woman, however, understands all too clearly how the lives of the younger women will turn out, for she is there already.

The text of the play is intricately crafted, and even before we become aware of the singularity of the character, the three women begin to comment upon each other's situation. The central themes of the play are conveyed in the narrative of the oldest character: she reflects upon her past life, missed opportunities, achievements, pleasures, and the pains. She recalls the best times of her life, her childhood and her marriage, and the worst, her husband's infidelity and her son's estrangement. The action of the play is static, but the energy is maintained in the sharp, often very funny dialogue. Here Albee returns to the device of the lengthy character monologue that he first explored effectively in THE ZOO STORY (1959).

The fourth character in the play is the mute figure of the son, whose silent comments and reactions to the unfolding story provide an unusual counterpoint to the main narrative. Perhaps Albee himself felt this same silent detachment and isolation in his own strained relationship with his mother. *Three Tall Women* is certainly dominated by several important autobiographical elements: the relationship between the play's protagonist and her gay son mirrors the author's own relationship with his adoptive mother, who was unable to accept his sexuality. Just as the son in the play leaves home to become his own person, so Albee did when he moved to Greenwich Village. He began to write this play one year after his mother died.

Albee's waning popularity in the early 1990s made it problematic to find an American producer willing to risk a production of this play. However, when the play finally opened in New York in January 1994, it was greeted by ecstatic critical response, including that of a critic from the *New York Times*, who wrote that the play is "so good it can only exist on the stage. A perfect illustration of why theatre is an indispensable art."

[*See also* United States]

FURTHER READING

Gussow, Mel. *Edward Albee: A Singular Journey*. London: Oberon Bks., 1999.

McCarthy, Gerry. *Edward Albee*. London: Macmillan, 1987.

Roudané, Matthew C. *Understanding Edward Albee*. Columbia: Univ. of South Carolina Press, 1987.

Paul E. Fryer

THE THUNDERSTORM

The Thunderstorm (Groza, 1859) is a drama in five acts by ALEKSANDR OSTROVSKY set in the imaginary town of Kalinov on the Volga River in RUSSIA. The heroine, Katerina, a sensitive young woman, is married to Tikhon, the obedient son of Kabanikha, a domestic tyrant. Katerina is pushed to desperation by her oppressive family environment, which Tikhon escapes by embarking on a business trip. In Tikhon's absence, his sister, Varvara—still unmarried and thus free to keep company with her friend Kudryash—steals a key so that Katerina and she can both go out to meet their lovers. Katerina has a brief affair with a young merchant, Boris, her first real love. But she is tormented by repentance and, during a storm on the Volga, feels impelled to confess her sin to her husband, as well as, incidentally, the townspeople who have taken shelter from the storm. Boris, who must obey his merchant uncle, Dikoy, is sent away as a punishment. Varvara and Kudryash go away together. Kabanikha and Tikhon make Katerina's life a misery, and she throws herself into the Volga.

The Thunderstorm renders vividly the gloom of the despotic family and the backwardness of a Russian provincial town. The mores of a river town, where Ostrovsky gathered material during his 1856 trip for the Maritime Ministry, are essential to the play. The town embodies elements of good and evil, with the gifted craftsman Kulygin and the irrepressible young lovers

Varvara and Kudryash representing the one, and with the monstrous Kabanikha and Dikoy standing for the other. The natural setting and the small-town environment also play an important part in the action. Ostrovsky uses the sweep of the river to denote the freedom of nature, in contrast to the women's confinement in chambers. Many scenes occur on a high bank overlooking the Volga River. The love scene is romantically set in a ravine at night, and the last act also exploits darkness. Music and sound effects enhance the play's emotional impact. In act 4 the climax is reached in an especially powerful scene of thunder and lightning.

According to Marc Slonim, "The character of Katerina, with her dreams and religious yearnings, transcends the narrow limits of a social phenomenon; and her dramatic conflict with her environment, enhanced by mystical forebodings and the eerie atmosphere of storm, lightning and thunder, is symbolic of the inevitable clash between the 'pure soul' and crude reality" (Slonim, 1961). Katerina has an emotional nature, not a rational one; her religiousness is exalted, and she is as subject to impulse and indecision as a Dostoevskian character. Critic Nikolai Dobrolyubov hailed Katerina's suicide as a protest against tyranny and hence "a ray of light" in the dark world of oppression. Ostrovsky won the Uvarov Prize for *The Thunderstorm*, and since its first performance in 1859, the play has remained a major classic of the Russian stage, with directors and actors offering ever-new interpretations of Katerina. Czech composer Leoš Janáček based his 1921 opera *Kátya Kabanová* on *The Thunderstorm*.

FURTHER READING

Hoover, Marjorie L. *Alexander Ostrovsky*. Boston: Twayne, 1981.

Ostrovsky, Aleksandr. *Groza* [The thunderstorm]. Ed. by Norman Henley. Letchworth: Bradda Books, 1963.

——. *The Storm*. In *Plays*, tr. by Margaret Wettlin. Moscow: Progress, 1974.

——. *The Storm*. Tr. by Frank McGuinness. London: Faber, 1998.

Peace, Richard. "A. N. Ostrovsky's *The Thunderstorm*: The Dramatization of Conceptual Ambivalence." *Modern Language Review* 84 (1990).

Rahman, Kate Sealey. *Ostrovsky: Reality and Illusion*. Birmingham Slavonic Monographs No. 30. Birmingham: Univ. of Birmingham, 1999.

Slonim, Marc. *Russian Theater from the Empire to the Soviets*. Cleveland: World Pub., 1961.

Liisa Byckling

TIAN HAN (1898–1968)

Chinese playwright and poet Tian Han was born Tian Shouchang in March 1898 in Changsha, Hunan Province. In 1916 he went to study in JAPAN, where he joined the Shaonian zhongguo xuehui (Society of Chinese Youth) founded by Li Dazhao and others. On his return to CHINA in 1921 he and several others founded the Chuang zao she (Creation Society), advocating ROMANTICISM for literature. Tian Han started playwriting in 1920 when he wrote his first play, *A Night in a Café* (*Kafei dian zhi yiye*). Afterwards he continued to write plays and founded the influential Nan guo she (South China Society), which became the forerunner in experimenting with and promoting modern drama in China. In 1930 Tian Han joined the Left-Wing Dramatists League, which marked the change of his political orientation. After 1949 Tian Han wrote fewer plays but assumed more administrative posts. The most important plays he wrote during this period include *Guan Hanqing* (1958), *Princess Wencheng* (*Wencheng gongzhu*, 1960), and *Xie Yaohuan* (1961). Tian was persecuted to death during the Cultural Revolution in December 1968.

As a man well versed in poetry and librettos, as well as drama, Tian Han spent about forty years in playwriting, which underwent, in his own words, three stages. His plays written before 1930 belonged to the first stage, which was marked by his embracing of the aesthetic proposition of art for art's sake. The poet seeking suicide for the sake of a dancer he salvaged in *The Sound from an Old Pond* (*Gu tan de shengyin*) and the manifestation of the protagonist shortly before her death in *Tragedy on the Lake* (*Hu shang de beiju*, 1928) are characteristic of Tian Han's ideas at this stage. Tian Han's self-criticism summarizing his theory and practice in drama, published in 1930, signaled his change to more realistic settings, which is best shown in *An Evening Talk in Suzhou* (*Suzhou yehua*), where Liu Shukang, an old painter, unexpectedly meets his lost daughter during the war. Liu's awakening self-reflection of his erstwhile indulgence in art is put in contrast with the realistic portraiture of the cruel reality of war. As Tian Han became more and more involved in the Left-Wing Dramatists League and advocated revolutionary ideology, his plays written at this time were considered to belong to the last stage of his playwriting, which was marked by the didactic overtone expressed in his plays, including his later historical plays such as *Guan Hanqing* (1958).

Tian Han's plays are generally not known for their well-made or intricate dramatic structure, but they excel in expository momentum and climactic mood, as well as artistic imagination. His use of lyric songs in his plays often adds to the success of the dramatic effect they produce.

[See also The White Snake]

SELECT PLAYS: *A Night in a Café* (*Kafei dian zhi yiye*, 1920); *The Night the Tiger Was Captured* (*Huo hu zhi ye*, 1924); *Tragedy on the Lake* (*Hu shang de beiju*, 1928); *Death of a Famous Actor* (*Ming you zhi si*, 1929); *The Rainy Season* (*Mei yu*, 1931); *The Moonlight Sonata in 1932* (*Yi jiu san er nian de yu guang qu*, 1932); *Seven Women in the Stormy Weather* (*Bao feng yu zhong de qi ge nüxing*, 1932); *Three Charming Ladies* (*Li ren xing*, 1947); *The White Snake* (*Bai she zhuan*, 1952); *Guan Hanqing* (1958); *Princess Wencheng* (*Wencheng gongzhu*, 1960); *Xie Yaohuan* (1961)

FURTHER READING

Chen, Xiaomei. *Acting the Right Part: Political Theater and Popular Drama in Contemporary China.* Honolulu: Univ. of Hawaii Press, 2002.

Dong, Jian. *Tian Han zhuan.* Beijing: Beijing shiyue wenyi chubanshe, 1996.

Kaplan, Randy Barbara. "The Pre-leftist One-Act Dramas of Tian Han (1898–1968)." Ph.D. diss., Ohio State Univ., 1986.

Tian, Benxiang, Wu Ge, and Song Baozhen. *Tian Han ping zhuan.* Chongqing: Chongqing chubanshe, 1998.

Zou, Ping. *Tian Han: Zhongguo hua ju di dian ji ren.* Shanghai: Shanghai Jiaoyu Chubanshe, 1999.

Hongchu Fu

TIANXIA DIYI LOU, HUAJU   See THE FIRST HOUSE OF BEIJING DUCK

TIANXIAN PEI, HUANGMEI XI   See MARRIED TO A CELESTIAL LADY

THE TICKET-OF-LEAVE MAN

THOMAS TAYLOR's *The Ticket-of-Leave Man* takes place in London, ENGLAND, between 1863 and 1868. Robert Brierly, a naïve Lancashire lad, gets mixed up with scoundrels James Dalton, also known as "the Tiger," and Melter Moss, Dalton's accomplice. Brierly unknowingly passes a counterfeit bill Dalton gives him, and he is sent to prison by Detective Hawkshaw. Released early for good behavior, Brierly receives a "ticket-of-leave," equivalent to today's early parole, and tries to rebuild his life with his faithful friend and later wife, May Edwards. Hoping to hound Brierly into a life of crime with them, Dalton and Moss again make trouble for Brierly by informing all his employers of his prison sentence. Eventually Brierly happens upon Dalton and Moss and is enlisted to break into a former employer's office. Brierly uses this opportunity to get his revenge on the two crooks and assists Hawkshaw in the capture of Dalton and Moss, proving that "there may be some good left in a 'Ticket-of-Leave-Man,' after all."

The Ticket-of-Leave Man is an adaptation from the French *La retour de Melun* by Edouard-Louis-Alexandre Brisebarre and Eugène Nus and was first produced in 1863 at the Olympic Theatre in London, where it ran for a record 407 continuous performances, followed the next year by another long run of performances in New York, making *The Ticket-of-Leave Man* fairly popular in its day. Unfortunately, the play has lost its acclaim today because of changing popular taste. Despite this, Detective Hawkshaw has remained a memorable character and is a precursor to Sherlock Holmes as the master sleuth. Since his first appearance in *The Ticket-of-Leave Man*, Hawkshaw has been re-created in various plays, movies, a ballet, and a Broadway musical.

Like many Victorian literary works, *The Ticket-of-Leave Man* carries deep moral overtones. While it denounces gambling and alcohol as the gateway to further sin and self-destruction, the overall battle between good and evil is portrayed through the fight for Brierly's moral conscience. Evil in all forms is denounced and demonstrated as corrosive, but still the play infers that the best men cannot be worn down through evil's constant harassment. Another issue of morality in the play is the applicability of past reputations to changed individuals. Should a man's past constantly affect others' perspective on that man? Hawkshaw recognizes the good in Brierly and sees him as having paid his debt to society, suggesting that people must be given a chance to prove that they can outlive their reputations, and when they do, society must also move past its prejudices against that individual.

Although too didactic by today's standards, at the time of its first production *The Ticket-of-Leave Man* appealed to its Victorian viewers, as evidenced by its many past performances. Today *The Ticket-of-Leave Man* receives little attention from critics and general drama enthusiasts alike, much like nearly all of Taylor's works. This lack of interest in one of the most prolific and popularly influential writers of the Victorian era demonstrates the continually transitioning general tastes in literature and drama.

FURTHER READING

Mackin, Dorothy. *Melodrama Classics: Six Plays and How to Stage Them.* New York: Sterling, 1982.

Moses, Montrose. *Representative British Dramas: Victorian and Modern.* Boston: Little, Brown, 1925.

Turner, Paul. *Victorian Poetry, Drama, and Miscellaneous Prose, 1832–1890.* Oxford: Oxford Univ. Press, 1990.

Chad Lawrence McClane

TILL DAMASKUS   See TO DAMASCUS

THE TIME OF YOUR LIFE

For its producers, the THEATRE GUILD, WILLIAM SAROYAN's *The Time of Your Life* did not have a propitious beginning. When the play started tryouts in New Haven, Connecticut, it was, according to Lawrence Langner (1951), "in a state of incredible chaos." No one knew what the play was about—actors, audience, even the reviewers. By the time the play opened in New York on October 25, 1939, the director had defected, to be replaced by a triumvirate of Eddie Dowling (who played Joe), Langner, and Saroyan himself; new actors had been hired (Gene Kelly as Harvey and Celeste Holme as Mary); and Saroyan, more problem than asset, had been banished from the stage. When Saroyan had difficulty ending the play, PHILIP BARRY suggested Joe's slow exit. Because Saroyan saw the climax of the play as the patriotic eruption of the pinball machine, Langner found a model maker to create just the right contraption for the desired effect. Brooks Atkinson called Saroyan the "imp of modern drama"; others called him a pain in the neck. Still, his lack of artistic discipline, mixed with his fondness for undistinguished people, somehow worked in the theater, where he received both the Pulitzer Prize and the Drama Critics' Circle Award for *The Time of Your Life*.

In Nick's waterfront honky-tonk in San Francisco, Joe, a generous person who seems to sit at a table all day and drink champagne, passes the time of his life. Into this bar come a great variety of people—common people mainly, although a society couple come slumming. At the end of the bar sits an Arab, who speaks one line, frequently repeated: "No foundation. All the way down the line." Harry is a dancer and a monologuist; Wesley plays the piano; Willie plays the pinball machine. Dudley R. Bostwick tries desperately to call Elsie Mandelspiegel on the telephone to ask her to marry him. Tom, who runs errands for Joe, falls in love with Kitty Duvall, a prostitute. Joe protects Kitty from the clutches of Blick from the vice squad and encourages Tom and Kitty to get married: "Go ahead," Joe tells Tom, "correct the errors of the world." Kit Carson tells fantastic stories of his past: "Ever try to herd cattle on a bicycle?" he asks Joe. A drunkard, a newsboy, and a good-time girl all play their parts in this "slice of life." Even a good cop gets to tell of his dreams, but the pivotal figure is Joe, who talks to everyone and has Tom give money to people for him and buy a gun for him. When Blick harasses Kitty, Joe tries to shoot him, but the gun does not fire. Then Nick announces that Blick is dead; Kit Carson explains: "I shot a man once. In San Francisco. In 1939, I think it was." Joe then gives him the revolver and walks slowly offstage. He waves; the marble game goes into its American routine again.

Throughout Saroyan's plays there is a strong feeling reminiscent of the RKO Keith vaudeville circuit. No vaudeville act was better than Mr. MacGregor playing the bugle in MY HEART'S IN THE HIGHLANDS; and scattered events from *The Time of Your Life* all suggest the vaudeville lineup: the storyteller, a dancer, a pianist, a pinball machine artist, a monologuist in the phone booth and at the bar, a drunkard's appeal, the comic social scene. This was the theater Saroyan enjoyed. Aram Saroyan, the dramatist's son, described his father as "the irrepressible old song-and-dance man" (1983). A fitting epitaph.

FURTHER READING

Dusenbury, Winifred L. *The Theme of Loneliness in Modern American Drama*. Gainesville: Univ. of Florida Press, 1960.

Langner, Lawrence. *The Magic Curtain*. New York: Dutton, 1951.

Nathan, George Jean. *The Magic Mirror*. New York: Knopf, 1960.

Saroyan, Aram. *William Saroyan*. San Diego, Harcourt, 1983.

Vernon, Granville. "The Time of Your Life." *Commonweal* 31 (November 19, 1939): 78.

Whitmore, Jon. *William Saroyan: A Research and Production Sourcebook*. Westport, Conn.: Greenwood Press, 1995.

Walter J. Meserve

TO, RAYMOND (1946–)

Raymond To (Kwok-wai) started his association with the performing arts at the early age of six when he participated in radio broadcasting. He has kept up that interest in the theater, films, and Cantonese opera since then. After graduation from the University of Hong Kong he took up teaching. During those years he promoted drama in school and started to write plays for performance. In 1992 he gave up teaching and held the post of playwright-in-residence of the Hong Kong Repertory Theatre for almost a decade.

To is a prolific playwright. He has written forty-six plays, many of which have been adapted into screenplays and television dramas. Many of his plays hark back with nostalgia to the experience, and celebrate the values, of earlier eras. His *Where Love Abides* (*Renjian youqing*, 1986) celebrates the warm interpersonal relationships of three generations in a family business over 100 years. *I Have a Date with Spring* (*Wo he chuntian you ge yuehui*, 1992), a musical that brings back nostalgic memories of the 1960s, was such a popular success that it ran for eighty performances and was made into a film. Other major works demonstrated To's affection for Cantonese opera. *Entrance on the P-side* (*Hudumen*, 1982) deals with the Cantonese opera milieu. *The Legend of the Mad Phoenix* (*Nanhai shisan lang*, 1993) is about the life of a legendary, eccentric, but brilliant Cantonese opera lyricist and composer. *A Sentimental Journey* (*Jian xue fusheng*, 1999) recounts the lives of two of the most popular Cantonese opera stars in the second half of the century. The subject matter, the values, and the warm affection in To's plays appealed to a wide audience, and the scripts attracted to the stage celebrities in films and television to act in those plays. The success of these major works created much excitement and changed stage performances from non-profit-making cultural events into popular and profitable Broadway-style shows. The box-office success of *I Have a Date with Spring* prompted To to found Springtime Production in October 1992. The company is still running as the only existing theater company in Hong Kong that operates on a commercial basis. Among To's works there are also plays that carry immediate political associations. *I Am Hong Kong* (*Wo xi xianggang ren*, 1985) was a prompt response to the 1984 signing of the Sino-British Joint Declaration. The play foregrounds a Hong Kong, rather than Chinese, identity for the Hong Kong people. It has received much critical acclaim. *A Foxy Tale* (*Liaozhai*, 1989) is an adaptation of a traditional ghost tale. The intricate love-hate relationship between the man and the fox depicted in the play is interpreted by many critics as the playwright's comment on the Tiananmen student movement. Raymond To has received the Hong Kong Artists' Guild Playwright of the Year Award (1989) and many other drama awards.

Raymond To works mainly in the local Cantonese cultural context and idiom and is able to bring popular support back to the theater with some of his major works. But To's contribution to drama is not recognized only in Hong Kong. The films based on his screenplays earned him an array of local and regional awards. He won the Golden Horse Film Award (1997) for the film *The Legend of the Mad Phoenix*, which also won a Hong Kong Film Award (1998). He received the honor of the Bronze Bauhinia in 1999 for his contribution to the arts.

[*See also* China]

SELECT PLAYS: *Entrance on the P-side* (Hudumen, 1982); *I Am Hong Kong* (Wo xi xianggang ren, 1985); *Where Love Abides* (Renjian youqing, 1986); *A Foxy Tale* (Liaozhai, 1989); *I Have a Date with Spring* (Wo he chuntian you ge yuehui, 1992); *The Legend of the Mad Phoenix* (Nanhai shisan lang, 1993); *A Sentimental Journey* (Jian xue fusheng, 1999)

FURTHER READING

Fong, Gilbert, and Hardy Tsoi, eds. *Xianggang huaju lunwen ji* [Essays on Hong Kong Theater]. Hong Kong: High Noon Production Co., 1992.

To, Raymond. *Where Love Abides*. Tr. by Y. P. Cheng. In *An Oxford Anthology of Contemporary Chinese Drama*, ed. by Martha P. Y. Cheung and Jane C. C. Lai. Hong Kong: Oxford Univ. Press, 1997. 665–749.

Jane Lai and Jessica Yeung

TO DAMASCUS

To Damascus (*Till Damaskus*, 1898, 1904) is a trilogy by AUGUST STRINDBERG. The first and most important part, in five acts, was written and published in 1898 and had its premiere at the Royal Dramatic Theater in Stockholm in 1900. The second part, in four acts, was written and published in 1898 and first performed, as an independent play, at the Lorensberg Theater in Gothenburg in 1924. The third part, in nine scenes, was written in 1901, published in 1904, and first performed at the Concert House in Stockholm in 1926.

The subject matter of *To Damascus* is largely based on Strindberg's experiences in his second marriage, with Frida Uhl, with whom he had a daughter; his stay with her family in AUSTRIA; his so-called Inferno crisis in Paris in the mid-1890s; his visits to a doctor friend in southern SWEDEN; and his considering joining a monastery in BELGIUM. For the description of the protagonist, fairy-tale figures such as Merlin and Robert le Diable, who both convert from evil to good and withdraw from the world, were also of importance.

The first part describes how the Stranger meets the Lady, abducts her from her husband, and marries her. Economic need drives the couple to seek refuge with her family, where they find a mixed reception. The Stranger leaves the Lady after she has read his latest book, which she had promised him not to read. Having wounded himself in a fall, the Stranger is brought to a sanctuary, where he undergoes a moral crisis. Retracing his steps, part of the time accompanied by the Lady, he discovers that he has treated many people unjustly. Returning to his point of departure, he finds a money order that had been awaiting him all this time at the post office. The play ends with his con-

clusion "It was my own stupidity—or meanness. . . . I didn't want to be made a fool of by life—and so I was!" and with his hesitant following the Lady into the church: "Well, I can pass through, of course, but I won't stay."

In a letter to his children Strindberg proudly describes the drama—not yet planned as part of a trilogy—as belonging to "a new genre, fantastic and brilliant as *Lucky Per* but with a contemporary setting and a completely real background." He explains its highly unusual structure to a colleague: "The art lies in the composition, which symbolizes the repetition Kierkegaard speaks of. The action unrolls forward to the Asylum; there it hits the 'point' and then is kicked back, the pilgrimage, the relearning, the ruminations; and then it starts anew in the same place where the game ends and where it began."

On his way to Damascus, Saul heard a voice speaking to him, saying: "Saul, Saul, why persecutest thou me? It is hard for thee to kick against the pricks" (Acts 26:14). This is what Strindberg refers to in the quoted passage. Just as Saul was converted into Paul, so the Stranger in the Asylum is converted from his earlier view that he is an innocent scapegoat to the view that he has continually trespassed against others. He now accepts that he must retrace his steps as a penitent pilgrim. That the road to Damascus is also a *via dolorosa* appears from the Mother's words: "My son, you have left Jerusalem and you are on your way to Damascus. Go there. The same way you came. And place a cross at each station, but stop at the seventh. You don't have fourteen, as He did."

With his *To Damascus* trilogy Strindberg launched dramas more subjective than any written before. Although the protagonist is not himself present in all the scenes, he is so indirectly, since many of the other characters are projections of his own self. Similarly, the scenery surrounding him represents not only an outer but even more an inner reality, the protagonist's mental state. The key word is half reality.

For all its novelty, *To Damascus* has much in common with the medieval morality play and its characters, named after the qualities they represent. Less didactic, Strindberg stresses the representativity of his characters by turning them into nameless types: the Lady, the Beggar, the Doctor, the Old Man, the Mother, and so on. More universal than any of these labels is the one given the protagonist: the Stranger, in Swedish *den Okände*, meaning literally the Unknown, that is, not knowing himself, a modern Everyman. His universality is ensured also through various historical and mythical analogies; in Evert Sprinchorn's words: "If the Stranger is Saul being persecuted by God, he is also Lucifer asserting his pride and Loki stirring up mischief. He is Jacob wrestling with God; he is Cain against whom every man's hand is raised; and he is Jesus who must suffer through the stations of the cross" (1982). The Stranger could also be compared with Dante Alighieri, who has to pass through Inferno and Purgatorio before he, guided by Beatrice, Strindberg's Lady, can reach Heaven.

To Damascus II shows the same struggle on the part of the Stranger as the first part. His closing speech to the Confessor—"Come, priest, before I change my mind!"—reveals that he has come only a bit farther on his road to Damascus. Truly dreamlike is the famous banquet-tavern scene in act 3 with its spectacular transformation of the set before the eyes of the audience.

In *To Damascus III* the Stranger finds himself in the vicinity of a monastery. He there encounters his double in the form of the Tempter, who does not disappear until the Stranger has found eternal rest in the white, nonsectarian monastery, where the key concepts are humanity and resignation.

The form of *To Damascus*, notably of its first part, is so innovative that a Swedish scholar has called it a mutation. Sprinchorn (1982) has predicted that it will soon be "a banality of criticism to say that twentieth-century drama begins with *To Damascus*. EXPRESSIONISM, SURREALISM and the theater of the absurd are all clearly adumbrated in this pioneering work."

[*See also* Religion and Drama]

FURTHER READING

Blackwell, Marilyn Johns. "Syn och subjektivitet i Till Damaskus I." *Strindbergiana* 15 (2000): 65–85.

Brandell, Gunnar. *Strindberg in Inferno.* Tr. by Barry Jacobs. Cambridge, Mass.: Harvard Univ. Press, 1974.

Karnick, Manfred. *Rollenspiel und Welttheater.* Munich: Fink, 1980.

Sprinchorn, Evert. *Strindberg as Dramatist.* New Haven: Yale Univ. Press, 1982.

Stockenström, Göran. *Ismael i öknen: Strindberg som mystiker.* Acta Universitatis Upsaliensis, Historia Litterarum, 5. Stockholm: Almqvist & Wiksell, 1972.

Törnqvist, Egil. *Strindbergian Drama: Themes and Structure.* Stockholm: Almqvist & Wiksell International, 1982.

Egil Törnqvist

TOKYO NOTES

Tokyo Notes (*Tōkyō Nōto,* 1994), a Japanese play that encapsulates HIRATA ORIZA's dramatic method, won the Kunio Kishida Drama Prize, JAPAN's top playwriting award, in 1995. Hirata's most successful work, it has also toured in North America (2000), Europe (2002), and AUSTRALIA (2004). The subject matter and style of this hyperrealistic play were inspired by Ozu Yasujirō's 1953 film *Tokyo Story;* as in Ozu's films (which many critics claim captured the essence of the Japanese), Hirata's characters demonstrate an aversion to conflict and strong displays of emotion; little is shown but much is suggested. Similarly, Hirata dislikes conventional plots and situations that other playwrights might exploit for dramatic effect. His desultory, laconic dialogue recalls the work of KUBOTA MANTARŌ.

The play is set in the year 2004, in the lobby of a suburban Tokyo art gallery, where the five Akiyama siblings and their in-laws have gathered to discuss what to do about their aging parents. Yumi, the oldest sister, looks after her parents back home, while her brothers and sisters live in the city. As in Ozu's

film, most of the children are too busy with their own lives and careers to be concerned with their old parents, but Hirata adds to this motif of family dissolution Yoshie's impending divorce from Yumi's little brother, Yūji.

The play's setting—the gallery where the Akiyamas meet is exhibiting works by Johannes Vermeer, evacuated from a war-torn Europe—questions the nature of Japan's relationship to the world. (In 1994, when Hirata wrote this play, the Bosnian war was threatening to spill beyond the borders of the former Yugoslavia, and Japan's role as a UN peacekeeper in CAMBODIA was a topic of hot debate.) Though several characters are involved with the war (as protestors, peacekeepers, or profiteers), the play critiques Japan's overall reluctance to take a moral position in international affairs.

Vermeer's paintings ask us how we view and represent reality, a dominant concern in Hirata's own theories on DRAMATURGY, direction, and ACTING, which are a reaction not only to the rational humanism of orthodox SHINGEKI ("new theater"), but also to the physicality and metatheatrical experimentation of ANGURA, the "underground" theater that TERAYAMA SHŪJI, KARA JŪRŌ, and SUZUKI TADASHI would define as the dominant tone for 1960s–1990s Japanese theater. Hirata advocates a return to REALISM and the well-made play, but rejects the use of drama as a medium to push an ideological message. Theater should provide "an objective sense of time as it is lived—quietly," he writes. Claiming that *shingeki*'s attempt to assimilate European modes of dramatic discourse actually distorted theatrical expression in Japan, he aims to reform stage dialogue to create a "contemporary colloquial theatre" reflecting how Japanese actually speak. *Tokyo Notes* is a manifesto of this new, "quiet" realism. Like Vermeer, Hirata is a realist who is nonetheless aware of the limits and tricks of representation. Art-loving Yumi points to this paradox when, casting doubt on Antoine de Saint-Exupéry's dictum that "what is essential is invisible to the eye," she asks, "How can you see with the heart? Everybody's hearts are different."

FURTHER READING

Hirata Oriza. *Engeki nyūmon* [Introduction to theater]. Tokyo: Kōdansha, 1998.

——. *Tokyo Notes.* Tr. by Rose-Marie Makino-Fayolle. Paris: Les Solitaires Intempestifs, 1998.

——. "Tokyo Notes: A Play by Hirata Oriza." Tr. by M. Cody Poulton. *Asian Theatre Journal* 19, no. 1 (Spring 2002): 1–120.

——. *Tōkyō Nōto.* Video recording with English subtitles by Cody Poulton. Tokyo: Kinokuniya Shoten, 1998.

M. Cody Poulton

TOLLER, ERNST (1893–1939)

Ernst Toller was born on December 1, 1893, in Samotschin, POLAND. His life was as turbulent as his dramas. Indeed, it has even provided the material for a play about him, Tankred Dorst's (1925–) *Toller* (1968). Toller began to write poetry and plays while still at school. When World War I started in 1914, he volunteered but was overcome psychologically by the horrors of trench warfare and was discharged in 1917 on medical grounds.

From then until his suicide in New York in 1939, Toller was relentless in struggling against militarism and social injustice. His first play, TRANSFIGURATION (*Die Wandlung: Das Ringen eines Menschen*, 1917), used the language and imagery of EXPRESSIONISM to shock audiences out of their steadfast patriotism. The play concludes with a call for "Revolution! Revolution!" When *Transfiguration* premiered to critical acclaim in 1919, Emperor William II (1859–1941) had already abdicated and the Weimar Republic had been proclaimed. The proclamation, however, did not put an end to political turmoil. For the Right the revolution had gone too far; for the Communists and Socialists it had not gone far enough because it brought no fundamental social changes.

Active in the Left, Toller played an important part in the fight to make Bavaria into a soviet republic to be governed by workers' councils. After the rebellion was quashed, he was sentenced to five years in prison for treason. While serving his sentence, Toller wrote most of his important plays: *Masses and Man: A Fragment of the Social Revolution of the Twentieth Century* (*Masse-Mensch: Ein Stück aus der sozialen Revolution des 20. Jahrhunderts*, 1920), *The Machine-Wreckers: A Drama of the English Luddites* (*Die Maschinenstürmer: Ein Drama aus der Zeit der Ludditenbewegung in England*, 1922), *Hinkemann: A Tragedy in Three Acts* (*Hinkemann: Eine Tragödie in drei Akten*, 1923), *Wotan Unleashed: A Comedy* (*Der entfesselte Wotan: Komödie*, 1924), and *The Scorned Lover's Revenge: Gallant Puppet Play After a Story by Cardinal Bandello* (*Die Rache des verhöhnten Liebhabers: Galantes Puppenspiel nach einer Geschichte des Kardinals Bandello*, 1925). After his release in 1924, Toller campaigned vigorously on behalf of other political prisoners. Several more plays followed: *Hoppla! Such Is Life!* (*Hoppla, wir leben! Ein Vorspiel und fünf Akte*, 1927), *Draw the Fires! A Historical Play* (*Feuer aus den Kesseln: Historisches Schauspiel*, 1930), *Mary Baker Eddy* (*Wunder in Amerika: Schauspiel*, with Hermann Kesten [1900–1996], 1931), and *The Blind Goddess* (*Die blinde Göttin: Schauspiel*, 1931). The manuscript for an adaptation of Molière's *Le Bourgeois gentilhomme* (1670) together with WALTER HASENCLEVER (1890–1940) and Hermann Kesten as *Bourgeois Remains Bourgeois* (*Bourgeois bleibt bourgeois*, 1929) is lost.

For the Nazis, who seized power in 1933, Toller was doubly anathema, because he was both Jewish and a leftist. In exile Toller was a leading figure in the international fight against fascism in Europe and after 1936 in North America. The two plays from this period, *No More Peace! A Thoughtful Comedy* (*Nie wieder Friede: Komödie*, 1937) and *Pastor Hall* (*Pastor Hall: Schauspiel*, 1939), were first published in English.

Against this background, it is no surprise that Toller's themes were political ones. The injustice, exploitation, and everyday cruelty that made drastic change urgent were depicted in *Transfiguration*, *The Machine-Wreckers*, *Hinkemann*, and *Hoppla! Such Is Life! Revolutions in process were analyzed in *Masses and Man* and *Draw the Fires!* The threats from the increasingly menacing Right were diagnosed in *Wotan Unleashed* and *Pastor Hall*.

Toller's enduring significance as a playwright comes from the way he explored possibilities for performance at a time when new media were emerging. Toller appropriated expressionist techniques such as masking to great effect, as in the scene of the dancing skeletons in *Transfiguration*. Dream sequences disrupt the illusion of REALISM, even in the polemical *No More Peace!* From his work with the spectacles of proletarian theater, Toller took the massed chorus heard in *Masses and Man*. For *Hoppla! Such Is Life!* Toller used film sequences and sound effects in one of the earliest multimedia events. Not until DARIO FO (1926–) would political theater again be so creative and exciting.

Toller's other contribution came from his insight that the isolation most people feel in their ordinary lives under capitalism is the stuff of modern TRAGEDY. Toller's most sophisticated analysis of how capitalism and technology reinforce each other and what happens to workers as a result comes in *The Machine-Wreckers*. Ostensibly set during the Luddite movement (1811–1816) when English textile workers tried to preserve their livelihoods by smashing power looms, the play reflects the impact of factory rationalization (Taylorism) in the 20th century. The rhythm of work is now determined by the machine, not by human beings. The rage of the workers is ineffective against the machines because their resistance is sporadic and unorganized. Instead of cooperating, the workers attack each other. Instead of learning the causes of their slide into pauperism, they are inspired by visionary language that cannot grasp the logic of advancing capitalism.

The alienation of ordinary life is captured poignantly at the opening of *Hinkemann*. The title character pities a songbird: "A mother! A mother put out the eyes of her goldfinch with a red-hot knitting needle because some newspaper wrote that blind birds sing better." The play follows the structure of Georg Büchner's (1813–1837) *Woyzeck* (written in 1836–1837, published in 1879). Eugen Hinkemann, emasculated in the war, loses his wife Grete to Paul Grosshahn (puns are possible: Hinkemann, "Limpman"; Grosshahn, "Bigcock"). Desperate to make money, Hinkemann takes a job at a freak show, where his trick will be to bite through the throats of rats and mice and drink their blood. The grotesque act distantly resembles the situation of Franz Kafka's (1883–1924) hunger artist, with the difference that here the inexorable economic forces pit two beings against each other. It is a cruel irony that Hinkemann must torture small creatures just as the goldfinch had been tortured for the sake of entertainment. Although he and his wife are reconciled at the end, she commits suicide because it all seems so hopeless. As the curtain falls, he is preparing to do likewise. Even those inured to the economy of pain will recognize themselves in Toller's plays.

SELECT PLAYS: Transfiguration (Die Wandlung: Das Ringen eines Menschen, 1917); Masses and Man: A Fragment of the Social Revolution of the Twentieth Century (Masse-Mensch: Ein Stück aus der sozialen Revolution des 20. Jahrhunderts, 1920); The Machine-Wreckers: A Drama of the English Luddites in a Prologue and Five Acts (Die Maschinenstürmer: Ein Drama aus der Zeit der Ludditenbewegung in England, 1922); Hinkemann: A Tragedy in Three Acts (Hinkemann: Eine Tragödie in drei Akten, 1923); Wotan Unleashed: A Comedy (Der entfesselte Wotan: Komödie, 1924); The Scorned Lover's Revenge: Gallant Puppet Play After a Story by Cardinal Bandello (Die Rache des verhöhnten Liebhabers: Galantes Puppenspiel nach einer Geschichte des Kardinals Bandello, 1925); Hoppla! Such Is Life! (Hoppla, wir leben! Ein Vorspiel und fünf Akte, 1927); Draw the Fires! A Historical Play (Feuer aus den Kesseln: Historisches Schauspiel, 1930); The Blind Goddess (Die blinde Göttin: Schauspiel, 1931); Mary Baker Eddy (Wunder in Amerika: Schauspiel, with Hermann Kesten, 1931); No More Peace! A Thoughtful Comedy (Nie wieder Friede: Komödie, 1937); Pastor Hall (Pastor Hall: Schauspiel, 1939)

FURTHER READING

Benson, Renate. German Expressionist Drama: Ernst Toller and Georg Kaiser. London: Macmillan, 1984.

Cafferty, Helen L. "Pessimism, Perspectivism, and Tragedy: Hinkemann Reconsidered." German Quarterly 54, no. 1 (1981): 44–58.

Davies, Cecil W. The Plays of Ernst Toller: A Revaluation. Amsterdam: Harwood Academic, 1996.

Dove, Richard. He Was a German: A Biography of Ernst Toller. London: Libris, 1990.

Ossar, Michael. Anarchism in the Dramas of Ernst Toller: The Realm of Necessity and the Realm of Freedom. Albany: State Univ. of New York Press, 1980.

Pittock, Malcolm. Ernst Toller. Boston: Twayne, 1979.

Arnd Bohm

TOLSTOY, LYOV (1828–1910)

Lyov Tolstoy's reputation as a novelist has obscured the significance of his dramatic output, which amounted to fifteen or so works, including unfinished plays. Apart from THE POWER OF DARKNESS (Vlast' t'my, 1888) and The Fruits of Enlightenment (Plody prosveshcheniya, 1889), very few have been consistently revived. Nevertheless, in his theoretical writings Tolstoy placed considerable importance on drama, especially its moralizing and didactic potential. In his What Is Art? (1897) he inveighs against traditional aesthetic theories characteristic of educated European taste and advocates a simple and straightforward realistic art of the people that is moral, educational, and intelligible. In many respects he echoes the sentiments of radical Russian utilitarians such as Nikolai Chernyshevsky, as well as anticipating the theories of socialist realist drama. This made his views popular with Vladimir Ilich Lenin, while his hostility to the likes of Johann Wolfgang von Goethe, RICHARD WAGNER, and even William Shakespeare has left others feeling rather bemused by his apparent eccentricity.

All that survives of Tolstoy's first dramatic efforts are fragments of a COMEDY, A Family of the Nobility (Dvoryanskoye semrtstvo, 1856), and a variant of the same play, A Practical Person (Prakticheskii chelovek, 1856), as well as scenes from two comedies on the same topic, An Uncle's Blessing (Dyadushkino blagosloveniye, 1856) and Free Love (Svobodnaya lyubov', 1856). He also wrote a farcical comedy for domestic performance about a group of radical students. The Nihilist (Nigilist, 1866). However, his first full-length work was An Infected Family (Zarazhyonnoye semeistvo, 1864), a comedy ridiculing newfangled ideas of "the emancipated woman" and the so-called nihilists who are also targeted in Ivan Turgenev's novel Fathers and Sons (1862). The First Distiller (Pervy vinokur, 1886) marks a change in dramatic direction after Tolstoy abandoned the Russian Orthodox faith for one of his own, based on moral self-perfection, sexual abstinence, temperance, pacifism, nonresistance to evil, and the cultivation of an idealized code of peasant values. The play is a kind of temperance tract, the first distiller of alcohol being the devil. Based on his own short story "The Imp and the Crust," the play shows how an imp employed by the devil suborns a group of peasants into distilling their own vodka, thereby corrupting their hitherto innocent way of life.

His most famous play, The Power of Darkness, has a distinctly religious theme, and while it reveals the spiritual darkness of the lives of Russian peasants, deriving from their impoverished environment, it concludes with the possibility of enlightenment and salvation, unlike the usual naturalistic plays of the period, which tended to be pessimistically determinist. Like many of his plays, this was initially banned, and productions of his other plays tended to be either posthumous or deferred. The Fruits of Enlightenment is an ironic satire at the expense of a landed gentry whose beliefs in spiritualism are shown to be more primitive than the supposed superstitions of their inferiors and who are outwitted by a serving girl into honoring an agreement to part with land to their peasants. The Living Corpse (Zhivoy trup, 1900) targets RUSSIA's judicial system, especially the laws on divorce, as well as its crude intrusion into private lives. The living corpse in question is a drunken husband who feigns suicide in order to allow his wife to make a better marriage, only to find himself, his wife, and her new husband dragged before the courts. He chooses to commit suicide for real, both to subvert the course of injustice and to liberate his wife. The Light Shineth in Darkness (I svet vo t'me svetit, 1900) is an autobiographical work derived from Tolstoy's own experience as someone who wished to turn over his estate to the peasants but was opposed by his own family. The play also refers to the plight of a dissident sect of "Spirit Wrestlers," the Dukhobors, who suffered persecution in Russia and whom Tolstoy assisted in emigrating to Canada. Another temperance play, The Cause of It All (Ot nyei vse kachestva, 1910), concerns a tramp with radical ideas who spends the night in a peasant hut and makes a moralizing, emancipatory appeal to a husband who returns in a drunken state and whose wife the tramp defends from abuse. The twist in the action occurs the following morning when the guest, who has also revealed a taste for the bottle, decamps with the couple's supply of tea and sugar, is apprehended by the peasant, but is offered forgiveness instead of a beating. In 1911 a sequence of twenty-one miniplays, *The Wisdom of Children* (*Detskaya mudrost'*, 1911), on subjects ranging from religion to war, capital punishment, art, science, and education, appeared posthumously.

Dramatized versions of Tolstoy's novels *Resurrection* (1899) and *Anna Karenina* (1878) were staged in FRANCE in 1902 and 1907, respectively, and during the 20th century dramatizations were made of *War and Peace* (1865–1869), as well as an operatic version by Sergei Prokofiev (1944). A stage version of *Kholstomer*, also known as *The Story of a Horse* (1886), was produced very successfully in Leningrad during the 1970s and was subsequently performed abroad.

[*See also* Religion and Drama]

PLAYS: *A Family of the Nobility* (*Dvoryanskoye semrtstvo*, 1856); *Free Love* (*Svobodnaya lyubov'*, 1856); *A Practical Person* (*Prakticheskii chelovek*, 1856); *An Uncle's Blessing* (*Dyadushkino blagosloveniye*, 1856); *An Infected Family*, also known as *A Contaminated Family* (*Zarazhyonnoye semeistvo*, 1864); *The Nihilist* (*Nigilist*, 1866); *Adaptation of the Legend of King Aggei*, also translated as *Dramatic Scenes About the Pan Who Became a Beggar* (*Dramaticheskaya abrabotka legendy ob Aggeye*, 1886); *The First Distiller; or, How the Imp Earned a Crust* (*Pervy vinokur, ili, Kak chertyonok kraiushku zasluzhil*, 1886); *Peter the Baker*, also known as *Peter the Publican* (*Pyotr khlebnik*, 1886); *The Power of Darkness; or, If the Claw Is Caught, the Whole Bird Is Lost* (*Vlast' t'my, ili, Kogotok uvyaz—vsey ptichke propast'*, 1888); *The Fruits of Enlightenment* (*Plody prosveshcheniya*, 1889); *The Living Corpse* (*Zhivoy trup*, 1900); *The Light Shineth in Darkness* (*I svet vo t'me svetit*, 1900); *The Newcomer and the Peasant* (*Priezzhii i krest' yanin*, 1909); *The Cause of It All* (*Ot nyei vse kachestva*, 1910); *The Wisdom of Children* (*Detskaya mudrost'*, 1911)

FURTHER READING

Christian, R. F. *Tolstoy: A Critical Introduction.* Cambridge: Cambridge Univ. Press, 1969.

Jones, Gareth W. "Tolstoy Staged in Paris, Berlin, and London." In *The Cambridge Companion to Tolstoy,* ed. by Donna Tussing Orwin. Cambridge: Cambridge Univ. Press, 2002.

Simmons, Ernest J. *Introduction to Tolstoy's Writings.* Chicago: Univ. of Chicago Press, 1968.

Tolstoy, Lyov. *Plays.* Tr. by Louise Maude and Aylmer Maude. 3d ed. London: Oxford Univ. Press, 1957. [Contains *The First Distiller, The Power of Darkness, The Fruits of Enlightenment, The Living Corpse, The Cause of It All,* and *The Light Shineth in Darkness.*]

——. *Plays, 1856–1886.* Tr. by Marvin Kantor with Tanya Tulchinsky. Evanston, Ill.: Northwestern Univ. Press, 1994.

——. *Stories and Dramas.* Tr. by Lydia Turin, Mrs. H. M. Lucas, and C. J. Hogarth. London: Dent, 1926.

——. "The Wisdom of Children." In *Father Sergius, and Other Stories,* ed. by Hagberg Wright. New York: Dodd, 1912.

Nick Worrall

TOMODACHI See FRIENDS

TONIGHT WE IMPROVISE

Tonight We Improvise (*Questa sera si recita a soggetto*) is a play in three acts by LUIGI PIRANDELLO completed in March 1929 during his self-imposed exile in Berlin. Between the successful premiere in remote Königsberg, GERMANY, on January 25, 1930, and the criticized Berlin opening at the Lessingtheater on May 31, 1930, Pirandello enjoyed a favorable reception in Turin, ITALY, on April 14, 1930, with Guido Salvini's company's performance. If with SIX CHARACTERS IN SEARCH OF AN AUTHOR (*Sei personoggi in cerca d'autore,* 1921) Pirandello began destroying the barrier between stage and audience, in *Tonight We Improvise* the barrier disappears: the performance takes place simultaneously on the stage, in the foyer, and amid the audience. More than bringing life into theater, with his play Pirandello brings theater into life. In this last part of his trilogy of "theater within the theater," Pirandello manipulates the balance of influences between the author, director, actors, and the audience. In *Six Characters in Search of an Author* Pirandello claims the greater role for authors, in *Each in His Own Way* (*Ciascuno a suo modo,* 1924) he acknowledges the audience's responsibility, and in *Tonight We Improvise* he grants the director primacy.

Doctor Hinkfuss, the Director, stages the performance of a play based on Pirandello's short story "Leonora, addio!" (1910). Hinkfuss informs the audience that Pirandello's work is not the center of the show, but a mere roll of paper. Hinkfuss becomes the creator of the play and its interpreter in its irreproducible performance.

Amid Hinkfuss's interruptions the actors continue acting the story: the life of a young woman humiliated by her husband as retribution for the lighthearted life she led with her three sisters and mother before her marriage. Rico Verri, the husband, impulsively married her to show the seriousness of his actions, but afterward he could not stand the thought of his wife's past. Held captive for years in her house, she dies while singing an aria to her two young daughters. The same night, returning home from the opera, Verri, repentant, finds her. Hinkfuss jumps onto the stage and extols the ending, so different from the short story that he has become the show.

Pirandello's experiences as director of Teatro d'Arte (1925–1928), staging his own plays and those of others, brought him to reflect on authors' limited authority on texts, theirs until they finish writing them. Texts are fixed, whereas the director has the power to make plays alive each time they are performed. Ahead of his time, Pirandello realizes that in the new century, authors' authority in theater diminishes in favor of the directors' aspiration to be its center. Actors recognize Hinkfuss's centrality and protest only when he denigrates their professionalism in front of the audience.

Perhaps Pirandello, in stressing Hinkfuss's exaggerated delirium of omnipotence, implicitly meant to criticize the directors' leaning toward mechanical spectacularization of scenes and to favor an approach that makes the actors' role more conspicuous. But never as in this play has Pirandello acknowledged the independence of theatrical production from a text. It was published in the United States in 1932, translated by Samuel Putnam; it opened in the United States at Vassar College produced by the Vassar College Experimental Theatre on December 11, 1936, with contrasting reviews. Because of the complexity of its production (with a large number of actors and an elaborate set design) and the conflicting criticism it generated, *Tonight We Improvise* has been seldom staged. It was part of the repertoire of THE LIVING THEATRE.

FURTHER READING

Bassnet McGuire, Susan. "Art and Life in Luigi Pirandello's *Questa sera si recita a soggetto*." *Themes in Drama*, no. 2 (1980): 81–102.

Pirandello, Luigi. *Pirandello's Love Letters to Marta Abba*. Ed. and tr. by Benito Ortolani. Princeton: Princeton Univ. Press, 1994.

——. *Tonight We Improvise and "Leonora, Addio!"* Tr. by J. Douglas Campbell and Leonard G. Sbrocchi. Pirandello Society of Canada Series, vol. 1. Ottawa: Canadian Society for Italian Studies, 1987.

Stefano Giannini

TOP GIRLS

> She's stupid, lazy and frightened, so what about her?
> —Joyce (referring to Angie), Act 3

First staged at the Royal Court Theatre in London in 1982, *Top Girls* transferred to New York the same year, where it won an Obie Award. The play is distinguished not only as one of CARYL CHURCHILL's most important and critically acclaimed works, but also as an enduring influence on feminist theater and scholarship. *Top Girls* was written between 1980 and 1982, when the recent election of the first female prime minister in Great Britain, Margaret Thatcher, seemed to evidence the significant advances made by women in society. But *Top Girls* critiques both the conservative government of Thatcher and the kind of feminism that encourages women to "get ahead" within existing social, political, and economic systems, with no attempt to change them and no regard for those left behind. As Churchill has said, "There's no such thing as right-wing feminism," a principle that drives her play. *Top Girls* is, therefore, an ironic title; it targets the hierarchical and patriarchal structure of capitalism, which rewards individuals whose skills and values equip them to climb the ladder of success, often supported by or stepping on those beneath them. The play also questions traditional (male) standards of achievement, marking the accomplishments of the "top" women it represents as partial or dubious and depicting the plight of those at the "bottom" as desperate. The stylistic innovations that enhance the dramatic—and feminist—impact of *Top Girls* include its female ensemble, nonlinear structure, transhistorical elements, double casting, and overlapping dialogue (a Churchill signature). Though *Top Girls*

is a work very much of its moment, it remains relevant decades later, posing social questions that transcend its original setting in a vital, theatrical style.

Top Girls' first act is an uproarious dinner party thrown by Marlene, managing director of the Top Girls Employment Agency, to celebrate her recent promotion. Marlene's guests, women from different historical periods and places, find some commonality, but are also divided by religious, class, and cultural differences. Act 2 consists of a series of short scenes at the agency, where women impose sexist double standards on one another, and in the backyard of Joyce, Marlene's working-class sister, who, it is gradually revealed, is raising Marlene's secret, illegitimate daughter, Angie. Marlene's "high-flying" career is, therefore, made possible partly by Joyce. Angie, who has dropped out of school, is depicted as "a bit thick, a bit funny." She suspects that her "Auntie" Marlene is really her mother, and surprises her at her office, hoping to stay. This is the last chronological event of the play, but not the final act. Subverting linear structure, Churchill sets act 3 one year earlier, in Joyce's kitchen. There Marlene and Joyce battle over their diametrically opposed personal and political positions. The personal is political in this play. Drawing a direct parallel between Marlene's attitudes and Margaret Thatcher's policies, Joyce (and Churchill) ask: What happens to people, like Angie, who have not "got what it takes" to survive in a heartless world? Marlene has already answered the question in the final lines of act 2 when she says, "She's not going to make it," dispassionately predicting a dismal future for her daughter. As a biting socialist and feminist critique of a capitalist, self-interested culture, *Top Girls* presents audiences with a dilemma, implicitly challenging them to search for solutions.

[*See also* England]

FURTHER READING

Aston, Elaine. *Caryl Churchill*. London: Northcote House, 1997.

——, and Janelle Reinelt, eds. *The Cambridge Companion to Modern British Playwrights*. New York: Cambridge Univ. Press, 2000.

Cousin, Geraldine. *Churchill the Playwright*. London: Methuen, 1989.

Fitzsimmons, Linda, comp. *File on Churchill*. London: Methuen, 1989.

Rosemary Malague

TOPOGRAPHY OF A NUDE

In more than one sense *Topography of a Nude* (*Topografía de un desnudo*, 1966) inaugurated a new phase in the prolific career of Jorge Díaz. The first play written from his new residence in Madrid, *Topography* introduced a number of AVANT-GARDE techniques hitherto unknown in Chilean theater while distinguishing Díaz from the European absurdist theater with which critics identified his earlier pieces. The play also prefigured an engagement with political reality in Latin America that powerfully crystallized in his later work, *All This Long Night* (*Toda esta larga noche*, 1976).

Set in a Brazilian favela and based on true events, *Topography* recounts the massacre of favela inhabitants by the police, charged with clearing the area to make room for a residential neighborhood. Here Díaz inverts the parable of the evangelist Luke to arrive at the exact opposite conclusion from the parable. San Lucas is the name of the police captain who assassinates Rufo, the site of the massacre is known as San Lázaro, and the prostitute's nickname is the Nun (La Monja). Here, unlike in the sacred book, the world of the poor is abandoned by the hand of God, and, as a result, all possibility of redemption is lost.

Sounding an alarm about the risks of progress at any cost, the play is a ferocious invective against the processes of modernization that various developing and Christian Democratic governments undertook in Latin America, beginning in the 1950s. In certain ways it also foretells the indiscriminate extermination that plagued the region as modernizing programs began to fail and the governments of these nations were replaced by military dictatorships.

Technically, the play is one of the most advanced in all Latin American theater. The action occurs around a circle of light into which the actors enter to become characters. When they are not acting, they remain in the semidarkness, forming an immobile chorus. A giant screen projects various texts and slides of the ragged poor, the military, corpses, and firearms. These images, along with a series of recorded sounds—such as gunshots and dog barks—complement the piece's atmosphere.

Díaz employs the devices of inversion and oxymoron to emphasize the sordidness and the moral decay of the favela. He upsets the spatial-temporal coordinates and transforms Rufo (initially a corpse) into the protagonist. The dead cry out, the living are silent. A man is killed like a dog, and a dog like a man—and indeed, the latter's death generates horror, while the former's is met with indifference. Even the characters' names allude to a strong ironic stance: the corrupt journalist is named Abel, and the instigator of the killing, Don Clemente. No one is noble or good in the world of San Lázaro, where apathy and violence reign supreme. Yet there remains a fundamental difference among the characters. The conduct of the poor, marked by denunciations and prostitution, comes from necessity and desperation, while that of the powerful—bureaucrats, politicians, the governor, the landowner—is the result of greed and corruption.

Perhaps the essential virtue of *Topography* consists in its desire to synthesize the principal currents of contemporary theater: from BERTOLT BRECHT it borrows the techniques of ALIENATION and the rejection of an Aristotelian unity; from the "HAPPENINGS" it derives the use of multimedia; from ANTONIN ARTAUD, the concept of cruelty's cathartic violence; and from PETER WEISS, its prevailing DOCUMENTARY nature. Undoubtedly, though, FRIEDRICH DÜRRENMATT serves as the play's fundamental inspiration, as much for the mixture of horror and the grotesque that he details in satires such as THE VISIT

OF THE OLD LADY and THE PHYSICISTS as for the parody of the police that is frequently found in the Swiss playwright's narrative pieces. Indeed, *Topography*'s subtitle is *Sketch of a Useless Investigation* (*Esquema para una indigación inútil*). It was a substantial transformation for someone who, until that time, was considered the Latin American disciple of EUGÈNE IONESCO.

FURTHER READING

Guerrero del Río, Eduardo. *Conversaciones: El teatro nuestro de cada Díaz.* Santiago, Chile: RIL, 1993. Reedited as *Jorge Díaz: Un pez entre dos agues.* Santiago, Chile: RIL, 2003.

Woodyard, George. "Jorge Díaz and the Liturgy of Violence." In *Dramatists in Revolt: The New Latin American Theater,* ed. by Leon F. Lyday and George W. Woodyard. Austin: Univ. of Texas Press, 1976. 59–76. [Includes a detailed analysis of *Topography of a Nude.*]

Norberto Cambiasso (Tr. by Gabriel Milner)

TOPOL, JOSEF (1935–)

Regarded as the most poetic of Czech playwrights writing in prose, Josef Topol (born on April 1, 1935, in Poříčí nad Sázavou, CZECHOSLOVAKIA) creates situations, characters, and dialogue that capture surface reality, but progressively probes more deeply into states of mind and feeling that reflect characters' personal crises, as well as universal desires and anxieties. Not infrequently his plays have also resonated with collective social and political stresses affecting Czech society since World War II.

At the age of twenty Topol gained immediate attention with his first play, *Midnight Wind* (*Půlnoční vítr*, 1955), produced by the major Czech director E. F. Burian in his Army Art Theatre. Drawing from Czech history and myth, the drama dealt with dynastic conflicts recalling those in William Shakespeare's chronicle plays. It was Topol's only play written in verse. In the late 1950s Topol began his significant relationship with director Otomar Krejča and DRAMATURG Karel Kraus in their playwriting workshop at the National Theatre. *Their Day* (*Jejich den*, 1959), the first product of this collaboration, reflected contemporary tensions between elders who represented the status quo of a repressive regime and idealistic youth who chafed under its restrictions. Episodically structured in many relatively short scenes and written in fresh, idiomatic prose, the play caught the spirit of a time that was seriously questioning an ideologically oppressive culture.

The equally contemporary *End of Carnival* (*Konec masopustu*, 1963), Topol's next work with Krejča, has been regarded as one of the most significant Czech plays of the century. Operating with relative objectivity on several levels with numerous characters, it presents the clash between forces of a new order and deeply rooted cultural traditions, specifically an individual landowner's resistance to the state-decreed collectivization of all agricultural activity, a deeply divisive program introduced by the new socialist government. Topol's play poetically and theatrically incorporates mythic elements in the form of ritual maskers celebrating the end of carnival, the death of the old and birth of the new. The action thereby acquires archetypal dimensions beyond the personal, familial, and social issues at stake.

A distinct shift of tone, theme, and scale marked Topol's next plays, all still emerging from the collaboration with Krejča. These are one-act chamber plays that center in a family or only two people rather than presenting a complex web of relationships. Two of them are closely related in theme and subject: *Cat on the Rails* (*Kočka na kolejích*, 1965) and *Hour of Love* (*Hodina lásky*, 1968). In *Cat* still-youthful Evi and Vena have been lovers for years but are now uncertain whether to continue their relationship. While waiting for a train at a rural stop as evening approaches, they reveal the insecurities underlying their feelings for each other in dialogue that is partly playful and often elusive. No central issue is confronted or problem posed, the external world is irrelevant, and no resolution is achieved at the play's end as they sit on the tracks with the sound of an approaching locomotive becoming progressively louder. In *Hour* the lovers, Ela and El, are older but similar to Evi and Vena; the setting is an interior, and a third character is added, Ela's ailing aunt. Ela and El behave as though they have one hour left before he must leave, perhaps forever. An interplay of sensibilities skirting painful recognitions is again the essence, but this time in a bleaker key and with a hint of death indirectly associated with the aunt. The other one-act play is *Nightingale for Supper* (*Slavík k večeři*, 1967), which Topol himself directed for Krejča's Theatre Beyond the Gate. A grotesque COMEDY of the absurd, it is reminiscent of works by HAROLD PINTER or AUGUST STRINDBERG'S THE GHOST SONATA with its destruction of vulnerable humanity by brutalizing forces.

Topol's last three plays were written during the period of forced "normalization" after the Soviet invasion, when none of his plays could be performed. The plays focus on older characters whose lives have entered their final phase with few, if any, vital inner resources or external supports. Although they never say it, love-as-life-force seems extinguished in their lives as they face the future, and illusions are a weak substitute.

Farewell, Socrates (*Zbohem, Sokrates*, 1976, not performed until 1991) takes place in the atelier of a sculptor on his fiftieth birthday, which is being celebrated as a masquerade party with a spectrum of guests who approximate a ship of fools, reflecting Topol's view of Czech society at the time. At the heart of the action is the sculptor's devoted wife as she faces the reality of her husband's terminal indifference and ultimately takes her own life. The masquerade theme is heightened by numerous symbols, the dialogue is tangential and ambivalent, and the ending includes no resolution of the complex relations within the work. It is a provocative, inner-directed study that some have compared to the films of INGMAR BERGMAN.

Almost ten years later, during which time he ran afoul of the regime and was forced into manual labor, Topol wrote *A Soul in Transit* (*Stěhování duší*, 1986, not produced until 1990). A one-woman monologue of an isolated, feisty old woman living in a cluttered basement, it recalls SAMUEL BECKETT'S KRAPP'S LAST TAPE or HAPPY DAYS in its free association of mostly painful memories. Her final line, "Life can be beautiful," is deeply ambivalent.

Topol's last play, *The Voices of Birds* (*Hlasy ptáků*, 1988, performed in 1989), is a wry, subdued TRAGICOMEDY that considers an aging actor's personal life, showing it to have been singularly lacking in meaningful human feelings. Overtly dramatic action is minimal, no important change occurs in any character, and the social context is irrelevant, but the inner lives of a number of people have been subtly revealed with spare objectivity. One might take the play as a depressing account of rather empty, barren souls or as a comedy of human inadequacies suggesting that what one gets from life is proportional to what one puts into it. Typically for Topol, the ending is open ended.

SELECT PLAYS: *Midnight Wind* (*Půlnoční vítr*, 1955); *Their Day* (*Jejich den*, 1959); *End of Carnival* (*Konec masopustu*, 1963); *Cat on the Rails* (*Kočka na kolejích*, 1965); *Nightingale for Supper* (*Slavík k večeři*, 1967); *Hour of Love* (*Hodina lásky*, 1968); *Two Nights with a Girl* (*Dvě noci s dívkou*, 1969); *Farewell, Socrates* (*Zbohem, Sokrates*, 1976)

FURTHER READING

Burian, Jarka M. *Modern Czech Theatre: Reflector and Conscience of a Nation.* Iowa City: Univ. of Iowa Press, 2000.

Czech Academy of Sciences. http://www.cas.cz/index.html.en.

Goetz-Stankiewicz, Marketa. *The Silenced Theatre: Czech Playwrights Without a Stage.* Toronto: Univ. of Toronto Press, 1979.

Trensky, Paul I. *Czech Drama Since World War II.* White Plains, N.Y.: M. E. Sharpe, 1978.

——. "The Playwrights of the Krejča Circle." In *Czech Literature Since 1956: A Symposium,* ed. by William E. Harkins and Paul I. Trensky. New York: Bohemica, 1980.

Jarka M. Burian

TOT, KTO POLUCHAET POSHCHECHINY See HE WHO GETS SLAPPED

THE TOTH FAMILY

In the mid-1960s the Hungarian government, installed by the Soviet tanks that crushed the 1956 revolution, began loosening constraints on artistic expression, and ISTVÁN ÖRKÉNY'S TRAGICOMEDY *The Toth Family* (*Tóték*, 1967) introduced Hungarian audiences to a new, grotesque view of the inhumanity and ambiguities of their recent history. It also influenced a generation of playwrights to examine the Hungarian condition in grotesque and absurd ways.

The play is set during World War II in a tranquil Hungarian village where the Toths live in contentment, disturbed only by concern over their son's military service at the front. Thus when the son's commanding officer, the Major, arrives for a few days in order to calm his shattered nerves, they eagerly extend their hospitality, hoping to induce him to assign the son to less life-threatening duty.

The Major's stay overturns the family's equilibrium. Step by step, in order to serve the Major's increasingly irrational requests, Mr. Toth forfeits his habits and loses his identity. His wife and daughter justify the Major's absurd whims as if they were perfectly natural. The complicit village folk further rob Toth of his sense of reality. Making cardboard boxes, with which the women used to supplement the family income, becomes one of the Major's obsessions. What began for him as a soothing routine becomes a mania that overwhelms the Toth family with sleepless nights and the stage with boxes. The women as mediators justify the exhausted and confused Toth's increasingly puzzling behavior to the Major. Thus, by degrees, the irrational and abnormal become the accepted norm. Reason, of which Toth preserves a spark, is forced to retreat. Indeed, Toth spends ever more time in the outhouse, his one refuge from this insane world.

But, characteristically of Örkény, coercion in this play is a complex issue. The Major himself is an ambivalent character in this regard. He is not an aggressive, cruel soldier, but a victim of fear. He lives in irrational dread of partisan attacks, even in this peaceful village. Nor are the Toths his unequivocal victims, since they volunteer for their role.

In an ironic twist, we learn from the postman at the end of the first act that he has taken it upon himself to keep bad news from the family by not delivering the announcement of the son's death at the front. From this point on, unbeknownst to the family, its self-sacrifice is pointless. When the tension is stretched to the limit, Toth kills the Major.

For much of the 20th century in Örkény's part of the world, those in power manipulated the people's natural self-interest, as well as the dissemination of information that would have allowed the people to act in their best interest. Örkény's parable, based on the Toths' concern for their son and their ignorance of his fate, encapsulates this condition. The killing of the Major not only restores Toth's authentic self, but demonstrates Örkény's characteristic balancing of the hopelessness of an absurd world with belief in man's capacity for taking action, or at least for starting over.

[See also Hungary]

FURTHER READING

Bécsy, Tamás. Kalandok a drámával: Magyar drámák, 1945–1989 [Adventures with drama: Hungarian dramas, 1945–1989]. Budapest: Balassi Kiadó, 1996.

P. Müller, Péter. A groteszk dramaturgiája [The dramaturgy of the grotesque]. Budapest: Magvető Könyvkiadó, 1990.

Radnóti, Zsuzsa. Lázadó dramaturgiák [Dramaturgies in revolt]. Budapest: Palatinus, 2003.

Eugene Brogyányi

A TOUCH OF THE POET

Faith, Patch Riley don't know it but he's playing a requiem for the dead.
—Sara, Act 4

A Touch of the Poet by EUGENE O'NEILL was first produced at the Dramatiska Teatern in Stockholm, SWEDEN, on March 29, 1957. Harold Clurman directed the American premiere on October 2, 1958, with Helen Hayes as Nora. José Quintero directed the 1977 revival with Jason Robards.

Set in 1828, the story revolves around Cornelius Melody, a "polished gentleman" who overplays the role that he believes too well. He preens in the mirror and tells himself, "Thank God, I still bear the unmistakable stamp of an officer and a gentleman. And so I will remain to the end, in spite of all fate can do to crush my spirit." He relishes the transformative magic of the actor, wearing the "brilliant scarlet full-dress uniform of a major in one of Wellington's dragoon regiments."

In Melody, O'Neill uses the figure of the actor as a metaphor for mankind. He challenges everyone—even himself—to solve the riddle of who he really is. His father kept a shebeen, and Melody himself was an upstart who rose in the British army but resigned his commission after fighting a duel and killing a Spanish nobleman whom he had cuckolded. Now he keeps a tavern in Massachusetts where even the mortgage does not spare his wife and daughter the ignominy of waiting tables and begging for credit.

Melody compels others to play roles; he asks Sara, his daughter, to play both wench and gentleman's child, Nora, his wife, to play both cook and lady, and his Irish cronies to play both subservient peasants and fellow soldiers. He must re-create others in order to re-create himself, for the strength of his identity depends on the reinforcement their belief offers. Yet Sara resists him, and his pub cronies play his game only when acquiescence will win them free drinks and a haven.

Sara loves Simon Harford, the son of an aristocratic family whose father sends a lawyer to negotiate an end to their relationship. Melody, deeply insulted, tries to challenge old Harford to a duel but ends brawling with the servants and thrown in jail. In despair over his crumbling self-image, Melody shoots his beloved mare.

Melody's progress through the play involves an implacable loss of self as he moves restlessly from role to role, trying in vain to maintain one identity and find fulfillment. We see him in the final scene as a beaten man, his costume in tatters and his resolve shattered; like the men in THE ICEMAN COMETH, he has faced the hollowness of his dream. Even Sara finally denies him, eradicating his past, as well as their relationship, by saying, "I heard someone. But it wasn't anyone I ever knew or want to know." In *The Nation* (October 25, 1958), Gore Vidal called it "a beautiful play."

With precision and—for him—economy, he sets the scene for his moral action which is the crushing of a man's false pride, his absorption into the main, his final realization that he has lived a bogus life, presuming a position both worldly and moral to which he has no right but the one—and this is significant—of wanting.

[*See also* United States, 1940–Present]

FURTHER READING

Bower, Martha Gilman. "Upstairs/Downstairs: Dueling Triangles in *A Touch of the Poet*." *Eugene O'Neill Review* 20 (Spring–Fall 1996): 97–101.

Manheim, Michael. "O'Neill's Transcendence of Melodrama in *A Touch of the Poet* and *A Moon for the Misbegotten*." *Comparative Drama* 16 (Fall 1982): 238–250.

Meade, Robert. "Incest Fantasy and the Hero in *A Touch of the Poet*." *Eugene O'Neill Review* 18 (Spring–Fall 1994): 79–94.

Miliora, Maria T. "Narcissistic Fantasies in *A Touch of the Poet*: A Self-Psychological Study." *Eugene O'Neill Review* 18 (Spring–Fall 1994): 95–107.

Porter, Laurin. "Bakhtin's Chronotope: Time and Space in *A Touch of the Poet* and *More Stately Mansions*." *Modern Drama* 34 (September 1991): 369–382.

———. *The Banished Prince: Time, Memory, and Ritual in the Late Plays of Eugene O'Neill*. Ann Arbor: UMI Res. Press, 1988.

Jeffrey D. Mason

TRAGEDY

The most familiar breakdown into dramatic genres—COMEDY, FARCE, tragedy, MELODRAMA, and TRAGICOMEDY—possibly goes back in part to the critical methods of Aristotle in his pioneering document on poetics. Some commentators believe that this pioneering document was compiled not from Aristotle's own lecture notes but from notes taken by the students in his classes. Today an Aristotelian analysis has several obvious shortcomings: one, it refers to theater written by Greek dramatists who had died before the father of criticism was born; two, in the nearly 2,400 years since his death in 384 B.C.E., later critics have reinterpreted his teachings, and these revisions are at variance with the originals and with each other; three, analysis by genre has, in the hands of these generations, crisscrossed (or clashed) with a plethora of dramatic writing styles and historical movements, such as neoclassicism, ROMANTICISM, lyrical verse, and EXPRESSIONISM, most of them over the past 300 years, while styles and movements have themselves come and gone almost as rapidly as fashionable political theories. Yet these transient shortcomings have brought benefits with them: they have spared scholars the unpleasant rigidity of rules and held out in their place the pleasures of witnessing other people's disagreements.

In everyday parlance and in slightly more rarefied theater talk, the word *tragedy* has several misleading implications. It does not denote a calamity or a sad accident—haphazard usage that belongs in proclamations of grief and regret for which we have to thank presidents, governors, mayors, police superintendents, and news announcers when they deplore a shoot-out, fire, explosion, flood, train crash, or earthquake, for which no perpetrator can be blamed and arrested. In more casual theater talk a tragedy is taken to mean a drama with a sorrowful or otherwise unsatisfying end. It often has reference also to a play that has strained pretensions or is viewed by the author or one of his friends as existing on a level of superiority that plays belonging to other genres could never match.

The exaggerated respect accorded the *idea* of tragedy may come from awestruck views of the oldest body of drama we have on record, the entire reworkings and fragments of Greek myths by Aeschylus, Sophocles, and Euripides, written and staged mostly in the 6th to 5th centuries B.C.E. They had a number of features rarely met with since. A chorus represented a Greek community and was located in the circular space known as the orchestra. Between one and three individual actors played multiple roles on a raised platform; they differentiated their parts by changing masks over their upper faces and adopting artificial voices. The three centers of most feverish and brutal Greek action consisted of Argos, the home of the Atridae, the ancestors and descendants of King Agamemnon; Thebes, where Labus, disregarding a warning of Apollo, begot a son, Oedipus, who set off a string of murders and other misdeeds by killing his father and marrying his mother; and Troy, an island on the far side of the Aegean Sea to which a mighty Greek army under its commander, Agamemnon, sailed in hopes of releasing the beauteous Helen, his sister-in-law.

Most Greek tragedies have come down to us in translations, adaptations, and fragments. Often a playwright or poet commissioned by a subsidized theater troupe to provide a new version of a Greek classic will, after some struggling to find an apt vocabulary and style, end up revising and retitling the original as his or her own. French authors in the 1920s–1940s found amazing affinities between Greek circumstances and theirs. The circumstances had to do largely with immersion in declared and undeclared wars, in which the playwrights pointed out resemblances between their days, the intermission between the 20th century's two world wars, and ancient times. JEAN COCTEAU wrote *Antigone* (1922), loosely drawn from the tragedy by Sophocles; *Orpheus* (1926), in which Orpheus seeks his wife Eurydice in the underworld; and THE INFERNAL MACHINE (1932), based on *King Oedipus*, also by Sophocles. JEAN GIRAUDOUX contributed THE TROJAN WAR WILL NOT TAKE PLACE (1935), known in CHRISTOPHER FRY's translation (1955) as *Tiger at the Gates*, drawn from several Greek plays, as well as the *Iliad*. JEAN-PAUL SARTRE's THE FLIES (1942) replaces the Eumenides from Aeschylus' *Oresteia*, a chorus of vengeful females, with the torturous buzzing of a cloud of flies who haunt Orestes after he slays his mother, Clytemnestra. JEAN ANOUILH modernized two tragic masterpieces, ANTIGONE (1944), after Sophocles again, and—a Shakespearean, not a Greek, entry—*Romeo and Jeannette* (1946).

When HENRIK IBSEN delved into the possibilities of conversational talk in his "middle" plays in the later 1870s, he clarified dramatic language. Critics noisily attacked him—GEORGE BERNARD SHAW was the great exception—for dispensing with rhetorical overstatement; but numerous playwrights, by contrast, admired and tried to mimic or even mirror his achievement. They seldom succeeded, because Ibsen evidently meant not merely to purify his dialogue but also to complicate it and, by introducing subtle symbolic hints, to enrich his characterizations and tragic structures. He fed the leading roles and some secondary roles lines that unconsciously betrayed them. They gave away their concealed feelings and especially their misgivings. Two Ibsen heroines, Helene Alving in GHOSTS and Hedda in HEDDA GABLER, look like their own worst enemies and, simultaneously, pitiful at that. Ibsen's plotting drives one of them into self-torture when Mrs. Alving blames herself for the imminent death of her son, while Hedda kills herself with a pistol that belonged to her father. Death, financial ruin, or some other downfall overtakes Ibsen's tragic victims. He unlocks a tormented past pointing forward to an intolerable future, and a helpless offense against oneself, even a crime, perhaps unmeant, against mankind or a group—or a sin against the gods and oneself.

AUGUST STRINDBERG's two most famous tragedies, THE FATHER and MISS JULIE, leaped all over Europe in the 1880s and 1890s and deposited thousandfold visual images and echoes. Early in his career Strindberg felt that he had the right to inspire principal parts, both male and female, by using characteristics drawn from his understanding of his own thoughts and feelings, such as "the Captain" in *The Father* and Julie in *Miss Julie*. In middle age he conceived his trilogy TO DAMASCUS as a modern journey, reminiscent of St. Paul's, across strange landscapes. These resembled the settings through which the unnamed protagonist (the Stranger) passed in his search for the person he would turn out to be, a figure not quite recognizable to himself.

Strindberg's dazzling array of theater does not lend itself to easy classification by genre. A DREAM PLAY and THE GHOST SONATA must have moved and shaken the pioneers of SURREAL-ISM and expressionism twenty or more years after those plays were written. With CREDITORS (1890), CRIMES AND CRIMES (1899), and THE DANCE OF DEATH (1901) one feels that, after writing bouts of ferocious quarreling in these domestic tragedies, the playwright advised his vehement inventions to sit back for a quiet break. Yet these plays do retain self-destructive elements, the essence of tragedies.

In America the plays most emphatically influenced by Ibsen and Strindberg, in addition to their ultimate sources, Greek tragedies, came from EUGENE O'NEILL, who transferred his Americanizing of DESIRE UNDER THE ELMS (1924, from the *Hippolytus* of Euripides and Jean Racine's *Phaedra*) and MOURNING BECOMES ELECTRA (1931, a trilogy from the *Oresteia* by Aeschylus) to New England, and specifically Connecticut. O'Neill's STRANGE INTERLUDE (1931) is a nine-act play whose principal, named Nina, seems like a comment on the play's length and may be a regeneration of a Greek goddess, possibly Aphrodite or another portrait of Phaedra, either Racine's or Lucius Annaeus Seneca's, or even Helen of Troy, who was actually Helen of Sparta and fled to Troy with Paris to escape from her husband. Nina attracts men, not nearly as many as Helen was reputed to have won, but in O'Neill's drama she settles for an unexciting but wealthy businessman and goes from being a vital, bubbling personality to becoming an unfulfilled Yankee matron, a fate that is in certain respects fulfilled, but semitragic at most. O'Neill is said to have written only one play that is comic, *Ah, Wilderness!* But that assertion is disputable. The rest of his dramatic output overflows with tragic material.

An approximate contemporary of O'Neill (1888–1953) and equally a Nobel Prize winner, WILLIAM BUTLER YEATS (1865–1939) also wrote many plays with tragic consequences. They were much shorter than most of O'Neill's and in verse, whereas O'Neill, a formidably patient craftsman, said more than once that he could not command more than "a touch of the poet." Yeats wrote poetry of the finest caliber. Some of his works were designed to be performed by dancers at the Abbey Theatre, of which he was a founder and contributing author. His most exquisitely tragic drama occurs in the encounter in *On Baile's Strand* (1904) between Cuchulain, a warrior-hero out of Irish myth, and a mysterious young man who challenges him and loses. The young man is the son of a woman whom Cuchulain loved dearly when they were both young; but Cuchulain had never met his opponent before and does not learn until too late that he killed his only son. Other dramatists who have worked the tragic vein include GERHARD HAUPTMANN, whose *The Family of Atreus* (1941) follows the fortunes and misfortunes of that house, and LYOV TOLSTOY, the novelist who, in THE POWER OF DARKNESS (1888), depicted the superstitious brutality of Russia's peasants.

Two esteemed American names after O'Neill's were those of ARTHUR MILLER and TENNESSEE WILLIAMS. Miller said that his plays are mythical; they are definitely less notable for their comic spirit than for their tragic heft. From ALL MY SONS (1947) and DEATH OF A SALESMAN (1949) through THE CRUCIBLE (1953) and A VIEW FROM THE BRIDGE (1955), Miller's work meets the definition of tragedy offered earlier and realizes scenes that hew to a level of superbly rich poetry, such as the spell Abigail casts on the other girls in the Salem church, whom she seems to have turned into wailing birds. Williams's plays, which he subjected to arduous revisions, avoided harshly tragic censuring of his protagonists by others, yet without shying away from the cruelty people unintentionally impose on those closest to them. In his most compelling artistic device he revived adroitly melodramatic solo speeches, such as Lord Byron's account of Percy Bysshe

Shelley's death by burning in CAMINO REAL (1953), except for Shelley's heart, which remained miraculously unscorched. The mechanics of forging passionate monologues and soliloquies have picked up many passengers in the last three or four decades; but Williams's two early works, THE GLASS MENAGERIE (1945) and A STREETCAR NAMED DESIRE (1947) not only proved popular in the UNITED STATES and Britain but also received enthusiastic welcomes in other parts of the world, as did *The Rose Tattoo* (1951), CAT ON A HOT TIN ROOF (1955), and THE NIGHT OF THE IGUANA (1961).

The ancient "blocking" of tragic acting, with a division of chorus and chorus leader (*choregos*) from the individual players (protagonist, antagonist, and deuteragonist), has disappeared, even in GREECE. The actor's disposition in the acting area, and often nowadays in the auditorium, is constantly revised. Some directors have returned to constructivist sets like the ones from the Soviet Union in the 1920s that encourage performers to fly through three dimensions like trapeze artists. Some stage designers have begun to favor water and pools onstage, as in a 2003 revival of Euripides's *Medea* that looked like a compromise between a splashing contest and a flooded basement.

FURTHER READING

Bentley, Eric. "Tragedy." In *The Life of the Drama*. New York: Atheneum, 1964.

Elsom, John. *Post-war British Theatre Criticism*. London: Routledge, 1981.

Guicharnaud, Jacques, with June Guicharnaud. *Modern French Theatre from Giraudoux to Genet*. New Haven: Yale Univ. Press, 1967.

Orr, John. *Tragic Drama and Modern Society*. Totowa, N.J.: Barnes & Noble, 1981.

Williams, Raymond. *Modern Tragedy*. Stanford, Calif.: Stanford Univ. Press, 1966.

Albert Bermel

TRAGICOMEDY

Is tragicomedy a comfortable and amusing piece of theater except that, toward its close, it heads bleakly in the direction of TRAGEDY, as in *The Misanthrope*? Or does it have a plot line that grows sorrowful for perhaps its first half but turns on itself and raises laughter and a reconciliation between embattled roles, as happens in most commercial plays? Or does it alternate between the opposed tendencies, so that the audience remains unsure until the end how to parse it, as with, say, TONY KUSHNER's two-part ANGELS IN AMERICA? This third type runs along the lines that Victor Hugo envisaged for the theater's future in his preface to *Cromwell*; he wanted to see more plays written as mixtures, as alternations, as examples of what he designated ROMANTICISM. In historical fact, all three types have made contributions to the genre we choose to call tragicomedy for want of a more precise name. (French theater often calls a tragicomedy a *drame*; the same word may also apply to a MELODRAMA.)

But the three types depend in large part on the nature of a play's ending. ANTON CHEKHOV, the most accomplished tragicomic dramatist of the modern theater, accused his director, KONSTANTIN STANISLAVSKY, of not giving enough emphasis to the COMEDY in his best-known plays. Yet from IVANOV (1889) to THE SEAGULL (1895–1898), UNCLE VANYA (1899), THREE SISTERS (1901), and THE CHERRY ORCHARD (1904), we do not find an unmistakable tone for the actors to sustain. Chekhov's life ended in 1904 when he was only forty-four years of age. If he had lived longer, he might have come down more definitively on one side or the other, as many authors do and as he had already done himself in the continuum of his work from early FARCE to later tragicomedy. In the stagings of Chekhov the genre still remains at the mercy of directors and actors. Stanislavsky may have left his efforts on the plays' behalf comically undernourished, but they invite a treatment that begins with plentiful comic effects that lean gradually more and more toward the serious (not the solemn) by demanding a sympathy from the audience that swells through nostalgia and at last into the sharing of sympathetic despair. In *Ivanov*, as in *The Seagull*, the leading man shoots himself; in *Three Sisters* Baron Tuzenbach, the man in love with Irina, the youngest sister, fights a duel, in which he is killed by his unbalanced army comrade, Solyony. In the two last plays old men speak the closing lines in a tone of hopelessness: in *Three Sisters*, Chebutykin; in *The Cherry Orchard*, Firs, who lies down on the floor to die.

Whether Chekhov faulted Stanislavsky—but playwrights are not always the most trustworthy judges of their work—few directors today play down Chekhovian laughs; they seek to maintain not so much a balance overall as a series of shifting moods that favor surprises, U-turns in the plotting. Something comparable happens in plays written by MAKSIM GORKY, for whom Chekhov became a model and who, for a few years after 1917, became one of the most revered artists of the Soviet revolution.

In FRANK WEDEKIND's SPRING AWAKENING one of a trio of young adults, Wendla, finds herself pregnant and submits to a treatment by what used to be called a backroom abortionist, who kills the fetus and Wendla. A second youngster, a shy and girlish boy named Moritz, shoots himself with a pistol that takes off his head; he becomes in death a hideous likeness of a "headless queen" about which he has been having prophetic nightmares. Or fulfilling wishes?

The third teenager, Melchior, who was the father of Wendla's unborn child and a close friend of Moritz, remains alive but feels responsible for the fate of the two others. This tragicomedy embraces the quasi-tragic doubts of fifteen-year-olds advised by ignorant parents and fuddy-duddy schoolteachers. *Spring Awakening* is, all in all, a sad tale of two wasted lives out of three. But Wedekind has charged its gloom with moments of sheer clownishness in scenes between Wendla and her mother, the teachers' meeting to determine how to punish the "erring" schoolchildren, and, at the end, a hilarious meeting in a graveyard between a disillusioned Melchior and the headless ghost of Moritz.

Two Swiss playwrights, MAX FRISCH and FRIEDRICH DÜRRENMATT, writing in German, came to Europe's front line in drama soon after World War II had concluded. Their country's neutrality during the war years had removed them from a defensive backward look at neutrality as a diplomatic posture. They each wrote with a committed social point of view. Dürrenmatt's THE VISIT OF THE OLD LADY (1956) presents a woman who had been spurned in marriage by a man who had gone on to become the mayor of a small town, which turned her out. She returns there years after, intent on a revenge that demands nothing less than his death by way of public humiliation, for which she can effortlessly pay, having become the widow of a millionaire. Perhaps the small town was meant to be Swiss and to mock the belief among its inhabitants that they could overlook sins in their collective past. But to a flood of cash there is no reply. Or, as a British comedian once proclaimed, "Money isn't everything. But what it isn't, it can buy." Frisch's plays have also delivered jabs to cozily settled opinions, such as the ones pierced by *The Firebugs* (1953). Some men walk into a bourgeois house and, after giving warning, set the home on fire. And they do so, as a number of European nations did symbolically when faced with German threats of invasion, by collaborating with the aggressor.

The most prolific tragicomic author from the 1920s through the 1960s was BERTOLT BRECHT, although his output also contains farces, comedies, and tragedies. Among the tragicomedies are *A Man's a Man* (1926), *The Seven Deadly Sins* (1933), THE GOOD WOMAN OF SETZUAN (1943), *Herr Puntila and His Servant Matti* (1948), and THE RESISTIBLE RISE OF ARTURO UI (1958), the last being a treatment of Adolf Hitler and his acolytes enacted as a bunch of Chicago hoodlums. The most ambitious tragicomedy produced by an American dramatist is most likely Tony Kushner's two-part *Angels in America* (1993), in which three of the maze of dazzling plots interconnect in the death of a protagonist by AIDS; the public career of Roy Cohn, one of the most disgustingly funny American villains of the 1900s; and appearances by an angel who, helmeted like Pallas Athena, the goddess of wisdom and protector of Athens, smashes through the ceiling and through the chandelier.

FURTHER READING

Bentley, Eric. "Tragicomedy." In *The Life of the Drama*. New York: Atheneum, 1964.

Bermel, Albert. *Comic Agony*. Evanston, Ill.: Northwestern Univ. Press. 1993.

Guthke, Karl S. *Modern Tragicomedy*. New York: Random House, 1966.

Kern, Edith. *The Absolute Comic*. New York: Columbia Univ. Press, 1980.

Albert Bermel

TRAINSPOTTING

Smack's an honest drug, . . . It doesnae alter your consciousness.
It jist gies ye a hit and a sense ay well-being. Eftir that, ye see the
misery ay the world as it is; ye cannae anaesthetize yirsel against it.
—Mark, Act 1

The play version of Irvine Welsh's novel *Trainspotting* was perhaps one of the most surprising theatrical successes in ENGLAND in the 1990s. The novel, about a group of heroin users in 1980s Edinburgh, was an international best-seller and a cult favorite of ravers, a subset of British youth culture who took ecstasy in order to dance and sweat the night away. While the book became known as the novel for people who did not read, Harry Gibson's adaptation (1994) became known as the play for those who did not attend the theater. Through its numerous productions across Britain, including two runs on London's West End, the play drew ravers and other members of club culture to the staid stalls of the British theater. Like JOHN OSBORNE's LOOK BACK IN ANGER, *Trainspotting* redefined the makeup of the British theatrical audience.

The stage play, which premiered before the Danny Boyle movie version, draws on the more memorable components of the novel. Gibson, though, writing for a cast of only four actors (three men, one woman), creatively refashioned the story by telescoping the novel's multiple story lines onto four main characters, Mark, Tommy, Franco, and Alison, all members of the previously unacknowledged subculture of the Scottish underclass.

The episodic play follows the exploits of the main narrator, the heroin addict Mark Renton, who is stuck in a continuing cycle of drug taking and then recovery, and his friends: Tommy, who becomes addicted to heroin after the breakup with his girlfriend; Alison, whose baby dies while she is shooting up; and Franco, who is the violent, unpredictable, and confrontational friend. One of the play's strengths relies on the characters' Scottish dialects, as well as their storytelling abilities, to convey viscerally and physically their bankrupt condition. In one monologue Mark relays his waking up in a bed covered in his own vomit, urine, and feces and his unsuccessful attempt to spirit the bed linen away from his girlfriend's home, and later Alison describes her revenge on a pack of obnoxious male customers by contaminating their meals with her menstrual blood, urine, and feces. One of the play's most powerful moments, though, does not rely on Welsh's language, as Gibson presents an addicted and demoralized Tommy shooting up in his penis.

The conclusion differs radically from those of the novel and movie, which end positively as Mark double-crosses his friends, stealing drug money for a new life in Amsterdam. In contrast, the play ends in an abandoned train station as Mark and Franco meet up with a bum, who turns out to be Franco's father. In ending this way, Gibson suggests that the fate of these characters is inescapable as Mark and Franco stare their future in the face.

The phenomenon of *Trainspotting* and Gibson's artfully constructed adaptation ensured the theatrical success of the play in

Britain, which led to productions around the world. In turn, other Welsh novels were adapted for the stage, and Welsh himself experimented with the dramatic genre by writing a play called *Headstate*.

FURTHER READING

Collin, Matthew. *Altered State: The Story of Ecstasy Culture and Acid House.* London: Serpent's Tail, 1997.

Dromgoole, Dominic. *The Full Room: An A–Z of Contemporary Playwriting.* London: Methuen, 2000.

Paget, Derek. "Speaking Out: The Transformations of *Trainspotting*." In *Adaptations: From Text to Screen, Screen to Text,* ed. by Deborah Cartmell and Imelda Whelehan. London: Routledge, 1999. 128–140.

Sierz, Aleks. *In-Yer-Face Theatre: British Drama Today.* London: Faber, 2001.

William C. Boles

TRANSFIGURATION

The translation of the title of ERNST TOLLER's (1893–1939) *Die Wandlung: Das Ringen eines Menschen* (1917) as *Transfiguration* has become established, but J. R. Ritchie's alternative, *Transformation*, would be more precise. *Transfiguration* directs attention too narrowly to the figure of Friedrich; *Transformation* underscores that a whole society, not just an individual, is shown undergoing change in the play. The process Toller depicts is the collapse of the social order in Europe under the impact of World War I and the death of millions of men in trench warfare. With them died the optimism and faith in God that had been felt by most people in the 19th century. Written in 1917, *Transfiguration* was remarkably prescient in its forecasting. The drama's last line consists of the cry for "Revolution! Revolution!" and the end of war brought just that to GERMANY. As it turned out, the play was not performed until September 30, 1919.

The problem of how to depict the complexity of social, economic, intellectual, and political forces undergoing change challenged conventional dramatic forms. Toller resorted to the structure of the "station drama," a series of scenes one after the other. The explicit heading "station" in the text takes on an added meaning, suggesting that Friedrich's progress resembles the movement of Christ through the stations of the cross. This analogy is strengthened by specific imagery, such as Friedrich lying on the prison floor "as though he had been crucified." Having rejected established religion, Friedrich becomes a secular messiah who espouses a new faith based in humanity.

As Friedrich and the audience proceed through the six stations, subdivided further into thirteen images, there is only a thin line holding everything together. Friedrich, dissatisfied with his middle-class life, jumps at the opportunity to fight in the colonies, where he is wounded. Back home, he tries to become a sculptor, but smashes the patriotic statue he is working on when he is confronted by a fellow veteran from the colo-nial wars who has been ravaged by syphilis. Friedrich's doubles then proceed through a variety of settings—a factory, a prison, and a public assembly—thereby revealing the material and spiritual exhaustion at every level of society. Not even erotic love has survived the degradation of the world. At the end Friedrich realizes that the old order has been destroyed and that he must assume leadership toward a new society. The measure of justice will have to come from human beings, since no one believes in God any longer.

Framing the stations is the allegorical prologue, which, according to the stage directions, could also be the epilogue. Two versions of death, death in war and death in peace, compare notes on how they are doing. The macabre scene is an overture for the play, which is haunted by death and dying. Toller's descriptions of the wounded soldiers are shocking, but at the same time undermine the conclusion of the play. The expressions of utopian desire at the end cannot erase the terrible images from our minds, and we are left with the sense that the future will not heal the past.

[*See also* Expressionism]

FURTHER READING

Benson, Renate. *German Expressionist Drama: Ernst Toller and Georg Kaiser.* London: Macmillan, 1984.

Kamla, Thomas. "Christianity and the Fatherland: The Problem of Community in Ernst Toller's *Die Wandlung*." *Germanic Notes* 15, nos. 3–4 (1984): 42–46.

Pittock, Malcolm. *Ernst Toller.* Boston: Twayne, 1979.

Arnd Bohm

TRANSLATIONS

We must learn those new names. . . . We must learn where we live. We must learn to make them our own. We must make them our new home.
—Hugh, Act 3

Translations is one of BRIAN FRIEL's most popular plays; it was also his most controversial. It premiered in Derry, Northern IRELAND, in November 1980 and was the first play produced by FIELD DAY THEATRE COMPANY, which Friel had co-founded with the actor Stephen Rea. It excited and delighted its first audiences, but Friel was accused by some commentators of historical inaccuracy and, more seriously, of having written a potentially inflammatory play at the height of the Northern Ireland Troubles.

The action is set in 1833 in a rural Irish "hedge school"—an unofficial school for Irish-speaking Catholics. As in many of Friel's plays, *Translations* is set at the end of summer—representing the fact that the community portrayed on stage is at the end of an era, about to move from prosperity to harsher times. In this case the transformation would be caused by the great Irish famine of the 1840s, which resulted in millions of deaths, mass emigration, and the near extinction of the Irish language.

The "translations" referred to in the title are carried out by a British mapping expedition, which is translating Irish place names into English—hence Baile Beag (in Irish, "little town"), where the play is set, is "translated" into English as "Ballybeg." The play is therefore an examination of the role of mapping—and education—in the extension of colonial power. Colonialism is also considered through a touching but doomed romance between the English sergeant Yolland and Maire, a young Irishwoman.

But there is another, highly theatrical, form of translation at work. Although the audience understands that many of the characters are speaking Irish to each other, all of the dialogue is presented in English. This is a daring theatrical device that often yields humorous results.

It is also a reflection of an important political reality. As a result of the historical situation that Friel is representing onstage, the majority of Irish people no longer understand the Irish language. Hence Friel must present his dialogue in English. By doing so, he shows that his English-speaking audience and his Irish-speaking characters share one important characteristic: both are Irish. This supports the play's argument that, painful as it might be, a civilization can and must develop—even to the point of abandoning one language and taking up another. This is a practical illustration of the argument advanced by many of the play's characters: a civilization that fails to move forward will fossilize, and "to remember everything is a form of madness."

The politics of Friel's play have frequently been misunderstood and occasionally misrepresented, much to his frustration. To the accusation of historical inaccuracy he has countered that his responsibility is to present artistic rather than historical truths. *Translations* is now one of Friel's most popular works and is frequently performed in Ireland and throughout the world, especially in regions where issues such as IDENTITY, territory, and language are contested.

FURTHER READING

Grene, Nicholas. *The Politics of Irish Drama.* Cambridge: Cambridge Univ. Press, 1999.

Pine, Richard. *Brian Friel and Ireland's Drama.* London: Routledge, 1990.

Steiner, George. *After Babel.* 3d ed. Oxford: Oxford Univ. Press, 1998.

Patrick Lonergan

TRAVESTIES

> *I learned three things in Zurich during the war. . . . Firstly, you're either a revolutionary or you're not, and if you're not you might as well be an artist as anything else. Secondly, if you can't be an artist, you might as well be a revolutionary. . . . I forget the third thing.*
> —Old Carr, Act 2

In an interview shortly before the premiere of *Travesties* (1974), TOM STOPPARD announced that he was trying to contrive "the perfect marriage between the play of ideas and FARCE or perhaps even high COMEDY." *Travesties* was first staged at the Aldwych Theatre in London in 1974 and was taken to New York one year later. Critical reactions were divided between enthusiastic praise for the play's highly allusive verbal fireworks and Kenneth Tynan's dismissal of the "triple-decker bus that isn't going anywhere." Literary criticism has alternately classified *Travesties* as a play or high comedy of ideas, a memory play, or a history play. Each of these labels seems appropriate, because the comedy actually thematizes and travesties (aesthetic) ideas, the function of memory or the role of history.

Travesties sets out from the coincidence that three revolutionaries resided at Zürich during World War I: Tristan Tzara, whose DADAISM aimed to overthrow traditional notions of art; James Joyce, whose *Ulysses* would epitomize the modernist revolution in literature; and Vladimir Ilich Lenin, planning his return to Russia. The protagonist of the play, Henry Carr, was actually a minor functionary at the Zürich consulate who had starred as Algernon in an amateur production of THE IMPORTANCE OF BEING EARNEST, directed by James Joyce, who—after an unsuccessful lawsuit with the amateur actor—had immortalized Carr in an unflattering footnote in *Ulysses*. Stoppard decided to use this marginal figure as the focal point of his play.

Old Carr is remembering himself in the role of the Zürich consul meeting Tzara, Joyce, and Lenin at Zürich. His memory being hopelessly unreliable, however, it turns out that he had neither been consul nor met any of the celebrities. Framed by his recollections of the performance of *The Importance of Being Earnest*, which provides a rudimentary plot for Stoppard's play, Carr confounds the historical characters with the fictional ones, casting Tzara as Jack Worthing, himself as Algernon, Joyce as Lady Bracknell, Lenin and his wife as Dr. Chasuble and Miss Prism, and his sister Gwendolen and the librarian Cecily as their namesakes in Wilde's play. Occasionally Carr's memory fails him altogether; in such "time slips" the play rewinds to an earlier passage in the dialogue, from which it resumes in a different direction.

Stoppard's comedy is a veritable echo chamber of styles, patching together Wildean dialogues, *Ulysses*, limericks, vaudeville songs, Shakespearean sonnets, and historical documents. Since Lenin's lines are quoted throughout from his own writings, some critics believe that his ontological status differs from that of the other characters. However, blurring the boundaries of history and fiction, the play also suggests that history does not consist in facts to be remembered, but is something created through memory—and that the Lenin plot makes no difference. The thematic core of the first act discusses the function of art, whereas the second act focuses on the role of the artist, especially his or her social responsibility toward society. As often in Stoppard's theater, it is hard, if not impossible, to claim which position is favored in the play—*Travesties* raises questions without giving answers.

[*See also* England]

FURTHER READING

Delaney, Paul. *Tom Stoppard: The Moral Vision of the Major Plays.* Basingstoke: Macmillan, 1990.

Haberer, Adolphe, ed. *De Joyce à Stoppard: Écritures de la modernité.* Lyon: Presses Universitaires de Lyon, 1991.

Sammells, Neil. *Tom Stoppard: The Artist as Critic.* Basingstoke: Macmillan, 1988.

Stoppard, Tom. "Ambushes for the Audience: Towards a High Comedy of Ideas; Interview with Roger Hudson, Catherine Itzin and Simon Trussler." *Theatre Quarterly* 14, no. 4 (1974): 3–17.

——. *Travesties.* London: Faber, 1975.

Whitaker, Thomas R. *Tom Stoppard.* Macmillan Modern Dramatists. Basingstoke: Macmillan, 1983.

Anja Müller

TREADWELL, SOPHIE (1885–1970)

Sophie Treadwell was born on October 3, 1885, in Stockton, California. She attended the University of California at Berkeley, where she participated in drama activities and wrote fiction and poetry before graduating in 1906. She earned fame as a journalist, most notably for a 1920 interview with Pancho Villa, the revolutionary Mexican bandit.

In 1915 Treadwell moved to New York, where her first two Broadway productions had short runs: *Gringo*, a MELODRAMA of Americans in Mexico, and *O'Nightingale*, an exuberant COMEDY depicting the adventures of a young aspiring actress. After spending three years researching and writing a play about Edgar Allan Poe, she sent a copy of *Poe* to John Barrymore, who told her in February 1921 that he loved the play and wanted to play the title role. He did not offer her a contract, and in August 1924 he informed her that he was going to produce a different Poe play written by his wife, Michael Strange. Suspicious, Treadwell met with Barrymore, and after hearing the other play read, she filed suit to stop production of Strange's play and to get her own script returned. A media frenzy over the suit cast Treadwell in an unfavorable light as the "unknown opportunist," but her public stand sparked considerable discussion in newspapers on the topic of plagiarism. Treadwell refused to drop the suit; Barrymore returned her script and eventually stopped plans for production of his wife's version. Treadwell's play was eventually produced in 1936 as *Plumes in the Dust* with Henry Hull in the title role, but it did not fare well with Depression-era audiences.

Treadwell attended the sensational 1927 trial of Ruth Snyder and Judd Gray, who conspired to kill Snyder's husband and were executed in 1928. Treadwell used the trial as the basis for MACHINAL, an expressionistic drama that became her greatest critical and commercial success, combining her concern for women's inequality with her journalistic ability to tell a topical story. In nine scenes Young Woman is compelled to submit to forces around her—her mother's wishes, her husband's ardor, the birth of an unwanted child, society's condemnation for her taking a lover, and the prison guard who shaves the crown of her head before she is electrocuted. Treadwell had four more Broadway productions, her last being *Hope for a Harvest*, concerning the loss of the American work ethic, a theme that did not go over with 1941 audiences.

Treadwell's most innovative work is *For Saxophone*, a "musical play" that uses constantly changing musical sound, lighting, and staging shifts, as well as unusual visual and verbal effects. In 1999 the piece was adapted for radio and aired on the BBC as *Intimations for Saxophone*. *Woman with Lilies* was produced at the University of Arizona under the title *Now He Doesn't Want to Play*. Her work has largely gone unappreciated, but recent revivals of *Machinal* have revitalized interest in her as a pioneering woman playwright willing to tackle new styles, subjects, and forms in over thirty plays. Treadwell died on February 20, 1970, in Tucson, Arizona.

[*See also* Expressionism; Feminist Drama in the United States; United States]

PLAYS: *Le Grand Prix* (1905); *Constance Darrow* (1908); *The Right Man* (1908); *The Settlement* (1911); *The Answer* (1918); *Claws* (1918); *Madame Bluff* (1918); *Trance* (1918); *Rights* (1921); *Gringo* (1922); *Love Lady* (previously *Old Rose*, 1924); *Many Mansions* (1925); *O'Nightingale* (1925; previously *Loney Lee*, 1923); *You Can't Have Everything* (1925); *Machinal* (1928); *Ladies Leave* (1929); *The Island* (1930); *Million Dollar Gate* (with William McGeehan, 1930); *Andrew Wells' Lady* (1931); *The Last Are First* (1933); *Lone Valley* (1933); *For Saxophone* (1934); *Plumes in the Dust* (1936); *Three* (1936); *Hope for a Harvest* (1941); *Highway* (1942); *The Last Border* (1947); *A String of Pearls* (1950); *Judgment in the Morning* (1952); *The Siren* (1953); *Garry* (1954); *Woman with Lilies* (produced as *Now He Doesn't Want to Play*, 1967)

FURTHER READING

Dickey, Jerry. *Sophie Treadwell: A Research and Production Sourcebook.* Westport, Conn.: Greenwood Press, 1997.

Engle, Sherry. "Desperately Seeking a Poe: Sophie Treadwell's *Plumes in the Dust.*" *American Drama* (Spring 1997): 25–42.

Heck-Rabi, Louise. "Sophie Treadwell: Agent for Change." In *Women in American Theatre*, ed. by Helen Krich Chinoy and Linda Walsh Jenkins. New York: Crown, 1981. 157–162.

Wynn, Nancy. "Sophie Treadwell: The Career of a Twentieth Century American Feminist Playwright." Ph.D. diss., City Univ. of New York, 1982.

Sherry D. Engle

TREMBLAY, MICHEL (1942–)

The most widely performed and translated Quebecois playwright, Michel Tremblay is acclaimed for sowing a metaphor of nationalist hope from intensely personal strife. Born on June

25, 1942, and raised in Montreal, CANADA's, impoverished Plateau Mont-Royal neighborhood, Tremblay rejected classical studies and their middle-class sensibilities. Calling his work "theatre of truth" and "photography," Tremblay came to prominence in 1968 with SISTERS-IN-LAW (Les belles–soeurs, 1968), a play that revolutionized dramatic language: the "sisters" speak in lower-class joual. Although the play was dismissed as "filthy" and "un-French," it signaled the emergence of a new Quebecois drama, thanks in part to the writer's solidarity with his own people: "One is never more universal than when one is local."

Tremblay's characters belong to one neighborhood, sometimes to one family, and, above all, to one species: they have been described as pathetic clowns, their days marked by despair and paralysis. Daily chores become ritualistic, and hope, as elusive as money, is replaced by "fun." They revel in bingo, television, drinking, magazines, even mayonnaise. Above all, the characters dream, and they recount their dreams with a lyricism that counters the crude, staccato sociolect in which they speak of mundane existence. Between these two discursive poles is a zone of noncommunication where monologues go unheeded and unheard. The perpetual stalemate of their lives leads characters to revel in animosity as masochists (taking pleasure in the martyrdom of their meager conditions) and sadists (characters repeatedly injure each other emotionally and physically). Women treat sex as bestial; they remain silent, ignorant, and afraid. Men lack virility; they are mad, disabled, or wicked. Tremblay ascribes this sexual and familial discordance to a Catholic deification of feminine dependence and obedience. His characters tend to replace family with conventionally censured relationships, including homosexuality and incest. Yet his same-sex couples hardly fare better: men refer to themselves in the feminine, and this self-identification is not trendy or casual. Tremblay's recurrent depictions of the transgendered create a political statement of social impotence, of a people who have renounced their identities in favor of disguise. For the playwright, the Quebecois have been "transvestites for 300 years."

Tremblay's plays are based on antithetical structures that represent the allure of escape and the wish to belong, the fear of madness and the joy of accepting it, the empowerment of selfishness and the desire to aid. The playwright recalls EUGÈNE IONESCO and SAMUEL BECKETT—a part of French literature, yet also a foreigner. His works blend Ionesco's quotidian awareness with Beckett's perverse psychology. Tremblay's characters, however, inhabit smaller, altered worlds within an external world of coherence and logic. In this sense his plays recall 19th–century dramatic NATURALISM, in which unseen forces predetermine characters' lives before they have the opportunity to live them. His unflinching portrayals of the resigned poor, in income as well as in spirit, are interpreted locally as a call for self-determination and a commitment to authentic Quebecois culture. Without them, implies Tremblay, we can only be paralyzed in our relationships and our communities. He was awarded the Chevalier de l'Ordre des Arts et des Lettres de France in 1984 and the Chevalier de l'Ordre National de Québec in 1992.

SELECT PLAYS: *The Train* (*Le train*, 1964); *Sisters-in-Law* (*Les belles-soeurs*, 1968); *The Duchess of Langeais* (*La Duchesse de Langeais*, 1969); *The Peacocks* (*Les paons*, 1969); *Johnny Mangana and His Astonishing Dogs* (*Trois petits tours*, 1971); *Tomorrow Morning, Montreal Awaits* (*Demain matin, Montréal m'attend*, 1972); *Forever Yours, Marie-Lou* (*A toi, pour toujours, ta Marie-Lou*, 1972); *Like Death Warmed Over* (*En pièces détachées*, 1973); *Hosanna* (1974); *Bonjour, la, Bonjour* (1975); *Surprise, Surprise!* (1975); *The Heroes of My Childhood* (*Les héros de mon enfance*, 1976); *Damned Manon, Holy Sandra* (*Damnée Manon, Sacrée Sandra*, 1978); *Saint Carmen of the Main* (*Sainte-Carmen de la Main*, 1978); *The Impromptu of Outremont* (*L'impromptu d'Outremont*, 1980); *Albertine in Five Times* (*Albertine, en cinq temps*, 1985); *The Real World?* (*Le vrai monde?* 1988); *The House Among the Stars* (*La maison suspendue*, 1990); *A Full Moon in Summer* (*Messe solenelle pour une pleine lune d'été*, 1995); *Marcel Pursued by the Hounds* (*Marcel poursuivi par les chiens*, 1997); *For the Pleasure of Seeing Her Again* (*Encore une fois si vous le permettez*, 1998); *Impromptu on Nuns' Island* (*L'état des lieux*, 2002)

FURTHER READING

Collet, Paulett. "Michel Tremblay: Le leitmotive de son théâtre" [The leitmotiv of his theater]. In *Le théâtre canadien-français*, ed. by Paul Wyczynski, Bernard Julien, and Hélène Beauchamp-Raule. Montreal: Fides, 1976. 597–615.

Piccione, Marie-Lyne. *Michel Tremblay, l'enfant multiple* [The complex child]. Talence, France: Presses Universitaires de Bordeaux, 1999.

Weiss, Jonathan M. *French-Canadian Theater*. Boston: Twayne, 1986.

Matt Di Cintio

TRETYAKOV, SERGEI (1892–1937)

Sergei Tretyakov was a Soviet playwright who was "in many ways, the representative figure of the revolutionary theatre . . . an artistic polymath whose contribution to the development of broadcast radio, journalism, documentary film and poetry are only beginning to be appreciated" (Leach, 1994). He was closely associated with VLADIMIR MAYAKOVSKY as joint leader of the leftist AVANT-GARDE during the 1920s; his contribution to agit-prop (AGITATION-PROPAGANDA) drama also involved working closely with Sergei Eisenstein and VSEVOLOD MEYERHOLD.

His first work for the theater involved an agit-prop adaptation of a 19th-century play by ALEKSANDR OSTROVSKY, *Enough Stupidity in Every Wise Man*, as an episodic "montage of attractions" staged by Eisenstein at the Proletkult (Proletarian Culture) Theater in Moscow in 1923. According to Eisenstein, an "attraction" (with its connotations of circus and fairground) consisted of "aggressive moments" designed to produce "emotional shocks" in the audience of an ideological nature. For this purpose, Tretyakov transferred the action of the play to contemporary Paris and turned the 19th-century characters into politically contentious types such as Benito Mussolini and capitalist speculators, describing the play as a "text montage." His next work, Gasmasks (Protivogazy, 1923), a "MELODRAMA," is set in a German gasworks, the owner of which has neglected both the plant and his workers' safety so that a gas leak has to be repaired without protective masks—a heroic act of self-sacrifice by the workers that involves the death of the director's own revolutionary son. Tretyakov's last play for the Proletkult, described as an "agit-guignol" (a reference to the French Grand Guignol), was Are You Listening, Moscow?! (Slyshish, Moskva?!, 1924). Also set in GERMANY and inspired by an actual workers' revolt in Hamburg, it concerns a count who has planned a festival in his own honor, only to find that his efforts have been subverted when, at the end of the play, a statue unveiled to the greater glory of his family is discovered to have been replaced by one of Vladimir Lenin.

Tretyakov's first work for Meyerhold involved the adaptation of a pacifist drama with a World War I setting as World Rampant (Zemlya dybom, 1923). The play was constructed as a series of propagandist episodes, using the device of choric speech, or "speech montage," and deploying revolutionary slogans projected onto screens, converting the psychological aspects of the original play into political posters in such a way that "the theatre show" was replaced by "the theatre blow" (Tretyakov). His second play for Meyerhold, Roar China! (Rychi, Kitay!, 1926), was based on an actual incident on the Yangtze river involving a British gunboat that threatened the destruction of a local town if those responsible for the drowning of an American business agent were not produced for summary execution. The play conforms to leftist demands for a "literature of fact" and sharply juxtaposes scenes involving the human Chinese against those depicting grotesque imperialists on HMS Cockchafer. Tretyakov's last and most controversial work, I Want a Baby (Khochu rebyonka, 1926), was rehearsed by Meyerhold but banned. Its theme of the selective breeding and rearing of children was designed to provoke discussion but proved too ambiguous for the censorship's taste and was described as "a hostile slander on the Soviet family." Tretyakov met BERTOLT BRECHT in 1930 and translated a handful of his plays before being arrested as an enemy of the people and committing suicide.

[See also Russia and the Soviet Union]

SELECT PLAYS: Gasmasks (Protivogazy, 1923); Immaculate Conception (Immaconcep, 1923); The Wise Man (Mudrets, adapted from Ostrovsky's Na vsyakogo mudretsa dovol'no prostoty, Enough Stupidity in Every Wise Man, also known as The Scoundrel, 1923); World Rampant, also known as Earth Rampant, Earth in Turmoil, The World Turned Upside-Down, and The World on Its Hind Legs (Zemlya dybom, 1923); Are You Listening, Moscow?!, also known as Do You Hear, Moscow?! (Slyshish, Moskva?!, 1924); I Want a Baby, also known as I Want a Child (Khochu rebyonka, 1926); Roar, China! (Rychi, Kitay!, 1926)

FURTHER READING

Kleberg, Lars. "Eisenstein's Potyomkan and Tretyakov's Rychi, Kitay." Scando-Slavica 23 (1977).

———. Theatre as Action: Soviet Avant-Garde Aesthetics. Tr. by Charles Rougle. Basingstoke: Macmillan, 1993.

Leach, Robert. Revolutionary Theatre. London: Routledge, 1994.

Tretyakov, Sergei. Roar China, an Episode in Nine Scenes. Tr. by F. Polianovska and Barbara Nixon. London: Martin Lawrence Ltd, 1931.

Nick Worrall

TRIANA, JOSÉ (1933–)

José Triana, Cuban playwright and poet, was a key figure in the short-lived theatrical renaissance that occurred in CUBA after the revolution of 1959. Born in Camagüey and raised in Bayamo, Triana left Cuba in 1955 to study in Madrid, SPAIN, where he remained until the end of Fulgencio Batista's dictatorship. In Madrid Triana wrote his first important play, The Major General Will Speak on Theogony (El mayor general hablará de teogonía, 1957), in which he first presented the themes and techniques that would define his drama: use of ritual and the presence of oppression. With the triumph of the revolution, Triana returned to Cuba and established himself in Havana with the successful debut in 1960 of Medea in the Mirror (Medea en el espejo, 1959), a modern urban version of Euripides' TRAGEDY. María, a mulatta scorned by her white lover Julián, takes revenge by killing their children. As Triana witnessed the revolutionary government's campaign to solidify its power, his next plays, El parque de la fraternidad (1962) and La muerte del Ñeque (1964), dealt with themes of oppression and violence as inevitable results of power struggles.

Triana's international fame is due largely to the success of his play Night of the Assassins (La noche de los asesinos, 1964). Because of this play, literary critics and theater groups began to recognize the artistry of Spanish-speaking theater, which had historically remained second-tier to the theater produced in Europe. Although the play won the coveted Casa de las Américas prize in 1965, the antirevolutionary interpretation of Night of the Assassins by Cuban critics provoked Triana's eventual social and intellectual ostracism from Cuban literary and political circles. Although he continued as editor at the Instituto del Libro, he was unable to publish any other literary work in Cuba because of his assumed political stance. In 1980 he left Cuba and settled in Paris with his wife, where he remains a prolific writer. Plays such as Ceremonial de guerra (1990), Revolico en el Campo de Marte (1995), Common Language (Palabras comunes, 1986), Cruzando el puente (1992), and La fiesta (1995) address the current Cuban and Cuban exile situation as the author continues to critically assess his country's past and present.

Triana cites the authors of Spain's generation of 1898 as an important influence in his work with their elements of tragedy, search for IDENTITY, and desire to better society. The use of violence and ritual, as well as Afro-Cuban cultural elements, characterizes the majority of his dramas. Triana recounts Cuba's "unofficial" history as his plays focus on marginalized people of diverse races and classes, demonstrating how society tragically affects their lives. In his plays an oppressive entity, either real or imagined, often presides over a suffocating stage space where victim and victimizer continually trade places through ritual. At their most decisive moments his antiheroic protagonists inevitably fail to move beyond the vicious cycle of interdependence because the power structure of society maintains their enslavement. Influenced by the Theater of the Absurd, cruelty, and ceremony, the seemingly illogical, incoherent, and violent situations depicted critically reflect the problematic elements that Triana believes to be at the root of the Cuban psyche, such as racism, sexism, corruption, and blind religious faith.

[See also Absurdism]

SELECT PLAYS: *The Major General Will Speak on Theogony* (*El mayor general hablará de teogonía*, 1957); *Medea in the Mirror* (*Medea en el espejo*, 1959); *El parque de la fraternidad* (1962); *La muerte del Ñeque* (1964); *Night of the Assassins* (*La noche de los asesinos*, 1964); *Common Language* (*Palabras comunes*, 1986); *Ceremonial de guerra* (1990); *Cruzando el puente* (1992); *La fiesta* (1995); *Revolico en el Campo de Marte* (1995); *Ahí están los Tarahumaras* (1997); *El último día del verano* (unpublished)

FURTHER READING

Campa, Román de la. *José Triana: Ritualización de la sociedad cubana.* Madrid: Catédra, 1979.

Dauster, Frank N. "The Game of Chance: The Theater of José Triana." In *Dramatists in Revolt: The New Latin American Theater,* ed. by Leon F. Lyday and George W. Woodyard. Austin: Univ. of Texas Press, 1976. 167–189.

Nigro, Kirsten, ed. *Palabras más que comunes: Ensayos sobre el teatro de José Triana.* Boulder, Colo.: Society of Spanish and Spanish-American Studies, 1994.

Taylor, Diana. "Framing the Revolution: Triana's *La noche de los asesinos* and *Ceremonial de guerra.*" *Latin American Theatre Review* 24 (Fall 1990): 81–92.

——, ed. *En busca de una imagen: Ensayos críticos sobre Griselda Gambaro y José Triana.* Ottawa, Canada: Girol Bks., 1989.

Vasserot, Christilla. "Siempre fui y seré un exiliado." *Encuentro con la Cultura Cubana* 4–5 (1997): 33–45.

I. Carolina Caballero

TRIBADERNAS NATT See THE NIGHT OF THE TRIBADES

TRIFLES

A model of the one-act form, SUSAN GLASPELL's *Trifles* (1916) exemplified modernist American DRAMATURGY for decades, holding the stage while serving as a touchstone text in playwriting manuals and appearing repeatedly in anthologies of short plays. Its equally noteworthy short-story counterpart, "A Jury of Her Peers" (1917), reemerged in the 1970s as a seminal text for Anglo-American feminist criticism. The two works reveal Glaspell's acute sensitivity to the social enforcement of gender roles, to sexual inequities in the U.S. legal system, and to the importance of foregrounding women's voices and women's experience in cultural production.

Glaspell later traced the genesis of the pieces to her early journalistic career, when she covered the Hossack murder trial of 1900 for the *Des Moines Daily News*. Glaspell filed twenty-six articles on the prosecution and conviction of Margaret Hossack for the murder of her husband, John. She did not return to the case for fifteen years, however, until the demand for new scripts for the theater company she co-founded, the Provincetown Players, prompted her to explore its theatrical potential.

Glaspell uses the structure and technical devices of the murder-mystery form to develop her narrative. John Wright has been killed in bed, and his wife Minnie has been arrested for the murder, before the play begins. Two sets of characters, grouped by sex, see the crime from different perspectives and use distinct strategies in their efforts to find evidence and reconstruct events. The men, who represent law and the social order, comb the offstage crime scene and the surrounding property for clues, to no avail. The wives of the sheriff and the neighbor who found Wright's body remain in the kitchen. This locale is of no interest to the men, who dismiss it and women's labor therein as unimportant. The women become amateur detectives, discussing Minnie's and their own lives empathically and thereby discovering, in the "trifles" of Minnie's daily routine, a possible motive for the crime. They forge meaningful ties with each other, and, through their identification with Minnie, they determine that their bonds as women outweigh their allegiance to the patriarchal judicial order. In the play's closing moments the women decide to hide the evidence they have found, operating as the "jury of her peers" that the exclusively male legal system precludes.

In *Trifles* Glaspell developed the device of "absent center" characters that would become a hallmark of her dramaturgy, recurring most notably in *Bernice* (1919) and her Pulitzer Prize–winning ALISON'S HOUSE (1930). These figures, who never appear onstage, ground her dramas and serve as foils through whom we come to know those we do see. The absent characters exemplify Glaspell's understanding of the constructedness of identity, in that we can only know them through their representation by others. Glaspell's conscious revision of cultural paradigms—her insistence on the significance of women's lives and her rejection of patriarchal conventions—established her as a maverick and a leading writer for the first wave of feminism in the UNITED STATES.

[See also Feminist Drama in the United States]

FURTHER READING

Gainor, J. Ellen. Susan Glaspell in Context: American Theater, Culture, and Politics, 1915–48. Ann Arbor: Univ. of Michigan Press, 2001.

Glaspell, Susan. Plays. Ed. by C. W. E. Bigsby. New York: Cambridge Univ. Press, 1987.

Ozieblo, Barbara. Susan Glaspell: A Critical Biography. Chapel Hill: Univ. of North Carolina Press, 2000.

Papke, Mary. Susan Glaspell: A Research and Production Sourcebook. Westport, Conn.: Greenwood Press, 1993.

J. Ellen Gainor

TRI SESTRY See THREE SISTERS

THE TROJAN WAR WILL NOT TAKE PLACE

A play in two acts, The Trojan War Will Not Take Place (La Guerre de Troie n'aura lieu, 1935) by JEAN GIRAUDOUX is generally considered his greatest dramatic achievement. Hector, a prince of Troy, returns from battle intent on closing the city's Gates of War, an act that will symbolize Troy's commitment to peace. But his brother Paris has caused a diplomatic incident by abducting Helen, the wife of the Greek king Menelaus, and there is talk of war; even the prophetess Cassandra is having bloody visions. Initially Hector smiles at Paris's dalliance, but his amusement fades as he discovers that the Trojans are more interested in keeping Helen than they are in keeping the peace. Beauty worth dying for, the pride of a nation, inspiration for a poet's couplet—Helen has come to represent all these things and more. In act 2 Ajax and Ulysses arrive to retrieve Helen; while the former is itching for a fight, the latter is charmed by Hector's wife, Andromache, and decides to return Helen to Greece without incident. But as the Greeks depart, a drunken Ajax insults Andromache, pushing Hector to the breaking point. When the Trojan poet Demokos bursts in to rail at him for betraying his country, Hector strikes Demokos, who, with his dying words, cries out that Ajax is his killer. The Trojans rush the Greek ship and kill Ajax in a frenzy as Hector, Andromache, and Cassandra look on in horror. As the curtain falls, the Gates of War slowly open.

At once a COMEDY of manners and a drama of ideas, a retelling of The Iliad and a critique of all war stories, The Trojan War Will Not Take Place was perhaps the ideal theatrical subject for Giraudoux's signature irony. Some critics have complained that his Boulevard style and apparent lack of moral commitment in other works rendered his drama pallid, if not precious. But in The Trojan War it is the principled Hector's very encounters with those seemingly indifferent or resigned to the impending conflict that fuel the play's mounting tension. As articulated by Ulysses in act 2, Giraudoux's play anatomizes how a "world's mood and atmosphere" can give "a kind of permission for war." What appear to be the subjects of comedy—Helen's narcissism, Ajax's boorishness, Priam's pompous nationalism—are revealed as deadly weapons, all the more so for their seeming inconsequence. Hector, perhaps Giraudoux's most appealing male protagonist, likely gives voice to the playwright's deeper feelings about combat; Giraudoux was wounded twice in World War I and was the first writer to be awarded the wartime Legion of Honor.

The Trojan War Will Not Take Place premiered in Paris on November 21, 1935, produced by Louis Jouvet. Critics understood the piece to be a trenchant commentary on Europe's strained political situation: GERMANY had just left the League of Nations and was about to occupy the Rhineland. A line spoken by Cassandra in the first act upon seeing Hector returning from battle would prove eerily prescient indeed: "This was the last war, the next one is waiting." CHRISTOPHER FRY's English adaptation of the play is titled Tiger at the Gates.

[See also France]

FURTHER READING

Body, Jacques. Jean Giraudoux: The Legend and the Secret. Rutherford, N.J.: Fairleigh Dickinson Univ. Press, 1991.

Giraudoux, Jean. Tiger at the Gates. Tr. by Christopher Fry. London: French, 1955.

Mankin, Paul. Precious Irony: The Theatre of Jean Giraudoux. The Hague: Mouton, 1971.

Charlotte Stoudt

TROMMELN IN DER NACHT See DRUMS IN THE NIGHT

TRUE WEST

There's no such thing as the West anymore! It's a dead issue!
—Austin, Scene 6

Although SAM SHEPARD's True West (1980) focuses on several familiar Shepard themes—the corruption of art by commerce, the spiritual death of the American family, and the vanished promise of the western frontier—it most closely examines the dynamics of the divided self. "I wanted to write a play about double nature, one that wouldn't be symbolic or metaphorical or any of that stuff," Shepard explained; "I've worked harder on this play than anything I've ever written. The play's down to the bone."

True West explores the relationship between two very different brothers. Austin, a preppy aspiring screenwriter, has left his wife and children "up north" to write in the quiet of his mother's suburban Southern California home while she vacations in Alaska. The older Lee, a renegade drifter and burglar who has spent the last three months in the desert, now crashes in on Mom's as well. Austin is trying to sell his "simple love story" to Saul Kimmer, a crass Hollywood producer, but Lee one-ups him and pitches Saul "a Western that'd knock yer lights out. . . . Contemporary Western. Based on a true story." Austin and Lee vie for Saul's approval, and, over a strong-armed golf game, Lee gets Saul to drop Austin's project and produce Lee's story. Austin at first refuses to write Lee's script, which he describes as "a bullshit story. . . . Two lamebrains chasing each other across Texas," but caves in when he realizes that it is the only way he will get his car keys back from Lee.

The heart of this two-act play is the scenes where the brothers trade roles: Lee attempts to dictate his script while Austin types, but in their brawling their roles deteriorate to the point that Austin quips, "We all sound alike when we're sloshed." Soon they have busted up Mom's kitchen, Lee mauls the typewriter with a golf club, and Austin has cat-burgled the neighborhood for all its toasters. But as the two brothers share stories about their "old man" losing his teeth and living broke and drunk in the Mexican desert, it becomes clear that they are both searching for something authentic. Each yearns for what the other has: Lee for Austin's legitimacy and stability, Austin for Lee's adventure and freedom. In the last scene of the play Mom comes home early, disappointed with Alaska, and, unable to deal with her rowdy sons and her vandalized home, she checks into a motel. At the play's end Austin and Lee are left in a dead-heat confrontation, circling each other, waiting for the next move.

True West was first produced in San Francisco by the Magic Theatre in 1980. Robert Woodruff directed, with Shepard in attendance at rehearsals; the play had a successful run. Woodruff then directed a new cast in a second production for the New York Shakespeare Festival's Public Theater, but was replaced after a dispute with the Public Theater's producer, Joseph Papp. Shepard disavowed the production. In 1982 the play enjoyed a long-running and critically acclaimed New York revival in a production by Chicago's Steppenwolf Theatre Company, which emphasized the black COMEDY of the play and featured John Malkovich as Lee and Gary Sinise as Austin. A television version of this production was also filmed for the Public Broadcasting Service's *American Playhouse*.

[*See also* United States, 1940–Present]

FURTHER READING

Bottoms, Stephen J. *The Theatre of Sam Shepard*. New York: Cambridge Univ. Press, 1998.

Marranca, Bonnie, ed. *American Dreams: The Imagination of Sam Shepard*. New York: Performing Arts Journal Publications, 1981.

Shepard, Sam. *True West*. In *Seven Plays*. New York: Bantam, 1981.

Mary Fleischer

THE TRUTH

In *The Truth* CLYDE FITCH played out his idea of a woman character who cannot help lying, writing what he described as "psychologically and technically" his "best play yet." After initial strong showings in Cleveland, Chicago, and Buffalo in the fall of 1906, *The Truth* opened in New York at the Criterion Theatre on January 7, 1907.

Becky Warder, a charming, vivacious, and lovable young woman, has been happily married to her adoring husband, Tom, for six years, but she has been meeting regularly Fred Lindon, the husband of her friend, Eva, from whom he is separated. Although she admits to Lindon that she enjoys his attention, Becky sees the meetings as harmless in her attempts to help the couple reconcile.

Eva, however, has hired detectives to follow her philandering husband, and, learning of the daily meetings between Becky and Fred, she becomes jealous and shows the reports to Tom. Warder refuses to believe the reports, but mentions them to Becky, who denies Eva's accusations and, at her husband's request, promises never to see Lindon again.

Early on, the likeable Becky is shown lying compulsively even over trivial matters, becoming increasingly enmeshed in her own falsehoods. Her husband returns home earlier than expected to find Lindon calling on his wife at her request; he also learns that she has sent her father money despite his adamant refusal to do so. When confronted by her husband about her broken promises, Becky denies and covers up, making things even worse. Although he has overlooked her mild prevarications in the past, Warder now finds her deception intolerable and leaves.

Becky goes to her father's shabby Baltimore apartment, where he has a friendship with Mrs. Crespigny, the coarse landlady to whom the old man owes back rent and holds off with vague hints of marriage. Roland's perpetual lying demonstrates the atmosphere in which Becky has been brought up. "I always hated the plain truth," he tells his daughter. "I liked to trim it up a little." To which Becky replies with a pathetic laugh, "Like me!" Roland, wanting his daughter to reconcile with her husband so they will resume their financial support, sends Warder a message that Becky is seriously ill. But when a worried Warder arrives, Becky refuses to go along, for now she "loathes" lies. She tells her husband the truth, and they happily reconcile.

New York reviews were initially unfavorable. In spite of a strong cast that included Clara Bloodgood, the chief complaint against the play was that there was too much conversation and "a paucity of action" until the last act. Even though positive reviews came later, the production did not recover from initial negative commentary.

The Truth, however, had enormous success abroad, beginning as a smash hit in London, with actress Marie Tempest, and running for 170 performances. Appreciative audiences throughout France, Germany, and Italy were drawn to the psychological aspects of the play; in Budapest *The Truth* became the first American play produced in Hungary.

[*See also* Realism; United States]

FURTHER READING

Bordman, Gerald. *The Oxford Companion to American Theatre*. 2d ed. New York: Oxford Univ. Press, 1992.

Moses, Montrose J., and Virginia Gerson. *Clyde Fitch and His Letters*. Boston: Little, Brown, 1924.

"Mr. Fitch's Play Ably Presented." *New York Times* (April 13, 1914): 11:3.

"Music and the Drama." *Chicago Chronicle* (October 24, 1906).

"The Truth." *Chicago Tribune* (October 23, 1906).

"The Truth." *New York Times* (January 8, 1907).

"The Truth." *New York Times* (January 13, 1907).

Sherry D. Engle

THE TRUTH ABOUT BLAYDS

Although perennially ignored by academics, *The Truth About Blayds* is the most serious play by A. A. MILNE. It was commercially and critically lauded—even Dorothy Parker, famous for her mockery of Milne's children's books, called *Blayds* "a fine and merciless and honest play." It was premiered on December 20, 1921, and 120 performances were staged at the Globe Theatre, London; major and minor American productions flourished—a young Katharine Hepburn played the male role of Oliver Blayds-Conway in one amateur show.

The play dramatizes the differing perspectives of the Blayds-Conway family: Oliver Blayds is a much-lauded, ninety-year-old literary giant; his eldest daughter, Marion, and her husband, William Conway, live fawningly in Blayds's shadow, as does his younger daughter, the devoted Isobel; the grandchildren, Oliver and Septima, resent the family's slavish devotion to the old man. The Samuel French "acting edition" of 1923 depicts the scenery that Milne stipulated: an imposing portrait of Blayds is placed in the center, while lush sofas, gentlemen's desks, ornate chandeliers, and a high ceiling stress the oddly austere opulence in which the Blayds-Conways exist. In the first act a number of "young writers" come to pay tribute at this altar to Oliver Blayds. Blayds is revealed to be a tired wreck of a man; the pompous choreographing of the visitors by Marion and William is embarrassing; Septima speaks of wishing to flee Blayds and the house, while her brother satirizes his own exploitation of his relative's name and scorns the prying relic hunting of Blayds's followers.

Unmourned by the audience, Blayds has died before act 2 begins. Isobel, Blayds's deathbed confidante, narrates the shocking "truth about Blayds": he did not write his literary works at all. A young friend of his, Jenkins, wrote all the works. When he died young, Blayds took possession of the manuscripts and promoted them as his own. The news is greeted with infuriated bitterness by the Blayds-Conways. In A. A. Milne's own words, the family is broken by the realization that they have worshiped someone who "is discovered to be a false god." In the third and final act Oliver makes a tongue-in-cheek, throwaway comment: Blayds must have been doting, hallucinating, when he "invented" the plagiarism story. Marion and William seize on this notion and determine to continue Blayds's deception even after his death. Isobel refuses to perpetuate the myth, but is won over by the promise of marriage to Blayds's chief admirer, A. L. Royce. This should, then, be a play that ends happily, as Isobel and Royce were frus-

trated lovers a generation previously. But Isobel herself states that Royce is probably in love with the teenage Isobel, not the one worn out by two decades of nursing the demanding old Blayds—and she will wind up nursing the now-middle-aged Royce. For the audience, the perpetuation of the lies about Blayds's genius grates, and the deference shown to esteemed characters such as Blayds by the family and by the "young writers" is seen to be simultaneously self-deluding and self-serving.

[*See also* England]

FURTHER READING

Haring-Smith, Tori. *A. A. Milne: A Critical Bibliography*. New York: Garland, 1982.

Mendelsohn, Michael J. "A. A. Milne." In *The Dictionary of Literary Biography*, vol. 10, pt. 2, *Modern British Dramatists, 1900–1945*, ed. by Stanley Weintraub. Detroit: Gale, 1982. 42–45.

Milne, A. A. *It's Too Late Now: The Autobiography of a Writer*. London: Methuen, 1939.

———. *Three Plays: The Dover Road, The Truth About Blayds, The Great Broxopp*. New York: Putnam, 1922; London: Chatto, 1923.

———. *The Truth About Blayds*. London: French, 1923.

Swann, Thomas Burnett. *A. A. Milne*. New York: Twayne, 1971.

Kevin De Ornellas

TSEGAYE GABRE-MEDHIN (1936–2006)

Ours, Africa's in general, or in this case, Ethiopia's in particular, is just another part of today's inquisitive generation that must be encouraged to come to terms with its historic past; even that historic past often torn and denied against him. And this, to a lesser or greater extent, may be achieved by a process of re-interpreting to himself, the human events of his past which, in a way is still responsible for his present conflicting awareness, if not for the shaping of his total future event. It is in this sense alone that a historical play becomes an instrument of history and change.

Another of AFRICA's prolific writers whose works are less known outside his country, largely owing to their publication mostly in Amharic, is Tsegaye Gabre-Medhin. Born in 1936 to parents of Amharic and Oromo parentage, Tsegaye wrote well over thirty-three plays, of which only *Oda-Oak Oracle*, written in 1965, and *Collision of Altars*, written in 1977, have been widely read in the English-speaking world; he also published several short stories, and newspaper columns and directed plays, some of which he translated into Amharic. Tsegaye is widely recognized in his country as poet laureate, winner of the Haile Selassie I prize in Amharic literature, and Ethiopia's most decorated playwright. A large number of Tsegaye's works were either censored or banned by various regimes in Ethiopia's turbulent political history, resulting in a short stay in jail for one of his plays that critiqued the military dictatorship of Mengitsu Haile Mariam.

Tsegaye began writing as a teenager. Though trained as a lawyer, he focused on writing and eventually won scholarships to study in the UNITED STATES, FRANCE, and ENGLAND. He was appointed the vice director of arts at the Haile Selassie Theatre on his return to Ethiopia in 1959. He and director Seyoum Sibhat began a systematic process of "Ethiopianizing" the theater's program, as opposed to a mostly European program. Tsegaye helped to translate plays by William Shakespeare and Molière into Amharic, directed some of them, and used his position to produce and showcase his works and those of other Ethiopians writing in the country's major languages.

A key characteristic of Tsegaye's plays is the centering of characters from lower classes and castes as protagonists of his plays. He wrote plays with titles such as *Blood Harvest* (Yedem Azmera), *Crown of Thorns* (Yeshoh Aklil), *Cheap Cigarettes* (Kosho Cigara), *The Ugly Girl* (Askeyami Ligagared), *Mumps* (Djoro Dgif), and *A Man of the People* (Ye Kermasow). This in itself was a radical departure from the norm in a society heavily invested in its aristocratic history and whose major literature sustained the culture of the monarchy. Such dissident representations eventually earned the displeasure and banning of his works by the monarch and subsequently by the various reformist regimes that overthrew the monarchy. His most popular play written in this vein is *Tewodros* (1987), which drew on the legacy of a former emperor of the same name to question the ideas of the monarchy and the clerical establishment that justified and sustained their divine right of rulership. Prior to such innovations, theater themes never focused on the plight of the commoners who constituted the majority of the population. Tsegaye's direction attracted different types of audiences to the theater and paved the way for a new populism that came to be adopted by younger playwrights and directors.

Beyond using poor people as subjects of his drama, Tsegaye's works constantly called for critical reforms to Ethiopia's religious and political history in order to stimulate a more democratic society. Tsegaye's earlier *Oda-Oak Oracle* (1965) and later *Collision of Altars* (1977) fully illustrate his desire to speak to the power of the dominant culture of Ethiopia while inviting the lower classes to consciousness of their subjectivity and citizenship. Tsegaye's leadership role in developing Ethiopian theater extended to pioneering the study of theater arts at the University of Addis Ababa, where he taught for a while. Tsegaye came to symbolize the voice of reason in a country with a turbulent political and cultural history. Tsegaye died on February 25, 2006, at age sixty-nine.

SELECT PLAYS: *Oda-Oak Oracle* (1965); *Collision of Altars* (1977); *Tewodros* (1987)

FURTHER READING

Mckinley, Jesse. "Tsegaye Gabre-Medhin Dies; Ethiopian Poet Laureate, 69." *New York Times* (March 9, 2006): C18.

Plastow, J. *African Theatre and Politics: The Evolution of Theatre in Ethiopia, Tanzania and Zimbabwe.* Amsterdam: Rodopi, 1996.

Tsegaye Gabre-Medhin. *Collision of Altars.* London: Rex Collins, 1977.

Awam Amkpa

TSUBOUCHI SHŌYŌ (1859–1935)

Tsubouchi Shōyō, a Japanese critic, theater reformer, playwright, and translator, is considered, with OSANAI KAORU, a founder of SHINGEKI. Tsubouchi entered Tokyo University in 1876, then taught at Waseda University from 1883. He framed his mission to modernize—not Westernize—Japanese literature and theater with two influential works, *The Essence of the Novel* (Shōsetsu Shinzui) in 1885, the first example of modern Japanese literary criticism, and the long essay "Wagakuni no Shigeki" (Japan's historical drama) in 1893–1894. Rejecting the prevailing neo-Confucian didacticism and set character types that dominated fiction and theater in his era, he urged instead REALISM, objectivity, and characters of psychological depth. He wanted to transform the then-current notion of theater as low-class, risqué, fanciful entertainment into one that was serious, elevated, and worthy of respect beyond JAPAN, just as William Shakespeare, HENRIK IBSEN, and ANTON CHEKHOV were respected outside their own countries. He envisioned combining the realism and character development in those playwrights with traditional Japanese elements, such as the stylized declamation and movement of *kabuki*.

Tsubouchi sought to realize his theories by founding, with the European-educated Shimamura Hōgetsu, the Literary Arts Society (Bungei Kyōkai) in 1906. He refused to work with *kabuki* actors, recruiting instead inexperienced young people whom he could train from scratch. He also attempted to write plays in the style he advocated. *A Paulownia Leaf* (Kiri hitoha) written in 1894–1895, laced with subtle structural borrowings from *Hamlet*, demonstrated that a *kabuki* text could be enjoyed for its literary and intellectual value. Not surprisingly, the play was attacked by traditionalists as going too far and by modernists as not going far enough. It went unstaged for nearly a decade but in time came to be regarded as a SHIN KABUKI classic. Perhaps his most successful play is EN THE ASCETIC (En no gyōja) written in 1916, which has distinct overtones of Shakespeare's *The Tempest*.

Unfortunately, Tsubouchi's practice as reformer and playwright lagged behind his vision for three reasons. First, without direct experience of theater outside Japan, he was, though gifted at declaiming lines, unable to shirk *kabuki* rhythms and tones, and his dutiful students emulated his every nuance; their productions were essentially *kabuki* recycled. Second, the only examples of new Japanese plays he showed his students were his own, but those, like his declamation, were more the work of a passionate intellectual than a professional actor or playwright and can wither under critical scrutiny. Third, the very success of his Shakespeare and Ibsen productions—*Hamlet* (1907 and 1910), *Julius Caesar* (1913), and *A Doll's House* (1911)—meant that Western theater, not Japanese, initially became the ideal modern theater in the minds of Japanese.

Still, Tsubouchi's unflagging commitment to reform shook the firmament of traditional Japanese theater and made accessible the idea of a modern theater. Perhaps his most enduring legacy is his complete translation of Shakespeare (he coined the Japanese word for COMEDY, kigeki), begun in 1884, completed in 1928. His enormous impact was acknowledged that year when the Tsubouchi Memorial Theatre Museum of Waseda University (modeled after the 16th-century Fortune Theatre in London) was built in his honor.

SELECT PLAYS: A Paulownia Leaf (Kiri hitoha, 1894–1895); The Sinking Moon Over the Lonely Castle Where the Cuckoo Cries (Hototogisu kojō no rakugetsu, 1897); The New Urashima (Shinkyoku Urashima, 1904); En the Ascetic (En no gyōja, 1916)

FURTHER READING
Ibaraki, Tadashi. Nihon shingeki shōshi [A short history of shingeki]. Tokyo: Miraisha, 1980.
Keene, Donald. Dawn to the West: Japanese Literature in the Modern Era; Poetry, Drama, Criticism. New York: H. Holt, 1984.
Ortolani, Benito. The Japanese Theatre: From Shamanistic Ritual to Contemporary Pluralism. Leiden: Brill, 1990.
Powell, Brian. Japan's Modern Theatre: A Century of Change and Continuity. London: Japan Library, 2002.
Rimer, J. Thomas. Toward a Modern Japanese Theatre: Kishida Kunio. Princeton: Princeton Univ. Press, 1974.
Tsubouchi, Shōyō. Ourashima: Légende dramatique en trois actes. Tr. by Takamatsu Yoshie. Paris: Roger, 1922.

John K. Gillespie

TSUKA KŌHEI (1948–)

Tsuka Kōhei is a Japanese playwright and director whom some believe to be the sole major playwright to emerge in JAPAN in the 1970s. Tsuka won the Kishida Kunio Prize for THE ATAMI MURDER CASE (Atami satsujin jiken, 1973) in 1974. Shortly after that he founded Tsuka Kōhei, Inc., and within two years a "Tsuka boom" began among young people who lined up at midsized commercial halls in Tokyo to see plays such as A Stripper's Tale (Sutorippaa monogatari, 1980) and The Fall Guy (Kamata kōshin–kyoku, 1981). Tsuka gave up writing drama after 1987, but his plays remain popular.

At the beginning of the 1970s younger theater practitioners faced two challenges: one was the high standard set by the little theater (SHŌGEKIJŌ) movement of the 1960s, and the other was the dissipation of political and artistic energy that resulted from the inability of the left wing to stop the renewal of the U.S.-Japan Security Treaty. After the treaty's renewal the left-wing coalition of resistance fell apart, and without a clear political objective little theater companies lost their dramatic focus.

Directors of the little theater movement such as KARA JŪRŌ and SUZUKI TADASHI tended to emphasize physicality, but the major influence on Tsuka was playwright BETSUYAKU MINORU, who was influenced in turn by SAMUEL BECKETT. Without a distrust of text, Tsuka's contribution in the 1970s was to revive

the status of words as a performative vehicle and the individual as a theme for drama. This fit the mood of youth seeking answers about themselves and disillusioned by politics.

Tsuka writes in Japanese and uses a Japanese pen name, but he is a second-generation resident Korean and does not hold Japanese citizenship. Although the political and social issues surrounding the marginalization of resident Koreans are addressed in later fiction and essays, they are not directly dealt with in his plays. However, the discrimination he experienced feeds his interest in the performative nature of human existence. Critic Senda Akihiko calls Tsuka's characters "actors" who choose their own role in life. Their excessive passion leads to bitterly humorous situations. This bitter laughter seems to have reflected the empty spiritual and political existence of youth in the 1970s. The Atami Murder Case reflects that emptiness. The play centers on three police officers who are more concerned about performance of their images and reputations than justice.

For My Father, Who Failed to Die in the War (Sensō de shinenakatta otōsan no tame ni, 1971) is a satirical treatment of how common people identified with the Japanese leadership's prosecution of World War II. In this play a man invents a military past in order to overcome the inadequacies he feels among his peers.

Revolution 101: Legend of the Hero (Shokyū kakumei kōza hiryūden, 1972), revised in 1974 as Legend of a Flying Dragon: And Then a Crow (Hiryūden: sore kara karasu) turns a scathing eye on hypocrisy within the left-wing political movements of the 1960s. Three characters from different sides look back at the political struggle. They give meaning to their empty memories by continuing to play at the game of class struggle.

In A Stripper's Tale Akemi, a stripper past her prime, slides into prostitution so her younger sister can study dance in New York. Akemi and her pimp, Shige, are in love, but he uses Akemi to further his political ambitions. Akemi's reward before her death is her sister's Broadway success.

Tsuka himself continues to pursue success in his various roles as stage director, novelist, screenwriter, theater educator, and resident foreigner in Japan.

SELECT PLAYS: Excuse Me Mr. Postman (Yūbinya-san chotto, 1970); For My Father Who Failed to Die in the War (Sensō de shinenakatta otōsan no tame ni, 1971); Revolution 101: Legend of the Hero (Shokyū kakumei kōza hiryūden, 1972); The Atami Murder Case (Atami satsujin jiken, 1973); A Stripper's Tale (Sutorippaa monogatari, 1980); The Fall Guy (Kamata kōshin-kyoku, 1981); Hotel Rose (Bara Hoteru, 1982); Tsuka's Chūshingura (Tsuka-ban Chūshingura, 1982); Disappearance of Youth (Seishun kakeochi, 1983); Kyōko (Kyōko, 1987)

FURTHER READING
Japan Playwrights Association, ed. Half a Century of Japanese Theater. Vol. 5, 1970s. Tokyo: Kinokuniya, 2003.
Kazama Ken. Shōgekijō no fūkei [The little theater landscape]. Tokyo: Chūō Kōronsha, 1992.

Powell, Brian. *Japan's Modern Theatre: A Century of Change and Continuity.* London: Japan Library, 2002.

Senda, Akihiko. *The Voyage of Contemporary Japanese Theatre.* Tr. by J. Thomas Rimer. Honolulu: Univ. of Hawaii Press, 1997.

John D. Swain

TUAN YUAN ZHI HOU, PUXIAN XI *See* AFTER THE REUNION

TUGHLAQ

Tughlaq (1964) was one of the most popular plays of the 1960s in INDIA. Although it presents the fictional story of Sultan Muhammad bin Tughlaq, who reigned from 1327 to 1332, GIRISH KARNAD wrote the play in 1964 because Tughlaq's history seemed very contemporary. Karnad has said that although Tughlaq was the most idealistic and intelligent ruler ever to come to power in India, his reign ended in chaos and bloodshed—a situation that mirrored India during Jawaharlal Nehru's last days. "In a sense," wrote Karnad, "the play reflected the slow disillusionment my generation felt with the new politics of independent India: the gradual erosion of the ethical norms that guided the movement for independence" (Karnad, 1994).

An idealistic young ruler takes the throne. He establishes laws that treat Hindus and Muslims equally. He introduces fair taxation policies. He introduces currency. Because his policies are so far ahead of their time, his subjects begin to refer to him as Muhammad the Mad, and they rebel. So Muhammad spends his time crushing rebellion after rebellion, and he begins to murder anyone who gets in the way of his goals—small sacrifices for the greater good of the kingdom. As time goes on and his policies fail, Tughlaq grows more and more vicious. A subplot of the play follows the character Aziz, who begins life as a common thief until he figures out how to make the most of Tughlaq's edicts. "Only a few months in Delhi," he says in scene 7, "and I have discovered a whole new world—politics. . . . It's a beautiful world—wealth, success, position, power." At the end of the play Aziz comes face-to-face with Tughlaq: "Since Your Majesty came to the throne, I have been your most devoted servant," he says. "I have studied your every order, followed every instruction, considered every measure of Your Majesty's with the greatest attention. I insist I am Your Majesty's true disciple." In Aziz, Tughlaq sees the corruption of every single one of his idealistic dreams.

The most famous production of *Tughlaq* was directed by Ebrahim Alkazi under the auspices of the National School of Drama in 1965, where it was staged as an environmental production at the Red Fort in Old Delhi. *Tughlaq* has also been produced in Bengali and Marathi, and Alyque Padamsee directed an English-language production in 1970. *Tughlaq* continues to be staged in schools and colleges all over India.

[*See also* Environmental Theater]

FURTHER READING

Dhanavel, P. *The Indian Imagination of Girish Karnad: Essays on "Hayavadana."* New Delhi: Prestige Bks., 2000.

Dodiya, Jaydipsinh, ed. *The Plays of Girish Karnad: Critical Perspectives.* New Delhi: Prestige Bks., 1999.

Karnad, Girish. *Collected Plays, Volume I (Tughlaq, Hayavadana, Bali: The Sacrifice, Naga-Mandala).* New Delhi: Oxford Univ. Press, 2005.

——. *Three Plays.* New York: Oxford Univ. Press, 1994.

Mukherjee, Tutun, ed. *Girish Karnad's Plays: Performance and Critical Perspectives.* Delhi: Pencraft International, 2006.

Pandey, Sudhakar, and Freya Barua, eds. *New Directions in Indian Drama.* New Delhi: Prestige Bks., 1994.

Erin B. Mee

TURKEY

While traditional Turkish drama revolves around several Oriental styles commonly known as *halk tiyatrosu* (people's drama), including *kukla oyunu* (puppet playing), *gölge oyunu* (shadow play), *meddah* (storyteller), and *orta oyunu* (a type of comic theater-in-the-round akin to commedia dell'arte), the roots of modern Turkish drama lie in the Westernization program of the Ottoman Empire in the 19th century. Modern Turkish drama has evolved in three successive waves, each corresponding to a defining sociopolitical epoch in Turkish history: Tanzimat (reform, 1839–1908), Meşrutiyet (constitutional monarchy, 1908–1923), and Cumhuriyet (republic, 1923–present).

When the Tanzimat Edict was issued in 1839, European drama had already penetrated the palace circles in Istanbul through the staging of Western plays at various foreign embassies. After Tanzimat these plays found an ever-growing audience among the nobility. The opening of the so-called Fransız Tiyatrosu (French Theater) in Istanbul in the early 19th century provided an opportunity for several European drama groups to visit the empire. Prominent plays were translated into the Turkish (Ottoman) language in this period. Written text was gradually accepted as the basis of theatrical activity. Tanzimat gave birth to the early examples of Turkish drama literature.

The first pioneers of Turkish drama were the Ottoman Armenians, who, thanks to their socioreligious links with Europe, were better suited to follow European developments in the arts and literature. The establishment of Gedikpaşa Theater in 1860 proved a turning point. Güllü Agop, an Armenian Ottoman, took over the theater in 1861 and eventually created a standing drama group called Osmanlı Tiyatrosu (Ottoman Theater) in 1868. Two years later Prime Minister Ali Paşa granted him the exclusive rights to stage Turkish plays in Istanbul. In return, Agop undertook to create Turkish theaters in different parts of the city.

Several students were sent abroad during Tanzimat to familiarize themselves with the entirely "new" European world. The discovery of the Western drama literature by these students manifested itself in their exploration of Western forms and patterns and especially in their translations of such playwrights as Molière, Jean Racine, William Shakespeare, and Victor Hugo. The translations/adaptations by Ahmet Vefik Paşa, Teodor Kasap, and Ali Bey of Molière's plays are especially worth noting. In fact, the Tanzimat drama continued to flourish under overall French influence, with vaudevilles, operettas, and modest comedies being the favorites of the masses. The Poet's Marriage (Şair Evlenmesi), a single-act comedy written by İbrahim Şinasi in 1860, is usually considered the first original Western-style Turkish play.

COMEDY was by no means the only attractive drama form for young Ottoman intellectuals. Such notable literary minds as Namık Kemal, Ahmet Mithat, Şemsettin Sami, Recaizade Mahmut Ekrem, Abdülhak Hamit, Muallim Naci, Ebuzziya Tevfik, Ali Süavi, Nabizade Nazım, and Ziya Paşa experimented with a wide array of themes and styles, including TRAGEDY and MELODRAMA. They considered theater a powerful tool for expressing their views on sociopolitical problems. Perhaps the most distinguished romantic text of the era is Namık Kemal's Homeland or Boatswain's Pipe (Vatan Yahut Silistre) of 1873. Kemal saw the state as the protector of both individual and collective liberties. His play called each citizen (an underdeveloped notion in the Ottoman Empire) to contribute to the collective protection of the state, so that individual freedoms could be protected as a natural consequence.

Istanbul theater companies, by touring other regions, slowly introduced modern drama to wider masses in Anatolia. The hopes, wishes, and disappointments of ordinary people began to find their expressions in drama texts. Yet theater was virtually out of reach for a crucial societal segment, namely, the women. As early as 1859, admission of women into theater buildings was prohibited. Twenty years later, when Agop built special protected boxes into his theater to attract female audiences, his radical attempt was frowned upon. Nonetheless, some plays were staged exclusively for women, and others did manage to attract women into those special boxes.

Tanzimat witnessed the first intellectual debates on the meaning and functions of drama. While some thinkers, such as Şinasi and Teodor Kasap, argued for the creation of an original Ottoman drama literature based on careful reconciliation of traditional cultural forms with novel Western ideas, others, such as Namık Kemal, maintained that modern drama simply would have to transcend the populistic and comedy-oriented halk tiyatrosu. Meanwhile, a new phenomenon emerged, largely due to the efforts of practitioners onstage. Traditional players incorporated into their own conventional technique such concepts of Western drama as stage, decor, and theme. The result was a highly successful drama style called tuluat. Pişekar Küçük İsmail, Agâh Efendi, Kavuklu Hamdi, and Büyük İsmail Efendi were among its creators.

Although tuluat put its mark on the late 19th and early 20th centuries, it gradually lost its popularity. Aside from the fact that the tuluat players were neither sufficiently organized nor capable of devising an original and systematic literary program, three political factors led to the demise of this genre. First, the oppressive reign of Abdülhamit II (1878–1908) was not at all conducive to a flourishing arts environment. Drama, in particular, found itself in dire straits. Second, the empire's continuous wars between the late 1870s and early 1920s considerably weakened popular involvement. Third, the Republic of Turkey, that is, the successor of the Ottoman Empire, made a conscious choice as early as 1923 to pursue a program of modernization in every aspect of life. As a natural outgrowth of this commitment, a modern Western approach to drama prevailed in Turkey. Ironically, though, the two most prominent masters of tuluat made their true reputation in the Republican era: Naşit and İsmail Dümbüllü.

The proclamation of 2. Meşrutiyet (the Second Constitutional Monarchy) in 1908 marked the end of Abdülhamit's censorship over intellectual works. Despite the sociopolitical chaos in the empire, notable poets and authors, including Cenap Şehabettin, Halit Ziya, Ali Ekrem, Mehmet Rauf, Hüseyin Rahmi, and Halit Fahri, produced several plays in the early 1900s. The period was especially rich in terms of romantic and historical plays. The establishment in 1914 of Darülbedayi, the first Turkish equivalent of a modern faculty of arts, is perhaps the most significant achievement of Meşrutiyet. Afife Jale, a student at Darülbedayi, performed Hüseyin Suat's Patches (Yamalar) in 1919 to become the first Muslim Turkish actress. However, this move proved a premature revolution at the time. Muslim women were banned from the stage in 1921. Fortunately, Turkey soon entered a new epoch, radically changing the entire status of and approach to women.

After the proclamation of the republic in 1923, Muhsin Ertuğrul, a thoroughly knowledgeable practitioner of European theater, was appointed head of Darülbedayi (1927). In search of financial and institutional stability, Darülbedayi was placed under the oversight of Istanbul Municipality in 1931 and given the status of "City Theater" in 1934. Several city theaters soon opened in different parts of Istanbul. Unlike earlier periods, the Republican era adopted Western drama literature as the unrivaled norm vis-à-vis traditional forms. The components of Western drama (in terms of ACTING, staging, DRAMATURGY, direction, and decor) were firmly integrated into the conception of "modern Turkish drama." The establishment of the so-called halkevleri (people's houses) in 1932 proved to be of enormous significance for the spread of a drama culture throughout Anatolia. Halkevleri were multifunctional local grassroots organizations and put considerable effort into building new theaters, educating young actors, promoting playwriting, and attracting audiences. The founding of the State Conservatory in 1936 under the direction of Carl Ebert—a first–rate artistic exile from

Adolf Hitler's GERMANY—was another significant move on the part of the new republic. These developments found their utmost support directly from the leader of the new Turkish regime, Kemal Atatürk. Both state and private theaters steadily grew in number. Female Turkish citizens (Muslim and non-Muslim alike) were now actively encouraged to contribute to the arts and literature. In this process Afife Jale not only reappeared onstage, but was joined by several other Muslim actresses, including Şaziye Moral, Nejla Sertel, Neyyire Neyir, and Bedia Muvahhit.

Although most examples of the early republican drama were under the influence of fresh memories, including the occupation by the Allied powers of Istanbul, a diversification in themes was slowly taking place, drawing attention to the moral degeneration in some societal segments, clashes between emerging ideological groups, and the dramatic effects of the transformation of the family as a social unit. Vedat Nedim Tör criticized social injustice and moral decay in such plays as The Unemployed (İşsizler, 1924), Without Roots (Köksüzler, 1937), and Between Three People (Üç Kişi Arasında, 1927), The Downpour (Sağanak, 1929), a play by Yakup Kadri Karaosmanoğlu, courageously explored the drama of people of differing convictions. Nazım Hikmet, a world-renowned socialist poet, used drama as an alternative means of communication in his plays titled The Skull (Kafatası, 1932), The House of the Morning (Bir Ölü Evi, 1932), and The Forgotten Man (Unutulan Adam, 1935). The interaction between psychological and social problems was examined by Cevdet Kudret in The River Flowing in Reverse (Tersine Akan Nehir, 1929), Wolves (Kurtlar, 1933), and The Living Dead (Yaşayan Ölüler, published posthumously 1994). Necip Fazıl Kısakürek focused on age-old moral dilemmas in Seed (Tohum, 1935), To Create a Man (Bir Adam Yaratmak, 1938), and Money (Para, 1942). Musahipzade Celal, on the other hand, successfully drew on traditional Ottoman drama and produced highly popular critiques in such plays as A Turban Has Fallen (Bir Kavuk Devrildi, 1930), The Judge of Mount Athos (Aynoroz Kadısı, 1927), and Monday–Thursday (Pazartesi–Perşembe, 1931).

Especially in the 1940s, in the wake of Turkey's uneasy neutrality during World War II, several writers revisited historical events. National heroism during the Turkish War of Independence, failures of the late Ottoman institutions, and sacrifices made by Turkish intellectuals were among the favorite subjects of Ahmet Kudsi Tecer, Aka Gündüz, Faruk Nafiz Çamlıbel, Behçet Kemal Çağlar, Yaşar Nabi Nayır, Halit Fahri Ozansoy, and Peyami Safa. At the same time, the 1940s introduced into Turkish drama the themes of "village reality" and societal dilemmas, as exemplified by Abidin Dino's Bald (Kel, 1944), Cevat Fehmi Başkut's The Little City (Küçük Şehir, 1945–1946), Ahmet Muhip Dranas's The Shadows (Gölgeler, 1946), and Ahmet Kudsi Tecer's Corner (Köşebaşı, 1947). This overall productivity, however, was accompanied by a didactic tone, eschewing in-depth character analyses and lacking in stylistic authority.

The passing of the Law on the State Theater and Opera in 1949 restructured the world of Turkish drama. Theater buildings were opened one after another in Ankara, Adana, Izmir, Bursa, and other cities. The introduction of special children's sections and plays was an innovative part of this reorganization. Turkey's first successful experiment with democracy in the 1950s created a hopeful atmosphere for the future of the arts. However, the country's internal sociopolitical contradictions, accompanied by external Cold War constraints, soon cast some doubts on these hopes. Halkevleri, for instance, were abolished as early as 1951 for entirely partisan reasons. New phenomena such as economic transformation, rapid urbanization, and changing rural life attracted particular attention in this period. For example, the changing sociopolitical dynamics were subjected to scrutiny in Selahattin Batu's Beautiful Helena (Güzel Helena, 1954), Yaşar Kemal's Tinplate (Teneke, 1955), and Refik Erduran's The Bicycle of Cengizhan (Cengizhan'ın Bisikleti, 1959). Turkish playwrights managed to develop, albeit slowly, their own drama styles and languages in the 1950s.

It is a well-known but ironic fact that the military coup d'etat in 1960 produced an unexpectedly liberal consitution for Turkey. The political freedoms of the 1960s, along with emerging social phenomena such as the Turkish guest workers in Germany and elsewhere, led to the diversification of the drama culture. A new realist approach with particular emphasis on the problems of rural life was either foreshadowed or explicitly developed in such plays as Necati Cumalı's The Dry Summer (Susuz Yaz, 1962), Yaşar Kemal's Iron Earth, Copper Sky (Yer Demir Gök Bakır, 1963), Recep Bilginer's Rebels (İsyancılar, 1964), Hidayet Sayın's A Woman Called Rosy (Pembe Kadın, 1965), Sermet Çağan's Foot Leg Factory (Ayak Bacak Fabrikası, 1965), Cahit Atay's Sultan Bride (Sultan Gelin, 1965), and Güngör Dilmen's The Sacrifice (Kurban, 1967). The fast–growing slum areas were scrutinized in Speckled Rooster (Çil Horoz, 1964) by Oktay Rifat, Snowbirds (İspinozlar, 1964) by Orhan Kemal, and Gültepe Plays (Gültepe Oyunları, 1968) by Cahit Atay. Orhan Kemal pointed to the problems of the working class in his Murtaza the Watchman (Bekçi Murtaza, 1965). Başar Sabuncu shared a similar concern in Goodwill (Şerefiye, 1969).

Although thematically diverse, several other plays also had something to say about the changing social complexion of Turkey in the 1960s. These include Fazilet Pharmacy (Fazilet Eczanesi, 1960) by Haldun Taner, The Guild (Ocak, 1962) by Turgut Özakman, The Linden Tree (Ihlamur Ağacı, 1962) by Vüs'at O. Bener, The Circles (Çemberler, 1964) by Çetin Altan, The Crack on the Roof (Çatıdaki Çatlak, 1964) by Adalet Ağaoğlu, The Corrupt Order (Bozuk Düzen, 1965) by Güner Sümer, The Feast at the Café (Kahvede Şenlik Var, 1966) by Sabahattin Kudret Aksal, The Sticks of the Mikado (Mikadonun Çöpleri, 1967) by Melih Cevdet Anday, and Oppressive Air (Yağmur Sıkıntısı, 1969) by Oktay Rıfat. At the same time, a new genre—Western–style musical plays—was discovered and used quite successfully as an effectual means of social criticism.

Leading examples include *Boulevard* (*Bulvar*, 1964) by Turgut Özakman, *Shrewish Zarife* (*Zilli Zarife*, 1966) by Haldun Taner, *In Direklerarası* (*Direkler Arasında*, 1965) by Refik Erduran, and *Hürmüz with Seven Husbands* (*Yedi Kocalı Hürmüz*, 1969) by Sadık Şendil. By the late 1960s new playwrights started to make a name for themselves, such as Tuncer Cücenoğlu, Ülker Köksal, Dinçer Sümer, Nezihe Araz, Bilgesu Erenus, Erhan Bener, Yılmaz Onay, Ferdi Merter, Ergun Sav, and Nezihe Meriç.

Another feature of the decade was the creation of visionary private theater companies, several of which were still functional as of the early 2000s. Companies such as Kent Oyuncuları, Ankara Sanat Tiyatrosu, and Dostlar Tiyatrosu developed alternative repertoires, gradually raising the level of popular consciousness about the art of drama. The latter two institutions, in particular, played a pioneering role in introducing BERTOLT BRECHT to Turkish audiences. Several Turkish authors started to adopt and successfully implement Brecht's EPIC drama methods. Haldun Taner's *The Legend of Keşanlı Ali* (*Keşanlı Ali Destanı*, 1964) and Vasıf Öngören's *How Will Asiye Be Rescued* (*Asiye Nasıl Kurtulur*, 1970) are arguably the most prominent examples. A number of other plays also experimented with Brecht's methods, although they did not clearly fall into the orbit of epic drama, including Turgut Özakman's *The Blue Fountain 1914* (*Sarıpınar 1914*, 1968), Haldun Taner's *The Cunning Wife of the Stupid Husband* (*Sersem Kocanın Kurnaz Karısı*, 1971), and Oktay Arayıcı's *Nickname Goncagül* (*Rumuz Goncagül*, 1977). Interestingly, other Western genres such as the absurd and abstract theaters would not attract comparable attention in the Turkish context.

In 1971 a military semicoup brought the liberal intellectual environment of the 1960s to an end. At the same time, political clashes among different ideological factions—nationalist, socialist, religious, liberal—created an especially sensitive social and cultural milieu. Throughout the 1970s "state" and "city" theaters, that is, the official and semiofficial representatives of Turkish drama, sought to maintain a neutral political stance in their activities. Consequently, their repertoires were chosen from among the Western classics and well-established Turkish plays of earlier periods. Evaluations of new social dynamics were carefully avoided. Instead, universal moral problems were given prominence. Plays and performances by private theater companies, on the other hand, were sometimes hindered or curtailed not only by direct and indirect governmental censorship, but also by intergroup political tensions. The entire experience in the 1970s demonstrated, implicitly but strongly, the linkages between the "theoretical" (playwriting, literary criticism) and the "practical" (performance, project management), on the one hand, and between the "political" (ideology, participation) and the "cultural" (act of writing, aesthetics), on the other. The realist approach continued to evolve under constant influence of leading Western trends, in such plays as *Memet of the Blackness* (*Karaların Memetleri*, 1971) by Cahit Atay, *German Notebook* (*Almanya*

Defteri, 1971) by Vasıf Öngören, *The Dead Want to Speak* (*Ölüler Konuşmak İsterler*, 1972), *Beware of the Dog* (*Dikkat Köpek Var*, 1972) and *Tomorrow at Another Meadow* (*Yarın Başka Koruda*, 1972) by Melih Cevdet Anday, and *Çiçu* (1979) and *You Aren't Black* (*Sen Gara Değilsin*, 1979) by Aziz Nesin.

In the 1960s and 1970s several playwrights utilized mythology, legend, and history to produce highly successful plays that drew strong parallels with contemporary social life: *Hürrem Sultan* (*Hürrem Sultan*, 1960) and *Gelgamesh* (*Gılgamış*, 1968) by Orhan Asena, *Murat IV* (*IV. Murat*, 1970) by Turan Oflazoğlu, *Pir Sultan Abdal* (*Pir Sultan Abdal*, 1970) by Erol Toy, and the *Midas* trilogy—including *The Ears of Midas* (*Midas'ın Kulakları*, 1965), *The Gold of Midas* (*Midas'ın Altınları*, 1970), and *The Knot of Midas* (*Midas'ın Kördüğümü*, 1975)—by Güngör Dilmen.

Turkey's third military coup d'etat took place in 1980. Unlike the previous three decades, the 1980s brought along a noticeable depoliticization in Turkey in all spheres of activity, including drama. This, however, did not slow the production of new plays in the subsequent two decades. Turgut Özakman's *The History of Ottoman Empire with Illustrations* (*Resimli Osmanlı Tarihi*, 1983), Mehmet Baydur's *Lemon* (*Limon*, 1987), *Woman Station* (*Kadın İstasyonu*, 1993), and *Girl of the Republic* (*Cumhuriyet Kızı*, 1990), and Murathan Mungan's *Mesopotamia* trilogy—consisting of *Mahmud and Yezida* (*Mahmud ile Yezida*, 1980), *Condolence* (*Taziye*, 1982), and *Deer Curses* (*Geyikler Lanetler*, 1992)—can be cited among the leading examples of the period. Numerous other practitioners, including active stage performers, experimented with the drama literature: Behiç Ak, Mehmet Akan, Çetin Altan, Ülkü Ayvaz, Coşkun Büktel, Erman Canatan, Civan Canova, Savaş Dinçel, Müjdat Gezen, Erhan Gökgücü, Oben Güney, Coşkun Irmak, Haluk Işık, Kenan Işık, İsmet Küntay, Güner Sümer, Kubilay Tuncer, Burak Mikail Uçar, Vasfi Uçkan, Özen Yula. Some actor-dramatists, such as Ferhan Şensoy, created unique writing and performance styles, bridging authentic themes and universal perspectives, and managed to gain wide popularity as well as intellectual respect.

Turkish drama since the early 1990s has been under the influence of changing internal and external sociopolitical dynamics. Turkey's efforts at European Union membership, the questions of IDENTITY and economic underdevelopment, the end of the bipolar world, and the post-9/11 world order are among the important factors that bear upon the social milieu within which theatrical activity takes shape. The (re)discovery of Turkish drama artists living abroad (famous playwrights, performers, and producers, such as Mehmet Ulusoy and Ayşe Emel Mestçi), along with the speedy proliferation of theater journals and networks, is perhaps the most crucial characteristic of this latest phase. "All its weaknesses and shortcomings aside," as Talat Halman observes, "the record of Turkish dramatic art is, by any objective criterion, impressive."

[In almost all cases the English translations of play titles have been directly borrowed from the Turkish Ministry of

Culture and Tourism website, although it is important to recognize that these are not official translations and are open to interpretation.]

[*See also* Absurdism]

FURTHER READING

And, Metin. *Cumhuriyet Dönemi Türk Tiyatrosu, 1923–1983.* Ankara: Türkiye İş Bankası Yayınları, 1983.

———. *Türk Tiyatro Tarihi.* Istanbul: İletişim Yayınları, 1992.

Cücenoğlu, Tuncer. "Cumhuriyetimizin 80inci Yılında Oyun Yazarlığımız." *Cumhuriyet* (November 11–12, 2003).

Erkoç, Gülayşe. "1960–1970 Dönemi Tiyatro Hareketleri." *Tiyatro Araştırmaları Dergisi,* no. 13 (June 2002).

Halman, Talat S., ed. "The Evolution of Turkish Drama." In *Modern Turkish Drama: An Anthology of Plays in Translation,* ed. by Talat S. Halman. Minneapolis: Bibliotheca Islamica, 1983.

Martinovich, Nicholas N. *The Turkish Theatre.* New York: B. Blom, 1968.

Önertoy, Olcay. "Cumhuriyet Dönemi Türk Edebiyatında Tiyatro." In *Çağdaş Türk Edebiyatı,* ed. by Canan İleri. Eskişehir: Anadolu Üniversitesi, 1998.

Pekman, Yavuz. "Tanzimat Dönemi Oyun Yazarlığında Batılılaşma Olgusu" [The notion of Westernization in the Tanzimat period playwriting]. *Tiyatro Araştırmaları Dergisi,* no. 14 (December 2002).

Republic of Turkey, Ministry of Culture and Tourism. *Encyclopedia of Turkish Authors.* http://www.kultur.gov.tr/EN/BelgeGoster .aspx?17A16AE30572D313D4AF1EF75F7A7968AD2159C2926A9E50.

Robson, Bruce. *The Drum Beats Nightly.* Tokyo: Centre for East Asian Cultural Studies, 1976.

Simin Aksu Erol

TURRINI, PETER (1944–)

> *Theater for me is first and foremost sensuality, cruelty: I want to distance myself from the principles of a boring dramaturgy permeated by psychology and artistry so that I can approach the depths of human nature.*
>
> —Peter Turrini, 1972

Peter Turrini—playwright, poet, essayist, opera LIBRETTIST, actor, and the author of novellas, radio and television plays, and filmscripts—is one of contemporary AUSTRIA's most politically engaged writers. Born on September 26, 1944, in St. Margarethen, the son of an Italian cabinetmaker who immigrated to Austria in the 1930s, Turrini has often remarked upon his father's repeated and ultimately unsuccessful attempts to integrate himself into Austrian village life. The son, in turn, has transformed his own experience of social alienation into the basis for an extensive and critically acclaimed body of work committed to realizing the democratic potential of Austria's social, cultural, and political institutions. In a post–World War II Austrian republic characterized by the consensus politics of the Social Partnership (an extragovernmental institution that brings together industrial, agrarian, and labor leaders to regulate socio-economic policy) and its desire to avoid conflict at all costs, Turrini has insisted upon an ongoing public confrontation with the nation's present and past. He has expanded his commitment to the theater as a lively forum for exploring pressing sociopolitical questions by giving frequent readings at schools and factories and by engaging in various forms of street theater. In response to the controversy surrounding the 1986 election of Kurt Waldheim (former UN secretary general and member of the German Wehrmacht) to the Austrian presidency, for example, Turrini and Alfred Hrdlicka (1928–), a famous Austrian sculptor, constructed a twelve-foot-tall wooden horse that they brought to Waldheim's public appearances to protest the president's refusal to answer truthfully questions about having joined a Nazi equestrian group shortly after the 1938 Anschluss of Austria by Nazi GERMANY. In the last decade of the 20th century Turrini devoted much of his political energy to campaigning against Jörg Haider, the charismatic radical-right leader of Austria's Freiheitliche Partei (Freedom Party), who made tremendous gains in popularity and power in the wake of the Waldheim affair. Haider, in turn, responded by repeatedly denouncing Turrini publicly as a "Nestbeschmutzer" (one who dirties his own nest).

Turrini's first play, *Shooting Rats* (*Rozznjogd*), was written entirely in dialect (Turrini "translated" the play into standard German [*Rattenjagd*] four years later) and premiered at Vienna's Volkstheater in 1971. Until the very last moments of the play, the cast consists of two people, "he" and "she," who travel to a garbage dump where they attempt to strip away both their clothes and the artifice of an increasingly affluent consumer society. Instead of finding each other, however, they find only death, because they are shot by two men who take the couple for rats. The men then take aim and begin shooting into the audience as the curtain falls.

The violence with which *Shooting Rats* ends escalates in *Swine* (*Sauschlachten,* 1971), which premiered in Munich in 1972. Set on a farm in the province of Carinthia, *Swine* examines fateful continuities between pre– and post–World War II Austrian society. The slaughter to which the title refers is that of the farmer's outcast son Valentin. Turrini subtitled *Swine* a "VOLKSSTÜCK" (popular drama), a designation that both harks back to a lively Austrian theatrical tradition and contributes to its postwar revival. But rather than uncritically resurrecting what was at times a socially affirmative form of popular entertainment, Turrini evokes conventions of the *Volksstück* (for example, the peasant milieu, the use of dialect, and the reinstitution of benevolent authority) only to subvert them. Turrini's DRAMATURGY shares more with ANTONIN ARTAUD's Theatre of Cruelty and BERTOLT BRECHT's EPIC THEATER than it does with most authors of the late 18th- and early 19th-century *Volksstück.* Accordingly, Turrini's work was central to the creation of a *bürgerliches Schocktheater* (a bourgeois theater of shock) in Austria in the 1960s and 1970s, a theater intended to shake Austrian audiences out of their postwar complacency by confronting them with issues such as the myth of Austrian innocence in World War II and the underside of their newfound economic affluence. Turrini remains intent on forcefully dramatizing the fates of those he considers the "losers," those groups and individuals disenfranchised and marginalized by Austria's postwar reconstruction.

The losers of the government's decision to privatize the Austrian steel industry take center stage in Turrini's *The Slackers* (*Die Minderleister*), which premiered at Vienna's Akademietheater in 1988 as part of the city's annual arts festival. The drama examines the plight of the unemployed in a society that defines itself primarily through work and production. Like many of Turrini's plays, *The Slackers* dramatizes the disastrous effects that occur when sociopolitical problems are individualized and privatized, when the victims of a market economy victimize those seemingly weaker than themselves. At various points in the play Turrini undercuts his largely realistic dramaturgy with surreal scenes, as when the television Quizmaster and his two assistants appear in Anna and Hans's living room and invite Hans to play "6 out of 45," a game that asks just how far unemployed workers are willing to go to win one of the few available jobs.

During the 1990s Turrini became the most frequently performed playwright on the German-language stage. His works of that decade include *Alpine Glow* (*Alpenglühen*, 1992), in which an "approximately seventy-year-old" blind man living in virtual isolation high in the Austrian Alps, who earns money by imitating the sounds of Alpine wildlife as groups of German tourists pass by his window at appointed times (Turrini has frequently referred to Austria as a touristic banana republic and likened the economic relationship between Austria and Germany to that of a whore and her john), receives a visit from Jasmine, "approximately fifty years old." In the course of the drama the two characters relate their lives in stories that are frequently contradictory. Jasmine may or may not be a prostitute, a secretary at the agency for the blind, and a (former) actress who has only wanted to play the part of William Shakespeare's Juliet. He, in turn, may or may not have lost his sight witnessing an atomic bomb test, had a promising career as a theater director, and been a committed National Socialist. "I was never a true Nazi," he remarks in scene 12, "I just imitated fascism." In what is perhaps Turrini's most metatheatrical play, the author reflects upon the role and power of theatrical fantasy in a nation whose recent history has been largely mythologized—or, to use Turrini's term, "theatricalized." Turrini currently lives in Vienna and Retz, Austria.

SELECT PLAYS: *Shooting Rats* (*Rozznjogd*, 1967); *Rattenjagd* (a standard German version of *Rozznjogd*, 1971); *Swine* (*Sauschlachten*, 1971); *A Crazy Day* (*Der tollste Tag*, an adaptation of Beaumarchais, 1972); *Infanticide* (*Kindsmord*, 1972); *The Innkeeper* (*Die Wirtin*, an adaptation of Goldoni, 1973); *Joseph and Mary* (*Joseph und Maria*, 1980); *A Social Engagement* (*Die Bürger*, 1981); *Campiello* (an adaptation of Goldoni, 1982); *The Slackers* (*Die Minderleister*, 1988); *Death and the Devil* (*Tod und Teufel*, 1990); *Alpine Glow* (*Alpenglühen*, 1992); *The Siege of Vienna* (*Die Schlacht um Wien*, 1995); *Love in Madagascar* (*Die Liebe in Madagaskar*, 1998); *I Love This Country* (*Ich liebe dieses Land*, 2001); *Da Ponte in Sante Fe* (2002); *The Giant from Steinfeld* (*Der Riese vom Steinfeld*, libretto, 2002)

FURTHER READING

Brzovic, Kathy, and Craig Decker. " 'Mir san a liebe Familie in an lieben Land . . .' (We're a Dear Family in a Dear Country): Fascism and the Family in Peter Turrini's *Sauschlachten*." *Modern Austrian Literature* 26, nos. 3/4 (1993): 183–197.

Landa, Jutta. " 'Minderleister': Problems of Audience Address in Peter Turrini's Plays." *Modern Austrian Literature* 24, nos. 3/4 (1991): 161–172.

———, ed. *"I Am Too Many People": Peter Turrini, Playwright, Poet, Essayist.* Riverside, Calif.: Ariadne Press, 1998.

Schuch, Wolfgang, and Klaus Siblewski, eds. *Peter Turrini: Texte, Daten, Bilder* [Peter Turrini: Texts, information, images]. Frankfurt/am Main: Luchterhand Literaturverlag, 1991.

Craig Decker

TUTTA CASA, LETTO E CHIESA See FEMALE PARTS

TWILIGHT CRANE

Twilight Crane (*Yūzuru*, 1949), a folktale play (*minwageki*) by KINOSHITA JUNJI (1914–), has become a universally esteemed lyrical masterpiece of the modern Japanese theater. Kinoshita's source was likely the ethnographer Yanagita Kunio's *A Compendium of Japanese Legends* (*Zenkoku mukashibanashi kiroku*), which he read during the war. *Twilight Crane*, incorporating aspects of Japanese mythology and folktales, was a distinct departure from the staid fourth-wall REALISM of mainstream SHINGEKI.

As the action unfolds, we learn that Yohyō, a rustic, has found a dying crane and nurtured it back to full vigor. The crane has become a beautiful woman, Tsū, who has visited the sincere, though plodding, rustic and become his wife. In gratitude for his tenderness, she has woven a wonderful fabric from her own feathers. While deeply appreciative, Yohyō has sensed the fabric's value and sold it. Now, goaded further by neighbors with visions of greater riches from sales in the city, he urges a reluctant Tsū to make more cloth. By so doing, Yohyō becomes the embodiment of greed and lost innocence. Yet his ever-loving wife weaves two last pieces, using all the feathers she can spare, then, ineffably saddened, becomes once again a crane and flies away. Yohyō finally realizes his wife's ultimate sacrifice and what he has forever lost.

The emotional impact of the play is intensified through the underlying Japanese folk wisdom on cranes as symbols of long life: by folding a thousand origami cranes, one can cure disease. *Twilight Crane*, articulating an overwhelming sense of loss, of nostalgia for a state of primordial innocence, for a kind of mythic homeland, renders powerful comment on the diseased condition of the Japanese people in the modern world. The play limns their feeling of being unmoored in a sea of mind-twisting change—urbanization, commodification—that the country has undergone and the consequent impact on the Japanese sense of morality and the question of identity.

In openly inviting the spectators to weigh a critical moral equation, the play calls to mind BERTOLT BRECHT'S LEARNING PLAYS (*Lehrstücke*). The famous actress Yamamoto Yasue, who was in the first production in 1950 and (before she died in 1993) performed the role of Tsū over 1,000 times, invariably highlighted the effort to balance the equation, to bring human sincerity and genuineness to a world of greed gone awry.

So popular was the original production that it has been cited as a catalyst in the widespread resurgence of interest in folktales and folk arts and crafts in early 1950s JAPAN. Indeed, *Twilight Crane* is so highly regarded that it has become integral to the mass acculturation process. It is among the most frequently performed plays in the postwar period and has been adapted for *kabuki*, NŌ, and opera. *Kabuki* female impersonators, or *onnagata*, such as the immensely popular Bandō Tamasaburō V, often play the role of Tsū. Cartoon (*manga*) versions exist both in print and for television. Performances are often arranged for children. It is widely read in junior high school, and the original folktale, *The Crane Returns a Debt of Gratitude* (*Tsuru no ongaeshi*) in elementary school.

FURTHER READING

Keene, Donald. *Dawn to the West: Japanese Literature in the Modern Era; Poetry, Drama, Criticism.* New York: H. Holt, 1984.

Kinoshita Junji. *Der Abendkranich* [Twilight crane]. Tr. by Jürgen Berndt. In *Japanische Dramen*. Berlin: Verlag Volk und Welt, 1968.

——. *Kinoshita Junji sakuhinshū* [Collected works]. 7 vols. Tokyo: Miraisha, 1962–1971.

——. *Twilight Crane*. Tr. by A. C. Scott. In *Playbook: 5 Plays for a New Theatre*. New York: New Directions, 1956.

Nihon Kindai Engekishi Kenkyūkai, ed. *Nijusseiki no gikyoku II: Gendai gikyoku no tenkai* [Twentieth-century plays II: The development of contemporary (Japanese) playwriting]. Tokyo: Shakai Hyōronsha, 2002.

Powell, Brian. *Japan's Modern Theatre: A Century of Change and Continuity.* London: Japan Library, 2002.

John K. Gillespie

THE TWISTING OF ANOTHER ROPE See THE QUARE FELLOW

UBU TRILOGY

In the character of Père Ubu, ALFRED JARRY made his lasting contribution to drama. Cowardly yet bloodthirsty, slothful yet ambitious, Ubu twists all logic to fit his personal narcissism. Created as a satire of the French bourgeoisie, Ubu and his wife Mère Ubu grew through the 20th century to become symbols for the mindlessly destructive potential of humanity. In his trilogy of plays featuring the couple—*Ubu the King* (*Ubu roi*) *Ubu the Cuckold* (*Ubu cocu*) and *Ubu Enchained* (*Ubu enchaîné*)—the target of Jarry's assault expands from the conventions of Boulevard theater to the foundations of Western philosophical thought.

In *Ubu the King* Père Ubu, "ex-King of Aragon" and Captain of Dragoons to King Wenceslas of Poland, is provoked by his wife into killing Wenceslas and seizing the throne. As king, Ubu imposes severe taxes, destroying all in his path in order to loot them. He begins with the aristocrats, but is soon massacring the peasants for their pocket money. The Czar of Russia invades Poland to restore Wenceslas's surviving son to the throne. While Ubu goes off to fight—or avoid—the Czar's army, Mère Ubu attempts to rob the Treasury, but is foiled by the arrival of Wenceslas's son and his supporters. She is reunited and reconciled with Ubu in a cave besieged by the Russians. After an escape they sail off to Paris, with Ubu announcing that he will declare himself "Minister of Phynance."

Ubu the Cuckold (uncompleted by Jarry and not published until 1944) takes the couple to France. Ubu carries his conscience around in a suitcase, bringing it out for consultation. When he is displeased with its advice, Ubu stuffs his conscience down the latrine, located upstage center.

In the third play of the trilogy (*Ubu Enchained*, published in 1900 but not produced until 1937), Ubu is depressed in the land of *liberté*, *egalité*, and *fraternité*. The only way to be an individual in a free land, he decides, is to become a slave. Working their way down to convicts and then galley slaves, Père and Mère Ubu convince the Free Men that slavery is preferable to the burden of free thought; they revolt and occupy the prisons and galleys, forcing Ubu and the convicts to run society.

Jarry began writing the Ubu plays as a schoolboy. *Ubu the King* began as a parody of an unpopular physics professor. After moving to Paris, Jarry persuaded the director Aurélien Lugné-Poë to produce a revised version of the play at his Théâtre de l'Oeuvre for two performances. The premiere, on December 10, 1896, provoked the greatest scandal on the French stage between the opening of Victor Hugo's *Hernani* in 1830 and the first performance of Igor Stravinsky's *The Rite of Spring* in 1913. After the first word (*merdre*, variously translated as "pschitt"

and "shittr"), the audience erupted in an uproar that stopped the play for fifteen minutes; disruptions continued throughout the performance.

Inspired by the rural performances he had witnessed in his youth, Jarry wrote with puppet performance in mind and supervised the production at the Théâtre de l'Oeuvre to reflect elements of this style, including grotesque costumes and masks, an artificial manner of speaking (which he later adopted for his public transformation into Ubu), and the use of a single painted backdrop featuring a fireplace in the middle of a landscape juxtaposing the Arctic with the tropics.

While it remains common to discount the plays (and their inversion of morality, reason, and even causality) as essentially adolescent parody, Jarry's impressive list of defenders (among them GUILLAUME APOLLINAIRE, JEAN COCTEAU, and ANTONIN ARTAUD) have claimed a positive, rather than negative, meaning in his aesthetic nihilism, often citing Père Ubu's epigraph to *Ubu Enchained* as the most direct evidence for this argument: "We shall not have succeeded in demolishing everything unless we demolish the ruins as well. But the only way I see of doing that is to use them to put up a lot of fine, well-designed buildings."

In Jarry's time the character of Ubu was quickly transformed into "art" and lost his ability to shock (a revival of *Ubu the King* performed by marionettes passed without controversy in 1898). However, Ubu's subversive influence has endured. Critics have seen traces of Ubu in the linguistic mayhem of COMEDY ranging from the Marx brothers, *Mad* magazine, and Monty Python's Flying Circus to the film *Airplane*. Ubu himself has reappeared as a satiric weapon: in the UNITED STATES and Europe during the Vietnam War, in Eastern Europe after the collapse of the iron curtain, and, in a recent South African adaptation, as a representative of the apartheid government.

FURTHER READING

Innes, Christopher. *Avant Garde Theatre, 1892–1992*. London: Routledge, 1993.

Jannarone, Kimberly. "Puppetry and Pataphysics: Populism and the Ubu Cycle." *New Theatre Quarterly* 17, no. 3 (2001): 239–253.

Jarry, Alfred. *The Ubu Plays*. Tr. by Cyril Connelly and Simon Watson Taylor. New York: Grove, 1969.

——. *The Ubu Plays*. Tr. and by Kenneth MacLeish. London: Nick Hern, 1997.

Shattuck, Roger. *The Banquet Years: The Origins of the Avant-Garde in France, 1885 to World War I*. Salem, N.H.: Ayer, 1984.

Walter Bilderback

UNCLE VANYA

The second of ANTON CHEKHOV's dramatic masterpieces, Uncle Vanya (Diadia Vania, 1895–1896), elaborates further the new poetics of drama the playwright had initiated in THE SEAGULL. By the time he wrote Uncle Vanya, Chekhov had abandoned the theatrical conventions of the so-called well-made play, opting instead for what has been called indirect action. He eschewed overt dramatic conflict and favored the dramatic tension of ordinary human interactions.

On the surface, Uncle Vanya appears to be merely a revision of Chekhov's earlier play The Wood Demon (Leshii, 1889), especially since the second and third acts of the two plays are strikingly similar; however, Chekhov insisted that Uncle Vanya was a new play and all but disowned The Wood Demon. In fact, he categorically refused an offer to stage the earlier play in 1900.

The differences between the two plays are telling. For example, Egor Voinitsky, the character who corresponds to Uncle Vanya, commits suicide at the juncture in The Wood Demon that parallels Uncle Vanya's homicidal pursuit of Professor Serebriakov in the later play. Egor's suicide is quite similar to the suicide of Ivanov in the eponymous play in that it is vehemently dramatic, but it is quite different from Treplev's suicide in THE SEAGULL, which seems an almost inevitable act of resignation that is unlikely to change the other characters. Likewise, Uncle Vanya's attempts to shoot Serebriakov, though wild and wildly irresponsible, prove fruitless, affecting those around him only superficially.

Chekhov remained dissatisfied with The Wood Demon because of deficiencies in its dramatic structure; from this point of view, Uncle Vanya represents a remarkable advance over the earlier play. To take but a single example, the last act of The Wood Demon centers around the happy ending of the romance between Mikhail Khrushchev, who corresponds to the Astrov character in Uncle Vanya, and Sonia, whose name remains the same in both plays, but whose character undergoes a metamorphosis. Their romance and the ending are both conventional and contrived. For good measure, Chekhov unites yet another couple before the curtain falls. The failure of the ending of The Wood Demon to grow out of its dramatic predicament stands in stark contrast to the ending of Uncle Vanya. The quiet optimism with which Sonia, Astrov, and Uncle Vanya handle the emotional devastation left in the wake of the Serebriakovs' departure grows organically out of long-held values that precipitated the play's dramatic action in the first place.

Uncle Vanya brings the eponymous Ivan Voinitsky to the foreground. In Vanya, Chekhov created an apotheosis of the so-called superfluous man, an ineffectual nobleman whose consciousness of his own inadequacy threatens to destroy him and those around him. Like Chekhov's earlier superfluous men, such as Ivanov, Vanya is a frustrated idealist who must come to terms with his own disillusionment; however, whereas Ivanov directs his frustration inward and ends up killing himself,

Vanya directs his anger at other people, principally at Serebriakov. In fact, the drama of Uncle Vanya grows out of the confrontation between the egotistical Serebriakovs, who live off other people both financially and emotionally, and those characters, such as Astrov and Sonia, who live and work for the benefit of others. Vanya belongs imperfectly to the latter group, and his recognition of his own shortcomings contributes to the play's pathos. Not unlike Treplev in The Seagull, Vanya is emotionally needy, and his need has an Oedipal dimension: He clearly longs for his mother's approval and affection, but neither is forthcoming. The failure of the characters to engage one another is a key theme in the play. From this point of view, Vanya's deceased sister plays an enormous role. Although rarely remarked on, she has left behind an emotional vacuum in her brother's life that has not been filled.

Chekhov gave Uncle Vanya the subtitle Scenes from Country Life in Four Acts, and the opposition of rural and city life informs the play in important ways. For example, although the environmental theme is much more strident in The Wood Demon, it nonetheless retains significance in Uncle Vanya. However, it is perhaps the theme of displacement, the opposition of the provinces to the city, that helps demarcate boundaries between characters. This theme, important in Nikolaí Gogol's COMEDIES, is taken up in all seriousness by Chekhov. The Serebriakovs are associated with the city as an intellectual center, and the professor has been in the habit of farming out work to his relatives in the provinces. The underlying inequity of this exploitation informs the confrontation between Vanya and Serebriakov over the sale of the estate in act 3.

The premiere of Uncle Vanya at the MOSCOW ART THEATRE on October 26, 1899, was a success, if not on the order of that of the Art Theatre's production of The Seagull. The cast included Chekhov's future wife Olga Knipper as Elena Serebriakova and KONSTANTIN STANISLAVSKY himself as Astrov.

[See also Russia and the Soviet Union]

FURTHER READING

Bentley, Eric. "Craftsmanship in Uncle Vanya." In Anton Chekhov's Plays, ed. by Eugene Bristow. New York: Norton, 1977. 349–368.

Bordinat, Philip. "Dramatic Structure in Chekhov's Uncle Vanya." In Chekhov's Great Plays: A Critical Anthology, ed. by Jean-Pierre Barricelli. New York: New York Univ. Press, 1981. 47–60.

Chekhov, Anton. The Wood Demon and Uncle Vanya. In The Oxford Chekhov, vol. 3. ed. by Ronald Hingley. London: Oxford Univ. Press, 1974.

Gilman, Richard. Chekhov's Plays: An Opening Into Eternity. New Haven: Yale Univ. Press, 1995.

Magarshack, David. Chekhov the Dramatist. New York: Hill & Wang, 1960.

Rayfield, Donald. Chekhov's "Uncle Vania" and "The Wood Demon." London: Bristol Classical Press, 1995.

Timothy C. Westphalen

UNCOMMON WOMEN AND OTHERS

Sometimes I know who I am when I feel attractive. Other times it makes me feel very shallow, like I'm not Rosie the Riveter. I suppose this isn't a very impressive sentiment, but I would really like to meet my prince. Even a few princes. And I wouldn't give up being a person. I'd still remember all the Art History dates. I just don't know why suddenly I'm supposed to know what I want to do.
—Muffet, Act 1

Begun as a one-act at the Yale School of Drama, *Uncommon Women and Others* (1977) announced the arrival of an important young female dramatist, WENDY WASSERSTEIN. With its sharp humor and frank depiction of female friendship and sexuality, the play gave voice on stage for the first time to the concerns of a new generation of American middle-class women, those raised after the social revolutions of the 1960s.

Framed by the reunion of five former college friends, the plot consists of a series of flashbacks to their student days at a prestigious "college for women" in New England, clearly modeled on Wasserstein's own alma mater, Mount Holyoke. An ensemble piece, the play shifts between the dilemmas and anxieties of its major characters rather than fashioning a single narrative. Kate, the most driven and respected of the group, struggles for her own identity despite the expectations raised by her physical beauty; Muffet is more conventional in embracing her looks and femininity but harbors no professional ambitions; the wide-eyed and affable Samantha gets engaged and forgoes career plans altogether; and Rita, a rebellious Daughters of the American Revolution (DAR) descendant, is the campus iconoclast, full of conspiracy theories and raunchy boasting. Less aggressively unconventional is Holly—the character autobiographically closest to Wasserstein—a disheveled dreamer, full of passion for many things, but unsettled about a definite career, even at the reunion. Together the girls mock the staid traditions of their school, debate their need for men or careers, and cling to each other's friendship to stave off the oncoming anxiety of graduation and adulthood.

In these reminiscences we meet three other classmates—including the would-be archeologist Leilah—as well as their housemother, Mrs. Plumm, who provides tea and fond memories of her own student days at the college during less liberated times. The only male presence in the play is a pompous offstage voice (presumably a commencement speaker or college president) extolling such virtues as training women to be fine secretaries or society hostesses, not full-fledged professionals on a par with their male Ivy League counterparts.

While the play's dialogue rarely gets explicitly political, Wasserstein's choice to focus on the interrelationships within an all-female world, exclusive of men, was received as a feminist gesture in itself. Yet the warm likeability of its characters and their amusing antics made it more successful and popular with large audiences than other more strident women's dramas of the time.

Uncommon Women was first produced by New York's Phoenix Theatre on November 21, 1977. Not only did it win Wasserstein wide acclaim and an Obie Award, but many in the young cast soon became household names as well, including Jill Eikenberry as Kate, Swoosie Kurtz as Rita, and Glenn Close as Leilah. The Public Broadcasting Service (PBS) filmed the production for television and broadcast it in May 1978 (Meryl Streep replaced Close in the television version). The play continues to enjoy a long life in regional theaters, drama schools, and colleges across the country.

[*See also* United States, 1940–Present]

FURTHER READING

Barnett, Claudia, ed. *Wendy Wasserstein: A Casebook.* New York: Garland, 1999.

Bryer, Jackson R., ed. *The Playwright's Art: Conversations with Contemporary American Dramatists.* New Brunswick, N.J.: Rutgers Univ. Press, 1995.

Kolin, Philip C., and Colby H. Kullman, eds. *Speaking on Stage: Interviews with Contemporary American Playwrights.* Tuscaloosa: Univ. of Alabama Press, 1996.

Schlueter, June, ed. *Modern American Drama: The Female Canon.* Rutherford, N.J.: Fairleigh Dickinson Univ. Press, 1990.

Wasserstein, Wendy. *The Heidi Chronicles, and Other Plays.* San Diego: Harcourt, 1990.

Garrett B. Eisler

THE UNDERPANTS

In CARL STERNHEIM's *The Underpants* (*Die Hose*, 1910) Luise Maske, the wife of Theobald Maske, loses her underpants as a crowd of people is watching Wilhelm II make an appearance on the streets of Berlin. Two strangers who witness the event, the writer Scarron and the barber Mandelbaum, begin to lust for Luise and show up at the Maskes' apartment to rent the two rooms the couple has advertised. With his pragmatic and materialist approach to life, Theobald fends off both the FRIEDRICH NIETZSCHE follower Scarron and the Jewish RICHARD WAGNER enthusiast Mandelbaum and uses their rent money to set about having children with Luise.

The play, a "bourgeois COMEDY," satirically inverts the tradition of the German bourgeois TRAGEDY (*bürgerliches Trauerspiel*), a dramatic form that arose in the 18th century as a means of bourgeois self-affirmation. In the 18th century it was noblemen from the nearby courts who put the virtues of bourgeois daughters at risk; in the early 20th century it is the bourgeois wife herself who is the seductress, hoping to escape the boredom of her marriage. In the 18th century the bourgeoisie asserted itself vis-à-vis the court on the basis of its virtue; at the Maskes' apartment the prospect of making extra money overcomes any moral trepidation. While the bourgeois family had previously reacted by distancing itself as much as possible from the corrupt court, in *The Underpants* the suitors move right in with the family. Empathy among the members of the bourgeois family has been replaced by scheming and material motives; bourgeois virtues have been reduced to the ability and desire to make oneself blend in as much as possible: "My inconspicuousness is the cloak of invisibility under which I can pursue my inclinations, my innermost nature," Theobald Maske proclaims.

In *The Underpants*, as well as in *The Snob* (*Der Snob*, 1914), 1913 (1915), and *The Fossil* (*Das Fossil*, 1922)—the plays that constitute *Scenes from the Heroic Life of the Middle Classes* (the Maske tetralogy *Aus dem bürgerlichen Heldenleben*)—Sternheim satirizes not only what has become of bourgeois virtues and their attending humanist ideals in a faceless mass society, but also their literary and cultural expressions from Gotthold Lessing to Wagner and Nietzsche, as well as by Sternheim's naturalist contemporaries. While the naturalists had attempted to show in the details of everyday life the misery and social polarization capitalism had created, Sternheim concentrates on the same aspects to show the banality and shallowness of bourgeois life. His plays resemble the work of writers such as Heinrich Mann (1871–1950) and Arnold Zweig (1887–1968) who characterize the Wilhelmine era as one concerned more with outward appearances (hence the name Maske [mask]) and the ideological mystification of the driving forces behind this period of rapid economic expansion and imperialist adventures: unfettered egotism and an exploitative lust for wealth, in the face of which traditional bourgeois values have only become a burden. In *The Underpants* even the Nietzschean *Übermensch* represented by the writer Scarron fails to conquer the fortress of bourgeois smugness as Theobald, during a night of heavy drinking, outlasts him and reclaims his place at the side of his wife.

[*See also* Germany; Naturalism]

FURTHER READING

Dedner, Burghard. *Carl Sternheim*. Boston: Twayne, 1982.

Myers, David. "Carl Sternheim: Satirist or Creator of Modern Heroes?" *Monatshefte* 65, no. 1 (1973): 39–47.

Rumold, Rainer. "Carl Sternheims Komödie 'Die Hose': Sprachkritik, Sprachsatire und der Verfremdungseffekt vor Brecht" [Carl Sternheim's comedy *Die Hose*: Language critique, language satire, and alienation effects before Brecht]. *Michigan German Studies* 4, no. 1 (1978): 1–16.

Friedemann J. Weidauer

UNDER THE GASLIGHT

Under the Gaslight was AUGUSTIN DALY's first successful play, and he directed its first production himself in 1867 at the New York Theatre. The production inaugurated "the victim on the tracks" scene in American and transatlantic MELODRAMA and thereby raised the stakes for scenographic innovation in the exploding genre of "sensation drama." *Under the Gaslight* brought onto the stage the very locomotive that symbolized industrialization, progress, and danger to mid-19th-century Americans. In his 1980 essay "Machines of the Visible" Jean Louis Comolli describes a "frenzy of the visible" that characterized antebellum spectacle culture; indeed, *Under the Gaslight* fueled that frenzy in theatergoing audiences.

The plot of *Under the Gaslight*, subtitled *Life and Love in These Times*, brings together members of high society and the urban slum, civilians and a Civil War veteran, immigrants and a magistrate in a topsy-turvy episodic intrigue of origins that resolves itself through revelations of cradle swapping at the play's end. The setting is New York City and its environs, the site of cosmopolitan fantasies and fears for midcentury Americans. Laura Courtland, virtuous fiancée of well-bred but doltish Ray Trafford, is discovered to be of lowly origins in the opening scene of the play. Banished from high society, Laura begins her journey into her rightful stratum of society. Through Laura's eyes the audience meets the clowns, innocents, and villains who dwell in the city's slums. The Dickensian predator, Byke, declares himself to be Laura's real father. Snorkey, a one-armed Union army veteran who always fights on the right side, pursues Byke on Laura's behalf. The infamous train-track spectacle occurs in the upstate town of the Courtland country home, where Byke, intent on blackmailing the family, discovers Snorkey at a train station and ties him to the tracks. Laura, hiding in the stationmaster's cabin, hacks her way out with an ax and unties Snorkey just as the train comes onstage. In a speedy resolution of the plot, Laura returns to Manhattan, her heartless sister Pearl is exposed as unvirtuous in behavior and birth, and Byke and his accomplice are taken into custody for baby swapping and extortion.

Joseph Daly, Augustin's brother and collaborator, describes the infamous disaster that befell the much-anticipated train-track effect on opening night. "The intensely wrought feelings of the spectators found vent in almost hysterical laughter when the 'railroad train' parted in the middle and disclosed the flying legs of the human motor who was propelling the first half of the express (1917)." The effect was fixed and improved upon thereafter. Indeed, *Under the Gaslight* was the inspiration for DION BOUCICAULT's play *After Dark* the next year in London, with its version of a train-track scene. Daly successfully sued Boucicault for stealing the effect; although Daly won the first judgment, countersuits continued for almost twenty years.

Under the Gaslight had many subsequent productions. American novelist Theodore Dreiser used the play as an organizing principle for his 1900 novel *Sister Carrie*, and the Biograph Company released a film version of the play in 1913.

[*See also* United States, 1860–1920]

FURTHER READING

Daly, Augustin. *Plays*. Ed. by Don B. Wilmeth and Rosemary Cullen. Cambridge: Cambridge Univ. Press, 1984.

Daly, Joseph F. *The Life of Augustin Daly.* New York: Macmillan, 1917.

Daly, Nicholas. "Blood on the Tracks: Sensation Drama, the Railway, and the Dark Face of Modernity." *Victorian Studies* 42 (1998/1999): 47–76.

Gerould, Daniel C., ed. *American Melodrama.* New York: Performing Arts Journal Publications, 1983.

McConachie, Bruce A. *Melodramatic Formations: American Theatre and Society, 1820–1870.* Iowa City: Univ. of Iowa Press, 1992.

Vardac, A. Nicholas. *Stage to Screen: Theatrical Method from Garrick to Griffith.* Cambridge, Mass.: Harvard Univ. Press, 1949.

Beth Cleary

UNDER THE WHALEBACK

RICHARD BEAN's black COMEDY *Under the Whaleback* won the 2002 George Devine Award and was first performed at the Royal Court Theatre Upstairs on April 10, 2003, directed by Richard Wilson. The play's United Kingdom regional premiere, in the playwright's native Hull, took place at the Hull Truck Theatre on February 26, 2004, and was directed by Gareth Tudor Price.

Under the Whaleback is set in the crew's living quarters of three trawlers (the "whaleback" is the curved deck under the ship's bow) and spans four decades, offering a glimpse into the lives of fishermen off the northeast coast of ENGLAND. The play explores the social and psychological context of the gradually decaying fishing industry around Hull and contemplates the present, in which the century-long tradition is on the verge of extinction. In the early 21st century, Bean argues, Hull's fishing heritage connotes unemployment and associated violent crime for those left to their own devices and hence disoriented and unable to embark on a new career. Bean is clearly angered by this state of affairs and by the transformation of former seagoing trawlers into sanitized museum pieces.

Structured in three acts, the play centers on a protagonist (Darrel) and his journey of self-discovery, survival, and reinvention. Darrel appears in these acts at different stages of his life: as a seventeen-year-old deckie learner in 1965, as an experienced deckhand in 1972, and as a retired fisherman working as the curator of a museum-ship in 2002. Throughout, the focus is on Darrel's interaction with his fellow crew members; bonding between the crew, however, is irreversibly connected to their constant struggle for survival. Most characters perish at sea, including Cassidy of scene 1 and the crew in scene 2, Darrel remaining the only one of his generation to tell their stories and to cope with the guilt of survival. Traditionally a profession inherited down the family line, fishing regularly juxtaposes fathers and sons, and Bean dramatizes the ways in which the sons deal with the legacies of their fathers.

Bean deliberately blurs the boundaries between biological and spiritual fathers and repeatedly puts the sons in situations to contemplate an alternative lineage. For instance, Darrel learns that he is Cassidy's son in scene 1 but only acknowledges it publicly in scene 2, while in scene 3 it is Darrel himself who breaks the news to a youth (Pat) that he is not the son of one fisherman dead at sea (Roc) but of another (Norman). To a similar end, Bean also doubles sons and fathers, casting the same actor for both roles in two such pairs, Cassidy and Darrel, Norman and Pat. As Cassidy, a legendary character referenced throughout the play, contends: "You gorra be born to this you know. It's the worst fucking job in the world and only those what is born to it, what has gorrit in the blood, can do it." Cassidy's remarks, as well as most of the play, are written in a rich and hearty Hull accent, intending to preserve for posterity not only the legacy of a now-extinct profession but also a regional flavor marginalized from mainstream discourse.

FURTHER READING

Bean, Richard. *Under the Whaleback.* London: Oberon Bks., 2003.

"Under the Whaleback." *Theatre Record* 23, no. 8 (May 13, 2003): 476–480. [Reviews of the 2003 Royal Court production.]

Jozefina Komporaly

UNIDENTIFIED HUMAN REMAINS AND THE TRUE NATURE OF LOVE

Unidentified Human Remains and the True Nature of Love by BRAD FRASER takes place in the Canadian city of Edmonton in 1989. The play follows the story of seven lonely people and their search for love and meaning in the jaded, cynical world of the late 1980s. As the characters try to accept their sexuality and find worthwhile relationships, their lives are affected by a serial killer who stalks the city. When the identity of the killer is revealed, the characters realize that he is no more lost or confused than they are. *Unidentified Human Remains* documents the "motion sickness of urban life" as it jumps from scene to scene, uncovering the characters' uncertainty with themselves and each other.

The main character, David, a former child star and now a waiter, seeks intimacy in brief sexual encounters with strangers. The twenty-nine-year old David begins a relationship with a seventeen-year-old boy, Kane, as a substitute for the man he can never have, his "straight" friend Bernie. Candy, David's roommate and former lover, also appears confused and desperate in her need for love. As Candy vacillates between her gym lesbian love affair with Jerry and her relationship with the bartender Robert, David and Bernie struggle with a more desperate form of love. The characters' troubles are all observed from the sidelines by David's clairvoyant friend and S&M prostitute, Benita.

The characters' hollow lives are mirrored by that of the serial killer in their midst; the killer's graphic violence echoes throughout the play. The scenes jump from one to the next and present an MTV-generation culture deeply cynical and distrustful of love or emotion due to excessive behavior. Deception, confusion, and lies permeate the dialogue while Benita tells urban legends to the audience, encapsulating the paranoia of a city caught in the shadow of a serial killer.

A jazzy, uncompromising story filled with violence, nudity, and strong language, the play is witness to the paranoia and confusion of a generation coming to terms with the AIDS crisis. The characters articulate their feeling of unease throughout the play; as David states, "I've never known anyone born after 1960 who wasn't incomplete somehow." Fraser desired to create characters that were caught in the emotional turmoil that Fraser found from his own experience and that of those around him. By making the characters speak the language of people he knew, and articulate the confusion that he felt, Fraser hoped to draw a different type of audience to the stage.

Playwright and screenwriter Brad Fraser has won awards for his work since his early years in Edmonton, CANADA. Fraser's plays are known for their explicit language and sexual activity, as well as their controversial view of homosexuality. Fraser has received the prestigious Chalmers Award (*Unidentified Human Remains*, 1990, and *Poor Super Man*, 1994) and was nominated for the Governor General's Award (*Poor Super Man*, 1996). *Unidentified Human Remains* was adapted into a film in 1994 by Denis Arcand. Fraser is also a co-producer and writer of the Showtime series *Queer as Folk* and hosts his own talk show, *Jawbreaker*.

FURTHER READING

Blumberg, Marcia. "Queer(y)ing the Canadian Stage: Brad Fraser's *Poor Super Man*." *Theatre Research in Canada* 17, no. 2 (Fall 1996): 175–187.

Dvorak, Maria. "Le Polar de la Génération X." *Canadian Studies/Etudes Canadiennes* (1998): 115–123.

Glaap, Albert-Reiner. *Anguished Human Relations and the Search for Love: Plays by Canadian Writers Brad Fraser, Judith Thompson, and Dianne Warren.* Trier: Germany Publications, 1998.

Holly Maples

UNITED STATES
1860–1929

From the Civil War to the Great Depression, changes in American society were seismic; they varied as the landscape of the nation was altered by factors ranging from dramatic population increases and movement from rural to urban centers to improved and more extensive transportation and to attitudinal shifts, albeit often subtle, toward social, moral, political, and economic matters. The war ended a romantic notion of American innocence. American dramatists responded haltingly to this and only slowly developed a meaningful engagement with an emerging new American society.

By 1860 the U.S. population had swelled to 31.4 million, with New York City's population of more than 800,000 people exceeding Philadelphia's—previously the theater heart of the country—which stood at 500,000. By 1900 the total U.S. population had risen to 76 million, and that of New York City, increasingly important for the theater, had climbed to 3.5 million. After the turbulence of a devastating war on U.S. soil, and despite some economic crises (the panics of 1873 and 1893), prosperity steadily increased largely unabated until the stock-market crash of 1929. Services provided by industry, transportation, and finance spread throughout much of the country, creating new opportunities, new tensions, and an increased optimism about the future. For the theater, and as fodder for playwrights, each factor was important, but none was more vital than the dramatic growth in railroads (by the mid-1880s four times the approximately 32,500 miles of track in 1860), increasing theatrical circuits, and the ease of movement to the West. This was especially increased with the completion of the transcontinental railroad in 1869.

By the late 1800s the United States began to flex its imperialistic, international power, which culminated in the brief Spanish-American War of 1898. By 1900 cities were industrial centers, thanks in large measure to sizable immigrations—almost 9 million between 1900 and 1910—and rural migrants swelling the unskilled and specialized labor force. The United States led the world in productivity. Part of this trend involved the theater. The Theatrical Syndicate (1896–1916), followed by a similar monopoly by the Shuberts (Lee, Sam S., and Jacob J.), who entered the picture in 1913 and sustained their control nationally until 1930 (and on Broadway until 1950), brought order to the chaos of booking and touring ("the Road") while at the same time controlling much of the material written for the stage.

The movement to provide women their voting rights was picking up steam and by 1912, a key year for significant changes in American theater as well. Conversely, racial issues would not begin to be solved in this period, but even the portrayal of blacks onstage gradually moved away from the earlier 19th-century grotesque image of the blackface minstrel to something a bit more realistic and sympathetic, especially after the Great Migration. In reality, the late 19th century and the first decade of the 20th century were a transitional era between the Victorian age and an emerging modern period. In the second decade of the new century the theater began to rebel against the commercialism and largely old-fashioned approaches to the drama current in American culture. Although profit-making attitudes, especially with an ever-growing Broadway theater district, have never died in the United States, for a decade or so a new dynamism and credo for new drama that could be categorized as an art form provoked experimentation that would help propel Americans into a more modernistic age. World War I, a major touchstone of the period, though not a cataclysmic event that affected directly all Americans, nonetheless added an ingredient to the mix and helped underscore the breakdown of American values.

Yet despite a seventy-year period of enormous evolution and change in American society, critics of the drama continue to suggest that as a serious form, drama in the United States is a product solely of the 20th century. A major historian of the early 20th century bemoaned in 1919 that by this period native drama had virtually ceased to exist, replaced by foreign imports, and HENRY JAMES criticized the drama as not having the same relationship to American society that the novel did; that is, it lacked an organic engagement with the values and experiences of the nation. There is some truth to both opinions, for American theater and even legitimate drama written for the stage have been largely profit driven, frequently satisfied if they served as a distraction or an amusement for the audience, often consciously anti-intellectual and drawing on often simplistic and formulaic structures of the past, such as light COMEDY or domestic MELODRAMA. James argued that the American audience did not want thoughtful, aesthetic, or subtle drama and was "very ignorant."

It is worth noting, however, that the situation was similar in this country to that in major Western European nations. Actors, popular entertainments (early musicals, minstrelsy, vaudeville, and the like), and spectacle largely dominated in the 19th century, and notable change in the drama did not begin to emerge until after HENRIK IBSEN, AUGUST STRINDBERG, and ANTON CHEKHOV exerted influence during the last two decades of the century. Popular forms continued to dominate on Broadway until the Depression.

It is important to recognize that the seeds for the emergence of a EUGENE O'NEILL and a MODERNIST DRAMA were nevertheless planted in the 19th century, and playwrights attempted to reflect the changing culture and its concerns. Consequently, in the United States, as elsewhere, the period from the turn of the century to 1929 was one of the most turbulent and dynamic in history, no less so in the struggling drama than in other venues of culture.

By the Civil War, the American theater had a strong mainstream tradition, yet reflecting discernible impulses from European traditions. After the war, and after a brief curtailment of theatrical growth in the East, there was a spurt of prosperity for the theater that lasted for over half a century. In the 1860s, with taste changing, the trend in dramatic writing was toward a more contemporary melodrama that offered the spectator excitement, emotional intensity, stereotypical characters, predictable morality, and sensationalized staging, led by the early melodramatic plays of former journalist AUGUSTIN DALY—UNDER THE GASLIGHT (1867), A Flash of Lightning (1868), and The Red Scarf (1868).

In 1871 Daly moved his melodramatic tendencies to the West with Horizon, a play inspired by the contemporary Indian wars and the fiction of BRET HARTE. Though not the first frontier melodrama, it was a more realistic picture with its combination of sensation and local color and inspired a new genre of frontier dramas, including Frank Murdoch's DAVY CROCKETT (1872), Harte's Two Men of Sandy Bar (1876), JOAQUIN MILLER's The Danites (1887), BARTLEY CAMPBELL's My Partner (1879),

AUGUSTUS THOMAS's Arizona (1899), and DAVID BELASCO's THE GIRL OF THE GOLDEN WEST (1905). WILLIAM VAUGHN MOODY, called the finest lyric poet of his generation, wrote in 1906 a frontier drama that would help alter the direction not only of this type of play but of American drama in general. His THE GREAT DIVIDE, one of the finest American plays of its time, blended somewhat realistic motivation with a poetic treatment of the myth of the East versus the West.

By the late 19th century and into the turn of the 20th century, even though melodrama as a form would persist well into the 20th century, there were general tendencies toward more realistic treatments of subject, but dramatic REALISM at the turn of the century remained relatively superficial, with the reality depicted grounded in location, action, and seemingly true-to-life characters or themes that nonetheless explored issues of greater seriousness than in the past. Both social comedy and drama moved ever so slowly away from FARCE and melodrama, yet because of the lack of effective copyright controls (there was no international agreement until 1891), most American playwrights were still forced to compete with translations or Americanized adaptations of European popular plays in order to survive. Even Daly and his contemporary, the Anglo-Irish writer DION BOUCICAULT, more successful original writers than most, were often reduced to such tactics for financial gain.

Yet by the 1870s there were indications that playwrights were beginning to turn away from subjects from the past and foreign imports (even if Americanized). In addition to frontier plays, themes and concerns of the day were ever more prominent, ranging from stock speculation and Wall Street machinations to marital difficulties and especially divorce. There was even a retrospective group of plays from the 1870s that, while ignoring causes and often issues, nonetheless dealt with the Civil War, more often than not from a romantic point of view.

Of the writers who dealt with social and cultural topics, none was more prominent than BRONSON HOWARD, termed the first professional American playwright and the author of several "businessman" plays, including The Banker's Daughter (1878); Young Mrs. Winthrop (1882); The Henrietta (1887), a melodramatic depiction of Wall Street, high finance, the consequences of an obsession with business, and romantic treachery; and Aristocracy (1892). Others followed suit: Belasco's and Henry C. DeMille's Men and Women (1890); CLYDE FITCH's The Climbers (1901); and LANGDON MITCHELL's THE NEW YORK IDEA (1906), the latter also the most effective sophisticated satire of the period on divorce.

Howard also authored a popular Civil War melodrama, SHENANDOAH (1888), one of several. Others of note are Boucicault's The Octoroon (1859) and Belle Lamar (1874); Daly's Norwood (1867); WILLIAM GILLETTE's Held by the Enemy (1886) and SECRET SERVICE (1896); and Fitch's Barbara Frietchie (1899). Fitch, though he died in his mid-forties, became a prolific writer with sixty plays to his credit, most dealing perceptively and humorously with topical American subjects. THE TRUTH (1907) and *The City* (1909), the latter demonstrating the deleterious effects the big city can have on weak individuals, are among his most effective, rich in "Fitchian" detail and effective dialogue.

Other writers late in the century brought new twists to old forms or, in a few rare instances, responded to the new realistic movement represented most notably by the work of Henrik Ibsen and encouraged by critics WILLIAM DEAN HOWELLS and Hamlin Garland (1860–1940). Yet Ibsen as a true model was still not possible, given the clear preferences of the American public for a drama that still contained melodramatic touches and romantic, happy, or at least upbeat endings.

EDWARD HARRIGAN, using farce and original songs, turned to ethnic urban types for his knockabout comedies, most prominently including Irish and African Americans but also German and Italian immigrants. Most popular were a series of "Mulligan guard" (1873–1880) plays built around a group of Irish immigrants who came to the Lower East Side of New York City's Manhattan after the famine of 1848, but also successful were such later plays as *Squatter Sovereignty* (1882), *Cordelia's Aspirations* (1883), and *Dan's Tribulations* (1884). Howells praised Harrigan's depiction of "the actual life of this city," yet Harrigan's work never fully developed into realism. In like manner, CHARLES HALE HOYT, like many 19th-century American playwrights trained in journalism, placed recognizable American types in farcical situations, such as his satire on Texas and congressmen, *A Texas Steer* (1890), and his mammoth hit, *A Trip to Chinatown* (1891), with its men-about-town. Like Harrigan, Hoyt wrote plays that offered transparent excuses for characters to sing and dance, for success and financial gain were foremost to him.

Other playwrights more consciously provided a transitional drama, beginning in the 1880s and moving into the early years of the 20th century. A few either sought a greater verisimilitude in their plays or chose to focus on the status of the individual in America. Most significant among these early, daring writers were the previously mentioned William Vaughn Moody, William Gillette, and Bronson Howard, STEELE MACKAYE (equally known as an actor, director, and visionary), Augustus Thomas, EDWARD SHELDON, JAMES A. HERNE, and, to a lesser extent, the prominent creator of an illusion of reality through his scenography and his meticulous direction, Belasco.

MacKaye's greatest success, HAZEL KIRKE (1880), essentially a domestic melodrama with realistic touches, combines a more natural portrayal of the titular character than its predecessors, the lack of a traditional villain, and a more realistic environment. Only one other MacKaye play held the stage, *Paul Kauvar; or, Anarchy* (1887), concerned with public politics and set during the French Revolution. MacKaye's contributions can also be seen in his staging and lighting innovations and his concern for a more believable acting style that brought greater emotional depth to stage characters. Augustus Thomas's notion of reality was centered on local color in plays such as *Alabama* (1891),

In Mizzoura (1893), *Arizona* (1899), *The Witching Hour* (1907), and *The Copperhead* (1918). Thomas also explored contemporary issues such as capital and labor (*New Blood*, 1894), politics (*The Capitol*, 1895), and mental healing (*As a Man Thinks*, 1911), among others. Edward Sheldon, trained in one of the earliest playwriting courses, GEORGE PIERCE BAKER's English 47 at Harvard, produced an early example of social realism in plays such as SALVATION NELL (1908); *The Nigger* (1909), considered one of the first serious plays after the abolition of slavery to represent a somewhat sympathetic portrait of African Americans' ongoing struggle; and *The Boss* (1911), concerned with labor-management confrontations.

Only James A. Herne of this group was able to produce a uniquely American type of realism during the last decade of the 19th century, stating his creed in an important 1897 essay, "Art for Truth's Sake in the Drama," in which he relates drama to other contemporary forms of literature and urges an emphasis on "humanity" and "large truth" in the drama. Although even Herne, after writing the landmark drama MARGARET FLEMING (1891), was forced to alter his emphasis to a degree for financial security, he nonetheless provided an example for the future in plays, in addition to *Margaret Fleming*, such as *Drifting Apart* (1888), SHORE ACRES (1892), and *The Reverend Griffith Davenport* (1899).

Belasco, a director-manager-playwright, was obsessed with the creation and execution of "real" stage effects. His plays invariably were written to emphasize startlingly real illusions, yet the texts themselves are marked by melodramatic action and sentimentally drawn and idealized characters, and none holds up well today. Nevertheless, from 1890 to 1915 his management was extraordinarily successful, frequently showcasing his own plays (he claimed to have written seventy), including *Madam Butterfly* (1900), *DuBarry* (1901), *The Darling of the Gods* (1902), the previously mentioned *The Girl of the Golden West* (1905), *The Rose of the Rancho* (1906), and *The Governor's Lady* (1912). One play produced by Belasco but not his own, and featuring the actual interior of a boardinghouse room, was Eugene Walter's (1874–1941) *The Easiest Way* (1909), considered by some too naturalistic and frank, with an unhappy ending, yet in fact, like most of Belasco's productions, thinly disguised melodrama.

Belasco's long career is closely intertwined with the trend toward monopoly that characterized much post–Civil War business, and that, in the American theater, had an immense impact on theatrical developments in myriad ways up to the Great Depression. In 1896, six theater owners, booking agents, or in one instance (Charles Frohman) a theater owner and producer combined forces with the objective, a natural and logical one for the times, of bringing order and a concentration of authority to a theater that was in desperate need of assistance. The end result was a monopoly of most first-class theater booking for twenty years, followed by similar control in the hands of the Shubert brothers. Belasco was a major producer dependent on the Syndicate until 1902, after which he broke away from it and actually prospered as a result, staging forty-two original productions and revivals up to 1915.

But most playwrights lacked Belasco's position and power, and the Syndicate has been accused of failing to encourage high-quality plays, a charge that has been exaggerated. Nevertheless, like most managements in the history of American theater, the Syndicate (and the Shuberts as well) was composed of businessmen who were in the theater for profit. Despite the production of plays by Herne, Fitch, and Belasco, in addition to classics and recent European plays by such writers as GEORGE BERNARD SHAW, J. M. BARRIE, and even Ibsen, the Syndicate was undeniably commercial in intent and consequently failed to stimulate experimentation and innovation in DRAMATURGY. This state of affairs, among many factors, led to a playwriting and production revolt that parallels the ongoing commercial dominance of Broadway during the teens and up to the end of the period under review.

Other than the position of actor, women's contributions to the American theater during the post–Civil War period and well into the 20th century were marginal, for the theater, like most pursuits outside the home, remained a male-dominated world. Even actresses were frequently considered by society little better than prostitutes. Nevertheless, one of the revolutions against the establishment was in the realm of women playwrights. Since early in the history of American theater there had been isolated examples of female writers in the theater, but only in the late 19th century did a group of women playwrights begin to emerge as part of the redefinition of women's position in society. Before 1915 a number of women playwrights began to have success on the American stage. These writers, though undeniably authors in the popular vein writing for the commercial theater, nevertheless prepared the way for the next, more innovative generation. They included Martha Morton (1865?–1925), the first to break through the Broadway gender barrier in 1891; Lottie Blair Parker (1898?–1937); Lillian Mortimer (c. 1880–1946), also an actor and manager; Rida Johnson Young (1875–1926); and Josephine Preston Peabody (1874–1922), author of the W. V. Moody–inspired poetic and fantasy drama The Piper in 1910, among others.

The most successful female writer in the commercial field was RACHEL CROTHERS, who began writing plays in 1906, continued until 1939, and also directed many of her works. Crothers's woman-centered plays that invariably deal with gender issues are a cut above most of the work of her contemporaries and contain true literary value, albeit aimed at a Broadway audience. As Gary Richardson notes in American Drama from the Colonial Period Through World War I (1993), it was not too surprising that women such as Crothers would begin to enter the male preserve of the theater and focus on gender concerns. He explains the motivations as follows: "The growth of women's educational opportunities after the Civil War, women's major roles in a host of reform projects, the entrance of women into the professional ranks and business, reformation of divorce laws, the persistent agitation for the franchise before 1920—all of these resulted in the redefining of American women and acute concern for their social, economic, and even moral status."

Crothers's plays often focus on the tension that early 20th-century women (the "New Woman") encountered when they pitted new rights and freedoms against old traditional values. Beginning with Three of Us in 1906, she wrote some thirty Broadway-produced plays, most notably A Man's World (1910), He and She (1911), Ourselves (1913), and Let Us Be Gay (1929). A Man's World was one of her most provocative efforts, dealing with the double standard facing women, in this case a successful feminist writer who rejects marriage with a man who insists that men can have a morality different from that of women. A year later Augustus Thomas, with little success, attempted to defend the double standard in a parody titled As a Man Thinks.

One of the most experimental plays of the 1920s was produced, former journalist SOPHIE TREADWELL's MACHINAL, a play that in nine expressionistic scenes depicts a woman victimized and dehumanized by the society around her. Furthermore, two of the most popular and commercially successful plays of the 1920s, a decade of record-setting numbers of Broadway productions and declining numbers of theaters outside New York City, were authored or co-authored by women. The Bat (1920), an old-fashioned mystery drama, was written by Mary Roberts Rinehart (1876–1958), based on her novel The Circular Staircase, and Avery Hopwood (1882–1928), one of the most popular playwrights of the day. At the time it was the second longest-running play in Broadway history (867 performances). Two years later Anne Nichols's ABIE's IRISH ROSE was an enormous success, running for 2,327 performances (closing in 1927), a fourteen-year record. Although the play is a predictable and sentimental telling of the collision of ethnic groups in the United States (the marriage of a Jewish boy and an Irish girl), it made a fortune for Nichols, who was never able to recapture this success.

But the female writer most able to ride the wave of meaningful revolt and to create innovative and unique dramas that placed her at the top of her profession was SUSAN GLASPELL. Her place in the development of American dramaturgy is best understood in the context of a revolt that began in the teens and had as its aim an art theater that could compete with and undercut the commercial dominance of American drama. Ultimately, this extraordinarily significant movement contributed to the emergence of the most important playwright before the Great Depression, Eugene O'Neill, whose life and plays are explored in some detail elsewhere in this encyclopedia.

The first decade of the 20th century, as noted, witnessed a number of efforts to revolt against commercialism, the Syndicate, and old-fashioned and stale dramaturgical formulas and staging techniques and to incorporate practices that had begun abroad and were beginning to infiltrate this country, especially efforts that were clearly artistic in intent. Inspiration for change was aroused in the 1910s by a visit by the Irish Players of the

Abbey Theatre in Dublin (1911); the German director MAX REINHARDT's production of the experimental *Sumurun* (1912), an example of what was being termed the "New Stagecraft" (in part a revolt against pictorial realism); innovative British director HARLEY GRANVILLE-BARKER's residency with the New Stage Society of New York in 1915; and the Paris company of director JACQUES COPEAU, the Vieux-Columbier, in New York (1917), among others. A few commercial producers dared to offer more challenging fare (plays by Shaw, for example), but it was an amateur and purposefully nonprofit revolt that ultimately brought change, or at least produced plays that marked a contrast and a new direction from the usual Broadway offerings.

Despite a few isolated efforts at alternative theaters at the turn of the century—notably the Hull-House Players in Chicago in 1897, persuaded that good plays performed by amateurs could have a salutary effect on the community—it was not until a decade later that the so-called Little Theater movement gained momentum with the catalyst of a symposium published in *Arena* magazine (1904), "A National Art Theatre for America"; a call for "constructive leisure" in PERCY MACKAYE's *The Civic Theatre* (1912); the founding in 1909 of the Drama League (still in existence), dedicated to the importance of theater as a social force through good plays; the establishment of the first university effort to train playwrights by George Pierce Baker in 1905; and the spur over the next decade of innovations and experiments in a few European theaters and foreign visitations. Dozens of small, adventurous amateur theaters cropped up throughout the nation in the 1910s and 1920s.

An additional factor in the changing tone and content of American plays dates from World War I in 1914. Although the United States did not enter the conflict until 1917, the aftereffects of the war had major consequences on the drama. Initially, very much like plays about the Civil War, as Ronald Wainscott illustrates in *The Emergence of the Modern American Theater, 1914–1929* (1997), the majority of war treatments onstage from 1919 to 1924 were "comic, farcical, or heroically melodramatic." American plays only began to explore "tragic, violent, and psychologically scathing material" in any concerted way with the more truthful portrayal of the horrors of war in WHAT PRICE GLORY? by MAXWELL ANDERSON and Laurence Stallings (1894–1968), considered the finest play inspired by World War I and an honest effort to reflect the senselessness of the Great War. From the outset of the war, however, until the Depression, there were at least 112 plays and revues, according to Wainscott, about World War I, and many of these, even before *What Price Glory?*, addressed the effect of the war at home and some of the wounds caused by its aftermath.

As many historians have noted, then, the period of the postwar, pre-Depression theater is unique in American history, for in the 1927–1928 Broadway season 264 different productions were staged, a record number never eclipsed, and, as significantly, the various revolts alluded to earlier led to some of the most exciting experimentation of the 20th century. Many of the most significant innovative developments are associated with two producing groups that emerged as part of the Little Theater movement, both prewar organizations founded in 1915: the Washington Square Players, whose purpose was to improve the level of drama seen in New York (though not necessarily to encourage native writers), which in 1919, after disbanding in 1918, was restructured as the THEATRE GUILD, arguably the most significant producing organization in New York City into the 1940s; and the Provincetown Players, founded on Cape Cod in Massachusetts by a group of eager amateurs led by the Iowan visionary George Cram Cook (1873–1924) with the avowed objective of encouraging new native playwrights. In 1916 a young Eugene O'Neill joined the latter group and that summer contributed his early work *Bound East for Cardiff*; in the fall the operation moved to New York's Greenwich Village, where it survived until the stock-market crash.

Two playwrights emerged as leading writers of the Providence Players, O'Neill and Cook's wife Susan Glaspell. O'Neill, who insisted on ignoring most stage conventions, was encouraged by Cook and others in his experimentation with form and style, ranging from realism and EXPRESSIONISM to costume drama, Strindbergian views of marriage, biblical fables, and even one comedy in 1932, *Ah, Wilderness!* Of the plays produced by the Players, the most noteworthy was THE EMPEROR JONES in 1920. For some critics, the most remarkable aspect of his early plays is their diversity, yet by 1922 he had written four of his most important and mature works: BEYOND THE HORIZON (1920), the previously mentioned *The Emperor Jones*, ANNA CHRISTIE (1921), and THE HAIRY APE (1922). O'Neill also associated with the Theatre Guild beginning in 1928, when his *Marco Millions* was staged, followed the same year by STRANGE INTERLUDE and the trilogy MOURNING BECOMES ELECTRA in 1931 (though the writing of his sprawling and Americanized version of *The Oresteia* began in 1929).

Glaspell's output was more modest than O'Neill's—she contributed eleven plays to the Players—yet she is considered second only to O'Neill in the establishment of an American drama that combined contemporary American ideas with European expressionistic techniques. As noted elsewhere in this encyclopedia, Glaspell never shied away from the new and the immediate, from her still-affecting examination of a woman's inner conflicts in TRIFLES (1916) to the controversial play *The Verge* (1921), her most symbolic and expressionistic drama.

Glaspell and O'Neill were not alone in their experimentation. A few of the poet DJUNA BARNES's AVANT-GARDE plays were also produced by the Provincetown Players, but with little success. ELMER RICE, who first gained attention with a popular drama titled *On Trial* in 1914, was most successful with the expressionistic THE ADDING MACHINE (1923) and its portrayal of a character's subjective perception of reality. Other plays of note in the experimental vein include GEORGE S. KAUFMAN and MARC CONNELLY's BEGGAR ON HORSEBACK (1924); JOHN

HOWARD LAWSON'S PROCESSIONAL (1925), a "JAZZ symphony of American life"; and the previously mentioned Machinal by Treadwell. The Adding Machine, Beggar on Horseback, and Processional were Theatre Guild productions.

Although the commercial Broadway theater in the 1920s largely catered to popular tastes, some notable playwrights emerged, and a few serious, traditional dramas made their impact. Among the writers of note were Kaufman, who began his long, successful career as a comic writer (predominantly in collaboration with others), with frequent barbs at contemporary society. His great success, however, came in the 1930s with collaborators MOSS HART and EDNA FERBER. GEORGE KELLY, also a comic writer, satirized the Little Theater movement in The Torchbearer (1922), followed by his most critically acclaimed play, The Show-Off in 1924. S. N. BEHRMAN (1893–1973) and PHILIP BARRY wrote their earliest fashionable comedies before the Depression, though, like Kaufman, their greatest successes came later, and Charles MacArthur (1895–1966) and fellow journalist Ben Hecht (1894–1964) concocted the most successful farce (with melodramatic overtones) of the day, THE FRONT PAGE (1928).

Finally, the late 1920s witnessed some early serious dramas by Maxwell Anderson (who with Harold Nickerson in 1928 wrote Gods of Lightning, based on the Nicola Sacco and Bartolomeo Vanzetti murder trial) and by ROBERT E. SHERWOOD (The Road to Rome in 1927). Few popular writers had the impact of SIDNEY HOWARD, a pivotal writer in moving American drama from a largely provincial and popular entertainment to a more respected literary reputation in provocative yet often comic plays that tackled subjects such as sex, prohibition, mother love, and psychiatry (based on Freudian ideas of family and sexual relationships). His best play, THEY KNEW WHAT THEY WANTED (1924), which preaches moral and sexual compromise, edged out What Price Glory? and DESIRE UNDER THE ELMS for the 1925 Pulitzer Prize in drama.

By the end of the 1920s the theater was undergoing decline and diminution as the country's major form of entertainment from which it could never recuperate, for in addition to the Great Depression, with its economic and political upheaval, mass forms of amusement had largely eclipsed live performance. From radio's first broadcast in 1920 until the end of the decade, an all-pervading new entertainment industry had evolved. And with the addition of sound to motion pictures in 1927, plays and musicals could be filmed in their entirety and shown to the American public for a modest cost. Significant new drama would be written in the near future, however, and certainly the concept of serious playwriting had been altered irreversibly, but the theater as an institution would remain largely marginal.

FURTHER READING

Bigsby, C. W. E. A Critical Introduction to Twentieth-Century American Drama. Vol. 1, 1900–1940. Cambridge: Cambridge Univ. Press, 1982.

Londré, Felicia Hardison, and Daniel J. Watermeier. The History of North American Theater. New York: Continuum, 1998.

Mason, Jeffrey D. Melodrama and the Myth of America. Bloomington: Indiana Univ. Press, 1993.

Miller, Jordan Y., and Winifred L. Frazer. American Drama Between the Wars: A Critical History. Boston: Twayne, 1991.

Richardson, Gary A. American Drama from the Colonial Period Through World War I: A Critical History. New York: Twayne, 1993.

Wainscott, Ronald H. The Emergence of the Modern American Theater, 1914–1929. New Haven: Yale Univ. Press, 1997.

Wilmeth, Don B., and Christopher Bigsby, eds. The Cambridge History of American Theatre. Vol. 1, Beginnings to 1870; vol. 2, 1870–1945. Cambridge: Cambridge Univ. Press, 1998, 1999.

Wilmeth, Don B., with Tice L. Miller, eds. Cambridge Guide to American Theatre. Updated ed. Cambridge: Cambridge Univ. Press, 1996.

Don B. Wilmeth

1929–1940

Analyses of American drama of the 1930s define the DRAMATURGY in terms of three or four distinct categories: POLITICAL THEATER, most notably that of CLIFFORD ODETS; poetic plays, almost exclusively represented by MAXWELL ANDERSON; the ubiquitous COMEDIES, exemplified by GEORGE S. KAUFMAN with MOSS HART and S. N. BEHRMAN; and, sometimes, musical theater. These labels obfuscate the interconnections and the tensions among the dramas and playwrights across the decade.

The decade can also be viewed in three socioeconomic and dramaturgical segments: the deep Depression years of 1930–1934; the apex of the decade, in terms of both politics (with the coalescence of the New Deal and the Popular Front) and dramatic literature (exemplified by WAITING FOR LEFTY) that occurred mid-decade in 1935; and the later years as World War II approached.

Corresponding with chronological and ideological stratifications are the dramatists' responses to cultural moments and to each other. So, while a combined sense of time and cultural condition is required to examine the plays, these "given circumstances" must remain porous, and the process must remain discursive, allowing the plays to resonate and reverberate off each other. The underlying story of the drama of the 1930s lies not in the surface turmoil or in a plodding progression from season to season, but in the fascinating intertextuality of the plays and their expression of the multifaceted and often conflicted "American spirit"—broken by the earlier stock-market crash, defiant in its confrontation with fascism, and self-reflexive in its examination of its own foibles and myths.

The notion of "American" must be reconsidered as we contemplate racial and ethnic boundaries of the time. Social and dramatic constructs must be wrestled within an attempt to critique "American values" in order to discern whether plays of the decade promulgate a mythologized America. The dramatic literature of the 1930s presents a complexity that defies categorizing simply by genre and interrogates both dramatic and social structure.

Marked by the crash and the depths of economic depression, consideration of communism as a panacea for the nation's hardships, the Popular Front, and the distinct rumblings of a second world war, the 1930s were an era of discontent, a time of confusion. No wonder, then, that the plays and playwrights of the period expressed both a social and a dramaturgical ambivalence.

In the cases of ROBERT SHERWOOD and ELMER RICE, the playwright's corpus clearly illustrates his changing sociopolitical attitudes and alliances. Sherwood moved from the symbolic REALISM of THE PETRIFIED FOREST to a pacifist political satire in IDIOT'S DELIGHT (1936) to the patriotic reflection of Franklin Delano Roosevelt in ABE LINCOLN IN ILLINOIS (1938). In the 1930s Rice, best remembered for the expressionism of THE ADDING MACHINE, switched genres to the realism of *We, the People* (1933), then to the nonrealistic manipulation of time and insertion of the folk hero in *American Landscape* (1939). Subtler dramaturgical variances are evidenced in other playwrights across the decade.

Although criticism of the dramatic literature of the 1930s typically uses a binary approach, considering the "political" versus the "nonpolitical," a close reading reveals two curious patterns: (1) that no play is exclusively political or nonpolitical, and (2) that, despite the plays' subject matter, age-old dramatic structures are continually co-opted or subverted by authors across the decade.

PANACHE: COMEDIES AND THE MUSICAL

Political discourse is apparent even in the seemingly light comedies, such as Kaufman and Hart's YOU CAN'T TAKE IT WITH YOU (1936), in which the character of Grandpa recalls the American "values" of ingenuity and wit, and *The Man Who Came to Dinner* (1938), in which the seemingly misanthropic Sheridan Whiteside has a soft spot in his heart for the sentimentality of the yuletide season. Political discourse is evident in the satirical musicals *Of Thee I Sing* (Kaufman, Morrie Ryskind, and Ira Gershwin, 1931), *Let 'Em Eat Cake* (1933), and I'D RATHER BE RIGHT! (Kaufman and Hart, 1937), which deftly lampoons the American government, but safely and at a time of adulation for Franklin Roosevelt. In a serious vein, DINNER AT EIGHT (Kaufman and EDNA FERBER, 1932) moves from the drawing room to despondency, and STAGE DOOR (Kaufman with Ferber, 1936) contrasts the malaise of the upper class with the dilemma of the poverty-stricken, unemployed Depression-era actor, including in the rank-and-file cast a character based on playwright Clifford Odets. S. N. Behrman covers his political discussions with a drawing-room veneer, rejecting pure propaganda as too obvious a vehicle, toying with traditional dramatic structure, and focusing on a subtle form of liberalism. His treatment results in dramas peopled by confused characters, at odds with their own ideologies.

The plays of the comic writers retain at their cores the structural traditions and character archetypes of comedy through the ages—the Aristophanic "happy idea," replete with agon, rising complications, and resolution in celebration; the Plautian characters of the juvenile and ingenue, paterfamilias, crotchety old man, and so on. The plays call into question the nature and purpose of comedy as well. The comic process operates via two strategies: "othering" or identifying. We laugh, on the one hand, because we can observe characters' behaviors from a distance and safely react, and/or we laugh because we can warmly respond, "Just like me." In American comedy of the 1930s both strategies may be present in the same play, reflecting the ambivalence of the time.

Kaufman provides us with kooky characters whose foibles we view from afar and with lovers in the commedia tradition. He throws into the mix all the characteristic elements of comedy that guarantee laughter—the slapstick, physical antics of FARCE, the verbal repartee of comedy of manners, the foolproof "rule of three," confusion and/or mistaken identities, and a fast pace matched by few. Kaufman's use of these machinations allows him to tinker with his themes, anarchy in *You Can't Take It with You*, critiquing American traditions such as "Mom's apple pie" in *Of Thee I Sing*, or questioning the wisdom of the Supreme Court and the efficacy of the FEDERAL THEATRE PROJECT in *I'd Rather Be Right*. For Kaufman, and for comedy of the 1930s in America, the medium may not, in fact, have been the message. Kaufman's comedies are marked with the ambivalent mood of the 1930s; they leave us wondering if his chiding of society was meant to incite change, to point out the fallacies of American myths, or to (re)instill in his audiences those romantic notions of Americana that keep us going when the going gets tough.

Although Kaufman remains the quintessential writer of American comedy of the 1930s (and beyond), Behrman used the same mechanisms of comedy to somewhat different ends. His pieces often end, not with the celebration so prized by theorist Francis Cornford, but in a surprise separation or dissolution. In this manner Behrman subverts the comic structure to reinscribe the ambiguity of the times. American comedy, in the 1930s, then, was serious (and often politicized) business.

POLITICS AND THE HOLY GRAIL

Seemingly purely political dramas of the 1930s use the set speeches of Marxist dogma, protagonists who are martyred, and requisite "call-to-action" endings; but, surprisingly, they reify distinctly American "values" of home and family. Clifford Odets's *Waiting for Lefty* endures, not because of its topicality or its political platform, but because of the manner in which the effect of the Depression is humanized, the way the play expresses the ramifications of economic deprivation on a specific family, on individuals who people the piece's vignettes. The same can be said of Odets's other more realistic works: AWAKE AND SING! (1935), *Paradise Lost* (1935), and GOLDEN BOY (1937). Odets finds his faith in the future of American youth, and he expresses promise in a fresh brand of (Jewish) American poetic dialogue. Unlike the more polemic playwrights of the era, Odets peopled his plays with characters whose underlying traits ring true—three-dimensional characters who, at the same time, proffer a poetic vision of a better world to come. Biblical allusion, extended metaphor, imagery, symbolism, and leitmotiv, the likes of which were not to be seen again until TENNESSEE WILLIAMS and ARTHUR MILLER, characterize the work of Odets. Structurally, like many playwrights of the era, Odets uses the underlying framework of MELODRAMA and the coincidences of the well-made play. Unlike some of his compatriots (such as Elmer Rice in We, the People), Odets hides the underpinnings of his plays beneath the surface of the action. Ultimately, Odets's canon is more accurately characterized as "social" rather than "political," for he explores socioeconomic issues in a more universal way than the purely political pieces of the time. Odets's plays remain vital some three-quarters of a century after their writing. Despite his membership in the Communist Party and his inclusion of rather "Red" characters and dialogue (such as the grandfather's reading material in Awake and Sing!), Odets crafted plays that transcend the topical, plays that foreshadowed Miller's social dramas.

The polemic playwrights of the 1930s whose works have not become canonized failed for the very reasons that Odets succeeded. Their dialogue is too strident or too topical to survive the test of time; the structural elements of their scripts are too obvious; and/or they fail to humanize the struggles of Depression-era Americans. The most egregious example is playwright JOHN HOWARD LAWSON, whose confused dramatic forms reflect his personal political dilemma. As he embraced communism and moved toward "Hollywood Ten" fame, Lawson lost the ability to create multifaceted characters and to sustain a believable plotline. Lawson never mastered the seamless meshing of medium and message. In both Success Story and Gentlewoman his characters became mouthpieces for his murky theorizing, and his dialogue cataloged the buzzwords of Marxist doctrine of the day. To a lesser degree SIDNEY KINGSLEY's melodramatic MEN IN WHITE (1934) falls prey to the same pitfalls. Plays by other playwrights in this vein, but more vituperative, are John Wexley's Steel (1931, revived 1937), Paul Peters and George Sklar's Stevedore (1934), Albert Bein's Let Freedom Ring (1935), and Albert Maltz's Black Pit (1935).

The socioeconomic conditions of the 1930s were ripe for docudramas. Although their relevance to a contemporary audience waned over time, these plays provide literary grist for the cultural materialist or New Historicist's mill. Included in this category are pieces on the Scottsboro case—Wexley's They Shall Not Die (1934) and Denis Donoghue's melodrama Legal Murder (1934). LANGSTON HUGHES's version of the story employs the workers' theater techniques of AGITATION-PROPAGANDA drama, and the German-speaking Prolet-Bühne staged a mass recitation version. Numerous plays emerged to depict the confrontation of workers with "management." Michael Denning's study The Cultural Front outlines the relationship between the Congress of Industrial Organizations (CIO) and the arts in the 1930s. Colette Hyman's Staging Strikes references numerous performances of "strike plays" about textile workers, dockworkers, coal miners, and workers in the automobile industry by the aforementioned playwrights and others. These plays, however, failed to capture the attention of future producers and playgoers. The holy grail of political playwriting of the 1930s, then, was the poetic depiction of "real-life" drama with a salient message.

An examination of American drama of the 1930s is incomplete without the works of LILLIAN HELLMAN. Like many of the literati of her day, the playwright became politicized as the Depression worsened and as war neared. Her most stridently polemical piece is Days to Come (1936), and it is her least successful play. In it Hellman mimics Waiting for Lefty, but she fails to pull in the reins on subplots and forces a dramatic structure that is out of keeping with her more engaging interpretations of the well-made play exhibited by THE CHILDREN'S HOUR (1934) and THE LITTLE FOXES (1939). Nonetheless, Hellman's plays of the 1930s respond to the socioeconomic milieu of the time. In The Little Foxes we see the ill effects of family members at odds with one another as they seek monetary gain and its attendant power. The basic tenets of capitalism are implicitly criticized in this piece set against the 1930s dilemma of the textile industry, as they are later in Watch on the Rhine (1941). The Children's Hour attained its notoriety for different reasons—still a staple among community and university theaters, the play was a courageous exploration of an alternative lifestyle, cast in a well-made-play format with some of the trappings of melodrama. Although Hellman's political activity per se seems to have transpired more offstage than on, her social dramas of the 1930s reflected the cultural moment.

Maxwell Anderson's work is an anomaly in the 1930s and constitutes the only commercially successful foray of American drama into the realm of poetic form. He stands alone as the successful writer of verse dramas in America. Anderson is woefully misunderstood and displaced in terms of the dramaturgy of the decade. His work is most often considered precious in the midst of a highly political time. In fact, Anderson's unwavering belief in the efficacy of verse drama was deliberately set within the socioeconomic constructs of his time, and the playwright is hardly without political presence.

ELIZABETH THE QUEEN (1930) and Mary of Scotland (1933) have been subsequently produced for their pageantry, and their pertinence to the social and political moments from which they sprang has been by and large forgotten. In truth, Anderson habitually critiqued the economic and political forces of his day by means of historicizing and poeticizing, allowing his audience the luxury of playing one cultural "text" against another. He used the myths of British history (and revolutionary America in *Valley Forge*, 1934) to promote images of strength and power. Sadly, Anderson so labored under the weight of his vast knowledge of history and literature that his efforts to draw contemporary parallels often became obscured. In *Drama and Commitment* Gerald Rabkin asserts that by the end of the 1930s Anderson deployed "history as prophecy" over "myth as history" (Rabkin, 1964). WINTERSET (1935), in its poetic interpretation of the Nicola Sacco-Bartolomeo Vanzetti case, is a unique blend of political docudrama and verse. It is, then, ironic that Anderson was awarded the Pulitzer Prize in 1933 for *Both Your Houses*, his political prose piece, because his reputation stands more squarely on his poetic dramas.

THE AMERICAN MYTH

One American myth that (re)surfaces in drama of the 1930s is that of the rugged individual, the "straight shooter," the independent thinker. Another is the concept of "American family values" that appears implicitly in plays across the decade. Nowhere, however, is America more clearly romanticized and mythologized than in three enduring plays from the decade's end—THORNTON WILDER's OUR TOWN (1939), Jack Kirkland's *Tobacco Road* (which ran at various New York theaters and toured from 1933 to 1941), and WILLIAM SAROYAN's THE TIME OF YOUR LIFE (1939). Each of these plays was reevaluated at the end of the 20th century with regard to the inherent racism and bigotry of the 1930s it depicts.

Our Town is deceptively simple in construct and theme. Noted for its minimalist stage conventions and its romanticized depiction of life in a small New England town, the piece problematizes American "values" of its day, presenting the human instinct to rush through everyday tasks without thinking, and pointing up the segregation and ethnic biases inherent in small-town life. At the end of the decade, when war loomed across the Atlantic, with an almost Buddhist philosophy, Wilder admonished his audience to "realize life while they live it." It may be argued that the play is the embodiment of pacifism.

Kirkland's *Tobacco Road* was touted as "DOCUMENTARY" in its time, a naturalistic depiction of the poverty inherent in the South during the Depression. As in the case of *Our Town*, there is more to the play than meets the eye. The piece immortalizes the stereotypical "Georgia cracker" and thus in a perverse manner romanticizes the notion of Southern poverty. Through the use of grotesque comedy the play simultaneously promotes racial profiling and economic marginalizing. *Tobacco Road*, throughout the 1930s, allowed its mainstream audience (by no means representative of characters the play depicts) an opportunity to assuage its guilt by paying homage to the deprivation of others.

Saroyan's *The Time of Your Life* appropriately concludes the decade and an assessment of its dramatic literature, for the play depicted the dreams and aspirations of its characters, thus idealizing America as well. In a Chekovian style that combines tragic and comic elements and examines the relationship between life and work, Saroyan upholds and questions American values. The play's action revolves around Joe, the inhabitant of a honky-tonk bar in San Francisco, who is independently wealthy but amassed his fortune at the expense of others. A crucial set speech on the American work ethic is presented by an itinerant pinball player who hopes to strike it rich; a prostitute acts out her fantasy of achieving the "American dream" of marriage to a doctor; and a Kit Carson figure arrives, inserting the mythology of the Wild West into Saroyan's already somewhat bizarre fictive world. Despite its seemingly incongruous characterizations, *The Time of Your Life* achieves a power and a poetry that epitomize America of the 1930s. Saroyan calls into question national beliefs in capitalism and the results of hard work in the wake of economic depression; yet he undercuts tragedy and sentimentality with humor in the face of fascism and the potential of a world war. (Interestingly, Saroyan refused to claim his Pulitzer Prize for the play, believing that the prize system constituted a reflection of the capitalism he opposed.)

American drama of the 1930s, then, presents a depth and a variety with which it is seldom fully credited. Playwrights grappled with the difficult issues of politics, poverty, and the potential of war that prevailed across the decade, and they did so with remarkable variety and nuance in terms of dramatic form.

FURTHER READING

Bigsby, C. W. E. *A Critical Introduction to Twentieth-Century American Drama.* Vol. 1, 1900–1940. Cambridge: Cambridge Univ. Press, 1982.

Denning, Michael. *The Cultural Front.* New York: Verso, 1998.

Fearnow, Mark. *The American Stage and the Great Depression.* New York: Cambridge Univ. Press, 1997.

Hyman, Colette. *Staging Strikes: Workers' Theatre and the American Labor Movement.* Philadelphia: Temple Univ. Press, 1997.

Mason, Jeffrey D. *Wisecracks: The Farces of George S. Kaufman.* Ann Arbor: UMI Res. Press, 1988.

Miller, Jordan Y., and Winifred L. Frazer. *American Drama Between the Wars: A Critical History.* Boston: Twayne, 1991.

Rabkin, Gerald. *Drama and Commitment: Politics in the American Theatre of the Thirties.* Bloomington: Indiana Univ. Press, 1964.

Smiley, Sam. *The Drama of Attack: Didactic Plays of the American Depression.* Columbia: Univ. of Missouri Press, 1972.

Anne Fletcher

1940–PRESENT

Drama in the United States has always occupied a position quite different from that of its sister forms in Europe, primarily because an understanding of drama as a central cultural resource has always been in conflict with the American sense of theater as primarily a commercial enterprise: a business proposition whose most important objective is to fill the seats of an auditorium. A contrasting sense of American drama as art was first fully articulated by the Little Theater movement in the 1920s, and from that point on, the conflict between drama-as-business and drama-as-art characterized American theater of the 20th century. In the decades from 1940 to the turn of the century the reciprocal influences of these two visions of American drama linked mainstream Broadway theater to OFF-BROADWAY, regional theater, off-off-Broadway, and, in an even more complex relationship, film and television.

For most of the 20th century Broadway was the nexus of American drama, the place where drama, live performance, and commerce achieved their most spectacular combinations. By 1940 Broadway had not only survived the Depression, but had witnessed the rise and fall of the most extensive art-theater venture in American history, the FEDERAL THEATRE PROJECT (FTP). The FTP demonstrated the possibilities of a countrywide, noncommercial, socially conscious, government-subsidized national theater. The shock of this suspiciously European-style venture and its apparently leftist politics led to its demise at the hands of the U.S. Congress, but its example of the power and accessibility of decentralized, noncommercial, experimental, and popular drama had established itself within the conscience and memory of American theater makers.

Mainstream American theater in 1940—by definition, Broadway theater—maintained its original connections to musical theater, spectacle, and COMEDY, but the legacy of EUGENE O'NEILL, ELMER RICE, and other playwrights whose works had migrated uptown from Greenwich Village was that enticing possibility of the serious American drama with commercial potential. Mirroring the developments of European drama from the first half of the century, serious American dramas were gingerly and tentatively stepping away from the reassuring dynamics of well-made play and MELODRAMA, although examples of those forms continued to be popular on American stages for the rest of the century.

By 1940 the dream of a legitimate American drama had been in part realized, and it included not only dramas of American character by O'Neill, but also expressly political plays by Rice and CLIFFORD ODETS. Moreover, an emerging tradition of American drama had been nurtured by collectives such as the THEATRE GUILD, Orson Welles's Mercury Theatre, Eva Le Gallienne's Civic Repertory Theatre, and the GROUP THEATRE. These earlier outgrowths of the Little Theater movement believed not only in supporting new American dramas, but also in new ways of ACTING in and designing for them.

One might argue that American drama in 1940 was in fact beginning a period of decline, because in sheer volume of work, the apex had already been reached in 1928, when over 260 new productions opened on Broadway. Because of increasing costs and competition from other media, Broadway saw its volume of productions gradually diminish over the next six decades to the point that in the 2003–2004 season only thirty-eight productions opened there, only eighteen of which were comedies or dramas. On the other hand, 1940 could also be considered the dawning of classic 20th-century American drama, because in the midst of an earthshaking war and attendant changes in the way the modern world would think and communicate, U.S. playwrights were about to articulate their ideas in characters and voices that would catch the moment in all its complexity.

American drama during World War II included a familiar mixture of comic and serious plays set among classic revivals, musicals, and revues. As one might expect, there was an emphasis on spirit-lifting entertainment, from Broadway revivals of *Twelfth Night* (1941), THREE SISTERS (1942), or *The Rivals* (1942) to mirth-inducing vaudeville-style revues such as *Keep 'Em Laughing* (1941). Although serious American drama of the Depression era had often included a social and political critique of American society, such perspectives were less welcome during the war years. ROBERT SHERWOOD's last play, *The Rugged Path* (1945), was a critique of war profiteers and deceitful journalists that failed at the box office; however, in the patriotic *Watch on the Rhine* (1941) LILLIAN HELLMAN turned her sense of American character and her ear for American voices to the conflict between democracy and fascism, here played out among rich Americans and European émigrés in Washington, D.C.

Other wartime dramas, such as PAUL OSBORN's *A Bell for Adano* (1944), made realistic drama about the American experience overseas, in this case the efforts of a noble American colonel to bring democracy to occupied Sicily. SIDNEY KINGSLEY's *The Patriots* (1943) was a costume drama about the American Revolution in which Thomas Jefferson pertinently declared, "I believe, indeed, I know this government is the world's best hope." Meanwhile, on the comic side, S. N. BEHRMAN's *Jacobowsky and the Colonel* (1944) managed to find character humor in the invasion of France, and JOHN VAN DRUTEN created a vastly popular romantic comedy about a soldier on leave in THE VOICE OF THE TURTLE (1941).

The era of the early 1940s was still influenced by an earlier genre of "Negro plays" written by white authors. Brooks Atkinson articulated some characteristics of the form in his *New York Times* review (October 26, 1940) of Lynn Root's "Negro fantasy" *Cabin in the Sky* (1940), writing optimistically (and without irony) that "Negroes can act with abandon and with infectious enjoyment when the occasion is right." The same wartime era also saw vaudeville icon Eddie Cantor in blackface makeup as a happy-go-lucky African American in *Banjo Eyes* (1941), a vestigial remnant of minstrel-show aesthetics. A more complex sense of African American drama was marked by a 1943 production of *Othello* starring Paul Robeson and by an all-black *Carmen Jones* that same year—Oscar Hammerstein II's revision of Georges Bizet's opera, modernized and shifted to a contemporary wartime setting in the Deep South.

The reassuring pleasure that *Cabin in the Sky* promised its Broadway audiences was a strong contrast to the discomfort delivered by a surprisingly strong array of dramas by African American writers who persisted in critiquing American society even while the war was on. Theodore Ward's 1940 *Big White Fog* was a slice of Harlem REALISM that Brooks Atkinson dismissed as a "communist" play; and the PAUL GREEN–Richard Wright collaboration *Native Son* (1941) presented veteran African American actor Canada Lee as fatally doomed Chicago chauffeur Bigger Thomas. Both dramas used realistic, violent, and ultimately tragic drama to bluntly criticize racism. However, despite their focus on social inequities, the fact of their appearance onstage (*Native Son* on Broadway, *Big White Fog* in Harlem) also represents the self-conscious sense of democratic possibility and openness that characterized American drama in the war years as a whole.

The slender persistence of experimental techniques in wartime drama was represented in these years by THORNTON WILDER, whose THE SKIN OF OUR TEETH (1942) was an epic history of mankind, seen as an archetypal middle-class New Jersey family. Wilder, in effect, echoed Kingsley's "world's best hope" sentiment of *The Patriots* by means of gentle, comic, and fantastic nonrealism, quite different from the confrontational radicalism that would characterize the AVANT-GARDE in the years to come.

Meanwhile, the sense of drama as an artistic entity with political resonance, which the Group Theatre had pioneered in the 1930s, lived on in the Dramatic Workshop, an institution created in 1939 at the New School for Social Research by expatriate director ERWIN PISCATOR. Piscator brought together such luminaries of the Group Theatre as Stella Adler and Lee Strasberg, but also historians John Gassner and Barrett Clark, critic Oliver Sayler, and designer Mordecai Gorelik. Piscator's students included Marlon Brando, TENNESSEE WILLIAMS, Judith Malina, Abram Hill, Miriam Colón (founder of the Puerto Rican Traveling Theatre), Vinnette Carroll, and Tony Randall, all of whom would have lasting effects on American drama as culturally essential art. Among other things, the Dramatic Workshop propelled Williams to produce his early play *Battle of Angels* with the Theatre Guild in 1940, but it also inspired playwright Abram Hill (who had been a script reader with the Federal Theatre Project) to found the American Negro Theatre (ANT) in 1940. For ANT, Hill adapted Philip Yordan's story of Polish immigrants, *Anna Lucasta*, as an African American social drama that opened in Harlem in 1944, but moved to Broadway for a successful run the same year.

The ever-more-popular medium of film represented a challenge and conundrum for American drama in the 1940s because movies expertly presented drama in all its popular forms: melodrama, well-made play, musical. In effect, the techniques of drama as text-based, dialogue-centered storytelling were realized far more successfully and economically in the film medium than they could be in live performance. In the 1940s Hollywood continued to lure writers and actors away from live theater to the more lucrative practice of writing and performing dramas for film. But perhaps more important, film and radio drama now clearly reached more Americans than live theater, which would never again function as a central forum of American performance. If the major issues, stories, characters, and sentiments of American life were now articulated to most of the country's citizens through electronic media, what role could live drama play? The end of the war in 1945 brought this question—an identity crisis of American drama—to the fore.

Although the role of theater in postwar American culture may have been far less consequential than that of electronic media—which now featured the colossus of television—the Cold War years of American drama in fact mark its golden age, a moment when the promise of American drama as both artistic and commercial success (suggested decades earlier by O'Neill and Odets) was fully achieved by Tennessee Williams, ARTHUR MILLER, and WILLIAM INGE. And this success was not achieved simply by updating the format of well-made drama to reflect postwar American life, but by incorporating new approaches to playwriting and play production. In 1955 Brooks Atkinson pointed out that the successful mainstream dramas of the postwar era "would have been regarded as 'experimental' a quarter of a century ago." Most of them, he added, "have broken with the old formula of the 'well-made play' in the interest of freer, more poetic, more subjective forms" (*New Voices*).

This was certainly true of Williams's 1945 Broadway hit THE GLASS MENAGERIE, which combined a modern American sensibility and precisely wrought "American" characters and voices with a HENRIK IBSEN–like sense of realistic melodrama, laced with all sorts of "EPIC" techniques that Williams had learned through Piscator. It is interesting to note that critic Lewis Nichols, writing in the *New York Times* (April 2, 1945), saw *The Glass Menagerie* as a particularly well-done actors' play, but bridled specifically at the kinds of dramaturgical innovations that made the play something quite different from straight prewar drama: "Mr. Williams' play is not all of the same caliber. A strict perfectionist could easily find a good many flaws. There are some unconnected odds and ends which have little to do with the story: Snatches of talk about the war, bits of psychology, occasional moments of rather flowery writing." In other words, for Nichols, the very things that made Williams's playwriting innovative—the narrator Tom's direct address to the audience, the way he contextualizes the story of his sister and mother as an aspect of Depression-era life in America, his articulation of the story as a nonrealistic "memory play"—all these "epic" elements marked Williams's drama as flawed, imperfect. Yet Williams's combination of exquisitely limned American characters, together with his penchant for nonrealistic storytelling techniques and his critique of American hostility to empathy and emotion, was a harbinger of American drama to come.

Williams, Miller, and Inge were the postwar triumvirate of American family drama, creating profoundly contemporary American characters whose faults and frustrations resonated with a society that was emerging from postwar euphoria into the years of Cold War anxiety and doubt. Their commercial success marked another successful wedding of experimental DRAMATURGY with mainstream popularity—in other words, dramatic techniques that had once been the domain of downtown theater were now accepted on Broadway. Miller, particularly in DEATH OF A SALESMAN, his 1949 Broadway hit and Pulitzer Prize winner, stretched the limits of stage realism by presenting Willy Loman's memories not simply as retrospective monologues, but as fully present, acted-out dreams. Inge's family dramas were more solidly centered on stage realism than Williams's or Miller's, but were marked by an overriding melancholia and a plot structure that eschewed the kind of "strict perfection" evoked by Lewis Nichols for composite stories that evoked character and emotion much more than a relentless march toward climax and resolution. In other words, Inge's plays avoided the kinds of well-made dramatic structure that were, for example, a hallmark of Hollywood movies. However, the epitome of postwar American family drama as classic realism was actually achieved by LORRAINE HANSBERRY, whose A RAISIN IN THE SUN (1959) presented the story of striving, middle-class Americans as the essence of African American life. Although Hansberry eschewed the nonrealistic experiments that characterized Miller's and Williams's work, her play was in a way much more radical because it presented its African Americans as complex human beings confronting the same kinds of challenges white Americans faced, although with the added encumbrance of racism. ALICE CHILDRESS also wrote realistic dramas about the African American experience beginning in the 1940s, but such plays as *Florence* (1949) were less sentimental than *A Raisin in the Sun*, and consequently less salable on Broadway.

Carson McCullers took an oblique approach to American family drama with *The Member of the Wedding* (1950), which, perhaps even more than Inge's work, focused on the articulation of character and emotion rather than traditional dramatic structure. The *New York Times* complained that the play "has no beginning, middle or end and never acquires dramatic momentum" (Brooks Atkinson, January 6, 1950), but what it did do was present black and white characters of the American South as complex outsiders. JANE BOWLES's equally innovative play IN THE SUMMER HOUSE (1954) depicted the conflicted and repressed feelings of three mother-daughter pairs. Its unusual primary focus on women, as well as its avoidance of a well-made plot, led to its middling success. Although Bowles and McCullers were out of step with mainstream Broadway drama, in retrospect their concerns can be seen as prescient.

"Strict perfectionist" playwriting of the postwar years was represented by scores of plays whose authors are, for the most part, much less known than Williams, Miller, and Inge. A particular success in straight-ahead postwar drama was GARSON KANIN, who returned from his service in the war to write and direct *Born Yesterday* (1946), a comedy about Washington politics and class and a Broadway showgirl turned, Pygmalion-like, into a socially conscious Washington sophisticate. Thomas Heggen and Joshua Logan's *Mister Roberts* (1948) was a straightforward drama looking back on the war with strong, mixed sentiments. Articulating what would become an increasingly popular postwar

theme, it told a seriocomic story of a crew of sailors—normal, everyday Americans—attempting to survive the injustices of an irrational captain. Herman Wouk's *The Caine Mutiny Court Martial* (1954) reprised the captain-crew conflict of *Mister Roberts* as melodrama. Robert Anderson's *Tea and Sympathy* (1953) also offered a traditionally structured drama about resistance to unreasonable authority, this time in a mildly scandalous but romantic story about a prep-school boy accused of homosexuality. Anderson's drama, like Arthur Miller's Puritan-era political drama THE CRUCIBLE of the same year, was a reflection of McCarthy-era anxieties. On the other hand, in 1959 William Gibson could write *The Miracle Worker*, a wildly popular historical drama about Helen Keller and the possibilities of learning.

Traditionally structured dramas had their more humorous counterpart in romantic comedies by such playwrights as JOHN PATRICK (*Teahouse of the August Moon*, 1953) and N. Richard Nash (*The Rainmaker*, 1954), whose works also reflected postwar situations. Patrick's tale of the foibles of American soldiers in occupied JAPAN and Nash's western about a confidence man and a would-be spinster represented a genre of postwar drama dedicated above all to audience entertainment. It is a telling marker of postwar American drama that such traditional plays that were commercially successful on Broadway were even bigger hits as Hollywood movies. Moreover, by 1948 over 1 million American homes had television sets, and that medium was on the way to supplanting not only live theater but also film as the major source of drama for American audiences. In the coming decade some of America's great dramatists (such as Rod Serling and Paddy Chayefsky) would write not for the live stage but for the cathode-ray tube, while others, including HORTON FOOTE and JEROME LAWRENCE, divided their efforts equally between Broadway and Hollywood.

Mainstream theater's appetite for lyrical whimsy, which Thornton Wilder had satisfied before the war with *The Skin of Our Teeth*, was now fed by such plays as ARCHIBALD MACLEISH's singular Broadway success, *J.B.* (1958), a modernized retelling of the tribulations of Job, here transformed into a successful businessman who never renounces God. MacLeish's play followed the more serious vein of T. S. ELIOT's *The Cocktail Party* (1950), which attempted to reintroduce verse drama as a modern form in a quasi-mystical story of contemporary English socialites who, mixed up by the competitive claims of religion and psychiatry, mull their spiritual destinies. These quirky Broadway successes were neither musicals nor straight dramas and, like the works of McCullers and Bowles, represented a certain experimentation with dramatic forms, but on the other hand, they were not entirely representative of the mainstream of alternative American drama. That development was, instead, taking form in a new arena for American theater: off-Broadway.

The rise of off-Broadway theater as the new center of serious American drama coincided with a general decline in the volume and artistic content of Broadway theater. Increased production costs and admission prices, as well as competition from television, led to sharp decreases in the number of Broadway productions. According to Brooks Atkinson (1970), postwar Broadway theater was "beginning to lose the confidence and drive it had before World War II," and even its most successful playwrights—Williams, Miller, and Inge—began to have trouble getting their works produced on Broadway. Some critics saw a falling off in the quality of the playwrights' work, but also the economics of Broadway had led it to become less adventurous about producing new drama, especially plays that experimented with new techniques and subjects. In any event, beginning in the 1950s, serious American drama, especially in its nonrealistic or avant-garde forms, began to appear more frequently off-Broadway than on Broadway. An example of the challenges facing innovative mainstream drama was the Experimental Theatre, founded in the late 1940s. It produced a brief Broadway run of BERTOLT BRECHT's THE LIFE OF GALILEO in 1947, with Charles Laughton in the title role, but this premiere production by one of the greatest playwrights of the century failed to attract an audience, and the Experimental Theatre itself ceased operations the following year.

The emergence of off-Broadway provided a viable (if less lucrative and popular) alternative for new American drama. Off-Broadway theater can be said to have truly begun in 1951 when a group of actors and directors founded the Circle in the Square theater in New York City's Greenwich Village. Circle in the Square helped define the nature of off-Broadway drama by producing a combination of adventurous new works and neglected classics. Its 1952 production of Williams's SUMMER AND SMOKE announced off-Broadway as a site of serious new drama, and its revival of O'Neill's THE ICEMAN COMETH (1956) initiated a rediscovery of that playwright as an American treasure.

The changing nature of 1950s drama was most apparent in Theater of the Absurd, a genre of mostly European playwriting influenced by JEAN-PAUL SARTRE's existentialist PHILOSOPHY and the sobering failures of modern society marked by the recently finished world war. ABSURDISM's signature drama, SAMUEL BECKETT's WAITING FOR GODOT, was in fact a 1956 Broadway success, although it seemed to have puzzled and challenged audiences more than it satisfied and amused. Atkinson's New York Times review (April 20, 1956) said that it told "melancholy truths about the hopeless destiny of the human race": hardly the function of typical Broadway fare. Indicating the shift of serious drama away from Broadway, Beckett's ENDGAME played off-Broadway at the Cherry Lane Theatre in 1958. Two years later Beckett's KRAPP'S LAST TAPE appeared (at the venerable Provincetown Playhouse in Greenwich Village), part of a double bill with THE ZOO STORY, a play by the United States' own emerging absurdist dramatist, EDWARD ALBEE, who set a tone of American existentialist shock and futility that would characterize much 1960s theater to come, including such off-Broadway plays as JACK RICHARDSON's Gallows Humor (1961).

The noncommercial, art-theater approach that characterized off-Broadway drama of the 1950s, and then off-off-Broadway theater of the 1960s, was articulated as a postwar phenomenon by the LIVING THEATRE, which Judith Malina began with Julian Beck in 1947 shortly after she graduated from Erwin Piscator's Dramatic Workshop in New York. Its initial performances, often in living rooms and lofts instead of theaters, were of plays by the mainstream European avant-garde: Brecht, GERTRUDE STEIN, FEDERICO GARCÍA LORCA, ALFRED JARRY, JEAN COCTEAU, and LUIGI PIRANDELLO. But it also performed plays by American poets (Kenneth Rexroth, Paul Goodman, Jackson MacLow) and then groundbreaking dramas by JACK GELBER (The Connection, 1959) and Kenneth Brown (The Brig, 1963).

The postwar shift of serious drama to off-Broadway happened in tandem with a concurrent development across the United States: regional theater. The advent of film had initiated a decline in the system of nationwide tours beyond Broadway, and consequently a dearth of live theater across the country. The regional theater movement, as Joseph Zeigler put it in Regional Theatre: The Revolutionary Stage (1973), was an effort to create a community-based, noncommercial drama as an alternative to "the commercial values" of Broadway: "a new world dedicated to the establishment of new theatrical values—permanence, the ensemble company of actors, classics on the stage, and art as a goal." Beginning in 1947 with Margo Jones's Theatre '47 in Dallas, the regional theater movement expanded across the United States throughout the 1950s and 1960s, including the Alley Theatre in Houston (1947), the Arena Stage in Washington (1950), the Actor's Workshop in San Francisco (1952), the Guthrie Theater in Minneapolis (1963), the Long Wharf Theatre in New Haven (1965), and the Mark Taper Forum in Los Angeles (1967). Although they began as alternatives to Broadway, the regional theaters actually continued the art-theater/commercial-theater symbiosis that had begun in the 1920s by developing plays that could end up on Broadway itself. In Theatre '47's first season, for example, Margo Jones directed Inge's The Dark at the Top of the Stairs and Williams's Summer and Smoke. In 1955 Jones produced Jerome Lawrence and Robert E. Lee's Inherit the Wind (a realistic historical drama about the John Scopes "monkey trial") in Dallas before the play moved on to Broadway and then film. In the mid-1960s at the Arena Stage director Zelda Fichandler developed Howard Sackler's The Great White Hope, a drama about the African American boxer Jack Johnson, into a Pulitzer Prize–winning Broadway success of 1968.

By the 1960s the Broadway-based system of proscenium theaters, realistic plays, and life-affirming musicals had become almost ancillary to the creation of new American drama. A successful Broadway dramatist such as NEIL SIMON (who also wrote for film and television) was almost a remnant of the earlier postwar era, whose ethos was evoked by his Manhattan-based comedies such as Come Blow Your Horn (1961), Barefoot in the Park (1963), or THE ODD COUPLE (1965). Production costs and ticket prices were steadily rising, television and film provided more popular entertainment, and American playwrights seemed uninterested in or unable to write mainstream dramas that could draw large, consistent audiences. Broadway's successes seemed to be limited to European imports, revivals, and the occasional sprightly musical, although innovative and often unsettling work did reach its way up from off-Broadway, off-off-Broadway, and regional theaters.

A model of the new American dramatist was Edward Albee. Despite his connections to Theater of the Absurd, Albee was unapologetically his own playwright, and a clearly American one at that. Nurtured in an off-Broadway world that welcomed the quirky and unusual, his often misanthropic plays refused to follow a formula for commercial success, and if one of his plays—such as WHO'S AFRAID OF VIRGINIA WOOLF? (1962)—did become a hit on Broadway, it was as much for its scandal as for its deft portrayal of American character and story. *Who's Afraid of Virginia Woolf?* appeared to follow the contours of the American family drama and could be performed on the same living-room set as *The Glass Menagerie*, *Death of a Salesman*, or *A Raisin in the Sun*. But Albee's dramaturgy was in no way the quasi-hopeful message of those postwar plays. Instead, Albee peopled his American living room with stunning combinations of fathomless cruelty, utter dysfunction, and—as a saving grace—humor. Audiences found his plays shocking, discomforting, and yet authentic.

Playwrights such as Albee were not necessarily focused on Broadway as an ultimate goal, although from time to time the prize of commercial success was awarded them. Instead, innovative dramatists of the 1960s worked within the established network of regional theaters and off- and off-off-Broadway houses, as well as with a burgeoning number of experimental theater companies. Some of these dramatists also devoted much of their energies to film and television work, which could support their less remunerative live-theater projects. Tennessee Williams's works were welcomed by this alternative matrix, as well as plays by new writers such as ARTHUR KOPIT, whose *Oh Dad, Poor Dad, Mamma's Hung You in the Closet and I'm Feelin' So Sad* revealed its unsettling truths about family on Broadway in 1962; and ISRAEL HOROWITZ, whose *The Indian Wants the Bronx* gained notice in 1968. Playwright PAUL ZINDEL might be considered typical: his mentor was Albee, and his realistic, semiautobiographical, caustic family drama *The Effect of Gamma Rays on Man-in-the-Moon Marigolds* premiered in Houston's Alley Theatre in 1964, moved to off-Broadway in 1970 and to Broadway in 1971, and then was released as a film in 1972.

In 1967 Joseph Papp's New York Shakespeare Festival found a permanent home in the old Astor Library in the East Village, now renamed the Public Theater, and its first production there was *Hair*, an upbeat, musical-theater version of the performance methods pioneered by the Living Theatre. The next year *Hair* moved to Broadway, announcing the arrival of hippie aesthetics, antiwar politics, rock music, and other elements determined

to shock and offend mainstream audiences. Papp also produced DAVID RABE's critical dramas about the Vietnam war, such as *The Basic Training of Pavlo Hummel* (1971) and *Streamers* (1976), but these plays made their weight felt without ever leaving the Public Theater.

Other playwrights expanded or redefined the American family drama in plays whose essence lay in a critique of traditional social norms. JOHN GUARE's *House of Blue Leaves* (produced off-Broadway in 1971) made a kitchen-sink Queens apartment the site of a profoundly critical satire of American sensibilities and values. MARK MEDOFF's *When You Comin' Back, Red Ryder?* was an off-Broadway success in 1973; and A. R. GURNEY's *Scenes from American Life* (1971) was the first of a series of dramatic insights into upper-class American families. WENDY WASSERSTEIN (*Any Woman Can't*, 1973) and MARSHA NORMAN (*Getting Out*, 1977) articulated similar concerns from a particularly feminist perspective. TERRENCE MCNALLY (*The Ritz*, 1975) and ALBERT INNAURATO (*Gemini*, 1977) crafted seriocomic dramas of American life that broached such subjects as homosexuality. Also in the 1970s ROMULUS LINNEY began to explore American history and morality with such plays as *Appalachia Sounding* (first produced in North Carolina in 1975); and the off-Broadway company Playwrights Horizons produced TED TALLY's *Hooters* (1978). At the same time, American playwright BERNARD POMERANCE found the London stage more receptive to his often historical dramas, but his *Elephant Man*, a critique of 19th-century society from the perspective of a hideously deformed man, achieved success both off-Broadway and on Broadway (both in 1979) before making its apparently inevitable transfer to film in 1980.

The heart of off-off-Broadway theater involved what *Village Voice* critic Michael Smith called "amateur theater done largely by professionals" and "theater with no resources but the most sophisticated audience in America" (introduction to *Eight Plays from Off-Off Broadway*, 1966). Centered around such producing entities as Ellen Stewart's La MaMa Experimental Theatre Company, the Judson Poets' Theater, the Caffé Cino, and Theatre Genesis, as well as individual theater companies such as the Living Theatre, the Open Theatre, the Performance Group, and Bread and Puppet Theater, off-off-Broadway theater fostered a much more radical critique of traditional theater than even its off-Broadway predecessor had.

Playwrights in the off-off-Broadway environment often worked in a different manner than traditional dramatists. The off-off Broadway playwrights often wrote in collaboration with actors and directors and might be performers in or directors of the plays they wrote. The Open Theatre, for example, supported playwrights Jean-Claude van Itallie (*America Hurrah!*, 1965), MARIA IRENE FORNES (*The Successful Life of Three*, 1965), MEGAN TERRY (*Viet Rock*, 1966), SUSAN YANKOWITZ (*Terminal*, 1969), and SAM SHEPARD (*Nightwalk*, 1975). Shepard's works also found support at such downtown theaters as La MaMa and the Judson Poets' Theater and then, depending upon their relative success, moved up the ladder to Broadway or across the country into the regional and local theaters. Dramatists such as LANFORD WILSON, whose portrait of a drag queen, *The Madness of Lady Bright*, opened at Caffé Cino in 1964, often experimented with far more radical dramaturgy off-off-Broadway than with later works, such as *Talley's Folly*, which was produced on Broadway in 1978. However, a ribald and shocking play such as ROCHELLE OWENS's *Futz*, about a farmer's romance with his pig, could start at a Guthrie Theater workshop in 1961, reach La MaMa in 1967, and then move uptown to a respectable off-Broadway theater the following year, more or less intact.

While much of off-off-Broadway was "radical" in its embrace of avant-garde techniques, many theater groups that formed in the 1960s also embraced a politically radical point of view, a part of the American activism that had begun during the civil rights movement and had blossomed into the anti–Vietnam War movement. Judith Malina had learned from Erwin Piscator in the mid-1940s that "the art theatre was always political," and the Living Theatre had itself taken up activist positions almost from its inception in 1947, a stance that only became stronger in the Vietnam War years. On the West Coast the San Francisco Mime Troupe began in 1959 as an attempt to rearticulate the acting style of commedia dell'arte, but its outdoor dramas also became more political during the 1960s, as did those of the Bread and Puppet Theater, founded in New York in 1963, and El Teatro Campesino, the Chicano theater that LUIS VALDEZ formed in 1965 after a short stint with the Mime Troupe. These were simply the best known of scores of POLITICAL THEATER groups across the United States that created dramas that, in addition to their attempts to create good political theater as an alternative to mainstream performance culture, also sought alternative venues (indoors, outdoors, on the streets), economics (pass-the-hat performances and communal living), and techniques (masks, physical theater, puppets).

In African American drama, the 1960s were marked by the Black Theater movement, inspired by the militancy of "Black Power" politics emerging from the civil rights struggle. While *A Raisin in the Sun* had been an attempt to explain African American middle-class ambitions to white audiences, playwrights such as AMIRI BARAKA and ED BULLINS saw Lorraine Hansberry's efforts to nurture empathy as a form of cultural appeasement that they rejected. Baraka's DUTCHMAN (1964) was a violent condemnation of white racism, featuring a villainous blonde seductress preying on a mild-mannered black man with middle-class aspirations; and Bullins's *Goin' a Buffalo* (1968) echoed the low-life realism of *The Connection* by dramatizing the lives of hustlers, prostitutes, and drug dealers in Los Angeles— a different type of American family drama.

ADRIENNE KENNEDY also emerged as an African American playwright in that same early 1960s moment, but she was inspired more by Beckett's abstract minimalism than by the possibilities of aggressive political drama. Her lyrical, surrealistically airy meditations on the meaning of racial and American IDENTITY, such as *Funnyhouse of a Negro* (1964), inspired audiences at Papp's Public Theater, but exasperated her male contemporaries in the Black Theater movement, who disparaged her apparent lack of interest in activist political theater. In the following decade a dramatist such as NTOZAKE SHANGE could bridge this gap by creating highly successful poetic dance-dramas such as *for colored girls who have considered suicide/when the rainbow is enuf* (1975), which articulated a feminist view of black women while maintaining a colorful and ultimately affirmative spectacle combining monologue, music, and dance.

The alternative venues and anticommercial pose of off-off-Broadway theater from the 1960s, as well as that period's activist social politics, encouraged the emergence of another aspect of American drama, the open and outright depiction of homosexuality as an essential component of American culture. Of course, homosexuality has always been a central element of theater making, but before the 1960s such homosexual playwrights as Williams, Inge, Bowles, or Albee were silent or circumspect about their sexual orientation and avoided the outright depiction of homosexual characters and society. The gay liberation movement of the late 1960s inspired MART CROWLEY to introduce a gay perspective to realistic American family drama with *The Boys in the Band* (1968), which brings together a group of homosexual men for a birthday party. Crowley's play (which achieved notable off-Broadway success) involves the same realistic, psychological probing that characterizes dramas by Miller, Inge, Williams, and Hansberry, but it culminates in a revelation that, for the most part, gay men in the United States lead extraordinarily unhappy lives. Crowley's soul-searching pessimism about gay American life was spectacularly contradicted by the emergence off-off-Broadway of "queer theater" (as Stefan Brecht coined the term): a rollicking, carnivalesque satire of everyday morality from the viewpoint of writers and performers who refused to define themselves by the clinically scientific and inherently pejorative appellation "homosexual," but instead used the blunt, gleefully outcast terms "gay" and "queer." Pulling the traditional aesthetics of homosexual performance up from their subculture status, queer theater celebrated drag queens and an outsider's critique of American culture. Dramatist, director, and actor CHARLES LUDLAM was the most successful figure to emerge from this coterie of theater makers, and his Ridiculous Theatrical Company achieved off-Broadway success in its own theater in Greenwich Village with such plays as *Camille* (1973), featuring Ludlam himself in the title role, his chest hairs peeking out through the décolletage of his ball gown. Off-off-Broadway, HARVEY FIERSTEIN created his *Torch Song Trilogy* as a comic and sentimental autobiographical saga dealing with the tribulations of gay life in New York. Fierstein himself starred in the Broadway production of *Trilogy*, which won a Tony Award for best play in 1983.

Perhaps the most radical addition to the aesthetics of postwar American drama was the development of avant-garde performance techniques connected to the dance and visual art worlds. A center for these innovations in the late 1940s was Black Mountain College in North Carolina, where émigré European artists met with open-minded Americans such as John Cage and Merce Cunningham to create multifaceted performances that could not be defined simply as "plays." Cage and Cunningham then migrated to New York, where, especially by means of Cage's classes at the New School, a whole new coterie of theater makers developed what would later be seen as a postmodern performance aesthetic. "Drama" is an inadequate term for what transpired in the rooms of such performance spaces as Greenwich Village's Judson Church, because the pieces were not always predicated on a dialogic text. Even the broader term "theater" seemed inadequate, for many of the developments in this area were music or dance pieces or ritual actions in which the performers simply produced action in front of an audience without embodying a fictitious character.

Within this vibrant downtown environment painter and sculptor Allan Kaprow created his tightly scripted, landmark production 18 Happenings in 6 Parts (1959) in a New York gallery, and other visual artists such as Carolee Schneemann followed suit with such HAPPENINGS as Meat Joy (1964), which brusquely confronted its audiences with female sexuality. The development of a new performance form that by definition lacked the kinds of rules and traditions pertinent to "the Drama" had an obvious appeal to all sorts of artists inspired by avant-garde traditions, and such a group included many who then made particular innovations in American drama, for example, Sam Shepard, Jack Smith (an inventor of queer theater), Peter Schumann (who founded Bread and Puppet Theater), and ROBERT WILSON (who transformed the spectacle aesthetics of the happening back into highbrow proscenium-arch theaters).

Although New York City remained the U.S. center for live theater throughout the second half of the 20th century, the innovations of off-off-Broadway theater from the 1960s onward were mirrored and reinforced by a resurgence of like-minded theaters throughout the country. One could term this a revival of regional theater, although such theaters as the Magic Theatre in San Francisco (begun in 1967) or Chicago's Steppenwolf Theatre Company (founded in 1974) were smaller, more poorly funded organizations than the regional theaters founded in the 1940s and 1950s. But the Magic Theatre nurtured such dramatists as the peripatetic Sam Shepard, who was playwright-in-residence there from 1975 to 1983; while Steppenwolf, part of a vibrant, young Chicago theater scene comprising many different companies and nourishing such playwrights as DAVID MAMET, produced powerful productions of new plays by Shepard, Lanford Wilson, and South African dramatist ATHOL FUGARD.

By the 1980s the actual center for text-based, dialogue-centered drama about realistic characters in realistic situations had long ago shifted from New York to Los Angeles, where dramatists wrote for film and television in various different genres: situation comedies, crime and detective melodramas, action films, docudramas, and biographies, as well as "serious" film and television dramas. This work had even evolved its own body of dramatic theory, epitomized by the work of Robert McKee, whose dramatic formulas (articulated in his popular book Story) amount to a rearticulation of Aristotle's Poetics for commercial film and television.

In the last two decades of the 20th century it was also clear that American drama as a live art form would never reassume the importance for U.S. culture that it had achieved in its 1920s heyday; instead, live drama had settled into a relatively comfortable, stable, and even occasionally profitable existence as a specialized, often rarefied and exclusive art form, supported by regional theaters around the United States and by energetic and committed theater companies and artists who did not necessarily expect to make a living directly from commercial success. In other words, the innovations in dramatic form and play production that had developed in the 1960s and 1970s were now institutionalized and functioned as the paradigms for most American theater. The 1990s renovation of New York City's Times Square into a kind of corporate-sponsored urban theme park helped solidify the ongoing shift of Broadway theater almost exclusively to blockbuster musicals and tried-and-true spectacles, and the appearance of comedies or "serious" dramas there was a cherished anomaly.

Although older dramatists such as Neil Simon and Edward Albee managed to maintain their status as Broadway playwrights during the 1980s and 1990s, the century's most important American playwright, Arthur Miller, could often get his newer works produced only outside the United States, especially in London. Meanwhile, successful younger American dramatists of these years, such as Sam Shepard and David Mamet, depended on the off-Broadway and regional theater network to develop works that did become popular on Broadway. Shepard combined a sure sense of America's violent Wild West past with an absurdist sense of futility to create striking family dramas in which dysfunction was the norm. Mamet's masterful ear for the rhythms of American speech and his own strict sense of well-made playmaking allowed him to create equally searing portraits of American hustlers (of all classes and kinds) and their motives. Highly politicized and openly gay writer TONY KUSHNER also draw upon the off-Broadway and regional theater system to develop Brecht-influenced popular dramas of historical social critique in a particularly American idiom, such as the two-part AIDS epic ANGELS IN AMERICA. All three of these authors were awarded Pulitzer Prizes for their theater work, but their dramas also reached larger audiences when they were shown on film and television. And while these playwrights came to Los Angeles after their work for live theater had already developed, the opposite trajectory was also possible: STEVE

TESICH, for example, gained attention on Broadway with such plays as *Division Street* (1980) only after his success as a Hollywood screenwriter. Other playwrights, such as LEE BLESSING, found Broadway success (*A Walk in the Woods*, 1988) to be an anomaly compared with finding consistent access to off-Broadway and regional theaters.

Other Broadway successes in the 1980s included playwrights whose clear articulation of a woman's point of view drew upon the development of FEMINIST DRAMA in the 1970s. Plays by Marsha Norman ('NIGHT MOTHER, 1982), Wasserstein (THE HEIDI CHRONICLES, 1989), BETH HENLEY (*Crimes of the Heart*, 1981), and TINA HOWE (*Coastal Disturbances*, 1987), all nurtured off-Broadway and in regional theaters, also had successful Broadway runs. In a similar fashion, openly gay playwrights such as Kushner, Wilson (*Talley's Folly*, 1980), and CRAIG LUCAS (*Prelude to a Kiss*, 1992) articulated a specifically gay perspective in their stage works for Broadway, while the venerable Albee became increasingly comfortable in allowing himself to be considered a gay playwright. The emergence of gay-identified playwrights on American stages took on a deeper significance with the arrival of the AIDS epidemic in the early 1980s (which, among thousands of other theater artists, took dramatist Charles Ludlam). Dramatist LARRY KRAMER, a founder of the AIDS activist groups Gay Men's Health Crisis and ACT UP, wrote *The Normal Heart* (produced off-Broadway at the Public Theater in 1985) as a realistic melodrama about a gay man's struggle to focus attention on the disease in the early years of the epidemic. Kramer's drama initiated a whole genre of "AIDS plays" that reached a popular culmination in the early 1990s when Kushner's *Angels in America* appeared on Broadway.

In the 1980s off-Broadway theater further solidified its position as the center for live American drama, and off-off-Broadway theater, despite increasingly harsh financial constraints, continued to nourish new plays and playwrights, many of whom were not even interested in making it to Broadway. Further off-center, hundreds of actors, writers, dancers, musicians, and puppeteers used the terms "performance" or "PERFORMANCE ART" to describe the works they developed in such venues as P.S. 122, the Kitchen, and other "performance spaces." In Chicago, San Francisco, Boston, and other American cities the parallel equivalents to these networks also thrived.

The various elements of this increasingly complex landscape of American drama flourished in a symbiotic fashion. Some playwrights, actors, directors, and producers might focus their energies exclusively on one particular area of performance (film, television, Broadway, off-Broadway, off-off-Broadway, or "avant-garde" performance), but others routinely alternated among the various theater worlds. For example, SPALDING GRAY began his professional career in the early 1970s acting in regional theater and then became involved in New York's experimental theater scene, working first with Richard Schechner's Performance Group and next pioneering the development of

avant-garde solo performance. Gray's work often took him to Los Angeles, where he worked as a film and television actor and also in popular movie versions of his monologues. This work did not prevent him from also performing on Broadway in such classics as *Our Town*, but the core of Gray's work continued to be his monologues, which he developed at such alternative venues as P.S. 122 in New York City's East Village.

By the 1980s a new coterie of venues began to emerge: Playwrights Horizons became an anchor of the nonprofit "Theatre Row" section of West 42nd Street in 1971; the Humana Festival was started in Louisville, Kentucky, in 1976; and New York Theatre Workshop began in 1979. These organizations joined now-venerable institutions such as Papp's Public Theater and the various regional theaters to encourage, develop, and produce new plays that above all else eschewed the varieties of American realism that had characterized pre–World War II drama (and that now dominated film and television writing), and instead embraced myriad versions of nonrealistic playwriting.

A good example of 1980s playwriting is WALLACE SHAWN, the author of seriocomic dramas such as *Aunt Dan and Lemon* (1985), whose unnerving depiction of the roots of fascism is mixed into a comedy of manners. Shawn's works were often first produced in London and then mounted in off-Broadway venues such as La MaMa, the Manhattan Theatre Club, or the Public Theater; *Aunt Dan and Lemon* even reached Broadway in 2003. ELIZABETH EGLOFF's plays appeared at the Humana Festival (*The Swan*, 1989) and New York Theatre Workshop (*The Devils*, 1994). Other playwrights who emerged in the 1980s, including ERIC OVERMYER, LEN JENKIN, JON ROBIN BAITZ, JOHN PATRICK SHANLEY, CHARLES MEE, and MAC WELLMAN, found success on off- and off-off-Broadway stages, but hardly ever on Broadway. In 1991 the Signature Theatre was created to devote an entire season to one playwright's works. It focused on plays by Lee Blessing, Horton Foote, Adrienne Kennedy, John Guare, Maria Irene Fornes, Lanford Wilson, and PAULA VOGEL (as well as the better-known Sam Shepard, Arthur Miller, and Edward Albee), thus helping establish a canon of late-century dramatists whose work was visible in the noncommercial theater scene. GEORGE C. WOLFE became director of the New York Public Theater in 1993 and continued its function as a home for substantial new plays by Tony Kushner, DAVID HENRY HWANG, SUZAN-LORI PARKS, Nilo Cruz, and others. As had been the case since the days of *Hair* and *A Chorus Line*, the Public Theater was sometimes able to shift its productions to Broadway (including the tap musical *Bring in 'Da Noise, Bring in 'Da Funk*, directed by Wolfe). The Broadway successes in part helped support the Public Theater's ongoing work, whose central focus remained the development of new American drama-as-art.

The structural stability of off- and off-off-Broadway theater in the 1980s and 1990s was paralleled by the changing nature of particular genres of American drama that had emerged in the 1960s and 1970s: African American, Asian American, Hispanic

American, gay, and feminist theater. The 1980s developments of these genres were more complex, less polemical, less overtly political, and more likely to resist taking on the mantle of a particular cause. In other words, the necessity of writing as a hyphenated American dramatist with one particular group in mind was somewhat diminished as "minority" interests were articulated more generally as aspects of mainstream American concerns.

For example, AUGUST WILSON, beginning with his play *Jitney* (1982), inaugurated a series of realistic dramas about black life in Pittsburgh that folded the politics of the earlier Black Theater movement back into the techniques of realistic American family drama. Although his multidecade play cycle brings to mind Miller's explorations of midcentury American morality, in fact, Wilson's work has its closest connections to Henrik Ibsen's series of social dramas depicting turn-of-the-century Europe, or to ANTON CHEKHOV's intense evocation of Russian character and society at the same moment. Wilson's Chekhovian depictions of 20th-century African American life made regular and successful appearances on Broadway throughout the 1980s. Later the radically avant-garde language of Suzan-Lori Parks's plays was also difficult to pinpoint as African American political theater, and her impressionistic visions of black life, such as *Top Dog/Underdog* (produced at the Public Theater and then on Broadway in 2002), had more in common with Adrienne Kennedy's work than with Amiri Baraka's. Similarly, numerous playwrights with Hispanic roots—Nilo Cruz, JOSÉ RIVERA, MIGDALIA CRUZ, and EDUARDO MACHADO—wrote dramas that articulated a Latino perspective, not with the confrontational politics of such 1960s playwrights as Luis Valdez, but instead in more subtle and nuanced styles, more in line with the similar approach of Valdez's contemporary Maria Irene Fornes.

The types of theater and performance that in the 1960s had been termed "avant-garde" or "experimental" had, by the 1980s, acquired a certain structural stability that like gay, feminist, and African American theater, was less overtly political and more explicitly concerned with particular theatrical styles developed from 1970s precedents. Thus playwright RICHARD FOREMAN (a surrealist heir of Gertrude Stein) maintained his Ontological-Hysteric Theater at St. Mark's Church in the Bowery, in New York's East Village, producing new works annually to general critical acclaim, and the Wooster Group (an outgrowth of Richard Schechner's late 1960s and early 1970s Performance Group) performed its signature brand of postmodern drama in its own theater in SoHo. PING CHONG, an Asian American performance artist originally associated with director Meredith Monk, directed his own works combining visual art, puppet theater, music, and dance. Similarly, director Robert Wilson, perhaps the most spectacular American theater artist to emerge in the 1970s, continued to direct (and, to some extent, write) his own works, although more often than not for European and Asian theaters instead of American venues. Younger

writer-directors, such as Iranian American Reza Abdoh, created theater pieces that deftly incorporated all sorts of stylistic elements of 1970s experiments, although, in Abdoh's case, these were combined with his own sense of global culture and American popular culture to produce searing critiques of American complacency in the age of AIDS and post–Cold War political violence.

Meanwhile, since Spalding Gray had initiated the genre of avant-garde monologue during his work with the Wooster Group, other artists, such as HOLLY HUGHES, Karen Finley, Paul Zaloom, Eric Bogosian, EVE ENSLER, ANNA DEAVERE SMITH, and Danny Hoch developed their own versions of the form as a new technique of late-century American playwriting.

A source of anxiety for early 20th-century critics of American drama was that the United States, because it was younger and foundationally different from Europe, needed to mature before it could claim that a truly American drama—and a truly artistic drama—existed. What makes American theater different from European dramatic traditions (and, for that matter, most Asian theater traditions) is that by definition the United States has to acknowledge its multiple ethnicity, its multiple cultural influences. And in fact, since the 19th century it has done so, although early on such differences emerged more often as racist stereotypes. The course of 20th-century American drama, and especially American drama from 1940 to the present, shows the gradual and often quite contested development of theater reflecting the United States' cultural heterogeneity. Ironically, the richness of American theater in these decades—which was noted and admired throughout the world—developed at the same time that live drama itself was overshadowed by mass-media performance, itself an intercultural, global phenomenon. In other words, the flowering of the various aspects of American drama by the end of the century coincided with some fundamental questions about whether live theater was itself relevant to a global culture that seemed to be defined by film, television, and the Internet. And yet, because of its existence as live art, drama persists as one of the few places where ideas, issues, and emotions can be articulated and experienced with unique freedom and spontaneity. From 1940 to the present the strength of American drama as live theater may have diminished economically, but it flowers as art.

FURTHER READING

Atkinson, Brooks. *Broadway*. New York: Macmillan, 1970.

———. Foreword to *New Voices in the American Theatre*. New York: Modern Library, 1955.

Brecht, Stefan. *Queer Theatre*. Frankfurt: Suhrkamp, 1978.

Cordell, Richard A., and Lowell Matson, eds. *The Off-Broadway Theatre*. New York: Random House, 1959.

Hatch, James V., and Ted Shine, eds. *Black Theatre U.S.A.: The Recent Period, 1935–Today*. New York: Free Press, 1996.

Orzel, Nick, and Michael Smith, eds. *Eight Plays from Off-Off Broadway*. Indianapolis: Bobbs-Merrill, 1966.

Sainer, Arthur. *The New Radical Theatre Notebook*. New York: Applause, 1997.

Ziegler, Joseph. *Regional Theatre: The Revolutionary Stage*. Minneapolis: Univ. of Minnesota Press, 1973.

John Bell

USIGLI, RODOLFO (1905–1979)

A multitalented author, Rodolfo Usigli is considered the playwright of the Mexican Revolution. He also wrote as a drama critic, historian, essayist, and poet. Usigli was born on November 17, 1905, in Mexico City. As a Rockefeller Foundation scholar at Yale, he studied alongside Xavier Villaurrutia and wrote several plays. He returned to Mexico City to teach at the university and direct the theater of the Ministry of Culture. During the 1930s Usigli was prolific. His political play *The President and the Ideal* (*El presidente y el ideal*) was performed in 1935, and *State of Secrecy* (*Estado de secreto*) and *The Last Door* (*La última puerta*) were performed in 1936. *Summer Night* (*Noche de estío*) was performed in 1950. This popular COMEDY used political satire and comic circumstances to expose political corruption.

Psychological drama also identified with the changing Mexican society. *The Boy and the Fog* (*El niño y la niebla*) was performed and published in 1951. A son is caught in a parental love triangle after his mother confesses about her lover. Her son then attempts to kill his father. Although the parents resolve their marriage, the son commits suicide. The public was intrigued by the complex characterization, despite the potential for MELODRAMA. *Janus Is a Girl* (*Jano es una muchacha*) was performed and published in 1952. Usigli's characterization of an innocent girl forced by circumstances into the underworld of a brothel scandalized the public. The drama criticized the double standard in the commercialization of sex and the stigma associated with women in the sex trade.

Usigli's most important plays were performed long after their writing. *The Imposter* (*El gesticulador*) was written in 1938 but not performed until 1947. It is now recognized as his masterpiece and the beginning of the modern era of Mexican theater. The drama overtly condemned corruption that was disintegrating Mexican society from within. It accurately portrayed his colleagues in governmental positions. Political rivals forced his resignation because of his overt criticism. Usigli's dramatic structure and hybrid style gave the play universal appeal. He disapproved of most English translations and international performances during his lifetime. Alejandro Usigli, his son, approved an English translation by Ramón Layera, *The Imposter*, produced in 1996 at Miami University of Ohio to critical acclaim.

Crown of Shadow (*Corona de sombra*), part of the CORONA TRILOGY, reinforced Usigli's international renown. His first historical drama of a trilogy explored the complex intermingling of cultures in Mexican society. He defined the plays as antihistorical because he focused on myths of MEXICO's origins and its evolving sense of nationhood rather than historical fact. In the first iconic image that defines Mexico, Emperor Maximilian is executed at the end of French occupation, and the lucid flashbacks of Empress Carlota reinterpret history in retrospect. The political intrigue between warring Mexican idealists, French and Austrian opportunists, and the Vatican has enduring dramatic impact. It was published in 1943 and performed in 1947 concurrently with *El gesticulador*. *Crown of Fire* (*Corona de fuego*) was performed in 1961 and published in 1966. The Spaniard Hernán Cortés and the Aztec Cuauhtémoc clash in the conquest of culture that initiates the saga. *Crown of Light* (*Corona de luz*) was published in 1965 and performed in 1969. The Virgin de Guadalupe appeared to the shepherd Juan Diego in this iconic drama.

Usigli intended to create a series of performance projects that would fulfill the project of performing "El gran teatro del Nuevo Mundo," or "the Great Theatre of the New World." Usigli did not complete his project, but his trilogy is the closest series to a more modest achievement of his goal. He died on June 18, 1979. The most important centers for Mexican theater scholarship and research are the Centro de Investigación Teatral Rodolfo Usigli (Rodolfo Usigli Center for Theater Research) in Mexico City and the Rodolfo Usigli Archive in the King Library of Miami University in Oxford, Ohio.

PLAYS: *The Impostor* (*El gesticulador*, 1937); *Crown of Shadow* (*Corona de sombra*, 1943); *Summer Night* (*Noche de estío*, 1950); *The Boy and the Fog* (*El niño y la niebla*, 1951); *Janus Is a Girl* (*Jano es una muchacha*, 1952); *One of these Days* (*Un día de éstos*, 1953); *Crown of Fire* (*Corona de fuego*, 1960); *Crown of Light* (*Corona de luz*, 1964); *The Great Circus of the World* (*El gran circo del mundo*, 1969); *The Flores Case* (*El caso Flores*, 1972); *Good Morning, Mr. President* (*Buenos días señor presidente*, 1972)

FURTHER READING

Donahue, Francis. "Toward a Mexican National Theater." *Revista/ Review Interamericana* 19 (Fall–Winter 1989): 29–40.

Kronick, John W. "Usigli's *El gesticulador* and the Fiction of Truth." *Latin American Theatre Review* 11, no. 1 (1977): 5–16.

Layera, Ramón. *Usigli en el teatro: Testimonio de sus contemporáneos, sucesores, y discípulos*. Mexico City: UNAM, 1996.

Perri, Dennis. "The Artistic Unity of *Corona de sombra*." *Latin American Theatre Review* 15, no. 1 (1981): 13–19.

Carole Anne Champagne

V

VALDEZ, LUIS (1940–)

I know that our work reaches into the streets. We attract young people, people who are confronted with rather stark realities. They have to hope for something, man. If they don't have the arts telling them about the essence and meaning of life, offering some kind of exploration of the positive and negative aspects of life, then there is no hope. I was a very angry young man not too many years ago, and I was able to channel that anger into the arts.

—Luis Valdez, 1985

Luis Valdez is a California-based playwright and director whose work is inevitably connected with El Teatro Campesino, the theater group he founded, and with which he initiated contemporary Chicano drama. Born on June 26, 1940, in Delano, California, into a family of Mexican American *campesinos* (farmworkers), Valdez grew up in the midst of Chicano culture and its continuing traditions of Catholic ritual performance and the aesthetics of popular traveling theater companies that performed in tents (CARPAS).

Valdez studied drama at San Jose State College, where his first full-length play, *The Shrunken Head of Pancho Villa*, was produced in 1964. Upon graduation in 1965 Valdez briefly joined the San Francisco Mime Troupe, but had already connected with Chicano activist César Chavez and decided to join the emerging farmworkers' movement. "I was a child of the '60s," he later said, "and so in that sense I wanted to change the world. I decided to go back to Delano and try to change this valley that treated Mexicans the way the south treated African Americans. We were fighting for our civil rights, for our humanity, and it seemed to me that using the arts, using humor, using masks, using theatre, was the way to do it."

Valdez started to make short skits, or *actos*, about *campesinos* and their struggles. Together with other Chicano performers Valdez created El Teatro Campesino, which began performing throughout central California at union rallies and on the backs of flatbed trucks. Plays such as *The Two Faces of the Owner* (*Las dos caras del patroncito*, 1965) or *Strikers* (*Huelguistas*, 1970) incorporated masks, commedia-style techniques, and the Chicano traditions of *carpa* theater, especially its wily trickster servants, or *pelados*.

In 1967 El Teatro Campesino won a Village Voice Obie Award for "demonstrating the politics of survival." Valdez and his company were considered the voice of the United Farm Workers, although its *actos* now also dealt with the Vietnam War and Chicano culture in general. El Teatro Campesino separated itself from the United Farm Workers in 1967, and Valdez began to see his role in broader terms, as a playwright of an emerging *teatro chicano*. Such dramas as *I Didn't Get Anything Out of School* (*No saco nada de la escuela*, 1969), while preserving the larger-than-life

theatrics of the *actos*, were broad-based satires about the entire scope of 1960s social and cultural issues—black militancy, "la Raza," white liberals, Ronald Reagan, education, and the ongoing Vietnam War—seen from a Chicano perspective.

In 1971 the company moved to the rural town of San Juan Bautista, and Valdez's plays reflected "greater spirituality." *The Dance of the Giants* (*El baile de los gigantes*, 1973) was a ritual performance based on Mayan beliefs and performed in MEXICO among ancient Mayan pyramids. Valdez termed such plays *mitos* because of their conscious connection to Chicano mythology and beliefs. Elements of the *mito* aesthetic played a role in *The Great Tent of the Underdogs* (*La gran carpa de los Rasquachis*, 1973) and *The End of the World* (*El fin del mundo*, 1975), which maintained the simplicity of *carpa*-style theatrics while incorporating Day of the Dead characters in striking mixtures of COMEDY and dread that analyzed the mid-1970s state of the world. El Teatro Campesino became world-famous through its tours of Europe, and in 1977 *The Great Tent of the Underdogs* was produced on California public television as *The Ballad* (*El corrido*).

Valdez's playwriting took yet another turn when *Zoot Suit*, his drama about the "Pachuco riots" in Los Angeles during World War II, opened in 1978 at the Mark Taper Forum and then moved to New York City, where it became the first Broadway play by a Chicano playwright, but failed to please critics or find an audience. Valdez began to focus more of his attention on screenwriting and had success with a film version of *Zoot Suit* (1981); *La Bamba* (1987), a biography of Chicano rock star Richie Valens; and numerous television specials about Chicano history and culture.

El Teatro Campesino continued its exploration of traditional Latino theater with annual performances of a miracle play, *The Virgin of Tepeyac* (*La Virgen del Tepeyac*) and a traditional shepherds' play, *The Pastoral* (*La pastorela*) in San Juan Bautista. Valdez wrote an "antimelodrama," *Bandit!* (*Bandido!* 1981), and a multimedia satire on the Reagan years, *I Don't Have to Show You No Stinking Badges!* (1986), but forsook live theater for film, television, and teaching from 1986 to 2000, when he returned to the stage with *The Mummified Deer*. This was followed by *Earthquake Sun* (2004), a mystical drama about a 21st-century musician who travels back and forth in time in search of his Chicano roots. Both plays were produced by the San Diego Repertory Theatre and marked Valdez's acceptance as an established American playwright.

[*See also* Political Theater in the United States;
United States, 1940–Present]

PLAYS: *Theft* (1961); *The Shrunken Head of Pancho Villa* (1964); *The Two Faces of the Owner* (*Las dos caras del patroncito*, 1965); *Three Grapes* (1965); *The Fifth Season* (*La quinta temporada*, 1966); *Dark Root of a*

Scream (1967); The Sellouis (Los vendidos, 1967); The Conquest of Mexico (La conquista de Mexico, 1968); Bernabe (1969); The Skull of Tiburcio Vásquez (La Calavera de Tiburcio Vásquez, 1969); The Militants (1969); I Didn't Get Anything Out of School (No saco nada de la escuela, 1969); Strikers (Huelguistas, 1970); Buck Private (Soldado Razo, 1970); Vietnam Peasant (Vietnam Campesino, 1970); The Virgin of Tepeyac (La el Virgen del Tepeyac, 1971); The Great Tent of the Underdogs (La gran carpa de los Rasquachis, 1971); Los olivos pits (1972); The Dance of the Giants (El baile de los gigantes, 1973); Serpentino Thought (Pensamiento serpentino, 1973); The End of the World (El fin del mundo, 1975); Zoot Suit (1978); World (Mundo, a touring version of The End of the World, 1980); Bandit! (Bandido!, 1981); Ballads (Corridos, 1982); I Don't Have to Show You No Stinking Badges! (1986); The Mummified Deer (2000); Earthquake Sun (2004)

FURTHER READING

Broyles-González, Yolanda. El Teatro Campesino: Theater in the Chicano Movement. Austin: Univ. of Texas Press, 1994.

Cardenas de-Dwyer, Carlota. "The Development of Chicano Drama and Luis Valdez's Actos." In Modern Chicano Writers: A Collection of Critical Essays, ed. by Joseph Sommers and Tomás Ybarra-Frausto. Englewood Cliffs, N.J.: Prentice-Hall, 1979.

Elam, Harry J. Taking It to the Streets: The Social Protest Theater of Luis Valdez and Amiri Baraka. Ann Arbor: Univ. of Michigan Press, 1997.

Kanellos, Nicolas. "Luis Miguel Valdez." In Dictionary of Literary Biography, vol. 122, Chicano Writers, Second Series, ed. by Francisco Lomelí and Carl R. Shirley. Detroit: Gale Res., 1992.

Shank, Theodore. American Alternative Theatre. London: Macmillan, 1982.

John Bell

VALLE-INCLÁN, RAMÓN MARÍA DEL (1866–1936)

Ramón María del Valle-Inclán was an enormously popular dramatist, novelist, poet, and journalist most famous for his iconoclastic plays that ridiculed early 20th-century Spanish society. He was born on October 28, 1866, in Villanueva de Arosa in Galicia, SPAIN. In 1886 Ramón del Valle-Peña, which was his actual name, began law school at the University of Santiago de Compostela, but he abandoned his studies in 1890. The restless Valle-Peña spent much of his time reading the works of AVANT-GARDE authors such as Jules BarBey d'Aurevilly and GABRIELE D'ANNUNZIO, who would make a major impact on Valle's work. In 1892 the author changed his name to Valle-Inclán, visited MEXICO and CUBA, and found work as a journalist.

He returned to Galicia in 1893 and complemented his journalistic endeavors with creative writing. Valle-Inclán moved to Madrid in 1896, and on the eve of the premiere of his first play, Ashes (Cenizas, 1899), a scuffle with his colleague Manuel Bueno resulted in a gangrenous wound on Valle's wrist that ultimately required the amputation of his left arm. Valle-Inclán was something of a spectacle himself as he adopted a bohemian appear-ance replete with a lavish purple cape and a conspicuously long beard.

During the first decade of the 20th century Valle-Inclán's subject matter was quite varied: a series of semiautobiographical novellas (Sonatas, 1902–1905) described the adventures of a Galician Don Juan, his Flower of Sainthood (Flor de santidad, 1904) dealt with peasants and religious pilgrims in Galicia, and The Carlist War (La Guerra Carlista, 1908–1909) dealt with the vicious civil war in Spain during the 1830s. Beginning with The Dragon's Head (La cabeza del dragón, 1910), Valle-Inclán gravitated toward FARCES and a literary genre called esperpento (grotesques), characterized by acid-tongued satire and the use of physically distorted characters to ridicule Spanish institutions. Valle-Inclán insisted that the 19th-century Spanish painter Francisco Goya was the founder of esperpento, and that he was aiming to put on stage what Goya illustrated.

The finest example of esperpento came with Valle-Inclán's signature play, BOHEMIAN LIGHTS (Luces de Bohemia, 1920), a fifteen-scene drama that details the funeral and last moments of the life of Max Estrella. Estrella—a character based on Alejandro Sawa, a contemporary of Valle—is a poet blinded by syphilis who struggles to gain literary recognition, only to be lied to, exploited, despised, and ultimately robbed as he lies drunk and dying on a Madrid street. Bohemian Lights illustrates life's absurdity, as well as that of men whose existence is an everyday struggle between practicality and idealism. With the declaration of the Second Spanish Republic in 1931 Valle-Inclán was named director of the Museum of Aranjuez, which was the traditional palace of the royal family driven into exile. Two years later he was named director of the Spanish Academy of Fine Arts in Rome, a post he was forced to abandon when a fatal blood disease led him back to his native Galicia, where he died on January 5, 1936, in the town of Santiago de Compostela.

PLAYS: Ashes (Cenizas, 1899); Dream Tragedy (Tragedia de ensueño, 1903); Dream Play (Comedia de ensueño, 1905); El Marqués de Bardomín (1906); The Heraldic Eagle (Águila de blasón, 1907); Ballad of the Wolves (Romance de lobos, 1908); The Dragon's Head (La cabeza del dragon, 1909); April Tale (Cuento de Abril, 1910); Epic Voices (Voces de gesta, 1911); La Duquesa Rosalinda (1912); The Bewitched (El embrujado, 1913); Divine Words (Divinas palabras, 1920); Farce and Licentiousness of the Noble Queen (Farsa y licencia de la reina castiza, 1920); Bohemian Lights (Luces de Bohemia, 1920); The Cuckolding of Don Friolera (Los cuernos de don Friolera, 1921); Silver Face (Cara de plata, 1922); The Dead Man's Best Suit (Las galas del difunto, 1924); Ligazón (1926); The Captain's Daughter (La hija del capitán, 1927); Paper Rose (La rosa de papel, 1927); Sacrilege (Sacrilegio, 1927)

FURTHER READING

Lima, Robert. Valle-Inclán: The Theatre of His Life. Columbia: Univ. of Missouri Press, 1988.

Valle-Inclán, Ramón María de. Lights of Bohemia (Luces de bohemia). Tr. by John Lyon. Warminster: Aris & Phillips, 1993.

Zahareas, Anthony N., ed. *Ramón del Valle-Inclán: An Appraisal of His Life and Works*. New York: Las Americas, 1968.

Enrique A. Sanabria

LE VALSE DES TORÉADORS   See THE WALTZ OF THE TOREADORS

VAN DRUTEN, JOHN (1901–1957)

John Van Druten was born in London, ENGLAND, on June 1, 1901, to English parents of Dutch extraction. His lifelong ability to create strong roles for women can be discerned in his first playwriting effort at age seven, when he created a slim script about Mary, Queen of Scots. Despite Van Druten's talent, however, his father discouraged his interest in a career he saw as financially insecure, and Van Druten instead studied law, qualifying as a solicitor of the Supreme Court Judicature in 1923. He became a lecturer of legal history at the University College of Wales in Aberystwyth, but continued to pursue writing for the theater as his true vocation. His play *Young Woodley*, produced in 1925 in London, gave him hope of ending his teaching career, but his story of a sensitive adolescent was banned for what was considered its daring depiction of the dark side of the British public school system. Fortunately, the play was successfully produced in the UNITED STATES in 1926, and, responding to the stateside recognition, Van Druten established residence in America in the same year, becoming a citizen in 1944. Van Druten soon moved to California to write screenplays for Hollywood movies, but the New York theater remained a major part of his life. In 1943 he enjoyed his greatest success there with THE VOICE OF THE TURTLE, a play considered daring for its time because of its celebratory depiction of a short-lived love affair between a young soldier and a free-spirited actress.

Van Druten's identity as both a gay man and a talented writer led to his becoming part of a circle of gay writers living in California gathered around British expatriate writer CHRISTOPHER ISHERWOOD. He adapted Isherwood's *Berlin Stories* into the play *I Am a Camera* (1951), which later became the basis for the musical *Cabaret* in 1966. *I Am a Camera*, featuring the quirky Sally Bowles, once again demonstrated Van Druten's gift for creating strong, near-magical female characters, a propensity that reached its apotheosis in *Bell, Book, and Candle* (1950), which centered on a powerful witch living secretly in the modern world.

Although noted for his polished and sophisticated romantic COMEDIES, Van Druten had a reflective spiritual side to his identity. He developed a strong interest in Christian Science and later joined the Vedanta Society. Although his plays were grounded in a realistic and even comfortably domestic context, his spiritual inclinations always enriched his work with a SUBTEXT of wonder and romance. In 1956 he developed heart problems and died on December 19, 1957, in Indio, California.

[*See also* Gay and Lesbian Drama]

SELECT PLAYS: *Young Woodley* (1925); *Leave Her to Heaven* (1940); *Old Acquaintance* (1940); *The Voice of the Turtle* (1943); *I Remember Mama* (1944); *The Mermaids Singing* (1946); *The Druid Circle* (1947); *Make Way for Lucia* (1949); *Bell, Book, and Candle* (1950); *I Am a Camera* (1951)

FURTHER READING

Isherwood, Christopher. *Lost Years: A Memoir, 1945–1951*. Ed. by Katherine Bucknell. New York: HarperCollins, 2000.

Mann, William J. *Behind the Screen: How Gays and Lesbians Shaped Hollywood, 1910–1969*. New York: Viking, 2001.

Van Druten, John. *Playwright at Work*. New York: Harper, 1953.

Margaret Boe Birns

VÅR ÆRE OG VÅR MAKT   See OUR POWER AND OUR GLORY

VAUTHIER, JEAN (1910–1992)

Jean Vauthier (born in Grâce-Berleur, BELGIUM) arrived on the French theater scene to great praise for his early plays, essentially tumultuous monologues, in which he sought, he said, to re-create the linguistic and intellectual energy of the English Elizabethan stage. Later in his career Vauthier sustained his reputation through the translation of foreign classics.

The first play to bring him major attention was *Captain Bada* in 1952. An emblematic portrait of the artist's creative struggle, it is also a stock battle of the sexes, carried out by Bada and Alice, whose frantic three-act coexistence in a sealed apartment corresponds to courtship, marriage, and old age together. We learn that Bada has "almost" written 18,000 pages, though we are never told of what. In a virtual monologue he vaunts himself to Alice as the quintessential artist; she is his perpetual servant, co-actor, and audience. "I am creation, creation itself made man!" he shouts. The pair's interactions swing from tenderness to abuse, and the playwright intends their relationship to be a sublime roller-coaster for the audience.

Vauthier returns to the same theme in *The Fighting Personage; or, Very Loud* (*Le personnage combattant, ou, Fortissimo*), produced in 1956. At the start of its forty-two "sequences" a bourgeois traveler takes a room in a seedy hotel, seeking inspiration to rewrite a novel begun in that very room years ago. He struggles with self-doubt in his long quasi-monologue, interrupted from time to time by hotel noises and a gruff bellboy. The situation is more naturalistic than that of *Bada*, but still Vauthier signals his dramaturgical insecurity by resorting, in his published text, to six levels of STAGE DIRECTIONS. These include paragraphs introducing each dialogued sequence, prose summaries for the sequences without dialogue, notes in two font sizes placed within the dialogue, marginal notes in vertical columns, and footnotes. There is little hierarchy of information among these six levels, and such directions do not guide production as much as they insist on meanings that cannot be inferred from the dialogue itself.

Vauthier was perhaps right to be insecure. Only two years later, in 1958, SAMUEL BECKETT would handle the issue of an artist's waning creativity and regrets in KRAPP'S LAST TAPE, a play that is much more powerful because it is much more laconic.

Vauthier's translations have lived longer than his original works. In 1952, the same year as *Captain Bada*, Vauthier's version of Niccolò Machiavelli's *Mandragola* was produced by Gérard Philipe, the actor whose charisma had first inspired Vauthier to write for the stage. Though the production was considered a failure, Vauthier continued to translate. His versions of William Shakespeare, Christopher Marlowe, and Lucius Annaeus Seneca were highly regarded and gave him a new way of bringing Elizabethan energy to the French stage. BERNARD-MARIE KOLTÈS said that seeing Maria Casarès perform in Vauthier's translation of Seneca's *Medea* shocked him into becoming a playwright. Though Vauthier's own verbose DRAMATURGY would lose out in midcentury to Beckett's concision, the legacy of Vauthier's monologues would reappear in Bernard-Marie Koltès through works such as *The Night Just Before the Forest (La nuit juste avant la forêt)*.

PLAYS: *The Impromptu of Arras (L'impromptu d'Arras*, 1951); *Captain Bada (Capitaine Bada*, 1952); *The Fighting Personage; or, Very Loud (Le personnage combattant, ou, Fortissimo*, 1956); *The Marvels (Les prodiges*, 1959); *The Dreamer (Le rêveur*, 1961); *The Depths (Les abysses*, screenplay, 1963); *More of Bada (Badadesques*, 1965); translation of Seneca's *Medea* (1967); *Blood (Le sang*, 1970); translation of Marlowe's *The Massacre at Paris* (1972); translation of Shakespeare's *Romeo and Juliet* (1973); *Your Name in Clouds of Fire, Elizabeth (Ton nom dans le feu des nuées, Élisabeth*, 1977); translation of Shakespeare's *Othello* (1979); translation of Shakespeare's *King Lear* (1984)

FURTHER READING

Beigbeder, Marc. *Le théâtre en France depuis la libération*. Paris: Bordas, 1959.

Guicharnaud, Jacques, with June Guicharnaud. *Modern French Theatre from Giraudoux to Genet*. New Haven: Yale Univ. Press, 1967.

Pronko, Leonard Cabell. *Avant-Garde: The Experimental Theater in France*. Berkeley: Univ. of California Press, 1962.

David Pelizzari

VENEZUELA

Historic MELODRAMAS based on the epic events of the independence wars (1810–1830), family FARCES, the ideals of personal freedom, and the burlesque were the themes that shaped Venezuelan drama between 1860 and 1900. The autocratic but progressivist government of Antonio Guzmán Blanco (1870–1888) transformed Caracas from a colonial into a modern city. He considered theater as an indispensable activity in modern society and in 1876 built the first opera house. During his period 120 new plays were staged, including Briceño Picón's *Aguirre, the Tyrannous (El tirano Aguirre*, 1872), Heraclio Martín de la Guardia's

Building on Sand (*Fabricar sobre arena*, 1873), Nicanor Bolet Peraza's Let Them Eat Cake (*A falta de pan buenas son tortas*, 1873), Manuel Dagnino's Home Angel (*El ángel del hogar*, 1874), José Antonio Arévalo Beluche's The Boor and the Coquette (*El palurdo y la coqueta*, 1875), Aníbal Dominici's A Woman's Honor (*La honra de la mujer*, 1880), and Vicente Fortoul's Twenty Thousand Pesos for a Fan (*Veinte mil pesos por un abanico*, 1880). In the 19th century women were represented by Carmen Brigué's Alone (*Sola*, 1894), Virginia Gil de Hermoso's Freedom (*Libertad*, 1895), and Margarita Agustini's Comic Toy (*Juguete cómico*, 1895).

The 20th century brought economic and social changes due to the country's transformation from an agrarian into an oil society. In this process drama disregarded romantic and melodramatic models and favored more contemporary approaches to life: social realism in Rómulo Gallegos's The Motor (*El motor*, 1910) and The Year's Miracle (*El milagro del año*, 1915), grotesque epic in Julio Planchart's Cain's Republic (*La república de Caín*, 1915), and SURREALISM in Arturo Uslar Pietri's E. Utreja (1927) and The Key (*La llave*, 1928). However, the dictatorships of Cipriano Castro (1899–1908) and Juan Vicente Gómez (1908–1936) censored plays with political or sexual content. Until 1916 the simple family life and the sanctification of poverty were the dominant topics in Manuel A. Díez's Perfect Shot (*Tiro seguro*, 1910) and Three Social Tableaus (Poverty, Well-Being, and Wealth) (*Tres cromos socials* [Pobreza, Bienestar, Riqueza], 1916), Simón Barceló's Cinderella (*La cenicienta*, 1907) and Christmas Tale (*Cuento de navidad*, 1909), and Salustio González Rincones's Dawn (*El alba*, 1909). Costumbrismo (a genre dealing with local custom) and NATURALISM merged in Rafael Benavides Ponce's The Arrival of Spring (*El retorno de la primavera*, 1912), Julio Rosales's Untraceable Path (*La senda inhallable*, 1912), and Angel Fuenmayor's Customary Love (*El amor de siempre*, 1914). Farcical COMEDIES proved to be the most popular genre in Rafael Ginand's The Break (*El rompimiento*, 1919) and I Am Also a Candidate (*Yo también soy candidato*, 1939), Leoncio Martínez's An Unexpected Mulatto Child (*El salto atrás*, 1925), and Leopoldo Ayala Michelena's Corroded Souls (*Almas descarnadas*, 1921), The Box Office (*La taquilla*, 1922), and Bagasse (*Bagazo*, 1934).

The clash between the urban and the rural that dominated Venezuelan drama until 1958 was first introduced in Andrés Eloy Blanco's The Christ of the Violets (*El Cristo de las violetas*, 1925). Other significant plays with a similar subject were Víctor Manuel Rivas's The Foundation (*El puntal*, 1933), Pablo Domínguez's Tremor (*Tremedal*, 1933), Guillermo Maneses's Nieves Marmol's Husband (*El marido de Nieves Mármol*, 1940), and Eduardo Calcaño's The Negative Pole (*El polo negativo*, 1942).

César Rengifo is considered the pioneer of Venezuelan modern drama because of the diversity of his themes and his use of innovative linguistic and dramatic models. In plays such as *Curayú* (1947), *Joaquina Sánchez* (1948), and *Manuelote* (1950) he combined the vernacular speech of the masses with philosophical reflections on the meaning of life. In works such as *Yuma* (1940), *The Canaries (Los canarios*, 1949), and *Armors of Smoke (Armaduras de* humo, 1951) Rengifo wittily portrayed the conflicts of the nascent urban middle class.

The arrival of Spanish director Alberto de Paz y Mateos (1945), Mexican actor Jesús Gómez Obregón (1947), and Argentine actress Juana Sujo (1949) introduced modern theater pedagogy in Venezuela. Gómez Obregón brought the KONSTANTIN STAN-ISLAVSKY method and the modern American theater. Sujo, with Carlos Márquez, founded the Venezuelan Theater Society, and Paz y Mateos taught the basics of experimental theater. Their teaching influenced Ramón Díaz Sánchez's *The House* (La casa, 1955), Ida Gramcko's *Belén Silveira* (1952), and *María Lionza* (1957), Elizabeth Schön's *Interval* (Intervalo, 1957), and Román Chalbaud's *The Adolescents* (Los adolescentes, 1952), *Horizontal Walls* (Muros horizontales, 1953), and *Cain Adolescent* (Caín adolescente, 1955).

The overthrow of Marcos Pérez Jiménez (1952–1958) inaugurated an era of democratic changes reflected in César Rengifo's *Rope of Fog* (Soga de niebla, 1958) and Román Chalbaud's *Requiem for an Eclipse* (Réquiem para un eclipse, 1958). Democracy witnessed the emergence of a new society and of original playwrights who portrayed contemporary realities without political and moral restraints. Román Chalbaud wrote about the underworld and the marginal urban community in *Sacred and Obscene* (Sagrado y obsceno, 1961), *Coffee and Orchids* (Café y orquídeas, 1962), *The Burning of Judas* (La quema de Judas, 1964), *The Terrible Angels* (Los ángeles terribles, 1967), and *The Smoking Fish* (El pez que fuma, 1968). Isaac Chocrón depicted the young urban middle class in *Monica and the Florentine* (Mónica y el florentino, 1959), *Ferocious Animals* (Animales feroces, 1963), *Asia and the Far East* (Asia y el lejano oriente, 1966), and *Okey* (1968). José Ignacio Cabrujas delved into the ideological imperfections of the political system in *Juan Francisco de León* (1959), *The Rebels* (Los insurgentes, 1960), *The Strange Voyage of Simon the Wicked* (El extraño viaje de Simón el malo, 1962), and *Fiésole* (1967). Chalbaud, Chocrón, and Cabrujas founded El Nuevo Grupo (1967–1988), which staged the works of more than thirty new Venezuelan playwrights and brought to audiences the best of modern world drama. Women playwrights were represented by Elizabeth Schön's *Melisa and the Self* (Melisa y el yo, 1961) and *The Village* (La aldea, 1966) and Elisa Lerner's *The Intelligent Belle* (La bella de inteligencia, 1960) and *Manhattan's Vast Silence* (El vasto silencio de Manhattan, 1964).

The 1970s brought stagings of spectacles with an elaborate mise-en-scène by Argentinean director Carlos Giménez. In 1971 he founded Rajatabla with his version of Luis Britto García's *Your Venezuela* (Venezuela tuya, 1971), followed by his interpretation of Rómulo Gallegos's novel *Reddish Lances* (Las lanzas coloradas, 1974) and Mariela Romero's *The Game* (El juego, 1976). Rodolfo Santana portrayed the violent contradictions between tradition and modernity during the oil boom under Carlos Andrés Pérez's government (1974–1979) in *End of the Round* (Fin de round, 1974), *The Firm Forgives a Moment of Madness* (La empresa perdona un momento de locura, 1975), *Tales of the Slums* (Historias de cerro arriba, 1975), *Thanks for the Favors* (Gracias por los favores recibidos, 1977), and *The Model Jail Chronicles* (Crónicas de la cárcel modelo, 1978), whereas Edilio Peña wrote an introspective and existential theater in *Resistance* (Resistencia, 1973), *The Circle* (El círculo, 1975), and *The Birds Go Away with Death* (Los pájaros se van con la muerte, 1978).

The 1980s saw the rise of collective and experimental theater in Marco Antonio Ettedgui's *Screams* (Gritos, 1980), Javier Vidal's *Salomé* (1981), José Simón Escalona's *Jav y Jos* (1986), and Xiomara Moreno's *White Pearl with Senorita's Ring* (Perlita blanca con sortija de señorita, 1986). Also, there was a surge of powerful feminist works in Carlota Martínez's *My God Have Her in Heaven* (Que Dios la tenga en su gloria, 1983), Thais Erminy's *Whisky & Cocaína* (1984), and Blanca Strepponi and Teotiste Gallegos's *Final Stroke* (Ultima recta final, 1989).

In the 1990s urgent topics took center stage: AIDS in Johnny Gavlovski's *Man* (Hombre, 1990) and *Habitant at the End of Time* (Habitante del fin de los tiempos, 1996), Elio Palencia's *Single Room for a Lonely Man* (Habitación independiente para hombre solo, 1990), Isaac Chocrón's *Written and Sealed* (Escrito y sellado, 1993), David Osorio Lovera's *The Decade's Last Brunch* (El último brunch de la década, 1993), Maritza Palencia's *AIDS and Genesis* (El sida y el génesis, 1993), Aminta de Lara's *End of the Century* (Fin de siglo, 1996), and Marcos Purroy's *Fingers/Dedos de goma* (1997); urban sexual and political violence in Román Chalbaud's *Mother-of-Pearl Vesicle* (Vesícula de nácar, 1992), Gustavo Ott's *I Never Said I Was a Good Girl* (Nunca dije que era una niña buena, 1992) and *Pornographic Heart* (Corazón pornográfico, 1994), Néstor Caballero's *Maladranzas* (1995), and Rodolfo Santana's *Encounter in a Dangerous Park* (Encuentro en el parque peligroso, 1996); women's intimate experiences in Fausto Verdial's *Don't Call Me Mad!* (¡Que no me llamen loca!, 1995), Basilio Alvarez's *Puttanesca Sunday* (Domingo a la puttanesca, 1996), and Mónica Montañés's *The Applause Goes Inside* (El aplauso va por dentro, 1996); and democracy's corruption in José Gabriel Núñez's *Mrs. Matos's Unbelievable Funeral* (El insólito funeral de la señora Matos, 1993) and Mariela Romero's *The Return of King Lear* (El regreso del rey Lear, 1996).

Recent playwrights have favored introspective works dealing with loneliness, loss, friendship, parenthood, and the dehumanization of society in Toti Vollmer's *Open Secret* (Secreto a voces, 2000), José Tomás Angola's *Folks in Bed* (Los seres sobre las camas, 2001), Orlando Urdaneta's *Men Getting a Divorce?* (¿Divorciarme yo?, 2002), and Gerardo Blanco's *A Citizen Called Teacher* (Un ciudadano llamado maestro, 2003). However, the course that Venezuelan theater will take in the new millennium is yet to be seen.

FURTHER READING

Azparren Giménez, Leonardo. *Documentos para la historia del teatro en Venezuela: Siglos XVI, XVII, XVIII* [Documents for Venezuela's theater history: 16th, 17th, and 18th centuries]. Caracas: Monte Avila, 1996.

———. *El teatro en Venezuela: Ensayos históricos* [Venezuelan theater: Historical essays]. Caracas: Alfadil, 1997.

Moreno Uribe, Edgard Antonio. *Teatro 93: Apuntes para su historia en Venezuela* [Theater 93: Notes for its history in Venezuela]. Caracas: Vadell Hermanos, 1994.

——. *Teatro 98: Apuntes para su historia en Venezuela*. Caracas: Kairos, 1998.

Varderi, Alejandro, Juan Calzadilla, and Elsa Flores, eds. *Ettedgui: Arte-información para la comunidad*. [Ettedgui: Art Information for the Community]. Caracas: Oxígeno, 1985.

Alejandro Varderi

VERDECCHIA, GUILLERMO (1962–)

This is the border zone and your papers are not in order.
—*Fronteras Americanas*, 1993

Playwright, director, translator, and actor Guillermo Verdecchia was born in Buenos Aires, ARGENTINA, in 1962. His family immigrated to CANADA and settled in southern Ontario. After a brief period studying at Ryerson University, Verdecchia began a successful career in theater. His plays, films, and radio pieces have been seen and heard across Canada, often to critical acclaim.

Verdecchia has taught playwriting and acting at the University of Guelph and Brock University (2001–2003) and was writer-in-residence at Memorial University of Newfoundland in 1999. In August 1999 he was appointed artistic director of Toronto's Cahoots Theatre Project, whose mission is the creation, development, promotion, and production of new Canadian theatrical works reflecting the country's ethnic and cultural diversity.

Verdecchia's work has won numerous accolades. These include Outstanding Theatre for Young Audience awards—a Dora Mavor Moore for *i.d.* (1989) and a Jessie for directing Dennis Foon's *War* (1995); Chalmers Canadian Play Awards for *i.d.* (1990), *The Noam Chomsky Lectures* (1992), *Fronteras Americanas: American Borders* (1993), and *A Line in the Sand* (1997); a place on the Governor General's Award shortlist for *Chomsky*, with an Award for Drama going to *Fronteras*; and numerous jury prizes at international film festivals.

A major element of Verdecchia's early works, particularly *Fronteras Americanas*, is an autobiographical element—the presence of the author within the work. In *Fronteras* several characters—including "Verdecchia" himself—all played by a single actor, describe revisiting their Argentinean homeland. The confrontation between cultures creates the central tension of the piece. Later works deal with an array of real and fictional characters projected onto the stage, forcing the audience to navigate its way through a series of challenges to the basic assumptions of Western culture.

For Verdecchia, the playwright is part detective, part oracle, part herald. The writer serves the community as one who reveals its hidden truths, the stories buried under "official versions" of events. His plays challenge the audience, confronting it with the cultural hypocrisies and contradictions of contemporary society. The theater, in his mind, should reflect Canada's cultural and ethnic diversity to accurately reflect the world.

To call his theater inherently political is not entirely accurate. Rather, his work deals with issues of culture, IDENTITY, home, and the conception of self as a global citizen. His work is highly critical of our media-saturated society. He writes on political issues, but rather than try to make the audience merely sympathize, he also tries to show how Western society is implicated in these issues.

For Verdecchia, political and personal identity are uncertain, and what he calls "totalizing myths"—stories we tell ourselves about ourselves and then apply to all people, everywhere—are bunk. Instead, he embraces the idea of identity as indeterminacy and process. His plays deal with shifting borders and transitions, the representation of minorities within the larger society, and the constant search for home.

SELECT PLAYS: *i.d.* (1989); *Final Decisions (War)* (1990); *The Noam Chomsky Lectures* (1991); *Fronteras Americanas: American Borders* (1993); *Twenty Steps to the Promised Land* (originally *Lo que cala son los filos* by Mauricio Jiménez) (1994); *True Lies* (1995); *A Line in the Sand* (1997); *Truth; or, The Terrible but Incomplete Journals of John D.* (1997); *Insomnia* (1999)

FURTHER READING

Benson, Eugene, and L. W. Conolly. *English-Canadian Theatre. Perspectives on Canadian Culture*. Toronto: Oxford Univ. Press, 1987.

Berry, J. W., and J. A. Laponce, eds. *Ethnicity and Culture in Canada: The Research Landscape*. Toronto: Univ. of Toronto Press, 1994.

Bowering, George, ed. *And Other Stories*. Vancouver: Talonbooks, 2001.

Burnet, Jean, and Howard Palmer. *Coming Canadians: An Introduction to a History of Canada's Peoples*. Toronto: McClelland & Stewart, 1988.

Francis, Daniel. *National Dreams: Myth, Memory, and Canadian History*. Vancouver: Arsenal Pulp Press, 1997.

Verdecchia, Guillermo. *Citizen Suárez*. Toronto: Talonbooks, 1998.

Vogt, Gordon. *Critical Stages: Canadian Theatre in Crisis*. Ottawa: Oberon Press, 1998.

Daniel Goldberg

VERGA, GIOVANNI (1840–1922)

Giovanni Verga, born in Catania, ITALY, in 1840, is the foremost representative of Italian *verismo* and a major Italian literary figure of the 19th century. Although he is known and valued primarily for his novels, especially *I Malavoglia* (1881) and *Mastro-don Gesualdo* (1889), and for his short stories, he wrote several plays, most of them adaptations of his short stories. *Rustic Chivalry* (*Cavalleria rusticana*) and *The She-Wolf* (*La lupa*) are the best known. *Rustic Chivalry*, set in Sicily and dealing with love, jealousy, infidelity, betrayal, and honor, premiered in Turin in 1884 with Eleonora Duse in the role of Santuzza and was an instant success, although it was destined for greater fame as an opera composed by Pietro Mascagni. *The She-Wolf*, a two-act play also set in Sicily, premiered in Turin in 1896. Like *Rustic Chivalry*, it is a drama in the veristic vein that rationalizes, as Luigi Ferrante notes in *Verga: La vita, il pensiero, i testi esemplari* (Verga The Life, the Thought, the Exemplary Texts), ancient myths of blood and love. Both plays lack the dramatic intensity of the short stories. In play form *Rustic Chivalry* focuses on Santuzza's pain and her revenge for having been wronged by Turiddu, while in the short story the violation of the sanctity of the family hearth by Turiddu's affair with the married Lola is a transgression that cannot go unpunished. In *The She-Wolf* Pina is no longer the central figure, and her passion for her son-in-law, central throughout the story, becomes a bland love affair secondary to ritual renderings, more imaginary than real, of folkloristic Sicilian peasant life made up of dances on the threshing floor and religious processions. In both plays Verga adjusts his plot to an urbane northern Italian audience uninterested in the customs and impulsiveness of the primitive Sicilian types that Verga the novelist holds dear.

Before these dramas, probably during the period 1873–1875, Verga wrote *Fading Roses* (*Rose caduche*), a three-act play reflective of the late romantic literary vein that attracted Verga before he turned his attention to *verismo*. This play deals with the mundane infatuations, gallantries, and duels associated with the self-indulgent high society of the time, for whom love is nothing more than a game, while intelligence and art are looked at cynically. In 1885 Verga adapted his short story "Il canarino del N. 15" into a two-act drama, *In the Porter's Lodge* (*In portineria*), which premiered in Milan and in which Verga relies on his observations of that city's suffering poor. *What's Yours Is Mine* (*Dal tuo al mio*), staged for the first time in Milan in 1903 and later published as a novel, concludes Verga's theatrical production. In this three-act play, perhaps his most innovative, Verga's focus is on progress and on the inevitable changes it brings as it favors some in society at the expense of others. The fall of Barone Navarra's family and the terrible condition of those who work in his sulfur mine are counterbalanced by the success of the modern-day entrepreneur, Mr. Rametta, a shrewd businessman who secures his wealth by exploiting without scruples. In this he finds an ally in Luciano, who, in his desire to climb the social ladder, marries the baron's daughter and takes up arms against the mine workers, for whom he had been their spokesperson in the past, who have staged a strike for better wages and improved living conditions.

Two other pieces, sketches rather than actual plays and with no documented performances, are *The Wolf Hunt* (*Caccia al lupo*) and *The Fox Hunt* (*Caccia alla volpe*).

SELECT PLAYS: *Fading Roses* (*Rose caduche*, 1873?); *Rustic Chivalry* (*Cavalleria Rusticana*, 1884); *In the Porter's Lodge* (*In Portineria*, 1885); *The She-Wolf* (*La Lupa*, 1886); *The Fox Hunt* (*Caccia alla volpe*, 1901); *The Wolf Hunt* (*La caccia al lupo*, 1902); *From Yours to Mine* (*Dal tuo al mio*, 1903)

FURTHER READING

Alexander, Alfred. *Giovanni Verga. A Great Writer and His World*. London: Grant & Cutler, 1972.

Amatangelo, Susan. *Figuring Women: A Thematic Study of Giovanni Verga's Female Character*. Madison, N.J.: Farleigh Dickinson Univ. Press, 2004.

Bergin, Thomas Goddard. *Giovanni Verga*. New Haven: Yale Univ. Press, 1931.

Ferrante, Luigi. *Verga: La vita, il pensiero, i testi esemplari* [Verga: The Life, the Thought, the Exemplary Texts]. Milan: Accademia, 1972.

Lucente, Gregory. "The Ideology of Form in Verga's La Lupa: Realism, Myth and the Passion of Control." In *The Narrative of Realism and Myth*. Baltimore: Johns Hopkins Univ. Press, 1979. 54–94.

Sansone, Matteo. "Verga, Puccini and La Lupa." *Italian Studies* 44 (1989): 65–76.

Nicholas Patruno

VESTIDO DE NOIVA See WEDDING GOWN

VIANNA FILHO ("VIANINHA"), ODUVALDO (1936–1974)

Oduvaldo Vianna Filho was the son of a well-known author of COMEDIES of the 1920s and 1930s. Vianinha, as he was called, was the leading voice of the politically engaged generation of dramatists of the 1960s and early 1970s in BRAZIL.

His main concern was investigating the country's social problems from the point of view of the Brazilian working class. This could not be done within the framework of conventional drama, and as a consequence he turned to the development of EPIC techniques, which allowed him to transcend the realm of individual conflicts and to focus on collective matters. The works of BERTOLT BRECHT and ERWIN PISCATOR were particularly influential in this respect.

Having grown up in a politically militant family, Vianinha was always extremely concerned with the discussion of the social role of culture. Theater, for him, was not only an instrument of artistic pleasure, but also a tool for the transformation of reality.

During his career he participated in theater groups directly involved in the renovation of the Brazilian drama of the day, such as the ARENA THEATER OF SÃO PAULO (Teatro de Arena de São Paulo, 1955–1960), the Centro Popular de Cultura da União Nacional dos Estudantes, organized after the production of his play *The Surplus Value Is Going to Finish, Mr. Edgar* (*A mais-valia vai acabar, seu Edgar*, 1960–1964), and the Opinião (1965–1967).

He started his career as a dramatist at the Arena Theater, where he also worked as an actor. His first play, *Chapetuba Football Club* (*Chapetuba Futebol Clube*, 1959), a realistic investigation of the political interests involved in a soccer championship, was welcomed by both the critics and the audience.

In 1960 he decided to leave the Arena, where the work was inevitably aimed at middle-class audiences. His intention of reaching proletarian spectators motivated him to join the organization of the street-theater department of Centro Popular de Cultura, where he participated in the collective creation of many political sketches dealing with the most crucial themes taken from the political debate. He also dedicated a series of three full-length plays, written between 1961 and 1963, to these themes: *Brazil Brazilian Version* (*Brasil versão brasileira*, 1962), *Four Pieces of Land* (*Quatro quadras de terra*, 1963) and *The Azeredos and the Benevides* (*Os Azeredo mais os Benevides*, 1963).

With the military dictatorship, implanted in 1964, and with a federal act promulgated in 1968 exacerbating censorship to an unprecedented level, Vianinha was forced to return to professional theater. All of the plays he wrote from this period on deal with the problems of middle-class intellectuals crucially divided between individualism and political consciousness.

Vianinha's most mature and well-developed plays include *Besieged Young Man* (*Moço em Estado de sítio*, 1965), *If You Run Away, the Beast Catches You, If You Stay, the Beast Eats You Up* (*Se correr o bicho pega, se ficar o bicho come*, 1965), *The Law Is Hard, for Your Hair, Use Only Gumex* (*Dura lex sed lex no cabelo só Gumex*, 1967), *Dictator Highirte* (*Papa Highirte*, 1968), *Our Life in the Family* (*Nossa vida em família*, 1972) and BREAK THE HEART (*Rasga coração*, 1974), considered his masterpiece.

He was also a talented author of television scripts, having written several television plays and the extremely successful television series *A grande família*. He died of lung cancer in 1974 at the age of thirty-seven. Many years were to pass until many of his plays, banned by the censorship, could finally be staged.

SELECT PLAYS: *Chapetuba Football Club* (*Chapetuba Futebol Clube*, 1959); *The Surplus Value Is Going to Finish, Mr. Edgar* (*A mais-valia vai acabar, Seu Edgar*, 1960); *The Act of the 99%* (*O Auto dos 99%*, 1962); *Brazil Brazilian Version* (*Brasil versão brasileira*, 1962); *The Azeredos and the Benevides* (*Os Azeredo mais os Benevides*, 1963); "*Opinion*" (*Show*) (*Show Opinião*, 1964); *Besieged Young Man* (*Moço em estado de sítio*, 1965); *If You Run Away, the Beast Catches You, If You Stay, the Beast Eats You Up* (*Se correr o bicho pega, se ficar o bicho come*, 1965); *Hand in Glove* (*Mão na luva*, 1966); *The Law Is Hard, for Your Hair, Use Only Gumex* (*Dura lex sed, lex, no cabelo só Gumex* [revue], 1967); *Dictator Highirte* (*Papa Highirte*, 1968); *Christal's Long Night* (*A longa noite de Cristal*, 1969); *Inner Struggle* (*Corpo a corpo* [monologue], 1970); *Frenzied Allegro* (*Allegro desbum*, 1972); *Mom, Dad Is Turning Purple* (*Mamãe, Papai está ficando roxo*, 1973); *Break the Heart* (*Rasga coração*, 1974)

FURTHER READING

Betti, Maria Silvia. *Oduvaldo Vianna Filho*. São Paulo: EDUSP, 1997.

Damasceno, Leslie. *Cultural Space and Theatrical Conventions in the Works of Oduvaldo Vianna Filho*. Detroit: Wayne State Univ. Press, 1996.

Guimarães, Carmelinda. *Um ato de resistência: O teatro de Oduvaldo Vianna Filho* [An Act of Resistance: The Theater of Oduvaldo Vianna Filho]. São Paulo: MG Editores, 1984.

Moraes, Dênis de. *Vianinha, cúmplice da paixão: Uma biografia de Oduvaldo Vianna Filho* [Vianinha, An Accomplice of Passion: A Biography of Oduvaldo Vianna Filho]. Rev. ed. Rio de Janeiro: Record, 2000.

Patriota, Rosângela. *Vianinha: Um dramaturgo no coração de seu tempo* [Vianinha: A Playwright in the Heart of His Own Age]. São Paulo: Hucitec, 1999.

Vianna, Deocélia. *Companheiros de viagem* [Travel Companions]. São Paulo: Brasiliense, 1984.

Maria Sílvia Betti

VIETNAM

The major stylized Vietnamese theaters are *tuong* or *hat boi*, a court form related to Chinese-style opera; *cai luong* (reformed song-and-dance theater) of the south; *cheo*, a folk opera of the northern region; and *mua roi nuoc* (water puppetry). These traditional genres continued to evolve in the 20th century.

Tuong was still a vital force in the early 20th century. *The Trung Queens* by Phan Boi Chau and Tong Phuoc Pho, which showed legendary women warriors defending Vietnam against Chinese imperialism, was among the most popular anticolonial scripts in the 1920s. Though *tuong* continues to be performed in northern and central Vietnam, it is considered old-fashioned by contemporary Vietnamese audiences. However, *tuong* companies are beginning to update productions to make them more appealing. Recent *tuong* productions in Hanoi have included an adaptation of William Shakespeare's *Othello* and a six-scene *tuong* variety show with English supertitles.

Cai luong was an attempt to modify *hat boi* for modern life. It began around 1916 with *Bui Kiem's Failure at the Exams* by the music group of Tong Huu Dinh. Infused with singing and MELODRAMA, it was popular in the south until the 1970s. Today the older generation attends annual festivals, but companies struggle to capture the younger audience. Repertoire has ranged from the 19th-century classical *Tale of Kieu*, which tells of a long-suffering courtesan, to cloak-and-dagger-type episodes of the 1930 and 1940s and contemporary tales. *The Suburbanite* (1980) by Minh Khoa shows a man who denies the Vietcong to save his daughter. He exonerates himself by leading the Vietcong to the American post. The story dealt with an issue for southern audiences—collaboration with Americans during the war.

Cheo's agrarian roots endeared it to northern audiences throughout the 19th and 20th centuries. Its proletarian potential gained the support of the Marxist government from the 1950s on. Traditional stories include *Thi Kinh, the Goddess of Mercy* (*Quan Am Thi Kinh*), the melodrama of a cast-out wife who disguises herself as a monk and raises a child she is accused of fathering. Modern scripts, such as *Return to the Barracks* (*Duron va tran dia*) by Tao Mat and Hoai Giao, are set in the 1970s war: a soldier is tested for loyalty by a militia woman.

Water puppetry (mua roi nuoc), a village art of the Red River area until the 1980s, has been reworked at the well-appointed Thang Long Theatre in Hanoi. Episodes evoke nostalgia for the agrarian life of the past and point to national pride at defeating foreign aggressors.

Kich noi is the spoken drama of Vietnam. Developed in the early 20th century as part of the New Poetry movement, it remains most popular in the north. Its textual emphasis contrasts with the traditional theater's use of music, song, and stylized movement. Flowering in the 1920s, it sought to emulate European models. Kich noi can be seen as undergoing three periods: the first is emulation of French models (1907–1920), in which both form and content are European; the second period is characterized by a self-reflexive but politically impotent critique of middle-class colonial life (1920–1945); the third period is linked to Vietnamese independence (1953–) after World War II and is characterized by a politically charged theater that ranges in content from revolutionary to propagandistic.

Vietnamese artists began by exploring Western models. Molière's Miser was staged in 1907, and other European translations followed. In 1920 To Gian, an author for Indochina Magazine, wrote Who Was That Killer? (Ai giet nguoi), and Pham Ngoc Khoi quickly followed with Being Choosy Turns Out Bad (Gia ken ken hom), which portrays a girl who abandons a good-hearted medical student to pursue a Westernized lover. Forced into prostitution, she is treated for venereal disease by the young doctor. Westernization bodes ill for those who embrace it.

A Cup of Poison (Chen thuoc doc, 1921) by Vu Dinh Long (1896–1960), presented at the Hanoi Grand Theatre, was the first fully developed play. A man is given to gambling; his wife and mother dabble in sorcery; and his unmarried sister is pregnant. He resolves to escape this degenerate life by drinking poison, but a sibling's financial assistance saves him. In this and other plays, such as Tribunal of Conscience (Toa an luong, 1923) and New Women (Dan ba moi, 1944), Vu Dinh Long probes the middle-class life of the colonial period and espouses a return to Confucian ethics. Another author who took up this theme was Vi Huyen Dac (1899–1976), who wrote twenty plays. In Money (Kim tien, 1938) an impoverished writer whose success in business brings no happiness contemplates the corrosive effect of wealth on family. One of the most successful plays of the colonial period was Nam Xuong's The Annamite Frenchman (Ong tay An-nam, 1931), which satirized francophile Vietnamese in a mode reminiscent of Molière's Bourgeois Gentleman.

Nguyen Huy Tuong (1912–1960) continued contemplation of Vietnamese life. But where characters of the colonial period seem trapped and passive, now we start to see politically active heroes altering their situation. Vu Nhu To (1943), a historical play, shows an architect who is forced to choose between self and service to the nation. Bac Son Village (1945) shows an evil French collaborator being slain by villagers after he kills his wife and her father. This writing anticipates independence.

From the 1950s through the 1970s, revolutionary themes and exemplary interpretations of history abounded. Training schools were established. Through Soviet and Eastern-bloc exchanges performers gained a strong base in KONSTANTIN STANISLAVSKY technique and Brechtian aesthetics. In 1952 director Thu Lu (1907–) and Nguyen Xuan Khoa founded the Central Spoken Drama Troupe, which remains a major company. SOCIALIST REALISM became the major artistic mode. Tahm Tam's Blood-Stained Banner was a paean to "those who have died for the red and gold." State-supported troupes communicated the message of the revolutionary government to the masses.

With the withdrawal of the U.S. military and the fall of Saigon in 1975, the painful rebuilding began. Southern intellectuals underwent "reeducation," but by the 1980s the doi moi (renovation) policy was opening the door to the Western bloc. Plays such as Seaside Summer (Mua he o bien, 1985) by Xuan Trinh expanded theatrical content. This play explored the contradictions between the old and the emerging generation. One of the most prolific writers of the postwar period was Luu Quang Vu, who created over thirty plays between 1981 and 1991. Truong Ba's Spirit in a Butcher's Body (Hon Truong Ba da hang thit, 1985) shows a gentle gardener who dies because of the carelessness of the gods and is reborn in a coarse butcher's body. The play deals with inefficiencies of the bureaucracy and the clash between traditional and modern values.

Though experimental work has emerged, theme and content remain circumspect. Whereas the modern drama in much of Southeast Asia is an openly political theater, attacking government and addressing the ravages of modern life, the theater of Vietnam follows a Marxist model. Theater is a didactic tool for inspiring people to ideologically and socially correct behavior.

FURTHER READING

Dinh Quang et al. Vietnamese Theater. Hanoi: Gioi, 1999.

Foley, Kathy. "The Metonomy of Art: Vietnamese Water Puppets." TDR (Winter 2001).

Foley, Kathy, and Krishen Jit. "Vietnam." In The Cambridge Guide to Asian Theatre, ed. by James Brandon. Cambridge: Cambridge Univ. Press, 1993. 245–251.

Mackerras, Colin. "Theatre in Vietnam." Asian Theatre Journal 4, no. 1 (1987).

Nguyen Huy Hong and Tran Trung Chinh. Vietnamese Traditional Water Puppetry. Hanoi: Gioi, 1996.

Viet Chung et al. "Vietnamese Modern Theatre." Vietnamese Studies 17, 87 (1987): 7–16.

Kathy Foley

A VIEW FROM THE BRIDGE

The one-act version of ARTHUR MILLER's A View from the Bridge opened on a double bill with A Memory of Two Mondays at the Coronet Theatre on September 29, 1955, where it played for 149 performances. A year later Miller reworked it as a play in two acts for Peter Brook's production in London. There was, as often with Miller's plays in the early 1950s, a swirl of extratheatrical conjecture about the climate in which it was produced. Miller had broken with his old friend Elia Kazan, the director of his first Broadway successes, because Kazan had testified as a friendly witness before the House Un-American Activities Committee, naming names that were already known to the committee. ERIC BENTLEY, reviewing the first production and the published play in the *New Republic*, assumed that *View* was an answer to Kazan's film *On the Waterfront* (1954), the latter proving that informing is good, the former that it is bad. Such a reading reduces the play to pettiness, but the gossip was so prevalent that Miller wrote a letter to the *New York Post*, protesting a remark in Murray Kempton's column and insisting that his play "is not about a political informer. When I write a play about a political informer he will be called a political informer." Still, it is a play about an informer, and plays—even Arthur Miller's plays—have been known to deal in analogies. More important, it is a play about a man in deep distress and fatal confusion. That was obvious in 1965 when an OFF-BROADWAY production, focusing on Eddie Carbone, ran for almost two years.

Carbone is unusual among early Miller protagonists, for he is a man who accepts the rules and prejudices of his society, an Italian neighborhood in Brooklyn, and dies because he violates them. Early in the play, warning his niece Catherine to be closemouthed about the illegal immigrants who are coming to live with them, he indicates his approval of the violent punishment a neighboring family visited on a boy who "snitched to the Immigration." By the end of the play, "passion that had moved into his body, like a stranger," as the ponderously pretentious narrator Alfieri says, leads him to become an informer. It is obvious from the beginning that Eddie's protective behavior toward his niece is unvoiced and unvoiceable sexual passion, and when she falls in love with Rodolpho, one of the illegals, he decides to remove the young man. His decision is so hedged with rationalization that he is never conscious of his motivation. Incapable of putting a label on his incestuous love for Catherine and his homosexual attraction to Rodolpho, he becomes an informer. Unable to accept that lesser label, he cries out "gimme my name" and rushes into a knife fight with Rodolpho's brother, asking for a lie that will let him live or, failing that, for death.

In 1999 Miller and Arnold Weinstein wrote the libretto for William Bolcom's opera version of *View*, a very effective work that indicated that what some critics in 1955 saw as melodramatic was, in fact, operatic.

[*See also* United States, 1940–Present]

FURTHER READING

Miller, Arthur. *The Theater Essays of Arthur Miller.* Ed. by Robert A. Martin. New York: Viking, 1978.

——. *Timebends: A Life.* New York: Grove, 1987.

Weales, Gerald. "Arthur Miller and the 1950s." *Michigan Quarterly Review* 37 (Fall 1998): 635–651.

Gerald Weales

VILDANDEN   See THE WILD DUCK

VINAVER, MICHEL (1927–)

Considered by many to be FRANCE's greatest living playwright, Michel Vinaver (pseudonym for Michel Grinberg) was born in Paris in 1927 to parents of Russian Jewish origin. During World War II they fled to the UNITED STATES, where in 1947 Vinaver received his bachelor's degree in English from Wesleyan University. Upon his subsequent return to France, Vinaver began a dual career as an author and businessman, writing plays while pursuing a career with the Gillette Corporation. Vinaver eventually became chief executive officer of Gillette Belgium, Gillette France, and Gillette's affiliate DuPont until 1979, when he quit business to focus exclusively on writing and teaching.

Vinaver's hallmark is his teasing, compelling, and exquisitely structured dramatic poetry. With his contemporaries, French playwrights ARMAND GATTI and ARTHUR ADAMOV, Vinaver shares an obsession with the dramatic potential of quotidian or "banal" dialogue and situations. Vinaver's mature style features seemingly desultory snippets of quotidian speech devoid of punctuation. Together these snippets form a continuous, rhythmic whole. The lack of punctuation unsettles the initial impression of NATURALISM, leaving the impression that a given character's words have no end point, no referent, that they signify nothing other than that character's own perceptions.

Vinaver demonstrates an extraordinarily full vision of postindustrial daily life, portraying Western society's alternating shock at and acceptance of its own reality. This dynamic is particularly French, and in it Vinaver perfectly captures the ongoing crisis of French national IDENTITY. His characters manifest both complacency and fortitude in their desperate attempts to navigate the tenuous separation between the marketplace and the home, the cultural mainstream and the fringe, the institutional narrative and the private experience. The result is an abstracted, musical form of tragicomic REALISM.

In *Overboard* (*Par-dessus bord*, produced 1969) the fate of French industry is symbolized by the debate of French toilet-paper executives as to whether the act of defecation is work or pleasure. In *High Places* (*L'Ordinaire*, produced 1981), American executives crash-land in the Andes and obsessively continue boardroom meetings while being forced to eat each other for survival. Such split purposes become less funny in Vinaver's more recent plays, *Portrait of a Woman* (*Portrait d'Une Femme*, produced 1984) and *The Television Program* (*L'Emission de télévision*, produced 1991). The institutional rapaciousness of the judicial, entertainment, and journalistic establishments separates individuals from their private experience of TRAGEDY, transforming it into facile fables for public consumption. This action becomes even sadder as the individuals themselves begin to subscribe to the public versions of their own lives.

Though some commentators have argued otherwise, Vinaver maintains that he is not a "political" playwright and that his work has no "message." He acknowledges being influenced by BERTOLT BRECHT's focus on contemporary society, but stronger influences may be found in the impressionism of ANTON CHEKHOV, which Vinaver has developed to a pointillist extreme; in the discontinuities of T. S. ELIOT's poetry; or in the recombinant Goldberg Variations of Johann Sebastian Bach.

Although such influential directors as Roger Planchon, Jacques Lasalle, and Alain Françon have staged Vinaver's plays, they have seen relatively few major productions because of their formal challenges. Vinaver remains extraordinarily active, continuing to publish new plays.

[See also Tragicomedy]

SELECT PLAYS (WITH DATES OF PUBLICATION): *The Koreans* (*Les Coréens*, 1956); *The Ushers* (*Les Huissiers*, 1958); *Iphigenia Hotel* (*Iphigénie Hotel*, 1960); *The Interview* (*La demande d'emploi*, 1972); *Overboard* (*Par-dessus bord*, 1969); *Dissident, It Goes Without Saying*, (*Dissident, il va sans dire*, 1976); *Nina, That's Something Else* (*Nina, c'est autre chose*, 1978); *Works and Days* (*Les travaux et les jours*, 1979); *Falling Over Backwards* (*A la renverse*, 1980); *High Places* (*L'Ordinaire*, 1981); *The Neighbors* (*Les Voisins*, 1986); *Portrait of a Woman* (*Portrait d'Une Femme*, 1984); *The Last Shock* (*Le Dernier sursaut*, 1990); *The Television Program* (*L'Emission de télévision*, 1991); *King* (1999); *September 11, 2001* (*11 Septembre 2001*, performed 2002); *The objecter* (dramatic version of his novel *L'Objecteur*, 2003)

FURTHER READING

Bradby, David. *The Theater of Michel Vinaver.* Ann Arbor: Univ. of Michigan Press, 1993.

Carmody, Jim. "'A Certain Music': Françon Revisits Vinaver's *Les Voisins.*" TheatreForum 22 (Winter/Spring 2003): 75–84.

Elstob, Kevin. *The Plays of Michel Vinaver: Political Theatre in France.* New York: P. Lang, 1992.

Lester, Gideon. "Industrial Art: The Theater of Michel Vinaver." Theater 28.1 (1997) 69–73.

Ubersfeld, Anne. *Vinaver dramaturge.* Paris: Librairie Théâtrale, 1989.

Scott Horstein

THE VIRGIN'S MASK

The Virgin's Mask (*Shōjo kamen*) is a Japanese drama by KARA JŪRŌ that won the prestigious Kishida Kunio Drama Prize. It is arguably his best play and incorporates most of the social, political, and theatrical elements that Kara concerned himself with in the 1960s, when JAPAN's theater was a leading force in the arts and society. Socially, Kara felt that Japanese traditions and culture were hollowed out through slavish imitation of the West. This

was not a new concern, but was perhaps felt acutely because of Japan's loss in World War II. At the same time, Kara and other leftists feared that politically Japan would return to militarism, a fear embodied in the government's push to renew the U.S.-Japan Security Treaty. Theatrically, Kara was trying to engage the audience through song and dance, elements inspired by *kabuki*, and by privileging the body of the actor.

The play centers around the efforts of a faded star from the all-female TAKARAZUKA REVUE COMPANY, Kasugano Yachiyo, to recover her popularity as Heathcliff in *Wuthering Heights*, which she toured to Manchuria at the height of the Japanese Empire. Kasugano now runs an underground coffee shop called the Body. To preserve her youth, Kasugano bathes daily in tears shed years ago by her virginal fans. Kasugano has been underground since the war and is ignorant of society's rapid modernization, or the subway construction headed straight for the Body. Inside, a ventriloquist and his dummy wage a debate about who has the right to speak for whom. As the ventriloquist dies of throat cancer, replicas take over for him and the dummy. Periodically an office worker, thirsting for what he cannot get from the scorched earth and barren modernization aboveground, rushes in begging for water. When the headwaiter of the Body kills the office worker, blood pours from the spigot that once gave water.

Into the Body come the aspiring actress Kai (Seashell) and her grandmother. Kai wonders if she has what it takes to be a "Zuka" (Takarazuka) girl, but perseveres on reassurances from her grandmother. After Kasugano casts Kai to play Catherine to her Heathcliff, the grandmother goes off to sell her dried cuttlefish.

The biggest stars of the Takarazuka Revue are the actors of male roles such as Kasugano. As with all-male *kabuki*, the cross-gender role-playing in Takarazuka has a characteristic eroticism. In *The Virgin's Mask* cross-gender eroticism was doubled in a later production when Kara played the role of Kasugano, a woman who plays men. That redoubling is one of the ways questions of the body are raised. The Body is buried and is conflated with the body of Catherine that Kasugano/Heathcliff wants to dig up and devour to make their flesh one. There are echoes of the Body as the "national body" (*kokutai*), a rallying cry during the war. Kara made the "privileged body" the center of his performance work, and questions of what "body" means infuse the play. The biggest question is whether or not the youthful Kai will become a replica of the "virginal" Kasugano, and what will happen to the "body" of Japanese culture and society.

FURTHER READING

Goodman, David. *Japanese Drama and Culture in the 1960's: The Return of the Gods.* Armonk, N.Y: M. E. Sharpe, 1988.

Ortolani, Benito. *The Japanese Theatre: From Shamanistic Ritual to Contemporary Pluralism.* Rev. ed. Princeton, N.J.: Princeton Univ. Press, 1995.

Powell, Brian. *Japan's Modern Theatre: A Century of Change and Continuity.* London: Japan Library, 2002.

Rolf, Robert T., and John K. Gillespie, eds. *Alternative Japanese Drama: Ten Plays.* Honolulu: Univ. of Hawaii Press, 1992.

John D. Swain

VISHNEVYI SAD   *See* THE CHERRY ORCHARD

THE VISIT OF THE OLD LADY

The world made me a whore. Now I'll make it into a brothel.
—Claire Zachanassian, Act 3

In FRIEDRICH DÜRRENMATT's *The Visit of the Old Lady* (*Der Besuch der alten Dame,* 1956) Kläri Wäscher, banished and branded a prostitute by the self-righteous burghers forty years earlier, has returned to her Swiss village Güllen as Claire Zachanassian, the richest woman in the world. The townspeople live in poverty, and Claire offers them a billion francs if they will kill Alfred Ill, the man who had caused her misery by impregnating her and bribing witnesses at his paternity trial. The town's initial solidarity with Ill dissolves gradually but perceptibly as the people, acting in the belief that Claire is only testing them, spend extravagantly and amass large debts. However, Claire is already in control of the town, having secretly bought and closed down all the industry. Trapped and hopelessly in debt, the people must kill their beloved neighbor. Two plot lines intersect: the damnation of a collective (Güllen) and the salvation of an individual (Ill). The townspeople spend most of the play in denial as greed wrestles with their humanistic ideals. Cognizant of the people's intentions before they are, Ill attempts to escape, but is anchored by his guilty conscience. Gradually he defeats his fears and dies a sacrificial death to atone for the misery he has caused. Ill becomes the scapegoat for the town, which bears a collective guilt in the injustice done to Claire. The townspeople, speaking in the style of a classical Greek chorus, close the play with a self-congratulatory encomium to virtue and possessions.

The sacrificial death and numerous biblical allusions have led scholars to suggest that *The Visit of the Old Lady* is a passion play. It is, in fact, a secular anti–passion play in which the sacrifice brings about the material prosperity but spiritual death of a community. It also has characteristics of a modern morality play in the tradition of Everyman, because all of Ill's friends and even his family abandon him in his greatest need. Dürrenmatt places the concept of justice under the closest scrutiny. Though her motivation is revenge, Claire insists upon calling it justice. Her manipulation of language allows the residents of Güllen to rationalize the deed and commit it with a collective clear conscience. This is the lower form of justice Dürrenmatt defines as resulting from guilt: justice that can be demanded and is therefore corruptible. The higher form, insight into guilt, can only be accomplished by the guilty. In judging himself guilty and offering atonement, Ill joins the ranks of Dürrenmatt's courageous individuals who restore the moral order within themselves while proving unable to effect the same change in society.

Premiering in Zürich on January 29, 1956, with Therese Giese in the role of Claire, *The Visit of the Old Lady* was Dürrenmatt's first international success. In 1958 Alfred Lunt and Lynn Fontanne starred in Maurice Valency's Broadway adaptation, which won the New York Drama Critics' Award the following year. Twentieth Century Fox filmed the story in 1964, starring Ingrid Bergman and Anthony Quinn, and in 1971 Gottfried von Einem premiered his operatic version in Vienna. *The Visit of the Old Lady* remains Dürrenmatt's best-known and most quoted play.

[*See also* Germany]

FURTHER READING

Crockett, Roger A. *Understanding Friedrich Dürrenmatt.* Columbia: Univ. of South Carolina Press, 1998.

Dufresne, Nicole. "Violent Homecoming: Liminality, Ritual and Renewal in *The Visit.*" In *Play Dürrenmatt,* ed. by Moshe Lazar and Ron Gottesman. Malibu: Undena, 1983. 39–53.

Jenny, Urs. *Dürrenmatt: A Study of His Plays.* Tr. by Keith Hamnett and Hugh Rorrison. London: Eyre Methuen, 1978.

Peppard, Murray. *Friedrich Dürrenmatt.* New York: Twayne, 1969.

Tiusanen, Timo. *Dürrenmatt: A Study in Plays, Prose, Theory.* Princeton: Princeton Univ. Press, 1977.

Whitton, Kenneth. *The Theatre of Friedrich Dürrenmatt: A Study in the Possibility of Freedom.* London: O. Wolff, 1980.

Roger A. Crockett

VITRAC, ROGER (1899–1952)

Roger Vitrac was perhaps the most accomplished playwright to employ surrealist principles in his writing. His dramatic oeuvre spans twenty-five years and sixteen plays, including works that embody SURREALISM and DADAISM and prefigure ABSURDISM. He was born on November 17, 1899, in Pinsac, FRANCE. He shared the general artistic spirit of the early 20th-century AVANT-GARDE: irreverence, a sharp wit, and an urgent need to disrupt the status quo. Vitrac enthusiastically greeted the arrival of the Dada movement in Paris in 1921. Having served in World War I, he grasped the importance of laying bare the ingrained patterns of language and thought that led to individual passivity. His early works, tentatively grouped together under the label "incendiary theater," relish dadaist principles of surprise, biting satire, humor, and a subversion of popular forms and attempt to change the nature of the relationship between the spectator and the stage.

Vitrac followed surrealism when it succeeded Dada, obeying his desire to explore the realm of dreams, automatic writing, and love. Born the year before Sigmund Freud's *The Interpretation of Dreams* was published, Vitrac grew up immersed in the possibilities that explorations of the unconscious unlocked. His plays merge interior and exterior reality within spaces that inextricably interweave spoken and scenic languages. Vitrac dubbed his first produced play, *The Mysteries of Love* (*Les Mystères de l'Amour*, 1923), "a surrealist drama," and its style—obeying dream logic and using intensely poetic images and dialogue—closely resembles that of automatic writing, in which the pen flows with the author's unedited thoughts. The tragicomic *Victor; or, The Children Take Power* (*Victor ou les Enfants au pouvoir*, 1928), exploits the banality of bourgeois existence by creating a COLLAGE of denunciatory clichés voiced by an ultra-precocious child. Its fantastically exaggerated drawing-room characters and subversion of everyday language anticipate the plays of EUGÈNE IONESCO and other absurdists.

Vitrac founded the Théâtre ALFRED JARRY in 1926 with Robert Aron and ANTONIN ARTAUD (for which Artaud directed the premieres of *The Mysteries of Love* and *Victor*), a theater intent upon channeling the disruptive force of Jarry's *Ubu roi the King*. A 1926 manifesto established their goal to create a theater that would "satisfy the most extreme demands of the imagination and the spirit." They met with little public support, and their efforts to sustain the theater concluded in 1930 with an essay (accompanied by a photo collage of them being dismembered) titled "The Alfred Jarry Theater and Public Hostility." Much of this "hostility" came from the now-estranged surrealists, who interrupted the theater's performances on several occasions on the grounds that theater was a commercial venture antithetical to a true spirit of revolution. This break, intensified by the surrealists' ideological shift to communism, embodies the uneasy relationship between artistic experiment and revolutionary politics that was being tested across Europe at the time. Vitrac believed in revolution but remained situated in the realm of the creative arts. His plays were not well known until JEAN ANOUILH directed a revival of *Victor* in 1962 to great critical success. A playwright whose works embody the almost impossible theatrical ideals of the surrealists, as well as pave the way for absurdist drama, Vitrac is an important dramatic innovator of early modernism. He died on June 22, 1952, in Paris.

PLAYS: *The Painter* (*Le peintre*, 1921); *Free Admission* (*Entrée libre*, 1922); *Mademoiselle Piège* (1922); *Monuments* (1922); *Poison* (1922); *The Mysteries of Love* (*Les mystères de l'amour*, 1923); *Victor; or, The Children Take Power* (*Victor, ou, Les enfants au pouvoir*, 1928); *The Ephemeral* (*L'éphémère*, 1929); *The Coup of Trafalgar* (*Le coup de Trafalgar*, 1930); *The Ladies of the Open Sea* (*Les demoiselles du large*, 1933); *The Werewolf* (*Le loup-garou*, 1934); *The Hawker* (*Le camelot*, 1936); *The Brawl* (*La bagarre*, 1938); *Médor* (1939); *The Sword of My Father* (*Le sabre de mon père*, 1945–1950); *The Condemned* (*Le condamné*, 1951)

FURTHER READING

Béhar, Henri. *Vitrac: Théâtre ouvert sur le rêve* [Theater open on the dream]. Lausanne: L'Age d'Homme, 1993.

Knapp, Bettina. *French Theatre, 1918–1939.* London: Macmillan, 1985.

Matthews, J. H. *Theatre in Dada and Surrealism.* Syracuse, N.Y.: Syracuse Univ. Press, 1974.

Kimberly Jannarone

VLAST' T'MY   *See* THE POWER OF DARKNESS

VOADEN, HERMAN (1903–1991)

Modern Canadian drama emerged from the debate—waged both in playwriting and polemic—between Herman Voaden and MERRILL DENISON (1893–1975). Denison introduced realist modernism to DRAMATURGY in CANADA with his volume of plays aptly titled *The Unheroic North* (1923). Voaden's response was both thematic and aesthetic: to create a wholly Canadian image of a "heroic north" by means of antirealist writing and stagecraft. In doing so, he became one of the first champions of "the Idea of North," which has been a central theme of Canadian art throughout the late 20th century, including such artists as Glenn Gould and Margaret Atwood and critics such as Northrop Frye. Voaden's influence on Canadian dramaturgy continued after World War II in his work as an advocate of government funding for the arts in Canada, including time spent as head of the Canadian Arts Council (1945–1948) and the Canadian Conference of the Arts (1966–1968).

Voaden was born in London, Ontario, on January 19, 1903. His primary influence was EXPRESSIONISM, most particularly the works of EUGENE O'NEILL in the 1920s, the subject of Voaden's master's thesis. The staging ideas of Edward Gordon Craig and Adalphe Appia were an additional influence, as were German plays such as ERNST TOLLER's *Masses and Man*. He studied playwriting at Yale with GEORGE PIERCE BAKER (who had also taught O'Neill) and modern dance in GERMANY with Kurt Jooss, the pioneer of *Tanzteater*, most famous for his antiwar ballet *The Green Room*.

Perhaps the strongest influence on the shape of his writing, however, was the Group of Seven, Canadian landscape painters who took the wild north shore of Lake Superior as their subject. Voaden attempted to make the landscape of western Ontario an active character in his plays. Toward this purpose, he created a style he called "symphonic expressionism," synthesizing the spoken word, music, lighting, dance, and choric speech (Voaden's work can be compared with that of U.S. playwright PAUL GREEN, who was creating what he called "symphonic drama," set outdoors and also combining all aspects of art, at the same time). The first major work in this style was *Symphony*, a work without words for orchestra and corps de ballet, co-written on a cross-country train journey with Loren Warriner, a young painter and protégé of the Group of Seven.

Although *Symphony* was never performed, Voaden succeeded in producing many of his plays between the late 1920s and 1942. These were produced first in Sarnia and later at Toronto's Central High School of Commerce, where Voaden was chair of the English Department until his retirement in 1964. These plays, including *Earth Song*, *Hill-Land*, *Murder Pattern*, and *Ascend as the Sun*, were generally well received by critics at the time. Their texts include very thorough STAGE DIRECTIONS on the quality of lighting used, choreography, and music: for example, *Earth Song* specifies precisely what sections (and recording) of Brahms's First Symphony are to be used at that time.

After *Ascend as the Sun*, however, playwriting and production became a secondary concern for Voaden. The demands of World War II intervened, and after the war Voaden's focus shifted to the campaign for government support for the arts. This shift, combined with the common feeling that Canadian work held second-class status to work from New York or London, and Voaden's self-confessed failure to publicize his own work to a larger (especially U.S.) critical audience, had the result that his plays disappeared from public consciousness until the 1970s, when he was rediscovered as a model for Canadian writers: for instance, *Murder Pattern* (1936), now considered his most important work, was not published until 1975.

Voaden's role as a leader in the development of Canadian drama also comes from his development of "the Sarnia Idea." A national drama could not wait for the development of a national professional theater, Voaden felt. Drawing on the inspiration of innovators such as ANDRÉ ANTOINE in Paris and J. T. Grein in London, he created a system for amateur production of plays using professional standards. He also created a "performance-based" system for teaching drama in secondary schools that was adopted nationwide in Canada. After Voaden's death in June 1991 in Toronto, his estate established the Herman Voaden National Playwriting Competition.

Voaden's critical reputation is based on his theatrical strength rather than the literary quality of his work. Like most symbolist and expressionist verse, Voaden's often feels overblown to a modern ear; and the multidisciplinary structure of the works requires great visual and aural imagination on the part of the reader. Their performative force, however, is apparent in the production photos, and the 1987 revival of *Murder Pattern* was heralded as "an important event in [Canadian] literary history (Grace, 1987)." *Murder Pattern* has received numerous revivals in Canada in the years since. Although Voaden felt that he had left no influence behind, his work is commonly considered an important early expression of the Idea of North, and in theater he has been seen as a precursor to writers such as JAMES REANEY, whose trilogy *The Donnellys* is often compared with *Murder Pattern*. His influence is also felt in the multimedia, imagistic theater that has arisen in Canada, especially Quebec, since the 1980s, such as the work of Robert Lepage. Gilles Maheu of Carbone-14 cites Voaden as a direct inspiration for his company's work.

PLAYS: *The White Kingdom* (1928); *Northern Storm* (1929); *Northern Song* (1930); *Symphony* (1930); *Fragment* (1931); *Western Wolf* (1931); *Wilderness* (1931; revised as *Rocks*, 1932); *Earth Song* (1932); *Hill-Land* (1933); *Murder Pattern* (1936); *Maria Chandelaine* (1937); *Ascend as the Sun* (1942); *The Miracle of the Valley of Dry Bones* (ballet scenario, 1942); *Masque of the Red Death* (1943); *The Prodigal Son* (libretto, 1944); *Decision* (1945); *Election Report* (1945); *Esther* (libretto, written

in 1948, premiered in 1952); *Dead and Gone, Lady* (1954); *Emily Carr* (1958, premiered in 1962); *The Poor Journey to Their City* (1971)

FURTHER READING
Grace, Sherrill. "Herman Voaden's *Murder Pattern*: 1936 and 1987." *Canadian Drama* 13., no. 1 (1987): 117–119.
Wagner, Anton, ed. *A Vision of Canada: Herman Voaden's Dramatic Works, 1928–1945*. Toronto: Simon & Pierre, 1993.

Walter Bilderback

VOGEL, PAULA (1951–)

I want to seduce the audience. If they can go along for the ride they wouldn't ordinarily take . . . then they might see highly charged political issues in a new and unexpected way.
—Paula Vogel, quoted in Steven Drukman's "A Playwright on the Edge," *New York Times* (March 16, 1997)

A playwright celebrated for her unconventional approach to controversial issues, Paula Vogel began writing in the 1970s. However, it was only with the success of her twenty-second play, THE BALTIMORE WALTZ (1992), that Vogel became recognized as a major figure in American theater.

Vogel was born on December 16, 1951, in Washington, D.C., into a working-class family. Her childhood was marred by her parents' divorce and the subsequent absence of a father whom she came to know only in adulthood, at the time when her older brother Carl was dying of AIDS. Vogel is a feminist and lesbian, and her personal experiences have led her to tackle subjects in her plays ranging from AIDS, prostitution, pedophilia, and pornography to homosexual parenting. Although these are contentious issues in themselves, her typical treatment of such subjects through bodily (and often bawdy) humor, plain speaking, and the chiaroscuro of morality has courted further controversy. In part, Vogel attributes the slow development of her career to her gender and nonconformist sensibilities. Her plays consistently present a female subject's viewpoint, revolve around strong women characters, and examine issues of female subjugation. Nevertheless, Vogel rejects the idea that her identity defines her as a playwright, instead asserting that her position has helped her empathize with widespread issues of marginalization. She considers playwriting a political act, but sees theater less as a platform for espousing her own ideological beliefs than as a powerful tool for communal exploration and understanding, for her own benefit as much as her audience's.

In approaching taboo political subjects, Vogel is interested in the questions surrounding an issue and believes that complex problems do not have simple answers. To ensure that her audience is engaged in an open dialogue with its culture, she typically structures her plays as journeys, taking spectators along for the ride and forcing them to examine the shades of gray in a situation and discard any absolutes. In her Pulitzer Prize–winning *How I Learned to Drive* (1997), a tale of a young woman whose adolescence in Maryland during the 1960s and 1970s is blighted by sexual molestation, Vogel avoids simply indicting the pedophilic uncle by presenting a character too complex to simply be designated a villain. Uncle Peck, who (according to Vogel) "should be played by an actor one might cast in the role of Atticus in *To Kill a Mockingbird*," is at once sinister and sympathetic. There is no question of the trauma his abuse inflicts on his niece L'il Bit. However, Vogel also emphasizes Peck's struggle to understand his sexuality, his compassion for L'il Bit, and his genuine efforts to warn her against himself, knowing that she is his only lifeline in a battle against despair.

Vogel's other plays are equally ambiguous. *The Mineola Twins* (1996) follows the lives of identical twins who differ only in their politics and chest size through three Republican administrations. At the end neither the antiestablishment nor the conservative character has the final word. In *Hot 'n' Throbbing* (1993), the story of a divorcée with a restraining order against her abusive ex-husband who writes soft-core erotica to support her children, the heroine is not only a victim of male objectification, but also complicit in it.

To challenge the audience to resist a single conditioned perspective, Vogel takes it on a voyage into the world of the strange and fantastical. In her plays the expected approach to an issue is often inverted, and the boundary between reality and fantasy is blurred. Painful subjects such as death and disease may be approached through satire and comedy, and alternative possibilities to the accepted attitude are presented when characters splinter or double and weave in and out of each other's stories. In addition, Vogel's narratives are filled with bizarre images and metatheatrical and literary allusions. *The Baltimore Waltz* (1992 Obie for Best Play) uses all these elements. Inspired by the death of Vogel's homosexual brother Carl, the play provides a fantastical and humorous alternative to what happened in real life. In the play's version of events, respectable kindergarten teacher Anna imagines that she is dying of acquired toilet disease (ATD)—Vogel's ironic answer to AIDS—and goes to Europe with her brother Carl and his stuffed rabbit in search of a potential cure from the Third Man.

Anna is not the only one of Vogel's characters who deals with life through the medium of fiction. Vogel fills her plays with fantasists who deliberately challenge the story assigned to them. In *Desdemona: A Play About a Handkerchief* (1978) William Shakespeare's heroine finds herself trapped in someone else's story and relieves herself of the burden of purity it has forced upon her by inventing her own fiction. In *And Baby Makes Seven* (1984) the trio in the gay household create imaginary children to help them through the fears of becoming actual parents. No matter how bizarre the fantasies in Vogel's plays, however, they can always be explained in the familiar and perennial realm of human need.

Paula Vogel is the Adele Kellenberg Seaver Professor of Creative Writing at Brown University, where she directs the master of fine arts playwriting program. In addition to her stage work, she has worked on film versions of *How I Learned to Drive* and *The Oldest Profession*, her 1981 play about five septuagenarian prostitutes. *The Long Christmas Ride Home* premiered at Trinity Repertory Theater in Providence in May 2003 and moved to the OFF-BROADWAY Vineyard Theatre in October 2004. The play, which integrates Bunraku puppetry with American theatrical COMEDY particularly indebted to THORNTON WILDER, continues Vogel's exploration of dysfunctional families using figurative and literal journeys as a segue to discovery.

[See also Feminist Drama in the United States; United States, 1940–Present]

SELECT PLAYS: *Swan Song of Sir Henry* (1974); *Meg* (1977); *Desdemona: A Play About a Handkerchief* (1978); *Apple-Brown Betty* (1979); *The Last Pat Epstein Show Before the Reruns* (1979); *Bertha in Blue* (1981); *And Baby Makes Seven* (1984); *The Oldest Profession* (1988); *The Baltimore Waltz* (1992); *Hot 'n' Throbbing* (1993); *The Mineola Twins* (1996); *How I Learned to Drive* (1997); *The Long Christmas Ride Home* (2003)

FURTHER READING

Bigsby, Christopher. *Contemporary American Playwrights*. Cambridge: Cambridge Univ. Press, 1999.

Vogel, Paula. *The Baltimore Waltz, and Other Plays*. New York: Theatre Communications Group, 1996.

——. *The Mammary Plays*. New York: Theatre Communications Group, 1998. [*How I Learned to Drive* and *The Mineola Twins*.]

Olivia Turnbull

THE VOICE OF THE TURTLE

The rain is over, the winter is past, and the voice of the turtle[dove] is heard in our land.
—Sgt. Bill Page, Act 2

Drawing its title from a Bible verse paraphrased by its lone male character, *The Voice of the Turtle* by English-born, naturalized American playwright JOHN VAN DRUTEN made its Broadway premiere on December 8, 1943, at the Morosco Theatre. Directed by the playwright and starring Margaret Sullavan, Audrey Christie, and Elliott Nugent, *The Voice of the Turtle* moved to the Martin Beck (later the Hirschfeld) in 1947 and subsequently to the Hudson, closing there on January 3, 1948, after 1,557 performances. A romantic COMEDY with three characters, *The Voice of the Turtle* was the first major Broadway success with a small cast and was also Van Druten's most successful play in a career that included *I Remember Mama*, *I Am a Camera* (the basis for the musical *Cabaret*), and *Bell, Book, and Candle*.

The plot concerns Sally Middleton, a naïve young actress from Joplin, Missouri, and Sgt. Bill Page, a soldier on leave, who fall in love over a three-day April weekend in World War II–era New York City. Sally's salty actress friend Olive Lashbrooke has stood up Bill, an out-of-town fling, so that she can pursue a higher-ranking catch. What begins as an unfortunate situation turns into a decidedly lucky one when Sally and Bill, after spending the weekend together primarily in Sally's sublet apartment, resolve ultimately to allow their blossoming relationship to flower into a serious, marriage-bound one.

The uncertainties and instabilities of the professional theater and a country immersed in a global war saturate and inform *The Voice of the Turtle*. Actresses Sally and Olive's jobs are short lived and sporadic, and their residences are impermanent; Bill, too, bounces from base to base, a player, however, in a greater and more real drama. The future is unclear, frightening, and somewhat bleak.

The playwright, however, infuses this dark landscape with the hope that all uncertainties will be abolished: by Sunday, beautiful spring weather has supplanted Friday's rainstorm; Sally, without a job on Friday, has found employment in a production opposite her favorite matinee idol; Sally and Bill emerge from the shadows of love affairs that had left them shell-shocked and embittered; and, most important, the prospect of a lifetime together incites them to seize love and commitment. These shifts bode, too, that the long war will soon end. Only Olive remains unchanged, jaded, and averse to marriage, which remains for her only an excuse to break a date and a poison that envenoms the gaiety of a successive string of sexual liaisons.

The Voice of the Turtle is provocative and ahead of its time in its handling of premarital sex, yet still contains the underlying messages that monogamy in the state of matrimony is desirable, and that men are expected and permitted to be more sexually promiscuous than women.

The play was made into a film in 1947, starring Ronald Reagan, Eleanor Parker, and Eve Arden.

[*See also* England; United States, 1940–Present]

FURTHER READING

Van Druten, John. *Playwright at Work*. New York: Harper, 1953.
——. *The Widening Circle*. New York: Scribner, 1957.

W. Douglas Powers

VOJNOVIĆ, IVO (1857–1929)

> *History is writing a play for us to perform,—the one and only, great and horrible!—And yet we should keep quiet and listen! Today, to write means, however, to give up our non possumus. When I write about Dubrovnik, it is like speaking about an unburied Corpse.*
>
> —Ivo Vojnović, 1917

A poet and writer of short prose works, Ivo Vojnović is the author of fourteen plays, the most important of which have made him the major representative of modern Croatian drama at the turn of the 20th century and the herald of its later developments. Born on October 9, 1857, in Dubrovnik, CROATIA, and raised in Split, Vojnović completed his studies in Zagreb and worked for several years as a civil service clerk in various Croatian towns until 1907. In 1911, after serving as literary adviser to the Croatian National Theatre in Zagreb, he became a professional writer, traveled around ITALY, and stayed in Prague, Budapest, and Belgrade. In 1914 he returned to Dubrovnik, where he was imprisoned for his Yugoslav nationalism, an ideology that informs his two verse plays generally held in low esteem, *The Death of the Mother of Jugovići* (*Smrt majke Jugovića*, 1907) and *The Resurrection of Lazarus* (*Lazarovo vaskrsenje*, 1913). After World War I he spent several years in Nice. By 1922 he was back in Dubrovnik and, almost blind, spent his last years in Belgrade, where he died on August 30, 1929.

Although some of his plays smack of decadent cosmopolitanism (*Psyche*, 1890; *A Lady with a Sunflower* [*Gospođa sa suncokretom*], 1912), and vague symbolism (*Imperatrix*, 1918), the central and most significant part of his oeuvre was devoted to the history and cultural IDENTITY of his native town, Dubrovnik, the former capital of the Dalmatian aristocratic republic, Ragusa, the autonomy of which was undone by Napoleon Bonaparte. With D'Annunzian emphasis Vojnović deplored but also penetratingly analyzed the reasons for the decline and fall of the republic. The recurring obsession with the myth of Dubrovnik earned him the label of a nostalgic political reactionary, prone to indulge in declamatory passages and necrophiliac imagery, but it is precisely in his imaginative historical chronicles that Vojnović succeeded in creating the most innovative dramaturgical work of the period. Having begun with a light comic well-made play (*Psyche*), he impressed the Zagreb intellectuals with his veristic slice of rural life *Equinox* (*Ekvinocijo*, 1895), which was followed by his naturalist-symbolist masterpiece, the psychologically dense Ibsenian historical fresco *The Ragusan Trilogy: Allons enfants, Twilight, On the Terrace* (*Dubrovačka trilogija: Allons enfants, Suton, Na taraci*, 1903). The metadramatic and multimedia experiments of his later Pirandellian phase, *Masquerades in the Attic* (*Maškarate ispod kuplja*, 1922) and *A Prologue to an Unwritten Play* (*Prolog nenapisane drame*, 1929), follow the same thematic line with a strikingly intentional dissolution of traditional plot and extensive commentaries on the process of artistic creation of an author faced with a director's impositions and a new medium, film. To these must be added a group of one-act lyric plays, grouped by scholars under the heading *The Little Trilogy* (*Mala trilogija*, 1926) not only because of the abiding interest in the history of Dubrovnik, but also in honor of a tendency of the playwright to present individual works as parts of larger wholes (thus *Equinox*, *The Death of the Mother of Jugovići*, *Imperatrix*, and *The Resurrection of Lazarus* form *The Maternal Tetralogy*).

A poet of the moribund and a skilled narrator in his profuse STAGE DIRECTIONS, permeated by learned references to other fields such as the plastic arts and music, Vojnović was also a successful public reader of his plays. His plays have at various times been translated into Czech, Slovak, Polish, Italian, German, French, Russian, and Chinese, and some of them, such as *Equinox*, have also been set to music. His best work for the stage continues to be produced in Croatia to this day.

PLAYS: *Psyche* (1890); *Equinox* (*Ekvinocijo*, 1895); *The Ragusan Trilogy: Allons enfants, Twilight, On the Terrace* (*Dubrovačka trilogija: Allons enfants, Suton, Na taraci*, 1903); *The Death of the Mother of Jugovići* (*Smrt majke Jugovića*, 1907); *A Lady with a Sunflower* (*Gospođa sa suncokretom*, 1912); *The Resurrection of Lazarus* (*Lazarovo vaskrsenje*, 1913); *Imperatrix* (1918); *Masquerades in the Attic* (*Maškarate ispod kuplja*, 1922); *The Little Trilogy: The Miracle of Saint Blasius. In the Last Moment, when Saint Mary went Walking Across Placa* (*Mala trilogija: Čudo Sv. Vlaha, U zadnjem času, Kad se Blažena Gospa prošetala preko Place*, 1926); *A Prologue to an Unwritten Play* (*Prolog nenapisane drame*, 1929)

FURTHER READING

Čale, Frano, ed. *O'djelu Iva Vojnovića* [Ivo Vojnović: His Life and Operas]. *Radovi Međunarodnog simpozija* [The Wade of Iva Vojnovića's Operas: Proceeding of the International Symposium]. Zagreb: JAZU, 1981.

Jovanović, Raško B. *Ivo Vojnović: Život i delo*. Belgrade: Institut za književnost i umetnost, 1974.

Suvin, Darko. "Dramatika Iva Vojnovića" [Playwright of Iva Vojnovića]. *Dubrovnik*, special issue 5–6 (1977).

Lada Cale Feldman

VOLKSSTÜCK

The term *Volksstück* is literally and mistakenly translated into English as "folk play." A more accurate translation would be "popular drama," an appellation that captures both the historical circumstances attending the genre's origins and the aesthetic impetus underlying its development. The form and content of the *Volksstück* have necessarily evolved as a consequence of the changing socioeconomic conditions that *Volkstück* dramatists seek to address. The stock characters and frequently coarse physical COMEDY of the early 19th century seem far removed from the depictions of physical and emotional brutality that came to characterize the genre in the late 20th century. In Ferdinand Raimund's *The King of the Alps* (*Der Alpenkönig und der Menschenfeind*, premiered 1828), for instance, the misanthropic protagonist Rappelkopf is ultimately cured through the benevolent intervention of Astragalus, the supernatural Alpine king, and Rappelkopf's cure results in multiple reconciliations and the reestablishment of social harmony. PETER TURRINI'S *Swine* (*Sauschlachten*, 1971), in contrast, culminates in the offstage slaughter of the farmer's son Valentin, an act sanctioned by the town dignitaries, physically committed by Valentin's extended family, and reconciling the characters with the traditions of AUSTRIA's Nazi past.

Despite thematic and formal variations, the *Volksstück* has always manifested an impulse to challenge and democratize both social institutions and aesthetic experience, constituting a form of theater intended to be thematically accessible and economically affordable to a broad and diverse audience. It is therefore not surprising that the three major phases in the development of the *Volksstück* occurred during periods in which questions of social, political, economic, and cultural democracy appeared particularly acute, that is, the mid-19th century, the 1920s and 1930s, and the 1960s and 1970s.

As the Biedermeier retreat into the private sphere gave way to the 1848 revolution, the works of Ferdinand Raimund (1790–1836) and Johann Nestroy (1801–1862) came to define the Viennese *Volksstück*. While Raimund's dramas always conclude with the reimposition of the status quo, the typically lower-class protagonists of Nestroy's FARCES and satires indict and subvert the bourgeois order.

Subsequent generations of 20th-century playwrights have consciously sought to rejuvenate the tradition of a popular and socially critical *Volksstück*. In the 1920s, as both Germans and Austrians struggled to establish democracies in the aftermath of World War I, BERTOLT BRECHT, MARIELUISE FLEIßER, ÖDÖN VON HORVÁTH, and CARL ZUCKMAYER attempted to create a *Volksstück* adequate to the interwar period. Amid the social upheavals of the 1960s and 1970s a new generation of *Volksstück* dramatists—including RAINER WERNER FASSBINDER, FRANZ XAVER KROETZ, Felix Mitterer, Martin Sperr, and Peter Turrini—emerged to question the ethical price of post–World War II affluence and confront the legacy of silence surrounding the Nazi past. Lacking the institutional support of a flourishing *Volkstheater*, these 20th-century playwrights have frequently turned to film and television as additional means to reach the broad audience they seek and thus reclaim for the *Volksstück* the popularity it enjoyed in 19th-century Vienna.

FURTHER READING

Aust, Hugo, Peter Haida, and Jürgen Hein. *Volksstück*. Munich: C. H. Beck, 1989.

Cocalis, Susan L. "The Politics of Brutality: Toward a Definition of the Critical Volksstück." *Modern Drama* 24, no. 3 (1981): 292–313.

Decker, Craig. "The Hermeneutics of Democracy: Nestroy, Horváth, Turrini and the Development of the 'Volksstück.'" *Seminar* 27, no. 3 (1991): 219–232.

Jones, Calvin N. *Negation and Utopia: The German Volksstück from Raimund to Kroetz*. New York: Peter Lang, 1993.

Craig Decker

VON MORGENS BIS MITTERNACHTS See FROM MORNING TO MIDNIGHT

VOR DEM RUHESTAND See EVE OF RETIREMENT

VOR SONNENAUFGANG See BEFORE DAYBREAK

LE VOYAGE DU COURONNEMENT See THE CORONATION VOYAGE

THE VOYSEY INHERITANCE

HARLEY GRANVILLE-BARKER's five-act realistic drama *The Voysey Inheritance* was first produced at the Court Theatre in London on November 7, 1905. The inheritance of the play's title is a Voysey family business secret. Mr. Voysey manages a successful financial firm, started by his father, that oversees the investments of several clients. In his old age Mr. Voysey has selected one of his six children, Edward, to become the next head of the firm, but passing on the business means divulging a history of transgression.

Years ago Edward's grandfather illegally spent most of the money deposited with the firm, and Mr. Voysey inherited the burden of quietly repairing this damage. Through bold investments he managed for years to pay the expected interest income to his clients, even though their capital had mostly vanished.

At first Edward refuses to stay with the business as a knowing co-conspirator, but he is persuaded by the nobility of working to replace all the stolen capital. He later discovers, however, that this has not exactly been his father's plan, and he confronts his father with the realization that the family's lifestyle has been built on stolen funds. "It's odd it never struck me until yesterday that my own pocket-money as a boy must have been drawn from some client's account."

Mr. Voysey dies, and Edward gives full disclosure of the business to his mother and siblings and suggests publicizing the embezzlement and giving the money left in Mr. Voysey's will to the firm's clients. He discovers that his family is far less eager than he to give restitution. Even Mr. Voysey's greatest victim, Mr. Booth, is more interested in financial gain than in morality. He conspires with the vicar, Rev. Colpus, and offers their conditional silence about the crimes as long as they financially benefit from the continued cover-up.

Eventually Edward learns that Mr. Voysey had managed, years earlier, to completely repair the effects of his father's misdeeds, but within a short time had started his own new embezzlements. The play ends with Edward vowing to stay at the firm and fix the worst of the client losses until the inevitable day that they are discovered. The audience is left to wonder if, like Mr. Voysey, Edward will clean the slate only to begin a new legacy of deception to pass on to the next generation.

Like his friend GEORGE BERNARD SHAW, Granville-Barker was interested in the British middle class and financial hypocrisy. *The Voysey Inheritance* is particularly reminiscent of Shaw's "new woman" play MRS. WARREN'S PROFESSION (1894), which likewise dramatizes respectable and gentle lives built on ill-gotten money. In both plays we see adult children who feel righteous indignation not so much at the discovery of their parents' crimes of necessity as at their persistence in behaving immorally after the necessity had evaporated. The social commentary is the same: that the English middle class is perfectly willing to accept immorality if it can benefit from it and retain its unstained reputations.

[*See also* England, 1860–1940]

FURTHER READING

Rijnbout, Frans A. "The 'New Woman' in Plays by Harley Granville Barker and His Contemporaries." Ph.D. diss., New York Univ., 1997.

Salenius, Elmer W. *Harley Granville Barker.* Boston: Twayne, 1982.

Stowell, S. "A Quaint and Comical Dismay—The Dramatic Strategies of Granville Barker's *The Voysey Inheritance.*" *Essays in Theatre/Etudes Théâtrales* 5, no. 2 (May 1987): 127–138.

DeAnna M. Toten Beard

VYROZUMENI *See* THE MEMORANDUM

W

WADA CHIREBANDI   *See* OLD STONE MANSION

WAGNER, RICHARD (1813–1883)

Richard Wagner (born on May 22, 1813, in Leipzig, GERMANY; died on February 13, 1883, in Venice, ITALY) is known primarily as one of the major composers of the 19th century. But he also exercised a great influence on the spoken drama, both through his operas and through his critical essays.

Unlike nearly all composers writing for the stage, Wagner wrote his own librettos. Not only were they crafted to complement the music beautifully; they were strikingly original examples of the dramatist's art. Although he was a great admirer and interpreter of Ludwig van Beethoven, Wagner wanted to go beyond what Beethoven had accomplished, which meant exceeding somehow the composer's monumental Ninth Symphony. There, in the last movement, Beethoven resorts to the human voice as a chorus sings Friedrich Schiller's "Ode to Joy." For Wagner, this transition from purely instrumental sound to a combination of voice and orchestra justified his belief (as a dramatist) that the most profound emotions must be given a cause, a motivation. This meant creating the dramatic situation that gave rise to the feelings. The outer world of causation and inner world of feeling were to be united. He scorned the term *opera* and thought of his works as music dramas (though that term did not satisfy him either), since he considered the text as vital as the music.

"In the highest conceivable work of art," he wrote, "the noblest inspiration of both composer and dramatist should exist as the very essence of the world thus revealed to us in the mirror of the world itself" ("Über die Bestimmung der Oper" [The Destiny of Opera], 1871). He said that he was attracted only to subject matter of which the "poetic and musical significance struck him simultaneously." In his best work there is a fusion of word and music unmatched in conventional opera. To accomplish this, he perfected the use of leitmotifs (a term coined not by Wagner but by Hans von Wolzogen). These are themes or fragments of themes that when woven together not only constitute the music of the drama but also underlie the story. What in straight drama is known as SUBTEXT wells up to the surface through Wagner's music.

For example, at the end of *Das Rheingold*, the first part of the cycle *Der Ring des Nibelungen*, a musical theme accompanying Alberich's renunciation of love is followed by a theme identified with the ring, establishing clearly the opposition of two forces, love and power, which will run through the whole Ring cycle.

Inspired mainly by Greek TRAGEDY, especially the *Oresteia* of Aeschylus, Wagner believed that the greatest drama was based on myth and legend. Being close to the people, the old stories, often retold, were, he believed, the repositories of the most profound truths. It was the task of the modern artist to recapture the essence of the ancient heroes. Stripped of irrelevant details, these elemental human beings revealed the underlying psychological and cultural forces at work.

In *Tannhäuser*, composed 1843–1845, he contrasted sacred with profane love. In *Lohengrin* (1850), he dealt with the betrayal of love (1850) and trust. In the *Ring* cycle, he pictured the whole history of human society as a struggle between love and power. *The Ring of the Nibelung* drew on material from the medieval poem *Nibelungenlied* and on the Scandinavian *Edda*. Begun as a single drama about the guiltless hero Siegfried, it was intended as a parable about 19th-century Germany, reflecting Wagner's radical, leftist views. Siegfried was to be the herald of a new society. But over the years, as Wagner became more disillusioned about politics, the single drama grew from 1848 to 1874 into a four-part cycle picturing in word and music the history of European civilization from its primal beginnings to the 19th century.

Wagner begins his story when human beings become divorced from nature. Alberich loves the Rhinemaidens, but when he is ridiculed by them for his ugliness, he forges the ring from the gold that they possess. The ring stands for power, the kind of power varying with its possessor. Wotan, chief of the gods who represent organized society, is willing to exchange love for political power. From then on there is a curse on the ring, and the history of the world is one of deceit and betrayal, ending eventually in the downfall, the twilight of the gods (*Götterdämmerung*, the last of the four operas in the cycle). The music critic Edward Downes hardly exaggerates when he wrote, "As *The Divine Comedy* of Dante sums up what Henry Adams called 'the thirteenth, greatest of centuries,' the peak of the Middle Ages, so Wagner's *Ring* epitomizes his age. Both works are rich in philosophical and political allegories. Both treat of first and last things, of basic human values, and the meaning of life itself."

In *Tristan and Isolde* (1865) Wagner depicted love as the passion that affords the only joy in a universe without purpose and meaning. Although the pessimistic PHILOSOPHY of Arthur Schopenhauer probably finds its fullest artistic expression in this work, Wagner differed from the philosopher on the question of love and sex.

Wagner's position is ambiguous. For Schopenhauer, love was a delusion arising from the conjunction of genitals. The love that Tristan and Isolde have for each other, however, is not presented as part of an ultimately pointless urge to procreate but as an irresistible drive to unite their souls. For Wagner, the union of the sexes meant a loss of egotism—hence, an overcoming of the will to propagate the species. Sex becomes an end in itself, and the music depicts rather explicitly foreplay and orgasm. (Or as GEORGE BERNARD SHAW, writing in the Victorian age, delicately put it, "an astonishingly intense and faithful translation into music of the emotions which accompany the union of a pair of lovers" [1898].) In the last scene the lovers, united in death, lose their individualities and surrender to the cosmos, the infinite universal energy. "Into the whirlwind of the universe, blowing round, sinking down, unconscious, highest bliss"—these are the final words of the drama. Music, like sex, unites the conscious and the unconscious, the individual and the world will.

Tristan is not only one of the most remarkable of all musical compositions, but it is a revolutionary dramatic work as well. Wagner deliberately dispensed with motivation and the complicated intrigues that are the basic material of almost all dramas. In his own words, he "immersed himself in the depths of events of the soul pure and simple, and out of this innermost center of the world fearlessly fashioned its outward form." He explained that "the copious detail that a historical poet has to employ in order to make the outer connections of his plot evident, to the detriment of a clear exposition of its inner motives, I now trusted myself to apply to these alone. Life and death, the whole significance and existence of the external world here turn on nothing but the inner movements of the soul" ("Zukunfsmusik" [Music of the Future]). Here was a new approach to drama that was to be a major influence on the symbolists at the end of the 19th century, a theory of a drama in which external action was reduced to a minimum, a virtual denial of drama in the conventional sense, a kind of drama in which Hamlet's soliloquies (set to music) would constitute the whole play.

In Parsifal (1882), which Wagner called a sacred festival drama, the musical motifs link religious and psychological life. The last of Wagner's works, it complements the Ring. In place of the ring as the central symbol (power), there is the holy grail (compassion). In its advocacy of asceticism, its borrowings from Eastern RELIGION, and its celebration of compassion for all living things, Parsifal is thoroughly Schopenhauerian. In these supreme works Wagner appears to have quite consciously and deliberately provided a world philosophy in three parts: political history in the Ring, sex and the unconscious in Tristan, and religion in Parsifal.

While the regular serious drama developed in the 19th century along scientific and materialistic lines, emphasizing factors such as environment and heredity, Wagner provided the alternative—the drama of the soul and of intuition, told through the use of parable and myth. Though his influence was mainly in the field of music, he provided the model for symbolist drama. As a theoretician, he was a major influence on FRIEDRICH NIETZSCHE, whose dichotomy of the Apollonian and the Dionysian, a staple of modern thought, derives mainly from Wagner's ideas and from Nietzsche's infatuation with Tristan.

His willful intrusion into politics and religion made him one of the most controversial artists of the modern era. He was an outspoken anti-Semite, and his essay "Judaism in Music" (1850) is extreme even for its time in its vehemence, going far beyond the conventional prejudices of mid-19th-century Europe. Wagner's racism, along with his glorification of Teutonic myth and legend, made him Adolf Hitler's favorite composer.

In his major works stretching from Lohengren to Parsifal, he not only composed music of unsurpassed power and originality; he also gave expression to most of the major ideas of his time. What he omitted or neglected can be found in the dramas of HENRIK IBSEN. Together they sum up and encompass nearly all that was significant in European culture in the 19th century. For his impact not only on music and drama but on politics and philosophy as well, Wagner has been arguably the single most influential creative genius since the titans of the Renaissance.

[See also Dramatic Structure; Symbolism]

FURTHER READING

Deathridge, John, and Carl Dahlhaus. The New Grove Wagner. London: Macmillan, 1984.

Köhler, Joachim. Richard Wagner, the Last of the Titans. Tr. by Stewart Spencer. New Haven, Conn.: Yale Univ. Press, 2004.

Magee, Bryan. Wagner and Philosophy. London: Penguin, 2000.

Millington, Barry, ed. The Wagner Compendium: A Guide to Wagner's Life and Music. New York: Schirmer, 1992.

Shaw, George Bernard. The Perfect Wagnerite. London: Grant Richards, 1898.

Tanner, Michael. Wagner. Princeton, N.J.: Princeton Univ. Press, 1996.

Wapnewski, Peter. "The Operas as Literary Works." In The Wagner Handbook, ed. by Ulrich Müller and Peter Wapnewski. Cambridge, Mass.: Harvard Univ. Press, 1992.

Evert Sprinchorn

WAITING FOR GODOT

Pozzo: [Suddenly furious.] Have you not done tormenting me with your accursed time! It's abominable! When! When! One day, is that not enough for you, one day like any other day, one day he went dumb, one day I went blind, one day we'll go deaf, one day we were born, one day we shall die, the same day, the same second, is that not enough for you? [Calmer.] They give birth astride of a grave, the light gleams an instant, then it's night once more. [He jerks the rope.] On!
—Act 2

SAMUEL BECKETT began writing Waiting for Godot (En attendant Godot) on October 9, 1948, and completed the manuscript on January 29, 1949. The evidence of the manuscript suggests that the play flowed smoothly in composition, with difficulties encountered mainly with the endings of each act. It is not yet known how many typescript versions it took for Beckett to achieve a "final" text. A year later the French actor and manager Roger Blin was actively seeking to stage the play but did not manage to achieve this until January 1953 at the Théâtre de Babylone in Paris. In the meantime, selected scenes from the play had been performed on

French radio in 1952, and the text of the play was published in October 1952. Beckett participated in the rehearsals for the first production by Blin, making cuts, adjustments, and changes to his text as required by the process of transfer from page to stage.

Within weeks of the Paris opening the play had been translated into German, with a little help from Beckett himself, and it was published and playing in numerous productions in GERMANY before Beckett finalized his translation of the play into English for first publication in New York in September 1954. The first English-language productions were given in London and Dublin in 1955, and the first American one opened in early 1956, a production Beckett called "the Miami fiasco."

From the outset it was recognized that Beckett's two-act play (it is called "a TRAGICOMEDY in two acts" on the title pages of English-language editions) was unconventional and subversive. It is virtually without plot—two men, Estragon (Gogo) and Vladimir (Didi), wait by a designated tree at the side of a country road for another man, Godot, who does not arrive but sends a messenger to say that "he will surely come tomorrow." The boredom of waiting is relieved in both acts by the arrival of Pozzo and Lucky, who tarry awhile before moving on. Both acts end with the same line, differently assigned, "Yes, let's go," followed by the stage direction, "They do not move. Curtain." This play (in which "nothing happens, twice," in Vivian Mercier's memorable phrase) ends in immobility rather than resolution; there is no dramatic outcome.

Not only did Beckett dispense with plot and story line; he also revolutionized the notion of character. We glean very little about the characters' past from the play: Estragon and Vladimir were "presentable" years ago; they worked at grape harvesting in the Macon country. At one time Estragon was a poet but is now reduced to begging and sleeping in ditches, as is Vladimir. They hope for some improvement in their situation from a charitable Godot, who may allow them to sleep in his warm hayloft. They recognize the pointlessness of trying to keep an appointment with a man who does not show up, but they are fearful he may punish them if they default. Pozzo and Lucky are even more enigmatic: they appear to be master and slave—Pozzo says in the first act that he is going to the fair to sell Lucky for whom he hopes to get a good price, but they return in the second act, much degraded—though Pozzo concedes that Lucky has taught him to appreciate "[b]eauty, grace, truth of the first water." Lucky, who has a rope around his neck, carries a bag, a picnic basket, a folding stool, and Pozzo's greatcoat and is "driven" by Pozzo, who carries only a whip and the end of the rope.

In place of the standard elements of plot and character, traditionally conceived, Beckett provides a rigorously structured set of repetitions and repetitions with variation in language that can move from the lyrical to the crude. The pattern of the first act is repeated in a shorter, compressed, and diminished way in the second. Thus, there is talk of suicide in both acts, but Didi and Gogo decide against it, twice. In the first act their decision is based on their suspicion that the tree would not bear their weight; in the second, they defer because they lack a serviceable piece of rope. The return of Pozzo and Lucky in the second act proves to be much less "entertaining" because this time Pozzo is blind and Lucky is dumb. The carrot Didi gives to Gogo in the first act dwindles to a black radish in the second.

The play provides startling images of destitution, neglect, despair, ill treatment, violence, and abuse—of human misery, in short. From these images Beckett contrives to wring some hilarious COMEDY. In the first act when Lucky has kicked Estragon in the shin as the latter performs a rare act of kindness, Vladimir reports to Pozzo that his friend is bleeding. Pozzo's response, "It's a good sign," is a signature Beckett effect—only the living bleed.

It is the abject Lucky who is given the most explicit passage in the play, in a speech he delivers for the entertainment of the others at the command of Pozzo. The "tirade" (Beckett's word) is assembled from the remains of various registers of language—literary, scientific, religious, philosophical. The point is that despite the best efforts of generations dedicated to human development, the fate of man is "to shrink and dwindle," "waste and pine"—to be born is to begin to die. The others resist this unpalatable truth, seeking to silence Lucky who struggles and shouts his text. It is a key moment because it reveals that all the actions of the play, the pastimes, comic turns and routines, the little "canters" the characters indulge in, have a common purpose, which is to prevent this truth from entering consciousness. But as the play goes on and the characters' store of ingenuity and invention diminishes, prevention becomes more difficult. Vladimir says, "How time flies when one has fun!" But the fun keeps breaking down into painful silence.

Waiting for Godot is the essential play of the latter half of the 20th century, and with it Beckett redefined the possibilities of theater. Its impact on playwrights in many languages is palpable and widely acknowledged.

[*See also* France]

FURTHER READING

Fahsenfeld, Martha, and Dougald McMillan. *Beckett in the Theatre.* London: John Calder, 1988.

Knowlson, James, and Dougald McMillan, eds. *The Theatrical Notebooks of Samuel Beckett.* Vol. 1, *Waiting for Godot.* New York: Grove, 1994.

Reid, Alec. *All I Can Manage, More Than I Could: An Approach to the Plays of Samuel Beckett.* Dublin: Dolmen Press, 1968.

States, Bert O. *The Shape of Paradox: An Essay on Waiting for Godot.* Berkeley: Univ. of California Press, 1978.

Gerry Dukes

WAITING FOR LEFTY

Not until the first work of CLIFFORD ODETS gained a professional Broadway production and a widespread audience did the Great

Depression–era drama of social protest achieve any meaningful success. Produced by the GROUP THEATRE in January 1935, by March it had moved to Broadway, where it was paired with Odets's less noteworthy Till the Day I Die on a regular daily basis.

Waiting for Lefty is unabashedly left-wing "agit-prop" (AGITATION-PROPAGANDA) drama holding to the Communist Party line. Its significance was Odets's success in presenting this message not to the "masses" but to the sophisticated Broadway audiences who, surprisingly, enthusiastically received it.

Much of the impact of Lefty lies in the overt THEATRICALITY that abandons nearly all conventional staging, while maintaining an intense sense of REALISM in setting and dialogue. The illusion of a union hiring hall is created by a semicircle of plain wooden chairs placed on a bare stage and facing the audience, which the actors address from time to time, with responses from "plants" in the auditorium. Traditional aesthetic distance is breached as viewers are drawn into the action. The climactic call of "Strike! Strike!" is fully intended to prompt the audience, psychologically at least, to rush into the street and man the barricades.

Most prominent among those seated onstage is the "porcine, well-fed," and confident union boss, Harry Fatt, who is trying to head off a strike of cab drivers. The personification of the bloated capitalist, he regards anyone opposed to him as "yellow" or a "damned Red." But of more immediate concern to the committee than Fatt's arguments are the whereabouts of the chairman, Lefty.

While the committee waits with increasing unease, within the circle is enacted a series of spotlighted vignettes spelling out the debilitating conditions of the workplace, which are forcing consideration of a walkout. A few examples: the young cabbie who tells his girlfriend that they cannot get married on five or six dollars a week; the intern who cannot hold a job because he is Jewish; discovery of a spy among the ranks of the laborers. The most direct political statement occurs when an actor seeking work is told by the office receptionist to read and follow the Communist Manifesto or, better yet, go to RUSSIA where you will be lifted out of the gutter and everybody calls you comrade.

The climax comes with the arrival through the audience of a breathless messenger with the news that Lefty has been found behind the car barns with a bullet through his head. The meeting erupts in the call to strike, and the entire audience is caught up in the emotional wave that sweeps through the theater.

Waiting for Lefty is radical theater at its best. Once presented, however, its mission is accomplished, and theoretically, it has no further life. But, of course, it is theater, and its message will continue night after night. While the impact of Odets's creation may be socially irrelevant in a different time and a different situation, the fact remains that it is tremendously effective. Its admixture of overt theatricality, consciously contrived, and the skilled illusion of reality makes it unsurpassed in the history of American social drama.

[See also Political Theater in the United States; United States, 1929–1940]

FURTHER READING

Clurman, Harold. The Fervent Years: The Story of the Group Theatre and the Thirties. 1945. New York: Hill & Wang, 1957.

Himelstein, Morgan Y. Drama Was a Weapon: The Left Wing Theatre in New York, 1929–1941. New Brunswick, N.J.: Rutgers Univ. Press, 1963.

Weales, Gerald. Clifford Odets, Playwright. New York: Pegasus, 1971.

Jordan Miller

WALCOTT, DEREK (1930–)

Playwright and poet Derek Walcott, born in Castries, Saint Lucia, on January 23, 1930, has achieved acclaim as both a West Indian and an international writer, earning the Nobel Prize for Literature in 1992. African and European literature and culture influence his work; therefore, his writing often engages issues of origin and the search for order in the world.

On a British government scholarship, Walcott received a bachelor of arts degree in 1953 from the University College of the West Indies in Mona, Jamaica. He taught in West Indian schools for four years, then studied theater in New York on a Rockefeller Foundation Fellowship in 1958. In 1959 he founded the Little Carib Theatre Workshop in Trinidad, which he ran until 1976. This company produced his plays, as well as work by writers as diverse as WOLE SOYINKA, EUGÈNE IONESCO, SAMUEL BECKETT, and EDWARD ALBEE. Walcott's own plays found inspiration in William Shakespeare, Japanese NŌ and kabuki, the films of Akiro Kurosawa, and most notably BERTOLT BRECHT's theater of the people, while also drawing on West Indian popular culture and myths, such as Trinidad's Carnival or Caribbean music and folktales. As a dramatist, Walcott wrote and produced plays in which everyone in the West Indies—not just the privileged colonial class—could participate, thus becoming instrumental in the development of a Caribbean theatrical tradition.

Walcott began writing plays and verse dramas in the 1940s, though he considers Henri Christophe (1950) his first play. In it, a former slave becomes a Haitian king, only to be overthrown by his people. Shakespeare's work figures as a preeminent influence here, as does a Jacobean poetic writing style. Later plays show Walcott using local, Caribbean language and motifs, such as in Ti-Jean and His Brothers (1958), a play based on a Caribbean folktale about three brothers who try to trick the devil.

Dream on Monkey Mountain (1967) continues Walcott's exploration of Caribbean cultural IDENTITY. This play incorporates elements of both European and African cultures, and through characters such as the protagonist, Makak, an imprisoned Afro-Caribbean Messiah, and Lestrade, a racially mixed defender of colonial order, Walcott suggests that all cultures, not just the cultures of the oppressed, have been creolized. This theme appears again in The Joker of Seville (1974), an adaptation of a 17th-century Don Juan play commissioned by Britain's Royal Shakespeare. The play—a musical collaboration with Galt MacDermot—draws on calypso music and American rhythm and blues while setting the European Don Juan legend in the Caribbean.

Walcott continued to work on musicals with MacDermot and ultimately collaborated with Paul Simon on the Broadway musical *The Capeman* (1998), which received poor reviews and had only a short run of sixty-nine shows. Later plays, such as *The Haytian Earth* (1984), demonstrate Walcott's ability as a playwright to engage Caribbean history and emphasize the importance of local history, language, and culture. Though he left the Little Carib Theater Company in 1976 and eventually became a professor at Boston University in 1981, Walcott retains a position as one of the most important Caribbean writers as well as an important world writer.

SELECT PLAYS: *Henri Christophe: A Chronicle in Seven Scenes* (1950); *The Sea at Dauphin: A Play in One Act* (1954); *Ione: A Play with Music* (1957); *Ti-Jean and His Brothers* (1958); *Dream on Monkey Mountain* (1967); *In a Fine Castle* (1970); *The Joker of Seville* (1974); *O Babylon!* (1976); *The Isle Is Full of Noises* (1982); *The Haytian Earth* (1984); *Odyssey: A Stage Version* (1993); *The Capeman: A Musical* (1998)

FURTHER READING
Baugh, Edward. *Derek Walcott: Memory as Vision.* London: Longman, 1979.
Colson, Theodore. "Derek Walcott's Plays: Outrage and Compassion." *World Literature Written in English* 12 (April 1973): 80–96.
Hamner, Robert D. "Derek Walcott." In *The Dictionary of Literary Biography.* Vol. 1, no. 117, *Twentieth Century Caribbean and Black African Writers First Series*, ed. by Bernth Lindors and Reinhard Sander. Detroit: Gale Res., 1992. 290–312.
King, Bruce. *Derek Walcott and West Indian Drama: "Not Only a Playwright But a Company—the Trinidad Theatre Workshop, 1959–1993."* Oxford: Oxford Univ. Press, 1995.
——. *Derek Walcott: A Caribbean Life.* Oxford: Oxford Univ. Press, 2000.
Thieme, John. *Derek Walcott.* New York: Manchester Univ. Press, 1999.

Gary Leising

WALKER, GEORGE F. (1947–)

George F. Walker, British CANADA's most acclaimed playwright of the late 20th century, was born in 1947 in Toronto's east end, where many of his later plays are set. He was working as a taxi driver in Toronto in 1970 when he saw an advertisement for new scripts and sent some plays to the fledgling Factory Theatre Lab. Ken Gass, founder and artistic director of Toronto's Factory Theatre Lab, quickly recognized a startlingly original talent in the unpretentious Walker. Walker's first six plays were all produced at the Factory Theatre Lab. Gass and Walker established a working relationship that continues to this day. Walker eventually became artistic director of the Factory Theatre Lab himself in 1978; and even after developing close relationships with other major theaters, such as becoming writer in residence at the New York Shakespeare Festival in 1981, he has returned to his roots at the Factory. He has written twenty-nine plays for the theater as well as several radio and television scripts. Among his numerous awards and recognitions, he has received the Governor General's Award for English-language drama twice.

Critic and historian of Canadian theater Craig Stewart Walker (2001) has argued that George F. Walker's first produced plays, *Prince of Naples* (1971) and *Ambush at Tether's End* (1971), are inspired by or even reworkings of absurdist plays by SAMUEL BECKETT and EUGÈNE IONESCO. Gass has also pointed out Walker's debt to "the French absurdists" but stresses that the mature Walker defies categorization.

Walker's work can be divided roughly into three categories: the early cartoon phase, the middle film noir phase, and the later REALISM phase. Although this division is not strictly chronological, it does reflect a development over time away from fantasy-based satire, passing through ironic reference to Hollywood genres, to a hybrid form combining the absurd with realism/NATURALISM.

Bagdad Saloon (1973), subtitled "a cartoon," *Beyond Mozambique* (1974), and *Ramona and the White Slaves* (1976) were all set in outrageous locales, such as an Arabian nights desert with cowboys, the Jungle, and Hong Kong, respectively. These works were entirely divorced from the urban, Canadian environment of the author and the company that produced them. During this "cartoon" phase, Walker seems to have been struggling against the claustrophobic nature of Canadian theater in the 1970s. This period was one of tremendous growth in Canadian theater and spawned an undeniable maturity of content and level of expertise in production values, but the bureaucratic demands from granting agencies and the Ministry of Culture, directly satirized in Walker's *The Art of War* (1982), also led to a dull, self-obsessed naturalism in many works. Walker's plays appeared on the scene as an antidote to this formula through sheer audacity of nonconformist locales, characters, and situations.

Despite the refreshingly non-Canadian quality of the cartoon plays, they attracted mainly a coterie, counterculture audience and got a lukewarm reception from the critics. Walker wanted to overcome the subculture ghetto of Canadian culture and reach a broader audience. In 1977 he wrote *Gossip* and ZASTROZZI, both produced at Toronto Free Theatre. These were the first of his plays to be premiered at a theater other than Factory Theatre Lab. Both plays were extremely successful, catapulting Walker to the mainstream of North American theater. *Gossip* introduced Walker's ironic version of Sam Spade in the character Tyrone Power, who would be the unlikely hero of two more, equally well received and popular plays: *Filthy Rich* (1979) and *The Art of War* (1982).

Gossip was set in an urban environment, less fantasy based than his earlier work, and represented the initiation of the film noir phase. *Zastrozzi* was based on a description of Percy Bysshe Shelley's romance of the same name. Walker claims not to have actually read Shelley when he wrote the play. *Zastrozzi* combined satisfying stage situations with a complex moral dilemma cum MELODRAMA. The title character seems to be the embodiment of evil, yet he is irresistible to most of the characters and the audience. The "good" characters cannot possibly defeat him because their idealism is unrealistic.

Chris Johnson (1980) has interpreted *Zastrozzi* as a thesis play promoting small-*c* conservative values. It is perhaps this kind of misreading that led Walker in his later work to move in a new naturalistic direction. In his *East End Plays* he explores territory much more familiar to his audience. The plays are set in kitchens, living rooms, and office spaces that contemporary people may live and work in. The influence of the absurd persists in the action and relationships of characters, but the use of fantasy and ironic quotations from film and nondramatic literature that run through his earlier work is almost entirely left behind. This experiment in simpler, more controlled storytelling is even more clearly the case in the *Suburban Motel* series, a collection of six plays set in the same motel room.

The play that stands apart from the tripartite formula of Walker's career is *Nothing Sacred* (1988), a free adaptation of Ivan Turgenev's novel *Fathers and Sons*. According to director Bill Glassco, Walker stressed that *Nothing Sacred* was a "Canadian comedy, not a Russian TRAGEDY," but its title is taken from an American movie from 1937 starring Carole Lombard and Fredric March. Perhaps the classic Hollywood title was an effort by Walker to form a bridge between this Russian social COMEDY of manners and Walker's previous, self-consciously low-culture lexicon. Whatever Walker's goals were in writing *Nothing Sacred*, it has proven to be one of his most successful plays internationally, surpassing even *Zastrozzi* in productions at important regional theaters and garnering him both the Dora Mavor Moore and Floyd S. Chalmers Awards.

With *Heaven*, produced at Canadian Stage Theatre in 2000, Walker appears to be exploring yet another path. He explores the banality of hatred and violence, specifically racism, but uses a fantasy mode akin to his earlier work. Characters transform unexpectedly, and reality and fantasy are as vaguely defined as they were in *Bagdad Saloon*.

In his introduction to *Shared Anxiety*, a representative collection of Walker plays, Stephen Haff (1994) writes: "Wherever they are—an unspecified jungle, a crumbling prison in turn-of-the-century Italy, a graveyard in the Paris of 1945, a cliff in Nova Scotia, an alley, a kitchen, a park—Walker's characters are in our world because they give us their mighty effort to survive in words full, direct and present, with bodies active, devoted and here." Haff's analysis reminds us that throughout Walker's experimenting with style, genre, content and form, his strength lies in his characters and their connection to the lives of the audience, however superficially otherworldly the situation onstage may be.

PLAYS: *Ambush at Tether's End* (1971); *Prince of Naples* (1971); *Sacktown Rag* (1972); *Bagdad Saloon* (1973); *Beyond Mozambique* (1974);

Demerit (1974); *Ramona and the White Slaves* (1976); *Gossip* (1977); *Zastrozzi* (1977); *Filthy Rich* (1979); *Rumours of Our Death* (1980); *Theatre of the Film Noir* (1981); *The Art of War* (1982); *Science and Madness* (1983); *Criminals in Love* (1984); *Better Living* (1986); *Beautiful City* (1987); *Nothing Sacred* (1988); *Love and Anger* (1989); *Escape from Happiness* (1991); *Tough!* (1993); *Adult Entertainment* (1997); *Criminal Genius* (1997); *Problem Child* (1997); *Risk Everything* (1997); *The End of Civilization* (1998); *Featuring Loretta* (1998); *Heaven* (2000)

FURTHER READING

De Raey, Daniel. "Chords: Lost and Vocal: An Introduction." In *Suburban Motel*. Vancouver: Talonbooks, 1999.

Gass, Ken. "Introduction." In *Three Plays*. Toronto: Coach House Press, 1978.

Gussow, Mel. "Turgenev, with License." *New York Times* (January 13, 1989): C5.

Haff, Steven. "Introduction." In *Shared Anxiety*, by George F. Walker. Toronto: Coach House Press, 1994. xi–xvii.

Johnson, Chris. "George F. Walker: B-Movies Beyond the Absurd." *Canadian Literature* 85 (Summer 1980): 82–103.

Walker, Craig Stewart. "George F. Walker: Postmodern City Comedy." In *The Buried Astrolabe: Canadian Dramatic Imagination and Western Tradition*. Montreal: McGill Univ. Press, 2001.

Donald Cameron McManus

WALLACE, NAOMI (1960–)

Naomi Wallace was born in 1960 in Prospect, Kentucky, and grew up on a farm within a largely working-class community. She credits growing up in the South and being privy to the stories of her neighbors and of her Dutch mother's World War II childhood with providing her the perspectives that inspire and inform her plays. Wallace's work has ranged widely in setting and subject matter, from class politics and quarantine in the 1665 London Plague to the sexual and racial politics of the Gulf War. All of her plays share a concern with questions of power, violence, and social justice, often filtered through the perspectives of those denied access to power and of those who struggle to change or escape their living and working conditions. Her plays have been more enthusiastically received in Britain than in the UNITED STATES. However, it was in Atlanta, Georgia, in 2001 that her work inspired a festival dedicated entirely to her writing and sponsored by twelve theater companies.

Wallace's Brechtian influences (such as audience ALIENATION and exposure of sociopolitical roles and structures) and her explorations of the eroticism of violence tie her to British playwrights like CARYL CHURCHILL, David Edgar, HAROLD PINTER, and SARAH KANE. However, Wallace herself has argued for the place of such political dialogue in the American theatrical tradition and locates its earlier expression in the work of CLIFFORD ODETS and ARTHUR MILLER and its current expression through such playwrights as TONY KUSHNER, Robert O'Hara, Kia Corthron, and SUZAN-LORI PARKS.

While it has been her playwriting that has earned her international acclaim, she turned to playwriting from poetry at the age of thirty-two. In the years that followed, she has been a prolific playwright and an engaged theater artist, receiving commissions from the Public Theater in New York and the Royal Shakespeare Company in ENGLAND and organizing two staged readings of new works by many playwrights, one in response to the capital conviction of Mumia Abu-Jamal and the other to protest the embargo of Iraq. She also launched an artistic exchange between American playwrights and Palestinian theater that took place throughout the West Bank in 2002 and is ongoing (the American playwrights' accounts of their trip were published in *American Theatre* magazine in the July–August and September–October 2002 issues).

Wallace's play *Things of Dry Hours* (2004) is based on the book *Hammer and Hoe* by Robin Kelley, about race relations and the Alabama Communist Party in the 1930s. She was awarded a MacArthur Fellowship in 1999 and has written a book of poetry (*To Dance a Stony Field*, 1995) and a film screenplay (*Lawn Dogs*, 2001).

PLAYS: *The War Boys* (1993); *In the Fields of Aceldama* (1993); *The Girl Who Fell Through a Hole In Her Jumper* (1993); *In the Heart of America* (1994); *One Flea Spare* (1995); *Slaughter City* (1996); *Birdy* (1997);*The Trestle at Pope Lick Creek* (1998); *The Inland Sea* (2002); *Two Into War* (2003); *Things of Dry Hours* (2004); *A State of Innocence* (2005)

FURTHER READING

Baley, Shannon. "Death and Desire, Apocalypse and Utopia: Feminist Gestus and the Utopian Performative in the Plays of Naomi Wallace." *Modern Drama* 47, no. 2 (Summer 2004): 237–249.

Barnett, Claudia. "Dialectic and the Drama of Naomi Wallace." In *Southern Women Playwrights: New Essays in Literary History and Criticism*, ed. by Robert L. McDonald and Linda Rohrer. Tuscaloosa: Univ. of Alabama Press, 2002.

Bell, Hilary. "The Landscape Remembers You: A Reflection by Hilary Bell from an Interview with Naomi Wallace." In *Trans-Global Readings: Crossing Theatrical Boundaries*, ed. by Caridad Svich. Manchester: Manchester Univ. Press, 2003.

Bilderback, Walter. "The Naomi Wallace Festival and 9/11." *Consciousness, Literature and the Arts* 4, no. 3 (December 2003).

Julian, Connie. "Naomi Wallace: Looking for Fire." *Revolutionary Worker*, no. 1232 (March 14, 2004).

Victoria Sams

THE WALTZ OF THE TOREADORS

General Saint-Pé has never abandoned his invalid wife Amélie, despite her shrewishness and feigned paralysis. For seventeen years, though, he has loved a woman with whom he once danced the Toreador waltz at a regimental ball. Now he loves Ghislaine so much he refuses to make her his mistress, preferring to wait for true marriage. As it so happens, Ghislaine has come into possession of a letter in which Amélie expresses love to her doctor; Saint-Pé has grounds for divorce from Amélie, leading to a bitter confrontation between the furious spouses in which the romantic waltz becomes a *danse macabre*. Saint-Pé's philandering, however, catches up with him: he cannot duel with his secretary Gaston for Ghislaine's hand because Gaston is his illegitimate son. The General can only soothe his desperate loneliness in the caresses of the new maid.

The Waltz of the Toreadors (*La valse des toréadors*, 1952) is considered JEAN ANOUILH's "blackest" COMEDY, the most successful expression of an intermediate style whose internal conflicts represent the playwright's preoccupation with incommunicability. As the Doctor says, "You must never understand your enemy—or your wife. . . . We must never understand anyone, in fact; we'll die from it." *The Waltz of the Toreadors* flopped in its initial staging at the Comédie des Champs-Elysées in 1952; its shifts in tone and genre, from vaudeville to TRAGEDY, from high comedy to MELODRAMA, from one scene to the next, led critics to accuse the play of incoherency and chaos. Indeed, the play was collected in *Pièces grinçantes* (Grating Plays, 1956), plays Anouilh termed "grating" because of their internal clashes of comedy and tragedy. Both play and playwright have been dismissed as outmoded and trivial; tonal discord, however, was Anouilh's domain of reflection. The progression from Amélie and Saint-Pé's brutality to the farcical denouement is one example of the playwright's delight in formal manipulation: centuries-old comic devices remain credible because they are preceded by unflinching combat. The protagonist recalls Molière's curmudgeons saddled with sickly wives and besieged by secondary characters rooted in commedia archetypes; Saint-Pé embodies Anouilh's most recurrent themes of nostalgic innocence, the tension between idealism and compromise, and the complexities of family relationships.

Believing in the value and power of stage artifice and convention, Anouilh saw drama as endlessly theatrical. While other writers depicted humanity doomed in the wake of war, he tempered his nihilism by positing comedy as crucial: "I'm through with tragedy. . . . Of course everything is sad. So what? Everyone knows it. The soul must be purged. By laughter" (Harvey, 1964). The General fears loneliness, he finds himself trapped in it, and it is heart-wrenching. By the end, however, we point and laugh. As Anouilh wrote in his own defense, "We live in a farcical universe, and we don't dare see it" (Harvey, 1964). If the play's burlesque ending undercuts our sympathy for the General, its comic tone is finally optimistic: ignobility exists—the General is destined to philander—but it is a requisite for grace, by way of guilt and even inspiration. Despite its cool reception in FRANCE, *The Waltz of the Toreadors* was a hit in both London and New York later in the decade; its 1962 film version starred Peter Sellars.

FURTHER READING

Della Fazia, Alba. *Jean Anouilh.* New York: Twayne, 1969.

Fowlie, Wallace. *Dionysus in Paris: A Guide to Contemporary French Theatre.* London: Gollancz, 1961.

Harvey, John. *Anouilh: A Study in Theatrics.* New Haven, Conn.: Yale Univ. Press, 1964.

McIntyre, H. G. *The Theatre of Jean Anouilh.* Totowa, N.J.: Barnes & Noble, 1981.

Pronko, Leonard Cabell. *The World of Jean Anouilh.* Berkeley: Univ. of California Press, 1961.

Matt Di Cintio

WANDOR, MICHELENE (1940–)

The British feminist playwright and critic Michelene Dinah Wandor was born into a Russian Jewish family in London on April 20, 1940. She was educated at Chingford Secondary Modern School, Essex (1954–1956), and Chingford County High School, Essex (1959–1962). Wandor spent four years in ISRAEL during her youth (1949–1954). She earned a B.A. (honours) at Newnham College, Cambridge (1962), an M.A. in sociology at the University of Essex, Colchester (1975), an LTCL and a DipTCL at the Trinity College of Music, London (1994), and an M.Mus at the University of London and Trinity College of Music (1997).

Wandor was poetry editor for *Time Out* magazine (1971–1982) and from 1972 to 1977 regularly contributed to *Spare Rib* magazine. She was playwright-in-residence at the University of Kent, Canterbury (1982–1983) and "Woman Writer in Residence" at Mainz University, GERMANY (2002). Her adaptation of William Luce's *The Belle of Amherst* for Thames TV won an International Emmy Award (1987).

During the 1970s and 1980s, Wandor worked with feminist collectives and fringe theater groups, such as Gay Sweatshop (1977, 1985), MONSTROUS REGIMENT (1977), the Women's Project Company (1978), and Mrs. Worthington's Daughters (1979). With *The Wandering Jew* (1987), a dramatization of a novel by Eugène Sue, Wandor was the first British woman playwright to have a mainstage production at the Royal National Theatre.

Wandor has consistently taken on topical, controversial issues such as the Miss World contest (*The Day After Yesterday*, 1972), prostitution (*Whores D'Oeuvres*, 1978), artificial insemination by donor (*AID Thy Neighbour*, 1978), and surrogacy (*Wanted*, 1988).

She also explores Jewish themes in her work, as in *Scissors* (1978), a Jewish family COMEDY set in ENGLAND in the 1970s, and *Wanted* (1988), which stars the biblical matriarch Sarah. Feminist issues and Jewish themes are also characteristic of her short fiction and poetry.

Wandor experiments with a variety of aesthetic forms, ranging from social REALISM and AGITATION-PROPAGANDA to comedy, COLLAGE, and the surreal. Wandor has proved to be a most versatile artist and has also distinguished herself as a poet, short-story writer, broadcaster, theater historian, and musician.

During the 1980s, Wandor edited the four-volume collection of women's plays in the *Plays by Women* series, and among the writers she worked with and introduced to a wider public were CARYL CHURCHILL, Pam Gems, LIZ LOCHHEAD, and Louise Page. Her studies *Understudies: Theatre and Sexual Politics* (1981, rev. as *Carry On, Understudies*, 1986) and *Look Back in Gender* (1987; 2001 rev. and updated as *Post-War British Drama: Looking Back in Gender*) are among the standard works of British feminism.

SELECT PLAYS: *You Two Can Be Ticklish* (1970); *The Day After Yesterday* (1972); *Mal de Mère* (1972); *Spilt Milk* (1972); *Friends and Strangers* (1974); *To Die Among Friends* (1974); *Sink Songs* (1975); *Care and Control* (1977); *Floorshow* (1977, with Caryl Churchill and Bryony Lavery); *The Old Wives' Tale* (1977); *Penthesilea* (1977, adaptation of Heinrich von Kleist's play); *AID Thy Neighbour* (1978); *Correspondence* (broadcast 1978, produced 1979); *Scissors* (1978); *Whores D'Oeuvres* (1978); *Aurora Leigh* (1979, adaptation of the poem by Elizabeth Barrett Browning); *Future Perfect* (1980, with Steve Gooch and Paul Thompson); *Rutherford and Son* (1980, adaptation of a play by Githa Sowerby); *The Blind Goddess* (1981, adaptation of a play by Ernst Toller); *Whose Greenham* (1986); *The Wandering Jew* (adapted from Eugène Sue's novel *Le Juif Errant* [The Wandering Jew, 1844–1845], 1987); *Wanted* (1988)

FURTHER READING

Goodman, Lizbeth. "Wandor, Michelene (Dinah)." In *Contemporary Women Dramatists*, ed. by Kate A. Berney. London: St. James Press, 1994. 255–259.

Goodman, Lizbeth, and Jane de Gay. "Interview with Michelene Wandor." In *Feminist Stages: Interviews with Women in Contemporary British Theatre*. London: Harwood Acad. Pubs., 1996. 90–93.

Keyssar, Helene. "Communities of Women in Drama: Pam Gems, Michelene Wandor, Ntozake Shange." In *Feminist Theatre: An Introduction to Plays of Contemporary British and American Women*. Basingstoke: Macmillan, 1984. 126–147.

Ulrike Behlau

WANG RENJIE (1942–)

Born a native of Quanzhou, Fujian Province, in 1942, Wang Renjie has mainly written *liyuanxi*, the regional music drama of his hometown and one of the oldest living theaters in CHINA, preserving the tradition of the early *nanxi* of the Song-Yuan period. His plays, which have been produced successfully on the *liyuanxi* stage since the late 1980s, are *The Lament of a Chaste Woman* (*Jiefu yin*, 1987), *Tutor Dong and Widow Li* (*Dong sheng yu Li shi*, 1993), *Love Under Evening Maple Trees* (*Fenglin wan*, 1985), *Chen Zhongzi and His Wife* (*Chen Zhongzi*, 1990), and *Woman Thief and Her Male Escort* (*Zaoli yu nuzei*, 1998). The first three plays are about widows of both traditional and contemporary societies. Wang was, therefore, nicknamed the "Three-Widow Playwright." *The Lament of a Chaste Woman* and *Tutor Dong and Widow Li* earned him two Cao Yu Awards for Dramatic Literature.

In *The Lament of a Chaste Woman*, Yan Shi, who has been widowed for ten years, shows her feeling for Shen Rong, her little son's tutor-in-residence, on the eve of his departure for the imperial examination. Though he cares for Yan Shi, Shen Rong rejects her, fearing that she will violate the chastity required of a widow. As the tutor rejects her, two of the widow's fingers are injured by the shutting door. Shamed by his rejection and her inability to control her feelings, she cuts her two fingers and vows to remain chaste for the rest of her life. Ten years later, her son, as a top winner in the imperial examination, asks the emperor to vest his mother with the imperial title of the chaste woman for her twenty years of utter devotion to her late husband and her son. But the incident of her two fingers' injury as the result of her onetime desire to be unchaste is revealed to the public by the tutor, although he is an unwilling teller. Despite imperial commendation, Yan Shi is so shamed by public gossip that she commits suicide.

The play is based on an anecdote recorded in a Ming dynasty book. Two prevailing themes in this play, as in some of Wang's other plays, are men's culturally imposed repression of themselves and women's yearning for freedom, which made the latter victims of the social norm.

Wang's *Tutor Dong and Widow Li* is a COMEDY that can be read as a DECONSTRUCTION of the TRAGEDY in *The Lament of a Chaste Woman* and a confirmation and realization of what the widow Yan has desired. In the second play, Widow Li wins over Tutor Dong, who had been hired by Li's late husband to watch over her chastity. Whether in a tragedy or in a comedy, Wang's sympathy for women's emancipation is carried out through vivid characterization, beautiful lyrics, and witty dialogues, which are somewhat characteristic of the liyuanxi genre.

As Wang became a well-known playwright, theatrical troupes of other *xiqu* forms commissioned him to write plays for their productions. He has adapted the complete version of Tang Xianzu's *Peony Pavilion* (*Mudan ting*) and Bai Juyi's ballad poetry *Pipa Song* (*Pipa xing*, 2001) into *kunqu* of the same titles for Shanghai Kunqu Opera Troupe. He has also written *Jasmine Flower* (*Suxin hua*, 1981) for folk opera (*geju*) as well as for Zhejiang *yueju*.

Wang is considered one of the most important *xiqu* playwrights since the late 1970s. A four-day symposium was held in December 2000 for the study of his plays. About 100 scholars and critics came from Beijing, Shanghai, Sichuan Province, Taiwan, and Hong Kong as well as from various places within Fujian Province to discuss his works. Thirty-six articles were presented, and some of them were later published in theater journals. The event marked a new trend in recognizing the contributions made by playwrights in the *xiqu* genres.

SELECT PLAYS: *Love Under Evening Maple Trees* (*Fenglin wan*, 1985); *The Lament of a Chaste Woman* (*Jiefu yin*, 1987); *Chen Zhongzi and His Wife* (*Chen Zhongzi*, 1990); *Tutor Dong and Widow Li* (*Dong sheng yu Li shi*, 1992); *Woman Thief and Her Male Escort* (*Zaoli yu nuzei*, 1998)

FURTHER READING

An Kui. "Wei chuantong er hou chaoyue—du Wang Renjie juzuo" [Respect and surpass the tradition: Reading Wang Renjie's plays]. *Juben* (Play Scripts) 3 (2001): 51–53.

Fu Jin. "Yuwang de qizhi: Wang Renjie juzuo de shehuixue jiedu" [The banner for desire: Sociological implications in Wang Renjie's plays]. *Zhongguo xiju* (Chinese Theatre) 2 (2001): 42–44.

Wang Renjie. *Sanwei zhai jugao* [A collection of plays of the Sanwei study]. Beijing: Zhongguo xiju chubanshe, 2000.

Zeitlin, Judith T. "My Year of Peonies." *Asian Theatre Journal* 19, no. 1 (Spring 2002): 124–133.

Wenwei Du

WAR BABIES

The most complex play by MARGARET HOLLINGSWORTH, one of CANADA's foremost dramatists of the 1980s, *War Babies* was also, according to critic Dorothy Parker (1988), "a consummation of all [Margaret] Hollingsworth's earlier technical, stylistic, and thematic explorations." Hollingsworth's work foregrounds female characters, often immigrant women, struggling with feelings of isolation and a precarious sense of IDENTITY. The protagonist Esme in *War Babies*, a writer traumatized by her pregnancy at age forty-two, feels estranged from her war correspondent husband and herself until she writes a surreal play that enacts her fears and fantasies. First produced in Vancouver in 1984, nominated for the 1986 Governor General's Award for Drama, and remounted in 1987 in Toronto, *War Babies* metatheatrically explores important issues of gender and creativity in fascinating ways.

Esme and her husband Colin have a fragile relationship during the late stages of her pregnancy. They only connect when playing what they call "war games," and she is anxious that he will leave her to go on assignment when she needs him most, ambivalent as he is about fatherhood and wedded to his job. She also fears a repeat of her first traumatic bout with motherhood fifteen years earlier that led to her giving up her son, Craig. Complicating matters, Craig was adopted by Esme's best friend, Barb, Colin's ex-girlfriend, who subsequently married Jack, Esme's first husband and Craig's father. Finally, Esme has discovered a secret that Colin has kept from her—that while covering a war in Sudan, he killed a young boy. Traditional gender roles predominate: the man is defined by work and violence; the woman is constrained by motherhood.

But Hollingsworth the playwright gives Esme the playwright the means to rewrite the script. Esme writes a sensationalistic play within the play (PWP) in which roles are ironically reversed. In it she overcomes her paralysis, buys a gun, and dresses in Colin's clothes to rob banks. Colin, in the PWP, who has renewed his affair with Barb, becomes increasingly housebound and is eventually arrested for the robberies. In a series of prison scenes he is brutalized by a young guard—Esme's grown son, Craig. Watching these scenes materialize as she writes them, the "real"

Esme gains strength, confidence, and self-awareness, finding a healthy middle ground between the extremes of her life and her theatrical revenge fantasies. *War Babies* ends in REALISM (the "real" Barb, Jack, and Craig are nothing like their PWP versions) and reconciliation. A girl-child is born, though ominously named Cassandra, and Esme makes peace with both Colin and Craig—although, as Colin says, "maybe it's only a cease-fire."

Praised for its intelligence, complexity, and theatrical sophistication, *War Babies* has also been criticized as overly ambitious, confusing, and soap operatic. But it remains one of the few plays of its era that deals seriously with a woman's subjective experience of childbirth as well as the dilemma of the female writer faced with the responsibilities of family. It powerful, imaginative presentation of psychological, emotional, and political issues makes *War Babies* an important play.

FURTHER READING

Hollingsworth, Margaret. *Willful Acts*. Rev. ed. Vancouver: Talonbooks, 1998.

Parker, Dorothy. "Alienation and Identity: The Plays of Margaret Hollingsworth." *Canadian Literature*, no. 118 (Autumn 1988): 97–113.

Rudakoff, Judith, and Rita Much. *Fair Play: 12 Women Speak (Conversations with Canadian Playwrights)*. Toronto: Simon & Pierre, 1990.

Zimmerman, Cynthia. *Playwriting Women: Female Voices in English Canada*. Toronto: Simon & Pierre, 1994.

Jerry Wasserman

WARIAT I ZAKONNICA   See THE MADMAN AND THE NUN

WASSERSTEIN, WENDY (1950–2006)

Feminism has affected me more in my writing than in a specifically political way. Sitting down to write a play that has three parts for women over forty, I think, is political. . . . My work is often thought of as lightweight commercial comedy, and I have always thought, no, you don't understand: this is in fact a political act. The Sisters Rosensweig had the largest advance in Broadway history, therefore nobody is going to turn down a play on Broadway because a woman wrote it or because it's about women.

—Wendy Wasserstein, in an interview with Laurie Winer, 1997

Wendy Wasserstein was not only one of the UNITED STATES's most commercially successful contemporary playwrights but also an especially important figure in the history of American female dramatists. While her couching of serious social commentary in witty banter and comfortable well-made plays has labeled her as a writer only of romantic COMEDIES, her work has consistently challenged gender stereotypes and given powerful voice to the concerns, professional and personal, of the post-1960s "liberated" woman.

Wasserstein was born on October 18, 1950, into an upper-middle-class Jewish family in Brooklyn, New York. She started writing seriously as an undergraduate at the all-female Mount Holyoke College; and after graduating in 1971, she entered a master's program in creative writing at City College of New York. Her first play, *Any Woman Can't*, was presented OFF-BROADWAY at Playwrights Horizons in 1973. Meanwhile Wasserstein went back to school, this time to the Yale School of Drama, where she developed her breakthrough play, UNCOMMON WOMEN AND OTHERS, about the friendship among five students at Mount Holyoke College confronting the oncoming dilemmas of marriage, career, and sexual liberation. Its premiere off-Broadway by the Phoenix Theatre in 1977 won an Obie Award for Best Play and went on to national fame when PBS (Public Broadcast Service) aired the production on television in 1978.

Her next play, *Isn't It Romantic* (final version, 1983), also portrayed the dynamics of female fellowship—this time between two twenty-something women—but also more explicitly examined the young professional woman's quest to "have it all." After various one-acts in the ensuing years (including an entry in the 1987 Chekhovian anthology *Orchards*), THE HEIDI CHRONICLES (1988) offered what many still consider Wasserstein's fullest expression of her themes, tracing the history of the women's movement from the 1960s to the 1980s, through the eyes of a brilliant yet conflicted female art historian. Transferring from a sold-out opening at Playwrights Horizons, the play became her Broadway debut and earned her both the Tony Award and the Pulitzer Prize for Best Play in 1989.

Wasserstein followed this critical triumph with the family comedy-drama *The Sisters Rosensweig* (1992), about a London reunion of three middle-aged Jewish American sisters, each fighting her own domestic battle against the backdrop of a changing post–Cold War world. She continued addressing political and social conditions more directly in the Washington drama *An American Daughter* (1997), inspired by the difficulties faced by women nominated for public office, and in *Old Money* (2000), which—in a bold stylistic experiment for Wasserstein—flashed back and forth between wealthy present-day New Yorkers and their ancestors a century earlier living in the same townhouse. Her final play, *Third* (2005), examined politics, ethics, and class in the relationship between a feminist professor and a male student she accuses of plagiarism.

While appreciating the erudite New York Jewish humor of Wasserstein's characters, critics have been less impressed by her more ambitious dramatic impulses, especially in her later work. Her champions, though, extol her as a pioneering woman writer whose success in a still male-dominated theater world opened a door for female dramatists to come. Wasserstein died January 30, 2006, from lymphoma.

Other nontheatrical writings include two collections of essays, *Bachelor Girls* (1990) and *Shiksa Goddess* (2001); a children's book, *Pamela's First Musical* (1996); a libretto for the three-part opera *Central Park* (1999); the screenplay for the romantic comedy *The Object of My Affection* (1998); and the posthumously published novel *Elements of Style* (2006).

[See also Feminist Drama in the United States]

SELECT PLAYS: *Any Woman Can't* (1973); *Uncommon Women and Others* (1977); *Isn't It Romantic* (1981–1983); *The Heidi Chronicles* (1988); *The Sisters Rosensweig* (1992); *An American Daughter* (1997); *Old Money* (2000); *Third* (2005)

FURTHER READING

Barnett, Claudia, ed. *Wendy Wasserstein: A Casebook*. New York: Garland, 1999.

Bigsby, C. W. E. *Contemporary American Playwrights*. New York: Cambridge Univ. Press, 1999.

Bryer, Jackson R., ed. *The Playwright's Art: Conversations with Contemporary American Dramatists*. Jefferson, N.C.: MacFarland, 1991.

Kolin, Philip C., and Colby H. Kullman, eds. *Speaking on Stage: Interviews with Contemporary American Playwrights*. Tuscaloosa: Univ. of Alabama Press, 1996.

Plimpton, George, ed. *Playwrights at Work: The Paris Review*. New York: Modern Library, 2000.

Savran, David. *The Playwright's Voice: American Dramatists on Memory, Writing and the Politics of Culture*. New York: Theatre Communications Group, 1999.

Wasserstein, Wendy. *Bachelor Girls*. New York: Knopf, 1990.

———. *Shiksa Goddess: Or, How I Spent my Forties: Essays by Wendy Wasserstein*. New York: Knopf, 2001.

Garrett Eisler

WASTE

It is unusual for a play to occupy an important place in theater history because of performances that never happened. That is the case, however, with HARLEY GRANVILLE-BARKER's *Waste* (1906). A review of the 1936 production of *Waste* in the *Observer* of December 6, 1936, summarizes the play's conflict-fraught history and provides a view of the play's role in debates about the state of British theater in the early 20th century:

> Written in 1906, refused the Censor's license, privately performed, much read and discussed, licensed as respectable in 1920, re-written in 1926, and at last publicly produced in 1936—the history of *Waste*—significant title!—gives melancholy confirmation to [GEORGE BERNARD] SHAW's opinion that the English theater is apt to be a generation behind the time.

Indeed, *Waste* provides a case study of the frustration that playwrights felt about the censorship exercised by the Examiner of Plays, which they perceived as one of the problems of Victorian theater that was continuing in the 20th century.

Waste tells the story of an abortion that jeopardizes a politician's career. Independent Member of Parliament Henry Trebell is on the brink of realizing his vision of disestablishing the church and using the recouped funds to create a utopian educational system. His career and life's work, however, ultimately are lost not because of the death of the married Amy Campbell after her abortion but for other political reasons. It is his consciousness of wasted life—

his own, because he will not be able to do his work, and that of his unborn child—that leaves him feeling "barren" and "empty . . . of all virtue" and leads to his suicide. It remains a matter of speculation whether the play was denied a license because of its frank treatment of sexuality or because of its political content.

Responding to the censor in an article in *Sketch* on October 23, 1907, Granville-Barker did not debate "whether he has done wisely or unwisely with regard to my play" but instead argued against the very principle of a censor. Granville-Barker suggested that theater managers, rather than plays, should be licensed and that any audience member could complain to a licensing committee "if [the manager] produced a play which was obscene, indecent, or objectionable." He advocated in favor of elected officials to govern the arts, rather than "one irresponsible individual who shelters himself behind the fact that he is a Court official, and, as a Court official, does not care a scrap for public opinion."

Reviews of the play's private performance by the Stage Society at the Imperial Theatre on November 24, 1907, credited *Waste* with being a play of ideas but also faulted the play for being overly elaborate in its treatment of politics. The play enjoys occasional revivals. Reviews of Sir Peter Hall's 1997 production of the play at London's Old Vic were split about whether it remained relevant in light of contemporary politics. Throughout its history, *Waste* has been best received by those who embrace its involvement in politics: both the role that it played in debates about the position of political officials in cultural life and its work in developing a theater of ideas.

[See also England, 1860–1940]

FURTHER READING

Billington, Michael. "Liars and Cheats." Review of the Old Vic's 1997 *Waste. Guardian, the Week* (March 15, 1997): 7.

Kennedy, Dennis. *Granville Barker and the Dream of Theatre*. New York: Cambridge Univ. Press, 1985.

Newey, Glen. "Balked Scraps from the Farmyard." Review of the Old Vic's 1997 *Waste*. TLS (April 4, 1997).

Salenius, Elmer W. *Harley Granville Barker*. Boston: Twayne, 1982.

Renata Kabetts Miller

WATANABE ERIKO (1955–)

Watanabe Eriko is a Japanese playwright, director, and actor, widely known for her acting in film and television but who established her reputation as a playwright by winning the Kishida Kunio Drama Prize in 1982 for *Kitarō the Ghost Buster* (*Gegege no Ge*). Watanabe began as a director and in 1978 cofounded with Kisaragi Koharu the 200 (Nijū-maru) company, changing the name to 300 (Sanjū-maru) in 1980. The Japanese pronunciations of the company's names do not mean 200 or 300 but rather two and three concentric circles. Watanabe thinks of circles as transcending the earth's contour, and she tries to create plays that transcend earthly forms.

In addition to *Kitarō*, 300 produced many of Watanabe's works such as *Shadows of the Night—A Gentle Ghost Story* (*Yoru no Kage—Yasashii Kaidan*, 1981), *The Forest of Wind* (*Kaze no Furu Mori*, 1989), and *TEMPO—Goodbye, Night!* (*TEMPO—Yoru yo Sayonara*, 1995). In 1987 Watanabe won the Kinokuniya Theatre Prize for 300's production of *A Girl with Eyelids* (*Mabuta no Me*, 1987). Watanabe's works premiered with other companies such as EN and Shinjuku Ryōzanpaku also have been well received. 300 disbanded in 1997. Watanabe became a freelance playwright, forming a production company in 2000.

Many of Watanabe's works are memory plays that shift seamlessly between the past and present. Her plays also reflect the influence of KARA JŪRŌ, using a mixture of reality and illusion, characters searching for meaning in their ordinary lives, songs, and other elements of spectacle. Although her plays are replete with the fantastic, Watanabe claims that the action of her plays is realistic because dreams and fantasy are contained within real life.

Kitarō the Ghost Buster combines a short story with characters from a popular comic. An introverted schoolboy, Makio, feels responsible for the deaths of his friend and his stillborn twin sister. He is bullied at school (the experience of Watanabe and her brother) and fantasizes about a friend to save him. Kitarō, hero of the comic *Gegege no Kitarō*, arrives, and they overcome the bullies, including Makio's teacher, who is actually Kitatō's comic-book nemesis Ratman. In Watanabe's theatrical fantasy world actors play dual characters. The old woman lying in bed (Watanabe originated the role) appears to be Makio's mother, but the schoolgirl, who is his worst tormentor, is her double.

A Gentle Ghost Story also centers on forces of dreams and fantasies but has heightened spectacle of character transformations and time slippages. The play shifts in time and space between contemporary JAPAN, 19th-century Europe, and a land of frozen tundra. Characters fly in and out on horses, climb up "beanstalks," and confront evil giants and the King of Hell. This all takes place in worlds that mirror each other and in which black is white and good is bad. As with many of Watanabe's plays, an older sister helps her younger brother overcome trials.

In *TEMPO* the character Shinji has to come to terms with the death of his brothers. In the fantasy/dreamscape of the play, chairs and refrigerators come to life à la Disney. In the end, Shinji acknowledges the world of dreams but knows life does not have a Disneyland happy ending.

PLAYS: *Shadows of the Night—A Gentle Ghost Story* (*Yoru no Kage—Yasashii Kaidan*, 1981); *Kitarō the Ghost Buster* (*Gegege no Ge*, 1982); *Secret of the Yellow Room* (*Kiiroi Heya no Himitsu*, 1983); *A Summer Crossing the River* (*Kawa o Wataru Natsu*, 1986); *A Girl with Eyelids* (*Mabuta no Me*, 1987); *Old Refrain* (*Ōrudo Rifurēn*, 1987); *The Night Swarming Star Calvary* (*Yoru ni Muragaru Hoshi no Kibatai*, 1988); *The Forest of Wind* (*Kaze no Furu Mori*, 1989); *The Legend of the Dancing Sand* (*Odoru Suna no Densetsu*, 1989); *Crayon Island* (*Kureyon no Shima*, 1991); *The Red Shoes* (*Akai Kutsu*, 1994); *TEMPO—Goodbye, Night!* (*TEMPO—Yoru yo Sayonara*, 1995); *Night Express* (*Shinya Tokkyū*, 1996); *Star Village* (*Hoshi no Mura*, 2001)

FURTHER READING

Japan Playwrights Association, ed. *Half a Century of Japanese Theater: III. 1980s, Part 1*. Tokyo: Kinokuniya, 2001.

Kazama Ken. *Shōgekijō no Fūkei* [The little theater landscape]. Tokyo: Chūō Kōronsha, 1992.

Uchino Tadashi. *Merodorama no Gyakushū: "Shiengeki" no 80 Nendai* [The revenge of melodrama: "Private theater" of the 80s]. Tokyo: Keisō Press, 1996.

John D. Swain

WATA PALWATA *See* ROUTES AND ESCAPE ROUTES

THE WATER STATION

The Water Station (*Mizu no Eki*, 1981), a Japanese play by ŌTA SHŌGO, the first of his Station trilogy, which includes *The Earth Station* (1985) and *The Wind Station* (1986). In the 1990s he added three more Station plays: *The Sand Station* (1993), *The Water Station 2* (1995), and *The Water Station 3* (1998). Ōta and his Theater of Transformation (*Tenkei Gekijō*, 1968–1988) won the Kinokuniya Theatre Award in the Group Division for *The Water Station* in 1984. It toured major cities in Europe and North America in the 1980s.

Ōta was inspired to experiment with silence and slow movement when he first produced *The Tale of Komachi Told by the Wind* on a NŌ stage in 1977. He refined his aesthetic in the Station plays. *The Water Station* is striking for the absence of dialogue; the slowed down, though natural, motion of the performers; and the use of basic elements such as water and space. Against a desolate landscape stands a faucet with a broken spigot, water trickling constantly. A pile of junk rises conspicuously in the barren scene. Travelers come by, interact, avail themselves of the water, and then move on. Nothing is said, and no new lasting relationships are formed. In this starkest of situations, the utter aloneness of each individual is revealed. In this way, Ōta creates an existential theater that prioritizes the species level over the individual level of existence and highlights the birth-to-death life cycle of the human race rather than human endeavors in society.

The Water Station illustrates in its purest form Ōta's theatrical code of divestiture. Distrust of language as the main tool of artistic expression led Ōta to look for a different kind of language, a body-centered code that applied the "power of passivity," the ability to create aesthetic distance by refraining from reaching out excessively to the audience—to do less, to explain less. The three aspects of his code are silence, slow movement, and empty space.

For Ōta, silence rather than speech is the normal human condition. He claims that we spend ninety percent of our life without talking. Silence as a divestiture of words creates distance from language-centered social activity. Slow movement contributes to an emphasis on the species level by luring both the actor's and viewer's attention away from culturally determined uses of the body. Ōta, furthermore, reduces social aspects by paring down the set to an elemental landscape.

One source of his bleak landscapes lies in his childhood experience during the 1945 repatriation of the Japanese in CHINA. On the long trek from Beijing to Tianjin, many Japanese discarded their belongings, which became mountains of junk by the wayside. Ōta remembers playing in the junkpile and then looking up to find himself alone, with the horizon stretching out before him.

[See also Japan]

FURTHER READING

Boyd, Mari. "Unaccommodated Man in Ōta Shōgo's Plays: A Study of Silence and Slow Movement in Mizu no Eki and Chi no Eki." Sophia International Review 9 (1987): 22–28.

Ōta Shōgo. The Water Station. Tr. by Mari Boyd. Asian Theater Journal 7, no. 2 (Fall 1990): 150–183.

Senda Akihiko. Nihon no Gendai Engeki [The modern theater of Japan]. Tokyo: Iwanami Shoten, 1995.

Mari Boyd

THE WAVE

UTPAL DUTT never had qualms about declaring himself a propagandist playwright. He firmly believed that theater needed to be an active agent in manufacturing consent in favor of a Marxist revolution in INDIA. To this effect, he wrote numerous plays based on meticulous research on Indian history (although impartial interpretation almost never marked his project), challenging the Gandhian history of India. Most of them were highly successful. Of these, The Wave (Kallol), written and produced in 1965, about a mutiny in the Indian Navy during the last days of the British Raj in 1946, is considered a masterpiece. One of many British ships that fought during World War II, the H.M.I.S. Khyber was the only one that did not return before its sailors suffered five months of torture at the hands of the Germans.

At the beginning of the play, Gunner Sardul Singh, leader of the Khyber crew, returns home to the slums of the Bombay waterfront. In the meantime, assuming the Khyber's absence meant the demise of its crew members, Sardul's fiancée Lakshmi became engaged to Subhash, who had saved her life when it was endangered by British soldiers. A heartbroken Sardul leaves Bombay to make the ship his home.

On February 18, 1946, Sardul and his crew turn against the British navy. Ignoring the Indian National Congress' call for nonviolent struggle, the Khyber crew takes up arms to rescue Castle Barracks, the headquarters of the Royal Indian Navy in Bombay, from an attack launched by the British Indian Army.

On land, the people of the waterfront slum defend themselves against the retaliation of the British forces. The British take Sardul's mother hostage, as a way of forcing the Khyber crew to negotiate with them. The British get the Khyber crew arrested, and Sardul, in his attempt to fight back, dies.

The play ran for 850 shows, creating a sensation in Kolkata and producing violent reactions both for and against. Dutt was jailed without trial, and the theater was attacked several times. For a while, newspapers, under governmental pressure, refused to carry advertisements of the play, but word-of-mouth and handbills were more than enough to draw the audience. A public meeting was held on the Kolkata Maidan (a sprawling Commons that is still a venue to big political rallies) to mark The Wave's 800th performance, which was attended by a million people. The Wave was a milestone production, not only for its adrenaline-laced political message and melodramatic plotline but also for its incredible stagecraft and lights. The Bengali professional theater had made many advances in staging illusions and had shown epic battle scenes and running trains onstage. But The Wave was the first to show the starboard of a gigantic warship. The Wave is also a landmark production in the history of Indian theater for the political uproar it caused in the late 1960s, just as Bengal was seeing the rise of a nascent Maoist revolution that Dutt initially endorsed. He revived the production in the 1980s with the People's Little Theatre.

FURTHER READING

Banerjee, Himani. The Mirror of Class: Essays on Bengali Theatre. Kolkata: Papyrus, 1998.

Bharucha, Rustom. "The Revolutionary Theater of Utpal Dutt." In Rehearsals of a Revolution: The Political Theater of Bengal. Honolulu: Univ. of Hawaii Press, 1983.

Bhatia, Nandi. "Colonial History and Postcolonial Interventions: Staging the 1857 Mutiny as 'The Great Rebellion.' " In Acts of Authority/Acts of Resistance: Theater and Politics in Colonial and Postcolonial India. Ann Arbor: Univ. of Mich. Press, 2004.

Datta, Utpal. Towards a Revolutionary Theatre. Calcutta: M.C. Sarkar & Sons Private Ltd., 1995.

Interview with Utpal Dutt. In Contemporary Indian Theatre: Interviews with Playwrights and Directors, ed. by Paul Jacob. New Delhi: Sangeet Natak Akademi, 1989.

Mukherjee, Sushil. The Story of the Calcutta Theatres. Calcutta: K. P. Bagchi & Co., 1982.

Sudipto Chatterjee

WE

During the Cultural Revolution in CHINA (1966–1976), twenty million "educated youth" from the cities were sent down to the countryside to be reeducated by the peasants and to be tempered in the crucible of revolution. Their trials and tribulations, hopes and despairs, are the subject of this play with the unusual title We (WM, huaju), by Wang Peigong and Wang Gui. Besides being an abbreviation of the pinyin spelling of the Chinese *Wo Men* (meaning "we"), these two letters also resemble a pictograph of two persons, one standing upright, the other on his head. This play is therefore about the collective experiences of the "sent-down" youth and their struggles to find their place in society and meaning in their lives.

SYMBOLISM in the play's title is matched by its structure with the four acts of "Winter," "Spring," "Summer," and "Autumn" each representing a phase in the lives of the characters. In the first act, the howling wind, the bitter cold, and the backbreaking labor create a powerful impression of life in the "collective household." The earthquake that concludes this act marks the end of the Cultural Revolution and the beginning of the seven characters' search for new identities. In order to get ahead in a rapidly changing society, they sacrifice friendship, love, and personal integrity, but when they meet again eight years later, they still have not found a purpose for their lives. Their disillusionment is symbolized by one of them, the only character that has kept his ideals, literally going blind. "The Song of the Young Pioneers," which they sing in act 1 and again at the end of the play, becomes a poignant reminder of their lost youth and lost hopes.

We has broken new ground both as dramatic literature and as performing art. Its language is refreshingly playful and irreverent, poking fun at political movements and communist leaders. Under the direction of Wang Gui, this play successfully combines realistic characterization with symbolic representation. On an almost bare stage, the actors' movements and gestures indicate time, place, and action. Symbolism is also used to convey the meaning of the play. In the earthquake scene, for example, all seven characters huddle together and look out through the frame of a window with fear and anticipation in their eyes. This tableau is a portrait of the Chinese nation awaking from the ten-yearlong nightmare of the Cultural Revolution.

The production of *We* in 1985 generated a great deal of controversy. Dramatists hailed it as a new chapter of modern Chinese spoken drama, but official reactions were definitely negative. The staging of this play coincided with the convening of the Communist Party Congress, which called for strengthening ideological education while promoting economic reform. Under such circumstances, the play was criticized for its lack of heroic characters, its gloomy outlook, and its negative social effect. After a few "internal showings" and short engagements, *We* was banned permanently. The Drama Troupe of the Chinese Air Force also dismissed Wang Peigong and Wang Gui. In 1990 in the aftermath of the Tiananmen incident, a summary of the controversies surrounding this play was republished with an additional warning that literature and art must toe the Party line.

Wang Peigong was born in Taikang, Henan Province, in 1943. After leaving the air force, Wang joined the Chinese Youth Art Theater. He is now a freelance writer, writing mostly for film and television.

FURTHER READING

Kang Hongxing. "Wang Gui daoyan yishu de meixue zhuiqiu" [The aesthetic pursuits of Wang Gui's art of directing]. *Xiju* (Drama) 3 (1987): 100–108.

Li Kehuan. "Bu'an de linghun reng zai qiusuo: *WM* (*Wo men*) duhou" [A restless soul is still searching: Thoughts after reading *We*]. *Juben* (Play Scripts) 9 (1985): 26–27.

Wang Peigong and Wang Gui. *WM* [*We*]. *Juben* (Play Scripts) 9 (1985): 6–23. English translation in Yu, Shiao-ling S., tr. and ed., *Chinese Drama After the Cultural Revolution, 1979–1989*. Lewiston: Edwin Mellen Press, 1996. 291–348.

Yi Ming. "*WM* (*Wo men*) fengbo shimo" [The whole story of the controversies about *We*]. *Juben* (Play Scripts) 11 (1990): 18–26.

Shiao-ling Yu

THE WEAVERS

Men are tortured slowly here.
In this chamber of torture
Sighs are heard everywhere
And bear witness to the despair.
—"The Weavers Song," Act 3

The Weavers (*Die Weber*) is GERHART HAUPTMANN's most influential play. Written in 1892 and first performed privately by Berlin's Freie Bühne in 1893, *The Weavers* created as much controversy as Hauptmann's first drama, BEFORE DAYBREAK (*Vor Sonnenaufgang*). With *The Weavers* it was not the moral but rather the political content that generated the storm. Many Social Democrats, led by the Marxist critic Franz Mehring, saw the play as the first truly revolutionary drama. The ruling elite perceived it similarly and responded by banning the play. Lengthy court procedures followed, and when the drama was first performed publicly in 1894 at Berlin's Deutsches Theater, Emperor Friedrich Wilhelm II canceled his subscription to the theater.

The Weavers is based on a historical event: the 1844 weaver uprising in Silesia that was brutally crushed by the military. The play has five acts but is far from a classical drama. There are no main characters, no climax, and no resolution. The play's loosely connected acts foreshadow the structure of both expressionist drama and the EPIC THEATER of BERTOLT BRECHT. The play begins in the home of the manufacturer Dreißiger. The weavers, emaciated and dressed in rags, are delivering their handwoven materials for which they receive alms. The second act portrays the miserable living conditions of an individual family. An outsider named Max Jäger enters the scene and recites the revolutionary "Weavers' Song." In act 3 the weavers rise up and sing the "Weavers' Song," which the authorities have forbidden. In the fourth act, the weavers are back in Dreißiger's house, this time looting and destroying everything in sight, forcing Dreißiger and his family to flee. The final act focuses on an old weaver named Hilse. He is a devout Christian who believes in God's divine plan and opposes violence. As the revolutionary weavers confront the approaching military, old Hilse, watching the conflict from his window, is fatally shot.

The Weavers is regarded as GERMANY's, and perhaps Europe's, best example of a naturalist play. The drama's materialist PHILOSOPHY and its sociopolitical content underscore such an interpretation. There is no individual hero or heroine; the leading role belongs to the proletariat. The extensive use of dialect (the first version of The Weavers was written entirely in dialect) and the detailed STAGE DIRECTIONS also exemplify a naturalist representation of reality. However, the success of The Weavers results from the fact that the play transcends the limitations of NATURALISM. The most strikingly antinaturalist element in the play is the ending. The appearance of the deeply religious Hilse functions as a counterpoint to the naturalist elements by introducing both the supernatural and the spiritual.

Commentaries of The Weavers have focused mainly on the play's ending and the extent to which the drama can be considered socialist. Theodor Fontane pointed out that Hilse's antirevolutionary stance contradicts a socialist interpretation of the play. Others have interpreted Hilse's death as a confirmation of socialist doctrine. With Hilse dies RELIGION, the opium of the people. Hauptmann himself considered the play social, not socialist, and many critics have pointed out that Hauptmann is driven primarily by compassion for the suffering weavers.

FURTHER READING
Findlay, Bill. "Silesian into Scots: Gerhart Hauptmann's The Weavers." Modern Drama 41, no. 1 (1998): 90–104.
Mehring, Franz. "On Hauptmann's 'The Weavers' (1893)." New Theatre Quarterly 11, no. 42 (1995): 184–189.
Williams, Kirk. "Anti-theatricality and the Limits of Naturalism." Modern Drama 44, no. 3 (2001): 284–299.

Kerstin T. Gaddy

DIE WEBER   See THE WEAVERS

THE WEDDING

The premiere of STANISŁAW WYSPIAŃSKI's The Wedding (Wesele) in Cracow on March 16, 1901, is one of the great events in the history of Polish theater and a landmark in the development of Polish drama. A prophetic work constantly restaged and reinterpreted, The Wedding has profound resonance for Polish audiences, drawing upon collective cultural memories and complex literary and theatrical traditions. It is a play about national destiny and IDENTITY, raising disturbing questions about guilt and responsibility, class conflict and solidarity, past and future.

The action of The Wedding takes place in a small village near Cracow. The political context is the longing for independence of a country that has long been occupied and sunk slowly into apathy. The motive force is the fashionable idealization of the peasant class by intellectuals who feel that only with the support of the peasants will it be possible to free the nation.

The actual event giving rise to the work was the marriage of Wyspiański's poet friend to a peasant girl in a union designed to unite the two classes and impart a sense of national purpose. The drama covers the wedding celebration in a farmhouse where the guests—local peasants and city intelligentsia—spend the night talking and drinking. Couples dance in and out like marionettes to hypnotic music played offstage. In a blend of native tradition and European modernism, Wyspiański utilizes the stylized movements of the szopka, the folk nativity play with its rod puppets.

In jest the Poet-Bridegroom invites the Mulch (a protective covering for the rosebush in the garden) to join the festivities. When midnight strikes, the straw man appears and presides as master of eerie ceremonies, pulling strings that make others dance to his tune and announcing the arrival of apparitions, dreams, and nightmares. As night grows deeper, these ghosts from the past (including the Cossack seer, Wernyhora, who has predicted the liberation of POLAND from RUSSIA) mingle with the living, until the human characters become engulfed in a phantasmagoric atmosphere halfway between waking and sleeping.

The excited guests imagine they see omens in the sky. Wernyhora declares the time has come to send a boy to fetch the mythic golden horn that will give the call to heroic action. The entire group, including peasants armed with scythes, looks down the road, waiting for the cock to crow and the message to arrive. The sound of hooves announces the boy's return, but he has lost the horn and forgotten the message.

In the blue light of dawn, the stupefied revelers, weary of waiting for a nonexistent message, begin a slow somnambulistic dance to creaking music played by the Mulch on a fiddle improvised out of two broken sticks. The whole puppet show, as though in a deep sleep, goes through its trancelike motions. Wyspiański's Mulch dance—denouement to The Wedding—is a powerful theatrical image of stagnation, despair, and death-in-life that is taken up again and again by Polish playwrights, novelists, and filmmakers throughout the rest of the 20th century.

FURTHER READING
Witoszek, Nina. "Polish Nuptial Dramas." In The Theatre of Recollection: A Cultural Study of the Modern Dramatic Tradition in Ireland and Poland. Stockholm: Stockholm Studies in English, Univ. of Stockholm, 1988. 113–139.
Wyspiański, Stanislaw. The Wedding. Tr. and intro. by Gerard T. Kapolka. Ann Arbor, Mich.: Ardis, 1990.
——. The Wedding. Tr. by Noel Clark and intro. by Jerzy Peterkiewicz. London: Oberon Bks., 1998.

Daniel Gerould

WEDDING DAY AT THE CRO-MAGNONS'

Why is the war so beautiful? Why can't I take my eyes off it? These fireworks! It's so enthralling mama, I'm kneeling, wide awake, at the open window, enraptured by the horror! Oh, it's so hard to keep my eyes closed! It's all so beautiful.

—Nelly

While Nelly may find the war beautiful, the audience will find it hard to ignore the vulgar, perverse, violent, grotesque, dehumanizing, and destabilizing effects of war. Indeed, after enduring the violence and profanity of this Lebanese family, the audience most likely will believe that war is hell.

The setting of WAJDI MOUAWAD's *Wedding Day at the Cro-Magnons'* (*Journée de noces chez les Cro-Magnons*, 1992) is not explicitly stated, but it is fair to assume the play's action is set in Beirut, Lebanon, during the Civil War of 1975–1990. The basic plot of the play is straightforward: against the backdrop of war, a Lebanese family is preparing for the wedding of its eldest daughter, Nelly, a narcoleptic who falls asleep whenever the atrocities of war intrude into her family's affairs. All the family members take part in the wedding preparations: Neyif, the father, brings home a live sheep and slaughters it with sewing scissors. Nazha, the mother, makes mashed potatoes that are too rotten to be fried. Neel, the youngest son, assists both his parents as he complains by spouting out violent expletives. As the play continues, it becomes apparent that there is no fiancé—the family simply is making it up, preparing for a wedding feast while knowing there is not going to be a wedding.

This absurdity is central to the play, as characters say and do ridiculous things that cannot be rationally explained. For example, Nelly tells Souhayla, the neighborhood friend, that she is ugly for no reason. These nonsensical actions of the characters in the play reveal a deep pathos of the human condition. The deep despair all the characters endure reveals how war can and does divide close family members. This closeness is revealed when Neel remembers a kindness his father had shown him in his youth. Sadly, Nayif responds by telling his son, "Oh shut up."

This despair that defines humankind is not so subtly implied throughout the play and also illuminates the title of the play. As Cro-Magnons are defined as an early form of modern human, the title of the play suggests that nothing has changed from the beginning of time to the present day—humanity still fights wars that reduce individuals to mere objects of wrath. And yet in spite of this, the play concludes with a magical occurrence. After the audience witnesses and endures the depths of despair and hopelessness of this family, a gentleman caller actually arrives for Nelly. Without explanation, this fiancé arrives to take Nelly away from the perversity that surrounds her.

There are several notable similarities between this play and TENNESSEE WILLIAMS's play THE GLASS MENAGERIE. Both have a daughter out of touch with reality and a family attempting to get her married. Unlike Laura, however, Nelly does find a mate—although Mouawad gives no real explanation about how that occurs.

FURTHER READING

Kourilsky, Françoise, ed. *Playwrights of Exile: An International Anthology.* New York: Ubu Repertory Theater Pubs., 1997.

Mouawad, Wajdi. *Wedding Day at the Cro-Magnons'.* Toronto: Playwrights Canada Press, 2001.

Thaddeus Wakefield

WEDDING GOWN

Wedding Gown (*Vestido de noiva*), by Brazilian playwright NELSON RODRIGUES, premiered on December 28, 1943, at Teatro Municipal, Rio de Janeiro, BRAZIL. The play marked the renovation of Brazilian drama and theater through an ingenious staging by Zbigniew Ziembinski, a Polish émigré director, whose mastery of European AVANT-GARDE expressionistic techniques enabled him to create a spectacle of remarkable impact. The author establishes a multilayered narrative unfolding in three dimensions clearly established in the script and onstage: reality, memory, and hallucination. The heroine, Alaíde, is dying in a hospital after being hit by a car. Most of the action takes place inside her traumatized mind. On the plane of memory, she reenacts an explosive triangular affair. Having married Pedro, her sister Lúcia's boyfriend, she sees husband and sister-in-law become lovers and plot against her life. She thus escapes into a world of morbid romantic fantasy through the diary of Madame Clessi, a famous cocotte of the turn of the century murdered by a seventeen-year-old lover. In her hallucination Alaíde encounters Clessi and her entourage, who help her reconstitute her life story. All such reminiscence and figments of imagination are framed by brief scenes on the plane of actuality: mostly newspapermen reporting the accident and hospital surgeons witnessing her agony with indifference. In the third act she eventually dies without having recovered consciousness. Reality takes over: her sister prepares to marry the widower. However, these final events are watched and commented on by the specters of the deceased and her protector, the courtesan Clessi. And as Lúcia, in her wedding gown, asks for the bridal bouquet, it is Alaíde, also dressed as a bride, who hands it over to her in a final striking image closing the play.

Playing with the disparate associations of the protagonist's delirious mind, Rodrigues, throughout the play, manages to reconstruct the events of her life and clarify the circumstances that drove her to the fatal accident. At the same time, the counterpoint of the hallucination plane, projecting Alaíde's fantasies of sex and death related to the story of Madame Clessi, illuminates the dark side of her psyche. The playwright displays a remarkable expertise in terms of dramatic construction. While maintaining the impression of psychic disorder, underneath the enmeshed web of facts, remembrances, and dreams, the fundamental elements of the drama are organized in a complex yet cohesive pattern.

The alternation of planes is very fluid. The narrative thread flows rapidly through the dimensions of time, space, and inner and outer reality, a technique totally unknown to Brazilian audiences and one of the main reasons for the play's overwhelming success.

In *Wedding Gown* we are struck by the moral baseness of the main characters showing beneath the strict principles of bourgeois righteousness. They are entirely devoid of spiritual nobility. Their motivations are selfish and perverse; their ends are petty and mean. Rodrigues's worldview, as shown in *Wedding Gown*, is utterly pessimistic. The low materialism of the world he puts onstage seems to infer a bitter complaint about the predatory quality of family and social relationships and the lack of transcendence in human life.

FURTHER READING

Clark, Fred M. *Impermanent Structures: Semiotic Readings of Nelson Rodrigues' Vestido de Noiva, Album de Familia, and Anjo Negro.* Chapel Hill: Univ. of North Carolina Press, 1991.

Souto, Carla. *Nelson "Tragico" Rodrigues* [Nelson "Tragic" Rodrigues]. Rio de Janeiro: Editora de Ilha, 2001.

Werneck, Maria Helena, and Victor Hugo Adler Pereira. "Dramaturgies and Theatricalities: Aspects of the Twentieth-Century Brazilian Literary Scene." In *Literary Cultures of Latin America: A Comparative History*, ed. by Mario J. Valdés and Djelai Kadir, 3 vols. New York: Oxford Univ. Press, 2004. Ch. 57.

Luiz Arthur Ferreira Freire Nunes

WEDEKIND, FRANK (1864–1918)

Frank Wedekind's literary creations are difficult to classify. His most productive years were around 1900, at the height of literary NATURALISM. However, Wedekind despised the naturalist imperative to reproduce social conditions with photographic accuracy, and he engaged in experiments with open dramatic forms, stylized and fragmented language, humor, the bizarre and the grotesque, and other potentially alienating techniques. His innovations were initially rejected or misunderstood but over time came to influence the expressionists as well as the Theater of the Absurd. BERTOLT BRECHT, ÖDÖN VON HORVÁTH, Heinrich Mann (1871–1950), Thomas Mann (1875–1955), FRIEDRICH DÜRRENMATT, and MAX FRISCH are among the many authors whose work contains noticeable traces of Wedekind's themes and formal techniques. Wedekind himself derived inspiration from Sturm und Drang authors and from Georg Büchner (1813–1837). While significantly concerned with how socioeconomic structures condition individuals, Wedekind focused his attention on the moral decay and hypocrisy of bourgeois society. A more "human" morality, Wedekind believed, one free of prejudice, would better acknowledge and serve man's natural instincts. Wedekind's cast of characters consists largely of outcasts: fallen women, misunderstood artists, and members of the underworld.

Benjamin Franklin Wedekind was born in 1864 in Hanover, after his parents returned to GERMANY from the UNITED STATES. Frank's father, a liberal sympathizer, had immigrated to the United States after the failure of the 1848 revolution. He met his wife, an actress and singer from southern Germany who was more than twenty years his junior, in San Francisco, where Frank was conceived. Back in Germany, the elder Wedekind found Bismarck's regime unacceptable, and in 1872 the family moved to Lenzburg near Aarau in SWITZERLAND. Frank grew up in affluence and attended school there.

Wedekind's literary production began early. He wrote a number of poems and a children's book while still in school and formed literary and philosophical reading circles with his school friends. His first published poem appeared in 1884, the year of his final secondary school examinations. That summer Wedekind began studying German and French literature at Lausanne, but at his father's insistence he subsequently enrolled at the University of Munich to study law.

While neglecting his legal studies, Wedekind continued to write poems, crafted his first novellas, and begin work on a play. After a conflict with his father in 1886, he moved to Zurich, where he worked in the advertising and press office of the food producer Maggi. He soon abandoned that job, however, and began writing for the *Neue Zürcher Zeitung*. In Zurich Wedekind joined the literary circle of Karl Henckell (1864–1929) and Carl Hauptmann (1858–1921). He later met GERHART HAUPTMANN, but this association soon became riddled with personal and literary conflicts. Wedekind was especially irritated when Hauptmann included Wedekind's private circumstances in his 1890 play *The Coming of Peace (Das Friedensfest)*.

Wedekind's career in journalism was short-lived. Following a father-son reconciliation, Frank agreed to resume his legal studies in Zurich in summer 1888. When his father abruptly died later that year, however, he stopped attending university. An inheritance from his father allowed Wedekind to travel to Berlin, Munich, London, and Paris. In 1889 he settled in Munich, where he developed contacts with the naturalists and other intellectual circles and worked on his plays. While drawn to the theater, Wedekind was also fascinated by other forms of the performing arts, especially the circus and the cabaret. He even participated in these venues, and they are richly represented in his dramatic works.

Wedekind's best-known dramas arose during this period: SPRING AWAKENING (*Frühlings Erwachen: Eine Kindertragödie*, 1891) and *Pandora's Box (Die Büchse der Pandora. Eine Monstertragödie*, 1893–1894). *Spring Awakening* dramatizes generational conflicts between a group of teenagers, their small-town bourgeois parents, and their conservative social institutions. Aware of the hypocritical nature of adult society, the adolescents develop their own philosophies of life. They follow their sexual instincts defiantly, but with liberation comes TRAGEDY: fatal abortion, reform school, and suicide. At the end of this "Childhood Tragedy," the youthful protagonist Melchior faces a choice: he can either follow his friend Moritz to the grave or the mysterious Masked Man to life. Melchior ultimately chooses the latter. MAX REINHARDT staged *Spring Awakening* for the first time in 1906 in Berlin. The performance caused considerable scandal, yet the play became a great success.

Pandora's Box engendered a number of legal challenges; the authorities deemed the drama offensive and immoral. Wedekind was forced into self-censorship, reworking the play's structure and content and supplementing it with explanatory notes. The play was divided into two parts, which were published separately. *Earth-Spirit* (*Erdgeist*, 1895), the first installment, consists of the first three acts of the original five-act "Monster Tragedy," with an additional act inserted between acts 2 and 3. The publication of the second part, titled *Pandora's Box* (1904), unleashed court proceedings in which the author and publisher were both convicted and acquitted. Eventually, the remaining copies of the play were seized and performances banned. In 1905, KARL KRAUS organized a closed premiere of *Pandora's Box* at the Trianon Theater in Vienna. Mathilde (Tilly) Newes, Wedekind's future wife, starred as Lulu; the playwright himself appeared as Jack the Ripper.

The tragedy tracks the fate of Lulu, a woman who believes in love. Lulu's circumstances change rapidly throughout both parts—from marriage to marriage, from wealth to indigence, from high social standing to anonymity, and from a career as a dancer to turning tricks in London streets. The corrupt society ridicules Lulu's passion but is apt to appropriate her body and freedom. She has had to play different roles for the different men on whom she has depended all her life; only the ever-present portrait of Lulu as Pierrot connects the protagonist's wildly divergent fortunes. The Pierrot, nailed to a wall in a London garret, is witness to Lulu's demise—at the hand of Jack the Ripper. One of the first lesbian characters onstage, Countess Geschwitz, utters the final lines in a work intended to shock bourgeois audiences. The Lulu plays inspired an opera by Alban Berg (1885–1935) and two film versions, in 1923 and 1929, respectively.

In 1896, Wedekind began writing for the satirical weekly *Simplicissimus*, published by Albert Langen (1869–1909). As a result of Wedekind's poems targeting Kaiser Friedrich Wilhelm II's visits to the Holy Land, the magazine offices were raided and a warrant issued for Wedekind's arrest on the grounds of *lèse majesté*. Wedekind left Germany for Zurich and then Paris but later returned and gave himself up to the police. He served a six-month prison sentence at the Königstein fortress near Dresden. Wedekind suspected Langen of having plotted the episode as a publicity stunt to boost circulation and subsequently portrayed the publisher unflatteringly in the plays *Hidalla* (1903–1904) and *Oaha* (1908).

While still in exile in Paris in 1900, Wedekind completed *The Marquis of Keith* (*Der Marquis von Keith*). The play was published in the magazine *Die Insel* (The Island) under the title *Scenes from Munich, Drawn from Life* (*Münchner Szenen. Nach dem Leben aufgezeichnet*). The title character is a confidence man who must manipulate members of various social circles to promote his enterprises.

Most of the time, his wealth and his reputation are based on an illusion, which Keith is able to sell to his advantage. What sets him apart from "reputable" society is the fact that Keith is conscious of his status and admits that his values are completely lacking in lofty ideals. As he engages in fund-raising for his life's project, the Fairyland Palace Theater, he himself is swindled out of a share in the enterprise by the respectable businessmen of Munich and is barely able to escape with his life in the end. Nevertheless, he seems to have fared better than his childhood friend Scholz, who arrives early in the play to learn from Keith how to be a sensualist. Scholz undergoes several shifts in his ideals, achieves none of them, and ultimately enters a mental asylum voluntarily. The tightrope walker Keith, in contrast, never had any ideals and will forever be confined to his balancing act.

In 1901, Wedekind appeared with the cabaret group Elf Scharfrichter (Eleven Executioners) in Munich. He sang and accompanied his own songs but soon grew disillusioned with this form of entertainment and with an audience unable to appreciate his true worth. A young Bertolt Brecht, however, was so inspired by Wedekind's persona that he based his first play, BAAL (1918), in part on it.

Wedekind's death came rather prematurely: he passed away on March 9, 1918, in Munich, after four unsuccessful appendix surgeries. His funeral attracted a strange mix of Munich bohemians and intellectuals.

Recognition, fame, and presence on the German stage came gradually to Wedekind. To the very end, he was subject to censorship. He also had to pursue a career as an actor in order to subsist and developed an ACTING style that was eerie yet memorable. Toward the end of his life, Wedekind had become a celebrated German playwright. At the outbreak of World War I he even embraced the German national cause but soon became a staunch pacifist. With the advent of the Weimar Republic the censoring of Wedekind's texts eased, leading to increased interest in his works. Once the National Socialists ascended to power, however, Wedekind's dramas disappeared from the German stage. The 1980s brought renewed interest in Wedekind's texts and significant growth in Wedekind scholarship.

SELECT PLAYS: *Spring's Awakening: A Children's Tragedy* (*Frühlings Erwachen. Eine Kindertragödie*, 1891); *Fritz Schwigerling—the Love Potion* (*Fritz Schwigerling—der Liebestrank*, 1891–1892); *Earth-Spirit: A Tragedy in Four Acts* (*Erdgeist*, 1893–1894); *Pandora's Box: A Tragedy in Three Acts with a Prologue* (*Die Büchse der Pandora*, 1893–1894); *The Court Singer* (*Der Kammersänger*, 1897); *The Marquis of Keith* (*Der Marquis von Keith*, 1900); *Such Is Life* (*König Nicolo oder So ist das Leben*, 1901); *Hidalla, or, Karl Hetmann, the Dwarf-Giant* (*Hidalla oder Karl Hetmann, der Zwergriese*, 1903–1904); *Death and Devil: A Death Dance in Three Scenes* (*Tod und Teufel*, 1905); *Music* (*Musik*, 1906); *Oaha, the Satire of the Satire* (*Oaha, die Satire der Satire*, 1908); *Castle Wetterstein: A Play in Three Acts* (*Schloss Wetterstein*, 1910); *Franziska* (1911); *Simson* (1913); *Bismarck* (1915); *Heracles* (*Herakles*, 1916–1917)

FURTHER READING

Best, Alan. *Frank Wedekind*. London: Wolff, 1975.

Boa, Elizabeth. *The Sexual Circus: Wedekind's Theatre of Subversion*. Oxford: Blackwell, 1987.

Gittleman, Sol. *Frank Wedekind*. New York: Twayne, 1969.

Lewis, Ward B. *The Ironic Dissident: Frank Wedekind in the View of His Critics*. Columbia, S.C.: Camden House, 1997.

Vinçon, Hartmut. *Frank Wedekind*. Stuttgart: Metzler, 1987.

Martins Masulis

WEI MINGLUN (1941–)

Contemporary Chinese playwright of Sichuan opera Wei Minglun was born in Zigong City, Sichuan Province, CHINA, in August 1941. With only four years of elementary schooling, Wei had to quit school to take on a full-time job in the Sichuan Opera Troupe of Zigong City at the age of nine. First as an actor in the troupe, Wei lost his voice at the age of thirteen when he overworked himself in a highly popular play at that time. Refusing to leave theater, Wei continued to work as a director and afterward as a playwright. Wei started his playwriting at the age of fourteen, but two years later, in 1957, he was criticized during the anti-Rightist political campaign launched by Mao Zedong. After the Cultural Revolution in 1976, Wei reemerged as a mature dramatist. *The Story of Yi Danda* (*Yi Danda*) and *The Fourth Daughter* (*Si guniang*) were the first two plays that both won him an award in 1981. Following the success, he quickly produced several influential plays such as *Scholar from Ba Mountain* (*Bashan xiucai*, 1983), *Pan Jinlian* (1985), and *Sunset at Qi Mountain* (*Xi zhao Qishan*, 1987). His most recent plays include *The Chinese Princess Turandot* (*Zhongguo gongzhu Du Landuo*, 1993) and *Good Woman, Bad Woman* (*Hao nuren, huai nuren*, 2002).

Wei's plays are characterized by his boldness at exploring new dramatic forms and techniques in expressing the contemporary audience aesthetic orientation. Claiming to change his tactics with each play, Wei is especially good at writing plays about women, to whose life he "has devoted all his attention and feelings" (Yu, 2006). The majority of his plays are about women, whether good or bad, but his most well known play was *Pan Jinlian*, which he described as "absurdist theater in the Sichuan opera style (*huangdan chuanju*)" (Wei, 1996). Deriving the story from the Ming dynasty novels *Water Margin* and *Golden Lotus* (*Jin Ping Mei*), it recreates the tragic life of Pan Jinlian, one of the most well known femme fatales in Chinese culture, from the modern feminist perspective. While condemning Pan's murder of her husband in collaboration with Ximen Qing, the play emphasizes the social and cultural impact on her motivation. In an attempt to reverse the traditional verdict on Pan, the play even invites characters, modern or historical, from different countries to comment on the fate of Pan Jinlian. In performance, the bold theme and the novel form of the play took the audience by surprise and were enthusiastically received across the nation and even abroad.

Wei's plays are often regarded as recreations of some stories or anecdotes already widely known to many. His most recent plays *The Chinese Princess Turandot* and *Good Woman, Bad Woman* are based on Giacomo Puccini's opera *Turandot* and BERTOLT BRECHT's play THE GOOD WOMAN OF SETZUAN, respectively. Because of Wei's playwriting tenet of "independent analysis, new discovery and unique way of expression (Yu, 2006)," his plays always tend to create those familiar characters anew from a new perspective with thought-provoking themes.

SELECT PLAYS: *The Story of Yi Danda* (*Yi Danda*, 1980); *The Fourth Daughter* (*Si guniang*, 1981); *Scholar from Ba Mountain* (*Bashan xiucai*, 1983); *Pan Jinlian* (1985); *Sunset at Qi Mountain* (*Xi zhao Qishan*, 1987); *The Chinese Princess Turandot* (*Zhongguo gongzhu Du Landuo*, 1993); *Changing Faces* (*Bian lian*, 1997); *Good Woman, Bad Woman* (*Hao nuren, huai nuren*, 2002)

FURTHER READING

Chen, Xiaomei. *Acting the Right Part: Political Theater and Popular Drama in Contemporary China*. Honolulu: Univ. of Hawaii Press, 2002.

Wei Minglun. *Wei Minglun wenji* [Collected Writings of Wei Mnglun]. Chengdu: Sichuan wenyi chubanshe, 1996.

Yan, Haiping, ed. *Theater & Society: An Anthology of Contemporary Chinese Drama*. Armonk, N.Y.: M. E. Sharpe, 1988 [contains a translation of Wei's play *Pan Jinlian*].

Yu Hua. "Wei Minglun bixia de hao nuren yu huai nuren" [Virtuous Women and Evil Women Written by Wei Minglun], *Zhongguo funu bao* at http://www.people.com.cn/GB/wenyu/66/134/20010425/451720.html

Yu, Shiao-ling. *Chinese Drama After the Cultural Revolution, 1979–1989: An Anthology*. Lewiston, N.Y.: Mellen Press, 1996 [contains a different English version of Wei's play *Pan Jinlian*].

Hongchu Fu

WEISS, PETER (1916–1982)

Because we know: a revolution of the social order must be accompanied by revolutionary art. It is, therefore, a contradiction if in some socialist countries art, because of its intrinsic power, is being kept down and condemned to colorlessness, while in the bourgeois countries, on account of its lack of commitment, it evolves to the point of anarchism.
—Peter Weiss, 1965

Both sides of this dilemma played a role in Peter Weiss's development as an author: artistic experimentation at the cost of social isolation, on the one hand, and on the other, the attempt to combine artistic experimentation with political activism that often met with criticism from those Weiss saw as his allies, that is to say, those in charge of cultural affairs in the so-called existing socialist countries like the German Democratic Republic. As an author committed both to socialist ideas and artistic innovation, Weiss did not please either side. The AVANT-GARDE of modern art saw his political activism as interfering with the aesthetic side of his works, while his political allies saw the explosiveness of Weiss's artistic innovations as a threat to SOCIALIST REALISM, the prevailing paradigm of art in socialist countries. Socialist cultural functionaries considered Weiss's work dangerously close to "formalism" and "decadence," the epithets used for (Western) art perceived as form for the sake of form without proper attention to content.

Weiss thus remained without a place he could call home, in a political as well as a geographic sense, for most of his life. While the dogmatists of the existing socialist countries resented his adherence to the concept of a "permanent revolution" of all aspects of life—and the cultural sphere in particular—the undogmatic Left of the West had problems with his sympathies for the existing socialist societies. While the GERMANY of his youth did not allow him to become a part of its culture and caused many displacements for the Weiss family as it attempted to find a safe place in the center of Europe, for most of Weiss's adult life he lived as if in double exile. He became a Swedish citizen but kept writing in German.

His work was widely discussed, especially after the staging of THE INVESTIGATION (Die Ermittlung, 1964), as that of a politically engaged author in a country whose system he despised, West Germany, while, at the same time, he was unable to find the recognition he had hoped for in that part of Germany he perceived as his political home, East Germany. Moreover, his peers in West Germany often treated him with a lack of respect, considering his political convictions naive, as typical of someone who, living in the relative political isolation of the fairly stable welfare system of a social democratically governed SWEDEN, was unable to understand the complications politically active West German authors experienced during the Cold War.

This became particularly evident in Weiss's debate with the West German author Hans Magnus Enzensberger (1929–) in the 1960s in which Weiss upheld the notion of class struggle as the decisive factor shaping historical events, while Enzensberger postulated that the working class of the industrialized world had long been paralyzed by the promises of a consumer society and that the decisive struggles would henceforth be waged between the industrialized countries and the rest of the world suffering under the poverty imposed by the industrialized nations.

Weiss was born on November 8, 1916, in Nowawes, Germany, a town near Berlin, as a citizen of the Austro-Hungarian monarchy. When the map of Europe was redrawn after World War I, Weiss became a Czech citizen. His businessman father was a Jew who converted to Christianity, the faith of his wife, while the family was living in Berlin from 1929 to 1935. Prior to those years in Berlin, the family resided in Bremen, and one can speculate about how, in Weiss's early childhood, he might have tried to reconcile his bourgeois family background with the revolutionary workers' councils he could see on the streets of Bremen at the

time. While in Berlin, Weiss began studying art but also attended commercial school, reflecting the tensions between the young man's artistic inclinations and the pressures from his family to play a part in the father's business. After a brief period in ENGLAND, the family settled in Varnsdorf, CZECHOSLOVAKIA, whence they fled the approaching Nazi occupation forces in October 1938. Following a short stay in SWITZERLAND, Weiss arrived in early 1939 in Sweden, the country that would become his permanent residence until his death on May 10, 1982, in Stockholm.

Weiss's biography can be seen as representative of the experiences of many others of his generation, experiences that offered the individual neither the comforts of geographic stability, of a home in the world, nor the support of a stable bourgeois family that was supposed to make up for external uncertainties. The family as such was under attack, from unexpected external catastrophes like Weiss's sister's death at the age of twelve in a car accident, as well as from tensions within, and both causes of uncertainty were intensified and magnified by the rise of political extremism in many European countries. Weiss explores the asymmetrical power and sexual relations within the threatened bourgeois family in his two psychoanalytically oriented prose texts Abschied von den Eltern (Leavetaking, 1960) and Fluchtpunkt (Vanishing Point, 1961). Transposing his personal experiences into literary forms that address matters beyond the purely personal, liberating the soul from the deformations it suffers in bourgeois society, and overcoming social ALIENATION by taking part in international political movements become the constants in Weiss's literary texts. In his last prose work, Die Ästhetik des Widerstands (The Aesthetics of Resistance, 1975–1981), the ties between the antifascist fighters across Europe in fact supplant the family for the protagonist who finds among his fellow freedom fighters the home the bourgeois family cannot provide, even as Europe is being torn apart by totalitarianism. This, however, also explains the string of disappointments Weiss experienced with those he considered his brothers-in-arms, as those he thought of as his allies received his literary productions with less than open arms. One must, however, suspect a certain naïveté or perhaps even exaggerated idealism on the part of an author who can portray Leon Trotsky (1879–1940) sympathetically in Trotsky in Exile (Trotzki im Exil, 1969) and still believe he will be welcomed by the successors of Trotsky's worst enemies in the German Democratic Republic and USSR.

In the West, however, Weiss's dramatic work continued to be successfully staged after he had become well known with the plays MARAT/SADE (Die Verfolgung und Ermordung Jean Paul Marats dargestellt durch die Schauspielgruppe des Hospizes zu Charenton unter Anleitung des Herrn de Sade, 1963) and The Investigation (1964), probably his two most important dramas. These two plays bring into clearer focus the surrealist antibourgeois and anticapitalist impetus of Weiss's earlier plays The Assurance (Die Versicherung, 1952) and Night with Guests (Nacht mit Gästen, 1963), supplanting nightmarish visions with systematic investigations into the oppression of the body and the people who call for a revolution of both the body and society.

The rest of Weiss's dramatic works parallels in a way the history of the Western European Left in the wake of the beginnings of the student movement: analyses of colonial and postcolonial power structures in *Song of the Lusitanian Bogey* (*Gesang vom lusitanischen Popanz*, 1967) and *Discourse on the Progress of the Prolonged War of Liberation in Viet Nam and the Events Leading Up to It as Illustration of the Necessity for Armed Resistance against Oppression and on the Attempts of the United States of America to Destroy the Foundations of Revolution* (*Diskurs über die Vorgeschichte und den Verlauf des lang andauernden Befreiungskrieges in Viet Nam als Beispiel für die Notwendigkeit des bewaffneten Kampfes der Unterdrückten gegen ihre Unterdrücker sowie über die Versuche der Vereinigten Staaten von Amerika die Grundlagen der Revolution zu vernichten*, 1968) that also reflect the Western student movement's exaggerated hopes that all oppressed peoples will join ranks and defeat the imperialists in a worldwide series of revolutions. Similarly, the play *How Mr. Mockinpott Was Cured of His Sufferings* (*Wie dem Herrn Mockinpott das Leiden ausgetrieben wird*, 1968) resembles the endless debates of the plethora of political groups at the time that were trying to find out what makes the supposed subject of the revolution, the wage laborer, tick and what might be preventing him from understanding his own oppression and taking up the political struggle that will end it. And just as toward the end of the student movement we find a somewhat melancholic inwardness that seeks to recover what might have been lost or suppressed among one's owns ranks in the political struggle with the "enemy," leaving no room for dreamers and utopian thinking, Weiss devotes two plays to "losers" in those battles, individuals who might have been the true visionaries yet were too far ahead of their own times to survive the Realpolitik of everyday life: *Trotsky in Exile* and *Hölderlin* (1971).

Weiss's most important contributions to modern dramatic forms are his experiments with DOCUMENTARY plays. His texts clearly demonstrate that using documents does not bring us closer to an objective truth. Rather, his plays show how even seemingly neutral materials take on a partisan perspective through the act of being unearthed, recorded, selected, edited, and put in a certain order by an author. Thus, in the tradition of Weiss, documentary dramas show the constructedness of what is mistaken for historical truth, and they offer their version of the truth as an antidote to that truth circulated by the mass media and those in power.

SELECT PLAYS: *The Tower* (*Der Turm*, 1949); *The Assurance* (*Die Versicherung. Ein Drama*, 1952); *Night with Guests* (*Nacht mit Gästen. Eine Moritat*, 1963); *The Persecution and Assassination of Jean-Paul Marat as Performed by the Inmates of the Asylum Charenton Under the Direction of the Marquis de Sade* (*Die Verfolgung und Ermordung Jean Paul Marats dargestellt durch die Schauspielgruppe des Hospizes zu Charenton unter Anleitung des Herrn de Sade. Drama in zwei Akten*, 1963); *The Investigation* (*Die Ermittlung. Oratorium in 11 Gesängen*, 1964); *Song of the Lusitanian Bogey* (*Gesang vom lusitanischen Popanz. Stück mit Musik in 2 Akten*, 1967); *Discourse on the Progress of the Prolonged War of Liberation in Viet Nam and the Events Leading Up to It as Illustration of the Necessity for Armed Resistance Against Oppression and on the Attempts of the United States of America to Destroy the Foundations of Revolution* (*Diskurs über die Vorgeschichte und den Verlauf des lang andauernden Befreiungskrieges in Viet Nam als Beispiel für die Notwendigkeit des bewaffneten Kampfes der Unterdrückten gegen ihre Unterdrücker sowie über die Versuche der Vereinigten Staaten von Amerika die Grundlagen der Revolution zu vernichten*, 1968); *How Mr. Mockinpott Was Cured of His Sufferings* (*Wie dem Herrn Mockinpott das Leiden ausgetrieben wird. Spiel in 11 Bildern*, 1968); *Trotsky in Exile* (*Trotzki im Exil. Stück in zwei Akten*, 1969); *Hölderlin* (*Hölderlin. Stück in zwei Akten*, 1971); *The Trial* (*Der Prozess. Stück in zwei Akten*, 1974)

FURTHER READING

Bathrick, David. "'The Theater of the White Revolution Is Over': The Third World in the Works of Peter Weiss and Heiner Müller." In *Blacks and German Culture*, ed. by Reinhold Grimm and Jost Hermand. Madison: Univ. of Wisconsin Press, 1986. 135–149.

Cohen, Robert. *Understanding Peter Weiss*. Columbia: Univ. of South Carolina Press, 1993.

Haiduk, Manfred. *Der Dramatiker Peter Weiss* [The dramatist Peter Weiss]. Berlin: Henschelverlag, 1977.

Friedemann J. Weidauer

WELLMAN, MAC (1945–)

What if we conceive of [disorder] not negatively, but positively, as the fundamental, unseen architect of all that is orderly, possesses a shape, boasts a fixed, structural configuration: the world of objects and their appearance? What if chaos should be the true determiner and shaper of representation itself? Whisper that . . . at the next meeting of the Board of Directors. . . . See how long it will take for those in charge to show you the door.

—Mac Wellman, "A Chrestomathy of 22 Answers to 22 Wholly Unaskable and Unrelated Questions Concerning Political and Poetic Theater," 1993

Chance brought Mac Wellman to the theater. Wellman was born on March 7, 1945, in Cleveland, Ohio. While pursuing a bachelor's degree in international relations at American University, he took a year abroad and while hitchhiking in Holland in 1965 caught a ride with the artistic director of an AVANT-GARDE theater. At her suggestion he began writing plays for Dutch radio, remaining in Europe for the next several years. The experimental theater he saw there contrasted sharply with what he later called the "conservatism" and "claustrophobia" of theater in the UNITED STATES, and it awakened Wellman's interest in the stage, which would be further affected by his discovery of the downtown New York theater scene of the mid-1970s. Relocating to New York, he saw the earliest works of Mabou Mines, RICHARD FOREMAN, and TADASHI SUZUKI; the last production of the

Open Theatre; and the Performance Group's *Tooth of Crime*. These 1970s productions introduced him to what he would later describe as a "theatre of excess" markedly different from the "penury and littleness and paucity and deprivation—spiritually, emotionally, ethically and theatrically" that he perceived in the mainstream (Savran, 1999). He began to write for the theater.

Nearly thirty years later Wellman has earned a reputation as an antinaturalist playwright of rich language and intellectual complexity; a harsh critic of mainstream American theater (its actor training, DRAMATURGY, and conditions of production); a passionate and articulate champion of poetic theater; and an active supporter of young, avant-garde playwrights. A prodigious writer, he has additionally published two novels, four volumes of poetry, and numerous essays and edited three collections of new American drama (*Theatre of Wonders*, *Slant 6*, and *Seven Different Plays*). He has been the recipient of multiple awards and honors and has been a three-time Village Voice Obie Award winner, including a 2003 Obie for lifetime achievement.

Wellman's work is often described as growing out of an American poetic and antirealist dramatic tradition, which began with GERTRUDE STEIN and continued in the 1960s with Richard Foreman, ADRIENNE KENNEDY, SAM SHEPARD, and MARIA IRENE FORNES. His plays also exhibit traces of the European and Russian avant-garde of the last century: a preference for montage and mosaic structures over psychorealist linearity, a fascination with the paradigms offered by contemporary science, a predilection for a THEATRICALITY "that is the repudiation of a split between presentation and representation, between performance and illusion, between making a show, and 'drama'" (Wellman, 1993). And they are political, if Wellman's antididactic brand of politics may be so termed; for Wellman, all political opinion, left or right, is suspect: white noise from a cacophony of *idées reçus*. Above all, Wellman's aesthetic project picks up where the absurdist playwrights left off: breaking apart and reconfiguring language, interrogating it, playing with it, creating it.

Wellman spent the 1980s forging what would become significant, long-term collaborations with such downtown companies as Ridge Theater (recent work with Ridge includes *Jennie Richee* [2000], which won eleven Obie Awards when it was performed at the Kitchen in New York City in 2001), BACA Downtown (where Wellman served as literary adviser from 1987 to 1991 and co-founded its New Works Project), and the site-specific production company En Garde Arts. By the end of the decade, he had begun to attract serious critical attention. The year 1989 saw his first regional production, *Albanian Softshoe*, at the San Diego Rep, as well as his first commercial success, the En Garde Arts production of *Crowbar* at the abandoned Victory Theatre on 42nd Street. The year 1990 brought his first Obie Award for *Bad Penny* (1989), *Terminal Hip* (1990), and *Crowbar*.

Wellman's work ranges across a broad spectrum of intellectually rich themes. Plays of the last two decades include *Harm's Way* (1985), a darkly comic anti-Western that touches on inter-related issues of vendetta, the violence of American language, national mythos, history, and foreign policy. *Sincerity Forever* (1990) and *7 Blowjobs* (1991) are both overtly political satires on the theme of moral hypocrisy. *The Difficulty of Crossing a Field* (1998) is an opera that tells, through seven different accounts at a legal inquest, of the abrupt disappearance "in the open and visible" of a slave owner while crossing a field, playing on the audience's building expectation of explanatory truths that are, however, never revealed. *Cat's-Paw* (1998) is "a meditation on the Don Juan story" in which Don Juan never appears and an all-female cast never discusses men. The heroine of Wellman's *Antigone* (2001) tells her tale into the ear of a puppet Sophocles at the beginning of time. *Swoop* (1994) is a Dracula play about the sexual oppression of Victorian women, and *Hypatia* (2000) is a drama about the 5th-century female mathematician Hypatia of Alexandria, who was beaten to death and mutilated by Christian monks.

SELECT PLAYS: *Fama Combinatoria* (1975); *The Memory Theatre of Giordano Bruno* (1976); *Starluster* (1979); *Dog in the Manger* (1982); *The Self-Begotten* (1982); *Phantomnation* (1983); *The Professional Frenchman* (1984); *Energumen* (1985); *Harm's Way* (1985); *Cleveland* (1986); *The Nain Rouge* (1986); *1951* (with Anne Bogart and Michael Roth, 1986); *Dracula* (1987); *Cellophane* (1988); *Peach Bottom Nuclear Reactor Full of Sleepers* (1988); *Albanian Softshoe* (1988–1989); *Without Colors* (1989); *Crowbar* (1990); *Sincerity Forever* (1990); *A Murder of Crows* (1991); *7 Blowjobs* (1991); *Coathanger* (1992); *The Land of Fog and Whistles* (1993); *Strange Feet* (1993); *Three Americanisms* (1993); *Absence of Mallets* (with David Van Tiegham, 1994); *The Hyacinth Macaw* (1994); *The Sandalwood Box* (1994); *Tigertigertiger* (1994); *Why the Y (in Ybor)* (1994); *The Distance to the Moon* (1995); *FNU LNU* (1996); *London (In 10 Cites)* (1996); *No Smoking Piece* (1996); *Second-Hand Smoke* (1996); *The Lesser Magoo* (1997); *My Old Habit of Returning to Places* (1997); *Cat's-Paw* (1998); *The Damned Thing* (1998); *The Difficulty of Crossing a Field* (1998); *I Don't Know Who He Was and I Don't Know What He Said* (1998); *Mac Wellman's Girl Gone* (1998); *The Porcupine Man* (1998); *The Sandalwood Box* (1998); *Hypatia* (2000); *Jennie Richee* (2000); *2 September* (2000); *Whiteness* (2000); *Antigone* (2001); *Anything's Dream* (2002); *The Fez* (2002); *Mister Original Bugg* (2002); *Bitter Bierce* (2003)

FURTHER READING

Overmeyer, Eric. "Mac Wellman's Horizontal Avalanches." *Theater* 21, no. 3 (Summer–Fall 1990): 54–56.

Perloff, Carey. "Seven Avenues Toward the Heart of a Mystery." *Theater* 27, nos. 2–3 (1997): 60–63.

Savran, David. "The World According to Wellman." *American Theater* 16, no. 2 (February 1999): 16–21.

Wellman, Mac. "A Chrestomathy of 22 Answers to 22 Wholly Unaskable and Unrelated Questions." *Theater* 24, no. 1 (March–April 1993): 43–51.

Kathryn Syssoyeva

WESELE See THE WEDDING

WESKER, ARNOLD (1932–)

Arnold Wesker was born on May 24, 1932, in the East End of London, ENGLAND, to Jewish immigrant parents. His career has spanned nearly five decades, and his works are frequently autobiographical and politically informed. Although his early plays receive the most attention, he has been prolifically active throughout. His first play, The Kitchen (1957), established a central theme in his work: the study of social and socialist concerns through character and experience-centered drama. Along with recollections of his family, this theme unifies his next three plays, collectively known as The Wesker Trilogy: Chicken Soup with Barley (1958), Roots (1959), and I'm Talking About Jerusalem (1960). Wesker followed this success with the popular Chips with Everything (1962).

During most of the 1960s he focused his energy on the ideological art project Centre 42. An organization dedicated to bringing art to the working classes, the center ultimately ended in dissolution and Wesker's frustration. Despite plays such as The Old Ones (1970) and The Journalists (1972), and continued success in Europe and elsewhere, Wesker's reception in Britain cooled significantly from the 1970s through the 1990s. Perhaps, in part, this might be blamed on his reluctance to embrace the niceties of the English theatrical scene: troubled relations with critics and a refusal to attend the Evening Standard Drama Awards were capped by turning down a Commander of the Order of the British Empire (CBE) nomination.

Nonetheless, Wesker will be remembered as a significant 20th-century British playwright. Perhaps nowhere is his contribution more vivid than in The Wesker Trilogy. Based on his own family, the sequence follows the Kahn family from the mid-1930s to 1959 as they struggle against loss and political tensions within the family and Britain. Chicken Soup sees the physical decline of the patriarch Harry play out alongside the ebbing of socialist principles in his circle. The play concludes with Harry's second stroke and the unsettling prospect of his son Ronny lapsing into the indifference and sloth of his father. In Roots the drama focuses on Beatie, Ronny's "simple" girlfriend whom he is trying to shape into a working-class intellectual. He abandons his efforts, ending the relationship by post while Beatie is visiting her family in Norfolk. Until the letter arrives in the final scene, Beatie's speech is largely made up of quotations from Ronny. However, once released, Beatie feels for the first time the personal and intellectual freedom Ronny had so tried to cultivate.

But this potentially uplifting tone is complicated in Jerusalem. Here Ada, the Kahn's daughter, has moved to the countryside where she and husband Dave are living the ideals of communism. Their efforts to escape the system and live as rural artisans ultimately fail, however, and despite their attempts to make real what others in The Trilogy have only talked about, they are drawn back to the city. Tellingly, the final scene opens with a radio announcement of General Election defeat for the Labour Party. Once again, Wesker provides us with a stage where individual TRAGEDIES and failures speak eloquently to the wider movements of the political world.

SELECT PLAYS: The Four Seasons (1965); Their Very Own and Golden City (1966); The Friends (1970); Shylock (previously called The Merchant, 1976); Lady Othello (1987); Beorhtel's Hill (1988); Blood Libel (1991); Denial (1997); Longitude (2002)

FURTHER READING

Dornan, Reade. Arnold Wesker Revisited. New York: Twayne, 1995.

Leeming, Glenda. Wesker: The Playwright. London: Methuen, 1983.

Wilcher, Robert. Understanding Arnold Wesker. Columbia: Univ. of South Carolina Press, 1991.

Paul Gleed

WEST, MAE (1892–1980)

I believe in censorship. After all, I made a fortune from it.
—Mae West, Interview with C. Robert Jennings, 1971

Born on August 17, 1892, In Brooklyn, New York, Mae West was the daughter of "Battling Jack" West, an ex-prizefighter and livery stable owner, and Matilda West, a former model. Taking to the stage at the age of eight, she performed child roles until she outgrew them. At seventeen, she teamed up with Frank Wallace, with whom she performed a touring song and dance act; in 1911 they were secretly married, but both the act and the marriage soon ended.

West began performing in vaudeville sketches, rewriting roles to get favorable attention from the audience and the press, which, more often than not, worked. Influenced by her father's "muscle" training, JAZZ, black performers, and vaudevilleans, she developed a signature style of dancing, singing, and sexual innuendo. In her first two plays, The Ruby Ring (1921) and The Hussy (1922), West wrote roles for herself as a gorgeous heroine irresistible to men and smart enough to find a rich husband by the end of the play. For her third play, she rewrote a third-rate sex play, Following the Fleet, by Jack Byrne. Renamed Sex, the play opened at Daly's Theatre on April 26, 1926.

Sex begins in the notorious red-light district of Montreal, in the "apartment" of Margy LaMont, a prostitute, and her pimp, Rocky Waldron. When Rocky brings in a society woman and drugs her, Margy helps her regain consciousness, only to be accused of stealing the woman's jewelry. Margy goes to Trinidad to continue her trade and perform at a popular cafe. Gregg, an English sailor who likes Margy, introduces her to Jimmy Stanton; the infatuated Jimmy proposes, and she accepts. But when Margy meets Jimmy's parents in Connecticut, she discovers that his mother is Clara, the society woman in Montreal. Despite the clash between the two women, Margy helps Clara fend off Rocky, who shows up to blackmail her. Gregg stops by on his way to AUSTRALIA and urges Margy to go with him. Margy, realizing she cannot hide from her past, tells Jimmy who she really is and departs with Gregg.

Mae West's role as Margy LaMont disrupted traditional DRAMATURGY and morals of the time, for here was a "bad woman" going off to start a new life. The show played for almost a year to packed houses before it was closed down for indecency, but West, who made a bundle of money from the play, scoffed at the $500 fine and ten-day jail term. Although *Sex* was prosecuted, it was really her next play, *The Drag* (1927), about homosexuality, that was under attack.

Embraced by the moviegoing public when she hit the big screen in 1933, West perfected the art of one-liners. In the 1970s she was reviled by feminists as a "reverse sexist" but was voted Woman of the Century by University of California at Los Angeles students in 1971 "in honor of her pioneering influence on sexual mores." West died on November 22, 1980, in Los Angeles.

[*See also* United States]

PLAYS: *The Ruby Ring* (1921); *The Hussy* (1922, with Adeline Leitzbach); *The Chick* (1924); *Sex* (1926); *The Drag* (1927); *The Wicked Age* (1927); *Diamond Lil* (1928, revised 1949); *The Pleasure Man* (1928); *Frisco Kate* (1930); *The Constant Sinner* (from novel *Babe Gordon*, 1931); *Catherine Was Great* (1944); *Sextette* (1952, revised 1961)

FURTHER READING

Hamilton, Marybeth. *When I'm Bad, I'm Better: Mae West, Sex and American Entertainment.* New York: HarperCollins, 1995.

Jefferson, Margo. "She Sidled Up to a Man's World and Made It Hers." *New York Times* (February 7, 2000): E2.

McCorkle, Susannah. "The Immortality of Mae West." *American Heritage* (September 2001): 48–58.

Schlissel, Lillian. *Three Plays by Mae West.* New York: Routledge, 1997.

Steyn, Mark. "Mae Days." *New Criterion* (March 2000): 42–47.

West, Mae. *Goodness Had Nothing to Do with It.* Englewood Cliffs, N.J.: Prentice-Hall, 1959.

Sherry D. Engle

WHALE RIDING WEATHER

Whale Riding Weather was the first BRYDEN MACDONALD–written play to be published. It is a considerable achievement for any young, unpublished playwright to have a play performed, so MacDonald's achievement of having so many significant productions of his play is notable. The eight-scene play, which dramatizes the slow but inevitable departure of a young twenty-something, Auto, from his lover and savior, the faded, middle-aged Lyle, was first directed by Annie Kidder at Toronto's Factory Theatre in October 1991. Another production—directed by MacDonald himself—flourished at Halifax's Neptune Theatre in February 1993; Roy Surette directed the Touchstone Theatre, Vancouver, production in the winter of 1993–1994. *Whale Riding Weather* has been produced in Britain, too: in May 1997, a production took place at London's Drill Hall, a venue renowned for staging contemporary gay theater. An April 2003 revival by the Great Canadian Theatre Company attracted good crowds and favorable comment: hoped-for revenue targets were surpassed.

MacDonald based the character of Lyle on an old, tearful homosexual whom he saw sitting friendless in a Montreal bar. The play, which is set in Lyle's dingy bachelor's apartment, excels for many reasons. These reasons include, but are not limited to, the funniness of much of the dialogue; the absurdity of Lyle's situation, which owes as much to SAMUEL BECKETT, EUGÈNE IONESCO, and HAROLD PINTER as it does to post-1980 developments in gay drama; the singularity of MacDonald's verse-based dialogue; and the unexpected rousing of Auto from the ennui that envelops Lyle. Lyle does nothing except talk to the disinterested Auto, indulge in paranoid fantasy, and imagine, falsely, that his lost son will visit. Lyle often considers activity, such as cooking—Auto notes ruefully that Lyle "has been threatening to roast that duck for five years." Lyle is defined by unhygienic, drink-sodden lethargy: a common stage direction for him is "*More sherry.*"

Lyle, however, can be eloquent. He remembers entertaining crowds in bygone years, telling Auto how to entertain at parties in one line of iambic tetrameter: "Just smile and watch and disagree." Such simple but unusual and effective verse is typical. When Auto has to question patiently the unfocussed Lyle, his steady slowness is conveyed by MacDonald's pace-controlling punctuation: "Which. Special. Drawer." Initially, Auto is as inactive as Lyle, drinking beer and chain smoking: "I don't do anything," he asserts. But soon he brings home a young man called Jude, who motivates Auto to forsake the squalid inertness of Lyle. Auto is, at first, reluctant to commit to Jude romantically—and Lyle strives to impede the couple's privacy. Gradually, Jude's emotional and sexual courtship of Auto gains force, and Lyle realizes that Auto will leave. After an agonizing farewell, Lyle is left alone. The walls and ceiling crack, and water pours in. The sound of whales overpowers Lyle and the audience. One of the many satisfactions of reading or attending a performance of *Whale Riding Weather* is speculating about the possible meanings of the whale sounds. MacDonald does not tell us what the whale represents—the implications are agreeably left for us to guess at.

[*See also* Canada; Gay and Lesbian Drama]

FURTHER READING

Crawford, Glen. "Playing the Outcast: Gay Playwright Keeps Coming Back to Ottowa." http://www.capitalxtra.on.ca/queercapital/cx106/cx106_storytellers.htm.

"Great Canadian Theatre Company Proudly Announces a Record-Breaking Season." http://gctc.ca/news/archives/2002–2003.html.

MacDonald, Bryden. *Whale Riding Weather.* Vancouver: Talonbooks, 1994.

"[Very Brief] Interview with Bryden MacDonald." http://www.talonbooks.com/Books/Whale_Riding_Weather.html.

Kevin De Ornellas

WHAT PRICE GLORY?

The premiere of *What Price Glory?* on September 3, 1924, produced by Arthur Hopkins and jointly authored by MAXWELL ANDERSON and Laurence Stallings, not only marked the reopening of the Plymouth Theatre in New York City but also could be said to have inaugurated the theater season that year, as Alexander Woollcott (1967) was to observe. In the latter's eyes, no war play written in the English language since World War I began had been "so true, so alive, so salty and so richly satisfying."

What Price Glory? is set in FRANCE during World War I. It concerns the immediate fortunes of a U.S. Marine company stationed in a small town that is partly held by the Germans. It begins ironically with three corporals discussing home and marriage, prospects that in most cases would not materialize. In contrast to that conventional premise of despair, Anderson and Stallings develop their main plot of raw yet indifferent heroism at a naturalistic level—the protracted conflict between Captain Flagg and Sergeant Quirt over scarlet women in battlefronts around the world. They grapple once more over Charmaine, whom the stage direction quaintly calls "a drab." Her father Pete Cognac, a tavern owner, almost succeeds in forcing Quirt—to the wry amusement of Flagg and with his official consent—to become the woman's unwilling bridegroom for allegedly having deflowered the lass.

In the somber second act the horrors of war are starkly revealed through its immediate and bloody consequences on soldiers like Captain Aldrich. And the entire illusion of glory in battle is cynically questioned in Captain Moore's hysterical speech, "What price glory now?" The price paid is no less than the abject annihilation of the lives of men and the dignity of women. The play draws to a conclusion with the desperate agreement by Flagg and Quirt to resolve the conflict over Charmaine through a game of cards. News that the battalion has been ordered to the front interrupts the Flagg-Quirt COMEDY. Flagg hesitates for a moment but never doubts that he will obey the order. Nor will Quirt be left behind; he exits with the famous curtain line, "Hey, Flagg, wait for baby!" Both head toward the possibility of death and a glory that no one really cares about.

The play's unique quality lay in its rigorous undermining of the tradition of romanticizing war and glorifying its protagonists and their ventures. What Stephen Crane had done in *The Red Badge of Courage* (Miller, 1991), GEORGE BERNARD SHAW in ARMS AND THE MAN, and E. E. CUMMINGS in *The Enormous Room*, Anderson and Stallings did for the American stage. The play's pacifist message struck a primary chord in the American psyche, which had undergone a total disillusionment with a war that had ended only six years earlier with an unforgettable history of decimated youth.

Though the play's lack of psychological depth has been criticized, its rigorous and original rendering through an unprecedented stage language made it unquestionably the dramatic success of the 1924–1925 season on Broadway.

FURTHER READING

Halline, Allan G. "Maxwell Anderson's Dramatic Theory." *American Literature* 1, no. 16 (May 1944): 66–81.

Miller, Jordan Y., and Winifred L. Frazer. *American Drama Between the Wars.* Boston: Twayne, 1991.

Shivers, Alfred S. *Maxwell Anderson.* Boston: Twayne, 1976.

Woollcott, Alexander. Review of *What Price Glory?* In *The American Drama as Seen by the Critics: 1752–1934,* ed. by Montrose J. Moses and John Mason Brown. New York: Cooper Square Pubs., 1967. 245–247.

Rupendra Guha-Majumdar

WHEN WE DEAD AWAKEN

When We Dead Awaken (*Når vi døde vågner,* 1899) is the very last play that HENRIK IBSEN wrote, and it is also his most personal play. Ibsen had in fact planned to write an autobiography, and *When We Dead Awaken* can be—and often is—regarded as an autobiograhical work about the relationship between art and life. The main character of the play, the sculptor Arnold Rubek, is—as was Ibsen himself—a famous artist just recently returned to his native country after a considerably long time abroad. The middle-aged Rubek and his younger wife Maja are staying at a health resort near the sea. Their marriage is not happy; Maja blames Rubek for idle promises of a new and happy life together with him, and Rubek complains that he is bored with Maja and unable to create art while living with her. During the play they both find themselves a new partner and a new life: Rubek, wanting to create art again, reunites with Irene, a strangely stiff and "dead" woman that he has known earlier in his life, when she sat for him while he was working on his masterpiece *The Day of Resurrection.* Maja joins Ulfhejm, a lively and cynical bear hunter, in order to live a life completely *without* art and artists. In the final scenes the two pairs climb up the mountain, and refusing to descend when the weather is getting really bad, Rubek and Irene are killed in an avalanche.

When We Dead Awaken is a highly symbolic drama in which life, death, and resurrection are central metaphors for the changing of values, IDENTITY, and life. A crucial point concerning the SYMBOLISM of the play is that Rubek has created a masterpiece, a sculpture—*The Day of Resurrection*—that has almost the same title as the drama he himself is part of: *When We Dead Awaken.* The work-in-progress version of the drama, was also titled *The Day of Resurrection.* What complicates this picture of similarity is that the sculpture, which is in fact a group of statues, contains a former version of itself, a single statue that is, confusingly, also referred to as *The Day of Resurrection* and the fact that the boundaries between the various images of resurrection are transgressed in the play: the characters resemble the statues of the sculpture and take up positions onstage that resemble the positions of the statues of the sculpture. In this way, the sculpture is brought to life by the drama it is itself a part of, even as the drama is frozen in the sculpture it thematizes. In the last act the resurrection of the drama is played out as an ascent into the mountains. When the main characters are seen physically to move upward into the mountain landscape, this both symbolizes resurrection and reflects the resurrection of the figures in the sculpture.

Partly because of its obvious and dense symbolism and lack of REALISM, *When We Dead Awaken* was more or less neglected until the 1960s. Some of the early critics even rejected it as an inferior work. Especially since the 1960s it has been considered one of Ibsen's masterpieces and in accordance with its subtitle—*A Dramatic Epilogue*—interpreted as an epilogue to Ibsen's own life and to his oeuvre. A central question in the literature about *When We Dead Awaken* is whether this drama represents a deeply disillusioned or pessimistic view of life or whether it also gives glimpses of optimism. There is a tendency in recent readings to see the "dead life" depicted in the drama as an unalterable state.

[*See also* Norway]

FURTHER READING

Joyce, James. "Ibsen's New Drama." Originally published in *Fortnightly Review*, no. 67 (April 1, 1900). Reprinted in Lisbeth Wærp, ed., *Livet på likstrå. Henrik Ibsens Når vi døde vågner. En antologi* [Dead life. Henrik Ibsen's *When We Dead Awaken*. An anthology]. Oslo: Cappelen Forlag, 1999.

McFarlane, James. "Drama and Individual Integrity: 1893–1899." In *Meaning & Evidence. Studies, Essays & Prefaces 1953–1987*. Norwich: Norvik Press, 1987.

Meyer, Michael. "The Top of a Cold Mountain: 1899." In *Ibsen: A Biography*. 1967. New York: Viking Penguin, 1985.

Lisbeth Pettersen Wærp

A WHISTLE IN THE DARK

A Whistle in the Dark was Irish dramatist TOM MURPHY's first professionally produced play. It premiered at Stratford East in 1961 and transferred to the West End, London, where it was hugely successful. The story of a brutal Irish family living in the English city of Coventry, its startling presentation of psychological and physical violence made it a groundbreaking play—but it was also formally traditional, written as a dramatic TRAGEDY in which a central character struggles heroically against a preordained fate.

The action takes place in the home of Michael Carney and his English wife Betty. Michael is an Irish immigrant to Britain, who has left his country to escape a family life that he found vicious and limiting. Unfortunately, that life proves inescapable: two of Michael's brothers have joined him in Coventry, and as the play opens, his father and youngest brother Des have also arrived.

The Carneys impose themselves brutally on their environment, arranging to fight another Irish family living nearby. Michael attempts to prevent Des from participating in this fight but is unsuccessful: violence is so essential a part of their family's life that Des finds it irresistible. Tragically, it is also an unavoidable aspect of Michael's own character: subjected to terrible pressure from his brothers, he attacks his wife, and as the play reaches an unbearably tense conclusion, he lapses further into violence, with fatal results.

The theme of exile dominates Irish theater: plays such as BRIAN FRIEL's PHILADELPHIA, HERE I COME! (1964) dramatize Irish characters' need to be free from the restrictions of rural Irish life. In *A Whistle in the Dark*, Murphy offers a caustic view of this tradition, showing that exile from IRELAND did not allow Michael to escape from himself.

The play also challenges traditional representations of violence on the Irish stage, where it is usually presented as a farcical upshot of drunkenness or as the product of an ideological belief. The Carneys fit neither tradition: they are thugs, motivated by tribal pride rather than any form of morality. While it is undoubtedly the case that such men did exist, this representation proved controversial. The play was originally submitted to the Abbey Theatre in Dublin, Ireland, which rejected it on the grounds that the Carneys could not exist. In contrast, some English critics took the play too literally, seeing the Carneys as representing an inherently Irish predisposition to violence. The play therefore provoked unusually strong responses when it was premiered in ENGLAND, being met with bewilderment, hostility, and even occasional racism.

Its representation of violence in the domestic sphere shocked English audiences, as did its treatment of a rural family's collision with urban life. These representations created a space for English writers to explore the same themes: elements of the work of David Rudkin, ARNOLD WESKER, EDWARD BOND, and many others can in some ways be traced back to Murphy. Indeed, HAROLD PINTER's THE HOMECOMING (1964) very closely resembles Murphy's play. Although Murphy has since failed to reproduce the success of *A Whistle in the Dark* in London, the play's influence on English drama cannot be overestimated.

FURTHER READING

Grene, Nicholas. *The Politics of Irish Drama: Plays in Context from Boucicault to Friel*. Cambridge: Cambridge Univ. Press, 1999.

——, ed. *Talking About Tom Murphy*. Dublin: Carysfort Press, 2002.

O'Toole, Fintan. *The Politics of Magic*. Dublin: New Island, 1995.

Patrick Lonergan

THE WHITE GUARD　*See* DAYS OF THE TURBINS

WHITE-HAIRED GIRL

White-Haired Girl (*Baimao nü, geju*) is the first full-scale *geju*, or song drama, a genre that has come to be very popular with the Chinese Communist Party (CCP). It is a type of opera that features song but is not in a traditional style of Chinese drama. It may be in a Western style, but Chinese-written song dramas virtually always include Chinese elements. Another major feature of *White-Haired Girl* is that it is highly political, following the prescriptions laid down by Mao Zedong (1893–1976) in his "Talks at the Yan'an Forum on Literature and the Arts" of May 1942 (FORCED UP MOUNT LIANG).

The words of *White-Haired Girl* are by He Jingzhi and Ding Yi, while Ma Ke and others composed the music. He Jingzhi claims to have taken the views of ordinary members of rehearsal audiences into account in reaching the final version. The premiere took place in April 1945 in conjunction with the CCP's Seventh National Congress in Yan'an, northern Shaanxi Province, which was the capital city of the CCP-controlled areas at the time. CCP chairman Mao Zedong saw and praised the play.

The story is based on a real incident in 1940, though the drama itself is set in the second half of the 1930s. The main protagonist is Xier, the seventeen-year-old daughter of a peasant tenant of wicked Landlord Huang, who lives in a village in Hebei Province, north CHINA. She works as a servant to the landlord's wife. The landlord rapes Xier while Mrs. Huang treats her cruelly, so she flees into the mountains. There she suffers privations so serious that her hair turns white, the local people calling her the White-Haired Goddess. The CCP's army, which is fighting against the Japanese, comes through the region, and a former village neighbor who has joined the army saves her. Finally, the army avenges her by arresting and charging Landlord Huang for his crimes.

The final chorus of act 5, scene 2 spells out the crux of the opera:

The old life forced men to turn into ghosts,
But the new life changes ghosts back into men,
It's saved our unhappy sister [Xier] here!

The music of *White-Haired Girl*, an opera that requires a full evening to perform, was based on the melodies of an ancient folk northern Shaanxi song-and-dance form called *yangge* (literally "seedling songs"). The accompanying orchestra includes both Western and Chinese instruments. The costuming and actions are in realistic style, totally unlike traditional Chinese theater. Characterization is quite stark: Xier and other peasants are portrayed in a positive light, but the landlord and his wife are cast as evil and deserving of their fate. The CCP and its army members are shown as heroes and saviors.

During the Cultural Revolution of 1966 to 1976, this song drama was banned, but the story was made into a ballet that became one of the model revolutionary dramas fashionable at the time. The song drama was repremiered in Beijing in February 1977.

FURTHER READING

Ebon, Martin, ed. *Five Chinese Communist Plays.* New York: John Day Co., 1975 [includes translation and commentary].

Ho Ching-Chih and Ting Yi. *The White-Haired Girl: An Opera in Five Acts.* Tr. by Yang Hsien-Yi and Gladys Yang. Peking: Foreign Languages Press, 1954.

Lopez, Manuel D. *Chinese Drama: An Annotated Bibliography of Commentary, Criticism and Plays in English Translation.* Metuchen, N.J.: Scarecrow, 1991.

Colin Mackerras

THE WHITE SNAKE

TIAN HAN (1898–1968) was one of the pioneers of modern spoken drama in CHINA. He called himself "a budding Chinese Ibsen" when he was a student in JAPAN in 1920. He was the first to coin the term *huaju* (spoken drama) in 1927, rechristening new plays in order to emphasize the medium's use of dialogue and its nonmusical nature (Hung, 1994). Tian made many endeavors to promote spoken drama in China—such as launching the *South China Fortnightly* (*Nanguo banyuekan*) in 1924 and establishing the South China Film and Drama Society (*Nanguo dianying jushe*; later renamed Nanguo She or the South China Society) in 1926. Although a pivotal figure in the modern spoken drama movement in China, Tian also breathed new life into traditional theater. He found classical plays ideal for promoting interaction with rural audiences with their enduring popularity, long tradition, and rich variety (Hung, 1994).

The White Snake (*Baishe zhuan*, *jingju*) was a Tang dynasty story recorded in *Taiping Guangji*. It was staged in theatrical performances in the Ming and Qing dynasties. The earliest Beijing Opera performance of the story was in the late Qing dynasty and was only a single act focusing on acrobatic fights. Tian created his Beijing Opera version of *The White Snake* in 1952. This script was an adapted continuation from his 1947 draft *The Story of Golden Urn* (*Jin Boji*), which was based on both Beijing Opera and Kunqu Opera accounts of the story. Wang Yaoqin, the so-called Godfather of Beijing Opera, arranged its melodic patterns.

It concerns a beautiful woman (in fact, a transformed white snake) who marries a young scholar. A Buddhist monk tries to break up the marriage and succeeds in imprisoning the woman in a pagoda. In the end the pagoda collapses, and she escapes. Tian's script is renowned for its elegantly poetic language and romantic spirit. Moreover, he attaches heroic sentiments and lofty ideals to the female protagonist and conjures up the elevated image of a strong-willed and emotionally rich woman. In some previous versions and renditions of this ancient story, the White Snake was portrayed as a female demon preying on men or as a more humanized complex figure, such as the version in the most famous literary version, a short story included in Feng Menglong's anthology *Stories to Startle the World* (1620), while the monk was a positive character and succeeded in foiling the plot of the snake. But in Tian's version, the White Snake is a powerful and good woman striving for freedom in love (McDougall and Louie, 1997). The monk is a symbol of feudalist superstition (Mackerras, 1990) and moral and religious conservatism (McDougall and Louie, 1997).

First performed in 1952, the premiere of the drama in Beijing starring Liu Xiurong was a sensational success. Later, Beijing

Opera stars such as Du Jinfang, Zhao Yanxia, Guan Sushuang, Yang Chunxia, and Li Bingshu also performed in the drama, which is believed to be the testing stone of ACTING skills for the female dan role. The performance of the legendary Beijing Opera female impersonator MEI LANFANG in the act of the Fallen Bridge (Duan Qiao) is considered a masterpiece. In 1980, Shanghai Film Studio created a film version of the Beijing Opera The White Snake and turned it into a common household name in China.

FURTHER READING

Chang, Donald, and William Packard, trans. The White Snake. In The Red Pear Garden: Three Great Dramas of Revolutionary China, ed. by John D. Mitchell. Boston: David Godine, 1973. 49–120.

Hung, Chang-tai. War and Popular Culture: Resistance in Modern China, 1937–1945. Berkeley: Univ. of California Press, 1994.

Mackerras, Colin. Chinese Drama: A Historical Survey. Beijing: New World Press, 1990.

McDougall, Bonnie S., and Kam Louie. The Literature of China in the Twentieth Century. New York: Columbia Univ. Press, 1997.

Hongwei Lu

WHITE HORSES   See ROSMERSHOLM

WHITING, JOHN (1917–1963)

John Whiting, born in 1917, was the son of an army captain. Unsurprisingly perhaps, many of his plays focus on the power of violence. Cherishing ambitions to be an actor, he attended the Royal Academy of Dramatic Art, London, ENGLAND, then pursued an acting career. Between 1939 and 1944 he served in the Royal Artillery and was commissioned in 1942.

He began writing seriously after the war: stories and plays for radio (Paul Southan, 1946), an unpublished novel (Not a Foot of Land), and then, with increasing skill and ability, a selection of plays. No More a-Roving was written in 1946, followed by Conditions of Agreement (1947). His major work, Saint's Day, was written in 1949, immediately followed by A Penny for a Song. Both were performed in 1951. A Penny for a Song appeared at the Haymarket and was generally ignored. Saint's Day, however, won the play competition for the Festival of Britain. This spotlight did not guarantee its critical success: in fact, it received a vindictive critical drubbing. This was due less to the play's quality than to its style: Whiting's work represented a serious break from "drawing room theater," very different from TERENCE RATTIGAN and NOËL COWARD. Among others, the play was championed by Kenneth Tynan, who sought to celebrate it as the harbinger of a new and more serious form of drama.

In 1954, when Marching Song was performed, Whiting was still regarded by intellectuals as Britain's new young hope. By the end of 1956, however, he was eclipsed by the new generation of playwrights at the Royal Court. This was followed by a period of theater writing and theorizing. He was held in high estimation by his contemporaries and invited to deliver the

1957 lecture at the Old Vic on "The Art of the Dramatist." Following his first mainstream success The Devils, performed in 1961 at the Aldwych, he became a reviewer for the London Magazine. He died on June 16, 1963, in London, of cancer.

Whiting is unusual as a playwright repeatedly accused of obscurantism by literary critics and reviewers yet celebrated by professionals of the theater. Typically, it was due to a commission by Peter Hall that his most celebrated work, The Devils, was produced. As a writer, he was heavily influenced by T. S. ELIOT and reacted against the lightheartedness of CHRISTOPHER FRY. His staccato style and tension-crackling dialogue foreshadow that of HAROLD PINTER. Tightly complex, his plays are rich in philosophical depth and detail. They often turn on a character's inner transformation. Perhaps surprisingly for a trained actor, Whiting could be scornful of the actor's and director's craft. In "The Writers' Theatre," published 1956, he wrote:

> A sad parting of the ways has occurred between the playwright and his interpretors. To the writer, drama is a basic form: the theatre is a toy, an ingenious piece of machinery. It exists for the interpretation of plays. To many actors and directors, it has become a thing in itself, tiresomely dependent on some form of content.

Given the strength of his plays, and his excessive unpopularity among critics, it is hard to help concluding that Whiting was a writer ahead of his time.

SELECT PLAYS: No More a-Roving (1946); Conditions of Agreement (1947); Saint's Day (1949, performed 1951); A Penny for a Song (1951); Marching Song (1954); The Gates of Summer (1956); The Devils (1961)

FURTHER READING

Salmon, Eric. The Dark Journey: John Whiting as Dramatist. London: Barrie & Jenkins, 1979.

Trussler, Simon. The Plays of John Whiting: An Assessment. London: Victor Gollancz, 1972.

Whiting, John. Whiting on Theatre. London: Alan Ross, 1966.

——. The Collected Plays of John Whiting. Ed. by Ronald Hayman. 2 vols. London: Heinemann, 1969.

Kerry Kidd

WHO'S AFRAID OF VIRGINIA WOOLF?

Who's Afraid of Virginia Woolf?—EDWARD ALBEE's most popular play—saw a return to theatrical REALISM from a playwright whose early output had established him in the forefront of the traditions of ABSURDISM and EXPRESSIONISM. It premiered on Broadway at the Billy Rose Theater in 1962.

The play is divided into three acts, subtitled "Fun and Games," "Walpurgisnacht," and "Exorcism," and graphically explores the marital strife and ritualized conflict that exists in the relationship between George, a New England history professor at fictional New Carthage College, and Martha, who is also the daughter of the college's president. George is an archetypal example of the mediocre academic whose career never took off and who, in spite of marrying the boss's daughter, has failed to come even close to the expectations of his wife or father-in-law. It is perhaps this failure that forms the basis of the utter contempt in which Martha now holds him.

By the beginning of the play, their increasingly loveless marriage has degenerated into an ever-more-frequent round of vituperative arguments. There is, however, one principal secret fiction in their lives, and it is this that will provoke the final outcome of the evening.

George returns home late from an inaugural college party to discover that Martha has unexpectedly invited the new, young, and handsome member of the science faculty, Nick, and his young, pregnant wife, Honey, back to their home for a nightcap. George is angry about this, and as the evening wears on, what at first seems to be familiar verbal sniping between the couple develops a more serious and damaging edge. Nick and Honey, initially confused and somewhat embarrassed by the increasing viciousness of the exchange, are gradually drawn into the conflict themselves. The seeming perfection of the young couple's marriage is a stark contrast, almost a mirror image, to their hosts'. The levels of complexity increase as it becomes more and more difficult for Nick and Honey—and also the audience—to distinguish between truth and invention. At one point George seems to imply that he may have been consciously responsible for the death of his parents: is this simply part of the fiction?

Although George attempts to steer the conversation in a different direction, Martha insists on revealing that they have a secret: they have a son, and he will shortly celebrate his twenty-first birthday. The verbal battle between the two protagonists increases in intensity: Martha openly and overtly flirts with Nick, while taunting her husband over the shortcomings of his career. Nick, however, seems unable to consummate this adultery, and George mounts a particularly vicious counterattack. He pretends that he has received a telegram with news that their son has been killed in an automobile crash.

In what is perhaps the most extraordinary and disturbing scene in the play, George encourages Martha to list all of the main events in their son's life, while he interjects with lines from the Requiem Mass. When the news of the son's death is finally revealed, Martha collapses in what appears to be genuine despair. The nature of her response, however, prompts Nick into the realization that the child is also a fiction, an invention created by this childless couple to give some semblance of a familial bond to their barren relationship. This lie appears to be the central thing that can hold them together.

At the end of the play, the young visitors leave, having acquired a painful awareness of the less-palatable side of married life. George and Martha, emotionally drained by the evening's excesses, are forced to face a new reality: now that the illusion at the center of their relationship has been publicly exorcised, they are faced with the possibility of being able to reshape their marriage.

One of the primary themes of this painfully emotional play is absence: the absence of love in a marriage built upon lies, the absence of the child, whose centrality to the marriage has necessitated his fictional replacement. Perhaps in this Albee, who was adopted as a young child, was exploring the pain of the absence and abandonment of his own birth parents.

In a 1976 *New York Times* review (April 11), critic Walter Kerr suggested that Albee used the imaginary child as an allegory for the American dream, "given spurious birth . . . hotly debated thereafter, now dead." Perhaps George and Martha are intended as contemporary images of their namesakes (General George Washington and his wife), but Albee has never confirmed this hypothesis. Critic Stephen J. Bottoms (2000) raises the issue that the play "not only demands to be performed, but is a play which is, fundamentally, all *about* performance and performativity." Certainly the central performance "staged" by George and Martha provides the catharsis not only for the characters onstage but also for the audience.

FURTHER READING

Bottoms, Stephen J. *Albee: Who's Afraid of Virginia Woolf?* New York: Cambridge Univ. Press, 2000.

Gussow, Mel. *Edward Albee: A Singular Journey.* London: Oberon Bks., 1999.

McCarthy, Gerald. *Edward Albee.* London: Macmillan Modern Dramatists, 1987.

Roudane, Mathew. *Understanding Edward Albee.* Columbia: Univ. of South Carolina Press, 1987.

Paul E. Fryer

WHY MARRY?

Marriage is woman's only true career.
—Lucy, Act 1

Published in 1914 under the title *And So They Were Married*, Jesse Lynch Williams's three-act COMEDY about the institution of marriage received amateur productions under that title until its Broadway premiere as *Why Marry?* on December 25, 1917, running for 120 performances and earning numerous accolades. While primarily remembered as the first drama to win the newly established Pulitzer Prize, *Why Marry?* was also praised for its bold confrontation of social norms as well as its fine THEATRICALITY, with *New York Times* critic John Corbin calling it "the most penetrating satire on social institutions yet written by an American" (Dec. 30, 1917). Gerald Bordman said that with *Why Marry?* "[m]any felt that Christmas night brought in the best present of all." In 1922, Williams wrote a companion piece (though not a sequel) about divorce titled *Why Not.*

Why Marry?—set on a September weekend gathering in "a country house not far away"—revolves around the relationship between Ernest, a brilliant young scientist, and his assistant

Helen, who are in love. However, Helen's brother John, the wealthy businessman owner of the estate, disdains her affiliation with a mere lower-rung scientist, preferring that she marry Rex, descendant of a family with name and privilege. Helen does not want to marry Ernest, fearing that the burden of a wife would impose on his career, saying that "we'll give up marriage but not each other." Moreover, Helen is determined to accompany Ernest to Paris to work, spurning claims that "marriage is woman's only true career." She notes that her sister Jean has become engaged to Rex, each of whom is in love with someone else and predicting a loveless marriage. In the end, however, Helen's Uncle Everett, a judge, tricks Helen and Ernest into acknowledging their love and pronounces them man and wife.

Corbin was the most contradictory critic of the play. Initially, he praised the rebirth of satire as a means of evaluating and critiquing social institutions, noting how Williams attacks the scales upon which "various services to the state are rewarded" (Bordman and Hischak, 2004). He also mentioned Williams's debt to GEORGE BERNARD SHAW, calling *Why Marry?* "as keenly satirical as Shaw at his best and . . . as amusing" and noting that in some respects "the play surpasses even Shaw" (*New York Times*, December 26, 1917). Yet in one review, Corbin praises *Why Marry?* as both an "admirable comedy" and "a good stage story," while in another he says that "as an embodiment of a normal situation in dramatic action [of] the play is quite futile" (*New York Times*, February 3, 1918). He also takes Williams to task for having the couple marry in the end, albeit unknowingly, claiming that after rejecting society's norms "they are quitters and immoralists" and accusing Williams of resorting "to the cover of orange blossoms" (*New York Times*, February 3, 1918).

Regardless, Williams—also a journalist, fiction writer, and novelist—boldly takes on what was at the time a shocking topic, exploring gender and institutional changes in the new century. Helen is referred to as a "New Woman," challenging marriage as the only option for females, exploring possibilities beyond the household, and rejecting the limitations imposed by men.

FURTHER READING

Adler, Thomas P. *Mirror on the Stage: The Pulitzer Plays as an Approach to American Drama.* West Lafayette, Ind.: Purdue Univ. Press, 1987.

Bonin, Jane F. *Major Themes in Prize-Winning American Drama.* Metuchen, N.J.: Scarecrow, 1975.

Bordman, Gerald, and Thomas S. Hischack. *The Oxford Companion to American Theatre.* 3rd ed. New York: Oxford Univ. Press, 2004.

Stephens, Judith L. "Why Marry? The 'New Woman' of 1918." *Theatre Journal* 34 (May 1982): 183–196.

Karen Blansfield

THE WIDOWING OF MRS. HOLROYD

It is rotten when you're tied to a life you don't like.
—Blackmore, Act 1

Based on an event that happened to D. H. LAWRENCE's family, *The Widowing of Mrs. Holroyd* takes place entirely in the dark kitchen of a small cottage, far away from the drawing-room settings of plays by many of his contemporaries, and depicts the crumbling marriage of Charles and Lizzie Holroyd. An orphan raised by a drunken uncle, Mrs. Holroyd married mainly to escape her rootless existence in which, as she says, "I felt I'd nowhere to go, I belonged to nowhere, and nobody cared about me." She went with "the first man that turned up," a strapping miner whom she now claims is "just his body and nothing else—nothing that keeps him, no anchor, no roots, nothing satisfying." The two are each miserable and, when the play opens, engaged in a game of cruelty, as she encourages a young electrician named Blackmore, who is smitten with her, and he stays out late after work and comes home drunk, feeling like "a dog in the house, an' not a man."

Frustration and recrimination infect the household, including their two children Jack and Minnie as well as Charles's mother. The final straw comes when Charles brings home what Lizzie calls two "trollops from Nottingham," and she begins to plot elopement to SPAIN with Blackmore, who recognizes that "it is rotten when you're tied to a life you don't like," especially when Lizzie realizes that Charles wants "a slave, not a wife." An unexpected accident at the mine the following evening (modeled after what happened to Lawrence's uncle) creates a macabre homecoming scene in which Charles's dead body is carried into the kitchen much as it was the previous night in an inebriated stupor. Charles's wife and mother begin to undress and clean the body; and in contrast to the liberation and happiness she envisioned after Charles's death earlier in the play, she experiences intense guilt and expresses her culpability in the TRAGEDY. Throughout the play, Lawrence's focus is as much the day-to-day trudgery of industrial folk as it is the stifling marital dynamics of the household.

More conventional in plot than his other "colliery" plays, *The Widowing of Mrs. Holroyd* was the first of Lawrence's plays to appear in print—drafted between 1910 and 1913 and published in 1914—and premiered in Los Angeles in 1916, not appearing onstage in ENGLAND until the 1920s. Focusing on the play's "every-day situation" rendered in "every-day" speech, the reviewers both lauded and criticized its form and content, in particular, its notorious and powerful final scene of body washing. Edwin Bjorkman (2002) marveled at the complexity of the characters, what he called the "psychological penetration" of Lawrence's written work. Although GEORGE BERNARD SHAW expressed admiration for the quality of his stage dialogue, Lawrence was not interested in writing what he called the "bony, bloodless drama" of the "rule and measure mathematical folk" produced by Royal Court playwrights (Eyre and Wright, 2000), choosing instead a style more akin to the DRAMATURGY of Irish writers like J. M. SYNGE and SEAN O'CASEY. While thematically similar to much of the New Drama, *Holroyd* provides a sharp contrast to representations of wealthier classes in Edwardian drama as well as its often more facile characterizations of working-class individuals. Juxtaposing symbolic elements with graphic naturalistic detail, including dialect, darkness, and even rats racing across the kitchen floor, the play presents, in addition, a complexity of structure that refuses melodramatic sentimentality and provides the audience with what John Worthen (1992) describes as "a REALISM [that ensures] no single one of the characters gains or maintains our sympathy throughout."

FURTHER READING

Bjorkman, Edwin. "Introduction" to The Widowing of Mrs. Holroyd. Philadelphia: Univ. of Pennsylvania, 2002. xiii–xvi.

Eyre, Richard, and Nicholas Wright. Changing Stages. New York: Alfred Knopf, 2001.

Sklar, Sylvia. The Plays of D. H. Lawrence: A Biographical and Critical Study. New York: Barnes & Noble, 1975.

Worthen, John. D. H. Lawrence, The Early Years, 1885–1912. Cambridge: Cambridge Univ. Press, 1992.

Christopher Wixson

WIEBE, RUDY (1934–)

Rudy Wiebe was born in 1934 in Fairholme, Saskatchewan, CANADA, the descendant of Mennonite German immigrants. Wiebe's ancestors lived in RUSSIA for many years and left what was then the Soviet Union when subjected to religious persecution. Wiebe did not speak English until he was six and spoke a combination of Low German (Plattdeutsch) and High German at home throughout his adolescence. Wiebe's family moved to Coaldale, Alberta, in 1947, where he attended the Mennonite High School. This experience provided the basis for his play Far as the Eye Can See (published 1977). Wiebe graduated from the University of Alberta in Edmonton in 1956. He studied with the writing teacher F. M. Salter. After traveling through Europe, Wiebe received his master's degree from Alberta in 1960. In 1958 he married Tena Isaak. He later studied and taught in the UNITED STATES and visited Mennonite settlements in Paraguay. He taught at Alberta from 1967 to 1992.

Wiebe's cultural background informs his writing, and he uses Mennonite themes and settings in much of his writing. But he is not seen as primarily an ethnic or religious writer, as he has written numerous fictional documentaries including The Temptations of Big Bear (1973), The Scorched-Wood People (1977), and A Discovery of Strangers (1994). In these fictional documentaries Wiebe rewrites the past from a Native point of view. Wiebe has also collaborated with Yvonne Johnson on Stolen Life: The Journey of a Cree Woman (1998). Stolen Life provokes troubling questions about the nature of this collaboration—assembled from hours of taped interviews and thousands of pages of Johnson's own writing—where the Native woman, sentenced to life in prison for her part in a brutal murder, appears not strictly as her own narrative voice but as the construction of the white author.

Wiebe is interested in groups that resist consensus. His style is not heartwarming and earnest but refractory and spiritual in a challenging way. Far as the Eye Can See refers to the prairies of Western Canada, but it also alludes to the potential for religious freedom in Canada for a Mennonite group so often oppressed. The play does not idealize Canada; rather, it examines corruption and pettiness in an Alberta small town and contains cameo appearances by such figures as Blackfoot chief Crowfoot; Social Credit leader William Aberhart; and Princess Louise, Queen Victoria's daughter and the wife of a Canadian governor general, the Marquess of Lorne. The play examines the Mennonites in a settled community in Canada, where they interact with others yet also adamantly preserve their own traditions. These are not just inherited maxims but actively exercised moral values. The play is not didactic. But part of its mission is to educate a general audience about the nature of the Mennonite community and its way of life. The last line, explicitly addressed to the audience, emblematizes this: "We have listened to you, and we have understood you. Thank you." The play was criticized for being too farcical, yet FARCE is arguably a key weapon in undermining any overly polemical tendencies.

PLAY: Far as the Eye Can See (published 1977)

FURTHER READING

Keith, W. J., ed. A Voice in the Land: Essays by and About Rudy Wiebe. Edmonton: NeWest Press, 1981.

Merrett, Robert James. "Communities." Canadian Literature, no. 85 (Summer 1980): 126–128.

van Toorn, Penny. Rudy Wiebe and the Historicity of the Word. Edmonton: Univ. of Alberta, 1995.

Nicholas Birns

WIJAYA, PUTU (1944–)

Putu Wijaya, born in 1944, an acclaimed Indonesian playwright, director, actor, and short-story writer, is an innovator of post-1968 theater in INDONESIA. He mixes Western and traditional Indonesian performance aesthetics and spirituality. Balinese-born, he moved to Yogyakarta to pursue a law degree. Disillusioned by the corruption of the Indonesian legal system, he turned to theater, performing with both RENDRA and ARIFIN C. NOER. In 1972 he formed his own company, Teater Mandiri, as the group's playwright and director. "Mandiri" is Javanese for "independent"—a guiding concept for the group whose motto is "to build from what is at hand."

By irreverently mixing fantasy and reality, Wijaya invokes "mental terror" in the hearts of his audiences, He attacks the monotonous rhythms of daily life and apathy toward the status quo. To create this sense of terror, he uses dozens of actors; deafening music and sound effects; jarring images; colorful costumes, sets, and props; loud delivery; burning incense; and nonrealistic situations. Wijaya refers to his plays as tontonan from the root "to watch." Indeed, his productions are feasts for the eye. Like the traditional Balinese performance from which he draws inspiration, productions are total theater combining drama, dialogue, music, dance, color, and smell. As playwright, he has introduced several important trends including the use of colloquial Indonesian. He plays with accepted conventions of modern and traditional performance aesthetics to subvert audience expectations.

In his first major play *Ouch* (*Aduh*, 1974), which won the prestigious Jakarta Arts Council annual playwriting contest, Wijaya initiated "stupid theater" (*teater bodoh*) by portraying a group of marginalized people facing disturbing moral, ethical, and social dilemmas in a simple reportage style, allowing the audience to draw their own conclusions. Often, his characters do not have individual names but are identified as "someone" or "committee member." The open structure of his plays is deliberately simple, allowing varying interpretations by performers. The structure is also practical since his theater company is composed mostly of transient nonactors who must adapt material to themselves. The open structure also served as a guerrilla tactic to circumvent strict censorship barring criticism of the government and social conditions during President Haji Mohammad Suharto's New Order regime (1966–1998).

In 1975, Wijaya issued a manifesto on "wounded theatre" (*teater luka*) as an explanation for his production of *Lo!* (*Lho*, 1975). This violent, nonnarrative PERFORMANCE ART piece ended with naked actors spouting political jargon while pretending to defecate in a fountain in front of the theater. His desire to unsettle audiences through jarring images that rip open seemingly tidy social systems has also been the main focus of his work since *YELL* (*YEL*, 1991), which toured the UNITED STATES during the Festival of Indonesia.

Wijaya has also performed throughout Asia and Europe, including Tokyo in 2000 and Hamburg in 2002. In Hamburg he staged THE COFFIN IS TOO BIG FOR THE HOLE, his first production by a playwright other than himself. The work was based on a play by Singaporean KUO PAO KUN.

PLAYS: *Ouch* (*Aduh*, 1974); *Whachumacallit* (*Anu*, 1974); *Lo!* (*Lho*, 1975); *Nil* (*Nol*, 1976); *Whatever* (*Entah*, 1976); *Hum-Pim-Pah* (1978); *Accelerate* (*Blong*, 1979); *Bang* (*Dor*, 1979); *Crazy* (*Edan*, 1980); *Watch It* (*Awas*, 1980); *Free* (*Los*, 1981); *Geez!* (*Gerr*, 1981); *Essence* (*Zat*, 1982); *Roar* (*Aum*, 1982); *Shit* (*Tai*, 1983); *The Front* (*Front*, 1985); *Shame* (*Aib*, 1988); *Gosh* (*Wah*, 1989); *YELL* (*YEL*, 1991); *Bore* (*Bor*, 1994); *Aware* (*Ngeh*, 1998); *Chaos* (*Keos*, 1998); *War* (2002)

FURTHER READING

Gillitt, Cobina. "Challenging Conventions and Crossing Boundaries: A New Tradition of Indonesian Theatre from 1968–1978." Ph.D. diss., New York Univ., 2001.

Gillitt Asmara, Cobina. "Tradisi Baru: A New Tradition of Indonesian Theatre." *Asian Theatre Journal* 12, no. 1 (1995): 164–174.

Morgan, Anne-Marie. "Three Approaches to Modern Theatre in Jakarta in the 1990s: Rendra, Putu Wijaya and Ratna Sarumpaet." *Australasian Drama Studies* 27 (1995): 70–85.

Rafferty, Ellen, ed. *Putu Wijaya in Performance: A Script and Study of Indonesian Theatre*. Madison: Univ. of Wisconsin Center for Southeast Asian Studies, 1989.

Cobina Gillitt

WILDCAT STAGE PRODUCTIONS

Dave MacLennan and Dave Anderson founded Wildcat Stage Productions in 1978 as an offshoot of the 7:84 (SCOTLAND) theater company. The development of this second company was spawned by a number of personal, political, and artistic differences emerging among members of the parent company during the late 1970s. As the driving force of popular political theater in Scotland during the 1970s and 1980s, 7:84, under the direction of JOHN MCGRATH, dedicated itself to the celebration of socialist ideals, targeting working-class audiences during tours throughout the Highland regions and cities of Scotland. Although 7:84 was well known for its populist style of theater involving aspects of Scottish music hall traditions, with song, humor, and the Indigenous *ceilidh* form of dance, as well as Brechtian agit-prop (AGITATION-PROPAGANDA), direct address, and DOCUMENTARY techniques, many of the band members of the original company felt that music should become a more important aspect of the group's work.

With Scottish Arts Council (SAC) funding to support them, the band broke away to create Wildcat, a company wholeheartedly devoted to a unique genre of political musical theater, distinct from the work of 7:84 (Scotland). Additionally, unlike conventional character and narrative-driven West End musicals, Wildcat more closely resembles the 1970s fringe company Cartoon Archetypal Slogan Theatre (CAST) in its use of rock opera–themed music to articulate and illuminate left-wing political and social issues. Notable performances include *Painted Bird* (1978), *Dummies* (1979), *1982/Any Minute Now* (1982), *Same Difference* (1984), *The Celtic Story* (1988), *Dead Liberty* (1990), and revivals of 7:84 productions such as *Border Warfare* (1990), *John Brown's Body* (1991), and *A Satire of the Four Estaites* (1996). Throughout its existence, Wildcat productions have presented new Scottish writing, concentrating on working-class experiences, popular culture, and left-wing political and social issues.

Unfortunately, an uneven record of successes, variable audience figures, and a certain amount of critically noted predictability led to financial difficulties and a conflict with the SAC. Ultimately, the company whose political fervor had engaged the emotions and imaginations of audiences during the eras of the Harold Wilson, Margaret Thatcher, and John Major political administrations became overshadowed by changes in post-Devolution Scottish theater and culture in the 1990s. Finally, during a major overhaul of subsidy practices and reallocation of funds, including the creation of fixed four-year grants to support touring companies in 1997, the SAC did not include Wildcat in the list of clients that were to receive new or continued financial support. Instead, the company's £200,000 annual subsidy was retracted. The four-year funding grants were allocated, instead, to those the SAC considered to be more forward looking, innovative, and cosmopolitan companies, reflecting a shift in dramatic tastes within Scotland and a response to the changing face of Scottish artistic and political culture at the end of the 20th century. After an exhausting and unsuccessful battle with the SAC to restore funding, Wildcat's artistic director Dave MacLennan resigned his post in favor of a return to previous writing interests. Dave Anderson took over responsibilities of artistic leadership, as the company continued rehearsals and productions on a project-by-project basis.

FURTHER READING

DiCenzo, Maria. *The Politics of Alternative Theatre in Britain, 1968–1990: The Case of 7:84 (Scotland)*. Cambridge: Cambridge Univ. Press, 1996.

MacLennan, Elizabeth. *The Moon Belongs to Everyone: Making Theatre with 7:84*. London: Methuen, 1990.

Maguire, Tom. "Still Cool for Cats? The Life and Times of Wildcat Stage Productions." *International Journal of Scottish Theatre* 1, no. 1 (June 2000). http://arts.qmuc.ac.uk/ijost/Volume1_no1/T_Maguire.htm.

Stevenson, Randall, and Gavin Wallace, eds. *Scottish Theatre Since the Seventies*. Edinburgh: Edinburgh Univ. Press, 1996.

Kristin A. Crouch

THE WILD DUCK

Take the lie out of any particular situation, and at once you take away happiness as well.
—Relling, Act 5

The Wild Duck (*Vildanden*), a play in five acts, was first performed at the Bergen Theater in January 1885. The play takes up themes one recognizes from HENRIK IBSEN's philosophical dramas of the 1860s, BRAND and PEER GYNT, dealing with contrary forms of self-realization. In *The Wild Duck* the opposition between "being oneself" and "being true to one's self enough" has been moved from the higher sphere of abstraction to a bourgeois sphere, in which Gregers Werle and Hjalmar Ekdal take over the agent positions of Brand and Peer Gynt. Due to an offense in the past, old Ekdal has served time in prison, while his business partner Haakon Werle avoided punishment. The Ekdals experienced a social decline, and as compensation for this, the rich merchant Werle has supported his former partner by employing him as copying clerk. At the same time, he has arranged for the marriage of Hjalmar, the son of old Ekdal, to his own former lover Gina, who has born an illegitimate child.

At the beginning of the play, Gina's daughter Hedvig is fourteen years old. The family is living together with old Ekdal in an apartment consisting of a living section, a photo atelier, and an attic. Domestic peace is threatened by Gregers's intrusion into the Ekdal family, presenting to his onetime school friend Hjalmar what he calls the "claim of the ideal." Eagerness to make up for the wrong his father has done to the Ekdals, father and son, he wants Hjalmar to be a truth witness, who is to cut through all lies and establish an existence based on ideal values. In his fundamentalist orientation, Gregers is related to Brand. Proceeding to make Hjalmar face the truth, he is not taking into account that Hjalmar is incapable of a life without illusions. With the assistance of Gregers's father, Hjalmar has established himself as a photographer specializing in portrait photography including the art of retouching. He is a master at recreating reality so that it appears in the way he would rather see it. His ambition is to become an inventor. This is simply empty rhetoric, however, and an excuse to spend time in the attic working on contraptions to improve the existence of the domesticated animals kept there.

The Wild Duck is a play about how one spends one's time nourishing the illusions that make life tolerable. Ibsen claimed that *The Wild Duck* occupies a special place in his dramatic production. The symbolic SUBTEXT beneath the realistic communication level seems to be more explicit than in his earlier plays. Hedvig finds the words to describe this deviating practice when she comments on Gregers Werle's way of expressing himself: "It was as if he meant something else than what he said." The attic itself—with the duck that has been wounded by a gunshot and captured—is the central symbol of the play. The duck is primarily symbolic of Hedvig, but together with the artificial surroundings in which it lives, it does have a symbolic reference to several of the characters in the play in that it articulates the difference between appearance and reality. Photography, lighting, visual communication, and the faculty of seeing constitute another continuous structural field with a number of symbolic references. Ibsen indirectly shows by means of inherited visual impairment that Hedvig is not Hjalmar's but Haakon Werle's daughter.

When Gregers informs Hjalmar of his suspicions about this paternity, Hjalmar is upset and rejects Hedvig in a way that makes her desperate to regain his love. Gregers suggests to her that shooting the duck would be a sacrifice that would convince Hjalmar of her unlimited affection for him. In the attic with a pistol, intending to shoot the bird, Hedvig overhears Hjalmar's rhetorical question to Gregers concerning whether she might be willing to prove her love for him by sacrificing the good life offered her by the Werle family. She misunderstands Hjalmar's self-pitying phrases, confusing his expression "good life" with "life," and in a self-sacrificing spontaneous reaction shoots herself.

Hedvig is the victim both of Hjalmar's pathetic rhetoric and Gregers's fanatical search for the truth. With Dr. Relling, Ibsen launched a character whose task it is to comment on characters and events from the position of a cynic. In direct opposition to Gregers and his self-imposed mission of uncompromising truth, Dr. Relling claims that the average human being, in order to be happy, is in need of a major illusion. Accordingly, as a doctor he is treating his fellow human beings by promoting "the life lie" of each individual, giving it therapeutic status as a remedy against all forms of moral and ideological fanaticism.

FURTHER READING

Johnston, Brian. "The Metaphoric Structure of *The Wild Duck*." *Contemporary Approaches to Ibsen* 1 (1966): 72–95.

Moi, Toril. " 'It was as if he meant something different from what he said—all the time': Language, Metaphysics and the Everyday in *The Wild Duck*." *Everyday Life*, special issue of *New Literary History* 33, no. 4 (2002): 655–686.

Reinert, Otto. "Sight Imagery in *The Wild Duck*." *The Journal of English and Germanic Philology* 55 (1956): 457–462.

Steene, Birgitta. "Can This Bird Fly? *The Wild Duck* on the Screen." *Edda* (1999): 31–39.

Van Laan, Thomas F. "The Novelty of *The Wild Duck*: The Author's Absence." *Journal of Dramatic Theory and Criticism* 1, no. 1 (1986): 17–33.

Knut Brynhildsvoll

WILDE, OSCAR (1854–1900)

The supreme vice is shallowness. Whatever is realised is right.
—De Profundis, 1905

A handbag?

—Lady Bracknell, Act 1, *The Importance of Being Earnest*

Oscar Wilde, born Fingal O'Flahertie Wills in Dublin, IRELAND, on October 10, 1854, was a celebrity wit, aesthete, poet, novelist, philosophical essayist, dramatist, and prison convict. He was the second son of Dr. William Wilde, a surgeon later knighted for his service as medical commissioner to the Irish census of 1841 and 1851, and Jane Francesca Wilde, a poet and folklorist, who wrote nationalist ballads under the pen name "Speranza." Dr. Wilde was a man of Victorian energy, writing books not just on medical subjects but on travels in the Mediterranean, the last years of Jonathan Swift, the archaeology of Ireland, and the history and geography of his beloved Lough Corrib in County Galway; he fathered three children outside of wedlock and was nearly ruined by an infamous libel suit involving a young female patient who accused him of taking liberties with her chloroformed body.

1874–1891

Wilde's larger-than-life parents held a salon for Dublin wits at 1 Merrion Square, near Trinity College, where Oscar enrolled after completing his schooling at Portora in County Fermanagh (which SAMUEL BECKETT later attended). Wilde, a brilliant student, caught the attention of John Pentland Mahaffy, author of *The Art of Conversation*. Professor Mahaffy wrote works of popular scholarship on the social life of the ancient Greeks, in which he did not wholly avoid the subject of the common practice of male homosexuality among the ancients. In 1874 Wilde chose to leave Trinity before graduation in order to complete his education at Oxford University.

Although affecting a bored superiority to the tasks set by tutors, Wilde was a naturally avid scholar, as his Oxford notebooks prove. His memoranda and responses to passages in German PHILOSOPHY are points of reckoning for the course of his future life. The great sages then on the faculty or in the university's orbit all had an influence on him. Walter Pater's devotion to Greek aestheticism and male friendship (as evident in *Studies in the History of the Renaissance*, 1873) was particularly attractive, but John Ruskin's commitment to the social practice of aestheticism—the ideal of making life beautiful for all—had a lasting impact as well. On one hand, he felt the charm of Cardinal Newman's devotion to the spiritual discipline of dogmatic Catholicism; on the other hand, he admired the individualist engagement with public matters displayed by the Protestant Matthew Arnold. Some of these influences—especially Pater's emphasis on fineness and intensity of feeling as the highest things in life—are apparent in Wilde's *Poems* (1881).

Carrying off the honors of a double first in "Greats" and the Newdigate Prize for poetry at Oxford, Wilde arrived in London in 1879. He became famous by accompanying celebrity actresses, giving interviews to journalists, wearing clothes even less utilitarian than those of women of fashion, and making no utterance that was not both quotable and memorable. Newspaper caricatures, gossip columns, and satirical operas made fun of this very large and outrageous Irishman, just down from Oxford, but Wilde gave to notoriety the same welcome he gave to fame: it was all publicity for himself.

In 1882 Wilde left for New York for a lecture tour across the UNITED STATES and CANADA, supposedly telling a customs officer, "I have nothing to declare but my genius." W. S. GILBERT and Arthur Sullivan's opera *Patience*, in which Wilde was caricatured, was on tour, and Wilde himself aimed to elaborate a profitable offstage fantasy of himself. He was businesslike both in offering himself as an effeminate laughingstock and in gaining the respect of listeners to his rather academic lectures on art and beauty.

On his return from North America, Wilde married Constance Lloyd. They had two sons, Cyril (born 1885) and Vivian (born 1886). With the assistance of a leading architect, Edward Godwin, and painter, James McNeill Whistler, the Wildes created a famously fashionable house at 16 Tite Street, Chelsea. From this address Wilde preached to others about "The House Beautiful" and made popular blue china and dados (a dado is a lining of the lower part of an interior wall of a different material from that of the upper part).

Only months after his marriage, Wilde began a lecture tour of cities in ENGLAND. In "Beauty, Taste, and Ugliness in Dress," a typical one, he told his listeners it would be better—more healthy and more beautiful—to have clothes for men and women hang from the shoulders rather than the waist, in the fashion of the ancients in togas rather than the Victorians in belted trousers and corseted gowns. To art students, he explained that pictures that make people exclaim, "How curious!" or "How sad!"

or "How interesting!" are all bad pictures; a good picture makes one exclaim only, "How beautiful."

As to literature itself, Wilde tried writing MELODRAMA (*Vera; or, The Nihilists*) and historical verse drama (*The Duchess of Padua*), but the first flopped in 1883, and the second had a similar fate in 1891. His talent emerged, however, in his superior reviews of inferior novels (one title is "Half-Hours with the Worst Authors"), elaborately clever letters to the editor, and accounts of painting exhibitions. Wilde's journalism is unique in its attention to precise diction and highly patterned sentence structure. Whatever he wrote was an expression of wit. Only with "The Portrait of Mr. W. H." in 1889, however, did he begin to show that he was not only a clever but a great writer. With a scholarly wit that foreshadows Jorge Luis Borges, the story tells of an effeminate young man in 19th-century England who has a theory about the identity of that "W. H." to whom William Shakespeare devoted his sonnets: the initials belonged to a boy-actor named Willie Hughes with whom the playwright was in love. Due to its elaborately arranged plausibility, the story was shocking: Shakespeare was a married man with two children, and yet he was sexually infatuated with a boy.

But all this was true in 1888 of Wilde himself. He had been seduced by Robert Ross, a Cambridge undergraduate he had met in 1886. Wilde then took a step into what thereafter had to be a secret life, for homosexuality was a criminal offense at the time. Hidden desires, false identities, the superficiality of custom and morality became the stuff of Wilde's personal life and subsequently of his fiction and plays. *The Picture of Dorian Gray* (1891), his one novel and a masterpiece, was immediately seen to concern the "filthy" desires of men. It certainly had a liberating effect on young men of similar temperament, such as Lionel Johnson, Max Beerbohm, Aubrey Beardsley, and John Gray, who looked upon Wilde as their hero. They became the "decadents" or "aesthetes" of the 1890s.

While it was apparent that *Dorian Gray* was crammed with sin and beauty, its moral and philosophical implications were unclear. For the instruction of those uncertain of his beliefs, Wilde published a number of profound if paradoxical essays at this time. "The Decay of Lying" (1889) made fun of honesty, a Victorian shibboleth, on the grounds that it censored and famished creativity. "The Soul of Man Under Socialism" (1891) surprisingly gave support for socialism, though for a kind of socialism based on the primacy of the individual (not the couple, the family, the masses, or the state). In a proper society, he thought that each individual should be as free from compulsion as every rich person. His most Nietzschean work—a classic of criticism—is "The Critic as Artist," a Platonic dialogue that refutes Matthew Arnold, saying that the real purpose of criticism is not to see the object as it really is; it is to see the object as it is not. The highest criticism, he proclaimed, is "the record of one's own soul."

Wilde's impact on theater followed his considerable achievements with other forms—poetry, journalism, short stories, a novel, philosophy, and criticism. In 1891, in Paris, he wrote a symbolist play about Salomé, who falls in love with the sexually pure John the Baptist, demands his head from her besotted stepfather Herod, and then lustfully dances with the severed head. The dialogue (in French) is encrusted with poetic imagery, slow moving, doom laden, and undramatic. In England, *Salomé* was denied a license for performance, but it became influential upon opera, upon the plays of W. B. YEATS, and after its 1896 production by Lugne-Poe at the Théatre de L'Oeuvre, on European symbolist theater in general.

1892–1900: FAMOUS, THEN INFAMOUS

Wilde's first COMEDY, LADY WINDERMERE'S FAN, opened at George Alexander's fashionable West End London theater on February 20, 1892, to a full house. The play appears to be a high-society melodrama, but everything is not what it appears. Mrs. Erlynne seems to be an immoral woman, come to blackmail a man for sins past. In fact, she does ask Lord Windermere for money for keeping it a secret that his puritanical wife is actually her daughter, by an affair that forced her out of good society. But Mrs. Erlynne ultimately intervenes to save her daughter from the imputation of immorality on her part and takes the blame upon herself, an expression of instinctive motherliness that she finds anything but pleasant. The foppish and witty Lord Darlington is the first of what became a common type in Wilde's plays: the wit who seems superficial but is actually moved by deep feeling and good sense.

A little more than a year later, on April 19, 1893, Wilde's second comedy, A WOMAN OF NO IMPORTANCE, opened in a production by Herbert Beerbohm Tree. Wilde told Tree that he took the plot from a family magazine, which had stolen it from a novel (his own!): "People love a wicked aristocrat who seduces a virtuous maid, and they love a virtuous maiden for being seduced. . . . I have given them what they like, so that they may learn to appreciate what I like to give them." There is much truth in this comment. With a blasé surrender to popular taste, Wilde did borrow plots from contemporary popular fiction and theater. He altered them here and there in small ways, so as to upset conventions. He also put into each play, even into the mouth of each character in each play, maxims on life that have devastatingly anarchic and satirical power. Such revolutionary one-sentence teachings are what he "liked to give" his hypocritical public. For example, explaining why women have more happiness and pleasure than men, Mrs. Allonby says, "There are far more things forbidden to us than are forbidden to them." Lord Illingworth is Wildean in his maxims: as Lady Hunstanton says, shaking her fan at Illingworth, "Everything you have said today seems to me excessively immoral. It has been most interesting, listening to you."

Jokes about temptation were not simply stage persiflage for Wilde. By the middle of 1892 he had embarked on a grand passion with an Oxford undergraduate of remarkable beauty, Lord Alfred Douglas, nicknamed "Bosie." For a second time, the author, husband, and father of two was "led astray" by a very young man. Bosie loved to spend money on restaurants, hotels, rent-boys, jewelry, and travels in England, FRANCE, and Algeria. With a lord's sense of being far above common society, he was reckless in the public display of unusual manners and morals. As Wilde was anyway one of the most famous men in England, whose face was well known through newspaper depictions, the couple could count on very little privacy for their love affair (and mutual love it was). In fact, they did not seek privacy; they sought celebrity instead, relishing outrage and danger.

It was difficult for Wilde to devote himself fully to writing while keeping this double life going. However, during a vacation by Bosie to the Continent, Wilde remained in England and rapidly wrote his two greatest plays, AN IDEAL HUSBAND and THE IMPORTANCE OF BEING EARNEST. The first opened on January 3, 1895. The prime minister, the prince of Wales, and many government ministers took box seats; the house was full. Society had come to expect from Wilde nothing but masterpieces, and nothing but masterpieces would he give them.

An Ideal Husband possessed elements that had become familiar in a Wilde play: an adventuress, an aristocratic wit with a fancy costume and a heart of gold, and a youthful sin that comes back to haunt the sinner. In this case, the sin was the sale of state secrets by Sir Robert Chiltern, now a cabinet minister of highest character, thought to be a future prime minister. The originality of the play, apart from its brilliant language, appears in its very modern and Nietzschean moral development. Chiltern refuses to be ashamed of his youthful misdeed. It got him the money that enabled him to enter both society and politics; everything good about his life follows from, and rests on, that act of misconduct. It took courage to sin, and he will not renounce it. While these ethics of a superman are not plainly endorsed in the play, they are made to seem superior to the high-toned moralism of Chiltern's wife, whose idealism comes off as cold and shallow.

The play broadly concerns a scandal of 1890s political life: the fall of Charles Stewart Parnell, who had been identified in a divorce suit by a fellow member of Parliament as the adulterous long-term lover of his wife, Katherine O'Shea. Parnell did not renounce his love. The Irish Catholic priests and English Protestant preachers all demanded that Parnell be dropped from the leadership of the Irish party and from any alliance with the ruling Liberal Party. Yet, by the logic of *An Ideal Husband*, Parnell's daring passion for O'Shea was not a sign of unfitness for office; it was an attribute inseparable from his greatness.

Wilde's relationship to Irish nationalism was complicated. Aristocratic and bohemian English society circles were his element; his manners were peerless. Yet his satire of English common sense, puritanism, snobbery, and hypocrisy was satire from an Irish point of view. When he appeared at the Southwark Irish Literary Club in 1887, at the start of the Irish Revival, the others were not pleased to see in their midst "the head centre of aestheticism," even if he were the son of "Speranza," a hero of Young

Ireland. Nonetheless, Wilde was friendly to their cause and to individual Irish writers. Yeats especially was grateful for Wilde's kindness and profoundly influenced by his work. That the Irish Revival became a kind of branch of aestheticism is the result of Wilde's influence.

In August and September of 1894, Wilde dashed off his greatest work, *The Importance of Being Earnest.* He was threatened by debt and, more seriously, by the dogged demands of the Marquess of Queensberry that Wilde see no more of his son "Bosie." Queensberry played the part of the righteous Victorian patriarch, but he was also a very unpleasant ruffian. While writing his play, Wilde kept all seriousness at bay. Its principle is to treat as trivial everything important (family, property, marriage) and to treat as important things that are trivial, such as cucumber sandwiches. At the heart of the play is Algernon's defense of the double life. He pretends to have a friend in the country named Bunbury, who is always falling ill. Whenever an unpleasant obligation appears in town, he dashes off supposedly to see Bunbury but actually to have riotous fun in country houses. The complications implicit in leading a double life lead to cock-ups all around. It had been Wilde's practice to employ somewhat silly and conventional plots, but in *The Importance of Being Earnest* the silliness was deliberately carried to zany lengths. While often farcical, Wilde realized that success onstage depended on a certain style of ACTING: rapid pace (like "a pistol shot"), indolent deadpan delivery, and perfect carriage. While rehearsing the actors, Wilde learned that the Marquess of Queensberry was planning a scandalous demonstration against Wilde's homosexuality during the first-night performance. Wilde had Queensberry's ticket canceled, and policemen stood at the theater door to bar his entry. On St. Valentine's Day of 1895, the play opened to immediate and unmarred success.

Only days later, Queensberry left a card with the porter of Wilde's club on which he had written, "To Oscar Wilde posing Somdomite" [sic]. The aim was to expose and humiliate Wilde among his friends. Wilde would have been better advised to tear up the card and treat it with amused triviality in the spirit of *The Importance of Being Earnest.* However, urged on by Bosie, he sued the Marquess of Queensberry for libel. This was a fatal mistake: Queensberry had for a long time employed detectives to follow Oscar and Bosie. By the time of the trial, a considerable number of male prostitutes and other men had given affadavits of having had sexual relations with Wilde. During the libel trial, Queensberry's defense was that the libel was true: Wilde was a homosexual. The jury decided against Wilde. As a result, a warrant of arrest was issued, and bravely if foolishly, Wilde declined to escape to France, as did most homosexual English aristocrats in flight from the police. Tried for sexual crimes, there was a hung jury; so he was tried again, found guilty, and sentenced to hard labor for two years.

In London, Wilde's crime and trial were the scandal of the decade, perhaps of the century. *An Ideal Husband* and *The Importance of Being Earnest*, both smash hits at first, were taken offstage, not to be revived for years. His name had become a dirty word, unmentionable. He was bankrupt. His wife divorced him. He was denied the chance to see his sons.

There were to be no more comedies from Oscar Wilde, but in prison he did write one more masterpiece, in the form of an immensely long letter to Lord Alfred Douglas, *De Profundis*. It is the autobiography of a disaster and a moving meditation on themes in the life of Jesus. Blame is mercilessly placed on Douglas, but love is expressed for him as well. After serving his sentence, Wilde was reunited with Douglas in Paris, where, writing no more, he died on November 30, 1900, evidently of an infection of the inner ear.

PLAYS: *Vera, or, The Nihilists* (1880); *The Duchess of Padua* (1883); *Lady Windermere's Fan* (1892); *Salomé* (1892); *A Woman of No Importance* (1893); *An Ideal Husband* (1895); *The Importance of Being Earnest* (1895)

FURTHER READING

Bloom, Harold, ed. *Oscar Wilde*. New York: Chelsea, 1985.

Ellmann, Richard. *Oscar Wilde*. New York: Knopf, 1988.

Gagnier, Regenia, ed. *Critical Essays on Oscar Wilde*. New York: Maxwell Macmillan, 1991.

Knox, Melissa. *Oscar Wilde: A Long and Lovely Suicide*. New Haven, Conn.: Yale Univ. Press, 1994.

Powell, Kerry. *Oscar Wilde and the Theatre of the 1890s*. Cambridge: Cambridge Univ. Press, 1990.

Adrian Frazier

WILDER, THORNTON (1897–1975)

Imaginative narration—the invention of souls and destinies—is to a philosopher an all but indefensible activity.

—Thornton Wilder, "Some Thoughts on Playwriting," 1941

The literary reputation of Thornton Wilder has not diminished in the decades since his death. His writings inject a calm yet stirring nostalgia unique to itself. His young life enveloped a far bigger world than most of his peers. Wilder was born in Madison, Wisconsin, on April 17, 1897. When he was eight years old, his family moved from the midwestern UNITED STATES to Hong Kong, where his father served as American consul general (1906–1908). After only six months in CHINA, Wilder was sent to school in California. In 1911 he returned to China, where he attended an English mission school at Chefoo. In 1912 Wilder attended Berkeley High School in California. From 1915 to 1917 he attended Oberlin College, where he wrote for the *Oberlin Literary Magazine*. In 1917 he transferred to his father's alma mater, Yale, where he published short plays and essays in the *Yale Literary Magazine*. In 1918 he served for a year in the Coast Artillery. He returned to Yale, earning his bachelor of arts degree in 1920. In 1920–1921 he spent ten months in Rome at the American Academy while beginning *The Cabala*, which the *New York Times* praised for its exquisite prose and "its jewels of charming observation and felicitous expression." From 1921 to 1928, Wilder

taught French at Lawrenceville School in New Jersey. Wilder earned his master's degree from Princeton University in 1926.

In 1927 the American Laboratory Theatre produced his play *The Trumpet Shall Sound*; but it was his 1928 Pulitzer Prize–winning novel *The Bridge of San Luis Rey* that made him a bestselling author. This skillful novel interlaces the personalities of one story in the destinies of another. Wilder's newly earned wealth allowed him to stop teaching and devote all of his energies to his writing. He bought a house in Connecticut for himself and his mother and culled from a group of previously written short plays *The Angel that Troubled the Waters* (1928). While traveling in Europe, he began writing *The Woman of Andros*. He taught at the University of Chicago from 1930 to 1936, while also writing Hollywood movie scripts. He adapted André Obey's *The Rape of Lucréce* (*Le Viol de Lucréce*). In 1935 Wilder's novel *Heaven's My Destination* was published, and by 1937 he completed his adaptation of HENRIK IBSEN'S A DOLL'S HOUSE.

In 1938 OUR TOWN opened on a Boston stage to poor reviews. Despite that, the show moved to New York, where it was a smashing success, earning Wilder his second Pulitzer Prize, making him the first writer to receive this award for both literature and drama. *Our Town* celebrated the miracles of birth, death, and the human spirit of American small-town life. In December 1938 *The Merchant of Yonkers* debuted but closed after three weeks. Four years later, Wilder wrote an Alfred Hitchcock movie, *The Shadow of a Doubt*.

In 1942 he enlisted in the air force where, despite very poor eyesight, he was commissioned a captain. While in the service, Wilder's 1942 smash hit THE SKIN OF OUR TEETH earned him the 1943 Pulitzer Prize in Drama. This fantastic parable deals with mankind's age-long struggle to achieve civilization. More shockingly controversial than the play were the accusations of Joseph Campbell and H. M. Robinson that Wilder had plagiarized from James Joyce's *Finnegan's Wake* (1939). This seems as absurd as accusing Arthur Laurents (*West Side Story*) of plagiarizing from *Romeo and Juliet*, or GEORGE BERNARD SHAW in PYGMALION of stealing from Ovid's *Metamorphoses*. Nevertheless, Wilder graciously acknowledged that he was "deeply indebted" to Joyce. About *The Skin of Our Teeth* Wilder states, "It was written on the eve of our entrance into the war and under strong emotion." This influential and vital drama has profoundly contributed to the American stage.

During World War II, Wilder served in AFRICA, ITALY, and the United States until September 1945. His 1948 novel *The Ides of March* centers on the assassination of Julius Caesar. Wilder then reworked *The Merchant of Yonkers*, a play based on Johann Nestroy's *He'll Have Himself a Good Time* (*Einen Jux will es sich Machen*, 1842), in turn based on John Oxenford's *A Day Well Spent* (1835). Newly titled, *The Matchmaker* (1954) was made into a motion picture in 1958 and later adapted in 1964 as the musical COMEDY *Hello Dolly!*—which was filmed in 1969.

At the Edinburgh Festival *The Alcestiad* was produced in 1955. *The Long Christmas Dinner*, a one-act play, was converted into an opera, performed at Mannheim in German in 1961, as was *The Alcestiad* in 1962. That same year three new one-act plays in two forms, *The Seven Deadly Sins* and *The Seven Ages of Man*, opened in New York. In 1967, Wilder published his longest novel, *The Eighth Day*. The title refers to a midwestern, 20th-century murder in which the falsely accused man (John Ashley) escapes. Wilder's last published work *Theophilus North* (1973) is a novel about the development of an artist (loosely based on Joyce's autobiographical novel *A Portrait of the Artist as a Young Man*, 1916). Theophilus explores nine career choices before realizing that being a writer incorporates all nine professions.

Wilder died of a heart attack in Hamden, Connecticut, on December 7, 1975, while living with his devoted sister Isabel, also a writer. He authored seven novels, many essays, scholarly articles, movie scripts, shorter works, and dozens of plays.

Wilder fashioned narrative prose into a physical medium harvested of the intellectual and chimerical. Wilder had an optimistic attitude about life and a genuine interest in people, especially the common person whose fibers are sinuous. Wilder's novels and plays vividly summon forth an often forgotten era in a style that is unique and incandescent. His themes are thoroughly human and impeccably simple. Paradoxically, they can only achieve their pricelessness when they are contrasted with the massive unimaginable events of history. It is only against such a background that the full individuality and poignancies of our personal microcosms become evident. His dramatic trademark involved creating extraordinarily stark sets where the individual stands out. Trivial people and events take on great relevance in Wilder's writings. Too often our lives involve misguided passions that are frequently sterile, self-seeking, and false. Wilder intermingles the serious with the comic, the sentimental with the harsh. His writings pay eloquent homage to the human race despite man's and nature's destructive powers, ignorance, follies, and shortcomings.

SELECT PLAYS: *The Trumpet Shall Sound* (1927); *The Angel that Troubled the Waters and Other Plays* (1928); *The Long Christmas Dinner and Other Plays* (1931); *Lucréce* (from a play by André Obey, 1932); *A Doll's House* (from a play by Ibsen, 1937); *The Merchant of Yonkers* (from a play by Johann Nestroy, 1938; revised as *The Matchmaker*, 1954); *Our Town* (1938); *The Skin of Our Teeth* (1942); *The Victors* (from a play by Sartre, 1949); *A Life in the Sun* (1955, published as *The Alcestiad* with *The Drunken Sisters: A Satyr Play*, 1977); *Plays for Bleecker Street* (1962)

FURTHER READING

Goldstein, Malcolm. *The Art of Thornton Wilder*. Lincoln: Univ. of Nebraska Press, 1965.

Haberman, Donald. *The Plays of Thornton Wilder: A Critical Study*. Middletown: Wesleyan Univ. Press, 1967.

Wilson, Edmund. *The Shores of Light*. Boston: Northeastern Univ. Press, 1952.

Meg Walters

WILLEMS, PAUL (1912–1997)

Paul Willems, the son of well-known Belgian novelist Marie Gevers, was born in 1912 in Edegem, BELGIUM, and lived his entire life in the family château, Missembourg, south of Antwerp. His family was of the old French-language bourgeoisie of Flanders, a breed that slowly but surely had become a vestigial appendage. Having done his studies in law, Willems was for many years the director of the Palais de Beaux Arts in Brussels, the principal performing arts center of the European capital. In addition to being a celebrated playwright, he wrote novels and short stories. He died in 1997 in Edegem.

Heir to the DRAMATURGY of his compatriots MAURICE MAETERLINCK, FERNAND CROMMELYNCK, and MICHEL DE GHELDERODE, his is an idiom of fantasy, dreams, and fables. At times one has the feeling that the dream world has broken in on the waking one or that there is no escape from a dream. While his theater may at first glance seem saccharine, particularly with his enormous hit *It's Raining in My House* (*Il pleut dans ma maison*, 1958), closer examination reveals a thick layer of grotesquerie, cynicism, feelings of loss, frustration, cruelty, and futility.

His early play *Mr. Nuche's Fine Wine* (*Le bon vin de m. Nuche*, 1949) is a love story about a pathetically cliché and fear-driven middle-class couple, the Nuches, who attempt to keep their adolescent daughter, Isabelle, safe from the possibility of love, a plan that backfires. Her natural drives triumph, as she falls in love with the very person her parents had thought was "safe" and whom they put over her as her minder. The COMEDY is replete with all the charm of a JEAN GIRAUDOUX or JEAN ANHOUILH bauble, such as *Ring Around the Moon*.

Life in a bubble is a recurring image in the Willems canon. The bubble may be a social barrier created by parents attempting to keep their daughter chaste as in *Mr. Nuche's Fine Wine* or one constructed by parents conniving to marry their daughter off to an aged, wealthy pretendant, as in *The Sailing City* (*La ville à voile*, 1967). But the bubble may also be a buffer from life's cruel realizations. A dotty family in *It's Raining in My House* is hiding out in their house with the leaking roof, surrounded by an extensive, overgrown, and neglected terrain. Their amiable world has its own logic, nicer and kinder than that outside their walls, and one in which all the potential suffering life holds has no part, including the menace of passing time. All interlopers forget their pragmatic purposes and fall prey to the household's aimless charm.

Reminiscent of Ghelderode and Maeterlinck, Willems's *The Weight of the Snow* (*Warna ou le poids de la neige*, 1962) is set in a medieval castle replete with a moat. Outside the plague is raging and has claimed the vast majority of the populace. Inside the middle-aged Countess Warna is keeping her consort Ernevelde in a velvet prison. The dangers outside the castle walls are too great to brave, but staying inside pursuing an unvarying routine with the domineering Warna whose love is suffocating has become intolerable. When Ernevelde ultimately attempts a getaway, Warna orders her minions to destroy a dangerous bear on the loose and has him shot. She opts to kill her coveted love, rather than suffer him living away from her.

Willems's late play *The Brief Life* (*La vita breve*, 1991) takes place on a ship, a bubble floating on an endless sea, in which fantasies promise to be realized but are disappointed. Josty, an aged roué suffering from an incurable disease, is attempting to arrest his doom by reviving his experience of young love with the sacrificial virgin, Anne-Marie. In this project, he overlooks Mesdemoiselles, a middle-aged companion, who would be more appropriate. The atmosphere in this play is even more surreal or Felliniesque than usual.

The more somber *She Confused Sleeping and Dying* (*Elle disait dormir pour mourir*, 1983) depicts the life of a woman whose father, to protect her from the war that is raging, has deposited his daughter in the House on the Marsh, a refuge meant to be unattainable from the dangerous outside world. Again, the heroine is trapped in a time bubble, one that is meant to protect her but that also arrests her development.

PLAYS: *Lamentable Julie* (1949); *Mr. Nuche's Fine Wine* (*Le bon vin de m. Nuche*, 1949); *Skin of the Bear* (*Peau d'ours*, 1951); *Tender and Barbarous Melody* (*Air barbare et tendre*, 1952); *Off and the Moon* (*Off et la lune*, 1954); *It's Raining in My House* (*Il pleut dans ma maison*, 1958); *Eel Beach* (*La plage aux anguilles*, 1959); *The Weight of the Snow* (*Warna ou le poids de la neige*, 1962); *The Early Morning Market* (*Le marché des petites heures*, 1964); *The Sailing City* (*La ville à voile*, 1967); *The Sun on the Sea* (*Le soleil sur la mer*, 1970); *The Mirrors of Ostend* (*Les miroirs d'Ostende*, 1974); *Night with Colored Shadows* (*Nuit avec ombres en couleurs*, 1983); *She Confused Sleeping and Dying* (*Elle disait dormir pour mourir*, 1983); *The Brief Life* (*La vita breve*, 1989); *Marceline* (1995)

FURTHER READING

Dieckman, Suzanne Burgoyne, ed. *Four Plays of Paul Willems*. New York: Garland, 1992.

Freidman, Donald Flanell, and Suzanne Burgoyne, eds. *Paul Willems' The Drowned Land and La Vita Breve*. New York: P. Lang, 1994.

Glasheen, Anne-Marie, ed. *Gambit, 42–43: Four Belgian Playwrights*. London: John Calder, 1986.

Van de Kerckhove, Fabrice, ed. *Paul Willems, L'enchanteur* [Paul Willems, the Enchanter]. New York: P. Lang, 2002.

David Paul Willinger

WILLIAMS, EMLYN (1905–1987)

George Emlyn Williams was born on November 26, 1905, in Flintshire, north Wales. At school he received particular encouragement from one teacher: Miss Cooke, the model for Miss Moffat in his best-known play THE CORN IS GREEN (1938). Coached by Miss Cooke, Williams was entered for an Open Scholarship at Christs Church, Oxford, which, to his surprise, he won. The transition from Flintshire to Oxford was extremely disorientating. However, Williams soon found himself relatively comfortable in this alien but intriguing world. He was less than absorbed by academic work but developed a conviction that his future lay in the theater. He became a member of the Oxford University Dramatic Society in 1924 and chose the professional name Emlyn Williams. ACTING stimulated Williams to write his own dramas. His obsession with theater and his disinterest in formal study combined with a brief love affair with another Oxford student led to a nervous breakdown. He returned home to recover. There, he quickly wrote a play called *Full Moon*, which was accepted for production in 1927 at the Oxford Playhouse by J. B. Fagan. Shortly afterward, Williams left his family home after an argument and caught a train to London. Fagan, the producer of *Full Moon*, arranged for him to take a walk-on part in his own play about Samuel Pepys, *And So to Bed*. Fagan thus launched Williams as playwright and actor. Immediately, Williams set to work on both aspects of his career. While acting, he wrote two new plays, *Glamour* (1929) and *A Murder Has Been Arranged* (1930).

In 1931 *A Murder Has Been Arranged* was given a single evening performance at the Strand Theatre, London. Reviewers were astonished by the originality of the piece: though in the relatively familiar form of the thriller, its setting in an allegedly haunted theater had a capacity genuinely to terrify audiences, with its sustained and increasingly intense atmosphere. The next day, eleven theaters made offers for the play. This was the turning point of Williams's career as dramatist, bringing him reputation and much-needed income. Over the next two decades Williams wrote some twelve further plays, mainly in a thriller or historical mode. His plays were very much well-made dramas and did not engage in MODERNIST experiment, but they were nevertheless original and serious.

Though they have largely not survived in the modern repertoire, all of his plays were effective and original, with a fluent command of theatrical devices and of dialogue. His best remembered plays are the thriller *Night Must Fall* (1935) and his most autobiographical play, *The Corn Is Green* (1938). *He Was Born Gay* (1937), a play about the exiled Louis XVII living in exile in Dover (and about the various imposters who claim to be the king) is a further good, if neglected, example of his work. Williams was also very well known for his one-man stage shows about DYLAN THOMAS and Charles Dickens. He died on September 25, 1987, in London, leaving a reputation as a talented dramatist and a distinguished actor in film and onstage.

PLAYS: *Vigil* (1926); *Full Moon* (1927); *Glamour* (1929); *A Murder Has Been Arranged* (1930); *Port Said* (1931); *Spring, 1600* (1934); *Night Must Fall* (1935); *He Was Born Gay* (1937); *The Corn Is Green* (1938); *The Druid's Rest* (1944); *The Winds of Heaven* (1945); *Trespass* (1947); *Accolade* (1950); *Someone Waiting* (1953)

FURTHER READING

Dale-Jones, Don. *Emlyn Williams*. Cardiff: Univ. of Wales Press and Welsh Arts Council, 1979.

Harding, James. *Emlyn Williams: A Life*. London: Weidenfield & Nicolson, 1993.

Stokes, Sewell. "Emlyn Williams." *Theatre Arts* 26 (1942): 697–705.

Williams, Emlyn. *George: An Early Autobiography.* London: Hamish Hamilton, 1961.

———. *Emlyn.* London: Penguin, 1976.

Chris Hopkins

WILLIAMS, TENNESSEE (1911–1983)

Tennessee Williams does not accuse; he describes. The social atmosphere of his plays is dramatized through characters in whom the social disorientation is mirrored in the frustrations of their love life. This is not the same thing as an obsession with sex: sex in Williams is the focal area at which the deeper trauma reveals itself. . . . The half-light in which Williams' stage seems to be plunged, as if he were writing of secret places of half-sinful and half-sacred sentiments, gives his plays their theatrical glow and appeal. There is a romantic mysteriousness in Williams' treatment of his characters, as if he took a peculiar pleasure in sharing the shadowy world in which they dwell. He is no stranger to their plight.

—Harold Clurman, "A Playwright's Symposium," 1969

Generally regarded as the foremost American dramatist of the post–World War II era, Tennessee Williams was a theatrical innovator equaled only by EUGENE O'NEILL. Honored with two Pulitzer Prizes (*A STREETCAR NAMED DESIRE*, and *CAT ON A HOT TIN ROOF*), Williams's poetic, often impressionistic, character-driven dramas probed repressed tensions and sexual confusions that occasionally shocked mid-20th-century audiences unaccustomed to the frankness and intense emotions characteristic of Williams. His plays initiated a period of renewed energy and excitement to post–World War II American drama, inspiring theatrical artists in both form and content.

EARLY CAREER, 1911–1944

Thomas Lanier Williams was born in 1911 in Columbus, Mississippi, to Cornelius Coffin ("C. C.") and Edwina Estelle (Dakin) Williams. His father was a traveling shoe salesman who ridiculed young Tom, a sickly and effeminate child who preferred books to sports. Williams's mother was the domineering, overprotective daughter of an Episcopalian minister, Walter Dakin, and she would provide a model for several of Williams's greatest dramatic characters, most particularly Amanda Wingfield of THE GLASS MENAGERIE. The marriage of Williams's parents was an unhappy one, and their frequent arguments deeply affected Williams and his sensitive sister, Rose. Much of his childhood was spent in various rectories where his grandfather presided.

Deeply interested in literature, Williams particularly admired the writing of D. H. LAWRENCE and ANTON CHEKHOV, both of whom he frequently acknowledged as significant influences on his own work. Williams achieved modest successes as a writer beginning in his teen years. He won third place ($5) in a national essay contest on the question "Can a good wife be a good sport?"

promoted by *The Smart Set* magazine in 1927. He also won a prize for a review of the Barbara Stanwyck film *Stella Dallas*. In 1928, Williams published a short story, "The Vengeance of Nitocris," in *Weird Tales*. The following year, he entered the University of Missouri, where attending a production of HENRIK IBSEN'S *GHOSTS* whetted his appetite to write for the stage. In 1930 Williams completed a one-act play, *Beauty Is the Word*, which won honorable mention from the University's Dramatic Arts Club, the first time such an honor was given to a freshman. Williams's education was abruptly interrupted by his father's insistence that he leave school to take a job as a typist at the International Shoe Company, a miserable experience he later chronicled in *The Glass Menagerie*. An even more significant trauma resulted from news of the deteriorating mental condition of his sister.

While working in St. Louis at the factory job, Williams enrolled in the University of Missouri at Columbia's School of Journalism. He managed to complete three years of college, but when he flunked ROTC training, his father compelled him to give up school once again and return to work at the shoe factory. Despite his dreary job, Williams continued to write. In 1933 his short story "Stella for Star" won first place in the St. Louis Writers Guild contest. When he collapsed from exhaustion resulting from his unhappiness at the shoe company, Williams spent the summer of 1935 with his grandparents in Memphis, Tennessee. There he wrote *Cairo! Shanghai! Bombay!*—his first play to be staged in a production by an amateur troupe in Memphis. In the fall of 1935 Williams returned to St. Louis and audited courses at Washington University. The following year, he was admitted to the university and worked on two plays, *Candles to the Sun* and *The Fugitive Kind*, both of which were produced early in 1937 by a St. Louis community troupe called the Mummers. With the financial support of his grandparents, Williams completed his education at the University of Iowa, where he studied playwriting with E. C. Mabie and E. P. Conkle. In that period he experimented with a "living newspaper" drama and completed another play, *Spring Storm* (1937), which was not well received when read to his playwriting class in early 1938. Graduating with a bachelor of arts degree in English in 1938, Williams returned to St. Louis in hopes that the Mummers might produce *Spring Storm*. When they refused, he commenced work on *Not About Nightingales* (1938), a drama inspired by newspaper accounts of inmates suffocated in a steam room at a Pennsylvania prison.

Finding little support for his work in St. Louis, Williams moved to New Orleans, where he was initially unsettled by the permissive sexual attitudes of its citizens. Williams eventually found the New Orleans environment comfortable as he slowly accepted his own homosexuality. During this time he supported himself as a waiter and continued to write, taking the first name "Tennessee" in acknowledgment of the prominence of his father's family in Tennessee history. The name change initiated an acceleration of his career: Williams engaged Audrey Wood as his agent, and she successfully placed his short story "The Field of

Blue Children" in *Story* magazine, his first published work under the name "Tennessee Williams." An important theatrical break came in 1939 when he won a $1,000 grant from the Rockefeller Foundation, which allowed him to polish his newest drama, *The Battle of Angels* (1940), and to move to New York, where he studied at ERWIN PISCATOR's Drama Workshop at the New School for Social Research. He also spent some time in Provincetown, Massachusetts, the setting for one of his last plays, the autobiographical *Something Cloudy, Something Clear* (1981). In Provincetown, Williams met and became romantically involved with a dancer named Kip Kiernan, the first significant homosexual relationship of his life.

The *Battle of Angels* went into production starring Miriam Hopkins under the direction of Margaret Webster, trying out in Boston in late December 1940. The ineffective production never made it to Broadway, closing in Boston in early January 1941. The THEATRE GUILD advanced Williams financial support to rewrite *The Battle of Angels* but ultimately rejected his revised script. Later that year, supporting himself as a cashier in a New Orleans restaurant, Williams completed a new play, *Stairs to the Roof* (1941). He worked on several projects during the subsequent two years, but he was devastated when his sister Rose was subjected to a frontal lobotomy at his mother's insistence in January 1943.

In New York, Williams found employment as an elevator operator, bellhop, and movie theater usher while living at the Young Men's Christian Association (YMCA). He returned to St. Louis to work on adapting his short story "Portrait of a Girl in Glass" to dramatic form, calling it *The Gentleman Caller*. Audrey Wood secured him a $250 a week position as a screenwriter for Metro-Goldwyn-Mayer. Unhappy with his assignments working on scripts for Lana Turner and child star Margaret O'Brien, Williams instead continued to polish *The Gentleman Caller*. When he submitted the script to his superiors, he was summarily fired for failing to fulfill the assignments he had been given.

Compounding this setback, in early 1944 Williams was distressed by the deaths of his grandmother Dakin and Kip Kiernan, who succumbed to a brain tumor. With a $1,000 grant from the American Academy of Arts and Letters, Williams retreated to Provincetown to complete *The Gentleman Caller*, renaming it *The Glass Menagerie*. The play, which was filled with autobiographical elements, was produced in Chicago in late December 1944, featuring a cast of four: Eddie Dowling, Julie Haydon, Anthony Ross, and the legendary stage star Laurette Taylor, who scored a personal triumph in the role of Amanda Wingfield, a character modeled on Williams's mother. A "memory play" narrated by Williams's alter ego Tom Wingfield, *The Glass Menagerie* explores the troubled relationship of Amanda with her two adult children, Tom and Laura. Laura is a delicate, hypersensitive creature clearly modeled on Williams's sister Rose. Laura retreats into an imaginary world of glass figurines, while Amanda plots ways to find her a "gentleman caller" who, she hopes, will secure Laura's future. Amanda also retreats into her own imaginary world,

recalling her past as a flirtatious Southern belle. Tom dreams of escaping his factory job to become a writer but feels obligated to support his mother and sister. Amanda nags Tom to bring a young man to meet Laura. When he does, Amanda's hopes are dashed when it turns out that the young man is engaged to another girl. Amanda and Tom argue bitterly, and Tom leaves, but he explains that despite geographic distance and the passage of time, he cannot put the memory of his sister out of his mind. After a successful run in Chicago, the play moved to Broadway, and most critics recognized it as a masterpiece and its author as a promising new voice in American drama. *The Glass Menagerie* won the New York Drama Critics' Circle Award and was filmed (for the first of four times) in 1950. The commercial success of *The Glass Menagerie* alleviated Williams's immediate financial needs, allowing him to focus full-time on his writing.

BROADWAY AND BEYOND, 1945–1960

As *The Glass Menagerie* ran triumphantly on Broadway, Williams continued a collaboration with a friend, Donald Windham, on a stage adaptation of a D. H. Lawrence story, *You Touched Me!* (1945), but it won only lukewarm response from critics and audiences. Following eye surgery, Williams went to MEXICO to recover and worked on a new play, initially titled *The Moth*. Renamed *Blanche's Chair in the Moon* and then *The Poker Night*, it eventually became *A Streetcar Named Desire*, a drama that consolidated his predominance among the newest generation of playwrights. A searing, lyrical drama illuminating the mental disintegration of the deeply troubled Blanche DuBois, *A Streetcar Named Desire* was optioned for production by Irene Selznick. At this time, Williams also worked on a new play, *Chart of Anatomy*, which would evolve into SUMMER AND SMOKE (1948), and he began work on a long one-act, *Ten Blocks on the Camino Real*, which he subsequently revised as CAMINO REAL for a Broadway production in 1953.

Directed by Elia Kazan in 1947, the cast of *A Streetcar Named Desire* was led by Jessica Tandy, whose acclaimed performance as Blanche exposed the complexities of a character at once fragile and strong, sensitive and cruel, damaged and poetic. Marlon Brando, in a star-making performance as the brutish Stanley Kowalski, Blanche's brother-in-law, also won acclaim. Blanche is horrified that her younger sister, Stella, has married a man she regards as beneath her social class. The passionate sexual bond between Stanley and Stella disturbs Blanche, and she is horrified when she learns that Stella is pregnant. Stanley's co-worker, Mitch, a gentle man attracted to Blanche's sensitivity and charm, courts her. When Blanche admits that Belle Reve, the family home, has been lost because of catastrophic expenses in caring for dying family members, Stanley secretly contacts a friend in Blanche's hometown and learns that she has been sexually promiscuous and was fired from her high school teaching job for becoming inappropriately involved with a student. Blanche is also haunted by the memory of her young husband, Alan, who killed himself when Blanche caught him in bed with a man. The animosity between Stanley and Blanche comes to a head when Stanley sexually assaults Blanche while Stella is in the hospital following the birth of her baby. Unhinged by this trauma, Blanche cannot convince Stella of the rape, and with nowhere to turn, the desperate Blanche falls victim to Stanley once again as he arranges for her to be institutionalized. This profoundly disturbing drama was awarded the 1948 Pulitzer Prize, the New York Drama Critics' Circle Award, and numerous other honors, and it was subsequently filmed with its original stage cast (which also included Karl Malden as Mitch and Kim Hunter as Stella) under Kazan's direction. Vivien Leigh, in an Academy Award–winning performance as Blanche (Malden and Hunter also won Oscars), replaced Tandy on screen, but Brando again played Stanley, and his performance launched him as one of the iconic stars of Hollywood films. A Streetcar Named Desire has been revived frequently, and there have been at least two other screen versions.

Among its many legacies, A Streetcar Named Desire explored sexuality at a level of frankness previously unseen in the American theater. Its inclusion of homosexual elements subtly acknowledged Williams's own conflicted feelings about his homosexuality. Stability was brought to his life at this time when he met Frank Merlo in 1948 and began a long-term relationship that ended when Merlo died of lung cancer in 1961. Merlo was central to Williams's life during his most productive and successful years as a dramatist, which, most critics acknowledge, began a precipitous decline about the time of Merlo's death.

Williams completed Summer and Smoke in late 1947, and it was produced in Dallas, Texas, under the direction of Margo Jones. Its 1948 New York production featured Margaret Phillips in the leading role of Alma Winemiller, a sexually repressed, small-town woman who finds liberation without redemption. The production was received respectfully if unenthusiastically by critics and audiences. Williams himself felt the production was inadequate, and he continued to revise Summer and Smoke over the course of nearly twenty years before it was produced again under the title Eccentricities of a Nightingale in the 1960s. Concerned for his sister's well-being, Williams arranged for her to receive half of the royalties of Summer and Smoke (he had done the same for his mother with the royalties of The Glass Menagerie). By 1949, Williams was beginning to fall victim to substance abuse, depending heavily on drugs and alcohol, but he continued to busy himself with new projects. These included his first novella, The Roman Spring of Mrs. Stone, which was published in 1950, and a new play, The Rose Tattoo, produced on Broadway in 1951 by Cheryl Crawford. Williams bought a house in Key West, and he also spent part of 1950 in Sicily attempting to pick up the local dialects for The Rose Tattoo, a robust play about the painful relationship of a proud Italian widow and a truck driver, played in the original Broadway production by Maureen Stapleton and Eli Wallach. The play won the Tony Award as Best Play that year, but Williams continued to abuse alcohol and drugs. After several attempts to find

a suitable environment for his sister, Williams settled Rose at Stony Lodge in Ossining, New York, where she lived for most of her remaining life.

Williams was pleased in 1952 when José Quintero staged a successful revival of Summer and Smoke at New York's Circle in the Square Theatre, starring Geraldine Page (who later appeared in the 1961 film version of the play). While working on a screenplay, "Hide and Seek," that would evolve into the controversial film Baby Doll, released in 1956, he completed his revision of Ten Blocks on the Camino Real as Camino Real. It was produced in New York in March 1953 to scathing reviews and a quick commercial failure. Williams was devastated by the response to this complex play that brought together a host of literary and mythical figures—Don Quixote, Casanova, Marguerite Gautier, Marcel Proust's Baron de Charlus, Kilroy—in a phantasmagoric setting in which the fragile and damaged beings of the world struggle to survive its harsh realities. Williams believed strongly in the play's worth and was proud of its ambition, points he made when he defended it against its critics in an essay published in the New York Times on March 15, 1953. In spite of its initial failure, Camino Real has continued to interest theatrical artists and perplex critics and audiences through revivals, television productions, and a proposed film version as yet unmade.

In 1953, Williams wrote "Man Bring This Up Road," a short story he later transformed into The Milk Train Doesn't Stop Here Anymore (1963). He also revised The Battle of Angels as Orpheus Descending, but it was not produced until 1957. Much of 1954 was spent on his next major project, Cat on a Hot Tin Roof. Elia Kazan, who had directed the original production of A Streetcar Named Desire, as well as its 1951 film version, was selected as director of Cat on a Hot Tin Roof, in which a Mississippi Delta family battles over the estate of its dying patriarch, Big Daddy. Williams focused the drama's attention on Brick, Big Daddy's son, a former athlete who has slipped into alcoholism. Trapped in his bedroom with a broken leg, Brick must face his former beauty queen wife, Maggie, who wants Brick to return to her bed. He is, however, struggling with doubts about his sexuality. Was his close relationship with his now-deceased teammate Skipper latently homosexual? Confronted by Big Daddy, Brick rejects the "mendacity" around him, including the machinations of his brother, Gooper, to become Big Daddy's heir. Painfully, Brick reveals the secret that the old man is dying of cancer. In the play's final act, Big Daddy comes to acceptance of his fate and urges Brick to get past his own struggles. When Maggie tells Big Daddy that she is expecting a child, Big Daddy makes it clear that Brick will inherit his fortune. Brick, moved by the comfort this lie has given Big Daddy, returns to Maggie's bed, where they intend to make their deception into a reality.

Cat on a Hot Tin Roof opened on Broadway on March 24, 1955, and scored a triumph with critics and audiences, winning the Pulitzer Prize for Drama, as well as the Drama Critics' Circle Award. Despite believing he was suffering from writer's block,

Williams was heartened by the reception of *Cat on a Hot Tin Roof*, as well as good reviews for the 1955 screen version of *The Rose Tattoo*, starring Anna Magnani (the celebrated Italian actress who had become one of Williams's close friends) and Burt Lancaster.

Williams completed the screenplay for *Baby Doll* in 1955, and it was filmed under the direction of Elia Kazan, starring Carroll Baker and Eli Wallach. The Catholic Church's Legion of Decency denounced *Baby Doll*'s unprecedented sexuality, and the subsequent controversy distressed Williams, although it helped make *Baby Doll* one of the most-talked-about films of 1956. During this turmoil Williams began work on a new play, *The Enemy: Time*. As he revised it over a two-year period, Williams changed its title to *Sweet Bird of Youth*. Meanwhile, 1957 brought a production of *Orpheus Descending* under the direction of Harold Clurman, but it received generally negative reviews and closed after a two-month run. Williams continued to treat his increasing depression with alcohol and drugs, as well as psychotherapy, but to little avail. During 1957, Williams also began work on SUDDENLY LAST SUMMER, a long one-act play about a battle of wills between Mrs. Venable, the imperious mother of a recently deceased poet, Sebastian, and her niece, Catherine Holly, who has witnessed Sebastian's death. Cannibalized by a mob of young men he had sexually exploited, Sebastian's horrific end leads his mother to attempt to have Catherine lobotomized so that her account of events will not prevail. A sympathetic surgeon draws the frightening story out of Catherine as Mrs. Venable sinks into madness. Produced OFF-BROADWAY on a double-bill titled *Garden District*, *Suddenly Last Summer* won critical approval. A film version was initiated, and under the direction of Joseph Mankiewicz, a stellar cast including Katharine Hepburn, Elizabeth Taylor, and Montgomery Clift was assembled. With a screenplay by Williams and his friend, Gore Vidal, the film version of *Suddenly Last Summer* was a success in 1959, as the screen adaptation of *Cat on a Hot Tin Roof* had been a year earlier, despite the fact that the filmmakers felt compelled to delete homosexual references from the script.

In early 1959, *Sweet Bird of Youth* was produced on Broadway under Elia Kazan's direction. Starring Geraldine Page and Paul Newman, its tale of a young hustler and a fading actress who use each other failed to interest most critics. Newman's screen popularity helped keep the play running, but Williams was disappointed by its critical failure. In 1960, Williams and Merlo journeyed to Key West where Williams completed two new plays, NIGHT OF THE IGUANA and *Period of Adjustment*. Merlo became ill with the cancer that would kill him within a year, and that situation, coupled with the tepid response to *Period of Adjustment* on Broadway, made for a distressing year. The only good news was the success of *The Fugitive Kind*, a screen version of *Orpheus Descending*, which starred Anna Magnani and Marlon Brando.

FRAGILE YEARS, 1961–1972

Williams sank further into depression in the early 1960s, believing that his skills as a writer were fading. At the end of 1961, *Night of the Iguana* opened on Broadway with a strong cast led by screen star Bette Davis, Margaret Leighton, and Patrick O'Neal. The play, a touching, nearly plotless drama about the search for spiritual redemption and the longing for various forms of freedom, won the Drama Critics' Circle Award. Williams was also recognized with a lifetime membership in the American Academy of Arts and Letters. He journeyed to the Spoleto Festival of Two Worlds in ITALY to see the premiere of *The Milk Train Doesn't Stop Here Anymore* but rushed back to the UNITED STATES when he learned that Merlo was fatally ill. *The Milk Train Doesn't Stop Here Anymore* managed only two months on Broadway beginning in January 1963, but Williams revised the play for a revival in early 1964. Preparations were interrupted when Merlo died of lung cancer in September 1963. After Merlo's funeral, a deeply depressed Williams traveled to Mexico to observe filming of the screen version of *Night of the Iguana*, directed by John Huston and starring Richard Burton, Deborah Kerr, and Ava Gardner.

Williams's depression was not helped by the mere three performances that the revised version of *The Milk Train Doesn't Stop Here Anymore* managed, despite a strong cast including Tallulah Bankhead, Tab Hunter, Ruth Ford, and Marian Seldes. To deal with his depressed state, Williams consulted Dr. Max Jacobson, the notorious "Dr. Feelgood," who provided Williams with a flow of drugs that undermined his health and mental condition. He later referred to this period as the "Stoned Age."

Despite his fragile state, Williams continued to write, working on a bill of two short plays, *The Gnädiges Fräulein* and *The Mutilated*, under the title *Slapstick Tragedy*. In late 1964 the film version of *Night of the Iguana* opened to positive reviews, as did a Broadway revival of *The Glass Menagerie* starring Maureen Stapleton. *The Milk Train Doesn't Stop Here Anymore* was revived again, this time in San Francisco, and it won positive critical response, while Williams also completed *The Eccentricities of a Nightingale*, his revision of *Summer and Smoke*.

When *Slapstick Tragedy* opened in New York in January 1966, it closed after only four performances. This distressing failure was only slightly assuaged by the moderate success of *This Property Is Condemned*, a film adaptation of one of Williams's early one-act plays. He worked on a screenplay of *The Milk Train Doesn't Stop Here Anymore*, which was filmed in 1967 in Sardinia with a stellar cast including Elizabeth Taylor, Richard Burton, and NOËL COWARD. Released under the title *Boom!*, it was not well received. In December 1967 a new Williams drama, *The Two-Character Play*, opened in London to a tepid critical response.

Williams continued to slide into an increased dependence on drugs. Considered mentally unstable by friends and family members, Williams continued to write and involve himself in productions of his plays. In February 1968, his *Kingdom of Earth* opened in Philadelphia, with a cast featuring Harry Guardino, Estelle Parsons, and Brian Bedford, prior to a Broadway opening on March 27, 1968, under a new title, *The Seven Descents of Myrtle*. Critics were not kind, and the play ran barely a month. For much of the rest of 1968, Williams worked on a revision of *The Two-Character Play* and a new play, *In the Bar of a Tokyo Hotel*, but his mental condition continued to disintegrate due to his addictions. He retreated to Key West, where his younger brother, Dakin, came and participated in Williams's conversion to Catholicism, although Williams later denied he had agreed to the conversion.

Despite his declining physical and mental state, Williams spent mid-1969 in New York, where he took over the direction of *In the Bar of a Tokyo Hotel*, but he was unable to save it. When the play opened on May 11, 1969, critics were unanimous in their condemnation, most viewing the play as a confused rehashing of old themes. Williams faced this sort of critical condemnation through the remainder of his career. Given that Williams became increasingly open about his homosexuality and that the plays often dealt with an exploration of sex, critics may well have been unduly harsh in response. These later Williams plays are generally small in scale and scope than his pre-1960 plays—more in the style of chamber pieces. Critics clearly preferred Williams's more operatic works and, as such, found that the later plays seemed to be striving for less than Williams had earlier. In fact, the later plays demonstrate a dramatist whose gifts may be waning but one who continued to experiment in the areas of structure, language, and characterization, as he plunged more deeply into the themes of his earlier works. In the years following Williams's death, critics and scholars began a reexamination of these later plays with some finding that they are of greater worth than earlier critics found.

Although his new plays found no favor, Williams continued to receive honors for the body of his work, including the National Institute of Arts and Letters gold medal and an honorary degree from the University of Missouri at Columbia, where he had been a student. Shortly after the failure of *In the Bar of a Tokyo Hotel*, Williams traveled to JAPAN to see a production of *A Streetcar Named Desire*, but his drug use caused him an increasing number of paranoic attacks. Dakin finally succeeded in persuading his brother to seek medical help. At Barnes Hospital in St. Louis, Williams was placed in the mental ward where he endured seizures and two heart attacks as he went through a difficult withdrawal from drugs.

In December 1969, Williams had recovered sufficiently from drug withdrawal to seek comfort in familiar surroundings in Key West. A revival of *Camino Real*, featuring Jessica Tandy and Al Pacino, brought him to New York, where he appeared on David Frost's television show and openly discussed his homosexuality. He spent much of the rest of the year traveling throughout Asia. In early 1970 *Out Cry*, Williams's revision of *The Two-Character Play*, was produced in Chicago with Donald Madden and Eileen Herlie, but the results were less than satisfying. Transforming the two young characters of *Out Cry* into a middle-aged pair did little to help the work, and Williams's editing made the complicated play more difficult to grasp. Unfortunately, Williams fell back into drug use, and a renewed paranoia inspired him to fire his longtime agent, Audrey Wood. He continued to write, completing a new play, *Small Craft Warnings* (1971), a character-driven chamber drama about a diverse group of troubled individuals who each have an opportunity to reveal their inner struggles. It was first performed in Philadelphia in February 1972, followed by an off-Broadway run in April. Despite critical apathy, the production eked out a run, partly because Williams agreed to step into the cast in the role of the down-and-out "Doc" in an attempt to attract an audience.

THE FINAL DECADE, 1973–1983

Williams, who had vaguely socialist leanings (he had voted for Norman Thomas in the 1930s), spoke out against America's military involvement in Vietnam, but his personal woes overwhelmed his political energies. In the spring of 1972 Williams was awarded an honorary degree by Indiana's Purdue University, and he worked on an autobiography, *Memoirs*. A retooled production of *Out Cry*, now starring two younger actors, Michael York and Cara Duff-MacCormick, opened on Broadway on March 1, 1973, but closed after twelve performances. Although his new works were not appreciated, Williams continued to write, and he worked on *The Red Devil Battery Sign* throughout 1973 and 1974. His early works, however, continued to build his reputation. An acclaimed 1974 Broadway revival of *Cat on a Hot Tin Roof*, starring Elizabeth Ashley, Keir Dullea, and Fred Gwynne, lifted his spirits, as did receiving the National Arts Club literary medal and the key to New York City.

In early 1975 Williams began work on a new play, *This Is (An Entertainment)*, and published a novel called *Moise and the World of Reason*, and *The Red Devil Battery Sign* was mounted for a Broadway production. Beginning its out-of-town tryout in Boston in June 1975, the production, starring Anthony Quinn and Claire Bloom, folded in less than two weeks. Williams's *Memoirs* was published, but critical reaction was decidedly mixed for this fragmented autobiography. These disappointments were somewhat allayed by well-received New York revivals of three Williams plays: *Sweet Bird of Youth*, *The Glass Menagerie*, and *Summer and Smoke*.

The January 1976 premiere of *This Is (An Entertainment)* in San Francisco generated little interest, but *Night of the Iguana* was successfully revived in London, and Williams was inducted into the American Academy of Arts and Letters. A new Williams play, *Vieux Carré*, premiered on Broadway in May 1977, but critical response was harsh, and the play closed after only five performances. The continuing disappointment from the long string of failures did not stop Williams from writing, and he pressed on with *Tiger Tail*, a stage adaptation of his screenplay for *Baby Doll*, and a new play, *Creve Coeur*. *Tiger Tail* flopped in a production in

Atlanta, Georgia, in early 1978, and *Creve Coeur*, retitled *A Lovely Sunday for Creve Coeur*, was produced at the Spoleto Festival in Charleston, South Carolina. When it moved to New York on January 1, 1979, it quickly closed. During 1979 Williams worked on yet another revision of *The Milk Train Doesn't Stop Here Anymore* and a new play, *Clothes for a Summer Hotel*, which dealt with madness and creativity by examining the lives of F. Scott and Zelda Fitzgerald. In September 1979, Williams's *Kirche, Kuchen, und Kinder* opened in New York to unenthusiastic response, but Williams was pleased to be one of the Kennedy Center Honors recipients in December 1979.

A new Williams play, *Will Mr. Merriwether Return from Memphis?*, was produced in Key West for the gala opening of the Tennessee Williams Performing Arts Center. After runs in Washington, D.C. and Chicago, Williams's *Clothes for a Summer Hotel*, starring Geraldine Page and Kenneth Haigh under José Quintero's direction, opened on Broadway on March 26, 1980. The play was not well received, but New York's Mayor Ed Koch declared the opening day, which was also Williams's birthday, "Tennessee Williams Day" in New York.

Williams's mother, Edwina, died on June 1, 1980, at the age of ninety-five and although Williams was frequently estranged from his brother Dakin, he continued to look after his sister Rose. That year, Williams spent time at Chicago's Goodman Theatre working on a bill of three one-act plays under the title *Tennessee Laughs*. Enjoying his connection with the Goodman, Williams worked on a new play, *A House Not Meant to Stand*, to be produced there. In March, it opened at the Goodman for a limited run. During the course of the year, Williams worked on two projects. The first, an adaptation of Anton Chekhov's THE SEAGULL, which he ultimately titled *The Notebook of Trigorin*, generated some small controversy with Chekhov purists because Williams freely adapted the play and invented a bisexual life for the character of Boris Trigorin. Williams deeply admired Chekhov, and *The Seagull* was his particular favorite among the great Russian playwright's work. He had hoped to direct *The Seagull* early in his career, when he identified with the artistic aspirations of Constantin Treplev, as well as the character's troubled relationship with his mother, Arkadina. By the time Williams worked on this adaptation, he identified more with the world-weariness and self-doubt of the established writer Trigorin.

The other Williams project in 1980 was an autobiographical drama, *Something Cloudy, Something Clear*, a "memory play" like *The Glass Menagerie*, which explored the events of the summer of 1940 when Williams had broken away from his St. Louis roots and was on the brink of theatrical success. The play's fractured reality allows August, the Williams alter ego, to view the events of 1940 from the perspective of 1980. *Something Cloudy, Something Clear* opened at New York's Jean Cocteau Repertory Theatre on August 24, 1981, for a limited run.

In February 1982, the Jean Cocteau Repertory revived *Something Cloudy, Something Clear*. A revised and expanded version of *A House Not Meant to Stand* opened in Chicago for a limited engagement in April 1982. That summer, Williams attended a series of his plays produced by the Williamstown Theatre Festival in Massachusetts, and he began work on a new play, *The Lingering Hour*, but was interrupted by a hospital stay to deal with a case of drug toxicity.

Williams spent the first weeks of 1983 at Key West before making a brief trip to Taormina, after which he returned to New York. The events of the last hours of Williams's life are not clear, but he died on February 24, 1983, of asphyxia, which was caused by choking on a plastic bottle cap. His funeral was held on March 5, 1983, at the St. Louis Cathedral, and he was buried beside his mother at the Calvary Cemetery in St. Louis.

Despite his tragic end, various addictions, and nearly two decades of poorly received plays, Williams's reputation as a dramatist has only grown in the decades following his death. The problems with alcohol and drugs inform his plays as well as his abuse of them surely made the task of writing them difficult. Williams's homosexuality similarly informs his work, and one can trace Williams's slow and often reluctant acceptance of his sexual proclivities through the course of his dramatic accomplishment. Despite his addictions, Williams proved to be a remarkably prolific writer—an experimenter in all forms of writing who excelled in the dramatic form and forever left his impression upon it. Williams's predominance in American theater is unchallenged, and audiences continue to enjoy revivals of his greatest plays while discovering both early and late works that were little seen during Williams's lifetime. These have contributed to a richer and more complex understanding of the experimentation of this most searching of American artists.

PLAYS: *Beauty Is the Word* (1930); *Cairo! Shanghai! Bombay!* (co-written with Doris Shapiro, 1935); *Candles to the Sun* (1936); *Headlines* (1936); *The Magic Tower* (1936); *The Fugitive Kind* (1937); *Spring Storm* (1937); *Not About Nightingales* (1938); *The Battle of Angels* (1940; later revised as *Orpheus Descending*); *The Long Goodbye* (one-act, 1940); *At Liberty* (one-act, 1941); *I Rise in Flame, Cried the Phoenix* (one-act, 1941); *Stairs to the Roof* (1941); *This Property Is Condemned* (1942); *You Touched Me!* (co-authored with Donald Windham, 1942); *The Glass Menagerie* (1945); *The Unsatisfactory Supper* (one-act, 1945; revised in 1948 as *The Long Stay Cut Short, or, The Unsatisfactory Supper*); *Auto-da-Fé* (one-act, 1946); *Hello from Bertha* (one-act, 1946); *The Lady of Larkspur Lotion* (one-act, 1946); *The Last of My Solid Gold Watches* (one-act, 1946); *The Long Goodbye* (one-act, 1946); *Lord Byron's Love Letter* (one-act, 1946); *Moony's Kid Don't Cry* (one-act, 1946); *Portrait of a Madonna* (one-act, 1946); *The Purification* (one-act, 1946); *The Strangest Kind of Romance* (one-act, 1946); *Ten Blocks on the Camino Real* (one-act, 1946; expanded into a full-length play, *Camino Real*); *27 Wagons Full of Cotton* (one-act, 1946); *A Streetcar Named Desire* (1947); *The Case of the Crushed Petunias* (one-act, 1948); *The Dark Room* (one-act, 1948); *The Long Stay Cut Short, or, The Unsatisfactory Supper* (one-act, 1948; revised from *The Unsatisfactory Supper*); *Summer and Smoke* (1948; revised in 1965 as *Eccentricities of a Nightingale*);

Ten Blocks on the Camino Real (one-act, 1948; later revised as full-length *Camino Real*); *The Rose Tattoo* (1951); *Camino Real* (1953; adapted from one-act *Ten Blocks on the Camino Real*); *Something Unspoken* (one-act, 1953); "*Something Wild*" (one-act, 1953); *Talk to Me Like the Rain and Let Me Listen* (one-act, 1953); *Cat on a Hot Tin Roof* (1955); *Three Players of a Summer Game* (one-act, 1955); *Orpheus Descending* (1957; revised from *Battle of Angels*); *The Enemy: Time* (one-act, 1958; revised as *Sweet Bird of Youth*); *The Perfect Analysis Given by a Parrot* (one-act, 1958); *Suddenly Last Summer* (1958); *Sweet Bird of Youth* (1959); *Period of Adjustment* (1960); *Night of the Iguana* (1961); *To Heaven in a Golden Coach* (one-act, 1961); *The Milk Train Doesn't Stop Here Anymore* (1963; revised 1964); *The Eccentricities of a Nightingale* (1965; revised from *Summer and Smoke*); *Slapstick Tragedy* (1966; bill of two one-acts, *The Gnädiges Fräulein* and *The Mutilated*);*The Two-Character Play* (1967; later revised as *Out Cry*); *The Seven Descents of Myrtle* (also titled *Kingdom of Earth*, 1968); *In the Bar of a Tokyo Hotel* (1969); *Confessional* (one-act, 1970; later revised as *Small Craft Warnings*); *The Frosted Glass Coffin* (one-act, 1970); *I Can't Imagine Tomorrow* (one-act, 1970); *Some Problems for the Moose Lodge* (one-act, 1970; later revised as *A House Not Meant to Stand*); *Out Cry* (1971; revised from *Two-Character Play*); *Small Craft Warnings* (1971); *The Red Devil Battery Sign* (1975); *Demolition Downtown: Count Ten in Arabic—Then Run* (1976); *This Is (An Entertainment)* (1976); *Lifeboat Drill* (1977); *Vieux Carré* (1977); *Tiger Tail* (1978); *A Lovely Sunday for Creve Coeur* (1979; originally titled *Creve Coeur*); *Clothes for a Summer Hotel* (1980); *Kirche, Kuchen, und Kinder* (1980); *Steps Must Be Gentle* (1980); *Will Mr. Merriwether Return from Memphis?* (1980); *Tennessee Laughs* (1980); *A House Not Meant to Stand* (1981; revised version of one-act *Some Problems for the Moose Lodge*); *The Notebook of Trigorin* (1981; free adaptation of Anton Chekhov's *The Seagull*); *Something Cloudy, Something Clear* (1981); *The Lingering Hour* (1982; unfinished); *The Remarkable Rooming-House of Mme Le Monde* (1983)

FURTHER READING

Clurman, Harold. "A Playwright's Symposium." In *The Playwrights Speak*, ed. by Walter Wager. New York: Longmans, 1969.

Crandell, George W., ed. *The Critical Response to Tennessee Williams*. Westport, Conn.: Greenwood Press, 1996.

Hayman, Ronald. *Tennessee Williams: Everyone Else Is an Audience*. New Haven, Conn.: Yale Univ. Press, 1993.

Leverich, Lyle. *Tom: The Unknown Tennessee Williams*. New York: Crown, 1995.

Rader, Dotson. *Tennessee, Cry of the Heart*. Garden City, N.Y.: Doubleday, 1985.

Roudané, Matthew C. *The Cambridge Companion to Tennessee Williams*. New York: Cambridge Univ. Press, 1997.

Saddik, Annette J. *Politics of Reputation: The Critical Reception of Tennessee Williams' Later Plays*. Rutherford, N.J.: Fairleigh Dickinson Univ. Press, 1999.

Savran, David. *Communists, Cowboys, and Queers: The Politics of Masculinity in the Works of Arthur Miller and Tennessee Williams*. Minneapolis: Univ. of Minnesota Press, 1992.

Spoto, Donald. *The Kindness of Strangers: The Life of Tennessee Williams*. Boston: Little, Brown, 1985.

Williams, Dakin, and Shepherd Mead. *Tennessee Williams: An Intimate Biography*. New York: Arbor House, 1983.

Williams, Edwina. *Remember Me to Tom*. As told to Lucy Freeman. New York: Putnam's, 1963.

James Fisher

WILLIAMSON, DAVID (1942–)

David Williamson, born in Melbourne, Victoria, AUSTRALIA, is a phenomenon in the Australian theater. By far its most popular and prolific playwright, he has been cleverly crafting images of contemporary Australian life for over thirty years, and in more than twenty plays. He received a bachelor's degree in English from Monash University in 1964 and once described himself as "a storyteller to the tribe." His affinity with his middle-class audiences seems undiminished.

Williamson became synonymous with box-office success in the subsidized theater; *The Club* in 1977 ran for eight weeks for the Melbourne Theatre Company at ninety-six percent capacity houses, and when the company gambled on a return season, it played for another eight weeks at ninety-eight percent capacity. Williamson's early, scandalous, "New Wave" dramas *The Coming of Stork* (1970), *The Removalists* (1972), and *Don's Party* (1973) violated most of the decorums governing what might be said and done on the stage; *The Removalists*, which deals with police and domestic violence, remains both physically and verbally a profoundly confronting play.

Increasingly, Williamson depicts relationships in the educated middle class. *A Handful of Friends* (1976) and *The Perfectionist* (1983) explore with a satirical but increasingly compassionate eye the messiness of contemporary marriage in the wake of feminism and an at least perceived openness in sexual behavior. *Travelling North* (1980) is a moving treatment of aging and death, juxtaposing the values of hedonistic north and morally serious south and recalling RAY LAWLER's classic *The Summer of the Seventeenth Doll*. In the 1990s, Williamson's dramatic subjects were placed a little higher on the social ladder, and plays like *Money and Friends* (1991) and *After the Ball* (1997) looked at the effects of affluence on close relationships.

Inevitably, when the characters supposedly at risk become remarkably comfortable people, there is some slackening of dramatic pressure in comparison with the unpredictable and uncompromising manner of the early work. But Williamson remains, always, a playwright with a keen interest in moral choices. Occasionally this has involved an expression of his own attitudes and values; in *Sons of Cain* (1985), with its treatment of journalistic ethics, and *Dead White Males* (1995), with its pillorying of the absurdities of literary theory as a form of prejudicial mantra, the playwright's views are unapologetically on display: a writer with strong opinions that he suspends in his investigation of the human COMEDY and with a focus on situational ethics rather than complex individual motivation. As people attempt to convince or deceive themselves and others, what they may believe is less consequential to the drama than why and how they profess it. This fascination with the dynamics of human interaction, which Williamson has traced to his early training as a social psychologist, has led him in some recent work to present highly structured (and intensely public) mediations of conflict; thus more than half of the action of *Brilliant Lies* (1993), about an allegation of sexual harassment, occurs in the artificially constrained formal negotiation setting, and *Face to Face* (1999) is set entirely in an industrial arbitration hearing. In the end, it may be as much Williamson's delight in the detail of social ritual as his uncanny ability to catch or anticipate the current preoccupations of his "tribe" that accounts for his unique place in Australian theater.

SELECT PLAYS: *The Coming of Stork* (1970); *The Removalists* (1972); *Don's Party* (1973); *A Handful of Friends* (1976); *The Club* (1977); *Travelling North* (1980); *The Perfectionist* (1983); *Sons of Cain* (1985); *Money and Friends* (1991); *Brilliant Lies* (1993); *Dead White Males* (1995); *After the Ball* (1997); *Face to Face* (1999)

FURTHER READING

Carroll, Dennis. *Australian Contemporary Drama from 1909.* 2d ed. Sydney: Currency Press, 1995.

Fitzpatrick, Peter. *Williamson.* Sydney: Currency Press, 1987.

Kiernan, Brian. *David Williamson—A Writer's Career.* Melbourne: Heinemann, 1990.

Peter Fitzpatrick

WILLS, FINGAL O'FLAHERTIE   See WILDE, OSCAR

WILSON, AUGUST (1945–2005)

Prolific playwright August Wilson has consistently and eloquently chronicled African American life in a series of critically acclaimed dramas, including MA RAINEY'S BLACK BOTTOM (1982), *Jitney* (1982), FENCES (1983), *Joe Turner's Come and Gone* (1984), THE PIANO LESSON (1986), *Two Trains Running* (1990), *Seven Guitars* (1994), *King Hedley II* (2002), and *Gem of the Ocean* (2002). Wilson is one of only seven American playwrights to win the Pulitzer Prize twice, and he is the only black playwright to have had two plays running on Broadway simultaneously. His plays have been performed on Broadway and in regional theaters across the country, and Wilson is considered one of the most important American playwrights of the 20th century.

Wilson was born Frederick August Kittel on April 27, 1945, in Pittsburgh, Pennsylvania, to his African American mother, Daisy Wilson, and his German immigrant father, Frederick Kittel, who never lived with the family. Wilson's mother raised him and his five siblings in Pittsburgh's Hill district, but during Wilson's teenage years, she married David Bedford, and the family moved

to the predominantly white suburban neighborhood of Hazelwood. The racial hostility they encountered there would shape Wilson's life in many important ways. The family was subject to violent acts during their time in Hazelwood: a brick was thrown into the window of their new home, and at school, white schoolmates often left notes on Wilson's desk reading "Nigger, go home." When his tenth-grade teacher accused Wilson of plagiarizing a twenty-page paper on Napoleon Bonaparte, he dropped out of school for good; it was months before he told his mother or stepfather. Each morning he would leave home, carrying his books as if he were going to school, but instead he would spend his day either playing basketball or reading the works of LANGSTON HUGHES, Richard Wright, JAMES BALDWIN, or Ralph Ellison in the "Negro section" of the public library. "These books were a comfort," Wilson remarked in a 1987 interview. "Just the idea black people would write books. I wanted my book up there, too. I used to dream about being a part of the Harlem Renaissance." In 1962, after a brief stint in the U.S. Army, he returned to Pittsburgh and civilian life. At the age of eighteen he began working a series of menial jobs that would later influence his writing.

On April 1, 1965, Wilson bought his first typewriter for $20, moved into his own apartment, and changed his name to August Wilson. "The first thing I wanted to type," he later said, "was my name." Reflecting on his youth, he described himself as "a 20-year-old poet wrestling with the world and his place in it." He supported himself working in a series of low-paying jobs for the next twelve years while at the same time founding two new institutions in Pittsburgh: the Center Avenue Poets Theatre Workshop and a theater, Black Horizons on the Hill, which he started with Rob Penny. Wilson's earliest plays, *Recycle* (1973) and *The Homecoming* (1979), were written for Black Horizons with the aim of exploring issues facing African Americans. Certain early influences played a key role in Wilson's development as a writer: "In terms of influence on my work, I have what I call the four B's: Romare Bearden, Amiri Baraka, Jorge Luis Borges and the biggest B of all, the blues." BARAKA's plays were also produced by Black Horizons and inspired Wilson to search for the roots of black theater. In a 1988 interview with scholar David Savran, Wilson described his goals for the theater: "I am trying to write plays that contain the sum total of black culture in America, and its difference from white culture. Once you put in the daily rituals of black life, the play starts to get richer and bigger." That year he wrote *The Homecoming*, a play that examines the mystery surrounding the death of Blind Willie Johnson, a character based on the blues legend Blind Lemon Jefferson. *The Homecoming* was staged by the Kunta Theatre, an amateur theater in Pittsburgh.

In the mid-1970s Wilson gave a reading of his epic poem *Black Bart and the Sacred Hills*, the story of a stagecoach robber in the Old West. Claude Perdy, a friend and stage director, urged Wilson to turn the poem into a play. The piece became a musical satire, complete with six songs Wilson wrote himself. It was first presented as a staged reading at the Inner City Cultural

Center in Los Angeles, but it ran over five hours, and the project's director cut the work to less than one hour without discussing the changes with Wilson. Upset by the experience, Wilson sent the script to Purdy, who had moved to St. Paul, Minnesota, to direct Penumbra, an African American theater. With Purdy's encouragement, Wilson rewrote the musical in 1977, and it was produced at Penumbra. With its large cast and rambling structure, *Black Bart* was not a success, and Wilson did not seek further productions. However, he did realize that he preferred St. Paul to his native Pittsburgh and thus decided to make it his home. For two years he worked for the Science Museum in Minneapolis as a writer of the diorama exhibits.

In 1980 Wilson was the recipient of a Jerome Fellowship at the Minneapolis Playwrights Center for his play *Jitney* (produced 1982). This realistic drama set in a gypsy cab station in Pittsburgh represented a significant change in Wilson's dramaturgical style. Wilson quit his job at the Science Museum to devote more time to writing. His next play was titled *Fullerton Street* (1980). Set in 1941, it explores the tension between rural southern and urban northern values. Wilson submitted both *Fullerton Street* and *Jitney* to the EUGENE O'NEILL Theatre Center's National Playwrights Conference in Connecticut. Neither play was accepted, but Wilson continued to write, and in 1982 he submitted *Ma Rainey's Black Bottom* to the O'Neill Center. It is the story of the legendary blues singer Ma Rainey and the musicians in her band. Set in Chicago in 1927, the play focuses on white record companies' exploitation of black musicians. It was accepted to the conference, and director Lloyd Richards staged a production of the play at the Yale Repertory Theatre just two years later.

Ma Rainey's Black Bottom marked the beginning of a longtime association between Wilson and Richards, who went on to direct six of Wilson's plays. From the beginning, Wilson associated the process of refining his plays with Richards, who was artistic director of both the Eugene O'Neill Theatre Center and the Yale Repertory Theatre. The two men became close, both creatively and personally. They both believed in the need to put the African American experience onstage. In a March 27, 1988 article in the *New York Times* titled "August Wilson's Voices From the Past," Richards said: "Black people are a disinherited nation, stripped of their lands and put into servitude in another land, where their culture was not so much a matter of choice as a matter of imposition." The two men respected each other's values and goals for the theater. Wilson says of Richards: "Our visions are the same. We come from the same place. I trust Lloyd's understanding of the characters." *Ma Rainey's Black Bottom* won several awards, including the New York Drama Critics' Circle Award for best play, a Tony nomination (1985), the League of New York Theatre and Producers Award (1985), and the Whiting Writers' Award from the Whiting Foundation (1986).

Wilson's career flourished in the following years as he wrote a series of plays chronicling African American life in successive decades of the 20th century: *Fences, Joe Turner's Come and Gone, The Piano Lesson, Two Trains Running, Seven Guitars, King Hedley II*, and *Gem of the Ocean. Fences*, written in 1983, is set in the 1950s and tells the story of a former athlete, Troy Maxson, who forbids his talented son, Corey, to accept an athletic scholarship to play baseball in college. Troy Maxson is based on Wilson's stepfather, David Bedford, a talented high school football player who had hoped for a career in medicine but was denied a college education. Troy is a big talker who often entertains friends with humorous stories and is hardworking but embittered by racism and discrimination. *Fences* was first staged at the O'Neill Theatre in 1983, was produced at the Yale Repertory Theatre in 1985, and opened on Broadway in 1987. That same year the *Chicago Tribune* named Wilson Artist of the Year, and *Fences* won the New York Drama Critics' Circle Award for Best Play, four Tony Awards, and the Pulitzer Prize for Drama.

Joe Turner's Come and Gone, set in the 1910s, opened on Broadway in 1988 while *Fences* was still running. This earned Wilson the distinction of being the first black American with two concurrent plays on Broadway. *Joe Turner's Come and Gone*, also set in Pittsburgh, focuses on the lingering effects of slavery, the flight of blacks from the South, and their attempts to assimilate in the urban North. It received several Tony nominations and a Drama Desk Award. *The Piano Lesson*, which appeared two years later, is set in 1969 in a local diner where the characters are dealing with issues of spiritual and economic empowerment; *The Piano Lesson* followed the same route as Wilson's other works, premiering on Broadway in 1990.

Two Trains Running, written in 1989 and produced at Yale in 1990, came to Broadway in 1991, to continue Wilson's cycle about African American life. Like many of Wilson's other plays, it also received the New York Drama Critics Award, was nominated for a Tony, and was awarded the American Theatre Critics' Association Award. Wilson's next play, *Seven Guitars*, recounts the fate of a Pittsburgh blues musician, Floyd "Schoolboy" Barton, who scores a hit record in Chicago but falls short of capitalizing on his success. *Newsweek* reviewer Jack Kroll described *Seven Guitars* as "a kind of JAZZ cantata for actors," with "a gritty, lyrical polyphony of voices that evokes the character and destiny of these men and women who can't help singing the blues even when they're just talking."

Wilson's 2002 play *King Hedley II* is an allegorical drama filled with metaphor and SYMBOLISM and tells the story of King Hedley, who lives with his mother Ruby and his wife Tonya. The play is set in a shared backyard occupied by the family of King himself and his slightly mad, Bible-bashing neighbor, Stool Pigeon. Pittsburgh in the 1980s is depicted as a violent and racist place to live; everybody carries a gun, and the life expectancy is short. *Gem of the Ocean*, which reached Broadway in 2004, actually constitutes the first chronological play in Wilson's cycle and is the imagistic story of a 285-year-old shamanist community matriarch, Aunt Ester, whose special powers allow Citizen

Barlow (in flight from the law) to see the past and envision a future of spiritual redemption in the "City of Bones."

Wilson was one of the most honored and prolific American playwrights of the 20th century, yet he continues to pressure himself to have a play in progress at all times. In April 1990 Wilson was quoted in the *New York Times* by Mervyn Rothstein as saying: "All those awards, all that stuff, I take them and I hang them on my wall. But then I turn around and my typewriter's sitting there, and it doesn't know from awards. I always tell people I'm a struggling playwright." Wilson is the recipient of the Bush, McKnight, Rockefeller, and Guggenheim Foundation fellowships in playwriting; he was elected to the American Academy of Arts and Sciences and inducted into the American Academy of Arts and Letters. In reflecting on Wilson's work, the *Chicago Tribune* wrote, "August Wilson has created the most complete cultural chronicle since Balzac wrote his vast 'Human Comedy'; an artistic whole that has grown even greater than its prize-winning parts."

What remains at the center of his work is his commitment to chronicling the experience of African Americans. In his preface to *Fences*, Wilson writes:

> Near the turn of the century, the destitute of Europe sprang on the city with tenacious claws and an honest and solid dream. The city grew. It nourished itself and offered each man a partnership limited only by his talent, his guile and his willingness and capacity for hard work. For the immigrants of Europe, a dream dared and won true. The descendants of African slaves were offered no such welcome or participation. They came from places called the Carolinas, the Virginias, Georgia, Alabama, Mississippi, and Tennessee. The city rejected them and they fled and settled along the riverbanks and under bridges in shallow, ramshackle houses made of sticks and tarp paper.

In his plays, Wilson gives voice to African Americans who have been previously denied a place on the mainstream American stage. In his speech "The Ground on Which I Stand," presented at the Theatre Communications Group National Conference at Princeton University, Wilson expressed his serious concerns about the American theater's lack of support for black artists.

Lloyd Richards describes Wilson as revolutionary in his aim to effect a change on the American stage. Always challenging the tradition handed down to him by white dramatists, Wilson's work is influenced by the African oral tradition and the lyricism of the blues and dramatizes the struggle of African Americans in the 20th century. He was interested in the impact of the past on the present. Wilson died on October 2, 2005, in Seattle, Washington.

PLAYS: *Recycle* (1973); *The Coldest Day of the Year* (1979); *The Homecoming* (1979); *Fullerton Street* (1980); *Black Bart and the Sacred Hills* (1981); *Jitney* (1982); *Ma Rainey's Black Bottom* (1982); *Fences* (1983); *The Mill Hand's Lunch Bucket* (1983); *Joe Turner's Come and Gone* (1984); *The Piano Lesson* (1986); *Two Trains Running* (1990); *Seven Guitars* (1994); *Gem of the Ocean* (2002); *King Hedley II* (2002)

FURTHER READING

Elam, Harry J., Jr. *The Past as Present in the Dramas of August Wilson*. Ann Arbor: Univ. of Michigan Press, 2004.

Harrington, Joan. *I Ain't Sorry for Nothin' I Done: August Wilson's Process of Playwriting*. New York: Limelight Ed., 1998.

Pereira, Kim. *August Wilson and the African-American Odyssey*. Urbana: Univ. of Illinois Press, 1995.

Wang, Qun. *An In-Depth Study of the Major Plays of African-American Playwright August Wilson: Vernacularizing the Blues on Stage*. Lewiston, N.Y.: Edwin Mellen Press, 1999.

Ellen Anthony-Moore and Christopher Moore

WILSON, LANFORD (1937–)

Having cut themselves off from the past by their cavalier treatment of their inheritance, they become rootless. The are from "somewhere else," as they live out their rootlessness in the Hotel Baltimores, Needle Parks and affluent living rooms of large American cities. Bitter indictments of humanity gone to seed in an American Eden.

—Lanford Wilson, quoted in Barnett, *Lanford Wilson*, 1987

Lanford Wilson's varied and extensive writings about contemporary American life led critic Frank Rich to class him as "one of the few artists who can truly make America sing" (*New York Times*, Oct. 18, 1982). Having received a strict Baptist upbringing, Wilson, born on April 13, 1937, in Lebanon, Missouri, discovered what he describes as his calling after taking a playwriting class at the University of Chicago. He now considers it sinful not to write. Since his first play, *So Long at the Fair*, was produced in 1963 at New York City's experimental Caffé Cino, Wilson has gone on to write seventeen full-length plays and over thirty one-acts, making him one of America's most prolific living playwrights.

If Caffé Cino gave him the opportunity to establish himself OFF-OFF-BROADWAY, Ellen Stuart's La Mama Experimental Theatre Club allowed him to write for more elaborate casts and sets. *Balm in Gilead* (1964) and *The Rimers of Eldritch* (1965) were first produced at La Mama to popular and critical acclaim. His first Broadway production, *The Gingham Dog* (1968), was less successful, closing after five performances. In 1969 Wilson was one of four founding members of the Circle Repertory Theatre in Greenwich Village, where he was resident playwright from 1969 to 1995. His long and successful collaboration with Circle Rep director Marshall Mason resulted in the production of many of Wilson's most acclaimed works. These included *The Hot l Baltimore* (1973), which ran for 1,166 performances (breaking the off-Broadway record for a nonmusical play), and *Talley's Folly*, for which Wilson was awarded the Pulitzer Prize in 1980.

Wilson has been the recipient of numerous theater awards, and many of his plays have been widely produced across the UNITED STATES and Europe. Nevertheless, his career has been uneven. In part, this can be explained by his experimentation with dramatic narrative and his interest in a broad cross section of American society. Wilson's anatomies of contemporary life have been explored in ways that extend from grittily naturalistic exposés of America's urban underbelly to self-consciously theatrical portraits of the nuclear family.

In style, Wilson's plays often involve extensive experimentation while retaining a traditional basis. His trilogy of Talley family plays illustrates these traits, combining Wilson's customary conversational dialogue with a variety of narrative techniques to chart the destruction and reconstruction of two generations of the Lebanon, Missouri, family. FIFTH OF JULY (1978), chronologically the last play in the series, was the first to be written and is a straightforward piece of REALISM. In *Talley's Folly* (1979) and *Talley and Son* (1985), Wilson moves back in time to explore how similar issues affected the previous generation. The realistic elements of these dramas—which take place in real time, involve some of the same characters, and occur simultaneously on different parts of the family estate—are offset by the deliberately artificial nature of the events. Both plays include engaged narrators who address the audience directly, commenting on the other characters and action and even divulging the running time and encouraging spectators to get refreshments. Such theatrical devices are taken further in other works. The highly experimental and autobiographical *Lemon Sky* (1968) plays with free-flowing time and memory and includes a character who is reminded by the narrator she has been dead for ten years since the events of the play took place. The domestic TRAGEDY *Serenading Louie* (1970) employs a fluid structure, eliding scenes through time and place by using a single location to represent the respective homes of two different couples.

Other dramas contrast just as sharply through Wilson's choice of mise-en-scène. The Tally saga is set in and around an elegant farmhouse in the playwright's home state and explores the issues devastating a small town's prominent and wealthy family. *The Hot l Baltimore* explores American life at the other end of the spectrum and is set in a decaying hotel populated by prostitutes, junkies, and other social misfits. An archeological dig provides the backdrop to a university professor's meditations on the past in *The Mound Builders* (1975); *Angels Fall* (1982) brings four strangers together to confront their own mortality in a small Catholic mission in New Mexico; a converted loft in New York sets the stage for finding love after death in *Burn This* (1987). Wilson is equally comfortable writing about grieving Manhattan yuppies and proud midwestern farmers and considers all people worthy of his attention and compassion. He has written for casts as large as thirty-two (*Balm in Gilead*, 1964) and as small as one (*The Madness of Lady Bright*, 1964).

No matter how eclectic his technique or subject, Wilson repeatedly returns to the same themes. At the heart of his work is the concern for the state of contemporary America and the decay of the nation, something realized through feelings of alienation, loneliness, and shattered dreams. Whether set amidst urban decay or in lush rural heartlands, the landscape,

like the country it represents, is revealed to be a mere shadow of its former self. The characters who live there are as spiritually destitute as the place, the victims of their own false hopes and the corrupted ideals of the previous generation. Emotionally displaced, they long to rediscover their roots and return to a loving home and family. It is a difficult ideal to attain. The society of Wilson's plays became restless and rootless in the social flux and economic revival that followed World War II. As critic Gene Barnett (1987) comments, "It is a society thoughtlessly turned destructive of a heritage it never learned to appreciate."

Wilson takes great pride in his heritage and is concerned to preserve it, something that applies as strongly to his craft as his homeland. The influences of such American icons as TENNESSEE WILLIAMS, LILLIAN HELLMAN, and THORNTON WILDER are explicitly and implicitly acknowledged in his works. Wilson's recent *Book of Days* (1998), for example, clearly recalls the stage manager from OUR TOWN, as the players gather onstage to set the scene. *Book of Days* was presented alongside his latest work, *Rain Dance* (2002), as part of Signature Theatre Company's 2002–2003 Wilson season and contains all of the playwright's trademarks. Directed by Marshall Mason, it uses Wilson's favorite technique of splintering the veneer of realism while remaining true to its essence and is set in the small town of Dublin, Missouri, where rot has set in beneath surface prosperity. T. S. ELIOT's aphorism "in my end is my beginning" seems to apply.

PLAYS : *So Long at the Fair* (1963); *Balm in Gilead* (1964); *Home Free!* (1964); *The Madness of Lady Bright* (1964); *No Trespassing* (1964); *Days Ahead* (1965); *Ludlow Fair* (1965); *The Rimers of Eldritch* (1965); *The Sand Castle* (1965); *Sex is Between Two People* (1965); *This Is the Rill Speaking* (1965); *Wandering* (1966); *Miss Williams: A Turn* (1967); *The Gingham Dog* (1968); *Lemon Sky* (1968); *Serenading Louie* (1970); *Sextet (YES)* (1970); *Stoop* (1970); *Ikke, Ikke, Nye, Nye, Nye* (1971); *The Family Continues* (1972); *The Hot l Baltimore* (1973); *Victory on Mrs. Dandywine's Island* (1973); *The Mound Builders* (1975); *Knock Knock* (1976); *Brontosaurus* (1977); *Gemini* (1977); *Fifth of July* (1978); *Bar Play* (1979); *The Great Nebula in Orion* (1979); *Talley's Folly* (1979); *A Tale Told* (1981); *Angels Fall* (1982); *Thymus Vulgaris* (1982); *A Betrothal* (1984); *The Sandcastle* (1984); *Unfinished Play* (1984); *As Is* (1985); *Say De Kooning* (1985); *Talley and Son* (1985); *Abstinence* (1986); *A Betrothal* (1986); *Sa-Hurt?* (1986); *Burn This* (1987); *Dying Breed* (1987); *Hall of North American Forests* (1987); *The Musical Comedy Murders of 1940* (1987); *A Poster of the Cosmos* (1987); *The Moonshot Tape* (1990); *Prelude to a Kiss* (1991); *Ukiah* (1991); *Redwood Curtain* (1992); *Master Class* (1995); *A Sense of Place* (1997); *Sympathetic Magic* (1997); *Three Sisters* (1997); *Book of Days* (1998); *Rain Dance* (2002)

FURTHER READING

Barnett, Gene. *Lanford Wilson*. New York: G. K. Hall, 1987.

Bryer, Jackson R., ed. *Lanford Wilson: A Casebook*. New York: Garland, 1994.

Busby, M. *Lanford Wilson*. Indiana: Boise State Univ. Press, 1987.

Dean, Anne M. *Discovery and Invention: The Urban Plays of Lanford Wilson*. Rutherford, N.J.: Fairleigh Dickinson Univ. Press, 1994.

Williams, Phillip Middleton. *A Comfortable House: Lanford Wilson, Marshall W. Mason, and the Circle Repertory Theatre*. Jefferson, N.C.: McFarland, 1993.

Olivia Turnbull

WILSON, ROBERT (1941–)

*[Wilson] is what we, from whom Surrealism was born,
dreamed would come after us and go beyond us.*

—Louis Aragon, 1971

The American director, writer, and performer Robert Wilson was born on October 4, 1941, in Waco, Texas. After studying architecture and design at the Pratt Institute in Brooklyn, New York, he studied painting in Paris, returning to New York City in the mid-1960s. In 1968 he established the Byrd Hoffman School of Byrds, an interdisciplinary group of artists that developed experimental pieces in Wilson's loft in Soho. His first major work premiered at the Brooklyn Academy of Music—*The Life and Times of Sigmund Freud* (1969), a "dance-play" in three acts in which the death of Freud's grandson was the axis around which swirled a profusion of polyvalent imagery. In 1970, Wilson achieved international acclaim with *Deafman Glance*, a "silent opera" inspired by his work in movement therapy for mentally- and hearing-impaired children and conceived as a vehicle for fifteen-year-old Raymond Andrews, a deaf-mute performer. The world premiere of *Einstein on the Beach* (1976), with music by Phillip Glass, at the Festival d'Avignon, secured his reputation internationally and was later revived in two world tours (1984 and 1992). Although the production's ostensible theme (as critic John Rockwell put it in 1976) was "consideration of the same moral and cosmic issues that concerned Einstein himself," the piece resists easy interpretation. Wilson's collaborators have included choreographer Meredith Monk, playwright HEINER MÜLLER, performance artist Laurie Anderson, musicians David Byrne and Tom Waits, writer William Burroughs, and many others. He is the recipient of numerous awards, including two Rockefeller and two Guggenheim fellowships.

While the ideas informing Wilson's productions are varied and eclectic, certain formal characteristics consistently obtain. His stage works are, in a sense, animated paintings or sculptures—or both—in which traditional dramatic concerns, such as plot, character development, psychological insight, metaphysical problems, social issues, and so on, are either subordinate to the visual and aural experience or entirely nonexistent. Lighting is employed with painterly precision and often mesmerizing effect; sculptured set pieces (sometimes simple, sometimes exceedingly complex) are moved with glacial slowness across the stage; actors engage in repetitive, highly stylized movements; dialogue and speech are treated as aspects of music and sound, which are always carefully controlled and often repetitious, hypnotic, and fragmentary. But despite his tendency to reduce language, as well as performers, to aspects of the mise-en-scène, during the last twenty-five years Wilson has mounted a number of established operas and dramatic texts, such as RICHARD WAGNER's *Parsifal* (1991) and Georg Buchner's *Woyzeck* (2000).

Wilson has been characterized as a "director/designer," but this is by no means delimiting or definitive. In addition, although he has scripted numerous original stage works, Wilson is not generally regarded as a playwright. Yet he is clearly the sole author of some of the late 20th century's most spectacular theater. Although he had no formal training in the performing arts, Wilson is nonetheless brilliantly capable of approaching theater holistically, without having to make sharp distinctions between the function and realization of the various components (text, set, light, sound, performer) of which theater is a synthesis.

[*See also* United States, 1940–Present]

SELECT PLAYS: *The King of Spain* (1969); *The Life and Times of Sigmund Freud* (1969); *Deafman Glance* (1970); *KA MOUNTAIN AND GUARDenia TERRACE* (1972); *The Life and Times of Joseph Stalin* (1973); *A Letter for Queen Victoria* (1974); *Einstein on the Beach* (1976); *Death Destruction & Detroit* (1980); *the CIVIL warS: a tree is best measured when it is down* (1983–1984); *The Forest* (1988); *Quartet* (1988); *The Black Rider* (1990); *Alice* (1992); *Monsters of Grace* (1998); *POEtry* (2000); *Prometheus* (2001); *Doctor Caligari* (2002)

FURTHER READING

Brecht, Stefan. *The Theatre of Visions: Robert Wilson. The Original Theatre of the City of New York from the Mid-60s to the Mid-70s, Book 1*. London: Methuen, 1985.

Holmberg, Arthur. *The Theatre of Robert Wilson*. New York: Cambridge Univ. Press, 1997.

Morey, Miguel, and Carmen Prado, eds. *Robert Wilson*. Barcelona: Ediciones Poligrafa, 2002.

Quadri, Franco, et al. *Robert Wilson*. New York: Rizzoli, 1984.

Shyer, Lawrence. *Robert Wilson and His Collaborators*. New York: Theatre Communications Group, 1989.

Wilson, Robert, and Byrd Hoffman Foundation. *Theater of Images*. 2d ed. New York: HarperCollins, 1984.

Bill Conte

WINTERSET

Winterset, a modern poetic TRAGEDY in blank verse with a contemporary setting, could only prove to be an experiment, a "new convention" to MAXWELL ANDERSON, as he remarks in his essay "Poetry in the Theater" (1947). In *Winterset*, which opened on Broadway on September 25, 1935, he was trying "to make tragic poetry out of the stuff of their own times" (Anderson, 1947). The play artistically reiterates within a romantic framework the Nicola Sacco-Bartolomeo Vanzetti case of 1921 that Anderson had touched upon in *Gods of the Lightning* (1928). Not only does the play possess a contemporary social relevance; it is "the product of a poet's brooding" (Krutch, 1957), turning it into his "most complex psychological drama" (Shivers, 1976), a commercial failure that "remains Anderson's masterpiece" (Miller and Frazer, 1991).

The setting of the play is a Manhattan slum neighborhood at the base of a gigantic bridge that arches high over the heads of the audience, symbolizing the alienated equations of wealth and poverty, centrality and marginality in the modern city. Here Mio enters, a Hamlet-like young man keen to square accounts about the injustice and death inflicted upon his father Romagna thirteen years earlier. The murder for which the latter paid with execution after being framed was actually committed by Trock Estralla, a seasoned gangster who was sentenced to jail on a different charge. Garth Esdras, son of a rabbi and Trock's accomplice, knows the truth but has never testified out of fear. But the moment arrives when Necessity, in the form of Mio, seeks Garth's cooperation in order to expose the truth. Trock, newly released, gets in the way of that move.

Into this picture comes Judge Gaunt, a King Lear–like figure who was the man responsible for convicting the innocent Romagna and whose unresolved guilt has turned his mind. In a mock trial conducted by Gaunt—reminiscent of Lear on the heath—Trock, in a state of shock, absolves Romagna by conceding the past.

The plot is complicated by the new love between Mio and Miriamne, Garth's sister. Mio realizes that his mission will endanger his beloved and her kin. He, therefore, relinquishes vengeance for the sake of the love that has been awakened in his heart. In a moving recognition scene Miriamne convinces Mio that his father's innocence has been vindicated and that violence may be replaced by faith: "I came here seeking / light in darkness, running, from the dawn, / and stumbled into a morning." All this in the presence of others like Shadow who has resurfaced, mutilated, like a macabre Banquo. "The essence of tragedy," as Anderson had observed, "is the spiritual awakening or regeneration of the hero." Caught in the crossfire of urban ambitions, the star-crossed lovers, like Romeo and Juliet, face death at the moment when they are most ready to create a new era of truth.

When the first Drama Critic's Circle Award was offered for *Winterset* in 1935, it was EUGENE O'NEILL who praised the group for choosing Anderson for his "splendid contribution . . . to what is finest in the American theatre."

[*See also* United States, 1929–1940]

FURTHER READING

Abernethy, Frances E. "*Winterset*: A Modern Revenge Tragedy." *Modern Drama*, 1, no. 7 (September 1964): 184–189.

Anderson, Maxwell. *Off Broadway: Essays About the Theater.* New York: William Sloane Assoc., 1947.

Brown, John Mason. *Dramatis Personae.* New York: Viking, 1929.

Jones, John Bush. "Shakespeare as Myth and Structure in *Winterset*." *Educational Theatre Journal* 25 (October 1954): 241–248.

Krutch, Joseph Wood. "The Poetic Drama: Maxwell Anderson." In *The American Drama Since 1918.* New York: Braziller, 1957.

Miller, Jordan Y., and Winifred L. Frazer. *American Drama Between the Wars: A Critical History.* Boston: Twayne, 1991.

Shivers, Alfred S. *Maxwell Anderson.* Boston: Twayne, 1976.

Rupendra Guha-Majumdar

WITKIEWICZ, STANISŁAW IGNACY (1885–1939)

Witkacy is by birth, by race, to the very marrow of his bones an artist. He lives exclusively by and for art. And his relationship to art is profoundly dramatic; he is one of those tormented spirits who in art seek the solution not to problems of success, but to the problem of their own being.

—Tadeusz Boy-Żeleński, 1921

Polish playwright, painter, novelist, and philosopher Stanisław Ignacy Witkiewicz, or Witkacy (his artistic persona), is now recognized as a major figure in 20th-century European AVANT-GARDE, but fame came only posthumously two decades after his suicide. He was born on February 24, 1885, in Warsaw in the Russian sector of partitioned POLAND. In 1890 his father, painter and cultural critic Stanisław Witkiewicz, for reasons of health retired to the picturesque resort Zakopane in the Tatras Mountains, where he educated his son at home to develop the boy's creative abilities and independence of mind. Witkacy, who wrote his first plays at eight, embarked upon a career as an artist but suffered doubts about his calling, underwent a mental crisis, and was treated by a Freudian psychoanalyst. After his fiancée's suicide in 1914, for which he felt responsible, he went to AUSTRALIA to attend a scientific congress with his lifelong friend, the anthropologist Bronisław Malinowski.

When World War I broke out, he volunteered to serve in the Czarist army, was wounded at the front, and witnessed the 1917 Revolution in St. Petersburg. Returning to Poland in 1918, he became active in the "Vanguard" group of painters called "Formists," while earning his living as a portraitist, which remained his wage-earning profession until his death.

Between 1918 and 1926, Witkacy wrote over thirty plays, many unpublished and unperformed; those staged had few performances and provoked largely hostile reactions. Highly distorted and ironic in their treatment of artistic and social conventions, Witkacy's plays were designed to support his theory, "Pure Form in the Theatre" (1920), an antinaturalistic doctrine that sought to liberate drama from storytelling and psychology and make it a formal construction—as in modern art and music—rather than an imitation of reality. Witkacy experimented with drugs and wrote about their impact on creativity. As in altered states of consciousness, the colors and shapes in his dramatic universe are intense, hyperbolic, and surprising.

Multitalented, he brought to the theater an unbridled visual imagination and a wide range of intellectual, artistic, and scientific interests.

He devoted the last ten years of his life to correspondence with professional philosophers and writing his own philosophical treatises. A proponent of biological monadology (derived from Gottfried Leibniz), Witkacy explored the ontological problem posed by the directly given feeling of the unity of each Individual Being (the "I" or self) as it confronts the plurality of all that lies outside it (the "non-I" or other). These existential premises gave rise to a tragic sense of life, composed of feelings of extreme loneliness and bewilderment, consciousness of the accidental character of everything, and recognition of the constant menace of nothingness. The function of art was to recapture the metaphysical feeling of the mystery of existence, which was in danger of being lost forever in the mechanized "happiness" of the coming anthill civilization.

Witkacy's plays, which portray "the experiences of a group of degenerate ex-people in the face of the growing mechanization of life," are characterized by grotesque humor, drug-induced dream logic, psychedelic colors, and spectacular stage effects. Some like *They* (*Oni*, written 1920, published 1962), *Gyubal Wahazar* (written 1921, published 1962), *The Crazy Locomotive* (*Szalona lokomotywa*, written 1923, published 1962), *The Mother* (*Matka*, written 1924, published 1962), and *The Shoemakers* (*Szewcy*, written 1927–1934, published 1948) paint an apocalyptic picture of a dystopian future where art and metaphysical feelings are becoming extinct. Others like *The Water Hen* (*Kurka Wodna*, written 1921, produced 1922), *Metaphysics of a Two-Headed Calf* (*Metafizyka dwugłowego cielęcia*, written 1921, produced 1928), and THE MADMAN AND THE NUN (*Wariat i zakonnica*, written 1923, produced 1924) portray the existential anguish felt by lonely human beings lost in an alien world. Artistic creativity is the major theme of plays such as *The Anonymous Work* (*Bezimienne dzieło*, written 1921, published 1962), *The Cuttlefish* (*Mątwa*, written 1922, published 1923), and *The Beelzebub Sonata* (*Sonata Belzebuba*, written 1925, published 1938).

Witkacy's heroes are often painters, poets, musicians, or sometimes scientists, thinkers, and social activists. At odds with the universe, with their society, and with themselves, these self-tormented pseudo-geniuses are filled with rage or despair and rendered absurdly helpless by their own unruly creativity. They must battle against state control, commercial exploitation, cultural leveling, self-doubts, and the theft of their work and IDENTITY.

At a period in European history when writers and artists were enrolling under various political banners, Witkacy remained skeptical, resisting all ideologies of either right or left. He saw the danger of mass movements fueled by slogans, and the picture of modern totalitarian regimes and crazed dictators contained in his dystopian fantasies has proved prophetic.

Witkacy created an autonomous scenic language, based on playfulness, CHANCE associations and random borrowings, verbal games, and a variety of parodied and quoted performance styles. Mockery and subversion are his tools.

Through parody and playfulness he called into question the grandiose mission accorded to the artist in Poland and challenged his own artistic importance by constantly clowning before the camera, staging hundreds of bizarre "auto-Witkacies"—his own version of PERFORMANCE ART (he was also a pioneer photographer, creating powerful metaphysical portraits). This aspect of Witkacy—the artist as prankster, displaying a fondness for jokes, tricks, and games—kept his contemporaries from treating him seriously. His plays are full of riddles, anagrams, and enigmas, beginning with the often bizarre titles. Literary allusions and appropriations abound; someone else's drama is enough to set Witkacy off on his own creative path, playing with the skeleton of a forbear and building his own structure out of the bones. Such "aesthetic irresponsibility," or creative playing, is a defining element of Witkacy's theater.

Witkacy's flamboyant life and uncompromising suicide on September 18, 1939, in Jeziory, Poland (now in Ukraine) in order to evade Nazis and Bolsheviks made him an artist hero to postwar intellectuals. Starting with Tadeusz Kantor's revival of *The Cuttlefish* in 1956, premieres of Witkacy's plays became major events in the formation of modern Polish theater. First discovered by the theatrical elite in their battle against Soviet-imposed SOCIALIST REALISM, Witkacy's "non-Euclidean dramas" gradually became accessible to the broad public and assimilated into popular culture in cabaret performance and rock musicals. With the fall of communism, he has become a classic avant-gardist and the most important Polish playwright-theorist of the 20th century. No longer forced into an antiregime mold, Witkacy—with his self-referential parody of modernism, strategies of appropriation, pastiche of different styles, blending of theory and practice, and mixture of high and low genres—can now be regarded as one of the first POST-MODERN playwrights.

SELECT PLAYS (with dates of composition): *The Pragmatists* (*Pragmatyści*, 1919); *Mister Price or Tropical Madness* (*Mister Price, czyli bzik tropikalny*, 1920); *They* (*Oni*, 1920); *Tumor Brainiowicz* (*Tumor Mózgowicz*, 1920); *Gyubal Wahazar or Along the Cliffs of the Absurd* (*Gyubal Wahazar, czyli na przełęczach absurdu*, 1921); *Metaphysics of a Two-headed Calf* (*Metafizyka dwugłowego cielęcia*, 1921); *The Water Hen* (*Kurka Wodna*, 1921); *The Cuttlefish or the Hyrcanic Worldview* (*Mątwa, czyli Hyrkaniczny światopogląd*, 1922); *Dainty Shapes and Hairy Apes, or the Green Pill* (*Nadobnisie i koczkodany, czyli zielona pigułka*, 1922); *The Crazy Locomotive* (*Szalona lokomotywa*, 1923); *Janulka, Daughter of Fizdejko* (*Janulka, córka Fizdejki*, 1923); *The Madman and the Nun, or There Is Nothing Bad Which Could Not Turn Into Something Worse* (*Wariat i zakonnica, czyli nie ma złego, coby na jeszcze gorsze nie wyszło*, 1923); *The Mother* (*Matka*, 1924); *The Beelzebub Sonata, or What Really Happened in Mordovar* (*Sonata Belzebuba, czyli prawdziwe zdarzenie w Mordowarze*, 1925); *The Shoemakers* (*Szewcy*, 1927–1934)

FURTHER READING

Gerould, Daniel. *Witkacy as an Imaginative Writer.* Seattle: Univ. of
    Washington Press, 1983.

Kiebuzinska, Christine Olga. *Revolutionaries in the Theater: Meyerhold,
    Brecht, and Witkiewicz.* Ann Arbor: UMI Res. Press, 1988.

Micińska, Anna. *Witkacy: Stanisław Ignacy Witkiewicz, Life and Work.*
    Tr. by Bogna Piotrowska. Warsaw: Interpress, 1990.

Seven Plays by Stanisław Ignacy Witkiewicz. Ed. and tr. by Daniel Gerould.
    New York: Martin E. Segal Theatre Center Pubs., 2004.

The Theatre in Poland. Special Witkiewicz issues. 3 (March 1970); 6–7
    (June–July 1978); 10–12 (October–December 1984).

The Witkiewicz Reader. Ed. and tr. by Daniel Gerould. Evanston:
    Northwestern Univ. Press, 1995.

                                                    Daniel Gerould

WM, HUAJU   *See* WE

WOLF, FRIEDRICH (1888–1953)

> Art is a weapon.
>
> —Friedrich Wolf, 1928

Like his contemporaries BERTOLT BRECHT and ERNST TOLLER,
Friedrich Wolf ranks among the leading socialist playwrights
in GERMANY. As a committed author who felt the poet's task
was to represent the conscience of society, Wolf had strong faith
in the vigor of the word and saw the theater as a powerful
weapon for social change. To this end, Wolf sought to produce a
didactic theater for the proletariat.

Born on December 23, 1888, in Neuwied, Germany, the son
of a Jewish merchant, Wolf studied medicine in Munich and
worked as a ship's doctor in 1913–1914. During World War I he
served in the medical corps until he was jailed as a conscientious objector. Before establishing himself as a playwright,
Wolf was well known for his manual of popular medicine. His
first drama, *Poor Conrad* (*Der arme Konrad*, produced 1924), depicts
the German peasant revolt of 1514 and exemplifies Wolf's commitment to bringing social problems onto the stage. Integrating the social complaints of the 20th-century worker with those
of the peasants of 1514, *Poor Conrad* represents the historical
power of the people and sets a precedent for revolution. Wolf
joined the Communist Party in 1928, and according to Lothar
Kahn (1993), none of Wolf's contemporaries were "more completely socialist, more completely communist" than he. Wolf's
scandalous breakthrough occurred in 1929 with the staging of
the controversial play *Cyanide* (*Cyankali*), the story of an unmarried, poor, and unemployed pregnant young woman who dies as
a result of an illegal, botched abortion. The play attacks Germany's antiabortion laws, in particular the infamous Paragraph
218. Soon after the premiere of *Cyanide*, the playwright and
medical doctor Wolf was imprisoned for violating the very same
paragraph. Following mass demonstrations in support of his
release, he was eventually freed.

After the great success of *Cyanide*, Wolf continued to practice
medicine and dramatize pressing social issues. *Sailors of Cattaro*
(*Die Matrosen von Cattaro*, produced 1930) is based on an Austro-
Hungarian naval mutiny and conveys Wolf's belief in the imminence of world revolution. The drama was performed successfully in New York in 1934–1935.

Among the many writers forced into exile by the Nazis (Wolf
spent 1933–1945 in Paris and Moscow), Wolf stands out as one of
the first to tackle anti-Semitism and Nazism with *Professor Mamlock* (produced 1934). The drama's title character is a Jewish war
veteran and surgeon who attempts to cope with the rise of Nazism
and its destruction of his life. Mamlock's fate is doomed by his
political ignorance, but hope remains in the conversion of a Nazi
to a Jewish sympathizer and in the relentless pamphleteering of
Mamlok's son. After World War II ended, Wolf returned to Germany in 1945 and settled in the Soviet Occupation Zone. He
worked there as a medical doctor, writer, and editor of the journal
Volk und Kunst (People and Art), remaining politically active until
his death on October 5, 1953, in Lehnitz, East Germany.

Wolf was a prolific writer whose complete works comprise
sixteen volumes. While widely accessible in German, the highly
topical nature of his texts has resulted in their limited availability in English translation.

SELECT PLAYS: *Mohammed* (1917); *The Absolute* (*Der Unbedingte*,
    1919); *This Is You* (*Das bist du*, 1919); *Black Sun* (*Die schwarze Sonne*,
    1921); *Poor Conrad* (*Der arme Konrad*, 1924); *Man in the Dark* (*Der Mann
    im dunkel*, 1925); *Kolonne Hund* (1927); *Koritke* (1927); *Cyanide*
    (*Cyankali*, 1929); *Boys of Mons* (*Die Jungens von Mons*, 1930); *Sailors of
    Cattaro* (*Die Matrosen von Cattaro*, 1930); *Tai Yang Awakes* (*Tai Yang
    erwacht*, 1930); *From New York to Shanghai* (*Von New York bis Schanghai*,
    1932); *How Are the Fronts?* (*Wie stehn die Fronten?* 1932); *Peasant Baetz*
    (*Bauer Baetz*, 1932); *Professor Mamlock* (1934); *Florisdorf* (1935);
    The Trojan Horse (*Das trojanische Pferd*, 1937); *Beaumarchais* (1941);
    Dr. Lilli Wanner (1944); *Mayor Anna* (*Bürgermeister Anna*, 1950);
    Thomas Münzer (1953)

FURTHER READING

Garten, H. F. *Modern German Drama.* London: Methuen, 1964.

Heizer, Donna K. *Jewish-German Identity in the Orientalist Literature of Else
    Lasker-Schüler, Friedrich Wolf, and Franz Werfel.* Columbia, S.C.:
    Camden House, 1996.

Kahn, Lothar. *Between Two Worlds. A Cultural History of German-Jewish
    Writers.* Ames: Iowa State Univ. Press, 1993.

Müller, Henning. *Friedrich Wolf. Weltbürger aus Neuwied* [Friedrich Wolf:
    Cosmopolitan from Neuwied]. Neuwied: Peter Kehrein, 1988.

                                        Maya Gerig and Cyrus M. Shahan

WOLFE, GEORGE C. (1954–)

Although he has arguably made his most lasting impact as a
director and producer, George C. Wolfe has also been an innovative and important playwright. He received his bachelor's

degree from Pomona College, where productions of his early plays *Up for Grabs* (1975) and *Block Party* (1976) received awards from the American College Theater Festival. Following graduation, he worked as a playwright, director, and actor in Los Angeles.

Wolfe relocated to New York in 1979, earning a master's degree in dramatic writing from New York University. The OFF-BROADWAY company Playwrights Horizons produced his musical *Paradise* in 1985, to largely negative reviews. However, his next effort, *The Colored Museum*, was both a critical and popular success when it debuted at New Jersey's Crossroads Theater in 1986. This satirical examination of black culture stirred up controversy because in it Wolfe dared to lampoon some of black America's most sacred cows. It also brought him to the attention of Joseph Papp, who transferred the play to New York's Public Theater.

Wolfe's next major work was *Spunk* (1989), adapted from three short stories by renowned black author ZORA NEALE HURSTON. In 1991, Wolfe wrote the book and was the co-lyricist for the Broadway musical *Jelly's Last Jam*, which he also directed. Based on the life of JAZZ musician "Jelly Roll" Morton, the show received ten Tony nominations, including Best Musical, Best Book, and Best Director.

Wolfe's continued work as a director, combined with his 1993 appointment as artistic director and producer of the New York Shakespeare Festival / Joseph Papp Public Theater prevented him from concentrating on his own playwriting for several years. However, in 1996, he conceived and directed the popular Broadway dance musical *Bring in 'da Noise, Bring in 'da Funk*, featuring a book by Reg E. Gaines and choreography by Savion Glover. Wolfe also co-wrote the book for Michael John LaChuisa's musical adaptation of *The Wild Party* in 2000, which debuted on Broadway under Wolfe's direction. His next solo playwriting effort was *Harlem Song* (2002), which he staged at the historic Apollo Theatre. Structured as a musical revue, the piece chronicles 100 years of Harlem's history, with special emphasis on the Harlem Renaissance of the 1920s.

In 1995 Wolfe was named a "living landmark" by the New York Landmarks Conservancy. His contributions to the American theater have been numerous. His plays and musical theater pieces range from irreverent satires to historical tributes and have heavily influenced the stage representation of African Americans. He has directed some of the most important theater works of the late 20th and early 21st century, including TONY KUSHNER's ANGELS IN AMERICA, Parts I and II, ANNA DEAVERE SMITH's *Twilight: Los Angeles, 1992*, and SUZAN-LORI PARKS's *Topdog/Underdog*. As head of the Public Theater, Wolfe diversified the choice of plays offered there, creating the legacy of a truly multiethnic theater.

[See also United States, 1940–Present]

SELECT PLAYS: *Up for Grabs* (1975); *Block Party* (1976); *Tribal Rites* (1978); *Back Alley Tales* (1979); *Paradise* (1985); *The Colored Museum* (1986); *Queenie Pie* (1987); *Over There* (1988); *Spunk* (1989); *Blackout* (1990); *Jelly's Last Jam* (1991); *Bring in 'da Noise, Bring in 'da Funk* (concept, 1996); *The Wild Party* (co-librettist, 2000); *Harlem Song* (2002)

FURTHER READING

Jackson, Pamela Faith, and Karimah, eds. *Black Comedy: Nine Plays, A Critical Anthology with Interviews and Essays.* New York: Applause, 1997.

Kroll, Jack. "Zapping Black Stereotypes." *Newsweek* (November 17, 1986): 84–85.

McKinley, Jesse. "Exiting the Public Stage." *New York Times* (May 29, 2005).

Rowell, Charles H. "'I Just Want to Keep Telling Stories': An Interview with George C. Wolfe." *Callaloo* 16, no. 3 (Summer 1993): 602–623.

Dan Bacalzo

WOLFF, EGON (1926–)

Born in Santiago, CHILE, in 1926, Egon Wolff was the son of German immigrants. Wolff began his career as a dramatist in 1958 with the debut of *Mansion of Owls* (*Mansión de luchazas*) and *Disciples of Fear* (*Discípulos del miedo*). In these two earliest pieces, he exhibits some of the obsessions that would come to characterize his later work: imprisonment, the rigidity of familial relations, the threat of the external world, and the conception of man's obscure psychological motivations as rooted in a repressed past. As a result, Wolff garnered attention as an adept investigator of the human psyche. *Groups of Clothes* (*Parejas de trapo*, 1960) is marked by a preoccupation with the concept of a false existence and the immoral compromises one must make when aspiring to a higher social level. It is the story of Jaime and the web of lies he must spin in order to sustain the way of life of his spouse Christina, the daughter of an elite upper-class Chilean family. As is often the case in the Wolffian universe, the moral comes from one of the play's more humble characters—in this case, a Czech immigrant who has suffered through some of the horrors of war.

The Invaders (*Los invasores*, 1963) solidified Wolff's position as an internationally successful playwright. Inspired by *Casa tomada* (*Drunken Home*), a story by the Argentine author Julio Cortázar, the play offers up a stark portrait of the guilty psychoses of the powerful and denounces the abysmal social practices that exacerbate class differences. In this work, Wolff introduces expressionist techniques that contrast sharply with the psychological REALISM of his earlier works.

Among his later plays, *Paper Flowers* (*Flores de papel*, 1970)—considered by many to be his masterpiece—and *The Pool of the Jellyfish* (*La Balsa de la medusa*, 1984)—similar in subject matter to Luis Buñuel's *The Exterminating Angel*—continue along similar lines. Thematically, they deal with the external threat—represented by individuals who have been condemned to the lowest rung of the social ladder—that perpetually hovers over the comfortable bourgeois world. In this way, reality is deconstructed until it becomes fantastical, marking the characters' moral decline.

Wolff's universe is vicious in its social criticisms, and during the 1960s his work was interpreted only within this rubric. Yet the strong Catholic influence he brings to his plays persists, saving them from any simplistic classification. Wolff's artistic obsessions have remained the same for almost a half century, serving as a sort of national conscience, alert to developments within Chilean society. He has continued to focus on an analysis of interpersonal relations within small groups, in particular, the family. Occasionally, as well, he has journeyed into the realms of FARCE (*The Blue Envelope* [*El sobre azul*, 1978]) and COMEDY (*Poplars on the Terrace* [*A lamos en la azotea*, 1981]).

SELECT PLAYS: *Mansion of Owls* (*Mansión de lechuzas*, 1958); *Disciples of Fear* (*Discípulos del miedo*, 1958); *Groups of Clothes* (*Parejas de trapo*, 1960); *Child-Mother* (*Niñamadre*, 1962); *The Invaders* (*Los invasores*, 1963); *Paper Flowers* (*Flores de papel*, 1970); (*Kindergarten* 1977); *The Blue Envelope* (*El sobre azul*, 1978); (*Minages Espejismos*, 1978); *José* (1980); *Poplars on the Terrace* (*Alamos en la azotea*, 1981); *The Pool of the Jellyfish* (*La balsa de la medusa*, 1984); *Speak to Me of Laura* (*Háblaime de Laura*, 1986); *Invitation to Eat* (*Invitación a come*, 1994) *Scars* (*Cicatrices*, 1994); *Chiaroscuro* (*Claroscuro*, 1995); *Crossroads* (*Encrucijada*, 2000); *Behind a Closed Door* (*Tras una puerta cerrada*, 2002); *The Recommendation* (*La recomendación*, 2003)

FURTHER READING

Bravo Elizondo, Pedro. *La dramaturgia de Egon Wolff: Interpretaciones críticas (1971–1981)* [The dramaturgy of Egon Wolff: Critical interpretations (1971–1981)]. Santiago, Chile: Editorial Nascimento, 1985.

Castedo Ellerman, Elena. "Variantes de Egon Wolff: fórumulas dramática y social" [Variants of Egon Wolff: Dramatic and social formulas]. *Hispamérica* 5, no. 15 (1976): 15–38.

López, Daniel. "Ambiguity in *Flores de Papel*." *Latin American Theatre Review* 12, no. 1 (Fall 1978): 43–50.

Sayers Peden, Margaret. "The Theater of Egon Wolff." In *Dramatists in Revolt: The New Latin American Theater*, ed. by Leon Lyday and George Woodyard. Austin: Univ. of Texas Press, 1976. 190–201.

Norberto Cambiasso (Tr. by Gabriel Milner)

A WOMAN'S LIFE

A Woman's Life (*Onna no Isshō*) is a Japanese SHINGEKI play written by MORIMOTO KAORU and first staged by the Literary Theater (Bungakuza) in April 1945. The action concerns Nunobiki Kei, orphaned by the Sino-Japanese War of 1894–1895 and adopted by the well-to-do Tsutsumi family. She shows gratitude by rendering unflagging service to the family for many years, then marries the eldest son. He lacks business sense, but Kei also shines in that arena and works vigilantly for the family's ongoing prosperity. Yet, in the measure that she is successful, she gradually loses the ready warmth and sensitivity that the rest of the family had grown to expect of her.

One by one, the family members move out—including her husband, who eventually dies—and she is left alone in the large house. The play ends with Kei, now fifty-nine, but looking considerably older, sitting alone in the ruins of the firebombed house. She encounters her brother-in-law Eiji and reflects, as if for the first time, on her life. Eiji attempts to suggest that the future will be better. Sugimura Haruko, the Literary Theater's foremost actress, played the lead.

Morimoto had worked often with Sugimura during the war and in fact crafted the play as a vehicle for her remarkable skills. Onstage virtually the whole time, she had to age more than forty years.

Curiously, the play had been commissioned by the military, ostensibly to shore up the home front during the increasingly dark days of the war. Yet Morimoto, with no overt political stance, did not create that sort of play. In fact, there are many sympathetic references to CHINA, which the censors inexplicably left untouched. In vividly portraying a woman who unreservedly sacrifices herself for her family but is dehumanized—even defeminized—in the process, Morimoto simply reflected the prevailing mood of futility and despair of a war-weary Japanese public.

Even without war as backdrop, this play had far wider appeal for the Japanese than the work of such Western playwrights as HENRIK IBSEN, whose plays, while popular, were peopled with self-assertive, aggressive heroes. Whether their theater is new or old, the Japanese appear to prefer characters, like Kei, whose inner strength is emphasized and made manifest by enduring the unendurable, not by rebelling against it.

Conditions for rehearsal and performance were dire. Air raids systematically strafed Tokyo, and the actors were not alone in fearing for their lives. Many theaters had been destroyed, and there were numerous restrictions on stage materials, lighting, and performance time. The play's premiere took place in a film theater. In spite of the dangerous atmosphere, however, performances were well attended. *A Woman's Life* was the Literary Theater's final production before JAPAN's defeat in August 1945. The play touched a chord with its audience and was a huge hit. It was Sugimura's path to glory for many years, with over 250 performances to the mid-1950s, and propelled her to superstar status onstage and in film.

FURTHER READING

Keene, Donald. *Dawn to the West: Japanese Literature in the Modern Era—Poetry, Drama, Criticism.* New York: Holt, 1984.

Nihon Kindai Engeki-shi Kenkyūkai, ed. *Nijusseiki no Gikyoku I: Nihon Kindai Gikyoku no Sekai* [Twentieth-century plays I: The world of modern Japanese plays]. Tokyo: Shakai Hyōronsha, 2002.

Powell, Brian. *Japan's Modern Theatre: A Century of Continuity and Change.* London: Japan Library, 2002.

Rimer, J. Thomas. *Toward a Modern Japanese Theatre: Kishida Kunio.* Princeton, N.J.: Princeton Univ. Press, 1974.

John K. Gillespie

THE WOMEN

I don't feel sorry for any woman who thinks the world owes her breakfast in bed.

—Miss Watts (Stephen Haines's secretary), Act 2

Although spoken by a minor character, the sentence quoted above is an apt expression of CLARE BOOTHE's view of the characters in *The Women*, her stinging satiric COMEDY of the way of life and social attitudes of a group of pampered women whose husbands' wealth protects them from the everyday concerns that beset most human beings of either sex. The play opened in New York on December 26, 1936, with, true to its title, a cast made up entirely of women. It won out over a barrage of critical complaints about the morality and manners of its characters to achieve a run of 657 performances.

The plot, as Boothe admitted in the introduction of the printed text of the play, is relatively simple. Mary Haines, married and the mother of two children, discovers, with "help" from her fiendish friend Sylvia Fowler, that her husband, Stephen, is having an affair with a salesclerk, Crystal Allen, who works behind the perfume counter at Saks' Fifth Avenue. Ignoring the sensible advice of her mother, whose husband had also failed to keep his marriage vows, Mary decides to get a divorce. She is a sympathetic character but, as Boothe also admitted, far from sparkling. As Crystal tells her in a high-keyed confrontation scene, she is "a hell of a *dull woman!*" But she is sharp enough to act swiftly to reclaim her man when, in the last of the play's twelve scenes, she discovers that Crystal is having an affair with the sexy young husband of a middle-aged woman, Countess de Lage. Sylvia too gets her comeuppence: she loses her very rich husband to an ex–chorus girl, Miriam Aarons.

Mary's travail and ultimate revenge provide Boothe with an opportunity to present a striking variety of locales and a diverse cast of characters. The settings include, among others, a hairdresser's salon, a hospital room, Mary's Reno hotel room, Crystal's absurdly luxurious bathroom, and finally, the "powder room" of a nightclub. Among the characters are representatives of virtually all social classes from Mary's Park Avenue friends down through the ranks to clerks, manicurists, mannequins, and domestic servants. The play's opening scene, which takes place in Mary's living room, strikes a note that will echo through all the action to the final curtain, as the women assembled chatter incessantly, and entertainingly, about marital infidelity, including Stephen's when Mary is not present. What has brought them together is a bridge party, an event that in itself offers an ironic comment on the intellectual limitations of this group. An exception, however, is Nancy Blake, a thoroughly undeceived and, incidentally, unmarried writer and perhaps, in her mordant remarks on womankind, a spokesperson for Boothe herself. She alone is insightful. The others in this set, apart from Mary and a very young woman, Peggy Day, are merely catty. The push and pull of their dialogue was the principal reason for the success of the play in its original production and accounts for its continuing popularity.

[*See also* United States, 1929–1940]

FURTHER READING

Chase, Ilka. *Past Imperfect*. Garden City, N.Y.: Doubleday, Doran, 1944
    [Chase played Sylvia Fowler in the original production].

Morris, Sylvia Jukes. *Rage for Fame: The Ascent of Clare Boothe Luce*.
    New York: Random House, 1997.

Shadegg, Stephen C. *Clare Boothe Luce: A Biography*. New York: Simon &
    Schuster, 1970.

Sheed, Wilfred. *Clare Boothe Luce*. New York: E. P. Dutton, 1982.

Malcolm Goldstein

WOOD, ELLEN (1814–1887)

Ellen Wood (born in Worcester, ENGLAND), who published under the name Mrs. Henry Wood, is best known as the author of the 1861 sensation novel EAST LYNNE. Significantly, she is not a playwright but has the distinction of having written a novel that spawned an entire theatrical industry. Her plot lent itself well to MELODRAMA, the most popular theatrical form in mid-Victorian England. *East Lynne* was adapted for the stage by dozens of playwrights beginning almost immediately after it was published until the craze died off early in the 20th century. Many accounts report that adaptations of *East Lynne* were nearly ubiquitous in the latter half of the 19th century. Wood herself once commented to her publisher on the prevalence of posters advertising productions of *East Lynne* on walls everywhere, especially in rural areas. She acknowledged, however, that the chief compensation for her novel being so often adapted was that the theatrical productions increased her book sales, for she never received any theater royalties.

Victorian audiences found her story bold and compelling in its exploration of domestic TRAGEDY, though some critics and readers felt she went too far in mediating her adulterous heroine's moral responsibility for her downfall. In creating a sympathetic portrait of a "fallen woman," Wood violated cultural notions that an adulterous woman was evil through and through.

Wood began her writing career publishing short stories and essays in British periodicals. *East Lynne*, however, was her first major success—as well as the biggest hit of her career. After the publication of *East Lynne*, she continued writing until her death, producing twenty more novels (now almost all out of print) over the succeeding twenty-five years. She wrote at a breakneck pace, often working on more than one novel at a time. Critically, her novels have been classified as mid-Victorian sensation fiction, a category of popular writing on the edge of what was considered appropriate for general audiences. Sensation fiction often explored the underside of proper domesticity with its references to secret sexual liaisons and dark psychological aspects of hidden criminality. As a result, readers and critics of sensation fiction found it both titillating and distressing.

[*See also* England, 1860–1940]

FURTHER READING

Booth, Michael R. *English Melodrama.* London: Jenkins, 1965.

Cross, Gilbert B. *Next Week—East Lynne: Domestic Drama in Performance 1820–1874.* Lewisburg, Pa.: Bucknell Univ. Press, 1976.

Scullion, Adrienne, ed. *Female Playwrights of the Nineteenth Century.* London: Dent, 1996.

Wood, Ellen. *East Lynne.* Ed. by Andrew Maunder. Orchard Park, N.Y.: Broadview, 2002.

Wynne, Deborah. "See What a Big Wide Bed It Is!: Mrs. Henry Wood and the Philistine Imagination." In *Feminist Readings of Victorian Popular Texts: Divergent Femininities,* ed. by Emma Liggins and Daniel Duffy. Brookfield, Vt.: Ashgate, 2001. 89–107.

Julianne Smith

THE WOOD CARVER'S WIFE

The Wood Carver's Wife, a one-act play in verse by MARJORIE PICKTHALL (1883–1922), was first published in 1920 in *University Magazine.* The scene is a rustic-log room, with a silent forest beyond. The wood carver Jean Marchant is carving a Pietà as an altar piece for the church on panels of red cedar wood. His wife, Dorette, sits as his model for the Madonna, as the pair is observed by the treacherous Indian lad Shagonas. Jean struggles with his carving because Dorette's face lacks the Virgin's expression of unutterable despair. Frustrated by his progress, Jean leaves with Shagonas for the church to observe the shrine where his carving will be placed. As Dorette kneels in prayer before the unfinished Pietà, her lover Louis De Lotbiniere joins her. The couple proclaims their love for one another, and Dorette persuades the faithful Louis to leave shortly before the return of the wood carver, who has been informed of his wife's adultery by Shagonas. Jean sends the Indian boy to murder Louis, and Shagonas returns with the dead man's sword, which he lays across Dorette's lap. She gazes at Louis's sword with a look of inconsolable grief, and the wood carver resumes his work.

The play initially received mixed praise, with critics both celebrating the beauty of Pickthall's verse and voicing concern with a perceived lack of dramatic interest and cumbersome dialogue. A popular poet of her age, Pickthall's single attempt at drama was seen by some as evidence of her great theatrical promise and a positive example of the development of a rich body of Canadian drama. Others, however, believed that the play suffered from staging difficulties and uneven flow of action.

Performed by various Canadian amateur theater companies in the early years after its publication, *The Wood Carver's Wife* is now out of print, although more recent stagings include a production at the University of British Columbia in April 2000. The play is an example of the age when Canadian theater was in transition, as it embodies the Victorian sensibilities evident in Pickthall's other literature, while simultaneously demonstrating the author's engagement with new MODERNIST approaches to theater.

With its striking SYMBOLISM and imagery, Pickthall's play is further evidence of her devotion to Canadian themes and her contribution to the development of a distinctly Canadian literature. Set in New France, the play explores themes of violence, RELIGION, artistic creation, sex, and femininity against a distinctly Canadian backdrop. Fraught with repressed emotions and desires, the play explores a violent act of artistic creation, as the suffering of both man and wife is reflected in the wood carver's brutal rendering of the Pietà. With its juxtaposition of the wood carver's wife and the Virgin Mary, Pickthall's drama explores the difficult expectations placed on women. Ultimately, the lovers are punished for their desires, and Dorette remains trapped in her role as the wood carver's wife, her inability to escape her existence being symbolized by the act of her likeness being carved in the "imprisoning dead cedar wood."

[*See also* Canada]

FURTHER READING

Badir, Patricia L. "'So entirely unexpected': The Modernist Dramaturgy of Marjorie Pickthall's *The Wood Carver's Wife.*" *Modern Drama* 43, no. 2 (2000): 216–245.

Logan, J. D. *Marjorie Pickthall: Her Poetic Genius and Art. An Appreciation and an Analysis of Aesthetic Paradox.* Halifax: T. C. Allen, 1922.

Pickthall, Marjorie L. C. *The Wood Carver's Wife and Later Poems.* Toronto: McClelland & Stewart, 1922.

Pierce, Lorne. *Marjorie Pickthall: A Book of Remembrance.* Toronto: Ryerson Press, 1925.

Relke, Diana M. A. "Killed Into Art: Marjorie Pickthall and *The Wood Carver's Wife.*" *Canadian Drama/L'Art Dramatique Canadien* 13, no. 2 (1987): 187–200.

Elizabeth Galway

THE WORD

> Give me the Word, the Word, Christ handed down to us from
> Heaven, the creative vitalizing Word. Give it to me now.
> —Johannes, Act 4

The Word (*Ordet;* written 1925; staged 1932) is KAJ MUNK's most original drama—a modern miracle play in a realist setting, far from the large gestures and pathos of his great historical dramas. *The Word* was written at the request of Professor Hans Brix, Munk's mentor and dramatic adviser at the Royal Theatre in Copenhagen, DENMARK. In 1925 he asked the young dramatist, who in his parsonage in Vederso impatiently awaited the performance of *An Idealist,* to pass the waiting time by writing a serious play about peasants. A few months later the first draft of *The Word* landed on Brix's desk.

The drama deals with the power of faith and takes place in a West Jutland milieu dominated by two competing religious movements: the liberal and broad-minded *grundtvigianism* and an evangelic fundamentalist sect, represented, respectively, by the old wealthy farmer Mikkel Borgen and the poor artisan Peter the Tailor. The two movements are confronted when Mikkel's youngest son, Anders, falls in love with the tailor's daughter. Mikkel decides to conquer his disgust for the sectarians and visits Peter to sanction the alliance between the two young people but is humiliated by Peter, who rejects his offer and asks God to put him under severe trials. At the very same moment Mikkel is told that his pregnant daughter-in-law, Inger, whose naive and nonconfessional belief and sunny disposition keep the family together, has become seriously ill, and he rushes home.

Inger's illness and following death confront Mikkel with the impotence of his faith. His prayers have no power as he has lost his trust in the miracle, for Munk the very core of Christianity. Everyone around the open coffin stands powerless. Inger's husband has no faith, the doctor has done what his science is capable of, and the representative of the official church has only empty phrases to offer. The only one with the right faith in God is Mikkel's son Johannes, who turned insane when his fiancée died and since then has believed himself to be an incarnation of Jesus Christ. When looking at the dead Inger, he regains his sanity and is now, with the help from Inger's child Maren and the power of his faith, able to do what he could not do when he lost his fiancée—to perform the miracle that brings Inger back to life.

In spite of Brix's warm recommendation, Munk's modern miracle play was never staged at the Royal Theatre. After the first performance of the play in the Betty Nansen Theatre in 1932, leading critic Frederik Schyberg blamed the National Theatre for its neglect and called the play "the most conquering sermon" he had ever heard. In 1955, Carl Th. Dreyer made *The Word* internationally famous with his adaptation for the screen, and in 2004 The Handcart Ensemble staged the play in New York on the basis of Dreyer's film.

FURTHER READING

Fujiwara, Chris *Ordet. The Criterion Collection*. http://www.criterionco
.com/asp/release.asp?id=126&eid=136&section=essay.
Munk, Kaj. *Five Plays*. New York: American Scandinavian Foundation, 1953.
Sandmann, Sandy. Review of *Ordet. CurtainUp*. http://www.curtainup
.com/ordet.html.

Kela Kvam

WRIGHT, DOUG (1962–)

You must save everything. And you must show it—auf Englisch, we say—"as is." It is a record, yes? Of living. Of lives.
—Charlotte Von Mahlsdorf, "On Curating" in Act 2, *I Am My Own Wife*

Doug Wright was born in Dallas, Texas, on December 20, 1962. He graduated from Yale University with a bachelor's degree in art history in 1985 and a master of fine arts degree in playwriting from New York University's Tisch School of the Arts in 1987, after which he resided in New York City.

Wright achieved early success when, as an undergraduate, his play *The Stonewater Rapture* (1983) was performed at SCOTLAND's Edinburgh Festival Fringe in August 1984. Subsequent plays have garnered significant awards, including the 1996 Obie Award for *Quills* (1995) and the 2004 Pulitzer Prize and Tony Award for Best Play for *I AM MY OWN WIFE* (2003). Wright has also penned several screenplays, including the screenplay for *Quills*, which was nominated for a Golden Globe Award and received the Paul Selvin Award from the Writer's Guild of America. (The film was named Best Picture by the National Board of Review and nominated for three Academy Awards.)

Wright's broad oeuvre ranges from spare one-act, bare-stage pieces to elaborate dramas, black COMEDIES, FARCES, and musicals. Many plays rework theatrical genres, from 1930s musicals in *Buzzsaw Berkeley* (1989) to the 19th-century Grand Guignol tradition of melodramatic horror in *Quills*. Even more characteristic is Wright's impressive ability to adapt conventions from other art forms. *Interrogating the Nude* (1989), for example, draws on AVANT-GARDE visual culture from the early 20th century, while *Lot 13: The Bone Violin*, one of the four one-act plays written between 1992 and 2001 that make up *Unwrap Your Candy*, is a "fugue for five actors" who perform behind music stands.

Despite this diversity, Wright's body of work is unified by its devotion to witty, nuanced language as well as its untiring exploration of the macabre, which Wright has called his "métier." In many plays, this fascination with the eccentric and grotesque materializes in his choice of historical or fictive protagonists from the extreme margins of society, such as the evangelist-wrestling manager and the country western superstar who battle over the site of a dinosaur theme park in *Dinosaurs* (1988), the iconoclastic artist Marcel Duchamp in *Interrogating the Nude*, the Marquis de Sade in *Quills*, the East German transvestite Charlotte von Mahlsdorf in *Wife*, and the eccentric Bouvier Beale family in *Grey Gardens* (2005). While Wright's plays induce audiences to see surprising aspects of themselves in these larger-than-life figures, his works just as often probe the uncanny facets of reality closer to home. *Watbanaland* (1993), for instance, explores unacknowledged fears aroused in parents by advances in reproductive science. Similarly, the hilarious one-act *Baby Talk*, part of *Unwrap Your Candy*, reveals the deeply weird aspects of "natural" human reproduction found in the celebrated emotional bonds between an expectant mother and her unborn child.

For all its whimsy and startling humor, however, Wright's predilection for the bizarre is infused with subtly fierce anger, kindled by "growing up gay in the Bible belt," as he has himself say onstage in *Wife*. That earlier state of siege has led to psychologically insightful, conceptually engaging, and wickedly charged theater that affirms the centrality of stories imagined—and lived—at the margins. Like von Mahlsdorf in *Wife*, his storytelling is its own act of survival.

PLAYS: *The Stonewater Rapture* (1983); *Dinosaurs* (1988); *Buzzsaw Berkeley* (1989); *Interrogating the Nude* (1989); *Unwrap Your Candy* (1992–2001); *Watbanaland* (1993); *Quills* (1995); *I Am My Own Wife* (2003); *Grey Gardens* (2005)

FURTHER READING

Bossler, Gregory. "Doug Wright." *Dramatist* 7, no. 2 (2004): 8–18.

Ryan, Kate Moira. "Adapting Biography for the Stage." *Dramatists Guild Quarterly* 32, no. 4 (1996): 24–29.

Wright, Doug. *I Am My Own Wife. Studies for a Play About Charlotte von Mahlsdorf.* With an introduction by the author. New York: Faber, 2004.

———. "Playwrights on Writing: The Outsider Within Us." *Los Angeles Times* (June 12, 2005): E33.

———. *Quills and Other Plays.* New York: Faber, 2005.

Jeffrey Schneider

WU ZUGUANG (1917–2003)

Wu Zuguang is one of modern CHINA's most eminent playwrights. He was born in Beijing on April 2, 1917, into an intellectual family originally from Changzhou, Jiangxu Province. From childhood, Wu was nurtured on Chinese art and literature. During his lifetime, he wrote scripts for a wide variety of art forms including Beijing Opera, Ping Opera, and modern spoken drama. He also directed several films and documentaries that recorded the performances and lives of prestigious Beijing Opera artists such as MEI LANFANG and Cheng Yanqiu. Wu earned the title "A Child Prodigy in Drama" when his successful launch onto the dramatic stage came at the age of nineteen with the publication of his first drama, *Phoenix City (Feng Huang Cheng)*, in the winter of 1937, which was at the beginning of the War of Resistance Against Japanese Aggression (1937–1945). The drama's instant rise to popularity owed much to its inspiring patriotic theme, which echoed the timely sentiments of the nation.

In the following two years, he produced several popular dramas inspired by the same patriotic theme, such as *The Song of Righteousness (Zheng qi ge,* c. 1938–1939), and *Children's Army (Hai zi jun,* c. 1938–1939), which extolled the courage of the Chinese people during the war and urged them to fight the Japanese invaders.

The period of 1937–1947 is regarded as the first high point of Wu's creativity. During this decade he produced eleven dramas. Among them, *Return Home on a Snowy Night (Feng xue ye gui ren,* 1942) came to be regarded as Wu's best work and established him as a dramatist of repute. The drama is a melodramatic story about the tragic love affair between a Beijing Opera star (Wei Liansheng) and a bureaucrat's concubine (Yu Chun) in an age of moral corruption. The drama was performed thousands of times on stages across the nation. Its popular appeal lies in part in its elaborate Beijing Opera setting, costuming, and singing and in part in its undertones of ambiguous sexuality.

In late 1947 Wu fled to Hong Kong to escape persecution at the hands of the Kuomintang, because two of his dramas— *Chang'e Flying to the Moon (Chang'e ben yue)* and *Catching the Devil (Zhuo gui zhuan)*—satirized governmental corruption at the time. During his three years of exile in Hong Kong, Wu produced and directed several films, including *Return Home on a Snowy Night* and *Waste Not Our Youth (Mo fu qing chun)*. In 1957 Wu was labeled a rightist and sent to the northeast by the communist regime.

On his return in 1960, Wu embarked on his second artistic high in the period of 1961–1965. In 1964 his lifelong interest in traditional theater inspired him to produce the well-known Pingju Opera *Flower as Our Matchmaker (Hua wei mei)* in which his wife, Xin Fengxia (1927–1998), a famous Pingju Opera singer, played the leading role. His 1979 modern spoken drama *Itinerant Performer (Chuang jiang hu)* is another popular favorite. It was based on the real life-experiences of Wu's wife.

The names of Wu and Xin, one a talented dramatist and the other a well-loved Pingju Opera star, were always spoken of as one. Wu died in Beijing on April 19, 2003.

PLAYS: *Phoenix City (Feng Huang Cheng,* 1937); *Children's Army (Ha zi jun,* c. 1938–1939); *The Song of Righteousness (Zheng qi ge,* c. 1938–1939); *The Cowhead and the Girl Weaver (Niu lang zhi nu,* 1942); *Return Home on a Snowy Night (Feng xue ye gui ren,* 1942); *Lin Chong (Li Chong ye ben,* 1943); *The Journey of the Boy (Shao nian you,* 1944); *Catching the Devil (Zhuo gui zhuan,* c. 1947); *Chang'e Flying to the Moon (Chang'e ben yue,* c. 1947); *Flower as Our Matchmaker (Hua wei mei,* 1964); *Itinerant Performer (Chuang jiang hu,* 1979)

FURTHER READING

McDougall, Bonnie S., and Kam Louie. *The Literature of China in the Twentieth Century.* New York: Columbia Univ. Press, 1997.

Wu Zuguan. *Wu Zuguang xuanji* [Selected works of Wu Zuguang]. Shijiazhvang: Hebei renmin chubanshe, 1995.

Xin Fengxia. *Wo yu Wu Zuguang* [Wu Zuguang and I]. Nanning: Guangxi jiaoyu chubanshe, 1994.

Hongwei Lu

WYSPIAŃSKI, STANISŁAW (1869–1907)

Son of a sculptor, Stanisław Wyspiański was born on January 15, 1869, in Cracow in the Austrian sector of partitioned POLAND. He was educated in Cracow, the ancient capital of Poland and center of its cultural life. All his works both as painter and playwright have deep roots in the artistic heritage of Cracow, which nurtured and shaped his visual imagination. There Wyspiański studied art, architecture, history, and literature; worked on church restorations; created stained glass windows, book illustrations, and stage designs; and in ten years wrote some twenty plays (plus fragments of incomplete works), adaptations of Pierre Corneille and Voltaire, two epic poems, lyric poetry, and a long essay on staging *Hamlet*.

Contact with European modernism set his creativity ablaze. Between 1890 and 1894 Wyspiański traveled three times to Western Europe, spending two and a half years in Paris, where he studied painting and was exposed to SYMBOLISM. Under the spell of RICHARD WAGNER and the Paris opera, he conceived of a poetic drama unifying all the arts (*Gesamstkunstwerk*) that would have a musical structure but transpose into visual imagery the power of operatic theater.

On returning to Cracow, Wyspiański worked as graphic artist for STANISŁAWA PRZYBYSZEWSKI's new MODERNIST journal *Życie* and became associated as designer and author with Teatr Miejski, where between 1898 and 1907 seven of his dramas were staged. His plays can conveniently be classified as historical, contemporary, classically inspired, and mythological-metaphysical. Each play has a powerfully visualized setting out of which the action grows. Wyspiański's sense of life was darkly tragic; he portrayed man's desperate battle with the invincible power of fate from an ironic and satiric viewpoint.

The November Uprising of 1830 against RUSSIA provides the subject of his early one-act *Warszawianka* (1898), a Maeterlinckian mood drama of ominous foreboding given a precise historical and political context. The popular song inspired by the insurrection, "La Varsovienne," recurs as a leitmotiv throughout the play, as a group of officers and the combatants' wives and daughters wait in growing terror for news of the outcome of a lost battle.

Wyspiański's most important contemporary drama, *The Wedding* (*Wesele*), was staged in 1901 with resounding success. Based on the marriage of his poet friend to a peasant girl, the drama evokes a heroic past through visions and dreams, satirizes a self-indulgent present, and bitterly mocks a future that refuses to be born. The same year Wyspiański adapted, published, and helped to mount the first production of Adam Mickiewicz's seminal romantic drama *Forefathers' Eve* (1820–1832).

As part of an ongoing dialogue of Polish drama with its own past, Wyspiański uses the device of theater-in-the-theater in *The Deliverance* (*Wyzwolenie*, 1903) and locates the action of the play on the bare stage of a contemporary Cracow theater, where Konrad, hero of *Forefathers' Eve*, has come to lead the nation to salvation. Konrad declares to the actors that there will be no play today, only a commedia improvisation to awaken the people from paralyzing dreams of past glory. In its theatricalist reckoning with masks of the past and settlement of accounts with romantic drama, *Deliverance* introduces techniques of parody, appropriation, and allusion characteristic of much 20th-century Polish drama.

Immersed in ancient Greek myth and Old Testament prophecy, Wyspiański brings the past alive in the present. *The Curse* (*Klątwa*, 1899) and *The Judges* (*Sędziowie*, 1907) are modern crime stories, rural *faits divers* (stories in the news) given high pictorial relief and elevated to the level of tragic fatality. Seeking the cause of a terrible drought that has blighted their crops, peasants in *The Curse* burn alive the mistress of their parish priest in order to bring rain. A family of Jewish country innkeepers in *Judges* calls down God's vengeance in condemning one of their own who has committed murder.

Turning to his beloved Homer, whose work he had illustrated, in *Achilles* (1903) Wyspiański reinterpreted the epic hero as a disillusioned and alienated opponent of the Trojan war, while he made his last play, *The Return of Odysseus* (*Powrót Odysa*, 1907), a sinister drama of the evil fate pursuing a violent, haunted man who cannot escape God's curse—a reflection of his own slow, agonizing death from syphilis contracted years earlier in Paris. He died on November 28, 1907 in Cracow.

In *November Night* (*Noc listopadowa*, 1904), his second drama about the 1830 uprising, Greek mythology animates Polish history. The entire action unfolds on the night of November 29 in the real places in Warsaw where the rebellion took place, but historical events are juxtaposed with the myth of Demeter and Persephone. The historical and supernatural become one; the soldiers engaged in the insurrection enact the roles of ancient warriors, playthings in the hands of Homeric gods, and the 1830 rebellion is transformed into an Eleusinian seasonal mystery of death and rebirth.

Influenced by Edouard Schuré's ideas about a "theatre of the soul," Wyspiański in *Acropolis* (1904) fashions a syncretism of Judaic, Greek, and Christian religious mythology. Set, on Easter eve, in the royal castle overlooking the city of Cracow and the river Vistula (which metaphorically become the Acropolis, Athens, and the Scamander), Wyspiański's visionary drama of death and resurrection has no human characters, only figures from sculpture, wall hangings, and architecture that, as the bells toll midnight, step down from their niches and tapestries to enact their stories from the Bible and *Iliad*. In the celebrated 1962 production by Jerzy Grotowski and Józef Szajna at the Laboratory Theatre, the action of *Acropolis* was transferred from the royal castle in Cracow to nearby Auschwitz.

Wyspiański's farsighted ideas about a new stagecraft, too advanced for his own day, became widely accepted and influential in the 1920s. Since then, Wyspiański's dramas have become a mainstay of the Polish repertory, constantly to be challenged and reinterpreted.

Wyspiański's language is impassioned and highly stylized, full of archaisms, folk dialect, and terse aphoristic sayings; his rhyming verse is richly allusive, containing antique motifs and manifold references to Polish history and art. His remarkable plays, which integrate the arts of poetry, painting, and music, have great power to stir the Polish cultural memory but remain almost impossible to translate or transpose to non-Polish dramatic traditions. For these reasons Wyspiański is an author who has not yet been estimated at his true worth outside Poland.

PLAYS: *Meleager* (1898); *Warszawianka* (1898); *The Curse* (*Klątwa*, 1899); *Lelewel* (1899); *Protesilas and Laodamia* (*Protesilas i Laodamia*, 1899); *Legion* (1900); *The Wedding* (*Wesele*, 1901); *Achillies* (1903); *Bolesław the Bold* (*Bolesław Śmiały*, 1903); *The Deliverance* (*Wyzwolenie*, 1903);

Acropolis (1904); Legenda (1904); November Night (Noc listopadowa, 1904); The Rock (Skałka, 1905); The Judges (Sędziowie, 1907); The Return of Odysseus (Powrót Odysa, 1907); Zygmunt August (1907)

FURTHER READING

"Profiles: Stanisław Wyspiański." www.culture.pl.[managed by Adam Mickiewicz Institute (AMI)]. http://www.culture.pl/en/culture/artykuly/os_wyspianski_stanislaw.

Schiller, Leon de Schildrenfeld. "The New Theatre in Poland: Stanisław Wyspiański." The Mask 2, nos. 1–3 (July 1909): 11–27; 2, nos. 4–6 (September 1909): 59–71.

Terlecka, Antonina Maria (Tola Korian). Stanisław Wyspiański and Symbolism. 27–28. Rome: Ex Antemurale, 1985–1986.

Terlecki, Tymon. Stanisław Wyspiański. Boston: Twayne, 1983.

Wyspiański, Stanislaw. The Return of Odysseus. Tr. and intro. by Howard Clark. Bloomington: Indiana Univ. Press, 1966.

Daniel Gerould

XENOPOULOS, GRIGORIOS (1867–1951)

A prolific playwright, novelist, and critic, Grigorios Xenopoulos dominated Greek cultural life for at least three decades. Xenopoulos was born in Istanbul (Constantinople) but spent his childhood and youth in the Ionian island of Zakynthos and all his adult life in Athens, GREECE. Already from his student years, he frequented literary circles of the capital, and he soon started working for the Press. His first attachment to theater came through criticism. In November 1894, in a speech preceding the first Greek performance of HENRIK IBSEN'S GHOSTS, he urged Greek playwrights to follow contemporary European developments and to embrace the vigorous realistic movement and especially Ibsen.

A year later, Xenopoulos wrote two plays influenced by the Norwegian dramatist: The Foster Father (O psychopateras, 1895) and The Third Man (O tritos, 1895). Nikolaos Lekatsas, the leading actor manager of the time, immediately performed both plays, which, despite their limited success onstage, initiated a thriving new career for their author and a whole new era for Greek DRAMATURGY. Xenopoulos's pieces were praised for their carefully constructed plot, the scrupulous but direct language, and the profound characterization. Moreover, they supplied directors and actors with intriguing plots and ingenious roles; most significantly, they advanced the tradition of middle-class drama in Greek theater.

Countess Valeraina's Secret (To mystiko tis Kontessas Valerainas), the drama Konstantinos Christomanos directed in 1904 at his pioneering independent theater in Athens, became a popular example of the new, realistic drama, for it recounted the departure from the ideals and principles upon which the nobility of the Ionian island had grounded its existence. The suppression of women and their right to love against patriarchal authority (Foteini Santri [1908] and Stella Violanti [1909]), the barriers that different religions and social classes raise between people (All Soul's Saturday [To psychosavvato, 1911] and Rachel [1909]), and the aspiring dreams and deadly conflicts that decide life for young students (The Students [Foititai, 1919]) are some of the subjects Xenopoulos discussed in his dramas, and they all manifest his intention to record aspects of contemporary life.

His COMEDIES also focused on the change in beliefs, mentality, and customs that Greek society was experiencing at the time. However, many of his plays are often accused of excessive sentimentality and a structure far too obedient to the stereotypes of the "well-made play" to be considered as a genuine part of the realistic tradition of the late 19th century. Xenopoulos's work, though, exactly demonstrates the way REALISM was initially embedded in Greek drama in order to reach contemporary audiences. The merging of realistic themes and perspective with earlier dramatic techniques facilitated the acceptance and presentation of these plays onstage, for it gave an appealing answer to a dominant question in Greek theater: the effects of foreign influences on national drama. Xenopoulos used previous trends that helped to attest Greekness to balance the "invasion" of the new trend. His success denotes not simply the limits of realism in the Greek drama of the time but also the unhurried path to the West that Greece was following.

SELECT PLAYS: The Foster Father (O psychopateras, 1895); The Third Man (O tritos, 1895); Countess Valeraina's Secret (To mystiko tis Kontessas Valerainas, 1904); Foteini Santri (1908); Rachel (1909); Stella Violanti (1909); The Temptation (O peirasmos, 1910); All Soul's Saturday (To psychosavvato, 1911); The Flower of Levant (To fioro tou Levante, 1914); It's Not Me (Den eimai ego, 1915); The Students (Foititai, 1919); The Plebeian (O popolaros, 1933)

FURTHER READING

"Grigorios Xenopoulos." Special issue of Nea Estia, no. 50 (Christmas 1951).

Spathis, Dimitris. "Grigorios Xenopoulos." In Istoria tou Neou Ellinismou [History of modern Hellenism]. Athens: Ellinika Grammata, 2004. 6:206.

Xenopoulos, Grigorios. I zoe mou san mythistorima [My life as a novel]. 1938–1939. Athens: Afoi Blassi, 1984.

Ioulia Pipinia

XIA YAN (1900–1995)

Xia Yan, whose original name was Shen Naixi, was one of the most prominent, influential, pioneering, and highly respected figures in the fields of modern drama, film, and literature in CHINA. He was awarded many official titles in the governing body of the Chinese cultural and literary worlds, including the associate chair of the Association of Chinese Literature and Arts. In 1965 he was harshly criticized for his assertions in literature and arts, removed from his official positions, and spent eight years in prison. He was rehabilitated in 1978, resumed his official posts, and was primarily in charge of the development of Chinese theater and filmmaking.

Born on October 30, 1900, in Zhejiang Province, China, at the age of twenty Xia Yan went to JAPAN, where he studied electronic engineering and participated in many leftist activities. After his return from Japan in 1927, he joined the Chinese Communist Party (CCP) and enthusiastically advocated "the proletarian drama," believing that drama of the time should represent the commoners and their lives. He translated many foreign literary theories and works into Chinese including MAKSIM GORKY'S novel Mat (Mother). In October 1929, he founded the Society of Shanghai Dramatists together with several new drama advocators and also became the chief editor of the leftist journal *The Arts*. In 1930, Xia helped to found the League of Left-Wing Writers and served as its first executive committee member.

As a witness of the turbulent events and tremendous social changes in Chinese society in the last century, Xia Yan passionately reflected his keen observations in his writings. His highly acclaimed play *Under the Eaves of Shanghai* (*Shanghai wuyan xia*, 1937) presented an innovative picture of the common people's struggle to survive against the backdrop of the impending national crisis of a Japanese invasion. Dramatizing the lives of five families residing in a typical house in Shanghai, Xia situated his three-set play in the early rainy summer and constituted the core of his theatrical tension on a revolutionist, Kuang Fu, and his homecoming after an eight-year imprisonment. Upon his return, he found his wife Cai Yu was living with his friend Lin Zhicheng and emotionally conflicted. The three of them nevertheless encountered the thorny issues of love, feeling, friendship, and grace accompanied by internal sorrow, frustration, despair, guilt, and the residuals of social turbulence. In the play, Xia also sketched a group of marginalized yet phenotypical and chromatic people—a discontented elementary school teacher, a sorrowful prostitute, a jobless clerk, a lonely senior news vendor who lost his son, and their unbearable and hopeless reality—and permitted the many individual problems of his characters to become the central problems of the play as a whole. He interwove such a love-triangle tale with multiple perspectives of individual character's depressing stories so as to evoke audience sympathy with them and to awake their desire for change. As a consequence of the Japanese invasion of Shanghai in 1937, *Under the Eaves of Shanghai* was not staged in Chongqing until 1939.

Xia Yan spent a great part of his life on the evolution of Chinese filmmaking. Many Chinese award-winning films were either scripted or adapted by him from successful stage performances and popular novels, including great modern Chinese writers Lu Xun's *Sacrifice* and Mao Dun's *The Shop of the Lin Family*.

In the People's Republic of China, it is customary to credit Xia Yan as a distinguished writer, journalist, translator, dramatist, screenwriter, film director, and film theorist. He died on February 6, 1995, in Beijing, China.

SELECT PLAYS: *Madam Sai Jinhua* (*Sai Jinhua*, 1936); *Under the Eaves of Shanghai* (*Shanghai wuyan xia*, 1937); *Free Soul/The Story of Qiu Jin* (*Ziyou hun/Qiu Jin zhuang*, 1937/1950); *In a Year/Paradise* (*Yi nian jian/Tian shang ren jian*, 1939/1944); *The Heart's Defense* (*Xin fang*, 1940); *The Account of Sorrow City* (*Chou cheng ji*, 1941); *The Fascist Bacillus* (*Faxisi xijun*, 1944); *The Fragrant Grass at the End of the World* (*Fang cao tian ya*, 1945); *The Test* (*Kaoyan*, 1955)

FURTHER READING

Chen Xiaomei. "Twentieth-Century Spoken Drama." In *The Columbia History of Chinese Literature*, ed. by Victor Mair. New York: Columbia Univ. Press, 2001.

Ge Yihon and Lu Fu, eds. *Zhongguo zuoyi xiju jia lianmeng shi liao ji* [Collected materials of the Chinese League of Left-Wing Dramatists]. Beijing: Zhongguo xiju chuban she, 1991.

Hui Lin, Chen Jian, and Shao Wu, eds. *Xia Yan yanjiu ziliao* [The materials of Xia Yan studies]. Beijing: Zhongguo xiju chuban she, 1983.

Tian Benxiang and Jiao Shangzhi. *Zhongguo huaju shi yanjiu kaishu* [An outline of Chinese spoken drama study]. Tianjin: Tianjin guji chuban she, 1993.

Xia Yan. *Under the Eaves of Shanghai: An Annotated Chinese Play*. Tr. by Richard Chang and William Lewis MacDonald. New Haven, Conn.: Far Eastern Publications, Yale Univ. Press, 1974.

Ping Fu

XIN JUZHANG LAI DAO ZHI QIAN, HUAJU
See BEFORE THE NEW BUREAU DIRECTOR CAME

XIONG FOXI (1900–1965)

Chinese playwright and educator Xiong Foxi was born in Fengcheng County, Jiangxi Province, CHINA, in 1900. He started schooling in a missionary school in Hankou, Hubei Province, where he often participated in its theatrical performances. From 1919 to 1922, Xiong studied education and Western literature at Yen-ching University, where he found his favorite authors in William Shakespeare, HENRIK IBSEN, GEORGE BERNARD SHAW, and others. In 1921 he joined the Literary Association, helped establish the People's Drama Society, and became an editor for the journal *Theater*. Xiong went on to do graduate work in drama and literature at Columbia University, New York City, in 1923. During that time he wrote *The First Day in the Year of Jiazi* (*Jiazi di yi tian*, 1926), *All from a Patriotic Heart* (*Yi pian aiguo xin*, 1925), and other plays. His first collection of plays was published in 1924 under the title *Sorrows of the Youth*. After his return to China in 1926, Xiong became a professor of dramatic arts at Beijing National Arts School, National Peking University, and Yen-ching University consecutively. During that time he wrote *Foxi on Drama*, *Principles of Playwriting*, and quite a few plays, of which *The Artist* (*Yishu jia*, 1928) and *The Tragedy of Lanzhi and Zhongqing* (*Lanzhi yu Zhongqing*, 1929) are more well known. At the invitation of the Chinese Society for Promoting Education among Common People in 1932, Xiong Foxi went to a rural experimental theater in Ding County of Hebei Province to engage in the experimentation and popularization of drama for the peasants.

During the Sino-Japanese War (1937–1945), Xiong served the Nationalist government as a theater director, president of Sichuan Provincial Drama School, and director of the Central Youth Theatrical Society. He went to various places to promote drama and wrote a number of anti-Japanese plays. After 1949, he was appointed a member of the National Association of Literature and Art and a member of the standing committee of the

Chinese Playwrights' Association, among other titles. He served as the first president of the Shanghai Drama School, later to be renamed Shanghai Institute of Drama. Meanwhile, Xiong Foxi continued to write plays and novels as well as short stories until his death on October 26, 1965, in Shanghai.

As an educator of drama, Xiong Foxi is primarily known for his role in promoting "amateur theater," along with Chen Dabei, Pu Boying, and OUYANG YUQIAN. Being quite versatile, he was good at producing COMEDIES of satire and FARCES, plays of parables, and social plays (All from a Patriotic Heart). All from a Patriotic Heart, a three-act play, was written in 1925 and published a year later. Centering on the issue of whether to sign a contract that betrayed Chinese coal mine rights, the play depicts a series of fundamental conflicts between Tang Huating, a revolutionary in the early republican period, and his Japanese wife Akiko, together with his son and daughter. Making use of the family conflict, the play successfully portrays a life-and-death struggle between the patriots and the traitors, eulogizing anti-imperialist patriotism. Besides its social significance, the play is also known for its vivid character portrayal, well-knit structure, and use of fluent vernacular. It is one of the most influential plays in Xiong Foxi's early playwriting.

SELECT PLAYS: Whose Fault Is This? (Zhe shi shui de cuo, 1921); Sorrows of the Youth (Qingchun di bei'ai, 1923); All from a Patriotic Heart (Yi pian aiguo xin, 1925); The First Day in the Year of Jiazi (Jiazi di yi tian, 1926); The Artist (Yishu jia, 1928); The Drunkard (Zuil, 1928); The Tragedy of Lanzhi and Zhongqing (Lanzhi yu Zhongqing, 1929); The Fruit of Love (Aiqing de jiejing, 1930); The Tragedy of a Poet (Shiren de beiju, 1930); The Chinese Descendants (Zhonghua minzu de zisun, 1938); Yuan Shikai (1942); The Spring in Shanghai (Shanghai tan de chuntian, 1956)

FURTHER READING

Chen Duo, et al. Xiandai xiju jia Xiong Foxi [The modern playwright Xiong Foxi]. Beijing: Zhongguo xiju chubanshe, 1985.

"Development of Peasants Drama." ChinaCulture.org. http://www .chinaculture.org/gb/en_artqa/2003-09/24/content_38624.htm.

Judd, Ellen R. "Cultural Articulation in the Chinese Countryside, 1937–1947." Modern China 16, no. 3 (July 1990): 269–308.

Sun Huizhu. "Xiong Foxi lingdao de dingxian nongmin xiju shiyan jiqi xianshi yiyi" [Xiong Foxi's experiment on peasant theater in Ding County and its social significance]. Xiju yishu (Theatre Arts) 1 (2001).

Xiong Foxi. The Artist. Translation of Yishu jia by Ku Tsong-nee. In Modern Chinese Plays, ed. and tr. by Ku Tsong-nee. Shanghai: Commercial Press, 1941. 119–137.

Hongchu Fu and Cai Xingshui

XU FEN (1933–)

Born in Chongqing in August 1933, Xu Fen was an actor in an army performance troupe from 1949 to 1954. She studied journalism at Beijing University, graduated in 1958, and was assigned to work in Sichuan Province. In 1961 she became the first female playwright in the history of chuanju (Sichuan Opera). Since then she has written more than thirty plays, mostly for the chuanju theater. She has been affiliated with the Chengdu Chuanju Troupe.

Her most representative work before the Cultural Revolution was Yanyan (1956), which promoted a revision, from a feminist point of view, of the characterization of the leading character of Guan Hanqing's Yuan zaju play A Girl Tricked Into Amorous Relations (Zha nizi tiao fengyue), in which Yanyan accepts her position as a concubine even after she had been taken advantage of, betrayed, and ridiculed by her man. Xu Fen could not accept such a fate for Yanyan; she turned the COMEDY into a TRAGEDY that calls for women's dignity by creating an unyielding and honest soul in Yanyan. Since the late 1970s, Xu's revision has been adapted into productions by troupes of different regional theaters and also produced on television.

In the same vein, she continued to write a series of plays, focusing on new portrayals of women, such as Sister Tian and Zhuang Zi (Tianjie yu Zhuang Zhou, 1986), Interrupted Dream of Red Chamber (Honglou jing meng, 1982), and Mulian's Mother (Mulian zhi mu, 1992). She has also turned to modern and contemporary themes, producing such plays as Billows out of Dead Waters (Sishui weilan, 1995), Governer's Wife: Dong Zhujun (Dudu furen Dong Zhujun, 2000), and Raging Tides in the Sea of Desire (Yuhai kuangchao, 1989). Billows out of Dead Waters, adapted from a novel of the same title, tells the story of a countrywoman who rebels against feudal ethics and pursues her own love in the ending years of the Qing Dynasty. Governer's Wife is based on an autobiography by Dong Zhujun, a woman entrepreneur, who had escaped from her occupation as a singsong girl at the age of fifteen and, after the failure of her marriage to one governor of Sichuan, started a restaurant of Sichuan cuisine in Shanghai, which later developed into the famous Jinjiang Hotel. Raging Tides in the Sea of Desire is adapted from EUGENE O'NEILL'S DESIRE UNDER THE ELMS, transforming the original story with a distinct Chinese environment. In this Sichuan Opera version, desire to possess permeates every character and brings everyone to ruin: the old landlord, his youngest son, his young wife, and the baby born out of the incestuous relationship. Xu Fen also wrote a one-act xiqu play, Lady Macbeth (Maikebai furen), joining the vogue of adapting Western classics onto the Chinese xiqu stage. Structurally, Xu Fen consciously reformed some of the chuanju conventions by quickening the pace of dramatic development, avoiding repetitions of similar plots, and replacing stock characters with those showing individual personalities.

Like WEI MINGLUN, Xu Fen has been writing mainly for Sichuan Opera. These two playwrights have been very innovative and, sometimes, controversial on the chuanju stage. Xu is undoubtedly one of the most important female playwrights on the contemporary scene. Her works have also appeared in Beijing

Opera (*The One and Only* [*Qiangu yiren*, 1996]), spoken drama (*The Tide of the 1911 Revolution* [*Xinhai chao*, 1990]), and dance drama (*Flowers of Distant Mountains* [*Yuanshan de huaduo*]).

[See also China]

SELECT PLAYS: *Yanyan* (1956); *The Story of a Scholar* (*Xiucai waizhuan*, 1960); *Wang Xifeng* (*Wang Xifeng*, 1963); *Interrupted Dream of Red Chamber* (*Honglou jing meng*, 1982); *Sister Tian and Zhuang Zi* (*Tianjie yu Zhuang Zhou*, 1986); *Raging Tides in the Sea of Desire* (*Yuhai kuangchao*, 1989); *The Tide of the 1911 Revolution* (*Xinhai chao*, 1990); *Mulian's Mother* (*Mulian zhi mu*, 1992); *Billows out of Dead Waters* (*Sishui weilan*, 1995); *The One and Only* (*Qiangu yiren*, 1996); *Governor's Wife: Dong Zhujun* (*Dudu furen Dong Zhujun*, 2000); *The Fall of Dust* (*Chen'ai luoding*, 2004); *Under the Mount Lanke* (*Lanke shanxia*, 2005)

FURTHER READING

"Chuanju Dudu furen Dong Zhujun zhuankan" [Special issue on the Sichuan Opera *Governor's Wife: Dong Zhujun*]. *Shanghai xiju* (Shanghai Drama) 11 (2001): 9–19.

Xu Fen. *Mulian zhi mu* [Mulian's Mother]. *Sichuan xiju* (Sichuan Drama) 4 (1993): 53–62.

———. *Sishui weilan* [Billows out of Dead Waters]. *Juben* (Play Scripts) 4 (1996): 2–18.

———. *Xu Fen xiju zuopin xuan* [Xu Fen's selected works of drama]. 2 vols. Chengdu: Sichuan wenyi chubanshe, 2001.

Wenwei Du

XU JIUJING SHENGGUAN JI, JINJU
See XU JIUJING'S PROMOTION

XU JIUJING'S PROMOTION
The Beijing Opera (*jingju*) *Xu Jiujing's Promotion* (*Xu Jiujing shengguan ji, jinju*), by Guo Dayou (1948–) and Xi Zhigan (1947–), belongs to a subgenre known as courtroom drama that dates back to the 13th century. (Guo Dayou and Xi Zhigan, both affiliated with the Beijing Opera Company of Hubei Province, write operas as well as film and television scripts.) As an embodiment of the Chinese conception of justice, *Xu Jiujing's Promotion* has been very popular with Chinese audiences since its premiere. In this modern version of the courtroom play (premiered in 1981), a low-ranking official, Xu Jiujing, is suddenly promoted to be the chief justice of the Supreme Court in order to try the case of a prince and a commander of the army suing each other, a case that the other justices are too afraid to take.

Unlike the judges in the traditional courtroom drama who mete out punishments to the others, Xu Jiujing must put his own conscience on trial as well. In the course of his investiga-

tion of this case, he discovers that the real culprit is the Prince's brother-in-law, not the Commander's son, as he had suspected. This turn of events is similar to the plot of "judgment reversal" plays in which the verdict of the first corrupt judge is overturned by that of the second. Xu now faces the moral dilemma of whether to repay the kindness of the Prince, who recommended him for the judgeship, or to rule in favor of the Commander, who is his political enemy. To maintain his original judgment or to overturn it becomes an ultimate test of his integrity and the focal point of the play. In the long aria "It's Hard to Be an Official," the playwrights display great verbal ingenuity by using the word *official* more than sixty times to highlight Xu's long-cherished ambition to climb the official ladder and the heavy price he must pay for it. Xu's self-revelation brings into sharp focus the conflict between his conscience and his self-interest. His inner struggle is further dramatized by two phantom images of himself, one urging him to follow his conscience, the other counseling him to look after his career. Emphasis on psychological conflict makes this opera different from the conventional courtroom drama.

Another innovation of this opera is to cast Xu Jiujing in the role of a clown (one of the four major role types in Beijing Opera) and to turn the solemn courtroom drama into a hilarious COMEDY. Xu's comic role also calls attention to the difficulty of upholding the rule of law. He succeeds in bringing the criminal to justice not by the power of law but through a ruse. The reward for his labor is not a promising official career but its termination. Despite the appearance of justice restored and the comic tone of the play, there is a note of resignation, as can be seen in Xu's exit poem: "The law of the land exists in vain. Common people have no recourse against power and rank. My official robe and cap I leave behind. You will find me under a crooked tree selling wine." Through this historical play, the playwrights expose the ills of contemporary Chinese society: official corruption and abuse of power in high places.

[See also China]

FURTHER READING

Guo Dayou and Xi Zhigan. *Xu Jiujing Shengguan ji* [Xu Jiujing's Promotion]. *Juben* (Play Scripts) 5 (1981): 2–24.

Hayden, George A. *Crime and Punishment in Medieval Chinese Drama: Three Judge Pao Plays*. Cambridge: Harvard Univ. Press, 1978.

Qi Zhixiang. "*Xu Jiujing shengguan ji guanju duanxiang*" [Thoughts on *Xu Jiujing's Promotion*]. *Juben* (Play Scripts) 5 (1981): 74–75.

Xu Jiujing's Promotion. In *Chinese Drama After the Cultural Revolution, 1979–1989*, tr. and ed. by Shiao-ling S. Yu. Lewiston, N.Y.: Edwin Mellen Press, 1996. 35–94.

Shiao-ling Yu

Y

YAMAMOTO YŪZŌ (1887–1974)

Yamamoto Yūzō (1887–1974), a Japanese SHINGEKI and SHINPA playwright, was born in Tochigi Machi, Tochigi Prefecture. His father was a dry-goods dealer, and Yamamoto, at the age of fifteen, started working at a dry-goods store in Tokyo. But he persuaded his father to let him attend school, and in 1909, at twenty-one, he entered the First Gymnasium in Tokyo. In the fall of that year, he saw HENRIK IBSEN's JOHN GABRIEL BORKMAN at the Free Theatre (Jiyū Gekijō), the first Ibsen performance in JAPAN, and was greatly moved. The next year, he wrote his first play, A Hole (Ana, 1911) which was performed by students of the Tokyo School of Actors a year later. A Hole was based on his own experience of visiting the Ashio Copper Mine, the subject of much contemporary criticism for mine pollution. The author's intention, however, was to draw a realistic picture of mining without any particular bias. This would be Yamamoto Yūzō's basic attitude throughout his playwriting career.

In 1912, Yamamoto entered Tokyo Imperial University, majoring in German literature. He began to translate German plays and write theater reviews. Graduating in 1915, Yamamoto joined the Inoue Masao Company but soon after moved to the Shinpa Triangular League (Shinpa Sankaku Dōmei) of Akizuki Keitarō, Kawakami Sadayakko, and Kitamura Rokurō, where he directed Mushakōji Saneatsu's Two Hearts and His Sister. In 1917 Yamamoto wrote Professor Tsumura (Tsumura Kyōju), now considered one of his best plays. It has been pointed out that AUGUST STRINDBERG's CREDITORS influenced this play, but Yamamoto had no sympathy with Strindberg's woman hating. He was much closer to the sentiment and morality of the Edo era (1603–1868). Professor Tsumura was produced by a kabuki actor, Morita Kan'ya XIII, at the Imperial Theatre (Teikoku Gekijō) in 1920. Shortly before that, Yamamoto's new play, The Crown of Life (Inochi no Kanmuri, 1920) was performed by the Inoue Company. Both productions were successful, and he firmly established his position as a promising young playwright. Thus, he was one of those contributing to the so-called Flowering Age of Taishō (1912–1923) Drama.

During the 1920s, most of Yamamoto's plays were performed by progressive young kabuki actors, such as Kan'ya, Onoe Kikugorō VI, and Matsumoto Kōshirō VII, or by talented shinpa actors, such as Inoue Masao, Mizutani Yaeko, and Hanayagi Shōtarō. In 1924 Yamamoto started a theater magazine, Engeki Shinchō, together with KIKUCHI KAN, OSANAI KAORU, and others but came to be in conflict with Osanai, who declared that he found no Japanese play good enough to be put onstage at his newly founded Tsukiji Little Theatre (Tsukiji Shōgekijō). Osanai's criticism of new Japanese plays was in a way justified, for young dra-

matists were mainly interested in commercial success in the traditional theater world. Yamamoto Yūzō was no doubt one of them. Even his best-known play, Baby-Killing (Eiji Goroshi, 1921) in which the author is sympathetic to a poor woman's baby killing, ends with the arrest of the woman.

Yamamoto wrote several historical plays, too, such as Sakazaki, Lord of Dewa (Sakazaki Dewa no Kami, 1921), Comrades (Dōshi no Hitobito, 1925), Saigō and Ōkubo (Saigō to Ōkubo, 1928), and The Sad Tale of a Woman, the Story of Chink Okichi (Nyonin Aishi, 1933), among others, all of which were performed by either kabuki or shinpa actors. In the Shōwa era (1926–1989), however, Yamamoto was primarily engaged with writing novels.

[See also Shin Kabuki]

SELECT PLAYS: A Hole (Ana, 1911); The Cluster-Amaryllis (Manjushage, published 1914); Professor Tsumura (Tsumura Kyōju, 1919); The Crown of Life (Inochi no Kanmuri, 1920); Baby-Killing (Eiji Goroshi, 1921); Sakazaki, Lord of Dewa (Sakazaki Dewa no Kami, 1921); Mother (Onna Oya, 1922); Shiman Story (Shiman Enngi, 1922); The Maid's Illness (Jochū no Byōki, published 1924); Monk Kumagai Renshō (Kumagai Renshō Bō, 1924); The Patron Saint (Honzon, 1924); Susanoo no Mikoto (published 1924); Umihiko and Yamahiko (Umihiko Yamahiko, 1924); Visiting Ōiso (Ōiso-Gayoi, published 1924); Comrades (Dōshi no Hitobito, 1925); Kamon and Hichirōemon (Kamon to Hichirōemon, 1927); Saigō and Ōkubo (Saigō to Ōkubo, 1928); Blind Brother (Mōmoku no Otōto, 1930); The Sad Tale of a Woman, the Story of Chink Okichi (Nyonin Aishi, 1933); Father (Chichioya, 1934); Hundred Bags of Rice (Kome Hyappō, 1943)

FURTHER READING

Keene, Donald. Dawn to the West: Japanese Literature in the Modern Era: Poetry, Drama, Criticism. New York: Henry Holt, 1984.

Yamamoto, Yūzō. Three Plays by Yamamoto Yūzō. Tr. by Glenn W. Shaw. Tokyo: Hokuseido, 1957.

——. Yamamoto Yūzō Zenshū [The collected works of Yamamoto Yūzō]. Tokyo: Iwanami Shoten, 1939–1941.

——. Yamamoto Yūzō Zenshū [The collected works of Yamamoto Yūzō]. Tokyo: Shinchōsha, 1976–1977.

INOUE Yoshie and Mitsuya Mori

YAMAZAKI MASAKAZU (1934–)

Yamazaki Masakazu (1934–), a Japanese SHINGEKI playwright, philosopher, critic, political adviser, and college president, was born in Manchuria while it was a Japanese colony. Writing in a wide range of styles, his constant theme is the shifts between reality and illusion, as individuals forge their identities through action (or inaction).

Often Yamazaki's plots revolve around a historic figure caught in a crucible of ambition, obligation, and faith: In *Zeami* (1963), Yamazaki explores the eponymous founder of classical Nō theater. The actor-director's struggle to achieve individual expression even while enjoying the protection of the shogun is depicted as "the tension between a total dedication to art and the human pressures of society, family, and the familiar world" (Rimer, 1980). Rather than transmit his art to an unworthy successor, Zeami refuses to divulge his secrets, content to be a shadow, fighting the darkness, following the light. Yamazaki's philosophical debates are skillfully interwoven with dance and song (*Zeami* later became a musical). The play is full of resonant symbols, such as a damask drum that makes a sound when struck.

Sanetomo Sets Sail (*Sanemoto Shuppan*, 1973) portrays the brief life of Minamoto Sanetomo (1192–1219), who attempted unsuccessfully to build a ship to sail to CHINA. Sanetomo's story is told by reluctant ghosts rehearsing their histories, gradually drawn into their roles by Sanetomo's charismatic force. J. Thomas Rimer hears echoes of *Hamlet* in the play's family intrigues and play-within-play framing, while Ted Takaya finds in Sanetomo's ambitious failure the need of an individual with a "profound spiritual vacuum . . . desperately trying to fill this void by immersing himself in feverish activity" (Takaya, 1979).

This Boat Is a Sailboat (*Fune wa Hansen yo*, 1973) has a contemporary setting, depicting the vague ambivalence of the postwar generation unable to feel passionately toward a career, marriage partner, or even a hobby. The style is semiabsurd, with mysterious visitors, elliptical conversations, and repetitions. At its end, the young company man antihero, who has changed jobs and residence every two years, disappears again. In a stunningly theatrical finale, the movers disassemble his room (the stage set) panel by panel, leaving a retired museum guard from the prewar generation alone on the bare stage, silent in an antique rocking chair.

Yamazaki demonstrates broad knowledge of both Western and Japanese history and literature. The musical *We Saw Rome* (*Roma o Mita*, 1989) follows the triumph and terror of the four young imperial envoys accompanying an Italian missionary to visit the pope in 1590, only to discover on their return to Japan that Christianity has been banned. The tensions between the great self-made shogun and his tea master are revealed in *Keeping a Lion: Rikyū and Hideyoshi* (*Shishi o Kau, Rikyū to Hideyoshi*, 1992). Modernity is viewed through the lens of the pioneering career of *Life* photographer Margaret Bourke-White in *20th Century* (*Nijū Seiki*, 2000).

Yamazaki's works are stimulating expressions of the postwar theater's continuing redefinition of individual freedom and responsibility as traditional values confront the pressures of modern institutions. His plays fuse Japanese sensitivity to the transience of material objects with a practical application of Western play craftsmanship.

[See also Absurdism; Japan]

SELECT PLAYS: *Castle of Cards* (*Karta no Shiro*, 1962); *Zeami* (1963); *Ambition and Summer Grass* (*Yabō to Natsugusa*, 1970); *Sanemoto Sets Sail* (*Sanemoto Shuppan*, 1973); *This Boat Is a Sailboat* (*Fune wa Hansen yo*, 1973); *We Saw Rome* (*Roma o Mita* [musical], 1989); *Zeami* ([musical] 1990); *Keeping a Lion: Rikyū and Hideyoshi* (*Shishi o Kau, Rikyū to Hideyoshi*, 1992); *20th Century* (*Nijū Seiki*, 2000)

FURTHER READING

Yamazaki Masakazu. *This Boat Is a Sailboat.* Tr. by Ted Takaya. In *Modern Japanese Drama: An Anthology*, ed. and tr. by Ted Takaya. New York: Columbia Univ. Press, 1979. 137–202.

——. *Zeami and Sanemoto.* Tr. by J. Thomas Rimer. In *Mask and Sword: Two Plays for the Contemporary Japanese Theater*, ed. by J. Thomas Rimer. New York: Columbia Univ. Press, 1980. 1–93; 98–181.

——. "The Aesthetics of Transformation: Zeami's Dramatic Theories." Tr. by Susan Matisoff. *Journal of Japanese Studies* 7 (Summer 1981): 215–358.

——. *Chōsakushū* [Collected plays]. 12 vols. Tokyo: Chūo Kōronsha, 1982.

——. *Individualism and the Japanese: An Alternative Approach to Cultural Comparison.* Tr. by Barbara Sugihara. Tokyo: Japan Echo, 2001.

Zeami Mtokiyo. *On the Art of Nō Drama: The Major Treatises of Zeami.* Tr. by J. Thomas Rimer and Masakazu Yamazaki. Princeton, N.J.: Princeton Univ. Press, 1984.

Jonah Salz

YANG LANCHUN (1921–)

Born in Wu'an, Hebei Province, in 1921, Yang Lanchun joined the Eighth Route Army in 1943, where he was engaged in educational activities through theatrical performances till 1948. After his demobilization from the army, he worked as head of the performing troupe (*wengongtuan*) of the Luoyang City, then as head of the Luoyang District of Henan Province. From 1950 to 1953, he studied in the Song and Dance Department of the Central Academy of Drama in Beijing. Then he was appointed the associate leader and director of the Henan Folk Opera Troupe (Henan Geju Tuan). In 1956 he was reassigned to the Henan Yuju Opera Troupe (Henan Yuju Yuan) as the leader of its third performance division (Henan Yuju Yuan San Tuan). Since then he has been professionally adapting and writing plays for *yuju*, one of the leading and most influential regional traditional theaters in CHINA. His troupe has been nationally influential as well. His reputation arose nationally when his *yuju* play *Chao Yang Village* (*Chao Yang Gou*) achieved huge success in 1958.

Chao Yang Village is a play in the traditional theatrical form but with a modern theme—belonging to a theatrical category termed in Chinese *xiqu xiandaixi* (*xiqu* plays of modern or contemporary themes). The genre was started in the 1950s when there was a national call for theatrical reforms on *xiqu* (traditional theater). The underlying reason for this reform was that the time had changed and the more than 300 forms of traditional theater should also depict the life and events of the contemporary people and society. Throughout the late 1950s and early 1960s, plays of modern and contemporary themes were one of the three major directions for *xiqu* playwriting and performances. *Chao Yang Village* has remained a classic in this direction, and its arias have been popularized through its later performances and the film it was made into in 1963.

It tells the story of Yinhuan, an educated city girl, following Shuanbao, her classmate and boyfriend, to Shuanbao's home village Chao Yang Gou (literally, Sun-facing Valley). Unaccustomed to the simple life and hard labor in the countryside, and pressured by her mother who looks down upon agricultural work, Yinhuan returns to her city temporarily. She later finds that her mother has pretended to be sick in order to lure her back to the city. At the same time, she is moved by Shuanbao and his villagers' boundless concern for her. She goes back to settle down in the countryside with Shuanbao as the first generation of peasants who have received education. The play develops through a series of tortuous but rewarding life experiences to reflect new images of educated youths in a vast agricultural field where they can also put their knowledge and strength to good use. The play was successfully revived after the Cultural Revolution. In 1982, Yang wrote its sequel, titled *Inside Story of Chao Yang Village* (*Chao Yang Gou neizhuan*).

Like *Chao Yang Village*, most of Yang Lanchun's plays focus on modern and contemporary themes, staged by his third division of the Henan Yuju Troupe. His major contribution as a playwright and director has been his successful advocacy and support of the modern plays of the *xiqu* form. Although his plays have been mainly of the *yuju* type, some of his plays have been adapted into other regional theaters as well, such as Beijing Opera, *pingju*, *lüju*, and *meihu*. The spirit and experience of his focus on modern plays have exerted significant influence on the whole movement of theater reform. He has served as vice chairman of the Association of Chinese Dramatists.

SELECT PLAYS: *Xiao Erhei's Marriage* (*Xiao Erhei jiehun*, *geju*, 1952; *yuju*, 1953); *Chao Yang Village* (*Chao Yang Gou*, *yuju*, 1958); *Spring Comes as Winter Goes* (*Dong qu chun lai*, *yuju*, 1959); *Li Shuangshuang* (*yuju*, 1963); *Apricot Flower Camp* (*Xinghua ying*, *yuju*, 1965); *Inside Story of Chao Yang Village* (*Chao Yang Gou neizhuan*, *yuju*, 1982); *Inside and Outside the Family* (*Jia li jia wai*, *yuju*, 1990)

FURTHER READING

Niu Qingpo. "Yang Lanchun xiandaixi chuangzuo qiantan" [Preliminary remarks on Yang Lanchun's creation of modern plays]. *Henan xiju* (Henan Drama) 12 (1984).

Wang Hongyu et al., eds. *Yang Lanchun bian dao yishu lun* [On the aesthetics of Yang Lanchun's playwriting and directing]. Beijing: Zhongguo xiju chubanshe, 1993.

Yang Lanchun. *Chao Yang Gou* [*Chao Yang Village*]. Juben (Play Scripts) 7 (1958).

Cai Xingshui and Wenwei Du

YANKOWITZ, SUSAN (1941–)

Playwright, screenwriter, and novelist Susan Yankowitz was born on February 20, 1941, in Newark, New Jersey. She earned her bachelor's degree from Sarah Lawrence College in 1963 and went on to earn her master's of fine arts degree in playwriting from the Yale School of Drama in 1968. Her first play, *The Cage*, was produced at Omar Khayyam Café in New York in 1965. *Nightmare* was produced at Yale in 1967, followed by *Old Rock-a-Bye* at Cooper Square Arts Theatre in 1968. Yankowitz's career as a writer thus began in the Yale–New York corridor of the mid-1960s, a time when the methods of the theatrical AVANT-GARDE included collaboration, political engagement, formal innovation, and risk taking.

Yankowitz began collaborating with the Open Theatre, directed by Joseph Chaikin, shortly after leaving Yale. Her abilities as a DRAMATURG and synthesizer of collaboratively generated material led to one of her best-known early works, *Terminal* (1969), with the Open Theatre. Yankowitz also was a founder and vigorous collaborator with other theater groups during this period: the Playwrights' Cooperative; the Cubiculo Theatre (where she wrote *The Ha-Ha Play* in 1970); Joseph Papp and the New York Shakespeare Festival, which produced her *Slaughterhouse Play* (1971); and the Westbeth Playwrights' Feminist Collective, where she wrote the one-act *Positions* (1972) and contributed to *The Wicked Women Revue* (1975). Yankowitz also gained recognition outside New York in this period with, for example, *The Lamb* (1973), at the Academy Theatre, Atlanta; *American Piece* (1974), for the Provisional Theatre in Los Angeles; and *Qui est Anna Marks?* (1979), at Théâtre l'Est Parisien in Paris.

FEMINIST concerns, social justice, civil rights issues, and the sources and effects of violence have been consistent themes in Yankowitz's work. "As a writer, I am almost always drawn to the drama of people in extreme situations, people pushed by fate or accident or character to the edge of some abyss, personal or political," Yankowitz explained in her introduction to *Night Sky* (1992).

Yankowitz's plays have had a significant production history in New York and throughout the UNITED STATES, and many of her dramas have been published and translated. Her play about a mass murderer, *A Knife in the Heart*, premiered at the EUGENE O'NEILL Theatre Center in 1982, was produced at Williamstown Theater Festival the following year, and was revived by Sledgehammer Theatre in San Diego in 2002. *Baby* opened at the Barrymore Theater in New York in 1983. The British company MONSTROUS REGIMENT commissioned her to write *Alarms*, a romp about Greek deities, fairy tales, and sexism, in 1986. *Night Sky*, about a woman astronomer who develops aphasia, was produced at Women's Project and Productions (1992). Yankowitz joined the 1996 reunion of Open Theatre members for a reconsideration of *Terminal*, writing *1969 Terminal 1996*, which premiered at Seven Stages Theatre in Atlanta. *Phaedra in Delirium* was co-produced by the Women's Project and Classic Stage Company in 1998 and again at Sledgehammer in 2003. *Cheri*, a musical with composer Michael Dellaira, premiered at Actors' Studio in New York in June 2003. Yankowitz has received National Endowment for the Arts, Guggenheim, and Rockefeller Foundation grants and awards and is a member of PEN and New Dramatists.

SELECT PLAYS: *The Cage* (1965); *Nightmare* (1967); *Old Rock-a-Bye* (1968); *Rats' Alley* (1969); *Terminal* (1969); *The Ha-Ha Play* (1970); *Slaughterhouse Play* (1971); *Boxes* (1972); *Positions* (1972); *The Lamb* (1973); *Wooden Nickels* (1973); *American Piece* (1974); *Portrait of a Scientist as a Dumb Broad* (1974); *Still Life* (1977); *True Romances* (1978); *Qui est Anna Marks?* (1979); *A Knife in the Heart* (1982); *Who Done It?* (1982); *Baby* (1983); *Alarms* (1986); *Night Sky* (1992); *1969 Terminal 1996* (1996); *Slain in the Spirit: The Promise of Jim Jones* (music by Taj Mahal, 1996); *Phaedra in Delirium* (1998); *Cheri* (music by Michael Dellaira, 2003)

FURTHER READING

Betsko, Kathleen, and R. Koenig, eds. *Interviews with Contemporary Women Playwrights*. New York: Beech Tree Bks., 1987.
Partnow, Elaine. *The Female Dramatist*. New York: Facts on File, 1998.
Sainer, Arthur. *The Radical Theatre Notebook*. New York: Avon Bks., 1975.

Beth Cleary

YAO YI-WEI (1922–1997)

Yao Yi-wei was born in Mainland CHINA. He received his bachelor's degree from the University of Xiamen in Mainland China in 1946. After graduation, he went to Taiwan. While working at the Bank of Taiwan, Yao devoted himself to drama education, playwriting, and theater activities.

In Taiwan, the beginning of the dynamic contemporary *huaju* theater can be traced back to *huaju* reform, which started in the 1960s and promoted pursuit of the arts rather than promotion of an anticommunist ideology. As a leading member of the Committee of Chinese Spoken Drama Appreciation, Yao held the five-year Experimental Drama Festival from 1980 to 1984, which made the LITTLE THEATER MOVEMENT successful in the 1980s and helped modernize Taiwan theater. In 1982, retired from the bank, he helped found the National Institute of the Arts (renamed as Taipei National University of the Arts in 2001), where he established the Department of Theatre. He

inspired and educated numerous talents and was called "the mentor of our time" (*yidai daoshi*).

Yao Yi-wei expanded the repertoire of locally written plays and took a more creative direction for spoken drama. He wrote fourteen plays and directed two productions—*Red Nose* (*Hong bizi*, co-directed with Chen Ling-ling, 1989) and *Re-Start* (*Chongxin kaishi*, 1995). His works deal with such themes as the existence of human beings, moral integrity, personal freedom, and the pursuit of artistic perfection.

Yao Yi-wei's *Red Nose*, the first stage play produced by a professional troupe, became a classic among local plays. After its 1970 debut by amateurs, the play was staged by professionals in Beijing in 1982 and JAPAN in 1987. In 1988, it was the first stage production produced by the new National Theater in Taipei. In *Red Nose*, Yao explored the issues of human nature, good deeds, pretense and truth, power and virtue, through the protagonist, who is playing a clown in a troupe. The clown, Red Nose, performs in the hotel with his circus team members in order to have shelter and food. Red Nose, who always wears a mask, not only brings laughter to the guests in the hotel but also takes care of his teamworkers as a spiritual supporter. His existence is symbolized as a Nobody, and yet he brings happiness to people in the world. It is only in the end that we (the troupe members, the hotel guests in the play, and the readers and spectators) find out that underneath the funny mask the person who plays the outgoing clown is in fact a shy white-collar bourgeois worker who has fled his previous life. He had disappeared for several years. At the play's climax, his wife, who has been looking for him, takes off his mask. Hidden in a small troupe, beneath the grotesque makeup, costume, ridiculous jokes, songs, and dance, the confident clown performer is actually her missing shy husband who was not happy with his former life. Yao's *Red Nose* gets at the core of human nature and discusses the essence of happiness and accomplishments.

Yao Yi-wei pointed out: "A great artist not only belongs to the people in his/her time, but also belongs to . . . mankind [a] thousand years later. [S]he not only belongs to a narrow area, but also belongs to the human beings in broad sense. Thus, [s]he must be the artist of the whole human beings." (*Yao Yi-wei*, 1968). Yao is also accomplished in aesthetic theories; literary, dramatic, and artistic criticism; and essays. Since the 1950s, Yao had participated in editing several important literary journals, such as *Literature Review* and *Modern Literature*. He is regarded by the literature world as "the person holding the light lamp at dark night."

PLAYS: *From Phoenix Town* (*Laizi fenghuangzhen de ren*, 1963); *Sun Feihu Robs the Bride* (*Sun Feihu qiang qin*, 1965); *The Emerald Bodhisativa* (*Nian yu Guanyin*, 1967); *Red Nose* (*Hong bizi*, 1969); *The Crown Prince Shen-Sheng* (*Shen sheng*, 1971); *A Suitcase* (*Yi kou xiangzi*, 1973); *Fu Qingzhu* (1978); *Let's Go and See Together* (*Women yitong zouzou kan*, 1979); *Zuo Botao* (1980); *Visitor* (*Fang ke*, 1984); *The Legend of the Tree*

God (*Da shu shen chuanqi*, 1985); *The Courier Station of Ma Wei* (*Ma Wei Yi*, 1987); *Miss X* (*X xiaojie*, 1991); *Re-start* (*Chongxin kaishi*, 1993)

FURTHER READING

Hwang Mei-shu. "Yao Yi-wei: A Modern Chinese Playwright." *Tamkang Review* 9, no. 2 (Winter 1978): 159–198.

Tian Benxiang. "Yao Yi-wei lun" [On Yao Yi-wei]. *Xiju yishu* (Theatre Art) 6 (2000): 81–87.

Yao Yi-wei. *The Secret of Art*. Taipei: Kai Ming, 1968.

——. *The Chest*. Tr. of *Yi kou xiangzi* by Mei-shu Hwang. *Tamkang Review* 9, no. 2 (Winter 1978): 199–232.

——. *Hong bizi* [Red Nose]. Tr. by Ying-chu Yeh. Master's thesis, Iowa State Univ., 1981.

Iris Hsin-chun Tuan

YEATS, W. B. (1865–1946)

What attracts me to drama is that it is, in the most obvious way, what all the arts are upon analysis. A farce and a tragedy are alike in this, that they are a moment of intense life. An action is taken out of all other actions; it is reduced to its simplest form. . . . The characters that are involved in it are freed from everything that is not a part of that action . . . it is an energy, an eddy of life, purified of everything but itself. The dramatist must picture life in acting . . . as the musician pictures it in sound and the sculptor in form.

—W. B. Yeats, 1904

William Butler (W. B.) Yeats, poet and playwright, was born on June 13, 1865, in Sandymount, County, Dublin, IRELAND, the eldest of four children of John Butler (J. B.) Yeats and Susan Pollexfen Yeats. His mother sank into decline as J. B. Yeats gave up the practice of law to become a painter and, going deeper with each year into debt, took his family to London, where W. B. Yeats went to school; his happiest days were summers in Sligo, where his mother's father and brothers were important figures in commerce and shipping. During the 1880s, Yeats entered art school in Dublin, but his real gift rapidly showed itself to be literary. By the 1890s, his mother was dead by a stroke, and his father was unable to support the family; Yeats had to make a living by his pen.

After meeting the beautiful insurrectionary Maud Gonne, in January 1889, Yeats began his first verse play, *The Countess Kathleen* (1892). Its central character is a wealthy Irish landowner who gives her wealth away and finally sells her soul to save a starving peasantry. Yeats's subsequent plays also drew upon his own life experience, symbolically transfigured. His first play to be staged was *The Land of Heart's Desire* at the Avenue Theatre, London, in 1894. Set in a peasant's cabin, in County Sligo, and based on folklore about Irish faeries, *The Land of Heart's Desire* became a model for other playwrights of the Irish Literary Revival.

While his reputation as a poet grew, Yeats longed to give himself and Ireland a forum for literary expression on an Irish stage. In 1897, Yeats, Edward Martyn, LADY GREGORY, and George Moore began to establish the Irish Literary Theatre (1899–1901). Yeats's *The Countess Kathleen* was produced during its first season, May 1899. It was condemned for its unorthodox presentation of Catholic beliefs and its favorable picture of an Irish landlord. In April 1902, CATHLEEN NI HOULIHAN, a one-act folkplay in prose, with Maud Gonne in the title role, and co-authored by Lady Gregory, was a great success. It was obvious propaganda for physical-force resistance to British rule in Ireland, and Yeats wrote no other plays quite like it.

In the summer of 1902, Yeats was elected president of the Irish National Theatre Society, a position he held until his last years. Yeats's aim as leader of the theater was not to propagandize for Irish Home Rule but to create an aesthetic and Irish alternative to HENRIK IBSEN'S REALISM and to London's drawing-room romances and COMEDIES. Yeats's ideals for theater were antimodern, antirealistic, and anti–middle class; he was in favor of a total theater, involving music, painting, poetry, and dancelike movement. On behalf of these aims, he engaged the support of an English heiress, Annie Horniman, who bought the Abbey Theatre for the Irish National Theatre Society and subsidized its actors. Yeats tried many innovative experiments at the Abbey, with nonrealistic lighting, sets, and costume designs by English artists such as Charles Ricketts and Gordon Craig, musical accompaniment by a stringed instrument called a psaltery, and various methods of producing dramatic verse. The chief successes of the theater by 1910, however, were its realistic plays by LENNOX ROBINSON and T. C. Murray.

In 1916, Yeats received new inspiration for playwriting from the NŌ plays of JAPAN, which combine poetic texts with masked actors, a chorus, dance, music, simple props, and no scenery. That nō performances were ceremonies for initiates also pleased Yeats, who was weary of failures to write down to the popular taste. The first performance of AT THE HAWK'S WELL (1916) was in the drawing room of a London mansion. The play resembles the concerns of his poetry and early dramatic work in that it gives a picture of the heroic life with great intensity, draws upon Irish myths, and foregrounds the speaking of beautiful verse, but the AVANT-GARDE adaptation of the Japanese form managed to escape the pseudo-Shakespearianism of Yeats's early work. Most of Yeats's later dramatic work follows from this formal experiment.

Two thematic elements of the nō plays that attracted Yeats—always interested in the occult and otherworldly beliefs—were the representation of ghosts who appear onstage to tell of the passions of their past lives and of demons who must be exorcised. Yeats's *The Only Jealousy of Emer* (1919) had both these elements: the appearance of the Ghost of Cuchulain, after he had died fighting the sea, and his possession by the demon Bricriu, who must be exorcised by Cuchulain's wife Emer. Because the play is so deeply involved with Yeats's conflicts over his recent marriage to George Hyde-Lees, and his forsaking of

Maud Gonne, the action is not easy to comprehend, but it is one of the most intensely beautiful of his theater pieces.

In November 1923 Yeats won the Nobel Prize; his speech of acceptance gave credit to "The Irish Dramatic Movement" as a whole. Yeats's contribution to the cultural movement in Ireland was also recognized by his election to the Senate of the Irish Free State (1923–1928). In February 1926, when the Abbey audience disrupted a performance of SEAN O'CASEY's THE PLOUGH AND THE STARS (felt to be an offense to those who died in the 1916 rebellion), Senator Yeats came before the curtain to denounce with great magnificence the disgraceful treatment of a work of art; the protestors were simply rocking "the cradle of genius," a phrase that became an epithet for the Abbey Theatre.

In May 1928 Yeats rejected for performance O'Casey's THE SILVER TASSIE, leading to a prolonged withdrawal by the Abbey Theatre's finest playwright. Yeats had little understanding of, and no sympathy for, EXPRESSIONISM, a style in which part of O'Casey's play was written. The same dislike caused Yeats to reject Denis Johnston's expressionist The Old Lady Says "No!" in 1928. Yet the poet had not become a theatrical traditionalist; he was simply interested in other kinds of experiment. In 1929, for instance, he rewrote The Only Jealousy of Emer as a ballet for Ninette de Valois, with avant-garde music scored by Ezra Pound's friend George Antheil.

Three of Yeats's most successful theater pieces were written in the 1930s, a period when he kept abreast of experiments in the writing of verse drama by W. H. AUDEN and T. S. ELIOT. The first of these successes—The Words Upon the Windowpane (1934)—was based on a modern séance (many of Yeats's plays are virtual séances themselves) in which the turbulent ghost of Jonathan Swift takes possession of the medium, an old woman named Mrs. Henderson. Swift is followed by the ghosts of his two lovers, Stella and Vanessa. The whole agonized drama of Swift's romantic, political, and medical life is then played out through Mrs. Henderson in front of guests who had hoped to contact departed friends and relatives. The drama manages to be spine-tingling and historically fascinating at once.

The second theatrical triumph of the poet in the 1930s was PURGATORY (1938), a horrifying one-act ghost play in which an old man tries by means of murder of his own son to free his mother from suffering in the next life. Its form is a very free adaptation from the nō tradition: centering on a remorseful ghost, but played without masks, the ritual unfolding of a curtain, attendant musicians, or a chorus. At the play's end, Yeats faced an Abbey audience for the last time, and after storms of applause (unusual in his experience), he said he had put into the play "my own beliefs about this world and the next." The Death of Cuchulain (1939) was being written right up to the death of Yeats. The fifth play about the Irish hero with whom the poet had come to identify, it depicts Cuchulain with mistress, wife, muse, and

the goddess of war, all of whom confront him at death's door. In the end, a blind man beheads the hero, bound and wounded, for a few pennies' reward. The dying man sees his soul take the shape of a bird, and Emer comes on to dance with his severed head. The play is weird, grand, brutal, and highly personal.

Yeats created a forum for the first subsidized national theater in the English-speaking world. He managed its affairs so that the Abbey became known worldwide for the quality of its dramatic writing and its focus on storytelling. Few playwrights had either the desire or ability to follow Yeats in the lyric and tragic qualities of his own plays, nor did those works—because of their strangeness, intensity, and limited plots—attract popular audiences. Playgoers continued to prefer what Yeats hated: realistic representations of modern life in conversational prose. Still, Yeats's verse plays are the best in English in the past two centuries. He influenced the dramatic work of T. S. Eliot, SAMUEL BECKETT, THOMAS KILROY, and others. His work presents one of the few alternatives to the central realist tradition of the modern stage. Yeats died January 28, 1939, at Cap Martin, Riviera, FRANCE.

SELECT PLAYS: *The Countess Kathleen* (1892); *The Land of Heart's Desire* (1894); *Cathleen ni Houlihan* (with Lady Gregory, 1902); *The Pot of Broth* (with Lady Gregory, 1902); *The King's Threshold* (1903); *On Baile's Strand* (1904); *Deirdre* (1906); *At the Hawk's Well* (1916); *The Dreaming of the Bones* (1919); *The Only Jealousy of Emer* (1919); *Calvary* (1920); *The Cat and the Moon* (1926); *Sophocles' King Oedipus* (1928); *The Resurrection* (1931); *The Words Upon the Windowpane* (1934); *Purgatory* (1938); *The Death of Cuchulain* (1939)

FURTHER READING

Cave, Richard Allen. "Yeats's Late Plays: 'A High Grave Dignity and Strangeness.'" *Proceedings of the British Academy* 68 (1982): 299–327.

Foster, R. F. *W. B. Yeats, a Life: The Apprentice Mage, 1865–1914.* Oxford: Oxford Univ. Press, 1997.

——. *W. B. Yeats, a Life: The Arch-poet, 1915–1939.* Oxford: Oxford Univ. Press, 2003.

Ure, Peter. *Yeats the Playwright: A Commentary on Character and Design in the Major Plays.* New York: Barnes & Noble, 1963.

Adrian Frazier

YERMA

Yerma, written in 1934, is the second rural TRAGEDY by FEDERICO GARCÍA LORCA. It centers on the life of Yerma, a rural middle-class woman, and her strong desire to beget a son. Yerma and her husband do not have sexual relations. But she seems to feel strongly attracted to Víctor, a shepherd working for her husband. As her desperation to have a baby grows deeper, Yerma ends up consulting a rural fortune teller who suggests that she go to a fertility pilgrimage. The husband finds her at the pilgrimage, and they engage in an argument where he tells her that, in spite of their inability to have a baby, he wants to have sex with her. He tries to kiss her, but she strangles him, after which she claims that she has just killed her son.

Birth in *Yerma* is represented on a sacred level, as Lorca establishes a clear relationship between the birth that Yerma aspires to and the Virgin Mary's childbirth. In fact, during the pilgrimage, Yerma and a chorus of six women say a prayer that contains direct allusions to the biblical scene of Annunciation, where the Archangel Gabriel announces the birth of Jesus to the Virgin Mary. However, unlike the original referent, the Archangel in *Yerma* has "las alas como tormentas" (the wings as storms) and "los ojos como agonías" (the eyes as agonies). Thus, God's messenger is represented as death's messenger announcing Yerma's destiny, that is, the killing of her husband, who she claims to be her own son. In some symbolic sense, then, Lorca is showing a Virgin Mary who kills her divine baby—or more profoundly, who kills the possibility of giving birth to him.

As in his previous play BLOOD WEDDING (1932), the topic of incest is also present in *Yerma*. Here it can be traced to the attraction that Yerma feels for Víctor, the shepherd. At the beginning of the play, Yerma dreams about a shepherd who is holding the hand of a child—the child she desires. Later in the play, we find out that Yerma is the daughter of Enrique "the shepherd." Therefore, in the dream (subconscious) of Yerma the figure of the shepherd is a fusion of the image of the father, of the man she feels attracted to, and the son she desires. And like the Mother and the Groom in Lorca's first tragedy, Yerma is also identified with the earth and does not maintain sexual relations with her husband or with the man she feels attracted to.

Considering the confusion Yerma herself creates when she says she has killed her son—when she has actually killed her husband—we can interpret her words as meaning that by killing her husband she really has killed her son. Thus, like in *Blood Wedding*, Yerma's sexual repression symbolically represents the prevention of incest. This shows how Lorca's women always prevent the completion of those rites that require or imply sexual consummation (weddings and childbirth). As Beth Wellington says in *Reflections on Lorca's Private Mythology* (1993), Lorca's rites are aborted rituals.

[See also Spain; Symbolism]

FURTHER READING

Feal, Carlos. *La idea del honor en las tragedias de Lorca.* Lanham, Md.: Univ. Press of America, 1988.

Fusco, Antonio, and Rosella Tomassoni. "A Psychological Outline of 'Yerma's Dream.'" *CLCWeb: Comparative Literature and Culture* 3, no. 3 (2001): 10.

Knapp, Bettina. "García Lorca's Yerma: A Woman's Mystery." In *Lorca's Legacy. Essays on Lorcas's Life, Poetry, and Theatre*, ed. by Manule Durán and Franchesca Collechia. New York: Peter Lang, 1991.

Lima, Robert. "Towards the Dionysiac: Pagan Elements and Rites in Yerma." In *Lorca's Legacy. Essays on Lorcas's Life, Poetry, and Theatre*, ed. by Manule Durán and Franchesca Collechia. New York: P. Lang, 1991.

Wellington, Beth. *Reflections on Lorca's Private Mythology: Once Five Years Pass and the Rural Plays.* New York: P. Lang, 1993.

Maribel Parra-Domínguez

YIDDISH THEATER

In the popular imagination, the modern Yiddish theater emerged full blown in 1876, when AVROM GOLDFADEN organized a small troupe in ROMANIA. In fact, Yiddish theater had already been centuries in the making—though mostly in an amateur capacity—and Goldfaden's dramas, like those of his contemporaries and successors, drew upon both Jewish and non-Jewish textual, musical, and performance traditions. These activities gave birth to one of the most popular cultural institutions in modern Jewish life; though its roots were Eastern European, its branches would span six continents.

PRECURSORS

Theatrical performances in Yiddish (a Germanic language written in Hebrew characters, with added linguistic components from Slavic and other languages) date back to the Middle Ages.

PURIMSHPIL

Jewish law prohibited women from performing in public and men from dressing in women's clothes, thus limiting the types of performances acceptable within the Jewish community—at least during most of the year. The exception was on Purim, a festive late-winter holiday celebrating the victory of Jews over deadly enemies in ancient Persia described in the Book of Esther; so light is the communal mood on Purim that Jews are encouraged to drink until they can no longer distinguish the hero of the Esther story from its villain. It was in this context that the PURIMSHPIL (plural: purimshpiln), or Purim play, was born.

Extant manuscripts of Yiddish poems about the Purim story date back to the 15th century, and printed versions as early as the 16th. The subject matter of the purimshpil was often, though by no means always, the Purim story itself. Other popular subjects included the sale of Joseph into slavery, the binding of Isaac, David, and Goliath, and Samson and Delilah. Some Purim plays also addressed contemporary issues and featured contemporary character types, but regardless of the subject matter, the performances exuded a spirit of irreverence befitting the holiday. The humor of these plays relied heavily on scatological and sexual jokes and puns, which not infrequently drew the wrath of religious and communal authorities.

The form of the purimshpil resembles the German Fastnachtspiel in many ways, including not only the aforementioned profanity and eroticism but the central role of a narrator (here known as the *loyfer, shrayber,* or *payats*). The traditional purimshpil was performed entirely by men and boys—often students from the yeshivas (religious seminaries). Since most performances took place in the homes of wealthy families, the plays needed to be short so that companies could make their rounds. Masks and primitive costumes were the norm, and extant early texts do not tend to indicate changes of costume or scenery. Beginning in the 16th century, purimshpiln gradually became more elaborate, and in some places, they expanded beyond the one-day festival itself, with performances being offered for up to two weeks on either side of the holiday. By the early 18th century, purimshpiln reflected many trends in the contemporary European theater in literary style, subject matter, and scene design. Nevertheless, the plays maintained a connection with Purim and were performed during the appropriate season.

THE JEWISH ENLIGHTENMENT

It would take a sea change in religious practice to allow theatrical performances to find a more regular place in Jewish life. Such a change came in the late 18th century in the form of the *Haskala*, or Jewish Enlightenment. The movement's proponents (*maskilim*) urged fellow Jews to become less insular, to integrate more fully into European society (at least to the extent that the law and their non-Jewish neighbors allowed), and reap the fruits of secular thought in politics, PHILOSOPHY, science, and the arts. While the movement initially met with fierce resistance from religious Jews, it would ultimately pave the way toward new forms of religious expression and a new orientation toward the non-Jewish world.

While no professional Jewish theater as yet existed, a number of *maskilim* took a strong interest in drama. Among them were two of the leading figures in Jewish Enlightenment circles in Berlin. The literary reputations of both Aaron Halle-Wolfssohn and Isaac Euchel rest in large part on works they wrote in Hebrew, and in genres other than drama, but each penned important Yiddish dramatic satires in the 1790s: Euchel's *Reb Henokh, or What Can Be Done With It?* (*Reb Henokh, oder vos tut men damit?*, c. 1792) and Wolfssohn's *Frivolity and False Piety* (*Leichtsinn und Frömmelei*, c. 1794). In subsequent decades, a number of other *maskilim* would write dramas—almost always COMEDIES. Among the most important were Solomon Ettinger's *Serkele* (*Serkele*, 1838); Avrom Ber Gottlober's *The Bridal Veil, or Two Weddings in One Night* (*Der dektukh, oder tsvey khupes in eyn nakht*, 1839); several comedies and MELODRAMAS by Israel Aksenfeld written in the 1830s and 1840s, including *The First Jewish Recruit in Russia* (*Der ershter yidisher rekrut in rusland*); the anonymous satire *The Duped World* (*Di genarte velt*); and S. Y. Abramovitsh's *The Tax* (*Di takse*, 1869).

BRODER SINGERS

The 1850s also saw the rise of a type of Yiddish performer who would directly influence later, more structured theatrical activity. The performers in question were called Broder Singers, after the Galician city of Brody, where the reputed "father" of the form, Berl Broder, had been active. Like the purimshpil, the performances of the Broder Singers became more elaborate over time. Initially, songs telling a story—often based on familiar character types and situations from everyday Jewish life—were accompanied by facial expressions and gestures. From there it was a short step to embedding the songs into theatrical situations with a couple of performers, quick changes of costume to suit the characters described in the lyrics, and the crudest of makeup.

As the Broder Singers' fame grew, so did their geographical reach. They spread throughout Galicia and Romania, and from there into RUSSIA. The most renowned of these figures, including Berl Broder and Velvl Zbarzher, would significantly influence the beginnings of professional Yiddish theater and develop close ties to writers like Goldfaden, Yisroel Yitskhok Linetski, and Eliakum Zunser, whose songs and sketches they performed.

THE BIRTH OF THE PROFESSIONAL YIDDISH THEATER

Though Yiddish companies managed to perform in places like Warsaw (in the 1830s and 1860s) during seasons completely unconnected to Purim, such efforts met with stiff resistance from Jewish community leaders and left no direct legacy. Avrom Goldfaden, on the other hand, would earn the title of "Father of the Yiddish Theater" by forming the first relatively stable professional Yiddish troupe and proceeding to write its plays and compose its music.

THE FATHER OF THE YIDDISH THEATER

Goldfaden's background prepared him in many ways for the task. He claimed to have begun composing songs as a young boy and was a published poet and dramatist by the time he completed his rabbinical studies in the 1860s. His first full-length play, *Aunt Sosya* (*Di mume Sosya*), bore the clear influence of Solomon Ettinger's comic melodrama *Serkele*—not entirely surprising, since Goldfaden had played the title role in a production staged at his seminary in Zhitomir in 1862. And one of Goldfaden's early teachers was none other than the noted satirical writer and dramatist Avrom Ber Gottlober.

After trying his hand at several different careers, Goldfaden assembled his first company (whose star performer, Yisroel Grodner, was a seasoned Broder Singer) in Jassy, Romania, in 1876. Over the next several years, the playwright would turn out a stream of vaudevilles, burlesques, and full-length comedies, including highly popular (and often controversial) works like *Shmendrik*, *The Two Kuni-Lemls* (*Di tsvey Kuni-leml*), and *The Sorceress* (*Di kishefmakherin*). Within the first year of its existence, Goldfaden's company hired its actress, and two rival troupes were formed, one led by Joseph Lateiner and the other by Moyshe Hurwitz. These two men would become Goldfaden's lifelong rivals. Though critics would always favor Goldfaden, Hurwitz and Lateiner would become as popular as they were prolific, each with an enormous number of musicals and melodramas to his credit. In addition to this trio, other playwrights who would contribute to the foundation of the professional repertoire were Nokhem-Meyer ("Shomer") Sheykevitsh and Yoysef-Yude Lerner.

WESTWARD EXODUS

The next sea change in Eastern European Jewish life followed the assassination of Tsar Alexander II in 1881. An outbreak of pogroms ensued, bringing with it a decline in the economic fortunes of Russian Jewry. These events sparked an exodus out of Russia, mostly to the West, and particularly to North America. The Yiddish theater would move with the masses. To be sure, it was given a firm push by the czarist authorities, who banned Yiddish theater in 1883. Though the ban would turn out to be capricious and inconsistent, it made a difficult business all the more precarious, and many performers and playwrights headed west. Companies were created or expanded in Eastern European cities like Warsaw and Lemberg (present-day Lwow), while new centers of Yiddish theater arose further west—most notably, at first, in London's East End and New York's Lower East Side. The repertoire in the first decade of activity in these new centers included the most popular plays from Eastern Europe, as well as new works written largely in the same vein: that is, primarily melodramas, musicals, and broad comedies. New writers emerging in the 1880s included Sigmund Feinman, Israel Barski, Rudolph Marks, and Reuben Weissman.

Such playwrights often irritated the critics in inverse proportion to how they pleased audiences. Reviewers constantly lamented the "low" taste of the Yiddish audience (pejoratively nicknamed "Moyshe") and the dominance of shund (popular theater; literally, "trash") in the repertoire. For these critics, a new ray of light burst through the clouds in the early 1890s in the person of JACOB GORDIN. Gordin, a new Russian immigrant to New York with a background in utopian politics and intellectual activity, also deplored the existing repertoire but was pleasantly surprised by the sophistication of performers like Jacob P. Adler, whom he met in the months after moving to New York's Lower East Side. Gordin was persuaded to write a play for Adler, and the result was Siberia, a work with its share of melodramatic touches but far more naturalistic than anything that had previously been shown in the Yiddish theater. Gordin would be hailed in many circles as the great reformer of Yiddish drama; works such as The Jewish King Lear (Der yidisher kenig Lir), Khasye the Orphan Girl (Khasye di yesoyme), God, Man, and Devil (Got, mentsh un tayvl), Mirele Efros, and many others would become staples in the Yiddish theatrical repertoire, and their main roles became proving grounds for leading men and women as well as character actors. Like the Europeans he emulated, including HENRIK IBSEN, GERHART HAUPTMANN, and MAKSIM GORKY, Gordin often sparked controversy for his treatment of delicate social issues.

Gordin's social engagement, as well as his dramaturgical technique, drew a following not just among audiences and critics but among a new generation of playwrights. Successful dramatists and their plays in turn-of-the-20th-century New York included Leon Kobrin's Yankl Boyle, Riverside Drive, Back to His People (Tsurik tsu zayn folk), and The Lady Next Door (Di nekst-dorike); Zalmen Libin's Hannele, or the Jewish Medea (Hanele oder di yidishe Medea) and Broken Hearts (Tsebrokhene hertser); Nokhem Rakov's The Idler (Der batlen), The Green Girl (Di grine moyd), and Khantshe in America (Khantshe in amerike); and Isidore Zolotarevsky's The Yeshiva Boy (Der yeshive bokher), The Jewish Anna Karenina (Di yidishe Ana Karenina), and The White Slave (Di vayse shklavin). Other popular playwrights of the time included Anshl and Moyshe Shor, Harry Sackler, and Moyshe Richter.

THE NEW YIDDISH DRAMATURGY

In New York, Gordin was often hailed as the great reformer of Yiddish drama. European critics like I. L. Peretz and Noyekh Prilutski had different standards and saw Gordin as little more than dressed-up shund.

EASTERN EUROPE

Peretz, one of the so-called classic Yiddish writers and the center of the Warsaw Yiddish literary universe in the early 1900s, turned his hand to drama among other genres, with grand symbolist works like A Night in the Old Marketplace (Baynakht afn altn mark) and The Golden Chain (Di goldene keyt) and naturalist one-act dramas like Sisters (Shvester) and It's Burning (Es brent). Fellow "classic" writer Sholem Aleichem, like Peretz better known for prose than for drama, also wrote a number of plays, including one-act comedies like People (Mentshn) and Mazl-tov and full-length comedies like Hard to Be a Jew (Shver tsu zayn a yid), The Jackpot (Dos groyse gevins), and Gold Diggers (Gold-greber). These authors had little success as dramatists in their own lifetimes, though a number of these works became successful in revivals and adaptations by such companies as the MOSCOW STATE YIDDISH THEATRE and the Yiddish Art Theatre in New York.

The greatest posthumous success—and arguably the most popular drama—in all of Yiddish theater history was S. Ansky's THE DYBBUK (Der dibek), which took Warsaw by storm when it premiered in 1920, shortly after the writer's death. Like many Yiddish writers who wrote plays, Ansky was not primarily a playwright; The Dybbuk, redolent with Eastern European Jewish folklore and superstition, grew out of a major ethnographic expedition Ansky led in the years before World War I. The play's wild success helped launch the Vilna Troupe, who staged it, to international prominence. Warsaw would also become home to other important ensembles during the interwar period, most notably Mikhl Weichert's Yung Teater and the Warsaw Yiddish Art Theatre (VYKT), run by the theatrical dynasty of the Turkow/Kaminska family. Other playwrights active in Warsaw between the world wars include Alter Kacyzne, Leib Malach, and Jacob Preger.

The formation of the Soviet Union would give rise to new theater ensembles in a number of cities, but none would attract more attention than the Moscow State Yiddish Theatre (better known by its Russian acronym, GOSET). The company revolutionized Yiddish theater with AVANT-GARDE productions of many of the Yiddish classics, including Goldfaden's The Sorceress,

Peretz's *A Night in the Old Marketplace*, Sholem Aleichem's *The Jackpot*, and a dramatization of S. Y. Abramovitsh's novel *The Travels of Benjamin III* (*Masoes Binyomin hashlishi*). It would also give voice to new writers, like Moyshe Kulbak (*Boytre*) and Dovid Bergelson (*The Deaf Man* [*Der toyber*], *Prince Reuveni*). Like Soviet Yiddish artists working in other genres, the company would encounter grave dangers from ideological enforcers. A number of important figures associated with GOSET, including the brilliant actors Solomon Mikhoels and Benjamin Zuskin, would meet their deaths under gruesome circumstances.

New York

As long as talented immigrants kept moving westward, New York would continue to assert itself as one of the world capitals of Yiddish theater. Almost all of the most important actors and performers in the American Yiddish theater would be foreign born, and many would start their careers in cultural centers like Warsaw and Odessa. Among the playwrights in this category were David Pinski and PERETZ HIRSCHBEIN. Both men were talented journalists and prose writers, and both generated a distinguished body of dramatic work as well. Pinski could write biting satires, like *The Treasure* (*Der oytser*), but often wrote in a darker vein, in dramas like *The Eternal Jew* (*Der eybiker yid*), *The Family Tsvi* (*Di familye Tsvi*), and *Isaac Sheftl* (*Ayzik Sheftl*). He also wrote popular dramas revolving around tempestuous human passions in works like *Yankl the Blacksmith* (*Yankl der shmid*) and *Gabri and the Women* (*Gabri un di froyen*). Hirschbein experimented with various dramatic modes and registers but is best known for his idylls of village life, relying more on deftly developed characters and convincing dialogue than on plot. These include *A Forsaken Nook* (*A farvorfn vinkl*), *The Idle Inn* (*Di puste kretshme*), and *Green Fields* (*Grine felder*). Other accomplished members of this new wave of dramatists working primarily in New York were writers like Osip Dimov (*Hear, O Israel* [*Shma yisroel*], *Bronx Express*, *Yoshke the Musician* [*Yoshke muzikant*]), H. Leivick (*Rags* [*Shmates*], *Shop*, *The Golem* [*Der goylem*]), and Fishl Bimko (*Thieves* [*Ganovim*], *Oaks* [*Dembes*]).

Playwrights like these would enrich the Yiddish repertoire, writing their material for performance by companies that would join the pantheon of the great Yiddish troupes. Foremost among them in New York was Maurice Schwartz's Yiddish Art Theatre, which subsisted on a diet of Western and Yiddish classics, new Yiddish dramas, and—most lucratively—adaptations of Yiddish novels, like Sholem Aleichem's *Tevye the Dairyman* (*Tevye der milkhiker*) and I. J. Singer's *Yoshe Kalb*, dramatized by Schwartz himself. Schwartz's company was in theory an ensemble, but in practice it belonged very much to the 19th-century star system. For true ensemble acting, New York Yiddish audiences went to Artef (from the Yiddish acronym for Workers' Theatre Collective), which opened its doors in 1928 with a production of Soviet Yiddish playwright Beynush Shteyman's *At the Gate* (*Bam toyer*). The company established itself as the avant-garde answer to commercial offerings with innovative productions of such works as Yisroel Aksenfeld's *Recruits* (*Der ershter yidisher rekrut in rusland*, also known as *Rekrutn*) and Sholem Aleichem's *200,000* (*Dos groyse gevins*).

Other Centers

The three great Yiddish cultural centers of Moscow, Warsaw, and New York had the highest concentration of Yiddish theaters, playwrights, and performers, but Yiddish speakers established theaters wherever they went, and Yiddish stars from major centers toured far and wide. In the countries with the largest Yiddish-speaking populations, numerous cities emerged as "provincial" centers: such as Minsk, Kharkov, and Kiev in the USSR; Cracow and Vienna in east-central Europe; and Philadelphia, Chicago, and Montreal in North America.

A number of other cities along the axes of Jewish migration emerged as important centers in their own right. The primary venue in Western Europe was London's East End, which spawned successful playwrights like Joseph Markovitsh and Shmuel Harendorf. In the Southern Hemisphere, AUSTRALIA and SOUTH AFRICA were small satellites of activity, while Buenos Aires was Latin America's important Yiddish theatrical center. Companies were also formed in MEXICO, Uruguay, Chile, and BRAZIL, but Buenos Aires was a popular touring destination for many American and European stars and generated its own companies and writers, most notably Jacob Botoshansky and Leib Malach. In ISRAEL, Yiddish cultural activity was initially suppressed, but these restrictions were ultimately loosened, leading to a flourishing of Yiddish theater beginning in the 1960s.

From its modest beginnings in the wine gardens of Romania, the Yiddish theater rapidly spread to other regions. Jewish emigrants from Eastern Europe took the Yiddish language and its cultural traditions with them, came in contact with other theatrical cultures, and planted Yiddish theater wherever they went. Yet much of this activity was cut short just as it was maturing. The main factor was the Holocaust, which wiped out much of Eastern European Jewish culture as it decimated those who created it. Yet Yiddish theater ultimately did not fare well in more hospitable climates, either. As audiences in such places as Western Europe and the Americas acculturated, they often abandoned cultural expression in Yiddish in favor of the local vernacular. At the start of the 21st century, efforts to produce Yiddish theater in centers like New York and Tel Aviv tend to arise out of a zealous commitment to the culture rather than—as in past decades—in response to a feverish demand from large audiences of Yiddish speakers.

FURTHER READING

Berkowitz, Joel, ed. *Yiddish Theatre: New Approaches*. London: Littman Library of Jewish Civilization, 2003.

Hoberman, J. *Bridge of Light: Yiddish Film Between Two Worlds*. New York: Museum of Modern Art and Schocken Books, 1991.

Nahshon, Edna. *Yiddish Proletarian Theatre: The Art and Politics of the Artef, 1925–1940*. Westport, Conn.: Greenwood Press, 1998.

Sandrow, Nahma. *Vagabond Stars: A World History of Yiddish Theater*. 1977. Syracuse: Syracuse Univ. Press, 1999.

Veidlinger, Jeffrey. *The Moscow State Yiddish Theatre.* Bloomington: Indiana Univ. Press, 2000.

Yidisher teater tsvishn beyde velt-milkhomes [Yiddish Theatre Between the Two World Wars]. 2 vols. New York: Congress for Jewish Culture, 1931–1969.

Zylbercweig, Zalmen. *Leksikon fun yidishn teater.* 6 vols. New York: Elisheva, 1931–1969.

Joel Berkowitz

YOU CAN'T TAKE IT WITH YOU

In *You Can't Take It With You,* by GEORGE S. KAUFMAN and MOSS HART, the Vanderhofs are a "slightly mad family" who maintain an idiosyncratic household where all are free to pursue their whims. Grandpa lives off his investments and genially declines to pay taxes, and the rest of his family is equally unconventional. Because they mean no harm, they cannot imagine why anyone would approach them with suspicion or hostility.

In order to juxtapose the Vanderhofs with the outside world, Kaufman and Hart employ the Menandrian (a comedic form derived from the comedies of the Greek playwright Menander) formula of a young man in love, a girl with a flaw (here, her family) that makes her unmarriageable, and the opposition of a stern older man. Alice Sycamore (Grandpa Vanderhof's older granddaughter) loves Tony Kirby, her boss's son, but she feels sure that she will never win the blessing of Mr. Kirby, a Wall Street financier, and she doubts that she and Tony could find domestic bless while living amidst the unpredictable Vanderhof clan. Nevertheless, the lovers arrange for the Kirbys to dine at the Vanderhof home, but Tony forces a spontaneous confrontation by bringing his parents on the wrong night. After the evening leads to general embarrassment and a mass arrest by the FBI, Alice resolves to leave home and never see anyone, including Tony, ever again, but the experience alters Kirby's perceptions and values so that he accepts not only Alice but the entire eccentric family. The love match unites two apparently irreconcilable points of view.

The contrast between the two families clarifies the comic potential of each. The Vanderhofs are active and free, while the Kirbys are restricted and sterile; that is, the Vanderhofs are what they *do*, while the Kirbys are what they do *not* do. Grandpa welcomes new experiences, while Mr. Kirby shies away from them, avoiding peculiar food and disapproving of unconventional behavior. The Vanderhofs include in their family a myriad of relatives, friends, and chance acquaintances, but the Kirbys remain a small, tight group that suspects outsiders. The Vanderhofs enjoy the eccentricities of such characters as Kolenkhov, the loud, Russian ballet teacher, but the Kirbys run from idiosyncrasy in confusion. The Kirbys are fettered by their preconceived notions of how people should behave, and their expectations are constantly undermined in the unpredictable Vanderhof home.

Kirby's experiences with the Vanderhofs may embarrass or humiliate him, but there is no malice intended. His night in jail leads him to a clearer understanding of himself and of his unique worth as an individual. For years, he has struggled to forget his youthful idealism and assume the trappings of convention to build up his business. Grandpa teaches him that a man can find security and a full life without the tension and indigestion of Wall Street. Kirby realizes that he has been wearing a mask, the product of values he has forced himself to accept, and that he is not really happy. He is reluctant to admit that he has always misunderstood himself, but Grandpa encourages him and finally Kirby relents.

Grandpa lives up to the American faith in individuality and freedom. He is an anachronism from America's earlier days, when backwoodsmen and pioneers created the law anew every day and kept a close, critical eye on it to see that it continued to serve them as they intended. Grandpa wants to know how he and his family will benefit before he awards his loyalty to convention, custom, or government. He is able to create the unique Vanderhof household because he is a maverick in the tradition of the American frontier, a loner who is not lonely, a man who lives his own life and revels in it.

The play opened on December 14, 1936, and won the Pulitzer Prize in 1937. In the *New York Times,* Brooks Atkinson hailed the play as the team's "most thoroughly ingratiating comedy, . . . a study in vertigo about a lovable family of hobby-horse riders, funny without being shrill, sensible without being earnest." Comparing it with the "machine-gun barrage of low comedy satire" that he remembered from their ONCE IN A LIFETIME (1930), he assured his readers that "you will find their current lark a much more spontaneous piece of hilarity; it is written with a dash of affection to season the humor and played with gayety and simple good spirit." He praised Kaufman and Hart as "fantastic humorists with a knack for extravagances of word and episode and an eye for hilarious incongruities" who may "have been more rigidly brilliant in the past, but they have never scooped up an evening of such tickling fun."

[*See also* Comedy; United States, 1929–1940]

FURTHER READING

Gaines, James R. *Wit's End: Days and Nights of the Algonquin Round Table.* New York: Harcourt Brace Jovanovich, 1977.

Goldstein, Malcolm. *George S. Kaufman: His Life, His Theater.* New York: Oxford Univ. Press, 1979.

Hart, Moss. *Act One.* New York: Random House–Vintage, 1959.

Mason, Jeffrey D. *Wisecracks: The Farces of George S. Kaufman.* Ann Arbor: UMI Res. Press, 1988.

Meredith, Scott. *George S. Kaufman and His Friends.* Garden City, N.Y.: Doubleday, 1974.

Teichmann, Howard. *George S. Kaufman: An Intimate Portrait.* New York: Atheneum, 1972.

Jeffrey D. Mason

YOUNG, DAVID (1946–)

David Young was born in Oakville, Ontario, CANADA, in 1946. He developed a leg infection as a child and had to be hospitalized for eighteen months. The sense of isolation he experienced during this time strongly informs the themes of some of his most successful plays. Young studied at the University of Western Ontario. In 1981 he joined the staff of Coach House Press, where he worked as an editor and eventually became president until 1996, when that company folded. During his tenure at Coach House, he worked on various writing projects. While there he also became acquainted with novelist MICHAEL ONDAATJE and eventually worked on the screenplay for the wildly successful adaptation of Ondaatje's novel *The English Patient*.

Early in his playwriting career, Young collaborated with writer Paul Ledoux. Their first collaboration, *Fire* (1983), received great acclaim across Canada, winning a Chalmers Award and receiving a nomination for a Dora Mavor Moore Award. The two also collaborated on *Love Is Strange* (1984) the following year. Young often uses true stories as the bases for his plays. For example, *Glenn* (1992) is based on the life of the famous pianist Glenn Gould; *Inexpressible Island* (1997) dramatizes the story of six men who took part in Robert Scott's ill-fated 1912 expedition to the South Pole; and *Love Is Strange* is based on the true story of a Saskatchewan man who stalked singer Anne Murray. Several of Young's plays have been developed and premiered at the Necessary Angel Theatre Company, a company known for its productions of challenging and innovative plays.

Even though Young often uses real stories as his basis, he uses very nonrealistic styles to present his subjects. Young's most successful play, *Glenn*, is a fantasy profile of the life of pianist Glenn Gould. The show presents the fractured psyche of the famous pianist by having him portrayed by four performers, each representing a different time period in his life. It is written in thirty-two small sections that Young structured to match the parts of Johann Sebastian Bach's *Goldberg Variations* in voice, tempo, and mood. The show premiered at the Necessary Angel Theatre Company in 1992 to great acclaim. It received seven Dora Mavor Moor Award nominations, in addition to a Governor General's Award nomination and Chalmers Award nomination. The play was revived at the Stratford Festival in 1999. This production proved wildly successful as well. Young's play *Clout* (2001) is also written in a challenging, expressionistic style. The play actually takes place in the mind of a dying hospital patient who is on a morphine drip. As the patient drifts in and out of consciousness, disjointed scenes of reality and fantasy intersect. Young says of the work, "The overriding impression should be of story elements drifting through each other like twists of smoke." His most recent play is *No Great Mischief* (2004), an adaptation of Alistair MacLeod's award-winning novel. Young has had a varied writing career, having written several novels, nonfiction books, screenplays, and tele-

plays. He is most well known, however, as the playwright who has written some of Canada's edgiest and most challenging plays.

SELECT PLAYS: *Fire* (with Paul Ledoux, 1983); *Love Is Strange: A Courtroom Romance* (with Paul Ledoux, 1984); *Glenn* (1992); *Inexpressible Island* (1997); *Cavies* (1999); *Preschool* (1999); *Two Beers For Three People* (1999); *Visions of Prostitutes* (1999); *Antarctica* (2001); *Clout* (2001); *No Great Mischief* (2004)

FURTHER READING

Connolly, Kevin. "What's Left: Playwright David Young Sorts Through the Rubble of '60s Radicalism in His New Comedy, *Clout*." *Eye Weekly* (February 15, 2001). http://www.eye.net/eye/issue/issue_02.15.01/arts/lead.php.

Hood, Sarah B. "Glenn, Again." *Performing Arts and Entertainment in Canada* 33, no. 2 (2000): 31–34.

Viccari, Ben. "Expressions of the Inexpressible." *Performing Arts and Entertainment in Canada* 32, no. 2 (1999): 36–37.

Young, David. *Clout*. Coach House Books. http://www.chbooks.com/archives/online_books/clout/. Accessed 8/26/04. [Contains the entire text of Young's play, *Clout*, as well as the playwright's notes and production photographs.]

Beth A. Kattelman

YUNG, DANNY N. T. (1943–)

Danny Yung (Ning-tsun) was born in 1943 in Shanghai but moved to Hong Kong with his family at the age of five. He studied architecture at the University of California, Berkeley, and urban design and urban planning at Columbia University. In 1979, he returned to Hong Kong and presented his structuralist theater work, *Broken Record #1*. In the following year, he produced his first performance series, *Journey to the East* (*Zhongguo lücheng*, 1980), in four parts, in Hong Kong. Its fifth part (*Hong Kong-Taipei-Hong Kong*) was staged in Taipei as the first production of Zuni Icosahedron, an art collective Yung founded with his friends in 1982. Since then, as a theater maker, he has coordinated, directed, and produced close to a hundred stage productions, including the *One Hundred Years of Solitude* (*Bainian guji*) series, the *Chronicle of Women* (*Lienü zhuan*) series, the *Opium War* (*Yapian Zhanzheng*) series, the *Journey to the East* series, the *Deep Structure of Chinese Culture* (*Zhongguo wenhua shenceng jiegou*) series, the *Two or Three Things About Hong Kong* (*Xianggang er san shi*) series, *The Book of Mountain and Ocean* (*Shanhai jing*), *Four Grand Inventions* (*Sida faming*), *Sigmund Freud in Search of Chinese Matter and Mind* (*Foluoyide xunzhao zhongguo qing yu shi*), and *In Search of Modern China* (*Xunzhao xin Zhongguo*).

In the provocative exploration of subjects such as history, gender, and cultural IDENTITY, politics, and ideology in the Zuni productions, Yung relies heavily on the orchestration of visual images, sound, movement, and the use of various media. In *Sigmund Freud*, a traditional Chinese theater female player in the male role is placed on one end of the stage in full costume, singing and enacting movements from a scene in *Peony Pavilion* (*Mudan ting*). She/he is then joined by a male player in his ordinary modern clothing on the other end of the stage, ACTING out the counterpart female character. The two players are aware of, but not interacting with, each other. Ample space is put between the lovers who are supposed to act intimately. This space is a visualization of the temporal distance of modern and traditional forms. The gender relationship between the players and the characters is destabilized. Then the players' singing is treated and given digitalized effects. Video clips are projected on the stage. This accentuates the discrepancy between the traditional and the modern. The scene concludes with an anarchic explosion of sounds and visual images of curves and shapes projected from digital video. The strong images are the main vocabulary of expression. This approach, puzzling to the more conservative theatergoers, is found to be challenging and attractive to a generation of young theater workers. This displacement of emphasis on language, together with the innovative perspective and critique in the content, makes the productions more accessible to non-Chinese audiences.

With the accentuation of cross-cultural elements, Yung's works are well received outside Hong Kong. Performance tours of his work with Zuni have visited Beijing, Brussels, London, Edinburgh, Munich, New York City, Los Angeles, Singapore, Taipei, Tokyo, and many other cities. Yung organized an eleven-week *Festival of Vision*—a cross-cultural festival and conference series in Berlin and Hong Kong, which involved 1,000 artists and cultural practitioners from some thirty-five cities in Asia and Europe. Yung is a political activist and works with groups attempting to affect cultural policy issues in Hong Kong.

[*See also* China]

SELECT PLAY: *Broken Record #1* (1979)

FURTHER READING

Cheung, Martha, and Jane Lai, eds. *An Oxford Anthology of Contemporary Chinese Drama*. New York: Oxford Univ. Press, 1997.

Lilley, Rozanna. *Staging Hong Kong Gender and Performance in Transition*. Richmond, Surrey, U.K.: Curzon Press, 1998.

Yung, Danny. *Chronicle of Women*. Tr. by Martha Cheung. In *An Oxford Anthology of Contemporary Chinese Drama*, ed. by Martha Cheung and Jane Lai. New York: Oxford Univ. Press, 1997. 825–873.

Jane Lai and Jessica Yeung

YU WU SHENG CHU See IN A LAND OF SILENCE

YŪZURU See TWILIGHT CRANE

ZAGAVOR CHUVSTV *See* A Conspiracy of Feelings

ZAPOLSKA, GABRIELA (1857–1921)

> *At times I have the urge to get married so as to stop working so hard. But I gave up the idea realizing that I'd be nothing more than a legal prostitute.*
>
> —Gabriela Zapolska

Gabriela Zapolska was an innovative playwright, actor, theater manager, teacher, journalist, and novelist, whose unconventional behavior and outspoken views provoked controversy and scandal. Born Gabriela Korwin Piotrowska on March 30, 1857, near Lwów in the Austrian sector of partitioned POLAND, Zapolska married at nineteen, abandoned her husband, and severed ties with her well-to-do family to embark on a precarious career as an actor in Warsaw amateur theaters. An affair with a theater manager left her with a child who died shortly thereafter. In 1882 she began her professional ACTING career in Cracow under the name of Zapolska.

In 1883, appearing as Nora in A DOLL'S HOUSE on tour in St. Petersburg, Zapolska introduced HENRIK IBSEN in RUSSIA. For the next five years she performed in Cracow and Lwów and toured the provinces, enduring a life of hardship. She published her first novel, *Małaszka*, in 1885, achieving notoriety for the frank treatment of sexuality. In 1888 she attempted suicide.

Forced by her outraged family to leave Poland in 1889, Zapolska moved to Paris, where she studied acting in hopes of achieving international stardom. While working as a cultural correspondent for Warsaw newspapers, she appeared in minor roles in boulevard theaters and at ANDRÉ ANTOINE's Théâtre Libre and in MAURICE MAETERLINCK's *Interior* and Ibsen's LITTLE EYOLF at Lugné-Poe's Théâtre de l'Oeuvre. As the lover of Paul Serusier, leader of the Nabis, she moved in AVANT-GARDE artistic circles and collected postimpressionist paintings including a Vincent Van Gogh, Paul Gauguin, and Georges Seurat.

Returning to Poland in 1894 as a proponent of NATURALISM with socialist sympathies, Zapolska continued her acting career (until 1900) and wrote many plays and novels, often sensational in form, about alcoholism, prostitution, venereal disease, class and ethnic conflicts, and oppression of women. She established a drama school and independent theater and, with her second husband, ran a company bearing her name. Under a pseudonym, she wrote successful patriotic social dramas. Her witty COMEDIES of sex and marriage—*The Little Frog* (*Żabusia*, 1897), *The Four of Them* (*Ich czworo*, 1907), and *The Secret of Skiz* (*Skiz*, 1908)—tear off the facade of respectability and reveal the erotic underpinnings of society.

Her satirical social dramas contain outstanding roles for women. *Małka Szwarcenkopf* (1897) depicts Jewish life in Warsaw; *Miss Maliczewska* (*Panna Maliczewska*, 1910) portrays the exploitation by men of a young dancer aspiring to be an actress. Her masterpiece, *Mrs. Dulska's Morality* (*Moralność Pani Dulskiej*, 1906), a "tragi-FARCE," exposes bourgeois hypocrisy embodied in the overbearing heroine (film scenario by the author, 1912).

Although denounced by the clergy and conservative critics, her plays were popular with audiences and constantly staged in all three sectors of Poland and in Central Europe (several were filmed), but it was difficult for Zapolska to collect royalties. Separated from her husband and in poor health, she was obliged to sell her valuable paintings and lived alone in poverty during World War I. On December 21, 1921, in Lwów, Poland, Zapolska died insolvent; her funeral expenses had to be paid out of municipal funds. In the 1920s her views on marriage and sexual equality made her a pioneer for women's rights. In 1927 her play *Tsarevitch* (*Carewicz*, 1917) was made into an operetta by Franz Lehar. New productions since 1989 reveal the continuing timeliness of Zapolska's satire.

SELECT PLAYS: *The First Ball* (*Pierwszy Bal*, 1883); *Małaszka* (1886); *Kate Caryatid* (*Kaśka Kariatyda*, 1895); *The Little Frog* (*Żabusia*, 1897); *Małka Szwarcenkopf* (1897); *Jojne Firułkes* (1898); *The Other* (*Tamten*, 1898); *Siberia* (*Sybir*, 1899); *A Virgin Evening* (*Dziewiczy wieczór*, 1899); *Life as a Jest* (*Życie na żart*, 1901); *A Man* (*Mężczyzna*, 1902); *The Trained Souls* (*Tresowane dusze*, 1902); *The Tsar Is Coming* (*Car jedzie*, 1902); *Misundersanding* (*Nieporozumienie*, 1903); *One Autumn Day* (*Jesiennym wieczorem*, 1903); *Mrs. Dulska's Morality* (*Moralność Pani Dulskiej*, 1906); *The Four of Them* (*Ich czworo*, 1907); *The Secret of Skiz* (*Skiz*, 1908); *Miss Maliczewska* (*Panna Maliczewska*, 1910); *Nervous Racket* (*Nerwowa awantura*, 1912); *A Woman Without a Blemish* (*Kobieta bez skazy*, 1912); *Outcasts* (*Pariasy*, 1914); *Tsarevitch* (*Carewicz*, 1917); *The Assistant* (*Asystent*, 1919)

FURTHER READING

Barr, Alan P. *Modern Women Playwrights of Europe*. New York: Oxford Univ. Press, 2000.

"Gabriela Zapolska." NEDWEB *Literature in Context*. http://www.ned.univie.ac.at/lic/autor.asp?paras=/lg;4/aut_id;26664/.

Rurawski, Józef. *Gabriela Zapolska*. Warsaw: Wiedza Powszechna, 1981.

Jadwiga Kosicka Gerould

ZARZUELA

Zarzuela is a Spanish lyric theater genre that mixes sung text with spoken dialogue. During the 17th and 18th centuries, zarzuela was essentially Italian opera (albeit without recitative) as written by Spanish composers for court entertainments. This form of zarzuela declined at the end of the 18th century as Italian composers became more popular. Modern zarzuela dates from the late 1840s; the revival of the form was due to an increasing interest in creating some form of Spanish opera. Although the musical style of early zarzuelas such as Emilio Arrieta's *Marina* (1855) and Francisco Asenjo Barbieri's *Bread and Bulls* (*Pan y toros*, 1864) was heavily derived from Italian opera, composers also self-consciously used Spanish folk music to turn the genre into a nationalist form of lyric theater. Zarzuela also turned to French *opéra-comique* for its plot devices—often plagiarizing librettos from French authors like Eugène Scribe—albeit adapting these devices to reflect Peninsular settings and Spanish historical events. During the 1870s and 1880s, zarzuela firmly cemented its identity as a popular and nationalistic entertainment, placing itself in opposition to Italian opera with its aristocratic supporters.

Beginning in the mid-1880s the form and content of zarzuela began to shift dramatically. Theaters in Madrid, SPAIN, had begun turning to the staging of one-act plays (the *género chico*) as a way of generating more money. Zarzuelas of the *género chico* placed more emphasis on the dialogue portions of the works than on the musical sections, and the music was almost exclusively drawn from urban dance hall idioms, such as the polka, the mazurka, or the schottische. The majority of *género chico* works were either satirical reviews, such as Federico Chueca's *The Grand Boulevard* (*La gran vía*, 1886), or COMEDIES of manners set among the working-class inhabitants of Madrid, of which Tómas Bretón's *The Festival of Our Lady of the Dove* (*La verbena de la paloma*, 1894) is the best known. The production of *género chico* works went into decline at the beginning of the 20th century, and in the decade after 1910 zarzuela became increasingly influenced by the popularity of Viennese operetta. Works such as José Serrano's *The Song of Oblivion* (*La canción del olvido*, 1916–1918) replaced the dance hall tunes and satirical plots of the *género chico* with lushly melodic music and romantic stories.

Zarzuela entered its heyday in the 1920s. This "silver age" of zarzuela was virtually a summation of the previous century of zarzuela: the traditions of Italian opera, the *género chico*, and Viennese operetta combined in a series of highly romantic and dramatic works such as Amadeo Vives's *Doña Francisquita* (1923) and Federico Moreno Torroba's *Luisa Fernanda* (1932). However, as a popular entertainment, zarzuela was losing ground against the increasing popularity of cinema (especially after the advent of sound film). The disruptions caused by the Spanish Civil War killed off zarzuela as a living theatrical genre. Although the Francisco Franco government attempted to revive interest in the genre through radio broadcasts of recordings and television productions of classic works, the genre remained moribund. Today zarzuela remains primarily a nostalgic entertainment, although there is increasing scholarly interest in the subject.

FURTHER READING

Alier, Roger. *La zarzuela*. Barcelona: Ma Non Troppo, 2002.

Casares Rodicio, Emilio, and Celsa Alonso González, eds. *La música española en el siglo XIX* [Spanish music in the 19th century]. Oviedo: Univ. of Oviedo, 1995.

Membrez, Nancy J. "The Teatro Por Horas: History, Dynamics, and Comprehensive Bibliography of a Madrid Industry, 1867–1922." Ph.D. diss., Univ. of California, Santa Barbara, 1987.

Stein, Louise K., and Roger Alier. "Zarzuela." In *The New Grove Dictionary of Music and Musicians*, ed. by Stanley Sadie and John Tyrrell. 2d ed. Vol. 27. London: Macmillan, 2001.

Webber, Christopher. *The Zarzuela Companion*. Lanham, Md.: Scarecrow, 2003.

Young, Clinton D. "Zarzuela; or, Lyric Theatre as Consumer Nationalism in Spain, 1874–1930." Ph.D. diss., Univ. of California, San Diego, 2006.

"Zarzuela!" http://www.zarzuela.net/index.htm.

Clinton D. Young

ZASTROZZI: THE MASTER OF DISCIPLINE

Written by GEORGE F. WALKER, *Zastrozzi: The Master of Discipline* premiered at Toronto's Free Theatre on November 2, 1977. It is a stylish black COMEDY in two acts about the obsessive pursuit of revenge and power. It has had over 100 productions in the English-speaking world.

Set in Europe, "probably ITALY," in 1893, the character known as Zastrozzi is an atheist and self-styled "master criminal of all Europe." He is also an agent of the fundamental disorder of life. He pursues the artist and dreamer Verezzi to avenge the murder of his mother but also for the sheer fun of the chase. In this pursuit he wreaks havoc with everyone he comes into contact with. He abandons his dark lover Matilda for the aristocratic and innocent Julia. When Matilda goes after Julia, Julia inadvertently kills her. Bernardo, Zastrozzi's henchman in love with Matilda, murders Julia. Zastrozzi makes short work of Bernardo and then Victor, Verrezzi's tutor. The play is a darkly comic series of violent encounters, in which everyone, except the arch enemies Zastrozzi and Verezzi, dies.

Its style is, as Walker intended, melodramatic. There is also a hint of the commedia dell'arte, ANTONIN ARTAUD's Theatre of Cruelty, and an underlying SURREALISM, creating a potent mix. Jerry Wasserman, in *Modern Canadian Plays* (1994), characterizes Walker's plays as "[a]voiding the subjects and styles that have come to characterize the Canadian theatrical mainstream"; he says they lie "somewhere between satire and parody." Certainly *Zastrozzi* is a prime example of this.

The era of the play's setting is crucial; the 19th century is coming to an end, and new ideas and philosophies are taking root. It is a time of shifting social and ideological milieus. In his opening monologue, Zastrozzi states: "I am disturbing social patterns and upsetting established cultures." In reality, he is attempting to retain control of a culture of absurd violence. Verezzi embodies the artistic and religious aspect of humanity, but he is insane and believes himself a messenger of God. It is this perverse innocence in juxtaposition with Zastrozzi's evil that provides the matrix for this drama to unfold. The women, Matilda and Julia, are also opposites of one another; one is sensuous, experienced, and cruel; the other naive and overly trusting: "a product of healthy civilization thrown into a jungle of the deranged." Yet it is Julia's defense of her life against Matilda's jealous attack that leads her to kill the older woman.

The wordplay in *Zastrozzi* is delightful and intelligent; the action is rambunctious: both create a strong counterpoint to the other. The result is a highly theatrical play, the kind that allows actors to make the grand and passionate gestures and an audience to delight in its strong cathartic possibilities.

[*See also* Canada; Melodrama]

FURTHER READING

Johnson, Chris. *Essays on George F. Walker: Playing with Anxiety.* Vancouver: Talonbooks, 1999.

Walker, Craig. "George F. Walker: Postmodern City Comedy." In *The Buried Astrolabe: Canadian Dramatic Imagination and Western Tradition.* Montreal: McGill-Queen's Univ. Press, 2001.

Wasserman, Jerry, ed. *Modern Canadian Plays: Volume II.* 3d ed. Vancouver: Talonbooks, 1994.

"Zastrozzi." *Canadian Theatre Encyclopedia.* http://www.canadiantheatre .com/dict.pl?term=Zastrozzi.

Valerie Senyk

ZE ŽIVOTA HMYZU See THE INSECT COMEDY

ZHIZN' CHELOVEKA See THE LIFE OF MAN

ZHENG HUAIXING (1948–)

Born in Xianyou, Fujian Province, CHINA, in 1948, Zheng Huaixing finished his second year of high school when the Cultural Revolution started in 1966 and disrupted the education for all youths in China. After serving in the army for two years, he returned to his hometown and first did farmwork for three years and then taught at a local school and worked as an editor for the local culture center. With the institutions of higher learning nationwide starting to take in students again in 1977, Zheng completed a three-year college program in political science. Upon his graduation in 1980, he began his career as a playwright for *puxianxi*, the traditional regional theater of his birthplace. Since then, he has written more than twenty plays, mostly for traditional theater. Seven of his plays have, respectively, received top prizes as the best plays in the Fujian Province. His *Tears of New Pavilion* (*Xinting lei,* 1981), *The Story of the Ugly Duck* (*Yazi chou xiaozhuan,* 1984), *Wang Zhaojun* (1999), and

Shangguan Wan'er (2002) have won national prizes for outstanding plays in different years.

His best-known play *Tears of New Pavilion* falls into a category termed "newly written historical play" (*xinbian lishi ju*). It is set in A.D. 322 of the Eastern Jin period. Based on real historical figures, it tells the story of how the imperial court of the Jin Yuan emperor is almost overthrown by its rebel general due to suspicion, jealousy, and internal strife among court officials, including the emperor himself. Of the major political players, Zhou Boren, minister of Official Personnel Affairs, is portrayed as an upright person who stands above his self-interest, with a strong sense of historical mission to restore the lost glory and unity of the Jin Dynasty. At two critical moments, he acts: to rescue the prime minister Wang Dao, the cousin of rebel general Wang Dun, from being executed by the emperor and later to protect the emperor from being overthrown by the rebel. But finally at New Pavilion, where Zhou used to drink with the Wang cousins, sharing their aspirations, he himself is killed by the rebel general, Zhou's own friend, based on the prime minister's suspicion of Zhou. The prime minister later learns that it was Zhou who once saved his life. Zhou's utter selflessness moves the prime minister to persuade his cousin general to retreat. Finally peace is restored.

The play was premiered in 1981 as a *puxianxi* music drama by the Li Sheng Troupe of the playwright's hometown and first published in 1982. The play has won several prizes at provincial and national levels and has been anthologized in at least five collections of plays. Apart from the beauty of its language and the superb performance of its *puxianxi* style, the play has political and social significance in that it reflects the historical reality of the ruling class and alludes to contemporary political and social issues. Zhou Boren, the protagonist, is the playwright's social call for a national spirit that will lead people to be concerned with the interests of the nation and its people.

As Zheng's reputation increases nationally, some of his plays have been adapted for other regional dramas such as *jingju, hanju, yueju, chaoju,* and *gaojiaxi.* In recent years, Zheng has also been engaged in writing scripts for television series.

SELECT PLAYS: *The Story of Lost Pearl* (*Yi zhu ji,* 1980); *Tears of New Pavilion* (*Xinting lei,* 1981); *The Trial of the Beggar* (*Shen qigai,* 1982); *The Cold Moon of the Jin Palace* (*Jin gong han yue,* 1983); *The Story of the Ugly Duck* (*Yazi chou xiaozhuan,* 1984); *The Story of Frogs* (*Qingwa ji,* 1986); *Borrowing the Bride* (*Jie xinniang,* 1989); *The Story of Sorcery* (*Xi wu ji,* 1991); *The Celestial Book of Qian You Shan* (*Qian you shan tian shu,* 1996); *Ye Liniang* (1998); *Wang Zhaojun* (1999); *Shangguan Wan'er* (2002)

FURTHER READING

An Kui. "Xunzhao tupo de bashe—shilun Zheng Huaixing de xiju chuanzuo" [Looking for breakthroughs: Comments on Zheng Huaixing's playwriting]. *Wenyi bao (Literature and Art Paper)* (December 29, 1990).

Liao Ben. "Zheng Huaixing juzuo de gexing jiqi chaoyue jiazhi" [The characteristics of Zheng Huaixing's plays and their tanscending value]. *Wenlun bao* (Literary Commentary) (June 11, 1987).

Wang Pingzhang. "Lun Zheng Huaixing de chuangzuo" [A study of Zheng Huaixing's Creation]. *Wenyi yanjiu* (Literature and Art Studies) 2 (1989).

Zheng Huaixing. *Xinting lei* [Tears of New Pavilion]. In *Zhongguo xiqu jingpin* [Best plays of the Chinese xiqu], ed. by Guo Hancheng and Wu Qianhao. Jinan: Shangdong jiaoyu chubanshe, 2002. 3: 125–184.

Cai Xingshui and Wenwei Du

ZINDEL, PAUL (1936–2003)

I see the world as a problem solving situation, and the solution of those problems through fiction seems to be the adventure that I've chosen for myself.

—Paul Janeczko, 1977

Paul Zindel won overnight recognition as a dramatist with the 1971 OFF-BROADWAY production of *The Effect of Gamma Rays on Man-in-the-Moon Marigolds*. It was awarded the Pulitzer Prize for Drama, but subsequent Zindel plays failed to build on the promise of this early work critics compared favorably to TENNESSEE WILLIAMS'S THE GLASS MENAGERIE. Despite the fact that he always considered himself first and foremost a playwright, Zindel spent much of his career as a pioneering writer of a new wave of young reader fiction focusing with greater REALISM on contemporary problems of teenage sexuality and drug use.

Born in 1936, in the fall of 1954 Zindel entered Wagner College, graduating in 1958 with a bachelor of science degree in chemistry. During his last year at Wagner, Zindel's father died, a loss that only intensified his difficult relationship with his mother. Following graduation, Zindel went to work as a technical writer for the Allied Chemical Company and continued his education at Wagner, completing a master's degree in education in 1959. At Wagner, Zindel took a writing course taught by dramatist EDWARD ALBEE, who encouraged him to continue writing. That same year, *Dimensions of Peacocks*, Zindel's first play, was produced. Zindel's fascination with dementia praecox is central to the play, as the youth attempts to understand his mother's disturbed behavior.

For the next decade, Zindel taught chemistry and physics at Staten Island's Tottenville High School, but he continued to write plays, including *A Dream of Swallows* (1964), which dealt with a mean-spirited drunk who finds pleasure in torturing inmates at an asylum she regularly visits, and most significantly, *Gamma Rays*, which had a successful first production at Houston's Alley Theatre in 1965. The play's positive reception encouraged Zindel to take a sabbatical from teaching during 1966–1967 to serve as playwright-in-residence at the Alley. During that time, National Education Television (NET) produced a short version of *Gamma Rays* along with another Zindel play, *Let Me Hear You Whisper* (1966) about dolphins.

The 1970 publication of *Gamma Rays* (with *Let Me Hear You Whisper*) inspired an off-Broadway production of *Gamma Rays* starring Sada Thompson, and the play won that year's Obie Award for Best Play. In 1971, *Gamma Rays* brought Zindel the Pulitzer Prize and established his reputation as perhaps the best writer of women's roles since Tennessee Williams, an image confirmed by his next important play, *And Miss Reardon Drinks a Little* (1967), produced on Broadway in 1971. Featuring Julie Harris in the leading role of Anna Reardon, a mentally disturbed high school girl, the plot is a vivid exploration of the interrelationships of the sisters and their uniquely individual characters. The play was only moderately successful but paved the way for the 1972 Broadway production of Zindel's *The Secret Affairs of Mildred Wild*, starring Maureen Stapleton. Focusing on another troubled middle-aged woman, Mildred, who escapes her squalid life by imagining herself in famous movie roles, the play failed despite critical acclaim for Stapleton's performance.

In 1973, Zindel's next major play, *The Ladies Should Be in Bed*, was published with *The Secret Affairs of Mildred Wild*. The play failed to garner critical approval. In 1975 Zindel's play *Ladies at the Alamo*, which dealt with a battle of wills among five strong women for control of a Texas theater, found no critical favor.

Zindel died of lung cancer in New York City in 2003. Although his obituaries commented on his plays, especially the Pulitzer Prize–winning *Gamma Rays*, Zindel was described as a prosperous writer of teenage fiction.

PLAYS: *Dimensions of Peacocks* (1959); *Euthanasia and the Endless Hearts* (1960); *A Dream of Swallows* (1962); *The Effect of Gamma Rays on Man-in-the-Moon Marigolds* (1964); *Let Me Hear You Whisper* (1966); *And Miss Reardon Drinks a Little* (1967); *The Secret Affairs of Mildred Wild* (1972); *Ladies Should Be in Bed* (1973); *Ladies at the Alamo* (1975); *Amulets Against the Dragon Forces* (1989; initially titled *A Destiny with Half Moon Street*); *Every Seventeen Minutes the Crowd Goes Crazy!* (2000); *Naughty Shrinks on Broadway* (2003, incomplete libretto for a musical)

FURTHER READING

Dace, Tish. "Paul Zindel." In *Contemporary American Dramatists*, ed. by K. A. Berney. London: St. James Press, 1994. 586–588.

Flately, Guy. ". . . And Gamma Rays Did It!" *New York Times* (April 19, 1970).

Forman, Jack Jacob. *Presenting Paul Zindel*. Boston, Mass.: Twayne, 1988.

Prideaux, Tom. "Man With a Bag of Marigold Dust." *Life* 69 (July 4, 1970): 8–9.

"Prizewinning Marigolds." *Time* 97 (May 17, 1971): 66.

Strickland, Ruth L. "Paul Zindel." In *Twentieth-Century American Dramatists*, ed. by John MacNicholas. 2 vols. Detroit, Mich: Gale, 1981.

James Fisher

ZŌ *See* THE ELEPHANT

ZOLA, ÉMILE (1840–1902)

Inspired by radical thinkers such as Charles Darwin and Hippolyte Taine, Émile Zola proclaimed that literature should reject ROMANTICISM for NATURALISM, which would adopt the methods of modern science and set up experiments; like the scientist, the writer's task was then to observe carefully and objectively record the results. The result would replace "metaphysical man" with "physiological man." Zola developed this theory in his novels, as well as critical writings on literature, painting, and the theater. His most enduring success was as a novelist; Zola's first literary success came with the novel THÉRÈSE RAQUIN (1867) and continued through the twenty volumes of the "Rougon-Macquart" series (including *L'Assommoir*, *Germinal*, and *Nana*). A tireless social reformer, he campaigned against literary and theatrical censorship and exposed the anti-Semitism of French society in *J'accuse* (*I Accuse*). He was born in Paris on April 2, 1840, and died of carbon monoxide poisoning on September 28, 1902. This happened under mysterious circumstances; allegations that he was murdered for his catalytic role in the Dreyfus Affair persist.

Zola's importance to the theater rests more on his critical writings than his plays. His first produced work, a stage adaptation of *Thérèse Raquin* (1873), is revived on occasion, but he remained unable to find a way to reveal his characters' psychological states through action; his characters recount their emotions for each other rather than embodying them.

Zola's theories on the theater appear in a chapter of *Le roman expérimental* (*The Experimental Novel*, 1879) and the books *Nos auteurs dramatiques* (*Our Dramatic Authors*) and *Le naturalisme au théâtre* (*Naturalism in the Theater*), both published in 1881. In place of the moralistic plots and character conventions established by playwrights such as VICTORIEN SARDOU and DUMAS FILS in their popular "thesis plays" that confirmed the preconceptions of a bourgeois audience, Zola called for the stage to match the scientific sophistication of the modern novel, replacing plot with "temperaments" and purging morals for observed facts. In place of ACTING directed to the audience, and costumes designed to reflect and set fashions, Zola advocated a style of acting where actors would concentrate on the other characters and the onstage reality, even if this meant turning their backs to the audience, and costumes would be merely clothes.

These theories had a great influence within and outside of FRANCE. AUGUST STRINDBERG's *MISS JULIE* and its preface reveal his debt to Zola's ideas on character and staging; GERHART HAUPTMANN's THE WEAVERS dramatically succeeds in replacing the individual protagonist with a social class. While Zola seems to have undervalued the work of these playwrights (as well as HENRIK IBSEN, another writer frequently compared to him in outlook), this did not prevent him from promoting the work of new playwrights to a French audience. In addition to writing an introduction to the French translation of Strindberg's THE FATHER, Zola championed the young director ANDRÉ ANTOINE, an important innovator in naturalistic staging and advocate for new playwrights. Zola's public support for Antoine's Théâtre Libre may have ensured its survival and influenced the breadth of its repertoire.

[*See also* France]

SELECT PLAYS: *Thérèse Raquin* (1873); *Rabourdin's Heirs* (*Les Héritiers Rabourdin*, from Ben Jonson's *Volpone*, 1874); *L'Assommoir* (adapted with Zola's collaboration by William Brusnach and Octave Gastineau, 1879); *Nana* (adapted with Zola's collaboration by Brusnach, 1881); *Messidor* (opera libretto, 1897)

FURTHER READING

Brown, Frederick. *Zola: A Life*. New York: Farrar Straus Giroux, 1995.

Carter, Lawson A. *Zola and the Theater*. New Haven, Conn.: Yale Univ. Press, 1963.

Richardson, Joanna. *Zola*. London: Weidenfeld & Nicolson, 1978.

Zola, Émile. "From *Naturalism in the Theatre*." In *The Theory of the Modern Stage*, ed. by Eric Bentley. 1968. Harmondsworth: Penguin, 1972. 352–372.

——. "Naturalism on the Stage." In *Dramatic Theory and Criticism: Greeks to Grotowski*, ed. by Bernard F. Dukore. New York: Harcourt Brace Jovanovich, 1974. 692–719.

Walter Bilderback

THE ZOO STORY

EDWARD ALBEE's first play *The Zoo Story* is a deceptively short one-act set in Central Park in New York City. It was first staged at the Schiller Theater in Berlin in 1959 and then at New York's Provincetown Playhouse the following year.

Peter, a middle-aged publisher, is sitting on a bench, reading. Jerry, a younger man who has just visited the Central Park Zoo, enters. Jerry engages Peter in an unwilling conversation in which he extracts many details of Peter's life: he is married with two daughters and lives in a house with cats and two parakeets. The parallel is drawn between Jerry's excursion and Peter's existence in a kind of domestic "zoo." Jerry, in turn, divulges details of his own life, providing a stark contrast with Peter: in a monologue that lasts almost for a quarter of the play, Jerry describes his relationship with his landlady's dog, which he hates and has attempted to poison.

Jerry's narrative turns to an account of his recent visit to the zoo, during which his actions become far more physically challenging to his unwilling listener. Peter begins to feel both threatened and angry but seems unable to respond effectively. Jerry draws a flick knife and throws it to Peter, who holds it as far away from himself as possible. But Jerry runs at him, impaling himself. Peter is horrified: suddenly Jerry's prediction, earlier in the scene, that their encounter would make the news, becomes horribly true. Peter escapes, returning to his own form of incarceration in his own version of the "zoo" from which Jerry has now permanently escaped.

The juxtaposition between the unfolding drama and the humor of the sharply constructed dialogue contributes to the deeply disturbing atmosphere that pervades Albee's first play and contributes in a major way to the construction of dramatic tension.

The play is unpredictable and confounds the audience's expectations by developing a shocking scenario from the most innocuous beginnings. Audiences would naturally identify with the very ordinariness of the character Peter, the classic innocent bystander caught up in an incident far from their own making. The unpredictability of Jerry's character threatens the conventional. The audience is made to feel uncomfortable by diverse and contrasting reactions to the characters and what they represent: Jerry is a bully and threatens physical violence; Peter seems unnaturally protective of what he perceives as his personal space: his park bench. Is this COMEDY or TRAGEDY? Should we laugh at or feel irritated by the absurdity of Peter's dilemma—he could just walk away—or be angered and disturbed by the apparent randomness of Jerry's violent actions, which threatens our accepted patterns of social behavior?

The convention of the long central monologue utilized by Albee, in which Jerry relates his relationship with the dog, seems to pay homage in equal part to both the stand-up storytelling traditions of American vaudeville and the soliloquies of the Shakespearian stage. Punctuated by asides, the monologue is balanced between the evidently comic and the distinctly cruel, a device later developed in WHO'S AFRAID OF VIRGINIA WOOLF? (1962).

How should the audience respond to this unpredictable situation, presented to them in an unconventional dramatic form (characters did not frequently perform monologues in plays of this period)? The Zoo Story seems to hover between comedy and tragedy, and the uncertainty of the audience can be an exhausting experience. In this play Albee confronts the audience with a kind of human zoo, in which the apparent passivity of Peter can have as dangerous and tragic an outcome as the apparent aggression of Jerry. Where does the audience stand in this? They are shocked and yet powerless observers having to make the choice of whether they should simply observe the action that passes before them or actively respond to the dilemma that develops from the seeming innocence of a few minutes sitting on a park bench and a trip to the zoo.

Over four decades after writing The Zoo Story, Albee returned to its difficult world with Homelife, which shows us Peter's relationship with his wife Ann immediately before he leaves for the park where he will meet Jerry. Homelife and The Zoo Story were performed together in 2004 at the Hartford Stage as acts 1 and 2 of Peter and Jerry.

[See also United States, 1940–Present]

FURTHER READING

Gussow, Mel. Edward Albee: A Singular Journey. London: Oberon Books, 1999.

McCarthy, Gerald. Edward Albee. London: Macmillan Modern Dramatists, 1987.

Roudane, Mathew. Understanding Edward Albee. Columbia: Univ. of South Carolina Press, 1987.

Paul E. Fryer

ZUCKMAYER, CARL (1896–1977)

The grand old man of German letters.
—Walter Killy

Although primarily known as a playwright, Carl Zuckmayer's work also encompasses prose fiction, lyric poetry, essays, adaptations for the stage, and film scripts such as The Blue Angel (Der blaue Engel, 1930). Zuckmayer was born on December 27, 1896, in Nackenheim, GERMANY, and began his career as a dramatist in the early 1920s with a play in the then current expressionist fashion, but he achieved his breakthrough with the Berlin premiere of the hugely popular The Merry Vineyard (Der fröhliche Weinberg, 1925). Zuckmayer dispensed with the bloodless abstractions and idealistic aspirations for a regeneration of humankind as espoused by expressionist drama in favor of unsophisticated humor, time-honored comedic devices, and down-to-earth characters who, imbued with a boundless zest for life, speak the dialect of his wine-growing home region on the Rhine. Owing to the immense appeal of the play, Zuckmayer was credited with almost single-handedly ending the vogue of EXPRESSIONISM on the stage and initiating a return to realistic representation by way of his revival of the VOLKSSTÜCK.

Schinderhannes (1927), a play named after a German Robin Hood–type figure from the late 1700s, and Katharina Knie (1928), a somewhat sentimental drama featuring a courageous circus artist as heroine, represent variations of the Volksstück. But Zuckmayer's best-known drama, which has become part of the theater canon, strikes out in a somewhat different direction. The plot of The Captain of Köpenick (Der Hauptmann von Köpenick, 1931) derives from a bizarre, well-documented 1906 incident: the impersonation of a captain in the imperial army by Wilhelm Voigt, an unemployed cobbler and ex-convict. Voigt managed to abscond with the municipal funds of the town of Köpenick (then outside the city limits of Berlin). The incident was widely construed to offer a prime example of the dominance of Prussian-German militarism in civil society, yet Zuckmayer's critique of the reliance on blind obedience and the veneration of the uniform is muted. He endows his play with fairy-tale elements by attributing magical powers to the uniform, powers that seem to derive from the ideas and principles underlying an oppressive regime and absolve uniform wearers from personal responsibility. The play ends on a conciliatory note when Voigt makes his peace with his former foes, the representatives of the state.

Zuckmayer's rather benign criticism of militarism was sufficient reason for the Nazis to put the playwright on their blacklist and, after Adolf Hitler's assumption of power in 1933, force him into exile. Until the Nazi annexation of AUSTRIA in 1938, Zuckmayer lived just outside Salzburg, then immigrated to the UNITED STATES. Banned from German stages, Zuckmayer concentrated on writing short prose fiction and film scripts. However, isolated on a remote farm in Vermont during World War II, he composed what became one of the most controversial and, at the same time, enormously successful dramas of the postwar years, *The Devil's General* (*Des Teufels General*, 1946). Protagonist General Harras of the Luftwaffe is faced with the moral predicament of despising Hitler, on the one hand, and of supporting Hitler's war effort via his expertise, on the other. In the end, he submits to "divine judgment" by flying a malfunctioning airplane and is killed in the ensuing crash. While Harras's case provides a partial explanation of Hitler's support among large segments of the population, it does not fully endorse the resistance movement, as is evident in Zuckmayer's ambivalent treatment of its chief representative. Despite its perceived shortcomings, the play, which features a host of characters espousing a broad spectrum of views on Nazism from principled opposition to wholesale acceptance, was instrumental in initiating an intense debate in postwar West Germany about coming to terms with the Nazi past.

Although Zuckmayer's subsequent plays tended to address topical issues related to World War II and the Cold War, they attracted limited public attention and little positive comment. *The Song of the Fiery Furnace* (*Der Gesang im Feuerofen*, 1950), a drama about resistance and betrayal in Nazi-occupied FRANCE, and *The Cold Light* (*Das kalte Licht*, 1955), a play about atomic espionage, subordinate political analysis to individualistic, humanitarian considerations. With his widely acclaimed autobiography *A Part of Myself* (*Als wär's ein Stück von mir*, 1966), Zuckmayer achieved a great success that his plays of the 1960s and 1970s could not match. In *The Life of Horace A. W. Tabor* (*Das Leben des Horace A. W. Tabor*, 1964) and *Dance of the Herons* (*Der Kranichtanz*, 1967), Zuckmayer chose his erstwhile host country, the United States, as his setting. He died on January 18, 1977, in Visp, SWITZERLAND.

SELECT PLAYS: *Crossroads* (*Kreuzweg*, 1920); *The Merry Vineyard* (*Der fröhliche Weinberg*, 1925); *Schinderhannes* (1927); *Katharina Knie* (1928); *The Captain of Köpenick* (*Der Hauptmann von Köpenick*, 1931); *The Devil's General* (*Des Teufels General*, 1946); *The Song of the Fiery Furnace* (*Der Gesang im Feuerofen*, 1950); *The Cold Light* (*Das kalte Licht*, 1955); *The Clock Strikes One* (*Die Uhr schlägt eins*, 1961); *The Life of Horace A. W. Tabor* (*Das Leben des Horace A. W. Tabor*, 1964); *Dance of the Herons* (*Der Kranichtanz*, 1967); *The Pied Piper* (*Der Rattenfänger*, 1975)

FURTHER READING

Mews, Siegfried. *Carl Zuckmayer*. Boston: Twayne, 1981.

Wagener, Hans. *Carl Zuckmayer Criticism: Tracing Endangered Fame*. Columbia, S.C.: Camden House, 1995.

Siegfried Mews

DIRECTORY OF CONTRIBUTORS

Aarseth, Asbjørn
Retired Professor of Scandinavian Literature, University of Bergen, Norway
Enemy of the People, An; Ghosts; Grieg, Nordahl; Ibsen, Henrik; Norway; Our Power and Our Glory; Peer Gynt; Pillars of Society

Abrams, Josh
Lecturer in Drama, Roehampton University, United Kingdom
Environmental Theater

Aksu Erol, Simin
PhD Candidate, Istanbul University, Turkey
Turkey

Alker, Gwendolyn
Associate Teacher of Theatre Studies, New York University
Cruz, Migdalia; Ensler, Eve; Fefu and Her Friends; Fornes, Maria Irene

Ametsbichler, Elizabeth
Professor of German, University of Montana
Anatol; Liebelei; Professor Bernhardi; Reigen; Schnitzler, Arthur

Amkpa, Awam
Associate Professor, Tisch School of the Arts, New York University
Africa; Blood Knot, The; Fugard, Athol; Onwueme, Tess; Osofisan, Femi; Sizwe Bansi Is Dead; Soyinka, Wole; Tsegaye Gabre-Medhin

Andrews, Jamie
Curator of Modern Literary Manuscripts, British Library, United Kingdom
Day in the Death of Joe Egg, A

Andrucki, Martin
Charles A. Dana Professor of Theater, Bates College
Baal; Caucasian Chalk Circle, The; Good Woman of Setzuan, The; Mother Courage and Her Children; Piscator, Erwin; Reinhardt, Max; Threepenny Opera, The

Anthony-Moore, Ellen
Assistant Professor, City University of New York; Ph.D. Candidate, The Graduate Center, City University of New York
Baldwin, James (w/ Christopher Moore); Blessing, Lee (w/ Christopher Moore); Bullins, Ed (w/ Christopher Moore); Fences (w/ Christopher Moore); Gurney, A. R. (w/ Christopher Moore); Kanin, Garson (w/ Christopher Moore); Ma Rainey's Black Bottom (w/ Christopher Moore); Medoff, Mark (w/ Christopher Moore); Piano Lesson, The (w/ Christopher Moore); Wilson, August (w/ Christopher Moore)

Applebaum, Jessica Kaplow
Independent Scholar and Production Dramaturg, New York, New York
Five Lesbian Brothers; Grimke, Angelina Weld; Split Britches

Arancibia, Juana
Lecturer, Department of Foreign Languages, California State University, Dominguez Hills
Halac, Ricardo (w/ Benito Gómez)

Armstrong, Jolene
Assistant Professor, Centre for Language and Literature, Athabasca University, Canada
Highway, Tomson; Maggie and Pierre; Marcel Pursued by Hounds; Sisters in Law

Arntzen, Even
Associate Professor, Department of Comparative Literature, University of Tromsø, Norway
Game of Life, The

Aronson-Lehavi, Sharon
Ph.D. Candidate in Theatre, The Graduate Center, City University of New York
Avant-Garde Drama, Israel-Palestine

Arrow, Michelle
Lecturer, Department of Modern History, Macquarie University, Australia
Australia, Women Playwrights Before 1970

Asensio, Paloma
Lecturer, Department of Spanish and Portuguese, Dartmouth College
Gambaro, Griselda; Information for Foreigners

Asiedu, Awo Mana
Lecturer, Department of Theater Arts, University of Ghana
Abdallah, Mohammed Ben; Aidoo, Ama Ata; Sutherland, Efua Theodora

Bacalzo, Dan
Adjunct Faculty, Tisch School of the Arts, New York University
Chong, Ping; Hughes, Holly; Hwang, David Henry; Wolfe, George C.

Baldwin, Jane
Full-time Faculty, Theatre Division, The Boston Conservatory
Henley, Beth; Howe, Tina

Ballesteros, Isolina
Assistant Professor, Department of Modern Languages and Comparative Literature, Baruch College, City University of New York
Theater of Urgency

Barlow, Judith E.
Professor, Department of English, University at Albany, State University of New York
Children's Hour, The; Gale, Zona; Hellman, Lillian; Little Foxes, The; Miss Lulu` Bett

Bar-On, Gefen
Postdoctoral Fellow, McGill University, Canada
Copenhagen

Basham, Rebecca R.
Assistant Professor, Department of English, Rider University
Arden, John

Baumrin, Seth
Department of Communication Skills, John Jay College of Criminal Justice, City University of New York
Poor Theater

Bay-Cheng, Sarah
Assistant Professor, Department of Theatre and Dance and Department of Media Study, University at Buffalo, The State University of New York
Avant-Garde Drama, Western Europe

Beeman, William O.
Professor of Anthropology, and Theatre, Speech and Dance, Brown University
Iran; Iraq

Beene, LynnDianne
Professor, Department of English Language and Literature, University of New Mexico
Madness of George III, The

Behlau, Ulrike
Department of English, Johannes Gutenberg University, Mainz, Germany
Wandor, Michelene

Bell, Barbara A. E.
Independent Scholar, Roxburghshire, United Kingdom
Bondagers; Cheviot, the Stag, and the Black, Black Oil, The; Glover, Sue; Maiden Stone, The; McGrath, John; Munro, Rona

Bell, John
Assistant Professor, Department of Performing Arts, Emerson College
Gray, Spalding; Off- and Off-Off-Broadway; Political Theater in the United States, Second Half 20th Century; United States, 1940–Present; Valdez, Luis

Bell, John M.
A.B.D., Southern Illinois University, Carbondale
Melodrama

Berkowitz, Joel
Associate Professor and Chair, Judaic Studies Department, University at Albany, State University of New York
Goldfaden, Avrom; Gordin, Jacob; Moscow State Yiddish Theatre; Yiddish Theater

Bermel, Albert
Professor of Theatre Emeritus, The Graduate Center, City University of New York
Comedy; Farce; Romanticism; Tragedy; Tragicomedy

Bernstein, Ana
Adjunct Faculty, College of Arts and Science, New Jersey City University
Candle King, The; Guarnieri, Gianfrancesco; They Don't Wear Black Tie

Betanzos, Lourdes
Associate Professor, Department of Foreign Languages and Literatures, Auburn University
Schmidhuber de la Mora, Guillermo

Bial, Henry
Assistant Professor, Department of Theatre and Film, University of Kansas
American Buffalo; Glengarry Glen Ross; Mamet, David; Oleanna; Sexual Perversity in Chicago

Bilderback, Walter
Dramaturg and Literary Manager, The Wilma Theater, Philadelphia, PA
Canada, English Language; Canada, French Language; Césaire, Aimé; Cocteau, Jean; Jarry, Alfred; League of Nathans, The; Reading Hebron; Romains, Jules; Sherman, Jason; Thérèse Raquin; Ubu Trilogy; Voaden, Herman; Zola, Émile

Billings, Brian C.
Independent Scholar, San Antonio, Texas
Blithe Spirit

Bird, Kym
Associate Professor, York University, Canada
Anderson, Clara Rothwell; Hayes, Kate Simpson; Mock Parliaments, The

Birns, Margaret Boe
Adjunct Assistant Professor, School of Continuing and Professional Studies, New York University
Van Druten, John

Birns, Nicholas
Professor, Department of English, New School University
Corker; Lill, Wendy; Occupation of Heather Rose, The; Reaney, James; Wiebe, Rudy

Bjørby, Pål
Associate Professor, Department of Scandinavian Studies, University of Bergen, Norway
Bankruptcy, A; Bjørnson, Bjørnstjerne

Bladel, Roderick
Librarian, Billy Rose Theatre Division, New York Public Library for the Performing Arts
Life with Father; Lindsay, Howard, and Russel Crouse

Blansfield, Karen
Adjunct Assistant Professor, Department of Dramatic Art, University of North Carolina at Chapel Hill
In Abraham's Bosom; Seven Keys to Baldpate; Why Marry?

Bloom, Arthur W.
Retired Dean, Visual and Performing Arts, Kutztown University
Rip Van Winkle

Boateng, Alex
Lecturer, Department of English, Southern Connecticut State University
Africa, West Africa

Bohm, Arnd
Associate Professor, Department of English Language and Literature, Carleton University, Canada
Andorra; Fear and Misery in the Third Reich; Frisch, Max; Hein, Christoph; Kokoschka, Oskar; Learning Play; Mother, The; New Objectivity; Resistible Rise of Arturo Ui, The; Sternheim, Carl; Toller, Ernst; Transfiguration

Boles, William C.
Professor, English Department, Rollins College
Butterfly Kiss; Trainspotting

Borja-Jimenez, Francisco
Independent Scholar, Rio Piedras, Puerto Rico
Dorr, Nicolás

Boyd, Mari
Chair, Department of Liberal Arts, Sophia University, Japan
Iwamatsu Ryō; Kishida Rio; Kōkami Shōji; Makino Nozomi; Ōta Shōgo; Water Station, The

Bramwell, Murray
Associate Professor, Department of Drama, Flinders University, Australia
Balodis, Janis; Nowra, Louis

Bredeson, Kate
Assistant Professor of Theatre, Dalhousie University, Canada
Antigone; Blacks, The; Gatti, Armand; Sarraute, Nathalie

Breitinger, Eckhard
Professor Emeritus, Institute for African Studies, Bayreuth University, Germany
Africa, Postcolonial Drama; Africa, East Africa

Brewer, Andrea
Graduate Student, Department of Philosophy, Princeton University
Kaspar

Brisbane, Katharine
Co-Founder and Publisher (1971–2001), Currency Press, Australia
Australia, 1860–1945

Brogyányi, Eugene
Artistic Director, Threshold Theater Company, New York City
Hungary; Molnár, Ferenc; Örkény, István; Páskándi, Géza; Spiró, György; Toth Family, The

Brousseau, Elaine
Special Lecturer of English, Providence College
Dear Brutus; Magistrate, The; Mid-Channel

Brown, Ian Jarvis
Independent Scholar, Australia
Cockroach Opera, The; Riantiarno, Nano

Brown, Lorraine A.
Professor of English, George Mason University
Federal Theatre Project

Brynhildsvoll, Knut
Professor, Centre for Ibsen Studies, University of Oslo, Norway
Hedda Gabler; Pretenders, The; Wild Duck, The

Brzovic, Kathy
Lecturer, Business Writing Program, California State University, Fullerton
Measures Taken, The

Burian, Jarka M.
Professor Emeritus, Department of Theatre, University at Albany, State University of New York
Čapek, Karel; Czechoslovakia; Fischerová, Daniela; Havel, Václav; Insect Comedy, The; Langer, František; Memorandum, The; R.U.R.; Steigerwald, Karel; Topol, Josef

Butler, Erik
Assistant Professor of German Studies, Emory University
Dadaism; Epic Theater

Byckling, Liisa
Ph.D. Researcher, Renvall-Institute, University of Helsinki, Finland
Forest, The; Moscow Art Theatre and Studios; Ostrovsky, Aleksandr; Scoundrel, The; Stanislavsky, Konstantin; Thunderstorm, The

Caballero, I. Carolina
Assistant Professor of Spanish, Regis University
Bufo Theater; Triana, José

Cai, Xingshui
Associate Professor, School of Performing Arts, Shanghai Institute of Visual Art, Fudan University, China
After the Reunion (w/ Hongchu Fu); Before the New Bureau Director Came (w/ Hongchu Fu); Liang Bingkun (w/ Li-hua Ying); Ma Zhongjun (w/ Hongchu Fu); Xiong Foxi (w/ Hongchu Fu); Yang Lanchun (w/ Wenwei Du); Zheng Huaixing (w/ Wenwei Du)

Čakare, Valda
Professor of Theatre and Drama, Latvian Academy of Culture
Latvia; Rainis

Cale Feldman, Lada
Professor of Theatre Studies, Department for Comparative Literature, Faculty of Philosophy, Zagreb, Croatia
Croatia; Krleža, Miroslav; Vojnović, Ivo

Cambiasso, Norberto
Professor of Social Communication, Universidad de Buenos Aires, Argentina
Bridge, The; Grotesco Criollo; Open Theater; Raznovich, Diana; Sánchez, Florencio; Topography of a Nude; Wolff, Egon

Campbell-Speltz, Heather
Academic Coordinator, Department of Hispanic Studies, University of Kentucky
Spain

Casey, Maryrose
ARC Postdoctoral Fellow, Monash University, Australia
Australia, Women Playwrights, 1980–1990s; Australia, Indigenous Performance; Australia, Indigenous Playwrights

Cassidy, Michael W.
Independent Researcher, Japan
Miyoshi Jūrō

Castelloe, Molly
Ph.D. Performance Studies, New York University; Adjunct Faculty, Tisch School of the Arts, New York University
Baraka, Amiri; *Dutchman*; Kennedy, Adrienne; Smith, Anna Deavere

Cervinka, Sarah
BA Spec. Honours, Theatre, York University, Canada
I Love You, Baby Blue; Thompson, Paul

Champagne, Carole Anne
Associate Professor of Modern Languages and Spanish Program Coordinator, University of Maryland Eastern Shore
Costa Rica; Cuba; Piñera, Virgilio; Puerto Rico; Usigli, Rodolfo

Charlton, Debra
Assistant Professor, Department of Theater and Dance, Texas State University
Richardson, Jack

Chatterjee, Sudipto
Assistant Professor, Department of Theatre, Dance, and Performance Studies, University of California, Berkeley
Dutt, Utpal; *Ebong Indrajit*; *Great Rebellion, The*; Hashmi, Safdar; Sircar, Badal; *Wave, The*

Chemers, Michael M.
Assistant Professor of Dramatic Literature and Head of Dramaturgy Program, Purnell Center for the Arts, Carnegie Mellon University
Barnes, Djuna; *Front Page, The*; Performance Art; Performance Studies

Chen, Xiaomei
Professor of Chinese Literature, University of California, Davis
Bai Fengxi; *Chronicles of Sangshuping, The*; Jin Yun; *Power Versus Law*

Chirico, Miriam M.
Associate Professor, English Department, Eastern Connecticut State University
Cummings, E. E. (w/ Jeffrey D. Mason)

Cleary, Beth
Associate Professor and Chair, Department of Theater and Dance, Macalester College
Under the Gaslight; Yankowitz, Susan

Cody, Gabrielle H.
Chair and Associate Professor, Department of Drama and Film, Vassar College
Duras, Marguerite

Conte, Bill
Department of Theater, The Graduate Center, City University of New York
Rabe, David; *Sticks and Bones*; Wilson, Robert

Cormier, J. Briggs
Ohio State University
Bogart, Anne; Donmar Warehouse; Joint Stock Theatre Group; Monstrous Regiment; SITI Company

Corsa, Lissette
Graduate Student, University of South Florida
Brazil

Costantino, Roselyn
Associate Professor of Spanish and Women's Studies, Pennsylvania State University Altoona
Rodríguez, Jesusa

Courtney, Angela
Librarian for English Literatures, Theater, Film Studies, and Philosophy, Indiana University
Jones, Henry Arthur; Robertson, Thomas William

Crockett, Roger A.
Chair, German and Russian Department, Washington and Lee University
Dürrenmatt, Friedrich; *Physicists, The*; *Visit of the Old Lady, The*

Crouch, Kristin A.
Assistant Professor of Drama, Trinity University
Shared Experience Theatre; Suspect Culture; Wildcat Stage Productions

Dahm, Jacobia
Doctoral Candidate in Film Studies, University of Mainz, Germany
Homecoming, The

Dassori, Emma
Ph.D. Candidate, Department of Drama and Dance, Tufts University; Adjunct Professor, Pine Manor College
'Night Mother; Norman, Marsha

Davis, Rick
Associate Dean, College of Visual and Performing Arts, George Mason University
Cyrano de Bergerac; Rostand, Edmond; *Scrap of Paper, A*

Däwes, Birgit
Ph.D., Lecturer of American Studies, University of Wuerzburg, Germany
Baby Blues, The; Taylor, Drew Hayden

Dean, Marla
Director of New Play Development, Remembrance Through the Performing Arts, Austin, Texas
Saved

Decker, Craig
Professor of German, Bates College
Austria; Horváth, Ödön von; *Tales from the Vienna Woods*; Turrini, Peter; *Volksstück*

Defraeye, Piet
Associate Professor, Department of Drama, University of Alberta, Canada
Happenings and Intermedia

Dent, Frank Lloyd
Director, Center for Arts and Church, First Presbyterian Church in the City of New York
Religion and Drama

De Ornellas, Kevin
Lecturer in English, University of Ulster, United Kingdom
Ackland, Rodney; Adventures of a Black Girl in Search of God; Bent; Charley's Aunt; Coward, Noël; Dangerous Corner; Dry Lips Oughta Move to Kapuskasing; Essex Girls; Guantanamo: "Honor Bound to Defend Freedom"; Hobson's Choice; Houghton, William Stanley; Luscombe, George; MacDonald, Bryden; Marchessault, Jovette; Maugham, William Somerset; Milner, Arthur; Normal; Ringwood, Gwen Pharis; Sears, Djanet; Serjeant Musgrave's Dance; Sherman, Martin; Sowerby, Githa; Stuff Happens; Talking Heads; Truth About Blayds, The; Whale Riding Weather

Dersofi, Nancy
Professor Emeritus of Italian and Comparative Literature, Bryn Mawr College
Bracco, Roberto; Praga, Marco

Di Cintio, Matt
Producing Director, Emigrant Theater, Minneapolis, Minnesota
Antoine, André; Becque, Henry; Brieux, Eugene; Copeau, Jacques; Illegitimate Son, The; Sardou, Victorien; Tremblay, Michel; Waltz of the Toreadors, The

Dickert, J. Nick
Assistant Professor of Theatre, Northeastern State University
Count of Monte Cristo, The

Dickinson, Peter
Assistant Professor and Associate/Undergraduate Chair, Department of English, Simon Fraser University, Canada
Hare, David

Dixon, Ros
Department of English, National University of Ireland, Galway
Russia and the Soviet Union, Set Design; Socialist Realism, Soviet Union

Dorney, Kate
Curator of Modern and Contemporary Performance, Victoria and Albert Theatre Museum, United Kingdom
England, 1960–1980; Entertaining Mr Sloane; Orton, Joe

Dorsey, Zachary A.
Ph.D. Candidate, Department of Theatre and Dance, University of Texas at Austin
Death and the Maiden; Dorfman, Ariel

Dovale, Leslie A.
Graduate Student, Department of English, Rutgers University
Pinero, Arthur

Du, Wenwei
Associate Professor of Chinese and Comparative Literature, and Chair, Chinese and Japanese Department, Vassar College
China; Guo Qihong; Luo Huaizhen; Wang Renjie; Xu Fen; Yang Lanchun (w/ Cai Xingshui); Zheng Huaixing (w/ Cai Xingshui)

Duffy, Meghan
Ph.D. Candidate, Theatre Department, The Graduate Center, City University of New York
McNally, Terrence; Owens, Rochelle; Terry, Megan

Dukes, Gerry
Independent Scholar and Writer, Dublin, Ireland
All That Fall; Beckett, Samuel; Beckett, Samuel: Short Plays and Dramaticules; Endgame; Happy Days; Krapp's Last Tape; Waiting for Godot

Dupuis, Chris
Independent Scholar, Ontario, Canada
Hosanna; Lilies

Durham, Leslie
Associate Professor, Department of Theatre Arts, Boise State University
Kane, Sarah

Dvergsdal, Alvhild
Professor, Department of Scandinavian Studies, University of Bergen, Norway
Beyond Human Power; Seagull Eaters

Dymond, Erica Joan
Ph.D. Candidate, Department of English, Lehigh University
Ondaatje, Michael

Earnest, Steve
Associate Professor, Department of Theater, Coastal Carolina University
Formalism; Socialist Realism Outside the U.S.S.R.

Edmond, Murray
Associate Professor in Drama and English, English Department, University of Auckland, New Zealand
New Zealand, 1960–1980

Einarsson, Sveinn
Theater Director, Iceland; Former Artistic Director of the National Theatre of Iceland
Iceland; Sigurjonsson, Johann

Eisler, Garrett
Freelance Drama Critic; Adjunct Professor, Tisch School of the Arts, New York University
Durang, Christopher; Heidi Chronicles, The; Lawrence, Jerome, and Robert E. Lee; Odd Couple, The; Simon, Neil; Uncommon Women and Others; Wasserstein, Wendy

Ellam, Julie
Freelance Writer, United Kingdom
Blood Relations

Elliott, Winter S.
Assistant Professor of English, Brenau University
Bouchard, Michel Marc; Coronation Voyage, The; Tale of Teeka, The

Engle, Sherry D.
Assistant Professor, Department of Speech, Communications and Theatre Arts, Borough of Manhattan Community College
Abie's Irish Rose; Crothers, Rachel; Fitch, Clyde; Machinal; Treadwell, Sophie; Truth, The; West, Mae

Estima, Christine L.
MA, Interdisciplinary Studies, York University, Canada; Playwright
Jewel

Ewert, Kevin
Associate Professor of Theatre, University of Pittsburgh at Bradford
Skriker, The

Farnsworth, May Summer
Lecturer in Spanish, University of North Carolina at Chapel Hill
D'Erzell, Catalina; Mondragón Aguirre, Magdalena; Ocampo, María Luisa; Sándor, Malena

Farrell, Joseph
Professor of Italian, University of Strathclyde, United Kingdom
Accidental Death of an Anarchist; Comic Mystery; Fo, Dario; Italy; Theater of the Grotesque

Feliciano, Wilma
Professor of Spanish and Latin American Studies, State University of New York at New Paltz
Casas, Myrna; Great USkranian Circus, The; Hands of God, The; Hernández, Luisa Josefina; Peru, Religious Theater; Royal Guests; Solórzano, Carlos

Ferrari, Rossella
Lecturer in Modern Chinese Culture and Language, School of Oriental and African Studies, University of London, United Kingdom
Avant-Garde Drama, China

Ferris, Lesley
Professor, Department of Theatre, Ohio State University
Horse and Bamboo Theatre; Matura, Mustapha

Finotti, Fabio
Professor of Italian Literature, University of Trieste, Italy
Giacosa, Giuseppe

Fisher, James
Professor of Theater, Wabash College
Angels in America: A Gay Fantasia on National Themes. Part One: Millennium Approaches; Camino Real; Cat on a Hot Tin Roof; Glass Menagerie, The; Inge, William; Kushner, Tony; Night of the Iguana, The; Patrick, John; Picnic; Streetcar Named Desire, A; Suddenly Last Summer; Summer and Smoke; Williams, Tennessee; Zindel, Paul

Fisler, Ben
Theatre Program Advisor, Harford Community College
Almighty Voice and His Wife; Aria; Gilbert, William Schwenck; Moses, Daniel David

Fitzpatrick, Peter
Professor and Head, Centre for Drama and Theatre Studies, Monash University, Australia
Lawler, Ray; Rayson, Hannie; Sewell, Stephen; Williamson, David

Flaherty, Jennifer
Graduate Student, Program of Comparative Literature, University of North Carolina at Chapel Hill
Goodnight Desdemona (Good Morning Juliet)

Fleischer, Mary
Professor of Theatre Arts, Marymount Manhattan College
Bowles, Jane; Buried Child; Curse of the Starving Class; Fool for Love; In the Summer House; Shepard, Sam; True West

Fletcher, Anne
Assistant Professor, Theater Department, Southern Illinois University, Carbondale
United States, 1929–1940

Fletcher, John
Assistant Professor of Theatre History, Louisiana State University
Community Theater

Foley, Kathy
Professor, Theater Arts Department, University of California, Santa Cruz
Burma; Cambodia; Hang Thun Hak; Ilagan, Bonifacio; Jacob, Malou; Joaquin, Nick; Laos; Lapeña-Bonifacio, Amelia; Philippine Educational Theater Association; Philippines; Vietnam

Frassica, Pietro
Professor of French and Italian, Princeton University
Pirandello, Luigi

Frazier, Adrian
Professor, English Department, National University of Ireland, Galway
At the Hawk's Well; Boucicault, Dionysius; Cathleen ni Houlihan; Colleen Bawn, The; Gregory, Lady; Importance of Being Earnest, The; In the Shadow of the Glen; Ireland; Lady Windermere's Fan; MacLiammóir, Micheál; Playboy of the Western World, The; Purgatory; Riders to the Sea; Robinson, Lennox; Spreading the News; Synge, John Millington; Wilde, Oscar; Yeats, W. B.

Freedman, John
Theatre Critic, The Moscow Times, Russia
Arbuzov, Aleksei; Conspiracy of Feelings, A; Erdman, Nikolai; Kharms, Daniil Ivanovich; Lunacharsky, Anatoly Vasilyevich; Lyubimov, Yury Petrovich; Olesha, Yury; Russia and the Soviet Union; Shvarts, Yevgeny Lvovich; Suicide, The

Frick, John W.
Professor, Department of Drama, University of Virginia
Mitchell, Langdon; New York Idea, The

Fryer, Paul E.
Programme Director, MA Theatre and Performance Studies, Rose Bruford College, United Kingdom
Albee, Edward; Three Tall Women; Who's Afraid of Virginia Woolf?; Zoo Story, The

Fu, Hongchu
Associate Professor of East Asian Languages and Literatures, Washington and Lee University
After the Reunion (w/ Cai Xingshui); Before the New Bureau Director Came (w/ Cai Xingshui); Cao Yu; Eight Revolutionary Model Plays; Hai Rui's Dismissal; Hong Shen; In a Land of Silence; Lao She; Ma Zhongjun (w/ Cai Xingshui); Mei Lanfang; Ouyang Yuqian; Tian Han; Wei Minglun; Xiong Foxi (w/ Cai Xingshui)

Fu, Ping
Visiting Assistant Professor, Film Studies and East Asian Studies, Dickinson College
Chen Baichen; Ding Xilin; Guo Moruo; Li Jianwu; On Guard Beneath the Neon Lights; Xia Yan

Fuchs, Elinor
Professor of Dramaturgy and Dramatic Criticism, Yale School of Drama
Apocalypse in Modern Drama

Gabriele, Tommasina
Professor and Coordinator of Italian Studies, Wheaton College, Massachusetts
Dreams of Clytemnestra, The; Female Parts; Maraini, Dacia; Rame, Franca

Gaddy, Kerstin T.
Assistant Professor for Professional Practice in German, The Catholic University of America
Before Daybreak; Brahm, Otto; Hauptmann, Gerhart; Sudermann, Hermann; Weavers, The

Gaensbauer, Deborah
Professor of French, Regis University
Absurdism

Gainor, J. Ellen
Professor of Theatre, Cornell University
Alison's House; Glaspell, Susan; Trifles

Gallimore, Daniel
D.Phil., Department of English, Japan Women's University
Fukuda Tsuneari

Galway, Elizabeth
Assistant Professor, Department of English, University of Lethbridge, Canada
Wood Carver's Wife, The

Gerig, Maya
Visiting Lecturer, Department of Germanic Languages and Literatures, University of North Carolina at Chapel Hill
Drums in the Night (w/ Cyrus M. Shahan); Wolf, Friedrich (w/ Cyrus M. Shahan)

Gerould, Daniel
Lucille Lantel Distinguished Professor of Theatre and Comparative Literature, The Graduate Center, City University of New York
Avant-Garde Drama, Eastern Europe; Avant-Garde Drama, Russia and the Soviet Union; Madman and the Nun, The; Monodrama; Mrożek, Sławomir; Poland (w/ Jadwiga

Kosicka Gerould); Wedding, The; Witkiewicz, Stanisław Ignacy; Wyspiański, Stanisław

Gerould, Jadwiga Kosicka
Independent Scholar, New York, New York
Danton Case, The; Poland (w/ Daniel Gerould); Przybyszewska, Stanisława; Różewicz, Tadeusz; Zapolska, Gabriela

Gianakaris, C. J.
Professor Emeritus of English and Theatre, Western Michigan University
Arcadia; Bond, Edward; Equus; Invention of Love, The; Look Back in Anger; Osborne, John; Pinter, Harold; Rosencrantz and Guildenstern Are Dead; Shaffer, Peter; Stoppard, Tom

Giannini, Stefano
Assistant Professor, Department of French, Italian and Spanish, University of Calgary, Canada
Enrico IV; Right You Are; Six Characters in Search of an Author; Tonight We Improvise

Gibbs, A. M.
Emeritus Professor of English, Division of Humanities, Macquarie University, Sydney, Australia
Arms and the Man; Back to Methuselah; Heartbreak House; John Bull's Other Island; Major Barbara; Man and Superman; Mrs. Warren's Profession; Pygmalion; Saint Joan; Shaw, George Bernard

Gibson, Melissa Dana
Associate Professor, Theatre Arts Department, California State University, Fresno
Ayckbourn, Alan; Lady's Not for Burning, The

Gillespie, John K.
President, Gillespie Global Group, New York
Betsuyaku Minoru; Elephant, The; En the Ascetic; Furuhashi Teiji; Inoue Hisashi; Kinoshita Junji; Morimoto Kaoru; Ohashi Yasuhiko; Sakate Yōji; Shimizu Kunio; Tsubouchi Shōyō; Twilight Crane; Woman's Life, A

Gillitt, Cobina
Adjunct Instructor of Drama, Tisch School of the Arts, New York University
Indonesia; Moths; Noer, Arifin C.; Rendra; Struggle of the Naga Tribe, The; Wijaya, Putu

Gleed, Paul
University at Buffalo, The State University of New York
Greig, David; Wesker, Arnold

Godiwala, Dimple
Ph.D., University of Oxford, United Kingdom
Bennett, Alan; Our Country's Good

Goldberg, Daniel
Department of Art History and Communication Studies, McGill University, Canada
Albertine in Five Times; Memoir; Simard, Andre; Verdecchia, Guillermo

Goldstein, Malcolm
 Professor Emeritus of English, Queens College and The Graduate Center, City University of New York
  Boothe, Clare; *Women, The*

Gómez, Benito
 Assistant Professor, Department of Foreign Languages, California State University, Dominguez Hills
  Catalan Experimental Theater (w/ Jorge Herreros); Dragún, Osvaldo (w/ Jorge Herreros); Gorostiza, Carlos (w/ Jorge Herreros); Halac, Ricardo (w/ Juana Arancibia); Martínez Sierra, Gregorio (w/ Jorge Herreros); *Posibilismo and Imposibilismo* (w/ Jorge Herreros)

González, Bernardo Antonio
 Professor, Department of Romance Languages and Literatures, Wesleyan University
  Benavente, Jacinto; García Lorca, Federico

Goodman, David G.
 Professor, Department of East Asian Languages and Cultures, University of Illinois at Urbana-Champaign
  Akimoto Matsuyo; *Angura and Shōgekijō*; Avant-Garde Drama, Japan; *Head of Mary*; Kubo Sakae; *Land of Volcanic Ash*; Satoh Makoto; *Shingeki*; Tanaka Chikao

Gordon, Eric A.
 Director, The Workmen's Circle/Arbeter Ring, Southern California District
  Blitzstein, Marc; *Cradle Will Rock, The*

Gordon, Kelly Carolyn
 Visiting Assistant Professor, Department of Theatre, University of North Carolina at Greensboro
  Guerrilla Theater

Graham-Jones, Jean
 Professor, Ph.D. Program in Theatre, The Graduate Center, City University of New York
  Avant-Garde Drama, Argentina

Gray, Frances
 Reader in Drama, Sheffield University, United Kingdom
  Albanesi, Meggie; *Loyalties*

Grehan, Helena
 Senior Lecturer in Theater and Creative Arts, Murdoch University, Australia
  Australia, Multicultural Identities in Drama; Davis, Jack

Gribben, Crawford
 Lecturer in Renaissance Literature, University of Manchester, United Kingdom
  Scotland

Grundmann, Heike
 Ph.D., Department of English and American Literature, University of Munich, Germany
  Blood, Sweat and Fears; Ravenhill, Mark

Guha-Majumdar, Rupendra
 Reader in English, Ramjas College, Delhi University, India

Anderson, Maxwell; *Beggar on Horseback*; Connelly, Marc; *Elizabeth the Queen*; *Green Pastures, The*; *What Price Glory?*; *Winterset*

Hacksley, Gregory
 Ph.D., Rhodes University, South Africa
  Birthday Party, The; Russell, Willy; *Song at Twilight, A*

Haney, Peter
 Visiting Assistant Professor of Anthropology, Colorado College
  Carpa

Hansen, Mei-Lin Te-Puea
 Ph.D., Department of English, University of Auckland, New Zealand
  Grace-Smith, Briar; Kouka, Hone; New Zealand, Maori Drama

Harding, James
 Associate Professor of English, University of Mary Washington Collage

Haynes, Robert
 Associate Professor of English, Texas A&M International University
  Bolt, Robert

He, Donghui
 Assistant Professor, Department of Modern Languages, University of Tennessee
  Gao Xingjian; Guo Shixing; Little Theater Movement; Sha Yexin

Herreros, Jorge
 Doctoral Student, Department of Spanish, Alcala de Henares University, Madrid, Spain
  Catalan Experimental Theater (w/ Benito Gómez); Dragún, Osvaldo (w/ Benito Gómez); Gorostiza, Carlos (w/ Benito Gómez); Martínez Sierra, Gregorio (w/ Benito Gómez); *Posibilismo and Imposibilismo* (w/ Benito Gómez)

Heteren, Lucia van
 Senior Lecturer, Department for Arts, Culture, and Media, Theatre Studies, Groningen University, Netherlands
  Heijermans, Herman; Netherlands

Hilger, Christine Marie
 Doctoral Student, Texas Women's University
  Ross, Cree Ian

Himelstein, Morgan Y.
 Professor of English Emeritus, Adelphi University
  Political Theater in the United States, Great Depression Roots

Hinton, KaaVonia
 Assistant Professor, Educational Curriculum and Instruction, Old Dominion University
  Oshodi, Maria

Hintz, Carrie
 Associate Professor of English, Queens College, City University of New York
  Peter Pan

Hischak, Thomas S.
Professor of Theatre, State University of New York College at Cortland
Librettists

Hohman, Valleri Robinson
Assistant Professor, School of Theatre Arts, University of Arizona
Futurism, Russian

Holm, Bent
Associate Professor, Department of Arts and Cultural Studies, University of Copenhagen, Denmark
Club, The; Denmark; Jepsen, Erling; Knutzon, Line; Ørnsbo, Jess; Saalbach, Astrid; Soon the Time Will Come

Honegger, Gitta
Professor of Theater, Arizona State University
Bernhard, Thomas; Eve of Retirement; Heldenplatz; Jelinek, Elfriede; Peymann, Claus

Hopkins, Chris
Professor of English Studies and Head of the Humanities Research Centre, Sheffield Hallam University, United Kingdom
Ascent of F6, The; Corn is Green, The; Williams, Emlyn

Horstein, Scott
Freelance Dramaturg, Los Angeles, CA
Vinaver, Michel

Hunter, Mary Ann
Lecturer in Drama Studies, University of Queensland, Australia
Australia, Drama for Young People

Iles, Lawrence I.
British Historian, UK Labour International Section; Independent Scholar Historian MLA
England, 1980–Present (w/ Betty L. McLane-Iles)

Inoue Yoshie
Kibi International University, Japan
Yamamoto Yūzō (w/ Mitsuya Mori)

Irwin, Derek
Lecturer, Department of English, Arts and Science Program, Lakehead University-Orillia Campus, Canada
Ryga, George

Jannarone, Kimberly
Assistant Professor of Theater Arts, University of California at Santa Cruz
Artaud, Antonin; Futurism, Italian; Salacrou, Armand; Surrealism; Vitrac, Roger

Jeffreys, Joe E.
Adjunct Instructor, Tisch School of the Arts, New York University and Department of Theatre Arts, Stony Brook University, State University of New York
Crowley, Mart; Fierstein, Harvey; Lucas, Craig; Ludlam, Charles

Jernigan, Daniel
Assistant Professor of English, Nanyang Technological University, Singapore
Mighton, John; Scientific Americans

Jiang, Jin
Professor of History, East China Normal University
Sister Xianglin

Johnsen-Neshati, Kristin
Associate Professor of Theater, George Mason University
Gide, André; Mnouchkine, Ariane; Théâtre du Grand-Guignol

Johnson, Jeff
Professor of English and Humanities, Brevard Community College
Lithuania

Johnson, Jerelyn
Assistant Professor of Spanish, College of Staten Island, City University of New York
Echegaray, José; Great Galeoto, The

Johnson, Katie N.
Associate Professor, Department of English, Miami University
Easiest Way, The; Salvation Nell

Johnson, Marlys H.
Graduate Student, Department of Theatre, University of Missouri-Columbia
Egloff, Elizabeth

Jones, Calvin N.
Professor of German, University of South Alabama
Fassbinder, Rainer Werner; Fleißer, Marieluise; Kroetz, Franz Xaver

Jortner, David
Visiting Assistant Professor, Department of Communication Arts and Theatre, Allegheny College
Abe Kōbō; Friends

Kallin, Britta
Assistant Professor of German, Georgia Institute of Technology
Loher, Dea; Strauss, Botho; Streeruwitz, Marlene

Kattelman, Beth A.
Associate Curator and Assistant Professor, Ohio State University Lawrence & Lee Theatre Research Institute
Jitters; Still Stands the House; Storey, Raymond; Young, David

Keele, Alan
Professor of German Literature, Brigham Young University
Borchert, Wolfgang; Grass, Günter

Kerr, David
Professor and Head of Department of Media Studies, University of Botswana
Africa, Central and Southern Africa

Kich, Martin
Professor of English, Wright State University
Afghanistan; al-Hakim, Tawfiq; Choukri, Mohamed; Cook, Michael; Dadie, Bernard; Dike, Fatima; Fennario, David; Frayn, Michael; Freeman, David; French, David; Gray, John; Khan-Din, Ayub; "Master Harold" . . . and the boys; Murrell, John; Nadeem, Shahid; Pakistan; South Africa; Storey, David

Kidd, Kerry
Wellcome Postdoctoral Research Fellow, University of Nottingham, United Kingdom
Jellicoe, Ann; *Knack, The*; Whiting, John

Kilpatrick, David
Assistant Professor, Literature, Language, and Communication, Mercy College
Barker, Howard; LaBute, Neil

Kilpatrick, David R.
Ph.D. Student, University of Missouri-Columbia
Overmyer, Eric

King, Lovalerie
Assistant Professor of English, Pennsylvania State University
Childress, Alice; Hansberry, Lorraine; *Raisin in the Sun, A*

Kinghorn, Michael
Playwright, Director, and Educator; Former Senior Dramaturg, Arena Stage, Washington, D.C., and the Alliance Theatre, Atlanta, Georgia
Grumberg, Jean-Claude; Pinget, Robert

Kirk, Connie Ann
Ph.D., Writer, Painted Post, New York
Milne, Alan Alexander

Kittang, Atle
Professor of Comparative Literature, University of Bergen, Norway; Professor, Centre for Ibsen Studies, University of Oslo, Norway
Brand; *John Gabriel Borkman*; *Master Builder, The*

Klett, Elizabeth
Lecturer, University of Houston
Blasted

Knowles, Joanne
Senior Lecturer, School of Media, Critical and Creative Arts, Liverpool John Moores University, United Kingdom
James, Henry

Kochhar-Lindgren, Kanta
Assistant Professor, Interdisciplinary Arts and Sciences Program, University of Washington Bothell
Boal, Augusto; *Identity Theater*

Koike, Misako
Professor of English, Ochanomizu University, Japan
Dinner at Eight; Ferber, Edna; *Stage Door*

Koger, Alicia Kae
Associate Professor of Drama, University of Oklahoma
Harrigan, Edward G.

Kominz, Laurence
Professor of Japanese Literature, Portland State University
Madame de Sade; Mishima Yukio

Komporaly, Jozefina
Senior Lecturer in Drama, School of English, Performance and Historical Studies, De Montfort University, Leicester, United Kingdom
Under the Whaleback

Krueger, Antonia Sophia
Ph.D., Independent Scholar, St. Paul, Minnesota
Browning Version, The; *Deep Blue Sea, The*; Page, Louise; Rattigan, Terence

Kuharski, Allen J.
Associate Professor and Chair, Department of Theater, Swarthmore College
Gombrowicz, Witold

Kuhn, John G.
Professor Emeritus of English and Theater, Rosemont College
Fall of the City, The; Heyward, Dorothy, and Heyward, Dubose; MacLeish, Archibald; *Porgy and Bess*

Kvam, Kela
Professor Emeritus, Institute of Theatre Studies, University of Copenhagen, Denmark
Abell, Kjeld; *Anna Sophie Hedvig*; Branner, Hans Christian; Drachmann, Holger; Madsen, Sven Åge; Munk, Kaj; Nathansen, Henri; Olsen, Ernst Bruun; *Parasites, The*; Soya, Carl Erik; *Word, The*

Lai, Jane
Honorary Professor, Department of English Language and Literature, Hong Kong Baptist University, China
Chan, Anthony (w/ Jessica Yeung); Chan, Joanna (w/ Jessica Yeung); To, Raymond (w/ Jessica Yeung); Yung, Danny N. T. (w/ Jessica Yeung)

Lamartina-Lens, Iride
Professor of Modern Languages and Cultures, Pace University
Diosdado, Ana; Resino, Carmen

Langås, Unni
Professor of Scandinavian Literature, Agder University College, Norway
Fosse, Jon; Løveid, Cecilie; *Name, The*

Lee, Amy
Assistant Professor, Department of English Language and Literature, Hong Kong Baptist University, China
Hay Fever

Lei, Daphne
Assistant Professor, Department of Drama, University of California, Irvine
Lai Sheng-ch'uan; Liu Ching-min

Leichman, Jeffrey M.
Department of French, Yale University
Copi

Leising, Gary
Assistant Professor, Department of English, Utica College
Walcott, Derek

Leiter, Samuel L.
Distinguished Professor Emeritus of Theatre, Brooklyn College and The Graduate Center, City University of New York
Kawatake Mokuami

Leonard, Candyce
  Associate Professor, Humanities Program, Wake Forest University
    Pedrero, Paloma

Levin, Laura
  Assistant Professor, Department of Theatre, York University, Canada
    Saga of the Wet Hens

Licastro, Emanuele
  Professor, Department of Romance Languages and Literatures, University at Buffalo, The State University of New York
    Betti, Ugo; Queen and the Rebels, The

Lindenblatt, Michelle
  Ph.D. Candidate, Department of Performance Studies, New York University
    MacLeod, Joan

Lomas-Sampedro, Esther
  Clinical Asistant Professor, Modern Languages Department, Fordham University
    Mihura, Miguel; Sanchis Sinisterra, José; Sastre, Alfonso

Lonergan, Patrick
  Lecturer, English Department, National University of Ireland, Galway
    Behan, Brendan; Carr, Marina; Field Day Theatre Company; Friel, Brian; Kilroy, Thomas; McDonagh, Martin; McGuinness, Frank; McPherson, Conor; Murphy, Tom; Observe the Sons of Ulster Marching Towards the Somme; Philadelphia, Here I Come; Quare Fellow, The; Translations; Whistle in the Dark, A

Longoria, Andrew
  Associate Professor and Director of Theatre, Mansfield University of Pennsylvania
    Howard, Sidney; They Knew What They Wanted

Longstaffe, Stephen
  Senior Lecturer in English, University of Cumbria, United Kingdom
    Bed; Cartwright, Jim; Road

Lord, Mark
  Associate Professor of Theater on the Theresa Helburn Fund, Bryn Mawr College
    Four Saints in Three Acts; Stein, Gertrude

Lu, Hongwei
  Assistant Professor, Asian Studies Program, University of Redlands
    Story of Butterfly Lovers, The; White Snake, The; Wu Zuguang

Lucero Baran, Nicole
  Graduate of University of California, Los Angeles, English Literature, 1994
    Architect and the Emperor of Assyria, The

MacCionnaith, Eric-Michael
  University of Oregon
    Boss, The

Mackerras, Colin
  Professor Emeritus, China Studies, Griffith University, Australia
    Dream of the Red Chamber; Fifteen Strings of Cash; Forced Up Mount Liang; Married to a Celestial Lady; Third Sister Liu; White-Haired Girl

Malague, Rosemary
  Senior Lecturer, Theatre Arts Program, University of Pennsylvania
    Churchill, Caryl; Cloud Nine; Top Girls

Malarcher, Jay
  Associate Professor of Theatre, West Virginia University
    Horovitz, Israel

Malick, Javed
  Reader, Department of English, Delhi University, India
    Agra Bazaar; Charandas the Thief; Tanvir, Habib

Maples, Holly
  Department of Drama, Trinity College Dublin
    Clark, Sally; Clothes They Stood Up In, The; Collected Works of Billy the Kid, The; Fraser, Brad; Gilbert, Sky; Unidentified Human Remains and the True Nature of Love

Marko, Marton
  Lecturer in German, Rensselaer Polytechnic Institute
    Handke, Peter

Marsh, Cynthia
  Professor of Russian Drama and Literature, University of Nottingham, United Kingdom
    Gorky, Maksim; Lower Depths, The; Summerfolk

Martin, Carol
  Associate Professor of Drama, Tisch School of the Arts, New York University
    Feminist Drama in the United States; Gelber, Jack; Mann, Emily; Shange, Ntozake

Masanovic, Natasa
  Assistant Professor and Coordinator of the German Language Program, University of Alaska Anchorage
    Hamletmachine; Müller, Heiner

Mason, Jeffrey D.
  Dean, College of Arts and Letters, and Professor of Theatre and Dance, California State University, Sacramento
    All God's Chillun Got Wings; Anna Christie; Baker, George Pierce; Beyond the Horizon; Campbell, Bartley; Cummings, E. E. (w/ Miriam M. Chirico); Desire Under the Elms; Emperor Jones, The; Gillette, William; Great God Brown, The; Hairy Ape, The; Harte, Bret; Howard, Bronson; Hughie; Iceman Cometh, The; Kaufman, George S.; Lazarus Laughed; Long Day's Journey Into Night; Long Voyage Home, The; Miller, Joaquin; Moon for the Misbegotten, A; Mourning Becomes Electra; My Partner; Once in a Lifetime; O'Neill, Eugene; Secret Service; Shenandoah; Strange Interlude; Touch of the Poet, A; You Can't Take it With You

Masor, Alyssa
  Graduate Student in Yiddish Studies, Columbia University
    Purimshpil

Masulis, Martins
Ph.D. Candidate, Department of German Studies, Cornell University
Earth Spirit; Spring Awakening; Wedekind, Frank

Maurer, Kate
English Instructor, Anoka-Ramsey Community College
Campbell, William Wilfred; Krizanc, John; Maillet,
Antonine

McDaniel, L. Bailey
Teaching Fellow, Department of English, Indiana University
MacDonald, Ann-Marie; Pollock, Sharon

McLane-Iles, Betty L.
Professor of French and Québécois Studies, Truman State University
England, 1980–Present (w/ Lawrence I. Iles)

McLane, Chad Lawrence
Brigham Young University-Idaho
Taylor, Thomas; Ticket-of-Leave Man, The

McLaren, Joseph
Professor of English, Hofstra University
Hughes, Langston; Little Ham; Mulatto

McManus, Donald Cameron
Assistant Professor of Theatre and Film, Franklin and Marshall College
Balconville; On the Job; Power Plays, The; Walker, George F.

McNulty, Charles
Chief Theater Critic, Los Angeles Times
Condemned of Altona, The; Flies, The; No Exit; Sartre,
Jean-Paul

Medenica, Ivan
Professor, Faculty of Drama Arts, Belgrade; Theater Critic, Vreme;
Artistic Director, Sterijino Pozorje Festival in Novi Sad, Serbia
Popović, Aleksandar; Serbia

Mee, Erin B.
Assistant Professor, Department of Theatre, Swarthmore College
Army Formation; Dattani, Mahesh; Ganguli, Usha;
Hayavadana; India; Karnad, Girish; On a Muggy Night in
Mumbai; Ottayan; Panikkar, Kavalam Narayana; Rudali;
Sharma, Tripurari; Theyyatheyyam; Thirty Days in September;
Thiyam, Ratan; Tughlaq

Meserve, Walter J.
Distinguished Professor Emeritus, Ph.D. Programs in Theatre and
English, The Graduate Center, City University of New York
Abe Lincoln in Illinois; Idiot's Delight; Millay, Edna St. Vincent;
My Heart's in the Highlands; Petrified Forest, The; Saroyan,
William; Sherwood, Robert E.; Time of Your Life, The

Meyrick, Julian
Associate Director and Literary Adviser, Melbourne Theatre
Company, Australia; Honorary Associate, Theatre and Drama
Program, La Trobe University, Australia
Australia, 1945–1969; Australia, New Wave Productions

Mews, Siegfried
Professor of German, University of North Carolina at Chapel Hill
Brecht, Bertolt; Germany; Zuckmayer, Carl

Miller, Gavin
Research Fellow, Institute for Advanced Studies in the Humanities,
University of Edinburgh, United Kingdom
Admirable Crichton, The; 7:84

Miller, Jordan
Professor Emeritus, Department of English, University of Rhode
Island
Awake and Sing!; Golden Boy; Group Theatre, The; Odets,
Clifford; Waiting for Lefty

Miller, Renata Kobetts
Assistant Professor, Department of English, City College of New York,
City University of New York
Caste; Waste

Milleret, Margo
Associate Professor of Portuguese and Spanish, University of New
Mexico
Arena Theater of São Paulo; Castro, Consuelo de

Milne, Geoffrey
Head of Program and Senior Lecturer, Theatre and Drama Program,
La Trobe University, Australia
Australia, New Wave Drama; Australia, Male Playwrights,
1980–1990s; Enright, Nick; Romeril, John

Montley, Patricia
Director of Theatre, Chatham College, 1983–2000
Bald Soprano, The; Caligula; Camus, Albert; Giraudoux,
Jean; Ondine

Moore, Christopher
Editor-in-Chief, Broadway Magazine, New York
Baldwin, James (w/ Ellen Anthony-Moore); Blessing, Lee
(w/ Ellen Anthony-Moore); Bullins, Ed (w/ Ellen Anthony-
Moore); Fences (w/ Ellen Anthony-Moore); Gurney, A. R.
(w/ Ellen Anthony-Moore); Kanin, Garson (w/ Ellen
Anthony-Moore); Ma Rainey's Black Bottom (w/ Ellen
Anthony-Moore); Medoff, Mark (w/ Ellen Anthony-
Moore); Piano Lesson, The (w/ Ellen Anthony-Moore);
Wilson, August (w/ Ellen Anthony-Moore)

Moore, Kerry
Visiting Assistant Professor of Drama, Vassar College
Brenton, Howard; Far Away; History Boys, The;
Hollingsworth, Michael; Margolin, Deb; Nagy, Phyllis;
Pillowman, The

Mori, Mitsuya
Professor of Theatre Sudies, Seijo University, Japan
Yamamoto Yūzō (w/ Inoue Yoshie)

Morillo, María Dolores
Graduate Student, Department of Spanish and Portuguese, Columbia
University
Bohemian Lights

Morra, Irene
Lecturer in English Literature, Cardiff University, United
Kingdom
Duncan, Ronald; England, 1940–1960

Morrison, Michael A.
Independent Scholar, New York, New York
Jones, Robert Edmond; Sheldon, Edward

Moser, Marlene
Associate Professor, Department of Dramatic Arts, Brock University, Canada
Crackwalker, The; Hollingsworth, Margaret; *Lion in the Streets*; MacIvor, Daniel; *Polygraph*; Thompson, Judith

Mounsef, Donia
Associate Professor of French and Theater Studies, Yale University
France; Koltès, Bernard-Marie; *Roberto Zucco*

Mufson, Daniel
Independent Scholar and Freelance Writer and Translator, Berlin, Germany
America Play, The; Claudel, Paul; Foreman, Richard; Maeterlinck, Maurice; Mee, Charles; Parks, Suzan-Lori

Müller, Anja
Assistant Professor, English Literature, University of Bamberg, Germany
Travesties

Murphy, A. Mary
Instructor, Department of English, The University of Winnipeg, Manitoba, Canada
Loot

Murphy, Brenda
Professor, Department of English, University of Connecticut
Howells, William Dean

Murray, Christopher
Professor Emeritus, School of English and Drama, University College Dublin, Ireland
Juno and the Paycock; O'Casey, Sean; *Plough and the Stars, The*; Shadow of a Gunman, The; Silver Tassie, The

Nadel, Norman
Author of A Pictorial History of the Theatre Guild (1969) and Retired Drama Critic
Theatre Guild

Nanney, Nancy
Chair, Humanities Division, West Virginia University at Parkersburg
Hassan, Noordin; Husain, Shaharom; *It Is Not the Tall Grass Blown By the Wind*; Leow Puay Tin; Malaysia

Nassar, Hala Khamis
Assistant Professor of Modern Arabic Culture and Literature and Director of Undergraduate Studies, Near Eastern Languages and Civilizations, and Women, Gender and Sexuality Studies, Yale University
Egypt; Palestine

Nath, Rajinder
Director, Shiram Centre New Delhi, India (1975, 1981, 1983, and 1989); Editor, Theatre India (1998–2003)
Halfway House; One Day in Asadh; Rakesh, Mohan

Ndung'u, Bantu
Ph.D. Candidate, Department of Performance Studies, New York University
Ngema, Mbongeni; Ngugi wa Thiong'o; Rugyendo, Mukotani; Serumaga, Robert

Nelson, Byron
Associate Professor, Department of English, West Virginia University
Entertainer, The

Nguyen, Lam-Thao
Visiting Instructor, Department of French, Classics and Italian, Michigan State University
Dubillard, Roland; *Season in the Congo, A*

Niemi, Irmeli
Retired Professor of Comparative Literature, Drama, and Film, University of Turku, Finland
Finland

Nunes, Luiz Arthur Ferreira Freire
Theatre Director, Rio de Janeiro and São Paulo, Brazil; Professor, Graduate Program in Theater, Universidade Federal do Estado do Rio de Janeiro, Brazil
Rodrigues, Nelson; *Wedding Gown*

Olid-Peña, Estefania
Graduate Student, Department of Modern and Classical Languages, Georgia State University
Akins, Zoë; Hart, Moss; *I'd Rather Be Right*; June Moon; Lardner, Ring

Olivares, Lissette
Ph.D. Student, History of Consciousness Graduate Program, University of California, Santa Cruz
Radrigán, Juan

Olsen, Chris
Assistant Professor of Drama, University of Puerto Rico
Philosophy and Drama, 1960-Present

Orenstein, Claudia
Associate Professor, Theatre Department, Hunter College and The Graduate Center, City University of New York
Agitation-Propaganda

Ormsby, Robert
Sessional Lecturer, University of Toronto, Canada
Brooks, Daniel

Orvis, David L.
Doctoral Student, Department of English, University of Arizona
Shape of Things, The

Paget, Derek
Reader in Theatre and Television, University of Reading, United Kingdom
Documentary Drama

Pandit, Maya
Professor, Central Institute of English and Foreign Languages, Hyderabad, India

Bhagat, Datta; Elkunchwar, Mahesh; *Ghashiram Kotwal*; *Old Stone Mansion*; *Routes and Escape Routes*; *Sakharam Binder*; Tendulkar, Vijay

Paris, Marta de
Independent Scholar, Buenos Aires, Argentina
Argentina

Parkin, Gil
Independent Scholar and Researcher, New York, New York
Doubt

Parra-Domínguez, Maribel
Harvard University
Blood Wedding; *House of Bernarda Alba, The*; *Yerma*

Patruno, Nicholas
Professor of Italian, Bryn Mawr College
Verga, Giovanni

Patterson, Jim
Distinguished Professor Emeritus, University of South Carolina
Morning's at Seven; Osborn, Paul

Peimer, David
Principal Tutor, University of the Witwatersrand, Johannesburg, South Africa; Guest Professor, Prague Division, New York University
Avant-Garde Drama, South Africa

Pelizzari, David
Educational and Cultural Programs, The Smithsonian Institution, Washington, D.C.
Balcony, The; Crommelynck, Fernand; Genet, Jean; Lenormand, Henri-René; Montherlant, Henry de; *Satin Slipper, The*; Tardieu, Jean; Vauthier, Jean

Pender, Judith Midyett
Associate Professor of Drama, University of Oklahoma
Barry, Philip; Green, Paul; *Holiday*; *Philadelphia Story, The*

Penner, James L.
Lecturer, English Department, University of Southern California
Marber, Patrick; Neilson, Anthony

Penuel, Suzanne
Doctoral Student, University of Texas at Austin
Fen

Peterson, William
Senior Lecturer in Drama and Theatre Studies, Monash University, Australia
Avant-Garde Drama, Southeast Asia; *Coffin Is Too Big for the Hole, The*; Kon, Stella; Kuo Pao Kun; Ong Keng Sen; Singapore

Picarazzi, Teresa
Teacher, Modern Language Department, Hopkins School, Connecticut
Ginzburg, Natalia

Pierce, Jason A.
Associate Professor of English, Mars Hill College
Bridie, James

Pipinia, Ioulia
Lecturer of Drama, Aristotle University of Thessaloniki, Greece
Greece; Kambanellis, Iakovos; Xenopoulos, Grigorios

Pizer, John D.
Professor of German and Comparative Literature, Louisiana State University
Kraus, Karl

Pizzato, Mark
Professor of Theatre, University of North Carolina at Charlotte
Psychoanalysis

Poulton, M. Cody
Associate Professor, Department of Pacific and Asian Studies, University of Victoria, Canada
Hirata Oriza; Izumi Kyōka; Kubota Mantarō; Mori Ōgai; Osanai Kaoru; Shinpa; Suzuki Senzaburō; *Tokyo Notes*

Pounders, Steven C.
Associate Professor, Department of Theatre Arts, Baylor University
Closer

Powell, Brian
Emeritus Fellow, Keble College, University of Oxford, United Kingdom
Father Returns, The; Fukuda Yoshiyuki; Hōjō Hideji; Japan; Katō Michio; Mayama Seika; Murayama Tomoyoshi; Okamato Kidō; Shin kabuki; *Tale of Shuzenji*

Powers, W. Douglas
Associate Professor, Department of Theatre, Susquehanna University
Fry, Christopher; *Voice of the Turtle, The*

Puchner, Martin
H. Gordon Garbedian Professor of English and Comparative Literature, Columbia University
Closet Drama; Modernist Drama

Pullen, Kirsten
Assistant Professor, Department of English, University of Calgary, Canada
Interculturalism

Quint, Alyssa
Princeton University
Dybbuk, The

Rähesoo, Jaak
Freelance Critic and Translator, Estonia
Estonia

Reilly, Kara
Postdoctoral Teaching Fellow, Stanford University
Avant-Garde Drama, United States; Postmodernism

Richardson, Stanley R.
Adjunct Professor of Dramaturgy, Emerson College
Baitz, Jon Robin; Bentley, Eric; Foote, Horton; Guare, John; Nelson, Richard; New Dramatists; Shawn, Wallace

Ridley, Clifford A.
Retired Theater Critic, Philadelphia Inquirer

Boy Meets Girl; Dead End; Kingsley, Sidney; Men in White; Spewack, Bella, and Spewack, Sam

Rimer, J. Thomas
Professor Emeritus of Japanese Literature, University of Pittsburgh
Suzuki Tadashi

Rogowski, Christian
Professor of German, Amherst College
Brasch, Thomas; Hofmannsthal, Hugo von

Romanska, Magda ·
Assistant Professor and Head of Theatre Studies, Department of Performing Arts, Emerson College
Boucher, Denise; Curzon, Sarah Anne; Denison, Merrill; Griffiths, Linda; Kerr, Lois Reynolds; Pickthall, Marjorie

Rosenberg, Ellen
Humanities Faculty, North Carolina School of the Arts
Guy Domville

Rosenthal, Cindy
Associate Professor of Drama and Dance, Hofstra University
Living Theatre

Rothkirch, Alyce von
Lecturer and Coordinator, M.A. Lifelong Learning, Department of Adult Continuing Education, University of Wales Swansea, United Kingdom
Edwards, Dic; House of America; Keep, The; Osborne, Alan; Thomas, Dylan; Thomas, Edward; Thomas, Gwyn; Rowlands, Ian

Ruppel, Richard R.
Professor of German and Chair, Department of Foreign Languages, University of Wisconsin, Stevens Point
Switzerland

Ryan, Delyse
Senior Lecturer in Drama, Australian Catholic University
Cusack, Dymphna; Gow, Michael

Sacca, Annalisa
Associate Professor of Italian, St. John's University
De Filippo, Eduardo

Sadock, Benjamin
Graduate Student, Department of Germanic Languages, Columbia University
Hirschbein, Peretz

Sæther, Astrid
Associate Professor, Centre for Ibsen Studies, University of Oslo, Norway
Lady from the Sea, The; Little Eyolf; Rosmersholm

Saivetz, Deborah
Associate Professor of Theatre, Baruch College, City College of New York
Me xihc co Teatro (MxTeatro); Morett, María

Sajko, Brian
Dean of Admissions and Financial Aid, Vice President of Admissions and Marketing, and Professor of Theatre Arts and Drama, Eureka College
Hoyt, Charles H.; Robins, Elizabeth

Salz, Jonah
Professor, Faculty of Intercultural Communication, Ryukoku University, Japan
Kawakami Otojirō; Nō and Kyōgen; Yamazaki Masakazu

Sams, Victoria
Assistant Professor of Modern Dramatic Literature, Dickinson College
Wallace, Naomi

Sanabria, Enrique A.
Assistant Professor of History, University of New Mexico
Buero Vallejo, Antonio; Pérez Galdós, Benito; Valle-Inclán, Ramón María del

Sanhueza, Ma. Teresa
Associate Professor of Romance Languages, Wake Forest University
Discépolo, Armando

Sauer, David
Professor, Languages and Literature Division, Spring Hill College
Behrman, S. N.; Biography; No Time for Comedy; Rain from Heaven

Scheeder, Louis
Arts Professor, Associate Dean of Faculty, Director of The Classical Studio, Tisch School of the Arts, New York University
Kopit, Arthur; Linney, Romulus; Tally, Ted

Schildcrout, Jordan
Assistant Professor, School of Theater, Ohio University
Gay and Lesbian Drama

Schneider, Jeffrey
Associate Professor of German, Vassar College
I Am My Own Wife; Offending the Audience; Wright, Doug

Schneider, Robert
Assistant Professor of Theater and Dance, Northern Illinois University
Ionesco, Eugene; Lesson, The; Reza, Yasmina; Screens, The; Terrible but Unfinished Story of Norodom Sihanouk, King of Cambodia, The

Schwartz, Michael
Ph.D. Candidate, University of Pittsburgh
It Pays to Advertise

Scullion, Adrienne
James Arnott Professor of Drama, University of Glasgow, United Kingdom
Circle, The; Constant Wife, The; Daphne Laureola; Journey's End; Sheppey; Sherriff, Robert Cedric

Seaton Brown, Robin
Doctoral Student, Department of English, University of North Carolina at Chapel Hill
Caretaker, The; Old Times

Sebesta, Juraj
Director of the City Library, Bratislava, Slovakia
Absolute Prohibition; Karvaš, Peter; Slovakia

Sejersted, Jørgen
Assistant Professor, Department of Scandinavian Studies, University of Bergen, Norway
Bird Lovers, The; Bjørneboe, Jens Ingvald

Sell, Mike
Associate Professor, Department of English, Indiana University of Pennsylvania
Avant-Garde Drama; Black Arts Movement; Chance; Jazz

Senyk, Valerie
Associate Professor of Theatre Arts, Thorneloe College, Laurentian University, Canada
Zastrozzi: The Master of Discipline

Shafer, Leah R.
Ph.D. Candidate, Theatre Studies, Cornell University
Davy Crockett; Great Divide, The; Moody, William Vaughn

Shahan, Cyrus M.
Graduate Student, Department of Germanic Languages, University of North Carolina at Chapel Hill
Drums in the Night (w/ Maya Gerig); Wolf, Friedrich (w/ Maya Gerig)

Shandell, Jonathan
Adjunct Instructor, Theater Studies, Tisch School of the Arts, New York University
Anouilh, Jean; Eurydice

Shantz, Jeff
York University, Toronto, Canada
Bean, Richard

Shastri, Sudha
Assistant Professor of English, Indian Institute of Technology, Bombay
Kureishi, Hanif

Sierz, Aleks
Visiting Research Fellow, Rose Bruford College, United Kingdom
Angry Young Men

Sílvia Betti, Maria
Professor, Area of Linguistic and Literary Studies in English, University of Sao Paulo, Brazil
Break the Heart; Vianna Filho ("Vianinha"), Oduvaldo

Skidmore, Jamie
Assistant Professor, Department of English, Memorial University of Newfoundland, Canada
Tamara

Slywka, Nikolai
Ph.D. Candidate, Department of English, Stanford University
Coast of Utopia, The; Real Thing, The

Smalls, Shanté T.
Ph.D. Candidate, Department of Performance Studies, New York University
Auden, Wystan Hugh; Barrie, J. M.; Galsworthy, John; Granville-Barker, Harley; Isherwood, Christopher; Lawrence, David Herbert; Nottage, Lynn

Smith, Julianne
Associate Professor of English, Pepperdine University
East Lynne; Wood, Ellen

Smith, Robert Lewis
AAssociate Professor of Theatre and Theatre Subgroup Chair, Department of Speech Communication and Theatre, Kutztown University of Pennsylvania
Strictly Dishonorable; Thomas, Augustus

Sollars, Michael D.
Assistant Professor of English, Texas Southern University
Betrayal; Delaney, Shelagh

Sorgenfrei, Carol Fisher
Professor, Department of Theater, University of California, Los Angeles
Hunchback of Aomori, The; Terayama Shūji

Southerland, Stacy
Professor of Spanish, University of Central Oklahoma
Garro, Elena; Lady on her Balcony, The

Spreizer, Christa
Assistant Professor, Department of European Languages and Literatures, Queens College, City University of New York
Bronnen, Arnolt; Chlumberg, Hans; Goll, Yvan; Hasenclever, Walter; Johst, Hanns; Kornfeld, Paul; Son, The; Sorge, Reinhard Johannes

Sprinchorn, Evert
Professor and Chairman Emeritus, Department of Drama, Vassar College
Acting; Days Without End; Directing Plays; Dramatic Criticism; Dramatic Cycles; Dramatic Dialogue; Dramatic Structure; Expressionism; Hamsun, Knut; Naturalism; Nietzsche, Friedrich; Philosophy and Drama, 1860–1960; Problem Play; Realism; Stage Directions and Stage Sets; Subtext; Symbolism; Wagner, Richard

Starrs, D. Bruno
School of Creative Arts, University of Melbourne, Australia
Needles and Opium; Seven Streams of the River Ota, The

Stefanova, Kalina
Associate Professor of Theatre Criticism, National Academy of Theatre and Film Arts, Bulgaria
Bulgaria

Stefanovski, Risto
Theatrologist, Macedonia
Macedonia; Stefanovski, Goran

Steinberger, Rebecca
Associate Professor, English Department, College Misericordia
Ervine, St. John

Stevens, Andrea R.
Ph.D. Candidate, English Department, University of Virginia
Billy Bishop Goes to War; Davies, Robertson; Princess Pocahontas and the Blue Spots

Stoudt, Charlotte
Dramaturg and Writer
Breasts of Tiresias, The; Cixous, Hélène; Infernal Machine, The; Jet of Blood, The; Maids, The; Orpheus; Trojan War Will Not Take Place, The

Suppes, Patricia
Instructor, Department of Foreign Languages, Elon University
Peru

Swain, John D.
Assistant Professor, Department of Theatre, California State University, Northridge
Atami Murder Case, The; Kara Jūrō; Kitamura Sō; Noda Hideki; Senda Koreya; Tsuka Kōhei; Virgin's Mask, The; Watanabe Eriko

Switzky, Lawrence
Harvard University
Priestley, John Boynton; Return of the Prodigal, The

Syssoyeva, Kathryn
Ph.D. Candidate, Department of Drama and Graduate Program in the Humanities, Stanford University
Pomerance, Bernard; Tesich, Steve; Wellman, Mac

Tait, Peta
Professor, Theater and Drama Program, La Trobe University, Australia
Australia, Gender and Sexuality in Drama and Physical Theater; De Groen, Alma; Hewett, Dorothy; Kemp, Jenny

Tanaka, Rokuo
Independent Scholar, Honolulu, Hawaii
Ariyoshi Sawako; Mafune Yutaka

Tautz, Birgit
Assistant Professor, Department of German, Bowdoin College
Tabori, George

Tharp, Richard K.
Ph.D. Candidate, Department of Theatre, University of Maryland, College Park
John Ferguson

Törnqvist, Egil
Professor Emeritus, Scandinavian Studies, University of Amsterdam, Netherlands
Advent; Bergman, Hjalmar; Bergman, Ingmar; Carl XII; Chamber Plays; Creditors; Crimes and Crimes; Dagerman, Stig; Dance of Death, The; Dream Play, A; Easter; Enquist, Per Olov; Erik XIV; Father, The; Forssell, Lars; Ghost Sonata, The; Gustav Vasa; Hangman, The; Lagerkvist, Pär; Master Olof; Miss Julie; Night is Mother to the Day, The; Night of the Tribades, The; Norén, Lars; Strindberg, August; Stronger, The; Sunday Promenade, The; Sweden; To Damascus

Toten Beard, DeAnna M.
Assistant Professor, Department of Theatre Arts, Baylor University
Adding Machine, The; Hazel Kirke; Lawson, John Howard; MacKaye, Percy; MacKaye, Steele; Processional; Rice, Elmer; Street Scene; Voysey Inheritance, The

Tuan, Iris Hsin-chun
Assistant Professor, Department of Humanities and Social Sciences, National Chiao Tung University, Taiwan
Hwang Mei-shu; Ma Sen; Yao Yi-wei

Turnbull, Olivia
Senior Lecturer, Department of Drama, Bath Spa University, United Kingdom
Baltimore Waltz, The; Fifth of July; Innaurato, Albert; Rivera, José; Shanley, John Patrick; Vogel, Paula; Wilson, Lanford

Tylee, Claire M.
Senior Lecturer, English Department, Brunel University, United Kingdom
Rutherford and Son

Urian, Dan
Professor, Department of Theater Arts, Tel Aviv University, Israel
Israel

Valentini, Daria
Associate Professor of Italian, Stonehill College
Marinetti, Filippo Tommaso

Varderi, Alejandro
Professor of Spanish, Borough of Manhattan Community College, City University of New York
Venezuela

Vargas, Margarita
Associate Professor, Department of Romance Languages and Literatures, University at Buffalo, The State University of New York
Berman, Sabina; Mexico

Vena, Michael
Professor of Foreign Languages, Southern Connecticut State University
Chiarelli, Luigi

Vey, Shauna
Assistant Professor of Humanities, New York City College of Technology
Daly, Augustin; Johnson, Georgia Douglas

Violanti, Heather Jeanne
Freelance Dramaturg and Writer
Apollinaire, Guillaume; Arrabal, Fernando; Audiberti, Jacques

Virulrak, Surapone
Member, Royal Institute, Bangkok, Thailand
Chandraprabha, Sompop; Rama V; Thailand

Wachter, David
Graduate Student, Department of Comparative Literature, Free University of Berlin, Germany
Art

Wærp, Lisbeth Pettersen
Associate Professor of Literature, University of Tromsø, Norway
Doll's House, A; Emperor and Galilean; When We Dead Awaken

Wakefield, Thaddeus
Instructor, Santa Rosa Junior College
Mouawad, Wajdi; Wedding Day at the Cro-Magnons'

Walters, Meg
  Former Director of Academics, Rosemont School of the Holy Child,
  Pennsylvania
    Our Town; Skin of Our Teeth, The; Wilder, Thornton

Wandor, Michelene
  Royal Literary Fund Fellowship, Birkbeck College, London University,
  United Kingdom
    Bagnold, Enid

Wasserman, Jerry
  Professor of English and Theatre, University of British Columbia,
  Canada
    War Babies

Weales, Gerald
  Emeritus Professor of English, University of Pennsylvania
    After the Fall; All My Sons; Crucible, The; Death of a Salesman;
    Miller, Arthur; Price, The; View from the Bridge, A

Weckwerth, Wendy A.
  Visiting Faculty, Department of Theater and Dance, Colby College
    Adamov, Arthur; Dumas fils; Ghelderode, Michel de

Weidauer, Friedemann J.
  Associate Professor of German, University of Connecticut
    Alienation Effect; Hochhuth, Rolf; Investigation, The;
    Kipphardt, Heinar; Life of Galileo, The; Marat/Sade;
    Underpants, The; Weiss, Peter

Weinstein, John B.
  Assistant Professor of Chinese and Asian Studies, Division of
  Languages and Literature, Simon's Rock College of Bard
    Lee Kuo-hsiu

Werner, Robin A.
  Ph.D., Instructor of English, University of New Orleans
    England, 1860–1940; Second Mrs. Tanqueray, The

West, Ron
  Ph.D., Metropolitan Community College
    Herne, James A.; Margaret Fleming; Saratoga; Shore Acres

Westphalen, Timothy C.
  Associate Professor and Director of Graduate Studies, Department of
  European Languages, Literatures, and Cultures, Stony Brook
  University, State University of New York
    Andreev, Leonid; Bathhouse, The; Bedbug, The; Blok,
    Aleksandr; Chekhov, Anton; Cherry Orchard, The; He Who
    Gets Slapped; Ivanov; Life of Man, The; Mayakovsky, Vladimir;
    Meyerhold, Vsevolod; Mystery-Bouffe; Platonov; Puppet Show,
    A; Russia and the Soviet Union, Russian Symbolist Drama;
    Seagull, The; Three Sisters; Uncle Vanya

Weyenberg, Astrid Van
  Amsterdam School for Cultural Analysis, University of Amsterdam,
  Netherlands
    Lochhead, Liz; Mary Queen of Scots Got Her Head Chopped Off

Whittaker, Robin C.
  Doctoral Candidate, Graduate Centre for Study of Drama, University
  of Toronto, Canada
    Saint Frances of Hollywood

Wichmann-Walczak, Elizabeth
  Professor and Director of Asian Theatre, Department of Theatre and
  Dance, University of Hawaii at Manoa
    Cao Cao and Yang Xiu

Wilcox, Dean
  Theatre History and Dramatic Literature, North Carolina School of
  the Arts
    Deconstruction

Willeke, Audrone B.
  Professor Emerita of German, Miami University
    From Morning to Midnight; Kaiser, Georg

Willinger, David Paul
  Professor of Theatre, City College of New York, City University of
  New York
    Belgium; Claus, Hugo; Jenkin, Len; Kalisky, René;
    Kramer, Larry; Machado, Eduardo; Willems, Paul

Willis, Craig
  Independent Scholar, Eugene, Oregon
    Kelly, George

Wilmeth, Don B.
  Asa Messer Emeritus Professor and Emeritus Professor of Theatre and
  English, Brown University
    United States, 1860–1929

Winet, Evan Darwin
  Assistant Professor, Theater and Dance Department, Macalester College
    Sarumpaet, Ratna

Witt, Gavin
  Resident Dramaturg, Center Stage, Maryland
    Feydeau, Georges; Flea in Her Ear, A

Wixson, Christopher
  Assistant Professor of English, Eastern Illinois University
    Cavalcade; Daughter in Law, The; Hindle Wakes; Private Lives;
    Widowing of Mrs. Holroyd, The

Woodhouse, John
  Fiat-Serena Professor of Italian Emeritus, Magdalen College,
  University of Oxford, United Kingdom
    D'Annunzio, Gabriele

Worrall, Nick
  Retired Principal Lecturer, Middlesex University, London
    Bulgakov, Mikhail; Days of the Turbins; Evreinov, Nikolai;
    Flight; Month in the Country, A; Optimistic Tragedy, An; Power
    of Darkness, The; Russia and the Soviet Union, Dramatic
    Criticism; Tretyakov, Sergei; Theatricality; Tolstoy, Lyov

Wyllie, Andrew
  Senior Lecturer, Department of Drama, University of the West of
  England, United Kingdom
    Design for Living; Inspector Calls, An

Yamanashi, Makiko
  Post Graduate, School of Asian Studies, University of Edinburgh,
  United Kingdom
    Takarazuka Revue Company

Yassur, Moshe
Off-Off-Broadway Director; Adjunct Faculty of Speech and Communication, School of New Resources, College of New Rochelle, New York
Caragiale, Ion Luca; Jonah; Naghiu, Iosif; Popescu, Dumitru Radu; Romania; Sorescu, Marin

Ybarra, Patricia
Assistant Professor of Theatre, Speech and Dance, Brown University
Corona Trilogy

Yeung, Jessica
Assistant Professor, Department of English Language and Literature, Hong Kong Baptist University, China
Chan, Anthony (w/ Jane Lai); Chan, Joanna (w/ Jane Lai); To, Raymond (w/ Jane Lai); Yung, Danny N. T. (w/ Jane Lai)

Ying, Li-hua
Associate Professor and Director of Chinese Program, Bard College
Liang Bingkun (w/ Cai Xingshui)

Young, Clinton D.
Visiting Assistant Professor, Department of History, Western Carolina University
Álvarez Quintero, Joaquín, and Serafín Alvarez Quintero; Sainete; Zarzuela

Young, Stuart
Associate Professor and Head of Theatre Studies Programme, University of Otago, New Zealand
Geary, David; Hall, Roger; Lord, Robert; Mason, Bruce; McGee, Greg; New Zealand, 1870–1960; New Zealand, 1980-Present; New Zealand, Feminist Drama; Renée; Thompson, Mervyn

Ystad, Vigdis
Professor, Centre for Ibsen Studies, University of Oslo, Norway
Heiberg, Gunnar

Yu, Shiao-ling
Associate Professor of Chinese Language and Literature, Oregon State University
First House of Beijing Duck, The; Li Longyun; We; Xu Jiujing's Promotion

Zelenak, Michael X.
Associate Professor, Department of Theatre Arts, Stony Brook University, State University of New York
Dramaturgy

Zhang, Lei
Doctoral Student, Texas Woman's University
Foon, Dennis

Zinman, Toby
Professor of English, University of the Arts
Eliot, Thomas Stearns; Family Reunion, The; Murder in the Cathedral

Zwerling, Philip
Assistant Professor of English and Creative Writing, Ursinus College
Belasco, David; Girl of the Golden West, The; Hurston, Zora Neale

SYNOPTIC OUTLINE OF CONTENTS

The outline presents entries organized by topics to help users navigate the contents. Entries are listed by countries; plays; playwrights; movements, forms, and genres; companies, groups, and theaters; and concepts and terms. The final section is a list of entries organized by country.

COUNTRIES

PLAYS

PLAYWRIGHTS

INDEX

Page numbers in **boldface type** indicate articles in which the index entry is the featured topic of discussion.
Arabic names beginning with the prefix "al-" are found in the As.
When looking up a subject, be sure to scan the column for entries beginning with the word in question. Subject entries do not
    include duplications of nearby titles. For example, "alienation" does not include *Alien Creature* among its subentries.